2003

Our Sunday Visitor's
CATHOLIC ALMANAC

Matthew Bunson
General Editor

Our Sunday Visitor Publishing Division
Our Sunday Visitor, Inc.
Huntington, Indiana 46750

STAFF OF *OUR SUNDAY VISITOR'S CATHOLIC ALMANAC*

Greg Erlandson
Publisher

Matthew E. Bunson
General Editor

Cathy Dee
Production Editor

Contributors to the 2003 Edition
Dr. John Borelli
Barbara Fraze
Dr. Eugene Fisher
Brother Jeffrey Gros, F.S.C.
Rev. C. Eugene Morris
Rev. Ronald Roberson, C.S.P.
William Ryan
Russell Shaw

Editorial Consultant
Jane Cavolina

Assistant
Carrie Bannister

ACKNOWLEDGMENTS: Catholic News Service, for coverage of news and documentary texts; *The Documents of Vatican II*, ed. W. M. Abbott (Herder and Herder, America Press: New York 1966), for quotations of Council documents; *Annuario Pontificio* (2002); *Statistical Yearbook of the Church* (2002); *L'Osservatore Romano* (English editions); *The Official Catholic Directory* — Excerpts of statistical data and other material, reprinted with permission of *The Official Catholic Directory*, © 2002 by Reed Reference Publishing, a division of Reed Publishing (USA), Inc. Trademark used under license from Reed Publishing (Nederland) B.V.; *The Papal Encyclicals*, 5 vols., ed. C. Carlen (Pierian Press, Ann Arbor, Mich.); Newsletter of the U.S. Bishops' Committee on the Liturgy; The United States Catholic Mission Assoc. (3029 Fourth St. N.E., Washington, D.C. 20017), for U.S. overseas-mission compilations and statistics; *Catholic Press Directory* (2001); *Annuaire Directiore*, Canadian Conference of Catholic Bishops, for latest available Canadian Catholic statistics; Rev. Thomas J. Reese, S.J., for names of dioceses for which U.S. bishops were ordained; other sources as credited in particular entries.
Special thanks are owed to His Excellency Most Reverend John P. Foley, President of the Pontifical Council for Social Communications; Bruce Egnew, Associate General Secretary, USCCB; Secretariat for Pro-Life Activities, USCCB; Rev. Mr. William Kokesch, Dir.-Communications Service, Canadian Conference of Catholic Bishops; Suzanne Lea.

2003 Catholic Almanac

Copyright © 2002 by Our Sunday Visitor Publishing Division, Our Sunday Visitor, Inc., 2003
Published annually by Our Sunday Visitor Publishing Division, Our Sunday Visitor, Inc., 200 Noll Plaza, Huntington, IN 46750
ISBN 1-931709-28-9
T16
Library of Congress Catalog Card No. 73-641001
International Standard Serial Number (ISSN) 0069-1208

Editorial Note: The Catholic Almanac is pleased to announce that a web site devoted to the *Almanac* is available at www.CatholicAlmanac.com. Readers are encouraged to visit the site, where they will find a searchable database of past "Special Reports," biographies of the "American Bishops of the Past," and "American Catholics of the Past." Comments, corrections, and suggestions should be addressed to the editorial offices of the *Catholic Almanac*: 2017 Scenic Sunrise Dr., Las Vegas, NV 89117; (702) 254-2678; E-mail: almanac@osv.com.

TABLE OF CONTENTS

4

In Remembrance

FATHER FELICIAN FOY, O.F.M.

Fr. Felician Foy, O.F.M., general editor of *Our Sunday Visitor's Catholic Almanac* for decades, passed away on Feb. 21, 2002. Father Foy was 83 at the time of his death. He had served as editor of the *Catholic Almanac* from 1952 to 1998 and as special consultant over the last years of his life.

Fr. Foy was asked to direct the *Catholic Almanac* in 1952. Founded in 1904, the Catholic Almanac was published by the St. Anthony's Guild when Fr. Foy became editor. He restructured the format and content of the *Catholic Almanac*, making it an invaluable, popular one-volume reference work on Catholic life. He revised the publication in response to the Second Vatican Council, arranged its transfer to Our Sunday Visitor in 1971, and oversaw its entry into the digital age in the 1990s.

Together with his assistant Miss Rose Avato, who died in 1997, Fr. Foy was personally involved in every aspect of the *Catholic Almanac* throughout his 45-year tenure. Working out of a small office in New Jersey, Fr. Foy and Rose each year assembled the treasure trove of data on the Catholic Church found in each edition. Fr. Foy was a hands-on editor, writing, proofreading and editing every section of the *Catholic Almanac*.

As Matthew Bunson, his successor as general editor, remembered him, "Fr. Felician was one of the unsung heroes of American Catholic journalism. He made his commitment to the *Almanac* one facet of his abiding love for the Church and service to others. He is a genuine inspiration for those who carry on his legacy with the *Almanac*."

Born on June 7, 1918 in Philadelphia, Fr. Foy was professed into the Franciscans on Aug. 13, 1942. He was ordained to the priesthood on June 14, 1947. He taught high school for several years until he received the unexpected appointment to serve as an editor.

In addition to his work on the *Catholic Almanac*, Fr. Foy was deeply involved in prison ministry, the direction of Third Order Franciscans, outreach programs for the growing Latino population in New Jersey, and chaplain work at St. Joseph's Hospital. An accomplished guitar player, Fr. Foy had also taught himself Spanish for his work in the Latino community in the Diocese of Paterson.

In 1996, Fr. Foy and Rose Avato were honored by a commendation from the Catholic Press Association for their decades of service through the *Catholic Almanac*. In 1998, Fr. Foy was awarded the *Pro Ecclesia et Pontifice* medal for his contributions to the life of the Church.

The 1999 edition of the *Catholic Almanac* was dedicated to Fr. Foy, and to the memory of Rose, who had died within days of completing work on the previous year's edition. At that time, Our Sunday Visitor honored both for their "Christian dedication, diligence and generosity."

Greg Erlandson, president of Our Sunday Visitor, best described Fr. Foy as "an indefatigable editor and writer who poured his heart and soul into this book for 45 years." He added that at the time of his death Fr. Foy had been working on a history of the publication to mark its 100th anniversary in 2004 and "up until the very end he continued to contribute" to each year's *Catholic Almanac*.

Fr. Foy was first and foremost a priest. Those at Our Sunday Visitor who were fortunate enough to work with him over the decades remember his Franciscan kindness and a practical spirituality that was evident in his every word and every page of the *Catholic Almanac*.

The *Catholic Almanac* today remains the legacy of this remarkable priest, whose journey with the *Catholic Almanac* spanned the papacies of Pius XII, John XXIII, Pope Paul VI, John Paul I and John Paul II. It was his work that documented in the *Catholic Almanac* an extraordinary half-century in the life of the Church, while reaffirming the eternal truths of the faith that was the very center of Fr. Felician Foy's life.

To know him was to be blessed.

Year In Review:
September 2001 to August 2002

SEPTEMBER 2001

Vatican

Murder of Missionary — Pope John Paul II extended sympathy to the Columban religious congregation and to the family members of the slain missionary priest, Rufus Halley. Father Halley was slain on Sept. 2 by a member of the Moro Islamic Liberation Front during an attempted kidnapping in Malabang, Philippines.

Marriage Repented — The Vatican announced on Sept. 2 that former archbishop Emmanuel Milingo regretted the suffering and embarrassment that he caused the Church by his Moon-sect marriage to Maria Sung in the public ceremony held by the sect. The former archbishop of Luseka, Zambia, repented this union and in a formal letter renounced the marriage and his ties to the Moon sect.

Catholic-Orthodox Dialogue — In a message sent to the 7th Inter-Christian Symposium, released on Sept. 3, Pope John Paul II stated that he prayed for genuine dialogue between Christian groups that stressed honesty, prudence and awareness. The pope has long advocated such dialogue between Catholics and members of the Orthodox Church.

Morality in Science — Pope John Paul II sent a message to the delegates of the World Day of the Sick meeting on Sept. 3, warning modern scientists that "the Church insists on the principle that not all that is technically feasible is morally admissible." In this message the pope added that human beings are "the custodians of life, not the proprietors."

New Eurocoins — The image of Pope John Paul II will probably be used on the new Vatican version of the cash currency being introduced as part of the Eurocoin program, it was announced on Sept. 3. The famed artist Veroi will design the new coins representing the Vatican in this monetary designation.

Matteo Ricci — Pope John Paul II addressed the members of the Italian-Chinese Institute on Sept. 5, declaring his interest in the life and virtues of Jesuit Father Matteo Ricci, the evangelizer of China. Commemorating the fourth centenary of the arrival of the Jesuit missionary in that land, the Institute members noted that Father Ricci is still revered in China today. The pope called Matteo Ricci a model in the mission field.

Aid to the Church in Need — On September 6, the Holy See provided details for the upcoming congress on Sept. 28-30, on the pastoral challenges of the Church. Three separate areas of study and review are anticipated. The first challenge to be discussed is the spread of Islam in Europe and Africa. The second challenge is the growth of non-Catholic religious movements and sects, especially in Latin American regions. The third challenge facing the Church in the world involves religious indifference, particularly in the West. Cardinal Francis Stafford, president of the Pontifical Council for the Laity, and other leaders will participate in this congress.

Appeal for Racial Accord — Responding to the discord demonstrated at the World Conference Against Racism, Pope John Paul II called for easing nationalism and racism on Sept. 6. He appealed to people of good will everywhere to promote human dignity, peace and harmony. The pope stated: "The Church reproves as contrary to God's will all discrimination or harassment of people due to race, color, condition of life or religion." Delegates from the United States and Israel withdrew from this conference when Israel was singled out as a racist nation.

Weak Need Protection — Addressing the new Irish ambassador to the Vatican, Bernard Davenport, on September 7, Pope John Paul II said that genuine development of countries in the world must include protections of the dignity, families and lives of all citizens. The pope welcomed the ambassador, praising Ireland, which has been cited as an economic miracle in the past decades.

Synod Theme — On Sept. 9, Pope John Paul II proposed a theme for the upcoming Synod of Bishops, scheduled for Sept. 30-Oct. 27. The theme recommended is "Put out into the deep." The Synod is expected to culminate efforts to promote the reforms of Vatican Council II, particularly those contained in the decree *Christus Dominus*.

Vatican Treasures — The Vatican announced Sept. 9 that it has begun an inventory of its vast collections and cultural treasures, a project expected to take two years of effort. In addition to the treasures contained in museums and libraries, this inventory will catalog the parks, residences and gardens of the Vatican. Remarkable and rare articles have been collected in the Vatican over the centuries, documenting cultural and artistic endeavors in historical eras.

St. Augustine a Model — Pope John Paul II sent a message to the Augustinian General Chapter on Sept. 10, citing St. Augustine of Hippo as a singular teacher for the modern age. The pope praised all of the saints and martyrs of the Augustinian Order.

Dark Day — On Sept. 12, Pope John Paul II called the massive terrorist attacks in New York and Washington, D.C., "a dark day in the history of humanity." The pope celebrated Mass for "the helpless victims of this tragedy." He added: "Let us beg the Lord that the spiral of hatred and violence will not prevail."

New U.S. Ambassador — Pope John Paul II welcomed James Nicholson, the recently appointed United States Ambassador to the Vatican, at Castel Gandolfo on Sept. 13. The pope noted that Ambassador Nicholson was beginning his mission "at a moment of intense tragedy," and he prayed with the ambassador for America. Ambassador Nicholson thanked the Holy Father for his "spiritual closeness" to the United States in this tragic period. Ambassador Nicholson expressed the gratitude of President George W. Bush and the American people.

Joint Statement — The Vatican announced on Sept. 13 that the Holy See and Muslim leaders have condemned the terrorist attacks on the United States. The Islamic-Catholic Liaison that issued this condemnation was formed in May 1998. Members include representatives of the Pontifical Council for Interreligious Dialogue, presided over by Cardinal Francis Arinze and representatives of the Al-Azhar Permanent Committee for Dialogue with Monotheistic Religions. The joint statement expresses "great sorrow at the number of victims" and condemns "the horrifying acts of terrorism."

Model of Unity and Service — Pope John Paul II met with the bishops of Haiti at Castel Gandolfo on Sept. 14, urging them to focus efforts on making the Church in Haiti a model of unity and service in a "fractured and desperate" society. The bishops of Haiti reported signs of hope in their homeland, despite ongoing crises.

Papal Condolences — Pope John Paul II sent a letter of condolence to Cardinal Theodore E. McCarrick of Washington, to be read at the Sept. 16 Mass for Healing and Peace in the Basilica of the National Shrine of the Immaculate Conception in Washington, D.C. In the letter the pope stated: "To all I solemnly repeat the Gospel injunction not to be conquered by evil, but to conquer evil with good (Rom. 12:21), to trust in the power of God's grace to transform human hearts and to work fearlessly to shape a future of justice, peace and security for the children of our world."

Deaconess Courses — A Vatican document prepared by the Vatican Congregations for the Doctrine of the Faith; for Divine Worship and for the Discipline of the Sacraments; and for the Clergy was announced on Sept. 17. This document condemns the formation of courses for women deaconesses, stating that such courses "are lacking in doctrinal foundation and, consequently, can generate pastoral confusion." The document stresses that it is not licit to implement initiatives that prepare candidates for an Order not available. The Vatican reminded the faithful that Church ministries are not about power but service. Bishops were asked to apply this directive to their dioceses and to make the ruling known in their jurisdictions.

New Biblical Faculty — The Vatican announced the establishment of the *Studium Biblicum Franciscum* of Jerusalem on Sept. 17. This institution is under the Pontificium Athenaeum Antonianum in Rome.

Papal Journey — Pope John Paul II visited Kazakstan and Armenia, Sept. 22-27, despite regional unrest and the ongoing U.S. attacks in Afghanistan.

(For details, see under **Papal Trips, 2001-2002**.)

Organ Transplants — The Vatican approved organ transplants from animals to humans as morally acceptable under certain circumstances, it was announced on Sept. 26. Such transplants should be used as a final "surgical therapy," following strict conditions that avoid animal suffering and protect the balance of species.

Papal Surprise — On the return trip to Rome from Armenia, on Sept. 28, Pope John Paul II invited members of the press corps to sit beside him, one by one, and to have photos taken. The members of the press filed to his side for this personal moment, which was greatly appreciated.

Pope Leaves Castel Gandolfo — On Sept. 29, Pope John Paul II bade farewell to Castel Gandolfo, the papal summer residence. Addressing a gathered populace, the pope said: "I continue to pray for the Lord's mercy for the deceased (of the Sept. 11 terrorist attacks on the United States), support and consolation for the survivors, and the precious gift of peace for all humanity."

Beatification of a Couple — Pope John Paul II beatified Luigi Beltrame Quattrocchi and Maria Corsini, the first spouses to be so honored as a couple. The ceremony was held in Rome on Sept. 30. In designating this couple as blessed, the pope renewed his appeal to families to defend values against disintegrative tendencies of the modern world and the threats of this new age of humanity. The beatification honored the 20th anniversary of *Familiaris Consortio*, which focused on the role of the family in the changing world.

Synod of Bishops — Pope John Paul II opened the 10th General Assembly on the Synod of Bishops on Sept. 30. The pope called the attending episcopal members of the synod to assume the role of heralds of the salvation of Christ. The synod was composed of 55 cardinals, 7 patriarchs, 70 archbishops, 106 bishops and 10 priests.

General Audience Topics:

• Reflection on the Lord, King of the Universe (Sept. 5).

International

Lutheran Convert — Michel Viot, a Lutheran Evangelical Church leader, converted to the Catholic Church in France. Word was released on Sept. 2 in Paris of Viot's decision to become a Catholic priest, an unprecedented event since the Reformation.

Peace Meeting — The 15th World Meeting of "Men and Religion" opened in Barcelona, Spain, on Sept. 2. The theme of the meeting was "The Frontiers of Dialogue: Religions and Civilizations in the New Century." Leaders of various religions gathered for the conference that will explore ecumenical responses to the perils and threats of the modern age.

Racism an Evil — Cardinal Wilfred Napier of Durban, South Africa, addressed delegates of the World Conference Against Racism on Sept. 2, urging Christians to abolish the evil and to heal fractured communities. He declared: "Racism is totally incompatible with the Christian faith."

Peruvian Safeguards — The Peruvian Health Minister, Luis Solari de la Fuente, announced on Sept. 2 new efforts to protect women against forced sterilization and other medical irregularities practiced over the past decade. A Japanese citizen is funding this health project, aimed particularly at women residing in the Amazon region. The forced sterilizations of women in provincial areas were part of former President Alberto Fujimori's population-control projects during his term of office.

World Summit for Children — The Catholic Family and Human Rights Institute announced on Sept. 2 that delegates from Latin American countries to the World Summit for Children are promoting abortions under the guise of "reproductive health services." The "Rio Group," a bloc of pro-life Latin American nations, will play a pivotal role in this summit, planned for Sept. 19-21.

Monasteries Revived — Mont-Saint-Michel, the great monastery on the Channel of La Mancha in France, is now serving as a haven for the Monastic Communities of Jerusalem, a group of religious monks and nuns founded in Paris in 1975. On Sept. 3, the foundation of the Monastic Communities of Jerusalem at Mont-Saint-Michel was announced. Other historical monasteries, such as the Abbey of Dombes, are accepting the modern communities into their ancient, understaffed structures. The *Chemin Neuf*, a Catholic movement founded in Lyon, France, in 1973, is another modern community involved in taking over the traditional monastic sites.

Mother Teresa's Sisters — The Missionaries of Charity, the congregation founded by Mother Teresa, marked their first anniversary in the Old City of Jerusalem on Sept. 3. This community works with sister houses in Amman, Gaqza and Nablus. The Missionaries of Charity care for the physically and mentally handicapped in these Arab societies.

Hanoi AIDS Center — The Daughters of Charity of St. Vincent de Paul opened a center northeast of Ho Chi Minh City, it was announced Sept. 3. This center will serve many AIDS patients. Vietnam has 35,767 patients suffering from AIDS, with 7,000 located in the area of the new center.

Scapular Anniversary — The general chapter of the Ancient Order of Carmel was held in Rome, Sept. 3-21. This gathering celebrated the 750th anniversary of the scapular, presented by the Blessed Virgin Mary to St. Simon Stock, an English Carmelite.

Bishop Sentenced — Bishop Pierre Pican of the Bayeux-Lisieux Diocese of France was sentenced to a three-month suspended jail term on Sept. 4. Facing a possible three years in prison before the sentencing, Bishop Pican was indicted and found guilty of failing to publicly denounce a priest who had sexually molested children. The priest was counseled by Bishop Pican and placed in a clinic, halting his activities in December 1996.

Mother Teresa Anniversary — On Sept. 5, the Missionaries of Charity marked the fourth anniversary of the death of Mother Teresa in Calcutta, India. Receiving the Nobel Prize in 1979 for her enduring care of India's sick and poor, her cause has been opened.

British Loss of Faith — Cardinal Cormac Murphy-O'Connor addressed a group at Leeds, England, on Sept. 6, declaring that Christianity is almost beaten in Britain. The cardinal cited modern music, the occult, consumerism, New Age, and the environmental movement as producing a new atheism in the British

Isles. A study indicates that 44% of all adults there have no religious affiliation, and younger individuals, from 18 to 24, are listed as two thirds unaffiliated. A prediction by a leading research specialist on church attendance suggested that in 40 years, Christian life will no longer be viable in Britain. Practicing Muslims now outnumber members of the Anglican Church in the U.K.

Slayers Forgiven — In Bogota, Colombia, the sister of a slain priest publicly forgave his slayers on Sept. 6. Father Hector Fabio Velez Jaramillo was tortured and stabbed to death by six men who entered and robbed his residence. In a public demonstration, the priest's sister, Noralba Velez, said that Christ is the only moral authority to judge the authors of such a crime.

Christian Artists Gather — The first International Seminar of European Christian Artists opened Sept. 7 at the Italian Shrine of Oropa, with 150 leaders of the arts attending. The shrine of Our Lady of Oropa dates to the era of St. Eusebius. This seminar is designed to foster the Christian vision and to sponsor emerging European artists who share that view of the world and eternity.

Dedicated Journalists — The World Congress of Catholic Journalists in Fribourg, Switzerland, was addressed by Archbishop John P. Foley, the president of the Pontifical Council for Social Communications on Sept. 17. Archbishop Foley opened with prayers for the victims of the terrorist attacks on the United States and then counseled young journalists to maintain an unwavering dedication to truth that is not hampered by ideology, prejudice, political correctness or social conformity. The archbishop also asked journalists to be instruments of peace and men and women of hope. The International Catholic Press Union organized the congress in Switzerland.

Papal Security — Kazakstan officials announced on Sept. 18 that "unprecedented" security measures will be in place for the safety of Pope John Paul II during his stay in that country. A large security force will guard the pope in Astana, the nation's capital. There are 300,000 Latin-rite Catholics in Kazakstan, along with six million Orthodox Catholics, some Greek Catholics and about 8 million Sunni Muslims.

Coexistence and Violence — A final statement of the Congress of the Council of Episcopal Conferences of Europe and the Council of Churches in Europe was issued on Sept. 18, making an appeal to the world not to justify violence in the name of religion. Leaders of the Catholic, Orthodox, Anglican, Evangelical and Lutheran communities gathered to discuss the effects of pluralist societies in Europe. The Grand Muftis of Moscow and Sarajevo, and other Muslim leaders supported the event.

Little Flower Relics — The relics of St. Thérèse of Lisieux began a tour of Canada on Sept. 18, scheduled to visit more than 100 locations. Canada is the 22nd nation hosting the reliquary containing the bones of the Little Flower. Canonized in 1925, St. Thérèse of Lisieux was declared a Doctor of the Church in 1997.

Annual Miracle — On Sept. 19, the faithful gathered in the cathedral of Naples to witness the annual liquefaction of St. Januarius's blood. The blood, kept in two small vials, liquefied during the service attended by Cardinal Michele Giordano. This miracle normally occurs three times a year, on Sept 19, the feast day of St. Januarius, on the first weekend in May, and on Dec. 16, the anniversary of the eruption of Mount Vesuvius in 1631. St. Januarius was the bishop of Benevento, Italy, and was martyred in 305. The eruption of Mount Vesuvius ended after the faithful begged his intercession on their behalf.

Young Missionaries — The Congregation of the Missionaries of the Divine Word announced on Sept. 26, in Steyl, Netherlands, 54 young men and women are setting out as worldwide temporary missionaries. Completing a nine-month course of preparation, 28 young men and 26 young women received their crosses and mandates to labor for Christ.

Ban on Cloning — A European Union effort being made to ban reproductive human cloning was announced on Sept. 28. The French and Germans are leading the efforts to see a United Nations ban on this process.

National

Pro-Life Ads Rejected — Advertisements of the U.S. Conference of Catholic Bishops for Pro-Life, part of the "Second Look Project," starting Sept. 1, were rejected by the city of Philadelphia. The ads were to be placed in bus shelters around the city to draw attention to the evils of abortion in modern society.

U.S.-Israeli Withdrawal — Delegates from the United States and Israel withdrew from the World Conference Against Racism, held at Durban, South Africa, on Sept. 3. Secretary of State Colin Powell stated that the U.S. withdrawal was prompted by the conference's focus on Israel as a "racist and apartheid state." Powell said that racism cannot be combated by conferences "that produce declarations containing hateful language."

Legalize Immigrants — The American Catholic bishops urged the legalization of undocumented Mexicans and other foreign residents in the U.S. Bishop Nicholas A. DiMarzio of Camden, New Jersey, the chairman of the U.S. Bishops' Committee on Migration, issued the statement on Sept. 4, in conjunction with the state visit of Mexican President Vicente Fox to Washington, D.C.

Shake the Nation — On Sept. 4 it was announced that a new campaign, Shake the Nation, was being adopted by a coalition of pro-life groups in the United States. Followers of the pro-life campaigns were asked to mail baby rattles to members of the United States Senate to encourage the culture of life and to demonstrate opposition to current abortion activities in the nation.

Confirmation Age — The new age for conferring the sacrament of confirmation in the United States Latin-rite dioceses was defined on Sept. 4 as between "the age of discretion and about 16 years of age." The decree of promulgation setting the age determination for the conferring of confirmation was originally issued on Aug. 21. The "age of discretion" is normally considered to be about 7 years of age.

Terrorist Attacks — On Sept. 11, the World Trade Center in New York and the Pentagon in Washington, D.C. were attacked by hijacked airliners. The New York towers collapsed following two impacts. Another plane, commandeered for a similar mission, crashed in Stony Creek Township in Pennsylvania, apparently as the result of American hostage-passengers resisting their captors. Cardinal Edward M. Egan of New York summed up the response of Americans when he announced: "For all of us this has been a terrible day, but we are not afraid...." (For full coverage on the attack and the war on terror, please see under **Special Reports**.)

Anti-Poverty Trust — The Catholic Campaign for Human Development announced on Sept. 12 that it would distribute $10 million to programs that combat poverty in America. The campaign is part of the domestic anti-poverty initiatives of the U.S. Catholic bishops, and the funds are raised in a national collection taken up in parishes each year.

Justice Meeting — The Pontifical Council for Justice and Peace convened Sept.13-15. St. John's University of New York and the University of St. Thomas in Minnesota acted as co-sponsors with other academic institutions. The council met on the 20th anniversary of Pope John Paul II's encyclical, *Laborem Exercens*. The pope sent a message asking members to focus on the needs of workers.

Knights' Fund — The Knights of Columbus announced a $1 million "Heroes Fund" on Sept. 14. Supreme Knight Carl A. Anderson said: "This gift is being offered along with our prayers." Scholarships will also be available.

Day of Prayer — President George W. Bush announced a national day of prayer and remembrance on Sept. 14. The victims of the terrorist attacks on Sept. 11 were honored with memorial services, bell ringing, candlelight vigils and other community observances. (See also under **Special Reports** for full coverage.)

Bishops-Muslim Statement — The U.S. Conference of Catholic Bishops and the American Muslim Council, along with other Islamic groups, issued a joint statement on Sept. 16, condemning the terrorist acts of Sept. 11. The groups also urged communities to promote peace.

Flags in Church — Discretion was urged on Sept. 16 in the display of the American flag at local parishes. The diocesan bishops have the discretion of regulating such patriotic measures, but the U.S. Bishops' Committee on the Liturgy urged pastors to display the flag outside of sanctuaries.

Fátima Secret — On Sept. 18, Archbishop John Favalora of Miami, Florida, declared that the "third secret of Fátima" currently being circulated on the Internet is false. The Internet version is a repeat of an earlier "secret" that predicted destruction and punishment. Archbishop Favalora pointed to the text made public by the Holy See on June 26, 2000, stating: "... the secret of Fátima is already known, and the world has not ended." The Vatican Congregation for the Doctrine of the Faith made the secret public in 2000.

Religious Liberty — It was announced on Sept. 27 that John V. Hanford is to be nominated as United States ambassador at large for international religious liberty.

St. Nicholas To Be Rebuilt — A Greek Orthodox Church, St. Nicholas, destroyed by the collapse of the World Trade Center during the terrorist attacks on America, will be rebuilt. On Sept. 27 it was announced that the administrators of St. Nicholas received a donation from the mayor of Bari, Italy, in the amount of $500,000, to aid in the planned reconstruction. St. Nicholas is the patron saint of Bari, Italy. The New York church was opened in 1916. The new building will honor the victims of the terrorist attack on Sept. 11.

OCTOBER 2001

Vatican

Caritas to Pakistan — Caritas, the confederation of Catholic relief agencies, is sending an emergency response team to Pakistan, the Vatican announced on Oct. 1. The Caritas team will aid Afghan refugees fleeing the bombing raids of Taliban-controlled areas of Afghanistan by American-led forces. Such attacks and impending starvation have forced entire villages to abandon their homeland and move to the Pakistan border. Caritas has been involved in Afghanistan in the past.

Pray the Rosary — Pope John Paul II asked people around the world to pray the rosary daily to save humanity from the "evil scourge" loose in this era. The pope sounded the Church's prophetic call for world peace on Oct. 1. He referred again to Sept. 11 as a "dark day in the history of humanity."

Synod of Bishops — About 250 bishops from around the world gathered for a Synod in the Vatican, Sept. 30-Oct. 27. Pope John Paul, addressing the gathered prelates, stated that bishops were called to be prophets who opposed modern sins from consumerism to hedonism. The bishops will focus on social ills and problems, particularly "religious illiteracy" among modern Catholics.

Globalization Environment — The speech of Archbishop Diarmuid Martin, permanent observer to the United Nations in Geneva, on the globalization of the environment, was made available by the Vatican on Oct. 3. The archbishop stated that environmental protection needs to go hand in hand with globalization. He also said that corporations must be accountable for actions imperiling human health and the natural environment. The papal observer was addressing a preparatory meeting of the World Summit on Sustainable Development, scheduled for Sept. 2002.

Roman Martyrology — After a two-decade revision, the new Vatican list of saints was released on Oct. 2. The work lists saints and blesseds by their feast days and is in Latin. It is expected that the various bishops' conferences will provide translations for their faithful. The martyrology was approved by Archbishop Francesco Pio Tamburrino, secretary of the Cong. for Divine Worship and the Sacraments.

Jerusalem Patriarch's Call — Jerusalem Latin-rite patriarch Michel Sabbah called upon the bishops of the Church on Oct. 3 to help humanity in the struggle against terrorism. He made the statement before Pope John Paul II and the nearly 250 bishops of the Vatican synod. Patriarch Sabbah said: "… the word of God starts from Jerusalem, war and peace also start from Jerusalem."

Former President Bush — Former U.S. Pres. George H. W. Bush met with Pope John Paul II at the Vatican on Oct. 4. The pope announced that the Vatican will join the prayer day on Oct. 11, and he assured former Pres. Bush that the synod of bishops, meeting in the Vatican at the time, "was feeling and living the suffering of the American people."

Pope as Model — Chaldean Archbishop Thomas Meram of Urmya, president of the bishops' conference of Iran, called Pope John Paul II a "living witness of happiness and hope." On Oct. 4, Archbishop Meram proposed the pope as a model for prelates attending the synod of bishops in Rome. Archbishop Meram added: "His presence gives spiritual peace and tranquility and causes in everyone an inner joy and hope. Why? Because you can feel the presence of Jesus Christ in the person of the Holy Father…."

Christian-Muslim Dialogue — The Holy Father received a telephone call from Iran's President Mohammed Khatami on Oct. 4, furthering Christian-Muslim dialogue. President Khatami expressed his hope that the Sept. 11 tragedy in New York would alert people of Islam and Christianity to the need for benevolent and close cooperation. He also stated that terrorist crimes have nothing to do with divine religions.

Respecting Eastern Heritage — Melkite Patriarch Gregoire III Laham of Antioch urged the synod of bishops on Oct. 4 to respect the traditions of Eastern Catholics. He stated that such reverence can enrich the entire church and aid unity with the Orthodox. Ukrainian Archbishop Stefan Soroka of Philadelphia added: "By valuing and preserving their ancient traditions and by promoting appreciation for the ancient heritage we share with our sister churches of the East, Eastern Catholic churches give tangible witness to the legitimate diversity that can and should exist within the Christian communion." Other Eastern leaders added their own comments to the subject.

Priestly Spirituality — Synod participants on Oct. 5 expressed concern about a lack of spirituality in many priestly formation programs and in adopted lifestyles. Some addressing the subject stressed the need for popular devotions in the seminary to foster intimate relationships with Christ. Others cited too much emphasis on social actions rather than spiritual maturity. Other matters discussed included liturgical translations, missionary assignments, and modern consumerist cultural tendencies.

Pope Beatifies Seven — On Oct. 8, Pope John Paul II beatified seven people. Among the new blesseds are: Sister Emilie Tavernier Gamelin, the foundress of the Canadian congregation, the Sisters of Providence; Ignatius Maloyan, an Armenian martyred by the Orttoman Turks in 1915; Nikolaus Gross, a German journalist who was tortured and slain by the Nazis in 1945; Eugenia Picco, who cared for the poor in World War II; Tommaso Maria Fusco, who founded a religious congregation for the care of orphans; Maria Euthymia Uffing, a German Mercy Sister who aided prisoners of war in World War II.

Pope Honors Annan — Pope John Paul II congratulated Kofi Annan, the U.N. Secretary-General, for receiving the Nobel Peace prize on Oct. 15. The pope wired his congratulations and his praise of the secretary-general's leadership in an era of international crises.

Papal Anniversary — On Oct. 16, the 23rd anniversary of his election as pontiff, Pope John Paul II was applauded by the members of the Synod of Bishops in Rome. Cardinal Bernard Agre of Abidjan, Ivory Coast, spoke for the synodal members, thanking the pope for being "a pilgrim of hope, a builder of dialogue and peace." The Vatican stated that Pope John Paul II has held 1,008 general audiences, with more than 16 million people attending. He also made 95 foreign trips and visited 128 countries.

Family Defense — Pope John Paul II called on the Church on Oct. 16 to launch a new series of initiations to defend the families of the world. Addressing the celebrations of the 20th Anniversary of *Familiaris Consortio*, the papal document dedicated to families, the pontiff sent a message to Cardinal Camillo Ruini. Pope John Paul II stated that family considerations should direct all political decisions. He added that the destiny of all people depends upon families.

Liturgical Responses — In a message to the Congregation for Divine Worship and Sacraments, released on Oct. 17, Pope John Paul II urged priests and the laity to display humility and reverence at the Mass celebration. He called for the transformation of all liturgies to reflect "a profound sense of the sacred."

Pope Pleads for Peace — Calling "in the name of God," Pope John Paul II begged for an end to violence in the Holy Land, it was announced on Oct. 17. The Holy Father mourned the death of 20 individuals in six Palestinian towns during an Israeli military operation. "War and death have arrived at the square of the Church of the nativity of Our Lord," the pope declared.

First Couple Beatified — On Oct. 21, Pope John Paul II beatified a married couple, the first wedded pair to be honored in the church's history. Luigi and Maria Beltrame Quattrocchi were beatified in St. Peter's Square, and they were called models for all Christians. The couple raised four children and lived during troubled times, having married in 1905. Luigi died in 1951, Maria in 1965.

Jordanian Visit — Prince El Hassan bin Talal of Jordan visited Pope John Paul II in the Vatican on Oct. 20. The prince supports Muslim-Christian dialogue and participated in the writing of "To Be a Muslim" by Alain Elkann. Prince El Hassan bin Talal is an uncle of Jordan's ruler, King Abdullah. He also gave an interview on Vatican Radio and took part in a meeting of Sant'Egidio Community, a Catholic organization that promotes interreligious dialogue for peace.

Vatican China Plea — Pope John Paul II apologized for any actions of Catholics in the past in a renewed plea for Vatican-Chinese dialogue. Addressing an Oct. 24 international conference in Rome celebrating the 400th anniversary of Jesuit Father Mateo Ricci's arrival in Beijing, the pontiff cited that missionary's courtesy and respect for the Chinese culture. Father Ricci is still honored in modern China.

Japanese Message — On Oct. 29, the new Japanese ambassador Mitsuhiro Nakamura met with Pope John Paul II at the Vatican. They discussed the present world condition and terrorism.

General Audience Topics:
• John Paul II Recalls Trip to Kazakstan and Armenia (Oct. 3).
• "God Wants to Make the Whole Man Happy" (Oct. 10).
• Evil Does Not Have the Last Word, John Paul II Says (Oct. 17).
• A Meditation on the *Miserere* (Oct. 24).
• Meditation at Audience Focuses on Isaiah 45. (Oct. 31).

International
Priest Released — Colombian Divine Word supe-

riors announced the release of Father Pavel Sochulak on Oct. 1. Colombian guerrillas had kidnapped the Divine Word missionary on Sept. 23. No word of the ransom payment to the National Arm of Liberation, one of the main guerrilla groups active in the region, was divulged. Father Sochulak was described as "safe and sound."

Terrorism Scapegoats — An international group of Christian and Muslim leaders attended a summit in Rome, Oct. 3-4, sponsored by the Rome-based Community of Sant'Egidio. The leaders warned against making all Muslims or members of a certain nation scapegoats for the terrorist attacks on the United States. Cardinal Roger Etchegaray, former president of the Pontifical Council for Justice and Peace, joined Muslim leaders in addressing the need for peace and good will between religious faiths. Cardinal Walter Kasper, president of the Pontifical Council for Promoting Christian Unity, also attended the summit.

Irish Abortion — The Irish government announced on Oct. 4 a referendum proposing to regulate and close a loophole in Irish law that allows abortion in cases where the mother threatens suicide. Cardinal Desmond Connell of Dublin has supported the wording of the referendum proposed by the Pro-Life Campaign. The new proposed legislation is designed to protect both women and the unborn. Ireland passed a constitutional amendment outlawing abortion in 1983.

Kazakstan Convert — On Oct. 9 Pope John Paul II received a letter from Sveta Barbassova, an interpreter for the papal visit to Kazakstan in September. Barbassova wrote that she had decided to be baptized into the Catholic Church. Pope John Paul II was the only Catholic encountered by Sveta, and her experience in his presence brought her to the faith. She was particularly moved by the Holy Father at an outdoor Mass in Astana, attended by 40,000 people.

Pakistani Protection — Pakistan President Pervez Musharraf promised on Oct. 9 to protect members of minority religious groups from Islamic fanatics. Catholic bishops and leaders met with Musharraf to express their appreciation following the Sept. 11 attacks in New York and received his assurances. The Pakistan government has placed police and military units at vulnerable sites to safeguard church properties and personnel.

Ecumenical Chapel — On Oct. 11, Catholic leaders welcomed the new ecumenical "Chapel for Europe," opened in Brussels, Belgium. Jesuit in origin, the new chapel serving staffers of the nearby European Union headquarters was prompted by Catholic concerns and a spirit of ecumenical openness.

Murderers Held — An El Salvador appeals court overturned a lesser court decision on Oct. 11 to recommend conditional parole for two convicted slayers of Maryknoll Sisters Ita Ford and Maureen Clark, Ursuline Sister Dorothy Kazel and lay missionary Jean Donovan in 1980. Three of the original five convicted slayers were released on conditional parole three years ago. The two being considered for parole now have been involved in prison offenses and disturbances.

Fátima Anniversary — About 200,000 people attended the Oct. 13 anniversary celebration at Fátima. The statue of the Virgin Mary was carried in procession to denote the 84th anniversary of the last Fátima apparitions in Portugal.

Priest Kidnapped — On Oct. 17, Sacred Heart of

Jesus Father Giuseppe Pierantoni was abducted in the southern Philippines. A missionary to Zamboanga del Sur, Fr. Pierantoni is expected to be "sold" to one of the major Islamic rebel groups on Mindanao. Fr. Pierantoni served the area for 10 years.

Cardinal Memorialized — The Church and government leaders in Poland are honoring Cardinal Stefan Wyszynski with a yearlong celebration, it was announced Oct. 19. The cardinal was a staunch foe of Communism, leading the Polish Catholics from 1949 until 1981. Pope John Paul II praised Cardinal Wyszynski for his "faith, heroic hope and limitless confidence in the Mother of God." The celebration will include conferences, exhibits, and school activities.

Patriarch Calls for Peace — Latin Patriarch Michel Sabbah of Jerusalem proclaimed the spiral of violence must end in a letter released on Oct. 21. "It is enough with the bloodshed; it is enough with the fighting," he declared. Bethlehem has been a pivotal site in the recent Palestinian-Israeli confrontation. Mayor Hanna Nasser, the mayor of Bethlehem, announced that life in the birthplace of Christ is now "overshadowed with fear, frustration and lack of food supplies, medicine, water, and fuel."

Counter Poverty — The Commission of Bishops' Conferences of the European Union, representing approximately 750 Catholic prelates, called for a global system to counter poverty. The report issued on Oct. 24 cited the September 11 terrorist attacks as a "decisive moment" in world affairs and stated that Pope John XXIII's plea for a "public authority with universal competence" (*Pacem in Terris*, 1963) was an inspiration. Various efforts and strategies for such programs were included in the report. The bishops said that the world and its peoples "need and deserve another, more coherent approach."

National

Messages of Condolence —Cardinals Theodore E. McCarrick of Washington and Edward Egan of New York received messages of condolence from over 80 prelates and public officials, it was announced on Oct. 1. The messages were sent after the terrorist attack on America on Sept. 11. Prelates from Jerusalem, Toronto, Northern Ireland, Nairobi, Kenya, Korea, Yugoslavia, England, Peru and France sent such messages. One of the most touching was the one-sentence e-mail from Cardinal Aloysius Ambrozic of Toronto that read: "Kindly allow us to join your tears and your prayers." The prelates attending the Synod of Bishops in Rome extended similar condolences. Cardinal Giovanni Battista Re stated: "We still have before our eyes the images of [New York's World Trade Center] twin towers collapsing after the gigantic terrorist attack."

New Catechism — A new catechism, compiled by Bishop Donald Wuerl of Pittsburgh, is being distributed by the publisher, Doubleday, it was announced on Oct. 1. The book, *The Catholic Way: Faith for Living Today*, is a paperback edition. Bishop Wuerl published the work to "translate" the teachings of the Church into popular language. The book evolved from a series composed for *Columbia* magazine over the past seven years and is being well received.

"Growing in Faith" — Archbishop Henry J. Flynn of the archdiocese of St. Paul and Minneapolis, said on Oct. 1 that the $115 million campaign "Growing in Faith" is about more than raising needed funds.

"Growing in Faith," the program instituted last fall in archdiocesan parishes, is designed to meet the ministerial, spiritual, and structural necessities and the challenges posed by an influx of immigrants into the cities. New parishes, education, and outreach projects will benefit. The program is also fostering a spiritual rebirth in the archdiocese.

Increasing Vocations — On Oct. 1, Fr. James Nash, vocations director of the diocese of Wilmington, Del., announced that the number of priestly vocations has tripled from five years ago. The diocese now educates the largest number of seminarians since 1985 and four other seminarians are expected to start priestly studies in the coming fall. The diocese serves the state of Delaware and nine counties on the eastern shore of Maryland. Fr. Nash credited the emphasis on vocations made by Bishop Michael A. Saltarelli and on an expanded awareness program and increased parental and family support.

Mother Angelica — Mother Angelica is back at work, it was announced on Oct. 1, after an absence of three weeks caused by a stroke. The founder of the Eternal Word Television Network in Birmingham, Alabama, is expected to recover fully. Mother Angelica, a 78-year-old Poor Clare of Perpetual Adoration, has been assured of her recovery.

Virginia History —A large volume that chronicles the Catholic Church in Virginia has been released. On Oct. 2, Bishop Walter F. Sullivan of Richmond, said that the book that he commissioned twelve years ago has been completed by Jesuit Father Gerlad P. Fogarty. The bishop describes the work as "a historical masterpiece." The book is titled *Commonwealth Catholicism: A History of the Catholic Church in Virginia*. It is available from Notre Dame Press.

U.N. Mass — On Oct. 1, a Mass for victims of the Sept. 11 attack on America was celebrated by Archbishop Renato R. Martino, the Vatican nuncio to the United Nations. The Mass commemorated all of the victims, with special attention to those of Italian ancestry. Giorgio Radicati, the Italian consul in New York and the Vatican U.N. mission, signified a new solidarity between Italy and the U.S., and honored New York Mayor Rudolph W. Giuliani, who addressed the U.N. General Assembly. Statements from the president and prime minister of Italy were also read.

Commitment to Life — October is designated as a time to confront contemporary culture with a recommitment to life, it was announced on Oct. 3. Cardinal William H. Keeler of Baltimore cited the response of Americans to the Sept. 11 attacks, pointing to acts that symbolized "humanity at its very best." Such activities define "the Christian message about human life in action." Respect Life Month is celebrated each year in October. Parishes, schools, and Catholic associations are receiving program materials.

Youth Prayer — Catholic young people in the United States are being urged to participate in organized prayer sessions, it was declared on Oct. 4. Such prayer sessions are scheduled for Oct. 11. The national Federation for Catholic Youth Ministry has prepared materials to aid organization of these gatherings. A theme, "We Remember, We Celebrate, We Believe," serves as a guide for the prayer services, which are nondenominational in many areas.

Vincent de Paul Society — On Oct. 4, the Society of St. Vincent de Paul issued an appeal for one million dollars to help victims of the Sept 11 terrorist attacks. The new campaign of the St. Louis-based society forwarded $125,000 to New York. Eugene B. Smith, national president of the 120,000 members, is directing the program. Last year, the society distributed $157 million in direct aid.

CARA Gathering — Fr. Paul J. Philibert addressed a group of Church leaders at the annual dinner of the Center for Applied Research in the Apostolate at Georgetown University on Oct. 3. Fr. Philibert described the new avenues of modern apostolates and the multiculturalism becoming evident in national parishes. American sociologist Fr. Raymond H. Potvin received the Louis J. Luzbetok Award from CARA at this event.

Bishops Enter Court Case — The U.S. Conference of Catholic Bishops filed an *amicus*, or friend of the court, brief in the case of Ernest McCarver's then-pending appeal before the U.S. Supreme Court, it was announced on Oct. 5. The American bishops opposed the right of civil authorities to execute mentally retarded individuals; another aspect is the constitutionality of school voucher programs; a third issue is the rights of migrant workers.

Cardinal Support War on Terror — Four cardinals of the United States announced measured support for the retaliatory military campaigns, adding concerns for the protection of innocents. Cardinal Theodore E. McCarrick of Washington, D.C., Cardinal Bernard F. Law of Boston, Cardinal Anthony J. Bevilacqua of Philadelphia, and Cardinal Adam J. Maida of Detroit prayed for the American service men and women in separate statements, released on Oct. 7 and 8.

Catholic-Jewish Accord — The Catholic Diocese of Camden and the southern New Jersey Jewish community leaders signed an agreement of cooperation, it was announced on Oct. 9. Bishop Nicholas A. DiMarzio of Camden and diocesan officials represented Catholics, and Michael Partnow, president of the Jewish Federation of Southern New Jersey, and the heads of other Jewish organizations signed the accord as well. The agreement promotes freedom of religion and conscience, cooperation in defending against bias and intolerance, the promotion of moral values in public education, and programs to discourage violence and prejudice. The Catholics and Jews of Rochester, New York, signed a similar pact in 1996.

Anti-Catholicism Probed — The nomination of John M. Klink as an assistant in the State Department by President George W. Bush appears to have released a firestorm of anti-Catholic protests by refugee advocates, it was announced on Oct. 9. Klink served with Catholic Relief Services, 1976-1986 and represented the Vatican at UNICEF from 1988-1999 and at the Cairo Conference in 1994. Critics rallied against Klink's Catholic connections and his stand on contraception, abortion, and related issues. Klink, who is a Knight of Malta and a Knight of the Holy Sepulchre, withdrew from the nomination.

Nuncio to the U.N. — Archbishop Renato Martino, the nuncio of the Holy See to the United Nations, announced on Oct. 9 that the horrors of Sept. 11 make people "realize the frailty of life." Addressing the U.N. General Assembly, Archbishop Martino continued his advocacy of the promotion and protection of the rights of children.

Russians at Catholic Hospital — A 10-member delegation from Russia, including six physicians and four health care administrators, toured St. Cloud Hospital, St. Benedict's Senior Community, and other sites in St. Cloud on Oct. 10. The physicians and administrators studied Church-related health facilities, planning to resurrect Russian charitable health services. Presently, three-quarters of Russian physicians are women.

Lumen Christi Award — The 2001 *Lumen Christi* Award, presented by the Catholic Extension of Chicago, was bestowed upon 91-year-old Marie Wilkinson on Oct. 11. She has served educational programs, migrant worker projects, and other charitable and advocacy measures over the years.

Basilica Renovation — The basilica of the national Shrine of the Immaculate Conception, Washington, D.C., announced on Oct. 15 that the first stages of pipe organ renovations have started. The organ, the largest in Washington, will undergo a four to eight year upgrading and repair.

World Food Day — The annual celebration of World Food Day, held on Oct. 16, will demonstrate the enormity of world hunger. An estimated 800 million people are chronically undernourished in the world. Events scheduled for World Food Day will provide speeches, films, communications, and promotions concerning international hunger. Patricia Young is the national coordinator of the U.S. National Committee for World Food Day.

Catholic Charities — Sharon Daly, Catholic Charities USA vice-president, testified on Oct. 11 before the U.S. Senate Finance Committee, relating the needs of the poor to the events of Sept. 11. Catholic Charities USA has submitted its economic and domestic relief programs and has asked for responsive national legislation. Tax relief, child support programs, child welfare, unemployment benefits, and access to Medicaid and state health insurance were all part of Catholic Charities USA's concepts for economical and social recovery.

Basilica Praised — On Oct. 17, Pope John Paul II cited the Basilica of the National Shrine of the Assumption of the Blessed Virgin Mary in Baltimore as "a worldwide symbol of religious freedom." The nearly 200-year old basilica is undergoing extensive restoration and renovation projects, according to Cardinal William H. Keeler of Baltimore. That city became the first U.S. diocese in 1789. Completion of restoration projects is scheduled for 2006.

Media Evangelization — On Oct. 19, Archbishop Patrick F. Flores addressed a San Antonio gathering of Catholic communicators and urged them to spread the faith with the dedication of the Franciscan missionaries of the past. The meeting was sponsored by UNDA-USA, the organization for Catholic radio and broadcasters and communication directors for local churches.

Baptist Catholic Dialogue — The U.S. Conference of Catholic Bishops and the Baptist Interfaith Witness Department announced the end of their current series of ecumenical discussions on Oct. 23. The series of conversations opened in 1995, and the ending should not be viewed as a sign of diminished commitment to ecumenical understanding. Other programs in social services, public policy concerns, and educational projects will continue.

NOVEMBER 2001

Vatican

All Saints — Pope John Paul II offered special prayers for the victims of recent violence while celebrating the feast of All Saints' on Nov. 1 and the feast of All Souls' on Nov. 2. The pope promised that he would also ask the Lord to comfort those bereaved because of recent tragedies.

Fátima Book — The Vatican announced Nov. 2 that it is publishing a work by Carmelite Sister Lucia dos Santos, the last surviving Fátima visionary. Sr. Lucia finished writing the meditations that comprise the book last summer, and a Portuguese translation was issued in summer 2001. Called *The Appeals of the Message of Fátima*, the book was also released in Italian. No release date for an English-language edition was disclosed.

Papal Films — Two recent popes will be depicted in movies now in production, it was reported Nov. 2. Veteran English actor Bob Hoskins and American actor Ed Asner will portray Pope Blessed John XXIII in separate films, scheduled to air as TV miniseries. The Greek director Constantin Costa-Gouras is also shooting a film attacking Pope Pius XII. This film is based on the book by German playwright Rolf Hochhuth, called an atrocious calumny by Catholic scholars.

Bulgarian Visit — Pope John Paul II will visit Bulgaria in May 2002, it was announced on Nov. 1. Solomon Pasi, the Bulgarian Foreign Minister, also said that he had received confirmation of the papal visit from the apostolic nuncio in Sofia, Archbishop Antonio Mennini. Such a visit is sought by the Bulgarians, still defending themselves against charges that they were involved in the 1981 assassination attempt on Pope John Paul II.

Beatified Honored — On Nov. 4, Pope John Paul II beatified eight priests and religious in Rome. The newly beatified included Bishop Pavol Peter Gojdic and Redemptorist priest Metod Dominik Trcka, both martyrs of the Communists. Others were Maria Pilar Izquierdo Albero, Gaetana Sterni, Paolo Manna, Luigi Tezza, Giovanni Antonio Farina, and Bartolomeu Fernandes dos Mártires. The pope called the new beati "living signs of God's love."

Papal Letter — Pope John Paul II sent a message, released on Nov. 5, to the pilgrims celebrating the centenary of the consecration of Our Lady of the Rosary Basilica in Lourdes. The Holy Father encouraged the pilgrims to pray the rosary to obtain a deeper knowledge of Christ. The French bishops attended the celebrations. Pope John Paul II called the basilica a "living parable of stone and light ... revealing the profound meaning of the rosary."

Evangelizing the Internet — On Nov. 6, it was announced by Archbishop John P. Foley that Pope John Paul II has chosen the Internet as a tool of evangelization. The theme, "Internet: A New Forum for Proclaiming the Gospel," will be used at the World Communications Day 2002. The communications observance is celebrated in most dioceses in May. (See **Special Reports**.)

Vatican Adopts Euro — It was announced on Nov. 7 that the Vatican will end minting the Vatican lira and will adopt the euro. The lira was used through six pontificates: Pius XI, Pius XII, John XXIII, Paul VI, John Paul I and John Paul II. The last lire denominations of coins have been issued, with runs of 26,000 each.

Papal Cartoon — Pope John Paul II is the subject of a new cartoon film, it was revealed on Nov. 6. This animated film was presented at the Genzano International Festival of Animated Cartoons. It is a homage to the pope and narrates his human and spiritual journey. The Italian artist, Mario Verger, conceived the idea.

Cultural Threats — The pope announced the members of the pontifical academies on Nov. 8 that globalization will have "human, cultural, and spiritual" implications on nations. The economy and the media can reduce human beings to market variables without identities. Cultures that give in to markets and fashions will lose their own originality and richness. The Holy Father said that "a careful and profound intellectual and theological discernment of the anthropological-cultural paradigm" are produced by the new globalization challenging concepts. He stated: "It is necessary to conquer all fear and address these challenges, trusting in the light and strength of the Spirit that the risen Lord continues to give to his Church."

True Religion — On Nov. 9, while addressing the Pontifical Council for Interreligious Dialogue, Pope John Paul II said that the tragedy of Sept. 11 must not be called "a veritable clash of religions." He said also: "A vital task before us is to show how religious belief inspires peace, encourages solidarity, promotes justice and upholds liberty."

U.N. Manual — The Vatican is protesting a United Nations field manual, it was announced on Nov. 9. U.N. personnel working with refugees are directed to promote abortion, contraception, and homosexual behavior. This manual was published in 1999 by the U.N. High Commissioner for Refugees. Vatican officials have noted that sterilization is presented as a simple form of contraception. Bishops have been alerted to this U.N. policy, especially as it impacts on adolescent development.

Pope Blesses Firefighters — A group of New York City firefighters met with Pope John Paul II on Nov. 10, and presented him with the helmet that belonged to Franciscan Fr. Mychal Judge, the fire department chaplain who died on Sept. 11 while administering the last rites to a fireman. The pope celebrated a Mass in St. Peter's Basilica and prayed for the heroic firefighters who died in that tragedy. Daniel Nigro, the newly appointed chief of the fire department, was among those attending the Mass in Rome.

Catholic Duties — Pope John Paul II met on Nov. 10 with bishops from Malaysia, Singapore and Brunei. The Holy Father also announced that Catholics have a duty to promote peace and human rights, working with other faiths. Each Catholic must be well-educated in the faith in order to defend Catholic beliefs and to recognize mutually shared values with other religions.

NATO at Vatican — Pope John Paul II met with uniformed members of the NATO Defense College on Nov. 14 at the Vatican. He urged the NATO personnel to serve peace and the common good in this era of turmoil. The pope recommended St. Albert the Great to the young people present in the audience, citing him as an agent of justice and reconciliation.

Family Role — Pope John Paul II met with the bishop of Thailand on Nov.16, addressing the problems of sexual exploitation in that nation. The pope recommended supporting families as the best antidote. Thailand is one of the world's sexual tourism destinations, resulting in the nation having the largest proportion of AIDS patients in Southeast Asia.

Pope Salutes Signis — Pope John Paul II met with members of Signis, the Catholic media association resulting from the fusion of the OCIC, the international Catholic media organizations of film, video, audio-visual, and UNDA (radio and television), on Nov. 20. He expressed hope that Signis would expand and influence evangelization through the media. Some 450 communicators participated in the Vatican Clementine Hall meeting with the pope. An international congress in Rome created Signis.

Video Conference — The Vatican announced on Nov. 20 that the Congregation for the Clergy would sponsor a video conference on "The Eschatology of Vatican Council II in Our Days" on Nov. 29. A theological debate on life after death will be the principal topic. The debate is available at www.clerus.org. *RealPlayer* is necessary to view the debate.

Internet Pope — Pope John Paul II made history on Nov. 22 when he published an official document on the Internet. The document, *Ecclesia in Oceania* ("The Church in Oceania"), was sent to the e-mail addresses of the dioceses of Oceania when the pope pressed the button to send the electronic message. Cardinals, bishops, priests, and religious were present in the Vatican Clementine Hall for this historic event.

Priest Pastors — Meeting with the plenary assembly of the Vatican Congregation for the Clergy on Nov. 23, Pope John Paul II stated that only an ordained minister can be a parish priest, although he encouraged lay collaboration in parishes. The plenary assembly had been called to discuss the topic, "The Priest: Pastor and Guide of the Parish Community." The pope warned against any activities that diminish the authority of the parish priest.

Canonizations — Pope John Paul canonized a bishop and three religious on Nov. 25: Giuseppe Marello (1844-1895), the founder of the Congregation of Oblates of St. Joseph; Paula Montal Fornés de San José de Calasanz (1799-1889), founder of the Institute of the Daughters of Mary (Pious Schools); Léonie Françoise de Sales Aviat (1844-1914), founder of the Congregation of Religious Oblates of St. Francis of de Sales; Maria Crescentia Höss (1682-1744), a religious of the Third Order of St. Francis. They were all canonized in St. Peter's basilica. The pope called them exemplary witnesses of evangelical life." (See under **Saints** for biographical information.)

General Audience Topics:

- Psalm 99[100]: A Hymn of Thanksgiving (Nov. 7).
- Meditation on Psalm 118[119] (Nov. 14).
- Meditation on Chapter of Exodus (Nov. 21).
- Meditation on the Shortest Psalm (Nov. 28).

International

Kenya Missions — Irish president Mary McAleese visited the Catholic missions in Kenya, it was announced Nov. 2, praising the missionaries, whom she called "Ireland's greatest unpaid ambassadors." President McAleese met modern Holy Ghost Fathers and toured the gravesite of Edel Quinn, the Legion of Mary lay missionary who died of tuberculosis in Nairobi's St. Mary's School. McAleese also visited Turkana and Bishop Patrick Harrington and was greeted by Carmelite Father Robert McCabe, who served on the Ethiopian border.

Chinese Clinic — China has allowed a Catholic religious congregation to open a facility for terminally ill patients, it was announced Nov. 4. The Hospitaller Order of St. John of God will open a center in the province of Jinin. An estimated 3,000 Chinese suffer from cancer in the city of Yanji. Five Hospitallers will operate the facility. The Chinese visited the Congregation's center for terminally ill cancer patients in the Korean city of Kwangju and were impressed enough to invite the Hospitallers to Jinin province.

Egyptian Trial — A new trial for 96 Egyptians accused of the January 2000 massacre of Christians and one Muslim was declared on Nov. 5. Twenty Coptic Christians were slain in the village of el-Kasheh, and the trial is taking place in the court at Sohaq. The court has to bring in the accused for the trial, as 15 of the 96 accused failed to appear in court. The accused are Muslims and Coptic Christians.

Abortion Debate — A new abortion law in France is being opposed by doctors, it was revealed Nov. 7. A doctor stated: "The law is the law, but the stomach rebels." The new abortion law became effective on July 7. Originally supportive of the law, French medical practitioners are now voicing opposition on moral, scientific and legal grounds.

"The Work" — The community founded in Belgium in 1938 by Mother Julia Verhaeghs has received pontifical recognition, it was announced on Nov. 9. Cardinal Joseph Ratzinger will celebrate a Mass in St. Peter's Basilica in thanksgiving for this new pontifical institute. The Work is based on biblical, sacramental, and ecclesial traditions and serves consecrated women, priests, deacons, and lay brothers. Mother Julia was inspired by the thoughts and writings of Cardinal John Henry Newman, the 19th century English convert to Catholicism.

Forum on Migration — The annual Caritas Europa Forum on Migration met on Nov. 9 in Prague to focus on ways to combat the trafficking and smuggling of human beings in the world. The three-day session heard reports on the estimated half million migrants smuggled into Western Europe.

Sant'Egidio Honored — The community of Sant'Egidio, a public association of laymen, has been proposed for the Nobel Peace prize, it was announced on Nov. 9. Founded in 1968 by Professor Andrea Riccardi and having 40,000 members in 60 countries, the community has been involved in projects and peace initiatives. Some 30 Italian parliamentarians requested that the Italian government present the candidacy of the Catholic movement officially.

Martyrs of Bahawalpur — The Catholic bishops of Pakistan issued a pastoral letter, it was revealed on Nov. 11, to honor the Christians and a Muslim slain in Bahawalpur at St. Dominic's Catholic Church. The letter reassured the Catholic minority of the country and asked for progress, prosperity, and peace. The Catholics and Muslim were slain by Islamic fundamentalists. Archbishop Paul Josef Cordes, a Special Envoy of Pope John Paul II, was in Pakistan soon after the massacre in Bahawalpur to demonstrate the pontiff's concerns and prayers. He read a message of condolence at the funeral of the martyrs. Critically injured survivors are in a hospital.

French Catholics — A survey revealed Nov. 13 indicates that only one in 10 Catholics in France attends Mass on Sundays. Declines in vocations are also evident, with fewer than 10,000 priests anticipated in 2003, compared to 45,000 in 1945. Adult baptisms, however, average 9,000 annually, and priestly ordinations increased in 2000 and 2001. Also noted were heavy increases in the numbers of French making retreats and visits to local monasteries and convents.

Iran President — Muhammad Khatami, the president of the Islamic Republic of Iran, addressed an inter-religious meeting at Seton Hall University in New Jersey, on Nov. 9. The session was part of the U.N. program called "Dialogue Among Civilizations," a program started by Khatami. He told his audience that the world is weary of war and violence. Cardinal Theodore E. McCarrick joined President Khatami in the meeting.

Panama TV — The Catholic Church in Panama is building the largest TV channel in Central America, it was announced on Nov. 12. The channel will cost $6.3 million and will sponsor live broadcasts from three studios. FETV-Channel 5 will be operational by February.

Missionary Freed — Fr. Giuseppe Pierantoni, an Italian Dehonian missionary in the Philippines, was freed by former members of the Moro Islamic Liberation Front, it was announced on Nov. 14. Muslims and Christians had worked together to effect this release. He was kidnapped by the Islamic group on Mindanao on Oct. 17. The kidnappers have become a kidnap-for-ransom group.

Senegal Ambush — Father Simeon Coly, a priest of the Casamance region of Senegal, was shot dead on Nov. 7 during an ambush on a bus. He was 40 and a parish priest, as well as director of the diocesan committee for Christian-Muslim relations. A rebel group claimed responsibility.

Franciscan Habits — The Franciscans of Assisi, Italy, have asked Elizabeth Bianchetti, a Milan fashion designer, to create new habits. The new religious garb is made of charcoal gray lightweight wool and was designed with breast pockets to hold mobile telephones. A debate in Assisi was sparked by the new habits.

Namibian Aid — The Namibian Catholic Bishops' Conference announced the launching of the Catholic Health Services Campaign on Nov. 20. Three dioceses are integrating their resources to improve care quality in this southern African nation.

Buddhist Converts — It was revealed on Nov. 22 that thousands of Dalit caste Hindus in India had renounced that religion and converted to Buddhism. The Dalits, the lower caste members, called untouchables and forced to assume degrading, menial labors for upper castes, were led by Udit Raj in their conversions. Raj gave up his Hindu name, Ram, on Nov. 4, taking Udit, meaning rebel. The mass conversion took place in New Delhi. The ceremony was an act of protest against the inequality and discrimination suffered by the lower castes in Indian society.

Nuns Targeted — The Missionaries of Charity of Calcutta founded by Mother Teresa, have been targeted by two Muslim groups linked to the al-Qaeda terrorist network, it was announced on Nov. 30. *Vidimus Dominum*, the information service of religious communities, verified the reports of the planned attacks on the sisters that were published in the local newspapers. The attacks are planned because the groups believe the missionaries receive U.S. funds to convert Muslims to Christianity.

National

Marianist Provincial — Marianist Brother Stephen Glodek has been appointed the first provincial of the new Marianist Province of the United States of America, it was announced on Nov. 1. A native of Chester, Pa., he also served as immediate past president of the Conference of major Superiors of Men.

Mail Resumed — The U.S. Conference of Catholic Bishops resumed mail service on Nov. 1, following the discovery of anthrax at the main Brentwood mail center of Washington, D.C. Deliveries were resumed at all areas, including the USCCB building.

Cardinal Bernardin Award — Jean Souffrant, a young Haitian-American Catholic of Miami, was named on Nov. 2 as the recipient of the Cardinal Bernardin New Leadership Award by the Catholic Campaign for Human Development, the national anti-poverty program of the U.S. Conference of Catholic Bishops. Jean Souffrant, 23, is a volunteer worker and youth minister in his parish and in Miami-Dade County. He arrived in the U.S. in 1991.

Stem-Cell Symposium — Archbishop Rembert G. Weakland of Milwaukee addressed a symposium on stem-cell research, it was announced on Nov. 2. The symposium was sponsored by the Jesuit Marquette University, the Archdiocese of Milwaukee and the Wisconsin Catholic Conference, with some 70 bishops, philosophers, scientists, and theologians. The symposium addressed the scientific breakthroughs and the ethical and moral issues accompanying them.

Blue Army Co-Founder — It was announced on Nov. 6 that John Mathias Haffert, co-founder of the Blue Army of Our Lady of Fátima, died on Oct. 31 from cancer. He was 86. A funeral Mass was celebrated for him on Nov. 3 in the Blessed Shrine of the Immaculate Heart of Mary in Washington. Carmelite Sr. Lucia dos Santos, the last surviving Fátima visionary, aided Haffert in developing the Blue Army Pledge in 1946. He hosted a television program and wrote extensively about Fátima.

Children Protected — Carmelite Sisters in East Chicago, Indiana, have undertaken the care of children of arrested individuals at Holy Innocents Center at the Carmelite Home for Girls in the area. The center can handle five children at a time, it was disclosed on Nov. 6. The children are referred to the Carmelites by the Indiana Department of Family and Children Services when their parents are arrested.

Ecumenical Patroness — St. Elizabeth Ann Seton has been chosen by the New York Catholic and Episcopal pastors as a "bridge" between their parishes. Fr. Peter K. Meehan, pastor of Our Lady of the Rosary Church and the Shrine of St. Elizabeth Ann Seton, received word of thanks from Rev. Daniel Paul Matthews, rector of Trinity Episcopal Church, on Nov. 4. Trinity parishioners have been holding services at Our Lady of the Rosary Church since the attack on the World Trade Center. The historic Episcopal Church was not damaged in the attack but was closed to the public after Sept. 11. Trinity Episcopal Church reopened on Nov. 4.

Praise for Ashcroft — Bishop Joseph A Fiorenza, then president of the U.S. Conference of Catholic Bishops, praised Attorney General John Ashcroft's policy of active prosecution of medical personnel assisting in patient suicides. In a letter to the Drug Enforcement Administration, released on Nov. 6, Ashcroft reversed former Attorney General Janet Reno's order of June 1998 that halted federal prosecutions of doctors who prescribed lethal doses under Oregon's assisted suicide law.

Pontifical Award — Pia de Solenni, a 29-year old American native of Crescent City, California, now residing in Washington, was awarded the 2001 Pontifical Academies' Prize by Pope John Paul II on Nov. 8. A $30,000 research grant comes with the award, which was given to Pia de Solenni for her work in Thomistic theology as it relates to modern feminism. She earned her doctorate from the University of the Holy Cross, sponsored by Opus Dei in Rome.

Campus Ministry — Bishop John M. D'Arcy of Fort Wayne-South Bend, Indiana, has been declared the annual Campus Ministry Exemplary Bishop, it was announced on Nov. 8 by the U.S. Conference of Catholic Bishops. Bishop D'Arcy has been active in establishing a Catholic presence in the state's colleges.

Catholic Relief — Catholic Relief Services is seeking $50 million for Afghan refugees and displaced persons according to a Nov. 9 statement. The agency hopes to aid some 100,000 Afghans immediately and 300,000 Afghans in the near future. CRS has an operation in Kabul and hopes to augment present programs with new supplies and services.

Retired Religious — The U.S. Conference of Catholic Bishops announced on Nov. 8 that Martin Sheen will do public service ads on radio and television to promote the yearly Catholic collection for retired religious. The collection was taken up in Catholic parishes across the U.S. on Dec. 8 and 9.

Msgr. Higgins Honored — Msgr. George Higgins was honored on Nov. 10 as America's foremost labor priest by 150 bishops, friends, and union leaders. The tribute was co-sponsored by the AFL-CIO and the U.S. Conference of Catholic Bishops and raised funds for the National Interfaith Committee for Worker Justice. Msgr. Higgins, 85, served the bishops' conference for 36 years in the fields of social action.

USCCB Meeting — On Nov. 12 the fall meeting of the U.S. Conference of Catholic Bishops opened in Washington, D.C. The meeting began by noting the mandate given to bishops to preach a message of hope amid the "destructive power of hate" loose in the world. Bishop Joseph Fiorenza, outgoing conference president, opened the sessions. Archbishop Gabriel Montalvo, apostolic nuncio to the U.S., also addressed the bishops, praising Americans for their solidarity following terrorist attacks. (See **News in Depth** for further details.)

New USCCB President — The election of Bishop Wilton D. Gregory, of Belleville, Ill., as president of the U.S. Conference of Catholic Bishops, the first African-American president on Nov. 13, is a sign of a new focus. Bishop Gregory said that he hopes his election demonstrates the American Church's commitment to policies of inclusiveness and multi-culturalism. He was elected on the first ballot. Bishop Gregory, who

served as vice-president of the USCCB for the past three years, is a Catholic convert from Chicago.

Catholic Charities — The Catholic Charities USA Fund to aid survivors of the Sept. 11 terrorist attacks has collected $14 million to date, it was announced on Nov. 13. These funds will address long-term problems and will aid 13 dioceses in the immediate vicinity of New York City.

Bishops' Mass — On Nov. 12, the U.S. bishops celebrated Mass in conjunction with their annual fall meeting in Washington, D.C., despite interruptions. A representative of the Women's Ordination Conference and a protester both interrupted the liturgy and were escorted from the basilica.

Catholic Digest — The University of St. Thomas, St. Paul, Minn., announced on Nov. 12 that it is selling the *Catholic Digest*, the largest paid-circulation Catholic magazine in America. Bayard, U.S.A., is the largest Catholic publisher in the world, located in Mystic, Conn., will purchase the magazine. Bayard is owned by the Congregation of the Augustinians of the Assumption. The sale was to be completed by the end of the year.

Bishop Chairmen — The U.S. bishops elected chairmen for nine national committees on Nov. 13 in Washington, D.C., during their annual meeting. The bishops also used an electronic voting system for the first time in order to speed up elections and tabulations. Bishops from across the nation chair the committees that function as part of the USCCB.

Liturgical Rules — On Nov. 13, the Catholic bishops of the U.S. discussed the new Vatican norms for liturgical translations during their annual fall meeting in Washington, D.C. The norms are contained in *Liturgiam Authenticam*, issued by the Congregation for Divine Worship and the Sacraments. The translation of the liturgy into local languages and the structures of international liturgical translation commissions are covered by the new norms.

Catholic Universities — Cardinal Avery Dulles challenged Catholic universities and colleges to proclaim their religious identities with enthusiasm. Receiving the John Henry Newman Award on Nov. 14, Cardinal Dulles said that American Catholic universities should end their apologetic approach to secular institutions and proudly proclaim the faith and abandon defensive positions. The Cardinal's award was bestowed by the Cardinal Newman Society, a group attempting to reverse secularism in the nation's institutions of Catholic education.

Bishops Pro-Life — On Nov. 14, the U.S. bishops at their meeting in Washington, D.C., approved a new pastoral Plan for Pro-Life Activities by a vote of 233-2. The new plan updates a 1985 program and concerns new areas such as stem-cell research and assisted suicides. The bishops hope to promote a consistent ethic of life in the U.S. Church. Another threat to human life being considered by the new plan is partial birth abortions and incorporates Pope John Paul II's encyclical *Evangelium Vitae*.

Day of Prayer — The U.S. bishops at their meeting in Washington, D.C., voted on Nov. 16 to designate Jan. 1, 2002, as a national day of prayer for peace as a response to Sept. 11. The Knights of Columbus in Kansas offered to fund devotional resources for this day of prayer. A "Rosary for Peace" has also been provided by the USCCB liturgical committee.

DECEMBER 2001

Vatican

Advent Aspirations — Pope John Paul II met with thousands of pilgrims on Dec. 2 to announce that Christians should prepare during Advent for Christmas, not as people awaiting "a faceless God," but with "concrete trust" in a loving God. The pilgrims were in St. Peter's Square to pray the Angelus.

Donations Planned — It was announced on Dec. 2 that the donations resulting from the Day of Fasting and Prayer, to be held on Dec. 14, will be distributed to victims of terrorism and war. *Cor Unum*, a Pontifical Council that coordinates charitable projects of the Church worldwide, will direct the distribution. Pope John Paul II proposed a day of fasting to make funds available to the poor, and to the sufferers of "the consequences of terrorism and war."

Domestic Refugees — On Dec. 2, Archbishop Renato Martino, permanent observer to the United Nations for the Holy See, expressed Pope John Paul II's concern for the 3.5 million refugees. Archbishop Martino encouraged the U.N. High Commission for Refugees to continue to aid the refugees, and to offer security and humanitarian aid, basic elements of caring for such displaced persons.

Polish Praise — Pope John Paul II, welcoming Poland's new ambassador to the Holy See on Dec. 3, praised Poland's economic and political progress since 1989 collapse of communism. The pope said that Poles should not be tempted to sideline the nation's thousand year tradition of the faith.

Gypsies and Nomads — Pope John Paul II praised the nomad populations of the world on Dec. 3. He extolled as well the gypsies, who defy modern consumerism. The pope addressed members of the Catholic Worldwide National Directors and Experts on the Pastoral Care of Nomads. These participants were invited to the international study by the Pontifical Council for the Pastoral Care of Migrants and Travelers. The pope stated that such nomadic populations "have found a place in the heart of the Church" since the pontificate of Pope Paul VI.

Volunteers Bring Hope — On Dec. 5, Pope John Paul II said that the volunteers are "a sign of hope" for this modern age, citing Maximilian Kolbe and Mother Teresa of Calcutta as the ultimate expressions of Christian commitments. The pope stated that as a volunteer, the Christian becomes a witness of divine love for the world. He addressed the close of the U.N. International Year of Volunteers.

Priestly Offenses — The Congregation for the Doctrine of the Faith took control of priestly pedophilia cases on Dec. 4 when a new set of norms was issued, giving the doctrinal congregation juridical authority over such cases. With these norms, the Vatican moved to centralize procedures and oversight on sexual abuse cases. Outlined in a letter to the world's bishops, the new procedures require local bishops to report probable cases of clerical sexual abuse against minors to the Holy See's doctrinal congregation. This congregation will then decide upon a proper course of action concerning diocesan tribunals or the congregation's tribunals. Cardinal Joseph Ratzinger heads the Congregation for the Doctrine of the Faith. (See **News in Depth** for further details.)

New Ambassadors — Pope John Paul II welcomed 10 new ambassadors to the Vatican on Dec. 6, receiving letters of credence from the representatives of Bangladesh, Djibouti, Eritrea, Finland, Georgia, Lesotho, Mali, Mauritius, Rwanda, and Switzerland. The pope asked the assembled diplomats and others around the world to foster peace on earth by overcoming poverty and the lack of education in many regions of the globe.

Fasting For Peace — Pastoral guidelines were issued on Dec. 6 by the Vatican for the Dec. 14 Day of Fasting and Prayer for Peace. Pope John Paul II called for this celebration and also initiated a major interfaith prayer gathering on Jan. 24 in Assisi. Children and the elderly can take part in this observance, as a variety of fasting methods are provided.

Turkey's Role — On Dec. 7, Pope John Paul II greeted the new ambassador for the Vatican from Turkey and delineated a unique role for that nation in modern times. The pope said that Turkey is a bridge between the Christian and Muslim worlds. Turkey is a Muslim nation with enduring ties to Christian history.

Pope's Christmas — The papal schedule for Christmas was released on Dec. 7 by the Vatican, revealing that Pope John Paul II would preside over the traditional liturgical celebrations. The papal program was published by the Office for Liturgical Celebrations of the Supreme Pontiff.

Renewed Holiness — Pope John Paul II proclaimed on Dec. 7 that holiness is the priority for Christians. Meeting with the Rogationists, the spiritual successors of Blessed di Francia, the pope declared that holiness is possible at this difficult time. He referred as well to the apostolic letter, *Tertio Millennio Ineunte*.

Saint Clement — On Dec. 7, it was announced that recent findings indicate that the Roman Catholic and Russian Orthodox Churches are linked by St. Clement, the second Bishop of Rome. St. Clement's Institute, the Pontifical Academy "Cultorum Martyrum" and the Pontifical Oriental Institute held an international congress on this pope, studying the continuing influence of St. Clement.

Weapons Against Hatred — On Dec. 9, Pope John Paul II declared that fasting and prayer are weapons that will overcome the hatred and violence of the modern age. Greeting pilgrims gathered in St. Peter's Square to recite the Angelus, the pontiff urged the faithful to mobilize energies so that love, peace, truth and forgiveness could triumph over hatred, war, falsehood, and revenge.

Immaculate Conception — Pope John Paul II entrusted the peace of the modern world to the Immaculate Conception on Dec. 9. In Rome's Piazza di Spagna, the pope recited a prayer on his knees before a statue of the Virgin Mary as the Immaculate Conception. More than 10,000 people attended the ceremony including city officials. The pope declared that dark clouds gather on the world horizon and that the faithful need to turn to the Immaculate Virgin.

Clergy Website — On Dec. 9, it was revealed that the Vatican has launched a web site dedicated to the ongoing formation of the clergy. "Missio-clerus.org Off Line" is a program that allows an individual to work within the electronic library at www.clerus.org without being connected to the Internet. Users may conduct research, reading the file of documents, articles, and books; finding the required page, the user can connect to the Internet and download the material desired. Books and documents are available in five languages.

Guadalupe Web Site — On Dec. 12, Pope John Paul II formally launched the official web site of Mexico's Basilica of Our Lady of Guadalupe on his laptop computer. The site can be visited at www.virgendeguadalupe.org.mx. The pope opened the web site at the end of his general audience.

Romanian Tree — Pope John Paul II accepted an 82-foot Christmas tree from Romanian president Ion Iliescu, on Dec. 17. The tree was from the forests of Transylvania and remained decorated during the holy season. On the same evening, the Romanian president and two Romanian bishops returned to the Vatican to hear two Romanian choirs. Cardinal Edmund C. Szoka, the American governor of the Vatican City State, welcomed the dignitaries as the tree was lighted.

New Saints — On Dec. 20, Pope John Paul II ordered the publication of decrees clearing the way for the canonizations of Blesseds Juan Diego, Padre Pio, and Josemaria Escriva de Balaguer, founder of Opus Dei. The decree lists miracles related to the intercessory prayers of the three blesseds. Dates will be set for the canonizations in early 2002. (See under **Saints** for other details.)

Papal Journey — On Dec. 21, Pope John Paul II told the new ambassador to the Holy See from Bulgaria that he would like to celebrate the Orthodox feast of St. Cyril and Methodius, May 24, in Bulgaria. The pope defined his intended visit as part of his ongoing pilgrimage to the origins of Christian communities.

Christmas Feast — On Dec. 21, it was announced that Sant'Egidio Community, a Rome-based lay group, will host a Christmas lunch for 1,500 poor, homeless and lonely in the Basilica of Santa Maria in Trastevere. Cardinal Roger Etchegeray, the former president of the Pontifical Council for Justice and Peace, will welcome the luncheon guests.

Roman Curia — Pope John Paul II met with the Roman Curia on Dec. 22 to review the pastoral achievements of the year, darkened by terrorism and war. The pope listed meetings with prelates from around the world, a consistory in February, a special consistory in May, a synod of bishops in October and his three foreign trips. Several hundred Vatican officials attended this meeting.

Victim Funds — People participating in the day of fasting and prayer on Dec. 14, as requested by Pope John Paul II, sent more than $650,000 to the Vatican to aid victims of war and terrorism, it was announced on Dec. 24. The Pontifical Council *Cor Unum* will distribute the funds.

New Year Goals — Pope John Paul II, addressing visitors to St. Peter's Square on Dec. 30, asked the faithful to put aside anger and to begin the New Year with thanks for the blessings they have received. The pope asked everyone to begin 2002 in the love and peace of Christ.

General Audience Topics:

• Christ Is Only Savior, Victorious Over Evil (Dec. 5)
• Meditation on the "Canticle of the Three Young Men" (Dec. 12)
• Jesus "Our Peace" Is Coming. (Dec. 19)

International

Christmas Canceled — It was announced on Dec. 3 that Christmas celebrations in Bethlehem would be canceled this year because of violence. Mayor Hanna Naser of Bethlehem made the announcement. This is the second consecutive year that Bethlehem declined secular or municipal celebrations, and only religious ceremonies will be conducted. Mayor Naser explained, "there is nothing to celebrate."

Gerhart Riegner — On Dec. 5, Vatican Radio honored Gerhart Riegner, the German lawyer who died at the age of 90 in Geneva. Riegner was a promoter of Jewish-Catholic dialogue and was among the first individuals to alert the world to the Nazi extermination programs. Exiled to Switzerland, Riegner learned about the Final Solution concerning the Jews and sent messages to the British and the United States. He became a high-ranking official of the Jewish World Congress after the war and maintained good relations with the Vatican.

Queen's Invitation — On Dec. 5, it was announced that Queen Elizabeth II invited Cardinal Cormac Murphy-O'Connor to stay at Sandringham Castle to preach to the royal family. This invitation marks a new relationship between the queen, who is the supreme head of the Church of England, and the Catholic hierarchy of the land. Queen Elizabeth is promoting ecumenical relations, started during the term of Cardinal Basil Hume, O.S.B., whom she designated as "my cardinal."

Priest Released — A Colombian priest, Fr. Guillermo Correa Ortiz, was released on Dec. 5 by an unknown guerilla group. He was kidnapped in Aug. 2000 while in the Huila region of Colombia. The priest is now ill but plans to return to his ministry when he recovers his health.

Men or Machines — Archbishop John P. Foley, president of the Pontifical Council for Social Communications, addressed an international congress on the cinema and culture on Dec. 6 in Rome. He addressed the topic of "Men or Machines" and called for a "new humanism" to provide authenticity to modern life. Cardinal Paul Poupard, president of the Pontifical Council for Culture, addressed the congress earlier, stressing the need for the cinema to serve as a sign of hope and to aid humanity in this critical era.

Culture of Peace — Archbishop Jean-Louis Tauran, the Vatican secretary for relations with States, addressed the Foreign Ministers of the Organization for security and Cooperation in Europe on Dec. 6 in Bucharest, Romania, stating that religion is too often used for political purposes. He said that the "international community needs to reflect on the way in which a culture of peace can be effectively promoted." OSCE is an institution composed of 55 states, and the ministers meeting in Bucharest concluded their efforts with a declaration of solidarity against terrorism.

Jewish Award — It was announced on Dec. 6 that Fernando Torreggiani, a jeweler of Gallarate, Italy, was given the Israeli "Righteous Among Nations" award for saving a Jewish family of six from a Nazi death camp. His daughter, Emilia, received the medal and certificate in Gallarate. Torregiani risked his life to save the family that was fleeing from German officers. The "Righteous Among Nations" award was instituted in 1952 by the Israeli Parliament.

Little Flower Relics — On Dec. 6 it was announced

that the visit of the relics of St. Thérèse of Lisieux has been the most successful Catholic event in Canada since the trip made there by Pope John Paul II in 1984. The visit opened in Vancouver in September, and more than two million venerated the relics across Canada. The visit ended on Dec. 17. St. Thérèse, called the Little Flower, was a French Carmelite nun who died in 1897 at age 24 .

Handicapped Pilgrimage — A group of 50 handicapped people will join a pilgrimage to the Holy Land, it was stated in Rome on Dec. 6. These pilgrims will pray and appeal for peace between Palestinians and Israelis. Initalsi, an Italian organization that arranges pilgrimages for patients to Lourdes, will sponsor the pilgrimage. The handicapped will go on the journey as "witnesses of an appeal for peace." The pilgrimage left Italy on Dec. 14.

Potential Genocide — On Dec. 4, Bishop Joseph Suwatan of Manado, Indonesia, called for U.N. intervention to prevent a potential genocide of Christians in the eastern part of his country. In Nov., some 10,000 Christians were displaced by Islamic assaults on the villages. The bishop called for security measures by the government and U.N. intervention against future attacks.

Youth Conference — The National Catholic Youth Conference held in Indianapolis, Ind., closed on Dec. 9 after three days of celebration. Almost 24,000 teenagers and adult chaperones were on hand to hear about their roles in the Church. The theme of the conference that was attended by 48 bishops was "Hope at the Crossroads."

Fátima Rumors — On Dec. 7, Archbishop Tarcisio Bertone, secretary of the Congregation for the Doctrine of the Faith, stated that Catholics devoted to Our Lady of Fátima have been disturbed by false rumors circulating concerning the link between the Fátima message and the Sept. 11 attacks on America. While visiting Carmelite Sister Lucia dos Santos, the archbishop said that this surviving Fátima visionary denied all of the rumors falsely attributed to her. The archbishop made his remarks during a Lisbon radio interview. He said the third Fátima secret did not include the announcement of the Sept. 11 terrorist attacks.

France's Future — On Dec. 7 the findings of the international congress held in the Regina Apostolorum Pontifical Athenaeum were announced concerning the future of the Church in France, traditionally called the "eldest daughter" of the Church. Mass attendance has dropped, vocations have declined, and the Church has endured media assaults, but there are signs of hope, according to Cardinal Paul Poupard, the president of the Pontifical Council for Culture. Marie Nicole Baiteau, a member of the Emmanuel Community, declared that French Catholics are more alive and active. The 1997 World Youth Day conducted by Pope John Paul II, an event that drew over one million participants, impacted on the French, alerting them to the vitality of the Church.

Neocatechumenal Way — A series of small communities, composed of diverse individuals and living within the parish structure, are about to receive papal approval in Spain. These communities now number 1,500, located in 800 dioceses and in 500 parishes. The group has also opened 40 seminaries. A young painter, Kiko Arguello, founded the first community. On Dec. 7, he reported that Pope John Paul II announced that the statues of the Neocatechumenal Way would be approved and praised the work of this growing approach to the Catholic apostolate.

Church in Africa — The Symposium of Episcopal Conferences of Africa and Madagascar announced on Dec. 9 that the Church is moving toward a greater role in combating AIDS. The Synod of Bishops for Africa propose using the concept of the sacredness of life, compassion, and solidarity as the fundamental values in commitments to the AIDS struggle. The bishops plan to share resources, time, food, money, and whatever is needed. AIDS is particularly devastating in Africa, claiming untold lives and imperiling social and economic security on the continent.

Woman of the Year — Chiara Castellani, a gynecologist-lay missionary in the Democratic Republic of the Congo, received the "Woman of the Year 2001" award, it was revealed on Dec. 10. The award is promoted by the Regional Council of Val d'Aosta under the patronage of the president of Italy and the European Parliament. Dr. Castellani began her mission work in Nicaragua at age 27. In 1989, she started working with the United Nations and was assigned to the Congo. She serves in a hospital without water, and is the only the doctor in Kimbau.

Priest Slain — It was announced on Dec. 10 that Fr. Michele D'Annucci, an Italian missionary near Pretoria, South Africa, was killed during a robbery. A member of the Congregation of the Sacred Wounds, he was shot when a group stole his car and mobile phone. He was the superior of his congregation in South Africa, Botswana, and Tanzania and worked in the area for 30 years.

Cuban Center — Fidel Castro, commemorating the visit of Pope John Paul II to Cuba, promoted the opening of an ecumenical center for spirituality in Havana, it was announced on Dec. 10. The Mother Abbess of the Bridgettine Order of the Most Holy Savior, Mother Tekle Famiglietti, met with Castro to discuss future plans. Castro asked that the center, designed to house eight religious, be opened within five months.

Mexican Nun — Sr. Alma del Carmen Murielde de la Torre received the "Volunteer of the Year" award from President Vicente Fox on Dec. 10. A member of the Sisters Auxiliaries of Purgatory, Sr. Muriel serves near Villahermosa in Mexico. She began her labors there 33 years ago. A native of Mexico City, Sr. Muriel remains dedicated to the poor and young of her region.

Chinese Harassment — On Dec. 10, it was announced that Bishop Bartholomew Yu Chengto of Hanzhong, China, has been restricted in his activities by the Chinese government. Three priests associated with him were put in a "re-education" program but refused to join the Chinese Catholic Patriotic Association and denounce the Vatican. These stalwart priests have been sent to remote provinces and placed under surveillance as a result of their loyalty to the pope.

Nun Slain — Sacred Heart Sr. Philomena Lyons, 67, was raped and murdered in Monaghan Co., Ireland, on Dec. 15. She was returning to Dublin from Ballybay when she was assaulted and slain. She was buried on Dec. 19.

National

Asian Pastoral — On Dec. 3 the U.S. Conference of Catholic Bishops issued a pastoral letter encouraging actions more hospitable to Asians and Pacific Islanders. The pastoral statement, "Asian and Pacific Presence: Harmony in Faith," was approved by a mail-in vote of the bishops. The document recognizes the valued presence of Asians and Pacific Islanders in the Church.

Habitat Home — The Catholic Daughters of America became one of the first women's organizations in the U.S. to build homes as part of the Habitat for Humanity. It was stated on Dec. 3 that six homes were erected in the first phase of operations, with others being built in ongoing projects.

Music Awards — On Dec. 1, the United Catholic Music and Video Association's Unity Awards were bestowed upon performers and musical composers. The song "Here I Am Lord" was chosen song of the year. The Benedictine monks of Santo Domingo de Silos, Spain, and other performers were also honored. This is the second award ceremony for the United Catholic Music and Video Association.

Radio Jesus — New York's first Hispanic-Catholic radio broadcasting station was inaugurated, it was announced on Dec. 2. Called "Radio Jesus," the station will broadcast 24 hours a day with programs dedicated to the family, catechetics, music, and art.

Religious Retirement — On Dec. 3, the Retirement Research Foundation awarded $200,000 for a two-year study of caring for retired religious to the Georgetown University-based Center for Applied Research on the Apostolate. The Commission of Religious Life and Ministry will direct the project.

Hilton Award — Dame Cecily Saunders was honored with the Conrad H. Hilton Foundation Humanitarian Prize at the Waldorf Astoria Hotel, it was announced on Dec. 3. Dame Cecily, an English physician who founded the modern hospice movement, received $1 million for St. Christopher's Hospice, established in London in 1967.

Hispanic Ministry — The U.S. bishops announced on Dec. 4 that the Committee on Hispanic Affairs has approved new pastoral directives for the Hispanic population. Training in leadership, greater integration, vocations and social and political issues will be part of the new program being adopted. A document, "A Pastoral Framework to Further Develop Hispanic Ministry" was approved for the directives.

Congressional Chaplain — Fr. Daniel Coughlin, chaplain of the U.S. House of Representatives, conducted a private prayer service for members on Dec. 4. Held in the Capitol rotunda on a National Day of Reconciliation, the service was well attended. The Protestant chaplain of the senate assisted Fr. Coughlin, who is the first Catholic Chaplain for the U.S. House of Representatives.

Housing Grant — St. Mary Parish, Lynn, Mass., was given a $2.9 million grant in federal funds on Dec. 6. The Dept. of Housing and Urban Development awarded the funds to the parish for a 32-unit transition housing facility for seniors needing temporary assistance. A vacant convent will be converted for the program. Part of the funds will include five years of rental subsidies.

Congressional Recognition — The Catholic Conference of Major Superiors of Men and the Leadership Conference of Women Religious were praised by the U.S. Representative Christopher H. Smith, R-N.J., on Dec. 7, for their roles in fighting human trafficking. His commendation was read into the Congressional Record and contains the text of a resolution adopted by these religious groups in August. The two conferences are working to end the trafficking of women and children for the purposes of sexual exploitation or labor around the world.

Epiphany Religious — A new religious congregation, the Community of the Epiphany, is being established in Venice, Fla., it was announced on Dec. 7. The group will be composed of religious sisters and lay men and women. Sr. Gilchrist Cottrill, a Sister of Notre Dame de Namur, is leading the new foundation. The community is a private association of the faithful, not yet approved canonically, and has 41 lay members and five preparing for sisterhood.

New Cathedral — On Dec. 9, more than 1,500 people joined in ceremonies to mark the dedication of the first U.S. cathedral in the new millennium in Dodge City, Kans. The date also commemorated the 50th anniversary of the Diocese of Dodge City. The cathedral is dedicated to Our Lady of Guadalupe.

Baltimore Restoration — The first major milestone was reached at the 180-year old Basilica of the National Shrine of the Assumption of the Blessed Virgin Mary in Baltimore, it was announced on Dec. 11. Four of the 24 skylights that originally circled the great dome have been reinstalled. The basilica was the first cathedral built in the United States.

Preaching Norms — On Dec. 19 it was announced that new U.S. Church norms for lay preaching and for expounding Catholic teaching on radio or television will take effect on Jan. 15, after approval by the Vatican. The U.S. Conference of Catholic Bishops promulgated the norms with decrees dated Dec. 13. These norms apply only to Latin Catholics.

Hero's Mass — The Midnight Mass at St. Patrick's Cathedral, New York, on Christmas was celebrated by Cardinal Edward M. Egan, surrounded by families of victims of Sept. 11. The archbishop of New York paid tribute to the fallen in his homily. The cardinal has been one of the most eloquent spokespersons for the victims of the Sept. 11 tragedy and earned wide acclaim for his pastoral labors on behalf of the city since the terrorist attack.

Mother Angelica — The Eternal Word Television Network of Birmingham, Ala., announced on Dec. 27 that Mother Angelica, 78, had undergone surgery to remove a blood clot from her brain after a second stroke in less than four months. The surgery was a success.

Women Religious — Sr. Carole Shinnick, provincial counselor of the School Sisters of Notre Dame from 1993 to 2001 has been named executive director of the Leadership Conference of Women Religious, it was announced on Dec. 28. She will assume this post in Feb., succeeding Sr. Mary Christine Fellerhoff of the Congregation of St. Agnes. Sr. Carole has a master's degree in American Studies and a master's in clinical social work.

Catholic Relief Services — Bishop Robert N. Lynch of St. Petersburg, Fla., has been named president and chairman of the board of Catholic Relief Services, it was announced on Dec. 31. Bishop Lynch was named to this post by Bishop Wilton D. Gregory of Belleville, Ill., president of the U.S. Conference of Catholic Bishops, which oversees CRS.

JANUARY 2002

Vatican

Peace call — Pope John Paul II proposed a global mobilization of consciences on Jan. 1 in his first appeal for peace in the New Year. He offered his proposal at the close of the Mass honoring the World Day of peace. He said: "In a globalized world where threats to justice and peace have large-scale repercussions to the detriment of the weakest, the global mobilization of consciences is an imperative."

Missionary Deaths — The Vatican missionary agency released data concerning mission deaths worldwide in 2001. Reporting on Jan. 1, Fides documented the deaths of 33 missionaries. Most died as a result of ethnic or religious fundamentalism, while others were victims of ethnic or religious cleansing. The new vulnerable status of missionaries reflects changes in fundamentalists and their aims. The spiritual values of the Catholic missionaries, once honored, are scorned by new religious and ethnic factions.

Altar Girls — Bishops cannot require priests to use female altar servers, the Congregation for Divine Worship and the Sacraments stated in an earlier document, it was revealed on Jan. 2. The Congregation also stated that the use of male servers should be especially encouraged because altar boys are a potential source of priestly vocations.

Russian Choir — A choir of 35 Russian young women, the Iubileum from Moscow, sang for Pope John Paul II at the Jan. 1 World Day of Peace Mass and at an evening gathering. Russian Orthodox Patriarch Alexei II had given his blessing to this unusual participation in Vatican events.

Anglican-Vatican Talks — Pope John Paul II welcomed Anglican Bishop Richard Gerrard to the Vatican on Jan 4. Bishop Gerrard is the representative of Archbishop George Carey of Canterbury, the spiritual leader of the Anglican Communion. The pontiff and Bishop Gerrard discussed ways in which close cooperation between Catholic and Anglicans can be advanced. Bishop Gerrard is the new director of the Anglican Center in Rome.

Epiphany Consecrations — Pope John Paul II celebrated the Feast of the Epiphany, Jan. 6, by consecrating 10 new bishops in St. Peter's Basilica. During the sermon, the pope said that the star that guided the Wise Men challenges the secularistic concepts of modern society. The asked: "Who does not feel the need of a star to guide him on the road of life on earth? Individuals and nations both feel this need." He stressed that Jesus is the star for all peoples.

Polish Invitation — On Jan. 6 it was revealed that Polish Prime Minister Leszek Miller has invited Pope John Paul II to make a pastoral visit to Poland. The Prime Minister made the invitation during a visit with the pope. They discussed Church-state relations in Poland, the international situation and European integration. The pope's return to Poland, possibly taking place in June, would be the Holy Father's eighth visit to his homeland during his pontificate.

Tatarstan Invitation — Pope John Paul II was invited by the Muslims of the autonomous Russian Republic of Tatarstan to visit their land in 2005. The invitation was revealed on Jan. 7. Pres. Mintimer Chaimievon also asked the Holy Father to return the image of Our Lady of Kazan, one of the most revered Russian Orthodox icons. Stolen from the cathedral of Kazan, the Tatar capital, in 1904, the icon was purchased by the American John Haffert, the founder of the Blue Army, and given to the Holy See so that it could be returned to Kazan. The icon was originally discovered in 1597 and is venerated for its miracles.

Priest Tribunals — Pope John Paul II decreed that some offenses committed by Catholic priests involving the sacrament of reconciliation and pederasty will be judged exclusively by the Tribunal of the Congregation for the Doctrine of the Faith, it was announced on Jan. 8. The document, *Sacramentorum Sanctitati Tutela*, was signed by the Holy Father last Apr. 30 and distributed to all bishops. Four "grave offenses" are listed in the document concerning the Eucharist, three against the sacrament of reconciliation, and one concerning pederasty, which is a crime against custom. (See also under **News in Depth**.)

Holy Childhood — On Jan. 8, the announcement was made of the title for the 2002 campaign of the Pontifical Missionary Society of Holy Childhood. "Enkindle Hope" will be the slogan for the campaign, which last year distributed grants amounting to $13 million throughout the world. Pope John Paul II launched the program.

Modern Challenges — Addressing the Vatican Diplomatic Corps, Pope John Paul II evaluated the international situation and the future of humankind. The challenges that the pope believed paramount were delineated in his speech, released on Jan. 10: the defense of the sacredness of human life, the promotion of the family, the elimination of poverty, respect for human rights, disarmament, ongoing research on the major human diseases, environmental protection, and the vigorous application of international law and conventions in ongoing confrontations.

Plenary Assembly — A four-day plenary assembly of the Congregation for the Doctrine of the Faith was announced on Jan. 14. Archbishop Tarcisio Bertone, secretary for the congregation, said that natural law and the relation of the Eucharist and the Church will be the main topics of the meeting, opening on the 15th. The assembly will also discuss *Dominus Iesus*, a declaration of Aug. 6, 2000, that treated the unique character of the salvation brought by Christ and his Church. Another topic will be the 1997 adoption of new norms to guarantee the rights and capacity for defense of theologians.

Putin Invitation — Russian Pres. Vladimir Putin said on Jan. 15 that he is willing to invite Pope John Paul II to Moscow at any time and encourages the Catholic and Russian Orthodox Churches to establish full relations. The relations between the Churches depends upon Alexei II, the orthodox Patriarch of Moscow. Mikhail Gorbachev and Boris Yeltsin also invited Pope John Paul II to Moscow.

Congo Volcano — Pope John Paul II made an appeal on Jan. 19 for the residents of Goma, a Congolese city partially buried by the eruption of Mount Nyiragongo volcano. The Holy Father said that the eruption decimated the region and made some 600,000 homeless and at risk.

Christian Unity — Pope John Paul II welcomed

an ecumenical delegation from Finland on Jan. 20, pledging that there would be "no turning back" on the road to Christian unity. The delegates were attending the annual Week of Prayer for Christian Unity.

Internet Evangelization — Pope John Paul II urged Catholics to use the Internet as a new forum for evangelization. He recommended using modern technology in his message for World Communications Day, celebrated on May 12. The Holy Father asked the entire Church to bravely cross "this new threshold," to serve peace and to spread the word of Christ.

Day of Prayer — On Jan. 24, the "Day of Prayer for Peace," more than 200 religious leaders of the world gathered at Assisi, Italy, with Pope John Paul II to dispel what the pope called the "dark clouds of terrorism, hatred, armed conflict." Thousands of pilgrims joined the representatives of the major faiths at Assisi. The theme of the gathering, considered the most representative interreligious meeting in history, is "Violence Never Again." The Holy Father also welcomed many young people, who spent the previous night in the Piazza San Francesco in Assisi in a prayer vigil. A great many Muslim leaders were in attendance. (See **Special Report** in the **News in Depth** section.)

Mexican Visit — On Jan. 25, Santiago Creel Miranda, an official of the Mexican government, disclosed that Pope John Paul II would arrive in Mexico on July 29 to canonize Blessed Juan Diego. Juan Diego was an Indian who saw apparitions of Our Lady of Guadalupe. The canonization was to be held in the basilica of Guadalupe.

Eliminate Leprosy — Pope John Paul II appealed on Jan. 27 for efforts to eradicate Hansen's Disease, leprosy, from the world. It is estimated that leprosy infects 2,000 new victims each day. He made his appeal on the World Day of Solidarity with Leprosy Sufferers on behalf of the eleven million lepers in the world. The disease can be controlled effectively, with a full treatment costing $112 per patient. The World Health Organization states that leprosy exists in 91 countries and is endemic in 25 nations. The Church operates 875 centers for leprosy patients throughout the world.

Magician's Patron — Hundreds of magicians attending the general audience of Pope John Paul II on Jan. 30 presented him with a petition requesting that St. John Bosco to be named patron saint of magicians and illusionists. The magicians also offered the pope a wand from India.

Beatification Opens — It was announced on Jan. 30 that the information process on the life and martyrdom of Minor Conventual Franciscan Nicole Placibo Corteses was requested by Bishop Eugenio Ravignani of Trieste, Italy. A director of *St. Anthony Messenger Magazine*, Fr. Cortese was considered a major threat by the Nazis in the Veneto area, and he was arrested on Oct. 8, 1944. He is called the "Italian Father Kolbe."

General Audience Topics:

- Intervention of divine providence (Jan 2)
- Meditation on Psalm 150 (Jan. 9)
- Address on Psalm 41-42 (42-43) (Jan. 16)
- Address on Sirach 36 (Jan 23)
- Address on Psalm 18(19) (Jan. 30)

International

Taize Youth — On Jan. 1, some 70,000 young people concluded a gathering of the Taize community in Budapest, Hungary. The Dec. 28-Jan. 1 conference drew participants from more than 60 countries. The head of Taize, Br. Roger Schutz, urged the young to overcome helplessness and to experience the miracle of forgiveness.

Forgotten War — Retired Candian Bishop Jean-Guy Hamelin of Rouyn-Noranda announced on Jan. 4 that he will lead a delegation to the Congo from Jan. 8-16. The delegation was organized by the Canadian Conference of Catholic Bishops and the Canadian Catholic Organization for Development and Peace. Bishop Hamelin and his group will focus on the situation in the Congo and attempt to aid in a peace process for the area. The ongoing disaster in the Congo is called the "forgotten war."

Iran at Assisi — On Jan. 6, Mustafa Borujerdi, the Iranian ambassador to the Vatican, notified Cardinal Francis Arinze, president of the Pontifical Council for Interreligious Dialogue, that a representative from Iran would participate in the Assisi World Prayer Meeting on Jan. 24. Iran and the Vatican will also organize the fourth Dialogue Forum between Islam and Catholicism to be held in Rome in 2003. Such a forum was held in Tehran in 2001.

Emmanuelle of Cairo — On Jan. 6, it was announced that Sr. Emmanuelle of Cairo received the French Legion of Honor. President Jacques Chirac signed the decree to honor this French religious. A member of the Congregation of Our Lady of Sion, Sr. Emmanuelle, 93, has served the poor and has established schools and hospitals in Cairo, the capital of Egypt, for more than two decades. Sr. Emmanuelle entered the congregation in 1931 and returned to France in 1993, when her superiors were concerned about her health. She has written books and gives interviews.

Moscow Revival — Moscow Patriarch Alexei II, head of the Russian Orthodox Church, stated on Jan. 6 that Russia is returning to the Christian faith. He said that the Orthodox "soul of the people" is vibrant and that the restoration of the Orthodox faith to its former strength "is near at hand." He exhorted the Russian people to "be not afraid, only believe."

Philippine Big Macs — Members of Immaculate Conception Cathedral in Balayan, Philippines, will have a McDonald's restaurant on the grounds of the cathedral, it was announced on Jan. 8. The congregation is sharply divided over the use of 480 square yards of cathedral property for this U.S. chain franchise. A cathedral priest explained that $1,400 monthly rental fee paid by McDonald's will fund a much-needed center.

Internet Knights — The Knights of Malta, the 900-year-old Sovereign Military Order, is now facing copycats on the Internet. It was revealed on Jan. 8 that new groups are forming on the Internet, using the symbols and names of this venerable and prestigious lay Catholic order. The Sovereign Military Hospitaller Order of St. John of Jerusalem of Rhodes and Malta, known as the Knights of Malta, is a sovereign state and a humanitarian organization, holding observer status at the United Nations and diplomatic relations with 92 countries.

Abortion Campaign — Vatican Radio reported on

Jan. 8 that the U.N. Population Fund has been conducting a campaign to promote abortion among Afghan refugees. The promotion of abortion has also been conducted by the U.N. in Pakistan. Refugees were not enthusiastic about the distribution of abortion kits when they expected food, water, blankets, and first-aid medications. Abortion is an offensive act under Islamic law.

World Youth Day — It was announced on Jan. 9 that the city of Cologne, Germany, will host the next World Youth Day, in August 2005. Pope John Paul II postponed the celebration for a year, to avoid competition with the Olympic Games in Athens in 2004, and to promote maximum participation.

Sudanese Suffering — Bishop Cesare Mazzolari, a Combonu Missionary, asked the international community to aid thousands of Sudan refugees who are dying of thirst, it was revealed on Jan. 10. The bishop declared that more than 7,000 families may die for lack of water in one county. Boreholes need to be dug by UNICEF and swiftly. The missionary is the bishop of Rumbek, an area affected by the flood of refugees caused by the political conditions in the Sudan.

Bishop to Moscow — Bishop Joseph Homeyer, the president of the Commission of the Bishops' Conference of the European Community, ended a two-day visit to Moscow on Jan. 10. Russian Orthodox Patriarch Alexei II invited Bishop Homeyer to discuss European unity and religious aspects. The bishop, from Hildesheim, Germany, also visited Catholicos Karekin II in Armenia.

Invitation Declined — It was announced on Jan. 11 that the Holy Synod, the collegial governing body of the Greek Orthodox Church, formally declined a papal invitation. Pope John Paul II had invited Archbishop Christodoulos, the head of the Greek Church, to visit the Vatican. The archbishop is in favor of a visit to Rome but bowed to the synod's decision.

Papal Envoy in Mexico — On Jan. 13, Cardinal Roger Etchegeray, a special envoy of Pope John Paul II, visited San Juan Chamula, Chiapas, Mexico, to encourage that troubled community to strengthen and purify their ancient traditions. Zapatista rebels rose up in 1994 in the area. The cardinal spent time talking to the people. The papal envoy's visit signals a new openness to the Catholic hierarchy in the region. The cardinal also visited Zinacantan. The area is part of the Tzozil Indian homeland, 450 miles southeast of Mexico City. Bishop Felipe Arizmendi of San Cristobal Diocese accompanied Cardinal Etchegeray on his visit.

Vietnam Catholics — The bishops of Vietnam, led by Cardinal Paul Joseph Pham Dinh Tung of Hanoi, announced on Jan. 15 that the Catholic Church has grown by 14% in their homeland over the past five years. Religious freedom is limited by the government, but the number of Catholics increased steadily, especially in the north. The bishops of Vietnam were in Rome on their *ad limina* visit to the Holy See.

Catholic Network — Cardinal Nicolaus de Jesus Lopez Rodriguez, the cardinal archbishop of Santo Domingo, said on Jan. 15 that he hoped to create a Catholic television network that will serve from Alaska to Argentina. The cardinal stressed the need for greater cooperation among Catholic media organizations on the American continent. He stated that "conditions are right for the international project to start taking shape."

Schism Ends — In an official ceremony held on Jan. 18 in San Salvador Cathedral, Campos, Brazil, the schism of the St. Jean Marie Vianney Fraternity ended. This group, with Lefebvrist leanings, was headed by Bishop Licino Rangel and flourished in the state of Rio de Janeiro in the Campos dos Goytacazes area. Cardinal Dario Castrillon Hoyos, prefect of the Vatican Congregation for the Clergy, served as the papal representative at the ceremony. The reunification process began in 2000 when the fraternity visited the Vatican. Members will recognize the authority of the pope.

Egyptian Meetings — Leaders of the Christian, Jewish, and Muslim religions gathered in Alexandria, Egypt, and released a declaration on Jan. 21, calling for an end to hatred. Latin Patriarch Michel Sabbah and Melkite Arcbhishop Pierre Mouallem of 'Akko were among the leaders present. All agreed that the traditions of the major faiths preach that the slaughter of innocents in the name of God is a desecration of the Holy name and defames religion in the world.

Holy Land — It was revealed on Jan. 23 that bishops from Europe and North America visited Jerusalem to study how Catholics communities worldwide can aid Christians in the Holy Land. The four-day session was called by Latin Patriarch Michel Sabbah of Jerusalem. This meeting followed the gathering in the Vatican, convoked by Pope John Paul II, on "The Future of Christians in the Holy Land."

Al-Jazeera — The television channel Al-Jazeera covered the Assisi Day of Prayer for Peace on Jan. 24. The Assisi event attracted 860 reporters. Al-Jazeera received and transmitted the controversial videos of Osama bin Laden in the first days of the anti-terrorist military operations in Afghanistan.

Kabul Mass — Having been banned for nine years, a Mass was celebrated on Jan. 27 in the Italian embassy of Kabul, the Afghanistan capital. Open to all, including the multinational force personnel, the Mass was celebrated by Father Ivan Lai, a military chaplain of the Italian contingent.

National

Bishops Retiring — An estimated 27 U.S. bishops will be eligible to retire this year, it was announced on Jan. 2. Retirement age is normally 75, and bishops are required to present resignations to the pope when reaching that birthday. The pope may refuse a resignation or delay accepting such an offer.

Family Center — The Fátima Family Center in Cleveland revealed on Jan. 2 that the Annie E. Casey Foundation had given the agency a $500,000 grant. Initially funded by the Missionary Servants of the Most Holy Trinity, the Fátima Family Center is now operating under the auspices of the Catholic Charities and the Diocese of Cleveland. The Fátima Family Center has served more than 6,000 families since opening its doors in 1973.

Grand Marshal — On Jan. 3 it was announced that Cardinal Edward M. Egan has been named grand marshal of this year's St. Patrick's Day Parade in New York. He was chosen by the unanimous vote of the officers and directors of the annual parade.

Cause Advocated — A candidate for sainthood, Fr. Emil Kapaun, is being promoted by a seminary classmate, it was revealed on Jan. 7. Fr. Kapaun was an Army chaplain who died in a North Korean prisoner of war camp. Msgr. Patrick J. Molloy, of St. Louis, is working with the U.S. archdiocese for the Military Services and the diocese of Wichita, Kans., Fr. Kapaum's home, to advance his cause.

Catechetical Directory — On Jan. 4 the first draft of a new *National Directory for Catechetics* was sent to the U.S. Bishops. This new publication defines processes and goals for religious education in the U.S. The document applies the *General Directory for Catechesis*, approved in 1997 by Pope John Paul II, and draws on the *Catechism of the Catholic Church* issued by the pope in 1992.

Anti-Violence Campaign — It was announced on Jan. 8 that "Stand Against Violence," a campaign sponsored by U.S. bishops, will open this year on Jan. 5 and will continue until Jan. 22. A resource packet is being distributed by the National Catholic Anti-Violence Working Group to provide guidelines to participating dioceses and their institutions.

Abortion Ruling — Judge Michael Allphin, of the 2nd District Court of Utah, ruled that the term "unborn child" refers to both viable and non-viable fetuses, according to to state legislation. The decision, handed down on Jan. 9, concerned the death of Susan MacGuire, a crime for which her husband, Roger MacGuire, is being prosecuted. The decision will probably send the case to the Utah Supreme Court.

Cardinal Law — On Jan. 9, Cardinal Bernard F. Law of Boston apologized for past sexual abuses of children in his diocese and stated that the archdiocese had adopted a "zero-tolerance policy" on such abuses. The archdiocese will also mandate all clergy employees and volunteers to report such activities to the civil authorities although Massachusetts law exempts clergy from such a mandate. (See additional coverage in **News in Depth**.)

Cuban Relief — Catholic Charities of Miami said on Jan 10 that it had sent 120,000 pounds of food and relief supplies to Cuba in the wake of destructive Hurricane Michelle. Valued at $25,000 two cargo flights of supplies were flown to Cuba on Dec. 19 and Dec. 21. The Nov. 4 hurricane killed five on the island and left thousands homeless.

Liturgical Academy — On Jan. 11 it was announced that 100 Catholic liturgists, members of the North American Academy of Liturgy, have formed the Catholic Academy of Liturgy. The new group will promote research and dialogue and will concern themselves with what they view as a "restorationist" movement that seeks to reverse liturgical changes resulting from the Second Vatican Council. Norbertine Fr. Andrew D. Ciferni was elected as convener of the group.

New Evangelization — On Jan. 12, Archbishop John P. Foley, president of the Pontifical Council for Social Communications, addressing a symposium sponsored by New Evangelization of America in Miami, remarked on the loss of public service time in the media. Such time was once available to religion on radio and television, but profit-geared organizations now neglect such services.

Indiana Desecration — On Jan. 15, it was announced that a Catholic cemetery in Gary, Ind., was vandalized for the seventh time in a year and for the second time in two days. St. John Kanty Cemetery was desecrated, with specific objects of devotion targeted. The total damage amounted to $7,500.

EWTN Appointment — It was announced on Jan. 16 that Fr. Mitch Pacwa, a Jesuit professor at the University of Dallas, would be taking over as host of two live programs for Mother Angelica, who is recovering from two strokes. Fr. Pacwa began his hosting duties in February.

Boston Charges — On Jan. 15, Fr. Kelvin E. Iguabita, of Haverhill, in the Boston archdiocese, pleaded innocent to two counts of rape of a minor. He was charged with raping and trying to rape a 15-year-old. A native of Colombia, Fr. Iguabita had not had an assignment in the archdiocese since July 2001. He was working at a private group home for the mentally ill when arrested.

Abortion Truths — Tens of thousands of marchers converged on Washington, D.C., for the annual March for Life on Jan. 22. This was the 29th annual observance of the U.S. Supreme Court's decision legalizing abortion. President George W. Bush greeted the marchers via telephone from West Virginia. Nellie Gray, founder of the March for Life, said that the marchers were in Washington "to tell America the truth about abortion."

Cardinal Law — During an assembly of priests of the archdiocese of Boston on Jan. 24, Cardinal Bernard Law announced that he would not resign in the wake of the sex abuse scandal in the archdiocese. His statement received a standing ovation from the priests assembled. The cardinal said that his resignation would not add to the solution of the current problem, which he intends to resolve successfully.

Herod's Death — The fatal illness of King Herod of Judea, the ruler who slew the Holy Innocents, has been analyzed at the University of Maryland medical school and diagnosed. Dr. Philip Mackowick announced on Jan. 25 that Herod's death in 4 A.D. was not pleasant. Mackowick, director of the Historical Clinicopathological Conference, stated that Herod probably died of kidney disease and gangrene of the genitals. The conference members apply their diagnostic skills to historical figures in order to solve mysterious or questionable demises.

Abuse Settlements — The diocese of Tucson announced on Jan. 29 that 11 civil suits over the sexual abuse of children have been settled for an undisclosed amount of money. Tucson bishop Manuel D. Moreno will give public and personal apologies as part of the settlement.

FEBRUARY 2002

Vatican

Indexed Aquinas — Pope John Paul II met with the Association for the Computerization of Lexicological Hermeneutical Analysis (CAEL) on Feb. 1, and encouraged the group to continue computerization services. CAEL is currently sponsoring the *Index Tomisticus*, a glossary of the nine million words taken from St. Thomas Aquinas' works. A CD-ROM will be produced by CAEL.

Pieta Rumor — The Vatican denied the rumor that Pope Paul VI had planned to sell Michelangelo's Pieta and to donate the proceeds to the poor. The Vatican statement on Feb. 1, based on a newspaper account of an antique dealer's memoirs, also included the instructions issued by Pope Paul VI that the marble masterpiece should never leave the Vatican without permission of the Holy Father.

Papal Retreat — Pope John Paul II announced on Feb. 1 that Brazilian Cardinal Claudio Hummes, O.F.M., would serve as the preacher of the papal Lenten retreat at the Vatican this year. The pope and Vatican officials will hear four reflections each day, from Feb. 17 to Feb. 23, from Cardinal Hummes, who heads the archdiocese of São Paulo, Brazil's largest archdiocese.

Pro-Life Day — Pope John Paul II addressed the faithful on Feb. 3, as Italians held Pro-Life Day in St. Peter's Square. The pope called for legal recognition of the human embryo and the preservation of life from the moment of conception.

Seminary Guidelines — On Feb. 4, Pope John Paul II commented on a document being prepared for seminary and vocation guidelines, using psychological studies for a more profound understanding of the priesthood. Addressing the plenary assembly of the Vatican Congregation for Catholic Education, the Holy Father stated that psychological procedures will foster a broader awareness and assist in discerning vocations and the human and spiritual dimensions of the priesthood. He also discussed the need for prayer, meditation, and personal asceticism in candidates.

Lenten Message — Pope John Paul II urged Christians to witness God's love with their lives in his Lenten Message on Feb. 5. The Holy Father stressed that life is a gift which must include generosity toward the poorest individuals.

Volunteers — Pope John Paul II stated on Feb. 7 that volunteer work can halt the modern trend of individualism and dominant economic interests. The Holy Father addressed his comments to the plenary assembly of the Pontifical Council *Cor Unum*. He added that volunteer work awakens the energies of the Church and the world. *Cor Unum* is currently studying volunteers and their labors. The pope thanked *Cor Unum* for its ongoing assistance to Afghanistan.

Sant'Egidio — On Feb. 8, Pope John Paul II met with 300 Catholic, Orthodox, and other religious leaders to celebrate this ecclesial movement's 34th anniversary. Sant'Egidio is also being proposed for the Nobel Peace Prize this year. The Holy Father praised the spirit and ongoing programs of the group, which include prayer services and care of the poor and suffering. The movement has more than 40,000 lay members in over 60 countries.

Day of Sick — Pope John Paul II greeted pilgrims on Feb. 10, the eve of the World Day of the Sick, declaring that illness and even death itself be open to life when seen through the eyes of faith. This year's observance will focus on the Shrine of Our Lady of Health in Vailankanny, Southern India. Visited by some 20 million pilgrims each year, the shrine is called the "Lourdes of the East." The pope also said, "Human suffering was assumed by Christ and is an integral part of this mystery of salvation."

Seminary Growth — During the pontificate of Pope John Paul II, the number of seminarians worldwide grew by 13%, it was announced on Feb. 11. The greatest increase is in Africa and Asia. The statistics are included in the *Annuario Pontificio*. The number of priests listed worldwide for 2002 is 405,000.

Papal Condolences — Pope John Paul II sent condolences to Britain's Queen Elizabeth II on the death of her sister, Princess Margaret, it was revealed on Feb. 11. Princess Margaret died of a stroke on Feb. 9. The Holy Father said that he commended the princess "to the God of all consolation" and prayed that she would find eternal life.

Call to Conversion — Cardinal Josef Tomko, prefect emeritus of the Congregation for Evangelization of Peoples, gave Pope John Paul II ashes on Ash Wednesday, Feb. 13. The Holy Father addressed worshippers in the Basilica of St. Sabina, calling to men and women to put aside "irresponsible egoism" and conversion to Christ.

Azerbaijan Visit — Pope John Paul II will visit Azerbaijan this coming spring, the Vatican announced on Feb. 14. This Muslim republic will be the first stop on the pontiff's journey, as he will also visit Bulgaria. A single Roman Catholic parish is in the capital of Azerbaijan, the city of Baku.

Pope Pius XII — The Vatican issued a statement on Feb. 15 that archival documents concerning Vatican-German relations and the efforts of Pope Pius XII to help prisoners during World War II will be opened ahead of schedule. These documents will be released as what Pope John Paul II calls an "exceptional gesture" in the face of "unjust and thankless speculation" concerning Pope Pius XII's activities. The announcement was made by officials of the Vatican Secret Archives and the Secretariat of State.

Child Catechesis — Pope John Paul II visited his 301st Roman parish on Feb. 17, urging parents there to be attentive to the religious education of their children. The Holy Father visited St. Henry's parish in Casal/Monastero, and he addressed the local families, stressing the need for improved catechesis throughout the school age years and proper preparation for the reception of the sacraments.

Theological Freedom — Pope John Paul II's address to the Pontifical Academy of Theology was released on Feb. 18, and illustrated a key principle of relationships between theologians and the Christian community. The pope declared that the theologian's freedom of research loses its ultimate objective when it separates one from the communion of the Church. The Academy of Theology was founded in 1695, and Pope John Paul II approved its new statutes in 1999.

Papal Condolences — Pope John Paul II sent condolences on Feb. 21 to Egypt, expressing his grief for victims of the worst train accident in that nation's history. The message was sent to the apostolic nunciature in Egypt.

Education of Priests — The Congregation for Clergy announced on Feb. 21 that monthly courses for the continuing education of priests are now conducted live from the Vatican and nine other cities around the world. These teleconferences and other programs can be downloaded from www.clerus.org. The material is being offered in five languages.

European Charter — Pope John Paul II said on Feb. 23 that the lack of reference to religion and the Judeo-Christian heritage of the region is "anti-historic and offensive." He made these comments while meeting with participants of an international forum concerned with the pope's teachings.

New Saints — On Feb. 26, it was announced that Pope John Paul II will proclaim nine new saints. The canonizations will be performed between May 1 and October, including during papal trips scheduled for Mexico and Guatemala. The future canonizations will be for Josémaria Escrivá Balaguer, in Rome, on October 6; Padre Pio, Rome, June 16; Juan Diego, Mexico City, July 30; Pedro de San José de Betancur, Guatemala, July 31; Pauline Amabile Visintainer, Rome, and Benedetta Bambiagio Frassinello, Rome, both on May 19; Alonso de Orozco, Ignazio Santhia (Lorenzo Belvisatti) and Umila da Bisignano (Luca Antonio Pirozzo), Rome, May 19.

Papal Tours — The Vatican announced on Feb. 26 that Pope John Paul II will visit Canada, Guatemala and Mexico in July. The eleven-day trip includes the World Youth Day activities in Canada and canonization and beatification ceremonies. Rumors abound that the Holy Father will include a visit to the United States in this tour, but the Vatican denies that possibility.

Communications Documents — On Feb. 28, the Vatican released two documents, "Ethics in Internet" and "The Church and the Internet." These were prepared by the Pontifical Council for Social Communications. The documents explore the benefits as well as dangers of modern Internet use. Archbishop John P. Foley, pres. of the Council, discussed the benefits and problems, including the digital divide between the technology-rich and those who lack such technology. The archbishop also thanked the American Russell Shaw for his key role in the writing of the document on ethics.

General Audience Topics:
• Address on Psalm 42(43) (Feb. 6)
• Canticle of King Hezekiah, in Isaiah (Feb. 13)

International

Embryo Imports — Cardinal Karl Lehmann, president of the German episcopal conference, and Manfred Koch, president of the council conference of German Evangelical churches, issued a joint statement condemning the German Parliament for approving the importation of embryonic stem cell for research. The statement was revealed on Feb. 1. Christians throughout Germany have expressed dismay over this legislative move that involves the death of embryos.

Eugenic Abortion — Bishop Abelardo Alvarado Alcántara, secretary-general of the episcopal conference of Mexico, opposed on Feb. 1 the Mexican Supreme Court's decision that allows the abortion of handicapped unborn babies. This is viewed as a prelude to future abortion legislation.

French Communications — The Christian communities of France are celebrating a week-long communications program from Feb. 1-7. Catholic and Protestant dioceses and groups are displaying their religious communication endeavor during this celebration.

Teen Suicides — Pastoral reflections from the French episcopal conference's Social Commission were revealed on Feb. 4 in Paris, directed toward preventing teen-age suicides in that country. Suicide is the second cause of death in France among youths between the ages of 15 and 20. The document also concerns funerals of suicides, care of surviving family members, and the obsession of the young with death.

Revised Figures — The Anglican Church of England revealed on Feb. 5 that 330,000 additional members have been uncovered by the use of a new method of counting attendance. The new total of 1.3 million Anglicans attending church on a weekly basis resulted from a parish head count in October. In 1999, the attendance figure was 970,000.

Body Returned — The body of Bishop Juan-Baptiste Pompallier, the first bishop of New Zealand, was returned to his adopted land, it was announced on Feb. 7. The New Zealanders asked as early as 1970 to have the remains, buried in Paris, returned to Wellington, part of Maori homeland. Bishop Pompallier arrived in New Zealand on Jan. 10, 1838, remaining there for 30 years with Marist missionaries.

Pope John XXIII — Ed Asner, the American actor, portrays Pope John XXIII in an Italian television series in Rome. Asner said, "… I think throughout his life he never abandoned the holiness the world sees in him…." in a Feb. 8 interview. The series will be seen in other countries.

New Russian Dioceses — Pope John Paul II created four new dioceses in Russia, it was announced on Feb. 11. The new dioceses are the Archdiocese of the Mother of God in Moscow, the Diocese of St. Clement in Saratow, the Diocese of the Transfiguration in Novosibirsk, and the Diocese of St. Joseph in Irkutsk. The pope also created an ecclesiastical province, with Moscow serving as the metropolitan see. The establishment of the dioceses was designed to regulate the Catholic Church in Russia, in accord with canonical procedures. The Diocese of St. Joseph in Irkutsk is 10 million square kilometers, an area larger than the United States. The Catholic presence in Russia is historical. There is a Daughter of St. Paul bookstore in downtown Moscow and a Jesuit television center in Novosibirsk. (See also the **International News section** in **News in Depth** for more on these developments.)

U.N. Protocol — The United Nations Protocol Prohibiting Child-Soldiers came into force, it was announced on Feb. 13. A ceremony held in a Geneva, Switzerland, park noted that 300,000 children are still engaged in armed conflict in the world. Ratification by 14 countries allowed the protocol, adopted last May, to be put into effect. The United States signed the agreement.

Death Penalty — Fiji announced on Feb. 13 that the death penalty for treason is being abolished. A trial of thirteen people involved in a coup was impacted by this ruling. The death penalty was removed from most criminal offenses in 1967, and this abolition eliminates treason as a capital offense. The last convicted individual in Fiji hanged for crimes died in the mid-1960s.

Carmelite Institute — Carmelite Fr. Patrick J. McMahon has been appointed president of the Rome-based Carmelite Institute, it was disclosed on Feb. 13. He is the second American to take that post since the institute's founding in 1951. The Carmelite Institute is a group of international scholars involved in Carmelite spiritual traditions as they relate to contemporary theological concerns.

Doctor Training — The Catholic Medical Mission Board of the United States has undertaken the training of 50 Lithuanian pediatricians in neurological disorders, it was announced on Feb. 13. Dr. Joan Day Mohr conducted a two-week program in Lithuania and more training sessions are scheduled.

French Accords — The Vatican praised the new era of Church-State relations in France on Feb. 15. Archbishop Jean-Louis Tauran, the Vatican secretary for relations with states, discussed this new era in a Vatican Radio address. France, now secular in tradition and with a left-of-center executive branch, has been a difficult place for normal Church-State relations, but contacts and dialogue are now addressing the situation.

Kosovo Aid — Caritas-Italy reported on Feb. 17 that 10,000 people received housing aid between the autumn of 1999 and the spring of 2001. The six-million-dollar project repaired damaged areas and restored entire villages. Italian dioceses contributed to the funding of Caritas-Italy's unusual program in Kosovo.

India Assault — On Feb. 17, a group of pro-Hindu Bajrang Dal attacked a Catholic Church near Mysore, India. Seven were injured by clubs and stones. Windows were smashed and the priest's room was ransacked. Children were attending catechism when the mob attacked. This was the second assault by the Hindu group.

Christians Released — On Feb. 22, eleven Church leaders were set free in Bulawayo, Zimbabwe. The 10 men and one woman had been arrested on Feb. 16 after a series of prayer meetings, forbidden by the military authorities. The ban is designed to halt critics of President Robert Mugabe and the ruling Zimbabwe African National Party.

Inquisition Studied — The Dominican Order conducted a three-day seminar on the Inquisition, it was announced on Feb. 24. The University of St. Thomas Aquinas, the Angelicum, in Rome, conducted the seminar, attended by 50 historians and theologians. This study is ongoing, as future seminars concerning the Inquisition are planned for 2004 and 2008.

Global Ban — A U.N. panel launched discussions on Feb. 25 to draft an international ban on cloning of human beings. France and Germany requested the ban as scientists began to declare their cloning goals. The draft is not expected to be completed in the near future.

World Slavery — The United Nations reported on Feb. 20 that an epidemic of trafficking in humans is taking place. UNDCP, the United Nations drug control and crime prevention agency, estimated that 700,000 people are enslaved every year. Crime organizations earn as much as seven billion dollars from economic and sexual slavery each year. Television public-service announcements are being produced in nine languages to disseminate information on this tragedy. In November 2000, the U.N. General Assembly adopted a protocol against human trafficking.

Presidential Plea — U.S. President George W. Bush asked China on Feb. 21 to release Catholic bishops being held in that nation's prisons. He cited the *Fides* list published earlier this month. *Fides* is the Vatican missionary agency. There are reportedly more than 30 bishops incarcerated at this time. Pres. Bush made the request directly to Chinese President Jiang Zemin. All of the Catholic bishops were arrested because they refused to deny papal authority.

Dutch Sanctions — A spokesman for the Dutch Diocese of Hertogenbosch confirmed on Feb. 21 that religious burials will not be provided for people who are euthanized. Guidelines are being prepared for priests who deal with such funerals.

National

Faith-Based Director — On Feb. 1, it was announced that James Towey, a former associate of Mother Teresa, has been chosen by President George W. Bush to oversee efforts to provide federal funds to religious charities in America. Towey succeeds John J. Dilulio, Jr. in this office.

NCCW Executive — Annette Kane, executive director of the National Council of Catholic Women, retired on Feb. 1 after sixteen years of leadership. The NCCW is a federation of 7,000 Catholic women's organizations of the United States.

Pastors Suspended — On Feb. 2, two pastors of the Boston archdiocese were suspended because of accusations of sexual misconduct with minors. Fr. Paul J. Finegan and Fr. Daniel M. Graham are the accused.

Youth and Religious — Young American Catholics have little knowledge of men and women religious, it was announced on Feb. 6, in conjunction with a study released at the World Day for Consecrated Life meeting, Feb. 2-3. Young adult Catholics have a positive view of religious in the U.S. but are unaware of vows, ordination requirements and roles. The study was commissioned by the Conference of Major Superiors of Men and the Leadership Conference of Women Religious and conducted by a Catholic University of America Sociologist.

Schools Reopened — Bishop J. Terry Steib of Memphis announced the reopening of three Catholic schools, it was announced on Feb. 5. The schools were closed decades ago but are reorganized as the foundation of all other schools in the diocese. The first will reopen in 2003 and the others will follow.

Catholic Charities — Bishop Michael P. Driscoll of Boise, Idaho, was named on Feb. 5 as episcopal liaison for Catholic Charities USA by the United States Conference of Catholic Bishops. Bishop Driscoll has a long history of leadership in Catholic Charities in various dioceses.

Tolkien Manuscripts — The original manuscripts for *The Lord of the Rings* and *The Hobbit*, the masterpieces written by devout Catholic author J.R.R. Tolkien, are at Marquette University's Memorial Library, it was revealed on Feb. 6. The Jesuit-operated university has a J.R.R. Tolkien Collection, visited by fans of the books and films.

Turn to Prayer — On Feb. 7, Pres. George W. Bush urged Americans to turn to prayer in these critical times. He made these recommendations at the National Prayer Breakfast, a half-century tradition that brings together lawmakers, foreign heads of state and spiritual leaders. President Bush declared: "… we have all been witnesses these past 21 weeks to the power of faith to see us through the hurt and loss that have come to the country."

Christopher Awards — On Feb. 7 it was revealed that the 2002 Christopher Awards will be bestowed upon former New York Mayor Rudy Giuliani, dancer Jacques d'Amboise, and Exxon/Mobil Masterpiece Theatre. The Christopher Awards were to be presented on Feb. 28. Mayor Giuliani will receive the first Christopher Leadership Award. Jacques d'Amboise will receive the James Keller Award, named after the Maryknoll founder, and the 2002 Special Christopher Award will be given to the Exxon/Mobil Masterpiece Theatre.

Catholic Campaign — The Catholic Campaign for Human Development announced on Feb. 7 that it will disperse $530,500 in grants for criminal justice reform and education projects. These grants are part of the second phase of the $1.5 million program of the U.S. Bishops to aid reforms in the U.S. criminal justice system. The first phase was completed in Nov. 2001.

NCCW Donation — The National Council of Catholic Women announced a donation of $289,000 for Catholic Relief Services on Feb. 11. The NCCW maintains the Works of Peace projects and Help-a-Child program that benefited El Salvador, Iran, Sudan, and India.

Terrorism Letter — On Feb. 12 an open letter in defense of the U.S. war on terrorism was disclosed. Signed by 60 prominent American intellectuals, the letter was published by the Institute for American Values.

Sacrament of Penance — It was announced on Feb. 14 that Pennsylvania Catholic bishops have released a new booklet, "A Guide to the Sacrament of Penance." This guide is in question-and-answer format and relates to the need for the sacrament, the forgiveness of sins and preparatory steps for receiving the sacrament. Some 600,000 copies have been ordered and are available from the Pennsylvania Catholic Conference.

Hostages Freed — On Feb. 13, Jesuit Father Aloysius P. Kelley, president of Fairfield University in Connecticut, thanked the university students, staff, and faculty for their response to a hostage situation on the previous day. Some 23 people were taken hostage for seven hours by a Fairfield graduate. The individual surrendered to police.

Black Catholics — On Feb. 18, Beverly A. Carroll, the executive director of the U.S. Bishops' Secretariat for African-American Catholics, urged participation in the upcoming National Black Catholic Congress IX, to be held on Aug. 29-Sept. 1. Addressing clergy and laity of the Newark Archdiocese, Carroll discussed the ongoing objectives of the Congress, which was founded in 1889 by Daniel Rudd.

Busted Halo — A Paulist Young Adult Ministries web site was announced on Feb. 18 in New York. Called "Busted Halo," the site targets young adults from 18 to 39 and treats relationships, spirituality, and work experiences. The sitec, at www.bustedhalo.com, also features bios on historical and contemporary religious figures.

Abuse Scandals — Bishop Wilton D. Gregory, president of the U.S. Conference of Catholic Bishops, issued a statement on Feb. 19 concerning the abuse scandals in the nation's dioceses. He said that the harm they have caused is "immeasurable," and he admitted that the priest abusers were not dealt with properly in the past. Bishop Gregory warned as well that such abuse scandals require new efforts to be on guard in the future.

Catholic Statistics — On Feb. 20 it was announced that there are 63,863,030 Catholics in the U.S., composing 23% of the population. These figures were released by the U.S. Conference of Catholic Bishops. There are 46,041 priests in the U.S., 30,655 diocesan clergy and 15,386 religious priests. Seminarians now number 4,917, permanent deacons, 13,348. There are also 79,462 religious sisters and 5,565 brothers. Elementary schools numbering 7,061 serve 1.94 million students. Some 680,947 students attend 1,596 high schools, and 235 Catholic colleges and universities are attended by 705,059 students.

New Priests — A sociological study of U.S. priests, released on Feb. 25, has determined that younger priests in 2001 have views on Church issues similar to older priests in 1970. Priests were happier in 2001 than in 1970, but they were also concerned about overwork and unrealistic demands of lay people. The 30-page report of the study was made available by Catholic University of America.

Vocation Support — The Knights of Columbus announced on Feb. 25 that $1,981,218 had been provided to seminarians and postulants by 2,050 councils of Knights. The "Refund Support Vocations Program" allows individual councils to raise money and to receive refunds for council use. The Knights of Columbus hope to adopt every seminarian in the United States and Canada and to provide each one with $500 for personal use.

St. Xavier's — The St. Xavier University of Chicago revealed on Feb. 26 that the Blanche Swift Morris Trust has given the institution a gift of $1.5 million. This is the largest cash donation ever released to St. Xavier's from a private donor. A residence hall will bear the name of Morris.

St. Katharine Drexel — It was announced on Feb. 26 that a life-size statue of St. Katharine Drexel has been installed at the basilica of the National Shrine of the Immaculate Conception in Washington, D.C. Two mosaics honoring Our Lady of China and Our Lady of La Salette have also been placed in the upper church area. A Hall of American Saints contains statues of St. Elizabeth Ann Seton, St. Francis Cabrini, St. Rose Philippine Duchesne, and Blessed Kateri Tekakwitha. St. Katherine Drexel was canonized by Pope John Paul II in Oct. 2000.

Canonization Cause — The diocese of Richmond, Va., announced on Feb. 28 that the cause for the possible canonization of Francis Joseph Parater III has been opened. He was a former diocesan seminarian who died at age 22 in 1920 while attending the North American College in Rome. Bishop Walter F. Sullivan, after consultation with other bishops of the Baltimore province, decreed Francis Joseph Parater III "a servant of God" and established a tribunal to examine his life.

MARCH 2002

Vatican

Media Challenge — Pope John Paul II, addressing the plenary assembly of the Pontifical Council for Social Communications on March 1, urged Catholics to make the Church recognized by the modern media. The Holy Father said that ways must be found to ensure that the voice of the Church is not marginalized or silenced in the modern media arena. He added that the Church must enter the great forum of the media with courage and confidence. Concrete planning and high standards of professionalism will be demanded by those who accept this challenge to keep the Gospel vibrant in the world.

Focolare Movement — Pope John Paul II met some 80 bishops who are involved in the Focolare Movement on March 1. The Holy Father urged the bishops to promote "the spirituality of communion" at this session. Chiara Lubich, the foundress of the Focolare Movement, was greeted personally by the pope during the session.

Internet Ethics — The Pontifical Council for Social Communications has published two documents concerning Ethics on the Internet, it was announced on March 1. The texts concern the opportunities and challenges of this new media system and propose specific guidelines for Catholic participation. (For other details, see under **Catholic Communications**.)

Human Slaves — Following the lead of U.S. President George W. Bush, Jim Nicholson, U.S. ambassador to the Holy See, is organizing an international congress on the traffic in human beings, it was announced on March 1. The congress will be held in May at the Gregorian University and will concern the estimated millions of people now in slavery in some nations.

Papal Greetings — Pope John Paul II sent feast-day greetings to Russian Orthodox Patriarch Alexei II of Moscow, the Vatican reported on March 1. The telegram included the Holy Father's prayers for an end to the present difficulties that resulted from the papal foundation of four dioceses in Russia. The telegram was reportedly sent on Feb. 23.

Film Restrictions — It was announced on March 1 that the Vatican has issued new guidelines forbidding the filming of movies on its property. The Pontifical Council for Social Communications, charged with control of media access to the Vatican, revised the 1964 regulations to handle increases in requests for access to the Vatican. Films based on fiction and using actors are especially noted in the new guidelines.

Peace Decalogue — Pope John Paul II sent a letter to the leaders of the world, it was revealed on March 4, providing them with the "Assisi Decalogue for Peace." The Holy Father assured the heads of nations that "violence and terrorism is incompatible with the authentic Spirit of religion." The text is designed to serve as a guideline for dealing with modern world conditions.

Roman Clergy — On March 4 the address given to a meeting of Roman priests by Pope John Paul II was released. Given on Feb. 14, the address concerned the vocations crisis in the Church. The Holy Father cited a growing weakening of the faith in the West and a lack of spiritual ardor. The pope called for a great commitment on all levels of the faithful and prayers to the Blessed Virgin Mary, the Mother of the Church.

Virtual Tours — The secretary of the Pontifical Council for Migrants and Travelers, Archbishop Agostino Marchetto, announced on March 5 that shrines across the world should make available virtual tours over the Internet. The Third European Congress on Shrines and Pilgrimages was in session at the Shrine of Monserrat and was considering methods by which 150 million annual shrine visitors can be accommodated. Virtual tours would enable many to visit a shrine in the only way possible, while others would see the tours and then visit the shrine personally.

Church Not a Democracy — On March 5, Cardinal Giovanni Battista Re addressed the meetings being held on "The Government of the Universal Church," stating that the Church is not a democratic structure in which the people are sovereign. As an instrument of God's mercy, the Church must be protected from the political and social mutations and competitions taking place in this era.

Communion Guide — The document "Communion Under Both Species" was released on March 8 by the Congregation for Divine Worship and the Discipline of the Sacraments. As a result, Catholics of the Roman rite will be able to receive Communion ordinarily under both species. It will be up to diocesan bishops to issue the norms.

Iranian Guest — Ayatollah Mehdi Karrubi, the president of the Iranian Parliament, visited Pope John Paul II, it was announced on March 11. A theologian and philosopher, Karrubi spent three days in Rome and presented the Holy Father with a Persian rug.

Famine Relief — Pope John Paul II has given $30,000 to the bishops of Malawi and Zambia, it was reported on March 12. These funds will aid the millions stricken by famine caused by low stockpiles, inflation and transportation difficulties.

Stations of the Cross — It was learned on March 15 that media correspondents accredited at the Vatican wrote meditations and prayers for Pope John Paul II's presentation of the Stations of the Cross on Good Friday in Rome. Journalists from Russia, Italy, Portugal, the United States, Austria, Poland, Mexico, and Spain were among those represented during the *Via Crucis*, the Way of the Cross, in the Roman Colosseum. Thousands of pilgrims attended these ceremonies.

Holy Thursday Collection — At the request of Pope John Paul II, the collections taken up on Holy Thursday will be designated to aid Latin American Indians and Mestizos. This designation was announced on March 15. The *Populorum Progressio* Foundation was organized to aid these Latin and Caribbean poor.

Orthodox Delegation — Pope John Paul II, it was reported on March 15, welcomed a delegation of Greek Orthodox to the Vatican. These delegates were sent by His Beatitude Christodoulos, Archbishop of Athens and All Greece. This was the first group visiting the Holy Father, and he expressed his joy and hope for future cooperation, stating that Catholics and Orthodox can collaborate in social, ecological, bioethical, and cultural areas in the modern world.

Archbishop's Murder — Pope John Paul II on March 17 condemned the murder of Archbishop Isaias Duarte Cancino of Cali, Colombia. The archbishop was an outspoken critic of drug traffickers, guerillas, and paramilitary forces in Colombia. He was murdered as he left Good Shepherd Church in Cali. Two men approached him and one shot him in the head and chest. (See also **Special Reports**.)

Roman Missal — On March 18, it was announced that the Vatican officials have presented Pope John Paul II with the *New Roman Missal*. The work has been in progress for seven years and includes new memorials of saints. Eucharistic prayers have also been added. The Vatican Congregation for Divine Worship and the Discipline of the Sacraments published the missal. Episcopal Conferences will be responsible for translation, which will have to be approved by the congregation.

Letter to Priests — The Vatican issued on March 21 Pope John Paul II's annual Holy Thursday Letter to priests world-wide. In the letter, he accused perpetrators of sexual abuse as betrayers of the priesthood who bring a "shadow of suspicion" over good priests serving faithfully. Each case, the Holy Father declared, must be handled in truth and justice. (See additional coverage of the letter in **News in Depth**.)

Lefebvrist Problem — The Vatican announced on March 22 that no quick resolution between the Holy See and the Lefebvrist St. Pius X Fraternity was on the horizon. Discussions with the main group of followers of the late Archbishop Marcel Lefebvre are continuing, but reconciliation with the Vatican is likely to be a long process, said Cardinal Jorge Medina Estevez. The cardinal is a member of the Pontifical Commission *Ecclesia Dei*, established by Pope John Paul II in 1988 to promote communion with the supporters of Archbishop Lefebvre after he was excommunicated for ordaining bishops. One of those ordained, Bishop Bernard Fellay, leads the Priestly Fraternity of St. Pius X, the main group of followers considered not in full communion with the Catholic Church.

Modern Martyrs — Pope John Paul II, on March 24, praised the modern missionary martyrs as models for the young. Some 33 Church workers in mission territories lost their lives in 2001. In 2002, three mission workers have already been murdered.

Prayers for Priests — On Holy Thursday, March 28, Pope John Paul II asked the faithful to pray for persecuted priests and for those clerics who are in crisis or have abandoned their ministries. Priests attending the Holy Father's Mass renewed the promises that they made at ordination. There are more than 400,000 priests in the world, and Pope John Paul II addressed each one in his homily.

Holy Land — *L'Osservatore Romano* depicted the violence raging in the Holy Land in its March 30 issue. An article concerning the destruction loosed in the region accompanied a picture of an Israeli tank in the front of the compound of Yasser Arafat, president of the Palestinian Authority. The contrast between the reconciliation brought by Christ and the modern conflict was noted.

War and Peace — In his Easter message to the world, Pope John Paul II announced on March 31 that it "seems that war has been declared on peace." Speaking in St. Peter's Square in Rome, the Holy Father imparted the *Urbi et Orbi* ("To the City of Rome and to the World") apostolic blessing. Thousands of pilgrims were in the square, and the message was carried to 50 countries by 63 television channels.

General Audience Topics:

- Meditation on Psalm 64 (65) (March 6)
- General Audience Address, on Psalm 76 (77) (March 13)
  - "Magnificat of the Old Testament" (March 20)
  - Paschal Triduum Is "Fulfillment of Human History" (March 27)

International

Harsh Response — Members of the Russian Orthodox Church in Moscow reacted to Pope John Paul II's video plans on March 1, protesting the linkage between the Vatican and the Catholic cathedral of Moscow. A spokesman for the Orthodox Church stated that the papal plans to allow the pope to lead Russian young people in prayers through a live video link demonstrate "the irrational persistence and determination" of the pope to make his presence felt in Russia.

Juan Diego — Mexican Catholic authorities announced on March 1 that the canonization of Juan Diego on July 30 is anticipated to be the largest mass in that nation's history. Some five million Mexicans are expected to attend the ceremony on the outskirts of Mexico City. The pope is also expected to beatify Juan Bautista and Jacinto de los Angeles, two other lay Indians, at this gathering.

Human Embryos — On March 1, the BBC reported in London that two licenses have been issued for medical experiments on human embryos. Guy's Hospital of London and Edinburgh University applied for and received permission from the British government to conduct stem cell research on embryos.

Princess Margaret — It was reported on March 1 in London that Princess Margaret, the sister of Queen Elizabeth II, had considered conversion to the Catholic Church. A new book by Noel Botham cited Princess Margaret's friendship with Derek Jennings, a convert and priest, and stated that she refrained from conversion out of loyalty to the Queen. Princess Margaret died on Feb. 9 at age 71.

Peace Prayers — On March 3, the Indian Catholic bishops met at the Indian-Pakistan border to pray for peace between the two nations. Cardinal Ivan Dias of Bombay led the prayers at the Wagah border gate. Some 140 bishops were in the peace group, traveling from their biennial plenary session in Jalandhar.

Canadian Debate — The Canadian federal guidelines on embryo stem-cell research have started a widespread ethical debate in Canada, it was reported on March 4. Scientists and political leaders are protesting that embryos must be protected and the vulnerable provided with legal safeguards.

Gospel Website — A Paris Internet site, the Daily Gospel (www.dailygospel.org), was announced on March 4. The service was started six months ago and is dedicated to using the modern tools available for evangelization. The Daily Gospel provides texts for the liturgy of each day and is staffed by volunteers.

Indian Catholics — The violence between religious groups in India harmed Catholics, it was reported on March 5. Two priests and two lay Catholics were attacked by members of a Hindu radical group, the Rashtriya Swayamsenek Sangh, RSS. A Divine Word Mission station was burned, and other Church-related programs were threatened. The bishops of India met for a day and fasting and prayer for the victims of the violence harming people of all faiths in the land.

Christian Vietnamese — It was announced on March 5 that 63 Christian Montagnards from Vietnam who sought asylum in Cambodia were forcibly repatriated to their homeland. Some 61 others were also returned to Vietnam, where tribal minorities have been protesting a lack of religious freedom and the loss of their lands. A military crackdown by the government resulted in more than 1,600 Christian Vietnamese fleeing into Cambodia. Many were returned to Vietnam when bounties were paid, and the U.N. High Commissioner for Refugees intervened with little success.

Brazilian Saint — Cardinal Claudio Hummes of São Paulo, Brazil said on March 6 that Mother Paulina do Coracao Agonizante de Jesus is truly Brazil's first saint. She will be canonized on May 19. Mother Paulina was born in Italy but is considered a native Brazilian because she was brought to Brazil as a child and spent her life there in service to the Church and the people. (For details of her life, see under **Canonizations and Beatifications 2001-2002**, under **Saints**.)

Church-State — A Norwegian religious panel announced March 8 that it has advised the Norwegian government to end the 465-year old state-church system. The Evangelical Lutheran Church has been Norway's official religion since 1537. The panel also recommended that all faiths should receive equal standing in the nation. It would take a constitutional amendment to end Norway's church-state system.

Guatemala Canonization — The nation of Guatemala announced its preparations to welcome Pope John Paul II as he planned to canonize Pedro San José de Betancur, July 31-Aug.1 during his visit to North and Central America. Pedro is called "the first Central American saint." (For details of his life, see under **Canonizations and Beatifications, 2001-2002** under **Saints**.)

EU — The European Parliament debated a report that condemned the Catholic Church for its moral position on abortion and other issues as well as its refusal to ordain women. Written by a Spanish Socialist, the report was supported by various radical women's organizations. The proposal would restrict the Church in proclaiming moral doctrine, despite the Charter of Fundamental Rights adopted by the European Parliament at its founding.

Madagascar Aid — On March 13, Fr. Cosimo Alvati of Radio Don Bosco appealed to the international community to intervene in Madagascar to end the rivalries and battles that have plagued the country. Pres. Didier Ratsiraka and a rival, Marc Ravalomanana, have been conducting strikes and civil unrest over the presidential office. Fr. Alvati asked for intervention before violence is unleashed in the nation.

Korean Anniversary — As part of the 40th anniversary of the establishment of the hierarchy in the Catholic Church in South Korea, it was announced on March 13 that a new revitalization program is planned. The South Korean hierarchy was established on March 10, 1962, when apostolic vicariates became dioceses. A program to foster communion between the clergy and laity, to elevate the status of women and to inspire native priests to holiness will begin as part of the celebrations.

Marian Statue — On March 14, a 120-year-old

statue of the Blessed Virgin Mary was hit by Israeli gunfire at a Bethlehem Church. The gunfire was called "unprovoked" and unnecessary. Israeli tanks at Bethlehem-Beit Jalla opened fire on the hospital and orphanage compound where the church is located.

Pakistan Attack — Two Americans died in an assault on a Protestant church in Islamabad, it was announced on March 17. An American woman and her daughter were among the five victims when grenades were thrown into the church. Earlier, fifteen worshippers and a police guard were killed in St. Dominic's in Bahawalpur. The Protestant church was inside the diplomatic enclave of Islamabad.

Lay Missionaries — Some 50,000 members of Missionary Youth and Family will spend Holy Week in rural and Indian communities of Mexico, it was announced on March 19. Called the "mega mission," this program will open with Masses and then the young missionaries will be sent to the most neglected areas of the country. The group was formed in 1993 in response to Pope John Paul II's appeal at World Youth Day. Besides evangelization, the missionaries will provide medical care. These missionaries are also active in Cuba, Colombia, Ireland, Germany, France, Poland, Hungary and Argentina, having already visited five million homes.

Interfaith Prayers — Cardinal Desmond Connell of Dublin, Ireland, organized on March 20 a gathering of different religions to pray for world peace at Clonliffe College. About 100 representatives, including Anglicans, Orthodox, Muslims, Hews, and Buddhists were present, including the Nuncio of the Holy See to Ireland.

Canadian Bankruptcy — It was announced on March 21 that the Edmonton-based Oblates of Mary Immaculate, Grandin Province, may join their Manitoba fellow religious in filing for bankruptcy. Native Americans who claim they were sexually, emotionally, and physically abused at Oblate residential schools have filed 1,200 lawsuits against the Oblates. Legal fees have also averaged about $380,000 a year over the matter, not counting other legal costs and damages.

Counter Suit — The auxiliary bishop of Paris, Bishop Jean-Michel di Falco, accused of sexual abuse 30 years ago, has decided to file a lawsuit for slander and false claims against his accuser. The bishop stated that the claims made against him were condemnable and without foundation. As a result, they were subject to legal action.

Priest Slain — On March 24, it was revealed that Fr. Declan O'Toole, a Mill Hill Missionary in Uganda, had criticized the Ugandan Army and was subsequently murdered by a uniformed soldier in Kotido, in northern Uganda. Two soldiers have since been arrested. An Anglican minister witnessed the slaying and escaped to report it. Fr. O'Toole labored among the Karamojong people of Uganda. An American Mill Hill priest, Fr. John Kaiser of Minnesota, was slain in Kenya two years ago.

Day of Unborn — On March 25, the people of Argentina celebrated the Day of the Unborn, on the feast of the Annunciation. This event was started in 1988, joined by similar activities in Nicaragua and Costa Rica. The motto of the event is "Let's Celebrate as a Family the Hope of New Life."

Chinese Persecution — Bishop Julius Jia Zhiguo

of Zhengding, China, was arrested by Communist authorities, it was reported on March 24. Bishop Jia has already spent over 20 years in various Chinese prisons, and he is customarily arrested on the eve of every major Catholic holy day in order to prevent him from celebrating Mass and taking part in the significant liturgical celebrations of the Church.

Congo Attack — It was revealed on March 25 that grenades had been thrown into a Palm Sunday procession of Catholic worshippers in Goma, Congo. A priest and a young girl of eight were killed. Fifteen others, including Bishop Faustin Ngabu of Goma, were injured in the attack. Suspects were arrested. Bishop Ngabu, despite his wounds, continued the celebration and led prayers for peace.

National

Ignatius Press — Ignatius Press announced on March 5 that it was forming Campion College. The move will be made as a result of the Vatican ruling in favor of the University of San Francisco's control of the St. Ignatius Institute, founded in 1976 by Jesuit Father Joseph Fessio. The new Campion College will offer a two-year program that will embody the spirit and curriculum of the St. Ignatius Institute. A donation of $500,000 has been made to promote the new college.

U.S. Catholic Publications — It was reported on March 6 that the total circulation for Catholic publications in the United States increased by nearly 380,000 in 2001. The Catholic Press Association made the new figure available in the 2002 *Catholic Press Directory*. The figures include magazines, newsletters, newspapers and foreign-language publications. The 2002 *Catholic Press Directory* reported a total of 640 periodicals in North America, with a circulation of 26.8 million. The figures included 217 newspapers, 243 magazines, 136 newsletters and 44 other-language periodicals (newspapers and magazines).

Women's Roles — A study conducted by the Leadership Conference of Women Religious reported on March 11 provided evidence that hundreds of U.S. Women perform in Church governance positions. The results of the study, conducted by the Leadership Conference of Women Religious, were published in a 152-page report titled "Women and Jurisdiction: An Unfolding Reality." It was released through a telephone news teleconference March 8, during the celebration of International Women's Day.

The study was based on surveys in late 2000 of U.S. women holding six kinds of positions in the church. Four are defined in canon law as ecclesiastical offices: diocesan chancellors, diocesan finance officers, judges on diocesan tribunals and pastoral directors of parishes. Before the new Code of Canon Law was issued in 1983, women were not permitted to hold those positions. The study identified 49 female chancellors, or slightly more than one-fourth of all chancellors in U.S. dioceses. It found 22 women who were diocesan finance officers, a bit more than one-tenth of the total. Women headed 71 Catholic Charities offices, or more than one-third of the total. The study also found that women religious accounted for 75 percent of the women surveyed. More than four-fifths of the chancellors and more than three-fifths of the finance directors were members of the bishop's Cabinet.

Protection Commission — The selection of members for the Boston Archdiocese Commission for the Protection of Children has been completed, it was announced on March 11. The members are experts and representatives of the archdiocese community. Experts are leaders in health, medical, child development and law enforcement. There are eight women and seven men on the Commission, chosen by Cardinal Bernard Law.

Social Security — It was reported March 12 that the School Sisters of St. Francis in Pennsylvania lost about $15,000 and future benefits when their SSA payments were reduced by the government. Lawyers representing the women religious say that the Social Security Administration is in the process of re-computing benefits owed to the sisters. These religious reside at Marian Hall Home in Bellevue.

Priest Slain — On March 12, a former employee of Our Lady of Peace Church in Lynbrook, N.Y., shot and killed Fr. Lawrence M. Penzes and a 73-year-old parishioner during the morning Mass. The suspected killer was captured after the police stormed his apartment nearby. The man had been dismissed from his custodian job in the parish.

Freedom of Religion — Rep. Walter Jones, Jr. (R-N.C.), offered a bill in the U.S. House of Representatives that will allow churches to become more involved politically. On March 15, Representative Jones announced that churches have the obligation to talk about moral issues facing the nation. He said that churches have been silenced in the recent past, and he is trying to bring back freedom of speech to the various faiths of America.

Sex Scandals — On March 18, it was reported that Archbishop John P. Foley, president of the Pontifical Council for Social Communications, stated that the real tragedy of clerical sex abuse is not embarrassment for the Church in America but the grave offense against God and children. The archbishop said that American Catholics are "living in sad days for the Church." He made these statements on March 10, at St. Charles Borromeo Seminary in Philadelphia.

Church Fire — On March 18, St. Michael's Church in Wheaton, Ill., was destroyed by a fire. The 44-year old church was beside a former convent, a rectory, and a parish school. Firefighters had to halt the blaze and hose down the adjacent buildings to protect them.

Buddhist Converts — It was announced on March 19 that a Laotian family of Buddhists converted to Catholicism in Little Rock, Ark., at the Easter Vigil Mass. The family migrated to the United States after the Vietnam War, and years of study and prayer brought them to the faith. There are nine in the family, which includes three couples and their children.

African-American "Angels" — A group of African-American Catholics have banded together in Jackson, Miss., it was reported on March 21. Serving in the "Be an Angel" campaign, these Catholics are working to support and sustain African-American Catholics schools in the diocese. A kick-off luncheon opened the fund-raising and outreach programs in the diocese.

Millions in Payments — It was reported on March 27 that the archdiocese of St. Louis has paid victims of clergy sexual misconduct about $1.6 million. The money was given to address the needs of victims. This amount was disbursed over the past two decades.

APRIL 2002

Vatican

Holy Week — Pope John Paul II focused on the continuing violence in the Holy Land during the Holy Week and Easter liturgical celebrations, it was revealed on Apr. 1. The Holy Father told visitors in St. Peter's Square that he prayed that the peace of the risen Christ would restore all who are suffering and oppressed.

Bethlehem Crisis — The Vatican on Apr. 3 expressed alarm over the Israeli siege and the Palestinian militia takeover of the Church of the Nativity in Bethlehem. Officials of the Holy See conducted a series of meetings to discuss the crisis and find ways to end the violence and desecration of holy sites.

Day of Prayer — Pope John Paul II held a World Day of Prayer on Apr. 7. The crisis in Bethlehem and the surrounding areas led the Holy Father to appeal to the whole church for prayers to alleviate the violence and suffering of the people involved.

Vatican Intercession — It was revealed on Apr. 7 that the Vatican was conducting unprecedented diplomatic sessions in order to promote peace in the Holy Land. A five-point program was organized and conveyed to representatives of the conflicting sides and the United States. The Vatican announced its (1) unequivocal condemnation of terrorism, from whatever side it may come; (2) disapproval of the conditions of injustice and humiliation imposed on the Palestinian people, as well as reprisals and retaliation, which only make the sense of frustration and hatred grow; (3) respect for the U.N. resolutions by all sides; (4) proportionality in the use of legitimate means of defense; (5) the duty for the parties in conflict to protect the sacred places, very significant for the three monotheistic religions and the patrimony of all humanity.

Popular Piety — On Apr. 9, the new Vatican Congregation for Divine Worship and the Sacraments issued "Directory on Popular Piety and Liturgy: Principles and Guidelines." The document defends popular piety, within certain limits. The statement also discussed the present trend to eliminate certain expressions of popular religiosity, noting that such purism implies a moral impoverishment for Christian life. Cardinal Jorge Medina Estévez, the prefect of the congregation, announced the new directory.

Elderly Care — The Vatican emphasized the value of elderly human beings on Apr. 9 at the United Nations World Assembly on aging in Madrid. The Church administers more than 13,000 centers for the care of the elderly. Archbishop Javier Lozano Barragán, president of the Pontifical Council for Health Care Workers, was the representative of Pope John Paul II.

Bishops' Meeting — On Apr. 9, Pope John Paul II held a working luncheon session with the leaders of the United States Bishops' Conference. The USCCB leaders had already visited Vatican offices, and their meeting with the Holy Father concerned the clerical sex-abuse scandals in the U.S.

Call to Buddhists — Cardinal Francis Arinze, in a message released on Apr. 9, called to Buddhists around the world to join Catholics in promoting respect for human life. He asked them also to oppose abortion and euthanasia. The letter was sent in honor of the Buddhist feast of Versakh.

Beatifications — On Apr. 14, Pope John Paul II beatified six servants of God. They were Gaetano Errico, Lodovico Pavoni, Luigi Variara, Maria del Transito de Jesus Sacramentado, Artemide Zatti, and Maria Romero Meneses. (For details on the beatifications, see under **Canonizations and Beatifications 2001-2002**, under **Saints**.)

Muslim-Catholic Accord — On Apr. 15, the Islamic Theological Center and the Vatican called for negotiations to end Middle East violence. The Committee of Islamic-Catholic Dialogue was created in May 1998 and includes the most prestigious theological representatives of Islam. The Al-Azhar Permanent Committee for Dialogue with Monotheist Religions, representing Al-Azhar University in Cairo, Egypt, and the members of the Pontifical Council for Interreligious Dialogue compose the committee.

Vocations Priority — Pope John Paul II sent a letter to the North American Congress on Vocations, it was announced on Apr. 19. Held in Montreal, the congress was attended by more than 1,200 delegates from the American continent. The Holy Father stated that the priesthood is unique and calls humans to act "*in persona Christi Capitis*, in the most sacred moments of his service to the Church." The congress is the third held worldwide at the invitation of the pope.

Call to Holiness — Pope John Paul II ordained 20 priests in St. Peter's Basilica on Apr. 21, reminding the newly ordained that their true vocation is a call to holiness. The Holy Father stated, "holiness is the perspective toward which the whole pastoral care of the Church must be directed." The ordinations are held annually on the World Day of Prayer for Vocations.

Islamic Impositions — On Apr. 23 it was reported that Pope John Paul II urged the Catholic bishops of Nigeria to oppose the enforced Islamic laws introduced in twelve states of their homeland. The Holy Father, addressing the bishops of Nigeria visiting Rome for the quinquennial *ad limina* visits, asked the bishops to speak out with courage to defend the Christian Nigerians. Nigeria is half Christian and half Muslim.

New Roman Missal — Pope John Paul II sent a message to the *Vox Clare* committee organized by the Congregation for Divine Worship and Sacraments, meeting on Apr. 22-24 in Rome. Composed of 12 English-speaking bishops and representing nine countries, the committee assisted in examining the new Roman Missal issued in the English language. The Holy Father said that he hoped that the vernacular would enable greater participation by the faithful at Mass.

Child Abuse — It was reported on Apr. 23 that Pope John Paul II labeled sexual abuse of children an "appalling sin" and a crime. He stated there is no place for such predators in the priesthood and the religious life. The Holy Father asked to be kept informed about the difficulties facing the American Church. The pope was addressing the American cardinals and bishops summoned to Rome because of the scandals.

Dominus Iesus — It was reported on Apr. 24 that the Vatican published a new book to offer an increased understanding of the document, *Dominus Iesus*, issued in August 2000. Available only in Italian, the book has a prologue by Cardinal Joseph Ratzinger. The document *Dominus Iesus* was a declaration on the unique and universal character of salvation offered by Christ and the Church. The new work will clarify and explain the document.

Russian Catholic Encyclopedia — Pope John Paul II received the first volume of the *Russian Catholic Encyclopedia*, it was announced on Apr. 25. Archbishop Tadeusz Kondrusiewicz, the metropolitan of the diocese of the Mother of God in Moscow and academics and professors who prepared the volume were received by the pontiff.

General Absolution — The Vatican announced on Apr. 26 that a decree on the sacrament of penance, an apostolic letter, *motu proprio*, entitled *Misericordia Dei*, would be released on May 2. (See also under **News in Depth**.)

Vatican-Turkey Agreement — The Vatican and Turkey have signed an unprecedented agreement to promote interreligious dialogue, it was revealed on Apr. 28. Cardinal Francis Arinze, president of the Pontifical Council for Interreligious Dialogue, and Mehmet Nuri Yelmaz, president of the Turkish Religious Affairs Office, signed the document. The intention is to promote a good understanding between Islam and Christianity and to support freedom of religion, belief, and conscience. Turkey is a primarily Islamic nation.

Seafarer Apostolate — On Apr. 29, Pope John Paul II addressed a plenary meeting of the Pontifical Council for Migrants and Travelers, saying that the great family of the sea deserves spiritual support. Tourists on cruise liners, merchant marine crews and immigrants need assistance from the seafarer apostolate.

General Audience Topics:

- Psalm 96 (97) (Apr. 3)
- God is Neither Asleep Nor Indifferent (Apr. 10)
- Reflection on a Canticle in Isaiah 12 (Apr. 17)
- Meditation on Psalm 80 (81) (Apr. 24)
- Interreligious Dialogue and Mission Aren't in Contradiction (Apr. 30)

International

Vietnam Cathedral — The groundbreaking for the new cathedral of Lang Son, Vietnam, is considered a true sign of recovery, it was revealed on Apr. 1. Bishop Joseph Ngo Quang Kiet of Lang Son heralded the event. The original cathedral was destroyed during the Vietnam War, in 1967, and was never rebuilt.

Queen Mother — Catholic leaders in the United Kingdom joined in the tributes paid to Queen Mother Elizabeth, who died on March 30. Pope John Paul II also sent a telegram of condolence to Queen Elizabeth II on the passing of her mother.

Nativity Church — On Apr. 2, 2002, a group of 200 Palestinian militia members entered the compound of the Church of Nativity in an effort to avoid Israeli troops besieging Bethlehem in response to terrorist bombings in Israel. The siege and standoff at the Church of the Nativity was resolved only on May 10 after extensive negotiations among the various parties, including the Holy See.

French Condemnation — On Apr. 4, the president of the French bishops' conference, Archbishop Jeanne-Pierre Ricard of Bordeaux, condemned the recent attacks on Jewish synagogues and cemeteries. He offered profound sympathy and solidarity on behalf of the Catholic Church in France. French Catholic leaders voiced their fraternity with the nation's Jewish communities.

Priest Slain — On Apr. 7, Fr. Juan Ramón Núñez and a layman were killed by gunmen in La Argentina, Colombia. Fr. Núñez was celebrating Mass in his parish church when gunmen approached the altar and fired at him. Police suspect the Revolutionary Armed Forces of Colombia (FARC) of conducting the attack. The layman, Joaquín Quebrada, was attending the Mass when he was slain.

Montagnard Asylum — It was announced on April 8 that 1,000 Vietnamese Montagnards, predominantly Christian, have the option to seek asylum in the U.S. The Montagnards are in Cambodia, where the U.N. High Commissioner for Refugees has jurisdiction for their welfare.

Dutch Documents — The Netherland's Catholic Bishops' Conference published a book on Apr. 8 containing collected documents on euthanasia from 1983-2001. The book was sent in English to the world's bishops' conferences and to other institutions to offer much-needed information on euthanasia. It is called *Euthanasia and Human Dignity* and opposes the Dutch efforts to legalize euthanasia.

New Salesian Superior — Fr. Pascuel Chávez Villanueva, a 51-year-old Mexican, was elected on Apr. 8 as the new rector major of the Society of St. Francis de Sales, called the Salesians. The 25th general chapter of the Salesians was held in Rome, and Fr. Chávez was elected on the first vote.

Priest Kidnapped — It was announced on Apr. 9 that two Colombian priests were kidnapped by guerrillas, while a third, a close collaborator of murdered Archbishop Isaías Duarte Cancino, has been forced to leave the country because of death threats. Fr. Saulo Carreño, parish priest of Saravena, and Fr. Teodore González of Arauca, were kidnapped by members of the National Liberation Army (NLA) during a humanitarian mission to the department of Arauca. The kidnappings occurred the same day that a priest, Juan Ramón Núñez, was murdered by gunmen while celebrating Mass in the southern village of La Argentina.

Visa denied — Fr. Stefano Caprio, a prominent Italian priest living and working in Moscow, Russia, reported on Apr. 10 that he had been stripped of his Russian visa. The move by Russian authorities was considered an Orthodox reprisal for the pope's creation of Roman Catholic dioceses in Russia. Fr. Caprio taught for 13 years in Moscow.

Padre Pio's Stigmata — The stigmata suffered by Blessed Padre Pio was analyzed by a scientific congress in Rome, it was announced on Apr. 12. The study will counter-attacks made by nonbelievers. Cardinal José Saraiva Martins, prefect of the Vatican Congregation for the Causes of Saints, addressed the congress. The congress was held at the Pontifical Athenaeum Regina Apostolorum in Rome. (For coverage of the canonization of Padre Pio, please see under **International News** in **News in Depth**.)

Madagascar Crisis — It was reported on Apr. 12 that Madagascar is suffering severe shortages of food and medicine, the result of divisive and contested elections. Catholic Relief Services announced that food shortages, roadblocks, and inflation have only deepened the humanitarian crisis. The 2,200 health centers in the country are empty of their supplies.

Madagascar Slayings — A Sacred Heart Brother, Joseph Roger Morin, 75, was killed on Apr. 12. He died in his room at Our Lady of the Sacred Heart Novitiate by gunfire during unrest triggered by disputes over the presidential election of December 2001. Morin made his religious profession in the Arthabaska Province of the congregation in Canada, in 1944. He had been a missionary in Madagascar for 51 years, serving as teacher, school principal, diocesan director of Catholic education, and formation director.

Bethlehem — Franciscan Fr. Giovanni Battistelli, the Franciscan Custodian of the Holy Land, met with U.S. Secretary of State Colin Powell on Apr. 14 to discuss the crisis gripping Bethlehem's Basilica of the Nativity, besieged by the Israeli army, ever since 200 Palestinians, many of them armed, invaded the sacred premises. At the end of the meeting between church leaders in the Holy Land and the U.S. secretary of state, Battistelli told Powell: "Don't leave us alone!"

Anglican Rebellion — The Anglican Forward in Faith, a group formed by the Church of England clergy, announced that they would go to Rome or seek some other form of faith owing to the ordination of women. Forward in Faith represents about 1,000 Anglican ministers and some 6,000 lay people in the Anglican community. The group's decision was reported on April 21.

Slaves Freed — The Christian Solidarity International (CSI), a group dedicated to rescuing African women and children from slavery, announced on Apr. 22 that some 6,000 slaves were freed in the Sudan. Half of these slaves were rescued from bondage in daring escapes and 3,000 were voluntarily freed by their masters in a treaty arranged by CSI between local Arabs and Africans. Some 700 slaves were also redeemed in the oil regions of the Western Upper Nile.

Hindu-Muslim Carnage — Some 20 people are dead and more than 100 injured after a two-day battle in Gujarat, India, it was reported on Apr. 22. The local Hindus and Muslims in Ahmadabad erupted in protests related to the Feb. 27 attack by radical Muslim groups on a train carrying Hindu pilgrims.

Russian Protests — On Apr. 26 a group of Russian intellectuals and authors issued a letter of protest over the expulsion of Catholic Bishop Jerzy Mazur of Irkutsk and Fr. Stefan Caprio. Some of Russia's most respected writers, poets, and intellectuals called the expulsions "worthy of the Soviet era."

Bavarian Expulsion — It was announced on Apr. 26 that the Teaching Sisters of Our Beloved Lady are being forced by the Bavarian German state and civil authorities to stop teaching in a local school. They are accused by parents of abusive teaching methods. Parents at Auerbach started complaining over the refusal of the nuns to use a state-approved book concerning biology and sex education. The Bavarian government demanded that the books be used. Some had been distributed to students with pages removed. When the nuns did not agree to the demands, they were notified of the expulsion.

Salesians in Kuwait — The Salesians opened their first school in Kuwait, it was revealed on Apr. 28. Located in Salamiya, The English Academy School will serve students from Egypt, Pakistan, the Philippines, Syria, and Yemen. The Salesians are serving the large foreign community involved in the oil industry in Kuwait.

Euthanasia Denied — The European Court of Human Rights ruled that a terminally-ill British woman does not have the right to commit suicide with the aid of her husband. This ruling was announced in Strasbourg, France, on Apr. 29. The case was brought before the court as an effort by Britain to allege violations of the European Convention on Human Rights, articles 2 and 3. The Netherlands had recently decriminalized euthanasia.

Tashkent Catholics — It was announced on Apr. 30 that a small group of young men were establishing a Catholic news site in Russian, with the aid of Franciscan Father Krysyztof Kukulka. Working every day, the young men are using the Internet sites for Catholic news, then translating items and posting them on web sites for Tashkent, Uzbekistan, viewers. They are also planning to open the world's premier Russian-language Catholics news service. Fr. Kukulka is a Polish Franciscan, fluent in Russian.

National

Legal Suicides — It was reported on Apr. 1 that Oregon lawyers attacked a U.S. Justice Department ruling that hindered suicides by terminally ill patients with the help of their physicians. Representing Oregon, the lawyers defended Oregon's law against rulings concerning federally regulated drugs.

Catholic Radio — *The Mission of Catholic Radio*, a new book and CD, is being released by the Atlanta-based Avila Radio, it was announced on Apr. 1. The booklet and CD offer counsel on starting radio projects and may be ordered on the Internet at www.avilaradio.com.

Defending Priests — Bishop John J. Nevins of Venice, Fla., asked on Apr. 2 that Catholics unite behind their priests in this crisis period. The bishop reminded the faithful that: "We've had rough times in the past, but we don't give up and we don't fall apart." His letter to the diocese, "The Priesthood and the Shadow of the Cross" asked Catholics to give priests support and encouragement.

Catholic Women — The National Council of Catholic Women celebrated its 20th year of serving elderly Americans, it was announced on Apr. 2. Representing more than 5,500 Catholic women's organizations, NCCW founded the Respite program in 1982, one of America's earliest projects for geriatric care.

Catholic Education — The National Catholic Education Association convention opened on Apr. 2 in Atlantic City, N.J. The conferences discussed the 9/11 disaster and the resulting changes in America. Teaching procedures, school violence, fund raising and other topics were included in convention workshops and meetings.

MIRA Awards — It was reported on Apr. 4 that Vanessa Williams and composer Elizabeth Swados had received the MIRA Awards, bestowed by the group Media and Religious Awareness. Williams portrayed Mother Henriette Delille of New Orleans in the Lifetime film *The Courage to Love*. Swados is being honored for choral drama, *The Missionaries*, depicting the four American Church women slain in El Salvador in 1980. The awards were given on Apr. 27 in New York.

Priest Suicide — Fr. Donald Rooney, a Cleveland diocesan priest, was found dead on Apr. 4, an apparent suicide. An associate pastor of St. Anthony of Padua Church in Parma, Ohio, he was found in a parking lot with a self-inflicted gunshot wound to the head. He had been accused on Apr. 1 of sexually abusing a child 22 years ago.

38

Seminary Increase — The Center for Applied Research in the Apostolate (CARA) announced on Apr. 9 that U.S. Catholic theological seminaries enrolled 101 more students this year. The figure rose from 3,483 in 2000-01 to 3,584 in 2001-02. This marks the fifth straight year of increases.

New Paper — On Apr. 9 it was announced that *El Spiritu Catolico*, a new Spanish-language newspaper, was launched in the archdiocese of St. Paul and Minneapolis. Some 6,000 copies of the paper were delivered to Hispanic-populated parishes in the archdiocese. The new publication will provide news coverage, columns and articles on matters of interest to Spanish-speaking Catholics.

Archbishop Chaput — In an address delivered on Apr. 5 to a national meeting of the Institute on Religious Life at the University of St. Mary of the Lake in Mundelein, Archbishop Charles J. Chaput of Denver stated in their efforts to be more open to the world since the Second Vatican Council, Catholics may have "been too comfortable and accommodating…. We've listened to the world too politely when it lies about abortion, or contraception, or divorce, or the death penalty, or our obligations to the poor, or the rights of undocumented workers, or the real meaning of pluralism, or our international responsibilities — and we haven't shouted out the truth."

Cloning Ban — President George W. Bush urged the U.S. Senate on Apr. 10 to pass legislation banning all cloning of humans. The Senate is expected to take up legislation on human cloning before it recesses for the summer. The House passed a bill last July that would ban all research in human cloning. One bill pending action in the Senate would prohibit research in cloning for reproductive purposes, but would permit research on cloned human embryos, which are destroyed after stem cells have been extracted. That version is unacceptable to the president. The Church is also adamantly opposed to human cloning.

Pentagon Memorial — The military chaplains, meeting on Apr. 10, designed and approved a stained-glass window, with assistance from an art studio. The window will commemorate the victims of the pentagon attack on September 11. The memorial will be placed in a new chapel being added to the Pentagon.

Norms Decreed — Bishop Wilton D. Gregory of Belleville, Ill., president of the U.S. Conference of Catholic Bishops, decreed on Apr. 15 new norms for the distribution and reception of Communion under the outward signs of both bread and wine by Catholics in the United States following Vatican approval. (See also coverage in **News in Depth** and in the **Sacraments** section.)

Ethics Award — Dr. Edmund D. Pellegrino, professor emeritus of medicine and medical ethics at Georgetown University Medical Center, was honored by both Marymount University in Arlington and a Washington-based Catholic lay ministry training program called Education, Parish and Service (EPS). The university presented Pellegrino with its 2002 Ethics Award March 25 in honor of his vision and leadership in fostering medical ethics. At an evening prayer service Apr. 10 on the campus of Trinity College in Washington, Pellegrino received the fifth annual EPS Service Award, which honors lay Catholic men and women who exemplify the lay vocation and mission to an exceptional degree by their witness, leadership and service. EPS is based at Trinity College, which is run by the Sisters of Notre Dame de Namur, and has a number of programs around the country.

St. Patrick's Suicide — On Apr. 15, Arem Gazaryan, a native of Armenia, died of the wounds he inflicted on himself at St. Patrick's Cathedral in New York on Apr. 3. Gazaryan shot himself in the face. He died in New York Presbyterian Hospital-Weill Cornell Medical Center.

Mission Societies — The four pontifical mission societies in the United States held a combined meeting in San Antonio, Tex., on Apr. 16-18. The groups are the Society for the Propagation of the Faith, the Holy Childhood Association, the Pontifical Missionary Union, and the Society of St. Peter Apostle. They are coordinated by the Vatican Congregation for the Evangelization of Peoples.

Apostleship of the Sea — The unique seafarer mission, Apostleship of the Sea, held a national convention in San Diego, it was reported on Apr. 17. More than two dozen chaplains attended. Fr. Gerard Troncke, international director of the apostolate and a member of the Pontifical Council for Migrants and Travelers in the Roman Curia, also took part. The Apostleship of the Sea conducts missions at 59 U.S. ports, including Samoa and Puerto Rico.

Rockford Newspaper — It was announced on Apr. 18 that the diocese of Rockford, Ill., had launched a Spanish-language newspaper, called *El Observer*.

Sex Abuse Meetings — An unprecedented gathering of U.S. cardinals and U.S. Church leaders with Vatican officials and the Holy Father was held on Apr. 23-24. The pope addressed the group at the end of their first morning session, which was led by Cardinal Angelo Sodano, Vatican secretary of state.

At the end of the summit, U.S. church leaders outlined a detailed plan of action, including a national policy to deal with priest-offenders and a special process for dismissing them from the priesthood. The proposals were described in a final statement from the Apr. 23-24 meeting. The proposals were then presented for consideration at the June meeting of bishops in Dallas. (For detailed coverage on the crisis, see under **National News** in **News in Depth**.)

Reproductive Technologies — On Apr. 25, Prof. Helen Alvaré, an associate professor of law at The Catholic University of America, termed the new reproductive technologies used by modern medicine the "silent killer of love and life." Addressing the annual convention of Legatus, the international organization of business leaders, Alvaré warned that Catholics do not understand the purpose of these new technologies and therefore do not defend the embryos being subjected to their use. Legatus met Apr. 18-20 in New Orleans.

Spanish Bible — An ad hoc committee formed by the Bishops' Administrative Committee was announced on Apr. 26. This committee, working with CELAM, the Latin American Bishops' Council and the Canadian Conference of Catholic Bishops, will explore the possibility of offering Spanish-speaking Catholics, estimated at 300 million in the Western Hemisphere, a Spanish translation of the Bible. Cultural and language differences as well as the need to have biblical scholars fluent in Spanish and national idioms make the task complex. Such references can help unify the Spanish-speaking Catholics in the hemisphere.

MAY 2002

Vatican

Misericordia Dei — On May 2, Cardinal Joseph Ratzinger announced in Rome that the apostolic letter *Misericordia Dei* ("The Mercy of God") was written by Pope John Paul II to provide insight into the personal character of the sacrament of penance. (See also coverage under **News in Depth**.)

Moroccan Ambassador — On May 3, the new ambassador of Morocco to the Vatican, Mohammed Sbihi, was welcomed by Pope John Paul II. The Holy Father noted that the ambassador's presence added weight to the truth that dialogue between cultures and religions is the most important challenge on the modern international scene. Pope John Paul II also reiterated his call to world leaders to put an end to violence.

Papal Vicar — On May 3, Cardinal Camillo Ruini, the papal vicar of Rome, announced the opening of the diocesan phase of the process to canonize Fr. Luigi Struzo, the founder of the Italian Popular Party. Fr. Sturzo, serving always as a priest in whatever political position that he held, was always granted a papal exemption from canon law to assume various offices. He was born in Italy in 1871 and died in Rome in 1959.

Basilica Siege — Pope John Paul II called on May 5 for prayers for the Holy Land as progress was reported in negotiations concerning the siege of the Basilica of the Nativity and the Franciscan Monastery in Bethlehem. The siege started on Apr. 2, when over 200 Palestinians stormed the holy site and refused to surrender to the Israeli troops that subsequently surrounded the church complex.

Pope in Ischia — Pope John Paul II traveled on May 5 to the Mediterranean island of Ischia, where he presided over a Mass for 15,000 worshippers. The Holy Father also met with 8,000 young people. Ischia's Ponte Square was the scene of the Mass, and there were 600 small boats just offshore, providing more room for the faithful. The people of Ischia asked the Holy Father to stay on the island to heal his ailing knee.

Pope Condemns Attack — The Holy Father issued a severe condemnation on May 6 against the attack by Colombian rebels against refugees in the Church of Bellavista in Bojaya.

Social Catechism — Cardinal François Xavier Nguyên Van Thuân announced on May 6 that a compendium of Catholic social doctrine will be published within a year. The cardinal is president of the Pontifical Council for Justice and Peace, and he directed attention to the beatitudes as modern moral guides. The document will clarify Church teaching in the wake of new terrorism and humanitarian focuses.

New Swiss Guards — Pope John Paul II greeted 28 new members of the Swiss Guards on May 6. The new "soldiers of the pope" met the Holy Father in the St. Damasus courtyard in the Apostolic Palace, having been accepted and trained to serve in the world's smallest army. The ceremony commemorates May 6 in 1527, when 147 Swiss Guards died protecting Pope Clement VII during the sack of Rome by the forces of the Holy Roman Empire under Emperor Charles V.

Catholic Gains — It was announced on May 6 that the number of Catholics in the world rose by 38% during the pontificate of Pope John Paul II. The *Annuarium Statisticum Ecclesiae* (*Statistical Yearbook of the Church*) compiled by the Vatican Secretariat of State and published by the *Libreria Editrice Vaticana* reported that the number of people baptized in the Catholic Church worldwide from 1978 to 2000 increased to 1.045 billion from 757 million.

Papal Admonition — Pope John Paul II, in a meeting with bishops from the Antilles on May 9, warned that the laity must not be given clerical powers and the clergy must not be laicized if the Church is to fulfill its mission.

Papal Birthday — At his May 15 general audience in St. Peter's Square, Pope John Paul II was greeted by 13,000 of the faithful, who offered him best wishes in anticipation of the Holy Father's 82nd birthday.

Orthodox Rapprochement — It was announced on May 16 that Cardinal Walter Kasper visited Yugoslavia and met with leaders of the Serbian Orthodox Church in a series of explorations of common bonds and differences. Kasper is president of the Pontifical Council for Promoting Christian Unity. He also met with Yugoslavian President Vojislava Kostunica and with Serbian Prime Minister Zoran Djindjic.

New Saints — On May 19, Pope John Paul II canonized five saints, including the first Brazilian saint, Paulina do Coracao Agonizante de Jesus (Amabile Visintainer) (1865-1942). The other saints are: Umile da Bisignano (Luca Antonio Pirozzo) (1582-1637); Ignazio da Santhia (Lorenzo Maurizio Belvisotti) (1686-1770); Benedetta Cambiagio Frassinello (1791-1858); and Alonso de Orozco (1500-1591). The Holy Father declared the new saints an eloquent sign of the Church's "perennial Pentecost."

World Mission Day — On May 20, Pope John Paul II announced that the theme for World Mission Day, Oct. 20, will be "Mission is Proclamation of Forgiveness." He appealed to Catholics to serve as missionaries of Christ's Gospel through dialogue and forgiveness. Forgiveness, the Holy Father instructed, creates real communion by opening hearts and healing the wounds of humanity from divisions and sins.

Mother Teresa — On May 21, Fr. Brian Kolodiejchuk, a Missionary of Charity priest, reported that Italian newspaper reports of a possibly early beatification for Mother Teresa of Calcutta could be true. Fr. Kolodiejchuk recently submitted a 5,000-page biography of Mother Teresa to the Congregation for the Causes of Saints in Rome. Known as a *positio*, the material will be reviewed by the congregation's officials and theologians.

Azerbaijan Visit — Pope John Paul II announced his purpose in Azerbaijan on May 22 as an ambassador of peace. He declared that as long he had breath he would cry out for peace. The Holy Father met Heidar Aliev, a former Communist and now the president of Azerbaijan in the Presidential Palace. Because there is no apostolic nunciature in Baku, the capital, the Holy Father stayed at the Irshad Hotel during his visit (this was the first time that a pope has stayed at a hotel during an apostolic visit).

Sofia Greeting — On May 23, Pope John Paul II addressed 5,000 Bulgarians and political leaders in Sofia, Bulgaria. In St. Alexander Novski Square, he was welcomed by Pres. Georgi Parvanov, Orthodox Patriarch Maxim, and Prime Minister Simeon Saxe-Coburg-Gotha.

Papal relic — Pope John Paul II gave the small

Catholic community of Bulgaria a very special gift on May 25. He presented a small piece of bone from the remains of Blessed Pope John XXIII (d. 1963). This was the first known relic of the recently beatified pontiff. During his years as a papal nuncio, the future pope, Angelo Roncalli, had served in Bulgaria as a papal representative.

Bulgarian Beati — Pope John Paul II beatified three Bulgarian martyrs in Alexander Battenberg Square in Plovdiv, Bulgaria, on May 26. A crowd of 25,000, including Catholics, Orthodox, and Muslims, attended the ceremony. The new beati are Kamen Vitchev, Pavel Djidjov, and Josaphat Chichkov, Augustinian religious of the Assumption. They were shot in a prison in Sofia on Nov. 11-12, 1952, by the Communist regime. Blessed Bishop Eugene Bossilkov, a Passionist, was martyred at the same time.

Seminary Training — On May 27, Pope John Paul II warned against lowering formation standards for priests in order to counteract a continuing decline in vocations in the first world. In a message to the superior general of the Congregation of the Holy Ghost, the Holy Father urged religious seminarians to prepare priests with a human, intellectual, pastoral, and spiritual formation that will aid the missions of the Church throughout the world.

Presidential Visit — Pres. George W. Bush had a second audience with Pope John Paul II on May 28 in the Vatican. Secretary of State Colin Powell met with Cardinal Angelo Sodano, Vatican Secretary of State and Archbishop Jean-Louis Tauran, Vatican Secretary for Relations with States. The Holy Father and Pres. Bush discussed a range of international problems, including the attack on Sept. 11 and the sex abuse scandal facing the Church in the United States. Pres. Bush, who views the Catholic Church as an incredibly important institution in the U.S., described Pope John Paul II as "a man of enormous dignity and compassion."

Missionary Superiors — The first meeting of general superiors of missionary institutes was held on May 28 by the Vatican Congregation for the Evangelization of Peoples. Cardinal Crescenzio Sepe, prefect of the congregation, addressed the gathering of 240 general superiors. The purpose of the gathering was to make the mission apostolate a vital aspect of the ongoing pastoral service of the Church in the modern world.

Worldwide Conference — It was announced on May 28 that a worldwide videoconference on the Blessed Virgin Mary in contemporary theology will be held in the Vatican. The ninth such videoconference, the broadcast will feature Cardinal Dario Castrillón Hoyos, prefect of the Vatican Congregation for the Clergy and other noted theologians.

General Audience Topics:

• Meditation on Psalm 50 (51), the *Miserere* (May 8)
•With God, Nightmares and Obstacles Disappear (May 15)
• Recollection of the Apostolic Pilgrimage to Azerbaijan and Bulgaria (May 29)

International

Malawi Famine — Predictions that as many as 80% of 10.5 million people are at risk to perish from malnutrition and related diseases were announced on May 1 in Malawi. A chronic corn shortage has brought about the deaths of hundreds already. Catholic missions in this southern African nation are in the forefront of relief efforts.

Ecumenical Care — Holy Family Hospital, operated by the Italian Brothers of St. John of God in Nazareth, Israel, has Arab and Jewish personnel working together, it was reported on May 2. Prayers, including the Our Father, are recited, and the Gospel is read aloud. The Holy Family Hospital was opened 120 years ago, under the auspices of the Hospitaller Order of St. John of God, and has emergency and other medical services.

Focolare Youths — Some 6,000 young people gathered in Loppiano, Italy, to dedicate themselves to world peace in the wake of Sept. 11. Representing 72 countries, the young people prayed and heard talks from others around the world. A petition asking European efforts and leadership in the Middle East was signed by 20,000 people, part of the Focolare efforts. Chiara Lubich, the foundress of the group, sent a message to the young people attending the gathering, it was reported on May 3.

Festival Attack — Archbishop Orlando Queveda of Catabato, Philippines, on May 3 condemned the grenade assault that killed seven and wounded 127 Catholic worshippers at St. Joseph the Worker parish. Celebrating the feast day, the parishioners and Muslim guests were attacked and endured "untold suffering." Reports concerning the attackers vary.

Brazil Debate — It was reported on May 7 that the Brazilian Senate, heeding words of caution expressed by Catholic bishops concerning moral values, has delayed ratification of the Optional Protocol of the Convention on the Elimination of All Forms of Discrimination Against Woman (CEDAW), known in Brazil as the "Woman's Convention." The bishops stated that CEDAW favors abortion and considers maternity a disgrace. CEDAW also advocates legalizing lesbianism. The U.N. General Assembly adopted the protocol for the convention of 1999.

Timor Advances — On May 6, Bishop Carlos Ximenes Belo of Dili, East Timor, addressed religious leaders in New York and spoke of his land's consciousness of democratic ideals. East Timor received full independence on May 20 after long being a colonial possession of Indonesia.

Martyr's Century — The 20th century claimed 65% of the Christian martyrs in history, it was reported on May 9 during a conference on "Anti-Christian Persecution in the 20th Century" held at the Pontifical Athenaeum Regina Apostolorum in Rome. Italian journalist Antonio Socci presented his new work, *The New Persecuted* (*I Nuovi Perseguitati*). According to Socci's research, in the two millennia of Christian history, about 70 million faithful have given their lives for the faith, and of these, 45.5 million — fully 65% — were in the last century. The major impetus for persecuting Christians can be seen in nations endorsing Muslim fundamentalism or Communism.

Sudan Victims — It was announced on May 12 that more than 470 Sudanese civilians were slain by Ugandan rebels, who assaulted women and girls and burned villages. Ugandan rebels are in the Sudan as are troops of Uganda. Bishop Akio Johnson Mutek of Torio appealed for international intervention.

Failed Petition — The Russian Duma, the nation's

legislative body, failed to pass a resolution asking Pres. Vladimir Putin to prohibit the Catholic Church from functioning in Russia, it was reported on May 16. The sponsors of the petition stated that the erection of four dioceses in Russia by the pope demonstrates that Pope John Paul II is seeking to dominate that nation.

Spiritual Rebirth — On May 17, it was reported that Cardinal Jaime Lucas Ortega, Archbishop of Havana, has noted a spiritual revival in Cuba since the visit of Pope John Paul II in January 1998. The cardinals reported that there are 250 missions and houses of prayer in Havana, and 83% of the Cubans declare themselves as believers.

Bahia Slaying — Fr. Alois Lintner, an Italian missionary in San Salvador de Bahia, Brazil, was reported shot to death on May 17. Laboring in the Brazilian missions since 1979, he was active in fighting local crime and was gunned down by two unidentified assailants. The attackers also took his car and drove over his body. He died on the way to the hospital.

Bishop Kidnapped — Catholic Bishop Everest Nduhirubusa of Ruyigi, Burundi, was kidnapped on May 18 by Hutu rebels. Two gendarmes, serving as his bodyguards, were slain in the attack. The bishop was taken alive by the Hutus, members of the Forces for the Defense of Democracy. The bishop was later released by his captors.

Misleading Tale — Marcos Musharaf, who confessed to murdering Msgr. Jorge Altafulla of Panama City, Panama, admitted on May 21 that he had charged the murdered priest with pedophilia in order to mislead the police. Musharaf killed the priest because he was resentful toward the Church.

Priest Scandals — Fr. Amedeo Cencini, a psychologist and educator of the Sons of Charity, said on May 27 that the priest abuse scandals are rooted in the modern trivialization of sex. Sexuality has been debased and made banal. Fr. Cencini added that in the modern world an intelligent and orderly management of sexuality does not exist. He also chided Americans for pursuing a favorable attitude toward the homosexual condition, as if it were entirely normal.

National

New Seminary — On May 1, Archbishop Gabriel Montalvo, the apostolic nuncio to the United States, presided over the blessing and dedication of a new seminary in Brownsville, Texas. The apostolic nuncio stated that the true treasures of the seminary are the students who will form the ministerial community for the diocese.

Moral Clarity — On May 1, Sen. Gordon Smith (R-Ore.) said he would vote to ban all human cloning. He was addressing an audience at the Catholic University of Portland when he praised the Church for its moral clarity concerning cloning and other life issues being debated in the country.

Mychal Judge Bio — Michael Ford, a British religious broadcaster, was commissioned to write a spiritual biography of the New York City Fire Department Chaplain, Franciscan Fr. Mychal Judge. The 160-page hardcover will cost $19.95, it was reported on May 1. Ford is the author of the 1999 book, *Wounded Prophet, the Life of Fr. Henri Nouwen*.

Priest Defense — The Knights of Columbus will begin an advertising campaign of prayer and support for priests, it was announced on May 2. Full-page newspaper ads and magazine advertisements will be part of the campaign. The Knights promote vocations through grants and scholarships.

Assisted Suicide — The Hawaii State Senate, by a vote of 14-11, rejected on May 2 proposed legislation that would allow physician-assisted suicides. The proposed bill was modeled on the Oregon legislation and was approved by the Hawaii House. Governor Ben Cayetano supported the bill.

Vocation Efforts — It was announced on May 3 that the archdiocese of Baltimore has started a 15-year plan to increase priestly vocations. This program will also enlist foreign-born priests and will streamline administrative procedures and parish clustering. The plan limits priests to being appointed pastors until they have served in the archdiocese for at least six years after ordination.

Volunteers of the Year — On May 7 it was announced that Tom and Kathy Gess of Baton Rouge, La., were named the Catholic Charities USA's 2002 volunteers of the year. The couple has served prison inmates, their families, and ex-offenders as part of the Catholic Community Services of Baton Rouge. The award will be bestowed on August 3.

Old Testament — At a May 7 conference in Washington, D.C., sponsored by the Catholic University of America, the U.S. Bishops' Secretariat for Ecumenical and Interrelgious Affairs and the Rabbinical Committee for Interreligious Dialogue, a Vatican document was praised for its contribution to Catholic-Jewish relations. The document, titled "The Jewish People and Their Sacred Scriptures in the Christian Bible," was prepared by the Pontifical Biblical Commission and made public in December 2001. It accepts as valid Jewish interpretations of Scripture that parallel Christian views. (See also under **Ecumenism** and **Interreligious Dialogue**.)

Unborn Needs — It was announced on May 8 that proposed regulatory changes would make unborn children eligible for care under the State Children's Health Insurance Program. The U.S. Department of Health and Human Services is proposing the changes to provide state care for the unborn and their mothers who are presently ineligible for prenatal coverage. The Bush administration has clarified the regulatory definition of a child for SCHIP coverage to include children under the age of 19, including the period from conception until birth.

Life Award — The five police and emergency medical staffs that responded to the Sept. 11 attack in New York received the annual Cardinal Cooke Right to Life Award on May 8. Representatives of each group accepted the awards, especially on behalf of those who gave their lives in the disaster.

Bishop Resigns — It was announced on May 8 that Bishop Paul Dudley, retired bishop of the diocese of Sioux Falls, S.D., withdrew from priestly ministry because of a pending investigation resulting from accusations that he was involved in sexual abuse. Bishop Dudley is 75.

Franciscan Web Sites — It was reported on May 13 that two web sites by the Franciscans are operating to allay damage caused by the current clergy sexual abuse scandal: www.AmericanCatholic.org and www.CatholicGreetings.org. The first offers links and discussions, and the second offers e-greetings support for priests.

American Hero — It was reported on May 14 that the cause of Fr. Emil J. Kapaun has been opened. He is best known for his compassion and sacrifice while a prisoner of war of the Chinese communists in North Korea in 1950-51. He died in captivity at the age of 35 on May 23, 1951. A Mass was celebrated on May 27 by Auxiliary Bishop Francis X. Roque at the U.S. Archdiocese for Military Services.

Priest Shot — On May 13, Fr. Maurice Blackwell, a priest of the archdiocese of Baltimore, was shot several times by Dontes Stokes. Stokes accused Fr. Blackwell of prior sexual abuse. The priest was hospitalized, and Stokes turned himself into the police for attempted homicide.

Peter's Pence — The theme for the 2002 Peter's Pence Collection for works of the Holy Father was announced on May 21 by Archbishop James P. Keleher of Kansas City, Kans. The theme is "A Listening Heart, A Helping Hand, A Better World." Archbishop Keleher reported also that the collection was scheduled for June 29-30 in U.S. parishes.

Chaldean Eparchy — Pope John Paul II created on May 21 the San Diego based Eparchy of St. Peter the Apostle in the western United States. Msgr. Sarhad Jammo, 61, pastor of St. Joseph Chaldean Parish in the Detroit suburb of Troy, Mich., was named the eparchy's first bishop. The new eparchy consists of the 19 westernmost United States: Alaska, Arizona, California, Colorado, Hawaii, Idaho, Kansas, Montana, Nebraska, Nevada, Oklahoma, New Mexico, North Dakota, Oregon, South Dakota, Texas, Utah, Washington and Wyoming.

Monks Investigated — On May 21 Stearns County Sheriff James Kostreba announced that he was "investigating some information that we had not investigated before" concerning one or more of the 13 monks who live under restricted conditions at St. John's Abbey because of alleged or admitted sexual misconduct. Kostreba would not elaborate on what the information was or on how many of the monks at the abbey in Collegeville were the subjects of investigation. The investigations are apparently in reference to two of the area's most notorious unsolved crimes: the 1974 murder of two St. Cloud girls and the 1989 disappearance of a St. Joseph boy.

Seminary Accusations — On May 22, Msgr. Helmut Hefner, the president-rector, and James Bevacqua, student body president, declared that a May 20 story in *Newsweek* magazine on "Gays and the Seminary" made "completely false" claims about the percentage of gays at St. John's Seminary in Camarillo. They claim that they were misquoted in the article, which stated, "Depending on whom you ask, gay and bisexual men make up 30 to 70 percent of the (St. John's) student body at the college and graduate levels." The article quoted Msgr. Hefner as saying that he "accepts that his gay enrollment may be as high as 50 percent." In a letter to the editor of *Newsweek*, Msgr. Hefner said he was "deeply disappointed that I was completely misquoted." He wrote, "In speaking for one hour with your reporter, I clearly and repeatedly stated that I believed that even the lowest estimated percentage (30 percent) of gay seminarians was highly inflated."

Holy Cross — Alumni of Holy Cross College in Worcester, Mass., announced on May 22 that they have formed a group to "restore" its Catholic identity. Called the Holy Cross Cardinal Newman Society, the alumni group is concerned about the current board of trustees, mostly lay people, who assumed administrative control when the Jesuits withdrew in 1970.

Mary's Role — Cardinal Avery Dulles, the noted theologian who teaches at Fordham University, gave the opening address for the May 22-25 annual meeting of the Mariological Society of America in New York. In his address, he defined the role of the Virgin Mary as permanent and irreplaceable. Cardinal Dulles spoke on "Mary Since Vatican II," noting the increasing prominence of the Mother of God in recent theological circles.

Mother Teresa — The Knights of Columbus Museum in New Haven is displaying a life-size bronze of Mother Teresa and other works by sculptor Tomasso Gismondi, it was reported on May 23.

U.S. Priesthood — Bishop Wilton D. Gregory of Belleville, the president of the U.S. Conference of Catholic Bishops, wrote in the May 24 issue of *The Messenger*, the Belleville diocesan paper, that, "The Catholic Church is not hopelessly corrupt — as many accounts would have you believe." He added, "The priesthood is not filled with child molesters and perverts — in spite of the horrendous behavior of a few grotesque clerics…. All bishops have not been negligent, deceitful or conniving in attempting to address this issue — though a number of terrible mistakes have been made by some of us."

Anti-Catholic Health Programs — Auxilary Bishop Joseph M. Sullivan of Brooklyn declared in an address on May 24 that the future of Catholic hospitals is threatened by efforts to end their access to public funds unless they provide services such as contraception and abortion that violate Catholic moral standards. He said Planned Parenthood and other organizations promoting reproductive services were working for state legislation requiring provision of these services by hospitals receiving Medicare and Medicaid, funding essential to hospital budgets. These "adversaries" of the Catholic approach to health care are starting in New York and California, with an expectation that other states will follow if success is achieved there, he said.

Weakland Resignation — Pope John Paul II accepted Milwaukee Archbishop Rembert G. Weakland's resignation on May 24, the day after the archbishop was publicly accused of making an unwanted sexual advance on a man more than 20 years ago. Weakland acknowledged a 1998 monetary settlement with the man but said, "I have never abused anyone." The archbishop requested that the Vatican "accelerate its acceptance" of his resignation, which he had already submitted on his 75th birthday on Apr. 2. Auxilary Bishop Timothy Dolan of St. Louis was appointed as successor to Archbishop Weakland on June 25.

Catholic Relief — It was reported on May 31 that the Catholic Relief Services has set up a program office in the United States for the first time in its nearly 60-year history. The relief and development agency of the USCCB is based in Baltimore, but program offices have always been located in the countries being served. In response to pastoral calls from dioceses on the U.S.-Mexico border, CRS opened an office in Tucson. The bishops decided CRS needed to have a Mexico program again, because of an increasingly difficult economic situation in the country.

JUNE 2002

Vatican

Eucharist on Sabbath — Pope John Paul II on June 2 urged the faithful to rediscover the meaning of the Sabbath and the Eucharist. Addressing thousands of pilgrims at the Midday Angelus, the Holy Father described the Eucharist as "the beating center" of the Christian world, calling that sacrament "its most precious treasure." Groups from Italy, Spain, and the Ukraine received greetings from the Holy Father at the ceremony.

Bolivian Leader — On June 3, Pope John Paul II met with Bolivian president Jorge Quiroga Ramirez in the private papal apartments of the Vatican. The audience lasted 20 minutes. The two exchanged gifts, and the president introduced his wife and members of his entourage to the Holy Father.

No Resignation — It was announced on June 4 that Pope John Paul II has no plans to resign because of health concerns. The announcement was made in response to a Czeh newspaper report that predicted that the Holy Father would resign in August while visiting Poland.

Prayer Day — The prefect of the Vatican Congregation for the Clergy, Cardinal Dario Castrillón Hoyos, announced on June 4 that the Holy See proposed a World Day of Prayer for the Sanctification of Priests to be observed on the Feast of the Sacred Heart. The cardinal addressed the more than 400,000 priests of the world in a letter dated May 8. He recommended devoting oneself to the Divine Mercy, as experienced by St. Faustina Kowalska. The majority of the world's dioceses supported the prayer day on the feast of the Sacred Heart.

Anglican Exhibit — It was reported on June 4 that an exhibition on the history of Anglicanism has been opened in the Vatican. "Anglicanism and the Western Church: Continuity and Change" is the name of the exhibit inaugurated by Cardinal Edmund Szoka, president of the Pontifical Commission for the Vatican City State. The display coincides with the 50th anniversary of the coronation of Queen Elizabeth II and is being offered in the Sistine Hall.

The Popemobile — Pope John Paul II received a new "popemobile," it was announced on June 5. Daimler-Chrysler provided the new vehicle, an M430 Mercedes-Benz. The vehicle is colored mother-of-pearl and has bulletproof glass. Older versions are on display in a Vatican Museum.

Apostolic Signature — It was reported on June 6 that Pope John Paul II has appointed five cardinals to the Supreme Tribunal of the Apostolic Signatura, including Cardinal Edward M. Egan of New York. Also appointed were Cardinal Josef Glemp of Warsaw and cardinals serving in Rome, Agostino Cacciavillan, Sergio Sebastiani, and Walter Kasper. The Apostolic Signatura serves as the highest court of appeals in the Church.

Malaysia Visitor — Dato Seri Mahathir bin Mohamad, the prime minister of Malaysia, was a Vatican guest on June 7. He met with Pope John Paul II and Vatican officials, the first prime minister of Malaysia to be received by the Holy See. Mahathir is also chairman of the Organization of the Islamic Conference, an international association formed in 1969.

Orthodox Patriarch — Patriarch Bartholomew I of Constantinople celebrated the Divine Liturgy in the Byzantine basilica of Ravenna on June 9. The celebration marked the first time that an Orthodox patriarch of Constantinople offered the Divine Liturgy there. In his sermon, the patriarch stated that he hoped the event would herald better relations between Catholics and Orthodox.

President of Ghana — It was reported on June 9 that Pope John Paul II received the president of Ghana, John Agyekum Kufuor. The Holy Father visited Ghana in 1980. There are 2.5 million Catholics there, served by 300 parishes and 2,500 mission stations, as well as 1,000 educational institutions.

Colombian President — Pope John Paul II received Colombian President Andrés Pastrana on June 10, as the head of that nation came to the Vatican to express his gratitude to the Holy Father for his support and pleas for solidarity. President Pastrana leaves office on Aug. 7. He introduced his wife and entourage during the audience.

AIDS Researcher — Pope John Paul II received a medical researcher, Dr. Luc Montagnier, in June 10. Montagnier and Dr. Robert Gallo are honored as the discoverers of the AIDS virus, and both are involved in efforts to speed the development of an AIDS vaccine.

Papal Envoy — It was announced on June 12 that Pope John Paul II has appointed Cardinal James Francis Stafford as his special envoy for the dedication of the new Los Angeles cathedral on Sept. 2. Cardinal Stafford is president of the Pontifical Council for the Laity. The original Los Angeles cathedral, St. Vibiana's, was condemned because of earthquake damage in 1996. New land was acquired for the cathedral complex of the Cathedral of Our Lady of the Angels.

Sri Lanka Visitor — On June 13, Pope John Paul II received Chandrika Bandaranaike Kumaratunga, the president of Sri Lanka. Catholics number some 1.2 million, and Sri Lanka has eleven dioceses, 374 parishes and 1000 diocesan centers. The majority of Sri Lankans are Buddhists.

Religious Life — It was reported on June 14 that the Vatican has published a document concerning the renewal of the religious life in the Church. Entitled "Restarting from Christ: A Renewed Commitment of the Consecrated Life in the Third Millennium," the document was formed at a plenary meeting of the Congregation for Institutes of Consecrated Life and Societies of Apostolic Life. Religious orders and congregations around the world face diminishing memberships and, in some areas, persecutions by local governments and members of other faiths. (For details, see under **Consecrated Life**.)

Congo President — On June 14, Congo President Joseph Kabila was received at the Vatican. Kabila took office after his father was assassinated. The Democratic Republic of Congo (formerly Zaire) is 41% Catholic. The president asked the Holy Father to continue to pray for the return of peace to that African land, which endures a war between armies of neighboring lands.

Padre Pio Canonized — On June 16, Pope John Paul II canonized Padre Pio of Pietrelcina before more than 300,000 pilgrims. The ceremony was televised worldwide, and Padre Pio Prayer Groups and other devotees watched the canonization. Padre Pio died in 1968, and the Holy Father said of him: "The new saint invites us to place God above all, and to consider him our sole and highest good." Padre Pio was the 462nd saint proclaimed by Pope John Paul II during his pontificate.

Papal Scholarship — Pope John Paul II provided a scholarship for an orphan of the September 11 terrorist attacks and $50,000 for medical care of terrorist victims, it was announced on June 18. The Pontifical Council *Cor Unum* also reported that the Holy Father gave about $6.2 million in disaster relief and development programs.

Liturgy Communal Prayer — Addressing the International Meeting on Jesuit Liturgy, Cardinal Godfried Danneels of Meschelen-Brussels, Belgium, on June 19 stated that the liturgy is a communal form of prayer. He said as well that the liturgy is not a showplace for "the creativity or the piety of any participant, whether celebrant or member of the congregation." The international gathering in Rome brought 122 Jesuits from 44 countries and Vatican officials together.

Hungarian President — On June 20, Pope John Paul II received Hungarian President Ferenc Madl. The Holy Father visited Hungary in June 1991. Of the country's 10 million inhabitants, 62% are Catholic.

Hindu Praise — On June 20, Pope John Paul II met with 40 Hindus who were attending a Focolare Movement symposium in Rome. The experience was monumental to the participants, including Hindu intellectuals, and was called a spiritual, not just an academic event. One Hindu leader said that Pope John Paul II "is the great saint."

Peace Award — Archbishop Renato Martino, the Holy See's nuncio to the United Nations, awarded Simeon Saxe-Coburg Gotha the annual Path to Peace Award on June 19. A former king of Bulgaria, Gotha became that nation's prime minister last year after a long exile. His sister, Princess Maria Luisa, accepted on his behalf. Also present was Archbishop Leonardo Sandri, Deputy for the General Affairs of the Vatican Secretariat of State.

Archbishop of Canterbury — Archbishop George C. Carey of Canterbury, the head of the Anglican Church, met with Pope John Paul II on June 21. The Archbishop plans to retire on Oct. 31 and was in Rome to say farewell to friends and Vatican officials. The Holy Father praised the archbishop's efforts for ecumenical union and at Mideast peace. In an interview over Vatican Radio following the audience, Archbishop Carey called Pope John Paul II the "spiritual leader of the whole of Christianity."

Quake Plea — Pope John Paul II made an appeal for international aid to victims of the earthquake in northern Iran. He made this appeal on June 23 after the recitation of the Angelus in St. Peter's Square. The Holy Father assured Iranians of his prayers. He sent a telegram to the apostolic nuncio in Tehran, Iran, conveying his sympathy and concern.

Order of Malta — Pope John Paul II met with Fra Andrew Bertie, Grand Master of the Sovereign Military Order of Malta, on June 23. The Order of Malta, an international hospitaller and relief organization, dates to 1050.

Iranian Official — On June 28, Pope John Paul gave an audience to Ayatollah Seyyed Mohammed Khamenei, president of the Molla Sadra Islamic Philosophy Foundation and the brother of Al Khamenei, Iran's highest religious authority. He brought six Iranian philosophers to visit the Holy Father.

General Audiences
- Meditation on Psalm 147 (June 6)
- Address on Psalm 91 (92) (June 12)
- Mosaic Canticle in Deuteronomy (June 19)
- Meditation on Psalm 8 (June 26)

International
Abortion Laws — In a referendum, Switzerland voted overwhelmingly to loosen the nation's laws on abortion on June 2. An estimated 72% of voters supported a proposal to allow abortions up to the 12th week of pregnancy. A proposal to ban all abortions was opposed by 81% of the Swiss voters. Some 12,000 to 13,000 abortions are performed in Switzerland annually.

U.S. President's Visit — U.S. President George W. Bush met with Archbishop Tadeusz Kondrusiewicz in Moscow on June 2. President Bush, aware of the problems of the Catholic Church in Russia, discussed the exiles of the faith, Bishop Jerzy Mazur and Fr. Stefano Caprio, who were expelled from Russia, and offered his concern and aid to the Vatican representative. Bush stressed the importance of religious rights and initiated the meeting with Archbishop Kondrusiewicz.

500th Anniversary — Cardinal Nicolas de Jesus Lopez Rodriguez, the cardinal primate of the Americas and Archbishop of Santo Domingo, Dominican Republic, was named the representative of Pope John Paul II for the 500th anniversary of the first Mass celebrated in the New World. This centenary was announced on June 2, taking place on August 14, in Tegulcigalpa, Honduras. Christopher Columbus's fourth trip brought him to Honduras on July 30, 1502, and there the first Mass in the Americas was celebrated.

Israeli Assault — On June 2, it was reported that the Israeli army damaged an old Orthodox Church near Ramallah on the West Bank. The Israeli army admitted splintering the doors of the church with dynamite, but declared the attack "a mistake." The Israeli army spokesman apologized to the local Palestinians. The structure was the medieval Church of St. Barbara, recently restored.

Romanian Properties — In response to an appeal by Pope John Paul II, the Romanian Parliament responded positively on June 3 to the prospect of returning Catholic property confiscated by the Communists. Some of these properties were given to the Orthodox. Prime Minister Adrian Nastase stated that the matter is a question of principle, not of favoring one church over another.

Oaxaca Massacre — Cardinal Norberto Rivera Carrera of Mexico condemned the massacre of 26 peasants in the state of Oaxaca on June 3. The archbishop primate of Mexico made the charge in the Corpus Christi celebration in the cathedral. The massacre resulted from a land dispute.

St. Padre Pio Church — It was announced on June 3 that the faithful in India will erect a church in honor of St. Padre Pio of Petrelcina. Bishop Giorgio Mamalassery of Thakimagre made the announcement, saying that construction will begin on June 16 and will take one year.

Church Unity — Cardinal Cormac Murphy-O'Connor, Archbishop of Westminster, and other English Church leaders signed a covenant in the presence of Queen Elizabeth II, it was announced on June 3. The various religious leaders vowed to work for unity at a ceremony in Windsor Castle. The signing was marked as a truly historic moment. The faiths will seek a common understanding of salvation, and will work for visible unity.

Religion Popular — A poll reported on June 4 indicates that Italian students choose Catholic topics for study. The poll was conducted in state schools in 196 Italian dioceses and records that in 2001-2002, 93.2% of Italian students chose religion classes as an option.

Churches Vandalized — It was announced on June 5 that churches and cathedrals in Britain are being vandalized, burglarized, and burned. Damage costing £7.3 million ($10.6 million) was assessed last year. Lack of respect for religious sites is on the rise in Britain. Churches are installing bulletproof glass and other security measures to deter damage. An estimated 1,850 attacks on places of worship were recorded in 1999.

Lithuanian Restoration — On June 5, it was reported that the famed Calvary of Vilnius, Lithuania, has been restored and reopened. The 35 stations, constructed as 18th century chapels, were dynamited by the Communists in 1962. All of the stations, situated in a pine forest, have been blessed by Cardinal Audrys Backis, Archbishop of Vilnius.

Siberian Dispute — It was reported on June 6 that the Russian government is appealing a court decision that allowed Fr. Michael Shields of the American archdiocese of Anchorage to remain at a Catholic parish in Eastern Siberia. He serves as pastor in Magadan, on the Sea of Okhotsk, having started his ministry there in 1994. The Justice Ministry of Russia wants the priest to give up his pastorate at Nativity of Jesus Parish.

St. Thomas More — A portrait of St. Thomas More, a copy of a Holbein painting, will hang in Chelsea Old Church, an Anglican parish, it was reported on June 10. St. Thomas and his first wife, Jane Colt, worshipped at the church. The Prince of Wales was scheduled to unveil the portrait as an act of reconciliation. Chelsea Old Church is near the Thames Embankment.

Rebel Victim — It was reported on June 10 that Filipino Catholics were mourning the death of Ediborah Yap, a nurse kidnapped by Muslim rebels in the southern Philippines. She sustained gunshot wounds on June 7 during a firefight in Zamboanga del Norte between the rebels and government troops. American Martin Burnham died in the same firefight, and his wife, Gracia, was wounded. The Muslim rebels are part of the Abu Sayyaf group.

Hope Village — It was reported on June 11 that the Adorer of the Blood of Christ, a religious congregation, have started construction of a "Village of Hope" in Dodoma, Tanzania. HIV-positive patients will be cared for there, and the institution will offer preventative programs for the disease. Children will be housed there, and clinics and a laboratory/observatory will aid the programs. The nuns of the Adorers of the Blood of Christ started the program in a rural area near Dodoma.

Fátima Prayers — More than 60,000 children took part in the annual pilgrimage for minors to Fátima on June 11. These children were called upon to construct a future of peace, and they prayed for peace at the Marian shrine.

Starvation Looming — The British Caritas office warned world leaders on June 12 of massive starvation in Southern Africa. Malawi, Zambia, and Angola will face exhausted food reserves. A report was made by CAFOD concerning the impending disaster. CAFOD is the Catholic Agency for Overseas Development.

Thailand Ecumenism — The World Council of Religious and Spiritual Leaders was inaugurated at a June 12-14 meeting in Nakhon Pathom, outside Bangkok. Catholic delegates were among the hundreds of religious representatives that included some 60 religious leaders and 1,200 delegates from 13 religions.

Nobel Nominee — It was announced on June 14 that a Czech foundation, People In Need, has initiated a campaign to promote the nomination of Cuban dissident Catholic Oswaldo Payá Sardinas for the Nobel Peace Prize. The group described Payá Sardinas as a person "of integrity and of solid democratic principles." He spent three years in forced labor camps for promoting the Christian Liberation Movement in Cuba and the Varela Project.

Ukraine University —The first Catholic university in the Ukraine was opened on June 29 in the city of Lviv. The opening marked the completion of a long period of construction that had its official beginning in June 2001 when Pope John Paul II blessed the cornerstone for the Ukrainian Catholic University.

Weapons for Bibles — The Dominican Republic's clergy, with the support of the government, are collecting bibles in a new program, "Arms for Bibles." Weapons will be gathered and exchanged for Bibles in the program, which coincides with the "Safe City" program, conducted by the national police and resulting in 1,046 arrests. The efforts are part of a campaign to end teenage violence and delinquency, it was announced on June 18.

Korean Novena — It was announced on June 18 that Korean Catholics were taking part in a novena for reconciliation that ended on June 22 in preparation for the Day of Prayer. A symposium on "The Role of the Catholic Church in the Search for a Solution to the Problem of Refugees in North Korea" is part of the prayer project.

Scottish Women Bishops — The Scottish Episcopal Church on June 18 voted overwhelmingly to begin the process for appointment of women bishops. The General Synod sent the motion to the seven Episcopal dioceses for debate; it is expected that the synod will vote on the measure next year.

IRA Leader — Gerry Adams, the pres. of Sinn Fein, the political wing for the Irish Republican Army, and Archbishop Jean-Louis Tauran, the Vatican foreign minister, met on June 21. The two met to discuss the Northern Ireland peace process.

Swiss Bishops — On June 21 the Catholic bishops of Switzerland criticized a national campaign in their country to legalize abortion. In a referendum on June 2, Switzerland voted overwhelmingly to loosen the nation's laws on abortion. Also, calling euthanasia "murder on demand," the bishops recommended "palliative care rather than death."

Siberian Carmelites — It was announced on June 25 that four Discalced Carmelite nuns had arrived in the city of Usole, in Siberia, where they will contribute to the work of the Carmelite men religious from the Warsaw Province who are already well-established in the region. Bishop Mazur, currently unable to return to his diocese owing to Russian opposition to his ministry, envisioned a series of facilities in Siberia, with a monastery, a convent of the Carmelites, and a sanctuary in the city, all named after St. Raphael.

Priest Slain — On June 27, Fr. Hilario Arango Serna was shot to death in Cali, Colombia, after an evening Mass. Fr. Serna was critical of the armed groups involved in Colombia's ongoing civil war. His death follows that of other priests and Archbishop Isaias Duarte Cancino of Cali.

National

New Morning — The National Interfaith Cable Coalition debuted a new series, "New Morning," on June 3, to explore faiths and religious perspectives. The cable coalition has nine hours of programming each week on the Hallmark Channel.

Medical Appeal — The U.S. Justice Department is appealing an Oregon ruling allowing medically assisted suicide, it was announced on June 3. The appeal will contest a court ruling by a federal judge in Portland allowing federally related drugs to be used by Oregon doctors to assist suicides.

U.S. Media — Cardinal Oscar Rodriguez Maradiaga of Honduras attacked Ted Turner and the U.S. media it was reported on June 9. The cardinal said that the media and especially Ted Turner are displaying "openly anti-Catholic" tactics in reporting the sex scandals in the Church. He added that it was brought about by the Catholic opposition to abortion, euthanasia, and the death penalty. Cardinal Maradiaga, speaking in Rome, define the media activities as a persecution against the Church.

Monastics Slain — On June 10, two members of Conception Benedictine Abbey monastery at Conception, Missouri, were slain by a 71-year old man, Lloyd Robert Jeffries, from Kearney, Mo., who was found dead in an abbey chapel. No motive for the shootings was immediately apparent. Fr. Philip Schuster, the retired chaplain of St. Francis Hospital in Maryville, was in his 80s when he was slain. Br. Damian Larson, 64, was the second victim. Abbot Gregory Polan said that the gunman was not known at the abbey.

Bishops Resign — On June 11 it was announced that Pope John Paul II accepted the resignation of Bishop Kendrick Williams of Lexington, Ky., who has been accused of sexual misconduct. While denying the accusations, Bishop Williams resigned to avoid diocesan scandal and unrest. Bishop Anthony O'Connell resigned as bishop of Palm Beach, Fla. in March, and Archbishop Rembert Weakland resigned in May for the same reasons.

Bishop Resigns — On June 11, the New York archdiocese announced that Auxilary Bishop James F. McCarthy resigned after admitting to affairs with several women. Bishop McCarthy was consecrated in June 1999 and served as regional vicar for the northern area of the archdiocese.

Gotti Burial — On June 12, the diocese of Brooklyn, N.Y., announced that John Gotti, the organized crime boss who had died on June 10, would not be allowed a funeral Mass. A Mass for the Dead was allowed some time after Gotti's burial, and a priest attended the wake and conducted a burial service.

Bishop's Charter — On June 14, the U.S. bishops at their summer meeting in Dallas approved a national "Charter for the Protection of Children and Young People." This document strips all priestly sexual offenders of any form of ordained ministry. Archbishop Harry Flynn, head of the bishops' ad hoc committee on sexual abuse, called the action "a defining moment." The charter will have to be approved by Rome. (For details, please see under **News in Depth**.)

Mission Web Site — It was announced on June 16 that American mission organizations have created a new web site for information and resources about the missionary work of the Church in the U.S. and abroad. The Maryknoll Fathers, Brothers, and Sisters, the Catholic Mission Forum, Glenmary Home Missioners, Glenmary Sisters, Society of St. Columban, and the U.S. Catholic Mission Association developed the site.

U.S. Bishop Board — On June 17, following the U.S. Bishops' Meeting in Dallas, Oklahoma Governor Frank Keating was named on June 17 to oversee the U.S. Bishops Review Board established by the national policy adopted earlier by the bishops. A former prosecutor and FBI agent, Gov. Keating will monitor the implementation of the proposed policy in all dioceses in the U.S.

Lakota Center — Bishop Blase J. Cupich of Rapid City, S.D., announced on June 19 the dedication of a new chapel at a Lakota retreat center. The bishop said: "We have been blessed with the Native Americans in our midst." The new chapel in the Sioux Spiritual Center near Howes was named *Woniya Wakan Oti* (House of the Holy Spirit).

Xavier University — Xavier University of Louisiana, the only historically black Catholic university in the United States, will share in nearly $3 million in grant money, it was reported on June 21. Tulane will also share in the grant. The funds will be used for the cooperative Tulane/Xavier Center for Substance Abuse and Prevention.

Ground Zero — Archbishop Leonardo Sandri, Deputy for the General Affairs of the Vatican Secretariat of State, prayed at the World Trade Center site, Ground Zero, on June 21. He was serving as an envoy of Pope John Paul II and was accompanied by Cardinal Edward Egan and Archbishop Renato Martino, the permanent observer of the Holy See to the U.N. Archbishop Sandri placed flowers at the base of the steel cross at Ground Zero.

Military Abortions — The U.S. Conference of Catholic Bishops protested on June 24 the U.S. Senate vote to allow military hospitals overseas to perform abortions that are privately funded. Abortions in military hospitals were prohibited in 1996.

School Vouchers — On June 27, the U.S. Supreme Court upheld a Cleveland voucher program in a 5-4 ruling, saying it is "entirely neutral with respect to religion." The majority opinion, written by Chief Justice William Rehnquist, said the program is therefore "a program of true private choice" and does not violate the Establishment Clause of the First Amendment. The decision was applauded by Church leaders and was also supported by the Bush administration.

JULY 2002

Vatican

Dialogue Necessary — On July 1, Pope John Paul II informed a delegation from the Ecumenical Orthodox Patriarchate of Constantinople that the Roman Catholic and Orthodox Churches must return to the theological dialogue that has been stalled for over 10 years. The delegation visited Rome to honor the feast of Sts. Peter and Paul, the patrons of the Holy See. A Vatican delegation visited Patriarch Bartholomew of Constantinople in Istanbul, Turkey, on the feast of St. Andrew.

Papal Sympathy — On July 2, Pope John Paul II expressed his sympathy and offered prayers in a telegram to Archbishop Giogio Zur, apostolic nuncio and Vatican representative to the Russian Federation. The Holy Father stated his prayerful condolences for victims of the air accident over southern Germany involving a chartered Russian airliner and a cargo plane over Lake Constance.

Papal Image — Cardinal Ersilio Tonini, Archbishop emeritus of Ravenna-Cervia, Italy, on July 2 said that Pope John Paul II would not allow his physical ailments to put an end to his ministry. The Cardinal, in an interview with the daily *La Repubblica*, stated that the Holy Father is a great witness of suffering. He is not ashamed to be seen as weak and tired. The Cardinal called for a halt to media speculations and predictions concerning the Holy Father's health and possible resignation.

Hungarian Visit — On July 4, Pope John Paul II received Peter Medgyessy, the Prime Minister of Hungary, in a private audience. Medgyessy reportedly planned to assure the Holy Father of his government's determination to guarantee legal and financial conditions for the Church's activities. The Prime Minister also met other Vatican officials.

World Day of Peace — Pope John Paul II was reported on July 4 as having chosen the theme for the next World Day of Peace, scheduled for Jan. 1, 2003. The celebration, the 36th over the years, will be dedicated to *Pacem in Terris*, the encyclical written by Blessed Pope John XXIII. The Holy Father declared the theme: "*Pacem in Terris*: A Constant Endeavor."

Miracles Accepted — Eight miracles were accepted by the Vatican's Congregation of the Causes of Saints, it was announced on July 5. The miracles open the way for eight new blessed, or beati, to be declared by the Holy Father. The candidates for beatification, the first step toward canonization, are Sigismond Felix Felinski (1822-95), John Adalbert Balicki (1869-1948), John Beyzym (1850-1912), Sanzia Szymkowiak (1910-42), Eugenia Ravasco (1845-1900), and Joanna Maria Cindesa Lluch (1862-1916). The miracle attributed to Prince Laszio Battkyany-Strattman (1870) was also approved.

Vatican Deficit — Cardinal Sergio Sebastiani, president of the Prefecture for the Economic Affairs of the Holy See, announced on July 5 that the Vatican has an operating deficit, the first in eight years. In presenting the financial statement for 2001, the cardinal linked the deficit to the Sept. 11 attacks, resulting economic factors, and the expenditures of assistance by the Holy See.

Indian Recruit — On July 9, it was reported that the newest recruit in the Vatican Swiss Guard is a naturalized Swiss citizen, born in India and adopted at age five. Dhani Baehmann, the new recruit, attracts considerable attention as he performs the duties of his probationary period. He is the first non-Caucasian member of the 500-year-old military unit of the Vatican.

Blasphemous Web Site — Five web sites in Italy were shut down after *L'Osservatore Romano*, the Vatican newspaper, made them public news on July 10. The sites blasphemed the Blessed Virgin Mary. A Roman businessman was also found involved in selling shirts proclaiming the same blasphemy.

Castel Gandolfo — Pilgrims gathered for the Angelus at Castel Gandolfo were surprised when Pope John Paul II walked into the courtyard to join them, it was reported on July 15. Tanned and using a cane, the Holy Father urged prayers for the sick and lonely. The pilgrims cheered when the pope appeared among them instead of using the balcony.

Cemetery Desecration — Pope John Paul II on July 19 condemned the desecration of graves in the Verano Cemetery in Rome's Jewish section. Cardinal Angelo Sodano, the Vatican Secretary of State, sent a telegram to Rome's chief rabbi to express the condolences of the Holy Father and to state the papal condemnation of such acts of violence.

Papal Letter — In a July 22 message to Saddam Hussein, Pope John Paul II expressed his prayers for peace. The Holy Father sent the letter on the 34th anniversary of the Baath Party's coming to power in Iraq.

Women Excommunicated — The seven women who were "ordained" on a pleasure boat in Austria were officially excommunicated on July 22 by the Vatican's Congregation for the Doctrine of the Faith. The women include four Germans, two Austrians, and an American, who call for feminist resistance to what they see is the patriarchal structure of the Church.

World Youth Day — Pope John Paul II expressed his hopes for World Youth Day when he arrived in Toronto, Canada on July 23. The Holy Father was welcomed by Canadian Prime Minister Jean Chrétien, along with Toronto Mayor Mel Lastman. The Holy Father went directly to Strawberry Island, a Basilian Fathers property, to rest after the flight from Rome.

Faithful Flock — Four hours after Pope John Paul II's plane took off for Toronto on July 23, a unique demonstration took place in St. Peter's Square. A flock of 8,681 homing pigeons were released to fly to cities and towns throughout Poland. The numbers of pigeons represents one for each day of the Holy Father's pontificate.

Czech-Vatican Treaty — On July 25, a key treaty on Church-State relations was signed in the Czech Republic to regulate the position of the Church and its institutions. The Czech Republic was the only Eastern European country without such an accord. The apostolic nuncio and the Czech Minister of Foreign Affairs signed the document. Among the nation's 10.2 million inhabitants, nearly 40% are Catholics.

Young at Heart — On July 26, Pope John Paul II gave his first address at World Youth Day, describing himself as "the aged Pope, full of years but still young at heart." The more than 200,000 young people on hand cheered and welcomed the World Youth Day cross into the celebration.

WYD Closing — Pope John Paul II on July 28 addressed a crowd of 800,000 in Downsview Park in Toronto, ending the celebration with mass. Some 600,000 young people had spent the night in the park. The night before the young people had gathered for a prayer vigil with the pope. He urged them to be builders of a civilization of love. The Holy Father also announced that the next World Youth Day will be held in Cologne, Germany, in 2005.

St. Pedro Betancur — On July 30, at a Mass attended by some 500,000 Guatemalans, Pope John Paul II proclaimed Pedro de San Jose Betancur the first Central American saint. The celebration was held at the Guatemala City racetrack. St. Pedro de San Jose Betancur was a 17th century missionary in Guatemala.

St. Juan Diego — On July 31, before hundreds of thousands of Mexicans, Pope John Paul II canonized Juan Diego, the Indian witness of the apparitions of Our Lady of Guadalupe. The celebration was held at the Basilica of Our Lady of Guadalupe in Mexico City. The Holy Father urged the Mexican people to follow the saint's testimony and to use brotherhood to build a nation of faith.

General Audience Topics

• Meditation on Psalm 92(93) (July 7)
• Meditation on a Canticle in Chapter 3 of Book of Daniel (July 10)
• Meditation on Psalm 148 (July 17)

International

First Ordination — The Dominicans who returned to Kiev, Russia, after the collapse of the Soviet regime, expressed satisfaction over the priestly ordination performed at the end of June, it was announced on July 1. The Dominicans arrived in Kiev in the mid-1200s. The site of the ordination was St. Alexander Parish, which was closed by the KGB in 1937, after they murdered the pastor. The parish was returned to Roman Catholics when the Ukraine became an independent state.

Orthodox Commission — The Holy Synod of the Greek Orthodox Church decided on July 2 to form a commission to examine sexual abuse charges made against the clergy. The Holy Synod said the charges would be discussed and presented to ecclesiastical courts.

Bethlehem Crisis — The meeting of the Works of Assistance to the Oriental Churches had an audience with Pope John Paul II as he appealed for aid to the Churches of the Holy Land on July 2. The Franciscan Custodian of the Holy Land, Fr. Giovanni Ballistelli, addressed the problems in a later interview, stating that the community in Bethlehem is at "zero level." Solidarity, an end to occupation, and dialogue are needed.

Ordination of Women — It was announced on July 2 that seven women who were ordained in a ceremony on a pleasure boat on the Danube River near Cologne, Germany, were not ordained by a Roman Catholic. The women were ordained by Archbishop Romulo Braschi of the Catholic-Apostolic Charismatic Church of Jesus the King, who was excommunicated and founded his own church in 1970. He admitted that he was a "Catholic but not Roman."

100th Anniversary — More than 60,000 worshippers traveled through the Abedare forest of central Kenya to take part in the 100th anniversary of the first Mass by the Consolata missionaries, it was reported on July 2. Tuthu, Kenya, was the site of the celebration, and there were so many vehicles on the road to the area that pilgrims had to walk to the mountain peak that serves as the Consolata mission site.

New Apostolic Prefecture — The Church in Mongolia was consolidated on July 8 by Pope John Paul II and established as an apostolic prefecture. The congregation of the Immaculate Heart of Mary has been serving in Ulan-Bator, and four priests are there.

Bin Laden — On July 9, it was reported that Osama Bin Laden, the head of the terrorist organization Al-Qaeda, was chosen as the model of Satan in Timisoara, Romania. Bin Laden is depicted on the wall of an Orthodox Church in Timisoara as holding a trident and challenging Christ. The artist, Ion Badila, chose bin Laden as "the most pure incarnation of evil."

Media Anti-Catholicism — Cardinal Norberto Rivera Carrera of Mexico City joined Latin American prelates in accusations against the U.S. media, it was reported on July 11. Cardinal Norberto Carrera said that the U.S. media is carrying out a systematic persecution of the Catholic Church in America, similar to the campaigns of ancient Rome and Nazi Germany. The coverage of clerical sex abuse has become a weapon in the hands of the media in the U.S., to dismantle the prestige of the Church and to remove it from any social relevance.

"We are Church" — The Spanish bishop's conference on July 12 condemned the "We are Church" group as a civil association with no ecclesial authorities. The group started in Austria and welcomes those who oppose the *magisterium* and the discipline of the Church. "We are Church" calls for a democratic Church and supports liberalization of moral doctrine, married clergy, and women's ordination.

Czech Trappists — A Trappist monastery was opened in Novy Duur, being the first monastic house to open in the Czech Republic since the Communist collapse. The Archbishop of Prague, Cardinal Miloslav Vlk, presided at the celebrations on July 12. The Trappists were formed at the abbey of Notre Dame, Sept-Fons, and six of them are Czechs.

Sudan Attacks — The Sudanese Air Force once again attacked Catholic buildings, it was reported on July 14. Church structures in the East Equatoria region were hit by twelve bombs. The new office of auxiliary bishop Akio Johnson Mutek and Torit diocesan holdings were targeted by the Khartoum government.

Lay Missionaries — The Lay Missionaries of Charity, founded by Mother Teresa of Calcutta and Fr. Vazhakala, held an international congress in Rome, it was announced on July 15. More than 1,000 people have consecrated themselves to the movement and several hundred are in formation. The group offers worship by their lives in prayer, penance, and works of mercy. A website is available: www.laymc.biz lands.com.

Canada Rejects — It was announced on July 15 that thousands of young worshippers were denied visas by the Canadian government and so were unable to attend the World Youth Day. About 6,000 visa applications from Third World countries, including Haiti, the Dominican Republic, Sudan, and Uganda were denied. The Canadians expressed concerns that the young people would migrate illegally to Canada once they had obtained their visas.

Hermano Pedro — The Church of San Francisco in Antigua, Guatemala, was reported on July 15 to be overwhelmed by pilgrims visiting the tomb of Hermano Pedro, Pedro de San Jose Betancur, whom Pope John Paul II canonized on July 30. Pilgrims from across Guatemala, Central America, and other parts of the globe came to visit the saint's remains and altar.

Nun Murdered — Sr. Marta Inés Vélez, 44, of Antioquia, Colombia, was murdered by two masked men on July 16. She was at the Marcelino Shelter of Mothers Institute in Mogotes when the masked men entered the house and asked if she was Sr. Marta. When she said yes, they shot her in the neck. A Poor Sister of St. Peter Claver, she was active in the community peace process that has sought an end to Colombia's political and social upheaval. She was the delegate of religious communities to the Constitutional Municipal Assembly, created in Mogotes to promote the peace process. The institution won the Nobel Peace Prize for the municipality in 1998.

Bethlehem Siege — A little known siege is being conducted by the Israelis against the Institute of the Daughters of Mary Most Holy of the Garden in Bethlehem, it was reported on July 17. The nuns operate a home for children and elderly, and for two months they have been surrounded by tanks and troops. The nuns are viewed as "suspicious" religious who aid Palestinians. The media attention of the past alleviated the situation, but now the nuns are at the mercy of the Israeli troops. The elderly patients are suffering because they cannot visit their families.

Benedictines Return — A group of Benedictines have started a monastery in Kelme, in northwestern Lithuania, it was announced on July 18. Expelled during the Czarist and then Soviet persecutions, the Benedictines were in Lithuania at the start of the 15th century. The new community was founded by the French Abbey of Solesmes, known for Gregorian Chant. The abbey church will be open to the public for Masses and liturgical hours.

Nun Jailed — On July 18, an Ursuline Sr. Bridhi Ekka was sentenced to six months in jail in Chhattisgarh state, central India. She was condemned for not reporting conversions to local authorities. The Catholic Bishops' Conference of India criticized the victimization of this controversial law. Sr. Bridhi was incarcerated soon after being sentenced. She converted over 90 Hindus.

Kazakstan Survivor — The only surviving Catholic Church in Kazakstan's Soviet era was reconsecrated, according to a July 22 report. Sacred Heart Church at Petropavlovsk, whose pastor was shot with five parishioners in 1922, is now an active parish, served by Polish Redemptorists. The Church was returned to the Church by the Kazakstan government.

Archbishop Named — It was announced on July 23 that Rowan Williams, a Welsh-born theologian, has been named to the office of archbishop of Canterbury, making him the head of the Anglican Church as successor to Archbishop George Carey. The new leader of Anglicans worldwide favors the ordination of women and other liberalizing policies, but he is also noted as one of England's most consistent pro-life advocates. Prime Minister Tony Blair named Williams, who has served as the Anglican Archbishop of Wales, after his nomination by Queen Elizabeth II in her capacity as head of the Church of England. The appointment was supported by the Society for the Protection of Unborn Children, one of Britain's leading pro-life groups. Some Anglicans, however, have expressed fears that the positions of the new Archbishop will further divide the Anglican Church. Williams has also assailed consumer society, entertainment giant Walt Disney, child talent shows, and violent computer games. Cardinal Murphy-O'Connor, archbishop of Westminster and president of the Catholic Bishops' Conference of England and Wales, welcomed the appointment of Williams, saying, "As a theologian of distinction, a man of deep spirituality and a gifted communicator he will, I have no doubt, prove to be a force for great good in this country and throughout the Christian world."

Children Arrested — Children in southwestern China were detained by police at summer catechetical classes, it was reported on July 25. About 40 children attending classes in a factory in Fuzhou were taken and then released. The nun who was responsible for organizing the classes was also arrested and sentenced to up to fifteen days of detention.

Priests Sentenced — Three Chinese Catholic priests were sentenced to three years of hard labor, it tried for carrying out their ministry without the consent of the Communist authorities. Some eighteen Catholics were also arrested for making a religious pilgrimage, considered illegal by the Communist regime.

National

Marianist Union — On July 1, the Society of Mary, the Marianists, announced that it had merged its four U.S. provinces into one. The provinces of Cincinnati, New York, St. Louis, and the Pacific, in which the Marianists serve more than 30 dioceses, were joined in St. Louis. The members who serve in India, Africa, Korea and Mexico will also be included in this new province.

New Mexico Shrine — It was reported on July 2 that El Santuario de Chimayo, a mission near Santa Fe in northern New Mexico, hosts about 300,000 pilgrims annually. The church has a special spiritual quality and attracts visitors, especially during Holy Week. El Santuario de Chimayo is located in the Sangre de Cristo Mountains and has been visited by the faithful for more than a century.

Spanish TV — A Burbank-based television station, ESNE (*El Sembrador Nueva Evangelizacion* — "The Sower New Evangelization") was announced on July 3. The station, supported by Cardinal Roger Mahony of Los Angeles, but will be independent. It plans to start airing programs on July 31.

Oregon Anti-Catholicism — It was reported on July 3 that a billboard on Interstate 5 in southern Oregon has finally been removed after weeks of controversy. The Rogue Valley Historic Seventh-Day Adventists had paid for the ad, but even after the contract for the sign ran out in early May, Medford-based Outdoor Media Dimensions had left up the billboard. The Rogue Valley Historic Seventh-Day Adventists group teaches that the Vatican is an agent of Satan.

Hispanic Image — On July 8 it was reported that the Catholic heritage of the growing Hispanic community must serve as a shield and symbol if the Hispanics are to make a difference in America. Auxiliary Bishop Jose H. Gomez of Denver expressed this sentiment as he and other members of the National

Catholic Council for Hispanic Ministry prepared for the Aug. 1-4 national meeting. Bishop Gomez stressed the fact that a "fundamental characteristic" of Hispanics is the fact that they are Catholic. Issues affecting Hispanics in the U.S. were on the national meeting agenda.

Abuse Cases — Archbishop Thomas C. Kelly of Louisville, Ky., was reported on July 9 to have sent a report to the more than 70,000 Catholic households of the archdiocese to explain the sexual abuse cases being handled there. More than 150 clergy sexual abuse lawsuits have been filed in Louisville. The Archbishop apologized for the way in which the abuse cases had been handled, adding, "I want to apologize on behalf of the church to all those who have been victimized, either directly or indirectly, by priests who have abused children."

U.S. Martyrs — Bishop Walter F. Sullivan of Richmond, Va., was reported on June 10 as opening a diocesan tribunal for the cause of eight Spanish Jesuits who were martyred in 1571 near modern Yorktown and Williamsburg. Authorization was received on March 2 from the Congregation for the Causes of Saints in Rome. Fr. Russell Smith was named postulator of the cause, and he is interested in hearing from anyone who has knowledge of miracles or favors granted through the intercession of the Jesuit martyrs.

Religious Priests — The charter for child protection adopted by the U.S. bishops does apply to the nation's religious order priests, some 15,000 in number. A Josephite priest was removed from ministry in Maryland, and other religious-order priests, subject to the powers of the bishops under Canon Law, have also been removed in Connecticut, Kentucky and Michigan.

Boys Town Chef — Pierre Bossant, a world-famous pastry chef, joined the Boys Town, Omaha, Neb., staff in 1962 and continues his work. On July 15 he was reported as being content there and has refused job offers. Chef Bossant lost his mother in World War II in France, and his father was taken prisoner by the Nazis.

Regnum Christi — On July 16 it was reported that more than 6,000 members of *Regnum Christi* had gathered in Baltimore for the annual Youth and Family Encounter conference. *Regnum Christi* has a worldwide membership of over 60,000, including lay people and priests called the Legionaries of Christ.

Priests Removed — Priests in the archdioceses of Chicago, Detroit, and Washington, as well as the diocese of Paterson, N.J., were reported on July 16 as having been removed from their posts. These priests were accused of sexual misconduct and were suspended or placed on leave.

Background Checks — The diocese of Paterson, N.J. has instituted criminal backgournd checks on all employees and volunteers, it was announced on July 19. The New Jersey Catholic Conference provided pastors, administrators, and agency heads with a guideline for making such mandatory inquiries.

Cancer Link Ad — The Virtue-Media, Inc. and Women's Resource Network have joined resources to produce a television commercial demonstrating a link between abortion and breast cancer, it was announced on July 19. The ad states that according to 28 medical studies, abortion can increase the risk of breast cancer by 50%. There has been a long debate concerning this linkage, although the media coverage tends to favor those positions against any link.

Withheld Funds — On July 22 it was announced that the Bush administration would withhold $34 million normally given to the United Nations family planning programs overseas. The UN agency tolerates the Chinese policy of forced abortions and sterilizations. The funds will be used instead for child survival and health programs of the U.S. Agency for International Development.

Georgia First — It was reported on July 23 that Southern Catholic College is now being constructed in Dawsonville, Georgia. The first Catholic college in Georgia, Southern Catholic will be an independent Catholic liberal arts college rooted in the values and intellectual tradition of the faith. The college will be erected on a 356-acre site some 40 miles north of Atlanta.

Review Board — It was announced on July 24 that eight new members had been named to the National Review Board of the U.S. Conference of Catholic Bishops to assist in matters concerning sexual abuse of minors. The full board will consist of 13 people. Four previous appointees, including review board chairman Gov. Frank Keating of Oklahoma, were named in June, immediately after the Bishops' Meeting in Dallas. The new members are: Leon E. Panetta, former White House chief of staff under Bill Clinton who now heads his own public policy institute in Monterey Bay, Calif.; President Alice Bourke Hayes of the University of San Diego; Dr. Paul R. McHugh, chairman of the department of psychiatry and behavioral sciences at the Johns Hopkins University School of Medicine; Nicholas P. Cafardi, dean of the Duquesne University Law School in Pittsburgh; William R. Burleigh, board chairman and former president of E.W. Scripps Co. in Union, Ky.; Jane J. Chiles, former director of the Catholic Conference of Kentucky; Pamela D. Hayes of New York, an attorney specializing in criminal defense and federal civil rights litigation; and Ray H. Siegfried II of Tulsa, Okla., chairman of the board of the NORDAM Group, an international aviation and manufacturing company.

Catechetical Sunday — The theme for Catechetical Sunday 2002 for Sept. 15 was announced by the U.S. Bishops' Department of Education on July 24. The theme is "Living for the Lord." Resource kits were made available to catechists and educators across the U.S., in English and in Spanish.

Carmelite Anniversary — It was announced on July 25 that the Discalced Carmelite monastery in Loretto, Pa. celebrated 75 years of prayerful service in the Diocese of Altoona-Johnstown. The monastery of St. Thérèse of Lisieux in Loretto is the only U.S. Discalced Carmelite house to have been founded by nuns from France. Bishop Joseph V. Adamec of Altoona-Johnstown celebrated an anniversary Mass of Thanksgiving. The Loretto Carmelites represent a unique branch of that order in the U.S. The monastery was founded in 1927.

John Paul II Center — The John Paul II Cultural Center in Washington, D.C., announced on July 26 that a Carmelite exhibit would remain open through the end of August. The exhibit included relics of St. Thérèse of Lisieux, St. Teresa of Ávila, St. Andrew Corsini, and the Carmelite nuns martyred in the French Revolution and the Spanish Civil War. Donated art and relics display the Carmelite tradition.

AUGUST 2002

Vatican

Foundation Awards — Pope John Paul II's foundation, *Populorum Progressio*, has awarded more than $1.8 million to 223 projects in 19 countries, it was announced on Aug. 1. *Populorum Progressio* was established in 1992 to aid the poorest people in the Caribbean and Latin America. The 2002 awards were announced recently. The administrative council of the foundation met in early July in Bolivia.

Mexican Beatifications — On Aug. 1, Pope John Paul II beatified two Zapotec Indians who were martyred in the state of Oaxaca. The new beati are Jacinto de Los Angeles and Juan Bautista, who were slain by a pagan mob in 1700. On Aug. 2 he canonized Juan Diego in Mexico City's Basilica of Our Lady of Guadalupe.

Special Tours — Pilgrims visiting the Vatican during the absence of the Holy Father were treated to a special tour, according to an Aug. 2 report. A gathering of 500 women-religious pilgrims celebrated St. Martha's feast by visiting the Vatican gardens. Visitors were searched, but metal detectors were not used. Msgr. Raffaello Lavagna inaugurated the St. Martha celebration for women religious who clean, cook and administer rectories and priests' households.

Plenary Indulgence — The Vatican announced on Aug. 3 that Pope John Paul II had authorized the recognition of a plenary indulgence for Catholics who participate in the Divine Mercy Devotion on the Sunday after Easter. The Apostolic Penitentiary, a Vatican court, made the announcement for the indulgence, which is a remission of the temporal punishment deserved for sins.

Women Excommunicated — The seven women who took part in an "ordination ceremony" on a pleasure boat on the Danube River incurred excommunication, it was announced on Aug. 5. The decree of excommunication was signed by Cardinal Joseph Ratzinger, prefect of the Congregation for the Doctrine of the Faith. The women claim to be ordained Catholic priests, having been ordained by the former Abp. Romulo Antonio Braschi, who founded the schismatic Catholic Apostolic Charismatic Church of Jesus the King. Braschi had already been condemned and excommunicated.

Knights Message — Pope John Paul II sent a message of appreciation on Aug. 6 to the Knights of Columbus for their support of U.S. priests and bishops during the sexual abuse scandal. The message was sent to the Knights 120th annual convention in Anaheim, Calif. The Holy Father said: "… I urge all the knights and their families to intensify their prayers for the authentic renewal of ecclesial life.…"

Pakistan Attacks — On Aug. 10, Pope John Paul II condemned terrorist attacks against a Christian school and hospital in Pakistan. In a telegram sent in the pope's name to the papal nuncio in Pakistan, Archbishop Alessandro D'Errico, the pope declared that such crimes should not be condoned or tolerated by the international community.

Middle East Condemnation — On Aug. 11 at Castel Gandolfo, Pope John Paul II issued his strongest condemnation of terrorist attacks and conflict in the Middle East. The pontiff declared, "There is no justification for indiscriminately killing defenseless civilians." The pope also condemned as a violation of basic human rights the Israeli curfew on Palestinian towns, as it prevents believers from attending churches and mosques.

International

Grisly Discovery — On Aug. 1, the Catholic monks of the Basilian Nativity of Christ Monastery in western Ukraine were reported as having made a horrifying discovery in the underground chambers of their community residence. Six priests and five monks now serve in the monastery, which was founded in the 17th century. A mass grave containing the skeletal remains of 226 people was uncovered in the cellar under the church and in a tunnel connecting the church to the monastery. The grave dates to the Soviet era.

Magsaysay Award — A Catholic nun, Sr. Ruth Pfau, 70, received the Ramon Magsaysay Award, it was announced on Aug. 2. Sr. Ruth received the Asian Nobel Prize for her work in the leper settlements of Pakistan. She is a member of the Congregation of the Daughters of the Heart of Mary. The award includes a certificate, a medallion, and $50,000.

Church Lands — The Indonesians started building homesteads on Church land in the district of Indonesia, prompting a protest from the archdiocese of Ende, it was reported on Aug. 2. Members of an advocacy group in the area informed the people that the land was taken from their ancestors during the Dutch colonial era. The Church has asked the Indonesian government to interfere in the land seizures.

New Refugees — Liberians are fleeing their war-ravaged country, it was announced on Aug. 6. About 50,000 people left Liberia and entered Sierra Leone, a report from the U.N. High Commissioner for Refugees claimed. Murders and rapes drove entire families into exile. Sierra Leone has welcomed the refugees but fears that the violence will spread into its own areas.

Civil War — Archbishop Oswald Gomis of Colombo, Sri Lanka, was reported as having urged his fellow countrymen to end the 19-year civil war, which has claimed the lives of 64,000. The archbishop addressed the nation at his installation in St. Lucia's Cathedral in Colombo. He predicted dire consequences if the fighting over a separate Tamil state continues to take its deadly toll on the populace.

Visa Revoked — Fr. Stanislaw Krajnak, a Slovakian priest, announced on Aug. 7 that the Russian government had revoked his visa, denying him a renewal. Fr. Krajnak had served in the city of Yaroslavl. His name was on a blacklist maintained by Russia's Federal Security Services, the modern successor of the Soviet KGB.

Edith Stein — The 60th anniversary of the death of Edith Stein, St. Teresa Benedicta of the Cross, was commemorated on Aug. 9 at Auschwitz, Poland, the death camp in which she was put to death by the Nazis. The event was sponsored by the archdiocese of Krakow, the diocese of Bielsko-Zywiec, and the Carmelite Province of Krakow. Edith Stein was canonized on Oct. 11, 1998, and named co-patroness of Europe by Pope John Paul II.

Shroud of Turin — Cardinal Severino Poletto of

Turin on Aug. 12 confirmed that conservation work had been undertaken on the Shroud of Turin. The cardinal also promised that a press conference and extensive documentation would be released in September detailing the restoration. According to reports, 30 fabric patches that had been sewn onto the shroud in 1534 to repair fire damage were removed in secret between late June and late July.

German Bishops — On Aug. 13, German bishops announced that they would fire church employees who take advantage of a new law allowing homosexuals to enter into "registered partnerships." The bishops' statement came in reaction to the new law that created an institution legally similar but not identical to marriage. It was passed a year ago and was upheld by the constitutional court on July 17.

Colombian Negotiations — On Aug. 14, Colombian cardinal Pedro Rubiano Saenz of Bogota, president of the Colombian bishops' conference, accepted a request by a Colombian official to mediate between the government of President Alvaro Uribe Velez and the rebel Revolutionary Armed Forces of Colombia, known as FARC. Cardinal Rubiano said Aug. 14 that he accepted the offer to mediate for "humanitarian" reasons to secure the release of the 12 congressmen kidnapped in June in the province of Cali.

National

Bishop Cleared — Cheyenne, Wyo., authorities cleared retired Cheyenne Bishop Joseph H. Hart of all sex abuse charges, it was reported on Aug. 1. Bishop Hart had claimed his innocence and was not surprised at the dismissal of the case, but he said that the entire matter has been "devastating" to him. He stated that his personal reputation was damaged by the media coverage.

Dismissed Priests — Under the provisions of the "Charter for the Protection of Children and Young People," approved by the U.S. bishops in Dallas in June, dismissed priests have an option under canon law to make appeal, it was announced on Aug. 1. A debate has been taking place concerning justice and proper handling of priests guilty of child abuse.

Small Communities — Over 600 people from 13 countries and 43 states gathered at St. Mary's University in San Antonio, Tx., from Aug. 1-4 for a convocation to discuss "Small Christian Communities, Society and Church: From Paul's Corinth to North America." Keynote Speaker Scott Appleby of the University of Notre Dame declared small communities indispensable to the future of the Church, seeing in recent events "an unprecedented opportunity and a 'new justification' for the growth and centrality of small Christian communities."

Alaskan Protest — The Alaska Catholic Conference announced on Aug. 2 that it is against the state or city government giving same-sex couples employment benefits that are currently restricted to married couples. The conference filed an *amicus*, or friend-of-the-court, brief in a case now before the Alaska

Supreme Court. The Alaska Civil Liberties Union is trying to secure the same health, pension and other benefits for the partners of homosexual government employees that are currently available to the spouses of married government workers.

Plenary Council — On Aug. 6, it was revealed that eight U.S. bishops sent a letter in July to their brother bishops asking them to consider convoking a national plenary council to promote holiness, priestly celibacy and sound sexual morality in the U.S. Catholic Church. Such a council would be the first in the United States since the Third Plenary Council of Baltimore in 1884. The purpose of the council would be to deal with "the root causes of this crisis."

Florida Vouchers – On Aug. 5, a state judge issued a surprise ruling striking down Florida's voucher law. Despite the recent ruling of the U.S. Supreme Court upholding vouchers, Florida Circuit Court Judge P. Kevin Davey said the state constitution is "clear and unambiguous" in prohibiting public money from going to churches or other "sectarian institutions."

Born-Alive Act – On Aug. 5, President Bush signed the Born-Alive Infants Protection Act into law. The law was supported strongly by Catholic leaders. The Act guarantees basic rights to children born alive during an abortion. (For details, see under **Life Issues** in **News in Depth**.)

Men Religious – The members of the Conference of Major Superiors of Men gathered from Aug. 7-10 in Philadelphia to establish means of complying with the U.S. bishops' charter to protect children, and to discuss other issues relevant to religious communities of men. At their meeting, the heads of the men's religious orders said they would embrace the bishops' policy barring priests who have sexually abused minors from any form of public ministry. They also passed instructions for other responses by religious orders that would be parallel to the policies adopted by the bishops for dioceses.

Plenary Council II – Only days after a proposal for a new plenary council of the U.S. church was revealed, a second appeal was issued on Aug. 8 by the New York-based National Pastoral Life Center in an editorial in its magazine, *Church*. The editorial argued that the present crisis in the Church in the United States cannot be addressed within ordinary structures, proposing a plenary council as provided for in canon law.

Jewish Evangelization – A new, joint, 12-page document, "Reflections on Covenant and Mission," was issued on Aug. 12 by the National Council of Synagogues and the U.S. Catholic bishops' Committee on Ecumenical and Interreligious Affairs. The document declared that "Campaigns that target Jews for conversion to Christianity are no longer theologically acceptable in the Catholic Church." Cardinal William H. Keeler of Baltimore, the bishops' moderator for Catholic-Jewish relations, called the reflection "a significant step forward in the dialogue between the Catholic Church and the Jewish community in this country."

DEATHS
AUGUST 2001 TO AUGUST 2002

Ahmann, Mathew, 70, Dec. 31, 2001, first head of National Catholic Conference for Interracial Justice and one of the most dedicated opponents of racial segregation in the Church during the 1960s; Catholic co-chairman of the 1963 March for Jobs and Freedom, later popularly known as the March on Washington (where the Rev. Martin Luther King, Jr., gave his famous "I have a dream" speech); the interracial justice conference's executive director from its founding in 1960 until 1968; exec. secr. of the National Conference on Religion and Race, held in January 1963 in Chicago; edited the book *Race: Challenge to Religion*, which won the National Mass Media Brotherhood Book Award from the National Council of Christians and Jews in 1964, and wrote the introduction to "Race Relations and the Catholic Press," a collection of papers delivered at the 1961 convention of the Catholic Press Association; died of cancer.

Begley, Bp. Michael J., 92, Feb. 9, 2002, founding bishop of Charlotte from 1972-84; born Mar. 12, 1909, Mattineague, Mass.; ord. priest, May 26, 1934; earned a master's in social work from the University of North Carolina in 1949; ord. first bp. of Charlotte, N.C., Jan. 12, 1972; chairman of the Commission on Religion in Appalachia; known for his care of the poor and his commitment to ecumenical dialogue; retired May 29, 1984.

Bertoli, Cardinal Paolo, 93, Nov. 8, 2001, Italian cardinal and former prefect of the Congregation for the Causes of Saints; ord. priest Aug. 15, 1930; entered diplomatic service of the Holy See, serving in nunciatures in Yugoslavia, France, Haiti and Switzerland; ord. titular Archbishop of Nicomedia, May 11, 1952; apostolic delegate to Turkey (1952-53), nuncio to Colombia (1953-59), Lebanon (1959-60), France (1960-69); cardinal Apr. 28, 1969; prefect of Congregation for Causes of Saints, 1969-73; entered order of cardinal bishops as titular bp. of Frascati, June 30, 1979; Chamberlain (*Camerlengo*) of Holy Roman Church, 1979-85; he had been a priest for more than 71 years and a bishop for almost 50 years.

Bethune, Ade, 88, May 1, 2002, artist and illustrator whose work appeared in *The Catholic Worker*; born Adelaide de Bethune in Schaerbeek, Belgium, she emigrated to the United States in 1928; her artwork has been part of *The Catholic Worker* newspaper's masthead since 1938; from 1933 to 1938, she was a close associate of Dorothy Day and Peter Maurin of the Catholic Worker movement; she died of complications from pneumonia and leukemia in Newport, R.I.

Billé, Cardinal Louis-Marie, 64, March 12, 2002, Cardinal and Archbishop of Lyons, as well as a Scripture scholar and former head of the French bishops' conference; b. Feb. 18, 1938, Fleury-lés-Aubrais, France; ord. priest, March 25, 1962; taught Scripture at Luçon major seminary; dir. of continuing formation for the clergy in La Roche-sur-Yon; dir. of the National Office for the Continuing Formation of the Clergy, 1978-81; episcopal vicar and archdeacon of Haut Bocage, 1980-84; app. bp. of Laval, March 10, 1984; app. Archbishop of Aix-en-Provence, May 5, 1995; pres. of the Bishops' Conference of France; app.

Archbishop of Lyons, July 10, 1998; cardinal, Feb. 21, 2001; titular church, St. Peter in Chains; died after a months-long battle with cancer.

Carter, Bp. Alexander, 92, Feb. 17, 2002, bishop of Sault Sainte Marie, Ont., from 1957-85, former head of the Canadian bishops' conference, and a participant in the Second Vatican Council; ord. in 1936, he was the brother of Cardinal G. Emmett Carter, retired archbishop of Toronto; one of 63 Canadians who made an oral presentation before the 1962-65 Second Vatican Council; he attended all four of its sessions; president of the Canadian Catholic Conference, the predecessor of the Canadian Conference of Catholic Bishops, during the conference's 1968 debate on the papal encyclical, *Humanae Vitae*.

Castelli, Jim, 55, July 6, 2002, longtime journalist, author, researcher and consultant on religion and public policy issues; a New York native and 1969 honors graduate of Iona College in New Rochelle, N.Y., he started his journalism career that year as an assistant editor at *The Catholic News*, then the New York archdiocesan newspaper; subsequently worked for the *National Catholic Reporter*, *National Catholic News Service*, now *Catholic News Service*, *The Washington Star*, *Our Sunday Visitor*, and *Time* magazine; among his books were two on religion in America co-written with George Gallup Jr., *The American Catholic People* in 1987 and *The People's Religion* in 1989; he also wrote *The Bishops and the Bomb* in 1983, on the development of the U.S. bishops' 1983 peace pastoral; *I'm Too Young to Have a Heart Attack* in 1990, reflecting on his life-changing 1985 heart attack; and *How I Pray* in 1994, interviewing 26 Americans on their spirituality and prayer life; with Msgr. Joseph Gremillion he co-wrote *The Emerging Parish* in 1988, a report on the massive Notre Dame study of U.S. Catholic parish life; died unexpectedly of an apparent heart attack.

Clarke, Sr. Sarah, 82, Feb. 4, 2002, Irish La Sainte Union sister and advocate for Irish prisoners in England, known as "the Joan of Arc of English prisons" because of her work investigating human rights abuses against Irish prisoners and their families; best remembered for her central role in freeing those wrongly convicted in the Birmingham Six, the Guildford Four, the Maguire family and Judith Ward cases; born in Eyrecourt, County Galway; joined the La Sainte Union sisters in 1939; taught in Athlone, Ireland, and at several schools in England; while at Highgate in north London, she became involved in the Northern Ireland Civil Rights Association, which led her to work with Irish prisoners and their families; undertook full-time pastoral work in the prisons in 1974 to assist Irish citizens arrested in Britain under the Prevention of Terrorism Act; authored a 1995 autobiography, *No Faith in the System*; awarded the *Pro Ecclesia et Pontifice* Cross in 2000.

Coniker, Gwen, 62, June 15, 2002, co-founder of the Apostolate for Family Consecration; b. in Chicago on Sept. 27, 1939; co-founded the apostolate with her husband, Jerome, to promote lay ecclesial teams to evangelize and catechize neighborhoods through the creative use of the media in homes, schools, churches and television; the apostolate's out-reach includes Familyland TV Network and Familyland Centers in the United States, Mexico and the Philippines, with training centers in Nigeria and Belgium; the 900-acre Catholic Familyland in Ohio also includes a camp; in April 1999, Pope John Paul II appointed Coniker and her husband, one of 20 couples worldwide, to be members of the Pontifical Council for the Family; the Conikers took part in the October 2000 Jubilee of Families as part of the jubilee year; last year, they received the *Pro Ecclesia et Pontifice* award in recognition of their service to the church; she is survived by her husband of nearly 43 years and their 12 children and 52 grandchildren.

Degenhardt, Cardinal Johannes Joachim, 76, July 25, 2002, German Cardinal, noted theologian, and Archbishop of Paderborn; b. Jan. 31, 1926, Schwelm, Germany; at the age of fifteen, he was arrested by the Gestapo and imprisoned for membership in the banned Catholic group, *Bund Neudeutschland*; ord. priest, Aug. 6, 1952; prefect of the Collegium, Leonianum, Paderborn, 1959; app. titular bp. of Vicus Pacati and aux. bp. of Paderborn Mar. 12, 1968; cons., May 1, 1968; app. Archbishop of Paderborn, Apr. 4, 1974; chair of Admin. Comm. of the Association of German Dioceses; cardinal, Feb. 21, 2001; titular church, St. Liborius; he died unexpectedly.

Diekmann, O.S.B., Fr. Godfrey, 93, Feb. 22, 2002, Benedictine priest and world-renowned liturgist who played a major role in the Second Vatican Council's reform of the liturgy; born Leo Diekmann (Godfrey was his religious name) on Apr. 7, 1908, in Roscoe, Minn.; joined the Benedictines; studied in Rome and Germany; took his final vows in 1929; ord. in Rome in 1931 and returned to Collegeville in 1933 after completing his doctorate in theology; worked closely with Benedictine Father Virgil Michel, editor of *Orate Fratres* and founder of the American liturgical movement; when Father Michel died in 1938, Father Diekmann was made editor of *Orate Fratres*; his work with the Vatican Council forced him to give up editorship of the journal in 1963, but he became editor-in-chief, a title he held until 1992, when he retired from teaching and became editor emeritus; at the council, he was a key figure in the drafting of *Sacrosanctum Concilium*, the Constitution on the Sacred Liturgy; he then served on the Consilium, the Vatican agency that oversaw the implementation of the council's liturgical reforms; involved in the founding of the International Commission on English in the Liturgy and the International Consultation on English Texts; also was a longtime consultor to the U.S. bishops' Committee on Liturgy; received 10 honorary degrees; in 1997 St. John's seminary and theology school established the Godfrey Diekmann, OSB, Center for Patristics and Liturgical Studies in his honor.

Frawley, Gerardine, 77, Sept. 6, 2001, publisher of the *National Catholic Register* and the *Catholic Twin Circle* for 20 years; a native of Vancouver, Canada, she suffered from tuberculosis when she was in her 20s and pregnant with her first child; Frawley died Sept. 6 in Los Angeles from lung disease at age 77.

Gottwald, Bp. George J., 87, Mar. 11, 2002; retired auxiliary bishop of St. Louis; b. May 12, 1914, St. Louis, Mo.; educ. Kenrick Seminary; ord. priest, June 9, 1940; ord. titular bp. of Cedamusa and aux. bp. of St. Louis, Aug. 8, 1961; attended sessions of the Second Vatican Council with Cardinal Joseph E. Ritter; administrator of the archdiocese for nearly a year after Ritter's death in 1967; resigned Aug. 2, 1988; as administrator, Bishop Gottwald joined the side of a St. Louis couple in their fair-housing case before the U.S. Supreme Court that asked that the court outlaw racial discrimination in housing by private real estate developers; in addition to his duties as an auxiliary, he continued as a parish pastor, first at the cathedral and later at Little Flower.

Grady, Bp. Thomas J., 87, Apr. 21, 2002, bishop of Orlando from 1974-89; b. Oct. 9, 1914, in Chicago, Ill.; studied at St. Mary-of-the-Lake Seminary, Gregorian Univ. in Rome, and Loyola Univ.; ord. priest Apr. 23, 1938; in 1956 appointed director at the National Shrine of the Immaculate Conception (now a basilica) in Washington, D.C.; then-Msgr. Grady was largely responsible for overseeing the construction of the shrine's superstructure in the late 1950s; app. aux. bp. of Chicago by Pope Paul VI in 1967, ord. titular bp. of Vamalla, Aug. 24, 1967; app. bp. of Orlando, Nov. 11, 1974, installed Dec. 16, 1974; resigned Dec. 12, 1989; as bishop in Orlando, he backed the treaties handing over control of the Panama Canal from the United States to Panama; in 2000, the Basilica of the National Shrine of the Immaculate Conception dedicated a sculpture, "Mary, Protector of Faith," to Bishop Grady in recognition of his efforts to complete the building of the shrine; died in his home in Altamonte Springs at age 87 following a long illness.

Haffert, John M., 86, Oct. 31, 2001, co-founder of the Blue Army of Our Lady of Fátima and lay director for decades, finally retiring in 1987; born on Aug. 23, 1915, to William Anthony and Louise Haffert in Sea Isle City, N.J.; he was one of four children. He received his high school and college education at Mount Carmel College, a Carmelite seminary; in 1946, worked with Carmelite Sister Lucia dos Santos, the last surviving Fátima visionary, to develop a "Fátima Message Pledge"; in 1948, joined his Brown Scapular Apostolate to the fledgling Blue Army Apostolate, which was founded in 1947 by Msgr. Harold Colgan; authored more than 20 Fátima-related books, as well as countless articles and leaflets; launched a magazine called *The Scapular* and founded and edited *Soul* magazine; helped construct The Blue Army's international headquarters; worked extensively on the National Blue Army Shrine of the Immaculate Heart of Mary in Washington, N.J., helped establish a religious community of sisters, the Handmaids of Mary Immaculate, on the shrine grounds.

Hajjar, Bp. Sleiman, 51, Mar. 10, 2002, Canadian Melkite Catholic leader since 1988; the head of Melkite Catholics in Canada, died suddenly in Fort Lauderdale while vacationing; b. May 13, 1950, in Jezzine, Lebanon; ord. priest on Aug. 4, 1979; opened a vocational school for the poor in his native country; served as an associate pastor for three years at Sts. Peter and Paul Parish in Ottawa, before his appointment as Melkite Catholic eparch in Canada; in July, 2001, he baptized Rene-Charles Angelil, the 6-month-old son of pop star Celine Dion.

Hargrove, Sr. Katharine Teresa, 92, Feb. 22, 2002, Sacred Heart sister and pioneer in Christian-Jewish relations; born in New York City in 1909, she entered the novitiate of the Sacred Heart in 1931 and made her final vows in 1939; earned master's degrees from The Catholic University of America in Washington and Providence College in Providence, R.I.; taught at Manhattanville College for 36 years, primarily as an associate professor of religion; from the 1960s until the 1990s, she was active in the National Conference of Christians and Jews and the International Council of Christians and Jews; she also worked with Vatican officials involved in interfaith relations; received the Edith Stein Award for Jewish-Christian relations and an award given by the Edith Stein Guild in 1966 to acknowledge efforts in fostering understanding between Christians and Jews; edited four books, including *The Star and the Cross, On the Other Side, The Paradox of Religious Secularity* and *Seeds of Reconciliation: Essays on Jewish-Christian Understanding.*

Higgins, Msgr. George, 86, May 1, 2002, the foremost labor priest in the United States for half a century; b. Jan. 21, 1916 in Chicago, IL; shortly after his ordination in Chicago in 1940, he was sent to Washington to earn a doctorate in economics; remained in Washington and devoted himself to labor relations, social justice and interracial, ecumenical and Catholic-Jewish relations; served the U.S. bishops' national conference as a social action official for 36 years, 1944-80, most of that time as department director. For decades he was the author of the bishops' annual Labor Day message; taught at The Catholic University of America as a lecturer on labor and social ethics, 1980-94, and as professor emeritus until 2000, when he moved to a nearby retirement home for priests; from 1945 to 2001, he wrote "The Yardstick," a Catholic press column syndicated by Catholic News Service; in 1984 he received the highest honor of the Catholic Press Association, the St. Francis de Sales Award, for "The Yardstick"; in 2000 he received the Presidential Medal of Freedom, the nation's highest civilian honor; in 2001 he was given the University of Notre Dame's prestigious Laetare Medal; died after a long illness May 1 in his childhood hometown of La Grange, Ill.

Karsh, Yousuf, 93, July 13, 2002, photographer who gained international fame through his portraits of world leaders, including 12 U.S. presidents, several popes, and a host of artists and other celebrities; he first rose to prominence with his 1941 portrait of Churchill, taken as Great Britain stood alone against Nazi Germany; his 1957 photo of Hemingway wearing a turtleneck sweater was the basis of a commemorative U.S. stamp honoring the acclaimed writer; his notable Catholic subjects included Pope John Paul II, Pope Pius XII and Archbishop Fulton J. Sheen; he also took portraits of Albert Einstein, Nikita Khrushchev, Mikhail Gorbachev, Fidel Castro and film stars Audrey Hepburn, Brigitte Bardot and Humphrey Bogart; born to an Armenian family in Turkey, he fled after massacres in his home town of Mardin; he arrived in Canada in 1924; originally planned to become a doctor, but studied under Boston portrait photographer John H. Garo, and in 1932 opened his first Ottawa photography studio; moved to Boston in the early 1990s; his photographs are included in permanent collections ranging from the Museum of Modern Art in New York to the National Por-

trait Gallery in London; he died in Boston but was buried in Ottawa's Notre Dame Cemetery.

Kienzle, William X., 73, Jan. 12, 2002, mystery author and former *Michigan Catholic* editor; a Detroit native, he served as a priest of the Archdiocese of Detroit from 1954 to 1974 and was editor of its archdiocesan newspaper, *The Michigan Catholic,* from 1962 to 1974; his first novel, *The Rosary Murders,* was published in 1979; authored 23 books, including *Death Wears a Red Hat, Mind Over Murder, Chameleon, Call No Man Father, Masquerade* and *Body Count;* his latest novel, *The Gathering,* was published in April.

Kuharic, Cardinal Franjo, 82, Mar. 11, 2002, Croatian cardinal, Archbishop of Zagreb from 1970 to 1997, and president of the Yugoslav bishops' conference; born Apr. 15, 1919, in Pribic, Croatia; ord. priest July 15, 1945; ord. titular bp. of Meta and aux. bp. of Zagreb, May 3, 1964; apostolic administrator of archdiocese of Zagreb, 1968-70; Archbishop of Zagreb, 1970-97; cardinal, Feb. 2, 1983; titular church, St. Jerome of the Croats. Archbishop emeritus of Zagreb; served as Archbishop and cardinal during a very difficult period of Communist rule; maintained generally good relations with Yugoslavia's communist government and sought to keep church life alive in predominantly Catholic Croatia. Pope John Paul II noted: "Under the communist regime and in the recent difficult period of national history, he worked with all his energy for the defense of the freedom and human dignity of the Croatian people."

Liu Hede, Bp. Victor, 90, Dec. 10, 2001, Chinese underground bishop who reconciled with his Communist government-approved counterpart; born in 1910; he entered the Franciscans in 1929 and was ordained in 1936; appointed administrator of Hankow Diocese in 1950, one year after the communist takeover; jailed in 1955 and sent to a labor camp during the Cultural Revolution; released during China's religion revival in the late 1970s and clandestinely ordained the bishop of Hankow in 1984; reconciled a decade ago with his Communist appointed counterpart, Bishop Bernardine Dong Guangqing of Hankow (Bishop Dong Guangqing celebrated Bishop Liu's funeral Mass Dec. 13); Bishop Liu moved into the Central and South China Seminary in Wuchang, giving spiritual guidance to seminarians, while Bishop Yang resided at the cathedral in Hankow until he died in 1999.

Longford, Lord, 95, Aug. 3, 2001, one of England's best-known Catholic politicians; born Francis Aungier Pakenham in Ireland, the son of aristocratic parents with strong military backgrounds; studied at Eton and Oxford University's New College and went on to teach at the London School of Economics; became a socialist and a backer of Irish republicans; converted to Catholicism at 35; in 1932, he switched to the Labor Party from the Conservative Party after seeing British fascists beat up a group of left-wing students; became known for championing the cause of social outcasts and unpopular causes; following World War II, he was asked to join the House of Lords, taking the title Baron Pakenham; inherited the title of Earl of Longford when his brother Edward died in 1961; in the late 1940s, served as a minister in the war office and later assumed responsibility for the British zones of occupation in Germany and Austria; worked for prison reform, often visiting prisons; fought to ban pornography; also wrote books: an autobiography, *Born to Believe* (1953), *The Causes of Crime* (1958), and *The Idea of Punishment* (1961); British Prime Minister Tony Blair said Lord Longford was "a man of passionate integrity and humanity and a great reformer committed to modernizing the law while also caring deeply for individuals." Cardinal Cormac Murphy-O'Connor celebrated his funeral Mass on Aug. 10.

Lowery, Fr. Daniel L., 72, Dec. 22, 2001, Redemptorist priest and former president of Liguori Publications; ord. June 29, 1955; in the early 1960s taught moral theology at The Catholic University of America in Washington; assoc. ed. of the *Liguorian* magazine, 1963-68, app. pres. of the Redemptorist seminary in Waterford, Wis., 1968; president-publisher of Liguori Publications from 1981 to 1987; wrote several books on religious and moral themes, including *Following Christ: How to Live a Moral Life*; from 1999 until his death, he was superior of the Liguori Mission House in Liguori, a residence for 18 Redemptorist priests and brothers; also served as provincial of the Redemptorists' Midwest province for six years; pastor of St. Alphonsus Parish in Minneapolis and St. Alphonsus Parish in Grand Rapids, Mich., for six years each; and president of Mount St. Alphonsus, the Redemptorist major seminary in Esopus, N.Y., for three years.

Lucker, Bp. Raymond A., 74, Sept. 19, 2001, retired bishop of New Ulm from 1976-2000; b. Feb. 24, 1927, St. Paul, Minn.; educ. St. Paul Seminary, University of Minnesota, and the Angelicum in Rome; ord. priest, June 7, 1952; dir. of USCC department of education, 1968-71; ord. titular bp. of Meta and aux. bp. of St. Paul and Minneapolis, Sept. 8, 1971; app. bp. of New Ulm, Dec. 23, 1975, installed Feb. 19, 1976; res. Nov. 17, 2000; was a nationally known pioneer in catechetical renewal and a founder of the Catechetical Forum; noted for his extensive efforts in social justice, peace, lay ministry and promotion of women in church and society; active member of Pax Christi USA and president of its Minnesota chapter for the past 20 years; received the national organization's highest honor, the Ambassador of Peace Award in July 2001; the author of five books, including a not-yet-published study of the pastoral letters of 19th-century Minnesota Bishop Thomas L. Grace, which he completed after his retirement.

McGann, Bp. John Raymond, 77, Jan. 29, 2002, bishop of Rockville Centre from 1976-2000; b. Dec. 2, 1924, Brooklyn, N.Y.; educ. Cathedral College, Immaculate Conception Seminary; ord. priest, June 3, 1950; ord. titular bp. of Morosbisdus and aux. bp. of Rockville Centre, Jan. 7, 1971; vicar general and episcopal vicar; app. bp. of Rockville Centre May 3, 1976, inst. June 24, 1976; res. Jan. 4, 2000.

Mahoney, Bp. James P., 76, June 1, 2002, aux. bp. of New York from 1972-97; b. Aug. 16, 1925, Kingston, N.Y.; ord. priest, May 19, 1951; served as a curate, pastor, high school teacher, Army chaplain and archdiocesan official, including vicar general; named a monsignor in 1964 and ordained aux. bp. of New York (titular bp. of Ipagro) Sept. 15, 1972; he served at St. John the Evangelist in Mahopac from 1974 to 1990; retired May 10, 1997, because of poor health; died June 1 at Calvary Hospital in the Bronx.

Mansfield, Sen. Mike, 98, Oct. 5, 2001, noted American diplomat, Senate majority leader a record 16 years, 1961-77, and elder statesman; born in N.Y. Mar. 16, 1903, to Irish-immigrant parents; when he was 3 years old, his mother died and his father, a hotel porter, sent him to live with an aunt and uncle in Great Falls, Mont.; a grade-school dropout, he enlisted in the Navy at the age of 14 during World War I and crossed the Atlantic seven times on the USS Minneapolis before the Navy discovered he was underage and discharged him; joined the Army for a year and the Marines for two years, serving in the Philippines, China and Siberia; returned to Montana in 1922 and started working in a copper mine in Butte; married Maureen Hayes in 1932; in 1933 he earned his high school diploma and graduated from the University of Montana in Missoula; earned a master's degree in 1934 and became a professor of Far Eastern and Latin American history; elected to the House of Representatives in 1942; ran for the Senate in 1952. In 1957 he became Senate majority whip and in 1961 majority leader; played a critical role in passage of the 1964 Civil Rights Act, the 1965 Voting Rights Act and far-reaching education, health and anti-poverty legislation in the Johnson administration; guided the passage in 1971 of the 26th Amendment, lowering the voting age to 18; became a leading congressional opponent of the Vietnam War; upon his retirement from the Senate, he was made U.S. ambassador to Japan, a post he held from 1977 to 1988 under Presidents Carter and Reagan; he served for 11 years, longer than any previous ambassador; when he retired from that post at the age of 85, he received a Presidential Medal of Freedom, the nation's highest civilian award.

Meaney, Msgr. John A., 86, Feb. 14, 2002, regional director in Beirut, Lebanon, for the Catholic Near East Welfare Association from 1978 to 1984; born in County Clare, Ireland, on July 24, 1915; graduated from University College in Dublin in 1940 and received a master's degree in English from New York University in 1952; after studies in Rome, he was ordained on Apr. 2, 1960, for the Archdiocese of Kingston, Jamaica; served as headmaster of St. Mary's College in Jamaica, 1960-65, and pastor of St. Ignatius Parish on Grand Cayman from 1984 to 1995, when he retired. He was named a monsignor in 1974; also served in the Caribbean as regional director for the Pontifical Mission Aid Societies.

Murphy, Fr. Francis X., 87, Apr. 11, 2002, Redemptorist Father best known as the mysterious Xavier Rynne whose *New Yorker* magazine articles on the Second Vatican Council in the 1960s provided a behind-the-scenes view of the council; born in New York City June 26, 1914; took vows as a Redemptorist in 1935 and was ordained in 1940; served as a church historian, moral theologian, military chaplain, and author of more than 20 books; "Letters From Vatican City," an intimate look at the council, were published in the *New Yorker* from 1962 to 1965; later published in book form; Murphy denied being Xavier Rynne until the late 1980s; taught moral theology at the Pontifical Lateran University and the Accademia Alfonsiana, the Redemptorist seminary in Rome from 1959-71; served as a *peritus* (theological expert) at the council from 1962-65; also served as a visiting professor at Princeton University, 1971-72; a fellow at the Woodrow Wilson Center for International Studies, 1972-73; and adjunct professor of politics at Johns Hopkins University, 1973-75; from 1975 to 1981 he was rector of Holy Redeemer College in Washington; died at Anne Arundel Medical Center in Annapolis, Md., of complications following cancer surgery.

Murphy, Fr. Roland, 85, July 20, 2002, a co-author of the *Jerome Biblical Commentary*, one of the top U.S. Scripture scholars of the 20th century, and Carmelite; a prolific author, he wrote more than 230 books and articles and more than 300 book reviews and was on the editorial boards of several scholarly publications; he is best known as a coauthor of the monumental *Jerome Biblical Commentary*, published in 1968, and an extensively revised version, the *New Jerome Biblical Commentary*, published in 1990; co-authors with him were two other giants in American Catholic Scripture scholarship, Jesuit Father Joseph A. Fitzmyer and the late Sulpician Father Raymond E. Brown; born in Chicago July 19, 1917, he was ordained a Carmelite priest in 1942 and began teaching at Whitefriars Hall, the Carmelite seminary in Washington, in the mid-1940s and was named to the Semitic languages faculty at Catholic University in 1948; his career included teaching positions at The Catholic University of America, 1948-70, Duke University Divinity School, 1971-86, Washington Theological Union; he also served as visiting professor at Yale and Princeton universities and at Pittsburgh Theological Seminary; elected president of the Catholic Biblical Association in 1968 and of the Society of Biblical Literature in 1984, he was editor-in-chief and a member of the editorial board of the *Catholic Biblical Quarterly*, 1959-65 and 1977-84; he received several honorary doctorates and numerous awards for his scholarship, teaching and ecumenical activities, including Washington Theological Union's highest honor, the Distinguished Achievement Award, in 1986.

O'Leary, Bp. Edward C., 81, Apr. 2, 2002, bishop of Portland, Maine, from 1974-88; b. Aug. 21, 1920, Bangor, Maine; studied at Holy Cross College, St. Paul's Seminary, Ottawa, Canada; ord. priest, June 15, 1946; ord. titular bp. of Moglena and aux. bp. of Portland, Maine, Jan. 25, 1971; served as assistant pastor, associate pastor, vice chancellor and chancellor; app. aux. bishop of Portland, Nov. 17, 1970, and ord. a bishop Jan. 25, 1971, taking as his motto, "One Who Serves"; app. bp. of Portland and installed Dec. 18, 1974; retired Sept. 27, 1988, because of a heart condition; credited with advancing ecumenical and interreligious relations in the state; died at St. Joseph Manor, Portland, after a lingering illness.

Riley, Bp. Lawrence J., 87, Dec. 2, 2001, auxiliary bishop of New York from 1972-1990; born Sept. 6, 1914; Boston, Mass.; educ. Boston College and St. John's Seminary, North American College and Gregorian Univ. in Rome, and Catholic Univ. of America; ord. priest, Sept. 21, 1940; ord. titular bp. of Daimlaig and aux. bp. of Boston, Feb. 2, 1972; retired Jan. 22, 1990; as a priest, served as chaplain to the Harvard Catholic Club at Harvard University, professor of theology at Emmanuel College, professor of moral theology and rector of St. John Seminary, secretary to then-Archbishop Richard Cushing, and pastor of Most Precious Blood Parish; president of the Catholic Theological Society of America and

president of the major seminary department of the National Catholic Educational Association.

Rodriguez, Bp. Miguel, 70, Aug. 13, 2001, bishop of Arecibo from 1974-1990; born Apr. 18, 1931, in Mayaguey; entered the Redemptorist order as a minor seminarian at the age of 15; ord. a Redemptorist priest in 1958; performed pastoral work in several Redemptorist parishes in Puerto Rico for 14 years and dir. of the Catholic University Center of Ponce and vicar of religious for the Arecibo diocese.

Ryan, Bp. James M., O.F.M., 89, July 12, 2002, retired bishop, Franciscan, and missionary who served the people of Brazil for nearly 60 years; Born Nov. 17, 1912, in Chicago, he joined the Franciscans in 1931; professed simple vows a year later and solemn vows on Aug. 20, 1935; first assigned to Brazil as a Franciscan missionary in 1943, he was named the first head of the prelature of Santarem in the Brazilian state of Para in 1958 (elevated to a diocese in 1979) and served until he retired in 1985; he continued to live there after his retirement; known as "Dom Tiago," Portuguese for "Father James"; he was a Franciscan for 71 years, a priest for 64 years, a bishop for 44 years and a missionary to the people of Brazil for 59 years

Schad, Bp. James L., 84, Mar. 27, 2002, retired auxiliary bishop of Camden, N.J., served from 1966-93, the first and so far only auxiliary bishop to be named to the diocese; b. July 20, 1917, in Philadelphia; studied at Augustinian Academy in New York, at St. Charles Seminary in Catonsville, Md., and St. Mary's College in Baltimore; ord. a priest on Apr. 10, 1943; served as a parish priest, Army chaplain, teacher, pastor and diocesan administrator; app. an aux. bp., but continued to hold various parish positions; was known for his special care of the poor and the mentally challenged.

Tertzakian, O.M.Ven., Bp. Hovhannes, 78, Jan. 28, 2001, Apostolic Exarchate for Armenian Catholics in the United States and Canada, 1995-2000, killed in a car accident; born Jan. 3, 1924, Aleppo, Syria; educ. Mekhitarist Monastery of St. Lazarus in Venice, Italy, Gregorian Univ. in Rome; entered Mekhitarist Order of Venice, 1938, final vows Oct. 24, 1945; ord. priest Sept. 8, 1948; rector of Moorat-Raphael College in Venice from 1970 to 1980, rector of Samuel-Moorat College in Sevres, France, from 1980 to 1984, and administrator at schools in Egypt and Syria; came to America in 1948 to establish a network of Armenian Catholic schools; Mekhitarists' abbot general and rector of the Armenian Catholic Cathedral of St. Ann in New York City in 1986, pro-exarch in 1989, and chancellor of the exarchate in 1990; ord. titular bp. of Trebizond for Armenians and apostolic exarch for Armenian Catholics in the United States and Canada, Apr. 29, 1995; struck by a car while walking back to the rectory of an Armenian Catholic church in Belmont, Mass., a Boston suburb.

Todea, Cardinal Alexandru, 89, May 22, 2002, Romanian cardinal, Archbishop of Fagaras, and a hero for his suffering for the faith; b. June 5, 1912, Teleac, Romania; ord. priest in the Byzantine Romanian rite Mar. 25, 1939; ord. bp. secretly (titular see of Cesaropoli), Nov. 19, 1950, by Archbishop Gerald P. O'Hara, Vatican representative to Romania; arrested, 1951, and sentenced to life imprisonment; after many years of intense persecution, he was granted amnesty in 1964; Archbishop of Fagaras and Alba Julia, 1990-94; cardinal June 28, 1991; titular church, St. Athanasius.

Toolan, S.J., Fr. David S., 66, July 16, 2002, Jesuit priest and associate editor of *America* magazine, the national Catholic weekly magazine sine 1989 after working at *Commonweal* for 10 years as an associate editor and book review editor; author of *Facing West from California: A Jesuit's Journey into New Age Consciousness* (1987) and *At Home in the Cosmos* (2001), which received a Catholic Press Association award.

Van de Vyver, Sr. Mary Francilene, 60, Dec. 31, 2001, Felician sister and president of Madonna University from 1976-2001; born Patricia Van de Vyver on Sept. 6, 1941, in Detroit to Hector and Irene (Zygailo) Van de Vyver; graduated from the Felician Academy in Detroit in 1959, and entered the order, pronouncing final vows in 1967; earned bachelor's degree from Madonna College and her master's and doctoral degrees from Wayne State University; taught in Catholic schools from 1962 to 1974, when she was appointed academic dean of Madonna College; appointed president two years later; during her tenure its enrollment doubled, to nearly 4,000, and it achieved university status; served on the boards of a number of local Catholic institutions and civic organizations; named one of the Outstanding Young Women in America in 1974, and as one of the 100 Most Effective College Presidents in the United States in 1987; died from pancreatic cancer.

Van Rensburg, Fr. Basil, 71, Mar. 31, 2002, South African priest who gained international recognition for fighting the forced removal of blacks under apartheid; served as a parish priest of St. Gabriel's Church in Guguletu, an impoverished black township in the Cape Town Archdiocese, and worked on a range of programs, including AIDS education; died in a Cape Town hospital from complications related to diabetes.

Walsh, Msgr. Bryan O., 71, Dec. 20, 2001, director of Catholic Community Services for the archdiocese of Miami and noted leader in providing immigrant services in southern Florida; started Operation Pedro Pan in 1960 to resettle in the United States unaccompanied children from Cuba whose parents could not leave the communist-ruled country; resettled 14,000 children who fled Cuba in the 1960s; more than 56 dioceses in 30 states cooperated in the program to provide housing and foster care for the children until they were adults or could be reunited with parents or relatives.

Walters, Ambassador Vernon A., 85, Feb. 10, 2002, distinguished Catholic layman, soldier and diplomat; born in New York City in 1917, he enlisted in the U.S. Army in 1941, beginning a career in various military and diplomatic positions; served as aide to Gen. Mark W. Clark during World War II, as assistant military attaché to Brazil, and as an aide to Averell Harriman as the Marshall Plan helped reshape Europe following the war; served in Vietnam in 1967 before going to Paris as U.S. military attaché to France; while in Paris, on orders from President Richard Nixon, he conducted secret negotiations with the North Vietnamese for three years; smuggled Henry Kissinger, then Nixon's national security adviser, into Paris; established contact with the Chinese commu-

nists in Paris, ultimately leading to Nixon's historic visit to China in 1972; came out of retirement in 1981 to serve as a senior adviser to the Reagan administration and then as ambassador at large, a position he held until 1985; retired for a second time in 1991; during his tenure at the United Nations, Walters had a private audience with Pope John Paul II in 1988; received the 1985 Brent Award for Distinguished Service from the Arlington Diocese and the Christendom College Medal for Distinguished Service in International Relations in 1992.

Whelan, Bp. Robert L., S.J., 89, Sept. 15, 2001, bp. of Fairbanks from 1968-1985; born Apr. 16, 1912, Wallace, Idaho; educ. St. Michael's College and Alma College; joined the Society of Jesus in 1931 and was ordained a Jesuit priest on June 17, 1944, in San Francisco; began serving in Alaska in 1946; parish priest for 22 years, director of the Newman Apostolate at Alaska Methodist University, chaplain for the Alaska Psychiatric Institute and director of Catholic Charities for the Archdiocese of Anchorage; ord. titular bp. of Sicilibba and coadjutor bp. of Fairbanks, Alaska, with right of succession, Feb. 22, 1968; bp. of Fairbanks, Nov. 30, 1968; retired June 1, 1985.

White, Justice Byron, 84, Apr. 15, 2002, retired Supreme Court Justice (served 1962-93) best remembered as a voice against abortion in the Roe vs Wade decision by the Supreme Court; b. Colorado; attended the University of Colorado where he became a college football star and was named an All-American player; entered the National Football League and was the highest-paid professional football player in the country, earning $15,800 for the 1938-39 season with the Pittsburgh Steelers; at the end of the season, he accepted a deferred Rhodes scholarship and left for England; after the start of World War II in Europe, he returned to the United States and entered Yale Law School; in 1942, he joined the Navy and served as an intelligence officer in the Pacific; met John F. Kennedy first in England, when the future president's father was ambassador to the Court of St. James; they met again later in the Navy, when White wrote an intelligence report on the sinking of Kennedy's ship, the PT-109; completed his law degree after the war, served as a clerk to Chief Justice Fred Vinson and then returned to Colorado and a law practice specializing in corporate and antitrust law; after working for Kennedy's election in 1960, White became deputy attorney general under the president's brother, Robert F. Kennedy. He was named to the Supreme Court in 1962; aside from Roe v. Wade, he voted to expand the powers of federal courts in ordering racial desegregation of public schools, and favored greater accommodation of religion by governments; he died of complications of pneumonia at his home in Denver.

White, Father Marcellus, 93, May 15, 2002, Passionist missionary who was imprisoned in solitary confinement in China during the 1950s; soon after ordination in 1934, he was sent to a Passionist mission in Yuanling, Hunan, China; during the war he also served as a chaplain with the U.S. military in China; he was arrested in January 1952 by Communist officials and kept in solitary confinement until he was released in November 1955; he lost more than 50 pounds while in jail; subsequently served in the Philippines from 1958-93; he died in Brockton, Mass. .

News In Depth

POPE JOHN PAUL II 2001-2002
PAPAL TRIPS

KAZAKSTAN AND ARMENIA, SEPT. 22-27, 2001
Pope John Paul II, on the 95th foreign trip of his pontificate, visited Kazakstan from Sept. 22-25 and Armenia from Sept. 25-27, 2001.

Itinerary
Sept. 22 (Astana)
Arrival at Astana International Airport. Welcoming ceremony, with speech by pope.
Visit to Monument for Victims of Totalitarian Regimes in Astana.
Sept. 23 (Astana)
Mass at Mother of the Homeland Square.
Courtesy visit to President Nursultan Nazarbayev.
Meeting with youths in Great Hall of Eurasia University.
Sept. 24 (Astana)
Mass with priests, religious and seminarians at Cathedral of the Virgin of Perpetual Help in Astana.
Meeting with representatives of the world of culture, arts and science.
Sept. 25 (Astana, Yerevan, Etchmiadzin)
Farewell ceremony, with greeting by pope.
Arrival at Zvartnotz International Airport in Yerevan. Welcoming ceremony, with speech by pope.
Meeting with Katholikos Karekin II in Great Hall of Apostolic Palace of Etchmiadzin.
Sept. 26 (Etchmiadzin, Yerevan)
Courtesy visit to President Robert Kocharian in Golden Room of Presidential Palace.
Visit to Memorial of Dzidzernagapert in Yerevan.
Official lunch with Katholikos Karekin II, with archbishops and bishops of Armenian Apostolic Church and cardinals and bishops of papal entourage in Apostolic Palace of Etchmiadzin.
Ecumenical celebration at new Apostolic Cathedral of St. Gregory the Illuminator in Yerevan.
Sept. 27 (Etchmiadzin, Yerevan)
Mass in Latin rite at the external grand altar of Etchmiadzin Sermon by pope.
Visit to monastery of Khor Virab. Prayer by pope, in chapel of "Dungeon of St. Gregory."
Departure ceremony at Zvartnotz International Airport.

Overview
The Holy Father's trip, coming only days after the terrorist attacks against the United States on Sept. 11, was dominated by his pleas for peace and his condemnation of terrorism. The pontiff appealed to all people for peace and made a special outreach to the majority Muslim population of Kazakstan, a former Soviet republic, to join with Christians in promoting the "civilization of love." The pope also stressed the value and need for interreligious dialogue and religious toleration. Among the most memorable moments was his visit to Eurasia University in Astana where he spoke to students.

The pope's visit to Armenia, a long-awaited journey, brought special tributes to the country's tragic history of suffering. The pontiff made the trip to help celebrate 1,700 years of Christianity in Armenia, the first nation to adopt Christianity as the national religion. He joined his Orthodox hosts in a prayer for Christian unity and had fruitful meetings with the Orthodox leaders of the country. The pope visited a memorial to massacre victims in Armenia, where he prayed for the dead and pleaded for the healing of "still open wounds" among Armenians. He also prayed at the hillside monument of Tsitsernagaberd, a memorial to the estimated 1.5 million Armenians, over half the Armenian population at the time, massacred by the Ottoman Turks from 1915-18 during World War I. With Katholikos Karekin II, head of the Armenian Apostolic Church, the pope dropped a red carnation next to an eternal flame in the center of a sloping, 12-sided basalt monument. In a prayer, he asked God to hear "the cry of innocent blood that pleads like the blood of Abel."

One other highlight was an outdoor Mass Sept. 27 at Etchmiadzin, outside the Armenian capital of Yerevan, attended by Armenia's tiny Catholic minority. Some 5,000 Armenian Catholics joined an equal number of Orthodox faithful. The pope extolled the Catholics, "As Armenians, with the same rights and duties of all Armenians, you are helping to rebuild the nation."

Excerpts from Addresses and Homilies

Kazakstan
September 22 — Welcome Ceremony, International Airport, Astana
I give thanks to God who has guided my steps to the city of Astana, capital of this noble and vast Country,

located in the heart of Eurasia. It is with affection that I kiss this Land, which has given rise to a multi-ethnic state, heir to numerous centuries-old spiritual and cultural traditions, and now on the move to new social and economic objectives. I have long desired this meeting and great is my joy at being able to hold all the citizens of Kazakstan in an admiring and affectionate embrace…. Thank you, Mr. President, for the invitation made to me at that time, and thank you for your commitment in making the arrangements for this visit, in all its complicated organizational aspects. I thank you also for the kind words of welcome which you addressed to me in the name of the Government and the Kazak people. I greet *the Islamic Leaders and faithful*, who boast a long religious tradition in this region. My good wishes go also to *all people of good will* who are engaged in promoting the moral and spiritual values that are capable of guaranteeing a future of peace for everyone….

This visit of mine is taking place *ten years after the proclamation of the independence of Kazakstan*, achieved following a long period of darkness and suffering. The date of 16 December 1991 is indelibly inscribed in the annals of your history. This regained freedom has rekindled in you a surer confidence in the future, and I am convinced that your past experience will provide a wealth of lessons from which to draw in order to move courageously towards new horizons of peace and progress. Kazakstan wishes to grow in brotherhood, dialogue and understanding; these are the indispensable requisites for building bridges of solidarity and cooperation with other peoples, nations and cultures…. Beloved peoples of Kazakstan! Having learned from the experiences of your ancient and recent past, and especially from the sad events of the twentieth century, you must see to it that your commitment to your country is always based on *the safeguarding of freedom,* the inalienable right and profound aspiration of every person. In particular, recognize *the right to religious freedom,* which enables people to express their most deeply held beliefs. When in a society citizens accept one another in their respective religious beliefs, it is easier to foster among them the effective recognition of other human rights and an understanding of the values on which a peaceful and productive coexistence is based. In fact, they feel a common bond in the awareness that they are brothers and sisters, because they are children of the one God, who created the universe.

September 23 — Mass at the Mother of the Homeland Square, Astana

"There is one God, and there is one mediator between God and men, the man Christ Jesus, who gave himself as a ransom for all" (1 Tim. 2:5).

These words from the Apostle Paul's First Letter to Timothy contain the central truth of Christian faith; and it is my joy to announce this truth to you today, dear Brothers and Sisters of Kazakstan. I come among you as an apostle of Christ and a witness to him; I come as a friend to all people of good will. To each and every one I come to offer the peace and love of God, the Father, the Son and the Holy Spirit.

I know your history. I know the sufferings to which many of you have been subjected, when the previous totalitarian regime took you from your lands of origin and deported you here in a situation of distress and deprivation. I am happy to be here today among you and to tell you that you are close to the Pope's heart….

Christianity does not lead to alienation from the tasks of this earth. If at times, in some quite particular situations, it gives this impression, that is because many Christians do not live as they should. But in truth, when it is lived as it should be, Christianity is a leaven in society, producing growth and maturity on the human level and opening society to the transcendent dimension of the Kingdom of Christ, in which the new humanity will be fully accomplished.

Youth meeting — Aula Magna of the Eurasia University, Astana

Dear Young People!

It is a great joy for me to meet with you, and I am deeply grateful for your warm welcome. I greet especially the Rector and the academic authorities of this new and already prestigious University. Its very name, Eurasia, indicates the particular mission which it has in common with your great nation which is a point of contact between Europe and Asia: a mission of linking two continents, their respective cultures and traditions, and the different ethnic groups who have mingled here through the centuries.

Indeed, yours is a country in which the world can see accord and harmony between different peoples as an eloquent sign of the vocation of all peoples to live together in peace, in mutual knowledge and openness, and an ever deeper discovery and appreciation of the distinctive traditions of each people. Kazakstan is a land of encounter, exchange and newness; a land which stirs in everyone the desire for new discoveries and makes it possible to experience difference not as a threat but as an enrichment.

Recognizing this, dear young people, I greet each one of you. To all of you I say as a friend: peace be with you, may peace fill your hearts! Know that you are called to be the builders of a better world. Be peace-makers, because a society solidly based on peace is a society with a future.

In preparing this visit, I asked myself what the young people of Kazakstan would want to hear from the Pope of Rome and what would they like to ask him. My experience of young people tells me that they are interested in the basic questions. Probably the first question you would want to put to me is this: "Who am I, Pope John Paul II, according to the Gospel that you proclaim? What is the meaning of my life? Where am I going?" My answer, dear young people, is simple but hugely significant: You are a thought of God, you are a heart-beat of God. To say this is like saying that you have a value which in a sense is infinite, that you matter to God in your completely unique individuality.

You understand then, dear young people, why I come among you this evening with respect and trepidation, and why I look to you with great affection and confidence. I am happy to meet you, the descendants of the noble Kazak people, proud of your indomitable yearning for freedom, which is as limitless as the steppe where you were born. You come from different backgrounds, in which suffering played a big part.

Here you sit side by side, in a spirit of friendship, not because you have forgotten the evil there has been in your history, but because you are rightly more interested in the good that you can build together. There is no true reconciliation which does not lead to generous shared commitment.

The Pope of Rome has come to say this to you: there is a God who has thought of you and given you life. He loves you personally and he entrusts the world to you. It is he who stirs in you the thirst for freedom and the desire for knowledge. Allow me to profess before you with humility and pride the faith of Christians: Jesus of Nazareth, the Son of God made man two thousand years ago, came to reveal to us this truth through his person and his teaching. Only in the encounter with him, the Word made flesh, do we find the fullness of self-realization and happiness. Religion itself, without the experience of wondrous discovery of the Son of God and communion with him who became our brother, becomes a mere set of principles which are increasingly difficult to understand, and rules which are increasingly hard to accept.

September 25 — Farewell Ceremony, International Airport, Astana

These three memorable days which have enabled me to meet so many people here in Astana and to experience at first hand the vitality of the Kazak people are coming to an end. The memory of my stay in this noble country, rich in history and cultural traditions, will be with me for a long time….

The words which I have heard in the various moments we have spent together remain impressed on my mind. I have in mind the hopes and expectations of this dear people, which I have come to know and respect more deeply: a people that has suffered years of harsh persecution, but has not hesitated to commit itself with enthusiasm to the path of development. A people seeking to build a serene future for its children, marked by solidarity, because it loves and seeks peace.

Kazakstan, a nation which has centuries of history behind it, knows how important and urgent peace is. Because of your geographical position, you are a frontier land and a land of encounter. Here, in these endless steppes, men and women of different races, cultures and religions have met and continue to meet in peace.

Kazakstan, may you with God's help grow in unity and solidarity! This is the heartfelt wish that I repeat as I recall the theme of this entire visit: "Love one another!" (Jn. 13:34). These demanding words of Jesus, uttered on the eve of his death on the Cross, have inspired and marked each stage of my pilgrimage….

In saying farewell to you, dear Kazak people, I wish to assure you that the Church will continue to be at your side. In close cooperation with the other religious communities and with all men and women of goodwill, Catholics will not fail to do their part to ensure that all together can build a common home which is ever more open and welcoming.

The quest for dialogue and harmony has characterized relations between Christianity and Islam here ever since the time of the formation of the Turkish Khanate in the endless spaces of your steppes, and this has enabled your country to become a junction between East and West on the great Silk Road. The younger generations too should follow this path with renewed commitment.

"Love one another!" This demanding saying of the Lord tests our credibility as Christians. Jesus himself warns: "By this all men will know that you are my disciples, if you have love for one another" (Jn. 13:35)….

Men and women of other religions who have the destiny of your people at heart, may you also be witnesses to love! Abai Kunanbai's question is directed to us all: "If I have been given the name of man, can I fail to love?" (*Poetry* 12). I am happy to echo this question now as I leave you: can a human being fail to love?

Armenia

September 25 — Welcome Ceremony in Armenia. Zvartnotz International Airport, Yerevan

I give thanks to Almighty God that today, for the first time, the Bishop of Rome stands on Armenian soil in this ancient and beloved land, of which your great poet Daniel Varujan once wrote: "From the villages to the far horizons / the land spreads forth as mother" (*The Call of the Lands*). For a long time I have awaited this moment of grace and joy – and most especially since the visits to the Vatican by yourself, Mr. President, and by Your Holiness, Supreme Patriarch and Katholikos of All Armenians.

Your Holiness, Katholikos Karekin, with fraternal love in the Lord I embrace you and the Church over which you preside. Without your encouragement I would not now be here, a pilgrim on a spiritual journey to honour the extraordinary witness of Christian life borne by the Armenian Apostolic Church through so many centuries, and not least in the Twentieth Century, which for you was a time of unspeakable terror and suffering. The whole Catholic Church shares your deep joy and the joy of all Armenians on the Seventeen Hundredth Anniversary of the proclamation of Christianity as the official religion of this cherished land….

I am deeply moved as I think of the glorious history of Christianity in this land, going back according to tradition to the preaching of the Apostles Thaddeus and Bartholomew. Later, through the witness and work of Saint Gregory the Illuminator, Christianity for the first time became the faith of an entire nation. For ever, the annals of the universal Church will say that the people of Armenia were the first as a whole people to embrace the grace and truth of the Gospel of our Lord Jesus Christ. Since those epic times, your Church has never ceased to sing the praises of God the Father, to celebrate the mystery of the Death and Resurrection of his Son Jesus Christ and to invoke the help of the Holy Spirit, the Consoler. You zealously guard the memory of your many martyrs: indeed, martyrdom has been the special mark of the Armenian Church and the Armenian people.

Armenia's past is inseparable from her Christian faith. Fidelity to the Gospel of Jesus Christ will contribute no less to the future which the nation is building beyond the devastations of the past century. Mr. President, dear Friends, you have just celebrated the tenth anniversary of independence. That was a significant step on the path towards a just and harmonious society in which all will feel fully at home and see their legitimate rights respected. Everyone, especially those responsible for public life, are called today to be genuinely committed to the common good, in justice and solidarity, putting the progress of the people ahead of any partial interests. This is also true in the urgent search for peace at the regional level. Peace will only be built on the solid foundations of mutual respect, justice in inter-community relations, and magnanimity on the part of the strong.

September 26 — Visit to the Memorial of Tzitzernagaberd, Yerevan
Prayer of John Paul II

O Judge of the living and the dead, have mercy
on us!

Listen, O Lord, to the lament that rises from this
place,

to the call of the dead from the depths of the
Metz Yeghérn,

the cry of innocent blood that pleads like the
blood of Abel,

like Rachel weeping for her children because
they are no more.

Listen, Lord, to the voice of the Bishop of Rome,
echoing the plea of his Predecessor Pope
Benedict XV,

when in 1915 he raised his voice in defence of
"the sorely afflicted Armenian people brought
to the brink of annihilation."

Look upon the people of this land
who put their trust in you so long ago,
who have passed through the great tribulation
and never failed in their faithfulness to you.

Wipe away every tear from their eyes
and grant that their agony in the twentieth
century

will yield a harvest of life that endures for ever.

We are appalled by the terrible violence done to
the Armenian people,

and dismayed that the world still knows such
inhumanity.

But renewing our hope in your promise, we
implore, O Lord,

rest for the dead in the peace which knows no
end,

and the healing of still open wounds through the
power of your love.

Our soul is longing for you, Lord, more than the
watchman for daybreak,

as we wait for the fullness of redemption won on
the Cross,

for the light of Easter which is the dawn of
invincible life,

for the glory of the new Jerusalem where death
shall be no more.

O Judge of the living and the dead, have mercy
on us all!

September 27 — Farewell Ceremony, Zvartnotz International Airport, Yerevan

The time has come to say farewell and to thank you,
Mr. President, and the members of the Government
for the wonderful hospitality I have found in Armenia. I am grateful to everyone, authorities and collaborators, civil and military, the men and women of
the media, to all who have given their time and skills
to make this visit a success.

With deep emotion I express my thanks to you, Your
Holiness, Supreme Patriarch and Katholikos, and to
the hierarchy and faithful of the Armenian Apostolic
Church for the spirit of brotherly love and communion which we have shared in these days.

Thank you, people of Armenia, for the warmth
of your friendship, for the prayer we have shared,
for your yearning for Christian unity. Thank you
most of all for the witness of your faith, a faith
you have not abandoned in dark times, a faith which

remains deeply rooted in your families and in your
national life.

Throughout history, Mount Ararat has been a symbol of stability and a source of confidence for the
Armenian people. Yet time and again that stability
and confidence were sorely tested by violence and
persecution. The Armenian people have paid dearly
for their frontier existence, so much so that the words
"holiness" and "martyrdom" have become almost
identical in your vocabulary. The terrible events at
the beginning of the last century which brought your
people "to the brink of annihilation", the long years
of totalitarian oppression, the devastation of a disastrous earthquake: none of these has been able to prevent the Armenian soul from regaining courage and
recovering its great dignity....

In saying farewell, I am filled with confidence, for
I have seen your resilience and the nobility of your
aspirations. May Armenian hearts ever repeat the
words of your great poet Hovhannès Tumaniàn about
the homeland:

"But still you live, standing erect in spite of all
your wounds

on the mysterious journey of time, past and
present,

still standing, wise and pensive, and sad, with
your God …

And the dawn of life's happiness will come,
its light at last in thousands upon thousands of
souls;

and on the sacred slopes of your Mount Ararat
will shine forth at last the flame of the time to
come.

Then, with the dawn, new songs and new poems
will be on the lips of the poets."

May Saint Gregory the Illuminator and the great
host of Armenian Martyrs and Saints watch over you
now and in the future! And may the Mother of Christ,
Ark of the New Covenant, guide Armenia to the peace
which lies beyond the great flood, the peace of God
who has set his bow in the clouds as a sign of his
everlasting love (cf. Gen 9:13).

AZERBAIJAN AND BULGARIA
MAY 22-26, 2002

Pope John Paul II, on the 96th foreign trip of his
pontificate, visited Azerbaijan from May 22-23 and
Bulgaria from May 23-26.

Azerbaijan — May 22 (Baku)

International Airport, Baku arrival: Welcome ceremony address of the Holy Father visit to the Monument for the Victims fallen in battle for the independence.

Courtesy visit to the president of the Republic.

Meeting with religious leaders and political, cultural
and arts representatives.

May 23 (Baku)

Mass: Homily of the Holy Father.

Lunch with the Salesian community and the members of the papal entourage.

Meeting with the Sheikh of the Caucasian muslims,
the Orthodox Eparch and the president of the Jewish
community.

Farewell ceremony.

Departure for Sofia.

Bulgaria, May 23 (Sofia)

Arrival.

St. Alexander Nevski Square in Sofia welcome ceremony: address of the Holy Father.

May 24 (Sofia)

Courtesy visit to the president of the Republic in the "Coat of Arms" Hall.

Visit to the patriarchal cathedral of St. Alexander Nevski, for the Feast of Sts. Cyril and Methodius.

Floral tribute at the monument to Sts. Cyril and Methodius.

Courtesy visit to His Beatitude Patriarch Maxim and to the Holy Synod; address of the Holy Father.

Lunch with the Catholic bishops of Bulgaria and the members of the papal entourage.

Meeting with representatives of the Jewish community.

Meeting with representatives of the worlds of culture, science and arts; address of the Holy Father.

May 25 (Sofia)

Departure by helicopter for Rila.

Heliport by the Holy Monastery of Rila arrival.

Address of the Holy Father.

Private meeting with the prime minister.

Meeting with the Grand Mùfti and representatives of the Muslim community.

Meeting with representatives of the evangelical churches.

Visit to the Latin Co-Cathedral.

Visit to the Byzantine-Slavonic Catholic Cathedral.

May 26 (Sofia)

Mass with beatifications; homily of the Holy Father

Recital of the *Angelus Domini*; words by the Holy Father.

Lunch with the Catholic bishops of Bulgaria and the members of the papal entourage.

Meeting with youth; address of the Holy Father.

Farewell ceremony.

Departure for Rome.

Overview

The demanding journey of the pontiff to Azerbaijan and Bulgaria was marked by his efforts at promoting ecumenical and interreligious dialogue. He urged continued progress in the Church's dialogue with Muslims and Orthodox Christians and used his visit to Bulgaria to encourage a much-desired meeting with Russian Orthodox Patriarch Alexei II of Moscow. The pope has now visited fifteen former Soviet republics or satellites since the fall of European communism

In Baku, Azerbaijan John Paul pleaded for religious tolerance around the globe and an end to violence in the name of God. In meeting with religious and cultural leaders, the pope said Christians, Muslims and Jews all share an essential belief in God, and should together "proclaim to the world: enough of wars in the name of God. No more profanation of his holy name."

The pontiff also addressed himself to the tiny community of Catholics in the country, numbering barely 120. He referred to the local Catholics as a "little flock" and celebrated Mass for them in a sports center normally used for volleyball and handball games. There is no church in Azerbaijan as Stalin ordered the basilica in Baku demolished in the 1930s.

The trip to Bulgaria was a significant achievement that permitted the pope to meet with the patriarch and governing body of the Bulgarian Orthodox Church

and to declare that it was time for both sides to make amends for past wrongs and work for closer relations.

The pope also proclaimed three new martyrs of 20th-century totalitarianism and brought spiritual comfort to a country still recovering from one of the most repressive of the communist regimes in Europe.

As a gesture of conciliation, the pope offered the Bulgarian Orthodox Church liturgical use of a church in central Rome and gave them a 1,700-year-old relic of a Christian martyred in Bulgaria. The pope met Bulgarian Orthodox Patriarch Maxim and the church's Holy Synod, or governing body, for more than an hour. In a surprise gift, the pope gave to the Bulgarians a relic of Blessed Pope John XXIII. The pontiff left a small piece of the late pontiff's bone, encased in a cross-shaped reliquary, with Sofia's Byzantine Catholic community for a new church under construction in Pope John's name. It was the first known relic of the late pope.

Pope John Paul II also announced that he never thought Bulgarian agents were involved in the assassination attempt in 1981 that nearly cost him his life.

Excerpts from Addresses and Homilies

Azerbaijan

May 22, Welcome Ceremony, International Airport, Baku

My respectful and cordial greetings to all of you. It was with sincere gratitude, Mr. President, that I accepted your repeated invitation to visit this noble country, and now I wish to express my joy that God has granted me the gift of coming to the land of the Azeri and meeting its people.

I thank you for your kind words of welcome. This visit takes place on the tenth anniversary of the beginning of diplomatic relations between Azerbaijan and the Holy See. In these years, your experience of independence, attained after a long period of foreign domination, has involved not a little difficulty and suffering, but you have never lost the hope of *building a better future in freedom*. The nation has seen its contacts with other peoples grow and be strengthened. This has led to a mutual enrichment which will surely bring good results in the years to come.

I arrive in this ancient land, with my heart filled with admiration for the *variety and richness of its culture*. Enriched by the many specific features of the Caucasus, your culture embraces elements of various civilizations, especially the Persian and Turanian. *Great religions* have been present and active in this land: *Zoroastrianism* lived side by side with the *Christianity* of the Albanian Church, which was so significant in antiquity. *Islam* then played a growing role, and today is the religion of the majority of the Azeri people. *Judaism* too, present here from very ancient times, has made its own specific contribution, which is esteemed to this day....

From this gateway of civilization which is Azerbaijan, I address today a *heartfelt appeal* to those lands experiencing the upheavals of conflict, which are bringing unspeakable suffering for their defenceless peoples. *Everyone must be committed to peace*. But it must be true peace, based on mutual respect, on the rejection of fundamentalism and every form of imperialism, on the pursuit of dialogue as the only effective means of resolving tensions, so that entire nations are saved from the cruelty of violence.

Meeting with Religious Leaders and Political, Cultural and Arts Representatives, Presidential Palace, Baku

One of your great poets wrote: "The word, new and at the same time old.... The word, which is like the spirit, is the treasurer of the riches of the invisible realm: it knows stories never heard, it reads books never written" (Nizami, *The Seven Effigies*). This image alludes to *something that is dear to the three great religions* present in this country: Jewish, Christian and Muslim. According to the teachings of each of them, the One God, shrouded in unapproachable mystery, has chosen to speak to man, inviting him to submit to his will.

Despite the differences between us, together we feel called to *foster ties of mutual esteem and benevolence*. I am aware of all that is being done by religious leaders in Azerbaijan to favour tolerance and mutual understanding. I am looking forward to the meeting tomorrow with the representatives of the three monotheistic religions, so that together we can affirm our conviction that religion must not serve to increase rivalry and hatred, but to promote love and peace.

From this country, which has held and still holds tolerance as a primary value of all wholesome life in society, we wish to proclaim to the world: *enough of wars in the name of God*! No more profanation of his holy name! I have come to Azerbaijan as an *ambassador of peace*. As long as I have breath within me I shall cry out: "Peace, in the name of God!" And when word joins word, a chorus is born, a symphony, which will spread to every soul, quench hatred, disarm hearts.

3. Praise to you, *followers of Islam* in Azerbaijan, for being open to hospitality, a cherished value of your religion and your people, and for having accepted the believers of other religions as brothers and sisters.

Praise to you, *Jewish people*, who, with courage and constancy, have kept your ancient traditions of good neighborliness, enriching this land with a contribution of great value and depth.

Praise to you, *Christians*, who have given so much, especially through the ancient Church of the Albans, in shaping the identity of this land. Praise especially to you, *Orthodox Church*, witness to God's friendship with man and a hymn extolling his beauty. When the fury of atheism was unleashed in this region, you welcomed the children of the Catholic Church who had lost their places of worship and their pastors, and put them into contact with Christ through the grace of the holy Sacraments.

May 23 — Mass in the Sports Palace, Baku

The universal Church pays tribute to all those who *succeeded in remaining faithful to their Baptismal commitments*. I am thinking in particular of those who live permanently in this country and who experienced *the tragedy of Marxist persecution*, and bore the consequences of their faithful attachment to Christ. Brothers and sisters, you saw your religion mocked as mere superstition, as an attempt to escape the responsibilities of engagement in history. For this reason you were regarded as second class citizens and were humiliated and marginalized in many ways....

Brothers and Sisters, beloved sons and daughters of the Catholic Church, *today the Pope is with you*. He too knows of your suffering, and has carried you in his heart during the years of wandering in the desert of persecution. Today he is here to share in your joy at freedom restored, and to support you on the journey which has as its final goal the promised land of Heaven, where the Lord of life will wipe away every tear: "death shall be no more, neither shall there be mourning nor crying nor pain any more, for the former things have passed away" (Rev. 21:4)....

O Church that prays, hopes and loves in this land of Azerbaijan, *the Pope invokes upon you the blessing of the Lord*. Take his blessing to your poor, sick and suffering. Take it to everyone, as an outpouring of grace and love. Never forget that you are called to be the leaven and the soul of the world, for the Lord is with you and he goes before you on your journey.

Bulgaria

May 23 — Welcome Ceremony, St. Alexander Nevski Square, Sofia

It is with emotion and deep joy that I find myself today in Bulgaria, addressing my warm greetings to you. I thank Almighty God for allowing me *to fulfill a desire* that I have long held in my heart.

Every year, on the Feast of Saints Cyril and Methodius, the Apostles to the Slavs, it is customary for me to receive in the Vatican representatives of the Bulgarian Government and Church. In a way therefore today, I am here *to repay those visits* and to meet in their own country the beloved Bulgarian people. At this moment, my thoughts turn to my predecessor Pope Adrian II, who went personally to meet the Holy Brothers of Thessalonica when they came to Rome to bring the relics of Saint Clement, Pope and Martyr (cf. *Life of Constantine*, XVII, 1), and to bear witness to the communion between the Church founded by them and the Church of Rome. Today *it is the Bishop of Rome who comes to you*, prompted by the same sentiments of communion in the love of Christ.

On this occasion, my thoughts turn also to another of my predecessors, Blessed Pope John XXIII, who was Apostolic Delegate in Bulgaria for ten years and remained always *deeply attached to this land and its people*. In memory of him, I greet everyone with affection and I say to all that *I have never ceased to love the Bulgarian people*, lifting them up always in my prayer to the Throne of the Most High: may my presence among you today be a clear sign of my sentiments of esteem and affection for this noble Nation and its children....

Bulgaria received the Gospel thanks to the preaching of Saints Cyril and Methodius, and down the centuries that seed planted in fertile soil has produced abundant fruits of Christian witness and holiness. Even during the long cold winter of the totalitarian system, which brought suffering to your country and to many other European nations, fidelity to the Gospel did not disappear, and numberless children of this people *remained heroically faithful to Christ*, in not a few cases to the point of sacrificing their lives.... Wounds must be healed, and the future needs to be planned with optimism. This is certainly not an easy road, nor one without obstacles, but *the united efforts of all sectors of the Nation* will make it possible to achieve the desired goals. At the same time, there is a need to move forward with wisdom, in accordance with law and safeguarding democratic institutions, sparing no sacrifice, maintaining and promoting *the values on which the greatness of the Nation is founded*: moral and intellectual honesty, the defence of the family, care of the needy, respect for human life from conception until natural death.

May 24 — Courtesy visit to His Beatitude Patriarch Maxim and to the Holy Synod, Patriarchal Palace, Sofia

Today the Lord enables us to meet personally and to exchange "the kiss of peace." I am grateful for the readiness with which Your Holiness and the Holy Synod permitted me to realize a deep desire which I have long nurtured in my heart. I come to you with a sense of esteem for the mission which the Orthodox Church of Bulgaria is undertaking, and I wish *to express my respect and appreciation* for your commitment to the good of the people of this land....

The fullness of communion between our Churches has suffered grievous wounds in the course of history, "for which, often enough, people of both sides were to blame" (*ibid.,* 3). "These sins of the past unfortunately still burden us and remain ever present temptations. It is necessary to make amends for them, and earnestly to beseech Christ's forgiveness" (Apostolic Letter, *Tertio Millennio Adveniente,* 34).

One thing, however, consoles us: the estrangement between Catholics and Orthodox has never extinguished in them *the desire to restore full ecclesial communion,* so that the unity for which the Lord prayed to the Father might be manifested more clearly. Today we can give thanks to God that the bonds between us have been much strengthened....

In broaching this theme, we cannot fail to look to *the example of unity* offered in the first millennium in very concrete ways by *the holy brothers Cyril and Methodius,* whose memory in your land is so vivid and legacy so profoundly felt. Their witness is relevant even to those who, in the field of politics, are working *to bring about European unification.* In searching for its own identity, the Continent cannot but return to its Christian roots. The whole of Europe, both West and East, expects *Catholics and Orthodox to work together* for the defence of peace and justice, human rights and the culture of life....

In a spirit of brotherhood, I assure you of my constant prayer, that the Lord will grant the Orthodox Church of Bulgaria to accomplish with courage, together with the Catholic Church, the mission of evangelization which he has entrusted to your Church in this land.

Meeting with representatives of the world of Culture, Science and Art, Palace of Culture, Sofia

This meeting is taking place *on a particularly significant day,* for Bulgaria today celebrates the feast of the Holy Brothers Cyril and Methodius, intrepid heralds of the Gospel of Christ and founders of the literary language and culture of the Slav peoples. Their liturgical memorial has a particular significance, since it is also the "feast of Bulgarian letters". This is not something which concerns the Orthodox and Catholic faithful alone, but is an opportunity for all to reflect on the cultural patrimony which originated with the activity of the two Holy Brothers of Thessalon-ica....

By introducing the Gospel to the culture of the peoples whom they evangelized, the Holy Brothers — with their brilliant creation of a new alphabet — achieved special merit. In order to respond to the needs of their apostolic ministry, they *translated the Sacred Books into the local language* for liturgical and catechetical purposes, and thus laid the foundations of literature in the languages of the Slav peoples. They are therefore rightly considered not only the *Apostles of the Slavs,* but also the *fathers of Slav culture.* Culture is *the expression, incarnate in history, of a people's identity*; it forges the soul of a nation, which identifies itself with specific values, expresses itself in precise symbols, and communicates by its own proper signs....

The work of Cyril and Methodius made *an outstanding contribution to forming the common Christian roots of Europe,* those roots which by their depth and vitality have created a solid cultural reference-point which cannot be ignored in any serious attempt to rebuild in a new and contemporary way the unity of the Continent....

Historical experience shows that the proclamation of the Christian faith has not *stifled* but rather *integrated and exalted* the authentic human and cultural values proper to the genius of the countries where it has been preached. It has also contributed to their *openness to one another* and helped them to overcome enmities and to create *a common spiritual and cultural heritage,* necessary for stable and constructive relations of peace....

In these troubling times there is an urgent need to affirm that, Europe, if it is to rediscover its own deepest identity, must necessarily return to its Christian roots, and in particular to the work of men like Benedict, Cyril and Methodius, whose witness offers an essential contribution for the spiritual and moral restoration of the Continent.

May 26 — Mass with Beatifications in the Central Square, Plovdiv

From the beginning of my service as the Successor of Peter, I have looked to you young people with great care and affection, because I am convinced that youth is *not just a time of transition* between adolescence and adulthood but a time of life given by God to each person *as a gift and a task.* It is a time to seek *the answer to fundamental questions,* like the young man in the Gospel (cf. *Mt* 16:20), and to discover not only the meaning of life but also a specific plan of life. Your personal, professional and social future will depend, dear young people, upon the choices you make in these years: youth is *the time to lay foundations*; an opportunity not to be missed, because it will never come again! ...

In this moment of your life, the Pope is happy to be with you in order *to listen respectfully* to your anxieties and cares, your expectations and hopes. He is here among you *to share with you the certainty which is Christ,* the truth which is Christ, the love which is Christ. The Church looks to you with the greatest care, because she sees in you her own future and she puts her hope in you....

Never forget, young friends: you are called to be the salt of the earth and the light of the world! Jesus does not ask you just to *say* or *do* something; Jesus asks you to *be* salt and light! And not just for a day, but for your whole life. It is a task that he puts before you every morning and in every setting. You must *be* salt and light with your family and friends; with other young people — Orthodox, Jewish, Muslim — with whom you have daily contact wherever you study, work or relax. It is also up to you to build a society where all people can find their proper place and where their dignity and freedom is recognized and respected. Do your part, so that day by day Bulgaria will be more and more *a land of hospitality, prosperity and peace.*

Farewell Ceremony — Airport, Plovdiv

My visit to the beloved land of Bulgaria, although brief, *has filled my heart with emotion and joy.* The Pope has been given the opportunity to meet the Bulgarian people, to admire their virtues and qualities, to appreciate their great talents and generous energies. I give thanks to God who has granted me the possibility of making this pilgrimage *during the very days on which the memory of the Holy Brothers Cyril and Methodius,* the Apostles of the Slav peoples, *is celebrated....*

My heartfelt thanks go also to *His Holiness Patriarch Maxim,* to the *Metropolitans* and *Bishops* of the Holy Synod, and to *all the faithful* of the Orthodox Church of Bulgaria. Not so long ago, both Catholics and Orthodox underwent harsh persecution for their fidelity to the Gospel: may so many sacrifices make the witness of Christians in this country bear much fruit and, with the grace of God, may they hasten the day when we shall be able to rejoice in the rediscovered fullness of unity among us!

One last word to *all the beloved Bulgarian people,* without distinction. A word that echoes what was said by my predecessor, Blessed Pope John XXIII, when he left this country in December 1934. On that occasion he referred to an Irish tradition according to which, on Christmas Eve, every house places a lighted candle in the window, as an indication to Joseph and Mary that inside there is a family awaiting them at the fireside. To the crowd that had come to bid him farewell, Archbishop Roncalli said: "If anyone from Bulgaria should ever pass by my house, at night, amid life's difficulties, he will always find the candle burning in my window. Let him knock, let him knock! He will not be asked whether he is Catholic or Orthodox: he is a Bulgarian brother and that is enough. Let him come in: two brotherly arms and a friend's warm heart will welcome him to the feast" (*Christmas Homily,* 25 December 1934)....

God bless Bulgaria, with the abundance of his grace may he make its people feel my affection and gratitude, and may he grant to the Nation days of progress, prosperity and peace.

WORLD YOUTH DAY — TORONTO, CANADA, GUATEMALA, AND MEXICO, JULY 23-AUG. 1, 2002

Pope John Paul II, on the 97th foreign trip of his pontificate, visited Toronto, Canada, for the celebration of the 17th World Youth Day from July 23-28, 2002; Guatemala City for the canonization of Blessed Pedro de San Jose de Betancur from July 29-30; and Mexico City for the beatification of the martyrs Juan Bautista and Jacinto de los Angeles and the canonization of Blessed Juan Diego Cuauhlatoatzin from July 31 to August 1.

Itinerary
July 23 — World Youth Day (Toronto)
Arrival: welcome ceremony.
Greeting of the Holy Father.
Departure for Strawberry Island.

July 24 (Strawberry Island)
Day of rest.

July 25 (Toronto)
Papal welcome ceremony to the young people.
Departure by helicopter for Strawberry Island.

July 26 (Strawberry Island)
Day of rest.

July 27 (Toronto)
Meetings with the governor general of Canada, prime minister of Canada, prime minister of Ontario, mayor of Toronto, and superior general and the Council of the Congregation of the Sisters of St. Joseph.
Recital of the *Angelus Domini.*
Lunch with the Catholic bishops of the Canadian Episcopal Conference and the members of the papal entourage.
Departure by helicopter for Downsview Park.
Prayer vigil with young people; departure by helicopter for Morrow Park.

July 28 (Toronto)
Departure by helicopter for Downsview Park.
Mass for the celebration of the 17th World Youth Day.
Recital of the *Angelus Domini.*
Departure by helicopter for Morrow Park.
Greeting of the Holy Father to the national organizing committee for World Youth Day 2002.

July 29 (Toronto)
Departure by helicopter for Lester B. Pearson International Airport.
Farewell ceremony.

Guatemala

July 29 (Guatemala City)
Arrival: Welcome Ceremony.
Greeting of the Holy Father.

July 30 (Guatemala City)
Mass and canonization of Blessed Hermano Pedro de San José de Betancurt.
Farewell ceremony.

Mexico City

July 30 (Mexico City)
Arrival: welcome ceremony.

July 31 (Mexico City)
Mass and canonization of Blessed Juan Diego Cuauhtlatoatzin.

Aug. 1 (Mexico City)
Liturgy of the word and beatification of the martyrs Juan Bautista and Jacinto de Los Angeles.
Departure for Rome.

Overview
The XVII World Youth Day was the first international gathering of young Catholics in the twenty-first century. It took place at a time when Canada is about to celebrate the four-hundredth anniversary of the first permanent French settlement in North America and in a city that is described as a microcosm of Canada's multicultural society, and one of the most multicultural cities in the world. The theme of World Youth Day 2002 was: "You are the salt of the earth. You are the light of the world" (Mt. 5: 13-14). These words are from the Sermon on the Mount.

Hundreds of thousands of young people from all over the world came to Toronto for several days of prayers and celebrations, and to visit with the 82-year-old pontiff who reminded them that real happiness is found in the Gospel, not in worldly success or the "fleeting pleasures of the senses."

The most memorable event of the several days was the celebration of the Eucharist on Sunday, July 28, at Downsview Park in Toronto. A crowd of 800,000 braved severe rain to hear the pontiff urge them to remain strong in their faith and not to be "discouraged by the sins and failings" of clergy accused of sex abuse.

Hundreds of thousands of World Youth Day pilgrims and local Catholics also gathered in downtown Toronto for a solemn celebration of the Way of the Cross. Four young people lit torches from the eternal flame in the Peace Park at Toronto's Nathan Philips Square. During his 1984 visit, Pope John Paul II lit the flame with an ember from the Peace Memorial Park in Hiroshima, Japan.

The pope journeyed to Guatemala to proclaim the first Central American saint, Pedro de San Jose Betancur, a 17th-century missionary who built hospitals, schools and shelters in the former Guatemalan capital now called Antigua. The Mass of canonization was attended by an estimated 500,000 Guatemalans. The pontiff stressed Betancur as a model for Christian mercy.

The pope's trip to Mexico, the fifth of his pontificate, was marked by a tumultuous welcome, enthusiastic crowds, the canonization of Juan Diego, North America's first indigenous saint, and the beatification of two indigenous martyrs. The pope was greeted by Mexican President Vicente Fox, a Catholic, his wife, Martha Sahagun, and Mexico City Cardinal Norberto Rivera Carrera.

The pope declared that he was proud to proclaim the first indigenous saint of the Americas, a "simple, humble Indian." He referred to Juan Diego, the Mexican peasant whose visions of Our Lady of Guadalupe in the 1500s helped establish the deepest devotion in Latin America. The pontiff stressed the fact that Juan Diego embraced the Catholic faith without surrendering his Indian identity, demonstrating the vital role of indigenous peoples in the Church. The liturgy for the canonization in the Basilica of Our Lady of Guadalupe was a powerful and joyous celebration that united Indian and European traditions.

The pope completed the trip by beatifying two Zapotec Indian martyrs from the southern state of Oaxaca. The pope ended the beatification service with the unscripted statement, "I may be going, but my heart stays with you. Beautiful Mexico, may God bless you."

Excerpts from Addresses and Homilies

Canada (World Youth Day)
July 23 — Welcome Ceremony, Lester B. Pearson International Airport, Toronto

Dear People of Canada, I have vivid memories of my first apostolic visit in 1984, and of my brief visit in 1987 to the First Nations in the land of Denendeh. This time I must be content to stay only in Toronto. From here I greet all Canadians. You are in my thankful prayers to God, who has so abundantly blessed your vast and beautiful country.

Young people from all parts of the world are gathering for the World Youth Day. With their gifts of intelligence and heart *they represent the future of the world*. But they also bear the marks of a humanity that too

often does not know peace, or justice.

Too many lives begin and end without joy, without hope. That is one of the principal reasons for the World Youth Day. Young people are coming together to commit themselves, in the strength of their faith in Jesus Christ, to the great cause of peace and human solidarity....

In a world of great social and ethical strains, and confusion about the very purpose of life, Canadians have an incomparable treasure to contribute — on condition that they preserve what is deep, and good and valid in their own heritage. I pray that the World Youth Day will offer all Canadians an opportunity to remember the values that are essential to good living and to human happiness.

July 27 — Prayer Vigil with the young people in Downsview Park, Toronto

This evening, together with you, I praise God and give thanks to him for the gift bestowed on the Church through the World Youth Days. Millions of young people have taken part, and as a result have become better and more committed Christian witnesses. I am especially thankful to you, who have responded to my invitation to come here to Toronto in order to "tell the world of the happiness you have found in meeting Jesus Christ, of your desire to know him better, of how you are committed to proclaiming the Gospel of salvation to the ends of the earth!" (Message for the 17th World Youth Day, No. 5).

The new millennium opened with *two contrasting scenarios*: one, the sight of multitudes of pilgrims coming to Rome during the Great Jubilee to pass through the Holy Door which is Christ, our Savior and Redeemer; and the other, the terrible terrorist attack on New York, an image that is a sort of icon of a world in which hostility and hatred seem to prevail.

The question that arises is dramatic: *on what foundations* must we build the new historical era that is emerging from the great transformations of the twentieth century? Is it enough to rely on the technological revolution now taking place, which seems to respond only to criteria of productivity and efficiency, without reference to the individual's spiritual dimension or to any universally shared ethical values? Is it right to be content with provisional answers to the ultimate questions, and to abandon life to the impulses of instinct, to short-lived sensations or passing fads?

The question will not go away: on what foundations, on what certainties should we build our lives and the life of the community to which we belong?

Dear Friends, spontaneously in your hearts, in the enthusiasm of your young years you know the answer, and you are saying it through your presence here this evening: *Christ alone is the cornerstone* on which it is possible solidly to build one's existence. Only Christ — known, contemplated and loved – is the faithful friend who never lets us down, who becomes our travelling companion, and whose words warm our hearts (cf. Lk. 24:13-35)....

This evening the Pope, along with all of you, young people from every continent, *reaffirms before the world the faith that sustains the life of the Church*. Christ is the light of the nations. He died and rose again in order to give back to those who journey through time the hope of eternity. *Nothing human is hurt by the Gospel*: every authentic value, in whatever culture it appears, is accepted and raised up by

Christ. Knowing this, Christians cannot fail to feel in their hearts the pride and responsibility of their call to be witnesses to the light of the Gospel.

Precisely for this reason I say to you this evening: let the light of Christ shine in your lives! *Do not wait until you are older in order to set out on the path of holiness*! Holiness is always youthful, just as eternal is the youthfulness of God....

Dear young people, I thank you for your presence in Toronto, in Wadowice and wherever you are spiritually united with the world's young people taking part in the 17th World Youth Day. I wish to assure you that in my heart and in my prayer I never cease to embrace each and every one of you, asking God that you may be the salt and the light of the earth, now and in your adult lives. God bless you!

July 28 — Mass for the celebration of the 17th World Youth Day in Downsview Park, Toronto

"*You are the salt of the earth! You are the light of the world*!" (Mt. 5:13-14)

On a hillside near the lake of Galilee, Jesus's disciples listened to his gentle and urgent voice; as *gentle* as the landscape of Galilee itself, as *urgent* as a call to choose between life and death, between truth and falsehood. The Lord spoke words of life that would echo forever in the hearts of his followers. Today he is speaking the same words to you, the young people of Toronto and Ontario, of the whole of Canada, of the United States, of the Caribbean, of Spanish-speaking America and Portuguese-speaking America, of Europe, Africa, Asia and Oceania. Listen to the voice of Jesus in the depths of your hearts! His words tell you *who you are as Christians*. They tell you *what you must do to remain in his love*.

But Jesus offers one thing, and the "spirit of the world" offers another. In today's Reading from the Letter to the Ephesians, Saint Paul tells us that Jesus leads us *from darkness into light* (cf. Eph. 5, 8). Perhaps the great Apostle is thinking of the light that blinded him, the persecutor of Christians, on the road to Damascus. When later he recovered his sight, *nothing was as before*. He had been born anew and nothing would ever take his new-found joy away from him. You too are called to be transformed. "Awake, O sleeper, arise from the dead, and Christ will give you light" (Eph. 5, 14), says Saint Paul.

The "spirit of the world" *offers many false illusions and parodies of happiness*. There is perhaps no darkness deeper than the darkness that enters young people's souls when false prophets extinguish in them the light of faith and hope and love. The greatest deception, and the deepest source of unhappiness, is *the illusion of finding life by excluding God*, of finding freedom by excluding moral truths and personal responsibility....

The world you are inheriting is a world which desperately needs a new sense of brotherhood and human solidarity. It is a world which needs to be touched and healed by the beauty and richness of God's love. *It needs witnesses to that love. The world needs salt. It needs you* — to be the salt of the earth and the light of the world....

You are young, and the Pope is old, 82 or 83 years of life is not the same as 22 or 23. But the Pope still fully identifies with your hopes and aspirations. Although I have lived through much darkness, under harsh totalitarian regimes, I have seen enough evidence to be unshakably convinced that no difficulty, no fear is so great that it can completely suffocate *the hope that springs eternal in the hearts of the young*. You are our hope, the young are our hope.

Do not let that hope die! Stake your lives on it! *We are not the sum of our weaknesses and failures*; we are the sum of the Father's love for us and our real capacity to become the image of his Son.

Guatemala

July 29 — Welcome Ceremony, International Airport of Ciudad de Guatemala

First of all I would like to express my great joy in coming to this beloved land of Guatemala for the third time as a pilgrim of love and hope. I thank God for permitting me to return here to celebrate the canonization of a figure you so deeply love and admire: Brother Pedro de San José de Betancurt, a son of Tenerife, one of the Canary Islands. Prompted by a great missionary spirit, he came to Guatemala and gave himself to the service of the poor and needy.

Tomorrow I will have the good fortune to canonize Brother Pedro de Betancurt, who embodied God's love for his people. This celebration should be a true moment of grace and renewal for Guatemala. In fact, the example of Brother Pedro's life and the eloquence of his message are a valuable contribution to building society, which is now opening to the challenges of the third millennium. I fervently hope that the noble Guatamalan people, who thirst for God and for spiritual values, who are anxious for peace, solidarity and justice, may live and enjoy the dignity which is theirs.

July 30 — Canonization Mass of Blessed Hermano Pedro de San José de Betancurt, Hippodrome, Guatemala City

Today, in adding Brother Pedro de San José de Betancurt to the list of the Saints, I am convinced of the present-day importance of his message. The new Saint, travelling with only his faith and his confidence in God, sailed across the Atlantic to care for the poor and indigenous people of America: first in Cuba, then in Honduras and finally in this blessed land of Guatemala, his "promised land."

Already in the land of his birth, as in every phase of his life, Brother Pedro was a deeply prayerful man, especially here where, at the hermitage of Calvary, he diligently sought God's will at every moment.

Thus he is an outstanding example for Christians today, whom he reminds that training in holiness "calls for a Christian life distinguished above all in the art of prayer" (*Novo millennio ineunte,* 32). I therefore renew my exhortation to all the Christian communities of Guatemala and other countries to be authentic schools of prayer where all activity is centered on prayer. An intensely devout life always bears abundant fruit.

Brother Pedro modelled his spirituality in this way, particularly in contemplation of the mysteries of Bethlehem and of the Cross. If, in the birth and childhood of Jesus, he immersed himself deeply in the fundamental event of the Incarnation of the Word — which led him to discover spontaneously, as it were, the face of God in man — then, in meditating on the Cross, he found the strength to practise mercy heroically with the lowliest and the most deprived.

Today, the new Saint represents also an urgent appeal to practise mercy in modern society, especially when so many are hoping for a helping hand. Let us think of the children and young people who are homeless or deprived of an education; of abandoned women with their many needs; of the hordes of social outcasts who live in the cities; of the victims of organized crime, of prostitution or of drugs; of the sick who are neglected and the elderly who live in loneliness.

Mexico

July 30 — Welcome Ceremony, International Airport of Mexico City

I am filled with great joy at being able to come to this hospitable land for the fifth time. It was here that I began my Apostolic travels which have taken me as the Successor of the Apostle Peter to so many parts of the world, bringing me close to many men and women to strengthen them in their faith in our Saviour, Jesus Christ.

After celebrating the 17th World Youth Day in Toronto, today I have had the good fortune to add to the list of saints a wonderful evangelizer from this continent: Brother Pedro de San José de Betancurt. Tomorrow, with deep joy I shall canonize Juan Diego, and on the following day I shall beatify two other compatriots of yours: Juan Bautista and Jacinto de los Ángeles, who will thus join these beautiful examples of holiness in these beloved American countries, where the Christian message has been welcomed with open hearts, permeating their cultures and bringing forth abundant fruit....

Dear Mexicans: thank you for your hospitality, for your constant affection, for your fidelity to the Church. Continue to be faithful on this journey, encouraged by the marvellous examples of holiness born in this noble nation. Be holy! Repeating what I said to you in the Basilica of Guadalupe in 1990, serve God, the Church and the nation, each one assuming personal responsibility for passing on the Gospel message and witnessing to a faith that is alive and active in society.

July 31 — Canonization Mass of Blessed Juan Diego Cuauhtlatoatzin at the Basilica of Our Lady of Guadalupe, Mexico City (*For details, see under Mexico*)

August 1 — Beatification of the Martyrs Juan Bautista and Jacinto de Los Angeles at the Basilica of Our Lady of Guadalupe, Mexico City

Faced with the human suffering that accompanies the journey of faith, Saint Peter urges: "*Rejoice insofar as you share Christ's sufferings, that you may also rejoice and be glad when his glory is revealed*" (1 Pt. 4:13). With this conviction, Juan Bautista and Jacinto de los Ángeles faced martyrdom, remaining faithful to their devotion to the true, living God and rejecting idols.

As they were being tortured, they were invited to renounce their Catholic faith and save themselves. But they answered bravely: "*Once we have professed Baptism, we shall always follow the true religion*": a beautiful example of how nothing, not even our life, should be put before our baptismal commitment. This is the same example given by the early Christians, who,born to new life through Baptism, abandoned all forms of idolatry (cf. Tertullian, *De baptismo*, 12,15).

These two indigenous Christians, whose personal and family life was irreproachable, suffered martyrdom for their fidelity to the Catholic faith, happy to have been baptized. They are an example to the lay faithful, who are called to sanctify themselves in the ordinary circumstances of everyday life.

With this beatification, the Church emphasizes the mission to proclaim the Gospel to all peoples. The new "Blesseds," fruit of the holiness of the First Evangelization among the Zapotec Indians, encourage indigenous people today to appreciate their cultures and languages, and above all their dignity as children of God. This dignity must be respected by others in the context of the Mexican nation, made up of peoples of many different origins but willing to build a common family in solidarity and justice.

The two "Blesseds" are an example of how, without regarding one's ancestral customs as myths, one can reach God without renouncing one's own culture but letting oneself be enlightened by the light of Christ, which renews the religious spirit of the best popular traditions.

POLAND, AUGUST 16-19, 2002

Pope John Paul II, on the 98th foreign trip of his pontificate, visited his homeland from Aug. 16-19, 2002.

Itinerary

August 16 (Krakow)
Welcome Ceremony: address of the Holy Father
August 17 (Krakow)
Mass and dedication of the Shrine of Divine Mercy in Kraków.
Meetings with the president of the Republic, the prime minister, and the local authorities.
August 18 (Krakow)
Mass with beatifications in Blonie Park.
Recital of the *Angelus Domini*.
Private visit to Wawel Cathedral.
Private visit to the tomb of his parents in the cemetery of Rakowice.
August 19 (Krakow)
Mass for the 400th anniversary of the dedication of the Shrine of Kalwaria Zebryzdowska.
Farewell ceremony.

Overview

In an emotional return to his homeland, Pope John Paul II journeyed to Poland to dedicate the Shrine of Divine Mercy in Krakow, beatify four Polish clergy and religious, and celebrate the 400th anniversary of the dedication of the Shrine of Kalwaria Zebryzdowska. The pope declared that the theme of his visit was to emphasize the divine mercy of God and the practice of mercy in daily life.

While those were the official reasons for his visit, the joyous welcome given the pope demonstrated the depth of love, regard and honor paid by the Polish people to the pontiff. The trip was made even more emotional by the possibility that this could be the last time the pope would visit Poland. The enthusiasm of the crowds and their outpouring of support clearly touched the pontiff who acknowledged their cheers and support.

Under the theme of Divine Mercy, on Aug. 17 the pope dedicated a new basilica next to the former convent of St. Faustina, the founder of the modern Divine Mercy movement. The next day, nearly two and a half million people attended a Beatification Mass.

The pontiff beatified four Poles — a bishop, two priests and a nun — who were proclaimed to be exemplars of the mercy in action that was so important to St. Faustina. The four new beati are: Archbishop Sigmund Felinski, Father John Balicki, Jesuit Father John Beyzym, and Sister Santia Szymkowiak.

On Aug. 19, Pope John Paul celebrated a final liturgy at Kalwaria Zebrzydowska, a 400-year-old shrine dedicated to Christ's passion and Mary's compassion. Located some 30 miles outside of Krakow, the shrine visited regularly by the future pope as a boy with his father. The pope also made a private visit to the Wawel Cathedral (where he celebrated his first Mass 56 years ago), and to the Krakow cemetery of Rakowice, where his mother, father and brother are buried.

Excerpts of Addresses and Homilies
August 16 — Arrival Ceremony, Krakow

Once again I greet Poland and all my countrymen. I do so with the very same sentiments of emotion and joy that I feel every time I return to my homeland....

This time I shall stay only in Krakow, but with affection I embrace the whole of Poland and all its people—.

Brothers and sisters! "God, rich in mercy." This is the motto of this pilgrimage. This is its proclamation. It comes from the encyclical *Dives in Misericordia*, but its source is here, in Krakow, at Lagiewniki. Because from here, thanks to the humble efforts of an unusual witness, — Saint Sister Faustina — the Gospel message of God's merciful love rings out. That is why the first stage of my pilgrimage and its chief purpose is my visit to the Shrine of Divine Mercy. I am happy to be able to dedicate the new building, which is becoming a world centre of devotion to the merciful Christ.

The mercy of God is reflected in human mercy. For centuries, Kraków has found glory in great figures who, trusting in God's love, bore witness to mercy through practical deeds of love of neighbour. It is enough to mention St. Hedwig, St. John of Kety, Fr. Piotr Skarga or St. Brother Albert. Today they will be joined by the Servants of God whom — with God's help — I shall have the joy of raising to the glory of the altars at Holy Mass in Blonie Park. The beatification of Zygmunt Szczesny Felinski, Jan Beyzym, Sancja Szymkowiak and Jan Balicki are the second reason for my pilgrimage. Already I hope that these new beati, who have given an example of the practice of mercy, will remind us of the great gift of God's love and predispose us for the daily practice of love of our neighbour.

There is also a third reason for my pilgrimage which I wish to mention. It is the prayer of thanksgiving for the 400 years of the Shrine of Kalwaria Zebrzydowska, which I have been associated with from childhood. It was there, praying as I walked along its paths, that I sought inspiration for my service of the Church in Kraków and in Poland, there that I made various difficult pastoral decisions. It was precisely there, among the faithful people at prayer, that I came to know the faith that guides me also on the Chair of Peter. Through the intercession of Our Lady of Kalwaria I want to thank God for this gift.

August 17 – Dedication of the Shrine of Divine Mercy, Krakow-Lagiewniki

"O inconceivable and unfathomable Mercy of God, Who can worthily adore you and sing your praises? O greatest attribute of God Almighty, You are the sweet hope of sinners" (Diary, 951).

Dear Brothers and Sisters!

Today I repeat these simple and straightforward words of Saint Faustina, in order to join her and all of you in adoring the inconceivable and unfathomable mystery of God's mercy. Like Saint Faustina, we wish to proclaim that apart from the mercy of God there is no other source of hope for mankind. We desire to repeat with faith: *Jesus, I trust in you!*

This proclamation, this confession of trust in the all-powerful love of God, is especially needed in our own time, when mankind is experiencing bewilderment in the face of many manifestations of evil . . .

I firmly believe that this new church will always be a place where people will come before God in Spirit and truth. They will come with the trust which accompanies all those who humbly open their hearts to the working of God's merciful love, to that love which is stronger than even the greatest sin. Here, in the fire of divine love, human hearts will burn with desire for conversion, and whoever looks for hope will find comfort....

August 18 – Beatification Mass in Blonie Park, Krakow

The call to be witnesses of mercy resounds with particular eloquence here, in my beloved Krakow, dominated by the Shrine of Divine Mercy of Lagiewniki and its new church which yesterday I had the joy of consecrating. Here this call sounds familiar, for it appeals to the age-old tradition of the City, which has always been known for its *readiness to assist those in need*. We cannot forget that this tradition includes the numerous Saints and Beati — priests, consecrated persons and laity — who devoted their lives to works of mercy. Beginning with Bishop Stanislaus, Queen Hedwig, John of Kety and Piotr Skarga, and continuing to Brother Albert, Angela Salawa and Cardinal Sapieha, this heritage of mercy has been passed down by generations of Christians in this City over many centuries. *Today this heritage has been placed in our hands and it must not be forgotten . . .*

The message of merciful love needs to resound forcefully anew. The world needs this love. The hour has come to bring Christ's message to everyone: to rulers and the oppressed, to those whose humanity and dignity seem lost in the *mysterium iniquitatis*. The hour has come when the message of Divine Mercy is able to fill hearts with hope and to become the spark of a new civilization: the civilization of love.

The Church desires tirelessly to proclaim this message, not only by convincing words, but by the ready practice of mercy. This is why she ceaselessly holds up stupendous examples of individuals *who out of love for God and for man "went forth and bore fruit"*. Today she adds four new Beati to their number. They lived at different times and led very different lives. But they are united by that particular feature of holiness which is *devotion to the cause of mercy*.

Blessed Sigismund Felix Felinski, Archbishop of Warsaw, during a difficult period marked by the lack of national freedom, urged everyone to persevere in generous service to the poor and to establish educational institutions and charitable works. He himself founded an orphanage and a school; he also brought the Sisters of Blessed Virgin Mary of Mercy to Warsaw and supported the work they began. After the failure of the insurrection of 1863, in a spirit of mercy towards his brothers and sisters he openly defended the persecuted. This fidelity cost him deportment to the interior of Russia, which lasted twenty years. Even there he continued to be mindful of the poor and distressed, showing them great love, patience and understanding....

August 19 – Mass for the 400th anniversary of the Dedication of the Shrine of Kalwaria Zebryzdowska.

Today I come to this Shrine as a pilgrim, as I used to come when I was a child and as a young man. I come before Our Lady of Calvary as I used to come as Bishop of Krakow to entrust to her the problems of the Archdiocese and of those whom God had entrusted to my pastoral care. I come here and, now as then, I repeat: Hail, Hail, Holy Queen, Mother of Mercy!

How many times have I seen that *the Mother of the Son of God turns her eyes of mercy upon the concerns of the afflicted*, that she obtains for them the grace to resolve difficult problems, and that they, in their powerlessness, come to a fuller realization of the amazing power and wisdom of Divine Providence? Has this not been the experience of the generations of pilgrims who have come here for four hundred years? Indeed it has. Otherwise today's celebration would not be taking place. You would not be here, dear friends, you who tread the Paths of Kalwaria, tracing the steps of Christ's Passion and Cross and following his Mother's journey of compassion and glory. This place wondrously helps the heart and mind to gain deeper insight into the mystery of that *bond which united the suffering Saviour and his co-suffering Mother*. At the centre of this mystery of love everyone who comes here rediscovers himself, his life, his daily existence, his weakness and, at the same time, the power of faith and hope: that power which springs up from the assurance that the Mother does not aban-

don her children at times of trouble, but leads them to her Son and entrusts them to his mercy . . .

In 1641 the Shrine of Kalwaria was enriched by a particular gift. Providence guided here the steps of Stanislaw Paszkowski of Brzezie, who wished to entrust to the custody of the Bernardine Fathers *the image of the Most Holy Mother*, which had already become famous for its graces when it was located in his house chapel. From that time on, and particularly after the day in 1887 when, with the approval of Pope Leo XIII, it was crowned by the Bishop of Krakow, Albin Sas Dunajewski, pilgrims have concluded their pilgrimage in her sight. At the beginning the pilgrims came here from all parts of Poland, but also from Lithuania, Rus', Slovakia, Bohemia, Hungary, Moravia and Germany. The natives of Silesia were especially devoted to her; it was they who offered the crown to Jesus and, from the day of the crowning until the present, they have taken part each year in the procession on the day of the Assumption of the Blessed Virgin Mary.

How important was this place for a Poland divided by the partitions!

August 19 – Farewell Ceremony, Kraków – Balice Airport

"Poland, my dear homeland, … God raises you up and treats you with special care, but you must show him gratitude" (*Diary*, 1038). With these words from Saint Faustina's Diary I wish to bid you farewell, dear Brothers and Sisters, my Compatriots!

The time having come when I must return to the Vatican, I look out once more upon you all with great joy, and I thank God who has permitted me to visit my Homeland yet again. My thoughts turn to the different stages of this three-day pilgrimage: Lagiewniki, B³onie in Krakow, Kalwaria Zebrzydowska. I shall not forget the crowds of the faithful gathered in prayer — living testimony of the faith of the Church in Poland and of your trust in the power of God's mercy. Taking leave of Poland, I wish to bid you all farewell, dear Compatriots. Many have waited for my coming. Many have wished to meet me, although not all were able to do so. Maybe next time . . .

PAPAL ACTIVITIES

DAY OF PEACE AT ASSISI

On Jan. 24, 2002, Pope John Paul II led an interreligious pilgrimage of more than 200 religious leaders to Assisi, birthplace of St. Francis, to promote peace. "In times of greater anxiety about the fate of the world," the pope declared in his welcome to the dignitaries, "we sense more clearly than ever the duty to commit ourselves personally to the defense and promotion of the fundamental good which is peace."

The pilgrimage brought together Christians from sixteen churches and communities, thirty Muslims clerics from eighteen nations, ten rabbis, and representatives from Buddhism, Tenrikyo, Shintoism, Jainism, Sikhism, Hinduism, Zoroastrianism, Confucianism and traditional African religions. The program was held in four parts:

• After arriving in Assisi, the Holy Father welcomed and greeted the representatives of the world religions in Piazza San Francesco; some of the representatives then read testimonies in favor of peace

• The second part was given to prayer. The representatives and their delegations, respecting their own religious convictions, prayed in different places. Christians of the various Churches and Ecclesial Communities prayed together in an ecumenical celebration in the Lower Basilica of Saint Francis.

• The third part consisted of a sign of communion and hospitality that included a fraternal meal for the representatives and their delegations in the Sacro Convento.

• The fourth part of the day took place in the afternoon, again in Piazza San Francesco. It comprised a reading by some of the representatives of a common text of commitment to peace, the sign of the lamp, the fraternal embrace and the Holy Father's farewell, urging renewed common witness to peace in today's world at the beginning of the third millennium.

At the morning gathering, Pope John Paul said he and other leaders of the world's religions share the anxiety of many of their faithful, but they also share a firm belief that God can grant the world peace:

"We are here, as representatives of different religions, to examine ourselves before God concerning our commitment to peace, to ask him for this gift, to bear witness to our shared longing for a world of greater justice and solidarity.

"We wish to do our part in fending off the dark clouds of terrorism, hatred, armed conflict, which in these last few months have grown particularly ominous on humanity's horizon. For this reason we wish to listen to one other: We believe that this itself is already a sign of peace. In listening to one another there is already a reply to the disturbing questions that worry us. This already serves to scatter the shadows of suspicion and misunderstanding."

The pope also offered a special greeting to Cardinal Edward M. Egan of New York, "the city so terribly affected by the tragic events of Sept. 11."

Ecumenical Patriarch Bartholomew, leader of the Greek Orthodox Church was the first of 11 religious leaders to speak. He said, "Today, once more, following horrendous holocausts and the slaughter of so many innocent victims, it is our duty to acknowledge the spiritual conditions for peace on earth, and not merely economic or other factors. "These conditions include righteousness and respect for the sacredness of the human person, for one's neighbor and for his freedom and dignity," the patriarch said.

"We must repent and turn back to God in full awareness of his holy will and in obedience to it. Only then will God hear our prayers and grant us and all mankind true peace on earth," he said.

Chief Amadou Gasseto, self-described high priest of followers of Avelekete Vodoo in Benin, reiterated the patriarch's point about personal behavior and its decisive role in creating peace or conflict.

"We must begin by achieving mastery over ourselves so as not to speak words which lead to feelings of opposition, exclusion or violence," he said. "It is good to invite people every year to a change of heart by renouncing hatred, violence and injustice."

Rabbi Israel Singer, secretary general of the World Jewish Congress, departed from his prepared text and told Pope John Paul, "You should tell your people and we should tell ours, all of us — all of us — to question whether land or places are more important than people's lives and, until we learn to do that, there will be no peace."

The rabbi was the only religious leader to speak directly about the events of September 11: "We are all too familiar with the way in which on Sept. 11 madmen who claimed to be acting in the name of religion plunged three airplanes into both towers of the World Trade Center and the Pentagon, killing thousands in only a few minutes, thus causing the first international military conflict of the 21st century. We must remember that in no religion are we commanded to kill indiscriminately, and those who have taught otherwise have done so by hijacking and distorting the religions in whose name they speak."

During the afternoon service, 10 religious leaders, reading in 10 different languages, recited 10 commitments they all promised to fulfill to help bring peace to the world.

The Rev. Konrad Raiser, secretary-general of the World Council of Churches, read the first pledge in German: "We commit ourselves to proclaiming our firm commitment that violence and terrorism are incompatible with the authentic spirit of religion and, as we condemn every recourse to violence and war in the name of God or religion, we commit ourselves to doing everything possible to eliminate the root causes of terrorism."

The leaders also promised to educate their faithful to respect others, to foster dialogue, to defend each person's right to live a decent life, to value differences, to be voices for the poor and defenseless and to promote friendship among peoples.

The Holy Father confirmed and concluded the shared commitment to peace in these words:

Violence never again!

War never again!

Terrorism never again!

In God's name, may all religions bring upon earth justice and peace, forgiveness, life and love!

CANONIZATION OF PADRE PIO

On June 16, 2002, Pope John Paul II canonized St. Pio of Pietrelcina, a Capuchin priest, spiritual advisor, and one of the most beloved of all modern saints. In a testament to the level of regard in which Padre Pio is held, the canonization was one of the largest liturgies in the Vatican's history. Padre Pio died in 1968 at the age of 81. More than 300,000 people, according to police, filled St. Peter's Square and surrounding streets in sweltering 90-degree heat.

Literally thousands of tour buses began delivering pilgrims to St. Peter's Square at 5 a.m. for the Mass, which began at 10. Pilgrims also arrived from all over Italy in 50 special trains. Tens of thousands other pilgrims watched the canonization by live audio link from a piazza in San Giovanni Rotondo, the southern Italian town where Padre Pio spent most of his life and is buried. At the moment when he was formally proclaimed a saint, they cheered and released thousands of blue and yellow balloons into the air. In his homily, the Holy Father declared:

"'For my yoke is easy and my burden light' (Mt. 11,30). Jesus' words to his disciples, which we just heard, help us to understand the most important message of this solemn celebration. Indeed, in a certain sense, we can consider them as a magnificent summary of the whole life of Padre Pio of Pietrelcina, today proclaimed a saint. The evangelical image of the 'yoke' recalls the many trials that the humble Capuchin of San Giovanni Rotondo had to face. Today we contemplate in him how gentle the 'yoke' of Christ is, and how truly light is his burden when it is borne with faithful love. The life and mission of Padre Pio prove that difficulties and sorrows, if accepted out of love, are transformed into a privileged way of holiness, which opens onto the horizons of a greater good, known only to the Lord.... Throughout his life, he always sought greater conformity with the Crucified, since he was very conscious of having been called to collaborate in a special way in the work of redemption. His holiness cannot be understood without this constant reference to the Cross.... Padre Pio was a generous dispenser of divine mercy, making himself available to all by welcoming them, by spiritual direction and, especially, by the administration of the sacrament of Penance. I also had the privilege, during my young years, of benefitting from his availability for penitents. The ministry of the confessional, which is one of the distinctive traits of his apostolate, attracted great crowds of the faithful to the monastery of San Giovanni Rotondo.... In fact, the ultimate reason for the apostolic effectiveness of Padre Pio, the profound root of so much spiritual fruitfulness can be found in that intimate and constant union with God, attested to by his long hours spent in prayer and in the confessional. He loved to repeat, 'I am a poor Franciscan who prays' convinced that 'prayer is the best weapon we have, a key that opens the heart of God.'" The pope departed at one point from his prepared homily text to recall that he, too, visited the Italian friar for the sacrament of reconciliation when he was a young theology student in 1947.

In extemporaneous remarks after the two-and-a-half-hour ceremony, the pope thanked the pilgrims for their "courage" and sacrifice in attending. The pope also announced at the end of the June 16 Mass that he was making Padre Pio's Sept. 23 feast day an "obligatory memorial" on the church's general liturgical calendar. The ranking of obligatory memorial accorded to Padre Pio means the celebration must be observed in Masses and the Liturgy of the Hours on the day it occurs unless an observance that takes precedence, a solemnity or feast, falls on the same day. St. Maximilian Kolbe, also in the Franciscan tradition, is the only other 20th-century saint whose memorial is obligatory.

The pope did not personally give first Communion as planned to Matteo Colella, the 8-year-old boy whose medically inexplicable cure from multiple organ failure in 2000 was deemed the miracle for Padre Pio's canonization.

Also among the pilgrims was Dr. Wanda Poltawska, a Polish woman for whom the future Pope John Paul asked Padre Pio's intercession in 1962. As an auxiliary bishop of Krakow, the future pope sent Padre Pio a letter asking him to pray for Poltawska, who had been diagnosed with malignant throat cancer. Eleven days later he wrote again to say the cancer had disappeared.

After the Mass, the pope traveled in his popemobile around the square and all the way down the Via della Conciliazione, the main street that leads from it, waving at the cheering crowds.

Later in the evening, pilgrims gathered for a musical performance in the Paul VI audience hall and watched a fireworks display over the Janiculum Hill next to the Vatican.

The canonization was the 45th canonization ceremony of Pope John Paul's nearly 24-year pontificate and brought to 461 the number of people he has proclaimed saints.

Biography of Saint Pio of Pietrelcina

Padre Pio was born on May 25, 1887, at Pietrelcina in the Archdiocese of Benevento, the son of Grazio Forgione and Maria Giuseppa De Nunzio. He was baptized the next day and given the name Francesco. At the age of twelve he received the Sacrament of Confirmation and made his First Holy Communion. On Jan. 6, 1903, at the age of sixteen, he entered the novitiate of the Capuchin Friars at Morcone, where on Jan. 22 he took the Franciscan habit and the name Brother Pio. At the end of his novitiate year he took simple vows, and on Jan. 27, 1907, made his solemn profession. After he was ordained priest on Aug. 10, 1910, at Benevento, he remained with his family until 1916 for health reasons. In September of that year he was sent to the friary of San Giovanni Rotondo and remained there until his death.

He committed himself to relieving the pain and suffering of many families, chiefly through the foundation of the Casa Sollievo della Sofferenza (House for the Relief of Suffering), opened on May 5, 1956. He was especially devoted to prayer, declaring: "In books we seek God, in prayer we find him. Prayer is the key which opens God's heart." In assisting the thousands who came to him for counsel, he demonstrated to an exemplary degree the virtue of prudence, acting and counseling in the light of God.

Padre Pio was investigated and cleared during several Vatican inquiries into charges of sexual misconduct and fraud. He accepted the investigations with humility and resignation. He died on Sept. 23, 1968, at the age of 81. Thousands attended his funeral, and eight million people visit his tomb annually. On May 2, 1999, Pope John Paul II beatified Padre Pio of Pietrelcina, naming September 23 as the date of his liturgical feast.

PAPAL DOCUMENTS AND ANNOUNCEMENTS

Indissolubility of Marriage

Following annual tradition, on the occasion of the inauguration of the judicial year, the Pope received the dean, prelate auditors, officials, and lawyers of the Tribunal of the Roman Rota on January 28, 2002. During the audience, the Holy Father spoke of the indissolubility of marriage as an asset for the spouses, for the children, for the Church, and for all of mankind.

"It is important to present in a positive way the indissoluble union," the Holy Father said, "in order to rediscover the good and the beauty of it. Above all, the vision of the indissolubility of marriage as a limit to the liberty of spouses and as a burden, sometimes unbearable, must be overcome. To this, it can be added the idea, widespread enough, that indissoluble marriage belongs only to believers, therefore they cannot 'impose' it on the civil society as a whole."

The Holy Father emphasized that the indissolubility of marriage "has an objective dimension. It is not merely a subjective fact. Consequently, the good of indissolubility is the good of marriage itself, and the incomprehension of this indissoluble nature constitutes the incomprehension of the essence of marriage.

"One must not surrender to the divorcing mentality: our trust in the natural and supernatural gifts of God to man prevents us. Pastoral activity must sustain and promote the indissolubility of marriage."

John Paul II noted, "Every right judgment of the validity or nullity of marriage is a contribution to the culture of indissolubility, not only within the Church but in the world.... Against the truth of a conjugal bond it is not correct to invoke the liberty of the spouses who, by freely assuming it, committed themselves to respect the objective needs of the marriage reality, which cannot be altered by human freedom.

"It would almost seem," the Pope went on, "that divorce is so much rooted in certain circles of society, that it is not worthwhile to go on opposing it by advocating a mentality of indissolubility in both social customs and civil legislation. Indeed it is worthwhile!"

The Holy Father added, "The essential testimony on the value of the indissolubility is given through the matrimonial life of the spouses, in the fidelity to their bond through the joys and the tests of life. The value of indissolubility cannot be thought to be the object of a simple private choice, it concerns one of the cornerstones of the whole of society.

"To the strong opposition to all legal and administrative measures introducing divorce or that make equal to marriage defacto unions, even homosexual union, it must be coupled a principle, throughout juridical measures, favoring the improvement of the social recognition of true matrimony in the sphere of legal system which unfortunately admits divorce."

On the other hand, civil lawyers "must avoid being personally involved in what could imply a cooperation to divorce. For judges this can be difficult, because the legal systems do not recognize an objection of the conscience that can exempt them from imposing judgment. Despite serious and well-grounded reasons judges can act according to the traditional principles of the actual cooperation to the bad. But they too must find effective means to favour the marriage union, above all by an operation of reconciliation wisely led.... Lawyers, as independent professionals must always decline to use their profession to an end contrary to justice, such as divorce. They should only collaborate to an action in this sense, when such action is, in the intention of the client, not aimed to the breaking of marriage, but to other legitimate purposes."

Misericordia Dei

On May 2, 2002, officials of the Roman Curia released a motu proprio *(an apostolic letter) by Pope John Paul II that calls for a "vigorous revitalization" of the sacrament of penance and asks bishops to adopt a stricter line on church law's "grave necessity" condition for general absolution.*

The 15-page letter, *Misericordia Dei* ("Mercy of God, On Certain Aspects of the Celebration of the Sacrament of Penance"), also requested bishops' conferences to submit national norms on general absolution to the Vatican for approval "as soon as possible."

At the press conference, Cardinal Joseph Ratzinger, prefect of the doctrinal congregation, said the duty to personally confess one's sins was instituted by Christ himself, "and even obligates the pope. It is not within the power of the church to substitute personal confession with general absolution."

He added that the incorrect use of general absolution was partly to blame for the general crisis facing the sacrament today. He characterized it as an "abuse that has contributed to the progressive disappearance of this sacrament (of penance) in certain parts of the church."

According to church law, individual confession is

the "sole ordinary means" of receiving absolution, but exceptions for "general absolution" are allowed in cases of imminent danger of death or "grave necessity," as determined by the local bishop.

In general absolution, a group of penitents receives forgiveness for their sins without first making an individual confession of sins. According to canon law, those who receive general absolution must confess their serious sins as soon as possible.

The pope's letter largely reiterates existing church law, but offers a six-point clarification of "grave necessity."

The pope further stipulates that bishops' conferences must send "the text of norms which they intend to issue or update in the light of this (letter)" to the Vatican's congregation for sacraments "as soon as possible." He cited a church law provision requiring Vatican "recognitio," or approval, of norms adopted by bishops' conferences.

The pope said it also would "be appropriate" for local bishops to inform their national conference whether or not cases of "grave necessity" have occurred in their dioceses, and then for the conferences to report to the Vatican's sacraments congregation "about the real situation in their regions and about any changes subsequently taking place."

The question of the use of general absolution has been a point of friction over the years between the Vatican and some bishops, especially in the English-speaking world, where it is also called the "third rite of penance." The following are excerpts from the *motu proprio*:

Down through history in the constant practice of the Church, the "ministry of reconciliation" (2 Cor. 5:18), conferred through the Sacraments of Baptism and Penance, has always been seen as an essential and highly esteemed pastoral duty of the priestly ministry, performed in obedience to the command of Jesus. Through the centuries, the celebration of the Sacrament of Penance has developed in different forms, but it has always kept the same basic structure: it necessarily entails not only the action of the minister — only a Bishop or priest, who judges and absolves, tends and heals in the name of Christ — but also the actions of the penitent: contrition, confession and satisfaction....

I ... encourage my Brother Bishops and earnestly appeal to them — and, through them, to all priests — to undertake a vigorous revitalization of the Sacrament of Reconciliation. This is a requirement of genuine charity and true pastoral justice, and we should remember that the faithful, when they have the proper interior dispositions, have the right to receive personally the sacramental gift.

In order that the minister of the Sacrament may know the dispositions of penitents with a view to granting or withholding absolution and imposing a suitable penance, it is necessary that the faithful, as well as being aware of the sins they have committed, of being sorry for them and resolved not to fall into them again, should also confess their sins....

It is a question of ensuring an ever more faithful, and thus more fruitful, celebration of the gift entrusted to the Church by the Lord Jesus after his Resurrection (cf. Jn. 20:19-23). This seems especially necessary, given that in some places there has been a tendency to abandon individual confession and wrongly to resort to "general" or "communal" absolution. In this case general absolution is no longer seen as an extraordinary means to be used in wholly exceptional situations. On the basis of an arbitrary extension of the conditions required for *grave necessity*, in practice there is a lessening of fidelity to the divine configuration of the Sacrament, and specifically regarding the need for individual confession, with consequent serious harm to the spiritual life of the faithful and to the holiness of the Church....

Given the fundamental importance of full harmony among the Bishops' Conferences of the world in a matter so essential to the life of the Church, the various Conferences, observing Can. 455 § 2 of the Code of Canon Law, shall send as soon as possible to the Congregation for Divine Worship and the Discipline of the Sacraments the text of the norms which they intend to issue or update in the light of this m*otu prop-*

rio on the application of Can. 961. This will help to foster an ever greater communion among the Bishops of the Church as they encourage the faithful everywhere to draw abundantly from the fountains of divine mercy which flow unceasingly in the Sacrament of Reconciliation.

In this perspective of communion it will also be appropriate for Diocesan Bishops to inform their respective Bishops' Conferences whether or not cases of *grave necessity* have occurred in their jurisdictions. It will then be the task of each Conference to inform the above-mentioned Congregation about the real situation in their regions and about any changes subsequently taking place.

(For coverage of recent documents on ethics and the Internet, please see under the section of **Catholic Communications.**)

SPECIAL REPORTS

INTERNATIONAL NEWS 2001-2002
SYNOD OF BISHOPS

(*By Russell Shaw*)

The tenth general assembly of the world Synod of Bishops brought together 247 bishops from around the world for a discussion of the theme "The Bishop: Servant of the Gospel of Jesus Christ for the Hope of the World." The meeting took place Sept. 30-Oct. 27 under the presidency of Pope John Paul II.

This general assembly of the Synod of Bishops was the first since 1994. Synod sessions that took place in the mid- to late-1990s were regional meetings held as part of the preparations for the Year 2000 Jubilee. But the general assembly of 2001, focusing on bishops themselves, marked the culmination of a series of sessions that considered various groups in the Church. Earlier assemblies had discussed priests, people in religious institutes and other forms of consecrated life, and the laity.

Four bishops from the United States elected by their peers attended: Bishop Joseph A. Fiorenza of Galveston-Houston, president of the United States Conference of Catholic Bishops, Bishop Wilton D. Gregory of Belleville, Ill., vice president, Cardinal William A. Keeler of Baltimore, and Cardinal Francis E. George, O.M.I., of Chicago. Three others were among a group appointed by the pope: Archbishop Justin F. Rigali of St. Louis, Archbishop Stefan Soroka, Metropolitan Archbishop of Philadelphia for the Ukrainians, and Auxiliary Bishop Robert P. Maginnis of Philadelphia.

Also participating were four American curial officials: Cardinal Edmund C. Szoka, governor of Vatican City State, Cardinal William W. Baum, Major Penitentiary, Cardinal James F. Stafford, president of the Pontifical Council for the Laity, and Archbishop John P. Foley, president of the Pontifical Council for Social Communications.

Cardinal Edward M. Egan of New York was named by the pope to serve as general reporter of the synod assembly responsible for summing up the deliberations at key points.

The world Synod of Bishops was instituted by the

Second Vatican Council (1962-65) as an expression of the collegial spirit. Explaining the doctrine of collegiality, *Lumen Gentium*, the Dogmatic Constitution on the Church, stated in part: "The order of bishops is the successor to the college of the apostles in their role as teachers and pastors, and in it the apostolic college is perpetuated. Together with their head, the Supreme Pontiff, and never apart from him, they have supreme and full authority over the universal Church; but this power cannot be exercised without the agreement of the Roman Pontiff (n. 22)."

Much of the discussion during the synod assembly focused on this doctrine of collegiality and on how it should be expressed in the life of the Church today. Pope John Paul alluded to this in his homily at the closing Mass, saying, "Only if the deep and convinced unity of the shepherds among themselves and with the successor of Peter is clearly perceptible ... can a credible answer be given to the challenges that come from today's social and cultural context."

Various views were expressed on how collegiality can best be expressed in practice. One suggested approach, supported by a number of speakers, is to place more authority in bishops' hands, either individually or collectively in their national episcopal conferences and in the world Synod of Bishops itself. Some criticized the Roman Curia for supposedly infringing on the authority of bishops.

Cardinal Keeler, a former president of the U.S. episcopal conference, was among those who spoke up on behalf of conferences of bishops. He described them as "indispensable as servants of communion" between local bishops and the universal Church. He also called for a "more profound" study of episcopal conferences going beyond a 1998 Vatican document which acknowledged that they have a teaching role while underlining the limits of their competence in this area.

The idea of subsidiarity — higher levels of authority should not do what lower levels are competent to do —also received attention from some speakers. Although subsidiarity is mainly a sociological concept, Bishop Fiorenza said it could be used to give "particular churches" and "regional churches" more authority to decide "matters which do not impinge on doctrinal issues." Like some others, he called for a study of the subject.

But other speakers took a more guarded view of these matters. Some, for example, cautioned that collective bodies like episcopal conferences should not be permitted to infringe on the rights of individual bishops or to interpose themselves between bishops and the Holy See.

Cardinal Joseph Ratzinger, prefect of the Congregation for the Doctrine Faith, told the assembly that decentralization in the Church would be an accomplished fact if bishops used the authority they already have to teach doctrine and correct error. "If bishops have the courage to judge and decide with authority in this battle for the Gospel, the so-called decentralization happens automatically," he said.

The discussion dealt at length with the office of bishop and how it should be exercised today. Citing the image of the bishop as a "good shepherd," Pope John Paul said bishops must "above all … have the courage to proclaim and defend healthy doctrine, even when this entails suffering."

Among the foundational principles that received attention during the assembly was the understanding of the Church as a communion. Speaking of this in an interview with *Our Sunday Visitor*, Cardinal George said:

"Ecclesial communion is the network of relationships that are created when the gifts of Christ are shared. The basis of communion is Christ's gifts to his people, the people of God….

"To the Reformation, the Church is only invisible. The Council of Trent responded by saying no — the Church is visible as well as invisible. But so much emphasis was placed on the visibility of the Church that she began to be considered just a society in her essence. It was Vatican Council II that, calling on scriptural models rather than societal models, was able to create a theology of communion that acknowledges that the Church is both visible and invisible—a fuller theology of the Church than we ever had before."

The assembly turned over nearly 70 recommendations to Pope John Paul for possible incorporation into an anticipated apostolic exhortation summing up the deliberations.

RUSSIAN DIOCESES

On Feb. 11, 2002, Pope John Paul II announced the creation of four new dioceses in Russia, elevating the new dioceses from four previous apostolic administrations. The decision was made over strenuous Orthodox objections and signaled a major step in the Catholic Church's post-communist restoration.

In reply to attacks by the Russian Orthodox Church, the Vatican described the decision as a "normal administrative act" and answered Orthodox criticism in a bluntly worded statement, saying the church has the right to care for all its members, even in countries where there is a majority of Orthodox:

"His Holiness John Paul II wants to respond concretely to the pastoral needs of those who have freely chosen the Catholic Church and recognize in it their 'home' or 'family,' " the Vatican statement said.

The Vatican rejected Orthodox accusations of a modern Catholic "invasion" of Russia, noting that the Catholic Church hierarchy was firmly established in the country many centuries ago.

"This is not really introducing new church structures into those territories, but rather restoring those that existed before," it said.

The move transforms the four existing apostolic administrations into three dioceses and one archdiocese.

The main Archdiocese of the Mother of God in Moscow, on which the other three dioceses will depend, is the former apostolic administration for Northern European Russia. The Moscow archdiocese will be headed by Archbishop Tadeusz Kondrusiewicz, who had been apostolic administrator there since 1991. The Diocese of St. Clement in Saratov is the former apostolic administration of Southern European Russia, headed by Bishop Clemens Pickel. In western Siberia, the Diocese of the Transfiguration in Novosibirsk will be headed by Bishop Joseph Werth. In Eastern Siberia, the Diocese of St. Joseph in Irkutsk will be headed by Bishop Jerzy Mazur.

The restructuring move and the negative Orthodox reaction created new tensions on the eve of an impor-

tant visit to Moscow by the Vatican's top ecumenist, Cardinal Walter Kasper, who was to meet Feb. 21-22 with leading Orthodox officials, including Russian Orthodox Patriarch Alexei II.

On Feb. 6, the Vatican's representative to the Russian Federation, Archbishop Giorgio Zur, explained the pastoral restructuring plans in a meeting with Orthodox Archbishop Clement of Kaluga and Borovsk, vice chairman of the Department of External Church Relations of the Moscow Patriarchate.

In a sharply worded statement, the Moscow Patriarchate said "the actions planned by the Vatican represent violations of canonical principles and norms of interchurch relations."

"Such actions will constitute serious obstacles for the development of dialogue between the two churches," it said.

In reply to the Orthodox, Vatican spokesman Joaquin Navarro-Valls emphasized several points:

• It was "normal" for apostolic administrations, which are temporary jurisdictions, eventually to become dioceses.

• Catholics in Russia had repeatedly requested the upgrade to dioceses.

• The Vatican was providing for Catholics in Russia only what Russian Orthodox faithful receive in the West — pastoral care in their own diocese. The Vatican spokesman cited the existence of Russian Orthodox dioceses in Vienna, Austria, Brussels, Belgium, and Berlin.

• The Russian civil authorities had no problem with the move, since they recognize international agreements on religious freedom.

• The Vatican hopes the reorganization will aid dialogue with the Russian Orthodox. Navarro-Valls noted that the Catholic Church, through agencies like Aid to the Church in Need, has donated more than $17 million to the Russian Orthodox Church over the last 10 years.

An accompanying unsigned Vatican statement rejected Orthodox accusations of proselytism.

"The current increase in the number of Catholics in the Russian Federation certainly is not occurring through passage from the Orthodox to the Catholic Church. The new Catholics come instead from environments traditionally distant from any religion.

"These people, having come into contact with the Catholic Church, asked to be baptized and join. That is enough to reject any accusation of proselytism, which often is formulated in a vague way, clearly based on an incorrect or partial reading of the facts," it said.

It said the small number of Catholic communities in Russia today have no intention and are in no position to "upset the cultural identity of a country that is traditionally considered Orthodox."

The Vatican statement provided a historical review of the Catholic Church's presence in Russia, to make it clear the current return of the church's hierarchy cannot be considered a form of invasion or interference.

It cited statistics of more than 112,000 Catholics in 1858 under the jurisdiction of the Archdiocese of Mohilev, with more than 30 parishes throughout the country. By the early 1920s, it said, that figure had grown to 1.6 million Catholics in four dioceses or jurisdictions and 580 parishes.

Much of the 20th-century increase in Catholics in Russia or Soviet territories was due to the forced migration of Poles, Germans and others across the country, the Vatican noted.

In 1991, after the Soviet breakup, the Vatican established two apostolic administrations to deal with pastoral reorganization, one in "European Russia" and one in Siberia. In 1999, each of those jurisdictions was split into two apostolic administrations.

The Vatican estimates the number of Catholics in Russian territory at approximately 1.4 million, about 1 million of them in western Siberia. In the parts of Russia closer to Europe, Catholics number about 300,000, according to official church statistics.

The tensions continued to remain palpable in the months following the announcement, becoming focused over the expulsion of Catholic Bishop Jerzy Mazur of Irkutsk and Fr. Stefan Caprio, an Italian priest who has spent many years laboring in Russia. The expulsion — on the basis of Mazur's Polish origins — was the subject of a letter of protest on April 26 by some of Russia's most respected writers, poets, and intellectuals who called the expulsions "worthy of the Soviet era." (For other details, see under **Ecumenism** and **Interreligious Dialogue**.)

IRELAND'S ABORTION REFERENDUM

On Mar. 6, 2002, Irish voters narrowly defeated an abortion referendum that was supported by the Irish bishops. The proposal was rejected by a margin of less than 1 percent in a lead up campaign that was sometimes confusing to voters.

The referendum sought to tighten Irish law pertaining to abortion, specifically including a measure to end the suicide provision that had been allowed in 1992 by the Irish Supreme Court that allowed abortion if a pregnant woman threatened to kill herself. Only about 43 percent of the electorate voted, and post-election analysis revealed an urban-rural divide, with voters in urban areas more likely to vote "no" and voters in rural areas more likely to vote "yes." Voter turnout in urban areas was far greater than rural areas.

Two factors were also cited in influencing the very narrow defeat of the referendum. The first was considerable voter confusion. While not a technically pro-life measure, the referendum was supported by Ireland's bishops and was termed in a leaflet distributed at Masses by Church officials in March, "An opportunity not to be missed." Individual bishops also distributed pastoral letters on the referendum that were read at Masses in early March. Supporters noted that if the referendum were passed the threat of suicide will no longer be a valid reason for a legal abortion. The proposal, however, was a complex one, and the fine details were often not understood by voters.

Adding to the confusion were divisions among pro-life campaigners in Ireland. The bishops and some pro-life advocates were in favor of the referendum, but others opposed it on the grounds that it did not go far enough. Contradictory campaign posters appeared side by side throughout the country, declaring "Defend the Unborn — Vote Yes" on one poster and "Babies Will Die — Vote Pro-Life — Vote No," on another.

Dana Rosemary Scallon, a former Catholic television personality and now an Independent member of the European Parliament, was against the referendum because it did not protect the fetus from the moment of conception. "The vote is a victory for the unborn child. If there had been a wording acceptable to the whole pro-life community, this would have been carried by a big majority," she said.

THE MURDER OF ARCHBISHOP DUARTE

On Mar. 16, 2002, Archbishop Isaias Duarte Cancino of Cali was shot to death after celebrating a wedding ceremony in a poor neighborhood of the city. The archbishop, 63, recently had spoken out against unnamed politicians he said were financing electoral campaigns through drug money and was revered by Colombian Catholics as a defender of the poor who was unafraid to speak bluntly to all factions in the country's civil strife.

Local Church officials and government investigators said drug criminals were the leading suspects in the archbishop's murder.

The following day, Pope John Paul II joined millions of Colombians who mourned the death of the archbishop. The pontiff declared that Duarte was "a pastor who was generous and brave in announcing the Good News, he paid the highest price for his energetic defense of human life, his firm opposition to every type of violence and his dedication to the social promotion." In a telegram of condolence, the pope asked the people and authorities of Colombia to decisively take up the way of peace and dialogue.

Archbishop Alberto Giraldo Jaramillo of Medellin, president of the Colombian bishops' conference, said in a statement that it was clear that "the clarity, sincerity and courage of Archbishop Duarte made many people uncomfortable."

In 1999 he excommunicated members of the National Liberation Army after they kidnapped parishioners leaving a Sunday Mass in Cali. "You do not fight for justice committing injustices. Nor do you attack innocent people to achieve peace," he had said.

Last December, Archbishop Duarte sent letters to the country's president and leaders of the largest guerrilla organizations proposing a five-year truce to negotiate a "real and thorough peace agreement." In his letter, the archbishop proposed the five years of peace so that "Colombians can concentrate on rebuilding the country, healing wounds and letting Colombians fearlessly decide what is best for the nation."

Recently, Duarte had spoken out against unnamed politicians he said were financing the Mar. 10 congressional elections with drug money. Although he did not name any candidates, he went public after several priests showed him evidence that drug cartels were buying votes in their neighborhoods.

Archbishop Duarte was born Feb. 15, 1939, in San Gil. After initial seminary studies in Colombia, he was sent to Rome where he received a degree in theology from the Gregorian University in Rome. He

was ordained in Rome in 1963 and then returned to Colombia as a priest of the Bucaramanga diocese. He was appointed archbishop of Cali in 1995. He started 45 parishes in poor areas and nine elementary schools in low-income neighborhoods. He also created the Commission for Life, Justice and Peace, which did studies on the victims of violence.

A suspect in the assassination was subsequently arrested on Apr. 10, 28-year-old Carlos Ramirez. According to police, Ramirez had been involved in a string of petty crimes and was arrested Mar. 12 as the alleged robber of a motorcycle and was placed in a Cali jail. He managed to get out several days later, allegedly to murder the archbishop. On May 30, however, Ramirez was shot in the head several times at a prison near Cali, presumably by another inmate or inmates. Police said they found a handgun and a grenade in Ramirez's cell and another handgun, believed to be the murder weapon, in a prison bathroom.

Sadly, Duarte's murder was another in a brutal history of assassinations and murder as a result of political violence in Colombia over the past 18 years. The political strife has taken the lives of two bishops, 36 priests, two male religious and two missionaries since 1984. Two bishops, five priests and a missionary have also been kidnapped.

BETHLEHEM AND THE CHURCH OF THE NATIVITY

On Apr. 2, 2002, a group of 200 Palestinian militia members entered the compound of the Church of the Nativity in an effort to avoid Israeli troops besieging Bethlehem in response to terrorist bombings in Israel. The siege and standoff at the Church of the Nativity was resolved on May 10 after extensive negotiations among the various parties, including the Holy See.

As part of what Israel described as a campaign to uproot terrorists, the Israeli army had moved into a number of Palestinian towns in late Mar., often searching house by house for suspected terrorists. Israeli tanks entered Bethlehem in early April, and when fighting began Apr. 2, Palestinian gunmen took refuge inside the Church of the Nativity and inside the convent of the Sisters of St. Brigid. The Palestinians left the convent early Apr. 3, but as of mid-afternoon several hundred were still inside the Church of the Nativity, which marks the place of Jesus' birth. Israeli representatives assured the Vatican that its army had "no intention whatsoever of opening fire" on the church or shelling the compound where some 30 Franciscan friars and sisters live.

Nevertheless, immediately after the incursion of the Palestinian gunmen into the compound, the Vatican issued a statement to Israeli, U.S. and Arab League representatives expressing its alarm over the situation.

Vatican spokesman Joaquin Navarro-Valls said the Vatican officials made five key points in its meetings with all of the parties involved:

• The unequivocal condemnation of terrorism, from whatever side it comes.
• Criticism of the conditions of injustice and humiliation imposed on the Palestinian people, as well as for the reprisals and retaliations, which do nothing but increase the sense of frustration and hatred.
• The need for Palestinians and Israelis to respect the resolutions of the United Nations aimed at bringing a cease-fire, promoting Palestinian statehood

and guaranteeing the security of Israel.
• The need to ensure "proportionality in the use of legitimate means of defense."
• The obligation the conflicting sides have to safeguard the holy places, which are very important for the three monotheistic religions and for the patrimony of all humanity.

Navarro-Valls added that Cardinal Angelo Sodano, Vatican secretary of state, had been in close contact with Latin Patriarch Michel Sabbah of Jerusalem and with the religious communities of men and women in Bethlehem, sending them assurance of "the solidarity of the Holy Father at this painful moment."

In the weeks that followed, negotiations proved unable to resolve the standoff. Complicating the situation was the Israeli siege of Ramallah and the headquarters of PLO Chairman Yasser Arafat. Following the resolution of that siege on May 1, the opportunity for he standoff to be concluded in Bethlehem increased. Representing the Vatican during the negotiations was Cardinal Roger Etchegaray who said in a statement released after his visit with Israeli President Moshe Katsav on May 2, "I come to ask that everything be done to settle as soon as possible the tragic situation of Bethlehem…. Everything can be hoped for when each person believes in the other and follows the path of love and not that of violence."

Intense negotiations finally ended the siege. On May 10, Israel's foreign minister, Shimon Peres, met with Cardinal Angelo Sodano, Vatican secretary of state, and with Archbishop Jean-Louis Tauran, Vatican foreign minister. The Vatican meeting took place as the last of some 180 Palestinians were leaving the church in Bethlehem, on the West Bank. Under the terms of a deal, 13 gunmen flew to Cyprus and were expected to take up residence in European countries; 26 other gunmen were released to the Gaza Strip, and 73 Palestinian policemen and civilians were allowed to go home.

Two days later, Cardinal Etchegaray celebrated Mass in St. Catherine Church, inside the Nativity compound.

Pope John Paul II, speaking at a noon blessing on May 12, offered thanks to all those who helped make sure that "this holy place was given back its true religious identity."

He expressed particular appreciation to the communities of Franciscans friars and nuns and Greek Orthodox and Armenian Orthodox monks who "with notable sacrifices remained faithful custodians of the sanctuary."

The pontiff added, "The universal message of Bethlehem is love, justice, reconciliation and peace. On this basis, a future can be built that respects the rights of the Israeli and Palestinian populations, in mutual trust."

NATIONAL NEWS 2001-2002

THE SEX-ABUSE SCANDAL IN THE U.S. CHURCH

The Catholic Church in the United States has been troubled profoundly in the last year by the severe crisis over the issue of sexual abuse of minors by members of the clergy. The following is a recapitulation of the events of the crisis, including the most significant documents and statements by Church authorities. Special thanks are offered to Russell Shaw for his kind assistance.

CLERGY SEX ABUSE

(By Russell Shaw)

Sex abuse of minors by some Catholic clergy has been a matter of public concern in the United States since the mid-1980s, when the case of Gilbert Gauthe first came to light. In the years that followed, other abuser-priests — Rudolph Kos, James Porter, Paul Shanley, and others — also were to become household names of a sort. Gauthe, a priest of the Diocese of Lafayette, La., at the time of his abusive acts, now is serving a prison term as are others.

Bishops at the diocesan and national levels sought to grapple with the sex abuse problem. In 1992, the National Conference of Catholic Bishops (now, the United States Conference of Catholic Bishops) adopted non-binding guidelines for dioceses. Although occasional reports of abuse by clerics continued to surface, it was assumed that the problem had been solved on the whole.

In January 2002, however, *The Boston Globe* began publishing detailed accounts in anticipation of the trial of John Geoghan, a laicized former Boston archdiocesan priest said to have abused well over a hundred of boys during the previous three decades. In February, Geoghan was convicted on one count of indecent assault on a 10-year-old boy and was sentenced to nine-to-10 years in prison.

Much of the public concern surrounding the Geoghan case centered on Cardinal Bernard Law of Boston, his predecessors, and other archdiocesan officials who did not notify the civil authorities about Geoghan and repeatedly gave him new parish assignments without telling the parishes of his background. Other, similar cases soon came to light in Boston and in other dioceses as the crisis escalated, fed by continuing media disclosures. Some called for the resignation of Cardinal Law and other bishops.

Bishops around the country began responding to the new pressures by turning over to the civil authorities diocesan records concerning priests accused of sex abuse, in some cases in the distant past. Numerous new lawsuits were filed against the Church. Up to this year abuse cases involving clerics were said already to have cost U.S. dioceses hundreds of millions of dollars — the actual figure is not known — in the preceding decade and a half.

At first, the problem commonly was said to involve pedophilia and the clergy involved were described as pedophiles. As the facts became clear, however, it also became clear that the vast majority of cases were not cases of pedophilia — the abuse of prepubescent children—but homosexual abuse of adolescent boys, sometimes referred to as "ephebophilia."

By mid-year, about 250 of the 45,700 U.S. priests had resigned or been suspended, according to one count. Several bishops resigned in the face of allegations of sexual misconduct. In March, Bishop Anthony O'Connell of Palm Beach, Fla., stepped down after admitting abuse of a student in a Missouri seminary where he had been rector 25 years earlier. In May, it was disclosed that Archbishop Rembert Weakland, O.S.B., of Milwaukee had paid $450,000 in archdiocesan funds to a man with whom he had had a relationship 20 years before; Archbishop Weakland had submitted his resignation to the Pope upon turning 75 a few weeks before, and the resignation now was accepted. In June, Bishop J. Kendrick Williams of Lexington, Ky., resigned in the face of allegations — which he denied — by three men. Also in June, Auxiliary Bishop James F. McCarthy of New York resigned after being accused of having abused a woman years before.

Faced with mounting calls for action, Pope John Paul II convened an April 23-24 meeting involving cardinals from the United States, Bishop Wilton D. Gregory of Belleville, Ill., and Bishop William S. Skylstad of Spokane, Wash., president and vice president respectively of USCCB, and leading Vatican officials. The Pope told the meeting there was "no place in the priesthood and religious life for those who would harm the young" but also stressed "the power of Christian conversion."

The meeting's final communiqué said the U.S. participants envisaged "a special process for the dismissal from the clerical state of a priest who has become notorious and is guilty of the serial, predatory sexual abuse of minors." These cases were distinguished from cases which were "not notorious" but which also would be subject to an unspecified special process if the diocesan bishop deemed this necessary to protect minors and avoid scandal.

Media speculation now focused on the question of whether USCCB, at its meeting scheduled in June in

Dallas, Tex., would adopt a policy of "zero tolerance" for even a single act of sex abuse. The task of developing a proposed policy was entrusted to the USCCB's Ad Hoc Committee on Sexual Abuse, reconstituted under the chairmanship of Archbishop Harry J. Flynn of St. Paul and Minneapolis.

With some 700 members of the media on hand, the bishops met June 13-15 in a downtown Dallas hotel under tight security and with an extraordinary agenda that included presentations by abuse victims, a mental health professional, and two designated lay representatives, as well as an executive session during which Cardinal Law reportedly apologized to his fellow bishops.

The major item before the bishops was the new policy on sex abuse. Archbishop Flynn's committee presented two documents: a "Charter for the Protection of Children and Young People" containing policy guidelines and a narrower set of "Essential Norms for Diocesan/Eparchial Policies Dealing With Sexual Abuse of Minors by Priests, Deacons or Other Church Personnel."

The norms, which are to be reviewed after two years, require approval (*recognitio*) by the Holy See to become "articular law" for the Church in the United States. Both documents were adopted after lengthy debate and amendment. The key vote approving the Charter was 239-13.

Among the amendments adopted by the bishops was a broad definition of sex abuse borrowed from a 1992 document of the Canadian bishops. It says that, as understood in the Charter, sex abuse "need not be a complete act of intercourse, nor should the term necessarily be equated with the definitions of sexual abuse or other crimes in civil law. 'Sexual abuse (includes) contacts or interactions between a child and an adult when the child is being used as an object of sexual gratification for the adult. A child is abused whether or not this activity involves explicit force, whether or not it involves genital or physical contact, whether or not it is initiated by the child, and whether or not there is discernible harmful outcome.' "

Other provisions of the policy include: Any allegation of abuse of a minor will be reported to the public authorities; alleged victims who are not minors will be encouraged to go the authorities themselves; no confidentiality agreements in settlements, unless there will be at a victim's request and for serious reasons; a priest found guilty of even one act of sex abuse in the past, present, or future will not be permitted to serve in any ministry, and will be expelled from the priesthood — laicized — unless "age and infirmity" dictate a regimen of prayer and penance, without publicly celebrating Mass or presenting himself as a priest; review boards with a majority of lay members will be established at the diocesan, provincial, and national levels; a child protection office will be established within USCCB and will compile an annual report on implementation of the policy by dioceses, naming dioceses that do not comply; the national board will commission studies of how dioceses handled the sex abuse issue and of its nature and scope.

Bishop Gregory appointed Oklahoma Gov. Frank Keating the national board's chairman. Others named were Washington attorney Robert Bennett and Justice Anne Burke of the Illinois Court of Appeals.

The bishops said they would welcome and cooperate with a proposed new apostolic visitation of U.S. seminaries to be carried out by the Holy See. A similar visitation of the seminaries was conducted in the late 1980s.

Ten days after the Dallas meeting Bishop Gregory and Msgr. William Fay, general secretary of USCCB, visited Rome, apparently to initiate the process of securing approval of the norms. The review process by the Holy See was expected to involve several offices of the Roman Curia and to take several months.

DOCUMENTS AND STATEMENTS

ADDRESS OF JOHN PAUL II TO THE U.S. CARDINALS

On April 23, 2002, Pope John Paul II opened the unprecedented meeting in the Vatican of 12 cardinals from the United States, the presidency of the Conference of Catholic Bishops of the U.S., and a number of officials of the Roman Curia, to discuss the sex abuse scandal.

Dear Brothers,

Let me assure you first of all that I greatly appreciate the effort you are making to keep the Holy See, and me personally, informed regarding the complex and difficult situation which has arisen in your country in recent months. I am confident that your discussions here will bear much fruit for the good of the Catholic people of the United States. You have come to the house of the Successor of Peter, whose task it is to confirm his brother Bishops in faith and love, and to unite them around Christ in the service of God's People. The door of this house is always open to you. All the more so when your communities are in distress.

Like you, I too have been deeply grieved by the fact that priests and religious, whose vocation it is to help people live holy lives in the sight of God, have themselves caused such suffering and scandal to the young.

Because of the great harm done by some priests and religious, the Church herself is viewed with distrust, and many are offended at the way in which Church's leaders are perceived to have acted in this matter. The abuse which has caused this crisis is by every standard wrong and rightly considered a crime by society; it is also an appalling sin in the eyes of God. To the victims and their families, wherever they may be, I express my profound sense of solidarity and concern.

It is true that a generalized lack of knowledge of the nature of the problem and also at times the advice of clinical experts led Bishops to make decisions which subsequent events showed to be wrong. You are now working to establish more reliable criteria to ensure that such mistakes are not repeated. At the same time, even while recognizing how indispensable these criteria are, we cannot forget the power of Christian conversion, that radical decision to turn away from sin and back to God, which reaches to the depths of a person's soul and can work extraordinary change.

Neither should we forget the immense spiritual, human and social good that the vast majority of priests and religious in the United States have done and are still doing. The Catholic Church in your country has always promoted human and Christian values with great vigor and generosity, in a way that has helped to consolidate all that is noble in the American people.

A great work of art may be blemished, but its beauty remains; and this is a truth which any intellectually honest critic will recognize. To the Catholic communities in the United States, to their Pastors and members, to the men and women religious, to teachers in Catholic universities and schools, to American missionaries in all parts of the world, go the wholehearted thanks of the entire Catholic Church and the personal thanks of the Bishop of Rome.

The abuse of the young is a grave symptom of a crisis affecting not only the Church but society as a whole. It is a deep-seated crisis of sexual morality, even of human relationships, and its prime victims are the family and the young. In addressing the problem of abuse with clarity and determination, the Church will help society to understand and deal with the crisis in its midst.

It must be absolutely clear to the Catholic faithful, and to the wider community, that Bishops and superiors are concerned, above all else, with the spiritual good of souls. People need to know that there is no place in the priesthood and religious life for those who would harm the young. They must know that Bishops and priests are totally committed to the fullness of Catholic truth on matters of sexual morality,

a truth as essential to the renewal of the priesthood and the episcopate as it is to the renewal of marriage and family life.

We must be confident that this time of trial will bring a purification of the entire Catholic community, a purification that is urgently needed if the Church is to preach more effectively the Gospel of Jesus Christ in all its liberating force. Now you must ensure that where sin increased, grace will all the more abound (cf. Rom. 5:20). So much pain, so much sorrow must lead to a holier priesthood, a holier episcopate, and a holier Church.

God alone is the source of holiness, and it is to him above all that we must turn for forgiveness, for healing and for the grace to meet this challenge with uncompromising courage and harmony of purpose. Like the Good Shepherd of last Sunday's Gospel, Pastors must go among their priests and people as men who inspire deep trust and lead them to restful waters (cf. Ps. 22:2).

I beg the Lord to give the Bishops of the United States the strength to build their response to the present crisis upon the solid foundations of faith and upon genuine pastoral charity for the victims, as well as for the priests and the entire Catholic community in your country. And I ask Catholics to stay close to their priests and Bishops, and to support them with their prayers at this difficult time.

The peace of the Risen Christ be with you!

STATEMENT BY U.S. CARDINALS IN ROME

Following the conclusion of the unprecedented meeting at the Vatican on Apr. 23-24, 2002, with 12 U.S. cardinals, the presidency of the Conference of Catholic Bishops of the U.S., and a number of officials of the Roman Curia, a three-page final communiqué, written in English, was released. Following are excerpts:

"The meeting was called with three goals in mind: on the part of the American Bishops, to inform the Holy See about the difficulties which they have faced in recent months, on the part of the Roman Dicasteries, to hear directly from the American Cardinals and the chief officials of the United States Conference of Catholic Bishops a general evaluation of the situation, and together to develop ways to move forward in addressing these issues."

"The participants first of all wish to express their unanimous gratitude to the Holy Father for his clear indications of direction and commitment for the future. In communion with the Pope they reaffirm certain basic principles:

"1) The sexual abuse of minors is rightly considered a crime by society and is an appalling sin in the eyes of God, above all when it is perpetrated by priests and religious whose vocation is to help persons to lead holy lives before God and men.

"2) There is a need to convey to the victims and their families a profound sense of solidarity and to provide appropriate assistance in recovering faith and receiving pastoral care.

"3) Even if the cases of true pedophilia on the part of priests and religious are few, all the participants recognized the gravity of the problem. In the meeting, the quantitative terms of the problem were discussed, since the statistics are not very clear in this regard. Attention was drawn to the fact that almost all the cases involved adolescents and therefore were not cases of true pedophilia.

"4) Together with the fact that a link between celibacy and pedophilia cannot be scientifically maintained, the meeting reaffirmed the value of priestly celibacy as a gift of God to the Church.

"5) Given the doctrinal issues underlying the deplorable behavior in question, certain lines of response have been proposed:

"a) the Pastors of the Church need clearly to promote the correct moral teaching of the Church and publicly to reprimand individuals who spread dissent and groups which advance ambiguous approaches to pastoral care;

"b) a new and serious Apostolic Visitation of seminaries and other institutes of formation must be made without delay, with particular emphasis on the need for fidelity to the Church's teaching, especially in the area of morality, and the need for a deeper study of the criteria of suitability of candidates to the priesthood.

"c) it would be fitting for the Bishops of the United States Conference of Catholic Bishops to ask the faithful to join them in observing a national day of prayer and penance, in reparation for the offenses perpetrated and in prayer to God for the conversion of sinners and the reconciliation of victims.

"6) All the participants … see the present time as a moment of grace…. We cannot underestimate, in the words of the Holy Father, 'the power of Christian conversion, that radical decision to turn away from sin and back to God,' … At the same time, as His Holiness also stated, 'People need to know that there is no place in the priesthood and religious life for those who would harm the young.'"

"Again in the Holy Father's words, 'neither should we forget the immense spiritual, human and social good that the vast majority of priests and religious in the United States have done and are still doing'."

"As part of the preparation for the June meeting of the American Bishops, the United States participants in the Rome meeting presented to the Prefects of the Roman Congregations the following proposals:

"1) We propose to send the respective Congregations of the Holy See a set of national standards which the Holy See will properly review ('*recognitio*'), in which essential elements for policies dealing with the sexual abuse of minors in Dioceses and Religious Institutes in the United States are set forth.

"2) We will propose that the United States Conference of Catholic Bishops recommend a special process for the dismissal from the clerical state of a priest who has become notorious and is guilty of the serial, predatory, sexual abuse of minors.

"3) While recognizing that the Code of Canon law already contains a judicial process for the dismissal of priests guilty of sexually abusing minors, we will also propose a special process for cases which are not notorious but where the Diocesan Bishop considers the priest a threat for the protection of children and young people, in order to avoid grave scandal in the future and to safeguard the common good of the Church.

"4) We will propose an Apostolic Visitation of seminaries and religious houses of formation, giving special attention to their admission requirements and the need for them to teach Catholic moral doctrine in its integrity.

"5) We will propose that the Bishops of the United States make every effort to implement the challenge of the Holy Father that the present crisis 'must lead to a holier priesthood, a holier episcopate, and a holier Church.' "

"6) We propose that the Bishops of the United States set aside a day for prayer and penance throughout the Church in the United States, in order to implore reconciliation and the renewal of ecclesial life."

MESSAGE TO THE PRIESTS OF THE U.S.

Following the conclusion of their unprecedented meeting in Rome with officials of the Holy See, the U.S. Cardinals in Rome and the presidency of Conference of Catholic Bishops of the United States issued the following message on Apr. 24, 2002, to the priests of the United States:

"We, the Cardinals of the United States and the Presidency of the National Conference of Catholic Bishops, gathered with our brother Cardinals of the Roman Curia around the Successor of Peter, wish to speak a special word to you, our brother priests who give yourselves so generously from day to day in service of God's people.

"At our meeting, you have been very much in our minds and hearts, for we know the heavy burden of sorrow and shame that you are bearing because some have betrayed the grace of Ordination by abusing those entrusted to their care.

"We regret that episcopal oversight has not been able to preserve the Church from this scandal. The entire Church, the Bride of Christ, is afflicted by this wound — the victims and their families first of all, but also you who have dedicated your lives to 'the priestly service of the Gospel of God' (Rom. 15:16).

"To all of you we express our deep gratitude for all that you do to build up the Body of Christ in holiness and love. We pledge to support you in every possible way through these troubled times, and we ask that you stay close to us in the bond of the priesthood as we make every effort to bring the healing grace of Christ to the people whom we serve.

"We are in complete harmony with the Holy Father when he said in his Address yesterday: 'Neither should we forget the immense spiritual, human and social good that the vast majority of priests and religious in the United States have done and are still doing.'

"As we look to the future, let us together beg the eternal High Priest for the grace to live this time of trial with courage and confidence in the Crucified Lord.... From the house of the Successor of Peter, who has confirmed us in our faith, we wish in turn to confirm you in the humble and exalted service of the Catholic priesthood to which we have been called. Peace be with you!"

CHARTER FOR THE PROTECTION OF CHILDREN AND YOUNG PEOPLE

Preamble

The Church in the United States is experiencing a crisis without precedent in our times. The sexual abuse of children and young people by some priests and bishops, and the ways in which we bishops addressed these crimes and sins, have caused enormous pain, anger, and confusion. Innocent victims and their families have suffered terribly. In the past, secrecy has created an atmosphere that has inhibited the healing process and, in some cases, enabled sexually abusive behavior to be repeated. As bishops, we acknowledge our mistakes and our role in that suffering, and we apologize and take responsibility for too often failing victims and our people in the past. We also take responsibility for dealing with this problem strongly, consistently, and effectively in the future. From the depths of our hearts, we bishops express great sorrow and profound regret for what the Catholic people are enduring.

We, who have been given the responsibility of shepherding God's people, will, with God's help and in full collaboration with our people, continue to work to restore the bonds of trust that unite us. Words alone cannot accomplish this goal. It will begin with the actions we take here in our General Assembly and at home in our dioceses/eparchies.

The damage caused by sexual abuse of minors is devastating and long-lasting. We reach out to those who suffer, but especially to the victims of sexual abuse and their families. We apologize to them for the grave harm that has been inflicted upon them, and we offer them our help for the future. In the light of so much suffering, healing and reconciliation are beyond human capacity alone. Only God's grace, mercy, and forgiveness can lead us forward, trusting Christ's promise: "for God all things are possible" (Mt. 19:26).

The loss of trust becomes even more tragic when its consequence is a loss of the faith that we have a sacred duty to foster. We make our own the words of our Holy Father: that sexual abuse of young people is "by every standard wrong and rightly considered a crime by society; it is also an appalling sin in the eyes of God" ("Address to the Cardinals of the United States and Conference Officers," Apr. 23, 2002).

The Conference of Bishops has been addressing the evil of sexual abuse of minors by a priest and, at its June 1992 meeting, established five principles to be followed (cf. Ad Hoc Committee on Sexual Abuse, National Conference of Catholic Bishops, *Restoring Trust*, November 1993). We also need to recognize that many dioceses and eparchies did implement in a responsible and timely fashion policies and procedures that have safeguarded children and young people. Many bishops did take appropriate steps to address clergy who were guilty of sexual misconduct.

Let there now be no doubt or confusion on anyone's part: For us, your bishops, our obligation to protect children and young people and to prevent sexual abuse flows from the mission and example given to us by Jesus Christ himself, in whose name we serve.

Jesus showed constant care for the vulnerable. He inaugurated his ministry with these words of the Prophet Isaiah:

The Spirit of the Lord is upon me,
because he has anointed me to bring glad tidings
   to the poor.
He has sent me to proclaim liberty to captives
   and recovery of sight to the blind,
to let the oppressed go free,
and to proclaim a year acceptable to the Lord (Lk 4:18).

In Matthew 25, the Lord made this part of his commission to his apostles and disciples when he told them that whenever they showed mercy and compassion to the least ones, they showed it to him.

Jesus extended this care in a tender and urgent way to children, rebuking his disciples for keeping them away from him: "Let the children come to me" (Mt. 19:14). And he uttered the grave warning about anyone who would lead the little ones astray, saying that it would be better for such a person "to have a great millstone hung around his neck and to be drowned in the depths of the sea" (Mt. 18:6).

We hear these words of the Lord as prophetic for this moment. With a firm determination to resolve this crisis, we bishops commit ourselves to a pastoral outreach to repair the breach with those who have suffered sexual abuse and with all the people of the Church. We renew our determination to provide safety and protection for children and young people in our church ministries and institutions. We pledge ourselves to act in a way that manifests our accountability to God, to his people, and to one another in this grave matter. We commit ourselves to do all we can to heal the trauma that victims/survivors and their families are suffering and the wound that the whole Church is experiencing. We acknowledge our need to be in dialogue with all Catholics, especially victims and parents, around this issue. By these actions, we want to demonstrate to the wider community that we comprehend the gravity of the sexual abuse of minors.

To fulfill these goals, our dioceses/eparchies and our national conference, in a spirit of repentance and renewal, will adopt and implement policies based upon the following.

To Promote Healing and Reconciliation with Victims/Survivors of Sexual Abuse of Minors

ARTICLE 1. Dioceses/eparchies will reach out to victims/survivors and their families and demonstrate a sincere commitment to their spiritual and emotional well-being. The first obligation of the Church with regard to the victims is for healing and reconciliation. Where such outreach is not already in place and operative, each diocese/eparchy is to develop an outreach to every person who has been the victim of sexual abuse* as a minor by anyone acting in the name of the Church, whether the abuse was recent or occurred many years in the past. This outreach will include provision of counseling, spiritual assistance, support groups, and other social services agreed upon by the victim and the diocese/eparchy. In cooperation with social service agencies and other churches, support groups for victims/survivors and others affected by abuse should be fostered and encouraged in every diocese/eparchy and in local parish communities.

Through pastoral outreach to victims and their families, the diocesan/eparchial bishop or his representative will offer to meet with them, to listen with patience and compassion to their experiences and concerns, and to share the "profound sense of solidarity and concern" expressed by our Holy Father in his Address to the Cardinals of the United States and Conference Officers. This pastoral outreach by the bishop or his delegate will also be directed to faith communities in which the sexual abuse occurred.

ARTICLE 2. Dioceses/eparchies will have mechanisms in place to respond promptly to any allegation where there is reason to believe that sexual abuse of a minor has occurred. Dioceses/eparchies will have a competent assistance coordinator to aid in the immediate pastoral care of persons who claim to have been sexually abused as minors by clergy or other church personnel. Dioceses/eparchies will also have a review board, the majority of whose members will be lay persons not in the employ of the diocese/eparchy. This board will assist the diocesan/eparchial bishop in assessing allegations and fitness for ministry, and will regularly review diocesan/eparchial policies and procedures for dealing with sexual abuse of minors. Also, the board can act both retrospectively and prospectively on these matters and give advice on all aspects of responses required in connection with these cases. The procedures for those making a complaint will be readily available in printed form and will be the subject of periodic public announcements.

ARTICLE 3. Dioceses/eparchies will not enter into confidentiality agreements except for grave and substantial reasons brought forward by the victim/survivor and noted in the text of the agreement.

To Guarantee an Effective Response to Allegations of Sexual Abuse of Minors

ARTICLE 4. Dioceses/eparchies will report an allegation of sexual abuse of a person who is a minor to the public authorities. They will cooperate in their investigation in accord with the law of the jurisdiction in question.

Dioceses/eparchies will cooperate with public authorities about reporting in cases when the person is no longer a minor.

In every instance, dioceses/eparchies will advise victims of their right to make a report to public authorities and will support this right.

ARTICLE 5. We repeat the words of our Holy Father in his Address to the Cardinals of the United States and Conference Officers: "There is no place in the priesthood or religious life for those who would harm the young."

When the preliminary investigation of a complaint (cc. 1717-1719) against a priest or deacon so indicates, the diocesan/eparchial bishop will relieve the alleged offender promptly of his ministerial duties (cf. c. 1722). The alleged offender will be referred for appropriate medical and psychological evaluation, so long as this does not interfere with the investigation by civil authorities. When the accusation has proved to be unfounded, every step possible will be taken to restore the good name of the priest or deacon.

Where sexual abuse by a priest or a deacon is admitted or is established after an appropriate investigation in accord with canon law, the following will pertain:

Diocesan/eparchial policy will provide that for even a single act of sexual abuse (see Article 1, note*) of a minor — past, present, or future — the offending priest or deacon will be permanently removed from ministry. In keeping with the stated purpose of this Charter, an offending priest or deacon will be offered professional assistance for his own healing and well-being, as well as for the purpose of prevention.

In every case, the processes provided for in canon law must be observed, and the various provisions of canon law must be considered (cf. *Canonical Delicts Involving Sexual Misconduct and Dismissal from the Clerical State*, 1995; cf. Letter from the Congregation for the Doctrine of the Faith, May 18, 2001). These provisions may include a request by the priest or deacon for dispensation from the obligation of holy orders and the loss of the clerical state, or a request by the bishop for dismissal from the clerical state even without the consent of the priest or deacon. For the sake of due process, the accused is to be encouraged to retain the assistance of civil and canonical counsel. When necessary, the diocese/eparchy will supply canonical counsel to a priest or deacon.

If the penalty of dismissal from the clerical state has not been applied (e.g., for reasons of advanced age or infirmity), the offender is to lead a life of prayer and penance. He will not be permitted to celebrate Mass publicly, to wear clerical garb, or to present himself publicly as a priest.

ARTICLE 6. While the priestly commitment to the virtue of chastity and the gift of celibacy is well known, there will be clear and well-publicized diocesan/eparchial standards of ministerial behavior and appropriate boundaries for clergy and for any other church personnel in positions of trust who have regular contact with children and young people.

ARTICLE 7. Each diocese/eparchy will develop a communications policy that reflects a commitment to transparency and openness. Within the confines of respect for the privacy and the reputation of the individuals involved, dioceses/eparchies will deal as openly as possible with members of the community. This is especially so with regard to assisting and supporting parish communities directly affected by ministerial misconduct involving minors.

To Ensure the Accountability of Our Procedures

ARTICLE 8. To assist in the consistent application of these principles and to provide a vehicle of accountability and assistance to dioceses/eparchies in this matter, we authorize the establishment of an Office for Child and Youth Protection at our national headquarters. The tasks of this Office will include (1) assisting individual dioceses/eparchies in the implementation of "safe environment" programs (see Article 12 below), (2) assisting provinces and regions in the development of appropriate mechanisms to audit adherence to policies, and (3) producing an annual public report on the progress made in implementing the standards in this Charter. This public report shall include the names of those dioceses/eparchies which, in the judgment of this Office, are not in compliance with the provisions and expectations of this Charter. This Office will have staffing sufficient to fulfill its basic purpose. Staff will consist of persons who are expert in the protection of minors; they will be appointed by the General Secretary of the Conference.

ARTICLE 9. The work of the Office for Child and Youth Protection will be assisted and monitored by a Review Board, including parents, appointed by the Conference President and reporting directly to him. The Board will approve the annual report of the implementation of this Charter in each of our dioceses/eparchies, as well as any recommendations that emerge from this review, before the report is submitted to the President of the Conference and published. To understand the problem more fully and to enhance the effectiveness of our future response, the National Review Board will commission a comprehensive study of the causes and context of the current crisis. The Board will also commission a descriptive study, with the full cooperation of our dioceses/eparchies, of the nature and scope of the problem within the Catholic Church in the United States, including such data as statistics on perpetrators and victims.

ARTICLE 10. The membership of the Ad Hoc Committee on Sexual Abuse will be reconstituted to include representation from all the episcopal regions of the country.

ARTICLE 11. The President of the Conference will inform the Holy See of this Charter to indicate the manner in which we, the Catholic bishops, together with the entire Church in the United States, intend to address this present crisis.

To Protect the Faithful in the Future

ARTICLE 12. Dioceses/eparchies will establish "safe environment" programs. They will cooperate with parents, civil authorities, educators, and community organizations to provide education and training for children, youth, parents, ministers, educators, and others about ways to make and maintain a safe environment for children. Dioceses/eparchies will make clear to clergy and all members of the community the standards of conduct for clergy and other persons in positions of trust with regard to sexual abuse.

ARTICLE 13. Dioceses/eparchies will evaluate the background of all diocesan/eparchial and parish personnel who have regular contact with minors. Specifically, they will utilize the resources of law enforcement and other community agencies. In addition, they will employ adequate screening and evaluative techniques in deciding the fitness of candidates for ordination (cf. National Conference of Catholic Bishops, *Program of Priestly Formation*, 1993, no. 513).

ARTICLE 14. When a cleric is proposed for a new assignment, transfer, residence in another diocese/eparchy or diocese/eparchy in a country other than the United States, or residence in the local community of a religious institute, the sending bishop or major superior will forward and the receiving bishop or major superior will review — before assignment — an accurate and complete description of the cleric's record, including whether there is anything in his background or service that would raise questions about his fitness for ministry (cf. National Conference of Catholic Bishops and Conference of Major Superiors of Men, *Proposed Guidelines on the Transfer or Assignment of Clergy and Religious*, 1993).

ARTICLE 15. The Ad Hoc Committee on Sexual Abuse and the Officers of the Conference of Major Superiors of Men will meet to determine how this Charter will be conveyed and established in the communities of religious men in the United States. Diocesan/eparchial bishops and major superiors of clerical institutes or their delegates will meet periodically to coordinate their roles concerning the issue of allegations made against a cleric member of a religious institute ministering in a diocese/eparchy.

ARTICLE 16. Given the extent of the problem of the sexual abuse of minors in our society, we are willing to cooperate with other churches and ecclesial communities, other religious bodies, institutions of learning, and other interested organizations in conducting research in this area.

ARTICLE 17. We pledge our complete cooperation with the Apostolic Visitation of our diocesan/eparchial seminaries and religious houses of formation recommended in the Interdicasterial Meeting with the Cardinals of the United States and the Conference Officers in April 2002. Unlike the previous visitation, these new visits will focus on the question of human formation for celibate chastity based on the criteria found in *Pastores Dabo Vobis* (1992). We look forward to this opportunity to strengthen our priestly formation programs so that they may provide God's people with mature and holy priests. Dioceses/eparchies will develop systematic ongoing formation programs in keeping with the recent Conference document *Basic Plan for the Ongoing Formation of Priests* (2001) so as to assist priests in their living out of their vocation.

Conclusion

In the midst of this terrible crisis of sexual abuse of young people by priests and bishops and how it has been dealt with by bishops, many other issues have been raised. In this Charter we focus specifically on the painful issue at hand. However, in this matter, we do wish to affirm our concern especially with regard to issues related to effective consultation of the laity and the participation of God's people in decision making that affects their well-being.

We must increase our vigilance to prevent those few who might exploit the priesthood for their own im-

moral and criminal purposes from doing so. At the same time, we know that the sexual abuse of young people is not a problem inherent in the priesthood, nor are priests the only ones guilty of it. The vast majority of our priests are faithful in their ministry and happy in their vocation. Their people are enormously appreciative of the ministry provided by their priests. In the midst of trial, this remains a cause for rejoicing. We deeply regret that any of our decisions have obscured the good work of our priests, for which their people hold them in such respect.

It is within this context of the essential soundness of the priesthood and of the deep faith of our brothers and sisters in the Church that we know that we can meet and resolve this crisis for now and the future.

An essential means of dealing with the crisis is prayer for healing and reconciliation, and acts of reparation for the grave offense to God and the deep wound inflicted upon his holy people. Closely connected to prayer and acts of reparation is the call to holiness of life and the care of the diocesan/eparchial bishop to ensure that he and his priests avail themselves of the proven ways of avoiding sin and growing in holiness of life.

By what we have begun here today and by what we have stated and agreed to,

We pledge most solemnly to one another and to you, God's people, that we will work to our utmost for the protection of children and youth.

We pledge that we will devote to this goal the resources and personnel necessary to accomplish it.

We pledge that we will do our best to ordain to the priesthood and put into positions of trust only those who share this commitment to protecting children and youth.

We pledge that we will work toward healing and reconciliation for those sexually abused by clerics.

We make these pledges with a humbling sense of our own limitations, relying on the help of God and the support of his faithful priests and people to work with us to fulfill them.

Above all we believe, in the words of St. Paul as cited by Pope John Paul II in April 2002, that "where sin increased, grace overflowed all the more" (Rm. 5:20). This is faith's message. With this faith, we are confident that we will not be conquered by evil but overcome evil with good (cf. Rm. 12:21).

This Charter is published for the dioceses/eparchies of the United States, and we bishops commit ourselves to its immediate implementation. It is to be reviewed in two years by the Conference of Bishops with the advice of the National Review Board created in Article 9 to ensure its effectiveness in resolving the problems of sexual abuse of minors by priests.

* Cf. c. 1395, §2. Notice that a sexual offense violative of §2 need not be a complete act of intercourse, nor should the term necessarily be equated with the definitions of sexual abuse or other crimes in civil law. "Sexual abuse [includes] contacts or interactions between a child and an adult when the child is being used as an object of sexual gratification for the adult. A child is abused whether or not this activity involves explicit force, whether or not it involves genital or physical contact, whether or not it is initiated by the child, and whether or not there is discernible harmful outcome" (Canadian Conference of Bishops, From Pain to Hope, 1992,

p. 20). If there is any doubt about whether a specific act fulfills this definition, the writings of recognized moral theologians should be consulted and, if necessary, the opinion of a recognized expert be obtained (*Canonical Delicts Involving Sexual Misconduct and Dismissal from the Clerical State*, 1995, p. 6). We also note that diocesan/eparchial policies must be in accord with the civil law.

ESSENTIAL NORMS FOR DIOCESAN/EPARCHIAL POLICIES DEALING WITH ALLEGATIONS OF SEXUAL ABUSE OF MINORS BY PRIESTS, DEACONS, OR OTHER CHURCH PERSONNEL

Preamble

On June 14, 2002, the United States Conference of Catholic Bishops approved a *Charter for the Protection of Children and Young People*. The charter addresses the Church's commitment to deal appropriately and effectively with cases of sexual abuse of minors by priests, deacons, and other church personnel (i.e., employees and volunteers). The bishops of the United States have promised to reach out to those who have been sexually abused as minors by anyone serving the Church in ministry, employment, or a volunteer position, whether the sexual abuse was recent or occurred many years ago. They stated that they would be as open as possible with the people in parishes and communities about instances of sexual abuse of minors, with respect always for the privacy and the reputation of the individuals involved. They have committed themselves to the pastoral and spiritual care and emotional well-being of those who have been sexually abused and of their families.

In addition, the bishops will work with parents, civil authorities, educators, and various organizations in the community to make and maintain the safest environment for minors. In the same way, the bishops have pledged to evaluate the background of seminary applicants as well as all church personnel, who have responsibility for the care and supervision of children and young people.

Therefore, to ensure that each diocese/eparchy in the United States of America will have procedures in place to respond promptly to all allegations of sexual abuse of minors, the United States Conference of Catholic Bishops decrees these norms for diocesan/eparchial policies dealing with allegations of sexual abuse of minors by priests, deacons, or other church personnel.

Norms

These norms, after approval by the Apostolic See, constitute particular law for all the dioceses/eparchies of the United States of America. Two years after recognitio has been received, these norms will be evaluated.

Each diocese/eparchy will have a written policy on the sexual abuse of minors by priests, deacons, or other church personnel. A copy of this policy will be filed with the United States Conference of Catholic Bishops within three months of the effective date of these norms. Copies of any eventual revisions of the written diocesan/eparchial policy are also to be filed with the United States Conference of Catholic Bishops within three months of such modifications.

Each diocese/eparchy will designate a competent assistance coordinator to aid in the immediate pastoral care of persons who claim to have been sexually abused when they were minors by priests, deacons, or other church personnel.

To assist the diocesan/eparchial bishop in his work, each diocese/eparchy will have a review board whose functions include:

• The assessment of allegations of sexual abuse of minors by priests, deacons, and other church personnel in order to advise the diocesan/eparchial bishop on whether or not the allegations appear to be credible; the assessment will be communicated to the victim and accused; the board can act both retrospectively and prospectively on these matters;

• The review of the diocesan/eparchial policy and procedures for dealing with these allegations at least every two years in order to recommend to the diocesan/eparchial bishop any modifications, if appropriate; and

• The recommendation concerning fitness for ministry in particular cases.

The review board, established by the diocesan/eparchial bishop, will be composed of at least five persons of outstanding integrity and good judgment. The majority of the review board members will be lay persons who are not in the employ of the diocese/eparchy; but at least one member should be a priest, and at least one member should have particular expertise in the treatment of the sexual abuse of minors. The members will be appointed for a term of five years, which can be renewed.

Each province will establish an appellate review board, to be composed of at least five persons of outstanding integrity and good judgment. The majority of the members will be lay persons; but at least one member should be a bishop, and at least one member should be a canon lawyer. The appellate review board's function will be to offer — upon request by the bishop, the alleged victim, or the accused — its advice to the diocesan/eparchial bishop on the case (cf. norm 4A). The request must be made within fifteen (15) days after the alleged victim or the accused has been notified of the assessment of the initial review board. Within sixty (60) days of its receiving the request, the appellate review board's advice will be communicated to those involved.

When a credible allegation of sexual abuse of a minor by priests, deacons, or other church personnel is made, the alleged offender will be relieved of any ecclesiastical ministry or function. An investigation in harmony with canon law will promptly commence. The accused will be encouraged to retain the assistance of civil and canonical counsel and will be promptly notified of the preliminary findings of the investigation.

If the credible allegation of sexual abuse of a minor involves a priest or deacon, the ordinary/hierarch will ask him to undergo appropriate medical and psychological evaluation and intervention, if possible.

Where sexual abuse by a priest or deacon is admitted or is established after an appropriate investigation in accord with canon law, the following will pertain:

Diocesan/eparchial policy will provide that for even a single act of sexual abuse of a minor — past, present, or future — the offending priest or deacon will be permanently removed from ministry.

In every case, the processes provided for in canon law must be observed, and the various provisions of canon law must be considered (cf. *Canonical Delicts Involving Sexual Misconduct and Dismissal from the Clerical State*, 1995; Letter from the Congregation for the Doctrine of the Faith, May 18, 2001). These provisions may include a request by the priest or deacon for dispensation from the obligations of holy orders and the loss of the clerical state, or a request by his diocesan/eparchial bishop for dismissal from the clerical state even without the consent of the priests or deacons. For the sake of due process, the accused is to be encouraged to retain the assistance of civil and canonical counsel. When necessary, the diocese/eparchy will supply canonical counsel to a priest.

If the penalty of dismissal from the clerical state has not been applied (e.g., for reasons of advanced age or infirmity), the offender is to lead a life of prayer and penance. He will not be permitted to celebrate Mass publicly, to wear clerical garb, or to present himself publicly as a priest.

The diocese/eparchy will report to the public authorities any allegation (unless canonically privileged) of sexual abuse of a person who is currently a minor and will cooperate in their investigation. It will cooperate with public authorities about reporting in cases when the person alleged to have been abused is no longer a minor. In every instance, the diocese/eparchy will advise and support a person's right to make a report to public authorities.

Before a priest or deacon is proposed to another diocese/eparchy for assignment, transfer, or residence, if there is anything in his background to indicate that he would be a danger to children or young people, an accurate and complete description of the priest's or deacon's record will be forwarded by his ordinary/hierarch to the local ordinary/hierarch of his new residence. This holds even if the priest or deacon will only reside in the local community of an institute of consecrated life or society of apostolic life (or, in the Eastern Churches, as a monk or other religious, in a society of common life according to the manner of religious, in a secular institute, or in another form of consecrated life or society of apostolic life).

Care will always be taken to protect the rights of all parties involved, particularly those of the person claiming to have been sexually abused and the person against whom the charge has been made. When the accusation has proved to be unfounded, every step possible will be taken to restore the good name of the person falsely accused.

These norms will become particular law after *recognitio* is received from the Holy See.

Note: For excerpts of Bishop Wilton Gregory's Address to the Bishops gathered in Dallas for their summer meeting, please see below under the **United States Conference of Catholic Bishops, Meetings of U.S. Bishops, 2001-2002.**

SEPTEMBER 11, 2001

(By Russell Shaw)

"Even if the forces of darkness appear to prevail, those who believe in God know that evil and death do not have the final say." With those words, spoken during an audience on September 12, 2001, Pope John Paul II summed up the reaction of millions of people around the world to what had happened less than 24 hours earlier in the United States.

At 8:48 a.m. on September 11, American Airlines Flight 11 bound from Boston to Los Angeles slammed into Tower One (the North Tower) of the 110-story World Trade Center in Lower Manhattan. Fifteen minutes later United Airlines Flight 175, also bound from Boston to Los Angeles, struck Tower Two (the South Tower). About 35 minutes later, American Airlines Flight 77, which had taken off a short time earlier from Dulles Airport outside Washington, D.C., en route to Los Angeles, struck the western side of the Pentagon. And, about 25 minutes after that, United Airlines Flight 93, originally bound for San Francisco out of Newark, but then apparently headed for Washington, went down in a rural area in Somerset County, Pa., after passengers battled hijackers who had taken over the plane.

More than 2,800 people died in these events; by comparison, between 2,300 and 2,400 were killed in the Japanese attack on Pearl Harbor, December 7, 1941. It was the first time since the War of 1812 a foreign enemy had attacked the U.S. mainland. The dead included all 265 on the four aircraft (33 crew members and 232 passengers including 19 hijackers), 125 at the Pentagon, 343 firefighters and 60 police killed when the World Trade Center towers collapsed, and people from more than 60 countries who were in the twin towers when they were struck. Thousands more were safely evacuated.

"Our nation saw evil" in the attacks, President Bush declared in televised address to the nation. Congress the same day adopted a resolution giving the administration expanded powers to act against terrorists and soon after appropriated $40 billion in emergency funding. The President pledged a "new kind of war" — a war on terrorism that would involve overt military action, covert activities, diplomatic and financial measures, and stepped up security.

The U.S. government quickly concluded that the attacks were the work of the al Qaeda terrorist organization headed by Osama bin Laden, a wealthy Saudi national holed up in a remote part of Afghanistan. Al Qaeda also was held responsible for attacks on U.S. embassies in Kenya and Tanzania in 1998 and on the USS Cole on a refueling stop in Yemen in 2000.

In the face of the emergency, the North Atlantic Treaty Organization invoked its mutual defense provision for the first time, and other nations, including Russia and China, promised cooperation. After the Taliban, the Islamic fundamentalist group in control of Afghanistan, refused to hand over bin Laden, the United States and Great Britain on October 7 began air attacks. Ground fighting soon followed, and by early in the new year al Qaeda had been dispersed and the Taliban regime overthrown, although bin Laden and other top leaders were not apprehended. As the war in Afghanistan continued, President Bush spoke of an "axis evil" consisting of Iraq, North Korea, and Iran, and suggested possible new military action, especially against Iraq.

At home, an Office of Homeland Security was established headed by former Pennsylvania Gov. Tom Ridge. Greatly increased security was apparent in airports and airline procedures as well as in other areas of life. There was widespread anxiety about possible new terrorist attacks, possibly involving weapons of mass destruction of a nuclear, chemical, or biological kind. Fears skyrocketed in October when several people died and others fell ill in several parts of the country from letters containing potentially deadly anthrax spores sent by an unknown person or persons.

The religious community in the United States responded strongly to the events of September 11. Many of those killed in the attacks, including many firefighters and police who died in rescue efforts at the World Trade Center, were Catholics, and funerals were a regular occurrence at New York-area parishes for several weeks. Special services were held in churches all over the country. Religious and government leaders participated in a September 14 service in the National Cathedral in Washington, and on September 16 Cardinal Edward Egan offered Mass for the victims at St. Patrick's cathedral in New York. Many statements by religious groups emphasized the importance of not blaming all Muslims for what had occurred.

Church attendance soared immediately after September 11 but apparently soon returned to its customary level. The Gallup organization reported that in the three decades between 39% and 43% of Americans regularly said they had attended church or synagogue the previous week; after September 11, the figure rose to 47%, but it declined to 42% by early October.

The U.S. bishops at their semiannual general meeting November 12-15 adopted a pastoral message, "Living With Faith and Hope After September 11," calling the terrorist threat "unique because of its global dimensions and the sheer magnitude of the terror its authors are willing and able to unleash." At the same time, they repudiated a view that would "attribute the extremism of a few to Islam as a whole."

Noting the fighting then underway in Afghanistan and the possibility of new military action elsewhere, the bishops said: "National leaders bear a heavy moral obligation to see that the full range of nonviolent means is employed. We acknowledge, however, the right and duty of a nation and the international community to use military force if necessary to defend the common good by protecting the innocent against mass terrorism.... Every military response must be in accord with sound moral principles, notably such norms of the just-war tradition as noncombatant immunity, proportionality, right intention and probability of success."

The bishops also urged the U.S. and other countries to address root causes of resentment and terrorism like poverty, injustice, and the longstanding Palestinian-Israeli conflict.

WAR ON TERROR

(By Russell Shaw)

At a White House ceremony on March 11 marking the six-month anniversary of the September 11 attacks on the World Trade Center and the Pentagon, President George W. Bush summed up the official U.S. view of the war on terror in these words:

"We face an enemy of ruthless ambition, unconstrained by law or morality. The terrorists despise other religions and have defiled their own. And they are determined to expand the scale and scope of their murder. The terror that targeted New York and Washington could next strike any center of civilization. Against such an enemy, there is no immunity, and there can be no neutrality."

The six months that had passed since the September 11 attacks were, the President said, "a short time in a long struggle."

Religious responses to the war on terror and to the military action by the United States and its allies against the al Qaeda terrorist group and the Taliban fundamentalist regime in Afghanistan have been mixed. But the U.S. effort in Afghanistan received support from the Holy See and the United States Conference of Catholic Bishops. This backing nevertheless fell far short of unconditional endorsement of whatever else the U.S. might choose to do in the name of fighting terrorism somewhere further down the line, such as a military assault on Iraq.

The first expression of support from the Vatican for a military response to September 11 came from Dr. Joaquin Navarro-Valls, director of the press office of the Holy See. In a September interview with the Reuters news agency he said a nation has a right to use force in self-defense. "The Pope understands the difficulties of a political leader who has to respond to such issues," he said.

Pope John Paul II himself spelled out his position in his message for the January 1, 2002, World Day of Peace, where he declared that "there exists...a right to defend oneself against terrorism." At the same time, he insisted, the right of defense "must be exercised with respect for moral and legal limits in the choice of ends and means.

"International cooperation in the fight against terrorist activities must also include a courageous and resolute political, diplomatic and economic commitment to relieving situations of oppression and marginalization which facilitate the designs of terrorists," the Pope added.

Earlier, on November 14 the U.S. bishops' conference adopted a pastoral message, concerning the military action in Afghanistan and the possibility of U.S. intervention elsewhere. It said in part:

"National leaders bear a heavy moral obligation to see that the full range of nonviolent means is employed. We acknowledge, however, the right and duty of a nation and the international community to use military force if necessary to defend the common good by protecting the innocent against mass terrorism.... Every military response must be in accord with sound moral principles, notably such norms of just-war tradition as noncombatant immunity, proportionality, right intention and probability of success."

Both the Pope and the bishops coupled their comments on the war on terror with appeals for a just settlement of the Israeli-Palestinian conflict, understood as a factor contributing to Arab hostility to the West. In a January 10 address to the diplomatic corps accredited to the Holy See, John Paul said:

"No one can remain indifferent to the injustice of which the Palestinian people have been victims for more than 50 years. No one can contest the right of the Israeli people to live in security.

"But neither can anyone forget the innocent victims who, on both sides, fall day after day under the blows of violence. Weapons and bloody attacks will never be the right means for making a political statement to the other side. Nor is the logic of the law of retaliation capable any longer of leading to paths of peace."

As he had done before, the Pope called for such steps as Israeli evacuation of the Occupied Territories and an "internationally guaranteed special status" for the holy places in Jerusalem.

A special challenge faced by Pope John Paul in addressing the issue of terrorism after September 11 was to defend religious faith against the charge of being a divisive force that can lead to violence.

His solution lay in singling out fundamentalism for condemnation as a source of conflict, while at the same time insisting that fundamentalism is a perversion of authentic faith. "Even when the truth has been reached—and this can happen only in a limited and imperfect way — it can never be imposed," he said in the World Peace Day message.

On several occasions, John Paul declared his conviction that "authentic" Islam is a religion of peace. But Islamic fundamentalism is another story, he made clear. In his remarks to the diplomatic corps he said: "Terrorism is often the outcome of that fanatic fundamentalism which springs from the conviction that one's own vision of the truth must be forced on everyone else.... No religious leader can condone terrorism, and much less preach it. It is a profanation of religion to declare oneself a terrorist in the name of God."

But the Pope's preferred emphasis clearly was upon what brings religions and religious people together in the quest for peace.

It found dramatic expression in his convening of a January 24 interreligious gathering in Assisi, similar to one that he organized and led in 1986. Two hundred religious leaders representing Catholicism, Protestantism, Orthodoxy, Judaism, Islam, Buddhism, Hinduism, and other faiths prayed separately, then came together with the Pope to declare their common commitment to peace.

"It is essential," John Paul said in his address to the group, "that religious people and communities should in the clearest and most radical way repudiate violence, all violence, starting with the violence that seeks to clothe itself in religion, appealing even to the most holy name of God in order to offend man.

"To offend against man is, most certainly, to offend against God. There is no religious goal which can possibly justify the use of violence by man against man."

SCHOOL VOUCHERS

On June 27, 2002, the U.S. Supreme Court upheld the Cleveland voucher program in a 5-4 ruling, saying it is "entirely neutral with respect to religion." The majority opinion, written by Chief Justice William Rehnquist, said the program is therefore "a program of true private choice" and does not violate the Establishment Clause of the First Amendment.

Cleveland established the voucher program in 1995 to help address problems in what was considered one of the worst public school systems in the country. The state legislature created the system after a federal judge declared the schools were being mismanaged and put them under the authority of the state superintendent of public instruction. The program provides for vouchers of up to $4,000 annually for children in low-income families to attend other public or private schools or pay for tutors. The vast majority of participants use their vouchers to pay tuition at church-affiliated schools, nearly all of them Catholic.

The case came to the Supreme Court after the 6th U.S. Circuit Court of Appeals ruled in 2000 that the program was unconstitutional because the vouchers are primarily used at religious schools. The U.S. Conference of Catholic Bishops in a friend-of-the-court brief argued that the program should not be considered unconstitutional because most voucher recipients choose to attend church schools.

Opponents of the program who filed briefs included the National Association for the Advancement of Colored People, an association of Ohio school boards and several groups of public schools from around the country. Opponents call vouchers a fraud meant to siphon tax money from struggling public schools. The Ohio school boards argued that the state has ignored its responsibility to provide a good education and is merely shifting the burden to religious schools.

Central to the court's reasoning was that children in the Cleveland program have a theoretical choice of attending religious schools, secular private academies, suburban public schools, or charter schools run by parents or others outside the education establishment. The fact that only a handful of secular schools and no suburban public schools have signed up to accept voucher students is not the fault of the program itself, Ohio authorities say. "We believe that the program challenged here is a program of true private choice," Chief Justice William H. Rehnquist wrote for himself and Justices Sandra Day O'Connor, Antonin Scalia, Anthony M. Kennedy and Clarence Thomas.

The Cleveland program goes too far toward state-sponsored religion, the dissenting justices said. It does not treat religion neutrally, as Rehnquist contended, wrote Justice David H. Souter. The majority is also wrong about the question of whether parents have a true choice among schools, Souter wrote for himself and Justices John Paul Stevens, Ruth Bader Ginsburg and Stephen Breyer. "There is, in any case, no way to interpret the 96.6% of current voucher money going to religious schools as reflecting a free and genuine choice by the families that apply for vouchers," Souter wrote.

President George W. Bush has been a staunch advocate of school vouchers, and emphasized the issue in his campaign for the White House. Congress last year shelved that effort, but Bush resurrected the idea, proposing in his 2003 budget to give families up to $2,500 per child in tax credits if they choose a private school rather than a failing neighborhood public school. Following the court's hearing on arguments in February, Education Secretary Rod Paige said he would continue advocating on behalf of both improved public schools and school choice. Republican lawmakers in Congress agreed with Bush's stance. The Bush administration sided with Ohio, arguing that the pro-gram is constitutional because parents control where the money goes. In Cleveland, the public money flows to parents, not directly to the church-run schools, the program's supporters noted.

MAJOR SUPREME COURT RULINGS ON CHURCH-STATE ISSUES

The following are some of the other major Supreme Court church-state rulings through recent history:

Chandler v. Siegelman (2001) — Court let stand a lower court ruling that students may participate in group prayers at school functions such as football games or graduations.

The Good News Club v. Milford Central Schools (2001) — Court ruled that if the Boy Scouts and 4-H can use a public school as a meeting hall, a children's Bible study class can too.

Brown v. Gilmore (2001) — Court declined to hear a challenge to Virginia's mandatory minute of silence in schools.

Children's Health Care is a Legal Duty Inc. v. McMullan (2001) — Turned down an appeal that claimed Medicare and Medicaid payments to church-run health centers violate the constitutional separation of church and state.

Gentala v. Tucson (2001) — Court ordered a federal appeals court to take another look at a case that asked whether taxpayers must cover $340 in expenses from a prayer rally in a city park, saying it should be reconsidered in light of the high court's earlier ruling that a Bible club cannot be excluded from meeting at a public school so long as other groups with a moral viewpoint are allowed to gather there.

Mitchell v. Helms (2000) — Court ruled that providing educational equipment to religious schools with taxpayer money does not violate the Constitution.

Agostini v. Felton (1997) — Court ruled that public school teachers providing supplemental, remedial instruction to disadvantaged students in religious schools is constitutional.

Mueller v. Allen (1983) — Court ruled that taxpayers can deduct from state income taxes tuition, textbooks, and transportation expenses that were incurred by attending private and religious schools.

Committee for Public Education v. Regan (1980) — Court ruled that states can reimburse religious schools for the cost of giving standardized tests.

Meek v. Pittenger (1975) — Court ruled that states can lend textbooks to religious schools but no other materials.

Committee v. Nyquist (1973) and **Sloan v. Lemon** (1973) — Court ruled that states cannot reimburse parents for sending their children to religious schools.

Lemon v. Kurtzman (1971) — Court ruled that state supplements to Catholic school teachers' salaries is unconstitutional.

Everson v. Board of Education (1947) — Court ruled that state reimbursement for bus fares to attend religious schools is constitutional.

Pierce v. Society of Sisters (1925) — Court invalidated an Oregon law that required 8-to-16-year-olds to attend public schools, saying it interfered with parents' right to oversee their children's education.

LIFE ISSUES 2001-02

Partial-Birth Abortion Ban Act

On July 24, 2002, the House of Representatives approved by a 274-151 vote the Partial-Birth Abortion Ban Act, intended to respond to concerns raised in the U.S. Supreme Court's Stenberg vs. Carhart decision in 2000.

The House Judiciary Committee approved the ban on July 17, 2002. The House has approved three bills banning partial-birth abortions, and the legislation passed Congress twice but was vetoed by Bill Clinton on both occasions. The Senate subsequently lacked sufficient votes to override the presidential veto. President Bush has said he would sign a bill to ban partial-birth abortion.

Cathleen Cleaver, director of planning and information for the U.S. bishops' Secretariat for Pro-Life Activities, urged the Senate to follow the House in approving a bill to ban partial-birth abortions. She declared, "Americans are appalled by partial-birth abortion, which they recognize as a cruel and barbaric procedure with no place in our society.

"Americans agree," she added, "partial-birth abortion has no place in a country which believes in compassion and dignity for all. Unborn children suffer terrible pain, and women suffer risks to their health. This procedure must be stopped."

In the case of Stenberg vs. Carhart, the high court said the Nebraska law lacked a precise definition of the targeted procedure and unconstitutionally limited access to abortion in general. The court majority also said it had to defer to evidence in the case record indicating that medical experts disagreed about whether the procedure being banned may sometimes be the only medical option when a pregnancy puts the woman's life or health at risk.

The new House bill includes a 2,500-word section of "findings," including one that asserts that, even among physicians who regularly perform other types of abortions, partial-birth abortion "remains a disfavored procedure."

The bill also seeks to counter the argument that the law needs an exception to preserve the health of the mother by citing testimony to the contrary and noting that Congress is not bound to accept the same "clearly erroneous" findings the court followed in Stenberg vs. Carhart that partial-birth abortion is as medically safe as other abortion procedures.

The bill defines partial-birth abortion as "an abortion in which a physician delivers an unborn child's body until only the head remains inside the womb, punctures the back of the child's skull with a sharp instrument, and sucks the child's brains out before completing delivery of the dead infant."

More than half the states have enacted laws to ban

partial-birth abortion, and polls have shown that at least 70 percent of Americans support such a ban.

Withdrawal of Funding For the U.N.

On July 22, 2002, the Bush administration announced that it was diverting $34 million set aside for the U.N. Population Fund this year to its own development arm on grounds the U.N. agency gave money to Chinese agencies running coercive abortion programs.

The brief announcement made by State Department spokesman Richard Boucher stated, "Secretary of State Colin Powell decided that … U.S. funds for family planning and reproductive health will be spent through the United States Agency for International Development programs and not through UNFPA." The decision was hailed by Bishop Wilton Gregory, Bishop of Belleville and President of the United States Conference of Catholic Bishops. The bishops wrote in a letter to President Bush:

"I commend you for your decision to withhold $34 million in U.S. funding from the U.N. Population Fund (UNFPA) due to its support for coercive population programs.

Despite many efforts to obfuscate this issue, it has always been about the rights and dignity of women, the lives of children, and our obligation to respect the law. Since 1985, Congress has forbidden the funding of any organization which, as determined by the President of the United States, 'supports or participates in the management of a program of coercive abortion or involuntary sterilization.' No one can plausibly deny that the Chinese population program uses these coercive means, or that the UNFPA supports and even helps manage the Chinese program. Therefore your responsibility was clear.

No less compelling are the humanitarian and human rights arguments for taking a clear and absolute stand against any involvement in coercive population programs. At the Nuremberg trials over fifty years ago, those who managed a program of coerced abortion were convicted of having committed a crime against humanity. More recently, the nations of the world condemned 'forced sterilization and forced abortion' as 'acts of violence against women' at the United Nations' World Conference on Women in 1995. It is tragic that one of the UN's own agencies has failed to appreciate that such policies assault the dignity of women as well as the lives of vulnerable unborn children. I hope the wise action you have taken will encourage the UNFPA to reconsider its involvement in such injustice. In the name of the Catholic Bishops of the United States, I thank you for taking this action in defense of women and children in developing nations."

Born-Alive Infants Protection Act

On Aug. 5, 2002, President Bush enthusiastically signed the Born-Alive Infants Protection Act. The bill had been sent to the president's desk after the U.S. Senate gave final congressional approval on July 18, 2002.

The bill, approved by unanimous consent in the Senate, guarantee certain rights under federal law to children born alive, even if birth occurs during an abortion. The House approved the legislation by a voice vote in March.

The Born-Alive Infants Protection Act amends the legal definitions of "person," "human being," "child" and "individual" to include a live birth that has occurred as part of an abortion procedure. The bill defines a child as "born alive" only if he or she displays a heartbeat, respiration and/or voluntary movements after "the complete expulsion or extraction from his or her mother."

In a statement last March, the Bush administration said it strongly supported the legislation which "would ensure that infants who are born alive, at any stage of development, are individual human beings who are entitled to the full protections of the law" and "would provide guaranteed legal protection whether or not the infant's delivery was natural or the result of an abortion."

HHS and Access to Prenatal Care

On May 8, 2002, the U.S. Department of Health and Human Services proposed a regulatory change that would make unborn children eligible for coverage under the State Children's Health Insurance Program.

In effect, the department's proposed rule would permit states to make unborn children and their mothers eligible for prenatal health care coverage under SCHIP.

The Bush administration has proposed using its rulemaking authority to clarify that the regulatory definition of a child eligible for SCHIP coverage includes children "under the age of 19 including the period from conception to birth."

The decision was immediately supported by the U.S. Conference of Catholic Bishops. Mark E. Chopko, USCCB general counsel, and Michael F. Moses, associate general counsel, wrote in a letter to the U.S. Department of Health and Human Services:

"Our support for the proposed rule is based on the importance of ensuring adequate health care for children, both before and after birth, and their mothers … The proposed rule serves this important goal, reflects the medical reality that the life of a child begins before birth at conception, and is thoroughly consistent with precedent according legal significance to, and protecting, the life of the unborn child.

"Unfortunately, some organizations with a political agenda regarding other issues affecting prenatal life have chosen to view the proposed rule through the lens of those issues and therefore greeted it with suspicion.

"It is far too late in the history of law and medicine to turn back the clock and urge our government to deny the reality of the patient in the womb — especially at the cost of sacrificing the health and well-being of both women and their unborn children."

Predictably, a coalition that included the National Abortion Federation, American Civil Liberties Union, American College of Obstetricians and Gynecologists, Religious Coalition for Reproductive Choice and a number of Protestant denominations and Jewish groups opposed the proposed change.

Bishops' Head Hails Government's Decision

(Courtesy: Secretariat for Pro-Life Activities United States Conference of Catholic Bishops.)

On November 6, 2001, Bishop Joseph A. Fiorenza, then President of the United States Conference of Catholic Bishops (USCCB), hailed a directive by the

U.S. Attorney General overturning a 1998 opinion which allowed federally controlled drugs to be used in physician-assisted suicide.

"This important directive not only ends the federal government's involvement in assisted suicide, but also promotes improved pain management for patients near the end of life," Bishop Fiorenza said.

This is the text of the statement by Bishop Fiorenza: "We applaud the Bush Administration's decision today to end the federal government's involvement in physician-assisted suicide. U.S. Attorney General John Ashcroft's directive overturns a June 1998 opinion by then-Attorney General Janet Reno, which allowed federally controlled drugs to be used for physician-assisted suicide in any state which permits the practice. Currently Oregon has the only state law allowing physician-assisted suicide. By stating that assisting suicide could be a 'legitimate medical purpose' for use of federally controlled drugs, the Reno opinion required the Drug Enforcement Administration to issue federal prescribing licenses to physicians who

would misuse them to help take patients' lives. With today's decision, federal law will again be correctly interpreted to forbid misuse of controlled substances to assist suicides. This important directive not only ends the federal government's involvement in assisted suicide, but also promotes improved pain management for patients near the end of life.

In other federal programs, and in states passing new laws against assisted suicide, use of controlled substances for pain control has dramatically improved once the law recognized a clear difference between intentional taking of life and the unintended side effects of necessary pain control. Attorney General Ashcroft's decision fully respects this medical, legal and ethical distinction. Suicide among the sick and elderly is not a 'medical' practice. It is a tragic public health problem that deserves our concern and caring response. Good medicine and good law call on physicians to kill pain, not patients. President Bush and Attorney General Ashcroft should be thanked for affirming this vitally important principle."

UNITED STATES CONFERENCE OF CATHOLIC BISHOPS

MEETINGS OF U.S. BISHOPS 2001-02

NOVEMBER 12-15, 2001

Presidential Address: Bishop Joseph A. Fiorenza of Galveston-Houston, outgoing president of the USCCB opened the annual bishops' meeting on Nov. 12. The bishop declared:

Since the June general assembly of our episcopal conference, there have been two events which have occupied our thoughts and prayers: One galvanized the world in horror as terrorists attacked the United States in an unprecedented destruction of lives and the symbols of our prosperity and military power; the other was the Synod of Bishops, which gathered bishops from around the world to consider our role as servants of the Gospel for the hope of the world. One event demonstrated the destructive power of hate, and the other was an evangelical summons for bishops to be prophets of hope, especially in a time of fear and confusion.

Within a few hours on a September morning which forever will be etched in our memory, a morning which the Holy Father described as "a dark moment in the history of humanity," the destructive power of hate cast its shadow across the face of the earth. We know the number killed or missing, and we have seen the enormity of the damage inflicted on lower Manhattan and the Pentagon, but still unmeasured is the extent of the emotional, psychological and economic harm both in the United States and around the world caused by the cruel terrorist attack. In the midst of this apocalyptic devastation we have been inspired and encouraged by the heroic efforts of firefighters, police, emergency medical workers, military personnel, and volunteers in the rescue and recovery efforts at ground zero in New York, the Pentagon and the site of the plane crash in Pennsylvania. Their heroism has equaled any feat of bravery recorded in our national history.

Perhaps we bishops should be especially inspired by the evidence which this tragedy has provided of the very large number of Catholics who enter these fields of public service and who risk and even sacrifice their

lives for others. Our faith's strong emphasis on the common good surely is one of the motivating factors in choosing these walks of life. The sacrifices we have seen over the last two months remind us all of the inherent nobility the church sees in such service....

The theme of the synod focused on the bishop whose service to the Gospel is a hope for the world. The final message of the synod reflected the unique mission of the church to testify before the world to the hope which is in Christ Jesus, who died and rose for us, defying all the evidence of his defeat on the cross. Now more than ever within our memory the world needs to hear the victory of hoping against hope. Who is more responsible than ourselves for giving people reasons for hope and living with confidence in God?

Agenda

The bishops attending the meeting in Washington, D.C., acted on the following issues:

• Elected Bp. Wilton D. Gregory of Belleville, Ill., as conference president and Bp. William S. Skylstad of Spokane, Wash., as vice president. Bp. Gregory is the first African-American to serve as president of the conference and the first convert.
• Issued a pastoral message on the current world situation, "Living With Faith and Hope After Sept. 11." (See below.)
• Adopted a revised, updated Pastoral Plan for Pro-Life Activities. (See under **Life Issues** above for other details.)
• Approved "A Call to Solidarity With Africa," increasing the U.S. church's commitment to Africa.
• Approved U.S. norms implementing general church law on lay preaching and on Catholics teaching doctrine on radio and television. (See below.)
• Revised special liturgical norms for U.S. dioceses in the wake of recent Vatican observations.
• Held extensive discussions on the new Vatican translation rules for liturgy.

- Discussed a pastoral statement on the growing Asian and Pacific presence in the U.S. church; a vote was not held on the statement as too many bishops had already left the meeting; those not present voted by mail. The pastoral statement was eventually passed.
- Heard a plea from Catholic Relief Services to raise some $50 million to aid Afghan refugees.
- Approved a $53.3 million budget for 2002.
- Elected a treasurer-elect and 22 committee chairmen or chairmen-elect.
- Used electronic voting for the first time.

DALLAS, JUNE 13-15, 2002

At their spring meeting in Dallas, the U.S. bishops focused almost exclusively on the crisis of clergy sexual abuse of minors in the U.S. Church.

President's Address

Bp. Wilton D. Gregory of Belleville, Ill., president of the USCCB, opened the bishops' spring meeting on June 13 with a speech titled, "A Catholic Response to Sexual Abuse: Confession, Contrition, Resolve." The following are excerpts of his address:

The Catholic Church in the United States is in a very grave crisis, perhaps the gravest we have faced. This crisis is not about a lack of faith in God. In fact, those Catholics who live their faith actively day-by-day will tell you that their faith in God is not in jeopardy; it has indeed been tested by this crisis, but it is very much intact. The crisis, in truth, is about a profound loss of confidence by the faithful in our leadership as shepherds, because of our failures in addressing the crime of the sexual abuse of children and young people by priests and church personnel. What we are facing is not a breakdown in belief, but a rupture in our relationship as bishops with the faithful. And this breakdown is understandable. We did not go far enough to ensure that every child and minor was safe from sexual abuse. Rightfully, the faithful are questioning why we failed to take the necessary steps. The unity for which the Lord prayed fervently for his disciples and his church on the night before he died — a unity that sadly has been broken too often in our history as a church — is in serious danger of being fractured again; this time within our beloved church in the United States…

Confession

The penance that is necessary here is not the obligation of the church at large in the United States, but the responsibility of the bishops ourselves. Both "what we have done" and "what we have failed to do" contributed to the sexual abuse of children and young people by clergy and church personnel. Moreover, our God-given duty as shepherds of the Lord's people holds us responsible and accountable to God and to the church for the spiritual and moral health of all of God's children, especially those who are weak and most vulnerable. It is we who need to confess; and so we do.

- We are the ones, whether through ignorance or lack of vigilance, or — God forbid — with knowledge, who allowed priest-abusers to remain in ministry and reassigned them to communities where they continued to abuse.
- We are the ones who chose not to report the criminal actions of priests to the authorities, because the law did not require this.
- We are the ones who worried more about the possibility of scandal than in bringing about the kind of openness that helps prevent abuse.
- And we are the ones who, at times, responded to victims and their families as adversaries and not as suffering members of the church.

Contrition

Our confession is matched by a heartfelt contrition.

To the victim-survivors, I want to say this … in my own name and in the name of all of the bishops, I express the most profound apology to each of you who have suffered sexual abuse by a priest or another official of the church. I am deeply and will be forever sorry for the harm you have suffered. We ask your forgiveness.

To the parents and families of the victim-survivors, I want to say this … I promise you this: Following the example of the Lord Jesus, today we bishops recommit ourselves to placing the protection of your children first, and I am confident that the work we will do together over the next few days here in Dallas and every day thereafter will confirm that promise with solid action to provide for the safety of your children in the church.

As a prelude to that work, in my own name and in the name of all of the bishops, I express a profound apology to each of you who have children or family members who have suffered sexual abuse by a priest or another representative of the church. I am deeply and will be forever sorry for the harm that you have suffered as a parent or loved one of a victim-survivor. We ask your forgiveness.

I need to say a word to the deacons, the religious and the laity … To each of you — and in the name of all the bishops — I offer a profound apology for the hurt and the embarrassment you have suffered. We ask your forgiveness.

To our faithful priests, I want to say this on behalf of the bishops. The Holy Spirit in the sacrament of orders unites us to you as our first collaborators in ministry and we love you as brothers. We are also proud of and grateful for the selfless way in which you serve the Lord and your brothers and sisters day after day. We bishops are profoundly sorry that mistakes we have made in dealing with priest-abusers have caused some to call into question your own good name and your reputation as priests. We are also sorry that failures in our leadership have led to a breakdown of trust between priests and bishops, brothers in ministry. We ask your forgiveness.

My brother bishops: There is a lot of anger among us in this room — righteous anger. Since 1985 — as a conference and individually as diocesan bishops — we have been working on the problem of sexual abuse to ensure, as much as is humanly possible, that the church would be a safe environment for our children. In 1992, after seven years of study and work that included listening sessions with victim-survivors and other members of the church, consultations with experts, and experimentation with policies on the diocesan level, we together adopted "Five Principles to Follow in Dealing with Accusations of Sexual Abuse." The vast majority of bishops embraced these principles, made them the standard for policies on sexual abuse in their dioceses and, therefore, contributed effectively to the protection of children in the church. These policies, however, were not implemented effectively in every diocese across this country….

Resolve

The resolve that we bishops bring to the work before us is nourished by a firm purpose of amendment. The failures of the past must not be repeated. Having faced and acknowledged our mistakes and expressed heartfelt sorrow for those failures, we bishops need to complete, once and for all, the work we began together almost 20 years ago to make our church as safe an environment as is humanly possible for our children and young people.

In order that our work might be on the surest footing, having dealt as honestly with the past as we are able, I would like to speak a brief word to three groups of people.

To victim-survivors. If there is anyone who has been a victim of sexual abuse by a priest or representative of the church in the United States and has not yet reported this fact, I ask you to report it to the bishop of your diocese and to the appropriate civil authorities. Though this may be a very difficult step for you, the church does love you and wants to help you find justice and healing.

To priests. If there is any priest who is responsible for the crime of the sexual abuse of a child or young person and your bishop is not aware of this fact, I ask you to come forward to your bishop and report this fact so that justice and the church will be served, and you will be able to live honestly with your own conscience.

To my brother bishops. If there is any bishop who has sexually abused a child or young person, I ask you to report this fact to the nunciature so that justice and the church will be served, and you will be able to live honestly with your own conscience.

During the past five months the sexual abuse of children and young people, especially by priests, has been a focus of the national and local media. In my own many encounters with the media, I have been treated usually, if not invariably, with consideration. I have a great respect for the power of the media to do good…. But I ask the media to allow me a moment of complete candor. During these last months, the image of Catholic hierarchy in this country has been distorted to an extent which I would not have thought possible six months ago. Sad and disturbing facts, often long in the past, have been readily presented in ways that create an erroneous image of the church in 2002 as neglectful and uncaring in a matter about which we bishops have cared a great deal for many years now….

I am not only proud to defend this body from the distortions; I do it as a matter of justice to set the record straight so that the work we bishops will be doing today and tomorrow will be seen in its proper perspective — as an important piece of work that we have been doing together for 20 years. There has indeed been some very thoughtful media coverage and editorial analysis alongside the hysterical and distorted coverage, analysis which has provided real insight into the issues….

When all is said and done, the Catholic Church in the United States remains the single largest private provider of services, care, formation and education for children throughout this nation. And we do that service well, effectively, and from the hearts of very faithful people. You who serve in the media have challenged us bishops well by calling us to better action in the fulfillment of our responsibilities. I extend the same courtesy to you and challenge you to do the same in the fulfillment of your own responsibilities.

The task that we bishops have before us these days in Dallas is enormous and daunting. We are called to put into place policies that will ensure the full protection of our children and young people and to bring an end to sexual abuse in the church. This we will do. Sadly, however, no decisions or policies that we make or put in place can save our children from human depravity. Our actions will have to be matched by an matched uncommon and persistent vigilance….

Agenda:

The bishops attending the Dallas meeting acted on these issues:

• Approved a far-reaching "Charter for the Protection of Children and Young People" that removes from all ministry any priest known to have abused a child. Most offenders will be laicized. The charter forms a national policy that sets new national structures and requires better diocesan structures to reach out to victims and assist them, end secrecy, report and remove abusers, and protect all children from future abuse.

• Adopted separate legal norms, which still need Vatican approval, to give legal teeth to the charter, requiring bishops by law to adhere to the national policy in areas where they would ordinarily be free to determine diocesan policy on their own.

• Set Aug. 14-15 as national days of penitence and prayer by the bishops in repentance for their failures to protect children adequately from child abusers in the past, and invited priests and laity to join them in their prayer.

• Devoted hours to listening to heart-rending stories of victim-survivors who suffered clerical sex abuse as children and to criticisms from nationally respected lay leaders and a specialist in child sex abuse trauma.

• Heard what at least one bishop described as a "profound apology" from Cardinal Bernard F. Law of Boston, where since January revelations of almost incomprehensible hierarchical toleration of known sex-abusing priests ignited the national scandal.

• Named Gov. Frank Keating of Oklahoma to head a new national review board that will oversee and monitor diocesan implementation of the bishops' new charter to protect children and oust sex-abusing priests.

• Spent a half-day of prayer and reflection June 15 on their role as bishops and their continuing need to respond pastorally and constructively to those sexually abused by priests.

• In their only business not related to the sex-abuse crisis, divided Region 4 of the bishops' conference, covering mid-Atlantic and Southeast dioceses, into two regions. The dioceses of the Carolinas, Georgia and Florida now form a new Region 14.

• Received more U.S. media coverage than ever in the history of the bishops' conference, with a record 750 media representatives accredited to cover the meeting.

(For detailed coverage of the "Charter for the Protection of Children and Young People" and the new norms, see under **News in Depth**.)

Doctrine of the Catholic Church

THE CATECHISM OF THE CATHOLIC CHURCH

(By Russell Shaw)

"The Catechism of the Catholic Church ... is a statement of the Church's faith and of Catholic doctrine, attested to or illumined by Sacred Scripture, the Apostolic Tradition, and the Church's Magisterium. I declare it to be a sure norm for teaching the faith and thus a valid and legitimate instrument for ecclesial communion."

Thus Pope John Paul II in the Apostolic Constitution Fidei Depositum ("The Deposit of Faith") formally presented the first official catechism or compendium of doctrine for the universal Church to have been published since the 16th century.

Fidei Depositum is dated October 11, 1992, the 30th anniversary of the opening of the Second Vatican Council (1962-65), and that date is significant. The predecessor of the Catechism of the Catholic Church is the Roman Catechism or Catechism of the Council of Trent, which was published by Pope St. Pius V in 1566 following the great reforming council held from 1545 to 1563. As the Roman Catechism sets forth the doctrine of the Church in light of the Council of Trent, so the Catechism of the Catholic Church sets forth the Church's teaching against the background of Vatican Council II.

History of the Catechism

In development since 1986, the definitive text of the *Catechism of the Catholic Church* was officially approved by Pope John Paul on June 25, 1992, with December 8 the date of formal promulgation.

Nine separate drafts of the *Catechism* were prepared. The document was written in French. In November 1989, the commission of cardinals sent a draft text to all the bishops of the world asking for their comments and suggestions. Although this consultation produced a reaction generally favorable to the text, more than 24,000 individual amendments were submitted by the bishops, and these were reviewed by the commission, and helped to shape the further revision of the document.

The pope in *Fidei Depositum* described the *Catechism* as "a sure and authentic reference text" both for the teaching of Catholic doctrine and particularly for the preparation of local catechisms; he said the *Catechism* was presented to "all the Church's Pastors and the Christian faithful" with these ends in view. Other purposes mentioned included helping Catholics to deepen their knowledge of the faith, supporting ecumenical efforts by "showing carefully the content and wondrous harmony of the Catholic faith," and providing authoritative answers to anyone who wishes to know "what the Catholic Church believes."

Structure and Contents of the Catechism

The *Catechism* adopts the four-fold division of the *Roman Catechism*. The four parts or "pillars" deal with the Creed; the Sacred Liturgy, with special emphasis on the sacraments; the Christian way of life, analyzed according to the Ten Commandments; and prayer, considered in the framework of the petitions of the Our Father.

Describing this organizational scheme, Pope John Paul said: "The four parts are related one to another: the Christian mystery is the object of faith (first part); it is celebrated and communicated in liturgical actions (second part); it is present to enlighten and sustain the children of God in their actions (third part); it is the basis of our prayer, the privileged expression of which is the Our Father, and it represents the object of our supplication, our praise and our intercession (fourth part)."

The pope also stressed the Christocentric nature of Christian faith as it is presented in the *Catechism*. "In reading the *Catechism of the Catholic Church* we can perceive the wonderful unity of the mystery of God, his saving will, as well as the central place of Jesus Christ, the only-begotten Son of God, sent by the Father, made man in the womb of the Blessed Virgin Mary by the power of the Holy Spirit, to be our Savior. Having died and risen, Christ is always present in his Church, especially in the sacraments; he is the source of our faith, the model of Christian conduct, and the Teacher of our prayer."

The text of the *Catechism of the Catholic Church*, with extensive cross-references and sectional summaries, consists of 2,865 numbered paragraphs. Passages in large print set out its more substantive contents, while passages in small print provide background information and explanations; there are numerous cross-references in the margins directing readers to other passages that treat the same theme or related themes. Among the features of the *Catechism* are the "In Brief" sections found throughout, which sum up the teaching of the preceding unit.

Outline of the Catechism

Prologue (1-25). The nature of catechesis is described, along with the aim of the present *Catechism* and its intended readership, its structure, its use, and the desirability of adaptations for different cultures, age groups, etc.

Part One: The Profession of Faith (26-1065)

Section One discusses the nature of faith. "Faith is man's response to God, who reveals himself and gives himself to man, at the same time bringing man a superabundant light as he searches for the ultimate meaning of his life. Thus we shall consider first that search (Chapter One), then the divine Revelation by which God comes to meet man (Chapter Two), and finally the response of faith (Chapter Three)" (26). The topics discussed include knowledge of God; Divine Revelation and its transmission; Sacred Scripture; and faith as the human response to God. "We do not believe in formulas, but in those realities they express, which faith allows us to touch.... All the same, we do approach these realities with the help of formulations of the faith which permit us to express the faith and to hand it on, to celebrate it in community, to assimilate and live on it more and more" (170).

Section Two deals with the profession of Christian faith, with the treatment organized according to the articles of the Creed. The Creed used is the Apostles' Creed; its "great authority," says the *Catechism*, quoting St. Ambrose, arises from its being "the Creed of the Roman Church, the See of Peter, the first of the apostles" (194). Among the doctrines covered in the three chapters of this section are the Trinity, creation, the angels, the creation of man, original sin, the Incarnation, the virgin birth, redemption, the Resurrection of Christ, the work of the Holy Spirit, the Church, the hierarchical constitution of the Church, the communion of saints, the Virgin Mary as Mother of Christ and Mother of the Church, the resurrection of the dead, judgment, heaven, and hell. "[T]he Creed's final 'Amen' repeats and confirms its first words: 'I believe.' To believe is to say 'Amen' to God's words, promises and commandments; to entrust oneself completely to him who is the 'Amen' of infinite love and perfect faithfulness. The Christian's everyday life will then be the 'Amen' to the 'I believe' of our baptismal profession of faith" (1064).

Part Two: The Celebration of the Christian Mystery (1066-1690)

Section One considers the sacramental economy. It explains that in this present "age of the Church," begun on Pentecost, "Christ now lives and acts in his Church, in a new way appropriate to this new age. He acts through the sacraments in what the common Tradition of the East and the West calls 'the sacramental economy'... the communication (or 'dispensation') of the fruits of Christ's Paschal Mystery in the celebration of the Church's 'sacramental' liturgy" (1076). Topics treated here are the Paschal Mystery and its sacramental celebration.

Section Two covers the seven sacraments of the Church. "Christ instituted the sacraments of the new law.... The seven sacraments touch all the stages and all the important moments of Christian life: they give birth and increase, healing and mission to the Christian's life of faith. There is thus a certain resemblance between the stages of natural life and the stages of the spiritual life" (1210). The presentation is organized in four chapters. These are: the sacraments of

Christian initiation (Baptism, Confirmation, the Eucharist) in chapter one; the sacraments of healing (Penance and Reconciliation, the Anointing of the Sick) in chapter two; the "sacraments at the service of communion" (Holy Orders and Matrimony) in chapter three; and sacramentals and Christian funerals in chapter four.

Part Three: Life in Christ (1691-2557)

Section One is entitled "Man's Vocation: Life in the Spirit." Its three chapters discuss the dignity of the human person, the human community, and "God's Salvation: Law and Grace" (the moral law, grace and justification, the Church as teacher of moral truth). "Catechesis has to reveal in all clarity the joy and the demands of the way of Christ.... The first and last point of reference of this catechesis will always be Jesus Christ himself, who is 'the way, and the truth, and the life' " (1697-1698).

Section Two reflects on the contents of Christian moral life. The treatment is organized according to the Ten Commandments, with a chapter devoted to each commandment and its concrete applications. While the commandments admit of what is traditionally called light matter (venial sin), nevertheless, the text says: "Since they express man's fundamental duties towards God and towards his neighbor, the Ten Commandments reveal, in their primordial content, grave obligations. They are fundamentally immutable, and they oblige always and everywhere. No one can dispense from them. The Ten Commandments are engraved by God in the human heart" (2072).

Part Four: Christian Prayer (2558-2865)

Section One considers prayer in Christian life, underlining the relationship of this topic to the rest of the *Catechism*: "The Church professes this mystery [of faith] in the Apostles' Creed (Part One) and celebrates it in the sacramental liturgy (Part Two), so that the life of the faithful may be conformed to Christ in the Holy Spirit to the glory of God the Father (Part Three). This mystery, then, requires that the faithful believe in it, that they celebrate it, and that they live from it in a vital and personal relationship with the living and true God. This relationship is prayer" (2558). The section then discusses the "revelation of prayer" in the Old Testament and now in the age of the Church, the tradition of prayer, and the life of prayer (kinds of prayer, problems and perseverance in prayer).

Section Two presents an extended reflection on the Our Father, considered as the model of prayer. Quoting Tertullian, the *Catechism* says: "The Lord's Prayer 'is truly the summary of the whole Gospel.' 'Since the Lord ... after handing over the practice of prayer, said elsewhere, 'Ask and you will receive,' and since everyone has petitions which are peculiar to his circumstances, the regular and appropriate prayer [the Lord's Prayer] is said first, as the foundation of further desires'" (2761).

Reception of the Catechism

Following the publication of the *Catechism of the Catholic Church*, Pope John Paul established an Interdicasterial Commission for the Catechism, under the chairmanship of Cardinal Ratzinger, responsible for overseeing translations of the volume and reviewing and approving suggested changes in the text. The commission approved the English translation of the *Catechism* in February 1994, and it was published on June 22 of that year — in the United States, under the auspices of the National Conference of Catholic Bishops.

Pope John Paul presented the *editio typica* or normative Latin version of the *Catechism* in a formal ceremony on September 8, 1997.

The following day, Cardinal Ratzinger presented the *editio typica* at a Vatican news conference. At the same time, he also introduced more than a hundred changes which had been approved for incorporation into the text. Most of the changes were of a minor, editorial nature. The most important was in paragraphs 2265-2267 of the *Catechism*, where the treatment of capital punishment had been strengthened to reflect the discussion of the same topic in Pope John Paul's 1995 encyclical letter *Evangelium Vitae* ("*The Gospel of Life*").

In the United States, the National Conference of Catholic Bishops in 1994 established an Ad Hoc Committee to Oversee the Use of the Catechism. It has an office and staff at NCCB headquarters in Washington, D.C.. The committee reviews and approves materials that seek to make substantial direct use of the text of the *Catechism of the Catholic Church*, and also reviews catechetical series for their conformity with the *Catechism*. In addition, the committee was mandated to conduct a feasibility study of a national catechism or catechetical series for the United States.

DOGMATIC CONSTITUTION ON THE CHURCH — *LUMEN GENTIUM*

Following are excerpts from the first two chapters of the "Dogmatic Constitution on the Church" (*Lumen Gentium*) promulgated by the Second Vatican Council. They describe the relation of the Catholic Church to the Kingdom of God, the nature and foundation of the Church, the People of God, the necessity of membership and participation in the Church for salvation. Additional subjects in the constitution are treated in other Almanac entries.

I. MYSTERY OF THE CHURCH

By her relationship with Christ, the Church is a kind of sacrament or sign of intimate union with God, and of the unity of all mankind (No. 1).

He (the eternal Father) planned to assemble in the holy Church all those who would believe in Christ. Already from the beginning of the world the foreshadowing of the Church took place. She was prepared for in a remarkable way throughout the history of the people of Israel and by means of the Old Covenant. Established in the present era of time, the Church was made manifest by the outpouring of the Spirit. At the end of time she will achieve her glorious fulfillment. Then all just men from the time of Adam, "from Abel, the just one, to the last of the elect," will be gathered together with the Father in the universal Church (No. 2).

When the work which the Father had given the Son to do on earth (cf. Jn. 17:4) was accomplished, the Holy Spirit was sent on the day of Pentecost in order that he might forever sanctify the Church, and thus all believers would have access to the Father through Christ in the one Spirit (cf. Eph. 2:18).

The Spirit dwells in the Church and in the hearts of the faithful as in a temple (cf. 1 Cor. 3:16; 6:19)…. The Spirit guides the Church into the fullness of truth (cf. Jn. 16:13) and gives her a unity of fellowship and service. He furnishes and directs her with various gifts, both hierarchical and charismatic, and adorns her with the fruits of His grace (cf. Eph. 4:11-12; 1 Cor. 12:4; Gal. 5:22). By the power of the Gospel he makes the Church grow, perpetually renews her, and leads her to perfect union with her Spouse (No. 4).

Foundation of the Church

The mystery of the holy Church is manifest in her very foundation, for the Lord Jesus inaugurated her by preaching the Good News, that is, the coming of God's Kingdom, which, for centuries, had been promised in the Scriptures…. In Christ's word, in his works, and in his presence this Kingdom reveals itself to men.

The miracles of Jesus also confirm that the Kingdom has already arrived on earth.

Before all things, however, the Kingdom is clearly visible in the very Person of Christ, Son of God and Son of Man.

When Jesus rose up again after suffering death on the cross for mankind, he manifested that he had been appointed Lord, Messiah, and Priest forever (cf. Acts 2:36; Heb. 5:6; 7:17-21), and he poured out on his disciples the Spirit promised by the Father (cf. Acts 2:33). The Church, consequently, equipped with the gifts of her Founder and faithfully guarding his precepts receives the mission to proclaim and to establish among all peoples the Kingdom of Christ and of God. She becomes on earth the initial budding forth of that Kingdom. While she slowly grows, the Church strains toward the consummation of the Kingdom and, with all her strength, hopes and desires to be united in glory with her King (No. 5).

Figures of the Church

In the Old Testament the revelation of the Kingdom had often been conveyed by figures of speech. In the same way the inner nature of the Church was now to be made known to us through various images.

The Church is a sheepfold … a flock … a tract of land to be cultivated, the field of God … his choice vineyard … the true vine is Christ … the edifice of God … the house of God … the holy temple (whose members are) living stones … this holy city … a bride … our Mother … the spotless spouse of the spotless Lamb … an exile (No. 6).

In the human nature which he united to himself, the Son of God redeemed man and transformed him into a new creation (cf. Gal. 6:15; 2 Cor. 5:17) by overcoming death through his own death and resurrection. By communicating his Spirit to his brothers, called together from all peoples, Christ made them mystically into his own body.

In that body, the life of Christ is poured into the believers, who, through the sacraments, are united in a hidden and real way to Christ who suffered and was glorified. Through baptism we are formed in the likeness of Christ.

Truly partaking of the body of the Lord in the breaking of the eucharistic bread, we are taken up into communion with him and with one another (No. 7).

One Body in Christ

As all the members of the human body, though they are many, form one body, so also are the faithful in Christ (cf. 1 Cor. 12:12). Also, in the building up of Christ's body there is a flourishing variety of members and functions. There is only one Spirit who distributes his different gifts for the welfare of the Church (cf. 1 Cor. 12:1-11). Among these gifts stands out the grace given to the apostles. To their authority, the Spirit himself subjected even those who were endowed with charisms (cf. 1 Cor. 14). The head of this body is Christ (No. 7).

Mystical Body of Christ

Christ, the one Mediator, established and ceaselessly sustains here on earth his holy Church, the community of faith, hope, and charity, as a visible structure. Through her he communicates truth and grace to all. But the society furnished with hierarchical agencies and the Mystical Body of Christ are not to be considered as two realities, nor are the visible assembly and the spiritual community, nor the earthly Church and the Church enriched with heavenly things. Rather they form one interlocked reality which is comprised of a divine and a human element. For this reason, this reality is compared to the mystery of the incarnate Word. Just as the assumed nature inseparably united to the divine Word serves him as a living instrument of salvation, so, in a similar way, does the communal structure of the Church serve Christ's Spirit, who vivifies it by way of building up the body (cf. Eph. 4:16).

This is the unique Church of Christ which in the Creed we avow as one, holy, catholic, and apostolic. After his Resurrection our Savior handed her over to Peter to be shepherded (Jn. 21:17), commissioning him and the other apostles to propagate and govern her (cf. Mt. 28:18, ff.). Her he erected for all ages as "the pillar and mainstay of the truth" (1 Tm. 3:15). This Church, constituted and organized in the world as a society, subsists in the Catholic Church, which is governed by the successor of Peter and by the bishops in union with that successor, although many elements of sanctification and of truth can be found outside of her visible structure. These elements, however, as gifts properly belonging to the Church of Christ, possess an inner dynamism toward Catholic unity.

The Church, embracing sinners in her bosom, is at the same time holy and always in need of being purified, and incessantly pursues the path of penance and renewal.

The Church, "like a pilgrim in a foreign land, presses forward, announcing the cross and death of the Lord until he comes" (cf. 1 Cor. 11:26) (No. 8).

II. THE PEOPLE OF GOD

At all times and among every people, God has given welcome to whosoever fears him and does what is right (cf. Acts 10:35). It has pleased God, however, to make men holy and save them not merely as individuals without any mutual bonds, but by making them into a single people, a people which acknowledges him in truth and serves him in holiness. He therefore chose the race of Israel as a people unto himself. With it he set up a covenant. Step by step he taught this people by manifesting in its history both himself and the decree of his will, and by making it holy unto himself. All these things, however, were done by way of preparation and as a figure of that new and small perfect covenant which was to be ratified in Christ.

Christ instituted this New Covenant, that is to say, the New Testament, in his blood (cf. 1 Cor. 11:25), by calling together a people made up of Jew and Gentile, making them one, not according to the flesh but in the Spirit.

This was to be the new People of God ... reborn ... through the Word of the living God (cf. 1 Pt. 1:23). from water and the Holy Spirit (cf. Jn. 3:5-6) ... "a chosen race, a royal priesthood, a holy nation, a purchased people. You who in times past were not a people, but are now the People of God" (1 Pt. 2:9-10).

That messianic people has for its head Christ. Its law is the new commandment to love as Christ loved us (cf. Jn. 13:34). Its goal is the Kingdom of God, which has been begun by God himself on earth, and which is to be further extended until it is brought to perfection by him at the end of time.

This messianic people, although it does not actually include all men, and may more than once look like a small flock, is nonetheless a lasting and sure seed of unity, hope, and salvation for the whole human race. Established by Christ as a fellowship of life, charity, and truth, it is also used by him as an instrument for the redemption of all, and is sent forth into the whole world as the light of the world and the salt of the earth (cf. Mt. 5:13-16).

Israel according to the flesh ... was already called the Church of God (Neh. 13:1; cf. Nm. 20:4; Dt. 23:1, ff.). Likewise the new Israel ... is also called the Church of Christ (cf. Mt. 16:18). For he has bought it for himself with his blood (cf. Acts 20:28), has filled it with his Spirit, and provided it with those means which befit it as a visible and social unity. God has gathered together as one all those who in faith look upon Jesus as the author of salvation and the source of unity and peace, and has established them as the Church, that for each and all she may be the visible sacrament of this saving unity (No. 9).

Priesthood

The baptized, by regeneration and the anointing of the Holy Spirit, are consecrated into a holy priesthood.

[All members of the Church participate in the priesthood of Christ, through the common priesthood of the faithful. *See* **Priesthood of the Laity**.]

Though they differ from one another in essence and not only in degree, the common priesthood of the faithful and the ministerial or hierarchical priesthood are nonetheless interrelated. Each of them in its own special way is a participation in the one priesthood of Christ (No. 10).

It is through the sacraments and the exercise of the virtues that the sacred nature and organic structure of the priestly community is brought into operation (No. 11). (See Role of the Sacraments.)

Prophetic Office

The holy People of God shares also in Christ's prophetic office. It spreads abroad a living witness to him, especially by means of a life of faith and charity and by offering to God a sacrifice of praise.... The body of the faithful as a whole, anointed as they are by the Holy One (cf. Jn. 2:20, 27), cannot err in matters of belief. Thanks to a supernatural sense of faith which characterizes the People as a whole, it manifests this unerring quality when, "from the bishops down to the last member of the laity," it shows universal agreement in matters of faith and morals.

God's People accepts not the word of men but the very Word of God (cf. 1 Thes. 2:13). It clings without fail to the faith once delivered to the saints (cf. Jude 3), penetrates it more deeply by accurate insights, and applies it more thoroughly to life. All this it does under the lead of a sacred teaching authority to which it loyally defers.

It is not only through the sacraments and Church ministries that the same Holy Spirit sanctifies and leads the People of God.... He distributes special graces among the faithful of every rank. By these gifts he makes them fit and ready to undertake the various tasks or offices advantageous for the renewal and upbuilding of the Church. These charismatic gifts ... are to be received with thanksgiving and consolation, for they are exceedingly suitable and useful for the needs of the Church.

Judgment as to their genuineness and proper use belongs to those who preside over the Church, and to whose special competence it belongs ... to test all things and hold fast to that which is good (cf. 1 Thes. 5:12; 19-21) (No. 12).

All Are Called

All men are called to belong to the new People of God. Wherefore this People, while remaining one and unique, is to be spread throughout the whole world and must exist in all ages, so that the purpose of God's will may be fulfilled. In the beginning God made human nature one. After his children were scattered, he decreed that they should at length be united again (cf. Jn. 11:52). It was for this reason that God sent his Son.... that he might be Teacher, King, and Priest of all, the Head of the new and universal People of the sons of God. For this God finally sent his Son's Spirit as Lord and Lifegiver. He it is who, on behalf of the whole Church and each and every one of those who believe, is the principle of their coming together and remaining together in the teaching of the apostles and in fellowship, in the breaking of bread and in prayers (cf. Acts 2:42) (No. 13).

One People of God

It follows that among all the nations of earth there is but one People of God, which takes its citizens from every race, making them citizens of a Kingdom which is of a heavenly and not an earthly nature. For all the faithful scattered throughout the world are in communion with each other in the Holy Spirit.... the Church or People of God foster(s) and take(s) to herself, insofar as they are good, the ability, resources and customs of each people. Taking them to herself, she purifies, strengthens, and ennobles them.... This characteristic of universality which adorns the People of God is a gift from the Lord himself. By reason of it, the Catholic Church strives energetically and constantly to bring all humanity with all its riches back to Christ its Head in the unity of his Spirit.

In virtue of this catholicity each individual part of the Church contributes through its special gifts to the good of the other parts and of the whole Church. Thus through the common sharing of gifts. The whole and each of the parts receive increase.

All men are called to be part of this catholic unity of the People of God. And there belong to it or are related to it in various ways, the Catholic faithful as well as all who believe in Christ, and indeed the whole of mankind. For all men are called to salvation by the grace of God (No. 13).

The Catholic Church

This sacred Synod turns its attention first to the Catholic faithful. Basing itself upon sacred Scripture and tradition, it teaches that the Church is necessary for salvation. For Christ, made present to us in his Body, which is the Church, is the one Mediator and the unique Way of salvation. In explicit terms he himself affirmed the necessity of faith and baptism (cf. Mk. 16:16; Jn. 3:5) and thereby affirmed also the necessity of the Church, for through baptism as through a door men enter the Church. Whosoever, therefore, knowing that the Catholic Church was made necessary by God through Jesus Christ, would refuse to enter her or to remain in her could not be saved.

They are fully incorporated in the society of the Church who, possessing the Spirit of Christ, accept her entire system and all the means of salvation given to her, and through union with her visible structure are joined to Christ, who rules her through the Supreme Pontiff and the bishops. This joining is effected by the bonds of professed faith, of the sacraments, of ecclesiastical government, and of communion. He is not saved, however, who, though he is part of the body of the Church, does not persevere in charity. He remains indeed in the bosom of the Church, but only in a "bodily" manner and not "in his heart."

Catechumens who, moved by the Holy Spirit, seek with explicit intention to be incorporated into the Church, are by that very intention joined to her. Mother Church already embraces them as her own (No. 14).

Other Christians, The Unbaptized

The Church recognizes that in many ways she is linked with those who, being baptized, are honored with the name of Christian, though they do not profess the faith in its entirety or do not preserve unity of communion with the successor of Peter.

We can say that in some real way they are joined with us in the Holy Spirit, for to them also he gives his gifts and graces, and is thereby operative among them with his sanctifying power (No. 15).

Finally, those who have not yet received the Gospel are related in various ways to the People of God. In the first place there is the people to whom the covenants and the promises were given and from whom Christ was born according to the flesh (cf. Rom. 9:4-5). On account of their fathers, this people remains most dear to God, for God does not repent of the gifts he makes nor of the calls he issues (cf. Rom. 11:28-29).

But the plan of salvation also includes those who acknowledge the Creator. In the first place among these are the Moslems. Nor is God himself far distant from those who in shadows and images seek the unknown God.

Those also can attain to everlasting salvation who through no fault of their own do not know the Gospel of Christ or his Church, yet sincerely seek God and, moved by grace, strive by their deeds to do his will as it is known to them through the dictates of conscience. Nor does divine Providence deny the help necessary for salvation to those who, without blame on their part, have not yet arrived at an explicit knowledge of God, but who strive to live a good life, thanks to his grace. Whatever goodness or truth is found among them is looked upon by the Church as a preparation for the Gospel. She regards such qualities as given by him who enlightens all men so that they may finally have life. (No. 16).

THE POPE, TEACHING AUTHORITY, COLLEGIALITY

The Roman Pontiff — the successor of St. Peter as the bishop of Rome and head of the Church on earth — has full and supreme authority over the universal Church in matters pertaining to faith and morals (teaching authority), discipline and government (jurisdictional authority).

The primacy of the pope is real and supreme power. It is not merely a prerogative of honor — that is, of his being regarded as the first among equals. Neither does primacy imply that the pope is just the presiding officer of the collective body of bishops. The pope is the head of the Church.

Catholic belief in the primacy of the pope was stated in detail in the dogmatic constitution on the Church, *Pastor Aeternus*, approved in 1870 by the fourth session of the First Vatican Council. Some elaboration of the doctrine was made in the Dogmatic Constitution on the Church which was approved and promulgated by the Second Vatican Council Nov. 21, 1964. The entire body of teaching on the subject is based on Scripture and tradition and the centuries-long experience of the Church.

Infallibility

The essential points of doctrine concerning infallibility in the Church and the infallibility of the pope were stated by the Second Vatican Council in the Dogmatic Constitution on the Church, as follows:

"This infallibility with which the divine Redeemer willed his Church to be endowed in defining a doctrine of faith and morals extends as far as extends the deposit of divine revelation, which must be religiously guarded and faithfully expounded. This is the infallibility which the Roman Pontiff, the head of the college of bishops, enjoys in virtue of his office, when, as the supreme shepherd and teacher of all the faithful who confirms his brethren in their faith (cf. Lk. 22:32), he proclaims by a definitive act some doctrine of faith or morals. Therefore his definitions, of themselves, and not from the consent of the Church, are justly styled irreformable, for they are pronounced with the assistance of the Holy Spirit, an assistance promised to him in blessed Peter. Therefore they need no approval of others, nor do they allow an appeal to any other judgment. For then the Roman Pontiff is not pronouncing judgment as a private person. Rather, as the supreme teacher of the universal Church, as one in whom the charism of the infallibility of the Church herself is individually present, he is expounding or defending a doctrine of Catholic faith.

"The infallibility promised to the Church resides also in the body of bishops when that body exercises supreme teaching authority with the successor of Peter. To the resultant definitions the assent of the Church can never be wanting, on account of the activity of that same Holy Spirit, whereby the whole flock of Christ is preserved and progresses in unity of faith.

"But when either the Roman Pontiff or the body of bishops together with him defines a judgment, they pronounce it in accord with revelation itself. All are obliged to maintain and be ruled by this revelation, which, as written or preserved by tradition, is transmitted in its entirety through the legitimate succession of bishops and especially through the care of the Roman Pontiff himself.

"Under the guiding light of the Spirit of truth, revelation is thus religiously preserved and faithfully expounded in the Church. The Roman Pontiff and the bishops, in view of their office and of the importance of the matter, strive painstakingly and by appropriate means to inquire properly into that revelation and to give apt expression to its contents. But they do not allow that there could be any new public revelation pertaining to the divine deposit of faith" (No. 25).

Authentic Teaching

The pope rarely speaks *ex cathedra* — that is, "from the chair" of St. Peter — for the purpose of making an infallible pronouncement. More often and in various ways he states authentic teaching in line with Scripture, tradition, the living experience of the Church, and the whole analogy of faith. Of such teaching, the Second Vatican Council said in its Dogmatic Constitution on the Church (No. 25):

"Religious submission of will and of mind must be shown in a special way to the authentic teaching authority of the Roman Pontiff, even when he is not speaking *ex cathedra*. That is, it must be shown in such a way that his supreme magisterium is acknowledged with reverence, the judgments made by him are sincerely adhered to, according to his manifest mind and will. His mind and will in the matter may be known chiefly either from the character of the documents, from his frequent repetition of the same doctrine, or from his manner of speaking."

Bishops "are authentic teachers, that is, teachers endowed with the authority of Christ, who preach to the people committed to them the faith they must believe and put into practice. By the light of the Holy Spirit, they make that faith clear, bringing forth from the treasury of revelation new things and old (cf. Mt. 13:52), making faith bear fruit and vigilantly warding off any errors which threaten their flock (cf. 2 Tm. 4:1-4).

"Bishops, teaching in communion with the Roman Pontiff, are to be respected by all as witnesses to divine and Catholic truth. In matters of faith and morals, the bishops speak in the name of Christ and the faithful are to accept their teaching and adhere to it with a religious assent of soul."

Magisterium — Teaching Authority

Responsibility for teaching doctrine and judging orthodoxy belongs to the official teaching authority of the Church.

This authority is personalized in the pope, the successor of St. Peter as head of the Church, and in the bishops together and in union with the pope, as it was originally committed to Peter and to the whole college of apostles under his leadership. They are the official teachers of the Church.

Others have auxiliary relationships with the magisterium: theologians, in the study and clarification of doctrine; teachers — priests, religious, lay persons — who cooperate with the pope and bishops in spreading knowledge of religious truth; the faithful, who by their sense of faith and personal witness contribute to the development of doctrine and the establishment of its relevance to life in the Church and the world.

The magisterium, Pope Paul VI noted in an address at a general audience Jan. 11, 1967, "is a subordinate and faithful echo and secure interpreter of the divine word." It does not reveal new truths, "nor is it superior to sacred Scripture." Its competence extends to the limits of divine revelation manifested in Scripture and tradition and the living experience of the Church, with respect to matters of faith and morals and related subjects. Official teaching in these areas is infallible when it is formally defined, for belief and acceptance by all members of the Church, by the pope, acting in the capacity of supreme shepherd of the flock of Christ; also, when doctrine is proposed and taught with moral unanimity of bishops with the pope in a solemn collegial manner, as in an ecumenical council, and/or in the ordinary course of events. Even when not infallibly defined, official teaching in the areas of faith and morals is authoritative and requires religious assent.

The teachings of the magisterium have been documented in creeds, formulas of faith, decrees and enactments of ecumenical and particular councils, various kinds of doctrinal statements, encyclical letters and other teaching instruments. They have also been incorporated into the liturgy, with the result that the law of prayer is said to be a law of belief.

Collegiality

The bishops of the Church, in union with the pope, have supreme teaching and pastoral authority over the whole Church in addition to the authority of office they have for their own dioceses.

This collegial authority is exercised in a solemn manner in an ecumenical council and can be exercised in other ways as well, "provided that the head of the college calls them to collegiate action, or at least so approves or freely accepts the united action of the dispersed bishops that it is made a true collegiate act."

This doctrine is grounded on the fact that: "Just as, by the Lord's will, St. Peter and the other apostles constituted one apostolic college, so in a similar way the Roman Pontiff as the successor of Peter, and the bishops as the successors of the apostles are joined together."

Doctrine on collegiality was stated by the Second Vatican Council in the Dogmatic Constitution on the Church (Nos. 22 and 23).

(For coverage of the *Role of Mary in the Mystery of Christ and the Church,* Chapter VIII, *Lumen Gentium,* see the section on the Blessed Virgin Mary.)

REVELATION

Following are excerpts from the "Dogmatic Constitution on Divine Revelation" (*Dei Verbum*) promulgated by the Second Vatican Council. They describe the nature and process of divine revelation, inspiration and interpretation of Scripture, the Old and New Testaments, and the role of Scripture in the life of the Church.

I. REVELATION ITSELF

God chose to reveal himself and to make known to us the hidden purpose of his will (cf. Eph. 1:9) by which through Christ, the Word made flesh, man has access to the Father in the Holy Spirit and comes to share in the divine nature (cf. Eph. 2:18; 2 Pt. 1:4). Through this revelation, therefore, the invisible God (cf. Col. 1:15; 1 Tm. 1:17). speaks to men as friends (cf. Ex. 33:11; Jn. 15:14-15) and lives among them (cf. Bar. 3:38) so that he may invite and take them into fellowship with himself. This plan of revelation is realized by deeds and words having an inner unity: the deeds wrought by God in the history of salvation manifest and confirm the teaching and realities signified by the words, while the words proclaim the deeds and clarify the mystery contained in them. By this revelation then, the deepest truth about God and the salvation of man is made clear to us in Christ, who is the Mediator and at the same time the fullness of all revelation (No. 2).

God from the start manifested himself to our first parents. Then after their fall his promise of redemption aroused in them the hope of being saved (cf. Gn. 3:15), and from that time on he ceaselessly kept the human race in his care, in order to give eternal life to those who perseveringly do good in search of salvation (cf. Rom. 2:6-7). He called Abraham in order to make of him a great nation (cf. Gn. 12:2). Through the patriarchs, and after them through Moses and the prophets, he taught this nation to acknowledge himself as the one living and true God and to wait for the Savior promised by him. In this manner he prepared the way for the Gospel down through the centuries (No. 3).

Revelation in Christ

Then, after speaking in many places and varied ways through the prophets, God "last of all in these days has spoken to us by his Son" (Heb. 1:1-2). Jesus perfected revelation by fulfilling it through his whole work of making himself present and manifesting himself: through his words and deeds, his signs and wonders, but especially through his death and glorious resurrection from the dead and final sending of the Spirit of truth. Moreover, he confirmed with divine testimony what revelation proclaimed: that God is with us to free us from the darkness of sin and death, and to raise us up to life eternal.

The Christian dispensation, therefore, as the new and definitive covenant, will never pass away, and we now await no further new public revelation before the glorious manifestation of our Lord Jesus Christ (cf. 1 Tm. 6:14; Ti. 2:13) (No. 4).

II. TRANSMISSION OF REVELATION

God has seen to it that what he had revealed for the salvation of all nations would abide perpetually in its full integrity and be handed on to all generations. Therefore Christ the Lord, in whom the full revelation of the supreme God is brought to completion (cf. 2 Cor. 1:20; 3:16; 4:6), commissioned the apostles to preach to all men that Gospel which is the source of all saving truth and moral teaching, and thus to impart to them divine gifts. This Gospel had been promised in former times through the prophets, and Christ himself fulfilled it and promulgated it with his own lips. This commission was faithfully fulfilled by the apostles who, by their oral preaching, by example, and by ordinances, handed on what they had received from Christ or what they had learned through the prompting of the Holy Spirit. The commission was fulfilled, too, by those apostles and apostolic men who under the inspiration of the same Holy Spirit committed the message of salvation to writing (No. 7).

Tradition

But in order to keep the Gospel forever whole and alive within the Church, the apostles left bishops as their successors, "handing over their own teaching role" to them. This sacred tradition, therefore, and sacred Scripture of both the Old and the New Testament are like a mirror in which the pilgrim Church on earth looks at God (No. 7).

The apostolic preaching, which is expressed in a special way in the inspired books, was to be preserved by a continuous succession of preachers until the end of time. Therefore the apostles, handing on what they themselves had received, warn the faithful to hold fast to the traditions which they have learned. Now what was handed on by the apostles includes everything which contributes to the holiness of life, and the increase in faith of the People of God; and so the Church, in her teaching, life, and worship, perpetuates and hands on to all generations all that she herself is, all that she believes (No. 8).

Development of Doctrine

This tradition which comes from the apostles develops in the Church with the help of the Holy Spirit. For there is a growth in the understanding of the realities and the words which have been handed down. This happens through the contemplation and study made by believers through the intimate understanding of spiritual things they experience, and through the preaching of those who have received through episcopal succession the sure gift of truth. For, as the centuries succeed one another, the Church constantly moves forward toward the fullness of divine truth until the words of God reach their complete fulfillment in her.

The words of the holy Fathers witness to the living presence of this tradition, whose wealth is poured into the practice and life of the believing and praying Church. Through the same tradition the Church's full canon of the sacred books is known, and the sacred writings themselves are more profoundly understood and unceasingly made active in her; ... and the Holy Spirit, through whom the living voice of the Gospel resounds in the Church, and through her, in the world, leads unto all truth those who believe and makes the word of Christ dwell abundantly in them (cf. Col. 3:16) (No. 8).

Tradition and Scripture

Hence there exist a close connection and communication between sacred tradition and sacred Scripture. For both of them, flowing from the same divine wellspring, in a certain way merge into a unity and tend toward the same end. For sacred Scripture is the word of God inasmuch as it is consigned to writing under the inspiration of the divine Spirit. To the successors of the apostles, sacred tradition hands on in its full purity God's word, which was entrusted to the apostles by Christ the Lord and the Holy Spirit. Thus, led by the light of the Spirit of truth, these successors can in their preaching preserve this word of God faithfully, explain it, and make it more widely known. Consequently, it is not from sacred Scripture alone that the Church draws her certainty about every thing which has been revealed. Therefore both sacred tradition and sacred Scripture are to be accepted and venerated with the same sense of devotion and reverence (No. 9).

Sacred tradition and sacred Scripture form one sacred deposit of the word of God, which is committed to the Church (No. 10).

Teaching Authority of Church

The task of authentically interpreting the word of God, whether written or handed on, has been entrusted exclusively to the living teaching office of the Church, whose authority is exercised in the name of Jesus Christ. This teaching office is not above the word of God, but serves it, teaching only what has been handed on ... it draws from this one deposit of faith everything which it presents for belief as divinely revealed.

It is clear, therefore, that sacred tradition, sacred Scripture, and the teaching authority of the Church ... are so linked and joined together that one cannot stand without the others, and that all together and each in its own way under the action of the one Holy Spirit contribute effectively to the salvation of souls (No. 10).

III. INSPIRATION, INTERPRETATION

Those revealed realities contained and presented in sacred Scripture have been committed to writing under the inspiration of the Holy Spirit. Holy Mother Church, relying on the belief of the apostles, holds that the books of both the Old and New Testament in their entirety, with all their parts, are sacred and canonical because, having been written under the inspiration of the Holy Spirit (cf. Jn. 20:31; 2 Tm. 3:16; 2 Pt. 1:19-21; 3:15-16) they have God as their author and have been handed on as such to the Church herself. In composing the sacred books, God chose men and, while employed by him, they made use of their powers and abilities, so that, with him acting in them and through them, they, as true authors, consigned to writing everything and only those things which he wanted (No. 11).

Inerrancy

Therefore, since everything asserted by the inspired authors or sacred writers must be held to be asserted by the Holy Spirit, it follows that the books of Scripture must be acknowledged as teaching firmly, faithfully, and without error that truth which God wanted put into the sacred writings for the sake of our salvation. Therefore "all Scripture is inspired by God and useful for teaching, for reproving, for correcting, for instruction in justice; that the man of God may be perfect, equipped for every good work" (2 Tm. 3:16-17) (No. 11).

Literary Forms

However, since God speaks in sacred Scripture through men in human fashion, the interpreter of sacred Scripture, in order to see clearly what God wanted to communicate to us, should carefully investigate what meaning the sacred writers really intended, and what God wanted to manifest by means of their words.

The interpreter must investigate what meaning the sacred writer intended to express and actually expressed in particular circumstances as he used contemporary literary forms in accordance with the situation of his own time and culture. For the correct understanding of what the sacred author wanted to assert, due attention must be paid to the customary and characteristic styles of perceiving, speaking, and narrating which prevailed at the time of the sacred writer, and to the customs men normally followed at that period in their everyday dealings with one another (No. 12).

Analogy of Faith

No less serious attention must be given to the content and unity of the whole of Scripture, if the meaning of the sacred texts is to be correctly brought to light. The living tradition of the whole Church must be taken into account along with the harmony which exists between elements of the faith. All of what has been said about the way of interpreting Scripture is subject finally to the judgment of the Church, which carries out the divine commission and ministry of guarding and interpreting the word of God (No. 12).

IV. THE OLD TESTAMENT

In carefully planning and preparing the salvation of the whole human race, the God of supreme love, by a special dispensation, chose for himself a people to whom he might entrust his promises. First he entered into a covenant with Abraham (cf. Gn. 15:18) and, through Moses, with the people of Israel (cf. Ex. 24:8). To this people which he had acquired for himself, he so manifested himself through words and deeds as the one true and living God that Israel came to know by experience the ways of God with men. The plan of salvation, foretold by the sacred authors, recounted and explained by them, is found as the true word of God in the books of the Old Testament: these books, therefore, written under divine inspiration, remain permanently valuable (No. 14).

Principal Purpose

The principal purpose to which the plan of the Old Covenant was directed was to prepare for the coming both of Christ, the universal Redeemer, and of the messianic Kingdom. Now the books of the Old Testament, in accordance with the state of mankind before the time of salvation established by Christ, re-

veal to all men the knowledge of God and of man and the ways in which God deals with men. These books show us true divine pedagogy (No. 15).

The books of the Old Testament with all their parts, caught up into the proclamation of the Gospel, acquire and show forth their full meaning in the New Testament (cf. Mt. 5:17; Lk. 24:27; Rom. 16:25-26; 2 Cor. 3:14-16) and in turn shed light on it and explain it (No. 16).

V. THE NEW TESTAMENT

The word of God is set forth and shows its power in a most excellent way in the writings of the New Testament. For when the fullness of time arrived (cf. Gal. 4:4), the Word was made flesh and dwelt among us in the fullness of grace and truth (cf. Jn. 12:32). This mystery had not been manifested to other generations as it was now revealed to his holy apostles and prophets in the Holy Spirit (cf. Eph. 3:4-6), so that they might preach the Gospel, stir up faith in Jesus, Christ and Lord, and gather the Church together. To these realities, the writings of the New Testament stand as a perpetual and divine witness (No. 17).

The Gospels and Other Writings

The Gospels have a special preeminence for they are the principal witness of the life and teaching of the incarnate Word, our Savior.

The Church has always and everywhere held and continues to hold that the four Gospels are of apostolic origin. For what the apostles preached afterwards they themselves and apostolic men, under the inspiration of the divine Spirit, handed on to us in writing: the foundation of faith, namely, the fourfold Gospel, according to Matthew, Mark, Luke, and John (No. 18).

The four Gospels ... whose historical character the Church unhesitatingly asserts, faithfully hand on what Jesus Christ, while living among men, really did and taught for their eternal salvation until the day he was taken up into heaven (see Acts 1:1-2). Indeed, after the ascension of the Lord the apostles handed on to their hearers what he had said and done. The sacred authors wrote the four Gospels, selecting some things from the many which had been handed on by word of mouth or in writing, reducing some of them to a synthesis, explicating some things in view of the situation of their churches, and preserving the form of proclamation but always in such fashion that they told us the honest truth about Jesus. For their intention in writing was that we might know "the truth" concerning those matters about which we have been instructed (cf. Lk. 1:2-4) (No. 19).

Besides the four Gospels, the canon of the New Testament also contains the Epistles of St. Paul and other apostolic writings, composed under the inspiration of the Holy Spirit. In these writings those matters which concern Christ the Lord are confirmed, his true teaching is more and more fully stated, the saving power of the divine work of Christ is preached, the story is told of the beginnings of the Church and her marvelous growth, and her glorious fulfillment is foretold (No. 20).

SCRIPTURE IN CHURCH LIFE

The Church has always venerated the divine Scriptures just as she venerates the body of the Lord. She has always regarded the Scriptures together with sacred tradition as the supreme rule of faith, and will ever do so. For, inspired by God and committed once and for all to writing, they impart the word of God himself without change, and make the voice of the Holy Spirit resound in the words of the prophets and apostles. Therefore, like the Christian religion itself, all the preaching of the Church must be nourished and ruled by sacred Scripture (No. 21).

Easy access to sacred Scripture should be provided for all the Christian faithful. That is why the Church from the very beginning accepted as her own that very ancient Greek translation of the Old Testament which is named after seventy men (the Septuagint); and she has always given a place of honor to other translations, Eastern and Latin, especially the one known as the Vulgate. But since the word of God should be available at all times, the Church with maternal concern sees to it that suitable and correct translations are made into different languages, especially from the original texts of the sacred books. And if, given the opportunity and the approval of Church authority, these translations are produced in cooperation with the separated brethren as well, all Christians will be able to use them (No. 22).

Biblical Studies, Theology

The constitution encouraged the development and progress of biblical studies "under the watchful care of the sacred teaching office of the Church."

It also noted: "Sacred theology rests on the written word of God, together with sacred tradition, as its primary and perpetual foundation," and that "the study of the sacred page is, as it were, the soul of sacred theology" (Nos. 23, 24).

(*See* separate article, **Interpretation of the Bible**.)

THE BIBLE

The Canon of the Bible is the Church's official list of sacred writings. These works, written by men under the inspiration of the Holy Spirit, contain divine revelation and, in conjunction with the tradition and teaching authority of the Church, constitute the rule of Catholic faith. The Canon was fixed and determined by the tradition and teaching authority of the Church.

The Catholic Canon

The Old Testament Canon of 46 books is as follows.
• **The Pentateuch**, the first five books: Genesis (Gn.), Exodus (Ex.), Leviticus (Lv.), Numbers (Nm.), Deuteronomy (Dt.).
• **Historical Books**: Joshua (Jos.), Judges (Jgs.), Ruth (Ru.) 1 and 2 Samuel (Sm.), 1 and 2 Kings (Kgs.), 1 and 2 Chronicles (Chr.), Ezra (Ezr.), Nehemiah (Neh.), Tobit (Tb.), Judith (Jdt.), Esther (Est.), 1 and 2 Maccabees (Mc.).
• **Wisdom Books**: Job (Jb.), Psalms (Ps.), Proverbs (Prv.), Ecclesiastes (Eccl.), Song of Songs (Song), Wisdom (Wis.), Sirach (Sir.).
• **The Prophets**: Isaiah (Is.), Jeremiah (Jer.), Lamentations (Lam.), Baruch (Bar.), Ezekiel (Ez.), Daniel (Dn.), Hosea (Hos.), Joel (Jl.), Amos (Am.), Obadiah (Ob.), Jonah (Jon.), Micah (Mi.), Nahum (Na.), Habakkuk (Hb.), Zephaniah (Zep.), Haggai (Hg.), Zechariah (Zec.) Malachi (Mal.).
The New Testament Canon of 27 books is as follows.
• **The Gospels**: Matthew (Mt.), Mark (Mk.), Luke (Lk.), John (Jn.).
• **The Acts of the Apostles** (Acts).
• **The Pauline Letters**: Romans (Rom.), 1 and 2 Corinthians (Cor.), Galatians (Gal.), Ephesians (Eph.), Philippians (Phil.), Colossians (Col.), 1 and 2 Thessalonians (Thes.) 1 and 2 Timothy (Tm.), Titus (Ti.), Philemon (Phlm.), Hebrews (Heb.).
• **The Catholic Letters**: James (Jas.), 1 and 2 Peter (Pt.), 1, 2, and 3 John (Jn.), Jude (Jude).
• **Revelation** (Rv.).

Developments

The Canon of the Old Testament was firm by the fifth century despite some questioning by scholars. It was stated by a council held at Rome in 382, by African councils held in Hippo in 393 and in Carthage in 397 and 419, and by Innocent I in 405.

All of the New Testament books were generally known and most of them were acknowledged as inspired by the end of the second century. The Muratorian Fragment, dating from about 200, listed most of the books recognized as canonical in later decrees. Prior to the end of the fourth century, however, there was controversy over the inspired character of several works — the Letter to the Hebrews, James, Jude, 2 Peter, 2 and 3 John and Revelation. Controversy ended in the fourth century and these books, along with those about which there was no dispute, were enumerated in the canon stated by the councils of Hippo and Carthage and affirmed by Innocent I in 405.

The Canon of the Bible was solemnly defined by the Council of Trent in the dogmatic decree *De Canonicis Scripturis*, Apr. 8, 1546.

Hebrew and Other Canons

The Hebrew Canon of sacred writings was fixed by tradition and the consensus of rabbis, probably by about 100 A.D. by the Synod or Council of Jamnia and certainly by the end of the second or early in the third century. It consists of the following works in three categories.
• **The Law** (Torah): the five books of Moses: Genesis, Exodus, Leviticus, Numbers, Deuteronomy.
• **The Prophets**: former prophets — Joshua, Judges, 1 and 2 Samuel, 1 and 2 Kings; latter prophets — Isaiah, Jeremiah, Ezekiel, and 12 minor prophets (Hosea, Joel, Amos, Obadiah, Jonah, Micah, Nahum, Habakkuk, Zephaniah, Haggai, Zechariah, Malachi).
• **The Writings**: 1 and 2 Chronicles, Ezra, Nehemiah, Job, Psalms, Proverbs, Ecclesiastes, Song of Songs, Ruth, Esther, Daniel.

This Canon, embodying the tradition and practice of the Palestine community, did not include a number of works contained in the Alexandrian version of sacred writings translated into Greek between 250 and 100 B.C. and in use by Greek-speaking Jews of the Dispersion (outside Palestine). The rejected works, called apocrypha and not regarded as sacred, are: Tobit, Judith, Wisdom, Sirach, Baruch, 1 and 2 Maccabees, the last six chapters of Esther and three passages of Daniel (3:24-90; 13; 14). These books have also been rejected from the Protestant Canon, although they are included in Bibles under the heading "Apocrypha."

The aforementioned books are held to be inspired and sacred by the Catholic Church. In Catholic usage, they are called deuterocanonical because they were under discussion for some time before questions about their canonicity were settled. Books regarded as canonical with little or no debate were called protocanonical. The status of both categories of books is the same in the Catholic Bible.

The Protestant Canon of the Old Testament is the same as the Hebrew.

The Old Testament Canon of some separated Eastern churches differs from the Catholic Canon. Christians are in agreement on the Canon of the New Testament.

Languages

Hebrew, Aramaic and Greek were the original languages of the Bible. Most of the Old Testament books were written in Hebrew. Portions of Daniel, Ezra, Jeremiah, Esther, and probably the books of Tobit and Judith were written in Aramaic. The Book of Wisdom, 2 Maccabees and all the books of the New Testament were written in Greek.

Manuscripts and Versions

The original writings of the inspired authors have been lost. The Bible has been transmitted through ancient copies called manuscripts and through translations or versions.

Authoritative Greek manuscripts include the Sinaitic and Vatican manuscripts of the fourth century and the Alexandrine of the fifth century A.D. The Septuagint and Vulgate translations are in a class by themselves.

The Septuagint version, a Greek translation of the Old Testament for Greek-speaking Jews, was begun about 250 and completed about 100 B.C. The work of several Jewish translators at Alexandria, it differed from the Hebrew Bible in the arrangement of books and included several, later called deuterocanonical, which were not acknowledged as sacred by the community in Palestine.

The Vulgate was a Latin version of the Old and New Testaments produced from the original languages by St. Jerome from about 383 to 404. It became the most widely used Latin text for centuries and was regarded as basic long before the Council of Trent designated it as authentic and suitable for use in public reading, controversy, preaching and teaching. Because of its authoritative character, it became the basis for many translations into other languages. A critical revision was completed by a pontifical commission in 1977.

Hebrew and Aramaic manuscripts of great antiquity and value have figured more significantly than before in recent scriptural work by Catholic scholars, especially since their use was strongly encouraged, if not mandated, in 1943 by Pius XII in the encyclical *Divino Afflante Spiritu.*

The English translation of the Bible in general use among Catholics until well into the 20th century was the Douay-Rheims, so-called because of the places where it was prepared and published, the New Testament at Rheims in 1582 and the Old Testament at Douay in 1609. The translation was made from the Vulgate text. As revised and issued by Bishop Richard Challoner in 1749 and 1750, it became the standard Catholic English version for about 200 years.

A revision of the Challoner New Testament, made on the basis of the Vulgate text by scholars of the Catholic Biblical Association of America, was published in 1941 in the United States under the sponsorship of the Episcopal Committee of the Confraternity of Christian Doctrine.

New American Bible

A new translation of the entire Bible, the first ever made directly into English from the original languages under Catholic auspices, was projected in 1944 and completed in the fall of 1970 with publication of the *New American Bible.* The Episcopal Committee of the Confraternity of Christian Doctrine sponsored the NAB. The translators were members of the Catholic Biblical Association of America and scholars of other faiths. The typical edition was produced by St. Anthony Guild Press, Paterson, N.J.

The *Jerusalem Bible,* published by Doubleday & Co., Inc., is an English translation of a French version based on the original languages.

Biblical translations approved for liturgical use by the National Conference of Catholic Bishops and the Holy See are the *New American Bible* (1970 edition), the *Revised Standard Version-Catholic Edition,* and the *Jerusalem Bible* (1966).

The Protestant counterpart of the *Douay-Rheims Bible* was the *King James Bible,* called the *Authorized Version* in England. Originally published in 1611 and in general use for more than three centuries, its several revisions include the *Revised Standard Version* and the *New Revised Standard Version.*

Biblical Federation

In November 1966, Pope Paul VI commissioned the Secretariat for Promoting Christian Unity to start work for the widest possible distribution of the Bible and to coordinate endeavors toward the production of Catholic-Protestant Bibles in all languages.

The World Catholic Federation for the Biblical Apostolate, established in 1969, sponsors a program designed to create greater awareness among Catholics of the Bible and its use in everyday life.

The U. S. Center for the Catholic Biblical Apostolate is related to the Secretariat for Pastoral Research and Practices, National Conference of Catholic Bishops, 3211 Fourth St. N.E., Washington, D.C. 20017.

APOCRYPHA

In Catholic usage, Apocrypha are books which have some resemblance to the canonical books in subject matter and title but which have not been recognized as canonical by the Church. They are characterized by a false claim to divine authority; extravagant accounts of events and miracles alleged to be supplemental revelation; material favoring heresy (especially in "New Testament" apocrypha); minimal, if any, historical value. Among examples of this type of literature itemized by J. McKenzie, S.J., in *Dictionary of the Bible* are: the Books of Adam and Eve, Martyrdom of Isaiah, Testament of the Patriarchs, Assumption of Moses, Sibylline Oracles; Gospel of James, Gospel of Thomas, Arabic Gospel of the Infancy, History of Joseph the Carpenter; Acts of John, Acts of

Paul, Acts of Peter, Acts of Andrew, and numerous epistles.

Books of this type are called "pseudepigrapha" by Protestants.

In Protestant usage, some books of the Catholic Bible (deuterocanonical) are called apocrypha because their inspired character is rejected.

DEAD SEA SCROLLS

The Qumran Scrolls, popularly called the Dead Sea Scrolls, are a collection of manuscripts, all but one of them in Hebrew, found since 1947 in caves in the Desert of Juda west of the Dead Sea.

Among the findings were a complete text of Isaiah dating from the second century, B.C., more or less extensive fragments of other Old Testament texts (including the deuterocanonical Tobit), and a commentary on Habakkuk. Until the discovery of these materials, the oldest known Hebrew manuscripts were from the 10th century A.D.

Also found were messianic and apocalyptic texts, and other writings describing the beliefs and practices of the Essenes, a rigoristic Jewish sect.

The scrolls, dating from about the first century before and after Christ, are important sources of information about Hebrew literature, Jewish history during the period between the Old and New Testaments, and the history of Old Testament texts. They established the fact that the Hebrew text of the Old Testament was fixed before the beginning of the Christian era and have had definite effects in recent critical studies and translations of the Old Testament. Together with other scrolls found at Masada, they are still the subject of intensive study.

BOOKS OF THE BIBLE

OLD TESTAMENT BOOKS

Pentateuch

The Pentateuch is the collective title of the first five books of the Bible. Substantially, they identify the Israelites as Yahweh's Chosen People, cover their history from Egypt to the threshold of the Promised Land, contain the Mosaic Law and Covenant, and disclose the promise of salvation to come. Principal themes concern the divine promise of salvation, Yahweh's fidelity and the Covenant. Work on the composition of the Pentateuch was completed in the sixth century.

Genesis: The book of origins, according to its title in the Septuagint. In two parts, covers: religious prehistory, including accounts of the origin of the world and man, the original state of innocence and the fall, the promise of salvation, patriarchs before and after the deluge, the Tower of Babel narrative, genealogies (first 11 chapters); the covenant with Abraham and patriarchal history from Abraham to Joseph (balance of the 50 chapters). Significant are the themes of Yahweh's universal sovereignty and mercy.

Exodus: Named with the Greek word for departure, is a religious epic which describes the oppression of the 12 tribes in Egypt and their departure, liberation or passover therefrom under the leadership of Moses; Yahweh's establishment of the covenant with them, making them his chosen people, through the mediation of Moses at Mt. Sinai; instructions concerning the tabernacle, the sanctuary and Ark of the Covenant; the institution of the priesthood. The book is significant because of its theology of liberation and redemption. In Christian interpretation, the Exodus is a figure of baptism.

Leviticus: Mainly legislative in theme and purpose, contains laws regarding sacrifices, ceremonies of ordination and the priesthood of Aaron, legal purity, the holiness code, atonement, the redemption of offerings and other subjects. Summarily, Levitical laws provided directives for all aspects of religious observance and for the manner in which the Israelites were to conduct themselves with respect to Yahweh and each other. Leviticus was the liturgical handbook of the priesthood.

Numbers: Taking its name from censuses recounted at the beginning and near the end, is a continuation of Exodus. It combines narrative of the Israelites' desert pilgrimage from Sinai to the border of Canaan with laws related to and expansive of those in Leviticus.

Deuteronomy: The concluding book of the Pentateuch, recapitulates, in the form of a testament of Moses, the Law and much of the desert history of the Israelites; enjoins fidelity to the Law as the key to good or bad fortune for the people; gives an account of the commissioning of Joshua as the successor of Moses. Notable themes concern the election of Israel by Yahweh, observance of the Law, prohibitions against the worship of foreign gods, worship of and confidence in Yahweh, the power of Yahweh in nature. The Deuteronomic Code or motif, embodying all of these elements, was the norm for interpreting Israelite history.

Joshua, Judges, Ruth

Joshua: Records the fulfillment of Yahweh's promise to the Israelites in their conquest, occupation and division of Canaan under the leadership of Joshua. It also contains an account of the return of Transjordanian Israelites and of a renewal of the Covenant. It was redacted in final form probably in the sixth century or later.

Judges: Records the actions of charismatic leaders, called judges, of the tribes of Israel between the death of Joshua and the time of Samuel, and a crisis of idolatry among the people. The basic themes are sin and punishment, repentance and deliverance; its purpose was in line with the Deuteronomic motif, that the fortunes of the Israelites were related to their observance or non-observance of the Law and the Covenant. It was redacted in final form probably in the sixth century.

Ruth: Named for the Gentile (Moabite) woman who, through marriage with Boaz, became an Israelite and an ancestress of David (her son, Obed, became his grandfather). Themes are filial piety, faith and trust in Yahweh, the universality of messianic salvation. Dates ranging from c. 950 to the seventh century have been assigned to the origin of the book, whose author is unknown.

Historical Books

These books, while they contain a great deal of factual material, are unique in their preoccupation with presenting and interpreting it, in the Deuteronomic manner, in primary relation to the Covenant on which the nation of Israel was founded and in accordance with which community and personal life were judged.

The books are: Samuel 1 and 2, from the end of Judges (c. 1020) to the end of David's reign (c. 961); Kings 1 and 2, from the last days of David to the start of the Babylonian exile and the destruction of the Temple (587); Chronicles 1 and 2, from the reign of Saul (c. 1020-1000) to the return of the people from the exile (538); Ezra and Nehemiah, covering the reorganization of the Jewish community after the exile (458-397); Maccabees 1 and 2, recounting the struggle against attempted suppression of Judaism (168-142).

Three of the books listed below — Tobit, Judith, and Esther — are categorized as religious novels.

Samuel 1 and 2: A single work in concept and contents, containing episodic history of the last two Judges, Eli and Samuel, the establishment and rule of the monarchy under Saul and David, and the political consequences of David's rule. The royal messianic dynasty of David was the subject of Nathan's oracle in 2 Sm. 7. The books were edited in final form probably late in the seventh century or during the exile.

Kings 1 and 2: Cover the last days of David and the career of Solomon, including the building of the Temple and the history of the kingdom during his reign; stories of the prophets Elijah and Elisha; the history of the divided kingdom to the fall of Israel in the North (721) and the fall of Judah in the South (587), the destruction of Jerusalem and the Temple. They reflect the Deuteronomic motif in attributing the downfall of the people to corruption of belief and practice in public and private life. They were completed probably in the sixth century.

Chronicles 1 and 2: A collection of historical traditions interpreted in such a way as to present an ideal picture of one people governed by divine law and united in one Temple worship of the one true God. Contents include genealogical tables from Adam to David, the careers of David and Solomon, coverage of the kingdom of Judah to the exile, and the decree of Cyrus permitting the return of the people and rebuilding of Jerusalem. Both are related to and were written about 400 by the same author, the Chronicler, who composed Ezra and Nehemiah.

Ezra and Nehemiah: A running account of the return of the people to their homeland after the exile and of practical efforts, under the leadership of Ezra and Nehemiah, to restore and reorganize the religious and political community on the basis of Israelite traditions, divine worship and observance of the Law. Events of great significance were the building of the second Temple, the building of a wall around Jerusalem and the proclamation of the Law by Ezra. This restored community was the start of Judaism. Both are related to and were written about 400 by the same author, the Chronicler, who composed Chronicles 1 and 2.

Tobit: Written in the literary form of a novel and having greater resemblance to wisdom than to historical literature, narrates the personal history of Tobit, a devout and charitable Jew in exile, and persons connected with him, viz., his son Tobiah, his kinsman Raguel and Raguel's daughter Sarah. Its purpose was to teach people how to be good Jews. One of its principal themes is patience under trial, with trust in divine Providence which is symbolized by the presence and action of the angel Raphael. It was written about 200.

Judith: Recounts, in the literary form of a historical novel or romance, the preservation of the Israelites from conquest and ruin through the action of Judith. The essential themes are trust in God for deliverance from danger and emphasis on observance of the Law. It was written probably during the Maccabean period.

Esther: Relates, in the literary form of a historical novel or romance, the manner in which Jews in Persia were saved from annihilation through the central role played by Esther, the Jewish wife of Ahasuerus; a fact commemorated by the Jewish feast of Purim. Like Judith, it has trust in Divine Providence as its theme and indicates that God's saving will is sometimes realized by persons acting in unlikely ways. It may have been written near the end of the fourth century.

Maccabees 1 and 2: While related to some extent because of common subject matter, are quite different from each other.

The first book recounts the background and events of the 40-year (175-135) struggle for religious and political freedom led by Judas Maccabaeus and his brothers against the Hellenist Seleucid kings and some Hellenophiles among the Jews. Victory was symbolized by the rededication of the Temple. Against the background of opposition between Jews and Gentiles, the author equated the survival of belief in the one true God with survival of the Jewish people, thus identifying religion with patriotism. It was written probably near the year 100.

The second book supplements the first to some extent, covering and giving a theological interpretation to events from 180 to 162. It explains the feast of the dedication of the Temple, a key event in the survival of Judaism which is commemorated in the feast of Hanukkah; stresses the primacy of God's action in the struggle for survival; and indicates belief in an afterlife and the resurrection of the body. It was completed probably about 124.

Wisdom Books

With the exceptions of Psalms and the Song of Songs, the titles listed under this heading are called "wisdom books" because their purpose was to formulate the fruits of human experience in the context of meditation on sacred Scripture and to present them as an aid toward understanding the problems of life. Hebrew wisdom literature was distinctive from pagan literature of the same type, but it had limitations; these were overcome in the New Testament, which added the dimensions of the New Covenant to those of the Old. Solomon was regarded as the archetype of the wise man.

Job: A dramatic, didactic poem consisting mainly of several dialogues between Job and his friends concerning the mystery involved in the coexistence of the just God, evil and the suffering of the just. It describes an innocent man's experience of suffering and conveys the truth that faith in and submission to God rather than complete understanding, which is impossible, make the experience bearable; also, that the justice of God cannot be defended by affirming that it is realized in this world. Of unknown authorship, it was composed between the seventh and fifth centuries.

Psalms: A collection of 150 religious songs or lyrics reflecting Israelite belief and piety dating from the time of the monarchy to the post-Exilic period, a span of well over 500 years. The psalms, which are a compendium of Old Testament theology, were used in the temple liturgy and for other occasions. They were of several types suitable for the king, hymns, lamentations, expressions of confidence and thanksgiving, prophecy, historical meditation and reflection, and the statement of wisdom. About one-half of them are attributed to David; many were composed by unknown authors.

Proverbs: The oldest book of the wisdom type in the Bible, consisting of collections of sayings attributed to Solomon and other persons regarding a wide variety of subjects including wisdom and its nature, rules of conduct, duties with respect to one's neighbor, the conduct of daily affairs. It reveals many details of Hebrew life. Its nucleus dates from the period before the exile. The extant form of the book dates probably from the end of the fifth century.

Ecclesiastes: A treatise about many subjects whose unifying theme is the vanity of strictly human efforts and accomplishments with respect to the achievement of lasting happiness; the only things which are not vain are fear of the Lord and observance of his commandments. The pessimistic tone of the book is due to the absence of a concept of afterlife. It was written by an unknown author probably in the third century.

Song of Songs: A collection of love lyrics reflecting various themes, including the love of God for Israel and the celebration of ideal love and fidelity between man and woman. It was written by an unknown author after the exile.

Wisdom: Deals with many subjects including the reward of justice; praise of wisdom, a gift of Yahweh proceeding from belief in him and the practice of his Law; the part played by him in the history of his people, especially in their liberation from Egypt; the folly and shame of idolatry. Its contents are taken from the whole sacred literature of the Jews and represent a distillation of its wisdom based on the law, beliefs and traditions of Israel. The last of the Old Testament books, it was written in the early part of the first century before Christ by a member of the Jewish community at Alexandria.

Sirach: Resembling Proverbs, is a collection of sayings handed on by a grandfather to his grandson. It contains a variety of moral instruction and eulogies of patriarchs and other figures in Israelite history. Its moral maxims apply to individuals, the family and community, relations with God, friendship, education, wealth, the Law, divine worship. Its theme is that true wisdom consists in the Law. (It was formerly called Ecclesiasticus, the Church Book, because of its extensive use by the Church for moral instruction.) It was written in Hebrew between 200 and 175, during a period of strong Hellenistic influence, and was translated into Greek after 132.

The Prophets

These books and the prophecies they contain "express judgments of the people's moral conduct, on the basis of the Mosaic alliance between God and Israel. They teach sublime truths and lofty morals. They contain exhortations, threats, announcements of punishment, promises of deliverance. In the affairs of men, their prime concern is the interests of God, especially in what pertains to the Chosen People through whom the Messiah is to come; hence their denunciations of idolatry and of that externalism in worship which exclude the interior spirit of religion. They are concerned also with the universal nature of the moral law, with personal responsibility, with the person and office of the Messiah, and with the conduct of foreign nations" (*The Holy Bible*, Prophetic Books, CCD Edition, 1961; Preface). There are four major (Isaiah, Jeremiah, Ezekiel, Daniel) and twelve minor prophets (distinguished by the length of books), Lamentations and Baruch. Earlier prophets, mentioned in historical books, include Samuel, Gad, Nathan, Elijah, and Elisha.

Before the exile, prophets were the intermediaries through whom God communicated revelation to the people. Afterwards, prophecy lapsed and the written word of the Law served this purpose.

Isaiah: Named for the greatest of the prophets whose career spanned the reigns of three Hebrew kings from 742 to the beginning of the seventh century, in a period of moral breakdown in Judah and threats of invasion by foreign enemies. It is an anthology of poems and oracles credited to him and a number of followers deeply influenced by him. Of special importance are the prophecies concerning Immanuel (6 to 12), including the prophecy of the virgin birth (7:14). Chapters 40 to 55, called Deutero-Isaiah, are attributed to an anonymous poet toward the end of the exile; this portion contains the Songs of the Servant. The concluding part of the book (56-66) contains oracles by later disciples. One of many themes in Isaiah concerned the saving mission of the remnant of Israel in the divine plan of salvation.

Jeremiah: Combines history, biography and prophecy in a setting of crisis caused by internal and external factors, viz., idolatry and general infidelity to the Law among the Israelites and external threats from the Assyrians, Egyptians and Babylonians. Jeremiah prophesied the promise of a new covenant as well as the destruction of Jerusalem and the Temple. His career began in 626 and ended some years after the beginning of the exile. The book, the longest in the Bible, was edited in final form after the exile.

Lamentations: A collection of five laments or elegies over the fall of Jerusalem and the fate of the people in exile, written by an unknown eyewitness. They convey the message that Yahweh struck the people because of their sins and reflect confidence in his love and power to restore his converted people.

Baruch: Against the background of the already-begun exile, it consists of an introduction and several parts: an exile's prayer of confession and petition for forgiveness and the restoration of Israel; a poem praising wisdom and the Law of Moses; a lament in which Jerusalem, personified, bewails the fate of her people and consoles them with the hope of blessings to come; and a polemic against idolatry. Although ascribed to Baruch, Jeremiah's secretary, it was written by several authors, probably in the second century.

Ezekiel: Named for the priest-prophet who prophesied in Babylon from 593 to 571, during the first phase of the exile. To prepare his fellow early exiles for the impending fall of Jerusalem, he reproached the Israelites for past sins and predicted woes to come upon them. After the destruction of the city, the burden of his message was hope and promise of restoration. Ezekiel had great influence on the religion of Israel after the exile.

Daniel: The protagonist is a young Jew, taken early to Babylon where he lived until about 538, who figured in a series of edifying stories which originated in Israelite tradition. The stories, whose characters are not purely legendary but rest on historical tradition, recount the trials and triumphs of Daniel and his three companions, and other episodes including those concerning Susannah, Bel, and the Dragon. The book is more apocalyptic than prophetic: it envisions Israel in glory to come and conveys the message that men of faith can resist temptation and overcome adversity. It states the prophetic themes of right conduct, divine control of men and events, and the final triumph of the kingdom. It was written by an unknown author in the 160s to give moral support to Jews during the persecutions of the Maccabean period.

Hosea: Consists of a prophetic parallel between Hosea's marriage and Yahweh's relations with his people. As the prophet was married to a faithless wife whom he would not give up, Yahweh was bound in Covenant with an idolatrous and unjust Israel whom he would not desert but would chastise for purification. Hosea belonged to the Northern Kingdom of Israel and began his career about the middle of the eighth century. He inaugurated the tradition of describing Yahweh's relation to Israel in terms of marriage.

Joel: Is apocalyptic and eschatological regarding divine judgment, the Day of the Lord, which is symbolized by a ravaging invasion of locusts, the judgment of the nations in the Valley of Josaphat and the outpouring of the Spirit in the messianic era to come. Its message is that God will vindicate and save Israel, in view of the prayer and repentance of the people, and will punish their enemies. It was composed about 400.

Amos: Consists of an indictment against foreign enemies of Israel; a strong denunciation of the people of Israel, whose infidelity, idolatry and injustice made them subject to divine judgment and punishment; and a messianic oracle regarding Israel's restoration. Amos prophesied in the Northern Kingdom of Israel, at Bethel, in the first half of the eighth century; chronologically, he was the first of the canonical prophets.

Obadiah: A 21-verse prophecy, the shortest and one of the sternest in the Bible, against the Edomites, invaders of southern Judah and enemies of those returning from the exile to their homeland. It was probably composed in the fifth century.

Jonah: A parable of divine mercy with the theme that Yahweh wills the salvation of all, not just a few, men who respond to his call. Its protagonist is a disobedient prophet; forced by circumstances beyond his control to preach penance among Gentiles, he is highly successful in his mission but baffled by the divine concern for those who do not belong to the Chosen People. It was written after the exile, probably in the fifth century.

Micah: Attacks the injustice and corruption of priests, false prophets, officials and people; announces judgment and punishment to come; foretells the restoration of Israel; refers to the saving remnant of Israel. Micah was a contemporary of Isaiah.

Nahum: Concerns the destruction of Nineveh in 612 and the overthrow of the Assyrian Empire by the Babylonians.

Habakkuk: Dating from about 605-597, concerns sufferings to be inflicted by oppressors on the people of Judah because of their infidelity to the Lord. It also sounds a note of confidence in the Lord, the Savior, and declares that the just will not perish.

Zephaniah: Exercising his ministry in the second half of the seventh century, during a time of widespread idolatry, superstition and religious degradation, he prophesied impending judgment and punishment for Jerusalem and its people. He prophesied too that a holy remnant of the people (*anawim*, mentioned also by Amos) would be spared. Zephaniah was a forerunner of Jeremiah.

Haggai: One of the first prophets after the exile, Haggai in 520 encouraged the returning exiles to reestablish their community and to complete the second Temple (dedicated in 515), for which he envisioned greater glory, in a messianic sense, than that enjoyed by the original Temple of Solomon.

Zechariah: A contemporary of Haggai, he prophesied in the same vein. A second part of the book, called Deutero-Zechariah and composed by one or more unknown authors, relates a vision of the coming of the Prince of Peace, the Messiah of the Poor.

Malachi: Written by an anonymous author, presents a picture of life in the post-Exilic community between 516 and the initiation of reforms by Ezra and Nehemiah about 432. Blame for the troubles of the community is placed mainly on priests for failure to carry out ritual worship and to instruct the people in the proper manner; other factors were religious indifference and the influence of doubters who were scandalized at the prosperity of the wicked. The vision of a universal sacrifice to be offered to Yahweh (1:11) is interpreted in Catholic theology as a prophecy of the sacrifice of the Mass. Malachi was the last of the minor prophets.

DATES OF THE OLD TESTAMENT

c. 1800 - c. 1600 B.C.: Period of the patriarchs (Abraham, Isaac, Jacob).

c. 1600: Israelites in Egypt.

c. 1250: Exodus of Israelites from Egypt.

c. 1210: Entrance of Israelites into Canaan.

c. 1210-c. 1020: Period of the Judges.

c. 1020-c. 1000: Reign of Saul, first king.

c. 1000-c. 961: Reign of David.

c. 961-922: Reign of Solomon. Temple built during his reign.

922: Division of the Kingdom into Israel (North) and Judah (South).

721: Conquest of Israel by Assyrians.

587-538: Conquest of Judah by Babylonians.

Babylonian Captivity and Exile. Destruction of Jerusalem and the Temple, 587. Captivity ended with the return of exiles, following the decree of Cyrus permitting the rebuilding of Jerusalem.

515: Dedication of the second Temple.

458-397: Restoration and reform of the Jewish religious and political community; building of the Jerusalem wall, 439. Leaders in the movement were Ezra and Nehemiah.

168-142: Period of the Maccabees; war against Syrians.

142: Independence granted to Jews by Demetrius II of Syria.

135-37: Period of the Hasmonean dynasty.

63: Beginning of Roman rule.

37-4: Period of Herod the Great.

NEW TESTAMENT BOOKS

Gospels

The term "Gospel" is derived from the Anglo-Saxon *god-spell* and the Greek *euangelion*, meaning good news, good tidings. In Christian use, it means the good news of salvation proclaimed by Christ and the Church, and handed on in written form in the Gospels of Matthew, Mark, Luke and John.

The initial proclamation of the coming of the kingdom of God was made by Jesus in and through his Person, teachings and actions, and especially through his Passion, death and resurrection. This proclamation became the center of Christian faith and the core of the oral Gospel tradition with which the Church spread the good news by apostolic preaching for some 30 years before it was committed to writing by the Evangelists.

Nature of the Gospels

The historical truth of the Gospels was the subject of an instruction issued by the Pontifical Commission for Biblical Studies Apr. 21, 1964.

• The sacred writers selected from the material at their disposal (the oral Gospel tradition, some written collections of sayings and deeds of Jesus, eyewitness accounts) those things which were particularly suitable to the various conditions (liturgical, catechetical, missionary) of the faithful and the aims they had in mind, and they narrated these things in such a way as to correspond with those circumstances and their aims.

• The life and teaching of Jesus were not simply reported in a biographical manner for the purpose of preserving their memory but were "preached" so as to offer the Church the basis of doctrine concerning faith and morals.

• In their works, the Evangelists presented the true sayings of Jesus and the events of his life in the light of the better understanding they had following their enlightenment by the Holy Spirit. They did not transform Christ into a "mythical" Person, nor did they distort his teaching. Passion narratives are the core of all the Gospels, covering the suffering, death and resurrection of Jesus as central events in bringing about and establishing the New Covenant. Leading up to them are accounts of the mission of John the Baptizer and the ministry of Jesus, especially in Galilee and finally in Jerusalem before the Passion. The infancy of Jesus is covered by Luke and Matthew with narratives inspired in part by appropriate Old Testament citations.

Matthew, Mark and Luke, while different in various respects, have so many similarities that they are called Synoptic; their relationships are the subject of the Synoptic Problem.

Matthew: Written probably between 80 and 100 for Jewish Christians with clear reference to Jewish background and identification of Jesus as the divine Messiah, the fulfillment of the Old Testament. Distinctive are the use of Old Testament citations regarding the Person, activity and teaching of Jesus, and the presentation of doctrine in sermons and discourses.

Mark: Most likely the first of the Gospels, dating from about 70. Written for Gentile Christians, it is noted for the realism and wealth of concrete details with which it reveals Jesus as Son of God and Savior more by his actions and miracles than by his discourses. Theologically, it is less refined than the other Gospels.

Luke: Written about 75 for Gentile Christians. It is noted for the universality of its address, the insight it provides into the Christian way of life, the place it gives to women, the manner in which it emphasizes Jesus' friendship with sinners and compassion for the suffering.

John: Edited and arranged in final form probably between 90 and 100, this is the most sublime and theological of the Gospels, and is different from the Synoptics in plan and treatment. Combining accounts of signs with longer discourses and reflections, it progressively reveals the Person and mission of Jesus — as Word, Way, Truth, Life, Light — in line with the purpose, "to help you believe that Jesus is the Messiah, the Son of God, so that through this faith you may have life in his name" (Jn. 20:31). There are questions about the authorship but no doubt about the Johannine authority and tradition behind the Gospel.

Acts of the Apostles

Written by Luke about 75 as a supplement to his Gospel. It describes the origin and spread of Christian communities through the action of the Holy Spirit from the resurrection of Christ to the time when Paul was placed in custody in Rome in the early 60s.

Letters (Epistles)

These letters, many of which antedated the Gospels, were written in response to existential needs of the early Christian communities for doctrinal and moral instruction, disciplinary action, practical advice, and exhortation to true Christian living.

Pauline Letters

These letters, which comprise approximately one-fourth of the New Testament, are primary and monumental sources of the development of Christian theology. Several of them may not have had Paul as their actual author, but evidence of the Pauline tradition behind them is strong. The letters to the Colossians, Philippians, Ephesians and Philemon have been called the "Captivity Letters" because of a tradition that they were written while Paul was under house arrest or another form of detention.

Romans: Written about 57, probably from Corinth, on the central significance of Christ and faith in him for salvation, and the relationship of Christianity to Judaism; the condition of mankind without Christ; justification and the Christian life; duties of Christians.

Corinthians 1: Written near the beginning of 57 from Ephesus to counteract factionalism and disorders, it covers community dissension, moral irregularities, marriage and celibacy, conduct at religious gatherings, the Eucharist, spiritual gifts (charisms) and their function in the Church, charity, the resurrection of the body.

Corinthians 2: Written later in the same year as 1

Cor., concerning Paul's defense of his apostolic ministry, and an appeal for a collection to aid poor Christians in Jerusalem.

Galatians: Written probably between 54 and 55 to counteract Judaizing opinions and efforts to undermine his authority, it asserts the divine origin of Paul's authority and doctrine, states that justification is not through Mosaic Law but through faith in Christ, insists on the practice of evangelical virtues, especially charity.

Ephesians: Written probably between 61 and 63, mainly on the Church as the Mystical Body of Christ.

Philippians: Written between 56 and 57 or 61 and 63 to warn the Philippians against enemies of their faith, to urge them to be faithful to their vocation and unity of belief, and to thank them for their kindness to him while he was being held in detention.

Colossians: Written probably while he was under house arrest in Rome from 61 to 63, to counteract the influence of self-appointed teachers who were watering down doctrine concerning Christ. It includes two highly important Christological passages, a warning against false teachers, and an instruction on the ideal Christian life.

Thessalonians 1 and 2: Written within a short time of each other probably in 51 from Corinth, mainly on doctrine concerning the *Parousia*, the second coming of Christ.

Timothy 1 and 2, Titus: Written between 65 and 67, or perhaps in the 70s, giving pastoral counsels to Timothy and Titus, who were in charge of churches in Ephesus and Crete, respectively. 1 Tm. emphasizes pastoral responsibility for preserving unity of doctrine; 2 Tm. describes Paul's imprisonment in Rome.

Philemon: A private letter written between 61 and 63 to a wealthy Colossian concerning a slave, Onesimus, who had escaped from him; Paul appealed for kind treatment of the man.

Hebrews: Dating from sometime between 70 and 96, a complex theological treatise on Christology, the priesthood and sacrifice of Christ, the New Covenant, and the pattern for Christian living. Critical opinion is divided as to whether it was addressed to Judaeo or Gentile Christians.

Catholic Letters

These seven letters have been called "catholic" because it was thought for some time, not altogether correctly, that they were not addressed to particular communities.

James: Written sometime before 62 in the spirit of Hebrew wisdom literature and the moralism of Tobit. An exhortation to practical Christian living, it is also noteworthy for the doctrine it states on good works and its citation regarding anointing of the sick.

Peter 1 and 2: The first letter may have been written between 64 and 67 or between 90 and 95; the second may date from 100 to 125. Addressed to Christians in Asia Minor, both are exhortations to perseverance in the life of faith despite trials and difficulties arising from pagan influences, isolation from other Christians and false teaching.

John 1: Written sometime in the 90s and addressed to Asian churches, its message is that God is made known to us in the Son and that fellowship with the Father is attained by living in the light, justice and love of the Son.

John 2: Written sometime in the 90s and addressed to a church in Asia, it commends the people for standing firm in the faith and urges them to perseverance.

John 3: Written sometime in the 90s, it appears to represent an effort to settle a jurisdictional dispute in one of the churches.

Jude: Written probably about 80, it is a brief treatise against erroneous teachings and practices opposed to law, authority and true Christian freedom.

Revelation

Written in the 90s along the lines of Johannine thought, it is a symbolic and apocalyptic treatment of things to come and of the struggle between the Church and evil combined with warning but hope and assurance to the Church regarding the coming of the Lord in glory.

INTERPRETATION OF THE BIBLE

According to the Dogmatic Constitution on Divine Revelation (*Dei Verbum*) issued by the Second Vatican Council, "the interpreter of Sacred Scripture, in order to see clearly what God wanted to communicate to us, should carefully investigate what meaning the sacred writers really intended, and what God wanted to manifest by means of their words" (No. 12).

Hermeneutics, Exegesis

This careful investigation proceeds in accordance with the rules of hermeneutics, the normative science of biblical interpretation and explanation. Hermeneutics in practice is called exegesis.

The principles of hermeneutics are derived from various disciplines and many factors which have to be considered in explaining the Bible and its parts. These include: the original languages and languages of translation of the sacred texts, through philology and linguistics; the quality of texts, through textual criticism; literary forms and genres, through literary and form criticism; cultural, historical, geographical and other conditions which influenced the writers, through related studies; facts and truths of salvation history; the truths and analogy of faith.

Distinctive to biblical hermeneutics, which differs in important respects from literary interpretation in general, is the premise that the Bible, though written by human authors, is the work of divine inspiration in which God reveals his plan for the salvation of men through historical events and persons, and especially through the Person and mission of Christ.

Textual, Form Criticism

Textual criticism is the study of biblical texts, which have been transmitted in copies several times removed from the original manuscripts, for the purpose of establishing the real state of the original texts. This purpose is served by comparison of existing copies; by application to the texts of the disciplines of philology and linguistics; by examination of related works of antiquity; by study of biblical citations in works of the Fathers of the Church and other authors; and by other means of literary study.

Since about 1920, the sayings of Christ have been a particular object of New Testament study, the purpose being to analyze the forms of expression used by the Evangelists in order to ascertain the words actually spoken by him.

Literary Criticism

Literary criticism aims to determine the origin and kinds of literary composition, called forms or genres, employed by the inspired authors. Such determinations are necessary for decision regarding the nature and purpose and, consequently, the meaning of biblical passages. Underlying these studies is the principle that the manner of writing was conditioned by the intention of the authors, the meaning they wanted to convey, and the then-contemporary literary style, mode or medium best adapted to carry their message — e.g., true history, quasi-historical narrative, poems, prayers, hymns, psalms, aphorisms, allegories, discourses. Understanding these media is necessary for the valid interpretation of their message.

Literal Sense

The key to all valid interpretation is the literal sense of biblical passages. Regarding this matter and the relevance to it of the studies and procedures described above, Pius XII wrote the following in the encyclical *Divino Afflante Spiritu:*

"What the literal sense of a passage is, is not always as obvious in the speeches and writings of ancient authors of the East as it is in the works of our own time. For what they wished to express is not to be determined by the rules of grammar and philology alone nor solely by the context; the interpreter must, as it were, go back wholly in spirit to those remote centuries of the East and with the aid of history, archeology, ethnology, and other sciences accurately determine what modes of writing, so to speak, the authors of that ancient period would be likely to use and in fact did use. In explaining the Sacred Scripture and in demonstrating and proving its immunity from all error [the Catholic interpreter] should make a prudent use of this means, determine to what extent the manner of expression or literary mode adopted by the sacred writer may lead to a correct and genuine interpretation; and let him be convinced that this part of his office cannot be neglected without serious detriment to Catholic exegesis."

The literal sense of the Bible is the meaning in the mind of and intended by the inspired writer of a book or passage of the Bible. This is determined by the application to texts of the rules of hermeneutics. It is not to be confused with word-for-word literalism.

Typological Sense

The typological sense is the meaning which a passage has not only in itself but also in reference to something else of which it is a type or foreshadowing. A clear example is the account of the Exodus of the Israelites: in its literal sense, it narrates the liberation of the Israelites from death and oppression in Egypt; in its typical sense, it foreshadowed the liberation of men from sin through the redemptive death and resurrection of Christ. The typical sense of this and other passages emerged in the working out of God's plan of salvation history. It did not have to be in the mind of the author of the original passage.

Accommodated Senses

Accommodated, allegorical and consequent senses are figurative and adaptive meanings given to books and passages of the Bible for moral and other purposes. Such interpretations involve the danger of stretching the literal sense beyond proper proportions. Hermeneutical principles require that interpretations like these respect the integrity of the literal sense of the passages in question.

In the Catholic view, the final word on questions of biblical interpretation belongs to the teaching authority of the Church. In other views, generally derived from basic principles stated by Martin Luther, John Calvin and other reformers, the primacy belongs to individual judgment acting in response to the inner testimony of the Holy Spirit, the edifying nature of biblical subject matter, the sublimity and simplicity of the message of salvation, the intensity with which Christ is proclaimed.

Biblical Studies

The first center for biblical studies, in some strict sense of the term, was the School of Alexandria, founded in the latter half of the second century. It was noted for allegorical exegesis. Literal interpretation was a hallmark of the School of Antioch.

St. Jerome, who produced the Vulgate, and St. Augustine, author of numerous commentaries, were the most important figures in biblical studies during the patristic period. By the time of the latter's death, the Old and New Testament canons had been stabilized. For some centuries afterwards, there was little or no progress in scriptural studies, although commentaries were written, collections were made of scriptural excerpts from the writings of the Fathers of the Church, and the systematic reading of Scripture became established as a feature of monastic life.

Advances were made in the 12th and 13th centuries with the introduction of new principles and methods of scriptural analysis stemming from renewed interest in Hebraic studies and the application of dialectics.

By the time of the Reformation, the Bible had become the first book set in movable type, and more than 100 vernacular editions were in use throughout Europe.

The Council of Trent

In the wake of the Reformation, the Council of Trent formally defined the Canon of the Bible; it also reasserted the authoritative role of tradition and the teaching authority of the Church as well as Scripture with respect to the rule of faith. In the heated atmosphere of the 16th and 17th centuries, the Bible was turned into a polemical weapon; Protestants used it to defend their doctrines, and Catholics countered with citations in support of the dogmas of the Church. One result of this state of affairs was a lack of substantial progress in biblical studies during the period.

Rationalists from the 18th century on and later Modernists denied the reality of the supernatural and doctrine concerning inspiration of the Bible, which they generally regarded as a strictly human production expressive of the religious sense and experience of mankind. In their hands, the tools of positive critical research became weapons for biblical subversion. The defensive Catholic reaction to their work had the temporary effect of alienating scholars of the Church from solid advances in archeology, philology, history, textual and literary criticism.

Catholic Developments

Major influences in bringing about a change in Catholic attitude toward use of these disciplines in biblical studies were two papal encyclicals and two institutes of special study, the *École Biblique*, founded in Jerusalem in 1890, and the Pontifical Biblical Institute established in Rome in 1909. The encyclical *Providentissimus Deus*, issued by Leo XIII in 1893, marked an important breakthrough; in addition to defending the concept of divine inspiration and the formal inspiration of the Scriptures, it encouraged the study of allied and ancillary sciences and techniques for a more fruitful understanding of the sacred writings. The encyclical *Divino Afflante Spiritu*, by Pope Pius XII 50 years later, gave encouragement for the use of various forms of criticism as tools of biblical research. A significant addition to documents on the subject is "The Interpretation of the Bible in the Church," published by the Pontifical Biblical Commission in November, 1993. It presents an overview of approaches to the Bible and probes the question: "Which hermeneutical theory best enables a proper grasp of the profound reality of which Scripture speaks and its meaningful expression for people today?"

The documents encouraged the work of scholars and stimulated wide communication of the fruits of their study.

Great changes in the climate and direction of biblical studies have occurred in recent years. One of them has been an increase in cooperative effort among Catholic, Protestant, Orthodox and Jewish scholars. Their common investigation of the Dead Sea Scrolls is well-known. Also productive has been the collaboration of Catholics and Protestants in turning out various editions of the Bible.

The development and results of biblical studies in this century have directly and significantly affected all phases of the contemporary renewal movement in the Church. Their influence on theology, liturgy, catechetics, and preaching indicate the importance of their function in the life of the Church.

APOSTLES AND EVANGELISTS

The Apostles were the men selected, trained, and commissioned by Christ to preach the Gospel, to baptize, to establish, direct and care for his Church as servants of God and stewards of his mysteries. They were the first bishops of the Church.

St. Matthew's Gospel lists the Apostles in this order: Peter, Andrew, James the Greater, John, Philip, Bartholomew, Thomas, Matthew, James the Less, Jude, Simon, and Judas Iscariot. Matthias was elected to fill the place of Judas. Paul became an Apostle by a special call from Christ. Barnabas was called an Apostle.

Two of the Evangelists, John and Matthew, were Apostles. The other two, Luke and Mark, were closely associated with the apostolic college.

Andrew: Born in Bethsaida, brother of Peter, disciple of John the Baptist, a fisherman, the first Apostle called; according to legend, preached the Gospel in northern Greece, Epirus and Scythia, and was martyred at Patras about 70; in art, is represented with an X-shaped cross, called St. Andrew's Cross; is honored as the patron of Russia and Scotland; Nov. 30.

Barnabas: Originally called Joseph but named Barnabas by the Apostles, among whom he is ranked because of his collaboration with Paul; a Jew of the Diaspora, born in Cyprus; a cousin of Mark and member of the Christian community at Jerusalem, influenced the Apostles to accept Paul, with whom he became a pioneer missionary outside Palestine and Syria, to Antioch, Cyprus, and southern Asia Minor; legend says he was martyred in Cyprus during the Neronian persecution; June 11.

Bartholomew (Nathaniel): A friend of Philip; according to various traditions, preached the Gospel in Ethiopia, India, Persia, and Armenia, where he was martyred by being flayed and beheaded; in art, is depicted holding a knife, an instrument of his death; Aug. 24 (Roman Rite), Aug. 25 (Byzantine Rite).

James the Greater: A Galilean, son of Zebedee, brother of John (with whom he was called a "Son of Thunder"), a fisherman; with Peter and John, witnessed the raising of Jairus's daughter to life, the transfiguration, the agony of Jesus in the Garden of Gethsemane; first of the Apostles to die, by the sword in 44 during the rule of Herod Agrippa; there is doubt about a journey legend says he made to Spain and also about the authenticity of relics said to be his at Santiago de Compostela; in art, is depicted carrying a pilgrim's bell; July 25 (Roman Rite), Apr. 30 (Byzantine Rite).

James the Less: Son of Alphaeus, called "Less" because he was younger in age or shorter in stature than James the Greater; one of the Catholic Epistles bears his name; was stoned to death in 62 or thrown from the top of the temple in Jerusalem and clubbed to death in 66; in art, is depicted with a club or heavy staff; May 3 (Roman Rite), Oct. 9 (Byzantine Rite).

John: A Galilean, son of Zebedee, brother of James the Greater (with whom he was called a "Son of Thunder"), a fisherman, probably a disciple of John the Baptist, one of the Evangelists, called the "Beloved Disciple"; with Peter and James the Greater, witnessed the raising of Jairus's daughter to life, the transfiguration, the agony of Jesus in the Garden of Gethsemane; Mary was commended to his special care by Christ; the fourth Gospel, three Catholic Epistles, and Revelation bear his name; according to various accounts, lived at Ephesus in Asia Minor for some time and died a natural death about 100; in art, is represented by an eagle, symbolic of the sublimity of the contents of his Gospel; Dec. 27 (Roman Rite), May 8 (Byzantine Rite).

Jude Thaddeus: One of the Catholic Epistles, the shortest, bears his name; various traditions say he preached the Gospel in Mesopotamia, Persia, and elsewhere, and was martyred; in art, is depicted with a halberd, the instrument of his death; Oct. 28 (Roman Rite), June 19 (Byzantine Rite).

Luke: A Greek convert to the Christian community, called "our most dear physician" by Paul, of whom he was a missionary companion; author of the third Gospel and Acts of the Apostles; the place — Achaia,

Bithynia, Egypt — and circumstances of his death are not certain; in art, is depicted as a man, a writer, or an ox (because his Gospel starts at the scene of temple sacrifice); Oct. 18.

Mark: A cousin of Barnabas and member of the first Christian community at Jerusalem; a missionary companion of Paul and Barnabas, then of Peter; author of the Gospel which bears his name; according to legend, founded the Church at Alexandria, was bishop there and was martyred in the streets of the city; in art, is depicted with his Gospel and a winged lion, symbolic of the voice of John the Baptist crying in the wilderness, at the beginning of his Gospel; Apr. 25.

Matthew: A Galilean, called Levi by Luke and John and the son of Alphaeus by Mark, a tax collector, one of the Evangelists; according to various accounts, preached the Gospel in Judea, Ethiopia, Persia and Parthia, and was martyred; in art, is depicted with a spear, the instrument of his death, and as a winged man in his role as Evangelist; Sept. 21 (Roman Rite), Nov. 16 (Byzantine Rite).

Matthias: A disciple of Jesus whom the faithful 11 Apostles chose to replace Judas before the Resurrection; uncertain traditions report that he preached the Gospel in Palestine, Cappadocia or Ethiopia; in art, is represented with a cross and a halberd, the instruments of his death as a martyr; May 14 (Roman Rite), Aug. 9 (Byzantine Rite).

Paul: Born at Tarsus, of the tribe of Benjamin, a Roman citizen; participated in the persecution of Christians until the time of his miraculous conversion on the way to Damascus; called by Christ, who revealed himself to him in a special way; became the Apostle of the Gentiles, among whom he did most of his preaching in the course of three major missionary journeys through areas north of Palestine, Cyprus, Asia Minor, and Greece; 14 epistles bear his name; two years of imprisonment at Rome, following initial arrest in Jerusalem and confinement at Caesarea, ended with martyrdom, by beheading, outside the walls of the city in 64 or 67 during the Neronian persecution; in art, is depicted in various ways with St. Peter, with a sword, in the scene of his conversion; June 29 (with St. Peter), Jan. 25 (Conversion).

Peter: Simon, son of Jonah, born in Bethsaida, brother of Andrew, a fisherman; called Cephas or Peter by Christ who made him the chief of the Apostles and head of the Church as his vicar; named first in the listings of Apostles in the Synoptic Gospels and the Acts of the Apostles; with James the Greater and John, witnessed the raising of Jairus's daughter to life, the transfiguration, the agony of Jesus in the Garden of Gethsemane; was the first to preach the Gospel in and around Jerusalem and was the leader of the first Christian community there; established a local church in Antioch; presided over the Council of Jerusalem in 51; wrote two Catholic Epistles to the Christians in Asia Minor; established his see in Rome where he spent his last years and was martyred by crucifixion in 64 or 65 during the Neronian persecution; in art, is depicted carrying two keys, symbolic of his primacy in the Church; June 29 (with St. Paul), Feb. 22 (Chair of Peter).

Philip: Born in Bethsaida; according to legend, preached the Gospel in Phrygia where he suffered martyrdom by crucifixion; May 3 (Roman Rite), Nov. 14 (Byzantine Rite).

Simon: Called the Cananean or the Zealot; according to legend, preached in various places in the Middle East and suffered martyrdom by being sawed in two; in art, is depicted with a saw, the instrument of his death, or a book, symbolic of his zeal for the Law; Oct. 28 (Roman Rite), May 10 (Byzantine Rite).

Thomas (Didymus): Notable for his initial incredulity regarding the Resurrection and his subsequent forthright confession of the divinity of Christ risen from the dead; according to legend, preached the Gospel in places from the Caspian Sea to the Persian Gulf and eventually reached India where he was martyred near Madras; Thomas Christians trace their origin to him; in art, is depicted kneeling before the risen Christ, or with a carpenter's rule and square; feast, July 3 (Roman Rite), Oct. 6 (Byzantine Rite).

Judas: The Gospels record only a few facts about Judas, the Apostle who betrayed Christ. The only non-Galilean among the Apostles, he was from Carioth, a town in southern Judah. He was keeper of the purse in the apostolic band. He was called a petty thief by John. He voiced dismay at the waste of money, which he said might have been spent for the poor, in connection with the anointing incident at Bethany. He took the initiative in arranging the betrayal of Christ. Afterwards, he confessed that he had betrayed an innocent man and cast into the Temple the money he had received for that action. Of his death, Matthew says that he hanged himself; the Acts of the Apostles states that he swelled up and burst open; both reports deal more with the meaning than the manner of his death — the misery of the death of a sinner.

The consensus of speculation over the reason why Judas acted as he did in betraying Christ focuses on disillusionment and unwillingness to accept the concept of a suffering Messiah and personal suffering of his own as an Apostle.

APOSTOLIC FATHERS, FATHERS, DOCTORS OF THE CHURCH

The writers listed below were outstanding and authoritative witnesses to authentic Christian belief and practice, and played significant roles in giving them expression.

Apostolic Fathers

The Apostolic Fathers were Christian writers of the first and second centuries whose writings echo genuine apostolic teaching. Chief in importance are: St. Clement (d. c. 97), bishop of Rome and third successor of St. Peter in the papacy; St. Ignatius (50-c. 107), bishop of Antioch and second successor of St. Peter in that see, reputed to be a disciple of St. John; St. Polycarp (69-155), bishop of Smyrna and a disciple of St. John. The authors of the Didache and the Epistle of Barnabas are also numbered among the Apostolic Fathers.

Other early ecclesiastical writers included: St. Justin, martyr (100-165), of Asia Minor and Rome, a layman and apologist; St. Irenaeus (130-202), bishop of Lyons, who opposed Gnosticism; and St. Cyprian (210-258), bishop of Carthage, who opposed Novatianism.

Fathers and Doctors

The Fathers of the Church were theologians and writers of the first eight centuries who were outstanding for sanctity and learning. They were such authoritative witnesses to the belief and teaching of the Church that their unanimous acceptance of doctrines as divinely revealed has been regarded as evidence that such doctrines were so received by the Church in line with apostolic tradition and Sacred Scripture. Their unanimous rejection of doctrines branded them as heretical. Their writings, however, were not necessarily free of error in all respects.

The greatest of these Fathers were: Sts. Ambrose, Augustine, Jerome, and Gregory the Great in the West; Sts. John Chrysostom, Basil the Great, Gregory of Nazianzus, and Athanasius in the East.

The Doctors of the Church were ecclesiastical writers of eminent learning and sanctity who have been given this title because of the great advantage the Church has derived from their work. Their writings, however, were not necessarily free of error in all respects.

Albert the Great, St. (c. 1200-1280): Born in Swabia, Germany; Dominican; bishop of Regensburg (1260-1262); wrote extensively on logic, natural sciences, ethics, metaphysics, Scripture, systematic theology; contributed to development of Scholasticism; teacher of St. Thomas Aquinas; canonized and proclaimed doctor, 1931; named patron of natural scientists, 1941; called *Doctor Universalis*, *Doctor Expertus*; Nov. 15.

Alphonsus Liguori, St. (1696-1787): Born near Naples, Italy; bishop of Saint Agatha of the Goths (1762-1775); founder of the Redemptorists; in addition to his principal work, *Theologiae Moralis*, wrote on prayer, the spiritual life and doctrinal subjects in response to controversy; canonized, 1839; proclaimed doctor, 1871; named patron of confessors and moralists, 1950; Aug. 1.

Ambrose, St. (c. 340-397): Born in Trier, Germany; bishop of Milan (374-397); one of the strongest opponents of Arianism in the West; his homilies and other writings — on faith, the Holy Spirit, the Incarnation, the sacraments and other subjects — were pastoral and practical; influenced the development of a liturgy at Milan which was named for him; Father and Doctor of the Church; Dec. 7.

Anselm, St. (1033-1109): Born in Aosta, Piedmont, Italy; Benedictine; archbishop of Canterbury (1093-1109); in addition to his principal work, *Cur Deus Homo*, on the atonement and reconciliation of man with God through Christ, wrote about the existence and attributes of God and defended the *Filioque* explanation of the procession of the Holy Spirit from the Father and the Son; proclaimed doctor, 1720; called Father of Scholasticism; Apr. 21.

Anthony of Padua, St. (1195-1231): Born in Lisbon, Portugal; first theologian of the Franciscan Order; preacher; canonized, 1232; proclaimed doctor, 1946; called Evangelical Doctor; June 13.

Athanasius, St. (c. 297-373): Born in Alexandria, Egypt; bishop of Alexandria (328-373); participant in the Council of Nicaea I while still a deacon; dominant opponent of Arians whose errors regarding Christ he refuted in *Apology Against the Arians*, Discourses against the Arians and other works; Father and Doctor of the Church; called Father of Orthodoxy; May 2.

Augustine, St. (354-430): Born in Tagaste, North Africa; bishop of Hippo (395-430) after conversion from Manichaeism; works include the autobiographical and mystical *Confessions*, *City of God*, treatises on the Trinity, grace, passages of the Bible and doctrines called into question and denied by Manichaeans, Pelagians, and Donatists; had strong and lasting influence on Christian theology and philosophy; Father and Doctor of the Church; called Doctor of Grace; Aug. 28.

Basil the Great, St. (c. 329-379): Born in Caesarea, Cappadocia, Asia Minor; bishop of Caesarea (370-379); wrote three books; *Contra Eunomium,* in refutation of Arian errors; a treatise on the Holy Spirit; many homilies, and several rules for monastic life, on which he had lasting influence; Father and Doctor of the Church; called Father of Monasticism in the East; Jan. 2.

Bede the Venerable, St. (c. 673-735): Born in Northumberland, England; Benedictine; in addition to his principal work, *Ecclesiastical History* of the English Nation (covering the period 597-731), wrote scriptural commentaries; regarded as probably the most learned man in Western Europe of his time; called Father of English History; May 25.

Bernard of Clairvaux, St. (c. 1090-1153): Born near Dijon, France; abbot; monastic reformer, called the second founder of the Cistercian Order; mystical theologian with great influence on devotional life; opponent of the rationalism brought forward by Abélard and others; canonized, 1174; proclaimed doctor, 1830; called Mellifluous Doctor because of his eloquence; Aug. 20.

Bonaventure, St. (c. 1217-1274): Born near Viterbo, Italy; Franciscan; bishop of Albano (1273-1274); cardinal; wrote *Itinerarium Mentis in Deum, De Reductione Artium ad Theologiam, Breviloquium*, scriptural commentaries, additional mystical works affecting devotional life, and a life of St. Francis of Assisi; canonized, 1482; proclaimed doctor, 1588; called Seraphic Doctor; July 15.

Catherine of Siena, St. (c. 1347-1380): Born in Siena, Italy; member of the Third Order of St. Dominic; mystic; authored a long series of letters, mainly concerning spiritual instruction and encouragement, to associates, and *Dialogue*, a spiritual testament in four treatises; was active in support of a crusade against the Turks and efforts to end war between papal forces and the Florentine allies; had great influence in inducing Gregory XI to return himself and the Curia to Rome in 1377, to end the Avignon period of the papacy; canonized, 1461; proclaimed the second woman doctor, Oct. 4, 1970; Apr. 29; named a co-patroness of Europe, with St. Edith Stein and St. Bridget of Sweden, on Oct. 1, 1999.

Cyril of Alexandria, St. (c. 376-444): Born in Egypt; bishop of Alexandria (412-444); wrote treatises on the Trinity, the Incarnation and other subjects, mostly in refutation of Nestorian errors; made key contributions to the development of Christology; presided at the Council of Ephesus, 431; proclaimed doctor, 1882; June 27.

Cyril of Jerusalem, St. (c. 315-386): Bishop of Jerusalem from 350; vigorous opponent of Arianism; principal work, *Catecheses*, a pre-baptismal explanation of the creed of Jerusalem; proclaimed doctor, 1882; Mar. 18.

Ephraem, St. (c. 306-373): Born in Nisibis, Mesopotamia; counteracted the spread of Gnostic and Arian errors with poems and hymns of his own composition; wrote also on the Eucharist and Mary; proclaimed doctor, 1920; called Deacon of Edessa and Harp of the Holy Spirit; June 9.

Francis de Sales, St. (1567-1622): Born in Savoy; bishop of Geneva (1602-1622); spiritual writer with strong influence on devotional life through treatises such as *Introduction to a Devout Life*, and *The Love of God*; canonized, 1665; proclaimed doctor, 1877; patron of Catholic writers and the Catholic press; Jan. 24.

Gregory Nazianzen, St. (c. 330-c. 390): Born in Arianzus, Cappadocia, Asia Minor; bishop of Constantinople (381-390); vigorous opponent of Arianism; in addition to five theological discourses on the Nicene Creed and the Trinity for which he is best known, wrote letters and poetry; Father and Doctor of the Church; called the Christian Demosthenes because of his eloquence and, in the Eastern Church, the Theologian; Jan. 2.

Gregory I, the Great, St. (c. 540-604): Born in Rome; pope (590-604): wrote many scriptural commentaries, a compendium of theology in the *Book of Morals* based on Job, Dialogues concerning the lives of saints, the immortality of the soul, death, purgatory, heaven and hell, and fourteen books of letters; enforced papal supremacy and established the position of the pope vis-á-vis the emperor; worked for clerical and monastic reform and the observance of clerical celibacy; Father and Doctor of the Church; Sept. 3.

Hilary of Poitiers, St. (c. 315-368): Born in Poitiers, France; bishop of Poitiers (c. 353-368); wrote *De Synodis*, with the Arian controversy in mind, and *De Trinitate*, the first lengthy study of the doctrine in Latin; introduced Eastern theology to the West; contributed to the development of hymnology; proclaimed doctor, 1851; called the Athanasius of the West because of his vigorous defense of the divinity of Christ against Arians; Jan. 13.

Isidore of Seville, St. (c. 560-636): Born in Cartagena, Spain; bishop of Seville (c. 600-636); in addition to his principal work, *Etymologiae*, an encyclopedia of the knowledge of his day, wrote on theological and historical subjects; regarded as the most learned man of his time; proclaimed doctor, 1722; Apr. 4.

Jerome, St. (c. 343-420): Born in Stridon, Dalmatia; translated the Old Testament from Hebrew into Latin and revised the existing Latin translation of the New Testament to produce the Vulgate version of the Bible; wrote scriptural commentaries and treatises on matters of controversy; regarded as Father and Doctor of the Church from the eighth century; called Father of Biblical Science; Sept. 30.

John Chrysostom, St. (c. 347-407): Born in Antioch, Asia Minor; archbishop of Constantinople (398-407); wrote homilies, scriptural commentaries and letters of wide influence in addition to a classical treatise on the priesthood; proclaimed doctor by the Council of Chalcedon, 451; called the greatest of the Greek Fathers; named patron of preachers, 1909; called Golden-Mouthed because of his eloquence; Sept. 13.

John Damascene, St. (c. 675-c. 749): Born in Dam-

ascus, Syria; monk; wrote Fountain of Wisdom, a three-part work including a history of heresies and an exposition of the Christian faith, three discourses against the Iconoclasts, homilies on Mary, biblical commentaries, and treatises on moral subjects; proclaimed doctor, 1890; called Golden Speaker because of his eloquence; Dec. 4.

John of the Cross, St. (1542-1591): Born in Old Castile, Spain; Carmelite; founder of Discalced Carmelites; one of the greatest mystical theologians, wrote *The Ascent of Mt. Carmel*; *The Dark Night of the Soul*, *The Spiritual Canticle*, *The Living Flame of Love*; canonized, 1726; proclaimed doctor, 1926; called Doctor of Mystical Theology; Dec. 14.

Lawrence of Brindisi, St. (1559-1619): Born in Brindisi, Italy; Franciscan (Capuchin); vigorous preacher of strong influence in the post-Reformation period; 15 tomes of collected works include scriptural commentaries, sermons, homilies and doctrinal writings; canonized, 1881; proclaimed doctor, 1959; July 21.

Leo I, the Great, St. (c. 400-461): Born in Tuscany, Italy; pope (440-461); wrote the *Tome* of Leo, to explain doctrine concerning the two natures and one Person of Christ, against the background of the Nestorian and Monophysite heresies; other works included sermons, letters and writings against the errors of Manichaeism and Pelagianism; was instrumental in dissuading Attila from sacking Rome in 452; proclaimed doctor, 1574; Nov. 10.

Peter Canisius, St. (1521-1597): Born in Nijmegen, Holland; Jesuit; wrote popular expositions of the Catholic faith in several catechisms which were widely circulated in 20 editions in his lifetime alone; was one of the moving figures in the Counter-Reformation period, especially in southern and western Germany; canonized and proclaimed doctor, 1925; Dec. 21.

Peter Chrysologus, St. (c. 400-450): Born in Imola, Italy; served as archbishop of Ravenna (c. 433-450); his sermons and writings, many of which were designed to counteract Monophysitism, were pastoral and practical; proclaimed doctor, 1729; July 30.

Peter Damian, St. (1007-1072): Born in Ravenna, Italy; Benedictine; cardinal; his writings and sermons, many of which concerned ecclesiastical and clerical reform, were pastoral and practical; proclaimed doctor, 1828; Feb. 21.

Robert Bellarmine, St. (1542-1621): Born in Tuscany, Italy; Jesuit; archbishop of Capua (1602-1605); wrote *Controversies*, a three-volume exposition of doctrine under attack during and after the Reformation, two catechisms and the spiritual work, *The Art of Dying Well*; was an authority on ecclesiology and Church-state relations; canonized, 1930; proclaimed doctor, 1931; Sept. 17.

Teresa of Jesus (Ávila), St. (1515-1582): Born in Ávila, Spain; entered the Carmelite Order, 1535; in the early 1560s, initiated a primitive Carmelite reform which greatly influenced men and women religious, especially in Spain; wrote extensively on spiritual and mystical subjects; principal works included her *Autobiography*, *Way of Perfection*, *The Interior Castle*, *Meditations on the Canticle*, *The Foundations*, *Visitation of the Discalced Nuns*; canonized, 1622; proclaimed first woman doctor, Sept. 27, 1970; Oct. 15.

Thérèse of Lisieux, St. (1873-1897): Born in Alençon, Normandy, France; entered the Carmelites at Lisieux in 1888, lived for only nine more years, dying on September 30, 1897 from tuberculosis. Trusting completely in God, a path she described as the "little way," she lived a seemingly ordinary life of a nun, but her spiritual advancement was such that her superiors instructed her to write an autobiography in 1895 (*The Story of a Soul*). One of the most popular and respected saints throughout the twentieth century, she was canonized on May 17, 1925. Pope John Paul II declared her the third woman doctor on Oct. 20, 1997 in the letter *Divini amoris scientia*; her relics also toured the United States, attracting huge crowds; Oct. 1.

Thomas Aquinas, St. (1225-1274): Born near Naples, Italy; Dominican; teacher and writer on virtually the whole range of philosophy and theology; principal works were *Summa contra Gentiles*, a manual and systematic defense of Christian doctrine, and *Summa Theologiae*, a new (at that time) exposition of theology on philosophical principles; canonized, 1323; proclaimed doctor, 1567; called *Doctor Communis, Doctor Angelicus*, the Great Synthesizer because of the way in which he related faith and reason, theology and philosophy (especially that of Aristotle), and systematized the presentation of Christian doctrine; named patron of Catholic schools and education, 1880; Jan. 28.

CREEDS

Creeds are formal and official statements of Christian doctrine. As summaries of the principal truths of faith, they are standards of orthodoxy and are useful for instructional purposes, for actual profession of the faith and for expression of the faith in the liturgy.

The classical creeds are the Apostles' Creed and the Creed of Nicaea-Constantinople. Two others are the Athanasian Creed and the Creed of Pius IV.

Apostles' Creed

Text: I believe in God, the Father almighty, Creator of heaven and earth.

And in Jesus Christ, his only Son, our Lord; who was conceived by the Holy Spirit, born of the Virgin Mary, suffered under Pontius Pilate, was crucified, died, and was buried. He descended into hell; the third day he arose again from the dead; he ascended into heaven, sits at the right hand of God, the Father almighty; from thence he shall come to judge the living and the dead.

I believe in the Holy Spirit, the holy Catholic Church, the communion of saints, the forgiveness of sins, the resurrection of the body, and life everlasting. Amen.

Background: The Apostles' Creed reflects the teaching of the Apostles but is not of apostolic origin. It probably originated in the second century as a rudimentary formula of faith professed by catechumens before the reception of baptism. Baptismal creeds in fourth-century use at Rome and elsewhere in the West closely resembled the present text, which was quoted in a handbook of Christian doctrine written between 710 and 724. This text was in wide use throughout the West by the ninth century. The Apostles' Creed is common to all Christian confessional churches in the West, but is not used in Eastern Churches.

Nicene Creed

The following translation of the Latin text of the Creed was prepared by the International Committee on English in the Liturgy.

Text: *We believe in one God, the Father, the Almighty, maker of heaven and earth, of all that is seen and unseen.*

We believe in one Lord, Jesus Christ, the only Son of God, eternally begotten of the Father, God from God, Light from Light, true God from true God, begotten, not made, one in Being with the Father. Through him all things were made. For us men and for our salvation he came down from heaven: by the power of the Holy Spirit he was born of the Virgin

Mary, and became man. For our sake he was crucified under Pontius Pilate; he suffered, died, and was buried. On the third day he rose again in fulfillment of the Scriptures; he ascended into heaven and is seated at the right hand of the Father. He will come again in glory to judge the living and the dead, and his kingdom will have no end.

We believe in the Holy Spirit, the Lord, the giver of life, who proceeds from the Father and the Son. With the Father and the Son he is worshipped and glorified. He has spoken through the prophets.

We believe in one holy catholic and apostolic Church. We acknowledge one baptism for the forgiveness of sins. We look for the resurrection of the dead, and the life of the world to come. Amen.

Background: The Nicene Creed (Creed of Nicaea-Constantinople) consists of elements of doctrine contained in an early baptismal creed of Jerusalem and enactments of the Council of Nicaea (325) and the Council of Constantinople (381).

Its strong trinitarian content reflects the doctrinal errors, especially of Arianism, it served to counteract. Theologically, it is much more sophisticated than the Apostles' Creed.

Since late in the fifth century, the Nicene Creed has been the only creed in liturgical use in the Eastern Churches. The Western Church adopted it for liturgical use by the end of the eighth century.

The Athanasian Creed

The Athanasian Creed, which has a unique structure, is a two-part summary of doctrine concerning the Trinity and the Incarnation-Redemption bracketed at the beginning and end with the statement that belief in the cited truths is necessary for salvation; it also contains a number of anathemas or condemnatory clauses regarding doctrinal errors. Although attributed to St. Athanasius, it was probably written after his death, between 381 and 428, and may have been authored by St. Ambrose. It is not accepted in the East; in the West, it formerly had place in the Roman-Rite Liturgy of the Hours and in the liturgy for the Solemnity of the Holy Trinity.

Creed of Pius IV

The Creed of Pius IV, also called the Profession of Faith of the Council of Trent, was promulgated in the bull *Injunctum Nobis*, Nov. 13, 1564. It is a summary of doctrine defined by the council concerning: Scripture and tradition, original sin and justification, the

Mass and sacraments, veneration of the saints, indulgences, the primacy of the See of Rome. It was slightly modified in 1887 to include doctrinal formulations of the First Vatican Council.

CHRISTIAN MORALITY

(By Fr. Alfred McBride, O.Praem.)

"Incorporated into Christ by Baptism, Christians are 'dead to sin and alive in Christ Jesus ... ' " (Rom 6:11).

CHRISTIAN MORALITY IS LIFE IN CHRIST

The third part of the *Catechism* focuses on Christian morality. After the Creed as faith professed, and sacraments as faith celebrated, the *Catechism* turns our attention to the faith lived. It deals with this issue in two major sections. The first section establishes the context for Christian morality. The second section analyzes the ten commandments. This approach preserves the *Catechism's* resolute insistence on the primacy of God's initiative through Revelation, salvation, and grace followed by our human response in faith, celebration, and Christian witness. Hence morality does not begin with the rules but with the call to life in Christ and the Holy Spirit. Covenant love comes first, then the response of Christian affection in the life of the commandments. This saves us both from legalism and from piety without practical witness.

The following excerpt from the *Catechism of the Catholic Church* sets the vision for the Christian moral life:

LIFE IN CHRIST

1691 "Christian, recognize your dignity and, now that you share in God's own nature, do not return to your former base condition by sinning. Remember who is your head and of whose body you are a member. Never forget that you have been rescued from the power of darkness and brought into the light of the Kingdom of God."[1]

1692 The Symbol of the faith confesses the greatness of God's gifts to man in his work of creation, and even more in redemption and sanctification. What faith confesses, the sacraments communicate: by the sacraments of rebirth, Christians have become "children of God,"[2] "partakers of the divine nature."[3] Coming to see in the faith their new dignity, Christians are called to lead henceforth a life "worthy of the gospel of Christ."[4] They are made capable of doing so by the grace of Christ and the gifts of his Spirit, which they receive through the sacraments and through prayer.

1693 Christ Jesus always did what was pleasing to the Father,[5] and always lived in perfect communion with him. Likewise Christ's disciples are invited to live in the sight of the Father "who sees in secret,"[6] in order to become "perfect as your heavenly Father is perfect."[7]

1694 Incorporated into Christ by Baptism, Christians are "dead to sin and alive to God in Christ Jesus" and so participate in the life of the Risen Lord.[8] Following Christ and united with him,[9] Christians can strive to be "imitators of God as beloved children, and walk in love"[10] by conforming their thoughts, words and actions to the "mind ... which is yours in Christ Jesus,"[11] and by following his example.[12]

1695 "Justified in the name of the Lord Jesus Christ and in the Spirit of our God,"[13] "sanctified ... [and] called to be saints,"[14] Christians have become the temple of the Holy Spirit.[15] This "Spirit of the Son" teaches them to pray to the Father[16] and, having become their life, prompts them to act so as to bear "the fruit of the Spirit"[17] by charity in action. Healing the wounds of sin, the Holy Spirit renews us interiorly through a spiritual transformation.[18] He enlightens and strengthens us to live as "children of light" through "all that is good and right and true."[19]

1696 The way of Christ "leads to life"; a contrary way "leads to destruction."[20] The Gospel parable of the two ways remains ever present in the catechesis of the Church; it shows the importance of moral decisions for our salvation: "There are two ways, the one of life, the other of death; but between the two, there is a great difference."[21]

1697 Catechesis has to reveal in all clarity the joy and the demands of the way of Christ.[22] Catechesis for the "newness of life"[23] in him should be:

• a catechesis of the Holy Spirit, the interior Master of life according to Christ, a gentle guest and friend who inspires, guides, corrects, and strengthens this life;

• a catechesis of grace, for it is by grace that we are saved and again it is by grace that our works can bear fruit for eternal life;

• a catechesis of the beatitudes, for the way of Christ is summed up in the beatitudes, the only path that leads to the eternal beatitude for which the human heart longs;

• a catechesis of sin and forgiveness, for unless man acknowledges that he is a sinner he cannot know the truth about himself, which is a condition for acting justly; and without the offer of forgiveness he would not be able to bear this truth;

• a catechesis of the human virtues which causes one to grasp the beauty and attraction of right dispositions towards goodness;

• a catechesis of the Christian virtues of faith, hope, and charity, generously inspired by the example of the saints; a catechesis of the twofold commandment of charity set forth in the Decalogue;

• an ecclesial catechesis, for it is through the manifold exchanges of "spiritual goods" in the "communion of saints" that Christian life can grow, develop, and be communicated.

1698 The first and last point of reference of this catechesis will always be Jesus Christ himself, who is "the way, and the truth, and the life."[24] It is by looking to him in faith that Christ's faithful can hope that he himself fulfills his promises in them, and that, by loving him with the same love with which he has loved them, they may perform works in keeping with their dignity: "I ask you to consider that our Lord Jesus Christ is your true head, and that you are one of his members. He belongs to you as the head belongs to its members; all that is his is yours: his spirit, his heart, his body and soul, and all his faculties. You must make use of all these as of your own, to serve, praise, love, and glorify God. You belong to him, as members belong to their head. And so he longs for you to use all that is in you, as if it were his own, for the service and glory of the Father."[25] "For to me, to live is Christ."[26]

FOOTNOTES

1. St. Leo the Great, Sermo 22 in nat. Dom. 3: PL 54, 192C. 2. Jn. 1:12; 1 Jn. 3:1. 3. 2 Pet. 1:4. 4. Phil. 1:27. 5. Cf. Jn. 8:29. 6. Mt. 6:6. 7. Mt. 5:48. 8, Rom. 6:11 and cf. 6:5; cf. Col. 2:12. 9. Cf. Jn. 15:5. 10. Eph. 5:1-2. 11. Phil. 2:5. 12. Cf. Jn. 13:12-16. 13. 1 Cor 6:11. 14. 1 Cor .1:2. 15. Cf. 1 Cor. 6:19. 16. Cf. Gal. 4:6. 17. Gal. 5:22, 25. 18. Cf. Eph. 4:23. 19. Eph. 5:8, 9. 20. Mt. 7:13; cf. Dt. 30: 15-20. 21. Didache 1, 1: SCh 248, 140. 22 .Cf. John Paul II, CT 29. 23. Rom. 6:4. 24. Jn. 14:6. 25. St. John Eudes, Tract. de admirabili corde Jesu, 1, 5. 26. Phil. 1:21.

THE TEN COMMANDMENTS

Any discussions of the commandments should begin with the scene at Sinai where God gave them to us. Read Ex. 19:3-6; 20:1-17. The first event is a covenant experience. God tells Moses how much he has loved the Israelites, in delivering them from slavery by "raising them up on eagles' wings," and is bringing them to freedom. God then offers them a binding covenant of love. He will be their only God and they will be his chosen people. It's like a marriage experience, an exchange of vows between God and Israel.

The next section shows God telling them how to live out the love they have pledged. He gives them the Ten Commandments as the means to live the covenant, to express the love they have promised. The *Catechism* points out that the Ten Commandments are privileged expressions of the natural law, made known to us by reason as well as Divine Revelation. We are obliged in obedience to observe these laws of love, both in serious and light matters. Love is in the details as well as the large matters. We must remember that what God has commanded, he makes possible by his grace.

Jesus set the tone for understanding the importance of the commandments. When a rich young man came to him and asked him what he should do to enter eternal life, Jesus replied, "if you wish to enter into life, keep the commandments" (Mt. 19:17). In another case, someone asked him which were the greatest commandments, Jesus replied, "you shall love the Lord, your God, with all your heart, with all your soul, and with all your mind. This is the greatest and first commandment. The second is like it: You shall love your neighbor as yourself" (Mt. 22:37-39). The first three commandments deal with Christ's call to God with all our being. The last seven commandments show us how to love our neighbors as we love ourselves.

The following excerpt from the *Catechism of the Catholic Church* shows how Jesus taught the importance of the Ten Commandments:

"Teacher, what must I do . . .?"

2052 "Teacher, what good deed must I do, to have eternal life?" To the young man who asked this ques-

tion, Jesus answers first by invoking the necessity to recognize God as the "One there is who is good," as the supreme Good and the source of all good. Then Jesus tells him: "If you would enter life, keep the commandments." And he cites for his questioner the precepts that concern love of neighbor: "You shall not kill, You shall not commit adultery, You shall not steal, You shall not bear false witness, Honor your father and mother." Finally Jesus sums up these commandments positively: "You shall love your neighbor as yourself."[1]

2053 To this first reply Jesus adds a second: "If you would be perfect, go, sell what you possess and give to the poor, and you will have treasure in heaven; and come, follow me."[2] This reply does not do away with the first: following Jesus Christ involves keeping the Commandments. The Law has not been abolished,[3] but rather man is invited to rediscover it in the person of his Master who is its perfect fulfillment. In the three synoptic Gospels, Jesus' call to the rich young man to follow him, in the obedience of a disciple and in the observance of the Commandments, is joined to the call to poverty and chastity.[4] The evangelical counsels are inseparable from the Commandments.

2054 Jesus acknowledged the Ten Commandments, but he also showed the power of the Spirit at work in their letter. He preached a "righteousness [which] exceeds that of the scribes and Pharisees"[5] as well as that of the Gentiles.[6] He unfolded all the demands of the Commandments. "You have heard that it was said to the men of old, 'You shall not kill.' ... But I say to you that every one who is angry with his brother shall be liable to judgment."[7]

2055 When someone asks him, "Which commandment in the Law is the greatest?"[8] Jesus replies: "You shall love the Lord your God with all your heart, and with all your soul, and with all your mind. This is the greatest and first commandment. And a second is like it: You shall love your neighbor as yourself. On these two commandments hang all the Law and the prophets."[9] The Decalogue must be interpreted in light of this twofold yet single commandment of love, he fullness of the Law: "The commandments: 'You shall not commit adultery, You shall not kill, You shall not steal, You shall not covet,' and any other commandment, are summed up in this sentence: 'You shall love your neighbor as yourself.' Love does no wrong to a neighbor; therefore love is the fulfilling of the law."[10]

FOOTNOTES

1. Mt. 19:16-19. 2. Mt. 19:21. 3. Cf. Mt. 5:17. 4. Cf. Mt. 19:6-12, 21, 23-29. 5. Mt. 5:20. 6.Cf. Mt. 5:46-47. 7. Mt. 5:21-22. 8. Mt. 22:36. 9. Mt. 22:37-40; cf. Dt. 6:5; Lv. 19:18. 10. Rom. 13:9-10.

In the traditional Catholic enumeration and according to Dt. 5:6-21, the Commandments are:
1. "I, the Lord, am your God You shall not have other gods besides me. You shall not carve idols."
2. "You shall not take the name of the Lord, your God, in vain."
3. "Take care to keep holy the Sabbath day."
4. "Honor your father and your mother."
5. "You shall not kill."
6. "You shall not commit adultery."

7. "You shall not steal."

8. "You shall not bear dishonest witness against your neighbor."

9. "You shall not covet your neighbor's wife."

10. "You shall not desire your neighbor's house or field, nor his male or female slave, nor his ox or ass, nor anything that belongs to him" (summarily, his goods).

Another version of the Commandments, substantially the same, is given in Ex. 20:1-17.

The traditional enumeration of the Commandments in Protestant usage differs from the above. Thus: two commandments are made of the first, as above; the third and fourth are equivalent to the second and third, as above, and so on; and the 10th includes the ninth and 10th, as above.

Love of God and Neighbor

The first three of the commandments deal directly with man's relations with God, viz.: acknowledgment of one true God and the rejection of false gods and idols; honor due to God and his name; observance of the Sabbath as the Lord's day.

The rest cover interpersonal relationships, viz.: the obedience due to parents and, logically, to other persons in authority, and the obligations of parents to children and of persons in authority to those under their care; respect for life and physical integrity; fidelity in marriage, and chastity; justice and rights; truth; internal respect for faithfulness in marriage, chastity, and the goods of others.

Perfection in Christian Life

The moral obligations of the Ten Commandments are complemented by others flowing from the two-fold law of love, the whole substance and pattern of Christ's teaching, and everything implied in full and active membership and participation in the community of salvation formed by Christ in his Church. Some of these matters are covered in other sections of the *Almanac* under appropriate headings.

Precepts of the Church

The purpose of the precepts of the Church, according to the *Catechism of the Catholic Church*, is "to guarantee to the faithful the indispensable minimum in the spirit of prayer and moral effort, in the growth and love of God and neighbor" (No. 2041).

1. Attendance at Mass on Sundays and holy days of obligation. (Observance of Sundays and holy days of obligation involves refraining from work that hinders the worship due to God.)

2. Confession of sins at least once a year. (Not required by the precept in the absence of serious sin.)

3. Reception of the Eucharist at least during the Easter season (in the U.S., from the first Sunday of Lent to Trinity Sunday).

4. Keep holy the holy days of obligation.

5. Observance of specified days of fasting and abstinence.

There is also an obligation to provide for the material needs of the Church.

CATHOLIC MORAL TEACHINGS OF POPE JOHN PAUL II

On Aug. 6, 1993, Pope John Paul II published his tenth encyclical, Veritatis Splendor *("The Splendor of the Truth") regarding the fundamental truths of the Church's moral teachings. On Mar. 25, 1995, he published his eleventh encyclical,* Evangelium Vitae *("The Gospel of Life"), concerning the value and inviolability of human life. The following material is adapted from* The Encyclicals of John Paul II, *with the kind permission of Rev. J. Michael Miller, C.S.B.*

Veritatis Splendor ("The Splendor of the Truth")

On Aug. 6, 1993, John Paul II signed his tenth encyclical, *Veritatis Splendor,* regarding certain fundamental truths of the Church's moral teaching.[1] Undoubtedly it is the pope's most complex and most discussed document. Since its publication, the encyclical has generated a great deal of comment in the media and among theologians. This is not surprising, since *Veritatis Splendor* is the first-ever papal document on the theological and philosophical foundations of Catholic moral teaching. In this encyclical the pope affirms that divine revelation contains "a specific and determined moral content, universally valid and permanent" (§37.1), which the Magisterium has the competence to interpret and teach.

Six years before, in the apostolic letter *Spiritus Domini* (1987), John Paul had publicly announced his intention to publish a document which would treat "more fully and more deeply the issues regarding the very foundations of moral theology" (§5.1). For several reasons the encyclical's preparation took longer than was first anticipated. First, the pope widely consulted bishops and theologians throughout the world, and various drafts were drawn up. Second, he thought that it was fitting for the encyclical "to be preceded by the *Catechism of the Catholic Church,* which contains a complete and systematic exposition of Christian moral teaching" (§5.3). The *Catechism,* published in 1992, gives a full presentation of the Church's moral doctrine, including that on particular questions, and expounds it in a positive way. *Veritatis Splendor,* on the other hand, limits itself to dealing with the fundamental principles underlying all moral teaching.

But why does John Paul think that an encyclical on moral issues will serve the Church and the world on the threshold of the third millennium? According to him, reflection on the ethical implications of Christian faith, lived from the beginning as the "way" (Acts 22:4), belongs to the full proclamation of the Gospel. Moreover, he is convinced that society is in the throes of a *"crisis of truth"* (§32.2). This crisis has the "most serious implications for the moral life of the faithful and for communion in the Church, as well as for a just and fraternal social life" (§5.2).

The dechristianization of many cultures involves not only a loss of faith but also *"a decline or obscuring of the moral sense"* (§106.2). This new moral situation brings with it "the *confusion between good and evil,* which makes it impossible to build up and to preserve the moral order" (§93.1). The ethical bewilderment of some Catholics has led to "the spread of numerous doubts and objections of a human and psychological, social and cultural, religious and even properly theological nature, with regard to the Church's moral teachings" (§4.2). In an increasingly secular world, believers are "making judgments and decisions [that] often appear extraneous or even contrary to those of the Gospel" (§88.2). Moreover, dissent from Catholic moral teaching often entails "an overall and systematic calling into question of traditional moral doctrine" (§4.2). Thus, as a service to the ethical and spiritual welfare of individuals and cultures, John Paul addresses the basic moral principles handed down by the Christian Tradition.

In order to meet his goal, the pope responds in a constructive way to the contemporary moral crisis by proclaiming "the splendor of the truth." When he announced the forthcoming publication of *Veritatis Splendor,* he described the encyclical's purpose: "It reaffirms the dignity of the human person, created in God's image, and proposes anew the genuine concept of human freedom, showing its essential and constitutive relationship with the truth in accordance with Christ's words: 'The truth will make you free!' (Jn 8:32)."[2] On another occasion, John Paul said that he intended the encyclical to be "a proclamation of truth and a hymn to freedom: values felt strongly by contemporary man and deeply respected by the Church."[3] His primary aim, then, is not to censure specific dissident moral opinions but to proclaim that Christ is "the true and final answer to the problem of morality" (§85).

John Paul sets several specific objectives for the encyclical. First, he wishes "*to reflect on the whole of the Church's moral teaching,*" with the precise goal of recalling certain fundamental truths of Catholic doctrine which, in the present circumstances, risk being distorted or denied" (§4.2, cf. §30.1). Second, he aims to show the faithful "the inviting splendor of that truth which is Jesus Christ himself" (§83.2). Christ alone is the answer to humanity's questions, "the only response fully capable of satisfying the desire of the human heart" (§7.1). Third, if the present crisis is to be successfully resolved, the Magisterium must authoritatively discern "*interpretations of Christian morality which are not consistent with 'sound teaching'*" (2 Tim 4:3)" (§29.4, cf. §27.4). This pastoral discernment of the pope and bishops is necessary as a way of assuring "*the right of the faithful*" to receive Catholic doctrine in its purity and integrity" (§113.2).

The pope addresses *Veritatis Splendor* specifically to his brother bishops. He intends them to be the first, but not exclusive, recipients of the encyclical. John Paul reminds them of their responsibility to safeguard and find "ever new ways of speaking with love and mercy" about "*the path of the moral life*" (§3.1,2).

John Paul II's training in ethics and moral theology is clearly evident in *Veritatis Splendor.* The encyclical's exposition is sometimes highly technical, especially in its analyses and responses to opinions contrary to Church teaching. While some commentators have voiced disagreement about the accuracy of the pope's descriptions of the ethical positions with which he disagrees, they respect his desire to be fair-minded. As we shall see, whenever John Paul deals with an opinion he disagrees with, he first takes great pains to point out what is positive in the view. Only after doing this does he then examine its weaknesses. When unmasking theological and philosophical ideas incompatible with revealed truth, he scrupulously avoids imposing "any particular theological system, still less a philosophical one" (§29.4).

Throughout the encyclical the pope repeatedly draws inspiration from the Bible. Chapter one, structured around the encounter of Jesus with the rich young man (Mt 19:16-21), establishes a biblical foundation for fundamental moral principles. In this chapter the pope wishes to apply the theological method proposed by the Second Vatican Council: "Sacred Scripture remains the living and fruitful source of the Church's moral doctrine" (§28.2, cf. §5.3). Chapter two, on the other hand, uses Scripture chiefly to corroborate positions advanced on the basis of the natural moral law. The beginning of chapter three returns to a more biblical approach; it discusses discipleship in terms of the Paschal Mystery and of martyrdom as the supreme expression of following Christ.

More so than in his other encyclicals, in *Veritatis Splendor* John Paul relies considerably on the teaching of Saint Thomas Aquinas, referring to him directly at least 20 times, and on the teaching of Saint Augustine, citing him 16 times. The pope also mines extensively the documents of Vatican II, especially *Gaudium et Spes,* which he cites more than 25 times. Except for one reference to Saint Alphonsus Liguori and a single direct citation of John Henry Newman, the pope mentions no moral philosopher or theologian after the Middle Ages.

FOOTNOTES

1. *Acta Apostolicae Sedis,* 85 (1993), 1133-1228. 2. *Angelus,* October 3, 1993, *L'Osservatore Romano,* 40 (1993), 1. 3. *Angelus,* October 17, 1993, *L'Osservatore Romano,* 42 (1993), 1.

Evangelium Vitae ("The Gospel of Life")

"The *Gospel of life* is at the heart of Jesus' message" (§1.1). With these words Pope John Paul II begins his eleventh encyclical, *Evangelium Vitae,* published on March 25, 1995.[1] He aptly chose the feast of the Annunciation, which celebrates Mary's welcoming of the Son of God who took flesh in her womb, to issue a document dedicated to the value and inviolability of human life. By taking up the cause of the "great multitude of weak and defenseless human beings" (§5.4), especially unborn children and those at the end of life, the pope continues the defense of human dignity dealt with in his three social encyclicals. *Evangelium Vitae* is an anguished and vigorous response to "*scientifically and systematically programmed threats*" against life (§17.2), assaults which have repercussions on Church teaching, touching upon "the core of her faith in the redemptive Incarnation of the Son of God" (§3.1).

For Pope John Paul II, the cause of life is the cause of the Gospel entrusted to the Church, which is dutybound to raise her voice in the defense of life. His encyclical is a "pressing appeal addressed to each and every person, in the name of God: *respect, protect, love and serve life, every human life!*" (§5.5).

Preparations for the encyclical began in April 1991, when the pope called a special meeting in Rome of the College of Cardinals to discuss current threats to human life. After their deliberations, the cardinals asked him "to reaffirm with the authority of the Successor of Peter the value of human life and its inviolability" (§5.1). As a first response to their request, the pope wrote a personal letter to every bishop, seeking contributions to the planned document. They replied with valuable suggestions, and he incorporated many of their proposals into the encyclical. *Evangelium Vitae*, then, is the fruit of genuine episcopal collegiality. By taking an active part in its preparation, the bishops "bore witness to their unanimous desire to share in the doctrinal and pastoral mission of the Church with regard to the *Gospel of life*" (§5.2).

Unlike *Veritatis Splendor*, which was directed primarily to bishops, John Paul intends *Evangelium Vitae* to be read also by the lay faithful, indeed by all people of good will. Concern for the sacredness of human life is not just a matter for Catholics. "The value at stake," writes the pope, "is one which every human being can grasp by the light of reason" (§101.2). The essential truths of the Gospel of life "are written in the heart of every man and woman," echoing in every human conscience "from the time of creation itself" (§29.3). He insists that anyone who is sincerely open to truth and goodness can discover "the sacred value of human life from its very beginning until its end, and can affirm the right of every human being to have this primary good respected to the highest degree" (§2.2).

The encyclical's style is typically Wojtylan. It intersperses rigorous analysis with prayers and exhortations. As can be seen from the more than three hundred biblical quotations and references, Scripture accompanies the pope's presentation from start to finish, giving *Evangelium Vitae* an inspirational tone and familiar style. He also relies heavily on the Church Fathers. The eighteen patristic quotations that appear in the encyclical reinforce the truths that God is the origin of life, that human beings share in divine life, and that Jesus gave his life so that others might live. As is customary, John Paul frequently cites the documents of the Second Vatican Council — here, more than 25 times. He also makes use of the *Catechism of the Catholic Church*, citing it on 10 occasions.

Of particular significance in *Evangelium Vitae* are the pope's three authoritative doctrinal pronouncements: on the direct and voluntary killing of innocent human life (cf. §57.4), on abortion (cf. §62.3), and on euthanasia (cf. §65.3). In each of these formal statements John Paul recalls, through his ordinary magisterium, that a specific proposition is taught infallibly by the ordinary and universal Magisterium of the College of Bishops in communion with the Successor of Peter. He does not, therefore, call upon the charism which belongs to the Petrine ministry to teach infallibly, as this was defined at the First Vatican Council (1870). Rather, the pope "confirms" or "declares" (as in the case of abortion) a doctrine already taught by the bishops as belonging to the Catholic faith. Thus, there is nothing "new" in the Pope's affirmations, but merely the reiteration of teaching about which a consensus exists in the Episcopal College.

FOOTNOTES

1. *Acta Apostolicae Sedis,* 87 (1995), 401-522.

CATHOLIC SOCIAL DOCTRINE

Nature of the Doctrine

Writing in *Christianity and Social Progress*, Pope John XXIII made the following statement about the nature and scope of the Church's social doctrine as stated in the encyclicals in particular and related writings in general:

"What the Catholic Church teaches and declares regarding the social life and relationships of men is beyond question for all time valid.

"The cardinal point of this teaching is that individual men are necessarily the foundation, cause, and end of all social institutions insofar as they are social by nature, and raised to an order of existence that transcends and subdues nature.

"Beginning with this very basic principle whereby the dignity of the human person is affirmed and defended, Holy Church — especially during the last century and with the assistance of learned priests and laymen, specialists in the field — has arrived at clear social teachings whereby the mutual relationships of men are ordered. Taking general norms into account, these principles are in accord with the nature of things and the changed conditions of man's social life, or with the special genius of our day. Moreover, these norms can be approved by all."

Background

While social concerns have always been a part of the Church's teachings, Catholic social doctrine has been the subject of much consideration since the end of the last century and has been formulated in a progressive manner in a number of authoritative documents starting with the encyclical *Rerum Novarum* ("On Capital and Labor") issued by Leo XIII in 1891. Owing to its significance, the encyclical was called by Pope John XXIII the *magna carta* of Catholic social doctrine.

Other outstanding examples are the encyclicals: *Quadragesimo Anno* ("On Reconstruction of the Social Order") by Pius XI in 1931; *Mater et Magistra* ("Christianity and Social Progress") and *Pacem in Terris* ("Peace on Earth"), by John XXIII in 1961 and 1963, respectively; *Populorum Progressio* ("Development of Peoples"), by Paul VI in 1967; *Laborem Exercens* ("On Human Work"), *Sollicitudo Rei Socialis* ("On Social Concerns") and *Centesimus Annus* ("The 100th Year") by John Paul II in 1981, 1987 and 1991, respectively. Among many other accomplishments of ideological importance in the social field, Pius XII made a distinctive contribution with his formulation of a plan for world peace and order in Christmas messages from 1939 to 1941, and in other documents.

Of particular significance to the contemporary application of social doctrine are the document *Gaudium et Spes* (Pastoral Constitution on the Church in the Modern World) issued by the Second Vatican Council and Pope John Paul II's encyclical letters, *Laborem Exercens* ("On Human Work"), *Sollicitudo Rei Socialis* ("On Social Concerns"), and *Centesimus Annus* ("The 100th Year").

These documents represent the most serious attempts in modern times to systematize the social implications of divine revelation as well as the socially relevant writings of the Fathers and Doctors of the Church. Their contents are theological penetrations into social life, with particular reference to human rights, the needs of the poor and those in underdeveloped countries, and humane conditions of life, freedom, justice and peace. In some respects, they read like juridical documents; essentially, however, they are Gospel-oriented and pastoral in intention.

Gaudium et Spes

Gaudium et Spes ("Pastoral Constitution on the Church in the Modern World") was the last document issued by Vatican Council II (Dec. 7, 1965). The document has as its purpose to search out the signs of God's presence and meaning in and through the events of this time in human history. Accordingly, it deals with the situation of men in present circumstances of profound change, challenge and crisis on all levels of life. It is evenly divided into two main parts: the Church's teaching on humanity in the modern era and urgent problems of the times.

Part One

The first part begins: "The joys and the hopes, the griefs and the anxieties of this age" (No. 1) — a clear indication that the Council Fathers were aware both of the positive nature of the modern world and its many dangers and travails. Further, the council places great emphasis throughout on the human existence, a stress that was quite innovative in its presentation: "According to the almost unanimous opinion of believers and unbelievers alike, all things on earth should be related to man as their center and crown" (No. 12). Having developed an analysis of humanity, the document then offered a thorough summary of traditional Church teaching on human life, complete with discussion of sin, the union of body and soul, and the moral conscience.

There is, as well, a genuinely realistic appraisal of contemporary society, noting the pervasiveness of atheism, adding that its spread can be attributed in part to the fault and carelessness of those within the Church whose actions and failures "must be said to conceal rather than reveal the authentic face of God and religion" (No. 19). Toward the fuller understanding of the place of the Church in the modern world, *Gaudium et Spes* emphasizes the harmony that should exist between the Catholic faith and scientific progress because "earthly matters and the concerns of faith derive from the same God" (No. 36). This does not mean, however, that there ought to be no qualifying elements or restraints to science; the Council Fathers add to this positive statement the provision that such

research, "within every branch of learning," must be "carried out in a genuinely scientific manner and in accord with moral norms" (No. 36). Finally, the first part makes an ecumenical gesture, noting that the Church "holds in high esteem the things which other Christian Churches or ecclesial communities have done...." (No. 40).

Part Two

Part Two offers the practical application of the Church's teaching and message enunciated in Part One. Most pressing is the council's concern for the family, and its treatment of family life and marriage is the most detailed and extensive in the history of the councils of the Church. This leads to study of the deeply troubling presence of contraception. The council reiterates Church instruction in an affirmation of opposition to contraception that would receive even fuller expression in three years in the encyclical *Humanae Vitae*. In the matter of abortion, the document states clearly: "... from the moment of its conception life must be guarded with the greatest care, while abortion and infanticide are unspeakable crimes" (No. 51). In its study of culture, in which the council reminds all humanity that culture and civilization are creations of man, it points out his responsibility over it and his duty to seek that which is above, which entails an "obligation to work with all men in constructing a more human world" (No. 57). Here we have a powerful preface or introduction to the next concerns voiced in *Gaudium et Spes*: the questions of economic life, political systems, and war. In building upon earlier social encyclicals, *Gaudium et Spes* discusses economics as vital to human progress and social development, striking the important balance (developed so masterfully in the later writings of Pope John Paul II) between the rights of an individual to possess goods and the obligation to aid the poor (Nos. 63-72). While declaring the autonomous and independent nature of the Church and politics, the Council Fathers do acknowledge: "There are, indeed, close links between earthly affairs and those aspects of man's condition which transcend this world. The Church herself employs the things of time to the degree that her own proper mission demands" (No. 76). The document goes on to state that "the arms race is an utterly treacherous trap for humanity" (No. 81) and "It is our clear duty, then, to strain every muscle as we work for the time when all war can be completely outlawed by international consent" (No. 82).

SOCIAL DOCTRINE UNDER POPE JOHN PAUL II

Background

Throughout his pontificate, Pope John Paul II has traveled the globe speaking out on all matters of the Church's social teachings and has written a number of important encyclicals that are reflective not only of the Church's traditions of social doctrine but that seek to utilize the teachings of the faith to offer specific points of reflection and solutions to the many pressing problems of the late 20th century. Rooted in Christian anthropology and

Tradition, Scripture, and Magisterium, John Paul's writings have encompassed economic ethics, the rights and dignity of the worker, the primacy of the human person, the place of the family in society and the Church, and the integrative teachings of the Church in the areas of moral and pastoral theology. The three main expressions of his social teachings have been the encyclicals: *Laborem Exercens* (1981); *Sollicitudo Rei Socialis* (1987); and *Centesimus Annus* (1991).

SOCIAL ENCYCLICALS OF POPE JOHN PAUL II

(The following material is adapted from The Encyclicals of John Paul II, *with the kind permission of the Rev. J. Michael Miller, C.S.B.)*

Laborem Exercens

Fascinated as he is by commemorative events, Pope John Paul II marked the ninetieth anniversary of Leo XIII's *Rerum Novarum* (1891) by publishing his first social encyclical, *Laborem Exercens,* on Sept. 14, 1981.[1] Before him, Pius XI in *Quadragesimo Anno* (1931), John XXIII in *Mater et Magistra* (1961), and Paul VI in *Octogesima Adveniens* (1971) had observed the anniversary of Leo's ground-breaking encyclical with documents of their own.

Laborem Exercens is a very personal document. The encyclical has solid roots in the pope's own experience as a worker. It reflects his familiarity with various worlds of work: in mines and factories, in artistic and literary production, in scholarship and pastoral ministry. More particularly, *Laborem Exercens* has its origins in the long debate carried on by the Archbishop of Kracow with Marxist intellectuals. The topics chosen, which include the struggle between capital and labor, ownership of the means of production, and solidarity, as well as the terminology of the encyclical, bear ample witness to this background of controversy. Here, however, he is less concerned with economic systems than with the human person as a "worker." Furthermore, John Paul intended his letter to encourage the Solidarity union movement, which in the early 1980s was the primary motor for effecting social and political change in a Poland under a totalitarian regime.

The style of encyclical is distinctively Wojtylan. It reveals the pope's preference for combining a phenomenological description of experience with philosophical-theological meditation. While he cites the Second Vatican Council's *Gaudium et Spes,* John Paul never directly quotes from any previous social encyclical, not even from *Rerum Novarum.* The encyclical's footnotes are almost entirely biblical, indicating that its primary inspiration is Sacred Scripture. As in his two previous encyclicals, *Redemptor Hominis* (1979) and *Dives in Misericordia* (1980), the pope relies heavily upon the plastic and descriptive language of the Bible, especially from the opening chapters of Genesis, to develop his theme. The encyclical unfolds the meaning of the human vocation to work in light of the biblical text on "subduing the earth" (cf. Gn 1:28). This call to exercise dominion is to be carried out by those created "in the image of God" (Gn 1:27) through their work, which the pope qualifies as "*one of the characteristics that distinguish* man from the rest of creatures" (preface).

Unlike earlier social encyclicals which dealt with a wide range of different questions, *Laborem Exercens* is sharply focused. John Paul chooses a very specific theme — the dignity and role of human work — and explores its many ramifications: "Through work man must earn his daily bread and contribute to the continual advance of science and technology and, above all, to elevating unceasingly the cultural and moral level of the society within which he lives in community with those who belong to the same family" (preface). At the present moment, he believes, the world is faced with important choices. It is "on the eve of new developments in technological, economic, and political conditions which, according to many experts, will influence the world of work and production no less than the industrial revolution of the last century" (§1.3).

A crisis in the meaning of human work is a crucial factor contributing to society's current plight. "Work, as human issue, is at the very center of the 'social question' " (§2.1). Moreover, the pope adds, "human work is *a key*, probably *the essential key*, to the whole social question" (§3.2). It is a problem with ramifications which extend beyond the so-called "working class"; the dimensions of the crisis are universal. Therefore he does not confine his encyclical to a reflection on the work only of industrial or agricultural workers. Instead, he extends it to encompass the work done by every sector of society: management, white-collar workers, scientists, intellectuals, artists, women in the home. "Each and every individual, to the proper extent and in an incalculable number of ways, takes part in the giant process whereby man 'subdues the earth' through his work" (§4.4). To use a favorite expression of the pope's, the world's "workbench" includes all those who labor for their daily bread — all men and women.

As in his two previous encyclicals, John Paul takes up the "way" of the human person, this time with regard to his fundamental activity of work. *Laborem Exercens* is yet another chapter in the pope's book on Christian anthropology. Moreover, since work is a great gift and good for humanity, his tone throughout the encyclical is constructive and exhortatory.

Footnote

1. *Acta Apostolicae Sedis,* 73 (1981), 577-647.

Sollicitudo Rei Socialis

Although signed on Dec. 30, 1987, Pope John Paul II's encyclical "on social concern" was not officially published until Feb. 19, 1988.[1] Like *Laborem Exercens* (1981), this second social encyclical commemorates a previous papal document. *Sollicitudo Rei Socialis* marks the twentieth anniversary of Paul VI's *Populorum Progressio* (1967). But more than merely recalling the relevance and doctrine of Pope Paul's encyclical, it highlights new themes and responds to the problems of development in the Third World which had emerged in the intervening twenty years.

John Paul writes as a teacher, explaining why the proclamation of the Church's social doctrine belongs to her evangelizing mission. He also writes as an informed witness to the increasing injustice and poverty in the world. Lastly, he writes as a defender of human dignity and inalienable rights, and of every person's transcendent vocation to communion with the Triune God.

In some ways *Sollicitudo Rei Socialis* echoes *Laborem Exercens* (1981). John Paul's use of Sacred Scripture, for example, is similar in that he frequently quotes from the opening chapters of Genesis. The differences between the two social encyclicals, however, are noteworthy. Whereas in *Laborem Exercens* (1981) the pope never directly cites *Rerum Novarum* (1891), the encyclical of Leo XIII which it commemorates, throughout *Sollicitudo Rei Socialis* John Paul quotes or refers to *Populorum Progressio* more than forty times. It is his constant point of reference. Second, to support his presentation, the pope marshals statements taken from earlier writings and discourses of his own pontificate, as well as the social teaching of the Second Vatican Council expressed in *Gaudium et Spes*. Third, more than in any other encyclical, John Paul makes use of documents published by the Roman Curia. Especially notable are his six references to the *Instruction on Christian Freedom and Liberation* (1986) issued by the Congregation for the Doctrine of the Faith. He also cites two publications of the Pontifical Commission "Iustitia et Pax": *At the Service of the Human Community: An Ethical Approach to the International Debt Question* (1986) and *The Church and the Housing Problem* (1987).

While *Sollicitudo Rei Socialis* perceptively analyzes the economic, political, social, and cultural dimensions of world development, its perspective is primarily ethical and theological. John Paul rereads *Populorum Progressio* through a moral-spiritual lens. His main concern is to form the consciences of individual men and women, to help them in their task of promoting authentic development "in the light of faith and of the Church's Tradition" (§41.7).

Footnote

1. *Acta Apostolicae Sedis,* 80 (1988), 513-586.

Centesimus Annus

Pope John Paul II issued his ninth encyclical, *Centesimus Annus,* on May 1, 1991.[1] Not surprisingly, the pope chose to mark the centenary of Leo XIII's *Rerum Novarum* (1891) with a document of his own. In the four years since the signing of *Sollicitudo Rei Socialis* (1987) the Berlin Wall had collapsed, and in the light of this event John Paul offers his "rereading" of *Rerum Novarum*. His purpose is twofold. He wishes to recall Leo's contribution to the development of the Church's social teaching and to honor the popes who drew upon the encyclical's "vital energies" in their social teaching.

Centesimus Annus has some interesting peculiarities. First, among all John Paul's encyclicals, it relies the least on citing Sacred Scripture. Its few biblical references are primarily exhortatory or illustrative. For his sources the pope depends mostly on *Rerum Novarum* and on the social encyclicals of his predecessors, as well as on earlier documents and discourses of his own Magisterium. Second, much of the encyclical's content is conditioned by current geopolitical affairs. Indeed, the encyclical reads as if the pope had *Rerum Novarum* in one hand and a diary of the 1989 events sweeping eastern Europe in the other.

Despite the opinions of some commentators, John Paul's primary interest is not to pass judgment on either failed socialism or contemporary capitalism. Above all, in keeping with his desire to articulate a Christian anthropology, he recalls the need for Catholic social doctrine to have a "*correct view of the human person* and of his unique value" (§11.3). Without such a view, he believes, it is impossible to solve today's social, economic, and political problems. The Church's distinctive contribution to meeting these challenges is her vision of the transcendent dignity of the human person created in God's image and redeemed by Christ's blood.

The pope's rereading of Leo XIII encompasses three time frames: "looking back" at *Rerum Novarum* itself, "looking around" at the contemporary situation, and "looking to the future" (§3.1). In looking back, John Paul confirms the enduring principles of Leo's encyclical, principles that belong to the Church's doctrinal inheritance. His "pastoral solicitude" also impels the pope to analyze recent political events from the perspective of the Gospel "in order to discern the new requirements of evangelization" (§3.5).

Even more clearly than in his two previous social encyclicals, *Laborem Exercens* (1981) and *Sollicitudo Rei Socialis* (1987), John Paul clearly distinguishes the authentic doctrine contained in the Church's social teaching from the analysis of contingent historical events. This analysis, he states, "is not meant to pass definitive judgments, since this does not fall *per se* within the Magisterium's specific domain" (§3.5). Whatever comes within the doctrinal sphere, however, "pertains to the Church's evangelizing mission and is an essential part of the Christian message" (§5.5).

Footnote

1. *Acta Apostolicae Sedis,* 83 (1991), 793-867.

SOCIO-ECONOMIC STATEMENTS BY U.S. BISHOPS

Over a period of nearly 80 years, the bishops of the United States have issued a great number of socioeconomic statements reflecting papal documents in a U.S. context.

One such statement, entitled "Economic Justice for All: Social Teaching and the U.S. Economy" was issued in November, 1986. It's contents are related in various ways with the subsequently issued encyclical letter, *Centesimus Annus.* Principles drawn from the bishops' document are given in the following excerpt entitled "A Catholic Framework for Economic Life." Another significant statement, entitled "The Harvest of Justice Is Sown in Peace" (1993) follows.

A Catholic Framework for Economic Life

As followers of Jesus Christ and participants in a powerful economy, Catholics in the United States, are called to work for greater economic justice in the face of persistent poverty, growing income gaps and increasing discussion of economic issues in the United States and around the world. We urge Catholics to use the following ethical framework for economic life as principles for reflection, criteria for judgment and directions for action. These principles are drawn directly from Catholic teaching on economic life.

1. The economy exists for the person, not the person for the economy.

2. All economic life should be shaped by moral principles. Economic choices and institutions must be judged by how they protect or undermine the life and dignity of the human person, support the family and serve the common good.

3. A fundamental moral measure of an economy is how the poor and vulnerable are faring.

4. All people have a right to life and to secure the basic necessities of life (e.g., food, clothing, shelter,

education, health care, safe environment, economic security).

5. All people have the right to economic initiative, to productive work, to just wages and benefits, to decent working conditions as well as to organize and join unions or other associations.

6. All people, to the extent they are able, have a corresponding duty to work, a responsibility to provide for the needs of their families and an obligation to contribute to the broader society.

7. In economic life, free markets have both clear advantages and limits; government has essential responsibilities and limitations; voluntary groups have irreplaceable roles, but cannot substitute for the proper working of the market and the just policies of the state.

8. Society has a moral obligation, including governmental action where necessary, to assure opportunity, meet basic human needs and pursue justice in economic life.

9. Workers, owners, managers, stockholders and consumers are moral agents in economic life. By our choices, initiative, creativity and investment, we enhance or diminish economic opportunity, community life and social justice.

10. The global economy has moral dimensions and human consequences. Decisions on investment, trade, aid and development should protect human life and promote human rights, especially for those most in need wherever they might live on this globe.

The Harvest of Justice Is Sown in Peace

The National Conference of Catholic Bishops, at a meeting Nov. 17, 1993, issued a statement entitled "The Harvest of Justice Is Sown in Peace," marking the 10th anniversary of their earlier pastoral letter, "The Challenge of Peace: God's Promise and Our Response."

The Challenge of Peace

"The challenge of peace today is different, but no less urgent" than in 1983, and the threat of global nuclear war "may seem more remote than at any time in the nuclear age." Questions of peace and war, however, cannot be addressed "without acknowledging that the nuclear question remains of vital political and moral significance."

The statement outlines an agenda for action to guide future advocacy efforts of the bishops' national conference. It also urges that the cause of peace be reflected constantly in liturgical prayers of petition, preaching and Catholic education at all levels.

Confronting the temptation to isolationism in U.S. foreign policy is among "the major challenges peacemakers face in this new era."

Factors in a vision for peace include a commitment to the universal common good and recognition of the imperative of human solidarity.

Nonviolent revolutions in some countries "challenge us to find ways to take into full account the power of organized, active nonviolence."

With respect to just war criteria, the statement says that "important work needs to be done in refining, clarifying and applying the just war tradition to the choices facing our decision-makers in this still violent and dangerous world."

Subjects of concern include humanitarian intervention, deterrence, conscientious objection and the development of peoples.

Presumption against Force

"Our conference's approach, as outlined in 'The Challenge of Peace,' can be summarized in this way:

"1) In situations of conflict our constant commitment ought to be, as far as possible, to strive for justice through nonviolent means.

"2) But when sustained attempts at nonviolent action fail to protect the innocent against fundamental injustice, then legitimate political authorities are permitted as a last resort to employ limited force to rescue the innocent and establish justice."

Lethal Force

"Whether lethal force may be used is governed by the following criteria:

• "Just cause: Force may be used only to correct a grave, public evil, i.e., aggression or massive violation of the basic rights of whole populations.

• "Comparative justice: While there may be rights and wrongs on all sides of a conflict, to override the presumption against the use of force, the injustice suffered by one party must significantly outweigh that suffered by the other.

• "Legitimate authority: Only duly constituted public authorities may use deadly force or wage war.

• "Right intention: Force may be used only in a truly just cause and solely for that purpose.

• "Probability of Success: Arms may not be used in a futile cause or in a case where disproportionate measures are required to achieve success.

• "Proportionality: The overall destruction expected from the use of force must be outweighed by the good to be achieved.

• "Last Resort: Force may be used only after all peaceful alternatives have been seriously tried and exhausted.

"These criteria [of just war], taken as a whole, must be satisfied in order to override the strong presumption against the use of force."

Just War

"The just-war tradition seeks also to curb the violence of war through restraint on armed combat between the contending parties by imposing the following moral standards for the conduct of armed conflict:

• "Noncombatant Immunity: Civilians may not be the object of direct attack, and military personnel must take due care to avoid and minimize indirect harm to civilians.

• "Proportionality: In the conduct of hostilities, efforts must be made to attain military objectives with no more force than is militarily necessary and to avoid disproportionate collateral damage to civilian life and property.

• "Right Intention: Even in the midst of conflict, the aim of political and military leaders must be peace with justice so that acts of vengeance and indiscriminate violence, whether by individuals, military units or governments, are forbidden."

Structures for Justice and Peace

Quoting an address given by Pope John Paul in August, 1993, in Denver, the statement said:

" 'The international community ought to establish more effective structures for maintaining and promoting justice and peace. This implies that a concept of strategic interest should evolve which is based on the full development of peoples — out of poverty and toward a more dignified existence, out of injustice and exploitation toward fuller respect for the human person and the defense of universal rights.'

"As we consider a new vision of the international community, five areas deserve special attention: (1) strengthening global institutions; (2) securing human rights; (3) promoting human development; (4) restraining nationalism and eliminating religious violence; and (5) building cooperative security."

Humanitarian Intervention

"Pope John Paul, citing the 'conscience of humanity and international humanitarian law,' has been outspoken in urging that 'humanitarian intervention is obligatory where the survival of populations and en-

tire ethnic groups is seriously compromised. This is a duty for nations and the international community.' He elaborated on this right and duty of humanitarian intervention in his 1993 annual address to the diplomatic corps (accredited to the Holy See):

" 'Once the possibilities afforded by diplomatic negotiations and the procedures provided for by international agreements and organizations have been put into effect, and that [sic], nevertheless, populations are succumbing to the attacks of an unjust aggressor, states no longer have a 'right to indifference.' It seems clear that their duty is to disarm this aggressor if all other means have proved ineffective. The principles of the sovereignty of states and of noninterference in their internal affairs — which retain all their value — cannot constitute a screen behind which torture and murder may be carried out.' "

THE BLESSED VIRGIN MARY

ROLE OF MARY IN THE MYSTERY OF CHRIST AND THE CHURCH

The following excerpts are from Chapter VIII of the Second Vatican Council's "Constitution on the Church," Lumen Gentium.

Preface

Wishing in his supreme goodness and wisdom to effect the redemption of the world, "when the fullness of time came, God sent his Son, born of a woman, that we might receive the adoption of sons" (Gal. 4:4-5). "He for us men, and for our salvation, came down from heaven, and was incarnate by the Holy Spirit from the Virgin Mary." This divine mystery of salvation is revealed to us and continued in the Church, which the Lord established as his own body. In this Church, adhering to Christ the head and having communion with all his saints, the faithful must also venerate the memory "above all of the glorious and perpetual Virgin Mary. Mother of our God and Lord Jesus Christ." (52)

At the message of the angel, the Virgin Mary received the Word of God in her heart and in her body, and gave Life to the world. Hence, she is acknowledged and honored as being truly the Mother of God and Mother of the Redeemer. Redeemed in an especially sublime manner by reason of the merits of her Son, and united to him by a close and indissoluble tie, she is endowed with the supreme office and dignity of being the Mother of the Son of God. As a result, she is also the favorite daughter of the Father and the temple of the Holy Spirit. Because of this gift of sublime grace, she far surpasses all other creatures, both in heaven and on earth.

At the same time, however, because she belongs to the offspring of Adam, she is one with all human beings in their need for salvation. Indeed, she is "clearly the Mother of the members of Christ since she cooperated out of love so that there might be born in the Church the faithful, who are members of Christ their head. Therefore, she is also hailed as a pre-eminent and altogether singular member of the Church, and as the Church's model and excellent exemplar in faith and charity. Taught by the Holy Spirit, the Catholic Church honors her with filial affection and piety as a

most beloved Mother. (53)

This sacred synod intends to describe with diligence the role of the Blessed Virgin in the mystery of the Incarnate Word and the Mystical Body. It also wishes to describe the duties of redeemed mankind toward the Mother of God, who is the Mother of Christ and Mother of men, particularly of the faithful.

The synod does not, however, have it in mind to give a complete doctrine on Mary, nor does it wish to decide those questions which have not yet been fully illuminated by the work of theologians. (54)

II. The Role of the Blessed Virgin in the Economy of Salvation

The Father of mercies willed that the consent of the predestined Mother should precede the Incarnation so that, just as a woman contributed to death, so also a woman should contribute to life. This contrast was verified in outstanding fashion by the Mother of Jesus. She gave to the world that very Life which renews all things, and she was enriched by God with gifts befitting such a role.

It is no wonder, then, that the usage prevailed among the holy Fathers whereby they called the Mother of God entirely holy and free from all stain of sin, fashioned by the Holy Spirit into a kind of new substance and new creature. Adorned from the first instant of her conception with the splendors of an entirely unique holiness, the Virgin of Nazareth is, on God's command, greeted by an angel messenger as "full of grace" (cf. Lk. 1:28). To the heavenly messenger she replies: "Behold the handmaid of the Lord; be it done to me according to thy word" (Lk. 1:38).

By thus consenting to the divine utterance, Mary, a daughter of Adam, became the Mother of Jesus. Embracing God's saving will with a full heart and impeded by no sin, she devoted herself totally as a handmaid of the Lord to the person and work of her Son. In subordination to him and along with him, by the grace of almighty God she served the mystery of redemption.

Rightly, therefore, the holy Fathers see her as used by God not merely in a passive way but as cooperating in the work of human salvation through free faith and obedience. (56)

This union of the Mother with the Son in the work of salvation was manifested from the time of Christ's virginal conception up to his death. It is shown first of all when Mary, arising in haste to go to visit Elizabeth, was greeted by her as blessed because of her belief in the promise of salvation, while the precursor leaped for joy in the womb of his mother (cf. Lk. 1:41-45). This association was shown also at the birth of our Lord, who did not diminish his Mother's virginal integrity but sanctified it, when the Mother of God joyfully showed her first-born Son to the shepherds and the Magi.

When she presented him to the Lord in the Temple, making the offering of the poor, she heard Simeon foretelling at the same time that her Son would be a sign of contradiction and that a sword would pierce the Mother's soul, that out of many hearts thoughts might be revealed (cf. Lk. 2:34-35). When the Child Jesus was lost and they had sought him sorrowing, his parents found him in the temple, taken up with things which were his Father's business. They did not understand the reply of the Son. But his Mother, to be sure, kept all these things to be pondered over in her heart (cf. Lk. 2:41-51). (57)

In the public life of Jesus, Mary made significant appearances. This was so even at the very beginning, when she was moved with pity at the marriage feast of Cana, and her intercession brought about the beginning of the miracles by Jesus the Messiah (Cf. Jn. 2:1-11). In the course of her Son's preaching, she received his praise when, in extolling a kingdom beyond the calculations and bonds of flesh and blood, he declared blessed (cf. Mk. 3:35 par.; Lk. 11:27-28) those who heard and kept the word of the Lord as she was faithfully doing (cf. Lk. 2:19, 51).

Thus, the Blessed Virgin advanced in her pilgrimage of faith and loyally persevered in her union with her Son unto the cross. There she stood, in keeping with the divine plan (cf. Jn. 19:25), suffering grievously with her only-begotten Son. There she united herself with a maternal heart to his sacrifice, and lovingly consented to the immolation of this Victim whom she herself had brought forth. Finally, the same Christ Jesus dying on the cross gave her as a mother to his disciple. This he did when he said: "Woman, behold your son" (Jn. 19:26-27). (58)

But since it pleased God not to manifest solemnly the mystery of the salvation of the human race until he poured forth the Spirit promised by Christ, we see the apostles before the day of Pentecost "continuing with one mind in prayer with the women and Mary, the Mother of Jesus, and with his brethren" (Acts 1:14). We see Mary prayerfully imploring the gift of the Spirit, who had already overshadowed her in the Annunciation.

Finally, preserved free from all guilt of original sin, the Immaculate Virgin was taken up body and soul into heavenly glory upon the completion of her earthly sojourn. She was exalted by the Lord as Queen of all, in order that she might be the more thoroughly conformed to her Son, the Lord of lords (cf. Rev. 19:16) and the conqueror of sin and death. (59)

III. The Blessed Virgin and the Church

We have but one Mediator, as we know from the words of the Apostle: "For there is one God, and one Mediator between God and men, himself man, Christ Jesus, who gave himself as a ransom for all" (1 Tim. 2:5-6). The maternal duty of Mary toward men in no way obscures or diminishes this unique mediation of Christ, but rather shows its power. For all the saving influences of the Blessed Virgin on men originate, not from some inner necessity, but from the divine pleasure. They flow forth from the superabundance of the merits of Christ, rest on his mediation, depend entirely on it, and draw all their power from it. In no way do they impede the immediate union of the faithful with Christ. Rather, they foster this union. (60)

In an utterly singular way, she (Mary) cooperated by her obedience, faith, hope and burning charity in the Savior's work of restoring supernatural life to souls. For this reason she is a mother to us in the order of grace. (61)

This maternity of Mary in the order of grace began with the consent which she gave in faith at the Annunciation and which she sustained without wavering beneath the cross. This maternity will last without interruption until the eternal fulfillment of all the elect. For, taken up to heaven, she did not lay aside this saving role, but by her manifold acts of intercession continues to win for us gifts of eternal salvation. By her maternal charity, Mary cares for the brethren of her Son who still journey on earth surrounded by dangers and difficulties until they are led to their happy fatherland. Therefore, the Blessed Virgin is invoked by the Church under the titles of Advocate, Auxiliatrix, Adjutrix and Mediatrix. These, however, are to be so understood that they neither take away nor add anything to the dignity and efficacy of Christ the one Mediator.

For no creature could ever be classed with the Incarnate Word and Redeemer. But, just as the priesthood of Christ is shared in various ways both by sacred ministers and by the faithful; and as the one goodness of God is in reality communicated diversely to his creatures: so also the unique mediation of the Redeemer does not exclude but rather gives rise among creatures to a manifold cooperation which is but a sharing in this unique source.

The Church does not hesitate to profess this subordinate role of Mary. She experiences it continuously and commends it to the hearts of the faithful so that, encouraged by this maternal help, they may more closely adhere to the Mediator and Redeemer. (62)

Through the gift and role of divine maternity, Mary is united with her Son, the Redeemer, and with his singular graces and offices. By these, the Blessed Virgin is also intimately united with the Church. As St. Ambrose taught, the Mother of God is a model of the Church in the matter of faith, hope and charity, and perfect union with Christ. For in the mystery of the Church, herself rightly called Mother and Virgin, the Blessed Virgin stands out in eminent and singular fashion as exemplar of both virginity and motherhood. (63)

In the most holy Virgin, the Church has already reached that perfection whereby she exists without spot or wrinkle (cf. Eph. 5:27). Yet, the followers of Christ still strive to increase in holiness by conquering sin. And so they raise their eyes to Mary who shines forth to the whole community of the elect as a model of the virtues. Devotedly meditating on her and contemplating her in the light of the Word made man, the Church with reverence enters more intimately into the supreme mystery of the Incarnation and becomes ever increasingly like her Spouse. (64)

The Church in her apostolic work looks to her who brought forth Christ, conceived by the Holy Spirit and born of the Virgin, so that through the Church Christ may be born and grow in the hearts of the faithful also. The Virgin Mary in her own life lived as an example of that maternal love by which all should be fittingly animated who cooperate in the apostolic mission of the Church on behalf of the rebirth of men. (65)

IV. Devotion to the Blessed Virgin in the Church

Mary was involved in the mystery of Christ. As the most holy Mother of God she was, after her Son, exalted by divine grace above all angels and men. Hence, the Church appropriately honors her with special reverence. Indeed, from most ancient times the Blessed Virgin has been venerated under the title of "Godbearer." In all perils and needs, the faithful; have fled prayerfully to her protection. Especially after the Council of Ephesus the cult of the people of God toward Mary wonderfully increased in veneration and love, in invocation and imitation, according to her own prophetic words: "All generations shall call me blessed; because he who is mighty has done great things for me" (Lk. 1:48).

As it has always existed in the Church, this cult (of Mary) is altogether special, Still, it differs essentially from the cult of adoration which is offered to the Incarnate Word, as well as to the Father and the Holy Spirit. Yet, devotion to Mary is most favorable to this supreme cult. The Church has endorsed many forms of piety toward the Mother of God, provided that they were within the limits of sound and orthodox doctrine. These forms have varied according to the circumstances of time and place, and have reflected the diversity of native characteristics and temperament among the faithful. While honoring Christ's Mother, these devotions cause her Son to be rightly known, loved and glorified, and all his commands observed. Through him all things have their beginning (cf. Col. 1: 15-16) and in him "it has pleased (the eternal Father) that all his fullness should dwell" (Col. 1:19). (66)

This most holy synod deliberately teaches this Catholic doctrine. At the same time, it admonishes all the sons of the Church that the cult, especially the liturgical cult, of the Blessed Virgin, be generously fostered. It charges that practices and exercises of devotion toward her be treasured as recommended by the teaching authority of the Church in the course of centuries.

This synod earnestly exhorts theologians and preachers of the divine word that, in treating of the unique dignity of the Mother of God, they carefully and equally avoid the falsity of exaggeration on the one hand and the excess of narrow-mindedness on the other.

Let the faithful remember, moreover, that true devotion consists neither in fruitless and passing emotion, nor in a certain vain credulity. Rather, it proceeds from the true faith, by which we are led to know the excellence of the Mother of God, and are moved to a filial love toward our Mother and to the imitation of her virtues. (67)

REDEMPTORIS MATER

Redemptoris Mater (Mother of the Redeemer), Pope John Paul II's sixth encyclical letter, is a "reflection on the role of Mary in the mystery of Christ and on her active and exemplary presence in the life of the Church." The letter was published Mar. 25, 1987.

Central to consideration of Mary is the fact that she is the Mother of God (*Theotokos*), since by the power of the Holy Spirit she conceived in her virginal womb and brought into the world Jesus Christ, the Son of God, who is of one being with the Father and the Holy Spirit.

Mary was preserved from original sin in view of her calling to be the Mother of Jesus. She was gifted in grace beyond measure. She fulfilled her role in a unique pilgrimage of faith. She is the Mother of the Church and the spiritual mother of all people.

The following excerpts are from the English text provided by the Vatican and circulated by the CNS Documentary Service, *Origins*, Apr. 9, 1987 (Vol. 16, No. 43). Subheads have been added. Quotations are from pertinent documents of the Second Vatican Council.

Mary's Presence in the Church

Mary, through the same faith which made her blessed, especially from the moment of the Annunciation, is present in the Church's mission, present in the Church's work of introducing into the world the kingdom of her Son.

This presence of Mary finds as many different expressions in our day just as it did throughout the Church's history. It also has a wide field of action: through the faith and piety of individual believers; through the traditions of Christian families or "domestic churches," of parish and missionary communities, religious institutes and dioceses; through the radiance and attraction of the great shrines where not only individuals or local groups, but sometimes whole nations and societies, even whole continents, seek to meet the Mother of the Lord, the one who is blessed because she believed, is the first among believers, and therefore became the Mother of Emmanuel.

This is the message of the land of Palestine, the spiritual homeland of all Christians, because it was the homeland of the Savior of the world and of his Mother.

This is the message of the many churches in Rome and throughout the world which have been raised up in the course of the centuries by the faith of Christians. This is the message of centers like Guadalupe, Lourdes, Fátima and others situated in the various countries. Among them, how could I fail to mention the one in my own native land, Jasna Gora? One could perhaps speak of a specific "geography" of faith and Marian devotion which includes all of these special places of pilgrimage where the people of God seek to meet the Mother of God in order to find, within the radius of the maternal presence of her "who believed," a strengthening of their own faith.

Mary and Ecumenism

"In all of Christ's disciples the Spirit arouses the desire to be peacefully united, in the manner determined by Christ, as one flock under one shepherd." The journey of the Church, especially in our own time, is marked by the sign of ecumenism: Christians are seeking ways to restore that unity which Christ implored from the Father for his disciples on the day before his passion.

Christians must deepen in themselves and each of their communities that "obedience of faith" of which Mary is the first and brightest example.

Christians know that their unity will be truly rediscovered only if it is based on the unity of their faith. They must resolve considerable discrepancies of doctrine concerning the mystery and ministry of the Church, and sometimes also concerning the role of Mary in the work of salvation.

Mary, who is still the model of this pilgrimage, is to lead them to the unity which is willed by their one Lord, and which is so much desired by those who are attentively listening to what "the Spirit is saying to the churches" today.

A Hopeful Sign

Meanwhile, it is a hopeful sign that these churches and ecclesial communities are finding agreement with the Catholic Church on fundamental points of Christian belief, including matters relating to the Virgin Mary. For they recognize her as the Mother of the Lord and hold that this forms part of our faith in Christ, true God and true man. They look to her who at the foot of the cross accepted as her son the Beloved Disciple (John), the one who in his turn accepted her as his Mother.

On the other hand, I wish to emphasize how profoundly the Catholic Church, the Orthodox Church and the ancient churches of the East feel united by love and praise of the *Theotokos*. Not only "basic dogmas of the Christian faith concerning the Trinity and God's Word made flesh of the Virgin Mary were defined in ecumenical councils held in the East," but also in their liturgical worship "the Eastern Christians pay high tribute, in very beautiful hymns, to Mary ever-Virgin. God's most holy Mother."

The churches which profess the doctrine of Ephesus proclaim the Virgin as "true Mother of God" since "our Lord Jesus Christ, born of the Father before time began according to his divinity, in the last days he himself, for our sake and for our salvation, was begotten of Mary the Virgin Mother of God according to his humanity." The Greek Fathers and the Byzantine tradition, contemplating the Virgin in the light of the Word made flesh, have sought to penetrate the depth of that bond which unites Mary, as the Mother of God, to Christ and the Church. The Virgin is a permanent presence in the whole reality of the salvific mystery.

Marian Mediation

The Church knows and teaches with St. Paul that there is only one mediator: "For there is one God, and there is one mediator between God and men, the man Christ Jesus, who gave himself as a ransom for all" (1 Tm. 2:5-6). "The maternal role of Mary toward people in no way obscures or diminishes the unique mediation of Christ, but rather shows its power." It is mediation in Christ.

The Church knows and teaches that "all the saving influences of the Blessed Virgin on mankind originate from the divine pleasure. They flow forth from the superabundance of the merits of Christ, rest on his mediation, depend entirely on it and draw all their power from it. In no way do they impede the immediate union of the faithful with Christ. Rather, they foster this union." This saving influence is sustained by the Holy Spirit, who, just as he overshadowed the Virgin Mary when he began in her the divine motherhood, in a similar way constantly sustains her solicitude for the brothers and sisters of her Son.

Mediation and Motherhood

In effect, Mary's mediation is intimately linked with her motherhood. It possesses a specifically maternal character, which distinguishes it from the mediation of the other creatures who in various and always subordinate ways share in the one mediation of Christ, although her own mediation is also a shared mediation. In fact, while it is true that "no creature could ever be classed with the Incarnate Word and Redeemer," at the same time "the unique mediation of the Redeemer does not exclude but rather gives rise among creatures a manifold cooperation which is but a sharing in this unique source." Thus "the one goodness of God is in reality communicated diversely also in his creatures."

Subordinate Mediation

The teaching of Vatican II presents the truth of Mary's mediation as "a sharing in the one unique source that is the mediation of Christ himself." Thus we read: "The Church does not hesitate to profess this subordinate role of Mary. She experiences it continuously and commends it to the hearts of the faithful so that, encouraged by this maternal help, they may more closely adhere to the Mediator and Redeemer."

This role is at the same time special and extraordinary. It flows from her divine motherhood and can be understood and lived in faith only on the basis of the full truth of this motherhood. Since by virtue of divine election Mary is the earthly Mother of the Father's consubstantial Son and his "generous companion" in the work of redemption, "she is a Mother to us in the order of grace." This role constitutes a real dimension of her presence in the saving mystery of Christ and the Church.

Mary is honored in the Church "with special reverence. Indeed, from most ancient times the Blessed Virgin Mary has been venerated under the title of 'God-bearer.' In all perils and needs, the faithful have fled prayerfully to her protection." This cult is altogether special; it bears in itself and expresses the profound link which exists between the Mother of Christ and the Church. As Virgin and Mother, Mary remains for the Church a "permanent model." It can therefore be said that, especially under this aspect, namely, as a model or rather as a "figure," Mary, present in the mystery of Christ, remains constantly present also in the mystery of the Church. For the Church too is "called mother and virgin," and these names have a profound biblical and theological justification.

Mary and Women

This Marian dimension of Christian life takes on special importance in relation to women and their status. In fact, femininity has a unique relationship with the Mother of the Redeemer, a subject which can be studied in greater depth elsewhere.... The figure of Mary of Nazareth sheds light on womanhood as such by the very fact that God, in the sublime event of the incarnation of his Son, entrusted himself to the ministry, the free and active ministry, of a woman.

... Women, by looking to Mary, find in her the secret of living their femininity with dignity and of achieving their own true advancement. In the light of Mary, the Church sees in the face of women the reflection of a beauty which mirrors the loftiest sentiments of which the human heart is capable: the self-offering totality of love; the strength that is capable of bearing the greatest sorrows; limitless fidelity and tireless devotion to work; the ability to combine penetrating intuition with words of support and encouragement.

APPARITIONS OF THE BLESSED VIRGIN MARY

Seven of the best-known apparitions are described.

Banneux, near Liège, Belgium: Mary appeared eight times between Jan. 15 and Mar. 2, 1933, to an 11-year-old peasant girl, Mariette Beco, in a garden behind the family cottage in Banneux. She called herself the Virgin of the Poor, and has since been venerated as Our Lady of the Poor, the Sick, and the Indifferent. A small chapel was blessed Aug. 15, 1933. Approval of devotion to Our Lady of Banneux was given in 1949 by Bishop Louis J. Kerkhofs of Liège, and a statue of that title was solemnly crowned in 1956.

Beauraing, Belgium: Mary appeared 33 times between Nov. 29, 1932, and Jan. 3, 1933, to five children in the garden of a convent school in Beauraing. A chapel was erected on the spot. Reserved approval of devotion to Our Lady of Beauraing was given Feb. 2, 1943, and final approbation July 2, 1949, by Bishop Charue of Namur (d. 1977).

Fátima, Portugal: Mary appeared six times between May 13 and Oct. 13, 1917, to three children (Lucia dos Santos, 10, who is now a Carmelite nun; Francisco Marto, 9, who died in 1919; and his sister Jacinta, 7, who died in 1920; Jacinta and Francisco were beatified by Pope John Paul II in 2000) in a field called Cova da Iria near Fátima. She recommended frequent recitation of the Rosary; urged works of mortification for the conversion of sinners; called for devotion to herself under the title of her Immaculate Heart; asked that the people of Russia be consecrated to her under this title, and that the faithful make a Communion of reparation on the first Saturday of each month.

The apparitions were declared worthy of belief in October 1930, and devotion to Our Lady of Fátima was authorized under the title of Our Lady of the Rosary. In October, 1942, Pius XII consecrated the world to Mary under the title of her Immaculate Heart. Ten years later, in the first apostolic letter addressed directly to the peoples of Russia, he consecrated them in a special manner to Mary. For more on the Third Secret of Fátima, see below.

Guadalupe, Mexico: Mary appeared four times in 1531 to an Indian, Juan Diego (declared Blessed in 1990), on Tepeyac hill outside of Mexico City, and instructed him to tell Bishop Zumarraga of her wish that a church be built there. The bishop complied with the request about two years later, after being convinced of the genuineness of the apparition by the evidence of a miraculously painted life-size figure of the Virgin on the mantle of the Indian. The mantle bearing the picture has been preserved and is enshrined in the Basilica of Our Lady of Guadalupe. The shrine church, originally dedicated in 1709 and subsequently enlarged, has the title of basilica.

Benedict XIV, in a 1754 decree, authorized a Mass and Office under the title of Our Lady of Guadalupe for celebration on Dec. 12, and named Mary the patroness of New Spain. Our Lady of Guadalupe was designated patroness of Latin America by St. Pius X in 1910 and of the Americas by Pius XII in 1945.

La Salette, France: Mary appeared as a sorrowing and weeping figure Sept. 19, 1846, to two peasant children, Melanie Matthieu, 15, and Maximin Giraud, 11, at La Salette. The message she confided to them, regarding the necessity of penance, was communicated to Pius IX in 1851 and has since been known as the "secret" of La Salette. Bishop de Bruillard of Grenoble declared in 1851 that the apparition was credible, and devotion to Mary under the title of Our Lady of La Salette was authorized. A Mass and Office with this title were authorized in 1942. The shrine church was given the title of minor basilica in 1879.

Lourdes, France: Mary, identifying herself as the Immaculate Conception, appeared 18 times between Feb. 11 and July 16, 1858, to 14-year-old Bernadette Soubirous (canonized in 1933) at the grotto of Massabielle near Lourdes. Her message concerned the necessity of prayer and penance for the conversion of peoples. Mary's request that a chapel be built at the grotto and spring was fulfilled in 1862. Devotion under the title of Our Lady of Lourdes was authorized, and a Feb. 11 feast commemorating the apparitions was instituted by Leo XIII. St. Pius X extended this feast throughout the Church in 1907. The Church of Notre Dame was made a basilica in 1870, and the Church of the Rosary was built later. The underground Church of St. Pius X, with a capacity of 20,000 persons, was consecrated Mar. 25, 1958. Plans were announced in 1994 for renovation and reconstruction of the Lourdes sanctuary.

Our Lady of the Miraculous Medal, France: Mary appeared three times in 1830 to Catherine Labouré (canonized in 1947) in the chapel of the motherhouse of the Daughters of Charity of St. Vincent de Paul, Rue de Bac, Paris. She commissioned Catherine to have made the medal of the Immaculate Conception, now known as the Miraculous Medal, and to spread devotion to her under this title. In 1832, the medal was struck.

THE THIRD SECRET OF FÁTIMA

(Courtesy Vatican Information Service.)

On June 26, 2000, the Holy See Press Office issued the document "The Message Of Fátima" that had been prepared by the Congregation for the Doctrine of the Faith and carried the signatures of Cardinal Joseph Ratzinger and Archbishop Tarcisio Bertone S.D.B., respectively prefect and secretary of the congregation.

The document, which is over 40 pages long, was published in English, French, Italian, Spanish, German, Portuguese and Polish. It was made up of an introduction by Archbishop Bertone; the first and second parts of the "secret" of Fátima in Sr. Lucia's original text dated August 31, 1941, and addressed to the bishop of Leiria-Fátima, and a translation; the photostatic reproduction of the original manuscript of the third part of the "secret" and a translation; John Paul II's letter to Sr. Lucia dated April 19, 2000, and a translation; a summary of Sr. Lucia's conversation with Archbishop Bertone and Bishop Serafim de Sousa Ferreira e Silva of Leiria-Fátima which took place on April 27, 2000, in the Carmel Monastery of St. Teresa of Coimbra, Portugal; the words of Cardinal Secretary of State Angelo Sodano at the end of the beatification of Jacinta and Francisco on May 13, 2000; a theological commentary by Cardinal Ratzinger.

In his introduction, Archbishop Bertone affirms that "Fátima is undoubtedly the most prophetic of modern apparitions.... In 1917 no one could have imagined all this: the three '*pastorinhos*' of Fátima see, listen and remember, and Lucia, the surviving witness, commits it all to paper when ordered to do so by the Bishop of Leiria and with Our Lady's permission."

He continues: "The third part of the 'secret' was written … on January 3, 1944. There is only one manuscript, which is here reproduced photostatically. The sealed envelope was initially in the custody of the Bishop of Leiria. To ensure better protection for the 'secret' the envelope was placed in the secret archives of the Holy Office on April 4, 1957. The Bishop of Leiria informed Sr. Lucia of this."

The secretary of the Congregation for the Doctrine of the Faith indicates that "according to the records of the Archives, the Commissary of the Holy Office, Fr. Pierre Paul Philippe O.P., with the agreement of

Cardinal Alfredo Ottaviani, brought the envelope containing the third part of the 'secret of Fátima' to Pope John XXIII on August 17, 1959. 'After some hesitation,' His Holiness said: 'We shall wait. I shall pray. I shall let you know what I decide.' In fact Pope John XXIII decided to return the sealed envelope to the Holy Office and not to reveal the third part of the 'secret.' Paul VI read the contents with the Substitute, Archbishop Angelo Dell'Acqua, on March 27, 1965, and returned the envelope to the Archives of the Holy Office, deciding not to publish the text. John Paul II, for his part, asked for the envelope containing the third part of the 'secret' following the assassination attempt on May 13, 1981," and this was given to Archbishop Eduardo Martinez Somalo, Substitute of the Secretariat of State, on July 18 of the same year. On August 11 it was returned to the Archives of the Holy Office.

"As is well known," added Archbishop Bertone, "Pope John Paul II immediately thought of consecrating the world to the Immaculate Heart of Mary and he himself composed a prayer for what he called an 'Act of Entrustment' which was to be celebrated in the Basilica of St. Mary Major on June 7 1981."

"In order to respond more fully to the requests of 'Our Lady,' the Holy Father desired to make more explicit during the Holy Year of the Redemption the Act of Entrustment of June 7, 1981, which had been repeated in Fátima on May 13, 1982."

"Sr. Lucia," continued the archbishop, "personally confirmed that this solemn and universal act of consecration corresponded to what Our Lady wished. Hence any further discussion or request is without basis."

Sr. Lucia had already hinted at the interpretation of the third part of the "secret" in a letter to the Holy Father dated May 12, 1982. That letter is also published in the document.

Finally, Archbishop Tarcisio Bertone indicates that "the decision of His Holiness Pope John Paul II to make public the third part of the 'secret' of Fátima brings to an end a period of history marked by tragic human lust for power and evil, yet pervaded by the merciful love of God and the watchful care of the Mother of Jesus and of the Church."

TRANSLATION OF THE THIRD SECRET OF FÁTIMA

On June 26, 2000, the Holy See issued the complete translation of the original Portuguese text of the third part of the secret of Fátima, revealed to the three shepherd children at Cova da Iria-Fátima on July 13, 1917, and committed to paper by Sr. Lucia on January 3, 1944:

"I write in obedience to you, my God, who command me to do so through his Excellency the Bishop of Leiria and through your Most Holy Mother and mine.

"After the two parts which I have already explained, at the left of Our Lady and a little above, we saw an Angel with a flaming sword in his left hand; flashing, it gave out flames that looked as though they would set the world on fire; but they died out in contact with the splendor that Our Lady radiated towards him from her right hand: pointing to the earth with his right

hand, the Angel cried out in a loud voice: 'Penance, Penance, Penance!'. And we saw in an immense light that is God: 'something similar to how people appear in a mirror when they pass in front of it' a Bishop dressed in White 'we had the impression that it was the Holy Father.' Other Bishops, Priests, men and women Religious going up a steep mountain, at the top of which there was a big Cross of rough-hewn trunks as of a cork-tree with the bark; before reaching there the Holy Father passed through a big city half in ruins and half trembling with halting step, afflicted with pain and sorrow, he prayed for the souls of the corpses he met on his way; having reached the top of the mountain, on his knees at the foot of the big Cross he was killed by a group of soldiers who fired bullets and arrows at him, and in the same way there died one after another the other Bishops, Priests, men and women Religious, and various lay people of different ranks and positions. Beneath the two arms of the Cross there were two Angels each with a crystal aspersorium in his hand, in which they gathered up the blood of the Martyrs and with it sprinkled the souls that were making their way to God."

EVENTS AT MEDJUGORJE

The alleged apparitions of the Blessed Virgin Mary to six young people of Medjugorje, Bosnia-Herzogovina, have been the source of interest and controversy since they were first reported in June 1981, initially in the neighboring hillside field, subsequently in the village church of St. James and even in places far removed from Medjugorje.

Reports say the alleged visionaries have seen, heard, and even touched Mary during visions, and that they have variously received several or all of 10 secret messages related to coming world events and urging a quest for peace through penance and personal conversion. An investigative commission appointed by former local Bishop Pavao Zanic of Mostar-Duvno reported in March 1984 that the authenticity of the apparitions had not been verified. He called the apparitions a case of "collective hallucination" exploited by local Franciscan priests at odds with him over control of a parish.

Former Archbishop Frane Franic of Split-Makarska, on the other hand, said in December 1985: "Speaking as a believer and not as a bishop, my personal conviction is that the events at Medjugorje are of supernatural inspiration." He based his conviction on the observations of spiritual benefits related to the reported events, such as the spiritual development of the six young people, the increases in Mass attendance and sacramental practice at the scene of the apparitions, and the incidence of reconciliation among people.

On Jan. 29, 1987, the bishops of Yugoslavia declared: "On the basis of research conducted so far, one cannot affirm that supernatural apparitions are involved" at Medjugorje. Currently, the events at Medjugorje are under on-going investigation by the Holy See to determine their authenticity. Nevertheless, the site of Medjugorje remains a popular destination for Catholic pilgrims from Europe and the United States.

THE CODE OF CANON LAW

Canon Law is the term that denotes the body of laws governing the Catholic Church. The name is derived from the Greek word *kanon* (rule, i.e., rule of practical direction), which, from the fourth century, was used to denote the ordinances and regulations promulgated by the various Church councils that were convened to discuss problems or important topics. The actual term "canon law" (*ius canonicum*) came into use in the 1100s and was intended to differentiate ecclesiastical law from civil law (*ius civile*).

History of Canon Law

In a practical sense, the laws and regulations began to take shape as early as apostolic times and were evident in their nascent form in the Didache, the Didscalia and the Apostolic Tradition. Owing to the persecution of the Church, however, there was little effort to gather laws together, and certainly less time was devoted to systematizing them.

The fourth century brought the Church freedom from persecution and the resulting rapid growth in membership that was a concomitant of the favors bestowed upon the faith by the rulers of the Roman Empire. New laws were naturally needed and desired. Local regulations were soon established through the decrees of the councils, although these most often had only a local authority and adherence. The general (or ecumenical) councils made laws for the whole Church, and the custom developed of carrying on the decrees of previous assemblies by having them read before the start of a new council. Collections of these laws or canons were then undertaken, but these did not bear the weight of being an official code as they were gathered under private authority.

The earliest efforts at collecting Church laws were centered around the private compilation of the decrees of the Eastern councils to which were added those of the Western Church. The councils of the African Church also made lasting contributions, the most significant coming out of the Seventeenth Council of Carthage (419), which accepted the book of canons later adopted into the canon law of both the Eastern and Western Churches. An official Code of Canon Law was recognized in the seventh century under the Isidorian Collection. Other important influences were the writings of monks in England and Ireland. The monks compiled lists of sins and various offenses to which confessors applied the proper fines or penances. The resulting books were called Penitentials, and they offer scholars an invaluable glimpse into the state of Church law in early medieval England and the development of moral theology.

The Carolingian Reforms of the Church under Charlemagne facilitated the enactment of much legislation that was beneficial to the faith, but it also signaled a long period of secular interference in ecclesiastical affairs. Two by-products of this lay intrusion were the creation of the forged but interesting False Decretals (collections of false canons and decrees of the popes used to falsify the Church's position) and the application of legal arguments by Churchmen that could protect the Church from abuse. Efforts at revitalization would become heightened under the Gregorian Reform, in particular with the reign of Pope St. Gregory VII (1073-1085). From that time, throughout the Middle Ages, laws from the Church would be centered in and produced by the papacy, assisted in running the administration of the Church by the Roman Curia.

Gradually, legal experts collected the decrees of popes, enactments of councils, and sources of older, ancient canons. To these were added glosses or commentaries, to assist in the teaching of the details of the subject. Still, the study of canon law was severely handicapped by the sheer number of collections, the contradiction between many points of law, and the inability to find specific laws because of the chronological arrangements of the material. Thus can be seen the major significance of the *Decretum* of Gratian, published around 1148 in Bologna. Compiled by the legal expert Gratian, the *Decretum* (in full, *Concordantia discordantum canonum*) was not a formal collection of canons but sought to provide a juridical system for its readers. Toward this end, though, Gratian examined (and excerpted) virtually every canon ever published. The *Decretum* was quickly adopted as the textbook of canon law, despite the fact that it was a private collection and not codified.

Over the next centuries, the popes added to the body of laws by giving rulings to those questions posed to them by bishops from around the Church. These decretal letters were then brought together and, for purposes of comprehensiveness, added to the *Decretum Gratiani*. The most important of these was the *Liber extra*, the collection made by St. Raymond Peñafort for Pope Gregory IX. This received official approval and was to be a vital source for the *Corpus Juris Canonici*. Other remarkable contributors to canon law in the late Middle Ages were Zenzelinus de Cassanis, Jean Chappuis, Guido de Baysio, John the Teuton (or Joannes Teutonicus), Stephen of Tournai, and most of all, Joannes Andreae (d. 1348).

Considerable activity was initiated by the Council of Trent (1545-1563), which sought to reform and reinvigorate the Church in the wake of the Protestant Reformation. The same century brought the formation in 1588 of the Sacred Congregation of the Curia by Pope Sixtus V (r. 1585-1590), which became the main means of implementing new laws and examining facets of established ones.

The final decision to codify the laws of the Church was made by Pope St. Pius X who, in 1903, issued *Arduum*, the *motu proprio* ordering the complete reform and codification of all canon law. It was completed and promulgated in 1917 as the *Codex Juris Canonici*, the first official guide to the laws of the Catholic Church. A new Code of Canon Law was issued by Pope John Paul II in 1983, the final result of a call for a new code dating back to Pope John XXIII (r. 1958-1963) and continued by Pope Paul VI (r. 1963-1978).

The 1983 Code of Canon Law

Pope John Paul II promulgated a revised Code of Canon Law for the Latin Rite on January 25, 1983, with the apostolic constitution *Sacrae Disciplinae Legis* ("Of the Sacred Discipline of Law") and ordered it into effect as of the following November 27. Promulgation of the Code marked the completion of the last major reform in the Church stemming from the Second Vatican Council.

The 1983 Code of Canon Law replaced the one which had been in effect since 1918. The new Code incorporates into law the insights of Vatican Council II. These 1,752 canons focus on the People of God and the threefold ministries of sanctifying, teaching and governance. Also included are general norms, temporalities, sanctions and procedures.

Guiding Principles

When Pope John XXIII announced on January 25, 1959, that he was going to convoke the Second Vatican Council, he also called for a revision of the existing Code of Canon Law. His successor, Paul VI, appointed a commission for this purpose in 1963 and subsequently enlarged it. The commission, which began its work after the conclusion of the Council in 1965, was directed by the 1967 Synod of Bishops to direct its efforts in line with 10 guiding principles. The bishops said the revised Code should:
• be juridical in character, not just a set of broad moral principles;
• be intended primarily for the external forum (regarding determinable fact, as opposed to the internal forum of conscience);
• be clearly pastoral in spirit;
• incorporate most of the faculties bishops need in their ministry;
• provide for subsidiarity or decentralization;
• be sensitive to human rights;
• state clear procedures for administrative processes and tribunals;
• be based on the principle of territoriality;
• reduce the number of penalties for infraction of law;
• have a new structure.

The commission carried out its mandate with the collegial collaboration of bishops all over the world and in consultation and correspondence with individuals and experts in canon law, theology, and related disciplines. The group finished its work in 1981 and turned its final draft over to Pope John Paul II at its final plenary meeting in October of that year.

Features

The revised code is shorter (1,752 canons) than the one it has replaced (2,414 canons) and has a number of important features:

It is more pastoral and flexible, as well as more theologically oriented than the former Code. It gives greater emphasis than its predecessor to a number of significant facets and concepts in church life.

In the apostolic constitution with which he promulgated the Code, Pope John Paul II called attention to its nature and some of its features, as follows:

Prime Legislative Document

"Since this is so, it seems clear enough that the Code in no way has its scope to substitute for faith, grace, the charisms, and especially charity in the life of the Church of the faithful. On the contrary, its end is rather to create such order in ecclesial society that, assigning primacy to love, grace and charisms, it at the same time renders more active their organic developments in the life both of the ecclesial society and of the individuals belonging to it. Inasmuch as it is the Church's prime legislative document, based on the juridical and legislative heritage of revelation and tradition, the Code must be regarded as the necessary instrument whereby due order is preserved in both individual and social life and in the Church's activity. Therefore, besides containing the fundamental elements of the hierarchical and organic structure of the Church, laid down by her divine Founder and founded on apostolic or at any rate most ancient tradition, and besides outstanding norms concerning the carrying out of the task mandated to the Church herself, the Code must also define a certain number of rules and norms of action."

Suits the Nature of the Church

"The instrument the Code is fully suits the Church's nature, for the Church is presented, especially through the magisterium of the Second Vatican Council, in her universal scope, and especially through the Council's ecclesiological teaching. In a certain sense, indeed, this new Code may be considered as a great effort to transfer that same ecclesiological or conciliar doctrine into canonical language. And, if it is impossible for the image of the Church described by the Council's teaching to be perfectly converted into canonical language, the Code nonetheless must always be referred to that very image, as the primary pattern whose outline the Code ought to express as well as it can by its own nature.

"From this derive a number of fundamental norms by which the whole of the new Code is ruled, of course within the limits proper to it as well as the limits of the very language befitting the material.

"It may rather be rightly affirmed that from this comes that note whereby the Code is regarded as a complement to the magisterium expounded by the Second Vatican Council.

"The following elements are most especially to be noted among those expressing a true and genuine image of the Church: the doctrine whereby the Church is proposed as the People of God and the hierarchical authority is propounded as service; in addition, the doctrine which shows the Church to be a 'communion' and from that lays down the mutual relationships which ought to exist between the particular and universal Church and between collegiality and primacy; likewise, the doctrine whereby all members of the People of God, each in the manner proper to him, share in Christ's threefold office of priest, prophet and king; to this doctrine is also connected that regarding the duties and rights of the Christian faithful, particularly the laity; then there is the effort which the Church has to make for ecumenism."

Code Necessary for the Church

"Indeed, the Code of Canon Law is extremely necessary for the Church ... The Church needs it for her hierarchichal and organic structure to be visible: so that exercise of the offices and tasks divinely entrusted to her, especially her sacred power and administration of the sacraments, should be rightly ordered; so that mutual relations of the Christian faithful may be carried out according to justice based on charity, with the rights of all being safeguarded and defined; so that we may then prepare and perform our common tasks, and that these, undertaken in order to live a Christian life more perfectly, may be fortified by means of the canonical laws.

"Thus, canonical laws need to be observed because of their very nature. Hence it is of the greatest importance that the norms be carefully expounded on the basis of solid juridical, canonical and theological foundations."

BOOKS OF THE CODE

Book I, General Norms (Canons 1-203):

Canons in this book cover Church laws, in general, custom and law, general decrees and instructions, administrative acts, statutes, physical and juridical persons, juridical acts, the power of governing, ecclesiastical offices, prescription (statutes of limitations), the reckoning of time.

Book II, The People of God (Canons 204-746):

Canons in Part I cover the obligations and rights of all the faithful, the obligations and rights of lay persons, sacred ministers and clerics, personal prelatures and associations of the faithful.

Canons in Part II cover the hierarchic constitution of the Church under the headings: the supreme authority of the Church and the college of bishops, diocesan churches and the authority constituted in them, councils of diocesan churches and the internal order of diocesan churches.

Canons in Part III cover institutes of consecrated life and societies of apostolic life.

Book III: The Teaching Office of the Church (Canons 747-833):

Canons under this heading cover: the ministry of the divine word, the missionary action of the Church, Catholic education, the instruments of social communication and books in particular, and the profession of faith.

Book IV, The Sanctifying Office of the Church (Canons 834-1252):

Canons under this heading cover each of the seven sacraments – baptism, confirmation, the Eucharist, penance, anointing of the sick, holy orders and matrimony; other acts of divine worship including sacramentals, the Liturgy of the Hours, ecclesiastical burial; the veneration of saints, sacred images and relics, vows and oaths.

Book V, Temporal Goods of the Church (Canons 1254-1310):

Canons under this heading cover: the acquisition and administration of goods, contracts, the alienation of goods, wills and pious foundations.

Book VI, Sanctions in the Church (Canons 1311-1399):

Canons in Part I cover crimes and penalties in general: the punishment of crimes in general, penal law and penal precept, persons subject to penal sanctions, penalties and other punishments, the application and cessation of penalties.

Canons in Part II cover penalties for particular crimes: crimes against religion and the unity of the Church; crimes against the authority of the Church and the liberty of the Church; the usurpation of Church offices and crimes in exercising office; false accusation of a confessor; crimes against special obligations; crimes against human life and liberty; a general norm regarding the punishment of external violations of divine law not specifically covered in the Code.

Book VII, Procedures (Canons 1400-1752):

Judicial proceedings are the principal subjects of canons under this heading: tribunals and their personnel, parties to proceedings, details regarding litigation and the manner in which it is conducted, special proceedings – with emphasis on matrimonial cases.

Glossary

A

Abbacy Nullius: A non-diocesan territory whose people are under the pastoral care of an abbot acting in general in the manner of a bishop.

Abbess: The female superior of a monastic community of nuns; e.g., Benedictines, Poor Clares, some others. Elected by members of the community, an abbess has general authority over her community but no sacramental jurisdiction.

Abbey: *See* **Monastery**.

Abbot: The male superior of a monastic community of men religious; e.g., Benedictines, Cistercians, some others. Elected by members of the community, an abbot has ordinary jurisdiction and general authority over his community. Eastern Rite equivalents of an abbot are a hegumen and an archimandrite. A regular abbot is the head of an abbey or monastery. An abbot general or archabbot is the head of a congregation consisting of several monasteries. An abbot primate is the head of the modern Benedictine Confederation.

Abiogenesis: The term used to describe the spontaneous generation of living matter from nonliving matter.

Ablution: A term derived from Latin, meaning washing or cleansing, and referring to the cleansing of the hands of a priest celebrating Mass, after the offering of gifts; and to the cleansing of the chalice with water and wine after Communion.

Abnegation: The spiritual practice of self-denial (or mortification), in order to atone for past sins or in order to join oneself to the passion of Christ. Mortification can be undertaken through fasting, abstinence, or refraining from legitimate pleasure.

Abortion: Abortion is not only "the ejection of an immature fetus" from the womb, but is "also the killing of the same fetus in whatever way at whatever time from the moment of conception it may be procured." (This clarification of Canon 1398, reported in the Dec. 5, 1988, edition of *L'Osservatore Romano*, was issued by the Pontifical Council for the Interpretation of Legislative Texts — in view of scientific developments regarding ways and means of procuring abortion.) Accidental expulsion, as in cases of miscarriage, is without moral fault. Direct abortion, in which a fetus is intentionally removed from the womb, constitutes a direct attack on an innocent human being, a violation of the Fifth Commandment. A person who procures a completed abortion is automatically excommunicated (Canon 1398 of the *Code of Canon Law*); also excommunicated are all persons involved in a deliberate and successful effort to bring about an abortion. Direct abortion is not justifiable for any reason, e.g.: therapeutic, for the physical and/or psychological welfare of the mother; preventive, to avoid the birth of a defective or unwanted child; social, in the interests of family and/or community. Indirect abortion, which occurs when a fetus is expelled during medical or other treatment of the mother for a reason other than procuring expulsion, is permissible under the principle of double effect for a proportionately serious reason; e.g., when a medical or surgical procedure is necessary to save the life of the mother. Such a procedure should not be confused with the purportedly "medical" procedure of the partial-birth abortion, a particularly cruel form of abortion.

Abrogation: The abolition or elimination of a law by some official action. In canon law, abrogation occurs through a direct decree of the Holy See or by the enactment of a later or subsequent law contrary to the former law.

Absolute: 1) A term in philosophy, first introduced at the end of the 18th century and used by Scholasticism, that signifies the "perfect being" (i.e., God), who relies upon no one for existence. Modern philosophical thought has added two new concepts: a) the Absolute is the sum of all being; b) the Absolute has no relationship with any other things; the Absolute is thus unknowable. These concepts are agnostic and contrary to Catholicism, which holds that God is the cause of all being (and hence not the sum) and is knowable by his creatures, at least in part. 2) Certain truths, revealed by God, which are unchanging.

Absolution, Sacramental: The act by which bishops and priests, acting as agents of Christ and ministers of the Church, grant forgiveness of sins in the sacrament of penance. The essential formula of absolution is: "I absolve you from your sins; in the name of the Father, and of the Son, and of the Holy Spirit. Amen." The power to absolve is given with ordination to the priesthood and episcopate. Priests exercise this power in virtue of authorization (faculties) granted by a bishop, a religious superior or canon law. Authorization can be limited or restricted regarding certain sins and penalties or censures. In cases of necessity, and also in cases of the absence of their own confessors, Eastern and Latin Rite Catholics may ask for and receive sacramental absolution from an Eastern or Latin Rite priest; so may Polish National Catholics, according to a Vatican decision issued in May 1993. Any priest can absolve a person in danger of death; in the absence of a priest with the usual faculties, this includes a laicized priest or a priest under censure. (*See* additional entry under **Sacraments**.)

Abstinence: 1) The deliberate deprivation by a person of meat or of foods prepared with meat on those days prescribed by the Church as penitential (Ash Wednesday, Good Friday, and all Fridays of the year which are not solemnities — in the United States, not all Fridays of the year but only the Fridays of Lent). Those 14 years of age and above are bound by the discipline. 2) Sexual abstinence is the willing refrain from sexual intercourse; total abstinence is observed in obedience to the Sixth Commandment by single persons and couples whose marriages are not recognized by the Church as valid; periodic abstinence or periodic continence is observed by a married couple for regulating conception by natural means or for ascetical motives.

Adoration: The highest act and purpose of religious worship, which is directed in love and reverence to God alone in acknowledgment of his infinite perfection and goodness, and of his total dominion over creatures. Adoration, which is also called latria, consists of internal and external elements, private and social prayer, liturgical acts and ceremonies, and especially sacrifice.

Adultery: Marital infidelity. Sexual intercourse between a married person and another to whom one is not married, a violation of the obligations of the marital covenant, chastity and justice; any sin of impurity (thought, desire, word, action) involving a married person who is not one's husband or wife has the nature of adultery.

Advent Wreath: A wreath of laurel, spruce, or similar foliage with four candles which are lighted successively in the weeks of Advent to symbolize the approaching celebration of the birth of Christ, the Light of the World, at Christmas. The wreath originated among German Protestants.

Agape: A Greek word, meaning love, love feast, designating the meal of fellowship eaten at some gatherings of early Christians. Although held in some places in connection with the Mass, the agape was not part of the Mass, nor was it of universal institution and observance. It was infrequently observed by the fifth century and disappeared altogether between the sixth and eighth centuries.

Age of Reason: 1) The time of life when one begins to distinguish between right and wrong, to understand an obligation and take on moral responsibility; seven years of age is the presumption in church law. 2) Historically, the 18th-century period of Enlightenment in England and France, the age of the Encyclopedists and Deists. According to a basic thesis of the Enlightenment, human experience and reason are the only sources of certain knowledge of truth; consequently, faith and revelation are discounted as valid sources of knowledge, and the reality of supernatural truth is called into doubt and/or denied.

Aggiornamento: An Italian word having the general meaning of bringing up-to-date; renewal, revitalization, descriptive of the processes of spiritual renewal and institutional reform and change in the Church; fostered by the Second Vatican Council.

Agnosticism: A theory which holds that a person cannot have certain knowledge of immaterial reality, especially the existence of God and things pertaining to him. Immanuel Kant, one of the philosophical fathers of agnosticism, stood for the position that God, as well as the human soul, is unknowable on speculative grounds; nevertheless, he found practical imperatives for acknowledging God's existence, a view shared by many agnostics. The First Vatican Council declared that the existence of God and some of his attributes can be known with certainty by human reason, even without divine revelation. The word "agnosticism" was first used, in the sense given here, by T. H. Huxley in 1869.

Agnus Dei: A Latin phrase, meaning Lamb of God. 1) A title given to Christ, the Lamb (victim) of the Sacrifice of the New Law (on Calvary and in Mass). 2) A prayer said at Mass before the reception of Holy Communion. 3) A sacramental. It is a round paschal-candle fragment blessed by the pope. On one side it bears the impression of a lamb, symbolic of Christ. On the reverse side, there may be any one of a number of impressions; e.g., the figure of a saint, the name and coat of arms of the reigning pope. The *agnus dei* may have originated at Rome in the fifth century. The first definite mention of it dates from about 820.

Akathist Hymn: The most profound and famous expression of Marian devotion in churches of the Byzantine Rite. It consists of 24 sections, 12 of which relate to the Gospel of the Infancy and 12 to the mysteries of the Incarnation and the virginal motherhood of Mary. In liturgical usage, it is sung in part in Byzantine churches on the first four Saturdays of Lent and in toto on the fifth Saturday; it is also recited in private devotion. It is of unknown origin prior to 626, when its popularity increased as a hymn of thanksgiving after the successful defense and liberation of Constantinople, which had been under siege by Persians and Avars. Akathist means "without sitting," indicating that the hymn is recited or sung while standing. Pope John Paul II, in a decree dated May 25, 1991, granted a plenary indulgence to the faithful of any rite who recite the hymn in a church or oratory, as a family, in a religious community or in a pious association — in conjunction with the usual conditions of freedom from attachment to sin, reception of the sacraments of penance and the Eucharist, and prayers for the intention of the pope (e.g., an Our Father, the Apostles' Creed and an aspiration). A partial indulgence can be gained for recitation of the hymn in other circumstances.

Alleluia: An exclamation of joy derived from Hebrew, "All hail to him who is, praise God," with various use in the liturgy and other expressions of worship.

Allocution: A formal type of papal address, as distinguished from an ordinary sermon or statement of views.

Alms: An act, gift or service of compassion, motivated by love of God and neighbor, for the help of persons in need; an obligation of charity, which is measurable by the ability of one person to give assistance and by the degree of another's need. Almsgiving, along with prayer and fasting, is regarded as a work of penance as well as an exercise of charity. (*See* **Mercy, Works of**.)

Alpha and Omega: The first and last letters of the Greek alphabet, used to symbolize the eternity of God (Rv. 1:8) and the divinity and eternity of Christ, the beginning and end of all things (Rv. 21:6; 22:13). Use of the letters as a monogram of Christ originated in the fourth century or earlier.

Amen: A Hebrew word meaning truly, it is true. In the Gospels, Christ used the word to add a note of authority to his statements. In other New Testament writings, as in Hebrew usage, it was the concluding word to doxologies. As the concluding word of prayers, it expresses assent to and acceptance of God's will.

Anamnesis: A prayer recalling the saving mysteries of the death and resurrection of Jesus, following the consecration at Mass in the Latin Rite.

Anaphora: A Greek term for the Canon or Eucharistic Prayer of the Mass.

Anathema: A Greek word with the root meaning of cursed or separated and the adapted meaning of excommunication, used in Church documents, especially the canons of ecumenical councils, for the condemnation of heretical doctrines and of practices opposed to proper discipline.

Anchorite: A kind of hermit living in complete isolation and devoting himself exclusively to exercises of religion and severe penance according to a rule and way of life of his own devising. In early Christian times, anchorites were the forerunners of the monastic life. The closest contemporary approach to the life of an anchorite is that of Carthusian and Camaldolese hermits.

Angels: Purely spiritual beings with intelligence and free will whose name indicates their mission as servants and messengers of God. They were created before the creation of the visible universe. Good angels enjoy the perfect good of the beatific vision. They can intercede for persons. The doctrine of guardian angels, although not explicitly defined as a matter of faith, is rooted in long-standing tradition. No authoritative declaration has ever been issued regarding choirs or various categories of angels: seraphim, cherubim, thrones, dominations, principalities, powers, virtues, archangels and angels. Archangels commemorated in the liturgy are: Michael, leader of the angelic host and protector of the synagogue; Raphael, guide of Tobiah and healer of his father; Gabriel, angel of the Incarnation. Fallen angels, the chief of whom is called the Devil or Satan, rejected the love of God and were therefore banished from heaven to hell. They can tempt persons to commit sin.

Angelus: A devotion which commemorates the Incarnation of Christ. It consists of three versicles, three Hail Marys and a special prayer, and recalls the announcement to Mary by the Archangel Gabriel that she was chosen to be the Mother of Christ, her acceptance of the divine will, and the Incarnation (Lk. 1:26-38). The Angelus is recited in the morning, at noon and in the evening. The practice of reciting the Hail Mary in honor of the Incarnation was introduced by the Franciscans in 1263. The *Regina Caeli*, commemorating the joy of Mary at Christ's Resurrection, replaces the Angelus during the Easter season.

Anger (Wrath): Passionate displeasure arising from some kind of offense suffered at the hands of another person, frustration or other cause, combined with a tendency to strike back at the cause of the displeasure; a violation of the Fifth Commandment, and one of the capital sins if the displeasure is out of proportion to the cause and/or if the retaliation is unjust.

Anglican Orders: Holy orders conferred according to the rite of the Anglican Church, which Leo XIII declared null and void in the bull *Apostolicae Curae*, Sept. 13, 1896. The orders were declared null because they were conferred according to a rite that was substantially defective in form and intent, and because of a break in apostolic succession that occurred when Matthew Parker became head of the Anglican hierarchy in 1559. In making his declaration, Pope Leo cited earlier arguments against validity made by Julius III in 1553 and 1554 and by Paul IV in 1555. He also noted related directives requiring absolute ordination, according to the Catholic ritual, of convert ministers who had been ordained according to the Anglican Ordinal.

Anglican Use Parishes: In line with Vatican-approved developments since 1980, several Anglican use parishes have been established in the United States with the right to continue using some elements of Anglican usage in their liturgical celebrations. A Vatican document dated Mar. 31, 1981, said: "In June 1980, the Holy See, through the Congregation for the Doctrine of the Faith, agreed to the request presented by the bishops of the United States of America in behalf of some clergy and laity formerly or actually belonging to the Episcopal (Anglican) Church for full communion with the Catholic Church. The Holy See's response to the initiative of these Episcopalians includes the possibility of a 'pastoral provision' which will provide, for those who desire it, a common identity reflecting certain elements of their own heritage."

Animals: Creatures of God, they are entrusted to human stewardship for appropriate care, use for human needs, as pets, for reasonable experimentation for the good of people. They should not be subject to cruel treatment.

Annulment: A decree issued by an appropriate Church authority or tribunal that a sacrament or ecclesiastical act is invalid and therefore lacking in all legal or canonical consequences.

Antichrist: The "deceitful one," the "antichrist" (2 Jn. 7), adversary of Christ and the kingdom of God, especially in the end time before the second coming of Christ. The term is also used in reference to anti-Christian persons and forces in the world.

Antiphon: 1) A short verse or text, generally from Scripture, recited in the Liturgy of the Hours before and after psalms and canticles. 2) Any verse sung or recited by one part of a choir or congregation in response to the other part, as in antiphonal or alternate chanting.

Anti-Semitism: A prejudice against Jews, and often accompanied by persecution. The prejudice has existed historically from the time of the ancient Persian Empire and survives even to the present day. It has been condemned consistently by the Church as being in opposition to scriptural principles and Christian charity.

Apologetics: The science and art of developing and presenting the case for the reasonableness of the Christian faith, by a wide variety of means including facts of experience, history, science, philosophy. The constant objective of apologetics, as well as of the total process of pre-evangelization, is preparation for response to God in faith; its ways and means, however, are subject to change in accordance with the various needs of people and different sets of circumstances.

Apostasy: 1) The total and obstinate repudiation of the Christian faith. An apostate automatically incurs a penalty of excommunication. 2)

Apostasy from orders is the unlawful withdrawal from or rejection of the obligations of the clerical state by a man who has received major orders. An apostate from orders is subject to a canonical penalty. 3) Apostasy from the religious life occurs when a Religious with perpetual vows unlawfully leaves the community with the intention of not returning, or actually remains outside the community without permission. An apostate from religious life is subject to a canonical penalty.

Apostolate: The ministry or work of an apostle. In Catholic usage, the word is an umbrella-like term covering all kinds and areas of work and endeavor for the service of God and the Church and the good of people. Thus, the apostolate of bishops is to carry on the mission of the Apostles as pastors of the people of God: of priests, to preach the word of God and to carry out the sacramental and pastoral ministry for which they are ordained; of religious, to follow and do the work of Christ in conformity with the evangelical counsels and their rule of life; of lay persons, as individuals and/or in groups, to give witness to Christ and build up the kingdom of God through practice of their faith, professional competence and the performance of good works in the concrete circumstances of daily life. Apostolic works are not limited to those done within the Church or by specifically Catholic groups, although some apostolates are officially assigned to certain persons or groups and are under the direction of church authorities. Apostolate derives from the commitment and obligation of baptism, confirmation, holy orders, matrimony, the duties of one's state in life, etc.

Apostolic Succession: Bishops of the Church, who form a collective body or college, are successors to the Apostles by ordination and divine right; as such they carry on the mission entrusted by Christ to the Apostles as guardians and teachers of the deposit of faith, principal pastors and spiritual authorities of the faithful. The doctrine of apostolic succession is based on New Testament evidence and the constant teaching of the Church, reflected as early as the end of the first century in a letter of Pope St. Clement to the Corinthians. A significant facet of the doctrine is the role of the pope as the successor of St. Peter, the vicar of Christ and head of the college of bishops. The doctrine of apostolic succession means more than continuity of apostolic faith and doctrine; its basic requisite is ordination by the laying on of hands in apostolic succession.

Archives: Documentary records, and the place where they are kept, of the spiritual and temporal government and affairs of the Church, a diocese, church agencies like the departments of the Roman Curia, bodies like religious institutes, and individual parishes. The collection, cataloguing, preserving, and use of these records are governed by norms stated in canon law and particular regulations. The strictest secrecy is always in effect for confidential records concerning matters of conscience, and documents of this kind are destroyed as soon as circumstances permit.

Ark of the Covenant: The sacred chest of the Israelites in which were placed and carried the tablets of stone inscribed with the Ten Commandments, the basic moral precepts of the Old Covenant (Ex. 25: 10-22; 37:1-9). The Ark was also a symbol of God's presence. The Ark was probably destroyed with the Temple in 586 B.C.

Asceticism: The practice of self-discipline. In the spiritual life, asceticism — by personal prayer, meditation, self-denial, works of mortification, and outgoing interpersonal works — is motivated by love of God and contributes to growth in holiness.

Ashes: Religious significance has been associated with their use as symbolic of penance since Old Testament times. Thus, ashes of palm blessed on the previous Sunday of the Passion are placed on the foreheads of the faithful on Ash Wednesday to remind them to do works of penance, especially during the season of Lent, and that they are dust and unto dust will return. Ashes are a sacramental.

Aspergillum: A vessel or device used for sprinkling holy water. The ordinary type is a metallic rod with a bulbous tip which absorbs the water and discharges it at the motion of the user's hand.

Aspersory: A portable metallic vessel, similar to a pail, for carrying holy water.

Aspiration (Ejaculation): Short exclamatory prayer; e.g., My Jesus, mercy.

Atheism: Denial of the existence of God, finding expression in a system of thought (speculative atheism) or a manner of acting (practical atheism) as though there were no God. The Second Vatican Council, in its Pastoral Constitution on the Church in the Modern World (*Gaudium et Spes*, Nos. 19 to 21), noted that a profession of atheism may represent an explicit denial of God, the rejection of a wrong notion of God, an affirmation of man rather than of God, an extreme protest against evil. It said that such a profession might result from acceptance of such propositions as: there is no absolute truth; man can assert nothing, absolutely nothing, about God; everything can be explained by scientific reasoning alone; the whole question of God is devoid of meaning.

Atonement: The redemptive activity of Christ, who reconciled man with God through his Incarnation and entire life, and especially by his suffering and Resurrection. The word also applies to prayer and good works by which persons join themselves with and take part in Christ's work of reconciliation and reparation for sin.

Attributes of God: Perfections of God. God possesses — and is — all the perfections of being, without limitation. Because he is infinite, all of these perfections are one, perfectly united in him. Because of the limited power of human intelligence, divine perfections — such as omnipotence, truth, love, etc. — are viewed separately, as distinct characteristics, even though they are not actually distinct in God.

Authority, Ecclesiastical: The authority exercised by the Church, and particularly by the pope and the bishops; it is delegated by Jesus Christ to St. Peter. This authority extends to all those matters entrusted to the Apostles by Christ, including teaching of the Faith, the liturgy and sacraments, moral guidance, and the administration of discipline.

Avarice (Covetousness): A disorderly and unreasonable attachment to and desire for material things; called a capital sin because it involves preoccupation with material things to the neglect of spiritual goods and obligations of justice and charity.

Ave Maria: See **Hail Mary**.

B

Baldacchino: A canopy over an altar.

Baptism: *See* **Sacraments**.

Beatification: A preliminary step toward canonization of a saint. It begins with an investigation of the candidate's life, writings and heroic practice of virtue, and, except in the case of martyrs, the certification of one miracle worked by God through his or her intercession. If the findings of the investigation so indicate, the pope decrees that the Servant of God may be called Blessed and may be honored locally or in a limited way in the liturgy. Additional procedures lead to canonization (*See* separate entry).

Beatific Vision: The intuitive, immediate and direct vision and experience of God enjoyed in the light of glory by all the blessed in heaven. The vision is a supernatural mystery.

Beatitude: A literary form of the Old and New Testaments in which blessings are promised to persons for various reasons. Beatitudes are mentioned 26 times in the Psalms, and in other books of the Old Testament. The best known Beatitudes — identifying blessedness with participation in the kingdom of God and his righteousness, and descriptive of the qualities of Christian perfection — are those recounted in Mt. 5:3-12 and Lk. 6:20-23. The Beatitudes are of central importance in the teaching of Jesus.

Benedictus: The canticle or hymn of Zechariah at the circumcision of St. John the Baptist (Lk. 1:68-79). It is an expression of praise and thanks to God for sending John as a precursor of the Messiah. The Benedictus is recited in the Liturgy of the Hours as part of the Morning Prayer.

Biglietto: A papal document of notification of appointment to the cardinalate.

Biretta: A stiff, square hat with three ridges on top worn by clerics in church and on other occasions.

Blasphemy: Any internal or external expression of hatred, reproach, insult, defiance or contempt with respect to God and the use of his name, principally, and to the Church, saints and sacred things, secondarily; a serious sin, directly opposed to the second commandment. Blasphemy against the Spirit is the deliberate refusal to accept divine mercy, rejection of forgiveness of sins and of the promise of salvation. The sin that is unforgivable because a person refuses to seek or accept forgiveness.

Blessing: Invocation of God's favor, by official ministers of the Church or by private individuals. Blessings are recounted in the Old and New Testaments, and are common in the Christian tradition. Many types of blessings are listed in the **Book of Blessings of the Roman Ritual**. Private blessings, as well as those of an official kind, are efficacious. Blessings are imparted with the Sign of the Cross and appropriate prayer.

Bride of Christ: A metaphorical title that denotes the intimate union that Christ enjoys with his Church; the title is mentioned specifically in the NT (2 Cor. 11:2).

Brief, Apostolic: A papal letter, less formal than a bull, signed for the pope by a secretary and impressed with the seal of the Fisherman's Ring. Simple apostolic letters of this kind are issued for beatifications and with respect to other matters.

Bull, Apostolic: Apostolic letter, a solemn form of papal document, beginning with the name and title of the pope (e.g., John Paul II, Servant of the Servants of God), dealing with an important subject, sealed with a *bulla* or red-ink imprint of the device on the *bulla*. Bulls are issued to confer the titles of bishops and cardinals, to promulgate canonizations, to proclaim Holy Years and for other purposes. A collection of bulls is called a *bullarium*.

Burial, Ecclesiastical: Interment with ecclesiastical rites, a right of the Christian faithful. The Church recommends burial of the bodies of the dead, but cremation is permissible if it does not involve reasons against church teaching. Ecclesiastical burial is in order for catechumens; for unbaptized children whose parents intended to have them baptized before death; and even, in the absence of their own ministers, for baptized non-Catholics unless it would be considered against their will.

Burse, Financial: A special fund maintained by a diocese, religious institute, or private foundation usually endowed by a private benefactor; it often has the purpose of making possible the education of candidates for the priesthood.

C

Calumny (Slander): Harming the name and good reputation of a person by lies; a violation of obligations of justice and truth. Restitution is due for calumny.

Calvary: A knoll about 15 feet high just outside the western wall of Jerusalem where Christ was crucified, so called from the Latin *calvaria* (skull), which described its shape.

Canon: A Greek word meaning rule, norm, standard, measure. 1) The word designates the Canon of Sacred Scripture, which is the list of books recognized by the Church as inspired by the Holy Spirit. 2) The term also designates the canons (Eucharistic Prayers, anaphoras) of the Mass, the core of the eucharistic liturgy. 3) Certain dignitaries of the Church have the title of Canon, and some religious are known as Canons. (*See* **Bible**.)

Canonization: An infallible declaration by the pope that a person, who died as a martyr and/or practiced Christian virtue to a heroic degree, is now in heaven and is worthy of honor and imitation by all the faithful. Such a declaration is preceded by the process of beatification and another detailed investigation concerning the person's reputation for holiness, writings, and (except in the case of martyrs) a miracle ascribed to his or her intercession after death. The pope can dispense from some of the formalities ordinarily required in canonization procedures (equivalent canonization), as Pope John XXIII did in the canonization of St. Gregory Barbarigo on May 26, 1960. A saint is worthy of honor in liturgical worship throughout the universal Church. From its earliest years the Church has venerated saints. Public official honor always required the approval of the bishop of the place. Martyrs were the first to be honored. St. Martin of Tours, who died in 397, was an early non-martyr venerated as a saint. The earliest canonization by a pope with positive documentation was that of St. Ulrich (Uldaric) of Augsburg by John XV in 993. Alexander III reserved the process of canonization to the Holy See in 1171. In 1588 Sixtus V established the Sacred

Congregation of Rites for the principal purpose of handling causes for beatification and canonization: this function is now the work of the Congregation for the Causes of Saints. The official listing of saints and blessed is contained in the Roman Martyrology (being revised and updated) and related decrees issued after its last publication. Butler's unofficial *Lives of the Saints* (1956) contains 2,565 entries. The Church regards all persons in heaven as saints, not just those who have been officially canonized. (*See* **Beatification, Saints, Canonizations by Leo XIII and His Successors.**)

Canon Law: The Code of Canon Law (*Corpus Iuris Canonici*) enacted and promulgated by ecclesiastical authority for the orderly and pastoral administration and government of the Church. A revised Code for the Latin Rite, effective Nov. 27, 1983, consists of 1,752 canons in seven books under the titles of general norms, the people of God, the teaching mission of the Church, the sanctifying mission of the Church, temporal goods of the Church, penal law, and procedural law. The antecedent of this Code was promulgated in 1917 and became effective in 1918; it consisted of 2,414 canons in five books covering general rules, ecclesiastical persons, sacred things, trials, crimes, and punishments. There is a separate Code of the Canons of Eastern Churches, in effect since Oct. 1, 1991.

Canticle: A scriptural chant or prayer differing from the psalms. Three of the canticles prescribed for use in the Liturgy of the Hours are: the *Magnificat*, the Canticle of Mary (Lk. 1:46-55); the *Benedictus*, the Canticle of Zechariah (Lk. 1:68-79); and the *Nunc Dimittis*, the Canticle of Simeon (Lk. 2:29-32).

Capital Punishment: Punishment for crime by means of the death penalty. The political community, which has authority to provide for the common good, has the right to defend itself and its members against unjust aggression and may in extreme cases punish with the death penalty persons found guilty before the law of serious crimes against individuals and a just social order. Such punishment is essentially vindictive. Its value as a crime deterrent is a matter of perennial debate. The prudential judgment as to whether or not there should be capital punishment belongs to the civic community. The U.S. Supreme Court, in a series of decisions dating from June 29, 1972, ruled against the constitutionality of statutes on capital punishment except in specific cases and with appropriate consideration, with respect to sentence, of mitigating circumstances of the crime. Pope John Paul II, in his encyclical letter *Evangelium Vitae* ("The Gospel of Life"), wrote: "There is a growing tendency, both in the Church and in civil society, to demand that it (capital punishment) be applied in a very limited way or even that it be abolished completely." Quoting the *Catechism of the Catholic Church*, the pope wrote: " 'If bloodless means are sufficient to defend human lives against an aggressor and to protect public order and the safety of persons, public authority must limit itself to such means, because they better correspond to the concrete conditions of the common good and are more in conformity to the dignity of the human person.' "

Capital Sins: Sins which give rise to other sins: pride, avarice, lust, wrath (anger), gluttony, envy, sloth.

Cardinal Virtues: The four principal moral virtues are prudence, justice, temperance and fortitude.

Casuistry: In moral theology, the application of moral principles to specific cases. Casuistry can be of assistance because it takes the abstract and makes it practical in a particular situation. It has definite limitations and does not replace the conscience in the decision-making process; additionally, it must be aligned with the cardinal virtue of prudence.

Catacombs: Underground Christian cemeteries in various cities of the Roman Empire and Italy, especially in the vicinity of Rome; the burial sites of many martyrs and other Christians.

Catechesis: The whole complex of church efforts to make disciples of Christ, involving doctrinal instruction and spiritual formation through practice of the faith.

Catechism: A systematic presentation of the fundamentals of Catholic doctrine regarding faith and morals. Sources are Sacred Scripture, tradition, the magisterium (teaching authority of the Church), the writings of Fathers and Doctors of the Church, liturgy. The new *Catechism of the Catholic Church*, published Oct. 11, 1992, consists of four principal sections: the profession of faith (the Creed), the sacraments of faith, the life of faith (the Commandments) and the prayer of the believer (the Lord's Prayer). The 16th-century Council of Trent mandated publication of the *Roman Catechism*. Catechisms such as these two are useful sources for other catechisms serving particular needs of the faithful and persons seeking admission to the Catholic Church.

Catechumen: A person preparing in a program (catechumenate) of instruction and spiritual formation for baptism and reception into the Church. The Church has a special relationship with catechumens. It invites them to lead the life of the Gospel, introduces them to the celebration of the sacred rites, and grants them various prerogatives that are proper to the faithful (one of which is the right to ecclesiastical burial). (*See* **Rite of Christian Initiation of Adults**, under **Baptism.**)

Cathedra: A Greek word for chair, designating the chair or seat of a bishop in the principal church of his diocese, which is therefore called a cathedral.

Cathedraticum: The tax paid to a bishop by all churches and benefices subject to him for the support of episcopal administration and for works of charity.

Catholic: A Greek word, meaning universal, first used in the title Catholic Church in a letter written by St. Ignatius of Antioch about 107 to the Christians of Smyrna.

Celebret: A Latin word, meaning "Let him celebrate," the name of a letter of recommendation issued by a bishop or other superior stating that a priest is in good standing and therefore eligible to celebrate Mass or perform other priestly functions.

Celibacy: The unmarried state of life, required in the Roman Church of candidates for holy orders and of men already ordained to holy orders, for the practice of perfect chastity and total dedication to the service of people in the ministry of the Church. Celibacy is enjoined as a condition for ordination by church discipline and law, not by dogmatic necessity. In the Roman Church, a consensus in favor of celibacy developed in the early centuries while the clergy included both celibates and men who had been married once. The first local legislation on the subject was enacted by a local council held in Elvira, Spain, about 306; it forbade bishops, priests, deacons and other ministers to have wives. Similar enactments were passed by other local councils from that time on, and by the 12th century particular laws regarded marriage by clerics in major orders to be not only unlawful but also null and void. The latter view was translated by the Second Lateran Council in 1139 into what seems to be the first written universal law making holy orders an invalidating impediment to marriage. In 1563 the Council of Trent ruled definitely on the matter and established the discipline in force in the Roman Church. Some exceptions to this discipline have been made in recent years. A number of married Protestant and Episcopalian (Anglican) clergymen who became converts and were subsequently ordained to the priesthood have been permitted to continue in marriage. Married men over the age of 35 can be ordained to the permanent diaconate. Eastern Church discipline on celibacy differs from that of the Roman Church. In line with legislation enacted by the Synod of Trullo in 692 and still in force, candidates for holy orders may marry before becoming deacons and may continue in marriage thereafter, but marriage after ordination is forbidden. Bishops of Eastern Catholic Churches in the U.S., however, do not ordain married candidates for the priesthood. Bishops of Eastern Catholic Churches are unmarried.

Cenacle: The upper room in Jerusalem where Christ ate the Last Supper with his Apostles.

Censer: A metal vessel with a perforated cover and suspended by chains, in which incense is burned. It is used at some Masses, Benediction of the Blessed Sacrament and other liturgical functions.

Censorship of Books: An exercise of vigilance by the Church for safeguarding authentic religious teaching. Pertinent legislation in a decree issued by the Congregation for the Doctrine of the Faith on Apr. 9, 1975, is embodied in the Code of Canon Law (Book III, Title IV). The legislation deals with requirements for pre-publication review and clearance of various types of writings on religious subjects. Permission to publish works of a religious character, together with the apparatus of reviewing them beforehand, falls under the authority of the bishop of the place where the writer lives or where the works are published. Clearance for publication is usually indicated by the terms *Nihil obstat* ("Nothing stands in the way") issued by the censor and *Imprimatur* ("Let it be printed") authorized by the bishop. The clearing of works for publication does not necessarily imply approval of an author's viewpoint or his manner of handling a subject.

Censures: Sanctions imposed by the Church on baptized Roman Catholics 18 years of age or older for committing certain serious offenses and for being or remaining obstinate therein: 1) excommunication (exclusion from the community of the faithful, barring a person from sacramental and other participation in the goods and offices of the community of the Church), 2) suspension (prohibition of a cleric to exercise orders) and 3) interdict (deprivation of the sacraments and liturgical activities). The intended purposes of censures are to correct and punish offenders; to deter persons from committing sins which, more seriously and openly than others, threaten the common good of the Church and its members; and to provide for the making of reparation for harm done to the community of the Church. Censures may be incurred automatically (*ipso facto*) on the commission of certain offenses for which fixed penalties have been laid down in church law (*latae sententiae*); or they may be inflicted by sentence of a judge (*ferendae sententiae*). Automatic excommunication is incurred for the offenses of abortion, apostasy, heresy and schism. Obstinacy in crime — also called contumacy, disregard of a penalty, defiance of church authority — is presumed by law in the commission of offenses for which automatic censures are decreed. The presence and degree of contumacy in other cases, for which judicial sentence is required, is subject to determination by a judge. Absolution can be obtained from any censure, provided the person repents and desists from obstinacy. Absolution may be reserved to the pope, the bishop of a place, or the major superior of an exempt clerical religious institute. In danger of death, any priest can absolve from all censures; in other cases, faculties to absolve from reserved censures can be exercised by competent authorities or given to other priests. The penal law of the Church is contained in Book VI of the Code of Canon Law.

Ceremonies, Master of: One who directs the proceedings of a rite or ceremony during the function.

Chamberlain (*Camerlengo*): 1) The Chamberlain of the Holy Roman Church is a cardinal with special responsibilities, especially during the time between the death of one pope and the election of his successor; among other things, he safeguards and administers the goods and revenues of the Holy See and heads particular congregations of cardinals for special purposes. (*See* also **Papal Election**.) 2) The Chamberlain of the College of Cardinals has charge of the property and revenues of the College and keeps the record of business transacted in consistories. 3) The Chamberlain of the Roman Clergy is the president of the secular clergy of Rome.

Chancellor: Notary of a diocese, who draws up written documents in the government of the diocese; takes care of, arranges and indexes diocesan archives, records of dispensations and ecclesiastical trials.

Chancery: 1) A branch of church administration that handles written documents used in the government of a diocese. 2) The administrative office of a diocese, a bishop's office.

Chant: A type of sacred singing. It is either recitative in nature with a short two-to-six tones for an accentus, or melodic in one of three styles (syllabic, neumatic, or melismatic).

Chapel: A building or part of another building used for divine worship; a portion of a church set aside for the celebration of Mass or for some special devotion.

Chaplain: A priest — or, in some instances, a properly qualified religious or lay person — serving the pastoral needs of particular groups of people and institutions, such as hospitals, schools, correctional facilities, religious communities, the armed forces, etc.

Chaplet: A term, meaning little crown, applied to a rosary or, more commonly, to a small string of beads used for devotional purposes; e.g., the Infant of Prague chaplet.

Chapter: A general meeting of delegates of religious orders for elections and the handling of other important affairs of their communities.

Charismatic Renewal: A movement which originated with a handful of Duquesne University students and faculty members in the 1966-67 academic year and spread from there to Notre Dame, Michigan State University, the University of Michigan, other campuses and cities throughout the U.S., and to well over 125 other countries. Scriptural keys to the renewal are: Christ's promise to send the Holy Spirit upon the Apostles; the description, in the Acts of the Apostles, of the effects of the coming of the Holy Spirit upon the Apostles on Pentecost; St. Paul's explanation, in the Letter to the Romans and 1 Corinthians, of the charismatic gifts (for the good of the Church and persons) the Holy Spirit would bestow on Christians; New Testament evidence concerning the effects of charismatic gifts in and through the early Church. The personal key to the renewal is baptism in the Holy Spirit. This is not a new sacrament but the personally experienced actualization of grace already sacramentally received, principally in baptism and confirmation. The experience of baptism in the Holy Spirit is often accompanied by the reception of one or more charismatic gifts. A characteristic form of the renewal is the weekly prayer meeting, a gathering which includes periods of spontaneous prayer, singing, sharing of experience and testimony, fellowship and teaching. (*See* also **Index**.)

Charisms: Gifts or graces given by God to persons for the good of others and the Church. Examples are special gifts for apostolic work, prophecy, healing, discernment of spirits, the life of evangelical poverty, here-and-now witness to faith in various circumstances of life. The Second Vatican Council made the following statement about charisms in the Dogmatic Constitution on the Church (No. 12): "It is not only through the sacraments and Church ministries that the same Holy Spirit sanctifies and leads the People of God and enriches it with virtues. Allotting his gifts 'to everyone according as he will' (1 Cor. 12:11), he distributes special graces among the faithful of every rank. By these gifts he makes them fit and ready to undertake the various tasks or offices advantageous for the renewal and upbuilding of the Church, according to the words of the Apostle: 'The manifestation of the Spirit is given to everyone for profit' (1 Cor. 12:7). These charismatic gifts, whether they be the most outstanding or the more simple and widely diffused, are to be received with thanksgiving and consolation, for they are exceedingly suitable and useful for the needs of the Church. Still, extraordinary gifts are not to be rashly sought after, nor are the fruits of apostolic labor to be presumptuously expected from them. In any case, judgment as to their genuineness and proper use belongs to those who preside over the Church, and to whose special competence it belongs, not indeed to extinguish the Spirit, but to test all things and hold fast to that which is good" (cf. 1 Thes. 5:12; 19-21).

Charity: Love of God above all things for his own sake, and love of one's neighbor as oneself because and as an expression of one's love for God; the greatest of the three theological virtues. The term is sometimes also used to designate sanctifying grace.

Chastity: Properly ordered behavior with respect to sex. In marriage, the exercise of the procreative power is integrated with the norms and purposes of marriage. Outside of marriage, the rule is self-denial of the voluntary exercise and enjoyment of the procreative faculty in thought, word or action. The vow of chastity, which reinforces the virtue of chastity with the virtue of religion, is one of the three vows professed publicly by members of institutes of consecrated life.

Chirograph or Autograph Letter: A letter written by a pope himself, in his own handwriting.

Chrism: A mixture of olive or other vegetable oil and balsam (or balm), that is consecrated by a bishop for use in liturgical anointings: baptism, confirmation, holy orders, the blessing of an altar.

Christ: The title of Jesus, derived from the Greek translation *Christos* of the Hebrew term Messiah, meaning the Anointed of God, the Savior and Deliverer of his people. Christian use of the title is a confession of belief that Jesus is the Savior.

Christianity: The sum total of things related to belief in Christ — the Christian religion, Christian churches, Christians themselves, society based on and expressive of Christian beliefs, culture reflecting Christian values.

Christians: The name first applied about the year 43 to followers of Christ at Antioch, the capital of Syria. It was used by the pagans as a contemptuous term. The word applies to persons who profess belief in the divinity and teachings of Christ and who give witness to him in life.

Circumcision: A ceremonial practice symbolic of initiation and participation in the covenant between God and Abraham.

Circumincession: The indwelling of each divine Person of the Holy Trinity in the others.

Clergy: Men ordained to holy orders and commissioned for sacred ministries and assigned to pastoral and other duties for the service of the people and the Church. 1) Diocesan or secular clergy are committed to pastoral ministry in parishes and in other capacities in a particular church (diocese) under the direction of their bishop, to whom they are bound by a promise of obedience. 2) Regular clergy belong to religious institutes (orders, congregations, societies — institutes of consecrated life) and are so called because they observe the rule (*regula*, in Latin) of their respective institutes. They are committed to the ways of life and apostolates of their institutes. In ordinary pastoral ministry, they are under the direction of local bishops as well as their own superiors.

Clericalism: A term generally used in a derogatory sense to mean action, influence and interference by the Church and the clergy in matters with which they allegedly should not be concerned. Anticlericalism is a reaction of antipathy, hostility, distrust and opposition to the Church and clergy arising from real and/or alleged faults of the clergy, over-extension of the role of the laity, or for other reasons.

Cloister: Part of a monastery, convent or other house of religious reserved for use by members of the institute. Houses of contemplative Religious have a strict enclosure.

Code: A digest of rules or regulations, such as the Code of Canon Law.

Code of Canon Law: *See* **Canon Law**.

Collegiality: A term in use especially since the Second Vatican Council to describe the authority exercised by the College of Bishops. The bishops of the Church, in union with and subordinate to the pope —

who has full, supreme and universal power over the Church which he can always exercise independently — have supreme teaching and pastoral authority over the whole Church. In addition to their proper authority of office for the good of the faithful in their respective dioceses or other jurisdictions, the bishops have authority to act for the good of the universal Church. This collegial authority is exercised in a solemn manner in an ecumenical council and can also be exercised in other ways sanctioned by the pope. Doctrine on collegiality was set forth by the Second Vatican Council in *Lumen Gentium* (the "Dogmatic Constitution on the Church"). (*See* separate entry.) By extension, the concept of collegiality is applied to other forms of participation and co-responsibility by members of a community.

Communicatio in Sacris: The reception of the Church's sacraments by non-members or the reception by Catholics of sacraments in non-Catholic Churches.

Communion of Saints: "The communion of all the faithful of Christ, those who are pilgrims on earth, the dead who are being purified, and the blessed in heaven, all together forming one Church; in this communion, the merciful love of God and his saints is always (attentive) to our prayers" (Paul VI, *Creed of the People of God*).

Communism: The substantive principles of modern communism, a theory and system of economics and social organization, were stated about the middle of the 19th century by Karl Marx, author of *The Communist Manifesto* and, with Friedrich Engels, *Das Kapital*. The elements of communist theory include: radical materialism; dialectical determinism; the inevitability of class struggle and conflict, which is to be furthered for the ultimate establishment of a worldwide, classless society; common ownership of productive and other goods; the subordination of all persons and institutions to the dictatorship of the collective; denial of the rights, dignity and liberty of persons; militant atheism and hostility to religion, utilitarian morality. Communism in theory and practice has been the subject of many papal documents and statements. Pius IX condemned it in 1846. Leo XIII dealt with it at length in the encyclical letters *Quod Apostolici Muneris* in 1878 and *Rerum Novarum* in 1891. Pius XI wrote on the same subject in the encyclicals *Quadragesimo Anno* in 1931 and *Divini Redemptoris* in 1937. These writings have been updated and developed in new directions by Pius XII, John XXIII, Paul VI and John Paul II.

Compline: The night prayer of the Church that completes the daily *cursus* (course) of the Liturgy of the Hours (Divine Office).

Concelebration: The liturgical act in which several priests, led by one member of the group, offer Mass together, all consecrating the bread and wine. Concelebration has always been common in churches of Eastern Rite. In the Roman Rite, it was long restricted, taking place only at the ordination of bishops and the ordination of priests. The Constitution on the Sacred Liturgy issued by the Second Vatican Council set new norms for concelebration, which is now relatively common in the Roman Rite.

Concordance, Biblical: An alphabetical verbal index enabling a user knowing one or more words of a scriptural passage to locate the entire text.

Concordat: A church-state treaty with the force of law concerning matters of mutual concern — e.g., rights of the Church, arrangement of ecclesiastical jurisdictions, marriage laws, education. Approximately 150 agreements of this kind have been negotiated since the Concordat of Worms in 1122.

Concupiscence: Any tendency of the sensitive appetite. The term is most frequently used in reference to desires and tendencies for sinful sense-pleasure.

Confession: Sacramental confession is the act by which a person tells or confesses his sins to a priest, who is authorized to give absolution in the sacrament of penance.

Confessor: A priest who administers the sacrament of penance. The title of confessor, formerly given to a category of male saints, was suppressed with publication of the calendar reform of 1969.

Confraternity: An association whose members practice a particular form of religious devotion and/or are engaged in some kind of apostolic work.

Congregation: 1) The collective name for the people who form a parish. 2) One of the chief administrative departments of the Roman Curia. 3) An unofficial term for a group of men and women who belong to a religious community or institute of consecrated life.

Conscience: Practical judgment concerning the moral goodness or sinfulness of an action (thought, word, desire). In the Catholic view, this judgment is made by reference of the action, its attendant circumstances and the intentions of the person to the requirements of moral law as expressed in the Ten Commandments, the summary law of love for God and neighbor, the life and teaching of Christ, and the authoritative teaching and practice of the Church with respect to the total demands of divine Revelation. A person is obliged to: 1) to obey a certain and correct conscience; 2) to obey a certain conscience even if it is inculpably erroneous; 3) not to obey, but to correct, a conscience known to be erroneous or lax; 4) to rectify a scrupulous conscience by following the advice of a confessor and by other measures; 5) to resolve doubts of conscience before acting. It is legitimate to act for solid and probable reasons when a question of moral responsibility admits of argument (*See* **Probabiliorism** and **Probabilism**).

Conscience, Examination of: Self-examination to determine one's spiritual state before God, regarding one's sins and faults. It is recommended as a regular practice and is practically necessary in preparing for the sacrament of penance. The particular examen is a regular examination to assist in overcoming specific faults and imperfections.

Consequentialism: A moral theory, closely associated with proportionalism and utilitarianism, that holds that the preferable action is one that brings about the best consequences. Preferred results, rather than the objective truth and intentionality, are the object of actions based on consequentialism. While traditional moral theology acknowledges that consequences are important in determining the rightness of an act, importance is also placed on the intrinsic morality of the act and the agent's intention.

Consistory: An assembly of cardinals presided over by the pope.

Constitution: 1) An apostolic or papal constitution is a document in which a pope enacts and promulgates law. 2) A formal and solemn document issued by an ecumenical council on a doctrinal or pastoral subject, with binding force in the whole Church; e.g., the four constitutions issued by the Second Vatican Council on the Church, liturgy, Revelation, and the Church in the modern world. 3) The constitutions of institutes of consecrated life and societies of apostolic life spell out details of and norms drawn from the various rules for the guidance and direction of the life and work of their members.

Consubstantiation: A theory which holds that the Body and Blood of Christ coexist with the substance of bread and wine in the Holy Eucharist. This theory, also called imputation, is incompatible with the doctrine of transubstantiation.

Contraception: Anything done by positive interference to prevent sexual intercourse from resulting in conception. Direct contraception is against the order of nature. Indirect contraception — as a secondary effect of medical treatment or other action having a necessary, good, non-contraceptive purpose — is permissible under the principle of the double effect. The practice of periodic continence is not contraception because it does not involve positive interference with the order of nature. (*See Humanae Vitae*, other entries.)

Contrition: Sorrow for sin coupled with a purpose of amendment. Contrition arising from a supernatural motive is necessary for the forgiveness of sin. 1) Perfect contrition is total sorrow for and renunciation of attachment to sin, arising from the motive of pure love of God. Perfect contrition, which implies the intention of doing all God wants done for the forgiveness of sin (including confession in a reasonable period of time), is sufficient for the forgiveness of serious sin and the remission of all temporal punishment due for sin. (The intention to receive the sacrament of penance is implicit — even if unrealized, as in the case of some persons — in perfect contrition.) 2) Imperfect contrition or attrition is sorrow arising from a quasi-selfish supernatural motive; e.g., the fear of losing heaven, suffering the pains of hell, etc. Imperfect contrition is sufficient for the forgiveness of serious sin when joined with absolution in confession, and sufficient for the forgiveness of venial sin even outside of confession.

Contumely: Personal insult, reviling a person in his presence by accusation of moral faults, by refusal of recognition or due respect; a violation of obligations of justice and charity.

Conversion: In a general sense, the turning away from someone or something and the moving toward another person or thing. In Christian belief, conversion is the embrace of Jesus Christ and a rejection of all that keeps one from God.

Corpus Iuris Canonici: *See* **Canon Law**.

Council: A formal meeting of Church leaders, summoned by a bishop or appropriate Church leader, with the general purpose of assisting the life of the Church through deliberations, decrees, and promulgations. Different councils include: **diocesan** councils (synod), a gathering of the officials of an individual diocese; **provincial** councils, the meeting of the bishops of a province; **plenary** councils, the assembly of the bishops of a country; and **ecumenical** councils, a gathering of all the bishops in the world under the authority of the Bishop of Rome.

Counsels, Evangelical: Gospel counsels of perfection, especially voluntary poverty, perfect chastity and obedience, which were recommended by Christ to those who would devote themselves exclusively and completely to the immediate service of God. Religious (members of institutes of consecrated life) bind themselves by public vows to observe these counsels in a life of total consecration to God and service to people through various kinds of apostolic works.

Counter-Reformation: The period of approximately 100 years following the Council of Trent (1545-63), which witnessed a reform within the Church to stimulate genuine Catholic life and to counteract effects of the Reformation.

Covenant: A bond of relationship between parties pledged to each other. God-initiated covenants in the Old Testament included those with Noah, Abraham, Moses, Levi, David. The Mosaic (Sinai) covenant made Israel God's Chosen People on terms of fidelity to true faith, true worship, and righteous conduct according to the Decalogue. The New Testament covenant, prefigured in the Old Testament, is the bond people have with God through Christ. All people are called to be parties to this perfect and everlasting covenant, which was mediated and ratified by Christ. The marriage covenant seals the closest possible relationship between a man and a woman.

Creation: The production by God of something out of nothing. The biblical account of creation is contained in the first two chapters of Genesis.

Creator: God, the supreme, self-existing Being, the absolute and infinite First Cause of all things.

Creature: Everything in the realm of being is a creature, except God.

Cremation: The reduction of a human corpse to ashes by means of fire. Cremation is not in line with Catholic tradition and practice, even though it is not opposed to any article of faith. The Congregation for the Doctrine of the Faith, under date of May 8, 1963, circulated among bishops an instruction which upheld the traditional practices of Christian burial but modified anti-cremation legislation. Cremation may be permitted for serious reasons, of a private as well as public nature, provided it does not involve any contempt of the Church or of religion, or any attempt to deny, question, or belittle the doctrine of the resurrection of the body. In a letter dated Mar. 21, 1997, and addressed to Bishop Anthony M. Pilla, president of the National Conference of Catholic Bishops, the Congregation for Divine Worship and the Discipline of the Sacraments granted "a particular permission to the diocesan bishops of the United States of America. By this, local Ordinaries (heads of dioceses) are authorized ... to permit that the funeral liturgy, including where appropriate the celebration of the Eucharist, be celebrated in the presence of the cremated remains instead of the natural body." Bishop Pilla asked bishops not to use this indult until appropriate texts and ritual directives are approved by the Vatican. (*See* **Burial, Ecclesiastical**).

Crib: Also crèche, a devotional representation of the birth of Jesus. The custom of erecting cribs is generally attributed to St. Francis of Assisi, who in 1223 obtained from Pope Honorius III permission to use a crib and figures of the Christ Child, Mary, St. Joseph, and others, to represent the mystery of the Nativity.

Crosier: The bishop's staff, symbolic of his pastoral office, responsibility and authority; used at liturgical functions.

Crypt: An underground or partly underground chamber; e.g., the lower part of a church used for worship and/or burial.

Cura Animarum: A Latin phrase, meaning care of souls, designating the pastoral ministry and responsibility of bishops and priests.

Curia: The personnel and offices through which 1) the pope administers the affairs of the universal Church, the Roman Curia (*See* p. 268), or 2) a bishop the affairs of a diocese, diocesan curia. The principal officials of a diocesan curia are the vicar general of the diocese, the chancellor, officials of the diocesan tribunal or court, examiners, consultors, auditors, notaries.

Custos: A religious superior who presides over a number of convents collectively called a custody. In some institutes of consecrated life a custos may be the deputy of a higher superior.

D

Dean: 1) A priest with supervisory responsibility over a section of a diocese known as a deanery. The post-Vatican II counterpart of a dean is an episcopal vicar. 2) The senior or ranking member of a group.

Decision: A judgment or pronouncement on a cause or suit, given by a church tribunal or official with judicial authority. A decision has the force of law for concerned parties.

Declaration: 1) An ecclesiastical document which presents an interpretation of an existing law. 2) A position paper on a specific subject; e.g., the three declarations issued by the Second Vatican Council on religious freedom, non-Christian religions, and Christian education.

Decree: An edict or ordinance issued by a pope and/ or by an ecumenical council, with binding force in the whole Church; by a department of the Roman Curia, with binding force for concerned parties; by a territorial body of bishops, with binding force for persons in the area; by individual bishops, with binding force for concerned parties until revocation or the death of the bishop. The nine decrees issued by the Second Vatican Council were combinations of doctrinal and pastoral statements with executive orders for action and movement toward renewal and reform in the Church.

Dedication of a Church: The ceremony whereby a church is solemnly set apart for the worship of God. The custom of dedicating churches had an antecedent in Old Testament ceremonies for the dedication of the Temple, as in the times of Solomon and the Maccabees. The earliest extant record of the dedication of a Christian church dates from early in the fourth century, when it was done simply by the celebration of Mass. Other ceremonies developed later. A church can be dedicated by a simple blessing or a solemn consecration. The rite of consecration is generally performed by a bishop.

Deposit of the Faith: The body of saving truth, entrusted by Christ to the Apostles and handed on by them to the Church to be preserved and proclaimed. As embodied in Revelation and Tradition the term is very nearly coextensive with objective revelation, in that it embraces the whole of Christ's teaching. But the term of deposit highlights particular features of the apostolic teaching implying that this teaching is an inexhaustible store that rewards and promotes reflection and study so that new insights and deeper penetration might be made into the mystery of the divine economy of salvation. Although our understanding of this teaching can develop, it can never be augmented in its substance; the teaching is a divine trust, that cannot be altered, modified, or debased. The term *depositum fidei* first entered official Catholic teaching with the Council of Trent, but its substance is well-attested in the Scriptures and the Fathers.

Despair: Abandonment of hope for salvation arising from the conviction that God will not provide the necessary means for attaining it, that following God's way of life for salvation is impossible, or that one's sins are unforgivable; a serious sin against the Holy Spirit and the theological virtues of hope and faith, involving distrust in the mercy and goodness of God and a denial of the truths that God wills the salvation of all persons and provides sufficient grace for it. Real despair is distinguished from unreasonable fear with respect to the difficulties of attaining salvation, from morbid anxiety over the demands of divine justice, and from feelings of despair.

Detraction: Revelation of true but hidden faults of a person without sufficient and justifying reason; a violation of requirements of justice and charity, involving the obligation to make restitution when this is possible without doing more harm to the good name of the offended party. In some cases, e.g., to prevent evil, secret faults may and should be disclosed.

Devil: 1) Lucifer, Satan, chief of the fallen angels who sinned and were banished from heaven. Still possessing angelic powers, he can cause such diabolical phenomena as possession and obsession, and can tempt men to sin. 2) Any fallen angel.

Devotion: 1) Religious fervor, piety; dedication. 2) The consolation experienced at times during prayer; a reverent manner of praying.

Devotions: Pious practices of members of the Church include not only participation in various acts of the liturgy but also in other acts of worship generally called popular or private devotions. Concerning these, the Second Vatican Council said in the Constitution on the Sacred Liturgy (*Sacrosanctum Concilium*, No. 13): "Popular devotions of the Christian people are warmly commended, provided they accord with the laws and norms of the Church. Such is especially the case with devotions called for by the Apostolic See. Devotions proper to the individual churches also have a special dignity. These devotions should be so drawn up that they harmonize with the liturgical seasons, accord with the sacred liturgy, are in some fashion derived from it, and lead the people to it, since the liturgy by its very nature far surpasses any of them." Devotions of a liturgical type are Exposition of the Blessed Sacrament, recitation of Evening Prayer and Night Prayer of the Liturgy of the Hours. Examples of paraliturgical devotion are a Bible service or vigil, and the Angelus, Rosary and Stations of the Cross, which have a strong scriptural basis.

Diocese: A particular church, a fully organized ecclesiastical jurisdiction under the pastoral direction of a bishop as local Ordinary.

Discalced: Of Latin derivation and meaning without shoes, the word is applied to religious orders or congregations whose members go barefoot or wear sandals.

Disciple: A term used sometimes in reference to the Apostles but more often to a larger number of followers (70 or 72) of Christ mentioned in Lk. 10:1.

Disciplina Arcani: A Latin phrase, meaning discipline of the secret and referring to a practice of the early Church, especially during the Roman persecutions, to: 1) conceal Christian truths from those who, it was feared, would misinterpret, ridicule and profane the teachings, and persecute Christians for believing them; 2) instruct catechumens in a gradual manner, withholding the teaching of certain doctrines until the catechumens proved themselves of good faith and sufficient understanding.

Dispensation: The relaxation of a law in a particular case. Laws made for the common good sometimes work undue hardship in particular cases. In such cases, where sufficient reasons are present, dispensations may be granted by proper authorities. Bishops, religious superiors and others may dispense from certain laws; the pope can dispense from all ecclesiastical laws. No one has authority to dispense from obligations of the divine law.

Divination: Attempting to foretell future or hidden things by means of things like dreams, necromancy, spiritism, examination of entrails, astrology, augury, omens, palmistry, drawing straws, dice, cards, etc. Practices like these attribute to created things a power which belongs to God alone and are violations of the First Commandment.

Divine Praises: Fourteen praises recited or sung at Benediction of the Blessed Sacrament in reparation for sins of sacrilege, blasphemy and profanity. Some of these praises date from the end of the 18th century: *Blessed be God. / Blessed be his holy Name. / Blessed be Jesus Christ, true God and true Man. / Blessed be the Name of Jesus. / Blessed be his most Sacred Heart. / Blessed be his most Precious Blood. / Blessed be Jesus in the most holy Sacrament of the Altar. / Blessed be the Holy Spirit, the Paraclete. / Blessed be the great Mother of God, Mary most holy. / Blessed be her holy and Immaculate Conception. / Blessed be her glorious Assumption. / Blessed be the name of Mary, Virgin and Mother. / Blessed be St. Joseph, her most chaste Spouse. / Blessed be God in his Angels and in his Saints.*

Double Effect Principle: Actions sometimes have two effects closely related to each other, one good and the other bad, and a difficult moral question can arise: Is it permissible to place an action from which two such results follow? It is permissible to place the action, if: the action is good in itself and is directly productive of the good effect; the circumstances are good; the intention of the person is good; the reason for placing the action is proportionately serious to the seriousness of the indirect bad effect.

Doxology: 1) The lesser doxology, or ascription of glory to the Trinity, is the Glory be to the Father. The first part dates back to the third or fourth century, and came from the form of baptism. The concluding words, "As it was in the beginning," etc., are of later origin. 2) The greater doxology, "Glory to God in the highest," begins with the words of angelic praise at the birth of Christ recounted in the Infancy Narrative

(Lk. 2:14). It is often recited at Mass. Of early Eastern origin, it is found in the Apostolic Constitutions in a form much like the present. 3) The formula of praise at the end of the Eucharistic Prayer at Mass, sung or said by the celebrant while he holds aloft the paten containing the consecrated host in one hand and the chalice containing the consecrated wine in the other.

Dulia: A Greek term meaning the veneration or homage, different in nature and degree from that given to God, paid to the saints. It includes honoring the saints and seeking their intercession with God.

Duty: A moral obligation deriving from the binding force of law, the exigencies of one's state in life, and other sources.

E

Easter Controversy: A three-phase controversy over the time for the celebration of Easter. Some early Christians in the Near East, called Quartodecimans, favored the observance of Easter on the 14th day of Nisan, the spring month of the Hebrew calendar, whenever it occurred. Against this practice, Pope St. Victor I, about 190, ordered a Sunday observance of the feast. The Council of Nicaea, in line with usages of the Church at Rome and Alexandria, decreed in 325 that Easter should be observed on the Sunday following the first full moon of spring. Uniformity of practice in the West was not achieved until several centuries later, when the British Isles, in delayed compliance with measures enacted by the Synod of Whitby in 664, accepted the Roman date of observance. Unrelated to the controversy is the fact that some Eastern Christians, in accordance with traditional calendar practices, celebrate Easter at a different time than the Roman and Eastern Churches.

Easter Duty: The serious obligation binding Catholics of Roman Rite, to receive the Eucharist during the Easter season (in the U.S., from the first Sunday of Lent to and including Trinity Sunday).

Easter Water: Holy water blessed with special ceremonies and distributed on the Easter Vigil; used during Easter Week for blessing the faithful and homes.

Ecclesiology: Study of the nature, constitution, members, mission, functions, etc., of the Church.

Ecology: The natural environment of the total range of creation — mineral, vegetable, animal, human — entrusted to people for respect, care and appropriate use as well as conservation and development for the good of present and future generations.

Ecstasy: An extraordinary state of mystical experience in which a person is so absorbed in God that the activity of the exterior senses is suspended.

Economy, Divine: The fulfillment of God's plan of salvation. It was fully developed in his divine mind from eternity, and fully revealed in Jesus Christ. Before the Incarnation it was known only obscurely, but after the ascension of Christ and the coming of the Holy Spirit at Pentecost, it became the substance of apostolic preaching and is preserved in its integrity for each new generation.

Ecumenism: The movement of Christians and their churches toward the unity willed by Christ. The Second Vatican Council called the movement "those activities and enterprises which, according to various needs of the Church and opportune occasions, are started and organized for the fostering of unity among Christians" ("Decree on Ecumenism," No. 4). Spiritual ecumenism, i.e., mutual prayer for unity, is the heart of the movement. The movement also involves scholarly and pew-level efforts for the development of mutual understanding and better interfaith relations in general, and collaboration by the churches and their members in the social area. (*See* **Index** for other entries.)

Elevation: The raising of the host after consecration at Mass for adoration by the faithful. The custom was introduced in the Diocese of Paris about the close of the 12th century to offset an erroneous teaching of the time which held that transubstantiation of the bread did not take place until after the consecration of the wine in the chalice. The elevation of the chalice following the consecration of the wine was introduced in the 15th century.

Encyclical: The highest form of papal teaching document. It is normally addressed to all the bishops and/or to all the faithful.

Envy: Sadness over another's good fortune because it is considered a loss to oneself or a detraction from one's own excellence; one of the seven capital sins, a violation of the obligations of charity.

Epiclesis: An invocation of the Holy Spirit, to bless the offerings consecrated at Mass; before the consecration in the Latin Rite, after the consecration in Eastern usage.

Epikeia: A Greek word meaning reasonableness and designating a moral theory and practice, a mild interpretation of the mind of a legislator who is prudently considered not to wish positive law to bind in certain circumstances.

Episcopate: 1) The office, dignity and sacramental powers bestowed upon a bishop at his ordination. 2) The body of bishops collectively.

Equivocation: 1) The use of words, phrases, or gestures having more than one meaning in order to conceal information which a questioner has no strict right to know. It is permissible to equivocate (have a broad mental reservation) in some circumstances. 2) A lie, i.e., a statement of untruth. Lying is intrinsically wrong. A lie told in joking, evident as such, is not wrong.

Eschatology: Doctrine concerning the last things: death, judgment, heaven and hell, and the final state of perfection of the people and kingdom of God at the end of time.

Eternity: The interminable, perfect possession of life in its totality without beginning or end; an attribute of God, who has no past or future but always is. Man's existence has a beginning but no end and is, accordingly, called immortal.

Ethics: Moral philosophy, the science of the morality of human acts deriving from natural law, the natural end of man, and the powers of human reason. It includes all the spheres of human activity — personal, social, economic, political, etc. Ethics is distinct from but can be related to moral theology, whose primary principles are drawn from divine revelation.

Euthanasia: Mercy killing, the direct causing of death for the purpose of ending human suffering. Euthanasia is murder and is totally illicit, for the natural law forbids the direct taking of one's own life or that of an innocent person. The use of drugs to re-lieve suffering in serious cases, even when this results in a shortening of life as an indirect and secondary effect, is permissible under conditions of the double-effect principle. It is also permissible for a seriously ill person to refuse to follow — or for other responsible persons to refuse to permit — extraordinary medical procedures even though the refusal might entail shortening of life.

Evangelization: Proclamation of the Gospel, the Good News of salvation in and through Christ, among those who have not yet known or received it; and efforts for the progressive development of the life of faith among those who have already received the Gospel and all that it entails. Evangelization is the primary mission of the Church, in which all members of the Church are called to participate.

Evolution: Scientific theory concerning the development of the physical universe from unorganized matter (inorganic evolution) and, especially, the development of existing forms of vegetable, animal and human life from earlier and more primitive organisms (organic evolution). Various ideas about evolution were advanced for some centuries before scientific evidence in support of the main-line theory of organic evolution, which has several formulations, was discovered and verified in the second half of the 19th century and afterwards. This evidence — from the findings of comparative anatomy and other sciences — confirmed evolution of species and cleared the way to further investigation of questions regarding the processes of its accomplishment. While a number of such questions remain open with respect to human evolution, a point of doctrine not open to question is the immediate creation of the human soul by God. For some time, theologians regarded the theory with hostility, considering it to be in opposition to the account of creation in the early chapters of Genesis and subversive of belief in such doctrines as creation, the early state of man in grace, and the fall of man from grace. This state of affairs and the tension it generated led to considerable controversy regarding an alleged conflict between religion and science. Gradually, however, the tension was diminished with the development of biblical studies from the latter part of the 19th century onwards, with clarification of the distinctive features of religious truth and scientific truth, and with the refinement of evolutionary concepts. So far as the Genesis account of creation is concerned, the Catholic view is that the writer(s) did not write as a scientist but as the communicator of religious truth in a manner adapted to the understanding of the people of his time. He used anthropomorphic language, the figure of days and other literary devices to state the salvation truths of creation, the fall of man from grace, and the promise of redemption. It was beyond the competency and purpose of the writer(s) to describe creation and related events in a scientific manner.

Excommunication: A penalty or censure by which a baptized Roman Catholic is excluded from the communion of the faithful, for committing and remaining obstinate in certain serious offenses specified in canon law; e.g. heresy, schism, apostasy, abortion. As by baptism a person is made a member of the Church in which there is a communication of spiritual goods, so by excommunication he is deprived of the same spiritual goods until he repents and receives absolution. Even though excommunicated, a person is still responsible for fulfillment of the normal obligations of a Catholic. (*See* **Censures**).

Ex Opere Operantis: A term in sacramental theology meaning that the effectiveness of sacraments depends on the moral rectitude of the minister or participant. This term was applied to rites of the OT in contrast with those of the NT when it was first advanced in the 13th century.

Ex Opere Operato: A term in sacramental theology meaning that sacraments are effective by means of the sacramental rite itself and not because of the worthiness of the minister or participant.

Exorcism: 1) Driving out evil spirits; a rite in which evil spirits are charged and commanded on the authority of God and with the prayer of the Church to depart from a person or to cease causing harm to a person suffering from diabolical possession or obsession. The sacramental is officially administered by a priest delegated for the purpose by the bishop of the place. Elements of the rite include the Litany of Saints; recitation of the Our Father, one or more creeds, and other prayers; specific prayers of exorcism; the reading of Gospel passages and use of the Sign of the Cross. On Jan. 26, 1999, the Congregation for Divine Worship and the Discipline of the Sacraments published a new rite of exorcism in the Roman Ritual. [*See* **Special Reports** for additional details.] 2) Exorcisms that do not imply the conditions of either diabolical possession or obsession form part of the ceremony of baptism and are also included in formulas for various blessings; e.g., of water.

Exposition of the Blessed Sacrament: "In churches where the Eucharist is regularly reserved, it is recommended that solemn exposition of the Blessed Sacrament for an extended period of time should take place once a year, even though the period is not strictly continuous. Shorter expositions of the Eucharist (Benediction) are to be arranged in such a way that the blessing with the Eucharist is preceded by a reasonable time for readings of the word of God, songs, prayers and a period for silent prayer." So stated Vatican directives issued in 1973.

F

Faculties: Grants of jurisdiction or authority by the law of the Church or superiors (pope, bishop, religious superior) for exercise of the powers of holy orders; e.g., priests are given faculties to hear confessions and officiate at weddings; bishops are given faculties to grant dispensations, etc.

Faith: In religion, faith has several aspects. Catholic doctrine calls faith the assent of the mind to truths revealed by God, the assent being made with the help of grace and by command of the will on account of the authority and trustworthiness of God revealing. The term "faith" also refers to the truths that are believed (content of faith) and to the way in which a person, in response to Christ, gives witness to and expresses belief in daily life (living faith). All of these elements, and more, are included in the following statement: " 'The obedience of faith' (Rom. 16:26; 1:5; 2 Cor. 10:5-6) must be given to God who reveals, an obedience by which man entrusts his whole self freely to God, offering 'the full submission of intellect and will to God who reveals' (First Vatican

Council, "Dogmatic Constitution on the Catholic Faith," Chap. 3), and freely assenting to the truth revealed by him. If this faith is to be shown, the grace of God and the interior help of the Holy Spirit must precede and assist, moving the heart and turning it to God, opening the eyes of the mind, and giving 'joy and ease to everyone in assenting to the truth and believing it' " (Second Council of Orange, Canon 7) (Second Vatican Council, "Constitution on Revelation," *Dei Verbum*, No. 5). Faith is necessary for salvation.

Faith, Rule of: The norm or standard of religious belief. The Catholic doctrine is that belief must be professed in the divinely revealed truths in the Bible and tradition as interpreted and proposed by the infallible teaching authority of the Church.

Fast, Eucharistic: Abstinence from food and drink, except water and medicine, is required for one hour before the reception of the Eucharist. Persons who are advanced in age or suffer from infirmity or illness, together with those who care for them, can receive Holy Communion even if they have not abstained from food and drink for an hour. A priest celebrating two or three Masses on the same day can eat and drink something before the second or third Mass without regard for the hour limit.

Father: A title of priests, who are regarded as spiritual fathers because they are the ordinary ministers of baptism, by which persons are born to supernatural life, and because of their pastoral service to people.

Fear: A mental state caused by the apprehension of present or future danger. Grave fear does not necessarily remove moral responsibility for an act, but may lessen it.

First Friday: A devotion consisting of the reception of Holy Communion on the first Friday of nine consecutive months in honor of the Sacred Heart of Jesus and in reparation for sin. (*See* **Sacred Heart, Promises**.)

First Saturday: A devotion tracing its origin to the apparitions of the Blessed Virgin Mary at Fátima in 1917. Those practicing the devotion go to confession and, on the first Saturday of five consecutive months, receive Holy Communion, recite five decades of the Rosary, and meditate on the mysteries for 15 minutes.

Fisherman's Ring: A signet ring (termed in Italian the *pescatorio*) engraved with the image of St. Peter fishing from a boat, and encircled with the name of the reigning pope. It is not worn by the pope. It is used to seal briefs, and is destroyed after each pope's death.

Forgiveness of Sin: Catholics believe that sins are forgiven by God through the mediation of Christ in view of the repentance of the sinner and by means of the sacrament of penance. (*See* **Penance, Contrition**).

Fortitude: Courage to face dangers or hardships for the sake of what is good; one of the four cardinal virtues and one of the seven gifts of the Holy Spirit.

Forty Hours Devotion: A Eucharistic observance consisting of solemn exposition of the Blessed Sacrament coupled with special Masses and forms of prayer, for the purposes of making reparation for sin and praying for God's blessings of grace and peace. The devotion was instituted in 1534 in Milan. St. John Neumann of Philadelphia was the first bishop in the U.S. to prescribe its observance in his diocese. For many years in this country, the observance was held annually on a rotating basis in all parishes of a diocese. Simplified and abbreviated Eucharistic observances have taken the place of the devotion in some places.

Forum: The sphere in which ecclesiastical authority or jurisdiction is exercised. 1) External: Authority is exercised in the external forum to deal with matters affecting the public welfare of the Church and its members. Those who have such authority because of their office (e.g., diocesan bishops) are called ordinaries. 2) Internal: Authority is exercised in the internal forum to deal with matters affecting the private spiritual good of individuals. The sacramental forum is the sphere in which the sacrament of penance is administered; other exercises of jurisdiction in the internal forum take place in the non-sacramental forum.

Freedom, Religious: The Second Vatican Council declared that the right to religious freedom in civil society "means that all men are to be immune from coercion on the part of individuals or of social groups and of any human power, in such wise that in matters religious no one is to be forced to act in a manner contrary to his own beliefs. Nor is anyone to be restrained from acting in accordance with his own beliefs, whether privately or publicly, whether alone or in association with others, within due limits" of requirements for the common good. The foundation of this right in civil society is the "very dignity of the human person" ("Declaration on Religious Freedom," *Dignitatis Humanae*, No. 2). The conciliar statement did not deal with the subject of freedom within the Church. It noted the responsibility of the faithful "carefully to attend to the sacred and certain doctrine of the Church" (No. 14).

Freemasons: A fraternal order that originated in London in 1717 with the formation of the first Grand Lodge of Freemasons. From England, the order spread to Europe and elsewhere. Its principles and basic rituals embody a naturalistic religion, active participation in which is incompatible with Christian faith and practice. Grand Orient Freemasonry, developed in Latin countries, is atheistic, irreligious and anticlerical. In some places, Freemasonry has been regarded as subversive of the state; in Catholic quarters, it has been considered hostile to the Church and its doctrine. In the United States, Freemasonry has been widely regarded as a fraternal and philanthropic order. For serious doctrinal and pastoral reasons, Catholics were forbidden to join the Freemasons under penalty of excommunication, according to church law before 1983. Eight different popes in 17 different pronouncements, and at least six different local councils, condemned Freemasonry. The first condemnation was made by Clement XII in 1738. Eastern Orthodox and many Protestant bodies have also opposed the order. In the U.S., there was some easing of the ban against Masonic membership by Catholics in view of a letter written in 1974 by Cardinal Franjo Seper, prefect of the Congregation for the Doctrine of the Faith. The letter was interpreted to mean that Catholics might join Masonic lodges which were not anti-Catholic. This was called erroneous in a declaration issued by the Doctrinal Congregation Feb. 17, 1981. The prohibition against Masonic membership was restated in a declaration issued by the Doctrinal Congregation Nov. 26, 1983, with the approval of Pope John Paul II, as follows. "The Church's negative position on Masonic associations remains unaltered, since their principles have always been regarded as irreconcilable with the Church's doctrine. Hence, joining them remains prohibited by the Church. Catholics enrolled in Masonic associations are involved in serious sin and may not approach Holy Communion. Local ecclesiastical authorities do not have the faculty to pronounce a judgment on the nature of Masonic associations which might include a diminution of the above-mentioned judgment." This latest declaration, like the revised Code of Canon Law, does not include a penalty of excommunication for Catholics who join the Masons. Local bishops are not authorized to grant dispensations from the prohibition. The foregoing strictures against Masonic membership by Catholics were reiterated in a report by the Committee for Pastoral Research and Practice, National Conference of Catholic Bishops, released through Catholic News Service June 7, 1985.

Free Will: The faculty or capability of making a reasonable choice among several alternatives. Freedom of will underlies the possibility and fact of moral responsibility.

Friar: Term applied to members of mendicant orders to distinguish them from members of monastic orders. (*See* **Mendicants**.)

Fruits of the Holy Spirit: Charity, joy, peace, patience, kindness, goodness, generosity, gentleness, faithfulness, modesty, self-control, chastity.

Fruits of the Mass: The spiritual and temporal blessings that result from the celebration of the Holy Sacrifice of the Mass. The general fruits are shared by all the faithful, living and departed, while the special fruits are applied to the priest who celebrates it, to those for whose intention it is offered, and to all those who participate in its celebration.

Fundamental Option: The orientation of one's life either to God by obedience or against Him through disobedience. Catholic Tradition acknowledges that one free and deliberate act with knowledge renders one at odds with God. A prevalent and vague moral theory today asserts that one act cannot change one's option to God — no matter how grave — unless the action comes from the person's "center." Pope John Paul II cautioned against this ambiguous position in the encyclical *Veritatis Splendor* (1993).

G

Gehenna: Greek form of a Jewish name, Gehinnom, for a valley near Jerusalem, the site of Moloch worship; used as a synonym for hell.

Genuflection: Bending of the knee, a natural sign of adoration or reverence, as when persons genuflect with the right knee in passing before the tabernacle to acknowledge the Eucharistic presence of Christ.

Gethsemani: A Hebrew word meaning oil press, designating the place on the Mount of Olives where Christ prayed and suffered in agony the night before he died.

Gifts of the Holy Spirit: Supernatural habits disposing a person to respond promptly to the inspiration of grace; promised by Christ and communicated through the Holy Spirit, especially in the sacrament of confirmation. They are: wisdom, understanding, counsel, knowledge, fortitude, piety, and fear of the Lord.

Glorified Body: The definitive state of humanity in eternity. The risen Christ calls humanity to the glory of his resurrection; this is a theological premise that presupposes that, like Christ, all of his brothers and sisters will be transformed physically.

Gluttony: An unreasonable appetite for food and drink; one of the seven capital sins.

God: The infinitely perfect Supreme Being, uncaused and absolutely self-sufficient, eternal, the Creator and final end of all things. The one God subsists in three equal Persons, the Father and the Son and the Holy Spirit. God, although transcendent and distinct from the universe, is present and active in the world in realization of his plan for the salvation of human beings, principally through Revelation, the operations of the Holy Spirit, the life and ministry of Christ, and the continuation of Christ's ministry in the Church. The existence of God is an article of faith, clearly communicated in divine Revelation. Even without this Revelation, however, the Church teaches, in a declaration by the First Vatican Council, that human beings can acquire certain knowledge of the existence of God and some of his attributes. This can be done on the bases of principles of reason and reflection on human experience. Non-revealed arguments or demonstrations for the existence of God have been developed from the principle of causality; the contingency of human beings and the universe; the existence of design, change and movement in the universe; human awareness of moral responsibility; widespread human testimony to the existence of God.

Goods of Marriage: Three blessings — children, faithful companionship, and permanence — that were first enumerated by St. Augustine in a work on marriage.

Grace: A free gift of God to persons (and angels), grace is a created sharing or participation in the life of God. It is given to persons through the merits of Christ and is communicated by the Holy Spirit. It is necessary for salvation. The principal means of grace are the sacraments (especially the Eucharist), prayer and good works. 1) **Sanctifying or habitual grace** makes persons holy and pleasing to God, adopted children of God, members of Christ, temples of the Holy Spirit, heirs of heaven capable of supernaturally meritorious acts. With grace, God gives persons the supernatural virtues and gifts of the Holy Spirit. The sacraments of baptism and penance were instituted to give grace to those who do not have it; the other sacraments, to increase it in those already in the state of grace. The means for growth in holiness, or the increase of grace, are prayer, the sacraments, and good works. Sanctifying grace is lost by the commission of serious sin. Each sacrament confers sanctifying grace for the special purpose of the sacrament; in this context, grace is called sacramental grace. 2) **Actual grace** is a supernatural help of God which enlightens and strengthens a person to do good and to avoid evil. It is not a permanent quality, like sanctifying grace. It is necessary for the performance of supernatural acts. It can be resisted and refused. Persons in the state of serious sin are given actual grace to lead them to repentance.

Grace at Meals: Prayers said before meals, asking a blessing of God, and after meals, giving thanks to God. In addition to traditional prayers for these purposes, many variations suitable for different occasions are possible, at personal option.

Guilt: The condition of an individual who has committed some moral wrong and is liable to receive punishment.

H

Habit: 1) A disposition to do things easily, given with grace (and therefore supernatural) and/or acquired by repetition of similar acts. 2) The garb worn by Religious.

Hagiography: Writings or documents about saints and other holy persons.

Hail Mary: A prayer addressed to the Blessed Virgin Mary; also called the *Ave Maria* (Latin equivalent of Hail Mary) and the Angelic Salutation. In three parts, it consists of the words addressed to Mary by the Archangel Gabriel on the occasion of the Annunciation, in the Infancy Narrative (*Hail Mary, full of grace, the Lord is with you, blessed are you among women.*); the words addressed to Mary by her cousin Elizabeth on the occasion of the Visitation (*Blessed is the fruit of your womb.*); a concluding petition (*Holy Mary, Mother of God, pray for us sinners now and at the hour of our death. Amen.*). The first two salutations were joined in Eastern-rite formulas by the sixth century, and were similarly used at Rome in the seventh century. Insertion of the name of Jesus at the conclusion of the salutations was probably made by Urban IV about 1262. The present form of the petition was incorporated into the breviary in 1514.

Heaven: The state of those who, having achieved salvation, are in glory with God and enjoy the beatific vision. The phrase, kingdom of heaven, refers to the order or kingdom of God, grace, salvation.

Hell: The state of persons who die in mortal sin, in a condition of self-alienation from God, which will last forever.

Heresy: The obstinate post-baptismal denial or doubt by a Catholic of any truth which must be believed as a matter of divine and Catholic faith (Canon 751, of the Code of Canon Law). Formal heresy involves deliberate resistance to the authority of God who communicates revelation through Scripture and tradition and the teaching authority of the Church. Heretics automatically incur the penalty of excommunication (Canon 1364 of the Code of Canon Law). Heresies have been significant not only as disruptions of unity of faith but also as occasions for the clarification and development of doctrine. Heresies from the beginning of the Church to the 13th century are described in **Dates and Events in Church History**.

Hermeneutics: *See* under the section **Interpretation of the Bible**.

Hermit: *See* **Anchorite**.

Heroic Act of Charity: The completely unselfish offering to God of one's good works and merits for the benefit of the souls in purgatory rather than for oneself. Thus a person may offer to God for the souls in purgatory all the good works he performs during life, all the indulgences he gains, and all the prayers and indulgences that will be offered for him after his death. The act is revocable at will, and is not a vow. Its actual ratification depends on the will of God.

Heroic Virtue: The exemplary practice of the four cardinal virtues and three theological virtues; such virtue is sought in persons considered for sainthood.

Heterodoxy: False doctrine teaching or belief; a departure from truth.

Hierarchy: The hierarchy of order who carry out the sacramental, teaching, and pastoral ministry of the Church; the hierarchy consists of the pope, bishops, priests, and deacons; the pope and the bishops give pastoral governance to the faithful.

Holy Father: A title used for the pope; it is a shortened translation of the Latin title *Beatissimus Pater*, "Most Blessed Father" and refers to his position as the spiritual father of all the Christian faithful.

Holy See: 1) The diocese of the pope, Rome. 2) The pope himself and/or the various officials and bodies of the Church's central administration at Vatican City — the Roman Curia — which act in the name and by authority of the pope.

Holy Spirit: God the Holy Spirit, third Person of the Holy Trinity, who proceeds from the Father and the Son and with whom he is equal in every respect; inspirer of the prophets and writers of sacred Scripture; promised by Christ to the Apostles as their advocate and strengthener; appeared in the form of a dove at the baptism of Christ and as tongues of fire at his descent upon the Apostles; soul of the Church and guarantor, by his abiding presence and action, of truth in doctrine; communicator of grace to human beings, for which reason he is called the sanctifier.

Holy Water: Water blessed by the Church and used as a sacramental, a practice which originated in apostolic times.

Holy Year: A year during which the pope grants the plenary Jubilee Indulgence to the faithful who fulfill certain conditions. For those who make a pilgrimage to Rome during the year, the conditions are reception of the sacraments of penance and the Eucharist, visits and prayer for the intention of the pope in the basilicas of St. Peter, St. John Lateran, St. Paul and St. Mary Major. For those who do not make a pilgrimage to Rome, the conditions are reception of the sacraments and prayer for the pope during a visit or community celebration in a church designated by the bishop of the locality. Pope Boniface VIII formally proclaimed the first Holy Year on Feb. 22, 1300, and the first three Holy Years were observed in 1300, 1350 and 1390. Subsequent ones were celebrated at 25-year intervals except in 1800 and 1850 when, respectively, the French invasion of Italy and political turmoil made observance impossible. Pope Paul II (1464-1471) set the 25-year timetable. In 1500, Pope Alexander VI prescribed the start and finish ceremonies — the opening and closing of the Holy Doors in the major basilicas on successive Christmas Eves. All but a few of the earlier Holy Years were classified as ordinary. Several — like those of 1933 and 1983-84 to commemorate the 1900th and 1950th anniversaries of the death and resurrection of Christ — were in the extraordinary category. Pope John Paul II designated Jubilee Year 2000 to be a Holy Year ending the second and beginning the third millennium of Christianity.

Homosexuality: The condition of a person whose sexual orientation is toward persons of the same rather than the opposite sex. The condition is not sinful in itself. Homosexual acts are seriously sinful in themselves; subjective responsibility for such acts, however, may be conditioned and diminished by compulsion and related factors.

Hope: The theological virtue by which a person firmly trusts in God for the means and attainment salvation.

Hosanna: A Hebrew word, meaning *O Lord, save, we pray*.

Host, The Sacred: The bread under whose appearances Christ is and remains present in a unique manner after the consecration which takes place during Mass. (*See* **Transubstantiation**.)

Human Dignity: The inherent worth of all human persons as they are made in God's image and likeness and they alone — of all God's creatures on earth — have an immortal soul.

Humanism: A world view centered on man. Types of humanism which exclude the supernatural are related to secularism.

Humility: A virtue which induces a person to evaluate himself or herself at his or her true worth, to recognize his or her dependence on God, and to give glory to God for the good he or she has and can do.

Hyperdulia: The special veneration accorded the Blessed Virgin Mary because of her unique role in the mystery of Redemption, her exceptional gifts of grace from God, and her pre-eminence among the saints. Hyperdulia is not adoration; only God is adored.

Hypostatic Union: The union of the human and divine natures in the one divine Person of Christ.

I

Icons: Byzantine-style paintings or representations of Christ, the Blessed Virgin and other saints, venerated in the Eastern Churches where they take the place of statues.

Idolatry: Worship of any but the true God; a violation of the First Commandment.

IHS: In Greek, the first three letters of the name of Jesus — *Iota, Eta, Sigma*.

Immaculate Conception: The doctrine that affirms that "the Blessed Virgin Mary was preserved, in the first instant of her conception, by a singular grace and privilege of God omnipotent and because of the merits of Jesus Christ the Savior of the human race, free from all stain of Original Sin," as stated by Pope Pius IX in his declaration of the dogma, Dec. 8, 1854. Thus, Mary was conceived in the state of perfect justice, free from Original Sin and its consequences, in virtue of the redemption achieved by Christ on the cross.

Immortality: The survival and continuing existence of the human soul after death.

Imprimatur: *See* **Censorship of Books**.

Impurity: Unlawful indulgence in sexual pleasure. (*See* **Chastity**.)

Imputability: A canonical term for the moral responsibility of a person for an act that he or she has performed.

Incardination: The affiliation of a priest to his diocese. Every secular priest must belong to a certain diocese. Similarly, every priest of a religious community must belong to some jurisdiction of his community; this affiliation, however, is not called incardination.

Incarnation: 1) The coming-into-flesh or taking of human nature by the Second Person of the Trinity. He became human as the Son of Mary, being miraculously conceived by the power of the Holy Spirit, without ceasing to be divine. His divine Person hypostatically unites his divine and human natures. 2) The supernatural mystery coextensive with Christ from the moment of his human conception and continuing through his life on earth; his sufferings and death; his resurrection from the dead and ascension to glory with the Father; his sending, with the Father, of the Holy Spirit upon the Apostles and the Church; and his unending mediation with the Father for the salvation of human beings.

Incense: A granulated substance which, when burnt, emits an aromatic smoke. It symbolizes the zeal with which the faithful should be consumed, the good odor of Christian virtue, the ascent of prayer to God. An incense boat is a small vessel used to hold incense which is to be placed in the censer.

Incest: Sexual intercourse with relatives by blood or marriage; a sin of impurity and also a grave violation of the natural reverence due to relatives. Other sins of impurity (desire, etc.) concerning relatives have the nature of incest.

Inculturation: The correct and entirely appropriate adaptation of the Catholic liturgy and institutions to the culture, language, and customs of an indigenous or local people among whom the Gospel is first proclaimed. Pope John Paul II on Feb. 15, 1982, at a meeting in Lagos with the bishops of Nigeria, proclaimed: "An important aspect of your own evangelizing role is the whole dimension of the inculturation of the Gospel into the lives of your people. The Church truly respects the culture of each people. In offering the Gospel message, the Church does not intend to destroy or to abolish what is good and beautiful. In fact, she recognizes many cultural values and, through the power of the Gospel, purifies and takes into Christian worship certain elements of a people's customs."

Index of Prohibited Books: A list of books which Catholics were formerly forbidden to read, possess or sell, under penalty of excommunication. The books were banned by the Holy See after publication because their treatment of matters of faith and morals and related subjects were judged to be erroneous or serious occasions of doctrinal error. Some books were listed in the Index by name; others were covered under general norms. The Congregation for the Doctrine of the Faith declared June 14, 1966, that the Index and its related penalties of excommunication no longer had the force of law in the Church. Persons are still obliged, however, to take normal precautions against occasions of doctrinal error.

Indifferentism: A theory that any one religion is as true and good — or false — as any other religion, and that it makes no difference, objectively, what religion one professes, if any. The theory is completely subjective, finding its justification entirely in personal choice without reference to or respect for objective validity. It is also self-contradictory, since it regards as equally acceptable — or unacceptable — the beliefs of all religions, which in fact are not only not all the same but are in some cases opposed to each other.

Indulgence: According to "The Doctrine and Practice of Indulgences," an apostolic constitution issued by Paul VI on Jan. 1, 1967, an indulgence is the remission before God of the temporal punishment due for sins already forgiven as far as their guilt is concerned, which a follower of Christ — with the proper dispositions and under certain determined conditions — acquires through the intervention of the Church. An indulgence is partial or plenary, depending on whether it does away with either part or all of the temporal punishment due for sin. Both types of indulgences can always be applied to the dead by way of suffrage; the actual disposition of indulgences applied to the dead rests with God. Only one plenary indulgence can be gained in a single day. The Apostolic Penitentiary issued a decree Dec. 14, 1985, granting diocesan bishops the right to impart — three times a year on solemn feasts of their choice — the papal blessing with a plenary indulgence to those who cannot be physically present but who follow the sacred rites at which the blessing is imparted by radio or television transmission. In July 1986, publication was announced of a new and simplified *Enchiridion Indulgentiarum*, in accord with provisions of the revised Code of Canon Law. A revised manual was issued by the Holy See on Sept. 17, 2000.

Indult: A favor or privilege granted by competent ecclesiastical authority, giving permission to do something not allowed by the common law of the Church.

Infallibility: 1) The inability of the Church to err in its teaching, in that she preserves and teaches the deposit of truth as revealed by Christ; 2) The inability of the Roman Pontiff to err when he teaches *ex cathedra* in matters of faith or morals, and indicates that the doctrine is to be believed by all the faithful; and 3) the inability of the college of bishops to err when speaking in union with the pope in matters of faith and morals, agreeing that a doctrine must be held by the universal Church, and the doctrine is promulgated by the pontiff.

Infused Virtues: The theological virtues of faith, hope, and charity; principles or capabilities of supernatural action, they are given with sanctifying grace by God rather than acquired by repeated acts of a person. They can be increased by practice; they are lost by contrary acts. Natural-acquired moral virtues, like the cardinal virtues of prudence, justice, temperance, and fortitude, can be considered infused in a person whose state of grace gives them supernatural orientation.

Inquisition: A tribunal for dealing with heretics, authorized by Gregory IX in 1231 to search them out, hear and judge them, sentence them to various forms of punishment, and in some cases to hand them over to civil authorities for punishment. The Inquisition was a creature of its time when crimes against faith, which threatened the good of the Christian community, were regarded also as crimes against the state, and when heretical doctrines of such extremists as the Cathari and Albigensians threatened the very fabric of society. The institution, which was responsible for many excesses, was most active in the second half of the 13th century.

Inquisition, Spanish: An institution peculiar to Spain and the colonies in Spanish America. In 1478, at the urging of King Ferdinand, Pope Sixtus IV approved the establishment of the Inquisition for trying charges of heresy brought against Jewish (*Marranos*) and Moorish (*Moriscos*) converts. It acquired jurisdiction over other cases as well, however, and fell into disrepute because of irregularities in its functions, cruelty in its sentences, and the manner in which it served the interests of the Spanish crown more than the accused persons and the good of the Church. Protests by the Holy See failed to curb excesses of the Inquisition, which lingered in Spanish history until early in the 19th century.

I N R I: The first letters of words in the Latin inscription atop the cross on which Christ was crucified: *(I)esus (N)azaraenus, (R)ex (I)udaeorum* — Jesus of Nazareth, King of the Jews.

Insemination, Artificial: The implanting of human semen by some means other than consummation of natural marital intercourse. In view of the principle that procreation should result only from marital intercourse, donor insemination is not permissible.

In Sin: The condition of a person called spiritually dead because he or she does not possess sanctifying grace, the principle of supernatural life, action and merit. Such grace can be regained through repentance.

Instruction: A document containing doctrinal explanations, directive norms, rules, recommendations, admonitions, issued by the pope, a department of the Roman Curia or other competent authority in the Church. To the extent that they so prescribe, instructions have the force of law.

Intercommunion, Eucharistic Sharing: The common celebration and reception of the Eucharist by members of different Christian churches; a pivotal issue in ecumenical theory and practice. Catholic participation and intercommunion in the Eucharistic liturgy of another church without a valid priesthood and with a variant Eucharistic belief is out of order. Under certain conditions, other Christians may receive the Eucharist in the Catholic Church. (*See* additional **Intercommunion** entry). Intercommunion is acceptable to some Protestant churches and unacceptable to others.

Interdict: A censure imposed on persons for certain violations of Church law. Interdicted persons may not take part in certain liturgical services, administer or receive certain sacraments.

Intinction: A method of administering Holy Communion under the dual appearances of bread and wine, in which the consecrated host is dipped in the consecrated wine before being given to the communicant. The administering of Holy Communion in this manner, which has been traditional in Eastern-Rite liturgies, was authorized in the Roman Rite for various occasions by the "Constitution on the Sacred Liturgy" promulgated by the Second Vatican Council.

Irenicism: Peace-seeking, conciliation, as opposed to polemics; an important element in ecumenism, provided it furthers pursuit of the Christian unity willed by Christ without degenerating into a peace-at-any-price disregard for religious truth.

Irregularity: A permanent impediment to the lawful reception or exercise of holy orders. The Church instituted irregularities — which include apostasy, heresy, homicide, attempted suicide — out of reverence for the dignity of the sacraments.

J

Jehovah: The English equivalent of the Hebrew *Adonai* ("my Lord") used out of fear and reverence for the Holy Name of Yahweh. *Jehovah* uses the consonants YHWH and the vowels of *Adonai* (a, o, a). Scholars today maintain that *Jehovah* is a false derivation.

Jesus: The name of Jesus, meaning "God saves," expressing the identity and mission of the second Person of the Trinity become man; derived from the Aramaic and Hebrew Yeshua and Joshua, meaning "Yahweh is salvation."

Jesus Prayer: A prayer of Eastern origin, dating back to the fifth century: *"Lord Jesus Christ, Son of God, have mercy on me (a sinner)."*

Judgment: 1) **Last or final judgment**: Final judgment by Christ, at the end of the world and the general resurrection. 2) **Particular judgment**: The judgment that takes place immediately after a person's death, followed by entrance into heaven, hell or purgatory.

Jurisdiction: Right, power, authority to rule. Jurisdiction in the Church is of divine institution; has pastoral service for its purpose; includes legislative, judicial and executive authority; can be exercised only by persons with the power of orders. 1) Ordinary jurisdiction is attached to ecclesiastical offices by law; the officeholders, called Ordinaries, have authority over those who are subject to them. 2) Delegated jurisdiction is that which is granted to persons rather than attached to offices. Its extent depends on the terms of the delegation.

Justice: One of the four cardinal virtues by which a person gives to others what is due to them as a matter of right. (*See* **Cardinal Virtues**.)

Justification: The act by which God makes a person just, and the consequent change in the spiritual status of a person, from sin to grace; the remission of sin and the infusion of sanctifying grace through the merits of Christ and the action of the Holy Spirit.

K

Kenosis: A term from the Greek for "emptying" that denotes Christ's emptying of himself in his free renunciation of his right to divine status, by reason of the Incarnation, particularly as celebrated in the kenotic hymn (Phil 2:6-11), where it is said that Christ "emptied himself," taking the form of a slave, born in the likeness of man totally integrated with his divinity.

Kerygma: Proclaiming the word of God, in the manner of the Apostles, as here and now effective for salvation. This method of preaching or instruction, centered on Christ and geared to the facts and themes of salvation history, is designed to dispose people to faith in Christ and/or to intensify the experience and practice of that faith in those who have it.

Keys, Power of the: Spiritual authority and jurisdiction in the Church, symbolized by the keys of the kingdom of heaven. Christ promised the keys to St. Peter, as head-to-be of the Church (Mt. 16:19), and commissioned him with full pastoral responsibility to feed his lambs and sheep (Jn. 21:15-17), The pope, as the successor of St. Peter, has this power in a primary and supreme manner. The bishops of the Church also have the power, in union with and subordinate to the pope. Priests share in it through holy orders and the delegation of authority. Examples of the application of the Power of the Keys are the exercise of teaching and pastoral authority by the pope and bishops, the absolving of sins in the sacrament of penance, the granting of indulgences, the imposing of spiritual penalties on persons who commit certain serious sins.

Kingdom of God: God's sovereign lordship or rule over salvation history, leading to the eschatological goal of eternal life with God.

Koinonia: A term from the Greek word for "community, fellowship, or association" that was used by St. Luke for the fellowship of believers who worshipped together and held all their possessions in common (Acts 2:42-47); it is also used of fellowship with God (1 Jn. 1:3, 6), with the Son (1 Cor. 1:9), and with the Holy Spirit (2 Cor. 13:13; Phil. 2:1). St. Paul used *koinonia* to denote the intimate union of the believer with Christ and the community that exists among all the faithful themselves (Rom. 15:26; 2 Cor. 6:14).

L

Laicization: The process by which a man ordained to holy orders is relieved of the obligations of orders and the ministry and is returned to the status of a lay person.

Languages of the Church: The languages in which the Church's liturgy is celebrated. These include Ge'ez, Syriac, Greek, Arabic, and Old Slavonic in the Eastern Churches. In the West, there is, of course, Latin and the various vernaculars. The Eastern Rites have always had the vernacular. The first language in church use, for divine worship and the conduct of ecclesiastical affairs, was Aramaic, the language of the first Christians in and around Jerusalem. As the Church spread westward, Greek was adopted and prevailed until the third century, when it was supplanted by Latin for official use in the West. In the Western Church, Latin prevailed as the general official language until the promulgation on Dec. 4, 1963, of the "Constitution on the Sacred Liturgy" (*Sacrosanctum Concilium*) by the second session of the Second Vatican Council. Since that time, vernacular languages have come into use in the Mass, administration of the sacraments, and the Liturgy of the Hours. Latin, however, remains the official language for documents of the Holy See, administrative and procedural matters.

Latria: Greek-rooted Latin term that refers to that form of praise due to God alone.

Law: An ordinance or rule governing the activity of things. 1) **Natural law**: Moral norms corresponding to man's nature, by which he orders his conduct toward God, neighbor, society and himself. This law, which is rooted in human nature, is of divine origin, can be known by the use of reason, and binds all persons having the use of reason. The Ten Commandments are declarations and amplifications of natural law. The primary precepts of natural law, to do good and to avoid evil, are universally recognized, despite differences with respect to understanding and application resulting from different philosophies of good and evil. 2) **Divine positive law**: That which has been revealed by God. Among its essentials are the twin precepts of love of God and love of neighbor, and the Ten Commandments. 3) **Ecclesiastical law**: That which is established by the Church for the spiritual welfare of the faithful and the orderly conduct of ecclesiastical affairs. (*See* **Canon Law**.) 4) **Civil law**: That which is established by a sociopolitical community for the common good.

Liberalism: A multi-phased trend of thought and movement favoring liberty, independence and progress in moral, intellectual, religious, social, economic and political life. Traceable to the Renaissance, it developed through the Enlightenment, the rationalism of the 19th century, and modernist- and existentialist-related theories of the 20th century. Evaluations of various kinds of liberalism depend on the validity of their underlying principles. Extremist positions — regarding subjectivism, libertinarianism, naturalist denials of the supernatural, and the alienation of individuals and society from God and the Church — were condemned by Gregory XVI in the 1830s, Pius IX in 1864, Leo XIII in 1899, and St. Pius X in 1907. There is, however, nothing objectionable about forms of liberalism patterned according to sound principles of Christian doctrine.

Liberation Theology: Deals with the relevance of Christian faith and salvation — and, therefore, of the mission of the Church — to efforts for the promotion of human rights, social justice and human development. It originated in the religious, social, political and economic environment of Latin America, with its contemporary need for a theory and corresponding action by the Church, in the pattern of its overall mission, for human rights and integral personal and social development. Some versions of liberation theology are at variance with the body of church teaching because of their ideological concept of Christ as liberator, and also because they play down the primary spiritual nature and mission of the Church. Instructions from the Congregation for the Doctrine of the Faith — "On Certain Aspects of the Theology of Liberation" (Sept. 3, 1984) and "On Christian Freedom and Liberation" (Apr. 5, 1986) — contain warnings against translating sociology into theology and advocating violence in social activism.

Life in Outer Space: Whether rational life exists on other bodies in the universe besides earth, is a question for scientific investigation to settle. The possibility can be granted, without prejudice to the body of revealed truth.

Limbo: The limbo of the fathers was the state of rest and natural happiness after death enjoyed by the just of pre-Christian times until they were admitted to heaven following the Ascension of Christ.

Litany: A prayer in the form of responsive petition; e.g., St. Joseph, pray for us, etc. Examples are the litanies of Loreto (Litany of the Blessed Mother), the Holy Name, All Saints, the Sacred Heart, the Precious Blood, St. Joseph, Litany for the Dying.

Logos: A Greek term for "word, speech, or reason." It is most commonly identified with the title given to Jesus in John's Gospel, though not exclusive to that Gospel; In the NT, however, the term reflects more the influence of Hellenistic philosophy: St. Paul uses logos as interchangeable with *sophia*, wisdom (1 Cor. 1:24). The *Logos* is the Wisdom of God made manifest in the Son. As a name for the Second Person of the Trinity, the Incarnate Word, the term receives new meaning in the light of the life, death, and resurrection of Jesus Christ.

Loreto, House of: A Marian shrine in Loreto, Italy, consisting of the home of the Holy Family which, according to an old tradition, was transported in a miraculous manner from Nazareth to Dalmatia and finally to Loreto between 1291 and 1294. Investigations conducted shortly after the appearance of the structure in Loreto revealed that its dimensions matched those of the house of the Holy Family missing from its place of enshrinement in a basilica at Nazareth. Among the many popes who regarded it with high honor was John XXIII, who went there on pilgrimage Oct. 4, 1962. The house of the Holy Family is enshrined in the Basilica of Our Lady.

Love: A devotion to a person or object that has been categorized by Greek philosophy into four types: *storge* (one loves persons and things close to him); *philia* (the love of friends); *eros* (sexual love and that of a spiritual nature); *agape* (a self-giving to one in need). Christian charity is love, but not all love is true charity.

Lust: A disorderly desire for sexual pleasure; one of the seven capital sins.

M

Magi: In the Infancy Narrative of St. Matthew's Gospel (2:1-12), three wise men from the East whose visit and homage to the Child Jesus at Bethlehem indicated Christ's manifestation of himself to non-Jewish people. The narrative teaches the universality of salvation. The traditional names of the Magi are Caspar, Melchior and Balthasar.

Magisterium: The Church's teaching authority, instituted by Christ and guided by the Holy Spirit, which seeks to safeguard and explain the truths of the faith. The Magisterium is exercised in two ways. The extraordinary Magisterium is exercised when the pope and ecumenical councils infallibly define a truth of faith or morals that is necessary for one's salvation and that has been constantly taught and held by the Church. Ordinary Magisterium is exercised when the Church infallibly defines truths of the Faith as taught universally and without dissent; which must be taught or the Magisterium would be failing in its duty; is connected with a grave matter of faith or morals; and which is taught authoritatively. Not everything taught by the Magisterium is done so infallibly; however, the exercise of the Magisterium is faithful to Christ and what He taught.

Magnificat: The canticle or hymn of the Virgin Mary on the occasion of her visitation to her cousin Elizabeth (Lk. 1:46-55). It is an expression of praise, thanksgiving and acknowledgment of the great blessings given by God to Mary, the Mother of the Second Person of the Blessed Trinity made Man. The *Magnificat* is recited in the Liturgy of the Hours as part of the Evening Prayer.

Martyr: A Greek word, meaning witness, denoting one who voluntarily suffered death for the faith or some Christian virtue.

Martyrology: A catalogue of martyrs and other saints, arranged according to the calendar. The Roman Martyrology contains the official list of saints venerated by the Church. Additions to the list are made in beatification and canonization decrees of the Congregation for the Causes of Saints.

Mass for the People: On Sundays and certain feasts throughout the year pastors are required to offer Mass for the faithful entrusted to their care. If they cannot offer the Mass on these days, they must do so at a later date or provide that another priest offer the Mass.

Materialism: Theory which holds that matter is the only reality, and everything in existence is merely a manifestation of matter; there is no such thing as spirit, and the supernatural does not exist. Materialism is incompatible with Christian doctrine.

Meditation: Mental, as distinguished from vocal, prayer, in which thought, affections, and resolutions of the will predominate. There is a meditative element to all forms of prayer, which always involves the raising of the heart and mind to God.

Mendicants: A term derived from Latin and meaning beggars, applied to members of religious orders without property rights; the members, accordingly, worked or begged for their support. The original mendicants were Franciscans and Dominicans in the early 13th century; later, the Carmelites, Augustinians, Servites and others were given the mendicant title and privileges, with respect to exemption from episcopal jurisdiction and wide faculties for preaching and administering the sacrament of penance. The practice of begging is limited at the present time, although it is still allowed with the permission of competent superiors and bishops. Mendicants are supported by free-will offerings and income received for spiritual services and other work.

Mercy, Divine: The love and goodness of God, manifested particularly in a time of need.

Mercy, Works of: Works of corporal or spiritual assistance, motivated by love of God and neighbor, to persons in need. 1) **Corporal works**: feeding the hungry, giving drink to the thirsty, clothing the naked, visiting the imprisoned, sheltering the homeless, visiting the sick, burying the dead. 2) **Spiritual works**: counseling the doubtful, instructing the ignorant, admonishing sinners, comforting the afflicted, forgiving offenses, bearing wrongs patiently, praying for the living and dead.

Merit: In religion, the right to a supernatural reward for good works freely done for a supernatural motive by a person in the state of and with the assistance of grace. The right to such reward is from God, who binds himself to give it. Accordingly, good works, as described above, are meritorious for salvation.

Metanoia: A term from the Greek *metanoein* ("to change one's mind, repent, be converted") that is used in the NT for conversion. It entails the repentance of sin and the subsequent turning toward the Lord. *Metanoia* is fundamental to the Christian life and is necessary for spiritual growth.

Metaphysics: The branch of philosophy (from the Greek *meta* — after + *physika* — physics) dealing with first things, including the nature of being (ontology), the origin and structure of the world (cosmology), and the study of the reality and attributes of God (natural theology). Metaphysics has long been examined by Catholic philosophers, most especially in the writings of St. Augustine and St. Thomas Aquinas.

Millennium: A thousand-year reign of Christ and the just upon earth before the end of the world. This belief of the Millenarians, Chiliasts, and some sects of modern times is based on an erroneous interpretation of Rv. 20.

Miracles: Observable events or effects in the physical or moral order of things, with reference to salvation, which cannot be explained by the ordinary operation of laws of nature and which, therefore, are attributed to the direct action of God. They make known, in an unusual way, the concern and intervention of God in human affairs for the salvation of men.

Mission: 1) Strictly, it means being sent to perform a certain work, such as the mission of Christ to redeem mankind, the mission of the Apostles and the

Church and its members to perpetuate the prophetic, priestly and royal mission of Christ. 2) A place where: the Gospel has not been proclaimed; the Church has not been firmly established; the Church, although established, is weak. 3) An ecclesiastical territory with the simplest kind of canonical organization, under the jurisdiction of the Congregation for the Evangelization of Peoples. 4) A church or chapel without a resident priest. 5) A special course of sermons and spiritual exercises conducted in parishes for the purpose of renewing and deepening the spiritual life of the faithful and for the conversion of lapsed Catholics.

Modernism: The "synthesis of all heresies," which appeared near the beginning of the 20th century. It undermines the objective validity of religious beliefs and practices which, it contends, are products of the subconscious developed by mankind under the stimulus of a religious sense. It holds that the existence of a personal God cannot be demonstrated, the Bible is not inspired, Christ is not divine, nor did he establish the Church or institute the sacraments. A special danger lies in modernism, which is still influential, because it uses Catholic terms with perverted meanings. St. Pius X condemned 65 propositions of modernism in 1907 in the decree *Lamentabili* and issued the encyclical *Pascendi* to explain and analyze its errors.

Monastery: The dwelling place, as well as the community thereof, of monks belonging to the Benedictine and Benedictine-related orders like the Cistercians and Carthusians; also, the Augustinians and Canons Regular. Distinctive of monasteries are: their separation from the world; the enclosure or cloister; the permanence or stability of attachment characteristic of their members; autonomous government in accordance with a monastic rule, like that of St. Benedict in the West or of St. Basil in the East; the special dedication of its members to the community celebration of the liturgy as well as to work that is suitable to the surrounding area and the needs of its people. Monastic superiors of men have such titles as abbot and prior; of women, abbess and prioress. In most essentials, an abbey is the same as a monastery.

Monk: A member of a monastic order — e.g., the Benedictines, the Benedictine-related Cistercians and Carthusians, and the Basilians, who bind themselves by religious profession to stable attachment to a monastery, the contemplative life and the work of their community. In popular use, the title is wrongly applied to many men Religious who really are not monks.

Monotheism: Belief in and worship of one God.

Morality: Conformity or difformity of behavior to standards of right conduct. (*See* **Moral Obligations**, **Commandments of God**, **Precepts of the Church**, **Conscience**, **Law**.)

Mortification: Acts of self-discipline, including prayer, hardship, austerities and penances undertaken for the sake of progress in virtue.

Motu Proprio: A Latin phrase designating a document issued by a pope on his own initiative. Documents of this kind often concern administrative matters.

Mystagogy: Experience of the mystery of Christ, especially through participation in the liturgy and the sacraments.

Mysteries of Faith: Supernatural truths whose existence cannot be known without revelation by God and whose intrinsic truth, while not contrary to reason, can never be wholly understood even after revelation. These mysteries are above reason, not against reason. Among them are the divine mysteries of the Trinity, Incarnation and Eucharist. Some mysteries — e.g., concerning God's attributes — can be known by reason without revelation, although they cannot be fully understood.

N

Natural Law: *See* **Law**.

Natural Theology: The field of knowledge that relies upon human reason and the observation of nature, instead of revelation, to determine the existence and attributes of God.

Necromancy: Supposed communication with the dead; a form of divination.

Neo-Scholasticism: A movement begun in the late 19th century that had as its aim the restoration of Scholasticism for use in contemporary philosophy and theology. Great emphasis was placed upon the writings of such Scholastic masters as Peter Lombard, St. Albert the Great, St. Anselm, St. Bonaventure, Bl. John Duns Scotus, and especially St. Thomas Aquinas. The movement began at the Catholic University of Louvain, in Belgium, and then found its way into theological centers in Italy, France and Germany. Particular attention was given to the philosophical and theological works of St. Thomas Aquinas, from which arose a particular school of neo-Thomism; the movement was strongly reinforced by Pope Leo XIII, who issued the encyclical *Aeterni Patris* (1879) mandating that Scholasticism, in particular Thomism, be the foundation for all Catholic philosophy and theology taught in Catholic seminaries, universities and colleges. Neo-Scholasticism was responsible for a true intellectual renaissance in 20th-century Catholic philosophy and theology. Among its foremost modern leaders were Jacques Maritain, Étienne Gilson, M. D. Chenu, Henri de Lubac and Paul Claudel.

Nihil Obstat: *See* **Censorship of Books**.

Non-Expedit: A Latin expression. It is not expedient (fitting, proper), used to state a prohibition or refusal of permission.

Novena: A term designating public or private devotional practices over a period of nine consecutive days; or, by extension, over a period of nine weeks, in which one day a week is set aside for the devotions.

Novice: A man or woman preparing, in a formal period of trial and formation called a novitiate, for membership in an institute of consecrated life. The novitiate lasts a minimum of 12 and a maximum of 24 months; at its conclusion, the novice professes temporary promises or vows of poverty, chastity and obedience. Norms require that certain periods of time be spent in the house of novitiate; periods of apostolic work are also required, to acquaint the novice with the apostolate(s) of the institute. A novice is not bound by the obligations of the professed members of the institute, is free to leave at any time, and may be discharged at the discretion of superiors. The superior of a novice is a master of novices or director of formation.

Nun: 1) Strictly, a member of a religious order of women with solemn vows (*moniales*). 2) In general, all women Religious, even those in simple vows, who are more properly called sisters.

Nunc Dimittis: The canticle or hymn of Simeon at the sight of Jesus at the Temple on the occasion of his presentation (Lk. 2:29-32). It is an expression of joy and thanksgiving for the blessing of having lived to see the Messiah. It is prescribed for use in the Night Prayer of the Liturgy of the Hours.

O

Oath: Calling upon God to witness the truth of a statement. Violating an oath, e.g., by perjury in court, or taking an oath without sufficient reason, is a violation of the honor due to God.

Obedience: Submission to one in authority. General obligations of obedience fall under the Fourth Commandment. The vow of obedience professed by religious is one of the evangelical counsels.

Obsession, Diabolical: The extraordinary state of one who is seriously molested by evil spirits in an external manner. Obsession is more than just temptation.

Occasion of Sin: A person, place, or thing that is a temptation to sin. An occasion may be either a situation that always leads to sin or one that usually leads to sin.

Octave: A period of eight days given over to the celebration of a major feast such as Easter.

Oils, Holy: The oils blessed by a bishop at the Chrism Mass on Holy Thursday or another suitable day, or by a priest under certain conditions. 1) The oil of catechumens (olive or vegetable oil), used at baptism; also, poured with chrism into the baptismal water blessed in Easter Vigil ceremonies. 2) Oil of the sick (olive or vegetable oil) used in anointing the sick. 3) Chrism (olive or vegetable oil mixed with balm), which is ordinarily consecrated by a bishop, for use at baptism, in confirmation, at the ordination of a priest and bishop, in the dedication of churches and altars.

Ontologism: A philosophical theory (the name is taken from the Greek for "being" and "study") that posits that knowledge of God is immediate and intuitive; it stipulates further that all other human knowledge is dependent upon this. It was condemned in 1861 by Pope Pius IX. (*See* also **Ontology**.)

Ontology: A branch of metaphysics that studies the nature and relations of existence.

Oratory: A chapel.

Ordinariate: An ecclesiastical jurisdiction for special purposes and people. Examples are military ordinariates for armed services personnel (in accord with provisions of the apostolic constitution *Spirituali militum curae*, Apr. 21, 1986) and Eastern-Rite ordinariates in places where Eastern-Rite dioceses do not exist.

Ordination: The consecration of sacred ministers for divine worship and the service of people in things pertaining to God. The power of ordination comes from Christ and the Church, and must be conferred by a minister capable of communicating it.

Organ Transplants: The transplanting of organs from one person to another is permissible provided it is done with the consent of the concerned parties and does not result in the death or essential mutilation of the donor. Advances in methods and technology have increased the range of transplant possibilities in recent years.

Original Sin: The sin of Adam (Gn. 2:8-3:24), personal to him and passed on to all persons as a state of privation of grace. Despite this privation and the related wounding of human nature and weakening of natural powers, original sin leaves unchanged all that man himself is by nature. The scriptural basis of the doctrine was stated especially by St. Paul in 1 Cor. 15:21ff., and Rom. 5:12-21. Original sin is remitted by baptism and incorporation in Christ, through whom grace is given to persons. Pope John Paul II, while describing original sin during a general audience Oct. 1, 1986, called it "the absence of sanctifying grace in nature which has been diverted from its supernatural end."

O Salutaris Hostia: The first three Latin words, *O Saving Victim*, of a Benediction hymn.

Ostpolitik: Policy adopted by Pope Paul VI in an attempt to improve the situation of Eastern European Catholics through diplomatic negotiations with their governments.

Oxford Movement: A movement in the Church of England from 1833 to about 1845 that had for its objective a threefold defense of the Church as a divine institution, the apostolic succession of its bishops, and the *Book of Common Prayer* as the rule of faith. The movement took its name from Oxford University and involved a number of intellectuals who authored a series of influential "Tracts for Our Times." Some of its leading figures — e.g., F. W. Faber, John Henry Newman and Henry Edward Manning — became converts to the Catholic Church. In the Church of England, the movement affected the liturgy, historical and theological scholarship, the status of the ministry, and other areas of ecclesiastical life.

P

Paganism: A term referring to non-revealed religions, i.e., religions other than Christianity, Judaism, and Islam.

Palms: Blessed palms are a sacramental. They are blessed and distributed on the Sunday of the Passion in commemoration of the triumphant entrance of Christ into Jerusalem. Ashes of the burnt palms are used on Ash Wednesday.

Pange Lingua: First Latin words, *Sing, my tongue*, of a hymn in honor of the Holy Eucharist, used particularly on Holy Thursday and in Eucharistic processions.

Pantheism: Theory that all things are part of God, divine, in the sense that God realizes himself as the ultimate reality of matter or spirit through being and/or becoming all things that have been, are, and will be. The theory leads to hopeless confusion of the Creator and the created realm of being, identifies evil with good, and involves many inherent contradictions.

Papal Election: The pope is elected by the College of Cardinals during a secret conclave that begins no sooner than 15 days and no later than 20 days after the death of his predecessor. Cardinals under the age of 80, totaling no more than 120, are eligible to take part in the election by secret ballot. Election is by a two-thirds vote of participating cardinals. New legislation regarding papal elections and church government during a vacancy of the Holy See was promulgated by Pope John Paul II on Feb. 23, 1996, in the apostolic constitution *Universi Dominici Gregis* ("Shepherd of the Lord's Whole Flock").

Paraclete: A title of the Holy Spirit meaning, in Greek, Advocate, Consoler.

Parental Duties: All duties related to the obligation of parents to provide for the welfare of their children. These obligations fall under the Fourth Commandment.

Parish: A community of the faithful served by a pastor charged with responsibility for providing them with full pastoral service. Most parishes are territorial, embracing all of the faithful in a certain area of a diocese: some are personal or national, for certain classes of people, without strict regard for their places of residence.

Parousia: The coming, or saving presence, of Christ that will mark the completion of salvation history and the coming to perfection of God's kingdom at the end of the world.

Particular Church: A term used since Vatican II that denotes certain divisions of the Universal Church. Examples include dioceses, vicariates, and prelatures.

Paschal Candle: A large candle, symbolic of the risen Christ, blessed and lighted on the Easter Vigil and placed at the altar until Pentecost. It is ornamented with five large grains of incense, representing the wounds of Christ, inserted in the form of a cross; the Greek letters Alpha and Omega, symbolizing Christ the beginning and end of all things, at the top and bottom of the shaft of the cross; and the figures of the current year of salvation in the quadrants formed by the cross.

Paschal Precept: Church law requiring reception of the Eucharist in the Easter season (*See* separate entry) unless, for a just cause, once-a-year reception takes place at another time.

Passion of Christ: Sufferings of Christ, recorded in the four Gospels.

Pastor: An ordained minister charged with responsibility for the doctrinal, sacramental and related service of people committed to his care; e.g., a bishop for the people in his diocese, a priest for the people of his parish.

Pater Noster: The initial Latin words, *Our Father*, of the Lord's Prayer.

Patriarch: 1) The leaders of the Israelite tribes and heads of prominent families who appear in Genesis from Adam to Joseph. Among the most significant patriarchs of the Old Testament are Abraham, Isaac and Jacob; the patriarchal narratives in Genesis associated with them constitute the prologue to Israel's salvation history, and the period during which they lived is known as the Age of the Patriarchs. It is noted that the title of patriarch that was used for David (Acts 2:29) was simply one of honor. 2) The head of a branch of the Eastern Church, corresponding to a province of the one-time Roman Empire. There are five official traditional patriarchal sees: Rome, Constantinople, Alexandria, Antioch, and Jerusalem. Presently, the autocephalous churches of the Orthodox Church comprise several of these traditional patriarchates.

Peace, Sign of: A gesture of greeting — e.g., a handshake — exchanged by the ministers and participants at Mass.

Pectoral Cross: A cross worn on a chain about the neck and over the breast by bishops and abbots as a mark of their office.

Penance or Penitence: 1) The spiritual change or conversion of mind and heart by which a person turns away from sin, and all that it implies, toward God, through a personal renewal under the influence of the Holy Spirit. Penance involves sorrow and contrition for sin, together with other internal and external acts of atonement. It serves the purposes of reestablishing in one's life the order of God's love and commandments, and of making satisfaction to God for sin. 2) Penance is a virtue disposing a person to turn to God in sorrow for sin and to carry out works of amendment and atonement. 3) The sacrament of penance and sacramental penance.

People of God: A name for the Church in the sense that it is comprised by a people with Christ as its head, the Holy Spirit as the condition of its unity, the law of love as its rule, and the kingdom of God as its destiny. Although it is a scriptural term, it was given new emphasis by the Second Vatican Council's "Dogmatic Constitution on the Church" (*Lumen Gentium*).

Perjury: Taking a false oath, lying under oath, a violation of the honor due to God.

Persecution, Religious: A campaign waged against a church or other religious body by persons and governments intent on its destruction. The best known campaigns of this type against the Christian Church were the Roman persecutions which occurred intermittently from about 54 to the promulgation of the Edict of Milan in 313. More Catholics have been persecuted in the 20th century than in any other period in history.

Personal Prelature: A special-purpose jurisdiction — for particular pastoral and missionary work, etc. — consisting of secular priests and deacons and open to lay persons willing to dedicate themselves to its apostolic works. The prelate in charge is an Ordinary, with the authority of office; he can establish a national or international seminary, incardinate its students and promote them to holy orders under the title of service to the prelature. The prelature is constituted and governed according to statutes laid down by the Holy See. Statutes define its relationship and mode of operation with the bishops of territories in which members live and work. Opus Dei is a personal prelature.

Peter's Pence: A collection made each year among Catholics for the maintenance of the pope and his works of charity. It was originally a tax of a penny on each house, and was collected on St. Peter's day, whence the name. It originated in England in the 8th century.

Petition: One of the four purposes of prayer. In prayers of petition, persons ask of God the blessings they and others need.

Pharisees: Influential class among the Jews, referred to in the Gospels, noted for their self-righteousness, legalism, strict interpretation of the Law, acceptance of the traditions of the elders as well as the Law of Moses, and beliefs regarding angels and spirits, the resurrection of the dead and judgment. Most of them were laymen, and they were closely allied with the Scribes; their opposite numbers were the Sadducees. The Pharisaic and rabbinical traditions had a lasting influence on Judaism following the destruction of Jerusalem in 70 A.D.

Pious Fund: Property and money originally accumulated by the Jesuits to finance their missionary work in Lower California. When the Jesuits were expelled from the territory in 1767, the fund was appropriated by the Spanish Crown and used to support Dominican and Franciscan missionary work in Upper and Lower California. In 1842 the Mexican government took over administration of the fund, incorporated most of the revenue into the national treasury, and agreed to pay the Church interest of six percent a year on the capital so incorporated. From 1848 to 1967 the fund was the subject of lengthy negotiations between the U.S. and Mexican governments because of the latter's failure to make payments as agreed. A lump-sum settlement was made in 1967 with payment by Mexico to the U.S. government of more than $700,000, to be turned over to the Archdiocese of San Francisco.

Polytheism: Belief in and worship of many gods or divinities, especially prevalent in pre-Christian religions.

Poor Box: Alms-box; found in churches from the earliest days of Christianity.

Pope: A title from the Italian word *papa* (from Greek *pappas*, father) used for the Bishop of Rome, the Vicar of Christ and successor of St. Peter, who exercises universal governance over the Church.

Portiuncula: 1) Meaning little portion (of land), the Portiuncula was the chapel of Our Lady of the Angels near Assisi, Italy, which the Benedictines gave to St. Francis early in the 13th century. He repaired the chapel and made it the first church of the Franciscan Order. It is now enshrined in the Basilica of St. Mary of the Angels in Assisi. 2) The plenary Portiuncula Indulgence, or Pardon of Assisi, was authorized by Honorius III. Originally, it could be gained for the souls in purgatory only in the chapel of Our Lady of the Angels; by later concessions, it could be gained also in other Franciscan and parish churches. The indulgence (applicable to the souls in purgatory) can be gained from noon of Aug. 1 to midnight of Aug. 2, once each day. The conditions are, in addition to freedom from attachment to sin: reception of the sacraments of penance and the Eucharist on or near the day and a half; a visit to a parish church within the day and a half, during which the Our Father, the Creed and another prayer are offered for the intentions of the pope.

Positivism: The philosophy that teaches that the only reality is that which is perceived by the senses; the only truth is that which is empirically verified. It asserts that ideas about God, morality, or anything else that cannot be scientifically tested are to be rejected as unknowable.

Possession, Diabolical: The extraordinary state of a person who is tormented from within by evil spirits who exercise strong influence over his powers of mind and body. (*See* also **Exorcism**.)

Postulant: One of several names used to designate a candidate for membership in a religious institute during the period before novitiate.

Poverty: 1) The quality or state of being poor, in actual destitution and need, or being poor in spirit. In the latter sense, poverty means the state of mind and disposition of persons who regard material things in proper perspective as gifts of God for the support of life and its reasonable enrichment, and for the service of others in need. It means freedom from unreasonable attachment to material things as ends in themselves, even though they may be possessed in small or large measure. 2) One of the evangelical counsels professed as a public vow by members of an institute of consecrated life. It involves the voluntary renunciation of rights of ownership and of independent use and disposal of material goods; or, the right of independent use and disposal, but not of the radical right of ownership. Religious institutes provide their members with necessary and useful goods and services from common resources. The manner in which goods are received and/or handled by religious is determined by poverty of spirit and the rule and constitutions of their institute.

Pragmatism: Theory that the truth of ideas, concepts and values depends on their utility or capacity to serve a useful purpose rather than on their conformity with objective standards; also called utilitarianism.

Prayer: The raising of the mind and heart to God in adoration, thanksgiving, reparation and petition. Prayer, which is always mental because it involves thought and love of God, may be vocal, meditative, private and personal, social, and official. The official prayer of the Church as a worshipping community is called the liturgy.

Precepts: Commands or orders given to individuals or communities in particular cases; they establish law for concerned parties. Preceptive documents are issued by the pope, departments of the Roman Curia and other competent authority in the Church.

Presence of God: A devotional practice of increasing one's awareness of the presence and action of God in daily life.

Presumption: A sin against hope, by which a person striving for salvation 1) either relies too much on his own capabilities or 2) expects God to do things which he cannot do, in keeping with his divine attributes, or does not will to do, according to his divine plan. Presumption is the opposite of despair.

Preternatural Gifts: Exceptional gifts, beyond the exigencies and powers of human nature, enjoyed by Adam in the state of original justice: immunity from suffering and death, superior knowledge, integrity or perfect control of the passions. These gifts were lost as the result of original sin; their loss, however, implied no impairment of the integrity of human nature.

Pride: Unreasonable self-esteem; one of the seven capital sins.

Prie-Dieu: A French phrase, meaning "pray God," designating a kneeler or bench suitable for kneeling while at prayer.

Priesthood: 1) The common priesthood of the non-ordained faithful. In virtue of baptism and confirmation, the faithful are a priestly people who participate in the priesthood of Christ through acts of worship, witness to the faith in daily life, and efforts to foster the growth of God's kingdom. 2) The ordained priesthood, in virtue of the sacrament of orders, of bishops, priests and deacons, for service to the common priesthood.

Primary Option: The life-choice of a person for or against God that shapes the basic orientation of moral conduct. A primary option for God does not preclude the possibility of serious sin.

Prior: A superior or an assistant to an abbot in a monastery.

Privilege: A favor, an exemption from the obligation of a law. Privileges of various kinds, with respect to ecclesiastical laws, are granted by the pope, departments of the Roman Curia and other competent authority in the Church.

Probabiliorism: The moral system asserting that the more probable opinion of a varied set of acceptable positions regarding the binding character of a law should be accepted. If the reasons for being free from a law are more probably true, one is freed from the law's obligations. Probabiliorism, however, maintained that if it was probable that the law did not bind, one still had to follow it unless it was more probable that the law did not bind.

Probabilism: A moral system for use in cases of conscience which involve the obligation of doubtful laws. There is a general principle that a doubtful law does not bind. Probabilism, therefore, teaches that it is permissible to follow an opinion favoring liberty, provided the opinion is certainly and solidly probable. Probabilism may not be invoked when there is question of: a certain law or the certain obligation of a law; the certain right of another party; the validity of an action; something which is necessary for salvation.

Pro-Cathedral: A church used as a cathedral.

Promoter of the Faith (*Promotor fidei*): An official of the Congregation for the Causes of Saints, whose role in beatification and canonization procedures is to establish beyond reasonable doubt the validity of evidence regarding the holiness of prospective saints and miracles attributed to their intercession.

Prophecy: 1) The communication of divine revelation by inspired intermediaries, called prophets, between God and his people. Old Testament prophecy was unique in its origin and because of its ethical and religious content, which included disclosure of the saving will of Yahweh for the people, moral censures and warnings of divine punishment because of sin and violations of the Law and Covenant, in the form of promises, admonitions, reproaches and threats. Although Moses and other earlier figures are called prophets, the period of prophecy is generally dated from the early years of the monarchy to about 100 years after the Babylonian Exile. From that time on, the written Law and its interpreters supplanted the prophets as guides of the people. Old Testament prophets are cited in the New Testament, with awareness that God spoke through them and that some of their oracles were fulfilled in Christ. John the Baptist is the outstanding prophetic figure in the New Testament. Christ never claimed the title of prophet for himself, although some people thought he was one. There were prophets in the early Church, and St. Paul mentioned the charism of prophecy in 1 Cor. 14:1-5. Prophecy disappeared after New Testament times. Revelation is classified as the prophetic book of the New Testament. 2) In contemporary non-scriptural usage, the term is applied to the witness given by persons to the relevance of their beliefs in everyday life and action.

Proportionalism: The moral theory that asserts that an action is judged on whether the evils resulting are proportionate to the goods that result. If the evils outweigh the goods, the act is objectionable; if the opposite is true, the act is permissible. Proportionalism differs from consequentialism in that the former admits that the inherent morality of the act and the agent's intention must also be considered. Proportionalism is rejected by critics as it does not offer an objective criterion for determining when evils are proportionate or disproportionate. It also fails to consider the intrinsic nature of human acts and does nothing to assist Christians to grow in virtue.

Province: 1) A territory comprising one archdiocese called the metropolitan see and one or more dioceses called suffragan sees. The head of the archdiocese, an archbishop, has metropolitan rights and responsibilities over the province. 2) A division of a religious order under the jurisdiction of a provincial superior.

Prudence: Practical wisdom and judgment regarding the choice and use of the best ways and means of doing good; one of the four cardinal virtues.

Punishment Due for Sin: The punishment which is a consequence of sin. It is of two kinds: 1) Eternal punishment is the punishment of hell, to which one becomes subject by the commission of mortal sin. Such punishment is remitted when mortal sin is forgiven. 2) Temporal punishment is a consequence of venial sin and/or forgiven mortal sin; it is not everlasting and may be remitted in this life by means of penance. Temporal punishment unremitted during this life is remitted by suffering in purgatory.

Purgatory: The state or condition of those who have died in the state of grace but with some attachment to sin, and are purified for a time before they are admitted to the glory and happiness of heaven. In this state and period of passive suffering, they are purified of unrepented venial sins, satisfy the demands of divine justice for temporal punishment due for sins, and are thus converted to a state of worthiness of the beatific vision.

Q

Quadragesima: From the Latin for fortieth, the name given to the forty penitential days of Lent.

Quinquennial Report: A report on the current state of a diocese that must be compiled and submitted by a bishop to the Holy See every five years in anticipation of the *ad limina* visit.

Quinque Viae: From the Latin for the "five ways," the five proofs for the existence of God that were proposed by St. Thomas Aquinas in his *Summa Theologiae* (Part I, question 2, article 3). The five ways are: 1) all the motion in the world points to an unmoved Prime Mover; 2) the subordinate agents in the world imply the First Agent; 3) there must be a Cause Who is not perishable and Whose existence is underived; 4) the limited goodness in the world must be a reflection of Unlimited Goodness; 5) all things tend to become something, and that inclination must have proceeded from some Rational Planner.

R

Racism: A theory which holds that any one or several of the different races of the human family are inherently superior or inferior to any one or several of the others. The teaching denies the essential unity of the human race, the equality and dignity of all persons because of their common possession of the same human nature, and the participation of all in the divine plan of redemption. It is radically opposed to the virtue of justice and the precept of love of neighbor. Differences of superiority and inferiority which do exist are the result of accidental factors operating in a wide variety of circumstances, and are in no way due to essential defects in any one or several of the branches of the one human race. The theory of racism, together with practices related to it, is incompatible with Christian doctrine.

Rash Judgment: Attributing faults to another without sufficient reason; a violation of the obligations of justice and charity.

Rationalism: A theory which makes the mind the measure and arbiter of all things, including religious truth. A product of the Enlightenment, it rejects the supernatural, divine revelation, and authoritative teaching by any church.

Recollection: Meditation, attitude of concentration or awareness of spiritual matters and things pertaining to salvation and the accomplishment of God's will.

Relativism: Theory which holds that all truth, including religious truth, is relative, i.e., not absolute, certain or unchanging; a product of agnosticism, indifferentism, and an unwarranted extension of the notion of truth in positive science. Relativism is based on the tenet that certain knowledge of any and all truth is impossible. Therefore, no religion, philosophy or science can be said to possess the real truth; consequently, all religions, philosophies and sciences may be considered to have as much or as little of truth as any of the others.

Relics: The physical remains and effects of saints, which are considered worthy of veneration inasmuch as they are representative of persons in glory with God. Catholic doctrine proscribes the view that relics are not worthy of veneration. In line with norms laid down by the Council of Trent and subsequent enactments, discipline concerning relics is subject to control by the Congregations for the Causes of Saints and for Divine Worship and the Discipline of the Sacraments.

Religion: The adoration and service of God as expressed in divine worship and in daily life. Religion is concerned with all of the relations existing between God and human beings, and between humans themselves because of the central significance of God. Objectively considered, religion consists of a body of truth which is believed, a code of morality for the guidance of conduct, and a form of divine worship. Subjectively, it is a person's total response, theoretically and practically, to the demands of faith; it is living faith, personal engagement, self-commitment to God. Thus, by creed, code and cult, a person orders and directs his or her life in reference to God and, through what the love and service of God implies, to all people and all things.

Reliquary: A vessel for the preservation and exposition of a relic; sometimes made like a small monstrance.

Reparation: The making of amends to God for sin committed; one of the four ends of prayer and the purpose of penance.

Requiem: A Mass offered for the repose of the soul of one who has died in Christ. Its name is derived from the first word of the Gregorian (Latin) entrance chant (or Introit) at Masses for the dead: *Requiem aeternam dona eis, Domine* ("Eternal rest grant unto them, O Lord"). The revised Rite for Funerals refers to the requiem as the Mass of Christian Burial; however, it would not be uncommon to hear people employ the former usage.

Rescript: A written reply by an ecclesiastical superior regarding a question or request; its provisions bind concerned parties only. Papal dispensations are issued in the form of rescripts.

Reserved Censure: A sin or censure, absolution from which is reserved to religious superiors, bishops, the pope, or confessors having special faculties. Reservations are made because of the serious nature and social effects of certain sins and censures.

Restitution: An act of reparation for an injury done to another. The injury may be caused by taking and/or retaining what belongs to another or by damaging either the property or reputation of another. The intention of making restitution, usually in kind, is required as a condition for the forgiveness of sins of injustice, even though actual restitution is not possible.

Ring: In the Church a ring is worn as part of the insignia of bishops, abbots, et al.; by sisters to denote their consecration to God and the Church. The wedding ring symbolizes the love and union of husband and wife.

Ritual: A book of prayers and ceremonies used in the administration of the sacraments and other ceremonial functions. In the Roman Rite, the standard book of this kind is the Roman Ritual.

Rogito: The official notarial act or document testifying to the burial of a pope.

Rosary: A form of mental and vocal prayer centered on mysteries or events in the lives of Jesus and Mary. Its essential elements are meditation on the mysteries and the recitation of a number of decades of Hail Marys, each beginning with the Lord's Prayer. Introductory prayers may include the Apostles' Creed, an initial Our Father, three Hail Marys and a Glory be to the Father; each decade is customarily concluded with a Glory be to the Father; at the end, it is customary to say the Hail, Holy Queen and a prayer from the liturgy for the feast of the Blessed Virgin Mary of the Rosary. The Mysteries of the Rosary, which are the subject of meditation, are: 1) *Joyful* — the Annunciation to Mary that she was to be the Mother of Christ, her visit to Elizabeth, the birth of Jesus, the presentation of Jesus in the Temple, the finding of Jesus in the Temple. 2) *Sorrowful* —Christ's agony in the Garden of Gethsemani, scourging at the pillar, crowning with thorns, carrying of the cross to Calvary, and crucifixion. 3) *Glorious* — the Resurrection and Ascension of Christ, the descent of the Holy Spirit upon the Apostles, Mary's Assumption into heaven and her crowning as Queen of angels and men. The complete Rosary, called the Dominican Rosary, consists of 15 decades. In customary practice, only five decades are usually said at one time. Rosary beads are used to aid in counting the prayers without distraction. The Rosary originated through the coalescence of popular devotions to Jesus and Mary from the 12th century onward. Its present form dates from about the 15th century. Carthusians contributed greatly toward its development; Dominicans have been its greatest promoters.

S

Sabbath: The seventh day of the week, observed by Jews and Sabbatarians as the day for rest and religious observance.

Sacrarium: A basin with a drain leading directly into the ground; standard equipment of a sacristy.

Sacred Heart, Enthronement of the: An acknowledgment of the sovereignty of Jesus Christ over the Christian family, expressed by the installation of an image or picture of the Sacred Heart in a place of honor in the home, accompanied by an act of consecration.

Sacred Heart, Promises: Twelve promises to persons having devotion to the Sacred Heart of Jesus, which were communicated by Christ to St. Margaret Mary Alacoque in a private revelation in 1675: 1) *I will give them all the graces necessary in their state in life.* 2) *I will establish peace in their homes.* 3) *I will comfort them in all their afflictions.* 4) *I will be their secure refuge during life and, above all, in death.* 5) *I will bestow abundant blessing upon all their undertakings.* 6) *Sinners shall find in my Heart the source and the infinite ocean of mercy.* 7) *By devotion to my Heart tepid souls shall grow fervent.* 8) *Fervent souls shall quickly mount to high perfection.* 9) *I will bless every place where a picture of my Heart shall be set up and honored.* 10) *I will give to priests the gift of touching the most hardened hearts.* 11) *Those who promote this devotion shall have their names written in my Heart, never to be blotted out.* 12) *I will grant the grace of final penitence to those who communicate (receive Holy Communion) on the first Friday of nine consecutive months.*

Sacrilege: Violation of and irreverence toward a person, place or thing that is sacred because of public dedication to God; a sin against the virtue of religion. Personal sacrilege is violence of some kind against a cleric or religious, or a violation of chastity with a cleric or religious. Local sacrilege is the desecration of sacred places. Real sacrilege is irreverence with respect to sacred things, such as the sacraments and sacred vessels.

Sacristy: A utility room where vestments, church furnishings and sacred vessels are kept and where the clergy vest for sacred functions.

Sadducees: The predominantly priestly party among the Jews in the time of Christ, noted for extreme conservatism, acceptance only of the Law of Moses, and rejection of the traditions of the elders. Their opposite numbers were the Pharisees.

Saints, Cult of: The veneration, called *dulia*, of holy persons who have died and are in glory with God in heaven; it includes honoring them and petitioning them for their intercession with God. Liturgical veneration is given only to saints officially recognized by the Church; private veneration may be given to anyone thought to be in heaven. The veneration of saints is essentially different from the adoration given to God alone; by its very nature, however, it terminates in the worship of God. (*See* also **Dulia** and **Latria**.)

Salvation: The liberation of persons from sin and its effects, reconciliation with God in and through Christ, the attainment of union with God forever in the glory of heaven as the supreme purpose of life and as the God-given reward for fulfillment of his will on earth. Salvation-in-process begins and continues in this life through union with Christ in faith professed and in action; its final term is union with God and the whole community of the saved in the ultimate perfection of God's kingdom. The Church teaches that: God wills the salvation of all men; men are saved in and through Christ; membership in the Church established by Christ, known and understood as the community of salvation, is necessary for salvation; men with this knowledge and understanding who deliberately reject this Church, cannot be saved. The Catholic Church is the Church founded by Christ. (*See* below, **Salvation Outside the Church**.)

Salvation History: The facts and the record of God's relations with human beings, in the past, present and future, for the purpose of leading them to live in accordance with his will for the eventual attainment after death of salvation, or everlasting happiness with him in heaven. The essentials of salvation history are: God's love for all human beings and will for their salvation; his intervention and action in the world to express this love and bring about their salvation; the revelation he made of himself and the covenant he established with the Israelites in the Old Testament; the perfecting of this revelation and the new covenant of grace through Christ in the New Testament; the continuing action-for-salvation carried on in and through the Church; the communication of saving grace to people through the merits of Christ and the operations of the Holy Spirit in the here-and-now circumstances of daily life and with the cooperation of people themselves.

Salvation Outside the Church: The Second Vatican Council covered this subject summarily in the following manner: "Those also can attain to everlasting salvation who through no fault of their own do not know the Gospel of Christ or his Church, yet sincerely seek God and, moved by grace, strive by their deeds to do his will as it is known to them through the dictates of conscience. Nor does divine Providence deny the help necessary for salvation to those who, without blame on their part, have not yet arrived at an explicit knowledge of God, but who strive to live a good life, thanks to his grace. Whatever good or truth is found among them is looked upon by the Church as a preparation for the Gospel. She regards such qualities as given by him who enlightens all men so that they may finally have life" ("Dogmatic Constitution on the Church," *Lumen Gentium*, No. 16).

Sanctifying Grace: *See* **Grace**.

Satanism: Worship of the devil, a blasphemous inversion of the order of worship which is due to God alone.

Scandal: Conduct which is the occasion of sin to another person.

Scapular: 1) A part of the habit of some religious orders like the Benedictines and Dominicans; a nearly shoulder-wide strip of cloth worn over the tunic and reaching almost to the feet in front and behind. Originally a kind of apron, it came to symbolize the cross and yoke of Christ. 2) Scapulars worn by lay persons as a sign of association with religious orders and for devotional purposes are an adaptation of monastic scapulars. Approved by the Church as sacramentals, they consist of two small squares of woolen cloth joined by strings and are worn about the neck. They are given for wearing in a ceremony of investiture or enrollment. There are nearly 20 scapulars for devotional use: the five principal ones are generally understood to include those of Our Lady of Mt. Carmel (the brown Carmelite Scapular), the Holy Trinity, Our Lady of the Seven Dolors, the Passion, and the Immaculate Conception.

Scapular Medal: A medallion with a representation of the Sacred Heart on one side and of the Blessed Virgin Mary on the other. Authorized by St. Pius X in 1910, it may be worn or carried in place of a scapular by persons already invested with a scapular.

Scapular Promise: According to a legend of the Carmelite Order, the Blessed Virgin Mary appeared to St. Simon Stock in 1251 at Cambridge, England, and declared that wearers of the brown Carmelite Scapular would be the beneficiaries of her special intercession. The scapular tradition has never been the subject of official decision by the Church. Essentially, it expresses belief in the intercession of Mary and the efficacy of sacramentals in the context of truly Christian life.

Schism: Derived from a Greek word meaning separation, the term designates formal and obstinate refusal by a baptized Catholic, called a schismatic, to be in communion with the pope and the Church. The canonical penalty is excommunication. One of the most disastrous schisms in history resulted in the definitive separation of the Church in the East from union with Rome about 1054.

Scholasticism: The term usually applied to the Catholic theology and philosophy which developed in the Middle Ages. (*See* also **Neo-Scholasticism**.)

Scribes: Hebrew intellectuals noted for their knowledge of the Law of Moses, influential from the time of the Exile to about 70 A.D. Many of them were Pharisees. They were the antecedents of rabbis and their traditions, as well as those of the Pharisees, had a lasting influence on Judaism following the destruction of Jerusalem in 70 A.D.

Scruple: A morbid, unreasonable fear and anxiety that one's actions are sinful when they are not, or more seriously sinful than they actually are. Compulsive scrupulosity is quite different from the transient scrupulosity of persons of tender or highly sensitive conscience, or of persons with faulty moral judgment.

Seal of Confession: The obligation of secrecy which must be observed regarding knowledge of things learned in connection with the confession of sin in the sacrament of penance. The seal covers matters whose revelation would make the sacrament burdensome. Confessors are prohibited, under penalty of excommunication, from making any direct revelation of confessional matter; this prohibition holds, outside of confession, even with respect to the person who made the confession unless the person releases the priest from the obligation. Persons other than confessors are obliged to maintain secrecy, but not under penalty of excommunication. General, non-specific discussion of confessional matter does not violate the seal.

Secularism: A school of thought, a spirit and manner of action which ignores and/or repudiates the validity or influence of supernatural religion with respect to individual and social life.

See: Another name for diocese or archdiocese.

Seminary: A house of study and formation for men, called seminarians, preparing for the priesthood. Traditional seminaries date from the Council of Trent in the middle of the 16th century; before that time, candidates for the priesthood were variously trained in monastic schools, universities under church auspices, and in less formal ways.

Sermon on the Mount: A compilation of sayings of Our Lord in the form of an extended discourse in Matthew's Gospel (5:1 to 7:27) and, in a shorter discourse, in Luke (6:17-49). The passage in Matthew, called the "Constitution of the New Law," summarizes the living spirit of believers in Christ and members of the kingdom of God. Beginning with the Beatitudes and including the Lord's Prayer, it covers the perfect justice of the New Law, the fulfillment of the Old Law in the New Law of Christ, and the integrity of internal attitude and external conduct with respect to love of God and neighbor, justice, chastity, truth, trust and confidence in God.

Seven Last Words of Christ: Words of Christ on the cross. 1) *"Father, forgive them; for they do not know what they are doing."* 2) To the penitent thief: *"I assure you: today you will be with me in Paradise."* 3) To Mary and his Apostle John: *"Woman, there is your son; There is your mother."* 4) *"My God, my God, why have you forsaken me?"* 5) *"I am thirsty."* 6) *"Now it is finished."* 7) *"Father, into your hands I commend my spirit."*

Shrine, Crowned: A shrine approved by the Holy See as a place of pilgrimage. The approval permits public devotion at the shrine and implies that at least one miracle has resulted from devotion at the shrine. Among the best known crowned shrines are those of the Virgin Mary at Lourdes and Fátima. Shrines with statues crowned by Pope John Paul in 1985 in South America were those of Our Lady of Coromoto, patroness of Venezuela, in Caracas, and Our Lady of Carmen of Paucartambo in Cuzco, Peru.

Shroud of Turin: A strip of brownish linen cloth, 14 feet, three inches in length and three feet, seven inches in width, bearing the front and back imprint of a human body. A tradition dating from the 7th century, which has not been verified beyond doubt, claims that the shroud is the fine linen in which the body of Christ was wrapped for burial. The early history of the shroud is obscure. It was enshrined at Lirey, France, in 1354 and was transferred in 1578 to Turin, Italy, where it has been kept in the cathedral down to the present time. Scientific investigation, which began in 1898, seems to indicate that the markings on the shroud are those of a human body. The shroud, for the first time since 1933, was placed on public view from Aug. 27 to Oct. 8, 1978, and was seen by an estimated 3.3 million people. Scientists conducted intensive studies of it thereafter, finally determining that the material of the shroud dated from between 1260 and 1390. The shroud, which had been the possession of the House of Savoy, was willed to Pope John Paul II in 1983.

Sick Calls: When a person is confined at home by illness or other cause and is unable to go to church for reception of the sacraments, a parish priest should be informed and arrangements made for him to visit the person at home. Such visitations are common in pastoral practice, both for special needs and for providing persons with regular opportunities for receiving the sacraments. If a priest cannot make the visitation, arrangements can be made for a deacon or Eucharistic minister to bring Holy Communion to the homebound or bedridden person.

Sign of the Cross: A sign, ceremonial gesture or movement in the form of a cross by which a person confesses faith in the Holy Trinity and Christ, and intercedes for the blessing of himself or herself, other persons and things. In Roman Rite practice, a person making the sign touches the fingers of the right hand to forehead, below the breast, left shoulder and right shoulder while saying: *"In the name of the Father, and of the Son, and of the Holy Spirit."* The sign is also made with the thumb on the forehead, the lips, and the breast. For the blessing of persons and objects, a large sign of the cross is made by movement of the right hand. In Eastern Rite practice, the sign is made with the thumb and first two fingers of the right hand joined together and touching the forehead, below the breast, the right shoulder and the left shoulder; the formula generally used is the doxology, *"O Holy God, O Holy Strong One, O Immortal One."* The Eastern manner of making the sign was general until the first half of the 13th century; by the 17th century, Western practice involved the whole right hand and the reversal of direction from shoulder to shoulder.

Signs of the Times: Contemporary events, trends and features in culture and society, the needs and aspirations of people, all the factors that form the context in and through which the Church has to carry on its saving mission. The Second Vatican Council spoke on numerous occasions about these signs and the relationship between them and a kind of manifestation of God's will, positive or negative, and about subjecting them to judgment and action corresponding to the demands of divine revelation through Scripture, Christ, and the experience, tradition and teaching authority of the Church.

Simony: The deliberate intention and act of selling and/or buying spiritual goods or material things so connected with the spiritual that they cannot be separated therefrom; a violation of the virtue of religion, and a sacrilege, because it wrongfully puts a material price on spiritual things, which cannot be either sold or bought. In church law, actual sale or purchase is subject to censure in some cases. The term is derived from the name of Simon Magus, who attempted to buy from Sts. Peter and John the power to confirm people in the Holy Spirit (Acts 8:4-24).

Sin: 1) Actual sin is the free and deliberate violation of God's law by thought, word or action. (a) Mortal sin — involving serious matter, sufficient reflection and full consent — results in the loss of sanctifying grace and alienation from God, and renders a person incapable of performing meritorious supernatural acts and subject to everlasting punishment. (b) Venial sin — involving less serious matter, reflection and consent — does not have such serious consequences. 2) Original sin is the sin of Adam, with consequences for all human beings. (*See* separate entry.)

Sins Against the Holy Spirit: Despair of salvation, presumption of God's mercy, impugning the known truths of faith, envy at another's spiritual good, obstinacy in sin, final impenitence. Those guilty of such sins stubbornly resist the influence of grace and, as long as they do so, cannot be forgiven.

Sins, Occasions of: Circumstances (persons, places, things, etc.) which easily lead to sin. There is an obligation to avoid voluntary proximate occasions of sin, and to take precautions against the dangers of unavoidable occasions.

Sins That Cry to Heaven for Vengeance: Willful murder, sins against nature, oppression of the poor, widows and orphans, defrauding laborers of their wages.

Sister: Any woman Religious, in popular speech; strictly, the title applies only to women Religious belonging to institutes whose members never professed solemn vows. Most of the institutes whose members are properly called Sisters were established during and since the 19th century. Women Religious with solemn vows, or belonging to institutes whose members formerly professed solemn vows, are properly called nuns.

Sisterhood: A generic term referring to the whole institution of the life of women Religious in the Church, or to a particular institute of women Religious.

Situation Ethics: A subjective, individualistic ethical theory which denies the binding force of ethical principles as universal laws and preceptive norms of moral conduct, and proposes that morality is determined only by situational conditions and considerations and the intention of the person. It has been criticized for ignoring the principles of objective ethics. (*See* also **Consequentialism** and **Proportionalism**.)

Slander: Attributing to a person faults which he or she does not have; a violation of the obligations of justice and charity, for which restitution is due.

Sloth (Acedia): One of the seven capital sins; spiritual laziness, involving distaste and disgust for spiritual things; spiritual boredom, which saps the vigor of spiritual life. Physical laziness is a counterpart of spiritual sloth.

Sorcery: A kind of black magic in which evil is invoked by means of diabolical intervention; a violation of the virtue of religion.

Soteriology: The division of theology which treats of the mission and work of Christ as Redeemer.

Species, Sacred: The appearances of bread and wine (color, taste, smell, etc.) which remain after the substance has been changed at the Consecration of the Mass into the Body and Blood of Christ. (*See* **Transubstantiation**.)

Spiritism: Attempts to communicate with spirits and departed souls by means of seances, table tapping, ouija boards, and other methods; a violation of the virtue of religion. Spiritualistic practices are noted for fakery.

Stational Churches, Days: Churches, especially in Rome, where the clergy and lay people were accustomed to gather with their bishop on certain days for the celebration of the liturgy. The 25 early titular or parish churches of Rome, plus other churches, each had their turn as the site of divine worship in practices which may have started in the third century. The observances were rather well developed toward the latter part of the 4th century, and by the 5th century they included a Mass concelebrated by the pope and attendant priests. On some occasions, the stational liturgy was preceded by a procession from another church called a *collecta*. There were 42 Roman stational churches in the 8th century, and 89 stational services were scheduled annually in connection with the liturgical seasons. Stational observances fell into disuse toward the end of the Middle Ages. Some revival was begun by John XXIII in 1959 and continued by Paul VI and John Paul II.

Stations (Way) of the Cross: A form of devotion commemorating the Passion and death of Christ, consisting of a series of meditations (stations): 1) his condemnation to death, 2) taking up of the cross, 3) the first fall on the way to Calvary, 4) meeting his Mother, 5) being assisted by Simon of Cyrene and 6) by the woman Veronica who wiped his face, 7) the second fall, 8) meeting the women of Jerusalem, 9) the third fall, 10) being stripped and 11) nailed to the cross, 12) his death, 13) the removal of his body from the cross and 14) his burial. Depictions of these scenes are mounted in most churches, chapels and in some other places, beneath small crosses. A person making the Way of the Cross passes before these stations, or stopping points, pausing at each for meditation. If the stations are made by a group of people, only the leader has to pass from station to station. A plenary indulgence is granted to the faithful who make the stations, under the usual conditions: freedom from all attachment to sin, reception of the sacraments of penance and the Eucharist, and prayers for the intentions of the pope. Those who are impeded from making the stations in the usual manner can gain the same indulgence if, along with the aforementioned conditions, they spend at least a half hour in spiritual reading and meditation on the passion and death of Christ. The stations originated remotely from the practice of Holy Land pilgrims who visited the actual scenes of incidents in the Passion of Christ. Representations elsewhere of at least some of these scenes were known as early as the 5th century. Later, the stations evolved in connection with and as a consequence of strong devotion to the Passion in the 12th and 13th centuries. Franciscans, who were given custody of the Holy Places in 1342, promoted the devotion widely; one of them, St. Leonard of Port Maurice, became known as the greatest preacher of the Way of the Cross in the 18th century. The general features of the devotion were fixed by Clement XII in 1731.

Statutes: Virtually the same as decrees (*see* separate entry), they almost always designate laws of a particular council or synod rather than pontifical laws.

Stigmata: Marks of the wounds suffered by Christ in his crucifixion, in hands and feet by nails, and side by the piercing of a lance. Some persons, called stigmatists, have been reported as recipients or sufferers of marks like these. The Church, however, has never issued any infallible declaration about their possession by anyone, even in the case of St. Francis of Assisi, whose stigmata seemed to be the best substantiated and may be commemorated in the Roman Rite liturgy. Ninety percent of some 300 reputed stigmatists have been women. Judgment regarding the presence, significance, and manner of causation of stigmata would depend, among other things, on irrefutable experimental evidence.

Stipend, Mass: An offering given to a priest for applying the fruits of the Mass according to the intention of the donor. The offering is a contribution to the support of the priest. The disposition of the fruits of the sacrifice, in line with doctrine concerning the Mass in particular and prayer in general, is subject to the will of God. Mass offerings and intentions were the subjects of a decree approved by John Paul II and made public Mar. 22, 1991: 1) Normally, no more than one offering should be accepted for a Mass; the Mass should be offered in accord with the donor's intention; the priest who accepts the offering should celebrate the Mass himself or have another priest do so. 2) Several Mass intentions, for which offerings have been made, can be combined for a "collective" application of a single Mass only if the previous and explicit consent of the donors is obtained. Such Masses are an exception to the general rule.

Stole Fee: An offering given on certain occasions; e.g., at a baptism, wedding, funeral, for the support of the clergy who administer the sacraments and perform other sacred rites.

Stoup: A vessel used to contain holy water.

Suffragan See: Any diocese, except the archdiocese, within a province.

Suicide: The taking of one's own life; a violation of God's dominion over human life. Ecclesiastical burial is denied to persons while in full possession of their faculties; it is permitted in cases of doubt.

Supererogation: Actions which go beyond the obligations of duty and the requirements enjoined by God's law as necessary for salvation. Examples of these works are the profession and observance of the evangelical counsels of poverty, chastity, and obedience, and efforts to practice charity to the highest degree.

Supernatural: Above the natural; that which exceeds and is not due or owed to the essence, exigencies, requirements, powers and merits of created nature. While human beings have no claim on supernatural things and do not need them in order to exist and act on a natural level, they do need them in order to exist and act in the higher order or economy of grace established by God for their salvation. God has freely given them certain things which are beyond the powers and rights of their human nature. Examples of the supernatural are: grace, a kind of participation by human beings in the divine life, by which they become capable of performing acts meritorious for salvation; divine revelation by which God manifests himself to them and makes known truth that is inaccessible to human reason alone; faith, by which they believe divine truth because of the authority of God who reveals it through Sacred Scripture and tradition and the teaching of his Church.

Suspension: A censure by which a cleric is forbidden to exercise some or all of his powers of orders and jurisdiction, or to accept the financial support of his benefices.

Syllabus, The: 1) When not qualified, the term refers to the list of 80 errors accompanying Pope Pius IX's encyclical *Quanta Cura*, issued in 1864. 2) The Syllabus of St. Pius X in the decree *Lamentabili*, issued by the Holy Office July 4, 1907, condemning 65 heretical propositions of modernism. This schedule of errors was followed shortly by that pope's encyclical *Pascendi*, the principal ecclesiastical document against modernism, issued Sept. 8, 1907.

Synod, Diocesan: Meeting of representative persons of a diocese — priests, religious, lay persons — with the bishop, called by him for the purpose of considering and taking action on matters affecting the life and mission of the Church in the diocese. Persons taking part in a synod have consultative status; the bishop alone is the legislator, with power to authorize synodal decrees. According to canon law, every diocese should have a synod every 10 years.

T

Tabernacle: The receptacle in which the Blessed Sacrament is reserved in churches, chapels, and oratories. It is to be immovable, solid, locked, and located in a prominent place.

Te Deum: The opening Latin words, *Thee, God*, of a

hymn of praise and thanksgiving prescribed for use in the Office of Readings of the Liturgy of the Hours on many Sundays, solemnities and feasts.

Temperance: Moderation, one of the four cardinal virtues.

Temptation: Any enticement to sin, from any source: the strivings of one's own faculties, the action of the devil, other persons, circumstances of life, etc. Temptation itself is not sin. Temptation can be avoided and overcome with the use of prudence and the help of grace.

Thanksgiving: An expression of gratitude to God for his goodness and the blessings he grants; one of the four ends of prayer.

Theism: A philosophy which admits the existence of God and the possibility of divine revelation; it is generally monotheistic and acknowledges God as transcendent and also active in the world. Because it is a philosophy rather than a system of theology derived from revelation, it does not include specifically Christian doctrines, like those concerning the Trinity, the Incarnation and Redemption.

Theodicy: From the Greek for God (*theos*) and judgment (*dike*), the study of God as he can be known by natural reason, rather than from supernatural revelation. First used by Gottfried Leibnitz (1646-1716), its primary objective is to make God's omnipotence compatible with the existence of evil.

Theological Virtues: The virtues which have God for their direct object: faith, or belief in God's infallible teaching; hope, or confidence in divine assistance; charity, or love of God. They are given to a person with grace in the first instance, through baptism and incorporation in Christ.

Theology: Knowledge of God and religion, deriving from and based on the data of divine Revelation, organized and systematized according to some kind of scientific method. It involves systematic study and presentation of the truths of divine Revelation in Sacred Scripture, tradition, and the teaching of the Church. Theology has been divided under various subject headings. Some of the major fields have been: dogmatic (systematic theology), moral, pastoral, historical, ascetical (the practice of virtue and means of attaining holiness and perfection), sacramental, and mystical (higher states of religious experience). Other subject headings include ecumenism (Christian unity, interfaith relations), ecclesiology (the nature and constitution of the Church), and Mariology (doctrine concerning the Blessed Virgin Mary), etc.

Theotokos: From the Greek for God-bearer, the pre-eminent title given to the Blessed Mother in the Oriental Church. This title has very ancient roots, stretching as far back as the third century but it did not became official in the Church until the Council of Ephesus in 431.

Thomism: The philosophy based on St. Thomas Aquinas (1224/5-1274), which is mandated to be the dominant philosophy used in Catholic educational institutions. (*See* also **Neo-Scholasticism** and **Scholasticism**.)

Tithing: Contribution of a portion of one's income, originally one-tenth, for purposes of religion and charity. The practice is mentioned 46 times in the Bible. In early Christian times, tithing was adopted in continuance of Old Testament practices of the Jewish people, and the earliest positive church legislation on the subject was enacted in 567. Catholics are bound in conscience to contribute to the support of their church, but the manner in which they do so is not fixed by law. Tithing, which amounts to a pledged contribution of a portion of one's income, has attracted new attention in recent years in the United States.

Titular Sees: Dioceses where the Church once flourished but which now exist only in name or title. Bishops without a territorial or residential diocese of their own; e.g., auxiliary bishops, are given titular sees. There are more than 2,000 titular sees; 16 of them are in the United States.

Transfinalization, Transignification: Terms coined to express the sign value of consecrated bread and wine with respect to the presence and action of Christ in the Eucharistic sacrifice and the spiritually vivifying purpose of the Eucharistic banquet in Holy Communion. The theory behind the terms has strong undertones of existential and "sign" philosophy, and has been criticized for its openness to interpretation at variance with the doctrine of transubstantiation and the abiding presence of Christ under the appearances of bread and wine after the sacrifice of the Mass and Communion have been completed. The terms, if used as substitutes for transubstantiation, are unacceptable; if they presuppose transubstantiation, they are acceptable as clarifications of its meaning.

Transubstantiation: "The way Christ is made present in this sacrament (Holy Eucharist) is none other than by the change of the whole substance of the bread into his Body, and of the whole substance of the wine into his Blood (in the Consecration at Mass), this unique and wonderful change the Catholic Church rightly calls transubstantiation" (encyclical *Mysterium Fidei* of Paul VI, Sept. 3, 1965). The first official use of the term was made by the Fourth Council of the Lateran in 1215. Authoritative teaching on the subject was issued by the Council of Trent.

Treasury of the Church: The superabundant merits of Christ and the saints from which the Church draws to confer spiritual benefits, such as indulgences.

Triduum: A three-day series of public or private devotions.

U-Z

Ultramontanism: The movement found primarily in France during the 19th century that advocated a strong sense of devotion and service to the Holy See. Generally considered a reaction to the anti-papal tendencies of Gallicanism, its name was derived from the Latin for "over the mountains," a reference to the Alps, beyond which rested Rome and the Holy See.

Unction: From the Latin, *ungere*, meaning to anoint or smear, a term used to denote the Sacrament of the Sick (or the Anointing of the Sick); it was more commonly termed Extreme Unction and was given as an anointing to a person just before death.

Universal Law: *See* **Law**.

Urbi et Orbi: A Latin phrase meaning "To the City and to the World" that is a blessing given by the Holy Father. Normally, the first *Urbi et Orbi* delivered by a pontiff is immediately after his election by the College of Cardinals. This is a blessing accompanied by a short address to the crowds in St. Peter's Square and to the world; frequently, as with Pope John Paul II in 1978, it is delivered in as many languages as possible. The pope also delivers an *Urbi et Orbi* each year at Christmas and at Easter.

Usury: Excessive interest charged for the loan and use of money; a violation of justice.

Vagi: A Latin word meaning wanderers that is used to describe any homeless person with no fixed residence.

Veni Creator Spiritus: A Latin phrase, meaning "Come, Creator Spirit" that is part of a hymn sung to the Holy Spirit. The hymn invokes the presence of the Holy Spirit and was perhaps first composed by Rabanus Maurus (776-856). The hymn is commonly sung as part of the Divine Office, papal elections, episcopal consecrations, ordinations, councils, synods, canonical elections, and confirmations.

Venial Sin: *See* under **Sin**.

Veronica: A word resulting from the combination of a Latin word for true, *vera*, and a Greek word for image, *eikon*, designating a likeness of the face of Christ or the name of a woman said to have given him a cloth on which he caused an imprint of his face to appear. The veneration at Rome of a likeness depicted on cloth dates from about the end of the 10th century; it figured in a popular devotion during the Middle Ages, and in the Holy Face devotion practiced since the 19th century. A faint, indiscernible likeness said to be of this kind is preserved in St. Peter's Basilica. The origin of the likeness is uncertain, and the identity of the woman is unknown. Before the 14th century, there were no known artistic representations of an incident concerning a woman who wiped the face of Christ with a piece of cloth while he was carrying the cross to Calvary.

Vespers: From the Latin for evening, the evening service of the Divine Office, also known as Evening Prayer, or among Anglicans as Evensong.

Viaticum: Holy Communion given to those in danger of death. The word, derived from Latin, means provision for a journey through death to life hereafter.

Vicar Forane: A Latin term meaning "deputy outside" that is applied to the priest given authority by the local bishop over a certain area or region of the diocese.

Vicar General: A priest or bishop appointed by the bishop of a diocese to serve as his deputy, with ordinary executive power, in the administration of the diocese.

Vicar, Judicial: The title given to the chief judge and head of the tribunal of a diocese.

Virginity: Observance of perpetual sexual abstinence. The state of virginity, which is embraced for the love of God by Religious with a public vow or by others with a private vow, was singled out for high praise by Christ (Mt. 19:10-12) and has always been so regarded by the Church. In the encyclical *Sacra Virginitas*, Pius XII stated: "Holy virginity and that perfect chastity which is consecrated to the service of God is without doubt among the most perfect treasures which the founder of the Church has left in heritage to the society which he established." Paul VI approved in 1970 a rite in which women can consecrate their virginity "to Christ and their brethren" without becoming members of a religious institute. The *Ordo Consecrationis Virginum*, a revision of a rite promulgated by Clement VII in 1596, is traceable to the Roman liturgy of about 50.

Virtue: A habit or established capability for performing good actions. Virtues are natural (acquired and increased by repeating good acts) and/or supernatural (given with grace by God).

Visions: A charism by which a specially chosen individual is able to behold a person or something that is naturally invisible. A vision should not be confused with an illusion or hallucination. Like other charisms, a vision is granted for the good of people; it should be noted, however, that they are not essential for holiness or salvation. Many saints throughout history have beheld visions, among them St. Thomas Aquinas, St. Teresa of Ávila, St. John of the Cross, and St. Francis of Assisi.

Vocation: A call to a way of life. Generally, the term applies to the common call of all persons, from God, to holiness and salvation. Specifically, it refers to particular states of life, each called a vocation, in which response is made to this universal call; viz., marriage, the religious life and/or priesthood, the single state freely chosen or accepted for the accomplishment of God's will. The term also applies to the various occupations in which persons make a living. The Church supports the freedom of each individual in choosing a particular vocation, and reserves the right to pass on the acceptability of candidates for the priesthood and religious life. Signs or indicators of particular vocations are many, including a person's talents and interests, circumstances and obligations, invitations of grace and willingness to respond thereto.

Vow: A promise made to God with sufficient knowledge and freedom, which has as its object a moral good that is possible and better than its voluntary omission. A person who professes a vow binds himself or herself by the virtue of religion to fulfill the promise. The best known examples of vows are those of poverty, chastity and obedience professed by Religious (*See* **Evangelical Counsels**, individual entries). Public vows are made before a competent person, acting as an agent of the Church, who accepts the profession in the name of the Church, thereby giving public recognition to the person's dedication and consecration to God and divine worship. Vows of this kind are either solemn, rendering all contrary acts invalid as well as unlawful; or simple, rendering contrary acts unlawful. Solemn vows are for life; simple vows are for a definite period of time or for life. Vows professed without public recognition by the Church are called private vows. The Church, which has authority to accept and give public recognition to vows, also has authority to dispense persons from their obligations for serious reasons.

Witness, Christian: Practical testimony or evidence given by Christians of their faith in all circumstances of life — by prayer and general conduct, through good example and good works, etc.; being and acting in accordance with Christian belief; actual practice of the Christian faith.

Zeal: The expression of charity that permits one to serve God and others fully with the objective of furthering the Mystical Body of Christ.

Zucchetto: A small skullcap worn by ecclesiastics, most notably prelates and derived from the popular Italian vernacular term *zucca*, meaning a pumpkin, and used as slang for head. The Holy Father wears a white zucchetto made of watered silk; cardinals use scarlet, and bishops use purple. Priests of the monsignorial rank may wear black with purple piping. All others may wear simple black.

The Church Calendar

The calendar of the Roman Church consists of an arrangement throughout the year of a series of liturgical seasons, commemorations of divine mysteries and commemorations of saints for purposes of worship.

The key to the calendar is the central celebration of the Easter Triduum, commemorating the supreme saving act of Jesus in his death and resurrection to which all other observances and acts of worship are related.

The purposes of this calendar were outlined in the Constitution on the Sacred Liturgy (*Sacrosanctum Concilium*, Nos. 102-105) promulgated by the Second Vatican Council.

"Within the cycle of a year ... (the Church) unfolds the whole mystery of Christ, not only from his incarnation and birth until his ascension, but also as reflected in the day of Pentecost, and the expectation of a blessed, hoped-for return of the Lord.

"Recalling thus the mysteries of redemption, the Church opens to the faithful the riches of her Lord's powers and merits, so that these are in some way made present at all times, and the faithful are enabled to lay hold of them and become filled with saving grace (No. 102).

"In celebrating this annual cycle of Christ's mysteries, holy Church honors with special love the Blessed Mary, Mother of God" (No. 103).

"The Church has also included in the annual cycle days devoted to the memory of the martyrs and the other saints (who) sing God's perfect praise in heaven and offer prayers for us. By celebrating the passage of these saints from earth to heaven the Church proclaims the paschal mystery as achieved in the saints who have suffered and been glorified with Christ; she proposes them to the faithful as examples who draw all to the Father through Christ, and through their merits she pleads for God's favors (No. 104).

"In the various seasons of the year and according to her traditional discipline, the Church completes the formation of the faithful by means of pious practices for soul and body, by instruction, prayer, and works of penance and mercy (No. 105)."

THE ROMAN CALENDAR

Norms for a revised calendar for the Western Church as decreed by the Second Vatican Council were approved by Paul VI in the *motu proprio Mysterii Paschalis* dated Feb. 14, 1969. The revised calendar was promulgated a month later by a decree of the Congregation for Divine Worship and went into effect Jan. 1, 1970, with provisional modifications. Full implementation of all its parts was delayed in 1970 and 1971, pending the completion of work on related liturgical texts. The U.S. bishops ordered the calendar into effect for 1972.

The Seasons

Advent: The liturgical year begins with the first Sunday of Advent, which introduces a season of four weeks or slightly less duration with the theme of expectation of the coming of Christ. During the first two weeks, the final coming of Christ as Lord and Judge at the end of the world is the focus of attention. From Dec. 17 to 24, the emphasis shifts to anticipation of the celebration of his Nativity on the solemnity of Christmas.

Advent has four Sundays. Since the 10th century, the first Sunday has marked the beginning of the liturgical year in the Western Church. In the Middle Ages, a kind of pre-Christmas fast was in vogue during the season.

Christmas Season: The Christmas season begins with the vigil of Christmas and lasts until the Sunday after Jan. 6, inclusive.

The period between the end of the Christmas season and the beginning of Lent belongs to the Ordinary Time of the year. Of variable length, the pre-Lenten phase of this season includes what were formerly called the Sundays after Epiphany and the suppressed Sundays of Septuagesima, Sexagesima and Quinquagesima.

Lent: The penitential season of Lent begins on Ash Wednesday, which occurs between Feb. 4 and Mar. 11, depending on the date of Easter, and lasts until the Mass of the Lord's Supper (Holy Thursday). It has six Sundays. The sixth Sunday marks the beginning of Holy Week and is known as Passion (formerly called Palm) Sunday.

The origin of Lenten observances dates back to the fourth century or earlier.

Easter Triduum: The Easter Triduum begins with evening Mass of the Lord's Supper and ends with Evening Prayer on Easter Sunday.

Easter Season: The Easter season whose theme is resurrection from sin to the life of grace, lasts for 50 days, from Easter to Pentecost. Easter, the first Sunday after the first full moon following the vernal equinox, occurs between Mar. 22 and Apr. 25. The terminal phase of the Easter season, between the solemnities of the Ascension of the Lord and Pentecost, stresses anticipation of the coming and action of the Holy Spirit.

Ordinary Time: The season of Ordinary Time begins on Monday (or Tuesday if the feast of the Baptism of the Lord is celebrated on that Monday) after the Sunday following Jan. 6 and continues until the day before Ash Wednesday, inclusive. It begins again on the Monday after Pentecost and ends on the Saturday before the first Sunday of Advent. It consists of 33 or 34 weeks. The last Sunday is celebrated as the Solemnity of Christ the King. The overall purpose of the season is to elaborate the themes of salvation history.

The various liturgical seasons are characterized in part by the scriptural readings and Mass prayers assigned to each of them. During Advent, for example, the readings are messianic; during the Easter season, from the Acts of the Apostles, chronicling the Resurrection and the original proclamation of Christ by the Apostles, and from the Gospel of John; during Lent, baptismal and penitential passages. Mass prayers reflect the meaning and purpose of the various seasons.

Commemorations of Saints

The commemorations of saints are celebrated concurrently with the liturgical seasons and feasts of our Lord. Their purpose is to illustrate the paschal mysteries as reflected in the lives of saints, to honor them as heroes of holiness, and to appeal for their intercession.

In line with revised regulations, some former feasts were either abolished or relegated to observance in particular places by local option for one of two reasons: (1) lack of sufficient historical evidence for observance of the feasts; (2) lack of universal significance.

The commemoration of a saint, as a general rule, is observed on the day of death (*dies natalis*, day of birth to glory with God in heaven). Exceptions to this rule include the feasts of St. John the Baptist, who is honored on the day of his birth; Sts. Basil the Great and Gregory Nazianzen, and the brother Saints, Cyril and Methodius, who are commemorated in joint feasts. Application of this general rule in the revised calendar resulted in date changes of some observances.

Sundays and Other Holy Days

Sunday is the original Christian feast day and holy day of obligation because of the unusually significant events of salvation history which took place and are commemorated on the first day of the week viz., the Resurrection of Christ, the key event of his life and the fundamental fact of Christianity; and the descent of the Holy Spirit upon the Apostles on Pentecost, the birthday of the Church. The transfer of observance of the Lord's Day from the Sabbath to Sunday was made in apostolic times. The Mass and Liturgy of the Hours (Divine Office) of each Sunday reflect the themes and set the tones of the various liturgical seasons.

Holy days of obligation are special occasions on which Catholics who have reached the age of reason are seriously obliged, as on Sundays, to assist at Mass: they are also to refrain from work and involvement with business which impede participation in divine worship and the enjoyment of appropriate rest and relaxation.

The holy days of obligation observed in the United States are: Christmas, the Nativity of Jesus, Dec. 25; Solemnity of Mary the Mother of God, Jan. 1; Ascension of the Lord; Assumption of Blessed Mary the Virgin, Aug. 15; All Saints' Day, Nov. 1; Immacu-

late Conception of Blessed Mary the Virgin, Dec. 8.

The precept to attend Mass is abrogated in the U.S. whenever the Solemnity of Mary, the Assumption, or All Saints falls on a Saturday or Monday (1991 decree of U.S. bishops; approved by Holy See July 4, 1992, and effective Jan. 1, 1993).

In addition to these, there are four other holy days of obligation prescribed in the general law of the Church which are not so observed in the U.S.: Epiphany, Jan. 6; St. Joseph, Mar. 19; Corpus Christi; Sts. Peter and Paul, June 29. The solemnities of Epiphany and Corpus Christi are transferred to a Sunday in countries where they are not observed as holy days of obligation.

Solemnities, Feasts, Memorials

Categories of observances according to dignity and manner of observance are: solemnities, principal days in the calendar (observance begins with Evening Prayer I of the preceding day; some have their own vigil Mass); feasts (celebrated within the limits of the natural day); obligatory memorials (celebrated throughout the Church); optional memorials (observable by choice).

Fixed observances are those which are regularly celebrated on the same calendar day each year.

Movable observances are those which are not observed on the same calendar day each year. Examples of these are Easter (the first Sunday after the first full moon following the vernal equinox), Ascension (40 days after Easter), Pentecost (50 days after Easter), Trinity Sunday (first after Pentecost), Christ the King (last Sunday of the liturgical year).

Weekdays, Days of Prayer

Weekdays are those on which no proper feast or vigil is celebrated in the Mass or Liturgy of the Hours (Divine Office). On such days, the Mass may be that of the preceding Sunday, which expresses the liturgical spirit of the season, an optional memorial, a votive Mass, or a Mass for the dead. Weekdays of Advent and Lent are in a special category of their own.

Days of Prayer: Dioceses, at times to be designated by local bishops, should observe "days or periods of prayer for the fruits of the earth, prayer for human rights and equality, prayer for world justice and peace, and penitential observance outside of Lent." So stated the Instruction on Particular Calendars (No. 331) issued by the Congregation for the Sacraments and Divine Worship June 24, 1970.

These days are contemporary equivalents of what were formerly called ember and rogation days.

Ember days originated at Rome about the fifth century, probably as Christian replacements for seasonal festivals of agrarian cults. They were observances of penance, thanksgiving, and petition for divine blessing on the various seasons; they also were occasions of special prayer for clergy to be ordained. These days were observed four times a year.

Rogation days originated in France about the fifth century. They were penitential in character and also occasions of prayer for a bountiful harvest and protection against evil.

Days and Times of Penance

Fridays throughout the year and the season of Lent are penitential times.

• **Abstinence:** Catholics in the United States, from the age of 14 throughout life, are obliged to abstain from meat on Ash Wednesday, the Fridays of Lent and Good Friday. The law forbids the use of meat, but not of eggs, the products of milk or condiments made of animal fat. Permissible are soup flavored with meat, meat gravy and sauces. The obligation to abstain from meat is not in force on days celebrated as solemnities (e.g., Christmas, Sacred Heart).

• **Fasting:** Catholics in the United States, from the day after their 18th birthday to the day after their 59th birthday, are also obliged to fast on Ash Wednesday and Good Friday. The law allows only one full meal a day, but does not prohibit the taking of some food in the morning and evening, observing as far as quantity and quality are concerned approved local custom. The order of meals is optional, i.e., the full meal may be taken in the evening instead of at midday. Also: (1) The combined quantity of food taken at the two lighter meals should not exceed the quantity taken at the full meal. (2) The drinking of ordinary liquids does not break the fast.

• **Obligation:** There is a general obligation to do penance for sins committed and for the remission of punishment resulting from sin. Substantial observance of fasting and abstinence, prescribed for the community of the Church, is a matter of serious obligation; it allows, however, for alternate ways of doing penance (e.g., works of charity, prayer and prayer-related practices, almsgiving).

Readings at Mass

Scriptural readings for Masses on Sundays and holy days are indicated under the appropriate dates in the calendar pages for the year 2002-03. The Year B cycle is prescribed for Sunday Masses in liturgical year 2003, beginning Dec. 1, 2002, to Nov. 23, 2003. The Year C cycle is prescribed for Masses on Sundays in liturgical year 2004, beginning Nov. 30, 2003, to Nov. 21, 2004.

The Year One cycle of weekday readings is prescribed for the year 2003.

Monthly Prayer Intentions

Intentions chosen and recommended by Pope John Paul II to the prayers of the faithful and circulated by the Apostleship of Prayer are given for each month of the calendar. He has expressed his desire that all Catholics make these intentions their own "in the certainty of being united with the Holy Father and praying according to his intentions and desires."

Celebrations in U.S. Particular Calendar

The General Norms for the Liturgical Year and the Calendar, issued in 1969 and published along with the General Roman Calendar for the Universal Church, noted that the calendar consists of the General Roman Calendar used by the entire Church and of particular calendars used in particular churches (nations or dioceses) or in families of religious.

The particular calendar for the U.S. contains the following celebrations. **January**: 4, Elizabeth Ann Seton; 5, John Neumann; 6, Bl. André Bessette. **March**: 3, Katharine Drexel. **May**: 10, Bl. Damien DeVeuster; 15, Isidore the Farmer. **July**: 1, Bl. Junípero Serra; 4, Independence Day; 14, Bl. Kateri Tekakwitha. **August**: 18, Jane Frances de Chantal. **September**: 9, Peter Claver. **October**: 6, Bl. Marie-Rose Durocher; 19, Isaac Jogues and John de Brébeuf and Companions; 20, Paul of the Cross. **November**: 13, Frances Xavier Cabrini; 18, Rose Philippine Duchesne; 23, Bl. Miguel Agustín Pro; Fourth Thursday, Thanksgiving Day. **December**: 9, Bl. Juan Diego; 12, Our Lady of Guadalupe.

| | | | | | Weeks of Ordinary Time | | | | |
| | | | | | Before Lent | | After Pent. | | First Sunday of Advent |
Year	Ash Wed.	Easter	Ascension	Pentecost	Week	Ends	Week	Ends	
2002	Feb. 13	Mar. 31	May 9	May 19	5	Feb. 12	7	May 20	Dec. 1
2003	Mar. 5	Apr. 20	May 29	June 8	8	Mar. 4	10	June 9	Nov. 30
2004	Feb. 25	Apr. 11	May 20	May 30	7	Feb. 24	9	May 31	Nov. 28
2005	Feb. 9	Mar. 27	May 5	May 15	5	Feb. 8	7	May 16	Nov. 27
2006	Mar. 1	Apr. 16	May 25	June 4	8	Feb. 28	9	June 5	Dec. 3
2007	Feb. 21	Apr. 8	May 17	May 27	7	Feb. 20	8	May 28	Dec. 2
2008	Feb. 6	Mar. 23	May 1	May 11	4	Feb. 5	6	May 12	Nov. 30
2009	Feb. 25	Apr. 12	May 21	May 31	7	Feb. 24	9	June 1	Nov. 29
2010	Feb. 17	Apr. 4	May 13	May 23	6	Feb. 16	8	May 24	Nov. 28
2011	Mar. 9	Apr. 24	June 2	June 12	9	Mar. 8	11	June 13	Nov. 27
2012	Feb. 22	Apr. 8	May 17	May 27	7	Feb. 21	8	May 28	Dec. 2
2013	Feb. 13	Mar. 31	May 9	May 19	5	Feb. 12	7	May 20	Dec. 1
2014	Mar. 5	Apr. 20	May 29	June 8	8	Mar. 4	10	June 9	Nov. 30
2015	Feb. 18	Apr. 5	May 14	May 24	6	Feb. 17	8	May 25	Nov. 29
2016	Feb. 10	Mar. 27	May 5	May 15	5	Feb. 9	7	May 16	Nov. 27
2017	Mar. 1	Apr. 16	May 25	June 4	8	Feb. 28	9	June 5	Dec. 3
2018	Feb. 14	Apr. 1	May 10	May 20	6	Feb. 13	7	May 21	Dec. 2
2019	Mar. 6	Apr. 21	May 30	June 9	8	Mar. 5	10	June 1	Dec. 1
2020	Feb. 26	Apr. 12	May 21	May 31	7	Feb. 25	9	June 1	Nov. 29
2021	Feb. 17	Apr. 4	May 13	May 23	6	Feb. 16	8	May 24	Nov. 28

TABLE OF MOVABLE FEASTS

2003 CALENDAR

January 2003

General Prayer Intention: "You are the salt of the earth and the light of the world" (cf. Mt. 5:13-14). That Christian communities may in this moment of our history ever more fully embrace the Lord's invitation to be the salt of the earth and the light of the world.

Missionary Prayer Intention: The Christian communities of China. That China's Christian communities may, in docility to the word of God, strengthen their ties and cooperate more effectively in spreading the Good News.

1   Wed. Octave of Christmas; Solemnity of the Blessed Virgin Mary, Mother of God; Holy day of obligation (Nm. 6: 22 -27; Gal. 4:4-7; Lk.2:16-21).
2   Thurs. Sts. Basil the Great and Gregory Nazianzus, bishops and doctors of the Church; memorial.
3   Fri. Weekday.
4   Sat. St. Elizabeth Ann Seton, religious; memorial.
5   Sun. Epiphany of Our Lord; solemnity (Is. 60:1-6; Eph. 3:2-3a, 5-6; Mt. 2:1-12).
6   Mon. Weekday. Bl. Andre Bessette, religious; optional memorial.
7   Tues. Weekday. St. Raymond of Penafort, priest; optional memorial.
8   Wed. Weekday.
9   Thurs. Weekday.
10   Fri. Weekday.
11   Sat. Weekday.
12   Sun. Baptism of the Lord; feast (Is 42:1-4,6-7; Acts 10:34-38; Mk. 1:7-11).
13   Mon. Weekday. St. Hilary, bishop-doctor; optional memorial (First Week in Ordinary Time).
14   Tues. Weekday.
15   Wed. Weekday.
16   Thurs. Weekday.
17   Fri. St. Anthony, abbot; memorial.
18   Sat. Weekday.
19   Sun. Second Sunday in Ordinary Time (1 Sam. 3:3b-10,19; 1 Cor. 6:13c-15a, 17-20; Jn.1:35-42).
20   Mon. Weekday. St. Fabian, pope-martyr; St. Sebastian, martyr; optional memorials.
21   Tues. St. Agnes, virgin and martyr; memorial.
22   Wed. Weekday. St. Vincent, deacon-martyr; optional memorial.
23   Thurs. Weekday.
24   Fri. St. Francis de Sales, bishop-doctor; memorial.
25   Sat. Conversion of St. Paul, apostle; feast.
26   Sun. Third Sunday in Ordinary Time (Jonah 3:1-5,10; 1 Cor. 7:29-31; Mk. 1:14-20).
27   Mon. Weekday. St. Angela Merici, virgin; optional memorial.
28   Tues. St. Thomas Aquinas, priest-doctor; memorial.
29   Wed. Weekday.
30   Thurs. Weekday.
31   Fri. St. John Bosco, priest; memorial.

Observances: World Day of Peace, Jan. 1. Customary ordination of bishops by the pope on the Solemnity of the Epiphany, Jan. 6. Week of Prayer for Christian Unity, Jan. 18-25. National Prayer Vigil for Life and March for Life in Washington, D.C., Jan. 21-22.

February 2003

General Prayer Intention: Bread and water for all the world. That all Christians, sensitive to the distressing conditions of the peoples who are still suffering from hunger and thirst, may be moved to greater solidarity with their brothers.

Missionary Prayer Intention: The Church in Malaysia, Singapore and Brunei. That the Church in Malaysia, Singapore, and Brunei may dialog with other religions while keeping faithful to its exacting evangelizing mission.

1   Sat. Weekday .
2   Sun. Presentation of the Lord, feast (Mal. 3:1-4; Heb. 2:14-18; Lk.2:22-40).
3   Mon. Weekday. St. Blase, bishop-martyr; St. Ansgar, bishop; optional memorial.
4   Tues. Weekday.
5   Wed. St. Agatha, virgin-martyr; memorial.
6   Thurs. St. Paul Miki, priest-martyr and companions, martyrs; memorial.
7   Fri. Weekday.
8   Sat. Weekday. St. Jerome Emiliani, priest; optional memorial.
9   Sun. Fifth Sunday in Ordinary Time (Job 7:1-4, 6-7; 1 Cor. 9:16-19, 22-23; Mk. 1:29-39).
10   Mon. St. Scholastica, virgin; memorial.
11   Tue. Weekday. Our Lady of Lourdes; optional memorial.
12   Wed. Weekday.
13   Thurs. Weekday.
14   Fri. Sts. Cyril, monk and Methodius, bishop; memorial.
15   Sat. Weekday.
16   Sun. Sixth Sunday in Ordinary Time (Lv. 13:1-2, 44-46; 1 Cor. 10:31-11:1; Mk. 1:40-45).
17   Mon. Weekday. Seven Holy Founders of the Order of Servites; optional memorial.
18   Tues. Weekday.
19   Wed. Weekday.
20   Thurs. Weekday.
21   Fri. St. Peter Damian, bishop-doctor; memorial.
22   Sat. Chair of St. Peter, apostle; feast.
23   Sun. Seventh Sunday in Ordinary Time (Isaiah 43:18-19, 21-22, 24b-25; 1 Cor. 1: 18-22; Mk. 2:1-12).
24   Mon. Weekday.
25   Tue. Weekday.
26   Wed. Weekday.
27   Thurs. Weekday.
28   Fri. Weekday.

Observances: The conclusion of Catholic Schools Week (Feb.1). The Presentation of the Child Jesus in the Temple, traditional day for the blessings of candles that will be used throughout the year. Optional memorial of St. Blase, bishop-martyr, whose intercession is sought against ailments of the throat and other evils. Optional memorial of Our Lady of Lourdes which also World Day of the Sick, a day of prayer, healing and anointing of those who are ill.

March 2003

General Prayer Intention: The sacrament of Reconciliation. That each one of us, the people of God and our pastors, may grow in the realization of the importance of God's merciful gift of love, the Sacrament of Reconciliation.

Missionary Prayer Intention: The local Churches of Africa. That Africa's local Churches, in the midst of their current difficult situations, may feel the urgency of announcing the Gospel coherently and courageously.

1 Sat. Weekday.
2 Sun. Eighth Sunday in Ordinary Time (Hos. 2:16b, 17b, 21-22; 1 Cor. 3:1b-6; Mk. 2:18-22).
3 Mon. Weekday. St. Katherine Drexel, virgin; optional memorial.
4 Tues. Weekday. St. Casimir; optional memorial.
5 Wed. Ash Wednesday (Jl. 2:12-18; 2 Cor. 5: 20-6:2; Mt. 6: 1-6, 16-18). Fast and abstinence.
6 Thurs. Lenten Weekday.
7 Fri. Lenten Weekday. Abstinence. Sts. Perpetua and Felicity, martyrs; optional memorial.
8 Sat. Lenten Weekday. St. John of God, religious; optional memorial.
9 Sun. First Sunday of Lent (Gn. 9:8-15; 1 Pt. 3:18-22; Mk. 1:12-15).
10 Mon. Lenten Weekday.
11 Tues. Lenten Weekday.
12 Wed. Lenten Weekday.
13 Thurs. Lenten Weekday.
14 Fri. Lenten Weekday. Abstinence.
15 Sat. Lenten Weekday.
16 Sun. Second Sunday of Lent (Gn. 22:1-2, 9a, 10-13, 15-18; Rom. 8:31b-34; Mk. 9:2-10).
17 Mon. Lenten Weekday. St. Patrick, bishop; optional memorial.
18 Tues. Lenten Weekday. St. Cyril of Jerusalem, bishop-doctor; optional memorial.
19 Wed. St. Joseph, husband of the Blessed Virgin Mary; solemnity.
20 Thurs. Lenten Weekday.
21 Fri. Lenten Weekday. Abstinence.
22 Sat. Lenten Weekday.
23 Sun. Third Sunday of Lent (Ex. 20:1-17; 1 Cor. 1:22-25; Jn. 2:13-25).
24 Mon. Lenten Weekday.
25 Tues. Annunciation of the Lord; solemnity.
26 Wed. Lenten Weekday.
27 Thurs. Lenten Weekday.
28 Fri. Lenten Weekday. Abstinence.
29 Sat. Lenten Weekday.
30 Sun. Fourth Sunday of Lent (Chronicles 36: 14-16, 19-23; Ephesians 2: 4-10; Jn.3:14-21).
31 Mon. Lenten Weekday.

Observances: The Lenten season begins with Ash Wednesday (Mar.5), when ashes are blessed and imposed on the forehead of the faithful to remind them of their obligation to do penance of sins, to seek spiritual renewal by means of prayer, fasting, good works and by bearing with patience and for God's purposes the trials and difficulties of everyday life. Catholics are reminded of the serious obligation to fast and abstain on those appointed days during the Lenten season as well as the opportunity for other acts of mortification and sacrifice. The Solemnity of St. Joseph, husband of Mary, is observed Mar. 19. The Solemnity of the Annunciation is observed Mar. 25.

April 2003

General Prayer Intention: Live according to the Spirit. That those who hold positions of responsibility in the Church may offer a shining example of a life always responsive to the guidance of the Spirit.

Missionary Prayer Intention: The universal call to holiness. That clergy, religious and laity, both men and women, who work in missionary lands, may live and bear witness to the universal call to holiness.

1 Tues. Lenten Weekday.
2 Wed. Lenten Weekday. St. Francis of Paola, hermit; optional memorial.
3 Thurs. Lenten Weekday.
4 Fri. Lenten Weekday. Abstinence. St. Isidore, bishop-doctor; optional memorial.
5 Sat. Lenten Weekday. St. Vincent Ferrer, priest; optional memorial.
6 Sun. Fifth Sunday of Lent (Jer. 31:31-34; Heb. 5:7-9; Jn.12:20-33).
7 Mon. Lenten Weekday. St. John Baptist de la Salle, priest; optional memorial.
8 Tues. Lenten Weekday.
9 Wed. Lenten Weekday.
10 Thurs. Lenten Weekday.
11 Fri. Lenten Weekday. Abstinence. St. Stanislaus, bishop-martyr; optional memorial.
12 Sat. Lenten Weekday.
13 Sun. Palm Sunday/The Lord's Passion (Mk. 11:1-10/Is. 50:4-7; Phil. 2:6-11; Mt. 26:14-27:66).
14 Mon. Monday of Holy Week.
15 Tue. Tuesday of Holy Week.
16 Wed. Wednesday of Holy Week
17 Thurs. Holy Thursday. Chrism Mass in the morning. The Easter Triduum begins with the evening Mass of the Lord's Supper.
18 Fri. Good Friday. The Lord's Passion. Fast and abstinence.
19 Sat. Holy Saturday. Easter Vigil.
20 Sun. Easter Sunday: Resurrection of the Lord; solemnity (Acts 10:34a, 37-43; Col. 3:1-4 or 1 Cor. 5:6b-8; Jn. 20:1-9 or Mt. 28:1-10 or (at an afternoon or evening Mass – Lk. 24:13-15]).
21 Mon. Easter Monday; solemnity.
22 Tues. Easter Tuesday; solemnity.
23 Wed. Easter Wednesday; solemnity.
24 Thurs. Easter Thursday; solemnity.
25 Fri. Easter Friday; solemnity.
26 Sat. Easter Saturday; solemnity.
27 Sun. Second Sunday of Easter (Acts 4:32-35; 1 Jn. 5:1-6; Jn.20:19-31).
28 Mon. Easter Weekday. St. Peter Chanel, priest-martyr; St. Louis Mary de Montfort; optional memorials.
29 Tues. St. Catherine of Siena, virgin-doctor; memorial.
30 Wed. Easter Weekday. St. Pius V, pope; optional memorial.

Observances: Holy Week: Passion Sunday, or Palm Sunday, begins these most solemn and holy celebrations of the Church year. Monday, Tuesday, and Wednesday of Holy Week are preparatory days leading to the Sacred Triduum. The morning of Holy Thursday is the celebration of the Mass of the Holy Chrism, when the oils used throughout the liturgical year are blessed by the diocesan bishops. During this Mass all priests renew their vows. Easter is the day when the Holy Father delivers the traditional *Urbi et Orbi* address.

May 2003

General Prayer Intention: Mary, Mother of Life. That children in difficulty and those who devote themselves to their care may find in Mary, Mother of Life, constant support and help.

Missionary Prayer Intention: The evangelization of Asia. That in the local Churches of Asia, the Holy Spirit may kindle renewed ardor for evangelizing the entire continent.

1 Thurs. Easter Weekday. St. Joseph the Worker; optional memorial.
2 Fri. St. Athanasius, bishop-doctor; memorial.
3 Sat. Sts. Philip and James, apostles; feast.
4 Sun. Third Sunday of Easter (Acts 3:13-15, 17-19; 1 Jn. 2:1-5a; Lk. 24:35-48).
5 Mon. Easter Weekday.
6 Tues. Easter Weekday.
7 Wed. Easter Weekday.
8 Thurs. Easter Weekday.
9 Fri. Easter Weekday.
10 Sat. Easter Weekday. Bl. Damien Joseph deVeuster of Molokai, priest; optional memorial.
11 Sun. Fourth Sunday of Easter (Acts 4:8-12; 1 Jn. 3:1-2; Jn.10: 11 -18).
12 Mon. Easter Weekday. Sts. Nereus and Achilleus, martyrs; St. Pancras, martyr; optional memorials.
13 Tues. Easter Weekday.
14 Wed. St. Mathias, apostle; feast.
15 Thurs. Easter Weekday. St. Isidore the farmer; optional memorial.
16 Fri. Easter Weekday.
17 Sat. Easter Weekday.
18 Sun. Fifth Sunday of Easter (Acts 9:26-31; 1 Jn. 3:18-24; Jn.15:1-8).
19 Mon. Easter Weekday.
20 Tues. Easter Weekday. St. Bernardine of Siena, priest; optional memorial.
21 Wed. Easter Weekday.
22 Thurs. Easter Weekday.
23 Fri. Easter Weekday.
24 Sat. Easter Weekday.
25 Sun. Sixth Sunday of Easter (Acts 10:25-26, 34-35, 44-48; 1 Jn. 4:7-10; Jn.15: 9-17).
26 Mon. St. Philip Neri, priest; memorial.
27 Tues. Easter Weekday. St. Augustine of Canterbury, bishop; optional memorial.
28 Wed. Easter Weekday.
29 Thurs. Ascension of our Lord; solemnity. Holy day of obligation (Acts 1:1-11; Eph. 4:1-13; Mk. 16:15-20).
30 Fri. Easter Weekday.
31 Sat. Visitation of the Blessed Virgin Mary to Elizabeth; feast.

Observances: The Solemnity of the Ascension celebrated May 29 (transferred to Sunday in some dioceses) is a holy day of obligation. Also, the month of May is traditionally dedicated to our Blessed Mother. Customary Marian devotions include the recitation of the Rosary and the Litany of Loretto, processions, the crowning of Mary and the celebration of votive masses dedicated to our Blessed Mother.

June 2003

General Prayer Intention: Respect of human values. That the faithful who hold responsible positions in public life may be guided by the Gospel and the Church's social teaching to promote respect for human values in every situation.

Missionary Prayer Intention: Testimony of full unity in the various Christians traditions of India. That the Christians of India, who belong to various traditions, may be drawn to offer together a testimony to full unity and communion in the one Spirit who guides them.

1 Sun. Seventh Sunday of Easter (Acts 1:15-17, 20a, 20c-26; 1 Jn. 4: 11-16; Mk. 17: 11b-19).
2 Mon. Easter Weekday. Sts. Marcellinus and Peter, martyrs; optional memorial.
3 Tues. St. Charles Lwanga, martyr, and Companions, martyrs; memorial.
4 Wed. Easter Weekday.
5 Thurs. St. Boniface, bishop-martyr; memorial.
6 Fri. Easter Weekday. St. Norbert, bishop; optional memorial.
7 Sat. Easter Weekday.
8 Sun. Pentecost Sunday; solemnity (Acts 2: 1-11; 1 Cor. 12: 3b-7, 12-13; or Gal. 5: 16-25; Jn.20: 19-23 or Jn.15: 26-27; 16: 12 -15).
9 Mon. Tenth Week in Ordinary Time. St. Ephrem, deacon-doctor; optional memorial.
10 Tues. Weekday.
11 Wed. St. Barnabas, apostle; memorial.
12 Thurs. Weekday.
13 Fri. St. Anthony of Padua, priest-doctor; memorial.
14 Sat. Weekday.
15 Sun. Most Holy Trinity; solemnity (Dt. 4:32-34, 39-40; Rom. 8:14-17; Mt. 28:16-20).
16 Mon. Eleventh Week in Ordinary Time. Weekday.
17 Tues. Weekday.
18 Wed. Weekday.
19 Thurs. Weekday. St. Romuald, abbot; optional memorial.
20 Fri. Weekday.
21 Sat. St. Aloysius Gonzaga, religious; memorial.
22 Sun. Most Holy Body and Blood of Christ (Corpus Christi); solemnity (Ex. 24:3-8; Heb. 9:11-15; Mk. 14: 12-16, 22-26).
23 Mon. Twelfth Week in Ordinary Time. Weekday.
24 Tues. Nativity of St. John the Baptist; solemnity.
25 Wed. Weekday.
26 Thurs. Weekday.
27 Fri. Most Sacred Heart of Jesus; solemnity.
28 Sat. St. Irenaeus, bishop-martyr; memorial.
29 Sun. Sts. Peter and Paul, apostles; solemnity (Acts 12: 1-11; 2 Tim. 4:6-8, 17-18; Mt. 16: 13-19).
30 Mon. Thirteenth Week of Ordinary Time. Weekday. First Martyrs of the Church of Rome; optional memorial.

Observances: Easter is completed with the celebration of the Feast of Pentecost. The Feast of the Most Holy Trinity is June 15. The Feast of the Body and Blood of Christ (Corpus Christi) is June 22. It is the custom in certain dioceses to gather for a Corpus Christi procession to venerate the Body of Christ at special altars prepared near the cathedral church. The Feast of the Sacred Heart is June 27 and the Feast of Sts. Peter and Paul on June 29.

July 2003

General Prayer Intention: An economy at the service of all. That governments and others responsible for the economies and finances of the world may seek modalities and conditions which guarantee all peoples the means necessary to live in a dignified way.

Missionary Prayer Intention: The sick people of Africa. That all the sick people of Africa — victims of AIDS and other serious diseases — may experience God's love and consolation, thanks to the doctors and others who take care of them.

1 Tue. Weekday. Bl. Junipero Serra, priest; optional memorial.
2 Wed. Weekday
3 Thurs. St. Thomas, apostle; feast.
4 Fri. Weekday St. Elizabeth of Portugal; optional memorial. Proper Mass for Independence Day.
5. Sat. Weekday. St. Anthony Maria Zaccaria, priest; optional memorial.
6 Sun. Fourteenth Sunday in Ordinary Time (Ez. 2:2-5; 1 Cor. 12: 7-10; Mk. 6:1-6).
7 Mon. Weekday.
8 Tues. Weekday.
9 Wed. Weekday.
10 Thurs. Weekday.
11 Fri. St. Benedict, abbot; memorial.
12 Sat. Weekday.
· 13 Sun. Fifteenth Sunday in Ordinary Time (Amos 7:12-15; Eph. 1:3-14; Mk. 6:7-13).
14 Mon. Bl. Kateri Tekakwitha, virgin; memorial.
15 Tues. St. Bonaventure, bishop-doctor; memorial.
16 Wed. Weekday. Our Lady of Mount Carmel; optional memorial.
17 Thurs. Weekday.
18 Fri. Weekday. St. Camillus de Lellis, priest; optional memorial.
19 Sat. Weekday.
20 Sun. Sixteenth Sunday in Ordinary Time (Jer. 23:1-6; Eph. 2:13-18; Mk. 6:30-34).
21 Mon. Weekday. St. Lawrence of Brandisi, priest-doctor; optional memorial.
22 Tues. St. Mary Magdalene; memorial.
23 Wed. Weekday. St. Bridget of Sweden; optional memorial.
24 Thurs. Weekday.
25 Fri. St. James, apostle; feast.
26 Sat. Sts. Joachim and Anne, parents of the Blessed Virgin Mary; memorial.
27 Sun. Seventeenth Sunday in Ordinary Time (2 Kgs. 4:42-44; Eph. 4:1-6; Jn.6:1-15).
28 Mon. Weekday.
29 Tues. St. Martha; memorial.
30 Wed. Weekday. St. Peter Chrysologus, bishop-doctor; optional memorial.
31 Thurs. St. Ignatius of Loyola, priest; memorial.

Observances: Blessed Juniper Serra, whose optional memorial may be celebrated July 1, found of the California Missions. St. Thomas the Apostle is observed on July 3; St. Maria Goretti, July 6; St. Benedict, the founder of western monasticism and patron saint of Europe, July 11; Blessed Kateri Tekakwitha, July 14; St. Bonaventure, called the second found of the Franciscan Order, July 15; St. Ignatius Loyola, founder of the Society of Jesus, July 31.

Independence Day, July 4, is observed with a special mass for celebration in the United States.

August 2003

General Prayer Intention: For a wise use of science and technology. That researches in science and technology may welcome the Church's incessant calls to make wise and responsible use of the successes they have attained.

Missionary Prayer Intention: The catechists of the Church. That the catechists of the young churches may bear witness faithfully to their adherence to the Gospel.

1 Fri. St. Alphonsus Liguori, bishop-doctor; memorial.
2 Sat. Weekday. St. Eusebius of Vercelli, bishop, and St. Peter Julian Eymard, priest; optional memorials.
3 Sun. Eighteenth Sunday in Ordinary Time (Ex. 16:2-4, 12-15; Eph. 4:17, 20-24; Jn.6:24-35).
4 Mon. St. John Mary Vianney, priest; memorial.
5 Tues. Weekday. Dedication of the Basilica of St. Mary Major in Rome; optional memorial.
6 Wed. Transfiguration of the Lord; feast.
7 Thurs. Weekday. St. Sixtus III, pope-martyr, and Companions, martyrs; St. Cajetan, priest; optional memorial.
8 Fri. St. Dominic, priest; memorial.
9 Sat. Weekday
10 Sun. Nineteenth Sunday in Ordinary Time (1Kgs. 19:4-8; Eph. 4:30-5:2; Jn.6:41-51).
11 Mon. St. Clare, virgin; memorial.
12 Tues. Weekday.
13 Wed. Weekday. St. Pontian, pope-martyr and St. Hippolytus, priest-martyr; optional memorials.
14 Thurs. St. Maximillian Mary Kolbe, priest-martyr; memorial.
15 Fri. Assumption of the Blessed Virgin Mary; solemnity. Holy Day of Obligation.
16 Sat. Weekday. St. Stephen of Hungary; optional memorial.
17 Sun. Twentieth Sunday in Ordinary Time (Proverbs 9:1-6; Eph. 5:15-20; Jn.6:51-58).
18 Mon. Weekday. St. Jane Frances de Chantal, religious; optional memorial.
19 Tues. Weekday. St. John Eudes, priest; optional memorial.
20 Wed. St. Bernard, abbot-doctor; memorial.
21 Thurs St. Pius X, pope; memorial.
22 Fri. Queenship of the Blessed Virgin Mary; memorial.
23 Sat. Weekday. St. Rose of Lima, virgin; optional memorial.
24 Sun. Twenty-first Sunday in Ordinary Time (Josh. 24:1-2a, 15-17, 18b; Eph. 5:21-32; Jn.6:60-69).
25 Mon. Weekday. St. Louis and St. Joseph Calasanz; optional memorials.
26 Tues. Weekday.
27 Wed. St. Monica; memorial.
28 Thurs. St. Augustine, bishop-doctor; memorial.
29 Fri. Martyrdom of St. John the Baptist; memorial.
30 Sat. Weekday.
31 Sun. Twenty-second Sunday of Ordinary Time (Dt. 4:1-2, 6-8; James 1:17-18, 21b-22, 27; Mk. 7:1-8, 14-15, 21-23).

Observances: The Feast of the Transfiguration of the Lord, Aug. 6; St. Dominic, Aug, 8; St. Clare, Aug. 11; The Feast of the Assumption of the Blessed Virgin Mary, Aug. 15; St. Augustine, Aug. 28.

September 2003

General Prayer Intention: The countries suffering because of war, terrorism and violence. That countries suffering from war, terrorism and violence may find the way of reconciliation, concord and peace.

Missionary Prayer Intention: The Christian communities of Central Asia. That the Christian communities of Central Asia who dwell among other religious traditions may be committed to spreading the good news of the kingdom through their lived faith.

1   Mon. Weekday. Labor Day. Special Mass for the Blessings of Human Labor.
2   Tues. Weekday.
3   Wed. St. Gregory the Great, pope-doctor; memorial.
4   Thurs. Weekday.
5   Fri. Weekday.
6   Sat. Weekday.
7   Sun. Twenty-third Sunday in Ordinary Time (Is. 35:4-7a; James 2:1-5; Mk. 7:31-37).
8   Mon. Birth of the Blessed Virgin Mary; feast.
9   Tues. St. Peter Claver, priest; memorial.
10 Wed. Weekday.
11 Thurs. Weekday.
12 Fri. Weekday
13 Sat. St. John Chrysostom, bishop-doctor; memorial.
14 Sun. Exaltation of the Holy Cross (Num. 21:4b-9; Philippians 2:6-11; Jn.3:13-17).
15 Mon. Our Lady of Sorrows; memorial.
16 Tues. Sts. Cornelius, pope-martyr and Cyprian, bishop-martyr; memorial.
17 Wed. Wednesday of the Twenty-fourth week in Ordinary Time. St. Robert Bellarmine, bishop-doctor; optional memorial.
18 Thurs. Weekday.
19 Fri. Weekday. St. Januarius, bishop-martyr; optional memorial.
20 Sat. Sts. Andrew Kim Taegon, priest-martyr, Paul Chong Hasang, martyr, and Companions, martyrs; memorial.
21 Sun. Twenty-fifth Sunday in Ordinary Time (Wisdom 2:12, 17-20; James 3:16 – 4:3; Mk. 9:30-37).
22 Mon. Weekday.
23 Tues. Weekday.
24 Wed. Weekday.
25 Thurs. Weekday.
26 Fri. Weekday. Sts. Cosmas and Damian, martyrs; optional memorial.
27 Sat. St. Vincent de Paul, priest; memorial.
28 Sun. Twenty-sixth Sunday in Ordinary Time (Num. 11:25-29; James 5:1-6; Mk. 9:38-43, 45, 47-48).
29 Mon. Michael, Gabriel, and Raphael, archangels; feast.
30 Tues. St. Jerome; memorial.

Observances: Birth of the Blessed Virgin Mary, Sept. 8; St. John Chrysostom, doctor of the Church, Sept. 13; Exaltation of the Holy Cross, Sept. 14; Our Lady of Sorrows, Sept. 15; St. Robert Bellarmine, doctor of the Church, Sept. 17. St. Matthew, apostle and evangelist Sept. 21; St. Vincent de Paul, founder of the Vincentians and Daughters of Charity, Sept. 27; Sts. Michael, Gabriel, and Raphael, archangels, Sept. 29,

Labor Day is celebrated Sept. 3 with a special mass.

October 2003

General Prayer Intention: To follow Christ with enthusiasm. That young people may follow Christ, the way, the truth and the life, with generous enthusiasm and bear witness to him in all the situations of their lives.

Missionary Prayer Intention: Pastors rich in wisdom and holiness. That God may mercifully provide his Church with pastors rich in wisdom and holiness and the readiness to defend the light of the Gospel to the ends of the earth.

1   Wed. St. Therese of the Child Jesus, virgin; memorial.
2   Thurs. Guardian Angels; memorial.
3   Fri. Weekday.
4   Sat. St. Francis of Assisi, religious; memorial.
5   Sun. Twenty-seventh of Ordinary Time (Gn. 2:18-24; Heb. 2:9-11; Mk. 10:2-16).
6   Mon. Weekday. St. Bruno, priest and Bl. Marie Rose Durocher, virgin; optional memorials.
7   Tues. Our Lady of the Rosary; memorial.
8   Wed. Weekday.
9   Thurs. Weekday. St. Denis, bishop-marytr; St. John Leonardi, priest; optional memorials.
10 Fri. Weekday.
11 Sat. Weekday.
12 Sun. Twenty-eighth Sunday in Ordinary Time (Wis. 7:7-11; Heb. 4:12-13; Mk. 10: 17-30).
13 Mon. Weekday.
14 Tues. Weekday. St. Callistus I, pope-martyr; optional memorial.
15 Wed. St. Theresa of Avila, virgin-doctor; memorial.
16 Thurs. Weekday. St. Hedwig, religious; St. Margaret Mary Alacoque, virgin; optional memorial.
17 Fri. St. Ignatius of Antioch, bishop-martyr; memorial.
18 Sat. St. Luke, evangelist; feast.
19 Sun. Twenty-ninth Sunday in Ordinary Time (Is. 53:10-11; Heb. 4:14-16; Mk. 10:35-45).
20 Mon. Weekday. St. Paul of the Cross; optional memorial.
21 Tues. Weekday.
22 Wed. Weekday.
23 Thurs. Weekday. St. John of Capistrano, priest; optional memorial.
24 Fri. Weekday. St. Anthony Mary Claret, bishop; optional memorial.
25 Sat. Weekday.
26 Sun. Thirtieth Sunday in Ordinary Time (Jer. 31:7-9; Heb. 5:1-6; Mk. 10:46-52).
27 Mon. Weekday.
28 Tues. Sts. Simon and Jude, apostles; feast.
29 Wed. Weekday.
30 Thurs. Weekday.
31 Fri. Weekday.

Observances: St. Therese of the Child Jesus, doctor of the Church, Oct.1; Guardian Angels, Oct. 2; St. Francis of Assisi, founder of the Franciscan Order, Oct. 4; St. Teresa of Jesus, doctor of the Church, reformer of the Carmelite Order, Oct. 15; The North American Martyrs, while not celebrated this year, are normally celebrated Oct. 19. St. Paul of the Cross, founder of the Congregation of the Passion, Oct. 20.

Mission Sunday is observed, with appeals for prayer and financial support for persons and projects involved in the ministry of evangelization at home and abroad.

November 2003

General Prayer Intention: The appreciation of the spirituality and liturgical traditions of the Oriental Churches. That the Christians of the West may continuously enhance their knowledge and appreciation of the spirituality and liturgical traditions of the Oriental Churches.

Missionary Prayer Intention: Second American Missionary Congress. That at the Second American Missionary Congress in Guatemala the Church in the Americas, may be inspired to evangelize even beyond its own borders.

1 Sat. All Saints'; solemnity.
2 Sun. Commemoration of All the Faithful Departed. All Souls' Day.
3 Mon. Weekday of the Thirty-first week in Ordinary Time. St. Martin de Porres, religious; optional memorial.
4 Tues. St. Charles Borromeo, bishop; memorial.
5 Wed. Weekday.
6 Thurs. Weekday.
7 Fri. Weekday.
8 Sat. Weekday.
9 Sun. Dedication of the Basilica of St. John Lateran in Rome; feast.
10 Mon. St. Leo the Great, pope-doctor; memorial.
11 Tues. St. Martin of Tours, bishop; memorial
12 Wed. St. Josaphat, bishop-martyr; memorial.
13 Thurs. St. Frances Xavier Cabrini; memorial.
14 Fri. Weekday.
15 Sat. Weekday. St. Albert the Great, bishop-doctor; optional memorial.
16 Sun. Thirty-third Sunday in Ordinary Time (Dn. 12:1-3; Heb. 10:11-14, 18; Mk. 13:24-32).
17 Mon. St. Elizabeth of Hungary, religious; memorial.
18 Tues. Weekday. St. Rose Philippine Duchesne, virgin; Dedication of the Basilicas of St. Peter and St. Paul, apostles, in Rome; optional memorials.
19 Wed. Weekday.
20 Thurs. Weekday.
21 Fri. Presentation of the Blessed Virgin Mary; memorial.
22 Sat. St. Cecilia, virgin-martyr; memorial.
23 Sun. Our Lord Jesus Christ the King; solemnity (Dn. 7:13-14; Rev. 1:5-8; Jn. 18:33b-37).
24 Mon. St. Andrew Dung-Lac, priest-martyr and Companions, martyrs; memorials.
25 Tues. Weekday.
26 Wed. Weekday.
27 Thurs. Thanksgiving Day; proper mass.
28 Fri. Weekday.
29 Sat. Weekday.
30 Sun. First Sunday of Advent (Jer. 33:14-16; Thes. 3:12-42; Lk. 21:25-28, 34-36).

Observances: All Saints' Day, Nov. 1; All Souls' Day, Nov. 2; Frances Xavier Cabrini, Nov. 13; St. Albert the Great, Nov. 15; Presentation of the Blessed Virgin Mary, Nov. 21; Christ the King, Nov. 23; Thanksgiving Day, Nov. 27; the beginning of the Church year, the first Sunday of Advent, Nov. 30.

The annual fall meeting of the bishops of the United States takes place this month in Washington, D.C. Its agenda covers a wide range of topics with particular attention given to doctrinal, pastoral and educational issues that impact the life of the Church in the U.S.

December 2003

General Prayer Intention: Inter-religious cooperation to alleviate human sufferings. That the members of all religions may cooperate to alleviate the human suffering of our time.

Missionary Prayer Intention: The Church in the totalitarian countries. That the Church in countries where totalitarian regimes reign may be given full freedom to carry out her spiritual mission.

1 Mon. Advent Weekday.
2 Tues. Advent Weekday.
3 Wed. St. Francis Xavier, priest; memorial.
4 Thurs. Advent Weekday. St. John Damascene, priest-doctor; optional memorial.
5 Fri. Advent Weekday.
6 Sat. Advent Weekday. St. Nicholas, bishop; optional memorial.
7 Sun. Second Sunday of Advent (Bar. 5:1-9; Phil. 1:4-6, 8-11; Lk. 3:1-6).
8 Mon. Immaculate Conception of the Blessed Virgin Mary; solemnity (Gn. 3:9-15, 20; Eph. 1:3-6, 11-12; Lk. 1:26-38). Not observed as a holy day of obligation.
9 Tues. Advent Weekday. St. Juan Diego; optional memorial.
10 Wed. Advent Weekday.
11 Thurs. Advent Weekday. St. Damasus, pope; optional memorial.
12 Fri. Our Lady of Guadalupe; feast.
13 Sat. St. Lucy, virgin-martyr; memorial.
14 Sun. Third Sunday of Advent (Zep. 3:14-18a; Phil. 4:4-7; Lk. 3:10-18).
15 Mon. Advent Weekday.
16 Tues. Advent Weekday.
17 Wed. Advent Weekday.
18 Thurs. Advent Weekday.
19 Fri. Advent Weekday.
20 Sat. Advent Weekday.
21 Sun. Fourth Sunday of Advent (Mi. 5:1-4a; Heb. 10:5-10; Lk. 1:39-45).
22 Mon. Advent Weekday.
23 Tues. Advent Weekday.
24 Wed. Advent Weekday.
25 Thurs. Nativity of the Lord, Christmas; solemnity; holy day of obligation. (Vigil Mass — Is. 62:1-5; Acts 13:16-17, 22-25; Mt. 1:1-25 or 1:18-25. Midnight Mass — Is.9:1-6; Ti. 2:11-14; Lk. 2:1-14. Mass at Dawn — Is. 62:11-12; Ti. 3:4-7; Lk. 2:15-20. Mass during the day — Is. 52:7-10; Heb. 1:1-6; Jn.1:1-18 or 1:1-5, 9-14).
26 Fri. St. Stephen, first martyr; feast.
27 Sat. St. John, apostle-evangelist; feast.
28 Sun. Holy Family of Jesus, Mary, and Joseph (Sir. 3:2-7, 12-14; Col. 3:12-21; Lk. 2:22-40).
29 Mon. Fifth Day in the Octave of Christmas. St. Thomas Becket, bishop-martyr; optional memorial.
30 Tues. Sixth Day in the Octave of Christmas.
31 Wed. Seventh Day in the Octave of Christmas. St. Sylvester, pope; optional memorial.

Observances: St. Francis Xavier, missionary, Dec. 3; Sts. John of Damascus, Ambrose, John of the Cross, Peter Canisius, doctors of the Church, Immaculate Conception, Dec. 8; St. Juan Diego, Dec. 9; Our Lady of Guadalupe, Dec. 12; Birth of our Lord, Dec. 25; St. Stephen, proto-martyr, Dec. 26; St. John, apostle-evangelist, Dec. 27; Holy Family, Dec. 28.

HOLY DAYS AND OTHER OBSERVANCES

The following list includes the six holy days of obligation observed in the United States and additional observances of devotional and historical significance. The dignity or rank of observances is indicated by the terms: **solemnity** (highest in rank); **feast; memorial** (for universal observance); **optional memorial** (for celebration by choice).

All Saints, Nov. 1, holy day of obligation, solemnity. Commemorates all the blessed in heaven, and is intended particularly to honor the blessed who have no special feasts. The background of the feast dates to the fourth century when groups of martyrs, and later other saints, were honored on a common day in various places. In 609 or 610, the Pantheon, a pagan temple at Rome, was consecrated as a Christian church for the honor of Our Lady and the martyrs (later all saints). In 835, Gregory IV fixed Nov. 1 as the date of observance.

All Souls, Commemoration of the Faithful Departed, Nov. 2. The dead were prayed for from the earliest days of Christianity. By the sixth century it was customary in Benedictine monasteries to hold a commemoration of deceased members of the order at Pentecost. A common commemoration of all the faithful departed on the day after All Saints was instituted in 998 by St. Odilo, of the Abbey of Cluny, and an observance of this kind was accepted in Rome in the 14th century.

Annunciation of the Lord (formerly, Annunciation of the Blessed Virgin Mary), Mar. 25, solemnity. A feast of the Incarnation which commemorates the announcement by the Archangel Gabriel to the Virgin Mary that she was to become the Mother of Christ (Lk. 1:26-38), and the miraculous conception of Christ by her. The feast was instituted about 430 in the East. The Roman observance dates from the seventh century, when celebration was said to be universal.

Ascension of the Lord, movable observance held 40 days after Easter, holy day of obligation, solemnity. Commemorates the Ascension of Christ into heaven 40 days after his Resurrection from the dead (Mk. 16:19; Lk. 24:51; Acts 1:2). The feast recalls the completion of Christ's mission on earth for the salvation of all people and his entry into heaven with glorified human nature. The Ascension is a pledge of the final glorification of all who achieve salvation. Documentary evidence of the feast dates from early in the fifth century, but it was observed long before that time in connection with Pentecost and Easter.

Ash Wednesday, movable observance, six and one-half weeks before Easter. It was set as the first day of Lent by Pope St. Gregory the Great (590-604) with the extension of an earlier and shorter penitential season to a total period including 40 weekdays of fasting before Easter. It is a day of fast and abstinence. Ashes, symbolic of penance, are blessed and distributed among the faithful during the day. They are used to mark the forehead with the Sign of the Cross, with the reminder: "Remember you are dust, and to dust you will return," or: "Turn away from sin and be faithful to the Gospel."

Assumption, Aug. 15, holy day of obligation, solemnity. Commemorates the taking into heaven of Mary, soul and body, at the end of her life on earth, a truth of faith that was proclaimed a dogma by Pius XII on Nov. 1, 1950. One of the oldest and most solemn feasts of Mary, it has a history dating back to at least the seventh century when its celebration was already established at Jerusalem and Rome.

Baptism of the Lord, movable, usually celebrated on the Sunday after January 6, feast. Recalls the baptism of Christ by John the Baptist (Mk. 1:9-11), an event associated with the liturgy of the Epiphany. This baptism was the occasion for Christ's manifestation of himself at the beginning of his public life.

Birth of Mary, Sept. 8, feast. This is a very old feast which originated in the East and found place in the Roman liturgy in the seventh century.

Candlemas Day, Feb. 2. See **Presentation of the Lord**.

Chair of Peter, Feb. 22, feast. The feast, which has been in the Roman calendar since 336, is a liturgical expression of belief in the episcopacy and hierarchy of the Church.

Christmas, Birth of Our Lord Jesus Christ, Dec. 25, holy day of obligation, solemnity. Commemorates the birth of Christ (Lk. 2:1-20). This event was originally commemorated in the East on the feast of Epiphany or Theophany. The Christmas feast itself originated in the West; by 354 it was certainly kept on Dec. 25. This date may have been set for the observance to offset pagan ceremonies held at about the same time to commemorate the birth of the sun at the winter solstice. There are texts for three Christmas Masses at midnight, dawn, and during the day.

Christ the King, movable, celebrated on the last Sunday of the liturgical year, solemnity. Commemorates the royal prerogatives of Christ and is equivalent to a declaration of his rights to the homage, service and fidelity of all people in all phases of individual and social life. Pius XI instituted the feast Dec. 11, 1925.

Conversion of St. Paul, Jan. 25, feast. An observance mentioned in some calendars from the 8th and 9th centuries. Pope Innocent III (1198-1216) ordered its observance with great solemnity.

Corpus Christi (The Body and Blood of Christ), movable, celebrated on the Thursday (or Sunday, as in the U.S.) following Trinity Sunday, solemnity. Commemorates the institution of the Holy Eucharist (Mt. 26:26-28). The feast originated at Liège in 1246 and was extended throughout the Church in the West by Urban IV in 1264. St. Thomas Aquinas composed the Liturgy of the Hours for the feast.

Cross, The Holy, Sept. 14, feast. Commemorates the finding of the Cross on which Christ was crucified, in 326 through the efforts of St. Helena, mother of Constantine; the consecration of the Basilica of the Holy Sepulchre nearly 10 years later: and the recovery in 628 or 629 by Emperor Heraclius of a major portion of the cross which had been removed by the Persians from its place of veneration at Jerusalem. The feast originated in Jerusalem and spread through the East before being adopted in the West. General adoption followed the building at Rome of the Basilica of the Holy Cross "in Jerusalem," so called because it was the place of enshrinement of a major portion of the cross of crucifixion.

Dedication of St. John Lateran, Nov. 9, feast. Commemorates the first public consecration of a church, that of the Basilica of the Most Holy Savior by Pope St. Sylvester about 324. The church, as well as the Lateran Palace, was the gift of Emperor Constantine. Since the 12th century it has been known as St. John Lateran, in honor of John the Baptist after whom the adjoining baptistery was named. It was rebuilt by Innocent X (1644-55), reconsecrated by Benedict XIII in 1726, and enlarged by Leo XIII (1878-1903). This basilica is regarded as the church of highest dignity in Rome and throughout the Roman rite.

Dedication of St. Mary Major, Aug. 5, optional memorial. Commemorates the rebuilding and dedication by Pope Sixtus III (432-40) of a church in honor of Blessed Mary the Virgin. This is the Basilica of St. Mary Major on the Esquiline Hill in Rome. An earlier building was erected during the pontificate of Liberius (352-66); according to legend, it was located on a site covered by a miraculous fall of snow seen by a nobleman favored with a vision of Mary.

Easter, movable celebration held on the first Sunday after the full moon following the vernal equinox (between Mar. 22 and Apr. 25), solemnity with an octave. Commemorates the Resurrection of Christ from the dead (Mk. 16:1-7). The observance of this mystery, kept since the first days of the Church, extends throughout the Easter season which lasts until the feast of Pentecost, a period of 50 days. Every Sunday in the year is regarded as a "little" Easter. The date of Easter determines the dates of movable feasts, such as Ascension and Pentecost, and the number of weeks before Lent and after Pentecost.

Easter Vigil, called by St. Augustine the "Mother of All Vigils," the night before Easter. Ceremonies are all related to the Resurrection and renewal-in-grace theme of Easter: blessing of the new fire, procession with the Easter Candle, singing of the Easter Proclamation (*Exsultet*), Liturgy of the Word with at least three Old Testament readings, the Litany of Saints, blessing of water, baptism of converts and infants, renewal of baptismal promises, Liturgy of the Eucharist. The vigil ceremonies are held after nightfall on Saturday.

Epiphany of the Lord, Jan. 6 or (in the U.S.) a Sunday between Jan. 2 and 8, solemnity. Commemorates the manifestations of the divinity of Christ. It is one of the oldest Christian feasts, with an Eastern origin traceable to the beginning of the third century and antedating the Western feast of Christmas. Originally, it commemorated the manifestations of Christ's divinity — or Theophany — in his birth, the homage of the Magi, and baptism by John the Baptist. Later, the first two of these commemorations were transferred to Christmas when the Eastern Church adopted that feast between 380 and 430. The central feature of the Eastern observance is the manifestation or declaration of Christ's divinity in his baptism and at the beginning of his public life. The Epiphany was adopted by the Western Church during the same period in which the Eastern Church accepted Christmas. In the Roman rite, commemoration is made in the Mass of the homage of the wise men from the East (Mt. 2:1-12).

Good Friday, the Friday before Easter, the second day of the Easter Triduum. Liturgical elements of the observance are commemoration of the Passion and Death of Christ in the reading of the Passion (according to John), special prayers for the Church and people of all ranks, the veneration of the Cross, and a Communion service. The celebration takes place in the afternoon, preferably at 3:00 p.m.

Guardian Angels, Oct. 2, memorial. Commemorates the angels who protect people from spiritual and physical dangers and assist them in doing good. A feast in their honor celebrated in Spain in the 16th century was placed in the Roman calendar in 1615 and Oct. 2 was set as the date of observance. Earlier, guardian angels were honored liturgically in conjunction with the feast of St. Michael.

Holy Family, movable observance on the Sunday after Christmas, feast. Commemorates the Holy Family of Jesus, Mary and Joseph as the model of domestic society, holiness and virtue. The devotional background of the feast was very strong in the 17th century. In the 18th century, in prayers composed for a special Mass, a Canadian bishop likened the Christian family to the Holy Family. Leo XIII consecrated families to the Holy Family. In 1921, Benedict XV extended the Divine Office and Mass of the feast to the whole Church.

Holy Innocents, Dec. 28, feast. Commemorates the infants who suffered death at the hands of Herod's soldiers seeking to kill the child Jesus (Mt. 2:13-18). A feast in their honor has been observed since the fifth century.

Holy Saturday, the day before Easter. The Sacrifice of the Mass is not celebrated, and Holy Communion may be given only as Viaticum. If possible the Easter fast should be observed until the Easter Vigil.

Holy Thursday, the Thursday before Easter. Commemorates the institution of the sacraments of the Eucharist and holy orders, and the washing of the feet of the Apostles by Jesus at the Last Supper. The Mass of the Lord's Supper in the evening marks the beginning of the Easter Triduum. Following the Mass, there is a procession of the Blessed Sacrament to a place of reposition for adoration by the faithful. Usually at an earlier Mass of Chrism, bishops bless oils (of catechumens, chrism, the sick) for use during the year. (For pastoral reasons, diocesan bishops may permit additional Masses, but these should not overshadow the principal Mass of the Lord's Supper.)

Immaculate Conception, Dec. 8, holy day of obligation, solemnity. Commemorates the fact that Mary, in view of her calling to be the Mother of Christ and in virtue of his merits, was preserved from the first moment of her conception from original sin and was filled with grace from the very beginning of her life. She was the only person so preserved from original sin. The present form of the feast dates from Dec. 8, 1854, when Pius IX defined the dogma of the Immaculate Conception An earlier feast of the Conception, which testified to long-existing belief in this truth, was observed in the East by the eighth century, in Ireland in the ninth, and subsequently in European countries. In 1846, Mary was proclaimed patroness of the U.S. under this title.

Immaculate Heart of Mary, Saturday following the second Sunday after Pentecost, memorial. On May 4, 1944, Pius XII ordered this feast observed throughout the Church in order to obtain Mary's intercession for "peace among nations, freedom for the Church, the conversion of sinners, the love of purity and the practice of virtue." Two years earlier, he consecrated the entire human race to Mary under this title. Devotion to Mary under the title of her Most Pure Heart originated during the Middle Ages. It was given great impetus in the 17th century by the preaching of St. John Eudes, who was the first to celebrate a Mass and Divine Office of Mary under this title. A feast, celebrated in various places and on different dates, was authorized in 1799.

Joachim and Ann, July 26, memorial. Commemorates the parents of Mary. A joint feast, celebrated Sept. 9, originated in the East near the end of the sixth century. Devotion to Ann, introduced in the eighth century at Rome, became widespread in Europe in the 14th century; her feast was extended throughout the Latin Church in 1584. A feast of Joachim was introduced in the West in the 15th century.

John the Baptist, Birth of, June 24, solemnity. The precursor of Christ, whose cousin he was, was commemorated universally in the liturgy by the fourth century. He is the only saint, except the Blessed Virgin Mary, whose birthday is observed as a feast. Another feast, on Aug. 29, commemorates his passion and death at the order of Herod (Mk. 6:14-29).

Joseph, Mar. 19, solemnity. Joseph is honored as the husband of the Blessed Virgin Mary, the patron and protector of the universal Church and workman. Devotion to him already existed in the eighth century in the East, and in the 11th in the West. Various feasts were celebrated before the 15th century when Mar. 19 was fixed for his commemoration; this feast was extended to the whole Church in 1621 by Gregory XV. In 1955, Pius XII instituted the feast of St. Joseph the Workman for observance May 1; this feast, which may be celebrated by local option, supplanted the Solemnity or Patronage of St. Joseph formerly observed on the third Wednesday after Easter. St. Joseph was proclaimed protector and patron of the universal Church in 1870 by Pius IX.

Michael, Gabriel and Raphael, Archangels, Sept. 29, feast. A feast bearing the title of Dedication of St. Michael the Archangel formerly commemorated on this date the consecration in 530 of a church near Rome in honor of Michael, the first angel given a liturgical feast. For a while, this feast was combined with a commemoration of the Guardian Angels. The separate feasts of Gabriel (Mar. 24) and Raphael (Oct. 24) were suppressed by the calendar in effect since 1970 and this joint feast of the three archangels was instituted.

Octave of Christmas, Jan. 1. See **Solemnity of Mary, Mother of God.**

Our Lady of Guadalupe, Dec. 12, feast (in the U.S.). Commemorates under this title the appearances of the Blessed Virgin Mary in 1531 to an Indian, Juan Diego, on Tepeyac hill outside Mexico City (see Apparitions of the Blessed Virgin Mary). The celebration, observed as a memorial in the U.S., was raised to the rank of feast at the request of the National Conference of Catholic Bishops. Approval was granted in a decree dated Jan. 8, 1988.

Our Lady of Sorrows, Sept. 15, memorial. Recalls the sorrows experienced by Mary in her association with Christ: the prophecy of Simeon (Lk. 2:34-35), the flight into Egypt (Mt. 2:13-21), the three-day separation from Jesus (Lk. 2:41-50), and four incidents connected with the Passion — her meeting with Christ on the way to Calvary, the crucifixion, the removal of Christ's body from the cross, and his burial (Mt. 27:31-

61; Mk. 15:20-47; Lk. 23:26-56; Jn. 19:17-42). A Mass and Divine Office of the feast were celebrated by the Servites, especially, in the 17th century, and in 1814 Pius VII extended the observance to the whole Church.

Our Lady of the Rosary, Oct. 7, memorial. Commemorates the Virgin Mary through recall of the mysteries of the Rosary which recapitulate events in her life and the life of Christ. The feast was instituted in 1573 to commemorate a Christian victory over invading the forces of the Ottoman Empire at Lepanto in 1571, and was extended throughout the Church by Clement XI in 1716.

Passion Sunday (formerly called Palm Sunday), the Sunday before Easter. Marks the start of Holy Week by recalling the triumphal entry of Christ into Jerusalem at the beginning of the last week of his life (Mt. 21:1-9). A procession and other ceremonies commemorating this event were held in Jerusalem from very early Christian times and were adopted in Rome by the ninth century, when the blessing of palm for the occasion was introduced. Full liturgical observance includes the blessing of palm and a procession before the principal Mass of the day. The Passion, by Matthew, Mark or Luke, is read during the Mass.

Pentecost, also called **Whitsunday**, movable celebration held 50 days after Easter, solemnity. Commemorates the descent of the Holy Spirit upon the Apostles, the preaching of Peter and the other Apostles to Jews in Jerusalem, the baptism and aggregation of some 3,000 persons to the Christian community (Acts 2:1-41). It is regarded as the birthday of the Catholic Church. The original observance of the feast antedated the earliest extant documentary evidence from the third century.

Peter and Paul, June 29, solemnity. Commemorates the martyrdoms of Peter by crucifixion and Paul by beheading during the Neronian persecution. This joint commemoration of the chief Apostles dates at least from 258 at Rome.

Presentation of the Lord (formerly called Purification of the Blessed Virgin Mary, also Candlemas), Feb. 2, feast. Commemorates the presentation of Jesus in the Temple — according to prescriptions of Mosaic Law (Lv. 12:2-8; Ex. 13:2; Lk. 2:22-32) — and the purification of Mary 40 days after his birth. In the East, where the feast antedated fourth century testimony regarding its existence, it was observed primarily as a feast of Our Lord; in the West, where it was adopted later, it was regarded more as a feast of Mary until the calendar in effect since 1970. Its date was set for Feb. 2 after the celebration of Christmas was fixed for Dec. 25, late in the fourth century. The blessing of candles, probably in commemoration of Christ who was the Light to enlighten the Gentiles, became common about the 11th century and gave the feast the secondary name of Candlemas.

Queenship of Mary, Aug. 22, memorial. Commemorates the high dignity of Mary as Queen of heaven, angels and men. Universal observance of the memorial was ordered by Pius XII in the encyclical *Ad Caeli Reginam*, Oct. 11, 1954, near the close of a Marian Year observed in connection with the centenary of the proclamation of the dogma of the Immaculate Conception and four years after the proclamation of the dogma of the Assumption. The original date of the memorial was May 31.

Resurrection. See **Easter**.

Sacred Heart of Jesus, movable observance held on the Friday after the second Sunday after Pentecost (Corpus Christi, in the U.S.), solemnity. The object of the devotion is the divine Person of Christ, whose heart is the symbol of his love for all people — for whom he accomplished the work of Redemption. The Mass and Office now used on the feast were prescribed by Pius XI in 1929. Devotion to the Sacred Heart was introduced into the liturgy in the 17th century through the efforts of St. John Eudes who composed an Office and Mass for the feast. It was furthered as the result of the revelations of St. Margaret Mary Alacoque after 1675 and by the work of St. Claude de la Colombière, S.J. In 1765, Clement XIII approved a Mass and Office for the feast, and in 1856 Pius IX extended the observance throughout the Roman rite.

Solemnity of Mary, Mother of God, Jan. 1, holy day of obligation, solemnity. The calendar in effect since 1970, in accord with Eastern tradition, reinstated the Marian character of this commemoration on the octave day of Christmas. The former feast of the Circumcision, dating at least from the first half of the sixth century, marked the initiation of Jesus (Lk. 2:21) in Judaism and by analogy focused attention on the initiation of persons in the Christian religion and their incorporation in Christ through baptism. The feast of the Solemnity supplants the former feast of the Maternity of Mary observed on Oct. 11.

Transfiguration of the Lord, Aug. 6, feast. Commemorates the revelation of his divinity by Christ to Peter, James and John on Mt. Tabor (Mt. 17:1-9). The feast, which is very old, was extended throughout the universal Church in 1457 by Callistus III.

Trinity, The Holy, movable observance held on the Sunday after Pentecost, solemnity. Commemorates the most sublime mystery of the Christian faith, i.e., that there are Three Divine Persons — Father, Son and Holy Spirit — in one God (Mt. 28:18-20). A votive Mass of the Most Holy Trinity dates from the seventh century; an Office was composed in the 10th century; in 1334, John XXII extended the feast to the universal Church.

Visitation, May 31, feast. Commemorates Mary's visit to her cousin Elizabeth after the Annunciation and before the birth of John the Baptist, the precursor of Christ (Lk. 1:39-47). The feast had a medieval origin and was observed in the Franciscan Order before being extended throughout the Church by Urban VI in 1389. It is one of the feasts of the Incarnation and is notable for its recall of the *Magnificat*, one of the few New Testament canticles, which acknowledges the unique gifts of God to Mary because of her role in the redemptive work of Christ. The canticle is recited at Evening Prayer in the Liturgy of the Hours.

Liturgical Life of the Church

The nature and purpose of the liturgy, along with norms for its revision, were the subject matter of *Sacrosanctum Concilium* (the Constitution on the Sacred Liturgy) promulgated by the Second Vatican Council. The principles and guidelines stated in this document, the first issued by the Council, are summarized here and/or are incorporated in other Almanac entries on liturgical subjects.

Nature and Purpose of Liturgy

The paragraphs under this and the following subhead are quoted directly from *Sacrosanctum Concilium* (Constitution on the Sacred Liturgy).

"It is through the liturgy, especially the divine Eucharistic Sacrifice, that 'the work of our redemption is exercised.' The liturgy is thus the outstanding means by which the faithful can express in their lives, and manifest to others, the mystery of Christ and the real nature of the true Church" (No. 2).

"The liturgy is considered as an exercise of the priestly office of Jesus Christ. In the liturgy the sanctification of man is manifested by signs perceptible to the senses, and is effected in a way which is proper to each of these signs; in the liturgy full public worship is performed by the Mystical Body of Jesus Christ, that is, by the Head and his members.

"From this it follows that every liturgical celebration, because it is an action of Christ the priest and of his Body the Church, is a sacred action surpassing all others. No other action of the Church can match its claim to efficacy, nor equal the degree of it" (No. 7).

"The liturgy is the summit toward which the activity of the Church is directed; at the same time it is the fountain from which all her power flows. For the goal of apostolic works is that all who are made sons of God by faith and baptism should come together to praise God in the midst of his Church, to take part in her sacrifice, and to eat the Lord's Supper.

"From the liturgy, therefore, and especially from the Eucharist, as from a fountain, grace is channeled into us; and the sanctification of men in Christ and the glorification of God, to which all other activities of the Church are directed as toward their goal, are most powerfully achieved" (No. 10).

Full Participation

"Mother Church earnestly desires that all the faithful be led to that full, conscious, and active participation in liturgical celebrations which is demanded by the very nature of the liturgy. Such participation by the Christian people as 'a chosen race, a royal priesthood, a holy nation, a purchased people' (1 Pt. 2:9; cf. 2:4-5), is their right and duty by reason of their baptism.

"In the restoration and promotion of the sacred liturgy, this full and active participation by all the people is the aim to be considered before all else; for it is the primary and indispensable source from which the faithful are to derive the true Christian spirit" (No. 14).

"In order that the Christian people may more securely derive an abundance of graces from the sacred liturgy, holy Mother Church desires to undertake with great care a general restoration of the liturgy itself. For the liturgy is made up of unchangeable elements divinely instituted, and elements subject to change. The latter not only may but ought to be changed with the passing of time if features have by chance crept in which are less harmonious with the intimate nature of the liturgy, or if existing elements have grown less functional.

"In this restoration, both texts and rites should be drawn up so that they express more clearly the holy things which they signify. Christian people, as far as possible, should be able to understand them with ease and to take part in them fully, actively, and as befits a community" (No. 21).

Norms

Norms regarding the reforms concern the greater use of Scripture; emphasis on the importance of the sermon or homily on biblical and liturgical subjects; use of vernacular languages for prayers of the Mass and for administration of the sacraments; provision for adaptation of rites to cultural patterns.

Approval for reforms of various kinds — in liturgical texts, rites, etc. — depends on the Holy See, regional conferences of bishops and individual bishops, according to provisions of law. No priest has authority to initiate reforms on his own. Reforms may not be introduced just for the sake of innovation, and any that are introduced in the light of present-day circumstances should embody sound tradition.

To assure the desired effect of liturgical reforms, training and instruction are necessary for the clergy, religious and the laity. The functions of diocesan and regional commissions for liturgy, music and art are to set standards and provide leadership for instruction and practical programs in their respective fields.

Most of the constitution's provisions regarding liturgical reforms have to do with the Roman rite. The document clearly respects the equal dignity of all rites, leaving to the Eastern Churches control over their ancient liturgies.

(For coverage of the Mystery of the Eucharist, see **The Mass**; **Other Sacraments**, see also separate entries.)

Sacramentals

Sacramentals, instituted by the Church, "are sacred signs which bear a resemblance to the sacraments: they signify effects, particularly of a spiritual kind, which are obtained through the Church's intercession. By them men are disposed to receive the chief effect of the sacraments, and various occasions in life are rendered holy" (No. 60).

"Thus, for well-disposed members of the faithful, the liturgy of the sacraments and sacramentals sanctifies almost every event in their lives; they are given access to the stream of divine grace which flows from the paschal mystery of the passion, death, and resurrection of Christ, the fountain from which all sacraments and sacramentals draw their power. There is hardly any proper use of material things which cannot thus be directed toward the sanctification of men and the praise of God" (No. 61).

Some common sacramentals are priestly blessings, blessed palm, candles, holy water, medals, scapulars, prayers and ceremonies of the Roman Ritual.

Liturgy of the Hours

The Liturgy of the Hours (Divine Office) is the public prayer of the Church for praising God and sanctifying the day. Its daily celebration is required as a sacred obligation by men in holy orders and by men and women religious who have professed solemn vows. Its celebration by others is highly commended and is to be encouraged in the community of the faithful.

"By tradition going back to early Christian times, the Divine Office is arranged so that the whole course of the day and night is made holy by the praises of God. Therefore, when this wonderful song of praise is worthily rendered by priests and others who are deputed for this purpose by Church ordinance, or by the faithful praying together with the priest in an approved form, then it is truly the voice of the bride addressing her bridegroom; it is the very prayer which Christ himself, together with his Body, addresses to the Father" (No. 84).

"Hence all who perform this service are not only fulfilling a duty of the Church, but also are sharing in the greatest honor accorded to Christ's spouse, for by offering these praises to God they are standing before God's throne in the name of the Church their Mother" (No. 85).

Revised Hours

The Liturgy of the Hours, revised since 1965, was the subject of Pope Paul VI's apostolic constitution *Laudis Canticum*, dated Nov. 1, 1970. The master Latin text was published in 1971; its four volumes have been published in authorized English translation since May 1975.

One-volume, partial editions of the Liturgy of the Hours containing Morning and Evening Prayer and other elements, have been published in approved English translation.

The revised Liturgy of the Hours consists of:

• Office of Readings, for reflection on the word of God. The principal parts are three psalms, biblical and non-biblical readings.

• Morning and Evening Prayer, called the "hinges" of the Liturgy of the Hours. The principal parts are a hymn, two psalms, an Old or New Testament canticle, a brief biblical reading, Zechariah's canticle (the *Benedictus*, morning) or Mary's canticle (the *Magnificat*, evening), responsories, intercessions and a concluding prayer.

• Daytime Prayer. The principal parts are a hymn, three psalms, a biblical reading and one of three concluding prayers corresponding to the time of day.

• Night Prayer. The principal parts are one or two psalms, a brief biblical reading, Simeon's canticle (*Nunc Dimittis*), a concluding prayer and an antiphon in honor of Mary.

In the revised Liturgy of the Hours, the hours are shorter than they had been, with greater textual variety, meditation aids, and provision for intervals of silence and meditation. The psalms are distributed over a four-week period instead of a week; some psalms, entirely or in part, are not included. Additional canticles from the Old and New Testaments are assigned for Morning and Evening Prayer. Additional scriptural texts have been added and variously arranged for greater internal unity, correspondence to readings at Mass, and relevance to events and themes of salvation history. Readings include some of the best material from the Fathers of the Church and other authors, and improved selections on the lives of the saints.

The book used for recitation of the *Office is the Breviary*.

For coverage of the Liturgical Year, see **Church Calendar**.

Sacred Music

"The musical tradition of the universal Church is a treasure of immeasurable value, greater even than that of any other art. The main reason for this pre-eminence is that, as sacred melody united to words, it forms a necessary or integral part of the solemn liturgy.

"Sacred music increases in holiness to the degree that it is intimately linked with liturgical action, winningly expresses prayerfulness, promotes solidarity, and enriches sacred rites with heightened solemnity. The Church indeed approves of all forms of true art, and admits them into divine worship when they show appropriate qualities" (No. 112).

The constitution decreed:

• Vernacular languages for the people's parts of the liturgy, as well as Latin, may be used.

• Participation in sacred song by the whole body of the faithful, and not just by choirs, is to be encouraged and brought about.

• Provisions should be made for proper musical training for clergy, religious and lay persons.

• While Gregorian Chant has a unique dignity and relationship to the Latin liturgy, other kinds of music are acceptable.

• Native musical traditions should be used, especially in mission areas.

• Various instruments compatible with the dignity of worship may be used.

Gregorian Chant: A form and style of chant called Gregorian was the basis and most highly regarded standard of liturgical music for centuries. It originated probably during the formative period of the Roman liturgy and developed in conjunction with Gallican and other forms of chant. Pope St. Gregory I the Great's connection with it is not clear, although it is known that he had great concern for and interest in church music. The earliest extant written versions of Gregorian Chant date from the ninth century. A thousand years later, the Benedictines of Solesmes, France, initiated a revival of chant which gave impetus to the modern liturgical movement.

Sacred Art and Furnishings

"Very rightly the fine arts are considered to rank among the noblest expressions of human genius. This judgment applies especially to religious art and to its highest achievement, which is sacred art. By their very nature both of the latter are related to God's boundless beauty, for this is the reality which these human efforts are trying to express in some way. To the extent that these works aim exclusively at turning men's thoughts to God persuasively and devoutly, they are dedicated to God and to the cause of his greater honor and glory" (No. 122).

The objective of sacred art is "that all things set apart for use in divine worship should be truly worthy, becoming, and beautiful, signs and symbols of heavenly realities. The Church has always reserved to herself the right to pass judgment upon the arts, deciding which of the works of artists are in accordance with faith, piety, and cherished traditional laws, and thereby suited to sacred purposes.

"Sacred furnishings should worthily and beautifully serve the dignity of worship" (No. 122).

According to the constitution:

• Contemporary art, as well as that of the past, shall "be given free scope in the Church, provided that it adorns the sacred buildings and holy rites with due honor and reverence" (No. 123).

• Noble beauty, not sumptuous display, should be sought in art, sacred vestments and ornaments.

• "Let bishops carefully exclude from the house of God and from other sacred places those works of artists which are repugnant to faith, morals, and Christian piety, and which offend true religious sense either by their distortion of forms or by lack of artistic worth, by mediocrity or by pretense.

• "When churches are to be built, let great care be taken that they be suitable for the celebration of liturgical services and for the active participation of the faithful" (No. 124).

• "The practice of placing sacred images in churches so that they may be venerated by the faithful is to be firmly maintained. Nevertheless, their number should be moderate and their relative location should reflect right order. Otherwise they may create confusion among the Christian people and promote a faulty sense of devotion" (No. 125).

• Artists should be trained and inspired in the spirit and for the purposes of the liturgy.

• The norms of sacred art should be revised. "These laws refer especially to the worthy and well-planned construction of sacred buildings, the shape and construction of altars, the nobility, location, and security of the Eucharistic tabernacle, the suitability and dignity of the baptistery, the proper use of sacred images, embellishments, and vestments" (No. 128).

RITES

Rites are the forms and ceremonial observances of

liturgical worship coupled with the total expression of the theological, spiritual and disciplinary heritages of particular churches of the East and the West.

Different rites have evolved in the course of church history, giving to liturgical worship and church life in general forms and usages peculiar and proper to the nature of worship and the culture of the faithful in various circumstances of time and place. Thus, there has been development since apostolic times in the prayers and ceremonies of the Mass, in the celebration of the sacraments, sacramentals and the Liturgy of the Hours, and in observances of the liturgical calendar. The principal sources of rites in present use were practices within the patriarchates of Rome (for the West) and Antioch, Alexandria and Constantinople (for the East). Rites are identified as Eastern or Western on the basis of their geographical area of origin in the Roman Empire.

Eastern and Roman Rites

Eastern rites are proper to Eastern Catholic Churches (see separate entry). The principal rites are Byzantine, Alexandrian, Antiochene, Armenian and Chaldean.

The Latin or Roman rite prevails in the Western Church. It was derived from Roman practices and the use of Latin from the third century onward, and has been the rite in general use in the West since the eighth century. Other rites in limited use in the Western Church have been the Ambrosian (in the Archdiocese of Milan), the Mozarabic (in the Archdiocese of Toledo), the Lyonnais, the Braga, and rites peculiar to some religious orders like the Dominicans, Carmelites and Carthusians.

The purpose of the revision of rites in progress since the Second Vatican Council is to renew them, not to eliminate the rites of particular churches or to reduce all rites to uniformity. The Council reaffirmed the equal dignity and preservation of rites as follows.

"It is the mind of the Catholic Church that each individual church or rite retain its traditions whole and entire, while adjusting its way of life to various needs of time and place. Such individual churches, whether of the East or of the West, although they differ somewhat among themselves in what are called rites (that is, in liturgy, ecclesiastical discipline and spiritual heritage), are, nevertheless, equally entrusted to the pastoral guidance of the Roman Pontiff, the divinely appointed successor of St. Peter in supreme government over the universal Church. They are, consequently, of equal dignity, so that none of them is superior to the others by reason of rite."

Determination of Rite

Determination of a person's rite is regulated by church law. Through baptism, a child becomes a member of the rite of his or her parents. If the parents are of different rites, the child's rite is decided by mutual consent of the parents; if there is lack of mutual consent, the child is baptized in the rite of the father. A candidate for baptism over the age of 14 can choose to be baptized in any approved rite. Catholics baptized in one rite may receive the sacraments in any of the approved ritual churches; they may transfer to another rite only with the permission of the Holy See and in accordance with other provisions of the Code of Canon Law.

MASS, EUCHARISTIC SACRIFICE AND BANQUET

Declarations of Vatican II

The Second Vatican Council made the following declarations among others with respect to the Mass:

"At the Last Supper, on the night when he was betrayed, our Savior instituted the Eucharistic Sacrifice of his Body and Blood. He did this in order to perpetuate the Sacrifice of the Cross throughout the centuries until he should come again, and so to entrust to his beloved spouse, the Church, a memorial of his death and resurrection: a sacrament of love, a sign of unity, a bond of charity, a paschal banquet in which Christ is consumed, the mind is filled with grace, and a pledge of future glory is given to us" (*Sacrosanctum Concilium*, Constitution on the Sacred Liturgy, No. 47).

"... As often as the Sacrifice of the Cross in which 'Christ, our Passover, has been sacrificed' (1 Cor. 5:7) is celebrated on an altar, the work of our redemption is carried on. At the same time, in the sacrament of the Eucharistic bread the unity of all believers who form one body in Christ (cf. 1 Cor. 10:17) is both expressed and brought about. All men are called to this union with Christ" (*Lumen Gentium*, Dogmatic Constitution on the Church, No. 3).

"... The ministerial priest, by the sacred power he enjoys, molds and rules the priestly people. Acting in the person of Christ, he brings about the Eucharistic Sacrifice, and offers it to God in the name of all the people. For their part, the faithful join in the offering of the Eucharist by virtue of their royal priesthood" (Ibid., No. 10).

Declarations of Trent

Among its decrees on the Holy Eucharist, the Council of Trent stated the following points of doctrine on the Mass.

1. There is in the Catholic Church a true sacrifice, the Mass instituted by Jesus Christ. It is the sacrifice of his Body and Blood, Soul and Divinity, himself, under the appearances of bread and wine.

2. This Sacrifice is identical with the Sacrifice of the Cross, inasmuch as Christ is the Priest and Victim in both. A difference lies in the manner of offering, which was bloody upon the Cross and is bloodless on the altar.

3. The Mass is a propitiatory Sacrifice, atoning for the sins of the living and dead for whom it is offered.

4. The efficacy of the Mass is derived from the Sacrifice of the Cross, whose superabundant merits it applies to men.

5. Although the Mass is offered to God alone, it may be celebrated in honor and memory of the saints.

6. Christ instituted the Mass at the Last Supper.

7. Christ ordained the Apostles priests, giving them power and the command to consecrate his Body and Blood to perpetuate and renew the Sacrifice.

ORDER OF THE MASS

The Mass consists of two principal divisions called the **Liturgy of the Word**, which features the proclamation of the Word of God, and the **Eucharistic Liturgy**, which focuses on the central act of sacrifice in the Consecration and on the Eucharistic Banquet in Holy Communion. (Formerly, these divisions were called, respectively, the **Mass of the Catechumens** and the **Mass of the Faithful**.) In addition to these principal divisions, there are ancillary introductory and concluding rites.

The following description covers the Mass as celebrated with participation by the people. This Order of the Mass was approved by Pope Paul VI in the apostolic constitution *Missale Romanum* dated Apr. 3, 1969, and promulgated in a decree issued Apr. 6, 1969, by the Congregation for Divine Worship. The assigned effective date was Nov. 30, 1969.

Introductory Rites

Entrance: The introductory rites begin with the singing or recitation of an entrance song consisting of one or more scriptural verses stating the theme of the mystery, season or feast commemorated in the Mass.

Greeting: The priest and people make the Sign of the Cross together. The priest then greets them in one of several alternative ways and they reply in a corresponding manner.

Introductory Remarks: At this point, the priest or another of the ministers may introduce the theme of the Mass.

Penitential Rite: The priest and people together acknowledge their sins as a preliminary step toward worthy celebration of the sacred mysteries.

This rite includes a brief examination of conscience, a general confession of sin and plea for divine mercy in one of several ways, and a prayer for forgiveness by the priest.

Glory to God: A doxology, a hymn of praise to God, sung or said on festive occasions.

Opening Prayer: A prayer of petition offered by the priest on behalf of the worshiping community.

I. Liturgy of the Word

Readings: The featured elements of this liturgy are readings of passages from the Bible. If three readings are in order, the first is usually from the Old Testament, the second from the New Testament (Letters, Acts, Revelation), and the third from one of the Gospels; the final reading is always a selection from a Gospel. The first reading(s) is (are) concluded with the formula, "The Word of the Lord" (effective Feb. 28, 1993; optional before that date), to which the people respond, "Thanks be to God." The Gospel reading is concluded with the formula, "The Gospel of the Lord," (effective as above), to which the people respond, "Praise to you, Lord Jesus Christ." Between the readings, psalm verses are sung or recited. A Gospel acclamation is either sung or omitted.

Homily: An explanation, pertinent to the mystery being celebrated and the special needs of the listeners, of some point in either the readings from sacred Scripture or in another text from the Ordinary or Proper parts of the Mass; it is a proclamation of the Good News for a response of faith.

Creed: The Nicene profession of faith, by priest and people, on certain occasions.

Prayer of the Faithful: Litany-type prayers of petition, with participation by the people. Called general intercessions, they concern needs of the Church, the salvation of the world, public authorities, persons in need, the local community.

II. Eucharistic Liturgy

Presentation and Preparation of Gifts: Presentation to the priest of the gifts of bread and wine, principally, by participating members of the congregation. Preparation of the gifts consists of the prayers and ceremonies with which the priest offers bread and wine as the elements of the sacrifice to take place during the Eucharistic Prayer and of the Lord's Supper to be shared in Holy Communion.

Washing of Hands: After offering the bread and wine, the priest cleanses his fingers with water in a brief ceremony of purification.

Pray, Brothers and Sisters: Prayer that the sacrifice to take place will be acceptable to God. The first part of the prayer is said by the priest; the second, by the people.

Prayer over the Gifts: A prayer of petition offered by the priest on behalf of the worshipping community.

Eucharistic Prayer

Preface: A hymn of praise, introducing the Eucharistic Prayer or Canon, sung or said by the priest following responses by the people. The Order of the Mass contains a variety of prefaces, for use on different occasions.

Holy, Holy, Holy; Blessed is He: Divine praises sung or said by the priest and people.

Eucharistic Prayer (Canon): Its central portion is the Consecration, when the essential act of sacrificial offering takes place with the changing of bread and wine into the Body and Blood of Christ. The various parts of the prayer, which are said by the celebrant only, commemorate principal mysteries of salvation history and include petitions for the Church, the living and dead, and remembrances of saints.

Doxology: A formula of divine praise sung or said by the priest while he holds aloft the chalice containing the consecrated wine in one hand and the paten containing the consecrated host in the other.

Communion Rite

Lord's Prayer: Sung or said by the priest and people.

Prayer for Deliverance from Evil: Called an embolism because it is a development of the final petition of the Lord's Prayer; said by the priest. It concludes with a memorial of the return of the Lord to which the people respond, "For the kingdom, the power, and the glory are yours, now and forever."

Prayer for Peace: Said by the priest, with corresponding responses by the people. The priest can, in accord with local custom, bid the people to exchange a greeting of peace with each other.

Lamb of God (*Agnus Dei*): A prayer for divine mercy sung or said while the priest breaks the consecrated host and places a piece of it into the consecrated wine in the chalice.

Communion: The priest, after saying a preparatory prayer, administers Holy Communion to himself and then to the people, thus completing the sacrifice-banquet of the Mass. (This completion is realized even if the celebrant alone receives the Eucharist.) On giving the Eucharist to each person under both species separately, the priest or eucharistic minister says, "The Body of Christ," "The Blood of Christ." The customary response is "Amen." If the Eucharist is given by intinction (in which the host is dipped into the consecrated wine), the priest says, "The Body and Blood of Christ."

Communion Song: Scriptural verses or a suitable hymn sung or said during the distribution of Holy Communion. After Holy Communion is received, some moments may be spent in silent meditation or in the chanting of a psalm or hymn of praise.

Prayer after Communion: A prayer of petition offered by the priest on behalf of the worshipping community.

Concluding Rite

Announcements: Brief announcements to the people are in order at this time.

Dismissal: Consists of a final greeting by the priest, a blessing, and a formula of dismissal. This rite is omitted if another liturgical action immediately follows the Mass; e.g., a procession, the blessing of the body during a funeral rite.

Some parts of the Mass are changeable with the liturgical season or feast, and are called the proper of the Mass. Other parts are said to be common because they always remain the same.

Additional Mass Notes

Catholics are seriously obliged to attend Mass in a worthy manner on Sundays and holy days of obligation. Failure to do so without a proportionately serious reason is gravely wrong.

It is the custom for priests to celebrate Mass daily whenever possible. To satisfy the needs of the faithful on Sundays and holy days of obligation, they are authorized to say Mass twice (**bination**) or even three times (**trination**). Bination is also permissible on weekdays to satisfy the needs of the faithful. On Christmas every priest may say three Masses.

The **fruits of the Mass**, which in itself is of infinite value, are: **general**, for all the faithful; **special (ministerial)**, for the intentions or persons specifically intended by the celebrant; **most special (personal)**, for the celebrant himself. On Sundays and certain other days pastors are obliged to offer Mass for their parishioners, or to have another priest do so. If a priest accepts a stipend or offering for a Mass, he is obliged in justice to apply the Mass for the intention of the donor. Mass may be applied for the living and the dead, or for any good intention.

Mass can be celebrated in several ways: e.g., with people present, without their presence (privately), with two or more priests as co-celebrants (concelebration), with greater or less solemnity.

Some of the various types of Masses are: **for the dead** (Funeral Mass or Mass of Christian Burial, Mass for the Dead — formerly called Requiem Mass); **ritual**, in connection with celebration of the sacraments, religious profession, etc.; **nuptial**, for married couples, with or after the wedding ceremony; **votive**, to honor a Person of the Trinity, a saint, or for some special intention.

Places, Altars for Mass

The ordinary place for celebrating the Eucharist is a church or other sacred place, at a fixed or movable altar.

The altar is a table at which the Eucharistic Sacrifice is celebrated.

A fixed altar is attached to the floor of the church. It should be of stone, preferably, and should be consecrated. The Code of Canon Law orders observance of the custom of placing under a fixed altar relics of martyrs or other saints.

A movable altar can be made of any solid and suitable material, and should be blessed or consecrated.

Outside of a sacred place, Mass may be celebrated in an appropriate place at a suitable table covered with a linen cloth and corporal. An altar stone containing the relics of saints, which was formerly prescribed, is not required by regulations in effect since the promulgation Apr. 6, 1969, of *Institutio Generalis Missalis Romani.*

LITURGICAL VESTMENTS

In the early years of the Church, vestments worn by the ministers at liturgical functions were the same as the garments in ordinary popular use. They became distinctive when their form was not altered to correspond with later variations in popular style. Liturgical vestments are symbolic of the sacred ministry and add appropriate decorum to divine worship.

Mass Vestments

Alb: A body-length tunic of white fabric; a vestment common to all ministers of divine worship.

Amice: A rectangular piece of white cloth worn about the neck, tucked into the collar and falling over the shoulders; prescribed for use when the alb does not completely cover the ordinary clothing at the neck.

Chasuble: Originally, a large mantle or cloak covering the body, it is the outer vestment of a priest celebrating Mass or carrying out other sacred actions connected with the Mass.

Chasuble-Alb: A vestment combining the features of the chasuble and alb; for use with a stole by concelebrants and, by way of exception, by celebrants in certain circumstances.

Cincture: A cord which serves the purpose of a belt, holding the alb close to the body.

Dalmatic: The outer vestment worn by a deacon in place of a chasuble.

Stole: A long, band-like vestment worn by a priest about the neck and falling to about the knees. A deacon wears a stole over the left shoulder, crossed and fastened at his right side.

The material, form and ornamentation of the aforementioned and other vestments are subject to variation and adaptation, according to norms and decisions of the Holy See and concerned conferences of bishops. The overriding norm is that they should be appropriate for use in divine worship. The customary ornamented vestments are the chasuble, dalmatic and stole.

The minimal vestments required for a priest celebrating Mass are the alb, stole, and chasuble.

Liturgical Colors

The colors of outer vestments vary with liturgical seasons, feasts and other circumstances. The colors and their use are:

Green: For the season of Ordinary Time; symbolic of hope and the vitality of the life of faith.

Violet (Purple): For Advent and Lent; may also be used in Masses for the dead; symbolic of penance. (See below, Violet for Advent.)

Red: For the Sunday of the Passion, Good Friday, Pentecost; feasts of the Passion of Our Lord, the Apostles and Evangelists, martyrs; symbolic of the supreme sacrifice of life for the love of God.

Rose: May be used in place of purple on the Third Sunday of Advent (formerly called Gaudete Sunday) and the Fourth Sunday of Lent (formerly called Laetare Sunday); symbolic of anticipatory joy during a time of penance.

White: For the seasons of Christmas and Easter; feasts and commemorations of Our Lord, except those of the Passion; feasts and commemorations of the Blessed Virgin Mary, angels, saints who are not martyrs, All Saints (Nov. 1), St. John the Baptist (June 24), St. John the Evangelist (Dec. 27), the Chair of St. Peter (Feb. 22), the Conversion of St. Paul (Jan. 25). White, symbolic of purity and integrity of the life of faith, may generally be substituted for other colors, and can be used for funeral and other Masses for the dead.

Options are provided regarding the color of vestments used in offices and Masses for the dead. The newsletter of the U.S. Bishops' Committee on the Liturgy, in line with No. 308 of the General Instruction of the Roman Missal, announced in July 1970: "In the dioceses of the United States, white vestments may be used, in addition to violet (purple) and black, in offices and Masses for the dead."

On more solemn occasions, better than ordinary vestments may be used, even though their color (e.g., gold) does not match the requirements of the day.

Violet for Advent: Violet is the official liturgical color for the season of Advent, according to the September 1988, edition of the newsletter of the U.S. Bishops' Committee on the Liturgy. Blue was being proposed in order to distinguish between the Advent season and the specifically penitential season of Lent. The newsletter said, however, that "the same effect can be achieved by following the official color sequence of the Church, which requires the use of violet for Advent and Lent, while taking advantage of the varying shades which exist for violet. Light blue vestments are not authorized for use in the United States."

Considerable freedom is permitted in the choice of colors of vestments worn for votive Masses.

Other Vestments

Cappa Magna: Flowing vestment with a train, worn by bishops and cardinals.

Cassock: A non-liturgical, full-length, close-fitting robe for use by priests and other clerics under liturgical vestments and in ordinary use; usually black for priests, purple for bishops and other prelates, red for cardinals, white for the pope. In place of a cassock, priests belonging to religious institutes wear the habit proper to their institute.

Cope: A mantle-like vestment open in front and fastened across the chest; worn by sacred ministers in processions and other ceremonies, as prescribed by appropriate directives.

Habit: The ordinary (non-liturgical) garb of members of religious institutes, analogous to the cassock of diocesan priests; the form of habits varies from institute to institute.

Humeral Veil: A rectangular vestment worn about the shoulders by a deacon or priest in Eucharistic processions and for other prescribed liturgical ceremonies.

Mitre: A headdress worn at some liturgical functions by bishops, abbots and, in certain cases, other ecclesiastics.

Pallium: A circular band of white wool about two inches wide, with front and back pendants, marked with six crosses, worn about the neck. It is a symbol of the fullness of the episcopal office. Pope Paul VI, in a document issued July 20, 1978, on his own initiative and entitled *Inter Eximia Episcopalis*, restricted its use to the pope and archbishops of metropolitan sees. In 1984, Pope John Paul II decreed that the pallium would ordinarily be conferred by the pope on the solemnity of Sts. Peter and Paul, June 29. The pallium is made from the wool of lambs blessed by the pope on the feast of St. Agnes (Jan. 21).

Rochet: A knee-length, white linen-lace garment of prelates worn under outer vestments.

Surplice: a loose, flowing vestment of white fabric with wide sleeves. For some functions, it is interchangeable with an alb.

Zucchetto: A skullcap worn by bishops and other prelates.

SACRED VESSELS, LINENS

Vessels

Paten and Chalice: The principal sacred vessels required for the celebration of Mass are the paten (plate) and chalice (cup) in which bread and wine, respectively, are offered, consecrated and consumed. Both should be made of solid and noble material which is not easily breakable or corruptible. Gold coating is required of the interior parts of sacred vessels subject to rust. The cup of a chalice should be made of non-absorbent material.

Vessels for containing consecrated hosts (see below) can be made of material other than solid and noble metal — e.g., ivory, more durable woods — provided the substitute material is locally regarded as noble or rather precious and is suitable for sacred use.

Sacred vessels should be blessed, according to prescribed requirements.

Vessels, in addition to the paten, for containing consecrated hosts are:

Ciborium: Used to hold hosts for distribution to the faithful and for reservation in the tabernacle.

Luna, Lunula, Lunette: A small receptacle which holds the sacred host in an upright position in the monstrance.

Monstrance, Ostensorium: A portable receptacle so made that the sacred host, when enclosed therein, may be clearly seen, as at Benediction or during extended exposition of the Blessed Sacrament.

Pyx: A watch-shaped vessel used in carrying the Eucharist to the sick.

Linens

Altar Cloth: A white cloth, usually of linen, covering the table of an altar. One cloth is sufficient. Three were used according to former requirements.

Burse: A square, stiff flat case, open at one end, in which the folded corporal can be placed; the outside is covered with material of the same kind and color as the outer vestments of the celebrant.

Corporal: A square piece of white linen spread on the altar cloth, on which rest the vessels holding the Sacred Species — the consecrated host(s) and wine — during the Eucharistic Liturgy. The corporal is used whenever the Blessed Sacrament is removed from the tabernacle; e.g., during Benediction the vessel containing the Blessed Sacrament rests on a corporal.

Finger Towel: A white rectangular napkin used by the priest to dry his fingers after cleansing them following the offering of gifts at Mass.

Pall: A square piece of stiff material, usually covered with linen, which can be used to cover the chalice at Mass.

Purificator: A white rectangular napkin used for cleansing sacred vessels after the reception of Communion at Mass.

Veil: The chalice intended for use at Mass can be covered with a veil made of the same material as the outer vestments of the celebrant.

THE CHURCH BUILDING

A church is a building set aside and dedicated for purposes of divine worship, the place of assembly for a worshipping community.

A Catholic church is the ordinary place in which the faithful assemble for participation in the Eucharistic Liturgy and other forms of divine worship.

In the early years of Christianity, the first places of assembly for the Eucharistic Liturgy were private homes (Acts 2:46; Rom. 16:5; 1 Cor. 16:5; Col. 4:15) and, sometimes, catacombs. Church building began in the latter half of the second century during lulls in persecution and became widespread after enactment of the Edict of Milan in 313, when it finally became possible for the Church to emerge completely from the underground. The oldest and basic norms regarding church buildings date from about that time.

The essential principle underlying all norms for church building was reformulated by the Second Vatican Council, as follows: "When churches are to be built, let great care be taken that they be suitable for the celebration of liturgical services and for the active participation of the faithful" (*Sacrosanctum Concilium*, Constitution on the Sacred Liturgy, No. 124).

This principle was subsequently elaborated in detail by the Congregation for Divine Worship in a document entitled *Institutio Generalis Missalis Romani*, which was approved by Paul VI Apr. 3 and promulgated by a decree of the congregation dated Apr. 6, 1969. Coverage of the following items reflects the norms stated in Chapter V of this document.

Main Features

Sanctuary: The part of the church where the altar of sacrifice is located, the place where the ministers of the liturgy lead the people in prayer, proclaim the word of God and celebrate the Eucharist. It is set off from the body of the church by a distinctive structural feature — e.g., elevation above the main floor — or by ornamentation. (The traditional communion rail, removed in recent years in many churches, served this purpose of demarcation.) The customary location of the sanctuary is at the front of the church; it may, however, be centrally located.

Altar: The main altar of sacrifice and table of the Lord is the focal feature of the sanctuary and entire church. It stands by itself, so that the ministers can move about it freely, and is so situated that they face the people during the liturgical action. In addition to this main altar, there may also be others; in new churches, these are ideally situated in side chapels or alcoves removed to some degree from the body of the church.

Adornment of the Altar: The altar table is covered with a suitable linen cloth. Required candelabra and a cross are placed upon or near the altar in plain sight of the people and are so arranged that they do not obscure their view of the liturgical action.

Seats of the Ministers: The seats of the ministers should be so arranged that they are part of the seating arrangement of the worshipping congregation and suitably placed for the performance of ministerial functions. The seat of the celebrant or chief concelebrant should be in a presiding position.

Ambo, Pulpit, Lectern: The stand at which scriptural lessons and psalm responses are read, the word of God preached, and the prayer of the faithful offered. It is so placed that the ministers can be easily seen and heard by the people.

Places for the People: Seats and kneeling benches (pews) and other accommodations for the people are so arranged that they can participate in the most appropriate way in the liturgical action and have freedom of movement for the reception of Holy Communion. Reserved seats are out of order.

Place for the Choir: Where it is located depends on the most suitable arrangement for maintaining the unity of the choir with the congregation and for providing its members maximum opportunity for carrying out their proper function and participating fully in the Mass.

Tabernacle: The best place for reserving the Blessed Sacrament is in a chapel suitable for the private devotion of the people. If this is not possible, reservation should be at a side altar or other appropriately adorned place. In either case, the Blessed Sacrament should be kept in a tabernacle, i.e., a safe-like, secure receptacle.

Statues: Images of the Lord, the Blessed Virgin Mary and the saints are legitimately proposed for the veneration of the faithful in churches. Their number and arrangement, however, should be ordered in such a way that they do not distract the people from the central celebration of the Eucharistic Liturgy. There should be only one statue of one and the same saint in a church.

General Adornment and Arrangement of Churches: Churches should be so adorned and fitted out that they serve the direct requirements of divine worship and the needs and reasonable convenience of the people.

Other Items

Ambry: A box containing the holy oils, attached to the wall of the sanctuary in some churches.

Baptistery: The place for administering baptism. Some churches have baptisteries adjoining or near the entrance, a position symbolizing the fact that persons are initiated in the Church and incorporated in Christ through this sacrament. Contemporary liturgical practice favors placement of the baptistery near the sanctuary and altar, or the use of a portable font in the same position, to emphasize the relationship of baptism to the Eucharist, the celebration in sacrifice and banquet of the death and resurrection of Christ.

Candles: Used more for symbolical than illuminative purposes, they represent Christ, the light and life of grace, at liturgical functions. They are made of beeswax. (See **Index: Paschal Candle**.)

Confessional, Reconciliation Room: A booth-like structure for the hearing of confessions, with separate compartments for the priest and penitents and a grating or screen between them. The use of confessionals became general in the Roman rite after the Council of Trent. Since the Second Vatican Council, there has been a trend in the U.S. to replace or supplement confessionals with small reconciliation rooms so arranged that priest and penitent can converse face-to-face.

Crucifix: A cross bearing the figure of the body of Christ, representative of the Sacrifice of the Cross.

Cruets: Vessels containing the wine and water used at Mass. They are placed on a credence table in the sanctuary.

Holy Water Fonts: Receptacles containing holy water, usually at church entrances, for the use of the faithful.

Sanctuary Lamp: A lamp which is kept burning continuously before a tabernacle in which the Blessed Sacrament is reserved, as a sign of the Real Presence of Christ.

LITURGICAL DEVELOPMENTS

The principal developments covered in this article are enactments of the Holy See and actions related to their implementation in the United States.

Modern Movement

Origins of the modern movement for renewal in the liturgy date back to the 19th century. The key contributing factor was a revival of liturgical and scriptural studies. Of special significance was the work of the Benedictine monks of Solesmes, France, who aroused great interest in the liturgy through the restoration of Gregorian Chant. St. Pius X approved their work in a *motu proprio* of 1903 and gave additional encouragement to liturgical study and development.

St. Pius X did more than any other single pope to promote early first Communion and the practice of frequent Communion, started the research behind a revised breviary, and appointed a group to investigate possible revisions in the Mass.

The movement attracted some attention in the 1920s and 30s but made little progress.

Significant pioneering developments in the U.S. during the 20s, however, were the establishment of the Liturgical Press, the beginning of publication of *Orate Fratres* (now Worship), and the inauguration of the League of the Divine Office by the Benedictines at St. John's Abbey, Collegeville, Minn. Later events of influence were the establishment of the Pius X School of Liturgical Music at Manhattanville College of the Sacred Heart and the organization of a summer school of liturgical music at Mary Manse College by the Gregorian Institute of America. The turning point toward real renewal was reached during and after World War II.

Pius XII gave it impetus and direction, principally through the background teaching in his encyclicals on the Mystical Body (*Mystici Corporis Christi*, 1943), Sacred Liturgy (*Mediator Dei*, 1947), and On Sacred Music (*Musicae sacrae*, 1955), and by means of specific measures affecting the liturgy itself. His work was continued during the pontificates of his successors. The Second Vatican Council, in virtue of *Sacrosanctum Concilium*, the Constitution on the Sacred Liturgy, inaugurated changes of the greatest significance.

Before and After Vatican II

The most significant liturgical changes made in the years immediately preceding the Second Vatican Council were the following:

1. Revision of the rites of Holy Week, for universal observance from 1956.
2. Modification of the Eucharistic fast and permission for afternoon and evening Mass, in effect from 1953 and extended in 1957.
3. The Dialogue Mass, introduced in 1958.
4. Use of popular languages in administration of the sacraments.
5. Calendar-missal-breviary reform, in effect from Jan. 1, 1961.
6. Seven-step administration of baptism for adults, approved in 1962.

The Constitution on the Sacred Liturgy, *Sacrosanctum Concilium*, approved (2,174 to 4) and promulgated by the Second Vatican Council Dec. 4, 1963, marked the beginning of a profound renewal in the Church's corporate worship. Implementation of some of its measures was ordered by Paul VI Jan. 25, 1964, in the *motu proprio Sacram Liturgiam*. On Feb. 29, a special commission, the Consilium for Implementing the Constitution on the Sacred Liturgy, was formed to supervise the execution of the entire program of liturgical reform. Implementation of the program on local and regional levels was left to bishops acting through their own liturgical commissions and in concert with their fellow bishops in national conferences.

Liturgical reform in the United States has been carried out under the direction of the Liturgy Committee, National Conference of Catholic Bishops. Its secretariat, established early in 1965, is located at 3211 Fourth St. N.E., Washington, DC 20017.

Stages of Development

Liturgical development after the Second Vatican Council proceeded in several stages. It started with the formulation of guidelines and directives, and with the translation into vernacular languages of virtually unchanged Latin ritual texts. Then came structural changes in the Mass, the sacraments, the calendar, the Divine Office and other phases of the liturgy. These revisions were just about completed with the publication of a new order for the sacrament of penance in February 1974. A continuing phase of development, in progress from the beginning, involves efforts to deepen the liturgical sense of the faithful, to increase their participation in worship and to relate it to full Christian life.

Recent Developments

On Nov. 14, 2001, the U.S. Bishops attending the annual fall meeting in Washington, approved revised U.S. adaptations in the liturgy by a vote of 207-7. The adaptations govern matters ranging from liturgical music and church furnishings to posture at Mass and how Communion is to be received.

The bishops had approved a complete set of adaptations at their spring meeting in June 2001, but the Vatican Congregation for Divine Worship and the Sacraments asked for modification of several of those and proposed a new approach that required editorial changes in all of them.

When completed, the U.S. adaptations are to be incorporated into the new General Instruction of the Roman Missal and have the same force of law in the United States as the rest of the general instruction.

New U.S. Norms for Distribution of Communion
Under Both Species

New norms for the distribution and reception of Communion under the outward signs of both bread and wine by Catholics in the United States were approved by the U.S. bishops on June 15, 2001, and confirmed by the Holy See on Mar. 22, 2002; they were subsequently published by Bishop Wilton D. Gregory of Belleville, Ill., president of the USCCB.

The norms, which replace the U.S. bishops' 1984 directory titled "This Holy and Living Sacrifice," give specific directives regarding liturgical roles, sacred vessels and the rites to be followed in distributing Communion under both kinds.

The first section of the new norms provides a theological summary of the church's teaching on Communion under both kinds, while the following section describes the authorized procedures by which such distribution can be accomplished at mass.

The U.S. adaptations are to be incorporated into the new General Instruction of the Roman Missal and have the same force of law in the United States as the rest of the general instruction. The General Instruction of the recently revised Roman Missal permits bishops' conferences to provide norms for the distribution of Communion under both kinds, meaning under the outward signs of both bread and wine.

Included among the norms is an indult — or exception to the general requirement — from the Vatican Congregation for Divine Worship and the Sacraments that provides for the cleansing of sacred vessels by special eucharistic ministers. The indult was promulgated as "particular law" for the dioceses of the United States at the same time as the norms and it became effective on Apr. 7.

However, the Vatican congregation declined to approve an indult authorizing special ministers to assist with the distribution of the consecrated blood to other chalices during the singing of the "Lamb of God."

In the letter confirming the norms, the congregation also made clear that special eucharistic ministers, or indeed any communicant, may assist in the consumption of what remains of the blood after distribution of Communion has been completed.

Texts and Translations

The master texts of all documents on liturgical reform are in Latin. Effective dates of their implementation have depended on the completion and approval of appropriate translations into vernacular languages. English translations were made by the International Committee for English in the Liturgy.

The principal features of liturgical changes and the effective dates of their introduction in the United States are covered below under topical headings. (For expanded coverage of various items, especially the sacraments, see additional entries.)

On May 7, 2001, the Congregation for Divine Worship and the Sacraments issued the new instruction, *Liturgiam Authenticam* ("The Authentic Liturgy"). The instruction set stricter rules for the translation of Latin liturgical texts into other languages and bears the subtitle, "On the Use of Vernacular Languages in the Publication of the Books of the Roman Liturgy." The instruction was welcomed by then-NCCB president, Bishop Joseph A. Fiorenza of Galveston-Houston, who said that it reflects long consultations between the Vatican and English-speaking bishops, adding that "It is now our hope and expectation that there will be a much quicker approval of liturgical texts" by the Vatican. The instruction was subsequently debated at the bishops' meeting in November 2001.

The Mass

A new Order of the Mass, supplanting the one authorized by the Council of Trent in the 16th century, was introduced in the U.S. Mar. 22, 1970. It had been approved by Paul VI in the apostolic constitution *Missale Romanum*, dated Apr. 3, 1969.

Preliminary and related to it were the following developments.

Mass in English: Introduced Nov. 29, 1964. In the same year, Psalm 42 was eliminated from the prayers at the foot of the altar.

Incidental Changes: The last Gospel (prologue of John) and vernacular prayers following Mass were eliminated Mar. 7, 1965. At the same time, provision was made for the celebrant to say aloud some prayers formerly said silently.

Rubrics: An instruction entitled *Tres Abhinc Annos*, dated May 4 and effective June 29, 1967, simplified directives for the celebration of Mass, approved the practice of saying the canon aloud, altered the Communion and dismissal rites, permitted purple instead of black vestments in Masses for the dead, discontinued wearing of the maniple, and approved in principle the use of vernacular languages for the canon, ordination rites, and lessons of the Divine Office when read in choir.

Eucharistic Prayers (Canons): The traditional Roman Canon in English was introduced Oct. 22, 1967. Three additional Eucharistic prayers, authorized May 23, 1968, were approved for use in English the following Aug. 15.

The customary Roman Canon, which dates at least from the beginning of the fifth century and has remained substantially unchanged since the seventh century, is the first in the order of listing of the Eucharistic prayers. It can be used at any time, but is the one of choice for most Sundays, some special feasts like Easter and Pentecost, and for feasts of the Apostles and other saints who are commemorated in the canon. Any preface can be used with it.

The second Eucharistic prayer, the shortest and sim-

plest of all, is best suited for use on weekdays and various special circumstances. It has a preface of its own, but others may be used with it. This canon bears a close resemblance to the one framed by St. Hippolytus about 215.

The third Eucharistic prayer is suitable for use on Sundays and feasts as an alternative to the Roman Canon. It can be used with any preface and has a special formula for remembrance of the dead.

The fourth Eucharistic prayer, the most sophisticated of them all, presents a broad synthesis of salvation history. Based on the Eastern tradition of Antioch, it is best suited for use at Masses attended by persons versed in Sacred Scripture. It has an unchangeable preface.

Five additional Eucharistic prayers — three for Masses with children and two for Masses of reconciliation — were approved in 1974 and 1975, respectively, by the Congregation for the Sacraments and Divine Worship.

Use of the Eucharistic Prayers for Various Needs and Occasions, was approved by the U.S. bishops in 1994, confirmed by the appropriate Vatican congregations May 9, 1995, and ratified for use beginning Oct. 1, 1995.

Lectionary: A new compilation of scriptural readings and psalm responsories for Mass was published in 1969. The Lectionary contains a three-year cycle of readings for Sundays and solemn feasts, a two-year weekday cycle, and a one-year cycle for the feasts of saints, in addition to readings for a variety of votive Masses, ritual Masses and Masses for various needs. There are also responsorial psalms to follow the first readings and gospel or alleluia versicles.

A second edition of the Lectionary, substantially the same as the first, was published in 1981. New features included an expanded introduction, extensive scriptural references and additional readings for a number of solemnities and feasts.

Volume One of a new Lectionary for the Mass was decreed by Bishop Anthony Pilla of Cleveland, president of the NCCB, as permissible for use as of the first Sunday of Advent, Nov. 29, 1998. The first new Lectionary since 1973, Volume One contains the readings for Sundays, solemnities and feasts of the Lord. Volume Two, containing the readings for weekdays, feasts of saints, and various other occasions, was given final approval on June 19, 1998, by the NCCB but still required confirmation by the Holy See.

Sacramentary (Missal): The Vatican Polyglot Press began distribution in June 1970, of the Latin text of a new Roman Missal, the first revision published in 400 years. The English translation was authorized for optional use beginning July 1, 1974; the mandatory date for use was Dec. 1, 1974.

The **Sacramentary** is the celebrant's Mass book of entrance songs, prayers, prefaces and Eucharistic prayers, including special common sets of texts for various commemorations and intentions — dedication of churches, Mary, the apostles, martyrs, doctors of the Church, virgins, holy men and women, the dead, other categories of holy persons, administration of certain sacraments, special intentions.

Study of the Mass: The Bishops' Committee on the Liturgy, following approval by the National Conference of Catholic Bishops in May 1979, began a study of the function and position of elements of the Mass, including the Gloria, the sign of peace, the penitential rite and the readings. Major phases of the study have been completed, and work is still under way toward completion of the project.

Mass for Special Groups: Reasons and norms for the celebration of Mass at special gatherings of the faithful were the subject of an instruction issued May 15, 1969. Two years earlier, the U.S. Bishops' Liturgy Committee went on record in support of the celebration of Mass in private homes under appropriate conditions.

Sunday Mass on Saturday: The Congregation for the Clergy, under date of Jan. 10, 1970, granted the request that the faithful, where bishops consider it pastorally necessary or useful, may satisfy the precept of participating in Mass in the late afternoon or evening hours of Saturdays and the days before holy days of obligation. This provision is stated in Canon 1248 of the Code of Canon Law.

Bination and Trination: Canon 905 of the Code of Canon Law provides that local ordinaries may permit priests to celebrate Mass twice a day (bination), for a just cause; in cases of pastoral need, they may permit priests to celebrate Mass three times a day (trination) on Sundays and holy days of obligation.

Mass in Latin: According to notices issued by the Congregation for Divine Worship June 1, 1971, and Oct. 28, 1974: (1) Bishops may permit the celebration of Mass in Latin for mixed-language groups; (2) bishops may permit the celebration of one or two Masses in Latin on weekdays or Sundays in any church, irrespective of mixed-language groups involved (1971); (3) priests may celebrate Mass in Latin when people are not present; (4) the approved revised Order of the Mass is to be used in Latin as well as vernacular languages; (5) by way of exception, bishops may permit older and handicapped priests to use the Council of Trent's Order of the Mass in private celebration of the holy Sacrifice. (See **Permission for Tridentine Mass**.)

Mass Obligation Waived: The Congregation for Bishops approved July 4, 1992, a resolution of the U.S. bishops to waive the Mass attendance obligation for the holy days of Mary, the Mother of God (Jan. 1), the Assumption of Mary (Aug. 15) and All Saints (Nov. 1) when these solemnities fall on Saturday or Monday.

Inter-Ritual Concelebration: The Apostolic Delegation (now Nunciature) in Washington, D.C., announced in June 1971, that it had received authorization to permit priests of Roman and Eastern rites to celebrate Mass together in the rite of the host church. It was understood that the inter-ritual concelebrations would always be "a manifestation of the unity of the Church and of communion among particular churches."

Ordo of the Sung Mass: In a decree dated June 24 and made public Aug. 24, 1972, the Congregation for Divine Worship issued a new *Ordo of the Sung Mass* — containing Gregorian chants in Latin — to replace the *Graduale Romanum*.

Mass for Children: Late in 1973, the Congregation for Divine Worship issued special guidelines for children's Masses, providing accommodations to the mentality and spiritual growth of pre-adolescents while retaining the principal parts and structures of the Mass. The Directory for Masses with Children was approved

by Paul VI Oct. 22 and was dated Nov. 1, 1973. Three Eucharistic prayers for Masses with children were approved by the congregation in 1974; English versions were approved June 5, 1975. Their use, authorized originally for a limited period of experimentation, was extended indefinitely Dec. 15, 1980.

Lectionary for Children: A lectionary for Masses with children, with an announced publication date of September 1993, was authorized for use by choice beginning Nov. 28, 1993.

Sacraments

The general use of English in administration of the sacraments was approved for the U.S. Sept. 14, 1964. Structural changes of the rites were subsequently made and introduced in the U.S. as follows.

Pastoral Care of the Sick: Revised rites, covering also administration of the Eucharist to sick persons, were approved Nov. 30, 1972, and published Jan. 18, 1973. The effective date for use of the provisional English prayer formula was Dec. 1, 1974. The mandatory effective date for use of the ritual, Pastoral Care of the Sick in English, was Nov. 27, 1983.

Baptism: New rites for the baptism of infants, approved Mar. 19, 1969, were introduced June 1, 1970.

Rite of Christian Initiation of Adults: Revised rites were issued Jan. 6, 1972, for the Christian initiation of adults — affecting preparation for and reception of baptism, the Eucharist and confirmation; also, for the reception of already baptized adults into full communion with the Church. These rites, which were introduced in the U.S. on the completion of English translation, nullified a seven-step baptismal process approved in 1962. On Mar. 8, 1988, the National Conference of Catholic Bishops was notified that the Congregation for Divine Worship had approved the final English translation of the Rite of Christian Initiation of Adults. The mandatory date for putting the rite into effect was Sept. 1, 1988.

Confirmation: Revised rites, issued Aug. 15, 1971, became mandatory in the U.S. Jan. 1, 1973. The use of a stole by persons being confirmed should be avoided, according to an item in the December 1984, edition of the Newsletter of the Bishops' Committee on the Liturgy. The item said: "The distinction between the universal priesthood of all the baptized and the ministerial priesthood of the ordained is blurred when the distinctive garb (the stole) of ordained ministers is used in this manner."

A decree regarding the proper age for confirmation, approved by the U.S. bishops in June 1993, was ratified by the Congregation for Bishops Feb. 8, 1994. The decree reads: "In accord with prescriptions of canon 891, the National Conference of Catholic Bishops hereby decrees that the sacrament of confirmation in the Latin rite shall be conferred between the age of discretion, which is about the age of seven, and 18 years of age, within the limits determined by the diocesan bishop and with regard for the legitimate exceptions given in canon 891, namely, when there is danger of death or where, in the judgment of the minister, grave cause urges otherwise." The decree became effective July 1, 1994, and continued in effect until July 1, 1999.

Special Ministers of the Eucharist: The designation of lay men and women to serve as special ministers of the Eucharist was authorized by Paul VI in an

"Instruction on Facilitating Communion in Particular Circumstances" (*Immensae Caritatis*), dated Jan. 29 and published by the Congregation for Divine Worship Mar. 29, 1973. Provisions concerning them are contained in Canons 230 and 910 of the Code of Canon Law.

Qualified laypersons may serve as special ministers for specific occasions or for extended periods in the absence of a sufficient number of priests and deacons to provide reasonable and appropriate service in the distribution of Holy Communion, during Mass and outside of Mass (to the sick and shut-ins). Appointments of ministers are made by priests with the approval of the appropriate bishop.

The Newsletter of the U.S. Bishops' Committee on the Liturgy stated in its February 1988, edition: "When ordinary ministers (bishops, priests, deacons) are present during a Eucharistic celebration, whether they are participating in it or not, and are not prevented from doing so, they are to assist in the distribution of Communion. Accordingly, if the ordinary ministers are in sufficient number, special ministers of the Eucharist are not allowed to distribute Communion at that Eucharistic celebration." Pope John Paul approved this decision and ordered it published June 15, 1987.

Holy Orders: Revised ordination rites for deacons, priests and bishops, validated by prior experimental use, were approved in 1970. The sacrament of holy orders underwent further revision in 1972 with the elimination of the Church-instituted orders of porter, reader, exorcist, acolyte and subdeacon, and of the tonsure ceremony symbolic of entrance into the clerical state. The former minor orders of reader and acolyte were changed from orders to ministries.

Matrimony: A revised rite for the celebration of marriage was promulgated by the Congregation for Divine Worship and the Discipline of the Sacraments Mar. 19, 1969, and went into effect June 1, 1970. A second typical edition of the order of celebration, with revisions in accord with provisions of the Code of Canon Law promulgated in 1983, was approved and published in 1990 (*Notitiae*, Vol. 26, No.6). The date for implementation was reported to be dependent on the completion of required translations and appropriate formalities.

Penance: Ritual revision of the sacraments was completed with the approval by Paul VI Dec. 2, 1973, of new directives for the sacrament of penance or reconciliation. The U.S. Bishops' Committee on the Liturgy set Feb. 27, 1977, as the mandatory date for use of the new rite. The committee also declared that it could be used from Mar. 7, 1976, after adequate preparation of priests and people. Earlier, authorization was given by the Holy See in 1968 for the omission of any reference to excommunication or other censures in the formula of absolution unless there was some indication that a censure had actually been incurred by a penitent.

Additional Developments

Music: An instruction on Music in the Liturgy, dated Mar. 5 and effective May 14, 1967, encouraged congregational singing during liturgical celebrations and attempted to clarify the role of choirs and trained singers. More significantly, the instruction indicated that a major development under way in the liturgy was a gradual erasure of the distinctive lines traditionally drawn between the sung liturgy and the spoken liturgy, between what had been called the high Mass and the low Mass.

In the same year, the U.S. Bishops' Liturgy Committee approved the use of contemporary music, as well as guitars and other suitable instruments, in the liturgy. The Holy See authorized in 1968 the use of musical instruments other than the organ in liturgical services, "provided they are played in a manner suitable to worship."

Calendar: A revised liturgical calendar approved by Paul VI Feb. 14 and made public May 9, 1969, went into effect in the U.S. in 1972. Since that time, memorials and feasts of beatified persons and saints have been added.

Communion in Hand: Since 1969, the Holy See has approved the practice of in-hand reception of the Eucharist in regions and countries where it had the approval of the appropriate episcopal conferences. The first grant of approval was to Belgium, in May 1969. Approval was granted the United States in June 1977.

Liturgy of the Hours: The background, contents, scope and purposes of the revised Divine Office, called the Liturgy of the Hours, were described by Paul VI in the apostolic constitution *Laudis Canticum*, dated Nov. 1, 1970. A provisional English version, incorporating basic features of the master Latin text, was published in 1971. The four complete volumes of the Hours in English have been published since May 1975. One-volume, partial editions have also been published in approved form. Nov. 27, 1977, was set by the Congregation for Divine Worship and the National Conference of Catholic Bishops as the effective date for exclusive use in liturgical worship of the translation of the Latin text of the Liturgy of the Hours approved by the International Committee on English in the Liturgy.

Holy Week: The English version of revised Holy Week rites went into effect in 1971. They introduced concelebration of Mass, placed new emphasis on commemorating the institution of the priesthood on Holy Thursday and modified Good Friday prayers for other Christians, Jews and other non-Christians.

In another action, the Congregation for Divine Worship released Feb. 20, 1988, a "Circular Letter concerning the Preparation and Celebration of the Easter Feasts." It called the feasts the "summit of the whole liturgical year," and criticized practices which dilute or change appropriate norms for their celebration. Singled out for blame for the abuse or ignorance of norms was the "inadequate formation given to the clergy and the faithful regarding the paschal mystery as the center of the liturgical year and of Christian life." The document set out the appropriate norms for the Lenten season, Holy Week, the Easter Triduum, Easter and the weeks following. It was particularly insistent on the proper celebration of the Easter Vigil, to take place after nightfall on Saturday and before dawn on Sunday.

Oils: The Congregation for Divine Worship issued a directive in 1971 permitting the use of other oils — from plants, seeds or coconuts — instead of the traditional olive oil in administering some of the sacraments. The directive also provided that oils could be blessed at other times than at the usual Mass of Chrism on Holy Thursday, and authorized bishops' conferences to permit priests to bless oils in cases of necessity.

Dancing and Worship: Dancing and worship was the subject of an essay which appeared in a 1975 edition of *Notitiae* (11, pp. 202-205), the official journal of the Congregation for the Sacraments and Divine Worship. The article was called a "qualified and authoritative sketch," and should be considered "an authoritative point of reference for every discussion of the matter."

The principal points of the essay were:
• "The dance has never been made an integral part of the official worship of the Latin Church."
• "If the proposal of the religious dance in the West is really to be made welcome, care will have to be taken that in its regard a place be found outside of the liturgy, in assembly areas which are not strictly liturgical. Moreover, the priests must always be excluded from the dance."

Mass for Deceased Non-Catholic Christians: The Congregation for the Doctrine of the Faith released a decree June 11, 1976, authorizing the celebration of public Mass for deceased non-Catholic Christians under certain conditions: "(1) The public celebration of the Masses must be explicitly requested by the relatives, friends, or subjects of the deceased person for a genuine religious motive. (2) In the Ordinary's judgment, there must be no scandal for the faithful."

Built of Living Stones: Art, Architecture, and Worship: At their November 2001 meeting in Washington, D.C., the Bishops approved this document by the U.S. Bishops' Committee on the Liturgy; it replaces the document *Environment and Art in Catholic Worship* issued in March 1978.

Doxology: The bishops' committee called attention in August 1978, to the directive that the Doxology concluding the Eucharistic Prayer is said or sung by the celebrant (concelebrants) alone, to which the people respond, "Amen."

Churches, Altars, Chalices: The Newsletter of the U.S. Bishops' Committee on the Liturgy reported in November 1978, that the Congregation for Divine Worship had given provisional approval of a new English translation of the rite of dedicating churches and altars, and of a new form for the blessing of chalices.

Eucharistic Worship: This was the subject of two documents issued in 1980. *Dominicae Coenae* was a letter addressed by Pope John Paul to bishops throughout the world in connection with the celebration of Holy Thursday; it was dated Feb. 24 and released Mar. 18. It was more doctrinal in content than the "Instruction on Certain Norms concerning Worship of the Eucharistic Mystery" (*Inaestimabile Donum*, "The Priceless Gift"), which was approved by the Pope Apr. 17 and published by the Congregation for the Sacraments and Divine Worship May 23. Its stated purpose was to reaffirm and clarify teaching on liturgical renewal contained in enactments of the Second Vatican Council and in several related implementing documents.

Tridentine Mass: The celebration of Mass according to the 1962 typical (master) edition of the Roman Missal — the so-called Tridentine Mass — was authorized by Pope John Paul under certain conditions. So stated a letter from the Congregation for Divine Worship, dated Oct. 3, 1984. The letter said the Pope wished to be responsive to priests and faithful who remained attached to the so-called Tridentine rite. The principal condition for the celebration was: "There

must be unequivocal, even public, evidence that the priest and people petitioning have no ties with those who impugn the lawfulness and doctrinal soundness of the Roman Missal promulgated in 1970 by Pope Paul VI." (This, in particular, with reference to the followers of dissident Archbishop Marcel Lefebvre.)

Six guidelines for celebration of the Tridentine Mass were contained in the letter regarding its "wide and generous" use, for two purposes: to win back Lefebvre followers and to clear up misunderstandings about liberal permission for use of the Tridentine rite. The letter, from the Pontifical Commission *Ecclesia Dei*, said in part:
• The Tridentine Mass can be celebrated in a parish church, so long as it provides a pastoral service and is harmoniously integrated into the parish liturgical schedule.
• When requested, the Mass should be offered on a regular Sunday and holy day basis, "at a central location, at a convenient time" for a trial period of several months, with "adjustment" later if needed.
• Celebrants of the Mass should make it clear that they acknowledge the validity of the postconciliar liturgy.
• Although the commission has the authority to grant use of the Tridentine rite to all groups that request it, the commission "would much prefer that such faculties be granted by the Ordinary himself so that ecclesial communion can be strengthened."
• While the new Lectionary in the vernacular can be used in the Tridentine Mass, as suggested by the Second Vatican Council, it should not be "imposed on congregations that decidedly wish to maintain the former liturgical tradition in its integrity."
• Older and retired priests who have asked permission to celebrate Mass according to the Tridentine rite should be given the chance to do so for groups that request it.

Spanish: In accord with decrees of the Congregation for Divine Worship, Spanish was approved as a liturgical language in the U.S. (Jan. 19, 1985). The *texto unico* of the Ordinary of the Mass became mandatory in the U.S. Dec. 3, 1989. Spanish translations of Proper-of-the-Mass texts proper to U.S. dioceses were approved Mar. 12, 1990. An approved Spanish version of the Rite for the Christian Initiation of Adults was published in 1991. The Institute of Hispanic Liturgy opened its national office June 1, 1995, on the campus of the Catholic University of America in Washington.

Funeral Rites: A revised Order of Christian Funerals became mandatory in the U.S. Nov. 2, 1989.

Permission for the presence of cremated human remains in the funeral liturgy, including the Eucharist, was granted in 1997 to local bishops in the U.S. by the Congregation for Divine Worship and the Discipline of the Sacraments. Adaptations to existing rites are under study.

Popular Piety and Liturgy: The relation of popular piety to the liturgy was the subject of remarks by Pope John Paul II at a meeting with a group of Italian bishops Apr. 24, 1986. He said, in part:

"An authentic liturgical ministry will never be able to neglect the riches of popular piety, the values proper to the culture of a people, so that such riches might be illuminated, purified and introduced into the liturgy as an offering of the people."

Extended Eucharistic Exposition: In response to queries, the Secretariat of the U.S. Bishops' Committee on the Liturgy issued an advisory stating that liturgical law permits and encourages in parish churches:

- Exposition of the Blessed Sacrament for an extended period of time once a year, with consent of the local Ordinary and only if suitable numbers of the faithful are expected to be present;
- Exposition ordered by the local Ordinary, for a grave and general necessity, for a more extended period of supplication when the faithful assemble in large numbers.

With regard to perpetual exposition, this form is generally permitted only in the case of those religious communities of men or women who have the general practice of perpetual Eucharistic adoration or adoration over extended periods of time.

The Secretariat's advisory appeared in the June-July 1986 edition of the Newsletter of the Bishops' Committee on the Liturgy.

Native American Languages: The Newsletter of the U.S. Bishops' Committee on the Liturgy reported in December 1986, and May 1987, respectively, that the Congregation for Divine Worship had authorized Mass translations in Navajo and Choctaw. Lakota was approved as a liturgical language in 1989.

Communion Guidelines: In 1986 and again in 1996, the U.S. bishops' approved the insertion of advisories in missalettes and similar publications, stating that: (1) The Eucharist is to be received by Catholics only, except in certain specific cases. (2) To receive Communion worthily, a person must be in the state of grace (i.e., free of serious sin)

and observe the eucharistic fast (See separate entry).

Unauthorized Eucharistic Prayers: The May 1987 Newsletter of the U.S. Bishops' Committee on the Liturgy restated the standing prohibition against the use of any Eucharistic Prayers other than those contained in the Sacramentary. Specifically, the article referred to the 25 unauthorized prayers in a volume entitled Spoken Visions.

Homilist: According to the Pontifical Commission for the Authentic Interpretation of Canon Law, the diocesan bishop cannot dispense from the requirement of Canon 767, par. 1, that the homily in the liturgy be reserved to a priest or deacon. Pope John Paul approved this decision June 20, 1987.

Concerts in Churches: In a letter released Dec. 5, 1987, the Congregation for Divine Worship declared that churches might be used on a limited basis for concerts of sacred or religious music, but not for concerts featuring secular music.

Blessings: A revised **Book of Blessings** was ordered into use beginning Dec. 3, 1989.

Litany of the Blessed Virgin Mary: "Queen of Families," a new invocation, was reported by the U.S. bishops in 1996, for insertion between "Queen of the Rosary" and "Queen of Peace."

Inclusive Language: "Criteria for the Evaluation of Inclusive Language Translations of Scriptural Texts Proposed for Liturgical Use" was issued by the U.S. bishops in November 1990. The criteria distinguish between non-use of vertical inclusiveness in references to God and use of horizontal, gender-inclusive terms (he/she, man/woman and the like) where appropriate in references to persons.

The Sacraments of the Church

The sacraments are actions of Christ and his Church (itself a kind of sacrament) which signify grace, cause it in the act of signifying it, and confer it upon persons properly disposed to receive it. They perpetuate the redemptive activity of Christ, making it present and effective. They infallibly communicate the fruit of that activity — namely grace — to responsive persons with faith. Sacramental actions consist of the union of sensible signs (matter of the sacraments) with the words of the minister (form of the sacraments).

Christ himself instituted the seven sacraments of the New Law by determining their essence and the efficacy of their signs to produce the grace they signify.

Christ is the principal priest or minister of every sacrament; human agents — an ordained priest, baptized persons contracting marriage with each other, any person conferring emergency baptism in a proper manner — are secondary ministers. Sacraments have efficacy from Christ, not from the personal dispositions of their human ministers.

Each sacrament confers sanctifying grace for the special purpose of the sacrament; this is, accordingly, called sacramental grace. It involves a right to actual graces corresponding to the purposes of the respective sacraments.

Baptism, confirmation and the Eucharist are sacraments of initiation; penance (reconciliation) and anointing of the sick, sacraments of healing; order and matrimony, sacraments for service.

While sacraments infallibly produce the grace they signify, recipients benefit from them in proportion to their personal dispositions. One of these is the intention to receive sacraments as sacred signs of God's saving and grace-giving action. The state of grace is also necessary for fruitful reception of the Holy Eucharist, confirmation, matrimony, holy orders and anointing of the sick. Baptism is the sacrament in which grace is given in the first instance and original sin is remitted. Penance is the secondary sacrament of reconciliation, in which persons guilty of serious sin after baptism are reconciled with God and the Church, and in which persons already in the state of grace are strengthened in that state.

Role of Sacraments

The Second Vatican Council prefaced a description of the role of the sacraments with the following statement concerning participation by all the faithful in the priesthood of Christ and the exercise of that priesthood by receiving the sacraments (Dogmatic Constitution on the Church, *Lumen Gentium*, Nos. 10 and 11).

"The baptized by regeneration and the anointing of the Holy Spirit are consecrated into a spiritual house and a holy priesthood. Thus through all those works befitting Christian men they can offer spiritual sacrifice and proclaim the power of him who has called them out of darkness into his marvelous light (cf. 1 Pt. 2:4-10).

"Though they differ from one another in essence and not only in degree, the common priesthood of the faithful and the ministerial or hierarchical priesthood (of those ordained to holy orders) are nonetheless interrelated. Each of them in its own special way is a participation in the one priesthood of Christ. The ministerial priest, by the sacred power he enjoys, molds and rules the priestly people. Acting in the Person of Christ, he brings about the Eucharistic Sacrifice, and offers it to God in the name of all the people. For their part, the faithful join in the offering of the Eucharist by virtue of their royal priesthood. They likewise exercise that priesthood by receiving the sacraments, by prayer and thanksgiving, by the witness of a holy life, and by self-denial and active charity."

"It is through the sacraments and the exercise of the virtues that the sacred nature and organic structure of the priestly community is brought into operation."

Baptism: "Incorporated into the Church through baptism, the faithful are consecrated by the baptismal character to the exercise of the cult of the Christian religion. Reborn as sons of God, they must confess before men the faith which they have received from God through the Church."

Confirmation: "Bound more intimately to the Church by the sacrament of confirmation, they are endowed by the Holy Spirit with special strength. Hence they are more strictly obliged to spread and defend the faith both by word and by deed as true witnesses of Christ."

Eucharist: "Taking part in the Eucharistic Sacrifice, which is the fount and apex of the whole Christian life, they offer the divine Victim to God, and offer themselves along with It. Thus, both by the act of oblation and through holy Communion, all perform their proper part in this liturgical service, not, indeed, all in the same way but each in that way which is appropriate to himself. Strengthened anew at the holy table by the Body of Christ, they manifest in a practical way that unity of God's People which is suitably signified and wondrously brought about by this most awesome sacrament."

Penance: "Those who approach the sacrament of penance obtain pardon from the mercy of God for offenses committed against him. They are at the same time reconciled with the Church, which they have wounded by their sins, and which by charity, example, and prayer seeks their conversion."

Anointing of the Sick: "By the sacred anointing of the sick and the prayer of her priests, the whole Church commends those who are ill to the suffering and glorified Lord, asking that he may lighten their suffering and save them (cf. Jas. 5:14-16). She exhorts them, moreover, to contribute to the welfare of the whole People of God by associating themselves freely with the passion and death of Christ (cf. Rom. 8:17; Col. 1:24; 2 Tm. 2:11-12; 1 Pt. 4:13)."

Holy Orders: "Those of the faithful who are consecrated by holy orders are appointed to feed the Church in Christ's name with the Word and the grace of God."

Matrimony: "Christian spouses, in virtue of the sacrament of matrimony, signify and partake of the mystery of that unity and fruitful love which exists between Christ and his Church (cf. Eph. 5:32). The spouses thereby help each other to attain to holiness in their married life and by the rearing and education of their children. And so, in their state and way of life, they have their own special gift among the People of God (cf. 1 Cor. 7:7).

"For from the wedlock of Christians there comes the family, in which new citizens of human society are born. By the grace of the Holy Spirit received in baptism these are made children of God, thus perpetuating the People of God through the centuries. The family is, so to speak, the domestic Church. In it parents should, by their word and example, be the first preachers of the faith to their children. They should encourage them in the vocation which is proper to each of them, fostering with special care any religious vocation.

"Fortified by so many and such powerful means of salvation, all the faithful, whatever their condition or state, are called by the Lord, each in his own way, to that perfect holiness whereby the Father himself is perfect."

Baptism

Baptism is the sacrament of spiritual regeneration by which a person is incorporated in Christ and made a member of his Mystical Body, given grace, and cleansed of original sin. Actual sins and the punishment due for them are remitted also if the person baptized was guilty of such sins (e.g., in the case of a person baptized after reaching the age of reason). The theological virtues of faith, hope and charity are given with grace. The sacrament confers a character on the soul and can be received only once.

The matter is the pouring of water. The form is: "I baptize you in the name of the Father and of the Son and of the Holy Spirit."

The minister of solemn baptism is a bishop, priest or deacon, but in case of emergency anyone, including a non-Catholic, can validly baptize. The minister pours water on the forehead of the person being baptized and says the words of the form while the water is flowing. The water used in solemn baptism is blessed during the rite.

Baptism is conferred in the Roman rite by immersion or infusion (pouring of water), depending on the directive of the appropriate conference of bishops, according to the Code of Canon Law. The Church recognizes as valid baptisms properly performed by non-Catholic ministers. The baptism of infants has always been considered valid and the general practice of infant baptism was well established by the fifth century. Baptism is conferred conditionally when there is doubt about the validity of a previous baptism.

Baptism is necessary for salvation. If a person cannot receive the baptism of water described above, this can be supplied by baptism of blood (martyrdom suffered for the Catholic faith or some Christian virtue) or by baptism of desire (perfect contrition joined with at least the implicit intention of doing whatever God wills that people should do for salvation).

A sponsor is required for the person being baptized. (See Godparents, below).

A person must be validly baptized before he or she can receive any of the other sacraments.

Christian Initiation of Infants: Infants should be solemnly baptized as soon after birth as conveniently possible. In danger of death, anyone may baptize an infant. If the child survives, the ceremonies of solemn baptism should be supplied.

The sacrament is ordinarily conferred by a priest or deacon of the parents' parish.

Catholics 16 years of age and over who have received the sacraments of confirmation and the Eucharist and are practicing their faith are eligible to be sponsors or godparents. Only one is required. Two, one of each sex, are permitted. A non-Catholic Christian cannot be a godparent for a Catholic child, but may serve as a witness to the baptism. A Catholic may not be a godparent for a child baptized in a non-Catholic religion, but may be a witness.

"Because of the close communion between the Catholic Church and the Eastern Orthodox churches," states the 1993 Directory on Ecumenism, "it is permissible for a just cause for an Eastern faithful to act as godparent together with a Catholic godparent at the baptism of a Catholic infant or adult, so long as there is provision for the Catholic education of the person being baptized and it is clear that the godparent is a suitable one.

"A Catholic is not forbidden to stand as godparent in an Eastern Orthodox Church if he/she is so invited. In this case, the duty of providing for the Christian education binds in the first place the godparent who belongs to the church in which the child is baptized."

The role of godparents in baptismal ceremonies is secondary to the role of the parents. They serve as representatives of the community of faith and with the parents request baptism for the child and perform other ritual functions. Their function after baptism is to serve as proxies for the parents if the parents should be unable or fail to provide for the religious training of the child.

At baptism every child should be given a name with Christian significance, usually the name of a saint, to symbolize newness of life in Christ.

Christian Initiation of Adults: According to the *Ordo Initiationis Christianae Adultorum* ("Rite of the Christian Initiation of Adults") issued by the Congregation for Divine Worship under date of Jan. 6, 1972, and put into effect in revised form Sept. 1, 1988, adults are prepared for baptism and reception into the Church in several stages:

• An initial period of inquiry, instruction and evangelization.

• The catechumenate, a period of at least a year of formal instruction and progressive formation in and familiarity with Christian life. It starts with a statement of purpose and includes a rite of election.

• Immediate preparation, called a period of purification and enlightenment, from the beginning of Lent to reception of the sacraments of initiation — baptism, confirmation, Holy Eucharist — during ceremonies of the Easter Vigil. The period is marked by scrutinies, formal giving of the creed and the Lord's Prayer, the choice of a Christian name, and a final statement of intention.

• A mystagogic phase whose objective is greater familiarity with Christian life in the Church through observances of the Easter season and association with the community of the faithful, and through extended formation for about a year.

National Statutes for the Catechumenate were approved by the National Conference of Catholic Bishops Nov. 11, 1986, and were subsequently ratified by the Vatican.

The priest who baptizes a catechumen can also administer the sacrament of confirmation.

A sponsor is required for the person being baptized.

The *Ordo* also provides a simple rite of initiation for adults in danger of death and for cases in which all stages of the initiation process are not necessary, and guidelines for: (1) the preparation of adults for the sacraments of confirmation and Holy Eucharist in cases where they have been baptized but have not received further formation in the Christian life; (2) for the formation and initiation of children of catechetical age.

The Church recognizes the right of anyone over the age of seven to request baptism and to receive the sacrament after completing a course of instruction and giving evidence of good will. Practically, in the case of minors in a non-Catholic family or environment, the Church accepts them when other circumstances favor their ability to practice the faith — e.g., well-disposed family situation, the presence of another or several Catholics in the family. Those who are not in such favorable circumstances are prudently advised to defer reception of the sacrament until they attain the maturity necessary for independent practice of the faith.

Reception of Baptized Christians: Procedure for the reception of already baptized Christians into full communion with the Catholic Church is distinguished from the catechumenate, since they have received some Christian formation. Instruction and formation are provided as necessary, however; and conditional baptism is administered if there is reasonable doubt about the validity of the person's previous baptism.

In the rite of reception, the person is invited to join the community of the Church in professing the Nicene Creed and is asked to state: "I believe and profess all that the holy Catholic Church believes, teaches, and proclaims as revealed by God." The priest places his hand on the head of the person, states the formula of admission to full communion, confirms (in the absence of a bishop), gives a sign of peace, and administers Holy Communion during a Eucharistic Liturgy.

Confirmation

Confirmation is the sacrament by which a baptized person, through anointing with chrism and the imposition of hands, is endowed with the fullness of baptismal grace; is united more intimately to the Church; is enriched with the special power of the Holy Spirit; is committed to be an authentic witness to Christ in word and action. The sacrament confers a character on the soul and can be received only once.

According to the apostolic constitution *Divinae Consortium Naturae* dated Aug. 15, 1971, in conjunction with the *Ordo Confirmationis* ("Rite of Confirmation"): "The sacrament of confirmation is conferred through the anointing with chrism on the forehead, which is done by the imposition of the hand (matter of the sacrament), and through the words: *'N, receive the seal of the Holy Spirit, the Gift of the Father'*" (form of the sacrament). On May 5, 1975, bishops' conferences in English-speaking countries were informed by the Congregation for Divine Worship that Pope Paul had approved this English version of the form of the sacrament: *"Be sealed with the gift of the Holy Spirit."*

The ordinary minister of confirmation in the Roman rite is a bishop. Priests may be delegated for the purpose. A pastor can confirm a parishioner in danger of death, and a priest can confirm in ceremonies of Christian initiation and at the reception of a baptized Christian into union with the Church.

Ideally, the sacrament is conferred during the Eucharistic Liturgy. Elements of the rite include renewal of the promises of baptism, which confirmation ratifies and completes, and the laying on of hands by the confirming bishop and priests participating in the ceremony.

"The entire rite," according to the *Ordo*, "has a twofold meaning. The laying of hands upon the candidates, done by the bishop and the concelebrating priests, expresses the biblical gesture by which the gift of the Holy Spirit is invoked. The anointing with chrism and the accompanying words clearly signify the effect of the Holy Spirit. Signed with the perfumed oil by the bishop's hand, the baptized person receives the indelible character, the seal of the Lord, together with the Spirit who is given and who conforms the person more perfectly to Christ and gives him the grace of spreading the Lord's presence among men."

A sponsor is required for the person being confirmed. Eligible is any Catholic 16 years of age or older who has received the sacraments of confirmation and the Eucharist and is practicing the faith. The baptismal sponsor, preferably, can also be the sponsor for confirmation. Parents may present their children for confirmation but cannot be sponsors.

In the Roman rite, it has been customary for children to receive confirmation within a reasonable time after first Communion and confession. There is a trend, however, to defer confirmation until later when its significance for mature Christian living becomes more evident. In the Eastern rites, confirmation is administered at the same time as baptism.

Eucharist

The Holy Eucharist is a sacrifice (see **The Mass**) and the sacrament in which Christ is present and is received under the appearances of bread and wine.

The matter is bread of wheat, unleavened in the Roman rite and leavened in the Eastern rites, and wine of grape. The form consists of the words of consecration said by the priest at Mass: "This is my body. This is the cup of my blood" (according to the traditional usage of the Roman rite).

Only a priest can consecrate bread and wine so they become the body and blood of Christ. After consecration, however, the Eucharist can be administered by deacons and, for various reasons, by religious and lay persons.

Priests celebrating Mass receive the Eucharist under the species of bread and wine. In the Roman rite, others receive under the species of bread only, i.e., the consecrated host, or in some circumstances they may receive under the species of both bread and wine. In Eastern-rite practice, the faithful generally receive a piece of consecrated leavened bread which has been dipped into consecrated wine (i.e., by intinction).

Conditions for receiving the Eucharist, commonly called Holy Communion, are the state of grace, the right intention and observance of the Eucharistic fast.

The faithful of Roman rite are required by a precept of the Church to receive the Eucharist at least once a year, ordinarily during the Easter time.

(See **Eucharistic Fast, Mass, Transubstantiation, Viaticum**.)

First Communion and Confession: Children are to be prepared for and given opportunity for receiving both sacraments (Eucharist and reconciliation, or penance) on reaching the age of discretion, at which time they become subject to general norms concerning confession and Communion. This, together with a stated preference for first confession before first Communion, was the central theme of a document entitled *Sanctus Pontifex* and published May 24, 1973, by the Congregation for the Discipline of the Sacraments and the Congregation for the Clergy, with the approval of Pope Paul VI.

What the document prescribed was the observance of practices ordered by St. Pius X in the decree *Quam Singulari* of Aug. 8, 1910. Its purpose was to counteract pastoral and catechetical experiments virtually denying children the opportunity of receiving both sacraments at the same time. Termination of such experiments was ordered by the end of the 1972-73 school year.

At the time the document was issued, two- or three-year experiments of this kind — routinely deferring reception of the sacrament of penance until after the first reception of Holy Communion — were in effect in more than half of the dioceses of the U.S. They have remained in effect in many places, despite the advisory from the Vatican.

One reason stated in support of such experiments is the view that children are not capable of serious sin at the age of seven or eight, when Communion is generally received for the first time, and therefore prior reception of the sacrament of penance is not necessary. Another reason is the purpose of making the distinctive nature of the two sacraments clearer to children.

The Vatican view reflected convictions that the principle and practice of devotional reception of penance are as valid for children as they are for adults, and that sound catechetical programs can avoid misconceptions about the two sacraments.

A second letter on the same subject and in the same vein was released May 19, 1977, by the aforementioned congregations. It was issued in response to the question:

" 'Whether it is allowed after the declaration of May 24, 1973, to continue to have, as a general rule, the reception of first Communion precede the reception of the sacrament of penance in those parishes in which this practice developed in the past few years.'

"The Sacred Congregations for the Sacraments and Divine Worship and for the Clergy, with the approval of the Supreme Pontiff, reply: Negative, and according to the mind of the declaration.

"The mind of the declaration is that one year after the promulgation of the same declaration, all experiments of receiving first Communion without the sacrament of penance should cease so that the discipline of the Church might be restored, in the spirit of the decree, *Quam Singulari.*"

The two letters from the Vatican congregations have not produced uniformity of practice in this country. Simultaneous preparation for both sacraments is provided in some dioceses where a child has the option of receiving either sacrament first, with the counsel of parents, priests and teachers. Programs in other dioceses are geared first to reception of Communion and later to reception of the sacrament of reconciliation.

Commentators on the letters note that: they are disciplinary rather than doctrinal in content; they are subject to pastoral interpretation by bishops; they cannot be interpreted to mean that a person who is not guilty of serious sin must be required to receive the sacrament of penance before (even first) Communion.

Canon 914 of the Code of Canon Law states that sacramental confession should precede first Communion.

Holy Communion under the Forms of Bread and Wine (by separate taking of the consecrated bread and wine or by intinction, the reception of the host dipped in the wine): Such reception is permitted under conditions stated in instructions issued by the Congregation for Divine Worship (May 25, 1967; June 29, 1970), the General Instruction on the Roman Missal (No. 242), and directives of bishops' conferences and individual bishops.

Accordingly, Communion can be administered in this way to: persons being baptized, received into communion with the Church, confirmed, receiving anointing of the sick; couples at their wedding or jubilee; religious at profession or renewal of profession; lay persons receiving an ecclesiastical assignment (e.g., lay missionaries); participants at concelebrated Masses, retreats, pastoral commission meetings, daily Masses and, in the U.S., Masses on Sundays and holy days of obligation.

A communicant has the option of receiving the Eucharist under the form of bread alone or under the forms of bread and wine. (See also **New U.S. Norms** in the **Liturgy** section.)

Holy Communion More Than Once a Day: A person who has already received the Eucharist may receive it (only) once again on the same day only during a Eucharistic celebration in which the person participates. A person in danger of death who has already received the Eucharist once or twice is urged to receive Communion again as Viaticum. Pope John Paul approved this decision, in accord with Canon 917, and ordered it published July 11, 1984.

Holy Communion and Eucharistic Devotion outside of Mass: These were the subjects of an instruction (*De Sacra Communione et de Cultu Mysterii Eucharistici extra Missam*) dated June 21 and made public Oct. 18, 1973, by the Congregation for Divine Worship.

Holy Communion can be given outside of Mass to persons unable for a reasonable cause to receive it during Mass on a given day. The ceremonial rite is modeled on the structure of the Mass, consisting of a penitential act, a scriptural reading, the Lord's Prayer, a sign or gesture of peace, giving of the Eucharist, prayer and final blessing. Viaticum and Communion to the sick can be given by extraordinary ministers (authorized lay persons) with appropriate rites.

Forms of devotion outside of Mass are exposition of the Blessed Sacrament (by men or women religious, especially, or lay persons in the absence of a priest; but only a priest can give the blessing), processions and congresses with appropriate rites.

Intercommunion: Church policy on intercommunion was stated in an "Instruction on the Admission of Other Christians to the Eucharist," dated June 1 and made public July 8, 1972, against the background of the Decree on Ecumenism approved by the Second Vatican Council, and the Directory on Ecumenism issued by the Secretariat for Promoting Christian Unity in 1967, 1970 and 1993.

Basic principles related to intercommunion are:
• "There is an indissoluble link between the mystery of the Church and the mystery of the Eucharist, or between ecclesial and Eucharistic communion; the celebration of the Eucharist of itself signifies the fullness of profession of faith and ecclesial communion" (1972 Instruction).
• "Eucharistic communion practiced by those who are not in full ecclesial communion with each other cannot be the expression of that full unity which the Eucharist of its nature signifies and which in this case does not exist; for this reason such communion cannot be regarded as a means to be used to lead to full ecclesial communion" (1972 Instruction).
• The question of reciprocity "arises only with those churches which have preserved the substance of the Eucharist, the sacrament of orders and apostolic succession" (1967 Directory).
• "A Catholic cannot ask for the Eucharist except from a minister who has been validly ordained" (1967 Directory).

The policy distinguishes between separated Eastern Christians and other Christians.

With Separated Eastern Christians (e.g., Orthodox): These may be given the Eucharist (as well as penance and anointing of the sick) at their request. Catholics may receive these same sacraments from priests of separated Eastern churches if they experience genuine spiritual necessity, seek spiritual benefit, and access to a Catholic priest is morally or physically impossible. This policy (of reciprocity) derives from the facts that the separated Eastern churches have apostolic succession through their bishops, valid priests, and sacramental beliefs and practices in accord with those of the Catholic Church.

With Other Christians (e.g., members of Reformation-related churches, others): Admission to the Eucharist in the Catholic Church, according to the Directory on Ecumenism, "is confined to particular cases of those Christians who have a faith in the sacrament in conformity with that of the Church, who

experience a serious spiritual need for the Eucharistic sustenance, who for a prolonged period are unable to have recourse to a minister of their own community and who ask for the sacrament of their own accord; all this provided that they have proper dispositions and lead lives worthy of a Christian." The spiritual need is defined as "a need for an increase in spiritual life and a need for a deeper involvement in the mystery of the Church and its unity."

Circumstances under which Communion may be given to other properly disposed Christians are danger of death, imprisonment, persecution, grave spiritual necessity coupled with no chance of recourse to a minister of their own community.

Catholics cannot ask for the Eucharist from ministers of other Christian churches who have not been validly ordained to the priesthood.

Penance

Penance is the sacrament by which sins committed after baptism are forgiven and a person is reconciled with God and the Church.

Individual and integral confession and absolution are the only ordinary means for the forgiveness of serious sin and for reconciliation with God and the Church.

(Other than ordinary means are perfect contrition and general absolution without prior confession, both of which require the intention of subsequent confession and absolution.)

A revised ritual for the sacrament — *Ordo Paenitentiae*, published by the Congregation of Divine Worship Feb. 7, 1974, and made mandatory in the U.S. from the first Sunday of Lent, 1977 — reiterates standard doctrine concerning the sacrament; emphasizes the social (communal and ecclesial) aspects of sin and conversion, with due regard for personal aspects and individual reception of the sacrament; prescribes three forms for celebration of the sacrament; and presents models for community penitential services.

The basic elements of the sacrament are sorrow for sin because of a supernatural motive, confession (of previously unconfessed mortal or grave sins, required; of venial sins also, but not of necessity), and reparation (by means of prayer or other act enjoined by the confessor), all of which comprise the matter of the sacrament; and absolution, which is the form of the sacrament.

The traditional words of absolution — *"I absolve you from your sins in the name of the Father, and of the Son, and of the Holy Spirit"* — remain unchanged at the conclusion of a petition in the new rite that God may grant pardon and peace through the ministry of the Church.

The minister of the sacrament is an authorized priest — i.e., one who, besides having the power of orders to forgive sins, also has faculties of jurisdiction granted by an ecclesiastical superior and/or by canon law.

The sacrament can be celebrated in three ways:
• For individuals, the traditional manner remains acceptable but is enriched with additional elements including: reception of the penitent and making of the Sign of the Cross; an exhortation by the confessor to trust in God; a reading from Scripture; confession of sins; manifestation of repentance; petition for

God's forgiveness through the ministry of the Church and the absolution of the priest; praise of God's mercy, and dismissal in peace. Some of these elements are optional.

• For several penitents, in the course of a community celebration including a Liturgy of the Word of God and prayers, individual confession and absolution, and an act of thanksgiving.

• For several penitents, in the course of a community celebration, with general confession and general absolution. In extraordinary cases, reconciliation may be attained by general absolution without prior individual confession as, for example, under these circumstances: (1) danger of death, when there is neither time nor priests available for hearing confessions; (2) grave necessity of a number of penitents who, because of a shortage of confessors, would be deprived of sacramental grace or Communion for a lengthy period of time through no fault of their own. Persons receiving general absolution are obliged to be properly disposed and resolved to make an individual confession of the grave sins from which they have been absolved; this confession should be made as soon as the opportunity to confess presents itself and before any second reception of general absolution.

Norms regarding general absolution, issued by the Congregation for the Doctrine of the Faith in 1972, are not intended to provide a basis for convoking large gatherings of the faithful for the purpose of imparting general absolution, in the absence of extraordinary circumstances. Judgment about circumstances that warrant general absolution belongs principally to the bishop of the place, with due regard for related decisions of appropriate episcopal conferences.

Communal celebrations of the sacrament are not held in connection with Mass.

The place of individual confession, as determined by episcopal conferences in accordance with given norms, can be the traditional confessional or another appropriate setting.

A precept of the Church obliges the faithful guilty of grave sin to confess at least once a year.

The Church favors more frequent reception of the sacrament not only for the reconciliation of persons guilty of serious sins but also for reasons of devotion. Devotional confession — in which venial sins or previously forgiven sins are confessed — serves the purpose of confirming persons in penance and conversion.

Penitential Celebrations: Communal penitential celebrations are designed to emphasize the social dimensions of Christian life — the community aspects and significance of penance and reconciliation.

Elements of such celebrations are community prayer, hymns and songs, scriptural and other readings, examination of conscience, general confession and expression of sorrow for sin, acts of penance and reconciliation, and a form of non-sacramental absolution resembling the one in the penitential rite of the Mass.

If the sacrament is celebrated during the service, there must be individual confession and absolution of sin.

(See **Absolution, Confession, Confessional, Confessor, Contrition, Faculties, Forgiveness of Sin, Power of the Keys, Seal of Confession, Sin.**)

(For details on the document *Misericordia Dei*, please see under **News in Depth**.)

Anointing of the Sick

This sacrament, promulgated by St. James the Apostle (Jas. 5:13-15), can be administered to the faithful after reaching the age of reason who begin to be in danger because of illness or old age. By the anointing with blessed oil and the prayer of a priest, the sacrament confers on the person comforting grace; the remission of venial sins and inculpably unconfessed mortal sins, together with at least some of the temporal punishment due for sins; and, sometimes, results in an improved state of health.

The matter of this sacrament is the anointing with blessed oil (of the sick — olive oil, or vegetable oil if necessary) of the forehead and hands; in cases of necessity, a single anointing of another portion of the body suffices. The form is: "Through this holy anointing and his most loving mercy, may the Lord assist you by the grace of the Holy Spirit so that, when you have been freed from your sins, he may save you and in his goodness raise you up."

Anointing of the sick, formerly called extreme unction, may be received more than once, e.g., in new or continuing stages of serious illness. Ideally, the sacrament should be administered while the recipient is conscious and in conjunction with the sacraments of penance and the Eucharist. It should be administered in cases of doubt as to whether the person has reached the age of reason, is dangerously ill or dead.

The sacrament can be administered during a communal celebration in some circumstances, as in a home for the aged.

Holy Orders

Order is the sacrament by which the mission given by Christ to the Apostles continues to be exercised in the Church until the end of time; it is the sacrament of apostolic mission. It has three grades: episcopacy, priesthood and diaconate. The sacrament confers a character on the soul and can be received only once. The minister of the sacrament is a bishop.

Order, like matrimony but in a different way, is a social sacrament. As the Second Vatican Council declared in *Lumen Gentium*, the Dogmatic Constitution on the Church:

"For the nurturing and constant growth of the People of God, Christ the Lord instituted in his Church a variety of ministries, which work for the good of the whole body. For those ministers who are endowed with sacred power are servants of their brethren, so that all who are of the People of God, and therefore enjoy a true Christian dignity, can work toward a common goal freely and in an orderly way, and arrive at salvation" (No. 18).

Bishop: The fullness of the priesthood belongs to those who have received the order of bishop. Bishops, in hierarchical union with the pope and their fellow bishops, are the successors of the Apostles as pastors of the Church: they have individual responsibility for the care of the local churches they serve and collegial responsibility for the care of the universal Church (see Collegiality). In the ordination or consecration of bishops, the essential form is the imposition of hands by the consecrator(s) and the assigned prayer in the preface of the rite of ordination.

"With their helpers, the priests and deacons, bishops have taken up the service of the community presiding in place of God over the flock whose shepherds they are, as teachers of doctrine, priests of sacred worship, and officers of good order" (No. 20).

Priests: A priest is an ordained minister with the power to celebrate Mass, administer the sacraments, preach and teach the word of God, impart blessings, and perform additional pastoral functions, according to the mandate of his ecclesiastical superior.

Concerning priests, the Second Vatican Council stated in *Lumen Gentium* (No. 28):

"The divinely established ecclesiastical ministry is exercised on different levels by those who from antiquity have been called bishops, priests, and deacons. Although priests do not possess the highest degree of the priesthood, and although they are dependent on the bishops in the exercise of their power, they are nevertheless united with the bishops in sacerdotal dignity. By the power of the sacrament of orders, and in the image of Christ the eternal High Priest (Heb. 5:1-10; 7:24; 9:11-28), they are consecrated to preach the Gospel, shepherd the faithful, and celebrate divine worship as true priests of the New Testament.

"Priests, prudent cooperators with the episcopal order as well as its aides and instruments, are called to serve the People of God. They constitute one priesthood with their bishop, although that priesthood is comprised of different functions."

In the ordination of a priest of Roman rite, the essential matter is the imposition of hands on the heads of those being ordained by the ordaining bishop. The essential form is the accompanying prayer in the preface of the ordination ceremony. Other elements in the rite are the presentation of the implements of sacrifice — the chalice containing the wine and the paten containing a host — with accompanying prayers.

Deacon: There are two kinds of deacons: those who receive the order and remain in it permanently, and those who receive the order while advancing to priesthood. The following quotation — from Vatican II's Dogmatic Constitution on the Church (*Lumen Gentium*, No. 29) — describes the nature and role of the diaconate, with emphasis on the permanent diaconate.

"At a lower level of the hierarchy are deacons, upon whom hands are imposed 'not unto the priesthood, but unto a ministry of service.' For strengthened by sacramental grace, in communion with the bishop and his group of priests, they serve the People of God in the ministry of the liturgy, of the word, and of charity. It is the duty of the deacon, to the extent that he has been authorized by competent authority, to administer baptism solemnly, to be custodian and dispenser of the Eucharist, to assist at and bless marriages in the name of the Church, to bring Viaticum to the dying, to read the sacred Scripture to the faithful, to instruct and exhort the people, to preside at the worship and prayer of the faithful, to administer sacramentals, and to officiate at funeral and burial services. (Deacons are) dedicated to duties of charity and administration.

"The diaconate can in the future be restored as a proper and permanent rank of the hierarchy. It pertains to the competent territorial bodies of bishops, of one kind or another, to decide, with the approval of the Supreme Pontiff, whether and where it is opportune for such deacons to be appointed for the care of souls. With the consent of the Roman Pontiff, this diaconate will be able to be conferred upon men of more mature age, even upon those living in the married state. It may also be conferred upon suitable young men. For them, however, the law of celibacy must remain intact" (No. 29).

The Apostles ordained the first seven deacons (Acts 6:1-6): Stephen, Philip, Prochorus, Nicanor, Timon, Parmenas, Nicholas.

Former Orders, Ministries: With the revision of the sacrament of order which began in 1971, the orders of subdeacon, acolyte, exorcist, lector and porter were abolished because they and their respective functions had fallen into disuse or did not require ordination. The Holy See started revision of the sacrament of order in 1971. In virtue of an indult of Oct. 5 of that year, the bishops of the United States were permitted to discontinue ordaining porters and exorcists. Another indult, dated three days later, permitted the use of revised rites for ordaining acolytes and lectors.

To complete the revision, Pope Paul VI abolished Sept. 14, 1972, the orders of porter, exorcist and subdeacon; decreed that laymen, as well as candidates for the diaconate and priesthood, can be installed (rather than ordained) in the ministries (rather than orders) of acolyte and lector; reconfirmed the suppression of tonsure and its replacement with a service of dedication to God and the Church; and stated that a man enters the clerical state on ordination to the diaconate.

The abolished orders were:

• Subdeacon, with specific duties in liturgical worship, especially at Mass. The order, whose first extant mention dates from about the middle of the third century, was regarded as minor until the 13th century; afterwards, it was called a major order in the West but not in the East.

• Acolyte, to serve in minor capacities in liturgical worship; a function now performed by Mass servers.

• Exorcist, to perform services of exorcism for expelling evil spirits; a function which came to be reserved to specially delegated priests.

• Lector, to read scriptural and other passages during liturgical worship; a function now generally performed by lay persons.

• Porter, to guard the entrance to an assembly of Christians and to ward off undesirables who tried to gain admittance; an order of early origin and utility but of present insignificance.

Permanent Diaconate

Restoration of the permanent diaconate in the Roman rite — making it possible for men to become deacons permanently, without going on to the priesthood — was promulgated by Pope Paul VI June 18, 1967, in a document entitled *Sacrum Diaconatus Ordinem* ("Sacred Order of the Diaconate").

The Pope's action implemented the desire expressed by the Second Vatican Council for reestablishment of the diaconate as an independent order in its own right not only to supply ministers for carrying on the work of the Church but also to complete the hierarchical structure of the Church of Roman rite.

Permanent deacons have been traditional in the Eastern Church. The Western Church, however, since the fourth or fifth century, generally followed the practice of conferring the diaconate only as a sacred order preliminary to the priesthood, and of restricting the ministry of deacons to liturgical functions.

The Pope's document, issued on his own initiative, provided:

• Qualified unmarried men 25 years of age or older may be ordained deacons. They cannot marry after ordination.

• Qualified married men 35 years of age or older may be ordained deacons. The consent of the wife of a prospective deacon is required. A married deacon cannot remarry after the death of his wife.

• Preparation for the diaconate includes a course of study and formation over a period of at least three years.

• Candidates who are not members of religious institutes must be affiliated with a diocese. Reestablishment of the diaconate among religious is reserved to the Holy See.

• Deacons will practice their ministry under the direction of a bishop and with the priests with whom they will be associated. (For functions, see also the description of deacon, under **Holy Orders**.)

Restoration of the permanent diaconate in the United States was approved by the Holy See in October 1968. Shortly afterwards the U.S. bishops established a committee for the permanent diaconate, which was chaired by Bishop Edward U. Kmiec of Nashville in 1997. The committee operates through a secretariat, with offices at 3211 Fourth St. N.E., Washington, DC 20017. Deacon John Pistone is executive director.

Status and Functions

The 2002 *Official Catholic Directory* reports that in the United States there were a total of 13,764 permanent deacons (the highest total by far for any single country), an increase of 416 from the previous year and an increase of 3,380 from 1992.

Training programs of spiritual, theological and pastoral formation are based on guidelines emanating from the National Conference of Catholic Bishops.

Deacons have various functions, depending on the nature of their assignments. Liturgically, they can officiate at baptisms, weddings, wake services and funerals, can preach and distribute Holy Communion. Some are engaged in religious education work. All are intended to carry out works of charity and pastoral service of one kind or another.

The majority of deacons, the majority of whom are married, continue in their secular work. Their ministry of service is developing in three dimensions: of liturgy, of the word, and of charity. Depending on the individual deacon's abilities and preference, he is assigned by his bishop to either a parochial ministry or to another field of service. Deacons are active in a variety of ministries including those to prison inmates and their families, the sick in hospitals, nursing homes and homes for the aged, alienated youth, the elderly and the poor, and in various areas of legal service to the indigent, of education and campus ministry.

National Association of Diaconate Directors: Membership organization of directors, vicars and other staff personnel of diaconate programs. Established in 1977 to promote effective communication and facilitate the exchange of information and resources of members; to develop professional expertise and promote research, training and self evaluation; to foster accountability and seek ways to promote means of implementing solutions to problems. The association is governed by an executive board of elected officers. Officers include Deacons: Maurice Reed of Green Bay, pres., 1997-98; Peter D'Heilly of St.Paul-Minneapolis, president-elect; Thomas Welch,

exec. dir. Office: 1337 W. Ohio St., Chicago, IL 60622.

Ordination of Women

The Catholic Church believes and teaches that, in fidelity to the will of Christ, it cannot ordain women to the priesthood. This position has been set out over the last quarter-century in a series of authoritative documents published by or with the authority of Pope Paul VI and Pope John Paul II.

The first of these, *Inter Insigniores* ("Among the Characteristics"), was issued by the Congregation for the Doctrine of the Faith in October 1976. Its central statement is: "The Sacred Congregation for the Doctrine of the Faith judges it necessary to recall that the Church, in fidelity to the example of the Lord, does not consider herself authorized to admit women to priestly ordination."

In support of this, the document cited the constant tradition of the Church, the fact that Christ called only men to be Apostles and the continuation of this practice by the Apostles themselves, and the sacramental appropriateness of a male priesthood acting *in persona Christi* — in the person of Christi.

Pope Paul reaffirmed the teaching set out in *Inter Insigniores* in an address the following year, calling it part of the Church's "fundamental constitution" as it is given by Christ.

In light of continuing discussion, Pope John Paul II returned to the subject in the apostolic letter *Ordinatio Sacerdotalis* ("Priestly Ordination"), issued May 29, 1994. He reaffirmed the position stated by Paul VI, and said the fact that the Blessed Virgin was not ordained a priest makes it clear that restricting ordination to men does not lessen the dignity of women or discriminate against them. Ordination is not a means of access to power, he pointed out; rather, the Church's hierarchical structure is entirely oriented to the "holiness of the faithful."

John Paul continued: "Wherefore, in order that all doubt may be removed regarding a matter of great importance, a matter which pertains to the Church's divine constitution itself, in virtue of my ministry of confirming the brethren (cf. Lk. 22.32) I declare that the Church has no authority whatsoever to confer priestly ordination on women and that this judgment is to be definitively held by all the Church's faithful."

The Congregation for the Doctrine of the Faith followed this on Oct. 28, 1995, with a response, published over the signature of its Prefect, Cardinal Joseph Ratzinger, to a bishop's inquiry concerning how "to be held definitively" should be understood. The response was:

"This teaching requires definitive assent, since, founded on the written Word of God and from the beginning constantly preserved and applied in the Tradition of the Church, it has been set forth infallibly by the ordinary and universal Magisterium (cf. Second Vatican Council, Dogmatic Constitution on the Church *Lumen Gentium*, 25, 2). Thus, in the present circumstances, the Roman Pontiff, exercising his proper office of confirming the brethren (cf. Lk. 22.32), has handed on this same teaching by a formal declaration, explicitly stating that it is to be held always, everywhere, and by all, as belonging to the deposit of faith."

Apparently it remains an open question at this time whether women could be ordained as deacons.

MATRIMONY

Coverage of the sacrament of matrimony is given in the following articles: **Marriage Doctrine**, *Humanae Vitae*, **Marriage Laws, Mixed Marriages**, and **Pastoral Ministry for Divorced and Remarried**.

Marriage Doctrine

The following excerpts, stating key points of doctrine on marriage, are from *Gaudium et Spes*, (Nos. 48 to 51) promulgated by the Second Vatican Council:

Conjugal Covenant

The intimate partnership of married life and love has been established by the Creator and qualified by his laws. It is rooted in the conjugal covenant of irrevocable personal consent.

God himself is the author of matrimony, endowed as it is with various benefits and purposes. All of these have a very decisive bearing on the continuation of the human race, on the personal development and eternal destiny of the individual members of a family, and on the dignity, stability, peace, and prosperity of the family itself and of human society as a whole. By their very nature, the institution of matrimony itself and conjugal love are ordained for the procreation and education of children, and find in them their ultimate crown.

Thus a man and a woman render mutual help and service to each other through an intimate union of their persons and of their actions. Through this union they experience the meaning of their oneness and attain to it with growing perfection day by day. As a mutual gift of two persons, this intimate union, as well as the good of the children, imposes total fidelity on the spouses and argues for an unbreakable oneness between them (No. 48).

Sacrament of Matrimony

Christ the Lord abundantly blessed this many-faceted love. The Savior of men and the Spouse of the Church comes into the lives of married Christians through the sacrament of matrimony. He abides with them thereafter so that, just as he loved the Church and handed himself over on her behalf, the spouses may love each other with perpetual fidelity through mutual self-bestowal.

Graced with the dignity and office of fatherhood and motherhood, parents will energetically acquit themselves of a duty which devolves primarily on them; namely, education, and especially religious education.

The Christian family, which springs from marriage as a reflection of the loving covenant uniting Christ with the Church, and as a participation in that covenant, will manifest to all men the Savior's living presence in the world, and the genuine nature of the Church (No. 48).

Conjugal Love

The biblical Word of God several times urges the betrothed and the married to nourish and develop their wedlock by pure conjugal love and undivided affection.

This love is an eminently human one since it is directed from one person to another through an affec-

tion of the will. It involves the good of the whole person. Therefore it can enrich the expressions of body and mind with a unique dignity, ennobling these expressions as special ingredients and signs of the friendship distinctive of marriage. This love the Lord has judged worthy of special gifts, healing, perfecting, and exalting gifts of grace and of charity.

Such love, merging the human with the divine, leads the spouses to a free and mutual gift of themselves, a gift proving itself by gentle affection and by deed. Such love pervades the whole of their lives. Indeed, by its generous activity it grows better and grows greater. Therefore it far excels mere erotic inclination, which, selfishly pursued, soon enough fades wretchedly away.

This love is uniquely expressed and perfected through the marital act. The actions within marriage by which the couple are united intimately and chastely are noble and worthy ones. Expressed in a manner which is truly human, these actions signify and promote that mutual self-giving by which spouses enrich each other with a joyful and a thankful will.

Sealed by mutual faithfulness and hallowed above all by Christ's sacrament, this love remains steadfastly true in body and in mind, in bright days or dark. It will never be profaned by adultery or divorce. Firmly established by the Lord, the unity of marriage will radiate from the equal personal dignity of wife and husband, a dignity acknowledged by mutual and total love.

The steady fulfillment of the duties of this Christian vocation demands notable virtue. For this reason, strengthened by grace for holiness of life, the couple will painstakingly cultivate and pray for constancy of love, largeheartedness, and the spirit of sacrifice (No. 49).

Fruitfulness of Marriage

Marriage and conjugal love are by their nature ordained toward the begetting and educating of children. Children are really the supreme gift of marriage and contribute very substantially to the welfare of their parents. God himself wished to share with man a certain special participation in his own creative work. Thus he blessed male and female, saying: "Increase and multiply" (Gn. 1:28).

Hence, while not making the other purposes of matrimony of less account, the true practice of conjugal love, and the whole meaning of the family life which results from it, have this aim: that the couple be ready with stout hearts to cooperate with the love of the Creator and the Savior, who through them will enlarge and enrich his own family day by day.

Parents should regard as their proper mission the task of transmitting human life and educating those to whom it has been transmitted. They should realize that they are thereby cooperators with the love of God the Creator, and are, so to speak, the interpreters of that love. Thus they will fulfill their task with human and Christian responsibility (No. 50).

Norms of Judgment

They will thoughtfully take into account both their own welfare and that of their children, those already born and those who may be foreseen. For this accounting they will reckon with both the material and the spiritual conditions of the times as well as of their state in life. Finally, they will consult the interests of the family group, of temporal society, and of the Church herself.

The parents themselves should ultimately make this judgment in the sight of God. But in their manner of acting, spouses should be aware that they cannot proceed arbitrarily. They must always be governed according to a conscience dutifully conformed to the divine law itself, and should be submissive toward the Church's teaching office, which authentically interprets that law in the light of the Gospel. That divine law reveals and protects the integral meaning of conjugal love, and impels it toward a truly human fulfillment.

Marriage, to be sure, is not instituted solely for procreation. Rather, its very nature as an unbreakable compact between persons, and the welfare of the children, both demand that the mutual love of the spouses, too, be embodied in a rightly ordered manner, that it grow and ripen. Therefore, marriage persists as a whole manner and communion of life, and maintains its value and indissolubility, even when offspring are lacking — despite, rather often, the very intense desire of the couple (No. 50).

Love and Life

This Council realizes that certain modern conditions often keep couples from arranging their married lives harmoniously, and that they find themselves in circumstances where at least temporarily the size of their families should not be increased. As a result, the faithful exercise of love and the full intimacy of their lives are hard to maintain. But where the intimacy of married life is broken off, it is not rare for its faithfulness to be imperiled and its quality of fruitfulness ruined. For then the upbringing of the children and the courage to accept new ones are both endangered.

To these problems there are those who presume to offer dishonorable solutions. Indeed, they do not recoil from the taking of life. But the Church issues the reminder that a true contradiction cannot exist between the divine laws pertaining to the transmission of life and those pertaining to the fostering of authentic conjugal love.

Church Teaching

For God, the Lord of Life, has conferred on men the surpassing ministry of safeguarding life — a ministry which must be fulfilled in a manner which is worthy of men. Therefore from the moment of its conception life must be guarded with the greatest care, while abortion and infanticide are unspeakable crimes. The sexual characteristics of man and the human faculty of reproduction wonderfully exceed the dispositions of lower forms of life. Hence the acts themselves which are proper to conjugal love and which are exercised in accord with genuine human dignity must be honored with great reverence (No. 51).

Therefore when there is question of harmonizing conjugal love with the responsible transmission of life, the moral aspect of any procedure does not depend solely on the sincere intentions or on an evaluation of motives. It must be determined by objective standards. These, based on the nature of the human person and his acts, preserve the full sense of mutual self-giving

and human procreation in the context of true love. Such a goal cannot be achieved unless the virtue of conjugal chastity is sincerely practiced. Relying on these principles, sons of the Church may not undertake methods of regulating procreation which are found blameworthy by the teaching authority of the Church in its unfolding of the divine law.

Everyone should be persuaded that human life and the task of transmitting it are not realities bound up with this world alone. Hence they cannot be measured or perceived only in terms of it, but always have a bearing on the eternal destiny of men (No. 51).

Humanae Vitae

Marriage doctrine and morality were the subjects of the encyclical letter *Humanae Vitae* ("Of Human Life"), issued by Pope Paul VI, July 29, 1968. *Humanae Vitae* was given reaffirmation and its teaching restated and defended by Pope John Paul II in his encyclical *Evangelium Vitae* (*The Gospel of Life*, 1995). Following are a number of key excerpts from *Humanae Vitae*, which was framed in the pattern of traditional teaching and statements by the Second Vatican Council.

Each and every marriage act ("*quilibet matrimonii usus*") must remain open to the transmission of life (No. 11).

Indeed, by its intimate structure, the conjugal act, while most closely uniting husband and wife, capacitates them for the generation of new lives according to laws inscribed in the very being of man and of woman. By safeguarding both these essential aspects, the unitive and the procreative, the conjugal act preserves in its fullness the sense of true mutual love and its ordination toward man's most high calling to parenthood (No. 12).

It is, in fact, justly observed that a conjugal act imposed upon one's partner without regard for his or her condition and lawful desires is not a true act of love, and therefore denies an exigency of right moral order in the relationships between husband and wife. Hence, one who reflects well must also recognize that a reciprocal act of love which jeopardizes the responsibility to transmit life — which God the Creator, according to particular laws, inserted therein — is in contradiction with the design constitutive of marriage and with the will of the Author of life. To use this divine gift, destroying, even if only partially, its meaning and its purpose, is to contradict the nature both of man and of woman and of their most intimate relationship, and therefore it is to contradict also the plan of God and his will (No. 13).

Forbidden Actions

The direct interruption of the generative process already begun, and, above all, directly willed and procured abortion, even if for therapeutic reasons, are to be absolutely excluded as licit means of regulating birth.

Equally to be excluded is direct sterilization, whether perpetual or temporary, whether of the man or of the woman. Similarly excluded is every action which, either in anticipation of the conjugal act, or in its accomplishment, or in the development of its natural consequences, proposes, whether as an end or as a means, to render procreation impossible.

To justify conjugal acts made intentionally infecund,

one cannot invoke as valid reasons the lesser evil, or the fact that such acts would constitute a whole together with the fecund acts already performed or to follow later and hence would share in one and the same moral goodness. In truth, if it is sometimes licit to tolerate a lesser evil in order to avoid a greater evil or to promote a greater good, it is not licit, even for the gravest reasons, to do evil so that good may follow therefrom; that is, to make into the object of a positive act of the will something which is intrinsically disorder, and hence unworthy of the human person, even when the intention is to safeguard or promote individual, family or social well-being.

Consequently, it is an error to think that a conjugal act which is deliberately made infecund, and so is intrinsically dishonest, could be made honest and right by the ensemble of a fecund conjugal life (No. 14).

If, then, there are serious motives to space out births, which derive from the physical or psychological conditions of husband and wife, or from external conditions, the Church teaches that it is then licit to take into account the natural rhythms immanent in the generative functions, for the use of marriage in the infecund periods only, and in this way to regulate birth without offending earlier stated principles (No. 16).

Pastoral Concerns

We do not at all intend to hide the sometimes serious difficulties inherent in the life of Christian married persons; for them, as for everyone else, "the gate is narrow and the way is hard that leads to life." But the hope of that life must illuminate their way, as with courage they strive to live with wisdom, justice and piety in this present time, knowing that the figure of this world passes away.

Let married couples then, face up to the efforts needed, supported by the faith and hope which "do not disappoint because God's love has been poured into our hearts through the Holy Spirit, who has been given to us." Let them implore divine assistance by persevering prayer; above all, let them draw from the source of grace and charity in the Eucharist. And, if sin should still keep its hold over them, let them not be discouraged but rather have recourse with humble perseverance to the mercy of God, which is poured forth in the sacrament of penance (No. 25).

Marriage Laws

The Catholic Church claims jurisdiction over its members in matters pertaining to marriage. which is a sacrament. Church legislation on the subject is stated principally in 111 canons of the Code of Canon Law.

Marriage laws of the Church provide juridical norms in support of the marriage covenant. In 10 chapters, the revised Code covers: pastoral directives for preparing men and women for marriage; impediments in general and in particular; matrimonial consent; form for the celebration of marriage; mixed marriages; secret celebration of marriage; effects of marriage; separation of spouses, and convalidation of marriage.

Catholics are bound by all marriage laws of the Church. Non-Catholics, whether baptized or not, are not considered bound by these ecclesiastical laws except in cases of marriage with a Catholic. Certain natural laws, in the Catholic view, bind all men and women, irrespective of their religious beliefs; accordingly, marriage is prohibited before the time of puberty, without knowledge and free mutual consent, in the case of an already existing valid marriage bond, in the case of antecedent and perpetual impotence.

Formalities

These include, in addition to arrangements for the time and place of the marriage ceremony, doctrinal and moral instruction concerning marriage and the recording of data which verifies in documentary form the eligibility and freedom of the persons to marry. Records of this kind, which are confidential, are preserved in the archives of the church where the marriage takes place.

Premarital instructions are the subject matter of Pre-Cana Conferences.

Marital Consent

Matrimonial consent can be invalidated by an essential defect, substantial error, the strong influence of force and fear, the presence of a condition or intention against the nature of marriage.

Form of Marriage

A Catholic is required, for validity and lawfulness, to contract marriage — with another Catholic or with a non-Catholic — in the presence of a competent priest or deacon and two witnesses.

There are two exceptions to this law. A Roman-rite Catholic (since Mar. 25, 1967) or an Eastern-rite Catholic (since Nov. 21, 1964) can contract marriage validly in the presence of a priest of a separated Eastern-rite Church, provided other requirements of law are complied with. With permission of the competent Roman-rite or Eastern-rite bishop, this form of marriage is lawful, as well as valid. (See **Eastern-rite Laws,** below.)

With these two exceptions, and aside from cases covered by special permission, the Church does not regard as valid any marriages involving Catholics which take place before non-Catholic ministers of religion or civil officials.

(An excommunication formerly in force against Catholics who celebrated marriage before a non-Catholic minister was abrogated in a decree issued by the Sacred Congregation for the Doctrine of the Faith on Mar. 18, 1966.)

The ordinary place of marriage is the parish of either Catholic party or of the Catholic party in case of a mixed marriage.

Church law regarding the form of marriage does not affect non-Catholics in marriages among themselves. The Church recognizes as valid the marriages of non-Catholics before ministers of religion and civil officials, unless they are rendered null and void on other grounds.

The canonical form is not to be observed in the case of a marriage between a non-Catholic and a baptized Catholic who has left the Church by a formal act.

Impediments

Diriment Impediments to marriage are factors which render a marriage invalid.

• Age, which obtains before completion of the 14th year for a woman and the 16th year for a man

• Impotency, if it is antecedent to the marriage and permanent (this differs from sterility, which is not an impediment)

• The bond of an existing valid marriage
• Disparity of worship, which obtains when one party is a Catholic and the other party is unbaptized
• Sacred orders
• Religious profession of the perpetual vow of chastity
• Abduction, which impedes the freedom of the person abducted
• Crime, variously involving elements of adultery, promise or attempt to marry, conspiracy to murder a husband or wife
• Blood relationship in the direct line (father-daughter, mother-son, etc.) and to the fourth degree inclusive of the collateral line (brother-sister, first cousins)
• Affinity, or relationship resulting from a valid marriage, in any degree of the direct line
•Public honesty, arising from an invalid marriage or from public or notorious concubinage; it renders either party incapable of marrying blood relatives of the other in the first degree of the direct line
• Legal relationship arising from adoption; it renders either party incapable of marrying relatives of the other in the direct line or in the second degree of the collateral line.

Dispensations from impediments: Persons hindered by impediments cannot marry unless they are dispensed therefrom in view of reasons recognized in canon law. Local bishops can dispense from the impediments most often encountered (e.g., disparity of worship) as well as others.

Decision regarding some dispensations is reserved to the Holy See.

Separation

A valid and consummated marriage of baptized persons cannot be dissolved by any human authority or any cause other than the death of one of the persons.

In other circumstances:

1. A valid but unconsummated marriage of baptized persons, or of a baptized and an unbaptized person, can be dissolved:

a. by the solemn religious profession of one of the persons, made with permission of the pope. In such a case, the bond is dissolved at the time of profession, and the other person is free to marry again.

b. by dispensation from the pope, requested for a grave reason by one or both of the persons. If the dispensation is granted, both persons are free to marry again.

Dispensations in these cases are granted for reasons connected with the spiritual welfare of the concerned persons.

2. A legitimate marriage, even consummated, of unbaptized persons can be dissolved in favor of one of them who subsequently receives the sacrament of baptism. This is the Pauline Privilege, so called because it was promulgated by St. Paul (1 Cor. 7:12-15) as a means of protecting the faith of converts. Requisites for granting the privilege are:

a. marriage prior to the baptism of either person;
b. reception of baptism by one person;
c. refusal of the unbaptized person to live in peace with the baptized person and without interfering with his or her freedom to practice the Christian faith. The privilege does not apply if the unbaptized person agrees to these conditions.

3. A legitimate and consummated marriage of a baptized and an unbaptized person can be dissolved by the pope in virtue of the Privilege of Faith, also called the Petrine Privilege.

Civil Divorce

Because of the unity and the indissolubility of marriage, the Church denies that civil divorce can break the bond of a valid marriage, whether the marriage involves two Catholics, a Catholic and a non-Catholic, or non-Catholics with each other.

In view of serious circumstances of marital distress, the Church permits an innocent and aggrieved party, whether wife or husband, to seek and obtain a civil divorce for the purpose of acquiring title and right to the civil effects of divorce, such as separate habitation and maintenance, and the custody of children. Permission for this kind of action should be obtained from proper church authority. The divorce, if obtained, does not break the bond of a valid marriage.

Under other circumstances — as would obtain if a marriage was invalid (see **Annulment**, below) — civil divorce is permitted for civil effects and as a civil ratification of the fact that the marriage bond really does not exist.

Annulment

This is a decision by a competent church authority — e.g., a bishop, a diocesan marriage tribunal, the Roman Rota — that an apparently valid marriage was actually invalid from the beginning because of the unknown or concealed existence, from the beginning, of a diriment impediment, an essential defect in consent, radical incapability for marriage, or a condition placed by one or both of the parties against the very nature of marriage.

Eastern-rite Laws

Marriage laws of the Eastern Church differ in several respects from the legislation of the Roman rite. The regulations in effect since May 2, 1949, were contained in the *motu proprio Crebre Allatae* issued by Pius XII the previous February.

According to both the Roman Code of Canon Law and the Oriental Code, marriages between Roman-rite Catholics and Eastern-rite Catholics ordinarily take place in the rite of the groom and have canonical effects in that rite.

Regarding the form for the celebration of marriages between Eastern Catholics and baptized Eastern non-Catholics, the Second Vatican Council declared:

"By way of preventing invalid marriages between Eastern Catholics and baptized Eastern non-Catholics, and in the interests of the permanence and sanctity of marriage and of domestic harmony, this sacred Synod decrees that the canonical 'form' for the celebration of such marriages obliges only for lawfulness. For their validity, the presence of a sacred minister suffices, as long as the other requirements of law are honored" (Decree on Eastern Catholic Churches, No. 18).

Marriages taking place in this manner are lawful, as well as valid, with permission of a competent Eastern-rite bishop.

The Rota

The Roman Rota is the ordinary court of appeal for

marriage, and some other cases, which are appealed to the Holy See from lower church courts. Appeals are made to the Rota if decisions by diocesan and archdiocesan courts fail to settle the matter in dispute. Pope John Paul II, at annual meetings with Rota personnel, speaks about the importance of the court's actions in providing norms of practice for other tribunals.

Mixed Marriages

"Mixed Marriages" (*Matrimonia Mixta*) was the subject of: a letter issued under this title by Pope Paul VI Mar. 31, 1970, and also a statement, "Implementation of the Apostolic Letter on Mixed Marriages," approved by the National Conference of Catholic Bishops Nov. 16, 1970.

One of the key points in the bishops' statement referred to the need for mutual pastoral care by ministers of different faiths for the sacredness of marriage and for appropriate preparation and continuing support of parties to a mixed marriage.

Pastoral experience, which the Catholic Church shares with other religious bodies, confirms the fact that marriages of persons of different beliefs involve special problems related to the continuing religious practice of the concerned persons and to the religious education and formation of their children.

Pastoral measures to minimize these problems include instruction of a non-Catholic party in essentials of the Catholic faith for purposes of understanding. Desirably, some instruction should also be given the Catholic party regarding his or her partner's beliefs.

Requirements

The Catholic party to a mixed marriage is required to declare his (her) intention of continuing practice of the Catholic faith and to promise to do all in his (her) power to share his (her) faith with children born of the marriage by having them baptized and raised as Catholics. No declarations or promises are required of the non-Catholic party, but he (she) must be informed of the declaration and promise made by the Catholic.

Notice of the Catholic's declaration and promise is an essential part of the application made to a bishop for permission to marry a baptized non-Catholic, or a dispensation to marry an unbaptized non-Catholic.

A mixed marriage can take place with a Nuptial Mass. (The bishops' statement added this caution: "To the extent that Eucharistic sharing is not permitted by the general discipline of the Church, this is to be considered when plans are being made to have the mixed marriage at Mass or not.")

The ordinary minister at a mixed marriage is an authorized priest or deacon, and the ordinary place is the parish church of the Catholic party. A non-Catholic minister may not only attend the marriage ceremony but may also address, pray with and bless the couple.

For appropriate pastoral reasons, a bishop can grant a dispensation from the Catholic form of marriage and can permit the marriage to take place in a non-Catholic church with a non-Catholic minister as the officiating minister. A priest may not only attend such a ceremony but may also address, pray with and bless the couple.

"It is not permitted," however, the bishops' statement declared, "to have two religious services or to have a single service in which both the Catholic marriage ritual and a non-Catholic marriage ritual are celebrated jointly or successively."

Pastoral Ministry for Divorced and Remarried

Ministry to divorced and remarried Catholics is a difficult field of pastoral endeavor, situated as it is in circumstances tantamount to the horns of a dilemma.

At Issue

On the one side is firm church teaching on the permanence of marriage and norms against reception of the Eucharist and full participation in the life of the Church by Catholics in irregular unions.

On the other side are men and women with broken unions followed by second and perhaps happier attempts at marriage which the Church does not recognize as valid and which may not be capable of being validated because of the existence of an earlier marriage bond.

Factors involved in these circumstances are those of the Church, upholding its doctrine and practice regarding the permanence of marriage, and those of many men and women in irregular second marriages who desire full participation in the life of the Church.

Sacramental participation is not possible for those whose first marriage was valid, although there is no bar to their attendance at Mass, to sharing in other activities of the Church, or to their efforts to have children baptized and raised in the Catholic faith.

An exception to this rule is the condition of a divorced and remarried couple living in a brother-sister relationship.

There is no ban against sacramental participation by separated or divorced persons who have not attempted a second marriage, provided the usual conditions for reception of the sacraments are in order.

Unverified estimates of the number of U.S. Catholics who are divorced and remarried vary between six and eight million.

Tribunal Action

What can the Church do for them and with them in pastoral ministry, is an old question charged with new urgency because of the rising number of divorced and remarried Catholics.

One way to help is through the agency of marriage tribunals charged with responsibility for investigating and settling questions concerning the validity or invalidity of a prior marriage. There are reasons in canon law justifying the Church in declaring a particular marriage null and void from the beginning, despite the short- or long-term existence of an apparently valid union.

Decrees of nullity (annulments) are not new in the history of the Church. If such a decree is issued, a man or woman is free to validate a second marriage and live in complete union with the Church.

The 2000 *Statistical Yearbook of the Church* (*Annuarium Statisticum Ecclesiae*, the most recent edition) reported that in 1999 U.S. tribunals issued 52,239 annulments (in ordinary and documentary processes). The canonical reasons were: invalid consent (39,298), impotence (161), other impediments (2,590), defect of form (11,190). Worldwide, 74,894 decrees or declarations of nullity were issued in 1999.

Reasons behind Decrees

Pastoral experience reveals that some married persons, a short or long time after contracting an apparently valid marriage, exhibit signs that point back to the existence, at the time of marriage, of latent and serious personal deficiencies which made them incapable of valid consent and sacramental commitment.

Such deficiencies might include gross immaturity and those affecting in a serious way the capacity to love, to have a true interpersonal and conjugal relationship, to fulfill marital obligations, to accept the faith aspect of marriage.

Psychological and behavioral factors like these have been given greater attention by tribunals in recent years and have provided grounds for numerous decrees of nullity.

Decisions of this type do not indicate any softening of the Church's attitude regarding the permanence of marriage. They affirm, rather, that some persons who have married were really not capable of doing so.

Serious deficiencies in the capacity for real interpersonal relationship in marriage were the reasons behind a landmark decree of nullity issued in 1973 by the Roman Rota, the Vatican high court of appeals in marriage cases. Pope John Paul referred to such deficiencies — the "grave lack of discretionary judgment," incapability of assuming "essential matrimonial rights and obligations," for example — in an address Jan. 26, 1984, to personnel of the Rota.

The tribunal way to a decree of nullity regarding a previous marriage, however, is not open to many persons in second marriages — because grounds are either lacking or, if present, cannot be verified in tribunal process.

Unacceptable Solutions

One unacceptable solution of the problem, called "good conscience procedure," involves administration of the sacraments of penance and the Eucharist to divorced and remarried Catholics unable to obtain a decree of nullity for a first marriage who are living in a subsequent marriage "in good faith."

This procedure, despite the fact that it has no standing or recognition in church law, is being advocated and practiced by some priests and remarried Catholics.

This issue was addressed by the Congregation for the Doctrine of the Faith in a letter to bishops dated Oct. 14, 1994, and published with the approval of Pope John Paul II. The letter said in part:

"Pastoral solutions in this area have been suggested according to which divorced-and-remarried members of the faithful could approach holy Communion in specific cases when they considered themselves authorized according to a judgment of conscience to do so. This would be the case, for example, when they had been abandoned completely unjustly although they sincerely tried to save the previous marriage; or when they are convinced of the nullity of their previous marriage although (they are) unable to demonstrate it in the external forum; or when they have gone through a long period of reflection and penance; or also when for morally valid reasons they cannot satisfy the obligation to separate.

"In some places it has also been proposed that, in order objectively to examine their actual situation, the divorced-and-remarried would have to consult a prudent and experienced priest. This priest, however, would have to respect their eventual decision in conscience to approach holy Communion, without this implying an official authorization.

"In these and similar cases, it would be a matter of a tolerant and benevolent pastoral solution in order to do justice to the different situations of the divorced-and-remarried.

"Even if analogous solutions have been proposed by a few fathers of the Church and in some measure were practiced, nevertheless these never attained the consensus of the fathers and in no way came to constitute the common doctrine of the Church nor to determine her discipline. It falls to the universal magisterium, in fidelity to sacred Scripture and tradition, to teach and to interpret authentically the deposit of faith."

Conditions for Receiving Communion

Practically speaking, "when for serious reasons — for example, for the children's upbringing — a man and a woman cannot satisfy the obligation to separate," they may be admitted to Communion if "they take on themselves the duty to live in complete continence, that is, by abstinence from the acts proper to married couples. In such a case they may receive holy Communion as long as they respect the obligation to avoid giving scandal."

The teaching of the Church on this subject "does not mean that the Church does not take to heart the situation of those faithful who, moreover, are not excluded from ecclesial communion. She is concerned to accompany them pastorally and invite them to share in the life of the Church in the measure that is compatible with the dispositions of divine law, from which the Church has no power to dispense. On the other hand, it is necessary to instruct these faithful so that they do not think their participation in the life of the Church is reduced exclusively to the question of the reception of the Eucharist. The faithful are to be helped to deepen their understanding of the value of sharing in the sacrifice of Christ in the Mass, or spiritual communion, of prayer, of meditation on the word of God, and of works of charity and justice."

The Communion of Saints

SAINTS OF THE CHURCH

Biographical sketches of additional saints and blesseds are found in other *Almanac* entries. See **Index**, under the name of each saint for the apostles, evangelists, Doctors of the Church, and Fathers of the Church. For beatification and canonization procedures, see those entries in the **Glossary**.

An asterisk with a feast date indicates that the saint is listed in the General Roman Calendar or the proper calendar for U.S. dioceses. For rank of observances, see listing in calendar for current year on preceding pages.

Adalbert (956-997): Born in Bohemia; bishop of Prague; Benedictine; missionary in Poland, Prussia and Hungary; martyred by Prussians near Danzig; Apr. 23.*

Adjutor (d. 1131): Norman knight; fought in First Crusade; monk-recluse after his return; Apr. 30.

Agatha (d. c. 250): Sicilian virgin-martyr; her intercession credited in Sicily with stilling eruptions of Mt. Etna; patron of nurses; Feb. 5.*

Agnes (d. c. 304): Roman virgin-martyr; martyred at age of 10 or 12; patron of young girls; Jan. 21.*

Aloysius Gonzaga (1568-1591): Italian Jesuit; died while nursing plague-stricken; canonized 1726; patron of youth; June 21.*

Amand (d. c. 676): Apostle of Belgium; b. France; established monasteries throughout Belgium; Feb. 6.

Andre Bessette, Bl. (Bro. Andre) (1845-1937): Canadian Holy Cross Brother; prime mover in building of St. Joseph's Oratory, Montreal; beatified May 23, 1982; Jan. 6* (U.S.).

Andre Grasset de Saint Sauveur, Bl. (1758-1792): Canadian priest; martyred in France, Sept. 2, 1792, during the Revolution; one of a group called the Martyrs of Paris who were beatified in 1926; Sept. 2.

Andrew Bobola (1592-1657): Polish Jesuit; joined Jesuits at Vilna; worked for return of Orthodox to union with Rome; martyred; canonized 1938; May 16.

Andrew Corsini (1302-1373): Italian Carmelite; bishop of Fiesoli; mediator between quarrelsome Italian states; canonized 1629; Feb. 4.

Andrew Dung-Lac and Companions (d. 18th-19th c.): Martyrs of Vietnam. Total of 117 included 96 Vietnamese, 11 Spanish and 10 French missionaries (8 bishops; 50 priests, including Andrew Dung-Lac; 1 seminarian, 58 lay persons). Canonized June 19, 1988; inscribed in General Roman Calendar, 1989, as a memorial. Nov. 24.*

Andrew Fournet (1752-1834): French priest; cofounder with St. Jeanne Elizabeth Bichier des Anges of the Daughters of the Holy Cross of St. Andrew; canonized 1933; May 13.

Andrew Kim, Paul Chong and Companions (d. between 1839-1867): Korean martyrs (103) killed in persecutions of 1839, 1846, 1866, and 1867; among them were Andrew Kim, the first Korean priest, and Paul Chong, lay apostle; canonized May 6, 1984, during Pope John Paul II's visit to Korea. Sept. 20.*

Angela Merici (1474-1540): Italian secular Franciscan; foundress of Company of St. Ursula, 1535, the first teaching order of women Religious in the Church; canonized 1807; Jan. 27.*

Angelico, Bl. (Fra Angelico; John of Faesulis) (1387-1455): Dominican; Florentine painter of early Renaissance; proclaimed blessed by John Paul II, Feb. 3, 1982; patron of artists; Feb. 18.

Anne Marie Javouhey, Bl. (1779-1851): French virgin; foundress of Institute of St. Joseph of Cluny, 1812; beatified 1950; July 15.

Ansgar (801-865): Benedictine monk; b. near Amiens; archbishop of Hamburg; missionary in Denmark, Sweden, Norway and northern Germany; apostle of Scandinavia; Feb. 3.*

Anthony (c. 251-c. 354): Abbot; Egyptian hermit; patriarch of all monks; established communities for hermits which became models for monastic life, especially in the East; friend and supporter of St. Athanasius in the latter's struggle with the Arias; Jan. 17.*

Anthony Claret (1807-1870): Spanish bishop; founder of Missionary Sons of the Immaculate Heart of Mary (Claretians), 1849; archbishop of Santiago, Cuba, 1851-57; canonized 1950; Oct. 24.*

Anthony Gianelli (1789-1846): Italian bishop; founded the Daughters of Our Lady of the Garden, 1829; bishop of Bobbio, 1838; canonized 1951; June 7.

Anthony Zaccaria (1502-1539): Italian priest; founder of Barnabites (Clerks Regular of St. Paul), 1530; canonized 1897; July 5.*

Apollonia (d. 249): Deaconess of Alexandria; martyred during persecution of Decius; her patronage of dentists and those suffering from toothaches probably rests on tradition that her teeth were broken by her persecutors; Feb. 9.

Augustine of Canterbury (d. 604 or 605): Italian missionary; apostle of the English; sent by Pope Gregory I with 40 monks to evangelize England; arrived there 597; first archbishop of Canterbury; May 27.*

Bartolomea Capitania (1807-1833): Italian

foundress with Vincenza Gerosa of the Sisters of Charity of Lovere; canonized 1950; July 26.

Beatrice da Silva Meneses (1424-1490): Foundress, b. Portugal; founded Congregation of the Immaculate Conception, 1484, in Spain; canonized 1976; Sept. 1.

Benedict Joseph Labré (1748-1783): French layman; pilgrim-beggar; noted for his piety and love of prayer before the Blessed Sacrament; canonized 1883; Apr. 16.

Benedict of Nursia (c. 480-547): Abbot; founder of monasticism in Western Europe; established monastery at Monte Cassino; proclaimed patron of Europe by Paul VI in 1964; July 11.*

Benedict the Black *(il Moro)* (1526-1589): Sicilian Franciscan; born a slave; joined Franciscans as lay brother; appointed guardian and novice master; canonized 1807; Apr. 3.

Bernadette Soubirous (1844-1879): French peasant girl favored with series of visions of Blessed Virgin Mary at Lourdes (see Lourdes Apparitions); joined Institute of Sisters of Notre Dame at Nevers, 1866; canonized 1933; Apr. 16.

Bernard of Montjoux (or Menthon) (d. 1081): Augustinian canon; probably born in Italy; founded Alpine hospices near the two passes named for him; patron of mountaineers; May 28.

Bernardine of Feltre, Bl. (1439-1494): Italian Franciscan preacher; a founder of *montes pietatis*; Sept. 28.

Bernardine of Siena (1380-1444): Italian Franciscan; noted preacher and missioner; spread of devotion to Holy Name is attributed to him; represented in art holding to his breast the monogram IHS; canonized 1450; May 20.*

Blase (d. c. 316): Armenian bishop; martyr; the blessing of throats on his feast day derives from tradition that he miraculously saved the life of a boy who had half-swallowed a fish bone; Feb. 3.*

Boniface (Winfrid) (d. 754): English Benedictine; bishop; martyr; apostle of Germany; established monastery at Fulda which became center of missionary work in Germany; archbishop of Mainz; martyred near Dukkum in Holland; June 5.*

Brendan (c. 489-583): Irish abbot; founded monasteries; his patronage of sailors probably rests on a legend that he made a seven-year voyage in search of a fabled paradise; called Brendan the Navigator; May 16.

Bridget (Brigid) (c. 450-525): Irish nun; founded religious community at Kildare, the first in Ireland; patron, with Sts. Patrick and Columba, of Ireland; Feb. 1.

Bridget (Birgitta) (c. 1303-1373): Swedish mystic; widow; foundress of Order of Our Savior (Brigittines); canonized 1391; patroness of Sweden; July 23.*

Bruno (1030-1101): German monk; founded Carthusians, 1084, in France; Oct. 6.*

Bridget (Birgitta) (c. 1303-1373): Swedish mystic; widow; foundress of Order of Our Savior (Brigittines); canonized 1391; patroness of Sweden; named a co-patroness of Europe, with St. Edith Stein and St. Catherine of Siena, on Oct. 1, 1999; July 23.*

Cabrini, Mother: See **Frances Xavier Cabrini**.

Cajetan (Gaetano) **of Thiene** (1480-1547): Italian lawyer; religious reformer; a founder of Oratory of Divine Love, forerunner of the Theatines; canonized 1671; Aug. 7.*

Callistus I (d. 222): Pope, 217-222; martyr; condemned Sabellianism and other heresies; advocated a policy of mercy toward repentant sinners; Oct. 14.*

Camillus de Lellis (1550-1614): Italian priest; founder of Camillians (Ministers of the Sick); canonized 1746; patron of the sick and of nurses; July 14.*

Casimir (1458-1484): Polish prince; grand duke of Lithuania; noted for his piety; buried at cathedral in Vilna, Lithuania; canonized 1521; patron of Poland and Lithuania; Mar. 4.*

Cassian of Tangier (d. 298): Roman martyr; an official court stenographer who declared himself a Christian; patron of stenographers; Dec. 3.

Catherine Labouré (1806-1876): French Religious; favored with series of visions soon after she joined Sisters of Charity of St. Vincent de Paul in Paris in 1830; first Miraculous Medal (see Index) struck in 1832 in accord with one of the visions; canonized 1947; Nov. 28.

Catherine of Bologna (1413-1463): Italian Poor Clare; mystic, writer, artist canonized 1712; patron of artists; May 9.

Cecilia (2nd-3rd century): Roman virgin-martyr; traditional patroness of musicians; Nov. 22.*

Charles Borromeo (1538-1584): Italian cardinal; nephew of Pope Pius IV; cardinal bishop of Milan; influential figure in Church reform in Italy; promoted education of clergy; canonized 1610; Nov. 4.*

Charles Lwanga and Companions (d. between 1885 and 1887): Twenty-two Martyrs of Uganda, many of them pages of King Mwanga of Uganda, who were put to death because they denounced his corrupt lifestyle; canonized 1964; first martyrs of black Africa; June 3.*

Charles of Sezze (1616-1670): Italian Franciscan lay brother who served in humble capacities; canonized 1959; Jan. 6.

Christopher (3rd cent.): Early Christian martyr inscribed in Roman calendar about 1550; feast relegated to particular calendars because of legendary nature of accounts of his life; traditional patron of travelers; July 25.

Clare (1194-1253): Foundress of Poor Clares; b. at Assisi; was joined in religious life by her sisters, Agnes and Beatrice, and eventually her widowed mother Ortolana; canonized 1255; patroness of television; Aug. 11.*

Claude de la Colombiere (1641-1682): French Jesuit; spiritual director of St. Margaret Mary Alacoque; instrumental in spreading devotion to the Sacred Heart; beatified, 1929; canonized May 31, 1992; Feb. 15.

Clement Hofbauer (1751-1820): Redemptorist priest, missionary; born in Moravia; helped spread Redemptorists north of the Alps; canonized 1909; Mar. 15.

Clement I (d. c. 100): Pope, 88-97; third successor of St. Peter; wrote important letter to Church in Corinth settling disputes there; venerated as a martyr; Nov. 23.*

Columba (521-597): Irish monk; founded monasteries in Ireland; missionary in Scotland; established monastery at Iona which became the center for conversion of Picts, Scots, and Northern English;

Scotland's most famous saint; patron saint of Ireland (with Sts. Patrick and Brigid); June 9.

Columban (545-615): Irish monk; scholar; founded monasteries in England and Brittany (famous abbey of Luxeuil), forced into exile because of his criticism of Frankish court; spent last years in northern Italy where he founded abbey at Bobbio; Nov. 23.*

Conrad of Parzham (1818-1894): Bavarian Capuchin lay brother; served as porter at the Marian shrine of Altotting in Upper Bavaria for 40 years; canonized 1934; Apr. 21.

Contardo Ferrini, Bl. (1859-1902): Italian secular Franciscan; model of the Catholic professor; beatified 1947; patron of universities; Oct. 20.

Cornelius (d. 253): Pope, 251-253; promoted a policy of mercy with respect to readmission of repentant Christians who had fallen away during the persecution of Decius (*lapsi*); banished from Rome during persecution of Gallus; regarded as a martyr; Sept. 16 (with Cyprian).*

Cosmas and Damian (d. c. 303): Arabian twin brothers, physicians; martyred during Diocletian persecution; patrons of physicians; Sept. 26.*

Crispin and Crispinian (3rd cent.): Early Christian martyrs; said to have met their deaths in Gaul; patrons of shoemakers, a trade they pursued; Oct. 25.

Crispin of Viterbo (1668-1750): Capuchin brother; canonized June 20, 1982; May 21.

Cyprian (d. 258): Early ecclesiastical writer; b. Africa; bishop of Carthage, 249-258; supported Pope St. Cornelius concerning the readmission of Christians who had apostatized in time of persecution; erred in his teaching that baptism administered by heretics and schismatics was invalid; wrote *De Unitate*; Sept. 16 (with St. Cornelius).*

Cyril and Methodius (9th century): Greek missionaries, bothers; venerated as apostles of the Slavs; Cyril (d. 869) and Methodius (d. 885) began their missionary work in Moravia in 863; developed a Slavonic alphabet; used the vernacular in the liturgy, a practice that was eventually approved; declared patrons of Europe with St. Benedict, Dec. 31, 1980; Feb. 14.*

Damasus I (d. 384): Pope, 366-384; opposed Arians and Apollinarians; commissioned St. Jerome to work on Bible translation; developed Roman liturgy; Dec. 11.*

Damian: See **Cosmas and Damian.**

Damien of Molokai (d. 1889): The so-called leper priest of Molokai; originally from Belgium, Damien devoted over twenty years to the care of the lepers in Hawaii, ultimately dying from the same disease. He was beatified by Pope John Paul II in 1996.

David (5th or 6th cent.): Nothing for certain known of his life; said to have founded monastery at Menevia; patron saint of Wales; Mar. 1.

Denis and Companions (d. 3rd cent.): Denis, bishop of Paris, and two companions identified by early writers as Rusticus, a priest, and Eleutherius, a deacon; martyred near Paris; Denis is popularly regarded as the apostle and a patron saint of France; Oct. 9.*

Dismas (1st cent.): Name given to repentant thief (Good Thief) to whom Jesus promised salvation (Lk. 23:40-43); regarded as patron of prisoners; Mar. 25 (observed on second Sunday of October in U.S. prison chapels).

Dominic (Dominic de Guzman) (1170-1221): Spanish priest; founded the Order of Preachers (Domini-

cans), 1215, in France; preached against the Albigensian heresy; a contemporary of St. Francis of Assisi; canonized 1234; Aug. 8.*

Dominic Savio (1842-1857): Italian youth; pupil of St. John Bosco; died before his 15th birthday; canonized 1954; patron of choir boys; May 6.

Duns Scotus, John (d. 1308): Scottish Franciscan; theologian; advanced theological arguments for doctrine of the Immaculate Conception; proclaimed blessed; cult solemnly confirmed by John Paul II, Mar. 20, 1993; Nov. 8.

Dunstan (c. 910-988): English monk; archbishop of Canterbury; initiated reforms in religious life; counselor to several kings; considered one of greatest Anglo-Saxon saints; patron of goldsmiths, locksmiths, jewelers (trades in which he is said to have excelled); May 19.

Dymphna (dates unknown): Nothing certain known of her life; according to legend, she was an Irish maiden murdered by her heathen father at Gheel near Antwerp, Belgium, where she had fled to escape his advances; her relics were discovered there in the 13th century; since that time cures of mental illness and epilepsy have been attributed to her intercession; patron of those suffering from mental illness; May 15.

Edith Stein, St. (1891-1942): German Carmelite (Teresa Benedicta of the Cross); born of Jewish parents; author and lecturer; baptized in Catholic Church, 1922; arrested with her sister Rosa in 1942 and put to death at Auschwitz; beatified 1987, by Pope John Paul II during his visit to West Germany. She was canonized by Pope John Paul II on Oct. 11, 1998 and named a co-patroness of Europe, with St. Bridget of Sweden and St. Catherine of Siena, on Oct. 1, 1999. Aug. 10.

Edmund Campion (1540-1581): English Jesuit; convert 1573; martyred at Tyburn; canonized 1970, one of the Forty English and Welsh Martyrs; Dec. 1.

Edward the Confessor (d. 1066): King of England, 1042-66; canonized 1161; Oct. 13.

Eligius (c. 590-660): Bishop; born in Gaul; founded monasteries and convents; bishop of Noyon and Tournai; famous worker in gold and silver; Dec. 1.

Elizabeth Ann Seton (1774-1821): American foundress; convert, 1805; founded Sisters of Charity in the U.S.; beatified 1963; canonized Sept. 14, 1975; the first American-born saint; Jan. 4 (U.S.).*

Elizabeth of Hungary (1207-1231): Became secular Franciscan after death of her husband in 1227; devoted life to poor and destitute; a patron of the Secular Franciscan Order; canonized 1235; Nov. 17.*

Elizabeth of Portugal (1271-1336): Queen of Portugal; b. Spain; retired to Poor Clare convent as a secular Franciscan after the death of her husband; canonized 1626; July 4.*

Emily de Rodat (1787-1852): French foundress of the Congregation of the Holy Family of Villefranche; canonized 1950; Sept. 19.

Emily de Vialar (1797-1856): French foundress of the Sisters of St. Joseph of the Apparition; canonized 1951; June 17.

Erasmus (Elmo) (d. 303): Life surrounded by legend; martyred during Diocletian persecution; patron of sailors; June 2.

Ethelbert (552-616): King of Kent, England; baptized by St. Augustine of Canterbury, 597; issued legal code; furthered spread of Christianity; Feb. 26.

Eusebius of Vercelli (283-370): Italian bishop; exiled from his see (Vercelli) for a time because of his opposition to Arianism; considered a martyr because of sufferings he endured; Aug. 2.*

Fabian (d. 250): Pope, 236-250; martyred under Decius; Jan. 20.*

Felicity: See **Perpetua and Felicity**.

Ferdinand III (1198-1252): King of Castile and Leon; waged successful crusade against Muhammadans in Spain; founded university at Salamanca; canonized 1671; May 30.

Fiacre (Fiachra) (d. c. 670): Irish hermit; patron of gardeners; Aug. 30.

Fidelis of Sigmaringen (Mark Rey) (1577-1622): German Capuchin; lawyer before he joined the Capuchins; missionary to Swiss Protestants; stabbed to death by peasants who were told he was agent of Austrian emperor; Apr. 24.*

Frances of Rome (1384-1440): Italian model for housewives and widows; happily married for 40 years; after death of her husband in 1436 joined community of Benedictine Oblates she had founded; canonized 1608; patron of motorists; Mar. 9.*

Frances Xavier Cabrini (Mother Cabrini) (1850-1917): American foundress; b. Italy; founded the Missionary Sisters of the Sacred Heart, 1877; settled in the U.S. 1889; became an American citizen at Seattle 1909; worked among Italian immigrants; canonized 1946, the first American citizen so honored; Nov. 13 (U.S.).*

Francis Borgia (1510-1572): Spanish Jesuit; joined Jesuits after death of his wife in 1546; became general of the Order, 1565; Oct. 10.

Francis Caracciolo (1563-1608): Italian priest; founder with Father Augustine Adorno of the Clerics Regular Minor (Adorno Fathers); canonized 1807; declared patron of Italian chefs, 1996; June 4.

Francis Fasani (1681-1742): Italian Conventual Franciscan; model of priestly ministry, especially in service to poor and imprisoned; canonized 1986; Nov. 27.

Francis of Assisi (Giovanni di Bernardone) (1181/82-1226): Founder of the Franciscans, 1209; received stigmata 1224; canonized 1228; one of best known and best loved saints; patron of Italy, Catholic Action and ecologists; Oct. 4.*

Francis of Paola (1416-1507): Italian hermit: founder of Minim Friars; Apr. 2.*

Francis Xavier (1506-1552): Spanish Jesuit; missionary to Far East; canonized 1602; patron of foreign missions; considered one of greatest Christian missionaries; Dec. 3.*

Francis Xavier Bianchi (1743-1815): Italian Barnabite; acclaimed apostle of Naples because of his work there among the poor and abandoned; canonized 1951; Jan. 31.

Gabriel of the Sorrowful Mother (Francis Possenti) (1838-1862): Italian Passionist; died while a scholastic; canonized 1920; Feb. 27.

Gaspar (Caspar) **del Bufalo** (1786-1836): Italian priest; founded Missionaries of the Precious Blood, 1815; canonized 1954; Jan. 2.

Gemma Galgani (1878-1903): Italian laywoman; visionary; subject of extraordinary religious experiences; canonized 1940; Apr. 11.

Genesius (d. c. 300): Roman actor; according to legend, was converted while performing a burlesque of Christian baptism and was subsequently martyred; patron of actors; Aug. 25.

Geneviève (422-500): French nun; a patroness and protectress of Paris; events of her life not authenticated; Jan. 3.

George (d. c. 300): Martyr, probably during Diocletian persecution in Palestine; all other incidents of his life, including story of the dragon, are legendary; patron of England; Apr. 23.*

Gerard Majella (1725-1755): Italian Redemptorist lay brother; noted for supernatural occurrences in his life including bilocation and reading of consciences; canonized 1904; patron of mothers; Oct. 16.

Gertrude (1256-1302): German mystic; writer; helped spread devotion to the Sacred Heart; Nov. 16.*

Gregory VII (Hildebrand) (1020?-1085): Pope, 1075-1085; Benedictine monk; adviser to several popes; as pope, strengthened interior life of Church and fought against lay investiture; driven from Rome by Henry IV; died in exile; canonized 1584; May 25.*

Gregory Barbarigo (1626-1697): Italian cardinal; noted for his efforts to bring about reunion of separated Christians; canonized 1960; June 18.

Gregory of Nyssa (c. 335-395): Bishop; theologian; younger brother of St. Basil the Great; Mar. 9.

Gregory Thaumaturgus (c. 213-268): Bishop of Neocaesarea; missionary, famed as wonder worker; Nov. 17.

Gregory the Illuminator (257-332): Martyr; bishop; apostle and patron saint of Armenia; helped free Armenia from the Persians; Sept. 30.

Hedwig (1174-1243): Moravian noblewoman; married duke of Silesia, head of Polish royal family; fostered religious life in country; canonized 1266; Oct. 16.*

Helena (250-330): Empress; mother of Constantine the Great; associated with discovery of the True Cross; Aug. 18.

Henry (972-1024): Bavarian emperor; cooperated with Benedictine abbeys in restoration of ecclesiastical and social discipline; canonized 1146; July 13.*

Herman Joseph (1150-1241): German Premonstratensian; his visions were the subjects of artists; writer; cult approved, 1958; Apr. 7.

Hippolytus (d. c. 236): Roman priest; opposed Pope St. Callistus I in his teaching about the readmission to the Church of repentant Christians who had apostatized during time of persecution; elected antipope; exiled to Sardinia; reconciled before his martyrdom; important ecclesiastical writer; Aug. 13* (with Pontian).

Hugh of Cluny (the Great) (1024-1109): Abbot of Benedictine foundation at Cluny; supported popes in efforts to reform ecclesiastical abuses; canonized 1120; Apr. 29.

Ignatius of Antioch (d. c. 107): Early ecclesiastical writer; martyr; bishop of Antioch in Syria for 40 years; Oct. 17.*

Ignatius of Laconi (1701-1781): Italian Capuchin lay brother whose 60 years of religious life were spent in Franciscan simplicity; canonized 1951; May 11.

Ignatius of Loyola (1491-1556): Spanish soldier; renounced military career after recovering from wounds received at siege of Pampeluna (Pamplona) in 1521; founded Society of Jesus (Jesuits), 1534, at Paris; wrote The Book of Spiritual Exercises; canonized 1622; July 31.*

Irenaeus of Lyons (130-202): Early ecclesiastical writer; opposed Gnosticism; bishop of Lyons; traditionally regarded as a martyr; June 28.*

Isidore the Farmer (d. 1170): Spanish layman; farmer; canonized 1622; patron of farmers; May 15 (U.S.).*

Jane Frances de Chantal (1572-1641): French widow; foundress, under guidance of St. Francis de Sales, of Order of the Visitation; canonized 1767; Dec. 12* (General Roman Calendar); Aug. 18* (U.S.).

Januarius (Gennaro) (d. 304): Bishop of Benevento; martyred during Diocletian persecution; fame rests on liquefaction of some of his blood preserved in a phial at Naples, an unexplained phenomenon which has occurred regularly several times each year for over 400 years; Sept. 19.*

Jeanne Delanoue (1666-1736): French foundress of Sisters of St. Anne of Providence, 1704; canonized 1982; Aug. 16.

Jeanne (Joan) **de Lestonnac** (1556-1640): French foundress; widowed in 1597; founded the Religious of Notre Dame 1607; canonized 1947; Feb. 2.

Jeanne de Valois (Jeanne of France) (1464-1505): French foundress; deformed daughter of King Louis XI; was married in 1476 to Duke Louis of Orleans who had the marriage annulled when he ascended the throne as Louis XII; Jeanne retired to life of prayer; founded contemplative Annonciades of Bourges, 1504; canonized 1950; Feb. 5.

Jeanne-Elizabeth Bichier des Ages (1773-1838): French Religious; co-founder with St. Andrew Fournet of Daughters of the Cross of St. Andrew, 1807; canonized 1947; Aug. 26.

Jeanne Jugan, Bl. (1792-1879): French Religious; foundress of Little Sisters of the Poor; beatified Oct. 3, 1982; Aug. 30.

Jerome Emiliani (1481-1537): Venetian priest; founded Somascan Fathers, 1532, for care of orphans; canonized 1767; patron of orphans and abandoned children; Feb. 8.*

Joan Antida Thouret (1765-1826): French Religious; founded, 1799, congregation now known as Sisters of Charity of St. Joan Antida; canonized 1934; Aug. 24.

Joan of Arc (1412-1431): French heroine, called The Maid of Orleans, La Pucelle; led French army in 1429 against English invaders besieging Orleans; captured by Burgundians the following year; turned over to ecclesiastical court on charge of heresy, found guilty and burned at the stake; her innocence was declared in 1456; canonized 1920; patroness of France; May 30.

Joaquina de Vedruna de Mas (1783-1854): Spanish foundress; widowed in 1816; after providing for her children, founded the Carmelite Sisters of Charity; canonized 1959; Aug. 28.

John I (d. 526): Pope, 523-526; martyr; May 18.*

John XXIII, Bl.: see under **Popes of the Twentieth Century** in **Papacy and the Holy See**.

John Baptist de la Salle (1651-1719): French priest; founder of Brothers of the Christian Schools, 1680; canonized 1900; patron of teachers; Apr. 7.*

John Berchmans (1599-1621): Belgian Jesuit scholastic; patron of Mass servers; canonized 1888; Aug. 13.

John (Don) Bosco (1815-1888): Italian priest; founded Salesians, 1859, for education of boys; co-founder of Daughters of Mary Help of Christians for education of girls; canonized 1934; Jan. 31.*

John Capistran (1386-1456): Italian Franciscan; preacher; papal diplomat; canonized 1690; declared patron of military chaplains, Feb. 10, 1984. Oct. 23.*

John de Ribera (1532-1611): Spanish bishop and statesman; archbishop of Valencia, 1568-1611, and viceroy of that province; canonized 1960; Jan. 6.

John Eudes (1601-1680): French priest; founder of Sisters of Our Lady of Charity of Refuge, 1642, and Congregation of Jesus-Mary (Eudists), 1643; canonized 1925; Aug. 19.*

John Fisher (1469-1535): English prelate; theologian; martyr; bishop of Rochester, cardinal; refused to recognize validity of Henry VIII's marriage to Anne Boleyn; upheld supremacy of the pope; beheaded for refusing to acknowledge Henry as head of the Church; canonized 1935; June 22 (with St. Thomas More).*

John Francis Regis (1597-1640): French Jesuit priest; preached missions among poor and unlettered; canonized 1737; patron of social workers, particularly medical social workers, because of his concern for poor and needy and sick in hospitals; July 2.

John Gualbert (d. 1073): Italian priest; founder of Benedictine congregation of Vallombrosians, 1039; canonized 1193; July 12.

John Kanty (Cantius) (1395-1473): Polish theologian; canonized 1767; Dec. 23.*

John Leonardi (1550-1609): Italian priest; worked among prisoners and the sick; founded Clerics Regular of the Mother of God; canonized 1938; Oct. 9.*

John Nepomucene (1345-1393): Bohemian priest; regarded as a martyr; canonized 1729; patron of Czechoslovakia; May 16.

John Nepomucene Neumann (1811-1860): American prelate; b. Bohemia; ordained in New York 1836; missionary among Germans near Niagara Falls before joining Redemptorists, 1840; bishop of Philadelphia, 1852; first bishop in U.S. to prescribe Forty Hours devotion in his diocese; beatified 1963; canonized June 19, 1977; Jan. 5 (U.S.).*

John of Ávila (1499-1569): Spanish priest; preacher; ascetical writer; spiritual adviser of St. Teresa of Jesus (Ávila); canonized 1970; May 10.

John of Britto (1647-1693): Portuguese Jesuit; missionary in India where he was martyred; canonized 1947; Feb. 4.

John of God (1495-1550): Portuguese founder; his work among the sick poor led to foundation of Brothers Hospitallers of St. John of God, 1540, in Spain; canonized 1690; patron of sick, nurses, hospitals; Mar. 8.*

John of Matha (1160-1213): French priest; founder of the Order of Most Holy Trinity, whose original purpose was the ransom of prisoners from the Muslims; Feb. 8.

John Ogilvie (1579-1615): Scottish Jesuit; martyr; canonized 1976, the first canonized Scottish saint since 1250 (Margaret of Scotland); Mar. 10.

John Vianney (Curé of Ars) (1786-1859): French parish priest; noted confessor, spent 16 to 18 hours a day in confessional; canonized 1925; patron of parish priests; Aug. 4.*

Josaphat Kuncevyc (1584-1623): Basilian monk; b. Poland; archbishop of Polotsk, Lithuania; worked for reunion of separated Eastern Christians with Rome; martyred by mob of schismatics; canonized 1867; Nov. 12.*

Josemaria Escrivá de Balaguer, Bl. (1902-75) Priest and Founder of Opus Dei; the society was designed to promote holiness among individuals in the world; beatified in 1992 and scheduled to be canonized on Oct. 6, 2002; May 17.

Joseph Benedict Cottolengo (1786-1842): Italian priest; established Little Houses of Divine Providence (*Piccolo Casa*) for care of orphans and the sick; canonized 1934; Apr. 30.

Joseph Cafasso (1811-1860): Italian priest; renowned confessor; promoted devotion to Blessed Sacrament; canonized 1947; June 23.

Joseph Calasanz (1556-1648): Spanish priest; founder of Piarists (Order of Pious Schools); canonized 1767; Aug. 25.*

Joseph of Cupertino (1603-1663): Italian Franciscan; noted for remarkable incidents of levitation; canonized 1767; Sept. 18.

Joseph Pignatelli (1737-1811): Spanish Jesuit; left Spain when Jesuits were banished in 1767; worked for revival of the Order; named first superior when Jesuits were reestablished in Kingdom of Naples, 1804; canonized 1954; Nov. 28.

Juan Diego (16th cent.): Mexican Indian, convert; indigenous name according to tradition Cuauhtlatohuac ("The eagle who speaks"); favored with apparitions of Our Lady (see Index: Our Lady of Guadalupe) on Tepeyac hill; beatified, 1990; canonized July 30, 2002; Dec. 9* (U.S.).

Julia Billiart (1751-1816): French foundress; founded Sisters of Notre Dame de Namur, 1804; canonized 1969; Apr. 8.

Juliana Falconieri (1270-1341): Italian foundress of the Servite Nuns; the niece of St. Alexis Falconieri; canonized in 1737; June 19.

Justin de Jacobis (1800-1860): Italian Vincentian; bishop; missionary in Ethiopia; canonized 1975; July 31.

Justin Martyr (100-165): Early ecclesiastical writer; Apologies for the Christian Religion, Dialog with the Jew Tryphon; martyred at Rome; June 1.*

Kateri Tekakwitha, Bl. (1656-1680): "Lily of the Mohawks." Indian maiden born at Ossernenon (Auriesville), N.Y.; baptized Christian, Easter, 1676, by Jesuit missionary Father Jacques de Lambertville; lived life devoted to prayer, penitential practices and care of sick and aged in Christian village of Caughnawaga near Montreal where her relics are now enshrined; beatified June 22, 1980; July 14* (in U.S.).

Katharine Drexel, St. (1858-1955): Philadelphia-born heiress; devoted wealth to founding schools and missions for Indians and Blacks; foundress of Sisters of Blessed Sacrament for Indians and Colored People, 1891; beatified 1988; canonized on Oct. 1, 2000; Mar. 3* (U.S.).

Ladislaus (1040-1095): King of Hungary; supported Pope Gregory VII against Henry IV; canonized 1192; June 27.

Lawrence (d. 258): Widely venerated martyr who suffered death, according to a long-standing but unverifiable legend, by fire on a gridiron; Aug. 10.*

Lawrence (Lorenzo) **Ruiz and Companions** (d. 1630s): Martyred in or near the city of Nagasaki, Japan; Lawrence Ruiz, first Filipino saint, and 15 companions (nine Japanese, four Spaniards, one Italian and one Frenchman); canonized 1987; Sept. 28.*

Leonard Murialdo (1828-1900): Italian priest; educator; founder of Pious Society of St. Joseph of Turin, 1873; canonized 1970; Mar. 30.

Leonard of Port Maurice (1676-1751): Italian Franciscan; ascetical writer; preached missions throughout Italy; canonized 1867; patron of parish missions; Nov. 26.

Leopold Mandic (1866-1942): Croatian-born Franciscan priest, noted confessor; spent most of his priestly life in Padua, Italy; canonized 1983; July 30.

Louis IX (1215-1270): King of France, 1226-1270; participated in Sixth Crusade; patron of Secular Franciscan Order; canonized 1297; Aug. 25.*

Louis de Montfort (1673-1716): French priest; founder of Sisters of Divine Wisdom, 1703, and Missionaries of Company of Mary, 1715; wrote True Devotion to the Blessed Virgin; canonized 1947; Apr. 28.*

Louis Zepherin Moreau, Bl. (d. 1901): Canadian bishop; headed St. Hyacinthe, Que., diocese, 1876-1901; beatified 1987; May 24.

Louise de Marillac (1591-1660): French foundress, with St. Vincent de Paul, of the Sisters of Charity; canonized 1934; Mar. 15.

Lucy (d. 304): Sicilian maiden; martyred during Diocletian persecution; one of most widely venerated early virgin-martyrs; patron of Syracuse, Sicily; invoked by those suffering from eye diseases; Dec. 13.*

Lucy Filippini (1672-1732): Italian educator, helped improve status of women through education; considered a founder of the Religious Teachers Filippini, 1692; canonized 1930; Mar. 25.

Madeleine Sophie Barat (1779-1865): French foundress of the Society of the Sacred Heart of Jesus; canonized 1925; May 25.

Malachy (1095-1148): Irish bishop; instrumental in establishing first Cistercian house in Ireland, 1142; canonized 1190; Nov. 3 (See Index: Prophecies of St. Malachy).

Marcellinus and Peter (d.c. 304): Early Roman martyrs; June 2.*

Margaret Clitherow (1556-1586): English martyr; convert shortly after her marriage; one of Forty Martyrs of England and Wales; canonized 1970; Mar. 25.

Margaret Mary Alacoque (1647-1690): French Religious; spread devotion to Sacred Heart in accordance with revelations made to her in 1675 (see Sacred Heart); canonized 1920; Oct. 16.*

Margaret of Cortona (1247-1297): Secular Franciscan; reformed her life in 1273 following the violent death of her lover; canonized 1728; May 16.

Margaret of Hungary (1242-1270): Contemplative; daughter of King Bela IV of Hungary; lived a life of self-imposed penances; canonized 1943; Jan. 18.

Margaret of Scotland (1050-1093): Queen of Scotland; noted for solicitude for the poor and promotion of justice; canonized 1250; Nov. 16.*

Maria Goretti (1890-1902): Italian virgin-martyr; a model of purity; canonized 1950; July 6.*

Mariana Paredes de Jesus (1618-1645): South American recluse; Lily of Quito; canonized, 1950; May 28.

Marie-Leonie Paradis, Bl. (1840-1912): Canadian Religious; founded Little Sisters of the Holy Family, 1880; beatified 1984; May 4.

Marie-Rose Durocher, Bl. (1811-1849): Canadian Religious; foundress of Sisters of Holy Names of Jesus and Mary; beatified 1982; Oct. 6* (in U.S.).

Martha (1st cent.): Sister of Lazarus and Mary of Bethany; Gospel accounts record her concern for homely details; patron of cooks; July 29.*

Martin I (d. 655): Pope, 649-55; banished from Rome by emperor in 653 because of his condemnation of Monothelites; considered a martyr; Apr. 13.*

Martin of Tours (316-397): Bishop of Tours; opposed Arianism and Priscillianism; pioneer of Western monasticism, before St. Benedict; Nov. 11.*

Mary Domenica Mazzarello (1837-1881): Italian foundress, with St. John Bosco, of the Daughters of Mary Help of Christians, 1872; canonized 1951; May 14.

Mary Josepha Rossello (1811-1881): Italian-born foundress of the Daughters of Our Lady of Mercy; canonized 1949; Dec. 7.

Mary Magdalen Postel (1756-1846): French foundress of the Sisters of Christian Schools of Mercy, 1807; canonized 1925; July 16.

Mary Magdalene (1st cent.): Gospels record her as devoted follower of Christ to whom he appeared after the Resurrection; her identification with Mary of Bethany (sister of Martha and Lazarus) and the woman sinner (Lk. 7:36-50) has been questioned; July 22.*

Mary Magdalene dei Pazzi (1566-1607): Italian Carmelite nun; recipient of mystical experiences; canonized 1669; May 25.*

Mary Michaeli Desmaisières (1809-1865): Spanish-born foundress of the Institute of the Handmaids of the Blessed Sacrament, 1848; canonized 1934; Aug. 24.

Maximilian Kolbe (1894-1941): Polish Conventual Franciscan; prisoner at Auschwitz who heroically offered his life in place of a fellow prisoner; beatified 1971, canonized 1982; Aug. 14.*

Methodius: See under Cyril and Methodius.

Miguel Febres Cordero (1854-1910): Ecuadorean Christian Brother; educator; canonized 1984; Feb. 9.

Miguel Pro, Bl. (1891-1927): Mexican Jesuit; joined Jesuits, 1911; forced to flee because of religious persecution; ordained in Belgium, 1925; returned to Mexico, 1926, to minister to people despite government prohibition; unjustly accused of assassination plot against president; arrested and executed; beatified 1988. Nov. 23* (U.S.).

Monica (332-387): Mother of St. Augustine; model of a patient mother; her feast is observed in the Roman calendar the day before her son's; Aug. 27.*

Nereus and Achilleus (d. c. 100): Early Christian martyrs; soldiers who, according to legend, were baptized by St. Peter; May 12.*

Nicholas of Flüe (1417-1487): Swiss layman; at the age of 50, with the consent of his wife and 10 children, he retreated from the world to live as a hermit; called Brother Claus by the Swiss; canonized 1947; Mar. 21.

Nicholas of Myra (4th cent.): Bishop of Myra in Asia Minor; one of most popular saints in both East and West; most of the incidents of his life are based on legend; patron of Russia; Dec. 6.*

Nicholas of Tolentino (1245-1305): Italian hermit; famed preacher; canonized 1446; Sept. 10.

Nicholas Tavelic and Companions (Deodatus of Aquitaine, Peter of Narbonne, Stephen of Cuneo) (d. 1391): Franciscan missionaries; martyred by Muslims in the Holy Land: canonized 1970; Nov. 14.

Norbert (1080-1134): German bishop; founded Canons Regular of Premontre (Premonstratensians, Norbertines), 1120; promoted reform of the clergy,

devotion to Blessed Sacrament; canonized 1582; June 6.*

Odilia (d. c. 720): Benedictine abbess; according to legend she was born blind, abandoned by her family and adopted by a convent of nuns where her sight was miraculously restored; patroness of blind; Dec. 13.

Oliver Plunket (1629-1681): Irish martyr; theologian; archbishop of Armagh and primate of Ireland; beatified 1920; canonized, 1975; July 1.

Pancras (d. c. 304): Roman martyr; May 12.*

Paola Frassinetti (1809-1882): Italian Religious; foundress, 1834, of Sisters of St. Dorothy; canonized 1984; June 11.

Paschal Baylon (1540-1592): Spanish Franciscan lay brother; spent life as door-keeper in various Franciscan friaries; defended doctrine of Real Presence in Blessed Sacrament; canonized 1690; patron of all Eucharistic confraternities and congresses, 1897; May 17.

Patrick (389-461): Famous missionary of Ireland; began missionary work in Ireland about 432; organized the Church there and established it on a lasting foundation; patron of Ireland, with Sts. Bridget and Columba; Mar. 17.*

Paul Miki and Companions (d. 1597): Martyrs of Japan; Paul Miki, Jesuit, and twenty-five other priests and laymen were martyred at Nagasaki; canonized 1862, the first canonized martyrs of the Far East; Feb. 6.*

Paul of the Cross (1694-1775): Italian Religious; founder of the Passionists; canonized 1867; Oct 19* (Oct. 20, U.S.*).

Paulinus of Nola (d. 451): Bishop of Nola (Spain); writer; June 22.*

Peregrine (1260-1347): Italian Servite; invoked against cancer (he was miraculously cured of cancer of the foot after a vision); canonized 1726; May 1.

Perpetua and Felicity (d. 203): Martyrs; Perpetua was a young married woman; Felicity was a slave girl; Mar. 7.*

Peter Chanel (1803-1841): French Marist; missionary to Oceania, where he was martyred; canonized 1954; Apr. 28.*

Peter Fourier (1565-1640): French priest; co-founder with Alice LeClercq (Mother Teresa of Jesus) of the Augustinian Canonesses of Our Lady, 1598; canonized 1897; Dec. 9.

Peter Gonzalez (1190-1246): Spanish Dominican; worked among sailors; court chaplain and confessor of King St. Ferdinand of Castile; patron of sailors; Apr. 14.

Peter Julian Eymard (1811-1868): French priest; founder of the Congregation of the Blessed Sacrament (men), 1856, and Servants of the Blessed Sacrament (women), 1864; dedicated to Eucharistic apostolate; canonized 1962; Aug. 2.*

Peter Nolasco (c. 1189-1258): Born in Langueduc area of present-day France; founded the Mercedarians (Order of Our Lady of Mercy), 1218, in Spain; canonized 1628; Jan. 31.

Peter of Alcantara (1499-1562): Spanish Franciscan; mystic; initiated Franciscan reform; confessor of St. Teresa of Jesus (Ávila); canonized 1669; Oct. 22 (in U.S.).

Philip Benizi (1233-1285): Italian Servite; noted preacher, peacemaker; canonized 1671; Aug. 23.

Philip Neri (1515-1595): Italian Religious; founded

Congregation of the Oratory; considered a second apostle of Rome because of his mission activity there; canonized 1622; May 26.*

Philip of Jesus (1517-157): Mexican Franciscan; martyred at Nagasaki, Japan; canonized 1862; patron of Mexico City; Feb. 6.*

Pio, Padre (1887-1968): Pio da Pietrelcina (Francesco Forgione), and Italian Capuchin Franciscan, mystic and stigmatic; assisted souls from all over the world who came to him for counsel and guidance; canonized on June 16, 2002; Sept. 23. (For other details, see **Special Reports**.)

Pius V (1504-1572): Pope, 1566-1572; enforced decrees of Council of Trent; organized expedition against Turks resulting in victory at Lepanto; canonized 1712; Apr. 30.*

Polycarp (2nd cent.): Bishop of Smyrna; ecclesiastical writer; martyr; Feb. 23.*

Pontian (d. c. 235): Pope, 230-235; exiled to Sardinia by the emperor; regarded as a martyr; Aug. 13 (with Hippolytus).*

Rafaela Maria Porras y Ayllon (1850-1925): Spanish Religious; founded the Handmaids of the Sacred Heart, 1877; canonized 1977; Jan. 6.

Raymond Nonnatus (d. 1240): Spanish Mercedarian; cardinal; devoted his life to ransoming captives from the Moors; Aug. 31.

Raymond of Peñafort (1175-1275): Spanish Dominican; confessor of Gregory IX; systematized and codified canon law, in effect until 1917; master general of Dominicans, 1238; canonized 1601; Jan. 7.*

Rita of Cascia (1381-1457): Widow; cloistered Augustinian Religious of Umbria; invoked in impossible and desperate cases; May 22.

Robert Southwell (1561-1595): English Jesuit; poet; martyred at Tyburn; canonized 1970, one of the Forty English and Welsh Martyrs; Feb. 21.

Roch (1350-1379): French layman; pilgrim; devoted life to care of plague-stricken; widely venerated; invoked against pestilence; Aug. 17.

Romuald (951-1027): Italian monk; founded Camaldolese Benedictines; June 19.*

Rose of Lima (1586-1617): Peruvian Dominican tertiary; first native-born saint of the New World; canonized 1671; Aug. 23.*

Scholastica (d. c. 559): Sister of St. Benedict; regarded as first nun of the Benedictine Order; Feb. 10.*

Sebastian (3rd cent.): Roman martyr; traditionally pictured as a handsome youth with arrows; martyred; patron of athletes, archers; Jan. 20.*

Seven Holy Founders of the Servants of Mary (Buonfiglio Monaldo, Alexis Falconieri, Benedict dell'Antello, Bartholomew Amidei, Ricovero Uguccione, Gerardino Sostegni, John Buonagiunta Monetti): Florentine youths who founded Servites, 1233, in obedience to a vision; canonized 1888; Feb. 17.*

Sharbel Makhlouf (1828-1898): Lebanese Maronite monk-hermit; canonized 1977; Dec. 24.

Sixtus II and Companions (d. 258): Sixtus, pope 257-258, and four deacons, martyrs; Aug. 7.*

Stanislaus (1030-1079): Polish bishop; martyr; canonized 1253; Apr. 11.*

Stephen (d. c. 33): First Christian martyr; chosen by the Apostles as the first of the seven deacons; stoned to death; Dec. 26.*

Stephen (975-1038): King; apostle of Hungary;

welded Magyars into national unity; canonized 1083; Aug. 16.*

Sylvester I (d. 335): Pope 314-335; first ecumenical council held at Nicaea during his pontificate; Dec. 31.*

Tarcisius (d. 3rd cent.): Early martyr; according to tradition, was martyred while carrying the Blessed Sacrament to some Christians in prison; patron of first communicants; Aug. 15.

Teresa Margaret Redi (1747-1770): Italian Carmelite; lived life of prayer and austere penance; canonized 1934; Mar. 11.

Teresa of Jesus Jornet Ibars (1843-1897): Spanish Religious; founded the Little Sisters of the Abandoned Aged, 1873; canonized 1974; Aug. 26.

Thérèse Couderc (1805-1885): French Religious; foundress of the Religious of Our Lady of the Retreat in the Cenacle, 1827; canonized 1970; Sept. 26.

Thomas Becket (1118-1170): English martyr; archbishop of Canterbury; chancellor under Henry II; murdered for upholding rights of the Church; canonized 1173; Dec. 29.*

Thomas More (1478-1535): English martyr; statesman, chancellor under Henry VIII; author of Utopia; opposed Henry's divorce, refused to renounce authority of the papacy; beheaded; canonized 1935; Pope John Paul II declared him patron of politicians on Oct. 31, 2000; June 22 (with St. John Fisher).*

Timothy (d. c. 97): Bishop of Ephesus; disciple and companion of St. Paul; martyr; Jan. 26.*

Titus (d. c. 96): Bishop; companion of St. Paul; recipient of one of Paul's epistles; Jan. 26.*

Titus Brandsma, Bl. (1881-1942): Dutch Carmelite priest; professor, scholar, journalist; denounced Nazi persecution of Jews; arrested by Nazis, Jan. 19, 1942; executed by lethal injection at Dachau, July 26, 1942; beatified 1985; July 26.

Valentine (d. 269): Priest, physician; martyred at Rome; legendary patron of lovers; Feb. 14.

Vicenta Maria Lopez y Vicuna (1847-1896): Spanish foundress of the Daughters of Mary Immaculate for domestic service; canonized 1975; Dec. 26.

Vincent (d. 304): Spanish deacon; martyr; Jan. 22.*

Vincent de Paul (1581?-1660): French priest; founder of Congregation of the Mission (Vincentians, Lazarists) and co-founder of Sisters of Charity; declared patron of all charitable organizations and works by Leo XIII; canonized 1737; Sept. 27.*

Vincent Ferrer (1350-1418): Spanish Dominican; famed preacher; Apr. 5.*

Vincent Pallotti (1795-1850): Italian priest; founded Society of the Catholic Apostolate (Pallottines), 1835; Jan. 22.

Vincent Strambi (1745-1824): Italian Passionist; bishop; reformer; canonized 1950; Sept. 25.

Vitus (d.c. 300): Martyr; died in Lucania, southern Italy; regarded as protector of epileptics and those suffering from St. Vitus Dance (chorea); June 15.

Walburga (d. 779): English-born Benedictine Religious; belonged to group of nuns who established convents in Germany at the invitation of St. Boniface; abbess of Heidenheim; Feb. 25.

Wenceslaus (d. 935): Duke of Bohemia; martyr; patron of Bohemia; Sept. 28.*

Zita (1218-1278): Italian maid; noted for charity to poor; patron of domestics; Apr. 27.

SAINTS — PATRONS AND INTERCESSORS

A patron is a saint who is venerated as a special intercessor before God. Most patrons have been so designated as the result of popular devotion and long-standing custom. In many cases, the fact of existing patronal devotion is clear despite historical obscurity regarding its origin. The Church has made official designation of relatively few patrons; in such cases, the dates of designation are given in parentheses in the list below. The theological background of the patronage of saints includes the dogmas of the Mystical Body of Christ and the Communion of Saints. Listed are patron saints of occupations and professions, and saints whose intercession is sought for special needs.

Academics: Thomas Aquinas.
Accomodations: Gertrude of Nivelles.
Accountants: Matthew.
Actors: Genesius.
Adopted children: Clotilde; Thomas More.
Advertisers: Bernardine of Siena (May 20, 1960).
Alcoholics: John of God; Monica.
Alpinists: Bernard of Montjoux (or Menthon) (Aug. 20, 1923).
Altar servers: John Berchmans.
Anesthetists: René Goupil.
Animals: Francis of Assisi.
Archaeologists: Damasus.
Archers: Sebastian.
Architects: Thomas, Apostle.
Art: Catherine of Bologna.
Artists: Luke, Catherine of Bologna, Bl. Angelico (Feb. 21, 1984).
Astronauts: Joseph Cupertino.
Astronomers: Dominic.
Athletes: Sebastian.
Authors: Francis de Sales.
Aviators: Our Lady of Loreto (1920), Thérèse of Lisieux, Joseph of Cupertino.
Bakers: Elizabeth of Hungary, Nicholas.
Bankers: Matthew.
Barbers: Cosmas and Damian, Louis.
Barren women: Anthony of Padua, Felicity.
Basket-makers: Anthony, Abbot.
Bees: Ambrose.
Birth: Margaret.
Beggars: Martin of Tours.
Blacksmiths: Dunstan.
Blind: Odilia, Raphael.
Blood banks: Januarius.
Bodily ills: Our Lady of Lourdes.
Bookbinders: Peter Celestine.
Bookkeepers: Matthew.
Booksellers: John of God.
Boy Scouts: George.
Brewers: Augustine of Hippo, Luke, Nicholas of Myra.
Bricklayers: Stephen.
Brides: Nicholas of Myra.
Bridges: John of Nepomucene.
Broadcasters: Gabriel.
Brushmakers: Anthony, Abbot.
Builders: Vincent Ferrer.
Bus drivers: Christopher.
Butchers: Anthony (Abbot), Luke.
Butlers: Adelelm.
Cabdrivers: Fiacre.
Cabinetmakers: Anne.

Cancer patients: Peregrine.
Canonists: Raymond of Peñafort.
Carpenters: Joseph.
Catechists: Viator, Charles Borromeo, Robert Bellarmine.
Catholic Action: Francis of Assisi (1916).
Catholic Press: Francis de Sales.
Chandlers: Ambrose, Bernard of Clairvaux.
Chaplains: John of Capistrano.
Charitable societies: Vincent de Paul (May 12, 1885).
Chastity: Thomas Aquinas.
Childbirth: Raymond Nonnatus; Gerard Majella.
Children: Nicholas of Myra.
Children of Mary: Agnes, Maria Goretti.
Choirboys: Dominic Savio (June 8, 1956), Holy Innocents.
Church: Joseph (Dec. 8, 1870).
Circus people: Julian the Hospitaller.
Clerics: Gabriel of the Sorrowful Mother.
Colleges: Thomas Aquinas.
Comedians: Vitus.
Communications personnel: Bernardine.
Confessors: Alphonsus Liguori (Apr. 26, 1950), John Nepomucene.
Converts: Helena; Vladimir.
Convulsive children: Scholastica.
Cooks: Lawrence, Martha.
Coopers: Nicholas of Myra.
Coppersmiths: Maurus.
Dairy workers: Brigid.
Dancers: Vitus.
Deaf: Francis de Sales.
Dentists: Apollonia.
Desperate situations: Gregory of Neocaesarea, Jude Thaddeus, Rita of Cascia.
Dietitians (in hospitals): Martha.
Diplomats: Gabriel.
Divorce: Helena.
Drug addiction: Maximilian Kolbe.
Dyers: Maurice, Lydia.
Dying: Joseph.
Ecologists: Francis of Assisi (Nov. 29, 1979).
Ecumenists: Cyril and Methodius.
Editors: John Bosco.
Emigrants: Frances Xavier Cabrini (Sept. 8, 1950).
Endurance: Pantaleon.
Engineers: Ferdinand III.
Epilepsy, Motor Diseases: Vitus, Willibrord.
Eucharistic congresses and societies: Paschal Baylon (Nov. 28, 1897).
Expectant mothers: Raymond Nonnatus, Gerard Majella.
Eye diseases: Lucy.
Falsely accused: Raymond Nonnatus.
Farmers: George, Isidore.
Farriers: John the Baptist.
Firemen: Florian.
Fire prevention: Catherine of Siena.
First communicants: Tarcisius.
Fishermen: Andrew.
Florists: Thérèse of Lisieux.
Forest workers: John Gualbert.
Foundlings: Holy Innocents.
Friendship: John the Divine.
Fullers: Anastasius the Fuller, James the Less.

Funeral directors: Joseph of Arimathea, Dismas.
Gardeners: Adelard, Tryphon, Fiacre, Phocas.
Glassworkers: Luke.
Goldsmiths: Dunstan, Anastasius.
Gravediggers: Anthony, Abbot.
Greetings: Valentine.
Grocers: Michael.
Grooms: King Louis IX of France.
Hairdressers: Martin de Porres.
Happy meetings: Raphael.
Hatters: Severus of Ravenna, James the Less.
Headache sufferers: Teresa of Jesus (Ávila).
Heart patients: John of God.
Homeless: Margaret of Cortona; Benedict Joseph Labré.
Horses: Giles; Hippolytus.
Housekeepers: Zita.
Hospital administrators: Basil the Great, Frances X. Cabrini.
Hospitals: Camillus de Lellis and John of God (June 22, 1886), Jude Thaddeus.
Housewives: Anne.
Hunters: Hubert, Eustachius.
Infantrymen: Maurice.
Innkeepers: Amand, Martha, Julian the Hospitaller.
Innocence: Hallvard.
Invalids: Roch.
Janitors: Theobald.
Jewelers: Eligius, Dunstan.
Journalists: Francis de Sales (Apr. 26, 1923).
Jurists: John Capistran.
Laborers: Isidore, James, John Bosco.
Lawyers: Ivo (Yves Helory), Genesius, Thomas More.
Learning: Ambrose.
Librarians: Jerome.
Lighthouse keepers: Venerius (Mar. 10, 1961).
Linguists: Gottschalk.
Locksmiths: Dunstan.
Lost souls: Nicholas of Tolentino.
Lovers: Raphael; Valentine.
Lunatics: Christina.
Maids: Zita.
Marble workers: Clement I.
Mariners: Michael, Nicholas of Tolentino.
Medical record librarians: Raymond of Peñafort.
Medical social workers: John Regis.
Medical technicians: Albert the Great.
Mentally ill: Dymphna.
Merchants: Francis of Assisi, Nicholas of Myra.
Messengers: Gabriel.
Metal workers: Eligius.
Military chaplains: John Capistran (Feb. 10, 1984).
Millers: Arnulph, Victor.
Missions, foreign: Francis Xavier (Mar. 25, 1904), Thérèse of Lisieux (Dec. 14, 1927).
Missions, black: Peter Claver (1896, Leo XIII), Benedict the Black.
Missions, parish: Leonard of Port Maurice (Mar. 17, 1923).
Monks: Benedict of Nursia.
Mothers: Monica.
Motorcyclists: Our Lady of Grace.
Motorists: Christopher, Frances of Rome.
Mountaineers: Bernard of Montjoux (or Menthon).
Musicians: Gregory the Great, Cecilia, Dunstan.
Mystics: John of the Cross.
Notaries: Luke, Mark.

Nuns: Bridget.
Nurses: Camillus de Lellis and John of God (1930, Pius XI), Agatha, Raphael.
Nursing and nursing service: Elizabeth of Hungary, Catherine of Siena.
Orators: John Chrysostom (July 8, 1908).
Organ builders: Cecilia.
Orphans: Jerome Emiliani.
Painters: Luke.
Paratroopers: Michael.
Pawnbrokers: Nicholas.
Plumbers: Vincent Ferrer.
Pharmacists: Cosmas and Damian, James the Greater.
Pharmacists (in hospitals): Gemma Galgani.
Philosophers: Justin.
Physicians: Pantaleon, Cosmas and Damian, Luke, Raphael.
Pilgrims: James the Greater.
Plasterers: Bartholomew.
Poets: David, Cecilia.
Politicians: Thomas More
Poison sufferers: Benedict.
Policemen: Michael.
Poor: Lawrence, Anthony of Padua.
Poor souls: Nicholas of Tolentino.
Popes: Gregory I the Great.
Porters: Christopher.
Possessed: Bruno, Denis.
Postal employees: Gabriel.
Priests: Jean-Baptiste Vianney (Apr. 23, 1929).
Printers: John of God, Augustine of Hippo, Genesius.
Prisoners: Dismas, Joseph Cafasso.
Protector of crops: Ansovinus.
Public relations: Bernardine of Siena (May 20, 1960).
Public relations (of hospitals): Paul, Apostle.
Publishers: John the Divine.
Race relations: Martin de Porres.
Radiologists: Michael (Jan. 15, 1941).
Radio workers: Gabriel.
Refugees: Alban.
Retreats: Ignatius Loyola (July 25, 1922).
Rheumatism: James the Greater.
Saddlers: Crispin and Crispinian.
Sailors: Cuthbert, Brendan, Eulalia, Christopher, Peter Gonzalez, Erasmus, Nicholas.
Scholars: Bede the Venerable; Brigid.
Schools, Catholic: Thomas Aquinas (Aug. 4, 1880), Joseph Calasanz (Aug. 13, 1948).
Scientists: Albert (Aug. 13, 1948).
Sculptors: Four Crowned Martyrs.
Seamen: Francis of Paola.
Searchers of lost articles: Anthony of Padua.
Secretaries: Genesius.
Secular Franciscans: Louis of France, Elizabeth of Hungary.
Seminarians: Charles Borromeo.
Servants: Martha, Zita.
Shepherds: Drogo.
Shoemakers: Crispin and Crispinian.
Sick: Michael, John of God and Camillus de Lellis (June 22, 1886).
Silversmiths: Andronicus.
Singers: Gregory, Cecilia.
Single mothers: Margaret of Cortona.
Single women: Catherine of Alexandria.
Skaters: Lidwina.
Skiers: Bernard of Montjoux (or Menthon).

Social workers: Louise de Marillac (Feb. 12, 1960).
Soldiers: Hadrian, George, Ignatius, Sebastian, Martin of Tours, Joan of Arc.
Speleologists: Benedict.
Stamp collectors: Gabriel.
Stenographers: Genesius, Cassian.
Stonecutters: Clement.
Stonemasons: Stephen.
Stress: Walter of Portnoise.
Students: Thomas Aquinas.
Surgeons: Cosmas and Damian, Luke.
Swimmers: Adjutor.
Swordsmiths: Maurice.
Tailors: Homobonus.
Tanners: Crispin and Crispinian, Simon.
Tax collectors: Matthew.
Teachers: Gregory the Great, John Baptist de la Salle (May 15, 1950).
Telecommunications workers: Gabriel (Jan. 12, 1951).
Television: Clare of Assisi (Feb. 14, 1958).
Television workers: Gabriel.
Thieves: Dismas.
Theologians: Augustine, Alphonsus Liguori.
Throat ailments: Blase.
Torture victims: Alban; Eustachius; Regina; Vincent; Victor of Marseilles.
Toymakers: Claude.
Travelers: Anthony of Padua, Nicholas of Myra, Christopher, Raphael.
Travel hostesses: Bona (Mar. 2, 1962).
Truck drivers: Christopher.
Universities: Blessed Contardo Ferrini.
Veterinarians: Blaise.
Vocations: Alphonsus.
Whales: Brendan the Voyager.
Watchmen: Peter of Alcantara.
Weavers: Paul the Hermit, Anastasius the Fuller, Anastasia.
Wine merchants: Amand.
Wineries: Morand; Vincent.
Women in labor: Anne.
Workingmen: Joseph.
Writers: Francis de Sales (Apr. 26, 1923), Lucy.
Yachtsmen: Adjutor.
Young girls: Agnes.
Youth: Aloysius Gonzaga (1729, Benedict XIII; 1926, Pius XI), John Berchmans, Gabriel of the Sorrowful Mother.

Patron Saints of Places

Albania: Our Lady of Good Counsel.
Alsace: Odilia.
Americas: Our Lady of Guadalupe, Rose of Lima.
Angola: Immaculate Heart of Mary (Nov. 21, 1984).
Argentina: Our Lady of Lujan.
Armenia: Gregory Illuminator.
Asia Minor: John, Evangelist.
Australia: Our Lady Help of Christians.
Belgium: Joseph.
Bohemia: Wenceslaus, Ludmilla.
Bolivia: Our Lady of Copacabana *"Virgen de la Candelaria."*
Borneo: Francis Xavier.
Brazil: Nossa Señora de Aparecida, Immaculate Conception, Peter of Alcantara.
Canada: Joseph, Anne.
Chile: James the Greater, Our Lady of Mt. Carmel.
China: Joseph.

Colombia: Peter Claver, Louis Bertran.
Corsica: Immaculate Conception.
Cuba: Our Lady of Charity.
Czechoslovakia: Wenceslaus, John Nepomucene, Procopius.
Denmark: Ansgar, Canute.
Dominican Republic: Our Lady of High Grace, Dominic.
East Indies: Thomas, Apostle.
Ecuador: Sacred Heart.
El Salvador: Our Lady of Peace (Oct. 10, 1966).
England: George.
Equatorial Guinea: Immaculate Conception (May 25, 1986).
Europe: Benedict (1964), Cyril and Methodius, co-patrons (Dec. 31, 1980); Sts. Catherine of Siena, Bridget of Sweden, and Edith Stein, co-patronesses (Oct. 1, 1999).
Finland: Henry.
France: Our Lady of the Assumption, Joan of Arc, Thérèse (May 3, 1944).
Germany: Boniface, Michael.
Gibraltar: Blessed Virgin Mary under title, "Our Lady of Europe" (May 31, 1979).
Greece: Nicholas, Andrew.
Holland: Willibrord.
Hungary: Blessed Virgin, "Great Lady of Hungary," Stephen, King.
Iceland: Thorlac (Jan. 14, 1984).
India: Our Lady of Assumption.
Ireland: Patrick, Brigid and Columba.
Italy: Francis of Assisi, Catherine of Siena.
Japan: Peter Baptist.
Korea: Joseph and Mary, Mother of the Church.
Lesotho: Immaculate Heart of Mary.
Lithuania: Casimir, Bl. Cunegunda.
Luxembourg: Willibrord.
Malta: Paul, Our Lady of the Assumption.
Mexico: Our Lady of Guadalupe.
Monaco: Devota.
Moravia: Cyril and Methodius.
New Zealand: Our Lady Help of Christians.
Norway: Olaf.
Papua New Guinea (including northern Solomon Islands): Michael the Archangel (May 31, 1979).
Paraguay: Our Lady of Assumption (July 13, 1951).
Peru: Joseph (Mar. 19, 1957).
Philippines: Sacred Heart of Mary.
Poland: Casimir, Bl. Cunegunda, Stanislaus of Krakow, Our Lady of Czestochowa.
Portugal: Immaculate Conception, Francis Borgia, Anthony of Padua, Vincent of Saragossa, George.
Russia: Andrew, Nicholas of Myra, Thérèse of Lisieux.
Scandinavia: Ansgar.
Scotland: Andrew, Columba.
Silesia: Hedwig.
Slovakia: Our Lady of Sorrows.
South Africa: Our Lady of Assumption (Mar. 15, 1952).
South America: Rose of Lima.
Solomon Islands: BVM, under title Most Holy Name of Mary (Sept. 4, 1991).
Spain: James the Greater, Teresa.
Sri Lanka (Ceylon): Lawrence.
Sweden: Bridget, Eric.
Tanzania: Immaculate Conception (Dec. 8, 1964).

United States: Immaculate Conception (1846).

Uruguay: Blessed Virgin Mary under title *"La Virgen de los Treinte y Tres"* (Nov. 21, 1963).

Venezuela: Our Lady of Coromoto.

Wales: David.

West Indies: Gertrude.

Emblems, Portrayals of Saints

Agatha: Tongs, veil.

Agnes: Lamb.

Ambrose: Bees, dove, ox, pen.

Andrew: Transverse cross.

Anne, Mother of the Blessed Virgin: Door.

Anthony of Padua: Infant Jesus, bread, book, lily.

Augustine of Hippo: Dove, child, shell, pen.

Bartholomew: Knife, flayed and holding his skin.

Benedict: Broken cup, raven, bell, crosier, bush.

Bernard of Clairvaux: Pen, bees, instruments of the Passion.

Bernardine of Siena: Tablet or sun inscribed with IHS.

Blase: Wax, taper, iron comb.

Bonaventure: Communion, ciborium, cardinal's hat.

Boniface: Oak, ax, book, fox, scourge, fountain, raven, sword.

Bridget of Sweden: Book, pilgrim's staff.

Bridget of Kildare: Cross, flame over her head, candle.

Catherine of Ricci: Ring, crown, crucifix.

Catherine of Siena: Stigmata, cross, ring, lily.

Cecilia: Organ.

Charles Borromeo: Communion, coat of arms with word "Humilitas."

Christopher: Giant, torrent, tree, Child Jesus on his shoulders.

Clare of Assisi: Monstrance.

Cosmas and Damian: A phial, box of ointment.

Cyril of Alexandria: Blessed Virgin holding the Child Jesus, pen.

Cyril of Jerusalem: Purse, book.

Dominic: Rosary, star.

Edmund the Martyr: Arrow, sword.

Elizabeth of Hungary: Alms, flowers, bread, the poor, a pitcher.

Francis of Assisi: Wolf, birds, fish, skull, the Stigmata.

Francis Xavier: Crucifix, bell, vessel.

Genevieve: Bread, keys, herd, candle.

George: Dragon.

Gertrude: Crown, taper, lily.

Gervase and Protase: Scourge, club, sword.

Gregory I (the Great): Tiara, crosier, dove.

Helena: Cross.

Ignatius of Loyola: Communion, chasuble, book, apparition of Our Lord.

Isidore: Bees, pen.

James the Greater: Pilgrim's staff, shell, key, sword.

James the Less: Square rule, halberd, club.

Jerome: Lion.

John Berchmans: Rule of St. Ignatius, cross, rosary.

John Chrysostom: Bees, dove, pen.

John of God: Alms, a heart, crown of thorns.

John the Baptist: Lamb, head on platter, skin of an animal.

John the Evangelist: Eagle, chalice, kettle, armor.

Josaphat Kuncevyc: Chalice, crown, winged deacon.

Joseph, Spouse of the Blessed Virgin: Infant Jesus, lily, rod, plane, carpenter's square.

Jude: Sword, square rule, club.

Justin Martyr: Ax, sword.

Lawrence: Cross, book of the Gospels, gridiron.

Leander of Seville: A pen.

Liberius: Pebbles, peacock.

Longinus: In arms at foot of the cross.

Louis IX of France: Crown of thorns, nails.

Lucy: Cord, eyes on a dish.

Luke: Ox, book, brush, palette.

Mark: Lion, book.

Martha: Holy water sprinkler, dragon.

Mary Magdalene: Alabaster box of ointment.

Matilda: Purse, alms.

Matthew: Winged man, purse, lance.

Matthias: Lance.

Maurus: Scales, spade, crutch.

Meinrad: Two ravens.

Michael: Scales, banner, sword, dragon.

Monica: Girdle, tears.

Nicholas: Three purses or balls, anchor or boat, child.

Patrick: Cross, harp, serpent, baptismal font, demons, shamrock.

Paul: Sword, book or scroll.

Peter: Keys, boat, cock.

Philip, Apostle: Column.

Philip Neri: Altar, chasuble, vial.

Rita of Cascia: Rose, crucifix, thorn.

Roch: Angel, dog, bread.

Rose of Lima: Crown of thorns, anchor, city.

Sebastian: Arrows, crown.

Simon Stock: Scapular.

Teresa of Jesus (Ávila): Heart, arrow, book.

Thérèse of Lisieux: Roses entwining a crucifix.

Thomas, Apostle: Lance, ax.

Thomas Aquinas: Chalice, monstrance, dove, ox, person trampled under foot.

Vincent de Paul: Children.

Vincent Ferrer: Pulpit, cardinal's hat, trumpet, captives.

CANONIZATIONS AND BEATIFICATIONS 2001-02

Pope John Paul II beatified and canonized the following individuals from September 2001 to August 2002. Included are the dates of the beatifications and canonizations as well as relevant biographical information.

Canonizations: 2001

Giuseppe Marello (1844-1895): Italian bishop and founder of the Oblates of St. Joseph. The religious community of priests and brothers was intended to assist bishops and clergy in evangelization. The members of the congregation arrived in the United States in 1929. In 1889, Giuseppe was consecrated the bishop of Asti. He died suddenly from a stroke. Pope John Paul II beatified Giuseppe in 1993 and canonized him on Nov. 25, 2001.

Léonie Françoise de Sales Aviat (1844-1914): Foundress of the Sister Oblates of Saint Francis of Sales with Fr. Brisson. The congregation had as its aim helping the plight of thousands of young woman trapped by the poverty and harsh life caused by the Industrial Revolution. By the time of her death, there were houses in Mexico and throughout many missionary lands. Pope John Paul II beatified her in 1992 and canonized her on Nov. 25, 2001. Her canonization miracle involved the healing of a 14-year-old Philadelphia girl with a spinal disease that had left her paralyzed.

Maria Crescentia Höss (1682-1744): Bavarian Franciscan tertiary nun. In 1703, she was permitted to enter the Franciscan tertiaries of Mayerhoff, in large measure because of the personal appeal of the town's Protestant mayor. Professed in 1704, she remained at Mayerhoff for the rest of her life. She endured frequent abuse from her fellow sisters, owing to the poor origins of her family. In 1741, she was elected superior of the community over her own protests. She was beatified in 1900 by Pope Leo XIII (r. 1878-1903) and canonized on Nov. 25, 2001.

Paula Montal Fornés de San José de Calasanz (1799-1889): Foundress of the Daughters of Mary, "the Pious School Sisters." The congregation received papal approval from Pope Pius IX (r. 1846-1878) in May 1860. Five years later, Queen Isabel II (r. 1833-1868) of Spain recognized the Daughters of Mary as well. The congregation arrived in the United States in 1954. Paula died at Olesa de Montserrat on Feb. 26, 1889. Pope John Paul II beatified Paula in 1993 and canonized her on Nov. 25, 2001.

Canonizations: 2002

Alonso de Orozco (1500-1591): A 16th-century Spanish Augustinian friar, who devoted most of his life to the poor. Known for his brilliant homilies, he was appointed "royal preacher" to the court of the emperor Charles V in 1554. He was also the author of many ascetical and mystical works. He was beatified by Pope Leo XIII on the January 15, 1882 and canonized on May 19, 2002.

Benedicta Cambiagio Frassinello (1791-1858): Italian foundress of the Benedictine Sisters of Providence. She married Giovanni Battista Frassinella in 1816 and lived as a married woman for two years; she then agreed with her husband to live chastely, as "brother and sister." The two eventually entered religious orders, and Benedetta founded her congregation to teach young girls. Pope John Paul II beatified Benedicta on May 10, 1987, and canonized her on May 19, 2002.

Ignazio da Santhiá (1686-1770) An 18th-century Italian Capuchin known for his ministry as a confessor and spiritual adviser. He was renowned for his gift of spiritual direction and concern for the spiritual life of the faithful. Pope Paul VI beatified him on Apr. 17, 1966, and Pope John Paul II canonized him on May 19, 2002.

Paulina do Coracao Agonizante de Jesus (Amabile Visintainer) (d. 1942): Italian-born founder of the Little Sisters of the Immaculate Conception; she is honored as the "first saint who grew up in Brazil." The congregation, dedicated to serving the poor, sick and elderly, was approved in 1885. Pope John Paul II beatified her in Florianopolis (São Paulo), Brazil, on Oct. 18, 1991, and canonized her on May 19, 2002.

Umile da Bisignano (1582-1637): Franciscan friar considered by contemporaries to be slow and seemingly dim-witted; in truth, he showed gifts of mysti-

cism and demonstrated a life of deep prayer up to the moment of his death. He was beatified by Leo XII on the Jan. 29, 1882 and canonized by Pope John Paul II on May 19, 2002.

Pio da Pietrelcina (Francesco Forgione): Canonized on June 16, 2002 (See above under **Saints**; for other details, see under **International News** in **Special Reports**).

Juan Diego Cuauhlatoatzin: Canonized on July 30, 2002. (See above under **Saints**).

Pedro de San Jose de Betancur (1616-1667): Franciscan missionary, called the "St. Francis of the Americas"; he entered the Third Order Franciscans in Guatemala and founded a hospital, a hostel, schools, and an oratory for the poor. He was beatified in 1980 and canonized on July 31, 2002, by Pope John Paul II.

Josemaria Escrivá de Balaguer: Scheduled to be canonized on Oct. 6, 2002. (See above under **Saints**).

Beatifications: 2001

Alfonso Maria Fusco (1839-1910): Italian priest and founder of the Congregation of the Baptistine Sisters of the Nazarene in 1878, with the purpose of spiritual and educational welfare of orphans and poor boys and girls. Beatified on Oct. 7, 2001.

Emilie Tavernier Gamelin (1800-1851): Canadian sister and founder of the Daughters of Charity, Servants of the Poor in 1843. Her congregation reflected her lifelong concern for the poor and the elderly; currently the congregation has sisters in Canada, the U.S., Chile, Cameroon, Argentina, Haiti, Egypt, El Salvador, and the Philippines. Beatified on Oct. 7, 2001.

Eugenia Picco (1867-1921): Italian sister and Superior General of the Congregation of the Little Daughters of the Sacred Hearts of Jesus and Mary. Beatified on Oct. 7, 2001.

Ignatius Maloyan (1869-1915): Turkish-born Armenian bishop and martyr. Maloyan was elected abp. of Mardin by a Bishops' Synod in Rome in 1911 after restoring the spiritual vitality of the diocese. Arrested in 1915 with his priests and many faithful during the pogrom against the Armenians by the Turks, he was tortured severely and finally executed on June 11. Beatified on Oct. 7, 2001.

Maria Euthymia Üffing (1914-1955): German sister and member of the Congregation of the Sisters of Charity. During World War II she cared for sick and infectious prisoners of war and foreign workers from various countries. Beatified on Oct. 7, 2001.

Nikolaus Gross (1898-1945): Layperson, father, union activist, opponent of the Nazi regime of Adolf Hitler, and martyr. As a member of the Catholic miners union, the St. Anthony's Miner Association (*Antonius Knappenverein*, KAB) and as editor-in-chief of its newspaper, the *Westdeutsche Arbeiterzeitung* (*West German Workers' Newspaper*), he resisted the rise of the Nazis. In Jan. 1945, the Nazis hanged him in Berlin. Beatified on October 7, 2001.

Tommaso Maria Fusco (1831-1891): Italian priest and founder of the Congregation of the Daughters of Charity of the Most Precious Blood in 1873 to care for and educate poor orphan girls. Beatified on Oct. 7, 2001.

Luigi Beltrame (1880-1951) and **Maria Quattrocchi** (1884-1965): Italian couple married for 50 years. They are considered a superb model for all

Christians who embrace the married state. They had four children, three of them in attendance at their beatification on Oct. 21, 2001.

Bartolomeu Fernandes dos Mártires, O.P. (1514-1590): Portuguese archbishop of Braga, Portugal. A member of the Dominicans, he was appointed archbishop in 1558. His time as archbishop was marked by his austerity, pastoral zeal, and commitment to evangelization. He also authored thirty-two books and was a vocal promoter of reform at the Council of Trent. Beatified on Nov. 4, 2001.

Gaetana Sterni (1827-1889): Italian sister and founder of the Sisters of the Divine Will. Initially a member of the Canossian Sisters, she left owing to the sudden death of her mother. In 1860, she founded the Sisters of the Divine Will to care for the poor and forgotten. Beatified on Nov. 4, 2001.

Giovanni Antonio Farina (1803-1888): Italian bishop of Treviso and Vicenza and founder of the Sisters Teachers of St. Dorothy. A gifted teacher, he sought to promote education among the poor by founding schools and the Sisters Teachers. He also ordained Giuseppe Sarto, the future Pope St. Pius X (r. 1903-14). Beatified on Nov. 4, 2001.

Luigi Tezza (1841-1923): Italian priest and founder of the Daughters of St. Camillus. A member of the Order of the Ministers of the Sick of St. Camillus, he labored for the congregation in France even after suppression of religious institutes in 1880. He founded the Daughters in 1892 (the institute was approved in 1931) and spent his last 23 years serving in Peru. Beatified on Nov. 4, 2001.

Maria Pilar Izquierdo Albero (1906-1945): Brazilian sister and founder of the Missionary Work of Jesus and Mary. Her congregation had as its apostolate the care of the poor; she also founded the Pious Union of Missionaries of Jesus, Mary and Joseph, and the Missionary Work of Jesus and Mary. Beatified on Nov. 4, 2001.

Metod Dominik Trcka, C.SS.R. (1886-1959): Slovakian Redemptorist superior and victim of Communist oppression. He worked as a missionary in eastern Slovakia and was one of leaders of the Redemptorists in Slovakia throughout World War II and under Communist rule. Arrested in 1950, he was sent to a concentration camp and died forgiving his persecutors. Beatified on Nov. 4, 2001.

Paolo Manna (1872-1952): Italian priest and missionary. After serving as a missionary in Burma, he returned to Italy where promoted the Mission Societies for the Propagation of the Faith and Holy Childhood and launched the Pontifical Missionary Union (PMU). In 1936 he started the Missionary Sisters of Immaculate Mary. Beatified on Nov. 4, 2001.

Pavol Peter Gojdic (1888-1960): Slovakian Greek Catholic bishop and victim of Communist oppression in Czechoslovakia. A priest of the Order of St. Basil the Great, he was appointed bishop of Presov, in Eastern Slovakia in 1940. During World War II, he aided refugees and defend the Church against the Nazis. Arrested by Communist officials in 1950, he suffered torture and humiliations until his death from cancer. Beatified on Nov. 4, 2001.

Beatifications: 2002

Artemide Zatti (1880-1951): Italian Salesian Brother. He devoted forty years of his life to running a hospital and pharmacy for the sick and poor in Viedma, Argentina. Beatified on Apr. 14, 2002.

Gaetano Errico (1791-1860): Founder of the Missionaries of the Sacred Hearts of Jesus and Mary. He established the Missionaries after receiving a vision of St. Alphonsus Liguori. The congregation was approved by Pope Bl. Pius IX in 1846. Beatified on Apr. 14, 2002.

Lodovico Pavoni (1784-1849): Italian priest and founder of the Congregation of the Sons of Mary Immaculate. His founded an orphanage and vocational school and the Congregation of the Sons of Mary Immaculate. Beatified on Apr. 14, 2002.

Luigi Variara (1875-1923): Italian Salesian Father and founder of the Institute of Daughters of the Sacred Hearts of Jesus and Mary. A native of Viarigi, Italy, he entered the Salesian Congregation at the age of twelve and met St. Don Bosco. He devoted himself to the care of the lepers in Colombia and founded the Institute to help the young patients in the leprosarium. Beatified on Apr. 14, 2002.

Maria del Tránsito de Jesus Sacramentado (1821-1885): Argentine sister and founder of the Congregation of Tertiary Franciscan Missionary Sisters of Argentina to teach poor and abandoned children in Argentina. Beatified on Apr. 14, 2002.

Maria Romero Meneses (1902-1977): Nicaraguan Salesian sister. She devoted most of her life to the care of poor and forgotten children in Costa Rica and founded a medical center, school, and villages. Beatified on Apr. 14, 2002.

Kamen Vitchev, Pavel Djidjov, and Josaphat Chichkov (d. Nov. 11-12, 1952): Three Bulgarian priests of the congregation of Augustinians of the Assumption who were executed by the Communist regime in 1952 along with Bishop Eugenio Bossilkov (who was beatified in 1998). Beatified on May 26, 2002, during Pope John Paul II's visit to Bulgaria.

Juan Bautista and Jacinto de los Ángeles (1660-1700): Mexican martyrs. Both were members of the Zapoteca tribe in Oaxaca and both served as attorneys general assisting the local converts to remain committed to the Catholic faith. They were martyred after tearing down pagan idols. Beatified on July 31, 2002.

Zygmunt Szczêsny Feliñski (1822-1895): Archbishop of Warsaw and founder of the Franciscan Sisters of the Family of Mary. He served as archbishop of Warsaw for 16 months, and then spent 20 years in exile in Siberia and 12 years in semi-exile as titular archbishop of Tarsus and parish priest. Beatified on Aug. 17, 2002.

Jan Beyzym (1850-1912): The apostle of the lepers of Madagascar. He was the first priest to live among the victims of Hansen's disease in the entire history of the mission of Madagascar. He spent 48 years as a missionary. Beatified on Aug. 17, 2002.

Sancja Szymkowiak (1910-1942): Polish member of the Congregation of the Daughters of Our Lady of Sorrows (the "Seraphic Sisters"). During World War II she helped care for English and French prisoners. She died from tuberculosis. Her motto was "God's will is my will." Beatified on Aug. 17, 2002.

Jan Adalbert Balicki (1869-1948): Polish priest, model for diocesan clergy, professor of theology, confessor, and a powerful influence in the formation of young priests. He is honored as an example for all priests of uniting the life of prayer with pastoral ministry. Beatified on Aug. 17, 2002.

Dates and Events in Catholic History

FIRST CENTURY

c. 33: First Christian Pentecost; descent of the Holy Spirit upon the disciples; preaching of St. Peter in Jerusalem; conversion, baptism and aggregation of some 3,000 persons to the first Christian community.

St. Stephen, deacon, was stoned to death at Jerusalem; he is venerated as the first Christian martyr.

c. 34: St. Paul, formerly Saul the persecutor of Christians, was converted and baptized. After three years of solitude in the desert, he joined the college of the apostles; he made three major missionary journeys and became known as the Apostle to the Gentiles; he was imprisoned twice in Rome and was beheaded there between 64 and 67.

39: Cornelius (the Gentile) and his family were baptized by St. Peter; a significant event signaling the mission of the Church to all peoples.

42: Persecution of Christians in Palestine broke out during the rule of Herod Agrippa; St. James the Greater, the first apostle to die, was beheaded in 44; St. Peter was imprisoned for a short time; many Christians fled to Antioch, marking the beginning of the dispersion of Christians beyond the confines of Palestine. At Antioch, the followers of Christ were called Christians for the first time.

49: Christians at Rome, considered members of a Jewish sect, were adversely affected by a decree of Claudius which forbade Jewish worship there.

51: The Council of Jerusalem, in which all the apostles participated under the presidency of St. Peter, decreed that circumcision, dietary regulations, and various other prescriptions of Mosaic Law were not obligatory for Gentile converts to the Christian community. The crucial decree was issued in opposition to Judaizers who contended that observance of the Mosaic Law in its entirety was necessary for salvation.

64: Persecution broke out at Rome under Nero, the emperor said to have accused Christians of starting the fire which destroyed half of Rome.

64 or 67: Martyrdom of St. Peter at Rome during the Neronian persecution. He established his see and spent his last years there after preaching in and around Jerusalem, establishing a see at Antioch, and presiding at the Council of Jerusalem.

70: Destruction of Jerusalem by Titus.

88-97: Pontificate of St. Clement I, third successor of St. Peter as bishop of Rome, one of the Apostolic Fathers. The First Epistle of Clement to the Corinthians, with which he has been identified, was addressed by the Church of Rome to the Church at Corinth, the scene of irregularities and divisions in the Christian community.

95: Domitian persecuted Christians, principally at Rome.

c. 100: Death of St. John, apostle and evangelist, marking the end of the Age of the Apostles and the first generation of the Church.

By the end of the century, Antioch, Alexandria and Ephesus in the East and Rome in the West were established centers of Christian population and influence.

SECOND CENTURY

c. 107: St. Ignatius of Antioch was martyred at Rome. He was the first writer to use the expression, "the Catholic Church."

112: Emperor Trajan, in a rescript to Pliny the Younger, governor of Bithynia, instructed him not to search out Christians but to punish them if they were publicly denounced and refused to do homage to the Roman gods. This rescript set a pattern for Roman magistrates in dealing with Christians.

117-38: Persecution under Hadrian. Many Acts of Martyrs date from this period.

c. 125: Spread of Gnosticism, a combination of elements of Platonic philosophy and Eastern mystery religions. Its adherents claimed that its secret-knowledge principle provided a deeper insight into Christian doctrine than divine revelation and faith. One gnostic thesis denied the divinity of Christ; others denied the reality of his humanity, calling it mere appearance (Docetism, Phantasiasm).

c. 144: Excommunication of Marcion, bishop and heretic, who claimed that there was total opposition and no connection at all between the Old Testament and the New Testament, between the God of the Jews and the God of the Christians; and that the Canon (list of inspired writings) of the Bible consisted only of parts of St. Luke's Gospel and 10 letters of St. Paul. Marcionism was checked at Rome by 200 and was condemned by a council held there about 260, but the heresy persisted for several centuries in the East and had some adherents as late as the Middle Ages.

c. 155: St. Polycarp, bishop of Smyrna and disciple of St. John the Evangelist, was martyred.

c. 156: Beginning of Montanism, a form of religious extremism. Its principal tenets were the imminent second coming of Christ, denial of the divine nature of the Church and its power to forgive sin, and excessively rigorous morality. The heresy, preached by Montanus of Phrygia and others, was condemned by Pope St. Zephyrinus (199-217).

161-80: Reign of Marcus Aurelius. His persecution, launched in the wake of natural disasters, was more violent than those of his predecessors.

165: St. Justin, an important early Christian writer, was martyred at Rome.

c. 180: St. Irenaeus, bishop of Lyons and one of the great early theologians, wrote *Adversus Haereses*. He stated that the teaching and tradition of the Roman See was the standard for belief.

196: Easter Controversy, concerning the day of celebration — a Sunday, according to practice in the West, or the 14th of the month of Nisan (in the Hebrew calendar), no matter what day of the week, according to practice in the East. The controversy was not resolved at this time.

The *Didache*, whose extant form dates from the second century, is an important record of Christian belief, practice and governance in the first century.

Latin was introduced as a liturgical language in the West. Other liturgical languages were Aramaic and Greek.

The Catechetical School of Alexandria, founded about the middle of the century, gained increasing influence on doctrinal study and instruction, and interpretation of the Bible.

THIRD CENTURY

202: Persecution under Septimius Severus, who wanted to establish a simple common religion in the Empire.

206: Tertullian, a convert since 197 and the first great ecclesiastical writer in Latin, joined the heretical Montanists; he died in 230.

215: Death of Clement of Alexandria, teacher of Origen and a founding father of the School of Alexandria.

217-35: St. Hippolytus, the first antipope; he was reconciled to the Church while in prison during persecution in 235.

232-54: Origen established the School of Caesarea after being deposed in 231 as head of the School of Alexandria; he died in 254. A scholar and voluminous writer, he was one of the founders of systematic theology and exerted wide influence for many years.

c. 242: Manichaeism originated in Persia: a combination of errors based on the assumption that two supreme principles (good and evil) are operative in creation and life, and that the supreme objective of human endeavor is liberation from evil (matter). The heresy denied the humanity of Christ, the sacramental system, the authority of the Church (and state), and endorsed a moral code which threatened the fabric of society. In the 12th and 13th centuries, it took on the features of Albigensianism and Catharism.

249-51: Persecution under Decius. Many of those who denied the faith (*lapsi*) sought readmission to the Church at the end of the persecution in 251. Pope St. Cornelius agreed with St. Cyprian that *lapsi* were to be readmitted to the Church after satisfying the requirements of appropriate penance. Antipope Novatian, on the other hand, contended that persons who fell away from the Church under persecution and/or those guilty of serious sin after baptism could not be absolved and readmitted to communion with the Church. The heresy was condemned by a Roman synod in 251.

250-300: Neo-Platonism of Plotinus and Porphyry gained followers.

251: Novatian, an antipope, was condemned at Rome.

256: Pope St. Stephen I upheld the validity of baptism properly administered by heretics, in the Rebaptism Controversy.

257: Persecution under Valerian, who attempted to destroy the Church as a social structure.

258: St. Cyprian, bishop of Carthage, was martyred.

c. 260: St. Lucian founded the School of Antioch, a center of influence on biblical studies.

Pope St. Dionysius condemned Sabellianism, a form of modalism (like Monarchianism and Patripassianism). The heresy contended that the Father, Son and Holy Spirit are not distinct divine persons but are only three different modes of being and self-manifestations of the one God. St. Paul of Thebes became a hermit.

261: Gallienus issued an edict of toleration which ended general persecution for nearly 40 years.

c. 292: Diocletian divided the Roman Empire into East and West. The division emphasized political, cultural and other differences between the two parts of the Empire and influenced different developments in the Church in the East and West. The prestige of Rome began to decline.

FOURTH CENTURY

303: Persecution broke out under Diocletian; it was particularly violent in 304.

305: St. Anthony of Heracles established a foundation for hermits near the Red Sea in Egypt.

c. 306: The first local legislation on clerical celibacy was enacted by a council held at Elvira, Spain; bishops, priests, deacons and other ministers were forbidden to have wives.

311: An edict of toleration issued by Galerius at the urging of Constantine the Great and Licinius officially ended persecution in the West; some persecution continued in the East.

313: The Edict of Milan issued by Constantine and Licinius recognized Christianity as a lawful religion in the Roman Empire.

314: A council of Arles condemned Donatism, declaring that baptism properly administered by heretics is valid, in view of the principle that sacraments have their efficacy from Christ, not from the spiritual condition of their human ministers. The heresy was condemned again by a council of Carthage in 411.

318: St. Pachomius established the first foundation of the cenobitic (common) life, as compared with the solitary life of hermits in Upper Egypt.

325: Ecumenical Council of Nicaea (I). Its principal action was the condemnation of Arianism, the most devastating of the early heresies, which denied the divinity of Christ. The heresy was authored by Arius of Alexandria, a priest. Arians and several kinds of Semi-Arians propagandized their tenets widely, established their own hierarchies and churches, and raised havoc in the Church for several centuries. The council contributed to formulation of the Nicene Creed (Creed of Nicaea-Constantinople); fixed the date for the observance of Easter; passed regulations concerning clerical discipline; adopted the civil divisions of the Empire as the model for the jurisdictional organization of the Church.

326: With the support of St. Helena, the True Cross on which Christ was crucified was discovered.

337: Baptism and death of Constantine.

c. 342: Beginning of a 40-year persecution in Persia.

343-44: A council of Sardica reaffirmed doctrine formulated by Nicaea I and declared also that bishops had the right of appeal to the pope as the highest authority in the Church.

361-63: Emperor Julian the Apostate waged an unsuccessful campaign against the Church in an attempt to restore paganism as the religion of the Empire.

c. 365: Persecution of orthodox Christians under Emperor Valens in the East.

c. 376: Beginning of the barbarian invasion in the West.

379: Death of St. Basil, the Father of Monasticism in the East. His writings contributed greatly to the development of rules for the life of Religious.

381: Ecumenical Council of Constantinople (I). It condemned various brands of Arianism as well as Macedonianism, which denied the divinity of the Holy Spirit; contributed to formulation of the Nicene Creed; approved a canon acknowledging Constantinople as the second see after Rome in honor and dignity.

382: The Canon of Sacred Scripture, the official list of the inspired books of the Bible, was contained in the Decree of Pope St. Damasus and published by a regional council of Carthage in 397; the Canon was formally defined by the Council of Trent in the 16th century.

382-c. 406: St. Jerome translated the Old and New Testaments into Latin; his work is called the Vulgate version of the Bible.

396: St. Augustine became bishop of Hippo in North Africa.

FIFTH CENTURY

410: Visigoths under Alaric sacked Rome and the last Roman legions departed Britain. The decline of imperial Rome dates approximately from this time.

430: St. Augustine, bishop of Hippo for 35 years, died. He was a strong defender of orthodox doctrine against Manichaeism, Donatism and Pelagianism. The depth and range of his writings made him a dominant influence in Christian thought for centuries.

431: Ecumenical Council of Ephesus. It condemned

Nestorianism, which denied the unity of the divine and human natures in the Person of Christ; defined *Theotokos* (Bearer of God) as the title of Mary, Mother of the Son of God made Man; condemned Pelagianism. The heresy of Pelagianism, proceeding from the assumption that Adam had a natural right to supernatural life, held that man could attain salvation through the efforts of his natural powers and free will; it involved errors concerning the nature of original sin, the meaning of grace and other matters. Related Semi-Pelagianism was condemned by a council of Orange in 529.

432: St. Patrick arrived in Ireland. By the time of his death in 461 most of the country had been converted, monasteries founded and the hierarchy established.

438: The Theodosian Code, a compilation of decrees for the Empire, was issued by Theodosius II; it had great influence on subsequent civil and ecclesiastical law.

451: Ecumenical Council of Chalcedon. Its principal action was the condemnation of Monophysitism (also called Eutychianism), which denied the humanity of Christ by holding that he had only one, the divine, nature.

452: Pope St. Leo the Great persuaded Attila the Hun to spare Rome.

455: Vandals under Geiseric sacked Rome.

484: Patriarch Acacius of Constantinople was excommunicated for signing the *Henoticon*, a document which capitulated to the Monophysite heresy. The excommunication triggered the Acacian Schism which lasted for 35 years.

494: Pope St. Gelasius I declared in a letter to Emperor Anastasius that the pope had power and authority over the emperor in spiritual matters.

496: Clovis, King of the Franks, was converted and became the defender of Christianity in the West. The Franks became a Catholic people.

SIXTH CENTURY

520: Irish monasteries flourished as centers for spiritual life, missionary training, and scholarly activity.

529: The Second Council of Orange condemned Semi-Pelagianism.

c. 529: St. Benedict founded the Monte Cassino Abbey. Some years before his death in 543 he wrote a monastic rule which exercised tremendous influence on the form and style of religious life. He is called the Father of Monasticism in the West.

533: John II became the first pope to change his name. The practice did not become general until the time of Sergius IV (1009).

533-34: Emperor Justinian promulgated the *Corpus Iuris Civilis* for the Roman world; like the Theodosian Code, it influenced subsequent civil and ecclesiastical law.

c. 545: Death of Dionysius Exiguus who was the first to date history from the birth of Christ, a practice which resulted in use of the B.C. and A.D. abbreviations. His calculations were at least four years late.

553: Ecumenical Council of Constantinople (II). It condemned the Three Chapters, Nestoriantainted writings of Theodore of Mopsuestia, Theodoret of Cyrus and Ibas of Edessa.

585: St. Columban founded an influential monastic school at Luxeuil.

589: The most important of several councils of Toledo was held. The Visigoths renounced Arianism, and St. Leander began the organization of the Church in Spain.

590-604: Pontificate of Pope St. Gregory I the Great. He set the form and style of the papacy which prevailed throughout the Middle Ages; exerted great influence on doctrine and liturgy; was strong in support of monastic discipline and clerical celibacy; authored writings on many subjects. Gregorian Chant is named in his honor.

596: Pope St. Gregory I sent St. Augustine of Canterbury and 40 monks to do missionary work in England.

597: St. Columba died. He founded an important monastery at Iona, established schools and did notable missionary work in Scotland. By the end of the century, monasteries of nuns were common; Western monasticism was flourishing; monasticism in the East, under the influence of Monophysitism and other factors, was losing its vigor.

SEVENTH CENTURY

613: St. Columban established the influential monastery of Bobbio in northern Italy; he died there in 615.

622: The *Hegira* (flight) of Mohammed from Mecca to Medina signalled the beginning of Islam which, by the end of the century, claimed almost all of the southern Mediterranean area.

628: Heraclius, Eastern Emperor, recovered the True Cross from the Persians.

649: A Lateran council condemned two erroneous formulas (Ecthesis and Type) issued by emperors Heraclius and Constans II as means of reconciling Monophysites with the Church.

664: Actions of the Synod of Whitby advanced the adoption of Roman usages in England, especially regarding the date for the observance of Easter. (See Easter Controversy.)

680-81: Ecumenical Council of Constantinople (III). It condemned Monothelitism, which held that Christ had only one will, the divine; censured Pope Honorius I for a letter to Sergius, bishop of Constantinople, in which he made an ambiguous but not infallible statement about the unity of will and/or operation in Christ.

692: Trullan Synod. Eastern-Church discipline on clerical celibacy was settled, permitting marriage before ordination to the diaconate and continuation in marriage afterwards, but prohibiting marriage following the death of the wife thereafter. Anti-Roman canons contributed to East-West alienation.

During the century, the monastic influence of Ireland and England increased in Western Europe; schools and learning declined; regulations regarding clerical celibacy became more strict in the East.

EIGHTH CENTURY

711: Muslims began the conquest of Spain.

726: Emperor Leo III, the Isaurian, launched a campaign against the veneration of sacred images and relics; called Iconoclasm (image-breaking), it caused turmoil in the East until about 843.

731: Pope Gregory III and a synod at Rome condemned Iconoclasm, with a declaration that the veneration of sacred images was in accord with Catholic tradition.

Venerable Bede issued his *Ecclesiastical History of the English People*.

732: Charles Martel defeated the Muslims at Poitiers, halting their advance in the West.

744: The Monastery of Fulda was established by St. Sturmi, a disciple of St. Boniface; it was influential in the evangelization of Germany.

754: A council of more than 300 Byzantine bishops endorsed Iconoclast errors. This council and its actions were condemned by the Lateran synod of 769.

Stephen II (III) crowned Pepin ruler of the Franks. Pepin twice invaded Italy, in 754 and 756, to defend the pope against the Lombards. His land grants to the papacy, called the Donation of Pepin, were later extended by Charlemagne (773) and formed part of the States of the Church.

c. 755: St. Boniface (Winfrid) was martyred. He was called the Apostle of Germany for his missionary work and organization of the hierarchy there.

781: Alcuin was chosen by Charlemagne to organize a palace school, which became a center of intellectual leadership.

787: Ecumenical Council of Nicaea (II). It condemned Iconoclasm, which held that the use of images was idolatry, and Adoptionism, which claimed that Christ was not the Son of God by nature but only by adoption. This was the last council regarded as ecumenical by Orthodox Churches.

792: A council at Ratisbon condemned Adoptionism.

The famous *Book of Kells* ("The Great Gospel of Columcille") dates from the early eighth or late seventh century.

NINTH CENTURY

800: Charlemagne was crowned Emperor by Pope Leo III on Christmas Day.

Egbert became king of West Saxons; he unified England and strengthened the See of Canterbury.

813: Emperor Leo V, the Armenian, revived Iconoclasm, which persisted until about 843.

814: Charlemagne died.

843: The Treaty of Verdun split the Frankish kingdom among Charlemagne's three grandsons.

844: A Eucharistic controversy involving the writings of St. Paschasius Radbertus, Ratramnus and Rabanus Maurus occasioned the development of terminology regarding the doctrine of the Real Presence.

846: Muslims invaded Italy and attacked Rome.

847-52: Period of composition of the False Decretals, a collection of forged documents attributed to popes from St. Clement (88-97) to Gregory II (714-731). The Decretals, which strongly supported the autonomy and rights of bishops, were suspect for a long time before being repudiated entirely about 1628.

848: The Council of Mainz condemned Gottschalk for heretical teaching regarding predestination. He was also condemned by the Council of Quierzy in 853.

857: Photius displaced Ignatius as patriarch of Constantinople. This marked the beginning of the Photian Schism, a confused state of East-West relations which has not yet been cleared up by historical research. Photius, a man of exceptional ability, died in 891.

865: St. Ansgar, apostle of Scandinavia, died.

869: St. Cyril died and his brother, St. Methodius (d. 885), was ordained a bishop. The Apostles of the Slavs devised an alphabet and translated the Gospels and liturgy into the Slavonic language.

869-70: Ecumenical Council of Constantinople (IV). It issued a second condemnation of Iconoclasm, condemned and deposed Photius as patriarch of Constantinople and restored Ignatius to the patriarchate. This was the last ecumenical council held in the East. It was first called ecumenical by canonists toward the end of the 11th century.

871-c. 900: Reign of Alfred the Great, the only English king ever anointed by a pope at Rome.

TENTH CENTURY

910: William, duke of Aquitaine, founded the Benedictine Abbey of Cluny, which became a center of monastic and ecclesiastical reform, especially in France.

915: Pope John X played a leading role in the expulsion of Saracens from central and southern Italy.

955: St. Olga, of the Russian royal family, was baptized.

962: Otto I, the Great, crowned by Pope John XII, revived Charlemagne's kingdom, which became the Holy Roman Empire.

966: Mieszko, first of a royal line in Poland, was baptized; he brought Latin Christianity to Poland.

988: Conversion and baptism of St. Vladimir and the people of Kiev which subsequently became part of Russia.

993: John XV was the first pope to decree the official canonization of a saint — Bishop Ulrich (Uldaric) of Augsburg — for the universal Church.

997: St. Stephen became ruler of Hungary. He assisted in organizing the hierarchy and establishing Latin Christianity in that country.

999-1003: Pontificate of Sylvester II (Gerbert of Aquitaine), a Benedictine monk and the first French pope.

ELEVENTH CENTURY

1009: Beginning of lasting East-West Schism in the Church, marked by dropping of the name of Pope Sergius IV from the Byzantine diptychs (the listing of persons prayed for during the liturgy). The deletion was made by Patriarch Sergius II of Constantinople.

1012: St. Romuald founded the Camaldolese Hermits.

1025: The Council of Arras, and other councils later, condemned the Cathari (Neo-Manichaeans, Albigenses).

1027: The Council of Elne proclaimed the Truce of God as a means of stemming violence; it involved armistice periods of varying length, which were later extended.

1038: St. John Gualbert founded the Vallombrosians.

1043-59: Constantinople patriarchate of Michael Cerularius, the key figure in a controversy concerning the primacy of the papacy. His and the Byzantine synod's refusal to acknowledge this primacy in 1054 widened and hardened the East-West Schism in the Church.

1047: Pope Clement II died; he was the only pope ever buried in Germany.

1049-54: Pontificate of St. Leo IX, who inaugurated a movement of papal, diocesan, monastic and clerical reform.

1054: Start of the Great Schism between the Eastern and Western Churches; it marked the separation of Orthodox Churches from unity with the pope.

1055: Condemnation of the Eucharistic doctrine of Berengarius.

1059: A Lateran council issued new legislation regarding papal elections; voting power was entrusted to the Roman cardinals.

1066: Death of St. Edward the Confessor, king of England from 1042 and restorer of Westminster Abbey.

Defeat, at Hastings, of Harold by William, Duke of Normandy (later William I), who subsequently exerted strong influence on the life-style of the Church in England.

1073-85: Pontificate of St. Gregory VII (Hildebrand). A strong pope, he carried forward programs of clerical and general ecclesiastical reform and struggled against German King Henry IV and other rulers to end the evils of lay investiture. He introduced the Latin liturgy in Spain and set definite dates for the observance of ember days.

1077: Henry IV, excommunicated and suspended from the exercise of imperial powers by Gregory VII, sought absolution from the pope at Canossa. Henry later repudiated this action and in 1084 forced Gregory to leave Rome.

1079: The Council of Rome condemned Eucharistic errors (denial of the Real Presence of Christ under the appearances of bread and wine) of Berengarius, who retracted.

1084: St. Bruno founded the Carthusians.

1097-99: The first of several Crusades undertaken between this time and 1265. Recovery of the Holy Places and gaining free access to them for Christians were the original purposes, but these were diverted to less worthy objectives in various ways. Results included: a Latin Kingdom of Jerusalem, 1099-1187; a military and political misadventure in the form of a Latin Empire of Constantinople, 1204-1261; acquisition, by treaties, of visiting rights for Christians in the Holy Land. East-West economic and cultural relationships increased during the period. In the religious sphere, actions of the Crusaders had the effect of increasing the alienation of the East from the West.

1098: St. Robert founded the Cistercians.

TWELFTH CENTURY

1108: Beginnings of the influential Abbey and School of St. Victor in France.

1115: St. Bernard established the Abbey of Clairvaux and inaugurated the Cistercian Reform.

1118: Christian forces captured Saragossa, Spain; the beginning of the Muslim decline in that country.

1121: St. Norbert established the original monastery of the Praemonstratensians near Laon, France.

1122: The Concordat of Worms (*Pactum Callixtinum*) was formulated and approved by Pope Callistus II and Emperor Henry V to settle controversy concerning the investiture of prelates. The concordat provided that the emperor could invest prelates with symbols of temporal authority but had no right to invest them with spiritual authority, which came from the Church alone, and that the emperor was not to interfere in papal elections. This was the first concordat in history.

1123: Ecumenical Council of the Lateran (I), the first of its kind in the West. It endorsed provisions of the Concordat of Worms concerning the investiture of prelates and approved reform measures in 25 canons.

1139: Ecumenical Council of the Lateran (II). It adopted measures against a schism organized by antipope Anacletus and approved 30 canons related to discipline and other matters; one of the canons stated that holy orders is an invalidating impediment to marriage.

1140: St. Bernard met Abelard in debate at the Council of Sens. Abelard, whose rationalism in theology was condemned for the first time in 1121, died in 1142 at Cluny.

1148: The Synod of Rheims enacted strict disciplinary decrees for communities of women Religious.

1152: The Synod of Kells reorganized the Church in Ireland.

1160: Gratian, whose *Decretum* became a basic text of canon law, died.

Peter Lombard, compiler of the Four Books of Sentences, a standard theology text for nearly 200 years, died.

1170: St. Thomas Becket, archbishop of Canterbury, who clashed with Henry II over church-state relations, was murdered in his cathedral.

1171: Pope Alexander III reserved the process of canonization of saints to the Holy See.

1179: Ecumenical Council of the Lateran (III). It enacted measures against Waldensianism and Albigensianism (see year 242 regarding Manichaeism), approved reform decrees in 27 canons, provided that popes be elected by a two-thirds vote of the cardinals.

1184: Waldenses and other heretics were excommunicated by Pope Lucius III.

THIRTEENTH CENTURY

1198-1216: Pontificate of Innocent III, during which the papacy reached its medieval peak of authority, influence and prestige in the Church and in relations with civil rulers.

1208: Innocent III called for a crusade, the first in Christendom itself, against the Albigensians; their beliefs and practices threatened the fabric of society in southern France and northern Italy.

1209: Verbal approval was given by Innocent III to a rule of life for the Order of Friars Minor, started by St. Francis of Assisi.

1212: The Second Order of Franciscans, the Poor Clares, was founded.

1215: Ecumenical Council of the Lateran (IV). It ordered annual reception of the sacraments of penance and the Eucharist; defined and made the first official use of the term transubstantiation to explain the change of bread and wine into the body and blood of Christ; adopted additional measures to counteract teachings and practices of the Albigensians and Cathari; approved 70 canons.

1216: Formal papal approval was given to a rule of life for the Order of Preachers, started by St. Dominic.

The Portiuncula Indulgence was granted by the Holy See at the request of St. Francis of Assisi.

1221: Rule of the Third Order Secular of St. Francis (Secular Franciscan Order) approved verbally by Honorius III.

1226: Death of St. Francis of Assisi.

1231: Pope Gregory IX authorized establishment of the Papal Inquisition for dealing with heretics. It was a creature of its time, when crimes against faith and heretical doctrines of extremists like the Cathari and Albigenses threatened the good of the Christian community, the welfare of the state and the very fabric of society. The institution, which was responsible for excesses in punishment, was most active in the second half of the century in southern France, Italy and Germany.

1245: Ecumenical Council of Lyons (I). It confirmed the deposition of Emperor Frederick II and approved 22 canons.

1247: Preliminary approval was given by the Holy See to a Carmelite rule of life.

1270: St. Louis IX, king of France, died.
Beginning of papal decline.

1274: Ecumenical Council of Lyons (II). It accomplished a temporary reunion of separated Eastern Churches with the Roman Church; issued regulations concerning conclaves for papal elections; approved 31 canons.

Death of St. Thomas Aquinas, Doctor of the Church, of lasting influence.

1280: Pope Nicholas III, who made the Breviary the official prayer book for clergy of the Roman Church, died.

1281: The excommunication of Michael Palaeologus by Pope Martin IV ruptured the union effected with the Eastern Church in 1274.

FOURTEENTH CENTURY

1302: Pope Boniface VIII issued the bull *Unam Sanctam*, concerning the unity of the Church and the temporal power of princes, against the background of a struggle with Philip IV of France; it was the most famous medieval document on the subject.

1309-77: For a period of approximately 70 years,

seven popes resided at Avignon because of unsettled conditions in Rome and other reasons; see separate entry.

1311-12: Ecumenical Council of Vienne. It suppressed the Knights Templar and enacted a number of reform decrees.

1321: Dante Alighieri died a year after completing the *Divine Comedy*.

1324: Marsilius of Padua completed *Defensor Pacis*, a work condemned by Pope John XXII as heretical because of its denial of papal primacy and the hierarchical structure of the Church, and for other reasons. It was a charter for conciliarism (an ecumenical council is superior to the pope in authority).

1337-1453: Period of the Hundred Years' War, a dynastic struggle between France and England.

1338: Four years after the death of Pope John XXII, who had opposed Louis IV of Bavaria in a years-long controversy, electoral princes declared at the Diet of Rhense that the emperor did not need papal confirmation of his title and right to rule. Charles IV later (1356) said the same thing in a *Golden Bull*, eliminating papal rights in the election of emperors.

1347-50: The Black Death swept across Europe, killing perhaps one-fourth to one-third of the total population; an estimated 40 per cent of the clergy succumbed.

1374: Petrarch, poet and humanist, died.

1377: Return of the papacy from Avignon to Rome. Beginning of the Western Schism; see separate entry.

FIFTEENTH CENTURY

1409: The Council of Pisa, without canonical authority, tried to end the Western Schism but succeeded only in complicating it by electing a third claimant to the papacy; see Western Schism.

1414-18: Ecumenical Council of Constance. It took successful action to end the Western Schism involving rival claimants to the papacy; rejected the teachings of Wycliff; condemned Hus as a heretic. One decree — passed in the earlier stages of the council but later rejected — asserted the superiority of an ecumenical council over the pope (conciliarism).

1431: St. Joan of Arc was burned at the stake.

1431-45: Ecumenical Council of Florence (also called Basle-Ferrara-Florence). It affirmed the primacy of the pope against the claims of conciliarists that an ecumenical council is superior to the pope. It also formulated and approved decrees of union with several separated Eastern Churches — Greek, Armenian, Jacobite — which failed to gain general or lasting acceptance.

1438: The Pragmatic Sanction of Bourges was enacted by Charles VII and the French Parliament to curtail papal authority over the Church in France, in the spirit of conciliarism. It found expression in Gallicanism and had effects lasting at least until the French Revolution.

1453: The fall of Constantinople to the Turks.

c. 1456: Gutenberg issued the first edition of the Bible printed from movable type, at Mainz, Germany.

1476: Pope Sixtus IV approved observance of the feast of the Immaculate Conception on Dec. 8 throughout the Church.

1478: Pope Sixtus IV, at the urging of King Ferdinand of Spain, approved establishment of the Spanish Inquisition for dealing with Jewish and Moorish converts accused of heresy. The institution, which was peculiar to Spain and its colonies in America, acquired jurisdiction over other cases as well and fell into disrepute because of its procedures, cruelty and the manner in which it served the Spanish crown, rather than the accused and the good of the Church. Protests by the Holy See failed to curb excesses of the Inquisition, which lingered in Spanish history until early in the 19th century.

1492: Columbus discovered the Americas.

1493: Pope Alexander VI issued a Bull of Demarcation which determined spheres of influence for the Spanish and Portuguese in the Americas.

The Renaissance, a humanistic movement which originated in Italy in the 14th century, spread to France, Germany, the Low Countries and England. A transitional period between the medieval world and the modern secular world, it introduced profound changes which affected literature and the other arts, general culture, politics and religion.

SIXTEENTH CENTURY

1512-17: Ecumenical Council of the Lateran (V). It stated the relation and position of the pope with respect to an ecumenical council; acted to counteract the Pragmatic Sanction of Bourges and exaggerated claims of liberty by the Church in France; condemned erroneous teachings concerning the nature of the human soul; stated doctrine concerning indulgences. The council reflected concern for abuses in the Church and the need for reforms but failed to take decisive action in the years immediately preceding the Reformation.

1517: Martin Luther signaled the beginning of the Reformation by posting 95 theses at Wittenberg. Subsequently, he broke completely from doctrinal orthodoxy in discourses and three published works (1519 and 1520); was excommunicated on more than 40 charges of heresy (1521); remained the dominant figure in the Reformation in Germany until his death in 1546.

1519: Zwingli triggered the Reformation in Zurich and became its leading proponent there until his death in combat in 1531.

1524: Luther's encouragement of German princes in putting down the two-year Peasants' Revolt gained political support for his cause.

1528: The Order of Friars Minor Capuchin was approved as an autonomous division of the Franciscan Order; like the Jesuits, the Capuchins became leaders in the Counter-Reformation.

1530: The Augsburg Confession of Lutheran faith was issued; it was later supplemented by the Smalkaldic Articles, approved in 1537.

1533: Henry VIII divorced Catherine of Aragon, married Anne Boleyn, was excommunicated. In

1534 he decreed the Act of Supremacy, making the sovereign the head of the Church in England, under which Sts. John Fisher and Thomas More were executed in 1535. Despite his rejection of papal primacy and actions against monastic life in England, he generally maintained doctrinal orthodoxy until his death in 1547.

1536: John Calvin, leader of the Reformation in Switzerland until his death in 1564, issued the first edition of Institutes of the Christian Religion, which became the classical text of Reformed (non-Lutheran) theology.

1540: The constitutions of the Society of Jesus (Jesuits), founded by St. Ignatius of Loyola, were approved.

1541: Start of the 11-year career of St. Francis Xavier as a missionary to the East Indies and Japan.

1545-63: Ecumenical Council of Trent. It issued a great number of decrees concerning doctrinal matters opposed by the Reformers, and mobilized the Counter-Reformation. Definitions covered the Canon of the Bible, the rule of faith, the nature of justification, grace, faith, original sin and its effects, the seven sacraments, the sacrificial nature of the Mass, the veneration of saints, use of sacred images, belief in purgatory, the doctrine of indulgences, the jurisdiction of the pope over the whole Church. It initiated many reforms for renewal in the liturgy and general discipline in the Church, the promotion of religious instruction, the education of the clergy through the foundation of seminaries, etc. Trent ranks with Vatican II as the greatest ecumenical council held in the West.

1549: The first Anglican Book of Common Prayer was issued by Edward VI. Revised editions were published in 1552, 1559 and 1662 and later.

1553: Start of the five-year reign of Mary Tudor who tried to counteract actions of Henry VIII against the Roman Church.

1555: Enactment of the Peace of Augsburg, an arrangement of religious territorialism rather than toleration, which recognized the existence of Catholicism and Lutheranism in the German Empire and provided that citizens should adopt the religion of their respective rulers.

1558: Beginning of the reign (to 1603) of Queen Elizabeth I of England and Ireland, during which the Church of England took on its definitive form.

1559: Establishment of the hierarchy of the Church of England, with the consecration of Matthew Parker as archbishop of Canterbury.

1563: The first text of the 39 Articles of the Church of England was issued. Also enacted were a new Act of Supremacy and Oath of Succession to the English throne.

1570: Elizabeth I was excommunicated. Penal measures against Catholics subsequently became more severe.

1571: Defeat of the Turkish armada at Lepanto staved off the invasion of Eastern Europe.

1577: The Formula of Concord, the classical statement of Lutheran faith, was issued; it was, generally, a Lutheran counterpart of the canons of the Council of Trent. In 1580, along with other formulas of doctrine, it was included in the Book of Concord.

1582: The Gregorian Calendar, named for Pope Gregory XIII, was put into effect and was eventually adopted in most countries: England delayed adoption until 1752.

SEVENTEENTH CENTURY

1605: The Gunpowder Plot, an attempt by Catholic fanatics to blow up James I of England and the houses of Parliament, resulted in an anti-Catholic Oath of Allegiance.

1610: Death of Matteo Ricci, outstanding Jesuit missionary to China, pioneer in cultural relations between China and Europe.
Founding of the first community of Visitation Nuns by Sts. Francis de Sales and Jane de Chantal.

1611: Founding of the Oratorians.

1613: Catholics were banned from Scandinavia.

1625: Founding of the Congregation of the Mission (Vincentians) by St. Vincent de Paul. He founded the Sisters of Charity in 1633.

1642: Death of Galileo, scientist, who was censured by the Congregation of the Holy Office for supporting the Copernican theory of the sun-centered planetary system. The case against him was closed in his favor in 1992.
Founding of the Sulpicians by Jacques Olier.

1643: Start of publication of the Bollandist *Acta Sanctorum*, a critical work on lives of the saints.

1648: Provisions in the Peace of Westphalia, ending the Thirty Years' War, extended terms of the Peace of Augsburg (1555) to Calvinists and gave equality to Catholics and Protestants in the 300 states of the Holy Roman Empire.

1649: Oliver Cromwell invaded Ireland and began a severe persecution of the Church there.

1653: Pope Innocent X condemned five propositions of Jansenism, a complex theory which distorted doctrine concerning the relations between divine grace and human freedom. Jansenism was also a rigoristic movement which seriously disturbed the Church in France, the Low Countries and Italy in this and the 18th century.

1673: The Test Act in England barred from public office Catholics who would not deny the doctrine of transubstantiation and receive Communion in the Church of England.

1678: Many English Catholics suffered death as a consequence of the Popish Plot, a false allegation by Titus Oates that Catholics planned to assassinate Charles II, land a French army in the country, burn London, and turn over the government to the Jesuits.

1682: The four Gallican articles, drawn up by Bossuet, asserted political and ecclesiastical immunities of France from papal control. The articles, which rejected the primacy of the pope, were declared null and void by Pope Alexander VIII in 1690.

1689: The Toleration Act granted a measure of freedom of worship to other English dissenters but not to Catholics.

EIGHTEENTH CENTURY

1704: Chinese Rites — involving the Christian adaptation of elements of Confucianism, veneration of ancestors and Chinese terminology in religion — were condemned by Clement XI.

1720: The Passionists were founded by St. Paul of the Cross.

1724: Persecution in China.

1732: The Redemptorists were founded by St. Alphonsus Liguori.

1738: Freemasonry was condemned by Clement XII and Catholics were forbidden to join, under penalty of excommunication; the prohibition was repeated by Benedict XIV in 1751 and by later popes.

1760s: Josephinism, a theory and system of state control of the Church, was initiated in Austria; it remained in force until about 1850.

1764: Febronianism, an unorthodox theory and practice regarding the constitution of the Church and relations between Church and state, was condemned for the first of several times. Proposed by an auxiliary bishop of Trier using the pseudonym Justinus Febronius, it had the effects of minimizing the office of the pope and supporting national churches under state control.

1773: Clement XIV issued a brief of suppression against the Jesuits, following their expulsion from Portugal in 1759, from France in 1764 and from Spain in 1767. Political intrigue and unsubstantiated accusations were principal factors in these developments. The ban, which crippled the society, contained no condemnation of the Jesuit constitutions, particular Jesuits or Jesuit teaching. The society was restored in 1814.

1778: Catholics in England were relieved of some civil disabilities dating back to the time of Henry VIII, by an act which permitted them to acquire, own and inherit property. Additional liberties were restored by the Roman Catholic Relief Act of 1791 and subsequent enactments of Parliament.

1789: Religious freedom in the United States was guaranteed under the First Amendment to the Constitution.

Beginning of the French Revolution which resulted in: the secularization of church property and the Civil Constitution of the Clergy in 1790; the persecution of priests, religious and lay persons loyal to papal authority; invasion of the Papal States by Napoleon in 1796; renewal of persecution from 1797-1799; attempts to dechristianize France and establish a new religion; the occupation of Rome by French troops and the forced removal of Pius VI to France in 1798.

This century is called the age of Enlightenment or Reason because of the predominating rational and scientific approach of its leading philosophers, scientists and writers with respect to religion, ethics and natural law. This approach downgraded the fact and significance of revealed religion. Also characteristic of the Enlightenment were subjectivism, secularism and optimism regarding human perfectibility.

NINETEENTH CENTURY

1801: Concordat between Napoleon and Pope Pius

VII is signed. It is soon violated by the Organic Articles issued by Napoleon in 1802.

1804: Napoleon crowns himself Emperor of the French with Pope Pius in attendance.

1809: Pope Pius VII was made a captive by Napoleon and deported to France where he remained in exile until 1814. During this time he refused to cooperate with Napoleon who sought to bring the Church in France under his own control, and other leading cardinals were imprisoned. The turbulence in church-state relations in France at the beginning of the century recurred in connection with the Bourbon Restoration, the July Revolution, the second and third Republics, the Second Empire and the Dreyfus case.

1814: The Society of Jesus, suppressed since 1773, was restored.

1817: Reestablishment of the Congregation for the Propagation of the Faith (Propaganda) by Pius VII was an important factor in increasing missionary activity during the century.

1820: Year's-long persecution, during which thousands died for the faith, ended in China. Thereafter, communication with the West remained cut off until about 1834. Vigorous missionary work got under way in 1842.

1822: The Pontifical Society for the Propagation of the Faith, inaugurated in France by Pauline Jaricot for the support of missionary activity, was established.

1829: The Catholic Emancipation Act relieved Catholics in England and Ireland of most of the civil disabilities to which they had been subject from the time of Henry VIII.

1832: Gregory XVI, in the encyclical *Mirari vos*, condemned indifferentism, one of the many ideologies at odds with Christian doctrine which were proposed during the century.

1833: Start of the Oxford Movement which affected the Church of England and resulted in some notable conversions, including that of John Henry Newman in 1845, to the Catholic Church.

Bl. Frederic Ozanam founded the Society of St. Vincent de Paul in France. The society's objectives are works of charity.

1848: *The Communist Manifesto*, a revolutionary document symptomatic of socio-economic crisis, was issued.

1850: The hierarchy was reestablished in England and Nicholas Wiseman made the first archbishop of Westminster. He was succeeded in 1865 by Henry Manning, an Oxford convert and proponent of the rights of labor.

1853: The Catholic hierarchy was reestablished in Holland.

1854: Pius IX proclaimed the dogma of the Immaculate Conception in the bull *Ineffabilis Deus*.

1858: The Blessed Virgin Mary appeared to St. Bernadette at Lourdes, France.

1864: Pius IX issued the encyclical *Quanta cura* and the *Syllabus of Errors* in condemnation of some 80 propositions derived from the scientific mentality and rationalism of the century. The subjects in question had deep ramifications in many areas of thought and human endeavor; in religion, they explicitly and/or implicitly rejected divine revelation and the supernatural order.

1867: The first volume of *Das Kapital* was published. Together with the Communist First International, formed in the same year, it had great influence on the subsequent development of communism and socialism.

1869: The Anglican Church was disestablished in Ireland.

1869-70: Ecumenical Council of the Vatican (I). It defined papal primacy and infallibility in a dogmatic constitution on the Church; covered natural religion, revelation, faith, and the relations between faith and reason in a dogmatic constitution on the Catholic faith.

1870-71: Victor Emmanuel II of Sardinia, crowned king of Italy after defeating Austrian and papal forces, marched into Rome in 1870 and expropriated the Papal States after a plebiscite in which Catholics, at the order of Pius IX, did not vote. In 1871, Pius IX refused to accept a Law of Guarantees. Confiscation of church property and hindrance of ecclesiastical administration by the regime followed.

1871: The German Empire, a confederation of 26 states, was formed. Government policy launched a *Kulturkampf* whose May Laws of 1873 were designed to annul papal jurisdiction in Prussia and other states and to place the Church under imperial control. Resistance to the enactments and the persecution they legalized forced the government to modify its anti-Church policy by 1887.

1878: Beginning of the pontificate of Leo XIII, who was pope until his death in 1903. Leo is best known for the encyclical *Rerum novarum*, which greatly influenced the course of Christian social thought and the labor movement. His other accomplishments included promotion of Scholastic philosophy and the impetus he gave to scriptural studies.

1881: The first International Eucharistic Congress was held in Lille, France.
Alexander II of Russia was assassinated. His policies of Russification — as well as those of his two predecessors and a successor during the century — caused great suffering to Catholics, Jews and Protestants in Poland, Lithuania, the Ukraine and Bessarabia.

1882: Charles Darwin died. His theory of evolution by natural selection, one of several scientific highlights of the century, had extensive repercussions in the faith-and-science controversy.

1887: The Catholic University of America was founded in Washington, D.C.

1893: The U.S. apostolic delegation was set up in Washington, D.C.

TWENTIETH CENTURY

1901: Restrictive measures in France forced the Jesuits, Benedictines, Carmelites and other religious orders to leave the country. Subsequently, 14,000 schools were suppressed; religious orders and congregations were expelled; the concordat was renounced in 1905; church property was confiscated in 1906. For some years the Holy See, refusing to comply with government demands for the control of bishops' appointments, left some ecclesiastical offices vacant.

1903-14: Pontificate of St. Pius X. He initiated the codification of canon law, 1904; removed the ban against participation by Catholics in Italian national elections, 1905; issued decrees calling upon the faithful to receive Holy Communion frequently and daily, and stating that children should begin receiving the Eucharist at the age of seven, 1905 and 1910, respectively; ordered the establishment of the Confraternity of Christian Doctrine in all parishes throughout the world, 1905; condemned Modernism in the decree *Lamentabili* and the encyclical *Pascendi*, 1907.

1908: The United States and England, long under the jurisdiction of the Congregation for the Propagation of the Faith as mission territories, were removed from its control and placed under the common law of the Church.

1910: Laws of separation were enacted in Portugal, marking a point of departure in church-state relations.

1911: The Catholic Foreign Mission Society of America — Maryknoll, the first U.S.-founded society of its type — was established.

1914: Start of World War I, which lasted until 1918.

1914-22: Pontificate of Benedict XV. Much of his pontificate was devoted to seeking ways and means of minimizing the material and spiritual havoc of World War I. In 1917 he offered his services as a mediator to the belligerent nations, but his pleas for settlement of the conflict went unheeded.

1917: The Blessed Virgin Mary appeared to three children at Fatima, Portugal.
A new constitution, embodying repressive laws against the Church, was enacted in Mexico. Its implementation resulted in persecution in the 1920s and 1930s.
Bolsheviks seized power in Russia and set up a communist dictatorship. The event marked the rise of communism in Russian and world affairs. One of its immediate, and lasting, results was persecution of the Church, Jews and other segments of the population.

1918: The Code of Canon Law, in preparation for more than 10 years, went into effect in the Western Church.

1919: Benedict XV stimulated missionary work through the decree *Maximum Illud*, in which he urged the recruiting and training of native clergy in places where the Church was not firmly established.

1920-22: Ireland was partitioned by two enactments of the British government which (1) made the six counties of Northern Ireland part of the United Kingdom in 1920 and (2) gave dominion status to the Irish Free State in 1922. The Irish Free State became an independent republic in 1949.

1922-39: Pontificate of Pius XI. He subscribed to the Lateran Treaty, 1929, which settled the Roman Question created by the confiscation of the Papal States in 1871; issued the encyclical *Casti connubii*, 1930, an authoritative statement on Christian marriage; resisted the efforts of Benito

Mussolini to control Catholic Action and the Church, in the encyclical *Non abbiamo bisogno*, 1931; opposed various fascist policies; issued the encyclicals *Quadragesimo anno*, 1931, developing the social doctrine of Leo XIII's *Rerum novarum*, and *Divini Redemptoris*, 1937, calling for social justice and condemning atheistic communism; condemned anti-Semitism, 1937.

1926: The Catholic Relief Act repealed virtually all legal disabilities of Catholics in England.

1931: Leftists proclaimed Spain a republic and proceeded to disestablish the Church, confiscate church property, deny salaries to the clergy, expel the Jesuits and ban teaching of the Catholic faith. These actions were preludes to the civil war of 1936-1939.

1933: Emergence of Adolf Hitler to power in Germany. By 1935 two of his aims were clear, the elimination of the Jews and control of a single national church. Six million Jews were killed in the Holocaust. The Church was subject to repressive measures, which Pius XI protested futilely in the encyclical *Mit brennender sorge* in 1937.

1936-39: Civil war in Spain between the leftist Loyalist and the forces of rightist leader Francisco Franco The Loyalists were defeated and one-man, one-party rule was established. Many priests, religious and lay persons fell victim to Loyalist persecution and atrocities.

1939-45: World War II.

1939-58: Pontificate of Pius XII. He condemned communism, proclaimed the dogma of the Assumption of Mary in 1950, in various documents and other enactments provided ideological background for many of the accomplishments of the Second Vatican Council. (See Twentieth Century Popes.)

1940: Start of a decade of communist conquest in more than 13 countries, resulting in conditions of persecution for a minimum of 60 million Catholics as well as members of other faiths.

Persecution diminished in Mexico because of non-enforcement of anti-religious laws still on record.

1950: Pius XII proclaimed the dogma of the Assumption of the Blessed Virgin Mary.

1957: The communist regime of China established the Patriotic Association of Chinese Catholics in opposition to the Church in union with the pope.

1958-63: Pontificate of Bl. John XXIII. His principal accomplishment was the convocation of the Second Vatican Council, the twenty-first ecumenical council in the history of the Church. (See Twentieth Century Popes.)

1962-65: Ecumenical Council of the Vatican (II). It formulated and promulgated 16 documents — two dogmatic and two pastoral constitutions, nine decrees and three declarations — reflect-

ing pastoral orientation toward renewal and reform in the Church, and making explicit dimensions of doctrine and Christian life requiring emphasis for the full development of the Church and the better accomplishment of its mission in the contemporary world.

1963-78: Pontificate of Paul VI. His main purpose and effort was to give direction and provide guidance for the authentic trends of church renewal set in motion by the Second Vatican Council. (See Twentieth Century Popes.)

1978: The thirty-four-day pontificate of John Paul I. Start of the pontificate of John Paul II; see Index.

1983: The revised Code of Canon Law, embodying reforms enacted by the Second Vatican Council, went into effect in the Church of Roman Rite.

1985: Formal ratification of a Vatican-Italy concordat replacing the Lateran Treaty of 1929.

1989-91: Decline and fall of communist influence and control in Middle and Eastern Europe and the Soviet Union.

1991: The Code of Canon Law for Eastern Churches went into effect.

1992: Approval of the new *Catechism of the Catholic Church*.

The Vatican officially closed the case against Galileo Galilei.

1994: Initiation of celebration preparations of the start of the third Christian millennium in the year 2000.

1997: Pope John Paul II issued an apology for any anti-Semitism by Catholics; a conference on anti-Semitism was also held in Rome and a number of Catholic leaders in Europe issued apologies for historical anti-Semitism.

1998: Pope John Paul II visited Cuba and secured the release of over 300 political prisoners.

The Vatican issued a white paper on Anti-Semitism, entitled: *We Remember: A Reflection on the Shoah*.

Twentieth anniversary of the pontificate of Pope John Paul II; he became the longest reigning pontiff elected in the 20th century.

2000: The Catholic Church celebrated the Holy Year 2000 and the Jubilee; commencement of the third Christian millennium.

Pope John Paul II issued apology for the sinful actions of the Church's members in the past. Pope John Paul II traveled to the Holy Land in an historic visit.

2001: Pope John Paul II traveled to Greece and Syria. He also named 44 new members to the College of Cardinals in an unprecedented consistory.

On September 11, the World Trade Center was destroyed and the Pentagon attacked by Islamic terrorists who hijacked several planes and used them as weapons of mass destruction. The attacks launched a global war on terror.

ECUMENICAL COUNCILS

An ecumenical council is an assembly of the college of bishops, with and under the presidency of the pope, which has supreme authority over the Church in matters pertaining to faith, morals, worship and discipline.

The Second Vatican Council stated: "The supreme authority with which this college (of bishops) is empowered over the whole Church is exercised in a solemn way through an ecumenical council. A council is never ecumenical unless it is confirmed or at least accepted as such by the successor of Peter. It is the prerogative of the Roman Pontiff to convoke these councils, to preside over them, and to confirm them" (Dogmatic Constitution on the Church, *Lumen Gentium*, No. 22).

Pope Presides

The pope is the head of an ecumenical council; he presides over it either personally or through legates. Conciliar decrees and other actions have binding force only when confirmed and promulgated by him. If a pope dies during a council, it is suspended until reconvened by another pope. An ecumenical council is not superior to a pope; hence, there is no appeal from a pope to a council.

Collectively, the bishops with the pope represent the whole Church. They do this not as democratic representatives of the faithful in a kind of church parliament, but as the successors of the Apostles with divinely given authority, care and responsibility over the whole Church.

All and only bishops are council participants with deliberative vote. The supreme authority of the Church can invite others and determine the manner of their participation.

Basic legislation concerning ecumenical councils is contained in Canons 337-41 of the Code of Canon Law. Basic doctrinal considerations were stated by the Second Vatican Council in the Dogmatic Constitution on the Church.

Background

Ecumenical councils had their prototype in the Council of Jerusalem in 51, at which the Apostles under the leadership of St. Peter decided that converts to the Christian faith were not obliged to observe all the prescriptions of Old Testament law (Acts 15). As early as the second century, bishops got together in regional meetings, synods or councils to take common action for the doctrinal and pastoral good of their communities of faithful. The expansion of such limited assemblies to ecumenical councils was a logical and historical evolution, given the nature and needs of the Church.

Emperors Involved

Emperors were active in summoning or convoking the first eight councils, especially the first five and the eighth. Among reasons for intervention of this kind were the facts that the emperors regarded themselves as guardians of the faith; that the settlement of religious controversies, which had repercussions in political and social turmoil, served the cause of peace in the state; and that the emperors had at their disposal ways and means of facilitating gatherings of bishops. Imperial actions, however, did not account for the formally ecumenical nature of the councils.

Some councils were attended by relatively few bishops, and the ecumenical character of several was open to question for a time. However, confirmation and de facto recognition of their actions by popes and subsequent councils established them as ecumenical.

Role in History

The councils have played a highly significant role in the history of the Church by witnessing to and defining truths of revelation, by shaping forms of worship and discipline, and by promoting measures for the ever-necessary reform and renewal of Catholic life. In general, they have represented attempts of the Church to mobilize itself in times of crisis for self-preservation, self-purification and growth.

The first eight ecumenical councils were held in the East; the other 13, in the West. The majority of separated Eastern Churches — e.g., the Orthodox — recognize the ecumenical character of the first seven councils, which formulated a great deal of basic doctrine. Other separated Eastern Churches acknowledge only the first two or first three ecumenical councils.

The 21 Councils

The 21 ecumenical councils in the history of the Church are listed below, with indication of their names or titles (taken from the names of the places where they were held); the dates; the reigning and/or approving popes; the emperors who were instrumental in convoking the eight councils in the East; the number of bishops who attended, when available; the number of sessions. Significant actions of the first 20 councils are indicated under appropriate dates in Dates and Events in Church History.

1. **Nicaea I**, 325: St. Sylvester I (Emperor Constantine I); attended by approximately 300 bishops; sessions held between May 20 or June 19 to near the end of August.

2. **Constantinople I**, 381: St. Damasus I (Emperor Theodosius I); attended by approximately 150 bishops; sessions held from May to July.

3. **Ephesus**, 431: St. Celestine I (Emperor Theodosius II); attended by 150 to 200 bishops; five sessions held between June 22 and July 17.

4. **Chalcedon**, 451: St. Leo I (Emperor Marcian); attended by approximately 600 bishops; 17 sessions held between Oct. 8 and Nov. 1.

5. **Constantinople II**, 553: Vigilius (Emperor Justinian I); attended by 165 bishops; eight sessions held between May 5 and June 2.

6. **Constantinople III**, 680-681: St. Agatho, St. Leo II (Emperor Constantine IV); attended by approximately 170 bishops; 16 sessions held between Nov. 7, 680, and Sept. 6, 681.

7. **Nicaea II**, 787: Adrian I (Empress Irene); attended by approximately 300 bishops: eight sessions held between Sept. 24 and Oct. 23.

8. **Constantinople IV**, 869-870: Adrian II (Emperor Basil I); attended by 102 bishops; six sessions held between Oct. 5, 869, and Feb. 28, 870.

9. **Lateran I**, 1123: Callistus II; attended by approximately 300 bishops; sessions held between Mar. 8 and Apr. 6.

10. **Lateran II**, 1139: Innocent II; attended by 900 to 1,000 bishops and abbots; three sessions held in April.

11. **Lateran III**, 1179: Alexander III; attended by at least 300 bishops; three sessions held between Mar. 5 and 19.

12. **Lateran IV**, 1215: Innocent III; sessions held between Nov. 11 and 30.

13. **Lyons I**, 1245: Innocent IV; attended by approximately 150 bishops; three sessions held between June 28 and July 17.

14. **Lyons II**, 1274: Gregory X; attended by approximately 500 bishops; six sessions held between May 7 and July 17.

15. **Vienne**, 1311-1312: Clement V; attended by 132 bishops; three sessions held between Oct. 16, 1311, and May 6, 1312.

16. **Constance**, 1414-1418: Gregory XII, Martin V; attended by nearly 200 bishops, plus other prelates and many experts; 45 sessions held between Nov. 5, 1414, and Apr. 22, 1418.

17. **Florence** (also called Basel-Ferrara-Florence), 1431-c. 1445: Eugene IV; attended by many Latin-Rite and Eastern-Rite bishops; preliminary sessions were held at Basel and Ferrara before definitive work was accomplished at Florence.

18. **Lateran V**, 1512-1517: Julius II, Leo X; 12 sessions held between May 3, 1512, and Mar. 6, 1517.

19. **Trent**, 1545-1563: Paul III, Julius III, Pius IV; 25 sessions held between Dec. 13, 1545, and Dec. 4, 1563.

20. **Vatican I**, 1869-1870: Pius IX; attended by approximately 800 bishops and other prelates; four public sessions and 89 general meetings held between Dec. 8, 1869, and Sept. 1, 1870.

VATICAN II

The Second Vatican Council, which was forecast by Pope John XXIII Jan. 25, 1959, was held in four sessions in St. Peter's Basilica.

Pope John convoked it and opened the first session, which ran from Oct. 11 to Dec. 8, 1962. Following John's death June 3, 1963, Pope Paul VI reconvened the council for the other three sessions which ran from Sept. 29 to Dec. 4, 1963; Sept. 14 to Nov. 21, 1964; Sept. 14 to Dec. 8, 1965.

A total of 2,860 Fathers participated in council proceedings, and attendance at meetings varied between 2,000 and 2,500. For various reasons, including the denial of exit from Communist-dominated countries, 274 Fathers could not attend.

The council formulated and promulgated 16 documents — two dogmatic and two pastoral constitutions, nine decrees and three declarations — all of which reflect its basic pastoral orientation toward renewal and reform in the Church. Given below are the Latin and English titles of the documents and their dates of promulgation.

Lumen Gentium (Dogmatic Constitution on the Church), Nov. 21, 1964.

Dei Verbum (Dogmatic Constitution on Divine Revelation), Nov. 18, 1965.

Sacrosanctum Concilium (Constitution on the Sacred Liturgy), Dec. 4, 1963.

Gaudium et Spes (Pastoral Constitution on the Church in the Modern World), Dec. 7, 1965.

Christus Dominus (Decree on the Bishops' Pastoral Office in the Church), Oct. 28, 1965.

Ad Gentes (Decree on the Church's Missionary Activity), Dec. 7, 1965.

Unitatis Redintegratio (Decree on Ecumenism), Nov. 21, 1964.

Orientalium Ecclesiarum (Decree on Eastern Catholic Churches), Nov. 21, 1964.

Presbyterorum Ordinis (Decree on the Ministry and Life of Priests), Dec. 7, 1965.

Optatam Totius (Decree on Priestly Formation), Oct. 28, 1965.

Perfectae Caritatis (Decree on the Appropriate Renewal of the Religious Life), Oct. 28, 1965.

Apostolicam Actuositatem (Decree on the Apostolate of the Laity), Nov. 18, 1965.

Inter Mirifica (Decree on the Instruments of Social Communication), Dec. 4, 1963.

Dignitatis Humanae (Declaration on Religious Freedom), Dec. 7, 1965.

Nostra Aetate (Declaration on the Relationship of the Church to Non-Christian Religions), Oct. 28, 1965.

Gravissimum Educationis (Declaration on Christian Education), Oct. 28, 1965.

The key documents were the four constitutions, which set the ideological basis for all the others. To date, the documents with the most visible effects are those on the liturgy, the Church, the Church in the world, ecumenism, the renewal of religious life, the life and ministry of priests, the lay apostolate.

The main business of the council was to explore and make explicit dimensions of doctrine and Christian life requiring emphasis for the full development of the Church and the better accomplishment of its mission in the contemporary world.

Enactments of the Second Vatican Council have been points of departure for a wide variety of developments in the internal life of the Church and its mission in the world at large. Much effort has been made in the pontificate of Pope John Paul II to provide the interpretation and implementation of the conciliar documents with a more uniform and universal structure.

The Papacy and the Holy See

POPE JOHN PAUL II

(Update courtesy of Russell Shaw; see many related entries under John Paul II in the Index.)

Cardinal Karol Wojtyla of Cracow was elected Bishop of Rome and 263rd successor of St. Peter as Supreme Pastor of the Universal Church on Oct. 16, 1978. He chose the name John Paul II in honor of his predecessor, Pope John Paul I, as well as Popes John XXIII and Paul VI. He was invested with the pallium, symbol of his office, on Oct. 22 in ceremonies attended by more than 250,000 people in St. Peter's Square.

From the start, Pope John Paul II has labored to keep the Church faithful to its tradition and to the teaching and spirit of Vatican Council II, while positioning it to meet the challenges of the Third Millennium. He is a staunch defender of the sanctity of human life — "from conception to natural death," he often says — and of marriage and the family. Opposition to totalitarianism and support for human rights make this activist, long-reigning pope a major figure on the world political scene.

He is the first non-Italian pope since Adrian VI (1522-23) and the first Polish pope ever. At his election, he was the youngest pope since Pius IX (1846-78). On May 24, 1998, he became the longest-reigning pope elected in the 20th century, surpassing the 19 years, seven months and seven days of Pius XII (1939-58). (Leo XIII, who died in 1903, was pope for 25 years.)

He is the most-traveled pope in history. Through September 2002, he had covered over 750,000 miles during 98 pastoral visits outside Italy, 140 within Italy, and 300 to the parishes of Rome. In all, he has visited over 130 countries and has held talks with 850 heads of state or government. Certainly he is the pope most prolific in literary output, having issued (through May 2002) 13 encyclicals, 12 apostolic exhortations, nine apostolic constitutions, and 37 apostolic letters. By his 82nd birthday John Paul had canonized over 450 saints and declared approximately 1,300 persons blessed; his 17 predecessors from Pope Clement VIII to Pope Paul VI canonized a total of 296 people. He had held eight consistories in which he created 203 cardinals. As of May 2002, the Holy Father has presided at 16 synods: the Particular Synod of Bishops of the Netherlands in 1980; five ordinary synods (1980, 1983, 1987, 1990, 1994); one extraordinary (1985) and eight special (1980, 1991, 1994, 1995, 1997, two in 1998, and the second synod for Europe in October 1999); the most recent synod was held in October 2001.

Early Life

Karol Josef Wojtyla was born May 18, 1920, in Wadowice, an industrial town near Cracow. His parents were Karol Wojtyla, who had been an adminstrative officer in the Austrian army and was a lieutenant in the Polish army until his retirement in 1927, and Emilia Kaczorowska Wojtyla. His mother died in 1929 of kidney and heart failure. His sister died a few days after birth; his older brother Edmund, a physician, died in 1932, and his father in 1941.

He attended schools in Wadowice and in 1938 enrolled in the faculty of philosophy of the Jagiellonian University in Cracow, moving there with his father that summer. At the university he also was active in the Studio 38 experimental theater group.

For young Wojtyla, as for countless others, life changed forever on Sept. 1, 1939, when World War II began. Nazi occupation forces closed the Jagiellonian University and the young man had to work in a quarry as a stone cutter and later in a chemical plant to avoid deportation to Germany. In Februrary 1940, he met Jan Tryanowski, a tailor who became his spiritual mentor and introduced him to the writings of St. John of the Cross and St. Teresa of Ávila. He also participated in underground theater groups, including the Rhapsodic Theater of Mieczyslaw Kotlarczyk.

In October 1942, he began studies for the priesthood in the underground seminary maintained by Cardinal Adam Sapieha of Cracow. He was struck by an automobile Feb. 29, 1944, and hospitalized until Mar. 12. In August of that year Cardinal Sapieha transferred him and the other seminarians to the Archbishop's Residence, where they lived and studied until war's end. Ordained a priest by the cardinal on Nov. 1, 1946, he left Poland Nov. 15 to begin advanced studies in Rome at the Angelicum University (the Pontifical University of St. Thomas Aquinas).

He subsequently earned doctorates in theology and philosophy and was a respected moral theologian and ethicist.

Bishop and Cardinal

On July 4, 1958, Pope Pius XII named him Auxiliary Bishop to Archbishop Eugeniusz Baziak, Apostolic Administrator of Cracow. His book *Love and Responsibility* was published in 1960. (Earlier, he published poetry and several plays.) Following Archbishop Baziak's death in 1962, he became Vicar Capitular and then on Jan. 13, 1964, Archbishop of Cracow — the first residential head of the See permitted by the communist authorities since Cardinal Sapieha's death in 1951.

Archbishop Wojtyla attended all four sessions of the Second Vatican Council, from 1962 to 1965, and helped draft Schema XIII, which became *Gaudium et Spes*, the Pastoral Constitution on the Church in the Modern World. He also contributed to *Dignitatis Humanae* (the Declaration on Religious Freedom) and on the theology of the laity.

Pope Paul VI created him a cardinal in the consistory of June 28, 1967, with the titular Roman church of S. Cesario in Palatio. Although scheduled to attend the first general assembly of the Synod of Bishops in September and October of that year, Cardinal Wojtyla did not go, as a sign of solidarity with Cardinal Stefan Wyszynski of Warsaw, Poland's primate, whom the communist government refused a passport. In October 1969, however, he participated in the first extraordinary assembly of the synod. Earlier that year, with approval of the statutes of the Polish bishops' conference, he became its vice president.

In 1971 he took part in the second general assembly of the synod and was elected to the council of the secretary general of the synod. He continued to participate in synod assemblies and to serve on the synod council up to his election as pope. May 8, 1972, saw the opening of the archdiocesan of synod of Cracow, which he had convened and would see conclude during his visit to Poland as Pope in 1979. Also in 1972 he published *Foundations of Renewal: A Study on the Implementation of the Second Vatican Council.*

Pope Paul died Aug. 6, 1978. Cardinal Wojtyla participated in the conclave that chose Cardinal Albino Luciani of Venice his successor on Aug. 26. When the new pope, who had taken the name John Paul I, died unexpectedly on Sept. 28, Cardinal Wojtyla joined 110 other cardinals in that year's second conclave. He emerged on the second day of voting, Oct. 16, as Pope John Paul II.

Pontificate

Pope John Paul set out the major themes and program of his pontificate in his first encyclical, *Redemptor Hominis (The Redeemer of Man)*, dated Mar. 4, 1979, and published Mar. 15. "The Redeemer of Man, Jesus Christ, is the center of the universe and of history," he wrote. Throughout his pontificate he has emphasized preparation for the year 2000—which he proclaimed a Jubilee Year — and for the Third Millennium of the Christian era, with the aim of fostering a renewed commitment to evangelization among Catholics. He also has produced a significant body of magisterial teaching in such areas as Christian anthropology, sexual morality, and social justice, while working for peace and human rights throughout the world.

His pontificate has been uncommonly active and filled with dramatic events. Among the most dramatic are those associated with the fall of communism in Eastern Europe. Many students of that complex event credit John Paul with a central role. His visits to his Polish homeland in 1979 (June 2-10) and 1983 (June 16-23) bolstered Polish Catholicism and kindled Polish resistance to communism, while his determined support for the Solidarity labor movement gave his countrymen a vehicle for their resistance. The result was a growing nonviolent liberation movement leading to the dramatic developments of 1989 — the collapse of communist regimes and the emergence of democracy in Poland and other countries, the fall of the Berlin Wall — and in time to the breakup of the Soviet Union and the end of the Cold War.

Dramatic in a much different way was the 1981 attempt on the Pope's life. At 5:19 p.m. on May 13, as he greeted crowds in St. Peter's Square before his Wednesday general audience, a Turkish terrorist named Mehmet Ali Agca shot John Paul at close range. Whether the assassin acted alone or at the behest of others — and which others — remain unanswered questions. Following a six-hour operation, John Paul was hospitalized for 77 days at Gemelli Hospital. He visited Ali Agca in the Rebibbia prison on Dec. 27, 1983.

Although he resumed his activities vigorously after his recuperation, the Pope's health and strength have declined over the years. In July 1992, he had colon surgery for the removal of a non-cancerous tumor; in November 1993, his shoulder was dislocated in a fall; he suffered a broken femur in another fall in April 1994; and in October 1996, he had an appendectomy. For several years, too, the effects have been apparent of what the Vatican acknowledges to be a neurological condition (many observers take the ailment to be Parkinson's disease). John Paul nevertheless maintains what is by any standards a highly demanding schedule. Clearly, he wishes to lead the Church into the new millennium.

Foreign Pastoral Visits

As noted, his pastoral visits have been a striking feature of his pontificate. Many have been to nations in the Third World. His 98 trips outside Italy (through September 2002) are as follows:

1979 Dominican Republic and Mexico, Jan. 5-Feb. 1; Poland, June 2-10; Ireland and the United States, Sept. 29-Oct. 7; Turkey, Nov. 28-30.

1980 Africa (Zaire, Congo Republic, Kenya, Ghana, Upper Volta, Ivory Coast), May 2-12; France, May 30-June 2; Brazil (13 cities), June 30-July 12; West Germany, Nov. 15-19.

1981 Philippines, Guam, and Japan, with stopovers in Pakistan and Alaska, Feb. 16-27.

1982 Africa (Nigeria, Benin, Gabon, Equatorial Guinea), Feb. 12-19; Portugal, May 12-15; Great Britain, May 28-June 2; Argentina, June 11-12; Switzerland, June 15; San Marino, Aug. 29; Spain, Oct. 31-Nov. 9.

1983 Central America (Costa Rica, Nicaragua, Panama, El Salvador, Guatemala, Belize, Honduras) and Haiti, Mar. 2-10; Poland, June 16-23; Lourdes, France, Aug. 14-15; Austria, Sept. 10-13.

1984 South Korea, Papua New Guinea, Solomon Islands, Thailand, May 12; Switzerland, June 12-17; Canada, Sept. 9-20; Spain, Dominican Republic, and Puerto Rico, Oct. 10-12.

1985 Venezuela, Ecuador, Peru, Trinidad and Tobago, Jan. 26-Feb. 6; Belgium, The Netherlands, and Luxembourg, May 11-21; Africa (Togo, Ivory Coast, Cameroon, Central African Republic, Zaire, Kenya, and Morocco), Aug. 8-19; Liechtenstein, Sept. 8.

1986 India, Feb. 1-10; Colombia and Saint Lucia, July 1-7; France, Oct. 4-7; Oceania (Australia, New Zealand, Bangladesh, Fiji, Singapore, and Seychelles), Nov. 18-Dec. 1.

1987 Uruguay, Chile, and Argentina, Mar. 31-Apr. 12; West Germany, Apr. 30-May 4; Poland, June 8-14; the United States and Canada, Sept. 10-19.

1988 Uruguay, Bolivia, Peru, and Paraguay, May 7-18; Austria, June 23-27; Africa (Zimbabwe, Botswana, Lesotho, Swaziland, and Mozambique), Sept. 10-19; France, Oct. 8-11.

1989 Madagascar, Reunion, Zambia, and Malawi, Apr. 28-May 6; Norway, Iceland, Finland, Denmark, and Sweden, June 1-10; Spain, Aug. 19-21; South Korea, Indonesia, East Timor, and Mauritius, Oct. 6-16.

1990 Africa (Cape Verde, Guinea Bissau, Mali, and Burkna Faso), Jan. 25-Feb. 1; Czechoslovakia, Apr. 21-22; Mexico and Curaçao, May 6-13; Malta, May 25-27; Africa (Tanzania, Burundi, Rwanda, and Ivory Coast), Sept. 1-10.

1991 Portugal, May 10-13; Poland, June 1-9; Poland and Hungary, Aug. 13-20; Brazil, Oct. 12-21.

1992 Africa (Senegal, The Gambia, Guinea), Feb. 10-26; Africa (Angola, São Tome, and Principe), June 4-10; Dominican Republic, Oct. 10-14.

1993 Africa (Benin, Uganda, Sudan), Feb. 2-10; Albania, Apr. 25; Spain, June 12-17; Jamaica, Mexico, Denver (United States), Aug. 9-15; Lithuania, Latvia, Estonia, Sept. 4-10.

1994 Zagreb, Croatia, Sept. 10.

1995 Philippines, Papua New Guinea, Australia, Sri Lanka, Jan. 12-21; Czech Republic and Poland, May 20-22; Belgium, June 3-4; Slovakia, June 30-July 3; Africa (Cameroon, South Africa, Kenya), Sept. 14-20; United Nations and United States, Oct. 4-8.

1996 Central America (Guatemala, Nicaragua, El Salvador), Feb. 5-11; Tunisia, Apr. 17; Slovenia, May 17-19; Germany, June 21-23; Hungary, Sept. 6-7; France, Sept. 19-22.

1997 Sarajevo, Apr. 12-13; Czech Republic, Apr. 25-27; Lebanon, May 10-11; Poland, May 31-June 10; France, Aug. 21-24; Brazil, Oct. 2-5.

1998 Cuba, Jan. 21-25; Nigeria, Mar. 21-23; Austria, June 19-21; Croatia, Oct. 3-4.

1999 Mexico, Jan. 22-25; St. Louis, United States, Jan. 26-27; Romania, May 2-5; Poland June, 5-17; Slovenia, Sept. 19; India, Nov. 6-7; Georgia, Nov. 8-9.

2000 Egypt and Mount Sinai, Feb. 24-26; Holy Land, Mar. 20-26; Fátima, May 12-13;

2001 Greece, Syria, and Malta, May 4-9; Ukraine, June 23-27; Kazakstan and Armenia, Sept. 22-27.

2002 Azerbaijan and Bulgaria, May 22-26; Toronto, Canada, July 23-28; Guatemala City, July 29-30; Mexico City, July 31-Aug. 2; Poland, Aug. 16-19.

(For details on the Holy Father's recent trips, please the **Papal Trips** section under **Special Reports**.)

Notable among the Pope's pastoral visits have been journeys to celebrate World Youth Day with young people, including the 2002 celebration in Toronto (see **Special Report**).

Encyclicals and Other Writings

As noted above, Pope John Paul's first encyclical, *Redemptor Hominis* (1979), set the tone for and in general terms indicated the subject matter of many of the documents to follow. These are infused with the Pope's distinctive personalism, which emphasizes the dignity and rights of the human person, most truly understood in the light of Christ, as the norm and goal of human endeavor.

His other encyclical letters to date are: **Dives in Misericordia** ("On the Mercy of God"), 1980; **Laborem Exercens** ("On Human Work"), 1981; **Slavorum Apostoli** ("The Apostles of the Slavs," honoring Sts. Cyril and Methodius), 1985; **Dominum et Vivificantem** ("Lord and Giver of Life, on the Holy Spirit"), 1986; **Redemptoris Mater** ("Mother of the Redeemer"), 1987; **Sollicitudo Rei Socialis** ("On Social Concerns"), 1988; **Redemptoris Missio** ("Mission of the Redeemer") and **Centesimus Annus** ("The Hundredth Year," on the anniversary of Leo XIII's **Rerum Novarum**), both 1991; **Veritatis Splendor** ("The Splendor of Truth"), 1993; **Evangelium Vitae** ("The Gospel of Life") and **Ut Unum Sint** ("That All May Be One"), 1995; **Fides et Ratio** ("Faith and Reason"), 1998.

Among his other publications are: *Catechesi Tradendae*, a post-synodal apostolic exhortation on catechesis, 1979; apostolic letter proclaiming Sts. Cyril and Methodius, together with St. Benedict, patrons of Europe, 1980; post-synodal apostolic exhortation *Familiaris Consortio*, on the family, 1981; apostolic letter *Caritatis Christi*, for the Church in China, 1982; letter for the 500th anniversary of the birth of Martin Luther, 1983; apostolic letter *Salvifici Doloris* ("On the Christian Meaning of Suffering"), apostolic exhortation *Redemptionis Donum*, to men and women religious, apostolic letters *Redemptionis Anno*, on Jerusalem, and *Les Grands Mysteres*, on Lebanon, and post-synodal apostolic exhortation *Reconciliatio et Poenitentia* ("Reconciliation and Penance"), all 1984.

Also: apostolic letter *Dilecti Amici*, on the occasion of the United Nations' International Year of Youth, 1985; apostolic letter *Euntes in Mundum*, for the millennium of Christianity in Kievan Rus', and apostolic letter *Mulieris Dignitatem* ("On the Dignity and Vocation of Women"), all 1988; post-synodal apostolic exhortation *Christifideles Laici* ("The Lay Members of Christ's Faithful People") and apostolic exhortation *Redemptoris Custos* ("On St. Joseph"), 1989; post-synodal apostolic exhortation *Pastores Dabo Vobis* ("I Give You Shepherds"), 1992; *Letter to Families*, for the International Year of the Family, Letter on the International Conference on Population and Development in Cairo, apostolic letter *Ordinatio Sacerdotalis* ("On Reserving Priestly Ordination to Men Alone"), apostolic letter *Tertio Millennio Adveniente*, on preparation for the Jubilee Year 2000, and *Letter to Children in the Year of the Family*, all 1994.

Also: apostolic letter *Orientale Lumen* ("The Light of the East"), on Catholic-Orthodox relations, *Letter to Women*, post-synodal apostolic exhortation *Ecclesia in Africa*, and apostolic letter for the fourth centenary of the Union of Brest, all 1995; apostolic constitution *Universi Dominici Gregis* ("On the Vacancy of the Apostolic See and the Election of the Roman Pontiff"), post-synodal apostolic exhortation *Vita Consecrata* ("On the Consecrated Life and Its Mission in the Church and in the World"), and apostolic letter on the 350th anniversary of the Union of Uzhorod, all 1996; post-synodal apostolic exhortation, *A New Hope for Lebanon*, 1997; *Incarnationis Mysterium*, Bull of Indiction of the Great Jubilee of the Year 2000, 1998; and the apostolic letter *Misericordia Dei* ("On Certain Aspects of the Celebration of the Sacrament of Penance"), 2002.

In his years as pope he also has published two books: *Crossing the Threshold of Hope* (1994) and *Gift and Mystery: On the Fiftieth Anniversary of My Priestly Ordination* (1996).

Issues and Activities

Doctrinal Concerns: The integrity of Catholic doctrine has been a major concern of Pope John Paul. On Nov. 25, 1981, he appointed Archbishop — later, Cardinal — Joseph Ratzinger of Munich-Freising, a prominent theologian, Prefect of the Congregation for the Doctrine of the Faith. The congregation under Cardinal Ratzinger has published important documents on bioethics, on liberation theology (1984 and 1986), and on the Church's inability to ordain women as priests, the latter affirming that the teaching on this matter has been "set forth infallibly" (1995).

Catechism: One of Pope John Paul's most important initiatives is the *Catechism of the Catholic Church*. The idea for this up-to-date compendium was broached at the extraordinary assembly of the Synod of Bishops held in 1985 to evaluate the implementation of Vatican Council II. The pope approved, and the project went forward under a commission of cardinals headed by Cardinal Ratzinger. Published in 1992 by authorization of John Paul II (the original was in French, with the English translation appearing in 1994 and the authoritative Latin *editio typica* in 1997), this first catechism for the universal Church in four centuries is crucial to the hoped-for renewal of catechesis.

Canon Law: John Paul oversaw the completion of the revision of the Code of Canon Law begun in 1959 at the direction of Pope John XXIII. He promulgated the new code on Jan. 25, 1983; it went into effect on Nov. 27 of that year. In *Sacrae Disciplinae Leges*, the apostolic constitution accompanying the revised code,

the Pope says it has "one and the same intention" as Vatican Council II — whose convening John XXIII announced at the same time — namely, "the renewal of Christian living."

On Apr. 18, 1990, John Paul promulgated the Code of Canons for the Eastern Churches. Although particular sections of the Eastern code appeared at various times dating back to 1949, this was the first time an integrated code of law for the Eastern Churches had been issued in its entirety.

Ecumenical and Interreligious Relations: Ecumenical and interreligious relations have received much attention from Pope John Paul II. Two of his major documents, the encyclical *Ut Unum Sint* and the apostolic letter *Orientale Lumen*, both published in 1995, deal with these matters. He has met frequently with representatives of other religious bodies, has spoken frequently about the quest for unity, and has called for Catholics and others to pray and work to this end.

Among the important actions in this area have been the signings of common declarations with the Ecumenical Patriarch of Constantinople His Holiness Dimitrios (Dec. 7, 1987) and his successor Bartholomew I (June 29, 1995), with the Archbishop of Canterbury and Primate of the Anglican Communion, Dr. Robert Runcie (May 29, 1982, in Canterbury Cathedral and again Oct. 2, 1989 in Rome) and his successor Dr. George Leonard Carey (Dec. 6, 1996), with the Supreme Patriarch and Catholicos of All Armenians, His Holiness Karekin I (Dec. 14, 1996), and with His Holiness Aram I Keshishian, Catholicos of Cilicia of the Armenians (Jan. 26, 1997). On Oct. 5, 1991, for the first time since the Reformation, two Lutheran bishops joined the Pope and the Catholic bishops of Stockholm and Helsinki in an ecumenical prayer service in St. Peter's Basilica marking the sixth centenary of the canonization of St. Bridget of Sweden.

Pope John Paul II has had Jewish friends since boyhood, and he has worked hard to strengthen Catholic-Jewish ties. The Holy See formally initiated diplomatic relations with the State of Israel at the level of apostolic nunciature and embassy on June 15, 1994. In March 1998, the Commission for Religious Relations with the Jews published an important document on the roots of the World War II Jewish Holocaust entitled *We Remember: A Reflection on the 'Shoah.'* In a letter dated Mar. 12 to the commission chairman, Cardinal Edward Idris Cassidy, the Pope expressed "fervent hope" that it would "help to heal the wounds of past misunderstandings and injustices."

On Sunday, Mar. 12, 2000, Pope John Paul II presided over a day of pardon for those sins committed by members of the Church over the centuries. The Holy Father issued a formal apology for the misdeeds of the members of the Church in the past, including a renewed apology for all anti-Semitic actions by Catholics. This apology was given even greater depth by the Holy Father's trip to the Holy Land in March 2000. During his historic visit to Israel, the pope placed a written apology to the Jewish People in the Wailing Wall in Jerusalem. He made further efforts at ecumenical dialogue with the Orthodox Churches during his visits to Greece, Syria, and Ukraine in 2001.

Women's Concerns: Pope John Paul's insistence that, in fidelity to the will of Christ, the Church is unable to ordain women as priests has put him at odds with some feminists, as has his opposition to abortion and contraception. But it is clear from his writings that he is unusually sensitive to women's issues, and he is a strong defender of women's dignity and rights, about which he often has spoken. In 1995 he appointed a woman, Professor Mary Ann Glendon of the Harvard University law school, head of the Holy See's delegation to the fourth United Nations conference on women, held in Beijing Sept. 4-15, the first time a woman had been named to such a post.

World Affairs: At least since Jan. of 1979, when he accepted a request for mediation in a border conflict between Argentina and Chile, John Paul II has worked for peace in many parts of the world. He has supported efforts to achieve reconciliation between conflicting parties in troubled areas like Lebanon, the Balkans, and the Persian Gulf, where he sought to avert the Gulf War of 1991. He has advocated religious liberty and human rights during pastoral visits to many countries, including Cuba and Nigeria in 1998. Among the notable ecumenical and interreligious events of the pontificate was the World Day of Prayer for Peace on Oct. 27, 1986, which he convoked in Assisi and attended along with representatives of numerous other churches and religious groups.

In 1984 the Holy See and the United States established diplomatic relations. (The pope has met with presidents Jimmy Carter, Ronald Reagan, George H.W. Bush, and Bill Clinton.) Relations with Poland were re-established in 1989. Diplomatic relations were established with the Soviet Union in 1990 and with the Russian Federation in 1992. Relations also have been established with other Eastern European countries and countries that were part of the former Soviet

Union, with Mexico, and with other nations including Jordan, South Africa, and Libya. Working contacts of a "permanent and official character" were begun with the Palestine Liberation Organization in 1994, leading to the signing of a formal Basic Agreement with the PLO on Feb. 15, 2000.

Administration: Under Pope John Paul II the long-term financial problems of the Holy See have been addressed and brought under control. Finances were on the agenda at the first plenary assembly of the College of Cardinals, Nov. 5-9, 1979, and subsequent meetings of that body. A council of cardinals for the study of organizational and economic problems of the Holy See was established in 1981. In 1988, the Holy See's financial report (for 1986) was published for the first time, along with the 1988 budget. In April 1991, a meeting of the presidents of episcopal conferences was held to discuss ways of increasing the Peter's Pence Collection taken in support of the Pope.

A reorganization of responsibilities of Vatican offices was carried out in 1984, and in 1988 an apostolic constitution, *Pastor Bonus*, on reform of the Roman Curia was issued. A Vatican labor office was instituted in 1989. Pope John Paul established a new Pontifical Academy of Social Sciences in 1994 and Pontifical Academy for Life in 1995. On Apr. 8, 1994, he celebrated Mass in the Sistine Chapel for the unveiling of the Michelangelo frescoes, which had been painstakingly cleaned and restored. The opening presentation of the Holy See's Internet site took place Mar. 24, 1997.

As Bishop of Rome, John Paul presided over a diocesan synod that concluded May 29, 1993. He also has visited numerous Roman parishes — close to 300 out of 328 by the time of his 82nd birthday.

POPES OF THE ROMAN CATHOLIC CHURCH

Information includes the name of the pope, in many cases his name before becoming pope, his birthplace or country of origin, the date of accession to the papacy, and the date of the end of reign that, in all but a few cases, was the date of death. Double dates indicate date of election and date of solemn beginning of ministry as Pastor of the universal Church.

Source: Annuario Pontificio.

St. Peter (Simon Bar-Jona): Bethsaida in Galilee; d. c. 64 or 67.
St. Linus: Tuscany; 67-76.
St. Anacletus (Cletus): Rome; 76-88.
St. Clement: Rome; 88-97.
St. Evaristus: Greece; 97-105.
St. Alexander I: Rome; 105-115.
St. Sixtus I: Rome; 115-125.
St. Telesphorus: Greece; 125-136.
St. Hyginus: Greece; 136-140.
St. Pius I: Aquileia; 140-155.
St. Anicetus: Syria; 155-166.
St. Soter: Campania; 166-175.
St. Eleutherius: Nicopolis in Epirus; 175-189.
  Up to the time of St. Eleutherius, the years indicated for the beginning and end of pontificates are not absolutely certain. Also, up to the middle of the 11th century, there are some doubts about the

exact days and months given in chronological tables.
St. Victor I: Africa; 189-199.
St. Zephyrinus: Rome; 199-217.
St. Callistus I: Rome; 217-222.
St. Urban I: Rome; 222-230.
St. Pontian: Rome; July 21, 230, to Sept. 28, 235.
St. Anterus: Greece; Nov. 21, 235, to Jan. 3, 236.
St. Fabian: Rome; Jan. 10, 236, to Jan. 20, 250.
St. Cornelius: Rome; Mar. 251, to June 253.
St. Lucius I: Rome; June 25, 253, to Mar. 5, 254.
St. Stephen I: Rome; May 12, 254, to Aug. 2, 257.
St. Sixtus II: Greece; Aug. 30, 257, to Aug. 6, 258.
St. Dionysius: birthplace unknown; July 22, 259, to Dec. 26, 268.
St. Felix I: Rome; Jan. 5, 269, to Dec. 30, 274.
St. Eutychian: Luni; Jan. 4, 275, to Dec. 7, 283.
St. Caius: Dalmatia; Dec. 17, 283, to Apr. 22, 296.
St. Marcellinus: Rome; June 30, 296, to Oct. 25, 304.
St. Marcellus I: Rome; May 27, 308, or June 26, 308, to Jan. 16, 309.
St. Eusebius: Greece; Apr. 18, 309, to Aug. 17, 309 or 310.
St. Melchiades (Miltiades): Africa; July 2, 311, to Jan. 11, 314.
St. Sylvester I: Rome; Jan. 31, 314, to Dec. 31, 335.

Most of the popes before St. Sylvester I were martyrs.

St. Marcus: Rome; Jan. 18, 336, to Oct. 7, 336.

St. Julius I: Rome; Feb. 6, 337, to Apr. 12, 352.

Liberius: Rome; May 17, 352, to Sept. 24, 366.

St. Damasus I: Spain; Oct. 1, 366, to Dec. 11, 384.

St. Siricius: Rome; Dec. 15, 22, or 29, 384, to Nov. 26, 399.

St. Anastasius I: Rome; Nov. 27, 399, to Dec. 19, 401.

St. Innocent I: Albano; Dec. 22, 401, to Mar. 12, 417.

St. Zozimus: Greece; Mar. 18, 417, to Dec. 26, 418.

St. Boniface I: Rome; Dec. 28 or 29, 418, to Sept. 4, 422.

St. Celestine I: Campania; Sept. 10, 422, to July 27, 432.

St. Sixtus III: Rome; July 31, 432, to Aug. 19, 440.

St. Leo I (the Great): Tuscany; Sept. 29, 440, to Nov. 10, 461.

St. Hilary: Sardinia; Nov. 19, 461, to Feb. 29, 468.

St. Simplicius: Tivoli; Mar. 3, 468, to Mar. 10, 483.

St. Felix III (II): Rome; Mar. 13, 483, to Mar. 1, 492. He should be called Felix II, and his successors of the same name should be numbered accordingly. The discrepancy in the numerical designation of popes named Felix was caused by the erroneous insertion in some lists of the name of St. Felix of Rome, a martyr.

St. Gelasius I: Africa; Mar. 1, 492, to Nov. 21, 496.

Anastasius II: Rome; Nov. 24, 496, to Nov. 19, 498.

St. Symmachus: Sardinia; Nov. 22, 498, to July 19, 514.

St. Hormisdas: Frosinone; July 20, 514, to Aug. 6, 523.

St. John I, Martyr: Tuscany; Aug. 13, 523, to May 18, 526.

St. Felix IV (III): Samnium; July 12, 526, to Sept. 22, 530.

Boniface II: Rome; Sept. 22, 530, to Oct. 17, 532.

John II: Rome; Jan. 2, 533, to May 8, 535. John II was the first pope to change his name. His given name was Mercury.

St. Agapitus I: Rome; May 13, 535, to Apr. 22, 536.

St. Silverius, Martyr: Campania; June 1 or 8, 536, to Nov. 11, 537 (d. Dec. 2, 537). St. Silverius was violently deposed in March 537, and abdicated Nov. 11, 537. His successor, Vigilius, was not recognized as pope by all the Roman clergy until his abdication.

Vigilius: Rome; Mar. 29, 537, to June 7, 555.

Pelagius I: Rome; Apr. 16, 556, to Mar. 4, 561.

John III: Rome; July 17, 561, to July 13, 574.

Benedict I: Rome; June 2, 575, to July 30, 579.

Pelagius II: Rome; Nov. 26, 579, to Feb. 7, 590.

St. Gregory I (the Great): Rome; Sept. 3, 590, to Mar. 12, 604.

Sabinian: Blera in Tuscany; Sept. 13, 604, to Feb. 22, 606.

Boniface III: Rome; Feb. 19, 607, to Nov. 12, 607.

St. Boniface IV: Abruzzi; Aug. 25, 608, to May 8, 615.

St. Deusdedit (Adeodatus I): Rome; Oct. 19, 615, to Nov. 8, 618.

Boniface V: Naples; Dec. 23, 619, to Oct. 25, 625.

Honorius I: Campania; Oct. 27, 625, to Oct. 12, 638.

Severinus: Rome; May 28, 640, to Aug. 2, 640.

John IV: Dalmatia; Dec. 24, 640, to Oct. 12, 642.

Theodore I: Greece; Nov. 24, 642, to May 14, 649.

St. Martin I, Martyr: Todi; July, 649, to Sept. 16, 655 (in exile from June 17, 653).

St. Eugene I: Rome; Aug. 10, 654, to June 2, 657. St. Eugene I was elected during the exile of St. Martin I, who is believed to have endorsed him as pope.

St. Vitalian: Segni; July 30, 657, to Jan. 27, 672.

Adeodatus II: Rome; Apr. 11, 672, to June 17, 676.

Donus: Rome; Nov. 2, 676, to Apr. 11, 678.

St. Agatho: Sicily; June 27, 678, to Jan. 10, 681.

St. Leo II: Sicily; Aug. 17, 682, to July 3, 683.

St. Benedict II: Rome; June 26, 684, to May 8, 685.

John V: Syria; July 23, 685, to Aug. 2, 686.

Conon: birthplace unknown; Oct. 21, 686, to Sept. 21, 687.

St. Sergius I: Syria; Dec. 15, 687, to Sept. 8, 701.

John VI: Greece; Oct. 30, 701, to Jan. 11, 705.

John VII: Greece; Mar. 1, 705, to Oct. 18, 707.

Sisinnius: Syria; Jan. 15, 708, to Feb. 4, 708.

Constantine: Syria; Mar. 25, 708, to Apr. 9, 715.

St. Gregory II: Rome; May 19, 715, to Feb. 11, 731.

St. Gregory III: Syria; Mar. 18, 731, to Nov., 741.

St. Zachary: Greece; Dec. 10, 741, to Mar. 22, 752.

Stephen II (III): Rome; Mar. 26, 752, to Apr. 26, 757. After the death of St. Zachary, a Roman priest named Stephen was elected but died (four days later) before his consecration as bishop of Rome, which would have marked the beginning of his pontificate. Another Stephen was elected to succeed Zachary as Stephen II. (The first pope with this name was St. Stephen I, 254-57.) The ordinal III appears in parentheses after the name of Stephen II because the name of the earlier elected but deceased priest was included in some lists. Other Stephens have double numbers.

St. Paul I: Rome; Apr. (May 29) 757, to June 28, 767.

Stephen III (IV): Sicily; Aug. 1 (7), 768, to Jan. 24, 772.

Adrian I: Rome; Feb. 1 (9), 772, to Dec. 25, 795.

St. Leo III: Rome; Dec. 26 (27), 795, to June 12, 816.

Stephen IV (V): Rome; June 22, 816, to Jan. 24, 817.

St. Paschal I: Rome; Jan. 25, 817, to Feb. 11, 824.

Eugene II: Rome; Feb. (May) 824, to Aug. 827.

Valentine: Rome; Aug. 827, to Sept. 827.

Gregory IV: Rome; 827, to Jan. 844.

Sergius II: Rome; Jan. 844 to Jan. 27, 847.

St. Leo IV: Rome; Jan. (Apr. 10), 847, to July 17, 855.

Benedict III: Rome; July (Sept. 29), 855, to Apr. 17, 858.

St. Nicholas I (the Great): Rome; Apr. 24, 858, to Nov. 13, 867.

Adrian II: Rome; Dec. 14, 867, to Dec. 14, 872.

John VIII: Rome; Dec. 14, 872, to Dec. 16, 882.

Marinus I: Gallese; Dec. 16, 882, to May 15, 884.

St. Adrian III: Rome; May 17, 884, to Sept. 885. Cult confirmed June 2, 1891.

Stephen V (VI): Rome; Sept. 885, to Sept. 14, 891.

Formosus: Bishop of Porto; Oct. 6, 891, to Apr. 4, 896.

Boniface VI: Rome; Apr. 896, to Apr. 896.

Stephen VI (VII): Rome; May 896, to Aug. 897.

Romanus: Gallese; Aug. 897, to Nov. 897.

Theodore II: Rome; Dec. 897, to Dec. 897.

John IX: Tivoli; Jan. 898, to Jan. 900.

Benedict IV: Rome; Jan. (Feb.) 900, to July 903.

Leo V: Ardea; July 903, to Sept. 903.

Sergius III: Rome; Jan. 29, 904, to Apr. 14, 911.

Anastasius III: Rome; Apr. 911, to June 913.

Landus: Sabina; July 913, to Feb. 914.

John X: Tossignano (Imola); Mar. 914, to May 928.

Leo VI: Rome; May 928, to Dec. 928.

Stephen VII (VIII): Rome; Dec. 928, to Feb. 931.

John XI: Rome; Feb. (Mar.) 931, to Dec. 935.

Leo VII: Rome; Jan. 3, 936, to July 13, 939.

Stephen VIII (IX): Rome; July 14, 939, to Oct. 942.

Marinus II: Rome; Oct. 30, 942, to May 946.

Agapitus II: Rome; May 10, 946, to Dec. 955.

John XII (Octavius): Tusculum; Dec. 16, 955, to May 14, 964 (date of his death).

Leo VIII: Rome; Dec. 4 (6), 963, to Mar. 1, 965.

Benedict V: Rome; May 22, 964, to July 4, 966.

Confusion exists concerning the legitimacy of claims to the pontificate by Leo VIII and Benedict V. John XII was deposed Dec. 4, 963, by a Roman council. If this deposition was invalid, Leo was an antipope. If the deposition of John was valid, Leo was the legitimate pope and Benedict was an antipope.

John XIII: Rome; Oct. 1, 965, to Sept. 6, 972.

Benedict VI: Rome; Jan. 19, 973, to June 974.

Benedict VII: Rome; Oct. 974, to July 10, 983.

John XIV (Peter Campenora): Pavia; Dec. 983, to Aug. 20, 984.

John XV: Rome; Aug. 985, to Mar. 996.

Gregory V (Bruno of Carinthia): Saxony; May 3, 996, to Feb. 18, 999.

Sylvester II (Gerbert): Auvergne; Apr. 2, 999, to May 12, 1003.

John XVII (Siccone): Rome; June 1003, to Dec. 1003.

John XVIII (Phasianus): Rome; Jan. 1004, to July 1009.

Sergius IV (Peter): Rome; July 31, 1009, to May 12, 1012.

The custom of changing one's name on election to the papacy is generally considered to date from the time of Sergius IV. Before his time, several popes had changed their names. After his time, this became a regular practice, with few exceptions; e.g., Adrian VI and Marcellus II.

Benedict VIII (Theophylactus): Tusculum; May 18, 1012, to Apr. 9, 1024.

John XIX (Romanus): Tusculum; Apr. (May) 1024, to 1032.

Benedict IX (Theophylactus): Tusculum; 1032 to 1044.

Sylvester III (John): Rome; Jan. 20, 1045, to Feb. 10, 1045.

Sylvester III was an antipope if the forcible removal of Benedict IX in 1044 was not legitimate.

Benedict IX (second time): Apr. 10, 1045, to May 1, 1045.

Gregory VI (John Gratian): Rome; May 5, 1045, to Dec. 20, 1046.

Clement II (Suitger, Lord of Morsleben and Hornburg): Saxony; Dec. 24 (25), 1046, to Oct. 9, 1047.

If the resignation of Benedict IX in 1045 and his removal at the Dec. 1046, synod were not legitimate, Gregory VI and Clement II were antipopes.

Benedict IX (third time): Nov. 8, 1047, to July 17, 1048 (d. c. 1055).

Damasus II (Poppo): Bavaria; July 17, 1048, to Aug. 9, 1048.

St. Leo IX (Bruno): Alsace; Feb. 12, 1049, to Apr. 19, 1054.

Victor II (Gebhard): Swabia; Apr. 16, 1055, to July 28, 1057.

Stephen IX (X) (Frederick): Lorraine; Aug. 3, 1057, to Mar. 29, 1058.

Nicholas II (Gerard): Burgundy; Jan. 24, 1059, to July 27, 1061.

Alexander II (Anselmo da Baggio): Milan; Oct. 1, 1061, to Apr. 21, 1073.

St. Gregory VII (Hildebrand): Tuscany; Apr. 22 (June 30), 1073, to May 25, 1085.

Bl. Victor III (Dauferius; Desiderius): Benevento; May 24, 1086, to Sept. 16, 1087. Cult confirmed July 23, 1887.

Bl. Urban II (Otto di Lagery): France; Mar. 12, 1088, to July 29, 1099. Cult confirmed July 14, 1881.

Paschal II (Raniero): Ravenna; Aug. 13 (14), 1099, to Jan. 21, 1118.

Gelasius II (Giovanni Caetani): Gaeta; Jan. 24 (Mar. 10), 1118, to Jan. 28, 1119.

Callistus II (Guido of Burgundy): Burgundy; Feb. 2 (9), 1119, to Dec. 13, 1124.

Honorius II (Lamberto): Fiagnano (Imola); Dec. 15 (21), 1124, to Feb. 13, 1130.

Innocent II (Gregorio Papareschi): Rome; Feb. 14 (23), 1130, to Sept. 24, 1143.

Celestine II (Guido): Citta di Castello; Sept. 26 (Oct. 3), 1143, to Mar. 8, 1144.

Lucius II (Gerardo Caccianemici): Bologna: Mar. 12, 1144, to Feb. 15, 1145.

Bl. Eugene III (Bernardo Paganelli di Montemagno): Pisa; Feb. 15 (18), 1145, to July 8, 1153. Cult confirmed Oct. 3, 1872.

Anastasius IV (Corrado): Rome; July 12, 1153, to Dec, 3, 1154.

Adrian IV (Nicholas Breakspear): England; Dec. 4 (5), 1154, to Sept. 1, 1159.

Alexander III (Rolando Bandinelli): Siena; Sept. 7 (20), 1159, to Aug. 30, 1181.

Lucius III (Ubaldo Allucingoli): Lucca; Sept. 1 (6), 1181, to Sept. 25, 1185.

Urban III (Uberto Crivelli): Milan; Nov. 25 (Dec. 1), 1185, to Oct. 20, 1187.

Gregory VIII (Alberto de Morra): Benevento; Oct. 21 (25), 1187, to Dec. 17, 1187.

Clement III (Paolo Scolari): Rome; Dec. 19 (20), 1187, to Mar. 1191.

Celestine III (Giacinto Bobone): Rome; Mar. 30 (Apr. 14), 1191, to Jan. 8, 1198.

Innocent III (Lotario dei Conti di Segni): Anagni; Jan. 8 (Feb. 22), 1198, to July 16, 1216.

Honorius III (Cencio Savelli): Rome; July 18 (24), 1216, to Mar. 18, 1227.

Gregory IX (Ugolino, Count of Segni): Anagni; Mar. 19 (21), 1227, to Aug. 22, 1241.

Celestine IV (Goffredo Castiglioni): Milan; Oct. 25 (28), 1241, to Nov. 10, 1241.

Innocent IV (Sinibaldo Fieschi): Genoa; June 25 (28), 1243, to Dec. 7, 1254.

Alexander IV (Rinaldo, House of Ienne): Ienne (Rome); Dec. 12 (20), 1254, to May 25, 1261.

Urban IV (Jacques Pantal,on): Troyes; Aug. 29 (Sept. 4), 1261, to Oct. 2, 1264.

Clement IV (Guy Foulques or Guido le Gros): France; Feb. 5 (15), 1265, to Nov. 29, 1268.

Bl. Gregory X (Teobaldo Visconti): Piacenza; Sept. 1, 1271 (Mar. 27, 1272), to Jan. 10, 1276. Cult confirmed Sept. 12, 1713.

Bl. Innocent V (Peter of Tarentaise): Savoy; Jan. 21 (Feb. 22), 1276, to June 22, 1276. Cult confirmed Mar. 13, 1898.

Adrian V (Ottobono Fieschi): Genoa: July 11, 1276, to Aug. 18, 1276.

John XXI (Petrus Juliani or Petrus Hispanus): Portugal; Sept. 8 (20), 1276, to May 20, 1277. There is confusion in the numerical designation of popes named John. The error dates back to the time of John XV.

Nicholas III (Giovanni Gaetano Orsini): Rome; Nov. 25 (Dec. 26), 1277, to Aug. 22, 1280.

Martin IV (Simon de Brie): France; Feb. 22 (Mar. 23), 1281, to Mar. 28, 1285. The names of Marinus 1 (882-84) and Marinus II (942-46) were construed as Martin. In view of these two pontificates and the earlier reign of St. Martin I (649-55), this pope was called Martin IV.

Honorius IV (Giacomo Savelli): Rome; Apr. 2 (May 20), 1285, to Apr. 3, 1287.

Nicholas IV (Girolamo Masci): Ascoli; Feb. 22, 1288, to Apr. 4, 1292.

St. Celestine V (Pietro del Murrone): Isernia; July 5 (Aug. 29), 1294, to Dec. 13, 1294; d. May 19, 1296. Canonized May 5, 1313.

Boniface VIII (Benedetto Caetani): Anagni; Dec. 24, 1294 (Jan. 23, 1295), to Oct. 11, 1303.

Bl. Benedict XI (Niccolo Boccasini): Treviso; Oct. 22 (27), 1303, to July 7, 1304. Cult confirmed Apr. 24, 1736.

Clement V (Bertrand de Got): France; June 5 (Nov. 14), 1305, to Apr. 20, 1314. (First of Avignon popes.)

John XXII (Jacques d'Euse): Cahors; Aug. 7 (Sept. 5), 1316, to Dec. 4, 1334.

Benedict XII (Jacques Fournier): France; Dec. 20, 1334 (Jan. 8, 1335), to Apr. 25, 1342.

Clement VI (Pierre Roger): France; May 7 (19), 1342, to Dec. 6, 1352.

Innocent VI (Etienne Aubert): France; Dec. 18 (30), 1352, to Sept. 12, 1362.

Bl. Urban V (Guillaume de Grimoard): France; Sept. 28 (Nov. 6), 1362, to Dec. 19, 1370. Cult confirmed Mar. 10, 1870.

Gregory XI (Pierre Roger de Beaufort): France; Dec. 30, 1370 (Jan. 5, 1371), to Mar. 26, 1378. (Last of Avignon popes.)

Urban VI (Bartolomeo Prignano): Naples; Apr. 8 (18), 1378, to Oct. 15, 1389.

Boniface IX (Pietro Tomacelli): Naples; Nov. 2 (9), 1389, to Oct. 1, 1404.

Innocent VII (Cosma Migliorati): Sulmona; Oct. 17 (Nov. 11), 1404, to Nov. 6, 1406.

Gregory XII (Angelo Correr): Venice; Nov. 30 (Dec. 19), 1406, to July 4, 1415, when he voluntarily resigned from the papacy to permit the election of his successor. He died Oct. 18, 1417. (See the Western Schism.)

Martin V (Oddone Colonna): Rome; Nov. 11 (21), 1417, to Feb. 20, 1431.

Eugene IV (Gabriele Condulmer): Venice; Mar. 3 (11), 1431, to Feb. 23, 1447.

Nicholas V (Tommaso Parentucelli): Sarzana; Mar. 6 (19), 1447, to Mar. 24, 1455.

Callistus III (Alfonso Borgia): Jativa (Valencia); Apr. 8 (20), 1455, to Aug. 6, 1458.

Pius II (Enea Silvio Piccolomini): Siena; Aug. 19 (Sept. 3), 1458, to Aug. 14, 1464.

Paul II (Pietro Barbo): Venice; Aug. 30 (Sept. 16), 1464, to July 26, 1471.

Sixtus IV (Francesco della Rovere): Savona; Aug. 9 (25), 1471, to Aug. 12, 1484.

Innocent VIII (Giovanni Battista Cibo): Genoa; Aug. 29 (Sept. 12), 1484, to July 25, 1492.

Alexander VI (Rodrigo Borgia): Jativa (Valencia); Aug. 11 (26), 1492, to Aug. 18, 1503.

Pius III (Francesco Todeschini-Piccolomini): Siena; Sept. 22 (Oct. 1, 8), 1503, to Oct. 18, 1503.

Julius II (Giuliano della Rovere): Savona; Oct. 31 (Nov. 26), 1503, to Feb. 21, 1513.

Leo X (Giovanni de' Medici): Florence; Mar. 9 (19), 1513, to Dec. 1, 1521.

Adrian VI (Adrian Florensz): Utrecht; Jan. 9 (Aug. 31), 1522, to Sept. 14, 1523.

Clement VII (Giulio de' Medici): Florence; Nov. 19 (26), 1523, to Sept. 25, 1534.

Paul III (Alessandro Farnese): Rome; Oct. 13 (Nov. 3), 1534, to Nov. 10, 1549.

Julius III (Giovanni Maria Ciocchi del Monte): Rome; Feb. 7 (22), 1550, to Mar. 23, 1555.

Marcellus II (Marcello Cervini): Montepulciano; Apr. 9 (10), 1555, to May 1, 1555.

Paul IV (Gian Pietro Carafa): Naples; May 23 (26), 1555, to Aug. 18, 1559.

Pius IV (Giovan Angelo de' Medici): Milan; Dec. 25, 1559 (Jan. 6, 1560), to Dec. 9, 1565.

St. Pius V (Antonio-Michele Ghislieri): Bosco (Alexandria); Jan. 7 (17), 1566, to May 1, 1572. Canonized May 22, 1712.

Gregory XIII (Ugo Buoncompagni): Bologna; May 13 (25), 1572, to Apr. 10, 1585.

Sixtus V (Felice Peretti): Grottammare (Ripatransone); Apr. 24 (May 1), 1585, to Aug. 27, 1590.

Urban VII (Giambattista Castagna): Rome; Sept. 15, 1590, to Sept. 27, 1590.

Gregory XIV (Niccolo Sfondrati): Cremona; Dec. 5 (8), 1590, to Oct. 16, 1591.

Innocent IX (Giovanni Antonio Facchinetti): Bologna; Oct. 29 (Nov. 3), 1591, to Dec. 30, 1591.

Clement VIII (Ippolito Aldobrandini): Florence; Jan. 30 (Feb. 9), 1592, to Mar. 3, 1605.

Leo XI (Alessandro de' Medici): Florence; Apr. 1 (10), 1605, to Apr. 27, 1605.

Paul V (Camillo Borghese): Rome; May 16 (29), 1605, to Jan. 28, 1621.

Gregory XV (Alessandro Ludovisi): Bologna; Feb. 9 (14), 1621, to July 8, 1623.

Urban VIII (Maffeo Barberini): Florence; Aug. 6 (Sept. 29), 1623, to July 29, 1644.

Innocent X (Giovanni Battista Pamfili): Rome; Sept. 15 (Oct. 4), 1644, to Jan. 7, 1655.

Alexander VII (Fabio Chigi): Siena; Apr. 7 (18), 1655, to May 22, 1667.

Clement IX (Giulio Rospigliosi): Pistoia; June 20 (26), 1667, to Dec. 9, 1669.

Clement X (Emilio Altieri): Rome; Apr. 29 (May 11), 1670, to July 22, 1676.

Bl. Innocent XI (Benedetto Odescalchi): Como; Sept. 21 (Oct. 4), 1676, to Aug. 12, 1689. Beatified Oct. 7, 1956.

Alexander VIII (Pietro Ottoboni): Venice; Oct. 6 (16), 1689, to Feb. 1, 1691.

Innocent XII (Antonio Pignatelli): Spinazzola (Venosa); July 12 (15), 1691, to Sept. 27, 1700.

Clement XI (Giovanni Francesco Albani): Urbino; Nov. 23, 30 (Dec. 8), 1700, to Mar. 19, 1721.

Innocent XIII (Michelangelo dei Conti): Rome; May 8 (18), 1721, to Mar. 7, 1724.

Benedict XIII (Pietro Francesco Vincenzo Maria Orsini): Gravina (Bari); May 29 (June 4), 1724, to Feb. 21, 1730.

Clement XII (Lorenzo Corsini): Florence; July 12 (16), 1730, to Feb. 6, 1740.

Benedict XIV (Prospero Lambertini): Bologna; Aug. 17 (22), 1740, to May 3, 1758.

Clement XIII (Carlo Rezzonico): Venice; July 6 (16), 1758, to Feb. 2, 1769.

Clement XIV (Giovanni Vincenzo Antonio Lorenzo Ganganelli): Rimini; May 19, 28 (June 4), 1769, to Sept. 22, 1774.

Pius VI (Giovanni Angelo Braschi): Cesena; Feb. 15 (22), 1775, to Aug. 29, 1799.

Pius VII (Barnaba Gregorio Chiaramonti): Cesena; Mar. 14 (21), 1800, to Aug. 20, 1823.

Leo XII (Annibale della Genga): Genga (Fabriano); Sept. 28 (Oct. 5), 1823, to Feb. 10, 1829.

Pius VIII (Francesco Saverio Castiglioni): Cingoli; Mar. 31 (Apr. 5), 1829, to Nov. 30, 1830.

Gregory XVI (Bartolomeo Alberto-Mauro-Cappellari): Belluno; Feb. 2 (6), 1831, to June 1, 1846.

Bl. Pius IX (Giovanni M. Mastai-Ferretti): Senigallia; June 16 (21), 1846, to Feb. 7, 1878.

Leo XIII (Gioacchino Pecci): Carpineto (Anagni); Feb. 20 (Mar. 3), 1878, to July 20, 1903.

St. Pius X (Giuseppe Sarto): Riese (Treviso); Aug. 4 (9), 1903, to Aug. 20, 1914. Canonized May 29, 1954.

Benedict XV (Giacomo della Chiesa): Genoa; Sept. 3 (6), 1914, to Jan. 22, 1922.

Pius XI (Achille Ratti): Desio (Milan); Feb. 6 (12), 1922, to Feb. 10, 1939.

Pius XII (Eugenio Pacelli): Rome; Mar. 2 (12), 1939, to Oct. 9, 1958.

Bl. John XXIII (Angelo Giuseppe Roncalli): Sotto il Monte (Bergamo); Oct. 28 (Nov. 4), 1958, to June 3, 1963.

Paul VI (Giovanni Battista Montini): Concessio (Brescia); June 21 (30), 1963, to Aug. 6, 1978.

John Paul I (Albino Luciani): Forno di Canale (Belluno); Aug. 26 (Sept. 3), 1978, to Sept. 28, 1978.

John Paul II (Karol Wojtyla): Wadowice, Poland; Oct. 16 (22), 1978.

ANTIPOPES

This list of men who claimed or exercised the papal office in an uncanonical manner includes names, birthplaces and dates of alleged reigns.

Source: Annuario Pontificio.

St. Hippolytus: Rome; 217-235; was reconciled before his death.

Novatian: Rome; 251.

Felix II: Rome; 355 to Nov. 22, 365.

Ursinus: 366-367.

Eulalius: Dec. 27 or 29, 418, to 419.

Lawrence: 498; 501-505.

Dioscorus: Alexandria; Sept. 22, 530, to Oct. 14, 530.

Theodore: ended alleged reign, 687.

Paschal: ended alleged reign, 687.

Constantine: Nepi; June 28 (July 5), 767, to 769.

Philip: July 31, 768; retired to his monastery on the same day.

John: ended alleged reign, Jan. 844.

Anastasius: Aug. 855, to Sept. 855; d. 880.

Christopher: Rome; July or Sept. 903, to Jan. 904.

Boniface VII: Rome; June 974, to July 974; Aug. 984, to July 985.

John XVI: Rossano; Apr. 997, to Feb. 998.

Gregory: ended alleged reign, 1012.

Benedict X: Rome; Apr. 5, 1058, to Jan. 24, 1059.

Honorius II: Verona; Oct. 28, 1061, to 1072.

Clement III: Parma; June 25, 1080 (Mar. 24, 1084), to Sept. 8, 1100.

Theodoric: ended alleged reign, 1100; d. 1102.

Albert: ended alleged reign, 1102.

Sylvester IV: Rome; Nov. 18, 1105, to 1111.

Gregory VIII: France; Mar. 8, 1118, to 1121.

Celestine II: Rome; ended alleged reign, Dec. 1124.

Anacletus II: Rome; Feb. 14 (23), 1130, to Jan. 25, 1138.

Victor IV: Mar. 1138, to May 29, 1138; submitted to Pope Innocent II.

Victor IV: Montecelio; Sept. 7 (Oct. 4), 1159, to Apr. 20, 1164; he did not recognize his predecessor (Victor IV, above).

Paschal III: Apr. 22 (26), 1164, to Sept. 20, 1168.

Callistus III: Arezzo; Sept. 1168, to Aug. 29, 1178; submitted to Pope Alexander III.

Innocent III: Sezze; Sept. 29, 1179, to 1180.

Nicholas V: Corvaro (Rieti); May 12 (22), 1328, to Aug. 25, 1330; d. Oct. 16, 1333.

Four antipopes of the Western Schism:

Clement VII: Sept. 20 (Oct. 31), 1378, to Sept. 16, 1394.

Benedict XIII: Aragon; Sept. 28 (Oct. 11), 1394, to May 23, 1423.

Alexander V: Crete; June 26 (July 7), 1409, to May 3, 1410.

John XXIII: Naples; May 17 (25), 1410, to May 29, 1415. (date of deposition by Council of Constance which ended the Western Schism; d. Nov. 22, 1419.)

Felix V: Savoy; Nov. 5, 1439 (July 24, 1440), to Apr. 7, 1449; d. 1451.

AVIGNON PAPACY

Avignon was the residence (1309-77) of a series of French popes (Clement V, John XXII, Benedict XII, Clement VI, Innocent VI, Urban V and Gregory XI). Prominent in the period were power struggles over the mixed interests of Church and state with the rulers of France (Philip IV, John II), Bavaria (Lewis IV), England (Edward III); factionalism of French and Italian churchmen; political as well as ecclesiastical turmoil in Italy, a factor of significance in prolonging the stay of popes in Avignon. Despite some positive achievements, the Avignon papacy was a prologue to the Western Schism that began in 1378.

GREAT WESTERN SCHISM

The Great Western Schism was a confused state of affairs that divided Christendom into two and then three papal obediences from 1378 to 1417.

It occurred some 50 years after Marsilius theorized that a general (not ecumenical) council of bishops and other persons was superior to a pope and nearly 30 years before the Council of Florence stated definitively that no kind of council had such authority. It was a period of disaster preceding the even more disastrous period of the Reformation.

Urban VI, following the return of the papal residence to Rome after approximately 70 years at Avignon, was elected pope Apr. 8, 1378, and reigned until his death in 1389. He was succeeded by Boniface IX (1389-1404), Innocent VII (1404-1406) and Gregory XII (1406-1415). These four are considered the legitimate popes of the period.

Some of the cardinals who chose Urban pope, dissatisfied with his conduct of the office, declared that his election was invalid. They proceeded to elect Clement VII, who claimed the papacy from 1378 to 1394. He was succeeded by Benedict XIII.

Prelates seeking to end the state of divided papal loyalties convoked the Council of Pisa (1409) which, without authority, found Gregory XII and Benedict XIII guilty in absentia on 30-odd charges of schism and heresy, deposed them, and elected a third claimant to the papacy, Alexander V (1409-1410). He was succeeded by John XXIII (1410-1415).

The schism was ended by the Council of Constance (1414-1418). Although originally called into session in an irregular manner, the council, acquired authority after being convoked by Gregory XII in 1415. In its early irregular phase, it deposed John XXIII whose election to the papacy was uncanonical anyway. After being formally convoked, it accepted the abdication of Gregory in 1415 and dismissed the claims of Benedict XIII two years later, thus clearing the way for the election of Martin V on Nov. 11, 1417. The Council of Constance also rejected the theories of John Wycliff and condemned John Hus as a heretic.

POPES OF THE TWENTIETH CENTURY

LEO XIII

Leo XIII (Gioacchino Vincenzo Pecci) was born May 2, 1810, in Carpineto, Italy. Although all but three years of his life and pontificate were of the 19th century, his influence extended well into the 20th century.

He was educated at the Jesuit college in Viterbo, the Roman College, the Academy of Noble Ecclesiastics, and the University of the Sapienza. He was ordained to the priesthood in 1837.

He served as an apostolic delegate to two States of the Church, Benevento from 1838 to 1841 and Perugia in 1841 and 1842. Ordained titular archbishop of Damietta, he was papal nuncio to Belgium from January 1843, until May 1846; in the post, he had controversial relations with the government over education issues and acquired his first significant experience of industrialized society.

He was archbishop of Perugia from 1846 to 1878. He became a cardinal in 1853 and chamberlain of the Roman Curia in 1877. He was elected to the papacy Feb. 20, 1878. He died July 20, 1903.

Canonizations: He canonized 18 saints and beatified a group of English martyrs.

Church Administration: He established 300 new dioceses and vicariates; restored the hierarchy in Scotland, set up an English, as contrasted with the Portuguese, hierarchy in India; approved the action of the Congregation for the Propagation of the Faith in reorganizing missions in China.

Encyclicals: He issued 86 encyclicals, on subjects ranging from devotional to social. In the former category were *Annum Sacrum*, on the Sacred Heart, in 1899, and 11 letters on Mary and the Rosary.

Social Questions: Much of Leo's influence stemmed from social doctrine stated in numerous encyclicals, concerning liberalism, liberty, the divine origin of authority; socialism, in *Quod Apostolici Muneris*, 1878; the Christian concept of the family, in *Arcanum*, 1880; socialism and economic liberalism, relations between capital and labor, in *Rerum Novarum*, 1891. Two of his social encyclicals were against the African slave trade.

Interfaith Relations: He was unsuccessful in unity overtures made to Orthodox and Slavic Churches. He declared Anglican orders invalid in the apostolic bull *Apostolicae Curae* Sept. 13, 1896.

International Relations: Leo was frustrated in seeking solutions to the Roman Question arising from the seizure of church lands by the Kingdom of Italy in 1870. He also faced anticlerical situations in Belgium and France and in the *Kulturkampf* policies of Bismarck in Germany.

Scholarship: In the encyclical *Aeterni Patris* of Aug. 4, 1879, he ordered a renewal of philosophical and theological studies in seminaries along scholastic, and especially Thomistic, lines, to counteract influential trends of liberalism and Modernism. He issued guidelines for biblical exegesis in *Providentissimus Deus* Nov. 18, 1893, and established the Pontifical Biblical Commission in 1902.

In other actions affecting scholarship and study, he opened the Vatican Archives to scholars in 1883 and established the Vatican Observatory.

United States: He authorized establishment of the apostolic delegation in Washington, D.C., Jan. 24, 1893. He refused to issue a condemnation of the Knights of Labor. With a document entitled *Testem Benevolentiae*, he eased resolution of questions concerning what was called an American heresy in 1899.

ST. PIUS X

St. Pius X (Giuseppe Melchiorre Sarto) was born in 1835 in Riese, Italy. Educated at the college of Castelfranco and the seminary at Padua, he was ordained to the priesthood Sept. 18, 1858. He served as a curate in Trombolo for nine years before beginning an eight-year pastorate at Salzano. He was chancellor of the Treviso diocese from November 1875, and bishop of Mantua from 1884 until 1893. He was cardinal-patriarch of Venice from that year until his election to the papacy by the conclave held from July 31 to Aug. 4, 1903.

Aims: Pius's principal objectives as pope were "to restore all things in Christ, in order that Christ may be all and in all," and "to teach (and defend) Christian truth and law."

Canonizations, Encyclicals: He canonized four saints and issued 16 encyclicals. One of the encyclicals was issued in commemoration of the 50th anniversary of the proclamation of the dogma of the Immaculate Conception of Mary.

Catechetics: He introduced a whole new era of religious instruction and formation with the encyclical *Acerbo Nimis* of Apr. 15, 1905, in which he called for vigor in establishing and conducting parochial programs of the Confraternity of Christian Doctrine.

Catholic Action: He outlined the role of official Catholic Action in two encyclicals in 1905 and 1906. Favoring organized action by Catholics themselves, he had serious reservations about interconfessional collaboration.

He stoutly maintained claims to papal rights in the anticlerical climate of Italy. He authorized bishops to relax prohibitions against participation by Catholics in some Italian elections.

Church Administration: With the *motu proprio Arduum Sane* of Mar. 19, 1904, he inaugurated the work that resulted in the Code of Canon Law; the code was completed in 1917 and went into effect the following year. He reorganized and strengthened the Roman Curia with the apostolic constitution *Sapienti Consilio* of June 29, 1908.

While promoting the expansion of missionary work, he removed from the jurisdiction of the Congregation for the Propagation of the Faith the Church in the United States, Canada, Newfoundland, England, Ireland, Holland and Luxembourg.

International Relations: He ended traditional prerogatives of Catholic governments with respect to papal elections, in 1904. He opposed anti-Church and anticlerical actions in several countries: Bolivia in 1905, because of anti-religious legislation; France in 1906, for its 1901 action in annulling its concordat with the Holy See, and for the 1905 Law of Separation by which it decreed separation of Church and state, ordered the confiscation of church property, and blocked religious education and the activities of religious orders; Portugal in 1911, for the separation of Church and state and repressive measures which resulted in persecution later.

In 1912 he called on the bishops of Brazil to work for the improvement of conditions among Indians.

Liturgy: "The Pope of the Eucharist," he strongly recommended the frequent reception of Holy Communion in a decree dated Dec. 20, 1905; in another decree, *Quam Singulari*, of Aug. 8, 1910, he called for the early reception of the sacrament by children. He initiated measures for liturgical reform with new norms for sacred music and the start of work on revision of the Breviary for recitation of the Divine Office.

Modernism: Pius was a vigorous opponent of "the synthesis of all heresies," which threatened the integrity of doctrine through its influence in philosophy, theology and biblical exegesis. In opposition, he condemned 65 of its propositions as erroneous in the decree *Lamentabili* July 3, 1907; issued the encyclical *Pascendi* in the same vein Sept. 8, 1907; backed both of these with censures; and published the Oath against Modernism in September 1910, to be taken by all the clergy. Ecclesiastical studies suffered to some extent from these actions, necessary as they were at the time.

Pius followed the lead of Leo XIII in promoting the study of scholastic philosophy. He established the Pontifical Biblical Institute May 7, 1909.

His death, Aug. 20, 1914, was hastened by the outbreak of World War I. He was beatified in 1951 and canonized May 29, 1954. His feast is observed Aug. 21.

BENEDICT XV

Benedict XV (Giacomo della Chiesa) was born Nov. 21, 1854, in Pegli, Italy.

He was educated at the Royal University of Genoa and Gregorian University in Rome. He was ordained to the priesthood Dec. 21, 1878.

He served in the papal diplomatic corps from 1882 to 1907; as secretary to the nuncio to Spain from 1882 to 1887, as secretary to the papal secretary of state from 1887, and as undersecretary from 1901.

He was ordained archbishop of Bologna Dec. 22, 1907, and spent four years completing a pastoral visitation there. He was made a cardinal just three months before being elected to the papacy Sept. 3, 1914. He died Jan. 22, 1922. Two key efforts of his pontificate were for peace and the relief of human suffering caused by World War I.

Canonizations: Benedict canonized three saints; one of them was Joan of Arc.

Canon Law: He published the Code of Canon Law, developed by the commission set up by St. Pius X, May 27, 1917; it went into effect the following year.

Curia: He made great changes in the personnel of the Curia. He established the Congregation for the Oriental Churches May 1, 1917, and founded the Pontifical Oriental Institute in Rome later in the year.

Encyclicals: He issued 12 encyclicals. Peace was the theme of three of them. In another, published two years after the cessation of hostilities, he wrote about child victims of the war. He followed the lead of Leo XIII in *Spiritus Paraclitus*, Sept. 15, 1920, on biblical studies.

International Relations: He was largely frustrated on the international level because of the events and attitudes of the war period, but the number of diplomats accredited to the Vatican nearly doubled, from 14 to 26, between the time of his accession to the papacy and his death.

Peace Efforts: Benedict's stance in the war was one of absolute impartiality but not of uninterested neutrality. Because he would not take sides, he was suspected by both the Allies and the Central Powers, and the seven-point peace plan he offered to all belligerents Aug. 1, 1917, was turned down. The points of the plan were: recognition of the moral force of right; disarmament; acceptance of arbitration in cases of dispute; guarantee of freedom of the seas; renunciation of war indemnities; evacuation and restoration of occupied territories; examination of territorial claims in dispute.

Relief Efforts: Benedict assumed personal charge of Vatican relief efforts during the war. He set up an international missing persons bureau for contacts between prisoners and their families, but was forced to close it because of the suspicion of warring nations that it was a front for espionage operations. He persuaded the Swiss government to admit into the country military victims of tuberculosis.

Roman Question: Benedict prepared the way for the meetings and negotiations which led to settlement of the question in 1929.

PIUS XI

Pius XI (Ambrogio Damiano Achille Ratti) was born May 31, 1857, in Desio, Italy.

Educated at seminaries in Seviso and Milan, and at the Lombard College, Gregorian University and Academy of St. Thomas in Rome, he was ordained to the priesthood in 1879.

He taught at the major seminary of Milan from 1882 to 1888. Appointed to the staff of the Ambrosian Library in 1888, he remained there until 1911, acquiring a reputation for publishing works on paleography and serving as director from 1907 to 1911. He then moved to the Vatican Library, of which he was prefect from 1914 to 1918. In 1919, he was named apostolic visitor to Poland in Apr., nuncio in June, and was made titular archbishop of Lepanto Oct. 28. He was made archbishop of Milan and cardinal June 13, 1921, before being elected to the papacy Feb. 6, 1922. He died Feb. 10, 1939.

Aim: The objective of his pontificate, as stated in the encyclical *Ubi Arcano*, Dec. 23, 1922, was to establish the reign and peace of Christ in society.

Canonizations: He canonized 34 saints, including the Jesuit Martyrs of North America, and conferred the title of Doctor of the Church on Sts. Peter Canisius, John of the Cross, Robert Bellarmine and Albertus Magnus.

Eastern Churches: He called for better understanding of the Eastern Churches in the encyclical *Rerum Orientalium* of Sept. 8, 1928, and developed facilities for the training of Eastern-Rite priests. He inaugurated steps for the codification of Eastern-Church law in 1929. In 1935 he made Syrian Patriarch Tappouni a cardinal.

Encyclicals: His first encyclical, *Ubi Arcano*, in addition to stating the aims of his pontificate, blueprinted Catholic Action and called for its development throughout the Church. *In Quas Primas*, Dec. 11, 1925, he established the feast of Christ the King for universal observance. Subjects of some of his other encyclicals were: Christian education, in *Rappresentanti in Terra*, Dec. 31, 1929; Christian marriage, in *Casti Connubii*, Dec. 31, 1930; social conditions and pressure for social change in line with the teaching in *Rerum Novarum*, in *Quadragesimo Anno*, May 15, 1931; atheistic Communism, in *Divini Redemptoris*, Mar. 19, 1937; the priesthood, in *Ad Catholici Sacerdotii*, Dec. 20, 1935.

Missions: Following the lead of Benedict XV, Pius called for the training of native clergy in the pattern of their own respective cultures, and promoted missionary developments in various ways. He ordained six native bishops for China in 1926, one for Japan in 1927, and others for regions of Asia, China and India in 1933. He placed the first 40 mission dioceses under native bishops, saw the number of native priests increase from about 2,600 to more than 7,000, and the number of Catholics in missionary areas more than double from nine million.

In the apostolic constitution *Deus Scientiarum Dominus* of May 24, 1931, he ordered the introduction of missiology into theology courses.

Interfaith Relations: Pius was negative to the ecumenical movement among Protestants but approved the Malines Conversations, 1921 to 1926, between Anglicans and Catholics.

International Relations: Relations with the Mussolini government deteriorated from 1931 on, as indicated in the encyclical *Non Abbiamo Bisogno*, when the regime took steps to curb liberties and activities of the Church; they turned critical in 1938 with the emergence of racist policies. Relations deteriorated also in Germany from 1933 on, resulting finally in condemnation of the Nazis in the encyclical *Mit Brennender Sorge*, March 1937. Pius sparked a revival of the Church in France by encouraging Catholics to work within the democratic framework of the Republic rather than foment trouble over restoration of a monarchy. Pius was powerless to influence developments related to the civil war that erupted in Spain in July 1936, sporadic persecution and repression by the Calles regime in Mexico, and systematic persecution of the Church in the Soviet Union. Many of the 10 concordats and two agreements reached with European countries after World War I became casualties of World War II.

Roman Question: Pius negotiated for two and one-half years with the Italian government to settle the Roman Question by means of the Lateran Agreement of 1929. The agreement provided independent status for the State of Vatican City; made Catholicism the official religion of Italy, with pastoral and educational freedom and state recognition of Catholic marriages, religious orders and societies; and provided a financial payment to the Vatican for expropriation of the former States of the Church.

PIUS XII

Pius XII (Eugenio Maria Giovanni Pacelli) was born Mar. 2, 1876, in Rome.

Educated at the Gregorian University and the Lateran University, in Rome, he was ordained to the priesthood Apr. 2, 1899.

He entered the Vatican diplomatic service in 1901, worked on the codification of canon law, and was appointed secretary of the Congregation for Ecclesiastical Affairs in 1914. Three years later he was ordained titular archbishop of Sardis and made apostolic nuncio to Bavaria. He was nuncio to Germany from 1920 to 1929, when he was made a cardinal, and took office as papal secretary of state in the following year. His diplomatic negotiations resulted in concordats between the Vatican and Bavaria (1924), Prussia (1929), Baden (1932), Austria and the German Republic (1933). He took part in negotiations that led to settlement of the Roman Question in 1929.

He was elected to the papacy Mar. 2, 1939. He died Oct. 9, 1958, at Castel Gandolfo after the 12th longest pontificate in history.

Canonizations: He canonized 34 saints, including Mother Frances X. Cabrini, the first U.S. citizen-saint.

Cardinals: He raised 56 prelates to the rank of cardinal in two consistories held in 1946 and 1953. There were 57 cardinals at the time of his death.

Church Organization and Missions: He increased the number of dioceses from 1,696 to 2,048. He established native hierarchies in China (1946), Burma (1955) and parts of Africa, and extended the native structure of the Church in India. He ordained the first black bishop for Africa.

Communism: In addition to opposing and condemning Communism on numerous occasions, he decreed in 1949 the penalty of excommunication for all Catholics holding formal and willing allegiance to the Communist Party and its policies. During his reign the Church was persecuted in some 15 countries that fell under communist domination.

Doctrine and Liturgy: He proclaimed the dogma of the Assumption of the Blessed Virgin Mary Nov. 1, 1950 (apostolic constitution, *Munificentissimus Deus*).

In various encyclicals and other enactments, he provided background for the *aggiornamento* introduced by his successor, John XXIII: by his formulations of doctrine and practice regarding the Mystical Body of Christ, the liturgy, sacred music and biblical studies; by the revision of the Rites of Holy Week; by initiation of the work which led to the calendar-missal-breviary reform ordered into effect Jan. 1, 1961; by the first of several modifications of the Eucharistic fast; by extending the time of Mass to the evening. He instituted the feasts of Mary, Queen, and of St. Joseph the Worker, and clarified teaching concerning devotion to the Sacred Heart.

His 41 encyclicals and nearly 1,000 public addresses made Pius one of the greatest teaching popes. His concern in all his communications was to deal with specific points at issue and/or to bring Christian principles to bear on contemporary world problems.

Peace Efforts: Before the start of World War II, he tried unsuccessfully to get the contending nations — Germany and Poland, France and Italy — to settle their differences peaceably. During the war, he offered his services to mediate the widened conflict, spoke out against the horrors of war and the suffering it caused, mobilized relief work for its victims, proposed a five-point program for peace in Christmas messages from 1939 to 1942, and secured a generally open status for the city of Rome. He has been criticized in some quarters for not doing enough to oppose the Holocaust. This is a matter of historical debate, but it is a fact that through his direct intercession many thousands of Jews in Rome and Italy were saved from certain death, and he resisted wherever possible the threat of Nazism to human rights. Such were his contributions to assisting Jews that the rabbi of Rome, Dr. Abraham Zolli was converted to Catholicism, and upon his death, Pius was praised by Golda Meir for his efforts. After the war, he endorsed the principles and intent of the United Nations and continued efforts for peace.

United States: Pius appointed more than 200 of the 265 American bishops resident in the U.S. and abroad in 1958, erected 27 dioceses in this country, and raised seven dioceses to archiepiscopal rank.

BLESSED JOHN XXIII

John XXIII (Angelo Roncalli) was born Nov. 25, 1881, at Sotte il Monte, Italy.

He was educated at the seminary of the Bergamo diocese and the Pontifical Seminary in Rome, where he was ordained to the priesthood Aug. 10, 1904.

He spent the first nine or 10 years of his priesthood as secretary to the bishop of Bergamo and as an instructor in the seminary there. He served as a medic and chaplain in the Italian army during World War I. Afterwards, he resumed duties in his own diocese until

he was called to Rome in 1921 for work with the Society for the Propagation of the Faith.

He began diplomatic service in 1925 as titular archbishop of Areopolis and apostolic visitor to Bulgaria. A succession of offices followed: apostolic delegate to Bulgaria (1931-1935); titular archbishop of Mesembria, apostolic delegate to Turkey and Greece, administrator of the Latin vicariate apostolic of Istanbul (1935-1944); apostolic nuncio to France (1944-1953). On these missions, he was engaged in delicate negotiations involving Roman, Eastern-Rite and Orthodox relations; the needs of people suffering from the consequences of World War II; and unsettling suspicions arising from wartime conditions.

He was made a cardinal Jan. 12, 1953, and three days later was appointed patriarch of Venice, the position he held until his election to the papacy Oct. 28, 1958. He died of stomach cancer June 3, 1963.

John was a strong and vigorous pope whose influence far out-measured both his age and the shortness of his time in the papacy. He was beatified by Pope John Paul II on Sept. 3, 2000.

Second Vatican Council: John announced Jan. 25, 1959, his intention of convoking the 21st ecumenical council in history to renew life in the Church, to reform its structures and institutions, and to explore ways and means of promoting unity among Christians. Through the council, which completed its work two and one-half years after his death, he ushered in a new era in the history of the Church.

Canon Law: He established a commission Mar. 28, 1963, for revision of the Code of Canon Law. The revised Code was promulgated in 1983.

Canonizations: He canonized 10 saints and beatified Mother Elizabeth Ann Seton, the first native of the U.S. ever so honored. He named St. Lawrence of Brindisi a Doctor of the Church.

Cardinals: He created 52 cardinals in five consistories, raising membership of the College of Cardinals above the traditional number of 70; at one time in 1962, the membership was 87. He made the college more international in representation than it had ever been, appointing the first cardinals from the Philippines, Japan and Africa. He ordered episcopal ordination for all cardinals. He relieved the suburban bishops of Rome of ordinary jurisdiction over their dioceses so they might devote all their time to business of the Roman Curia.

Eastern Rites: He made all Eastern-Rite patriarchs members of the Congregation for the Oriental Churches.

Ecumenism: He assigned to the Second Vatican Council the task of finding ways and means of promoting unity among Christians. He established the Vatican Secretariat for Promoting Christian Unity June 5, 1960. He showed his desire for more cordial relations with the Orthodox by sending personal representatives to visit Patriarch Athenagoras I June 27, 1961; approved a mission of five delegates to the General Assembly of the World Council of Churches which met in New Delhi, India, in November 1961; removed a number of pejorative references to Jews in the Roman-Rite liturgy for Good Friday.

Encyclicals: Of the eight encyclicals he issued, the two outstanding ones were *Mater et Magistra* ("Christianity and Social Progress"), in which he recapitulated, updated and extended the social doctrine stated earlier by Leo XIII and Pius XI; and *Pacem in Terris* ("Peace on Earth"), the first encyclical ever addressed to all men of good will as well as to Catholics, on the natural-law principles of peace.

Liturgy: In forwarding liturgical reforms already begun by Pius XII, he ordered a calendar-missal-breviary reform into effect Jan. 1, 1961. He authorized the use of vernacular languages in the administration of the sacraments and approved giving Holy Communion to the sick in afternoon hours. He selected the liturgy as the first topic of major discussion by the Second Vatican Council.

Missions: He issued an encyclical on the missionary activity of the Church; established native hierarchies in Indonesia, Vietnam and Korea; and called on North American superiors of religious institutes to have one-tenth of their members assigned to work in Latin America by 1971.

Peace: John spoke and used his moral influence for peace in 1961 when tension developed over Berlin, in 1962 during the Algerian revolt from France, and later the same year in the Cuban missile crisis. His efforts were singled out for honor by the Balzan Peace Foundation. In 1963, he was posthumously awarded the U.S. Presidential Medal of Freedom.

PAUL VI

Paul VI (Giovanni Battista Montini) was born Sept. 26, 1897, at Concesio in northern Italy. Educated at Brescia, he was ordained to the priesthood May 29, 1920. He pursued additional studies at the Pontifical Academy for Noble Ecclesiastics and the Pontifical Gregorian University. In 1924 he began 30 years of service in the Secretariat of State; as undersecretary from 1937 until 1954, he was closely associated with Pius XII and was heavily engaged in organizing informational and relief services during and after World War II. He declined the offer of the cardinalate by Pope Pius XII.

Ordained archbishop of Milan Dec. 12, 1954, he was inducted into the College of Cardinals Dec. 15, 1958 by Pope John XXIII. Trusted by John, he was a key figure in organizing the first session of Vatican Council II and was elected to the papacy June 21, 1963, two days after the conclave began. He died of a heart attack Aug. 6, 1978.

Second Vatican Council: He reconvened the Second Vatican Council after the death of John XXIII, presided over its second, third and fourth sessions, formally promulgated the 16 documents it produced, and devoted the whole of his pontificate to the task of putting them into effect throughout the Church. The main thrust of his pontificate — in a milieu of cultural and other changes in the Church and the world — was toward institutionalization and control of the authentic trends articulated and set in motion by the council.

Canonizations: He canonized 84 saints. They included groups of 22 Ugandan martyrs and 40 martyrs of England and Wales, as well as two Americans — Elizabeth Ann Bayley Seton and John Nepomucene Neumann.

Cardinals: He created 144 cardinals, and gave the Sacred College a more international complexion than it ever had before. He limited participation in papal elections to 120 cardinals under the age of 80.

Collegiality: He established the Synod of Bishops

in 1965 and called it into session five times. He stimulated the formation and operation of regional conferences of bishops, and of consultative bodies on other levels.

Creed and Holy Year: On June 30, 1968, he issued a Creed of the People of God in conjunction with the celebration of a Year of Faith. He proclaimed and led the observance of a Holy Year from Christmas Eve of 1974 to Christmas Eve of 1975.

Diplomacy: He met with many world leaders, including Soviet President Nikolai Podgorny in 1967, Marshal Tito of Yugoslavia in 1971 and President Nicolai Ceausescu of Romania in 1973. He worked constantly to reduce tension between the Church and the intransigent regimes of Eastern European countries by means of a detente type of policy called *Ostpolitik*. He agreed to significant revisions of the Vatican's concordat with Spain and initiated efforts to revise the concordat with Italy. More than 40 countries established diplomatic relations with the Vatican during his pontificate.

Encyclicals: He issued seven encyclicals, three of which are the best known. In *Populorum Progressio* ("Development of Peoples") he appealed to wealthy countries to take "concrete action" to promote human development and to remedy imbalances between richer and poorer nations; this encyclical, coupled with other documents and related actions, launched the Church into a new depth of involvement as a public advocate for human rights and for humanizing social, political and economic policies. In *Sacerdotalis Caelibatus* ("Priestly Celibacy") he reaffirmed the strict observance of priestly celibacy throughout the Western Church. In *Humanae Vitae* ("Of Human Life") he condemned abortion, sterilization and artificial birth control, in line with traditional teaching and in "defense of life, the gift of God, the glory of the family, the strength of the people."

Interfaith Relations: He initiated formal consultation and informal dialogue on international and national levels between Catholics and non-Catholics — Orthodox, Anglicans, Protestants, Jews, Muslims, Buddhists, Hindus, and unbelievers. He and Greek Orthodox Patriarch Athenagoras I of Constantinople nullified in 1965 the mutual excommunications imposed by their respective churches in 1054.

Liturgy: He carried out the most extensive liturgical reform in history, involving a new Order of the Mass effective in 1969, a revised church calendar in 1970, revisions and translations into vernacular languages of all sacramental rites and other liturgical texts.

Ministries: He authorized the restoration of the permanent diaconate in the Roman Rite and the establishment of new ministries of lay persons.

Peace: In 1968, he instituted the annual observance of a World Day of Peace on New Year's Day as a means of addressing a message of peace to all the world's political leaders and the peoples of all nations. The most dramatic of his many appeals for peace and efforts to ease international tensions was his plea for "No more war!" before the United Nations Oct. 4, 1965.

Pilgrimages: A "Pilgrim Pope," he made pastoral visits to the Holy Land and India in 1964, the United Nations and New York City in 1965, Portugal and Turkey in 1967, Colombia in 1968, Switzerland and

Uganda in 1969, and Asia, Pacific islands and Australia in 1970. While in Manila in 1970, he was stabbed by a Bolivian artist.

Roman Curia: He reorganized the central administrative organs of the Church in line with provisions of the apostolic constitution, *Regimini Ecclesiae Universae*, streamlining procedures for more effective service and giving the agencies a more international perspective by drawing officials and consultors from all over the world. He also instituted a number of new commissions and other bodies. Coupled with curial reorganization was a simplification of papal ceremonies.

JOHN PAUL I

John Paul I (Albino Luciani) was born Oct. 17, 1912, in Forno di Canale (now Canale d'Agordo) in northern Italy. Educated at the minor seminary in Feltre and the major seminary of the Diocese of Belluno, he was ordained to the priesthood July 7, 1935. He pursued further studies at the Pontifical Gregorian University in Rome and was awarded a doctorate in theology. From 1937 to 1947 he was vice rector of the Belluno seminary, where he taught dogmatic and moral theology, canon law and sacred art. He was appointed vicar general of his diocese in 1947 and served as director of catechetics.

Ordained bishop of Vittorio Veneto Dec. 27, 1958, he attended all sessions of the Second Vatican Council, participated in three assemblies of the Synod of Bishops (1971, 1974 and 1977), and was vice president of the Italian Bishops' Conference from 1972 to 1975.

He was appointed archbishop and patriarch of Venice Dec. 15, 1969, and was inducted into the College of Cardinals Mar. 5, 1973.

He was elected to the papacy Aug. 26, 1978, on the fourth ballot cast by the 111 cardinals participating in the largest and one of the shortest conclaves in history. The quickness of his election was matched by the brevity of his pontificate of 33 days, during which he delivered 19 addresses. He died of a heart attack Sept. 28, 1978.

JOHN PAUL II

See separate entry.

PAPAL ENCYCLICALS — BENEDICT XIV (1740) TO JOHN PAUL II

(*Source:* The Papal Encyclicals *[5 vols.],* Claudia Carlen, I.H.M.; Pieran Press, Ann Arbor, Mich. Used with permission.)

An encyclical letter is a pastoral letter addressed by a pope to the whole Church. In general, it concerns matters of doctrine, morals or discipline, or significant commemorations. Its formal title consists of the first few words of the official text. Some encyclicals, notably *Pacem in terris* by John XXIII, *Ecclesiam Suam* by Paul VI and several by John Paul II, have been addressed to people of good will in general as well as to bishops and the faithful in communion with the Church.

An encyclical epistle resembles an encyclical letter but is addressed only to part of the Church. The authority of encyclicals was stated by Pius XII in the encyclical *Humani generis* Aug. 12, 1950: "Nor must it be thought that what is contained in encyclical letters does not of itself demand assent, on the pretext that the popes do not exercise in them the supreme power of their teaching authority. Rather, such teachings belong to the ordinary magisterium, of which it is true to say: 'He who hears you, hears me' (Lk. 10:16); for the most part, too, what is expounded and inculcated in encyclical letters already appertains to Catholic doctrine for other reasons."

The Second Vatican Council declared: "Religious submission of will and of mind must be shown in a special way to the authentic teaching authority of the Roman Pontiff, even when he is not speaking *ex cathedra*. That is, it must be shown in such a way that his supreme magisterium is acknowledged with reverence, the judgments made by him are sincerely adhered to, according to his manifest mind and will. His mind and will in the matter may be known chiefly either from the character of the documents (one of which could be an encyclical), from his frequent repetition of the same doctrine, or from his manner of speaking" (Dogmatic Constitution on the Church, *Lumen Gentium,* No. 25).

The following list contains the titles and indicates the subject matter of encyclical letters and epistles.

The latter are generally distinguishable by the limited scope of their titles or contents.

Benedict XIV
(1740-1758)

1740: *Ubi primum* (On the duties of bishops), Dec. 3.

1741: *Quanta cura* (Forbidding traffic in alms), June 30.

1743: *Nimiam licentiam* (To the bishops of Poland: on validity of marriages), May 18.

1745: *Vix pervenit* (To the bishops of Italy: on usury and other dishonest profit), Nov. 1.

1748: *Magnae Nobis* (To the bishops of Poland: on marriage impediments and dispensations), June 29.

1749: *Peregrinantes* (To all the faithful: proclaiming a Holy Year for 1750), May 5.

Apostolica Constitutio (On preparation for the Holy Year), June 26.

1751: *A quo primum* (To the bishops of Poland: on Jews and Christians living in the same place), June 14.

1754: *Cum Religiosi* (To the bishops of the States of the Church: on catechesis), June 26.

Quod Provinciale (To the bishops of Albania: on Christians using Mohammedan names), Aug. 1.

1755: *Allatae sunt* (To missionaries of the Orient: on the observance of Oriental rites), July 26.

1756: Ex quo primum (To bishops of the Greek rite: on the Euchologion), Mar. 1.

Ex omnibus (To the bishops of France: on the apostolic constitution, *Unigenitus*), Oct. 16.

Clement XIII
(1758-1769)

1758: *A quo die* (Unity among Christians), Sept. 13.

1759: Cum primum (On observing canonical sanctions), Sept. 17.

Appetente Sacro (On the spiritual advantages of fasting), Dec. 20.

1761: In Dominico agro (On instruction in the faith), June 14.

1766: Christianae republicae (On the dangers of anti-Christian writings), Nov. 25.

1768: Summa quae (To the bishops of Poland: on the Church in Poland), Jan. 6.

Clement XIV
(1769-1774)

1769: *Decet quam maxime* (To the bishops of Sardinia: on abuses in taxes and benefices), Sept. 21.

Inscrutabili divinae sapientiae (To all Christians: proclaiming a universal jubilee), Dec.12.

Cum summi (Proclaiming a universal jubilee), Dec. 12.

1774: *Salutis nostra* (To all Christians: proclaiming a universal jubilee), Apr. 30.

Pius VI
(1775-1799)

1775: *Inscrutabile* (On the problems of the pontificate), Dec. 25.

1791: *Charitas* (To the bishops of France: on the civil oath in France), Apr. 13.

Pius VII
(1800-1823)

1800: *Diu satis* (To the bishops of France: on a return to Gospel principles), May 15.

Leo XII
(1823-1829)

1824: *Ubi primum* (To all bishops: on Leo XII's assuming the pontificate), May 5.

Quod hoc ineunte (Proclaiming a universal jubilee), May 24.

1825: *Charitate Christi* (Extending jubilee to the entire Church), Dec. 25.

Pius VIII
(1829-1830)

1829: *Traditi humilitati* (On Pius VIII's program for the pontificate), May 24.

Gregory XVI
(1831-1846)

1832: *Summo iugiter studio* (To the bishops of Bavaria: on mixed marriages), May 27.

Cum primum (To the bishops of Poland: on civil obedience), June 9.

Mirari vos (On liberalism and religious indifferentism), Aug. 15.

1833: *Quo graviora* (To the bishops of the Rhineland: on the "pragmatic Constitution"), Oct. 4.

1834: *Singulari Nos* (On the errors of Lammenais), June 25.

1835: *Commissum divinitus* (To clergy of Switzerland: on Church and State), May 17.

1840: *Probe nostis* (On the Propagation of the Faith), Sept. 18.

1841: *Quas vestro* (To the bishops of Hungary: on mixed marriages), Apr. 30.

1844: *Inter praecipuas* (On biblical societies), May 8.

Pius IX
(1846-1878)

1846: *Qui pluribus* (On faith and religion), Nov. 9.

1847: *Praedecessores Nostros* (On aid for Ireland), Mar. 25.

Ubi primum (To religious superiors: on discipline for religious), June 17.

1849: *Ubi primum* (On the Immaculate Conception), Feb. 2.

Nostis et Nobiscum (To the bishops of Italy: on the Church in the Pontifical States), Dec. 8.

1851: *Exultavit cor Nostrum* (On the effects of jubilee), Nov. 21.

1852: *Nemo certe ignorat* (To the bishops of Ireland: on the discipline for clergy), Mar. 25.

Probe noscitis Venerabiles (To the bishops of Spain: on the discipline for clergy), May 17.

1853: *Inter multiplices* (To the bishops of France: pleading for unity of spirit), Mar. 21.

1854: *Neminem vestrum* (To clergy and faithful of Constantinople: on the persecution of Armenians), Feb. 2.

Optime noscitis (To the bishops of Ireland: on the proposed Catholic university for Ireland), Mar. 20.

Apostolicae Nostrae caritatis (Urging prayers for peace), Aug. 1.

1855: *Optime noscitis* (To the bishops of Austria: on episcopal meetings), Nov. 5.

1856: *Singulari quidem* (To the bishops of Austria: on the Church in Austria), Mar. 17.

1858: *Cum nuper* (To the bishops of the Kingdom of the Two Sicilies: on care for clerics), Jan. 20.

Amantissimi Redemptoris (On priests and the care of souls), May 3.

1859: *Cum sancta mater Ecclesia* (Pleading for public prayer), Apr. 27.

Qui nuper (On Pontifical States), June 18.

1860: *Nullis certe verbis* (On the need for civil sovereignty), Jan. 19.

1862: *Amantissimus* (To bishops of the Oriental rite: on the care of the churches), Apr. 8.

1863: *Quanto conficiamur moerore* (To the bishops of Italy: on promotion of false doctrines), Aug. 10.

Incredibili (To the bishops of Bogota: on persecution in New Granada), Sept. 17.

1864: *Maximae quidem* (To the bishops of Bavaria: on the Church in Bavaria), Aug. 18.

Quanta cura (Condemning current errors), Dec. 8.

1865: *Meridionali Americae* (To the bishops of South America: on the seminary for native clergy), Sept. 30.

1867: *Levate* (On the afflictions of the Church), Oct. 27.

1870: *Respicientes* (Protesting the taking of the Pontifical States), Nov. 1.

1871: *Ubi Nos* (To all bishops: on Pontifical States), May 15.

Beneficia Dei (On the twenty-fifth anniversary of his pontificate), June 4.

Saepe Venerabiles Fratres (On thanksgiving for twenty-five years of pontificate), Aug. 5.

1872: *Quae in Patriarchatu* (To bishops and people of Chaldea: on the Church in Chaldea), Nov. 16.

1873: *Quartus supra* (To bishops and people of the Armenian rite: on the Church in Armenia), Jan. 6.

Etsi multa (On the Church in Italy, Germany and Switzerland), Nov. 21.

1874: *Vix dum a Nobis* (To the bishops of Austria: on the Church in Austria), Mar. 7.

Gravibus Ecclesiae (To all bishops and faithful: proclaiming a jubilee for 1875), Dec. 24.

1875: *Quod nunquam* (To the bishops of Prussia: on the Church in Prussia), Feb. 5.

Graves ac diuturnae (To the bishops of Switzerland: on the Church in Switzerland), Mar. 23.

Leo XIII
(1878-1903)

1878: *Inscrutabili Dei consilio* (On the evils of society), Apr. 21.

Quod Apostolici muneris (On socialism), Dec. 28.

1879: *Aeterni Patris* (On the restoration of Christian philosophy), Aug. 4.

1880: *Arcanum* (On Christian marriage), Feb. 10.

Grande munus (On Sts. Cyril and Methodius), Sept. 30.

Sancta Dei civitas (On mission societies), Dec. 3.

1881: *Diuturnum* (On the origin of civil power), June 29.

Licet multa (To the bishops of Belgium: on Catholics in Belgium), Aug. 3.

1882: *Etsi Nos* (To the bishops of Italy: on conditions in Italy), Feb. 15.

Auspicato concessum (On St. Francis of Assisi), Sept. 17.

Cum multa (To the bishops of Spain: on conditions in Spain), Dec. 8.

1883: *Supremi Apostolatus officio* (On devotion to the Rosary), Sept. 1.

1884: *Nobilissima Gallorum gens* (To the bishops of France: on the religious question), Feb. 8.

Humanum genus (On Freemasonry), Apr. 20.

Superiore anno (On the recitation of the Rosary), Aug. 30.

1885: *Immortale Dei* (On the Christian constitution of states), Nov. 1.

Spectata fides (To the bishops of England: on Christian education), Nov. 27.

Quod auctoritate (Proclamation of extraordinary Jubilee), Dec. 22.

1886: *Iampridem* (To the bishops of Prussia: on Catholicism in Germany), Jan. 6.

Quod multum (To the bishops of Hungary: on the liberty of the Church), Aug. 22.

Pergrata (To the bishops of Portugal: on the Church in Portugal), Sept. 14.

1887: *Vieben noto* (To the bishops of Italy: on the Rosary and public life), Sept. 20.

Officio sanctissimo (To the bishops of Bavaria: on the Church in Bavaria), Dec. 22.

1888: *Quod anniversarius* (On his sacerdotal jubilee), Apr. 1.

In plurimis (To the bishops of Brazil: on the abolition of slavery), May 5.

Libertas (On the nature of human liberty), June 20.

Saepe Nos (To the bishops of Ireland: on boycotting in Ireland), June 24.

Paterna caritas (To the Patriarch of Cilicia and the archbishops and bishops of the Armenian people: on reunion with Rome), July 25.

Quam aerumnosa (To the bishops of America: on Italian immigrants), Dec. 10.

Etsi cunctas (To the bishops of Ireland: on the Church in Ireland), Dec. 21.

Exeunte iam anno (On the right ordering of Christian life), Dec. 25.

1889: *Magni Nobis* (To the bishops of the United States: on the Catholic University of America), Mar. 7.

Quamquam pluries (On devotion to St. Joseph), Aug. 15.

1890: *Sapientiae Christianae* (On Christians as citizens), Jan. 10.

Dall'alto Dell'Apostolico seggio (To the bishops and people of Italy: on Freemasonry in Italy), Oct. 15.

Catholicae Ecclesiae (On slavery in the missions), Nov. 20.

1891: *In ipso* (To the bishops of Austria: on episcopal reunions in Austria), Mar. 3.

Rerum novarum (On capital and labor), May 15.

Pastoralis (To the bishops of Portugal: on religious union), June 25.

Pastoralis officii (To the bishops of Germany and Austria: on the morality of dueling), Sept. 12.

Octobri mense (On the Rosary), Sept. 22.

1892: *Au milieu des sollicitudes* (To the bishops, clergy and faithful of France: on the Church and State in France), Feb. 16.

Quarto abeunte saeculo (To the bishops of Spain, Italy, and the two Americas: on the Columbus quadricentennial), July 16.

Magnae Dei Matris (On the Rosary), Sept. 8.

Inimica vis (To the bishops of Italy: on Freemasonry), Dec. 8.

Custodi di quella fede (To the Italian people: on Freemasonry), Dec. 8.

1893: *Ad extremas* (On seminaries for native clergy), June 24.

Constanti Hungarorum (To the bishops of Hungary: on the Church in Hungary), Sept. 2.

Laetitiae sanctae (Commending devotion to the Rosary), Sept. 8.

Non mediocri (To the bishops of Spain: on the Spanish College in Rome), Oct. 25.

Providentissimus Deus (On the study of Holy Scripture), Nov. 18.

1894: *Caritatis* (To the bishops of Poland: on the Church in Poland), Mar. 19.

Inter graves (To the bishops of Peru: on the Church in Peru), May 1.

Litteras a vobis (To the bishops of Brazil: on the clergy in Brazil), July 2.

Iucunda semper expectatione (On the Rosary), Sept. 8.

Christi nomen (On the propagation of the Faith and Eastern churches), Dec. 24.

1895: *Longinqua* (To the bishops of the United States: on Catholicism in the United States), Jan. 6.

Permoti Nos (To the bishops of Belgium: on social conditions in Belgium), July 10.

Adiutricem (On the Rosary), Sept. 5.

1896: *Insignes* (To the bishops of Hungary: on the Hungarian millennium), May 1.

Satis cognitum (On the unity of the Church), June 29.

Fidentem piumque animum (On the Rosary), Sept. 20.

1897: *Divinum illud munus* (On the Holy Spirit), May 9.

Militantis Ecclesiae (To the bishops of Austria, Germany, and Switzerland: on St. Peter Canisius), Aug. 1.

Augustissimae Virginis Mariae (On the Confraternity of the Holy Rosary), Sept. 12.

Affari vos (To the bishops of Canada: on the Manitoba school question), Dec. 8.

1898: *Caritatis studium* (To the bishops of Scotland: on the Church in Scotland), July 25.

Spesse volte (To the bishops, priests, and people of Italy: on the suppression of Catholic institutions), Aug. 5.

Quam religiosa (To the bishops of Peru: on civil marriage law), Aug. 16.

Diuturni temporis (On the Rosary), Sept. 5.

Quum diuturnum (To the bishops of Latin America: on Latin American bishops' plenary council), Dec. 25.

1899: *Annum Sacrum* (On consecration to the Sacred Heart), May 25.

Depuis le jour (To the archbishops, bishops, and clergy of France: on the education of the clergy), Sept. 8.

Paternae (To the bishops of Brazil: on the education of the clergy), Sept. 18.

1900: *Omnibus compertum* (To the Patriarch and bishops of the Greek-Melkite rite: on unity among the Greek Melkites), July 21.

Tametsi futura prospicientibus (On Jesus Christ the Redeemer), Nov. 1.

1901: *Graves de communi re* (On Christian democracy), Jan. 18.

Gravissimas (To the bishops of Portugal: on religious orders in Portugal), May 16.

Reputantibus (To the bishops of Bohemia and Moravia: on the language question in Bohemia), Aug. 20.

Urbanitatis Veteris (To the bishops of the Latin church in Greece: on the foundation of a seminary in Athens), Nov. 20.

1902: *In amplissimo* (To the bishops of the United States: on the Church in the United States), Apr. 15.

Quod votis (To the bishops of Austria: on the proposed Catholic University), Apr. 30.

Mirae caritatis (On the Holy Eucharist), May 28.

Quae ad Nos (To the bishops of Bohemia and Moravia: on the Church in Bohemia and Moravia), Nov. 22.

Fin dal principio (To the bishops of Italy: on the education of the clergy), Dec. 8.

Dum multa (To the bishops of Ecuador: on marriage legislation), Dec. 24.

St. Pius X
(1903-1914)

1903: *E supremi* (On the restoration of all things in Christ), Oct. 4.

1904: *Ad diem illum laetissimum* (On the Immaculate Conception), Feb. 2.

Iucunda sane (On Pope Gregory the Great), Mar. 12.

1905: *Acerbo nimis* (On teaching Christian doctrine), Apr. 15.

Il fermo proposito (To the bishops of Italy: on Catholic Action in Italy), June 11.

1906: *Vehementer Nos* (To the bishops, clergy, and people of France: on the French Law of Separation), Feb. 11.

Tribus circiter (On the Mariavites or Mystic Priests of Poland), Apr. 5.

Pieni l'animo (To the bishops of Italy: on the clergy in Italy), July 28.

Gravissimo officio munere (To the bishops of France: on French associations of worship), Aug. 10.

1907: *Une fois encore* (To the bishops, clergy, and

people of France: on the separation of Church and State), Jan. 6.

Pascendi dominici gregis (On the doctrines of the Modernists), Sept. 8.

1909: *Communium rerum* (On St. Anselm of Aosta), Apr. 21.

1910: Editae saepe (On St. Charles Borromeo), May 26.

1911: Iamdudum (On the Law of Separation in Portugal), May 24.

1912: Lacrimabili statu (To the bishops of Latin America: on the Indians of South America), June 7.

Singulari quadam (To the bishops of Germany: on labor organizations), Sept. 24.

Benedict XV
(1914-1922)

1914: Ad beatissimi Apostolorum (Appeal for peace), Nov. 1.

1917: Humani generis Redemptionem (On preaching the Word of God), June 15.

1918: Quod iam diu (On the future peace conference), Dec. 1.

1919: *In hac tanta* (To the bishops of Germany: on St. Boniface), May 14.

Paterno iam diu (On children of central Europe), Nov. 24.

1920: *Pacem, Dei munus pulcherrimum* (On peace and Christian reconciliation), May 23.

Spiritus Paraclitus (On St. Jerome), Sept. 15.

Principi Apostolorum Petro (On St. Ephrem the Syrian), Oct. 5.

Annus iam plenus (On children of central Europe), Dec. 1.

1921: *Sacra propediem* (On the Third Order of St. Francis), Jan. 6.

In praeclara summorum (To professors and students of fine arts in Catholic institutions of learning: on Dante), Apr. 30.

Fausto appetente die (On St. Dominic), June 29.

Pius XI
(1922-1939)

1922: *Ubi arcano Dei consilio* (On the peace of Christ in the Kingdom of Christ), Dec. 23.

1923: *Rerum omnium perturbationem* (On St. Francis de Sales), Jan. 26.

Studiorum Ducem (On St. Thomas Aquinas), June 29.

Ecclesiam Dei (On St. Josaphat), Nov. 12.

1924: *Maximam gravissimamque* (To the bishops, clergy, and people of France: on French diocesan associations), Jan. 18.

1925: *Quas primas* (On the feast of Christ the King), Dec. 11.

1926: *Rerum Ecclesiae* (On Catholic missions), Feb. 28.

Rite expiatis (On St. Francis of Assisi), Apr. 30.

Iniquis afflictisque (On the persecution of the Church in Mexico), Nov. 18.

1928: *Mortalium animos* (On religious unity), Jan. 6.

Miserentissimus Redemptor (On reparation to the Sacred Heart), May 8.

Rerum Orientalium (On the promotion of Oriental Studies), Sept. 8.

1929: *Mens Nostra* (On the promotion of Spiritual Exercises), Dec. 20.

Quinquagesimo ante (On his sacerdotal jubilee), Dec. 23.

Rappresentanti in terra (On Christian education), Dec. 31. [Latin text, *Divini illius magistri*, published several months later with minor changes.]

1930: *Ad salutem* (On St. Augustine), Apr. 20.

Casti connubii (On Christian Marriage), Dec. 31.

1931: *Quadragesimo anno* (Commemorating the fortieth anniversary of Leo XIII's *Rerum novarum*: on reconstruction of the soical order), May 15.

Non abbiamo bisogno (On Catholic Action in Italy), June 29.

Nova impendet (On the economic crisis), Oct. 2.

Lux veritatis (On the Council of Ephesus), Dec. 25.

1932: *Caritate Christi compulsi* (On the Sacred Heart), May 3.

Acerba animi (To the bishops of Mexico: on persecution of the Church in Mexico), Sept. 29.

1933: *Dilectissima Nobis* (To the bishops, clergy, and people of Spain: on oppression of the Church in Spain), June 3.

1935: *Ad Catholici sacerdotii* (On the Catholic priesthood), Dec. 20.

1936: *Vigilanti cura* (To the bishops of the United States: on motion pictures), June 29.

1937: *Mit brennender Sorge* (To the bishops of Germany: on the Church and the German Reich), Mar. 14.

Divini Redemptoris (On atheistic communism), Mar. 19.

Nos es muy conocida (To the bishops of Mexico: on the religious situation in Mexico), Mar. 28

Ingravescentibus malis (On the Rosary) Sept. 29.

Pius XII

(1939-1958)

1939: *Summi Pontificatus* (On the unity of human society), Oct. 20.

Sertum laetitiae (To the bishops of the United States: on the 150th anniversary of the establishment of the hierarchy in the United States), Nov. 1.

1940: *Saeculo exeunte octavo* (To the bishops of Portugal and its colonies: on the eighth centenary of the independence of Portugal), June 13.

1943: *Mystici Corporis Christi* (On the Mystical Body of Christ), June 29.

Divino afflante Spiritu (On promoting biblical studies, commemorating the fiftieth anniversary of *Providentissimus Deus*), Sept. 30.

1944: *Orientalis Ecclesiae* (On St. Cyril, Patriarch of Alexandria), Apr. 9.

1945: *Communium interpretes dolorum* (To the bishops of the world: appealing for prayers for peace during May), Apr. 15.

Orientales omnes Ecclesias (On the 350th anniversary of the reunion of the Ruthenian Church with the Apostolic See), Dec. 23.

1946: *Quemadmodum* (Pleading for the care of the world's destitute children), Jan. 6.

Deiparae Virginis Mariae (To all bishops: on the possibility of defining the Assumption of the Blessed Virgin Mary as a dogma of faith), May 1.

1947: *Fulgens radiatur* (On St. Benedict), Mar. 21.

Mediator Dei (On the sacred liturgy), Nov. 20.

Optatissima pax (Prescribing public prayers for social and world peace), Dec. 18.

1948: *Auspicia quaedam* (On public prayers for world peace and solution of the problem of Palestine), May 1.

In multiplicibus curis (On prayers for peace in Palestine), Oct. 24.

1949: *Redemptoris nostri cruciatus* (On the holy places in Palestine), Apr. 15.

1950: *Anni Sacri* (On the program for combatting atheistic propaganda throughout the world), Mar. 12.

Summi maeroris (On public prayers for peace), July 19.

Humani generis (Concerning some false opinions threatening to undermine the foundations of Catholic doctrine), Aug. 12.

Mirabile illud (On the crusade of prayers for peace), Dec. 6.

1951: *Evangelii praecones* (On the promotion of Catholic missions), June 2.

Sempiternus Rex Christus (On the Council of Chalcedon), Sept. 8.

Ingruentium malorum (On reciting the Rosary), Sept. 15.

1952: *Orientales Ecclesias* (On the persecuted Eastern Church), Dec. 15.

1953: *Doctor Mellifluus* (On St. Bernard of Clairvaux, the last of the fathers), May 24.

Fulgens corona (Proclaiming a Marian Year to commemorate the centenary of the definition of the dogma of the Immaculate Conception), Sept. 8.

1954: *Sacra virginitas* (On consecrated virginity), Mar. 25.

Ecclesiae fastos (To the bishops of Great Britain, Germany, Austria, France, Belgium, and Holland: on St. Boniface), June 5.

Ad Sinarum gentem (To the bishops, clergy, and people of China: on the supranationality of the Church), Oct. 7.

Ad Caeli Reginam (Proclaiming the Queenship of Mary), Oct. 11.

1955: *Musicae sacrae* (On sacred music), Dec. 25.

1956: *Haurietis aquas* (On devotion to the Sacred Heart), May 15.

Luctuosissimi eventus (Urging public prayers for peace and freedom for the people of Hungary), Oct. 28.

Laetamur admodum (Renewing exhortation for prayers for peace for Poland, Hungary, and especially for the Middle East), Nov. 1.

Datis nuperrime (Lamenting the sorrowful events in Hungary and condemning the ruthless use of force), Nov. 5.

1957: *Fidei donum* (On the present condition of the Catholic missions, especially in Africa), Apr. 21.

Invicti athletae (On St. Andrew Bobola), May 16.

Le pelerinage de Lourdes (Warning against materialism on the centenary of the apparitions at Lourdes), July 2.

Miranda prorsus (On the communications field: motion picture, radio, television), Sept. 8.

1958: *Ad Apostolorum Principis* (To the bishops of China; on Communism and the Church in China), June 29.

Meminisse iuvat (On prayers for persecuted Church), July 14.

John XXIII

(1958-1963)

1959: *Ad Petri Cathedram* (On truth, unity, and peace, in a spirit of charity), June 29.

Sacerdotii Nostri primordia (On St. John Vianney), Aug. 1.

Grata recordatio (On the Rosary: prayer for the Church, missions, international and social problems), Sept. 26.

Princeps Pastorum (On the missions, native clergy, lay participation), Nov. 28.

1961: *Mater et Magistra* (On Christianity and social progress), May 15.

Aeterna Dei sapientia (On fifteenth centenary of the death of Pope St. Leo I: the see of Peter as the center of Christian unity), Nov. 11.

1962: *Paenitentiam agere* (On the need for the practice of interior and exterior penance), July 1.

1963: *Pacem in terris* (On establishing universal peace in truth, justice, charity, and liberty), Apr. 11.

Paul VI
(1963-1978)

1964: *Ecclesiam Suam* (On the Church), Aug. 6.

1965: *Mense maio* (On prayers during May for the preservation of peace), Apr. 29.

Mysterium Fidei (On the Holy Eucharist), Sept. 3.

1966: *Christi Matri* (On prayers for peace during Oct.), Sept. 15.

1967: *Populorum progressio* (On the development of peoples), Mar. 26.

Sacerdotalis caelibatus (On the celibacy of the priest), June 24.

1968: *Humanae vitae* (On the regulation of birth), July 25.

John Paul II
(1978-)

1979: *Redemptor hominis* (On redemption and dignity of the human race), Mar. 4

1980: *Dives in misericordia* (On the mercy of God), Nov. 30.

1981: *Laborem exercens* (On human work), Sept. 14.

1985: *Slavorum Apostoli* (Commemorating Sts. Cyril and Methodius, on the eleventh centenary of the death of St. Methodius), June 2.

1986: *Dominum et Vivificantem* (On the Holy Spirit in the life of the Church and the world), May 18.

1987: *Redemptoris Mater* (On the role of Mary in the mystery of Christ and her active and exemplary presence in the life of the Church), Mar. 25.

Sollicitudo Rei Socialis (On social concerns, on the twentieth anniversary of *Populorum progressio*), Dec. 30.

1991: *Redemptoris missio* (On the permanent validity of the Church's missionary mandate), Jan. 22.

Centesimus annus (Commemorating the centenary of *Rerum novarum* and addressing the social question in a contemporary perspective), May 1.

1993: *Veritatis Splendor* (Regarding fundamental questions on the Church's moral teaching), Aug. 6.

1995: *Evangelium Vitae* (On the value and inviolability of human life), Mar. 25.

Ut Unum Sint (On commitment to ecumenism), May 25.

1998: *Fides et Ratio* (On Faith and Reason), Oct. 1, 1998.

CANONIZATIONS BY LEO XIII AND HIS SUCCESSORS

Canonization (see entry in **Glossary**) is an infallible declaration by the pope that a person who suffered martyrdom and/or practiced Christian virtue to a heroic degree is in glory with God in heaven and is worthy of public honor by the universal Church and of imitation by the faithful.

Biographies of some of the saints listed below are given elsewhere in the Almanac. See Index.

Leo XIII
(1878-1903)

1881: Clare of Montefalco (d. 1308); John Baptist de Rossi (1698-1764); Lawrence of Brindisi (d. 1619).

1883: Benedict J. Labre (1748-1783).

1888: Seven Holy Founders of the Servite Order; Peter Claver (1581-1654); John Berchmans (1599-1621); Alphonsus Rodriguez (1531-1617).

1897: Anthony M. Zaccaria (1502-1539); Peter Fourier of Our Lady (1565-1640).

1900: John Baptist de La Salle (1651-1719); Rita of Cascia (1381-1457).

St. Pius X
(1903-1914)

1904: Alexander Sauli (1534-1593); Gerard Majella (1725-1755).

1909: Joseph Oriol (1650-1702); Clement M. Hofbauer (1751-1820).

Benedict XV
(1914-1922)

1920: Gabriel of the Sorrowful Mother (1838-1862);

Margaret Mary Alacoque (1647-1690); Joan of Arc (1412-1431).

Pius XI
(1922-1939)

1925: Thérèse of Lisieux (1873-1897); Peter Canisius (1521-1597); Mary Magdalen Postel (1756-1846); Mary Magdalen Sophie Barat (1779-1865); John Eudes (1601-1680); John Baptist Vianney (Curé of Ars) (1786-1859).

1930: Lucy Filippini (1672-1732); Catherine Tomas (1533-1574); Jesuit North American Martyrs; Robert Bellarmine (1542-1621); Theophilus of Corte (1676-1740).

1931: Albert the Great (1206-1280) (equivalent canonization).

1933: Andrew Fournet (1752-1834); Bernadette Soubirous (1844-1879).

1934: Joan Antida Thouret (1765-1826); Mary Michaeli (1809-1865); Louise de Marillac (1591-1660); Joseph Benedict Cottolengo (1786-1842); Pompilius M. Pirotti, priest (1710-1756); Teresa Margaret Redi (1747-1770); John Bosco (1815-1888); Conrad of Parzham (1818-1894).

1935: John Fisher (1469-1535); Thomas More (1478-1535).

1938: Andrew Bobola (1592-1657); John Leonardi (c. 1550-1609); Salvatore of Horta (1520-1567).

Pius XII
(1939-1958)

1940: Gemma Galgani (1878-1903); Mary Euphrasia Pelletier (1796-1868).

1943: Margaret of Hungary (d. 1270) (equivalent canonization).

1946: Frances Xavier Cabrini (1850-1917).

1947: Nicholas of Flüe (1417-1487); John of Britto (1647-1693); Bernard Realini (1530-1616); Joseph Cafasso (1811-1860); Michael Garicoits (1797-1863); Jeanne Elizabeth des Ages (1773-1838); Louis Marie Grignon de Montfort (1673-1716); Catherine Labouré (1806-1876).

1949: Jeanne de Lestonnac (1556-1640); Maria Josepha Rossello (1811-1880).

1950: Emily de Rodat (1787-1852); Anthony Mary Claret (1807-1870); Bartolomea Capitanio (1807-1833); Vincenza Gerosa (1784-1847) Jeanne de Valois (1461-1504); Vincenzo M. Strambi (1745-1824); Maria Goretti (1890-1902); Mariana Paredes of Jesus (1618-1645).

1951: Maria Domenica Mazzarello (1837-1881); Emilie de Vialar (1797-1856); Anthony M. Gianelli (1789-1846); Ignatius of Laconi (1701-1781); Francis Xavier Bianchi (1743-1815).

1954: Pope Pius X (1835-1914); Dominic Savio (1842-1857); Maria Crocifissa di Rosa (1813-1855); Peter Chanel (1803-1841); Gaspar del Bufalo (1786-1837); Joseph M. Pignatelli (1737-1811).

1958: Herman Joseph, O. Praem. (1150-1241) (equivalent canonization).

John XXIII
(1958-1963)

1959: Joaquina de Vedruna de Mas (1783-1854); Charles of Sezze (1613-1670).

1960: Gregory Barbarigo (1625-1697) (equivalent canonization); John de Ribera (1532-1611).

1961: Bertilla Boscardin (1888-1922).

1962: Martin de Porres (1579-1639); Peter Julian Eymard (1811-1868); Anthony Pucci, priest (1819-1892); Francis Mary of Camporosso (1804-1866).

1963: Vincent Pallotti (1795-1850).

Paul VI
(1963-1978)

1964: Charles Lwanga and Twenty-One Companions, Martyrs of Uganda (d. between 1885-1887).

1967: Benilde Romacon (1805-1862).

1969: Julia Billiart (1751-1816).

1970: Maria Della Dolorato Torres Acosta (1826-1887); Leonard Murialdo (1828-1900); Therese Couderc (1805-1885); John of Ávila (1499-1569); Nicholas Tavelic, Deodatus of Aquitaine, Peter of Narbonne and Stephen of Cuneo, martyrs (d. 1391); Forty English and Welsh Martyrs (d. 16th cent.).

1974: Teresa of Jesus Jornet Ibars (1843-1897).

1975: Vicenta Maria Lopez y Vicuna (1847-1890); Elizabeth Bayley Seton (1774-1821); John Masias (1585-1645); Oliver Plunket (1629-1681); Justin de Jacobis (1800-1860); John Baptist of the Conception (1561-1613).

1976: Beatrice da Silva (1424 or 1426-1490); John Ogilvie (1579-1615).

1977: Rafaela Maria Porras y Ayllon (1850-1925); John Nepomucene Neumann (1811-1860); Sharbel Makhlouf (1828-1898).

John Paul II
(1978-)

1982: Crispin of Viterbo (1668-1750); Maximilian

Kolbe (1894-1941); Marguerite Bourgeoys (1620-1700); Jeanne Delanoue (1666-1736).

1983: Leopold Mandic (1866-1942).

1984: Paola Frassinetti (1809-1892); 103 Korean Martyrs (d. between 1839-1867); Miguel Febres Cordero (1854-1910).

1986: Francis Anthony Fasani (1681-1742); Giuseppe Maria Tomasi (1649-1713).

1987: Giuseppe Moscati (d. 1927); Lawrence (Lorenzo) Ruiz and Fifteen Companions, Martyrs of Japan (d. 1630s).

1988: Eustochia Calafato (1434-1485); 117 Martyrs of Vietnam (96 Vietnamese, 11 Spanish, 10 French; included 8 bishops, 50 priests, 1 seminarian, 58 lay persons); Roque Gonzalez (1576-1628), Alfonso Rodriguez (1598-1628) and Juan de Castillo (1596-1628), Jesuit martyrs of Paraguay; Rose Philippine Duchesne (1796-1852); Simon de Rojas (1552-1624); Magdalen of Canossa (1774-1835); Maria Rosa Molas y Vollve (d. 1876).

1989: Clelia Barbieri (1847-1870); Gaspar Bertoni (1777-1853); Richard Pampuri, religious (1897-1930); Agnes of Bohemia (1211-1282); Albert Chmielowski (1845-1916); Mutien-Marie Wiaux (1841-1917).

1990: Marguerite D'Youville (1701-1777).

1991: Raphael (Jozef) Kalinowski (1835-1907).

1992: Claude La Colombiere (1641-1682); Ezequiel Moreno y Diaz (1848-1905).

1993: Marie of St. Ignatius (Claudine Thevenet) (1774-1837); Teresa "de los Andes" (Juana Fernandez Solar) (1900-20); Enrique de Ossó y Cervelló (1840-96).

1995: Jan Sarkander (1576-1620), Zdislava of Lemberk (d. 1252); Marek Krizin (1588-1619), Stefan Pongracz (1582-1619), Melichar Grodziecky (1584-1619), martyrs of Kosice; Eugene de Mazenod (1782-1861).

1996: Jean-Gabriel Perboyre (1802-40), Juan Grande Roman (1546-1600) and Bro. Egidio Maria of St. Joseph (1729-1812).

1997: Hedwig (1371-1399), John Dukla, O.F.M. (d. 1484).

1998: Edith Stein (d. 1942).

1999: Marcellin Joseph Benoit Champagnat (1789-1840), Giovanni Calabria (1873-1954), Agostina Livia Pietrantonio (1864-1894), Sr. Kunegunda Kinga (1224-92); Cirilo Bertrán and eight companion Brothers of the Christian Schools (d. Oct. 9, 1934); Inocencio de la Immaculada (d. Oct. 9, 1934); St. Jaime Hilario Barbal (1889-1937); Benedetto Menni (1841-1914); Tommaso da Cori (1655-1729).

2000: Mary Faustina Kowalska (1905-1938); María Josefa of the Heart of Jesus Sancho de Guerra (1842-1912); Cristóbal Magallanes and 24 Companions (d. 1915-28); José Maria de Yermo y Parres (1851-1904); Maria de Jesús Sacramentado Venegas (1868- 1959); 120 Martyrs of China (17th-20th centuries); Katherine Drexel (1858-1955); Josephine Bakhita (d. 1947).

2001: Luigi Scrosoppi (1804-1884); Agostino Roscelli (1818-1902); Bernardo da Corleone (1605-1667); Teresa Eustochio Verzeri (1801-1852); Rafqa Petra Choboq Ar-Rayes (1832-1914); Giuseppe Marello (1844-1895); Paula Montal Fornés de San José de Calasanz (1799-1889);

Léonie Françoise de Sales Aviat (1844-1914); Maria Crescentia Höss (1682-1744).
2002: Alonso de Orozco (1500-1591); Ignazio da Santhia (Lorenzo Maurizio Belvisotti) (1686-1770); Umile da Bisignano (Luca Antonio Pirozzo) (1582-1637); Paulina do Coracao Agonizante de Jesus (Amabile Visintainer) (1865-1942); Benedetta Cambiagio Frassinello (1791-1858); Pio da Pietrelcina (Padre Pio, 1887-1968); Juan Diego Cuauhlatoatzin (16th cent); Pedro de San Jose de Betancur (1619-1667). (For biographies of all new saints for 2001-02, please see **Saints**.)

BEATIFICATIONS BY POPE JOHN PAUL II, 1979-2002

1979: Margarret Ebner (Feb. 24); Francis Coll, O.P., Jacques Laval, S.S.Sp. (Apr. 29); Enrique de Ossó y Cervelló (Oct. 14).

1980: José de Anchieta, Pedro de San Jose Betancur, Francois de Montmorency Laval, Kateri Tekakwitha, Marie Guyart of the Incarnation (June 22); Don Luigi Orione, Bartolomea Longo, Maria Anna Sala (Oct. 26).

1981: Sixteen Martyrs of Japan (Lorenzo Ruiz and Companions) (Feb 18); Maria Repetto, Alan de Solminihac, Richard Pampuri, Claudine Thevenet, Aloysius (Luigi) Scrosoppi (Oct. 4).

1982: Peter Donders, C.SS.R., Marie Rose Durocher, Andre Bessette, C.S.C., Maria Angela Astorch, Marie Rivier (May 23); Fra Angelico (equivalent beatification) (July); Jeanne Jugan, Salvatore Lilli and 7 Armenian Companions (Oct. 3); Sr. Angela of the Cross (Nov. 5).

1983: Maria Gabriella Sagheddu (Jan. 25); Luigi Versiglia, Callisto Caravario (May 15); Ursula Ledochowska (June 20); Raphael (Jozef) Kalinowski, Bro. Albert (Adam Chmielowski), T.O.R. (June 22); Giacomo Cusmano, Jeremiah of Valachia, Domingo Iturrate Zubero (Oct. 30); Marie of Jesus Crucified (Marie Bouardy) (Nov. 13).

1984: Fr. William Repin and 98 Companions (Martyrs of Angers during French Revolution), Giovanni Mazzucconi (Feb. 19); Marie Leonie Paradis (Sept. 11); Federico Albert, Clemente Marchisio, Isidore of St. Joseph (Isidore de Loor), Rafaela Ybarra de Villalongo (Sept. 30); José Manyanet y Vives, Daniel Brottier, C.S.Sp., Sr. Elizabeth of the Trinity (Elizabeth Catez) (Nov. 25).

1985: Mercedes of Jesus (Feb. 1); Ana de los Angeles Monteagudo (Feb. 2); Pauline von Mallinckrodt, Catherine Troiani (Apr. 14); Benedict Menni, Peter Friedhofen (June 23); Anwarite Nangapeta (Aug. 15); Virginae Centurione Bracelli (Sept. 22); Diego Luis de San Vitores, S.J., Jose M. Rubio y Peralta, S.J., Francisco Garate, S.J. (Oct. 6); Titus Brandsma, O.Carm. (Nov. 3); Pio Campidelli, C.P., Marie Teresa de Jesus Gerhardinger, Rafqa Ar-Rayes (Nov. 17).

1986: Alphonsa Mattathupandatu of the Immaculate Conception, Kuriakose Elias Chavara (Feb. 8); Antoine Chevrier (Oct. 4); Teresa Maria of the Cross Manetti (Oct. 19).

1987: Maria Pilar of St. Francis Borgia, Teresa of the Infant Jesus, Maria Angeles of St. Joseph, Cardinal Marcellis Spinola y Maestre, Emmanuel Domingo y Sol (Mar. 29); Teresa of Jesus "de los Andes" (Apr. 3); Edith Stein (Teresa Benedicta of the Cross) (May 1); Rupert Meyer, S.J. (May 3); Pierre-Francois Jamet, Cardinal Andrea Carlo Ferrari, Benedetta Cambiagio Frassinello, Louis Moreau (May 10); Carolina Kozka, Michal Kozal (June 10); George Matulaitis (Matulewicz) (June 28); Marcel Callo, Pierino Morosini, Antonia Mesina (Oct. 4); Blandina Marten, Ulricke Nische, Jules Reche (Bro. Arnold) (Nov. 1); 85 Martyrs (d. between 1584-1689) of England, Scotland and Wales (Nov. 22).

1988: John Calabria, Joseph Nascimbeni (Apr. 17); Pietro Bonilli, Kaspar Stangassinger, Francisco Palau y Quer, Savina Petrilli (Apr. 24), Laura Vicuna (Sept. 3); Joseph Gerard (Sept. 11); Miguel Pro, Giuseppe Benedetto Dusmet, Francisco Faa di Bruno, Junipero Serra, Frederick Jansoone, Josefa Naval Girbes (Sept. 25); Bernardo Maria Silvestrelli, Charles Houben, Honoratus Kozminski (Oct. 16); Niels Stensen (Nicolaus Steno) (Oct. 23); Katharine Drexel, 3 Missionary Martyrs of Ethiopia (Liberato Weiss, Samuel Marzorati, Michele Pio Fasoli) (Nov. 20).

1989: Martin of Saint Nicholas, Melchior of St. Augustine, Mary of Jesus of the Good Shepherd, Maria Margaret Caiani, Maria of Jesus Siedliska, Maria Catherine of St. Augustine (Apr. 23); Victoria Rasoamanarivo (Apr. 30); Bro. Scubilionis (John Bernard Rousseau) (May 2); Elizabeth Renzi, Antonio Lucci (June 17); Niceforo de Jesus y Maria (Vicente Diez Tejerina and 25 Companions, martyred in Spain), Lorenzo Salvi, Gertrude Caterina Comensoli, Francisca Ana Cirer Carbonell (Oct. 1); 7 Martyrs from Thailand (Philip Sipong, Sr. Agnes Phila, Sr. Lucia Khambang, Agatha Phutta, Cecilia Butsi, Bibiana Khampai, Maria Phon), Timothy Giaccardo, Mother Maria of Jesus Deluil-Martiny (Oct. 22); Giuseppe Baldo (Oct. 31).

1990: 9 Martyrs of Asturias during Spanish Civil War (De la Salle Brothers Cyrill Bertran, Marciano Jose, Julian Alfredo, Victoriano Pio, Benjamin Julian, Augustino Andres, Benito de Jesus, Aniceto Adolfo; and Passionist priest Innocencio Inmaculada), Mercedes Prat, Manuel Barbal Cosan (Brother Jaime), Philip Rinaldi (Apr. 29); Juan Diego (confirmation of Apr. 9 decree), 3 Child Martyrs (Cristobal, Antonio and Juan), Fr. Jose Maria de Yermo y Parres (May 6); Pier Giorgio Frassati (May 20); Hanibal Maria Di Francia, Joseph Allamano (Oct. 7); Marthe Aimee LeBouteiller, Louise Therese de Montaignac de Chauvance, Maria Schinina, Elisabeth Vendramini (Nov. 4).

1991: Annunciata Cocchetti, Marie Therese Haze, Clara Bosatta (Apr. 21); Jozef Sebastian Pelczar (June 2); Boleslava Lament (June 5); Rafael Chylinski (June 9); Angela Salawa (Aug. 13); Edoardo Giuseppe Rosaz (July 14, Susa, Italy); Pauline of the Heart of Jesus in Agony Visentainer (Oct. 18, Brazil); Adolph Kolping (Oct. 27).

1992: Josephine Bakhita, Josemaria Escriva de Balaguer (May 17); Francesco Spinelli (June 21,

Caravaggio, Italy); 17 Irish Martyrs, Rafael Arnáiz Barón, Nazaria Ignacia March Mesa, Léonie Françoise de Sales Aviat, and Maria Josefa Sancho de Guerra (Sept. 27); 122 Martyrs of Spanish Civil War, Narcisa Martillo Morán (Oct. 25); Cristóbal Magellanes and 24 companions, Mexican martyrs, and Maria de Jesús Sacramentado Venegas (Nov. 22).

1993: Dina Belanger (Mar. 20); John Duns Scotus (Mar. 20, cult solemnly recognized); Mary Angela Truszkowska, Ludovico of Casoria, Faustina Kowalska, Paula Montal Fornés (Apr. 18); Stanislaus Kazimierczyk (Apr. 18, cult solemnly recognized); Maurice Tornay, Marie-Louise Trichet, Columba Gabriel and Florida Cevoli (May 16); Giuseppe Marello (Sept. 26); Eleven martyrs of Almeria, Spain, during Spanish Civil War (2 bishops, 7 brothers, l priest, l lay person); Victoria Diez y Bustos de Molina, Maria Francesca (Anna Maria) Rubatto; Pedro Castroverde, Maria Crucified (Elisabetta Maria) Satellico (Oct. 10).

1994: Isidore Bakanja, Elizabeth Canori Mora; Dr. Gianna Beretta Molla (Apr. 24); Nicolas Roland, Alberto Hurtado Cruchaga, Maria Rafols, Petra of St. Joseph Perez Florida, Josephine Vannini (Oct. 16); Magdalena Caterina Morano (Nov. 5); Hyacinthe Marie Cormier, Marie Poussepin, Agnes de Jesus Galand, Eugenia Joubert, Claudio Granzotto (Nov. 20).

1995: Peter ToRot (Jan. 17); Mother Mary of the Cross MacKillop (Jan. 19); Joseph Vaz (Jan. 21); Rafael Guizar Valencia, Modestino of Jesus and Mary, Genoveva Torres Morales, Grimoaldo of the Purification (Jan. 29); Johann Nepomuk von Tschiderer (Apr. 30); Maria Helena Stollenwerk, Maria Alvarado Cordozo, Giuseppina Bonino, Maria Domenica Brun Barbantini, Agostino Roscelli (May 7); Damien de Veuster (June 4); 109 Martyrs (64 from French Revolution – Martyrs of La Rochelle – and 45 from Spanish Civil War), Anselm Polanco Fontecha, Felipe Ripoll Morata, and Pietro Casini (Oct. 1); Mary Theresa Scherer, Maria Bernarda Butler and Marguerite Bays (Oct. 29).

1996: Daniel Comboni and Guido Maria Conforti (Mar. 17); Cardinal Alfredo Ildefonso Schuster, O.S.B., Filippo Smaldone and Gennaro Sarnelli (priests) and Candida Maria de Jesus Cipitria y Barriola, Maria Raffaella Cimatti, Maria Antonia Bandres (religious) (May 12); Bernhard Lichtenberg and Karl Leisner (June 23), Wincenty Lewoniuk and 12 companions, Edmund Rice, Maria Ana Mogas Fontcuberta and Marcelina Darowska (Oct 6); Otto Neururer, Jakob Gapp and Catherine Jarrige (Nov. 24).

1997: Bishop Florentino Asensio Barroso, Sr. Maria Encarnacion Rosal of the Sacred Heart, Fr. Gaetano Catanoso, Fr. Enrico Rebuschini and Ceferino Gimenez Malla, first gypsy beatified (May 4); Bernardina Maria Jablonska, Maria Karlowska (June 6); Frédéric Ozanam (Aug. 22); Bartholomew Mary Dal Monte (Sep. 27); Elías del Socorro Nieves, Domenico Lentini, Giovanni

Piamarta, Emilie d'Hooghvorst, Maria Teresa Fasce (Oct. 12); John Baptist Scalabrini, Vilmos Apor, María Vicenta of St. Dorothy Chávez Orozco (Nov. 9).

1998: Bishop Vincent Bossilkov, María Sallés, Brigida of Jesus (Mar. 15); Fr. Cyprian Tansi (Mar. 22); Nimatullah al-Hardini, 11 Spanish nuns (May 10); Secondo Polla (May 23); Giovanni Maria Boccardo, Teresa Grillo Chavez, Teresa Bracco (May 24); Jakob Kern, Maria Restituta Kafka, and Anton Schwartz (June 21); Giuseppe Tovini (Sept. 20); Cardinal Alojzije Stepinac (Oct. 3); Antônio de Sant'Anna Galvão, Faustino Miguez, Zeferino Agostini, Mother Theodore Guérin (Oct. 25).

1999: Vicente Soler, and six Augustinian Recollect Companions, Manuel Martin Sierra, Nicolas Barre, Anna Schaeffer (Mar. 7); Padre Pio (May 2); Fr. Stefan Wincenty Frelichowski (June 7); 108 Polish Martyrs, Regina Protmann, Edmund Bojanowski (June 13); Bishop Anton Slomsek (Sept. 19); Ferdinando Maria Baccilieri, Edward Maria Joannes Poppe, Arcangelo Tadini, Mariano da Roccacasale, Diego Oddi, Nicola da Gesturi (Oct. 3).

2000: André de Soveral, Ambrósio Francisco Ferro and 28 Companions, Nicolas Bunkerd Kitbamrung, Maria Stella Mardosewicz and 10 Companions, Pedro Calungsod and Andrew of Phú Yên (Mar. 5); Mariano de Jesus Euse Hoyos, Francis Xavier Seelos, Anna Rosa Gattorno, Maria Elisabetta Hesselblad, Mariam Thresia Chiramel Mankidiyan (Apr. 9); Jacinta and Francisco Marto of Fatima (May 13);   Pope Pius IX, Pope John XXIII, Tommaso Reggio, Guillaume-Joseph Chaminade, Columba Marmion (Sept. 3).

2001: José Aparicio Sanz and 232 Companions of the Spanish Civil War (Mar. 11); Manuel Gonzalez Garcia, Marie-Anne Blondin, Caterina Volpicelli, Caterina Cittadini, Carlos Manuel Cecilio Rodriguez Santiago (Apr. 29); George Preca, Ignatius Falzon, Maria Adeodata Pisani (May 9); Abp. Jósef Bilczewski and Fr. Sygmunt Gorazdowski, Ukrainian Martyrs (June 27); Ignatius Maloyan, Nikolaus Gross, Alfonso Maria Fusco, Tommaso Maria Fusco, Emilie Tavernier Gamelin, Eugenia Picco, Maria Euthymia Uffing (Oct. 7); Luigi Beltrame Quattrocchi and Maria Corsini (Oct. 21); Pavol Peter Gojdic, Metod Dominik Trcka, Giovanni Antonio Farina, Bartolomeu Fernandes dos Mártires, Luigi Tezza, Paolo Manna, Gaetana Sterni, Maria Pilar Izquierdo Albero (Nov. 4).

2002: Gaetano Errico, Lodovico Pavoni, Luigi Variara, Maria del Transito de Jesus Sacramentado, Artemide Zatti, Maria Romero Meneses (Apr. 14); Kamen Vitchev, Pavel Djidjov, Josaphat Chichkov (May 26); Juan Bautista and Jacinto de Los Angeles (July 31); Zygmunt Szczesny Felinski, Jan Balicki, Jan Beyzym, Sancja Szymkowiak (Aug. 17).

(For biographical details of all those beatified in 2001-2002, please see under **Saints**.)

ROMAN CURIA

The Roman Curia is the Church's network of central administrative agencies (called dicasteries) serving the Vatican and the local churches, with authority granted by the pope.

The Curia evolved gradually from advisory assemblies or synods of the Roman clergy with whose assistance the popes directed church affairs during the first 11 centuries. Its original office was the Apostolic Chancery, established in the fourth century to transmit documents. The antecedents of its permanently functioning agencies and offices were special commissions of cardinals and prelates. Its establishment in a form resembling what it is now dates from the second half of the 16th century.

Pope Paul VI initiated a four-year reorganization study in 1963 that resulted in the constitution *Regimini Ecclesiae Universae.* The document was published Aug. 18, 1967, and went into full effect in Mar. 1968. Pope John Paul II, in the apostolic constitution *Pastor Bonus,* published June 28, 1988, and effective Mar. 1, 1989, ordered modifications of the Curia based on the broad outline of Paul VI's reorganization.

In accordance with Pope John Paul II's reform effective Mar. 1, 1989, and later revisions, the Curia consists of the Secretariat of State, nine congregations (governing agencies), three tribunals (judicial agencies), 11 councils (promotional agencies) and three offices (specialized service agencies). All have equal juridical status with authority granted by the Pope.

SECRETARIAT OF STATE

The Secretariat of State, *Palazzo Apostolico Vaticano,* Vatican City. Cardinal Angelo Sodano, Secretary of State; Most Rev. Leonardo Sandri, Deputy for General Affairs; Most Rev. Jean-Louis Tauran, Secretary for Relations with States.

The Secretariat of State provides the pope with the closest possible assistance in the care of the universal Church. It consists of two sections:

· The Section for General Affairs assists the Pope in expediting daily business of the Holy See. It coordinates curial operations; prepares drafts of documents entrusted to it by the pope; has supervisory duties over the *Acta Apostolicae Sedis, Annuario Pontificio,* the Vatican Press Office and the Central Statistics Office.

· The Section for Relations with States (formerly the Council for Public Affairs of the Church, a separate body) handles diplomatic and other relations with civil governments. Attached to it is a council of Cardinals and Bishops.

Background: Evolved gradually from secretarial offices (dating back to the 15th century) and the Congregation for Extraordinary Ecclesiastical Affairs (dating back to 1793; restructured as the Council for the Public Affairs of the Church by Paul VI in 1967). John Paul II gave it its present form in his June 28, 1988, reform of the Curia.

CONGREGATIONS

Congregation for the Doctrine of the Faith: Piazza del S. Uffizio 11, 00193 Rome, Italy. Cardinal Joseph Ratzinger, prefect; Most Rev. Tarcisio Bertone, S.D.B., secretary.

Has responsibility to safeguard the doctrine of faith and morals. Accordingly, it examines doctrinal questions; promotes studies thereon; evaluates theological opinions and, when necessary and after prior consultation with concerned bishops, reproves those regarded as opposed to principles of the faith; examines books on doctrinal matters and can reprove such works, if the contents so warrant, after giving authors the opportunity to defend themselves. It examines matters pertaining to the Privilege of Faith (Petrine Privilege) in marriage cases, and safeguards the dignity of the sacrament of penance. Attached to the congregation are the Pontifical Biblical Commission and the Theological Commission.

Background: At the beginning of the 13th century, legates of Innocent III were commissioned as the Holy Office of the Inquisition to combat heresy; the same task was entrusted to the Dominican Order by Gregory IX in 1231 and to the Friars Minor by Innocent IV from 1243 to 1254. On July 21, 1542 (apostolic constitution *Licet*), Paul III instituted a permanent congregation of cardinals with supreme and universal competence over matters concerning heretics and those suspected of heresy. Pius IV, St. Pius V and Sixtus V further defined the work of the congregation. St. Pius X changed its name to the Congregation of the Holy Office. Paul VI (*motu proprio Integrae Servandae,* Dec. 7, 1965), began reorganization of the Curia with this body, to which he gave the new title, Congregation for the Doctrine of the Faith. Its orientation is not merely negative, in the condemnation of error, but positive, in the promotion of orthodox doctrine.

Congregation for the Oriental Churches: Palazzo del Bramante, Via della Conciliazione 34, 00193 Rome, Italy. Cardinal Ignace Moussa I Daoud, prefect; Most Rev. Antonio Maria Vegliò, secretary. Members include all patriarchs of the Eastern Catholic Churches and major archbishops.

Has competence in matters concerning the persons and discipline of Eastern Catholic Churches. It has jurisdiction over territories in which the majority of Christians belong to Eastern Churches (i.e., Egypt, the Sinai Peninsula, Eritrea, Northern Ethiopia, Southern Albania, Bulgaria, Cyprus, Greece, Iran, Iraq, Lebanon, Palestine, Syria, Jordan, Turkey, Afghanistan); also, over minority communities of Eastern Church members no matter where they live.

Background: Established by Pius IX Jan. 6, 1862 (apostolic constitution *Romani Pontifices*), and united with the Congregation for the Propagation of the Faith. The congregation was made autonomous by Benedict XV May 1, 1917 (*motu proprio Dei Providentis*), and given wider authority by Pius XI Mar. 25, 1938 (*motu proprio Sancta Dei Ecclesia*).

Congregation for Divine Worship and the Discipline of the Sacraments: Piazza Pio XII 10, 00193 Rome, Italy. Cardinal Jorge Arturo Medina Estévez, prefect; Most Rev. Francesco Pio Tamburrino, O.S.B., secretary.

Supervises everything pertaining to the promotion and regulation of the liturgy, primarily the sacraments, without prejudice to the competencies of the Congregation for the Doctrine of the Faith. Attached to the congregation are special commissions treating causes of nullity of sacred ordinations and dispensations from obligations of sacred ordination of deacons and priests.

Background: Originally two separate congregations: the Congregation for Divine Worship (instituted by Paul VI, May 8, 1969) and the Congregation for the Discipline of the Sacraments (established by St. Pius X, June 29, 1908, to replace the Congregation of Rites instituted by Pope Sixtus V in 1588). They were united by Paul VI, July 11, 1975, as the Congregation for the Sacraments and Divine Worship; reestablished as separate congregations by John Paul II in an autograph letter of Apr. 5, 1984, and reunited anew by the same Pope, June 28, 1988 (apostolic constitution *Pastor Bonus*) as the Congregation for Divine Worship and the Discipline of the Sacraments.

Congregation for the Causes of Saints: Piazza Pio XII 10, 00193 Rome, Italy. Cardinal José Saraiva Martins, C.F.M., prefect; Most Rev. Edward Nowak, secretary.

Handles matters connected with beatification and canonization causes (in accordance with revised procedures decreed in 1983), and the preservation of relics.

Background: Established by Sixtus V in 1588 as the Congregation of Rites; affected by legislation of Pius XI in 1930; title changed and functions defined by Paul VI, 1969 (apostolic constitution *Sacra Rituum Congregatio*). It was restructured and canonization procedures were revised by John Paul II in 1983 (apostolic constitution *Divinus Perfectionis Magister*).

Congregation for Bishops: Piazza Pio XII 10, 00193 Rome, Italy. Cardinal Giovanni Battista Re, prefect; Most Rev. Francesco Monterisi, secretary.

Has functions related in one way or another to bishops and the jurisdictions in which they serve. It supervises the Pontifical Commission for Latin America. Attached to the congregation are a central coordinating office for Military Vicars (established Feb. 2, 1985) and an office for coordinating *ad limina* visits (established June 29, 1988).

Background: Established by Sixtus V Jan. 22, 1588 (apostolic constitution *Immensa*); given an extension of powers by St. Pius X June 20, 1908, and Pius XII Aug. 1, 1952 (apostolic constitution *Exsul Familia*); given present title (was known as Consistorial Congregation) by Paul VI (Aug. 1, 1967); competencies redefined by John Paul II, June 28, 1988.

Congregation for the Evangelization of Peoples: Piazza di Spagna 48, 00187 Rome, Italy. Cardinal Crescenzio Sepe, prefect; Most Rev. Robert Sarah, secretary; Most Rev. Patabendige Don Albert Malcom Ranjith, adjunct secretary.

Directs and coordinates missionary work throughout the world. Accordingly, it has competence over those matters which concern all the missions established for the spread of Christ's kingdom without prejudice to the competence of other congregations. These include: fostering missionary vocations; assigning missionaries to fields of work; establishing ecclesiastical jurisdictions and proposing candidates to serve them as bishops and in other capacities; encour-

aging the recruitment and development of indigenous clergy; mobilizing spiritual and financial support for missionary activity.

To promote missionary cooperation, the congregation has a Supreme Council for the Direction of Pontifical Missionary Works composed of the Missionary Union of the Clergy and Religious, the Society for the Propagation of the Faith, the Society of St. Peter the Apostle for Native Clergy, the Society of the Holy Childhood, and the International Center of Missionary Animation.

Background: Originated as a commission of cardinals by St. Pius V and Gregory XII for missions in East and West Indies, Italo-Greeks and for ecclesiastical affairs in Protestant territories of Europe; Clement VIII instituted a Congregation of the Propagation of the Faith in 1599 which ceased to exist after several years. Erected as a stable congregation by Gregory XV June 22, 1622 (apostolic constitution *Inscrutabili Divinae*); its functions were redefined by John Paul II, June 28, 1988.

Congregation for the Clergy: Piazza Pio XII 3, 00193 Rome, Italy. Cardinal Darío Castrillón Hoyos, prefect; Most Rev. Csaba Ternyák, secretary.

Has three offices with competencies concerning the life, discipline, rights and duties of the clergy; the preaching of the Word, catechetics, norms for religious education of children and adults; preservation and administration of the temporal goods of the Church. Attached to it are the International Council for Catechetics (established in 1973 by Paul VI) and the Institute *Sacrum Ministerium* for the permanent formation of the clergy (established in line with John Paul II's 1992 apostolic exhortation *Pastores Dabo Vobis*).

Background: Established by Pius IV Aug. 2, 1564 (apostolic constitution *Alias Nos*), under the title, Congregation of the Cardinals Interpreters of the Council of Trent; affected by legislation of Gregory XIII and Sixtus V; known as Congregation of the Council until Aug. 15, 1967, when Paul VI renamed it the Congregation for the Clergy and redefined its competency; John Paul II gave it added responsibilities June 28, 1988.

Congregation for Institutes of Consecrated Life and Societies of Apostolic Life: Piazza Pio XII 3, 00193 Rome, Italy. Cardinal Eduardo Martinez Somalo, prefect; Most. Rev. Piergiorgio Silvano Nesti, C.P., secretary.

Has competence over institutes of Religious, secular institutes, societies of the apostolic life and third (secular) orders. With two sections, the congregation has authority in matters related to the establishment, general direction and suppression of the various institutes; general discipline in line with their rules and constitutions; the movement toward renewal and adaptation of institutes in contemporary circumstances; the setting up and encouragement of councils and conferences of major religious superiors for intercommunication and other purposes.

Background: Founded by Sixtus V May 27, 1586, with the title, Congregation for Consultations of Regulars; confirmed by the apostolic constitution *Immensa* Jan. 22, 1588; made part of the Congregation for Consultations of Bishops and other Prelates in 1601; made autonomous by St. Pius X in 1908 as Congregation of Religious; title changed to Congregation for Religious and Secular Institutes by Paul VI in 1967; given present title by John Paul II, June 28, 1988.

Congregation for Catholic Education (for Seminaries and Institutes of Study): Piazza Pio XII 3, 00193 Rome, Italy. Cardinal Zenon Grocholewski, pro-prefect; Most Rev. Giuseppe Pittau, S.J., secretary.

Has supervisory competence over institutions and works of Catholic education. It carries on its work through three offices. One office handles matters connected with the direction, discipline and temporal administration of seminaries, and with the education of diocesan clergy, religious and members of secular institutes. A second office oversees Catholic universities, faculties of study and other institutions of higher learning inasmuch as they depend on the authority of the Church; encourages cooperation and mutual assistance among Catholic institutions, and the establishment of Catholic hospices and centers on campuses of non-Catholic institutions. A third office is concerned in various ways with all Catholic schools below the college-university level, with general questions concerning education and studies, and with the cooperation of conferences of bishops and civil authorities in educational matters. The congregation supervises Pontifical Works for Priestly Vocations.

Background: The title (Congregation of Seminaries and Universities) and functions of the congregation were defined by Benedict XV Nov. 4, 1915; Pius XI, in 1931 and 1932, and Pius XII, in 1941 and 1949, extended its functions; Paul VI changed its title to Congregation for Catholic Education in 1967; given its present title by Pope John Paul II, June 28, 1988. Its work had previously been carried on by two other congregations erected by Sixtus V in 1588 and Leo XII in 1824.

Inter-Agency Curia Commissions

In accordance with provisions of the apostolic constitution *Pastor Bonus,* John Paul II established the following interdepartmental permanent commissions to handle matters when more than one agency of the Curia is involved in activities:

• For matters concerning appointments to local Churches and the setting up and alteration of them and their constitution (Mar. 22, 1989). Members include officials of the Secretariat of State and Congregation for Bishops. President, Cardinal Angelo Sodano, Secretary of State.

• For matters concerning members, individually or as a community, of Institutes of Consecrated Life founded or working in mission territories (Mar. 22, 1989). Members include officials of the Congregations for the Evangelization of Peoples and for Institutes of Consecrated Life and Societies of Apostolic Life. President: Cardinal Crescenzio Sepe, prefect of the Congregation for the Evangelization of Peoples.

• For the formation of candidates for Sacred Orders (Mar. 22, 1989). Members include officials of the Congregations for Catholic Education, for Institutes of Consecrated Life and Societies of Apostolic Life, for Evangelization of Peoples, for Oriental Churches. President: Cardinal Zenon Grocholewski, prefect of the Congregation for Catholic Education.

• For promoting a more equitable distribution of priests throughout the world (July 20, 1991). Members include secretaries of congregations for Evan-gelization of Peoples, for the Clergy, Catholic Education, for the Institutes of Consecrated Life and Societies of Apostolic Life; and vice-president of Commission for Latin America. President: Card. Zenon Grocholewski, Prefect of the Congregation for Catholic Education.

• For the Church in Eastern Europe (Jan. 15, 1993), replacing the Pontifical Commission for Russia which was terminated. The commission is concerned with both Latin and Eastern-rite churches in territories of the former Soviet Union and other nations affected by the historical circumstances resulting from atheistic communism. It is responsible for promoting the apostolic mission of the Church and fostering ecumenical dialogue with the Orthodox and other Churches of the Eastern tradition. Members, under presidency of Cardinal Secretary of State, include the secretary and undersecretary of the Section for Relations with States and secretaries of Congregations for the Oriental Churches, for the Clergy, for Institutes of Consecrated Life and Societies of Apostolic Life, secretary of the Pontifical Council for Promoting Christian Unity. President: Cardinal Angelo Sodano.

Tribunals

Apostolic Penitentiary: Piazza della Cancelleria 1, 00186 Rome, Italy. Most Rev. Luigi de Magistris, major penitentiary; regent, Rev. P. Gianfranco Girotti, O.F.M. Conv.

Has jurisdiction for the internal forum only (sacramental and non-sacramental). It issues decisions on questions of conscience; grants absolutions, dispensations, commutations, sanations and condonations; has charge of non-doctrinal matters pertaining to indulgences.

Background: Origin dates back to the 12th century; affected by the legislation of many popes; radically reorganized by St. Pius V in 1569; jurisdiction limited to the internal forum by St. Pius X; Benedict XV annexed the Office of Indulgences to it Mar. 25, 1917.

Apostolic Signatura: Piazza della Cancelleria 1, 00186 Rome, Italy. Cardinal Mario Francesco Pompedda, prefect; Most Rev. Francesco Saverio Salerno, secretary.

The principal concerns of this supreme court of the Church are to resolve questions concerning juridical procedure and to supervise the observance of laws and rights at the highest level. It decides the jurisdictional competence of lower courts and has jurisdiction in cases involving personnel and decisions of the Rota. It is the supreme court of the State of Vatican City.

Background: A permanent office of the Signatura has existed since the time of Eugene IV in the 15th century; affected by the legislation of many popes; reorganized by St. Pius X in 1908 and made the supreme tribunal of the Church.

Roman Rota: Piazza della Cancelleria 1, 00186 Rome, Italy. Msgr. Raffaello Funghini, Dean.

The ordinary court of appeal for cases appealed to the Holy See. It is best known for its competence and decisions in cases involving the validity of marriage.

Background: Originated in the Apostolic Chancery; affected by the legislation of many popes; reorganized by St. Pius X in 1908; further revised by Pius XI in 1934; new norms approved and promulgated by John Paul II in 1982 and 1987.

PONTIFICAL COUNCILS

Pontifical Council for the Laity: Piazza S. Calisto 16, 00153 Rome, Italy. Cardinal James Francis Stafford, president; Most Rev. Stanislaw Rylko, secretary; Prof. Guzman Carriquiry, undersecretary.

Its competence covers the apostolate of the laity and their participation in the life and mission of the Church. Members are mostly lay people from different parts of the world and involved in different apostolates.

Background: Established on an experimental basis by Paul VI Jan. 6, 1967; given permanent status Dec. 10, 1976 (*motu proprio Apostolatus Peragendi*).

Pontifical Council for Promoting Christian Unity: Via dell' Erba 1, 00193 Rome, Italy. Cardinal Walter Kasper, president; Most Rev. P. Marc Ouellet, S.S., secretary.

Handles relations with members of other Christian ecclesial communities; deals with the correct interpretation and execution of the principles of ecumenism; initiates or promotes Catholic ecumenical groups and coordinates on national and international levels the efforts of those promoting Christian unity; undertakes dialogue regarding ecumenical questions and activities with churches and ecclesial communities separated from the Apostolic See; sends Catholic observer-representatives to Christian gatherings, and invites to Catholic gatherings observers of other churches; orders into execution conciliar decrees dealing with ecumenical affairs. The **Commission for Religious Relations with the Jews** is attached to the secretariat.

Background: Established by John XXIII June 5, 1960, as a preparatory secretariat of the Second Vatican Council; raised to commission status during the first session of the council in the fall of 1962; status as a secretariat confirmed and functions defined by Paul VI in 1966 and 1967; made a pontifical council by John Paul II, June 28, 1988.

Pontifical Council for the Family: Piazza S. Calisto 16, 00153 Rome, Italy. Cardinal Alfonso López Trujillo, president; Most Rev. Karl Josef Romer, secretary.

Is concerned with promoting the pastoral care of families so they may carry out their educative, evangelizing and apostolic mission and make their influence felt in areas such as defense of human life and responsible procreation according to the teachings of the Church. Members, chosen by the Pope, are married couples and men and women from all parts of the world and representing different cultures. They meet in general assembly at least once a year.

Background: Instituted by John Paul II May 9, 1981, replacing the Committee for the Family established by Paul VI Jan. 11, 1973.

Pontifical Council for Justice and Peace: Piazza S. Calisto 16, 00153 Rome, Italy. Cardinal François Xavier Nguyên Van Thuân, president; Most Rev. Giampaolo Crepaldi, secretary.

Its primary competence is to promote justice and peace in the world according to the Gospels and social teaching of the Church.

Background: Instituted by Paul VI Jan. 6, 1967, on an experimental basis; reconstituted and made a permanent commission Dec. 10, 1976; its competence was redefined and it was made a pontifical council June 28, 1988, by John Paul II.

Pontifical Council "*Cor Unum*": Piazza S. Calisto 16, 00153 Rome, Italy. Most Rev. Paul Josef Cordes, president; secretary, Msgr. Karel Kasteel.

Its principal aims are to provide informational and coordinating services for Catholic aid and human development organizations and projects on a worldwide scale. Attached to the council are the John Paul II Foundation for the Sahel and "*Populorum Progressio.*"

Background: Instituted by Paul VI July 15, 1971.

Pontifical Council for Pastoral Care of Migrants and Itinerant Peoples: Piazza S. Calisto 16, 00153 Rome, Italy. Most Rev. Stephen Fumio Hamao president; Most Rev. Agostino Marchetto, secretary.

Is concerned with pastoral assistance to migrants, nomads, tourists, sea and air travelers.

Background: Instituted by Paul VI and placed under general supervision of Congregation for Bishops, Mar. 19, 1970; made autonomous as a pontifical council and renamed by John Paul II, June 28, 1988.

Pontifical Council for Pastoral Assistance to Health Care Workers: Via della Conciliazione 3, 00193 Rome, Italy. Most Rev. Javier Lozano Barragán, president; Most Rev. José Luis Redrado Marchite, O.H., secretary.

Its functions are to stimulate and foster the work of formation, study and action carried out by various international Catholic organizations in the health care field.

Background: Established in 1985 as a commission by John Paul II; made a council June 28, 1988.

Pontifical Council for the Interpretation of Legislative Texts: Piazza Pio XII 10, 00193 Rome, Italy. Most Rev. Julián Herranz, president; Most Rev. Bruno Bertagna, secretary.

Primary function is the authentic interpretation of the universal laws of the Church.

Background: Established by John Paul II, Jan. 2, 1984, as the Pontifical Commission for the Authentic Interpretation of the Code of Canon Law; name changed and given additional functions June 28, 1988. Its competency was extended in 1991 to include interpretation of Code of Canon Law of Oriental Church that was promulgated in 1990.

Pontifical Council for Interreligious Dialogue: Via dell' Erba 1, 00193 Rome, Italy. Cardinal Francis Arinze, president; Most Rev. Michael Louis Fitzgerald, M. Afr., secretary.

Its function is to promote studies and dialogue for the purpose of increasing mutual understanding and respect between Christians and non-Christians. The Commission for Religious Relations with Muslims is attached to the council.

Background: Established by Paul VI May 19, 1964, as the Secretariat for Non-Christians; given present title and functions by John Paul II, June 28, 1988.

Pontifical Council for Culture: Piazza S. Calisto 16, 00153 Rome, Italy. Cardinal Paul Poupard, president; Very Rev. Bernard Ardura, O. Praem., secretary.

Its functions are to foster the Church's and the Holy See's relations with the world of culture and to establish dialogue with those who do not believe in God or who profess no religion provided these are open to sincere cooperation. It consists of two sections: (1) faith and culture; (2) dialogue with cultures. Attached to it is the Coordinating **Council for Pontifical Academies**.

Background: Present council with expanded functions was instituted by John Paul II (*motu proprio* of Mar. 25, 1993) through the merger of the Pontifical Council for Culture (established May 20, 1982, by John Paul II) and the Pontifical Council for Dialogue with Non-Believers (established by Paul VI Apr. 9, 1965, as the secretariat for Non-Believers).

Pontifical Council for Social Communications: Palazzo S. Carlo, 00120 Vatican City. Most Rev. John P. Foley, president; Most Rev. Pierfranco Pastore, secretary.

Engaged in matters pertaining to instruments of social communication so that through them the message of salvation and human progress is fostered and carried forward in civil culture and mores.

Background: Instituted on an experimental basis by Pius XII in 1948; reorganized three times in the 1950s; made permanent commission by John XXIII Feb. 22, 1959; established as council and functions restated by John Paul II June 28, 1988.

OFFICES

Apostolic Camera: Palazzo Apostolico, 00120 Vatican City. Cardinal Eduardo Martinez Somalo, chamberlain of the Holy Roman Church; Most Rev. Ettore Cunial, vice-chamberlain.

Administers the temporal goods and rights of the Holy See between the death of one pope and the election of another (*sede vacante*), in accordance with special laws.

Background: Originated in the 11th century; reorganized by Pius XI in 1934; functions redefined (especially of *camerlengo*) by subsequent legislation in 1945, 1962 and 1975.

Administration of the Patrimony of the Apostolic See: Palazzo Apostolico, 00120 Vatican City. Cardinal Agostino Cacciavillan, president; Most Rev. Claudio Maria Celli, secretary.

Handles the estate of the Apostolic See under the direction of papal delegates acting ith ordinary or extraordinary authorization.

Background: Some of its functions date back to 1878; established by Paul VI Aug. 15, 1967.

Prefecture for the Economic Affairs of the Holy See: Largo del Colonnato 3, 00193 Rome, Italy. Cardinal Sergio Sebastiani, President; Most Rev. Franco Croci, secretary.

A financial office that coordinates and supervises administration of the temporalities of the Holy See. Membership includes Cardinal Roger M. Mahony.

Background: Established by Paul VI Aug. 15, 1967; functions redefined by John Paul II, June 28, 1988.

Other Curia Agencies

Prefecture of the Papal Household: Most Rev. James M. Harvey, prefect; Most Rev. Stanislaw Dziwisz, adjunct-prefect.

Oversees the papal chapel — which is at the service of the pope in his capacity as spiritual head of the Church — and the pontifical family — which is at the service of the pope as a sovereign. It arranges papal audiences, has charge of preparing non-liturgical elements of papal ceremonies, makes all necessary arrangements for papal visits and trips outside the Vatican, and settles questions of protocol connected with papal audiences and other formalities.

Background: Established by Paul VI Aug. 15, 1967,

under the title, Prefecture of the Apostolic Palace; it supplanted the Sacred Congregation for Ceremonies founded by Sixtus V Jan. 22, 1588. The office was updated and reorganized under the present title by Paul VI, Mar. 28, 1968.

Office for Liturgical Celebrations of the Supreme Pontiff: Palazzo Apostolico Vaticano, 00120 Vatican City. Most Rev. Piero Marini, Master of Ceremonies.

Prepares everything necessary for liturgical and other sacred celebrations by the Pope or in his name; directs everything in accordance with prescriptions of liturgical law.

Background: Evolved gradually from the early office of Apostolic Master of Ceremonies; affected by legislation of Pope Paul IV in 1563 and Benedict XV in 1917; restructured by Paul VI in 1967; given its present title (formerly known as Prefecture of Pontifical Ceremonies) and constituted as an autonomous agency of the Roman Curia by John Paul II, June 28, 1988.

Vatican Press Office: Via della Conciliazione 54, 00120 Vatican City. Joaquin Navarro-Valls, director.

Established Feb. 29, 1968, to replace service agencies formerly operated by *L'Osservatore Romano* and an office created for press coverage of the Second Vatican Council. New directives were issued in 1986.

Vatican Information Service (VIS): Via della Conciliazione 54, 00120 Vatican City.

Established Mar. 28, 1990, within the framework but distinct from the Vatican Press Office. Furnishes information, in English, French and Spanish, on pastoral and magisterial activity of the Pope through use of electronic mail and fax.

Central Statistics Office: Palazzo Apostolico, 00120 Vatican City.

Established by Paul VI Aug. 15, 1967; attached to the Secretariat of State. Compiles, systematizes and analyzes information on the status and condition of the Church.

COMMISSIONS AND COMMITTEES

Listed below are non-curial institutes that assist in the work of the Holy See. Some are attached to curial agencies, as indicated. Other institutes are listed elsewhere in the Almanac; see Index.

Pontifical Commission for the Cultural Heritage of the Church: Established by John Paul II, June 28, 1988, as Pontifical Commission for Preserving the Church's Patrimony of Art and History and attached to the Congregation for the Clergy; made autonomous and given present title Mar. 25, 1993. Vacant, president.

Pontifical Commission for Sacred Archeology: Instituted by Pius IX Jan, 6, 1852. Vacant, president.

Pontifical Biblical Commission: Instituted by Leo XIII Oct. 30, 1902; completely restructured by Paul VI June 27, 1971; attached to the Congregation for the Doctrine of the Faith. Cardinal Joseph Ratzinger, president.

Pontifical Commission for Latin America: Instituted by Pius XII Apr. 19, 1958; attached to the Congregation for Bishops July, 1969; restructured by John Paul II in 1988. Cardinal Giovanni Battista Re, president.

Pontifical Commission for the Revision and Emendation of the Vulgate: Established in 1984 by John Paul II to replace the Abbey of St. Jerome instituted by Pius XI in 1933. Rev. Jean Mallet, O.S.B., director.

Pontifical Commission "*Ecclesia Dei*": Established by John Paul II, July 2, 1988, to facilitate the return to full ecclesial communion of priests, seminarians and religious who belonged to the fraternity founded by Marcel Lefebvre. Cardinal Darío Castrillón Hoyos, president.

International Theological Commission: Instituted by Paul VI Apr. 11, 1969, as an advisory adjunct of no more than 30 theologians to the Congregation for the Doctrine of the Faith; definitive statutes promulgated by John Paul II, Aug. 6, 1982. Cardinal Joseph Ratzinger, president; Rev. Georges Cottier, O.P., general secretary.

Commission for Religious Relations with the Jews: Instituted by Paul VI, Oct. 22, 1974, to promote and foster relations of a religious nature between Jews and Christians; attached to the Council for Promoting Christian Unity. Cardinal Walter Kasper, president.

Commission for Religious Relations with Muslims: Instituted by Paul VI, Oct. 22, 1974, to promote, regulate and interpret relations between Catholics and Muslims; attached to the Council for Interreligious Dialogue. Cardinal Francis Arinze, president.

Pontifical Committee for International Eucharistic Congresses: Instituted, 1879, by Pope Leo XIII; established as a pontifical committee with new statutes by John Paul II, Feb. 11, 1986. Card. Jozef Tomko, president.

Pontifical Committee for Historical Sciences: Instituted by Pius XII Apr. 7, 1954, as a continuation of a commission dating from 1883. Msgr. Walter Brandmüller, president.

Vatican II Archives: Preserves the documents of the Second Vatican Council.

Disciplinary Commission of the Roman Curia: Most Rev. Julián Herranz, president.

Council of Cardinals for Study of Organizational and Economic Problems of the Holy See: Council established in 1981 by Pope John Paul II; composed of approximately 15 cardinals from countries throughout the world. American members of the council include Cardinals Bernard Law, Roger Mahony, and Edward Egan.

Commission for the Protection o0f the Historical and Artistic Monuments of the Holy See: Instituted by Pius XI in 1923, reorganized by Paul VI in 1963. Vacant, president.

Institute for Works of Religion: Instituted by Pius XII June 27, 1942, to bank and administer funds for works of religion; replaced an earlier administration established by Leo XIII in 1887; reorganized by John Paul II (chirograph of Mar. 1, 1990). Headed by a commission of Cardinals, including Cardinal Angelo Sodano.

Fabric of St. Peter: Administration, care and preservation of Vatican Basilica. Abp. Francesco Marchisano, Archpriest of the Patriarchal Vatican Basilica, president.

Office of Papal Charities (Apostolic Almoner): Distributes alms and aid to those in need in the name of the Pope. Most Rev. Oscar Rizzato, almoner.

Labor Office of the Apostolic See (ULSA-*Ufficio del Lavoro della Sede Apostolica*): Has competence in regard to those who work for the Apostolic See; charged with settling labor issues. Instituted by John Paul II (*motu proprio* of Jan. 1, 1989); functions reaffirmed and definitive text of statutes approved by John Paul II (*motu proprio* of Sept. 30, 1994). Cardinal Jan Schotte, C.I.C.M., president.

Internationalization

As of May 15, 2002, principal officials of the Roman Curia were from the following countries: Italy (Cards. Antonetti, Cacciavillan, Cheli, Fagiolo, Felici, Laghi, Monduzzi, Noè, Pompedda,Ré, Sebastiani, Sepe, Silvestrini, Sodano; Abps. Bertone, Celli, Crepaldi, Cunial, de Magistris, Marchetto, Marchisano, Monterisi, Nesti, Salerno, Sandri, Tamburinno, Vegliò; Bps. Bertagna, Marini, Pastore); France (Cards. Etchegaray, Poupard, Abp. Tauran); United States (Cards. Baum, Stafford, Szoka, Abp. Foley, Bp. Harvey); Spain (Card. Martinez Somalo; Abps. Gil Hellín, Herranz, Redrado Marchite); Argentina (Card. Mejía); Germany (Cards. Kasper, Ratzinger, Bp. Cordes); Poland (Card. Grocholewski, Abps. Nowak, Rylko, Bp. Dziwisz); Belgium (Card. Schotte); Brazil (Abp. Agnelo); Canada (Abp. Ouellet); Chile (Card. Medina Estévez); Colombia (Cards. Castrillón Hoyos, Lopez Trujillo); England (Bp. Fitzgerald); French Guinea (Abp. Sarah); Hungary (Ternyák); Mexico (Abp. Lozano Barrágan); Nigeria (Card. Arinze); Portugal (Card. Saraiva Martins); Slovakia (Card. Tomko); Sri Lanka (Abp. Ranjith); Switzerland (Card. Agustoni); Syria (Card. Moussa I Daoud); Ukraine (Abp. Marusyn); Vietnam (Card. Nguyên Van Thuân); Japan (Abp. Hamao).

VATICAN CITY STATE

The State of Vatican City (*Stato della Città del Vaticano*) is the territorial seat of the papacy. The smallest sovereign state in the world, it is situated within the city of Rome, embraces an area of 108.7 acres, and includes within its limits the Vatican Palace, museums, art galleries, gardens, libraries, radio station, post office, bank, astronomical observatory, offices, apartments, service facilities, St. Peter's Basilica, and neighboring buildings between the Basilica and Viale Vaticano. The extraterritorial rights of Vatican City extend to more than 10 buildings in Rome, including the major basilicas and office buildings of

various congregations of the Roman Curia, and to the papal villas at **Castel Gandolfo** 15 miles southeast of the City of Rome. Castel Gandolfo is the summer residence of the Holy Father.

The government of Vatican City is in the hands of the reigning pope, who has full executive, legislative and judicial power. The administration of affairs, however, is handled by the **Pontifical Commission for the State of Vatican City** under Cardinal Edmund Casimir Szoka. The legal system is based on Canon Law; in cases where this code does not obtain, the laws of the City of Rome apply. The City is an absolutely neutral state and enjoys all the rights and privileges of a sovereign power. The citizens of Vatican City, and they alone, owe allegiance to the pope as a temporal head of state. On Nov. 26, 2000, Pope John Paul II promulgated the new Fundamental Law of the Vatican City State. The new law replaced that first established in 1929 by Pope Pius XI.

Cardinals of the Roman Curia residing outside Vatican City enjoy the privileges of extraterritoriality. The Secretary General for the Governatorate of the Vatican City State is Most. Rev. Gianni Danzi.

The normal population is approximately 1,000. While the greater percentage is made up of priests and religious, there are several hundred laypersons living in Vatican City. They are housed in their own apartments in the City and are engaged in secretarial, domestic, trade and service occupations. Approximately 3,400 laypersons are employed by the Vatican.

Services of honor and order are performed by the Swiss Guards, who have been charged with responsibility for the personal safety of popes since 1506. Additional police and ceremonial functions are under the supervision of a special office. These functions were formerly handled by the Papal Gendarmes, the Palatine Guard of Honor, and the Guard of Honor of the Pope (Pontifical Noble Guard); the units were disbanded by Pope Paul VI on Sept. 14, 1970.

The **Basilica of St. Peter**, built between 1506 and 1626, is the largest church in Christendom (with the exception of the Basilica of Our Lady Queen of Peace in Ivory Coast) and the site of most papal ceremonies. The pope's own patriarchal basilica, however, is **St. John Lateran**, whose origins date back to 324.

St. Ann's, staffed by Augustinian Fathers, is the parish church of Vatican City. Its pastor is appointed by the pope, following the recommendation of the prior general of the Augustinians and the archpriest of the Vatican Basilica.

The Church of **Santa Susanna** was designated as the national church for Americans in Rome by Pope Benedict XV Jan. 10, 1922, and entrusted to the Paulist Fathers, who have served there continuously since then except for several years during World War II.

Pastoral care in Vatican City State, which is separate from the diocese of Rome, is entrusted to the archpriest of St. Peter's Basilica, who is also vicar general for Vatican City and the papal villas at Castel Gandolfo (chirograph of Pope John Paul II, Jan. 14, 1991). Abp. Francesco Marchisano was appointed to the posts in April 2002. He succeeded Cardinal Virgilio Noè, who had held the posts since 1991.

The **Vatican Library** (00120 Vatican City; Rev. Raffaele Farina, S.D.B., prefect; Dr. Ambrogio Piazzoni, vice-prefect) has among its holdings 150,000 manuscripts, about 1,000,000 printed books, and 7,500 incunabula. The **Vatican Secret Archives** (00120 Vatican City; Rev. Sergio Pagano, prefect), opened to scholars by Leo XIII in 1881, contain central church documents dating back to the time of Innocent III (1198-1216). Cardinal Jorge María Mejía is librarian and archivist of the Holy Roman Church.

The independent temporal power of the pope, which is limited to the confines of Vatican City and small areas outside, was for many centuries more extensive than it is now. As late as the nineteenth century, the pope ruled 16,000 square miles of Papal States across the middle of Italy, with a population of over 3,000,000. In 1870 forces of the Kingdom of Italy occupied these lands that, with the exception of the small areas surrounding the Vatican and Lateran in Rome and the Villas of Castel Gandolfo, became part of the Kingdom by the Italian law of May 13, 1871.

The **Roman Question**, occasioned by this seizure and the voluntary confinement of the pope to the Vatican, was settled with ratification of the Lateran Agreement June 7, 1929, by the Italian government and Vatican City. The agreement recognized Catholicism as the religion of Italy and provided, among other things, a financial indemnity to the Vatican in return for the former Papal States; it became Article 7 of the Italian Constitution Mar. 26, 1947. The Lateran Agreement was superseded by a new concordat given final approval by the Italian Chamber of Deputies Mar. 20 and formally ratified June 3, 1985.

Papal Flag

The papal flag consists of two equal vertical stripes of yellow and white, charged with the insignia of the papacy on the white stripe-triple crown or tiara over two crossed keys, one of gold and one of silver, tied with a red cord and two tassels. The divisions of the crown represent the teaching, sanctifying and ruling offices of the pope. The keys symbolize his jurisdictional authority.

The papal flag is a national flag inasmuch as it is the standard of the Supreme Pontiff as the sovereign of the state of Vatican City. It is also universally accepted by the faithful as a symbol of the supreme spiritual authority of the Holy Father.

Vatican Radio

The declared purpose of Vatican Radio Station HVJ is "that the voice of the Supreme Pastor may be heard throughout the world by means of the ether waves, for the glory of Christ and the salvation of souls." Designed by Guglielmo Marconi, the inventor of radio, and supervised by him until his death, the station was inaugurated by Pope Pius XI in 1931. The original purpose has been extended to a wide variety of programming.

Vatican Radio operates on international wave lengths, transmits programs in 37 languages, and serves as a channel of communication between the Vatican, church officials and listeners in general in many parts of the world. The station broadcasts about 400 hours a week throughout the world.

The daily English-language program for North America is broadcast on 6095, 7305, 9600 kilohertz as well as via satellite INTELSAT 325,5° East (Atlantic) — 4097.75 Mhz — LHCP polarization.

Frequencies, background information and audio files can be obtained via the World Wide Web homepages www.wrn.org/vatican-radio and www.vatican.va.

The staff of 415 broadcasters and technicians includes 30 Jesuits. Studios and offices are at Palazzo Pio, Piazza Pia, 3, 00193 Rome. The transmitters are situated at Santa Maria di Galeria, a short distance north of Rome. President Cardinal Roberto Tucci, S.J.; Director General Rev. Pasquale Borgomeo, S.J.

2002 Vatican Stamps and Coins

The Vatican Philatelic and Numismatic Office (00120 Vatican City) scheduled the following issues of stamps and coins for the year 2002:

Stamps
• The Madonna in the Vatican Basilica
• The Restored Sistine Chapel: The Masterpieces of XV Century (3rd and last issue)
• Europa 2002: The Circus
• 150th Anniversary of the first Pontifical State Stamp
• Millenary of the Birth of St. Leo IX
• Third Centenary of the Ecclesiastical Pontifical Academy
• Seventh Centenary of the Death of Cimabue
• The Journeys of H.H. Pope John Paul II in the World
• Holy Christmas (joint issue with New Zealand)
• Automatic Vending Stamps – The Four Evangelists

Postal Stationery
Aerogram
Postcards

Publications
Vaticano 2002

Coins
• Series for XXIV year (2002) of the Pontificate of John Paul II; in eight values (1, 2, 5, 10, 20, 50 Eurocent, 1 Euro and 2 Euro). Minting: B.U. and Mirror Proof (with a Silver Medal).
• First Silver Celebrative Coin — Subject: Europe, a project of peace and brotherhood.
• Second Silver Celebrative Coin — Subject: Message of H.H. John Paul II on the Occasion of World Peace Day, Jan. 1, 2002.
• Two Celebrative Gold Coins — Subject: The Bible: The Roots of Faith – Noah's Ark and Abraham's Sacrifice.

Papal Audiences

General audiences are scheduled weekly, on Wednesday.

In Vatican City, they are held in the Audience Hall on the south side of St. Peter's Basilica or, weather permitting, in St. Peter's Square. The hall, which was opened in 1971, has a seating capacity of 6,800 and a total capacity of 12,000. Audiences have been held during the summer at Castel Gandolfo when the pope is there on a working vacation.

General audiences last from about 60 to 90 minutes, during which the pope gives a talk and his blessing. A résumé of the talk, which is usually in Italian, is given in several languages. Arrangements for papal audiences are handled by an office of the Prefecture of the Apostolic Household.

American visitors can obtain passes for general audiences by applying to the Bishops' Office for United States Visitors to the Vatican, Casa Santa Maria, Via dell'Umilita, 30, 00187 Rome. Private and group audiences are reserved for dignitaries of various categories and for special occasions.

Publications

Acta Apostolicae Sedis, 00120 Vatican City: The only "official commentary" of the Holy See, was established in 1908 for the publication of activities of the Holy See, laws, decrees and acts of congregations and tribunals of the Roman Curia. The first edition was published in Jan., 1909. St. Pius X made AAS an official organ in 1908. Laws promulgated for the Church ordinarily take effect three months after the date of their publication in this commentary. The publication, mostly in Latin, is printed by the Vatican

Press. The immediate predecessor of this organ was *Acta Sanctae Sedis,* founded in 1865 and given official status by the Congregation for the Propagation of the Faith in 1904.

Annuario Pontificio, 00120 Vatican City: The yearbook of the Holy See. It is edited by the Central Statistics Office of the Church and is printed in Italian, with some portions in other languages, by the Vatican Press. It covers the worldwide organization of the Church, lists members of the hierarchy, and includes a wide range of statistical information. The publication of a statistical yearbook of the Holy See dates back to 1716, when a volume called *Notizie* appeared. Publication under the present title began in 1860, was suspended in 1870, and resumed again in 1872 under the title *Catholic Hierarchy*. This volume was printed privately at first, but has been issued by the Vatican Press since 1885. The title *Annuario Pontificio* was restored in 1912, and the yearbook was called an "official publication" until 1924.

L'Osservatore Romano, Via del Pellegrino, 00120 Vatican City: The daily newspaper of the Holy See. It began publication July 1, 1861, as an independent enterprise under the ownership and direction of four Catholic laymen headed by Marcantonio Pacelli, vice minister of the interior under Pope Pius IX and a grandfather of the late Pius XII. Leo XIII bought the publication in 1890, making it the "pope's" own newspaper.

The only official material in *L'Osservatore Romano* is that which appears under the heading, "*Nostre Informazioni*." This includes notices of appointments by the Holy See, the texts of papal encyclicals and addresses by the Holy Father and others, various types of documents, accounts of decisions and rulings of administrative bodies, and similar items. Additional material includes news and comment on developments in the Church and the world. Italian is the language most used. The editorial board is directed by Prof. Mario Agnes. A staff of about 15 reporters covers Rome news sources. A corps of correspondents provides foreign coverage.

A weekly roundup edition in English was inaugurated in 1968 (Msgr. Richard Malone, is editor). Other weekly editions are printed in French (1949), Italian (1950), Spanish (1969), Portuguese (1970) and German (1971). The Polish edition (1980) is published monthly. *L'Osservatore della Domenica* is published weekly as a supplement to the Sunday issue of the daily edition.

Vatican Television Center (*Centro Televisivo Vaticano*, CTV), Palazzo Belvedere, 00120 Vatican City: Instituted by John Paul II Oct. 23, 1983, with the rescript, *Ex Audentia*. Dr. Emilio Rossi is president of the administrative council.

Vatican Press, 00120 Vatican City: The official printing plant of the Vatican. The Vatican press was conceived by Marcellus II and Pius IV but was actually founded by Sixtus V on Apr. 27, 1587, to print the Vulgate and the writings of the Fathers of the Church and other authors. A Polyglot Press was established in 1626 by the Congregation for the Propagation of the Faith to serve the needs of the Oriental Church. St. Pius X merged both presses under the title Vatican Polyglot Press. It was renamed Vatican Press July 1, 1991, by John Paul II following restructuring. The plant has facilities for the printing of a wide variety of material in about

30 languages. Director Rev. Elio Torrigiani, S.D.B.
Vatican Publishing House (*Libreria Editrice Vaticana*), Piazza S. Pietro, 00120 Vatican City: Formerly an office of the Vatican Press to assist in the circulation of the liturgical and juridical publications of the Apostolic See, the congregations and later the *Acta Apostolicae Sedis*. In 1926, with the expansion of publishing activities and following the promulgation of the 1917 Code, the office was made an independent entity. An administrative council and editorial commission were instituted in 1983; in 1988 *Pastor Bonus* listed it among institutes joined to the Holy See; new statutes were approved by the Secretariat of State July 1, 1991. Chairman, Most Rev. Giovanni De Andrea.

Activities of the Holy See: An annual documentary volume covering the activities of the pope and of the congregations, commissions, tribunals and offices of the Roman Curia.

Statistical Yearbook of the Church (*Annuarium Statisticum Ecclesiae*): Issued by the Central Statistics Office of the Church, it contains principal data concerning the presence and work of the Church in the world. The first issue was published in 1972 under the title *Collection of Statistical Tables, 1969*. It is printed in corresponding columns of Italian, French, and Latin. Some of the introductory material is printed in other languages.

DIPLOMATIC ACTIVITIES OF THE HOLY SEE

REPRESENTATIVES OF THE HOLY SEE

Representatives of the Holy See and their functions were the subject of a document entitled *Sollicitudo Omnium Ecclesiarum* which Pope Paul VI issued on his own initiative under the date of June 24, 1969.

Delegates and Nuncios

Papal representatives "receive from the Roman Pontiff the charge of representing him in a fixed way in the various nations or regions of the world.

"When their legation is only to local churches, they are known as apostolic delegates. When to this legation, of a religious and ecclesial nature, there is added diplomatic legation to states and governments, they receive the title of nuncio, pro-nuncio, and internuncio." An apostolic nuncio has the diplomatic rank of ambassador extraordinary and plenipotentiary. Traditionally, because the diplomatic service of the Holy See has the longest uninterrupted history in the world, a nuncio has precedence among diplomats in the country to which he is accredited and serves as dean of the diplomatic corps on state occasions. Since 1965 pro-nuncios, also of ambassadorial rank, have been assigned to countries in which this prerogative is not recognized. In recent years, the Vatican has phased out the title of pro-nuncio. The title of nuncio (with an asterisk denoting he is not dean of the diplomatic corps) has been given to the majority of appointments of ambassadorial rank. See also: Other Representatives.

Service and Liaison

Representatives, while carrying out their general and special duties, are bound to respect the autonomy of local churches and bishops. Their service and liaison responsibilities include the following:

• Nomination of Bishops: To play a key role in compiling, with the advice of ecclesiastics and lay persons, and submitting lists of names of likely candidates to the Holy See with their own recommendations.
• Bishops: To aid and counsel local bishops without interfering in the affairs of their jurisdictions.
• Episcopal Conferences: To maintain close relations with them and to assist them in every possible way.

(Papal representatives do not belong to these conferences.)
• Religious Communities of Pontifical Rank: To advise and assist major superiors for the purpose of promoting and consolidating conferences of men and women religious and to coordinate their apostolic activities.
• Church-State Relations: The thrust in this area is toward the development of sound relations with civil governments and collaboration in work for peace and the total good of the whole human family. The mission of a papal representative begins with appointment and assignment by the pope and continues until termination of his mandate. He acts "under the guidance and according to the instructions of the cardinal secretary of state to whom he is directly responsible for the execution of the mandate entrusted to him by the Supreme Pontiff." Normally representatives are required to retire at age 75.

NUNCIOS AND DELEGATES

(Sources: *Annuario Pontificio*, *L'Osservatore Romano*, *Acta Apostolicae Sedis*, Catholic News Service.). As of July 30, 2002: country, rank of legation (corresponding to rank of legate unless otherwise noted), name of legate (archbishop unless otherwise noted) as available. An asterisk indicates a nuncio who is not presently dean of the diplomatic corps.

Delegate for Papal Legations: Archbishop Carlo M. Viganò, titular archbishop of Ulpiana. The post was instituted in 1973 to coordinate papal diplomatic efforts throughout the world. The office entails responsibility for "following more closely through timely visits the activities of papal representatives … and encouraging their rapport with the central offices" of the Secretariat of State.

Albania: Tirana, Nunciature; Giovanni Bulaitis.*
Algeria: Algiers, Nunciature; Augustine Kasujja* (also Nuncio* to Tunisia).
Andorra: Nunciature; Manuel Monteiro de Castro (also Nuncio to Spain).
Angola: Luanda, Nunciature; Giovanni Angelo Becciu* (also Nuncio* to São Tome and Principe). (Diplomatic relations established in 1997.)

Antigua and Barbuda: Nunciature; Emil Paul Tscherrig* (resides in Port of Spain, Trinidad).

Antilles: Apostolic Delegation; Emil Paul Tscherrig (resides in Port of Spain, Trinidad).

Arabian Peninsula: Apostolic Delegation; Luigi Gatti (also Nuncio in Kuwait and Lebanon; resides in Lebanon).

Argentina: Buenos Aires, Nunciature; Abril y Castelló Santos.

Armenia: Nunciature; Claudio Gugerotti* (resides in Tbilisi, Georgia; also nuncio* to Georgia and Azerbaijan). (Diplomatic relations established in 1992.)

Australia: Canberra, Nunciature; Francesco Canalini.

Austria: Vienna, Nunciature; Donato Squicciarini.

Azerbaijan: Nunciature; Claudio Gugerotti* (resides in Tbilisi, Georgia; also nuncio* to Georgia and Armenia). (Diplomatic relations established in 1992.)

Bahamas: Nunciature; Emil Paul Tscherrig* (resides in Port of Spain, Trinidad).

Bahrain: Manama; Nunciature; Giuseppe De Andrea (Diplomatic relations established Jan. 12, 2000).

Bangladesh: Dhaka, Nunciature; vacant.*

Barbados: Nunciature; Emil Paul Tscherrig* (resides in Port of Spain, Trinidad).

Belarus: Nunciature; Ivan Jurkovic.*

Belgium: Brussels, Nunciature; Pier Luigi Celata (also Nuncio to Luxembourg).

Belize: Nunciature; Giacinto Berloco* (resides in Port of Spain, Trinidad).

Benin (formerly Dahomey): Nunciature; André Dupuy* (resides in Accra, Ghana).

Bolivia: La Paz, Nunciature; Ivo Scapolo.

Bosnia and Herzegovina: Sarajevo; Nunciature; Giuseppe Leanza*

Botswana: See **South Africa**.

Brazil: Brasilia, Nunciature; Alfio Rapisarda.

Brunei: See **Malaysia** and **Brunei**.

Bulgaria: Sofia, Nunciature (reestablished in 1990);Vladimir Gradev.*

Burkina Faso: Ouagadougou, Nunciature; Mario Zenari*(resides in Abidjan, Côte d'Ivoire).

Burma: See **Myanmar**.

Burundi: Bujumbura, Nunciature; Michael Aidan Courtney.*

Cambodia: Nunciature; Adriano Bernardini* (resides in Bangkok, Thailand). (Diplomatic relations established in 1994.)

Cameroon: Yaounde, Nunciature; Félix del Blanco Prieto* (also Nuncio to Equatorial Guinea).

Canada: Ottawa, Nunciature; Luigi Ventura.*

Cape Verde, Republic of: Nunciature; Giuseppe Pinto* (resides in Dakar, Senegal).

Central African Republic: Bangui, Nunciature; Joseph Chennoth* (also Nuncio* to Chad).

Chad: Nunciature; Joseph Chennoth* (resides in Bangui, Central African Republic).

Chile: Santiago, Nunciature; Aldo Cavalli.

China, Republic of: Taipei (Taiwan), Nunciature; vacant.

Colombia: Bogota, Nunciature; Beniamino Stella.

Comoros: See **Madagascar**: (formerly Zaire)

Congo (formerly Zaire): Kinshasa-Gombe, Nunciature; Giovanni d'Aniello.*

Congo: Brazzaville, Nunciature; Roberto Cassari* (also Nuncio* to Gabon).

Costa Rica: San Jose, Nunciature; Antonio Sozzo.

Côte d'Ivoire (Ivory Coast): Abidjan, Nunciature; Mario Zenari (also Nuncio* to Niger and Burkina Faso).

Croatia: Zagreb, Nunciature; Franjo Zenko.

Cuba: Havana, Nunciature; Luiz Robles Díaz.*

Cyprus: Nicosia, Nunciature; Pietro Sambi (also Nuncio to Israel), Pro-Nuncio.

Czech Republic: Prague, Nunciature; Erwin Josef Ender.

Denmark: Copenhagen, Nunciature; Piero Biggio* (also Nuncio* to Finland, Iceland, Norway and Sweden).

Djibouti: Nunciature (established May 2000); Silvano Tomasi, C.S. (resides in Addis Ababa, Ethiopia).

Dominica: Nunciature; Emil Paul Tscherrig* (resides in Port-of-Spain, Trinidad).

Dominican Republic: Santo Domingo, Nunciature; Timothy P. Broglio (also serves as Apostolic Delegate to Puerto Rico).

East Timor: Díli, Nunciature;Nunciature; vacant. (Diplomatic relations established on May 20, 2002).

Ecuador: Quito, Nunciature; Alain Lebeaupin.

Egypt: Cairo, Nunciature; Marco Dino Brogi, O.F.M. (also delegate to the Organization of the League of Arab States).*

El Salvador: San Salvador, Nunciature; Giacinto Berloco.

Equatorial Guinea: Santa Isabel, Nunciature; Felix del Blanco Prieto* (resides in Yaounde, Cameroon).

Eritrea: Nunciature: Silvano Tomasi, C.S.* (resides in Ethiopia). (Diplomatic relations established in 1995.)

Estonia: Nunciature; Peter Stephan Zurbriggen* (resides in Vilna, Lithuania).

Ethiopia: Addis Ababa, Nunciature; Silvano Tomasi, C.S.* (also Nuncio* to Eritrea and apostolic delegate to Djibouti).

European Community: Brussels, Belgium, Nunciature; Faustino Sainz Muñoz.

Fiji: Nunciature; Patrick Coveney* (resides in Wellington, New Zealand).

Finland: Helsinki, Nunciature; Piero Biggio * (resides in Denmark).

France: Paris, Nunciature; Fortunato Baldelli.

Gabon: Libreville, Nunciature; Roberto Cassari* (resides in Congo).

Gambia: Nunciature; Alberto Bottari de Castello* (resides in Freetown, Sierra Leone).

Georgia: Tbilisi, Nunciature; Claudio Gugerotti* (also Nuncio* to Armenia and Azerbaijan). (Diplomatic relations established in 1992.)

Germany: Bonn, Nunciature; Giovanni Lajolo.

Ghana: Accra, Nunciature; George Kocherry * (also Nuncio to Benin and Togo).

Great Britain: London, Nunciature; Pablo Puente* (also papal representative to Gibraltar).

Greece: Athens, Nunciature; Paul Fouad Tabet.*

Grenada: Nunciature; vacant* (resides in Port of Spain, Trinidad).

Guatemala: Guatemala City, Nunciature; Ramiro Moliner Inglés.

Guinea: Conakry, Nunciature; Alberto Bottari de Castello* (resides in Freetown, Sierra Leone).

Guinea Bissau: Nunciature; Giuseppe Pinto* (resides at Dakar, Senegal).

Guyana: Nunciature; Emil Paul Tscherrig (resides in Port of Spain, Trinidad).

Haiti: Port-au-Prince, Nunciature; Luigi Bonazzi.

Honduras: Tegucigalpa, Nunciature; George Panikulam.

Hungary: Budapest, Nunciature; Karl-Josef Rauber (also Nuncio* to Moldova).

Iceland: Nunciature; Piero Biggio * (resides in Denmark).

India: New Delhi, Nunciature; Lorenzo Baldisseri* (also Nuncio* to Nepal).

Indonesia: Jakarta, Nunciature; Renzo Fratini*.

Iran: Teheran, Nunciature; Angelo Mottola.*

Iraq: Baghdad, Nunciature; Fernando Filoni * (also Nuncio to Jordan).

Ireland: Dublin, Nunciature; Giuseppe Lazzarotto.

Israel: Nunciature; Pietro Sambi (also Nuncio to Cyprus). (Diplomatic relations established June 1994.)

Italy: Rome, Nunciature; Paolo Romeo (also Nuncio to San Marino).

Ivory Coast: See Côte d'Ivoire.

Jamaica: Nunciature; Emil Paul Tscherrig, Pro-Nuncio (resides in Port of Spain, Trinidad).

Japan: Tokyo, Nunciature; Ambrose de Paoli*.

Jerusalem and Palestine: Apostolic Delegation (also Nuncio to Israel): Pietro Sambi.

Jordan: Nunciature; Fernando Filoni* (also Nuncio to Iraq).

Kazakstan: Almaty, Nunciature; Józef Wesolowski* (also Nuncio* to Kyrgyzstan, Tajikistan and Uzbekistan).

Kenya: Nairobi, Nunciature; Giovanni Tonucci.*

Kiribati: Nunciature; Patrick Coveney* (resides in Wellington, New Zealand).

Korea: Seoul, Nunciature; Giovanni Battista Morandini* (also Nuncio* to Mongolia).

Kuwait: Al Kuwait, Nunciature; Giuseppe De Andrea* (resides in Lebanon).

Kyrgyzstan: Nunciature; Józef Wesolowski * (resides in Kazakstan; also Nuncio* to Kyrgyzstan, Tajikistan and Uzbekistan).

Laos: Apostolic Delegation; Adriano Bernardini, (resides in Bangkok, Thailand).

Latvia: Nunciature; Peter Stephan Zurbriggen* (resides in Vilna, Lithuania).

Lebanon: Beirut, Nunciature; Luigi Gatti (also Nuncio* to Kuwait and apostolic delegate to Arabian Peninsula).

Lesotho: Maseru, Nunciature; Blasco Francisco Collaço (also Nuncio to South Africa, Namibia, and Swaziland; resides in Pretoria, South Africa).

Liberia: Monrovia, Nunciature; Alberto Bottari de Castello* (resides in Freetown, Sierra Leone).

Libya: Nunciature; Luigi Conti* (resides in Malta). (Diplomatic relations established in 1997.)

Liechtenstein: Nunciature; Pier Giacomo De Nicolò (resides in Bern, Switzerland).

Lithuania: Vilnius, Nunciature; Peter Stephan Zurbriggen* (also Nuncio to Estonia and Latvia.).

Luxembourg: Nunciature; Pier Luigi Celata (resides in Brussels, Belgium).

Macedonia: Nunciature; Marian Oles* (also Nuncio to Slovenia; resides in Slovenia).

Madagascar: Antananarivo, Nunciature; Bruno Musarò* (also Nuncio* to Seychelles, and Mauritius and Apostolic Delegate to Comoros and Reunion).

Malawi: Lilongwe, Nunciature; Orlando Antonini* (resides in Lusaka, Zambia).

Malaysia and Brunei: Apostolic Delegation; Adriano Bernardini (resides in Bangkok, Thailand).

Mali: Nunciature; Giuseppe Pinto* (resides in Dakar, Senegal).

Malta: La Valletta, Nunciature; Luigi Conti (also Nuncio* to Libya).

Marshall Islands: Nunciature; Patrick Coveney* (resides in Wellington, New Zealand).

Mauritania: Nouakchott, Apostolic Delegation; Giuseppe Pinto (resides in Dakar, Senegal).

Mauritius: Port Louis, Nunciature; Bruno Musarò* (resides in Antananarivo, Madagascar).

Mexico: Mexico City, Nunciature; Giuseppe Bertello.* (Diplomatic relations established in 1992).

Micronesia, Federated States of: Nunciature; Patrick Coveney* (resides in Wellington, New Zealand).

Moldova: Nunciature; Karl-Josef Rauber* (resides in Budapest, Hungary). (Diplomatic relations established in 1992.)

Mongolia: Nunciature; Giovanni Battista Morandini* (resides in Seoul, South Korea).

Morocco: Rabat, Nunciature; Domenico De Luca.*

Mozambique: Maputo, nunciature; Juliusz Janusz.* (Diplomatic relations established in 1995.)

Myanmar (formerly Burma): Apostolic Delegation; Adriano Bernardini (resides in Bangkok, Thailand).

Namibia: Nunciature; Blasco Francisco Collaço* (resides in Pretoria, South Africa).

Nauru: Nunciature; Patrick Coveney* (resides in Wellington, New Zealand).

Nepal: Nunciature; Lorenzo Baldisseri* (resides in New Delhi, India).

Netherlands: The Hague, Nunciature; François Bacqué.*

New Zealand: Wellington, Nunciature; Patrick Coveney.* (also Nuncio* to Fiji, Kiribati, Marshall Islands, Federated States of Micronesia, Tonga, Vanuatu and Western Samoa; Apostolic Delegate to Pacific Islands).

Nicaragua: Managua, Nunciature; Jean-Paul Gobel.

Niger: Niamey, Nunciature; Mario Zenari* (resides in Abidjan, Côte d'Ivoire.)

Nigeria: Lagos, Nunciature; Osvaldo Padilla*.

Norway: Nunciature; Piero Biggio* (resides in Denmark).

Pacific Islands: Apostolic Delegation; Patrick Coveney (resides in Wellington, New Zealand).

Pakistan: Islamabad, Nunciature; Alessandro D'Errico.

Palau, Republic of: Palau, Nunciature; Patrick Coveney.*

Panama: Panama City, Nunciature; Giacomo Ottonello.

Papua New Guinea: Port Moresby; Nunciature; Adolfo Tito Yllana* (also Nuncio* to Solomon Islands).

Paraguay: Asuncion, Nunciature; Antonio Lucibello.

Peru: Lima, Nunciature; Rino Passigato.

Philippines: Manila, Nunciature; Antonio Franco.

Poland: Warsaw, Nunciature; Hanna Suchoka.

Portugal: Lisbon, Nunciature; Edoardo Rovida.

Puerto Rico: See **Dominican Republic**.

Reunion: See **Madagascar**.

Romania: Bucharest, Nunciature. Jean-Claude Périsset.*

Russia (Federation of): Moscow, Nunciature; Giorgio Zur; Nuncio appointed Representative of the Holy See to Russian Federation, 1994.

Rwanda: Kigali, Nunciature. Salvatore Pennacchio.

Saint Vincent and the Grenadines: Nunciature; Emil Paul Tscherrig, Pro-Nuncio (resides in Port of Spain, Trinidad).

San Marino: Nunciature; Paolo Romeo.

Santa Lucia: Nunciature; Emil Paul Tscherrig* (resides in Port of Spain, Trinidad).

São Tome and Principe: Nunciature; Giovanni Angelo Becciu* (also Nuncio* to Angola, where he resides).

Senegal: Dakar, Nunciature; Giuseppe Pinto* (also Nuncio* to Cape Verde, Guinea-Bissau and Mali; Apostolic Delegate to Mauritania.)

Seychelles Islands: Nunciature; Bruno Musarò* (resides in Antananrivo, Madagascar).

Sierra Leone: Freetown, Nunciature (1996); Alberto Bottari de Castello* (also Nuncio* to Gambia, Guinea and Liberia).

Singapore: Nunciature; Adriano Bernardini* (He is also Nuncio to Cambodia and Thailand and apostolic delegate to Laos, Malaysia and Brunei, and Myanmar.)

Slovakia: Nunciature; Henryk Jozef Nowacki.

Slovenia: Ljubljana, Nunciature; Marian Oles (also Nuncio to Macedonia).

Solomon Islands: Nunciature; Adolfo Tito Yllana (resides in Port Moresby, Papua New Guinea).

Somalia: Apostolic Delegation (est. 1992); Dominique Mamberti (resides in Sudan).

South Africa: Pretoria, Nunciature; Blasco Francisco Collaço.* (also Nuncio* to Namibia and Swaziland and apostolic delegate to Botswana.)

Spain: Madrid, Nunciature; Manuel Monteiro de Castro.

Sri Lanka: Colombo, Nunciature; Thomas Yeh Sheng-nan.*

Sudan: Khartoum, Nunciature; Dominique Mamberti* (also Apostolic Delegate to Somalia).

Suriname: Nunciature; vacant* (resides in Port of Spain, Trinidad).

Swaziland: Nunciature; Blasco Francisco Collaço* (resides in Pretoria, South Africa).

Sweden: Nunciature; Piero Biggio* (resides in Denmark).

Switzerland: Bern, Nunciature; Pier Giacomo De Nicolò (also Nuncio to Liechtenstein).

Syria: (Syrian Arab Republic): Damascus, Nunciature, Diego Causero.*

Tajikistan: Nunciature (1996); Józef Wesolowski* (resides in Kazakstan; also Nuncio* to Kyrgyzstan, Kazakstan, and Uzbekistan).

Tanzania: Dar-es-Salaam, Nunciature; Luigi Pezzuto.*

Thailand: Bangkok, Nunciature; Adriano Bernardini* (also Nuncio* to Cambodia and Singapore and Apostolic Delegate to Laos, Malaysia, Brunei, Myanmar).

Togo: Lome, Nunciature; George Kocherry* (resides in Accra, Ghana).

Tonga: Nunciature; Patrick Coveney* (resides in Wellington, New Zealand).

Trinidad and Tobago: Port of Spain, Trinidad, Nunciature; Emil Paul Tscherrig, Pro-Nuncio (also Pro-Nuncio to Antigua and Barbuda, Bahamas,

Barbados, Belize, Dominica, Grenada, Jamaica, Saint Lucia, Saint Vincent and the Grenadines, Suriname and Apostolic Delegate to Antilles).

Tunisia: Tunis, Nunciature; Augustine Kasujja* (resides in Algiers, Algeria).

Turkey: Ankara, Nunciature; Edmond Farhat.*

Turkmenistan: Nunciature (1996); Edmond Farhat* (resides in Ankara, Turkey.)

Ukraine: Kiev, Nunciature; Nikola Eterovic.*

Uganda: Kampala, Nunciature; Pro-Nuncio, Christophe Pierre.

United States of America: Washington, D.C., Nunciature;Gabriel Montalvo.*

Uruguay: Montevideo, Nunciature; Janusz Bolonek.

Uzbekistan: Nunciature; Józef Wesolowski* (resides in Kazakhstan; also Nuncio* to Kazakstan, Kyrgyzstan, and Tajikistan).

Vanuatu: Nunciature; Patrick Coveney* (resides in Wellington, New Zealand).

Venezuela: Caracas, Nunciature; André Dupuy.

Vietnam: Apostolic Delegation; vacant.

Western Samoa: Nunciature; Patrick Coveney* (resides in Wellington, New Zealand).

Yemen: San'a, Nunciature; Giuseppe De Andrea* (relations established in 1998).

Yugoslavia: Belgrade, Nunciature; Eugenio Sbarbaro.

Zaire: See Congo: Lusaka, Nunciature; Giuseppe Leanza* (also Nuncio* to Malawi).

Zambia: Lusaka, Nunciature; Orlando Antonini* (also Nuncio* to Malawi).

Zimbabwe: Harare, Nunciature; Edward Joseph Adams.*

The Current Nuncio to the U.S.

The representative of the Pope to the Church in the United States is Archbishop Gabriel Montalvo, J.C.D. Archbishop Montalvo was born Jan. 27, 1930, in Bogota, Colombia. Ordained to the priesthood Jan. 18, 1953, he earned a doctorate in canon law and entered the Vatican diplomatic service in 1957, serving in nunciatures in Bolivia, Argentina, and El Salvador. From 1964 to 1974, Archbishop Montalvo served in the Secretariat of State, Vatican City, where he dealt with matters affecting the Churches in Eastern Europe. In 1974, he was named Apostolic Nuncio in Honduras and Nicaragua. He was named Titular Archbishop of Celene on June 30, 1974. In 1980, Archbishop Montalvo was named Pro-Nuncio in Algeria and Tunisia and Apostolic Delegate in Libya. In 1986, Archbishop Montalvo was named Apostolic Pro-Nuncio in Yugoslavia and subsequently Apostolic Nuncio in Belarus. In 1993 he was appointed President of the Pontifical Ecclesiastical Academy where diplomats in service to the Holy See are trained. On Dec. 7, 1998, Archbishop Montalvo was appointed nuncio to the United States and permanent observer to the Organization of American States, succeeding Archbishop Agostino Cacciavillan.

The U.S. Apostolic Nunciature is located at 3339 Massachusetts Ave., N.W., Washington, DC 20008-3687; (202) 333-7121.

A Nuncio represents the Holy Father to both the hierarchy and Church of a particular nation and to that nation's civil government.

From 1893 to 1984, papal representatives to the Church in the U.S. were apostolic delegates (all archbishops): Francesco Satolli (1893-96), Sebastiano Martinelli, O.S.A., (1896-1902), Diomede Falconio,

O.F.M. (1902-1911), Giovanni Bonzano (1911-22), Pietro Fumasoni-Biondi (1922-33), Amleto Cicognani (1933-58), Egidio Vagnozzi (1958-67), Luigi Raimondi (1967-73), Jean Jadot (1973-80), and Pio Laghi (1980-90) who was the first to hold the title Pro-Nuncio, beginning in 1984 (See Index, U.S.-Vatican Relations). Archbishop (now Cardinal) Agostino Cacciavillan was Pro-Nuncio and permanent observer to the Organization of American States from 1990 to 1998.

Other Representatives

(*Sources:* Annuario Pontificio; *Catholic News Service.*)

The Holy See has representatives to or is a regular member of a number of quasi-governmental and international organizations. Most Rev. Ernesto Gallina was appointed delegate to International Governmental Organizations Jan. 12, 1991.

Governmental Organizations: United Nations (Abp. Renato Raffaele Martino, permanent observer); UN Office in Geneva and Specialized Institutions (Abp. Diarmuid Martin, permanent observer); International Atomic Energy Agency (Msgr. Leo Boccardi, permanent representative); UN Office at Vienna and UN Organization for Industrial Development (Msgr. Leo Boccardi, permanent observer); UN Food and Agriculture Organization (Msgr. Renato Volante, permanent observer); UN Educational, Scientific and Cultural Organization (Msgr. Francesco Follo, permanent observer); World Organization of Commerce (Abp. Diarmuid Martin); Council of Europe (Msgr. Paul Richard Gallagher, special representative with function of permanent observer); Council for Cultural Cooperation of the Council of Europe (Msgr. Paul Richard Gallagher, delegate); Organization of American States (Abp.Gabriel Montalvo, permanent observer, with personal title of Apostolic Nuncio); Organization for Security and Cooperation in Europe (Msgr. Leo Boccardi, permanent representative); International Institute for the Unification of Private Law (Prof. Giuseppe dalla Torre del Tiempo di Sanguinetto Conte, delegate); International Committee of Military Medicine (Rev. Luc De Maere, delegate), World Organization of Tourism (Msgr. Piero Monni, permanent observer).

Non-Governmental Organizations: International Committee of Historical Sciences (Msgr. Walter Brandmüller); International Committee of the History of Art (Dr. Francesco Buranelli); International Committee of Anthropological and Ethnological Sciences; Committee for the Neutrality of Medicine; International Center of Study for the Preservation and Restoration of Cultural Goods (Dr. Francesco Buranelli); International Council of Monuments and Sites (Msgr. Lorenzo Frana, delegate); International Alliance on Tourism; World Association of Jurists (Abp. Gabriel Montalvo); International Commission of the Civil State (Msgr. Paul Richard Gallagher); International Astronomical Union; International Institute of Administrative Sciences; International Technical Committee for Prevention and Extinction of Fires; World Medical Association; International Archives Council; World Trade Organization.

DIPLOMATS TO THE HOLY SEE

(*Sources:* Annuario Pontificio, L'Osservatore Romano).

Listed below are countries maintaining diplomatic relations with the Holy See, dates of establishment (in some cases) and names of Ambassadors (as of Aug. 30, 2002). Leaders (. . . . .) indicate the post was vacant.

The senior member of the diplomatic corps at the Vatican is Jean Wagner of Luxembourg who was appointed in Nov. 7, 1981, and presented his credentials Jan. 18, 1982.

Albania (1991): Zef Bushati.
Algeria (1972): Mohamed-Salah Dembri.
Andorra (1995): Manuel Mas Ribó.
Angola (1997): José Bernardo Domingos Quiosa.
Antigua and Barbuda (1986): . . . . .
Argentina: Vicente Espeche Gil.
Armenia (1992): Edward Nalbandian.
Australia (1973): Robert George Halverson.
Austria: Walter Greinert.
Azerbaijan (1992): . . . . .
Bahamas (1979): . . . . .
Bahrain (2000): . . . . .
Bangladesh (1972):Toufiq Ali.
Barbados (1979): Peter Patrick Kenneth Simmons.
Belarus (1992): Vladimir R. Korolev.
Belgium (1835): Thierry Muûls.
Belize (1983): . . . . .
Benin (formerly Dahomey) (1971): Euloge Hinvi.
Bolivia: Pedro José Rivera Saavedra.
Bosnia and Herzegovina (1992): Dr. Vlatko Kraljevic.
Brazil: Oto Agripino Maia.
Bulgaria (1990): Dr. Svetlozar Dimitrov Raev.
Burkina Faso (1973): Felipe Savadogo.
Burundi (1963): Aloys Mbonayo.
Cambodia (1994): . . . . .
Cameroon (1966): Jean Melaga.
Canada (1969): Wilfred-Guy Licari.
Cape Verde (1976): Teófilo de Figueiredo Almeida.
Central African Republic (1975): . . . . .
Chad (1988): Mahmoud Hissein Mahmoud.
Chile: Maximo Pacheco Gómez.
China, Republic of (Taiwan) (1966): Raymond R.M. Tai.
Colombia: Dr. Guillermo León Escobar-Herrán.
Congo (formerly Zaire) (1963): . . . . .
Congo (1977): Henri Marie Joseph Lopes.
Costa Rica: Javier Guerra Laspiur.
Côte d'Ivoire (Ivory Coast) (1971): Louis Esmel.
Croatia (1992): Dr. Marijan Sunjic.
Cuba: Isidro Gómez Santos.
Cyprus (1973): Christos N. Psilogenis.
Czech Republic (1929-50, reestablished, 1990, with Czech and Slovak Federative Republic; reaffirmed, 1993): Martin Stropnicky.
Denmark (1982): Bjarne Bladbjerg.
Djibouti: (2000): Barkat Gourad Hamadou (Diplomatic relations established May 20, 2000).
Dominica (1981): . . . . .
Dominican Republic: Victor A.Hidlago Justo.
East Timor (2002): . . . . (Diplomatic relations established on May 20, 2002).
Ecuador: Marcelo Fernández de Córdoba Ponce.
Egypt (1966): Farouk Hussein Raafat
El Salvador: Roberto José Simán Jacir.
Equatorial Guinea (1981): . . . . .
Eritrea (1995): Zemede Tekle Woldetatios.
Estonia (1991): Indrek Tarand.

Ethiopia (1969): Mulugeta Eteffa.
Fiji (1978): Filimone Jitoko.
Finland (1966): Antti Hynninen.
France: Alain Dejammet.
Gabon (1967): Bonaventure Ndong-Ekomie.
Gambia, The (1978): Gibril Seman Joof.
Georgia (1992): Amiran Kavadze.
Germany: Wilhelm Hans-Theodor Wallau.
Ghana (1976): Harry Osei Blavo.
Great Britain (1982): Mark Pellew.
Greece (1980): Stelios Rocanas.
Grenada (1979): . . . . .
Guatemala: Aciscio Valladares Molina.
Guinea (1986): Abraham Doukouré.
Guinea-Bissau (1986): . . . . .
Guyana (Cooperative Republic of): Laleshwar Kumar
   Narayan Singh.
Haiti: Marc A. Trouillot.
Honduras: Alejandro Emilio Valladares Lanza.
Hungary (1990): Pál Tar.
Iceland (1976): Hördur H. Bjarnason.
India: Niranjan Natverlal Desai.
Indonesia (1965): Widodo Sutiyo.
Iran (1966): Mostafa Borujerdi.
Iraq (1966): Wissam Chawkat Al-Zahawi.
Ireland: Bernard Davenport.
Israel (1994): Yosef Neville Lamdan.
Italy: Raniero Avogardo.
Ivory Coast: See Côte d'Ivoire.
Jamaica (1979): Peter Carlisle Black.
Japan (1966): Mitsuhiro Nakamura.
Jordan (1994): Dina Kawar.
Kazakstan (1992): Nurlan Danenov.
Kenya (1965): Boaz Kidiga Mbaya.
Kiribati: Diplomatic relations established Apr. 1995.
Korea (1966): Seo Hyun-Seop.
Kuwait (1969): Ahmad Abdulkarim Al-Ebrahim.
Kyrgyzstan (1992): Apas Dschumagulov
Latvia (1991): Atis Sjanits.
Lebanon (1966): Fouad Aoun.
Lesotho (1967): Seymour Rehaulele Kikine.
Liberia (1966): . . . . .
Libya: (1997): Husein-Fuad Mustafa Kabazi.
Liechtenstein (1985): Nikolaus de Liechtenstein.
Lithuania: Kazys Lozoraitis.
Luxembourg (1955): Jean Wagner.
Macedonia (1994): Ivan Angelov.
Madagascar (1967): Malala-Zo Raolison
   Randrianjoa Ramahatafandry.
Malawi (1966): Silas Samuel Ncozana.
Mali (1979): Moussa Coulibaly.
Malta (1965): James Farrugia.
Marshall Islands (1993): . . . . .
Mauritius: Mohunlall Goburdhun.
Mexico (personal representative, 1990; diplomatic
   relations, 1992): Fernando Estrada Sámano.
Micronesia, Federated States (1994): . . . . .
Moldova (1992): . . . . .
Monaco: Jean- Claude Michel.
Mongolia (1992): Chuluuny Batjargal.
Morocco: Mohammed Sbihi.
Mozambique: Diplomatic relations established Dec.
   1995.
Namibia: Diplomatic relations established Sept.
   1995.
Nauru (1992): . . . . .
Nepal (1983): Balram Singh Malla.

Netherlands (1967): Baron Hendrik Volkier Bentinck
   van Schoonheten.
New Zealand (1973): Christine Heather Bogle.
Nicaragua: Luvy Salerni Navas.
Niger (1971): Amadou Touré.
Nigeria (1976): Samuel Otuyelu.
Norway (1982): Bengt O. Johansen.
Order of Malta (see Index): Alberto Leoncini Bartoli.
Pakistan (1965): Tayyab Siddiqui.
Palau, Republic of (1998): . . . . .
Panama: Edda Victoria Martinelli de Dutari.
Papua New Guinea (1977): . . . . .
Paraguay: Blanca Elida Zuccolillo de Rodríguez
   Alcalá.
Peru: Alberto Montagne Vidal.
Philippines (1951): Francisco A. Alba
Poland (1989): Hanna Suchocka.
Portugal: Pedro José Ribeiro de Menezes.
Romania (1920; broken off, 1948; reestablished,
   1990): Mihail Dobre.
Rwanda (1964): Christine Nyinawumwami Umutoni.
Saint Lucia (1984): Desmond Arthur McNamara.
Saint Vincent and the Grenadines (1990): . . . . .
San Marino (1986): Giovanni Galassi.
São Tome and Principe (1984): . . . . .
Senegal (1966): Henri Antoine Turpin.
Seychelles (1984): . . . . .
Sierra Leone: Diplomatic relations established July
   1996.
Singapore (1981): Ampalavanar Selverajah.
Slovak Republic (1993; when it became independent
   republic): Dr. Marián Servátka.
Slovenia (1992): Karl Bonutti.
Solomon Islands (1984): . . . . .
South Africa (1994): Patricia Nozipho January-
   Bardill.
Spain: Carlos Abella y Ramallo.
Sri Lanka (1975): Prasad Kariyawasam.
Sudan (1972): Abdelbasit Badawi Ali Elsanosi.
Suriname (1994): Evert G. Azimullah.
Swaziland (1992): H.R.H. Prince David M. Dlamini.
Sweden (1982): Fredrik Vahlquist.
Switzerland (1992): Hansrudolf Hoffmann, Ambas-
   sador with special mission to Holy See.
Syria (Arab Republic) (1966): Elias Najmeh.
Tajikistan: Diplomatic relations established June
   1996.
Tanzania (1968): Andrew Mhando Daraja.
Thailand (1969): Jullapong Nonsirchai.
Togo (1981): . . . . .
Tonga (1994): . . . . .
Trinidad and Tobago (1978): . . . . .
Tunisia (1972): Saïda Chtioui.
Turkey (1966): Filiz Dinçmen.
Turkmenistan: Diplomatic relations established July
   1996.
Uganda (1966): Tibamanya Mwene Mushanga.
Ukraine (1992): Nina Kovalska.
United States (1984):James Nicholson..
Uruguay: Julio César Lupinacci.
Uzbekistan (1992): . . . . .
Vanuatu (1994): . . . . .
Venezuela: Ignacio Quintana.
Western Samoa (1994): . . . . .
Yemen: (1998): Mohy Al-Dhabbi.
Yugoslavia: Darko Tanaskovic.
Zaire: See Congo.

Zambia (1965): Silumelume Kufunduka Mubukwanu.
Zimbabwe (1980): Joey Mazorodze Bimha.
Special Representatives
Russia (Federation of) (1989): Vitaly Litvin, Ambassador Extraordinary and Plenipotentiary.
United Nations (Center of Information of UN at the Holy See): Shalini Dewan, Director.
Office of the League of Arab States: Mohammad Ali Mohammad.
United Nations High Commission for Refugees: Ana Liria-Franch, delegate.
Organization for the Liberation of Palestine: Afif E. Safieh, director.

U.S. - HOLY SEE RELATIONS

The United States and the Holy See announced Jan. 10, 1984, the establishment of full diplomatic relations, thus ending a period of 117 years in which there was no formal diplomatic relationship. The announcement followed action by the Congress in November 1983, to end a prohibition on diplomatic relations enacted in 1867.

William A. Wilson, President Reagan's personal representative to the Holy See from 1981, was confirmed as the U.S. ambassador by the Senate, on Mar. 7, 1984. He presented his credentials to Pope John Paul II on Apr. 9, 1984, and served until May 1986, when he resigned. He was succeeded by Frank Shakespeare, 1986-89, and Thomas P. Melady, 1989-93. Raymond L. Flynn, Mayor of Boston, was appointed by Bill Clinton and confirmed by the Senate in July, 1993. He served until 1997 when he was succeeded by Corinne Claiborne "Lindy" Boggs. She presented her credentials to Pope John Paul II on Dec. 16, 1997. The present U.S. Ambassador to the Holy See is James Nicholson.

Archbishop (now Cardinal) Pio Laghi, apostolic delegate to the U.S. since 1980, was named first pronuncio by the Pope on Mar. 26, 1984. He served until 1990, when he was named prefect of the Congregation for Catholic Education; Archbishop Agostino Cacciavillan was appointed pro-nuncio on June 13, 1990. He served until he was named president of the Administration of the Patrimony of the Apostolic See (APSA) and was succeeded on Dec. 7, 1998 by Archbishop Gabriel Montalvo, the present nuncio.

Nature of Relations

The nature of relations was described in nearly identical statements by John Hughes, a State Department spokesman, and the Holy See. Hughes said: "The United States of America and the Holy See, in the desire to further promote the existing mutual friendly relations, have decided by common agreement to establish diplomatic relations between them at the level of embassy on the part of the United States of America, and nunciature on the part of the Holy See, as of today, Jan. 10, 1984."

The Holy See statement said: "The Holy See and the United States of America, desiring to develop the mutual friendly relations already existing, have decided by common accord to establish diplomatic relations at the level of apostolic nunciature on the side of the Holy See and of embassy on the side of the United States beginning today, Jan. 10, 1984."

The establishment of relations was criticized as a violation of the separation-of-church-and-state principle by spokesmen for the National Council of Churches, the National Association of Evangelicals, the Baptist Joint Committee on Public Affairs, Seventh Day Adventists, Americans United for Separation of Church and State, and the American Jewish Congress.

Legal Challenge Dismissed

U.S. District Judge John P. Fullam, ruling May 7, 1985, in Philadelphia, dismissed a legal challenge to U.S.-Holy See relations brought by Americans United for Separation of Church and State. He stated that Americans United and its allies in the challenge lacked legal standing to sue, and that the courts did not have jurisdiction to intervene in foreign policy decisions of the executive branch of the U.S. government. Parties to the suit brought by Americans United were the National Association of Laity, the National Coalition of American Nuns and several Protestant church organizations. Bishop James W. Malone, president of the U.S. Catholic Conference, said in a statement: "This matter has been discussed at length for many years. It is not a religious issue but a public policy question which, happily, has now been settled in this context."

Russell Shaw, a conference spokesman, said the decision to send an ambassador to the Holy See was not a church-state issue and "confers no special privilege or status on the Church."

Earlier Relations

Official relations for trade and diplomatic purposes were maintained by the United States and the Papal States while the latter had the character of and acted like other sovereign powers in the international community.

Consular relations developed in the wake of an announcement, made by the papal nuncio in Paris to the American mission there Dec. 15, 1784, that the Papal States had agreed to open several Mediterranean ports to U.S. shipping.

U.S. consular representation in the Papal States began with the appointment of John B. Sartori, a native of Rome, in June, 1797. Sartori's successors as consuls were: Felix Cicognani, also a Roman, and Americans George W. Greene, Nicholas Browne, William C. Sanders, Daniel LeRoy, Horatio V. Glentworth, W.J. Stillman, Edwin C. Cushman, David M. Armstrong.

Consular officials of the Papal States who served in the U.S. were: Count Ferdinand Lucchesi, 1826 to 1829, who resided in Washington; John B. Sartori, 1829 to 1841, who resided in Trenton, N.J.; Daniel J. Desmond, 1841 to 1850, who resided in Philadelphia; Louis B. Binsse, 1850 to 1895, who resided in New York.

U.S. recognition of the consul of the Papal States did not cease when the states were absorbed into the Kingdom of Italy in 1871, despite pressure from Baron Blanc, the Italian minister. Binsse held the title until his death Mar. 28, 1895. No one was appointed to succeed him.

Diplomatic Relations

The U.S. Senate approved a recommendation, made by President James K. Polk in December 1847, for the establishment of a diplomatic post in the Papal States. Jacob L. Martin, the first charge d'affaires, arrived in Rome Aug. 2, 1848, and presented his credentials to Pius IX Aug. 19. Martin, who died within a month, was succeeded by Lewis Cass, Jr. Cass became minister resident in 1854 and served in that capacity until his retirement in 1858.

John P. Stockton, who later became a U.S. Senator from New Jersey, was minister resident from 1858 to 1861. Rufus King was named to succeed him but, instead, accepted a commission as a brigadier general in the Army. Alexander W. Randall of Wisconsin took the appointment. He was succeeded in August 1862, by Richard M. Blatchford who served until the following year. King was again nominated minister resident and served in that capacity until 1867 when the ministry was ended because of objections from some quarters in the U.S. and failure to appropriate funds for its continuation. J. C. Hooker, a secretary, remained in the Papal States until the end of March 1868, closing the ministry and performing functions of courtesy.

Personal Envoys

Myron C. Taylor was appointed by President Franklin D. Roosevelt in 1939 to serve as his personal representative to Pope Pius XII and continued serving in that capacity during the presidency of Harry S. Truman until 1951. Henry Cabot Lodge was named to the post by President Richard M. Nixon in 1970, served also during the presidency of Gerald Ford, and represented President Carter at the canonization of St. John Neumann in 1977. Miami attorney David Walters served as the personal envoy of President Jimmy Carter to the Pope from July 1977, until his resignation Aug. 16, 1978. He was succeeded by Robert F. Wagner who served from October 1978, to the end of the Carter presidency in January 1981. William A. Wilson, appointed by President Ronald Reagan in February 1981, served as his personal envoy until 1984 when he was named ambassador to the Holy See.

None of the personal envoys had diplomatic status. President Harry S. Truman nominated Gen. Mark Clark to be ambassador to the Holy See in 1951, but withdrew the nomination at Clark's request because of controversy over the appointment.

None of Truman's three immediate successors — Dwight D. Eisenhower, John F. Kennedy and Lyndon B. Johnson — had a personal representative to the pope.

PONTIFICAL ACADEMIES

Pontifical Academy of Sciences

(*Sources:* Annuario Pontificio, *Catholic News Service.*)

The Pontifical Academy of Sciences was constituted in its present form by Pius XI Oct. 28, 1936, in virtue of *In Multis Solaciis,* a document issued on his own initiative.

The academy is the only supranational body of its kind in the world with a pope-selected, life-long membership of outstanding mathematicians and experimental scientists regardless of creed from many countries. The normal complement of 70 members was increased to 80 in 1985-86 by John Paul II. There are additional honorary and supernumerary members.

The academy traces its origin to the *Linceorum Academia* (Academy of the Lynxes — its symbol) founded in Rome Aug. 17, 1603. Pius IX reorganized this body and gave it a new name — *Pontificia Accademia dei Nuovi Lincei* — in 1847. It was taken over by the Italian state in 1870 and called the *Accademia Nazionale dei Lincei.* Leo XIII reconstituted it with a new charter in 1887. Pius XI designated the Casina of Pope Pius IV in the Vatican Gardens as the site of academy headquarters in 1922 and gave it its present title and status in 1936. In 1940, Pius XII gave the title of Excellency to its members; John XXIII extended the privilege to honorary members in 1961.

Members in U.S.

Scientists in the U.S. who presently hold membership in the Academy are listed below according to year of appointment. Nobel prizewinners are indicated by an asterisk.

Franco Rasetti, professor emeritus of physics at Johns Hopkins University, Baltimore, Md. (Oct 28, 1936); Christian de Duve,* professor of biochemistry at the International Institute of Cellular and Molecular Pathology at Brussels, Belgium, and Rockefeller University, New York (Apr. 10, 1970);

Marshall Warren Nirenberg,* director of Laboratory on genetics and biochemistry at the National Institutes of Health, Bethesda, Md. (June 24, 1974).

George Palade,* professor of cellular biology at University of California, San Diego and Victor Weisskopf, professor of physics at the Massachusetts Institute of Technology, Cambridge, Mass. (Dec. 2, 1975); David Baltimore,* professor of biology at the Massachusetts Institute of Technology, Cambridge, Mass.; Har Gobind Khorana,* professor of biochemistry, and Alexander Rich, professor of biophysics — both at the Massachusetts Institute of Technology, Cambridge, Mass. (Apr. 17, 1978).

Charles Townes,* professor emeritus of physics at the University of California at Berkeley (Jan. 26, 1983). Beatrice Mintz, senior member of the Cancer Research Institute of Philadelphia and Maxine Singer, biochemist, president of Carnegie Institution, Washington, D.C. (June 9, 1986).

Roald Z. Sagdeev, professor of physics at University of Maryland, College Park and Peter Hamilton Raven, professor of biology at the Missouri Botanical Garden of St. Louis, Mo. (Oct 4, 1990); Luis Angel Caffarelli, professor of mathematics at New York University and Luigi Luca Cavalli-Sforza, professor of genetics at Stanford University (Aug. 2, 1994).

Joshua Lederberg, professor of genetics at Rockefeller Univ., New York (Mar. 4, 1996), Joseph Edward Murray, professor of plastic surgery at Harvard Medical School, Cambridge, Mass., Paul Berg, professor of biochemistry at Stanford Univ. and Vera C. Rubin, professor of astronomy at Carnegie

Institution of Washington (June 25, 1996); Gary S. Becker,* professor of economics at the University of Chicago (Mar. 3, 1997); Chen-ning Yang,* professor of physics and director of the Institute of Theoretical Physics at the State University of New York at Stoney Brook (Apr. 18,1997); Frank Press, professor of geophysics and director of the Washington Advisory Group (Sept. 3, 1999); Ahmed Zewail, professor of Chemistry and Physics, California Institute of Technology of Pasadena (Sept. 3, 1999); Mario Jose Molina, professor of atmospheric chemistry at the Massachusetts Institute of Technology (Nov. 9, 2000); Günter Blobel,* professor of cellular biology of the Rockefeller University of New York (Sept. 28, 2001). There are also two honorary members from the U.S.: Stanley L, Jaki, O.S.B., professor of physics, history and philosophy at Seton Hall University, South Orange (Sept. 5, 1990) and Robert J. White, professor of neurosurgery at Case Western Reserve University, Cleveland (Mar. 29, 1994).

Members in Other Countries

Listing includes place and date of selection. Nobel prizewinners are indicated by an asterisk.

Armenia: Rudolf M. Muradian (Oct. 16, 1994).

Austria: Hans Tuppy (Apr. 10, 1970); Walter Thirring (June 9, 1986).

Belgium: Paul Adriaan Jan Janssen (June 25, 1990); Thierry Boon-Falleur (Apr. 9, 2002).

Brazil: Carlos Chagas, former president of the academy (Aug. 18, 1961); Johanna Döbereiner (Apr. 17, 1978); Crodowaldo Pavan (Apr. 17, 1978); Rudolf Muradian (Oct. 16, 1994).

Canada: John Charles Polanyi* (June 9, 1986).

Chile: Héctor Rezzio Croxatto (Dec. 2, 1975); Rafael Vicuna (Nov. 10, 2000).

Congo (formerly Zaire): Felix wa Kalengo Malu (Sept. 26, 1983).

Denmark: Aage Bohr* (Apr. 17, 1978).

France: André Blanc-LaPierre (Apr. 17, 1978); Paul Germain (June 9, 1986); Jacques-Louis Lions (Oct. 4, 1990), Jean-Marie Lehn (May 30, 1996); Claude Cohen-Tannoudji (May 17, 1999); Nicole M. Le Douarin (Sept. 3, 1999); Pierre Jean Léna (Jan. 18, 2001).

Germany: Rudolf L. Mössbauer* (Apr. 10, 1970); Manfred Eigen* (May 12, 1981); Wolf Joachim Singer (Sept. 18, 1992), Paul Joseph Crutzen (June 25, 1996), Yuri Ivanovich Manin (June 26, 1996).

Ghana: Daniel Adzei Bekoe (Sept. 26, 1983).

Great Britain: Hermann Alexander Brück (Apr. 5, 1955); George Porter* (June 24, 1974); Max Ferdinand Perutz* (May 12, 1981); Stephen William Hawking (Jan. 9, 1986); Martin John Rees (June 25, 1990); Sir Richard Southwood (Sept. 18, 1992); Raymond Hide (June 25, 1996).

India: Mambillikalathil Govind Kumar Menon (May 12, 1981); Chintamani N.R. Rao (June 25, 1990).

Israel: Michael Sela (Dec. 2, 1975).

Italy: Giampietro Puppi (Apr. 17, 1978); Nicola Cabibbo (June 9, 1986), President; Nicola Dallaporta (Oct. 5, 1989; honorary member); Bernardo Maria Colombo (Sept. 18, 1992); Antonino Zichichi (Nov. 9, 2000); Enrico Berti (Sept. 28, 2001).

Japan: Minoru Oda (Sept. 18, 1992).

Kenya: Thomas R. Odhiambo (May 12, 1981).

Mexico: Marcos Moshinsky (June 9, 1986).

Nigeria: Thomas Adeoye Lambo (June 24, 1974).

Poland: Stanislaw Lojasiewicz (Jan. 28, 1983); Czeslaw Olech (June 9, 1986); Michal Heller (Oct. 4, 1990); Andrzej Szezeklik (Oct. 16, 1994).

Russia: Vladimir Isaakovich Keilis-Borok (Oct. 16, 1994); Sergei Petrovich Novikov (June 25, 1996; also teaches at University of Maryland, U.S.A.).

Spain: Manuel Lora-Tamayo (Sept. 24, 1964).

Sweden: Sune Bergström* (Dec. 14, 1985); Kai Siegbahn* (Dec. 14, 1985).

Switzerland: Werner Arber* (May 12, 1981); Carlo Rubbia* (Dec. 14, 1985); Albert Eschenmoser (June 9, 1986).

Taiwan: Te-tzu Chang (Apr. 18, 1997).

Vatican City State: Cottier, Rev. George, O.P. (Oct. 28, 1992; honorary member); Rev. Enrico do Rovasenda, O.P. (Nov. 13, 1968; honorary member).

Venezuela: Marcel Roche (Apr. 10, 1970).

Ex officio members: Rev. George V. Coyne, S.J., director of Vatican Observatory (Sept. 2, 1978); Very Rev. Raffaele Farina, S.D.B., prefect of the Vatican Library (May 24, 1997); Very Rev. Sergio B. Pagano, prefect of the Secret Vatican Archives (Jan. 7, 1997). President: Nicola Cabibbo, professor of theoretical physics at Univ. of Rome (app. Apr. 6, 1993). Chancellor: Most Rev. Marcelo Sánchez Sorondo.

Honorary members: Cardinal Joseph Ratzinger, Prefect of the Congregation for the Doctrine of the Faith and Cardinal Carlo Maria Martini, Archbishop of Milan.

PONTIFICAL ACADEMY OF SOCIAL SCIENCES

Founded by John Paul II, Jan. 1, 1994 (*motu proprio Socialium scientiarum investigationes*), to promote the study and the progress of social sciences, to advise the Vatican on social concerns and to foster research aimed at improving society. The number of members is not less than 20 nor more than 40. Two of the thirty members of the Academy (as of Jan. 1, 2002) were from the United States: Kenneth J. Arrow of Stanford University and Mary Ann Glendon of Harvard University. President, Prof. Edmond Malinvaud of France; Chancellor, Most Rev. Marcelo Sánchez Sorondo. Address: Casino Pio IV, Vatican Gardens.

PONTIFICAL ACADEMY FOR LIFE

Established by John Paul II, Feb. 11, 1994 (*motu proprio Vitae Mysterium*), "to fulfill the specific task of study, information and formation on the principal problems of biomedicine and law relative to the promotion and defense of life, especially in the direct relationship they have with Christian morality and the directives of the Church's magisterium."

Members, appointed by the Pope without regard to religion or nationality, represent the various branches of "the biomedical sciences and those that are most closely related to problems concerning the promotion and protection of life." Membership, as of Jan. 1, 2002, included seven from the United States:

Prof. Carl Anderson, Vice-President of the Pontifical John Paul II Institute for Studies of Marriage and the Family; Mrs. Mercedes Arzu-Wilson, founder and president of the Foundations Family of the Americas and founder and director of the Commission at the World Organization for the Family; Dr. Thomas Hilgers, founder and director of the Institute "Paul VI,"

Omaha, Neb.; Mrs. Christine de Vollmer, president of the World Organization for the Family; Dr. Denis Cavanaugh, professor of obstetrics and gynecology at the University of South Florida College of Medicine; Prof. John M. Finnis, professor of philosophy of law, University of Oxford and Notre Dame University; Prof. Edmund Pellegrino, director of the Center for Advanced Studies in Ethics at Georgetown University, Washington, D.C., honorary member; President: Prof. Juan de Dios Vial Correa, physician and biologist.

EXCERPTS FROM THE MESSAGE OF HIS HOLINESS POPE JOHN PAUL II FOR THE CELEBRATION OF THE WORLD DAY OF PEACE

"No Peace Without Justice, No Justice Without Forgiveness"

The World Day of Peace (Jan. 1, 2002) this year is being celebrated in the shadow of the dramatic events of 11 September last. On that day, a terrible crime was committed: in a few brief hours thousands of innocent people of many ethnic backgrounds were slaughtered. Since then, people throughout the world have felt a profound personal vulnerability and a new fear for the future. Addressing this state of mind, the Church testifies to her hope, based on the conviction that evil, the *mysterium iniquitatis,* does not have the final word in human affairs....

Peace: the work of justice and love

... I have often paused to reflect on the persistent question: *how do we restore the moral and social order subjected to such horrific violence?* My reasoned conviction, confirmed in turn by biblical revelation, is that the shattered order cannot be fully restored except by a response that combines justice with forgiveness. *The pillars of true peace are justice and that form of love which is forgiveness.*

But in the present circumstances, how can we speak of justice and forgiveness as the source and condition of peace? *We can and we must,* no matter how difficult this may be.... But forgiveness is the opposite of resentment and revenge, not of justice....

True peace therefore is the fruit of justice, that moral virtue and legal guarantee which ensures full respect for rights and responsibilities, and the just distribution of benefits and burdens. But because human justice is always fragile and imperfect, subject as it is to the limitations and egoism of individuals and groups, it must include and, as it were, be completed by the *forgiveness which heals and rebuilds troubled human relations from their foundations....*

... The World Day of Peace this year offers all humanity, and particularly the leaders of nations, the opportunity to reflect upon the demands of justice and the call to forgiveness in the face of the grave problems which continue to afflict the world, not the least of which is *the new level of violence introduced by organized terrorism.*

The reality of terrorism

It is precisely peace born of justice and forgiveness that is under assault today by international terrorism....

...Terrorism springs from hatred, and it generates isolation, mistrust and closure. Violence is added to violence in a tragic sequence that exasperates successive generations, each one inheriting the hatred which divided those that went before. *Terrorism is built on contempt for human life....* It is itself *a true crime against humanity.*

There exists therefore a right to defend oneself against terrorism, a right which, as always, must be exercised with respect for moral and legal limits in the choice of ends and means.... International cooperation in the fight against terrorist activities must also include a courageous and resolute political, diplomatic and economic commitment to relieving situations of oppression and marginalization which facilitate the designs of terrorists....

You shall not kill in God's name!

...Terrorists hold that the truth in which they believe or the suffering that they have undergone are so absolute that their reaction in destroying even innocent lives is justified. ... *Terrorism exploits not just people, it exploits God:* it ends by making him an idol to be used for one's own purposes.

Consequently, no religious leader can condone terrorism, and much less preach it. It is a profanation of religion to declare oneself a terrorist in the name of God, to do violence to others in his name....

The need for forgiveness

But what does forgiveness actually mean? And why should we forgive? A reflection on forgiveness cannot avoid these questions. Returning to what I wrote in my Message for the 1997 World Day of Peace ("Offer Forgiveness and Receive Peace"), I would reaffirm that forgiveness inhabits people's hearts before it becomes a social reality....

Forgiveness, the high road

... Forgiveness in fact always involves an *apparent* short-term loss for a *real* long-term gain. Violence is the exact opposite; opting as it does for an apparent short-term gain, it involves a real and permanent loss....

Interreligious understanding and cooperation

... The various Christian confessions, as well as the world's great religions, need to work together to eliminate the social and cultural causes of terrorism. They can do this by teaching the greatness and dignity of the human person, and by spreading *a clearer sense of the oneness of the human family....*

In particular, I am convinced that Jewish, Christian and Islamic religious leaders must now take the lead in publicly condemning terrorism and in denying terrorists any form of religious or moral legitimacy....

Prayer for peace

No peace without justice, no justice without forgiveness: this is what in this Message I wish to say to believers and non-believers alike, to all men and women of good will who are concerned for the good of the human family and for its future....

From the Vatican, Dec. 8, 2001

Hierarchy of the Catholic Church

ORGANIZATION AND GOVERNMENT

As a structured society, the Catholic Church is organized and governed along lines corresponding mainly to the jurisdictions of the pope and Bishops. The pope is the supreme head of the Church. He has primacy of jurisdiction as well as honor over the entire Church. Bishops, in union with and in subordination to the pope, are the successors of the Apostles for care of the Church and for the continuation of Christ's mission in the world. They serve the people of their own dioceses, or particular churches, with ordinary authority and jurisdiction. They also share, with the pope and each other, common concern and effort for the general welfare of the whole Church.

Bishops of exceptional status are patriarchs of Eastern Catholic Churches who, subject only to the pope, are heads of the faithful belonging to their rites throughout the world.

Subject to the Holy Father and directly responsible to him for the exercise of their ministry of service to people in various jurisdictions or divisions of the Church throughout the world are: resident archbishops and metropolitans (heads of archdioceses), diocesan bishops, vicars and prefects apostolic (heads of vicariates apostolic and prefectures apostolic), certain abbots and prelates, apostolic administrators. Each of these, within his respective territory and according to the provisions of canon law, has ordinary jurisdiction over pastors (who are responsible for the administration of parishes), priests, religious and lay persons.

Also subject to the Holy Father are titular archbishops and bishops, religious orders and congregations of pontifical right, pontifical institutes and faculties, papal nuncios and apostolic delegates.

Assisting the pope and acting in his name in the central government and administration of the Church are cardinals and other officials of the Roman Curia.

THE HIERARCHY

The ministerial hierarchy is the orderly arrangement of the ranks and orders of the clergy to provide for the spiritual care of the faithful, the government of the Church, and the accomplishment of the Church's total mission in the world.

Persons belong to this hierarchy by virtue of ordination and canonical mission.

The term hierarchy is also used to designate an entire body or group of bishops; for example, the hierarchy of the Church, the hierarchy of the United States.

Hierarchy of Order: Consists of the pope, bishops, priests and deacons. Their purpose, for which they are ordained to holy orders, is to carry out the sacramental and pastoral ministry of the Church.

Hierarchy of Jurisdiction: Consists of the pope and bishops by divine institution, and other church officials by ecclesiastical institution and mandate, who have authority to govern and direct the faithful for spiritual ends.

The Pope

His Holiness the Pope is the Bishop of Rome, Vicar of Jesus Christ, successor of St. Peter, Prince of the Apostles, Supreme Pontiff of the Universal Church, Patriarch of the West, Primate of Italy, Archbishop and Metropolitan of the Roman Province, Sovereign of the State of Vatican City, Servant of the Servants of God.

Cardinals
(See Index)

Patriarchs

Patriarch, a term which had its origin in the Eastern Church, is the title of a bishop who, second only to the pope, has the highest rank in the hierarchy of jurisdiction. He is the incumbent of one of the sees listed below. Subject only to the pope, a patriarch of the Eastern Church is the head of the faithful belonging to his rite throughout the world. The patriarchal sees are so called because of their special status and dignity in the history of the Church.

The Council of Nicaea (325) recognized three patriarchs — the Bishops of Alexandria and Antioch in the East, and of Rome in the West. The First Council of Constantinople (381) added the bishop of Constantinople to the list of patriarchs and gave him rank second only to that of the pope, the bishop of Rome and patriarch of the West; this action was seconded by the Council of Chalcedon (451) and was given full recognition by the Fourth Lateran Council (1215). The Council of Chalcedon also acknowledged patriarchal rights of the bishop of Jerusalem.

Eastern patriarchs are as follows: one of Alexandria, for the Copts; three of Antioch, one each for the Syrians, Maronites and Greek Melkites (the latter also has the personal title of Greek Melkite patriarch of Alexandria and of Jerusalem). The patriarch of

Babylonia, for the Chaldeans, and the patriarch of Sis, or Cilicia, for the Armenians, should be called, more properly, *Katholikos* — that is, a prelate delegated for a universality of causes. These patriarchs are elected by bishops of their churches: they receive approval and the pallium, symbol of their office, from the pope.

Latin Rite patriarchates were established for Antioch, Jerusalem, Alexandria and Constantinople during the Crusades; afterwards, they became patriarchates in name only. Jerusalem, however, was reconstituted as a patriarchate by Pius IX, in virtue of the bull *Nulla Celebrior* of July 23, 1847. In 1964, the Latin titular patriarchates of Constantinople, Alexandria and Antioch, long a bone of contention in relations with Eastern Churches, were abolished.

As of Aug. 15, 2002, the patriarchs in the Church were:

The Pope, Bishop of Rome, Patriarch of the West; Cardinal Stephanos II Ghattas, C.M., of Alexandria, for the Copts; Ignace Pierre VIII Abdel-Ahad, of Antioch, for the Syrians; Gregory III Laham, of Antioch, for the Greek Melkites (the patriarch also has personal titles of Alexandria and Jerusalem for the Greek Melkites); Cardinal Nasrallah Pierre Sfeir, of Antioch, for the Maronites; Michael Sabbah, of Jerusalem, for the Latin Rite; Raphaël I Bidawid, of Babylon, for the Chaldeans; Nerses Bedros XIX Tarmouni, of Cilicia, for the Armenians. (For biographical information on the patriarchs, please under the **Eastern Catholic** section.)

The titular patriarchs (in name only) of the Latin Rite were: Cardinal José da Cruz Policarpo of Lisbon; Archbishop Angelo Scola of Venice; Archbishop Raul Nicolau Gonsalves of the East Indies (archbishop of Goa and Damao, India); and Archbishop Michel Sabbah of Jerusalem. The patriarchate of the West Indies has been vacant since 1963.

Major Archbishops

An archbishop with the prerogatives but not the title of a patriarch. As of May 15, 2002, there were two major archbishops: Cardinal Lubomyr Husar of the major archbishopric of Lviv of the Ukrainian Catholic Church (Ukraine) and Cardinal Varkey Vithayathil, C.SS.R. of the major archbishopric of Ernakulam-Angomaly of the Syro-Malabar Church (India).

Archbishops, Metropolitans

Archbishop: A bishop with the title of an archdiocese.

Coadjutor Archbishop: An assistant archbishop with right of succession.

Metropolitan: Archbishop of the principal see, an archdiocese, in an ecclesiastical province consisting of several dioceses. He has the full powers of bishop in his own archdiocese and limited supervisory jurisdiction and influence over the other (suffragan) dioceses in the province. The pallium, conferred by the pope, is the symbol of his status as a metropolitan.

Titular Archbishop: Has the title of an archdiocese that formerly existed in fact but now exists in title only. He does not have ordinary jurisdiction over an archdiocese. Examples are archbishops in the Roman Curia, papal nuncios, apostolic delegates.

Archbishop *ad personam*: A title of personal honor and distinction granted to some bishops. They do not

have ordinary jurisdiction over an archdiocese.

Primate: A title of honor given to the ranking prelate of some countries or regions.

Bishops

Diocesan Bishop: A bishop in charge of a diocese.

Coadjutor Bishop: An assistant (auxiliary) bishop to a diocesan bishop, with right of succession to the see.

Titular Bishops: A bishop with the title of a diocese that formerly existed in fact but now exists in title only; an assistant (auxiliary) bishop to a diocesan bishop.

Episcopal Vicar: An assistant, who may or may not be a bishop, appointed by a residential bishop as his deputy for a certain part of a diocese, a determined type of apostolic work, or the faithful of a certain rite.

Eparch, Exarch: Titles of bishops of Eastern churches.

Nomination of Bishops: Nominees for episcopal ordination are selected in several ways. Final appointment and/or approval in all cases is subject to decision by the pope.

In the U.S., bishops periodically submit the names of candidates to the archbishop of their province. The name are then considered at a meeting of the Bishops of the province, and those receiving a favorable vote are forwarded to the pro-nuncio for transmission to the Holy See. Normally, three names are submitted. Bishops are free to seek the counsel of priests, religious and lay persons with respect to nominees.

Eastern Catholic churches have their own procedures and synodal regulations for nominating and making final selection of candidates for episcopal ordination. Such selection is subject to approval by the pope. The Code of Canon Law concedes no rights or privileges to civil authorities with respect to the election, nomination, presentation or designation of candidates for the episcopate.

***Ad Limina* Visit:** Diocesan bishops and apostolic vicars are obliged to make an *ad limina* visit ("to the threshold" of the Apostles) every five years to the tombs of Sts. Peter and Paul, have audience with the Holy Father and consult with appropriate Vatican officials. They are required to send a report on conditions in their jurisdiction to the Congregation for bishops approximately six — and not less than three — months in advance of the scheduled visit.

Others with Ordinary Jurisdiction

Ordinary: One who has the jurisdiction of an office: the pope, diocesan bishops, vicars general, prelates of missionary territories, vicars apostolic prefects apostolic, vicars capitular during the vacancy of a see, superiors general, abbots primate and other major superiors of men religious.

Some prelates and abbots, with jurisdiction like that of diocesan bishops, are pastors of the people of God in territories (prelatures and abbacies) not under the jurisdiction of diocesan bishops.

Vicar Apostolic: Usually a titular bishop who has ordinary jurisdiction over a mission territory.

Prefect Apostolic: Has ordinary jurisdiction over a mission territory.

Apostolic Administrator: Usually a bishop appointed to administer an ecclesiastical jurisdiction temporarily. Administrators of lesser rank are also appointed on occasion and have more restricted supervisory duties.

Vicar General: A bishop's deputy for the administration of a diocese. Such a vicar does not have to be a bishop.

Prelates Without Jurisdiction

The title of protonotary apostolic was originally given by the fourth century or earlier to clergy who collected accounts of martyrdom and other church documents, or who served the Church with distinction in other ways. Other titles — e.g., domestic prelate, papal chamberlain, prelate of honor — are titles of clergy in service to the pope and the papal household, or of clergy honored for particular reasons. All prelates without jurisdiction are appointed by the pope, have designated ceremonial privileges and the title of Rev. Monsignor.

SYNOD OF BISHOPS

The Synod of Bishops was chartered by Pope Paul VI Sept. 15, 1965, in a document he issued on his own initiative under the title, *Apostolica Sollicitudo*. Provisions of this *motu proprio* are contained in Canons 342 to 348 of the Code of Canon Law. According to major provisions of the Synod charter:

• The purposes of the Synod are: "to encourage close union and valued assistance between the Sovereign Pontiff and the Bishops of the entire world; to insure that direct and real information is provided on questions and situations touching upon the internal action of the Church and its necessary activity in the world of today; to facilitate agreement on essential points of doctrine and on methods of procedure in the life of the Church."

• The Synod is a central ecclesiastical institution, permanent by nature.

• The Synod is directly and immediately subject to the Pope, who has authority to assign its agenda, to call it into session, and to give its members deliberative as well as advisory authority.

• In addition to a limited number of ex officio members and a few heads of male religious institutes, the majority of the members are elected by and representative of national or regional episcopal conferences. The Pope reserved the right to appoint the general secretary, special secretaries and no more than 15 per cent of the total membership.

The Pope is president of the Synod. The secretary general is Cardinal Jan Schotte, C.I.C.M., of Belgium. Address: Palazzo del Bramante, Via della Concilizione 34, 00193 Rome, Italy.

An advisory council of 15 members (12 elected, three appointed by the pope) provides the secretariat with adequate staff for carrying on liaison with episcopal conferences and for preparing the agenda of synodal assemblies. Cardinal William H, Keeler, archbishop of Baltimore, is a member of the secretariat.

Assemblies

1. First Assembly: The first assembly was held from Sept. 29 to Oct. 29, 1967. Its objectives, as stated by Pope Paul VI, were "the preservation and strengthening of the Catholic faith, its integrity, its force, its development, its doctrinal and historical coherence." One result was a recommendation for the establishment of an international commission of theologians to assist the Congregation for the Doctrine of the Faith and to broaden approaches to theological research. Pope Paul set up the commission in 1969.

2. Pope-Bishop Relations: The second assembly held Oct. 11 to 28, 1969, was extraordinary in character. It opened the way toward greater participation by bishops with the pope and each other in the governance of the Church. Proceedings were oriented to three main points: (1) the nature and implications of collegiality; (2) the relationship of bishops and their conferences to the pope; (3) the relationships of bishops and their conferences to each other.

3. Priesthood and Justice: The ministerial priesthood and justice in the world were the principal topics under discussion at the second ordinary assembly, Sept. 30 to Nov. 6, 1971. In one report, the Synod emphasized the primary and permanent dedication of priests in the Church to the ministry of word, sacrament and pastoral service as a full-time vocation. In another report, the assembly stated: "Action on behalf of justice and participation in the transformation of the world fully appear to us as a constitutive dimension of the preaching of the Gospel; or, in other words, of the Church's mission for the redemption of the human race and its liberation from every oppressive situation."

4. Evangelization: The assembly of Sept. 27 to Oct. 26, 1974, produced a general statement on evangelization of the modern world, covering the need for it and its relationship to efforts for total human liberation from personal and social evil. The assembly observed: "The Church does not remain within merely political, social and economic limits (elements which she must certainly take into account) but leads towards freedom under all its forms — liberation from sin, from individual or collective selfishness — and to full communion with God and with men who are like brothers. In this way the Church, in her evangelical way, promotes the true and complete liberation of all men, groups and peoples."

5. Catechetics: The fourth ordinary assembly, Sept. 30 to Oct. 29, 1977, focused attention on catechetics, with special reference to children and young people. The participants issued a "Message to the People of God," the first synodal statement issued since inception of the body, and also presented to Pope Paul VI a set of 34 related propositions and a number of suggestions.

6. Family: "A Message to Christian Families in the Modern World" and a proposal for a "Charter of Family Rights" were produced by the assembly held Sept. 26 to Oct. 25, 1980. The assembly reaffirmed the indissolubility of marriage and the contents of the encyclical letter *Humanae Vitae* (see separate entry), and urged married couples who find it hard to live up to "the difficult but loving demands" of Christ not to be discouraged but to avail themselves of the aid of divine grace. In response to synodal recommendation, Pope John Paul issued a charter of family rights late in 1983.

7. Reconciliation: Penance and reconciliation in the mission of the Church was the theme of the assembly held Sept. 29 to Oct. 29, 1983. Sixty-three propositions related to this theme were formulated on a wide variety of subjects, including: personal sin and so-called systemic or institutional sin; the nature of serious sin; the diminished sense of sin and of the need of redemption, related to decline in the administration and reception of the sacrament of penance; general absolution; individual and social reconciliation; violence and violations of human rights; reconciliation as the basis of peace and justice in society. In a statement issued Oct. 27, the Synod stressed the need of the world to become, increasingly, "a reconciled community of peoples," and said that "the Church, as sacrament of reconciliation to the world, has to be an effective sign of God's mercy."

8. Vatican II Review: The second extraordinary assembly was convened Nov. 24 to Dec. 8, 1985, for the purposes of: recalling the Second Vatican Council; evaluating the implementation of its enactments during the 20 years since its conclusion; and seeking ways and means of promoting renewal in the Church in accordance with the spirit and letter of the council. At the conclusion of the assembly the bishops issued two documents. In "A Message to the People of God," they noted the need for greater appreciation of the enactments of Vatican II and for greater efforts to put them into effect, so that all members of the Church might discharge their responsibility of proclaiming the good news of salvation. In a "Final Report," the first of its kind published by a synodal assembly, the bishops reflected on lights and shadows since Vatican II, stating that negative developments had come from partial and superficial interpretations of conciliar enactments and from incomplete or ineffective implementation thereof. The report also covered a considerable number of subjects discussed during the assembly, including the mystery of the Church, inculturation, the preferential (but not exclusive) option for the poor, and a suggestion for the development of a new universal catechism of the Catholic faith.

9. Vocation and Mission of the Laity in the Church and in the World 20 years after the Second Vatican Council: The seventh ordinary assembly, Oct. 1 to 30, 1987, said in a "Message to the People of God": "The majority of the Christian laity live out their vocation as followers and disciples of Christ in all spheres of life which we call 'the world': the family, the field of work, the local community and the like. To permeate this day-to-day living with the spirit of Christ has always been the task of the lay faithful; and it should be with still greater force their challenge today. It is in this way that they sanctify the world and collaborate in the realization of the kingdom of God." The assembly produced a set of 54 propositions which were presented to the Pope for consideration in the preparation of a document of his own on the theme of the assembly. He

responded with the apostolic exhortation, *Christifideles Laici*, "The Christian Faithful Laity," released by the Vatican Jan. 30, 1989.

10. Formation of Priests in Circumstances of the Present Day: The eighth general assembly, Sept. 30 to Oct. 28, 1990, dealt principally with the nature and mission of the priesthood; the identity, multi-faceted formation and spirituality of priests; and, in a "Message to the People of God," the need on all levels of the Church for the promotion of vocations to the priesthood. Forty-one proposals were presented to the Pope for his consideration in preparing a document of his own on the theme of the assembly. Pope John Paul issued an apostolic exhortation entitled *Pastores Dabo Vobis* ("I Will Give You Shepherds") Apr. 7, 1992, in response to the Synods' recommendations.

11. The Consecrated Life and Its Role in the Church and in the World: The ninth general assembly was held Oct. 2 to 29, 1994. Pope John Paul's reflections on the proceedings of the assembly and the recommendations of the Bishops were the subjects of his apostolic exhortation entitled *Vita Consecrata* ("Consecrated Life"), issued Mar. 25, 1996. The document dealt with various forms of consecrated life: contemplative institutes, apostolic religious life, secular institutes, societies of apostolic life, mixed institutes and new forms of evangelical life.

12. The Bishop: Servant of the Gospel of Jesus Christ for the Hope of the World: The tenth ordinary general assembly was held from September 30 to October 27, 2001. Pope John Paul II's reflections on the proceedings of the assembly and the recommendations of the Bishops will be the subject of an apostolic exhortation.

Recent special assemblies of the Synod of Bishops: Special Synods have been held for Europe (Nov. 28 to Dec. 14, 1991; on the theme "So that we might be witnesses of Christ who has set us free"); for Africa (Apr. 10 to May 8, 1994; on the theme "The Church in Africa and Her Evangelizing Mission Towards the Year 2000: 'You Shall Be My Witnesses' (Acts 1:8)"); for Lebanon (Nov. 27 to Dec. 14, 1995; on the theme "Christ is Our Hope: Renewed by His Spirit, in Solidarity We Bear Witness to His Love"); the Americas (Nov. 16 to Dec. 12, 1997; on the theme, "Encounter with the Living Jesus Christ: Way to Conversion, Community and Solidarity"); for Asia (Apr. 19 to May 14, 1998 on the theme "Jesus Christ the Savior and His Mission of Love and Service in Asia: '... That They May Have Life, and Have it Abundantly' (Jn. 10:10)"); for Oceania (Nov. 12 to Dec. 12, 1998, with the theme "Jesus Christ and the Peoples of Oceania: Walking His Way, Telling His Truth, Living His Life"); and a special assembly for Europe (Oct. 1 to 23, 1999), on the theme "Jesus Christ, Alive in His Church, Source of Hope for Europe."

COLLEGE OF CARDINALS

Cardinals are chosen by the pope to serve as his principal assistants and advisers in the central administration of church affairs. Collectively, they form the College of Cardinals. Provisions regarding their selection, rank, roles and prerogatives are detailed in Canons 349 to 359 of the Code of Canon Law.

History of the College

The College of Cardinals was constituted in its present form and categories of membership in the 12th century. Before that time the pope had a body of advisers selected from among the bishops of dioceses neighboring Rome, priests and deacons of Rome. The college was given definite form in 1150, and in 1179 the selection of cardinals was reserved exclusively to the pope. Sixtus V fixed the number at 70, in 1586. John XXIII set aside this rule when he increased membership at the 1959 and subsequent consistories. The number was subsequently raised by Paul VI and by John Paul II. The number of cardinals entitled to participate in papal elections was limited to 120 by Paul VI in 1973. The limit on the number of cardinals was set aside by Pope John Paul II twice, in 1998 and again in 2001. As of Aug. 15, 2002, 118 of the 174 cardinals were eligible to vote.

In 1567 the title of cardinal was reserved to members of the college; previously it had been used by priests attached to parish churches of Rome and by the leading clergy of other notable churches. The Code of Canon Law promulgated in 1918 decreed that all cardinals must be priests. Previously there had been cardinals who were not priests (e.g., Cardinal Giacomo Antonelli, d. 1876, Secretary of State to Pius IX, was a deacon). John XXIII provided in the *motu proprio Cum Gravissima* Apr. 15, 1962, that cardinals would henceforth be bishops; this provision is included in the revised Code of Canon Law.

Age Limits

Pope Paul VI placed age limits on the functions of cardinals in the apostolic letter *Ingravescentem Aetatem,* dated Nov. 21, 1970, and effective as of Jan. 1, 1971. At 80, they cease to be members of curial departments and offices, and become ineligible to take part in papal elections. They retain membership in the College of Cardinals, however, with relevant rights and privileges.

Three Categories

All cardinals except Eastern patriarchs are aggregated to the clergy of Rome. This aggregation is signified by the assignment to each cardinal, except the patriarchs, of a titular church in Rome. The three categories of members of the college are cardinal Bishops, cardinal priests and cardinal deacons.

Cardinal Bishops include the six titular bishops of the suburbicarian sees and Eastern patriarchs. First in rank are the titular bishops of the suburbicarian sees, neighboring Rome: Ostia, Palestrina, Porto-Santa Rufina, Albano, Velletri-Segni, Frascati, Sabina-Poggio Mirteto. The dean of the college holds the title of the See of Ostia as well as his other suburbicarian see. These cardinal bishops are engaged in full-time service in the central administration of church affairs in departments of the Roman Curia.

Full recognition is given in the revised Code of Canon Law to the position of Eastern patriarchs as the heads of sees of apostolic origin with ancient liturgies. They are assigned rank among the cardinals in order of seniority, following the suburbicarian titleholders.

Cardinal priests, who were formerly in charge of leading churches in Rome, are bishops whose dioceses are outside Rome.

Cardinal deacons, who were formerly chosen according to regional divisions of Rome, are titular bishops assigned to full-time service in the Roman Curia.

The dean and sub-dean of the college are elected by the cardinal bishops — subject to approval by the pope — from among their number. The dean, or the sub-dean in his absence, presides over the college as the first among equals. Cardinals Bernardin Gantin, June 4, 1993 (papal approval June 5, 1993), and Joseph Ratzinger, Nov. 6, 1998 (papal approval Nov. 9, 1998), were elected dean and vice-dean, respectively. The Secretary to the College of Cardinals is Archbishop Francesco Monterisi.

Selection and Duties

Cardinals are selected by the pope and are inducted into the college in appropriate ceremonies. Cardinals under the age of 80: elect the pope when the Holy See becomes vacant (see Index: Papal Election); and are major administrators of church affairs, serving in one or more departments of the Roman Curia. Cardinals in charge of agencies of the Roman Curia and Vatican City are asked to submit their resignation from office to the pope on reaching the age of 75. All cardinals enjoy a number of special rights and privileges. Their title, while symbolic of high honor, does not signify any extension of the powers of holy orders. They are called princes of the Church.

A cardinal *in pectore (petto)* is one whose selection has been made by the pope but whose name has not been disclosed; he has no title, rights or duties until such disclosure is made, at which time he takes precedence from the time of the secret selection.

BIOGRAPHIES OF CARDINALS

Biographies of the cardinals, as of Aug. 15, 2002, are given below in alphabetical order. For historical notes, order of seniority and geographical distribution of cardinals, see separate entries. An asterisk indicates cardinals ineligible to take part in papal elections.

Agré, Bernard: b. March 2, 1926, Monga, Côte d'Ivoire; ord. priest, July 20, 1953; headmaster in Dabou; vicar general of Abidjan archdiocese; app. bp. of Man, June 8, 1968; app. first bp. of Yamoussoukro, March 6, 1992; app. abp. of Abidjan, Dec. 19, 1994; pres. of the Episcopal Conferences of Francophone West Africa (CERAO) and chair of the Pan-African Episcopal Committee for Social Communications (CEPACS); cardinal, Feb. 21, 2001; titular church, St. John Chrysostom in Monte Sacro Alto. Abp. of Abidjan. *Curial membership:* Evangelization of Peoples (congregation); Justice and Peace, Family, Social Communications (councils).

Agustoni,* Gilberto: b. July 26, 1922, Schaffhausen, Switzerland; ord. priest Apr. 20, 1946; called to Rome in 1950 to work under Cardinal Ottaviani in the Congregation for the Holy Office; a Prelate Auditor of the Roman Rota, 1970-86; ord. titular abp. of Caorle, Jan. 6, 1987; sec. of the Congregation for the Clergy, 1986-92; pro-prefect of the Apostolic Signatura, 1992-94; cardinal Nov. 26, 1994; deacon Sts. Urban and Laurence at Prima Porta. Prefect of Supreme Tribunal of Apostolic Signatura, 1994-98. Prefect emeritus of Supreme Tribunal of Apostolic Signatura. *Curial membership:* Bishops, Education (congregations); Supreme Tribunal of the Apostolic Signatura (tribunal); Interpretation of Legislative Texts (council); APSA (office).

Álvarez Martínez, Francisco: b. July 14, 1925, Santa Eulalia de Ferroñes Llanera, Spain; ord. priest, June 11, 1950; personal secretary to Abp. Lauzurica y Torralba of Oviedo; chancellor and secretary of archdiocesan curia; chaplain of the university students at Teresian Institute; app. bp. of Tarazona, April 13, 1973; cons., June 3, 1973; bp. of Calahorra and La Calzado-Logroño, Dec. 20, 1976; transferred to Orihuela-Alicante, May 12, 1989; app. abp. of Toledo, June 23, 1995; member of the Standing Committee and the Executive Committee of the Spanish Episcopal Conference; cardinal, Feb. 21, 2001; titular church, St. Mary *Regina Pacis* in Monte Verde. Abp. of Toledo. *Curial membership:* Christian Unity, Laity (councils).

Ambrozic, Aloysius M.: b. Jan. 27, 1930, Gabrje, Slovenia (emigrated to Austria, 1945, and Canada, 1948); ord. priest, June 4, 1955; taught Scripture, St. Augustine's Seminary, 1960-67; taught NT exegesis, Toronto School of Theology, 1970-76; aux. bp. of Toronto, March 26, 1976; co-adjutor of Toronto, May 22, 1986; abp. of Toronto, March 17, 1990; cardinal, Feb. 21, 1998; titular church, Sts. Marcellinus and Peter. *Curial membership:* Oriental Churches, Sacraments, Clergy (congregation); Pastoral Care of Migrants and Itinerant People, Culture (councils).

Angelini,* Fiorenzo: b. Aug. 1, 1916, Rome, Italy; ord. priest Feb. 3, 1940; master of pontifical ceremonies, 1947-54; ord. bp. (titular see of Messene) July 29, 1956, and head of Rome Vicariate's section for apostolate to health care workers; abp, 1985; pres. of newly established Curia agency for health care workers; cardinal June 28, 1991, deacon, Holy Spirit (in Sassio). President of Pontifical Council for Pastoral Assistance to Health Care Workers, 1986-96.

Antonetti,* Lorenzo: b. July 31, 1922, Romagnano Sesia, Italy; ord. priest, May 26, 1945; entered diplomatic service and served in Lebanon, Venezuela, first section for Extraordinary Affairs of the Secretariat of State, U.S., and France; ord. titular abp. of Roselle, May 12, 1968; apostolic nuncio to Nicaragua and Honduras, 1968-1973, and Zaire, 1973-77; secretary of the Administration of the Patrimony of the Apostolic See (APSA), 1977-88; apostolic nuncio to France, 1988-95; pro-president Admin. of the Patrimony of the Apostolic See, 1995-1998; pres. Administration of the Patrimony of the Apostolic See (APSA)., Feb. 23, 1998; cardinal, Feb. 21, 1998; deaconry, St. Agnes in Agone. President emeritus Administration of the Patrimony of the Apostolic See. *Curial membership:* Evangelization of Peoples (congregations); Economic Affairs of the Holy See, APSA (prefectures); Vatican City (commission).

Aponte Martínez,* Luis: b. Aug. 4, 1922, Lajas, Puerto Rico; ord. priest Apr. 10, 1950; parish priest at Ponce; ord. titular bp. of Lares and aux. of Ponce, Oct. 12, 1960; bp. of Ponce, 1963-64; abp. of San Juan, Nov. 4, 1964-99; cardinal Mar. 5, 1973; titular church, St. Mary Mother of Providence (in Monte Verde). Abp. emeritus of San Juan.

Aramburu,* Juan Carlos: b. Feb. 11, 1912, Reduccion, Argentina; ord. priest in Rome, Oct. 28, 194; ord. titular bp. of Plataea and aux. of Tucuman, Argentina, Dec. 15, 1946; bp., 1953, and first abp., 1957, of Tucuman; titular abp. of Torri di Bizacena and coadj. abp. of Buenos Aires, June 14, 1967; abp. of Buenos Aires, Apr. 22, 1975 (resigned July 10,

1990); cardinal May 24, 1976; titular church, St. John Baptist of the Florentines. Abp. emeritus of Buenos Aires.

Arinze, Francis: b. Nov. 1, 1932, Eziowelle, Nigeria; ord. priest Nov. 23, 1958; ord. titular bp. of Fissiana and aux. bp. of Onitsha, Aug. 29, 1965; abp. of Onitsha, 1967-84; pro-president of Secretariat for Non-Christians (now the Council for Interreligious Dialogue), 1984; cardinal May 25, 1985; deacon, St. John (della Pigna); transferred to the order of cardinal priests Jan. 29, 1996. President of Council for Interreligious Dialogue, 1985. *Curial membership:* Doctrine of the Faith, Oriental Churches, Evangelization of Peoples, Causes of Saints (congregations); Laity, Christian Unity, Culture (councils); International Eucharistic Congresses (committee).

Arns,* Paulo Evaristo, O.F.M.: b. Sept. 14, 1921, Forquilhinha, Brazil; ord. priest Nov. 30, 1945; held various teaching posts; director of *Sponsa Christi*, monthly review for religious, and of the Franciscan publication center in Brazil; ord. titular bp. of Respetta and aux. bp. of São Paulo, July 3, 1966; abp. of São Paulo, Oct. 22, 1970-98; cardinal Mar. 5, 1973, titular church, St. Anthony of Padua (in Via Tuscolana). Abp. emeritus of São Paulo.

Backis, Audrys Juozas: b. Feb. 1, 1937, Kaunas, Lithuania; ord. priest, March 18, 1961; entered Holy See diplomatic service in 1964 and posted to the Philippines, Costa Rica, Turkey, Nigeria, and the Council for the Public Affairs of the Church; underscretary to the Council for the Public Affairs of the Church, 1979-88; app. titular abp. of Meta and nuncio to the Netherlands, Aug. 5, 1988; app. abp. of Vilnius Dec. 24, 1991; pres. of the Lithuanian Bishops' Conference; cardinal, Feb. 21, 2001; titular church, Nativity of Our Lord Jesus Christ in Via Gallia. Abp. of Vilnius. *Curial membership:* Education (congregation); Social Communication (council); Cultural Heritage of the Church (commission).

Bafile,* Corrado: b. July 4, 1903, L'Aquila, Italy; practiced law in Rome for six years before beginning studies for priesthood; ord. priest Apr. 11, 1936; served in Vatican secretariat of state, 1939-59; ord. titular abp. of Antiochia in Pisidia, Mar. 19, 1960; apostolic nuncio to Germany, 1960-75; pro-prefect of Congregation for Causes of Saints, July 18, 1975; cardinal May 24, 1976; deacon, S. Maria (in Portico); transferred to order of cardinal priests, June 22, 1987; prefect of Congregation for Causes of Saints, 1976-80.

Baum, William Wakefield: b. Nov. 21, 1926, Dallas, Tex.; moved to Kansas City, Mo., at an early age; ord. priest (Kansas City-St. Joseph diocese) May 12, 1951; executive director of U.S. Bishops commission for ecumenical and interreligious affairs, 1964-69; attended Second Vatican Council as *peritus* (expert adviser); ord. bp. of Springfield-Cape Girardeau, Mo., Apr. 6, 1970; abp. of Washington, D.C., 1973-80; cardinal May 24, 1976; titular church, Holy Cross on the Via Flaminia; prefect of Congregation for Catholic Education (Seminaries and Institutes of Study), 1980-90. Major Penitentiary, 1990-2001; res. Nov. 22, 2001. *Curial membership:* Bishops, Oriental Churches, Consecrated Life and Societies of Apostolic Life, Evangelization of Peoples (congregations); APSA (office).

Bergoglio, S.J., Jorge Mario: b. Dec. 17, 1936,

Buenos Aires, Argentina; ord. priest for the Jesuits, Dec. 13, 1969; novice master in the Theological Faculty of San Miguel; Jesuit provincial for Argentina, 1973-79; rector of the Philosophical and Theological Faculty of San Miguel, 1980-86; completed doctoral dissertation in Germany and served as confessor and spiritual director in Córdoba; app. titular bp. of Auca and aux. bp. of Buenos Aires, May 20, 1992; cons., June 27, 1992; app. coadj. abp. of Buenos Aires, June 3, 1997; succeeded as abp. of Buenos Aires, Feb. 28, 1998; also serves as Ordinary for Eastern-Rite faithful in Argentina who lack their own ordinary and second vice-pres. of the Argentine Episcopal Conference; cardinal, Feb. 21, 2001; titular church, St. Robert Bellarmine. Abp. of Buenos Aires. *Curial membership*: Sacraments, Clergy, Institutes of Consecrated Life and Societies of Apostolic Life (congregations); Family (council).

Bevilacqua, Anthony Joseph: b. June 17, 1923, Brooklyn N.Y.; ord. priest (Brooklyn diocese) June 11, 1949; ord. titular bp. of Aquae Albae in Byzacena and aux. bp. of Brooklyn, Nov. 24, 1980; bp. of Pittsburgh Oct. 7, 1983, installed Dec. 12, 1983; abp. of Philadelphia, Feb. 11, 1988; cardinal June 28, 1991; titular church, Most Holy Redeemer and St. Alphonsus (on Via Merulana). Abp. of Philadelphia. *Curial membership*: Clergy, Causes of Saints (congregations); "Cor Unum," Migrants and Itinerant People (councils); Institute for Works of Religion (commission).

Biffi, Giacomo: b. June 13, 1928, Milan, Italy; ord. priest Dec. 23, 1950; ord. titular bp. of Fidene and aux. of Milan, Jan. 11, 1976; abp. of Bologna, Apr. 19, 1984; cardinal May 25, 1985; titular church, Sts. John the Evangelist and Petronius. Archbp. of Bologna. *Curial membership*: Clergy, Catholic Education, Evangelization (congregations).

Cacciavillan, Agostino: b. Aug. 14, 1926, Novale de Valdagno (Vicenza), Italy; ord. priest, June 26, 1949; attended Pont. Ecclesiastical Academy; entered Holy See diplomatic service; posted to the Philippines, Spain, Portugal, and Secretariat of State; pro-nuncio in Kenya and apostolic delegate to Seychelles, 1976; titular abp. of Amiternum, Feb. 28, 1976; nuncio to India, 1981; pro-nuncio to Nepal, 1985; nuncio to United States and permanent observer at the Org. of American States, 1990; pres. Admin. of the Patrimony of the Apostolic See (APSA), Nov. 5, 1998; cardinal, Feb. 21, 2001; titular church, Deaconry of the Holy Guardian Angels in Città Giardino. Pres. Admin. of the Patrimony of the Apostolic See. *Curial membership*: Bishops, Oriental Churches, Evangelization of Peoples, Causes of Saints (congregations); Texts, (council); Latin America, Vatican City State (commissions).

Canestri,* Giovanni: b. Sept. 30, 1918, Castelspina, Italy; ord. priest Apr. 12, 1941; spiritual director of Rome's seminary, 1959; ord. titular bp. of Tenedo and aux. to the cardinal vicar of Rome, July 30, 1961; bp. of Tortona, 1971-75; titular bp. of Monterano (personal title of abp.) and vice regent of Rome, 1975-84; abp. of Cagliari, 1984-87; abp. of Genoa, July 6, 1987-95; cardinal June 28, 1988; titular church, St. Andrew of the Valley. Abp. emeritus of Genoa.

Caprio,* Giuseppe: b. Nov. 15, 1914, Lapio, Italy; ord. priest Dec. 17, 1938; served in diplomatic missions in China (1947-51, when Vatican diplomats were expelled by communists), Belgium (1951-54), and South Vietnam (1954-56); internuncio in China with residence at Taiwan, 1959-67; ord. titular abp. of Apollonia, Dec. 17, 1961; pro-nuncio in India, 1967-69; secretary, 1969-77, and president, 1979-81, of Administration of Patrimony of Holy See; substitute secretary of state, 1977-79; cardinal deacon June 30, 1979; transferred to order of cardinal priests, Nov., 1990; titular church, St. Mary of Victory; president of Prefecture of Economic Affairs of the Holy See, 1981-90. Grand Master of Equestrian Order of the Holy Sepulchre, 1988-95.

Carles Gordó, Ricardo Maria: b. Sept. 24, 1926, Valencia, Spain; ord. priest June 29, 1951; ord. bp. of Tortosa, Aug. 3, 1969; abp. of Barcelona, Mar. 23, 1990; cardinal Nov. 26, 1994; titular church, St. Mary of Consolation in Tiburtino. Abp. of Barcelona. *Curial membership*: Catholic Education (congregation); Economic Affairs of the Holy See (office).

Carter,* Gerald Emmett: b. Mar. 1, 1912, Montreal, Canada; ord. priest May 22, 1937; founder and president of St. Joseph Teachers' College and co-founder and director of Thomas More Institute for adult education; ord. titular bp. of Altiburo and aux. bp. of London, Ont., Feb. 2, 1962; bp. of London, Ont., 1964-78; vice president, 1971-73, and president, 1975-77, of Canadian Conference of Catholic Bishops; abp. of Toronto, 1978-90; cardinal June 30, 1979; titular church, St. Mary (in Traspontina). Archbp. emeritus of Toronto.

Cassidy, Edward Idris: b. July 5, 1924, Sydney, Australia; ord. priest July 23, 1949; entered Vatican diplomatic service in 1955; served in nunciatures in India, Ireland, El Salvador and Argentina; ord. titular bp. of Amantia with personal title of abp., Nov. 15, 1970; pro-nuncio to Republic of China (Taiwan), 1970-79 and pro-nuncio to Bangladesh and apostolic delegate in Burma, 1973-79; pro-nuncio to Lesotho and apostolic delegate to southern Africa, 1979-84; pro-nuncio to the Netherlands, 1984-88; substitute of the Secretary of State for General Affairs, 1988-89; pres. of Pontifical Council for Promoting Christian Unity, 1989-2001; cardinal June 28, 1991; deacon, St. Mary (in via Lata). President emeritus of Pontifical Council for Promoting Christian Unity. *Curial membership*: Divine Worship and Sacraments, Bishops, Oriental Churches, Evangelization of Peoples (congregations); Interreligious Dialogue (councils); APSA (office).

Castillo Lara,* Rosalio José, S.D.B.: b. Sept. 4, 1922, San Casimiro, Venezuela; ord. priest Sept. 4, 1949; ord. titular bp. of Precausa, May 24, 1973; coadj. bp. of Trujillo, 1973-76; abp. May 26, 1982; pro-pres. of Pontifical Commission for Revision of Code of Canon Law, 1982-84; pro-pres. of Commission for Authentic Interpretation of Code of Canon Law, 1984-85; cardinal May 25, 1985; deacon, Our Lady of Coromoto (in St. John of God); transferred to order of cardinal priests Jan. 29, 1996; pres. of Administration of Patrimony of the Holy See, 1989-95. President of the Pontifical Commission for the State of Vatican City State, 1990-97. *Curial membership*: Consecrated Life and Societies of Apostolic Life (congregation); Institute for Works of Religion (commission).

Castrillón Hoyos, Darío: b. July 4, 1929, Medellín, Colombia; ord. priest Oct. 26, 1952; served as curate in two parishes; dir. local Cursillo Movement; delegate for Catholic Action; taught canon law at the Free Civil University; gen. sec. of the Colombian Bishops' Conference; coadj. bp. of Pereira, June 2, 1971; bp. of Pereira, 1976-1992; gen. sec. of Latin American Episcopal Council (CELAM) 1983-87; pres. CELAM, 1987-91; abp. of Bucaramanga, 1992-96; pro-prefect Cong. for the Clergy, 1996-98; Pref. Cong. for the Clergy, 1998; cardinal, Feb. 21, 1998; deaconry, Holy Name of Mary on the Forum Traiani. Prefect of the Congregation for the Clergy. *Curial membership*: Bishops, Evangelization of Peoples, Education, Divine Worship and Sacraments (congregations); Social Communications, Texts (councils); APSA (office); Latin America (commission).

Cé, Marco: b. July 8, 1925, Izano, Italy; ord. priest Mar. 27, 1948; taught sacred scripture and dogmatic theology at seminary in his home diocese of Crema; rector of seminary, 1957; presided over diocesan liturgical commission, preached youth retreats; ord. titular bp. of Vulturia, May 17, 1970; aux. bp. of Bologna, 1970-76; gen. ecclesiastical assistant of Italian Catholic Action, 1976-78; patriarch of Venice, 1978-2001; ret. Jan. 5, 2002; cardinal June 30, 1979; titular church, St. Mark. Patriarch emeritus of Venice. *Curial membership*: Oriental Churches (congregations).

Cheli,* Giovanni: b. Oct. 4, 1918, Turin, Italy; ord. priest, June 21, 1942; entered Secretariat of State and diplomatic service; second secretary, apostolic nunciature in Guatemala, 1952-55; first secretary, apostolic nunciature in Madrid, Spain, 1955-62; counselor, nunciature in Rome, 1962-67; Council for Public Affairs of the Church, Vatican City, 1967-73; Permanent Observer of the Holy See to the United Nations, 1973-86; ord. titular abp. of Santa Giusta, Sept. 16, 1978; pres. Pontifical Council for the Pastoral Care of Migrants and Itinerant People, 1986-98; cardinal, Feb. 21, 1998; deaconry, Sts. Cosmas and Damian. President Emeritus Pontifical Council for the Pastoral Care of Migrants and Itinerant People.

Cipriani Thorne, Juan Luis: b. Dec. 28, 1943, Lima, Peru; champion basketball player and student in industrial engineering, he joined Opus Dei in 1962; ord. for the prelature Aug. 21, 1977; after earning a doctorate in theology at the University of Navarre and pastoral work in Lima, he taught moral theology at the Pontifical Faculty of Theology, Lima and was regional vicar for Peru and vice-chancellor of the University of Piura; app. titular bp. of Turuzi and aux. bp. of Ayacucho May 23, 1988; cons. July 3, 1988; app. abp. of Ayacucho May 13, 1995; tried to negotiate a peaceful resolution to the siege of the Japanese ambassador's residence in Lima, December 1996-April 1997 and ministered to Japanese and Peruvian hostages; app. abp. of Lima Jan. 9, 1999; cardinal priest Feb. 21, 2001; titular church St. Camillus de Lellis. Abp. of Lima. *Curial membership*: Sacraments, Causes of Saints (congregation); Latin America (commission).

Clancy, Edward Bede: b. Dec. 13, 1923, Lithgow, New South Wales, Australia; ord. priest July 23, 1949; ord. titular bp. of Ard Carna and aux. of Sydney, Jan. 19, 1974; abp. of Canberra, 1978-83; abp. of Sydney, Feb. 12, 1983; res., March 26, 2001; cardinal June 28, 1988; titular church, Holy Mary of Vallicella. Abp. emeritus of Sydney. *Curial membership*: Secretariat of State (second section).

Colasuonno, Francesco: b. Jan. 2, 1925, Grumo Appulia, Italy; ord. priest Sep. 28, 1947; taught in seminary of archdiocese of Bari; entered diplomatic service in 1958; served in section for Extraordinary Ecclesiastical Affairs of the Secretariat of State and in nunciatures in U.S., India, and Taiwan; ord. titular abp. of Truentum, Dec. 6, 1974; first apostolic delegate to Mozambique, 1974-81; apostolic delegate to Zimbabwe, 1981-85; apostolic pro-nuncio to Yugoslavia, 1985-86; headed Holy See delegation for permanent working contacts with Poland, 1986-90; representative to the USSR, 1990-94; nuncio to Italy, 1994-98, and San Marino, 1995-98; cardinal, Feb. 21, 1998. *Curial membership*: Oriental Churches (congregation); Promoting Christian Unity, Justice and Peace (councils).

Connell, Desmond: b. March 24, 1926, Phibsboro, Ireland; ord. priest, May 19, 1951; taught at University College Dublin, 1953-72; dean of the faculty of Philosophy and Sociology, 1983; awarded degree of D.Litt. by National University of Dublin, 1981; chaplain to the Poor Clares in Donnybrook and Carmelites in Drumcondra and Blackrock; app. abp. of Dublin, Jan. 21, 1988; cons., March 6, 1988; cardinal, Feb. 21. 2001; titular church, St. Sylvester *in Capite*. Abp. of Dublin. *Curial membership*: Doctrine of the Faith, Bishops (congregations); Laity (council).

Corripio Ahumada,* Ernesto: b. June 29, 1919, Tampico, Mexico; ord. priest Oct. 25, 1942, in Rome, where he remained until almost the end of World War II; taught and held various positions in local seminary of Tampico, 1945-50; ord. titular bp. of Zapara and aux. bp. of Tampico, Mar. 19, 1953; bp. of Tampico, 1956-67; abp. of Antequera, 1967-76; abp. of Puebla de los Angeles, 1976-77; abp. of Mexico City and primate of Mexico, July 19, 1977-1994; cardinal June 30, 1979; titular church, Mary Immaculate al Tiburtino. Abp. emeritus of Mexico City.

Daly,* Cahal Brendan: b. Oct. 1, 1917, Loughguile, Northern Ireland; ord. priest June 22, 1941; earned advanced degrees in philosophy and theology; 30 years of priestly life dedicated to teaching; attended Second Vatican Council as a theological adviser to members of Irish hierarchy; outspoken critic of violence in Northern Ireland; ord. bp. of Ardagh, July 16, 1967; bp. of Down and Connor, 1982-90; abp. of Armagh and primate of All Ireland, 1990-96; cardinal June 28, 1991; titular church, St. Patrick. Abp. emeritus of Armagh.

Danneels, Godfried: b. June 4, 1933, Kanegem, Belgium; ord. priest Aug. 17, 1957; professor of liturgy and sacramental theology at Catholic University of Louvain, 1969-77; ord. bp. of Antwerp Dec. 18, 1977; app. abp. of Mechelen-Brussel, Dec. 19, 1979; installed Jan. 4, 1980; cardinal Feb. 2, 1983; titular church, St. Anastasia. Abp. of Mechelen-Brussel, military ordinary of Belgium. *Curial membership*: Secretariat of State (second section); Oriental Churches, Divine Worship and Sacraments, Evangelization of Peoples, Education (congregations).

Darmaatmadja, Julius Riyadi, S.J.: b. Dec. 20, 1934, Muntilan, Mageland, Central Java, Indonesia; entered Society of Jesus in 1957; ord. priest Dec. 18, 1969; ord. abp. of Semarang, June 29, 1983 (transferred to Jakarta Jan. 11, 1996); cardinal Nov. 26, 1994; titular church, Sacred Heart of Mary. Abp. of Jakarta, military ordinary of Indonesia (1984). *Cu-*

rial membership: Evangelization of Peoples (congregation); Interreligious Dialogue (council).

de Giorgi, Salvatore: b. Sep. 6, 1930 Vernole, Italy; ord. priest June 28, 1953; diocesan chaplain to the Teachers' Movement of Catholic Action; dir. Diocesan Pastoral Office; app. titular bp. of Tulana and aux. bp. of Oria, Nov. 21, 1973; bp. of Oria, March 17, 1978; abp. of Foggia, Apr. 4, 1981; abp. of Taranto, Oct. 10, 1987 (resigned, 1990); general president of Catholic Action, 1990-96; abp. of Palermo, Apr. 4, 1996; president of the Sicilian Episcopal Conference; cardinal Feb. 21, 1998; titular church, St. Mary in Ara Caeli. Abp. of Palermo. *Curial membership*: Clergy (congregations); Laity, Family (councils).

Deskur, Andrzej Maria: b. Feb. 29, 1924, Sancygniow, Poland; ord. priest Aug. 20, 1950, in France; assigned to Vatican secretariat of state, 1952; undersecretary and later secretary of Pontifical Commission for Film, Radio and TV (Social Communications), 1954-73; ord. titular bp. of Tene, June 30, 1974; abp., 1980; president of Pontifical Commission for Social Communications, 1974-84; cardinal May 25, 1985; deacon, St. Cesario (in Palatio); transferred to order of cardinal priests Jan. 29, 1996. President emeritus of Council for Social Communications. *Curial membership*: Divine Worship and Sacraments, Causes of Saints (congregations); Health Care Workers (council); State of Vatican City (commission).

Dias, Ivan: b. April 14, 1936, Bandra, India; ord. priest, Dec. 8, 1958; entered the Holy See diplomatic service and was posted to Indonesia, Madagascar, Reunion, the Comorros, Mauritius, and Secretariat of State; app. titular abp. of Rusubisir and pro-nuncio in Ghana, Togo and Benin, May 8, 1982; cons., June 19, 1982; nuncio in Korea, 1987-91; nuncio in Albania, 1991-97; app. abp. of Bombay, Jan. 22, 1997; cons., March 13, 1997; cardinal, Feb. 21, 2001; titular church, Holy Spirit in Ferratella. Abp. of Bombay. *Curial membership*: Doctrine of the Faith, Sacraments, Education (congregations); Culture (council); Cultural Heritage of the Church (commission).

do Nascimento, Alexandre: b. Mar. 1, 1925, Malanje, Angola; ord. priest Dec. 20, 1952, in Rome; professor of dogmatic theology in major seminary of Luanda, Angola; editor of *O Apostolada*, Catholic newspaper; forced into exile in Lisbon, Portugal, 1961-71; returned to Angola, 1971; active with student and refugee groups; professor at Pius XII Institute of Social Sciences; ord. bp. of Malanje, Aug. 31, 1975; abp. of Lubango and apostolic administrator of Onjiva, 1977-86; held hostage by Angolan guerrillas, Oct. 15 to Nov. 16, 1982; cardinal Feb. 2, 1983; titular church, St. Mark in Agro Laurentino. Abp. of Luanda, 1986. *Curial membership*: Catholic Education (congregations).

Dulles,* Avery, S.J.: b. Aug. 24, 1918, Auburn, New York; the son of U.S. Secretary of State John Foster Dulles; raised a Protestant, he converted to the Catholic faith while a student at Harvard; served in U.S. Navy and then entered the Jesuits; ord. priest for the Jesuits, June 16, 1956; earned a doctorate in theology at the Gregorian University, Rome; taught theology at Woodstock College, 1960-74, and Catholic University of America, 1974-88; visiting professor at numerous other institutions; author of 21 books and over 650 articles; pres. of the Catholic Theologi-

cal Society of America; member of the International Theological Commission and the U.S. Lutheran/Roman Catholic Dialogue; consultor to the U.S. Bishops' Committee on Doctrine; currently the Laurence J. McGinley Professor of Religion and Society at Fordham University; cardinal, Feb. 21, 2001; titular church, Deaconry of the Most Holy Names of Jesus and Mary in Via Lata.

Egan, Edward Michael: b. Apr. 2, 1932, Oak Park, IL; ord. priest, Dec. 15, 1957, in Rome; sec. to Cardinal Albert Meyer, 1958-60; assistant vice-rector of the North American College, 1960-64; vice-chancellor of the archdiocese of Chicago, 1964-68; co-chancellor for human relations and ecumenism, 1968-72; judge of Roman Rota, 1972-85; ord. titular bp. of Allegheny and aux. bp. of New York, May 22, 1985; app. bp. of Bridgeport, Nov. 5, 1988; abp. of New York, May 11, 2000, inst., June 19, 2000; cardinal, Feb. 21, 2001; titular church, St. John and Paul. Abp. of New York. *Curial membership*: Family (council).

Errázuriz Ossa, Francisco Javier: b. Sept. 5, 1933, Santiago, Chile; ord. for the Schönstatt Fathers, July 16, 1961; chaplain to students and professionals of the Schönstatt Movement and regional superior; elected superior general of the Schönstatt Fathers, 1974; app. titular abp. of Hólar and sec. of the Cong. For Institutes of Consecrated Life and Societies of Apostolic Life, Dec. 22, 1990; app. abp. of Valparaiso, Sept. 24, 1996; transferred to archdiocese of Santiago, April 24, 1998; pres. of the Episcopal Conference of Chile and first vice-pres. of CELAM; cardinal, Feb. 21, 2001; titular church, St. Mary of Peace. Abp. of Santiago. *Curial membership*: Consecrated Life and Societies of Apostolic Life (congregation); Family (council); Latin America (commission).

Etchegaray,* Roger: b. Sept. 25, 1922, Espelette, France; ord. priest July 13, 1947; deputy director, 1961-66, and secretary general, 1966-70, of French Episcopal Conference; ord. titular bp. of Gemelle di Numidia and aux. of Paris, May 27, 1969; abp. of Marseilles, 1970-84; prelate of Mission de France, 1975-82; president of French Episcopal Conference, 1979-81; cardinal June 30, 1979; titular church, St. Leo I; president of Council *Cor Unum*, 1984-95. President of Council for Justice and Peace (1984-98) and President of Central Committee for the Jubilee of the Holy Year 2000 (1994-98); transferred to order of cardinal bishops, June 24, 1998 (suburbicarian see of Porto-Santa Rufina). President of the Central Committee for the Jubilee of the Holy Year 2000. *Curial membership*: Oriental Churches, Evangelization of Peoples, Education (congregations); Laity, Christian Unity, Interreligious Dialogue (councils).

Etsou-Nzabi-Bamungwabi, Frédéric, C.I.C.M.: b. Dec. 3, 1930, Mazalonga, Zaire; ord. priest July 13, 1958; educ. Catholic Institute of Paris (degree in sociology) and "Lumen Vitae" in Belgium (degree in pastoral theology); ord. titular bp. of Menefessi and coadj. abp. of Mbandaka-Bikora, Nov. 7, 1976; abp. of Mbandaka-Bikora, 1977-90; abp. of Kinshasa, July 7, 1990; cardinal June 28, 1991; titular church, St. Lucy (a Piazza d'Armi). Abp. of Kinshasa. *Curial membership*: Evangelization of Peoples (congregation); Family (council).

Falcão, José Freire: b. Oct. 23, 1925, Erere, Brazil; ord. priest June 19, 1949; ord. titular bp. of Vardimissa and coadj. of Limoeiro do Norte, June 17, 1967; bp.

of Limoeiro do Norte, Aug. 19, 1967; abp. of Teresina, Nov. 25, 1971; abp. of Brasilia, Feb. 15, 1984; cardinal June 28, 1988; titlar church, St. Luke (Via Prenestina). Abp. of Brasilia. *Curial membership*: Health Care Workers (council).

Felici,* Angelo: b. July 26, 1919, Segni, Italy; ord. priest Apr. 4, 1942; in Vatican diplomatic service from 1945; ord. titular bp. of Cesariana, with personal title of abp., Sept. 24, 1967; nuncio to Netherlands, 1967-76, Portugal, 1976-79, France, 1979-88; cardinal June 28, 1988; deacon, Sts. Blaise and Charles in Catinari, promoted to cardinal priest, Jan. 9, 1999. Prefect of Congregation for Causes of Saints, 1988-95. President of Pontifical Commission "Ecclesia Dei," 1995.

Fernandes de Araújo, Serafim: b. Aug. 13, 1924 Minas Novas, Brazil; ord. priest March 12, 1949; taught canon law at provincial seminary of Diamantina; titular bp. of Verinopolis and aux. bp. of Belo Horizonte, Jan. 19, 1959; co-adjutor abp. of Belo Horizonte, 1982; abp. Belo Horizonte Feb. 5, 1986; co-president of the Fourth General Conference of the Latin American Episcopate, 1992; cardinal, Feb. 21, 1998; titular church, St. Louis Marie Grignion de Montfort. Abp. of Belo Horizonte. *Curial membership*: Bishops (congregation); Latin America (commission), Justice and Peace (council).

Fresno Larraín,* Juan Francisco: b. July 26, 1914, Santiago, Chile; ord. priest Dec. 18, 1937; ord. bp. of Copiapo, Aug. 15, 1958; abp. of La Serena, 1967-83; abp. of Santiago, May 3, 1983-90; cardinal May 25, 1985; titular church, St. Mary Immaculate of Lourdes (a Boccea). Abp. emeritus of Santiago.

Furno,* Carlo: b. Dec. 2, 1921, Bairo Canavese, Italy; ord. priest June 25, 1944; entered diplomatic service of the Holy See in the 1950s; served in Colombia, Ecuador and Jerusalem; worked in Secretariat of State for 11 years and taught at Pontifical Ecclesiastical Academy, 1966-73; ord. titular bp. of Abari with personal title of abp., Sept. 16, 1973; nuncio in Peru, 1973-78, Lebanon, 1978-82, Brazil, 1982-92, Italy, 1992-94; cardinal Nov. 26, 1994; deacon, Sacred Heart of Christ the King. Grand Master of the Equestrian Order of the Holy Sepulchre, 1995; pontifical delegate for Patriarchal Basilica of St. Francis in Assisi, 1996; archpriest of the patriarchal basilica of Santa Maria Maggiore, Rome, 1998.

Gagnon,* Edouard, P.S.S.: b. Jan. 15, 1918, Port Daniel, Que., Canada; ord. priest Aug. 15, 1940; ord. bp. of St. Paul in Alberta Mar. 25, 1969 (resigned May 3, 1972); rector of Canadian College in Rome, 1972-77; vice president-secretary of Vatican Committee for the Family, 1973-80; titular abp. of Giustiniana Prima, July 7, 1983; pro-president of Pontifical Council for the Family, 1983; cardinal May 25, 1985; deacon, St. Elena (fuori Porta Prenestina); transferred to order of cardinal priests Jan. 29, 1996; titular church St. Marcellus; president of Pontifical Council for the Family, 1985-90. President of Pontifical Committee for International Eucharistic Congresses, 1991-2000.

Gantin,* Bernardin: b. May 8, 1922, Toffo, Dahomey (now Benin); ord. priest Jan. 14, 1951; ord. titular bp. of Tipasa di Mauritania and aux. bp. of Cotonou, Feb. 3, 1957; abp. of Cotonou, 1960-71; associate secretary (1971-73) and secretary (1973-75) of Congregation for Evangelization of Peoples; vice-president (1975) and president (1976-84) of Pontifical Commission for Justice and Peace; cardinal dea-

con June 27, 1977; transferred to order of priests June 25, 1984; titular church, Sacred Heart of Christ the King; titular bp. of suburbicarian see of Palestrina Sept 29, 1986, when he entered the order of cardinal bishops, and of Ostia June 5, 1993, when he became dean of the college of cardinals. Prefect of Congregation for Bishops, 1984-98; president of commission for Latin America, 1984-98; dean of college of cardinals, 1993. *Curial membership*: Causes of Saints, Evangelization of Peoples, Oriental Churches, Institutes of Consecrated Life and Societies of Apostolic Life, Catholic Education (congregations); Apostolic Signatura (tribunal).

George, Francis E., O.M.I.: b. Jan. 16, 1937, Chicago, Ill.; ord. priest Dec. 21, 1963; provincial of central region of Oblates of Mary Immaculate, 1973-74, vicar general, 1974-86; ord. bp. of Yakima, Sept. 21, 1990; abp. of Portland, Ore., Apr. 30, 1996, installed May 27, 1996; abp. of Chicago, Apr. 8, 1997, installed May 7, 1997; cardinal Feb. 21, 1998; titular church, St. Bartholomew on Tiber Island. Abp. of Chicago. *Curial membership*: Divine Worship and the Discipline of the Sacraments, Oriental Churches, Evangelization, Institutes of Consecrated Life and Societies of Apostolic Life (congregations); "Cor Unum" (council); Cultural Heritage of the Church (commission).

Giordano, Michele: b. Sept. 26, 1930, S. Arcangelo, Italy; ord. priest July 5, 1953; ord. titular bp. of LariCastello and aux. of Matera, Feb. 5, 1972; abp. of Matera and Irsina, 1974-87; abp. of Naples, May 9, 1987; cardinal June 28, 1988; titular church, St. Joachim. Abp. of Naples. *Curial membership*: Clergy (congregation); Health Care Workers (council).

Glemp, Józef: b. Dec. 18, 1929, Inowroclaw, Poland; assigned to forced labor on German farm in Rycerzow during Nazi occupation; ord. priest May 25, 1956; studied in Rome, 1958-64; received degree in Roman and canon law from Pontifical Lateran University; secretary of primatial major seminary at Gniezno on his return to Poland, 1964; spokesman for secretariat of primate of Poland and chaplain of primate for archdiocese of Gniezno, 1967; ord. bp. of Warmia, Apr. 21, 1979; abp. of Gniezno, 1981-92, with title of abp. of Warsaw and primate of Poland; cardinal Feb. 2, 1983; titular church, St. Mary in Trastevere. Abp. of Warsaw (Mar. 25, 1992), primate of Poland, ordinary for Eastern-Rite faithful in Poland who do not have ordinaries of their own rites. *Curial membership*: Oriental Churches (congregation); Culture (council).

González Martin,* Marcelo: b. Jan. 16, 1918, Villanubla, Spain; ord. priest June 29, 1941; taught theology and sociology at Valladolid diocesan seminary; founded organization for construction of houses for poor; ord. bp. of Astorga, Mar. 5, 1961; titular abp. of Case Mediane and coadj. of Barcelona, Feb. 21, 1966; abp. of Barcelona, 1967-71; abp. of Toledo, 1971-95; cardinal Mar. 5, 1973; titular church, St. Augustine. Abp. emeritus of Toledo.

González Zumárraga, Antonio José: b. March 18, 1925, Pujilí (Cotopaxi), Ecuador; ord. priest June 29, 1951; taught at the Pontifical Catholic University of Ecuador; chancellor of the Curia, 1964; rector of Our Mother of mercy College; app. titular bp. of Tagarata and aux. bp. of Quito; apostolic admin. of Machala, March 1976; bp. of Machata, Jan. 30, 1978; coadj.

abp. of Quito, June 28, 1980; abp. of Quito June 1, 1985; served two terms as pres. of the Ecuadorean Episcopal Conference; cardinal priest Feb. 21, 2001; titular church, St. Mary *in Via*. Abp. of Quito. *Curial membership*: Laity (council); Latin America (commission).

Grocholewski, Zenon: b. Oct. 11, 1939, Bródki, Poland; ord. priest, May 26, 1963; earned a doctorate in canon law; served in the Supreme Tribunal of the Apostolic Signatura, 1972-1999; prefect of the Supreme Tribunal of the Apostolic Signatura; member of the commission studying the 1983 *Code of Canon Law*; titular bp. of Agropoli, Dec. 21, 1982; titular abp., Dec. 16, 1991; prefect of the Cong. for Catholic Education, Nov. 15, 1999; titular church, Deaconry of St. Nicholas *in Carcere*. Prefect of the Congregation for Catholic Education. *Curial membership*: Doctrine of the Faith Bishops (congregations); Texts (council).

Gröer,* Hans Hermann, O.S.B.: b. Oct. 13, 1919, Vienna, Austria; ord. priest Apr. 12, 1942; abp. of Vienna, 1986-95; cardinal June 28, 1988; titular church, Sts. Joachim and Anne al Tuscolano.

Gulbinowicz, Henryk Roman: b. Oct. 17, 1928, Szukiszki, Poland; ord. priest June 18, 1950; ord. titular bp. of Acci and apostolic administrator of Polish territory in Lithuanian archdiocese of Vilnius (Vilna), Feb. 8, 1970; abp. of Wroclaw, Poland, Jan. 3, 1976; cardinal May 25, 1985; titular church, Immaculate Conception of Mary (a Grottarosa). Abp. of Wroclaw. *Curial membership*: Oriental Churches (congregations).

Hickey,* James A.: b. Oct. 11, 1920, Midland, Mich.; ord. priest (Saginaw diocese) June 15, 1946; ord. titular bp. of Taraqua and aux. of Saginaw, Apr. 14, 1967; rector of North American College, Rome, 1969-74; bp. of Cleveland, 1974-80; app. abp. of Washington, D.C., June 17, 1980, installed Aug. 5, 1980; cardinal June 28, 1988; titular church, St. Mary Mother of the Redeemer; ret. Nov. 2000. Abp. emeritus of Washington, D.C.

Honoré,* Jean: b. Aug. 13, 1920; ord. priest, June 29, 1943; authored doctoral dissertation under the direction of Jean Daniélou at the *Institute Catholique*, Paris; taught at St. Vincent's College in Rennes and in Saint-Malo; worked for six years at the National Religious Education Centre (CNEC); rector of the Catholic University of Angers; app. bp. of Evreux, Oct. 24, 1972; cons., Dec. 17, 1972; app. abp. of Tours, Aug. 13, 1981; participated in the preparation of the *Catechism*, following the 1985 Synod of Bishops; res. as abp. of Tours, July 22, 1997; cardinal, Feb. 21, 2001; titular church, St. Mary of Health in Primavalle. Abp. emeritus of Tours.

Hummes, O.F.M., Cláudio: b. Aug. 8, 1934, Montenegro, Brazil; ord. priest for the Franciscans, Aug. 3, 1958; specialist in ecumenism; taught philosophy at the Franciscan seminary in Garibaldi, at the major seminary of Viamão and the Pontifical Catholic University of Porto Alegre; adviser for ecumenical affairs to the National Bishops' Conference of Brazil; Provincial of Rio Grande do Sul, 1972-75; pres. of the Union of Latin American Conferences of Franciscans; app. coadj. bp. of Santo André, March 22, 1975; cons., May 25, 1975; succeeded to see, Dec. 29, 1975; app. abp. of Fortaleza, July 21, 1996; transferred to São Paulo, May 23, 1998; cardinal, Feb. 21,

2001; titular church, St. Anthony of Padua in Via Merulana. Abp. of São Paulo. *Curial membership*: Sacraments (congregation); Family, *Cor Unum*, Culture, Interreligious Dialogue, Laity (councils); Latin America (commission).

Husar, Lubomyr, M.S.U.: b. Feb. 26, 1933, Lviv, Ukraine; family fled to Austria because of the war and then to the U.S.; ord. for the eparchy of Stamford for Ukrainians, USA, March 30, 1958; entered the Studite Monks after completing a doctorate in theology in Rome; superior of the Studion in Grottaferrata, Italy; ord. bp. on April 2, 1977; app. archimandrite of Studite Monks residing outside Ukraine; organized a new Studite monastery in Ternopil, Ukraine, 1994; elected exarch of Kyiv-Vyshorod, 1995; app. aux. bp. to major abp. of Lviv, 1996; elected major abp. of Lviv for Ukrainians, Jan. 25, 2001; cardinal, Feb. 21, 2001; titular church, Holy Wisdom in Via Boccea. Major Abp. of Lviv for Ukrainians. *Curial membership*: Oriental Churches (congregation); Christian Unity, Texts (council).

Innocenti,* Antonio: b. Aug. 23, 1915, Poppi, Italy; ord. priest July 17, 1938; held curial and diplomatic positions; ord. titular bp. of Eclano with personal title of abp., Feb. 18, 1968; nuncio to Paraguay, 1967-73; secretary of Congregation for Causes of Saints, 1973-75; secretary of Congregation for Sacraments and Divine Worship, 1975-80; nuncio to Spain, 1980-85; cardinal deacon May 25, 1985; transferred to order of cardinal priests Jan. 29, 1996; titular church, St. Marie (in Aquiro); prefect of Congregation for the Clergy, 1986-91; president of Pontifical Commission for Preservation of Artistic Patrimony of the Church, 1988-91; president of Pontifical Commission "Ecclesia Dei," 1991-95.

Javierre Ortas,* Antonio María, S.D.B.: b. Feb. 21, 1921, Sietamo, Spain; ord. priest Apr. 24, 1949; leading European writer on ecumenism; ord. titular bp. of Meta with personal title of abp., June 29, 1976; Secretary of Congregation for Catholic Education, 1976-88; cardinal June 28, 1988; deacon (Santa Maria Liberatrice a Monte Testaccio), promoted to cardinal priest, Jan. 9, 1999 (Santa Maria Liberatrice a Monte Testaccio; raised to presbyteral title). Librarian and Archivist of the Holy Roman Church, 1988-92. Prefect of Congregation for Divine Worship and the Sacraments, 1992-96.

Jaworski, Marian: b. Aug. 21, 1926, Lwów, Poland (modern Lviv, Ukraine); ord. priest, June 25, 1950; taught at the Catholic Theological Academy in Warsaw and Pontifical Theological faculty of Kraków; first rector of the Pontifical Theological Academy, Kraków, 1981-87; app. titular bp. of Lambaesis and apostolic admin. of Lubaczów, May 21, 1984; cons., June 23, 1984; app. abp. of Lviv for Latins, Jan. 16, 1991; pres. of the Ukrainian Episcopal Conference, 1992; cardinal (*in pectore*), Feb. 21, 1998; titular church, St. Sixtus. Abp. of Lviv for Latins. *Curial membership*: Clergy (congregation); Family (council).

Kasper, Walter: b. March 5, 1933, Heidenheim/ Brenz, Germany; ord. priest, April 6, 1957; taught theology and was later dean of the theological faculty in Münster and Tübingen; app. bp. of Rottenburg-Stuttgart, April 17, 1989, cons. June 17, 1989; co-chair of the International Commission for Lutheran/Catholic Dialogue, 1994; sec. of the Pontifical Council for Promoting Christian Unity, June 1, 1999; pres. Pontifical Council for Promoting Christian Unity, 2001; cardinal deacon, Feb. 21, 2001; titular church, Deaconry of All Saints in Via Appia Nuova. President of the Pontifical Council for Promoting Christian Unity. *Curial membership:* Doctrine of the Faith, Oriental Churches (congregations); Culture (council).

Keeler, William Henry: b. Mar. 4, 1931, San Antonio, Tex.; ord. priest (Harrisburg diocese) July 17, 1955; secretary to Bp. Leech at Vatican II, named *peritus* by Pope John XXIII; ord. titular bp. of Ulcinium and aux. bp. of Harrisburg, Sept. 21, 1979; bp. of Harrisburg, Nov. 10, 1983, installed Jan. 4, 1984; abp. of Baltimore, Apr. 6, 1989; cardinal Nov. 26, 1994; titular church, St. Mary of the Angels. Abp. of Baltimore. *Curial membership*: Oriental Churches (congregation); Christian Unity (council).

Kim Sou-hwan,* Stephen: b. May 8, 1922, Tae Gu, Korea; ord. priest Sept. 15, 1951; ord. bp. of Masan, May 31, 1966; abp. of Seoul, Apr. 9, 1968 (resigned May 29, 1998); cardinal Apr. 28, 1969; titular church, St. Felix of Cantalice (Centocelle). Abp. emeritus of Seoul, apostolic administrator emeritus of Pyeong Yang.

Kitbunchu, Michael Michai: b. Jan. 25, 1929, Samphran, Thailand; ord. priest Dec. 20, 1959, in Rome; rector of metropolitan seminary in Bangkok, 1965-72; ord. abp. of Bangkok, June 3, 1973; cardinal Feb. 2, 1983, the first from Thailand; titular church, St. Laurence in Panisperna. Abp. of Bangkok. *Curial membership*: Evangelization of Peoples, Sacraments (congregation).

König,* Franz: b. Aug. 3, 1905, Rabenstein, Lower Austria; ord. priest Oct. 29, 1933; ord. titular bp. of Livias and coadj. bp. of Sankt Poelten, Aug. 31, 1952; abp. of Vienna, May 10, 1956-85; cardinal Dec. 15, 1958; titular church, St. Eusebius; president of Secretariat (now Council) for Dialogue with Non-Believers, 1965-80. Abp. emeritus of Vienna.

Korec, Ján Chryzostom, S.J.: b. Jan. 22, 1924, Bosany, Slovakia; entered Society of Jesus in 1939; ord. priest Oct. 1, 1950; ord. bp. secretly Aug. 24, 1951; sentenced to 12 years in prison in 1960 for helping seminarians with their study and ordaining priests; paroled in 1968; appointed bp. of Nitra Feb. 6, 1990; cardinal June 28, 1991; titular church, Sts. Fabian and Venantius (a Villa Forelli). Bp. of Nitra. *Curial membership*: Clergy, Institutes of Consecrated Life and Societies of Apostolic Life (congregation); Culture (council).

Kozlowiecki,* Adam, S.J.: b. Apr. 1, 1911, Huta Komorowska, Poland; ord. priest June 24, 1937; arrested by Nazi Gestapo with 24 fellow priests in Kraków in 1939 and sent to Auschwitz concentration camp; moved to Dachau six months later where he suffered throughout the war; sent to Rhodesia after the war and taught until 1950; appointed apostolic administrator of prefecture of Lusaka, 1950; appointed bp. and vicar apostolic, Sept. 11, 1955; appointed abp. of Lusaka, 1959; resigned, 1969, to allow a native African to receive the post; member Congregation for the Evangelization of People, 1970-91; cardinal, Feb. 21, 1998; titular church, St. Andrew on the Quirinal.

Laghi,* Pio: b. May 21, 1922, Castiglione, Italy; ord. priest Apr. 20, 1946; entered diplomatic service of the Holy See in 1952; served in Nicaragua, the U.S. (as secretary of the apostolic delegation, 1954-61) and India; recalled to Rome and served on Council for Public Affairs of the Church; ord. titular abp. of Mauriana June 22, 1969; apostolic delegate to Jerusalem and Palestine, 1969-74; nuncio to Argentina, 1974-80; apostolic delegate, 1980-84, and first pro-nuncio, 1984-90 to the U.S.; pro-prefect of Congregation for Catholic Education, 1990-91; cardinal June 28, 1991; deacon, St. Mary Auxiliatrix (in Via Tuscolana). Prefect of Congregation for Catholic Education, 1991-99. Grand chancellor of Pontifical Gregorian University. Patron of Sovereign Military Order of Malta, 1993. Protodeacon, 1999-2002. *Curial membership*: Secretariat of State (second section); Bishops, Oriental Churches, Evangelization of Peoples, Causes of Saints, Consecrated Life and Societies of Apostolic Life, Clergy (congregations); Texts (council).

Law, Bernard F.: b. Nov. 4, 1931, Torreon, Mexico, the son of U.S. Air Force colonel; ord. priest (Jackson diocese) May 21, 1961; editor of Natchez-Jackson, Miss., diocesan paper, 1963-68; director of NCCB Committee on Ecumenical and Interreligious Affairs, 1968-71; ord. bp. of Springfield-Cape Girardeau, Mo., Dec. 5, 1973; abp. of Boston, Jan. 11, 1984; cardinal May 25, 1985; titular church, St. Susanna. Abp. of Boston. *Curial membership*: Bishops, Oriental Churches; Divine Worship and Sacraments, Consecrated Life and Societies of Apostolic Life, Evangelization of Peoples, Clergy, Education (congregations); Culture, Family (councils).

Lehmann, Karl: b. May 16, 1936, Sigmaringen, Germany; ord. priest, Oct. 10, 1963; earned doctorates in theology and philosophy; assistant to Fr. Karl Rahner at University of Münster; taught dogmatic theology at the Johannes Gutenberg University, Mainz; member of the Central Committee of German Catholics and the Jaeger-Stählin Ecumenical Circle; taught at the Albert Ludwig University, Freiburg im Breisgau; member of the International Theological Commission; edited the official publication of the documents of the Joint Synod of the Dioceses in the Federal Republic of Germany, Synod of Würzburg, 1971-75; app. bp. of Mainz, June 21, 1983; cons. Oct. 2, 1983; pres. of the German Bishops' Conference; cardinal, Feb. 21, 2001; titular church, St. Leo I. Bp. of Mainz. *Curial membership*: Bishops, Oriental Churches (congregations); APSA (office).

López Rodriguez, Nicolás de Jesús: b. Oct. 31, 1936, Barranca, Dominican Republic; ord. priest Mar. 18, 1961; sent to Rome for advanced studies at the Angelicum and Gregorian Univ.; served in various diocesan offices after returning to his home diocese of La Vega; ord. first bp. of San Francisco de Macoris Feb. 25, 1978; abp. of Santo Domingo, Nov. 15, 1981; cardinal June 28, 1991; titular church, St. Pius X (alla Balduina). Abp. of Santo Domingo and Military Ordinary for Dominican Republic. *Curial membership*: Clergy, Institutes of Consecrated Life and Societies of Apostolic Life (congregations); Social Communications (council); Latin America (commission) .

López Trujillo, Alfonso: b. Nov. 8, 1935, Villahermosa, Colombia; ord. priest Nov. 13, 1960, in Rome; returned to Colombia, 1963; taught at major seminary; was pastoral coordinator for 1968 International Eucharistic Congress in Bogota; vicar general of Bogota, 1970-72; ord. titular bp. of Boseta,

Mar. 25, 1971; aux. bp. of Bogota, 1971-72; secretary-general of CELAM, 1972-78; helped organize 1979 Puebla Conference in which Pope John Paul II participated; app. coadj. abp. of Medellin, May 22, 1978; abp. of Medellin, June 2, 1979 (resigned Jan 9, 1991); president of CELAM, 1979-83; cardinal Feb. 2, 1983; titular church, St. Prisca; promoted to cardinal bishop, Nov. 17, 2001; suburbicarian see, Frascati. Abp. emeritus of Medellin. President of the Pontifical Council for the Family, 1990. *Curial membership*: Bishops, Doctrine of the Faith, Causes of Saints, Evangelization of Peoples (congregations); Latin America (commission).

Lorscheider, Aloisio, O.F.M.: b. Oct. 8, 1924, Estrela, Brazil; received in Franciscan Order, Feb. 1, 1942; ord. priest Aug. 22, 1948; professor of theology at the Antonianum, Rome, and director of Franciscan international house of studies; ord. bp. of Santo Angelo, Brazil, May 20, 1962; abp. of Fortaleza, 1973-95; president of CELAM, 1975-79; cardinal May 24, 1976; titular church, S. Pietro (in Montorio). Abp. of Aparecida, July 12, 1995. *Curial membership*: Consecrated Life and Societies of Apostolic Life (congregation).

Lourdusamy, D. Simon: b. Feb. 5, 1924, Kalleri, India; ord. priest Dec. 21, 1951; ord. titular bp. of Sozusa and aux. of Bangalore, Aug. 22, 1962; titular abp. of Filippi and coadj. abp. of Bangalore, Nov. 9, 1964; abp. of Bangalore, 1968-71; associate secretary, 1971-73, and secretary, 1973-85, of Congregation for Evangelization of Peoples; cardinal May 25, 1985; deacon, St. Mary of Grace; transferred to the order of cardinal priests Jan. 29, 1996; prefect of Congregation for Oriental Churches, 1985-91. *Curial membership*: Evangelization of Peoples, Causes of Saints, (congregations); Apostolic Signatura (tribunal); Interreligious Dialogue, Family (councils); International Eucharistic Congresses (commission).

Lustiger, Jean-Marie: b. Sept. 17, 1926, Paris, France, of Polish-Jewish parents who emigrated to France after World War I; taken in by Catholic family in Orleans when his parents were deported during Nazi occupation (his mother died in 1943 at Auschwitz); convert to Catholicism, baptized Aug. 25, 1940; active in Young Christian Students during university days; ord. priest Apr. 17, 1954; ord. bp. of Orleans, Dec. 8, 1979; abp. of Paris, Jan. 31, 1981; cardinal Feb. 2, 1983; titular church, St. Louis of France. Abp. of Paris, ordinary for Eastern-Rite faithful in France without ordinaries of their own. *Curial membership*: Secretariat of State (second section); Bishops, Clergy, Consecrated Life and Societies of Apostolic Life, Oriental Churches, (congregations); Culture (council).

Macharski, Franciszek: b. May 20, 1927, Kraków, Poland; ord. priest Apr. 2, 1950; engaged in pastoral work, 1950-56; continued theological studies in Fribourg, Switzerland, 1956-60; taught pastoral theology at the Faculty of Theology in Kraków, 1970; app. rector of archdiocesan seminary at Kraków, 1970; ord. abp. of Kraków, Jan. 6, 1979, by Pope John Paul II; cardinal priest June 30, 1979; titular church, St. John at the Latin Gate. Abp. of Kraków. *Curial membership*: Secretariat of State (second section); Bishops, Clergy, Consecrated Life and Societies of Apostolic Life, Education, Evangelization of Peoples (congregations).

Mahony, Roger M.: b. Feb. 27, 1936, Hollywood,

Calif.; ord. priest (Fresno diocese) May 1, 1962; ord. titular bp. of Tamascani and aux. bp. of Fresno, Mar. 19, 1975; bp. of Stockton, Feb. 15, 1980, installed Apr. 25, 1980; abp. of Los Angeles, July 16, 1985, installed Sept. 5, 1985; cardinal June 28, 1991; titular church, Four Crowned Saints. Abp. of Los Angeles. *Curial membership*: Social Communications (council); Economic Affairs (office).

Maida, Adam Joseph: b. Mar. 18, 1930, East Vandergrift, Pa.; ord. priest (Pittsburgh diocese) May 26, 1956; ord. bp. of Green Bay, Jan. 25, 1984; app. abp. of Detroit, Apr. 28, 1990, installed June 12, 1990; cardinal Nov. 26, 1994; titular church, Sts. Vitalis, Valeria, Gervase and Protase. Abp. of Detroit. *Curial membership*: Clergy, Education (congregations); Migrants and Itinerant Peoples (council); Institute for Works of Religion (commission).

Majella Agnelo, Geraldo: b. Oct. 19, 1933, Juiz de Fora, Brazil; ord. priest, June 29, 1957; taught at the seminary of Aparecida, Immaculate Conception Seminary, and Pius XI Theological Institute; rector of Our Lady of the Assumption Seminary; bp. of Toledo May 5, 1978; cons. Aug. 6, 1978; app. abp. of Londrina Oct. 27, 1982; pres. of the Brazilian Bishops' Liturgical Commission; app. sec. of the Cong. For Divine Worship and the Discipline of Sacraments Sept. 16, 1991; app. abp. of São Salvador da Bahia Jan. 13, 1999; cardinal priest Feb. 21, 2001; titular church, St. Gregory the Great in Magliana Nuova. Abp. of São Salvador da Bahia. *Curial membership*: Pastoral Care of Migrants and Itinerant People (council); Cultural Heritage of the Church (commission).

Margéot,* Jean: b. Feb. 3, 1916, Quatre-Bornes, Mauritius; ord. priest Dec. 17, 1938; ord. bp. of Port Louis, 1969-93; cardinal June 28, 1988; titular church, St. Gabriel the Archangel all'Acqua Traversa. Bp. emeritus of Port Louis.

Martinez Somalo, Eduardo: b. Mar. 31, 1927, Baños de Rio Tobia, Spain; ord. priest Mar. 19, 1950; ord. titular bp. of Tagora with personal title of abp., Dec. 13, 1975; in secretariat of state from 1956; substitute (assistant) secretary of state, 1979-88; cardinal June 28, 1988; deacon, Most Holy Name of Jesus (raised *pro hac vice* to presbyteral title); promoted to cardinal priest, Jan. 9, 1999; prefect of Congregation for Divine Worship and Sacraments, 1988-92. Prefect of Congregation for Institutes of Consecrated Life and Societies of Apostolic Life, Jan. 21, 1992; Chamberlain (Camerlengo) of the Holy Roman Church, Apr. 5, 1993; Protodeacon 1996-99. *Curial membership*: Secretariat of State (second section); Bishops, Causes of Saints, Clergy, Divine Worship and Sacraments, Education, Evangelization of Peoples (congregations); Texts (council); Latin America, Institute for Works of Religion (commissions).

Martini, Carlo Maria, S.J.: b. Feb. 15, 1927, Turin, Italy; entered Jesuits Sept. 25, 1944; ord. priest July 13, 1952; biblical scholar; seminary professor, Chieri, Italy, 1958-61; professor and later rector, 1969-78, of Pontifical Biblical Institute; rector of Pontifical Gregorian University, 1978-79; author of theological, biblical and spiritual works; abp. of Milan, 1980-2002; cardinal Feb. 2, 1983; titular church, St. Cecilia. Abp. emeritus of Milan. *Curial membership*: Consecrated Life and Societies of Apostolic Life, Education Oriental Churches (congregations); Culture (council); Cultural Heritage of the Church (commission).

Mayer,* Paul Augustin, O.S.B.: b. May 23, 1911, Altötting, Germany; ord. priest Aug. 25, 1935; rector of St. Anselm's Univ., Rome, 1949-66; secretary of Congregation for Religious and Secular Institutes, 1972-84; ord. titular bp. of Satriano with personal title of abp., Feb. 13, 1972; pro-prefect of Congregations for Sacraments and Divine Worship, 1984; cardinal May 25, 1985; deacon, St. Anselm; transferred to order of cardinal priests Jan. 29, 1996. Prefect of Congregation for Divine Worship and Sacraments, 1985-88; president of Pontifical Commission "Ecclesia Dei," 1988-91.

McCarrick, Theodore E.: b. July 7, 1930, New York, NY; ord. priest May 31, 1958; dean of students Catholic Univ. of America, 1961-63; pres., Catholic Univ. of Puerto Rico, 1965-69; secretary to Cardinal Cooke, 1970; ord. titular bp. of Rusubisir and aux. bp. of New York, June 29, 1977; app. first bp. of Metuchen, NJ, Nov. 19, 1981, installed Jan. 31, 1982; app. abp. of Newark, June 3, 1986, installed July 25, 1986; abp. of Washington, Nov. 21, 2000; ins. Jan. 3, 2001, cardinal priest Feb. 21, 2001; titular church, Sts. Nereus and Achilleus. Abp. of Washington. *Curial membership*: Justice and Peace (council); APSA.

Medina Estévez, Jorge Arturo: b. Dec. 23, 1926, Santiago, Chile; ord. priest June 12, 1954; ord. abp. Jan. 6, 1985, Santiago, Chile; appointed pro-prefect, Congregation for Divine Worship and the Discipline of the Sacraments 1996-98; prefect of the Congregation for Divine Worship and the Discipline of the Sacraments, 1998; cardinal, Feb. 21, 1998; deaconry, St. Sabas. Prefect of the Congregation for Divine Worship and the Discipline of the Sacraments. *Curial membership*: Bishops, Clergy, Doctrine of the Faith (congregations); Family, Texts (councils); Latin America (commission).

Meisner, Joachim: b. Dec. 25, 1933, Breslau, Silesia, Germany (present-day Wroclaw, Poland); ord. priest Dec. 22, 1962; regional director of Caritas; ord. titular bp. of Vina and aux. of apostolic administration of Erfurt-Meiningen, E. Germany, May 17, 1975; bp. of Berlin, 1980-88; cardinal Feb. 2, 1983; titular church, St. Prudenziana. Abp. of Cologne, Dec. 20, 1988. *Curial membership*: Bishops, Clergy, Divine Worship and Sacraments (congregations); Economic Affairs of Holy See (office).

Mejía, Jorge María: b. Jan. 31, 1923, Buenos Aires, Argentina; ord. priest, Sept. 22, 1945; prof. of Old Testament studies at Catholic University of Buenos Aires; *peritus* at Second Vatican Council; sec. of CELAM's Department of Ecumenism, 1967-77; sec. of Pontifical Commission for Religious Relations with Jews, 1977-86; vice-president of the Pontifical Commission Justice and Peace and titular bp. of Apollonia, April 12, 1986; sec. of the Cong. for Bishops and titular abp., March 1994; Archivist and Librarian of the Holy Roman Church, 1998; cardinal deacon, Feb. 21, 2001; titular church, Deaconry of St. Jerome *della Carità*. Archivist and Librarian of the Holy Roman Church. *Curial membership*: Causes of Saints (congregation); Culture, Justice and Peace, Interreligious Dialogue (councils); Cultural Heritage of the Church (commission).

Monduzzi,* Dino: b. Apr. 2, 1922, Brisighella, Italy; ord. priest July 22, 1945; director of Catholic Action in Calabria and Sardinia; served in Agrarian Reform Agency in Fucino; sec. in the Office of the Maestro di Camera 1959-67; sec. and regent of the Apostolic Palace 1967-86; ord. titular bp. of Capri Jan. 6, 1987; prefect of the Papal Household 1986-1998; cardinal, Feb. 21, 1998; deaconry, St. Sebastian on the Palatine. *Curial membership*: Causes of Saints, Divine Worship and the Discipline of the Sacraments (congregations).

Moussa I Daoud, Ignace: b. Sept. 18, 1930, Meskaneh, Syria; ord. priest, Oct. 17, 1954; elected July 2, 1977 bp. of Cairo, Egypt by Syrian Patriarchal Synod; cons. Sept. 18, 1977; member of the commission for the revision of the Eastern Code of Canon Law and chaired the commission that translated the Code of Canons of the Eastern Churches into Arabic; promoted abp. of Homs for Syrians, Syria, July 6, 1994; elected patriarch of Antioch for Syrians, Oct. 13, 1998; app. prefect of the Cong. for the Oriental Churches, Nov. 25, 2000; cardinal Feb. 21, 2001 (as patriarch, he has no titular church). Prefect of the Congregation for the Oriental Churches. *Curial membership*: Doctrine of the Faith, Causes of Saints (congregations), Christian Unity, Legislative Texts (councils).

Murphy-O'Connor, Cormac: b. Aug. 24, 1932, Reading, Great Britain; ord. priest, Oct. 28, 1956; dir. of vocations and secretary to the bp.; rector of the Venerable English College, Rome, 1971-77; app. bp. of Arundel and Brighton, Nov. 17, 1977; cons., Dec. 21, 1977; co-chairman of the Anglican-Roman Catholic International Commission (ARCIC), 1982-2000; chairman of several committees of the Bishop's Conference of England and Wales; app. abp. of Westminster, Feb. 15, 2000; cardinal, Feb. 21, 2001; titular church, St. Mary *sopra Minerva*. Abp. of Westminster. *Curial membership*: Sacraments (congregation); Family, Culture (councils); APSA (office).

Napier, O.F.M., Wilfrid Fox: b. March 8, 1941, Swartberg, South Africa; ord. priest for the Franciscans, July 25, 1970; app. apostolic admin. of Kokstad, 1978; app. bp. of Kokstad, Nov. 29, 1980; cons., Feb. 28, 1981; deeply involved in the mediation and negotiations surrounding the ending of apartheid in South Africa and subsequent South African politics; pres. of the Southern African Catholic Bishops' Conference, 1987-94; app. abp. of Durban, May 29, 1992; apostolic admin. *sede vacante et ad nutum Sanctae Sedis* of Umzimkulu, 1994; cardinal, Feb. 21, 2001; titular church, St. Francis of Assisi in Acilia. Abp. of Durban. *Curial membership*: Evangelization of Peoples, Institutes of Consecrated Life and Societies of Apostolic Life (congregations); Cultural Heritage of the Church (commission).

Neves, Lucas Moreira, O.P.: b. Sept. 16, 1925, São Joao del Rei, Brazil; ord. priest July 9, 1950; ord. titular bp. of Feradi maggiore and aux. of São Paulo, Aug. 26, 1967; assigned to Vatican, 1974; vice president of Pontifical Commission for Laity, 1974-79; abp. Oct. 15, 1979; secretary of Congregation for Bishops, 1979-87; assigned titular see of Vescovia, Jan. 3, 1987; abp. of São Salvador da Bahia, 1987-98; cardinal June 28, 1988; titular church, Sts. Boniface and Alexius; Prefect of Congregation of Bishops, 1998-2000; transferred to order of cardinal bishops, June 25, 1998 (suburbicarian see of Sabina-Poggio Mireto). Prefect emeritus of Congregation of Bishops. *Curial membership*: Clergy, Consecrated Life and Societies of Apostolic Life, Education, Evangelization of Peoples, Oriental Churches (congregations); Family, Culture (councils).

Nguyên Van Thuân, François Xavier: b. April 17, 1928, Huê, Viet Nam; ord. priest, June 11, 1953; app. bp. of Nha Trang, April 13, 1967, cons. June 24, 1967; co-adj. abp. of Saigon (now Ho Chi Minh City), April 24, 1975; arrested by Communists, Aug. 15, 1975; imprisoned without trial for thirteen years, nine years in solitary confinement; released Nov. 21, 1988; vice-pres. Pont. Council for Justice and Peace, Nov. 24, 1994; pres., Pont. Council for Justice and Peace, June 24, 1998; cardinal, Feb. 21, 2001; titular church, Deaconry of St. Mary della Scala. Pres. of the Pont. Council for Justice and Peace. *Curial membership*: Evangelization of Peoples, Sacraments (congregations); Laity (council).

Noè,* Virgilio: b. Mar. 30, 1922, Zelata di Bereguardo, Italy; ord. priest Oct. 1, 1944; master of pontifical ceremonies and undersecretary of Congregation for Sacraments and Divine Worship, 1970-82; ord. titular bp. of Voncario with personal title of abp., Mar. 6, 1982; coadj. Archpriest of St. Peter's Basilica, 1989-2002; vicar general of Vatican City State, 1991-2002; cardinal June 28, 1991; deacon, St. John Bosco (in Via Tuscolana). Archpriest emeritus of St. Peter's Basilica, Vicar General emeritus of Vatican City State and President emeritus of the Fabric of St. Peter, 1991. *Curial membership*: Causes of Saints, Divine Worship and Sacraments (congregations).

Obando Bravo, Miguel, S.D.B.: b. Feb. 2, 1926, La Libertad, Nicaragua; ord. priest Aug. 10, 1958; ord. titular bp. of Puzia di Bizacena and aux. of Matagalpa, Mar. 31, 1968; abp. of Managua, Feb. 16, 1970; cardinal May 25, 1985; titular church, St. John the Evangelist (a Spinaceta). Abp. of Managua. *Curial membership*: Clergy, Consecrated Life and Societies of Apostolic Life, Divine Worship and Sacraments, (congregations); Latin America (commission).

Ortega y Alamino, Jaime Lucas: b. Oct. 18, 1936, Jagüey Grande, Cuba; ord. priest Aug. 2, 1964 detained in work camps (UMAP) 1966-67; parish priest; ord. bp. of Pinar del Rio, Jan. 14, 1979; app. abp. of Havana, Nov. 20, 1981; cardinal Nov. 26, 1994; titular church, Sts. Aquila and Priscilla. Abp. of Havana. *Curial membership*: Clergy (congregation); Health Care Workers (council); Latin America (commission).

Otunga, Maurice Michael: b. Jan., 1923, Chebukwa, Kenya; son of pagan tribal chief; baptized 1935, at age of 12; ord. priest Oct. 3, 1950, at Rome; taught at Kisumu major seminary for three years; attaché in apostolic delegation at Mombasa, 1953-56; ord. titular bp. of Tacape and aux. of Kisumu, Feb. 25, 1957; bp. of Kisii, 1960-69; titular abp. of Bomarzo and coadj. of Nairobi, Nov. 15, 1969; abp. of Nairobi, Oct. 24, 1971 (resigned May 14, 1997); cardinal Mar. 5, 1973; titular church, St. Gregory Barbarigo. Abp. emeritus of Nairobi, military ordinary of Kenya, 1981. *Curial membership*: Consecrated Life and Societies of Apostolic Life (congregations).

Pappalardo,* Salvatore: b. Sept. 23, 1918, Villafranca Sicula, Sicily; ord. priest Apr. 12, 1941; entered diplomatic service of secretariat of state, 1947; ord. titular abp. of Miletus, Jan. 16, 1966; pro-nuncio in Indonesia, 1966-69; president of Pontifical Ecclesiastical Academy, 1969-70; abp. of Palermo, Oct. 17, 1970-96; cardinal Mar. 5, 1973; titular church, St.

Mary Odigitria of the Sicilians. Abp. emeritus of Palermo.

Paskai, László, O.F.M.: b. May 8, 1927, Szeged, Hungary; ord. priest Mar. 3, 1951; ord. titular bp. of Bavagaliana and apostolic administrator of Veszprem, Apr. 5, 1978; bp. of Veszprem Mar. 31, 1979; coadj. abp. of Kalocsa, Apr. 5, 1982; abp. of Esztergom (renamed Esztergom-Budapest, 1993), Mar. 3, 1987; cardinal June 28, 1988; titular church, St. Theresa (al Corso d'Italia). Abp. of Esztergom-Budapest. *Curial membership*: Consecrated Life and Societies of Apostolic Life, Oriental Churches (congregations); Texts (council).

Pengo, Polycarp: b. Aug. 5, 1944, Mwayze, Tanzania; ord. priest Aug. 5, 1971; taught moral theology at the major seminary in Kipalapala, Tanzania, 1977; rector of the major seminary in Segerea, 1978-83; ord. bp. of Nachingwea, Jan. 6, 1984; bp. of Tunduru-Masasi 1986-90; co-adjutor abp. of Dar-es-Salaam, Jan. 22, 1990; abp. of Dar-es-Salaam, July 22,1992, in succession to Laurean Cardinal Rugambwa; cardinal Feb. 21, 1998; titular church, Our Lady of La Salette. Abp. of Dar-es-Salaam. *Curial membership*: Evangelization of Peoples (congregation); Interreligious Dialogue (council).

Pham Dinh Tung,* Paul Joseph: b. June 15, 1919, Binh-Hoa, Vietnam; ord. priest June 6, 1949; ord. bp. of Bac Ninh, Aug. 15, 1963; apostolic administrator of Hanoi, June 18, 1990; abp. of Hanoi, Mar. 23, 1994; cardinal Nov. 26, 1994; titular church, St. Mary Queen of Peace in Ostia mare. Abp. of Hanoi.

Pimenta,* Simon Ignatius: b. Mar. 1, 1920, Marol, India; ord. priest Dec. 21, 1949; ord. titular bp. of Bocconia and aux. of Bombay, June 29, 1971; coadj. abp. of Bombay, Feb. 26, 1977; abp. of Bombay, Sept. 11, 1978; cardinal June 28, 1988; titular church, Mary, Queen of the World (a Torre Spaccata). Abp. emeritus of Bombay (resigned Nov. 8, 1996).

Piovanelli, Silvano: b. Feb. 21, 1924, Ronta di Mugello, Italy; ord. priest July 13, 1947; ord. titular bp. of Tubune di Mauretania and aux. of Florence, June 24, 1982; abp. of Florence, 1983-2001; cardinal May 25, 1985; titular church, St. Mary of Graces (Via Trionfale). Abp. emeritus of Florence.

Poggi,* Luigi: b. Nov. 25, 1917, Piacenza, Italy; ord. priest July 28, 1940; studied diplomacy at the Pontifical Ecclesiastical Academy, 1944-46; started to work at Secretariat of State; ord. titular bp. of Forontoniana with personal title of abp., May 9, 1965; apostolic delegate for Central Africa., 1965; nuncio in Peru; recalled to Rome, 1973; negotiated with various Eastern bloc governments to improve situation of the Church; named head of Holy See's delegation for permanent contact with government of Poland, 1974; nuncio in Italy, 1986-92; pro-librarian and pro-archivist of the Holy Roman Church, 1992; cardinal Nov. 26, 1994; protodeacon, Feb. 2002; titular church, Diaconate of St. Mary in Domnica. Archivist and librarian emeritus of the Holy Roman Church.

Poletto, Severino: b. March 18, 1933, Salgareda (Treviso), Italy; ord. priest, June 29, 1957; pref. of discipline at the diocesan seminary and vocation director; founded the Diocesan Centre for Family Ministry, 1973; coordinated the city mission for the 500th Anniversary of the foundation of the diocese of Casale Monferrato; app. coadj. bp. of Fossano, April 3, 1980; cons., May 17, 1980; succeeded to see on Oct. 29,

1980; app. bp. of Asti, March 16, 1989; app. abp. of Turin, June 19, 1999; cardinal, Feb. 21, 2001; titular church, St. Joseph in Via Trionfale. Abp. of Turin. *Curial membership*: *Clergy* (congregation); Economic Affairs of the Holy See (office); Cultural Heritage of the Church (commission).

Policarpo, José Da Cruz: b. Feb. 26, 1936, Alvorninha, Portugal; ord. priest, Aug. 15, 1961; dir. of the seminary in Penafirme, rector of the seminary in Olivais and dean of the Theological Faculty of the Portuguese Catholic University; served two terms as rector of the Portuguese Catholic University, 1988-96; app. titular bp. of Caliabria and aux. bp. of Lisbon, May 26, 1978; cons., June 29, 1978; app. coadj. abp. of Lisbon, March 5, 1997; succeeded as patriarch of Lisbon, March 24, 1998; grand chancellor of the Portuguese Catholic University, pres. of the Portuguese Episcopal Conference; cardinal, Feb. 21, 2001; titular church, St. Anthony in Campo Formio. Patriarch of Lisbon. *Curial membership:* Education (congregation), Culture, Laity (councils).

Pompedda, Mario Francesco: b. April 18, 1929, Ozieri (Sardinia), Italy; ord. priest, Dec. 23, 1951 for Vatican clergy; app. to Tribunal of the Roman Rota, 1955 and held a variety of posts, including Defender of the Bond, prelate auditor, 1969, and dean, 1993; pres. of the Appellate Court of Vatican City State; app. titular abp. of Bisarcio, Nov. 29, 1997 and ord. by Holy Father, Jan. 6, 1998; app. prefect of the Supreme Tribunal of the Apostolic Signatura and pres. of the Court of Cassation of Vatican City State; cardinal, Feb. 21, 2001; titular church, Deaconry of the Annunciation of the Blessed Virgin Mary in Via Ardeatina. Prefect of the Supreme Tribunal of the Apostolic Signatura and President of the Court of Cassation of Vatican City State. *Curial membership*: Sacraments (congregation); Texts (council).

Poupard, Paul: b. Aug. 30, 1930, Bouzille, France; ord. priest Dec. 18, 1954; scholar; author of a number of works; ord. titular bp. of Usula and aux. of Paris, Apr. 6, 1979; title of abp. and pro-president of the Secretariat for Non-Believers, 1980; cardinal deacon May 25, 1985; transferred to order of cardinal priests Jan. 29, 1996; titular church, St. Praxedes, president of Pontifical Council for Dialogue with Non-Believers, 1985-93. President of Pontifical Council for Culture, 1988. *Curial membership*: Divine Worship and Sacraments, Education, Evangelization of Peoples (congregations); Interreligious Dialogue (council).

Primatesta,* **Raúl Francisco**: b. Apr. 14, 1919, Capilla del Senor, Argentina; ord. priest Oct. 25, 1942, at Rome; taught at minor and major seminaries of La Plata; contributed to several theology reviews; ord. titular bp. of Tanais and aux. of La Plata, Aug. 15, 1957; bp. of San Rafael, 1961-65; abp. of Cordoba, 1965-98; cardinal Mar. 5, 1973; titular church, Blessed Mary Sorrowful Virgin. Abp. emeritus of Cordoba, Argentina.

Pujats, Janis: b. Nov. 14, 1930, the Rezekne district of Latvia; ord. priest March 29, 1951; taught art history and liturgy at the catholic Theological Seminary, Riga; vicar general in the Metropolitan Curia, Riga, 1979-84; declared *persona non grata* by the KGB, 1984; app. abp. of Riga, May 8, 1991, cons., June 1, 1991; pres. of the Latvian Bishops' Conference; cardinal priest (*in pectore*), Feb. 21, 1998, titu-

lar church, St. Sylvia. Abp. of Riga. *Curial membership*: Causes of Saints (congregation).

Puljic, Vinko: b. Sept. 8, 1945, Prijecani, Bosnia-Herzegovina; ord. priest June 29, 1970; spiritual director of minor seminary of Zadar, 1978-87; parish priest; app. vice-rector of Sarajevo major seminary, 1990; ord. abp. of Vrhbosna (Sarajevo), Jan. 6, 1991, in Rome; cardinal Nov. 26, 1994; titular church, St. Clare in Vigna Clara. Abp. of Sarajevo. *Curial membership*: Evangelization of Peoples (congregation); Interreligious Dialogue (council).

Ratzinger, Joseph: b. Apr. 16, 1927, Marktl am Inn, Germany; ord. priest June 29, 1951; professor of dogmatic theology at University of Regensburg, 1969-77; member of International Theological Commission, 1969-80; ord. abp. of Munich-Freising, May 28, 1977 (resigned Feb. 15, 1982); cardinal June 27, 1977; titular church, St. Mary of Consolation (in Tiburtina); transferred to order of cardinal bishops as titular bp. of suburbicarian see of Velletri-Segni, Apr. 5, 1993. Prefect of Congregation for Doctrine of the Faith, 1981; president of Biblical and Theological Commissions. Vice-dean of the Sacred College of Cardinals (Nov. 6, 1998, appr. Nov. 9, 1998). *Curial membership*: Secretariat of State (second section); Bishops, Divine Worship and Sacraments, Education, Evangelization of Peoples, Oriental Churches (congregations); Christian Unity, Culture (councils); *Ecclesia Dei*, Latin America (commissions).

Razafindratandra, Armand Gaétan: b. Aug. 7, 1925, Ambohimalaza, Madagascar; ord. priest July 27, 1954; ord. bp. of Mahajanga, July 2, 1978; app. abp. of Antananarivo, Feb. 3, 1994, installed May 15, 1994; cardinal Nov. 26, 1994; titular church, Sts. Sylvester and Martin ai Monti. Abp. of Antananarivo and apostolic administrator of Miarinarivo. *Curial membership*: Evangelization of Peoples (congregation); Laity (council).

Re, Giovanni Battista: b. Jan. 30, 1934, Borno (Brescia), Italy; ord. priest March 3, 1957; earned doctorate in canon law and taught in the Brescia Seminary; entered Holy See diplomatic service; served in Panama and Iran; recalled for service in Secretariat of State; sec. for Cong. for Bishops, 1987; titular abp., Nov. 7, 1987; *sostituto* for Secretariat of State, 1989; prefect of the Cong. of Bishops and pres. of the Pont. Comm. for Latin America, Sep. 16, 2000; cardinal Feb. 21, 2001; titular church, Twelve Holy Apostles. Prefect of the Cong. of Bishops. *Curial membership*: Secretariat of State (second section); Doctrine of the Faith (congregation); Vatican City State (commission).

Rivera Carrera, Norberto: b. June 6, 1942, La Purísima, Mexico; ord. priest July 3, 1966; taught dogmatic theology at the major seminary of Mexico City; professor of ecclesiology at Pontifical University of Mexico; bp. of Tehuacán, Nov. 5, 1985; abp. of Mexico City, June 13,1995; cardinal Feb. 21, 1998; titular church, St. Francis of Assisi at *Ripa Grande*. Abp. of Mexico City. *Curial membership*: Clergy, Divine Worship and the Discipline of Sacraments (congregation); Family (council); Latin America (commission).

Rodríguez Maradiaga, S.D.B., Oscar Andrés: b. Dec. 29, 1942, Tegucigalpa, Honduras; ord. priest for the Salesians June 28, 1870; taught in various Salesian colleges in El Salvador, Honduras and Guatemala;

prof. at the Salesian Theological Institute, Guatemala and rector of the Salesian Philosophical Institute, Guatemala; app. titular bp. of Pudentiana and aux. bp. of Tegucigalpa Oct. 28, 1978; app. abp. of Tegucigalpa Jan. 8, 1993; pres. of CELAM, 1995-99; pres. of the Episcopal Conference of Honduras; cardinal priest Feb. 21, 2001; titular church, St. Mary of Hope. Abp. of Tegucigalpa. *Curial membership*: Clergy (congregation); Justice and Peace, Social Communication (councils); Latin America (commission).

Rossi,* Opilio: b. May 14, 1910, New York, N.Y.; holds Italian citizenship; ord. priest for diocese of Piacenza (now Piacenza-Bobbio), Italy, Mar. 11, 1933; served in nunciatures in Belgium, The Netherlands, and Germany, 1938-53; ord. titular abp. of Ancyra, Dec. 27, 1953; nuncio in Ecuador, 1953-59, Chile, 1959-61, Austria 1961-76; cardinal deacon May 24, 1976; transferred to order of cardinal priests, June 22, 1987; titular church, St. Lawrence (in Lucina); president of Pontifical Committee for International Eucharistic Congresses, 1983-90; president of Commission for the Sanctuaries of Pompeii, Loreto and Bari, 1984-93.

Rouco Varela, Antonio María: b. Aug. 24, 1936, Villalba, Spain; ord. priest March 28, 1959; taught fundamental theology and canon law at the Mondoñedo seminary; adjunct professor at the University of Munich; taught ecclesiastical law at Pontifical University of Salamanca; vice-rector of Pontifical University of Salamanca; titular bp. of Gergis and aux. bp. of Santiago de Compostela, Sep. 17, 1976; abp. of Santiago de Compostela, My 9,1984; abp. of Madrid June 29, 1994; cardinal, Feb. 21, 1998, titular church, St. Laurence *in Damaso*. Abp. of Madrid. *Curial membership*: Bishops, Clergy, Education (congregations); "Cor Unum," Culture, Texts (councils).

Rubiano Sáenz, Pedro: b. Sept. 13, 1932, Cartago, Colombia; ord. priest July 8, 1956; chaplain to Marco Fidel Suárez Air Force Academy, St. Liberata National College, and Our Lady of Remedies Clinic; app. bp. of Cúcuta June 2, 1971; cons. June 11, 1971; app. coadj. abp. of Cali Marh 26, 1983; abp. of Cali Feb. 7, 1985; apost. admin. of Popayán; pres. of the Episcopal Conference of Colombia; app. December 27, 1994; cardinal priest Feb. 21, 2001; titular church, Transfiguration of Our Lord Jesus Christ. Abp. of Bogotá. *Curial membership*: Education (congregation); Pastoral Care of Migrants and Itinerant Peoples (council).

Ruini, Camillo: b. Feb. 19, 1931, Sassuolo, Italy; ord. priest Dec. 8, 1954; taught at seminaries in central Italy; ord. titular bp. of Nepte and aux. bp. of Reggio Emilia and Guastella, June 29, 1983; secretary general of Italian Bishops' Conference, 1986-91; abp. Jan. 17, 1991 and pro-vicar general of the Pope for the Rome diocese; pro-Archpriest of Patriarchal Lateran Archbasilica; cardinal June 28, 1991; titular church, St. Agnes outside the Wall. Vicar General of the Pope for the Diocese of Rome and Archpriest of Patriarchal Lateran Basilica, July 1, 1991; Grand Chancellor of Pontifical Lateran University; President of the Peregrinatio ad Petri Sedem, 1992-96. *Curial membership*: Bishops (congregation).

Sabattani,* Aurelio: b. Oct. 18, 1912, Casal Fiumanese, Italy; ord. priest July 26, 1935; jurist; served in various assignments in his native diocese of Imola and as judge and later an official of the regional ecclesiastical tribunal of Bologna; called to Rome in 1955 as prelate auditor of the Roman Rota; ord. titular abp. of Justinian Prima, July 25, 1965; prelate of Loreto, 1965-71; secretary of Supreme Tribunal of Apostolic Signatura and consultor of Secretariat of State, 1971; pro-prefect of Apostolic Signatura, 1982-83; cardinal deacon Feb. 2, 1983; transferred to order of cardinal priests Apr. 5, 1993; titular church, St. Apollinaris; prefect of Apostolic Signatura, 1983-88; archpriest of Patriarchal Vatican Basilica and president of the Fabric of St. Peter, 1983-91; former vicar general of the Pope for Vatican City.

Saldarini, Giovanni: b. Dec. 11, 1924, Cantu, Italy; ord. priest May 31, 1947; respected scripture scholar; taught scripture at Milan archdiocesan seminary, 1952-67; ord. titular bp. of Guadiaba and aux. bp. of Milan, Dec. 7, 1984; abp. of Turin Jan. 31, 1989; cardinal June 28, 1991 (resigned, June 19, 1999); titular church, Sacred Heart of Jesus (a Castro Pretorio). Abp. emeritus of Turin.

Sales*, Eugênio de Araújo: b. Nov. 8, 1920, Acari, Brazil; ord. priest Nov. 21, 1943; ord. titular bp. of Tibica and aux. bp. of Natal, Aug. 15, 1954; abp. of São Salvador, 1968-71; cardinal Apr. 28, 1969; titular church, St. Gregory VII. Abp. of Rio de Janeiro (1971), ordinary for Eastern Rite Catholics in Brazil without ordinaries of their own rites. *Curial membership*: Secretariat of State (second section).

Sánchez,* José T.: b. Mar. 17, 1920, Pandan, Philippines; ord. priest May 12, 1946; ord. titular bp. of Lesvi and coadj. bp. of Lucena, May 12, 1968; bp. of Lucena, 1976-82; abp. of Nueva Segovia Jan. 12, 1982 (resigned Mar. 22, 1986); secretary of Congregation for Evangelization of Peoples, 1985-91; cardinal June 28, 1991; deacon, St. Pius V (a Villa Carpegna); president of Commission for Preservation of Artistic and Historic Patrimony of the Holy See, 1991-93. Prefect of Congr. for the Clergy, 1991-96.

Sandoval Íñiguez, Juan: b. Mar. 28, 1933, Yahualica, Mexico; ord. priest Oct. 27, 1957; ord. coadj. bp. of Ciudad Juárez, Apr. 30, 1988; bp. of Ciudad Juarez, July 11, 1992; app. abp. of Guadalajara, Apr. 21, 1994; cardinal Nov. 26, 1994; titular church, Our Lady of Guadalupe and St. Philip the Martyr on Via Aurelia. Abp. of Guadalajara. *Curial membership*: Institutes of Consecrated Life and Societies of Apostolic Life, Catholic Education (congregations); Latin America (commission); Economic Affairs of the Holy See (office); Laity, Latin America (councils).

Santos, Alexandre José Maria dos, O.F.M.: b. Mar. 18, 1924, Zavala, Mozambique; ord. priest July 25, 1953; first Mozambican black priest; ord. abp. of Maputo, Mar. 9, 1975; cardinal June 28, 1988; titular church, St. Frumentius (ai Prati Fiscali). Abp. of Maputo. *Curial membership*: Sacraments (congregation).

Saraiva Martins, José, C.M.F.: b. Jan. 6, 1932, Gagos do Jarmelo, Portugal; ord. priest for the Claretians, March 16, 1957; taught at Claretian seminary in Marino, Italy; taught at Claretianum, Rome; taught at the Pontifical Urbanian University and served as rector, 1977-80, 1980-83, 1986-88; sec. of the Cong. for Catholic Education and titular abp. of Thuburnica, May 26, 1988; cons. abp., July 2, 1988; pref. of Cong. for the Causes of Saints, May 30, 1998;

cardinal, Feb. 21, 2001; titular church, Deaconry of Our Lady of the Sacred Heart. Prefect of the Congregation for the Causes of Saints. *Curial membership*: Bishops, Sacraments (congregations); Health Care (council).

Scheffczyk,* Leo: b. Feb. 21, 1920, Beuthen (modern Bytom), Poland; ord. priest, June 29, 1947; named vice-rector of the seminary in Königstein (Taunus) for seminarians from then East Germany; studied under Michael Schmaus; taught at Tübingen University and was professor of dogmatic theology at the Ludwig Maximilian University of Münich, 1965-85; author of over 80 books, 500 papers, 400 book reviews, and countless articles; edited the *Münchener Theologisches Zeitschrift*, 1966-84; consultor to the Pontifical Council for the Family and the Commission on Faith of the German Bishops' Conference; cardinal, Feb. 21, 2001; titular church, Deaconry of St. Francis Xavier in Garbatella. Theologian.

Schönborn, Christoph, O.P.: b. Jan. 22, 1945, Skalsko, Bohemia (fled to Austria in Sept. 1945); entered Dominican Order in 1963; ord. priest, 1970; student pastor in Graz University, 1973-75; associate professor of dogma in the University of Fribourg, 1976; professor for theology, 1978; professor for dogmatic theology, 1981-91; member of the Orthodox-Roman Catholic Dialogue Commission of Switzerland, 1980-87; member International Theological Commission, 1980-; member of the foundation, "Pro Oriente" since 1984; Secretary for the Draft-Commission of the *Catechism of the Catholic Church*, 1987-1992; ord. aux. bp. (Sutri) of Vienna, Sept. 29, 1991; co-adjutor of Vienna, Apr. 13, 1995; abp. of Vienna, Sept. 14, 1995; cardinal, Feb. 21, 1998; titular church, Jesus the Divine Worker. Abp. of Vienna. *Curial membership*: Doctrine of the Faith, Education, Oriental Churches (congregations); Culture (council); Cultural Heritage of the Church (commission).

Schotte, Jan Pieter, C.I.C.M.: b. Apr. 29, 1928, Beveren-Leie, Belgium; entered Congregation of the Immaculate Heart of Mary (Scheut Missionaries) in 1946; ord. priest Aug. 3, 1952; taught canon law at Louvain and was rector of community's seminary in Washington, D.C.; general secretary of Congregation of the Immaculate Heart of Mary in Rome, 1967-72; secretary (1980) and vice-president (1983) of the Pontifical Commission of Justice and Peace; ord. titular bp. of Silli, Jan. 6, 1984; promoted to titular abp., Apr. 24, 1985; cardinal Nov. 26, 1994; deacon St. Julian of the Flemings. Secretary general of the Synod of Bishops since 1985; president of the Labor Office of the Holy See, 1989. *Curial membership*: Bishops, Causes of Saints, Evangelization of Peoples (congregations); Apostolic Signatura (tribunal); Latin America (commission).

Schwery, Henri: b. June 14, 1932, Saint-Leonard, Switzerland; ord. priest July 7, 1957; director of minor seminary and later rector of the College in Sion; ord. bp. of Sion, Sept. 17, 1977; cardinal June 28, 1991; titular church, Protomartyrs (a via Aurelia Antica). Bp. emeritus of Sion (retired Apr. 1, 1995). *Curial membership*: Causes of Saints (congregation); Social Communications (council).

Sebastiani, Sergio: b. April 11, 1931, Montemonaco (Ascoli Piceno), Italy; ord. priest, 1956; studied at Lateran University and Pontifical Ecclesiastical Academy; entered Holy See diplomatic service and posted

to Peru, Brazil, and Chile; recalled to Secretariat of State; app. titular abp. of Caesarea in Mauretania and pro-nuncio in Madagascar and Mauritius and apostolic delegate to Reunion and Comorros; nuncio to Turkey, 1985; sec. to Central Committee for the Great Jubilee of the Year 2000, 1994; pres. Prefecture for the Economic Affairs of the Holy See, Nov. 3, 1997; card. Feb. 21, 2001; titular church, Deaconry of St. Eustace. President of the Prefecture for the Economic Affairs of the Holy See. *Curial membership*: Bishops, Clergy, Causes of Saints (congregations); Christian Unity, Interreligious Dialogue (councils).

Sepe, Crescenzio: b. June 2, 1943, Carinaro (Caserta), Italy; ord. priest, Marh 12, 1967; taught at Lateran and Urbanian Universities; studied at Pontifical Ecclesiastical Academy; entered Holy See diplomatic service and posted to Brazil; recalled to Secretariat of State, 1987; pres. of Commission for Vatican Telecommunications; app. titular abp. of Grado and sec. of the Cong. for the Clergy, April 2, 1992; cons. April 26, 1992; General Secretary of the Central Committee for the Great Jubilee of the Year 2000, 1997-2001; Pref. Cong. for the Evangelization of Peoples, April 9, 2001; cardinal deacon Feb. 21, 2001; titular church, Deaconry of God the Merciful Father. Prefect of the Cong. for the Evangelization of Peoples. *Curial membership*: Clergy (congregation); Interreligious Dialogue, Social Communication (council).

Sfeir,* Nasrallah Pierre: b. May 15, 1920, Reyfoun, in Maronite diocese of Sarba, Lebanon; ord. priest May 7, 1950; secretary of Maronite patriarchate, 1956-61; taught Arabic literature and philosophy at Marist Fathers College, Jounieh, 1951-61; ord. titular bp. of Tarsus for the Maronites, July 16, 1961; elected Patriarch of Antioch for Maronites, Apr. 19, 1986, granted ecclesial communion by John Paul II May 7, 1986; cardinal Nov. 26, 1994. Patriarch of Antioch for Maronites. *Curial membership*: Oriental Churches (congregation); Health Care (council).

Shan Kuo-hsi, Paul, S.J.: b. Dec. 2, 1923, Puyang, China; ord. priest March 18, 1955; director of the Chinese section of the Sacred Heart School in Cebu; socius of the novice master in Thu-duc, Vietnam; novice master and rector of Manresa House, Chanhua, Taiwan; rector of St. Ignatius High School, Taipei, Taiwan; bp. of Hualien, Nov. 15, 1979; bp. of Kaohsiung, Taiwan, 1991; cardinal, Feb. 21, 1998; titular church, St. Chrysogonus. Bp. of Kaohsiung. *Curial membership*: Evangelization of Peoples (congregation); Interreligious Dialogue, Social Communications (councils).

Shirayanagi, Peter Seiichi: b. June 17, 1928, Hachioji City, Japan; ord. priest Dec. 21, 1954; ord. titular bp. of Atenia and aux. bp. of Tokyo, May 8, 1966; titular abp. of Castro and coadj. abp. of Tokyo, Nov. 15, 1969; succeeded to see, Feb. 21, 1970; cardinal Nov. 26, 1994; titular church, St. Emerentiana in Tor Fiorenza; res. June 12, 2000. Abp. emeritus of Tokyo. *Curial membership*: Family (council); Cultural Heritage of the Church (commission).

Silvestrini, Achille: b. Oct. 25, 1923, Brisighella, Italy; ord. priest July 13, 1946; official in Secretariat of State from 1953; ord. titular bp. of Novaliciana with personal title of abp., May 27, 1979; undersecretary, 1973-79, and secretary, 1979-88, of the Council for Public Affairs of the Church (now the second section of the Secretariat of State); cardinal

June 28, 1988; deacon, St. Benedict Outside St. Paul's Gate, promoted to cardinal priest, Jan. 9, 1999; prefect of Apostolic Signatura, 1988-91. Prefect of Congregation for Oriental Churches, 1991-2001; Grand Chancellor of Pontifical Oriental Institute. Prefect emeritus of Congregation for Oriental Churches. *Curial membership*: Secretariat of State (second section); Bishops, Causes of Saints, Doctrine of the Faith, Education, Evangelization of Peoples (congregations); Christian Unity, Texts, Interreligious Dialogue (councils).

Simonis, Adrianus J.: b. Nov. 26, 1931, Lisse, Netherlands; ord. priest June 15, 1957; ord. bp. of Rotterdam, Mar. 20, 1971; coadj. abp. of Utrecht, June 27, 1983; abp. of Utrecht, Dec. 3, 1983; cardinal May 25, 1985; titular church, St. Clement. Abp. of Utrecht. *Curial membership*: Consecrated Life and Societies of Apostolic Life, Education (congregations); Christian Unity (council).

Sin, Jaime L.: b. Aug. 31, 1928, New Washington, Philippines; ord. priest Apr. 3, 1954; diocesan missionary in Capiz, 1954-57; app. first rector of the St. Pius X Seminary, Roxas City, 1957; ord. titular bp. of Obba and aux. bp. of Jaro, Mar. 18, 1967; apostolic administrator of archdiocese of Jaro, June 20, 1970; titular abp. of Massa Lubrense and coadj. abp. of Jaro, Jan. 15, 1972; abp. of Jaro, 1972-74; abp. of Manila, Jan. 21, 1974; cardinal May 24, 1976; titular church, S. Maria (ai Monti). Abp. of Manila. *Curial membership*: Clergy, Consecrated Life and Societies of Apostolic Life, Divine Worship and Sacraments (congregations).

Sodano, Angelo: b. Nov. 23, 1927, Isola d'Asti, Italy; ord. priest Sept. 23, 1950; entered diplomatic service of the Holy See in 1959; served in Ecuador and Uruguay; ord. titular abp. of Nova di Cesare, Jan. 15, 1978; nuncio to Chile, 1978-88; secretary of the Council for Relations with States, 1988-90; pro-Secretary of State, 1990 (Dec. 1)-1991; cardinal June 28, 1991; titular church, S. Maria Nuova; transferred to order of cardinal Bishops, Jan 10, 1994, as titular bp. of suburbicarian see of Albano (while retaining title to S. Maria Nuova). Secretary of State, June 29, 1991. *Curial membership*: Bishops, Doctrine of the Faith, Oriental Churches (congregations); Vatican City State, Institute for Works of Religion (commission).

Stafford, James Francis: b. July 26, 1932, Baltimore, Md.; ord. priest (Baltimore*) Dec. 15, 1957; ord. titular bp. of Respetta and aux. bp. of Baltimore, Feb. 29, 1976; app. bp. of Memphis, Nov. 17, 1982; app. abp. of Denver, June 3, 1986, installed July 30, 1986; app. President of Pontifical Council for the Laity, Aug. 20, 1996; cardinal Feb. 21, 1998; titular church, the church of Jesus, the Good Shepherd at Montagnola. President of Pontifical Council for the Laity. *Curial membership*: Bishops, Doctrine of the Faith, Causes of Saints (congregations); Texts (council).

Stéphanos II Ghattas, C.M.*: b. Jan. 16, 1920, Sheikh Zein-el-Dine, Egypt; ord priest, March 25, 1944; taught philosophy and dogmatic theology at the major seminary in Tahta; joined Congregation of the Mission, 1952; worked in Lebanon and served as Vincentian econome and superior in Alexandria; elected by the Coptic Catholic Synod bp. of Thebes-Luxor, May 8, 1967; named apostolic admin. of the patriarchate to substitute for the ailing Patriarch Stéphanos I Sidarous; elected unanimously by the Coptic Catholic Synod patriarch of Alexandria for Copts; changed name from Andraos Ghattas to Stéphanos II in honor of his predecessor; cardinal, Feb. 21, 2001; as a patriarch, he did not receive a titular church. Patriarch emeritus of Alexandria for Copts. *Curial membership:* Oriental Churches (congregation).

Sterzinsky, Georg Maximilian: b. Feb. 9, 1936, Warlack, Germany; ord. priest June 29, 1960; vicar general to the apostolic administrator of Erfurt-Meiningen, 1989; ord. bp. of Berlin, Sept. 9, 1989; cardinal, June 28, 1991; titular church, St. Joseph (all'Aurelio). Abp. of Berlin (June 27, 1994). *Curial membership*: Catholic Education (congregation); Migrants and Itinerant People (council).

Stickler,* Alfons, S.D.B.: b. Aug. 23, 1910, Neunkirchen, Austria; ord. priest Mar. 27, 1937; director of the Vatican Library, 1971; ord. titular bp. of Bolsena, Nov. 1, 1983, with personal title of abp.; Pro-Librarian and Pro-Archivist, 1984; cardinal May 25, 1985; deacon, St. George (in Velabo); transferred to order of cardinal priests Jan. 29, 1996. Librarian and Archivist of the Holy Roman Church, 1985-88.

Suárez Rivera, Adolfo Antonio: b. Jan. 9, 1927, San Cristobal, Mexico; ord. priest Mar. 8, 1952; ord. bp. of Tepic, Aug. 15, 1971; bp. of Tlalnepantla, May 8, 1980; app. abp. of Monterrey, Nov. 8, 1983; cardinal Nov. 26, 1994; titular church, Our Lady of Guadalupe on Monte Mario. Abp. of Monterrey. *Curial membership*: Clergy (congregation).

Suquía Goicoechea,* Angel: b. Oct. 2, 1916, Zaldivia, Spain; ord. priest July 7, 1940; ord. bp. of Almeria, July 16, 1966; bp. of Malaga, 1969-73; abp. of Santiago de Compostela, 1973-83; abp. of Madrid, Apr. 12, 1983-94; cardinal May 25, 1985; titular church, Great Mother of God. Abp. emeritus of Madrid.

Swiàtek,* Kazimierz: b. Oct. 21, 1914, Walga, in apostolic administration of Estonia; ord. priest (of Pinsk, Belarus, clergy) Apr. 8, 1939; arrested by KGB Apr. 21, 1941, and imprisoned on death row until June 22, when he escaped during confusion of German invasion and returned to his parish; arrested again by KGB and imprisoned in Minsk until 1945; sentenced to 10 years of hard labor in concentration camps; released June 16, 1954; resumed pastoral work in cathedral parish in Pinsk; ord. abp. of Minsk-Mohilev, Belarus, May 21, 1991, and also appointed apostolic administrator of Pinsk; cardinal Nov. 26, 1994; titular church, St. Gerard Majella. Abp. of Minsk-Mohilev; apostolic administrator of Pinsk.

Szoka, Edmund C.: b. Sept. 14, 1927, Grand Rapids, Mich.; ord. priest (Marquette diocese), June 5, 1954; ord. first bp. of Gaylord, Mich., July 20, 1971; abp. of Detroit, 1981-90; cardinal June 28, 1988; titular church, Sts. Andrew and Gregory (al Monte Celio). President of Prefecture for Economic Affairs of the Holy See, 1990-97. Pres. Pont. Comm. for Vatican City State, 1997. *Curial membership*: Secretariat of State (second section); Bishops, Causes of Saints, Clergy, Evangelization of Peoples, Consecrated Life and Societies of Apostolic Life (congregations).

Taofinu'u, Pio, S.M.: b. Dec. 9, 1923, Falealupo, W. Samoa; ord. priest Dec. 8, 1954; joined Society of Mary, 1955; ord. bp. of Apia (Samoa and Tokelau), May 29, 1968, the first Polynesian bp.; cardinal Mar.

5, 1973; titular church, St. Humphrey. Abp. of Sa-moa-Apia and Tokelau, Sept. 10, 1982 (title of see changed to Samoa-Apia, June 26, 1992).

Terrazas Sandoval, C.SS.R., Julio: b. March 7, 1936, Vallegrande, Bolivia; ord. priest for the Redemptorists July 29, 1962; superior of the Redemptorist community in Vallegrande and vicar forane; app. aux. bp. of La Paz and cons. April 15, 1978; transferred to the see of Oruro Jan. 9, 1982; pres. of the Bolivian Episcopal Conference in 1985 and 1988; app. abp. of Santa Cruz Feb. 6, 1991; cardinal priest Feb. 21, 2001; titular church, St. John Baptist Rossi. Abp. of Santa Cruz. *Curial member-ship*: Laity (council); Latin America (commission).

Tettamanzi, Dionigi: b. March 14, 1934, Renate, Italy; ord. priest June 28, 1957; taught fundamental theology at the major seminary of Lower Venegono, pastoral theology at the Priestly Institute of Mary Immaculate and the Lombard Regional Institute of Pastoral Ministry, Milan; rector of the Pontifical Lombard Seminary, Rome; abp. of Ancona-Osimo July 1,1989 (resigned 1991); general secretary of the Italian Episcopal Conference 1991-95; Vice-president of the Italian Episcopal Conference May 25, 1995; abp. of Genoa Apr. 20, 1995; cardinal Feb. 21, 1998; titular church, Sts. Ambrose and Charles; app. abp. of Milan, July 11, 2002. *Curial membership*: Clergy, Doctrine of the Faith, Education, Oriental Churches (congregations); Social Communications (council); Economic Affairs of the Holy See (office).

Thiandoum,* Hyacinthe: b. Feb. 2, 1921, Poponguine, Senegal; ord. priest Apr. 18, 1949; stud-ied at Gregorian University, Rome, 1951-53; returned to Senegal, 1953; ord. abp. of Dakar, May 20, 1962, res. June 16, 2000; cardinal May 24, 1976; titular church, S. Maria (del Popolo). Abp. emeritus of Dakar.

Tomko, Jozef: b. Mar. 11, 1924, Udavske, Slovakia; ord. priest Mar. 12, 1949; ord. titular abp. of Doclea, Sept, 15, 1979; secretary-general of the Synod of Bishops, 1979-85; cardinal deacon May 25, 1985; transferred to order of cardinal priests Jan. 29, 1996; titular church, St. Sabina. Prefect of the Congrega-tion for the Evangelization of Peoples, 1985-2001; Grand Chancellor of Pontifical Urban University. President of Pontifical Committee for International Eucharistic Congresses, 2001. *Curial membership*: Secretariat of State (second section); Bishops, Clergy, Consecrated Life and Societies of Apostolic Life, Divine Worship and Sacraments, Doctrine of the Faith, Education (congregations); Christian Unity, Interre-ligious Dialogue, Culture, Texts (councils); Latin America, State of Vatican City (commissions).

Tonini,* Ersilio: b. July 20, 1914, Centovera di San Giorgio Piacentino, Italy; ord. priest Apr. 18, 1937; vice-rector and later rector of the Piacenza seminary; taught Italian, Latin and Greek; editor of diocesan weekly; ord. bp. of Macerata-Tolentino, June 2, 1969; abp. of Ravenna-Cervia, Nov. 22, 1975-90; cardinal Nov. 26, 1994; titular church, Most Holy Redeemer in Val Melaina. Abp. emeritus of Ravenna-Cervia.

Tucci,* Roberto, S.J.: b. April 19, 1921, Naples, Italy; ord. priest for the Jesuits, Aug. 24, 1950; editor of *La Civiltà Cattolica*; member of the Preparatory Commission on the *Apostolate of the Laity* for Vati-can II and *peritus* involved in drafting *Ad Gentes* and *Gaudium et Spes*; consultor to the Pontifical Council for Social Communications, 1965-89; member of the

editorial committee for the Pastoral Instruction *Communio et Progressio*; vice-pres. of the Italian Catholic Union of the Press, 1961-82; general sec. of the Italian Province of the Jesuits, 1967-69; app. gen-eral manager of Vatican Radio, 1973; since 1982, he has been responsible for all papal visits outside Italy; app. chairman of the Administrative Committee of Vatican Radio, 1986; cardinal, Feb. 21, 2001; titular church, Deaconry of St. Ignatius Loyola in Campo Marzio. Chairman of the Administrative Committee of Vatican Radio.

Tumi, Christian Wiyghan: b. Oct. 15, 1930, Kikaikelaki, Cameroon; ord. priest Apr. 17, 1966; ord. bp. of Yagoua, Jan. 6, 1980; coadj. abp. of Garoua, Nov. 19, 1982; abp. of Garoua, 1984-91; cardinal June 28, 1988; titular church, Martyrs of Uganda (a Poggio Ameno). Abp. of Douala, Aug. 31, 1991. *Curial mem-bership*: Education, Evangelization of Peoples (con-gregations); *Cor Unum*, Culture (councils).

Turcotte, Jean-Claude: b. June 26, 1936, Montreal, Canada; ord. priest May 24, 1959; ord. titular bp. of Suas and aux. of Montreal, June 29, 1982; abp. of Montreal, Mar. 17, 1990; cardinal Nov. 26, 1994; titu-lar church, Our Lady of the Blessed Sacrament and the Holy Canadian Martyrs. Abp. of Montreal. *Cu-rial membership*: Causes of Saints (congregation); Social Communications (council).

Tzadua*, Paulos: b. Aug. 25, 1921, Addifini, Ethio-pia; ord. priest Mar. 12, 1944; ord. titular bp. of Abila di Palestina and aux. of Addis Ababa, May 20, 1973; abp. of Addis Ababa, Feb. 24, 1977-98; cardinal May 25, 1985; titular church, Most Holy Name of Mary (a Via Latina). Abp. emeritus of Addis Ababa.

Ursi,* Corrado: b. July 26, 1908, Andria, Italy; ord. priest July 25, 1931; vice-rector and later rector of the Pontifical Regional Seminary of Molfetta, 1931-51; ord. bp. of Nardo, Sept. 30, 1951; abp. of Acerenza, Nov. 30, 1961; abp. of Naples, May 23, 1966-87; cardinal June 26, 1967; titular church, St. Callistus. Abp. emeritus of Naples.

Vachon,* Louis-Albert: b. Feb. 4, 1912, Saint-Frederic-de-Beauce, Que., Canada; ord. priest June 11, 1938; ord. titular bp. of Mesarfelta and aux. of Quebec, May 14, 1977; abp. of Quebec, Mar. 20, 1981 (resigned Mar. 17, 1990); cardinal May 25, 1985; titu-lar church, St. Paul of the Cross (a Corviale). Abp. emeritus of Quebec.

Velasco García, S.D.B., Ignacio Antonio: b. Jan. 17, 1929, Acarigua, Venezuela; ord. priest for the Salesians Dec. 17, 1955; worked as a catechist and taught at the major Salesian seminary in Altamira; rector of various Salesian colleges and member of the Salesian General Council with responsibility for Latin America, Caribbean, and Pacific; app. titular bp. of Utimmira and vicar apostolic of Puerto Ayacucho Oct. 23, 1989; cons. by the pope on Jan. 6, 1990; app. apostolic admin. *ad nutum Sanctae Sedis* of San Fernando de Apure; abp. of Caracas May 27, 1995; cardinal priest Feb. 21, 2001; titular church, St. Maria Domenica Mazzarello. Abp. of Caracas. *Curial membership*: Evangelizaton of Peoples (con-gregation); *Cor Unum* (council); Latin America (com-mission).

Vidal, Ricardo J.: b. Feb. 6, 1931, Mogpoc, Philip-pines; ord. priest Mar. 17, 1956; ord. titular bp. of Claterna and coadj. of Melalos, Nov. 30, 1971; abp. of Lipa, 1973-81; coadj. abp. of Cebu, Apr. 13, 1981;

abp. of Cebu, Aug. 24, 1982; cardinal May 25, 1985; titular church, Sts. Peter and Paul (in Via Ostiensi). Abp. of Cebu. *Curial membership*: Education, Evangelization of Peoples (congregations); Health Care Workers, Family (councils).

Vithayathil, C.SS.R., Varkey: b. May 29, 1927, North Paravur, India; ord. priest for the Redemptorists June 12, 1954; taught canon law for twenty-five years at the Redemptorist major seminary in Bangalore; served as provincial for Redemptorists in India and Sri Lanka, 1978-84; pres. of the Conference of Religious, India, 1984-85; apostolic administrator of the Asirvanum Benedictine Monastery, Bangalore, 1990-96; app. titular abp. of Ohrid and apostolic administrator of the vacant see of Ernakulam-Angamaly for Syro-Malabars; cons. by the pope, Jan. 6, 1997; app. major abp. of Ernakulam-Angamaly for Syro-Malabars Dec. 18, 1999; cardinal Feb. 21, 2001; titular church, St. Bernard at the Baths. Major abp. of Ernakulam-Angamaly for Syro-Malabars. *Curial membership:* Oriental Churches (congregation); Texts (council).

Vlk, Miloslav: b. May 17, 1932, Lisnice, Czech Republic; during communist persecution when theological studies were impossible he studied archival science at Charles University and worked in various archives in Bohemia; ord. priest June 23, 1968, during "Prague Spring"; sent to isolated parishes in Bohemian Forest by State authorities in 1971; state authorization to exercise his priestly ministry was cancelled in 1978; from then until 1986 he worked as a window-washer in Prague, carrying out his priestly ministry secretly among small groups. In 1989, he was permitted to exercise his priestly ministry for a "trial" year; the situation changed with the "velvet revolution"; ord. bp. of Ceske Budejovice, Mar. 31, 1990; abp. of Prague, Mar. 27, 1991; cardinal Nov. 26, 1994; titular church, Holy Cross in Jerusalem. Abp. of Prague, President of the Council of European Episcopal Conferences, 1993-. *Curial membership*: Oriental Churches (congregation); Social Communications (council).

Wamala, Emmanuel: b. Dec. 15, 1926, Kamaggwa, Uganda; ord. priest Dec. 21, 1957; ord. bp. of Kiyinda-Mityana, Nov. 22, 1981; coadj. abp. of Kampala, June 21, 1988; abp. of Kampala, Feb. 8, 1990; cardinal Nov. 26, 1994; titular church, St. Hugh. Abp. of Kampala. *Curial membership*: Evangelization of Peoples (congregation); "Cor Unum" (council).

Wetter, Friedrich: b. Feb. 20, 1928, Landau, Germany; ord. priest Oct. 10, 1953; ord. bp. of Speyer, June 29, 1968; abp. of Munich and Freising, Oct. 28, 1982; cardinal May 25, 1985; titular church, St. Stephen (al Monte Celio). Abp. of Munich and Freising. *Curial membership*: Education, Evangelization of Peoples (congregations).

Willebrands,* Johannes: b. Sept. 4, 1909, Bovenkarspel, The Netherlands; ord. priest May 26, 1934; ord. titular bp. of Mauriana, June 28, 1964; secretary of Secretariat for Christian Unity, 1960-69; cardinal Apr. 28, 1969; titular church, St. Sebastian (alle Catacombe); abp. of Utrecht, 1975-83; president of Council for Christian Unity, 1969-89. President emeritus of the Council for Promoting Christian Unity.

Williams, Thomas Stafford: b. Mar. 20, 1930, Wellington, New Zealand; ord. priest Dec. 20, 1959, in Rome; studied in Ireland after ordination, receiving degree in social sciences; served in various pastoral assignments on his return to New Zealand; missionary in Western Samoa to 1976; ord. abp. of Wellington, New Zealand, Dec. 20, 1979; cardinal Feb. 2, 1983; titular church, Jesus the Divine Teacher (at Pineda Sacchetti). Abp. of Wellington; Military Ordinary for New Zealand (1995). *Curial membership*: Evangelization of Peoples (congregation).

Wu Cheng-chung, John Baptist: b. Mar. 26, 1925, Shui-Tsai, mainland China; ord. priest (for Hsinchu, Taiwan, diocese) July 6, 1952; ord. bp. of Hong Kong, July 25, 1975; cardinal June 28, 1988; titular church, Blessed Virgin Mary of Mount Carmel (a Mostacciano). Bp. of Hong Kong. *Curial membership*: Divine Worship and the Sacraments, Evangelization of Peoples (congregation).

CATEGORIES OF CARDINALS

As of Aug. 20, 2002.

Information below includes categories of cardinals and dates of consistories at which they were created. Seniority or precedence usually depends on order of elevation.

One of these 174 cardinals one was named by John XXIII (consistory of Dec. 15, 1958); 18 by Paul VI (consistories of June 26, 1967, Apr. 28, 1969, Mar. 5, 1973, May 24, 1976, and June 27, 1977); 155 by John Paul II (consistories of June 30, 1979, Feb. 2, 1983, May 25, 1985, June 28, 1988, June 28, 1991, Nov. 26, 1994, Feb. 21, 1998, and Feb. 21, 2001).

Order of Bishops

Titular Bishops of Suburbicarian Sees: Bernardin Gantin, dean (June 27, 1977, Ostia and Palestrina); Joseph Ratzinger sub-dean (June 27, 1977, Velletri-Segni); Angelo Sodano (June 28, 1991, Albano); Roger Etchegaray (June 24, 1998, Porto-Santa Rufina); Lucas Moreira Neves, O.P. (June 25, 1998, Sabina-Poggio Mireto); Alfonso López Trujillo (Nov.

17, 2001, Frascati). Eastern Rite Patriarchs: Nasrallah Pierre Sfeir (Nov. 26, 1994); Ignace Moussa I Daoud (Feb. 21, 2001); Stephanos II Ghattas (Feb. 21, 2001).

Order of Priests

1958 (Dec. 15): Franz König.

1967 (June 26): Corrado Ursi.

1969 (Apr. 28): Stephen Sou-hwan Kim, Eugênio de Araújo Sales, Johannes Willebrands.

1973 (Mar. 5): Luis Aponte Martinez, Raúl Francisco Primatesta, Salvatore Pappalardo, Marcelo González Martin, Maurice Otunga, Paulo Evaristo Arns, O.F.M., Pio Taofinu'u.

1976 (May 24): Opilio Rossi, Juan Carlos Aramburu, Corrado Bafile, Hyacinthe Thiandoum, Jaime L. Sin, William W. Baum, Aloisio Lorscheider.

1979 (June 30): Giuseppe Caprio, Marco Cé, Ernesto Corripio Ahumada, Gerald Emmett Carter, Franciszek Macharski.

1983 (Feb. 2): Aurelio Sabattani, Michael Michai Kitbunchu, Alexandre do Nascimento, Alfonso

López Trujillo (promoted to cardinal-bishop on Nov. 17, 2001), Godfried Danneels, Thomas Stafford Williams, Carlo Maria Martini, Jean-Marie Lustiger, József Glemp, Joachim Meisner.

1985 (May 25): Juan Francisco Fresno Larraín, Miguel Obando Bravo, S.D.B., Angel Suquía Goicoechea, Ricardo Vidal, Henryk Roman Gulbinowicz, Paulus Tzadua, Louis-Albert Vachon, Friedrich Wetter, Silvano Piovanelli, Adrianus J. Simonis, Bernard F. Law, Giacomo Biffi, Simon D. Lourdusamy, Francis A. Arinze, Antonio Innocenti, Paul Aug.in Mayer, Jozef Tomko, Andrzej Maria Deskur, Paul Poupard, Rosalio José Castillo Lara, S.D.B., Edouard Gagnon, P.S.S., Alfons Stickler, S.D.B.

1988 (June 28): José Freire Falcão, Michele Giordano, Alexandre José Maria dos Santos, O.F.M., Giovanni Canestri, Simon Ignatius Pimenta, Edward Bede Clancy, James Aloysius Hickey, Edmund C. Szoka, László Paskai, O.F.M., Christian Wiyghan Tumi, Hans Hermann Gröer, O.S.B., Jean Margéot, John Baptist Wu Cheng-chung.

1991 (June 28): Frédéric Etsou-Nzabi-Bamungwabi, C.I.C.M., Nicolás de Jesús López Rodriguez, Roger Mahony, Anthony J. Bevilacqua, Giovanni Saldarini, Cahal Brendan Daly, Camillo Ruini, Ján Chryzostom Korec, S.J., Henri Schwery, Georg Sterzinsky.

1994 (Nov. 26): Miloslav Vlk, Peter Seiichi Shirayanagi, Adolfo Antonio Suárez Rivera, Jaime Lucas Ortega y Alamino, Julius Riyadi Darmaatmadja, S.J., Emmanuel Wamala, William Henry Keeler, Jean-Claude Turcotte, Ricardo Maria Carles Gordó, Adam Joseph Maida, Vinko Puljic, Armand Gaétan Razafindratandra, Paul Joseph Pham Dính Tung, Juan Sandoval Íñiguez, Kazimierz Swiàtek, Ersilio Tonino.

1998 (Feb. 21): Aloysius Ambrozic, Salvatore de Giorgi, Serafim Fernandes de Araújo, Francis George, O.M.I., Adam Kozlowiecki, S.J., Paul Shan Kuo-hsi, S.J., Marian Jaworski, Polycarp Pengo, Janis Pujats, Norberto Rivera Carrera, Antonio Maria Rouco Varela, Christoph Schönborn, O.P., Dionigi Tettamanzi.

2001 (Feb. 21): Bernard Agré, Francisco Álvarez Martínez, Audrys Juozas Backis, Jorge Mario Bergoglio, S.J., Desmond Connell, Ivan Dias, Edward Michael Egan, Francisco Javier Errázuriz Ossa, Antonio Jose Gonzalez Zumarraga, Jean Honoré, Cláudio Hummes, O.F.M., Lubomyr Husar, Karl Lehmann, Theodore E. McCarrick, Geraldo Majella Agnelo, Cormac Murphy-O'Connor, Wilfrid Fox Napier, O.F.M., José Da Cruz Policarpo, Severino Poletto, Giovanni Battista Re, Oscar Andres Rodríguez Maradiaga, S.D.B., Pedro Rubiano Sáenz, Juan Julio Terrazas Sandoval, C.SS.R., Luis Cipriani Thorne, Ignacio Antonio Velasco García, S.D.B., Varkey Vithayathil, C.SS.R.

Order of Deacons

1988 (June 28): Eduardo Martinez Somalo, Achille Silvestrini, Angelo Felici, Antonio Maria Javierre Ortas, S.D.B.

1991 (June 28): Pio Laghi, Edward I. Cassidy, José T. Sánchez, Virgilio Noè, Fiorenzo Angelini.

1994 (Nov. 26): Carlo Furno, Jan Pieter Schotte, C.I.C.M., Gilberto Agustoni.

1998 (Feb. 21): Lorenzo Antonetti, Darío Castrillón Hoyos, Giovanni Cheli, Francesco Colasuonno, Jorge Medina Estévez, Dino Monduzzi, James Francis Stafford.

2001 (Feb. 21): Agostino Cacciavillan, Avery Dulles, S.J., Zenon Grocholewski, Walter Kasper, Jorge María Mejía, François Xavier Nguyên Van Thuân, Mario Francesco Pompedda, José Saraiva Martins, C.M.F., Leo Scheffczyk, Sergio Sebastiani, Crescenzio Sepe, Roberto Tucci, S.J..

DISTRIBUTION OF CARDINALS

As of Aug. 15, 2002, there were 174 cardinals from more than 60 countries or areas. Listed below are areas, countries, number and last names.

Europe — 87

Italy (37): Angelini, Antonetti, Bafile, Biffi, Cacciavillan, Canestri, Caprio, Cé, Cheli, Colasuonno, de Giorgi, Felici, Furno, Giordano, Innocenti, Laghi, Martini, Monduzzi, Noè, Pappalardo, Piovanelli, Poggi, Poletto, Pompedda, Re, Rossi, Ruini, Sabattani, Saldarini, Sebastiani, Silvestrini, Sepe, Sodano, Tettamanzi, Tonini, Tucci, Ursi.

Germany (8): Kasper, Lehmann, Mayer, Meisner, Ratzinger, Scheffczyk, Sterzinsky, Wetter.

Spain (7): Alvarez Martinez, Carles Gordó, Gonzalez Martin, Javierre Ortas, Martinez Somalo, Rouco Varela, Suquia Goicoechea.

Poland (6): Deskur, Glemp, Grocholewski, Gulbinowicz, Kozlowiecki, Macharski.

France (4): Etchegaray, Honore, Lustiger, Poupard.

Austria (4): Gröer, König, Schönborn, Stickler.

Belgium (2): Danneels, Schotte.

Ireland (2): Connell, Daly

Lithuania (2): Backis, Pujats.

Netherlands (2): Simonis, Willebrands.

Portugal (2): Policarpo, Saraiva Martins

Slovakia (2): Korec, Tomko.

Switzerland (2): Agustoni, Schwery.

Ukraine (2): Husar, Jaworski

One from each of the following countries: Belarus, Swiatek; Bosnia-Herzegovina, Puljic; Czech Republic, Vlk; England, Murphy-O'Connor; Hungary, Paskai.

Asia — 17

India (4): Dias, Lourdusamy, Pimenta, Vithayathil.

Philippines (3): Sánchez, Sin, Vidal.

Vietnam (2): Nguyen Van Thuan, Pham Dinh Tung

One from each of the following countries: Indonesia, Darmaatmadja; Japan, Shirayanagi; Korea, Kim; Lebanon, Sfeir; People's Republic of China, Wu Cheng-chung (Hong Kong); Syria, Moussa I Daoud; Taiwan, Shan Kuo-hsi; Thailand, Kitbunchu;.

Oceania — 4

Australia (2): Cassidy, Clancy.

One each from: New Zealand, Williams; Pacific Islands (Samoa), Taofinu'u.

Africa — 16

One from each of the following countries: Angola, do Nascimento; Benin, Gantin; Cameroon, Tumi; Congo (formerly Zaire), Etsou-Nzabi-Bamungwabi; Egypt, Stephanos II Ghattas; Ethiopia, Tzadua; Ivory

Coast, Agre; Kenya, Otunga; Madagascar, Razafindratandra; Mauritius, Margeot; Mozambique, Santos; Nigeria, Arinze; Senegal, Thiandoum; South Africa, Napier; Tanzania, Pengo; Uganda, Wamala.

North America – 23

United States (13): Baum, Bevilacqua, Dulles, Egan, George, Hickey, Keeler, Law, Mahony, Maida, McCarrick, Stafford, Szoka.
Canada (5): Ambrozic, Carter, Gagnon, Turcotte, Vachon.
Mexico (4): Corripio Ahumada, Rivera Carrera, Sandoval Iñiguez, Suárez Rivera.
Puerto Rico (1): Aponte Martinez.

Central and South America – 27

Brazil (8): Arns, Falcão, Fernandes de Araújo, Hummes, Lorscheider, Majella Agnelo, Neves, Sales.
Argentina (4): Aramburu, Bergoglio, Mejia, Primatesta.
Chile (3): Errazuriz Ossa, Fresno Larraín, Medina Estévez.
Colombia (3): Castrillón Hoyos, Lopez Trujillo, Rubiano Saenz.
Venezuela (2): Castillo Lara, Velasco Garcia.
One each from the following countries: Bolivia, Sandoval; Cuba, Ortega y Alamino; Dominican Republic, Lopez Rodriguez; Ecuador, Gonzalez Zumarraga; Honduras, Rodriguez Maradiaga; Nicaragua, Obando Bravo; Peru, Thorne.

Ineligible to Vote

As of Sept. 15, 2002, 56 of the 174 cardinals were ineligible to take part in a papal election in line with the apostolic letter *Ingravescentem Aetetem* effective Jan. 1, 1971, which limited the functions of cardinals after completion of their 80th year.
Cardinals affected are: Agustoni, Angelini, Antonetti, Aponte Martínez, Aramburu, Arns, Bafile, Canestri, Caprio, Carter, Castillo Lara, Cheli, Corripio Ahumada, Daly, Dulles, Felici, Fresno Larrain, Furno, Gagnon, Gantin, González Martin, Gröer, Hickey, Honoré, Innocenti, Javierre Ortas, Kim Sou-hwan, König, Kozlowiecki, Laghi, Margéot, Mayer, Monduzzi, Noè, Pappalardo, Pham Dinh Tung, Pimenta, Poggi, Primatesta, Rossi, Sabattani, Sales, Sánchez, Scheffczyk, Sfeir, Stephanos II Ghattas, Stickler, Suguía Goicoechea, Swiatek, Thiandoum, Tonini, Tucci, Tzadua, Ursi, Vachon, Willebrands.
Cardinals who complete their 80th year in 2002

and who become ineligible to vote: Etchegaray.

Cardinals of the United States

As of Aug. 15, 2002, the following cardinals were in service, according to their years of elevation (for biographies, see under the **College of Cardinals** above):
1976: William W. Baum (major penitentiary emeritus); 1985: Bernard F. Law (abp. of Boston); 1988: James A. Hickey (abp. emeritus of Washington), Edmund C. Szoka (governor of the Vatican City State); 1991: Roger M. Mahony (abp. of Los Angeles), Anthony M. Bevilacqua (abp. of Philadelphia); 1994: William H. Keeler (abp. of Baltimore), Adam J. Maida (abp. of Detroit); 1998: Francis E. George, O.M.I. (abp. of Chicago), James F. Stafford (president of the Pontifical Council for the Laity); 2001: Edward M. Egan (abp. of New York), Theodore McCarrick (abp. of Washington), Avery Dulles, S.J. (theologian). Cardinal Lubomyr Husar, M.S.U., major abp. of Lviv for Ukrainians, is also an American citizen.
U.S. Cardinals of the Past (according to year of elevation; for biographical data, see **American Catholics of the Past at www.CatholicAlmanac.com**):
1875: John McCloskey; 1886: James Gibbons; 1911: John Farley, William O'Connell; 1921: Dennis Dougherty; 1924: Patrick Hayes, George Mundelein; 1946: John Glennon, Edward Mooney, Francis Spellman, Samuel Stritch; 1953: James F. McIntyre; 1958: John O'Hara, C.S.C., Richard Cushing; 1959: Albert Meyer, Aloysius Muench; 1961: Joseph Ritter; 1965: Lawrence J. Shehan; 1967: Francis Brennan, John P. Cody, Patrick A. O'Boyle, John J. Krol; 1969: John J. Wright, Terence J. Cooke, John F. Dearden, John J. Carberry; 1973: Humberto S. Medeiros, Timothy Manning; 1983: Joseph L. Bernardin; 1985: John J. O'Connor. (Myroslav Lubachivsky, major abp. of Lviv of the Ukrainians (Ukraine), was made a cardinal in 1985. He was a citizen of the United States and was metropolitan of the Philadelphia Ukrainian Rite Archeparchy, from 1979-81.)
Prelates who became cardinals after returning to their native countries: John Lefebvre de Chevrus, first bp. of Boston (1808-23) and apostolic administrator of New York (1810-15), elevated to the cardinalate, 1836, in France. Ignatius Persico, O.F.M. Cap., bp. of Savannah (1870-72), elevated to the cardinalate, 1893, in Italy; Diomede Falconio, O.F.M. ord. a priest in Buffalo, N.Y.; missionary in U.S.; apostolic delegate to the U.S. (1902-11), elevated to cardinalate, 1911, in Italy.

ELECTING THE POPE: THE CONCLAVE

One of the primary duties of the Cardinals of the Catholic Church is the election of the Bishop of Rome who becomes thereby the Supreme Pontiff of the Church. The election is held in what is termed the conclave. The name is derived from the Latin *cum* (with) and *clavis* (key), and implies the fact that the cardinals are locked together in a room until a new pontiff has been chosen. This form of papal election began in 1274 and is considered the third period in the historical evolution of choosing the successor to St. Peter. Central to the full understanding of the con-

clave is the firm belief that the entire process of election is guided by the Holy Spirit.
In the early Church, new Bishops of Rome were chosen in the manner customarily used in the other dioceses, that is, the clergy, with the people of the diocese, elected or chose the new bishop in the presence of the other bishops in the province. This was a simple method, but it became impractical as the Christian population grew in size and there arose rival claimants and hostility between the upper classes (the patricians) and the lower classes (the plebeians), each

of whom had their own candidates. This situation created considerable upheaval in Rome as demonstrated by the riots accompanying the contested elections of Pope St. Damasus I (366-384) and the antipope Ursinus in 366. Such was the violence that the prefect of the city was called in to restore order.

On the basis of these disturbances, the Roman emperors began to involve themselves in the elections by guaranteeing proper procedure and ensuring free voting by the clergy in cases where two claimants had emerged. This intervention launched a long period of secular interference that would continue, to various degrees, until 1903. The so-called barbarian kings often supervised elections until the sixth century when the Byzantines reconquered Italy. The emperors not only demanded tribute from the popes but also retained the right of confirmation, a practice that routinely created long delays, as word would have to be sent to Constantinople (later Ravenna) to request approval. The last pope to seek confirmation from imperial authorities was Gregory III in 731. After this time, the popes sought the protection of the Franks, and in 769, Pope Stephen III convened a synod at Rome that confirmed the decree of 502 (under Symmachus) that laypeople should no longer vote for the popes and that only higher clerics should be considered eligible.

A major reform was achieved in 1059 when Pope Nicholas II decreed that the cardinal bishops should choose the popes, a procedure modified by the Third Lateran Council (1179), which declared an end to distinctions among the three orders of cardinals in terms of voting, and requiring that a candidate receive a two-thirds majority.

The new need of a majority complicated many elections as a two-thirds plurality would often be quite difficult to reach owing to competing international interests among the cardinals. After the death of Pope Clement IV in 1268, for example, three years passed until the eighteen cardinals gathered at Viterbo could agree on Pope Gregory X (r. 1271-1276). Gregory introduced changes through the Second Council of Lyons (1272) to speed up elections, inaugurating the system of the conclave. It remained essentially unchanged until 1975. In that year, Pope Paul VI issued the apostolic constitution *Romano Pontifici Eligendo* (October 1) that stipulated various requirements for the conclave. Among these were: only cardinals may be electors; their number is limited to one hundred twenty, with each cardinal allowed to bring two or three assistants; while not essential for validity, it is the recognized form of election; three forms are acceptable: acclamation (*acclamatio*), compromise (by which certain cardinals are named delegates and are given power to act on behalf of the others); and balloting; if the person chosen is not a bishop, he is to be ordained to the episcopacy immediately (if a bishop, he is pope at once); secrecy is to be carefully observed; all ecumenical councils are immediately adjourned; and, if no one is elected after three days, one day is to be spent in prayer and meditation. New legislation regarding papal elections and church government during a vacancy of the Holy See was promulgated by Pope John Paul II on Feb. 23, 1996, in the apostolic constitution *Universi Dominici Gregis* ("Shepherd of the Lord's Whole Flock"). Among the changes that were introduced was the call for heightened security in preventing electronic surveillance and the provision that after a set number of unsuccessful ballots, the cardinals may elect the new pope by a simple majority vote.

The last election not held in the Vatican (the Sistine Chapel) was in 1846 (Pius IX), which took place at the Quirinal Palace. The last pope not a cardinal at the time of his election was Urban VI (1378-1389); the last by compromise was John XXII (r. 1316-1334); and the last by acclamation was Gregory XV (1621-1623).

The Universal Church

THE CHURCH IN COUNTRIES THROUGHOUT THE WORLD

(Principal sources for statistics: Annuarium Statisticum Ecclesiae, Statistical Yearbook of the Church, 2000 — *the most recent edition;* Annuario Pontificio, 2002; *and* Agenzia Internazionale FIDES. *Figures are as of Jan. 1, 2001, except for cardinals (as of Aug. 30, 2002) and others which are indicated. For 2001 developments, see* **Index** *entries for individual countries.)*

An asterisk indicates that the country has full diplomatic relations with the Holy See (see Diplomats to the Holy See in the Holy See section).

Abbreviations (in order in which they appear): archd. – archdiocese; dioc. – diocese; ap. ex. – apostolic exarchate; prel. – prelature; abb. – abbacy; v.a. – apostolic vicariate; p.a. – apostolic prefecture; a.a. – apostolic administration; mil. ord. – military ordinariate; card. – cardinal; abp. – archbishops; bp. – bishops (diocesan and titular); priests (dioc. – diocesan or secular priests; rel. – those belonging to religious orders); p.d. – permanent deacons; sem. – major seminarians, diocesan and religious; bros. – brothers; srs. – sisters; bap. – baptisms; Caths. – Catholic population; tot. pop. – total population; (AD) – apostolic delegate (see Index: Papal Representatives).

Afghanistan

Republic in south-central Asia; capital, Kabul. Christianity antedated Muslim conquest in the seventh century but was overcome by it. All inhabitants are subject to the law of Islam. Under Afghan's Taliban regime, religious freedom was severely restricted, and proselytizing was forbidden. In January 2002, Italian and English chaplains celebrated the first public Mass in nearly 10 years in Kabul, at the Italian Embassy.

Albania*

Archd., 2; dioc., 4; a.a., 1; abp., 3; bp., 3; parishes, 113; priests, 122 (38 dioc., 84 rel.); p.d.,1; sem., 58; bros., 15; srs., 381; bap., 5,792; Caths., 513,000 (18.4%); tot. pop., 3,130,000.

Republic in the Balkans, bordering the Adriatic Sea; capital, Tirana. Christianity was introduced in apostolic times. The northern part of the country remained faithful to Rome while the South broke from unity following the schism of 1054. A large percentage of the population was to become Muslim following the invasion (15th century) and long centuries of occupation by the Ottoman Turks. Many Catholics fled to southern Italy, Sicily and Greece. In 1945, at the time of the communist takeover, an estimated 68 percent of the population was Muslim; 19 percent was Orthodox and 13 percent Roman Catholic. The Catholic Church prevailed in the North. During 45 years of communist dictatorship, the Church fell victim, as did all religions, to systematic persecution: non-Albanian missionaries were expelled; death, prison sentences and other repressive measures were enacted against Church personnel and laity; Catholic schools and churches were closed and used for other purposes, and lines of communication with the Holy See were cut off.

In 1967, the government, declaring it had eliminated all religion in the country, proclaimed itself the first atheist state in the world. The right to practice religion was restored in late 1990. In March 1991, a delegation from the Vatican was allowed to go to Albania; later in the year diplomatic relations were established with the Holy See at the request of the Albanian prime minister. Pope John Paul II made a one-day visit to the country Apr. 25, 1993, during which he ordained four bishops appointed by him in December 1992 to fill long-vacant sees. Restoration of the Church is a slow and difficult process. The first Albanian cardinal was named in November 1994.

Although Catholics are a minority, they are well respected, including for their work in the education and health fields. Albanians welcomed hundreds of thousands of ethnic Albanians from Kosovo during Yugoslav persecution in 1999.

Algeria*

Archd., 1; dioc., 3; abp., 2; bp., 3; parishes, 39; priests, 108 (39 dioc., 69 rel.); p.d., 1; sem., 1; bros., 16; srs., 191; bap., 5; Caths., 3,000 (.01%); tot. pop., 30,290,000.

Republic in northwest Africa: capital, Algiers. Christianity, introduced at an early date, succumbed to Vandal devastation in the fifth century and Muslim conquest in 709, but survived for centuries in small communities into the 12th century. Missionary work was unsuccessful except in service to traders, military personnel and captives along the coast. Church organization was established after the French gained control of the territory in the 1830s. A large number of Catholics were among the estimated million Europeans who left the country after it secured independence from France July 5, 1962. Islam is the state religion.

Armed Islamic militants and guerrillas have caused terror and unrest in Algeria since 1992. Among the more than 80,000 people killed were seven Trappist monks and the Catholic bishop of Oran, all in 1996.

Andorra*

Parishes, 7; priests, 18 (12 dioc., 6 rel.); srs., 10; bap., 447; Caths., 64,000 (94%); tot. pop., 68,000.

Parliamentary state (1993) in the Pyrenees; capital, Andorra la Vella. From 1278-1993, it was a co-principality under the rule of the French head of state and the bishop of Urgel, Spain, who retain their titles. Christianity was introduced at an early date. Catholicism is the state religion. Ecclesiastical jurisdiction is under the Spanish Diocese of Urgel. The constitution calls for freedom of religion, but also guarantees "the Roman Catholic Church free and public exercise of its activities and the preservation of the relations of special cooperation with the state."

Angola*

Archd., 3; dioc., 13; card., 1; abp., 5; bp., 18; parishes, 239; priests, 543 (247 dioc., 296 rel.); sem., 1,057; bros., 107; srs., 1,642; catechists, 27,389; bap., 173,716; Caths., 7,737,000 (58.9%); tot. pop., 13,130,000.

Republic in southwest Africa; capital, Luanda. Evangelization by Catholic missionaries from Portugal, dating from 1491, reached high points in the 17th and 18th centuries. Independence from Portugal in 1975 and the long civil war that followed (peace accord signed in 1991) left the Church with a heavy loss of personnel through the departure of about half of the foreign missionaries and the persecution and martyrdom experienced by the Church during the war. Renewed fighting following elections in late 1992 brought repeated appeals for peace from the nation's bishops and religious in 1993 and 1994.

Despite another peace accord signed by the rebels and the government in late 1994, conditions have remained unsettled. One effect of the fighting was to cut off Church leaders from large groups of the faithful. In an attempt to encourage peace efforts, the Vatican established diplomatic relations with Angola in 1997. Attacks on Church workers, however, continued in 1998 and 1999. In 2000 Church leaders began an active peace movement, holding national and diocesan congresses and beginning a consultation with Angolan political leaders. Government and rebel representatives signed a peace agreement in 2002, after the government killed rebel leader Jonas Savimbi, and the Church offered humanitarian aid and helped to rebuild the country.

Antigua and Barbuda*

Dioc., 1; bp., 1; parishes, 2; priests, 6 (2 dioc., 4 rel.); p.d., 4; sem., 1; bros., 4; srs., 9; bap., 99; Caths., 8,000 (12.5%); tot. pop., 64,000.

Independent (1981) Caribbean island nation; capital, St. John's, Antigua. The Diocese of St. John's-Basseterre includes Antigua and Barbuda, St. Kitts and Nevis, Anguilla, the British Virgin Islands and Montserrat.

Argentina*

Archd., 14; dioc., 50; prel., 3; ap. ex., 2 (for Armenians of Latin America); mil. ord., 1; card., 4; abp., 24; bp., 81; parishes, 2,694; priests, 5,866 (3,608 dioc., 2,260 rel.); p.d., 510; sem., 2,020; bros., 822; srs.,

9,829; bap., 554,190; catechists, 83,173; Caths., 33,549,000 (90%); tot. pop., 37,030,000

Republic in southeast South America, bordering on the Atlantic; capital, Buenos Aires. Priests were with the Magellan exploration party and the first Mass in the country was celebrated April 1, 1519. Missionary work began in the 1530s, diocesan organization in the late 1540s, and effective evangelization about 1570. Independence from Spain was proclaimed in 1816. Since its establishment in the country, the Church has been influenced by Spanish cultural and institutional forces, antagonistic liberalism, government interference and opposition; the latter reached a climax during the last five years of the first presidency of Juan Peron (1946-55).

Widespread human rights violations, including the disappearance of thousands of people, marked the "Dirty War," the period of military rule from 1976 to December 1983, when an elected civilian government took over. In 1996 the Argentine bishops said they did not do enough to stop human rights violations during the "Dirty War." In the late 1990s, the bishops spoke out against government corruption and a severe government economic program.

Armenia*

Ord., 1 (for Catholic Armenians of Eastern Europe, with seat in Armenia); parishes, 18; abp., 1; priests, 4 (rel.); sem., 12; bros., 1; srs., 16; bap., 794; Caths., 150,000 (4%); tot. pop., 3,800,000.

Republic in Asia Minor; capital Yerevan. Part of the USSR from 1920 until it declared its sovereignty in September 1991. Ancient Armenia, which also included territory annexed by Turkey in 1920, was Christianized in the fourth century. Diplomatic relations were established with the Holy See May 23, 1992. Pope John Paul II visited Armenia in late September 2001 to help mark the 1,700th anniversary of Christianity in the nation. The small Catholic community in Armenia has good relations with the predominant Armenian Apostolic Church, an Oriental Orthodox Church.

Australia*

Archd., 7; dioc., 24; mil. ord., 1; card., 2; abp., 11; bp., 47; parishes, 1,407; priests, 3,318 (1,977 dioc., 1,341 rel.); p.d., 47; sem., 247; bros., 1,164; srs., 8,147; catechists, 8,147; bap., 66,789; Caths., 5,316,000 (28.7%); tot. pop. 19,160,000.

Commonwealth; island continent southeast of Asia; capital, Canberra. The first Catholics in the country were Irish under penal sentence, 1795-1804; the first public Mass was celebrated May 15, 1803. Official organization of the Church dates from 1820. The country was officially removed from mission status in March 1976.

As the 20th century neared its end, the Church in Australia was rocked by allegations of sexual abuse from previous decades. In 1996 the Australian bishops published a plan for dealing with such cases. In 1998 the bishops also apologized to aboriginal children, saying their support of government policy in the 1970s might have contributed to separation of the children from their families.

In an unusual move, in mid-November 1998, just before the Synod of Bishops for Oceania at the Vatican and after the Australian bishops' "ad limina" visits, Vatican officials met with Church leaders from Australia to discuss doctrinal and pastoral issues. In December, 1998, the Vatican and representatives of Australian Church leaders signed a document, later endorsed by the Australian bishops' conference, that spoke of a "crisis of faith" in the Catholic Church on the continent.

Austria*

Archd., 2; dioc., 7; abb., 1; ord., 1; mil. ord., 1; card., 4; abp., 4; bp., 14; parishes, 3,063; priests, 4,469 (2,701 dioc., 1,768 rel.); p.d., 428; sem., 392; bros., 376; srs., 6,038; catechists, 2,916; bap., 62,983; Caths., 6,027,000 (74.4%); tot. pop., 8,100,000.

Republic in central Europe; capital, Vienna. Christianity was introduced by the end of the third century, strengthened considerably by conversion of the Bavarians from about 600, and firmly established in the second half of the eighth century. Catholicism survived and grew stronger as the principal religion in the country in the post-Reformation period, but suffered from Josephinism in the 18th century. Although liberated from much government harassment in the aftermath of the Revolution of 1848, the Church came under pressure again some 20 years later in the *Kulturkampf*. The Church faced strong opposition from Socialists after World War I and suffered persecution from 1938 to 1945 during the Nazi regime. Some Church-state matters are regulated by a concordat originally concluded in 1934.

In recent years, the Church in Austria has been beset by internal difficulties, including the launch of a global movement seeking more lay participation in Church decision-making and changes in Church policy on ordination of women and priestly celibacy. In 1995, Cardinal Hans Hermann Gröer resigned as archbishop of Vienna amid charges of sexual misconduct. His successor, Cardinal Christoph Schönborn, has worked to restore a sense of unity to the Church.

Azerbaijan*

Independent republic (1991) on the Caspian Sea; formerly part of the USSR; capital, Baku. Islam is the prevailing religion. Soviet rulers destroyed Baku's one Catholic church in the late 1930s. A small Catholic community of Polish and Armenian origin near the capital is ministered to by missionaries. Latin-rite Catholics are under the apostolic administration of Caucasus (seat in Georgia), established in December 1993.

Bahamas*

Dioc., 1; bp., 1; parishes, 30; priests, 27 (12 dioc., 15 rel.); p.d., 14; sem., 6; srs., 30; catechists, 202; bap., 925; Caths., 48,000 (16%); tot. pop., 298,000.

Independent (July 10, 1973) island group consisting of some 700 (30 inhabited) small islands southeast of Florida and north of Cuba; capital, Nassau. On Oct. 12, 1492, Columbus landed on one of these islands, where the first Mass was celebrated in the New World. Organization of the Catholic Church in the Bahamas dates from about the middle of the 19th century.

Bahrain*

Parish, 1; priests, 3 (2 dioc., 1 rel.); srs., 6; bap., 214; Caths., 30,000 (4.3%); tot. pop., 690,000. (AD)

Island state in Persian Gulf; capital, Manama. Population is Muslim; Catholics are foreign workers. Under ecclesiastical jurisdiction of Arabia apostolic vicariate. Diplomatic relations were established between Bahrain and the Holy See in January 2000.

Bangladesh*

Archd., 1; dioc., 5; abp., 2; bp., 7; parishes, 78; priests, 276 (139 dioc., 137 rel.); sem., 108; bros., 64; srs., 977; catechists, 1,381; bap., 6,917; Caths., 264,000 (.20%); tot. pop. 137,440,000.

Formerly the eastern portion of Pakistan. Officially constituted as a separate nation Dec. 16, 1971; capital, Dhaka. Islam, the principal religion, was declared the state religion in 1988; freedom of religion is granted. Jesuit, Dominican and Augustinian missionaries were in the area in the 16th century. An apostolic vicariate (of Bengali) was established in 1834; the hierarchy was erected in 1950. Church-run humanitarian and development agencies have been instrumental in responding to natural disasters, such as flooding. The bishops have emphasized inculturation and Church social doctrine.

Barbados*

Dioc., 1; bp., 2; parishes, 6; priests, 8 (3 dioc., 5 rel.); p.d., 1; srs., 11; bap., 185; sem., 3; Caths., 10,000 (3.8%); tot. pop., 260,000.

Parliamentary democracy (independent since 1966), easternmost of the Caribbean islands; capital, Bridgetown. About 70 percent of the population are Anglican.

Belarus*

Archd., 1; dioc., 3; card., 1; abp., 1; bp., 5; parishes, 368; priests, 309 (162 dioc., 147 rel.); sem., 210; bros., 15; srs., 327; bap., 6,832; Caths., 1,059,000 (10%); tot. pop., 10,190,000.

Independent republic (1991) in eastern Europe; former Soviet republic (Byelorussia); capital, Minsk. Slow recovery of the Church was reported after years of repression in the Soviet Union, although in the mid-1990s under the authoritarian rule of President Alexander Lukashenka, the Church encountered tensions, especially in refusal of permits for foreign religious workers. In December 2000, the nation's bishops asked forgiveness for the "human weaknesses" of Church members throughout the centuries and said the Church forgave acts of Soviet-era persecution.

Belgium*

Archd., l; dioc., 7; mil. ord., 1; card., 2; abp., 4; bp., 18; parishes, 3,949; priests, 8,070 (4,978 dioc., 3,092 rel.); p.d., 543; sem., 260; bros., 1,215; srs., 15,801; catechists, 8,108; bap., 77,355; Caths., 8,105,000 (79%); tot. pop., 10,250,000.

Constitutional monarchy in northwestern Europe; capital, Brussels. Christianity was introduced about the first quarter of the fourth century and major evangelization was completed about 730. During the rest of the medieval period the Church had firm diocesan and parochial organization, generally vigorous monastic life and influential monastic and cathedral schools. Lutherans and Calvinists made some gains during the Reformation period but there was a strong Catholic restoration in the first half of the 17th century, when the country was under Spanish rule.

Jansenism disturbed the Church from about 1640 into the 18th century. Josephinism, imposed by an Austrian regime, hampered the Church late in the same century. Repressive and persecutory measures were enforced during the Napoleonic conquest. Freedom came with separation of Church and state in the wake of the Revolution of 1830, which ended the reign of William I. Thereafter, the Church encountered serious problems with philosophical liberalism and political socialism.

Catholics have long been engaged in strong educational, social and political movements. In 1990, in an unprecedented political maneuver, King Baudouin temporarily gave up his throne, saying his Catholic conscience would not allow him to sign a law legalizing abortion. In the mid- and late-1990s, Church leaders expressed concern that the Church was characterized by indifference toward the papacy and dissent from Church teachings. Therapeutic in vitro fertilization for stable married couples continued at a leading Belgian Catholic hospital despite Vatican objections.

Belize*

Dioc., 1; bp., 1; parishes, 13; priests, 43 (16 dioc., 27 rel.); p.d., 1; sem., 4; bros., 5; srs., 66; catechists, 608; bap., 2,686; Caths., 133,000 (52%); tot. pop., 250,000.

Independent (Sept. 21, 1981) republic on eastern coast of Central America; capital, Belmopan. Its history has points in common with Guatemala, where evangelization began in the 16th century. The Church in Belize worked with refugees during the decades of Central American civil wars.

Benin*

Archd., 2; dioc., 8; card., 1; abp., 2; bp., 10; parishes, 185; priests, 418 (305 dioc., 113 rel.); sem., 376; bros., 73; srs., 722; catechists, 8,875; bap., 46,864; Caths., 1,493,000 (24%); tot. pop., 6,170,000.

Democratic republic in West Africa, bordering on the Atlantic; capital, Porto Novo. Missionary work was very limited from the 16th to the 18th centuries. Effective evangelization dates from 1861. The hierarchy was established in 1955. In the 1970s, Benin's Marxist-Leninist government nationalized Catholic schools, expelled foreign missionaries and jailed some priests. After the government dropped the one-party system in 1989, Archbishop Isidore de Souza of Cotonou presided over the 1990 national conference that drew up a new constitution and prepared the way for elections. One challenge facing the Church as it entered the 21st century was maintaining peace with people of other faiths.

Bermuda

Dioc., 1; bp., 2; parishes, 6; priests, 6 (rel.); sem., 1; srs., 3; bap., 96; Caths., 9,000 (16%); tot. pop., 62,000. (AD)

British dependency, consisting of 360 islands (20 of them inhabited), nearly 600 miles east of Cape Hatteras; capital, Hamilton. Catholics were not permitted until about 1800. Occasional pastoral care was provided the few Catholics there by visiting priests during the 19th century. Early in the 1900s priests from Nova Scotia began serving the area. An apostolic prefecture was set up in 1953. The first bishop

assumed jurisdiction in 1956, when it was made an apostolic vicariate; diocese established, 1967.

Bhutan

Parish; catechist, 2; bap., 4; Caths., 400 (approx.); tot. pop., 2,090,000.

Kingdom in the Himalayas, northeast of India; capital, Thimphu. Buddhism is the state religion; citizens of other faiths have freedom of worship but may not proselytize. Jesuits (1963) and Salesians (1965) were invited to country to direct schools. Salesians were expelled in February 1982, on disputed charges of proselytism. The only Catholic missionary allowed to stay in the country was Canadian Jesuit Father William Mackey, who served Catholics there from 1963 until his death in 1995. Ecclesiastical jurisdiction is under the Darjeeling (India) Diocese, which ordained the first native Bhutanese priest in 1995.

Bolivia*

Archd., 4; dioc., 6; prel., 2; mil. ord., 1; v.a., 5; card., 1; abp., 7; bp., 26; parishes, 565; priests, 1,056 (453 dioc., 603 rel.); p.d., 62; sem., 714; bros., 212; srs., 2,463; catechists, 10,243; bap., 119,131; Caths., 7,246,000 (87%); tot. pop., 8,330,000.

Republic in central South America; capital, Sucre; seat of government, La Paz. Catholicism, the official religion, was introduced in the 1530s, and the first diocese was established in 1552. Effective evangelization among the Indians, slow to start, reached high points in the middle of the 18th and the beginning of the 19th centuries and was resumed about 1840. Independence from Spain was proclaimed in 1825, at the end of a campaign that started in 1809. Church-state relations are regulated by a 1951 concordat with the Holy See. In recent years, Catholics have worked against social poverty and corruption. In 1996, Pope John Paul II urged Bolivia to put its drug-trafficking "merchants of death" out of business.

Bosnia and Herzegovina*

Archd., 1; dioc., 2; card., 1; abp., 1; bp., 3; parishes, 281; priests, 609 (258 dioc., 351 rel.); sem., 136; p.d., 1; bros., 16; srs., 501; bap., 6,186; Caths., 459,000 (12%); tot. pop., 3,980,000.

Independent republic (1992) in southeastern Europe; formerly part of Yugoslavia; capital, Sarajevo. During the three years of fighting that erupted after Bosnia-Herzegovina declared its independence, some 450,000 Catholics were driven from their homes; many fled to Croatia or southern Bosnia. Sarajevo Cardinal Vinko Puljic, named a cardinal in 1994, has led the bishops in calls for the safe return of all refugees from the war and acknowledged that in some areas Croatian Catholics were responsible for atrocities. In 1999 the Vatican and Franciscan officials formally agreed to the handover of seven parishes in the Diocese of Mostar, but the agreement was greeted in some areas with violence, and Church officials said many local people did not immediately accept the situation. The parish in Medjugorje, site of alleged Marian apparitions in 1981, remained the responsibility of the Franciscans.

Botswana

Dioc., 1; v.a., 1; bp., 2; parishes, 28; priests, 41 (9 dioc., 41 rel.); p.d., 1; sem., 12; bros., 5; srs., 69; catechists, 376; bap., 1,415; Caths., 78,000 (4.8%); tot. pop., 1,650,000. (AD)

Republic (independent since 1966) in southern Africa; capital, Gaborone. The first Catholic mission was opened in 1928 near Gaborone; earlier attempts at evangelization dating from 1879 were unsuccessful. The Church in Botswana gave strong support to tens of thousands of South African refugees from apartheid. As Botswana's diamond industry grew, Church leaders worked to minimize the effects of social changes such as pockets of unemployment and competition for jobs.

Brazil*

Archd., 39; dioc., 210; prel., 14; abb., 2; exarch., 1; mil. ord., 1; card., 8; abp., 54; bp., 343; parishes, 8,732; priests, 16,598 (9,240 dioc., 7,358 rel.); p.d., 1,157; sem., 8,215; bros., 2,421; srs., 35,365; catechists, 428,836; bap., 2,163,086; Caths., 143,900,000 (86%); tot. pop., 167,720,000.

Federal republic in northeastern South America; capital, Brasilia. One of several priests with the discovery party celebrated the first Mass in the country Apr. 26, 1500. Evangelization began some years later, and the first diocese was erected in 1551. During the colonial period, which lasted until 1822, evangelization made some notable progress — especially in the Amazon region between 1680 and 1750 — but was seriously hindered by government policy and the attitude of colonists regarding Amazon Indians the missionaries tried to protect from exploitation and slavery. The Jesuits were suppressed in 1782 and other missionaries expelled as well. Liberal anti-Church influence grew in strength. The government exercised maximum control over the Church. After the proclamation of independence from Portugal in 1822 and throughout the regency, government control was tightened and the Church suffered greatly from dissident actions of ecclesiastical brotherhoods, Masonic anticlericalism and general decline in religious life. Church and state were separated by the constitution of 1891, proclaimed two years after the end of the empire.

The Church carried into the 20th century problems associated with increasingly difficult political, economic and social conditions affecting the majority of the population. Many Afro-Brazilians indiscriminately mixed African-based rites such as candomble with Catholic rituals. In the second half of the 20th century, the bishops became known for their liberal stances on social and some theological issues. In the 1980s, Vatican officials had a series of meetings with Brazilian bishops to discuss liberation theology and other issues. The Brazilian bishops' conference took the lead in advocating for land reform in the country. Members of the Church's Pastoral Land Commission often faced threats, harassment and murder. The Church-founded Indigenous Missionary Council worked for the rights of the country's Indians. Each year, the bishops' Lenten campaign targeted a social issue, such as women's rights or economic reform.

Brunei

P.a., 1; parishes, 3; priests, 3 (2 dioc., 1 rel); sem., 3; bap., 193; Caths., 2,500 (0.7%); tot. pop., 331,000.

Independent state (1984) on the northern coast of Borneo; formal name, Brunei Darussalam; capital, Bandar Seri Begawan. Islam is the official religion; other religions are allowed with some restrictions. Most of the Catholics are technicians and skilled workers from other countries who are not permanent residents; under ecclesiastical jurisdiction of Miri Diocese, Malaysia.

Bulgaria*

Dioc., 2; ap. ex., 1; abp., 2; bp., 3; parishes, 54; priests, 51 (17 dioc., 34 rel.); sem., 10; bros., 2; srs., 86; bap., 444; Caths., 80,000 (1%), tot. pop., 7,950,000.

Republic in southeastern Europe on the eastern part of the Balkan peninsula; capital, Sofia. Most of the population is Orthodox. Christianity was introduced before 343 but disappeared with the migration of Slavs into the territory. The baptism of Boris I about 865 ushered in a new period of Christianity, which soon became involved in switches of loyalty between Constantinople and Rome. Through it all the Byzantine, and later Orthodox, element remained stronger and survived under the rule of Ottoman Turks into the 19th century. The Byzantines are products of a reunion movement of the 19th century.

In 1947 the constitution of the new republic decreed the separation of Church and state. Catholic schools and institutions were abolished and foreign religious banished in 1948. A year later the apostolic delegate was expelled. Ivan Romanoff, vicar general of Plovdiv, died in prison in 1952. Bishop Eugene Bossilkoff, imprisoned in 1948, was sentenced to death in 1952; his fate remained unknown until 1975, when the Bulgarian government informed the Vatican that he had died in prison shortly after being sentenced. He was beatified in 1998. Latin- and Eastern-rite apostolic vicars were permitted to attend the Second Vatican Council. All Church activity was under surveillance and/or control by the government, which professed to be atheistic. Pastoral and related activities were strictly limited. There was some improvement in Bulgarian-Vatican relations in 1975. In 1979, the Sofia-Plovdiv apostolic vicariate was raised to a diocese, and a bishop was appointed for the vacant see of Nicopoli. Diplomatic relations with the Holy See were established in 1990. In the late 1990s, the government instituted religion classes in state schools, but Church leaders complained they had no input into the curriculum and that teachers were predominantly Orthodox. In 2002, Pope John Paul II visited Bulgaria, one of several trips to predominantly Orthodox Soviet-bloc countries, and said Catholics and Orthodox should work for closer relations.

Burkina Faso*

Archd., 3; dioc., 9; abps., 2; bp., 13; parishes, 123; priests, 624 (481 dioc., 143 rel.); sem., 409; bros., 189; srs., 1,078; catechists, 9,584; bap., 64,823; Caths., 1,324,000 (11.4%); tot. pop., 11,540,000.

Republic inland in West Africa; capital, Ouagadougou. Missionaries of Africa started the first missions in 1900 and 1901. Their sisters began work in 1911. A minor and a major seminary were established in 1926 and 1942, respectively. The first indigenous bishop in modern times from West Africa was ordained in 1956 and the first cardinal created in 1965. The hierarchy was established in 1955. In 1980 and 1990, Pope John Paul II's visits to the country were used to launch appeals for an end to desertification of sub-Saharan Africa and an end to poverty in the region. In later years, the pope encouraged increased evangelization and interreligious harmony.

Burma (See Myanmar)

Burundi*

Archd., 1; dioc., 6; abp., 3; bp., 9; parishes, 144; priests, 351 (270 dioc., 81 rel.); p.d., 1; sem., 367; bros., 137; srs., 1,062; catechists, 4,794; bap., 157,660; Caths., 3,991,000 (63 %); tot. pop., 6,360,000.

Republic (1966), near the equator in east-central Africa; capital, Bujumbura. The first permanent Catholic mission station was established late in the 19th century. Large numbers were received into the Church following the ordination of the first Burundi priests in 1925. The first indigenous bishop was appointed in 1959.

In 1972-73, the country was torn by tribal warfare between the Tutsis, the ruling minority, and the Hutus. In 1979, the government began expelling foreign missionaries, and in 1986, seminaries were nationalized. A gradual resumption of Church activity since 1987 has been hampered by continuing ethnic violence, which began in 1993 and left more than 150,000 Burundians dead. The bishops repeatedly have called for peace and for an end to sanctions imposed by the Organization of African Unity in 1996. Missionaries continued to be the target of violent attacks.

Cambodia*

V.a., 1; p.a., 2; bp., 2; parishes, 31 (there were also 22 mission stations without resident priests); priests, 46 (16 dioc., 30 rel.); sem., 9; bros., 4; srs., 68; catechists, 139; baptisms, 483; Caths., 20,000 (.15%); tot. pop., 13,100,000.

Republic in Southeast Asia; capital, Phnom Penh. Evangelization dating from the second half of the 16th century had limited results, more among Vietnamese than Khmers. Thousands of Catholics of Vietnamese origin were forced to flee in 1970 because of Khmer hostility. Most indigenous priests and nuns were killed under the 1975-79 Pol Pot regime. During those years, the Vietnamese invasion in 1979 and the long civil war that followed, foreign missionaries were expelled, local clergy and religious were sent to work the land and a general persecution followed. Religious freedom was re-established in 1990. Diplomatic relations with the Holy See were established in March 1994. Despite a lack of vocations, many Catholics maintain their faith through basic Christian communities led by lay catechists.

Cameroon*

Archd., 5; dioc., 18; card., 1; abp., 6; bp., 22; parishes, 630; priests, 1,270 (787 dioc., 483 rel.); p.d., 18; sem., 1,023; bros., 205; srs., 1,581; catechists, 15,512; bap., 85,158; Caths., 3,920,000 (26.3%); tot. pop., 14,880,000.

Republic in West Africa; capital, Yaounde. Effective evangelization began in 1890, although Catholics had been in the country long before that time. In the 40-year period from 1920 to 1960, the number of Catholics increased from 60,000 to 700,000. The first black priests were ordained in 1935. Twenty years later

the first indigenous bishops were ordained and the hierarchy established. The first Cameroonian cardinal (Christian Wiyghan Tumi) was named in 1988. Around that same time, unknown people began persecuting Church personnel. Among those murdered was Archbishop Yves Plumy of Garoua in 1991. Some felt the government did not do enough to investigate.

Canada* (See Catholic Church in Canada; see also Statistics of the Church in Canada)

Cape Verde*

Dioc., 1; bp., 1; parishes, 31; priests, 47 (12 dioc., 35 rel.); sem., 27; bros., 5; srs., 123; catechists, 3,420; bap., 15,833; Caths., 409,000 (94%); tot. pop., 434,000.

Independent (July 5, 1975) island group in the Atlantic 300 miles west of Senegal; formerly a Portuguese overseas province; capital, Praia, São Tiago Island. Evangelization began some years before the establishment of a diocese in 1532. The Church languished from the 17th to the 19th centuries, and for two long periods there was no resident bishop. Portugal's anti-clerical government closed the only minor seminary in 1910. Missionaries returned in the 1940s. Cape Verde has faced massive emigration of youth because of perennial drought and a weak economy.

Central African Republic*

Archd., 1; dioc., 7; abp., 2; bp., 9; parishes, 122; priests, 268 (134 dioc., 134 rel.); sem., 120; bros., 64; srs., 380; catechists, 4,769; bap., 24,316; Caths., 718,000 (19%); tot. pop., 3,720,000.

Former French colony (independent since 1960) in central Africa; capital, Bangui. Effective evangelization dates from 1894. The region was organized as a mission territory in 1909. The first native priest was ordained in 1938. The hierarchy was organized in 1955. Pope John Paul II has urged the country's bishops to give hope to a people ruled by corrupt dictatorships and the military. The Church in the country also has expressed concern about the growing number of sects.

Chad*

Archd., 1; dioc., 6; p.a., 1; abp., 1; bp., 7; parishes, 110; priests, 223 (102 dioc., 121 rel.); sem., 98; bros., 30; srs., 302; catechists, 8,076; bap., 17,303; Caths., 905,000 (11.4%); tot. pop., 7,890,000.

Republic (independent since 1960) in north-central Africa; former French possession; capital, N'Djamena. Evangelization began in 1929, leading to firm organization in 1947 and establishment of the hierarchy in 1955. Many catechists, who often were local community leaders, were killed during Chad's 1982-87 civil war. The Vatican established diplomatic relations with Chad in 1988. After the government established more freedoms in the early 1990s, the Church worked to teach people, including Catholics, that solidarity must extend across religious, ethnic and regional boundaries.

Chile*

Archd., 5; dioc., 18; prel., 2; v.a., 1; mil. ord., 1; card., 3; abp., 9; bp., 36; parishes, 951; priests, 2,298

(1,113 dioc., 1,185 rel.); p.d., 568; sem., 773; bros., 382; srs., 5,574; catechists, 53,143; bap., 192,189; Caths., 11,426,000 (75.2%); tot. pop., 15,210,000.

Republic on the southwest coast of South America; capital, Santiago. Priests were with the Spanish on their entrance into the territory early in the 16th century. The first parish was established in 1547 and the first diocese in 1561. Overall organization of the Church took place later in the century. By 1650, most of the peaceful Indians in the central and northern areas were evangelized. Missionary work was more difficult in the southern region. Church activity was hampered during the campaign for independence, 1810-18, and through the first years of the new government, to 1830. Later gains were made, into this century, but hindering factors were shortages of indigenous clergy and religious and attempts by the government to control Church administration through the patronage system in force while the country was under Spanish control. Separation of Church and state was decreed in the constitution of 1925.

Church-state relations were strained during the regime of Marxist President Salvador Allende (1970-73). In the mid-1970s, the Archdiocese of Santiago established the Vicariate of Solidarity to counter human-rights abuses under the rule of Gen. Augusto Pinochet. The Chilean bishops issued numerous statements strongly critical of human rights abuses by the military dictator, who remained in power until 1990, when an elected president took office. The Church was praised for its role in educating and registering voters in the 1988 plebiscite that rejected another term for Pinochet. In 1999, when a British court ruled that Pinochet could be extradited from Britain to Spain to face trial for torture and murder, some Chilean bishops said the ruling damaged the Chilean democracy they had fought so hard to get.

China, People's Republic of

Archd., 20; dioc., 92; p.a., 29. No Roman Catholic statistics are available. In 1949 there were between 3,500,000-4,000,000 Catholics, about .7 per cent of the total population; current total is unknown. Tot. pop. 1,275,724,000. **Hong Kong:** Dioc., 1; card., 1; bp., 1; parishes, 55; priests, 325 (70 dioc., 255 rel.); p.d., 3; sem., 17; bros., 67; srs., 532; catechists, 981; bap., 4,116; Caths., 371,000 (3.7%); tot. pop., 6,800,000.

People's republic in eastern part of Asia; capital, Beijing. Christianity was introduced by Nestorians who had some influence on part of the area from 635 to 845 and again from the 11th century until 1368. John of Monte Corvino started a Franciscan mission in 1294; he was ordained an archbishop about 1307. Missionary activity involving more priests increased for a while thereafter, but the Franciscan mission ended in 1368. Jesuit Matteo Ricci initiated a remarkable period of activity in the 1580s. The Chinese-rites controversy, concerning the adaptation of rituals and other matters to Chinese traditions and practices, ran throughout the 17th century, ending in a negative decision by mission authorities in Rome. Francis de Capillas, the Dominican protomartyr of China, was killed in 1648. Persecution occurred several times in the 18th century and resulted in the departure of most missionaries from the country.

The Chinese door swung open again in the 1840s,

and progress in evangelization increased with an extension of legal and social tolerance. At the turn of the 20th century, however, Christian missionary activity helped provoke the Boxer Rebellion.

Missionary work in the 1900s reached a new high. The hierarchy was instituted by Pope Pius XII, Apr. 11, 1946 (Apostolic Constitution *Quotidie Nos*). Then followed persecution initiated by communists, before and especially after they established the republic in 1949. The government began a savage persecution as soon as it came into power. Among its results were outlawed missionary work and pastoral activity; the expulsion of more than 5,000 foreign missionaries, 510 of whom were American; the arrest, imprisonment and harassment of Chinese Church officials; the forced closing of more than 4,000 schools, institutions and homes; denial of the free exercise of religion; the detention of hundreds of priests, religious and lay people in jail and their employment in slave labor; the proscription of Catholic movements for "counterrevolutionary activities" and "crimes against the new China."

The government formally established the Chinese Catholic Patriotic Association, independent of the Holy See, in July 1957. Relatively few priests and lay people joined the organization, which was condemned by Pius XII in 1958. The government formed the nucleus of what it hoped might become the hierarchy of a schismatic Chinese Church in 1958 by "electing" 26 bishops and having them consecrated validly but illicitly between Apr. 13, 1958, and Nov. 15, 1959, without the permission or approval of the Holy See. Additional bishops were subsequently ordained. Officially, members of the Patriotic Association spurn ties with the Vatican.

Hong Kong Church leaders say more than two-thirds of the government-approved bishops in the Patriotic Association have secretly reconciled with the Vatican, and that the Vatican often approves the ordination of government-appointed bishops as long as the ordinations are conducted by the reconciled bishops. After China insisted on ordaining bishops Jan. 6, 2000, the same day the pope ordained bishops at the Vatican, bishops and clergy of the Patriotic Association began trying to distance themselves from the government.

Growth of the underground church has been reported for several years, despite sometimes intense persecution. The underground church's most senior leader, Cardinal Ignatius Kung Pin-mei, died Mar. 12, 2000, in Stamford, CT, where, because of failing health, he had lived for years with his nephew.

The Vatican's diplomatic relations with Taiwan remain one of the biggest stumbling blocks to Sino-Vatican ties.

Colombia*

Archd., 12; dioc., 48; v.a., 10; mil. ord., 1; card., 3; abp., 18; bp., 82; parishes, 3,614; priests, 7,851 (5,470 dioc., 2,381 rel.); p.d., 161; sem., 4,505; bros., 1,069 srs., 17,347; catechists, 39,537; bap., 719,737; Caths., 37,723,000 (89%); tot. pop., 42,320,000.

Republic in northwest South America; capital, Bogotá. Evangelization began in 1508. The first two dioceses were established in 1534. Vigorous development of the Church was reported by the middle of the 17th century despite obstacles posed by the multiplicity of Indian languages, government interference through patronage rights, rivalry among religious orders and the small number of native American priests among the predominantly Spanish clergy. Some persecution, including the confiscation of property, followed in the wake of the proclamation of independence from Spain in 1819. Guerrilla warfare aimed at Marxist-oriented radical social reform and redistribution of land, along with violence related to drug traffic, has plagued the country since the 1960s, posing problems for the Church, which backed reforms but rejected actions of radical groups. In the late 20th and early 21st centuries, the Church has often worked as a mediator between the government and guerrillas, but Church leaders still suffer threats and attacks, and sometimes death, including from paramilitaries. For example, on Mar. 16, 2002, Abp. Isaias Duarte Cancino of Cali was shot to death for speaking out about the political situation.

Comoros

A.a., 1; parishes, 2; missions, 4; priests, 4 (1 dioc., 3 rel.); srs., 4; catechists, 12; bap., 19; Caths., 2,000 (.02%); tot. pop., 688,000. (AD)

Consists of main islands of Grande Comore, Anjouan and Moheli in Indian Ocean off southeast coast of Africa; capital, Moroni, Grande Comore Island. Former French territory; independent (July 6, 1975). The majority of the population is Muslim. An apostolic administration was established in 1975.

Congo, Democratic Republic of *

Archd., 6; dioc., 41; card., 1; abp., 6; bp., 55; parishes, 1,296; priests, 3,937 (2,685 dioc., 1,252 rel.); p.d., 5; sem., 2,901; bros., 1,442; srs., 6,652; catechists, 64,883; bap., 439,512; Caths., 27,067,000 (53%); tot. pop., 50,950,000.

Republic in south central Africa; capital, Kinshasa. Christianity was introduced in 1484 and evangelization began about 1490. The first bishop from black Africa was ordained in 1518. Subsequent missionary work was hindered by factors including 18th- and 19th-century anticlericalism. Modern evangelization started in the second half of the 19th century. The hierarchy was established in 1959. In the civil disorders that followed independence in 1960, some missions and other Church installations were abandoned, thousands of people reverted to tribal religions and many priests and religious were killed.

Church-state tensions developed in the late 1980s and 1990s because of the Church's criticism of President Mobutu Sese Seko, who called a 1990 bishops' pastoral letter seditious. In 1992, after troops fired on thousands of protesters and killed 13, the government blamed priests who organized the march. In 1992, Archbishop Laurent Monswengo Pasinya was named president of a council charged with drafting a new constitution and overseeing a transition to democracy, but Mobutu supporters blocked effective change, and the archbishop resigned in 1994. As government and rebel forces battled in the Bukavu region of the country in 1996, Archbishop Christophe Munzihirwa Mwene Ngabo was killed in unclear circumstances. In the ensuing years of civil war, in which neighboring countries became involved, Church authorities worked to meet humanitarian needs and to promote peace through dialogue, but often were targeted for their work. Rebels forced one bishop into exile and house arrest for seven months.

Congo, Republic of *

Archd., 1; dioc., 5; p.a., 1; abp., 2; bp., 5; parishes, 141; priests, 298 (213 dioc., 85 rel.); sem., 245; bros., 49; srs., 227; catechists, 2,957; bap., 13,456; Caths., 1,719,000 (56%); tot. pop., 3,020,000.

Republic (independent since 1960) in west central Africa; former French possession; capital, Brazzaville. Small-scale missionary work with little effect preceded modern evangelization dating from the 1880s. The work of the Church has been affected by political instability, communist influence, tribalism and hostility to foreigners. The hierarchy was established in 1955. In 1992 Bishop Ernest Kombo of Owando was appointed chief organizer of the country's parliamentary elections. In 1994, the Church canceled independence day celebrations after more than 142 Catholics, mostly children, were crushed or suffocated in a rain-induced stampede at a Catholic church in Brazzaville. During renewed violence in the late 1990s, the bishops appealed for peace and stability.

Costa Rica*

Archd., 1; dioc., 6; abp., 2; bp., 8; parishes, 258; priests, 770 (547 dioc., 223 rel.); sem., 318; p.d., 2; bros., 47; srs., 888; catechists, 25,945; bap., 63,056; Caths., 3,346,000 (88%); tot. pop., 3,820,000.

Republic in Central America; capital, San José. Evangelization began about 1520 and proceeded by degrees to real development and organization of the Church in the 17th and 18th centuries. The republic became independent in 1838. Twelve years later Church jurisdiction also became independent with the establishment of a diocese in the present capital.

Côte d'Ivoire (Ivory Coast)*

Archd., 4; dioc., 10; card., 1; abp., 5; bp., 11; parishes, 259; priests, 823 (570 dioc., 253 rel.); p.d., 6; sem., 614; bros., 317; srs., 938; catechists, 14,939; bap., 54,424; Caths., 2,605,000 (15.8%); tot. pop., 16,400,000.

Republic in western Africa; capital, Abidjan. The Holy Ghost Fathers began systematic evangelization in 1895. The first priests from the area were ordained in 1934. The hierarchy was set up in 1955; the first indigenous cardinal (Bernard Yago) was named in 1983. In 1990 Pope John Paul II consecrated the continent's biggest, most costly and most controversial cathedral in Yamoussoukro. The pope only agreed to accept the cathedral after convincing the country's president to build an adjacent hospital and youth center.

Croatia*

Archd., 4; dioc., 10; mil. ord., 1; abp., 9; bp., 17; parishes, 1,533; priests, 2,259 (1,449 dioc., 810 rel.); sem., 434; bros., 98; srs., 3,464; catechists, 1,512; bap., 41,984; Caths., 3,745,000 (84%); tot. pop., 4,650,000.

Independent (1991) republic in southeastern Europe; capital Zagreb; formerly a constituent republic of Yugoslavia. Christianity was introduced in the seventh century. On-again, off-again fighting from 1991 to 1995 pitted mostly Catholic Croats against mostly Orthodox Serbs. In 1995, Croatian bishops issued guidelines for rebuilding the nation including suppressing feelings of vengeance toward Serbs. However, in 1996 the head of Croatia's Helsinki human rights committee criticized the bishops for taking a weak stance on Croat abuses after the 1995 Croatian recapture of the Serb-occupied Krajina region. Pope John Paul II's 1998 beatification of Croatian Cardinal Alojzije Stepinac generated controversy among some Serb and Jewish leaders, who considered the cardinal a Nazi sympathizer.

Cuba*

Archd., 3; dioc., 8; card., 1; abp., 3; bp., 12; parishes, 264; priests, 296 (166 dioc., 130 rel.); p.d., 48; sem., 101; bros., 36; srs., 500; catechists, 4,577; bap., 74,164; Caths. 6,179,000 (55.2%); tot. pop., 11,190,000.

Republic under Communist dictatorship, south of Florida; capital, Havana. Effective evangelization began about 1514, leading eventually to the predominance of Catholicism on the island. Vocations to the priesthood and religious life were unusually numerous in the 18th century but declined in the 19th. The island became independent of Spain in 1902 following the Spanish-American War.

Fidel Castro took control of the government Jan. 1, 1959. In 1961, after Cuba was officially declared a socialist state, the University of Villanueva was closed, 350 Catholic schools were nationalized and 136 priests expelled. A greater number of foreign priests and religious had already left the country. Freedom of worship and religious instruction were limited to Church premises and no social action was permitted by the Church, which survived under surveillance. A new constitution approved in 1976 guaranteed freedom of conscience but restricted its exercise. Small improvements in Church-state relations occurred in the late 1980s and early 1990s. In December 1997, just before Pope John Paul II's historic visit, the government allowed public celebration of Christmas, banned for 30 years. Although the pope's January 1998 visit was seen as a new dawn for the Church on the islands, Cuban Catholics say change has come slowly.

Cyprus*

Archd., 1 (Maronite); abp., 1; parishes, 13; priests, 22 (11 dioc., 11 rel.); bros., 7; srs., 43; bap., 82; Caths., 17,000 (2.2%); tot. pop., 780,000.

Republic in the eastern Mediterranean; capital, Nicosia. Christianity was preached on the island in apostolic times and has a continuous history from the fourth century. Latin and Eastern rites were established but the latter prevailed and became Orthodox after the schism of 1054. Christians have suffered under many governments, particularly during the period of Turkish dominion from late in the 16th to late in the 19th centuries, and from differences between the 80 percent Greek majority and the Turkish minority. About 80 percent of the population are Orthodox. Catholics are under the jurisdiction of the Maronite Archdiocese of Cipro, based in Nicosia.

Czech Republic*

Archd., 2; dioc., 6; ap. ex., 1; card., 1; abp., 3; bp., 13; parishes, 3,135; priests, 1,959 (1,364 dioc., 595 rel.); p.d., 141; sem., 359; bros., 101; srs., 2,297; catechists, 1,364; bap., 26,321; Caths., 4,307,000 (42%); tot. pop., 10,270,000.

Independent state (Jan. 1, 1993); formerly part of Czechoslovakia; capital, Prague. The martyrdom of Prince Wenceslaus in 929 triggered the spread of Christianity. Prague has had a continuous history as a diocese since 973. A parish system was organized about the 13th century in Bohemia and Moravia. Mendicant orders strengthened relations with the Latin rite in the 13th century. In the next century the teachings of John Hus in Bohemia brought trouble to the Church in the forms of schism and heresy and initiated a series of religious wars that continued for decades following his death at the stake in 1415. So many of the faithful joined the Bohemian Brethren that Catholics became a minority.

In the 1560s, a Counter-Reformation got under way and led to a gradual restoration through the thickets of Josephinism, the Enlightenment, liberalism and troubled politics. St. Jan Sarkander, a priest killed by Protestants in 1620, was accused by Protestants of helping an invading Polish army. (His 1995 canonization caused strains with the Protestant community.)

In 1920, two years after the establishment of the Republic of Czechoslovakia, the schismatic Czechoslovak Church was proclaimed at Prague, resulting in numerous defections from the Catholic Church in the Czech region. Following the accession of the Gottwald regime to power early in 1948, persecution began in the Czech part of Czechoslovakia. Hospitals, schools and property were nationalized and Catholic organizations were liquidated. A puppet organization was formed in 1949 to infiltrate the Church and implement an unsuccessful plan for establishing a schismatic church. In the same year Archbishop Josef Beran of Prague was placed under house arrest. A number of theatrical trials of bishops and priests were staged in 1950. Pressure was applied on Eastern Catholics in Slovakia to join the Orthodox Church. Diplomatic relations with the Holy See were terminated in 1950. In the following decade, thousands of priests were arrested and hundreds were deported, and attempts were made to force government-approved "peace priests" on the people. Pope Pius XII granted the Czech Church emergency powers to appoint clergy during the communist persecution.

From January to October 1968, Church-state relations improved to some extent under the Dubcek regime: a number of bishops were reinstated; some priests were still barred from priestly work; the "peace priests" organization was disbanded. The Eastern Catholic Church was re-established. In 1969, rehabilitation trials for priests and religious ended, but there was no wholesale restoration of priests and religious to their proper ways of life and work. Government restrictions continued to hamper the work of priests and nuns. Signatories of the human rights declaration Charter 77 were particular objects of government repression and retribution.

In December 1983, the Czechoslovakian foreign minister met with the pope at Vatican City; it was the first meeting of a high Czech official with a pope since the country had been under communist rule. In 1988, three new bishops were ordained in Czechoslovakia, the first since 1973. The communist government fell in late 1989. In 1990, bishops were appointed to fill vacant sees; diplomatic relations between the Holy See and Czechoslovakia were re-established, and Pope John Paul II visited the country.

In 1997 the issue of married Czech priests secretly ordained under communist rule was resolved when they began work in the country's new Eastern Catholic jurisdiction. Under a 1949 communist decree, declaring priests Culture Ministry employees, Czech priests were still paid by the state. A Church spokesman said confiscation of Church property under communist rule left priests still financially dependent on the state.

Denmark*

Dioc., 1; abp., 1; bp., 2; parishes, 49; priests, 91 (41 dioc., 50 rel.); p.d., 3; sem., 6; bros., 3; srs., 229; bap., 656; Caths., 34,000 (.6%); tot. pop., 5,340,000.

Includes the Faroe Islands and Greenland. Constitutional monarchy in northwestern Europe; capital, Copenhagen. Christianity was introduced in the ninth century and the first diocese for the area was established in 831. Intensive evangelization and full-scale organization of the Church occurred from the second half of the 10th century and ushered in a period of great development and influence in the 12th and 13th centuries. Decline followed, resulting in almost total loss to the Church during the Reformation, when Lutheranism became the national religion. A few Catholic families practiced the faith secretly until religious freedom was legally assured in the mid-1800s. Since then, immigration has increased the number of Catholics. About 95 percent of the population are Evangelical Lutherans.

Catholicism was introduced in Greenland, a Danish island province northeast of North America, about 1000. The first diocese was established in 1124 and a line of bishops dated from then until 1537. The first known Churches in the Western Hemisphere, dating from about the 11th century, were on Greenland. The departure of Scandinavians and spread of the Reformation reduced the Church to nothing. The Moravian Brethren evangelized the Inuit from the 1720s to 1901. By 1930 the Danish Church — Evangelical Lutheran — was in full possession. Since 1930, priests have been in Greenland, which is part of the Copenhagen Diocese.

Djibouti*

Dioc., 1; bp., 1; parishes, 5; priests, 6 (2 dioc., 4 rel.); sem., 1; bros., 5; srs., 19; catechists, 16; bap., 15; Caths., 7,000 (1%); tot. pop., 630,000. (AD)

Independent (1977) republic in East Africa; capital, Djibouti. Christianity in the area, formerly part of Ethiopia, antedated but was overcome by the Arab invasion of 1200. Modern evangelization, begun in the latter part of the 19th century, had meager results. The hierarchy was established in 1955. Formal diplomatic relations with the Holy See were established in May 2000.

Dominica*

Dioc., 1; bp., 1; parishes, 15; priests, 48 (6 dioc., 42 rel.); sem., 1; bros., 8; srs., 27; catechists, 485; bap., 923; Caths., 60,000 (79%); tot. pop., 75,000.

Independent (Nov. 3, 1978) state in Caribbean; capital, Roseau. Evangelization began in 1642.

Dominican Republic*

Archd., 2; dioc., 9; mil. ord., 1; card., 1; abp., 1; bp., 17; parishes, 485; priests, 817 (390 dioc., 427 rel.); p.d., 227; sem., 493; bros., 78; srs., 1,644; catechists, 27,721; bap., 108,702; Caths., 7,475,000 (87.7%); tot. pop., 8,520,000.

Caribbean republic on the eastern two-thirds of the island of Hispaniola, bordering on Haiti; capital, Santo Domingo. Evangelization began shortly after discovery by Columbus in 1492 and Church organization, the first in America, was established by 1510. Catholicism is the state religion. Pope John Paul II visited the country in 1992 to mark the quincentennial celebrations of Columbus's discovery. The pope also opened the Fourth General conference of the Latin American Episcopate there. Church leaders worked to end social injustices, including the plight of mistreated sugar cane workers.

East Timor*

Dioc., 2; bp., 2; parishes, 31; priests, 101 (44 dioc., 57 rel.); sem., 151; p.d., 1; bros., 15; srs., 284; catechists, 1,513; bap., 22,910; Caths., 750,000 (94%); tot. pop., 794,000.

Independent (May 2002) state; capital, Dili. Predominantly Catholic former Portuguese colony invaded by Indonesia in 1975 and annexed the following year. Most countries did not recognize the annexation. The Catholic Church worked to bring peace between the Indonesian government and guerrilla forces seeking independence. Bishop Carlos Filipe Ximenes Belo, apostolic administration of Dili, was a co-winner of the 1996 Nobel Peace Prize for his peace efforts. In 1999, dozens of civilians were killed — including more than two dozen at a Catholic church — during a terror campaign waged by pro-Indonesia paramilitaries in the run-up to an August vote on independence for East Timor. Indonesian troops withdrew, and in August 2001 East Timor held elections for a transitional government. The church has worked on peace and reconciliation issues and at raising awareness of social issues.

Ecuador*

Archd., 4; dioc., 11; v.a., 7; p.a., 1; mil. ord., 1; card., 1; abp., 6; bp., 29; parishes, 1,151; priests, 1,836 (1,019 dioc., 817 rel.); p.d., 69; sem., 728; bros., 339; srs., 4,894; catechists, 34,985; bap., 272,350; Caths., 11,623,000 (92%); tot. pop., 12,650,000.

Republic on the west coast of South America, includes Galápogos Islands; capital, Quito. Evangelization began in the 1530s. The first diocese was established in 1545. Multi-phased missionary work, spreading from the coastal and mountain regions into the Amazon, made the Church highly influential during the colonial period. The Church was practically enslaved by the constitution enacted in 1824, two years after Ecuador, as part of Colombia, gained independence from Spain. Some change for the better took place later in the century, but from 1891 until the 1930s the Church labored under serious liabilities imposed by liberal governments. Foreign missionaries were barred from the country for some time; the property of religious orders was confiscated; education was taken over by the state; traditional state support was refused; legal standing was denied; attempts to control Church offices were made through insistence on rights of patronage. A period of harmony and independence for the Church began after agreement was reached on Church-state relations in 1937.

In 1998, the Church was actively involved in peace talks that ended a border dispute of some 170 years standing with Peru. As the 20th century came to a close, Ecuador's bishops were working to fight social turmoil and the results of severe economic austerity measures.

Egypt*

Patriarchates, 2 (Alexandria for the Copts and for the Melkites); dioc., 10; v.a., 1; ex., 1; patriarch, 1; card., 1; abp., 2; bp., 11; parishes, 219; priests, 473 (210 dioc., 263 rel.); p.d., 12; sem., 129; bros., 50; srs., 1,413; catechists, 1,586; bap., 3,006; Caths., 237,000 (.37%); tot. pop., 63,980,000.

Arab Republic in northeastern Africa; capital, Cairo. Alexandria was the influential hub of a Christian community established by the end of the second century; it became a patriarchate and the center of the Coptic Church and had great influence on the spread of Christianity in various parts of Africa. Monasticism developed from desert communities of hermits in the third and fourth centuries. Arianism was first preached in Egypt in the 320s. In the fifth century, the Coptic Church went Monophysite through failure to accept doctrine formulated by the Council of Chalcedon in 451 with respect to the two natures of Christ. The country was thoroughly Arabized after 640 and was under the rule of Ottoman Turks from 1517 to 1798.

Islam, the religion of some 90 percent of the population, is the state religion. The tiny Catholic minority has a dialogue with the Muslims, but sometimes each side treats the other warily and with mistrust. Pope John Paul II's visit to Cairo and Mount Sinai in 2000 was considered to have given impetus to interreligious dialogue.

El Salvador*

Archd., 1; dioc., 7; mil. ord., 1; abp., 2; bp., 9; parishes, 376; priests, 663 (430 dioc., 233 rel.); p.d., 3; sem., 379; bros., 82; srs., 1,542; catechists, 5,247; bap., 97,023; Cath., 4,986,000 (79%); tot. pop., 6,280,000.

Republic in Central America; capital, San Salvador. Evangelization affecting the whole territory followed Spanish occupation in the 1520s. The country was administered by the captaincy general of Guatemala until 1821, when independence from Spain was declared and it was annexed to Mexico. El Salvador joined the Central American Federation in 1825, declared independence in 1841 and became a republic formally in 1856.

During the country's 1980-92 civil war, Church leaders worked to achieve social justice. The San Salvador Archdiocese's human rights office, *Tutela Legal*, documented abuses and political killings and offered legal support to victims, despite Church persecution. Archbishop Oscar Romero of San Salvador, peace advocate and outspoken champion of human rights, was murdered on Mar. 24, 1980, while celebrating Mass. Four U.S. Church women were murdered the same year. Six Jesuits and two lay women were assassinated Nov. 16, 1989, at Central American University in El Salvador. Church leaders, particularly Archbishop Romero's successor, Archbishop Arturo Rivera Damas, were active in the peace process. In the 1990s, Church-government relations cooled. Church leaders often urged the U.S. government not to deport the hundreds of thousands of Salvadoran refugees who lived, often illegally, in the United States, sending money to their families in El Salvador. The situation worsened after the destruction caused by Hurricane Mitch in 1999.

England

Archd., 4; dioc., 15; ap. ex., 1; mil. ord. (Great Britain), 1; card., 1; abp., 4; bp., 35; parishes, 2,515; priests, 4,793 (3,288 dioc., 1,505 rel.); p.d., 494; sem., 217; bros., 2,140; srs., 6,827; bap., 65,567; Caths., 4,034,960 (8.5%); tot. pop., 47,212,853 (tot. pop. for Great Britain: 55,269,750). (Figures from 2002 *Annuario Pontificio*) Note: England and Wales share a joint Episcopal Conference; see also Scotland and Wales.

Center of the United Kingdom of Great Britain (England, Scotland, Wales) and Northern Ireland, off the northwestern coast of Europe; capital, London. The arrival of St. Augustine of Canterbury and a band of monks in 597 marked the beginning of evangelization. Real organization of the Church took place some years after the Synod of Whitby, held in 663. Heavy losses were sustained in the wake of the Danish invasion in the 780s, but recovery starting from the time of Alfred the Great and dating especially from the middle of the 10th century led to Christianization of the whole country and close Church-state relations. The Norman Conquest of 1066 opened the Church in England to European influence. The Church began to decline in numbers in the 13th century. In the 14th century, John Wycliff presaged the Protestant Reformation.

Henry VIII, failing in 1529 to gain annulment of his marriage to Catherine of Aragon, refused to acknowledge papal authority over the Church in England, had himself proclaimed its head, suppressed all houses of religious, and persecuted people — Sts. Thomas More and John Fisher, among others — for not subscribing to the Oath of Supremacy and Act of Succession. He held the line on other-than-papal doctrine, however, until his death in 1547. Doctrinal aberrations were introduced during the reign of Edward VI (1547-53), through the Order of Communion, two books of Common Prayer, and the Articles of the Established Church. Mary Tudor's attempted Catholic restoration (1553-58) was a disaster, resulting in the deaths of more than 300 Protestants. Elizabeth (1558-1603) firmed up the established Church with the aid of Matthew Parker, archbishop of Canterbury, with formation of a hierarchy, legal enactments and multiphased persecution. More than 100 priests and 62 lay persons were among the casualties of persecution during the underground Catholic revival that followed the return to England of missionary priests from France and the Lowlands.

Several periods of comparative tolerance ensued after Elizabeth's death. The first of several apostolic vicariates was established in 1685; this form of Church government was maintained until the restoration of the hierarchy and diocesan organization in 1850. The revolution of 1688 and subsequent developments to about 1781 subjected Catholics to a wide variety of penal laws and disabilities in religious, civic and social life. The situation began to improve in 1791, and from 1801 Parliament frequently considered proposals for the repeal of penal laws against Catholics.

The Act of Emancipation restored citizenship rights to Catholics in 1829. Restrictions remained in force for some time afterward, however, on public religious worship and activity. The hierarchy was restored in 1850. Since then the Catholic Church, existing side by side with the established Churches of England and Scotland, has followed a general pattern of growth and development. After the Church of England began ordaining women priests in 1994, more than 200 Anglican priests and four Anglican bishops were received into the Catholic Church, although many said ordination of women was not their primary reason for leaving. In the late 20th and early 21st centuries, the Church was active in the prolife movement and was outspoken on bioethical issues. (See also Ireland, Northern)

Equatorial Guinea*

Archd., 1; dioc., 2; abp., 1; bp., 2; parishes, 66; priests, 103 (49 dioc., 54 rel.); p.d. 1; sem., 73; bros., 27; srs., 214; catechists, 1,934; bap., 9,832; Caths., 385,000 (94%); tot. pop., 407,000.

Republic on the west coast of Africa, consisting of Rio Muni on the mainland and the islands of Bioko and Annobon in the Gulf of Guinea: capital, Malabo. Evangelization began in 1841. The country became independent of Spain in 1968. The Church was severely repressed during the 11-year rule of President Macias Nguema. Developments since his overthrow in 1979 indicated some measure of improvement. An ecclesiastical province was established in October 1982.

In the 1990s, bishops worked to educate Catholics about the need for social justice and respect for human rights. In mid-1998, the government expelled three foreign missionaries involved in development programs partially funded by the United States.

Eritrea*

Dioc., 3; bp., 3; parishes, 97; priests, 254 (52 dioc., 202 rel); sem., 104; bros., 27; srs., 460; catechists, 139; bap., 4,036; Caths., 133,000 (3.6%); tot. pop., 3,670,000.

Independent state (May 24, 1993) in northeast Africa; formerly a province of Ethiopia. Christianity was introduced in the fourth century. Population is evenly divided between Christians and Muslims. Catholics form a small minority; most of the population is Orthodox or Muslim. In 1995, two new dioceses were established, but because of three decades of civil war, the dioceses had no facilities and little staffing. In 1998 the government announced plans to take over private schools and health clinics, most of which were run by the Church. Eritrean bishops form an episcopal conference with Ethiopia, and the bishops of the two countries frequently appealed for peace during their governments' border war.

Estonia*

A.a., 1; abp., 1 (nuncio is apostolic administrator); parishes, 5; priests, 9 (5 dioc., 4 rel); sem., 4; srs., 19; bap., 84; Caths., 4,000 (.27%); tot. pop., 1,390,000.

Independent (1991) Baltic republic; capital, Tallinn. (Forcibly absorbed by the USSR in 1940, it regained independence in 1991.) Catholicism was introduced in the 11th and 12th centuries. Jurisdiction over the area was made directly subject to the Holy See in 1215. Lutheran penetration was general in the Reformation period, and Russian Orthodox influence was strong from early in the 18th century until 1917, when independence was attained. The first of several apostolic administrators was appointed in 1924. The small Catholic community was hard-hit during the 1940-91 Soviet occupation (not recognized by the Holy See or the United States). Since its independence, the small Catholic community in Estonia has worked to re-establish Catholic theology and education. In 1999 the Holy See and government of Estonia reached agreement on a number of issues, including guarantees that the Church could name its own bishops and that priests from abroad would be able to continue to work in the country.

Ethiopia*

Archd., 1; dioc., 1; v.a., 5; p.a., 2; card., 1; abp., 2; bp., 8; parishes, 216; priests, 439 (162 dioc., 277 rel.); p.d., 1; sem., 323; bros., 69; srs., 696; catechists, 1,756; bap., 17,528; Caths., 443,000 (.7%); tot. pop., 63,490,000.

People's republic in northeast Africa; capital, Addis Ababa. The country was evangelized by missionaries from Egypt in the fourth century and had a bishop by about 340. Following the lead of its parent body, the Egyptian (Coptic) Church, the Church in the area succumbed to the Monophysite heresy in the sixth century. An apostolic delegation was set up in Addis Ababa in 1937 and several jurisdictions were organized, some under Vatican congregations. The northern Church jurisdictions follow the Alexandrian rite, while the southern part of the country is Latin rite. The small Church has good relations with Orthodox and Protestant Churches, all of which face the task of helping people move from a rural society to a more modern society without losing Christian identity. Although the constitution calls for religious freedom, treatment of the churches can vary in different localities. The bishops share an episcopal conference with the Eritrean bishops, and the bishops of the two countries frequently appealed for peace during their governments' border war.

Falkland Islands

P.a., 1; parish, 1; priests, 2 (rel.); bros., 1; srs., 1; bap., 3; Caths., 1,000 (approx.) (25%); tot. pop., 4,000 (approx.).

British colony off the southern tip of South America; capital, Port Stanley. The islands are called Islas Malvinas by Argentina, which also claims sovereignty.

Fiji*

Archd., 1; abp., 1; parishes, 35; priests, 126 (29 dioc., 97 rel.); sem., 59; bros., 61; srs., 172; bap., 1,372; catechists, 466; Caths., 83,000 (10%); tot. pop., 816,000.

Independent island group (100 inhabited) in the southwest Pacific; capital, Suva. Marist missionaries began work in 1844 after Methodism had been firmly established. An apostolic prefecture was organized in 1863. The hierarchy was established in 1966.

Finland*

Dioc., 1; bp., 1; parishes, 7; priests, 21 (6 dioc., 15 rel.); p.d., 3; sem., 2; srs., 49; bap., 158; Caths., 8,000 (.01%); tot. pop., 5,180,000.

Republic in northern Europe; capital, Helsinki. Swedes evangelized the country in the 12th century. The Reformation swept the country, resulting in the prohibition of Catholicism in 1595, general reorganization of ecclesiastical life and affairs, and dominance of the Evangelical Lutheran Church. Catholics were given religious liberty in 1781 but missionaries and conversions were forbidden by law. The first Finnish priest since the Reformation was ordained in 1903 in Paris. An apostolic vicariate for Finland was erected in 1920 (made a diocese in 1955). A law on religious liberty, enacted in 1923, banned the foundation of monasteries.

France*

Archd., 19; dioc.,75; prel., 1; ap. ex., 2; mil. ord., 1; card., 4; abp., 31; bp., 137; parishes, 22,156; priests, 25,353 (19,234 dioc., 6,119 rel.); p.d., 1,622; sem., 1,596; bros., 3,456; srs., 48,499; catechists, 74,769; bap., 401,054; Caths., 46,823,000 (79%); tot. pop., 58,890,000.

Republic in western Europe; capital, Paris. Christianity was known around Lyons by the middle of the second century. By 250 there were 30 dioceses. The hierarchy reached a fair degree of organization by the end of the fourth century. Vandals and Franks subsequently invaded the territory and caused barbarian turmoil and doctrinal problems because of their Arianism. The Frankish nation was converted following the baptism of Clovis about 496. Christianization was complete by some time in the seventh century. From then on the Church, its leaders and people, figured in virtually every important development — religious, cultural, political and social — through the periods of the Carolingians, feudalism, the Middle Ages and monarchies to the end of the 18th century. The University of Paris became one of the intellectual centers of the 13th century. Churchmen and secular rulers were involved with developments surrounding the Avignon residence of the popes and curia from 1309 until near the end of the 14th century and with the disastrous Western Schism that followed.

Strong currents of Gallicanism and conciliarism ran through ecclesiastical and secular circles in France; the former was an ideology and movement to restrict papal control of the Church in the country, the latter sought to make the pope subservient to a general council. Calvinism entered the country about the middle of the 16th century and won a strong body of converts. Jansenism appeared in the next century, to be followed by the highly influential Enlightenment. The Revolution, which started in 1789 and was succeeded by the Napoleonic period, completely changed the status of the Church, taking a toll of numbers by persecution and defection and disenfranchising the Church in practically every way. Throughout the 19th century the Church was caught up in the whirl of imperial and republican developments and was made the victim of official hostility, popular indifference and liberal opposition.

In the 20th century, the Church struggled with problems involving the heritage of the Revolution and its aftermath, the alienation of intellectuals, liberalism, the estrangement of the working classes because of the Church's former identification with the ruling class, and the massive needs of contemporary society. In the 1990s, French bishops fought a racist backlash that resulted from large-scale immigration from Africa.

Gabon*

Archd., 1; dioc., 3; abp., 2; bp., 4; parishes, 63; priests, 111 (47 dioc., 64 rel.); p.d., 1; sem., 141; bros., 31; srs., 168; catechists, 855; bap., 7,623; Caths., 643,000 (53%); tot. pop., 1,210,000.

Republic on the west coast of central Africa; capital Libreville. Sporadic missionary effort took place before 1881 when effective evangelization began. The hierarchy was established in 1955. In 1993, Gabon's president defeated a Catholic priest in presidential elections. In the late 1990s, the government and the Holy See signed an agreement setting out the rights of the Church in society.

Gambia*

Dioc., 1; bp., 1; parishes, 56; priests, 24 (12 dioc., 12 rel.); sem., 4; bros., 13; srs., 56; bap., 1,844; Caths., 30,000 (2%); tot. pop., 1,390,000.

Republic (1970) on the northwestern coast of Africa; capital, Banjul. Christianity was introduced by Portuguese explorers in the 15th century; effective evangelization began in 1822. The country was under the jurisdiction of an apostolic vicariate until 1931. The hierarchy was established in 1957. Pope John Paul II has encouraged Catholics to dialogue with the majority Muslims.

Georgia*

A.a., 1; parishes, 27; bp., 1; priests, 16 (3 dioc., 13 rel); sem., 8; srs., 27; bap, 192; Caths., 100,000 (1.9%); tot. pop., 5,270,000

Independent (1991) state in the Caucasus; former Soviet republic; capital, Tbilisi. Christianity came to the area under Roman influence and, according to tradition, was spread through the efforts of St. Nino (or Christiana), a maiden who was brought as a captive to the country and is venerated as its apostle. The apostolic administration of the Caucasus (with seat in Georgia) was established in December 1993 for Latin-rite Catholics of Armenia, Azerbaijan and Georgia. Chaldean- and Armenian-rite Catholics also are present. Differences between Catholicism and Orthodoxy often are blurred on the parish level. The Catholic Church and the Armenian Orthodox Church have been unable to secure the return of Churches closed during the Soviet period, many of which were later given to the Georgian Orthodox Church. Early in the 21st century, many denominations, including Catholics, reported attacks and harassment from Orthodox mobs.

Germany*

Archd., 7; dioc., 20; ap. ex., 1; mil. ord., 1; card., 9; abp., 6; bp., 90; parishes, 12,466; priests, 19,290 (14,682 dioc., 4,608 rel.); p.d., 2,218; sem., 1,423; bros., 1,606; srs., 38,400; catechists, 23,524; bap., 234,010; Caths., 27,455,000 (34.3%); tot. pop., 82,020,000.

Country in northern Europe; capital, Berlin. From 1949-90 it was partitioned into the Communist German Democratic Republic in the East (capital, East Berlin) and the German Federal Republic in the West (capital, Bonn). Christianity was introduced in the third century, if not earlier. Trier, which became a center for missionary activity, had a bishop by 400. Visigoth invaders introduced Arianism in the fifth century but were converted in the seventh century by the East Franks, Celtic and other missionaries. St. Boniface, the apostle of Germany, established real ecclesiastical organization in the eighth century.

Beginning in the Carolingian period, bishops began to act in dual roles as pastors and rulers, a state of affairs that inevitably led to confusion and conflict in Church-state relations and perplexing problems of investiture. The Church developed strength and vitality through the Middle Ages but succumbed to abuses that antedated and prepared the ground for the Reformation. Martin Luther's actions from 1517 made Germany a confessional battleground. Religious strife continued until the conclusion of the Peace of Westphalia at the end of the Thirty Years' War in 1648. Nearly a century earlier the Peace of Augsburg (1555) had been designed, without success, to assure a degree of tranquillity by recognizing the legitimacy of different religious confessions in different states, depending on the decisions of princes. The implicit principle that princes should control the churches emerged in practice into the absolutism and Josephinism of subsequent years. St. Peter Canisius and his fellow Jesuits spearheaded a Counter Reformation in the second half of the 16th century. Before the end of the century, however, 70 percent of the population of north and central Germany were Lutheran. Calvinism also had established a strong presence.

The Church suffered some impoverishment as a result of shifting boundaries and the secularization of property shortly after 1800. It came under direct attack in the *Kulturkampf* of the 1870s but helped to generate the opposition that resulted in a dampening of the campaign of Bismarck against it. Despite action by Catholics on the social front and other developments, discrimination against the Church spilled over into the 20th century and lasted beyond World War I. Catholics in politics struggled with others to pull the country through numerous postwar crises. The dissolution of the Center Party, agreed to by the bishops in 1933 without awareness of the ultimate consequences, contributed in part to the rise of Hitler to supreme power. Church officials protested the Nazi anti-Church and anti-Semitic actions, but to no avail.

After World War II East Germany, compelled to communism under Soviet domination, initiated a program of control and repression of the Church. The regime eliminated religious schools, curtailed freedom for religious instruction and formation, and restricted the religious press. Beginning in the mid-1950s, the communists substituted youth initiation and Communist ceremonies for many sacraments. Bishops were generally forbidden to travel outside the Republic. The number of priests decreased, partly because of reduced seminary enrollments ordered by the East German government.

The official reunification of Germany took place Oct. 3, 1990, and the separate episcopal conferences were merged to form one conference in November. During the 1990s, the united German bishops fought against introduction of the former East Germany's more liberal abortion law. When a high-court decision allowed a woman to obtain an abortion after visiting a state-approved counseling center and obtaining proof she had been counseled, German church leaders searched for a compromise position, since they ran more than 250 such centers. In 1999, Pope John Paul II asked the German bishops to include a line on the proof-of-counseling certificate that said it could not be used for abortion, but some German states said they would not consider the line valid. Eventually, most of the bishops withdrew from the system. As the 20th century came to an end, German Church leaders also spoke on behalf of immigrants, refugees and asylum seekers and against a surge in racist and anti-Semitic attacks.

Ghana*

Archd., 3; dioc., 15; abp., 4; bp., 17; parishes, 318; priests, 918 (747 dioc., 171 rel.); p.d., 2; sem., 659; bros., 169; srs., 774; catechists, 5,715; bap., 75,138; Caths., 2,242,000 (12%); tot. pop., 18,410,000.

Republic on the western coast of Africa; capital, Accra. Priests visited the country in 1482, 11 years after discovery by the Portuguese, but missionary effort, hindered by the slave trade and other factors, was slight until 1880 when systematic evangelization began. An apostolic prefecture was set up in 1879. The hierarchy was established in 1950.

In 1985, the government shut down the Church's newspaper, *The Catholic Standard*, for criticizing the government; in 1989 the government ordered religious bodies to register. However, in 1992 the paper resumed publication, and five new dioceses were established in 1995. In 1997 the bishops issued a pastoral letter urging an end to political corruption and ethnic tension.

Gibraltar

Dioc., 1; bp., 2; parishes, 5; priests, 15 (14 dioc., 1 rel.); sem., 1; srs., 5; bap., 361; Caths., 23,000 (85%); tot. pop., 27,000.

British dependency on the tip of the Spanish Peninsula on the Mediterranean. Evangelization took place after the Moors were driven out near the end of the 15th century. The Church was hindered by the British, who acquired the colony in 1713. Most of the Catholics were, and are, Spanish and Italian immigrants and their descendants. An apostolic vicariate was organized in 1817. The diocese was erected in 1910.

Great Britain (See separate entries for England, Scotland, Wales, Northern Ireland)

Greece*

Archd., 4; dioc., 4; v.a., 1; ap. ex., 2; abp., 6; bp., 3; parishes, 70; priests, 92 (50 dioc., 42 rel.); p.d., 2; sem., 6; bros., 31; srs., 133; bap., 640; Caths., 55,000 (.6%); tot. pop., 11,000,000.

Republic in southeastern Europe on the Balkan Peninsula; capital, Athens. St. Paul preached the Gospel at Athens and Corinth on his second missionary journey and visited the country again on his third tour. Other Apostles may have passed through. Two bishops from Greece attended the First Council of Nicaea. After the division of the Roman Empire, the Church remained Eastern in rite and later broke ties with Rome as a result of the schism of 1054. A Latin-rite jurisdiction was set up during the period of the Latin Empire of Constantinople, 1204-1261, but crumbled afterward. Unity efforts of the Council of Florence had poor results and failed to save the Byzantine Empire from conquest by the Ottoman Empire in 1453. The country now has Latin, Byzantine and Armenian rites. The Greek Orthodox Church is predominant. The Catholic Church continues to work to obtain full legal rights. In May 2001, during the first papal visit to Greece since the eighth century, Pope John Paul II apologized for past wrongs against the Orthodox, including the 13th-century sack of Constantinople.

Greenland (Numbers for Greenland are included in Denmark)

Grenada*

Dioc., 1; bp., 1; parishes, 20; priests, 22 (5 dioc., 17 rel.); p.d., 5; sem., 5; bros., 5; srs., 31; catechists, 123; bap., 553; Caths., 55,000 (59%); tot. pop., 93,000.

Independent island state in the West Indies; capital, St. George's.

Guam

Archd., 1; abp., 1; parishes, 24; priests, 437 (31 dioc., 16 rel.); p.d., 7; sem., 19; bro., 1; srs., 125; bap., 2,272; catechists, 471; Caths., 151,000 (90%); tot. pop., 167,000.

Outlying area of U.S. in the southwest Pacific; capital, Agana. The first Mass was offered in the Mariana Islands in 1521. The islands were evangelized by the Jesuits, from 1668, and other missionaries. The first Micronesian bishop was ordained in 1970. The Agana Diocese, which had been a suffragan of San Francisco, was made a metropolitan see in 1984.

Guatemala*

Archd., 2; dioc., 10; prel., 1; v.a., 2; abp., 3; bp., 17; parishes, 434; priests, 970 (360 dioc., 610 rel.); p.d., 6; sem., 396; bros., 172; srs., 2,070; catechists, 43,318; bap., 518,310; Caths. 9,471,000 (83%); tot. pop. 11,390,000.

Republic in Central America; capital, Guatemala City. Evangelization dates from the beginning of Spanish occupation in 1524. The first diocese, for all Central American territories administered by the captaincy general of Guatemala, was established in 1534. The country became independent in 1839, following annexation to Mexico in 1821, secession in 1823 and membership in the Central American Federation from 1825. In 1870, a government installed by a liberal revolution repudiated the concordat of 1853 and took active measures against the Church. Separation of Church and state was decreed; religious orders were suppressed and their property seized; priests and religious were exiled; schools were secularized. Full freedom was subsequently granted.

During the nation's 36-year civil war, which ended in 1996, Church officials spoke out against atrocities and illegal drafting of youths and often were persecuted. The Guatemala City archbishop's human rights office, established after decades of war, was one of the few agencies able to document abuses. Bishops participated in the country's peace process, at times withdrawing in an effort to force government and guerrilla leaders back to the table.

After the war, the archbishop's human rights office began an extensive project to help document abuses

during the war. Two days after the report was released in April 1998, Auxiliary Bishop Juan Gerardi Conedera of Guatemala City, who headed the project, was murdered. In 2001, a priest who lived with the bishop and three military officers were convicted of involvement in the murder but said they would appeal the decision.

Guinea*

Archd., 1; dioc., 2; abp., 1; bp., 3; parishes, 54; priests, 96 (70 dioc., 26 rel.); sem., 31; bros., 27; srs., 100; catechists, 562; bap., 2,384; Caths., 134,000 (1.6%); tot. pop., 8,150,000.

Republic on the west coast of Africa; capital, Conakry. Occasional missionary work followed exploration by the Portuguese about the middle of the 15th century; organized effort dates from 1877. The hierarchy was established in 1955. Following independence from France in 1958, Catholic schools were nationalized, youth organizations banned and missionaries restricted. Foreign missionaries were expelled in 1967. Archbishop Raymond-Marie Tchidimbo of Conakry, sentenced to life imprisonment in 1971 on a charge of conspiring to overthrow the government, was released in August 1979; he resigned his see. Private schools, suppressed by the government for more than 20 years, again were authorized in 1984.

Guinea-Bissau*

Dioc., 2; bp., 1; parishes, 22; priests, 66 (13 dioc., 53 rel.); sem., 20; bros., 8; srs., 94; bap., 1,500; catechists, 615; Caths., 136,000 (11.5%); tot. pop., 1,140,000.

Independent state on the west coast of Africa; capital, Bissau. Catholicism was introduced in the second half of the 15th century but limited missionary work, hampered by the slave trade, had meager results. Missionary work in the 20th century began in 1933. An apostolic prefecture was made a diocese in 1977. In 1998, Bishop Settimio Ferrazzetta of Bissau worked to mediate a crisis between the government and military leaders.

Guyana

Dioc., 1; bp., 1; parishes, 24; priests, 51 (5 dioc., 46 rel.); sem., 3; bros., 5; srs., 49; catechists, 571; bap., 1,323; Caths., 88,000 (10.2%); tot. pop., 800,000.

Republic on the north coast of South America; capital, Georgetown. In 1899 the Catholic Church and other churches were given equal status with the Church of England and the Church of Scotland. Most of the Catholics are Portuguese. The Georgetown Diocese was established in 1956, 10 years before Guyana became independent of England. The first indigenous bishop was appointed in 1971. Schools were nationalized in 1976. In the late 1970s and in the 1980s, *The Catholic Standard* newspaper was cited by the Inter-American Press Association as the "sole independent voice" in Guyana.

Haiti*

Archd., 2; dioc., 7; abp., 4; bp., 10; parishes, 266; priests, 611 (340 dioc., 271 rel.); p.d., 5; sem., 342; bros., 295; srs., 1,037; catechists, 5,607; bap., 143,381; Caths., 6,778,000 (85%); tot. pop., 7,960,000.

Caribbean republic on the western third of

Hispaniola adjacent to the Dominican Republic; capital, Port-au-Prince. Evangelization followed discovery by Columbus in 1492. Capuchins and Jesuits did most of the missionary work in the 18th century. From 1804, when independence was declared, until 1860, the country was in schism. Relations were regularized by a concordat concluded in 1860, when an archdiocese and four dioceses were established.

In the second half of the 20th century, the Church worked to develop the small nation, considered among the poorest in the Western Hemisphere. In the 1980s and 1990s, priests and religious often were targets of political violence, which resulted in a series of coups. The Church was sometimes seen as the lone voice for the people and, at times, was seen as backing the government. A Salesian priest, Father Jean-Bertrand Aristide, known for his fiery, anti-government sermons, won the December 1990 president election, considered the first genuinely democratic vote in Haitian history. A 1991 military coup forced him into exile for three years and resulted in an international trade embargo against Haiti. Aristide was laicized by the Vatican and married in January 1996. In the late 1990s, the Church continued its service in the social field through programs in basic literacy and operation of schools and health facilities.

Honduras*

Archd., 1; dioc., 6; card., 1; abp., 3; bp., 6; parishes, 169; priests, 382 (168 dioc., 214 rel.); p.d., 1; sem., 111; bros., 35; srs., 561; catechists, 13,092; bap., 83,403; Caths., 5,362,000 (84%); tot. pop., 6,420,000.

Republic in Central America; capital, Tegucigalpa. Evangelization preceded establishment of the first diocese in the 16th century. Under Spanish rule and after independence from 1823, the Church held a favored position until 1880, when equal legal status was given to all religions. Harassment of priests and nuns working among indigenous peasants and Salvadoran refugees was reported during the years of Central American civil unrest in the late 20th century. In 1998 Hurricane Mitch killed more than 6,000 Hondurans and forced more than 2 million in the country to evacuate their homes. The Church took a lead role in post-hurricane relief and development efforts.

Hungary*

Archd., 4; dioc., 9; abb., 1; ap. ex., 1; mil. ord. 1; card., 1; abp., 7; bp., 20; parishes, 2,223; priests, 2,472 (1,915 dioc., 557 rel.); p.d., 46; sem., 547; bros., 81; srs., 1,515; catechists, 3,444; bap., 55,084; Caths., 6,231,000 (62%); tot. pop., 10,020,000.

Republic in east central Europe; capital, Budapest. The early origins of Christianity in the country, whose territory was subject to a great deal of change, is not known. Magyars accepted Christianity about the end of the 10th century. St. Stephen I promoted its spread and helped to organize some of its historical dioceses. Bishops became influential in politics as well as in the Church.

For centuries the country served as a buffer for the Christian West against barbarians from the East, notably the Mongols in the 13th century. Hussites and Waldensians prepared the way for the Reformation, which struck at almost the same time as the Turks. The Reformation made considerable progress after 1526, resulting in the conversion of large numbers to

Lutheranism and Calvinism by the end of the century. Most of them or their descendants returned to the Church later, but many Magyars remained staunch Calvinists. Turks repressed the Churches, Protestant as well as Catholic, during a reign of 150 years, but they managed to survive. Domination of the Church was one of the objectives of government policy during the reigns of Maria Theresa and Joseph II in the second half of the 18th century; their Josephinism affected Church-state relations until World War I.

Secularization increased in the second half of the 19th century, which also witnessed the birth of many new Catholic organizations and movements. Catholics were involved in the social chaos and anti-religious atmosphere of the years following World War I, struggling with their compatriots for religious as well as political survival.

After World War II, the communist campaign against the Church started with the disbanding of Catholic organizations in 1946. In 1948, Caritas, the Catholic charitable organization, was taken over, and all Catholic institutions were suppressed. Interference in Church administration and attempts to split the bishops preceded the arrest of Cardinal Jozsef Mindszenty Dec. 26, 1948, and his sentence to life imprisonment in 1949. (He was free for a few days during the unsuccessful uprising of 1956. He then took up residence at the U.S. Embassy in Budapest, where he remained until September 1971, when he was permitted to leave the country. He died in 1975 in Vienna.)

In 1950, religious orders and congregations were suppressed and 10,000 religious were interned. Several dozen priests and monks were assassinated, jailed or deported. About 4,000 priests and religious were confined in jail or concentration camps. The government sponsored a national "Progressive Catholic" Church and captive organizations for priests. Despite a 1964 agreement with the Holy See regarding episcopal appointments, bishops remained subject to government surveillance and harassment.

On Feb. 9, 1990, an accord was signed between the Holy See and Hungary re-establishing diplomatic relations. Pope John Paul II reorganized the ecclesiastical structure of the country in May 1993. In 1997, the Vatican and Hungary signed an agreement that restored some Church property confiscated under communism and provided some sources of funding for Church activities. Hungary's bishops have said social conflicts, political changes and economic strains have put new pressures on the Church.

Iceland*

Dioc., 1; bp., 1; parishes, 4; priests, 12 (6 dioc., 6 rel.); srs., 37; bap., 82; Caths., 4,000 (1.4%); tot. pop., 283,000.

Island republic between Norway and Greenland; capital, Rekjavik. Irish hermits were there in the eighth century. Missionaries subsequently evangelized the island and Christianity was officially accepted about 1000. The first bishop was ordained in 1056. The Black Death had dire effects, and spiritual decline set in during the 15th century. Lutheranism was introduced from Denmark between 1537 and 1552 and made the official religion. Some Catholic missionary work was done in the 19th century. Religious freedom was granted to the few Catholics in 1874. A vicariate was erected in 1929 and was made a diocese in 1968.

India*

Patriarchate, 1 (titular of East Indies); major archbishopric (Syro-Malabar), 1; archd., 24; dioc., 118; card., 4; patr., 1; abp., 32; bp., 150; parishes, 8,200; priests, 19,404 (11,004 dioc., 8,400 rel.); p.d., 21; sem., 10,058; bros., 2,471; srs., 81,551; catechists, 59,963; bap., 352,474; Caths., 16,516,000 (1.6%); tot. pop. 1,002,140,000.

Republic on the subcontinent of south central Asia; capital, New Delhi. Long-standing tradition credits the Apostle Thomas with the introduction of Christianity in the Kerala area. Evangelization followed the establishment of Portuguese posts and the conquest of Goa in 1510. Jesuits, Franciscans, Dominicans, Augustinians and members of other religious orders figured in the early missionary history. An archdiocese for Goa, with two suffragan sees, was set up in 1558.

Missionaries had some difficulties with the British East India Co., which exercised virtual government control from 1757 to 1858. They also had trouble because of a conflict that developed between policies of the Portuguese government, which pressed its rights of patronage in episcopal and clerical appointments, and the Vatican Congregation for the Propagation of the Faith, which sought greater freedom of action in the same appointments. This struggle resulted in the schism of Goa between 1838 and 1857. In 1886, when the number of Catholics was estimated to be 1 million, the hierarchy for India and Ceylon was restored.

Jesuits contributed greatly to the development of Catholic education from the second half of the 19th century. A large percentage of the Catholic population is located around Goa and Kerala and farther south. The country is predominantly Hindu. Anti-conversion laws in effect in several states have had a restrictive effect on pastoral ministry and social service.

Recent years have seen tensions within the Syro-Malabar rite over liturgy and tradition. In addition, there have been tensions between the Latin-rite and Eastern-rite Catholic churches in India over the care of Catholics outside the traditional boundaries of their rites. The Vatican has investigated several Jesuits in India for teaching relativism, which refrains from proclaiming Christ as the world's savior out of respect for other religions. From 1998 to mid-2001 more than 150 cases of anti-Christian violence were recorded in western India. An independent commission probing the violence said right-wing Hindus were responsible.

Indonesia*

Archd., 8; dioc., 26; mil. ord. 1; card., 1; abp., 9; bps., 31; parishes, 1,044; priests, 2,883 (1,114 dioc., 1,769 rel.); p.d., 14; sem., 2,720; bros., 874; srs., 6,889; catechists, 21,763; bap., 196,559; Caths., 6,284,000 (3%); tot. pop., 210,490,000. Note: East Timor was granted independence in May 2002. See under Timor, East, for statistical details.

Republic in the Malay Archipelago, consisting of some 3,000 islands; capital, Jakarta. Evangelization by the Portuguese began about 1511. St. Francis Xavier spent some 14 months in the area. Christianity was strongly rooted in some parts of the islands by 1600. Islam's rise to dominance began at this time. The Dutch East Indies Co., which gained effective control in the 17th century, banned evangelization by Catholic missionaries for some time, but Dutch secular and religious priests managed to resume the work. A vicariate of Batavia for all the Dutch East Indies was set up in 1841. About 90 percent of the population is Muslim. The hierarchy was established in 1961.

From 1981 to about 1996, Catholics and Protestants clashed more than 40 times over what Catholics perceived as Communion host desecration. At least three Protestants died from beatings by Catholics after the incidents.

In the late 1990s, as the Indonesian economy took a nose-dive, Muslim-Christian violence increased, especially in the Molucca Islands. Church leaders continued to urge calm and dialogue.

Iran*

Archd., 4; dioc., 2; abp., 4; bp., 2; parishes, 18; priests, 11 (4 dioc., 7 rel.); p.d., 16; sem., 4; srs., 31; bap., 68; Caths., 25,000 (.02%); tot. pop., 63,660,000.

Islamic republic (Persia until 1935) in southwestern Asia; capital, Teheran. Some of the earliest Christian communities were established in this area outside the Roman Empire. They suffered persecution in the fourth century and were then cut off from the outside world. Nestorianism was generally professed in the late fifth century. Islam became dominant after 640. Some later missionary work was attempted but without success. Religious liberty was granted in 1834, but Catholics were the victims of a massacre in 1918. Islam is the religion of perhaps 98 percent of the population. Catholics belong to the Latin, Armenian and Chaldean rites.

After Iran nationalized many Church-run social institutions in 1980, about 75 Catholic missionaries left the country, by force or by choice. In recent years, however, Iranian authorities have shown more cooperation regarding entry visas for Church personnel. Although freedom of worship is guaranteed in Iran, Church sources said Catholic activities are monitored carefully by authorities. Since Pope John Paul II and Iranian President Mohammed Khatami met in 1999, the Holy See and Iran have had several high-level diplomatic exchanges.

Iraq*

Patriarchate, 1; archd., 9; dioc., 5; ap. ex., 2; patriarch, 1; abp., 10; bp., 2; parishes, 92; priests, 135 (115 dioc., 20 rel.); p.d., 7; sem., 87; bros., 9; srs., 293; catechists, 1,041; bap., 3,543; Caths., 281,000 (1%); tot. pop., 22,950,000.

Republic in southwestern Asia; capital, Baghdad. Some of the earliest Christian communities were established in the area, whose history resembles that of Iran. Catholics belong to the Armenian, Chaldean, Latin and Syrian rites; Chaldeans are most numerous. Islam is the religion of some 90 percent of the population. Iraq's Chaldean Catholic patriarch has been outspoken against the international embargo against Iraq, saying it especially hurts children and the sick.

Ireland*

Archd., 4; dioc., 22; card., 2; abp., 9; bp., 40; parishes, 1,367; priests, 5,642 (3,336 dioc., 2,306 rel.); p.d., 2; sem., 295; bros., 950; srs., 9,254; bap., 62,600 (preceding figures include Northern Ireland); Caths., 4,666,000 (75%); tot. 6,121,000 (population numbers include Northern Ireland; in Republic of

Ireland, Catholics comprise 95% of the population).

Republic in the British Isles; capital, Dublin. St. Patrick, who is venerated as the apostle of Ireland, evangelized parts of the island for some years after the middle of the fifth century. Conversion of the island was not accomplished, however, until the seventh century or later. Celtic monks were the principal missionaries. The Church was organized along monastic lines at first, but a movement developed in the 11th century for the establishment of jurisdiction along episcopal lines. By that time many Roman usages had been adopted. The Church gathered strength during the period from the Norman Conquest of England to the reign of Henry VIII despite a wide variety of rivalries, wars, and other disturbances.

Henry introduced an age of repression of the faith, which continued for many years under several of his successors. The Irish suffered from proscription of the Catholic faith, economic and social disabilities, subjection to absentee landlords and a plantation system designed to keep them from owning property, and actual persecution which took an uncertain toll of lives up until about 1714. Some penal laws remained in force until emancipation in 1829. Nearly 100 years later Ireland was divided in two, making Northern Ireland, consisting of six counties, part of the United Kingdom (1920) and giving dominion status to the Irish Free State, made up of the other 26 counties (1922). This state (Eire, in Gaelic) was proclaimed the Republic of Ireland in 1949. The Catholic Church predominates but religious freedom is guaranteed for all. The Irish Republic and Northern Ireland share a bishops' conference, which has worked for peace in Northern Ireland. Recent years have witnessed a decrease in vocations and growing turmoil over issues such as priestly pedophilia, divorce, and abortion.

Ireland, Northern

Tot. pop., 1,610,000; Catholics comprise more than one third. (Other statistics are included in Ireland).

Part of the United Kingdom, it consists of six of the nine counties of Ulster in the northeast corner of Ireland; capital, Belfast. Early history is given under Ireland.

Nationalist-unionist tensions fall primarily along Catholic-Protestant lines, with nationalists, mainly Catholics, advocating an end to British rule. Violence and terrorism began in the late 1960s and, by the late 1990s, more than 3,000 people had been killed. Catholic-Protestant tensions are highlighted each year during the Protestant marching season, when members of the Protestant Orange Order parade through Catholic neighborhoods, culminating in a march to commemorate the 1690 Battle of the Boyne, when Protestant King William of Orange defeated Catholic King James II. Catholics see the marches as signs of triumphalism.

On Apr. 10, 1998, the governments of the Irish Republic and Great Britain and the political parties of Northern Ireland reached an agreement known as the Good Friday agreement. Irish archbishops supported it, and it was endorsed by the voters in Ireland and Northern Ireland. However, decommissioning of weapons for the outlawed, primarily Catholic Irish Republican Army remained a stumbling block to peace.

Catholics have claimed discrimination in the work-place and harassment from the Royal Ulster Constabulary, Northern Ireland's police force. Although Catholics make up about 47 percent of Northern Ireland's population, they make up only 7 percent of the force. Former Hong Kong Gov. Chris Patten headed an independent review of the constabulary. In early 2000, Britain announced sweeping changes in the force.

Israel*

Patriarchates, 2 (Jerusalem for Latins; patriarchal vicariate for Greek-Melkites); archd., 2; ap.ex., 5; patriarch, 1; abp., 5; bp., 4; parishes, 78; priests, 379 (78 dioc., 301 rel.); p.d., 6; sem., 145; bros., 162; srs., 1,038; bap., 1,558; Caths., 118,000 (1.9%); tot. pop., 6,040,000.

Parliamentary democracy in the Middle East; capitals, Jerusalem and Tel Aviv (diplomatic). Israel was the birthplace of Christianity, the site of the first Christian communities. Some persecution was suffered in the early Christian era and again during the several hundred years of Roman control. Muslims conquered the territory in the seventh century and, except for the period of the Kingdom of Jerusalem established by Crusaders, remained in control most of the time up until World War I. The Church survived in the area, sometimes just barely, but it did not prosper greatly or show any notable increase in numbers. The British took over the protectorate of the area after World War I.

Partition into Israel for the Jews and Palestine for the Arabs was approved by the United Nations in 1947. War broke out a year later with the proclamation of the Republic of Israel. The Israelis won the war and 50 percent more territory than they had originally been ceded. War broke out again for six days in June 1967, and in October 1973, resulting in a Middle East crisis.

Judaism is the faith professed by about 85 percent of the inhabitants; approximately one-third of them are considered observant. Israeli-Holy See relations improved in 1994 with the implementation of full diplomatic relations, and the Church gained legal status in 1997.

The Holy See repeatedly has asked for an internationally guaranteed statute to protect the sacred nature of Jerusalem, which is holy to Christians, Muslims and Jews. It has underlined that this means more than access to specific holy places and that the political and religious dimensions of Jerusalem are interrelated. During the Palestinian intifada, the Vatican and Holy Land church leaders defended Israeli rights to live without the threat of terrorism and the Palestinians' right to a homeland, saying both would only be achieved through a negotiated settlement.

Italy*

Patriarchate, 1 (Venice); archd. 60 (40 are metropolitan sees); dioc., 156; prel., 3; abb., 7; mil. ord. 1; pat., 1 (Venice); card., 37; abp., 175; bps., 281 (hierarchy includes 223 residential, 25 coadjutors or auxiliaries, 119 in Curia offices, remainder in other offices or retired); parishes, 25,865; priests, 54,920 (36,117 dioc., 18,803 rel.); p.d., 2,439; sem., 6,445; bros., 3,947; srs., 113,295; catechists, 182,552; bap., 487,935; Caths., 55,877,000 (97%); tot. pop., 57,530,000.

Republic in southern Europe; capital, Rome. A

Christian community was formed early in Rome, probably by the middle of the first century. St. Peter established his see there. He and St. Paul suffered death for the faith in the 60s. The early Christians were persecuted at various times, as in other parts of the empire, but the Church developed in numbers and influence, gradually spreading out from towns and cities in the center and south to rural areas and the north.

Church organization, in the process of formation in the second century, developed greatly between the fifth and eighth centuries. By the latter date the Church had already come to grips with serious problems, including doctrinal and disciplinary disputes that threatened the unity of faith, barbarian invasions, and the need for the pope and bishops to take over civil responsibilities because of imperial default. The Church has been at the center of life on the peninsula throughout the centuries. It emerged from underground in 313, with the Edict of Milan, and rose to a position of prestige and lasting influence. It educated and converted the barbarians, preserved culture through the early Middle Ages and passed it on to later times, suffered periods of decline and gained strength through recurring reforms, engaged in military combat for political reasons and intellectual combat for the preservation and development of doctrine, saw and patronized the development of the arts, experienced all human strengths and weaknesses in its members.

From the fourth to the 19th centuries, the Church was a temporal as well as spiritual power. In the 1870s, the Papal States were annexed by the Kingdom of Italy. The 1929 Lateran Pacts included a treaty recognizing the Vatican as an independent state, a financial agreement by which Italy agreed to compensate the Vatican for loss of the papal states, and a concordat regulating Church-state relations. In 1984 the Vatican and Italy signed a revised concordat, reducing some of the Church's privileges and removing Catholicism as the state religion.

The Church strongly opposed Italy's abortion law in 1978 and forced a 1981 referendum on the issue. Abortion remained legal, and the Italian Church has taken a more low-profile stance. The Church has been active in social issues, including helping unprecedented numbers of illegal immigrants in the late 1990s. Church leaders have expressed concern about Italy's low birth rate.

In 1997, a double earthquake destroyed a large section of the ceiling of the Basilica of St. Francis in Assisi, killing four people. Restoration experts began work almost immediately on the basilica, one of the Italian Church's largest tourism sites. The upper basilica was reopened in November 1999.

Jamaica*

Archd., 1; dioc., 2; abp., 2; bp., 2; parishes, 87; priests, 90 (49 dioc., 41 rel.); p.d., 32; sem., 20; bros., 51; srs., 177; catechists, 436; bap., 1,369; Caths., 116,000 (4.4%); tot. pop., 2,590,000.

Republic in the West Indies; capital, Kingston. Franciscans and Dominicans evangelized the island from about 1512 until 1655. Missionary work was interrupted after the English took possession but was resumed by Jesuits about the turn of the 19th century. An apostolic vicariate was organized in 1837. The

hierarchy was established in 1967. In the late 1990s, Church leaders spoke out against violence; more than 800 people were murdered in Jamaica in 1997 alone.

Japan*

Archd., 3; dioc., 13; p.a., 1; card., 1; abp., 5; bp., 20; parishes, 871; priests, 1,749 (549 dioc., 1,200 rel.); p.d., 8; sem., 219; bros., 253; srs., 6,552; catechists, 1,294; bap., 9,938; Caths., 513,000 (.39%); tot. pop., 126,870,000.

Archipelago in the northwest Pacific; capital, Tokyo. Jesuits began evangelization in the middle of the 16th century and about 300,000 converts, most of them in Kyushu, were reported at the end of the century. The Nagasaki Martyrs were victims of persecution in 1597. Another persecution took some 4,000 lives between 1614 and 1651. Missionaries, banned for two centuries, returned about the middle of the 19th century and found Christian communities still surviving in Nagasaki and other places in Kyushu. A vicariate was organized in 1866. Religious freedom was guaranteed in 1889. The hierarchy was established in 1891. Several Japanese bishops at the 1998 Synod of Bishops for Asia said Catholicism has grown slowly in the region because the Church is too Western.

Since the 1980s, on several occasions Church leaders have apologized and asked forgiveness for the Church's complicity in the nation's aggression during the 1930s and 1940s. At the end of the 20th century, bishops and religious superiors suggested that during the 21st century the Japanese Church focus on pastoral care for migrant workers, concern for the environment and interreligious dialogue.

Jordan*

Archd., 1; ex. pat., 1; abp., 1; bp., 1; parishes, 62; priests, 75 (59 dioc., 16 rel.); sem., 3; bros., 9; srs., 256; bap., 1,100; Caths., 72,000 (1%); tot. pop., 4,910,000.

Constitutional monarchy in the Middle East; capital, Amman. Christianity there dates from apostolic times. Survival of the faith was threatened many times under the rule of Muslims from 636 and Ottoman Turks from 1517 to 1918, and in the Islamic Emirate of Trans-Jordan from 1918 to 1949. In the years following the creation of Israel, some 500,000 Palestinian refugees, including Christians, moved to Jordan. In the 1990s, Jordan cared for some 130,000 Iraqi refugees, including some 30,000 Chaldean Catholics. Islam is the state religion, but religious freedom is guaranteed for all. The Greek Melkite Archdiocese of Petra and Filadelfia is located in Jordan. Latin-rite Catholics are under the jurisdiction of the Latin Patriarchate of Jerusalem. Jordan established diplomatic relations with the Holy See in 1994.

Kazakstan*

Dioc., 1; a.a., 3; abp., 1; bp., 3; parishes, 37, priests, 59 (37 dioc., 22 rel.); sem., 10; bros., 2; srs., 62; bap., 1,116; Caths., 180,000 (1.2%); tot. pop., 16,170,000.

Independent republic (1991); formerly part of USSR; capital, Astana. About 47 percent of the population is Muslim, and about 44 percent is Orthodox. The Catholic population is mainly of German, Polish and Ukrainian origin, descendants of those deported during the Stalin regime. A Latin-rite apostolic administration was established in 1991. In 1998, the

Vatican and the Kazak government signed an agreement guaranteeing the Church legal rights. Diocesan structure was established in 1999. Pope John Paul II visited the country in 2001, saying he believed the post-communist era offered an evangelizing opportunity for the Catholic Church.

Kenya*
Archd. 4; dioc., 19; v.a., 1; mil. ord., 1; card., 1; abp. 5; bp., 23; parishes, 642; priests, 1,865 (989 dioc., 876 rel.); p.d., 2; sem., 1,536; bros., 690; srs., 4,082; catechists, 9,582; bap., 258,302; Caths., 7,654,000 (25%); tot. pop., 30,670,000.

Republic in East Africa on the Indian Ocean; capital, Nairobi. Systematic evangelization by the Holy Ghost Missionaries began in 1889, nearly 40 years after the start of work by Protestant missionaries. The hierarchy was established in 1953. Three metropolitan sees were established in 1990. Kenyan Catholics were in the forefront of ministering to victims of the 1998 explosion at the U.S. Embassy in Nairobi. The Kenyan bishops have been very outspoken against ethnic violence, poverty, government corruption and mismanagement, and the need for a constitutional review.

Kiribati*
Dioc., 1; bp., 1; parishes, 23; priests, 26 (12 dioc., 14 rel.); p.d. 1; sem., 22; bros., 23; srs., 92; catechists, 222; bap., 1,679; Caths., 46,000 (54.2%); tot. pop., 83,000.

Former British colony (Gilbert Islands) in Oceania; became independent July 12, 1979; capital, Bairiki on Tarawa. French Missionaries of the Sacred Heart began work in the islands in 1888. A vicariate for the islands was organized in 1897. The hierarchy was established in 1966.

Korea, North
Tot. pop., 22,270,000. No recent Catholic statistics available; there were an estimated 100,000 Catholics reported in 1969.

Northern part of peninsula in eastern Asia; formal name Democratic People's Republic of Korea (May 1, 1948); capital, Pyongyang. See South Korea for history before country was divided. After liberation from Japan in 1945, the Soviet regime in the North systematically punished all religions. After the 1950-53 Korean war, Christian worship was not allowed outside of homes until 1988, when the country's one Catholic Church was built in Pyongyang. A 1999 South Korean government report said North Korea clearly restricts religious practices, and churches in the North exist only for show.

Korea, South*
Archd., 3; dioc., 11; mil. ord. 1; card., 1; abp., 5; bp., 20; parishes, 1,152; priests, 2,731 (2,299 dioc., 432 rel.); sem., 1,882; bros., 616; srs., 7,938; catechists, 12,067; bap., 170,397; Caths., 4,047,000 (8.5%); tot. pop., 47,270,000.

Southern part of peninsula in eastern Asia; formal name, Republic of Korea (1948); capital, Seoul. Some Catholics may have been in Korea before it became a "hermit kingdom" toward the end of the 16th century and closed its borders to foreigners. The modern introduction to Catholicism came in 1784 through lay converts. A priest arriving in the country in 1794 found 4,000 Catholics there who had never seen a priest. A vicariate was erected in 1831 but was not manned for several years thereafter. There were 15,000 Catholics by 1857. Four persecutions in the 19th century took a terrible toll; several thousand died in the last one, 1866-69. (Pope John Paul II canonized 103 martyrs of this period during his 1984 visit to South Korea.) Freedom of religion was granted in 1883, when Korea opened its borders. During World War II, most foreign priests were arrested and expelled, seminaries were closed and churches were taken over. After liberation from Japan in 1945, the Church in the South had religious freedom. Since the 1950-53 Korean war, the Church in South Korea has flourished. Church leaders in the South have worked at reconciliation with the North and to alleviate famine in the North.

Kuwait*
V.a., 1; pat. ex., 1; bp., 1; parishes, 5; priests, 9 (3 dioc., 6 rel.); p.d., 1; bros., 13; bap., 571; Caths., 154,000 (.8%); tot. pop., 2,190,000.

Constitutional monarchy (sultanate or sheikdom) in southwest Asia bordering on the Persian Gulf. Remote Christian origins probably date to apostolic times. Islam is the predominant and official religion. Catholics are mostly foreign workers; the Church enjoys religious freedom.

Kyrgyzstan*
Mission, 1; parishes, 7; priests, 6 (rel.); bros., 1; srs., 4; bap., 8; Caths., 30,000; tot. pop., 4,900,000.

Independent republic bordering China; former Soviet republic; capital, Bishkek (former name, Frunze). Most of the people are Sunni Muslim. Established diplomatic relations with the Holy See in August 1992.

Laos
V.a., 4; bp., 3; parishes, 111; priests, 13 (12 dioc., 1 rel.); p.d., 1; sem., 18; srs., 149; catechists, 278; bap., 1,060; Caths., 38,000 (.6%); tot. pop., 5,280,000. (AD)

People's republic in southeast Asia; capital, Vientiane. Systematic evangelization by French missionaries started about 1881; earlier efforts ended in 1688. The first mission was established in 1885 by Father Xavier Guégo. An apostolic vicariate was organized in 1899. Most of the foreign missionaries were expelled following the communist takeover in 1975. Catholic schools remain banned, and the government lets foreign missionaries into the country only as "social workers." A Laotian bishop at the 1998 Synod of Bishops for Asia said religious practice was nearly normal in two of the country's four apostolic vicariates, but elsewhere was more controlled and sometimes difficult. Buddhism is the state religion.

Latvia*
Archd., 1; dioc., 3; abp., 1; bp., 5; parishes, 243; priests, 116 (95 dioc., 21 rel.); p.d., 1; sem., 55; srs., 86; catechist, 284; bap., 5,894; Caths., 408,000 (16.6%); tot. pop., 2,430,000.

Independent (1991) Baltic republic; capital, Riga. (Forcibly absorbed by the USSR in 1940; it regained independence in 1991). Catholicism was introduced late in the 12th century. Lutheranism became the dominant religion after 1530. Catholics were free to practice their faith during the long period of Russian control and during independence from 1918 to 1940. The relatively small Catholic community in Latvia was repressed during the 1940-91 Soviet takeover, which was not recognized by the Holy See or the United States. After Latvia declared its independence, the Church began to flourish, including among people who described themselves as nonreligious. In the late 1990s, one archbishop urged the Russian government not to interfere in disputes over citizenship for the country's ethnic Russians, who make up about one-third of the country's population.

Lebanon*

Patriarchates, 3; achd., 12 (1 Armenian, 4 Maronite, 7 Greek Melkite); dioc., 8 (1 Chaldean, 6 Maronite); v.a., 1 (Latin); card., 1 (patriarch of the Maronites); patriarchs, 3 (patriarchs of Antioch of the Maronites, Antioch of the Syrians and Cilicia of the Armenians who reside in Lebanon); abp., 20; bp., 15; parishes, 1,029; priests, 1,370 (730 dioc., 640 rel.); p.d., 4; sem., 450; bros., 210; srs., 2,625; catechists, 585; bap., 11,975; Caths., 1,819,000 (52%); tot. pop., 3,500,000.

Republic in the Middle East; capital, Beirut. Christianity, introduced in apostolic times, was firmly established by the end of the fourth century and has remained so despite heavy Muslim influence since early in the seventh century. The country is the center of the Maronite rite. In the 1980s, the country was torn by violence and often heavy fighting among rival political-religious factions drawn along Christian-Muslim lines. Pope John Paul II convened a synod of bishops for Lebanon in 1995 to urge Lebanese to forgive and forget the wounds of the war. Synod members provoked controversy by directly criticizing Israeli occupation of southern Lebanon and Syria's continued deployment of troops in the area. In 1999, Lebanon was the site of a historic meeting of Mideast and North African Church leaders, who discussed the future of the Catholic Church in the Arab world.

Lesotho*

Archd., 1; dioc., 3; abp., 1; bp., 3; parishes, 81; priests, 146 (61 dioc., 85 rel.); sem., 74; bros., 41; srs., 676; catechists, 1,627; bap., 24,914; Caths., 894,000 (44%); tot. pop., 2,040,000.

Constitutional monarchy, an enclave in the southeastern part of South Africa; capital, Maseru. Oblates of Mary Immaculate, the first Catholic missionaries in the area, started evangelization in 1862. Father Joseph Gerard, whom Pope John Paul II beatified in 1988, worked 10 years before he made his first conversion. An apostolic prefecture was organized in 1894. The hierarchy was established in 1951. Under the military government of the late 1980s, Lesotho's Catholics pressed for democratic reforms. In the 1990s, they gave special pastoral care to families whose breadwinners had to travel to South Africa to work, often for weeks at a time.

Liberia*

Archd., 1; dioc., 2; abp., 1; bp., 1; parishes, 48; priests, 52 (31 dioc., 21 rel.); p.d., 3; sem., 42; bros., 18; srs., 48; catechists, 433; bap. 10,205; Caths., 142,000 (4.8%); tot. pop., 2,910,000.

Republic in West Africa; capital, Monrovia. Missionary work and influence, dating intermittently from the 16th century, were slight before the Society of African Missions undertook evangelization in 1906. The hierarchy was established in 1982. Fighting within the country, which began in 1989, culminated in 1996 and resulted in the evacuation of most Church workers and the archbishop of Monrovia. The war claimed the lives of 150,000 and made refugees of or displaced another million. Most Church institutions in Monrovia were destroyed.

Libya*

V.a., 3; p.a., 1; abp., 1; bp., 2; parishes, 4; priests, 14 (4 dioc., 10 rel.); sem. 2; srs., 62; bap., 112; Caths., 77,000 (1.5%); tot. pop., 5,290,000.

Arab state in North Africa; capital, Tripoli. Christianity was probably preached in the area at an early date but was overcome by the spread of Islam from the 630s. Islamization was complete by 1067, and there has been no Christian influence since then. Almost all Catholics are foreign workers. Islam is the state religion. After implementation of a U.N. embargo against the country in 1992, the government removed most limitations on entry of Catholic religious orders, especially health care workers. Libya established diplomatic relations with the Holy See in 1997.

Liechtenstein*

Archd. 1; abp., 1; parishes, 10; priests, 30 (19 dioc., 11 rel); sem., 16; srs., 69; bap., 322; Caths., 25,000 (80%); tot. pop., 32,000.

Constitutional monarchy in central Europe; capital, Vaduz. Christianity in the country dates from the fourth century; the area has been under the jurisdiction of Chur, Switzerland, since about that time. The Reformation had hardly any influence in the country. Catholicism is the state religion, but religious freedom for all is guaranteed by law.

Lithuania*

Archd., 2; dioc., 5; mil. ord., 1; card., 2; abp., 3; bp., 11; parishes, 676; priests, 774 (670 dioc., 104 rel.); p.d., 3; sem., 259; bros., 28; srs., 743; catechists, 2,077; bap., 32,072; Caths., 2,828,000 (80%); tot. pop., 3,690,000.

Baltic republic forcibly absorbed and under Soviet domination from 1940; regained independence, 1991; capital, Vilnius. Catholicism was introduced in 1251 and a short-lived diocese was established by 1260. Effective evangelization took place between 1387 and 1417, when Catholicism became the state religion. Losses to Lutheranism in the 16th century were overcome. Efforts of czars to "russify" the Church between 1795 and 1918 were strongly resisted. Concordat relations with the Vatican were established in 1927, nine years after independence from Russia and 13 years before Russia annexed Lithuania. The Russians closed convents and seminaries; in Kaunas, men needed government approval to attend the seminary. Priests were restricted in pastoral ministry and subject to appointment by government officials; no religious services were allowed outside churches; religious press and instruction were banned. Two bishops — Vincentas Sladkevicius and Julijonas Steponavicius — were forbidden to act as bishops and relegated to remote parishes in 1957 and 1961, respectively. Some bishops and hundreds of priests and laity were imprisoned or detained in Siberia between 1945 and 1955. Despite such conditions, a vigorous underground Church flourished in Lithuania.

In the 1980s, government pressure eased, and some bishops were allowed to return to their dioceses. In 1989 Pope John Paul II appointed bishops in all six Lithuanian dioceses. The Church strongly supported the 1990 independence movement, and Lithuanian independence leaders urged young men to desert the Russian army and seek sanctuary in churches. However, communist rule nearly destroyed the Church's infrastructure. In 2000 the Church and government signed a series of agreements regularizing the Church's position.

Luxembourg*

Archd., 1; abp., 2; parishes, 275; priests, 279 (207 dioc., 72 rel.); p.d., 7; sem., 7; bros., 20; srs., 650; catechism, 460; bap., 3,185; Caths. 378,000 (89%); tot. pop., 436,000.

Constitutional monarchy in western Europe; capital, Luxembourg. Christianity, introduced in the fifth and sixth centuries, was firmly established by the end of the eighth century. A full-scale parish system was in existence in the ninth century. Monastic influence was strong until the Reformation, which had minimal influence in the country. The Church experienced some adverse influence from the currents of the French Revolution. In recent years, the Church has restructured its adult formation program to involve more lay workers.

Macau

Dioc., 1; bp., 1; parishes, 6; priests, 72 (27 dioc., 45 rel.); bros., 17; srs., 176; bap., 437; catechists, 5,273; Caths., 29,000; tot. pop., 438,000.

Former Portuguese-administered territory in southeast Asia across the Pearl River estuary from Hong Kong; reverted to Chinese control Dec. 20, 1999. Christianity was introduced by the Jesuits in 1557. Diocese was established in 1576. Macau served as a base for missionary work in Japan and China. Portuguese and Chinese Catholics remained somewhat segregated throughout the more than 400 years of Portuguese rule. Bishop Domingos Lam Ka Tseung became the first Chinese bishop of Macau in 1988 and launched a lay formation plan that included Chinese and Portuguese language training. The Church has been prominent in education. A Catholic priest was among three religious leaders named to the committee to prepare for the enclave's return to Chinese rule in December 1999. Church leaders said the transition proceeded smoothly.

Macedonia*

Dioc., 1; bp., 2; parishes, 7; priests, 13 (12 dioc., 1 rel.); srs., 32; bap., 128; Caths., 10,000 (.9%); tot. pop., 2,030,000.

Former Yugoslav Republic of Macedonia; declared independence in 1992; capital, Skopje. The Diocese of Skopje-Prizren includes the Yugoslav province of Kosovo, so the Macedonian Church was intimately involved with ethnic Albanians during the period of ethnic cleansing by Serb forces and retaliatory NATO air strikes.

Madagascar*

Archd., 3; dioc., 17; card., 1; abp., 4; bp., 21; parishes, 310; priests, 1,111 (436 dioc., 675 rel.); sem., 827; bros., 467; srs., 3,584; catechists, 16,382; bap., 153,941; Caths., 4,147,000 (26%); tot. pop. 15,970,000.

Republic (Malagasy Republic) off the eastern coast of Africa; capital, Antananarivo. Missionary efforts were generally fruitless from early in the 16th century until the Jesuits were permitted to start open evangelization about 1845. An apostolic prefecture was set up in 1850 and an apostolic vicariate in the North was placed in charge of the Holy Ghost Fathers in 1898. There were 100,000 Catholics by 1900. The first native bishop was ordained in 1936. The hierarchy was established in 1955. In the late 1980s and early 1990s, the Church joined opposition calls for renewal of social institutions. Today, the Church in Madagascar runs hundreds of schools and dozens of orphanages and is active in the island's social justice concerns; some consider it the largest landowner, after the government.

Malawi*

Archd., 1; dioc., 6; abp., 1; bp., 8; parishes, 150; priests, 398 (269 dioc., 129 rel.); sem., 222; bros., 82; srs., 725; catechists, 7,174; bap., 112,491; Caths., 2,680,000 (24%); tot. pop., 11,310,000.

Republic in the interior of East Africa; capital, Lilongwe. Missionary work, begun by Jesuits in the late 16th and early 17th centuries, was generally ineffective until the end of the 19th century. The Missionaries of Africa (White Fathers) arrived in 1889 and later were joined by others. A vicariate was set up in 1897. The hierarchy was established in 1959. In the late 1980s, the Church in Malawi helped hundreds of thousands of refugees from the war in Mozambique. Malawi's churches, especially the Catholic Church, were instrumental in bringing about the downfall of President Hastings Kamuzu Banda, who ruled for 30 years. A 1992 bishops' pastoral letter criticized Banda's rule and the nation's poverty and galvanized Malawians into pro-democracy protests. Banda responded by summoning the country's bishops, seizing copies of the letter and expelling an Irish member of the Malawi hierarchy. Western donors called off aid, and in 1994 Banda was forced to call multi-party elections, which he lost. In 2002, church officials were outspoken against plans by Banda's successor, President Bakili Muluzi, to seek a third term of office; church officials said they were threatened and attacked for that criticism.

Malaysia

Archd., 2; dioc., 6; abp., 3; bp., 8; parishes, 140; priests, 244 (188 dioc., 56 rel.); p.d., 1; sem., 67; bros., 68; srs., 540; catechists, 2,841; bap., 24,098; Caths., 752,000 (3%); tot. pop., 23,260,000. (AD)

Parliamentary democracy in southeast Asia; capital, Kuala Lumpur. Christianity, introduced by Portuguese colonists about 1511, was confined almost exclusively to Malacca until late in the 18th century. The effectiveness of evangelization increased from then on because of the recruitment and training of indigenous clergy. Singapore (see separate entry), founded in 1819, became a center for missionary work. Effective evangelization in Sabah and Sarawak began in the second half of the 19th century. The hierarchy was established in 1973. In accordance with government wishes for Bahasa Malaysia to be the national language, the Church has tried to introduce it into its liturgies. For more than a decade, Church leaders campaigned against the Internal Security Act, which allows renewable 30-day detentions without trial. Proselytizing Muslims is illegal, but the government allows conversions from other religions.

Maldives

Republic, an archipelago 400 miles southwest of India and Ceylon; capital, Male. No serious attempt was ever made to evangelize the area, which is completely Muslim. Population, 290,000.

Mali*

Archd., 1; dioc., 5; abp., 1; bp., 5; parishes, 38; priests, 154 (74 dioc., 80 rel.); sem., 27; bros., 22; srs., 264; catechists, 958; bap., 4,041; Caths., 211,000 (.2%); tot. pop., 11,350,000.

Republic, inland in western Africa; capital, Bamako. Catholicism was introduced late in the second half of the 19th century. Missionary work made little progress in the midst of the predominantly Muslim population. A vicariate was set up in 1921. The hierarchy was established in 1955. In recent years, the Church has promoted the role of women in society. Catholics have cordial relations with Muslims.

Malta*

Archd., 1; dioc., 1; abp., 3; bp., 2; parishes, 79; priests, 931 (496 dioc., 435 rel.); sem., 84; bros., 77; srs., 1,248; catechists, 1,215; bap., 4,177; Caths., 364,000 (92%); tot. pop., 380,000.

Republic south of Sicily; capital, Valletta. Early catacombs and inscriptions are evidence of the early introduction of Christianity. St. Paul was shipwrecked on Malta in 60. Saracens controlled the islands from 870 to 1090, a period of difficulty for the Church. The line of bishops extends from 1090 to the present. Church-state conflict developed in recent years over passage of government-sponsored legislation affecting Catholic schools and Church-owned property. An agreement reached in 1985 ended the dispute and established a joint commission to study other Church-state problems.

Marshall Islands*

P.a., 1; parishes, 4; priests, 6 (rel.); p.d., 2; sem., 2; srs., 17; bap., 537; Caths., 5,000 (12.5%); tot. pop., 51,000.

Island republic in central Pacific Ocean; capital, Majura. Formerly administered by United States as part of U.N. Trust Territory of the Pacific; independent nation, 1991. An apostolic prefecture was erected May 25, 1993 (formerly part of Carolines-Marshall Diocese), with U.S. Jesuit Rev. James Gould as first apostolic prefect.

Mauritania*

Dioc., 1; bp., 1; parishes, 6; priests, 10 (1 dioc., 9 rel.); srs., 32; bap., 34; Caths., 5,000 (.2%); tot. pop., 2,670,000. (AD)

Islamic republic on the northwest coast of Africa; capital, Nouakchott. With few exceptions, the Catholics in the country are foreign workers. At the 1994

Synod of Bishops for Africa, a bishop from Mauritania reported increasing problems with fundamentalist Muslims, but cautioned Church leaders against generalizing about Muslims.

Mauritius*

Dioc., 1; card., 1; bp., 1; parishes, 52; priests, 99 (59 dioc., 39 rel.); sem., 14; bros., 30; srs., 249; catechists, 807; bap., 4,236; Caths., 288,000 (25%); tot. pop., 1,180,000.

Island republic in the Indian Ocean; capital, Port Louis. Catholicism was introduced by Vincentians in 1722. Port Louis, made a vicariate in 1819 and a diocese in 1847, was a jumping-off point for missionaries to Australia, Madagascar and South Africa. During a 1989 visit to Mauritius, Pope John Paul II warned against sins that accompanied its rapid economic development and booming tourism industry.

Mexico* (See Catholic Church in Mexico; see also Statistics of the Church in Mexico)

Micronesia*

Dioc., 1; bp., 2; parishes, 23; priests, 23 (11 dioc., 12 rel.); p.d., 39; sem., 10; bros., 1; srs., 47; catechists, 113; bap., 1,920; Caths., 62,000 (53%); tot. pop., 117,000.

Federated States of Micronesia (Caroline archipelago) in southwest Pacific; capital, Palikir; former U.N. trust territory under U.S. administration; became independent nation September 1991. Effective evangelization began in the late 1880s. The government established diplomatic relations with the Holy See in 1994.

Moldova*

Dioc., 2; bp., 1; parishes, 11; priests, 15 (8 dioc., 7 rel.); p.d., 1; sem., 7; bros., 2; srs., 26; bap., 98; Caths., 20,000 (.34%); tot. pop., 4,340,000.

Independent republic, former constituent republic of the USSR; capital, Kishinev. The majority of people belong to the Orthodox Church. Catholics are mostly of Polish or German descent.

Monaco*

Archd., 1; abp., 1; parishes, 6; priests, 22 (14 dioc., 8 rel.); p.d., 1; sem., 2; bros., 1; srs., 18; bap., 162; Caths., 29,000 (90%); tot. pop., 32,000.

Constitutional monarchy, an enclave on the Mediterranean coast of France; capital, Monaco-Ville. Christianity was introduced before 1000. Catholicism is the official religion but freedom is guaranteed for all.

Mongolia*

Parish; priests, 7 (2 dioc., 5 rel.); sem., 2; bros., 1; srs., 14; bap., 8; Caths., 1,000 (.04%); tot. pop., 2,530,000.

Republic in north central Asia; formerly under communist control; capital Ulan Bator. Christianity was introduced by Oriental Orthodox. Some Franciscans were in the country in the 13th and 14th centuries, en route to China. Freedom of worship is guaranteed under the new constitution, which went into effect in 1992. The government established relations with the Holy See in 1992 and indicated that missionaries would be welcome to help rebuild the country. The first Catholic parish was established in 1994, and by 1997 the Church had extended its work beyond the capital.

Morocco*

Archd., 2; abp., 4; parishes, 35; priests, 62 (19 dioc., 43 rel.); p.d., 1; bros., 16; srs., 270; bap., 49; Caths., 24,000 (.08%); tot. pop., 28,710,000.

Constitutional monarchy in North Africa; capital, Rabat. Christianity was known in the area by the end of the third century. Bishops from Morocco attended a council at Carthage in 484. Catholic life survived under Visigoth and, from 700, Arab rule; later it became subject to influence from the Spanish, Portuguese and French. Islam is the state religion. The hierarchy was established in 1955. Pope John Paul II visited in 1985.

Mozambique

Archd., 3; dioc., 9; card., 1; abp. 3; bp., 11; parishes, 271; priests, 447 (139 dioc., 308 rel.); sem., 293; bros., 84; srs., 988; catechists, 64,269; bap., 131,957; Caths., 3,737,000 (21%); tot. pop., 17,690,000. (AD)

Republic in southeast Africa; capital, Maputo. Christianity was introduced by Portuguese Jesuits about the middle of the 16th century. Evangelization continued from then until the 18th century, when it went into decline largely because of the Portuguese government's expulsion of the Jesuits. Conditions worsened in the 1830s, improved after 1881, but deteriorated again during the anticlerical period from 1910 to 1925. Conditions improved in 1940, the year Portugal concluded a new concordat with the Holy See and the hierarchy was established. Missionaries' outspoken criticism of Portuguese policies in Mozambique resulted in Church-state tensions in the years immediately preceding independence. The first two indigenous bishops were ordained Mar. 9, 1975. Two ecclesiastical provinces were established in 1984. Mozambican bishops and members of the Rome-based Sant' Egidio Community were official mediators in the talks that ended 16 years of civil war in 1992. Since then, Church participation has flourished, with high attendance at Mass, a boom in vocations and active catechists at the parish level.

Myanmar

Archd., 3; dioc., 9; abp., 3; bp., 12; parishes, 272; priests, 483 (461 dioc., 22 rel.); sem., 269; bros., 100; srs., 1,294; catechists, 2,840; bap., 22,518; Caths., 600,000 (1.2%); tot. pop., 47,750,000. (AD)

Socialist republic in southeast Asia, formerly Burma; name changed to Myanmar in 1989; capital, Yangon (Rangoon). Christianity was introduced about 1500. Small-scale evangelization had limited results from the middle of the 16th century until the 1850s, when effective organization of the Church began. The hierarchy was established in 1955. Buddhism was declared the state religion in 1961, but the state is now officially secular. In 1965, Church schools and hospitals were nationalized. In 1966, all foreign missionaries who had entered the country for the first time after 1948 were forced to leave when the government refused to renew their work permits. The Church is involved primarily in pastoral and social activities.

Namibia*

Archd., 1; dioc., 1; v.a., 1; abp., 1; bp., 3; parishes, 92; priests, 77 (17 dioc., 60 rel.); p.d., 42; sem., 37; bros., 25; srs., 266; catechists, 1,251; bap., 5,494; Caths., 307,000 (17%); tot. pop., 1,820,000. (AD)

Independent (Mar. 21, 1990) state in southern Africa; capital, Windhoek. The area shares the history of South Africa. The hierarchy was established in 1994. The Church is hindered by a lack of priests.

Nauru*

Parish, 1; priest, 1 (rel); p.d., 2; srs., 3; bap., 95; Caths., 4,000 (50%); tot. pop., 8,000.

Independent republic in western Pacific; capital, Yaren. Forms part of the Tarawa and Nauru Diocese (Kiribati). Established diplomatic relations with the Holy See in 1992.

Nepal*

P.a., 1; parishes, 35; priests, 51 (11 dioc.; 40 rel.); sem., 35; bros., 1; srs., 104; bap., 143; Caths., 6,000 (2.7%); tot. pop., 22,900,000.

Constitutional monarchy, the only Hindu kingdom in the world, in central Asia; capital, Katmandu. Little is known of the country before the 15th century. Some Jesuits passed through from 1628 and some sections were evangelized in the 18th century, with minimal results, before the country was closed to foreigners. Conversions from Hinduism, the state religion, are not recognized in law and are punishable by imprisonment.

Netherlands*

Archd., 1; dioc., 6; mil ord., 1; card., 2; abp., 1; bp., 20; parishes, 1,492; priests 3,876 (1,588 dioc., 2,288 rel.); p.d., 214; sem., 218; bros., 1,464; srs., 11,350; bap., 44,536; Caths., 5,365,000 (34.6%); tot. pop., 15,860,000.

Constitutional monarchy in northwestern Europe; capital, Amsterdam (seat of government, The Hague). Evangelization, begun about the turn of the sixth century by Irish, Anglo-Saxon and Frankish missionaries, resulted in Christianization of the country by 800 and subsequent strong influence on the Lowlands. Invasion by French Calvinists in 572 brought serious losses to the Catholic Church and made the Reformed Church dominant. Catholics suffered a practical persecution of official repression and social handicap in the 17th century. The schism of Utrecht occurred in 1724. Only one-third of the population was Catholic in 1726. The Church had only a skeletal organization from 1702 to 1853, when the hierarchy was reestablished.

Despite this upturn, cultural isolation was the experience of Catholics until about 1914. From then on new vigor came into the life of the Church, and a whole new climate of interfaith relations began to develop. Before and for some years following the Second Vatican Council, the thrust and variety of thought and practice in the Dutch Church moved it to the vanguard position of "progressive" renewal. A synod of Dutch bishops held at the Vatican in January 1980 discussed ideological differences among Catholics with the aim of fostering unity and restoring some discipline within the nation's Church. However, even into the 1990s Church leaders spoke of a polarization among Catholics over issues such as sexual morality, ministries for women and priestly celibacy. The bishops also spoke out against permissive laws on euthanasia and assisted suicide.

New Zealand*

Archd., 1; dioc., 5; mil. ord., 1; card., 1; abp., 1; bp., 10; parishes, 272; priests, 554 (339 dioc., 215 rel.); p.d., 2; sem., 30; bros., 184; srs., 1,096; bap., 7,671; Caths. 457,000 (12%); tot. pop., 3,816,000.

Parliamentary democracy in southwestern Pacific Ocean; capital, Wellington. Protestant missionaries were the first evangelizers. On North Island, Catholic missionaries started work before the establishment of two dioceses in 1848; their work among the Maoris was not organized until about 1881. On South Island, whose first resident priest arrived in 1840, a diocese was established in 1869. These three jurisdictions were joined in a province in 1896. The Marists were the predominant Catholic missionaries in the area. The first Maori bishop was named in 1988. In 1998, Pope John Paul II urged New Zealand's bishops not to allow the Church to fall prey to the practices and values of prevailing culture. However, the president of the bishops' conference used the same occasion to express the bishops' concern to the pope about inconsistency in the way the Vatican exercises its authority.

Nicaragua*

Archd., 1; dioc., 6; v.a., 1; card., 1; abp., 1; bp., 10; parishes, 243; priests, 418 (247 dioc., 171 rel.); p.d., 30; sem., 301; bros., 99; srs., 977; catechists, 11,625; bap., 81,221; Caths., 4,518,000 (89%); tot. pop., 5,070,000.

Republic in Central America: capital, Managua. Evangelization began shortly after the Spanish conquest, about 1524, and eight years later the first bishop took over jurisdiction of the Church in the country. Jesuits were leaders in missionary work during the colonial period, which lasted until the 1820s. Evangelization endeavor increased after establishment of the republic in 1838. In this century it was extended to the Atlantic coastal area, where Protestant missionaries began work about the middle of the 1900s.

Many Church leaders, clerical and lay, supported the aims but not necessarily all the methods of the revolution, which forced the resignation and flight July 17, 1979, of Anastasio Somoza, whose family had controlled the government since the early 1930s. During the Sandinista period that followed, four priests accepted government posts. Some Nicaraguan Catholics threw their energies behind the Sandinista program of land reform and socialism, forming what some called a "popular church" based on liberation theology, while others strongly opposed the government. Managua Cardinal Miguel Obando Bravo helped mediate cease-fire talks during the war between the Sandinistas and U.S.-backed guerrillas. Land distribution, exacerbated by a wide gap in incomes, continued to be an issue, and in the late 1990s the Nicaraguan bishops continued to call for compromise between the government and former government officials. Despite an influx of aid after Hurricane Mitch killed more than 2,500 Nicaraguans and forced 900,000 to evacuate, Church leaders predicted an increase in poverty for the nation.

Niger*

Dioc., 1; bp., 3; parishes, 22; priests, 48 (7 dioc., 41 rel.); sem., 11; bros., 6; srs., 92; catechists, 340; bap., 344; Caths., 20,000 (.2%); tot. pop., 10,830,000.

Republic in west central Africa; capital, Niamey. The first mission was set up in 1831. An apostolic prefecture was organized in 1942, and the first diocese was established in 1961. The country is predominantly Muslim. The Church is active in the fields of health and education.

Nigeria*

Archd., 9; dioc., 36; v.a., 2; p.a., 1; card., 1; abp., 10; bp., 41; parishes, 1,752; priests, 3,597 (2,995 dioc., 602 rel.); p.d., 5; sem., 3,912; bros., 501; srs., 3,464; catechists, 26,560; bap., 566,324; Caths., 16,579,000 (14.3%); tot. pop., 115,220,000.

Republic in West Africa; capital, Lagos. The Portuguese introduced Catholicism to the coastal region in the 15th century. Capuchins did some evangelization in the 17th century but systematic missionary work did not get under way along the coast until about 1840. A vicariate for this area was organized in 1870. A prefecture was set up in 1911 for missions in the northern part of the country, where Islam was strongly entrenched. From 1967, when Biafra seceded, until early in 1970 the country was torn by civil war. The hierarchy was established in 1950. Six dioceses were made metropolitan sees in 1994; four new dioceses were established as in 1995. Under the 1993-99 rule of Gen. Sani Abacha, Church leaders spoke out on behalf of human rights and democracy. After Abacha announced elections, the bishops said the country needed "new leading actors and fresh vision." As the 21st century began, bishops spoke out against imposition of Islamic law in individual states within the country.

Norway*

Dioc., 1; prel., 2; bp., 3; parishes, 32; priests, 69 (31 dioc., 38 rel.); p.d., 3; sem., 7; bros., 3; srs., 184; bap., 709; Caths., 53,000 (1%); tot. pop., 4,490,000.

Constitutional monarchy in northern Europe; capital, Oslo. Evangelization begun in the ninth century by missionaries from England and Ireland put the Church on a firm footing about the turn of the 11th century. The first diocese was set up in 1153 and development of the Church progressed until the Black Death in 1349 inflicted losses from which it never recovered. Lutheranism, introduced from outside in 1537 and furthered cautiously, gained general acceptance by about 1600 and was made the state religion. Legal and other measures crippled the Church, forcing priests to flee the country and completely disrupting normal activity. Changes for the better came in the 19th century, with the granting of religious liberty in 1845 and the repeal of many legal disabilities in 1897. Norway was administered as a single apostolic vicariate from 1892 to 1932, when it was divided into three jurisdictions.

Oman

Parishes, 4; priests, 8 (1 dioc., 7 rel.); bap., 198; Caths., 66,000 (2.6%); tot. pop., 2,540,000.

Independent monarchy in eastern corner of Arabian Peninsula; capital, Muscat. Under ecclesiastical jurisdiction of Arabia apostolic vicariate.

Pakistan*

Archd., 2; dioc., 4; p.a., 1; abp., 1; bp., 6; parishes, 112; priests, 266 (136 dioc., 130 rel.); sem., 125; p.d., 3; bros., 51; srs., 711; catechists, 522; bap., 19,679; Caths., 1,237,000 (.09%); tot. pop., 137,500,000.

Islamic republic in southwest Asia; capital, Islamabad. Islam, firmly established in the eighth century, is the state religion. Christian evangelization of the native population began about the middle of the 19th century, years after earlier scattered attempts. The hierarchy was established in 1950. A series of death sentences against Christians accused of blasphemy resulted in acquittals during appeal processes, but in 1998 Bishop John Joseph of Faisalabad committed suicide to protest the strict blasphemy laws, which continued to be used as reasons for Christian arrests. In early 2002, the government did away with the system under which religious minorities, such as Catholics, could only vote for in elections for members of their religious group.

Palau*

Parishes, 3; priests, 5 (2 dioc., 3 rel.); p.d., 1; bros., 2; srs., 6; bap., 191; Caths., 8,000 (42%); tot. pop., 19,000.

Independent (1994) nation in western Pacific; capital, Koror; part of Caroline chain of Islands. Under ecclesiastical jurisdiction of diocese of Caroline Islands, Federated States of Micronesia.

Panama*

Archd., 1; dioc., 5; prel., 1; v.a., 1; abp., 2; bp., 8; parishes, 176; priests, 392 (181 dioc., 211 rel.); p.d., 66; sem., 166; bros., 53; srs., 566; catechists, 2,130; bap., 28,241; Caths., 2,434,000 (85%); tot. pop., 2,860,000.

Republic in Central America; capital, Panama City. Catholicism was introduced by Franciscan missionaries and evangelization started in 1514. The Panama Diocese, oldest in the Americas, was set up at the same time. The Catholic Church has favored status and state aid for missions, charities and parochial schools, but religious freedom is guaranteed to all religions. In May 1989, Panama's bishops accused the government of thwarting the presidential elections and of attempting to intimidate the Church. The elections' legitimate leader, Guillermo Endara, temporarily sought refuge at the Vatican Embassy in Panama City. After increasing unrest and violence, on Dec. 24, 1989, the country's dictator, Gen. Manuel Noriega, sought refuge at the Vatican Embassy. Ten days later, after U.S. troops spent days blasting the embassy with loud rock music and after meetings with Church diplomatic officials, Noriega surrendered.

Papua New Guinea*

Archd., 4; dioc., 14; abp., 6; bp., 23; parishes, 342; priests, 547 (175 dioc., 372 rel.); p.d., 8; sem., 339; bros., 254; srs., 851; catechists, 2,970; bap., 34,542; Caths., 1,630,000 (34%); tot. pop., 4,810,000.

Independent (Sept. 16, 1975) republic in southwest Pacific; capital, Port Moresby. Marists began evangelization about 1844 but were handicapped by many factors, including "spheres of influence" laid out for Catholic and Protestant missionaries. An apostolic prefecture was set up in 1896 and placed in charge of the Divine Word Missionaries. The territory suffered greatly during World War II. Hierarchy was established for New Guinea and adjacent islands in 1966. A decade-long war that began in the Bougainville area in the late 1980s left many churches, schools and health centers destroyed. At the end of the century, the Church fought social disintegration marked by violence, poverty and corruption.

Paraguay*

Archd., 1; dioc., 11; v.a., 2; mil. ord. 1; abp., 3; bp., 18; parishes, 358; priests, 783 (355 dioc., 428 rel.); p.d., 120; sem., 354; bros., 118; srs., 2,132; bap., 88,927; catechists, 54,359; Caths., 4,708,000 (86%); tot. pop., 5,500,000.

Republic in central South America; capital, Asunción. Catholicism was introduced in 1542, evangelization began almost immediately. A diocese erected in 1547 was occupied for the first time in 1556. On many occasions thereafter, dioceses in the country were left unoccupied because of political and other reasons. Jesuits who came into the country after 1609 devised the reductions system for evangelizing the Indians, teaching them agriculture, husbandry, trades and other arts, and giving them experience in property use and community life. The reductions were communes of Indians only, an average population of 3,000-4,000, under the direction of the missionaries. At their peak, some 30 reductions had a population of 100,000. Political officials regarded the reductions with disfavor because they did not control them and feared that the Indians trained in them might foment revolt and upset the established colonial system under Spanish control. The reductions lasted until about 1768, when the Jesuits were expelled.

Church-state relations following independence from Spain in 1811 were often tense because of government efforts to control the Church through continued exercise of Spanish patronage rights and by other means. The Church as well as the whole country suffered during the War of the Triple Alliance from 1865-70. After that time, the Church had the same kind of experience in Paraguay as in the rest of Latin America, with forces of liberalism, anticlericalism, massive educational needs, poverty, a shortage of priests and other personnel.

In the 1980s, Church-state tensions increased as Catholic leaders spoke out against President Alfredo Stroessner's decades of one-man rule. A 1988 papal visit seemed to increase the Church's confidence, as bishops repeatedly spoke out against him. The army general who overthrew Stroessner in 1989 said he did so in part to defend the Catholic Church.

Peru

Archd., 7; dioc., 18; prel., 11; v.a., 8; mil. ord. 1; card., 1; abp., 12; bp., 48; parishes, 1,426; priests, 2,790 (1,401 dioc., 1,389 rel.); p.d., 51; sem., 1,742; bros., 639; srs., 5,537; catechists, 42,489; bap., 351,904; Caths., 23,020,000 (90%); tot. pop., 25,660,000.

Republic on the west coast of South America; capital, Lima. An effective diocese became operational in 1537, five years after the Spanish conquest. Evangelization, already under way, developed for some time after 1570 but deteriorated before the end of the colonial period in the 1820s. The first American saint of the new world was a Peruvian, Rose of Lima, a

Dominican tertiary who died in 1617 and was canonized in 1671.

In the new republic founded after the wars of independence the Church experienced problems of adjustment, government efforts to control it through continuation of the patronage rights of the Spanish crown; suppression of houses of religious and expropriation of Church property; religious indifference and outright hostility. In the 20th century, liberation theology was born in Peru under the leadership of Father Gustavo Gutierrez. In the 1980s and early 1990s, the Maoist Sendero Luminoso guerrillas often targeted Church workers, who also found themselves prone to false charges of terrorism. A Peruvian cardinal was credited with much of the success of an early 1990s government effort to win the surrender of the rebels. When the government initiated a drastic economic program in 1990, Peruvian Church leaders worked to help feed and clothe the poor. In the late '90s, the Church successfully fought a government program of sterilization.

Philippines*

Archd., 16; dioc., 50; prel., 6; v.a., 7; mil. ord. 1; card., 3; abp., 17; bp., 90; parishes, 2,795; priests, 7,521 (5,013 dioc., 2,508 rel.); p.d., 17; sem., 6,531; bros., 664; srs., 10,798; catechists, 95,566; bap., 1,642,371; Caths., 63,025,000 (83%); tot. pop., 76,320,000.

Republic, an archipelago of 7,000 islands off the southeast coast of Asia; capital, Manila. Systematic evangelization was begun in 1564 and resulted in the establishment of the Church by the 19th century. During the period of Spanish rule, which lasted from the discovery of the islands by Magellan in 1521 to 1898, the Church experienced difficulties with the patronage system under which the Spanish crown tried to control ecclesiastical affairs through episcopal and other appointments. This system ended in 1898 when the United States gained possession of the islands and instituted a policy of separation of Church and state. Anticlericalism flared late in the 19th century. The Aglipayan schism, an attempt to set up a nationalist Church, occurred in 1902.

Church leaders and human rights groups constantly criticized abuses under former president and dictator Ferdinand Marcos. Church newspapers were among those censored or closed after he declared martial law, and religious and lay people were arrested and held without formal charges for long periods of time. After Marcos declared himself the victor in the 1986 elections and international observers declared his win a fraud, the Philippine bishops' call for a nonviolent struggle for justice was seen as the catalyst for the nation's "people power" revolution. Corazon Aquino, Marcos' successor, took refuge with Carmelite nuns during the revolution. At the turn of the century, Church workers often found themselves unintentional victims of violence spurred by Muslim separatists' fight for autonomy in the southern Philippines. Church social action focused on the poor, overseas workers, ecology and a fight against the death penalty.

Poland*

Archd., 15; dioc., 26; mil. ord., 1; ordinariate, 1; cards., 6; abps., 17; bps., 101; parishes, 9,966; priests,

27,458 (21,280 dioc., 6,178 rel.); p.d., 13; sem., 6,818; bros., 1,297; srs., 23,945; catechists, 14,776; bap., 379,371; Caths., 37,002,000 (96%); tot. pop., 38,610,000.

Republic in eastern Europe; capital, Warsaw. The first traces of Christianity date from the second half of the ninth century. Its spread was accelerated by the union of the Slavs in the 10th century. The first diocese was set up in 968. Some tensions with the Orthodox were experienced. The Reformation, supported mainly by city dwellers and the upper classes, peaked from about the middle of the 16th century, resulting in numerous conversions to Lutheranism, the Reformed Church and the Bohemian Brethren. A successful Counter-Reformation, with the Jesuits in a position of leadership, was completed by about 1632. The movement served a nationalist as well as a religious purpose; in restoring religious unity to a large degree, it united the country against potential invaders, the Swedes, Russians and Turks. The Counter-Reformation had bad side effects, leading to the repression of Protestants long after it was over and to prejudice against Orthodox who returned to allegiance with Rome in 1596 and later. The Church, in the same manner as the entire country, was adversely affected by the partitions of the 18th and 19th centuries. Russification hurt the Eastern- and Latin-rite Catholics.

In the republic established after World War I the Church reorganized itself, continued to serve as a vital force in national life, and enjoyed generally harmonious relations with the state. Progressive growth was strong until 1939, when German and Russian forces invaded and World War II began. In 1945, seven years before the adoption of a Soviet-type of constitution, the communist-controlled government initiated a policy that included a constant program of atheistic propaganda; a strong campaign against the hierarchy and clergy; the imprisonment in 1948 of 700 priests and even more religious; rigid limitation on the activities of the Catholic press and religious movements.

Regular contacts on a working level were initiated by the Vatican and Poland in 1974; regular diplomatic relations were established in 1989. Cardinal Karol Wojtyla of Krakow was elected to the papacy in 1978. Church and papal support was strong for the independent labor movement, Solidarity, which was recognized by the government in August 1980 but outlawed in December 1981, when martial law was imposed (martial law was suspended in 1982). In May 1989, following recognition of Solidarity and a series of political changes, the Catholic Church was given legal status for the first time since the communists took control of the government in 1944. In 1990, a new constitution was adopted declaring Poland a democratic state. In 1992, the pope restructured the Church in Poland, adding 13 new dioceses. A new concordat between the Polish government and the Holy See was signed in 1993.

Since the end of communist rule, Poland's Church has struggled with anti-Semitism among some clergy. A dispute over a Carmelite convent outside the former Nazi death camp at Auschwitz resulted in the convent's removal, but several years later the Church was forced to speak against Catholic protesters who posted hundreds of crosses outside the camp. A nearly eight-year national synod process concluded in 1999 with calls for priests to live less luxurious lifestyles and to keep parishes finances open. The Polish Church continued to be a source of missionary priests in more than 90 countries.

Portugal*

Patriarchate (Lisbon), 1; archd., 2; dioc., 17; mil. ord., 1; patriarch, 1; card., 2; abp., 6; bp., 41; parishes, 4,362; priests, 4,237 (3,159 dioc., 1,078 rel.); p.d., 125; sem., 585; bros., 341; srs., 6,446; catechists, 54,327; bap., 98,139; Caths., 9,404,000 (94%); tot. pop., 10,010,000.

Republic in the western part of the Iberian peninsula; capital, Lisbon. Christianity was introduced before the fourth century. From the fifth century to early in the eighth century the Church experienced difficulties from the physical invasion of barbarians and the intellectual invasion of doctrinal errors in the forms of Arianism, Priscillianism and Pelagianism. The Church survived under the rule of Arabs from about 711 and of the Moors until 1249. Ecclesiastical life was fairly vigorous from 1080 to 1185, and monastic influence became strong. A decline set in about 1450. Several decades later Portugal became the jumping-off place for many missionaries to newly discovered colonies. The Reformation had little effect in the country.

In the early 1700s, King John V broke relations with Rome and required royal approval of papal acts. His successor, Joseph I, expelled the Jesuits from Portugal and the colonies. Liberal revolutionaries with anti-Church policies made the 19th century a difficult one for the Church. Similar policies prevailed in Church-state relations in the 20th century until the accession of Premier Antonio de Oliveira Salazar to power in 1928; the hierarchy was seen as closely aligned with him. In 1940 Salazar concluded a concordat with the Holy See that regularized Church-state relations but still left the Church in a subservient condition.

In 1930, after lengthy investigation, the Church authorized devotion to Our Lady of Fátima, who appeared to three Portuguese children in 1917. In 1971 several priests were tried for subversion for speaking out against colonialism and for taking part in guerrilla activities in Angola. A military coup Apr. 25, 1974, ended the dictatorship and led to democratic socialism. Pope John Paul II, who credited Our Lady of Fátima with saving his life during a 1981 assassination attempt on her feast day, visited Portugal several times, including in May 2000 to beatify two of the Fátima visionaries. At that time, he had his Secretary of State, Cardinal Angelo Sodano, announce that the so-called third secret of Fátima would be published and that he believed part of it was a direct reference to the assassination attempt.

Puerto Rico

Archd., 1; dioc., 4; card., 1; abp., 1; bp., 9; parishes, 354; priests, 761 (374 dioc., 387 rel.); p.d., 418; sem., 96; bros., 69; srs., 1,152; catechists, 9,944; bap., 34,516; Caths., 3,045,000 (78%); tot. pop., 3,880,000. (AD)

A U.S. commonwealth, the smallest of the Greater Antilles, 885 miles southeast of the southern coast of Florida; capital, San Juan. Following its discovery by Columbus in 1493, the island was evangelized by Spanish missionaries and remained under Spanish ecclesiastical as well as political control until 1898, when it became a possession of the United States. The original diocese, San Juan, was erected in 1511. The present hierarchy was established in 1960.

Qatar

Parish, 1; priest, 1 (dioc.); p.d., 2; bap., 119; Caths., 65,000 (11.8%); tot. pop., 550,000.

Independent state in the Persian Gulf; capital, Doha. Under ecclesiastical jurisdiction of Arabia apostolic vicariate.

Réunion

Dioc., 1; bp., 1; parishes, 75; priests, 108 (56 dioc., 52 rel.); p.d., 13; sem., 17; bros., 28; srs., 505; catechists, 500; bap., 11,157; Caths., 595,000 (85.5%); tot. pop., 645,000. (AD)

French overseas department, 450 miles east of Madagascar; capital, Saint-Denis. Catholicism was introduced in 1667 and some intermittent missionary work was done through the rest of the century. An apostolic prefecture was organized in 1712. Vincentians began work there in 1817 and were joined later by Holy Ghost Fathers. In 1998 the bishops joined their counterparts in Guadeloupe, French Guiana and Martinique to call slavery "an immense collective sin."

Romania*

Archd., 3; dioc., 8; ord., 1; ex., 1; abp., 7; bp., 11; parishes, 1,770; priests, 1,686 (1,475 dioc., 211 rel.); p.d., 3; sem., 985; bros., 84; srs., 1,232; bap., 12,816; Caths., 2,032,000 (9.5%); tot. pop., 22,440,000.

Republic in southeastern Europe; capital, Bucharest. Latin Christianity, introduced in the third century, all but disappeared during the barbarian invasions. The Byzantine rite was introduced by the Bulgars about the beginning of the eighth century and established firm roots. It eventually became Orthodox, but a large number of its adherents returned later to union with Rome.

Communists took over the government following World War II, forced the abdication of Michael I in 1947, and enacted a Soviet type of constitution in 1952. By that time a campaign against religion was already in progress. In 1948 the government denounced a concordat concluded in 1929, nationalized all schools and passed a law on religions that resulted in the disorganization of Church administration. The 1.5 million-member Romanian Byzantine-rite Church, by government decree, was incorporated into the Romanian Orthodox Church, and Catholic properties were given to the Orthodox. Five of the six Latin-rite bishops were immediately disposed of by the government, and the last was sentenced to 18 years' imprisonment in 1951. Religious orders were suppressed in 1949.

Some change for the better in Church-state relations was reported after the middle of the summer of 1964, although restrictions were still in effect. The Eastern Church regained liberty in 1990 with the change of government. The hierarchy was restored and diplomatic relations with the Holy See were re-established. Today, most Latin-rite Catholics are ethnic Hungarians residing in Transylvania.

Pope John Paul II visited Romania May 7-9, 1999,

but remained in Bucharest; he split time between visits with Catholics and Orthodox and did not visit Transylvania, despite an invitation from the region's bishops. To facilitate the visit, Eastern Catholics gave up their demands for the return of all former Church properties and agreed to work on committees with Orthodox to discuss each case individually. Church leaders said the historic visit led to a deeper openness and understanding between Catholics and Orthodox.

Russia*

Archd., 1; dioc. 4 (2 for European Russia, 2 for Siberia); ap. ex., 1; abp., 2; bp., 7; parish, 306; priests, 309 (122 dioc., 187 rel.); p.d., 3; sem., 106; bros., 15; srs, 282; bap., 1,568; Caths., 1,304,000 (.09%); tot. pop., 145,490,000.

Federation in Europe and Asia; capital, Moscow. The Orthodox Church has been predominant in Russian history. It developed from the Byzantine Church before 1064. Some of its members subsequently established communion with Rome as the result of reunion movements, but most remained Orthodox. The government has always retained some kind of general or particular control of this Church.

From the beginning of the Communist government in 1917, all churches of whatever kind became the targets of official campaigns designed to negate their influence on society and/or to eliminate them entirely. An accurate assessment of the situation of the Catholic Church in Russia was difficult to make. Research by a Polish priest, reported in 1998, documented the arrests, trials and fabricated confessions of priests in the 1920s and 1930s. A report by a team of research specialists made public by the Judiciary Committee of the U.S. House of Representatives in 1964 said: "The fate of the Catholic Church in the USSR and countries occupied by the Russians from 1917 to 1959 shows the following: (a) the number killed: 55 bishops; 12,800 priests and monks; 2.5 million Catholic believers; (b) imprisoned or deported: 199 bishops; 32,000 priests and 10 million believers; (c) 15,700 priests were forced to abandon their priesthood and accept other jobs; and (d) a large number of seminaries and religious communities were dissolved; 1,600 monasteries were nationalized, 31,779 churches were closed. 400 newspapers were prohibited, and all Catholic organizations were dissolved." Several Latin-rite churches were open in places like Moscow, Leningrad, Odessa and Tiflis. Despite repression, Lithuania and Ukraine remained strongholds of Catholicism.

During his 1985-91 presidency, Soviet President Mikhail Gorbachev met twice with Pope John Paul II — meetings later credited with the return of religious freedom in the Soviet Union. In 1991, the pope established two Latin-rite apostolic administrations in the Russian Republic: one in Moscow and one based in Novosibirsk, Siberia. Both administrations later were divided, so that the country had four Latin-rite jurisdictions.

Catholic communities in Europe and the United States have been instrumental in helping to rebuild the Church in Russia. Under a 1997 religion law, every religious organization in Russia had to register on a national level, then re-register each parish by the end of 1999 to enjoy full legal benefits such as owning property and publishing religious literature. The apostolic administrations registered with no problems, but after the Russian government rejected the Jesuits' registration application, they were forced to take the matter to the country's constitutional court, which ruled that they qualified.

The Vatican's upgrading of the four apostolic administrations to dioceses in early 2002 provoked new tensions with the Orthodox, who accused the Catholic Church of trying to convert its members. Russian authorities refused to readmit two prominent Church leaders, including one bishop, after they left the country.

Rwanda*

Archd., 1; dioc., 8; abp., 2; bp., 9; parishes, 132; priests, 485 (366 dioc., 119 rel.); sem., 344; p.d., 2; bros., 134; srs., 1,217; catechists, 3,455; bap., 162,241; Caths., 3,628,000 (47%); tot. pop., 7,610,000.

Republic in east central Africa; capital, Kigali. Catholicism was introduced about the turn of the 20th century. The hierarchy was established in 1959. Intertribal warfare between the ruling Hutus (90 percent of the population) and the Tutsis (formerly the ruling aristocracy) plagued the country for a number of years. In April 1994, the deaths of the presidents of Rwanda and Burundi in a suspicious plane crash sparked the outbreak of a ferocious civil war. Among the thousands of victims — mostly Tutsis — were three bishops and about 25 percent of the clergy. Many more thousands fled the country.

Although in 1996 Pope John Paul II said that all members of the Church who participated in the genocide must face the consequences, in 1997 the Vatican donated $50,000 to help ensure that certain people — including priests and religious — received fair trials. Two nuns accused of participating in the genocide were sent to prison in Belgium, but a bishop was acquitted after a nine-month trial in Rwanda. The bishop later said Marian apparitions in his diocese in the 1980s foretold the genocide.

Saint Lucia*

Archd., 1; abp., 1; parishes, 22; priests, 29 (16 dioc., 13 rel.); p.d., 8; bros., 6; srs., 42; catechists, 400; bap., 1,862; Caths., 116,000 (79%); tot. pop., 147,000.

Independent (Feb. 22, 1979) island state in West Indies; capital, Castries.

Saint Vincent and the Grenadines*

Dioc., 1; bp., 1; parishes, 6; priests, 6 (3 dioc., 3 rel.); srs., 14; catechists, 62; bap., 149; Caths., 10,000 (9%); tot. pop., 107,000.

Independent state (1979) in West Indies; capital, Kingstown. The Kingstown diocese (St. Vincent) was established in 1989; it was formerly part of Bridgetown-Kingstown Diocese with see in Barbados. The Vatican established diplomatic relations with St. Vincent and the Grenadines in 1990. The Church is recognized for its role in education and health care.

Samoa, American

Dioc., 1; bp., 1; parishes, 11; priests, 13 (10 dioc., 3 rel.); p.d., 16; sem., 13; srs., 14; bap., 481; Caths., 12,000 (16%); tot. pop., 62,000.

Unincorporated U.S. territory in southwestern Pacific, consisting of six small islands; seat of government, Pago Pago on the Island of Tutuila. Samoa-Pago Pago Diocese established in 1982.

Samoa, Western*

Archd., 1; card., 1; parishes, 29; priests, 50 (29 dioc., 21 rel.); p.d., 24; sem., 15; bros., 20; srs., 71; catechists, 133; bap., 1,469; Caths., 30,000 (16%); tot. pop., 183,000.

Independent state in the southwestern Pacific; capital, Apia. Catholic missionary work began in 1845. Most of the missions now in operation were established by 1870 when the Catholic population numbered about 5,000. Additional progress was made in missionary work from 1896. The first Samoan priest was ordained in 1892. A diocese was established in 1966; elevated to a metropolitan see in 1982.

San Marino

Parishes, 12; priests, 31 (12 dioc., 19 rel.); p.d. 1; bro. 1; srs, 20; bap, 275; Caths., 26,000 (99%); tot, pop., 26,000.

Republic, a 24-square-mile enclave in northeastern Italy; capital, San Marino. The date of initial evangelization is not known, but a diocese was established by the end of the third century. Ecclesiastically, it forms part of the Diocese of San Marino-Montefeltro in Italy.

São Tome and Principe*

Dioc., 1; bp., 1; parishes, 12; priests, 12 (2 dioc., 10 rel.); sem. 11; bros., 2; srs., 44; catechists, 438; bap., 2,153; Caths., 109,000 (83%); tot. pop., 131,000.

Independent republic (July 12, 1975), consisting of two islands off the western coast of Africa in the Gulf of Guinea; former Portuguese territory; capital, São Tome. Evangelization was begun by the Portuguese who discovered the islands in 1471-72. The São Tome Diocese was established in 1534. In a 1992 visit to São Tome, a major transport center for slaves until the mid-1800s, Pope John Paul II condemned slavery as "a cruel offense" to African dignity.

Saudi Arabia

Parishes, 4; priests, 5 (1 dioc., 4 rel.); p.d., 1; srs., 15.; bap., 504; Caths., 900,000; total pop., 20,350,000.

Monarchy occupying four-fifths of Arabian peninsula; capital, Riyadh. Population is Muslim; all other religions are banned. Christians in the area are workers from other countries. The Church falls under the ecclesiastical jurisdiction of the Arabian apostolic vicariate. In May 1999, Pope John Paul II met with the crown prince of Saudi Arabia at the Vatican.

Scotland

Archd., 2; dioc., 6; abp., 2; bp., 7; parishes, 458; priests, 791 (631 dioc., 160 rel.); p.d., 24; sem., 45; bros., 262; srs., 644; bap., 9,051; Caths., 690,076 (14%); tot. pop., 4,979,600.

Part of the United Kingdom, in the northern British Isles; capital, Edinburgh. Christianity was introduced by the early years of the fifth century. St. Ninian's arrival in 397 marked the beginning of Christianity in Scotland. The arrival of St. Columba and his monks in 563 inaugurated a new era of evangelization that reached into remote areas by the end of the sixth century. He was extremely influential in determining the character of the Church, which was tribal, monastic, and in union with Rome. Considerable disruption of Church activity resulted from Scandinavian invasions in the late eighth and ninth centuries. By 1153 the Scottish Church took a turn away from its insularity and was drawn into closer contact with the European community. Anglo-Saxon religious and political relations, complicated by rivalries between princes and ecclesiastical superiors, were not always the happiest.

From shortly after the Norman Conquest of England to 1560 the Church suffered adverse effects from the Hundred Years' War, the Black Death, the Western Schism and other developments. In 1560 Parliament abrogated papal supremacy over the Church in Scotland and committed the country to Protestantism in 1567. The Catholic Church was proscribed, to remain that way for more than 200 years, and the hierarchy was disbanded. Defections made the Church a minority religion from that time on. Presbyterian Church government was ratified in 1690. Priests launched the Scottish Mission in 1653, incorporating themselves as a mission body under an apostolic prefecture and working underground to serve the faithful in much the same way their confreres did in England. About 100 heather priests, trained in clandestine places in the heather country, were ordained by the early 19th century. Catholics got some relief from legal disabilities in 1793 and more relief later. Many left the country about that time. Some of their numbers were filled subsequently by immigrants from Ireland. The hierarchy was restored in 1878. Scotland, though predominantly Protestant, has a better record for tolerance than Northern Ireland. In a 1997 message to celebrations marking 1,600 years of Christianity in Scotland, Pope John Paul II urged Catholics to make new efforts at evangelization and ecumenism.

Senegal*

Archd., 1; dioc., 6; card., 1; abp., 2; bp., 6; parishes, 98; priests, 396 (254 dioc., 142 rel.); p.d., 1; sem., 189; bros., 181; srs., 714; catechists, 2,435; bap., 9,231; Caths., 483,000 (5%); tot. pop., 9,520,000.

Republic in West Africa; capital, Dakar. The country had its first contact with Catholicism through the Portuguese some time after 1460. Some incidental missionary work was done by Jesuits and Capuchins in the 16th and 17th centuries. A vicariate for the area was placed in charge of the Holy Ghost Fathers in 1779. More effective evangelization efforts were accomplished after the Senegambia vicariate was erected in 1863; the hierarchy was established in 1955. During a 1992 trip to the predominantly Muslim country, Pope John Paul II praised the small Catholic community for its contributions, especially in the areas of health care and education.

Seychelles*

Dioc., 1; bp., 1; parishes, 17; priests, 15 (9 dioc., 6 rel.); p.d., 1; sem., 4; srs., 58; catechists, 365; bap., 1,245; Caths., 69,000 (85%); tot. pop., 81,000.

Independent (1976) group of 92 islands in the Indian Ocean; capital, Victoria. Catholicism was introduced in the 18th century. An apostolic vicariate was organized in 1852. All education in the islands was conducted under Catholic auspices until 1954. In

1991, Bishop Felix Paul of Port Victoria said the country's one-party socialist government was an affront to the rights and dignity of its people, but President France-Albert René continued to lead the government into the 21st century. Pope John Paul II has warned Seychelles to beware of the dark side of tourism, a main industry in the country.

Sierra Leone*

Archd., 1; dioc., 2; abp., 2; bp., 2; parishes, 38; priests, 121 (44 dioc., 77 rel.); p.d., 3; sem., 54; bros., 31; srs., 15; catechists, 334; bap., 3,365; Caths., 72,000 (2%); tot. pop., 4,523,000.

Republic on the west coast of Africa; capital, Freetown. Catholicism was introduced in 1858. Members of the African Missions Society, the first Catholic missionaries in the area, were joined by Holy Ghost Fathers in 1864. Protestant missionaries were active in the area before their Catholic counterparts. Educational work had a major part in Catholic endeavor. The hierarchy was established in 1950. Most of the inhabitants are followers of traditional African religions.

Church leaders suffered at the hands of rebel soldiers in the late 1990s, when a military coup ousted the country's democratically elected government. Although some Church workers fled to neighboring Guinea, some remained. Rebels kidnapped several foreign missionaries and, shortly before West African intervention forces ousted them from power in 1998, they forced the archbishop of Freetown to strip naked while they plundered his office. As the war lessened and later ended, the Church worked for reconciliation, to rehabilitate child soldiers and to rebuild damaged church property.

Singapore*

Archd., 1; abp., 1; parishes, 30; priests, 131 (69 dioc., 62 rel.); sem., 19; bros., 49; srs., 221; catechists, 1,375; bap., 4,234; Caths., 152,000 (3.7%); tot. pop., 4,020,000.

Independent island republic off the southern tip of the Malay Peninsula; capital, Singapore. Christianity was introduced in the area by Portuguese colonists about 1511. Singapore was founded in 1819; the first parish Church was built in 1846. Freedom of religion is generally respected, although in the late 1980s nearly a dozen people involved in Catholic social work were arrested and detained without trial under the Internal Security Act.

Slovakia*

Archd., 2; dioc., 5; ap. ex., 1; card., 2; abp., 2; bp., 15; parishes, 1,480; priests, 2,508 (1,893 dioc., 615 rel.); p.d., 21; sem., 974; bros., 226; srs., 2,895; catechists, 1,793 bap., 45,508; Caths., 3,659,000 (68%); tot. pop., 5,400,000.

Independent state (Jan. 1, 1993); formerly part of Czechoslovakia; capital, Bratislava. Christianity was introduced in Slovakia in the eighth century by Irish and German missionaries, and the area was under the jurisdiction of German bishops. In 863, Sts. Cyril and Methodius began pastoral and missionary work in the region, ministering to the people in their own language. A diocese established at Nitra in 880 had a continuous history (except for one century ending in 1024). The Church in Slovakia was severely tested by the Reformation and political upheavals. After World War I, when it became part of the Republic of Czechoslovakia, it was 75 percent Catholic.

Vigorous persecution of the Church began in Slovakia in 1944, when communists mounted an offensive against bishops, priests and religious. In 1945, Church schools were nationalized, youth organizations were disbanded, the Catholic press was curtailed, the training of seminarians was seriously impeded. Msgr. Josef Tiso, a Catholic priest who served as president of the Slovak Republic from 1939-45, was tried for "treason" in December 1946 and was executed the following April.

In 1972, the government ordered the removal of nuns from visible but limited apostolates to farms and mental hospitals. In 1973, the government allowed the ordination of three bishops in the Slovak region. Reports from Slovakia late in the same year stated that authorities there had placed severe restrictions on the education of seminarians and the work of priests.

When Slovakia split from Czechoslovakia in 1993, the country slid into economic difficulties. Churchstate tensions increased, and the Slovakian government eventually apologized to Bishop Rudolf Balaz of Banska Bystrica, whose house had been raided in a government investigation of stolen art. In an attempt to fight the effects of decades of communism, in 1996 the bishops said all adult Catholics who had not received confirmation must undergo a special two-year catechism course. In 2000, the government and Vatican signed an accord establishing the Church's legal status.

Slovenia*

Archd., 1; dioc., 2; abp., 3; bp., 9; parishes, 805; priests, 1,150 (855 dioc., 295 rel.); p.d., 9; sem., 165; bros., 40; srs., 787; catechists, 509; bap., 14,169; Caths., 1,622,000 (81.9%); tot. pop., 1,990,000.

Independent republic (1991) in southeastern Europe; formerly part of Yugoslavia; capital, Ljubljana. Established diplomatic relations with the Holy See in 1992. After independence, Church leaders found themselves in repeated skirmishes with Slovenia's governing coalition over religious education, restitution of Church property and the Church's proper social role.

Solomon Islands*

Archd., 1; dioc., 2; abp., 1; bp., 3; parishes, 27; priests, 57 (25 dioc., 32 rel.); sem., 32; bros., 21; srs., 95; catechists, 1,073; bap., 2,586; Caths., 83,000 (19%); tot. pop., 440,000.

Independent (July 7, 1978) island group in Oceania; capital, Honiara, on Guadalcanal. After violence interrupted the Marists' evangelization of the Southern Solomons, they resumed their work in 1898. An apostolic vicariate was organized in 1912. A similar jurisdiction was set up for the Western Solomons in 1959. World War II caused a great deal of damage to mission installations.

Somalia

Dioc., 1; parish, 1; priests, 4 (1 dioc., 3 rel.); bros., 1; srs., 3; Caths., 100; tot. pop., 8,780,000. (AD)

Republic on the eastern coast of Africa; capital, Mogadishu. The country has been Muslim for centuries. Pastoral activity has been confined to immigrants. Schools and hospitals were nationalized in 1972, resulting in the departure of some foreign missionaries.

South Africa*

Archd., 4; dioc., 21; v.a., 1; mil. ord., 1; card., 1; abp., 7; bp., 29; parishes, 729; priests, 1,077 (401 dioc., 676 rel.); p.d., 217; sem., 452; bros., 189; srs., 2,658; catechists, 12,101; bap., 54,536; Caths., 3,081,000 (7.0%); tot. pop., 43,690,000.

Republic in the southern part of Africa; capitals, Cape Town (legislative), Pretoria (administrative) and Bloemfontein (judicial). Christianity was introduced by the Portuguese who discovered the Cape of Good Hope in 1488. Boers, who founded Cape Town in 1652, expelled Catholics from the region. There was no Catholic missionary activity from that time until the 19th century. After a period of British opposition, a bishop established residence in 1837, and evangelization got under way thereafter among the Bantus and white immigrants. The hierarchy was established in 1951.

Under South Africa's apartheid regime, the Church found itself the victim of attacks, from the parish level to the headquarters of the bishops' conference in Pretoria. Some Church leaders were detained, tortured and deported, particularly in the 1970s and 1980s. However, in a 1997 statement to South Africa's Truth Commission, the Catholic Church said the complicity of some Catholics with apartheid was in "acts of omission rather than commission." Since the end of apartheid, Catholic leaders have spoken out against an increase in violence and anti-Muslim sentiment and have worked to combat the growing AIDS problem.

Spain*

Archd., 14; dioc., 53; mil. ord., 1; card., 7; abp., 19; bp., 95; parishes, 22,618; priests, 27,281 (18,439 dioc., 8,842 rel.); p.d., 231; sem., 2,908; bros., 5,073; srs., 60,525; catechists, 101,995; bap., 309,996; Caths., 37,152,000 (94%); tot. pop., 39,470,000.

Constitutional monarchy on the Iberian peninsula in southwestern Europe; capital, Madrid. Christians were on the peninsula by 200; some of them suffered martyrdom during persecutions of the third century. A council held in Elvira about 305 enacted the first legislation on clerical celibacy in the West. Vandals invaded the peninsula in the fifth century, bringing with them an Arian brand of Christianity that they retained until their conversion following the baptism of their king, Reccared, in 589.

In the seventh century, Toledo was established as the primatial see. The Visigoth kingdom lasted to the time of the Arab invasion, 711-14. The Church survived under Muslim rule but experienced some doctrinal and disciplinary irregularities as well as harassment. Reconquest of most of the peninsula was accomplished by 1248; unification was achieved during the reign of Ferdinand and Isabella. The discoveries of Columbus and other explorers ushered in an era of colonial expansion in which Spain became one of the greatest mission-sending countries in history. In 1492, in repetition of anti-Semitic actions of 694, the expulsion of unbaptized Jews was decreed, leading to mass baptisms but a questionable number of

real conversions in 1502. Activity by the Inquisition followed. Spain was not seriously affected by the Reformation. Ecclesiastical decline set in about 1650.

Anti-Church actions authorized by a constitution enacted in 1812 resulted in the suppression of religious and other encroachments on the leaders, people and goods of the Church. Political, religious and cultural turmoil recurred during the 19th century and into the 20th. A revolutionary republic was proclaimed in 1931, triggering a series of developments that led to civil war from 1936 to 1939. During the conflict, which pitted leftist Loyalists against the forces of Francisco Franco, more than 6,600 priests and religious and an unknown number of lay people were massacred. One-man, one-party rule, established after the civil war and with rigid control policies with respect to personal liberties and social and economic issues, continued for more than 35 years before giving way after the death of Franco to democratic reforms. Since the 1970s, the Catholic Church has not been the established religion; the constitution guarantees freedom for other religions as well. In the late 20th century, Spanish Church leaders fought a growing feeling of indifference among many Catholics.

Sri Lanka*

Archd., 1; dioc., 10; abp., 2; bp., 14; parishes, 376; priests, 941 (604 dioc., 337 rel.); sem., 443; p.d. 2; bros., 246; srs., 2,232; catechists, 9,257; bap., 28,737; Caths., 1,300,000 (6.7%); tot. pop., 19,360,000.

Independent socialist republic, island southeast of India; capital, Colombo. The Portuguese began evangelizing in the 16th century. In 1638, the Dutch began forcing Portuguese from the coastal areas. The Dutch outlawed Catholicism, banished priests and confiscated buildings, forcing people to become Calvinists. Blessed Joseph Vaz, an Oratorian priest, is credited with almost single-handedly reviving the Catholic Church toward the end of the 17th century. Anti-Catholic laws were repealed by the British in 1806. The hierarchy was established in 1886; the country gained independence in 1948. Sri Lankan bishops repeatedly have called for reconciliation in the nearly two-decade war between the Liberation Tigers of Tamil Eelam and the Sinhalese-dominated government. In an unusual move in January 1998, Archbishop Nicholas M. Fernando of Colombo, authorized by the Vatican Congregation for the Doctrine of the Faith, lifted the excommunication of a prominent Sri Lankan theologian, Oblate Father Tissa Balasuriya.

Sudan*

Archd., 2; dioc., 7; ap. ex., 1; abp., 3; bp., 11; parishes, 164; priests, 323 (205 dioc., 118 rel.); p.d., 4; sem., 253; bros., 74; srs., 326; catechists, 3,945; bap., 52,305; Caths., 3,810,000 (12%); tot. pop., 31,100,000.

Republic in northeastern Africa, the largest country on the continent; capital Khartoum. Christianity was introduced from Egypt and gained acceptance in the sixth century. Under Arab rule, it was eliminated in the northern region. No Christians were in the country in 1600.

Evangelization attempts begun in the 19th century in the south yielded hard-won results. By 1931 there were nearly 40,000 Catholics there, and considerable progress was made by missionaries after that time. In

1957, a year after the republic was established, Catholic schools were nationalized. An act restrictive of religious freedom went into effect in 1962, resulting in the harassment and expulsion of foreign missionaries. By 1964 all but a few Sudanese missionaries had been forced out of the southern region. The northern area, where Islam predominates, is impervious to Christian influence.

Late in 1971 some missionaries were allowed to return to work in the South. The hierarchy was established in 1974. The most recent fighting, which began in 1983, originally pitted the mostly Arab and Muslim North against the mostly black African Christian and animist South, but it has since evolved into a nationwide conflict fuelled by religion, ethnicity, oil and ideology. The imposition of Islamic penal codes in 1984 was a cause of concern to all Christian Churches. Recent government policies have denied Christians the right to places of worship and authorization to gather for prayer. Bishops from the South have condemned human rights violations — aggravated by famine and war — in their area. They have said they want peace but cannot accept an Islamic state.

Surinam*

Dioc., 1; bp., 1; parishes, 31; priests, 20 (6 dioc., 14 rel.); sem., 1; bros., 7; srs., 18; bap., 2,138; Caths., 100,000 (23%); tot. pop., 436,000.

Independent (Nov. 25, 1975) state in northern South America; capital, Paramaribo, Catholicism was introduced in 1683. Evangelization began in 1817.

Swaziland*

Dioc., 1; bp., 1; parishes, 15; priests, 40 (9 dioc., 31 rel.); sem., 13; bros., 6; srs., 57; bap., 468; Caths., 53,000 (5.4%); tot. pop., 990,000.

Monarchy in southern Africa; almost totally surrounded by South Africa; capital, Mbabane. Missionary work was entrusted to the Servites in 1913. An apostolic prefecture was organized in 1923. The hierarchy was established in 1951. Swaziland established diplomatic relations with the Holy See in 1992. In the 1990s, Swazi Catholics worked to help transform the country to a democracy but to retain the traditions of the people.

Sweden*

Dioc., 1; bp., 3; parishes, 40; priests, 147 (71 dioc., 76 rel.); p.d., 17; sem., 11; bros., 12; srs., 236; catechists, 455; bap., 1,152; Caths., 97,000 (1.8%); tot. pop., 8,870,000.

Constitutional monarchy in northwestern Europe; capital, Stockholm. Christianity was introduced by St. Ansgar, a Frankish monk, in 829-830. The Church became well-established in the 12th century and was a major influence at the end of the Middle Ages. Political and other factors favored the introduction and spread of the Lutheran Church, which became the state religion in 1560. The Augsburg Confession of 1530 was accepted by the government; all relations with Rome were severed; monasteries were suppressed; the very presence of Catholics in the country was forbidden in 1617. A decree of tolerance for foreign Catholics was issued about 1781. Two years later an apostolic vicariate was organized for the country. In 1873 Swedes were given the legal right to leave the Lutheran Church and join another Christian Church. Membership in the Lutheran Church is presumed by law unless notice is given of membership in another church. Since 1952 Catholics have enjoyed almost complete religious freedom. The hierarchy was re-established in 1953. Hindrances to growth of the Church are the strongly entrenched established church, limited resources, a clergy shortage and the size of the country. In the 1960s, an influx of guest workers increased the number of Catholics, and in the 1970s and 1980s, refugees helped increase Church numbers. In 1998, the pope named the first Swedish bishop in more than 400 years. Reforms due to be implemented by the year 2004 will give the Church and other minority faiths the right to operate as legal entities, including owning property.

Switzerland*

Dioc., 6; abb., 2; card., 2; abp., 4; bp., 19; parishes, 1,695; priests, 3,126 (1,882 dioc., 1,244 rel.); p.d., 139; sem., 231; bros., 454; srs., 5,924; catechists, 1,842; bap., 31,800; Caths., 3,169,000 (44%); tot. pop., 7,170,000.

Confederation in central Europe; capital, Bern. Christianity was introduced in the fourth century or earlier and was established on a firm footing before the barbarian invasions of the sixth century. Constance, established as a diocese in the seventh century, was a stronghold of the faith against the pagan Alamanni, in particular, who were not converted until some time in the ninth century. During this period of struggle with the barbarians, a number of monasteries of great influence were established.

The Reformation in Switzerland was triggered by Zwingli in 1519 and furthered by him at Zurich until his death in battle against the Catholic cantons in 1531. Calvin set in motion the forces that made Geneva the international capital of the Reformation and transformed it into a theocracy. Catholics mobilized a Counter-Reformation in 1570, six years after Calvin's death. Struggle between Protestant and Catholic cantons was a fact of Swiss life for several hundred years. The Helvetic Constitution enacted at the turn of the 19th century embodied anti-Catholic measures and consequences, among them the dissolution of 130 monasteries. The Church was reorganized later in the century to meet the threats of liberalism, radicalism and the *Kulturkampf*. In the process, the Church, even though on the defensive, gained the strength and cohesion that characterizes it to the present time. In 1973, constitutional articles banning Jesuits from the country and prohibiting the establishment of convents and monasteries were repealed. In the 1990s, Swiss bishops battled internal divisions and sought forgiveness for any anti-Semitism on behalf of the Church.

Syria*

Patriarchates, 1 (Greek Melkites; patriarchs of Antioch of Maronites and Syrians reside in Lebanon); archd., 12 (1 Armenian, 2 Maronite, 5 Greek Melkite, 4 Syrian); dioc., 3 (Armenian, Chaldean, Maronite); v.a., 1 (Latin); ap.ex., 1; patriarch, 1; card., 1; abp., 17; bp., 4; parishes, 203; priests, 253 (178 dioc., 75 rel.); p.d., 12; sem., 82; bros., 9; srs., 371; catechists, 1,698; bap., 2,906; Caths., 335,000 (2%); tot. pop., 16,320,000.

Arab socialist republic in southwest Asia; capital, Damascus. Christian communities were formed in apostolic times. It is believed that St. Peter established a see at Antioch before going to Rome. Damascus became a center of influence. The area was the place of great men and great events in the early history of the Church. Monasticism developed there in the fourth century; so did the Monophysite and Monothelite heresies to which a portion of the Church succumbed. Byzantine Syrians who remained in communion with Rome were given the name Melkites. Christians of various persuasions — Jacobites, Orthodox and Melkites — were subject to various degrees of harassment from the Arabs who took over in 638 and from the Ottoman Turks who isolated the country and remained in control from 1516 to the end of World War II.

Syrian Catholics are members of the Armenian, Chaldean, Greek-Melkite, Latin, Maronite and Syrian rites. During a visit to Syria in May 2001, Pope John Paul II became the first pontiff in history to enter a mosque.

Taiwan

Archd., 1; dioc., 7; card., 1; abp., 3; bp., 11; parishes, 460; priests, 699 (254 dioc., 445 rel.); sem., 113; bros., 84; srs., 1,055; catechists, 640; bap., 3,838; Caths., 309,000 (1.3%); tot. pop., 23,180,000.

Democratic island state, 100 miles off the southern coast of mainland China; capital, Taipei. Attempts to introduce Christianity in the 17th century were unsuccessful. Evangelization in the 19th century resulted in some 1,300 converts in 1895. Missionary endeavor was hampered by the Japanese, who occupied the island following the Sino-Japanese war of 1894-95. Great progress was made in missionary endeavor among the Chinese who emigrated to the island (seat of the Nationalist Government of the Republic of China) following the Communist takeover of the mainland in 1949. The hierarchy was established in 1952. Many Taiwanese Catholics have worked to form a bridge to Catholics in mainland China. China has said the Vatican's diplomatic relations with Taiwan form the biggest stumbling block to Sino-Vatican relations.

Tajikistan*

Mission, 3; parishes, 2; priests, 4 (1 dioc., 3 rel.); srs., 4; bap., 65; Cath., 2000; tot. pop. 6,170,000.

Independent republic (1992) in Asia; formerly part of the USSR; capital, Dushanbe. The majority of the population is Sunni Muslim. When the Vatican established diplomatic relations in 1996, Church officials estimated most of the country's Catholics had fled. In 1997, the Vatican decided to establish a mission in the country.

Tanzania*

Archd., 5; dioc., 25; card., 1; abp., 5; bp., 32; parishes, 792; priests, 2,067 (1,359 dioc., 708 rel.); p.d. 1; sem., 1,027; bros., 630; srs., 7,128; catechists, 12,044; bap., 303,975; Caths., 9,470,000 (27%); tot. pop., 35,120,000.

Republic on and off the eastern coast of Africa; capital, Dar es Salaam. The first Catholic mission in the former Tanganyikan portion of the republic was manned by Holy Ghost Fathers in 1868. The hierar-

chy was established there in 1953. Zanzibar was the landing place of Augustinians with the Portuguese in 1499. Some evangelization was attempted between then and 1698 when the Arabs expelled all priests from the territory. There was no Catholic missionary activity from then until the 1860s. The Holy Ghost Fathers arrived in 1863 and were entrusted with the mission in 1872. Zanzibar was important as a point of departure for missionaries to Tanganyika, Kenya and other places in East Africa. A vicariate for Zanzibar was set up in 1906.

In the late 20th century the Church in Tanzania saw an increase in vocations and an active Church life. The bishops assisted hundreds of thousands of refugees from Rwanda, Burundi and Mozambique.

Thailand*

Archd., 2; dioc., 8; card., 1; abp., 2; bp., 10; parishes, 350; priests, 642 (406 dioc., 236 rel.); p.d., 1; sem., 262; bros., 129; srs., 1,454; catechists, 1,812; bap., 7,254; Caths., 273,000 (.04%); tot. pop., 62,320,000.

Constitutional monarchy in southeast Asia; capital, Bangkok. The first Christians in the region were Portuguese traders who arrived early in the 16th century. A number of missionaries began arriving in the mid-1500s, but pastoral care was confined mostly to the Portuguese until the 1660s, when evangelization began. A seminary was organized in 1665, a vicariate was set up four years later, and a point of departure was established for China. Persecution and death for some of the missionaries ended evangelization efforts in 1688. It was resumed, however, and made progress from 1824 onward. In 1881 missionaries were sent from Siam to neighboring Laos. The hierarchy was established in 1965. Archbishop Michael Michai Kitbunchu was named the first Thai cardinal in 1983. The Church is recognized for its social justice efforts, including work with refugees.

Togo*

Archd., 1; dioc., 6; abp., 1; bp., 5; parishes, 133; priests, 377 (259 dioc., 118 rel.); sem., 230; bros., 168; srs., 625; catechists, 4,606; bap., 36,239; Caths., 1,259,000 (28%); tot. pop., 4,530,000.

Republic on the west coast of Africa; capital, Lome. The first Catholic missionaries in the area, where slave raiders operated for nearly 200 years, were members of the African Missions Society who arrived in 1563. They were followed by Divine Word Missionaries in 1914, when an apostolic prefecture was organized. At that time the Catholic population numbered about 19,000. The African Missionaries returned after their German predecessors were deported following World War I. The first indigenous priest was ordained in 1922. The hierarchy was established in 1955. In the early 1990s, Archbishop Philippe Fanoko Kossi Kpodzro of Lome served as president of the transitional legislative assembly.

Tonga*

Dioc., 1; bp., 1; parishes, 10; priests, 21 (12 dioc., 9 rel.); sem., 34; bros., 8; srs., 47; bap., 516; Caths., 15,000 (14.5%); tot. pop., 95,000.

Polynesian monarchy in the southwestern Pacific, consisting of about 150 islands; capital, Nuku'alofa. Marists started missionary work in 1842, some years after Protestants had begun evangelization. By 1880 the Catholic population numbered about 1,700. A vicariate was organized in 1937. The hierarchy was established in 1966. Tonga established diplomatic relations with the Holy See in 1994.

Trinidad and Tobago*

Archd., 1; abp., 1; bp., 1; parishes, 61; priests, 110 (44 dioc., 66 rel.); sem., 19; bros., 8; srs., 175; bap., 4,639; Caths., 383,000 (30%); tot. pop., 1,278,000.

Independent nation, consisting of two islands in the Caribbean; capital, Port-of-Spain. The first Catholic Church in Trinidad was built in 1591, years after several missionary ventures had been launched and a number of missionaries killed. Capuchins were there from 1618 until about 1802. Missionary work continued after the British gained control early in the 19th century. Cordial relations have existed between the Church and state, both of which have manifested their desire for the development of indigenous clergy. In 1999, Church leaders protested reinstatement of the death penalty.

Tunisia*

Dioc., 1; abp., 1; parishes, 12; priests, 33 (12 dioc., 21 rel.); bros., 7; sem., 4; srs., 165; bap., 28; Caths., 22,000 (.02%); tot. pop., 9,560,000.

Republic on the northern coast of Africa; capital, Tunis. Ancient Carthage, now a site outside the capital city of Tunis, hosted early Church councils and was home to Church fathers like St. Augustine. Carthage was devastated by Vandals in the fifth century and invaded by Muslims in the seventh century, after which it had few Christians until the 19th century. An apostolic vicariate was organized in 1843, and the Carthage Archdiocese was established in 1884. The Catholic population in 1892 consisted of most of the approximately 50,000 Europeans in the country. When Tunis became a republic in 1956, most of the Europeans left the country. A 1964 agreement with the Vatican and Holy See suppressed the Archdiocese of Carthage and replaced it with the Territorial Prelature of Tunis. In 1995 the prelature was made a diocese.

Today Tunisia's Catholics are predominantly foreign nationals. The Church's social presence is seen in schools, hospitals and institutions for the disabled.

Turkey*

Archd., 3; v.a., 2; ord., 1; ap. ex., 1; abp., 4; bp., 2; parishes, 52; priests, 59 (15 dioc., 44 rel.); p.d., 4; sem., 11; bros., 12; srs., 114; bap., 97; Caths., 32,000 (.05%); tot. pop., 67,380,000.

Republic in Asia Minor and southeastern Europe; capital, Ankara. Christian communities were established in apostolic times, as attested in the Acts of the Apostles, some of the Letters of St. Paul and Revelation. The territory was the scene of heresies and ecumenical councils, the place of residence of Fathers of the Church, the area in which ecclesiastical organization reached the dimensions of more than 450 sees in the middle of the seventh century. The region remained generally Byzantine except for the period of the Latin occupation of Constantinople from 1204 to 1261, but was conquered by the Ottoman Turks in 1453 and remained under their domination until establishment of the republic in 1923. Christians, al-

ways a minority, numbered more Orthodox than Catholics; they all were under some restrictions during the Ottoman period. They suffered persecution in the 19th and 20th centuries, the Armenians being the most numerous victims. Turkey is overwhelmingly Muslim. Catholics are tolerated to a degree.

Turkmenistan*

Mission, 1; parish, 1; priests, 3 (rel.); bap., 10; Caths., 1,000; tot. pop., 4,740,000.

Former constituent republic of USSR; independent, 1991; capital, Ashgabat. Almost all the population is Sunni Muslim. The Vatican established diplomatic relations with the country in 1996 and set up a mission in 1997.

Tuvalu

Mission, 1; parish, 1; priest, 1 (rel.); bap., 2; Caths., 100; tot. pop., 10,000.

Independent state (1978) in Oceania, consisting of 9 islands; capital, Funafuti.

Uganda*

Archd., 4; dioc., 15; mil. ord., 1; card., 1; abp., 3; bp., 22; parishes, 424; priests, 1,590 (1,263 dioc., 327 rel.); p.d., 1; sem., 806; bros., 475; srs., 2,711; catechists, 12,021; bap., 320,451; Caths., 10,057,000 (45%); tot. pop., 22,210,000.

Republic in East Africa; capital, Kampala. The Missionaries of Africa (White Fathers) were the first Catholic missionaries, starting in 1879. Persecution broke out from 1885 to 1887, taking a toll of 22 Catholic martyrs, who were canonized in 1964, and a number of Anglican victims. (Pope Paul VI honored all those who died for the faith during a visit to Kampala in 1969.) By 1888, there were more than 8,000 Catholics. Evangelization was resumed in 1894, after being interrupted by war, and proceeded thereafter. The first African bishop was ordained in 1939. The hierarchy was established in 1953.

The Church was suppressed during the erratic regime of President Idi Amin, who was deposed in the spring of 1979. Guerrilla activity in northern and southwestern Uganda has hampered Church workers, and Church leaders have called for peace so the country can develop. The Church has devoted much of its resources to caring for the many victims of HIV/AIDS in the country.

Ukraine*

Major archbishopric, 1 (Ukrainian); archd., 3 (Metropolitans); dioc., 11; a.a., 1; pat. ex., 1; card., 2; abp., 2; bp., 20; parishes, 3,676; priests, 2,522 (2,140 dioc., 382 rel.); p.d., 14; sem., 1,247; bros., 124; srs., 970; catechists, 869; bap., 28,658; Caths., 4,611,000 (10%); tot. pop., 49,570,000.

Independent republic bordering on the Black Sea; former USSR republic; capital, Kiev. The baptism of Vladimir and his people in 988 marked the beginning of Christianity in the territory of Kievan Rus, which is included in today's Ukraine. The 1596 Union of Brest brought the Ukrainian Byzantine-rite community back into communion with Rome. The Eastern Catholic Church was officially suppressed and underground in the USSR from the late 1940s; all of its bishops were killed or imprisoned and its property seized by the government and given to the Orthodox.

Some Catholic priests continued to minister clandestinely under communist rule.

As the Eastern Church regained its legal status under Soviet President Mikhail Gorbachev, serious tensions arose with the Orthodox over ownership of property and the allegiance of priests and lay people. Latin-rite dioceses were re-established in 1991. In the late 1990s, rising inflation and weakening currency, aggravated by the government's and some companies' failure to pay wages, led Ukrainian Church leaders to fight homelessness and hunger. Despite opposition from Ukraine's largest Orthodox Church, Pope John Paul II visited Ukraine in June 2001. He challenged Ukrainians to talk to each other and focus on unity, despite religious, ethnic and political tensions.

United Arab Emirates

V.a, 1; bp., 1; parishes, 5; priests, 17 (3 dioc., 14 rel.); srs., 32; bap., 1,325; Caths., 336,000 (.8%); tot. pop., 2,610,000.

Independent state along Persian Gulf; capital, Abu Dhabi. The apostolic vicariate of Arabia has its seat in Abu Dhabi. It includes the states of Bahrain, Oman, Qatar, Saudi Arabia and Yemen (see separate entries) as well as United Arab Emirates.

United States* (See Catholic Church in the United States; see also Catholic History in the United States and Statistics of the Church in the United States)

Uruguay*

Archd., 1; dioc., 9; abp., 3; bp., 11; parishes, 229; priests, 498 (221 dioc., 277 rel.); p.d., 63; sem., 92; bros., 97; srs., 1,281; catechists, 3,320; bap., 31,372; Caths., 2,507,000 (75%); tot. pop., 3,330,000.

Republic on the southeast coast of South America; capital, Montevideo. The Spanish established a settlement in 1624 and evangelization followed. Missionaries followed the reduction pattern to reach the Indians, form them in the faith and train them in agriculture, husbandry, other arts, and the experience of managing property and living in community. Montevideo was made a diocese in 1878. The constitution of 1830 made Catholicism the religion of the state and subsidized some of its activities, principally the missions to the Indians. Separation of Church and state was provided for in the constitution of 1917. In 1997, despite a court decision halting further investigations, the Church pledged to make one last effort to help search for people who remained missing from the 1973-85 military dictatorship.

Uzbekistan*

Mission, 1; parishes, 3; priests, 9 (2 dioc., 7 rel.); bros., 2; srs., 8; bap., 24 Caths. 3,000; tot. pop. 24,750,000.

Former republic of USSR; independent, 1991; capital, Tashkent. The majority of the population is Sunni Muslim. A small number of Catholics live in Tashkent. The Vatican established a mission in 1997.

Vanuatu*

Dioc., 1; bp., 1; parishes, 18; priests, 29 (16 dioc., 13 rel.); p.d., 1; sem., 8; bros., 23; srs., 63; bap., 620; Caths., 29,000 (16%); tot. pop., 190,000.

Independent (July 29, 1980) island group in the southwest Pacific; capital, Vila. Effective, though slow, evangelization by Catholic missionaries began about 1887. An apostolic vicariate was set up in 1904. The hierarchy was established in 1966.

Vatican City State (See separate entry)

Venezuela*

Archd., 9; dioc., 22; ord.; v.a., 4; ap. ex., 2; mil. ord. 1; card., 3; abp., 12; bp., 43; parishes, 1,185; priests, 2,320 (1,364 dioc., 956 rel.); p.d., 104; sem., 1,037; bros., 284; srs.,3,812; catechists, 21,442; bap., 436,695; Caths., 21,414,000 (89%); tot. pop., 24,170,000.

Republic in northern South America; capital, Caracas. Evangelization began in 1513-14 and involved members of a number of religious orders who worked in assigned territories, developing missions into pueblos or villages of Indian converts. Nearly 350 towns originated as missions. The first diocese was established in 1531.

Fifty-four missionaries met death by violence from the start of missionary work until 1817. Missionary work was seriously hindered during the wars of independence in the second decade of the 19th century and continued in decline through the rest of the century as dictator followed dictator in a period of political turbulence. Restoration of the missions got under way in 1922. In the 1990s, the Church worked at reconciliation in the country but condemned government corruption and violent crime. Church leaders also called for respect for human rights.

Vietnam

Archd., 3; dioc., 22; card., 2; abp., 2; bp., 33; parishes, 2,570; priests, 2,443 (1,993 dioc., 450 rel.); p.d., 11; sem., 1,862; bros., 1,455; srs., 9,672; catechists, 37,859; bap., 157,127; Caths., 5,301,000 (6.8%); tot. pop., 77,690,000.

Country in southeast Asia, reunited officially July 2, 1976, as the Socialist Republic of Vietnam; capital, Hanoi.

Catholicism was introduced in 1533, but missionary work was intermittent until 1615, when Jesuits arrived to stay. Two vicariates were organized in 1659. A seminary was set up in 1666, and two Vietnamese priests were ordained two years later. A congregation of native women religious formed in 1670 is still active. Severe persecution broke out in 1698, three times in the 18th century, and again in the 19th. Up to 300,000 people suffered in some way from persecution during the 50 years before 1883, when the French moved in to secure religious liberty for the Catholics. Most of the 117 beatified Martyrs of Vietnam were killed during this 50-year period. After the French were forced out of Vietnam in 1954, the country was partitioned at the 17th parallel. The North became Communist and the Viet Cong, joined by North Vietnamese regular army troops in 1964, fought to gain control of the South. In 1954 there were approximately 1.1 million Catholics in the North and 480,000 in the South. More than 650,000 fled to the South to avoid the government repression. In South Vietnam, the Church continued to develop during the war years. After the end of the war in 1975, the government exercised control over virtually all aspects of Church life. In the late 1980s, bishops noted some softening of the government's hard line. In the 1990s, the Vatican and Vietnam held intermittent talks on Church-state issues, with sporadic progress reported, but in 1997, the government censored the section of the "Catechism of the Catholic Church" that dealt with human rights. Although at times the Vatican was forced to wait years for government approval of bishops' appointments, in July 2001, just one month after Vatican officials visited Vietnam, Pope John Paul II named three new bishops.

Virgin Islands (U.S.)

Dioc., 1 (St. Thomas, suffragan of Washington, D.C.); bp., 2; parishes, 8; priests, 16 (9 dioc., 7 rel.); p.d., 18; sem., 10; bros., 11; srs., 17; bap., 336; Caths., 30,000 (29%); tot. pop., 102,000.

Organized unincorporated U.S. territory in Atlantic Ocean; capital, Charlotte Amalie on St. Thomas (one of the three principal islands). The islands were discovered by Columbus in 1493 and named for St. Ursula and her virgin companions. Missionaries began evangelization in the 16th century. A church on St. Croix dates from about 1660; another, on St. Thomas, from 1774. The Baltimore Archdiocese had jurisdiction over the islands from 1804 to 1820, when it was passed on to the first of several places in the Caribbean area. Some trouble arose over a pastoral appointment in the 19th century, resulting in a small schism. The Redemptorists took over pastoral care in 1858; normal conditions have prevailed since.

Wales

Archd., 1; dioc., 2; abp., 2; bp., 3; parishes, 184; priests, 258 (148 dioc., 110 rel.); p.d., 11; sem., 10; bros., 122; srs., 434; bap, 2,016; Caths., 140,797 (.5%); tot. pop., 3,077,297

Part of the United Kingdom, on the western part of the island of Great Britain. Celtic missionaries completed evangelization by the end of the sixth century, the climax of what has been called the age of saints. Welsh Christianity received its distinctive Celtic character at this time. Some conflict developed when attempts were made — and proved successful later — to place the Welsh Church under the jurisdiction of Canterbury; the Welsh opted for direct contact with Rome.

The Church made progress despite the depredations of Norsemen in the eighth and ninth centuries. Norman infiltration occurred near the middle of the 12th century, resulting in a century-long effort to establish territorial dioceses and parishes to replace the Celtic organizational plan of monastic centers and satellite churches. The Western Schism produced split views and allegiances. Actions of Henry VIII in breaking away from Rome had serious repercussions. Proscription and penal laws crippled the Church, resulted in heavy defections and touched off a 150-year period of repression. Methodism prevailed by 1750. Modern Catholicism came to Wales with Irish immigrants in the 19th century, when the number of Welsh Catholics was negligible. Catholic emancipation was granted in 1829. The hierarchy was restored in 1850. Wales shares a bishops' conference with England.

Yemen*

Parishes, 4; priests, 4 (rel.); srs., 27; bap., 19; Caths., 4,000; tot. pop., 18,300,000.

Republic on southern coast of Arabian peninsula; capital, San'a. Formerly North Yemen (Arab Republic of Yemen) and South Yemen (People's Republic of Yemen); formally reunited in 1990. Christians perished in the first quarter of the sixth century. Muslims have been in control since the seventh century. The state religion is Islam; the Church is under the ecclesiastical jurisdiction of Arabia apostolic vicariate. In the early 1990s, Salesians reported some harassment of Church workers in the South. In early 1998, three Missionaries of Charity nuns were murdered. The Vatican established diplomatic relations with Yemen in October 1998.

Yugoslavia*

Archd., 2; dioc., 3; a.a., 1; abp., 5; bp., 4; parishes, 287; priests, 271 (227 dioc., 44 rel.); p.d., 7; sem., 51; bros., 6; srs., 356; bap., 4,957; Caths., 553,000 (5%); tot. pop., 10,640,000.

Republic in southeastern Europe formed in 1992, consisting of Serbia and Montenegro; capital, Belgrade. The four other republics (Croatia, Slovenia, Bosnia-Herzegovina, and Macedonia) which made up the federation of Yugoslavia created after World War II, proclaimed their independence in 1991-92; see separate entries.

Christianity was introduced from the seventh to ninth centuries in the regions combined to form the nation after World War I. Since these regions straddled the original line of demarcation for the Western and Eastern Empires (and churches), and since the Reformation had little lasting effect, the Christians are nearly all either Latin- or Eastern-rite Catholics or Orthodox. Yugoslavia was proclaimed a Socialist republic in 1945, and persecution of the church began.. In an agreement signed June 25, 1966, the government recognized the Holy See's spiritual jurisdiction over the Church in the country and guaranteed to bishops the possibility of maintaining contact with Rome in ecclesiastical and religious matters. During the split of the Yugoslav republic, Catholic leaders joined Orthodox and, in some cases, Muslim leaders in calling for peace.

Zambia*

Archd., 2; dioc., 8; abp., 4; bp., 7; parishes, 256; priests, 575 (240 dioc., 335 rel.); p.d., 3; sem., 429; bros., 167; srs., 1,475; catechists, 20,170; bap., 88,678; Caths., 3,012,000 (28%); tot. pop., 10,720,000.

Republic in central Africa; capital, Lusaka. Portuguese priests did some evangelizing in the 16th and 17th centuries but no results of their work remained in the 19th century. Jesuits began work in the South in the 1880s and White Fathers in the North and East in 1895. Evangelization of the western region began for the first time in 1931. The number of Catholics doubled in the 20 years following World War II.

Zambian Catholics have welcomed tens of thousands of refugees from the region. During a 1989 visit, Pope John Paul II praised Zambians for their generosity and offered encouragement as they faced poverty. Zambian Catholics told the pope about fundamentalist sects and why Vatican teaching on marriage faced problems in a polygamous culture. In the 1990s, Zambian Church leaders worked caring for victims of HIV/AIDS and spoke out against foreign debt.

CATHOLIC WORLD STATISTICS

(*Principal sources:* Statistical Yearbook of the Church, 2000, *the latest edition; figures are as of Jan. 1, 2001 unless indicated otherwise.*)

	Africa	North America[1]	South America	Asia	Europe	Oceania	WORLD TOTALS
Patriarchates[2]	2	-	-	8	2	-	12
Archdioceses	84	86	96	116	169	18	569
Dioceses	380	356	406	313	505	54	2,014
Prelatures	-	7	32	6	6	-	51
Abbacies	-	-	2	-	11	-	13
Exarchates/Ords.	-	1	5	1	16	-	23
Military Ords.	3	4	9	3	13	2	34
Vicariates Apostolic	15	5	37	18	1	-	76
Prefectures	7	-	2	6	-	1	16
Apostolic Admin.	1	-	-	5	7	-	13
Independent Missions	1	2	-	5	1	2	11
Cardinals [3]	16	27	23	17	87	4	174
Patriarchs [2]	1	-	-	8	2	-	1
Archbishops	115	127	148	150	350	24	914[4]
Bishops	473	671	720	458	1,059	94	3,475[4]
Priests	27,165	78,836	42,005	43,566	208,659	4,947	405,178
Diocesan	16,962	50,859	24,262	25,716	145,268	2,714	265,781
Religious	10,203	27,977	17,743	17,850	63,391	2,233	139,397
Perm.Deacons	361	15,457	2,885	128	8,813	180	27,306
Brothers	7,256	10,217	6,398	7,659	21,691	1,836	55,057
Sisters	52,583	144,611	88,375	138,195	366,326	11,095	801,185
Maj. Seminarians	20,383	15,421	20,971	26,006	26,879	923	110,583
Sec. Inst. Mbrs. (Men)	26	62	130	79	421	1	719
Sec. Inst. Mbrs. (Women)	418	1,640	3,948	1,378	22,540	44	29,968
Lay Missionaries	1,222	5,176	114,406	3,597	1,857	107	126,365
Catechists	385,897	707,501	772,834	260,961	502,352	12,343	2,641,888
Parishes	11,022	33,698	20,984	20,543	129,565	2,384	218,196[5]
Kindergartens	11,672	8,353	6,725	10,905	23,528	661	61,844
Students	1,147,902	473,642	857,416	1,369,762	1,681,039	37,051	5,566,812
Elem./PrimarySchools	30,245	14,540	9,320	14,625	18,006	2,721	89,457
Students	10,158,438	3,850,310	3,704,341	4,668,907	3,099,393	615,746	26,097,135
Secondary Schools	7,297	3,764	5,647	7,976	10,226	651	35,559
Students	2,267,086	1,507,047	2,290,520	4,017,422	3,593,830	350,784	14,026,685
Students in Higher Insts.[6]	24,806	385,322	132,210	795,744	221,768	8,777	1,568,637
Social Service Facilities	14,196	15,393	20,973	20,525	30,808	1,522	103,417
Hospitals	819	1,049	897	1,584	1,330	174	5,853
Dispensaries	4,715	2,627	2,597	3,427	2,893	186	16,445
Leprosariums	378	16	39	348	4	2	787
Homes for Aged/Handic.	890	1,730	1,735	1,548	7,679	351	13,933
Orphanages	859	1,141	1,375	2,851	2,411	58	8,695
Nurseries	1,760	1,056	2,944	2,849	1,939	92	10,640
Matrimonial Advice Ctrs.	1,503	1,845	2,595	945	4,434	280	11,602
Social Educ.Ctrs.	2,105	4,721	6,096	6,084	8,514	239	25,759
Other Institutions	1,167	1,208	2,695	889	1,604	140	7,703
Baptisms	3,574,219	4,498,166	4,935,004	2,701,555	2,571,180	127,952	18,408,076
Under Age 7	2,265,897	4,189,742	4,400,277	2,256,942	2,463,112	114,062	15,690,032
Over Age 7	1,308,322	308,424	534,727	444,613	108,068	13,890	2,718,044
Marriages	368,653	861,168	743,519	696,840	1,033,709	27,023	3,730,912
Between Catholics	326,173	768,567	725,230	635,898	960,918	16,211	3,432,997
Mixed Marriages	42,480	92,601	18,289	60,942	72,791	10,812	297,915
Catholic Pop.[7]	130,018,000	221,936,000	297,455,000	107,302,000	280,144,000	8,202,000	1,045,057,000
World Population	789,455,000	483,194,000	343,360,000	3,698,043,000	702,661,000	30,566,000	6,047,279,000

1. Includes Central America. 2. For listing and description, see **Index**. 3. As of Aug. 30, 2002. 4. Figures for the hierarchy (cardinals, archbishops and bishops) included 2,649 ordinaries, 625 coadjutors or auxiliaries, 251 with offices in the Roman Curia, 25 in other offices, 991 retired. 5. 162,467 have parish priests; 51,141 are administered by other priests; 326 are entrusted to permanent deacons; 237 to brothers; 940 to women religious; 1,630 to lay people; 1,781 vacant. 6. There are also approximately 200,889 in universities for ecclesiastical studies and 2,934,681 other university students. 7. Percentages of Catholics in world population: Africa, 16.4; North America (Catholics 76,815,000; tot. pop., 312,294,000), 24.5; Central America (Catholics, 145,121,000; tot. pop., 170,900,000), 84.9; South America, 86.6; Asia, 2.9; Europe, 39.8; Oceania, 26.8; World, 17.3. (Catholic totals do not include those in areas that could not be surveyed, estimated to be approximately 6 million.)

Zimbabwe*

Archd., 2; dioc., 6; abp., 4; bp., 7; parishes, 152; priests, 414 (166 dioc., 248 rel.); p.d., 12; sem., 313; bros., 114; srs., 1,095; catechists, 5,008; bap., 38,292; Caths., 1,172,000 (9%); tot. pop., 12,630,000.

Independent republic (1980) in south central Africa; capital, Harare. Earlier unsuccessful missionary ventures preceded the introduction of Catholicism in 1879. Missionaries began to make progress after 1893. The hierarchy was established in 1955; the first black bishop was ordained in 1973.

In 1969, four years after the government of Ian Smith made a unilateral declaration of independence from England, a new constitution was enacted for the purpose of assuring continued white supremacy over the black majority. Catholic and Protestant prelates in the country criticized the constitution and related enact-

ments as opposed to human rights of the blacks and restrictive of the Church's freedom to carry out its pastoral, educational and social service functions. The Smith regime was ousted in 1979 after seven years of civil war in which at least 25,000 people were killed.

In 1997, the bishops published a report detailing more than 7,000 cases of killings, torture and human rights abuses by government troops in western Zimbabwe from 1981-87. As the Church entered the 21st century, it was devoting tremendous resources toward palliative care of AIDS victims and work with AIDS orphans. However, the Church was sometimes criticized for not doing enough to prevent the spread of AIDS, which Church and health-care workers said was exacerbated by poverty and cultural beliefs. Church leaders were outspoken against a government-backed campaign of violence against white landowners.

EPISCOPAL CONFERENCES

(*Principal sources:* Annuario Pontificio *and Catholic Almanac survey.*)

Episcopal conferences, organized and operating under general norms and particular statutes approved by the Holy See, are official bodies in and through which the bishops of a given country or territory act together as pastors of the Church.

Listed below according to countries or regions are titles and addresses of conferences, telephone numbers (where possible), and names and sees of presidents.

Africa, Northern: *Conference Episcopale Regionale du Nord de l'Afrique* (CERNA), 13 rue Khelifa-Boukhalfa, 16000 Algiers, Algeria; (02) 64-53-88. Abp. Henri Teissier (Algiers).

Africa, Southern: Southern African Catholic Bishops' Conference (SACBC), 140 Visagie St., P.O. Box 941, Pretoria 0001, S. Africa; (021) 65-35-62. Cardinal Wilfrid Napier, O.F.M. (Durban, South Africa).

Albania: *Conferenza Episcopale dell'Albania*, Tirane, Rruga Don Bosco 1, Kulia Postare 2950; (042) 47-159. Abp. Angelo Massafra, O.F.M. (Shkodre, Albania).

Angola and São Tome: *Conferencia Episcopal de Angola e HR Tome* (CEAST), C.P. 87 Luanda, Angola; (02) 34-36-86. Archbishop Zacarias Kamwenho (Lubango).

Antilles: Antilles Episcopal Conference (AEC), P.O. Box 3086, St. James (Trinidad and Tobago), W.I.; (868) 622-2932. Abp. Roland Clarke Edgerton (Kingston).

Arab Countries: *Conférence des Evêques Latins dans les Régions Arabes* (CELRA), Latin Patriarchate, P.O. Box 14152, Jerusalem (Old City); (02) 628-85-54. Patriarch Michel Sabbah (Jerusalem).

Argentina: *Conferencia Episcopal Argentina* (CEA), C.C. 3175, Calle Suipacha 1034, 1008 Buenos Aires; (011) 4328-09-93. Abp. Estanislao Esteban Karlic (Paraná).

Australia: Australian Catholic Bishops' Conference, 63 Currong St., Braddon, A.C.T. 2601; (02) 6201-9845; www.catholic.org.au. Abp. Francis Patrick Carroll (Canberra, Australia).

Austria: *Österreichische Bischofskonferenz*, Wollzeile 2, A-1010 Vienna; 43-1-51552-3723. Cardinal Christoph Schönborn, O.P. (Vienna).

Bangladesh: Catholic Bishops' Conference of Bangladesh (CBCB), P.O. Box 3, Dhaka-1000; (02)

40-88-79. Abp. Michael Rozario (Dhaka).

Belgium: *Bisschoppenconferentie van België-Conférence Episcopale de Belgique*, Rue Guimard 1, B-1040 Brussel; (32) 2-509-96-93; www.catho.be; www.kerknet.be. Card. Godfried Danneels (Mechelen-Brussel).

Belarus: *Conferentia Episcoporum Catholicorum*, 220030 Minsk, pl. Swobody 9; (017) 26.61.27. Card. Kazimierz Swiàtek (Minsk-Mohilev).

Benin: *Conférence Episcopale du Bénin*, Cotonou, 01 B.P. 491; 30.01.45. Abp. Nestor Assogba (Dhaka).

Bolivia: *Conferencia Episcopal Boliviana* (CEB), Casilla 2309, Calle Potosi 814, La Paz; (02) 32-12-54. Card. Julio Terrazas Sandoval, C.SS.R. (Santa Cruz de la Sierra).

Bosnia and Herzegovina: *Biskupska Konferencija Bosne i Hercegovine* (B.K. B.i.H.), *Nadbiskupski Ordinariat*, Kaptol 7, 71000 Sarajevo; (387) 71-664-784. Card. Vinko Puljic, (Vrhbosna, Sarajevo).

Brazil: *Conferência Nacional dos Bispos do Brasil* (CNBB), C.P. 02067, SE/Sul Quadra 801, Conjunto "B," 70259-970 Brasilia, D.F.; (061) 313-8300. Bishop Jayme Henrique Chemello (Pelotas).

Bulgaria: *Mejduritual Episcopska Konferenzia vâv Bâlgaria*, Ul. Liulin Planina 5, 1606 Sofia; (0) 540-406. Bp. Christo Proykov (Briula, titular see).

Burkina Faso and Niger: *Conférence des Evêques de Burkina Faso et du Niger*, B.P. 1195, Ouagadougou, Burkina Faso; 30-60-26. Bp. Philippe Ouédraogo (Ouahigouya).

Burma: See **Myanmar**.

Burundi: *Conférence des Evêques catholiques du Burundi* (C.E.CA.B.), B. P. 1390, 5 Blvd. de l'Uprona, Bujumbura; 257-22-32-63. Archbishop Simon Ntamwana (Gitega).

Cameroon: *Conférence Episcopale Nationale du Cameroun* (CENC), BP 807, Yaoundé. Bp. Cornelius Fontem Esua (Kumbo).

Canada: See **Canadian Conference of Catholic Bishops** in the section on the **Catholic Church in Canada**.

Central African Republic: *Conférence Episcopale Centrafricaine* (CECA), B.P. 1518, Bangui; 50-24-84. Bp. Paulin Pomodimo (Bossangoa).

Chad: *Conférence Episcopale du Tchad*, B.P. 456, N'Djaména; (235) 51-74-44. Abp. Charles Vandame, S.J. (N'Djamena).

Chile: *Conferencia Episcopal de Chile* (CECH), Casilla 517-V, Correo 21, Cienfuegas 47, Santiago; (02) 671-77-33. Card. Francisco Javier Erráruiz Ossa (Santiago de Chile).

China: Chinese Regional Episcopal Conference, 34 Lane 32, Kuang-Fu South Rd., Taipeh 10552, Taiwan; (02) 578-2355. Card. Paul Shan Kuo-hsi, S.J. (Kaohsiung).

Colombia: *Conferencia Episcopal de Colombia*, Apartado 7448, Carrera 8ª 47, N. 84-85, Santafé de Bogotá D.E.; (91) 311-42-77. Abp. Alberto Giraldo Jaramillo, P.S.S. (Medellin).

Congo: *Conférence Episcopale du Congo*, B.P. 200, Brazzaville; (83) 06-29. Abp. Anatole Milandou (Brazzaville).

Congo, Democratic Republic (formerly Zaire): *Conférence Episcopale du Zaïre* (CEZ), B.P. 3258, Kinshasa-Gombe. Card. Frédéric Etsou-Nzabi-Bamungwabi C.I.C.M. (Kinshasa).

Costa Rica: *Conferencia Episcopal de Costa Rica* (CECOR), Apartado 497, 1000 San Jose; 221-30-53. Abp. Román Arrieta Villalobos (San Jose de Costa Rica).

Côte d'Ivoire: *Conference Episcopale de la Côte d'Ivoire*, B.P. 1287, Abidjan 01. Abp. Vital Komenan Yao (Bouaké).

Croatia: *Hrvatska Biskupska Konferencija*, Kaptol 22, HR-10000 Zagreb; 385-01-481-18-93; www.hbk.hr. Abp. Josip Bozanic (Zagreb).

Cuba: *Conferencia de Obispos Católicos de Cuba* (COCC), Apartado 594, Calle 26 n. 314 Miramar, 10100 Havana 1; (07) 22-3868. Card. Jaime Lucas Ortega y Alamino (Havana).

Czech Republic: *Ceská Biskupská Konference*, Sekretariat, Thakurova 3, 160 00 Praha (Prague) 6; (02) 33-15-421. Bp. Jan Graubner (Olomouc).

Dominican Republic: *Conferencia del Episcopado Dominicano* (CED), Apartado 186, Santo Domingo; (809) 685-3141. Card. Nicolás de Jesús López Rodriguez (Santo Domingo).

Ecuador: *Conferencia Episcopal Ecuatoriana*, Apartado 1081, Avenida América 1805 y Lagasca, Quito; (02) 52-45-68. Abp. José Mario Ruiz Navas (Portoviejo).

El Salvador: *Conferencia Episcopal de El Salvador* (CEDES). 15 Av. Norte 1420, Col. Layco, Apartado 1310, San Salvador; 25-8997. Abp. Fernando Sáenz Lacalle (San Salvador).

Equatorial Guinea: *Conferencia Episcopal de Guinea Ecuatorial*, Apartado 106, Malabo. Abp. Ildefonso Obama Obono (Malabo).

Ethiopia: Ethiopian Episcopal Conference, P.O. Box 21322, Addis Ababa; (01) 55-03-00. Abp. Berhane-Yesus Demerew Souraphiel, C.M. (Addis Ababa).

France: *Conférence des Evêques de France*, 106 rue du Bac, 75341 Paris CEDEX 07; 33-01-45-49-69-70; www.cef.fr. Abp. Jean-Pierre Ricard (Bordeaux).

Gabon: *Conférence Episcopale du Gabon*, B.P. 2146, Libreville; 72-20-73. Bp. Basile Mvé Engone, S.D.B. (Oyem).

Gambia, Liberia and Sierra Leone: Inter-Territorial Catholic Bishops' Conference of the Gambia, Liberia and Sierra Leone (ITCABIC), Santanno House, P.O. Box 893, Freetown, Sierra Leone; (022) 22-82-40. Abp. Joseph Henry Ganda (Freetown).

Germany: *Deutsche Bischofskonferenz*, Postfach 2962, Kaiserstrasse 163, D-53019 Bonn; (0049) 228-103-290. Card. Karl Lehmann (Mainz).

Ghana: Ghana Bishops' Conference, National Catholic Secretariat, P.O. Box 9712 Airport, Accra; (021) 500-491. Bp. Peter Kodwo Appiah Turkson (Cape Coast).

Great Britain: Bishops' Conference of England and Wales, General Secretariat, 39 Eccleston Square, London, SWIV IBX; (020) 7630-8220. Card. Cormac Murphy-O'Connor.

Greece: *Conferentia Episcopalis Graeciae*, Odos Homirou 9, 106 72 Athens; (01) 3642-311. Abp. Nikólaos Fóscolos (Athens).

Guatemala: *Conferencia Episcopal de Guatemala* (CEG), Apartado 1698, 01901 Ciudad de Guatemala; 543-18-27/8. Abp. Victor Hugo Martinez Contreras (Los Altos, Quetzaltenango-Totonicapán).

Guinea: *Conférence Episcopale de la Guinée*, B.P. 2016; (224) 41-32-70. Conakry. Vacant.

Guinea-Bissau: See **Senegal**.

Haiti: *Conférence Episcopale de Haïti* (CEH). B.P. 1572, Angle rues Piquant et Lammarre, Port-au-Prince; 222-5194. Bp. Hubert Constant, O.M.I. (Fort-Liberté).

Honduras: *Conferencia Episcopal de Honduras* (CEH), Apartado 3121, Los Laureles Tegucigalpa; (504) 229-1111. Abp. Oscar Andrés Rodríguez Maradiaga (Tegucigalpa).

Hungary: *Magyar Katolikus Püspöki Konferencia*, H-1071 Budapest VII, Városligeti fasor 45; 1-342-69-59. Abp. István Seregély (Eger).

India: Catholic Bishops' Conference of India (CBCI), CBCI Centre, Ashok Place, Goldakkhana, New Delhi-110001; (011) 334-44-70; Abp. Cyril Baseolios Malancharuvil, O.I.C. (Trivandrum). Conference of Catholic Bishops of India — Latin Rite (CCBI-L.R.), Divya Deepti Sadan, Second Floor, P.B. 680, 9-10 Bhai Vir Singh Marg; (011) 336-42-22; Abp. Henry Sebastian D'Souza (Calcutta).

Indian Ocean: *Conférence Episcopale de l'Océan Indien* (CEDOI) (includes Islands of Mauritius, Seychelles, Comore and La Réunion), 13 rue Msgr. Gonin, Port Louis, Mauritius; (230) 208-3068. Bp. Maurice Piat, C.S.Sp. (Port Louis) .

Indonesia: *Konperensi Waligereja Indonesia* (KWI), Jl. Cut Mutiah 10, Tromolpos 3044, Jakarta 10002; (021) 33-64-22. Card. Julius Riyadi Darmaatmadja, S.J. (Jakarta).

Ireland: Irish Episcopal Conference, "Ara Coeli," Armagh BT61 7QY; 028-3752-2045. Abp. Sean B. Brady (Armagh).

Italy: *Conferenza Episcopale Italiana* (CEI), Circonvallazione Aurelia, 50, 00165 Rome; 06-663-981. Card. Camillo Ruini (Vicar General, Rome).

Ivory Coast: See **Côte d'Ivoire**.

Japan: Catholic Bishops' Conference of Japan, Shiomi 2-10-10, Koto-Ku, Tokyo, 135; (03) 56324411. Bp. Augustinus Junichi Nomura (Nagoya).

Kenya: Kenya Episcopal Conference (KEC), The Kenya Catholic Secretariat, P.O. Box 13475, Nairobi; (02) 44-31-33. Bp. John Njue (Embu).

Korea: Catholic Bishops' Conference of Korea, Box 16, Seoul 100-600; (02) 466-3417. Bp. Michael Pak Jeong-il (Masan).

Laos and Cambodia: *Conférence Episcopale du Laos et du Cambodge*, c/o Msgr. Pierre Bach, Paris Foreign Missions, 254 Silom Rd., Bangkok 10500; (02) 234-1714. Bp. Jean Khamsé Vithavong, O.M.I. (Moglena).

Latvia: *Latvijas Biskapu Konference*, Maza Pils iela 2/a, LV-1050, Riga; (7) 22-72-66. Card. Janis Pujats (Riga).

Lesotho: Lesotho Catholic Bishops' Conference, Catholic Secretariat, P.O. Box 200, Maseru 100; (0501) 31-25-25. Abp. Bernard Mohlalisi, O.M.I. (Maseru).

Liberia: Catholic Bishops' Conference of Liberia, 1000 Monrovia 10, P.O. Box 10-2078; 227-245. Abp. Francis Michael Kpakala (Monrovia).

Lithuania: *Conferentia Episcopalis Lituaniae*, Sventaragio, 4, 2001 Vilnius; (2) 22-54-55. Abp. Sigitas Tamkevicius (Kaunas).

Madagascar: *Conférence Episcopale de Madagascar*, 102 bis Av. Maréchal Joffre, Antanimena, B. P 667, Antananarivo; (02) 2220-478. Card. Armand Gaétan Razafindratandra (Antananarivo).

Malawi: Episcopal Conference of Malawi, Catholic Secretariat of Malawi, P.O. Box 30384, Lilongwe 3; 782-066. Bp. Tarcisius Gervazio Ziyaye (Blantyre).

Malaysia-Singapore-Brunei: Catholic Bishops' Conference of Malaysia, Singapore and Brunei (BCMSB), Xavier Selangor Darul Ehsan, 46000 Petaling Jaya, Malaysia; (03) 758-1371. Abp. Anthony Soter Fernandez (Kuala Lampur).

Mali: *Conférence Episcopale du Mali*, B.P. 298, Bamako; 225-499. Bp. Jean-Gabriel Diarra.

Malta: *Konferenza Episkopali Maltija*, Archbishop's Curia, Floriana; (356) 234317; www.maltachurch.org.mt. Abp. Joseph Mercieca (Malta).

Mexico: See the *Conferencia del Episcopado Mexicano* (CEM), under the section on the Catholic Church in Mexico.

Mozambique: *Conferência Episcopal de Moçambique* (CEM), Av. Paulo Samuel Kankhomba 188/RC, C.P. 286; (01) 49-07-66. Bp. Francisco João Silota, M.Afr. (Chimoio).

Myanmar: Myanmar Catholic Bishops' Conference (MCBC), 292 Pyi Rd., P.O. Box 1080, Yangon; (01) 23-71-98. Bp. Bo Charles Maung, S.D.B. (Pathein).

Namibia: Namibian Catholic Bishops' Conference (NCBC). P.O. Box 11525 W., Windhoek; (061) 22-47-98. Abp. Bonifatius Haushiku (Windhoek).

Netherlands: *Nederlandse Bisschoppenconferentie*, Postbus 13049, NL-3507 LA, Utrecht; (31)-30-232-69-00; www.omroep.nl/rkk. Card. Adrianus J. Simonis (Utrecht).

New Zealand: New Zealand Catholic Bishops Conference, P.O. Box 1937, Wellington 6015; (04) 496-1747. Bp. Peter James Culliname (Palmerston North).

Nicaragua: *Conferencia Episcopal de Nicaragua* (CEN), Apartado Postal 2407, de Ferretería Lang 1 cuadro al Norte y 1 cuadro al Este, Managua; (02) 666-292. Cardinal Miguel Odando Bravo, S.D.B. (Managua).

Niger: See **Burkina Faso**.

Nigeria: Catholic Bishops Conference of Nigeria, P.O. Box 951, 6 Force Rd., Lagos; (01) 263-58-49. Abp. Albert K. Obiefuna (Onitsha).

Pacific: *Conferentia Episcopalis Pacifici* (CE PAC), P.O. Box 289, Suva (Fiji); 300-340. Abp. Michel Marie Bernard Calvet, S.M. (Noumea, New Caledonia).

Pakistan: Pakistan Episcopal Conference, P.O. Box 909, Lahore 54000; (042) 6366-137. Abp. Simeon Anthony Pereira (Karachi).

Panama: *Conferencia Episcopal de Panamá* (CEP),

Apartado 870033, Panama 7; 223-0075. Abp. José Luis Lacunza Maestrojuán, O.A.R. (David).

Papua New Guinea and Solomon Islands: Catholic Bishops' Conference of Papua New Guinea and Solomon Islands, P.O. Box 398, Waigani, N.C.D., Papua New Guinea; 25-9577. Bp. Stephen Joseph Reichert, O.F.M. Cap. (Mendi).

Paraguay: *Conferencia Episcopal Paraguaya* (CEP), Alberdi 782, Casilla Correo 1436, Asunción; (021) 490-920. Bp. Jorge Adolfo Carlos Livieres Banks (Encarnación).

Peru: *Conferencia Episcopal Peruana*, Apartado 310, Rio de Janeiro 488, Lima 100; (01) 463-10-10. Bp. Luis Armando Bambarén Gastelumendi, S.J. (Chimbote).

Philippines: Catholic Bishops' Conference of the Philippines (CBCP), P.O. Box 3601, 470 General Luna St., 1099 Manila; (02) 527-4054. Abp. Orlando Quevedo, O.M.I. (Cotabato).

Poland: *Konferencja Episkopatu Polski*, Skwer Kardynala Stefana Wyszynskiego 6, 01-015 Warsaw; (022) 838-92-51. Card. Józef Glemp (Warsaw).

Portugal: *Conferência Episcopal Portuguesa*, Campo dos Mártires da Pátria, 43-1 Esq., 1100 Lisbon; 21-885-21-23. Abp. José da Cruz Policarpo (Lisbon).

Puerto Rico: *Conferencia Episcopal Puertorriqueña* (CEP), P.O. Box 40682, Estacion Minillas, San Juan 00940-0682; (787) 728-1650. Abp. Roberto Octavio Gonzalez Nieves, O.F.M. (San Juan de Puerto Rico).

Romania: *Conferinte Episcopala România*, Via Popa Tatu 58, Bucharest; (01) 311-12-89. Abp. Ioan Robu (Bucharest).

Russian Federation: Conference of Catholic Bishops of the Russian Federation (C.V.C.F.R.), 101031 Moskva, Via Pietrovka, d. 19 str., 5Kv. 35; (095) 923-16-97. Abp. Tadeusz Kondrusiewicz (Archdiocese of the Mother of God).

Rwanda: *Conférence Episcopale du Rwanda* (C.Ep.R.), B.P. 357, Kigali; 75439. Abp. Thadée Ntihinyurwa (Kigali).

Scandinavia: *Conferentia Episcopalis Scandiae*, Trollbärsvägen 16, S-426 55 Västra Frölunda (Sweden); (031) 709-64-87. Bp. Gerhard Schwenzer, S.S.C.C. (Oslo).

Scotland: Bishops' Conference of Scotland, 64 Aitken St., Airdrie, ML6; 44-1236-764-061. Vacant.

Senegal, Mauritania, Cape Verde and Guinea Bissau: *Conférence des Evêques du Sénégal, de la Mauritanie, du Cap-Vert et de Guinée-Bissau*, B.P. 941, Dakar, Senegal. Abp. Théodore-Adrien Sarr (Dakar).

Sierra Leone: See **Gambia**, **Liberia** and **Sierra Leone**.

Slovakia: *Biskupská Konferencia Slovenska*, Kapitulská 11, 81521 Bratislava; (07) 733-54-50. Bp. Frantisek Tondra (Spis).

Slovenia: *Slovenska Skofovska Konferenca*, Ciril-Metodov trg 4, p.p.1990, 1001 Ljubljana; (386) 1-2342612. Abp. Franc Rodé, C.M. (Ljubljana).

Spain: *Conferencia Episcopal Española*, Apartado 29075, Calle Añastro 1, 28033 Madrid; 91-343-96-15. Cardinal Antonio María Rouco Varela (Madrid).

Sri Lanka: Catholic Bishops' Conference of Sri Lanka, 19 Balcombe Place, Cotta Rd., Borella, Colombo 8; (01) 95-091; 59-70-62. Bp. Oswald Thomas Colman Gomis (Anuradhapura).

Sudan: Sudan Catholic Bishops' Conference

(SCBC), P.O. Box 6011, Khartoum; (011) 225-075-9. Abp. Paulino Lukudu Loro, M.C.C.I. (Juba).

Switzerland: *Conférence des Evêques Suisses*, Secretariat, C.P. 22, av. Moléson 21, CH-1706 Fribourg; (026) 322-47-94; www.kath.ch. Bp. Amédée Grab, O.S.B. (Chur).

Tanzania: Tanzania Episcopal Conference (TEC), P.O. Box 2133, Mansfield St., Dar-es-Salaam; (022) 51-075. Bp. Severine Niwemugizi (Rulenge).

Thailand: Bishops' Conference of Thailand, 122-6-7 Soi Naaksuwan, Nonsi Road, Yannawa, Bangkok; 02-6815361-8. Card. Michael Michai Kitbunchu (Bangkok).

Togo: *Conférence Episcopale du Togo*, B.P. 348, Lomé; 21-22-72. Abp. Philippe Fanoko Kossi Kpodzro (Lomé).

Turkey: Turkish Episcopal Conference, Ölçek Sokak 83, Harbiye, 80230 Istanbul; (212) 248-07-75. Bp. Ruggero Franceschini, O.F.M. Cap. (Sicilibba).

Uganda: Uganda Episcopal Conference, P.O. Box 2886, Kampala; (041) 268-175. Bp. Paul L. Kalanda (Fort Portal).

Ukraine: Ukraine Episcopal Conference, Obrzadku Laciñskiego, pl. Katedralna 1, 290008 Lviv; (0322) 76-94-15. Card. Marian Jaworski (Lviv of Latins).

United States: See **National Conference of Catholic Bishops**.

Uruguay: *Conferencia Episcopal Uruguaya* (CEU), Avenida Uruguay 1319, 11100 Montevideo; (02) 900-26-42. Bp. carlos Maria Collazzi Irazábal, S.D.B. (Mercedes).

Venezuela: *Conferencia Episcopal de Venezuela* (CEV), Apartado 4897, Torre a Madrices, Edificio Juan XXIII, Piso 4, Caracas 1010-A; (02) 442-20-77. Abp. Baltazar Porras Cardozo (Mérida).

Vietnam: *Conferenza Episcopale del Viêt Nam*, Nha Trang, Khán Hòa, 22 Tran Phu; (058) 822-842. Bp. Paul Nguyen Van Hòa (Nha Trang).

Yugoslavia: *Biskupska Konferencija Savezne Republike Jugoslavije*, 11000 Beograd, Visegradska 23; (011) 642-280. Abp. Stanislav Hocevar, S.D.B. (Beograd).

Zambia: Zambia Epscopal Conference, P.O. Box 31965, 10101 Lusaka; 260-122-7854. Bp. Joseph Mazombwe Medardo (Lusaka).

Zimbabwe: Zimbabwe Catholic Bishops' Conference (ZCBC), Causeway, P.O. Box 8135, Harare; (14) 705-368. Bp. Alexio Churu Muchabaiwa (Mutare).

Regional Conferences

(*Sources: Almanac survey; Annuario Pontificio.*)

Africa: Symposium of Episcopal Conferences of Africa and Madagascar (SECAM) (*Symposium des Conférences Episcopales d'Afrique et de Madagascar*, SCEAM): Abp. Laurent Monsengwo Pasinya, abp. of Kisangani, president. Address: Secretariat, P.O. Box 9156 Airport, Accra, Ghana.

Association of Episcopal Conferences of Central Africa (*Association des Conférences Episcopales de l'Afrique Centrale*, ACEAC): Comprises Burundi, Rwanda and Zaire. Bp. Frédéric Rubwejanga, bp. of Kibungo, president. Address: B.P. 20511, Kinshasa, Democratic Republic of Congo.

Association of Episcopal Conferences of the Region of Central Africa (*Association des Conférences Episcopales de la Région de l'Afrique Central*, ACERAC): Comprises Cameroon, Chad, Congo,

Equatorial Guinea, Central African Republic and Gabon. Bp. Anacleto Sima Ngua, bp. of Bata, president. Address: Secretariat, B.P. 200, Brazzaville, Republic of the Congo.

Association of Episcopal Conferences of Anglophone West Africa (AECAWA): Comprises Gambia, Ghana, Liberia, Nigeria and Sierra Leone. Bp. John Olorunfemi Onaiyekan, abp. of Abuja, president. Address: P.O. Box 11, Santasi, Ghana.

Association of Member Episcopal Conferences in Eastern Africa (AMECEA): Represents Eritrea, Ethiopia, Kenya, Malawi, Sudan, Tanzania, Uganda and Zambia. Affiliate members: Seychelles (1979), Somalia (1994). Bp. Josaphat L. Lebulu, bp. of Arusha, president. Address: P.O. Box 21191, Nairobi, Kenya.

Regional Episcopal Conference of French-Speaking West Africa (*Conférence Episcopale Régionale de l'Afrique de l'Ouest Francophone*, CERAO): Comprises Benin, Burkina Faso, Cape Verde, Côte d'Ivoire, Guinea, Guinea-Bissau, Mali, Mauritania, Niger, Senegal and Togo. President: vacant. Address: Secretariat General, B.P.470 CIDEX 1, Abidjan-Côte d'Ivoire.

Inter-Regional Meeting of Bishops of Southern Africa (IMBISA): Bishops of Angola, Botswana, Lesotho, Mozambique, Namibia, São Tome e Principe, South Africa, Swaziland and Zimbabwe. Bp. Louis Ncamiso Ndlovu, O.S.M., bp. of Manzini, president. Address: 88 Broadlands Rd. Avondale Harare, Zimbabwe.

Asia: Federation of Asian Bishops' Conferences (FABC): Represents 14 Asian episcopal conferences and four independent jurisdictions (Hong Kong, Macau, Nepal, Mongolia) as regular members (excluding the Middle East). Established in 1970; statutes approved experimentally Dec. 6, 1972. Abp. Oswald Thomas Colman Gomis, bp. of Anuradhapura, secretary general. Address: 16 Caine Road, Hong Kong; 25258021; www.fabc.org.ph.

Oceania: Federation of Catholic Bishops' Conferences of Oceania (FCBCO). Statutes approved Dec. 25, 1997. Bp. Soane Lilo Foliaki, S.M., bishop of Tonga, president. Address: CEPAC Secretariat, P.O. Box 289, Suva, Fiji Islands.

Europe: Council of European Bishops' Conferences (Consilium Conferentiarum Episcoporum Europae, CCEE): Amédé Grab, bp. of Chur, president. Address of secretariat: Gallusstrasse 24, CH-9000 Sankt Gallen, Switzerland; (0041) 71-227-33-74; www.kath.ch/ccee. Reorganized in 1993 in accordance with suggestions made during the 1991 Synod of Bishops on Europe.

Commission of the Episcopates of the European Community (*Commissio Episcopatuum Communitatis Europaeae*, COMECE): Established in 1980; represents episcopates of states belonging to European Community. Bp. Josef Homeyer, bp. of Hildesheim, Germany, president. Address of secretariat: 42, Rue Stévin, B-1000 Brussels, Belgium; (02) 230-73-16.

Central and South America: Latin American Bishops' Conference (*Consejo Episcopal Latino-Americano*, CELAM): Established in 1956; statutes approved Nov. 9, 1974. Represents 22 Latin American national bishops' conferences. Bp. Jorge Enrique Jiménez Carvajal, C.I.M., president. Address of the secretariat: Carrera 5 No. 118-31, Usaquén, Bogotá, Colombia; (91) 612-16-20.

Episcopal Secretariat of Central America and Panama (*Secretariado Episcopal de America Central y Panama*, SEDAC): Statutes approved experimentally Sept. 26, 1970. Bp. Leonel Ramazzini Imeri Alvaro, bp. of San Marcos, president. Address of secretary general: Calle 20 y Av Mexico 24-45, Apartado 6386, Panama 5, Panama; 262-7802.

INTERNATIONAL CATHOLIC ORGANIZATIONS

(*Principal sources: Sr. Dorothy Farley, Executive Director, ICO Information Center; Pontifical Council for the Laity; Catholic Almanac survey.*)

Guidelines

International organizations wanting to call themselves "Catholic" are required to meet standards set by the Vatican's Council for the Laity and to register with and get the approval of the Papal Secretariat of State, according to guidelines dated Dec. 3 and published in *Acta Apostolicae Sedis* under the date of Dec. 23, 1971.

Among conditions for the right of organizations to "bear the name Catholic" are:

• Leaders "will always be Catholics," and candidates for office will be approved by the Secretariat of State

• Adherence by the organization to the Catholic Church, its teaching authority and the teachings of the Gospel

• Evidence that the organization is really international with a universal outlook and that it fulfills its mission through its own management, meetings and accomplishments.

The guidelines also stated that leaders of the organizations "will take care to maintain necessary reserve as regards taking a stand or engaging in public activity in the field of politics or trade unionism. Abstention in these fields will normally be the best attitude for them to adopt during their term of office."

The guidelines were in line with a provision stated by the Second Vatican Council: "No project may claim the name 'Catholic' unless it has obtained the consent of the lawful Church authority."

They made it clear that all organizations are not obliged to apply for recognition, but that the Church "reserves the right to recognize as linked with her mission and her aims those organizations or movements which see fit to ask for such recognition."

Conference of International Catholic Organizations

A permanent body for collaboration among various organizations the conference seeks to promote the development of international life along the lines of Christian principles. Eleven international Catholic organizations participated in its foundation and first meeting in 1927 at Fribourg, Switzerland. In 1951, the conference established its general secretariat and adopted governing statutes that were approved by the Vatican Secretariat of State in 1953.

The permanent secretariat is located at 37-39 rue de Vermont, CH-1202 Geneva, Switzerland. Other office addresses are: 1 rue Varembe, CH-1211 Geneva 20, Switzerland (International Catholic Center of Geneva); 9, rue Cler, F-75007 Paris, France (International Catholic Center for UNESCO); ICO Information Center, 323 East 47th St., New York, NY 10017.

Charter

According to its charter (adopted in November 1997), the conference "responds to the challenge of *Christifideles Laici:* Open to the saving power of Christ the frontiers of States, economic and political systems, the vast domains of culture, civilization and development (no. 34)."

In a universal vision of those problems, these organizations have the following responsibilities to their members:

• To make them increasingly aware of the compexities of the situations in which they live and work

• To help them to grow in discernment and critical analysis

• To facilitate the search for solutions to concrete difficulties.

The Conference is open to any organization which is acting and is involved recognizably Catholic in its work in the international world, which accepts the present Charter, respects its principles in practice and adheres to its Statutes. The Conference witnesses to the organized presence of Catholics in the international world.

Fundamental Convictions

• Their desire to announce Jesus Christ to the women and men of our time, and their vocation to serve the world, are indivisible; faith calls for action

• Their wish to contribute to the building of the Kingdom of God is demonstrated by solidarity with all women and men of good will

• Their desire for participation in decision-making in the Church in areas which concern their competence and in which they are involved.

A unique spirituality

In its desire to live fully its faith in Jesus Christ, the Cnference stresses:

• The need to be rooted in reality, through a relationship with God lived out in the world

• An experience of community nourished by group sharing and exchange

• Openness to the international dimension, validated by experiences at local level to which it gives meaning

• Adaptation to different human groups and to different sensibilies

• The witness of Christian freedom to initiate, as well as willingness to live in "solid and strong communion" with the Church

• Desire to serve the universal Church through insertion in the local Churches by respecting diverse pastoral programmes, but also to participate in major events in the life of the universal Church.

Members

Members of the Conference of International Catholic Organizations are listed below. Information includes name, date and place of establishment (when available), address of general secretariat. Approximately 30 of the organizations have consultative status with other international or regional non-governmental agencies.

Caritas Internationalis (1951, Rome, Italy): Piazza San Calisto 16, I-00153, Rome, Italy. Coordinates and represents its 146 national member organizations (in 194 countries) operating in the fields of development, emergency aid, social action.

Catholic International Education Office (1952): 60, rue des Eburons, B-1000 Brussels, Belgium.

Catholic International Union for Social Service (1925, Milan, Italy): rue de la Poste 111, B-1210 Brussels, Belgium (general secretariat).

Christian Life Community (CVX) (1953): Borgo Santo Spirito 8, C.P. 6139, I-00195 Rome, Italy. First Sodality of Our Lady founded in 1563.

International Ascent, The: 84, rue Charles Michels, F-93206 Saint Denis Cedex, France. Member of ICO.

International Association of Charities (1617, Chatillon les Dombes, France): Rue Joseph Brand, 118, B-1030 Brussels, Belgium.

International Catholic Child Bureau (1948, in Paris): 63, rue de Lausanne, CH-1202 Geneva, Switzerland.

International Catholic Committee of Nurses and Medico-Social Assistants (ICCN) (1933): Square Vergote, 43, B-1040 Brussels, Belgium.

International Catholic Conference of Scouting (1948): Piazza Pasquale Paoli, 18, I-00186 Rome, Italy.

International Catholic Migration Commission (1951): 37-39 rue de Vermont, C.P. 96, CH-1211 Geneva 20, Switzerland. Coordinates activities worldwide on behalf of refugees and migrants, both administering programs directly and supporting the efforts of national affiliated agencies.

International Catholic Organization for Cinema and Audiovisual (1928, The Hague, The Netherlands): Rue du Saphir, 15, B-1040 Brussels, Belgium (general secretariat). Federation of National Catholic film offices.

International Catholic Society for Girls (1897): 37-39, rue de Vermont, CH-1202 Geneva, Switzerland.

International Catholic Union of the Press: 37-39 rue de Vermont, Case Postale 197, CH-1211 Geneva 20 CIC, Switzerland. Coordinates and represents at the international level the activities of Catholics and Catholic federations or associations in the field of press and information. Has seven specialized branches: International Federation of Catholic Journalists; International Federation of Dailies; International Federation of Periodicals; International Federation of Catholic News Agencies; International Catholic Federation of Teachers and Researchers in the Science and Techniques of Information; International Federation of Church Press Associations; and International Federation of Book Publishers.

International Conference of Catholic Guiding (1965): c/o Mlle Francoise Parmentier, rue de la Tour 64, 75016 Paris. Founded by member bodies of interdenominational World Association of Guides and Girl Scouts.

International Coordination of Young Christian Workers (YCYCW): via dei Barbieri 22, I00186 Rome, Italy.

International Council of Catholic Men (ICCM) (Unum Omnes) (1948): Wahringer Str. 2-4, A.1090 Vienna IX, Austria.

International Federation of Catholic Medical Associations (1954): Palazzo San Calisto, I-00120 Vatican City.

International Federation of Catholic Parochial Youth Communities (1962, Rome, Italy): St. Kariliquai 12, 6000 Lucerne 5, Switzerland.

International Federation of Catholic Pharmacists (1954): Bosdorf 180, 9190 Stekene, Belgium.

International Federation of Rural Adult Catholic Movements (1964, Lisbon, Portugal): Rue Jaumain 15, B-5330 Assesse, Belgium.

International Federation of Catholic Universities (1949): 21, rue d'Assas, F-75270 Paris Cedex 06, France.

International Federation of the Catholic Associations of the Blind: Avenue Dailly 90, B-1030 Brussels, Belgium. Coordinates actions of Catholic groups and associations for the blind and develops their apostolate.

International Independent Christian Youth (IICY): 11, rue Martin Bernard, F-75013 Paris, France.

International Military Apostolate (1967): Breite Strasse 25. D-53111 Bonn, Germany. Comprised of organizations of military men.

International Movement of Apostolate of Children (1929, France): 24, rue Paul Rivet, F-92350 Le Plessis Robinson, France.

International Movement of Apostolate in the Independent Social Milieux (MIAMSI) (1963): Piazza San Calisto 16, 00153 Rome, Italy.

International Movement of Catholic Agricultural and Rural Youth (1954, Annevoie, Belgium): 53, rue J. Coosemans, B-1030 Brussels, Belgium (permanent secretariat).

International Young Catholic Students (1946, Fribourg, Switzerland; present name, 1954): 171 rue de Rennes, F-75006 Paris, France.

Pax Romana (1921, Fribourg, Switzerland, divided into two branches, 1947): **Pax Roman-IMCS (International Movement of Catholic Students)** (1921): 171, rue de Rennes, F-75006, Paris, France, or undergraduates; **Pax Romana-ICMICA (International Catholic Movement for Intellectual and Cultural Affairs)** (1947): rue du Grand Bureau 15, CH-1227 Geneva, Switzerland. For Catholic intellectuals and professionals.

Society of St. Vincent de Paul (1833, Paris): 5, rue du Pré-aux-Clercs, F-75007 Paris, France.

Unda: International Catholic Association for Radio and Television (1928, Cologne, Germany): rue de l'Orme, 12, B-1040 Brussels, Belgium.

World Movement of Christian Workers (1961): Blvd. du Jubilé 124, 1080 Brussels, Belgium.

World Organization of Former Pupils of Catholic Education (1967, Rome): 48, rue de Richelieu, F-75001 Paris, France.

World Union of Catholic Teachers (1951): Piazza San Calisto 16, 00153 Rome, Italy.

World Union of Catholic Women's Organizations (1910): 18, rue Notre Dame des Champs, F-75006 Paris, France.

Other Catholic Organizations

Apostleship of Prayer (1849): Borgo Santo Spirito 5, I-00193 Rome, Italy. National secretariat in most countries.

Apostolatus Maris (Apostleship of the Sea) (1922, Glasgow, Scotland): Pontifical Council for Migrants and Itinerant People, Piazza San Calisto 16, 00153 Rome, Italy. (See Index.)

L'Arche Communities: B.P. 35, 60350 Cuise Lamotte, France.

Associationes Juventutis Salesianae (Associations of Salesian Youth) (1847): Via della Pisana, 1111, 00163 Rome, Italy.

Blue Army of Our Lady of Fatima: P.O. Box 976, Washington, NJ, 07882.

Catholic International Federation for Physical and Sports Education (1911; present name, 1957): 5, rue Cernuschi, F-75017 Paris, France.

Christian Fraternity of the Sick and Handicapped: 9, Avenue de la Gare, CH-1630, Bulle, Switzerland.

"Communione e Liberazione" Fraternity (1955, Milan, Italy): Via Marcello Malpighi 2, 00161 Rome, Italy. Catholic renewal movement.

"Focolare Movement" or "Work of Mary" (1943, Trent, Italy): Via di Frascati, 306, I-00040 Rocca di Papa (Rome), Italy.

Foi et Lumiere: 8 rue Serret, 75015 Paris, France.

Franciscans International: 345 E. 47th St., New York, NY 10017. A non-governmental organization at the UN.

Inter Cultural Association (ICA, 1937, Belgium) and **Association Fraternelle Internationale** (AFI): 91, rue de la Servette, CH-1202 Geneva, Switzerland.

International Association of Children of Mary (1847): 67 rue de Sèvres, F-75006 Paris, France.

International Catholic Rural Association (1962, Rome): Piazza San Calisto, 00153 Rome, Italy. International body for agricultural and rural organizations. Invited member of ICO.

International Catholic Union of Esperanto: Via Berni 9, 00185 Rome, Italy.

International Centre for Studies in Religious Education LUMEN VITAE (1934-35, Louvain, Belgium, under name Catechetical Documentary Centre; present name, 1956): 184, rue Washington, B-1050 Brussels, Belgium. Also referred to as Lumen Vitae Centre; concerned with all aspects of religious formation.

International Young Christian Workers (1925, Belgium): 11, rue Plantin, B-1070 Brussels, Belgium. Associate member of ICO.

Legion of Mary (1921, Dublin, Ireland): De Montfort House, North Brunswick St., Dublin, Ireland. (See **Index**.)

Medicus Mundi Internationalis (1964, Bensberg, Germany FR): P.O. Box 1547, 6501 BM Nijmegen, Netherlands. To promote health and medico-social services, particularly in developing countries; recruit essential health and medical personnel for developing countries; contribute to training of medical and auxiliary personnel; undertake research in the field of health.

NOVALIS, Marriage Preparation Center: University of St. Paul, 1 rue Stewart, Ottawa 2, ON Canada.

Our Lady's Teams (Equipes Notre-Dame) (1937, France): 49, rue de la Glacière, F-75013 Paris, France. Movement for spiritual formation of couples.

Pax Christi International (1950): rue du Vieux Marché aux grains 21, B-1000 Brussels, Belgium. International Catholic peace movement. Originated in Lourdes, France, in 1948 by French and German Catholics to reconcile enemies from World War II; spread to Italy and Poland and acquired its international title when it merged with the English organization Pax. Associate member of ICO.

Pro Sanctity Movement: Piazza S. Andrea della Valle 3, 00166 Rome, Italy.

St. Joan's International Alliance (1911, in England, as Catholic Women's Suffrage Society): Quai Churchill 19-Boite 061, B-4020 Liège, Belgium. Associate member of ICO.

Salesian Cooperators (1876, Turin, Italy): **Salesian Cooperators**: Founded by St. John Bosco; for lay men and women and diocesan clergy. A public association of the faithful, members commit themselves to apostolates in the local Church, especially on behalf of the young, in the Salesian spirit and style. Address: 114 Filors Lane, Stony Point, NY 10980-2645; (845) 947-2200.

Secular Franciscan Order (1221, first Rule approved): Via Piemonte, 70, 00187, Rome, Italy.

Secular Fraternity of Charles de Foucauld: Katharinenweg 4, B4700 Eupen, Belgium.

Serra International (1953, in U.S.): 65 E. Wacker Pl. Suite 1210, Chicago, IL 60601.

Unio Internationalis Laicorum in Servitio Ecclesiae (1965, Aachen, Germany): Postfach 990125, Am Kielshof 2, 5000 Cologne, Germany 91. Consists of national and diocesan associations of persons who give professional services to the Church.

Union of Adorers of the Blessed Sacrament (1937): Largo dei Monti Parioli 3, I-00197, Rome, Italy.

World Catholic Federation for the Biblical Apostolate (1969, Rome): Mittelstrasse, 12, P.O. Box 601, D-7000, Stuttgart 1, Germany.

Regional Organizations

European Federation for Catholic Adult Education (1963, Lucerne, Switzerland): Hirschengraben 13, P.B. 2069, CH-6002 Lucerne, Switzerland.

European Forum of National Committees of the Laity (1968): 169, Booterstown Av., Blackrock, Co. Dublin, Ireland.

Movimiento Familiar Cristiano (1949-50, Montevideo and Buenos Aires): Carrera 17 n. 4671, Bogotá, D.E., Colombia. Christian Family Movement of Latin America.

Eastern Catholic Churches

(*Sources: Rev. Ronald Roberson, C.S.P., Associate Director, Ecumenical and Interreligious Affairs, USCCB.; Annuario Pontificio*; Official Catholic Directory.)

The Second Vatican Council, in its Decree on Eastern Catholic Churches (*Orientalium Ecclesiarum*), stated the following points regarding Eastern heritage, patriarchs, sacraments and worship.

Venerable Churches: The Catholic Church holds in high esteem the institutions of the Eastern Churches, their liturgical rites, ecclesiastical traditions, and Christian way of life. For, distinguished as they are by their venerable antiquity, they are bright with that tradition which was handed down from the Apostles through the Fathers, and which forms part of the divinely revealed and undivided heritage of the universal Church (No. 1). That Church, Holy and Catholic, which is the Mystical Body of Christ, is made up of the faithful who are organically united in the Holy Spirit through the same faith, the same sacraments, and the same government and who, combining into various groups held together by a hierarchy, form separate Churches or rites. It is the mind of the Catholic Church that each individual Church or rite retain its traditions whole and entire, while adjusting its way of life to the various needs of time and place (No. 2).

Such individual Churches, whether of the East or of the West, although they differ somewhat among themselves in what are called rites (that is, in liturgy, ecclesiastical discipline, and spiritual heritage) are, nevertheless, equally entrusted to the pastoral guidance of the Roman Pontiff, the divinely appointed successor of St. Peter in supreme government over the universal Church. They are consequently of equal dignity, so that none of them is superior to the others by reason of rite (No. 3).

Eastern Heritage: Each and every Catholic, as also the baptized of every non-Catholic Church or community who enters into the fullness of Catholic communion, should everywhere retain his proper rite, cherish it, and observe it to the best of his ability (No. 4). The Churches of the East, as much as those of the West, fully enjoy the right, and are in duty bound, to rule themselves. Each should do so according to its proper and individual procedures (No. 5). All Eastern rite members should know and be convinced that they can and should always preserve their lawful liturgical rites and their established way of life, and that these should not be altered except by way of an appropriate and organic development (No. 6)

Patriarchs: The institution of the patriarchate has existed in the Church from the earliest times and was recognized by the first ecumenical Synods. By the name Eastern Patriarch is meant the bishop who has jurisdiction over all bishops (including metropolitans), clergy, and people of his own territory or rite, in accordance with the norms of law and without prejudice to the primacy of the Roman Pontiff (No. 7). Though some of the patriarchates of the Eastern Churches are of later origin than others, all are equal in patriarchal dignity. Still the honorary and lawfully established order of precedence among them is to be preserved (No. 8). In keeping with the most ancient tradition of the Church, the Patriarchs of the Eastern Churches are to be accorded exceptional respect, since each presides over his patriarchate as father and head. This sacred Synod, therefore, decrees that their rights and privileges should be re-established in accord with the ancient traditions of each Church and the decrees of the ecumenical Synods. The rights and privileges in question are those which flourished when East and West were in union, though they should be somewhat adapted to modern conditions.

The Patriarchs with their synods constitute the superior authority for all affairs of the patriarchate, including the right to establish new eparchies and to nominate bishops of their rite within the territorial bounds of the patriarchate, without prejudice to the inalienable right of the Roman Pontiff to intervene in individual cases (No. 9).

What has been said of Patriarchs applies as well, under the norm of law, to major archbishops, who preside over the whole of some individual Church or rite (No. 10).

Sacraments: This sacred Ecumenical Synod endorses and lauds the ancient discipline of the sacraments existing in the Eastern Churches, as also the practices connected with their celebration and administration (No. 12).

With respect to the minister of holy chrism (confirmation), let that practice be fully restored which existed among Easterners in most ancient times. Priests, therefore, can validly confer this sacrament, provided they use chrism blessed by a Patriarch or bishop (No. 13).

In conjunction with baptism or otherwise, all Eastern-Rite priests can confer this sacrament validly on all the faithful of any rite, including the Latin; licitly, however, only if the regulations of both common and particular law are observed. Priests of the Latin rite, to the extent of the faculties they enjoy for administering this sacrament, can confer it also on the faithful of Eastern Churches, without prejudice to rite.

They do so licitly if the regulations of both common and particular law are observed (No. 14).

The faithful are bound on Sundays and feast days to attend the divine liturgy or, according to the regulations or custom of their own rite, the celebration of the Divine Praises. That the faithful may be able to satisfy their obligation more easily, it is decreed that this obligation can be fulfilled from the Vespers of the vigil to the end of the Sunday or the feast day (No. 15). Because of the everyday intermingling of the communicants of diverse Eastern Churches in the same Eastern region or territory, the faculty for hearing confession, duly and unrestrictedly granted by his proper bishop to a priest of any rite, is applicable to the entire territory of the grantor, also to the places and the faithful belonging to any other rite in the same territory, unless an Ordinary of the place explicitly decides otherwise with respect to the places pertaining to his rite (No. 16).

This sacred Synod ardently desires that where it has fallen into disuse the office of the permanent diaconate be restored. The legislative authority of each individual church should decide about the subdiaconate and the minor orders (No. 17).

By way of preventing invalid marriages between Eastern Catholics and baptized Eastern non-Catholics, and in the interests of the permanence and sanctity of marriage and of domestic harmony, this sacred Synod decrees that the canonical 'form' for the celebration of such marriages obliges only for lawfulness. For their validity, the presence of a sacred minister suffices, as long as the other requirements of law are honored (No. 18).

Worship: Henceforth, it will be the exclusive right of an ecumenical Synod or the Apostolic See to establish, transfer, or suppress feast days common to all the Eastern Churches. To establish, transfer, or suppress feast days for any of the individual Churches is within the competence not only of the Apostolic See but also of a patriarchal or archiepiscopal synod, provided due consideration is given to the entire region and to other individual Churches (No. 19). Until such time as all Christians desirably concur on a fixed day for the celebration of Easter, and with a view meantime to promoting unity among the Christians of a given area or nation, it is left to the Patriarchs or supreme authorities of a place to reach a unanimous agreement, after ascertaining the views of all concerned, on a single Sunday for the observance of Easter (No. 20). With respect to rules concerning sacred seasons, individual faithful dwelling outside the area or territory of their own rite may conform completely to the established custom of the place where they live. When members of a family belong to different rites, they are all permitted to observe sacred seasons according to the rules of any one of these rites (No. 21). From ancient times the Divine Praises have been held in high esteem among all Eastern Churches. Eastern clerics and religious should celebrate these Praises as the laws and customs of their own traditions require. To the extent they can, the faithful too should follow the example of their forebears by assisting devoutly at the Divine Praises (No. 22).

Restoration of Ancient Practices

An "Instruction for the Application of the Liturgical Prescriptions of the Code of Canons of the Eastern Churches" was published in Italian by the Congregation for Eastern-Rite Churches in January, 1996. Msgr. Alan Detscher, executive director of the U.S. bishops' Secretariat for the Liturgy, said it was the first instruction on liturgical renewal of the Eastern Catholic Churches since the Second Vatican Council (1962-65).

JURISDICTIONS AND FAITHFUL OF THE EASTERN CATHOLIC CHURCHES

Introduction

The Church originated in Palestine, whence it spread to other regions of the world where certain places became key centers of Christian life with great influence on the local churches in their respective areas. These centers developed into the ancient patriarchates of Constantinople, Alexandria, Antioch and Jerusalem in the East, and Rome in the West. The main lines of Eastern Church patriarchal organization and usages were drawn before the Roman Empire became two empires, East (Byzantine) and West (Roman), in 292. Other churches with distinctive traditions grew up beyond the boundaries of the Roman Empire in Persia, Armenia, Syria, Egypt, Ethiopia, and India. The "nestorian" church in Persia, known today as the Assyrian Church of the East, broke communion with the rest of the church in the wake of the Council of Ephesus (431) whose teachings it did not accept. The "monophysite" churches of Armenia, Syria, Egypt, Ethiopia, Eritrea and India (known today as the Oriental Orthodox Churches) did not accept the christological teachings of the Council of Chalcedon (451) and so broke away from the church within the Roman Empire. And finally, in the wake of the mutual excommunications of 1054 between the Patriarch of Constantinople and the papal legate, the church within the empire divided into what would become the Catholic Church in the West and the Orthodox Church in the East. This was a lengthy process of estrangement that culminated only in 1204 and the sack of Constantinople by the Latin Crusaders.

In the following centuries, attempts to overcome these divisions took place, most notably at the Second Council of Lyons in 1274 and the Council of Ferrara-Florence in 1438-39. Both failed. Subsequently, the Catholic Church began to send missionaries to work with separated Eastern Christians, and some groups within those churches spontaneously asked to enter into full communion with Rome. Thus began the formation of the Eastern Catholic Churches, which retained most of the liturgical, canonical, spiritual and theological patrimony of their non-Catholic counterparts.

The Code of Canons of the Eastern Churches groups these churches today into four categories: patriarchal, major archepiscopal, metropolitan, and other churches *sui iuris*.

STATISTICS

(Principal source: Annuario Pontificio.*)*

The following statistics are the sum of those reported for Eastern Catholic jurisdictions only, and do not include Eastern Catholics under the jurisdiction of Latin bishops. Some of the figures reported are only approximate. The churches are grouped according to their liturgical traditions.

PATRIARCHS

The current six Patriarchs of the Eastern Catholic Churches (as of Aug. 15, 2002) are as follows:

Abdel-Ahad, Ignatius Peter VIII: b. June 28, 1930; ord. Oct. 17, 1954; cons. bp. June 21, 1997; Patriarch of Antioch of the Syrians, Feb. 16, 2001; granted "ecclesiastical communion" with Pope John Paul II, Feb. 20, 2001.

Bidawid, Raphaël I: b. Apr. 17, 1922; ord. Oct. 22, 1944; patriarch of Babylon of the Chaldeans, May 21, 1989; granted "ecclesiastical communion" with Pope John Paul II, June 11, 1989.

Ghattas, Stéphanos II, C.M.: Patriarch of Alexandria; for details, see under Cardinals, College of.

Laham, Gregory III: b. Dec. 15, 1933; ord. Feb. 15, 1959; cons. bp., Nov. 27, 1981; patriarch of Greek Melkites, Nov. 29, 2000; granted "ecclesiastical communion" with Pope John Paul II, Dec. 5, 2000.

Sfeir, Nasrallah Pierre: Patriarch of Antioch of the Maronites; for details, see under Cardinals, College of.

Tarmouni, Nerses XIX Bedros: b. Jan. 17, 1940, in Cairo, Egypt; ord. Aug. 15, 1965; patriarch of Cilicia of the Armenians, Oct. 7, 1999; granted "ecclesiastical communion" with the Pope John Paul II, Oct. 13, 1999.

ALEXANDRIAN

The liturgical tradition of Egypt, in particular that of the early Greek Patriarchate of Alexandria. In the Egyptian desert monasteries the rite evolved in a distinctive way and eventually became that of the Coptic Orthodox Church. The Greek Patriarchate of Alexandria adopted the Byzantine rite by the 12th century. The Coptic rite, with its Alexandrian origins, spread to Ethiopia in the 4th century where it underwent substantial modifications under strong Syrian influence. The Catholic Churches in this group are:

The **Coptic Catholic Church** (Patriarchate): Six dioceses in Egypt, 212,668.

Catholic missionaries were present since the 17th century. The Patriarchate was established first in 1824 and renewed in 1895. Liturgical languages are Coptic and Arabic.

The **Ethiopian Catholic Church** (Metropolitanate): Two dioceses in Ethiopia and three in Eritrea; 199,909. Catholic missionary activity began in the 19th century, and the present ecclesiastical structure dates from 1961. The liturgical languages are Ge'ez and Amharic.

ANTIOCHIAN

The liturgical tradition of Antioch, one of the great centers of the early Christian world, also known as West Syrian. In Syria it developed under strong influence of Jerusalem, especially the Liturgy of St. James, into the form used by today's Syrian Orthodox and Catholics in the Middle East and India. The Maronites of Lebanon developed their own liturgical traditions under the influence of both the Antiochian and Chaldean rites.

The Catholic Churches of this group are:

The **Syro-Malankara Catholic Church** (Metropolitanate): Four diocese in India; 450,400.

Began in 1930 when two bishops, a priest, a deacon and a layman of the Malankara Orthodox Church were received into full communion with Rome. The liturgical language is Malayalam.

The **Maronite Catholic Church (Patriarchate)**: Ten dioceses in Lebanon, three in Syria, two in the United States, and one each in Cyprus, Egypt, Argentina, Brazil, Australia, Canada, and Mexico, plus patriarchal exarchates in Jordan and Jerusalem; 3,035,054.

Founded by St. Maron in the 4th century, the Maronites claim to have always been in communion with Rome. They have no counterpart among the separated Eastern churches. The patriarchate dates to the 8th century, and was confirmed by Pope Innocent III in 1216. Liturgical language is Arabic.

The **Syrian Catholic Church (Patriarchate)**: Four dioceses in Syria, two in Iraq, and one each in Lebanon, Egypt, and North America, and patriarchal exarchates in Turkey and Iraq/Kuwait; 132,114.

Catholic missionary activity among the Syrian Orthodox began in the 17th century, and there has been an uninterrupted series of Catholic patriarchs since 1783. The liturgical languages are Syriac/Aramaic and Arabic.

ARMENIAN

The liturgical tradition of the Armenian Apostolic and Catholic Churches. It contains elements of the Syriac, Jerusalem, and Byzantine rites. From the 5th to the 7th centuries there was strong influence from Syria and Jerusalem. More Byzantine usages were adopted later, and in the Middle Ages elements of the Latin tradition were added.

The **Armenian Catholic Church (Patriarchate)**: Two dioceses in Syria, one each in Lebanon, Iran, Iraq, Egypt, Turkey, Ukraine, France and Argentina. Apostolic Exarchate for the United States, and Ordinariates in Greece, Romania, and Eastern Europe (Armenia); 369,374.

Catholic missionaries had been working among the Armenians since the 14th century, and an Armenian Catholic patriarchate was established in Lebanon in 1742. The liturgical language is classical Armenian. His Beatitude Nerses Bedros XIX Tarmouni, canonically elected as patriarch of Cilicia of the Armenians, by the Synod of Bishops of the Armenian Catholic Church was approved by Pope John Paul II on October 18, 1999.

BYZANTINE

The tradition of the Eastern Orthodox and Byzantine Catholic Churches which originated in the Orthodox Patriarchate of Constantinople (Byzantium). Its present form is a synthesis of Constantinopolitan and Palestinian elements that took place in the monasteries between the 9th and 14th centuries. It is by far the most widely used Eastern liturgical tradition. The Catholic Churches of this group are:

Albanians: One apostolic administration in southern Albania; 2,655. Very small groups of Albanian Orthodox became Catholic in 1628 and again in 1900; liturgical language is Albanian.

Belarusans (formerly Byelorussian, also known as White Russian): No hierarchy. Most Belarusan Orthodox became Catholic with the Union of Brest in 1595-6, but this union was short lived. A modest revival has taken place since the end of communism. The liturgical language is Belarusan.

The Bulgarian Catholic Church: One apostolic exarchate in Bulgaria; 15,000. Originated with a group of Bulgarian Orthodox who became Catholic in 1861; liturgical language is Old Slavonic.

Eparchy of Krizevci: One diocese located in Croatia with jurisdiction over all of former Yugoslavia; 42,579. A bishop for former Serbian Orthodox living in Catholic Croatia was first appointed in 1611; liturgical languages are Old Slavonic and Croatian.

The Greek Catholic Church: Apostolic exarchates in Greece and Turkey; 2,345. Catholic missionaries in Constantinople formed a small group of Byzantine Catholics there in the mid-19th century. Most of them moved to Greece in the 1920s. The liturgical language is Greek.

The Hungarian Catholic Church: One diocese and one apostolic exarchate in Hungary: 278,000.

Descendants of groups of Orthodox in Hungary who became Catholic in the 17th century and after. The liturgical language is Hungarian.

The Italo-Albanian Catholic Church: Two dioceses, one territorial abbey in Italy; 61,198.

Descended mostly from Albanian Orthodox who came to southern Italy and Sicily in the 15th century and eventually became Catholic; liturgical languages are Greek and Italian.

The Melkite Greek Catholic Church (Patriarchate): Five dioceses in Syria, seven in Lebanon, one each in Jordan, Israel, Brazil, US, Canada, Mexico, and Australia. Apostolic Exarchate in Venezuela, and patriarchal exarchates in Iraq and Kuwait; 1,283,304.

Catholic missionaries began work within the Greek Orthodox Patriarchate of Antioch in the mid-17th century. In 1724 it split into Catholic and Orthodox counterparts, the Catholics becoming known popularly as Melkites. Liturgical languages are Greek and Arabic.

The Romanian Greek Catholic Church (Metropolitanate): Five dioceses in Romania and one in the US; 781,704.

Romanian Orthodox in Transylvania formally entered into union with Rome in 1700; the liturgical language is Romanian.

Russians: No hierarchy. An apostolic exarchate was established for Russia in 1917 and for Russians in China in 1928, but neither is functioning today. Five parishes exist in the diaspora.

The Ruthenian Catholic Church (Metropolitanate in the United States): One diocese in Ukraine, four in the United States, and an apostolic exarchate in the Czech Republic. Originated with the reception of 63 Orthodox priests into the Catholic Church at the Union of Uzhhorod in 1646. Liturgical languages are Old Slavonic and English; 683,539.

The Slovak Catholic Church: One diocese and one apostolic exarchate in Slovakia, and one diocese in Canada; 255,292.

Also originated with the Union of Uzhhorod in 1646; diocese of Presov was established for them in 1818. Liturgical languages are Old Slavonic and Slovak.

The Ukrainian Greek Catholic Church (Major Archbishopric): Six dioceses and one archepiscopal exarchate in Ukraine, two dioceses in Poland, five dioceses in Canada, four in the United States, one

each in Australia, Brazil and Argentina, apostolic exarchates in Great Britain, Germany, and France; 4,127,760.

Originated with the Union of Brest between the Orthodox Metropolitanate of Kiev and the Catholic Church in 1595-6. Liturgical languages are Old Slavonic and Ukrainian.

CHALDEAN

Also called East Syrian, the liturgical tradition of the Chaldean Catholic and Syro-Malabar Catholic Churches as well as the Assyrian Church of the East. Descends from the ancient rite of the church of Mesopotamia in the Persian Empire. It is celebrated in the eastern dialect of classical Syriac. The Catholic Churches of this tradition are:

The Chaldean Catholic Church (Patriarchate): Ten dioceses in Iraq, three in Iran, two in the U.S., one each in Lebanon, Egypt, Syria, and Turkey; 344,473.

A group of disaffected members of the ("nestorian") Assyrian Church of the East asked for union with Rome in 1553. In that year Pope Julius III ordained their leader a bishop and named him Patriarch; liturgical languages are Syriac, Arabic.

The Syro-Malabar Catholic Church (Major Archbishopric): 22 dioceses in India, one in the U.S.; 3,546,198.

Descended from Thomas Christians of India who became Catholic in the wake of Portuguese colonization; the diocese of Ernakulam-Angamaly was raised to Major Archepiscopal status in 1993; the liturgical language is Malayalam.

EASTERN JURISDICTIONS

For centuries Eastern Churches were identifiable with a limited number of nationality and language groups in certain countries of the Middle East, Eastern Europe, Asia and Africa. The persecution of religion in the former Soviet Union since 1917 and in communist-controlled countries for more than 40 years following World War II — in addition to decimating and destroying the Church in those places — resulted in the emigration of many Eastern Catholics from their homelands. This forced emigration, together with voluntary emigration, has led to the spread of Eastern Churches to many other countries.

Europe

(Bishop Krikor Ghabroyan, of the Armenian Eparchy of Sainte-Croix-de-Paris, France, is apostolic visitator for Armenian Catholics in Western Europe who do not have their own bishop. Bishop Youssef Ibrahim Sarraf of Cairo of the Chaldeans is apostolic visitator for Chaldeans in Europe. Bishop Samis Mazloum is apostolic visitator for Maronites in Western and Northern Europe.)

Albania: Byzantine apostolic administration.

Austria: Byzantine ordinariate.

Bulgaria: Bulgarian apostolic exarchate

Croatia: Eparchy of Krizevci.

Czech Republic: Ruthenian apostolic exarchate.

France: Ukrainian apostolic exarchate. Armenian eparchy (1986). Ordinariate for all other Eastern Catholics.

Germany: Ukrainian apostolic exarchate.

Great Britain: Ukrainian apostolic exarchate.

Greece: Byzantine apostolic exarchate. Armenian ordinariate.

Hungary: Hungarian Byzantine eparchy, apostolic exarchate

Italy: Two Italo-Albanian eparchies, one abbacy.

Poland: Ukrainian metropolitan see (1996), one eparchy. Ordinariate for all other Eastern Catholics.

Romania: Romanian Byzantine metropolitan, four eparchies; Armenian ordinariate.

Russia: Russian apostolic exarchate (for Byzantine Catholics in Moscow).

Slovakia: Slovak Byzantine eparchy, one apostolic exarchate.

Ukraine: Armenian archeparchy; Ruthenian eparchy; Ukrainian major archbishopric, seven eparchies.

Asia

Armenia: Armenian ordinariate (for Armenians of Eastern Europe).

China: Russian Byzantine apostolic exarchate.

Cyprus: Maronite archeparchy.

India: Syro-Malankara metropolitan see, three eparchies.

Syro-Malabar major archbishopric (1993), three metropolitan sees (1995), 18 eparchies.

Iran: Two Chaldean metropolitan sees, one archeparchy, one eparchy; Armenian eparchy.

Iraq: Two Syrian archeparchies; Melkite patriarchal exarchate; Chaldean patriarchate, two metropolitan sees, three archeparchies and five eparchies; Armenian archeparchy.

Israel (including Jerusalem): Syrians patriarchal exarchate; Maronite archeparchy; Melkite archeparchy, patriarchal exarchate; Chaldean patriarchal exarchate; Armenian patriarchal exarchate.

Jordan: Melkite archeparchy.

Kuwait: Melkite patriarchal exarchate; Syrian patriarchate exarchate.

Syria: Two Maronite archeparchies, one eparchy; two Syrian metropolitan and two archeparchal sees; Melkite patriarchate, four metropolitan sees, one archeparchy; Chaldean eparchy; Armenian archeparchy, one eparchy.

Turkey: Syrian patriarchal exarchate; Greek apostolic exarchate; Chaldean archeparchy; Armenian archeparchy.

Oceania

Australia: Ukrainian eparchy; Melkite eparchy (1987); Maronite eparchy.

Africa

Egypt: Coptic patriarchate, five eparchies; Maronite eparchy; Syrian eparchy; Melkite patriarchal dependency; Chaldean eparchy; Armenian eparchy.

Eritrea: Three Ethiopian eparchies.

Ethiopia: Ethiopian metropolitan see, one eparchy.

Sudan: Melkite patriarchal dependency.

North America

Canada: One Ukrainian metropolitan, four eparchies; Slovak eparchy; Melkite eparchy; Armenian apostolic exarchate for Canada and the U.S. (New York is see city); Maronite eparchy.

United States: Two Maronite eparchies; Syrian eparchy (1995); one Ukrainian metropolitan see, three eparchies; one Ruthenian metropolitan see, three eparchies; Melkite eparchy; Romanian eparchy; a new Syro-Malabar eparchy based in Chicago; Belarusan apostolic visitator; Armenian apostolic exarchate for Canada and U.S. (New York is see city); two Chaldean eparchies; other Eastern Catholics are under the jurisdiction of local Latin bishops. (See Eastern Catholics in the United States.)

Mexico: Melkite eparchy; Maronite eparchy (1995).

South America

Armenian Catholics in Latin America (including Mexico and excluding Argentina) are under the jurisdiction of an apostolic exarchate (see city, Buenos Aires, Argentina).

Argentina: Ukrainian eparchy; Maronite eparchy; Armenian eparchy; ordinariate for all other Eastern Catholics.

Brazil: Maronite eparchy; Melkite eparchy; Ukrainian eparchy; ordinariate for all other Eastern Catholics.

Venezuela: Melkite apostolic exarchate.

Synods, Assemblies

These assemblies are collegial bodies that have pastoral authority over members of the Eastern Catholic Churches. (Canons 102-113, 152-153, 322 of Oriental Code of Canon Law.)

Patriarchal Synods:

Synod of the Coptic Catholic Church: Stephanos II Ghattas, C.M., patriarch of Alexandria of the Copts.

Synod of the Greek-Melkite Catholic Church: Gregory III Laham, patriarch of Antioch of the Greek Catholics-Melkites.

Synod of the Syrian Catholic Church: Ignatius Peter VIII, patriarch of Antioch of the Syrians.

Synod of the Maronite Church: Cardinal Nasrallah Pierre Sfeir, patriarch of Antioch of the Maronites.

Synod of the Chaldean Church: Raphaël I Bidawid, patriarch of Babylonia of the Chaldeans.

Synod of the Armenian Catholic Church: Nerses Bedros XIX Tarmouni, patriarch of Cilicia of the Armenians.

Major Archiepiscopal Synods:

The Synod of the Ukrainian Catholic Church (raised to major archiepiscopal status Dec. 23, 1963): Cardinal Lubomir Husar, major archbishop of Lviv of the Ukrainians, president.

The Synod of the Syro-Malabar Church (raised to major archiepiscopal status, Jan. 29, 1993): Cardinal Varkey Vithayathil, C.SS.R., major archbishop of Ernakulam-Angamaly of the Syro-Malabars, president.

Councils, Assemblies, Conferences

Council of Ethiopian Churches: Most Rev. Berhane-Yesus Demerew Souraphiel, C.M. of Addis Ababa, president.

Council of Romanian Churches: Abp. Lucian Muresan of Fagaras and Alba Julia, president.

Council of Ruthenian Churches, U.S.A.: Metropolitan of Pittsburgh of the Byzantines, presently vacant, president.

Council of Syro-Malankarese Churches: Abp.

Cyril Baselios Malancharuvil, O.I.C., of Trivandrum of the Syro-Malankarese, president.

Assembly of the Catholic Hierarchy of Egypt (Dec. 5, 1983): Cardinal Stéphanos II Ghattas, C.M., patriarch of Alexandria of the Copts, president.

Assembly of Catholic Patriarchs and Bishops of Lebanon: Cardinal Nasrallah Pierre Sfeir, patriarch of Antioch of the Maronites, president.

Assembly of Ordinaries of the Syrian Arab Republic: Maximos V Hakim, patriarch of Antioch of the Greek Catholics-Melkites, president.

Assembly of Catholic Ordinaries of the Holy Land (Jan. 27, 1992): Michel Sabbah, patriarch of Jerusalem of the Latins, president.

Interritual Union of the Bishops of Iraq: Raphaël I Bidawid, patriarch of Babylonia of the Chaldeans, president.

Iranian Episcopal Conference (Aug. 11, 1977): Most Rev. Vartan Tékéyan, bishop of Ispahan of the Armenians of the Armenians, president.

Episcopal Conference of Turkey (Nov. 30, 1987): Most Rev. Louis A. Pelâtre, A.A., vicar apostolic of Istanbul, president.

EASTERN CATHOLIC CHURCHES IN U.S.

(*Statistics, from the* Annuario Pontificio *unless noted otherwise, are membership figures reported by Eastern jurisdictions. Additional Eastern Catholics are included in statistics for Latin dioceses.*)

Byzantine Tradition

Ukrainians: There were 104,300 reported in four jurisdictions in the U.S.: the metropolitan see of Philadelphia (1924, metropolitan 1958) and the suffragan sees of Stamford, Conn. (1956), St. Nicholas of Chicago (1961) and St. Josaphat in Parma (1983).

Ruthenians: There were 116,539 reported in four jurisdictions in the U.S.: the metropolitan see of Pittsburgh (est. 1924 at Pittsburgh; metropolitan and transferred to Munhall, 1969; transferred to Pittsburgh, 1977) and the suffragan sees of Passaic, N.J. (1963), Parma, Ohio (1969) and Van Nuys, Calif. (1981). Hungarian and Croatian Byzantine Catholics in the U.S. are also under the jurisdiction of Ruthenian bishops.

Melkites: There were 27,934 reported under the jurisdiction of the Melkite eparchy of Newton, Mass. (established as an exarchate, 1965; eparchy, 1976).

Romanians: There were 5,000 reported in 15 Romanian Catholic Byzantine Rite parishes in the U.S., under the jurisdiction of the Romanian eparchy of St. George Martyr, Canton, Ohio (established as an exarchate, 1982; eparchy, 1987).

Belarusans: One parish in the U.S. — Christ the Redeemer, Chicago, IL.

Russians: Have parishes in California (St. Andrew, El Segundo, and Our Lady of Fatima Center, San Francisco); New York (St. Michael's Chapel of St. Patrick's Old Cathedral). They are under the jurisdiction of local Latin bishops.

Alexandrian Tradition

Copts: Have a Catholic Chapel — Resurrection, in Brooklyn, N.Y., and St. Mary's Coptic Catholic parish, Los Angeles, CA.

Antiochian Tradition

Maronites: There were 54,658 reported in two jurisdictions in the U.S.: the eparchy of St. Maron, Brooklyn (established at Detroit as an exarchate, 1966; eparchy, 1972; transferred to Brooklyn, 1977) and the eparchy of Our Lady of Lebanon of Los Angeles (resident in St. Louis, MO, established Mar. 1, 1994).

Syrians: The eparchy of Our Lady of the Deliverance of Newark with 12,180 faithful (see city, Newark, N.J.) was established in 1995 for Syrian Catholics of the U.S. and Canada.

Malankarese: Have a mission in Chicago.

Armenian Tradition

An apostolic exarchate for Canada and the United States (see city, New York) was established July 3, 1981; 36,000 in the two countries.

Chaldean Tradition

Chaldeans: There were 85,800 reported under the jurisdictions of the eparchy of St. Thomas the Apostle of Detroit (established as an exarchate, 1982; eparchy, 1986) and the eparchy of St. Peter the Apostle of San Diego (established on May 21, 2002).

Syro-Malabarese (Malabar): Have an eparchy based in Chicago and several other cities. Estimated 200,000 faithful with 50 priests.

Eastern Catholic Associates

Eastern Catholic Associates is the association of all Eastern Catholic bishops and their equivalents in law in the United States, representing the Armenian, Chaldean, Maronite, Melkite, Syriac, Romanian, Ruthenian and Ukrainian churches. The Syro-Malabar and Russian churches are also represented even though they do not have bishops in the U.S. President: Bishop Robert M. Moskal, Eparch of St. Josaphat, P.O. Box 347180, Parma, OH 44134. The Vice President is Bishop Basil Schott, OFM, Metropolitan Apb. of Pittsburgh.

The association meets at the same time as the National Conference of Catholic Bishops in the fall of each year.

BYZANTINE DIVINE LITURGY

The Divine Liturgy in all rites is based on the consecration of bread and wine by the narration-reactualization of the actions of Christ at the Last Supper, and the calling down of the Holy Spirit. Aside from this fundamental usage, there are differences between the Roman (Latin) Rite and Eastern Rites, and among the Eastern Rites themselves. Following is a general description of the Byzantine Divine Liturgy which is in widest use in the Eastern Churches.

In the Byzantine, as in all Eastern Rites, the bread and wine are prepared at the start of the Liturgy. The priest does this in a little niche or at a table in the sanctuary. Taking a round loaf of leavened bread stamped with religious symbols, he cuts out a square host and other particles while reciting verses expressing the symbolism of the action. When the bread and wine are ready, he says a prayer of offering and in-censes the oblations, the altar, the icons and the people.

Liturgy of the Catechumens: At the altar a litany for all classes of people is sung by the priest. The congregation answers, "Lord, have mercy." The Little Entrance comes next. In procession, the priest leaves the sanctuary carrying the Book of the Gospels, and then returns. He sings prayers especially selected for the day and the feast. These are followed by the sol-emn singing of the prayer, "Holy God, Holy Mighty One, Holy Immortal One." The Epistle follows. The Gospel is sung or read by the priest facing the people at the middle door of the sanctuary.

An interruption after the Liturgy of the Catechu-mens, formerly an instructional period for those learn-ing the faith, is clearly marked. Catechumens, if present, are dismissed with a prayer. Following this are a prayer and litany for the faithful.

Great Entrance: The Great Entrance or solemn Offertory Procession then takes place. The priest first says a long silent prayer for himself, in preparation for the great act to come. Again he incenses the obla-tions, the altar, the icons and people. He goes to the table on the Gospel side for the veil-covered paten and chalice. When he arrives back at the sanctuary door, he announces the intention of the Mass in the prayer: "May the Lord God remember all of you in his kingdom, now and forever." After another litany, the congregation recites the Nicene Creed.

Consecration: The most solemn portion of the sac-rifice is introduced by the preface, which is very much like the preface of the Roman Rite. At the beginning of the last phrase, the priest raises his voice to intro-duce the singing of the Sanctus. During the singing he reads the introduction to the words of consecra-tion. The words of consecration are sung aloud, and the people sing "Amen" to both consecrations. As the priest raises the Sacred Species in solemn offering, he sings: "Thine of Thine Own we offer unto Thee in behalf of all and for all." A prayer to the Holy Spirit is followed by the commemorations, in which special mention is made of the all-holy, most blessed and glo-rious Lady, the Mother of God and ever-Virgin Mary. The dead are remembered and then the living.

Holy Communion: A final litany for spiritual gifts precedes the Our Father. The Sacred Body and Blood are elevated with the words, "Holy Things for the Holy." The Host is then broken and commingled with the Precious Blood. The priest recites preparatory prayers for Holy Communion, consumes the Sacred Species, and distributes Holy Communion to the people under the forms of both bread and wine. Dur-ing this time the choir or congregation sings a com-munion verse.

The Liturgy closes quickly after this. The conse-crated Species of bread and wine are removed to the side table to be consumed later by the priest. A prayer of thanksgiving is recited, a prayer for all the people is said in front of the icon of Christ, a blessing is in-voked upon all, and the people are dismissed.

BYZANTINE CALENDAR

The Byzantine calendar has many distinctive fea-tures of its own, although it shares common elements with the Roman calendar — e.g., general purpose, commemoration of the mysteries of faith and of the saints, identical dates for some feasts. Among the dis-tinctive things are the following. The liturgical year begins on Sept. 1, the Day of Indiction, in contrast with the Latin or Roman start on the First Sunday of Advent late in November or early in December. The Advent season begins on Dec. 10.

Cycles of the Year

As in the Roman usage, the dating of feasts follows the Gregorian Calendar. Formerly, until well into this century, the Julian Calendar was used. (The Julian Calendar, which is now about 13 days late, is still used by some Eastern Churches.) The year has sev-eral cycles, which include proper seasons, the feasts of saints, and series of New Testament readings. All of these elements of worship are contained in liturgi-cal books of the rite. The ecclesiastical calendar, called the *Menologion,* explains the nature of feasts, other observances and matters pertaining to the liturgy for each day of the year. In some cases, its contents in-clude the lives of saints and the history and meaning of feasts.

The Divine Liturgy (Mass) and Divine Office for the proper of the saints, fixed feasts, and the Christ-mas season are contained in the *Menaion.* The *Triodion* covers the pre-Lenten season of preparation for Easter; Lent begins two days before the Ash Wednesday observance of the Roman Rite. The Pentecostarion contains the liturgical services from Easter to the Sunday of All Saints, the first after Pen-tecost. The *Evangelion* and *Apostolos* are books in which the Gospels, and Acts of the Apostles and the Epistles, respectively, are arranged according to the order of their reading in the Divine Liturgy and Di-vine Office throughout the year.

The cyclic progression of liturgical music through-out the year, in successive and repetitive periods of eight weeks, is governed by the *Oktoechos*, the *Book of Eight Tones.*

Sunday Names

Many Sundays are named after the subject of the Gospel read in the Mass of the day or after the name of a feast falling on the day — e.g., Sunday of the Publican and Pharisee, of the Prodigal Son, of the Samaritan Woman, of St. Thomas the Apostle, of the Fore-Fathers (Old Testament Patriarchs).

Other Sundays are named in the same manner as in the Roman calendar e.g., numbered Sundays of Lent and after Pentecost.

Holy Days

The calendar lists about 28 holy days. Many of the major holy days coincide with those of the Roman calendar, but the feast of the Immaculate Conception is observed on Dec. 9 instead of Dec. 8, and the feast of All Saints falls on the Sunday after Pentecost rather than on Nov. 1. Instead of a single All Souls' Day, there are five All Souls' Saturdays. According to regu-lations in effect in the Byzantine (Ruthenian) Archeparchy of Pittsburgh and its suffragan sees of Passaic, Parma and Van Nuys, holy days are obliga-tory, solemn and simple, and attendance at the Di-vine Liturgy is required on five obligatory days — the feasts of the Epiphany, the Ascension, Sts. Peter and Paul, the Assumption of the Blessed Virgin Mary, and Christmas. Although attendance at the liturgy is not obligatory on 15 solemn and seven simple holy days, it is recommended. In the Byzantine (Ukrainian) Archeparchy of Philadelphia and its suffragan sees of St. Josaphat in Parma, St. Nicholas (Chicago) and Stamford, the obligatory feasts are the Epiphany, Annunciation, Ascension, SS. Peter & Paul, Dormition, and Christmas.

Lent

The first day of Lent — the Monday before Ash Wednesday of the Roman Rite — and Good Friday are days of strict abstinence for persons in the age bracket of obligation. No meat, eggs, or dairy products may be eaten on these days. All persons over the age of 14 must abstain from meat on Fridays during Lent, Holy Saturday, and the vigils of the feasts of Christmas and Epiphany; abstinence is urged, but is not obligatory, on Wednesdays of Lent. The abstinence obligation is not in force on certain "free" or "privileged" Fridays.

Synaxis

An observance without a counterpart in the Roman calendar is the synaxis. This is a commemoration, on the day following a feast, of persons involved with the occasion for the feast — e.g., Sept. 9, the day following the feast of the Nativity of the Blessed Virgin Mary, is the Synaxis of Joachim and Anna, her parents.

Holy Week

In the Byzantine Rite, Lent is liturgically concluded with the Saturday of Lazarus, the day before Palm Sunday, which commemorates the raising of Lazarus from the dead. On the following Monday, Tuesday and Wednesday, the Liturgy of the Presanctified is prescribed.

On Holy Thursday, the Liturgy of St. Basil the Great is celebrated together with Vespers.

The Divine Liturgy is not celebrated on Good Friday. On Holy Saturday, the Liturgy of St. Basil the Great is celebrated along with Vespers.

BYZANTINE FEATURES

Art: Named for the empire in which it developed, Byzantine art is a unique blend of imperial Roman and classic Hellenic culture with Christian inspiration. The art of the Greek Middle Ages, it reached a peak of development in the 10th or 11th century. Characteristic of its products, particularly in mosaic and painting, are majesty, dignity, refinement and grace. Its sacred paintings, called icons, are reverenced highly in all the Eastern Churches of the Byzantine tradition.

Church Building: The classical model of Byzantine church architecture is the Church of the Holy Wisdom (*Hagia Sophia*), built in Constantinople in the first half of the sixth century and still standing. The square structure, extended in some cases in the form of a cross, is topped by a distinctive onion-shaped dome and surmounted by a triple-bar cross. The altar is at the eastern end of building, where the wall bellies out to form an apse. The altar and sanctuary are separated from the body of the church by a fixed or movable screen, the iconostas, to which icons or sacred pictures are attached (see below).

Clergy: The Byzantine Churches have married as well as celibate priests. In places other than the U.S.,

where married candidates have not been accepted for ordination since about 1929, men already married can be ordained to the diaconate and priesthood and can continue in marriage after ordination. Celibate deacons and priests cannot marry after ordination; neither can a married priest remarry after the death of his wife. Bishops must be unmarried.

Iconostasis: A large screen decorated with sacred pictures or icons that separates the sanctuary from the nave of a church; its equivalent in the Roman Rite, for thus separating the sanctuary from the nave, is an altar rail. An iconostas has three doors through which the sacred ministers enter the sanctuary during the Divine Liturgy: smaller (north and south) Deacons' Doors and a large central Royal Door. The Deacons' Doors usually feature the icons of Sts. Gabriel and Michael; the Royal Door, the icons of the Evangelists—Matthew, Mark, Luke and John. To the right and left of the Royal Door are the icons of Christ the Teacher and of the Blessed Virgin Mary with the Infant Jesus. To the extreme right and left are the icons of the patron of the church and St. John the Baptist (or St. Nicholas of Myra). Immediately above the Royal Door is a picture of the Last Supper. To the right are six icons depicting the major feasts of Christ, and to the left are six icons portraying the major feasts of the Blessed Virgin Mary. Above the picture of the Last Supper is a large icon of Christ the King. Some icon screens also have pictures of the 12 Apostles and the major Old Testament prophets surmounted by a crucifixion scene.

Liturgical Language: In line with Eastern tradition, Byzantine practice has favored the use of the language of the people in the liturgy. Two great advocates of the practice were Sts. Cyril and Methodius, apostles of the Slavs, who devised the Cyrillic alphabet and pioneered the adoption of Slavonic in the liturgy.

Sacraments: Baptism is administered by immersion, and confirmation (Chrismation) is conferred at the same time. The Eucharist is administered by intinction, i.e., by giving the communicant a piece of consecrated leavened bread that has been dipped into the consecrated wine. When giving absolution in the sacrament of penance, the priest holds his stole over the head of the penitent. Distinctive marriage ceremonies include the crowning of the bride and groom. Ceremonies for anointing the sick closely resemble those of the Roman Rite. Holy orders are conferred by a bishop.

Sign of the Cross: The sign of the cross in conjunction with a deep bow expresses reverence for the presence of Christ in the Blessed Sacrament. (See also entry in **Glossary**.)

VESTMENTS, APPURTENANCES

Antimension: A silk or linen cloth laid on the altar for the Liturgy; it may be decorated with a picture of the burial of Christ and the instruments of his passion; the relics of martyrs are sewn into the front border.

Asteriskos: Made of two curved bands of gold or silver which cross each other to form a double arch; a star depends from the junction, which forms a cross; it is placed over the *diskos* holding the consecrated bread and is covered with a veil.

Diskos: A shallow plate, which may be elevated on

a small stand, corresponding to the Roman-Rite paten.

Eileton: A linen cloth that corresponds to the Roman-Rite corporal.

Epimanikia: Ornamental cuffs; the right cuff symbolizing strength, the left, patience and good will.

Epitrachelion: A stole with ends sewn together, having a loop through which the head is passed; its several crosses symbolize priestly duties.

Lance: A metal knife used for cutting up the bread to be consecrated during the Liturgy.

Phelonion: An ample cape, long in the back and sides and cut away in front; symbolic of the higher gifts of the Holy Spirit.

Poterion: A chalice or cup that holds the wine and Precious Blood.

Spoon: Used in administering Holy Communion by intinction; consecrated leavened bread is dipped into consecrated wine and spooned onto the tongue of the communicant.

Sticharion: A long white garment of linen or silk with wide sleeves and decorated with embroidery; formerly the vestment for clerics in minor orders, acolytes, lectors, chanters, and subdeacons; symbolic of purity.

Veils: Three are used, one to cover the *poterion*, the second to cover the *diskos*, and the third to cover both.

Zone: A narrow clasped belt made of the same material as the *epitrachelion*; symbolic of the wisdom of the priest, his strength against enemies of the Church and his willingness to perform holy duties.

CODE OF CANONS OF THE EASTERN CHURCHES

Just as the Latin Catholics are governed by a specific set of universal laws, so too are the Eastern Catholics. The Code of Canons of the Eastern Churches serves as the legal corpus for the Eastern Churches, providing the legal principles for the preservation of the rich heritage of these Churches. The overarching theological structure for the Code was enunciated by the Second Vatican Council in its declaration in *Orientalium Ecclesiarum* (3):

"These individual Churches, whether of the East or the West, although they differ somewhat among themselves in rite (to use the current phrase), that is, in liturgy, ecclesiastical discipline, and spiritual heritage, are, nevertheless, each as much as the others, entrusted to the pastoral government of the Roman Pontiff, the divinely appointed successor of St. Peter in primacy over the universal Church. They are consequently of equal dignity, so that none of them is superior to the others as regards rite and they enjoy the same rights and are under the same obligations, also in respect of preaching the Gospel to the whole world (cf. Mark 16:15) under the guidance of the Roman Pontiff."

Background

The creation and promulgation of the Code for the Eastern Churches began during the pontificate of Pope Pius XI (1922-39) when he established a commission of cardinals in 1929 to examine the requirements for a code. This preparatory commission was succeeded in 1935 by a new commission with the task of undertaking the actual composition of the Code. What followed was a gradual process of promulgations. Pope Pius XII (1939-58) issued a series of apostolic letters as different elements of the Eastern Code were completed. This method of promulgation continued until 1972 when Pope Paul VI (1963-78) established the Pontifical Commission for the Revision of the Code of Eastern Canon Law.

The commission approached the initial stages of its work quite deliberately. Extensive consultation was made with canonists as well as many bishops of the Eastern Churches. These efforts culminated in November 1988 with the unanimous vote of the commission's members accepting the draft of the new Code. On October 18, 1990, Pope John Paul II officially promulgated the Code of Canons of the Eastern Churches. The Code became effective on October ber 1, 1991. As the decree makes clear, in accordance with this universal legislation, each Eastern Catholic Church is to develop its own particular law. This stands in contrast to the Code of Canon Law that applies only to the single Latin Church.

Contents and Structure

The *Code of Canons of the Eastern Churches* marked a significant milestone in the history of Church law. It represented the long process in the development of Canon Law for the Eastern Churches throughout the 20th century and was an eloquent means of both respecting and preserving the proper discipline of those Churches. It was noted from the start that the Code for the Eastern Catholics was organized differently in comparison with the Code of Canon Law for the Latin Rite. There are different elements to Eastern Law, and the Code presents the independence of these laws from the Latin Rite, save, of course, for those canons that give reference to the Pope. Nevertheless, while safeguarding the centuries' old traditions and heritage of the Eastern Catholic Churches, the differences are not disruptive to the unity of the Church. Rather, the Code is an instrument in moving toward appropriate unity. As the 1996 document, "Applying the Liturgical Prescriptions of the Code of Canons of the Eastern Catholic Churches" (9), by the Congregation for the Eastern Churches states:

"The *Code of Canons of the Eastern Churches*, in can. 28 § 1 which refers to *Lumen Gentium*, n. 23, and *Orientalium Ecclesiarum*, n. 3, elucidates the important areas which articulate the heritage of each of the Churches *sui iuris*: liturgy, theology, spirituality and discipline. It is necessary to note that these particular fields penetrate and condition one another in turn inside a global vision of divine revelation which pervades all life and which culminates in the praise of the most holy Trinity. Such articulations imply the idea of a history, of a culture, of conceptions and uses specific to each Church, and likewise constitute the rays originating in the one Lord, the sun of justice which illumines every man (cf. Jn. 1:9) and brings him to live in communion with him. Every one of these rays, received by each individual Church *sui iuris*, has value and infinite dynamism and constitutes a part of the universal heritage of the Church."

The Catholic Church In the United States

U.S. CATHOLIC HISTORY

(*Update courtesy Rev. Clyde Crews, Ph.D.*)

The starting point of the mainstream of Catholic history in the United States was in Baltimore at the end of the Revolutionary War. Long before that time, however, Catholic explorers had traversed much of the country and missionaries had done considerable work among Indians in the Southeast, Northeast and Southwest. (See also Index: Chronology of Church in U.S.)

Spanish and French Missions

Missionaries from Spain evangelized Indians in Florida (which included a large area of the Southeast), New Mexico, Texas and California. Franciscan Juan de Padilla, killed in 1542 in what is now central Kansas, was the first of numerous martyrs among the early missionaries. The city of St. Augustine, settled by the Spanish in 1565, was the first permanent settlement in the United States and also the site of the first parish, established the same year with secular Father Martin Francisco Lopez de Mendoza Grajales as pastor. Italian Jesuit Eusebio Kino (1645-1711) established Spanish missions in lower California and southern Arizona, where he founded San Xavier del Bac mission in 1700. Bl. Junípero Serra (1713-84), who established nine of the famous chain of 21 Franciscan missions in California, was perhaps the most noted of the Spanish missionaries. He was beatified in 1988.

French missionary efforts originated in Canada and extended to parts of Maine, New York and areas around the Great Lakes and along the Mississippi River as far south as Louisiana. Sts. Isaac Jogues, René Goupil and John de Brébeuf, three of eight Jesuit missionaries of New France martyred between 1642 and 1649 (canonized in 1930), met their deaths near Auriesville, New York. Jesuit explorer Jacques Marquette (1637-75), who founded St. Ignace Mission at the Straits of Mackinac in 1671, left maps and a diary of his exploratory trip down the Mississippi River with Louis Joliet in 1673. Claude Allouez (1622-89), another French Jesuit, worked for 32 years among Indians in the Midwest, baptizing an estimated 10,000. French Catholics founded the colony in Louisiana in 1699. In 1727, Ursuline nuns from France founded a convent in New Orleans, the oldest in the United States.

English Settlements

Catholics were excluded by penal law from English settlements along the Atlantic coast.

The only colony established under Catholic leadership was Maryland, granted to George Calvert (Lord Baltimore) as a proprietary colony in 1632; its first settlement at St. Mary's City was established in 1634 by a contingent of Catholic and Protestant colonists who had arrived from England on the "Ark and the Dove." Jesuits Andrew White and John Altham, who later evangelized Indians of the area, accompanied the settlers. The principle of religious freedom on which the colony was founded was enacted into law in 1649 as the Act of Toleration. It was the first such measure passed in the colonies and, except for a four-year period of Puritan control, remained in effect until 1688, when Maryland became a royal colony, and the Anglican Church was made the official religion in 1692. Catholics were disenfranchised and persecuted until 1776.

The only other colony where Catholics were assured some degree of freedom was Pennsylvania, founded by the Quaker William Penn in 1681.

One of the earliest permanent Catholic establishments in the English colonies was St. Francis Xavier Mission, Old Bohemia, in northern Maryland, founded by the Jesuits in 1704 to serve Catholics of Delaware, Maryland and southeastern Pennsylvania. Its Bohemia Academy, established in the 1740s, was attended by sons of prominent Catholic families in the area.

Catholics and the Revolution

Despite their small number, which accounted for about one percent of the population, Catholics made significant contributions to the cause for independence from England.

Father John Carroll (1735-1815), who would later become the first bishop of the American hierarchy, and his cousin, Charles Carroll (1737-1832), a signer of the Declaration of Independence, were chosen by the Continental Congress to accompany Benjamin Franklin and Samuel Chase to Canada to try to secure that country's neutrality. Father Pierre Gibault (1737-1804) gave important aid in preserving the Northwest Territory for the revolutionaries. Thomas FitzSimons (1741-1811) of Philadelphia gave financial support to the Continental Army, served in a number of campaigns and later, with Daniel Carroll of Maryland, became one of the two Catholic signers of the Constitution. John Barry (1745-1803), commander of the Lexington, the first ship commissioned by Congress, served valiantly and is considered a founder of the U.S. Navy. There is no record of the number of Catholics who served in Washington's armies, although 38 to 50 percent had Irish surnames.

Casimir Pulaski (1748-79) and Thaddeus Kosciusko (1746-1817) of Poland served the cause of the Revolution. Assisting also were the Catholic nations of France, with a military and naval force, and Spain with money and the neutrality of its colonies.

Acknowledgment of Catholic aid in the war and the founding of the Republic was made by General Washington in his reply to a letter from prominent Catholics seeking justice and equal rights: "I presume your fellow citizens of all denominations will not forget the patriotic part which you took in the accomplishment of our Revolution and the establishment of our government or the important assistance which they received from a nation [France] in which the Roman Catholic faith is professed."

In 1789, religious freedom was guaranteed under the First Amendment to the Constitution. Discriminatory laws against Catholics remained in force in many of the states, however, until well into the 19th century.

Beginning of Organization

Father John Carroll's appointment as superior of the American missions on June 9, 1784, was the first step toward organization of the Church in this country. According to a report he made to Rome the following year, there were 24 priests and approximately 25,000 Catholics, mostly in Maryland and Pennsylvania, in a general population of four million. Many of them had been in the Colonies for several generations. For the most part, however, they were an unknown minority laboring under legal and social handicaps.

Establishment of the Hierarchy

Father Carroll was named the first American bishop in 1789 and placed in charge of the Diocese of Baltimore, whose boundaries were coextensive with those of the United States. He was ordained in England Aug. 15, 1790, and installed in his see the following Dec. 12.

Ten years later, Father Leonard Neale became his coadjutor and the first bishop ordained in the United States. Bishop Carroll became an archbishop. in 1808 when Baltimore was designated a metropolitan see and the new dioceses of Boston, New York, Philadelphia and Bardstown (now Louisville) were established. These jurisdictions were later subdivided, and by 1840 there were, in addition to Baltimore, 15 dioceses, 500 priests and 663,000 Catholics in the general population of 17 million.

Priests and First Seminaries

The original number of 24 priests noted in Bishop Carroll's 1785 report was gradually augmented with the arrival of others from France and other countries. Among arrivals from France after the Civil Constitution of the Clergy went into effect in 1790, were Jean Louis Lefebvre de Cheverus and Sulpicians Ambrose Maréchal, Benedict Flaget and William Dubourg, who later became bishops.

The first seminary in the country was St. Mary's, established in 1791 in Baltimore, and placed under the direction of the Sulpicians. French seminarian Stephen T. Badin (1768-1853), who fled to the U.S. in 1792 and became a pioneer missionary in Kentucky, Ohio and Michigan, was the first priest ordained (1793) in the U.S. Demetrius Gallitzin (1770-1840), a Russian prince and convert to Catholicism who did pioneer missionary work in western Pennsylvania, was ordained to the priesthood in 1795; he was the first to receive all his orders in the U.S. By 1815, St. Mary's Seminary had 30 ordained alumni.

Two additional seminaries — Mt. St. Mary's at Emmitsburg, Md., and St. Thomas at Bardstown, Ky. — were established in 1809 and 1811, respectively. These and similar institutions founded later played key roles in the development and growth of the American clergy.

Early Schools

Early educational enterprises included the establishment in 1791 of a school at Georgetown which later became the first Catholic university in the U.S.; the opening of a secondary school for girls, conducted by Visitation Nuns, in 1799 at Georgetown; and the start of a similar school in the first decade of the 19th century at Emmitsburg, Md., by Sr. Elizabeth Ann Seton.

By the 1840s, which saw the beginnings of the present public school system, more than 200 Catholic elementary schools, half of them west of the Alleghenies, were in operation. From this start, the Church subsequently built the greatest private system of education in the world.

Sisterhoods

Institutes of women Religious were largely responsible for the development of educational and charitable institutions. Among them were Ursuline Nuns in Louisiana from 1727 and Visitation Nuns at Georgetown in the 1790s.

The first contemplative foundation in the country was established in 1790 at Fort Tobacco, Md., by three American-born Carmelites trained at an English convent in Belgium.

The first community of American origin was that of the Sisters of Charity of St. Joseph, founded in 1808 at Emmitsburg, Md., by Mother Elizabeth Ann Bayley Seton (canonized in 1975). Other early American communities were the Sisters of Loretto and the Sisters of Charity of Nazareth, both founded in 1812 in Kentucky, and the Oblate Sisters of Providence, a black community founded in 1829 in Baltimore by Mother Mary Elizabeth Lange.

Among pioneer U.S. foundresses of European communities were Mother Rose Philippine Duchesne (canonized in 1980), who established the Religious of the Sacred Heart in Missouri in 1818, and Mother Theodore Guérin, who founded the Sisters of Providence of St.-Mary-of-the-Woods in Indiana in 1840.

The number of sisters' communities, most of them branches of European institutes, increased apace with needs for their missions in education, charitable service and spiritual life.

Trusteeism

The initial lack of organization in ecclesiastical affairs, nationalistic feeling among Catholics and the independent action of some priests were factors involved in several early crises.

In Philadelphia, some German Catholics, with the reluctant consent of Bishop Carroll, founded Holy

Trinity, the first national parish in the U.S. They refused to accept the pastor appointed by the bishop and elected their own. This and other abuses led to formal schism in 1796, a condition that existed until 1802 when they returned to canonical jurisdiction. Philadelphia was also the scene of the Hogan Schism, which developed in the 1820s when Father William Hogan, with the aid of lay trustees, seized control of St. Mary's Cathedral. His movement, for churches and parishes controlled by other than canonical procedures and run in extralegal ways, was nullified by a decision of the Pennsylvania Supreme Court in 1822.

Similar troubles seriously disturbed the peace of the Church in other places, principally New York, Baltimore, Buffalo, Charleston and New Orleans.

Dangers arising from the exploitation of lay control were gradually diminished with the extension and enforcement of canonical procedures and with changes in civil law about the middle of the century.

Anti-Catholicism

Bigotry against Catholics waxed and waned during the 19th century and into the 20th. The first major campaign of this kind, which developed in the wake of the panic of 1819 and lasted for about 25 years, was mounted in 1830 when the number of Catholic immigrants began to increase to a noticeable degree. Nativist anti-Catholicism generated a great deal of violence, represented by climaxes in loss of life and property in Charlestown, Mass., in 1834, and in Philadelphia 10 years later. Later bigotry was fomented by the Know-Nothings, in the 1850s; the Ku Klux Klan, from 1866; the American Protective Association, from 1887, and the Guardians of Liberty. Perhaps the last eruption of virulently overt anti-Catholicism occurred during the campaign of Alfred E. Smith for the presidency in 1928. Observers feel the issue was muted to a considerable extent in the political area with the election of John F. Kennedy to the presidency in 1960.

The Catholic periodical press had its beginnings in response to the attacks of bigots. The *U.S. Catholic Miscellany* (1822-61), the first Catholic newspaper in the U.S., was founded by Bishop John England of Charleston to answer critics of the Church. This remained the character of most of the periodicals published in the 19th and into the 20th century.

Growth and Immigration

Between 1830 and 1900, the combined factors of natural increase, immigration and conversion raised the Catholic population to 12 million. A large percentage of the growth figure represented immigrants: some 2.7 million, largely from Ireland, Germany and France, between 1830 and 1880; and another 1.25 million during the 1880s when Eastern and Southern Europeans came in increasing numbers. By the 1860s the Catholic Church, with most of its members concentrated in urban areas, was probably the largest religious body in the country.

The efforts of progressive bishops to hasten the acculturation of Catholic immigrants occasioned a number of controversies, which generally centered around questions concerning national or foreign-language parishes. One of them, called Cahenslyism, arose from complaints that German Catholic immigrants were not being given adequate pastoral care.

Eastern-Rite Catholics

The immigration of the 1890s included large numbers of Eastern-Rite Catholics with their own liturgies and tradition of a married clergy, but without their own bishops. The treatment of their clergy and people by some of the U.S. (Latin-Rite) hierarchy and the prejudices they encountered resulted in the defection of thousands from the Catholic Church.

In 1907, Basilian monk Stephen Ortynsky was ordained the first bishop of Byzantine-rite Catholics in the U.S. Eventually jurisdictions were established for most Byzantine- and other Eastern-rite Catholics in the country.

Councils of Baltimore

The bishops of the growing U.S. dioceses met at Baltimore for seven provincial councils between 1829 and 1849.

In 1846, they proclaimed the Blessed Virgin Mary patroness of the United States under the title of the Immaculate Conception, eight years before the dogma was proclaimed in Rome.

After the establishment of the Archdiocese of Oregon City in 1846 and the elevation to metropolitan status of St. Louis, New Orleans, Cincinnati and New York, the first of the three plenary councils of Baltimore was held.

The first plenary assembly was convoked on May 9, 1852, with Abp. Francis P. Kenrick of Baltimore as papal legate. The bishops drew up regulations concerning parochial life, matters of church ritual and ceremonies, the administration of church funds and the teaching of Christian doctrine.

The second plenary council, meeting from Oct. 7 to 21, 1866, under the presidency of Abp. Martin J. Spalding, formulated a condemnation of several current doctrinal errors and established norms affecting the organization of dioceses, the education and conduct of the clergy, the management of ecclesiastical property, parochial duties and general education.

Abp. (later Cardinal) James Gibbons called into session the third plenary council which lasted from Nov. 9 to Dec. 7, 1884. Among highly significant results of actions taken by this assembly were the preparation of the line of Baltimore catechisms which became a basic means of religious instruction in this country; legislation that fixed the pattern of Catholic education by requiring the building of elementary schools in all parishes; the establishment of the Catholic University of America in Washington, D.C., in 1889; and the determination of six holy days of obligation for observance in this country.

The enactments of the three plenary councils have had the force of particular law for the Church in the United States.

The Holy See established the Apostolic Delegation in Washington, D.C., on Jan. 24, 1893.

Slavery

In the Civil War period, as before, Catholics reflected attitudes of the general population with respect to the issue of slavery. Some supported it, some opposed it, but none were prominent in the Abolition Movement. Gregory XVI had condemned the slave trade in 1839, but no contemporary pope or American bishop published an official document on slavery itself. The issue did not split Catholics in schism as it did Baptists, Methodists and Presbyterians.

Catholics fought on both sides in the Civil War. Five hundred members of 20 or more sisterhoods served the wounded of both sides.

One hundred thousand of the four million slaves emancipated in 1863 were Catholics; the highest concentrations were in Louisiana, about 60,000, and Maryland, 16,000. Three years later, their pastoral care was one of the subjects covered in nine decrees issued by the Second Plenary Council of Baltimore. The measures had little practical effect with respect to integration of the total Catholic community, predicated as they were on the proposition that individual bishops should handle questions regarding segregation in churches and related matters as best they could in the pattern of local customs.

Long entrenched segregation practices continued in force through the rest of the 19th century and well into the 20th. The first effective efforts to alter them were initiated by Cardinal Joseph Ritter of St. Louis in 1947, Cardinal (then Abp.) Patrick O'Boyle of Washington in 1948, and Bishop Vincent Waters of Raleigh in 1953.

Friend of Labor

The Church became known during the 19th century as a friend and ally of labor in seeking justice for the working man. Cardinal Gibbons journeyed to Rome in 1887, for example, to defend and prevent a condemnation of the Knights of Labor by Leo XIII. The encyclical *Rerum Novarum* (1891) was hailed by many American bishops as a confirmation, if not vindication, of their own theories. Catholics have always formed a large percentage of union membership, and some have served unions in positions of leadership.

Americanism

Near the end of the century some controversy developed over what was characterized as Americanism or the phantom heresy. It was alleged that Americans were discounting the importance of contemplative virtues, exalting the practical virtues, and watering down the purity of Catholic doctrine for the sake of facilitating convert work.

The French translation of Father Walter Elliott's *Life of Isaac Hecker*, which fired the controversy, was one of many factors that led to the issuance of Leo XIII's *Testem Benevolentiae* in January 1899, in an attempt to end the matter. It was the first time the orthodoxy of the Church in the U.S. was called into question.

Schism

In the 1890s, serious friction developed between Poles and Irish in Scranton, Buffalo and Chicago, resulting in schism and the establishment of the Polish National Catholic Church. A central figure in the affair was Father Francis Hodur, who was excommunicated by Bishop William O'Hara of Scranton in 1898. Nine years later, his ordination by an Old Catholic Abp. of Utrecht gave the new church its first bishop.

Another schism of the period led to formation of the American Carpatho-Russian Orthodox Greek Catholic Church.

Coming of Age

In 1900, there were 12 million Catholics in the total U.S. population of 76 million, 82 dioceses in 14 provinces, and 12,000 priests and members of about 40 communities of men Religious. Many sisterhoods, most of them of European origin and some of American foundation, were engaged in Catholic educational and hospital work, two of their traditional apostolates.

The Church in the United States was removed from mission status with promulgation of the apostolic constitution *Sapienti Consilio* by Pope St. Pius X on June 29, 1908.

Before that time, and even into the early 1920s, the Church in this country received financial assistance from mission-aid societies in France, Bavaria and Austria. Already, however, it was making increasing contributions of its own. At the present time, it is one of the major national contributors to the worldwide Society for the Propagation of the Faith.

American foreign missionary personnel increased from 14 or less in 1906 to an all-time high in 1968 of 9,655 priests, brothers, sisters, seminarians, and lay persons. The first missionary seminary in the U.S. was in operation at Techny, Ill., in 1909, under the auspices of the Society of the Divine Word. Maryknoll, the first American missionary society, was established in 1911 and sent its first priests to China in 1918. Despite these contributions, the Church in the U.S. has not matched the missionary commitment of some other nations.

Bishops' Conference

A highly important apparatus for mobilizing the Church's resources was established in 1917 under the title of the National Catholic War Council. Its name was changed to National Catholic Welfare Conference several years later, but its objectives remained the same: to serve as an advisory and coordinating agency of the American bishops for advancing works of the Church in fields of social significance and impact — education, communications, immigration, social action, legislation, youth and lay organizations.

The forward thrust of the bishops' social thinking was evidenced in a program of social reconstruction they recommended in 1919. By 1945, all but one of their 12 points had been enacted into legislation — including many later social security programs.

The NCWC was renamed the United States Catholic Conference (USCC) in November 1966, when the hierarchy also organized itself as a territorial conference with pastoral-juridical authority under the title, National Conference of Catholic Bishops. The USCC carried on the functions of the former NCWC until July, 2001 when it merged with the National Conference of Catholic Bishops to create the USCCB.

Catholic Press

The establishment of the National Catholic News Service (NC) — now the Catholic News Service (CNS) — in 1920 was an important event in the development of the Catholic press, which had its beginnings about a hundred years earlier. Early in the 20th century there were 63 weekly newspapers. The 2002 *Catholic Press Directory*, published by the Catholic Press Association, reported a total of 640 periodicals in North America, with a circulation of 26.8 million. The figures included 217 newspapers, 243 magazines, 136 newsletters, and 44 other-language periodicals (newspapers and magazines).

Lay Organizations

A burst of lay organizational growth occurred from the 1930s onwards with the appearance of Catholic Action types of movements and other groups and associations devoted to special causes, social service and assistance for the poor and needy. Several special apostolates developed under the aegis of the National Catholic Welfare Conference (now the United States Catholic Conference); the outstanding one was the Confraternity of Christian Doctrine.

Nineteenth-century organizations of great influence included: The St. Vincent de Paul Society, whose first U.S. office was set up in 1845 in St. Louis; the Catholic Central Union (*Verein*), dating from 1855; the Knights of Columbus, founded in 1882; the Holy Name Society, organized in the U.S. in 1870; the Rosary Society (1891) and scores of chapters of the Sodality of the Blessed Virgin Mary.

Pastoral Concerns

The potential for growth of the Church in this country by immigration was sharply reduced but not entirely curtailed after 1921 with the passage of restrictive federal legislation. As a result, the Catholic population became more stabilized and, to a certain extent and for many reasons, began to acquire an identity of its own.

Some increase from outside has taken place in the past 50 years, however; from Canada, from Central and Eastern European countries, and from Puerto Rico and Latin American countries since World War II. This influx, while not as great as that of the 19th century and early 20th, has enriched the Church here with a sizable body of Eastern-Rite Catholics for whom 12 ecclesiastical jurisdictions have been established. It has also created a challenge for pastoral care of millions of Hispanics in urban centers and in agricultural areas where migrant workers are employed.

The Church continues to grapple with serious pastoral problems in rural areas, where about 600 counties have no priests in ministry. The National Catholic Rural Life Conference was established in 1922 in an attempt to make the Catholic presence felt on the land, and the Glenmary Society since its foundation in 1939 has devoted itself to this single apostolate. Religious communities and diocesan priests are similarly engaged.

Other challenges lie in the cities and suburbs where 75 percent of the Catholic population lives. Conditions peculiar to each segment of the metropolitan area have developed in recent years as the flight to the suburbs has not only altered some traditional aspects of parish life but has also, in combination with many other factors, left behind a complex of special problems in inner city areas.

A Post-War World

In the year after the Second World War, Catholics increasingly assumed a mainline role in American life. This was evidenced especially in the 1960 election of John F. Kennedy as the nation's first Catholic president. Catholic writers and thinkers were making a greater impact in the nation's life. One example of this was Trappist Thomas Merton's runaway best-selling book of 1948, *The Seven Storey Mountain*; another was the early television success of Bishop Fulton Sheen's "Life is Worth Living" series, begun in 1952. Meanwhile, lay leader Dorothy Day, founder of the Catholic Worker movement, continued to challenge American society with her views on pacifism and evangelical poverty.

A Post-Conciliar World

Catholic life in the United States was profoundly affected by the Second Vatican Council (1962-65). In the post-conciliar generation, American Catholicism grew both in numbers and complexity. Lay ministry and participation expanded; extensive liturgical changes (including the use of English) were implemented; and the numbers of priests, vowed religious and seminarians declined.

The Church has taken a high profile in many social issues. This has ranged from opposition to abortion, capital punishments and euthanasia to support for civil rights, economic justice and international peace and cooperation. Meanwhile Catholics have been deeply involved in inter-faith and ecumenical relationships. And the bishops have issued landmark pastoral statements, including "The Challenge of Peace" (1983) and "Economic Justice for All" (1986).

In these years after the Council, the Catholics in America have known something of alienation, dissent and polarity. They also found new intensity and maturity. New U.S. saints have been declared by the universal church, such as Elizabeth Ann Seton (1975), John Nepomucene Neumann (1977), and Rose Philippine Duchesne (1988). Especially at the time of visits to America by Pope John Paul II (e.g., in 1979, 1987, 1993, 1995, and 1999), U.S. Catholics have given evidence – in their personal and corporate lives – of the ongoing power of faith, liturgy and the primal call of the Gospel in its many dimensions.

CHURCH-STATE RELATIONS IN THE UNITED STATES

CHURCH-STATE DECISIONS OF THE SUPREME COURT

(Among sources of this selected listing of U.S. Supreme Court decisions was *The Supreme Court on Church and State*, Joseph Tussman, editor; Oxford University Press, New York, 1962.)

Watson v. Jones, 13 Wallace 679 (1872): The Court declared that a member of a religious organization may not appeal to secular courts against a decision made by a church tribunal within the area of its competence.

Reynolds v. United States, 98 US 145 (1879); Davis v. Beason, 133 US 333 (1890); Church of Latter-Day Saints v. United States, 136 US 1 (1890): The Mormon practice of polygamy was at issue in three decisions and was declared unconstitutional.

Bradfield v. Roberts, 175 US 291 (1899): The Court denied that an appropriation of government funds for an institution (Providence Hospital, Washington, D.C.) run by Roman Catholic sisters violated the No Establishment Clause of the First Amendment.

Pierce v. Society of Sisters, 268 US 510 (1925):

The Court denied that a state can require children to attend public schools only. The Court held that the liberty of the Constitution forbids standardization by such compulsion, and that the parochial schools involved had claims to protection under the Fourteenth Amendment.

Cochran v. Board of Education, 281 US 370 (1930): The Court upheld a Louisiana statute providing textbooks at public expense for children attending public or parochial schools. The Court held that the children and state were beneficiaries of the appropriations, with incidental secondary benefit going to the schools.

United States v. MacIntosh, 283 US 605 (1931): The Court denied that anyone can place allegiance to the will of God above his allegiance to the government since such a person could make his own interpretation of God's will the decisive test as to whether he would or would not obey the nation's law. The Court stated that the nation, which has a duty to survive, can require citizens to bear arms in its defense.

Everson v. Board of Education, 330 US 1 (1947): The Court upheld the constitutionality of a New Jersey statute authorizing free school bus transportation for parochial as well as public school students. The Court expressed the opinion that the benefits of public welfare legislation, included under such bus transportation, do not run contrary to the concept of separation of Church and State.

McCollum v. Board of Education, 333 US 203 (1948): The Court declared unconstitutional a program for releasing children, with parental consent, from public school classes so they could receive religious instruction on public school premises from representatives of their own faiths.

Zorach v. Clauson, 343 US 306 (1952): The Court upheld the constitutionality of a New York statute permitting, on a voluntary basis, the release during school time of students from public school classes for religious instruction given off public school premises.

Torcaso v. Watkins, 367 US 488 (1961): The Court declared unconstitutional a Maryland requirement that one must make a declaration of belief in the existence of God as part of the oath of office for notaries public.

McGowan v. Maryland, 81 Sp Ct 1101; **Two Guys from Harrison v. McGinley**, 81 Sp Ct 1135; **Gallagher v. Crown Kosher Super Market**, 81 Sp Ct 1128; **Braunfield v. Brown**, 81 Sp Ct 1144 (1961): The Court ruled that Sunday closing laws do not violate the No Establishment of Religion Clause of the First Amendment, even though the laws were religious in their inception and still have some religious overtones. The Court held that, "as presently written and administered, most of them, at least, are of a secular rather than of a religious character, and that presently they bear no relationship to establishment of religion as those words are used in the Constitution of the United States."

Engel v. Vitale, 370 US 42 (1962): The Court declared that the voluntary recitation in public schools of a prayer composed by the New York State Board of Regents is unconstitutional on the ground that it violates the No Establishment of Religion Clause of the First Amendment.

Abington Township School District v. Schempp

and **Murray v. Curlett, 83 Sp Ct 1560** (1963): The Court ruled that Bible reading and recitation of the Lord's Prayer in public schools, with voluntary participation by students, are unconstitutional on the ground that they violate the No Establishment of Religion Clause of the First Amendment.

Chamberlin v. Dade County, 83 Sp Ct 1864 (1964): The Court reversed a decision of the Florida Supreme Court concerning the constitutionality of prayer and devotional Bible reading in public schools during the school day, as sanctioned by a state statute which specifically related the practices to a sound public purpose.

Board of Education v. Allen, No. 660 (1968): The Court declared constitutional the New York school book loan law which requires local school boards to purchase books with state funds and lend them to parochial and private school students.

Walz v. Tax Commission of New York (1970): The Court upheld the constitutionality of a New York statute exempting church-owned property from taxation.

Earle v. DiCenso, Robinson v. DiCenso, Lemon v. Kurtzman, Tilton v. Richardson (1971): In Earle v. DiCenso and Robinson v. DiCenso, the Court ruled unconstitutional a 1969 Rhode Island statute that provided salary supplements to teachers of secular subjects in parochial schools; in Lemon v. Kurtzman, the Court ruled unconstitutional a 1968 Pennsylvania statute that authorized the state to purchase services for the teaching of secular subjects in nonpublic schools. The principal argument against constitutionality in these cases was that the statutes and programs at issue entailed excessive entanglement of government with religion. In Tilton v. Richardson, the Court held that this argument did not apply to a prohibitive degree with respect to federal grants, under the Higher Education Facilities Act of 1963, for the construction of facilities for nonreligious purposes by four church-related institutions of higher learning, three of which were Catholic, in Connecticut.

Yoder, Miller and Yutzy (1972): In a case appealed on behalf of Yoder, Miller and Yutzy, the Court ruled that Amish parents were exempt from a Wisconsin statute requiring them to send their children to school until the age of 16. The Court said in its decision that secondary schooling exposed Amish children to attitudes, goals and values contrary to their beliefs, and substantially hindered "the religious development of the Amish child and his integration into the way of life of the Amish faith-community at the crucial adolescent state of development."

Committee for Public Education and Religious Liberty, et al., v. Nyquist, et al., No. 72-694 (1973): The Court ruled that provisions of a 1972 New York statute were unconstitutional on the grounds that they were violative of the No Establishment Clause of the First Amendment and had the "impermissible effect" of advancing the sectarian activities of church-affiliated schools. The programs ruled unconstitutional concerned: (1) maintenance and repair grants, for facilities and equipment, to ensure the health, welfare and safety of students in nonpublic, non-profit elementary and secondary schools serving a high concentration of students from low income families; (2) tuition reimbursement ($50 per grade school child, $100 per high school student) for parents (with income less than $5,000) of children attending nonpublic elementary or secondary schools; tax deduction from adjusted gross income for parents failing to qualify under the above reimbursement plan, for each child attending a nonpublic school.

Sloan, Treasurer of Pennsylvania, et al., v. Lemon, et al., No. 72-459 (1973): The Court ruled unconstitutional a Pennsylvania Parent Reimbursement Act for Nonpublic Education which provided funds to reimburse parents (to a maximum of $150) for a portion of tuition expenses incurred in sending their children to nonpublic schools. The Court held that there was no significant difference between this and the New York tuition reimbursement program (above), and declared that the Equal Protection Clause of the Fourteenth Amendment cannot be relied upon to sustain a program held to be violative of the No Establishment Clause.

Levitt, et al., v. Committee for Public Education and Religious Liberty, et al., No. 72-269 (1973): The Court ruled unconstitutional the Mandated Services Act of 1970 under which New York provided $28 million ($27 per pupil from first to seventh grade, $45 per pupil from seventh to 12th grade) to reimburse nonpublic schools for testing, recording and reporting services required by the state. The Court declared that the act provided "impermissible aid" to religion in contravention of the No Establishment Clause.

In related decisions handed down June 25, 1973, the Court: (1) affirmed a lower court decision against the constitutionality of an Ohio tax credit law benefiting parents with children in nonpublic schools; (2) reinstated an injunction against a parent reimbursement program in New Jersey; (3) affirmed South Carolina's right to grant construction loans to church-affiliated colleges, and (4) dismissed an appeal contesting its right to provide loans to students attending church-affiliated colleges (Hunt v. McNair, Durham v. McLeod).

Wheeler v. Barrera (1974): The Court ruled that nonpublic school students in Missouri must share in federal funds for educationally deprived students on a comparable basis with public school students under Title I of the Elementary and Secondary Education Act of 1965.

Norwood v. Harrison (93 S. Ct. 2804): The Court ruled that public assistance which avoids the prohibitions of the "effect" and "entanglement" tests (and which therefore does not substantially promote the religious mission of sectarian schools) may be confined to the secular functions of such schools.

Wiest v. Mt. Lebanon School District (1974): The Court upheld a lower court ruling that invocation and benediction prayers at public high school commencement ceremonies do not violate the principle of separation of Church and State.

Meek v. Pittenger (1975): The Court ruled unconstitutional portions of a Pennsylvania law providing auxiliary services for students of nonpublic schools; at the same time, it ruled in favor of provisions of the law permitting textbook loans to students of such schools. In denying the constitutionality of auxiliary services, the Court held that they had the "primary effect of establishing religion" and involved "excessive entanglement" of Church and state officials with respect to supervision; objection was also made against providing such services only on the premises of nonpublic schools and only at the request of such schools.

TWA, Inc., v. Hardison, 75-1126; International Association of Machinists and Aero Space Workers v. Hardison, 75-1385 (1977): The Court ruled that federal civil rights legislation does not require employers to make more than minimal efforts to accommodate employees who want a particular working day off as their religion's Sabbath Day, and that an employer cannot accommodate such an employee by violating seniority systems determined by a union collective bargaining agreement. The Court noted that its ruling was not a constitutional judgment but an interpretation of existing law.

Wolman v. Walter (1977): The Court ruled constitutional portions of an Ohio statute providing tax-paid textbook loans and some auxiliary services (standardized and diagnostic testing, therapeutic and remedial services, off school premises) for nonpublic school students. It decided that other portions of the law, providing state funds for nonpublic school field trips and instructional materials (audio-visual equipment, maps, tape recorders), were unconstitutional.

Byrne v. Public Funds for Public Schools (1979): The Court decided against the constitutionality of a 1976 New Jersey law providing state income tax deductions for tuition paid by parents of students attending parochial and other private schools.

Student Bus Transportation (1979): The Court upheld a Pennsylvania law providing bus transportation at public expense for students to nonpublic schools up to 10 miles away from the boundaries of the public school districts in which they lived.

Reimbursement (1980): The Court upheld the constitutionality of a 1974 New York law providing direct cash payment to nonpublic schools for the costs of state-mandated testing and record-keeping.

Ten Commandments (1980): The Court struck down a 1978 Kentucky law requiring the posting of the Ten Commandments in public school classrooms in the state.

Widmar v. Vincent (1981): The Court ruled that the University of Missouri at Kansas City could not deny student religious groups the use of campus facilities for worship services. The Court also, in Brandon v. Board of Education of Guilderland Schools, declined without comment to hear an appeal for reversal of lower court decisions denying a group of New York high school students the right to meet for prayer on public school property before the beginning of the school day.

Lubbock v. Lubbock Civil Liberties Union (1983): By refusing to hear an appeal in this case, the Court upheld a lower court ruling against a public policy of permitting student religious groups to meet on public school property before and after school hours.

Mueller v. Allen (1983): The Court upheld a Minnesota law allowing parents of students in public and nonpublic (including parochial) schools to take a tax deduction for the expenses of tuition, textbooks and transportation. Maximum allowable deductions were $500 per child in elementary school and $700 per child in grades seven through 12.

Lynch v. Donnelly (1984): The Court ruled 5-to-4 that the First Amendment does not mandate "complete separation of church and state," and that, therefore, the sponsorship of a Christmas nativity scene by the City of Pawtucket, R.I., was not unconstitutional. The case involved a scene included in a display of Christmas symbols sponsored by the city in a park owned by a non-profit group. The majority opinion said "the Constitution (does not) require complete separation of church and state; it affirmatively mandates accommodation, not merely tolerance, of all religions and forbids hostility toward any. Anything less" would entail callous indifference not intended by the Constitution. Moreover, "such hostility would bring us into 'war with our national tradition as embodied in the First Amendment's guaranty of the free exercise of religion.' " (The additional quotation was from the 1948 decision in McCollum v. Board of Education.)

Christmas Nativity Scene (1985): The Court upheld a lower court ruling that the Village of Scarsdale, N.Y., must make public space available for the display of privately sponsored nativity scenes.

Wallace v. Jaffree, No. 83-812 (1985): The Court ruled against the constitutionality of a 1981 Alabama law calling for a public-school moment of silence that specifically included optional prayer.

Grand Rapids v. Ball, No. 83-990, and Aguilar v. Felton, No. 84-237 (1985): The Court ruled against the constitutionality of programs in Grand Rapids and New York City allowing public school teachers to teach remedial entitlement subjects (under the Elementary and Secondary Education Act of 1965) in private schools, many of which were Catholic.

Bender v. Williamsport Area School District (1986): The Court let stand a lower federal court decision allowing a public high school Bible study group the same "equal access" to school facilities as that enjoyed by other extracurricular clubs. A similar decision was handed down in 1990 in Board of Education v. Mergens, involving Westside High School in Omaha.

County of Allegheny v. American Civil Liberties Union (1989): The Court ruled (1) that the display of a Christmas nativity scene in the Allegheny County Courthouse in Pittsburgh, Pa., violated the principle of separation of church and state because it appeared to be a government-sponsored endorsement of Christian belief; (2) and that the display of a Hanukkah menorah outside the Pittsburgh-Allegheny city-county building was constitutional because of its "particular physical setting" with secular symbols.

Unemployment Division v. Smith (1990): The Court ruled that religious use of the hallucinogenic cactus peyote is not covered by the First Amendment protection of religious freedom.

Lee v. Weisman (1992): The Court banned officially organized prayer at public school graduation ceremonies.

Lamb's Chapel v. Center Moriches Union School District (1993): The Court reversed a ruling by the 3rd U.S. Circuit Court of Appeals, declaring that the school district was wrong in prohibiting the congregation of Lamb's Chapel from using public school meeting space after hours to show a film series addressing family problems from a religious perspective. In view of the variety of organizations permitted to use school property after school hours, said the Court's opinion: "There would have been no realistic danger that the community would think that the district was endorsing religion or any particular creed,

and any benefit to religion or to the church would have been no more than incidental."

5th U.S. Circuit Court of Appeals (1993): The Court let stand a ruling by the 5th U.S. Circuit Court of Appeals, permitting students in Texas, Mississippi and Louisiana to include student-organized and student-led prayers in graduation exercises.

Church of Lukumi Babalu Aye v. City of Hialeah (1993): The Court ruled that municipal laws that effectively prohibit a single church from performing its religious rituals are unconstitutional. The ordinances at issue singled out one religion, Santeria, for the purpose of restricting its members from the practice of ritual animal sacrifices.

Zobrest v. Catalina Foothills School District (1993): The Court ruled that a public school district may provide a sign-language interpreter for a deaf student attending a Catholic school without violating constitutional separation of church and state. The majority opinion said: "Handicapped children, not sectarian schools are the primary beneficiaries of the Disabilities Education Act; to the extent sectarian schools benefit at all from (the act), they are only incidental beneficiaries."

Fairfax County, Va., school district (1994): The Court upheld lower court rulings against a Fairfax County, Va., school district's practice of charging churches more rent than other entities for the use of school buildings.

Board of Education of Kiryas Joel Village School District v. Grumet (1994): The Court ruled in 1994 that a school district created to meet the special education needs of an Hasidic Jewish community violated the Establishment Clause of the Constitution. The Court said the New York Legislature effectively endorsed a particular religion when it established a public school district for the Satmar Hasidic Village of Kiryas Joel.

Agostino v. Felton (1997): The court reversed, 5 to 4, its 1985 Aguilar v. Felton ruling, which had declared it unconstitutional for teachers employed by public school districts to hold Title I remedial programs for low-income students on the property of church-related schools.

Boerne v. Flores (1997): The court ruled, 6 to 3, that the Religious Freedom Restoration Act (1993) was unconstitutional because Congress overstepped its constitutional authority in enacting the law. Congress "has been given the power to 'enforce,' not the power to determine what constitutes a constitutional violation," said the majority opinion.

Mitchell v. Helms (2000): The court ruled, 6 to 3, that a Louisiana parish can distribute money for instructional equipment — including computers, books, maps, and film strip projectors — to private schools as long as it is done in a "secular, neutral and non-ideological" way. The court's decision overturns two previous Supreme Court bans on giving public materials to parochial schools.

Santa Fe Independent School District v. Doe (2000): The court affirmed a lower court ruling that said prayer in public schools must be private and that such prayers at high school football games violate the constitutionally required separation of church and state. At issue in the Santa Fe case was a Texas school policy which permitted students selected by their peers to deliver an inspirational message of their own design at football games and the graduation ceremony. In 1999, the Santa Fe policy was struck down by the U.S. Court of Appeals for the Fifth Circuit. The Court of Appeals held that the policy violated the Establishment Clause of the First Amendment, even though the government played no role in creating the message or selecting the messenger.

RELIGION IN PUBLIC SCHOOLS
(*Based on a Catholic News Service article by Carol Zimmermann.*)

A diverse group of religious and civil rights organizations issued a joint statement Apr. 13, 1995, in an effort to clarify the confusing issue of prayer and religious observances or discussions in public schools. Their six-page statement outlines what is and what is not currently permissible in expressing religious beliefs in public schools.

The statement says, for example: "Students have the right to pray individually or in groups, or to discuss their religious views with their peers so long as they are not disruptive." But, the statement specifies that such prayers or discussions do not include "the right to have a captive audience listen or to compel other students to participate."

Prayer at Graduations
Regarding prayer at graduation ceremonies, the document says school officials may not mandate or organize prayer, but hardly sets the record straight about student-led prayer at these services.

"The courts have reached conflicting conclusions under the federal Constitution" in this area, says the statement, recommending that schools consult their lawyers for the rules that apply to them, "until the issue is authoritatively resolved."

Since the Supreme Court's 1992 Lee v. Weisman opinion prohibited school authorities from even arranging for a speaker to present a prayer, lower courts in different states have made various rulings about student-led prayer at commencement exercises.

In Virginia, the state's Attorney General and the Board of Education proposed guidelines in mid-April to allow student-led prayer at graduations, despite a 1994 ruling by a U.S. district judge banning all prayer at graduations.

Religion in the Classroom
"It is permissible and desirable to teach objectively about the role of religion in the history of the United States and other countries," but public school teachers may not specifically teach religion.

The same rules apply to the recurring controversy surrounding theories of evolution. Teachers may discuss explanations of the beginnings of life, but only within the confines of classes on religion or social studies. Public school teachers are required, according to the statement, to teach only scientific explanations of life's beginnings in science classes. And, just as teachers may not advance a religious view, they should not ridicule a student's religious belief.

Constitutional Protection
The statement says that students' expressions of religious beliefs in reports, homework or artwork are constitutionally protected. Likewise, students have the right to speak to and attempt to persuade their peers

on religious topics. "But school officials should intercede to stop student religious speech if it turns into religious harassment aimed at a student or a small group of students."

The statement also says:
• Students have the right to distribute religious literature to their schoolmates, subject to reasonable restrictions for any non-school literature.
• Student religious clubs in secondary schools "must be permitted to meet and to have equal access" to school media for announcing their events.
• Religious messages on T-shirts and the like cannot be singled out for suppression.
• Schools can use discretion about dismissing students for off-site religious instruction.

The 35 organizations that endorsed the statement included the National Association of Evangelicals, the American Jewish Congress, the Christian Legal Society, the National Council of Churches, the Baptist Joint Committee on Public Affairs, the American Muslim Council, the Presbyterian Church (USA) and the American Civil Liberties Union.

Purpose of the Statement
"By making this document available," said Phil Baum, executive director of the American Jewish Congress, "the organizations are attempting to clarify what has become one of the most divisive issues of our time: religion in the public schools."

He said the document attempts to "ensure that the rights of all students are respected in the public schools."

Baum noted that the American Jewish Congress, which initiated the effort to draft the statement, had a long-standing commitment to ensuring that public schools are themselves religiously neutral.

"We believe, however, that it is inconsistent with that historic commitment to ask the public schools to root out private expressions of religious faith."

CHURCH TAX EXEMPTION
The exemption of church-owned property was ruled constitutional by the U.S. Supreme Court May 4, 1970, in the case of Walz v. The Tax Commission of New York.

Suit in the case was brought by Frederick Walz, who purchased in June 1967, a 22-by-29-foot plot of ground in Staten Island valued at $100 and taxable at $5.24 a year. Shortly after making the purchase, Walz instituted a suit in New York State, contending that the exemption of church property from taxation authorized by state law increased his own tax rate and forced him indirectly to support churches in violation of his constitutional right to freedom of religion under the First Amendment. Three New York courts dismissed the suit, which had been instituted by mail. The Supreme Court, judging that it had probable jurisdiction, then took the case.

In a 7-1 decision affecting Church-state relations in every state in the nation, the Court upheld the New York law under challenge.

For and Against
Chief Justice Warren E. Burger, who wrote the majority opinion, said that Congress from its earliest days had viewed the religion clauses of the Constitution as authorizing statutory real estate tax exemption to re-

ligious bodies. He declared: "Nothing in this national attitude toward religious tolerance and two centuries of uninterrupted freedom from taxation has given the remotest sign of leading to an established church or religion, and on the contrary it has operated affirmatively to help guarantee the free exercise of all forms of religious beliefs."

Justice William O. Douglas wrote in dissent that the involvement of government in religion as typified in tax exemption may seem inconsequential but: "It is, I fear, a long step down the establishment path. Perhaps I have been misinformed. But, as I read the Constitution and the philosophy, I gathered that independence was the price of liberty."

Burger rejected Douglas' "establishment" fears. If tax exemption is the first step toward establishment, he said, "the second step has been long in coming."

The basic issue centered on the following question: Is there a contradiction between federal constitutional provisions against the establishment of religion, or the use of public funds for religious purposes, and state statutes exempting church property from taxation? In the Walz decision, the Supreme Court ruled that there is no contradiction.

Legal Background

The U.S. Constitution makes no reference to tax exemption. There was no discussion of the issue in the Constitutional Convention nor in debates on the Bill of Rights.

In the Colonial and post-Revolutionary years, some churches had established status and were state-supported. This changed with enactment of the First Amendment, which laid down no-establishment as the federal norm. This norm was adopted by the states which, however, exempted churches from tax liabilities.

No establishment, no hindrance, was the early American view of Church-State relationships.

This view, reflected in custom law, was not generally formulated in statute law until the second half of the 19th century, although specific tax exemption was provided for churches in Maryland in 1798, in Virginia in 1800, and in North Carolina in 1806.

The first major challenge to church property exemption was initiated by the Liberal League in the 1870s. It reached the point that President Grant included the recommendation in a State of the Union address in 1875, stating that church property should bear its own proportion of taxes. The plea fell on deaf ears in Congress, but there was some support for the idea at state levels. The exemption, however, continued to survive various challenges.

About 36 state constitutions contain either mandatory or permissive provisions for exemption. Statutes provide for exemption in all other states.

There has been considerable litigation challenging this exemption, but most of it focused on whether a particular property satisfied statutory requirements. Few cases before Walz focused on the strictly constitutional question, whether directly under the First Amendment or indirectly under the Fourteenth.

Objections

Objectors to the tax exempt status of churches feel that churches should share, through taxation, in the cost of the ordinary benefits of public services they enjoy, and/or that the amount of "aid" enjoyed through exemption should be proportionate to the amount of social good they do.

According to one opinion, exemption is said to weaken the independence of churches from the political system that benefits them by exemption.

In another view, exemption is said to involve the government in decisions regarding what is and what is not religion.

The Wall of Separation

Thomas Jefferson, in a letter written to the Danbury (Conn.) Baptist Association Jan. 1, 1802, coined the metaphor, "a wall of separation between Church and State," to express a theory concerning interpretation of the religion clauses of the First Amendment: "Congress shall make no law respecting an establishment of religion or prohibiting the free exercise thereof."

The metaphor was cited for the first time in judicial proceedings in 1879, in the opinion by Chief Justice Waite in Reynolds v. United States. It did not, however, figure substantially in the decision.

Accepted as Rule

In 1947 the wall of separation gained acceptance as a constitutional rule, in the decision handed down in Everson v. Board of Education. Associate Justice Black, in describing the principles involved in the No Establishment Clause, wrote:

"Neither a state nor the Federal Government can set up a church. Neither can pass laws which aid one religion, aid all religions, or prefer one religion over another. Neither can force nor influence a person to go to or to remain away from church against his will or force him to profess a belief or disbelief in any religion. No person can be punished for entertaining or professing religious beliefs or disbeliefs, for church attendance or non-attendance. No tax in any amount, large or small, can be levied to support any religious activities or institutions, whatever they may be called, or whatever form they may adopt to teach or practice religion. Neither a state nor the Federal Government can, openly or secretly, participate in the affairs of any religious organizations or groups and vice versa. In the words of Jefferson, the clause against establishment of religion by law was intended to erect 'a wall of separation between Church and State.' "

Mr. Black's associates agreed with his statement of principles, which were framed without reference to the Freedom of Exercise Clause. They disagreed, however, with respect to application of the principles, as the split decision in the case indicated. Five members of the Court held that the benefits of public welfare legislation — in this case, free bus transportation to school for parochial as well as public school students — did not run contrary to the concept of separation of Church and State embodied in the First Amendment.

MISSIONARIES TO THE AMERICAS

An asterisk with a feast date indicates that the saint or blessed is listed in the General Roman Calendar or the proper calendar for U.S. dioceses.

Allouez, Claude Jean (1622-1689): French Jesuit; missionary in Canada and midwestern U.S.; preached to 20 different tribes of Indians and baptized over 10,000; vicar general of Northwest.

Altham, John (1589-1640): English Jesuit; missionary among Indians in Maryland.

Anchieta, José de, Bl. (1534-1597): Portuguese Jesuit, born Canary Islands; missionary in Brazil; writer; beatified 1980; feast, June 9.

Andreis, Felix de (1778-1820): Italian Vincentian; missionary and educator in western U.S.

Aparicio, Sebastian, Bl. (1502-1600): Franciscan brother, born Spain; settled in Mexico, c. 1533; worked as road builder and farmer before becoming Franciscan at about the age of 70; beatified, 1787; feast, Feb. 25.

Badin, Stephen T. (1768-1853): French missioner; came to U.S., 1792, when Sulpician seminary in Paris was closed; ordained, 1793, Baltimore, the first priest ordained in U.S.; missionary in Kentucky, Ohio and Michigan; bought land on which Notre Dame University now stands; buried on its campus.

Baraga, Frederic (1797-1868): Slovenian missionary bishop in U.S.; studied at Ljubljana and Vienna, ordained, 1823; came to U.S., 1830; missionary to Indians of Upper Michigan; first bishop of Marquette, 1857-1868; wrote Chippewa grammar, dictionary, prayer book and other works.

Bertran, Louis, St. (1526-1581): Spanish Dominican; missionary in Colombia and Caribbean, 1562-69; canonized, 1671; feast, Oct. 9.

Betancur, Pedro de San José, Bl. (1626-1667): Secular Franciscan, born Canary Islands; arrived in Guatemala, 1651; established hospital, school and homes for poor; beatified 1980; feast, Apr. 25.

Bourgeoys, Marguerite, St. (1620-1700): French foundress, missionary; settled in Canada, 1653; founded Congregation of Notre Dame, 1658; beatified, 1950; canonized 1982; feast, Jan. 12.

Brébeuf, Jean de, St. (1593-1649): French Jesuit; missionary among Huron Indians in Canada; martyred by Iroquois, Mar. 16, 1649; canonized, 1930; one of Jesuit North American martyrs; feast, Oct. 19* (U.S.).

Cancer de Barbastro, Louis (1500-1549): Spanish Dominican; began missionary work in Middle America, 1533; killed at Tampa Bay, Fla.

Castillo, John de, St. (1596-1628): Spanish Jesuit; worked in Paraguay Indian mission settlements (reductions); martyred; beatified, 1934; canonized, 1988; feast, Nov. 16.

Catala, Magin (1761-1830): Spanish Franciscan; worked in California mission of Santa Clara for 36 years.

Chabanel, Noel, St. (1613-1649): French Jesuit; missionary among Huron Indians in Canada; murdered by renegade Huron, Dec. 8, 1649; canonized, 1930; one of Jesuit North American martyrs; feast, Oct. 19* (U.S.).

Chaumonot, Pierre Joseph (1611-1693): French Jesuit; missionary among Indians in Canada.

Claver, Peter, St. (1581-1654): Spanish Jesuit; missionary among Negroes of South America and West Indies; canonized, 1888; patron of Catholic missions among black people; feast, Sept. 9*.

Daniel, Anthony, St. (1601-1648): French Jesuit; missionary among Huron Indians in Canada; martyred by Iroquois, July 4, 1648; canonized, 1930; one of Jesuit North American martyrs; feast, Oct. 19* (U.S.).

De Smet, Pierre Jean (1801-1873): Belgian-born Jesuit; missionary among Indians of northwestern U.S.; served as intermediary between Indians and U.S. government; wrote on Indian culture.

Duchesne, Rose Philippine, St. (1769-1852): French nun; educator and missionary in the U.S.; established first convent of the Society of the Sacred Heart in the U.S., at St. Charles, Mo.; founded schools for girls; did missionary work among Indians; beatified, 1940; canonized, 1988; feast, Nov. 18* (U.S.).

Farmer, Ferdinand (family name, Steinmeyer) (1720-1786): German Jesuit; missionary in Philadelphia, where he died; one of the first missionaries in New Jersey.

Flaget, Benedict J. (1763-1850): French Sulpician bishop; came to U.S., 1792; missionary and educator in U.S.; first bishop of Bardstown, Ky. (now Louisville), 1810-32; 1833-50.

Gallitzin, Demetrius (1770-1840): Russian prince, born The Hague; convert, 1787; ordained priest at Baltimore, 1795; frontier missionary, known as Father Smith; Gallitzin, Pa., named for him.

Garnier, Charles, St. (c. 1606-1649): French Jesuit; missionary among Hurons in Canada; martyred by Iroquois, Dec. 7, 1649; canonized, 1930; one of Jesuit North American martyrs; feast, Oct. 19* (U.S.).

Gibault, Pierre (1737-1804): Canadian missionary in Illinois and Indiana; aided in securing states of Ohio, Indiana, Illinois, Michigan and Wisconsin for the Americans during Revolution.

Gonzalez, Roch, St. (1576-1628): Paraguayan Jesuit; worked in Paraguay Indian mission settlements (reductions); martyred; beatified, 1934; canonized, 1988; feast, Nov. 16.

Goupil, René, St. (1607-1642): French lay missionary; had studied surgery at Orleans, France; missionary companion of St. Isaac Jogues among the Hurons; martyred, Sept. 29, 1642; canonized, 1930; one of Jesuit North American martyrs; feast, Oct. 19* (U.S.).

Gravier, Jacques (1651-1708): French Jesuit; missionary among Indians of Canada and midwestern U.S.

Hennepin, Louis (d. c. 1701): Belgian-born Franciscan missionary and explorer of Great Lakes region and Upper Mississippi, 1675-81, when he returned to Europe.

Jesuit North American Martyrs: Isaac Jogues, Anthony Daniel, John de Brébeuf, Gabriel Lalemant, Charles Garnier, Noel Chabanel (Jesuit priests), and René Goupil and John Lalande (lay missionaries) who were martyred between Sept. 29, 1642, and Dec. 9, 1649, in the missions of New France; canonized June 29, 1930; feast, Oct. 19* (U.S.). See separate entries.

Jogues, Isaac, St. (1607-1646): French Jesuit; missionary among Indians in Canada; martyred near present site of Auriesville, N.Y., by Mohawks, Oct. 18, 1646; canonized, 1930; one of Jesuit North American martyrs; feast, Oct. 19* (U.S.).

Kino, Eusebio (1645-1711): Italian Jesuit; missionary and explorer in U.S.; arrived Southwest, 1681; established 25 Indian missions, took part in 14 exploring expeditions in northern Mexico, Arizona and southern California; helped develop livestock raising and farming in the area. He was selected in 1965 to represent Arizona in Statuary Hall.

Lalande, John, St. (d. 1646): French lay missionary, companion of Isaac Jogues; martyred by Mohawks at Auriesville, N.Y., Oct. 19, 1646; canonized, 1930; one of Jesuit North American martyrs; feast, Oct. 19* (U.S.).

Lalemant, Gabriel, St. (1610-1649): French Jesuit; missionary among the Hurons in Canada; martyred by the Iroquois, Mar. 17, 1649; canonized, 1930; one of Jesuit North American martyrs; feast, Oct. 19* (U.S.).

Lamy, Jean Baptiste (1814-1888): French prelate; came to U.S., 1839; missionary in Ohio and Kentucky; bishop in Southwest from 1850; first bishop (later Abp.) of Santa Fe, 1850-1885. He was nominated in 1951 to represent New Mexico in Statuary Hall.

Las Casas, Bartolome (1474-1566): Spanish Dominican; missionary in Haiti, Jamaica and Venezuela; reformer of abuses against Indians and black people; bishop of Chalapas, Mexico, 1544-47; historian.

Laval, Françoise de Montmorency, Bl. (1623-1708): French-born missionary bishop in Canada; named vicar apostolic of Canada, 1658; first bishop of Québec, 1674; jurisdiction extended over all French-claimed territory in New World; beatified 1980; feast, May 6.

Manogue, Patrick (1831-1895): Missionary bishop in U.S., born Ireland; migrated to U.S.; miner in California; studied for priesthood at St. Mary's of the Lake, Chicago, and St. Sulpice, Paris; ordained, 1861; missionary among Indians of California and Nevada; coadj. bishop, 1881-84, and bishop, 1884-86, of Grass Valley; first bishop of Sacramento, 1886-1895, when see was transferred there.

Margil, Antonio, Ven. (1657-1726): Spanish Franciscan; missionary in Middle America; apostle of Guatemala; established missions in Texas.

Marie of the Incarnation, St. (Marie Guyard Martin) (1599-1672): French widow; joined Ursuline Nuns; arrived in Canada, 1639; first superior of Ursulines in Québec; missionary to Indians; writer; beatified 1980; feast, Apr. 30.

Marquette, Jacques (1637-1675): French Jesuit; missionary and explorer in America; sent to New France, 1666; began missionary work among Ottawa Indians on Lake Superior, 1668; accompanied Joliet down the Mississippi to mouth of the Arkansas, 1673, and returned to Lake Michigan by way of Illinois River; made a second trip over the same route; his diary and map are of historical significance. He was selected in 1895 to represent Wisconsin in Statuary Hall.

Massias (Macias), John de, St. (1585-1645): Dominican brother, a native of Spain; entered Dominican Friary at Lima, Peru, 1622; served as doorkeeper until his death; beatified, 1837; canonized 1975; feast, Sept. 16.

Mazzuchelli, Samuel C. (1806-1864): Italian Dominican; missionary in midwestern U.S.; called builder of the West; writer. A decree advancing his beatification cause was promulgated July 6, 1993.

Membre, Zenobius (1645-1687): French Franciscan; missionary among Indians of Illinois; accompanied LaSalle expedition down the Mississippi (1681-1682) and Louisiana colonizing expedition (1684) which landed in Texas; murdered by Indians.

Mozcygemba, Leopold (1824-1891): Polish Franciscan priest and missionary, the patriarch of American Polonia; labored as a missionary in Texas and 11 other states for nearly 40 years; co-founded the Polish seminary of Sts. Cyril and Methodius in Detroit (1885) and served as confessor at Vatican Council I.

Nerinckx, Charles (1761-1824): Belgian priest; missionary in Kentucky; founded Sisters of Loretto at the Foot of the Cross.

Nobrega, Manoel (1517-1570): Portuguese Jesuit; leader of first Jesuit missionaries to Brazil, 1549.

Padilla, Juan de (d. 1542): Spanish Franciscan; missionary among Indians of Mexico and southwestern U.S.; killed by Indians in Kansas; protomartyr of the U.S.

Palou, Francisco (c. 1722-1789): Spanish Franciscan; accompanied Junípero Serra to Mexico, 1749; founded Mission Dolores in San Francisco; wrote history of the Franciscans in California.

Pariseau, Mother Mary Joseph (1833-1902): Canadian Sister of Charity of Providence; missionary in state of Washington from 1856; founded first hospitals in northwest territory; artisan and architect. Represents Washington in National Statuary Hall.

Peter of Ghent (d. 1572): Belgian Franciscan brother; missionary in Mexico for 49 years.

Porres, Martin de, St. (1579-1639): Peruvian Dominican oblate; his father was a Spanish soldier and his mother a black freedwoman from Panama; called wonder worker of Peru; beatified, 1837; canonized, 1962; feast, Nov. 3*.

Quiroga, Vasco de (1470-1565): Spanish missionary in Mexico; founded hospitals; bishop of Michoacan, 1537.

Ravalli, Antonio (1811-1884): Italian Jesuit; missionary in far-western United States, mostly Montana, for 40 years.

Raymbaut, Charles (1602-1643): French Jesuit; missionary among Indians of Canada and northern U.S.

Richard, Gabriel (1767-1832): French Sulpician; missionary in Illinois and Michigan; a founder of University of Michigan; elected delegate to Congress from Michigan, 1823; first priest to hold seat in the House of Representatives.

Rodriguez, Alfonso, St. (1598-1628): Spanish Jesuit; missionary in Paraguay; martyred; beatified, 1934; canonized, 1988; feast, Nov. 16.

Rosati, Joseph (1789-1843): Italian Vincentian; missionary bishop in U.S. (vicar apostolic of Mississippi and Alabama, 1822; coadj. of Louisiana and the Two Floridas, 1823-26; administrator of New Orleans, 1826-29; first bishop of St. Louis, 1826-1843).

Sahagun, Bernardino de (c. 1500-1590): Spanish Franciscan; missionary in Mexico for over 60 years; expert on Aztec archaeology.

Seelos, Francis X. (1819-1867): Redemptorist missionary, born Bavaria; ordained, 1844, at Baltimore; missionary in Pittsburgh and New Orleans.

Seghers, Charles J. (1839-1886): Belgian missionary bishop in North America; Apostle of Alaska; Abp. of Oregon City (now Portland), 1880-1884; murdered by berserk companion while on missionary journey.

Serra, Junípero, Bl. (1713-1784): Spanish Franciscan; born Majorca; missionary in America; arrived Mexico, 1749, where he did missionary work for 20 years; began work in Upper California in 1769 and established nine of the 21 Franciscan missions along the Pacific coast; baptized some 6,000 Indians and confirmed almost 5,000; a cultural pioneer of California. Represents California in Statuary Hall. He was declared venerable May 9, 1985, and was beatified Sept. 25, 1988; feast, July 1* (U.S.).

Solanus, Francis, St. (1549-1610): Spanish Franciscan; missionary in Paraguay, Argentina and Peru; wonder worker of the New World; canonized, 1726; feast, July 14.

Sorin, Edward F. (1814-1893): French priest; member of Congregation of Holy Cross; sent to U.S. in 1841; founder and first president of the University of Notre Dame; missionary in Indiana and Michigan.

Todadilla, Anthony de (1704-1746): Spanish Capuchin; missionary to Indians of Venezuela; killed by Motilones.

Turibius de Mogrovejo, St. (1538-1606): Spanish Abp. of Lima, Peru, c. 1580-1606; canonized 1726; feast, Mar. 23*.

Twelve Apostles of Mexico (early 16th century): Franciscan priests; arrived in Mexico, 1524: Fathers Martin de Valencia (leader), Francisco de Soto, Martin de la Coruna, Juan Suares, Antonio de Ciudad Rodrigo, Toribio de Benevente, Garcia de Cisneros, Luis de Fuensalida, Juan de Ribas, Francisco Ximenes; Brothers Andres de Coroboda, Juan de Palos.

Valdivia, Luis de (1561-1641): Spanish Jesuit; defender of Indians in Peru and Chile.

Vasques de Espiñosa, Antonio (early 17th century): Spanish Carmelite; missionary and explorer in Mexico, Panama and western coast of South America.

Vieira, Antonio (1608-1687): Portuguese Jesuit; preacher; missionary in Peru and Chile; protector of Indians against exploitation by slave owners and traders; considered foremost prose writer of 17th-century Portugal.

White, Andrew (1579-1656): English Jesuit; missionary among Indians in Maryland.

Wimmer, Boniface (1809-1887): German Benedictine; missionary among German immigrants in the U.S.

Youville, Marie Marguerite d', St. (1701-1771): Canadian widow; foundress of Sisters of Charity (Grey Nuns), 1737, at Montréal: beatified, 1959; canonized 1990, first native Canadian saint; feast, Dec. 23.

Zumarraga, Juan de (1468-1548): Spanish Franciscan; missionary; first bishop of Mexico; introduced first printing press in New World, published first book in America, a catechism for Aztec Indians; extended missions in Mexico and Central America; vigorous opponent of exploitation of Indians; approved of devotions at Guadalupe; leading figure in early church history in Mexico.

FRANCISCAN MISSIONS

The 21 Franciscan missions of Upper California were established during the 54-year period from 1769 to 1822. Located along the old El Camino Real, or King's Highway, they extended from San Diego to San Francisco and were the centers of Indian civilization, Christianity and industry in the early history of the state.

Junípero Serra (beatified 1988) was the great pioneer of the missions of Upper California. He and his successor as superior of the work, Fermin Lasuen, each directed the establishment of nine missions. One hundred and 46 priests of the Order of Friars Minor, most of them Spaniards, labored in the region from 1769 to 1845; 67 of them died at their posts, two as martyrs. The regular time of mission service was 10 years.

The missions were secularized by the Mexican government in the 1830s but were subsequently restored to the Church by the U.S. government. They are now variously used as the sites of parish churches, a university, houses of study and museums.

The names of the missions and the order of their establishment were as follows:

San Diego de Alcala, San Carlos Borromeo (El Carmelo), San Antonio de Padua, San Gabriel Arcangel, San Luis Obispo de Tolosa, San Francisco de Asis (Dolores), San Juan Capistrano; Santa Clara de Asis, San Buenaventura, Santa Barbara, La Purisima Concepcion de Maria Santisima, Santa Cruz, Nuestra Señora de la Soledad, San José de Guadalupe; San Juan Bautista, San Miguel Arcangel, San Fernando Rey de España, San Luis Rey de Francia, Santa Iñes, San Rafael Arcangel, San Francisco Solano de Sonoma (Sonoma).

American Catholics of the Past

Readers will find this material available at the Catholic Almanac Web site: www.CatholicAlmanac.com.

CATHOLICS IN THE U.S. GOVERNMENT

CATHOLICS IN PRESIDENTS' CABINETS

From 1789 to 1940, nine Catholics were appointed to cabinet posts by six of 32 presidents. The first was Roger Brooke Taney (later named first Catholic Supreme Court Justice) who was appointed in 1831 by Pres. Andrew Jackson. Catholics have been appointed to cabinet posts from the time of Pres. Franklin D. Roosevelt to the present.

Listed below in chronological order are presidents, Catholic cabinet officials, posts held, dates.

Andrew Jackson — Roger B. Taney, Attorney General, 1831-33, Secretary of Treasury, 1833-34.

Franklin Pierce — James Campbell, Postmaster General, 1853-57.

James Buchanan — John B. Floyd, Secretary of War, 1857-61.

William McKinley — Joseph McKenna, Attorney General, 1897-98.

Theodore Roosevelt — Robert J. Wynne, Postmaster General, 1904-05; Charles Bonaparte, Secretary of Navy, 1905-06, Attorney General, 1906-09.

Franklin D. Roosevelt — James A. Farley, Postmaster General, 1933-40; Frank Murphy, Attorney General, 1939-40; Frank C. Walker, Postmaster General, 1940-45.

Harry S. Truman — Robert E. Hannegan, Postmaster General, 1945-47; J. Howard McGrath, Attorney General, 1949-52; Maurice J. Tobin, Secretary of Labor, 1948-53; James P. McGranery, Attorney General, 1952-53.

Dwight D. Eisenhower — Martin P. Durkin, Secretary of Labor, 1953; James P. Mitchell, Secretary of Labor, 1953-61.

John F. Kennedy — Robert F. Kennedy, Attorney General, 1961-63; Anthony Celebrezze, Secretary of Health, Education and Welfare, 1962-63; John S. Gronouski, Postmaster General, 1963.

Lyndon B. Johnson — (Robert F. Kennedy, 1963-64, Anthony Celebrezze, 1963-65, and John S. Gronouski, 1963-65, reappointed to posts held in Kennedy Cabinet, see above.) John T. Connor, Secretary of Commerce, 1965-67; Lawrence O'Brien, Postmaster General, 1965-68.

Richard M. Nixon — Walter J. Hickel, Secretary of Interior, 1969-71; John A. Volpe, Secretary of Transportation, 1969-72; Maurice H. Stans, Secretary of Commerce, 1969-72; Peter J. Brennan, Secretary of Labor, 1973-74; William E. Simon, Secretary of Treasury, 1974.

Gerald R. Ford — Peter J. Brennan, 1974-75, and William E. Simon, 1974-76, reappointed to posts held above.

Jimmy Carter — Joseph Califano, Jr., Secretary of Health, Education and Welfare, 1977-79; Benjamin Civiletti, Attorney General, 1979-81; Moon Landrieu, Secretary of Housing and Urban Development, 1979-81; Edmund S. Muskie, Secretary of State, 1980-81.

Ronald Reagan — Alexander M. Haig, Secretary of State, 1981-82; Raymond J. Donovan, Secretary of Labor, 1981-84; Margaret M. Heckler, Secretary of Health and Human Services, 1983-85; William J. Bennett, Secretary of Education, 1985-88; Ann Dore McLaughlin, Secretary of Labor, 1988-89; Lauro F. Cavazos, Secretary of Education, 1988-89; Nicholas F. Brady, Secretary of Treasury, 1988-89.

George Bush — Lauro F. Cavazos (reappointed), Secretary of Education, 1989-90; Nicholas F. Brady (reappointed), Secretary of Treasury, 1989-93; James D. Watkins, Secretary of Energy, 1989-93; Manuel Lujan, Jr., Secretary of Interior, 1989-93; Edward J. Derwinski, Secretary of Veteran Affairs, 1989-92; Lynn Martin, Secretary of Labor, 1990-93; Edward Madigan, Secretary of Agriculture, 1991-93; William P. Barr, Attorney General, 1991-93.

Bill Clinton — Henry G. Cisneros, Secretary of Housing and Urban Development, 1993-97; Federico F. Peña, Secretary of Transportation, 1993-97; Donna Shalala, Secretary of Health and Human Services, 1993-2001; William M. Daley, Secretary of Commerce, 1997-2000; Andrew Cuomo, Secretary of Housing and Urban Development, 1997-2001; Alexis H. Herman, Secretary of Labor, 1997-2001.

George W. Bush — Paul O'Neill, Secretary of the Treasury, 2001-; Tommy Thompson, Secretary of Health and Human Services, 2001-; Mel Martinez, Secretary of Housing and Urban Development, 2001-; Anthony Principi, Secretary of Veterans Affairs, 2001-.

Cabinet members who became Catholics after leaving their posts were: Thomas Ewing, Secretary of Treasury under William A. Harrison, and Secretary of Interior under Zachary Taylor; Luke E. Wright, Secretary of War under Theodore Roosevelt; Albert B. Fall, Secretary of Interior under Warren G. Harding.

Catholics in the 107th Congress

At of the start of the 107th Congress in 2001, there were 152 Catholic members. There are presently 128 Catholics in the House and 24 Catholics in the Senate, a difference of one fewer senator from the 106th Congress and a decline by one from two years ago. The number of Catholics is distributed essentially the same as it was for the 106th Congress, with 93 Democrats and 59 Republicans this term. There are two fewer Democrats and one more Republican than two years ago.

CATHOLIC SUPREME COURT JUSTICES

Roger B. Taney, Chief Justice 1836-64; app. by Andrew Jackson.

Edward D. White, Associate Justice 1894-1910, app. by Grover Cleveland; Chief Justice 1910-21, app. by William H. Taft.

Joseph McKenna, Associate Justice 1898-1925; app. by William McKinley.

Pierce Butler, Associate Justice 1923-39; app. by Warren G. Harding.

Frank Murphy, Associate Justice 1940-49; app. by Franklin D. Roosevelt.

William Brennan, Associate Justice 1956-90; app. by Dwight D. Eisenhower.

Antonin Scalia, Associate Justice 1986-; app. by Ronald Reagan.

Anthony M. Kennedy, Associate Justice 1988-; app. by Ronald Reagan.

Clarence Thomas, Associate Justice 1991- ; app. by George Bush.

Sherman Minton, Associate Justice from 1949 to 1956, became a Catholic several years before his death in 1965.

CATHOLICS IN STATUARY HALL

Statues of 13 Catholics deemed worthy of national commemoration are among those enshrined in National Statuary Hall and other places in the U.S. Capitol. The Hall, formerly the chamber of the House of Representatives, was erected by Act of Congress July 2, 1864.

Donating states, names and years of placement are listed.

Arizona: Rev. Eusebio Kino, S. J., missionary, 1965.

California: Rev. Junípero Serra, O. F. M. missionary, 1931. (Beatified 1988.)

Hawaii: Father Damien, missionary, 1969. (Beatified 1995.)

Illinois: Gen. James Shields, statesman, 1893.

Louisiana: Edward D. White, Justice of the U.S. Supreme Court (1894-1921), 1955.

Maryland: Charles Carroll, statesman, 1901.

Nevada: Patrick A. McCarran, statesman, 1960.

New Mexico: Dennis Chavez, statesman, 1966. (Abp. Jean B. Lamy, pioneer prelate of Santa Fe, was nominated for Hall honor in 1951.)

North Dakota: John Burke, U.S. treasurer, 1963.

Oregon: Dr. John McLoughlin, pioneer, 1953.

Washington: Mother Mary Joseph Pariseau, pioneer missionary and humanitarian.

West Virginia: John E. Kenna, statesman, 1901.

Wisconsin: Rev. Jacques Marquette, S.J., missionary, explorer, 1895.

United States Hierarchy

U.S. CATHOLIC JURISDICTIONS, HIERARCHY, STATISTICS

The organizational structure of the Catholic Church in the United States consists of 33 provinces with as many archdioceses (metropolitan sees); 152 suffragan sees (dioceses); five Eastern Church jurisdictions immediately subject to the Holy See — the eparchies of St. Maron and Our Lady of Lebanon of Los Angeles (Maronites), Newton (Melkites), St. Thomas Apostle of Detroit (Chaldeans), St. Thomas of Chicago (Syro-Malabars, created on March 13, 2001) and St. George Martyr of Canton, Ohio (Romanians); and the Military Services Archdiocese. The current number of suffragan sees reflects the creation of the new diocese of Laredo, TX on July 3, 2000 and the eparchy of Saint Peter the Apostle of San Diego of the Chaldeans on May 21, 2002. The eparchy of Our Lady of Deliverance of Newark for Syrian-rite Catholics in the U.S. and Canada has its seat in Newark, N.J. An Armenian apostolic exarchate for the United States and Canada has its seat in New York. Each of these jurisdictions is under the direction of an archbishop or bishop, called an ordinary, who has apostolic responsibility and authority for the pastoral service of the people in his care.

The structure includes the territorial episcopal conference known as the United States Conference of Catholic Bishops (USCCB). In and through this body, which is an amalgamation of the National Conference of Catholic Bishops (NCCB) and the United States Catholic Conference (USCC), the bishops exercise their collegiate pastorate over the Church in the entire country (see **Index**).

The representative of the Holy See to the Church in the United States is an Apostolic Nuncio (presently Archbishop Gabriel Montalvo).

ECCLESIASTICAL PROVINCES

(*Sources*: The Official Catholic Directory, *Catholic News Service*.)

The 33 ecclesiastical provinces bear the names of archdioceses, i.e., of metropolitan sees.

Anchorage: Archdiocese of Anchorage and suffragan sees of Fairbanks, Juneau. Geographical area: Alaska.

Atlanta: Archdiocese of Atlanta (Ga.) and suffragan sees of Savannah (Ga.); Charlotte and Raleigh (NC), Charleston (SC). Geographical area: Georgia, North Carolina, South Carolina.

Baltimore: Archdiocese of Baltimore (Md.) and suffragan sees of Wilmington (Del.); Arlington and Richmond (Va.); Wheeling-Charleston (W. Va.). Geographical area: Maryland (except five counties), Delaware, Virginia, West Virginia.

Boston: Archdiocese of Boston (Mass.) and suffragan sees of Fall River, Springfield and Worcester (Mass.); Portland (Me.); Manchester (N.H.); Burlington (Vt.). Geographical area: Massachusetts, Maine, New Hampshire, Vermont.

Chicago: Archdiocese of Chicago and suffragan sees of Belleville, Joliet, Peoria, Rockford, Springfield. Geographical area: Illinois.

Cincinnati: Archdiocese of Cincinnati and suffragan sees of Cleveland, Columbus, Steubenville, Toledo, Youngstown. Geographical area: Ohio.

Denver: Archdiocese of Denver (Colo.) and suffragan sees of Colorado Springs and Pueblo (Colo.); Cheyenne (Wyo.). Geographical area: Colorado, Wyoming.

Detroit: Archdiocese of Detroit and suffragan sees of Gaylord, Grand Rapids, Kalamazoo, Lansing, Marquette, Saginaw. Geographical area: Michigan.

Dubuque: Archdiocese of Dubuque and suffragan sees of Davenport, Des Moines, Sioux City. Geographical area: Iowa.

Hartford: Archdiocese of Hartford (Conn.) and suffragan sees of Bridgeport and Norwich (Conn.); Providence (R.I.). Geographical area: Connecticut, Rhode Island.

Indianapolis: Archdiocese of Indianapolis and suffragan sees of Evansville, Fort Wayne-South Bend, Gary, Lafayette. Geographical area: Indiana.

Kansas City (Kans.): Archdiocese of Kansas City and suffragan sees of Dodge City, Salina, Wichita. Geographical area: Kansas.

Los Angeles: Archdiocese of Los Angeles and suffragan sees of Fresno, Monterey, Orange, San Bernardino, San Diego. Geographical area: Southern and Central California.

Louisville: Archdiocese of Louisville (Ky.) and suffragan sees of Covington, Lexington and Owensboro (Ky.); Knoxville, Memphis and Nashville

(Tenn.). Geographical area: Kentucky, Tennessee.

Miami: Archdiocese of Miami and suffragan sees of Orlando, Palm Beach, Pensacola-Tallahassee, St. Augustine, St. Petersburg, Venice. Geographical area: Florida.

Milwaukee: Archdiocese of Milwaukee and suffragan sees of Green Bay, La Crosse, Madison, Superior. Geographical area: Wisconsin.

Mobile: Archdiocese of Mobile, Ala., and suffragan sees of Birmingham (Ala.); Biloxi and Jackson (Miss.). Geographical area: Alabama, Mississippi.

Newark: Archdiocese of Newark and suffragan sees of Camden, Metuchen, Paterson, Trenton. Geographical area: New Jersey.

New Orleans: Archdiocese of New Orleans and suffragan sees of Alexandria, Baton Rouge, Houma-Thibodaux, Lafayette, Lake Charles and Shreveport. Geographical area: Louisiana.

New York: Archdiocese of New York and suffragan sees of Albany, Brooklyn, Buffalo, Ogdensburg, Rochester, Rockville Centre, Syracuse. Geographical area: New York.

Oklahoma City: Archdiocese of Oklahoma City (Okla.) and suffragan sees of Tulsa (Okla.) and Little Rock (Ark.). Geographical area: Oklahoma, Arkansas.

Omaha: Archdiocese of Omaha and suffragan sees of Grand Island, Lincoln. Geographical area: Nebraska.

Philadelphia: Archdiocese of Philadelphia and suffragan sees of Allentown, Altoona-Johnstown, Erie, Greensburg, Harrisburg, Pittsburgh, Scranton. Geographical area: Pennsylvania.

Philadelphia (Byzantine, Ukrainians): Metropolitan See of Philadelphia (Byzantine) and Eparchies of St. Josaphat in Parma (Ohio), St. Nicholas of the Ukrainians in Chicago and Stamford, Conn. The jurisdiction extends to all Ukrainian Catholics in the U.S. from the ecclesiastical province of Galicia in the Ukraine.

Pittsburgh (Byzantine, Ruthenians): Metropolitan See of Pittsburgh, Pa. and Eparchies of Passaic (N.J.), Parma (Ohio), Van Nuys (Calif.).

Portland: Archdiocese of Portland (Ore.) and suffragan sees of Baker (Ore.); Boise (Ida.); Great Falls-Billings and Helena (Mont.). Geographical area: Oregon, Idaho, Montana.

St. Louis: Archdiocese of St. Louis and suffragan sees of Jefferson City, Kansas City-St. Joseph, Springfield-Cape Girardeau. Geographical area: Missouri.

St. Paul and Minneapolis: Archdiocese of St. Paul and Minneapolis (Minn.) and suffragan sees of Crookston, Duluth, New Ulm, St. Cloud and Winona (Minn.); Bismarck and Fargo (ND); Rapid City and Sioux Falls (SD). Geographical area: Minnesota, North Dakota, South Dakota.

San Antonio: Archdiocese of San Antonio (Tex.) and suffragan sees of Amarillo, Austin, Beaumont, Brownsville, Corpus Christi, Dallas, El Paso, Fort Worth, Galveston-Houston, Laredo, Lubbock, San Angelo, Tyler and Victoria (Tex.). Geographical area: Texas.

San Francisco: Archdiocese of San Francisco (Calif.) and suffragan sees of Oakland, Sacramento, San Jose, Santa Rosa and Stockton (Calif.); Honolulu (Hawaii); Reno (Nev.); Las Vegas (Nev.); Salt Lake City (Utah). Geographical area: Northern California, Nevada, Utah, Hawaii.

Santa Fe: Archdiocese of Santa Fe (N.M.) and suffragan sees of Gallup and Las Cruces (N.M.); Phoenix and Tucson (Ariz.). Geographical area: New Mexico, Arizona.

Seattle: Archdiocese of Seattle and suffragan sees of Spokane, Yakima. Geographical area: Washington.

Washington: Archdiocese of Washington, D.C., and suffragan see of St. Thomas (Virgin Islands). Geographical area: District of Columbia, five counties of Maryland, Virgin Islands.

ARCHDIOCESES, DIOCESES, ARCHBISHOPS, BISHOPS

(*Sources:* Official Catholic Directory; *Catholic News Service;* L'Osservatore Romano. *As of Aug. 20, 2002.*)

Information includes name of diocese, year of foundation (as it appears on the official document erecting the see), present ordinaries (year of installation), auxiliaries and former ordinaries (for biographies, see **Index**).

Archdioceses are indicated by an asterisk.

Albany, N.Y. (1847): Howard J. Hubbard, bishop, 1977.

Former bishops: John McCloskey, 1847-64; John J. Conroy, 1865-77; Francis McNeirny, 1877-94; Thomas M. Burke, 1894-1915; Thomas F. Cusack, 1915-18; Edmund F. Gibbons, 1919-54; William A. Scully, 1954-69; Edwin B. Broderick, 1969-76.

Alexandria, La. (1853): Sam G. Jacobs, bishop, 1989.

Established at Natchitoches, transferred to Alexandria 1910; title changed to Alexandria-Shreveport, 1977; redesignated Alexandria, 1986, when Shreveport was made a diocese.

Former bishops: Augustus M. Martin, 1853-75;

Francis X. Leray, 1877-79, administrator, 1879-83; Anthony Durier, 1885-1904; Cornelius Van de Ven, 1904-32; Daniel F. Desmond, 1933-45; Charles P. Greco, 1946-73; Lawrence P. Graves, 1973-82; William B. Friend, 1983-86; John C. Favalora, 1986-89.

Allentown, Pa. (1961): Edward P. Cullen, 1997.

Former bishop: Joseph McShea, 1961-83; Thomas J. Welsh, 1983-97.

Altoona-Johnstown, Pa. (1901): Joseph V. Adamec, bishop, 1987.

Established as Altoona, name changed, 1957.

Former bishops: Eugene A. Garvey, 1901-20; John J. McCort, 1920-36; Richard T. Guilfoyle, 1936-57; Howard J. Carroll, 1958-60; J. Carroll McCormick, 1960-66; James J. Hogan, 1966-86.

Amarillo, Tex. (1926): John W. Yanta, bishop, 1997.

Former bishops: Rudolph A. Gerken, 1927-33; Robert E. Lucey, 1934-41; Laurence J. Fitzsimon, 1941-58; John L. Morkovsky, 1958-63; Lawrence M. De Falco, 1963-79; Leroy T. Matthiesen, 1980-97.

Anchorage,* Alaska (1966): Roger Lawrence Schwietz O.M.I., archbishop, 2001.

Former archbishop: Joseph T. Ryan, 1966-75; Francis T. Hurley, 1976-2001.

Arlington, Va. (1974): Paul S. Loverde, bishop, 1999.

Former bishop: Thomas J. Welsh, 1974-83, John R. Keating, 1983-98.

Atlanta,* Ga. (1956; archdiocese, 1962): John F. Donoghue, archbishop, 1993.

Former ordinaries: Francis E. Hyland, 1956-61; Paul J. Hallinan, first archbishop, 1962-68; Thomas A. Donnellan, 1968-87; Eugene A. Marino, S.S.J., 1988-90; James P. Lyke, 1991-92.

Austin, Tex. (1947): Gregory Michael Aymond bishop, 2001.

Former bishops: Louis J. Reicher, 1947-71; Vincent M. Harris, 1971-86; John E. McCarthy, 1986-2001.

Baker, Ore. (1903): Robert Francis Vasa, bishop, 2000.

Established as Baker City, name changed, 1952.

Former bishops: Charles J. O'Reilly, 1903-18; Joseph F. McGrath, 1919-50; Francis P. Leipzig, 1950-71; Thomas J. Connolly, 1971-99.

Baltimore,* Md. (1789; archdiocese, 1808): Cardinal William H. Keeler, archbishop, 1989. Gordon D. Bennett, S.J., P. Francis Murphy, William C. Newman, W. Francis Malooly, auxiliaries.

Former ordinaries: John Carroll, 1789-1815, first archbishop; Leonard Neale, 1815-17; Ambrose Marechal, S.S., 1817-28; James Whitfield, 1828-34; Samuel Eccleston, S.S., 1834-51; Francis P. Kenrick, 1851-63; Martin J. Spalding, 1864-72; James R. Bayley, 1872-77; Cardinal James Gibbons, 1877-1921; Michael J. Curley, 1921-47; Francis P. Keough, 1947-61; Cardinal Lawrence J. Shehan, 1961-74; William D. Borders, 1974-89.

Baton Rouge, La. (1961): Robert W. Muench, bishop, 2001.

Former bishops: Robert E. Tracy, 1961-74; Joseph V. Sullivan, 1974-82; Stanley J. Ott, 1983-93; Alfred C. Hughes, 1993-2001.

Beaumont, Tex. (1966): Curtis J. Guillory, S.V.D., bishop, 2000.

Former bishops: Vincent M. Harris, 1966-71; Warren L. Boudreaux, 1971-77; Bernard J. Ganter, 1977-93; Joseph A. Galante, 1994-2000.

Belleville, Ill. (1887): Wilton D. Gregory, bishop, 1994.

Former bishops: John Janssen, 1888-1913; Henry Althoff, 1914-47; Albert R. Zuroweste, 1948-76; William M. Cosgrove, 1976-81; John N. Wurm, 1981-84; James P. Keleher, 1984-93.

Biloxi, Miss. (1977): Thomas John Rodi, bishop, 2001.

Former bishop: Joseph Lawson Howze, 1977-2001.

Birmingham, Ala. (1969): David E. Foley, bishop, 1994.

Former bishops: Joseph G. Vath, 1969-87; Raymond J. Boland, 1988-93.

Bismarck, N. Dak. (1909): Paul A. Zipfel, bishop, 1996.

Former bishops: Vincent Wehrle, O.S.B., 1910-39; Vincent J. Ryan, 1940-51; Lambert A. Hoch, 1952-56; Hilary B. Hacker, 1957-82; John F. Kinney, 1982-95.

Boise, Ida. (1893): Michael P. Driscoll, 1999.

Former bishops: Alphonse J. Glorieux, 1893-1917; Daniel M. Gorman, 1918-27; Edward J. Kelly, 1928-

56; James J. Byrne, 1956-62; Sylvester Treinen, 1962-88; Tod David Brown, 1989-98.

Boston,* Mass. (1808; archdiocese, 1875): Cardinal Bernard F. Law, archbishop, 1984. John P. Boles, William F. Murphy, John B. McCormack, Francis Xavier Irwin, Emilio Allué, S.D.B., Richard Joseph Malone, Walter James Edyvean, Richard Gerard Lennon, auxiliaries.

Former ordinaries: John L. de Cheverus, 1810-23; Benedict J. Fenwick, S.J., 1825-46; John B. Fitzpatrick, 1846-66; John J. Williams, 1866-1907, first archbishop; Cardinal William O'Connell, 1907-44; Cardinal Richard Cushing, 1944-70; Cardinal Humberto Medeiros, 1970-83.

Bridgeport, Conn. (1953): William Edward Lori, 2001.

Former bishops: Lawrence J. Shehan, 1953-61; Walter W. Curtis, 1961-88; Edward M. Egan, 1988-2000.

Brooklyn, N.Y. (1853): Thomas V. Daily, bishop, 1990. Joseph M. Sullivan, Rene A. Valero, Ignatius Catanello, auxiliaries.

Former bishops: John Loughlin, 1853-91; Charles E. McDonnell, 1892-1921; Thomas E. Molloy, 1921-56; Bryan J. McEntegart, 1957-68; Francis J. Mugavero, 1968-90.

Brownsville, Tex. (1965): Raymundo J. Peña, bishop, 1995.

Former bishops: Adolph Marx, 1965; Humberto S. Medeiros, 1966-70; John J. Fitzpatrick, 1971-91; Enrique San Pedro, S.J., 1991-94.

Buffalo, N.Y. (1847): Henry J. Mansell, bishop, 1995. Edward M. Grosz, auxiliary.

Former bishops: John Timon, C.M., 1847-67; Stephen V. Ryan, C.M., 1868-96; James E. Quigley, 1897-1903; Charles H. Colton, 1903-15; Dennis J. Dougherty, 1915-18; William Turner, 1919-36; John A. Duffy, 1937-44; John F. O'Hara, C.S.C., 1945-51; Joseph A. Burke, 1952-62; James McNulty, 1963-72; Edward D. Head, 1973-95.

Burlington, Vt. (1853): Kenneth A. Angell, bishop, 1992.

Former bishops: Louis De Goesbriand, 1853-99; John S. Michaud, 1899-1908; Joseph J. Rice, 1910-38; Matthew F. Brady, 1938-44; Edward F. Ryan, 1945-56; Robert F. Joyce, 1957-71; John A. Marshall, 1972-91.

Camden, N.J. (1937): Nicholas A. Di Marzio, 1999.

Former bishops: Bartholomew J. Eustace, 1938-56; Justin J. McCarthy, 1957-59; Celestine J. Damiano, 1960-67; George H. Guilfoyle, 1968-89, James T. McHugh, 1989-98.

Charleston, S.C. (1820): Robert J. Baker, bishop, 1999.

Former bishops: John England, 1820-42; Ignatius W. Reynolds, 1844-55; Patrick N. Lynch, 1858-82; Henry P. Northrop, 1883-1916; William T. Russell, 1917-27; Emmet M. Walsh, 1927-49; John J. Russell, 1950-58; Paul J. Hallinan, 1958-62; Francis F. Reh, 1962-64; Ernest L. Unterkoefler, 1964-90; David B. Thompson, 1990-99.

Charlotte, N.C. (1971): William G. Curlin, bishop, 1994.

Former bishops: Michael J. Begley, 1972-84; John F. Donoghue, 1984-93.

Cheyenne, Wyo. (1887): David Laurin Ricken, bishop, 2001.

Former bishops: Maurice F. Burke, 1887-93; Thomas M. Lenihan, 1897-1901; James J. Keane, 1902-11; Patrick A. McGovern, 1912-51; Hubert M. Newell, 1951-78; Joseph Hart, 1978-2001.

Chicago,* Ill. (1843; archdiocese, 1880): Cardinal Francis E. George, archbishop, 1997. Thad J. Jakubowski, John R. Gorman, Raymond E. Goedert, Edwin M. Conway, John R. Manz, Joseph N. Perry, Jerome E. Listecki, auxiliaries.

Former ordinaries: William Quarter, 1844-48; James O. Van de Velde, S.J., 1849-53; Anthony O'Regan, 1854-58; James Duggan, 1859-70; Thomas P. Foley, administrator, 1870-79; Patrick A. Feehan, 1880-1902, first archbishop; James E. Quigley, 1903-15; Cardinal George Mundelein, 1915-39; Cardinal Samuel Stritch, 1939-58; Cardinal Albert Meyer, 1958-65; Cardinal John Cody, 1965-82; Cardinal Joseph L. Bernardin, 1982-96.

Cincinnati,* Ohio (1821; archdiocese, 1850): Daniel E. Pilarczyk, archbishop, 1982. Carl K. Moeddel, auxiliary.

Former ordinaries: Edward D. Fenwick, O.P., 1822-32; John B. Purcell, 1833-83, first archbishop; William H. Elder, 1883-1904; Henry Moeller, 1904-1925; John T. McNicholas, O.P., 1925-50; Karl J. Alter, 1950-69; Paul F. Leibold, 1969-72; Joseph L. Bernardin, 1972-82.

Cleveland, Ohio (1847): Anthony M. Pilla, bishop, 1980. A. James Quinn, Roger W. Gries, O.S.B., Martin John Amos, auxiliaries.

Former bishops: L. Amadeus Rappe, 1847-70; Richard Gilmour, 1872-91; Ignatius F. Horstmann, 1892-1908; John P. Farrelly, 1909-21; Joseph Schrembs, 1921-45; Edward F. Hoban, 1945-66; Clarence G. Issenmann, 1966-74; James A. Hickey, 1974-80.

Colorado Springs, Colo. (1983): Richard C. Hanifen, bishop, 1984; Michael J. Sheridan, co-adjutor.

Columbus, Ohio (1868): James A. Griffin, bishop, 1983.

Former bishops: Sylvester H. Rosecrans, 1868-78; John A. Watterson, 1880-99; Henry Moeller, 1900-03; James J. Hartley, 1904-44; Michael J. Ready, 1944-57; Clarence Issenmann, 1957-64; John J. Carberry, 1965-66; Clarence E. Elwell, 1968-73; Edward J. Herrmann, 1973-82.

Corpus Christi, Tex. (1912): Edmond Carmody, bishop, 2000.

Former bishops: Paul J. Nussbaum, C.P., 1913-20; Emmanuel B. Ledvina, 1921-49; Mariano S. Garriga, 1949-65; Thomas J. Drury, 1965-83; Rene H. Gracida, 1983-97. Roberto O. Gonzalez, O.F.M., 1997-99.

Covington, Ky. (1853): Roger J. Foys, bishop, 2002.

Former bishops: George A. Carrell, S.J., 1853-68; Augustus M. Toebbe, 1870-84; Camillus P. Maes, 1885-1914; Ferdinand Brossart, 1916-23; Francis W. Howard, 1923-44; William T. Mulloy, 1945-59; Richard Ackerman, C.S.Sp., 1960-78; William A. Hughes, 1979-95; Robert W. Muench, 1996-2001.

Crookston, Minn. (1909): Victor H. Balke, bishop, 1976.

Former bishops: Timothy Corbett, 1910-38; John H. Peschges, 1938-44; Francis J. Schenk, 1945-60; Laurence A. Glenn, 1960-70; Kenneth J. Povish, 1970-75.

Dallas, Tex. (1890): Charles V. Grahmann, bishop, 1990; Joseph Galante, coadjutor, 2000.

Established 1890, as Dallas, title changed to Dallas-Ft. Worth 1953; redesignated Dallas, 1969, when Ft. Worth was made diocese.

Former bishops: Thomas F. Brennan, 1891-92; Edward J. Dunne, 1893-1910; Joseph P. Lynch, 1911-54; Thomas K. Gorman, 1954-69; Thomas Tschoepe, 1969-90.

Davenport, Ia. (1881): William E. Franklin, bishop, 1993.

Former bishops: John McMullen, 1881-83; Henry Cosgrove, 1884-1906; James Davis, 1906-26; Henry P. Rohlman, 1927-44; Ralph L. Hayes, 1944-66; Gerald F. O'Keefe, 1966-93.

Denver,* Colo. (1887; archdiocese, 1941): Charles J. Chaput, O.F.M. Cap., archbishop, 1997. José H. Gomez, auxiliary.

Former ordinaries: Joseph P. Machebeuf, 1887-89; Nicholas C. Matz, 1889-1917; J. Henry Tihen, 1917-31; Urban J. Vehr, 1931-67, first archbishop; James V. Casey, 1967-86; J. Francis Stafford, 1986-96.

Des Moines, Ia. (1911): Joseph L. Charron, C.PP.S., bishop, 1993.

Former bishops: Austin Dowling, 1912-19; Thomas W. Drumm, 1919-33; Gerald T. Bergan, 1934-48; Edward C. Daly, O.P., 1948-64; George J. Biskup, 1965-67; Maurice J. Dingman, 1968-86; William H. Bullock, 1987-93.

Detroit,* Mich. (1833; archdiocese, 1937): Cardinal Adam J. Maida, archbishop, 1990. Thomas J. Gumbleton, Moses B. Anderson, S.S.E., Kevin M. Britt, Allen H. Vigernon, Leonard P. Blair, Earl Boyea, auxiliaries.

Former ordinaries: Frederic Rese, 1833-71; Peter P. Lefevere, administrator, 1841-69; Caspar H. Borgess, 1871-88; John S. Foley, 1888-1918; Michael J. Gallagher, 1918-37; Cardinal Edward Mooney, 1937-58, first archbishop; Cardinal John F. Dearden, 1958-80; Cardinal Edmund C. Szoka, 1981-90.

Dodge City, Kans. (1951): Ronald M. Gilmore, bishop, 1998.

Former bishops: John B. Franz, 1951-59; Marion F. Forst, 1960-76; Eugene J. Gerber, 1976-82; Stanley G. Schlarman, bishop, 1983-98.

Dubuque,* Iowa (1837; archdiocese, 1893): Jerome Hanus, O.S.B., archbishop, 1995.

Former ordinaries: Mathias Loras, 1837-58; Clement Smyth, O.C.S.O., 1858-65; John Hennessy, 1866-1900, first archbishop; John J. Keane, 1900-11; James J. Keane, 1911-29; Francis J. Beckman, 1930-46; Henry P. Rohlman, 1946-54; Leo Binz, 1954-61; James J. Byrne, 1962-83; Daniel W. Kucera, O.S.B., 1984-95.

Duluth, Minn. (1889): Dennis M. Schnurr, 2001.

Former bishops: James McGolrick, 1889-1918; John T. McNicholas, O.P., 1918-25; Thomas A. Welch, 1926-59; Francis J. Schenk, 1960-69; Paul F. Anderson, 1969-82; Robert H. Brom, 1983-89; Roger L. Schwietz, O.M.I., 1990-2000.

El Paso, Tex. (1914): Armando X. Ochoa, bishop, 1996.

Former bishops: Anthony J. Schuler, S.J., 1915-42; Sidney M. Metzger, 1942-78. Patrick F. Flores, 1978-79; Raymundo J. Pena, 1980-95.

Erie, Pa. (1853): Donald W. Trautman, bishop, 1990.

Former bishops: Michael O'Connor, 1853-54; Josue M. Young, 1854-66; Tobias Mullen, 1868-99; John E. Fitzmaurice, 1899-1920; John M. Gannon, 1920-

66; John F. Whealon, 1966-69; Alfred M. Watson, 1969-82; Michael J. Murphy, 1982-90.

Evansville, Ind. (1944): Gerald A. Gettelfinger, bishop, 1989.

Former bishops: Henry J. Grimmelsman, 1944-65; Paul F. Leibold, 1966-69; Francis R. Shea, 1970-89.

Fairbanks, Alaska (1962): Donald Kettler, ,bishop, 2002.

Former bishops: Francis D. Gleeson, S.J., 1962-68; Robert L. Whelan, S.J., 1968-85; Michael J. Kaniecki, S.J., 1985-2000.

Fall River, Mass. (1904): Vacant.

Former bishops: William Stang, 1904-07; Daniel F. Feehan, 1907-34; James E. Cassidy, 1934-51; James L. Connolly, 1951-70; Daniel A. Cronin, 1970-91; Sean O'Malley, O.F.M. Cap., bishop, 1992-2002,.

Fargo, N. Dak. (1889): Samuel J. Aquila, bishop, 2002.

Established at Jamestown, transferred, 1897.

Former bishops: John Shanley, 1889-1909; James O'Reilly, 1910-34; Aloysius J. Muench, 1935-59; Leo F. Dworschak, 1960-70; Justin A. Driscoll, 1970-84; James S. Sullivan, bishop, 1985-2002.

Fort Wayne-South Bend, Ind. (1857): John M. D'Arcy, bishop, 1985.

Established as Fort Wayne, name changed, 1960.

Former bishops: John H. Luers, 1858-71; Joseph Dwenger, C.Pp. S., 1872-93; Joseph Rademacher, 1893-1900; Herman J. Alerding, 1900-24; John F. Noll, 1925-56; Leo A. Pursley, 1957-76; William E. McManus, 1976-85.

Fort Worth, Tex. (1969): Joseph P. Delaney, bishop, 1981.

Former bishop: John J. Cassata, 1969-80.

Fresno, Calif. (1967): John T. Steinbock, bishop, 1991.

Formerly Monterey-Fresno, 1922.

Former bishops (Monterey-Fresno): John J. Cantwell, administrator, 1922-24; John B. MacGinley, first bishop, 1924-32; Philip G. Sher, 1933-53; Aloysius J. Willinger, 1953-67.

Former bishops (Fresno): Timothy Manning, 1967-69; Hugh A. Donohoe, 1969-80; Joseph J. Madera, M.Pp.S., 1980-91.

Gallup, N. Mex. (1939): Donald Pelotte, S.S.S., bishop, 1990.

Former bishops: Bernard T. Espelage, O.F.M., 1940-69; Jerome J. Hastrich, 1969-90.

Galveston-Houston, Tex. (1847): Joseph A. Fiorenza, bishop, 1985. Vincent M. Rizzotto, José S. Vasquez, auxiliaries.

Established as Galveston, name changed, 1959.

Former bishops: John M. Odin, C.M., 1847-61; Claude M. Dubuis, 1862-92; Nicholas A. Gallagher, 1892-1918; Christopher E. Byrne, 1918-50; Wendelin J. Nold, 1950-75; John L. Morkovsky, 1975-84.

Gary, Ind. (1956): Dale J. Melczek, bishop, 1996. Former bishops: Andrew G. Grutka, 1957-84; Norbert F. Gaughan, 1984-96.

Gaylord, Mich. (1971): Patrick R. Cooney, bishop, 1989, installed 1990.

Former bishops: Edmund C. Szoka, 1971-81; Robert J. Rose, 1981-89.

Grand Island, Neb. (1912): Lawrence J. McNamara, bishop, 1978.

Established at Kearney, transferred, 1917.

Former bishops: James A. Duffy, 1913-31;

Stanislaus V. Bona, 1932-44; Edward J. Hunkeler, 1945-51; John L. Paschang, 1951-72; John J. Sullivan, 1972-77.

Grand Rapids, Mich. (1882): Robert J. Rose, bishop, 1989.

Former bishops: Henry J. Richter, 1883-1916; Michael J. Gallagher, 1916-18; Edward D. Kelly, 1919-26; Joseph G. Pinten, 1926-40; Joseph C. Plagens, 1941-43; Francis J. Haas, 1943-53; Allen J. Babcock, 1954-69; Joseph M. Breitenbeck, 1969-89.

Great Falls-Billings, Mont. (1904): Anthony M. Milone, bishop, 1988.

Established as Great Falls; name changed, 1980.

Former bishops: Mathias C. Lenihan, 1904-30; Edwin V. O'Hara, 1930-39; William J. Condon, 1939-67; Eldon B. Schuster, 1968-77; Thomas J. Murphy, 1978-87.

Green Bay, Wis. (1868): Robert J. Banks, bishop, 1990. Robert F. Morneau, auxiliary.

Former bishops: Joseph Melcher, 1868-73; Francis X. Krautbauer, 1875-85; Frederick X. Katzer, 1886-91; Sebastian G. Messmer, 1892-1903; Joseph J. Fox, 1904-14; Paul P. Rhode, 1915-45; Stanislaus V. Bona, 1945-67; Aloysius J. Wycislo, 1968-83; Adam J. Maida, 1984-90.

Greensburg, Pa. (1951): Anthony G. Bosco, bishop, 1987.

Former bishops: Hugh L. Lamb, 1951-59; Willam G. Connare, 1960-87.

Harrisburg, Pa. (1868): Nicholas C. Dattilo, bishop, 1990.

Former bishops: Jeremiah F. Shanahan, 1868-86; Thomas McGovern, 1888-98; John W. Shanahan, 1899-1916; Philip R. McDevitt, 1916-35; George L. Leech, 1935-71; Joseph T. Daley, 1971-83; William H. Keeler, 1984-89.

Hartford,* Conn. (1843; archdiocese, 1953): Daniel A. Cronin, archbishop, 1991, installed, 1992. Peter A. Rosazza, Christie A. Macaluso, auxiliaries.

Former ordinaries: William Tyler, 1844-49; Bernard O'Reilly, 1850-56; F. P. MacFarland, 1858-74; Thomas Galberry, O.S.A., 1876-78; Lawrence S. McMahon, 1879-93; Michael Tierney, 1894-1908; John J. Nilan, 1910-34; Maurice F. McAuliffe, 1934-44; Henry J. O'Brien, 1945-68, first archbishop; John F. Whealon, 1969-91.

Helena, Mont. (1884): Robert C. Morlino, 1999.

Former bishops: John B. Brondel, 1884-1903; John P. Carroll, 1904-25; George J. Finnigan, C.S.C., 1927-32; Ralph L. Hayes, 1933-35; Joseph M. Gilmore, 1936-62; Raymond Hunthausen, 1962-75; Elden F. Curtiss, 1976-93; Alexander J. Brunett, 1994-97.

Honolulu, Hawaii (1941): Francis X. DiLorenzo (apostolic administrator, 1993), bishop, 1994.

Former bishops: James J. Sweeney, 1941-68; John J. Scanlan, 1968-81; Joseph A. Ferrario, 1982-93.

Houma-Thibodaux, La. (1977): C. Michael Jarrell, bishop, 1993.

Former bishop: Warren L. Boudreaux, 1977-92.

Indianapolis,* Ind. (1834; archdiocese, 1944): Daniel M. Buechlein, O.S.B., archbishop, 1992.

Established at Vincennes, transferred, 1898.

Former ordinaries: Simon G. Bruté, 1834-39; Celestine de la Hailandiere, 1839-47; John S. Bazin, 1847-48; Maurice de St. Palais, 1849-77; Francis S. Chatard, 1878-1918; Joseph Chartrand, 1918-33; Joseph E. Ritter, 1934-46, first archbishop; Paul C.

Schulte, 1946-70; George J. Biskup, 1970-79; Edward T. O'Meara, 1980-92.

Jackson, Miss. (1837): William R. Houck, bishop, 1984.

Established at Natchez; title changed to Natchez-Jackson, 1956; transferred to Jackson, 1977 (Natchez made titular see).

Former bishops: John J. Chanche, S.S., 1841-52; James Van de Velde, S.J., 1853-55; William H. Elder, 1857-80; Francis A. Janssens, 1881-88; Thomas Heslin, 1889-1911; John E. Gunn, S.M., 1911-24; Richard O. Gerow, 1924-67; Joseph B. Brunini, 1968-84.

Jefferson City, Mo. (1956): John R. Gaydos, bishop, 1997.

Former bishops: Joseph Marling, C.Pp.S., 1956-69; Michael F. McAuliffe, 1969-97.

Joliet, Ill. (1948): Joseph L. Imesch, bishop, 1979. Roger L. Kaffer, James Fitzgerald auxiliaries.

Former bishops: Martin D. McNamara, 1949-66; Romeo Blanchette, 1966-79.

Juneau, Alaska (1951): Michael W. Warfel, bishop, 1996.

Former bishops: Dermot O'Flanagan, 1951-68; Joseph T. Ryan, administrator, 1968-71; Francis T. Hurley, 1971-76, administrator, 1976-79; Michael H. Kenny, 1979-95.

Kalamazoo, Mich. (1971): James A. Murray, bishop, 1997.

Former bishop: Paul V. Donovan, 1971-94; Alfred J. Markiewicz, 1995-97.

Kansas City,* Kans. (1877; archdiocese, 1952): James P. Keleher, archbishop, 1993.

Established as vicariate apostolic, 1850, became Diocese of Leavenworth, 1877, transferred to Kansas City 1947.

Former ordinaries: J. B. Miege, vicar apostolic, 1851-74; Louis M. Fink, O.S.B., vicar apostolic, 1874-77, first bishop, 1877-1904; Thomas F. Lillis, 1904-10; John Ward, 1910-29; Francis Johannes, 1929-37; Paul C. Schulte, 1937-46; George J. Donnelly, 1946-50; Edward Hunkeler, 1951-69, first archbishop; Ignatius J. Strecker, 1969-93.

Kansas City-St. Joseph, Mo. (Kansas City, 1880; St. Joseph, 1868; united 1956): Raymond J. Boland, bishop, 1993.

Former bishops: John J. Hogan, 1880-1913; Thomas F. Lillis, 1913-38; Edwin V. O'Hara, 1939-56; John P. Cody, 1956-61; Charles H. Helmsing, 1962-77; John J. Sullivan, 1977-93.

Former bishops (St. Joseph): John J. Hogan, 1868-80, administrator, 1880-93; Maurice F. Burke, 1893-1923; Francis Gilfillan, 1923-33; Charles H. Le Blond, 1933-56.

Knoxville, Tenn. (1988): Joseph E. Kurtz, 1999.

Former bishops: Anthony J. O'Connell, bishop, 1988-98.

La Crosse, Wis. (1868): Raymond L. Burke, bishop, 1995.

Former bishops: Michael Heiss, 1868-80; Kilian C. Flasch, 1881-91; James Schwebach, 1892-1921; Alexander J. McGavick, 1921-48; John P. Treacy, 1948-64; Frederick W. Freking, 1965-83; John J. Paul, 1983-94.

Lafayette, Ind. (1944): William L. Higi, bishop, 1984.

Former bishops: John G. Bennett, 1944-57; John J.

Carberry, 1957-65; Raymond J. Gallagher, 1965-82; George A. Fulcher, 1983-84.

Lafayette, La. (1918): Edward J. O'Donnell, bishop, 1994.

Former bishops: Jules B. Jeanmard, 1918-56; Maurice Schexnayder, 1956-72; Gerard L. Frey, 1973-89; Harry J. Flynn, 1989-94.

Lake Charles, La. (1980): Edward Braxton, bishop, 2000.

Former bishop: Jude Speyrer, 1980-2000.

Lansing, Mich. (1937): Carl F. Mengeling, bishop, 1995; installed 1996.

Former bishops: Joseph H. Albers, 1937-65; Alexander Zaleski, 1965-75; Kenneth J. Povish, 1975-95.

Laredo, Tx. (2000): James A. Tamayo, bishop, 2000.

Las Cruces, N. Mex. (1982): Ricardo Ramirez, C.S.B., bishop, 1982.

Las Vegas, Nev. (1995): Joseph Pepe, 2001.

Formerly Reno-Las Vegas, 1976; made separate diocese 1995.

Former bishops: Daniel F. Walsh, 1995-2000.

Lexington, Ky. (1988): Vacant.

Former bishops: James Kendrick Williams, 1988-2002.

Lincoln, Neb. (1887): Fabian W. Bruskewitz, bishop, 1992.

Former bishops: Thomas Bonacum, 1887-1911; J. Henry Tihen, 1911-17; Charles J. O'Reilly, 1918-23; Francis J. Beckman, 1924-30; Louis B. Kucera, 1930-57; James V. Casey, 1957-67; Glennon P. Flavin, 1967-92.

Little Rock, Ark. (1843): James Peter Sartain, bishop, 2000.

Former bishops: Andrew Byrne, 1844-62; Edward Fitzgerald, 1867-1907; John Morris, 1907-46; Albert L. Fletcher, 1946-72; Andrew J. McDonald, 1972-2000.

Los Angeles,* Calif. (1840; archdiocese, 1936): Cardinal Roger M. Mahony, archbishop, 1985. Thomas J. Curry, Joseph M. Sartoris, Gerald E. Wilkerson, Gabino Zavala, Edward William Clark, auxiliaries.

Founded as diocese of Two Californias, 1840; became Monterey diocese, 1850; Baja California detached from Monterey diocese, 1852; title changed to Monterey-Los Angeles, 1859; Los Angeles-San Diego, 1922; became archdiocese under present title, 1936 (San Diego became separate see).

Former ordinaries: Francisco Garcia Diego y Moreno, O.F.M., 1840-46; Joseph S. Alemany, O.P., 1850-53; Thaddeus Amat, C.M., 1854-78; Francis Mora, 1878-96; George T. Montgomery, 1896-1903; Thomas J. Conaty, 1903-15; John J. Cantwell, 1917-47, first archbishop; Cardinal James McIntyre, 1948-70; Cardinal Timothy Manning, 1970-85.

Louisville,* Ky. (1808; archdiocese, 1937): Thomas C. Kelly, O.P., archbishop, 1982.

Established at Bardstown, transferred, 1841.

Former ordinaries: Benedict J. Flaget, S.S., 1810-32; John B. David, S.S., 1832-33; Benedict J. Flaget, S.S., 1833-50; Martin J. Spalding, 1850-64; Peter J. Lavialle, 1865-67; William G. McCloskey, 1868-1909; Denis O'Donaghue, 1910-24; John A. Floersh, 1924-67, first archbishop; Thomas J. McDonough, 1967-81.

Lubbock, Tex. (1983): Placido Rodriguez, C.M.F., bishop, 1994.

Former bishop: Michael J. Sheehan, 1983-93.

Madison, Wis. (1946): William H. Bullock, bishop, 1993. George O. Wirz, auxiliary.

Former bishops: William P. O'Connor, 1946-67; Cletus F. O'Donnell, 1967-92.

Manchester, N.H. (1884): John B. McCormack, bishop, 1998; Francis J. Christian, auxiliary.

Former bishops: Denis M. Bradley, 1884-1903; John B. Delany, 1904-06; George A. Guertin, 1907-32; John B. Peterson, 1932-44; Matthew F. Brady, 1944-59; Ernest J. Primeau, 1960-74; Odore J. Gendron, 1975-90; Leo E. O'Neil, 1990-97.

Marquette, Mich. (1857): James H. Garland, bishop, 1992.

Founded as Sault Ste. Marie and Marquette; changed to Marquette, 1937.

Former bishops: Frederic Baraga, 1857-68; Ignatius Mrak, 1869-78; John Vertin, 1879-99; Frederick Eis, 1899-1922; Paul J. Nussbaum, C.P., 1922-35; Joseph C. Plagens, 1935-40; Francis Magner, 1941-47; Thomas L. Noa, 1947-68; Charles A. Salatka, 1968-77; Mark F. Schmitt, 1978-92.

Memphis, Tenn. (1970): J. Terry Steib, S.V.D., bishop, 1993.

Former bishops: Carroll T. Dozier, 1971-82; J. Francis Stafford, 1982-86; Daniel M. Buechlein, O.S.B.,1987-92.

Metuchen, N.J. (1981): Paul G. Bootkoski, bishop, 2002.

Former bishops: Theodore E. McCarrick, 1981-86; Edward T. Hughes, 1987-97; Vincent DePaul Breen, 1997-2002.

Miami,* Fla. (1958; archdiocese, 1968): John C. Favalora, archbishop, 1994. Agustin A. Roman, Gilberto Fernandez, Thomas G. Wenski, auxiliaries.

Former ordinaries: Coleman F. Carroll, 1958-77, first archbishop; Edward A. McCarthy, 1977-94.

Milwaukee,* Wis. (1843; archdiocese, 1875): Timothy M. Dolan, archbishop, 2002. Richard J. Sklba, auxiliary.

Former ordinaries: John M. Henni, 1844-81, first archbishop; Michael Heiss, 1881-90; Frederick X. Katzer, 1891-1903; Sebastian G. Messmer, 1903-30; Samuel A. Stritch, 1930-39; Moses E. Kiley, 1940-53; Albert G. Meyer, 1953-58; William E. Cousins, 1959-77; Rembert G. Weakland, O.S.B., 1977-2002.

Mobile,* Ala. (1829; archdiocese, 1980): Oscar H. Lipscomb, first archbishop, 1980.

Founded as Mobile, 1829; title changed to Mobile-Birmingham, 1954; redesignated Mobile, 1969.

Former bishops: Michael Portier, 1829-59; John Quinlan, 1859-83; Dominic Manucy, 1884; Jeremiah O'Sullivan, 1885-96; Edward P. Allen, 1897-1926; Thomas J. Toolen, 1927-69; John L. May, 1969-80.

Monterey in California (1967): Sylvester D. Ryan, bishop, 1992.

Formerly Monterey-Fresno, 1922. (Originally established in 1850, see Los Angeles listing.)

Former bishops (Monterey-Fresno): John J. Cantwell, administrator, 1922-24; John B. MacGinley, first bishop, 1924-32; Philip G. Sher, 1933-53; Aloysius J. Willinger, 1953-67.

Former bishops (Monterey): Harry A. Clinch, 1967-82; Thaddeus A. Shubsda, 1982-91.

Nashville, Tenn. (1837): Edward U. Kmiec, bishop, 1992.

Former bishops: Richard P. Miles, O.P., 1838-60; James Whelan, O.P., 1860-64; Patrick A. Feehan, 1865-80; Joseph Rademacher, 1883-93; Thomas S. Byrne, 1894-1923; Alphonse J. Smith, 1924-35; William L. Adrian, 1936-69; Joseph A. Durick, 1969-75; James D. Niedergeses, 1975-92.

Newark,* N.J. (1853; archdiocese, 1937): John J. Myers, 2001. David Arias, O.A.R., Charles J. McDonnell, Arthur J. Serratelli, auxiliaries.

Former ordinaries: James R. Bayley, 1853-72; Michael A. Corrigan, 1873-80; Winand M. Wigger, 1881-1901; John J. O'Connor, 1901-27; Thomas J. Walsh, 1928-52, first archbishop; Thomas A. Boland, 1953-74; Peter L. Gerety, 1974-86; Theodore E. McCarrick, 1986-2000.

New Orleans,* La. (1793; archdiocese, 1850): Alfred Hughes, 2002. Dominic Carmon, S.V.D., auxiliary.

Former ordinaries: Luis Penalver y Cardenas, 1793-1801; John Carroll, administrator, 1805-15; W. Louis Dubourg, S.S., 1815-25; Joseph Rosati, C.M., administrator, 1826-29; Leo De Neckere, C.M., 1829-33; Anthony Blanc, 1835-60, first archbishop; Jean Marie Odin, C.M., 1861-70; Napoleon J. Perche, 1870-83; Francis X. Leray, 1883-87; Francis A. Janssens, 1888-97; Placide L. Chapelle, 1897-1905; James H. Blenk, S.M., 1906-17; John W. Shaw, 1918-34; Joseph F. Rummel, 1935-64; John P. Cody, 1964-65; Philip M. Hannan, 1965-88; Francis B. Schulte, 1988-2002.

Newton, Mass. (Melkite) (1966; eparchy, 1976): John A. Elya, B.S.O., eparch, 1993; installed, 1994. Nicholas Samra, auxiliary.

Former ordinaries: Justin Najmy, exarch, 1966-68; Joseph Tawil, exarch, 1969-76, first eparch, 1976-89; Ignatius Ghattas, B.S.O., 1990-92.

New Ulm, Minn. (1957): John Clayton Nienstedt, bishop, 2001.

Former bishop: Alphonse J. Schladweiler, 1958-75; Raymond A. Lucker, 1975-2000.

New York,* N.Y. (1808; archdiocese, 1850): Cardinal Edward M. Egan, archbishop, 2000. Robert A. Brucato, Robert J. Iriondo, Dominick J. Lagonegro, Timothy A. McDowell, auxiliaries.

Former ordinaries: Richard L. Concanen, O.P., 1808-10; John Connolly, O.P., 1814-25; John Dubois, S.S., 1826-42; John J. Hughes, 1842-64, first archbishop; Cardinal John McCloskey, 1864-85; Michael A. Corrigan, 1885-1902; Cardinal John Farley, 1902-18; Cardinal Patrick Hayes, 1919-38; Cardinal Francis Spellman, 1939-67; Cardinal Terence J. Cooke, 1968-83; Cardinal John J. O'Connor, 1984-2000.

Norwich, Conn. (1953): Daniel A. Hart, bishop, 1995.

Former bishops: Bernard J. Flanagan, 1953-59; Vincent J. Hines, 1960-75; Daniel P. Reilly, 1975-94.

Oakland, Calif. (1962): John S. Cummins, bishop, 1977.

Former bishop: Floyd L. Begin, 1962-77.

Ogdensburg, N.Y. (1872): Gerald Michael Barbarito, 1999.

Former bishops: Edgar P. Wadhams, 1872-91; Henry Gabriels, 1892-1921; Joseph H. Conroy, 1921-39; Francis J. Monaghan, 1939-42; Bryan J. McEntegart, 1943-53; Walter P. Kellenberg, 1954-57; James J. Navagh, 1957-63; Leo R. Smith, 1963; Thomas A. Donnellan, 1964-68; Stanislaus J. Brzana, 1968-93; Paul S. Loverde, 1993-99.

Oklahoma City,* Okla. (1905; archdiocese, 1972): Eusebius J. Beltran, archbishop, 1993.
Former ordinaries: Theophile Meerschaert, 1905-24; Francis C. Kelley, 1924-48; Eugene J. McGuinness, 1948-57; Victor J. Reed, 1958-71; John R. Quinn, 1971-77, first archbishop; Charles A. Salatka, 1977-92.

Omaha,* Nebr. (1885; archdiocese, 1945): Elden F. Curtiss, archbishop, 1993.
Former ordinaries: James O'Gorman, O.C.S.O., 1859-74, vicar apostolic; James O'Connor, vicar apostolic, 1876-85, first bishop, 1885-90; Richard Scannell, 1891-1916; Jeremiah J. Harty, 1916-27; Francis Beckman, administrator, 1926-28; Joseph F. Rummel, 1928-35; James H. Ryan, 1935-47, first archbishop; Gerald T. Bergan, 1948-69; Daniel E. Sheehan, 1969-93.

Orange, Calif. (1976): Tod D. Brown, bishop, 1998; Jaime Soto, auxiliary.
Former bishop: William R. Johnson, 1976-86. Norman F. McFarland, 1986-98.

Orlando, Fla. (1968): Norbert M. Dorsey, C.P., bishop, 1990.
Former bishops: William Borders, 1968-74; Thomas J. Grady, 1974-89.

Our Lady of Deliverance of Newark (for Syrianrite Catholics of the U.S. and Canada) (1995): Joseph Younan, bishop, 1996.

Our Lady of Lebanon of Los Angeles, Calif. (Maronite) (1994): Robert J. Shaheen, 2000.
Former eparch: John G. Chedid, 1994-2000.

Owensboro, Ky. (1937): John J. McRaith, bishop, 1982.
Former bishops: Francis R. Cotton, 1938-60, Henry J. Soenneker, 1961-82.

Palm Beach, Fla. (1984): Sean O'Malley, O.F.M. Cap., bishop, 1992.
Former bishop: Thomas V. Daily, 1984-90; J. Keith Symons, 1990-98; Anthony J. O'Connell, 1998-2002.

Parma, Ohio (Byzantine, Ruthenian) (1969): John Kudrick, bishop, 2002.
Former bishops: Emil Mihalik, 1969-84; Andrew Pataki, 1984-95; Basil Schott, O.F.M., 1996-2002.

Passaic, N.J. (Byzantine, Ruthenian) (1963): Andrew Pataki, eparch, 1996.
Former bishops: Stephen Kocisko, 1963-68; Michael J. Dudick, 1968-95.

Paterson, N.J. (1937): Frank J. Rodimer, bishop, 1978.
Former bishops: Thomas H. McLaughlin, 1937-47; Thomas A. Boland, 1947-52; James A. McNulty, 1953-63; James J. Navagh, 1963-65; Lawrence B. Casey, 1966-77.

Pensacola-Tallahassee, Fla. (1975): John H.Ricard, S.S.J., bishop, 1997.
Former bishops: Rene H. Gracida, 1975-83; J. Keith Symons, 1983-90; John M. Smith, 1991-95.

Peoria, Ill. (1877): Daniel R. Jenky, C.S.C., bishop, 2002.
Former bishops: John L. Spalding, 1877-1908; Edmund M. Dunne, 1909-29; Joseph H. Schlarman, 1930-51; William E. Cousins, 1952-58; John B. Franz, 1959-71; Edward W. O'Rourke, 1971- 90; John J. Myers, 1990-2001.

Philadelphia,* Pa. (1808; archdiocese, 1875): Cardinal Anthony J. Bevilacqua, archbishop, 1988. Edward P. Cullen, Robert P. Maginnis, Joseph F. Martino, Michael F. Burbidge, auxiliaries.

Former ordinaries: Michael Egan, O.F.M., 1810-14; Henry Conwell, 1820-42; Francis P. Kenrick, 1842-51; John N. Neumann, C.SS.R., 1852-60; James F. Wood, 1860-83, first archbishop; Patrick J. Ryan, 1884-1911; Edmond F. Prendergast, 1911-18; Cardinal Dennis Dougherty, 1918-51; Cardinal John O'Hara, C.S.C., 1951-60; Cardinal John Krol, 1961-88.

Philadelphia,* Pa. (Byzantine, Ukrainian) (1924; metropolitan, 1958): Stephen Soroka, archbishop, 2001.
Former ordinaries: Stephen Ortynsky, O.S.B.M., 1907-16; Constantine Bohachevsky, 1924-61; Ambrose Senyshyn, O.S.B.M., 1961-76; Joseph Schmondiuk, 1977-78; Myroslav J. Lubachivsky, 1979-80, apostolic administrator, 1980-81; Stephen Sulyk, 1981-2000.

Phoenix, Ariz. (1969): Thomas J. O'Brien, bishop, 1982.
Former bishops: Edward A. McCarthy, 1969-76; James S. Rausch, 1977-81.

Pittsburgh,* Pa. (Byzantine, Ruthenian) (1924; metropolitan, 1969): Basil Schott, O.F.M., archbishop, 2002.
Former ordinaries: Basil Takach 1924-48; Daniel Ivancho, 1948-54; Nicholas T. Elko, 1955-67; Stephen J. Kocisko, 1968-91, first metropolitan; Thomas V. Dolinay, 1991-93; Judson M. Procyk, 1995-2001.

Pittsburgh, Pa. (1843): Donald W. Wuerl, bishop, 1988. William J. Winter, David A. Zubic, auxiliaries.
Former bishops: Michael O'Connor, 1843-53, 1854-60; Michael Domenec, C.M., 1860-76; J. Tuigg, 1876-89; Richard Phelan, 1889-1904; J.F. Regis Canevin, 1904-20; Hugh C. Boyle, 1921-50; John F. Dearden, 1950-58; John J. Wright, 1959-69; Vincent M. Leonard, 1969-83; Anthony J. Bevilacqua, 1983-88.

Portland, Me. (1853): Joseph J. Gerry, O.S.B., bishop, 1989. Michael R. Cote, auxiliary.
Former bishops: David W. Bacon, 1855-74; James A. Healy, 1875-1900; William H. O'Connell, 1901-06; Louis S. Walsh, 1906-24; John G. Murray, 1925-31; Joseph E. McCarthy, 1932-55; Daniel J. Feeney, 1955-69; Peter L. Gerety, 1969-74; Edward C. O'Leary, 1974-88.

Portland,* Ore. (1846): John G. Vlazny, archbishop, 1997. Kenneth D. Steiner, auxiliary.
Established as Oregon City, name changed, 1928.
Former ordinaries: Francis N. Blanchet, 1846-80 vicar apostolic, first archbishop; Charles J. Seghers, 1880-84; William H. Gross, C.SS.R., 1885-98; Alexander Christie, 1899-1925; Edward D. Howard, 1926-66; Robert J. Dwyer, 1966-74; Cornelius M. Power, 1974-86; William J. Levada, 1986-95; Francis E. George, 1996-97.

Providence, R.I. (1872): Robert E. Mulvee, bishop, 1997. Robert McManus, auxiliary.
Former bishops: Thomas F. Hendricken, 1872-86; Matthew Harkins, 1887-1921; William A. Hickey, 1921-33; Francis P. Keough, 1934-47; Russell J. McVinney, 1948-71; Louis E. Gelineau, 1972-97.

Pueblo, Colo. (1941): Arthur N. Tafoya, bishop, 1980.
Former bishops: Joseph C. Willging, 1942-59; Charles A. Buswell, 1959-79.

Raleigh, N.C. (1924): F. Joseph Gossman, bishop, 1975.
Former bishops: William J. Hafey, 1925-37; Eugene

J. McGuinness, 1937-44; Vincent S. Waters, 1945-75.
Rapid City, S. Dak. (1902): Blase Cupich, bishop, 1998.

Established at Lead, transferred, 1930.

Former bishops: John Stariha, 1902-09; Joseph F. Busch, 1910-15; John J. Lawler, 1916-48; William T. McCarty, C.SS.R., 1948-69; Harold J. Dimmerling, 1969-87; Charles J. Chaput, O.F.M. Cap., 1988-97.
Reno, Nev. (1931): Phillip F. Straling, bishop, 1995.

Established at Reno, 1931; title changed to Reno-Las Vegas, 1976; redesignated Reno, 1995, when Las Vegas was made a separate diocese.

Former bishops (Reno/Reno-Las Vegas): Thomas K. Gorman, 1931-52; Robert J. Dwyer, 1952-66; Joseph Green, 1967-74; Norman F. McFarland, 1976-86; Daniel F. Walsh, 1987-95.
Richmond, Va. (1820): Walter F. Sullivan, bishop, 1974.

Former bishops: Patrick Kelly, 1820-22; Ambrose Marechal, S.S., administrator, 1822-28; James Whitfield, administrator, 1828-34; Samuel Eccleston, S.S., administrator, 1834-40; Richard V. Whelan, 1841-50; John McGill, 1850-72; James Gibbons, 1872-77; John J. Keane, 1878-88; Augustine Van de Vyver, 1889-1911; Denis J. O'Connell, 1912-26; Andrew J. Brennan, 1926-45; Peter L. Ireton, 1945-58; John J. Russell, 1958-73.
Rochester, N.Y. (1868): Matthew H. Clark, bishop, 1979.

Former bishops: Bernard J. McQuaid, 1868-1909; Thomas F. Hickey, 1909-28; John F. O'Hern, 1929-33; Edward F. Mooney, 1933-37; James E. Kearney, 1937-66; Fulton J. Sheen, 1966-69; Joseph L. Hogan, 1969-78.
Rockford, Ill. (1908): Thomas G. Doran, bishop, 1994.

Former bishops: Peter J. Muldoon, 1908-27; Edward F. Hoban, 1928-42; John J. Boylan, 1943-53; Raymond P. Hillinger, 1953-56; Loras T. Lane, 1956-68; Arthur J. O'Neill, 1968-94.
Rockville Centre, N.Y. (1957): William Francis Murphy, bishop, 2001. John C. Dunne, Emil A. Wcela, auxiliaries.

Former bishop: Walter P. Kellenberg, 1957-76; John R. McGann, 1976-2000; James McHugh, 2000.
Sacramento, Calif. (1886): William K. Weigand, bishop, 1993; installed, 1994. Richard J. Garcia, auxiliary.

Former bishops: Patrick Manogue, 1886-95; Thomas Grace, 1896-1921; Patrick J. Keane, 1922-28; Robert J. Armstrong, 1929-57; Joseph T. McGucken, 1957-62; Alden J. Bell, 1962-79; Francis A. Quinn, 1979-93.
Saginaw, Mich. (1938): Kenneth E. Untener, bishop, 1980.

Former bishops: William F. Murphy, 1938-50; Stephen S. Woznicki, 1950-68; Francis F. Reh, 1969-80.
St. Augustine, Fla. (1870): Victor Benito Galeone, bishop, 2001.

Former bishops: Augustin Verot, S.S., 1870-76; John Moore, 1877-1901; William J. Kenny, 1902-13; Michael J. Curley, 1914-21; Patrick J. Barry, 1922-40; Joseph P. Hurley, 1940-67; Paul F. Tanner, 1968-79; John J. Snyder, 1979-2000.
St. Cloud, Minn. (1889): John F. Kinney, bishop, 1995.

Former bishops: Otto Zardetti, 1889-94; Martin Marty, O.S.B., 1895-96; James Trobec, 1897-1914; Joseph F. Busch, 1915-53; Peter Bartholome, 1953-68; George H. Speltz, 1968-87; Jerome Hanus, O.S.B.,1987-94.
St. George's in Canton, Ohio (Byzantine, Romanian) (1982; eparchy, 1987): John Michael Botean, bishop, 1996.

Former bishop: Vasile Louis Puscas, 1983-93.
St. Josaphat in Parma, Ohio (Byzantine, Ukrainians) (1983): Robert M. Moskal, bishop, 1984.
St. Louis,* Mo. (1826; archdiocese, 1847): Justin F. Rigali, archbishop, 1994. Joseph F. Naumann, auxiliary.

Former ordinaries: Joseph Rosati, C.M., 1827-43; Peter R. Kenrick, 1843-95, first archbishop; John J. Kain, 1895-1903; Cardinal John Glennon, 1903-46; Cardinal Joseph Ritter, 1946-67; Cardinal John J. Carberry, 1968-79; John L. May, 1980-92.
St. Maron, Brooklyn, N.Y. (Maronite) (1966; diocese, 1971): Hector Y. Doueihi, eparch, 1997.

Established at Detroit; transferred to Brooklyn, 1977.

Former eparch: Francis Zayek, exarch 1966-72, first eparch 1972-97
St. Nicholas in Chicago (Byzantine Eparchy of St. Nicholas of the Ukrainians) (1961): Vacant.

Former bishops: Jaroslav Gabro, 1961-80; Innocent H. Lotocky, O.S.B.M., 1981-93; Michael Wiwchar, C.SS.R., 1993-2000.
St. Paul and Minneapolis,* Minn. (1850; archdiocese, 1888): Harry J. Flynn, archbishop, 1995. Frederick F. Campbell, Richard Edmund Pates, auxiliaries.

Former ordinaries: Joseph Cretin, 1851-57; Thomas L. Grace, O.P., 1859-84; John Ireland, 1884-1918, first archbishop; Austin Dowling, 1919-30; John G. Murray, 1931-56; William O. Brady, 1956-61; Leo Binz, 1962-75; John R. Roach, 1975-95.
St. Peter the Apostle of San Diego (Chaldean) (May 21, 2002, eparchy): Sarhad Jammo, first eparch, 2002.
St. Petersburg, Fla. (1968): Robert N. Lynch, bishop, 1996.

Former bishops: Charles McLaughlin, 1968-78; W. Thomas Larkin, 1979-88; John C. Favalora, 1989-94.
St. Thomas the Apostle of Detroit (Chaldean) (1982; eparchy, 1985): Ibrahim N. Ibrahim, exarch, 1982; first eparch, 1985.
St. Thomas of the Syro-Malabars of Chicago (Syro-Malabars) (2001, eparchy): Jacob Angadiath, first eparch, 2001.
Salina, Kans. (1887): George K. Fitzsimons, bishop, 1984.

Established at Concordia, transferred, 1944.

Former bishops: Richard Scannell, 1887-91; John J. Hennessy, administrator, 1891-98; John F. Cunningham, 1898-1919; Francis J. Tief, 1921-38; Frank A. Thill, 1938-57; Frederick W. Freking, 1957-64; Cyril J. Vogel, 1965-79; Daniel W. Kucera, O.S.B., 1980-84.
Salt Lake City, Utah (1891): George H. Niederauer, bishop, 1995.

Former bishops: Lawrence Scanlan, 1891-1915; Joseph S. Glass, C.M., 1915-26; John J. Mitty, 1926-32; James E. Kearney, 1932-37; Duane G. Hunt, 1937-60; J. Lennox Federal, 1960-80; William K. Weigand, 1980-93.

San Angelo, Tex. (1961): Michael D. Pfeifer, O.M.I., bishop, 1985.

Former bishops: Thomas J. Drury, 1962-65; Thomas Tschoepe, 1966-69; Stephen A. Leven, 1969-79; Joseph A. Fiorenza, 1979-84.

San Antonio,* **Tex.** (1874; archdiocese, 1926): Patrick F. Flores, archbishop, 1979. Thomas J. Flanagan, Patrick J. Zurek, auxiliaries.

Former ordinaries: Anthony D. Pellicer, 1874-80; John C. Neraz, 1881-94; John A. Forest, 1895-1911; John W. Shaw, 1911-18; Arthur Jerome Drossaerts, 1918-40, first archbishop; Robert E. Lucey, 1941-69; Francis Furey, 1969-79.

San Bernardino, Calif. (1978): Gerald R. Barnes, bishop, 1995. Dennis P. O'Neil, auxiliary.

Former bishop: Phillip F. Straling, 1978-95.

San Diego, Calif. (1936): Robert H. Brom, bishop, 1990. Gilbert Espinoza Chavez, Salvatore Cordileone, auxiliaries.

Former bishops: Charles F. Buddy, 1936-66; Francis J. Furey, 1966-69; Leo T. Maher, 1969-90.

San Francisco,* **Calif.** (1853): William J. Levada, archbishop, 1995. John C. Wester, auxiliary.

Former ordinaries: Joseph S. Alemany, O.P., 1853-84; Patrick W. Riordan, 1884-1914; Edward J. Hanna, 1915-35; John Mitty, 1935-61; Joseph T. McGucken, 1962-77; John R. Quinn, 1977-95.

San Jose, Calif. (1981): Patrick J. McGrath, bishop, 1999.

Former ordinaries: R. Pierre DuMaine, 1981-98.

Santa Fe*, N. Mex. (1850; archdiocese, 1875): Michael J. Sheehan, archbishop, 1993.

Former ordinaries: John B. Lamy, 1850-85; first archbishop; John B. Salpointe, 1885-94; Placide L. Chapelle, 1894-97; Peter Bourgade, 1899-1908; John B. Pitaval, 1909-18; Albert T. Daeger, O.F.M., 1919-32; Rudolph A. Gerken, 1933-43; Edwin V. Byrne, 1943-63; James P. Davis, 1964-74; Robert F. Sanchez, 1974-93.

Santa Rosa, Calif. (1962): Daniel Walsh, 2000.

Former bishops: Leo T. Maher, 1962-69; Mark J. Hurley, 1969-86; John T. Steinbock, 1987-91; G. Patrick Ziemann, 1992-99.

Savannah, Ga. (1850): John Kevin Boland, bishop, 1995.

Former bishops: Francis X. Gartland, 1850-54; John Barry, 1857-59; Augustin Verot, S.S., 1861-70; Ignatius Persico, O.F.M. Cap., 1870-72; William H. Gross, C.SS.R., 1873-85; Thomas A. Becker, 1886-99; Benjamin J. Keiley, 1900-22; Michael Keyes, S.M., 1922-35; Gerald P. O'Hara, 1935-59; Thomas J. McDonough, 1960-67; Gerard L. Frey, 1967-72; Raymond W. Lessard, 1973-95.

Scranton, Pa. (1868): James C. Timlin, bishop, 1984. John M. Dougherty, auxiliary.

Former bishops: William O'Hara, 1868-99; Michael J. Hoban, 1899-1926; Thomas C. O'Reilly, 1928-38; William J. Hafey, 1938-54; Jerome D. Hannan, 1954-65; J. Carroll McCormick, 1966-83; John J. O'Connor, 1983-84.

Seattle,* **Wash.** (1850; archdiocese, 1951): Alexander J. Brunett, archbishop, 1997.

George L. Thomas, auxiliary. Established as Nesqually, name changed, 1907.

Former ordinaries; Augustin M. Blanchet, 1850-79; Aegidius Junger, 1879-95; Edward J. O'Dea, 1896-1932; Gerald Shaughnessy, S.M., 1933-50; Thomas

A. Connolly, first archbishop, 1950-75; Raymond G. Hunthausen, 1975-91; Thomas J. Murphy, 1991-97.

Shreveport, La. (1986): William B. Friend, bishop, 1986.

Sioux City, Ia. (1902): Daniel N. DiNardo, bishop, 1998.

Former bishops: Philip J. Garrigan, 1902-19; Edmond Heelan, 1919-48; Joseph M. Mueller, 1948-70; Frank H. Greteman, 1970-83; Lawrence D. Soens, 1983-98.

Sioux Falls, S. Dak. (1889): Robert J. Carlson, bishop, 1995.

Former bishops: Martin Marty, O.S.B., 1889-94; Thomas O'Gorman, 1896-1921; Bernard J. Mahoney, 1922-39; William O. Brady, 1939-56; Lambert A. Hoch, 1956-78; Paul V. Dudley, 1978-95.

Spokane, Wash. (1913): William S. Skylstad, bishop, 1990.

Former bishops: Augustine F. Schinner, 1914-25; Charles D. White, 1927-55; Bernard J. Topel, 1955-78; Lawrence H. Welsh, 1978-90.

Springfield, Ill. (1853): George J. Lucas, 1999.

Established at Quincy, transferred to Alton 1857; transferred to Springfield 1923.

Former bishops: Henry D. Juncker, 1857-68; Peter J. Baltes, 1870-86; James Ryan, 1888-1923; James A. Griffin, 1924-48; William A. O'Connor, 1949-75; Joseph A. McNicholas, 1975-83; Daniel L. Ryan, bishop, 1984-99.

Springfield, Mass. (1870): Thomas L. Dupre, bishop, 1995.

Former bishops: Patrick T. O'Reilly, 1870-92; Thomas D. Beaven, 1892-1920; Thomas M. O'Leary, 1921-49; Christopher J. Weldon, 1950-77; Joseph F. Maguire, 1977-91; John A. Marshall, 1991-94.

Springfield-Cape Girardeau, Mo. (1956): John J. Leibrecht, bishop, 1984.

Former bishops: Charles Helmsing, 1956-62; Ignatius J. Strecker, 1962-69; William Baum, 1970-73; Bernard F. Law, 1973-84.

Stamford, Conn. (Byzantine, Ukrainian) (1956); Basil Losten, eparch, 1977.

Former eparchs: Ambrose Senyshyn, O.S.B.M., 1956-61; Joseph Schmondiuk, 1961-77.

Steubenville, Ohio (1944): Robert Daniel Conlon, 2002.

Former bishops: John K. Mussio, 1945-77; Albert H. Ottenweller, 1977-92; Gilbert I. Sheldon, 1992-2002.

Stockton, Calif. (1962): Stephen E. Blaire, bishop, 1999.

Former bishops: Hugh A. Donohoe, 1962-69; Merlin J. Guilfoyle, 1969-79; Roger M. Mahony, 1980-85; Donald W. Montrose, 1986-99.

Superior, Wis. (1905): Raphael M. Fliss, bishop, 1985.

Former bishops: Augustine F. Schinner, 1905-13; Joseph M. Koudelka, 1913-21; Joseph G. Pinten, 1922-26; Theodore M. Reverman, 1926-41; William P. O'Connor, 1942-46; Albert G. Meyer, 1946-53; Joseph Annabring, 1954-59; George A. Hammes, 1960-85.

Syracuse, N.Y. (1886): James M. Moynihan, bishop, 1995. Thomas J. Costello, auxiliary.

Former bishops: Patrick A. Ludden, 1887-1912; John Grimes, 1912-22; Daniel J. Curley, 1923-32; John A. Duffy, 1933-37; Walter A. Foery, 1937-70;

David F. Cunningham, 1970-76; Frank J. Harrison, 1976-87; Joseph T. O'Keefe, 1987-95.

Toledo, Ohio (1910): James R. Hoffman, bishop, 1980. Robert W. Donnelly, auxiliary.

Former bishops: Joseph Schrembs, 1911-21; Samuel A. Stritch, 1921-30; Karl J. Alter, 1931-50; George J. Rehring, 1950-67; John A. Donovan, 1967-80.

Trenton, N.J. (1881): John M. Smith, bishop, 1997. Former bishops: Michael J. O'Farrell, 1881-94; James A. McFaul, 1894-1917; Thomas J. Walsh, 1918-28; John J. McMahon, 1928-32; Moses E. Kiley, 1934-40; William A. Griffin, 1940-50; George W. Ahr, 1950-79; John C. Reiss, 1980 -97.

Tucson, Ariz. (1897): Manuel D. Moreno, bishop, 1982; Gerald F. Kicanas, coadjutor, 2002.

Former bishops: Peter Bourgade, 1897-99; Henry Granjon, 1900-22; Daniel J. Gercke, 1923-60; Francis J. Green, 1960-81;.

Tulsa, Okla. (1972): Edward J. Slattery, bishop, 1993.

Former bishops: Bernard J. Ganter, 1973-77; Eusebius J. Beltran, 1978-92.

Tyler, Tex. (1986): Alvaro Corrada del Rio, S.J., 2000.

Former bishop: Charles E. Herzig, 1987-91; Edmond Carmody, 1992-2000.

Van Nuys, Calif. (Byzantine, Ruthenian) (1981): William C. Skurla, 2002.

Former bishop: Thomas V. Dolinay, 1982-90; George M. Kuzma, 1991-2000.

Venice, Fla. (1984): John J. Nevins, bishop, 1984.

Victoria, Tex. (1982): David E. Fellhauer, bishop, 1990.

Former bishop: Charles V. Grahmann, 1982-89.

Washington,* D.C. (1939): Cardinal Theodore E. McCarrick, archbishop, 2000. Leonard Olivier, S.V.D., Kevin J. Farrell, Francisco González Valer, S.F, auxiliaries.

Former ordinaries: Michael J. Curley, 1939-47; Cardinal Patrick O'Boyle, 1948-73; Cardinal William Baum, 1973-80; Cardinal James A. Hickey, 1980-2000.

Wheeling-Charleston, W. Va. (1850): Bernard W. Schmitt, bishop, 1989.

Established as Wheeling; name changed, 1974.

Former bishops: Richard V. Whelan, 1850-74; John J. Kain, 1875-93; Patrick J. Donahue, 1894-1922; John J. Swint, 1922-62; Joseph H. Hodges, 1962-85; Francis B. Schulte, 1985-88.

Wichita, Kans. (1887): Thomas J. Olmsted, bishop, 2001.

Former bishops: John J. Hennessy, 1888-1920; Augustus J. Schwertner, 1921-39; Christian H.

Winkelmann, 1940-46; Mark K. Carroll, 1947-67; David M. Maloney, 1967-82; Eugene J. Gerber, 1982-2001.

Wilmington, Del. (1868): Michael A. Saltarelli, bishop, 1995.

Former bishops: Thomas A. Becker, 1868-86; Alfred A. Curtis, 1886-96; John J. Monaghan, 1897-1925; Edmond Fitzmaurice, 1925-60; Michael Hyle, 1960-67; Thomas J. Mardaga, 1968-84; Robert E. Mulvee, 1985-95.

Winona, Minn. (1889): Bernard J. Harrington, 1998.

Former bishops: Joseph B. Cotter, 1889-1909; Patrick R. Heffron, 1910-27; Francis M. Kelly, 1928-49; Edward A. Fitzgerald, 1949-69; Loras J. Watters, 1969-86; John G. Vlazny, 1987-97.

Worcester, Mass. (1950): Daniel P. Reilly, bishop, 1994.George E. Rueger, auxiliary.

Former bishops: John J. Wright, 1950-59; Bernard J. Flanagan, 1959-83; Timothy J. Harrington, 1983-94.

Yakima, Wash. (1951):Carlos A. Sevilla, S.J., bishop, 1996

Former bishops: Joseph P. Dougherty, 1951-69; Cornelius M. Power, 1969-74; Nicolas E. Walsh, 1974-76; William S. Skylstad, 1977-90; Francis E. George, O.M.I., 1990-96.

Youngstown, Ohio (1943): Thomas J. Tobin, bishop, 1995; installed 1996.Former bishops: James A. McFadden, 1943-52; Emmet M. Walsh, 1952-68; James W. Malone, 1968-95.

Apostolic Exarchate for Armenian Catholics in the United States and Canada, New York, N.Y. (1981): Manuel Batakian, exarch, 2000.

Former exarch: Nerses Mikael Setian, 1981-93; Hovhannes Tertzakian, O.M. Ven., 1995-2000.

Archdiocese for the Military Ordinariate, U.S.A., Washington, D.C. (1957; restructured, 1985): Archbishop Edwin F. O'Brien, military ordinary, 1997. Francis X. Roque, Joseph J. Madera, M.Pp.S., John J. Kaising, auxiliaries.

Military vicar appointed, 1917; canonically established, 1957, as U.S. Military Vicariate under jurisdiction of New York archbishop; name changed, restructured as independent jurisdiction, 1985.

Former military vicars: Cardinal Patrick Hayes, 1917-38; Cardinal Francis Spellman, 1939-67; Cardinal Terence J. Cooke, 1968-83; Cardinal John J. O'Connor, apostolic administrator, 1984-85.

Former military ordinaries: Archbishop Joseph T. Ryan, 1985-91; Joseph T. Dimino, 1991-97.

(Note: For coverage of Missionary Bishops, see under Missionary Activity of the Church of the U.S.)

CHANCERY OFFICES OF U.S. ARCHDIOCESES AND DIOCESES

A chancery office, under this or another title, is the central administrative office of an archdiocese or diocese. (Archdioceses are indicated by asterisk.)

Albany, NY: Pastoral Center, 40 N. Main Ave. 12203. (518) 453-6611; www.rcda.org.

Alexandria, LA: The Chancery Office, P.O. Box 7417, 71306. (318) 445-2401; www.diocesealex.org.

Allentown, PA: The Chancery Office, P.O. Box F. 18105-1538. (610) 437-0755.

Altoona-Johnstown, PA: The Chancery, 126 Logan Blvd., Hollidaysburg. 16648. (814) 695-5579;

www.diocesealtjtn.org.

Amarillo, TX: Pastoral Center, 1800 N. Spring St., P.O. Box 5644. 79117-5644. (806) 383-2243.

Anchorage,* AK: The Chancery Office, 225 Cordova St., Anchorage 99501. (907) 297-7700; www.archdioceseofanchorage.org

Arlington, VA: The Chancery Office, Suite 914, 200 N. Glebe Rd. 22203. (703) 841-2500.

Atlanta,* GA: Catholic Center, 680 W. Peachtree St. N.W. 30308. (404) 888-7802; www.archatl.com.

Austin, TX: The Chancery Office, 1600 N. Congress Ave., P.O. Box 13327. 78711. (512) 476-4888; www.austindiocese.org.

Baker, OR: Diocesan Pastoral Office, P.O. Box 5999, Bend. 97708. (541) 388-4004; users bendnet.com/diocbakr/.

Baltimore,* MD: The Chancery Office, 320 Cathedral St. 21201. (410) 547-5446; www.archbalt.org.

Baton Rouge, LA: Catholic Life Center, P.O. Box 2028. 70821-2028. (225) 387-0561; www.diobr.org.

Beaumont, TX: Diocesan Pastoral Office, 703 Archie St., P.O. Box 3948. 77704-3948. (409) 838-0451.

Belleville, IL: The Chancery, 222 S. Third St. 62220-1985. (618) 277-8181; www.diobelle.org.

Biloxi, MS: Administration Offices, P.O. Box 6489 39522-6489. (228) 702-2100; www.biloxidiocese.org.

Birmingham, AL: Catholic Life Center, P.O. Box 12047. 35202-2047. (205) 838-8322.

Bismarck, ND: The Chancery Office, 420 Raymond St., Box 1575. 58502-1575. (701) 223-1347.

Boise, ID: The Chancery Office, 303 Federal Way. 83705-5925. (208) 342-1311

Boston,* MA: The Chancery Office, 2121 Commonwealth Ave., Brighton. 02135. (617) 254-0100; www.rcab.org

Bridgeport, CT: The Catholic Center, 238 Jewett Ave. 06606-2892. (203) 372-4301

Brooklyn, NY: The Chancery Office, 75 Greene Ave., P.O. Box C. 11238. (718) 399-5970.

Brownsville, TX: The Catholic Pastoral Center, P.O. Box 2279, 1910 E. Elizabeth St. 78522-2279. (956) 542-2501; www.cdob.org.

Buffalo, NY: The Chancery Office, 795 Main St. 14203. (716) 847-5500; www.buffalodiocese.org

Burlington, VT: The Chancery Office, 351 North Ave., P.O. Box 526. 05401-0526. (802) 658-6110; www.vermontcatholic.org.

Camden, NJ: Camden Diocesan Center, 631 Market St., P.O. Box 708, 08101. (609) 756-7900.

Charleston, SC: The Chancery Office, 119 Broad St., P.O. Box 818. 29402. (843) 723-3488; www.catholic-doc.org.

Charlotte, NC: The Pastoral Center, P.O. Box 36776. 28236. (704) 370-6299; www.charlotte diocese.org.

Cheyenne, WY: The Chancery Office, Box 1468. 82003-0426. (307) 638-1530.

Chicago,* IL: Pastoral Center, P.O. Box 1979. 60690. (312) 751-7999; www.archdiocese-chgo.org.

Cincinnati,* OH: The Chancery Office, 100 E. 8th St. 45202. (513) 421-3131; www.archdiocese-cinti.org.

Cleveland, OH: The Chancery Office, 1027 Superior Ave. 44114. (216) 696-6525; www.cle-dioc.org

Colorado Springs, CO: The Chancery Office, 29 W. Kiowa. 80903-1498. (719) 636-2345.

Columbus, OH: The Chancery Office, 198 E. Broad St. 43215-3766. (614) 224-2251.

Corpus Christi, TX: The Chancery Office, 620 Lipan St. P.O. Box 2620. 78403-2620. (512) 882-6191; www.diocesecc.org.

Covington, KY: The Catholic Center, P.O. Box 18548, Erlanger 41018-0548. (859) 283-6200; www.dioofcovky.org.

Crookston, MN: The Chancery Office, 1200 Memorial Dr., P.O. Box 610. 56716. (218) 281-4533; www.crookston.org.

Dallas, TX: The Chancery Office, 3725 Blackburn, P.O. Box 190507. 75219. (214) 528-2240; www.cathdal.org.

Davenport, IA: The Chancery Office, St. Vincent Center, 2706 N. Gaines St. 52804-1998. (319) 324-1911; www.davenportdiocese.org.

Denver,* CO: Catholic Pastoral Center, 1300 South Steele St. 80210. (303) 715-2000; www.archden.org/archden.

Des Moines, IA: The Chancery Office, P.O. Box 1816. 50306. (515) 243-7653; www.dmdiocese.org.

Detroit,* MI: The Chancery Office, 1234 Washington Blvd. 48226. (313) 237-5816.

Dodge City, KS: The Chancery Office, 910 Central Ave., P.O. Box 137. 67801-0137. (316) 227-1500; www.dcdiocese.org.

Dubuque,* IA: The Chancery Office, P.O.Box 479. 52004-0479. (319) 556-2580; www.archdio cese.dbq.pvt.k12.ia.us.

Duluth, MN: Pastoral Center, 2830 E. 4th St. 55812. (218) 724-9111; www.dioceseduluth.org.

El Paso, TX: The Chancery Office, 499 St. Matthews St. 79907. (915) 595-5000; www.elpaso diocese.org.

Erie, PA: St. Mark Catholic Center, P.O. Box 10397. 16514-0397. (814) 824-1111; www.eriecd.org.

Evansville, IN: The Chancery Office, P.O. Box 4169. 47724-0169. (812) 424-5536; www.evansville-diocese.org.

Fairbanks, AK: The Chancery Office, 1316 Peger Rd. 99709. (907) 474-0753; www.cbna.org.

Fall River, MA: The Chancery Office, Box 2577. 02722. (508) 675-1311.

Fargo, ND: The Chancery Office, 1310 Broadway, Box 1750. 58107. (701) 235-6429; www.fargo diocese.org.

Fort Wayne-South Bend, IN: The Chancery Office, P.O. Box 390, Fort Wayne. 46801. (219) 422-4611; www.diocesefwsb.org.

Fort Worth, TX: Catholic Center, 800 W. Loop 820 South. 76108. (817) 560-3300; www.fwdioc.org.

Fresno, CA: The Chancery Office, 1550 N. Fresno St. 93703-3788. (559) 488-7400.

Gallup, NM: The Chancery Office, 711 S. Puerco Dr., P.O. Box 1338. 87305. (505) 863-4406.

Galveston-Houston, TX: The Chancery Office, P.O. Box 907. 77001. (713) 659-5461.

Gary, IN: The Chancery Office, 9292 Broadway, Merrillville. 46410. (219) 769-9292; www.dcgary.org.

Gaylord, MI: Diocesan Pastoral Center, 611 North St. 49735. (517) 732-5147.

Grand Island, NE: The Chancery Office, 311 W. 17th St., P.O. Box 996. 68802. (308) 382-6565.

Grand Rapids, MI: The Chancery Office, 660 Burton St., S.E. 49507. (616) 243-0491; www.dioceseof grandrapids.org.

Great Falls-Billings, MT: The Chancery Office, P.O. Box 1399, Great Falls. 59401. (406) 727-6683; www.mcn.net/~dioceseofgfb.

Green Bay, WI: The Chancery Office, P.O. Box 23825. 54305-3825. (920) 437-7531; www.gbdioc.org.

Greensburg, PA: The Chancery Office, 723 E. Pittsburgh St. 15601. (724) 837-0901; www.catholic gbg.org.

Harrisburg, PA: The Chancery Office, P.O. Box 2153. 17105-2153. (717) 657-4804; www.hbg diocese.org.

Hartford,* CT: The Chancery Office, 134 Farmington Ave. 06105-3784. (860) 541-6491; www.archdiocese-hartford.org.

Helena, MT: The Chancery Office, 515 North Ewing, P.O. Box 1729. 59624-1729. (406) 442-5820.

Honolulu, HI: The Chancery Office, 1184 Bishop St. 96813. (808) 585-3342; www.pono.net.

Houma-Thibodaux, LA: The Chancery Office, P.O. Box 505, Schriever, La. 70395. (504) 868-7720; www.htdiocese.org.

Indianapolis,* IN: The Archbishop Edward T. O'Meara Catholic Center, 1400 N. Meridian St. 46206. (317) 236-1403; www.archindy.org.

Jackson, MS: The Chancery Office, 237 E. Amite St., P.O. Box 2248. 39225-2248. (601) 969-1880; www.jacksondiocese.org.

Jefferson City, MO: Chancery Office, 605 Clark Ave., P.O. Box 417. 65102-0417. (573) 635-9127; www.diojeffcity.org.

Joliet, IL: The Chancery Office, 425 Summit St. 60435. (815) 722-6606.

Juneau, AK: The Chancery Office, 419 6th St., No. 200. 99801. (907) 586-2227; www.juneaudiocese.addr.com.

Kalamazoo, MI: The Chancery Office, 215 N. Westnedge Ave. 49007-3760. (616) 349-8714.

Kansas City,* KS: The Chancery Office, 12615 Parallel Pkwy. 66109. (913) 721-1570; www.arch kck.org.

Kansas City-St. Joseph, MO: The Chancery Office, P.O. Box 419037, Kansas City. 64141-6037. (816) 756-1850; www.diocese-kcsj.org.

Knoxville, TN: The Chancery Office, 805 Northshore Dr., P.O. Box 11127. 37939-1127. (865) 584-3307.

La Crosse, WI: The Chancery Office, 3710 East Ave. S., Box 4004. 54602-4004. (608) 788-7700; www.dioceseoflacrosse.com

Lafayette in Indiana: The Bishop's Office, P.O. Box 260. 47902-0260. (765) 742-0275; www.diocese oflafayette.org.

Lafayette, LA: The Chancery Office, 1408 Carmel Ave. 70501. (337) 261-5614; www.dol-louisiana.org.

Lake Charles, LA: The Chancery Office, P.O. Box 3223. 70602. (318) 439-7400; lcdiocese.laol.net

Lansing, MI: The Chancery Office, 300 W. Ottawa St. 48933-1577. (517) 342-2440.

Laredo, Tx.: Diocesan Pastoral Center, P.O. Box 2247, 78044. (956) 727-2140.

Las Cruces, NM: The Chancery Office, 1280 Med Park Dr., 88005. (505) 523-7577; www.zianet.com/ diocese.

Las Vegas, NV: Chancery Office, P.O. Box 18316. 89114-8316. (702) 735-3500.

Lexington, KY: Catholic Center, 1310 Main St. 40508-2040. (606) 253-1993; www.cdlex.org.

Lincoln, NE: The Chancery Office, P.O. Box 80328. 68501-0328. (402) 488-0921.

Little Rock, AR: The Chancery Office, 2415 N. Tyler St. P.O. Box 7239. 72217. (501) 664-0340.

Los Angeles,* CA: Archdiocesan Catholic Center, 3424 Wilshire Blvd. 90010-2241. (213) 637-7000; www.LA-Archdiocese.org.

Louisville,* Ky.: Chancery Office, 212 E. College St., P.O. Box 1073. 40201-1073. (502) 585-3291; www.archlou.org.

Lubbock, TX: The Catholic Center, P.O. Box 98700.

79499. (806) 792-3943; www.catholiclubbock.org.

Madison, WI: Bishop O'Connor Catholic Pastoral Center, P.O. Box 44983, 3577 High Point Road. 53744-4983. (608) 821-3000; www.madison diocese.org.

Manchester, NH: The Chancery Office, 153 Ash St., P.O. Box 310. 03105-0310. (603) 669-3100; www.diocesemanch.org.

Marquette, MI: The Chancery Office, 444 S. Fourth St., P.O. Box 550. 49855. (906) 225-1141.

Memphis, TN: The Catholic Center, 5825 Shelby Oaks Dr., P.O. Box 341669. 38184-1669. (901) 373-1200; www.cdom.org.

Metuchen, NJ: The Chancery Office, P.O. Box 191. 08840. (732) 283-3800; www.diometuchen.org.

Miami,* FL: The Chancery Office, 9401 Biscayne Blvd., Miami Shores. 33138. (305) 757-6241; www.archdioceseofmiami.org.

Milwaukee,* WI: The Chancery Office, P.O. Box 07912. 53207-0912. (414) 769-3340; www.arch mil.org.

Mobile,* AL: The Chancery Office, 400 Government St., P.O. Box 1966. 36633. (334) 434-1585

Monterey, CA: The Chancery Office, P.O. Box 2048. 93942-2048. (831) 373-4345; www.diocese ofmonterey.org.

Nashville, TN: The Chancery Office, 2400 21st Ave. S. 37212-5387. (615) 383-6393; www.serve.com/ dionash/.

Newark,* NJ: Chancery Office, P.O. Box 9500. 07104-0500. (973) 497-4000; www.rcan.org.

New Orleans,* LA: The Chancery Office, 7887 Walmsley Ave. 70125. (504) 861-9521; www.cath olic.org/neworleans/.

Newton, MA (Melkite): The Chancery Office, 158 Pleasant St., Brookline. 02446. (617) 566-4511; www.melkite.org.

New Ulm, MN: Catholic Pastoral Center, 1400 Sixth St. N., 56073-2099. (507) 359-2966; www.dnu.org.

New York,* NY: The Chancery Office, 1011 First Ave. 10022-4134. (212) 371-1000; www.ny-archdiocese.org.

Norwich, CT: The Chancery Office, 201 Broadway, P.O. Box 587. 06360-0587. (860) 887-9294; www.norwichdiocese.org.

Oakland, CA: The Chancery Office, 2900 Lakeshore Ave. 94610. (510) 893-4711.

Ogdensburg, NY: The Chancery Office, 604 Washington St., P.O. Box 369. 13669. (315) 393-2920.

Oklahoma City,* OK: The Chancery Office, P.O. Box 32180. 73123. (405) 721-5651.

Omaha,* NE: The Chancery Office, 100 N. 62nd St. 68132-2795. (402) 558-3100; www.oarch.org.

Orange, CA: The Chancery Office, 2811 E. Villa Real Dr., P.O. Box 14195. 92863-1595. (714) 282-3000; www.rcbo.org.

Orlando, FL: The Chancery Office, P.O. Box 1800. 32802-1800. (407) 246-4800; www.orlando diocese.org.

Our Lady of Deliverance of Newark, for Syrian rite Catholics of the U.S. and Canada: P.O. Box 8366, Union City, NJ 07087-8262. (201) 583-1067; www.syriac-catholic.org.

Our Lady of Lebanon of Los Angeles, CA (Maronite): The Chancery Office, P.O. Box 16397, Beverly Hills 90209. (310) 247-8322; www.eparchyla.org.

Owensboro, KY: The Catholic Pastoral Center, 600 Locust St. 42301-2130. (502) 683-1545; www.owens borodio.org.

Palm Beach, FL: Pastoral Center, P.O. Box 109650, Palm Beach Gardens 33410-9650. (561) 775-9500; www.diocese.maco.net.

Parma, OH (Byzantine): The Chancery Office, 1900 Carlton Rd. 44134-3129. (216) 741-8773; www.parma.com.

Passaic, NJ (Byzantine): The Chancery Office, 445 Lackawanna Ave., W. Paterson. 07424. (973) 890-7777; members.aol.com/byzruth/index/htm.

Paterson, NJ: Diocesan Pastoral Center, 777 Valley Rd., Clifton. 07013. (973) 777-8818; www.patersondiocese.org.

Pensacola-Tallahassee, FL: Pastoral Center, P.O. Drawer 17329, Pensacola. 32522. (904) 432-1515; www.cfi.net/ptdiocese/pt.html.

Peoria, IL: The Chancery Office, 607 N.E. Madison Ave., P.O. Box 1406. 61655. (309) 671-1550.

Philadelphia,* PA: The Chancery Office, 222 N. 17th St. 19103. (215) 587-4538; www.archdiocese-phl.org.

Philadelphia,* PA (Byzantine): The Chancery Office, 827 N. Franklin St. 19123-2097. (215) 627-0143.

Phoenix, AZ: The Chancery Office, 400 E. Monroe St. 85004-2376. (602) 257-0030; www.catholic sun.org.

Pittsburgh,* PA (Byzantine): The Chancery Office, 66 Riverview Ave. 15214-2253. (412) 231-4000.

Pittsburgh, PA: Pastoral Center, 111 Blvd. of the Allies. 15222-1618. (412) 456-3000; www.diopitt.org.

Portland, ME: The Chancery Office, 510 Ocean Ave., P.O. Box 11559. 04104-7559. (207) 773-6471.

Portland, OR*: Pastoral Center, 2838 E. Burnside St., Portland, OR 97214. (503) 234-5334; www.archdpdx.org/.

Providence, RI: The Chancery Office, One Cathedral Sq. 02903-3695. (401) 278-4500; www.dioceseofprovidence.com.

Pueblo, CO: Catholic Pastoral Center, 1001 N. Grand Ave. 81003-2948. (719) 544-9861; www.pueblo-diocese.com.

Raleigh, NC: Catholic Center, 715 Nazareth St. 27606-2187. (919) 821-9700; www.raldioc.org.

Rapid City, SD: The Chancery Office, 606 Cathedral Dr., P.O. Box 678, 57709. (605) 343-3541.

Reno, NV: Pastoral Center, P.O. Box 1211. 89504-1211. (775) 329-9274; www.catholicreno.com.

Richmond, VA: The Chancery Office, 811 Cathedral Pl., 23220-4801. (804) 359-5661; www.dio cric.org.

Rochester, NY: The Pastoral Center, 1150 Buffalo Rd. 14624. (716) 328-3210; www.dor.org.

Rockford, IL: The Chancery Office, 1245 N. Court St., P.O. Box 7044. 61126-7044. (815) 962-3709; www.rockforddiocese.org.

Rockville Centre, NY: The Chancery Office, 50 N. Park Ave. 11570-4184. (516) 678-5800; www.drvc.org.

Sacramento, CA: Pastoral Center, 2110 Broadway. 95818-2541. (916) 733-0100; www.diocese-sacramento.org.

Saginaw, MI: The Chancery Office, 5800 Weiss St. 48603-2799. (517) 799-7910; www.dioceseof saginaw.org.

St. Augustine, FL: Catholic Center, P.O. Box 24000,

Jacksonville, FL 32241-4000. (904) 262-3200; staugustine.ml.org/diocese.

St. Cloud, MN: The Chancery Office, P.O. Box 1248. 56302. (320) 251-2340; www.stcdio.org.

St. George's in Canton, OH (Byzantine, Romanian): The Chancery Office, 1121 44th St. N.E., Canton. 44714-1297. (330) 492-4086; www.Romanian Catholic.org.

St. Josaphat in Parma, OH (Byzantine): The Chancery Office, P.O. Box 347180, Parma. 44134-7180. (440) 888-1522.

St. Louis,* MO: The Catholic Center, 4445 Lindell Blvd. 63108-2497. (314) 633-2222; www.archstl.org.

St. Maron of Brooklyn (Maronite): The Pastoral Center, 294 Howard Ave., Staten Island, NY 10301-4409. (718) 815-0436.

St. Nicholas in Chicago (Byzantine): The Chancery Office, 2245 W. Rice St. 60622. (312) 276-5080.

St. Paul and Minneapolis,* MN: The Chancery Office, 226 Summit Ave., St. Paul. 55102-2197. (651) 291-4400; www.mtn.org/archcom/.

St. Peter the Apostle of San Diego (Chaldean)

St. Petersburg, FL: The Chancery Office, P.O. Box 40200. 33743-0200. (727) 344-1611; www.diocese ofstpete.org.

St. Thomas of Chicago (Syro-Malabar): Diocesan Office, 717 N. Eastland, Elmhurst, IL 60126. (630) 530-8399.

St. Thomas the Apostle of Detroit (Chaldean Catholic Diocese-USA): The Chancery Office, 25603 Berg Rd., Southfield, MI 48034. (248) 351-0440.

Salina, KS: The Chancery Office, P.O. Box 980. 67402-0980. (785) 827-8746.

Salt Lake City, UT: The Chancery Office, 27 C St. 84103-2397. (801) 328-8641; www.utahcatholic diocese.org.

San Angelo, TX: The Chancery Office, P.O. Box 1829. 76902-1829. (915) 651-7500; www.san-angelo-diocese.org.

San Antonio,* TX: The Chancery Office, P.O. Box 28410. 78228-0410. (210) 734-2620; www.arch diosa.org.

San Bernardino, CA: The Chancery Office, 1201 E. Highland Ave. 92404. (909) 475-5300; www.sb diocese.org.

San Diego, CA: Pastoral Center, P.O. Box 85728. 92186-5728. (619) 490-8200; www.diocese-sdiego.org.

San Francisco,* CA: The Chancery Office, 445 Church St. 94114. (415) 565-3609; www.sfarch diocese.org

San Jose, CA: The Chancery Office, 900 Lafayette St., Suite 301, Santa Clara 95050-4966. (408) 983-0100; www.dsj.org.

Santa Fe,* NM: Catholic Center, 4000 St. Joseph's Pl. N.W., Albuquerque. 87120. (505) 831-8100.

Santa Rosa, CA: The Chancery Office, P.O. Box 1297. 95402-1297. (707) 545-7610; www.santa rosacatholic.org.

Savannah, GA: Catholic Pastoral Center, 601 E. Liberty St. 31401-5196. (912) 238-2320; www.dioceseofsavannah.org.

Scranton, PA: The Chancery Office, 300 Wyoming Ave. 18503-1279. (570) 207-2216; www.diocese ofscranton.org.

Seattle,* WA: The Chancery Office, 910 Marion St. 98104-1299. (206) 382-4560; www.seattlearch.org.

Shreveport, LA: Catholic Center, 3500 Fairfield Ave. 71104. (318) 868-4441; www.dioshpt.org.

Sioux City, IA: The Chancery Office, P.O. Box 3379. 51102-3379. (712) 255-7933; www.sc diocese.org.

Sioux Falls, SD: Catholic Pastoral Center, 523 N. Duluth Ave. 57104-2714. (605) 334-9861; Diocese-of-Sioux-Falls.org.

Spokane, WA: Catholic Pastoral Center, Catholic Diocese of Spokane, P.O. Box 1453. 99210-1453. (509) 358-7300; www.dioceseofspokane.org.

Springfield, IL: Catholic Pastoral Center, 1615 West Washington, P.O. Box 3187. 62708-3187. (217) 698-8500.

Springfield, MA: The Chancery Office, P.O. Box 1730. 01101. (413) 732-3175; www.dio springfield.org.

Springfield-Cape Girardeau, MO: The Catholic Center, 601 S. Jefferson Ave., Springfield. 65806-3143. (417) 866-0841; www.diocspfdcape.org.

Stamford, CT (Byzantine): The Chancery Office, 14 Peveril Rd. 06902-3019. (203) 324-7698

Steubenville, OH: The Chancery Office, P.O. Box 969. 43952. (740) 282-3631; www.diosteub.org.

Stockton, CA: The Chancery Office, 1125 N. Lincoln St.. 95203. (209) 466-0636.

Superior, WI: The Chancery Office, 1201 Hughitt Ave., Box 969. 54880. (715) 392-2937.

Syracuse, NY: The Chancery Office, P.O. Box 511. 13201-0511. (315) 422-7203; wwwsyrdioc.org.

Toledo, OH: The Chancery Office, P.O. Box 985. 43697-0895. (419) 244-6711; www.toledo diocese.org.

Trenton, NJ: Chancery Office, 701 Lawrenceville Rd., P.O. Box 5147. 08638. (609) 406-7400.

Tucson, AZ: The Chancery Office, 192 S. Stone Ave., Box 31. 85702. (520) 792-3410; www.azstar net.com/~rccdot.

Tulsa, OK: The Chancery Office, P.O. Box 690240. 74169. (918) 294-1904.

Tyler, TX: The Chancery Office, 1015 E.S.E. Loop 323. 75701-9663. (903) 534-1077.

Van Nuys, CA (Byzantine): The Chancery Office, 8131 N. 16th St., Phoenix, AZ 85020. (602) 861-9778; eparchy-of-van-nuys.org.

Venice, FL: The Catholic Center, P.O. Box 2006. 34284. (941) 484-9543; www.dioceseofvenice.org.

Victoria, TX: The Chancery Office, P.O. Box 4070. 77903. (361) 573-0828.

Washington,* DC: Archdiocesan Pastoral Center, P.O. Box 29260. 20017. (301) 853-4500.

Wheeling-Charleston, WV: The Chancery Office, 1300 Byron St., P.O. Box 230, Wheeling. 26003. (304) 233-0880; www.dwc.org.

Wichita, KS: The Chancery Office, 424 N. Broadway. 67202. (316) 269-3900.

Wilmington, DE: The Chancery Office, P.O. Box 2030. 19899-2030. (302) 573-3100; www.cdow.org.

Winona, MN: The Chancery Office, P.O. Box 588. 55987. (507) 454-4643; www.dow.org.

Worcester, MA: The Chancery Office, 49 Elm St. 01609-2597. (508) 791-7171; www.worcester diocese.org.

Yakima, WA: The Chancery Office, 5301-A Tieton Dr. 98908. (509) 965-7117.

Youngstown, OH: The Chancery Office, 144 W. Wood St. 44503. (330) 744-8451; www.doy.org.

Military Archdiocese: P.O. Box 4469, Washington, D.C. 20017-0469; 3311 Toledo Terrace, Suite A201, Hyattsville, MD 20782-4135. (301) 853-0400; www.milarch.org.

Armenian Apostolic Exarchate for the United States and Canada: 110 E. 12th St., New York, NY 10003. (212) 477-2030.

CATHEDRALS, BASILICAS, AND SHRINES IN THE U.S.

CATHEDRALS IN THE UNITED STATES

*A cathedral is the principal church in a diocese, the one in which the bishop has his seat (*cathedra*). He is the actual pastor, although many functions of the church, which usually serves a parish, are the responsibility of a priest serving as the rector. Because of the dignity of a cathedral, the dates of its dedication and its patronal feast are observed throughout a diocese.*

The pope's cathedral, the Basilica of St. John Lateran, is the highest-ranking church in the world.

(Archdioceses are indicated by asterisk.)

Albany, N.Y.: Immaculate Conception.
Alexandria, La.: St. Francis Xavier.
Allentown, Pa.: St. Catherine of Siena.
Altoona-Johnstown, Pa.: Blessed Sacrament (Altoona); St. John Gualbert (Johnstown).
Amarillo, Tex.: St. Laurence.
Anchorage,* Alaska: Holy Family.
Arlington, Va: St. Thomas More.
Atlanta,* Ga.: Christ the King.
Austin, Tex.: St. Mary (Immaculate Conception).
Baker, Ore.: St. Francis de Sales.
Baltimore,* Md.: Mary Our Queen; Basilica of the

National Shrine of the Assumption of the Blessed Virgin Mary (Co-Cathedral).
Baton Rouge, La.: St. Joseph.
Beaumont, Tex.: St. Anthony (of Padua).
Belleville, Ill.: St. Peter.
Biloxi, Miss.: Nativity of the Blessed Virgin Mary.
Birmingham, Ala.: St. Paul.
Bismarck, N.D.: Holy Spirit.
Boise, Id.: St. John the Evangelist.
Boston,* Mass.: Holy Cross.
Bridgeport, Conn.: St. Augustine.
Brooklyn, N.Y.: St. James (Minor Basilica).
Brownsville, Tex.: Immaculate Conception.
Buffalo, N.Y.: St. Joseph.
Burlington, Vt.: Immaculate Conception; St. Joseph (Co-Cathedral).
Camden, N.J.: Immaculate Conception.
Charleston, S.C.: St. John the Baptist.
Charlotte, N.C.: St. Patrick.
Cheyenne, Wyo.: St. Mary.
Chicago,* Ill.: Holy Name (of Jesus).
Cincinnati,* Ohio: St. Peter in Chains.
Cleveland, Ohio: St. John the Evangelist.

Colorado Springs, Colo: St. Mary.
Columbus, Ohio: St. Joseph.
Corpus Christi, Tex.: Corpus Christi.
Covington, Ky.: Basilica of the Assumption.
Crookston, Minn.: Immaculate Conception.
Dallas, Tex.: Cathedral-Santuario de Guadalupe.
Davenport, Ia.: Sacred Heart.
Denver,* Colo.: Immaculate Conception (Minor Basilica).
Des Moines, Ia.: St. Ambrose.
Detroit,* Mich.: Most Blessed Sacrament.
Dodge City, Kans.: Our Lady of Guadalupe.
Dubuque,* Ia.: St. Raphael.
Duluth, Minn.: Our Lady of the Rosary.
El Paso, Tex.: St. Patrick.
Erie, Pa.: St. Peter.
Evansville, Ind.: Most Holy Trinity (Pro-Cathedral).
Fairbanks, Alaska: Sacred Heart.
Fall River, Mass.: St. Mary of the Assumption.
Fargo, N.D.: St. Mary.
Fort Wayne-S. Bend, Ind.: Immaculate Conception (Fort Wayne); St. Matthew (South Bend).
Fort Worth, Tex.: St. Patrick.
Fresno, Calif.: St. John (the Baptist).
Gallup, N.M.: Sacred Heart.
Galveston-Houston, Tex.: St. Mary (Minor Basilica, Galveston); Sacred Heart Co-Cathedral (Houston).
Gary, Ind.: Holy Angels.
Gaylord, Mich.: St. Mary, Our Lady of Mt. Carmel.
Grand Island, Nebr.: Nativity of Blessed Virgin Mary.
Grand Rapids, Mich.: St. Andrew.
Great Falls-Billings, Mont.: St. Ann (Great Falls); St. Patrick Co-Cathedral (Billings).
Green Bay, Wis.: St. Francis Xavier.
Greensburg, Pa.: Blessed Sacrament.
Harrisburg, Pa.: St. Patrick.
Hartford,* Conn.: St. Joseph.
Helena, Mont.: St. Helena.
Honolulu, Hawaii: Our Lady of Peace; St. Theresa of the Child Jesus (Co-Cathedral).
Houma-Thibodaux, La.: St. Francis de Sales (Houma); St. Joseph Co-Cathedral (Thibodaux).
Indianapolis,* Ind.: Sts. Peter and Paul.
Jackson, Miss.: St. Peter.
Jefferson City, Mo.: St. Joseph.
Joliet, Ill.: St. Raymond Nonnatus.
Juneau, Alaska: Nativity of the Blessed Virgin Mary.
Kalamazoo, Mich.: St. Augustine.
Kansas City,* Kans.: St. Peter the Apostle.
Kansas City-St. Joseph, Mo.: Immaculate Conception (Kansas City); St. Joseph Co-Cathedral (St. Joseph).
Knoxville, Tenn.: Sacred Heart of Jesus.
La Crosse, Wis.: St. Joseph the Workman.
Lafayette, Ind.: St. Mary.
Lafayette, La.: St. John the Evangelist.
Lake Charles, La.: Immaculate Conception.
Lansing, Mich.: St. Mary.
Laredo, Tex.: San Augustin.
Las Cruces, N. Mex.: Immaculate Heart of Mary.
Las Vegas, Nev.: Guardian Angel.
Lexington, Ky.: Christ the King.
Lincoln, Nebr.: Cathedral of the Risen Christ.
Little Rock, Ark.: St. Andrew.
Los Angeles,* Calif.: Cathedral of Our Lady of the Angels of Los Angeles.

Louisville,* Ky.: Assumption.
Lubbock, Tex.: Christ the King.
Madison, Wis.: St. Raphael.
Manchester, N.H.: St. Joseph.
Marquette, Mich.: St. Peter.
Memphis, Tenn.: Immaculate Conception.
Metuchen, N.J.: St. Francis (of Assisi).
Miami,* Fla.: St. Mary (Immaculate Conception).
Milwaukee,* Wis.: St. John.
Mobile,* Ala.: Immaculate Conception (Minor Basilica).
Monterey, Calif.: San Carlos Borromeo.
Nashville, Tenn.: Incarnation.
Newark,* N.J.: Sacred Heart (Minor Basilica).
New Orleans,* La.: St. Louis. (Minor Basilica)
Newton, Mass. (Melkite): Our Lady of the Annunciation (Boston).
New Ulm, Minn.: Holy Trinity.
New York,* N.Y.: St. Patrick.
Norwich, Conn.: St. Patrick.
Oakland, Calif.: St. Francis de Sales.
Ogdensburg, N.Y.: St. Mary (Immaculate Conception).
Oklahoma City,* Okla.: Our Lady of Perpetual Help.
Omaha,* Nebr.: St. Cecilia.
Orange, Calif.: Holy Family.
Orlando, Fla.: St. James.
Our Lady of Deliverance of Newark, New Jersey for Syrian Rite Catholics in the U.S. and Canada: Our Lady of Deliverance.
Our Lady of Lebanon of Los Angeles, Calif. (Maronite): Our Lady of Mt. Lebanon-St. Peter.
Owensboro, Ky.: St. Stephen.
Palm Beach, Fla.: St. Ignatius Loyola, Palm Beach Gardens.
Parma, Ohio (Byzantine): St. John the Baptist.
Passaic, N.J. (Byzantine): St. Michael.
Paterson, N.J.: St. John the Baptist.
Pensacola-Tallahassee, Fla.: Sacred Heart (Pensacola); Co-Cathedral of St. Thomas More (Tallahassee).
Peoria, Ill.: St. Mary.
Philadelphia,* Pa.: Sts. Peter and Paul (Minor Basilica).
Philadelphia,* Pa. (Byzantine): Immaculate Conception of Blessed Virgin Mary.
Phoenix, Ariz.: Sts. Simon and Jude.
Pittsburgh,* Pa. (Byzantine): St. John the Baptist, Munhall.
Pittsburgh, Pa.: St. Paul.
Portland, Me.: Immaculate Conception.
Portland,* Ore.: Immaculate Conception.
Providence, R.I.: Sts. Peter and Paul.
Pueblo, Colo.: Sacred Heart.
Raleigh, N.C.: Sacred Heart.
Rapid City, S.D.: Our Lady of Perpetual Help.
Reno, Nev.: St. Thomas Aquinas.
Richmond, Va.: Sacred Heart.
Rochester, N.Y.: Sacred Heart.
Rockford, Ill.: St. Peter.
Rockville Centre, N.Y.: St. Agnes.
Sacramento, Calif.: Blessed Sacrament.
Saginaw, Mich.: St. Mary.
St. Augustine, Fla.: St. Augustine (Minor Basilica).
St. Cloud, Minn.: St. Mary.
St. George's in Canton, Ohio (Byzantine, Romanian): St. George.

St. Josaphat in Parma, Oh. (Byzantine): St. Josaphat.

St. Louis,* Mo.: St. Louis.

St. Maron, Brooklyn, N.Y. (Maronite): Our Lady of Lebanon.

St. Nicholas in Chicago (Byzantine): St. Nicholas.

St. Paul and Minneapolis,* Minn.: St. Paul (St. Paul); Basilica of St. Mary Co-Cathedral (Minneapolis).

St. Petersburg, Fla.: St. Jude the Apostle.

St. Thomas the Apostle of Detroit (Chaldean): Our Lady of Chaldeans Cathedral (Mother of God Church), Southfield, Mich.

St. Thomas of Chicago (Syro-Malabar): Mar Thoma Shleeha Church.

Salina, Kans.: Sacred Heart.

Salt Lake City, Utah: The Madeleine.

San Angelo, Tex.: Sacred Heart.

San Antonio,* Tex.: San Fernando.

San Bernardino, Calif: Our Lady of the Rosary.

San Diego, Calif.: St. Joseph.

San Francisco,* Calif.: St. Mary (Assumption).

San Jose, Calif.: St. Joseph (Minor Basilica); St. Patrick, Proto-Cathedral.

Santa Fe,* N.M.: San Francisco de Asis.

Santa Rosa, Calif.: St. Eugene.

Savannah, Ga.: St. John the Baptist.

Scranton, Pa.: St. Peter.

Seattle,* Wash.: St. James.

Shreveport, La.: St. John Berchmans.

Sioux City, Ia.: Epiphany.

Sioux Falls, S.D.: St. Joseph.

Spokane, Wash.: Our Lady of Lourdes.

Springfield, Ill.: Immaculate Conception.

Springfield, Mass.: St. Michael.

Springfield-Cape Girardeau, Mo.: St. Agnes (Springfield): St. Mary (Cape Girardeau).

Stamford, Conn. (Byzantine): St. Vladimir.

Steubenville, Ohio: Holy Name.

Stockton, Calif: Annunciation.

Superior, Wis.: Christ the King.

Syracuse, N.Y.: Immaculate Conception.

Toledo, Ohio: Queen of the Most Holy Rosary.

Trenton, N.J.: St. Mary (Assumption).

Tucson, Ariz.: St. Augustine.

Tulsa, Okla.: Holy Family.

Tyler, Tex.: Immaculate Conception.

Van Nuys, Calif. (Byzantine): St. Mary (Patronage of the Mother of God), Van Nuys; St. Stephen's (Pro-Cathedral), Phoenix, Ariz.

Venice, Fla: Epiphany.

Victoria, Tex.: Our Lady of Victory.

Washington,* D.C.: St. Matthew.

Wheeling-Charleston, W. Va.: St. Joseph (Wheeling); Sacred Heart (Charleston).

Wichita, Kans.: Immaculate Conception.

Wilmington, Del.: St. Peter.

Winona, Minn.: Sacred Heart.

Worcester, Mass.: St. Paul.

Yakima, Wash.: St. Paul.

Youngstown, Ohio: St. Columba.

Apostolic Exarchate for Armenian Catholics in the U.S. and Canada: St. Ann (110 E. 12th St., New York, N.Y. 10003).

BASILICAS IN THE UNITED STATES

Basilica is a title assigned to certain churches because of their antiquity, dignity, historical importance or significance as centers of worship. Major basilicas have the papal altar and holy door, which is opened at the beginning of a Jubilee Year; minor basilicas enjoy certain ceremonial privileges.

Among the major basilicas are the patriarchal basilicas of St. John Lateran, St. Peter, St. Paul Outside the Walls and St. Mary Major in Rome; St. Francis and St. Mary of the Angels in Assisi, Italy. The patriarchal basilica of St. Lawrence, Rome, is a minor basilica. The dates in the listings below indicate when the churches were designated as basilicas.

Minor Basilicas in U.S., Puerto Rico, Guam

Alabama: Mobile, Cathedral of the Immaculate Conception (Mar. 10, 1962).

Arizona: Phoenix, St. Mary's (Immaculate Conception) (Sept. 11, 1985).

California: San Francisco, Mission Dolores (Feb. 8, 1952); Carmel, Old Mission of San Carlos (Feb. 5, 1960); Alameda, St. Joseph (Jan. 21, 1972); San Diego, Mission San Diego de Alcala (Nov. 17, 1975); San Jose, St. Joseph (Jan. 28, 1997).

Colorado: Denver, Cathedral of the Immaculate Conception (Nov. 3, 1979).

District of Columbia: National Shrine of the Immaculate Conception (Oct. 12, 1990).

Florida: St. Augustine, Cathedral of St. Augustine (Dec. 4, 1976).

Illinois: Chicago, Our Lady of Sorrows (May 4, 1956), Queen of All Saints (Mar. 26, 1962).

Indiana: Vincennes, Old Cathedral (Mar. 14, 1970). Notre Dame, Parish Church of Most Sacred Heart, Univ. of Notre Dame (Nov. 23, 1991).

Iowa: Dyersville, St. Francis Xavier (May 11, 1956); Des Moines, St. John the Apostle (Oct. 4, 1989).

Kentucky: Trappist, Our Lady of Gethsemani (May 3, 1949); Covington, Cathedral of Assumption (Dec. 8, 1953).

Louisiana: New Orleans, St. Louis King of France (Dec. 9, 1964).

Maryland: Baltimore, Assumption of the Blessed Virgin Mary (Sept. 1, 1937; designated national shrine, 1993); Emmitsburg, Shrine of St. Elizabeth Ann Seton (Feb. 13, 1991).

Massachusetts: Roxbury, Perpetual Help ("Mission Church") (Sept. 8, 1954); Chicopee, St. Stanislaus (June 25, 1991).

Michigan: Grand Rapids, St. Adalbert (Aug. 22, 1979).

Minnesota: Minneapolis. St. Mary (Feb. 1, 1926).

Missouri: Conception, Basilica of Immaculate Conception (Sept. 14, 1940); St. Louis, St. Louis King of France (Jan. 27, 1961).

New Jersey: Newark, Cathedral Basilica of the Sacred Heart (Dec. 22, 1995).

New York: Brooklyn, Our Lady of Perpetual Help (Sept. 5, 1969), Cathedral-Basilica of St. James (June 22, 1982); Lackawanna, Our Lady of Victory (1926); Youngstown, Blessed Virgin Mary of the Rosary of Fatima (Oct. 7, 1975).

North Carolina: Asheville, St. Lawrence (Apr. 6,

1993; ceremonies, Sept. 5, 1993); Belmont, Our Lady Help of Christians (July 27, 1998)..

North Dakota: Jamestown, St. James (Oct. 26, 1988).

Ohio: Carey, Shrine of Our Lady of Consolation (Oct. 21, 1971).

Pennsylvania: Latrobe, St. Vincent Basilica, Benedictine Archabbey (Aug. 22, 1955); Conewago, Basilica of the Sacred Heart (June 30, 1962); Philadelphia, Sts. Peter and Paul (Sept. 27, 1976); Danville, Sts. Cyril and Methodius (chapel at the motherhouse of the Sisters of Sts. Cyril and Methodius) (June 30, 1989); Loretto, St. Michael the Archangel (September 9, 1996); Scranton, National Shrine of St. Ann (Oct. 18, 1997).

Texas: Galveston, St. Mary Cathedral (Aug. 11, 1979).

Virginia: Norfolk, St. Mary of the Immaculate Conception (July 9, 1991).

Wisconsin: Milwaukee, St. Josaphat (Mar. 10, 1929).

Puerto Rico: San Juan, Cathedral of San Juan (Jan. 25, 1978).

Guam: Agana, Cathedral of Dulce Nombre de Maria (Sweet Name of Mary) (1985).

BASILICA OF THE NATIONAL SHRINE OF THE IMMACULATE CONCEPTION

The Basilica of the National Shrine of the Immaculate Conception is dedicated to the honor of the Blessed Virgin Mary, declared patroness of the United States under this title in 1846, eight years before the proclamation of the dogma of the Immaculate Conception. The church was designated a minor basilica by Pope John Paul II Oct. 12, 1990. The church is the eighth largest religious building in the world and the largest Catholic church in the Western Hemisphere, with numerous special chapels and with normal seating and standing accommodations for 6,000 people. Open daily, it is adjacent to The Catholic University of America, at Michigan Ave. and Fourth St. N.E., Washington, D.C. 20017; (202) 526-8300; www.national shrine.com. Rev. Msgr. Michael J. Bransfield is the rector.

SHRINES AND PLACES OF HISTORIC INTEREST IN THE U.S.

(Principal source: Catholic Almanac *survey.)*

Listed below, according to state, are shrines, other centers of devotion and some places of historic interest with special significance for Catholics. The list is necessarily incomplete because of space limitations.

Information includes: name and location of shrine or place of interest, date of foundation, sponsoring agency or group, and address for more information.

Alabama: St. Jude Church of the City of St. Jude, Montgomery (1934; dedicated, 1938); Mobile Archdiocese. Address: 2048 W. Fairview Ave., Montgomery 36108; (334) 265-1390..

• Shrine of the Most Blessed Trinity, Holy Trinity (1924); Missionary Servants of the Most Blessed Trinity. Address: Holy Trinity 36859.

Arizona: Chapel of the Holy Cross, Sedona (1956); Phoenix Diocese: P.O. Box 1043, W. Sedona 86339.

• Mission San Xavier del Bac, near Tucson (1692); National Historic Landmark; Franciscan Friars and Tucson Diocese; Address: 1950 W. San Xavier Rd., Tucson 85746-7409; (520) 294-2624.

• Shrine of St. Joseph of the Mountains, Yarnell (1939); erected by Catholic Action League; currently maintained by Board of Directors. Address: P.O. Box 267, Yarnell 85362.

California: Mission San Diego de Alcala (July 16, 1769); first of the 21 Franciscan missions of Upper California; Minor Basilica; National Historic Landmark; San Diego Diocese. Address: 10818 San Diego Mission Rd., San Diego 92108; (619) 283-7319.

• Carmel Mission Basilica (Mission San Carlos Borromeo del Rio Carmelo), Carmel by the Sea (June 3, 1770); Monterey Diocese. Address: 3080 Rio Rd., Carmel 93923; (831) 624-1271.

• Old Mission San Luis Obispo de Tolosa, San Luis Obispo (Sept. 1, 1772); Monterey Diocese (Parish Church). Address: Old Mission Church, 751 Palm St., San Luis Obispo 93401.

• San Gabriel Mission, San Gabriel (Sept. 8, 1771); Los Angeles Archdiocese (Parish Church, staffed by Claretians). Address: 537 W. Mission, San Gabriel 91776.

• Mission San Francisco de Asis (Oct. 9, 1776) and Mission Dolores Basilica (1860s); San Francisco Archdiocese. Address: 3321 Sixteenth St., San Francisco 94114.

• Old Mission San Juan Capistrano, San Juan Capistrano (Nov. 1, 1776); Orange Diocese. Address: P.O. Box 697, San Juan Capistrano 92693; (949) 248-2026; www.missionsjc.com.

• Old Mission Santa Barbara, Santa Barbara (Dec. 4, 1786); National Historic Landmark; Parish Church, staffed by Franciscan Friars. Address: 2201 Laguna St., Santa Barbara 93105; (805) 682-4713.

• Old Mission San Juan Bautista, San Juan Bautista (June 24, 1797); National Historic Landmark; Monterey Diocese (Parish Church). Address: P.O. Box 400, San Juan Bautista 95045.

• Mission San Miguel, San Miguel (July 25, 1797); Parish Church, Monterey diocese; Franciscan Friars. Address: P.O. Box 69, San Miguel 93451; (805) 467-3256.

• Old Mission Santa Inés, Solvang (1804); Historic Landmark; Los Angeles Archdiocese (Parish Church, staffed by Capuchin Franciscan Friars). Address: P.O. Box 408, Solvang 93464 (805) 688-4815; www.missionsantaines.org.

Franciscan Friars founded 21 missions in California. (See Index: Franciscan Missions.)

• Shrine of Our Lady of Sorrows, Sycamore (1883); Sacramento Diocese. Address: c/o Our Lady of Lourdes Church, 745 Ware Ave., Colusa 95932.

Colorado: Mother Cabrini Shrine, Golden; Missionary Sisters of the Sacred Heart. Address: 20189 Cabrini Blvd., Golden 80401.

Connecticut: Shrine of Our Lady of Lourdes, Litchfield (1958); Montfort Missionaries. Address: P.O. Box 667, Litchfield 06759.

• Shrine of the Infant of Prague, New Haven (1945); Dominican Friars. Address: P.O. Box 1202, 5 Hillhouse Ave., New Haven 06505.

District of Columbia: Mount St. Sepulchre, Franciscan Monastery of the Holy Land (1897; church dedicated, 1899); Order of Friars Minor. Address:

1400 Quincy St. N.E., Washington, D.C. 20017.
• Basilica of the National Shrine of the Immaculate Conception. See Index for separate entry.

Florida: Mary, Queen of the Universe Shrine, Orlando (1986, temporary facilities; new shrine dedicated, 1993); Orlando diocese. Address: 8300 Vineland Ave., Orlando, 32821; (407) 239-6600; www.maryqueenoftheuniverse.org.
• Our Lady of La Leche Shrine (Patroness of Mothers and Mothers-to-be) and Mission of Nombre de Dios, Saint Augustine (1565); Angelus Crusade Headquarters. St. Augustine Diocese. Address: 30 Ocean Ave., St. Augustine 32084.

Illinois: Holy Family Log Church, Cahokia (1799; original log church erected 1699); Belleville Diocese (Parish Church). Address: 116 Church St., Cahokia 62206; (618) 337-4548.
• Marytown/Shrine of St. Maximilian Kolbe and Retreat Center, Libertyville; Our Lady of the Blessed Sacrament Sanctuary of Perpetual Eucharistic Adoration (1930 and Archdiocesan Shrine to St. Maximilian Kolbe (1989), conducted by Conventual Franciscan Friars, 1600 West Park Ave., Libertyville 60048; (847) 367-7800.
• National Shrine of Our Lady of the Snows, Belleville (1958); Missionary Oblates of Mary Immaculate. Address: 442 S. De Mazenod Dr., Belleville 62223.
• National Shrine of St. Jude, Chicago (1929); located in Our Lady of Guadalupe Church, founded and staffed by Claretians. Address: 3200 E. 91st St., Chicago 60617; (312) 236-7782.
• National Shrine of St. Therese and Museum, Darien (1930, at St. Clara's Church, Chicago; new shrine, 1987, after original destroyed by fire); Carmelites of Most Pure Heart of Mary Province. Address: Carmelite Visitor Center, 8501 Bailey Rd., Darien 60561; (630) 969-3311; www.saint-therese.org.
• Shrine of St. Jude Thaddeus, Chicago (1929) located in St. Pius V Church, staffed by Dominicans, Central Province. Address: 1909 S. Ashland Ave., Chicago 60608; (312) 226-0020; www.op.org/domcentral/places/stjude.

Indiana: Our Lady of Monte Cassino Shrine, St. Meinrad (1870); Benedictines. Address: Saint Meinrad Archabbey, Indiana StateHighway 62, St. Meinrad 47577; (812) 357-6585; www.saint meinrad.edu/abbey/shrine.
• Old Cathedral (Basilica of St. Francis Xavier), Vincennes (1826, parish records go back to 1749); Evansville Diocese. Minor Basilica, 1970. Address: 205 Church St., Vincennes 47591; (812) 882-5638.

Iowa: Grotto of the Redemption, West Bend (1912); Sioux City Diocese. Life of Christ in stone. Mailing address: P.O. Box 376, West Bend 50597; (515) 887-2371; www.aw-cybermail.com/grotto.htm.

Louisiana: National Votive Shrine of Our Lady of Prompt Succor, New Orleans (1810); located in the Chapel of the Ursuline Convent (a National Historic Landmark). Address: 2635 State St., New Orleans 70118.
• Shrine of St. Ann. Mailing address: 4920 Loveland St., Metaire 70006; (504) 455-7071.
• Shrine of St. Roch, New Orleans (1876); located in St. Roch's Campo Santo (Cemetery); New Orleans Archdiocese. Address: 1725 St. Roch Ave., New Orleans 70117.

Maryland: Basilica of the National Shrine of the Assumption of the Blessed Virgin Mary, Baltimore (1806). Mother Church of Roman Catholicism in the U.S. and the first metropolitan cathedral. Designed by Benjamin Henry Latrobe (architect of the Capitol) it is considered one of the finest examples of neoclassical architecture in the world. The church hosted many of the events and personalities central to the growth of Roman Catholicism in the U.S. Address: Cathedral and Mulberry Sts., Baltimore, MD 21201.
• National Shrine Grotto of Our Lady of Lourdes, Emmitsburg (1809, Grotto of Our Lady; 1875, National Shrine Grotto of Lourdes); Public oratory, Archdiocese of Baltimore. Address: Mount St. Mary's College and Seminary, Emmitsburg 21727; (301) 447-5318; www.msmary.edu/grotto/.
• National Shrine of St. Elizabeth Ann Seton, Emmitsburg. Religious/Historical. Foundation of Sisters of Charity (1809); first parochial school in America (1810); dedicated as Minor Basilica (1991); Address: 333 South Seton Ave., Emmitsburg 21727; (301) 447-6606; www.setonshrine.org.
• St. Francis Xavier Shrine, "Old Bohemia", near Warwick (1704), located in Wilmington, Del., Diocese; restoration under aupices of Old Bohemia Historical Society, Inc. Address: P.O. Box 61, Warwick 21912.

Massachusetts: National Shrine of Our Lady of La Salette, Ipswich (1945); Missionaries of Our Lady of La Salette. Address: 251 Topsfield Rd., Ipswich 01938.
• Our Lady of Fatima Shrine, Holliston (1950); Xaverian Missionaries. Address: 101 Summer St., Holliston 01746; (508) 429-2144.
• St. Anthony Shrine, Boston (1947); downtown Service Church with shrine; Boston Archdiocese and Franciscans of Holy Name Province. Address: 100 Arch St., Boston 02107.
• Saint Clement's Eucharistic Shrine, Boston (1945); Boston Archdiocese, staffed by Oblates of the Virgin Mary. Address: 1105 Boylston St., Boston 02215.
• National Shrine of The Divine Mercy, Stockbridge (1960); Congregation of Marians. Address: National Shrine of The Divine Mercy, Eden Hill, Stockbridge 01262.

Michigan: Cross in the Woods-Parish, Indian River (1947); Gaylord diocese; staffed by Franciscan Friars of Sacred Heart Province, St. Louis. Address: 7078 M-68, Indian River 49749; (231) 238-8973; www.rc.net/gaylord/crossinwoods.
• Shrine of the Little Flower, Royal Oak (c. 1929, by Father Coughlin); Detroit archdiocese. Address: 2123 Roseland, Royal Oak 48073.

Missouri: Memorial Shrine of St. Rose Philippine Duchesne, St. Charles; Religious of the Sacred Heart of Jesus. Address: 619 N. Second St., St. Charles 63301; (314) 946-6127..
• National Shrine of Our Lady of the Miraculous Medal, Perryville; located in St. Mary of the Barrens Church (1837); Vincentians. Address: 1811 W. St. Joseph St., Perryville 63775; (573) 547-8343; www.amm.org.
• Old St. Ferdinand's Shrine, Florissant (1819, Sacred Heart Convent; 1821, St. Ferdinand's Church); Friends of Old St. Ferdinand's, Inc. Address: No. 1 Rue St. Francois, Florissant 63031.
• Shrine of Our Lady of Sorrows, Starkenburg (1888;

shrine building, 1910); Jefferson City Diocese. Address: c/o Church of the Risen Savior, 605 Bluff St., Rhineland 65069; (573) 236-4390.

Nebraska: The Eucharistic Shrine of Christ the King (1973); Lincoln diocese and Holy Spirit Adoration Sisters. Address: 1040 South Cotner Blvd., Lincoln 68510; (402) 489-0765.

New Hampshire: Shrine of Our Lady of Grace, Colebrook (1948); Missionary Oblates of Mary Immaculate. Address: R.R. 1, Box 521, Colebrook 03576-9535; (603) 237-5511.
• Shrine of Our Lady of La Salette, Enfield (1951); Missionaries of Our Lady of La Salette. Address: Rt. 4A, P.O. Box 420, Enfield 03748.

New Jersey: Blue Army Shrine of the Immaculate Heart of Mary (1978); National Center of the Blue Army of Our Lady of Fatima, USA, Inc. Address: Mountain View Rd. (P.O. Box 976), Washington 07882-0976; (908) 689-1701; www.bluearmy.com
• Shrine of St. Joseph, Stirling (1924); Missionary Servants of the Most Holy Trinity. Address: 1050 Long Hill Rd., Stirling 07980; (908) 647-0208; www.STShrine.org

New Mexico: St. Augustine Mission, Isleta (1613); Santa Fe Archdiocese. Address: P.O. Box 463, Isleta, Pueblo 87022.
• Santuario de Nuestro Senor de Esquipulas, Chimayo (1816); Santa Fe archdiocese, Sons of the Holy Family; national historic landmark, 1970. Address: Santuario de Chimayo, P.O. Box 235; Chimayo 87522.

New York: National Shrine of Bl. Kateri Tekakwitha, Fonda (1938); Order of Friars Minor Conventual. Address: P.O. Box 627, Fonda 12068.
• Marian Shrine (National Shrine of Mary Help of Christians), West Haverstraw (1953); Salesians of St. John Bosco. Address: 174 Filors Lane, Stony Point, NY 10980-2645; (845) 947-2200; www.Marian Shrine.org.
• National Shrine Basilica of Our Lady of Fatima, Youngstown (1954); Barnabite Fathers. Address: 1023 Swann Rd., Youngstown 14174; (716) 754-7489. Designated a national shrine in 1994.
• Original Shrine of St. Ann in New York City (1892); located in St. Jean Baptiste Church; Blessed Sacrament Fathers. Address: 184 E. 76th St., New York 10021; (212) 288-5082.
• Our Lady of Victory National Shrine, Lackawanna (1926); Minor Basilica. Address: 767 Ridge Rd., Lackawanna 14218.
• Shrine Church of Our Lady of Mt. Carmel, Brooklyn (1887); Brooklyn Diocese (Parish Church). Address: 275 N. 8th St., Brooklyn 11211; (718) 384-0223.
• Shrine of Our Lady of Martyrs, Auriesville (1885); Society of Jesus. Address: Auriesville 12016; (518) 853-3033; www.klink.net/~jesuit.
• Shrine of Our Lady of the Island, Eastport (1975); Montfort Missionaries. Address: Box 26, Eastport, N.Y., 11941; (516) 325-0661.
• Shrine of St. Elizabeth Ann Seton, New York City (1975); located in Our Lady of the Rosary Church. Address: 7 State St., New York 10004.
• Shrine of St. Frances Xavier Cabrini, New York (1938; new shrine dedicated 1960); Missionary Sisters of the Sacred Heart. Address: 701 Fort Washington Ave., New York 10040; (212) 923-3536; www.cabrinishrineny.org

Ohio: Basilica and National Shrine of Our Lady of Consolation, Carey (1867); Minor Basilica; Toledo Diocese; staffed by Conventual Franciscan Friars. Address: 315 Clay St., Carey 43316; (419) 396-7107.
• National Shrine of Our Lady of Lebanon, North Jackson (1965); Eparchy of Our Lady of Lebanon of Los Angeles. Address: 2759 N. Lipkey Rd., N. Jackson 44451; (330) 538-3351; www.nationalshrine.org.
• National Shrine and Grotto of Our Lady of Lourdes, Euclid (1926); Sisters of the Most Holy Trinity. Address: 21281 Chardon Rd., Euclid 44117-2112; (216) 481-8232.
• Our Lady of Czestochowa Shrine, Garfield Heights (1939); Sisters of St. Joseph, Third Order of St. Francis. Address: 12215 Granger Rd., Garfield Hts. 44125; (216) 581-3535.
• Our Lady of Fatima, Ironton (1954); Old Rt. 52, Haverhill, Ohio. Mailing address: St. Joseph Church, P.O. Box 499, Ironton 45638-0499; (740) 429-2144.
• St. Anthony Shrine, Cincinnati (1888); Franciscan Friars, St. John Baptist Province. Address: 5000 Colerain Ave., Cincinnati 45223; .
• Shrine and Oratory of the Weeping Madonna of Mariapoch, Burton (1956); Social Mission Sisters. Parma Diocese (Byzantine). Address: 17486 Mumford Rd., Burton 44021.
• Shrine of the Holy Relics (1892); Sisters of the Precious Blood. Address: 2291 St. Johns Rd., Maria Stein 45860; (419) 925-4532.
• Sorrowful Mother Shrine, Bellevue (1850); Society of the Precious Blood. Address: 4106 State Rt. 269, Bellevue 44811; (419) 483-3435.

Oklahoma: National Shrine of the Infant Jesus of Prague, Prague (1949); Oklahoma City Archdiocese. Address: P.O. Box 488, Prague 74864.

Oregon: The Grotto (National Sanctuary of Our Sorrowful Mother), Portland (1924); Servite Friars. Address: P.O. Box 20008, Portland 97294; www.thegrotto.com.

Pennsylvania: Basilica of the Sacred Heart of Jesus, Conewago Township (1741; present church, 1787); Minor Basilica; Harrisburg Diocese. Address: 30 Basilica Dr., Hanover 17331.
• National Shrine Center of Our Lady of Guadalupe, Allentown (1974); located in Immaculate Conception Church; Allentown Diocese. Address: 501 Ridge Ave., Allentown 18102; (610) 433-4404.
• National Shrine of Our Lady of Czestochowa (1955); Order of St. Paul the Hermit (Pauline Fathers). Address: P.O. Box 2049, Doylestown 18901.
• National Shrine of St. John Neumann, Philadelphia (1860); Redemptorist Fathers, St. Peter's Church. Address: 1019 N. 5th St., Philadelphia 19123.
• National Shrine of the Sacred Heart, Harleigh (1975); Scranton Diocese. Address: P.O. Box 500, Harleigh (Hazleton) 18225; (570) 455-1162.
• Old St. Joseph's National Shrine, Philadelphia (1733); Philadelphia Archdiocese (Parish Church). Address: 321 Willings Alley, Philadelphia 19106; (215) 923-1733; www.oldstjoseph.org.
• St. Ann's Basilica Shrine, Scranton (1902); Passionist Community. Designated a minor basilica Aug. 29, 1996. Address: 1230 St. Ann's St., Scranton 18504; (570) 347-5691.
• St. Anthony's Chapel, Pittsburgh (1883); Pittsburgh Diocese. Address: 1700 Harpster St., Pittsburgh 15212.

• Shrine of St. Walburga, Greensburg (1974); Sisters of St. Benedict. Address: 1001 Harvey Ave., Greensburg 15601; (724) 834-3060.

Texas: National Shrine of Our Lady of San Juan Del Valle, San Juan (1949); Brownsville Diocese; staffed by Oblates of Mary Immaculate. Mailing address: P.O. Box 747, San Juan 78589; (956) 787-0033.

Vermont: St. Anne's Shrine, Isle La Motte (1666); Burlington Diocese, conducted by Edmundites. Address: West Shore Rd., Isle La Motte 05463; (802) 928-3362.

Wisconsin: Holy Hill - National Shrine of Mary, Help of Christians (1857); Discalced Carmelite Friars. Address: 1525 Carmel Rd., Hubertus 53033.

• National Shrine of St. Joseph, De Pere (1889); Norbertine Fathers. Address: 1016 N. Broadway, De Pere 54115.

• Shrine of Mary, Mother Thrice Admirable Queen and Victress of Schoenstatt (1965), Address: W284 N698 Cherry Lane, Waukesha 53188-9402; (414) 547-7733.

THE CATHEDRAL OF OUR LADY OF THE ANGELS

On Sept. 2, 2002, the Cathedral of Our Lady of the Angels was dedicated and opened for the archdiocese of Los Angeles. Cardinal Roger M. Mahony, archbishop of Los Angeles, was the chief celebrant in a dedication liturgy that was attended by most of the cardinals in the United States, dozens of bishops, hundreds of clergy, and several thousand people. Also present was Cardinal James Francis Stafford, prefect of the Pontifical Council for the Laity in Rome, the official representative of Pope John Paul II.

The cathedral took six years to build and cost over $190 million. It is three times larger than the former cathedral, St. Vibiana's, torn down because of earthquake damage. Cardinal Mahony broke ground with a ceremonial shovel in 1999, starting the lengthy and sometimes controversial process of building Our Lady of the Angels. The designs for the cathedral and its extensive plaza were conceived by Spanish architect José Rafael Moneo; construction was undertaken by contractor Morley Builders. Moneo is noted for his style of combining classic architectural themes with modern designs. The square, 11-story cathedral thus utilizes an asymmetrical design and a lack of right angles, with a heavy emphasis on lighting and making the liturgy the central focus of the interior. The sandstone-colored walls are intended to evoke California's history of Spanish missions. At 58,000 square feet, the cathedral is 1,000 square feet smaller than Notre Dame in Paris but one foot longer that St. Patrick's in New York.Cardinal Stafford read a message from the pontiff that declared: "May this cathedral always remain an eloquent symbol of communion and fraternity, of mutual respect and understanding; may it be an enduring monument to Christian faith, hope and love, to Christian holiness.... May those who enter this house of prayer reflect on Mary's example and holiness and treasure in their hearts the Mystery of Salvation and God's boundless love for all people."

Following are excerpts from Cardinal Roger M. Mahony's homily:

"It is truly fitting that we begin today's celebration at a site alongside the El Camino Real. The 18th-century Spanish Franciscans trod up and down that fabled road, as California's first evangelizers. They inaugurated God's active plan of salvation for all who, ultimately, came North and West to make their home in this golden State....

"We celebrate the Liturgical Dedication of the Altar and the Cathedral of Our Lady of the Angels in our State's most diverse and decidedly most global city.

"Today, we offer our praise to God for this new Cathedral Church. Yet we do not gather here simply to celebrate its architectural and artistic achievements.

These give homage to God and, together, we speak our thanks for the inspiration and artistry engraved in this soaring edifice. But we gather here mainly to reflect more deeply on the significance of this Cathedral Church....

"Today, the Cathedral of Our Lady of the Angels joins the storied ranks of the early missions, the first permanent structures built across the California landscape. It sinks its foundations in the very heart of the City of Los Angeles, astride today's El Camino Real — today's less colorfully named Hollywood Freeway — where it will stand and soar for many centuries as a sign of God's enduring presence in our lives and community....

"A Cathedral achieves its destiny when the mystery of the Church is fully lived out: in the gathering of God's People; in the celebration of the Eucharist and the sacramental life of the Church. Every Eucharist is both a gathering and a sending, and both are only possible by the prior action of God....

"It is the one and same Spirit who led the 18th-century Franciscans to evangelize California, carrying the Gospel message as they trod the Camino Real. It is the Spirit of God, Spirit of Christ, who has challenged and consoled generation after generation of Catholics throughout Southern California, and today has gathered us here for the dedication liturgy of the Cathedral of Our Lady of the Angels.

It is the same Spirit who is stirring now in our hearts as we ready to make the Profession of Faith for the first time in the Cathedral, our voices rising in proclamation of a living faith from the time of the apostolic church until now, at this time and in this place. Let our proclamation echo to the ends of the earth: We believe in one, holy, catholic and apostolic Church. We stand amidst that blessed communion of saints, women and men, young and old, heroic and humble, sung and unsung, as we prepare to invoke their names in litany. Hallowing the altar with the relics of Saints and Blesseds we are unceasingly reminded of the faith of those who have gone before us, leading us onward, interceding for us and strengthening us in our call to holiness.

And as we lift up our hearts in the prayer of dedication of the Cathedral altar, we enter more fully into the mystery of Christ's Church, a Church fruitful, holy, favored, and exalted. For the Church is the very Body of Christ — member for member — a living sacrifice of praise to the glory of God the Father. Transformed by the Word, strengthened by the celebration of the Sacraments, we, the Body, become a spiritual house, a living temple of the Lord, more radiant still than the hallowed ground on which we stand, and even more resplendent than the grandeur which today we behold."

Biographies of American Bishops

(*Sources:* Catholic Almanac *survey,* The Official Catholic Directory, Annuario Pontificio, *Catholic News Service. As of Aug. 20, 2002. For notable former bishops of the U.S., see under* **American Catholics of the Past.**)
Information includes: date and place of birth; educational institutions attended; date of ordination to the priesthood with, where applicable, name of archdiocese (*) or diocese in parentheses; date of episcopal ordination; episcopal appointments; date of resignation/retirement.

A

Adamec, Joseph V.: b. Aug. 13, 1935, Bannister, MI; educ. Michigan State Univ. (East Lansing), Nepomucene College and Lateran Univ. (Rome); ord. priest (for Nitra diocese, Slovakia), July 3, 1960; served in Saginaw diocese; ord. bp. of Altoona-Johnstown, May 20, 1987.

Adams, Edward J.: b. Aug. 24, 1944. Philadelphia, PA; educ. St. Charles Borromeo Seminary (Philadelphia), Pontifical Ecclesiastical Academy (Rome); ord. priest (Philadelphia*), May 16, 1970; in Vatican diplomatic service from 1976; ord. titular abp. of Scala Oct. 23, 1996; papal nuncio to Bangladesh.

Ahern, Patrick V.: b. Mar. 8, 1919, New York, NY; educ. Manhattan College and Cathedral College (New York City), St. Joseph's Seminary (Yonkers, NY), St. Louis Univ. (St. Louis, MO), Notre Dame Univ. (Notre Dame, IN); ord. priest (New York*) Jan. 27, 1945; ord. titular bp. of Naiera and aux. bp. of New York, Mar. 19, 1970; retired Apr. 26, 1994.

Allué, Emilio S., S.D.B.: b. Feb. 18, 1935, Huesca, Spain; educ. Salesain schools (Huesca, Spain) Don Bosco College/Seminary (Newton, NJ); Salesian Pontifical Univ. (Rome), Fordham Univ. (New York); ord. priest Dec. 22, 1966, in Rome; ord. titular bp. of Croe and aux. bp. of Boston, Sept. 17, 1996.

Amos, Martin J.: b. Dec. 8, 1941, Cleveland; educ. St. Mary Seminary Cleveland; ord. priest (Cleveland) May 25, 1968; app. aux. bp. of Cleveland April 3, 2001, ord. June 7, 2001.

Anderson, Moses B., S.S.E.: b. Sept. 9, 1928, Selma, AL; educ. St. Michael's College (Winooski, VT), St. Edmund Seminary (Burlington, VT), Univ. of Legon (Ghana); ord. priest May 30, 1958; ord. titular bp. of Vatarba and aux. bp. of Detroit, Jan. 27, 1983.

Angadiath, Jacob: b. Oct. 26, 1945, Periappuram, Kerala, India; educ. St. Thomas Apostolic Seminary, Vadavathoor, Kottayam, India, Univ. of Kerala, India, Univ. of Dallas (USA); ord. priest (Palai, Kerala)

Jan. 5, 1972; Director, Syro-Malabar Catholic Mission, Archdiocese of Chicago, 1999-2001; app. bp. of Eparchy of St. Thomas of Chicago of the Syro-Malabarians and Permanent Apostolic Visitator in Canada, March 13, 2001; inst. July 1, 2001.

Angell, Kenneth A.: b. Aug. 3, 1930, Providence, RI; educ. St. Mary's Seminary (Baltimore, MD); ord. priest (Providence) May 26, 1956; ord. titular bp. of Septimunicia and aux. bp. of Providence, RI, Oct. 7, 1974; bp. of Burlington, Oct. 6, 1992; installed Nov. 9, 1992.

Apuron, Anthony Sablan, O.F.M. Cap.: b. Nov. 1, 1945, Agana, Guam; educ. St. Anthony College and Capuchin Seminary (Hudson, NH), Capuchin Seminary (Garrison, NY), Maryknoll Seminary (New York), Notre Dame Univ. (Notre Dame, IN); ord. priest Aug. 26, 1972, in Guam; ord. titular bp. of Muzuca in Proconsulari and aux. bp. of Agana, Guam (unicorporated U.S. territory), Feb. 19, 1984; abp. of Agana, Mar. 10, 1986.

Aquila, Samuel J.: b. Sept. 24, 1950, Burbank, CA; educ. St. Thomas Seminary, Denver, San Anselmo (Rome); ord. priest (Denver*) June 5, 1976; rector, St. John Vianney Seminary (Denver) 1999-2001; app. coadjutor bp. of Fargo, June 12, 2001; ord. Aug. 24, 2001; bp. of Fargo, March 19, 2002.

Arias, David, O.A.R.: b. July 22, 1929, Leon, Spain; educ. St. Rita's College (San Sebastian, Spain), Our Lady of Good Counsel Theologate (Granada, Spain), Teresianum Institute (Rome, Italy); ord. priest May 31, 1952; ord. titular bp. of Badie and aux. bp. of Newark, Apr. 7, 1983; episcopal vicar for Hispanic affairs.

Arzube, Juan A.: b. June 1, 1918, Guayaquil, Ecuador; educ. Rensselaer Polytechnic Institute (Troy, NY), St. John's Seminary (Camarillo, CA); ord. priest (Los Angeles*) May 5, 1954; ord. titular bp. of Civitate and aux. bp. of Los Angeles, Mar. 25, 1971; retired Sept 7, 1993.

Aymond, Gregory M.: b. Nov. 12, 1949, New Orleans, LA; educ. St. Joseph Seminary College, Notre Dame Seminary (New Orleans, LA); ord. priest (New Orleans*) May 10, 1975; ord. titular bp. of Acolla and aux. bp. of New Orleans, Jan. 10, 1997; co-adjutor bp. of Austin, June 2, 2000, ins. Aug. 3, 2000; bp. of Austin, Jan. 2, 2001.

B

Baker, Robert J.: b. June 4, 1944, Fostoria, OH; educ. Pontifical College Josephinum, Columbus, OH, Gregorian Univ., Rome; ordained (St. Aug.ine) March 21, 1970; app. bp of Charleston, July 13, 1999; ord. Sept. 29, 1999.

Balke, Victor H.: b. Sept. 29, 1931, Meppen, IL; educ. St. Mary of the Lake Seminary (Mundelein, IL), St. Louis Univ. (St. Louis, MO); ord. priest (Springfield, IL) May 24, 1958; ord. bp. of Crookston, Sept. 2, 1976.

Baltakis, Paul Antanas, O.F.M.: b. Jan. 1, 1925, Troskunai, Lithuania; educ. seminaries of the Franciscan Province of St. Joseph (Belgium); ord. priest Aug. 24, 1952, in Belgium; served in U.S. as director of Lithuanian Cultural Center, New York, and among Lithuanian youth; head of U.S. Lithuanian Franciscan Vicariate, Kennebunkport, ME, from 1979; ord. titular bp. of Egara, Sept. 24, 1984; assigned to pastoral assistance to Lithuanian Catholics living outside Lithuania (resides in Brooklyn).

Banks, Robert J.: b. Feb. 26, 1928, Winthrop, MA; educ. St. John's Seminary (Brighton, MA), Gregorian Univ., Lateran Univ. (Rome); ord. priest (Boston*) Dec. 20, 1952, in Rome; rector of St. John's Seminary, Brighton, MA, 1971-81; vicar general of Boston archdiocese, 1984; ord. titular bp. of Taraqua and aux. bp. of Boston, Sept. 19, 1985; bp. of Green Bay, Oct. 16, 1990, installed Dec. 5, 1990.

Barbarito, Gerald M.: b. Jan. 4, 1950, Brooklyn, NY; educ. Cathedral College (Douglaston, NY), Immaculate Conception Seminary (Huntington, NY), Catholic University (Washington, DC); ord. priest (Brooklyn) Jan. 31, 1976; ord. titular bp. of Gisipa and aux. bp. of Brooklyn, Aug. 22, 1994; bp. of Ogdensburg, Oct. 27, 1999; ins. Jan. 7, 2000.

Barnes, Gerald R.: b. June 22, 1945, Phoenix, AZ, of Mexican descent; educ. St. Leonard Seminary (Dayton, OH), Assumption-St. John's Seminary (San Antonio, TX); ord. priest (San Antonio*) Dec. 20, 1975; ord. titular bp. of Montefiascone and aux. bp. of San Bernardino, Mar. 18, 1992; bp. of San Bernardino, Dec. 28, 1995.

Batakian, Manuel: b. Nov. 5, 1929, Greece; moved with his family to Lebanon during World War II; educ. philosophy and theology studies in Rome; ord. priest (as a member of the Institute of the Clergy of Bzommar, an Armenian patriarchal religious order, Dec.8, 1954; patriarchal vicar of the Institute and superior of its motherhouse in Bzommar, 1978-84; pastor of the Armenian Catholic Cathedral, Paris, 1984-90; rector of the Armenian Pontifical College, Rome, 1990-94; elected auxiliary of the patriarchate Dec. 8, 1994, ordained bishop March 12, 1995.

Baum, William W.: (See **Cardinals, Biographies.**)

Beltran, Eusebius J.: b. Aug. 31, 1934, Ashley, PA; educ. St. Charles Seminary (Philadelphia, PA); ord. priest (Atlanta*) May 14, 1960; ord. bp. of Tulsa, Apr. 20, 1978; app. abp. of Oklahoma City, Nov. 24, 1992; installed Jan 22, 1993.

Bennett, Gordon D., S.J.: b. Oct. 21, 1946, Denver; educ. Mount St. Michael's, Spokane, WA, Jesuit School of Theology, Berkeley, CA, Fordham Univ., NY; entered Society of Jesus, 1966; ord priest June 14, 1975; app. titular bp. of Nesqually and aux. bp. of Baltimore, Dec. 23, 1997, ord. Mar 3, 1998.

Bevilacqua, Anthony J.: (See **Cardinals, Biographies.**)

Blair, Leonard P.: b. Dec. 12, 1949, Detroit; educ. Sacred Heart Seminary, Detroit, Pontifical North American College, Gregorian University, and the Angelicum, Rome; ord. priest (Detroit*) June 26, 1976; at Vatican Secretariat of State, 1986-1991, Secretary to the President of the Prefecture for the Economic Affairs of the Holy See, 1994-1997; app. aux. of Detroit, July 9, 1999, ord. Aug. 24, 1999.

Blaire, Stephen E.: b. Dec. 22, 1941, Los Angeles, CA; educ. St. John's Seminary (Camarillo, CA); ord. priest (Los Angeles*) Apr. 29, 1967; ord. titular bp. of Lamzella and aux. of Los Angeles, May 31, 1990; app. bp. of Stockton, Jan. 19, 1999, ins. March 16, 1999.

Boland, Ernest B., O.P.: b. July 10, 1925, Providence, RI; educ. Providence College (RI), Dominican Houses of Study (Somerset, OH; Washington, DC); ord. priest June 9, 1955; ord. bp. of Multan, Pakistan, July 25, 1966; resigned Oct. 20, 1984.

Boland, J.(John) Kevin: b. Apr. 25, 1935, Cork, Ireland (brother of Bp. Raymond J. Boland); educ. Christian Brothers School (Cork, Ire.), All Hallows Seminary (Dublin); ord. priest (Savannah), June 14, 1959; ord. bp. of Savannah, Apr. 18, 1995.

Boland, Raymond J.: b. Feb. 8, 1932, Tipperary, Ireland; educ. National Univ. of Ireland and All Hallows Seminary (Dublin); ord. priest (Washington*) June 16, 1957, in Dublin; vicar general and chancellor of Washington archdiocese; ord. bp. of Birmingham, AL, Mar. 25, 1988; app. bp. of Kansas City-St. Joseph, MO, June 22, 1993.

Boles, John P.: b. Jan. 21, 1930, Boston, MA; educ. St. John Seminary, Boston College (Boston, MA); ord. priest (Boston*) Feb. 2, 1955; ord. titular bp. of Nova Sparsa and aux. bp. of Boston, May 21, 1992.

Bootkoski, Paul G: b. July 4, 1940, Newark, NJ; educ. Seton Hall Univ. (South Orange, NJ), Immaculate Conception Seminary (Darlington, NJ); ord. priest (Newark*) May 29, 1966; ord. titular bp. of Zarna and aux. bp. of Newark, Sept. 5, 1997; app. bp. of Metuchen, Jan. 4, 2002.

Borders, William D.: b. Oct. 9, 1913, Washington, IN; educ. St. Meinrad Seminary (St. Meinrad, IN), Notre Dame Seminary (New Orleans, LA), Notre Dame Univ. (Notre Dame, IN); ord. priest (New Orleans*) May 18, 1940; ord. first bp. of Orlando, June 14, 1968; app. abp. of Baltimore, Apr. 2, 1974, installed June 26, 1974; retired Apr. 11, 1989.

Bosco, Anthony G.: b. Aug. 1, 1927, New Castle, PA; educ. St. Vincent Seminary (Latrobe, PA), Lateran Univ. (Rome); ord. priest (Pittsburgh) June 7, 1952; ord. titular bp. of Labicum and aux. of Pittsburgh, June 30, 1970; app. bp. of Greensburg, Apr. 14, 1987, installed June 30, 1987.

Botean, John Michael: b. July 9, 1955, Canton, OH; educ. St. Fidelis Seminary (Herman, PA), Catholic University of America (Washington, DC), St. Gregory Melkite Seminary (Newton Centre, Mass), Catholic Theological Union (Chicago, IL); ord. priest (Romanian rite St. George's in Canton), May 18, 1986; ord. bp. of Saint George's in Canton for Romanians Aug. 24, 1996.

Boyea, Earl: b. April 10, 1951, Pontiac, Mich.; educ., Sacred Heart Seminary (Detroit), North American College and Pontifical Gregorian University (Rome), Wayne State University (Detroit), Catholic University of America (Washington, D.C.); ord. May 20, 1978 (Detroit*); rector and president of the Pontifical College *Josephinum* (Columbus, Ohio), 2000-2002; app. titular bp. of Siccenna and aux. bp. of Detroit, July 22, 2002.

Boyle, Paul M., C.P.: b. May 28, 1926, Detroit, MI; educ. Passionist houses of study, Lateran Univ.

(Rome); professed in Congregation of the Passion July 9, 1946; ord. priest May 30, 1953; president of Conference of Major Superiors of Men, 1969-74; superior general of Passionists, 1976-88; ord. titular bp. of Canapium and first vicar apostolic of Mandeville, Jamaica, July 9, 1991.

Braxton, Edward K.: b. June 28, 1944, Chicago, IL; educ. Loyola Univ. of Chicago, Univ. of St. Mary of the Lake and Mundelein Seminary (Chicago), Louvain Univ. (Belgium); ord. priest (Chicago*) May 13, 1970; ord. titular bp. of Macomades rusticiana and aux. bp. of St. Louis, May 17, 1995; app. bp. of Lake Charles, Dec. 11, 2000; ins. Feb. 22, 2001.

Breen, Vincent DePaul: b. Dec. 24, 1936, Brooklyn, NY; educ. Cathedral College of Immaculate Conception (Brooklyn, NY), North American College, Gregorian Univ. (Rome); ord. priest (Brooklyn) July 15, 1962, in Rome; vicar of education for diocese of Brooklyn; app. bp. of Metuchen, July 8, 1997; res. Jan. 4, 2002.

Breitenbeck, Joseph M.: b. Aug. 3, 1914, Detroit, MI; educ. University of Detroit, Sacred Heart Seminary (Detroit, MI), North American College and Lateran Univ. (Rome), Catholic Univ. (Washington, DC); ord. priest (Detroit*) May 30, 1942; ord. titular bp. of Tepelta and aux. bp. of Detroit, Dec. 20, 1965; app. bp. of Grand Rapids, Oct. 15, 1969, installed Dec. 2, 1969; retired July 11, 1989.

Britt, Kevin Michael: b. Nov. 19, 1944, Detroit, MI; educ. Sacred Heart Seminary, St. John Provincial Seminary, Universtiy of Detroit Mercy (Detroit, MI), Lateran Univ. (Rome); ord. priest (Detroit*) June 28, 1970; ord. titular bp. of Esco and aux. of Detroit, Jan. 6, 1994.

Broderick, Edwin B.: b. Jan. 16, 1917, New York, NY; educ. Cathedral College (Douglaston, NY), St. Joseph's Seminary (Yonkers, NY), Fordham Univ. (New York City); ord. priest (New York*) May 30, 1942; ord. titular bp. of Tizica and aux. of New York, Apr. 21, 1967; bp. of Albany, 1969-76; executive director of Catholic Relief Services, 1976-82. Bp. emeritus of Albany.

Broglio, Timothy M.: b. Dec. 22, 1951, Cleveland, OH; educ. Boston College (Boston, MA), North American College and Gregorian Univ. (Rome); ord. May 19, 1977; graduate of the Pontifical Ecclesiastical Academy; entered the diplomatic corps in 1983; chief of staff to the Vatican Secretary of State; app. titular abp. (Amiternum) and papal nuncio to the Dominican Republic and apostolic delegate to Puerto Rico, Feb. 27, 2001; ord. Mar. 19, 2001.

Brom, Robert H.: b. Sept. 18, 1938, Arcadia, WI; educ. St. Mary's College (Winona, MN), Gregorian Univ. (Rome); ord. priest (Winona) Dec. 18, 1963, in Rome; ord. bp. of Duluth, May 23, 1983; coadjutor bp. of San Diego, May, 1989; bp. of San Diego, July 10, 1990.

Brown, Tod D.: b. Nov. 15, 1936, San Francisco, CA; educ. St. John's Seminary (Camarillo, CA), North American College (Rome); ord. priest (Monterey-Fresno) May 1, 1963; ord. bp. of Boise, Apr. 3, 1989; app. bp. of Orange, June 30, 1998.

Brucato, Robert A.: b. Aug. 14, 1931, New York, NY educ. Cathedral College (Douglaston, NY), St. Joseph's Seminary (Dunwoodie, NY), Univ. of Our Lady of the Lake (San Antonio, TX); ord. priest (New York*) June 1, 1957; air force chaplain for 22 years;

ord. titular bp. of Temuniana and aux. of New York, Aug. 25, 1997.

Brunett, Alexander J.: b. Jan. 17, 1934, Detroit, MI; educ. Gregorian Univ. (Rome), Sacred Heart Seminary, University of Detroit (Detroit, MI), Marquette Univ. (Milwaukee, WI); ord. priest (Detroit*), July 13, 1958; ord. bp. of Helena, July 6, 1994; app.Abp. of Seattle Oct. 28, 1997, installed Dec. 18, 1997.

Bruskewitz, Fabian W.: b. Sept. 6, 1935, Milwaukee, WI; educ. North American College, Gregorian Univ. (Rome); ord. priest (Milwaukee*) July 17, 1960; ord. bp. of Lincoln, May 13, 1992.

Buechlein, Daniel M., O.S.B.: b. Apr. 20, 1938; educ. St. Meinrad College and Seminary (St. Meinrad, IN), St. Anselm Univ. (Rome); solemn profession as Benedictine monk, Aug. 15, 1963; ord. priest (St. Meinrad Archabbey) May 3, 1964; ord. bp. of Memphis, Mar. 2, 1987; app. abp. of Indianapolis, July 14, 1992; installed Sept. 9, 1992.

Bukovsky, John, S.V.D.: b. Jan. 18, 1924, Cerova, Slovakia; educ. Slovakia, Divine Word Seminary (Techny, IL), Catholic Univ. (Washington, DC), Univ. of Chicago, Gregorian Univ. (Rome); ord. priest Dec. 3, 1950; became U.S. citizen 1958; worked at East European desk of Secretariat of State; ord. titular abp. of Tabalta, Oct. 13, 1990; nuncio to Romania, 1990-94; app. papal representative to Russia, Dec. 20, 1994-99.

Bullock, William H.: b. Apr. 13, 1927, Maple Lake, MN; educ. St. Thomas College and St. Paul Seminary (St. Paul, MN), Notre Dame Univ. (Notre Dame, IN); ord. priest (St. Paul-Minneapolis*) June 7, 1952; ord. titular bp. of Natchez and aux. bp. of St. Paul and Minneapolis, Aug. 12, 1980; app. bp. of Des Moines, Feb. 10, 1987; app. bp. of Madison, WI, Apr. 13, 1993.

Burbidge, Michael F.: b. June 16, 1957, Philadelphia; educ. St. Charles Borromeo Seminary; ord. priest (Philadelphia*) May 19, 1984; app. titular bp. of Cluain Iraird and aux. bp. of Philadelphia June 21, 2002.

Burke, John J., O.F.M.: b. Mar. 16, 1935, River Edge, NJ; educ. St. Joseph Seminary (Callicoon, NY), St. Bonaventure Univ. (St. Bonaventure, NY), Holy Name College (Washington, DC); solemnly professed in Franciscan Order, Aug. 20, 1958; ord. priest Feb. 25, 1961; missionary in Brazil from 1964; ord. coadjutor bp. of Miracema do Tocantins, Brazil, Mar. 25, 1995; bp. of Miracema do Tocantins, Feb. 14, 1996.

Burke, Raymond L.: b. June 30, 1948, Richland Center, WI; educ. Holy Cross Seminary (La Crosse, WI), Catholic Univ. (Washington, DC), North American College and Gregorian Univ. (Rome); ord. priest (La Crosse) June 29, 1975; ord. bp. of La Crosse Jan. 6, 1995, installed Feb. 22, 1995.

Buswell, Charles A.: b. Oct. 15, 1913, Homestead, OK; educ. St. Louis Preparatory Seminary (St. Louis, MO), Kenrick Seminary (Webster Groves, MO), American College, Univ. of Louvain (Belgium); ord. priest (Oklahoma City*) July 9, 1939; ord. bp. of Pueblo, Sept. 30, 1959; resigned Sept. 18, 1979.

C

Camacho, Tomas Aguon: b. Sept. 18, 1933, Chalon Kanoa, Saipan; educ. St. Patrick's Seminary (Menlo Park, CA); ord. priest June 14, 1961; ord. first bp. of

Chalan Kanoa, Northern Marianas (U.S. Commonwealth), Jan. 13, 1985.

Campbell, Frederick F.: b. Aug. 5, 1943, Elmira, NY; educ. Ohio State Univ., St. Paul Seminary, St. Paul, MN; ord. priest (St. Paul and Minneapolis*) May 31, 1980; app. titular bp. of Afufenia and aux. bp. of St. Paul and Minneapolis, March 2, 1999, ord. May 14, 1999.

Carlson, Robert J.: b. June 30, 1944, Minneapolis, MN; educ. Nazareth Hall and St. Paul Seminary (St. Paul, MN), Catholic Univ. (Washington, DC): ord. priest (St. Paul-Minneapolis*) May 23, 1970; ord. titular bp. of Avioccala and aux. bp. of St. Paul and Minneapolis, Jan. 11, 1984; app. coadjutor bp. of Sioux Falls, Jan. 13, 1994; succeeded as bp. of Sioux Falls, Mar. 21, 1995.

Carmody, Edmond: b. Jan. 12, 1934, Ahalena, Kerry, Ireland; educ. St. Brendan's College (Killarney), St. Patrick Seminary (Carlow, Ire.); ord. priest (San Antonio*) June 8, 1957; missionary in Peru 1984-89; ord. titular bp. of Mortlach and aux. bp. of San Antonio, Dec. 15, 1988; app. bp. of Tyler, 1992-2000; app. bp. of Corpus Christi, Feb. 3, 2000; inst. March 17, 2000.

Carmon, Dominic, S.V.D.: b. Dec. 13, 1930, Opelousas, LA; entered Society of Divine Word, 1946; ord. priest Feb. 2, 1960; missionary in Papua-New Guinea, 1961-68; ord. titular bp. of Rusicade and aux. bp. of New Orleans, Feb. 11, 1993.

Casey, Luis Morgan: b. June 23, 1935, Portageville, MO; ord. priest (St. Louis*) Apr. 7, 1962; missionary in Bolivia from 1965; ord. titular bp. of Mibiarca and aux. of La Paz, Jan. 28, 1984; vicar apostolic of Pando, Bolivia, Jan. 18, 1988 and apostolic administrator (1995) of La Paz.

Catanello, Ignatius A.: b. July 23, 1938, Brooklyn, NY; educ. Cathedral Preparatory Seminary and St. Francis College (Brooklyn, NY), Catholic Univ. (Washington, DC); St. John's University (Jamaica, NY), New York University; ord. priest (Brooklyn) May 28, 1966; ord. titular bp. of Deulto and aux. bp. of Brooklyn, Aug. 22, 1994.

Chaput, Charles J., O.F.M. Cap.: b. Sept. 26, 1944, Concordia, KS; educ. St. Fidelis College (Herman, PA), Capuchin College and Catholic Univ. (Washington, DC), Univ. of San Francisco; solemn vows as Capuchin, July 14, 1968; ord. priest Aug. 29, 1970; ord. bp. of Rapid City, SD, July 26, 1988, the second priest of Native American ancestry (member of Prairie Band Potawatomi Tribe) ordained a bp. in the U.S.; app abp. of Denver, installed Apr. 7, 1997.

Charron, Joseph L., C.PP.S.: b. Dec. 30, 1939, Redfield, SD; educ. St. John's Seminary (Collegeville, MN); ord. priest June 3, 1967; ord. titular bp. of Bencenna and aux. bp. of St. Paul and Minneapolis, Jan. 25, 1990; app. bp. of Des Moines, Nov. 12, 1993.

Chavez, Gilbert Espinoza: b. May 9, 1932, Ontario, CA; educ. St. Francis Seminary (El Cajon, CA), Immaculate Heart Seminary (San Diego), Univ. of CA; ord. priest (San Diego) Mar. 19, 1960; ord. titular bp. of Magarmel and aux. bp. of San Diego, June 21, 1974.

Chedid, John: b. July 4, 1923, Eddid, Lebanon; educ. seminaries in Lebanon and Pontifical Urban College (Rome); ord. priest Dec. 21, 1951, in Rome; ord. titular bp. of Callinico and aux. bp. of St. Maron of Brooklyn for the Maronites, Jan. 25, 1981; app. first bp. of Eparchy of Our Lady of Lebanon of Los Angeles for the Maronites, Mar. 1, 1994; res. Dec. 5, 2000.

Christian, Francis J.: b. Oct. 8, 1942, Peterborough, NH; educ. St. Anselm College (Manchester, NH), St. Paul Seminary (Ottawa), American College in Louvain (Belgium); ord. priest (Manchester) June 29, 1968; ord titular bp. of Quincy and aux. of Manchester May 14, 1996.

Clark, Edward W.: b. Nov. 30, 1946, Minneapolis; educ. Our Lady Queen of Angels Seminary (San Fernando, CA), St. John's Seminary College (Camarillo, CA), Gregorian University (Rome); ord. priest (Los Angeles*) May 9, 1972; President/Rector, St. John's Seminary College (Camarillo, CA) 1994-2001; app. titular bp. of Gardar and aux. bp. of Los Angeles, Jan. 16, 2001, ord. Mar. 26, 2001.

Clark, Matthew H.: b. July 15, 1937, Troy, NY; educ. St. Bernard's Seminary (Rochester, NY), Gregorian Univ. (Rome); ord. priest (Albany) Dec. 19, 1962; ord. bp. of Rochester, May 27, 1979; installed June 26, 1979.

Clinch, Harry A.: b. Oct. 27, 1908, San Anselmo, CA; educ. St. Joseph's College (Mountain View, CA), St. Patrick's Seminary (Menlo Park, CA); ord. priest (Monterey-Fresno) June 6, 1936; ord. titular bp. of Badiae and aux. bp. of Monterey-Fresno, Feb. 27, 1957; app. first bp. of Monterey in CA, Oct. 16, 1967; resigned Jan. 19, 1982.

Conlon, Robert D.: b. Dec. 4, 1948, Cincinnati; educ. Mount St. Mary's Seminary of the West, University of St. Paul, Ottawa; ord. priest (Cincinnati*) Jan. 15, 1977; app. bp. of Steubenville, May 31, 2002.

Connolly, Thomas J.: b. July 18, 1922, Tonopah, NV; educ. St. Patrick's Seminary (Menlo Park, CA), Catholic Univ. (Washington, DC), Lateran Univ. (Rome); ord. priest (Reno-Las Vegas) Apr. 8, 1947; ord. bp. of Baker, June 30, 1971; res. Nov. 19, 1999.

Connors, Ronald G., C.SS.R.: b. Nov. 1, 1915, Brooklyn, NY; ord. priest June 22, 1941; ord. titular bp. of Equizetum and coadjutor bp. of San Juan de la Maguana, Dominican Republic, July 20, 1976; succeeded as bp. of San Juan de la Maguana, July 20, 1977; retired Feb. 20, 1991.

Conway, Edwin M.: b. Mar. 6, 1934, Chicago, IL; educ. St. Mary of the Lake Seminary (Chicago), Loyola in Chicago; ord. priest (Chicago*) May 3, 1960; ord. titular bp. of Auguro and aux. of Chicago, Mar. 20, 1995.

Cooney, Patrick R.: b. Mar. 10, 1934, Detroit, MI; educ. Sacred Heart Seminary (Detroit), Gregorian Univ. (Rome), Notre Dame Univ. (Notre Dame, IN); ord. priest (Detroit*) Dec. 20, 1959; ord. titular bp. of Hodelm and aux. bp. of Detroit, Jan. 27, 1983; app. bp. of Gaylord, Nov. 6, 1989; installed Jan. 28, 1990.

Cordileone, Salvatore: b. June 5, 1956, San Diego, Calif.; educ. Saint Francis Seminary (San Diego), University of San Diego (San Diego), North American College (Rome), Pontifical Gregorian University (Rome); ord. July 9, 1982; official of the Supreme Tribunal of the Apostolic Signatura in Roma, 1995-2002 and vice-director of Villa Stritch in Rome; app. titular bp. of Natchez and aux. bp. of San Diego, July 5, 2002.

Corrada del Rio, Alvaro, S.J.: b. May 13, 1942, Santurce, Puerto Rico; entered Society of Jesus, 1960, at novitiate of St. Andrew-on-Hudson (Poughkeepsie, NY); educ. Jesuit seminaries, Fordham Univ. (New

York), Institut Catholique (Paris); ord. priest July 6, 1974, in Puerto Rico; pastoral coordinator of Northeast Catholic Hispanic Center, New York, 1982-85; ord. titular bp. of Rusticiana and aux. bp. of Washington, DC, Aug. 4, 1985; app. apostolic administrator of Caguas, Puerto Rico, Aug. 5, 1997 (retained his title as aux. bp. of Washington); app. bp. of Tyler, Dec. 5, 2000; ins. Jan. 30, 2001.

Coscia, Benedict Dominic, O.F.M.: b. Aug. 10, 1922, Brooklyn, NY; educ. St. Francis College (Brooklyn, NY), Holy Name College (Washington, DC); ord. priest June 11, 1949; ord. bp. of Jatai, Brazil, Sept. 21, 1961.

Costello, Thomas J.: b. Feb. 23, 1929, Camden, NY; educ. Niagara Univ. (Niagara Falls, NY), St. Bernard's Seminary (Rochester, NY), Catholic Univ. (Washington, DC); ord. priest (Syracuse) June 5, 1954; ord. titular bp. of Perdices and aux. bp. of Syracuse Mar. 13, 1978.

Cote, Michael R.: b. June 19, 1949, Sanford, ME; educ. Our Lady of Lourdes Seminary (Cassadaga, NY), St. Mary's Seminary College (Baltimore, MD); Gregorian Univ. (Rome), Catholic Univ. (Washington, DC); ord. priest (Portland, ME.) June 29, 1975 by Pope Paul VI in Rome; secretary, 1989-94 at apostolic nunciature, Washington; ord. titular bp. of Cebarades and aux. of Portland, ME, July 27, 1995.

Cotey, Arnold R., S.D.S.: b. June 15, 1921, Milwaukee, WI; educ. Divine Savior Seminary (Lanham, MD), Marquette Univ. (Milwaukee, WI); ord. priest June 7, 1949; ord. first bp. of Nachingwea (now Lindi), Tanzania, Oct. 20, 1963; retired Nov. 11, 1983.

Cronin, Daniel A.: b. Nov. 14, 1927, Newton, MA; educ. St. John's Seminary (Boston, MA), North American College and Gregorian Univ. (Rome); ord. priest (Boston*) Dec. 20, 1952; attaché apostolic nunciature (Addis Ababa), 1957-61; served in papal Secretariat of State, 1961-68; ord. titular bp. of Egnatia and aux. bp. of Boston, Sept. 12, 1968; bp. of Fall River, Dec. 16, 1970; abp. of Hartford, Dec. 10, 1991.

Crowley, Joseph R.: b. Jan. 12, 1915, Fort Wayne, IN; educ. St. Mary's College (St. Mary, KY), St. Meinrad Seminary (St. Meinrad, IN); served in US Air Force, 1942-46; ord. priest (Ft. Wayne-S. Bend) May 1, 1953; editor of *Our Sunday Visitor* 1958-67; ord. titular bp. of Maraguis and aux. bshop of Fort Wayne-South Bend, Aug. 24, 1971; retired May 8, 1990.

Cullen, Edward P.: b. Mar. 15, 1933, Philadelphia, PA; educ. St. Charles Borromeo Seminary (Overbrook, PA), Univ. of Pennsylvania and LaSalle Univ. (Philadelphia), Harvard Graduate School of Business; ord. priest (Philadelphia*) May 19, 1962; ord. titular bp. of Paria in Proconsolare and aux. of Philadelphia, Feb. 8, 1994; app. bp. of Allentown, Dec. 16, 1997, ord. Feb. 9, 1998.

Cummins, John S.: b. Mar. 3, 1928, Oakland, CA; educ. St. Patrick's Seminary (Menlo Park, CA), Catholic Univ. (Washington, DC), Univ. of CA; ord. priest (San Francisco*) Jan. 24, 1953; executive director of the CA Catholic Conference 1971-76; ord. titular bp. of Lambaesis and aux. bp. of Sacramento, May 16, 1974; app. bp. of Oakland, installed June 30, 1977.

Cupich, Blase: b. Mar. 19, 1949, Omaha, NE; educ. College of St. Thomas (St. Paul, MN), Gregorian Univ. (Rome), Catholic University of America (Washing-

ton, DC); ord. priest (Omaha*), Aug. 16, 1975; service at the apostolic nunciature, Washington, DC, 1981-87; rector, Pontifical College Josephinum (Columbus, OH) 1989-97; app. bp. of Rapid City, SD, July 7, 1998; installed Sept. 21, 1998.

Curlin, William G.: b. Aug. 30, 1927, Portsmouth, Va.; educ. Georgetown Univ. (Washington, DC), St. Mary's Seminary (Baltimore, MD); ord. priest (Washington*), May 25, 1957; ord. titular bp. of Rosemarkie and aux. bp. of Washington, Dec. 20, 1988; app. bp. of Charlotte, Feb. 22, 1994.

Curry, Thomas J.: b. Jan. 17, 1943, Drumgoon, Ireland; educ. Patrician College (Ballyfin, Ire.), All Hallows Seminary (Dublin, Ire.); ord. priest (Los Angeles*) June 17, 1967; ord. titular bp. of Ceanannus Mór and aux. of Los Angeles, Mar. 19, 1994.

Curtiss, Elden F.: b. June 16, 1932, Baker, OR; educ. St. Edward Seminary College and St. Thomas Seminary (Kenmore, WA); ord. priest (Baker) May 24, 1958; ord. bp. of Helena, MT, Apr. 28, 1976; app. abp. of Omaha, NE, May 4, 1993.

D

Daily, Thomas V.: b. Sept. 23, 1927, Belmont, MA; educ. Boston College, St. John's Seminary (Brighton, MA); ord. priest (Boston*) Jan. 10, 1952; missionary in Peru for five years as a member of the Society of St. James the Apostle; ord. titular bp. of Bladia and aux. bp. of Boston, Feb. 11, 1975; app. first bp. of Palm Beach, FL, July 17, 1984; app. bp. of Brooklyn, Feb. 20, 1990; installed Apr. 18, 1990.

Daly, James: b. Aug. 14, 1921, New York, NY; educ. Cathedral College (Brooklyn, NY), Immaculate Conception Seminary (Huntington, L.I.); ord. priest (Brooklyn) May 22, 1948; ord. titular bp. of Castra Nova and aux. bp. of Rockville Centre, May 9, 1977; retired July 1, 1996.

D'Antonio, Nicholas, O.F.M.: b. July 10, 1916, Rochester, NY; educ. St. Anthony's Friary (Catskill, NY); ord. priest June 7, 1942; ord. titular bp. of Giufi Salaria and prelate of Olancho, Honduras, July 25, 1966; resigned 1977; vicar general of New Orleans archdiocese and episcopal vicar for Spanish Speaking, 1977-91.

D'Arcy, John M.: b. Aug. 18, 1932, Brighton, MA; educ. St. John's Seminary (Brighton, MA), Angelicum Univ. (Rome); ord. priest (Boston*) Feb. 2, 1957; spiritual director of St. John's Seminary; ord. titular bp. of Mediana and aux. bp. of Boston, Feb. 11, 1975; app. bp. of Fort Wayne-South Bend, Feb. 26, 1985, installed May 1, 1985.

Dattilo, Nicholas C.: b. Mar. 8, 1932, Mahoningtown, PA; educ. St. Vincent Seminary (Latrobe, PA), St. Charles Borromeo Seminary (Philadelphia, PA); ord. priest (Pittsburgh) May 31, 1958; ord. bp. of Harrisburg, Jan. 26, 1990.

Delaney, Joseph P.: b. Aug. 29, 1934, Fall River, MA; educ. Cardinal O'Connell Seminary (Boston, MA), Theological College (Washington, DC), North American College (Rome), Rhode Island College (Providence, RI); ord. priest (Fall River) Dec. 18, 1960; ord. bp. of Fort Worth, TX, Sept. 13, 1981.

De Palma, Joseph A., S.C.J.: b. Sept. 4, 1913, Walton, NY; ord. priest May 20, 1944; superior general of Congregation of Priests of the Sacred Heart, 1959-67; ord. first bp. of De Aar, South Africa, July 19, 1967; retired Nov. 18, 1987.

De Paoli, Ambrose: b. Aug. 19, 1934, Jeannette, PA, moved to Miami at age of nine; educ. St. Joseph Seminary (Bloomfield, CT), St. Mary of the West Seminary (Cincinnati, OH), North American College and Lateran Univ. (Rome); ord. priest (Miami*) Dec. 18, 1960, in Rome; served in diplomatic posts in Canada, Turkey, Africa and Venezuela; ord. titular abp. of Lares, Nov. 20, 1983, in Miami; apostolic pro-nuncio to Sri Lanka, 1983-88; apostolic delegate in southern Africa and pro-nuncio to Lesotho, 1988; first apostolic nuncio to South Africa, 1994; apostolic nuncio to Japan.

De Simone, Louis A.: b. Feb. 21, 1922, Philadelphia, PA; educ. Villanova Univ. (Villanova, PA), St. Charles Borromeo Seminary (Overbrook, PA); ord. priest (Philadelphia*) May 10, 1952; ord. titular bp. of Cillium and aux. bp. of Philadelphia, Aug. 12, 1981; retired Apr. 5, 1997.

Di Lorenzo, Francis X.: b. Apr. 15, 1942, Philadelphia, PA; educ. St. Charles Borromeo Seminary (Philadelphia), Univ. of St. Thomas (Rome); ord. priest (Philadelphia*) May 18, 1968; ord. titular bp. of Tigia and aux. bp. of Scranton, Mar. 8, 1988; app. apostolic administrator of Honolulu, Oct. 12, 1993; bp. of Honolulu, Nov. 29, 1994.

DiMarzio, Nicholas: b. June 16, 1944, Newark, NJ; educ. Seton Hall University (South Orange, NJ), Immaculate Conception Seminary (Darlington, NJ), Catholic Univ. (Washington, DC), Fordham Univ. (New York), Rutgers Univ. (New Brunswick, NJ); ord. priest (Newark*) May 30, 1970; ord. titular bp. of Mauriana and aux. bp. of Newark, Oct. 31, 1996, app. Bishop of Camden, June 8, 1999, installed July 22, 1999.

Dimino, Joseph T.: b. Jan. 7, 1923, New York, NY; educ. Cathedral College (Douglaston, NY), St. Joseph's Seminary (Yonkers, NY), Catholic Univ. (Washington, DC); ord. priest (New York*) June 4, 1949; ord. titular bp. of Carini and aux. bp. of the Military Services archdiocese, May 10, 1983; app. ordinary of Military Services archdiocese, May 14, 1991; retired Aug. 12, 1997.

DiNardo, Daniel N.: b. May 23, 1949, Steubenville, OH; educ. Catholic Univ. of America (Washington, DC) North American College, (Rome), Gregorian Univ. (Rome); ord. priest (Pittsburgh) July 16, 1977; app. Coadjutor Bp. of Sioux City Aug. 19, 1997, ord. Oct. 7, 1997, Bp. of Sioux City Nov. 28, 1998.

Dion, George E., O.M.I.: b. Sept. 25, 1911, Central Falls, RI; educ. Holy Cross College (Worcester, MA), Oblate Juniorate (Colebrook, NH), Oblate Scholasticates (Natick, MA, and Ottawa, Ont.); ord. priest June 24, 1936; ord. titular bp. of Arpaia and vicar apostolic of Jolo, Philippines Apr. 23, 1980; retired Oct. 11, 1991; titular bp. of Arpaia.

Dolan, Timothy M.: b. Feb. 6, 1950, St. Louis; educ. St. Louis Preparatory Seminary, Cardinal Glennon College, North American College, Pontifical Univ. of St. Thomas (Rome), the Catholic University of America (Washington, D.C.); ord. priest (St. Louis*) June 19, 1976; served on staff of Apostolic Nunciature, (Washington); rector, North American College (Rome) 1994-2001; app. titular bp. of Natchez and aux. bp. of St. Louis, June 19, 2001; ord. Aug. 15, 2001; app. abp. of Milwaukee, June 25, 2002; inst. Aug. 28, 2002..

Donnelly, Robert William: b. Mar. 22, 1931, To-

ledo, OH; educ. St. Meinrad Seminary College (St. Meinrad, IN), Mount St. Mary's in the West Seminary (Norwood, OH); ord. priest (Toledo) May 25, 1957; ord. titular bp. of Garba and aux. bp. of Toledo, May 3, 1984.

Donoghue, John F.: b. Aug. 9, 1928, Washington, DC; educ. St. Mary's Seminary (Baltimore, MD); Catholic Univ. (Washington, DC); ord. priest (Washington*) June 4, 1955; chancellor and vicar general of Washington archdiocese, 1973-84; ord. bp. of Charlotte, NC, Dec. 18, 1984; app. abp. of Atlanta, June 22, 1993; installed Aug. 19, 1993.

Donovan, Paul V.: b. Sept. 1, 1924, Bernard, IA; educ. St. Gregory's Seminary (Cincinnati, OH), Mt. St. Mary's Seminary (Norwood, OH), Lateran Univ. (Rome); ord. priest (Lansing) May 20, 1950; ord. first bp. of Kalamazoo, MI, July 21, 1971; retired Nov. 22, 1994.

Doran, Thomas George: b. Feb. 20, 1936, Rockford, IL; educ. Loras College (Dubuque, IA), Gregorian Univ. (Rome), Rockford College (Rockford, IL); ord. priest (Rockford) Dec. 20, 1961; ord. bp. of Rockford, June 24, 1994.

Dorsey, Norbert M., C.P.: b. Dec. 14, 1929, Springfield, MA; educ. Passionist seminaries (eastern U.S. province), Pontifical Institute of Sacred Music and Gregorian Univ. (Rome, Italy); professed in Passionists, Aug. 15, 1949; ord. priest Apr. 28, 1956; assistant general of Passionists, 1976-86; ord. titular bp. of Mactaris and aux. bp. of Miami, Mar. 19, 1986; app. bp. of Orlando, Mar. 20, 1990, installed May 25, 1990.

Doueihi, Stephen Hector: b. June 25, 1927, Zghorta, Lebanon; educ. University of St. Joseph (Beirut, Lebanon), Propaganda Fide, Gregorian Univ. and Institute of Oriental Study (Rome); ord. priest Aug. 14, 1955; came to U.S. in 1973; eparch of Eparchy of St. Maron of Brooklyn, Jan 11, 1997

Dougherty, John Martin: b. Apr. 29, 1932, Scranton, PA; educ. St. Charles College (Catonsville, MD), St. Mary's Seminary (Baltimore), Univ. of Notre Dame (South Bend); ord. priest (Scranton) June 15, 1957; ord. titular bp. of Sufetula and aux. bp. of Scranton, Mar. 7, 1995.

Driscoll, Michael P.: b. Aug. 8, 1939, Long Beach, CA; educ. St. John Seminary (Camarillo, CA), Univ. of Southern CA; ord. priest (Los Angeles*) May 1, 1965; ord. titular bp. of Massita and aux. bp. of Orange, Mar. 6, 1990; app. bp. of Boise, Jan. 19, 1999, ins. Mar. 18, 1999.

Dudick, Michael J.: b. Feb. 24, 1916, St. Clair, PA; educ. St. Procopius College and Seminary (Lisle, IL); ord. priest (Passaic, Byzantine Rite) Nov. 13, 1945; ord. bp. of Byzantine Eparchy of Passaic, Oct. 14, 1968; retired Nov. 6, 1995.

Dudley, Paul V.: b. Nov. 27, 1926, Northfield, MN; educ. Nazareth College and St. Paul Seminary (St. Paul, MN); ord. priest (St. Paul-Minneapolis*) June 2, 1951; ord. titular bp. of Ursona and aux. bp. of St. Paul and Minneapolis, Jan. 25, 1977; app. bp. of Sioux Falls, installed Dec. 13, 1978; retired Mar. 21, 1995.

Duffy, Paul, O.M.I.: b. July 25, 1932, Norwood, MA; educ Oblate houses of study in Canada and Washington, DC; ord. priest 1962; missionary in Zambia from 1984; app. first bp. of Mongu, Zambia, July 1, 1997.

Duhart, Clarence James, C.SS.R.: b. Mar. 23,

1912, New Orleans, LA; ord. priest June 29, 1937; ord. bp. of Udon Thani, Thailand, Apr. 21, 1966; resigned Oct. 2, 1975.

DuMaine, (Roland) Pierre: b. Aug. 2, 1931, Paducah, KY; educ. St. Joseph's College (Mountain View, CA), St. Patrick's College and Seminary (Menlo Park, CA), Univ. of CA (Berkeley), Catholic Univ. (Washington, DC); ord. priest (San Francisco) June 15, 1957; ord. titular bp. of Sarda and aux. bp. of San Francisco, June 29, 1978; app. first bp. of San Jose, Jan. 27, 1981; inst. Mar. 18, 1981; res. Nov. 27, 1999.

Dunne, John C.: b. Oct. 30, 1937, Brooklyn, NY; educ. Cathedral College (Brooklyn, NY). Immaculate Conception Seminary (Huntington, NY), Manhattan College (New York); ord. priest (Rockville Centre) June 1, 1963; ord. titular bp. of Abercorn and aux. bp. of Rockville Centre, Dec. 13, 1988. Vicar for Central Vicariate.

Dupre, Thomas L.: b. Nov. 10, 1933, South Hadley Falls, MA; educ. College de Montreal, Assumption College (Worcester, MA), Catholic Univ. (Washington, DC), ord. priest (Springfield, MA) May 23, 1959; ord. titular bp. of Hodelm and aux. bp. of Springfield, MA, May 31, 1990; bp. of Springfield, Mar. 14, 1995.

Durning, Dennis V., C.S.Sp.: b. May 18, 1923, Germantown, PA; educ. St. Mary's Seminary (Ferndale, CT); ord. priest June 3, 1949; ord. first bp. of Arusha, Tanzania, May 28, 1963; resigned Mar. 6, 1989.

E

Edyvean, Walter J.: b. Oct. 18, 1938, Medford, MA; educ. Boston College, St. John's Seminary (Brighton, MA), the North American College and the Gregorian Univ. (Rome); ord. priest (Boston*) Dec. 16, 1964; served on staff of Congregation for Catholic Education, 1990-2001; app. titular bp. of Elie and aux. bp. of Boston, June 29, 2001, ord. Sept. 12, 2001.

Egan, Edward M.: (See **Cardinals, Biographies**.)

Elya, John A., B.S.O.: b. Sept. 16, 1928, Maghdouche, Lebanon; educ. diocesan monastery (Sidon, Lebanon), Gregorian Univ. (Rome, Italy); professed as member of Basilian Salvatorian Order, 1949; ord. priest Feb. 17, 1952, in Rome; came to U.S., 1958; ord. titular bp. of Abilene of Syria and aux. bp. of Melkite diocese of Newton, MA, June 29, 1986; app. bp. of Newton (Melkites), Nov. 25, 1993.

F

Farrell, Kevin J.: b. Dublin, Ireland, Sept. 2, 1947; educ. University of Salamanca (Spain), Gregorian University and University of St. Thomas Aquinas (Rome), University of Notre Dame (South Bend, IN); ord. priest (of the Legionaries of Christ) Dec. 24, 1978; incardinated into Archdiocese of Washington, 1984; app. titular bp. of Rusuccuru and aux. bp. of Washington, Dec. 28, 2001.

Favalora, John C.: b. Dec. 5, 1935, New Orleans, LA; educ. St. Joseph Seminary (St. Benedict, LA), Notre Dame Seminary (New Orleans, LA), Gregorian Univ. (Rome), Catholic Univ. of America (Washington, DC), Xavier Univ. and Tulane Univ. (New Orleans); ord. priest (New Orleans*) Dec. 20, 1961; ord. bp. of Alexandria, LA, July 29, 1986; bp. of St. Petersburg, Mar. 14, 1989; app. abp. of Miami, installed Dec. 20, 1994.

Fellhauer, David E.: b. Aug. 19, 1939, Kansas City, MO; educ. Pontifical College Josephinum (Worthington, OH), St. Paul Univ. (Ottawa, Ont.); ord. priest (Dallas), May 29, 1965; ord. bp. of Victoria, May 28, 1990.

Fernandez, Gilberto: b. Feb. 13, 1935, Havana, Cuba; educ. El Buen Pastor Seminary (Havana); ord. priest (Havana*), May 15, 1959; came to U.S. 1967; app. titular bp. of Irina and aux. of Miami, June 24, 1997.

Ferrario, Joseph A.: b. Mar. 3, 1926, Scranton, PA; educ. St. Charles College (Catonsville, MD), St. Mary's Seminary (Baltimore, MD), Catholic Univ. (Washington, DC); Univ. of Scranton; ord. priest (Honolulu) May 19, 1951; ord. titular bp. of Cuse and aux. bp. of Honolulu, Jan. 13, 1978; bp. of Honolulu, May 13, 1982; retired Oct. 12, 1993.

Fiorenza, Joseph A.: b. Jan. 25, 1931, Beaumont, TX; educ. St. Mary's Seminary (LaPorte, TX); ord. priest (Galveston-Houston) May 29, 1954; ord. bp. of San Angelo, Oct. 25, 1979; app. bp. of Galveston-Houston, Dec. 18, 1984, installed Feb. 18, 1985 vice president, NCCB/USCC, 1995-1998, President, 1998-2001.

Fitzgerald, James: b. Dec. 30, 1938, Chicago; educ. Conception Seminary, Conception, MO; app. titular bp. of Walla Walla and aux. bp. of Joliet, Jan. 11, 2002, ord. March 19, 2002.

Fitzpatrick, John J.: b. Oct. 12, 1918, Trenton, Ont., Canada; educ. Urban Univ. (Rome), Our Lady of the Angels Seminary (Niagara Falls, NY); ord. priest (Buffalo) Dec. 13, 1942; ord. titular bp. of Cenae and aux. bp. of Miami, Aug. 28, 1968; bp. of Brownsville, TX, May 28, 1971; retired Nov. 30, 1991.

Fitzsimons, George K.: b. Sept. 4, 1928, Kansas City, MO; educ. Rockhurst College (Kansas City, MO), Immaculate Conception Seminary (Conception, MO); ord. priest (Kansas City-St. Joseph) Mar. 18, 1961; ord. titular bp. of Pertusa and aux. bp. of Kansas City-St. Joseph, July 3, 1975; app. bp. of Salina, Mar. 28, 1984, installed May 29, 1984.

Flanagan, Thomas Joseph: b: Oct. 23, 1930, Rathmore, Ireland; educ. St. Patrick's College, Thurles, Ireland; ord priest (San Antonio*) June 10, 1956; app. titular bp. of Bavagaliana and aux. bp. of San Antonio, Jan. 5, 1998, ord. Feb. 16, 1998.

Fliss, Raphael M.: b. Oct. 25, 1930, Milwaukee, WI; educ. St. Francis Seminary (Milwaukee, WI), Catholic University (Washington, DC), Pontifical Lateran Univ. (Rome); ord. priest (Milwaukee*) May 26, 1956; ord. coadjutor bp. of Superior with right of succession, Dec. 20, 1979; bp. of Superior, June 27, 1985.

Flores, Patrick F.: b. July 26, 1929, Ganado, TX; educ. St. Mary's Seminary (Houston, TX); ord. priest (Galveston-Houston) May 26, 1956; ord. titular bp. of Itolica and aux. bp. of San Antonio, May 5, 1970 (first Mexican-American bp.); app. bp. of El Paso, Apr. 4, 1978, installed May 29, 1978; app. abp. of San Antonio 1979; installed Oct. 13, 1979.

Flynn, Harry J.: b. May 2, 1933, Schenectady, NY; educ. Siena College (Loudonville, NY), Mt. St. Mary's College (Emmitsburg, MD); ord. priest (Albany) May 28, 1960; ord. coadjutor bp. of Lafayette, LA, June 24, 1986; bp. of Lafayette, LA, May 15, 1989; app. coadjutor abp. of St. Paul and Minneapolis, Feb. 24, 1994, installed Apr. 27, 1994;

abp. of St. Paul and Minneapolis, Sept. 8, 1995.

Foley, David E.: b. Feb. 3, 1930, Worcester, MA; educ. St. Charles College (Catonsville, MD), St. Mary's Seminary (Baltimore, MD); ord. priest (Washington*) May 26, 1952; ord. titular bp. of Octaba and aux. bp. of Richmond, June 27, 1986; app. bp. of Birmingham, Mar. 22, 1994.

Foley, John Patrick: b. Nov. 11, 1935, Sharon Hill, PA; educ. St. Joseph's Preparatory School (Philadelphia, PA), St. Joseph's College (now University) (Philadelphia, PA), St. Charles Borromeo Seminary (Overbrook, PA), St. Thomas Univ. (Rome), Columbia School of Journalism (New York); ord. priest (Philadelphia*) May 19, 1962; assistant editor (1967-70) and editor (1970-84) of *The Catholic Standard and Times*, Philadelphia archdiocesan paper; ord. titular abp. of Neapolis in Proconsulari, May 8, 1984, in Philadelphia; app. president of the Pontifical Council for Social Communications, Apr. 5, 1984.

Forst, Marion F.: b. Sept. 3, 1910, St. Louis, MO; educ. St. Louis Preparatory Seminary (St. Louis, MO), Kenrick Seminary (Webster Groves, MO); ord. priest (St. Louis*) June 10, 1934; ord. bp. of Dodge City, Mar. 24, 1960; app. titular bp. of Scala and aux. bp. of Kansas City, KS, Oct. 16, 1976; retired Dec. 23, 1986. Titular bp. of Leavenworth.

Foys, Roger J.: b. July 27, 1945, Chicago; educ. University of Steubenville, St. John Vianney Seminary, Bloomingdale, Ohio, the Catholic University of America, Washington, D.C.; ord. priest (Steubenville), May 16, 1973; Knight Commander of the Equestrian Order of the Holy Sepulchre of Jerusalem, 1986; app. bp. of Covington, May 31, 2002.

Franklin, William Edwin: b. May 3, 1930, Parnell, IA; educ. Loras College and Mt. St. Bernard Seminry (Dubuque, IA); ord. priest (Dubuque*) Feb. 4, 1956; ord. titular bp. of Surista and aux. bp. of Dubuque, Apr. 1, 1987; app. bp. of Davenport, Nov. 12, 1993, installed Jan. 20, 1994.

Franzetta, Benedict C.: b. Aug. 1, 1921, East Liverpool, OH; educ. St. Charles College (Catonsville, MD), St. Mary Seminary (Cleveland, OH); ord. priest (Youngstown) Apr. 29, 1950; ord. titular bp. of Oderzo and aux. bp. of Youngstown, Sept. 4, 1980; retired Sept. 4, 1996.

Frey, Gerard L.: b. May 10, 1914, New Orleans, LA; educ. Notre Dame Seminary (New Orleans, LA); ord. priest (New Orleans*) Apr. 2, 1938; ord. bp. of Savannah, Aug. 8, 1967; app. bp. of Lafayette, LA, Nov. 7, 1972, installed Jan, 7, 1973; retired May 15, 1989.

Friend, William B.: b. Oct. 22, 1931, Miami, FL; educ. St. Mary's College (St. Mary, KY), Mt. St. Mary Seminary (Emmitsburg, MD), Catholic Univ. (Washington, DC), Notre Dame Univ. (Notre Dame, IN); ord. priest (Mobile*) May 7, 1959; ord. titular bp. of Pomaria and aux. bp. of Alexandria-Shreveport, LA, Oct. 30, 1979; app. bp. of Alexandria-Shreveport, Nov. 17, 1982, installed Jan 11, 1983; app. first bp. of Shreveport, June, 1986; installed July 30, 1986.

G

Galante, Joseph A.: b. July 2, 1938, Philadelphia, PA; educ. St. Joseph Preparatory School, St. Charles Seminary (Philadelphia, PA); Lateran Univ., Angelicum, North American College (Rome); ord. priest (Philadelphia*) May 16, 1964; on loan to dio-

cese of Brownsville, TX, 1968-72, where he served in various diocesan posts; returned to Philadelphia, 1972; assistant vicar (1972-79) and vicar (1979-87) for religious; undersecretary of Congregation for Institutes of Consecrated Life and Societies of Apostolic Life (Rome), 1987-92; ord. titular bp. of Equilium and aux. bp. of San Antonio, Dec. 11, 1992; app. bp. of Beaumont, Apr. 5, 1994; app. co-adjutor bp. of Dallas, Nov. 23, 1999.

Galeone, Victor Benito: b. Sept. 13, 1935, Philadelphia; educ. St. Charles College (Baltimore), North American College, Pontifical Gregorian University (Rome), ord. priest (Baltimore*) Dec. 18, 1960; served as missionary in Peru 1970-75, 1978-85; app. bp. of St. Augustine, June 25, 2001, ord. Aug. 21, 2001.

Garcia, Richard J.: b. Apr. 24, 1947, San Francisco; educ. St. Patrick's Seminary (Menlo Park, CA); ord priest (San Francisco*) May 13, 1973; app. Titular bp. of Bapara and aux. bp. of Sacramento, Nov. 25, 1997, ord. Jan. 28, 1998.

Garland, James H.: b. Dec. 13, 1931, Wilmington, OH; educ. Wilmington College (OH), Ohio State Univ. (Columbus, OH); Mt. St. Mary's Seminary (Cincinnati, OH), Catholic Univ. (Washington, DC); ord. priest (Cincinnati*) Aug. 15, 1959; ord. titular bp. of Garriana and aux. bp. of Cincinnati, July 25, 1984; app. bp. of Marquette, Oct. 6, 1992; installed Nov. 11, 1992.

Garmendia, Francisco: b. Nov. 6, 1924, Lozcano, Spain; ord. priest June 29, 1947, in Spain; came to New York in 1964; became naturalized citizen; ord. titular bp. of Limisa and aux. bp. of New York, June 29, 1977. Vicar for Spanish pastoral development in New York archdiocese; res. Oct. 31, 2001.

Garmo, George: b. Dec. 8, 1921, Telkaif, Iraq; educ. St. Peter Chaldean Patriarchal Seminary (Mossul, Iraq), Pontifical Urban Univ. (Rome); ord. priest Dec. 8, 1945; pastor of Chaldean parish in Detroit archdiocese, 1960-64, 1966-80; ord. abp. of Chaldean archdiocese of Mossul Iraq, Sept. 14, 1980.

Gaydos, John R.: b. Aug. 14, 1943, St. Louis, MO; educ Cardinal Glennon College (St. Louis, MO), North American College, Gregorian Univ. (Rome); ord. priest (St. Louis*) Dec. 20, 1968; ord. bp. of Jefferson City, Aug. 27, 1997.

Gelineau, Louis E.: b. May 3, 1928, Burlington, VT; educ. St. Michael's College (Winooski, VT), St. Paul's Univ. Seminary (Ottawa, Ont.), Catholic Univ. (Washington, DC); ord. priest (Burlington) June 5, 1954; ord. bp. of Providence, RI, Jan. 26, 1972; retired June 11, 1997.

Gendron, Odore J.: b. Sept. 13, 1921, Manchester, NH; educ. St. Charles Borromeo Seminary (Sherbrooke, Que., Canada), Univ. of Ottawa, St. Paul Univ. Seminary (Ottawa, Ont., Canada); ord. priest (Manchester) May 31, 1947; ord. bp. of Manchester, Feb. 3, 1975; resigned June 12, 1990.

George, Cardinal Francis E., O.M.I.: (See **Cardinals, Biographies**).

Gerber, Eugene J.: b. Apr. 30, 1931, Kingman, KS; educ. St. Thomas Seminary (Denver, CO), Wichita State Univ.; Catholic Univ. (Washington, DC), Angelicum (Rome); ord. priest (Wichita) May 19, 1959; ord. bp. of Dodge City, Dec. 14, 1976; app. bp. of Wichita, Nov. 17, 1982, installed Feb. 9, 1983; re. Oct. 4, 2001.

Gerety, Peter L.: b. July 19, 1912, Shelton, CT; educ. Sulpician Seminary (Paris, France); ord. priest (Hartford*) June 29, 1939; ord. titular bp. of Crepedula and coadjutor bp. of Portland, ME, with right of succession, June 1, 1966; app. apostolic administrator of Portland, 1967; bp. of Portland, ME, Sept. 15, 1969; app. abp. of Newark, Apr. 2, 1974; installed June 28, 1974; retired June 3, 1986.

Gerry, Joseph J., O.S.B.: b. Sept. 12, 1928, Millinocket, ME; educ. St. Anselm Abbey Seminary (Manchester, NH), Univ. of Toronto (Canada), Fordham Univ. (New York); ord. priest June 12, 1954; abbot of St. Anselm Abbey, Manchester, NH, 1972; ord. titular bp. of Praecausa and aux. of Manchester, Apr. 21, 1986; bp. of Portland, ME, Dec. 27, 1988, installed Feb. 21, 1989.

Gettelfinger, Gerald A.: b. Oct. 20, 1935, Ramsey, IN; educ. St. Meinrad Seminary (St. Meinrad, IN), Butler Univ. (Indianapolis, IN); ord. priest (Indianapolis*) May 7, 1961; ord. bp. of Evansville, Apr. 11, 1989.

Gilbert, Edward J., C.SS.R.: b. Dec. 26, 1936, Brooklyn, NY; educ. Mt. St. Alphonsus Seminary (Esopus, NY), Catholic Univ. (Washington, DC); ord. priest (Redemptorists, Baltimore Province) June 21, 1964; ord. bp. of Roseau, Dominica, Sept. 7, 1994.

Gilmore, Ronald W.: b. Apr. 23, 1942, Wichita, KS; educ. University Seminary (Ottawa), St. Paul University (Ottawa); ord. priest (Wichita), June 7, 1969; app. Bp. of Dodge City, May 11, 1998, ord. July 16, 1998.

Glynn, John J.: b. Aug. 6, 1926, Boston, MA; educ. St. John's Seminary (Brighton, MA); ord. priest (Boston*), Apr. 11, 1951; Navy chaplain, 1960-85; ord. titular bp. of Monteverde and aux. bp. of Military Services archdiocese, Jan. 6, 1992; res. Aug. 13, 2002.

Goedert, Raymond E.: b. Oct. 15, 1927, Oak Park, IL; educ. Quigley Preparatory Seminary (Chicago, IL), St. Mary of the Lake Seminary and Loyola Univ. (Chicago, IL), Gregorian Univ. (Rome); ord. priest (Chicago*), May 1, 1952; ord. titular bp. of Tamazeni and aux. bp. of Chicago, Aug. 29, 1991; res. Aug. 12, 2002.

Gomez, José H.: b. Dec. 26, 1951, Monterrey, Mexico (became U.S. citizen 1995); educ. National University, Mexico, University of Navarre (Spain); ord. priest of the Prelature of Opus Dei, Aug. 15, 1978; Vicar of Opus Dei for State of Texas, 1999-2001; app. titular bp. of Belali and aux. bp of Denver Jan. 23, 2001, ord. Mar. 26, 2001.

Gonzalez, Roberto O., O.F.M., b. June 2, 1950, Elizabeth, NJ; educ. St. Joseph Seminary (Callicoon, NY), Siena College, (Loudonville, NY), Washington Theological Union (Silver Spring, MD), Fordham Univ. (New York, NY); solemnly professed in Franciscan Order, 1976; ord. priest May 8, 1977; ord. titular bp. of Ursona and aux. bp. of Boston, Oct. 3, 1988; app. coadjutor bp. of Corpus Christi, May 16, 1995; bishop of Corpus Christi, Apr. 1, 1997; app. abp. of San Juan de Puerto Rico, Mar. 26, 1999, ord. May 8, 1999.

Gonzalez Valer, S.F., Francisco: b. Arcos de Jalon, Spain, May 22, 1939; educ. Missionary Seminary of the Holy Family, Barcelona (Spain), Catholic University of America (Washington, DC); ord. priest (of the Congregation of the Sons of the Holy Family) May 1, 1964; Episcopal Vicar for Hispanic Catholics, Archdiocese of Washington, 1997; app. titular bp. of Lamfua and aux. bp. of Washington, Dec. 28, 2001.

Gorman, John R.: b. Dec. 11, 1925, Chicago, IL; educ, St. Mary of the Lake Seminary (Mundelein, IL), Loyola Univ. (Chicago, IL); ord. priest (Chicago*) May 1, 1956; ord. titular bp. of Catula and aux. bp. of Chicago, Apr. 11, 1988.

Gossman, F. Joseph: b. Apr. 1, 1930, Baltimore, MD; educ. St. Charles College (Catonsville, MD), St. Mary's Seminary (Baltimore, MD), North American College (Rome), Catholic Univ. (Washington, DC); ord. priest (Baltimore*) Dec. 17, 1955; ord. titular bp. of Agunto and aux. bp. of Baltimore, Sept. 11, 1968; app. bp. of Raleigh Apr. 8, 1975.

Gracida, Rene H.: b. June 9, 1923, New Orleans, LA; educ. Rice Univ. and Univ. of Houston (Houston, TX), Univ. of Fribourg (Switzerland); ord. priest (Miami*) May 23, 1959; ord. titular bp. of Masuccaba and aux. bp. of Miami, Jan. 25, 1972; app. first bp. of Pensacola-Tallahassee, Oct. 1, 1975, installed Nov. 6, 1975; app. bp. of Corpus Christi, May 24, 1983, installed July 11, 1983; retired Apr. 1, 1997.

Grahmann, Charles V.: b. July 15, 1931, Halletsville, TX; educ. The Assumption-St. John's Seminary (San Antonio, TX); ord. priest (San Antonio*) Mar. 17, 1956; ord. titular bp. of Equilium and aux. bp. of San Antonio, Aug. 20, 1981; app. first bp. of Victoria, TX, Apr. 13, 1982; app. coadjutor bp. of Dallas, Dec. 9, 1989; bp. of Dallas, July 14, 1990.

Gregory, Wilton D.: b. Dec. 7, 1947, Chicago, IL; educ. Quigley Preparatory Seminary South, Niles College of Loyola Univ. (Chicago, IL), St. Mary of the Lake Seminary (Mundelein, IL), Pontifical Liturgical Institute, Sant' Anselmo (Rome); ord. priest (Chicago*) May 9, 1973; ord. titular bp. of Oliva and aux. bp. of Chicago, Dec. 13, 1983; app. bp. of Belleville, Dec. 29, 1993; installed Feb. 10, 1994 vice president, NCCB/USCC, 1998-2001; President, USCCB, 2001-.

Gries, Roger W., O.S.B.: b. Mar. 26, 1937, Cleveland; educ. St. John Univ., Collegeville, MN, St. Joseph's Seminary, Cleveland, Loyola Univ., Chicago; ord. priest (Order of St. Benedict) May 16, 1963; Abbot, St. Andrew Abbey, Cleveland, 1981-2001; app. aux. bp. of Cleveland, April 3, 2001, ord. June 7, 2001.

Griffin, James A.: b. June 13, 1934, Fairview Park, OH; educ. St. Charles College (Baltimore, MD), Borromeo College (Wicklife, OH); St Mary Seminary (Cleveland, OH); Lateran Univ. (Rome); Cleveland State Univ.; ord. priest (Cleveland) May 28, 1960; ord. titular bp. of Holar and aux. bp. of Cleveland, Aug. 1, 1979; app. bp. of Columbus, Feb. 8, 1983.

Grosz, Edward M.: b. Feb. 16, 1945, Buffalo, NY; educ. St. John Vianney Seminary (East Aurora, NY), Notre Dame Univ. (Notre Dame, IN); ord. priest (Buffalo) May 29, 1971; ord. titular bp. of Morosbisdus and aux. bp. of Buffalo, Feb. 2, 1990.

Guillory, Curtis J., S.V.D.: b. Sept. 1, 1943, Mallet, LA; educ. Divine Word College (Epworth, IA), Chicago Theological Union (Chicago), Creighton Univ. (Omaha, NE); ord. priest Dec. 16, 1972; ord. titular bp. of Stagno and aux. bp. of Galveston-Houston, Feb. 19, 1988; bp. of Beaumont, June 2, 2000, ins. July 28, 2000.

Gumbleton, Thomas J.: b. Jan. 26, 1930, Detroit, MI; educ. St. John Provincial Seminary (Detroit, MI), Pontifical Lateran Univ. (Rome); ord. priest (Detroit*) June 2, 1956; ord. titular bp. of Ululi and aux. bp. of Detroit, May 1, 1968.

H

Ham, J. Richard, M.M.: b. July 11, 1921, Chicago, IL; educ. Maryknoll Seminary (NY); ord. priest June 12, 1948; missionary to Guatemala, 1958; ord. titular bp. of Puzia di Numidia and aux. bp. of Guatemala, Jan. 6, 1968; resigned see 1979; aux. bp. of St. Paul and Minneapolis, Oct., 1980; retired Oct. 29, 1990.

Hanifen, Richard C.: b. June 15, 1931, Denver, CO; educ. Regis College and St. Thomas Seminary (Denver, CO), Catholic Univ. (Washington, DC), Lateran Univ. (Rome); ord. priest (Denver*) June 6, 1959; ord. titular bp. of Abercorn and aux. bp. of Denver, Sept. 20, 1974; app. first bp. of Colorado Springs, Nov. 10, 1983; installed Jan. 30, 1984.

Hannan, Philip M.: b. May 20, 1913, Washington, DC; educ. St. Charles College (Catonsville, MD), Catholic Univ. (Washington, DC), North American College (Rome); ord. priest (Washington*) Dec. 8, 1939; ord. titular bp. of Hieropolis and aux. bp. of Washington, DC, Aug. 28, 1956; app. abp. of New Orleans, installed Oct. 13, 1965; retired Dec. 6, 1988.

Hanus, Jerome George, O.S.B.: b. May 25, 1940, Brainard, NE; educ. Conception Seminary (Conception, MO), St. Anselm Univ. (Rome), Princeton Theological Seminary (Princeton, NJ); ord. priest (Conception Abbey, MO) July 30, 1966; abbot of Conception Abbey, 1977-87; president of Swiss American Benedictine Congregation, 1984-87; ord. bp. of St. Cloud, Aug. 24, 1987; app. coadjutor abp. of Dubuque, Aug. 23, 1994; abp. of Dubuque, Oct. 16, 1995.

Harrington, Bernard J.: b. Sept. 6, 1933, Detroit, MI; educ. Sacred Heart Seminary (Detroit), St. John's Provincial Seminary (Plymouth, MI), Catholic Univ. of America (Washington, DC), University of Detroit; ord. priest (Detroit*) June 6, 1959; ord. titular bp. of Uzali and aux. bp. of Detroit, Jan. 6, 1994; app. Bp. of Winona, Nov. 5, 1998, ordained Jan. 6, 1999.

Harrison, Frank J.: b. Aug. 12, 1912; Syracuse, NY; educ. Notre Dame Univ. (Notre Dame, IN), St. Bernard's Seminary (Rochester, NY), ord. priest (Syracuse) June 4, 1937; ord. titular bp. of Aquae in Numidia and aux. of Syracuse, Apr. 22, 1971; app. bp. of Syracuse, Nov. 9, 1976, installed Feb. 6, 1977; retired June 16, 1987.

Hart, Daniel A.: b. Aug. 24, 1927, Lawrence, MA; educ. St. John's Seminary (Brighton, MA); ord. priest (Boston*) Feb. 2, 1953; ord. titular bp. of Tepelta and aux. bp. of Boston, Oct. 18, 1976; bp. of Norwich Sept. 12, 1995.

Hart, Joseph: b. Sept. 26, 1931, Kansas City, MO; educ. St. John Seminary (Kansas City, MO), St. Meinrad Seminary (Indianapolis, IN); ord. priest (Kansas City-St. Joseph) May 1, 1956; ord. titular bp. of Thimida Regia and aux. bp. of Cheyenne, WY, Aug. 31, 1976; app. bp. of Cheyenne, installed June 12, 1978; ret., Sept. 26, 2001.

Harvey, James M.: b. Oct. 20, 1949, Milwaukee, WI; educ. De Sales Preparatory Seminary and St. Francis De Sales College, Milwaukee, North American College and Gregorian Univ. (Rome); ord. priest (Milwaukee*) June 29, 1975; entered Vatican diplomatic service, 1980; Apostolic Nunciature, Dominican Republic, 1980-82; transferred to the Vatican Secretariat of State, 1982; named assessor of the Secretariat, 1997; named titular bp. of Memphis and pre-fect of the papal household, Feb. 7, 1998; ordained bp. Mar. 19, 1998.

Head, Edward D.: b. Aug. 5, 1919, White Plains, NY; educ. Cathedral College, St. Joseph's Seminary, Columbia Univ. (New York City); ord. priest (New York*) Jan. 27, 1945; director of New York Catholic Charities; ord. titular bp. of Ardsratha and aux. bp. of New York, Mar. 19, 1970; app. bp. of Buffalo, Jan. 23, 1973, installed Mar. 19, 1973; retired Apr. 18, 1995.

Heim, Capistran F., O.F.M.: b. Jan. 21, 1934, Catskill, NY; educ. Franciscan Houses of Study; ord. priest Dec. 18, 1965; missionary in Brazil; ord. first bp. of prelature of Itaituba, Brazil, Sept. 17, 1988; installed Oct. 2, 1988.

Hermes, Herbert, O.S.B.: b. May 25, 1933, Scott City, KS; ord. priest (St. Benedict Abbey, Atchison, KS), May 26, 1960; missionary in Brazil; ord. bp. of territorial prelature of Cristalandia, Brazil, Sept. 2, 1990.

Hickey, James A.: (See **Cardinals, Biographies**.)

Higi, William L.: b. Aug. 29, 1933, Anderson, IN; educ. Our Lady of the Lakes Preparatory Seminary (Wawasee, IN), Mt. St. Mary of the West Seminary and Xavier Univ. (Cincinnati, OH); ord. priest (Lafayette, IN) May 30, 1959; ord. bp. of Lafayette, IN, June 6, 1984.

Hoffman, James R.: b. June 12, 1932, Fremont, OH; educ. Our Lady of the Lake Minor Seminary (Wawasee, IN), St. Meinrad College (St. Meinrad, IN), Mt. St. Mary Seminary (Norwood, OH), Catholic Univ. (Washington, DC); ord. priest (Toledo) July 28, 1957; ord. titular bp. of Italica and aux. bp. of Toledo, June 23, 1978; bp. of Toledo, Dec. 16, 1980.

Hogan, James J.: b. Oct. 17, 1911, Philadelphia, PA; educ. St. Charles College (Catonsville, MD), St. Mary's Seminary (Baltimore), Gregorian Univ. (Rome), Catholic Univ. (Washington, DC); ord. priest (Trenton) Dec. 8, 1937; ord. titular bp. of Philomelium and aux. bp. of Trenton, Feb. 25, 1960; app. bp. of Altoona-Johnstown, installed July 6, 1966; retired Nov. 4, 1986.

Houck, William Russell: b. June 26, 1926, Mobile, AL; educ. St. Bernard Junior College (Cullman, AL), St. Mary's Seminary College and St. Mary's Seminary (Baltimore, MD), Catholic Univ. (Washington, DC); ord. priest (Mobile*) May 19, 1951; ord. titular bp. of Alessano and aux. bp. of Jackson, MS, May 27, 1979, by Pope John Paul II; app. bp. of Jackson, Apr. 11, 1984, installed June 5, 1984.

Howze, Joseph Lawson: b. Aug. 30, 1923, Daphne, AL; convert to Catholicism, 1948; educ. St. Bonaventure Univ. (St. Bonaventure, NY); ord. priest (Raleigh) May 7, 1959; ord. titular bp. of Massita and aux. bp. of Natchez-Jackson, Jan. 28, 1973; app. first bp. of Biloxi, MS, Mar. 8, 1977; installed June 6, 1977; res. May 15, 2001.

Hubbard, Howard J.: b. Oct. 31, 1938, Troy, NY; educ. St. Joseph's Seminary (Dunwoodie, NY); North American College and Gregorian Univ. (Rome), Catholic Univ. (Washington, DC); ord. priest (Albany) Dec. 18, 1963; ord. bp. of Albany, Mar. 27, 1977.

Hughes, Alfred C.: b. Dec. 2, 1932, Boston, MA; educ. St. John Seminary (Brighton, MA), Gregorian Univ. (Rome); ord. priest (Boston*) Dec. 15, 1957, in Rome; ord. titular bp. of Maximiana in Byzacena and aux. bp. of Boston, Sept. 14, 1981; app. bp. of Baton

Rouge, Sept. 7, 1993; co-adj. abp. of New Orleans, Feb. 16, 2001; abp. of New Orleans, Jan. 3, 2002.

Hughes, Edward T.: b. Nov. 13, 1920, Lansdowne, PA; educ. St. Charles Seminary, Univ. of Pennsylvania (Philadelphia); ord. priest (Philadelphia*) May 31, 1947; ord. titular bp. of Segia and aux. bp. of Philadelphia, July 21, 1976; app. bp. of Metuchen, Dec. 11, 1986, installed Feb. 5, 1987; retired July 8, 1997.

Hughes, William A.: b. Sept. 23, 1921, Youngstown, OH; educ. St. Charles College (Catonsville, MD), St. Mary's Seminary (Cleveland, OH), Notre Dame Univ. (Notre Dame, IN); ord. priest (Youngstown) Apr. 6, 1946; ord. titular bp. of Inis Cathaig and aux. bp. of Youngstown, Sept. 12, 1974; app. bp. of Covington, installed May 8, 1979. Retired July 4, 1995.

Hunthausen, Raymond G.: b. Aug. 21, 1921, Anaconda, MT; educ. Carroll College (Helena, MT), St. Edward's Seminary (Kenmore, WA), St. Louis Univ. (St. Louis, MO), Catholic Univ. (Washington, DC), Fordham Univ. (New York City), Notre Dame Univ. (Notre Dame, IN); ord. priest (Helena) June 1, 1946; ord. bp. of Helena, Aug. 30, 1962; app. abp. of Seattle, Feb. 25, 1975; retired Aug. 21, 1991.

Hurley, Francis T.: b. Jan. 12, 1927, San Francisco, CA; educ. St. Patrick's Seminary (Menlo Park, CA), Catholic Univ. (Washington, DC); ord. priest (San Francisco*) June 16, 1951; assigned to NCWC in Washington, DC, 1957; assistant (1958) and later (1968) associate secretary of NCCB and USCC; ord. titular bp. of Daimlaig and aux. bp. of Juneau, AK, Mar. 19, 1970; app. bp. of Juneau, July 20, 1971, installed Sept. 8, 1971; app. abp. of Anchorage, May 4, 1976, installed July 8, 1976; res. March 3, 2001.

I-J

Ibrahim, Ibrahim N.: b. Oct. 1, 1937, Telkaif, Mosul, Iraq.; educ. Patriarchal Seminary (Mosul, Iraq), St. Sulpice Seminary (Paris, France); ord. priest Dec. 30, 1962, in Baghdad, Iraq; ord. titular bp. of Anbar and apostolic exarch for Chaldean Catholics in the United States, Mar. 8, 1982, in Baghdad; installed in Detroit, Apr. 18, 1982; app. first eparch, Aug. 3, 1985, when exarchate was raised to eparchy of St. Thomas Apostle of Detroit.

Imesch, Joseph L.: b. June 21, 1931, Detroit, MI; educ. Sacred Heart Seminary (Detroit, MI), North American College, Gregorian Univ. (Rome); ord. priest (Detroit*) Dec. 16, 1956; ord. titular bp. of Pomaria and aux. bp. of Detroit, Apr. 3, 1973; app. bp. of Joliet, June 30, 1979.

Iriondo, Robert J.: b. Dec. 19, 1938, Legazti, Spain; educ. Collegio San Vittore and Pontifical Gregorian University, Rome; ord. priest (of the Canons Regular of the Lateran) Dec. 22, 1962; incardinated into Archdiocese of New York, 1996; Vicar for Hispanics, 1997; ord. titular bp. of Alton and aux. of New York, Dec. 12, 2001.

Irwin, Francis X.: b. Jan 9, 1934, Medford, MA; educ. Boston College High School, Boston College, St. John's Seminary (Brighton, MA), Boston College School of Social Service; ord. priest (Boston*) Feb. 2, 1960; ord. titular bp. of Ubaza and aux. bp. of Boston, Sept. 17, 1996.

Jacobs, Sam Galip: b. Mar. 4, 1938, Greenwood, MS; educ. Immaculata Seminary (Lafayette, LA), Catholic Univ. (Washington, DC); ord. priest (Lafayette) June 6, 1964; became priest of Lake Charles diocese, 1980, when that see was established; ord. bp. of Alexandria, LA, Aug. 24, 1989.

Jakubowski, Thad J.: b. Apr. 5, 1924, Chicago, IL; educ. Mundelein Seminary, St. Mary of the Lake Univ., Loyola Univ. (Chicago); ord priest (Chicago*) May 3, 1950; ord. titular bp. of Plestia and aux. bp. of Chicago, Apr. 11, 1988.

Jammo, Sarhad: b. March 14, 1941, Baghdad, Iraq; educ. Patrarchal Seminary of Mosul, Urban College of the Propaganda Fide Pontifical Oriental Institute (Rome); ord. priest (Baghdad*) Dec. 19, 1964; Rector, Chaldean Seminary, Baghdad; after service in Iraq, transferred in 1977 to the Eparchy of Saint Thomas the Apostle of Detroit for Chaldeans; pastor, Mother of God parish, Detroit, 1980; Vicar General of the Chaldean Exarchate established in 1982; app. first eparch of the eparchy of St. Peter the Apostle of San Diego (Chaldean), May 21, 2002.

Jarrell, C. Michael: b. May 15, 1940, Opelousas, LA; educ. Immaculata Minor Seminary (Lafayette, LA); Catholic Univ. (Washington, DC); ord. priest (Lafayette, LA) June 3, 1967; ord. bp. of Houma-Thibodaux, Mar. 4, 1993.

Jenky, Daniel R.: b. Mar. 3, 1947, Chicago; educ. University of Notre Dame; ord. priest Apr. 6, 1974; Religious Superior of the Holy Cross religious at Notre Dame, 1985-1990; app. Titular Bp. of Amanzia and Aux. of Fort Wayne-South Bend, Oct. 21, 1997, ord. Dec. 16, 1997, bp. of Peoria, Feb. 12, 2002, inst. Apr. 10, 2002.

K

Kaffer, Roger L.: b. Aug. 14, 1927, Joliet, IL; educ. Quigley Preparatory Seminary (Chicago, IL), St. Mary of the Lake Seminary (Mundelein, IL), Gregorian Univ. (Rome); ord. priest (Joliet) May 1, 1954; ord. titular bp. of Dusa and aux. bp. of Joliet, June 26, 1985.

Kaising, John. J.: b. March 3, 1936, Cincinnati; educ. Seminary of Cincinnati, Xavier University; ord. priest (Cincinnati*) Dec. 22, 1962; military chaplain in the Army 1970-1998, exec. assist. to the Chief of Chaplains of the Army, 1994-1998; app. titular bp. of Orreacelia and aux. bp. of the Archdiocese for the Military Services, Feb. 21, 2000, ord. April 11, 2000.

Kalisz, Raymond P., S.V.D.: b. Sept. 25, 1927, Melvindale, MI; educ. St. Mary's Seminary (Techny, IL); ord. priest Aug. 15, 1954; ord. bp. of Wewak, Papua New Guinea, Aug. 15, 1980.

Keeler, Cardinal William Henry: (See **Cardinals, Biographies.**)

Keleher, James P.: b. July 31, 1931, Chicago, IL; educ. Quigley Preparatory Seminary (Chicago, IL), St. Mary of the Lake Seminary (Mundelein, IL); ord. priest (Chicago*) Apr. 12, 1958; ord. bp. of Belleville, Dec. 11, 1984; app. abp. of Kansas City, KS, June 28, 1993.

Kelly, Thomas C., O.P.: b. July 14, 1931, Rochester, NY; educ. Providence College (Providence, RI), Immaculate Conception College (Washington, DC), Angelicum (Rome); professed in Dominicans, Aug. 26, 1952; secretary, apostolic delegation, Washington, DC, 1965-71; associate general secretary, 1971-77, and general secretary, 1977-81, NCCB/USCC; ord. titular bp. of Tusurus and aux. bp. of Washington, DC, Aug. 15, 1977; app. abp. of Louisville, Dec. 28, 1981, installed Feb. 18, 1982.

Kettler, Donald J.: b. Nov. 26, 1944, Minneapolis: educ. St. John's Seminary Collegeville, Minnesota; ord. priest (Sioux Falls) May 29, 1970; app. bp. of Fairbanks, Alaska, June 7, 2002.

Kicanas, Gerald F.: b. Aug. 18, 1941, Chicago, IL; educ. Quigley Preparatory Seminary, St. Mary of the Lake Seminary and Loyola University in Chicago; ord. priest (Chicago*) Apr. 27, 1967; ord. titular bp. of Bela and aux. of Chicago, Mar. 20, 1995; app. coadj. bp. of Tucson, Oct. 30, 2001; inst. as coadj. bp. of Tuscon, Jan. 17, 2002.

Kinney, John F.: b. June 11, 1937, Oelwein, IA; educ. Nazareth Hall and St. Paul Seminaries (St. Paul, MN); Pontifical Lateran University (Rome); ord. priest (St. Paul-Minneapolis*) Feb. 2, 1963; ord. titular bp. of Caorle and aux. bp. of St. Paul and Minneapolis, Jan. 25, 1977; app. bp. of Bismarck June 30, 1982; app. bp. of St. Cloud, May 9, 1995.

Kmiec, Edward U.: b. June 4, 1936, Trenton, NJ; educ. St. Charles College (Catonsville, MD), St. Mary's Seminary (Baltimore, MD), Gregorian Univ. (Rome); ord. priest (Trenton) Dec. 20, 1961; ord. titular bp. of Simidicca and aux. bp. of Trenton, Nov. 3, 1982; app. bp. of Nashville, Oct. 13, 1992; installed Dec. 3, 1992.

Kucera, Daniel W., O.S.B.: b. May 7, 1923, Chicago, IL; educ. St. Procopius College (Lisle, IL), Catholic Univ. (Washington, DC); professed in Order of St. Benedict, June 16, 1944; ord. priest May 26, 1949; abbot, St. Procopius Abbey, 1964-71; pres. Illinois Benedictine College, 1959-65 and 1971-76; ord. titular bp. of Natchez and aux. bp. of Joliet, July 21, 1977; app. bp. of Salina, Mar. 5, 1980; app. abp. of Dubuque, installed Feb. 23, 1984; retired Oct. 16, 1995.

Kuchmiak, Michael, C.SsR.: b. Feb. 5, 1923, Obertyn, Horodenka, Western Ukraine; left during World War II; educ. St. Josaphat Ukrainian Seminary (Rome, Italy), St. Mary's Seminary (Meadowvale, Ont., Canada); ord. priest May 13, 1956; in the U.S. from 1967; ord. titular bp. of Agathopolis and aux. bp. of Ukrainian metropolitan of Philadelphia, Apr. 27, 1988; exarch of apostolic exarchate for Ukrainian Catholics in Great Britain, June 24, 1989.

Kudrick, John M.: b. Dec. 23, 1947, Lloydell, PA; educ. Third Order Regular of St. Francis, 1967; ord. priest May 3, 1975; granted bi-ritual faculties for service in the Byzantine Rite, 1978; app. bp. of Parma May 3, 2002

Kupfer, William F., M.M.: b. Jan. 28, 1909, Brooklyn, NY; educ. Cathedral College (Brooklyn, NY), Maryknoll Seminary (Maryknoll, NY); ord. priest June 11, 1933; missionary in China; app. prefect apostolic of Taichung, Taiwan, 1951; ord. first bp. of Taichung, July 25, 1962; retired Sept. 3, 1986.

Kurtz, Joseph E.: b. Aug. 18, 1946, Shenandoah, PA.; educ. St. Charles Borromeo Seminary, Philadelphia, Marywood College, Scranton; ord. priest (Allentown) Mar. 18, 1972; app. bishop of Knoxville, Oct. 26, 1999, ord. Dec. 8, 1999.

Kurtz, Robert, C.R.: b. July 25, 1939, Chicago, IL; ord. priest Mar. 11, 1967; ord. bp. of Hamilton, Bermuda, Sept. 15, 1995.

Kuzma, George M.: b. July 24, 1925, Windber, PA; educ. St. Francis Seminary (Loretto, PA), St. Procopius College (Lisle, IL), Sts. Cyril and Methodius Byzantine Catholic Seminary, Duquesne

Univ. (Pittsburgh, PA); ord. priest (Pittsburgh*, Byzantine Rite), May 5, 1955; ord. titular bp. of Telmisso and aux. bp. of Byzantine eparchy of Passaic, 1987; app. bp. of Byzantine diocese of Van Nuys, CA, Oct. 23, 1990, inst. Jan. 15, 1991; res. Dec. 5, 2000.

L

Lagonegro, Dominick J.: b. Mar. 6, 1943, White Plains, NY; educ. Cathedral College, Douglaston, St. Joseph Seminary, Yonkers; ord. priest (New York*) May 31, 1969; ord. titular bp. of Modrus and aux. of New York, Dec. 12, 2001.

Lambert, Francis, S.M.: b. Feb. 7, 1921, Lawrence, MA; educ. Marist Seminary (Framingham, MA); ord. priest, June 29, 1946; served in Marist missions in Oceania; provincial of Marist Oceania province, 1971; ord. bp. of Port Vila, Vanuatu (New Hebrides), Mar. 20, 1977; retired Nov. 30, 1996.

Larkin, W. Thomas: b. Mar. 31, 1923, Mt. Morris, NY; educ. St. Andrew Seminary and St. Bernard Seminary (Rochester, NY); Angelicum Univ. (Rome); ord. priest (St. Augustine) May 15, 1947; ord. bp. of St. Petersburg, May 27, 1979; retired Nov. 29, 1988.

Law, Bernard F.: (See **Cardinals, Biographies.**)

Leibrecht, John J.: b. Aug. 30, 1930, Overland, MO; educ. Catholic Univ. (Washington, DC); ord. priest (St. Louis*) Mar. 17, 1956; superintendent of schools of St. Louis archdiocese, 1962-1981; ord. bp. of Springfield-Cape Girardeau, MO, Dec. 12, 1984.

Lennon, Richard G.: b. Mar. 26, 1947, Arlington, (MA); educ. St. John's Seminary, Brighton; ord. priest (Boston*) May 19, 1973; rector, St. John's Seminary 1999-2001; app. titular bp. of Sufes and aux. bp. of Boston, June 29, 2001, ord. Sept. 12, 2001.

Lessard, Raymond W.: b. Dec. 21, 1930, Grafton, N.D.; educ. St. Paul Seminary (St. Paul, MN), North American College (Rome); ord. priest (Fargo) Dec. 16, 1956; served on staff of the Congregation for Bps. in the Roman Curia, 1964-73; ord. bp. of Savannah, Apr. 27, 1973; retired Feb. 7, 1995.

Levada, William J.: b. June 15, 1936, Long Beach, CA; educ. St. John's College (Camarillo, CA), Gregorian Univ. (Rome); ord. priest (Los Angeles*) Dec. 20, 1961; ord. titular bp. of Capri and aux. bp. of Los Angeles, May 12, 1983; app. abp. of Portland, OR, July 3, 1986; coadj. abp. of San Francisco, Aug. 17, 1995; abp. of San Francisco Dec. 27, 1995.

Lipscomb, Oscar H.: b. Sept. 21, 1931, Mobile, AL; educ. McGill Institute, St. Bernard College (Cullman, AL), North American College and Gregorian Univ. (Rome), Catholic Univ. (Washington, DC); ord. priest (Mobile*) July 15, 1956; ord. first abp. of Mobile, Nov. 16, 1980.

Listecki, Jerome E.: b. March 12, 1949, Chicago; educ. Loyola University and St. Mary of the Lake Seminary, Mundelein, IL, De Paul University College of Law, University of St. Thomas Aquinas and Pontifical Gregorian University, Rome; ord. priest (Chicago*) June 1, 1975, app. titular bp. of Nara and aux bp. of Chicago, Nov. 7, 2000, ordained Jan. 8, 2001.

Lohmuller, Martin N.: b. Aug. 21, 1919, Philadelphia, PA; educ. St. Charles Borromeo Seminary (Philadelphia, PA), Catholic Univ. (Washington, DC); ord. priest (Philadelphia*) June 3, 1944; ord. titular bp. of Ramsbury and aux. bp. of Philadelphia, Apr. 2, 1970; retired Oct. 11, 1994.

Lori, William E.: b. May 6, 1951, Louisville, KY; educ. St. Pius X College (Covington, KY), Mount St. Mary's Seminary (Emmitsburg, MD), Catholic Univ. (Washington, DC); ord. priest (Washington*) May 14, 1977; ord. titular bp. of Bulla and aux. bp. of Washington, DC, Apr. 20, 1995; Bp. of Bridgeport, Jan. 23, 2001; ins. Mar. 19, 2001.

Losten, Basil: b. May 11, 1930, Chesapeake City, MD; educ. St. Basil's College (Stamford, CT), Catholic University (Washington, DC); ord. priest (Philadelphia*, Ukrainian Byzantine) June 10, 1957; ord. titular bp. of Arcadiopolis in Asia and aux. bp. of Ukrainian archeparchy of Philadelphia, May 25, 1971; app. apostolic administrator of archeparchy, 1976; app. bp. of Ukrainian eparchy of Stamford, Sept. 20, 1977.

Lotocky, Innocent Hilarius, O.S.B.M.: b. Nov. 3, 1915, Petlykiwci, Ukraine; educ. seminaries in Ukraine, Czechoslovakia and Austria; ord. priest Nov. 24, 1940; ord. bp. of St. Nicholas of Chicago for the Ukrainians, Mar. 1, 1981; retired July 15, 1993.

Loverde, Paul S.: b. Sept. 3, 1940, Framingham, MA; educ. St. Thomas Seminary (Bloomfield, CT), St. Bernard Seminary (Rochester, NY), Gregorian Univ. (Rome), Catholic Univ. (Washington, DC); ord. priest (Norwich), Dec. 18, 1965; ord. titular bp. of Ottabia and aux. bp. of Hartford, Apr. 12, 1988; app. bp. of Ogdensburg, Nov. 11, 1993; installed Jan. 17, 1994; app. bp. of Arlington, Jan. 25, 1999, ins. Mar. 25, 1999.

Lucas, George J.: b. June 12, 1949, St. Louis, MO; educ. Major Seminary of St. Louis, Univ. of St. Louis; ord. priest (St. Louis*) May 24, 1975; rector, Kenrick-Glennon Seminary, 1995-1999; app. bishop of Springfield in Illinois, Oct. 19, 1999, ord. Dec. 14, 1999.

Lynch, George E.: b. Mar. 4, 1917, New York, NY; educ. Fordham Univ. (NY), Mt. St. Mary's Seminary (Emmitsburg, MD), Catholic Univ. (Washington, DC); ord. priest (Raleigh) May 29, 1943; ord. titular bp. of Satafi and aux. of Raleigh Jan. 6, 1970; retired Apr. 16, 1985.

Lynch, Robert N.: b. May 27, 1941, Charleston, WV; educ. Pontifical College Josephinum (Columbus, OH); John XXIII National Seminary (Weston, MA); ord. priest (Miami*) May 13, 1978; associate general secretary (1984-89) and general secretary (1989-95) of the NCCB/USCC; app. bp. of St. Petersburg, Dec. 5, 1995; ord. and installed Jan. 26, 1996; app. apostolic administrator of Palm Beach (while continuing as bp. of St. Petersburg), June 2, 1998.

Lyne, Timothy J.: b. Mar. 21, 1919, Chicago, IL; educ. Quigley Preparatory Seminary, St. Mary of the Lake Seminary (Mundelein, IL); ord. priest (Chicago*) May 1, 1943; ord. titular bp. of Vamalla and aux. bp. of Chicago, Dec. 13, 1983; retired Jan. 24, 1995.

M

Macaluso, Christie Albert: b. June 12, 1945, Hartford, CT; educ. St. Thomas Seminary (Bloomfield, CT), St. Mary's Seminary (Baltimore, Md), Trinity College (Hartford, CT), New York University; ord. priest (Hartford*) May 21, 1971; ord. titular bp. of Grass Valley and aux. bp. of Hartford, June 10, 1997.

Madera, Joseph J., M.Sp.S.: b. Nov. 27, 1927, San Francisco, CA; educ. Domus Studiorum of the Missionaries of the Holy Spirit (Coyoacan, D.F. Mexico); ord. priest June 15, 1957; ord. coadjutor bp. of Fresno, Mar. 4, 1980; bp. of Fresno, July 1, 1980; app. titular bp. of Orte and aux. of Military Services archdiocese, June 30, 1991.

Maginnis, Robert P.: b. Dec. 22, 1933, Philadelphia, PA; educ. St. Charles Borromeo Seminary (Overbrook, PA); ord. priest (Philadelphia*) May 13, 1961; ord. titular bp. of Siminina and aux. bp. of Philadelphia, Mar. 11, 1996.

Maguire, Joseph F.: b. Sept. 4, 1919, Boston, MA; educ. Boston College, St. John's Seminary (Boston, MA); ord. priest (Boston*) June 29, 1945; ord. titular bp. of Macteris and aux. bp. of Boston, Feb. 2, 1972; app. coadjutor bp. of Springfield, MA, Apr. 13, 1976; succeeded as bp. of Springfield, MA, Oct. 15, 1977; retired Dec. 27, 1991.

Mahony, Roger M.: (See **Cardinals, Biographies**.)

Maida, Adam J.: (See **Cardinals, Biographies**.)

Malone, Richard J.: b. March 19, 1946, Salem, MA; educ. St. John's Seminary, Brighton, Boston University, ord. priest (Boston*) May 20, 1972; app. titular bp. of Aptuca and aux. bp. of Boston, Jan. 27, 2000, ord. March 1, 2000.

Maloney, Charles G.: b. Sept. 9, 1912, Louisville, KY; educ. St. Joseph's College (Rensselaer, IN), North American College (Rome); ord. priest (Louisville*) Dec. 8, 1937; ord. titular bp. of Capsa and aux. bp. of Louisville, Feb. 2, 1955; resigned Jan. 8, 1988; transferred to Bardstown, 1995, when it was reestablished as a titular see.

Malooly, W.(William) Francis: b. Jan. 18, 1944, Baltimore; educ. St. Charles Minor Seminary, St. Mary's Seminary (Baltimore); ord priest (Baltimore*) May 7, 1970, app. titular bp. of Flumenzer and aux. bp. of Baltimore, Dec. 12, 2000, ord. March 1, 2001.

Manning, Elias (James), O.F.M. Conv.: b. Apr. 14, 1938, Troy, NY; educ. Sao José Seminary (Rio de Janeiro, Brazil); ord. priest Oct. 30, 1965, in New York; ord. bp. of Valenca, Brazil, May 13, 1990.

Manning, Thomas R., O.F.M.: b. Aug. 29, 1922, Baltimore, MD; educ. Duns Scotus College (Southfield, MI), Holy Name College (Washington, DC); ord. priest June 5, 1948; ord. titular bp. of Arsamosata, July 14, 1959 (resigned titular see Dec. 30, 1977); prelate of Coroico, Bolivia, July 14, 1959; became first bp., 1983, when prelature was raised to diocese; retired Oct. 9, 1996.

Mansell, Henry J.: b. Oct. 10, 1937, New York, NY; educ. Cathedral College, St. Joseph's Seminary and College (New York); North American College, Gregorian Univ. (Rome); ord. priest (New York*) Dec. 19, 1962; ord. titular bp. of Marazane and aux. bp. of New York, Jan. 6, 1993, by John Paul II in Vatican City; app. bp. of Buffalo, Apr. 18, 1995; installed June 12, 1995.

Manz, John R.: b. Nov. 14, 1945, Chicago, IL; educ. Niles College Seminary (Niles, IL), Univ. of St. Mary of the Lake-Mundelein Seminary (Chicago); ord. priest (Chicago*) May 12, 1971; ord. titular bp. of Mulia and aux. bp. of Chicago, Mar. 5, 1996.

Marcinkus, Paul C.: b. Jan. 15, 1922, Cicero, IL; ord. priest (Chicago*) May 3, 1947; served in Vatican secretariat from 1952; ord. titular bp. of Orta, Jan. 6, 1969; secretary (1968-71) and president (1971-89) of Institute for Works of Religion (Vatican Bank); titular abp., Sept. 26, 1981; former pro-president of Pontifical Commission for the State of Vatican City; resigned in 1990.

Marconi, Dominic A.: b. Mar. 13, 1927, Newark, NJ; educ. Seton Hall Univ. (S. Orange, NJ), Immaculate Conception Seminary (Darlington, NJ), Catholic Univ. (Washington, DC); ord. priest (Newark*) May 30, 1953; ord. titular bp. of Bure and aux. bp. of Newark, June 25, 1976; res. July 1, 2002.

Martino, Joseph F.: b. May 1, 1946, Philadelphia, PA; educ. St. Charles Borromeo Seminary (Overbrook, PA), Gregorian Univ. (Rome); ord. priest (Philadelphia*) Dec. 18, 1970; ord. titular bp. of Cellae in Mauretania and aux. bp. of Philadelphia, Mar. 11, 1996.

Matthiesen, Leroy Theodore: b. June 11, 1921, Olfen, TX; educ. Josephinum College (Columbus, OH), Catholic Univ. (Washington, DC), Register School of Journalism; ord. priest (Amarillo) Mar. 10, 1946; ord. bp. of Amarillo, May 30, 1980; retired Jan. 21, 1997.

McAuliffe, Michael F.: b. Nov. 22, 1920, Kansas City, MO; educ. St. Louis Preparatory Seminary (St. Louis, MO), Catholic Univ. (Washington, DC): ord. priest (Kansas City-St. Joseph) May 31, 1945; ord. bp. of Jefferson City, Aug. 18, 1969; ret., June, 1997.

McCarrick, Theodore E.: (See **Cardinals, Biographies.**)

McCarthy, Edward A.: b. Apr. 10, 1918, Cincinnati, OH; educ. Mt. St. Mary Seminary (Norwood, OH), Catholic Univ. (Washington, DC), Lateran and Angelicum (Rome); ord. priest (Cincinnati*) May 29, 1943; ord. titular bp. of Tamascani and aux. bp. of Cincinnati, June 15, 1965; first bp. of Phoenix, AZ, Dec. 2, 1969; app. coadjutor abp. of Miami, FL, July 7, 1976; succeeded as abp. of Miami, July 26, 1977; retired Nov. 3, 1994.

McCarthy, James F.: b. July 9, 1942, Mount Kisco, NY; educ. Cathedral College and St. Joseph's Seminary, New York; ord. priest (New York*) June 1, 1968; app. titular bp. of Veronna and aux. bp. of New York, May 11, 1999, ins. June 29, 1999; res. June 12, 2002.

McCarthy, John E.: b. June 21, 1930, Houston, TX; educ. Univ. of St. Thomas (Houston, TX); ord. priest (Galveston-Houston) May 26, 1956; assistant director Social Action Dept. USCC, 1967-69; executive director Texas Catholic Conference; ord. titular bp. of Pedena and aux. bp. of Galveston-Houston, Mar. 14, 1979; app. bp. of Austin, Dec. 19, 1985, installed Feb. 25, 1986; res. Jan. 2, 2001.

McCormack, John B.: b Aug. 12, 1935, Winthrop, MA; educ. St. John Seminary College and St. John Seminary Theologate (Boston, MA); ord. priest (Boston*) Feb. 2, 1960; ord. titular bp. of Cerbali and aux. bp. of Boston, Dec. 27, 1995; app. bp. of Manchester, NH, July 21, 1998, installed Sept. 22, 1998.

McCormack, William J.: b. Jan. 24, 1924, New York, NY; educ. Christ the King Seminary, St. Bonaventure Univ. (St. Bonaventure, NY); ord. priest (New York*) Feb. 21, 1959; national director of Society for the Propagation of the Faith, 1980; ord. titular bp. of Nicives and aux. bp. of New York, Jan. 6, 1987; res. Oct. 31, 2001..

McDonald, Andrew J.: b. Oct. 24, 1923, Savannah, GA; educ. St. Mary's Seminary (Baltimore, MD), Catholic Univ. (Washington, DC), Lateran Univ. (Rome); ord. priest (Savannah) May 8, 1948; ord. bp. of Little Rock, Sept. 5, 1972; res. Jan. 4, 2000.

McDonnell, Charles J.: b. July 7, 1928, Brooklyn, NY; educ. Seton Hall Univ. (South Orange, NJ), Immaculate Conception Seminary (Darlington, NJ), Long Island Univ. (Brooklyn, NY); ord. priest (Newark*) May 29, 1954; U.S. Army Chaplain, 1965-89; retired from active duty with rank of Brigadier General; ord. titular bp. of Pocofelto and aux. bp. of Newark, May 12, 1994.

McDonnell, Timothy A.: b. Dec. 23, 1937, New York City; educ. St. Joseph Seminary, Yonkers, Iona College, New Rochelle; ord. priest (New York*) June 1, 1963; ord. titular bp. of Semina and aux. bp. of New York, Dec. 12, 2001.

McDonough, Thomas J.: b. Dec. 5, 1911, Philadelphia, PA; educ. St. Charles Seminary (Overbrook, PA), Catholic Univ. (Washington, DC); ord. priest (Philadelphia*) May 26, 1938; ord. titular bp. of Thenae and aux. bp. of St. Aug.ine, Apr. 30, 1947; app. aux. bp. of Savannah, Jan. 2, 1957; named bp. of Savannah, installed Apr. 27, 1960; app. abp. of Louisville, installed May 2, 1967; resigned Sept. 29, 1981. Died Aug. 4, 1998.

McDowell, John B.: b. July 17, 1921, New Castle, PA; educ. St. Vincent College, St. Vincent Theological Seminary (Latrobe, PA), Catholic Univ. (Washington, DC); ord. priest (Pittsburgh) Nov. 4, 1945; superintendent of schools, Pittsburgh diocese, 1955-70; ord. titular bp. of Tamazuca, and aux. bp. of Pittsburgh, Sept. 8, 1966; retired Sept. 9, 1996.

McFarland, Norman F.: b. Feb. 21, 1922, Martinez, CA; educ. St. Patrick's Seminary (Menlo Park, CA), Catholic Univ. (Washington, DC); ord. priest (San Francisco*) June 15, 1946; ord. titular bp. of Bida and aux. bp. of San Francisco, Sept. 8, 1970; apostolic adminstrator of Reno, 1974; app. bp. of Reno, Feb. 10, 1976, installed Mar. 31, 1976; title of see changed to Reno-Las Vegas; app. bp. of Orange, CA, Dec. 29, 1986; installed Mar. 31, 1976; resigned June 30, 1998.

McGarry, Urban, T.O.R.: b. Nov. 11, 1911, Warren, PA; ord. priest Oct. 3, 1942, in India; prefect apostolic of Bhagalpur, Aug. 7, 1956; ord. first bp. of Bhagalpur, India, May 10, 1965; resigned Nov. 30, 1987.

McGrath, Patrick J.: b. July 11, 1945, Dublin, Ire.; educ. St. John's College Seminary (Waterford, Ire.), Lateran Univ. (Rome, Italy); ord. priest in Ireland June 7, 1970; came to U.S. same year and became San Francisco archdiocesan priest; ord. titular bp. of Allegheny and aux. bp. of San Francisco, Jan. 25, 1989; app. coadj. bp. of San Jose, June 30, 1998; bp. of San Jose, Nov. 29, 1999.

McKinney, Joseph C.: b. Sept. 10, 1928, Grand Rapids, MI: educ. St. Joseph's Seminary (Grand Rapids, MI), Seminaire de Philosophie (Montreal, Canada), Urban Univ. (Rome, Italy); ord. priest (Grand Rapids) Dec. 20, 1953; ord. titular bp. of Lentini and aux. bp. of Grand Rapids, Sept. 26, 1968; res. Oct. 2, 2001.

McLaughlin, Bernard J.: b. Nov. 19, 1912, Buffalo, NY; educ. Urban Univ. (Rome, Italy); ord. priest (Buffalo) Dec. 21, 1935, at Rome; ord. titular bp. of Mottola and aux. bp. of Buffalo, Jan. 6, 1969; resigned Jan. 5, 1988.

McManus, Robert J.: b. July 5, 1951, Warwick, RI; educ. Our Lady of Providence Seminary, Catholic Univ. (Washington, DC), Seminary of Toronto,

Canada, Pontifical Gregorian Univ. (Rome); ord. priest (Providence) May 27, 1978; diocesan Vicar for Education and Rector of Our Lady of Providence; app. titular bp. of Allegheny and aux. of Providence, Dec. 1, 1998, ord. Feb. 22, 1999.

McNabb, John C., O.S.A.: b. Dec. 11, 1925, Beloit, WI; educ. Villanova Univ. (Villanova, PA), Augustinian College and Catholic Univ. (Washington, DC), De Paul Univ. (Chicago, IL); ord. priest May 24, 1952; ord. titular bp. of Saia Maggiore, June 17, 1967 (resigned titular see, Dec. 27, 1977); prelate of Chulucanas, Peru, 1967; first bp. of Chulucanas, Dec. 12, 1988.

McNamara, Lawrence J.: b. Aug. 5, 1928, Chicago, IL; educ. St. Paul Seminary (St. Paul, MN), Catholic Univ. (Washington, DC); ord. priest (Kansas City-St. Joseph) May 30, 1953; executive director of Campaign for Human Development 1973-77; ord. bp. of Grand Island, NE, Mar. 28, 1978.

McNaughton, William J., M.M.: b. Dec. 7, 1926, Lawrence, MA; educ. Maryknoll Seminary (Maryknoll, NY); ord. priest June 13, 1953; ord. titular bp. of Thuburbo Minus and vicar apostolic of Inchon, Korea, Aug. 24, 1961; first bp. of Inchon, Mar. 10, 1962, when vicariate was raised to diocese.

McRaith, John Jeremiah: b. Dec. 6, 1934, Hutchinson, MN; educ. St. John Preparatory School (Collegeville, MN), Loras College, St. Bernard Seminary (Dubuque, IA); ord. priest (New Ulm) Feb. 21, 1960; exec. dir. of Catholic Rural Life Conference, 1971-78; ord. bp. of Owensboro, KY, Dec. 15, 1982.

Melczek, Dale J.: b. Nov. 9, 1938, Detroit, MI; educ. St. Mary's College (Orchard Lake, MI), St. John's Provincial Seminary (Plymouth, MI), Univ. of Detroit; ord. priest (Detroit*) June 6, 1964; ord. titular bp. of Trau and aux. bp. of Detroit, Jan. 27, 1983; apostolic administrator of Gary, Aug. 19, 1992; coadjutor bp. of Gary, Oct. 28, 1995; bp. of Gary, June 1, 1996.

Mengeling, Carl F.: b. Oct. 22, 1930, Hammond, IN; educ. St. Meinrad College and Seminary (St. Meinrad, IN), Alphonsianum Univ. (Rome); ord. priest (Gary) May 25, 1957; ord. bp. of Lansing Jan. 25, 1996.

Mestice, Anthony F.: b. Dec. 6, 1923, New York, NY; educ. St. Joseph Seminary (Yonkers, NY); ord. priest (New York*) June 4, 1949; ord. titular bp. of Villa Nova and aux. bp. of New York, Apr. 27, 1973; ret. Oct. 31, 2001.

Michaels, James E., S.S.C.: b. May 30, 1926, Chicago, IL; educ. Columban Seminary (St. Columban, NE), Gregorian Univ. (Rome); ord. priest Dec. 21, 1951; ord. titular bp. of Verbe and aux. bp. of Kwang Ju, Korea, Apr. 14, 1966; app. aux. bp. of Wheeling, Apr. 3, 1973 (title of see changed to Wheeling-Charleston, 1974); resigned Sept. 22, 1987.

Milone, Anthony M.: b. Sept. 24, 1932, Omaha, NE; educ. North American College (Rome); ord. priest (Omaha*) Dec. 15, 1957, in Rome; ord. titular bp. of Plestia and aux. bp. of Omaha, Jan. 6, 1982; app. bp. of Great Falls-Billings, Dec. 14, 1987, installed Feb. 23, 1988.

Minder, John, O.S.F.S.: b. Nov. 1, 1923, Philadelphia, PA; educ. Catholic Univ. (Washington, DC); ord. priest June 3, 1950; ord. bp. of Keimos (renamed Keimos-Upington, 1985), South Africa, Jan. 10, 1968.

Moeddel, Carl K.: b. Dec. 28, 1937, Cincinnati,

OH; educ. Athenaeum of Ohio, Mt. St. Mary's Seminary (Cincinnati); ord. priest (Cincinnati*) Aug. 15, 1962; ord. titular bp. of Bistue and aux. bp. of Cincinnati, Aug. 24, 1993.

Montrose, Donald W.: b. May 13, 1923, Denver, CO; educ. St. John's Seminary (Camarillo, CA); ord. priest (Los Angeles*) May 7, 1949; ord. titular bp. of Forum Novum and aux. bp. of Los Angeles, May 12, 1983; app. bp. of Stockton, Dec. 17, 1985, installed Feb. 20, 1986; res. Jan. 19, 1999.

Moreno, Manuel D.: b. Nov. 27, 1930, Placentia, CA; educ. Univ. of CA (Los Angeles), Our Lady Queen of Angels (San Fernando, CA), St. John's Seminary (Camarillo, CA); ord. priest (Los Angeles*) Apr. 25, 1961; ord. titular bp. of Tanagra and aux. bp. of Los Angeles, Feb. 19, 1977; bp. of Tucson, Jan. 12, 1982, installed Mar. 11, 1982.

Morlino, Robert C.: b. Dec. 31, 1946, Scranton, PA; educ. Fordham Univ., University of Notre Dame, Weston School of Theology, Cambridge, MA, Gregorian University, Rome; ord. priest for the Society of Jesus, Maryland Province, June 1, 1974, incardinated into the Diocese of Kalamazoo, MI, Oct. 26, 1983, app. bp. of Helena, July 6, 1999, ins. Sept. 21, 1999.

Morneau, Robert F.: b. Sept. 10, 1938, New London, WI; educ. St. Norbert's College (De Pere, WI), Sacred Heart Seminary (Oneida, WI), Catholic Univ. (Washington, DC); ord. priest (Green Bay) May 28, 1966; ord. titular bp. of Massa Lubrense and aux. bp. of Green Bay, Feb. 22, 1979.

Moskal, Robert M.: b. Oct. 24, 1937, Carnegie, PA; educ. St. Basil Minor Seminary (Stamford, CT), St. Josaphat Seminary and Catholic Univ. (Washington, DC); ord. priest (Philadelphia*, Byzantine Ukrainian) Mar. 25, 1963; ord. titular bp. of Agatopoli and aux. bp. of the Ukrainian archeparchy of Philadelphia, Oct. 13, 1981; app. first bp. of St. Josaphat in Parma, Dec. 5, 1983.

Moynihan, James M.: b. July 16, 1932, Rochester, NY; educ. St. Bernard's Seminary (Rochester, NY), North American College and Gregorian Univ. (Rome); ord. priest (Rochester) Dec. 15, 1957, in Rome; ord. bp. of Syracuse May 29, 1995.

Muench Robert W.: b. Dec. 28, 1942, Louisville, KY; educ. St. Joseph Seminary and Notre Dame Seminary (New Orleans, LA), Catholic Univ. (Washington, DC); ord. priest (New Orleans*) June 18, 1968; ord. titular bp. of Mactaris and aux. bp. of New Orleans, June 29, 1990; app. bp. of Covington Jan., 1996; installed Mar. 19, 1996; app. bp. of Baton Rouge, Dec. 15, 2001.

Mulvee, Robert E.: b. Feb. 15, 1930, Boston, MA; educ. St. Thomas Seminary (Bloomfield, CT), University Seminary (Ottawa, Ont., Canada), American College (Louvain, Belgium), Lateran Univ. (Rome); ord. priest (Manchester) June 30, 1957; ord. titular bp. of Summa and aux. bp. of Manchester, NH, Apr. 14, 1977; app. bp. of Wilmington, Del., Feb. 19, 1985; app. coadjutor bp. of Providence, Feb. 9, 1995; bp. of Providence, June 11, 1997.

Mundo, Miguel P.: b. July 25, 1937, New York, NY; educ. Fordham Univ. (Bronx, NY), St. Jerome's College (Kitchener, Ont., Canada), St Francis Seminary (Loretto, PA); ord. priest (Camden) May 19, 1962; missionary in Brazil from 1963; ord. titular bp. of Blanda Julia and aux. bp. of Jatai, Brazil, June 2, 1978.

Murphy, Michael J.: b. July 1, 1915, Cleveland, OH; educ. Niagara Univ. (Niagara Falls, NY); North American College (Rome), Catholic Univ. (Washington, DC); ord. priest (Cleveland) Feb. 28, 1942; ord. titular bp. of Ariendela and aux. bp. of Cleveland, June 11, 1976; app. coadjutor bp. of Erie, Nov. 20, 1978; bp. of Erie, July 16, 1982; retired June 12, 1990.

Murphy, William F.: b. May 14, 1940, Boston MA; educ. Boston Latin School (Boston), Harvard College, St. John's Seminary (Boston), Gregorian Univ. (Rome); ord. priest (Boston*) Dec. 16, 1964; ord. titular bp. of Saia Maggiore and aux. bp. of Boston, Dec. 27, 1995; app. bp. of Rockville Centre, June 25, 2001, ord. Sept. 5, 2001.

Murray, James A.: b. July 5, 1932, Jackson, MI; educ. Sacred Heart Seminary Detroit, St. John Provincial Seminary (Plymouth, MI), Catholic Univ. of America; ord. priest (Lansing) June 7, 1958; app. bp. of Kalamazoo, Nov. 18, 1997, ord. Jan. 27, 1998.

Murry, George V., S.J.: b. Dec. 28, 1948, Camden, NJ; educ. St. Joseph's College (Philadelphia, PA), St. Thomas Seminary (Bloomfield, CT), St. Mary Seminary (Baltimore, MD), Jesuit School of Theology (Berkeley, Calif), George Washington Univ. (Washington, DC); entered Jesuits 1972; ord. priest June 9, 1979; ord. titular bp. of Fuerteventura and aux. bp. of Chicago, Mar. 20, 1995; app. co-adjutor of St. Thomas in the Virgin Islands, May 5, 1998; bp. of St. Thomas in the Virgin Islands, June 30, 1999.

Myers, John Joseph: b. July 26, 1941, Ottawa, IL; educ. Loras College (Dubuque, IA), North American College and Gregorian Univ. (Rome), Catholic Univ. of America (Washington, DC); ord. priest (Peoria) Dec. 17, 1966, in Rome; ord. coadjutor bp. of Peoria, Sept. 3, 1987; bp. of Peoria, Jan. 23, 1990; app. abp. of Newark, July 24, 2001.

N

Naumann, Joseph F.: b. June 4, 1949, St. Louis, MO; educ. Cardinal Glennon Seminary College and Kenrick Seminary (St. Louis, MO); ord. priest (St. Louis*) 1975; app. titular bp. of Caput Cilla and aux. bp. of St. Louis, July 9, 1997.

Nevins, John J.: b. Jan. 19, 1932, New Rochelle, NY; educ. Iona College (New Rochelle, NY), Catholic Univ. (Washington, DC); ord. priest (Miami*) June 6, 1959; ord. titular bp. of Rusticana and aux. bp. of Miami, Mar. 24, 1979; app. first bp. of Venice, FL, July 17, 1984; installed Oct. 25, 1984.

Newman, William C.: b. Aug. 16, 1928, Baltimore, MD; educ. St. Mary Seminary (Baltimore, MD), Catholic Univ. (Washington, DC), Loyola College (Baltimore, MD); ord. priest (Baltimore*) May 29, 1954; ord. titular bp. of Numluli and aux. bp. of Baltimore, July 2, 1984.

Neylon, Martin J., S.J.: b. Feb. 13, 1920, Buffalo, NY; ord. priest June 18, 1950; ord. titular bp. of Libertina and coadjutor vicar apostolic of the Caroline and Marshall Islands, Feb. 2, 1970; vicar apostolic of Caroline and Marshall Is., Sept. 20, 1971; first bp. of Carolines-Marshalls when vicariate apostolic was raised to diocese, 1979; title of see changed to Caroline Islands, Apr. 23, 1993; retired Mar. 25, 1995.

Niederauer, George H.: b. June 14, 1936, Los Angeles, CA; educ. St. John's Seminary (Camarillo, CA), Catholic Univ. (Washington, DC), Loyola Univ. of Los Angeles, Univ. of Southern CA, Loretta Heights College (Denver, CO); ord. priest (Los Angeles*) Apr. 30, 1962; app. bp. of Salt Lake City, Nov. 3, 1994, ord. Jan. 25, 1995.

Niedergeses, James D.: b. Feb. 2, 1917, Lawrenceburg, TN; educ. St. Bernard College (St. Bernard, AL), St. Ambrose College (Davenport, IA), Mt. St. Mary Seminary of the West and Athenaeum (Cincinnati, OH); ord. priest (Nashville) May 20, 1944; ord. bp. of Nashville, May 20, 1975; retired Oct. 13, 1992.

Nienstedt, John C.: b. Mar. 18, 1947, Detroit, MI; educ. Sacred Heart Seminary (Detroit), North American College, Gregorian Univ., Alphonsianum (Rome); ord. priest (Detroit*) July 27, 1974; served in Vatican Secretariat of State, 1980-86; rector of Sacred Heart Seminary (Detroit), 1988-94; pastor of the Shrine of the Little Flower (Royal Oak, MI), 1994; ord. titular bp. of Alton and aux. bp. of Detroit, July 9, 1996; app. bp. of New Ulm, June 12, 2001, inst. Aug. 6, 2001.

Novak, Alfred, C.SS.R.: b. June 2, 1930, Dwight, NE; educ. Immaculate Conception Seminary (Oconomowoc, WI); ord. priest July 2, 1956; ord. titular bp. of Vardimissa and aux. bp. of Sao Paulo, Brazil, May 25, 1979; bp. of Paranagua, Brazil, Mar. 14, 1989.

O

O'Brien, Edwin F.: b. Apr. 8, 1939, Bronx, NY; educ. St. Joseph's Seminary (Yonkers, NY), Angelicum (Rome); ord. priest (New York*) May 29, 1965; ord. titular bp. of Tizica and aux. bp. of New York, Mar. 25, 1996; app. coadjutor abp. for Military Services Archdiocese, Apr. 8, 1997; abp. of Military Services Archdiocese, Aug. 12, 1997.

O'Brien, Thomas Joseph: b. Nov. 29, 1935, Indianapolis, IN; educ. St. Meinrad High School Seminary, St. Meinrad College Seminary (St. Meinrad, IN); ord. priest (Tucson) May 7, 1961; ord. bp. of Phoenix, Jan. 6, 1982.

Ochoa, Armando: b. Apr. 3, 1943, Oxnard, CA; educ. Ventura College (Ventura, CA), St. John's College and St. John's Seminary (Camarillo, CA); ord. priest (Los Angeles*) May 23, 1970; ord. titular bp. of Sitifi and aux. bp. of Los Angeles, Feb. 23, 1987; app. bp. of El Paso, Apr. 1, 1996; installed June 26, 1996.

O'Connell, Anthony J.: b. May 10, 1938, Lisheen, Co. Clare, Ireland; came to U.S. at age 20; educ. Mt. St. Joseph College (Cork), Mungret College (Limerick), Kenrick Seminary (St. Louis); ord. priest (Jefferson City) Mar. 30, 1963; ord. First Bp. of Knoxville, TN, Sept. 8, 1988; app. bp. of Palm Beach, Nov. 12, 1998, ord. Jan. 14, 1999; res. March 8, 2002.

O'Donnell, Edward J.: b. July 4, 1931, St. Louis, MO; educ. St. Louis Preparatory Seminary and Kenrick Seminary (St. Louis, MO); ord. priest (St. Louis*) Apr. 6, 1957; ord. titular bp. of Britania and aux. bp. of St. Louis Feb. 10, 1984; app. bp. of Lafayette, LA, installed Dec. 16, 1994.

Olivier, Leonard J., S.V.D.: b. Oct. 12, 1923, Lake Charles, LA; educ. St. Augustine Major Seminary (Bay St. Louis, MS), Catholic Univ. (Washington, DC), Loyola Univ. (New Orleans, LA); ord. priest June 29, 1951; ord. titular bp. of Leges in Numidia and aux. bp. of Washington, Dec. 20, 1988.

Olmsted, Thomas J.: b. Jan. 21, 1947, Oketo, Kansas; educ. St. Thomas Seminary (Denver), North American College and Pontifical Gregorian University (Rome); ord. priest (Lincoln) July 2, 1973; served in Vatican Secretariat of State, 1979-1988; Dean of Formation, Pontifical College Josephinum, Columbus, OH, 1993, President and Rector, Pontifical College, Josephinum, 1997; app. coadjutor bp. of Wichita, Feb. 16, 1999, ord. Apr. 20, 1999; bp. of Wichita Oct. 4, 2001.

O'Malley, Sean, O.F.M.Cap.: b. June 29, 1944, Lakewood, OH; educ. St. Fidelis Seminary (Herman, PA), Capuchin College and Catholic Univ. (Washington, DC); ord. priest Aug. 29, 1970; episcopal vicar of priests serving Spanish speaking in Washington archdiocese, 1974-84; executive director of Spanish Catholic Center, Washington, from 1973; ord. coadjutor bp. of St. Thomas, Virgin Islands, Aug. 2, 1984; bp. of St. Thomas, Oct. 16, 1985; app. bp. of Fall River, June 16, 1992; app. bp. of Palm Beach, Fla., Sept. 3, 2002.

O'Neil, Dennis P.: b. Jan. 16, 1940, Fremont, NE.; educ. St. John's Seminary College (Camarillo, CA.), ord. priest (Los Angeles*) 1966; on assignment in Diocese of Juneau (AK) 1979-1984; app. titular bp. of Macon and aux. bp. of San Bernardino, Jan. 16, 2001, ord. Mar. 27, 2001.

O'Neill, Arthur J.: b. Dec. 14, 1917, East Dubuque, IL; educ. Loras Collge (Dubuque, IA), St. Mary's Seminary (Baltimore, MD); ord. priest (Rockford) Mar. 27, 1943; ord. bp. of Rockford, Oct. 11, 1968; retired Apr. 19, 1994.

Ottenweller, Albert H.: b. Apr. 5, 1916, Stanford, MT; educ. St. Joseph's Seminary (Rensselaer, IN), Catholic Univ. (Washington, DC); ord. priest (Toledo) June 19, 1943; ord. titular bp. of Perdices and aux. bp. of Toledo, May 29, 1974; app. bp. of Steubenville, OH, Oct. 11, 1977, installed Nov. 22, 1977; retired Jan. 28, 1992.

P

Paska, Walter: b. Nov. 29, 1923, Elizabeth, NJ; educ. St. Charles Seminary (Catonsville, MD), Catholic Univ. (Washington, DC), Fordham Univ. (New York); ord. priest (Philadelphia of Ukrainians*) June 2, 1947; ord. titular bp. of Tigilava and aux. of Ukrainian archdiocese of Philadelphia, Mar. 19, 1992; res. Nov. 29, 2000.

Pataki, Andrew: b. Aug. 30, 1927, Palmerton, PA; educ. St. Vincent College (Latrobe, PA), St. Procopius College, St. Procopius Seminary (Lisle, IL), Sts. Cyril and Methodius Byzantine Catholic Seminary (Pittsburgh, PA), Gregorian Univ. and Oriental Pontifical Institute (Rome, Italy); ord. priest (Pittsburgh,* Ruthenian Byzantine) Feb. 24, 1952; ord. titular bp. of Telmisso and aux. bp. of Byzantine diocese of Passaic, Aug. 23, 1983; app. bp. of Ruthenian Byzantine diocese of Parma, July 3, 1984; app. bp. of Ruthenian Byzantine diocese of Passaic, Nov. 6, 1995; installed Feb. 8, 1996.

Pates, Richard E.: b. Feb. 12, 1943, St. Paul; educ. St. Paul Seminary, North American College (Rome); ord. priest (St. Paul and Minneapolis*) Dec. 20, 1968; staff, Apostolic Nunciature, Washington, 1975-81; app. titular bp. of Suacia and aux. bp. of St. Paul and Minneapolis, Dec. 22, 2000, ordained March 26, 2001.

Paul, John J.: b. Aug. 17, 1918, La Crosse, WI; educ. Loras College (Dubuque, IA), St. Mary's Semi-

nary (Baltimore, MD), Marquette Univ. (Milwaukee, WI), ord. priest (Lincoln) Jan. 24, 1943; ord. titular bp. of Lambaesis and aux. bp. of La Crosse, Aug. 4, 1977; app. bp. of La Crosse, Oct. 18, 1983, installed Dec. 5, 1983; retired Dec. 10, 1994.

Pearce, George H., S.M.: b. Jan. 9, 1921, Brighton, MA; educ. Marist College and Seminary (Framington, MA); ord. priest Feb. 2, 1947; ord. titular bp. of Attalea in Pamphylia and vicar apostolic of the Samoa and Tokelau Islands, June 29, 1956; title changed to bp. of Apia, June 21, 1966; app. abp. of Suva, Fiji Islands, June 22, 1967; resigned Apr. 10, 1976.

Pelotte, Donald E., S.S.S.: b. Apr. 13, 1945, Waterville, ME; educ. Eymard Seminary and Junior College (Hyde Park, NY), John Carroll Univ. (Cleveland, OH), Fordham Univ. (Bronx, NY); ord. priest Sept. 2, 1972; ord. coadjutor bp. of Gallup, May 6, 1986 (first priest of Native American ancestry to be named U.S. bp.); bp. of Gallup, Mar. 20, 1990.

Peña, Raymundo J.: b. Feb. 19, 1934, Robstown, TX; educ. Assumption Seminary (San Antonio, TX); ord. priest (Corpus Christi) May 25, 1957; ord. titular bp. of Trisipa and aux. bp. of San Antonio, Dec. 13, 1976; app. bp. of El Paso, Apr. 29, 1980; app. bp. of Brownsville, May 23, 1995.

Pepe, Joseph A.: : b. June 18, 1942, Philadelphia; educ. St. Charles Borromeo Seminary, University of St. Thomas (Rome); ord. priest (Philadelphia*) May 16, 1970; app. bp. of Las Vegas April 6, 2001, ordained May 31, 2001.

Perry, Joseph N.: b. Apr. 18, 1948, Chicago, IL; educ. Capuchin Seminary of St. Lawrence, (Milwaukee), St. Mary Capuchin Seminary, Crown Point, (Indiana), St. Francis Seminary (Milwaukee), Catholic Univ. of America (Washington, DC); ord. priest (Milwaukee*), May 24, 1975; app. titular bp. of Lead and aux. bp. of Chicago, May 5, 1998; ord. June 29, 1998.

Pevec, A. Edward: b. Apr. 16, 1925, Cleveland, OH; educ. St. Mary's Seminary, John Carroll Univ. (Cleveland, OH); ord. priest (Cleveland) Apr. 29, 1950; ord. titular bp. of Mercia and aux. bp. of Cleveland, July 2, 1982; res. Apr. 3, 2001.

Pfeifer, Michael, O.M.I.: b. May 18, 1937, Alamo, TX; educ. Oblate school of theology (San Antonio, TX); ord. priest Dec. 21, 1964; provincial of southern province of Oblates of Mary Immaculate, 1981; ord. bp. of San Angelo, July 26, 1985.

Pilarczyk, Daniel E.: b. Aug. 12, 1934, Dayton, OH; educ. St. Gregory's Seminary (Cincinnati, OH), Urban Univ. (Rome), Xavier Univ. and Univ. of Cincinnati (Cincinnati, OH); ord. priest (Cincinnati*) Dec. 20, 1959; ord. titular bp. of Hodelm and aux. bp. of Cincinnati, Dec. 20, 1974; app. abp. of Cincinnati, Oct. 30, 1982; installed Dec. 20, 1982; president of NCCB/USCC, 1989-92.

Pilla, Anthony M.: b. Nov. 12, 1932, Cleveland, OH; educ. St. Gregory College Seminary (Cincinnati, OH), Borromeo College Seminary (Wickliffe, OH), St. Mary Seminary and John Carroll Univ. (Cleveland, OH); ord. priest (Cleveland) May 23, 1959; ord. titular bp. of Scardona and aux. bp. of Cleveland, Aug. 1, 1979; app. apostolic administrator of Cleveland, 1980; bp. of Cleveland, Nov. 13, 1980. President of NCCB/USCC, 1995-98.

Popp, Bernard F.: b. Dec. 6, 1917, Nada, TX; educ. St. John's Seminary and St. Mary's Univ. (San Antonio, TX); ord. priest (San Antonio*) Feb. 24, 1943;

ord. titular bp. of Capsus and aux. bp. of San Antonio, July 25, 1983; retired Mar. 23, 1993.

Potocnak, Joseph J., S.C.J.: b. May 13, 1933, Berwick, PA; educ. Dehon Seminary (Great Barrington, MA), Kilroe Seminary (Honesdale, PA), Sacred Heart (Hales Corners, WI); ord. priest Sept 21, 1966; missionary in South Africa from 1973; ord. bp. of De Aar, South Africa, May 1, 1992.

Povish, Kenneth J.: b. Apr. 19, 1924, Alpena, MI; educ. St. Joseph's Seminary (Grand Rapids, MI), Sacred Heart Seminary (Detroit, MI), Catholic Univ. (Washington, DC); ord. priest (Saginaw) June 3, 1950; ord. bp. of Crookston, Sept. 29, 1970; app. bp. of Lansing, Oct. 8, 1975, installed Dec. 11, 1975; retired Nov. 7, 1995.

Puscas, Vasile Louis: b. Sept. 13, 1915, Aurora, IL; educ. Quigley Preparatory Seminary (Chicago, IL), seminary in Oradea-Mare (Romania), Propaganda Fide Seminary (Rome), Illinois Benedictine College (Lisle, IL); ord. priest (Erie) May 14, 1942; ord. titular bp. of Leuce and first exarch of apostolic exarchate for Byzantine Romanians in the U.S., June 26, 1983 (seat of the exarchate, Canton, OH); app. first eparch, Apr. 11, 1987, when exarchate was raised to eparchy of St. George's in Canton; retired July 15, 1993.

Q

Quinn, Alexander James: b. Apr. 8, 1932, Cleveland, OH; educ. St. Charles College (Catonsville, MD), St. Mary Seminary (Cleveland, OH), Lateran Univ. (Rome), Cleveland State Univ.; ord. priest (Cleveland) May 24, 1958; ord. titular bp. of Socia and aux. bp. of Cleveland, Dec. 5, 1983.

Quinn, Francis A.: b. Sept. 11, 1921, Los Angeles, CA; educ. St. Joseph's College (Mountain View, CA), St. Patrick's Seminary (Menlo Park, CA), Catholic Univ. (Washington, DC); Univ. of CA (Berkeley); ord. priest (San Francisco*) June 15, 1946; ord. titular bp. of Numana and aux. bp. of San Francisco, June 29, 1978; app. bp. of Sacramento Dec. 18, 1979; retired Nov. 30, 1993.

Quinn, John R.: b. Mar. 28, 1929, Riverside, CA; educ. St. Francis Seminary (El Cajn, CA), North American College (Rome); ord. priest (San Diego) July 19, 1953; ord. titular bp. of Thisiduo and aux. bp. of San Diego, Dec. 12, 1967; bp. of Oklahoma City and Tulsa, Nov. 30, 1971; first abp. of Oklahoma City, Dec. 19, 1972; app. abp. of San Francisco Feb. 22, 1977, installed Apr. 26, 1977; president NCCB/USCC, 1977-80; resigned see Dec. 27, 1995.

R

Ramirez, Ricardo, C.S.B.: b. Sept. 12, 1936, Bay City, TX; educ. Univ. of St. Thomas (Houston, TX), Univ. of Detroit (Detroit, MI), St. Basil's Seminary (Toronto, Ont.), Seminario Concilium (Mexico City, Mexico), East Asian Pastoral Institute (Manila, Philippines); ord. priest Dec. 10, 1966; ord titular bp. of Vatarba and aux. of San Antonio, Dec. 6, 1981; app. first bp. of Las Cruces, N. Mex., Aug. 17, 1982; installed Oct. 18, 1982.

Raya, Joseph M.: b. July 20, 1917, Zahle, Lebanon; educ. St. Louis College (Paris, France), St. Anne's Seminary (Jerusalem); ord. priest July 20, 1941; came to U.S., 1949, became U.S. citizen; ord. abp. of Acre, Israel, of the Melkites, Oct. 20, 1968; resigned Aug.

20, 1974; assigned titular metropolitan see of Scytopolis (resides in Canada).

Reichert, Stephen J., O.F.M. Cap.: b. May 14, 1943, Leoville, KS; educ. Capuchin minor seminary (Victoria, KS), St. Fidelis College (Hermann, PA), Capuchin College (Washington, DC); ord. priest Sept. 27, 1969; missionary in Papua New Guinea since 1970; ord. bp. of Mendi, Papua New Guinea, May 7, 1995.

Reilly, Daniel P.: b. May 12, 1928, Providence, RI; educ. Our Lady of Providence Seminary (Warwick, RI), St. Brieuc Major Seminary (Cotes du Nord, France); ord. priest (Providence) May 30, 1953; ord. bp. of Norwich, Aug. 6, 1975; app. bp. of Worcester, Oct. 27, 1994, installed Nov. 8, 1994.

Reiss, John C.: b. May 13, 1922, Red Bank, NJ; educ. Catholic Univ. (Washington, DC), Immaculate Conception Seminary (Darlington, NJ); ord. priest (Trenton) May 31, 1947; ord. titular bp. of Simidicca and aux. bp. of Trenton, Dec. 12, 1967; app. bp. of Trenton, Mar. 11, 1980; retired July 1, 1997.

Riashi, Georges, B.C.O.: b. Nov. 25, 1933, Kaa-el-Rim, Lebanon; ord. priest Apr. 4, 1965; parish priest of Our Lady of Redemption Parish, Warren, MI (Newton Greek-Catholic Melkite eparchy); U.S. citizen; ord. first bp. of eparchy of St. Michael's of Sydney (Australia) for Greek-Catholic Melkites, July 19, 1987; app. abp. of archeparchy of Tripoli of Lebanon for Greek-Melkites, Aug. 5, 1995.

Ricard, John H., S.S.J.: b. Feb. 29, 1940, Baton Rouge, LA; educ. St. Joseph's Seminary (Washington, DC), Tulane Univ. (New Orleans, LA); ord. priest May 25, 1968; ord. titular bp. of Rucuma and aux. of Baltimore, July 2, 1984; urban vicar, Baltimore; app. bp. of Pensacola-Tallahassee, Jan 21, 1997.

Ricken, David L.: b. Nov. 9, 1952, Dodge City, Kansas; educ. Conception Seminary College, MO, Univ. of Louvain (Belgium), Pontifical Gregorian Univ., Rome; ord. priest (Pueblo) Sept. 12, 1980; official of the Congregation for the Clergy, 1996-1999; app. Coadjutor Bishop of Cheyenne, Dec. 14, 1999, ord. bp. by Pope John Paul II at the Vatican, Jan. 6, 2000; bp. of Cheyenne, Sept. 26, 2001.

Rigali, Justin F.: b. Apr. 19, 1935, Los Angeles, CA; educ. St. John's Seminary (Camarillo, CA); ord. priest (Los Angeles*) Apr. 25, 1961; in Vatican diplomatic service from 1964; ord. titular abp. of Bolsena, Sept. 14, 1985, by Pope John Paul II; president of the Pontifical Ecclesiastical Academy, 1985-89; secretary of Congregation for Bps., 1989-94, and the College of Cardinals, 1990-94; app. abp. of St. Louis, Jan. 25, 1994, installed Mar. 16, 1994.

Rizzotto, Vincent M.: b. Sept. 9, 1931, Houston; educ. St. Mary Seminary (Houston), the Catholic University of America (Washington, D.C.), ord. priest (Galveston, now Galveston-Houston) May 26, 1956; Vicar General of Galveston-Houston, 1994; app. titular bp. of Lamasba and aux. bp. of Galveston-Houston June 22, 2001, ord. July 31, 2001.

Roach, John R.: b. July 31, 1921, Prior Lake, MN; educ. St. Paul Seminary (St. Paul, MN), Univ. of Minnesota (Minneapolis); ord. priest (St. Paul and Minneapolis*) June 18, 1946; ord. titular bp. of Cenae and aux. bp. of St. Paul and Minneapolis, Sept. 8, 1971; app. abp. of St. Paul and Minneapolis, May 28, 1975; president of NCCB/USCC, 1980-83; retired Sept 8, 1995.

Rodi, Thomas J: b. March 27, 1949, New Orleans; educ. Georgetown University (Washington, D.C.), Tulane University School of Law (New Orleans), Notre Dame Seminary (New Orleans); ord. priest (New Orleans*) May 20, 1978; app. bp. of Biloxi, May 15, 2001, ord. July 2, 2001.

Rodimer, Frank J.: b. Oct. 25, 1927, Rockaway, NJ; educ. Seton Hall Prep (South Orange, NJ), St. Charles College (Catonsville, MD), St. Mary's Seminary (Baltimore, MD), Immaculate Conception Seminary (Darlington, NJ), Catholic Univ. (Washington, DC); ord. priest (Paterson) May 19, 1951; ord. bp. of Paterson, Feb. 28, 1978.

Rodriguez, Migúel, C.SS.R.: b. Apr. 18, 1931, Mayaguez, P.R.; educ. St. Mary's Minor Seminary (North East, PA), Mt. St. Alphonsus Major Seminary (Esopus, NY); ord. priest June 22, 1958; ord. bp. of Arecibo, P.R., Mar. 23, 1974; resigned Mar. 20, 1990.

Rodriguez, Placido, C.M.F.: b. Oct. 11, 1940, Celaya, Guanajuato, Mexico; educ. Claretian Novitate (Los Angeles, CA), Claretville Seminary College (Calabasas, CA), Catholic Univ. (Washington, DC), Loyola Univ. (Chicago, IL); ord. priest May 23, 1968; ord. titular bp. of Fuerteventura and aux. bp. of Chicago, Dec. 13, 1983; app. bp. of Lubbock, TX, Apr. 5, 1994.

Roman, Agustin A.: b. May 5, 1928, San Antonio de los Banos, Havana, Cuba; educ. San Alberto Magno Seminary (Matanzas, Cuba), Missions Etrangeres (Montreal, Canada), Barry College (Miami, FL); ord. priest July 5, 1959, Cuba; vicar for Spanish speaking in Miami archdiocese, 1976; ord. titular bp. of Sertei and aux. bp. of Miami, Mar. 24, 1979.

Roque, Francis X.: b. Oct. 9, 1928, Providence RI; educ. St. John's Seminary (Brighton, MA); ord. priest (Providence) Sept. 19, 1953; became chaplain in U.S. Army 1961; ord. titular bp. of Bagai and aux. bp. of Military Services archdiocese, May 10, 1983.

Rosazza, Peter Anthony: b. Feb. 13, 1935, New Haven, CT; educ. St. Thomas Seminary (Bloomfield, CT), Dartmouth College (Hanover, NH), St. Bernard's Seminary (Rochester, NY), St. Sulpice (Issy, France); ord. priest (Hartford*) June 29, 1961; ord. titular bp. of Oppido Nuovo and aux. bp. of Hartford, June 24, 1978.

Rose, Robert John: b. Feb. 28, 1930, Grand Rapids, MI; educ. St. Joseph's Seminary (Grand Rapids, MI), Seminaire de Philosophie (Montreal, Canada), Urban University (Rome), Univ. of Michigan (Ann Arbor); ord. priest (Grand Rapids) Dec. 21, 1955; ord. bp. of Gaylord, Dec. 6, 1981; app. bp. of Grand Rapids, installed Aug. 30, 1989.

Rueger, George E.: b. Sept. 3, 1933, Framingham, Mass; educ. Holy Cross College (Worcester, MA), St. John's Seminary (Brighton), Harvard University (Cambridge, MA); ord. priest (Worcester), Jan. 6, 1958; ord. titular bp. of Maronana and aux. bp. of Worcester, Feb. 25, 1987.

Ryan, Daniel L.: b. Sept. 28, 1930, Mankato, MN; educ. St. Procopius Seminary (Lisle, IL), Lateran Univ. (Rome); ord. priest (Joliet) May 3, 1956; ord. titular bp. of Surista and aux. bp. of Joliet, Sept. 30, 1981; app. bp. of Springfield, IL, Nov. 22, 1983, inst. Jan. 18, 1984; res. Oct. 19, 1999.

Ryan, James C., O.FM.: b. Nov. 17, 1912, Chicago, IL; educ. St. Joseph's Seraphic Seminary (Westmont, IL), Our Lady of the Angels Seminary (Cleveland, OH); ord. priest June 24, 1938; ord. titular bp. of Margo and prelate of Santarem, Brazil, Apr. 9, 1958; first bp. of Santarem, Dec. 4, 1979; retired Nov. 27, 1985.

Ryan, Sylvester D.: b. Mar. 3, 1930, Catalina Is., CA; educ. St. John's Seminary (Camarillo, CA); ord. priest (Los Angeles*) May 3, 1957; ord. titular bp. of Remesiana and aux. bp. of Los Angeles, May 31, 1990; app. bp. of Monterey, Jan. 28, 1992.

S

Salatka, Charles A.: b. Feb. 26, 1918, Grand Rapids, MI; educ. St. Joseph's Seminary (Grand Rapids, MI), Catholic Univ. (Washington, DC), Lateran Univ. (Rome); ord. priest (Grand Rapids) Feb. 24, 1945; ord. titular bp. of Cariana and aux. bp. of Grand Rapids, MI, Mar. 6, 1962; app. bp. of Marquette, installed Mar. 25, 1968; app. abp. of Oklahoma City, Sept. 27, 1977; retired Nov. 24, 1992.

Saltarelli, Michael A.: b. Jan. 17, 1932, Jersey City, NJ; educ. Seton Hall College and Immaculate Conception Seminary (S. Orange, NJ); ord. priest (Newark*), May 28, 1960; ord. titular bp. of Mesarfelta and aux. bp. of Newark, July 30, 1990; app. bp. of Wilmington, Nov. 21, 1995; installed Jan. 23, 1996.

Samra, Nicholas J.: b. Aug. 15, 1944, Paterson, NJ; educ. St. Anselm College (Manchester, NH), St. Basil Seminary (Methuen, MA), St. John Seminary (Brighton, MA); ord. priest (Newton) May 10, 1970; ord. titular bp. of Gerasa and aux. bp. of Melkite diocese of Newton, July 6, 1989.

Sanchez, Robert F.: b. Mar. 20, 1934, Socorro, NM; educ. Immaculate Heart Seminary (Santa Fe, NM), Gregorian Univ. (Rome), Catholic Univ. (Washington, DC); ord. priest (Santa Fe*) Dec 20, 1959; ord. abp. of Santa Fe, NM, July 25, 1974; resigned Apr. 6, 1993.

Sartain, James P.: b. June 6, 1952, Memphis, TN; educ. St. Meinrad Seminary, (Indiana), North American College, (Rome), Pontifical University of St. Thomas (the Angelicum), Pontifical Institute of St. Anselm (Rome); ord. priest (Memphis) July 15, 1978; app. bp. of Little Rock, Jan. 4, 2000, ord. March 6, 2000.

Sartoris, Joseph M.: b. July 1, 1927, Los Angeles, CA; educ. St. John's Seminary (Camarillo, CA); ord. priest (Los Angeles*) May 30, 1953; ord. titular bp. of Oliva and aux. bp. of Los Angeles, Mar. 19, 1994. San Pedro regional bp.

Scarpone Caporale, Gerald, O.F.M.: b. Oct. 1, 1928, Watertown, MA; ord. priest June 24, 1956; ord. coadjutor bp. of Comayagua, Honduras, Feb. 21, 1979; succeeded as bp. of Comayagua, May 30, 1979.

Schlarman, Stanley Gerard: b. July 27, 1933, Belleville, IL; educ. St. Henry Prep Seminary (Belleville, IL), Gregorian Univ. (Rome), St. Louis Univ. (St. Louis, MO); ord. priest (Belleville) July 13, 1958, Rome; ord. titular bp. of Capri and aux. bp. of Belleville, May 14, 1979; app. bp. of Dodge City, Mar. 1, 1983; resigned May 12, 1998.

Schleck, Charles A., C.S.C.: b. July 5, 1925, Milwaukee, WI; educ. Univ. of Notre Dame (IN), Pontifical Univ. of St. Thomas (Rome); ord. priest Dec. 22, 1951; ord. titular abp. of Africa (Mehdia), Apr. 1, 1995; adjunct secretary of Congregation for Evangelization of Peoples; president of the superior council of the Pontifical Mission Societies.

Schmidt, Firmin M., O.F.M. Cap.: b. Oct. 12, 1918, Catherine, KS; educ. Catholic Univ. (Washington, DC); ord. priest June 2, 1946; app. prefect apostolic of Mendi, Papua New Guinea, Apr. 3, 1959; ord. titular bp. of Conana and first vicar apostolic of Mendi, Dec.15, 1965; became first bp. of Mendi when vicariate apostolic was raised to a diocese, Nov. 15, 1966; retired Feb. 22, 1995.

Schmitt, Bernard W.: b. Aug. 17, 1928, Wheeling, WV; educ. St. Joseph College (Catonsville, MD), St. Mary's Seminary (Baltimore), Ohio Univ. (Athens, OH); ord. priest (Wheeling-Charleston) May 28, 1955; ord. titular bp. of Walla Walla and bp. of Wheeling-Charleston, Aug. 1, 1988; bp. of Wheeling-Charleston, Mar. 29, 1989.

Schmitt, Mark F.: b. Feb. 14, 1923, Algoma, WI; educ. Salvatorian Seminary (St. Nazianz, WI), St. John's Seminary (Collegeville, MN); ord. priest (Green Bay) May 22, 1948; ord. titular bp. of Ceanannus Mor and aux. bp. of Green Bay, June 24, 1970; app. bp. of Marquette, Mar. 21, 1978, installed May 8, 1978; retired Oct. 6, 1992.

Schmitz Simon, Paul, O.F.M. Cap.: b. Dec. 4, 1943, Fond du Lac, WI; ord. priest Sept. 3, 1970; missionary in Nicaragua from 1970; superior of vice province of Capuchins in Central America (headquartered in Managua), 1982-84; ord. titular bp. of Elepla and aux. of the vicariate apostolic of Bluefields, Nicaragua, Sept. 17, 1984; app. bp. of vicariate apostolic of Bluefields, Aug. 17, 1994.

Schnurr, Dennis M.: b. June 21, 1948, Sheldon, Iowa; educ. Loras College (Dubuque), Gregorian University (Rome), Catholic University of America (Washington, D.C.); ord. priest (Sioux City) July 20, 1974; Staff, Apostolic Nunciature, Washington, D.C., 1985-1989; Associate General Secretary, National Conference of Catholic Bishops/United States Catholic Conference (NCCB/USCC), 1989-1995; National Executive Director, World Youth Day 1993, Denver, 1991-1993; General Secretary, NCCB/USCC, 1995-2001; app. bp. of Duluth, Jan. 18, 2001, ord. Apr. 2, 2001.

Schoenherr, Walter J.: b. Feb. 28, 1920, Detroit, MI; educ. Sacred Heart Seminary (Detroit, MI), Mt. St. Mary Seminary (Norwood, OH); ord. priest (Detroit*) Oct. 27, 1945; ord. titular bp. of Timidana and aux. bp. of Detroit, May 1, 1968; retired Mar. 7, 1995.

Schott, Basil, O.F.M.: b. July 21, 1939, Freeland, PA; entered Byzantine Franciscans, professed Aug. 4, 1959; educ. Immaculate Conception College (Troy, NY), St. Mary's Seminary (Norwalk, CT) and Post Graduate Center (New York, NY); ord. priest Aug. 29, 1965; ord. bp. of Byzantine eparchy of Parma, July 11, 1996; app. metropolitan abp. of Pittsburgh (Byzantine Ruthenian), May 3, 2002.

Schulte, Francis B.: b. Dec. 23, 1926, Philadelphia, PA; educ. St. Charles Borromeo Seminary (Overbrook, PA); ord. priest (Philadelphia*) May 10, 1952; ord. titular bp. of Afufenia and aux. bp. of Philadelphia, Aug. 12, 1981; app. bp. of Wheeling-Charleston, June 4, 1985; abp. of New Orleans, Dec. 6, 1988, installed Feb. 14, 1989; ret. Jan. 3, 2002.

Schwietz, Roger L., O.M.I.: b. July 3, 1940, St. Paul, MN; educ. Univ. of Ottawa (Canada), Gregorian Univ. (Rome); ord. priest Dec. 20, 1967; ord. bp. of Duluth Feb. 2, 1990; bp. of Duluth, 1990-2000; coadj. abp. of Anchorage, Jan. 18, 2000; abp. of Anchorage, March 3, 2001.

Serratelli, Arthur J.: b. April 18, 1944, Newark, NJ; educ. Seton Preparatory School (NJ), Seton Hall University (NJ), North American College and Gregorian University (Rome), Pontifical Biblical Istitute (Rome); ord. priest (Newark*) Dec. 20, 1968; prof. of Sacred Scripture, Immaculate Conception Seminary; rector of the College Seminary, Seton Hall University; prelate of honor, 1998; app. titular bp. of Enera and aux. bp. of Newark, July 3, 2000.

Setian, Nerses Mikail: b. Oct. 18,1918, Sebaste, Turkey; educ. Armenian Pontifical College and Gregorian Univ. (Rome); ord. priest Apr. 13, 1941, in Rome; ord. titular bp. of Ancira of the Armenians and first exarch of the apostolic exarchate for Armenian Catholics in Canada and the United States (see city New York), Dec. 5, 1981; retired Nov. 24, 1993.

Sevilla, Carlos A., S.J.: b. Aug. 9, 1935, San Francisco, CA; entered Jesuits Aug. 14, 1953; educ. Gonzaga Univ. (Spokane, WA), Santa Clara Uiv. (Santa Clara, CA), Jesuitenkolleg (Innsbruck, Austria), Catholic Institute of Paris (France); ord. priest June 3, 1966; ord. titular bp. of Mina and aux. bp. of San Francisco, Jan. 25, 1989; bp. of Yakima, Dec. 31, 1996.

Shaheen, Robert J.: b. June 3, 1937, Danbury, Conn.; ord. May 2, 1964; elected eparch of Our Lady of Lebanon of Los Angeles of the Maronites (U.S.A.), Dec. 5, 2000.

Sheehan, Michael J.: b. July 9, 1939, Wichita, KS; educ. Assumption Seminary (San Antonio, TX), Gregorian Univ. and Lateran Univ. (Rome); ord. priest (Dallas) July 12, 1964; ord. first bp. of Lubbock, TX, June 17, 1983; apostolic administrator of Santa Fe, Apr. 6, 1993; app. abp. of Santa Fe, Aug. 17, 1993.

Sheets, John R., S.J.: b. Sept. 21, 1922, Omaha, NE; joined Jesuits, 1940; educ. St. Louis Univ. (St. Louis, MO), St. Mary's College (St. Mary's, KS), Univ. of Innsbruck (Austria); ord. priest June 17, 1953; final profession of vows as Jesuit, Aug. 15, 1957; ord. titular bp. of Murcona and aux. bp. of Fort Wayne-South Bend, IN, June 25, 1991; ret., Sept. 23, 1997.

Sheldon, Gilbert I.: b. Sept. 20, 1926, Cleveland, OH; educ. John Carroll Univ. and St. Mary Seminary (Cleveland, OH); ord. priest (Cleveland) Feb. 28, 1953; ord. titular bp. of Taparura and aux. bp. of Cleveland, June 11, 1976; app. bp. of Steubenville, Jan. 28, 1992, ret. May 31, 2002.

Sheridan, Michael J.: b. Mar. 4, 1945, St. Louis, MO; educ. Glennon College, Kenrick Seminary (St. Louis, MO), Angelicum (Rome); ord. priest (St. Louis*) 1971; app. titular bp. of Thibiuca and aux. bp. of St. Louis, July 9, 1997; co-adjutor bp. of Colorado Springs, Dec. 4, 2001.

Sheridan, Patrick J.: b. Mar. 10, 1922, New York, NY; educ. St. Joseph's Seminary (Yonkers, NY), University of Chicago; ord. priest (New York*) Mar. 1, 1 20, 1959; ord. titular bp. of Castra and aux. bp. of Milwaukee, Dec. 19, 1979.

Skurla, William C.: b. June 1, 1956, Duluth; educ. Columbia Univ., New York, Mary Immaculate Seminary, Northhampton, PA; ord. priest (Franciscan) 1987; incardinated into Eparchy of Van Nuys, 1996; app. bp. of Van Nuys Byzantine Catholic Eparchy in California, Feb. 19, 2002.

Skylstad, William S.: b. Mar. 2, 1934, Omak, WA; educ. Pontifical College Josephinum (Worthington, OH), Washington State Univ. (Pullman, WA),

Gonzaga Univ. (Spokane, WA); ord. priest (Spokane) May 21, 1960; ord. bp. of Yakima, May 12, 1977; app. bp. of Spokane, Apr. 17, 1990; vice-pres. of USCCB, 2001-.

Slattery, Edward J.: b. Aug. 11, 1940, Chicago, IL; educ. Quigley Preparatory, St. Mary of the Lake Seminary (Mundelein, IL), Loyola Univ. (Chicago); ord. priest (Chicago*) Apr. 26, 1966; vice president, 1971-76, and president, 1976-94, of the Catholic Church Extension Society; ord. bp. of Tulsa, Jan. 6, 1994.

Smith, John M.: b. June 23, 1935, Orange, NJ; educ. Immaculate Conception Seminary (Darlington, NJ), Seton Hall Univ. (South Orange, NJ), Catholic Univ. (Washington, DC); ord. priest (Newark*) May 27, 1961; ord. titular bp. of Tre Taverne and aux. bp. of Newark, Jan. 25, 1988; app. bp. of Pensacola-Tallahassee, FL, June 25, 1991; app. coadjutor bp. of Trenton, Nov. 21, 1995; bp. of Trenton, July 1, 1997.

Smith, Philip F., O.M.I.: b. Oct. 16, 1924, Lowell, MA; ord. priest Oct. 29, 1950; ord. titular bp. of Lamfua and vicar apostolic of Jolo, Philippine Islands, Sept. 8, 1972; app. coadjutor abp. of Cotabato, Philippines, Apr. 11, 1979; abp. of Cotabato, Mar. 14, 1980.

Snyder, John J.: b. Oct. 25, 1925, New York, NY; educ. Cathedral College (Brooklyn, NY), Immaculate Conception Seminary (Huntington, NY); ord. priest (Brooklyn) June 9, 1951; ord. titular bp. of Forlimpoli and aux. bp. of Brooklyn, Feb. 2, 1973; app. bp. of St. Aug.ine, installed Dec. 5, 1979; res. Dec. 11, 2000.

Soens, Lawrence D.: b. Aug. 26, 1926, Iowa City, IA; educ. Loras College (Dubuque, IA), St. Ambrose College (Davenport, IA), Kenrick Seminary (St. Louis, MO), Univ. of Iowa; ord. priest (Davenport) May 6, 1950; ord. bp. of Sioux City, Aug. 17, 1983, resigned Nov. 28, 1998.

Soroka, Stephen: b. Nov. 13, 1951, Winnipeg, Manitoba; educ. Univ. of Manitoba, Ukrainian Seminary, Washington, D.C., Catholic Univ. of America, ordained (Ukrainian Archdiocese of Winnipeg*) June 13, 1982; Chancellor and financial administrator of the Winnipeg archdiocese, 1994, auxiliary bishop, Winnipeg, 1996; metropolitan abp. of Philadelphia for the Ukrainians, Nov. 29, 2000; inst. Feb. 27, 2001.

Soto, Jaime: b. Dec. 31, 1955, Inglewood, CA; educ. St. John's Seminary, Camarillo, CA, Columbia University School of Social Work, New York; ord. priest (Orange) June 12, 1982; Episcopal Vicar for Hispanic Ministry, 1989; app. titular bp. of Segia and aux. bp. of Orange, Mar. 23, 2000, ord. May 31, 2000.

Sowada, Alphonse A., O.S.C.: b. June 23, 1933, Avon, MN; educ. Holy Cross Scholasticate (Fort Wayne, IN), Catholic Univ. (Washington, DC), ord. priest May 31, 1958; missionary in Indonesia from 1958; ord. bp. of Agats, Indonesia, Nov. 23, 1969.

Speltz, George H.: b. May 29, 1912, Altura, MN; educ. St. Mary's College, St. Paul's Seminary (St. Paul, MN), Catholic Univ. (Washington, DC); ord. priest (St. Cloud) June 2, 1940; ord. titular bp. of Claneus and aux. bp. of Winona, Mar. 25, 1963; app. coadjutor bp. of St. Cloud, Apr. 4, 1966; bp. of St. Cloud, Jan. 31, 1968; retired Jan. 13, 1987.

Speyrer, Jude: b. Apr. 14, 1929, Leonville, LA; educ. St. Joseph Seminary (Covington, LA), Notre Dame Seminary (New Orleans, LA), Gregorian Univ.

(Rome), Univ. of Fribourg (Switzerland); ord. priest (Lafayette, LA) July 25, 1953; ord. first bp. of Lake Charles, LA, Apr. 25, 1980; res. Dec. 11, 2000.

Stafford, James Francis: (See **Cardinals, Biographies**).

Steib, J. (James) Terry, S.V.D.: b. May 17, 1940, Vacherie, LA; educ. Divine Word seminaries (Bay St. Louis, MS, Conesus, NY, Techny, IL), Xavier Univ. (New Orleans, LA); ord. priest Jan. 6, 1967; ord. titular bp. of Fallaba and aux. bp. of St. Louis, Feb. 10, 1984; app. bp. of Memphis, Mar. 24, 1993.

Steinbock, John T.: b. July 16, 1937, Los Angeles, CA; educ. Los Angeles archdiocesan seminaries; ord. priest (Los Angeles*) May 1, 1963; ord. titular bp. of Midila and aux. bp. of Orange, CA, July 14, 1984; app. bp. of Santa Rosa, Jan. 27, 1987; app. bp. of Fresno, Oct. 15, 1991.

Steiner, Kenneth Donald: b. Nov. 25, 1936, David City, NE; educ. Mt. Angel Seminary (St. Benedict, OR), St. Thomas Seminary (Seattle, Wash); ord. priest (Portland,* OR) May 19, 1962; ord. titular bp. of Avensa and aux. bp. of Portland, OR, Mar. 2, 1978.

Straling, Phillip F.: b. Apr. 25, 1933, San Bernardino, CA; educ. Immaculate Heart Seminary, St. Francis Seminary, Univ. of San Diego and San Diego State University (San Diego, CA), North American College (Rome); ord. priest (San Diego) Mar. 19, 1959; ord. first bp. of San Bernardino, Nov. 6, 1978; app. first bp. of Reno, Mar. 21, 1995, when Reno-Las Vegas diocese was made two separate dioceses.

Strecker, Ignatius J.: b. Nov. 23, 1917, Spearville, KS; educ. St. Benedict's College (Atchison, KS), Kenrick Seminary (Webster Groves, MO), Catholic Univ. (Washington, DC); ord. priest (Wichita) Dec. 19, 1942; ord. bp. of Springfield-Cape Girardeau, MO, June 20, 1962; abp. of Kansas City, KS, Oct. 28, 1969; retired June 28, 1993.

Sullivan, James S.: b. July 23, 1929, Kalamazoo, MI; educ. Sacred Heart Seminary (Detroit, MI), St. John Provincial Seminary (Plymouth, MI); ord. priest (Lansing) June 4, 1955; ord. titular bp. of Siccessi and aux. bp. of Lansing, Sept. 21, 1972; app. bp. of Fargo, Apr. 2, 1985; installed May 30, 1985; ret. March 19, 2002.

Sullivan, Joseph M.: b. Mar. 23, 1930, Brooklyn, NY; educ. Immaculate Conception Seminary (Huntington, NY), Fordham Univ. (New York); ord. priest (Brooklyn) June 2, 1956; ord. titular bp. of Suliana and aux. bp. of Brooklyn, Nov. 24, 1980.

Sullivan, Walter F.: b. June 10, 1928, Washington, DC; educ. St. Mary's Seminary (Baltimore, MD), Catholic Univ. (Washington, DC); ord. priest (Richmond) May 9, 1953; ord. titular bp. of Selsea and aux. bp. of Richmond, Va., Dec. 1, 1970; app. bp. of Richmond, June 4, 1974.

Sulyk, Stephen: b. Oct. 2, 1924, Balnycia, Western Ukraine; migrated to U.S. 1948; educ. Ukrainian Catholic Seminary of the Holy Spirit (Hirschberg, Germany), St. Josaphat's Seminary and Catholic Univ. (Washington, DC); ord. priest (Philadelphia,* Byzantine) June 14, 1952; ord. abp. of the Ukrainian archeparchy of Philadelphia, Mar. 1, 1981; res. Nov. 29, 2000.

Symons, J. Keith: b. Oct. 14, 1932, Champion, MI; educ. St. Thomas Seminary (Bloomfield, CT), St. Mary Seminary (Baltimore, MD); ord. priest (St. Augustine) May 18, 1958; ord. titular bp. of

Siguitanus and aux. bp. of St. Petersburg, Mar. 19, 1981; app. bp. of Pensacola-Tallahassee, Oct. 4, 1983, installed Nov. 8, 1983; app. bp. of Palm Beach, June 12, 1990; resigned, June 2, 1998.

Szoka, Edmund C.: (See **Cardinals, Biographies.**)

T

Tafoya, Arthur N.: b. Mar. 2, 1933, Alameda, NM; educ. St. Thomas Seminary (Denver, CO), Conception Seminary (Conception, MO); ord. priest (Santa Fe*) May 12, 1962; ord. bp. of Pueblo, Sept. 10, 1980.

Tamayo, James A.: b. Oct. 23, 1949, Brownsville, TX; educ. Del Mar College (Corpus Christi, TX), Univ. of St. Thomas and Univ. of St. Thomas School of Theology (Houston); ord. priest (Corpus Christi) June 11, 1976; ord. titular bp. of Ita and aux. bp. of Galveston-Houston, Mar. 10, 1993; app. first bp. of Laredo, TX, July 3, 2000, ins. Aug. 9, 2000.

Thomas, Elliott G.: b. July 15, 1926, Pittsburgh, PA; educ. Howard Univ. (Washington, DC), Gannon Univ. (Erie, PA), St. Vincent de Paul Seminary (Boynton Beach, FL); ord. priest (St. Thomas, Virgin Islands) June 6, 1986; ord. bp. of St. Thomas in the Virgin Islands, Dec. 12, 1993; resigned June 30, 1999.

Thomas, George L.: b. May 19, 1950, Anaconda, MT, educ. St. Thomas Seminary, Seattle, Univ. of Washington, Seattle; ord. priest (Seattle*) May 22, 1976; chancellor and vicar general, 1988-1999, diocesan administrator of Seattle, 1996-1997; app. titular bp. of Vagrauta and aux. bp. of Seattle, Nov. 19, 1999, rec. Jan. 28, 2000.

Thompson, David B.: b. May 29, 1923, Philadelphia, PA; educ. St. Charles Seminary (Overbrook, PA), Catholic Univ. (Washington, DC); ord. priest (Philadelphia*) May 27, 1950; ord. coadjutor bp. of Charleston, May 24, 1989; bp. of Charleston, Feb. 22, 1990; res. July 13, 1999

Timlin, James C.: b. Aug. 5, 1927, Scranton, PA; educ. St. Charles College (Catonville, MD), St. Mary's Seminary (Baltimore, MD), North American College (Rome); ord. priest (Scranton) July 16, 1951; ord. titular bp. of Gunugo and aux. bp. of Scranton, Sept. 21, 1976; app. bp. of Scranton, Apr. 24, 1984.

Tobin, Thomas J.: b. Apr. 1, 1948, Pittsburgh, PA; educ. St. Mark Seminary High School, Gannon Univ. (Erie, PA), St. Francis College (Loretto, PA), North American College (Rome); ord. priest (Pittsburgh) July 21, 1973; ord. titular bp. of Novica and aux. bp. of Pittsburgh, Dec. 27, 1992; app. bp. of Youngstown Dec. 5, 1995; installed Feb. 2, 1996.

Trautman, Donald W.: b. June 24, 1936, Buffalo, NY; educ. Our Lady of Angels Seminary (Niagara Falls, NY), Theology Faculty (Innsbruck, Austria), Pontifical Biblical Institute (Rome), Catholic Univ. (Washington, DC); ord. priest (Buffalo) Apr. 7, 1962, in Innsbruck; ord. titular bp. of Sassura and aux. of Buffalo, Apr. 16, 1985; app. bp. of Erie, June 12, 1990.

Tschoepe, Thomas: b. Dec. 17, 1915, Pilot Point, TX; educ. Pontifical College Josephinum (Worthington, OH); ord. priest (Dallas) May 30, 1943; ord. bp. of San Angelo, TX, Mar. 9, 1966; app. bp. of Dallas, TX, Aug. 27, 1969; retired July 14, 1990.

Turley Murphy, Daniel T., O.S.A.: b. Jan. 25, 1943, Chicago, IL; ord. priest Dec. 21, 1961; ord. coadjutor bp. of Chulucanas, Peru, Aug. 17, 1996.

U-V

Untener, Kenneth E.: b. Aug. 3, 1937, Detroit, MI; educ. Sacred Heart Seminary (Detroit, MI), St. John's Provincial Seminary (Plymouth, MI), Gregorian Univ. (Rome); ord. priest (Detroit*) June 1, 1963; ord. bp. of Saginaw, Nov. 24, 1980.

Valero, René A.: b. Aug. 15, 1930, New York, NY; educ. Cathedral College, Immaculate Conception Seminary (Huntington, NY), Fordham Univ. (New York); ord. priest (Brooklyn) June 2, 1956; ord. titular bp. of Turris Vicus and aux. bp. of Brooklyn, Nov. 24, 1980.

Vasa, Robert F.: b. May 7, 1951, Lincoln, NE, educ. St. Thomas Seminary, Denver, Holy Trinity Seminary, Dallas, Pontifical Gregorian Univ. (Rome, Italy); ord. priest (Lincoln) May 22,1976; Vicar General and Moderator of the Curia, 1996; app. bp. of Baker, OR Nov. 19, 1999, ins. Jan. 26, 2000.

Vasquez, José S.: b. July 9, 1957, Stamford, Texas; educ. St. Mary Seminary, Houston, University of St. Thomas, North American College and Pontifical Gregorian University (Rome); ord. priest (San Angelo) June 30, 1984; app. titular bp. of Cova and aux. of Galveston-Houston, Nov. 30, 2001, ordained Jan. 23, 2002.

Veigle, Adrian J.M., T.O.R.: b. Sept. 15, 1912, Lilly, PA; educ. St. Francis College (Loretto, PA), Pennsylvania State College; ord. priest May 22, 1937; ord. titular bp. of Gigthi June 9, 1966 (resigned titular see May 26, 1978); prelate of Borba, Brazil, 1966; retired July 6, 1988.

Vigernon, Allen H.: b. Oct. 21, 1948, Detroit, MI; educ. Sacred Heart Seminary (Detroit, MI), North American College, Gregorian Univ. (Rome) Catholic Univ.(Washington, DC); ord. priest (Detroit*) July 26, 1975; served in Vatican Secretariat of State, 1991-94; rector of Sacred Heart Seminary (Detroit), 1994; ord. titular bp. of Sault Sainte Marie and aux. bp. of Detroit, July 9, 1996.

Vlazny, John G.: b. Feb. 22, 1937, Chicago, IL; educ. Quigley Preparatory Seminary (Chicago, IL), St. Mary of the Lake Seminary (Mundelein, IL), Gregorian Univ. (Rome), Univ. of Michigan, Loyola Univ. (Chicago, IL); ord. priest (Chicago*) Dec. 20, 1961; ord. titular bp. of Stagno and aux. bp. of Chicago, Dec. 13, 1983; app. bp. of Winona, MN, May 19, 1987; app. abp. of Portland in Oregon, Oct. 28, 1997, installed Dec. 19, 1997.

W

Walsh, Daniel Francis: b. Oct. 2, 1937, San Francisco, CA; educ. St. Joseph Seminary (Mountain View, CA), St. Patrick Seminary (Menlo Park, CA) Catholic Univ. (Washington, DC); ord. priest (San Francisco*) Mar. 30, 1963; ord. titular bp. of Tigia and aux. bp. of San Francisco, Sept. 24, 1981; app. bp. of Reno-Las Vegas, June 9, 1987; app. first bp. of Las Vegas Mar. 21, 1995, when the Reno-Las Vegas diocese was made two separate dioceses; app. bp. Santa Rosa, Apr. 11, 2000.

Ward, John J.: b. Sept. 28, 1920, Los Angeles, CA; educ. St. John's Seminary (Camarillo, CA), Catholic Univ. (Washington, DC); ord. priest (Los Angeles*) May 4, 1946; ord. titular bp. of Bria and aux. of Los Angeles, Dec. 12, 1963; retired May 7, 1996; titular bp. of CA.

Warfel, Michael William: b. Sept 16, 1948, Elkhart,

IN; educ. Indiana Univ, St. Gregory's College Seminary, Mt. St. Mary's Seminary of the West (Cincinnati, OH); ord. priest Apr. 26, 1980; ord. bp. of Juneau, Dec. 17, 1996.

Watters, Loras J.: b. Oct. 14, 1915, Dubuque, IA; educ. Loras College (Dubuque, IA), Gregorian Univ. (Rome), Catholic Univ. (Washington, DC); ord. priest (Dubuque*) June 7, 1941; ord. titular bp. of Fidoloma and aux. bp. of Dubuque, Aug. 26, 1965; bp. of Winona, installed Mar. 13, 1969; retired Oct. 14, 1986.

Watty Urquidi, Ricardo, M.Sp.S.: b. July 16, 1938, San Diego, CA; ord. priest June 8, 1968; ord. titular bp. of Macomedes and aux. bp. of Mexico City, July 19, 1980; app. first bp. of Nuevo Laredo, Mexico, Nov. 6, 1989.

Wcela, Emil A.: b. May 1, 1931, Bohemia, NY; educ. St. Francis College (Brooklyn, NY), Immaculate Conception Seminary (Huntington, NY), Catholic Univ. (Washington, DC), Pontifical Biblical Institute (Rome, Italy); ord. priest (Brooklyn) June 2, 1956; ord. titular bp. of Filaca and aux. bp. of Rockville Centre, Dec. 13, 1988.

Weakland, Rembert G., O.S.B.: b. Apr. 2, 1927, Patton, PA; joined Benedictines, 1945; ord. priest June 24, 1951; abbot-primate of Benedictine Confederation, 1967-77; ord. abp. of Milwaukee, Nov. 8, 1977; res. May 24, 2002.

Weigand, William K.: b. May 23, 1937, Bend, OR; educ. Mt. Angel Seminary (St. Benedict, OR), St. Edward's Seminary and St. Thomas Seminary (Kenmore, WA); ord. priest (Boise) May 25, 1963; ord. bp. of Salt Lake City, Nov. 17, 1980; app. bp. of Sacramento, Nov. 30, 1993, installed Jan. 27, 1994.

Weitzel, John Quinn, M.M.: b. May 10, 1928, Chicago, IL; educ. Maryknoll Seminary (Maryknoll, NY); ord. priest Nov. 5, 1955; missionary to Samoa, 1979; ord. bp. of Samoa-Pago Pago, American Samoa, Oct. 29, 1986.

Welsh, Thomas J.: b. Dec. 20, 1921, Weatherly, PA; educ. St. Charles Borromeo Seminary (Philadelphia, PA), Catholic Univ. (Washington, DC); ord. priest (Philadelphia*) May 30, 1946; ord. titular bp. of Scattery Island and aux. bp. of Philadelphia, Apr. 2, 1970; app. first bp. of Arlington, Va., June 4, 1974; app. bp. of Allentown, Feb. 8, 1983, installed Mar. 21, 1983. Retired: Dec. 16, 1997.

Wenski, Thomas G.: b. Oct. 18, 1950, West Palm Beach, FL; educ. St. John Vianney College Seminary, St. Vincent de Paul Regional Seminary, Fordham Univ.; ord. priest (Miami*) May 15, 1976; director of Miami Haitian Apostolate; app.titular bp. of Kearney and aux. of Miami, June 24, 1997.

Wester, John Charles: b. Nov. 5, 1950, San Francisco; educ.St. John's Seminary, Camarillo, CA, St. Patrick's Seminary, Menlo Park, CA, Univ. of San Francisco; ord. priest (San Francisco*) May 15, 1976; app. titular bp. of Lamiggiga and aux. bp. of San Francisco, June 30, 1998.

Wilkerson, Gerald E.: b. Oct. 21, 1939, Des Moines, IA; educ. St. John's Seminary (Camarillo, CA); ord. priest (Los Angeles*) Jan. 5, 1965; app. Titular Bp. of Vincennes and aux. bp. of Los Angeles, Nov. 5, 1997, ord. Jan. 21, 1998.

Williams, James Kendrick: b. Sept. 5, 1936, Athertonville, KY; educ. St. Mary's College (St. Mary's, KY), St. Maur's School of Theology (South Union, KY); ord. priest (Louisville*) May 25, 1963;

ord. titular bp. of Catula and aux. bp. of Covington, June 19, 1984; first bp. of Lexington, KY, installed Mar. 2, 1988; res. June 11, 2002.

Winter, William J.: b. May 20, 1930, Pittsburgh, PA; educ. St. Vincent College and Seminary (Latrobe, PA), Gregorian Univ. (Rome, Italy); ord. priest (Pittsburgh), Dec. 17, 1955; ord. titular bp. of Uthina and aux. bp. of Pittsburgh, Feb. 13, 1989.

Wirz, George O.: b. Jan. 17, 1929, Monroe, WI; educ. St. Francis Seminary and Marquette Univ. (Milwaukee, WI); Cath. Univ. (Washington, DC); ord. priest (Madison) May 31, 1952; ord. titular bp. of Municipa and aux. bp. of Madison, Mar. 9, 1978.

Wiwchar, Michael, C.SS.R.: b. May 9, 1932, Komarno, Manitoba, Can.; educ. Redemptorist Seminary (Windsor, Ontario); made solemn vows as Redemptorist, 1956; ord. priest, June 28, 1959; pastor St. John the Baptist Parish, Newark, NJ, 1990-93; ord. bp. of St. Nicholas of Chicago for the Ukrainians, Sept. 28, 1993; bp. of Saskatoon of Ukrainians, Nov. 29, 2000.

Wuerl, Donald W.: b. Nov. 12, 1940, Pittsburgh, PA; educ. Catholic Univ. (Washington, DC), North American College, Angelicum (Rome); ord. priest (Pittsburgh) Dec. 17, 1966, in Rome; ord. titular bp. of Rosemarkie Jan. 6, 1986, in Rome; aux. bp. of Seattle, 1986-87; app. bp. of Pittsburgh Feb. 11, 1988, installed Mar. 25, 1988.

Wycislo, Aloysius John: b. June 17, 1908, Chicago, IL; educ. St. Mary's Seminary (Mundelein, IL), Catholic Univ. (Washington, DC); ord. priest (Chicago*) Apr. 4, 1934; ord. titular bp. of Stadia and aux. bp. of Chicago, Dec. 21, 1960; app. bp. of Green Bay, installed Apr. 16, 1968; resigned May 10, 1983.

Y-Z

Yanta, John W.: b. Oct. 2, 1931, Runge, TX; educ. St. John's Preparatory Seminary and Assumption Seminary (San Antonio); ord. priest (San Antonio*) Mar. 17, 1956; ord. titular bp. of Naratcata and aux. bp. of San Antonio Dec. 30, 1994; app. bp. of Amarillo, Jan. 21,1997, installed Mar. 17, 1997.

Younan, Joseph: b. Nov. 15, 1944, Hassakeh, Syria; educ. Our Lady of Deliverance Seminary (Charfet, Lebanon), Pontifical College of the Propagation of the Faith (Rome); ord. priest Sept. 12, 1971; came to U.S., 1986; served Syrian Catholics in U.S.; ord. first bp. Our Lady of Deliverance of Newark for Syrian Catholics in the U.S. and Canada, Jan. 7, 1996, in Kamisly, Syria.

Zavala, Gabino: b. Sept. 7, 1951, Guerrero, Mexico; became U.S. citizen, 1976; educ. St. John's Seminary (Los Angeles), Catholic Univ. (Washington, DC); ord. priest (Los Angeles*) May 28, 1977; ord. titular bp. of Tamascani and aux. bp. of Los Angeles, Mar. 19, 1994.

Zayek, Francis: b. Oct. 18, 1920, Manzanillo, Cuba; ord. priest Mar. 17, 1946; ord. titular bp. of Callinicum and aux. bp. for Maronites in Brazil, Aug. 5, 1962; named apostolic exarch for Maronites in U.S., with headquarters in Detroit; installed June 11. 1966; first eparch of St. Maron of Detroit, Mar. 25, 1972; see transferred to Brooklyn, June 27, 1977; given personal title of abp., Dec. 22, 1982; retired Nov. 23, 1996.

Ziemann, G. Patrick: b. Sept. 13, 1941, Pasadena, CA; educ. St. John's College Seminary and St. John's

Seminary (Camarillo, CA), Mt. St. Mary's College (Los Angeles, CA); ord. priest (Los Angeles*) Apr. 29, 1967; ord. titular bp. of Obba and aux. bp. of Los Angeles, Feb. 23, 1987; app. bp. of Santa Rosa, July 14, 1992; resigned, July 22, 1999.

Zipfel, Paul A.: b. Sept. 22, 1935, St. Louis, MO; educ. Cardinal Glennon College, Kenrick Seminary (St. Louis, MO), Catholic Univ. (Washington, DC), St. Louis Univ. (St. Louis, MO); ord. priest (St. Louis*) Mar. 18, 1961; ord. titular bp. of Walla Walla and aux. bp. of St. Louis, June 29, 1989; app. bp. of Bismarck, Dec. 31, 1996.

Zubic, David A.: b. Sept. 4, 1949, Sewickley, PA; educ. St. Paul Seminary-Duquesne Univ. (Pittsburgh), St. Mary's Seminary (Baltimore), Duquesne Univ. (Pittsburgh); ord. priest (Pittsburgh) May 3, 1975; ord. titular bp. of Jamestown and aux. of Pittsburgh, Apr. 6, 1997.

Zurek, Patrick J.: b. Aug. 17, 1948, Wallis, TX; educ. Univ.of St. Thomas (Houston), Angelicum and Alphonsian Academy (Rome); ord priest (Austin) June -9, 1975; app. titular bp. of Tamugadi and aux. bp. of San Antonio, Jan. 5, 1998, ord. Feb. 16, 1998.

BISHOP-BROTHERS

(The asterisk indicates brothers who were bishops at the same time.)

There have been 10 pairs of brother-bishops in the history of the U.S. hierarchy.

Living: Francis T. Hurley,* abp. of Anchorage and Mark J. Hurley,* bp. emeritus of Santa Rosa. Raymond J. Boland,* bp. of Kansas City-St. Joseph, MO and John Kevin Boland,* bp. of Savannah.

Deceased: Francis Blanchet* of Oregon City (Portland) and Aug.in Blanchet* of Walla Walla; John S. Foley of Detroit and Thomas P. Foley of Chicago; Francis P. Kenrick,* apostolic administrator of Philadelphia, bp. of Philadelphia and Baltimore, and Peter R. Kenrick* of St. Louis; Matthias C. Lenihan of Great Falls and Thomas M. Lenihan of Cheyenne; James O'Connor, vicar apostolic of Nebraska and bp. of Omaha, and Michael O'Connor of Pittsburgh and Erie; Jeremiah F. and John W. Shanahan, both of Harrisburg; Sylvester J. Espelage, O.F.M.* of Wuchang, China, who died 10 days after the ordination of his brother, Bernard T. Espelage, O.F.M.* of Gallup; Coleman F. Carroll* of Miami and Howard Carroll* of Altoona-Johnstown.

U.S. BISHOPS OVERSEAS

Cardinal William W. Baum, major penitentiary; Cardinal Edmund C. Szoka, President, Pontifical Commission for Vatican City State; Cardinal James Francis Stafford, president of the Pontifical Council for the Laity; Abp. John P. Foley, president of Pontifical Commission for Social Communications; Abp. Ambrose de Paoli, apostolic nuncio to Japan; Abp. Charles A. Schleck, C.S.C., former adjunct secretary of the Congregation for the Evangelization of Peoples; Abp. Edward Joseph Adams, nuncio in Bangladesh; Abp. Timothy P. Broglio, apostolic nuncio to the Dominican Republic and apostolic delegate to Puerto Rico; Abp. George Riashi, B.C.O., abp. of archeparchy of Tripoli of Lebanon (Lebanon) for Greek-Catholic Melkites; Bp. James M. Harvey, prefect of the Papal Household; Bp. Michael R. Kuchmiak, exarch of apostolic exarchate of Great Britain for Ukrainian Catholics; Bp. Joseph Pelletier, M.S., bp. of Morondava, Madagascar; Bp. David Albin Zywiec, O.F.M.Cap., bp. of Bluefields, Nicaragua; Abp. John Bukovsky, S.V.D. (naturalized U.S. citizen), former papal representative to Russia. (See also Missionary Bishops.)

RETIRED/RESIGNED U.S. PRELATES

Information, as of Aug. 20, 2002, includes name of the prelate and see held at the time of retirement or resignation; abps. are indicated by an asterisk. Most of the prelates listed below resigned their sees because of age in accordance with church law. See Index: Biographies, U.S. Bishops.

Forms of address of retired residential prelates (unless they have a titular see): Abp. or Bp. Emeritus of (last see held); Former Abp. or Bp. of (last see held).

Patrick V. Ahern (New York, aux.), Juan Arzube (Los Angeles, aux.), Ernest B. Boland, O.P. (Multan, Pakistan), William D. Borders* (Baltimore), Vincent D. Breen (Metuchen), Joseph M. Breitenbeck (Grand Rapids), Edwin B. Broderick (Albany), Charles A. Buswell (Pueblo).

John Chedid (Our Lady of Lebanon), Harry A. Clinch (Monterey), John W. Comber, M.M. (Foratiano, titular see), Thomas Connolly (Baker), Ronald G. Connors, C.SS.R. (San Juan de la Maguana, Dominican Republic), Arnold R. Cotey, S.D.S. (Nachingwea, now Lindi, Tanzania), Joseph R. Crowley (Ft. Wayne-S. Bend, aux.), James J. Daly (Rockville Centre, aux.), Nicholas D'Antonio, O.F.M. (Olancho, Honduras).

Joseph A. DePalma, S.C.J. (DeAar, South Africa), Louis A. DeSimone (Philadelphia, aux.), Joseph T. Dimino* (Military Services archdiocese), George Dion, O.M.I. (titular see, Arpaia), Paul V. Donovan (Kalamazoo), Michael J. Dudick (Passaic, Byzantine rite), Paul V. Dudley (Sioux Falls), Roland Pierre DuMaine (San Jose), Dennis V. Durning, C.S.Sp. (Arusha, Tanzania), J. Lennox Federal (Salt Lake City), Joseph A. Ferrario (Honolulu), John J. Fitzpatrick (Brownsville), Marion F. Forst (Dodge City), Benedict C. Franzetta (Youngstown, aux.), Gerard L. Frey (Lafayette, LA).

Francisco Garmendia (New York, aux.), Louis E. Gelineau (Providence), Odore Gendron (Manchester), Peter L. Gerety* (Newark), John J. Glynn (Military Services Archdiocese), Rene H. Gracida (Corpus Christi), J. Richard Ham, M.M. (St. Paul and Minneapolis, aux.), Philip M. Hannan* (New Orleans), Frank J. Harrison (Syracuse), Edward D. Head (Buffalo), Joseph Hart (Cheyenne), Cardinal James A. Hickey* (Washington, D.C.).

James J. Hogan (Altoona-Johnstown), Joseph L. Hogan (Rochester), Joseph Lawson Howze (Biloxi), Edward T. Hughes (Metuchen), William A. Hughes (Covington), Raymond G. Hunthausen* (Seattle), Daniel W. Kucera, O.S.B.* (Dubuque), William F. Kupfer, M.M. (Taichung, Taiwan), George Kuzma (Van Nuys), Francis Lambert, S.M. (Port Vila, Vanuatu), W. Thomas Larkin (St. Petersburg) Raymond W. Lessard (Savannah), Martin N. Lohmuller (Philadelphia, aux.), Innocent Hilarius Lotocky, O.S.B.M. (St. Nicholas of Chicago for Ukrainians), George E. Lynch (Raleigh, aux.), Timothy J. Lyne (Chicago, aux.).

Michael F. McAuliffe (Jefferson City), Edward A. McCarthy* (Miami), James F. McCarthy (New York, aux.) John McCarthy (Austin), William J. McCormack (New York, aux.), Andrew McDonald (Little Rock), Thomas J. McDonough* (Louisville), John B. McDowell (Pittsburgh, aux.), Norman McFarland (Orange, CA), Urban McGarry, T.O.R. (Bhagalpur, India), Bernard J. McLaughlin (Buffalo, aux.), Joseph F. Maguire (Springfield, MA), Charles G. Maloney (Louisville, aux.), Thomas R. Manning, O.F.M. (Coroico, Bolivia), Paul C. Marcinkus* (titular see of Orta), Dominic Anthony Marconi (Newark, aux.), Leroy T. Matthiesen (Amarillo), Anthony F. Mestice (New York, aux.), James E. Michaels (Wheeling-Charleston, aux.), Donald W. Montrose (Stockton), Michael J. Murphy (Erie), Martin J. Neylon, S.J. (Caroline Islands), James D. Niedergeses (Nashville), Anthony J. O'Connell (Palm Beach), Arthur J. O'Neill (Rockford).

Albert H. Ottenweller (Steubenville), Walter Paska (Philadelphia, Ukrainians, aux.), John J. Paul (La Crosse), George H. Pearce, S.M.* (Suva, Fiji Islands), Edward Pevec (Cleveland, aux.), Bernard F. Popp (San Antonio, aux.), Kenneth J. Povish (Lansing), Vasile Louis Puscas (St. George's in Canton of the Romanians), Francis A. Quinn (Sacramento), John R. Quinn* (San Francisco), Joseph M. Raya* (Acre), John C. Reiss (Trenton), John R. Roach* (St. Paul and Minneapolis), Daniel Ryan (Springfield, IL).

Charles A. Salatka* (Oklahoma City), Robert F. Sanchez* (Santa Fe), Stanley G. Schlarman (Dodge City), Firmin M. Schmidt, O.F.M. Cap. (Mendi, Papua New Guinea), Mark Schmitt (Marquette), Walter J. Schoenherr (Detroit, aux.), Francis B. Schulte* (New Orleans), Nerses Mikail Setian (Armenian Exarchate), Daniel E. Sheehan* (Omaha), John R. Sheets, SJ (Fort Wayne-South Bend, aux.), Gilbert I. Sheldon (Steubenville), Patrick Sheridan (New York, aux.), John Snyder (St. Augustine), Jude Speyrer (Lake Charles), George H. Speltz (St. Cloud), Ignatius J. Strecker* (Kansas City, KS), Stephen Sulyk* (Philadelphia, Ukrainians).

Elliott Thomas (Virgin Islands), David B. Thompson (Charleston), Thomas Tschoepe (Dallas), Adrian Veigle, T.O.R. (Borba, Brazil, Prelate), John J. Ward (Los Angeles, aux.), Loras J. Watters (Winona), Rembert G. Weakland, O.S.B.* (Milwaukee), Thomas J. Welsh (Allentown), James Kendrick Williams (Lexington), Aloysius J. Wycislo (Green Bay), Francis Zayek (St. Maron of Brooklyn); G. Patrick Ziemann (Santa Rosa).

American Bishops of the Past: For *Almanac* coverage of the deceased Bishops who served in the United States, please consult the *Almanac* pages at www.CatholicAlmanac.com.

The United States Conference of Catholic Bishops

(*Courtesy USCCB*)

When the bishops merged their two national organizations into the United States Conference of Catholic Bishops (USCCB) on July 1, 2001, it marked the latest chapter in the evolution of the bishops' national structure that was established 82 years ago in the aftermath of World War I.

Like its immediate predecessors — the National Conference of Catholic Bishops (NCCB) and United States Catholic Conference (USCC) — the USCCB is an organization staffed by lay people, priests, and members of religious orders, but whose members are the bishops of the United States, and it is the bishops who direct its activities.

The concept of the bishops acting together on matters of mutual interest can be traced back to 1919 when, in their first national meeting since 1884, they agreed to meet annually and to form the National Catholic Welfare Council (NCWC) to serve as their organized voice on the national scene. The word "Council" was replaced by the word "Conference" in 1922.

In 1966, following the Second Vatican Council, NCWC was reorganized into two parallel conferences. The National Conference of Catholic Bishops — sometimes referred to as the canonical arm — would deal with matters connected to the internal life of the Church, such as liturgy and priestly life and ministry. The U.S. Catholic Conference — in effect the civil arm — would represent the bishops as they related to the "secular" world, in areas such as social concerns, education, communications, and public affairs.

During the period from 1992 to 1996, a Conference committee on mission and structure, headed by the late Cardinal Joseph L. Bernardin of Chicago, led the bishops in extensive consultation on restructuring. A primary purpose of this undertaking was to provide more of the nation's approximately 300 bishops with an opportunity to be directly involved in the work of the Conference, which operates primarily through a committee structure.

In 1997 the bishops voted to combine NCCB-USCC into one conference, to be called the U.S. Conference of Catholic Bishops. They decided that in the future only bishops would be voting members of committees, but non-bishops could serve on some committees as consultants or advisers. A new committee on statutes and bylaws, headed by Archbishop Daniel E. Pilarczyk of Cincinnati, which was formed to lead the rest of the reorganization process, completed its work last year. The new statutes and bylaws were subsequently approved by the Holy See.

It is unlikely that persons outside the Bishops' Conference will notice any immediate difference in the new structure. Many of the same concerns that motivated the Bishops in 1919 — like the welfare of immigrants, communicating through the Catholic press, and defending the legal rights of the Church — are still pressing today, as evidenced in the departments which carry out these functions, though many others have been added as well. In a May 23, 2001, letter sent to organizations which have dealings with the Conference, its General Secretary, Monsignor William P. Fay, said the renaming "will not affect any change in the activities or programs of the Conference but simply how the Conference is identified."

Mission Statement

The United States Conference of Catholic Bishops is a permanent institute composed of Catholic Bishops of the United States of America in and through which the bishops exercise in a communal or collegial manner the pastoral mission entrusted to them by the Lord Jesus of sanctification, teaching, and leadership, especially by devising forms and methods of the apostolate suitably adapted to the circumstances of the times. Such exercise is intended to offer appropriate assistance to each bishop in fulfilling his particular ministry in the local Church, to effect a commonality of ministry addressed to the people of the United States of America, and to foster and express communion with the Church in other nations within the Church universal, under the leadership of its chief pastor, the pope.

Administration

The principal officers of the conference are: Wilton D. Gregory, president; William S. Skylstad, vice president; Bishop Henry J. Mansell, treasurer; Bishop William B. Friend, secretary. General Secretary: Msgr. William Fay, Ph.D. Headquarters of the conferences are located at 3211 Fourth St. N.E., Washington, DC 20017. (202) 541-3000; www.usccb.org.

USCCB REGIONS

I. Maine, Vermont, New Hampshire, Massachusetts, Rhode Island, Connecticut. II. New York. III. New Jersey, Pennsylvania. IV. Delaware, District of Columbia, Florida, Georgia, Maryland, North Carolina, South Carolina, Virgin Islands, Virginia, West Virginia. V. Alabama, Kentucky, Louisiana, Mississippi, Tennessee. VI. Michigan, Ohio. VII. Illinois, Indiana, Wisconsin. VIII. Minnesota, North Dakota, South Dakota. IX. Iowa, Kansas, Missouri, Nebraska. X.

Arkansas, Oklahoma, Texas. XI. California, Hawaii, Nevada. XII. Idaho, Montana, Alaska, Washington, Oregon. XIII. Utah, Arizona, New Mexico, Colorado, Wyoming.

Pastoral Council

The conference, one of many similar territorial conferences envisioned in the conciliar "Decree on the Pastoral Office of Bishops in the Church" (No. 38), is "a council in which the bishops of a given nation or territory [in this case, the United States] jointly exercise their pastoral office to promote the greater good which the Church offers mankind, especially through the forms and methods of the apostolate fittingly adapted to the circumstances of the age."

Its decisions, "provided they have been approved legitimately and by the votes of at least two-thirds of the prelates who have a deliberative vote in the conference, and have been recognized by the Apostolic See, are to have juridically binding force only in those cases prescribed by the common law or determined by a special mandate of the Apostolic See, given either spontaneously or in response to a petition of the conference itself."

All bishops who serve the Church in the U.S., its territories and possessions, have membership and voting rights in the USCCB. Retired bishops cannot be elected to conference offices nor can they vote on matters which by law are binding by two-thirds of the membership. Only diocesan bishops can vote on diocesan quotas, assessments or special collections.

Officers, Committees

The conference operates through a number of bishops' committees with functions in specific areas of work and concern. Their basic assignments are to prepare materials on the basis of which the bishops, assembled as a conference, make decisions, and to put suitable action plans into effect.

The principal officers are: Bishop Wilton D. Gregory, president; Bishop William S. Skylstad, vice president; Bishop Henry J. Mansell, treasurer; Bishop William B. Friend, secretary.

These officers, with several other bishops, hold positions on executive-level committees — Executive Committee, the Committee on Budget and Finance, the Committee on Personnel, and the Committee on Priorities and Plans. They also, with other bishops, serve on the USCCB Administrative Committee.

The standing committees and their chairmen (cardinals, archbishops and bishops) are as follows (names in parentheses are chairmen-elect who will take office in November 2002):

African-American Catholics: J. Terry Steib, S.V.D. (Gordon D. Bennett)
American College, Louvain: Edward K. Braxton
Bishops' Welfare Emergency Relief: Joseph Fiorenza
Boundaries of Dioceses and Provinces: Joseph Fiorenza
Canonical Affairs: A. James Quinn (Thomas G. Doran)
Communications: Joseph A. Galante
Consecrated Life: Sean P. O'Malley, O.F.M. Cap.
Diaconate: Robert C. Morlino
Doctrine: Donald W. Trautmann

Domestic Policy: Theodore E. Cardinal McCarrick
Ecumenical and Interreligious Affairs: Tod D. Brown (Stephen E. Blaire)
Education: Donald W. Wuerl (Bernard J. Harrington)
Evangelization: Michael Warfel (Edward J. Slattery)
Hispanic Affairs: Arthur N. Tafoya (James A. Tamayo)
Home Missions: Paul A. Zipfel
International Policy: John H. Ricard
Laity: John J. McRaith (Dale J. Melczek)
Latin America: Edmond Carmody
Lay Ministry, Subcommittee: Joseph P. Delaney
Lay Ministry, Subcommittee on Youth: Kevin M. Britt
Liturgy: Francis E. Cardinal George
Marriage and Family Life: J. Kevin Boland
Migration: Thomas G. Wenski
North American College, Rome: Daniel Cronin
Pastoral Practices: James R. Hoffman
Priestly Formation: George H. Niederauer (John C. Nienstedt)
Priestly Life and Ministry: John R. Gaydos
Pro-Life Activities: Anthony J. Cardinal Bevilacqua
Relationship between Eastern and Latin Catholic Churches: Basil H. Losten (Basil Schott)
Sapientia Christiana: John P. Boles
Science and Human Values: John S. Cummins (Francis X. DiLorenzo)
Selection of Bishops: Joseph A. Fiorenza
Vocations: Kevin M. Britt
Women in Society and in the Church: Edward P. Cullen
World Missions: Gregory M. Aymond
Ad hoc committees and their chairmen are as follows:
Agricultural Issues: William Skylstad
Aid to the Church in Central and Eastern Europe: Cardinal Adam Maida
Bishops Life and Ministry: William S. Skylstad
Catechism, Oversee the Use of the: Daniel M. Buechlein, O.S.B.
Catholic Charismatic Renewal: Sam G. Jacobs
Diocesan Audits: Joseph P. Delaney
Economic Concerns of the Holy See: James P. Keleher
Forum on the Principles of Translation: Jerome G. Hanus, O.S.B.
Health Care Issues and the Church: Joseph L. Charron, C.P.P.S.
Mandatum: Daniel E. Pilarczyk
Native American Catholics: Donald E. Pelotte, S.S.S.
Nomination of Conference Officers: Jerome Hanus, O.S.B.
Review of Scripture Translations: Richard J. Sklba
Sexual Abuse: John B. McCormack
Shrines: James P. Keleher
Stewardship: Sylvester Ryan

STATE CATHOLIC CONFERENCES

These conferences are agencies of bishops and dioceses in the various states. Their general purposes are to develop and sponsor cooperative programs designed to cope with pastoral and common-welfare needs, and to represent the dioceses before governmental bodies, the public, and in private sectors. Their membership consists of representatives from the dioceses in the states — bishops, clergy and lay persons in various capacities.

The National Association of State Catholic Conference Directors maintains liaison with the general secretariat of the United States Conference of Catholic Bishops. President: Robert J. Castagna, executive director of Oregon Catholic Conference.

Alaska Catholic Conference, 225 Cordova, Anchorage, AK 99501; (907) 297-7738; contact person, Robert Flint.

Arizona Catholic Conference, 400 E. Monroe St., Phoenix, AZ 85004-2376; (602) 257-5597; Exec. Dir., Rev. Msgr. Edward J. Ryle.

California Catholic Conference, 1119 K St., 2nd Floor, Sacramento, CA 95814; (916) 443-4851; Exec. Dir., Edward Dolejsi.

Colorado Catholic Conference, 1535 Logan St., Denver, CO 80203; (303) 894-8808; Exec. Dir., James P. Tatten.

Connecticut Catholic Conference, 134 Farmington Ave., Hartford, CT 06105; (860) 524-7882; Exec. Dir., Dr. Marie T. Hilliard.

Florida Catholic Conference, 313 S.Calhoun St., Tallahassee, FL 32301; (850) 222-3803; Exec. Dir., D. Michael McCarron, Ph.D.

Georgia Catholic Conference, Office Bldg., 3200 Deans Bridge Rd., Augusta, GA 30906; (404) 798-1719; Exec. Dir., Cheatham E. Hodges, Jr.

Hawaii Catholic Conference, St. Stephen Diocesan Center, 6301 Pali Hwy., Kaneohe, HI 96744; (808) 263-8844; Exec. Dir., Errol J. Christian.

Illinois, Catholic Conference of, 65 E. Wacker Pl., Ste. 1620, Chicago, IL 60601; (312) 368-1066; 108 E. Cook, Springfield, IL 62701; (217) 528-9200; Exec. Dir., Doug Delaney.

Indiana Catholic Conference, 1400 N. Meridian St., P.O. Box 1410, Indianapolis, IN 46206; (317) 236-1455; Exec. Dir., M. Desmond Ryan, Ph.D.

Iowa Catholic Conference, 505 Fifth Ave., Suite No. 818, Des Moines, IA 50309-2393; (515) 243-6256; Exec. Dir., Dr. Thomas Feld.

Kansas Catholic Conference, 6301 Antioch, Merriam, KS 66202; (913) 722-6633; Exec. Dir., Michael P. Farmer.

Kentucky, Catholic Conference of, 1042 Burlington Lane, Frankfort, KY 40601; (502) 875-4345; Exec. Dir., Jane J. Chiles.

Louisiana Catholic Conference, 3423 Hundred Oaks Ave., Baton Rouge, LA 70808; (225) 344-7120; Exec. Dir., Kirby J. Ducote.

Maryland Catholic Conference, 188 Duke of Gloucester St., Annapolis, MD 21401; (410) 269-1155; Exec. Dir., Richard J. Dowling, Esq.

Massachusetts Catholic Conference, 150 Staniford St., West End Pl., Boston, MA 02114; (617) 367-6060; Exec. Dir., Gerald D. D'Avolio, Esq.

Michigan Catholic Conference, 505 N. Capitol Ave., Lansing, MI 48933; (517) 372-9310; President and CEO, Sr. Monica Kostielney, R.S.M.

Minnesota Catholic Conference, 475 University Ave. W., St. Paul, MN 55103; (651) 227-8777; Interim Exec. Dir., Thomas J. Pearson.

Missouri Catholic Conference, P.O. Box 1022, 600 Clark Ave., Jefferson City, MO 65102; (573) 635-7239; Exec. Dir., Lawrence A. Weber.

Montana Catholic Conference, P.O. Box 1708, Helena, MT 59624; (406) 442-5761; www.mt.net/~mcc; Exec. Dir., Sharon Hoff-Brodowy.

Nebraska Catholic Conference, 215 Centennial Mall South, Suite 410, Lincoln, NE 68508; (402) 477-7517; Exec. Dir., James R. Cunningham.

Nevada Catholic Conference, 290 South Arlington Ave., Ste. 200, Reno, NV 89501-1713; (775) 326-9416; Exec. Dir., Robert Payant.

New Jersey Catholic Conference, 211 N. Warren St., Trenton, NJ 08618; (609) 599-2110; Exec. Dir., William F. Bolan, Jr., J.D.

New York State Catholic Conference, 465 State St., Albany, NY 12203; (518) 434-6195; www.nys catholicconference.org; interim Exec. Dir., Richard E. Barnes.

North Dakota Catholic Conference, 227 West Broadway, Suite No. 2, Bismarck, ND 58501; (701) 223-2519; www.ndcatholic.org; Exec. Dir., Christopher T. Dodson.

Ohio, Catholic Conference of, 9 E. Long St., Suite 201, Columbus, OH 43215; (614) 224-7147; Exec. Dir., Timothy V. Luckhaupt.

Oregon Catholic Conference, 2838 E. Burnside, Portland, OR 97214; (503) 233-8387; General Counsel and Exec. Dir., Robert J. Castagna.

Pennsylvania Catholic Conference, 223 North St., Box 2835, Harrisburg, PA 17105; (717) 238-9613; (717) 238-9613; Exec. Dir., Robert J. O'Hara, Jr.

Texas Catholic Conference, 1625 Rutherford Lane, Bldg. D, Austin, TX 78754; (512) 339-9882; Exec. Dir., Bro. Richard Daly, C.S.C.

Washington State Catholic Conference, 508 2nd Ave. West, Seattle, WA 98119-3928; (206) 301-0556; Exec. Dir., Sr. Sharon Park, O.P.

West Virginia State Catholic Conference, P.O. Box 230, Wheeling, WV 26003; (304) 233-0880; Dir., Very Rev. John R. Gallagher.

Wisconsin Catholic Conference, 30 W. Mifflin St., Suite 302, Madison, WI 53703; (608) 257-0004; Exec. Dir., John A. Huebscher.

Background

The National Conference of Catholic Bishops (NCCB) was established by action of the U.S. hierarchy Nov. 14, 1966, as a strictly ecclesiastical body with defined juridical authority over the Church in this country. It was set up with the approval of the Holy See and in line with directives from the Second Vatican Council. Its constitution was formally ratified during the November 1967 meeting of the U.S. hierarchy. The NCCB developed from the Annual Meeting of the Bishops of the United States, whose pastoral character was originally approved by Pope Benedict XV, Apr. 10, 1919.

The USCC, as of Jan. 1, 1967, took over the general organization and operations of the former National Catholic Welfare Conference, Inc., whose origins dated back to the National Catholic War Council of 1917. The council underwent some change after World War I and was established on a permanent basis on Sept. 24, 1919, as the National Catholic Welfare Council, to serve as a central agency for organizing and coordinating the efforts of U.S. Catholics in carrying out the social mission of the Church in this country. In 1923, its name was changed to National Catholic Welfare Conference, Inc., and clarification was made of its nature as a service agency of the bishops and the Church rather than as a conference of bishops with real juridical authority in ecclesiastical affairs.

The Official Catholic Directory stated that the USCC assisted "the bishops in their service to the Church in this country by uniting the people of God where voluntary collective action on a broad interdiocesan level is needed. The USCC provided an organizational structure and the resources needed to insure coordination, cooperation, and assistance in the public, educational and social concerns of the Church at the national, regional, state and, as appropriate, diocesan levels."

CATHOLIC RELIEF SERVICES

Catholic Relief Services is the official overseas aid and development agency of U.S. Catholics; it is a separately incorporated organization of the U.S. Conference of Catholic Bishops.

CRS was founded in 1943 by the bishops of the United States to help civilians in Europe and North Africa caught in the disruption and devastation of World War II. As conditions in Europe improved in the late 1940s and early 1950s, the works conducted by CRS spread to other continents and areas — Asia, Africa and Latin America.

Although best known for its record of disaster response, compassionate aid to refugees and commitment to reconstruction and rehabilitation, CRS places primary focus on long-term development projects designed to help people to help themselves and to determine their own future. Administrative funding for CRS comes largely from the American Bishops' Overseas Appeal (ABOA). Major support is derived from private, individual donors and through a program of sacrificial giving called Operation Rice Bowl.

Kenneth F. Hackett is Executive Director. CRS headquarters are located at 209 W. Fayette St., Baltimore, MD 21201; (410) 625-2220; www.catholicrelief.org.

2002 LABOR DAY STATEMENT

On Sept. 2, 2002, Cardinal Theodore McCarrick, Archbishop of Washington and Chairman of the Domestic Policy Committee for the USCCB, issued the 2002 Labor Day Statement on behalf of the Bishops of the United States. The focus of the statement was the life and work of the famed labor priest, Msgr. George Higgins. Following are excerpts from the statement:

As we approach Labor Day 2002, we face many challenges as a nation and as a Church....

In tough times like these, we look to people of courage and candor, fidelity and wisdom. Last May, we lost just such a person in Monsignor George G. Higgins. After 62 years of service to the Church and several months of illness, he died at home in Illinois bringing to an end decades of principled service and faithful ministry to his Church and the labor movement.

For decades he was the author of our Conference's "Labor Day Statement." I am both awed and honored to continue this tradition. At a memorial service in his honor, sponsored by our Bishops Conference and the AFL-CIO, I called him a "giant," and quoted Bishop Joseph Fiorenza, the former President of the Bishops' Conference, who referred to him as "the most respected priest in America." While consistently loyal, he challenged the two institutions he cared most about — the Catholic Church and the American Labor Movement — to be faithful to their ideals and values. His work continues to be a source of wisdom and guidance for all of us, especially in these tough times.

In his priestly ministry, Msgr. Higgins built bridges between the Catholic Church and the labor movement in the United States. He developed and maintained communication between Catholics and Jews.... He shared and interpreted the words and vision of the Second Vatican Council....

Long remembered for his ministry with working men and women, Monsignor Higgins died, most fittingly, on the feast of St. Joseph the Worker. Our yearly commemoration of workers should remind us of his insistence that most people fulfill their vocation, their calling, by the work they do day in and day out.... Msgr. Higgins' life and words remind us of the connection between work and holiness, between what most people do for a living, our employment, and fulfilling God's purpose, our call to holiness....

Work has a special place in our Catholic tradition. It is much more than just a job. While it is the way most people meet their material needs and provide for their families, it is also a way to contribute to the community. As we participate in our own small way in God's continuing creation, our work promotes the common good and reflects our human dignity. For too many Americans, especially those at the bottom of the economic ladder, decent work is not available or does not meet their family's basic needs....

This is not the way it should be. Work should strengthen our family life, providing resources and respect, benefits and health care for families. Work should enhance our family, community, and spiritual lives. Work should allow a family to live in dignity. As we perform our work, our contribution to the continuation of God's creation, we need to recognize that even the simplest thing we do can be a contribution to the common good. The decisions we make at work can in small ways help shape the fabric and ethics of our society.

As we approach Labor Day, we should reflect on how we bring holiness and wholeness to the work we do. Let us remember the lessons of Msgr. George Higgins and the rich legacy he left us. Let us continue his efforts to secure a living wage and greater respect for the dignity and rights of workers. In telling the truth, in building bridges among peoples, in standing with the poor, and in solidarity with Church's teaching on the importance of the labor movement, Msgr. Higgins calls us to reform and renewal, to leadership and service.

No one can fill Monsignor Higgins' shoes, but all of us are called to carry forward his legacy by sharing and acting on the Church's teaching on work and workers' rights. This Labor Day, let us remember the work of an extraordinary priest and commit ourselves, each in our own way, to continue his mission and share his message.

Hispanic, African-American, and Native-American Catholics

HISPANIC CATHOLICS IN THE UNITED STATES

The nation's Hispanic population totaled 22.4 million in 1990, according to figures reported by the U.S. Census Bureau. It is estimated that 80 percent of the Hispanics were baptized Catholics. It is estimated that perhaps 100,000 Catholic Hispanics a year were being lost, principally to fundamentalist and pentecostal sects.

Pastoral Patterns

Pastoral ministry to Hispanics varies, depending on differences among the people and the availability of personnel to carry it out. The pattern in cities with large numbers of Spanish-speaking people is built around special and bilingual churches, centers or other agencies where pastoral and additional forms of service are provided in a manner suited to the needs, language and culture of the people. Services in some places are extensive and include legal advice, job placement, language instruction, recreational and social assistance, specialized counseling, replacement services. In many places, however, even where there are special ministries, the needs are generally greater than the means available to meet them.

Some urban dwellers have been absorbed into established parishes and routines of church life and activity. Many Spanish-speaking communities remain in need of special ministries. An itinerant form of ministry best meets the needs of the thousands of Hispanic migrant workers who follow the crops.

Pastoral ministry to Hispanics was the central concern of three national meetings, Encuentros, held in 1972, 1977 and 1985.

The third National Encuentro in 1985 produced a master pastoral plan for ministry which the National Conference of Catholic Bishops approved in 1987. Its four keys are collaborative ministry; evangelization; a missionary option regarding the poor, the marginalized, the family, women and youth; the formation of lay leadership. A National Encuentro was held in 2000.

The U.S. bishops, at their annual meeting in November 1983, approved and subsequently published a pastoral letter on Hispanic Ministry under the title, "The Hispanic Presence: Challenge and Commit-

ment." (For text, see pp. 46-49 of the 1985 *Catholic Almanac*.)

Bishops

As of Aug. 1, 2002, there were 26 (22 active) bishops of Hispanic origin in the United States; all were named since 1970 (for biographies, see Index). Twelve were heads of archdioceses or dioceses: Archbishop Patrick F. Flores (San Antonio); Bishops Raymundo J Peña (Brownsville), James A. Tamayo (Laredo), Ricardo Ramirez, C.S.B. (Las Cruces), Alvaro Corrada del Rio, S.J. (Tyler), Arthur N. Tafoya (Pueblo), Manuel D. Moreno (Tucson), Placido Rodriguez, C.M.F. (Lubbock), Gerald R. Barnes (San Bernardino), Armando Ochoa (El Paso), Carlos A. Sevilla, S.J. (Yakima), and Victor Benito Galeone (St. Augustine). Fourteen were auxiliary bishops: Gabino Zavala (Los Angeles), José H. Gomez (Denver), Gilbert Espinoza Chavez (San Diego), Joseph J. Madera (Military Services), Francisco Garmendia (New York), Agustin Roman (Miami), Rene Valero (Brooklyn), David Arias, O.A.R. (Newark), Dominick J. Lagonegro (New York), Emilio Simeon Allué (Boston), Richard J. Garcia (Sacramento), Francisco Gonzalez Valer, S.F. (Washington, D.C.), José S. Vasquez (Galveston-Houston), and Gilberto Fernandez (Miami). Resigned/retired prelates: Archbishop Robert F. Sanchez (Santa Fe), Bishop Juan Arzube (Los Angeles, auxiliary), Bishop Rene H. Gracida (Corpus Christi). Bishop Roberto O. Gonzalez, O.F.M. (Corpus Christi), was appointed archbishop of San Juan de Puerto Rico on Mar. 26, 1999, by Pope John Paul II.

Hispanic priests and nuns in the U.S. number about 1,600 and 2,000, respectively, according to an estimate made in June 1988 by Father Gary Riebe Estrella, S.V.D., director of a Hispanic vocational recruitment program.

Secretariat for Hispanic Affairs

The national secretariat was established by the U.S. Catholic Conference for service in promoting and coordinating pastoral ministry to the Spanish-speaking. Its basic orientation is toward integral evangelization, combining religious ministry with development efforts in programs geared to the culture and needs of Hispanics. Its concerns are urban and migrant Spanish-speaking people; communications and publications in line with secretariat purposes and the service of people; bilingual and bicultural religious and general education; liaison for and representation of Hispanics with church, civic and governmental agencies.

The Secretariat states that its mission is:

"To assist the Catholic Church in its efforts to serve the large Catholic Hispanic/Latino population in the United States and in the New Evangelization as we approach the Great Jubilee of the Year 2000.

To coordinate Hispanic ministry efforts in the Catholic Church through regional and diocesan offices, pastoral institutes, secular and ecclesial organizations, and apostolic movements.

To promote the implementation of the National Pastoral Plan for Hispanic Ministry, *Ecclesia in America, Many Faces in God's House: A Catholic Vision for the Third Millennium*, and other church documents, as well as the development of small ecclesial communities.

To integrate the Hispanic presence into the life of the Catholic Church and society."

The secretariat publishes a newsletter, *En Marcha*, available to interested parties.

Ronaldo M. Cruz is executive director of the national office at 3211 Fourth St. N.E., Washington, D.C. 20017; (202) 541-3000; www.usccb.org.

The secretariat works in collaboration with regional and diocesan offices and pastoral institutes throughout the country.

The Northeast Regional Office, officially the Northeast Hispanic Catholic Center, was established in 1976 under the auspices of the bishops in 12 states from Maine to Virginia. It has established the Conference of Diocesan Directors of the Hispanic Apostolate, the Association of Hispanic Deacons, a Regional Youth Task Force and a Regional Committee of Diocesan Coordinators of Religious Educators for the Hispanics. The office is the official publishing house for the Hispanic Lectionary approved by the National Conference of Catholic Bishops for the United States. The center has liturgical, evangelization and youth ministry departments and an office of cultural affairs. Mario J. Paredes is executive director. The center is located at 1011 First Ave., New York, NY 10022; (212) 751-7045.

The Southeast Regional Office serves 26 dioceses in Tennessee, North and South Carolina, Florida, Georgia, Mississippi, Alabama and Louisiana. Father Mario Vizcaino, Sch. P., is director of the region and institute. The office is located at 7700 S.W. 56 St., Miami, FL 33155; (305) 279-2333. The Southeast Pastoral Institute serves as the educational arm of the regional office by providing formation programs for the development of leadership skills focused on ministry among Hispanics, at the Miami site and in the various dioceses of the region.

In the Southwest, the Mexican American Cultural Center serves as convener of diocesan directors and representatives of Hispanic ministry in Arkansas, Oklahoma and Texas.

A regional office serving the Mountain States (Arizona, New Mexico, Utah, Colorado and Wyoming) is under the coordination of Deacon Germán Toro, 27 C St., Salt Lake City, UT 84103.

The Northwest Regional Office for Hispanic Affairs serves 11 dioceses in Alaska, Montana, Washington, Oregon and Idaho. Father Heliodoro Lucatero is president. The office is located at 2838 Burnside, Portland, OR 97214. It serves as convener for regional workshops, retreats, formation programs and social advocacy.

The National Pastoral Plan for Hispanic Ministry

The National Pastoral Plan for Hispanic Ministry was approved by the NCCB in November 1987. This plan is addressed to the entire Church in the United States. It focuses on the pastoral needs of the Hispanic Catholic, but it challenges all Catholics as members of the Body of Christ.

General Objective: To live and promote by means of a *Pastoral de Conjunto*, a model of Church that is: communitarian, evangelizing, and missionary, incarnate in the reality of the Hispanic people and open to the diversity of cultures, a promoter and example of justice ... that develops leadership through integral education ... that is leaven for the Kingdom of God in society.

Specific Dimensions: *Pastoral de Conjunto*: To develop a *Pastoral de Conjunto*, which through pastoral agents and structures, manifests communion in integration, coordination in servicing, and communication of the Church's pastoral action, in keeping with the general objective of this plan. Evangelization: To recognize, develop, accompany and support small ecclesial communities and other church groups (e.g., *Cursillos de Cristiandad, Movimiento Familiar Cristiano*, RENEW, Charismatic Movement, prayer groups, etc.) which in union with the bishop are effective instruments of evangelization for the Hispanic people. These small ecclesial communities and other groups within the parish framework promote experiences of faith and conversion, prayer life, missionary outreach and evangelization, interpersonal relations and fraternal love, and prophetic questioning and actions for justice. They are a prophetic challenge for the renewal of our Church and humanization of our society. Missionary Option: To promote faith and effective participation in Church and societal structures on the part of these priority groups (the poor, women, families, youth) so that they may be agents of their own destiny (self-determination) and capable of progressing and becoming organized. Formation: To provide leadership formation adapted to the Hispanic culture in the United States that will help people to live and promote a style of Church that will be leaven of the Kingdom of God in society.

National Hispanic Priests Association

The National Association of Hispanic Priests of the USA (ANSH - *La Asociación Nacional de Sacerdotes Hispanos*, EE. UU.) was established in September 1989 with a representation of about 2,400 Hispanic priests residing and ministering in the United States. The association came into its present form after a 20 year process of organization by different groups of Hispanic priests around the country. By 1985, the first National Convention of Hispanic Priests was organized in New York City, and in 1989 the Association was established in Miami, Florida, as a non-profit Corporation for priestly fraternity and support for Hispanic priests in the United States. Among the multiple objectives are: to help members develop their priestly identity in the United States and encourage a genuine spirituality; to provide a national forum of Hispanic priests to help solve the problems that arise in the Hispanic community; to promote vocations to the priesthood among Hispanics; to pray and ask for more Hispanic bishops in the U.S., for the growing needs of the Catholic Hispanic community; and to cooperate with the Bishops and the laity in implementing the National Pastoral Plan for Hispanic Ministry. The Association publishes a quarterly Newsletter and holds an annual national convention. The president is Rev. José H. Gomez, S.T.D. 2472 Bolsover, Suite 442, Houston, TX 77005; (713) 528-6517.

National Catholic Council for Hispanic Ministry (NCCHM)

The council is a volunteer federation of Roman Catholic organizations, agencies and movements committed to the development of Hispanics/Latinos in Church and society. It was established June 17, 1990, at a gathering at Mundelein College, Chicago; its by-laws were adopted in January 1991 at Mercy Center, Burlingame, CA. The council convokes a national gathering every three years called Raices y Alas (Roots and Wings). With funding from foundations NCCHM has designed and piloted a leadership development program that links contemporary understandings of leadership with experiences and insights from faith and Hispanic cultures. NCCHM has 53 member organizations. It publishes Puentes, a newsletter. Exec. Dir., Rosa Maria Sanchez, 2025 Chickasau Ave., Los Angeles, CA 90041; (213) 344-9153.

Mexican American Cultural Center

This national center, specializing in pastoral studies and language education, was founded in 1972 to provide programs focused on ministry among Hispanics and personnel working with Hispanics in the U.S. Courses — developed according to the see-judge-act methodology — include culture, faith development, Scripture, theology, and praxis; some are offered in Spanish, others in English. Intensive language classes are offered in Spanish, with emphasis on pastoral usage.

The center also conducts workshops for the development of leadership skills and for a better understanding of Hispanic communities. Faculty members serve as resource personnel for pastoral centers, dioceses and parishes throughout the U.S. The center offers master-degree programs in pastoral ministry in cooperation with Incarnate Word College, Boston College, the Oblate School of Theology, St. Mary's University and Loyola University, New Orleans and other educational institutions.

The center is a distribution agency for the circulation of bilingual pastoral materials in the U.S. and Latin America. Sister Maria Elena Gonzalez, R.S.M., is president of the center, which is located at 3019 W. French Place, San Antonio, TX 78228.

Institute of Hispanic Liturgy

Spanish-speaking communities in the U.S. are served by the Institute of Hispanic Liturgy, a national organization of liturgists, musicians, artists and pastoral agents, funded in part by the U.S. Bishops. The institute promotes the study of liturgical texts, art, music and popular religiosity in an effort to develop liturgical spirituality among Hispanics. It works closely with the U.S. Bishops' Committee on the Liturgy, and has published liturgical materials. Rev. Heliodoro Lucatero, is the president; Sr. Doris Mary Turek, S.S.N.D., is executive director. Address: P.O. Box 29387, Washington, D.C. 20017; (202) 319-6450.

Statistics

(Courtesy, Secretariat for Hispanic Affairs, USCCB.)

The official 1990 Census estimates a population of nearly 23 million Hispanics, or about 12 percent of the total population. The nation's Hispanic population (not including Puerto Rico) totaled 27 million in 1994, an increase of 28 percent since 1990. The total U.S. population grew at a much slower rate, increasing by only 6 percent during the 4-year period. As a result, about 1 in 10 Americans today are Hispanic.

Four states had over a million Hispanic residents in 1990: California, 7.7 million; Texas, 4.3 million; New York, 2.2 million; and Florida, 1.6 million. The ten cities with the largest Hispanic populations are: New York, Los Angeles, Chicago, San Antonio, Houston, El Paso, San Diego, Miami, Dallas, and San Jose.

Approximately one half of the Hispanic population lived in just two states: California and Texas. In three states, Hispanics made up one-fourth or more of the state's total population: New Mexico, 38 percent; and California and Texas, each 26 percent.

Current U.S. Census figures reveal a Hispanic growth rate that is five times that of non-Hispanics. While the non-Hispanic population showed a growth rate of 8 percent since 1980, Hispanics demonstrated a growth rate of 39 percent. New York City had the largest Hispanic population of any city in 1990, with 1.8 million Hispanic residents. The other city with more than a million Hispanics was Los Angeles.

Hispanics comprised 11.4 of the population in the year 2000; they will be 13.8 percent in 2010; and 24 percent in the year 2050.

Data demonstrate that the Hispanic population in the United States is young. Approximately 50 percent is under the age of 26 years. Of this number, approximately 20 percent are under five years of age. Only four percent of Hispanics are over the age of 65 years.

The higher birth rate has resulted in an increase in the proportion of the nation's children. In Los Angeles, over 50 percent of the births in 1992 were to Hispanics. The poverty rate in the general population went up from 12.4 percent in 1979 to 13.1 percent in 1989, while the number of persons in poverty rose from 27.4 million in 1979 to 31.7 million in 1989. In the Hispanic community the poverty rate is at 25.3 percent, or approximately 5.4 million people.

Based on the 1990 Census's "Comparison of Principal Fertility, Mortality, and New Immigration Assumption" and based on new legislation and the impact IRCA will have on the continued flow of immigrants, the following projections have been made regarding the Hispanics population:

By the second decade of the next century, the Church in the United States will very likely be comprised by a population that is over 50 percent Hispanic.

Hispanics were projected to be 33 percent of the population growth of the United States by the year 2000, 37 percent by the year 2010, 42 percent between the years 2010 and 2030, and over 50 percent between the years 2030 and 2050.

Although three-quarters of the population was non-Hispanic white in 1992, this group will contribute only 30 percent of the total population growth between 1992 and 2000, 21 percent from 2000 to 2010, and 13 percent from 2010 to 2030. This group will contribute nothing to population growth after 2030 because the non-Hispanic group would be declining in size. The population increase in the United States by the total white population after 2029 will be entirely due to growth in the number of white Hispanics.

AFRICAN-AMERICAN CATHOLICS IN THE UNITED STATES

Secretariat for African American Catholics

(*Courtesy, Secretariat for African American Catholics, USCCB.*)

The Secretariat for African American Catholics is the officially recognized voice of the African American Catholic community as it articulates the needs and aspirations regarding ministry, evangelization, social justice issues, and worship.

The USCCB *Secretariat for African American Catholics* supports the Bishops' Committee for African American Catholics through identification and communication of the socio-cultural dimension of the African American Community. The vastness of this dimension encompasses historical, social and cultural elements at work within African American communities. The Secretariat's role is consultative. It is often the voice of conscience, as we, a people of faith, grow toward a truly universal church.

The Secretariat for African American Catholics serves as the chief advisor to the National Conference of Catholic Bishops and the United States Catholic Conference in fulfilling its ministry to African American Catholics in the United States. The Secretariat has as its function the coordination of responses regarding ministry, evangelization, and worship in the African American Community on the national level. The work of the Secretariat is guided by the Bishop's Committee on African American Catholics whose primary mission is to encourage the development and assist in the implementation of pastoral programs in relation to evangelization and incorporation into the local church of racial, ethnic, cultural and language groups within the National Conference of Catholic Bishops.

It also serves as a liaison to the National Black Catholic Clergy Caucus, the National Black Catholic Seminarians Association, the National Black Sisters' Conference, National Black Catholic Administrators, Knights of St. Peter Claver and Ladies Auxiliary, the National Black Catholic Congress, and the National Black Catholic Theological Society. The Secretariat for African American Catholics is under the executive direction of Beverly Carroll. The committee and secretariat have offices at 3211 Fourth St. N.E., Washington, D.C. 20017; (202) 541-3000; www. usccb.org/saac.

USCCB Committee

The Committee on African American Catholics, established by the National Conference of Catholic Bishops in 1987, is chaired by Bishop George V. Murry, S.J., auxiliary of Chicago. The purpose of the committee is to assist the bishops in their evangelization efforts to the African American community by initiating, encouraging and supporting programs which recognize and respect African American genius and values. Priorities of the Committee include implementation of the National Black Catholic Pastoral Plan of 1987, inculturation of liturgy and ministry, and increasing lay leadership and vocations.

The Secretariat for African American Catholics was established as a service agency to the committee.

National Office for Black Catholics

The National Office for Black Catholics, organized in July 1970 is a central agency with the general purposes of promoting active and full participation by black Catholics in the Church and of making more effective the presence and ministry of the Church in the black community.

Its operations are in support of the aspirations and calls of black Catholics for a number of objectives, including the following:

• representation and voice for blacks among bishops and others with leadership and decision-making positions in the Church

• promoting vocations to the priesthood and religious life

• sponsoring programs of evangelization, pastoral ministry, education and liturgy on a national level

• recognition of the black heritage in liturgy, community life, theology and education.

Walter T. Hubbard is executive director of NOBC. The NOBC office is located at 3025 Fourth St. N.E., Washington, D.C. 20017; (202) 635-1778.

National Black Catholic Clergy Caucus

The National Black Catholic Clergy Caucus, founded in 1968 in Detroit, is a fraternity of several hundred black priests, permanent deacons and brothers pledged to mutual support in their vocations and ministries.

The Caucus develops programs of spiritual, theological, educational and ministerial growth for its members, to counteract the effects of institutionalized racism within the Church and American society. A bimonthly newsletter is published. The NBCCC office is located at 321 N. Walnut St., P.O. Box 1088, Opelousas, LA 70571; (318) 942-2392. Other peer and support groups are the National Black Sisters' Conference and the National Black Catholic Seminarians Association.

National Black Catholic Congress

The National Black Catholic Congress, Inc., was formed in 1985 exclusively to assist in the development of the Roman Catholic Church in the African American community and to devise effective means of evangelization of African American peoples in the United States. Its fundamental purpose is the formation and development of concrete approaches toward the evangelization of African Americans through revitalization of African American Catholic life.

The Congress is under the sponsorship of the African American Roman Catholic bishops of the United States, the National Black Catholic Clergy Caucus, the National Black Sisters' Conference, the National Association of Black Catholic Administrators and the Knights of Peter Claver and the Ladies Auxiliary Knights of Peter Claver. The Congress is also in consultation with African American clergy and vowed religious women communities. The Congress sponsors "Pastoring in African American Parishes," an annual workshop first held in 1988 and an African American Catholic Ministries Program, a week-long curriculum presented twice a year, usually in January and June.

The National Black Catholic Congress sponsored the seventh assembly of African-American Catholics and those serving in African American communities, July 9 to 12, 1992, in New Orleans. The most recent National Congress convened in Baltimore, Aug. 27 to 31, 1997. The Congress is sponsoring construction of "Our Mother of Africa Chapel" at the Basilica of the National Shrine of the Immaculate Conception in Washington, D.C. The office of the Congress is located at the Archdiocese of Baltimore Catholic Center, 309 Cathedral St., 3rd Floor, Baltimore, MD 21201; the executive director is Dr. Hilbert D. Stanley; (410) 547-8496; www.nbccongress.org

Josephite Pastoral Center

The Josephite Pastoral Center was established in September 1968 as an educational and pastoral service agency for the Josephites in their mission work, specifically in the black community, subsequently to all those who minister in the African-American community. St. Joseph's Society of the Sacred Heart, the sponsoring body, has about 134 priests and 11 brothers in 64 mostly southern parishes in 17 dioceses. The staff of the center includes Father John G. Harfmann, S.S.J., director, and Maria M. Lannon, administrator. Address: Josephite Pastoral Center 1200 Varnum St. N.E., Washington, D.C. 20017; (202) 526-9270.

African-American Evangelization

The National Black Catholic Pastoral Plan adopted by the National Black Catholic Congress in May 1987 was approved and recommended for implementation by the National Conference of Catholic Bishops in November 1989.

Following is an account of several points in the bishops' statement, based on coverage by the CNS Documentary Service, *Origins*, Dec. 28, 1989 (Vol. 19, No. 30).

"Evangelization," wrote the bishops, "would not be complete if it did not take account of the unceasing interplay of the Gospel and of man's concrete life, both personal and social. Evangelization involves an explicit message, adapted to the different situations constantly being realized, about the rights and duties of every human being, about family life, without which personal growth and development are hardly possible, about life in society, about international life, peace, justice and development — a message especially energetic today about liberation."

Three Areas

The pastoral plan "embraces three broad areas: 1) the Catholic identity of African-American Catholics; 2) ministry and leadership within the African-American community; and 3) the responsibility of this community to reach out to the broader society. Within these areas are such issues as culture, family, youth, spirituality, liturgy, ministry, lay leadership, parishes, education, social action and community development."

Reflecting a recommendation of the pastoral plan, the bishops encourage African-American Catholics to "discover their past" since "the possession of one's history is the first step in an appreciation of one's culture."

Bishops

There were 13 (11 active) black bishops as of Sept. 1, 2002. Six were heads of dioceses: Bishops Wilton D. Gregory (Belleville, President of the USCCB), Curtis J. Guillory, S.V.D. (Beaumont), George V. Murry, S.J. (St. Thomas, Virgin Islands), John H. Ricard, S.S.J. (Pensacola-Tallahassee), Edward K. Braxton (Lake Charles), J. Terry Steib, S.V.D. (Memphis). Five were auxiliary bishops: Moses Anderson, S.S.E. (Detroit), Gordon D. Bennett, S.J. (Baltimore), Dominic Carmon, S.V.D. (New Orleans), Leonard J. Olivier, S.V.D. (Washington), Joseph N. Perry (Chicago). Elliott G. Thomas, of St. Thomas, Virgin Islands, resigned June 30, 1999, and Joseph L. Howze, of Biloxi, resigned May 15, 2001. Bishop Wilton Gregory was elected President of the USCCB in November 2001.

African-American Bishops of the Past: James August Healy (1830-1900); Joseph A. Francis, S.V.D. (1923-1997); Eugene A. Marino, S.S.J. (1934-2000); Raymond Rodly Caeser, S.V.D. (1932-1987); James Lyke, O.F.M. (1939-1992); Carl A. Fisher, S.S.J. (1945-1993); Emerson J. Moore (1938-1995); Harold R. Perry, S.V.D. (1916-1991).

Statistics

The Secretariat for African American Catholics reports that there are presently approximately 2.3 million African American Catholics in the United States. They are served by 1,300 parishes and 75 African American pastors. There are approximately 250 African American priests, 300 African American sisters, and 380 African American deacons.

NATIVE-AMERICAN CATHOLICS IN THE UNITED STATES

The Kateri Tekakwitha Conference is so named in honor of Blessed Kateri Tekakwitha, "Lily of the Mohawks," who was born in 1656 at Ossernenon (Auriesville), NY, in 1656, baptized in 1676, lived near Montreal, died in 1680, and was beatified in 1980.

The conference was established in 1939 as a missionary-priest advisory group in the Diocese of Fargo. It was a missionary-priest support group from 1946 to 1977. Since 1977 it has been a gathering of Catholic Native peoples and the men and women — clerical, religious and lay persons — who minister to Native Catholic communities.

The primary focus of conference concern and activity is evangelization, with specific emphasis on development of Native ministry and leadership. Other priorities include catechesis, liturgy, family life, social justice ministry, chemical dependency, youth ministry, spirituality and Native Catholic dialogue. Conferences and local Kateri Circles serve as occasions for the exchange of ideas, prayer and mutual support. Since 1980, the national center has promoted and registered 130 Kateri Circles in the U.S. and Canada. Publications include a quarterly newsletter.

The conference has a board of 12 directors, the majority of whom are Native people. Archbishop Charles Chaput, O.F.M. Cap., is the episcopal moderator. Address: Tekakwitha Conference National Center,

P.O. Box 6768, Great Falls, MT 59406; (406) 727-0147.

STATISTICS

According to 1999 estimates from the Population Estimate Program of the U.S. Census Bureau, there are approximately 2,026,000 Native American, Eskimo, Aleuts, non-Hispanic people in the United States, making up 0.7 percent of the U.S. population. It is estimated by the Bureau of Catholic Indian Missions that of the Native Americans in the United States approximately one quarter are baptized Catholics. It is expected that these numbers will change with the 2000 census.

MISSIONARY ACTIVITY OF THE U.S. CHURCH

OVERSEAS MISSIONS

Sources: U.S. Catholic Mission Handbook 2000: Mission Inventory 1998-1999 *(the most recent issue), reproduced with permission of the United States Catholic Mission Council, 3029 Fourth St. N.E., Washington, DC.*

Field Distribution, 1998-1999

Africa: 714 (395 men; 319 women). Largest numbers in Kenya, 172; Tanzania, 105; Ghana, 72; Nigeria, 56; Zambia, 53; South Africa, 42.

Asia: 837 (580 men; 257 women). Largest numbers in Philippines, 193; Japan, 169; Taiwan, 107; China PRC-Hong Kong SAR, 85; India, 68; Korea, 58. (Those present in China were there for professional services.)

Caribbean: 368 (198 men; 170 women). Largest numbers in Puerto Rico, 110; Belize, 55; Haiti, 49; Jamaica, 47; Dominican Republic 38.

Eurasia (Kazakhstan, Russia, Siberia): 17 (13 men; 4 women). Largest group, Russia, 15.

Europe: 158 (78 men; 80 women). Largest numbers in Italy, 43; Ireland, 19; England, 16; France, 11.

Latin America: 1,423 (739 men; 684 women). Largest numbers in Peru, 267; Brazil, 241; Mexico, 224; Guatemala, 146; Bolivia, 131.

Middle East: 55 (41 men; 14 women). Largest numbers in Israel, 25; Sudan, 12.

North America (Canada and United States): 2109 (527 men; 1582 women). Largest number in the United States, 2040.

Oceania: 202 (136 men; 66 women). Largest numbers in Papua New Guinea,79; Micronesia, 44; Australia, 18; Guam, 14; Marshall Island, 14.

TOTAL: 5,883 (2,707 men; 3,176 women).

Missionary Personnel, 1998-1999

Bishops: See below.

Religious Priests: 67 mission-sending groups had 1,875 priests in overseas assignments. Listed below are those with 15 or more members abroad.

Jesuits, 375; Maryknoll Fathers and Brothers, 286; Franciscans (O.F.M.), 137; Redemptorists, 119; Society of Divine Word, 108; Oblates of Mary Immaculate, 86; Franciscans (O.F.M. Cap), 67; Holy Cross Fathers, 45; Columbans, 41; Vincentians, 37; Dominicans, 36; Passionists, 23; Franciscans (O.F.M. Conv.), 20; Comboni Missionaries, 20; Congregation of Sacred Heart, 17; Spiritans, 17; Marianists, 16; Xaverian Missionaries, 16; Benedictines-Cassinese Cong., 16;

Legionaries of Christ, 15; Salesians, 15; Oblates of St. Francis de Sales, 15.

Diocesan Priests: There were 166 priests from 68 dioceses The majority were in Latin American countries.

Religious Brothers: 45 mission-sending groups had 370 brothers in overseas assignments. Those with 15 or more members:

Christian Brothers (Brothers of the Christian Schools), 91; Marianists, 36; Holy Cross Brothers, 35; Franciscans (O.F.M.), 26; Maryknoll Priests and Brothers, 24; Jesuits, 16.

Religious Sisters: 189 mission-sending communities of women Religious had 2,693 sisters in overseas missions. Those with 15 or more members:

Maryknoll Mission Sisters, 319; School Sisters of Notre Dame,198; Blessed Sacrament Sisters, 111; Dominicans, 94; Missionaries of Charity, 75; Sisters of Mercy (various communities), 70; Sisters of Notre Dame de Namur, 64; Congregation of Sisters of St. Agnes, 62; Medical Mission Sisters, 61; Society of the Sacred Heart, 55; Presentation Sisters, 45; St. Joseph Sisters, 45; Marist Missionary Sisters, 44; Benedictine Sisters, 42; Holy Cross, Cong. Of Sisters, 38; Daughters of Charity, 36; Sisters of St. Joseph of Carondelet, 35; Cong. of St. Joseph, 29; Medical Missionaries of Mary, 28; Charity Sisters, 28; Franciscan Sisters of Atonement, 28; Sacred Heart of Jesus Sisters, 27; Franciscan Sisters of Charity, 25; School Sisters of St. Francis, 25; Franciscan Sisters of Philadelphia, 23; Bernardine Franciscan Sisters, 23; Missionary Sisters of Our Lady of Africa, 23; Mission Sisters of the Immaculate Heart of Mary, 23; Sisters of St. Mary of Namur, 19; Little Sisters of the Poor, 18; Daughters of the Holy Spirit, 18; Mission Sisters of the Immaculate Conception, 18; Ursulines, 17; Franciscan Sisters of Little Falls, 17; Missionary Benedictine Sisters, 16; Immaculate Heart of Mary Sisters of Monroe, 16.

Lay Persons: 79 mission sending groups had 739 members in overseas missions. Those with 15 or more members:

Maryknoll Mission Associates, 118; Jesuit Volunteers International, 63; Mercy Corps, 38; Jesuit Volunteer Corps, 35; Vincentian Service Corps, 27; Salesian Lay Missionaries, 21; Franciscan Volunteer Ministry, 16.

Seminarians: There were 11 from 6 groups.

Legionaries of Christ, 3; Society of Our Lady of the Most Holy Trinity, 1; Holy Cross Fathers, 2; Jesuits,

3; Annunciation House, 1; Glenmary Home Missioners, 1.

MISSIONARY BISHOPS
Africa
South Africa: Keimoes-Upington (diocese), John B. Minder, O.S.F.S.; De Aar (diocese), Joseph J. Potocnak, S.C.J.

Zambia: Mongu (diocese), Paul Duffy, O.M.I.
Asia
Indonesia: Agats (diocese), Alphonse A. Sowada, O.S.C.

Iraq: Mossul (Chaldean-rite archdiocese), George Garmo.

Kazakstan: Almaty (apostolic admin.), Henry Howaniec, O.F.M.

Korea: Inchon (diocese), William J. McNaughton, M.M.

Philippines: Cotabato (archdiocese), Philip F. Smith, O.M.I. (emeritus; resigned, May 30, 1998).
Central America, West Indies
Honduras: Comayagua (diocese), Gerald Scarpone Caporale, O.F.M.

Jamaica: Mandeville (diocese), Paul M. Boyle, C.P.

Nicaragua: Bluefields (vicariate apostolic), Bp. David Albin Zywiec, O.F.M.Cap.

Trinidad and Tobago: Port of Spain (archdiocese), Edward J. Gilbert, C.SS.R.

Virgin Islands: St. Thomas (diocese), Elliott G. Thomas, bishop, 1993.
North America
Bermuda: Hamilton (diocese), Robert Kurtz, C.R.

Mexico: Nuevo Laredo (diocese), Ricardo Watty Urquidi, M.Sp.S., first bishop.
Oceania
American Samoa: Samoa-Pago Pago (diocese), John Quinn Weitzel, M.M.

Papua New Guinea: Mendi (diocese), Stephen J. Reichert, O.F.M.Cap.; Wewak (diocese), Raymond P. Kalisz, S.V.D.

Solomon Islands: Gizo (diocese), Christopher Cardone, O.P., aux. bp
South America
Bolivia: Pando (vicariate apostolic), Luis Morgan Casey.

Brazil: Cristalandia (prelacy), Herbert Hermes, O.S.B.; Jatai (diocese), Benedito Domingos Coscia, O.F.M.; Itaituba (prelacy), Capistran Heim, O.F.M.; Jataí (diocese), Miguel P. Mundo aux. bishop; Miracema do Tocantins (diocese), John J. Burke, O.F.M.; Paranagua (diocese), Alfred Novak, C.Ss.R.; Valença (diocese), Elias James Manning, O.F.M. Conv.

Peru: Chulucanas (diocese), John C. McNabb, O.S.A.; Daniel Thomas Turley Murphy, O.S.A., coadjutor.

U.S. CATHOLIC MISSION ASSOCIATION

This is a voluntary association of individuals and organizations for whom the missionary presence of the universal Church is of central importance. It is a nonprofit religious, educational and charitable organization which exists to promote global missions. Its primary emphasis is on cross-cultural evangelization and the promotion of international justice and peace. The association is also responsible for gathering and publishing annual statistical data on U.S. missionary personnel overseas. President: William J. Morton, S.S.C.; Executive Director, Sister Rosanne Rustemeyer, S.S.N.D. Address: 3029 Fourth St. NE, Washington, DC 20017; (202) 832-3112; www.uscatholic mission.org

Mission Statement
In its 1996-97 handbook, the association included the following in a mission statement.

"In the Church, our understanding of the mission of evangelization is evolving to embrace dialogue, community building, struggles for justice, efforts to model justice and faith in our lifestyles, activities and structures, in addition to the teaching/preaching/witnessing role traditionally at the heart of the mission enterprise. Still, the contemporary 'identity-confusion' about 'mission' stands forth as a major challenge for USCMA as we move toward the 21st century.

"The larger context of mission is the Spirit moving in the Signs of our Times: the liberation movements, the women's movements, the economy movements, the rising awareness and celebration of cultural diversity, the search for ways to live peacefully and creatively with great pluralism, rapid technological change, the emergence of the global economy, the steady increase in poverty and injustice, the realign-ing of the global political order - and the many ripples radiating out from each of these."

Home Missions
The expression "home missions" is applied to places in the U.S. where the local church does not have its own resources, human and otherwise, which are needed to begin or, if begun, to survive and grow. These areas share the name "missions" with their counterparts in foreign lands because they too need outside help to provide the personnel and means for making the Church present and active there in carrying out its mission for the salvation of people.

Dioceses in the Southeast, the Southwest, and the far West are most urgently in need of outside help to carry on the work of the Church. Millions of persons live in counties in which there are no resident priests. Many others live in rural areas beyond the reach and influence of a Catholic center. According to recent statistics compiled by the Glenmary Research Center, there are more than 500 priestless counties in the United States.

Mission Workers
A number of forces are at work to meet the pastoral needs of these missionary areas and to establish permanent churches and operating institutions where they are required. In many dioceses, one or more missions and stations are attended from established parishes and are gradually growing to independent status. Priests, brothers and sisters belonging to scores of religious institutes are engaged full-time in the home missions. Lay persons, some of them in affiliation with special groups and movements, are also involved.

The Society for the Propagation of the Faith, which conducts an annual collection for mission support in all parishes of the U.S., allocates 40 per cent of this sum for disbursement to home missions through the American Board of Catholic Missions.

Various mission-aid societies frequently undertake projects on behalf of the home missions.

The Glenmary Home Missioners, founded by Father W. Howard Bishop in 1939, is the only home mission society established for the sole purpose of carrying out the pastoral ministry in small towns and rural districts of the United States. Glenmary serves in many areas where at least 20 per cent of the people live in poverty and less than one per cent are Catholic. With 61 priests and 19 professed brothers as of January 1998 the Glenmary Missioners had missions in the archdioceses of Atlanta and Cincinnati, and in the dioceses of Birmingham, Charlotte, Covington, Jackson, Lexington, Little Rock, Nashville, Owensboro, Richmond, Savannah, Tulsa, Tyler and Wheeling-Charleston. National headquarters are located at 4119 Glenmary Trace, Fairfield, Ohio. The mailing address is P.O. Box 465618, Cincinnati, Ohio 45246; (513) 874-8900.

Organizations

Black and Indian Mission Office (The Commission for Catholic Missions among the Colored People and the Indians): Organized officially in 1885 by decree of the Third Plenary Council of Baltimore. Provides financial support for religious works among Blacks and Native Americans in 133 archdioceses and dioceses through funds raised by an annual collection in all parishes of the U.S. on the first Sunday of Lent, the designated Sunday. In 2001, $8,707,657 was raised; disbursements amounted to $8,584,000 for Black missions and for Native American evangelization programs.

Bureau of Catholic Indian Missions (1874): Established as the representative of Catholic Indian missions before the federal government and the public; made permanent organization in 1884 by Third Plenary Council of Baltimore. After a remarkable history of rendering important services to the Indian people, the bureau continues to represent the Catholic Church in the U.S. in her apostolate to the American Indian. Concerns are evangelization, catechesis, liturgy, family life, education, advocacy. Address: 2021 H Street NW, Washington, DC 20006-4207; (202) 331-8542.

Catholic Negro-American Mission Board (1907): Supports priests and sisters in southern states and provides monthly support to sisters and lay teachers in the poorest Black schools.

Board of Directors of the three organizations above are: Cardinal Anthony Bevilacqua, president; Cardinal William Keeler; Msgr. Paul A. Lenz, secretary-treasurer; Patricia L. O'Rourke, D.St.G.G., assistant secretary/treasurer. Address: 2021 H Street NW, Washington, DC 20006-4207; (202) 331-8542.

The Catholic Church Extension Society (1905): Established with papal approval for the purpose of preserving and extending the Church in rural and isolated parts of the U.S. and its dependencies through the collection and disbursement of funds for home mission work. Since the time of its founding, more than $300 million has been received and distributed for this purpose. Works of the society are supervised by a 14-member board of governors: Cardinal Francis George of Chicago, chancellor; Rev. Msgr. Kenneth Velo, president; three archbishops, three bishops and six lay people. Headquarters: 150 S. Wacker Drive, 20th Floor, Chicago, IL 60601; (312) 236-7240.

National Catholic Rural Life Conference: Founded in 1923 through the efforts of Bishop Edwin V. O'Hara. Applies the Gospel message to rural issues through focus on rural parishes and the provision of services including distribution of educational materials development of prayer and worship resources, advocacy for strong rural communities. Bishop Raymond L. Burke of LaCrosse, president; Brother David G. Andrews C.S.C., exec. dir. National headquarters: 4625 Beaver Ave., Des Moines, IA 50310; (515) 270-2634; www.ncrle.com.

U.S. Catholic Statistics

U.S. STATISTICAL SUMMARY

(*Principal sources:* The Official Catholic Directory, 2002; *Bill Ryan, USCCB Dept. of Communications. Comparisons, where given, are with figures reported in the previous edition of the* Directory. *Totals below do not include statistics for outlying areas of the U.S. These are given in tables on the preceding pages and elsewhere in the* Catholic Almanac; *see **Index**.*)

Catholic Population: 65,270,444; increase, 1,581,414. Percent of total population: 22.9%.

Jurisdictions: 34 archdioceses (includes 33 metropolitan sees and the Military Archdiocese), 152 dioceses (includes St. Thomas, Virgin Islands, and the eparchy of Our Lady of Deliverance of Newark for Syrians of the U.S. and Canada), 1 apostolic exarchate (New York-based Armenian exarchate for U.S. and Canada). The current number of dioceses reflects the creation on July 3, 2000, of the new diocese of Laredo. There are also the eparchies of St. Maron and Our Lady of Lebanon of Los Angeles (Maronites), Newton (Melkites), St. Thomas Apostle of Detroit (Chaldeans), St. George Martyr of Canton, Ohio (Romanians), St. Thomas of Chicago (Syro-Malabars) which was created on March 13, 2001 and the Eparchy of St. Peter the Apostle of San Diego which was created on May 21, 2002. The eparchy of Our Lady of Deliverance of Newark, N.J. has its seat in Newark, N.J. The Armenian apostolic exarchate for the United States and Canada has its seat in New York. Vacant jurisdictions (as of Aug. 15, 2002): Knoxville, Palm Beach, St. Nicholas of Chicago.

Cardinals: 14 (8 head archiepiscopal sees in U.S.; 2 are Roman Curia officials; three are retired, including Puerto Rico; one is a theologian). As of July 10, 2002.

Archbishops: 47. Diocesan, in U.S., 27 (does not include cardinals); retired, 18; there are also 2 archbishops serving outside U.S. (As of Aug. 24, 2002.)

Bishops: 377. Heads of Dioceses in U.S. and VirginIslands: 160; auxiliaries: 90; coadjutors: 3; retired 103; serving outside the U.S.: 21. (As of Aug. 24, 2002.)

Priests: 45,673; decrease, 368. Diocesan, 30,429 (decrease, 226); religious order priests (does not include those assigned overseas), 15,244 (decrease, 142). There were 479 newly ordained priests, a decrease of 57.

Permanent Deacons: 13,764; increase, 416.

Brothers: 5,690; increase, 125.

Sisters: 75,500; decrease, 3,962.

Seminarians: 4,719. Diocesan seminarians, 3,359; religious order seminarians, 1,360.

Receptions into Church: 1,168,848. Includes 1,007,716 infant baptisms; 79,892 adult baptisms and 81,240 already baptized persons received into full communion with the Church.

First Communions: 892,532.

Confirmations: 628,141.

Marriages: 256,563.

Deaths: 572,795.

Parishes: 19,496.

Seminaries, Diocesan: 78.

Religious Seminaries: 122.

Colleges and Universities: 238. Students, 724,065.

High Schools: 1,343. Students, 691,456.

Elementary Schools: 6,949. Students, 2,005,573.

Non-Residential Schools for Handicapped: 82. Students, 18,696.

Teachers: 176,088 (priests, 1,899; brothers, 1,194; scholastics, 58; sisters, 8,233; laity, 164,704).

Public School Students in Religious Instruction Programs: 4,314,232. High school students, 766,754; elementary school students, 3,547,478.

Hospitals: 597; patients treated, 82,395,935.

Health Care Centers: 483; patients treated, 5,811,381.

Specialized Homes: 1,431; patients assisted, 1,166,984.

Residential Care of Children (Orphanages): 176; children assisted, 94,101.

Day Care and Extended Day Care Centers: 1,077; children assisted, 111,186.

Special Centers for Social Services: 2,450; assisted annually, 23,541,687.

PERCENTAGE OF CATHOLICS IN TOTAL POPULATION IN U.S.

(*Source:* The Official Catholic Directory, 2002; *figures are as of Jan. 1, 2002. Total general population figures at the end of the table are U.S. Census Bureau estimates for Jan. 1 of the respective years. Archdioceses are indicated by an asterisk; for dioceses marked +, see Dioceses with Interstate Lines.*)

State Diocese	Catholic Pop.	Total Pop.	Cath. Pct.
Alabama	**157,402**	**4,447,080**	**3.5**
*Mobile	65,480	1,640,683	3.9
Birmingham	91,922	2,806,397	3.2
Alaska	**54,2686**	**24,478**	**8.6**
*Anchorage	31,112	395,951	7.8
Fairbanks	17,700	155,225	11.0
Juneau	5,456	73,302	7.4
Arizona	**808,780**	**5,104,501**	**15.8**
Phoenix	478,163	3,651,780	13.0
Tucson	330,617	1,452,721	22.7
Arkansas			
Little Rock	100,820	2,673,400	3.7
California	**10,110,452**	**34,225,970**	**29.5**
*Los Angeles	4,197,635	10,985,200	38.2
*San Francisco	425,210	1,744,050	24.3
Fresno	338,040	2,404,750	14.0
Monterey	315,902	957,279	32.9
Oakland	428,466	2,392,557	17.9
Orange	1,110,508	2,846,289	39.0
Sacramento	500,097	3,125,610	15.9
San Bernardino	943,898	3,254,821	28.9
San Diego	901,172	2,956,195	28.9
San Jose	584,000	1,682,585	34.7
Santa Rosa	148,605	753,893	19.7
Stockton	216,919	1,122,741	19.3
Colorado	**604,667**	**4,293,890**	**14.0**
*Denver	376,514	2,907,890	12.9
Colorado Springs	120,000	785,000	15.3
Pueblo	108,153	601,000	17.9
Connecticut	**1,309,871**	**3,405,565**	**38.4**
*Hartford	719,953	1,863,384	38.6
Bridgeport	362,569	882,567	41.0
Norwich+	227,349	659,614	34.4
Delaware			
Wilmington	215,000	1,179,504	18.2
District of Columbia			
*Washington+	551,436	2,528,235	21.8
Florida	**2,214,107**	**16,043,542**	**13.8**
*Miami	830,366	3,955,969	20.9
Orlando	353,342	3,360,319	10.5
Palm Beach	246,040	1,599,467	15.3
Pensacola-Tallahassee	56,939	1,274,000	4.4
St. Augustine	143,413	1,674,910	8.5
St. Petersburg	384,259	2,561,727	14.9
Venice	199,748	1,617,150	12.3
Georgia	**394,933**	**8,150,497**	**4.8**
*Atlanta	321,978	5,300,000	6.0
Savannah	72,955	2,850,497	2.5
Hawaii			
Honolulu	145,453	1,211,537	12.0
Idaho			
Boise	130,750	1,213,362	10.7
Illinois	**3,839,333**	**12,413,690**	**30.9**
*Chicago	2,442,000	6,052,000	40.3
Belleville	104,022	845,906	12.2
Joliet	609,252	1,647,914	36.9
Peoria	151,413	1,452,688	10.4
Rockford	375,185	1,309,058	28.6
Illinois, cont.			
Springfield	157,461	1,106,124	14.2
Indiana	**776,441**	**6,042,007**	**12.8**
*Indianapolis	233,171	2,430,606	9.5
Evansville	89,087	491,121	18.1
Ft.Wayne-S.Bend	170,290	1,178,520	14.4
Gary	187,000	765,024	24.4
Lafayette	96,893	1,176,736	8.2
Iowa	**519,916**	**2,794,849**	**18.6**
*Dubuque	213,555	927,161	23.0
Davenport	112,156	728,048	15.4
Des Moines	97,306	671,091	14.4
Sioux City	96,899	468,549	20.6
Kansas	**406,628**	**2,658,618**	**15.2**
*Kansas City	197,752	1,174,5000	16.8
Dodge City	44,093	212,332	20.7
Salina	49,246	325,112	15.1
Wichita	115,537	946,674	12.2
Kentucky	**384,596**	**3,957,444**	**9.7**
*Louisville	197,283	1,220,070	16.1
Covington	89,121	464,629	19.1
Lexington	47,583	1,436,583	3.3
Owensboro	50,609	836,162	6.0
Louisiana	**1,317,838**	**4,447,999**	**29.6**
*New Orleans	488,004	1,360,436	35.8
Alexandria	48,0503	92,639	12.2
Baton Rouge	208,574	853,165	24.4
Houma-Thibodaux	130,000	205,000	63.4
Lafayette	331,186	568,154	58.2
Lake Charles	72,768	283,429	25.6
Shreveport	39,256	758,176	4.9
Maine			
Portland	213,680	1,274,923	16.7
Maryland			
*Baltimore	497,424	2,944,407	16.8
Massachusetts	**2,987,473**	**5,991,817**	**49.8**
*Boston	2,069,225	3,857,751	53.6
Fall River	350,570	590,911	59.3
Springfield	262,748	792,195	33.1
Worcester	304,930	750,960	40.6
Michigan	**2,265,678**	**9,803,731**	**23.1**
*Detroit	1,465,918	4,441,551	33.0
Gaylord	78,430	476,244	16.4
Grand Rapids	161,525	1,167,900	13.9
Kalamazoo	116,740	937,037	12.4
Lansing	233,201	1,739,241	13.4
Marquette	70,200	317,616	22.1
Saginaw	139,664	724,142	19.2
Minnesota	**1,266,513**	**4,908,762**	**25.8**
*St. Paul and Minneapolis	785,584	2,899,361	27.0
Crookston	40,429	235,145	17.1
Duluth	71,531	430,852	16.6
New Ulm	70,039	286,617	24.4
St. Cloud	147,849	499,103	29.6
Winona	150,081	557,684	27.0
Mississippi	**119,438**	**2,739,684**	**4.3**
Biloxi	70,630	759,659	9.2

State / Diocese	Catholic Pop.	Total Cath. Pop.	Pct.
Mississippi, cont.			
Jackson	48,808	1,980,025	2.4
Missouri	**865,238**	**5,395,115**	**16.0**
*St. Louis	555,750	2,100,000	26.4
Jefferson City	86,011	841,455	10.2
Kansas City-St. Joseph	161,689	1,394,054	11.5
Springfield-Cape Girardeau	61,788	1,059,606	5.8
Montana	**123,208**	**900,799**	**13.6**
Great Falls-Billings	55,405	391,360	14.1
Helena	67,803	509,439	13.3
Nebraska	**364,434**	**1,687,824**	**21.5**
*Omaha	219,897	853,300	25.7
Grand Island	55,206	295,176	18.7
Lincoln	89,331	539,348	16.5
Nevada	**539,519**	**2,053,920**	**26.2**
Las Vegas	464,164	1,478,230	31.3
Reno	75,355	575,690	13.0
New Hampshire			
Manchester	325,674	1,201,000	31.8
New Jersey	**3,359,769**	**7,881,326**	**42.6**
*Newark	1,319,558	2,809,267	46.9
Camden	441,482	1,329,206	33.2
Metuchen	446,794	1,272,078	35.1
Paterson	411,578	1,103,427	37.2
Trenton	740,357	1,367,348	54.1
New Mexico	**474,975**	**1,997,706**	**23.7**
*Santa Fe	287,055	1,083,069	26.5
Gallup	55,274	430,000	12.8
Las Cruces	132,646	484,637	27.3
New York	**7,779,305**	**19,225,524**	**40.4**
*New York	2,471,742	5,492,762	44.9
Albany	400,000	1,340,450	29.8
Brooklyn	1,815,752	4,694,705	38.6
Buffalo	713,752	1,591,708	44.8
Ogdensburg	143,760	462,000	31.1
Rochester	340,000	1,490,891	22.8
Rockville Centre	1,548,623	2,978,121	52.0
Syracuse	345,736	1,174,887	29.4
North Carolina	**303,310**	**7,980,378**	**3.8**
Charlotte	131,147	4,168,955	3.1
Raleigh	172,163	3,811,423	74.5
North Dakota	**166,376**	**645,426**	**25.7**
Bismarck	67,416	254,426	26.4
Fargo	98,960	391,000	25.3
Ohio	**2,149,632**	**11,353,137**	**18.9**
*Cincinnati	516,470	2,932,047	17.6
Cleveland	820,110	2,855,129	28.7
Columbus	207,328	2,332,887	8.9
Steubenville	40,859	515,672	7.9
Toledo	319,280	1,489,769	21.4
Youngstown	245,585	1,227,633	20.0
Oklahoma	**164,213**	**3,829,163**	**4.2**
*Oklahoma City	103,213	2,268,480	4.5
Tulsa	61,000	1,560,683	3.9
Oregon	**388,319**	**3,409,347**	**11.3**
*Portland	351,164	2,969,847	11.8
Baker	37,155	439,500	8.4
Pennsylvania	**3,686,036**	**12,280,572**	**30.0**
*Philadelphia	1,488,316	3,849,647	38.6
Allentown	268,609	1,161,932	23.1
Altoona-J'town	112,426	645,268	17.4
Erie	227,162	874,057	25.9
Pennsylvania, cont.			
Greensburg	188,301	680,152	7.6
Harrisburg	242,726	2,027,835	11.9
Pittsburgh	793,417	1,975,373	40.1
Scranton	365,079	1,066,308	34.2
Rhode Island			
Providence	639,962	1,048,319	61.0
South Carolina			
Charleston	130,696	4,012,012	3.2
South Dakota	**155,472**	**766,532**	**20.2**
Rapid City	30,266	227,211	13.3
Sioux Falls	125,206	539,321	23.2
Tennessee	**182,609**	**5,703,751**	**3.2**
Knoxville	48,185	2,141,075	2.2
Memphis	64,944	1,455,808	4.4
Nashville	69,480	2,106,868	3.2
Texas	**5,329,077**	**20,732,428**	**25.7**
*San Antonio	640,186	1,906,519	33.5
Amarillo	56,361	402,862	13.9
Austin	400,156	2,056,550	19.4
Beaumont	94,145	588,265	16.0
Brownsville	831,613	978,369	85.0
Corpus Christi	250,000	548,196	45.6
Dallas	843,167	3,200,064	26.3
El Paso+	646,340	799,843	80.8
Fort Worth	253,087	2,670,972	9.4
Galveston-Houston	947,312	4,704,532	20.1
Laredo	64,724	286,457	22.5
Lubbock	55,701	451,995	12.3
San Angelo	82,522	683,043	12.0
Tyler	54,879	1,242,826	4.4
Victoria	108,884	211,935	51.3
Utah			
Salt Lake City	120,000	2,233,000	5.2
Vermont			
Burlington	148,813	608,827	24.4
Virginia	**576,583**	**7,078,515**	**8.1**
Arlington	368,575	2,403,540	15.3
Richmond	208,008	4,674,975	4.4
Washington	**680,902**	**5,808,631**	**11.7**
*Seattle	535,500	4,655,100	11.5
Spokane	75,791	691,931	10.9
Yakima	69,611	461,600	15.0
West Virginia			
Wheeling-Charleston	69,614	1,806,928	3.8
Wisconsin	**1,634,599**	**5,371,211**	**30.4**
*Milwaukee	689,519	2,236,283	30.8
Green Bay	375,708	951,159	39.5
La Crosse	215,573	848,455	25.4
Madison	266,396	917,645	29.0
Superior	87,403	417,669	20.9
Wyoming			
Cheyenne	45,060	493,782	9.1
Eastern Churches	422,284	-	-
Military			
Archdiocese ('99)	1,194,000	-	-
Outlying Areas	3,073,562	4,344,617	70.7
Total 2002	65,270,444	284,972,437	22.9
Total 2001	63,683,030	278,849,034	22.8
Total 1992	58,267,424	254,476,684	22.8

Note: These statistics do not include the Eparchy of St. Peter the Apostle of San Diego which was created on May 21, 2002.

CATHOLIC POPULATION OF THE UNITED STATES

(*Source:* The Official Catholic Directory, 2002; *figures as of Jan. 1, 2002. Archdioceses are indicated by an asterisk; for dioceses marked +, see Dioceses with Interstate Lines.*)

State Diocese	Cath. Pop.	Dioc. Priests	Rel. Priests	Total Priests	Perm. Deac.	Bros.	Sisters	Par- ishes
Alabama	**157,402**	**186**	**79**	**265**	**80**	**38**	**300**	**131**
*Mobile	66,480	108	36	144	36	11	179	76
Birmingham	91,922	78	43	121	44	27	121	55
Alaska	**54,268**	**34**	**32**	**66**	**58**	**6**	**69**	**72**
*Anchorage	31,112	18	14	32	18	2	46	20
Fairbanks	17,700	6	16	22	35	4	17	41
Juneau	5,456	10	2	12	5	-	6	11
Arizona	**808,780**	**250**	**169**	**419**	**328**	**22**	**464**	**158**
Phoenix	478,163	136	101	237	204	13	225	87
Tucson	330,617	114	68	182	124	9	239	71
Arkansas, Little Rock	**100,820**	**77**	**59**	**136**	**78**	**31**	**278**	**90**
California	**10,110,452**	**2,077**	**1,515**	**3,592**	**792**	**449**	**4,771**	**1,067**
*Los Angeles	4,197,635	583	597	1,180	198	161	1,831	287
*San Francisco	425,210	215	183	398	74	50	794	90
Fresno	338,040	117	29	146	9	3	132	86
Monterey	315,902	71	26	97	3	35	102	46
Oakland	428,466	161	99	260	97	30	360	87
Orange	1,110,508	159	95	254	52	12	360	56
Sacramento	500,097	165	59	224	115	24	179	98
San Bernardino	943,898	139	106	245	85	16	151	97
San Diego	901,172	191	104	295	78	20	345	98
San Jose	584,000	118	189	307	8	59	394	48
Santa Rosa	148,605	90	13	103	39	35	69	42
Stockton	216,919	68	15	83	34	4	54	32
Colorado	**604,667**	**267**	**184**	**451**	**189**	**31**	**629**	**198**
*Denver	376,514	160	125	285	148	22	404	113
Colorado Springs	120,000	36	27	63	26	2	125	33
Pueblo	108,153	71	32	103	15	7	100	52
Connecticut	**1,309,871**	**778**	**244**	**1,022**	**452**	**74**	**1,634**	**383**
*Hartford	719,953	374	129	503	308	50	901	218
Bridgeport	362,569	266	58	324	87	-	481	87
Norwich+	227,349	138	57	195	57	24	252	78
Delaware, Wilmington+	**215,000**	**125**	**91**	**216**	**73**	**25**	**231**	**56**
D.C.,*Washington+	**551,436**	**315**	**682**	**997**	**237**	**137**	**752**	**140**
Florida	**2,214,107**	**889**	**448**	**1,337**	**573**	**172**	**1,232**	**456**
*Miami	830,366	273	111	384	148	59	323	110
Orlando	353,342	124	42	166	130	15	124	72
Palm Beach	246,040	102	49	151	46	4	147	49
Pensacola- Tallahassee	56,939	76	13	89	52	7	53	50
St. Augustine	143,413	88	26	114	29	3	112	51
St. Petersburg	384,259	128	131	259	93	52	353	73
Venice	199,748	98	76	174	75	32	120	51
Georgia	**394,933**	**223**	**94**	**317**	**188**	**10**	**243**	**129**
*Atlanta	321,978	154	67	221	138	1	118	77
Savannah	72,955	69	27	96	50	9	125	52
Hawaii, Honolulu	**145,453**	**72**	**56**	**128**	**50**	**43**	**161**	**66**
Idaho, Boise	**130,750**	**85**	**12**	**97**	**52**	**5**	**97**	**57**
Illinois	**3,839,333**	**1,749**	**1,121**	**72,966**	**1,040**	**496**	**5,016**	**1,054**
*Chicago	2,442,000	874	918	1,792	621	338	2,967	378
Belleville	104,022	136	35	171	32	13	238	124
Joliet	609,252	196	109	305	174	87	655	120
Peoria	151,413	239	48	287	91	12	246	165
Rockford	375,185	165	48	213	117	17	249	105
Springfield	157,461	139	59	198	5	29	661	162
Indiana	**776,441**	**592**	**338**	**930**	**87**	**182**	**1,846**	**425**
*Indianapolis	233,171	158	102	260	-	53	731	139
Evansville	89,087	100	7	107	21	2	304	70
Ft. Wayne- South Bend	170,290	94	166	260	22	108	617	79

State Diocese	Cath. Pop.	Dioc. Priests	Rel. Priests	Total Priests	Perm. Deac.	Bros.	Sisters	Par- ishes
Indiana, cont.								
Gary	187,000	122	44	166	39	17	109	75
Lafayette	96,893	118	19	137	5	2	85	62
Iowa	**519,916**	**647**	**42**	**689**	**221**	**32**	**1,187**	**503**
*Dubuque	213,555	240	28	268	68	28	861	210
Davenport	112,156	144	2	146	43	1	130	85
Des Moines	97,306	101	11	112	73	7	102	84
Sioux City	96,899	162	1	163	37	-	94	124
Kansas	**406,628**	**335**	**94**	**429**	**8**	**16**	**1,324**	**352**
*Kansas City	197,752	100	64	164	-	15	677	119
Dodge City	44,093	41	7	48	9	-	105	49
Salina	49,246	65	16	81	-	1	211	92
Wichita	115,537	129	7	136	2	-	331	92
Kentucky	**384,596**	**419**	**109**	**528**	**166**	**96**	**1,691**	**297**
*Louisville	197,283	180	65	245	106	79	941	111
Covington	89,121	108	2	110	24	8	393	47
Lexington	47,583	50	20	70	36	4	143	60
Owensboro	50,609	81	22	103	-	5	214	79
Louisiana	**1,317,838**	**688**	**323**	**1,011**	**357**	**184**	**1,201**	**488**
*New Orleans	488,004	228	186	414	190	128	787	142
Alexandria	48,050	65	12	77	5	4	49	48
Baton Rouge	208,574	81	38	119	26	12	111	70
Houma-Thibodaux	130,000	75	8	83	31	6	29	39
Lafayette	331,186	150	55	205	75	27	148	121
Lake Charles	72,768	48	10	58	24	1	23	36
Shreveport	39,256	41	14	55	6	6	54	32
Maine, Portland	**213,680**	**176**	**46**	**222**	**23**	**28**	**406**	**136**
Maryland, *Baltimore	**497,424**	**285**	**238**	**523**	**172**	**72**	**1,160**	**162**
Massachusetts	**2,987,473**	**1,550**	**1,005**	**2,555**	**403**	**270**	**3,991**	**718**
*Boston	2,069,225	912	732	1,644	218	149	2,606	362
Fall River	350,570	178	122	300	60	34	303	103
Springfield	262,748	220	40	260	59	7	604	127
Worcester	304,930	240	111	351	66	80	478	126
Michigan	**2,265,678**	**1,093**	**401**	**1,494**	**310**	**143**	**3,090**	**804**
*Detroit	1,465,918	485	300	785	147	122	1,911	310
Gaylord	78,430	72	13	85	13	2	50	81
Grand Rapids	161,525	120	22	142	18	2	283	90
Kalamazoo	116,740	61	11	72	20	1	173	46
Lansing	233,201	147	32	179	73	16	488	95
Marquette	70,200	99	10	109	25	-	61	74
Saginaw	139,664	109	13	122	14	-	124	108
Minnesota	**1,266,513**	**807**	**304**	**1,111**	**273**	**145**	**2,443**	**720**
*St.Paul & Minneapolis	785,584	347	170	517	190	45	949	222
Crookston	40,429	50	2	52	10	1	157	69
Duluth	71,531	77	11	88	29	2	161	93
New Ulm	70,039	80	1	81	2	-	85	80
St. Cloud	147,849	135	111	246	36	76	631	138
Winona	151,081	118	9	127	6	21	460	118
Mississippi	**119,438**	**124**	**63**	**187**	**27**	**40**	**278**	**119**
Biloxi	70,630	59	29	88	20	27	56	45
Jackson	48,808	65	34	99	7	13	222	74
Missouri	**865,238**	**784**	**528**	**1,312**	**371**	**259**	**2,464**	**465**
*St. Louis	555,750	478	349	827	246	151	1,996	220
Jefferson City	86,011	110	8	118	56	5	89	95
Kansas City-St. Joseph	161,689	120	102	222	59	32	271	85
Springfield-Cape Girardeau	61,788	76	69	145	10	71	108	65
Montana	**123,208**	**160**	**19**	**179**	**38**	**1**	**124**	**124**
Great Falls-Billings	55,405	70	13	83	3	1	78	47
Helena	67,803	90	6	96	35	-	46	58
Nebraska	**364,434**	**443**	**108**	**551**	**157**	**28**	**580**	**314**
*Omaha	219,897	216	99	315	155	22	361	138
Grand Island	55,206	77	-	77	-	-	86	41
Lincoln	89,331	150	9	159	2	6	133	135
Nevada	**539,519**	**53**	**34**	**87**	**14**	**6**	**59**	**51**

State Diocese	Cath. Pop.	Dioc. Priests	Rel. Priests	Total Priests	Perm. Deac.	Bros.	Sisters	Par- ishes
Nevada, cont.								
Las Vegas	464,164	32	24	56	5	3	23	23
Reno	75,355	21	10	31	9	3	36	28
New Hampshire,								
Manchester	**325,674**	**235**	**85**	**320**	**25**	**26**	**688**	**131**
New Jersey	**3,359,769**	**1,746**	**544**	**2,290**	**938**	**263**	**3,255**	**707**
*Newark	1,319,558	742	227	969	248	104	1,276	235
Camden	441,482	312	48	360	122	21	325	127
Metuchen	466,794	200	44	244	130	21	392	108
Paterson	411,578	253	182	435	162	45	829	111
Trenton	740,357	239	43	282	276	72	433	126
New Mexico	**474,975**	**204**	**155**	**359**	**195**	**105**	**419**	**192**
*Santa Fe	287,055	116	82	198	143	93	246	92
Gallup	55,274	58	22	80	27	10	125	56
Las Cruces	132,646	30	51	81	25	2	48	44
New York	**7,779,305**	**3,155**	**1,567**	**4,722**	**1,181**	**790**	**8,426**	**1,652**
*New York	2,471,742	743	913	1,656	346	303	2,267	411
Albany	400,000	284	105	389	94	94	934	182
Brooklyn	1,815,752	624	210	834	145	187	1,177	217
Buffalo	713,752	414	174	588	103	46	1,317	266
Ogdensburg	143,700	159	12	171	57	11	168	119
Rochester	340,000	247	61	308	132	38	647	154
Rockville Centre	1,548,623	402	32	434	231	95	1,419	134
Syracuse	345,736	282	60	342	73	16	497	169
North Carolina	**303,310**	**195**	**116**	**311**	**96**	**15**	**186**	**144**
Charlotte	131,147	109	62	171	73	7	109	68
Raleigh	172,163	86	54	140	23	8	77	76
North Dakota	**166,376**	**238**	**36**	**274**	**87**	**26**	**349**	**222**
Bismarck	67,416	71	27	98	63	22	140	62
Fargo	98,960	167	9	176	24	4	209	160
Ohio	**2,149,632**	**1,465**	**522**	**1,987**	**658**	**262**	**4,001**	**922**
*Cincinnati	516,470	320	240	560	145	165	1,200	230
Cleveland	820,110	460	134	594	179	59	1,428	235
Columbus	207,328	190	41	231	70	3	359	107
Steubenville	40,859	107	29	136	5	8	95	73
Toledo	319,280	206	55	261	191	7	689	161
Youngstown	245,583	182	23	205	68	20	230	116
Oklahoma	**164,213**	**192**	**44**	**236**	**119**	**17**	**254**	**152**
*Oklahoma City	103,213	117	23	140	60	11	149	72
Tulsa	61,000	75	21	96	59	6	105	80
Oregon	**388,319**	**194**	**188**	**382**	**39**	**82**	**554**	**161**
*Portland	351,164	155	182	337	25	81	527	125
Baker	37,155	39	6	45	14	1	27	36
Pennsylvania	**3,686,036**	**2,503**	**883**	**3,386**	**511**	**206**	**7,663**	**1,266**
*Philadelphia	1,488,316	751	392	1,143	196	122	3,547	282
Allentown	268,609	249	80	329	99	-	510	153
Altoona-Johnstown	112,426	152	62	214	29	4	87	100
Erie	227,162	234	14	248	23	2	459	126
Greensburg	188,301	143	83	226	-	26	285	105
Harrisburg	242,726	159	36	195	59	-	492	89
Pittsburgh	793,417	475	122	597	54	38	1,560	216
Scranton	365,079	340	94	434	51	14	723	195
Rhode Island,								
Providence	**639,962**	**306**	**105**	**411**	**96**	**129**	**655**	**157**
South Carolina,								
Charleston	**130,696**	**87**	**34**	**121**	**70**	**29**	**151**	**93**
South Dakota	**155,472**	**167**	**66**	**233**	**54**	**16**	**450**	**248**
Rapid City	30,266	46	30	76	28	5	58	97
Sioux Falls	125,206	121	36	157	26	11	392	151
Tennessee	**182,609**	**171**	**52**	**223**	**128**	**62**	**287**	**137**
Knoxville	48,185	53	18	71	22	14	33	44
Memphis	64,944	66	9	75	53	46	78	42
Nashville	69,480	52	25	77	53	2	176	51
Texas	**5,329,077**	**1,195**	**824**	**2,059**	**1,411**	**231**	**2,875**	**1,010**
*San Antonio	640,186	151	188	339	298	91	903	138

State Diocese	Cath. Pop.	Dioc. Priests	Rel. Priests	Total Priests	Perm. Deac.	Bros.	Sisters	Par- ishes
Texas, cont.								
Amarillo	56,361	62	9	71	51	1	134	35
Austin	400,156	131	53	184	177	46	111	101
Beaumont	94,145	45	26	71	30	1	45	44
Brownsville	831,613	58	40	98	67	13	128	64
Corpus Christi	250,000	113	43	156	63	26	209	66
Dallas	843,167	104	75	179	152	4	154	66
El Paso	646,340	86	37	123	11	14	253	58
Fort Worth	253,087	60	60	120	61	13	96	88
Galveston-Houston	947,312	196	226	462	299	9	503	150
Laredo	64,724	15	20	35	24	8	88	25
Lubbock	55,701	35	7	42	49	-	28	34
San Angelo	82,522	39	16	55	39	-	28	49
Tyler	54,879	43	16	59	65	5	60	42
Victoria	108,884	57	8	65	25	-	135	50
Utah, Salt Lake City	**120,000**	**59**	**29**	**85**	**46**	**12**	**58**	**47**
Vermont, Burlington	**148,813**	**127**	**46**	**173**	**39**	**15**	**195**	**86**
Virginia	**576,583**	**322**	**111**	**433**	**76**	**29**	**348**	**211**
Arlington	368,575	157	78	235	44	19	161	67
Richmond	208,008	165	33	198	32	10	187	144
Washington	**680,902**	**332**	**222**	**554**	**149**	**31**	**820**	**258**
*Seattle	535,500	180	107	287	74	13	492	139
Spokane	75,791	81	103	184	52	11	281	78
Yakima	69,611	71	12	83	23	7	47	41
West Virginia								
Wheeling-Charleston	**69,614**	**120**	**65**	**185**	**30**	**20**	**255**	**112**
Wisconsin	**1,634,599**	**1,075**	**479**	**1,554**	**356**	**174**	**4,234**	**832**
*Milwaukee	689,519	438	291	729	175	125	2,683	226
Green Bay	375,708	215	135	350	92	34	621	188
La Crosse	215,573	194	26	220	35	6	493	168
Madison	266,396	152	13	165	4	8	330	137
Superior	87,403	76	14	90	50	1	107	113
Wyoming, Cheyenne+	**45,060**	**49**	**10**	**59**	**14**	**1**	**23**	**36**
EASTERN CHURCHES	**422,284**	**575**	**105**	**680**	**119**	**31**	**293**	**574**
*Philadelphia	67,800	56	5	61	7	-	85	74
St. Nicholas	10,000	20	13	33	12	-	2	36
Stamford	16,600	64	13	77	7	3	32	52
St. Josaphat (Parma)	11,224	42	2	44	7	10	10	38
*Pittsburgh	60,686	64	9	73	-	4	102	86
Parma	12,482	37	2	39	5	-	14	37
Passaic	24,504	82	10	92	15	2	18	90
Van Nuys	3,016	18	5	23	4	7	3	19
St. Maron (Maronites)	30,000	61	12	73	12	5	2	33
Our Lady of Lebanon (Maronites)	25,336	30	10	40	9	-	7	30
Newton (Melkites)	28,026	46	16	62	36	-	3	35
St. Thomas Apostle of Detroit (Chaldean)	90,000	23	-	23	-	-	-	14
St. George Martyr (Romanian)	5,000	15	2	17	-	-	-	15
Our Lady of Deliverance (Syrians, U.S.-Canada)	12,610	12	-	12	4	-	-	8
Armenian Ex.(U.S.-Canada)	25,000	5	6	11	1	-	15	7
MILITARY ARCHDIOCESE ('99)	**1,194,000**	-	-	-	-	-	-	-
OUTLYING AREAS								
Puerto Rico	2,729,000	346	380	726	414	70	1,143	326
Samoa-Pago Pago	11,850	9	3	12	19	-	11	12
Caroline Islands	72,940	14	13	27	43	2	33	26
Chalan Kanoa (N. Mariana Is.)	53,066	15	1	16	2	-	-	11
Guam, *Agana	150,500	36	16	52	7	1	124	24
Marshall Islands	4,512	6	6	12	2	-	12	4
Virgin Islands, St. Thomas	30,000	14	6	20	20	4	17	8
TOTAL 2002	**65,270,444**	**30,429**	**15,244**	**45,713**	**13,764**	**5,690**	**75,500**	**19,496**
TOTAL 2001	**63,683,030**	**30,655**	**15,386**	**46,075**	**13,348**	**5,565**	**79,462**	**19,544**
TOTAL 1992	**58,267,424**	**34,288**	**17,989**	**52,277**	**10,384**	**6,603**	**99,337**	**19,971**

[1] Priest chaplains are on loan from their dioceses or religious community. The 2002 *Annuario Pontificio* reported 839 diocesan and 221 religious order chaplains in the United States. **Note:** These statistics do not include the Eparchy of St. Peter the Apostle of San Diego, created on May 21, 2002.

RECEPTIONS INTO THE CHURCH IN THE UNITED STATES

(*Source:* The Official Catholic Directory, 2002; *figures as of Jan. 1, 2002. Archdioceses are indicated by an asterisk; for dioceses marked +, see Dioceses with Interstate Lines. Information includes infant and adult baptisms and those received into full communion.*)

State Diocese	Infant Baptisms	Adult Bapts.	Rec'd into Full Comm.	State Diocese	Infant Baptisms	Adult Bapts.	Rec'd into Full Comm.
Alabama	**2,853**	**487**	**954**	**Indiana, cont.**			
*Mobile	1,145	225	342	Ft.Wayne-S. Bend	2,810	540	552
Birmingham	1,708	262	612	Gary	2,237	170	304
Alaska	**1,009**	**124**	**121**	Lafayette	2,141	322	339
*Anchorage	536	81	85	**Iowa**	**8,770**	**781**	**1,271**
Fairbanks	364	18	20	*Dubuque	3,344	164	431
Juneau	109	25	16	Davenport	1,681	271	242
Arizona	**18,286**	**953**	**1,566**	Des Moines	2,069	228	388
Phoenix	11,398	619	1,080	Sioux City	1,676	118	210
Tucson	6,888	334	486	**Kansas**	**8,760**	**1,241**	**1,490**
Arkansas, Little Rock	**2,439**	**314**	**543**	*Kansas City	4,124	406	767
California	**201,894**	**8,655**	**9,296**	Dodge City	1,193	346	119
*Los Angeles	99,066	2,023	2,647	Salina	982	98	199
*San Francisco	7,144	478	338	Wichita	2,461	391	405
Fresno	15,419	544	643	**Kentucky**	**6,043**	**1,183**	**1,287**
Monterey	6,200	206	378	*Louisville	3,026	469	658
Oakland	9,497	532	584	Covington	1,318	430	175
Orange	16,077	769	723	Lexington	691	123	231
Sacramento	8,907	585	773	Owensboro	1,008	161	223
San Bernardino	10,542	903	622	**Louisiana**	**19,107**	**1,223**	**1,835**
San Diego	11,345	1,513	1,017	*New Orleans	6,526	392	335
San Jose 8,550	644	495		Alexandria	675	81	127
Santa Rosa	3,254	125	187	Baton Rouge	2,847	263	356
Stockton	5,893	333	889	Houma-Thibodaux	1,766	61	225
Colorado	**13,631**	**1,002**	**2,296**	Lafayette	5,330	163	310
*Denver	10,395	686	1,489	Lake Charles	1,434	118	250
Colorado Springs	1,404	154	343	Shreveport	529	145	232
Pueblo	1,832	162	464	**Maine,** Portland	**2,806**	**313**	**346**
Connecticut	**18,555**	**613**	**845**	**Maryland,** *Baltimore	7,490	629	1,006
*Hartford	9,803	265	322	**Massachusetts**	**40,242**	**1,085**	**1,423**
Bridgeport	5,713	199	97	*Boston	27,325	712	348
Norwich+	3,039	149	426	Fall River	4,722	94	121
Delaware, Wilmington+	**2,905**	**288**	**378**	Springfield	3,717	141	670
District of Columbia				Worcester	4,478	138	284
*Washington+	6,612	973	632	**Michigan**	**28,364**	**3,215**	**3,408**
Florida	**39,696**	**3,071**	**4,053**	*Detroit	15,875	1,381	1,656
*Miami	17,517	808	957	Gaylord	1,014	137	160
Orlando	5,905	580	786	Grand Rapids	3,048	402	-
Palm Beach	4,656	357	424	Kalamazoo	1,580	315	293
Pensacola-				Lansing	4,035	621	954
Tallahassee	967	146	272	Marquette	921	72	119
St. Augustine	2,296	317	486	Saginaw	1,891	287	226
St. Petersburg	4,895	634	600	**Minnesota**	**18,338**	**772**	**2,160**
Venice	3,460	229	528	*St. Paul and			
Georgia	**10,520**	**1,034**	**1,378**	Minneapolis	11,312	507	1,399
*Atlanta	8,868	787	953	Crookston	709	19	86
Savannah	1,652	247	425	Duluth	1,014	39	131
Hawaii, Honolulu	**3,006**	**530**	**619**	New Ulm	1,039	43	111
Idaho, Boise	**2,599**	**380**	**210**	St. Cloud	2,341	79	213
Illinois	**62,340**	**3,889**	**3,920**	Winona	1,923	85	220
*Chicago	39,041	2,245	1,515	**Mississippi**	**1,681**	**574**	**517**
Belleville	1,624	306	287	Biloxi	855	472	250
Joliet	10,665	355	718	Jackson	826	102	267
Peoria	2,502	371	410	**Missouri**	**11,938**	**1,717**	**1,912**
Rockford	5,980	254	539	*St. Louis	7,796	532	920
Springfield	2,528	358	451	Jefferson City	1,344	307	281
Indiana	**12,864**	**1,884**	**2,290**	Kansas City-St. Jos.	2,052	323	481
*Indianapolis	4,317	711	884	Springfield-			
Evansville	1,359	141	211	Cape Girardeau	746	555	230

State / Diocese	Infant Baptisms	Adult Bapts.	Rec'd into Full Comm.
Montana	**1,554**	**559**	**340**
Great Falls-Billings	896	146	220
Helena	658	413	120
Nebraska	**6,734**	**663**	**903**
*Omaha	4,132	420	567
Grand Island	1,170	106	166
Lincoln	1,432	137	170
Nevada	**7,057**	**430**	**322**
Las Vegas	5,415	237	194
Reno	1,642	193	128
New Hampshire			
Manchester	**4,587**	**191**	**-**
New Jersey	**49,573**	**1,798**	**2,157**
*Newark	17,001	480	578
Camden	6,553	602	608
Metuchen	6,885	126	208
Paterson	8,688	199	318
Trenton	10,446	391	445
New Mexico	**9,508**	**734**	**945**
*Santa Fe	6,106	327	640
Gallup	825	254	197
Las Cruces	2,577	153	108
New York	**96,791**	**3,997**	**4,174**
*New York	32,095	991	895
Albany	4,650	150	259
Brooklyn	19,789	886	811
Buffalo	6,865	557	467
Ogdensburg	1,565	152	117
Rochester	4,937	330	657
Rockville Centre	21,731	697	517
Syracuse	5,159	234	451
North Carolina	**8,218**	**559**	**421**
Charlotte	3,819	291	-
Raleigh	4,399	268	421
North Dakota	**2,107**	**106**	**256**
Bismarck	1,065	59	256
Fargo	1,042	47	-
Ohio	**30,136**	**3,590**	**4,464**
*Cincinnati	7,984	902	976
Cleveland	10,470	1,058	978
Columbus	4,050	515	871
Steubenville	774	221	138
Toledo	3,811	587	961
Youngstown	3,047	307	540
Oklahoma	**3,368**	**540**	**829**
*Oklahoma City	2,105	350	521
Tulsa	1,263	190	308
Oregon	**6,477**	**845**	**816**
*Portland	5,661	717	704
Baker	816	128	112
Pennsylvania	**42,633**	**3,106**	**3,058**
*Philadelphia	17,052	1,255	725
Allentown	3,624	217	-
Altoona-Johnstown	1,448	126	211
Erie	2,102	252	266
Greensburg	1,956	149	349
Harrisburg	3,249	393	506
Pittsburgh	8,372	384	646
Scranton	4,830	330	355
Rhode Island			
Providence	**5,398**	**201**	**312**
South Carolina			
Charleston	2,198	616	-
South Dakota	**2,258**	**153**	**401**
Rapid City	605	73	84

State / Diocese	Infant Baptisms	Adult Bapts.	Rec'd into Full Comm.
South Dakota, cont.			
Sioux Falls	1,653	80	317
Tennessee	**3,582**	**886**	**883**
Knoxville	946	237	228
Memphis	928	429	269
Nashville	1,708	220	386
Texas	**82,059**	**9,779**	**7,010**
*San Antonio	12,324	712	721
Amarillo	1,277	112	91
Austin	7,494	573	1,074
Beaumont	1,268	118	337
Brownsville	4,608	4,148	420
Corpus Christi	3,634	219	253
Dallas	14,574	1,000	602
El Paso	9,260	140	280
Fort Worth	5,606	469	1,364
Galveston-Houston	12,020	1,639	973
Laredo	2,999	78	179
Lubbock	1,629	157	217
San Angelo	1,907	165	235
Tyler	1,859	201	163
Victoria	1,600	48	101
Utah, Salt Lake City	**3,367**	**513**	**326**
Vermont, Burlington	**1,571**	**144**	**163**
Virginia	**11,014**	**1,293**	**1,590**
Arlington	7,141	854	578
Richmond	3,873	439	1,012
Washington	**10,711**	**1,495**	**978**
*Seattle	6,956	1,198	662
Spokane	919	191	163
Yakima	2,836	106	153
West Virginia			
Wheeling-Chas.	**995**	**220**	**321**
Wisconsin	**20,278**	**1,102**	**1,927**
*Milwaukee	8,768	387	754
Green Bay	4,561	187	309
La Crosse	2,858	125	287
Madison	3,101	147	449
Superior	990	256	128
Wyoming, Cheyenne+	**866**	**170**	**160**
Eastern Churches	**4,034**	**183**	**381**
*Philadelphia	207	25	30
St. Nicholas	255	5	7
Stamford	175	4	-
St. Josaphat (Parma)	119	6	-
*Pittsburgh	277	29	69
Parma	105	12	42
Passaic	285	22	39
Van Nuys	95	15	18
St. Maron (Maronites)	468	15	52
Our Lady of Lebanon (Maronites)	451	21	-
Newton (Melkites)	358	8	20
St. Thomas Apostle of Detroit (Chaldeans)	1,058	12	-
St. George Martyr (Romanian)	19	-	16
Our Lady of Deliverance (Syrians,U.S.-Can.)	82	4	4
Armenian Ex. (U.S.-Can.)	79	5	84
Military Archdiocese	**4,299**	**764**	**381**
Outlying Areas	**33,595**	**8,325**	**2,101**
Total 2002	**1,007,716**	**79,892**	**81,240**
Total 2001	**1,031,243**	**83,234**	**95,299**

Note: These statistics do not include the Eparchy of St. Peter the Apostle of San Diego, created on May 21, 2002.

The Catholic Church in Canada

Background

The first date in the remote background of the Catholic history of Canada was July 7, 1534, when a priest in the exploration company of Jacques Cartier celebrated Mass on the Gaspe Peninsula.

Successful colonization and the significant beginnings of the Catholic history of the country date from the foundation of Québec in 1608 by Samuel de Champlain and French settlers. Montréal was established in 1642.

The earliest missionaries were Franciscan Récollets (Recollects) and Jesuits who arrived in 1615 and 1625, respectively. They provided some pastoral care for the settlers but worked mainly among the 100,000 Indians — Algonquins, Hurons and Iroquois — in the interior and in the Lake Ontario region. Eight of the Jesuit missionaries, killed in the 1640s, were canonized in 1930. (See Index: Jesuit North American Martyrs.) Sulpician Fathers, who arrived in Canada late in the 1640s, played a part in the great missionary period which ended about 1700.

Kateri Tekakwitha, "Lily of the Mohawks," who was baptized in 1676 and died in 1680, was declared "Blessed" on June 22, 1980.

The communities of women religious with the longest histories in Canada are the Canonesses of St. Augustine and the Ursulines, since 1639; and the Hospitallers of St. Joseph, since 1642. Communities of Canadian origin are the Congregation of Notre Dame, founded by St. Marguerite Bourgeoys in 1658, and the Grey Nuns, formed by St. Marie Marguerite d'Youville in 1737.

Mother Marie (Guyard) of the Incarnation, an Ursuline nun, was one of the first three women missionaries to New France; called "Mother of the Church in Canada," she was declared "Blessed" on June 22, 1980.

Start of Church Organization

Ecclesiastical organization began with the appointment in 1658 of François De Montmorency-Laval, "Father of the Church in Canada," as vicar apostolic of New France. He was the first bishop of Québec from 1674 to 1688, with jurisdiction over all French-claimed territory in North America. He was declared "Blessed" on June 22, 1980.

In 1713, the French Canadian population numbered 18,000. In the same year, the Treaty of Utrecht ceded Acadia, Newfoundland and the Hudson Bay Territory to England. The Acadians were scattered among the American Colonies in 1755.

The English acquired possession of Canada and its 70,000 French-speaking inhabitants in virtue of the Treaty of Paris in 1763. Anglo-French and Anglican-Catholic differences and tensions developed. The pro-British government at first refused to recognize the titles of church officials, hindered the clergy in their work and tried to install a non-Catholic educational system. Laws were passed which guaranteed religious liberties to Catholics (Québec Act of 1774, Constitutional Act of 1791, legislation approved by Queen Victoria in 1851), but it took some time before actual respect for these liberties matched the legal enactments. The initial moderation of government antipathy toward the Church was caused partly by the loyalty of Catholics to the Crown during the American Revolution and the War of 1812.

Growth

The 15 years following the passage in 1840 of the Act of Union, which joined Upper and Lower Canada, were significant. New communities of men and women religious joined those already in the country. The Oblates of Mary Immaculate, missionaries par excellence in Canada, advanced the penetration of the West which had been started in 1818 by Abbé Provencher. New jurisdictions were established, and Québec became a metropolitan see in 1844. The first Council of Québec was held in 1851. The established Catholic school system enjoyed a period of growth.

Laval University was inaugurated in 1854 and canonically established in 1876.

Archbishop Elzear-Alexandre Taschereau of Québec was named Canada's first cardinal in 1886.

The apostolic delegation to Canada was set up in 1899. It became a nunciature October 16, 1969, with the establishment of diplomatic relations with the Vatican. The present Apostolic Nuncio is Archbishop Luigi Ventura, appointed on June 22, 2001.

Early in this century, Canada had eight ecclesiastical provinces, 23 dioceses, three vicariates apostolic, 3,500 priests, 2 million Catholics, about 30 communities of men religious, and 70 or more communities of women religious. The Church in Canada was phased out of mission status and removed from the jurisdiction of the Congregation for the Propagation of the Faith in 1908.

Diverse Population

The greatest concentration of Catholics is in the eastern portion of the country. In the northern and western portions, outside metropolitan centers, there are some of the most difficult parish and mission areas in the world. Bilingual (English-French) differences in the general population are reflected in the

Church; for example, in the parallel structures of the Canadian Conference of Catholic Bishops, which was established in 1943. Québec is the center of French cultural influence. Many language groups are represented among Catholics, who include more than 257,000 members of Eastern Rites in one metropolitan see, seven eparchies and an apostolic exarchate.

Education, a past source of friction between the Church and the government, is administered by the civil provinces in a variety of arrangements authorized by the Canadian Constitution. Denominational schools have tax support in one way in Québec and Newfoundland, and in another way in Alberta, Ontario and Saskatchewan. Several provinces provide tax support only for public schools, making private financing necessary for separate church-related schools.

ECCLESIASTICAL JURISDICTIONS OF CANADA

Provinces

Names of ecclesiastical provinces and metropolitan sees in bold face; suffragan sees in parentheses.

Edmonton (Calgary, St. Paul).

Gatineau-Hull (Amos, Mont-Laurier, Rouyn Noranda).

Grouard-McLennan (Mackenzie-Ft. Smith, Prince George, Whitehorse).

Halifax (Antigonish, Charlottetown, Yarmouth).

Keewatin-LePas (Churchill-Hudson Bay, Labrador-Schefferville, Moosonee).

Kingston (Alexandria-Cornwall, Peterborough, Sault Ste. Marie).

Moncton (Bathurst, Edmundston, St. John).

Montréal (Joliette, St. Jean-Longueuil, St. Jerome, Valleyfield).

Ottawa (Hearst, Pembroke, Timmins).

Québec (Chicoutimi, Ste. Anne-de-la-Pocatiere, Trois Rivieres).

Regina (Prince Albert, Saskatoon, Abbey of St. Peter).

Rimouski (Baie-Comeau, Gaspe).

St. Boniface (no suffragan).

St. John's (Grand Falls, St. George).

Sherbrooke (Nicolet, St. Hyacinthe).

Toronto (Hamilton, London, St. Catharines, Thunder Bay).

Vancouver (Kamloops, Nelson, Victoria).

Winnipeg-Ukrainian (Edmonton, New Westminster, Saskatoon, Toronto).

Jurisdictions immediately subject to the Holy See: Roman-Rite Archdiocese of Winnipeg, Byzantine Eparchy of Sts. Cyril and Methodius for Slovaks, Byzantine Eparchy of St. Sauveur de Montréal for Greek Melkites; Antiochene Eparchy of St. Maron of Montréal for Maronites.

JURISDICTIONS, HIERARCHY

(Principal sources: Information office, Canadian Conference of Catholic Bishops; Rev. Mr. William Kokesch, Dir., Communications Service, Canadian Conference of Catholic Bishops; Annuaire, Conférence des Évêques Catholiques du Canada; Catholic Almanac survey; Annuario Pontificio; L'Osservatore Romano; Catholic News Service. As of June 1, 2002.)

Information includes names of archdioceses (indicated by asterisk) and dioceses, date of foundation, present ordinaries and auxiliaries; addresses of chancery office/bishop's residence; cathedral.

Alexandria-Cornwall, Ont. (1890 as Alexandria; name changed to Alexandria-Cornwall, 1976): Paul-André Durocher, bishop, 2002.

Diocesan Center: 220, chemin Montréal, C.P. 1388, Cornwall, Ont. K6H 5V4; (613) 938-1138; www.diocese-alex-cnwl.on.ca/. Cathedral: St. Finnans (Alexandria); Nativity Co-Cathedral (Cornwall).

Amos, Qué. (1938): Gérard Drainville, bishop, 1978.

Bishop's Residence: 450, rue Principale Nord, Amos, Qué. J9T 2M1; (819) 732-6515; www3.sympatico.ca/dioceseamos. Cathedral: St. Teresa of Ávila.

Antigonish, N.S. (Arichat, 1844; transferred, 1886): Colin Campbell, bishop, 1987.

Chancery Office: 168 Hawthorne St., P.O. Box 1330, Antigonish, N.S., B2G 2L7; (902) 863-3335; www.antigonishdiocese.com/title.htm. Cathedral: St. Ninian.

Baie-Comeau, Qué. (p.a., 1882; v.a., 1905; diocese Gulf of St. Lawrence, 1945; name changed to Hauterive, 1960; present title, 1986): Pierre Morissette, bishop, 1990.

Bishop's Residence: 639, rue de Bretagne, Baie-Comeau, Qué., G5C 1X2; (418) 589-5744; www.diocese-bc.org. Cathedral: Paroisse St. Jean-Eudes.

Bathurst, N.B. (Chatham, 1860; transferred, 1938): Valéry Vienneau, bishop, 2002.

Bishop's Residence: 645, avenue Murray, C.P. 460, Bathurst, N.B., E2A 3Z4; (506) 546-1420. Cathedral: Sacred Heart of Jesus.

Calgary, Alberta. (1912): Frederick Henry, bishop, 1997.

Address: Room 290, The Iona Building, 120 17 Ave. SW, Calgary, Alberta. T2S 2T2; (403) 218-5526; www.rcdiocese-calgary.ab.ca. Cathedral: St. Mary.

Charlottetown, P.E.I. (1829): Joseph Vernon Fougere, bishop, 1992.

Bishop's Residence: P.O. Box 907, Charlottetown, P.E.I., C1A 7L9; (902) 368-8005; www.dioceseof charlottetown.com. Cathedral: St. Dunstan's.

Chicoutimi, Qué. (1878): Jean-Guy Couture, bishop, 1979. Roch Pedneault, aux.

Bishop's Residence: 602, Racine Est, Chicoutimi, Qué. G7H 6J6; (418) 543-0783; www.evechedechicoutimi.qc.ca. Cathedral: St. Francois-Xavier.

Churchill-Hudson Bay, Man. (p.a., 1925; v.a. Hudson Bay, 1931; diocese of Churchill, 1967; present title, 1968): Reynald Rouleau, O.M.I., bishop, 1987.

Diocesan Office: P.O. Box 10, Churchill, Man. R0B 0E0; (204) 675-2252. Cathedral: Holy Canadian Martyrs.

Edmonton,* Alberta. (St. Albert, 1871; archdiocese, transferred Edmonton, 1912): Thomas C. Collins, archbishop, 1999.

Archdiocese Office: 8421-101 Avenue, Edmonton, Alta. T6A 0L1; (780) 469-1010; www.edmonton

catholic-church.com. Cathedral: Basilica of St. Joseph.

Edmonton, Alberta. (Ukrainian Byzantine) (ap. ex. of western Canada, 1948; eparchy, 1956): Lawrence Daniel Huculak, O.S.B.M., eparch, 1997.

Eparch's Residence: 9645 108th Ave., Edmonton, Alta. T5H 1A3; (780) 424-5496. Cathedral: St. Josaphat.

Edmundston, N.B. (1944): François Thibodeau, C.J.M., bishop, 1994.

Diocesan Center: 60, rue Bouchard, Edmundston, N.B. E3V 3K1; (506) 735-5578; www.francophone.net/diocese. Cathedral: Immaculate Conception.

Gaspé, Qué. (1922): Vacant, bishop.

Bishop's House: 172, rue Jacques-Cartier, Gaspé, Qué. G4X 1M9; (418) 368-2274; www.gaspesie.net/diocesegaspe. Cathedral: Christ the King.

Gatineau-Hull,* Qué. (1963, as Hull; name changed, 1982; archdiocese, 1990): Roger Ébacher, bishop, 1988; first archbishop, Oct. 31, 1990.

Diocesan Center: 180 Boulevard Mont-Bleu, Hull, Qué. J8Z 3J5; (819) 771-8391; www.diocesegatineauhull.qc.ca.

Grand Falls, Nfld. (Harbour Grace, 1856; present title, 1964): Martin W. Currie, bishop, 2000.

Chancery Office: 8A Church Rd., P.O. Box 771, Grand Falls-Windsor, Nfld. A2A 2M4; (709) 489-2778; home.thezone.net/~rcecgf/. Cathedral: Immaculate Conception.

Grouard-McLennan,* Alberta (v.a. Athabaska-Mackenzie, 1862; Grouard, 1927; archdiocese Grouard-McLennan, 1967); Arthé Guimond, archbishop, 2000.

Archbishop's Residence: C.P. 388, McLennan, Alberta. T0H 2L0; (780) 324-3820. Cathedral: St. Jean-Baptiste (McLennan).

Halifax,* N.É. (1842; archdiocese, 1852): Terrence Prendergast, S.J., archbishop, 1998.

Chancery Office: 1531 Grafton St., P.O. Box 1527, Halifax, N.É. B3J 2Y3; (902) 429-9800; www.catholichalifax.org.

Hamilton, Ont. (1856): Anthony Tonnos, bishop, 1984. Matthew Ustrzycki, auxiliary.

Chancery Office: 700 King St. West, Hamilton, Ont. L8P 1C7; (905) 528-7988; www.hamilton diocese.com/. Cathedral: Christ the King.

Hearst, Ont. (p.a., 1918; v.a., 1920; diocese, 1938): André Vallée, P.M.É., bishop, 1996.

Bishop's Residence: 76 7e rue, C.P. 1330, Hearst, Ont. P0L 1N0; (705) 362-4903; www.diocese hearst.com. Cathedral: Notre Dame de l'Assumption.

Joliette, Qué. (1904): Gilles Lussier, bishop, 1991.

Bishop's Residence: 2 rue Saint-Charles-Borromée Nord, C.P. 470, Joliette, Qué. J6E 6H6; (450) 753-7596. Cathedral: St. Charles Borromeo.

Kamloops, B.C. (1945): David Monroe, bishop, 2002.

Bishop's Residence: 635-A Tranquille Rd., Kamloops, B.C. V2B 3H5; (250) 376-3351. Cathedral: Sacred Heart.

Keewatin-Le Pas,* Man. (v.a., 1910; archdiocese, 1967): Peter-Alfred Sutton, O.M.I., archbishop, 1986.

Archbishop's Residence: 76 1st St. W., P.O. Box 270, The Pas, Man. R9A 1K4; (204) 623-6152. Cathedral: Our Lady of the Sacred Heart.

Kingston,* Ont. (1826; archdiocese, 1889): Anthony Meagher, archbishop, 2002.

Chancery Office: 390 Palace Rd., Kingston, Ont. K7L 4T3; (613) 548-4461; www.roman catholic.kingston.on.ca. Cathedral: St. Mary of the Immaculate Conception.

Labrador City-Schefferville, Qué. (v.a. Labrador, 1946; diocese, 1967): Douglas Crosby, O.M.I., bishop, 1997.

Bishop's Residence: Sutton House, 320 avenue Elizabeth, C.P. 545, Labrador City, Labrador, Nfld. A2V 2L3; (709) 944-2046. Cathedral: Our Lady of Perpetual Help.

London, Ont. (1855; transferred Sandwich, 1859; London, 1869): Ronald P. Fabbro, C.S.B., bishop, 2002.

Bishop's Residence: 1070 Waterloo St., London, Ont. N6A 3Y2; (519) 433-0658; www.rcec.lon don.on.ca. Cathedral: St. Peter's Cathedral Basilica.

Mackenzie-Fort Smith, N.W.T. (v.a. Mackenzie, 1902; diocese Mackenzie-Fort Smith, 1967): Denis Croteau, O.M.I., bishop, 1986.

Diocesan Office: 5117-52nd St., Yellowknife, N.T. X1A 1T7; (867) 920-2129. Cathedral: St. Joseph (Ft. Smith).

Moncton,* N.B. (1936): Ernest Léger, archbishop, 1997.

Archbishop's Residence: 452, rue Amirault, Dieppe, N.B. E1A 1G3; (506) 857-9531. Cathedral: Our Lady of the Assumption.

Mont-Laurier, Qué. (1913): Vital Massé, bishop, 2001.

Bishop's Residence: 435, rue de la Madone, Mont-Laurier, Qué. J9L 1S1; (819) 623-5530. Cathedral: Notre Dame de Fourvières.

Montréal,* Qué. (1836; archdiocese, 1886): Cardinal Jean-Claude Turcotte, archbishop, 1990. Anthony Mancini, Louis Dicaire, Jude Saint-Antoine, André Rivest, auxiliaries.

Archbishop's Residence: 2000, rue Sherbrooke Ouest, Montréal, Qué. H3H 1G4; (514) 931-7311; www.archeveche-mtl.qc.ca. Cathedral: Basilica of Mary Queen of the World and Saint James.

Montréal, Qué. (Sauveur de Montréal, Eparchy of Greek Melkites) (ap. ex. 1980; eparchy, 1984): Vacant.

Address: 34 rue Maplewood, Montréal, Qué. H2V 2MI; (514) 272-6430.

Montréal, Que. (St. Maron of Montréal, Maronites) (1982): Joseph Khoury, eparch, 1996.

Chancery Office: 12475 rue Grenet, Montréal, Qué. H4J 2K4; (514) 331-2807. Cathedral: St. Maron.

Moosonee, Ont. (v.a. James Bay, 1938; diocese Moosonee, 1967): Vincent Cadieux, O.M.I., bishop, 1992.

Bishop's Residence: 6 Bay Rd., C.P. 40, Moosonee, Ont. P0L 1Y0; (705) 336-2908. Cathedral: Christ the King.

Nelson, B.C. (1936): Eugene J. Cooney, bishop, 1996.

Bishop's Residence: 402 West Richards St., Nelson, B.C. VIL 3K3; (250) 354-4740; www.diocese.nel son.bc.ca/. Cathedral: Mary Immaculate.

New Westminster, B.C. (Ukrainian Byzantine) (1974): Severian Stephen Yakymyshyn, O.S.B.M., eparch, 1995.

Eparch's address: 502 5th Ave., New Westminster,

B.C. V3L 1S2; (604) 524-8824; www.vcn.bc.ca/ucepnw.

Nicolet, Qué. (1885): Raymond Saint-Gelais, bishop, 1989.

Bishop's Residence: 49, rue Mgr Brunault, Nicolet, Qué. J3T 1X7; (819) 293-4696. Cathedral: St. Jean-Baptiste.

Ottawa,* Ont. (Bytown, 1847, name changed, 1854; archdiocese, 1886): Marcel A.J. Gervais, archbishop, 1989.

Archbishop's Residence: 1247 Place Kilborn, Ottawa, Ont. K1H 6K9; (613) 738-5025; www.ecclesia-ottawa.org. Cathedral: Basilica of Notre Dame-of-Ottawa.

Pembroke, Ont. (v.a. 1882; diocese, 1898): Richard Smith, bishop, 2002.

Bishop's Residence: 188 Renfrew St., P.O. Box 7, Pembroke, Ont. K8A 6X1; (613) 732-7933. Cathedral: St. Columbkille.

Peterborough, Ont. (1882): James L. Doyle, bishop, 1976.

Bishop's Residence: 350 Hunter St. West, P.O. Box 175, Peterborough, Ont. K9J 6Y8; (705) 745-5123. Cathedral: St. Peter-in-Chains.

Prince Albert, Sask. (v.a., 1890; diocese, 1907): Blaise Morand, bishop, 1983.

Address: 1415 4th Ave. West, Prince Albert, Sask. S6V 5H1; (306) 922-4747; www.padiocese.sk.ca. Cathedral: Sacred Heart.

Prince George, B.C. (p.a., 1908; v.a. Yukon and Prince Rupert, 1944; diocese Prince George, 1967): Gerald Wiesner, O.M.I., bishop, 1993.

Chancery Office: P.O. Box 7000, 2935 Highway 16 West, Prince George, B.C. V2N 3Z2; (250) 964-4424; www.pgdiocese.bc.ca. Cathedral: Sacred Heart.

Québec,* Qué. (v.a., 1658; diocese, 1674; archdiocese, 1819; metropolitan, 1844; primatial see, 1956): Maurice Couture, S.V., archbishop, 1990. Jean Pierre Blais, Eugène Tremblay, Jean Gagnon, auxiliaries.

Chancery Office: 1073, boul. René-Lévesque ouest, Québec, Qué. G1S 4R5; (418) 688-1211; www.diocesequebec.qc.ca/. Cathedral: Notre-Dame-de-Québec (Basilica).

Regina,* Sask. (1910; archdiocese, 1915): Peter Mallon, archbishop, 1995.

Chancery Office: 445 Broad St. North, Regina, Sask. S4R 2X8; (306) 352-1651; www.archregina.sk.ca. Cathedral: Our Lady of the Most Holy Rosary.

Rimouski,* Qué. (1867; archdiocese, 1946): Bertrand Blanchet, archbishop, 1992.

Archbishop's Residence: 34, rue de l'Évêché Ouest, C.P. 730, Rimouski, Qué. G5L 7C7; (418) 723-3320; www.dioceserimouski.com.

Rouyn-Noranda, Qué. (1973): Dorylas Moreau, bishop, 2001.

Bishop's Residence: 515, avenue Cuddihy, C.P. 1060, Rouyn-Noranda, Qué. J9X 4C5; (819) 764-4660; www.dioc-cath-rouyn-noranda.org. Cathedral: St. Michael the Archangel.

Saint-Boniface,* Man. (1847; archdiocese, 1871): Emilius Goulet, P.S.S..

Archbishop's Residence: 151, avenue de la Cathedrale, Saint-Boniface, Man. R2H 0H6; (204) 237-9851. Cathedral: Basilica of St. Boniface.

St. Catharine's, Ont. (1958): James M. Wingle, bishop, 2001.

Bishop's Residence: P.O. Box 875, St. Catharines,

Ont. L2R 6Y3; (905) 684-0154; www.roman catholic.niagara.on.ca. Cathedral: St. Catherine of Alexandria.

St. George's, Nfld. (p.a., 1870; v.a., 1890; diocese, 1904): Raymond J. Lahey, bishop, 1986.

Bishop's Residence: 13 Mount Bernard, Corner Brook, Nfld. A2H 6K6; (709) 639-7073; www.rcchurch.com. Cathedral: Most Holy Redeemer and Immaculate Conception.

Saint-Hyacinthe, Qué. (1852): François Lapierre, P.M.E., bishop, 1998.

Bishop's Residence: 1900, rue Girouard Ouest, C.P. 190, Saint-Hyacinthe, Qué. J2S 7B4; (450) 773-8581; www.diocese-st-hyacinthe.qc.ca. Cathedral: St. Hyacinthe the Confessor.

Saint-Jean-Longueuil, Qué. (1933 as St.-Jean-de-Québec; named changed, 1982): Jacques Berthelet, C.S.V., bishop, 1996.

Bishop's Residence: 740, boulevard Sainte-Foy, C.P. 40, Longueuil, Qué. J4K 4X8; (450) 679-1100; www.diocese-st-jean-longueuil.org. Cathedral: St. John the Evangelist.

St. Jérôme, Qué. (1951): Gilles Cazabon, O.M.I., bishop, 1998.

Bishop's Residence: 355, rue Saint-Georges, Saint-Jerome, Qué. J7Z 5A9; (450) 432-9742; www.diocese-stjerome.qc.ca. Cathedral: St. Jerome.

Saint John, N.B. (1842): Joseph Faber MacDonald, bishop, 1998.

Chancery Office: 1 Bayard Dr., Saint John, N.B. E2L 3L5; (506) 653-6800; www.brunnet.net/dsj/. Cathedral: Immaculate Conception.

St. John's,* Nfld. (p.a., 1784; v.a., 1796; diocese, 1847; archdiocese, 1904): Brendan Michael O'Brien, archbishop, 2000.

Chancery Office: P.O. Box 37, St. John's, Nfld. A1C 5N5; (709) 726-3660; www.stjohnsarchdiocese.nf.ca. Cathedral: St. John the Baptist.

St. Paul in Alberta (1948): Joseph Luc André Bouchard, bishop, 2001.

Bishop's Residence: 4410, 51e avenue, Saint Paul, Alta. T0A 3A2; (780) 645-3277. Cathedral: St. Paul.

Sainte-Anne-de-la-Pocatière, Qué. (1951): Clément Fecteau, bishop, 1996.

Bishop's Residence: 1200, 4e avenue, C.P. 430, La Pocatière, Qué. G0R 1Z0; (418) 856-1811. Cathedral: St. Anne.

Saskatoon, Sask. (1933): Albert LeGatt, 2001.

Chancery Office: 100-5th Ave. North, Saskatoon, Sask. S7K 2N7; (306) 242-1500; www.rcdiocese sktn.sk.ca. Cathedral: St. Paul.

Saskatoon, Sask. (Ukrainian Byzantine) (ap. ex., 1951; diocese, 1956): Michael Wiwchar, CSSR, 2000.

Address: 866 Saskatchewan Crescent East, Saskatoon, Sask. S7N 0L4; (306) 653-0138.

Sault Ste. Marie, Ont. (1904): Jean-Louis Plouffe, bishop, 1990.

Chancery Office: 30, chemin Ste. Anne, Sudbury, ON, P3C 5E1, (705) 674-2727; www.isys.ca/cathcom.htm. Cathedral: Pro-Cathedral of the Assumption, North Bay.

Sherbrooke,* Qué. (1874; archdiocese, 1951); André Gaumond, archbishop, 1996.

Archbishop's Residence: 130, rue de la Cathédrale, C.P. 430, Sherbrooke, Qué. J1H 5K1; (819) 563-9934; www.diocesesherbrooke.org. Cathedral: St. Michel.

Thunder Bay, Ont. (Ft. William, 1952; transferred, 1970): Frederick J. Colli, bishop, 1999.

Bishop's Office: 1222 Reaume St., P.O. Box 10400, Thunder Bay, Ont. P7B 6T8; (807) 343-9313; www.dotb.baynet.net. Cathedral: St. Patrick.

Timmins, Ont. (v.a. Temiskaming, 1908; diocese Haileybury, 1915; present title, 1938): Paul Marchand, S.M.M., bishop, 1999.

Address: 65, Ave. Jubilee Est, Timmins, Ont. P4N 5W4; www.nt.net/~dioctims/. Cathedral: St. Anthony of Padua.

Toronto,* Ont. (1841; archdiocese, 1870): Cardinal Aloysius M. Ambrozic, archbishop, 1990. Nicola De Angelis, C.F.I.C., John A. Boissonneau, Richard Grecco, auxiliaries.

Chancery Office: Catholic Pastoral Centre, 1155 Yonge St., Toronto, Ont. M4T 1W2; (416) 934-0606; www.archtoronto.org. Cathedral: St. Michael.

Toronto, Ont. (Eparchy for Slovakian Byzantine) (1980): John Pazak, C.SS.R., 2000.

Eparch's Residence: 223 Carlton Rd., Unionville, Ont. L3R 3M2; (905) 477-4867.

Toronto, Ont. (Eparchy for Ukrainian Byzantine) (ap. ex., 1948; eparchy, 1956): Isidore Borecky (exarch 1948-56), first eparch, 1956. Cornelius Pasichny, O.S.B.M., eparch, 1998.

Chancery Office: 3100-A Weston Rd., Weston, Ont. M9M 2S7; (416) 746-0154; www.ucet.ca. Cathedral: St. Josaphat.

Trois-Rivières, Qué. (1852): Martin Veillette, bishop, 1996.

Bishop's Residence: 362, rue Bonaventure, C.P. 879, Trois-Rivières, Qué. G9A 5J9; (819) 374-9847; www.diocese-tr.qc.ca/. Cathedral: The Assumption.

Valleyfield, Qué. (1892): Luc Cyr, bishop, 2001.

Bishop's Residence: 11, rue de l'Eglise, Salaberry-de-Valleyfield, Qué. J6T 1J5; (450) 373-8122; www.rocler.qc.ca/diocese-valleyfield/. Cathedral: St. Cecilia.

Vancouver,* B. C. (v.a. British Columbia, 1863; diocese New Westminster, 1890; archdiocese Vancouver, 1908): Adam Exner, O.M.I., archbishop, 1991.

Chancery Office: 150 Robson St., Vancouver, B.C. V6B 2A7; (604) 683-0281; www.rcav.bc.ca. Cathedral: Holy Rosary.

Victoria, B.C. (diocese Vancouver Is., 1846; archdiocese, 1903; diocese Victoria, 1908): Raymond Roussin, S.M., bishop, 1999.

Chancery Office: Diocesan Pastoral Centre, #1-4044 Nelthorpe St., Victoria, B.C. V8X 2A1; (250) 479-1331; www.rcdvictoria.org. Cathedral: St. Andrew.

Whitehorse,Y.T. (v.a., 1944; diocese 1967): Vacant.

Chancery Office: 5119 5th Ave., Whitehorse, Yukon Y1A 1L5; (867) 667-2052. Cathedral: Sacred Heart.

Winnipeg,* Man. (1915): James V. Weisberger, archbishop, 2000.

Chancery Office: Catholic Centre, 1495 Pembina Highway, Winnipeg, Man., R3T 2C6; (204) 452-2227; www.manitobacatholic.net. Cathedral: St. Mary.

Winnipeg,* Man. (Ukrainian Byzantine) (Ordinariate of Canada, 1912; ap. ex. Central Canada, 1948; ap. ex. Manitoba, 1951; archeparchy Winnipeg, 1956): Michael Bzdel, C.Ss.R., archeparch, 1993; David Motiuk, auxiliary.

Archeparchy Office: 233 Scotia St., Winnipeg, Man. R2V 1V7; (204) 338-7801; www.escape.ca/~mwinn. Cathedral: Sts. Vladimir and Olga.

Yarmouth, N.É. (1953): Vacant.

Address: C.P. 278, 53 rue Park, Yarmouth, N.É. B5A 4B2; (902) 742-7163; www.dioceseyarmouth.org Cathedral: St. Ambrose.

Military Ordinariate of Canada (1951):Donald J. Thériault, bishop, 1998.

Address: Canadian Forces Support Unit (Ottawa), Uplands Site – Bldg. 469, Ottawa, Ont. K1A 0K2; (613) 998-8747.

An Apostolic Exarchate for Armenian-Rite Catholics in Canada and the United States was established in July 1981 with headquarters in New York City (110 E. 12th St., New York, NY 10003); (212) 477-2030. Manuel Batakian, exarch, 1995.

The Eparchy of Our Lady of Deliverance of Newark for Syrian-rite Catholics in the United States and Canada was established Nov. 6, 1995. Address: 502 Palisade Ave., Union City, NJ 08087; (201) 583-1067; www.Syriac-Catholic.org. Joseph Younan, bishop.

Hungarian Emigrants throughout the world, resides in Canada: Most Rev. Attila Mikloshazy, S.J., titular bishop of Castel Minore. Address: 2661 Kingston Rd., Scarborough, Ont. M1M 1M3; (416) 261-7207.

Note: The diocese of Gravelbourg, in Saskatchewan, was dissolved in September 1998 as part of a reorganization of Canadian dioceses. The regions under the jurisdiction of Gravelbourg were integrated into the neighboring dioceses of Regina and Saskatoon. The Territorial Abbacy of St. Peter, Muenster, Sask., was also dissolved.

Dioceses with Interprovincial Lines

The following dioceses, indicated by + in the table, have interprovincial lines.

Churchill-Hudson Bay includes part of Northwest Territories.

Keewatin-LePas includes part of Manitoba and Saskatchewan provinces.

Labrador City-Schefferville includes the Labrador region of Newfoundland and the northern part of Québec province.

Mackenzie-Fort Smith, Northwest Territories, includes part of Alberta and Saskatchewan provinces.

Moosonee, Ontario, includes part of Québec province.

Pembroke, Ontario, includes one county of Québec province.

Whitehorse, Yukon Territory, includes part of British Columbia.

CANADIAN CONFERENCE OF CATHOLIC BISHOPS

The Canadian Conference of Catholic Bishops was established Oct. 12, 1943, as a permanent voluntary association of the bishops of Canada, was given official approval by the Holy See in 1948, and acquired the status of an episcopal conference after the Second Vatican Council.

The CCCB acts in two ways: (1) as a strictly ecclesiastical body through which the bishops act together with pastoral authority and responsibility for the Church throughout the country; (2) as an operational secretariat through which the bishops act on a wider scale for the good of the Church and society.

At the top of the CCCB organizational table are the president, an executive committee, a permanent council and a plenary assembly. The membership consists of all the bishops of Canada.

Departments and Offices

The CCCB's work is planned and coordinated by the Programmes and Priorities Committee composed of the six chairmen of the national episcopal commissions and the two general secretaries. It is chaired by the vice-president of the CCCB.

The CCCB's 12 episcopal commissions undertake study and projects in special areas of pastoral work. Six serve nationally (social affairs; canon law/interrite; relations with associations of clergy, consecrated life and laity; evangelization of peoples; ecumenism; theology); three relate to French sectors (*communications sociale, éducation Chrétienne, liturgie*); and three relate to corresponding English sectors (social communications, Christian education, liturgy).

The general secretariat consists of a general secretary and assistants and directors of public relations. The current general secretary is Msgr. Peter Schonenbach, P.H.

Administrative services for purchasing, archives and library, accounting, personnel, publications, printing and distribution are supervised by directors who relate to the general secretaries.

Various advisory councils and committees with mixed memberships of lay persons, religious, priests and bishops also serve the CCCB on a variety of topics.

Operations

Meetings for the transaction of business are held at least once a year by the plenary assembly, six times a year by the executive committee, and four times a year by the permanent council.

Bishop Jacques Berthelet, C.S.V. of Saint-Jean-Longueuil, is president of the CCCB and Bishop Brendan O'Brien, of Saint John's, is vice president, for the 2002-2003 term.

The Secretariat headquarters is located at 90 Parent Ave., Ottawa, K1N 7B1, Canada; (613) 241-9461; www.cccb.ca.

CANADIAN SHRINES

Our Lady of the Cape (Cap de la Madeleine), Queen of the Most Holy Rosary: The Three Rivers, Québec, parish church, built of fieldstone in 1714 and considered the oldest stone church on the North American continent preserved in its original state, was rededicated June 22, 1888, as a shrine of the Queen of the Most Holy Rosary. Thereafter, the site increased in importance as a pilgrimage and devotional center, and in 1904 St. Pius X decreed the crowning of a statue of the Blessed Virgin which had been donated 50 years earlier to commemorate the dogma of the Immaculate Conception. In 1909, the First Plenary Council of Québec declared the church a shrine of national pilgrimage. In 1964, the church at the shrine was given the status and title of minor basilica.

St. Anne de Beaupre: The devotional history of this shrine in Québec began with the reported cure of a cripple, Louis Guimont, on Mar. 16, 1658, the starting date of construction work on a small chapel of St. Anne. The original building was successively enlarged and replaced by a stone church which was given the rank of minor basilica in 1888. The present structure, a Romanesque-Gothic basilica, houses the shrine proper in its north transept. The centers of attraction are an eight-foot-high oaken statue and the great relic of St. Anne, a portion of her forearm.

St. Joseph's Oratory: The massive oratory basilica standing on the western side of Mount Royal and overlooking the city of Montréal had its origin in a primitive chapel erected there by Blessed André Bessette, C.S.C., in 1904. Eleven years later, a large crypt was built to accommodate an increasing number of pilgrims, and in 1924 construction work was begun on the large church. A belfry, housing a 60-bell carillon and standing on the site of the original chapel, was dedicated May 15, 1955, as the first major event of the jubilee year observed after the oratory was given the rank of minor basilica.

Martyrs' Shrine: A shrine commemorating several of the Jesuit Martyrs of North America who were killed between 1642 and 1649 in the Ontario and northern New York area is located on the former site of old Fort Sainte Marie. Before its location was fixed near Midland, Ont., in 1925, a small chapel had been erected in 1907 at old Mission St. Ignace to mark the martyrdom of Fathers Jean de Brebeuf and Gabriel Lalemant. This sanctuary has a U.S. counterpart in the Shrine of the North American Martyrs near Auriesville, N.Y., under the care of the Jesuits.

Others

Other shrines and historic churches in Canada:

In Québec City: the Basilica of Notre Dame, dating from 1650, once the cathedral of a diocese stretching from Canada to Mexico; Notre Dame des Victoires, on the waterfront, dedicated in 1690; the Ursuline Convent, built in 1720, on du Parloir St.

In Montréal: Notre Dame Basilica, patterned after the famous basilica of the same name in Paris, constructed in 1829; the Shrine of Mary, Queen of All Hearts.

Near Montréal: the Chapel of St. Marie Marguerite d'Youville, foundress of the Grey Nuns; Notre Dame de Lourdes, at Rigaud.

STATISTICAL SUMMARY OF THE CATHOLIC CHURCH IN CANADA

(*Principal source:* 2002 Directory of the Canadian Conference of Catholic Bishops; *figures as of Jan. 2002*); Catholic population statistics are those reported in the 1991 Canadian Census. Archdioceses are indicated by an asterisk. For dioceses marked +, see Canadian Dioceses with Interprovincial Lines.

Canada's 10 civil provinces and two territories are divided into 18 ecclesiastical provinces consisting of 18 metropolitan sees (archdioceses) and 45 suffragan sees; there are also eight Oriental Rite dioceses, one archdiocese and three eparchies immediately subject to the Holy See, and the Military Ordinariate.

This table presents a regional breakdown of Catholic statistics. In some cases, the totals are approximate because diocesan boundaries fall within several civil provinces.

Civil Province Diocese	Cath. Pop.	Dioc. Priests	Rel. Priests	Total Priests	Perm. Deacs.	Bro- thers	Sis- ters	Lay Assts.	Par- ishes[1]
Newfoundland	213,055	95	22	117	2	7	326	28	229
St. John's*	119,260	35	9	44	-	6	231	2	73
Grand Falls	37,940	31	-	31	1	-	34	5	73
Labrador- Schefferville+	13,550	1	11	12	1	1	22	17	25
St. George's	42,305	28	2	30	-	-	39	4	58
Prince Edward Island									
Charlottetown	60,625	53	2	55	1	-	157	3	57
Nova Scotia	450,270	217	23	250	27	4	643	53	237
Halifax*	152,515	54	21	75	25	2	287	30	75
Antigonish	138,990	137	12	149	1	2	330	14	123
Yarmouth	39,505	26	0	26	1	-	26	9	39
New Brunswick	386,480	224	63	287	4	30	845	188	250
Moncton*	105,775	60	30	90	1	23	320	88	60
Bathurst	115,560	59	9	68	1	5	236	14	63
Edmundston	52,435	39	9	48	-	1	119	18	32
St. John	112,710	66	15	81	2	1	170	68	95
Québec	6,057,315	2,696	1,809	4,505	398	1,726	15,295	1,749	1,798
Gatineau-Hull*	216,725	56	37	93	2	5	217	99	61
Montréal*	1,656,297	560	796	1,356	102	532	5,169	91	267
Québec*	902,545	511	341	852	85	265	3,771	290	235
Rimouski*	152,565	137	19	156	10	38	688	29	118
Sherbrooke*	235,145	213	107	320	20	88	1,090	84	116
Amos	103,890	27	22	49	-	11	112	128	62
Baie Comeau	93,715	45	17	62	8	9	83	27	45
Chicoutimi	275,580	200	47	247	35	56	645	120	96
Gaspé	94,645	60	6	66	3	5	166	25	66
Joliette	177,138	78	53	131	6	105	254	62	57
Mont Laurier	72,755	38	15	53	-	12	65	52	58
Montréal, St. Maron (Maronites)	80,000	10	7	17	1	-	3	-	13
Montréal, St. Sauveur (Greek-Melkites)	38,000	5	9	14	1	-	-	-	8
Nicolet	177,620	160	22	182	25	79	556	41	85
Rouyn-Noranda	56,475	27	7	34	-	2	82	24	44
Ste-Anne-de-la- Pocatière	87,865	116	1	117	6	-	177	59	54
St.-Hyacinthe	330,515	160	77	237	34	184	840	146	108
St.-Jean-Longueuil	524,150	110	46	156	3	115	391	160	90
St. Jérôme	353,310	91	90	181	17	105	262	137	72
Trois Rivières	243,085	116	65	81	30	92	628	116	80
Valleyfield	185,295	76	25	101	10	23	96	59	63
Ontario	3,575,065	1,539	871	2,410	386	137	3,333	216	1,269
Kingston*	102,650	69	4	73	-	-	186	-	72
Ottawa*	364,285	165	103	268	48	12	886	4	114
Toronto*	1,420,395	403	470	873	129	71	757	-	223
Alexandria-Cornwall	56,020	41	7	48	18	4	56	5	34
Hamilton	480,695	133	101	234	2	19	322	46	149

Civil Province Diocese	Cath. Pop.	Dioc. Priests	Rel. Priests	Total Priests	Perm. Deacs.	Bro-thers	Sis-ters	Lay Assts.	Par-ishes[1]
Ontario, cont.									
Hearst	34,840	31	-	31	-	4	15	24	28
London	414,285	210	72	282	2	5	444	89	169
Moosonee+	3,905	-	3	3	1	3	3	3	18
Pembroke+	64,925	71	3	74	7	3	174	7	67
Peterborough	83,680	106	11	117	13	-	101	5	70
St. Catharine's	145,850	60	34	94	1	5	48	14	48
Sault Ste. Marie	218,850	102	32	134	108	4	253	2	117
Thunder Bay	78,480	29	15	44	31	-	28	-	42
Timmins	55,195	26	3	29	7	5	33	16	34
Toronto (Ukrainians)	41,010	89	9	98	19	2	27	1	76
Toronto (Slovaks, Sts. Cyril and Methodius)	10,000	4	4	8	-	-	-	-	8
Manitoba	346,180	190	112	302	50	15	535	137	389
Keewatin-Le Pas*+	35,195	5	12	17	-	2	17	14	49
St. Boniface*	101,920	83	56	139	17	13	329	9	105
Winnipeg*	170,590	64	26	90	17	3	153	4	91
Winnepeg (Ukrainians)*	33,490	38	10	48	16	-	34	-	127
Churchill-Hudson Bay+	4,985	-	8	8	-	-	2	110	17
Saskatchewan+	301,335	162	78	250	10	27	472	56	490
Regina*#	129,500	76	11	87	3	5	145	10	167
Prince-Albert	57,580	22	9	31	2	1	89	4	86
Saskatoon#	90,908	42	48	90	-	16	236	12	108
Saskatoon (Ukrainians)	20,080	22	10	32	5	2	18	-	129
Alberta	665,870	218	199	417	17	49	611	67	387
Edmonton*	294,935	74	116	190	-	39	415	46	146
Grouard-McLennan*	40,715	5	18	23	2	-	2	16	67
Calgary	250,605	89	49	138	6	10	124	-	74
Edmonton (Ukrainians)	26,250	27	14	41	8	-	35	-	87
St. Paul	53,365	23	2	25	1	-	17	5	13
British Columbia	600,175	185	136	321	5	36	286	258	304
Vancouver*	340,775	87	90	177	1	28	138	-	94
Kamloops	47,010	12	10	22	1	3	16	-	71
Nelson	63,570	36	10	46	-	-	18	10	53
New Westminster (Ukrainians)	7,555	11	2	13	2	-	2	-	16
Prince George	51,200	11	7	18	1	2	22	248	41
Victoria	90,065	28	17	45	-	3	90	-	29
Yukon Territory									
Whitehorse+	8,235	3	11	14	1	1	8	12	22
Northwest Territories									
MacKenzie-Ft. Smith+	19,745	3	4	7	1	-	15	20	40
Military Ordinariate	75,183	33*	3**	36	2	-	-	35	24**
TOTALS	12,637,006[2]	5,718	3,340	9,058	913	2,028	22,542	2,792	5,496

1. Denotes both parishes and missions.

2. Catholics comprise about 44% of the total population. According to the 2000 *Annuarium Statisticum Ecclesiae* (the most recent edition), there were 138,057 baptisms and 35,626 marriages.

* The Canadian Military Ordinariate does not incardinate clerics.

** Not included in the total.

The Catholic Church In Mexico

BACKGROUND

Start of Church Organization

The history of the Catholic Church in Mexico began in 1519 with the capture of Mexico's native civilization, the Aztec Empire, by the Spanish *conquistadores* under Hernándo Cortés. The Spanish army besieged the Aztec capital of Tenochtitlan, massacred most of the inhabitants, strangled the Aztec emperor Montezuma, and crushed the rest of the empire. Mexico City became the chief city of New Spain and the cultural and religious center of colonial Mexico; it was declared a diocese in 1530.

The record of Colonial Spanish treatment of the native peoples of Mexico is a grim one. The Indians suffered exploitation, slavery, and rapid depletion of their population from disease; they were forced to labor in inhuman conditions in mines and endured servitude in the *encomienda* system.

In sharp contrast to the treatment of the natives by the government was the effort to evangelize Mexico by the religious orders who followed the command of Pope Alexander VI in the 1494 Treaty of Tordesillas to convert all peoples who should be encountered in the coming age of exploration. A papal bull, dated Apr. 25, 1521, gave to the Franciscans the permission of the Holy See to preach in New Spain. They were joined by the Dominicans and, later, by the Jesuits. The missionary orders soon distinguished themselves by their resistance to the brutal enslavement of the Indians, their mastery of native languages, and their willingness to endure enormous hardships in bringing the faith to the distant corners of Mexico.

As the Church became more established, however, the missionary priests and friars came increasingly into conflict with the secular clergy, who desired full control over ecclesiastical affairs, resented the extensive powers of religious orders, and normally identified closely with the interests of the crown. The government thus decreed that the missionaries were to have ten years in which to convert the Indians after which control should pass to the diocesan clergy. This was protested by the missionary orders, and the conflict was resolved in favor of the diocesan priests in 1640 thanks to the efforts of Bishop Juan de Palafox de Mendoza of Puebla.

The alliance of the secular clergy with the government was a reflection of the control enjoyed by the Spanish crown over the Church in Mexico. The Holy See had granted to the kings of Spain royal patronage over the Church in Mexico, and the practice of the *Patronato Real* meant that the king nominated all Church officials in New Spain and held authority over the Church's temporal concerns. A major element in this policy was the forced conversion of the local peoples. Coerced into adopting the faith, many Indians were insincere or hesitant to embrace a faith that was forced upon them. To insure the full embrace of the faith, Spanish authorities received permission from King Philip II in 1569 to introduce the Inquisition to Mexico. Indians who had survived the mines, diseases, and brutality of the colonial rulers were now subjected to tribunals to test their faith. This practice was eventually ended when authorities decided that the natives were not culpable because of limited intelligence. Nevertheless, the close identification of the diocesan clergy with the interests and policies of the Spanish crown created a hostility toward the Church in Mexico by the lower classes that endures today.

On the positive side, the Church did much through its missionaries to save many Indians from death and enslavement and to preserve vital portions of Mesoamerican culture, art, and history. Equally, friars traveled to northern Mexico and beyond, bringing the faith into California, Texas, and New Mexico.

The native peoples were given a profound encouragement to embrace the Catholic faith in 1531 by the appearance of Our Lady of Guadalupe to the farmer Juan Diego (canonized in 2002 by Pope John Paul II) on the Tepeyac hill just outside of Mexico City. The shrine built in her honor remains the most important religious site in Mexico. Enshrined within it is the mantle brought by Juan Diego to Bishop Zumaragga to convince him of the genuine nature of the apparition. Miraculously emblazoned upon it is the life-size image of the Virgin Mary.

MEXICAN INDEPENDENCE

The Spanish domination of Mexico endured for nearly three centuries, deteriorating gradually throughout the 1700s as the gulf widened between the Spanish ruling class and the native classes that were joined by the *mestizos* and *creoles* (descendants of Native Americans and Europeans). Unrest broke out into a full-scale rebellion in 1810 with the uprising of many priests led by Father Miguel Hidalgo y Costilla and, after his execution, by Father José Maria Morelos y Pavón. While suppressed in 1816 by the colonial regime with the support of the upper classes and most of the diocesan clergy, it proved only the first of several revolts, culminating in the 1821 declaration of Mexican independence. By the terms of the independence, the Church received a special status and had enormous sway in political life.

A republic was proclaimed in 1834 and various liberal regimes came to power. Anticlericalism became commonplace, made even more strident by the lingering hostility over the Church's activities with Spanish colonial government. Much influenced by the ideals of the European revolutions then taking place, the Mexican republican movements were strongly anti-Catholic. For more than a decade, power was in the hands of Antonio López de Santa Anna (of the Alamo fame) and Valentín Gómez Farías. After the Mexican-American War (1846-1848), the political instability led to the dictatorship of Santa Anna.

Santa Anna was toppled in 1855 by a liberal regime whose anti-Church legislation sparked an armed struggle called the War of the Reform (1858-1861). The laws issued by the government included the *Ley Juárez*, abolishing all ecclesiastical courts, and the *Ley Lerdo*, forcing the Church to sell all of its lands. Deprived of its properties, the Church lost control of education and schools, and Mexico's educational system became often bitterly anti-Catholic.

While the liberal forces won the War of the Reform, the conflict had so debilitated Mexico that the French were able to intervene in 1861 and install their puppet, the Austrian duke Maximilian, on the Mexican throne. As the United States was embroiled in its own civil war from 1861-1865, it was unable to respond to French imperialist ambitions in Mexico. Maximilian initially enjoyed the support of the conservative elements and the Church, but his liberal reforms alienated the mistrustful conservatives and he soon clung to power only with French support. When France finally withdrew its troops in 1867, Maximilian was deposed by republican forces and executed.

MODERN MEXICO

The fall of Emperor Maximilian signaled a restoration of the anticlerical constitution of 1857 and the elevation of Benito Juárez — the republican leader long recognized by the United States — as president. His successor, Sebastián Lerdo de Tijada, was toppled in 1876 by Porfirio Diáz, who remained dictator for thirty-four years. A civil war ended his regime, and more bloodshed ensued. Finally, a constitution was issued in 1917 that placed severe restrictions on the Church: there could be no criticism of the government, only Mexicans could be clergy, the Church was not permitted to own property, and any privileges were stripped away.

The situation became worse after 1923, when the papal legate was expelled. The administration of Plutarco Calles (1924-1928) launched a wave of persecution that sparked a popular but ultimately unsuccessful uprising called the Cristero Rebellion. Coupled with the repressive measures of local governments, the Calles regime and its successors forced the Church into very difficult circumstances, with only a few priests remaining in the country. The tragedy was deepened by the execution of dozens of priests and nuns by republican forces for assorted and imaginary crimes or for speaking out on behalf of the poor or oppressed Catholics. A number of the executed clergy have been beatified and canonized since the tragedy, most so during the pontificate of Pope John Paul II. The persecution prompted Pope Pius XI to issue the encyclicals *Iniquis afflictisque* (1926) and *Acerba animi* (1932).

An easing of the situation began in 1940 as the rigid anticlerical laws ceased to be enforced with enthusiasm. A rapprochement was visible in the 1958 elections, when the Church received conciliatory gestures from the ruling Revolutionary Party and its presidential candidate Adolfo López Mateos. The Church continued to exist under numerous legal disabilities and was oppressed in a number of the Mexican states.

Gradual improvement in relations between Mexico and the Holy See led to the exchange in 1990 of personal representatives between the Mexican president and Pope John Paul II. The Holy Father's efforts to build a further diplomatic bridge culminated in the establishment of full diplomatic ties in 1992. This was followed by the final easing of many of the handicaps under which the Church had long suffered.

The faith of the Mexican people is profoundly deep, as was seen in the nearly frenzied greeting given to Pope John Paul II in 1979, 1990, 1993, and 1999. However, social unrest, poverty, economic challenges, the violence of drug cartels, and corruption still plague the country. Church leaders — especially religious orders — have been outspoken in their criticism of government human rights abuses and corruption. During the mid-1990s, the Jesuits said they were the target of a "campaign of intimidation" because of their human rights work.

On May 24, 1993, Cardinal Juan Jesus Posadas Ocampo of Guadalajara was killed during a supposed shoot-out among rival drug cartels. The murder remained unsolved, although Cardinal Posadas' successor, Cardinal Juan Sandoval Íñiguez, continued to claim that high-ranking officials, including the Mexican attorney general at the time, lied to protect others involved in a plot. In 2001 Cardinal Sandoval said he would seek a reopening of the case because he had new evidence contradicting the findings of the official investigation; he also claimed he had been almost fatally poisoned in 1999 during a dinner with federal officials angry with his insistence that the murder was not accidental.

In the 1970s and 1980s, one of Mexico's most prominent proponents of liberation theology was Bishop Samuel Ruiz Garcia of San Cristobal de las Casas. In the early 1990s the Vatican began investigating his views, but because he had the trust of indigenous peasants, in 1994 he was thrown into the role of mediator between the government and the mostly native Zapatista National Liberation Army in Chiapas. He continued that role until 1998, when he resigned after accusing the government of "dismantling any possible means or effort to solve the crisis in Chiapas." Mexico's bishops said at that time that they would provide support to the peace process but would not seek to mediate the conflict.

On July 2, 2000, Vicente Fox Quesada, head of the National Action Party and a practicing Catholic, won the Mexican presidential election, marking the first time since 1929 that the country was not ruled by the Institutional Revolutionary Party. Mexico City Cardinal Norberto Rivera Carrera told reporters the election was "not a miracle, as some have suggested, but it is an extraordinary act." Church officials emphasized that they expected no special privileges from the new government, but the general climate was one of optimism for an improvement in church-state relations.

Within weeks, Fox — with news cameras flashing — received Communion in his hometown parish. However, in July 2001, the Vatican said he failed to have his first marriage annulled before marrying his spokeswoman in a civil ceremony; thus, he would be prohibited from receiving the sacraments. In June 2001, federal and state officials participated in a public Mass at the Basilica of Our Lady of Guadalupe, breaking a taboo on government officials publicly practicing their religion.

ORGANIZATION

Presently, the Church in Mexico is organized into 14 provinces. There are 14 archdioceses, 59 dioceses (including the April 2000 creation of two new suffragan dioceses of the archdiocese of Xalapa), 6 prelacies, and 1 vicariate apostolic. As of August 15, 2002, there were four Mexican members of the College of Cardinals: Ernesto Corripio Ahumada, Norberto Rivera Carrera, Juan Sandoval Íñiguez, and Adolfo Antonio Suárez Rivera. (For statistical information on the Church in Mexico, see below.)

The current apostolic delegation to Mexico was set up in 1992 as a nunciature with the establishment of renewed formal diplomatic relations with the Vatican. The present Apostolic Nuncio is Archbishop Giuseppe Bertolli, appointed in December 2000.

ECCLESIASTICAL JURISDICTIONS
Provinces

Names of ecclesiastical provinces and metropolitan sees in bold face: suffragan sees in parentheses.

Acapulco (Ciudad Lázaro Cárdenas, Chilpancingo-Chilapa, Ciudad Altamirano, Tlapa).

Chihuahua (Ciudad Juárez, Cuauhtémoc-Madera, Parral, Tarahumara).

Durango (Culiacán, Mazatlán, Torreón, El Salto).

Guadalajara (Aguascalientes, Autlán, Ciudad Guzmán, Colima, San Juan de los Lagos, Tepic, Zacatecas; Prelature of Jesús Maria del Nayar).

Hermosillo (Ciudad Obregón, La Paz, Mexicali, Tijuana).

México (Atlacomulco, Cuernavaca, Toluca, Tula, Tulancingo).

Monterrey (Ciudad Valles, Ciudad Victoria, Linares, Matamoros, Nuevo Laredo, Saltillo, Tampico, Nuevo Casas Grandes).

Morelia (Apatzingán, Tacámbaro, Zamora).

Oaxaca, Antequera (San Cristóbal de las Casas, Tapachula, Tehuantepec, Tuxtla Gutiérrez, Tuxtepec; Prelacies of Mixes and Huautla).

Puebla de los Angeles (Huajuapan de León, Huejutla, Tehuacán, Tlaxcala).

San Luis Potosi (Celaya, León, Querétaro, Matehuala).

Tlalnepantla (Texcoco, Cuautitlán, Netzahualcóyotl, Ecatepec).

Xalapa (Papantla, San Andrés Tuxtla, Coatzacoalcos, Tuxpan, Veracruz, Orizaba, Cordoba).

Yucatán (Campeche, Tabasco, Prelacy of Cancún-Chetumal; Eparchy of Nuestra Señora del Paraiso).

Jurisdictions, Hierarchy

(*Principal sources: Information office, Mexican Conference of Catholic Bishops;* Catholic Almanac *survey;* Annuario Pontificio; L'Osservatore Romano; Catholic News Service. *As of June 1, 2002; addresses and phone numbers are provided by the* Annuario Pontificio.)

Information includes names of archdioceses (indicated by asterisk) and dioceses, date of foundation, present ordinaries and auxiliaries; addresses of chancery office/bishop's residence.

Acapulco* (1958; promoted to archdiocese, 1983): Felipe Aguirre Franco, archbishop, 2001.

Diocesan Address: Apartado Postal 201, Quebrada 16, 39850 Acapulco, Guerrero; (748) 2-07-63.

Aguascalientes (1899): Ramón Godinez Flores, bishop, 1998.

Diocesan Address: Apartado 628, Galeana 105 Norte, 20000 Aquascalientes, Aquascalientes; (49) 15-32-61.

Apatzingán (1962): Miguel Patiño Velázquez, M.S.F., bishop, 1981.

Diocesan Address: Calle Esteban Vaca Calderón 100, 60600 Apatzingán, Mich.; (453)-41787.

Atlacomulco (1984): Constancio Miranda Weckmann, bishop, 1998.

Diocesan Address: Hidalgo Sur 1, Apartado 22, 50450 Atlacomulco, Méx.; (712) 2-05-53.

Autlán (1961): Lázaro Pérez Jiménez, bishop, 1991.

Diocesan Address: Apartado 8, Hidalgo 74, 48900 Autlán, Jal., Mex.; (338) 2-12-28.

Campeche (1895): José Luis Amezcua Melgoza, bishop, 1995.

Diocesan Address: Calle 16 y Alvaro Obregón s/n, Col. Santa Lucia, n. 5, Apartado 127, 24000 Campeche, Camp.; (981) 6-03-39.

Cancún-Chetumal, Prelacy of (1970, as Chetumal; name changed in 1996): Jorge Bernal Vargas, bishop, 1978.

Diocesan Address: Apartado Postal 165, Othón P. Blanco 150, 77000 Chetumal, Quintana Roo; (983) 2-06-38.

Celaya (1973): Jesús Humberto Velázquez Garay, bishop, 1988.

Diocesan Address: Curia Diocesana, Apartado 207, Manuel Doblado 110, 38000 Celaya, Gto.; (461)-2-48-35.

Chihuahua* (1891; promoted to archdiocese, 1958): José Fernández Arteaga, archbishop, 1991.

Diocesan Address: Av. Cuauhtémoc, Apartado Postal 7, 31020 Chihuahua, Chihuahua; (14) 10-32-03.

Chilpancingo-Chilapa (1863 as Chilpancingo; name changed to Chilpancingo-Chilapa, 1989): Efrén Ramos Salazar, bishop, 1990.

Diocesan Address: Apartado Postal #185, 39000 Chilpancingo, Gro.; (747) 1-05-92.

Ciudad Altamirano (1964): Carlos Garfias Merlos, bishop, 1996.

Diocesan Address: Juárez 18 Oriente, Centro, Apdo 17, 40680 Ciudad Altamirano, Gro.; (767) 2-17-74.

Ciudad Guzmán (1972): Braulio Rafael León Villegas, bishop, 1999.

Diocesan Address: Ramón Corona 26, Apartado 86, 49000 Ciudad Guzman, Jal.; (341) 2-19-94.

Ciudad Juárez (1957): Renato Ascencio León, bishop, 1994.

Diocesan Address: Apartado Postal 188, 32000 Cuidad Juárez, Chih.; (16) 15-09-22.

Ciudad Lázaro Cárdenas (1985): Salvador Flores Huerta, bishop, 1993.

Diocesan Address: Apartado 500, Andador Ciudad del Carmen #4, Fideicomiso 2° Sector, 60950 Lázaro Cardenas, Mich.; (753) 2-34-88.

Ciudad Obregón (1959): Vicente Garcia Bernal, bishop, 1988.

Diocesan Address: Apartado 402, Sonora 161 Norte, 85000 Ciudad Obregón, Son.; (641) 3-20-98.

Ciudad Valles (1960): Roberto Octavio Balmori Cinta, M.J., bishop, 2002.

Diocesan Address: 16 de Septiembre 726, Apartado 170, 79000 Ciudad Valles, S.L.P.; (138) 2-25-97

Ciudad Victoria (1964): Antonio González Sánchez, bishop, 1995.

Diocesan Address: 15 Hidalgo y Juárez, Centro, Apartado Postal #335, 87000 Ciudad Victoria, Tamps.; (131) 2-87-16.

Coatzacoalcos (1984): Carlos Talavera Ramírez, bishop, 1984.

Diocesan Address: Apartado 513, Aldama 502, 96400 Coatzacoalcos, Ver.; (921) 2-23-99.

Colima (1881): Gilberto Valbuena Sánchez, bishop, 1989.

Diocesan Address: Hidalgo 135, Apartado 1, 28000 Colima, Colima; (331) 2-02-62.

Cordoba (2000): Eduardo Porfirio Patiño Leal, bishop, 2000.

Diocesan Address: Avenida 11-1300, Esquina cin Calle 13, Apartado 154, Zona Centro, 94500 Cordoba, Ver., Mexico.

Cuauhtémoc-Madera (1966): Juan Guillermo López Soto, bishop, 1995.

Diocesan Address: Apartado Postal 209, 31500 Cuauhtemoc, Chih.; (158) 2-11-97.

Cuautitlán (1979): Manuel Samaniego Barriga, bishop, 1979.

Diocesan Address: Apartado 14-21, Sor Juana Inés de la Cruz 208, Anexo a Catedral, 54800 Cuautitlán de Romero Rubio; (5) 872-19-96

Cuernavaca (1891): Florencio Olvera Ochoa, bishop, 2002.

Diocesan Address: Apartado 13, Hidalgo #2, 62000 Cuernavaca, Mor.; (73) 18-96-46.

Culiacán (1883 as Sinaloa; name changed 1959): Benjamin Jiménez Hernández, bishop, 1993.

Diocesan Address: Apartado Postal 666, Av. Las Palmas #26 Oriente, 80220 Culiacán, Sinaloa; (67) 12-14-97.

Durango* (1620, promoted to archdiocese, 1891): Vacant, archbishop; Juan de Dios Caballero Reyes, aux.

Diocesan Address: Apartado Postal 116, 34000 Durango, Durango; (18) 11-42-42.

Ecatepec (1995): Onésimo Cepeda Silva, bishop, 1995.

Diocesan Address: Plaza Principal s/n, San Cristóbal Centro, Apartado Postal 95, 55000 Ecatepec de Morelos; (5) 116-09-76.

El Salto, Prelacy of (1968): Manuel Mireles Vaquera, bishop, 1988.

Prelature Address: Apartado Postal 58, 34950 El Salto, Durango; (187) 6-00-70.

Guadalajara* (1548; promoted to archdiocese, 1863): Cardinal Juan Sandoval Íñiguez, archbishop, 1994; Benjamin Castillo Plascencia, José Trinidad González Rodriguez, Miguel Romano Gómez, Rafael Martínez Sainz, José María De la Torre Martín, auxiliaries.

Diocesan Address: Arzobispado, Apartado Postal 1-331, Calle Liceo 17, 44100 Guadalajara, Jal.; (3) 614-55-04; www.arquidiocesisgdl.org.mx.

Hermosillo* (1779, as Sonora, promoted to an archdiocese, 1963): José Ulises Macias Salcedo, archbishop, 1996.

Diocesan Address: Apartado 1, Dr. Paliza 81, 83260 Hermosillo, Son.; (62) 13-21-38.

Huajuapan de Leon (1903): Teodoro Enrique Pino Miranda, 2000.

Diocesan Address: Apartado 43, Anexos de Catedral, 69000 Huajuapan de León, Oax.; (953) 2-07-97.

Huautla, Prelacy of (1972): Hermengildo Ramirez Sánchez, M.J., bishop, 1978.

Diocesan Address: Casa Prelaticia, Apartado 2, 68500 Huautla de Jiménez, Oaxaca; (237) 8-00-19.

Huejutla (1922): Salvador Martínez Pérez, bishop, 1994.

Diocesan Address: Obispado, Apartado 8, Ave. Corona del Rosal s/n, Col. Tecoluco, 43000 Huejutla, Hgo.; (789) 6-01-85.

Jesús María of Nayar, Prelature of (1962): José Antonio Pérez Sánchez, O.F.M., bishop, 1992.

Diocesan Address: Curia Prelaticia de Jesús María, Belén #24, Apartado 33-B, 63150 Tepic, Nayar; (32) 3-38-80.

La Paz en la Baja California Sur (1988): Miguel Angel Alba Díaz, 2001.

Diocesan Address: Apartado 25, Revolución y 5 de Mayo, 23000 La Paz, B.C.S.; (112) 2-25-96.

León (1863): José Guadalupe Martin Rábago, bishop, 1995.

Diocesan Address: Pedro Moreno #312, Apartado 108, 37000 León, Gto.; (47) 13-10-58; www.diocesisleon.org.mx.

Linares (1962): Ramón Calderón Batres, bishop, 1988.

Diocesan Address: Morelos y Zaragoza s/n, Apartado 70, 67700 Linares, N.L.; (821) 2-00-54.

Matamoros (1958): Francisco Javier Chavolla Ramos, bishop, 1991.

Diocesan Address: Apartado 70, Calle 5 y Morelos, 87351 Matamoros, Tamps.; (88) 13-55-11; www.communion.org.mx.

Matehuala (1997): Rodrigo Aguilar Martínez, bishop, 1997.

Diocesan Address: Júarez 512 Sur, Apartado 40, 78700 Matehuala, S.L.P.; (01) 488-2-51-42.

Mazatlán (1958): Rafael Barraza Sánchez, bishop, 1981.

Diocesan Address: Apartado Postal 1, Canizales y Benito Juárez s/n, 82000 Mazatlán, Sin.; (69) 81-33-52.

Mexicali (1966): José Isidro Guerrero Macías, bishop, 1997.

Diocesan Address: Av. Morelos #192, Col. Primera sección, Apartado 3-547, 21100 Mexicali, B.C. Norte; (65)52-4009.

México* (1530, promoted to an archdiocese, 1546): Cardinal Norberto Rivera Carrera, archbishop, 1995; Abelardo Alvarado Alcántara, José de Jesús Martinez Zepeda, Marcelino Hernández Rodríguez, Luis Fletes Santana, Rodrigo Guillermo Ortiz Mondragón, Felipe Tejeda Garcia, M.Sp.S., Francisco Clavel Gil, Rogelio Esquivel Medina, Jonás Guerrero Corona, auxiliaries.

Diocesan Address: Curia Arzobispal, Apartado Postal 24-433, Durango 90, Col. Roma, 06070 México, D.F.; (5) 525-11-10, 208-3200; www.arzobispadomexico.org.mx.

Mixes, Prelacy of (1964): Braulio Sánchez Fuentes, S.D.B., bishop, 1978.

Diocesan Address: Casa del Señor Obispo, 70283, Ayutla, Mixes, Oax.; (956) 8-03-54.

Monterrey* (1777, as Linares o Nuevo León, promoted to an archdiocese, 1891; name changed 1922): Cardinal Adolfo Antonio Suárez Rivera, archbishop, 1983; José Lizares Estrada, Gustavo Rodríguez Vega, auxiliaries.

Diocesan Address: Apartado 7, Zuazua 1110 Sur con Ocampo, 64000 Monterrey, N.L.; (83) 45-24-66; www.pixel.com.mx/info-gral/info-nl/religion/catolica/arqui.html.

Morelia* (1536, as Michoacan, promoted to an archdiocese 1863, name changed in 1924): Alberto Suárez Inda, archbishop, 1995; Leopoldo González González, aux.

Diocesan Address: Apartado 17, 58000 Morelia, Mich.; (43) 12-05-23.

Netzahualcóyotl (1979): José María Hernández González, bishop, 1989.

Diocesan Address: Apartado 89, 4 Avenida esq. Bellas Artes, Col. Evolución, 57700 Cuidad Netzahualcóyotl; (5) 797-61-32.

Nuestra Señora del Paraiso, Eparchy of (Greek Melkites, 1988): vacant.

Diocesan Address: Matías Romero 1014, Dpto. 601, Col. Del Valle, 3100 Mexico, D.F.; (5) 542-0225.

Nuevo Casas Grandes (1977): Hilario Chávez Joya, M.N.M., bishop, 2000.

Diocesan Address: Apartado Postal 198, Av. Hidalgo #105, 31700 Nuevo Casas Grandes, Chih.; (169) 4-05-20.

Nuevo Laredo (1989): Ricardo Watty Urquidi, M.Sp.S., bishop, 1989.

Diocesan Address: Saltillo 206, Apartado Postal #20-B, Col. México, 88280 Nuevo Laredo, Tamps.; (871) 5-29-28.

Oaxaca* (Also Antequera, 1535, promoted to archdiocese, 1891): Hector González Martínez, archbishop, 1993; Miguel Ángel Alba Díaz, aux.

Diocesan Address: Apartado Postal # 31, Garcia Vigil #600, 68000 Oaxaca, Oax.; (951) 6-20-49.

Orizaba (2000): Hipolito Reyes Larios, bishop, 2000.

Papantla (1922): Lorenzo Cárdenas Aregullin, bishop, 1980.

Diocesan Address: Apartado 27, Juárez 1102, 73800 Teziutlán, Pue.; (231) 3-24-30.

Parral (1992): José Andrés Corral Arredondo, bishop, 1992.

Diocesan Address: Apartado Postal 313, Fray Bartolomé de las Casas #13, 33800 Parral, Chih.; (152) 2-03-71.

Puebla de los Angeles* (1525, as Tlaxcala, renamed in 1903): Rosendo Huesca Pacheco, archbishop, 1977.

Diocesan Address: Apartado 235, Av. 2, Sur N. 305, 72000 Puebla, Pue.; (2) 232-62-12.

Querétaro (1863): Mario de Gasperín Gasperín, bishop, 1989.

Diocesan Address: Apartado Postal 49, Reforma #48, 76000 Querétaro, Qro.; (42) 12-10-33.

Saltillo (1891): Raul Vera López, O.P., bishop, 1999.

Diocesan Address: Hidalgo Sur 166, Apartado 25, 25000 Saltillo, Coah.; (84) 12-37-84.

San Andrés Tuxtla (1959): Guillermo Ranzahuer González, bishop, 1969.

Diocesan Address: Constitución y Morelos, 95700 San Andrés Tuxtla, Ver.; (294) 2-12-45.

San Cristóbal de las Casas (1539, as Chiapas, renamed in 1964): Felipe Arizmendi Esquivel, bishop, 2000.

Diocesan Address: Av. 20 de Noviembre n. 1, 29000 San Cristóbal de las Casas, Chia.; (967) 8-00-53; www.laneta.apc.org/curiasc.

San Juan de los Lagos (1972): Javier Navarro Rodríguez, bishop, 1999.

Diocesan Address: Morelos 30, Apartado #1, 47000 San Juan de los Lagos, Jal.; (378) 5-05-70; www.redial.com.mx/obispado/index.htm.

San Luis Potosí* (1854, promoted to an archdiocese, 1988): Luis Morales Reyes, archbishop, 1999.

Diocesan Address: Calle Francisco Madero N. 300, Apartado N. 1, 17800 San Luis Potosí, S.L.P.; (48) 12-45-55.

Tabasco (1880): Vacant, bishop.

Diocesan Address: Apartado Postal 97, Fidencia 502, 86000 Villahermosa, Tab.; (93) 12-13-97.

Tacámbaro (1913): Vacant.

Diocesan Address: Apartado 4, Enrique Aguilar 49, 61650 Tacámbaro, Mich.; (459) 6-00-44.

Tampico (1870, as Ciudad Victoria o Tamaulipas, renamed in 1958): Rafael Gallardo Garcia, bishop, 1987.

Diocesan Address: Apartado 545, Altamira 116 Oriente, 89000 Tampico, Tamps.; (12) 12-28-02.

Tapachula (1957): Rogelio Cabrera López, 2001.

Diocesan Address: Apartado 70, Av. Primera Sur 1, 30700 Tapachula, Chiapas; (962) 6-15-03; www.diocesis-tapachula.org.mx.

Tarahumara (1958, as a vicariate apostolic, promoted to diocese, 1993): José Luis Dibildox Martinez, bishop, 1994.

Diocesan Address: Apartado Postal 11, Av. López Mateos #7, 33190 Guachochi, Chih.; (154) 3-02-07.

Tehuacán (1962): Mario Espinosa Contreras, bishop, 1996.

Diocesan Address: Apartado Postal 137, Agustin A. Cacho 107, 75700 Tehuacán, Pue.; (238) 3-20-00.

Tehuantepec (1891): Felipe Padilla Cardona, bishop, 2000.

Diocesan Address: Apartado Postal 93, Matamoros 36, 70760 Tehuantepec, Oax.; (971) 5-00-60.

Tepic (1891): Alfonso Humberto Robles Cota, bishop, 1981.

Diocesan Address: Apartado 15, Av. de las Flores 10, Fracciónamiento Residencial La Loma, 63137 Tepic, Nay.; (321) 4-46-45.

Texcoco (1960): Carlos Aguiar Retes, bishop, 1997; Juan Manuel Mancilla Sanchez, auxiliary.

Diocesan Address: Apartado Postal 35, Fray Pedro de Gante 2, 56100 Texcoco, Méx.; (595) 4-08-69.

Tijuana (1963): Rafael Romo Muñoz, bishop, 1996.

Diocesan Address: Apartado 226, Calle Décima y Av. Ocampo #1049, 22000 Tijuana, B.C.N.; (66) 84-84-12; www.iglesiatijuana.org.

Tlalnepantla* (1964, promoted to archdiocese, 1989): Ricardo Guizar Díaz, archbishop, 1996; Francisco Ramírez Navarro, auxiliary.

Diocesan Address: Apartado 268 y 270, Av. Juárez

42, 54000 Tlalnepantla, Méx.; (95) 565-39-44.

Tlapa (1992): Alejo Zavala Castro, bishop, 1992.
Diocesan Address: Anexo Catedral, Centro, 41300 Tlapa de Comonfort, Gro.; (747) 6-08-35.

Tlaxcala (1959): Jacinto Guerrero Torres bishop, 2001.
Diocesan Address: Apartado 84, Lardizábal 45, 90000 Tlaxcala, Tlax.; (246) 2-07-23.

Toluca (1950): Francisco Robles Ortega, bishop, 1996.
Diocesan Address: Apartado 82, Portal Reforma Norte 104, 50000 Toluca, Méx.; (72) 15-25-35; www.diocesistoluca.org.mx.

Torreón (1957): vacant.
Diocesan Address: Apartado Postal 430, Av. Morelos 46 Poniente, 27000 Torreón, Coah.; (17) 12-30-43.

Tula (1961): Octavio Villegas Aguilar, bishop, 1994.
Diocesan Address: 5 de Mayo, #5, Apartado 31, 42800 Tula de Allende, Hgo.; (773) 2-02-75.

Tulancingo (1863): Pedro Aranda Díaz-Muñoz, bishop, 1975.
Diocesan Address: Apartado #14, Plaza de la Constitución, 43600 Tulancingo, Hgo.; (775) 3-10-10.

Tuxpan (1962): Domingo Díaz Martínez, bishop, 2002.
Diocesan Address: Independencia #56, 92870 Tuxpan, Ver.; (783) 4-16-36.

Tuxtepec (1979): José de Jesús Castillo Rentería, M.N.M., bishop, 1979.
Diocesan Address: Apartado Postal 9, Guerrero

164, 68300 Tuxtepec, Oax.; (287) 5-00-42.

Tuxtla Gutiérrez (1964): José Luis Chávez Botello, 2001.
Diocesan Address: 1/a Poniente Norte 236, Anexo Santo Domingo, 29000 Tuxtla Gutiérrez, Chis.; (961) 2-21-54; www.chisnet.com.mx/~cosi/obispado.

Veracruz (1962): Luis Gabriel Cuara Méndez, bishop, 2000.
Diocesan Address: Insurgentes Veracruzanos #470, Paseo del Malecón, 91700 Veracruz, Ver.; (29) 32-20-26.

Xalapa* (1962; originally Veracruz and Xalapa, 1863; promoted to archdiocese, 1951): Sergio Obeso Rivera, archbishop, 1979.
Diocesan Address: Apartado 359, Av. Manuel Avila Camacho #73, 91000 Xalapa, Ver.; (28) 17-29-35.

Yucatán* (1561, promoted to archdiocese, 1906): Emilio Carlos Berlie Belaunzarán, archbishop, 1995.
Diocesan Address: Calle 58 N. 501, 97000 Mérida, Yuc.; (99) 23-79-83; www.geocities.com/SoHo/207/principa.html.

Zacatecas (1863): Fernando Chávez Ruvalcaba, bishop, 1999.
Diocesan Address: Apartado #1, Miguel Auza #219, 98000 Zacatecas, Zacatecas; (492) 2-65-37; www.logicnet.com.mx/obispado.

Zamora (1863): Carlos Suárez Cázares, bishop, 1994.
Diocesan Address: Altos de Catedral (Calle Hidalgo), Apartado Postal #18, 59600 Zamora, Mich.; (351) 2-12-08.

CONFERENCIA DEL EPISCOPADO MEXICANO

(Sources: Annuario Pontificio; *Rev. Luis Barrera Flores, Adjunct Secretary,* Conferencia del Episcopado Mexicano; Conferencia del Episcopado Mexicano, Directorio, 2001-2003; *translation courtesy Suzanne Lea.)*

STRUCTURE

The Mexican Conference of Bishops (CEM, *Conferencia del Episcopado Mexicano*) is the permanent body of Mexican bishops. The bishops adhere to the guidelines of the conference in specific fulfillment of their pastoral labors. They do this in order to obtain the greatest good for the people that the church can achieve. The conference proposes:

1) To study the problems that occur in pastoral work, and to seek solutions; 2) To initiate, with a common end in mind and a common course of action, the forms and methods of preaching that best suit the needs of the country; 3) In regard to the collective salvific mission of the Church: To look for and to teach the best way in which the respective activities of the deacons, priests, religious, and lay person will be most efficient; 4) To facilitate relations with the civil authority and with other organizations in specific cases; 5) To write to the Episcopal commission regarding patrimonial and proprietary matters, and give counsel on determined financial or labor related points.

All those elected to the body of the CEM will have three years of service and will not be reelected to the same position after two three-year sessions have been completed consecutively.

The address of the conference headquarters is: Prolongación Misterios No. 24 PB, Col. Tepeyac-

Insurgentes, Apartado Postal 118-055, México, D.F. 07020; 01 (5) 781-84-62; www.cem.org.mx.

Permanent Assembly

The Permanent Assembly is the representative arm of the bishops belonging to the CEM. Its function is to ensure the continuation of the works of the conference and the fulfillment of its accords.

The Permanent Assembly is comprised of the Presidential Assembly and the Assembly of Pastoral Regions. It meets four times per year in ordinary session. It meets in extraordinary sessions whenever the majority of its members or those of the Presidential Assembly determine it to be necessary.

A session is valid if two-thirds of the members are present.

Officers

President: Bishop Luis Morales Reyes of San Luis Potosí.

Vice-President: Bishop José Guadalupe Martin Rábago of Léon.

Secretary General: Bishop Abelardo Alvarado Alcántara, aux. of Mexico.

General Treasurer: Bishop José Guadalupe Galván Galindo of Ciudad Valles.

Vocals: Bishop Ricardo Watty Urquidi, M.Sp.S. of Nuevo Laredo; Bishop Javier Navarro Rodríguez of San Juan de los Lagos.

Commissions, Section One:

Biblical Studies: Bishop Rogelio Cabrera López.
Doctrine: Bishop Lázaro Pérez Jiménez.

Culture: Archbishop Rosenda Huesca Pacheco.
Education: Bishop Francisco Robles Ortega.
Evangelization: Bishop José Luis Chávez Botello.
Liturgy: Bishop Mario de Gasperín Gasperín.
Missions: Archbishop Ricardo Guizar Díaz.
Pastoral Sanctuaries: Bishop Efren Ramos Salazar.
Preaching: Bishop José Lizares Estrada.
Social Communications: Bishop Rodrigo Guillermo Ortiz Mondragón.
Social Justice: Bishop Jacinto Guerreo Torres.

Commissions, Section Two:
Clergy: Archbishop Alberto Suárez Inda.
Consecrated Life: Bishop Ricardo Watty Urquidi, M.Sp.S.
Lay Apostolates: Bishop Carlos Talavera Ramírez.
Lay Ministry and Diaconate: Bishop José de Jesus Martinez Zepeda.
Priestly Formation: Bishop Benjamin Jiménez Hernández.
Seminaries and Vocations: Bishop Carlos Suárez Cázares.

CANONIZATION OF ST. JUAN DIEGO CUAUHTLATOATZIN

On July 31, 2002, during his pastoral visit to Mexico, Pope John Paul II canonized St. Juan Diego. The pontiff was on his fifth visit to the country and received another boisterous welcome from the Mexican people. The canonization was celebrated in the Basilica of Our Lady of Guadalupe in Mexico City. Juan Diego is the first indigenous saint of the American continent.

The Life of Juan Diego

A figure of considerable historical mystery and interest, Juan Diego was born probably in 1474 with the name "Cuauhtlatoatzin" ("the talking eagle") in Cuautlitlán, today part of Mexico City, Mexico. He was a member of the Chichimeca people, one of the indigenous communities that resided in the Anáhuac Valley. Little is known about his life prior to conversion, but when he was 50 years old he received baptism by a Franciscan priest, Fr Peter da Gand, one of the first Franciscan missionaries in Mexico.

On December 9, 1531, Juan Diego was on his way to morning Mass when the Blessed Mother appeared to him on Tepeyac Hill. She asked him to go to the bishop and request in her name that a shrine be built at Tepeyac. There, she promised, she would pour out her grace upon those who invoked her. The bishop, not surprisingly, did not believe Juan Diego, and demanded some kind of proof that the apparition was true. On December 12, Juan Diego returned to Tepeyac. The Blessed Mother appeared again and instructed him to climb the hill and to pick the flowers that he would find there. Juan Diego obeyed, and although it was winter, he found magnificent roses in bloom. He gathered up the flowers and carried them to Our Lady. She placed them in his mantle and told him to take them to the Bishop as the proof that had been demanded.

Juan Diego went back to the skeptical bishop with the roses hidden in his mantle. When he opened his mantle, the flowers fell on the ground. Even more remarkable was the mantle, for where the flowers had been wrapped there was now impressed an image of the Blessed Mother.

The bishop accepted without question the claim of Juan Diego, granting permission for Juan Diego to live the rest of his life as a hermit in a small hut near the chapel where the bishop had commanded the miraculous image to be preserved. Juan Diego devoted his remaining life to the care for the church and the many pilgrims who came to visit and pray to Our Lady.

Juan Diego died in 1548 and was buried in the first chapel dedicated to the Virgin of Guadalupe. He was beatified on May 6, 1990, by Pope John Paul II in the Basilica of Our Lady of Guadalupe.

Homily of Pope John Paul II

Following are excerpts from the homily of the Holy Father for the canonization on July 31:

"With deep joy I have come on pilgrimage to this Basilica of Our Lady of Guadalupe, the Marian heart of Mexico and of America, to proclaim the holiness of Juan Diego Cuauhtlatoatzin, the simple, humble Indian who contemplated the sweet and serene face of Our Lady of Tepeyac, so dear to the people of Mexicoduring his pastoral visit to Mexico....

"Today I address a very affectionate greeting to the many indigenous people who have come from the different regions of the country, representing the various ethnic groups and cultures which make up the rich, multifaceted Mexican reality. The Pope expresses his closeness to them, his deep respect and admiration, and receives them fraternally in the Lord's name....

" 'The Guadalupe Event,' as the Mexican Episcopate has pointed out, 'meant the beginning of evangelization with a vitality that surpassed all expectations. Christ's message, through his Mother, took up the central elements of the indigenous culture, purified them and gave them the definitive sense of salvation" (May 14, 2002, No. 8). Consequently Guadalupe and Juan Diego have a deep ecclesial and missionary meaning and are a model of perfectly inculturated evangelization....

"The noble task of building a better Mexico, with greater justice and solidarity, demands the cooperation of all. In particular, it is necessary today to support the indigenous peoples in their legitimate aspirations, respecting and defending the authentic values of each ethnic group. Mexico needs its indigenous peoples and these peoples need Mexico!...

"Blessed Juan Diego, a good, Christian Indian, whom simple people have always considered a saint! We ask you to accompany the Church on her pilgrimage in Mexico, so that she may be more evangelizing and more missionary each day....

"Happy Juan Diego, true and faithful man! We entrust to you our lay brothers and sisters so that, feeling the call to holiness, they may imbue every area of social life with the spirit of the Gospel. Bless families, strengthen spouses in their marriage, sustain the efforts of parents to give their children a Christian upbringing. Look with favour upon the pain of those who are suffering in body or in spirit, on those afflicted by poverty, loneliness, marginalization or ignorance. May all people, civic leaders and ordinary citizens, always act in accordance with the demands of justice and with respect for the dignity of each person, so that in this way peace may be reinforced....

STATISTICAL SUMMARY OF THE CATHOLIC CHURCH IN MEXICO

(*Principal sources:* Annuario Pontificio, 2002; Conferencia del Espicopado Mexicano, Directorio, 2000-2002; *figures as of January 2002; Catholic population statistics are those reported in the most recent Annuario population estimates. Archdioceses are indicated by an asterisk.*)

Current ecclesiastical organization includes 14 provinces: 14 archdioceses, 59 dioceses, 6 prelacies, and 1 vicariate apostolic. The Catholic population of Mexico comprises approximately 90% of the overall Mexican population of 139,442,580 (in 2001 there were 2,002,515 baptisms and 396,019 marriages). This table presents a provincial breakdown of Catholic statistics. In some cases, the totals are approximate because diocesan estimates are often considered unreliable owing to difficulties in adequate assessment of demographics and population distribution.

Province Diocese	Cath. Pop.	Dioc. Priests	Rel. Priests	Total Priests	Perm. Deacs.	Bro- thers	Sis- ters	Par- ishes
Acapulco	**5,363,600**	**289**	**57**	**346**	**17**	**60**	**404**	**249**
Acapulco*	2,795,000	82	18	100	16	30	200	82
Chilpancingo-Chilapa	825,000	106	14	120	-	14	28	91
Ciudad Lázaro Cárdenas	660,600	25	12	37	1	14	72	22
Ciudad Altamirano	660,000	53	3	56	-	6	83	26
Tlapa	423,000	23	10	33	-	10	21	28
Chihuahua	**4,517,551**	**263**	**124**	**387**	**30**	**168**	**645**	**191**
Chihuahua*	973,503	77	31	108	8	44	189	62
Ciudad Juárez	2,300,000	84	34	118	10	43	176	59
Cuauhtémoc-Madera	311,231	22	15	37	-	18	71	25
Nuevo Casas Grandes	169,859	28	10	38	-	10	27	14
Parral	497,638	39	12	51	12	19	68	17
Tarahumara	265,320	13	22	35	-	34	114	14
Durango	**6,679,886**	**506**	**73**	**579**	**-**	**115**	**983**	**268**
Durango*	2,157,812	199	19	218	-	46	387	105
Culiacán	2,215,974	134	5	139	-	10	308	68
El Salto	295,000	17	-	17	-	-	22	13
Mazatlán	682,100	68	8	76	-	9	135	38
Torreón	1,329,000	88	41	129	-	50	131	44
Guadalajara	**12,016,201**	**1,927**	**393**	**2,320**	**5**	**1,037**	**5,888**	**819**
Guadalajara*	5,733,000	924	286	1,210	2	783	3,633	365
Aguascalientes	1,472,500	225	45	270	-	99	595	79
Autlán	283,426	95	-	95	2	-	156	42
Ciudad Guzmán	470,000	108	12	120	-	17	181	54
Colima	621,152	124	9	133	-	14	212	52
San Juan los Lagos	1,007,745	259	16	275	-	58	427	64
Tepic	1,068,671	195	7	202	-	15	275	66
Zacatecas	1,200,000	187	5	192	-	32	403	97
Jesús Maria of Nayar, Prelature of	160,000	10	13	23	1	19	6	15
Hermosillo	**5,918,970**	**492**	**158**	**650**	**15**	**302**	**1,045**	**277**
Hermosillo*	1,020,000	122	11	133	1	15	95	59
Ciudad Obregón	835,000	107	14	121	1	29	90	56
La Paz	378,000	33	28	61	-	31	189	25
Mexicali	1,085,082	96	27	123	1	45	150	49
Tijuana	2,600,888	134	78	212	12	182	521	88
Mexico	**15,955,658**	**1,367**	**742**	**2,109**	**79**	**1,823**	**5,270**	**838**
Mexico*	7,283,712	712	635	1,347	77	1,630	4,251	425
Atlacomulco	834,350	77	10	87	1	26	86	50
Cuernavaca	1,829,341	125	53	178	1	87	383	116
Toluca	3,015,555	243	32	275	-	55	315	124
Tula	1,052,700	55	10	65	-	15	85	40
Tulancingo	1,940,000	155	2	157	-	10	150	83
Monterrey	**10,693,630**	**809**	**237**	**1,046**	**9**	**339**	**1,743**	**457**
Monterrey*	4,500,000	321	134	455	6	205	755	155
Ciudad Valles	859,500	52	12	64	-	12	116	41

Province Diocese	Cath. Pop.	Dioc. Priests	Rel. Priests	Total Priests	Perm. Deacs.	Bro- thers	Sis- sters	Par- ishes
Monterey, cont.								
Ciudad Victoria	400,000	32	15	47	-	18	112	32
Linares	202,210	33	2	35	-	2	55	21
Matamoros	1,505,495	89	7	96	-	8	80	47
Nuevo Laredo	787,000	39	15	54	1	20	96	32
Saltillo	1,322,815	143	38	181	2	53	365	71
Tampico	1,116,610	100	14	114	-	21	164	58
Morelia	**5,555,998**	**888**	**162**	**1,050**	**-**	**336**	**2,206**	**425**
Morelia*	2,940,000	479	132	611	-	245	1,107	251
Apatzingán	630,000	50	3	53	-	7	115	25
Tacámbaro	367,152	86	2	88	-	2	140	32
Zamora	1,618,846	273	25	298	-	82	844	121
Oaxaca	**7,097,544**	**430**	**142**	**572**	**392**	**186**	**1,036**	**325**
Oaxaca*	1,900,730	148	39	187	19	47	290	130
San Cristobal	995,322	28	34	62	337	44	191	37
Tapachula	1,125,450	69	9	78	-	9	110	38
Tehuantepec	1,135,602	67	8	75	-	12	120	33
Tuxtepec	615,000	27	12	39	17	13	31	25
Tuxtla Gutiérrez	1,010,000	81	12	93	-	22	259	39
Huautla, Prel of	120,440	5	4	9	-	8	5	7
Mixes, Prel of	195,000	5	24	29	19	31	30	16
Puebla de los Angeles	**7,609,751**	**791**	**175**	**966**	**2**	**305**	**1,943**	**470**
Puebla de los Angeles*	4,709,106	395	133	528	1	246	1,190	242
Huajuapan de León	611,200	108	-	108	-	-	157	71
Huejutla	486,560	75	10	85	-	10	65	38
Tehuacán	904,885	84	12	96	-	13	159	55
Tlaxcala	898,000	129	20	149	1	36	372	64
San Luis Potosi	**8,046,340**	**787**	**345**	**1,132**	**9**	**515**	**4,110**	**362**
San Luis Potosi*	1,693,498	180	46	226	9	65	539	80
Celaya	1,137,456	152	59	211	-	79	527	62
León	3,364,864	252	137	389	-	145	1,528	115
Matehuala	271,688	29	3	32	-	3	36	17
Querétaro	1,578,834	174	100	274	-	223	1,480	88
Tlalnepantla	**21,917,169**	**759**	**199**	**958**	**41**	**452**	**1,189**	**505**
Tlalnepantla*	3,119,079	230	73	303	8	141	314	140
Cuautitlan	3,395,000	145	58	203	-	214	333	80
Ecatepec	3,500,000	97	10	107	19	18	136	82
Netzahualcóyotl	8,995,699	158	38	196	-	48	150	128
Texcoco	2,907,391	129	20	149	14	31	256	75
Xalapa	**8,899,185**	**603**	**45**	**648**	**48**	**56**	**1,226**	**358**
Xalapa*	1,022,143	131	4	135	-	6	296	56
Coatzacoalcos	849,469	44	6	50	4	15	75	24
Cordoba	605,555	66	-	66	-	-	146	40
Orizaba	490,000	49	7	56	-	7	185	35
Papantla	1,752,667	83	1	84	1	1	151	44
San Andrés Tuxtla	844,351	71	3	74	32	3	82	43
Tuxpan	1,300,000	77	-	77	3	-	68	48
Veracruz	2,035,000	82	24	106	8	24	223	68
Yucatán	**3,878,521**	**297**	**113**	**410**	**21**	**209**	**797**	**218**
Yucatán*	1,467,459	156	43	199	16	90	393	95
Campeche	531,992	40	11	51	1	31	129	35
Tabasco	1,056,570	95	15	110	-	17	185	52
Cancún-Chetumal, Prelacy of	820,000	5	43	48	2	71	89	35
Nuestra Señora del Paraiso, Eparchy of	2,500	1	1	2	-	1	-	1
Totals:	**124,150,004**	**10,208**	**2,965**	**13,173**	**668**	**6,491**	**28,485**	**5,762**

Consecrated Life

INSTITUTES OF CONSECRATED LIFE

Religious institutes and congregations are special societies in the Church — institutes of consecrated life — whose members, called Religious, commit themselves by public vows to observance of the evangelical counsels of poverty, chastity and obedience in a community kind of life in accordance with rules and constitutions approved by church authority.

Secular institutes (covered in their own *Almanac* entries) are also institutes of consecrated life.

The particular goal of each institute and the means of realizing it in practice are stated in the rule and constitutions proper to the institute. Local bishops can give approval for rules and constitutions of institutes of diocesan rank. Pontifical rank belongs to institutes approved by the Holy See. General jurisdiction over all Religious is exercised by the Congregation for Institutes of Consecrated Life and Societies of Apostolic Life. General legislation concerning Religious is contained in Canons 573 to 709 in Book II, Part III, of the Code of Canon Law.

All institutes of consecrated life are commonly called religious orders, despite the fact that there are differences between orders and congregations. The best known orders include the Benedictines, Trappists, Franciscans, Dominicans, Carmelites and Augustinians, for men; and the Carmelites, Benedictines, Poor Clares, Dominicans of the Second Order and Visitation Nuns, for women. The orders are older than the congregations, which did not appear until the 16th century.

Contemplative institutes are oriented to divine worship and service within the confines of their communities, by prayer, penitential practices, other spiritual activities and self-supporting work. Examples are the Trappists and Carthusians, the Carmelite and Poor Clare nuns. Active institutes are geared for pastoral ministry and various kinds of apostolic work. Mixed institutes combine elements of the contemplative and active ways of life. While most institutes of men and women can be classified as active, all of them have contemplative aspects.

Clerical communities of men are those whose membership is predominantly composed of priests.

Non-clerical or lay institutes of men are the various brotherhoods.

"The Consecrated Life and Its Role in the Church and in the World," was the topic of the ninth general assembly of the Synod of Bishops held Oct. 2 to 29, 1994.

Societies of Apostolic Life

Some of the institutes listed below have a special kind of status because their members, while living a common life like that which is characteristic of Religious, do not profess the vows of Religious. Examples are the Maryknoll Fathers, the Oratorians of St. Philip Neri, the Paulists and Sulpicians. They are called societies of apostolic life and are the subject of Canons 731 to 746 in the Code of Canon Law.

RELIGIOUS INSTITUTES OF MEN IN THE UNITED STATES

(*Sources:* Annuario Pontificio, The Official Catholic Directory; Catholic Almanac *survey. As of June 1, 2002.*)

Africa, Missionaries of, M. Afr.: Founded 1868 at Algiers by Cardinal Charles M. Lavigerie; known as White Fathers until 1984. Generalate, Rome, Italy; U.S. headquarters, 1624 21st St. N.W., Washington, DC 20009, (202) 232-5154. Missionary work in Africa.

African Missions, Society of, S.M.A.: Founded 1856, at Lyons, France, by Bishop Melchior de Marion Brésillac. Generalate, Rome, Italy; American province (1941), 23 Bliss Ave., Tenafly, NJ 07670; (201) 567-9085. Missionary work.

Alexian Brothers, C.F.A.: Founded 14th century in western Germany and Belgium during the Black Plague. Motherhouse, Aachen, Germany; generalate,

198 James Blvd., Signal Mountain, TN 37377, (423) 886-0380. Hospital and general health work.

Assumptionists (Augustinians of the Assumption), A.A.: Founded 1845, at Nimes, France, by Rev. Emmanuel d'Alzon; in U.S., 1946. General house, Rome, Italy; U.S. province, 330 Market St., Brighton, MA 02135, (617) 783-0400, www.assumptionists.com. Educational, parochial, ecumenical, retreat, foreign mission work.

Atonement, Franciscan Friars of the, S.A.: Founded as an Anglican Franciscan community in 1898 at Garrison, NY, by Rev. Paul Wattson. Community corporately received into the Catholic Church in 1909. Generalate, St. Paul's Friary, Graymoor, Rte. 9, P.O. Box 300, Garrison, NY 10524, (914) 424-2113. Ecumenical, mission, retreat and charitable works.

Augustinian Recollects, O.A.R.: Founded 1588: in

U.S., 1944. General motherhouse, Rome, Italy. St. Augustine Province (1944), 29 Ridgeway Ave., W. Orange, NJ 07052, (973) 731-0616; www.augustinian recollects.org. St. Nicholas of Tolentino Province (U.S. Delegation), St. Anselm's Church, 685 Tinton Ave., Bronx, NY, 10455, (718) 585-8666. Missionary, parochial, education work.

Augustinians (Order of St. Augustine), O.S.A.: Established canonically in 1256 by Pope Alexander IV; in U.S., 1796. General motherhouse, Rome, Italy. 214 Ashwood Rd. P.O. Box 340, Villanova, PA 19085-0338, (610) 527-3330, www.augustinians.org., (1796); Our Mother of Good Counsel Province (1941), Tolentine Center, 20300 Governors Hwy., Olympia Fields, IL 60461-1081, (708) 748-9500, www.midweststaugustinians.org. St. Augustine, Province of (1969), 1605 28th St., San Diego, CA 92102-1417, (619) 235-0247.

Barnabites (Clerics Regular of St. Paul), C.R.S.P.: Founded 1530, in Milan, Italy, by St. Anthony M. Zaccaria; approved 1533; in U.S., 1952. Historical motherhouse, Church of St. Barnabas (Milan). Generalate, Rome, Italy; North American province, 981 Swann Rd, P.O. Box 167, Youngstown, NY 14174, (716) 754-7489; www.catholic-church.org/barnabites. Parochial, educational, mission work.

Basil the Great, Order of St. (Basilian Order of St. Josaphat), O.S.B.M.: General motherhouse, Rome, Italy; U.S. province, 31-12 30th St., Long Island City, NY 11106, (718) 278-6626. Parochial work among Byzantine Ukrainian Rite Catholics.

Basilian Fathers (Congregation of the Priests of St. Basil), C.S.B.: Founded 1822, at Annonay, France. General motherhouse, Toronto, Ont., Canada. U.S. address: 1910 W. Alabama, Houston, TX 77098, (713) 522-1736. Educational, parochial work.

Basilian Salvatorian Fathers, B.S.O.: Founded 1684, at Saida, Lebanon, by Eftimios Saifi; in U.S., 1953. General motherhouse, Saida, Lebanon; American headquarters, 30 East St., Methuen, MA 01844. Educational, parochial work among Eastern Rite peoples.

Benedictine Monks (Order of St. Benedict), O.S.B.: Founded 529, in Italy, by St. Benedict of Nursia; in U.S., 1846.

• **American Cassinese Congregation (1855).** Pres., Rt. Rev. Melvin J. Valvano, O.S.B., Newark Abbey, 528 Dr. Martin Luther King Blvd., Newark, NJ 07102, (973) 733-2822. Abbeys and Priories belonging to the congregation:

St. Vincent Archabbey, 300 Fraser Purchase Rd., Latrobe, PA 15650, (724) 539-9761, www.benedic tine.stvincent.edu; Saint John's Abbey, P.O. Box 2015, Collegeville, MN 56321, (320) 363-2548, www.saintjohnsabbey.org; St. Benedict's Abbey, Atchison, KS 66002, (913) 367-7853, www.benedictine.edu/abbey/index.html; St. Mary's Abbey, 230 Mendham Rd., Morristown, NJ 07960, (973) 538-3231, www.osbmonks.org; Newark Abbey, 528 Dr. Martin Luther King, Jr., Blvd., Newark, NJ 07102, (973) 643-4800; Belmont Abbey, 100 Belmont-Mt. Holly Rd., Belmont, NC 28012, (704) 825-6675, www.bac.edu/monastery; St. Bernard Abbey, Cullman, AL 35055, (256) 734-8291; St. Procopius Abbey, 5601 College Rd., Lisle, IL 60532, (630) 969-6410, www.procopius.org; St. Gregory's Abbey, 1900 W. MacArthur, Shawnee, OK 74804,

(405) 878-5491, www.sgc.edu; St. Leo Abbey, St. Leo, FL 33574, (352) 588-8626, www.saintleoabbey.org; Assumption Abbey, P.O. Box A, Richardton, ND 58652, (701) 974-3315; St. Bede Abbey, Peru, IL 61354, (815) 223-3140, www.theramp.net/stbede/index.html; St. Martin's Abbey, 5300 Pacific Ave. S.E., Lacey, WA 98503-1297, (360) 438-4440, www.stmartin.edu; Holy Cross Abbey, P.O. Box 1510, Canon City, CO 81215, (719) 275-8631, www.holy crossabbey.org; St. Anselm's Abbey, 100 St. Anselm Dr., Manchester, NH 03102, (603) 641-7285, www.anselm.edu; St. Andrew Abbey, 10510 Buckeye Rd., Cleveland, OH 44104-3725, (216) 721-5300, www.bocohio.org; Holy Trinity Priory, P.O. Box 990, Butler, PA 16003, (724) 287-4461; St. Maur Priory, 4615 N. Michigan Rd., Indianapolis, IN 46208, (317) 925-9095; Benedictine Priory, 6502 Seawright Dr., Savannah, GA 31406, (912) 356-3520, www.bcc adets.org; Woodside Priory, 302 Portola Rd., Portola Valley, CA 94028, (415) 851-8220; Mary Mother of the Church Abbey, 12829 River Rd., Richmond, VA 23233, (804) 784-3508, www.richmondmonks.org; Abadia de San Antonio Abad, P.O. Box 729, Humacao, PR 00792, (787) 852-1616.

• **Swiss-American Congregation (1870).** Abbeys and priory belonging to the congregation:

St. Meinrad Archabbey, 100 Hill Dr., St. Meinrad, IN 47577-1003, (812) 357-6514, www.saint meinrad.edu; Conception Abbey, P.O. Box 501, Conception, MO 64433-0501, (660) 944-2823, www.conceptionabbey.org; Mt. Michael Abbey, 22520 Mt. Michael Rd., Elkhorn, NE 68022-3400, (402) 289-2541; Subiaco Abbey, Subiaco, AR 72865, (501) 934-4295; St. Joseph's Abbey, St. Benedict, LA 70457, (504) 892-1800; Mt. Angel Abbey, St. Benedict, OR 97373, (503) 845-3030; Marmion Abbey, Butterfield Rd., Aurora, IL 60504, (630) 897-7215.

St. Benedict's Abbey, 12605 224th Ave., Benet Lake, WI 53102, (888) 482-1044, www.benetlake.org; Glastonbury Abbey, 16 Hull St., Hingham, MA 02043, (781) 749-2155, www.glastonburyabbey.org; Blue Cloud Abbey, Marvin, SD 57251-0098, (605) 398-9200, www.bluecloud.org; Corpus Christi Abbey, 101 South Vista Dr., Sandia, TX 78383, (361) 547-3257, www.geocities.com/Athens/styx/8125/ccabbey.html; Prince of Peace Abbey, 650 Benet Hill Rd., Oceanside, CA 92054, (760) 430-1305; St. Benedict Abbey, 254 Still River Rd., PO Box 22, Still River (Harvard), MA 01467, (978) 456-8017.

• **Congregation of St. Ottilien for Foreign Missions:** St. Paul's Abbey, P.O. Box 7, 289 Rt. 206 South, Newton, NJ 07860, (973) 383-2470; Christ the King Priory, P.O. Box 528, Schuyler, NE 68661, (402) 352-2177, www.megavision.net/benedict.

• **Congregation of the Annunciation**, St. Andrew Abbey, P.O. Box 40, Valyermo, CA 93563-0040, (661) 944-2178; www.valyermo.com.

• **English Benedictine Congregation**: St. Anselm's Abbey, 4501 S. Dakota Ave. N.E., Washington, DC 20017, (202) 269-2300; Abbey of St. Gregory the Great, Cory's Lane, Portsmouth, RI 02871-1352, (401) 683-2000; Abbey of St. Mary and St. Louis, 500 S. Mason Rd., St. Louis, MO 63141, (314) 434-2557, www.priory.org, www.stlouisabbey.org.

• **Houses not in Congregations**: Mount Saviour Monastery, 231 Monastery Rd., Pine City, NY 14871-

9787, (607) 734-1688, www.servtech.com/ ~msaviour; Weston Priory, 58 Priory Hill Rd., Weston, VT 05161-6400, (802) 824-5409, www.weston priory.org.

Benedictines, Camaldolese Hermits of America, O.S.B. Cam.: Founded 1012, at Camaldoli, near Arezzo, Italy, by St. Romuald; in U.S. 1958. General motherhouse, Arezzo, Italy; U.S. foundation, New Camaldoli Hermitage, 62475 Highway 1, Big Sur, CA 93920, (831) 667-2456, www.contemplation.org.

Benedictines, Olivetan, O.S.B.: General motherhouse, Siena, Italy. U.S. monasteries, Our Lady of Guadalupe Abbey, Pecos, NM 87552, (505) 757-6600, www.pecosabbey.org; Holy Trinity Monastery, P.O. Box 298, St. David, AZ 85630-0298, (520) 720-4642, www.holytrinitymonastery.org; Monastery of the Risen Christ, P.O. Box 3931, San Luis Obispo, CA 93403-3931, (805) 544-1810; Benedictine Monastery of Hawaii, P.O. Box 490, Waialua, HI 96791, (808) 637-7887, www.catholichawaii.com/religious/ benedictine.

Benedictines, Subiaco Congregation, O.S.B.: Independent priory, 1983. Monastery of Christ in the Desert, Abiquiu, NM 87510, (505) 470-4515; St. Mary's Monastery, P.O. Box 345, Petersham, MA 01366, (978) 724-3350.

Benedictines, Sylvestrine, O.S.B.: Founded 1231, in Italy by Sylvester Gozzolini. General motherhouse, Rome, Italy; U.S. foundations: 17320 Rosemont Rd., Detroit, MI 48219, (313) 532-6064; 2711 E. Drahner Rd., Oxford, MI 48051, (248) 628-2249; 1697 State Highway 3, Clifton, NJ 07012, (201) 778-1177.

Blessed Sacrament, Congregation of the, S.S.S.: Founded 1856, at Paris, France, by St. Pierre Julien Eymard; in U.S., 1900. General motherhouse, Rome, Italy; U.S. province, 5384 Wilson Mills Rd., Cleveland, OH 44143-3092, (440) 442-6311, www.blessedsacrament.com. Eucharistic apostolate.

Brigittine Monks (Order of the Most Holy Savior), O.Ss.S.: Monastery of Our Lady of Consolation, 23300 Walker Lane, Amity, OR 97101, (503) 835-8080; www.brigittine.org.

Camaldolese Hermits of the Congregation of Monte Corona, Er. Cam.: Founded 1520, from Camaldoli, Italy, by Bl. Paul Giustiniani. General motherhouse, Frascati (Rome), Italy; U.S. foundation, Holy Family Hermitage, 1501 Fairplay Rd., Bloomingdale, OH 43910-7971, (740) 765-4511.

Camillian Fathers and Brothers (Order of St. Camillus; Order of Servants of the Sick), O.S.Cam.: Founded 1582, at Rome, by St. Camillus de Lellis; in U.S., 1923. General motherhouse, Rome, Italy; North American province, 10101 W. Wisconsin Ave., Wauwatosa, WI 53226, (414) 259-4511.

Carmelites (Order of Our Lady of Mt. Carmel), O. Carm.: General motherhouse, Rome, Italy. Most Pure Heart of Mary Province (1864), 1317 Frontage Rd., Darien, IL 60559, (630) 971-0050. North American Province of St. Elias (1931), P.O. Box 3079, Middletown, NY 10940-0890, (845) 344-2225. Mt. Carmel Hermitage, Pineland, R.R. 1, Box 330 C, Bolivar, PA, 15923, (724) 238-0423. Educational, charitable work.

Carmelites, Order of Discalced, O.C.D.: Established 1562, a Reform Order of Our Lady of Mt. Carmel; in U.S., 1924. Generalate, Rome, Italy. Western Province (1983), 926 E. Highland Ave., P.O. Box

2178, Redlands, CA 92373, (909) 793-0424. Province of St. Thérèse (Oklahoma,1935), 515 Marylake Dr., Little Rock AR 72206, (501) 888-5827. Immaculate Heart of Mary Province (1947), 1233 S. 45th St., Milwaukee, WI 53214, (414) 672-7212. Our Lady of Mt. Carmel Monastery, 1628 Ridge Rd., Munster, IN 46321, (219) 838-7111. Spiritual direction, retreat, parochial work.

Carmelites of Mary Immaculate, C.M.I.: Founded 1831, in India, by Bl. Kuriakose Elias Chavara and two other Syro-Malabar priests; canonically established, 1855. Generalate, Kerala, India; North American headquarters, Holy Family Church, 21 Nassau Ave., Brooklyn, NY 11222, (718) 388-4866.

Carthusians, Order of, O. Cart.: Founded 1084, in France, by St. Bruno; in U.S., 1951. General motherhouse, St. Pierre de Chartreuse, France; U.S., Charterhouse of the Transfiguration, Carthusian Monastery, 1800 Beartown Rd., Arlington, VT 05250, (802) 362-2550, www.chartreux.org. Cloistered contemplatives; semi-eremitic.

Charity, Brothers of, F.C.: Founded 1807, in Belgium, by Canon Peter J. Triest. General motherhouse, Rome, Italy: American District (1963), 7720 Doe Lane, Laverock, PA 19038.

Charity, Servants of (Guanellians), S.C.: Founded 1908, in Italy, by Bl. Luigi Guanella. General motherhouse, Rome, Italy; U.S. headquarters, St. Louis School, 16195 Old U.S. 12, Chelsea, MI 48118, (734) 475-8430, www.stlouiscenter.org.

Christ, Society of, S.Ch.: Founded 1932. General Motherhouse, Poznan, Poland; U.S.-Canadian Province, 3000 Eighteen Mile Rd., Sterling Heights, MI 48311.

Christian Brothers, Congregation of, C.F.C. (formerly Christian Brothers of Ireland): Founded 1802 at Waterford, Ireland, by Bl. Edmund Ignatius Rice; in U.S., 1906. General motherhouse, Rome, Italy. American Province, Eastern U.S. (1916), 33 Pryer Terr., New Rochelle, NY 10804, (914) 636-6194. Brother Rice Province, Western U.S. (1966), 958 Western Ave., Joliet, IL 60435, (815) 723-5464. Educational work.

Christian Instruction, Brothers of (La Mennais Brothers), F.I.C.: Founded 1817, at Ploermel, France, by Abbe Jean Marie de la Mennais and Abbe Gabriel Deshayes. General motherhouse, Rome, Italy; American province, Notre Dame Institute, P.O. Box 159, Alfred, ME 04002, (207) 324-0067.

Christian Schools, Brothers of the (Christian Brothers), F.S.C.: Founded 1680, at Reims, France, by St. Jean Baptiste de la Salle. General motherhouse, Rome, Italy; U.S. Conference, 4351 Garden City Dr., Suite 200, Landover, MD 20785, (301) 459-9410, www.cbconf.org. Baltimore Province (1845), Box 29, Adamstown, MD 21710-0029, (301) 874-5188; www.fscbaltimore.org. Brothers of the Christian Schools (Midwest Province) (1995), 7650 S. County Line Rd., Burr Ridge, IL 60527-4718, (630) 323-3725; www.cbmidwest.org. New York Province (1848), 800 Newman Springs Rd., Lincroft, NJ 07738, (732) 842-7420. Long Island-New England Province (1957), Christian Brothers Center, 635 Ocean Rd., Narragansett, RI 02882-1314, (401) 789-0244. San Francisco Province (1868), P.O. Box 3720, Napa, CA 94558, (707) 252-0222. New Orleans-Santa Fe Province (1921), De La Salle Christian Brothers, 1522

Carmel Dr., Lafayette, LA 70501, (337) 234-1973. Educational, charitable work.

Cistercians, Order of, O.Cist.: Founded 1098, by St. Robert. Headquarters, Rome, Italy. Our Lady of Spring Bank Abbey, 17304 Havenwood Rd., Sparta, WI 54656-8177, (608) 269-8138. Our Lady of Dallas Monastery, 1 Cistercian Rd., Irving, TX 75039, (972) 438-2044. Cistercian Monastery of Our Lady of Fatima, 564 Walton Ave., Mt. Laurel, NJ 08054, (856) 235-1330. Cistercian Conventual Priory, St. Mary's Priory, R.D. 1, Box 206, New Ringgold, PA 17960, (717) 943-2645.

Cistercians of the Strict Observance, Order of (Trappists), O.C.S.O.: Founded 1098, in France, by St. Robert; in U.S., 1848. Generalate, Rome, Italy. Our Lady of Gethsemani Abbey (1848), Trappist, KY 40051, (502) 549-3117. Our Lady of New Melleray Abbey (1849), 6500 Melleray Circle, Peosta, IA 52068, (319) 588-2319. St. Joseph's Abbey (1825), Spencer, MA 01562, (508) 885-8700. Holy Spirit Monastery (1944), 2625 Hwy. 212 S.W., Conyers, GA 30208, (770) 483-8705. Our Lady of Guadalupe Abbey (1947), P.O. Box 97, Lafayette, OR 97127, (503) 852-7174, www.trappistabbey.org. Our Lady of the Holy Trinity Abbey (1947), 1250 South 9500 East, Huntsville, UT 84317, (801) 745-3784, www.xmission.com~hta. Abbey of the Genesee (1951), P.O. Box 900, Piffard, NY 14533, (585) 243-0660; www.geneseeabbey.org. Mepkin Abbey (1949), 1098 Mepkin Abbey Rd., Moncks Corner, SC 29461-4796, (843) 761-8509, www.mepkinabbey.org. Our Lady of the Holy Cross Abbey (1950), 901 Cool Spring Lane, Berryville, VA 22611, (540) 955-5277; www.holycrossabbeybrryville.org. Assumption Abbey (1950), Rt. 5, Box 1056, Ava, MO 65608, (417) 683-5110. Abbey of New Clairvaux (1955), Vina, CA 96092, (530) 839-2161, www.maxinet.com/trappist. St. Benedict's Monastery (1956), 1012 Monastery Rd., Snowmass, CO 81654, (970) 927-3311.

Claretians (Missionary Sons of the Immaculate Heart of Mary), C.M.F.: Founded 1849, at Vich, Spain, by St. Anthony Mary Claret. General headquarters, Rome, Italy. Western Province, 1119 Westchester Pl., Los Angeles, CA 90019-3523, (323) 734-1824. Eastern Province, 400 N. Euclid Ave. Oak Park, IL 60302, (708) 848-2076. Missionary, parochial, educational, retreat work.

Clerics Regular Minor (Adorno Fathers) C.R.M.: Founded 1588, at Naples, Italy, by Ven. Augustine Adorno and St. Francis Caracciolo. General motherhouse, Rome, Italy; U.S. address, 575 Darlington Ave., Ramsey, NJ 07446, (201) 327-7375, members.tripod.com/~adornofathers.

Columban, Society of St. (St. Columban Foreign Mission Society), S.S.C.: Founded 1918. General headquarters, Dublin, Ireland. U.S. headquarters., P.O. Box 10, St. Columbans, NE 68056, (402) 291-1920, www.columban.org. Foreign mission work.

Comboni Missionaries of the Heart of Jesus (Verona Fathers), M.C.C.J.: Founded 1867, in Italy by Bl. Daniel Comboni; in U.S., 1939. General motherhouse, Rome, Italy; North American headquarters, Comboni Mission Center, 8108 Beechmont Ave., Cincinnati, OH 45255, (513) 474-4997. Mission work in Africa and the Americas.

Consolata Missionaries, I.M.C.: Founded 1901, at Turin, Italy, by Bl. Joseph Allamano. General

motherhouse, Rome, Italy; U.S. headquarters, P.O. Box 5550, 2301 Rt. 27, Somerset, NJ 08875, (732) 297-9191.

Crosier Fathers (Canons Regular of the Order of the Holy Cross), O.S.C.: Founded 1210, in Belgium by Bl. Theodore De Celles. Generalate, Rome, Italy; U.S. Province of St. Odilia, 3510 Vivian Ave., Shoreview, MN 55126-3852, (651) 486-7456, www.crosier.org. Mission, retreat, educational work.

Cross, Brothers of the Congregation of Holy, C.S.C.: Founded 1837, in France, by Rev. Basil Moreau; U.S. province, 1841. Generalate, Rome, Italy. Midwest Province (1841), Box 460, Notre Dame, IN 46556, (219) 251-2221, www.hcc-nd.edu/mwp/. Southwest Province (1956), 1101 St. Edward's Dr., Austin, TX 78704-6512, (512) 442-7856, www.stedwards.edu/holycross/. Eastern Province (1956), 85 Overlook Circle, New Rochelle, NY 10804, (914) 632-4468. Educational, social work, missions.

Cross, Congregation of Holy, C.S.C.: Founded 1837, in France; in U.S., 1841. Generalate, Rome, Italy. Indiana Province (1841), 54515 State Rd. 933, North, P.O. Box 1064, Notre Dame, IN 46556-1064, (574) 631-6196). Eastern Province (1952), 835 Clinton Ave., Bridgeport, CT 06604-2393, (203) 367-7252, www.holycross.org. Southern Province (1968), 2111 Brackenridge St., Austin, TX 78704, (512) 443-3886, www.southerncsc.org. Educational and pastoral work; home missions and retreats; foreign missions; social services and apostolate of the press.

Divine Word, Society of the, S.V.D.: Founded 1875, in Holland, by Bl. Arnold Janssen. General motherhouse, Rome, Italy. North American Province founded 1897 with headquarters in Techny, IL. Province of Bl. Joseph Freinademetz (Chicago Province) (1985, from merger of Eastern and Northern provinces), 1985 Waukegan Rd., Techny, IL 60082, (847) 272-2700. St. Augustine (Southern Province) (1940), 201 Ruella Ave., Bay St. Louis, MS 39520, (228) 467-4322; www.svdsouth.com. St. Therese of the Child Jesus (Western Province) (1964), 2737 Pleasant St., Riverside, CA 92507, (323) 735-8130.

Dominicans (Order of Friars Preachers), O.P.: Founded early 13th century by St. Dominic de Guzman. General headquarters, Santa Sabina, Rome, Italy. Eastern Province of St. Joseph (1805), 869 Lexington Ave., New York, NY 10021-6680, (212) 737-5757, www.op-stjoseph.org. Most Holy Name of Jesus (Western) Province (1912), 5877 Birch Ct., Oakland, CA 94618, (510) 658-8722; www.op.org/opwest. St. Albert the Great (Central) Province (1939), 1909 S. Ashland Ave., Chicago, IL 60608, (312) 666-3244. St. Martin de Porres Province (1979), 1421 N. Causeway Blvd., Suite 200, Metairie, LA 70001-4144, (504) 837-2129; www.opsouth.org. Spanish Province, U.S. foundation (1926), P.O. Box 279, San Diego, TX 78384, (512) 279-3596. Preaching, teaching, missions, research, parishes.

Edmund, Society of St., S.S.E.: Founded 1843, in France, by Fr. Jean Baptiste Muard. General motherhouse, Edmundite Generalate, 270 Winooski Park, Colchester, VT 05439-0270, (802) 654-3400, www.sse.org. Educational, missionary work.

Eudists (Congregation of Jesus and Mary), C.J.M.: Founded 1643, in France, by St. John Eudes. General motherhouse, Rome, Italy; North American province, 6125 Premiere Ave., Charlesbourg, Que. G1H 2V9, Canada, (418) 626-6494; U.S. community, 36 Flohr Ave., Seneca, N.Y. 14224, (716) 825-4475. Parochial, educational, pastoral, missionary work.

Francis, Brothers of Poor of St., C.F.P.: Founded 1857. Motherhouse, Aachen, Germany; U.S. province, P.O. Box 35, Wever, IA 52658-0035; (319) 752-4000; www.brothersofthepoorofstfrancis.org. Educational work, especially with poor and neglected youth.

Francis, Third Order Regular of St., T.O.R.: Founded 1221, in Italy; in U.S., 1910. General motherhouse, Rome, Italy. Most Sacred Heart of Jesus Province (1910), 128 Woodshire Dr., Pittsburgh, PA 15215-1714, (412) 781-8333. Immaculate Conception Province (1925), 3811 Emerson Ave. N., Minneapolis, MN 55412, (763) 227-3600, www.sanpedro center.org. Franciscan Commissariat of the Spanish Province, 1924), 301 Jefferson Ave., Waco, TX 76701-1419, (254) 752-8434. Educational, parochial, missionary work.

Francis de Sales, Oblates of St., O.S.F.S.: Founded 1871, by Fr. Louis Brisson. General motherhouse, Rome, Italy. Wilmington-Philadelphia Province (1906), 2200 Kentmere Parkway, Wilmington, DE 19806; (302) 656-8529; www.oblates.org. Toledo-Detroit Province (1966), 2056 Parkwood Ave., Toledo, OH 43620, (419) 243-5105. Educational, missionary, parochial work.

Francis Xavier, Brothers of St. (Xaverian Brothers), C.F.X.: Founded 1839, in Belgium, by Theodore J. Ryken. Generalate, Twickenham, Middlesex, England. Generalate, 4409 Frederick Ave., Baltimore, MD, 21229, (410) 644-0034. Educational work.

Franciscan Brothers of Brooklyn, O.S.F.: Founded in Ireland; established at Brooklyn, 1858. Generalate, 135 Remsen St., Brooklyn, NY 11201, (718) 858-8217, www.franciscanbros.org. Educational work.

Franciscan Brothers of Christ the King, O.S.F.: Founded 1961. General motherhouse, 7329 E. Eastwood Ave., Indianapolis, IN 46239, (317) 862-9211.

Franciscan Brothers of the Holy Cross, F.F.S.C.: Founded 1862, in Germany. Generalate, Hausen, Linz Rhein, Germany; U.S. region, 2500 St. James Rd., Springfield, IL 62707, (217) 747-5947. Educational work.

Franciscan Brothers of the Third Order Regular, O.S.F.: Generalate, Mountbellew, Ireland; U.S. region, 2117 Spyglass Trail W., Oxnard, CA 93030, (805) 485-5002. (Mailing address: 4522 Gainsborough Ave., Los Angeles, CA 90029.)

Franciscan Friars of the Immaculate, F.F.I: Founded 1990, Italy. General motherhouse, Benevento, Italy. U.S. addresses, 600 Pleasant St., New Bedford, MA. 02740; 22 School Hill Rd., Baltic, CT 06330, (508) 996-8274.

Franciscan Friars of the Renewal, C.F.R.: Community established under jurisdiction of the archbishop of New York. Central House, St. Crispin Friary, 420 E. 156th St., Bronx, NY 10455, (718) 665-2441.

Franciscan Missionary Brothers of the Sacred Heart of Jesus, O.S.F.: Founded 1927, in the St. Louis archdiocese. Motherhouse, St. Joseph Rd., Eureka, MO 63025, (314) 587-3661. Care of aged, infirm, homeless men and boys.

Franciscans (Order of Friars Minor), O.F.M.: A family of the First Order of St. Francis (of Assisi) founded in 1209 and established as a separate jurisdiction in 1517; in U.S., 1844. General headquarters, Rome, Italy. English-speaking conference: 1615 Vine St., Cincinnati, OH 45210-1200, (513) 721-4700.

Immaculate Conception Province (1855), 125 Thompson St., New York, NY 10012, (212) 674-4388. Sacred Heart Province, Franciscan Missionary Union (1858), 3140 Meramec St., St. Louis, MO 63118, (314) 353-3421. Assumption of the Blessed Virgin Mary Province (1887), P.O. Box 100, 165 East Pulaski St., Pulaski, WI 54162-0100. Most Holy Name of Jesus Province (1901), 126 W. 32nd St., New York, NY 10001, (212) 967-6300, www.hnp.org. St. Barbara Province (1915), 1500 34th Ave., Oakland, CA 94601, (510) 536-3722.

Our Lady of Guadalupe Province (1985), 1350 Lakeview Rd. S.W., Albuquerque, NM 87105, (505) 877-5425. Commissariat of the Holy Cross (1912), 14246 Main St., P.O. Box 608, Lemont, IL 60439, (630) 257-2494. Most Holy Savior Vice-Province, 232 S. Home Ave., Pittsburgh, PA 15202, (412) 761-2550. Mt. Alverna Friary, 517 S. Belle Vista Ave., Youngstown, OH 44509, (330) 799-1888. Holy Family Croatian Custody (1926), 4848 S. Ellis Ave., Chicago, IL 60615, (773) 536-0552.

St. Casimir Lithuanian Vice-Province, P.O. Box 980, Kennebunkport, ME 04046, (207) 967-2011. Holy Gospel Province (Mexico), U.S. foundation, 2400 Marr St., El Paso, TX 79903, (915) 565-2921. Commissariat of the Holy Land, Mt. St. Sepulchre, 1400 Quincy St. N.E., Washington, DC 20017, (202) 269-5430. Holy Dormition Friary, Byzantine Slavonic Rite, P.O. Box 270, Rt. 93, Sybertsville, PA 18251, (570) 788-1212; www.holydorm.com; Academy of American Franciscan History, 1712 Euclid Ave., Berkeley, CA 94709. Preaching, missionary, educational, parochial, charitable work.

Franciscans (Order of Friars Minor Capuchin), O.F.M. Cap.: A family of the First Order of St. Francis (of Assisi) founded in 1209 and established as a separate jurisdiction in 1528. St. Joseph Province (1857), 1740 Mt. Elliott Ave., Detroit, MI 48207, (313) 579-2100. Province of St. Augustine (1873), 220 37th St., Pittsburgh, PA 15201, (412) 682-6011, www.capuchin.com. St. Mary Province (1952), 30 Gedney Park Dr., White Plains, NY 10605, (914) 761-3008. Province of the Stigmata of St. Francis (1918), P.O. Box 809, Union City, NJ 07087-0809, (201) 865-0611. Western American Capuchin Province, Our Lady of the Angels, 1345 Cortez Ave., Burlingame, CA 94010, (650) 342-1489, www.beafriar.com.

St. Stanislaus Friary (1948), 2 Manor Dr., Oak Ridge, NJ 07438, (973) 697-7757. Province of Mid-America (1977), 3553 Wyandot St., Denver, CO 80211, (303) 477-5436, www.midamcaps.org. Vice-Province of Texas, 604 Bernal Dr., Dallas, TX 75212, (214) 631-1937. St. John the Baptist Vice-Province, P.O. Box 21350, Rio Piedras, Puerto Rico 00928-1350, (787) 764-3090. General motherhouse, Rome, Italy. Missionary, parochial work, chaplaincies.

Franciscans (Order of Friars Minor Conventual), O.F.M. Conv.: A family of the First Order of St. Francis (of Assisi) founded in 1209 and established as a separate jurisdiction in 1517; first U.S. foundation, 1852. General curia, Rome, Italy. Immaculate Conception Province (1852), Immaculate Conception

Friary, P.O. Box 629, Rensselaer, NY 12144, (518) 472-1000, www.franciscanseast. St. Anthony of Padua Province (1906), 12300 Folly Quarter Rd., Ellicott City, MD 21042, (410) 531-9200; www.stanthony province.org. St. Bonaventure Province (1939), 6107 Kenmore Ave., Chicago, IL 60660, (773) 274-7681. Our Lady of Consolation Province (1926), 101 St. Anthony Dr., Mt. St. Francis, IN 47146, (812) 923-8444. St. Joseph of Cupertino Province (1981), P.O. Box 820, Arroyo Grande, CA 93421, (805) 489-1012. Missionary, educational, parochial work.

Glenmary Missioners (The Home Missioners of America): Founded 1939, in U.S., general headquarters, P.O. Box 465618, Cincinnati, OH 45246, (513) 874-8900, www.glenmary.org. Home mission work.

Good Shepherd, Little Brothers of the, B.G.S.: Founded 1951, by Bro. Mathias Barrett. Foundation House, P.O. Box 389, Albuquerque, NM 87103, (505) 243-4238. General headquarters, Hamilton, Ont., Canada. Operate shelters and refuges for aged and homeless; homes for handicapped men and boys, alcoholic rehabilitation center.

Holy Eucharist, Brothers of the, F.S.E.: Founded in U.S., 1957. Generalate, P.O. Box 25, Plaucheville, LA 71362, (318) 922-3630. Teaching, social, clerical, nursing work.

Holy Family, Congregation of the Missionaries of the, M.S.F.: Founded 1895, in Holland, by Rev. John P. Berthier. General motherhouse, Rome, Italy; U.S. provincialate, 3014 Oregon Ave., St. Louis, MO, 63118-1498. Belated vocations for the missions.

Holy Family, Sons of the, S.F.: Founded 1864, at Barcelona, Spain, by Bl. Jose Mañanet y Vives; in U.S., 1920. General motherhouse, Barcelona, Spain; U.S. address, 401 Randolph Rd., P.O. Box 4138, Silver Spring, MD 20914, (301) 622-1184, www.hometown.aol.com/holyfamsem/index.htm.

Holy Ghost Fathers, C.S.Sp.: Founded 1703, in Paris, by Claude Francois Poullart des Places; in U.S., 1872. Generalate, Rome, Italy. Eastern Province (1872), 6230 Brush Run Rd., Bethel Park, PA 15102, (412) 831-0302; www.spiritans.org.Western Province (1964), 1700 W. Alabama St., Houston, TX 77098, (713) 522-2882, www.spiritans.org. Missions, education.

Holy Ghost Fathers of Ireland: Founded 1971. U.S. delegates: 4849 37th St., Long Island City, NY 11101 (East); St. Dunstan's Church, 1133 Broadway, Mill Brae, CA 94030 (West).

Holy Spirit, Missionaries of the, M.Sp.S.: Founded 1914, at Mexico City, Mexico, by Felix Rougier. General motherhouse, Mexico City; U.S. headquarters, Our Lady of Guadalupe, 500 N. Juanita Ave., P.O. Box 272, Oxnard, CA 93032-1091, (805) 483-0987. Missionary work.

Immaculate Heart of Mary, Brothers of the, I.H.M.: Founded 1948, at Steubenville, Ohio, by Bishop John K. Mussio. Villa Maria Generalate, 609 N. 7th St., Steubenville, OH 43952, (740) 283-2462. Educational, charitable work.

Jesuits (Society of Jesus), S.J.: Founded 1534, in France, by St. Ignatius of Loyola; received papal approval, 1540; suppressed in 1773 and revived in 1814 by Pope Pius VII; first U.S. province, 1833. The Jesuits remain the largest single order in the Church. Generalate, Rome, Italy; U.S. national office, Jesuit Conference, 1616 P Street, Suite 300, Washington,

DC 20036, (202) 462-0400, www.jesuit.org. Maryland Province (1833), 5704 Roland Ave., Baltimore, MD 21210, (410) 532-1400; www.marprov jesuits.org. New York Province (1943), 39 East 83rd St., New York, NY 10028, (212) 774-5500, www.nysj.org. Missouri Province (1863), 4511 W. Pine Blvd., St. Louis, MO 63108-2191, (314) 361-7765. New Orleans Province (1907), 500 S. Jefferson Davis Pkwy., New Orleans, LA 70119, (504) 821-0334.

California Province (1909), 300 College Ave., P.O. Box 519, Los Gatos, CA 95031, (408) 354-6143, www.calprov.org. New England Province (1926), 771 Harrison Ave., Boston, MA 02118, (617) 266-7233. Chicago Province (1928), 2050 N. Clark St., Chicago, IL 60614, (773) 975-6363, www.jesuits-chi.org. Oregon Province (1932), 2222 N.W. Hoyt, Portland, OR 97210, (503) 226-6977. Detroit Province (1955), 7303 W. Seven Mile Rd., Detroit, MI 48221-2121, (313) 861-7500, www.jesuitdet.org. Wisconsin Province (1955), PO Box 080288, Milwaukee, WI 53208-0288, (414) 937-6949, www.jesuitwisprov.org. Province of the Antilles (1947), U.S. address, 12725 S.W. 6th St., Miami, FL 33184; (305) 559-9044. Missionary, educational, literary work.

John of God, Brothers of the Hospitaller Order of St., O.H.: Founded 1537, in Spain. General motherhouse, Rome, Italy; American province, 2425 S. Western Ave., Los Angeles, CA 90018, (323) 734-0233. Nursing work and related fields.

Joseph, Congregation of St., C.S.J.: General motherhouse, Rome, Italy; U.S. vice province, 338 North Grand Ave., San Pedro, CA 90731-2006, (310) 547-2969. Parochial, missionary, educational work.

Joseph, Oblates of St., O.S.J.: Founded 1878, in Italy, by Bl. Joseph Marello; in U.S., 1929. General motherhouse, Rome, Italy. Our Lady of Sorrows Province, 1880 Hwy 315, Pittston, PA 18640, (570) 654-7542. California Province, 544 W. Cliff Dr., Santa Cruz, CA 95060, (831) 457-1868. Parochial, educational work.

Josephite Fathers, C.J.: General motherhouse, Ghent, Belgium; U.S. foundation, 180 Patterson Rd., Santa Maria, CA 93455, (805) 937-5378.

Josephites (St. Joseph's Society of the Sacred Heart), S.S.J.: Established 1893, in U.S. as American congregation (originally established in U.S. in 1871 by Mill Hill Josephites from England). General motherhouse, 1130 N. Calvert St., Baltimore, MD 21202, (410) 727-3386, www.josephite.com. Evangelization in African-American community.

LaSalette, Missionaries of Our Lady of, M.S.: Founded 1852, by Msgr. de Bruillard; in U.S., 1892. Motherhouse, Rome, Italy. Province of Mary, Mother of the Americas (1934), 915 Maple Ave., Hartford, CT 06114, (860) 956-8870.

Lateran, Canons Regular of the, C.R.L.: General house, Rome, Italy; U.S.: 2317 Washington Ave., Bronx, NY 10458, (212) 295-9600.

Legionaries of Christ, L.C.: Founded 1941, in Mexico, by Rev. Marcial Maciel; in U.S., 1965. General headquarters, Rome, Italy; U.S. headquarters, 393 Derby Ave., Orange, CT 06477, (203) 795-2800; novitiate, 475 Oak Ave., Cheshire, CT 06410, (203) 271-0805, www.legionofchrist.org.

Little Brothers of St. Francis, L.B.S.F.: Founded 1970 in Archdiocese of Boston by Bro. James Curran.

General fraternity, 785-789 Parker St., Roxbury (Boston), MA 02120-3021, (617) 442-2556. Combine contemplative life with evangelical street ministry.

Mariannhill, Congregation of the Missionaries of, C.M.M.: Trappist monastery, begun in 1882 by Abbot Francis Pfanner in Natal, South Africa, became an independent modern congregation in 1909; in U.S., 1920. Generalate, Rome, Italy; U.S.-Canadian province (1938), Our Lady of Grace Monastery, 23715 Ann Arbor Trail, Dearborn Hts., MI 48127-1449, (313) 561-7140, www.rc.net/detroit/marianhill. Foreign mission work.

Marians of the Immaculate Conception, Congregation of, M.I.C.: Founded 1673; U.S. foundation, 1913. General motherhouse, Rome, Italy. St. Casimir Province (1913), 6336 S. Kilbourn Ave., Chicago, IL 60629-5588, (773) 582-8191, www.marians.org. St. Stanislaus Kostka Province (1948), Eden Hill, Stockbridge, MA 01262, (413) 298-3931. Educational, parochial, mission, publication work.

Marist Brothers, F.M.S.: Co-founded 1817, in France, by St. Marcellin Champagnat. General motherhouse, Rome, Italy. Esopus Province, 1241 Kennedy Blvd., Bayonne, NJ 07002, (201) 823-1115. Poughkeepsie Province, 26 First Ave., Pelham, NY 10803, (914) 738-0740. Educational, social, catechetical work.

Marist Fathers (Society of Mary), S.M.: Founded 1816, at Lyons, France, by Jean Claude Colin; in U.S., 1863. General motherhouse, Rome, Italy. Atlanta Province, P.O. Box 81144, Atlanta, GA 30366-1144, (770) 458-1435, www.maristsociety.org. Boston Province (1924), 27 Isabella St., Boston, MA 02116, (508) 879-7223. Educational, foreign mission, pastoral work.

Maronite Lebanese Missionaries, Congregation of, C.M.L.M.: Founded in Lebanon 1865; established in the U.S., 1991. U.S. foundation, Our Lady of the Cedars Maronite Mission, 11935 Bellfort Village, Houston, TX 77031, (281) 568-6800.

Mary, Society of (Marianist Fathers and Brothers; Brothers of Mary), S.M.: Founded 1817, at Bordeaux, France, by Rev. William-Joseph Chaminade; in U.S., 1849. General motherhouse, Rome, Italy. Cincinnati Province (1849), 4435 E. Patterson Rd., Dayton, OH 45430-1095, (937) 429-0794. St. Louis Province (1908), 4425 W. Oine Blvd., St. Louis, MO 63108, (314) 533-1207. Pacific Province (1948), PO Box 1775, Cupertino, CA 95015, (408) 253-4841. New York Province (1961), 4301 Roland Ave., Baltimore, MD 21210, (410) 366-1300, www.marianists.org. Province of Meribah (1976), 240 Emory Rd., Mineola, NY 11501, (516) 292-0200. Educational work.

Mary Immaculate, Missionary Oblates of, O.M.I.: Founded 1816, in France, by St. Charles Joseph Eugene de Mazenod; in U.S., 1849. General house, Rome, Italy. U.S. Province: 391 Michigan Ave., N.E., Washington, D.C., 20017, (202) 529-4505; Southwest Area, 327 Oblate Dr., San Antonio, TX 78216-6602, (210) 349-1475; www.omiusa.org. Parochial, foreign mission, educational work, ministry to marginal.

Maryknoll (Catholic Foreign Mission Society of America), M.M.: Founded 1911, in U.S., by Frs. Thomas F. Price and James A. Walsh. General Center, Maryknoll, NY 10545, (914) 941-7590.

Mercedarians (Order of Our Lady of Mercy), O. de M.: Founded 1218, in Spain, by St. Peter Nolasco. General motherhouse, Rome, Italy; U.S. headquarters, 7758 E. Main Rd., LeRoy, NY, 14482, (716) 768-7110.

Mercy, Brothers of, F.M.M.: Founded 1856, in Germany. General motherhouse, Montabaur, Germany. American headquarters, 4520 Ransom Rd., Clarence, NY 14031, (716) 759-8341. Hospital work.

Mercy, Brothers of Our Lady, Mother of, C.F.M.M.: Founded 1844, in The Netherlands by Abp. Jan Zwijsen. Generalate, Tilburg, The Netherlands; U.S. region, 2336 S. C St., Oxnard, CA 93033-3501, (805) 486-3692.

Mercy, Congregation of Priests of (Fathers of Mercy), C.P.M.: Founded 1808, in France, by Rev. Jean Baptiste Rauzan; in U.S., 1839. General mission house, South Union, KY 42283, (502) 542-4164. Mission work.

Mill Hill Missionaries (St. Joseph's Society for Foreign Missions), M.H.M.: Founded 1866, in England, by Cardinal Vaughan; in U.S., 1951. International headquarters, London, England; American headquarters, 222 W. Hartsdale Ave., Hartsdale, N.Y. 10530, (914) 682-0645.

Minim Fathers, O.M.: General motherhouse, Rome, Italy. North American delegation (1970), 3431 Portola Ave., Los Angeles, CA 90032, (213) 223-1101.

Missionaries of St. Charles, Congregation of the (Scalabrinians), C.S.: Founded 1887, at Piacenza, Italy, by Bl. John Baptist Scalabrini. General motherhouse, Rome, Italy. St. Charles Borromeo Province (1888), 27 Carmine St., New York, NY 10014, (212) 675-3993. St. John Baptist Province (1903), 546 N. East Ave., Oak Park, IL 60302, (708) 386-4430.

Missionaries of the Holy Apostles, M.Ss.A.: Founded 1962, Washington, D.C., by Very Rev. Eusebe M. Menard. North American headquarters, 24 Prospect Hill Rd., Cromwell, CT 06416, (860) 632-3039.

Missionary Servants of Christ, M.S.C.: Founded 1979 in U.S. by Bro. Edwin Baker. Headquarters, P.O. Box 270, 305 S. Lake St., Aurora, IL 60507, (630) 892-2371, www.misacor-usa.org.

Missionhurst-CICM (Congregation of the Immaculate Heart of Mary): Founded 1862, at Scheut, Brussels, Belgium, by Very Rev. Theophile Verbist. General motherhouse, Rome, Italy; U.S. province, 4651 N. 25th St., Arlington, VA 22207, (703) 528-3800; www.missionhurst.org. Home and foreign mission work.

Montfort Missionaries (Missionaries of the Company of Mary), S.M.M.: Founded 1715, by St. Louis Marie Grignon de Montfort; in U.S., 1948. General motherhouse, Rome, Italy; U.S. province, 101-18 104th St., Ozone Park, NY 11416, (718) 849-5885. Mission work.

Mother Co-Redemptrix, Congregation of, C.M.C.: Founded 1953 at Lein-Thuy, Vietnam (North), by Fr. Dominic Mary Tran Dinh Thu; in U.S., 1975. General house, Hochiminhville, Vietnam; U.S. provincial house, 1900 Grand Ave., Carthage, MO 64836, (417) 358-7787, www.dongcong.net. Work among Vietnamese Catholics in U.S.

Oblates of the Virgin Mary, O.M.V.: Founded

1815, in Italy; in U.S., 1976; Generalate, Rome, Italy; U.S. provincialate: 2 Ipswich St., Boston, MA 02215, (617) 536-4141.

Oratorians (Congregation of the Oratory of St. Philip Neri), C.O.: Founded 1575, at Rome, by St. Philip Neri. A confederation of autonomous houses. U.S. addresses: P.O. Box 11586, Rock Hill, SC 29731, (803) 327-2097, www.rockhilloratory.org; P.O. Box 1688, Monterey, CA 93940, (831) 373-0476; 4450 Bayard St., Pittsburgh, PA 15213, (412) 681-3181; P.O. Drawer II, Pharr, TX 78577, (956) 843-8217; 109 Willoughby St., Brooklyn, NY 11201, (718) 875-2096.

Pallottines (Society of the Catholic Apostolate), S.A.C.: Founded 1835, at Rome, by St. Vincent Pallotti. Generalate, Rome, Italy. Immaculate Conception Province (1953), P.O. Box 979, South Orange, NJ 07079, (201) 762-2926. Mother of God Province (1946), 5424 W. Blue Mound Rd., Milwaukee, WI 53208, (414) 259-0688. Irish Province (1909), U.S. address: 3352 4th St., Wyandotte, MI 48192. Queen of Apostles Province (1909), 448 E. 116th St., New York, NY 10029, (212) 534-0681. Christ the King Province, 3452 Niagara Falls, Blvd., N. Tonawanda, NY 14120, (716) 694-4313. Charitable, educational, parochial, mission work.

Paraclete, Servants of the, s.P.: Founded 1947, Santa Fe, N.M., archdiocese. Generalate and U.S. motherhouse, 18161 State Hwy. 4, Jemez Springs, NM 87025-0010, (505) 829-3586. Devoted to care of priests.

Paris Foreign Missions Society, M.E.P.: Founded 1662, at Paris, France. Headquarters, Paris, France; U.S. establishment, 930 Ashbury St., San Francisco, CA 94117, (415) 664-6747. Mission work and training of native clergy.

Passionists (Congregation of the Passion), C.P.: Founded 1720, in Italy, by St. Paul of the Cross. General motherhouse, Rome, Italy. St. Paul of the Cross Province (Eastern Province) (1852), 80 David St., South River, NJ 08882, (732) 257-7177. Holy Cross Province (Western Province), 5700 N. Harlem Ave., Chicago, IL 60631, (773) 631-6336.

Patrician Brothers (Brothers of St. Patrick), F.S.P.: Founded 1808, in Ireland, by Bishop Daniel Delaney; U.S. novitiate, 7820 Bolsa Ave., Midway City, CA 92655, (714) 897-8181. Educational work.

Patrick's Missionary Society, St., S.P.S.: Founded 1932, at Wicklow, Ireland, by Msgr. Patrick Whitney; in U.S., 1953. International headquarters, Kiltegan Co., Wicklow, Ireland. U.S. foundations: 70 Edgewater Rd., Cliffside Park, NJ 07010, (201) 943-6575; 19536 Eric Dr., Saratoga, CA 95070, (408) 253-3135; 1347 W. Granville Ave., Chicago, IL 60660, (773) 973-3737.

Pauline Fathers (Order of St. Paul the First Hermit), O.S.P.P.E.: Founded 1215; established in U.S., 1955. General motherhouse, Czestochowa, Jasna Gora, Poland; U.S. province, P.O. Box 2049, Doylestown, PA 18901, (215) 345-0607.

Pauline Fathers and Brothers (Society of St. Paul for the Apostolate of Communications), S.S.P.: Founded 1914, by Very Rev. James Alberione; in U.S., 1932. Motherhouse, Rome, Italy; New York province (1932), P.O. Box 139, Ellsworth, OH 44416-0139, (330) 533-7427. Social communications work.

Paulists (Missionary Society of St. Paul the

Apostle), C.S.P.: Founded 1858, in New York, by Fr. Isaac Thomas Hecker. Motherhouse: 86-11 Midland Pkwy, Jamaica Estates, N.Y. 11432; (718) 291-5995. Missionary, ecumenical, pastoral work.

Piarists (Order of the Pious Schools), Sch.P.: Founded 1617, at Rome, Italy, by St. Joseph Calasanctius. General motherhouse, Rome, Italy. U.S. province, 363 Valley Forge Rd., Devon, PA 19333, (610) 688-7337. New York-Puerto Rico vice-province (Calasanzian Fathers), P.O. Box 118, Playa Sta., Ponce, PR 00734, (809) 840-0610. California vice province, 3940 Perry St., Los Angeles, CA 90063, (323) 261-1386. Educational work.

Pius X, Brothers of St., C.S.P.X.: Founded 1952, at La Crosse, WI, by Bishop John P. Treacy. Motherhouse, P.O. Box 217, De Soto, WI 54624. Education.

Pontifical Institute for Foreign Missions, P.I.M.E.: Founded 1850, in Italy, at request of Pope Pius IX. General motherhouse, Rome, Italy; U.S. province, 17330 Quincy Ave., Detroit, MI 48221, (313) 342-4066, www.pimeusa.org work.

Precious Blood, Society of, C.P.P.S.: Founded 1815, in Italy, by St. Gaspar del Bufalo. General motherhouse, Rome, Italy. Cincinnati Province, 431 E. Second St., Dayton, OH 45402, (937) 228-9263, www.cpps-preciousblood.org. Kansas City Province, P.O. Box 339, Liberty, MO 64068, (816) 781-4344. Pacific Province, 2337 134th Ave. W., San Leandro, CA 94577, (510) 357-4982. Atlantic Province, 13313 Niagara Pkwy, Niagara Falls, ON L2E 6S6, (905) 382-1118, www.preciousblood.org.

Premonstratensians (Order of the Canons Regular of Premontre; Norbertines), O. Praem.: Founded 1120, at Premontre, France, by St. Norbert; in U.S., 1893. Generalate, Rome, Italy. St. Norbert Abbey, 1016 N. Broadway, DePere, WI 54114, (920) 337-4300; www.snc.edu/norbertines. Daylesford Abbey, 220 S. Valley Rd., Paoli, PA 19301, (610) 647-2530, www.daylesford.org. St. Michael's Abbey, 19292 El Toro Rd., Silverado, CA 92676, (949) 858-0222. Immaculate Conception Priory (1997), 3600 Philadelphia Pike, Claymont, DE 19703, (302) 792-2791. Educational, parish work.

Priestly Fraternity of St. Peter, F.S.S.P.: Founded and approved Oct. 18, 1988; first foundation in U.S., 1991. U.S. headquarters, Our Lady of Guadalupe Seminary, Griffin Rd., P.O. Box 196, Elmhurst, PA 18416, (570) 842-4000; www.fssp.com.

Providence, Sons of Divine, F.D.P.: Founded 1893, at Tortona, Italy, by Bl. Luigi Orione; in U.S., 1933. General motherhouse, Rome, Italy; U.S. address, 111 Orient Ave., E. Boston, MA 02128, (617) 569-2100.

Redemptorist Fathers and Brothers (Congregation of the Most Holy Redeemer), C.SS.R.: Founded 1732, in Italy, by St. Alphonsus Mary Liguori. Generalate, Rome, Italy. Baltimore Province (1850), 7509 Shore Rd., Brooklyn, NY 11209, (718) 833-1900. Redemptorist-Denver Province (1875), Box 300399, Denver, CO 80203-0399, (303) 370-0035; www.redemptorists-denver.org. New Orleans Vice-Province, 5354 Plank Rd., P.O. Box 53900, Baton Rouge, LA 70892, (225) 355-2600. Richmond Vice-Province (1942), 313 Hillman St., P.O. Box 1529, New Smyrna Beach, FL 32170, (904) 427-3094. Mission work.

Resurrectionists (Congregation of the Resurrec-

tion), C.R.: Founded 1836, in France, under direction of Bogdan Janski. Motherhouse, Rome, Italy. U.S. Province, 7050 N. Oakley Ave., Chicago, IL 60645-3426, (773) 465-8320, www.crusa.org. Ontario Kentucky Province, U.S. address, 338 N. 25th St., Louisville, KY 40212, (502) 772-3694.

Rogationist Fathers, R.C.J.: Founded by Bl. Annibale (Hannibal) di Francia, 1887. General motherhouse, Rome, Italy. U.S. delegation: 2688 S. Newmark Ave., Sanger, CA 91343, (209) 875-5808. Charitable work.

Rosary, Brothers of Our Lady of the Holy, F.S.R.: Founded 1956, in U.S. Motherhouse and novitiate, 232 Sunnyside Dr., Reno, NV 89503-3510, (775) 747-4441.

Rosminians (Institute of Charity), I.C.: Founded 1828, in Italy, by Antonio Rosmini-Serbati. General motherhouse, Rome, Italy; U.S. address, 2327 W. Heading Ave., Peoria, IL 61604, (309) 676-6341. Charitable work.

Sacred Heart, Brothers of the, S.C.: Founded 1821, in France, by Rev. Andre Coindre. General motherhouse, Rome, Italy. New Orleans Province (1847), 4540 Elysian Fields Ave., New Orleans, LA 70122, (504) 282-5693. New England Province (1945), 685 Steere Farm Rd., Pascoag, RI 02859-4601, (401) 769-0313, www.brothersofthesacredheart.org. New York Province (1960), 141-11 123 Ave., South Ozone Park, NY 11436-1426, (718) 322-3309. Educational work.

Sacred Heart, Missionaries of the, M.S.C.: Founded 1854, by Rev. Jules Chevelier. General motherhouse, Rome, Italy; U.S. province, 305 S. Lake St., Aurora, IL 60507-0271, (630) 892-8400.

Sacred Heart of Jesus, Congregation of the (Sacred Heart Fathers and Brothers), S.C.J.: Founded 1877, in France. General motherhouse, Rome, Italy; U.S. provincial office, P.O. Box 289, Hales Corners, WI 53130-0289, (414) 425-6910; www.scj.org. Educational, preaching, mission work.

Sacred Hearts of Jesus and Mary, Congregation of (Picpus Fathers), SS.CC.: Founded 1805, in France, by Fr. Coudrin. General motherhouse, Rome, Italy. Eastern Province (1946), 77 Adams St. (Box 111), Fairhaven, MA 02719, (508) 993-2442. Western Province (1970), 2150 Damien Ave., La Verne, CA 91750, (909) 593-5441. Hawaii Province, Box 797, Kaneohe, Oahu, HI 96744, (808) 247-5035. Mission, educational work.

Sacred Hearts of Jesus and Mary, Missionaries of the, M.SS.CC.: Founded 1833, in Naples, Italy, by Cajetan Errico. General motherhouse, Rome, Italy; U.S. headquarters, 2249 Shore Rd., Linwood, NJ 08221, (609) 927-5600.

Salesians of St. John Bosco (Society of St. Francis de Sales), S.D.B.: Founded 1859, by St. John (Don) Bosco. Generalate, Rome, Italy. St. Philip the Apostle Province (1902), 148 Main St., P.O. Box 639, New Rochelle, NY 10802-0639, (914) 636-4225. San Francisco Province (1926), 1100 Franklin St., San Francisco, CA 94109, (415) 441-7144.

Salvatorians (Society of the Divine Savior), S.D.S.: Founded 1881, in Rome, by Fr. Francis Jordan; in U.S., 1896. General headquarters, Rome, Italy; U.S. province, 1735 Hi-Mount Blvd., Milwaukee, WI 53208-1720, (414) 258-1735. Educational, parochial, mission work; campus ministries, chaplaincies.

Scalabrinians: *See* **Missionaries of St. Charles**.

Servites (Order of Friar Servants of Mary), O.S.M.: Founded 1233, at Florence, Italy, by Seven Holy Founders. Generalate, Rome, Italy. United States Province (1967), 3121 W. Jackson Blvd., Chicago, IL 60612, (773) 533-0360. General apostolic ministry.

Somascan Fathers, C.R.S.: Founded 1534, at Somasca, Italy, by St. Jerome Emiliani. General motherhouse, Rome, Italy; U.S. address, Pine Haven Boys Center, River Rd., P.O. Box 162, Suncook, NH 03275, (603) 485-7141, www.somascans.org.

Society of Our Lady of the Most Holy Trinity, S.O.L.T.: Headquarters, Casa San Jose, 109 W. Avenue F, P.O. Box 152, Robstown, TX 78380, (512) 387-2754.

Sons of Mary Missionary Society (Sons of Mary, Health of the Sick), F.M.S.I.: Founded 1952, in the Boston archdiocese, by Rev. Edward F. Garesche, S.J. Headquarters, 567 Salem End Rd., Framingham, MA 01702, (508) 879-2541; www.sonsofmary.com.

Stigmatine Fathers and Brothers (Congregation of the Sacred Stigmata), C.S.S.: Founded 1816, by St. Gaspar Bertoni. General motherhouse, Rome, Italy; North American Province, 554 Lexington St., Waltham, MA 02452-3097, (781) 209-3060; www.stigmatines.com. Parish work.

Sulpicians (Society of Priests of St. Sulpice), S.S.: Founded 1641, in Paris, by Rev. Jean Jacques Olier. General motherhouse, Paris, France; U.S. province, 5408 Roland Ave., Baltimore, MD 21210, (410) 323-5070, www.sulpicians.org. Education of seminarians and priests.

Theatines (Congregation of Clerics Regular), C.R.: Founded 1524, in Rome, by St. Cajetan. General motherhouse, Rome, Italy; U.S. headquarters, 1050 S. Birch St., Denver, CO 80246, (303) 756-5522.

Trappists: *See* **Cistercians of the Strict Observance**.

Trinitarians (Order of the Most Holy Trinity), O.SS.T.: Founded 1198, by St. John of Matha; in U.S., 1911. General motherhouse, Rome, Italy; U.S. headquarters, P.O. Box 5742, Baltimore, MD 21282, (410) 486-5171.

Trinity Missions (Missionary Servants of the Most Holy Trinity), S.T.: Founded 1929, by Fr. Thomas Augustine Judge. Generalate, P.O. Box 7130, Silver Springs, MD 20907-7130, (301) 434-6761; www.trinitymissions.org. Home mission work.

Viatorian Fathers (Clerics of St. Viator), C.S.V.: Founded 1831, in France, by Fr. Louis Joseph Querbes. General motherhouse, Rome, Italy. Province of Chicago (1882), 1212 E. Euclid St., Arlington Hts., IL 60004, (847) 398-1354. Educational work.

Vincentians (Congregation of the Mission; Lazarists), C.M.: Founded 1625, in Paris, by St. Vincent de Paul; in U.S., 1818. General motherhouse, Rome, Italy. Eastern Province (1867), 500 E. Chelten Ave., Philadelphia, PA 19144, (215) 848-1985. Midwest Province (1888), 13663 Rider Trail North, Earth City, MO 63045, (314) 344-1184. New England Province (1975), 234 Keeney St., Manchester, CT 06040-7048, (860) 643-2828. American Italian Branch, Our Lady of Pompei Church, 3600 Claremont St., Baltimore, MD 21224, (410) 675-7790. American Spanish Branch (Barcelona, Spain), 234 Congress St., Brooklyn, NY 11201, (718) 624-3425. American Spanish

Branch (Zaragoza, Spain), Holy Agony Church, 1834 3rd Ave., New York, NY 10029, (212) 289-5589. Western Province (1975), 420 Date St., Montebello, CA 90640, (323) 721-5486. Southern Province (1975), 3826 Gilbert Ave., Dallas, TX 75219, (214) 526-0234, www.cmsouth.org. Educational work.

Vocationist Fathers (Society of Divine Vocations), S.D.V.: Founded 1920, in Italy; in U.S., 1962.

Generalate, Rome, Italy; U.S. headquarters, 90 Brooklake Rd., Florham Park, NJ 07932, (973) 966-6262, www.vocationist.org.

Xaverian Missionary Fathers, S.X.: Founded 1895, by Bl. Guido Conforti, at Parma, Italy. General motherhouse, Rome, Italy; U.S. province, 12 Helene Ct., Wayne, NJ 07470, (973) 942-2975, www.xaviermissionaries.org. Foreign mission work.

MEMBERSHIP OF RELIGIOUS INSTITUTES OF MEN

(*Principal source:* Annuario Pontificio. *Statistics as of Jan. 1, 2002, unless indicated otherwise.*) Listed below are world membership statistics of institutes of men of pontifical right with 500 or more members; the number of priests is in parentheses. Also listed are institutes with less than 500 members with houses in the United States.

Jesuits (14,935)	21,147
Franciscans (Friars Minor) (11,266)	16,958
Salesians (11,234)	17,056
Franciscans (Capuchins) (7,705)	11,321
Benedictines (4,571)	7,995
Society of the Divine Word (3,799)	6,003
Brothers of Christian Schools	6,487
Dominicans (4,707)	6,359
Redemptorists (4,232)	5,730
Marist Brothers	4,867
Oblates of Mary Immaculate (3,432)	4,760
Franciscans (Conventuals) (2,826)	4,523
Vincentians (3,174)	4,105
Discalced Carmelites (O.C.D.) (2,521)	3,942
Claretians (2,015)	3,065
Holy Spirit (Holy Ghost), Vincentians Congregation of (2,220)	3,005
Augustinians (2,158)	2,889
Passionists (1,786)	2,356
Priests of the Sacred Heart (1,679)	2,394
Trappists (1,008)	2,310
Missionaries of the Sacred Pallottines (1,578)	2,305
Heart of Jesus (1,476)	2,141
Combonian Missionaries of the Heart of Jesus (1,312)	2,218
Missionaries of Africa (1,731)	2,068
Carmelites (O.Carm.) (1,399)	2,108
Carmelites of BVM (1,281)	1,947
Legionaries of Christ (434)	1,745
Holy Cross, Congregation of (787)	1,704
Christian Brothers	1,598
Marianists (496)	1,556
Piarists (1,067)	1,476
Cistercians (Common Observance) (741)	1,468
Hospitallers of St. John of God (143)	1,420
Marists (1,114)	1,321
Brothers of the Sacred Heart (44)	1,335
Premonstratensians (940)	1,331
Congregation of the Immaculate Heart of Mary (Missionhurst; Scheut Missionaries) (959)	1,220
Augustinians (Recollects) (1,006)	1,283
Brothers of Christian Instruction of St. Gabriel (28)	1,266
Salvatorians (802)	1,232
Brothers of Christian Instruction of Ploërmel (7)	1,159
Society of St. Paul (582)	1,139
Little Workers of Divine Providence (732)	1,056
Ministers of the Sick (Camillians) (689)	1,077

Sacred Hearts, Congregation (Picpus) (849)	1,062
Montfort Missionaries (729)	1,037
Society of African Missions (868)	1,010
Missionaries of St. Francis de Sales of Annecy (556)	1,089
Consolata Missionaries (771)	1,004
Servants of Mary (719)	940
Blessed Sacrament, Congregation of (677)	979
Missionaries of the Holy Family (676)	950
Assumptionists (630)	946
LaSalette Missionaries (667)	941
Xaverian Missionaries (683)	877
Franciscans (Third Order Regular) (559)	847
Canons Regular of St. Augustine (633)	767
Scalabrinians (617)	773
Viatorians (312)	740
Mercedarians (532)	743
Order of St. Basil the Great (Basilians of St. Josaphat) (300)	691
Columbans (583)	684
Oblates of St. Francis de Sales (510)	656
Missionaries of the Mill Hill (457)	626
Congregation of St. Joseph (515)	663
Most Precious Blood (458)	619
Maryknollers (506)	610
Oratorians (417)	556
Brothers of Charity (Ghent)	550
Pontifical Institute for Foreign Missions (499)	567
Trinitarians (389)	547
Marian Fathers and Brothers (358)	542
Eudists (411)	519
Somascans (353)	520
Oblates of St. Joseph (332)	508
Society of Christ (390)	493
Crosiers (Order of Holy Cross) (304)	464
Order of St. Paul the First Hermit (277)	463
Servants of Charity (327)	449
Stigmatine Fathers and Brothers (316)	416
Resurrection, Congregation of the (337)	410
Missionaries of the Holy Spirit (264)	397
Barnabites (303)	392
Mariannhill Missionaries (211)	393
St. Patrick's Mission Society (336)	383
Paris Foreign Mission Society (356)	356
Rogationists (226)	366
Carthusians (161)	356
Maronite Order of Lebanon (267)	357
Sulpicians (352)	352
Rosminians (221)	329

RELIGIOUS INSTITUTES OF WOMEN IN THE UNITED STATES

(*Sources:* The Official Catholic Directory; Catholic Almanac *survey.*)

Adorers of the Blood of Christ, A.S.C.: Founded 1834, in Italy; in U.S., 1870. General motherhouse, Rome, Italy. U.S. provinces: 2 Pioneer Lane, Red Bud, IL 62278, (618) 282-6229; 1400 South Sheridan, Wichita, KS 67213, (316) 943-1203; 3950 Columbia Ave., Columbia, PA 17512, (717) 285-4536. Education, retreats, social services, pastoral ministry.

Africa, Missionary Sisters of Our Lady of (Sisters of Africa), M.S.O.L.A.: Founded 1869, at Algiers, Algeria, by Cardinal Lavigerie; in U.S., 1929. General motherhouse, Rome, Italy; U.S. headquarters, 47 W. Spring St., Winooski, VT 05404-1397, (802) 655-4003. Medical, educational, catechetical and social work in Africa.

Agnes, Sisters of St., C.S.A.: Founded 1858, in U.S., by Rev. Caspar Rehrl. General motherhouse, 320 County Rd., Fond du Lac, WI 54935, (920) 907-2321. Education, health care, social services.

Ann, Sisters of St., S.S.A.: Founded 1834, in Italy; in U.S., 1952. General motherhouse, Rome, Italy; U.S. headquarters, Mount St. Ann, Ebensburg, PA 15931, (814) 472-9354.

Anne, Sisters of St., S.S.A.: Founded 1850, at Vaudreuil, Quebec, Canada; in U.S., 1866. General motherhouse, Lachine, Quebec, Canada; U.S. address, 720 Boston Post Rd., Marlboro, MA 01752, (508) 481-4934, www.sistersofsaintanne.org. Retreat work, pastoral ministry, religious education.

Anthony, Missionary Servants of St., M.S.S.A.: Founded 1929, in U.S., by Rev. Peter Baque. General motherhouse, 100 Peter Baque Rd., San Antonio, TX 78209, (210) 824-4553. Social work.

Antonine Maronite Sisters: Founded in Beirut, Lebanon; Motherhouse, Couvent Mar-Doumith, Roumieh, El-Metn, B.P. 84, Borumana, Lebanon; U.S. house, 2691 North Lipkey Rd., North Jackson, OH 44451, (330) 538-9822.

Assumption, Little Sisters of the, L.S.A.: Founded 1865, in France; in U.S., 1891. General motherhouse, Paris, France; U.S. provincialate, 100 Gladstone Ave., Walden, NY 12586, (914) 778-0667. Social work,

nursing, family life education.

Assumption, Religious of the, R.A.: Founded 1839, in France; in U.S., 1919. Generalate, Paris, France; North American province, 11 Old English Rd., Worcester, MA 01609, (508) 793-1954.

Assumption of the Blessed Virgin, Sisters of the, S.A.S.V.: Founded 1853, in Canada; in U.S., 1891. General motherhouse, Nicolet, Quebec, Canada; U.S. province, 316 Lincoln St., Worcester, MA 01605, (508) 856-9450. Education, mission, pastoral ministry.

Augustinian Nuns of Contemplative Life, O.S.A.: Established in Spain in 13th century; U.S. foundation, Convent of Our Mother of Good Counsel, 440 Marley Rd., New Lenox, IL, 60451, (815) 463-9662.

Augustinian Sisters, Servants of Jesus and Mary, Congregation of, O.S.A.: Generalate, Rome, Italy; U.S. foundation, St. John School, 513 E. Broadway, Brandenburg, KY 40108, (270) 422-2088, www.stjohnonline.org.

Basil the Great, Sisters of the Order of St. (Byzantine Rite), O.S.B.M.: Founded fourth century, in Cappadocia, by St. Basil the Great and his sister, St. Macrina; in U.S., 1911. Generalate, Rome, Italy; U.S. motherhouses: Philadelphia Ukrainian Byzantine Rite, 710 Fox Chase Rd., Philadelphia, PA 19046-4198, (215) 342-4222; Pittsburgh Ruthenian Byzantine Rite, Mount St. Macrina, P.O. Box 878, Uniontown, PA 15401, (724) 438-8644. Education, health care.

Benedict, Sisters of the Order of St., O.S.B.: Our Lady of Mount Caritas Monastery (founded 1979, Ashford, CT), 54 Seckar Rd., Ashford, CT 06278, (860) 429-7457. Contemplative.

Benedictine Nuns, O.S.B.: St. Scholastica Priory, Box 606, Petersham, MA 01366, (978) 724-3213. Cloistered.

Benedictine Nuns of the Congregation of Solesmes, O.S.B.: U.S. establishment, 1981, in Burlington diocese. Monastery of the Immaculate Heart of Mary, 4103 Vt. Rte 100, Westfield, VT 05874, (802) 744-6525. Cloistered, papal enclosure.

Benedictine Nuns of the Primitive Observance,

O.S.B.: Founded c. 529, in Italy; in U.S., 1948. Abbey of Regina Laudis, Flanders Rd., Bethlehem, CT 06751, (203) 266-7727. Cloistered.

Benedictine Sisters, O.S.B.: Founded c. 529, in Italy; in U.S., 1852. General motherhouse, Eichstatt, Bavaria, Germany. U.S. addresses: St. Emma Monastery, Motherhouse and Novitiate, 1001 Harvey Ave., Greensburg, PA 15601, (724) 834-3060, www.stemma.org; Abbey of St. Walburga, 32109 N. U.S. Highway 287, Virginia Dale, CO 80536, (970) 472-0612; www.walburga.org.

Benedictine Sisters (Regina Pacis), O.S.B.: Founded 1627, in Lithuania as cloistered community; reformed 1918 as active community; established in U.S. 1957, by Mother M. Raphaela Simonis. Regina Pacis, 333 Wallace Rd., Bedford, NH 03102, (603) 472-3239.

Benedictine Sisters, Missionary, O.S.B.: Founded 1885. Generalate, Rome, Italy; U.S. motherhouse, 300 N. 18th St., Norfolk, NE 68701, (402) 371-3438, www.norfolkosb.org.

Benedictine Sisters, Olivetan, O.S.B.: Founded 1887, in U.S. General motherhouse, Holy Angels Convent, P.O. Drawer 130, Jonesboro, AR 72403, (870) 935-5810, www.olivben.org. Educational, hospital work.

Benedictine Sisters of Perpetual Adoration of Pontifical Jurisdiction, Congregation of the, O.S.B.: Founded in U.S., 1874, from Maria Rickenbach, Switzerland. General motherhouse, 8300 Morganford Rd., St. Louis, MO 63123, (314) 638-6427.

Benedictine Sisters of Pontifical Jurisdiction, O.S.B.: Founded c. 529, in Italy. No general motherhouse in U.S. Three federations:

• **Federation of St. Scholastica** (1922). Pres., Sister Esther Fangman, O.S.B., 3741 Forest Ave., Kansas City, MO 64109, (816) 753-2514. Motherhouses belonging to the federation:

Mount St. Scholastica, 801 S. 8th St., Atchison, Kans. 66002, (913) 360-6200, www.mountosb.org; Benedictine Sisters of Elk Co., St. Joseph's Monastery, St. Mary's, PA 15857, (814) 834-2267; Benedictine Sisters of Erie, 6101 E. Lake Rd., Erie, PA 16511, (814) 899-0614, www.eriebene dictines.org; Benedictine Sisters of Chicago, St. Scholastica Priory, 7430 N. Ridge Blvd., Chicago, IL 60645, (773) 764-2413, www.benedictine-sisters.org; Benedictine Sisters of the Sacred Heart, 1910 Maple Ave., Lisle, IL 60532-2164, (630) 969-7040, www.shmlisle.org; Benedictine Sisters of Elizabeth, St. Walburga Monastery, 851 N. Broad St., Elizabeth, NJ 07208-2593, (201) 352-4278, www.catholicforum.com/bensisnj; Benedictine Sisters of Pittsburgh, 4530 Perrysville Ave., Pittsburgh, PA 15229, (412) 931-2844, www.osbpgh.org;

Red Plains Monastery, 728 Richland Rd. S.W., Piedmont, OK 73078, (405) 373-4565, www.geocities.com/redplains; St. Joseph's Monastery, 2200 S. Lewis, Tulsa, OK 74114, (918) 742-4989, www.tulsaosb.org; St. Gertrude's Monastery, 14259 Benedictine Lane, Ridgely, MD 21660, (410) 634-2497; St. Walburga Monastery, 2500 Amsterdam Rd., Villa Hills, KY 41017, (606) 331-6324; Sacred Heart Monastery, P.O. Box 2040, Cullman, AL 35056, (256) 734-4622, www.shmon.org; Benedictine Sisters of Virginia, 9535 Linton Hall Rd., Bristow, VA 20136, (703) 361-0106;

St. Scholastica Convent, 416 W. Highland Dr., Boerne, TX 78006, (830) 249-2645; St. Lucy's Priory, 19045 E. Sierra Madre Ave., Glendora, CA 91741, (626) 335-1682; Benedictine Sisters of Florida, Holy Name Monastery, P.O. Box 2450, St. Leo, FL 33574-2450, (352) 588-8320, www.floridabenedictines.org; Benet Hill Monastery, 2555 N. Chelton Rd., Colorado Springs, CO 80909, (719) 633-0655; Queen of Heaven Monastery (Byzantine Rite), 8640 Squires Lane N.E., Warren, OH 44484, (330) 856-1813, www.benedictine byzantine.org; Queen of Angels Monastery, 23615 N.E. 100th St., Liberty, MO 64068, (816) 750-4618.

• **Federation of St. Gertrude the Great** (1937). Office: St. Benedict of Ferdinand, Indiana, 802 E. 10th St., Ferdinand, IN 47532, (812) 367-1411; www.thedome.org. Pres., Sister Kathryn Huber, O.S.B. Motherhouses belonging to the federation:

Mother of God Monastery, 110 28th Ave., S.E., Watertown, SD 57201, (605) 882-6633, www.monastery@dailypost.com; Sacred Heart Monastery, 1005 W. 8th St., Yankton, SD 57078, (605) 668-6000, www.yanktonbenedictines@mtmc.edu; Mt. St. Benedict Monastery, 620 E. Summit Ave., Crookston, MN 56716, (218) 281-3441; Sacred Heart Monastery, P.O. Box 364, Richardton, ND 58652, (701) 974-2121, www.sacredheartmonastery.com; Convent of St. Martin, 2110-C St. Martin's Dr., Rapid City, SD 57702, (605) 343-8011, www.catholic-church.org/stmartin; Monastery of Immaculate Conception, 802 E. 10th St., Ferdinand, IN 47532, (812) 367-2313; Monastery of St. Gertrude, HC3, Box 121, Cottonwood, ID 83522, (208) 962-3224, www.stgertrudes.org;

Monastery of St. Benedict Center, Box 5070, Madison, WI 53705, (608) 836-1631; Queen of Angels Monastery, 840 S. Main St., Mt. Angel, OR 97362, (503) 845-6141, www.benedictine-srs.org; St. Scholastica Monastery, P.O. Box 3489, Fort Smith, AR 72913, (479) 783-4147, www.scholastica fortsmith.org; Our Lady of Peace Monastery, 3710 W. Broadway, Columbia, MO 65203, (573) 446-2300, www.benedictinesister.org; Queen of Peace Monastery, Box 370, Belcourt, ND 58316, (701) 477-6167; Our Lady of Grace Monastery, 1402 Southern Ave., Beech Grove, IN 46107, (317) 787-3287, www.benedictine.com; Holy Spirit Monastery, 22791 Pico St., Grand Terrace, CA 92324, (909) 783-4446; Spirit of Life Monastery, 10760 W. Glennon Dr., Lakewood, CO 80226, (303) 986-9234; St. Benedict's Monastery 225 Masters Ave., Winnipeg, MB, R4A 2A1, Canada, (204) 338-4601, www.mts.net/~stbens; The Dwelling Place Monastery, 150 Mt. Tabor Rd., Martin, KY 41649, (606) 886-9624.

• **Federation of St. Benedict** (1947). Pres., Sister Colleen Haggerty, O.S.B., St. Benedict Convent, 104 Chapel Lane, St. Joseph, MN 56374-0220, (320) 363-7100; www.sbm.osb.org. Motherhouses in U.S. belonging to the federation:

St. Benedict's Convent, St. Joseph, MN 56374, (320) 363-7100; St. Scholastica Monasstery, 1001 Kenwood Ave., Duluth, MN 55811-2300, (218) 723-7001, www.duluthbenedictines.org; St. Bede Monastery, 1190 Priory Rd., Eau Claire, WI 54702, (715) 834-3176, www.saintbede.org; St. Mary Monastery, Nauvoo, IL 62354, (217) 453-2227; Annunciation Monastery, 7520 University Dr., Bismarck, ND 58504, (701) 255-1520, www.annunciation

monastery.org; St. Paul's Monastery, 2675 Larpenteur Ave. E., St. Paul, MN 55109, (651) 777-8181, www.osb.org/spm; St. Placid Priory, 500 College St. N.E., Lacey, WA 98516, (360) 438-1771, www.stplacid.org; Mount Benedict Monastery, 6000 South 1075 East, Ogden, UT 84405-4945, (801)479-6030, www.mbutah.org.

Bethany, Sisters of, C.V.D.: Founded 1928, in El Salvador; in U.S. 1949. General motherhouse, Santa Tecla, El Salvador; U.S. address: 850 N. Hobart Blvd., Los Angeles, CA 90029, (213) 669-9411.

Bethlemita Sisters, Daughters of the Sacred Heart of Jesus (Beth.): Founded 1861, in Guatemala. Motherhouse, Bogota, Colombia; U.S. address, St. Joseph Residence, 330 W. Pembroke St., Dallas, TX 75208, (214) 948-3597.

Bon Secours, Congregation of, C.B.S.: Founded 1824, in France; in U.S., 1881. Generalate, Rome, Italy; U.S. provincial house, 1525 Marriottsville Rd., Marriottsville, MD 21104, (410) 442-1333, www.bonsecours.org. Hospital work.

Brigid, Congregation of St., C.S.B.: Founded 1807, in Ireland; in U.S., 1953. U.S. regional house, 5118 Loma Linda Dr., San Antonio, TX 78201, (210) 733-0701.

Brigittine Sisters (Order of the Most Holy Savior), O.SS.S.: Founded 1344, at Vadstena, Sweden, by St. Bridget; in U.S., 1957. General motherhouse, Rome, Italy; U.S. address, Vikingsborg, 4 Runkenhage Rd., Darien, CT 06820, (203) 655-1068.

Canossian Daughters of Charity (Fd.C.C.): Founded 1808 in Verona, Italy, by St. Magdalen of Canossa. General motherhouse, Rome, Italy; U.S. provincial house, 5625 Isleta Blvd. S.W., Albuquerque, NM 87105, (505) 873-2854, www.fdcc.org.

Carmel, Congregation of Our Lady of Mount, O. Carm.: Founded 1825, in France; in U.S., 1833. Generalate, P.O. Box 476, Lacombe, LA 70445, (504) 882-7577, www.mountcarmel.home.minsdpring.com. Education, social services, pastoral ministry, retreat work.

Carmel, Institute of Our Lady of Mount, O. Carm.: Founded 1854, in Italy; in U.S., 1947. General motherhouse, Rome, Italy; U.S. novitiate, 5 Wheatland St., Peabody, MA 01960, (978) 531-4733. Apostolic work.

Carmelite Community of the Word, C.C.W.: Motherhouse and novitiate, 394 Bem Rd., Gallitzin, PA 16641, (814) 886-4098 (fax).

Carmelite Nuns, Discalced, O.C.D.: Founded 1562, Spain. First foundation in U.S. in 1790, at Charles County, MD; this monastery was moved to Baltimore. Monasteries in U.S. are listed below by state.

Alabama: 716 Dauphin Island Pkwy., Mobile 36606, (334) 471-3991. Arkansas: 7201 W. 32nd St., Little Rock 72204, (501) 565-5121, www.aristotle.net/~carmelitenunslr.org. California: 215 E. Alhambra Rd., Alhambra 91801, (626) 282-2387, www.carmelites.org/teresacarmel; 27601 Highway 1, Carmel 93923, (831) 624-3043; 68 Rincon Rd., Kensington 94707; 6981 Teresian Way, Georgetown 95634, (530) 333-1617; 5158 Hawley Blvd., San Diego 92116, (619) 280-5424; 721 Parker Ave., San Francisco 94118; 530 Blackstone Dr., San Rafael 94903, (415) 479-6872; 1000 Lincoln St., Santa Clara 95050-5285, (408) 296-8412.

Colorado: 6138 S. Gallup St., Littleton 80120, (303)

798-4176. Georgia: Coffee Bluff, 11 W. Back St., Savannah 31419, (912) 925-8505. Hawaii: 6301 Pali Hwy., Kaneohe 96744, (808) 261-6542; Illinois: 1101 N. River Rd., Des Plaines 60016, (847) 298-4241. Indiana: 2500 Cold Spring Rd., Indianapolis 46222, (317) 926-5654; 59 Allendale Pl., Terre Haute 47802, (812) 299-1410. Iowa: 17937 250th St., Eldridge 52748, (319) 285-8387; 2901 S. Cecilia St., Sioux City 51106, (712) 276-1680. Kentucky: 1740 Newburg Rd., Louisville 40205, (502) 451-6796. Louisiana: 1250 Carmel Ave., Lafayette 70501, (337) 232-4651; 73530 River Rd., Covington 70435.

Maryland: 1318 Dulaney Valley Rd., Towson, Baltimore 21286, (410) 823-7415, www.geocities.com/baltimorecarmel; 5678 Mt. Carmel Rd., La Plata, 20646. Massachusetts: 61 Mt. Pleasant Ave., Roxbury, Boston 02119, (617) 442-1411; 15 Mt. Carmel Rd., Danvers 01923, (978) 774-3008. Michigan: 4300 Mt. Carmel Dr. NE, Ada 49301, (616) 691-8306; 35750 Moravian Dr., Clinton Township 48035, (586) 790-7255, www.rc.net/detroit/carmelite; U.S. 2 Highway, P.O. Box 397, Iron Mountain 49801, (906) 774-0561; 3501 Silver Lake Rd., Traverse City 49684, (231) 946-4960. Minnesota: 8251 De Montreville Trail N., Lake Elmo 55042-9547, (651) 777-3882. Mississippi: 2155 Terry Rd., Jackson 39204, (601) 373-1460.

Missouri: 2201 W. Main St., Jefferson City 65101, (573) 636-3364; 9150 Clayton Rd., Ladue, St. Louis Co. 63124, (314) 993-3494, www.stormpages.com/mtcarmel; 424 E. Monastery Rd., Springfield 65807, (417) 881-2115. Nevada: 1950 La Fond Dr., Reno 89509-3099, (775) 323-3236. New Hampshire: 275 Pleasant St., Concord, 03301-2590, (603) 225-5791. New Jersey: 26 Harmony School Rd., Flemington 08822; 189 Madison Ave., Morristown 07960, (973) 539-0773. New Mexico: 49 Mt. Carmel Rd., Santa Fe 87505-0352, (505) 983-7232. New York: c/o Chancery Office, Diocese of Brooklyn, 75 Greene Ave., Brooklyn 11238, (718) 399-5990; 89 Hiddenbrook Dr., Beacon, 12508, (914) 831-5572; 75 Carmel Rd., Buffalo 14214, (716) 837-6499; 1931 W. Jefferson Rd., Pittsford 14534, (716) 427-7094; 428 Duane Ave., Schenectady 12304.

Ohio: 3176 Fairmount Blvd., Cleveland Heights 44118, (216) 321-6568. Oklahoma: 20,000 N. County Line Rd., Piedmont 73078, (405) 348-3947. Oregon: 87609 Green Hill Rd., Eugene 97402, (541) 345-8649. Pennsylvania: 70 Monastery Rd., Elysburg 17824-9697, (570) 672-2935; 510 E. Gore Rd., Erie 16509, (814) 825-0846; R.D. 6, Box 28, Center Dr., Latrobe 15650, (724) 539-1056; P.O. Box 57, Loretto 15940, (814) 472-8620; Byzantine Rite, R.R. No. 1, Box 1336, Sugarloaf 18249, (570) 788-1205; 66th and Old York Rd., Philadelphia 19126, (215) 424-6143. Rhode Island: 25 Watson Ave., Barrington 02806, (401) 245-3421. South Dakota: 221 5th St., W., Alexandria, 57311.

Texas: 600 Flowers Ave., Dallas 75211; 5801 Mt. Carmel Dr., Arlington 76017, (817) 468-1781; 1100 Parthenon Pl., Roman Forest, New Caney 77357-3039, (281) 399-0270, www.icansurf.com/ocdnewcaney; 6301 Culebra and St. Joseph Way, San Antonio 78238-4909, (210) 680-1834. Utah: 5714 Holladay Blvd., Salt Lake City 84121, (801) 277-6075. Vermont: 94 Main St., Montpelier, 05601, (914) 831-5572. Washington: 2215 N.E. 147th St., Shoreline 98155, (206) 365-7335 (fax). Wisconsin: W267

N2517 Meadowbrook Rd., Pewaukee 53072, (262) 691-0336, www.geocities.com/pewaukeecarmel.org; 4047 Chapel Dr., New Franken 54229, (920) 866-2571.

Carmelite Nuns of the Ancient Observance (Calced Carmelites), O. Carm.: Founded 1452, in The Netherlands; in U.S., 1930, from Naples, Italy, convent (founded 1856). U.S. monasteries: Carmelite Monastery of St. Therese, 3551 Lanark Rd., Coopersburg, PA 18036; Carmel of Mary, Wahpeton, ND 58075; Our Lady of Grace Monastery, 6200 CR 339 Via Maria, Christoval, TX 76935, (915) 853-1722; Carmel of the Sacred Heart, 430 Laurel Ave., Hudson, WI 54016, (715) 862-2156, www.pres senter.com~carmelit. Papal enclosure.

Carmelite Sisters (Corpus Christi), O. Carm.: Founded 1908, in England; in U.S., 1920. General motherhouse, Tunapuna, Trinidad, W.I. U.S. address: Mt. Carmel Home, 412 W. 18th St., Kearney, NE 68847, (308) 237-2287. Home and foreign mission work.

Carmelite Sisters for the Aged and Infirm, O. Carm.: Founded 1929, at New York, by Mother M. Angeline Teresa, O. Carm. Motherhouse, 600 Woods Rd., Avila-on-Hudson, Germantown, NY 12526, (518) 537-5000. Social work, nursing and educating in the field of gerontology.

Carmelite Sisters of Charity, C.a.Ch.: Founded 1826 at Vich, Spain, by St. Joaquina de Vedruna. Generalate, Rome, Italy; U.S. address, 701 Beacon Rd., Silver Spring, MD 20903, (301) 434-6344.

Carmelite Sisters of St. Therese of the Infant Jesus, C.S.T.: Founded 1917, in U.S. General motherhouse, 1300 Classen Dr., Oklahoma City, OK 73103, (405) 232-7926. Educational work.

Carmelite Sisters of the Divine Heart of Jesus, Carmel D.C.J.: Founded 1891, in Germany; in U.S., 1912. General motherhouse, Sittard Netherlands. U.S. provincial houses: Northern Province, 1230 Kavanaugh Pl., Milwaukee, WI 52313 (414) 453-4040, www.carmelitedcjnorth.org; Central Province, 10341 Manchester Rd., St. Louis, MO 63122, (314) 965-7616, www.carmelitesdcj.org; South Western Province, 8585 La Mesa Blvd., La Mesa, CA 92041 (619) 466-3116. Social services, mission work.

Carmelite Sisters of the Most Sacred Heart of Los Angeles, O.C.D.: Founded 1904, in Mexico. General motherhouse and novitiate, 920 E. Alhambra Rd., Alhambra, CA 91801, wwwcarmelgener alate.homestead.com. Social services, retreat and educational work.

Carmelites, Calced, O. Carm.: Founded 1856 in Naples, Italy. U.S. address: Carmelite Monastery of St. Therese, 3551 Lanark Rd., Coopersburg, PA 18036.

Carmelites of St. Theresa, Congregation of Missionary, C.M.S.T.: Founded 1903, in Mexico. General motherhouse, Mexico City, Mexico; U.S. foundation, 9548 Deer Trail Dr., Houston, TX 77038, (281) 445-5520.

Casimir, Sisters of St., S.S.C.: Founded 1907, in U.S., by Mother Maria Kaupas. General motherhouse, 2601 W. Marquette Rd., Chicago, IL 60629, (773) 776-1324. Education, missions, social services.

Cenacle, Congregation of Our Lady of the Retreat in the, R.C.: Founded 1826, in France; in U.S., 1892. Generalate, Rome, Italy. Eastern Province,

Cenacle Rd., Lake Ronkonkoma, NY 11779, (516) 471-6270; Midwestern Province, 513 Fullerton Pkwy., Chicago, IL 60614, (773) 528-6300.

Charity, Daughters of Divine, F.D.C.: Founded 1868, at Vienna, Austria; in U.S., 1913. General motherhouse, Rome, Italy; U.S. province: 205 Major Ave., Staten Island, NY 10305, (718) 720-4377, www.godslovefdc.org. Education, social services.

Charity, Missionaries of, M.C.: Founded 1950, in Calcutta, India, by Mother Teresa; first U.S. foundation, 1971. General motherhouse, 54A Lower Circular Road, Calcutta 700016, India. U.S. address, 335 E. 145th St., Bronx, NY 10451, (718) 292-0019. Service of the poor.

Charity, Religious Sisters of, R.S.C.: Founded 1815, in Ireland; in U.S., 1953. Motherhouse, Dublin, Ireland; U.S. headquarters, 206 N. Edgemont St., Los Angeles, CA 90029, (310) 559-0176.

Charity, Sisters of (of Seton Hill), S.C.: Founded 1870, at Altoona, PA, from Cincinnati foundation. Generalate, De Paul Center, 463 Mt. Thor Rd., Greensburg, PA 15601, (724) 836-0406, www.sosh.org. Educational, hospital, social, foreign mission work.

Charity, Sisters of (Grey Nuns of Montréal), S.G.M.: Founded 1737, in Canada, by St. Marie Marguerite d'Youville; in U.S., 1855. General administration, Montréal, Que. H2Y 2L7, Canada; U.S. provincial house, 10 Pelham Rd., Ste. 1000, Lexington, MA 02421, (781) 862-4700, www.sqmlex.org.

Charity, Sisters of (of Leavenworth), S.C.L.: Founded 1858, in U.S. Motherhouse, 4200 S. 4th St., Leavenworth, KS 66048, (913) 758-6508, www.scls.org/

Charity, Sisters of (of Nazareth), S.C.N.: Founded 1812, in U.S. General motherhouse, SCN Center, P.O. Box 172, Nazareth, KY 40048, (502) 348-1568, www.scnazareth.org. Education, health services.

Charity, Sisters of (of St. Augustine), C.S.A.: Founded 1851, at Cleveland, Ohio. Motherhouse, 5232 Broadview Rd., Richfield, OH 44286, (330) 659-5100, www.srsofcharity.org.

Charity, Sisters of Christian, S.C.C.: Founded 1849, in Paderborn, Germany, by Bl. Pauline von Mallinckrodt; in U.S., 1873. Generalate, Rome, Italy. U.S. provinces: Mallinckrodt Convent, 350 Bernardsville Rd., Mendham, NJ 07945, (973) 543-6528, www.scceast.org; 2041 Elmwood Ave., Wilmette, IL 60091, (847) 920-9341, www.sccwilmette.org. Education, health services, other apostolic work.

Charity, Vincentian Sisters of, V.S.C.: Founded 1835, in Austria; in U.S., 1902. General motherhouse, 8200 McKnight Rd., Pittsburgh, PA 15237, (412) 364-3000, www.vincentiansrspgh.org.

Charity, Vincentian Sisters of, V.S.C.: Founded 1928, at Bedford, Ohio. General motherhouse, 1160 Broadway, Bedford, OH 44146, (440) 232-4755.

Charity of Cincinnati, Ohio, Sisters of, S.C.: Founded 1809; became independent community, 1852. General motherhouse, 5900 Delhi Rd., Mt. St. Joseph, OH 45051, (513) 347-5200, www.srcharitycinti.org. Educational, hospital, social work.

Charity of Ottawa, Sisters of (Grey Nuns of the Cross), S.C.O.: Founded 1845, at Ottawa, Canada; in U.S., 1857. General motherhouse, Ottawa, Canada;

U.S. provincial house, 559 Fletcher St., Lowell, MA 01854, (978) 453-4993. Educational, hospital work, extended health care.

Charity of Our Lady, Mother of Mercy, Sisters of, S.C.M.M.: Founded 1832, in Holland; in U.S., 1874. General motherhouse, Den Bosch, Netherlands; U.S. provincialate, 520 Thompson Ave., East Haven, CT 06512, (203) 469-7872.

Charity of Our Lady, Mother of the Church, S.C.M.C: U.S. foundation, 1970. General motherhouse, 520 Thompson Ave., East Haven, CT 06512, (203) 469-7872.

Charity of Our Lady of Mercy, Sisters of, O.L.M.: Founded 1829, in Charleston, SC. Generalate and motherhouse, 424 Fort Johnson Rd., P. O. Box 12410, Charleston, SC 29422, (843) 795-6083. Education, campus ministry, social services.

Charity of Quebec, Sisters of (Grey Nuns), S.C.Q.: Founded 1849, at Quebec; in U.S., 1890. General motherhouse, 2655 Le Pelletier St., Beauport, Que. GIC 3X7, Canada; U.S. address, 359 Summer St., New Bedford, MA 02740, (508) 996-6751. Social work.

Charity of St. Elizabeth, Sisters of (Convent Station, N.J.), S.C.: Founded 1859, at Newark, N J. General motherhouse, P.O. Box 476, Convent Station, NJ 07961-0476, (973) 290-5335. Education, pastoral ministry, social services.

Charity of St. Hyacinthe, Sisters of (Grey Nuns), S.C.S.H.: Founded 1840, at St. Hyacinthe, Canada; in U.S., 1878. General motherhouse, 16470 Avenue Bourdages, SUD, St. Hyacinthe, Que. J2T 4J8, Canada; U.S. regional house, 98 Campus Ave., Lewiston, ME 04240, (207) 797-8607.

Charity of St. Joan Antida, Sisters of, S.C.S.J.A.: Founded 1799, in France; in U.S., 1932. General motherhouse, Rome, Italy; U.S. provincial house, 8560 N. 76th Pl., Milwaukee, WI 53223, (414) 354-9233, www.scsja.org.

Charity of St. Louis, Sisters of, S.C.S.L.: Founded 1803, in France; in U.S., 1910. Generalate, Rome, Italy; U.S. provincialate, 4907 S. Catherine St., Plattsburgh, NY 12901, (518) 563-0383.

Charity of St. Vincent de Paul, Daughters of, D.C.: Founded 1633, in France; in U.S. 1809, at Emmitsburg, MD, by St. Elizabeth Ann Seton. General motherhouse, Paris, France. U.S. provinces: 333 South Seton Ave., Emmitsburg, MD 21727, (301) 447-2900, www.setonhs.org/Eburg/eburg.htm; 7800 Natural Bridge Rd., St. Louis, MO 63121, (314) 382-2800; 9400 New Harmony Rd., Evansville, IN 47720-8912, (812) 963-3341, www.doc-ecp.org; 96 Menands Rd., Albany, NY 12204; 26000 Altamont Rd., Los Altos Hills, CA 94022, (650) 941-4490.

Charity of St. Vincent de Paul, Sisters of, V.Z.: Founded 1845, in Croatia; in U.S., 1955. General motherhouse, Zagreb, Croatia; U.S. foundation, 171 Knox Ave., West Seneca, NY 14224, (716) 825-5859.

Charity of St. Vincent de Paul, Sisters of, Halifax, S.C.: Founded 1856, at Halifax, N. S., from Emmitsburg foundation. Generalate, Mt. St. Vincent, Halifax, N.S., Canada. U.S. addresses: Commonwealth of Massachusetts, 125 Oakland St., Wellesley Hills, MA 02481, (781) 237-2161; Boston Province, 26 Phipps St., Quincy, MA 02169, (617) 773-6085; New York Province, 84-32 63rd Ave., Middle Village, NY 11379, (718) 651-1685. Educational, hospital, social work.

Charity of St. Vincent de Paul, Sisters of, New York, SC.: Founded 1817, from Emmitsburg foundation. General motherhouse, Mt. St. Vincent on Hudson, 6301 Riverdale Ave., Bronx, NY 10471, (718) 549-9200, www.scny.org. Educational, hospital work.

Charity of the Blessed Virgin Mary, Sisters of, B.V.M.: Founded 1833, in U.S. by Mary Frances Clarke. General motherhouse, BVM Center, 1100 Carmel Dr., Dubuque, IA 52002, (563) 588-2351. Education, pastoral ministry, social services.

Charity of the Immaculate Conception of Ivrea, Sisters of, S.C.I.C.: Founded 18th century, in Italy; in U.S., 1961. General motherhouse, Rome, Italy; U.S. address, Immaculate Virgin of Miracles Convent, Box 348, Mt. Pleasant, PA 15666, (724) 887-6753.

Charity of the Incarnate Word, Congregation of the Sisters of, C.C.V.I.: Founded 1869, at San Antonio, Tex., by Bishop C. M. Dubuis. Generalate, 4709 Broadway, San Antonio, TX 78209, (210) 828-0020.

Charity of the Incarnate Word, Congregation of the Sisters of (Houston, Tex.), C.C.V.I.: Founded 1866, in U.S., by Bishop C. M. Dubuis. General motherhouse, P.O. Box 230969, Houston, TX 77223, (713) 928-6053. Educational, hospital, social work.

Charity of the Sacred Heart, Daughters of, F.C.S.C.J.: Founded 1823, at La Salle de Vihiers, France; in U.S., 1905. General motherhouse, La Salle de Vihiers, France; U.S. address, Sacred Heart Province, Grove St., P.O. Box 642, Littleton, NH 03561, (603) 444-5346.

Charles Borromeo, Missionary Sisters of St. (Scalabrini Srs.): Founded 1895, in Italy; in U.S., 1941. American novitiate, 1414 N. 37th Ave., Melrose Park, IL 60160, (708) 343-2162.

Child Jesus, Sisters of the Poor, P.C.J.: Founded 1844, at Aix-la-Chapelle, Germany; in U.S., 1924. General motherhouse, Simpelveld, Netherlands; American provincialate, 4567 Olentangy River Rd., Columbus, OH 43214, (614) 451-3900.

Chretienne, Sisters of Ste., S.S.Ch.: Founded 1807, in France; in U.S., 1903. General motherhouse, Metz, France; U.S. provincial house, 297 Arnold St., Wrentham, MA 02093, (508) 384-8066. Educational, hospital, mission work.

Christ the King, Missionary Sisters of, M.S.C.K.: Founded 1959 in Poland; in U.S., 1978. General motherhouse, Poznan, Poland; U.S. address, 3000 18-Mile Rd., Sterling Heights, MI 48314.

Christ the King, Sister Servants of, S.S.C.K.: Founded 1936, in U.S. General motherhouse, Loretto Convent, N8114 Calvary St., Mt. Calvary, WI 53057, (920) 753-3211. Social services.

Christian Doctrine, Sisters of Our Lady of, R.C.D.: Founded 1910, in New York. Central office, 23 Haskell Ave., Suffern, NY 10901, (914) 357-0046.

Christian Education, Religious of, R.C.E.: Founded 1817, in France; in U.S., 1905. General motherhouse, France; U.S. provincial residence, 55 Parkwood Dr., Milton, MA 02186, (617) 696-7732.

Cistercian Nuns, O. Cist.: Headquarters, Rome, Italy; U.S. address, Valley of Our Lady Monastery, E. 11096 Yanke Dr., Prairie du Sac, WI 53578, (608) 643-3520, www.cistercianorder.org.

Cistercian Nuns of the Strict Observance, Order of, O.C.S.O.: Founded 1125, in France, by St. Stephen Harding; in U.S., 1949. U.S. addresses: Mt. St. Mary's

Abbey, 300 Arnold St., Wrentham, MA 02093, (508) 528-1282; HC 1, Box 929, Sonoita, AZ 85637, (520) 455-5595, www.santaritaabbey.org; Our Lady of the Redwoods Abbey, 18104 Briceland Thorn Rd., Whitethorn, CA 95589, (707) 986-7419. Our Lady of the Mississippi Abbey, 8400 Abbey Hill Rd., Dubuque, IA 52003, (319) 582-2595, www.mississippiabbey.org/; Our Lady of the Angels Monastery, 3365 Monastery Dr., Crozet, VA 22932, (434) 823-1452, www.olamonastery.org.

Clare, Sisters of St., O.S.C.: General motherhouse, Dublin, Ireland; U.S. foundation, St. Francis Convent, 1974 Cherrywood St., Vista, CA 92083, (760) 945-8040.

Claretian Missionary Sisters (Religious of Mary Immaculate), R.M.I.: Founded 1855, in Cuba; in U.S., 1956. Generalate, Rome, Italy; U.S. address, 9600 W. Atlantic Ave., Delray Beach, FL 33446.

Clergy, Congregation of Our Lady, Help of the, C.L.H.C.: Founded 1961, in U.S. Motherhouse, Maryvale Convent, 2522 June Bug Rd., Vale, NC 28168, (704) 276-2626.

Clergy, Servants of Our Lady Queen of the, S.R.C.: Founded 1929, in Canada; in U.S., 1934. General motherhouse, 57 Jules A. Brillant, Rimouski, Que. G5L 1X1 Canada, (418) 724-0508. Domestic work.

Colettines: *See* **Franciscan Poor Clare Nuns**.

Columban, Missionary Sisters of St., S.S.C.: Founded 1922, in Ireland; in U.S., 1930. General motherhouse, Wicklow, Ireland; U.S. region, 73 Mapleton St., Brighton, MA 02135, (617) 782-5683.

Comboni Missionary Sisters (Missionary Sisters of Verona), C.M.S.: Founded 1872, in Italy; in U.S., 1950. U.S. address, 5405 Loch-Raven Blvd., Baltimore, MD 21239, (410) 323-1469.

Consolata Missionary Sisters, M.C.: Founded 1910, in Italy, by Bl. Giuseppe Allamano; in U.S., 1954. General motherhouse, Turin, Italy; U.S. headquarters, 6801 Belmont Rd., Belmont, MI 49306 (616) 361-9609, www.consolatasisters.org.

Cross, Daughters of the, D.C.: Founded 1640, in France; in U.S., 1855. General motherhouse, 411 E. Flournoy-Lucas Rd., Shreveport, LA 71115, (318) 797-0887. Educational work.

Cross, Daughters of, of Liege, F.C.: Founded 1833, in Liege, Belgium; in U.S., 1958. U.S. address, 165 W. Eaton Ave., Tracy, CA 95376.

Cross, Sisters of the Holy, C.S.C.: Founded 1841, at Le Mans, France; established in Canada, 1847; in U.S., 1881. General motherhouse, St. Laurent, Montreal, Que., Canada; U.S. regional office, 377 Island Pond Rd., Manchester, NH 03109, (603) 622-9504. Educational work.

Cross, Sisters of the Holy, Congregation of, C.S.C.: Founded 1841, at Le Mans, France; in U.S., 1843. General motherhouse, 100 Lourdes Hall-Saint Mary's, Notre Dame, IN 46556, (574) 284-5572. Education, health care, social services, pastoral ministry.

Cross and Passion, Sisters of the (Passionist Sisters), C.P.: Founded 1852; in U.S., 1924. Generalate, Northampton, England; U.S. address: Holy Family Convent, One Wright Lane, N. Kingstown, RI 02852, (401) 294-3554.

Cyril and Methodius, Sisters of Sts., SS.C.M.: Founded 1909, in U.S., by Rev. Matthew Jankola. General motherhouse, Villa Sacred Heart, Danville,

PA 17821, (570) 275-3581, www.sscm.org. Education, care of aged.

Disciples of the Lord Jesus Christ, D.L.J.C.: Founded 1972; canonically erected 1991. Address, P.O. Box 17, Channing, TX 79018, (806) 534-2312; www.dljc.org.

Divine Compassion, Sisters of, R.D.C.: Founded 1886, in U.S. General motherhouse, 52 N. Broadway, White Plains, NY 10603, (914) 949-2950. Education, other ministries.

Divine Love, Daughters of, D.D.L.: Founded 1969, in Nigeria; in U.S., 1990. General house, Enugu, Nigeria; U.S. regional house, 140 North Ave., Highwood, IL 60040, (847) 432-4946.

Divine Spirit, Congregation of the, C.D.S.: Founded 1956, in U.S., by Archbishop John M. Gannon. Motherhouse, 409 W. 6th St., Erie, PA 16507, (814) 455-3590. Education, social services.

Divine Zeal, Daughters of, F.D.Z.: Founded 1887 in Italy by Bl. Hannibal Maria DiFrancia; in U.S., 1951. Generalate, Rome; U.S. headquarters, Hannibal House Spiritual Center, 1526 Hill Rd., Reading, PA 19602, (610) 375-1738.

DOMINICANS

Nuns of the Order of Preachers (Dominican Nuns), O.P.: Founded 1206 by St. Dominic at Prouille, France. Cloistered, contemplative. Two branches in the United States:

• **Dominican Nuns having perpetual adoration.** First monastery established 1880, in Newark, NJ, from Oullins, France, foundation (1868). Autonomous monasteries:

Monastery of St. Dominic, 375 13th Ave., Newark, NJ 07103-2124, (973) 622-6622; Corpus Christi Monastery, 1230 Lafayette Ave., Bronx, NY 10474, (718) 328-6996; Blessed Sacrament, 29575 Middlebelt Rd., Farmington Hills, MI 48334-2311, (248) 626-8321; Monastery of the Angels, 1977 Carmen Ave., Los Angeles, CA 90068, (323) 466-2186; Corpus Christi, 215 Oak Grove Ave., Menlo Park, CA 94025, (650) 221-1801, www.op.org/nunsmenlo; Infant Jesus, 1501 Lotus Lane, Lufkin, TX 75904-2699, (936) 634-4233.

• **Dominican Nuns devoted to the Perpetual Rosary.** First monastery established 1891, in Union City, NJ, from Calais, France, foundation (1880). Autonomous monasteries (some also observe perpetual adoration):

Dominican Nuns of Perpetual Rosary, 14th and West Sts., Union City, NJ 07087; 217 N. 68th St., Milwaukee, WI 53213, (414) 258-0579, www.dsopr. home.mindspring.com; Perpetual Rosary, 1500 Haddon Ave., Camden, NJ 08103; Our Lady of the Rosary, 335 Doat St., Buffalo, NY 14211; Our Lady of the Rosary, 543 Spingfield Ave., Summit, NJ 07901, (908) 273-1228, www.op.org/nunsopsummit; Monastery of the Mother of God, 1430 Riverdale St., W. Springfield, MA 01089-4698, (413) 736-3639; Perpetual Rosary, 802 Court St., Syracuse, NY 13208; Immaculate Heart of Mary, 1834 Lititz Pike, Lancaster, PA 17601-6585, (717) 569-2104; Mary the Queen, 1310 W. Church St., Elmira, NY 14905, (607) 734-9506, www.oporg/maryqueen; St. Jude, Marbury, AL 36051, (205) 755-1322; Our Lady of Grace Monastery, 11 Race Hill Rd., North Guilford, CT 06437, (203) 345-0599, www.op-stjoseph.org/nuns/olgrace/

olgrace.htm; St. Dominic's Monastery, 4901 16th St. N.W., Washington, DC 20011; (202) 726-2107.

Dominican Sisters of Charity of the Presentation, O.P.: Founded 1696, in France; in U.S., 1906. General motherhouse, Tours, France; U.S. headquarters, 3012 Elm St., Dighton, MA 02715, (508) 669-5425, www.dominicansistersofthepresentation.org. Hospital work.

Dominican Sisters of Hope, O.P.: Formed 1995 through merger of Dominican Sisters of the Most Holy Rosary, Newburgh, NY, Dominican Sisters of the Sick Poor, Ossining, NY, and Dominican Sisters of St. Catherine of Siena, Fall River, MA. General Offices: 229 N. Highland Ave., Ossining, NY 10562, (914) 941-4420, www.ophope.org.

Dominican Sisters of Our Lady of the Rosary and of St. Catherine of Siena (Cabra): Founded 1644 in Ireland. General motherhouse, Cabra, Dublin, Ireland. U.S. regional house, 1930 Robert E. Lee Rd., New Orleans, LA 70122, (504) 288-1593.

Dominican Sisters of the Perpetual Rosary, O.P.: 217 N. 68th St., Milwaukee, WI 53213. Cloistered, contemplative.

Dominican Sisters of the Roman Congregation of St. Dominic, O.P.: Founded 1621, in France; in U.S., 1904. General motherhouse, Rome, Italy; U.S. province, 18 Tampa St., Lewiston, ME 04240, (207) 782-7480. Educational work.

Eucharistic Missionaries of St. Dominic, O.P.: Founded 1927, in Louisiana. General motherhouse, 3801 Canal St., Suite 400, New Orleans, LA 70119, (504) 486-1133; www.emdsisters.org. Parish work, social services.

Religious Missionaries of St. Dominic, O.P.: General motherhouse, Rome, Italy. U.S. address (Spanish province), 2237 Waldron Rd., Corpus Christi, TX 78418, (361) 939-8102.

Sisters of St. Dominic, O.P.: Names of congregations are given below, followed by the date of foundation, and location of motherhouse. St. Catherine of Siena, 1822. 2645 Bardstown Rd., St. Catharine, KY 40061, (606) 336-9303; St. Mary of the Springs, 1830. 2320 Airport Dr., Columbus, OH 43219, (614) 252-2137; Most Holy Rosary, 1847. Sinsinawa, WI 53824, (608) 748-4411; Most Holy Name of Jesus, 1850. 1520 Grand Ave., San Rafael, CA 94901, (415) 453-8303, www.sanrafaelop.org; Holy Cross, 1853. 555 Albany Ave., Amityville, NY 11701, (631) 842-6000, www.amityvilleop.org; St. Cecilia, 1860. 801 Dominican Dr., Nashville, TN 37228, (615) 256-5486, www.nashvilledominican.org.

St. Mary, 1860. 7300 St. Charles Ave., New Orleans, LA 70118, (504) 861-8183; St. Catherine of Siena, 1862. 5635 Erie St., Racine, WI 53402, (262) 639-4100, www.racinedominicans.org; Sacred Heart Convent, 1873. 1237 W. Monroe St., Springfield, IL 62704, (217) 787-0481, www.springfieldop.org; Sisters of Our Lady of the Rosary, Dominican Convent, 175 Route 340, Sparkill, NY 10976, (845) 359-6400, www.sparkill.org, 1876; Queen of the Holy Rosary, 1876. P.O. Box 3908, Mission San Jose, CA 94539, (510) 657-2468, www.msjdominicans.org; Most Holy Rosary, 1892. 1257 Siena Heights Dr., Adrian, MI 49221, (517) 266-3570.

Our Lady of the Sacred Heart, 1877. 2025 E. Fulton St., Grand Rapids, MI 49503, (616) 459-2910; St. Dominic, 1878. 496 Western Hwy., Blauvelt, NY 10913, (845) 359-0696, www.opblauvelt.org; St. Catherine de Ricci, 1880. 750 Ashbourne Rd., Elkins Park, PA 19027, (215) 635-6027; Sisters of St. Dominic, 1881. 1 Ryerson Ave., Caldwell, NJ 07006, (973) 403-3331; Dominican Sisters of Houston, 1882. 6501 Almeda Rd., Houston, TX 77021-2095, (713) 747-3310, www.op.org/houstonop; Tacoma Dominican Center, 1888. 935 Fawcett Ave., Tacoma, WA 98402, (253) 272-9688; Holy Cross, 1890. P.O. Box 280, Edmonds, WA 98020, (206) 542-3212, www.opedmonds.org.

St. Rose of Lima (Servants of Relief for Incurable Cancer) 1896. 600 Linda Ave., Hawthorne, NY 10532, (914) 769-0114, www.hawthorne-dominicans.org; Dominican Sisters of Great Bend, 1902. 3600 Broadway, Great Bend, KS 67530, (316) 792-1232, www.ckan.com/ksdom; Mission Center, 1911. Box 1288, Kenosha, WI 53141, (262) 694-2067; St. Rose of Lima, 1923. 775 Drahner Rd., #204, Oxford, MI 48371, (248) 628-2872, www.op.org/oxford; Immaculate Conception, 1929. 9000 W. 81st St., Justice, IL 60458, (708) 458-3040; Immaculate Heart of Mary, 1929. 1230 W. Market St., Akron, OH 44313, (330) 836-4908, www.elms.k12.oh.us; Dominican Sisters of Oakford (St. Catherine of Siena), 1889. Motherhouse, Oakford, Natal, South Africa; U.S. regional house, 1965. 980 Woodland Ave., San Leandro, CA 94577, (510) 638-2822.

(END OF LISTING FOR DOMINICANS)

Dorothy, Institute of the Sisters of St., S.S.D.: Founded 1834, in Italy, by St. Paola Frassinetti; in U.S., 1911. General motherhouse, Rome, Italy; U.S. provincialate, Mt. St. Joseph, 13 Monkeywrench Lane, Bristol, RI 02809, (401) 253-7835.

Eucharist, Religious of the, R.E.: Founded 1857, in Belgium; in U.S., 1900. General motherhouse, Belgium; U.S. foundation, 2907 Ellicott Terr., N.W., Washington, DC 20008, (202) 966-3111.

Felix, Congregation of the Sisters of St. (Felician Sisters), C.S.S.F.: Founded 1855, in Poland by Bl. Mary Angela Truszkowska; in U.S., 1874. General motherhouse, Rome, Italy. U.S. provinces: 36800 Schoolcraft Rd., Livonia, MI 48150, (734) 591-1730; 600 Doat St., Buffalo, NY 14211, (716) 892-4141; 3800 W. Peterson Ave., Chicago, IL 60659, (773) 463-3020; 260 South Main St., Lodi, NJ 07644, (973) 473-7447, www.felician.edu/cssf.htm; 1500 Woodcrest Ave., Coraopolis, PA 15108, (412) 264-2890; 1315 Enfield St., Enfield, CT 06082, (860) 745-7791; 4210 Meadowlark Lane, S.E., Rio Rancho, NM 87124-1021, (505) 892-8862.

Filippini, Religious Teachers, M.P.F.: Founded 1692, in Italy; in U.S., 1910. General motherhouse, Rome, Italy; U.S. provinces: St. Lucy Filippini Province, Villa Walsh, Morristown, NJ 07960, (973) 538-2886; Queen of Apostles Province, 474 East Rd., Bristol, CT 06010, (860) 584-2138, www.queenofapostles.com. Educational work.

Francis de Sales, Oblate Sisters of St., O.S.F.S.: Founded 1866, in France; in U.S., 1951. General motherhouse, Troyes, France; U.S. headquarters, Villa Aviat Convent, 399 Childs Rd., MD 21916, (410) 398-3699. Educational, social work.

FRANCISCANS

Bernardine Sisters of the Third Order of St.

Francis, O.S.F.: Founded 1457, at Cracow, Poland; in U.S., 1894. Generalate, 403 Allendale Rd., King of Prussia, PA 19406, (610) 337-3864. Educational, hospital, social work.

Capuchin Poor Clares, O.S.C. Cap: U.S. establishment, 1981, Amarillo diocese. Convent of the Blessed Sacrament and Our Lady of Guadalupe, 4201 N.E. 18th St., Amarillo, TX 79107, (806) 383-9877. Cloistered.

Congregation of the Servants of the Holy Child Jesus, O.S.F.: Founded 1855, in Germany; in U.S., 1929. General motherhouse, Würzburg, Germany; American motherhouse, Villa Maria, 641 Somerset St., North Plainfield, NJ 07060-4909, (908) 757-3050.

Congregation of the Third Order of St. Francis of Mary Immaculate, O.S.F.: Founded 1865, in U.S., by Fr. Pamphilus da Magliano, O.F.M. General motherhouse, 520 Plainfield Ave., Joliet, IL 60435, (815) 727-3686. Educational and pastoral work.

Daughters of St. Francis of Assisi, D.S.F.: Founded 1894, in Hungary; in U.S., 1946. Provincial motherhouse, 507 N. Prairie St., Lacon, IL 61540, (309) 246-2175. Nursing, CCD work.

Eucharistic Franciscan Missionary Sisters, E.F.M.S.: Founded 1943, in Mexico. Motherhouse, 943 S. Soto St., Los Angeles, CA 90023, (323) 264-6556.

Franciscan Handmaids of the Most Pure Heart of Mary, F.H.M.: Founded 1916, in U.S. General motherhouse, 15 W. 124th St., New York, NY 10027, (212) 289-5655. Educational, social work.

Franciscan Hospitaller Sisters of the Immaculate Conception, F.H.I.C.: Founded 1876, in Portugal; in U.S., 1960. General motherhouse, Lisbon, Portugal; U.S. novitiate, 300 S. 17th St., San Jose, CA 95112, (408) 998-3407.

Franciscan Missionaries of Mary, F.M.M.: Founded 1877, in India; in U.S., 1904. General motherhouse, Rome, Italy; U.S. provincialate, 3305 Wallace Ave., Bronx, NY 10467, (718) 547-4693, www.fmmusa.org. Mission work.

Franciscan Missionaries of Our Lady, O.S.F.: Founded 1854, at Calais, France; in U.S., 1913. General motherhouse, Desvres, France; U.S. provincial house, 4200 Essen Lane, Baton Rouge, LA 70809, (225) 926-1627. Hospital work.

Franciscan Missionaries of St. Joseph (Mill Hill Sisters), F.M.S.J.: Founded 1883, at Rochdale, Lancashire, England; in U.S., 1952. Generalate, Manchester, England; U.S. headquarters, Franciscan House, 1006 Madison Ave., Albany, NY 12208, (518) 482-1991.

Franciscan Missionary Sisters for Africa, O.S.F.: American foundation, 1953. Generalate, Ireland; U.S. headquarters, 172 Foster St., Brighton, MA 02135, (617) 254-4343.

Franciscan Missionary Sisters of Assisi, F.M.S.A.: First foundation in U.S., 1961. General motherhouse, Assisi, Italy; U.S. address, St. Francis Convent, 1039 Northampton St., Holyoke, MA 01040, (413) 536-0853.

Franciscan Missionary Sisters of Our Lady of Sorrows, O.S.F.: Founded 1939, in China, by Bishop Rafael Palazzi, O.F.M.; in U.S., 1949. U.S. address, 3600 S.W. 170th Ave., Beaverton, OR 97006, (503) 649-7127. Educational, social, domestic, retreat and foreign mission work.

Franciscan Missionary Sisters of the Divine Child, F.M.D.C.: Founded 1927, at Buffalo, NY, by Bishop William Turner. General motherhouse, 6380 Main St., Williamsville, NY 14221, (716) 632-3144. Educational, social work.

Franciscan Missionary Sisters of the Infant Jesus, F.M.I.J.: Founded 1879, in Italy; in U.S., 1961. Generalate, Rome, Italy; U.S. provincialate, 1215 Kresson Rd., Cherry Hill, NJ 08003, (609) 428-7930.

Franciscan Missionary Sisters of the Sacred Heart, F.M.S.C.: Founded 1860, in Italy; in U.S., 1865. Generalate, Rome, Italy; U.S. provincialate, 250 South St., Peekskill, NY 10566, (914) 737-5409. Educational and social welfare apostolates.

Franciscan Poor Clare Nuns (Poor Clares, Order of St. Clare, Poor Clares of St. Colette), P.C., O.S.C., P.C.C.: Founded 1212, at Assisi, Italy, by St. Francis of Assisi; in U.S., 1875. Proto-monastery, Assisi, Italy. Addresses of autonomous motherhouses in U.S. are listed below.

8650 Russell Ave., S., Minneapolis, MN 55431, (952) 881-4766, www.poorclare.com; 3626 N. 65th Ave., Omaha, NE 68104-3299, (402) 558-4916, www.poorclare.org/omaha; 720 Henry Clay Ave., New Orleans, LA 70118-5891, (504) 895-2019, www.poorclarenuns.com; 6825 Nurrenbern Rd., Evansville, IN 47712-8518, (812) 425-4396; 1310 Dellwood Ave., Memphis, TN 38127, (901) 357-6662, www.poorclare.org/memphis; 920 Centre St., Jamaica Plain, MA 02130, (617) 524-1760, www.st anthonyshrine.org/poorclares; 327 S. Broad St., Trenton, NJ 08608, (609) 392-7673; 1271 Langhorne-Newtown Rd., Langhorne, PA 19047, (215) 968-5775; 4419 N. Hawthorne St., Spokane, WA 99205, (509) 327-4479; 86 Mayflower Ave., New Rochelle, NY, 10801-1615, (914) 632-5227; 421 S. 4th St., Sauk Rapids, MN 56379-1898, (612) 251-3556; 3501 Rocky River Dr., Cleveland, OH 44111, (216) 941-2820;

1671 Pleasant Valley Rd., Aptos, CA 95001, (831) 761-9659; 2111 S. Main St., Rockford, IL 61102, (815) 963-7343; 215 E. Los Olivos St., Santa Barbara, CA 93105, (805) 682-7670; 445 River Rd., Andover, MA 01810, (978) 683-7599; 809 E. 19th St., Roswell, NM 88201, (505) 622-0868; 28210 Natoma Rd., Los Altos Hills, CA 94022, (650) 948-2947; 1916 N. Pleasantburg Dr., Greenville, SC 29609-4080, (864) 244-4514; 28 Harpersville Rd., Newport News, VA 23601, (804) 596-5942; 1175 N. 300 W., Kokomo, IN 46901-1799, (765) 457-5743; 3900 Sherwood Blvd., Delray Beach, FL 33445, (561) 498-3294; 200 Marycrest Dr., St. Louis, MO 63129, (314) 846-2618; 6029 Estero Blvd., Fort Myers Beach, FL 33931, (239) 463-5599, www.poorclaresfmb.org; 9300 Hwy 105, Brenham, TX 77833, (409) 836-2444.

Franciscan Sisters, Daughters of the Sacred Hearts of Jesus and Mary, O.S.F.: Founded 1860, in Germany; in U.S., 1872. Generalate, Rome, Italy; U.S. motherhouse, P.O. Box 667, Wheaton, IL 60189, (630) 462-7422, wwwfranciscanswheaton.org. Educational, hospital, foreign mission, social work.

Franciscan Sisters Daughters of Mercy, F.H.M.: Founded 1856, in Spain; in U.S., 1962. General motherhouse, Palma de Mallorca, Spain; U.S. address, 612 N. 3rd St., Waco, TX 76701, (254) 753-5565.

Franciscan Sisters of Allegany, O.S.F.: Founded

1859, at Allegany, N.Y., by Fr. Pamphilus da Magliano, O.F.M. General motherhouse, P.O. Box W.115 East Main St., Allegany, NY 14706, (716) 373-0200, www.fsalleg.org. Educational, hospital, foreign mission work.

Franciscan Sisters of Baltimore, O.S.F.: Founded 1868, in England; in U.S., 1881. General motherhouse, 3725 Ellerslie Ave., Baltimore, MD 21218, (410) 235-0139. Educational work; social services.

Franciscan Sisters of Chicago, O.S.F.: Founded 1894, in U.S., by Mother Mary Therese (Josephine Dudzik). General motherhouse, 14700 Main St., Lemont, IL 60439, (630) 257-7776. Educational work, social services.

Franciscan Sisters of Christian Charity, O.S.F.: Founded 1869, in U.S. Motherhouse, Holy Family Convent, 2409 S. Alverno Rd., Manitowoc, WI 54220, (920) 682-7728. Educational, hospital work.

Franciscan Sisters of Little Falls, MN, O.S.F.: Founded 1891, in U.S. General motherhouse, Little Falls, MN 56345, (320) 632-2981, www.fslf.org. Health, education, social services, pastoral ministry, mission work.

Franciscan Sisters of Mary, F.S.M.: Established, 1987, through unification of the Sisters of St. Mary of the Third Order of St. Francis (founded 1872, St. Louis) and the Sisters of St. Francis of Maryville, MO. (founded 1894). Address of general superior: 1100 Bellevue Ave., St. Louis, MO 63117-1883, (314) 768-1833. Health care, social services.

Franciscan Sisters of Mary Immaculate of the Third Order of St. Francis of Assisi, F.M.I.: Founded 16th century, in Switzerland; in U.S., 1932. General motherhouse, Bogota, Colombia; U.S. provincial house, 4301 N.E. 18th Ave., Amarillo, TX 79107-7220, (806) 383-5769. Education.

Franciscan Sisters of Our Lady of Perpetual Help, O.S.F.: Founded 1901, in U.S., from Joliet, IL, foundation. General motherhouse, 335 South Kirkwood Rd., St. Louis, MO 63122, (314) 965-3700, www.franciscansisters-olph.org. Educational, hospital work.

Franciscan Sisters of Peace, F.S.P.: Established 1986, in U.S., as archdiocesan community, from Franciscan Missionary Sisters of the Sacred Heart. Congregation Center, 20 Ridge St., Haverstraw, NY 10927, (845) 942-2527, www.fspnet.org.

Franciscan Sisters of Ringwood, F.S.R.: Founded 1927, at Passaic, New Jersey. General motherhouse, Mt. St. Francis, 474 Sloatsburg Rd., Ringwood, NJ 07456, (973) 962-7411. Educational work.

Franciscan Sisters of St. Elizabeth, F.S.S.E.: Founded 1866, at Naples, Italy, by Bl. Ludovico of Casorio; in U.S., 1919. General motherhouse, Rome, Italy; U.S. delegate house, 499 Park Rd., Parsippany, NJ 07054, (973) 539-3797, www.franciscan sisters.com. Educational work, social services.

Franciscan Sisters of St. Joseph, F.S.S.J.: Founded 1897, in U.S. General motherhouse, 5286 S. Park Ave., Hamburg, NY 14075, (716) 649-1205. Educational, hospital work.

Franciscan Sisters of St. Joseph (of Mexico): U.S. foundation, St. Paul College, 3015 4th St. N.E., Washington, DC 20017, (202) 832-6262.

Franciscan Sisters of the Atonement (Graymoor Sisters), S.A.: Founded 1898, in U.S., as Anglican community; entered Church, 1909. General motherhouse, St. Francis Convent-Graymoor, 41 Old Highland Turnpike, Garrison, NY 10524, (914) 424-3624. Mission work.

Franciscan Sisters of St. Paul, MN, O.S.F.: Founded 1863, at Neuwied, Germany (Franciscan Sisters of the Blessed Virgin Mary of the Holy Angels); in U.S., 1923. General motherhouse, Rhine, Germany; U.S. motherhouse, 1388 Prior Ave. S., St. Paul, MN 55116, (516) 690-1501. Educational, hospital, social work.

Franciscan Sisters of the Immaculate Conception, O.S.F.: Founded in Germany; in U.S., 1928. General motherhouse, Kloster, Bonlanden, Germany; U.S. province, 291 North St., Buffalo, NY 14201, (716) 881-2323.

Franciscan Sisters of the Immaculate Conception, O.S.F.: Founded 1874, in Mexico; in U.S., 1926. U.S. provincial house, 11306 Laurel Canyon Blvd., San Fernando, CA 91340, (818) 365-2582.

Franciscan Sisters of the Immaculate Conception, Missionary, M.F.I.C.: Founded 1873, in U.S. General motherhouse, Rome, Italy; U.S. address, 790 Centre St., Newton, MA 02158, (617) 527-1004. Educational work.

Franciscan Sisters of the Immaculate Conception and St. Joseph for the Dying, O.S.F.: Founded 1919, in U.S. General motherhouse, 1249 Joselyn Canyon Rd., Monterey, CA 93940, (408) 372-3579.

Franciscan Sisters of the Poor, S.F.P.: Founded 1845, at Aachen, Germany, by Bl. Frances Schervier; in U.S., 1858. Congregational office, 133 Remsen St., Brooklyn, NY 11201, (718) 643-1919, www.fran ciscansisters.org. Hospital, social work and foreign missions.

Franciscan Sisters of the Sacred Heart, O.S.F.: Founded 1866, in Germany; in U.S., 1876. General motherhouse, St. Francis Woods, 9201 W. St. Francis Rd., Frankfort, IL 60423, (815) 469-4895. Education, health care, other service ministries.

Hospital Sisters of the Third Order of St. Francis, O.S.F.: Founded 1844, in Germany; in U.S., 1875. General motherhouse, Muenster, Germany; U.S. motherhouse, 4849 La Verna Rd., Springfield, IL 62707, (217) 522-3386. Hospital work.

Institute of the Franciscan Sisters of the Eucharist, F.S.E.: Founded 1973. Motherhouse, 405 Allen Ave., Meriden, CT 06451, (203) 237-0841.

Little Franciscans of Mary, P.F.M.: Founded 1889, in U.S. General motherhouse, Baie St. Paul, Quebec, Canada; U.S. region, 55 Moore Ave., Worcester, MA 01602, (508) 755-0878. Educational, hospital, social work.

Missionary Sisters of the Immaculate Conception of the Mother of God, S.M.I.C.: Founded 1910, in Brazil; in U.S., 1922. U.S. provincialate, P.O. Box 3026, Paterson, NJ 07509, (973) 279-3790. Mission, educational, health work, social services.

Mothers of the Helpless, M.D.: Founded 1873, in Spain; in U.S., 1916. General motherhouse, Valencia, Spain; U.S. address, Sacred Heart Residence, 432 W. 20th St., New York, NY 10011, (212) 929-5790.

Poor Clares of Perpetual Adoration, P.C.P.A.: Founded 1854, at Paris, France; in U.S., 1921, at Cleveland, Ohio. U.S. monasteries: 4200 N. Market Ave., Canton, OH 44714; 2311 Stockham Lane, Portsmouth, OH 45662-3049, (740) 353-4713; 4108 Euclid

Ave., Cleveland, OH 44103, (216) 361-0783; 3900 13th St. N.E., Washington, DC 20017, (202) 526-6808; 5817 Old Leeds Rd., Birmingham, AL 35210, (205) 271-2917. Contemplative, cloistered, perpetual adoration.

St. Francis Mission Community, O.S.F.: Autonomous province of Franciscan Sisters of Mary Immaculate. Address: 4305 54th St., Lubbock, TX 79413, (806) 793-9859.

School Sisters of St. Francis, O.S.F.: Founded 1874, in U.S. General motherhouse, 1501 S. Layton Blvd., Milwaukee, WI 53215, (414) 384-4105.

School Sisters of St. Francis, (Pittsburgh, PA), O.S.F.: Established 1913, in U.S. Motherhouse, Mt. Assisi Convent, 934 Forest Ave., Pittsburgh, PA 15202, (412) 761-2855, www.franciscansisters-pa.org. Education, health care services and related ministries.

School Sisters of the Third Order of St. Francis (Bethlehem, PA), O.S.F.: Founded in Austria, 1843; in U.S., 1913. General motherhouse, Rome, Italy; U.S. province, 395 Bridle Path Rd., Bethlehem, PA 18017, (610) 866-2597. Educational, mission work.

School Sisters of the Third Order of St. Francis (Panhandle, TX), O.S.F.: Established 1931, in U.S., from Vienna, Austria, foundation (1845). General motherhouse, Vienna, Austria; U.S. center and novitiate, P.O. Box 906, Panhandle, TX 79068, (806) 537-3182. Educational, social work.

Sisters of Mercy of the Holy Cross, S.C.S.C.: Founded 1856, in Switzerland; in U.S. 1912. General motherhouse, Ingenbohl, Switzerland; U.S. provincial residence, 501 S. Center Ave., Merrill, WI 54452, (715) 539-5000, www.pcpros.net/~hcross.

Sisters of Our Lady of Mercy (Mercedarians), S.O.L.M.: General motherhouse, Rome, Italy; U.S. addresses: Most Precious Blood, 133 27th Ave., Brooklyn, NY 11214.

Sisters of St. Francis (Clinton, IA), O.S.F.: Founded 1868, in U.S. General motherhouse, 588 N. Bluff Blvd., Clinton, IA 57232-3953, (563) 242-7611. Educational, hospital, social work.

Sisters of St. Francis (Millvale, Pa.), O.S.F.: Founded 1865, Pittsburgh. General motherhouse, 146 Hawthorne Rd., Millvale P.O., Pittsburgh, PA 15209, (412) 821-2200. Educational, hospital work.

Sisters of St. Francis (Hastings-on-Hudson), O.S.F.: Founded 1893, in New York. General motherhouse, 49 Jackson Ave., Hastings-on-Hudson, NY 10706-3217, (914) 478-3932. Education, parish ministry, social services.

Sisters of St. Francis of Assisi, O.S.F.: Founded 1849, in U.S. General motherhouse, 3221 S. Lake Dr., St. Francis, WI 53235-3799, (414) 744-3150, www.lakeosfs.org. Education, other ministries.

Sisters of St. Francis of Christ the King, O.S.F.: Founded 1864, in Austria; in U.S., 1909. General motherhouse, Rome, Italy; U.S. provincial house, 13900 Main St., Lemont, IL 60439, (630) 257-7495. Educational work, home for aged.

Sisters of St. Francis of Penance and Christian Charity, O.S.F.: Founded 1835, in Holland; in U.S., 1874. General motherhouse, Rome, Italy. U.S. provinces: 4421 Lower River Rd., Stella Niagara, NY 14144, (716) 754-2193; 2851 W. 52nd Ave., Denver, CO 80221, (303) 458-6270; 3910 Bret Harte Dr., P.O. Box 1028, Redwood City, CA 94064, (650) 369-1725.

Sisters of St. Francis of Philadelphia, O.S.F.: Founded 1855, at Philadelphia, by Mother Mary Francis Bachmann and St. John N. Neumann. General motherhouse, Convent of Our Lady of the Angels, Aston, PA 19014, (610) 558-7701, www.osfphila.org. Education, health care, social services.

Sisters of St. Francis of Savannah, MO, O.S.F.: Founded 1850, in Austria; in U.S., 1922. Provincial house, La Verna Heights, Box 488, 104 E. Park, Savannah, MO 64485-0488, (816) 324-3179. Educational, hospital work.

Sisters of St. Francis of the Congregation of Our Lady of Lourdes, O.S.F.: Founded 1916, in U.S. General motherhouse, 6832 Convent Blvd., Sylvania, OH 43560-2897, (419) 824-3606, www.sistersosf.org. Education, health care, social services, pastoral ministry.

Sisters of St. Francis of the Holy Cross, O.S.F.: Founded 1881, in U.S., by Rev. Edward Daems, O.S.C. General motherhouse, 3025 Bay Settlement Rd., Green Bay, WI 54311, (920) 468-1828, www.gbfranciscansisters.org. Educational, nursing work, pastoral ministry, foreign missions.

Sisters of St. Francis of the Holy Eucharist, O.S.F.: Founded 1378, in Switzerland; in U.S., 1893. General motherhouse, 2100 N. Noland Rd., Independence, MO 64050, (816) 252-1673. Education, health care, social services, foreign missions.

Sisters of St. Francis of the Holy Family, O.S.F.: U.S. foundation, 1875. Motherhouse, Mt. St. Francis, 3390 Windsor Ave., Dubuque, IA 52001, (319) 583-9786, www.osfdbq.org. Varied apostolates.

Sisters of St. Francis of the Immaculate Conception, O.S.F.: Founded 1890, in U.S. General motherhouse, 2408 W. Heading Ave., West Peoria, IL 61604-5096, (309) 674-6168. Education, care of aging, pastoral ministry.

Sisters of St. Francis of the Immaculate Heart of Mary, O.S.F.: Founded 1241, in Bavaria; in U.S., 1913. General motherhouse, Rome, Italy; U.S. motherhouse, 102 6th St., S.E., Hankinson, ND 58041, (701) 242-7195, www.fargodiocese.org/sfc/index.htm. Education, social services.

Sisters of St. Francis of the Martyr St. George, O.S.F.: Founded 1859, in Germany; in U.S., 1923. General motherhouse, Thuine, Germany; U.S. provincial house, St. Francis Convent, 2120 Central Ave., Alton, IL 62002, (618) 463-2750. Education, social services, foreign mission work.

Sisters of St. Francis of the Perpetual Adoration, O.S.F.: Founded 1863, in Germany; in U.S., 1875. General motherhouse, Olpe, Germany. U.S. provinces: Box 766, Mishawaka, IN 46546, (574) 259-5427, www.ssfpa.org; 7665 Assisi Heights, Colorado Springs, CO 80919, (719) 598-5486, www.st francis.org.

Sisters of St. Francis of the Providence of God, O.S.F.: Founded 1922, in U.S., by Msgr. M. L. Krusas. General motherhouse, 3603 McRoberts Rd., Pittsburgh, PA 15234, (412) 885-7407. Education, varied apostolates.

Sisters of St. Joseph of the Third Order of St. Francis, S.S.J.: Founded 1901, in U.S. Administrative office, 1300 Maria Dr., Stevens Pt., WI 54481-0305, (715) 341-8457, www.ssj-tosf.org. Education, health care, social services.

Sisters of the Infant Jesus, I.J.: Founded 1662, at Rouen, France; in U.S., 1950. Motherhouse, Paris, France. Generalate, Rome, Italy. U.S. address: 20 Reiner St., Colma, CA 94014.

Sisters of the Sorrowful Mother (Third Order of St. Francis), S.S.M.: Founded 1883, in Italy; in U.S., 1889. General motherhouse, Rome, Italy; U.S. address: 17600 E. 51st St., Broken Arrow, OK 74012, (918) 355-1148, (918) 355-1148. Educational, hospital work.

Sisters of the Third Franciscan Order, O.S.F.: Founded 1860, at Syracuse, N.Y. Generalate offices, 2500 Grant Blvd., Syracuse, NY 13208, (315) 425-0115.

Sisters of the Third Order of St. Francis, O.S.F.: Founded 1877, in U.S., by Bishop John L. Spalding. Motherhouse, 1175 St. Francis Lane, E. Peoria, IL 61611-1299, (309) 699-7215. Hospital work.

Sisters of the Third Order of St. Francis (Oldenburg, IN), O.S.F.: Founded 1851, in U.S. General motherhouse, Sisters of St. Francis, Oldenburg, IN 47036-0100, (812) 934-2475, oldenburgfranciscans.org. Education, social services, pastoral ministry, foreign missions.

Sisters of the Third Order of St. Francis of Penance and Charity, O.S.F.: Founded 1869, in U.S., by Rev. Joseph Bihn. Motherhouse, 200 St. Francis Ave., Tiffin, OH 44883, (419) 447-0435, www.tiffinohio.com/stfrancis. Education, social services.

Sisters of the Third Order of St. Francis of the Perpetual Adoration, F.S.P.A.: Founded 1849, in U.S. Generalate, 912 Market St., La Crosse, WI 54601, (608) 782-5610, www.fspa.org. Education, health care.

Sisters of the Third Order Regular of St. Francis of the Congregation of Our Lady of Lourdes, O.S.F.: Founded 1877, in U.S. General motherhouse, Assisi Heights, Rochester, MN 55901, (507) 282-7441. Education, health care, social services.

(END OF LISTING FOR FRANCISCANS)

Good Shepherd Sisters (Servants of the Immaculate Heart of Mary), S.C.I.M.: Founded 1850, in Canada; in U.S., 1882. General motherhouse, Quebec, Canada; in U.S., Provincial House, Bay View, 313 Seaside Ave., Saco, Maine 04072, (207) 283-3433. Educational, social work.

Good Shepherd, Sisters of Our Lady of Charity of the, R.G.S.: Founded 1835, in France, by St. Mary Euphrasia Pelletier; in U.S., 1843. Generalate, Rome, Italy. U.S. provinces: 2108 Hatmaker St., Cincinnati, OH 45204, (513) 921-5923; 82-31 Doncaster Pl., Jamaica, NY 11432, (718) 380-3270, www.good shepherdsistersna.org; 504 Hexton Hill Rd., Silver Spring, MD 20904, (301) 384-1169; 7654 Natural Bridge Rd., St. Louis, MO 63121, (314) 381-3400, www.goodshepherdsisters.org; 5100 Hodgson Rd., St. Paul, MN 55112, (651) 482-5251. Active and contemplative (Contemplative Sisters of the Good Shepherd, C.G.S.).

Graymoor Sisters: See **Franciscan Sisters of the Atonement.**

Grey Nuns of the Sacred Heart, G.N.S.H.: Founded 1921, in U.S. General motherhouse, 1750 Quarry Rd., Yardley, PA 19067-3998, (215) 968-4236, www.greynun.org.

Guadalupan Missionaries of the Holy Spirit,

M.G.Sp.S.: Founded 1930 in Mexico by Rev. Felix de Jesus Rougier, M.Sp.S. General motherhouse, Mexico; U.S. delegation: 2483 S.W. 4th St. Miami, FL 33135, (305) 642-9544.

Guardian Angel, Sisters of the, S.A.C.: Founded 1839, in France. General motherhouse, Madrid, Spain; U.S. foundation, 1245 S. Van Ness, Los Angeles, CA 90019, (213) 732-7881.

Handmaids of the Precious Blood, Congregation of, H.P.B.: Founded 1947, at Jemez Springs, NM. Motherhouse and novitiate, Cor Jesu Monastery, P.O. Box 90, Jemez Springs, NM 87025, (505) 829-3906.

Helpers, Society of, H.H.S.: Founded 1856, in France; in U.S., 1892. General motherhouse, Paris, France; American province, 3206 S. Aberdeen, Chicago, IL 60657, (773) 523-8638.

Hermanas Catequistas Guadalupanas, H.C.G.: Founded 1923, in Mexico; in U.S., 1950. General motherhouse, Mexico; U.S. addresses: 4110 S. Flores, San Antonio, TX 78214, (210) 533-9344.

Hermanas Josefinas, H.J.: General motherhouse, Mexico; U.S. foundation, Assumption Seminary, 2600 W. Woodlawn Ave., P.O. Box 28240, San Antonio, TX 78284, (210) 734-0039. Domestic work.

Holy Child Jesus, Society of the, S.H.C.J.: Founded 1846, in England; in U.S., 1862. General motherhouse, Rome, Italy; U.S. province, 460 Shadeland Ave., Drexel Hill, PA 19026, (610) 626-1400, www.shcj.org.

Holy Faith, Congregation of the Sisters of the, C.H.F.: Founded 1856, in Ireland; in U.S., 1953. General motherhouse, Dublin, Ireland; U.S. province, 12322 S. Paramount Blvd., Downey, CA 90242, (562) 869-6092.

Holy Family, Congregation of the Sisters of the, S.S.F.: Founded 1842, in Louisiana, by Henriette Delille and Juliette Gaudin. General motherhouse, 6901 Chef Menteur Hwy., New Orleans, LA 70126, (504) 242-8315, www.sistersoftheholyfamily, hospital work.

Holy Family, Little Sisters of the, P.S.S.F.: Founded 1880, in Canada; in U.S., 1900. General motherhouse, Sherbrooke, Quebec, Canada. U.S. novitiate, 285 Andover St., Lowell, MA 01852, (508) 454-7481.

Holy Family, Sisters of the, S.H.F.: Founded 1872, in U.S. General motherhouse, P.O. Box 3248, Fremont, CA 94539, (510) 624-4596, www.holyfamilysisters.com. Educational, social work.

Holy Family of Nazareth, Sisters of the, C.S.F.N.: Founded 1875, in Italy; in U.S., 1885. General motherhouse, Rome, Italy; U.S. provinces: Sacred Heart, 310 N. River Rd., Des Plaines, IL 60016, (847) 298-6760; Immaculate Conception BVM, 4001 Grant Ave., Torresdale, Philadelphia, PA 19114, (215) 637-6464; St. Joseph, 285 Bellevue Rd., Pittsburgh, PA 15229, (412) 931-4778, www.geocities\csfn_pgh; Immaculate Heart of Mary, Marian Heights, 1428 Monroe Turnpike, Monroe, CT 04648, (203) 268-7646; Bl. Frances Siedliska Provincialate, 1814 Egyptian Way, Box 530959, Grand Prairie, TX 75053, (972) 641-4496, www.csfn.org.

Holy Heart of Mary, Servants of the, S.S.C.M.: Founded 1860, in France; in U.S., 1889. General motherhouse, Montreal, Quebec, Canada; U.S. province, 485 W. Merchant St., Kankakee, IL 60901, (815) 937-2380, www.inil.com/users/hatton. Educational, hospital, social work.

Holy Names of Jesus and Mary, Sisters of the, S.N.J.M.: Founded 1843, in Canada by Bl. Marie Rose Durocher; in U.S., 1859. Generalate, Longueuil Quebec, Canada. U.S. addresses: Oregon Province, Box 25, Marylhurst, OR 97036, (503) 675-2449; California Province, P.O. Box 907, Los Gatos, CA 95031, (408) 395-5150; New York Province, 1061 New Scotland Rd., Albany, NY 12208, (518) 489-5469; Washington Province, 2911 W. Ft. Wright Dr., Spokane, WA 99224, (509) 328-7470, www.snjm.org, www.holynames.net.

Holy Spirit, Community of the, C.H.S.: Founded 1970 in San Diego, CA. Address: 6151 Rancho Mission Rd., No. 205, San Diego, CA 92108, (619) 584-0809.

Holy Spirit, Daughters of the, D.H.S.: Founded 1706, in France; in U.S., 1902. Generalate, Bretagne, France; U.S. motherhouse, 72 Church St., Putnam, CT 06260, (860) 928-0891. Educational work, district nursing, pastoral ministry.

Holy Spirit, Mission Sisters of the, M.S.Sp.: Founded 1932, at Cleveland, OH. Motherhouse, 1030 N. River Rd., Saginaw, MI 48603, (517) 781-0934.

Holy Spirit, Missionary Sisters, Servants of the: Founded 1889, in Holland; in U.S., 1901. Generalate, Rome, Italy; U.S. motherhouse, Convent of the Holy Spirit, Techny, IL 60082 .

Holy Spirit, Sisters of the, C.S.Sp.: Founded 1890, in Rome, Italy; in U.S. as independent diocesan community, 1929. General motherhouse, 10102 Granger Rd., Garfield Hts., OH 44125. Educational, social, nursing work.

Holy Spirit, Sisters of the, S.H.S.: Founded 1913, in U.S., by Most Rev. J. F. Regis Canevin. General motherhouse, 5246 Clarwin Ave., Ross Township, Pittsburgh, PA 15229-2208, (412) 931-1917. Educational, nursing work, care of aged.

Holy Spirit and Mary Immaculate, Sisters of, S.H.Sp.: Founded 1893, in U.S. Motherhouse, 301 Yucca St., San Antonio, TX 78203, (210) 533-5149. Education, hospital work.

Holy Spirit of Perpetual Adoration, Sister Servants of the, S.Sp.S.deA.P.: Founded 1896, in Holland; in U.S., 1915. Generalate, Bad Driburg, Germany; U.S. novitiate, 2212 Green St., Philadelphia, PA 19130, (215) 567-0123.

Holy Union Sisters, S.U.S.C.: Founded 1826, in France; in U.S., 1886. Generalate, Rome, Italy. U.S. provinces: P.O. Box 410, Milton, MA 02186-0006, (617) 696-8765; Box 993, Main St., Groton, MA 01450, (978) 448-6049. Varied ministries.

Home Mission Sisters of America (Glenmary Sisters), G.H.M.S.: Founded 1952, in U.S. Glenmary Center, P.O. Box 22264, Owensboro, KY 42304-2264, (270) 686-8401.

Home Visitors of Mary, Sisters, H.V.M.: Founded 1949, in Detroit, MI. Motherhouse, 121 E. Boston Blvd., Detroit, MI 48202, (313) 869-2160.

Humility of Mary, Congregation of, C.H.M.: Founded 1854, in France; in U.S., 1864. U.S. address, Humility of Mary Center, Davenport IA, 52804, (319) 323-9466, www.chmiowa.org.

Humility of Mary, Sisters of the, H.M.: Founded 1854, in France; in U.S., 1864. U.S. address, Villa Maria Community Center, Villa Maria, PA 16155, (724) 964-8861.

Immaculate Conception, Little Servant Sisters of the, L.S.I.C.: Founded 1850, in Poland; in U.S., 1926. General motherhouse, Poland; U.S. provincial house, 1000 Cropwell Rd., Cherry Hill, NJ 08003, (609) 424-1962. Education, social services, African missions.

Immaculate Conception, Sisters of the, R.C.M.: Founded 1892, in Spain; in U.S., 1962. General motherhouse, Madrid, Spain; U.S. address, 2230 Franklin, San Francisco, CA 94109, (415) 474-0159.

Immaculate Conception, Sisters of the, C.I.C.: Founded 1874, in U.S. General motherhouse, P.O. Box 50426, New Orleans, LA 70185, (504) 486-7426.

Immaculate Conception of the Blessed Virgin Mary, Sisters of the (Lithuanian): Founded 1918, at Mariampole, Lithuania; in U.S., 1936. U.S. headquarters, Immaculate Conception Convent, 600 Liberty Hwy., Putnam, CT 06260, (860) 928-7955.

Immaculate Heart of Mary, Missionary Sisters, I.C.M.: Founded 1897, in India; in U.S., 1919. Generalate, Rome, Italy; U.S. province, 283 E. 15th St., New York, NY 10003, (212) 254-0658. Educational social, foreign mission work.

Immaculate Heart of Mary, Sisters of the, I.H.M.: Founded 1848, in Spain; in U.S., 1878. General motherhouse, Rome, Italy; U.S. province, 4100 Sabino Canyon Rd., Tucson, AZ 85750, (520) 886-4273. Educational work.

Immaculate Heart of Mary, Sisters, Servants of the, I.H.M.: Founded 1845. SSIHM Leadership Council, 610 W. Elm, Monroe, MI 48162, (734) 340-9700, www.sistersihm.org.

Immaculate Heart of Mary, Sisters, Servants of the, I.H.M.: Founded 1845; established in Scranton, PA, 1871. General motherhouse, 2300 Adams Ave., Scranton, PA 18509, (570) 346-5404, ihm.marywood.edu.

Immaculate Heart of Mary, Sisters Servants of the, I.H.M.: Founded 1845; established in West Chester, PA., 1872. General motherhouse, Villa Maria, Immaculata, PA 19345, (610) 647-2160.

Immaculate Heart of Mary of Wichita, Sisters of, I.H.M.: Established at Wichita, 1979. Address: 605 N. Woodchuck, Wichita, KS 67212, (316) 722-9316; www.sistersof wichita.org.

Incarnate Word, Religious of, C.V.I.: General motherhouse, Mexico City, Mexico; U.S. address, 153 Rainier Ct., Chula Vista, CA 92011, (619) 420-0231.

Incarnate Word and Blessed Sacrament, Congregation of, C.V.I.: Founded 1625, in France; in U.S., 1853. Incarnate Word Convent, 3400 Bradford Pl., Houston, TX 77025, (713) 668-0423.

Incarnate Word and Blessed Sacrament, Congregation of the, I.W.B.S.: Motherhouse, 1101 Northeast Water St., Victoria, TX 77901, (361) 575-2266, www.catholic-forum.com/iwbsvictoria.

Incarnate Word and Blessed Sacrament, Congregation of the, I.W.B.S.: Motherhouse, 2930 S. Alameda, Corpus Christi, TX 78404, (361) 882-5413, www.iwbscc.org.

Incarnate Word and Blessed Sacrament, Sisters of the, S.I.W.: Founded 1625, in France; in U.S. 1853. Motherhouse, 6618 Pearl Rd., Parma Heights, Cleveland, OH 44130, (216) 886-6440, wwwincarnate wordorder.org.

Infant Jesus, Congregation of the (Nursing Sisters of the Sick Poor), C.I.J.: Founded 1835, in France; in U.S., 1905. General motherhouse, 310 Prospect Park W., Brooklyn, NY 11215, (718) 965-7300.

Institute of the Blessed Virgin Mary (Loretto Sisters), I.B.V.M.: Founded 17th century in Belgium; in U.S., 1954. Motherhouse, Rathfarnham, Dublin, Ireland; U.S. address: 2521 W. Maryland Ave., Phoenix, AZ 85017, (602) 242-2544.

Institute of the Blessed Virgin Mary (Loretto Sisters), I.B.V.M.: Founded 1609, in Belgium; in U.S., 1880. U.S. address, Loretto Convent, Box 508, Wheaton, IL 60189, (630) 665-3814. Educational work.

Jesus, Daughters of (*Filles de Jesus*), F.J.: Founded 1834, in France; in U.S., 1904. General motherhouse, Kermaria, Locmine, France; U.S. address, 4209 3rd Ave. S., Great Falls, MT 59405, (406) 452-7231. Educational, hospital, parish and social work.

Jesus, Little Sisters of, L.S.J.: Founded 1939, in Sahara; in U.S., 1952. General motherhouse, Rome, Italy; U.S. headquarters, 400 N. Streeper St., Baltimore, MD 21224, www.rc.net/org/littlesisters.

Jesus, Society of the Sisters, Faithful Companions of, F.C.J.: Founded 1820, in France; in U.S., 1896. General motherhouse, Kent, England; U.S. province, St. Philomena Convent, Cory's Lane, Portsmouth, RI 02871, (401) 683-2000, www.portsmouthabbey.org.

Jesus and Mary, Little Sisters of, L.S.J.M.: Founded 1974 in U.S. Address: Joseph House, P.O. Box 1755, Salisbury, MD 21802, (410) 543-1645.

Jesus and Mary, Religious of, R.J.M.: Founded 1818, at Lyons, France; in U.S., 1877. General motherhouse, Rome, Italy; U.S. province, 3706 Rhode Island Ave., Mt. Ranier, MD 20712, (301) 277-3594. Educational work.

Jesus Crucified, Congregation of: Founded 1930, in France; in U.S., 1955. General motherhouse, Brou, France; U.S. foundation: Benedictines of Jesus Crucified, Monastery of the Glorious Cross, 61 Burbin Dr., Branford, CT 06405-4003, (203) 315-9964.

Jesus Crucified and the Sorrowful Mother, Poor Sisters of, C.J.C.: Founded 1924, in U.S., by Rev. Alphonsus Maria, C.P. Motherhouse, 261 Thatcher St., Brockton, MA 02402. Education, nursing homes, catechetical centers.

Jesus, Mary and Joseph, Missionaries of, M.J.M.J.: Founded 1942, in Spain; in U.S., 1956. General motherhouse, Madrid, Spain; U.S. regional house, 12940 Leopard St., Corpus Christi, TX 78410, (361) 241-1955.

John the Baptist, Sisters of St., C.S.J.B.: Founded 1878, in Italy; in U.S., 1906. General motherhouse, Rome, Italy; U.S. provincialate, 3308 Campbell Dr., Bronx, NY 10465, (718) 518-7820, www.home.att.net/~baptistines. Education, parish and retreat work; social services.

Joseph, Poor Sisters of St., P.S.S.J.: Founded 1880, in Argentina. General motherhouse, Muniz, Buenos Aires, Argentina; U.S. addresses, Casa Belen, 305 E. 4th St., Bethlehem, PA 78015, (610) 867-4030; Casa Nazareth, 5321 Spruce St., Reading, PA 19602, (610) 378-1947; St. Gabriel Convent, 4319 Sano St., Alexandria, VA 22312, (703) 354-0395 .

Joseph, Religious Daughters of St., F.S.J.: Founded 1875, in Spain. General motherhouse, Spain; U.S. foundation, 319 N. Humphreys Ave., Los Angeles, CA 90022.

Joseph, Servants of St., S.S.J.: Founded 1874, in Spain; in U.S., 1957. General motherhouse, Salamanca, Spain; U.S. address, 203 N. Spring St., Falls Church, VA 22046, (703) 533-8441.

Joseph, Sisters of St., C.S.J. or S.S.J.: Founded 1650, in France; in U.S., 1836, at St. Louis. Independent motherhouses in U.S.: 637 Cambridge St., Brighton, MA 02135, (617) 783-9090; 1515 W. Ogden Ave., La Grange Park, IL, 60526, (708) 354-9200, www.ministryofhearts.org; 480 S. Batavia St., Orange, CA 92668, (714) 633-8121. St. Joseph Convent, 1725 Brentwood Rd., Brentwood, NY 11717-5587, (516) 273-4531; 23 Agassiz Circle, Buffalo, NY 14214, (716) 838-4400; 7 Clement Rd., Rutland, VT 05701, (802) 775-0665; 3430 Rocky River Dr., Cleveland, OH 44111, (216) 252-0440; 1440 W. Division Rd., Tipton, IN 46072, (765) 675-6203; Motherhouse and novitiate, Nazareth, MI 49074, (616) 381-6290; 1425 Washington St., Watertown, NY 13601, (315) 782-3460; 1020 State St., Baden, PA 15005, (724) 869-2151, www.stjoseph-baden.org; 5031 W. Ridge Rd., Erie, PA 16506, (814) 838-4100; 4095 East Ave., Rochester, NY 14618, (585) 641-8119, www.ssjvolunteers; Mont Marie, 34 Lower Westfield Rd. Ste. 1, Holyoke, MA 01040, (413) 536-0853; Pogue Run Rd., Wheeling, WV 26003, (304) 232-8160; 3700 E. Lincoln St., Wichita, KS 67218, (316) 686-7171, www.feist.com/~wichitacsj/

Joseph, Sisters of St. (Lyons, France), C.S.J.: Founded 1650, in France; in U.S., 1906. General motherhouse, Lyons, France; U.S. provincialate, 93 Halifax St., Winslow, ME 04901, (207) 873-4512; www.e-livingwater.org. Educational, hospital work.

Joseph, Sisters of St., of Peace, C.S.J.P.: Founded 1884, in England; in U.S. 1885. Generalate, 3043 Fourth St., N.E., Washington, DC 20017, (202) 832-5333. Educational, hospital, social service work.

Joseph of Carondelet, Sisters of St., C.S.J.: Founded 1650, in France; in U.S., 1836, at St. Louis, MO. U.S. headquarters, 2307 S. Lindbergh Blvd., St. Louis, MO 63131.

Joseph of Chambery, Sisters of St.: Founded 1650, in France; in U.S., 1885. Generalate, Rome, Italy; U.S. provincial house, 27 Park Rd., West Hartford, CT 06119, (860) 233-5126. Educational, hospital, social work.

Joseph of Chestnut Hill, Sisters of St., S.S.J.: Founded 1650; Philadelphia foundation, 1847. Motherhouse, Mt. St. Joseph Convent, 9701 Germantown Ave., Chestnut Hill, PA 19118, (215) 248-7200, www.ssjphila.org.

Joseph of Cluny, Sisters of St., S.J.C.: Founded 1807, in France. Generalate, Paris, France; U.S. provincial house, Brenton Rd., Newport, RI 02840, (401) 846-4757.

Joseph of Medaille, Sisters of, C.S.J.: Founded 1650, in France; in U.S., 1855. Became an American congregation Nov. 30, 1977. Central office, 1821 Summit Rd., Suite 210, Cincinnati, OH 45237, (513) 761-2888.

Joseph of St. Augustine, Florida, Sisters of St., S.S.J.: General motherhouse, 241 St. George St., P.O. Box 3506, St. Augustine, FL 32085, (904) 824-1752. Educational, hospital, pastoral, social work.

Joseph of St. Mark, Sisters of St., S.J.S.M.: Founded 1845, in France; in U.S., 1937. General motherhouse, 21800 Chardon Rd., Euclid, Cleveland, OH 44117; (216) 531-7426. Nursing homes.

Joseph the Worker, Sisters of St., S.J.W.: General motherhouse, St. William Convent, 1 St. Joseph Lane, Walton, KY 41094, (859) 485-4256.

Lamb of God, Sisters of the, A.D.: Founded 1945, in France; in U.S., 1958. General motherhouse, France; U.S. address, 2063 Wyandotte Ave., Owensboro KY 42301, (502) 281-5450.

Life, Sisters of, S.V. (Sorer Vitae): Founded by Cardinal John J. O'Connor, 1991, to protect life. Address: St. Frances de Chantal Convent, 198 Hollywood Ave., Bronx, NY 10465, (718) 863-2264; Our Lady of New York, 1955 Needham Ave., Bronx, NY, 10466, (718) 881-8008; Sacred Heart Convent, 450 W. 51st St., NY, NY, (212) 397-1386.

Little Sisters of the Gospel, L.S.G.: Founded 1963 in France by Rev. Rene Voillaume; in U.S., 1972. U.S. address, Box 305, Mott Haven Sta., Bronx, NY 10454, (718) 292-2867.

Little Workers of the Sacred Hearts, P.O.S.C.: Founded 1892, in Italy; in U.S., 1948. General house, Rome, Italy; U.S. address, Our Lady of Grace Convent, 635 Glenbrook Rd., Stamford, CT 06906, (203) 348-5531.

Living Word, Sisters of the, S.L.W.: Founded 1975, in U.S. Motherhouse, Living Word Center, 800 N. Fernandez Ave. B, Arlington Heights, IL 60004-5316, (847) 577-5972, www.slw.org. Education, hospital, parish ministry work.

Loretto at the Foot of the Cross, Sisters of, S.L.: Founded 1812 in U.S., by Rev. Charles Nerinckx. General motherhouse, Nerinx, KY 40049, (270) 865-5811. Educational work.

Louis, Juilly-Monaghan, Congregation of Sisters of St., S.S.L.: Founded 1842, in France; in U.S., 1949. General motherhouse, Monaghan, Ireland; U.S. regional house, 22300 Mulholland Dr., Woodland Hills, CA 91364, (818) 883-1678. Educational, medical, parish, foreign mission work.

Lovers of the Holy Cross Sisters (Phat Diem), L.H.C.: Founded 1670, in Vietnam; in U.S. 1976. U.S. address, Holy Cross Convent, 14700 South Van Ness Ave., Gardena, CA 90249, (310) 516-0271.

Mantellate Sisters, Servants of Mary, of Blue Island, O.S.M.: Founded 1861, in Italy; in U.S., 1916. Generalate, Rome, Italy; U.S. motherhouse, 13811 S. Western Ave., Blue Island, IL 60406, (708) 385-2103. Educational work.

Mantellate Sisters Servants of Mary, of Plainfield, O.S.M.: Founded 1861 in Italy; in U.S., 1916. Address:16949 S. Drauden Rd., Plainfield, IL 60544, (815) 436-5796.

Marian Sisters of the Diocese of Lincoln: Founded 1954. Marycrest Motherhouse, R.R. 1, Box 108, Waverly, NE 68462, (402) 786-2750.

Marianites of Holy Cross, Congregation of the Sisters, M.S.C.: Founded 1841, in France; in U.S., 1843. Motherhouse, Le Mans, Sarthe, France. North American headquarters, 1011 Gallier St., New Orleans, LA 70117, (504) 945-1620, www.marianites.org.

Marist Sisters, Congregation of Mary, S.M.: Founded 1824, in France. General motherhouse, Rome, Italy; U.S. foundation: 810 Peach, Abilene, TX 79602, (915) 675-5806.

Mary, Company of, O.D.N.: Founded 1607, in France; in U.S., 1926. General motherhouse, Rome, Italy; U.S. motherhouse, 16791 E. Main St., Tustin, CA 92680-4034, (714) 541-3125.

Mary, Daughters of the Heart of, D.H.M.: Founded 1790, in France; in U.S., 1851. Generalate, Paris, France; U.S. provincialate, 1339 Northampton St., Holyoke, MA 01040, (413) 532-7406. Education, retreat work.

Mary, Missionary Sisters of the Society of (Marist Sisters), S.M.S.M.: Founded 1845, at St. Brieuc, France; in U.S., 1922. General motherhouse, Rome, Italy; U.S. provincial house, 349 Grove St., Waltham, MA 02154, (781) 893-0149. Foreign missions.

Mary, Servants of, O.S.M.: Founded 13th century, in Italy; in U.S., 1893. General motherhouse, England; U.S. provincial motherhouse, 7400 Military Ave., Omaha, NE 68134, (402) 571-2547.

Mary, Servants of (Servite Sisters), O.S.M.: Founded 13th century, in Italy; in U.S., 1912. General motherhouse, Servants of Mary Convent, 1000 College Ave., Ladysmith, WI 54848, (715) 532-3364.

Mary, Sisters of St., of Oregon, S.S.M.O.: Founded 1886, in Oregon, by Bishop William H. Gross, C.Ss.R. General motherhouse, 4440 S.W. 148th Ave., Beaverton, OR 97007, (503) 644-9181, www.ssmo.org. Educational, nursing work.

Mary, Sisters of the Little Company of, L.C.M.: Founded 1877, in England; in U.S., 1893. Generalate, London, England; U.S. provincial house, 9350 S. California Ave., Evergreen Park, IL 60805, (708) 229-5490.

Mary, Sisters Servants of (Trained Nurses), S.M.: Founded 1851, at Madrid, Spain; in U.S., 1914. General motherhouse, Rome, Italy; U.S. motherhouse, 800 N. 18th St., Kansas City, KS 66102. Home nursing.

Mary and Joseph, Daughters of, D.M.J.: Founded 1817, in Belgium; in U.S., 1926. Generalate, Rome, Italy; American provincialate, 5300 Crest Rd., Rancho Palos Verdes, CA 90274, (310) 541-8194.

Mary Help of Christians, Daughters of (Salesian Sisters of St. John Bosco), F.M.A.: Founded 1872, in Italy, by St. John Bosco and St. Mary Dominic Mazzarello; in U.S., 1908. General motherhouse, Rome, Italy; U.S. provinces, 655 Belmont Ave., Haledon, NJ 07508, (937) 790-7963; 6019 Buena Vista St., San Antonio, TX 78237, (210) 432-0090. Education, youth work.

Mary Immaculate, Daughters of (Marianist Sisters), F.M.I.: Founded 1816, in France, by Very Rev. William-Joseph Chaminade. General motherhouse, Rome, Italy; U.S. foundation, 251 W. Ligustrum Dr., San Antonio, TX 78228, (210) 433-5501. Educational work.

Mary Immaculate, Religious of, R.M.I.: Founded 1876, in Spain; in U.S., 1954. Generalate, Rome, Italy; U.S. foundation, 719 Augusta St., San Antonio, TX 78215, (210) 226-0025.

Mary Immaculate, Sisters Minor of, S.M.M.I.: Established in U.S., 1989. Address: 138 Brushy Hill Rd., Danbury, CT 06818, (203) 744-8041.

Mary Immaculate, Sisters of, S.M.I.: Founded 1948, in India, by Bishop Louis LaRavoire Morrow; in U.S., 1981. General motherhouse, Bengal, India; U.S. address, R.D. 5, Box 1231, Leechburg, PA 15656, (724) 845-2828.

Mary Immaculate, Sisters Servants of, S.S.M.I.: Founded 1878 in Poland. General motherhouse, Mariowka-Opoczynska, Poland; American provincialate, 1220 Tugwell Dr., Catonsville, MD 21228, (410) 747-1353.

Mary Immaculate, Sisters Servants of, S.S.M.I: Founded 1892, in Ukraine; in U.S., 1935. General motherhouse, Rome, Italy; U.S. address, 9 Emmanuel Dr., P.O. Box 9, Sloatsburg, NY 10974, (845) 753-2840. Educational, hospital work.

Mary of Namur, Sisters of St., S.S.M.N.: Founded 1819, at Namur, Belgium; in U.S., 1863. General motherhouse, Namur, Belgium. U.S. provinces: 250 Bryant, Buffalo, NY 14222, (716) 884-8221, www.ssmn.org; 909 West Shaw St., Ft. Worth, TX 76110, (817) 923-8393.

Mary of Providence, Daughters of St., D.S.M.P.: Founded 1872, at Como, Italy; in U.S., 1913. General motherhouse, Rome, Italy; U.S. provincial house, 4200 N. Austin Ave., Chicago, IL 60634, (773) 545-8300. Special education for mentally handicapped.

Mary of the Immaculate Conception, Daughters of, D.M.: Founded 1904, in U.S., by Msgr. Lucian Bojnowski. General motherhouse, 314 Osgood Ave., New Britain, CT 06053, (860) 225-9406. Educational, hospital work.

Mary Queen, Congregation of, C.M.R.: Founded in Vietnam; established in U.S., 1979. U.S. region, 625 S. Jefferson, Springfield, MO 65806.

Mary Reparatrix, Society of, S.M.R.: Founded 1857, in France; in U.S., 1908. Generalate, Rome, Italy. U.S. province, 225 E. 234th St., Bronx NY 10470.

Maryknoll Sisters, M.M.: Founded in 1912 in U.S. by Mother Mary Joseph. General motherhouse: P.O. Box 311, Maryknoll, NY 10545-0311, (914) 941-7575; www.maryknoll.org.

Medical Mission Sisters (Society of Catholic Medical Missionaries, Inc.), M.M.S.: Founded 1925, in U.S., by Mother Anna Dengel. Generalate, London, England; U.S. headquarters, 8400 Pine Rd., Philadelphia, PA 19111, (215) 742-6100, www.medicalmissionsisters.org. Medical work, health education, especially in mission areas.

Medical Missionaries of Mary, M.M.M.: Founded 1937, in Ireland, by Mother Mary Martin; in U.S., 1950. General motherhouse, Dublin, Ireland; U.S. headquarters, 563 Minneford Ave., City Island, Bronx, NY 10464, (718) 885-0945. Medical aid in missions.

Medical Sisters of St. Joseph, M.S.J.: Founded 1946, in India; first U.S. foundation, 1985. General motherhouse, Kerala, S. India; U.S. address, 3435 E. Funston, Wichita, KS 67218, (316) 686-4746. Health care apostolate.

Mercedarian Sisters of the Blessed Sacrament, H.M.S.S.: Founded 1910, in Mexico; first U.S. foundation, 1926. Regional House, 222 W. Cevallos St., San Antonio, TX 78204, (210) 223-5013.

Mercy, Daughters of Our Lady of, D.M.: Founded 1837, in Italy, by St. Mary Joseph Rossello; in U.S., 1919. General motherhouse, Savona, Italy; U.S. motherhouse, Villa Rossello, 1009 Main Rd., Newfield, NJ 08344, (856) 697-2983. Educational, hospital work.

Mercy, Missionary Sisters of Our Lady of, M.O.M.: Founded 1938, in Brazil; in U.S., 1955. General motherhouse, Brazil; U.S. address, 388 Franklin St., Buffalo, NY 14202, (716) 854-5198.

Mercy, Religious Sisters of, R.S.M.: Founded 1973 in U.S. Motherhouse, 1835 Michigan Ave., Alma, MI 48801, (517) 463-6035.

Mercy, Sisters of, of the Americas: Formed in July, 1991, through union of 9 provinces and 16 regional communities of Sisters of Mercy which previously were independent motherhouses or houses which formed the Sisters of Mercy of the Union. Mother Mary Catherine McAuley founded the Sisters of Mercy in Dublin, Ireland, in 1831; first established in the U.S., 1843, in Pittsburgh. Address of administrative office: 8300 Colesville Rd., No. 300, Silver Spring, MD 20910, (301) 587-0423. Pres., Sr. Marie Chin, R.S.M. Total in congregation 5,840.

Mill Hill Sisters: *See* **Franciscan Missionaries of St. Joseph.**

Minim Daughters of Mary Immaculate, C.F.M.M.: Founded 1886, in Mexico; in U.S., 1926. General motherhouse, Leon, Guanajuato, Mexico; U.S. address, 555 Patagonia Hwy., Nogales, AZ 85628, (520) 287-3377.

Misericordia Sisters, S.M.: Founded 1848, in Canada; in U.S., 1887. General motherhouse, 12435 Ave. Misericorde, Montreal H4J 2G3, Canada; U.S. address, 225 Carol Ave., Pelham, 10803. Social work with unwed mothers and their children; hospital work.

Mission Helpers of the Sacred Heart, M.H.S.H.: Founded 1890, in U.S. General motherhouse, 1001 W. Joppa Rd., Baltimore, MD 21204, (410) 823-8585. Religious education, evangelization.

Missionary Catechists of the Sacred Hearts of Jesus and Mary (Violetas), M.C.S.H.: Founded 1918, in Mexico; in U.S., 1943. Motherhouse, Tlalpan, Mexico; U.S. address, 805 Liberty St., Victoria, TX 77901, (512) 578-9302.

Missionary Daughters of the Most Pure Virgin Mary, M.D.P.V.M.: Founded in Mexico; in U.S., 1916. Address: 919 N. 9th St., Kingsville, TX 78363, (512) 595-1087.

Mother of God, Missionary Sisters of the, M.S.M.G.: Byzantine, Ukrainian Rite, Stamford. Motherhouse, 711 N. Franklin St., Philadelphia, PA 19123, (215) 627-7808.

Mother of God, Sisters Poor Servants of the, S.M.G.: Founded 1869, in London, England; in U.S., 1947. General motherhouse, Maryfield, Roehampton, London. U.S. address: Maryfield Nursing Home, Greensboro Rd., High Point, NC 27260, (336) 886-2444, www.greensboro.com/mnh. Hospital, educational work.

Nazareth, Poor Sisters of, P.S.N.: Founded in England; U.S. foundation, 1924. General motherhouse, Hammersmith, London, England; U.S. novitiate, 3333 Manning Ave., Los Angeles, CA 90064, (310) 839-2361. Social services, education.

Notre Dame, School Sisters of, S.S.N.D.: Founded 1833, in Germany; in U.S., 1847. General motherhouse, Rome, Italy. U.S. provinces: 13105 Watertown Plank Rd., Elm Grove, WI 53122-2291, (262) 782-9850; 6401 N. Charles St., Baltimore, MD 21212, (410) 377-7774; 320 E. Ripa Ave., St. Louis, MO 63125, (314) 544-0455; 170 Good Counsel Dr., Mankato, MN 56001-3138, (507) 389-4210, www.ssndmankato.org; 345 Belden Hill Rd., Wilton, CT 06897, (203) 762-1220; P.O. Box 227275, Dallas, TX 75222, (214) 330-9152, www.ssnd.org; 1431 Euclid Ave., Berwyn, IL 60402, (708) 749-1380.

Notre Dame, Sisters of, S.N.D.: Founded 1850, at Coesfeld, Germany; in U.S., 1874. General motherhouse, Rome, Italy. U.S. provinces: 13000 Auburn Rd., Chardon, OH 44024, (440) 286-7101;

1601 Dixie Highway, Covington, KY 41011, (606) 291-2040; 3837 Secor Rd., Toledo, OH 43623, (419) 474-5485; 1776 Hendrix Ave., Thousand Oaks, CA 91360, (805) 496-3243.

Notre Dame, Sisters of the Congregation of, C.N.D.: Founded 1658, in Canada, by St. Marguerite Bourgeoys; in U.S., 1860. General motherhouse, Montréal, Qué., Canada; U.S. province, 223 West Mountain Rd., Ridgefield, CT 06877, (203) 438-3115, www.cnd-m.com. Education.

Notre Dame de Namur, Sisters of, S.N.D.deN.: Founded 1804, in France; in U.S., 1840. General motherhouse, Rome, Italy. U.S. provinces: 351 Broadway, Everett, MA 02149, (617) 387-1303 (fax), www.SNDdeN.org; 30 Jeffrey's Neck Rd., Ipswich, MA 01938, (978) 356-4381; 468 Poquonock Ave., Windsor, CT 06095-2473, (860) 688-1832, www.sndden.org; 1531 Greenspring Valley Rd., Stevenson, MD 21153, (410) 486-5599; 305 Cable St., Baltimore, MD 21210, (410) 243-1993, www.sndden.org; 701 E. Columbia Ave., Cincinnati, OH 45215, (513) 761-7636; 14800 Bohlman Rd., Saratoga, CA 95070, (408) 741-0324; SND Base Communities, 3037 Fourth St. N.E., Washington, DC 20017, (202) 832-8770. Educational work.

Notre Dame de Sion, Congregation of, N.D.S.: Founded 1850, in France; in U.S., 1892. Generalate, Rome, Italy; U.S. province, 3823 Locust St., Kansas City, MO 64109, (816) 531-1374. Creation of better understanding and relations between Christians and Jews.

Notre Dame Sisters: Founded 1853, in Czechoslovakia; in U.S., 1910. General motherhouse, Javornik, Czech Republic; U.S. motherhouse, 3501 State St., Omaha, NE 68112, (402) 455-2994, www.notre damesisters.org. Educational work.

Oblates of the Mother of Orphans, O.M.O. Founded 1945, in Italy. General motherhouse, Milan, Italy; U.S. address, 20 E. 72nd St., New York, NY 10021.

Our Lady of Charity, North American Union of Sisters of, Eudist Sisters (Sisters of Our Lady of Charity of the Refuge), N.A.U.-O.L.C.: Founded 1641, in Caen, France, by St. John Eudes; in U.S., 1855. Autonomous houses were federated in 1944 and in March 1979 the North American Union of the Sisters of Our Lady of Charity was established. General motherhouse and administrative center, 154 Edgington Ln., Wheeling, WV 26003, (304) 242-0042. Primarily devoted to re-education and rehabilitation of women and girls in residential and non-residential settings.

Independent houses: 1125 Malvern Ave., Hot Springs, AR 71901, (501) 623-9651, www.lightof mary.org; 4500 W. Davis St., Dallas, TX 75211, (214) 331-1754.

Our Lady of Sorrows, Sisters of, O.L.S.: Founded 1839, in Italy; in U.S., 1947. General motherhouse, Rome, Italy; U.S. headquarters, 9894 Norris Ferry Rd., Shreveport, LA 71106.

Our Lady of the Holy Rosary, Daughters of, F.M.S.R. (*Filiae Mariae Sacri Rosarii*): Founded 1946, in North Vietnam; foundation in U.S., 1968. General Motherhouse, Saigon, Vietnam; U.S. Province, 1492 Moss St., New Orleans, LA 70119, (504) 486-0039.

Our Lady of Victory Missionary Sisters,

O.L.V.M.: Founded 1922, in U.S. Motherhouse, Victory Noll, 1900 W. Park Dr., P.O. Box 109, Huntington, IN 46750, (260) 356-0628, www.olv.org. Educational, social work.

Pallottine Missionary Sisters (Missionary Sisters of the Catholic Apostolate), S.A.C.: Founded in Rome, 1838; in U.S., 1912. Generalate, Rome, Italy; U.S. provincialate, 15270 Old Halls Ferry Rd., Florissant, MO 63034, (314) 837-7100, www.geveities.com/pallottinerenewal.org.

Pallottine Sisters of the Catholic Apostolate, C.S.A.C.: Founded 1843, at Rome, Italy; in U.S., 1889. General motherhouse, Rome; U.S. motherhouse, St. Patrick's Villa, Harriman Heights, Harriman, NY 10926, (914) 783-9007. Educational work.

Parish Visitors of Mary Immaculate, P.V.M.I.: Founded 1920, in New York. General motherhouse, Box 658, Monroe, NY 10950, (845) 783-2251. Mission work.

Passion of Jesus Christ, Religious of (Passionist Nuns), C.P.: Founded 1771, in Italy, by St. Paul of the Cross; in U.S., 1910. U.S. convents: 2715 Churchview Ave., Pittsburgh, PA 15227, (412) 881-1155; 631 Griffin Pond Rd., Clarks Summit, PA 18411, (570) 586-2791; 8564 Crisp Rd., Whitesville, KY 42378, (270) 233-4571, www.passionistnuns.org; 1151 Donaldson Hwy., Erlanger, KY 41018, (606) 371-8568; 15700 Clayton Rd., Ellisville, MO 63011, (314) 227-5275.Contemplatives.

Passionist Sisters: *See* **Cross and Passion, Sisters of the**.

Paul, Daughters of St. (Missionary Sisters of the Media of Communication), D.S.P.: Founded 1915, at Alba, Piedmont, Italy; in U.S., 1932. General motherhouse, Rome, Italy; U.S. provincial house, 50 St. Paul's Ave., Boston, MA 02130, (617) 522-8911, www.pauline.org. Apostolate of the communications arts.

Paul of Chartres, Sisters of St., S.P.C.: Founded 1696, in France. General house, Rome, Italy; U.S. address, 1300 County Rd. 492, Marquette, MI 49855, (906) 226-3932, members.aol.com/spcmqt/index.htm.

Perpetual Adoration of Guadalupe, Sisters of, A.P.G.: U.S. foundation, 2403 W. Travis, San Antonio, TX 78207, (210) 227-7785.

Peter Claver, Missionary Sisters of St., S.S.P.C.: Founded 1894 in Austria by Bl. Maria Teresa Ledochowska; in U.S., 1914. General motherhouse, Rome, Italy; U.S. address, 667 Woods Mill Rd. S., Chesterfield, MO 63006, (314) 434-8084.

Pious Disciples of the Divine Master, P.D.D.M.: Founded 1924 in Italy; in U.S., 1948. General motherhouse, Rome, Italy; U.S. headquarters, 60 Sunset Ave., Staten Island, NY 10314, (718) 494-8597.

Pious Schools, Sisters of, Sch. P.: Founded 1829 in Spain; in U.S., 1954. General motherhouse, Rome, Italy; U.S. headquarters, 17601 Nordhoff St., Northridge, CA 91325, (818) 882-5265.

Poor, Little Sisters of the, L.S.P.: Founded 1839, in France, by Bl. Jeanne Jugan; in U.S., 1868. General motherhouse, St. Pern, France. U.S. provinces: 110-30 221st St., Queens Village, NY 11429, (718) 464-1800; 601 Maiden Choice Lane, Baltimore, MD 21228, (410) 744-9367; 80 W. Northwest Hwy., Palatine, IL 60067, (847) 358-5700. Care of aged.

Poor Clare Missionary Sisters (Misioneras Clarisas), M.C.: Founded in Mexico. General motherhouse, Rome, Italy; U.S. novitiate, 1019 N. Newhope, Santa Ana, CA 92703, (714) 554-8850.

Poor Clare Nuns: *See* **Franciscan Poor Clare Nuns.**

Poor Handmaids of Jesus Christ (Ancilla Domini Sisters), P.H.J.C.: Founded 1851, in Germany by Bl. Mary Kasper; in U.S., 1868. General motherhouse, Dernbach, Westerwald, Germany; U.S. motherhouse, Ancilla Domini Convent, Donaldson, IN 46513, (219) 936-9936. Educational, hospital work, social services.

Precious Blood, Daughters of Charity of the Most, D.C.P.B.: Founded 1872, at Pagani, Italy; in U.S., 1908. General motherhouse, Rome, Italy; U.S. convent, 1482 North Ave., Bridgeport, CT 06604, (203) 334-7000.

Precious Blood, Missionary Sisters of the, C.P.S.: Founded 1885, at Mariannhill, South Africa; in U.S., 1925. Generalate, Rome, Italy; U.S. novitiate, P.O. Box 97, Reading, PA 19607, (610) 777-1624. Home and foreign mission work.

Precious Blood, Sisters Adorers of the, A.P.B.: Founded 1861, in Canada; in U.S., 1890. General motherhouse, Canada. U.S. autonomous monasteries: 54th St. and Fort Hamilton Pkwy., Brooklyn, NY 11219, (718) 438-6371; 700 Bridge St., Manchester, NH 03104, (603) 623-4264; 166 State St., Portland, ME 04101; 1106 State St., Lafayette, IN 47905, (765) 742-8227; 400 Pratt St., Watertown, NY 13601, (315) 788-1669. Cloistered, contemplative.

Precious Blood, Sisters of the, C.PP.S.: Founded 1834, in Switzerland; in U.S., 1844. Generalate, 4000 Denlinger Rd., Dayton, OH 45426, (937) 837-3302. Education, health care, other ministries.

Precious Blood, Sisters of the Most, C.PP.S.: Founded 1845, in Steinerberg, Switzerland; in U.S., 1870. General motherhouse, 204 N. Main St., O'Fallon, MO 63366, (636) 240-3420. Education, other ministries.

Presentation, Sisters of Mary of the, S.M.P.: Founded 1829, in France; in U.S., 1903. General motherhouse, Broons, Côtes-du-Nord, France. U.S. address, Maryvale Novitiate, 11550 River Rd., Valley City, ND 58072, (701) 845-2864. Educational, hospital work.

Presentation of Mary, Sisters of the, P.M.: Founded 1796, in France by Bl. Marie Rivier; in U.S., 1873. General motherhouse, Castel Gandolfo, Italy. U.S. provincial houses: 495 Mammoth Rd., Manchester, NH 03104, (603) 669-1080, www.presentation ofmary.com; 209 Lawrence St., Methuen, MA 01844, (978) 687-1369; www.presmarymethuen.org.

Presentation of the B.V.M., Sisters of the, P.B.V.M.: Founded 1775, in Ireland; in U.S., 1854, in San Francisco. U.S. motherhouses: 2360 Carter Rd., Dubuque, IA 52001, (563) 588-2008, www.dubuque presentations.org; 880 Jackson Ave., New Windsor, NY 12553, (914) 564-0513; 2340 Turk Blvd., San Francisco, CA 94118, (415) 751-0406, www.presentationsisterssf.org; St. Colman's Convent, Watervliet, NY 12189, (518) 273-4911; 1101 32nd Ave., S., Fargo ND 58103, (701) 237-4857; Presentation Convent, Aberdeen, SD 57401, (605) 229-8419, www.sistersonline.org; Leominster, MA 01453; 419 Woodrow Rd., Staten Island, NY 10312, (718) 356-2121.

Presentation of the Blessed Virgin Mary, Sisters of, of Union: Founded in Ireland, 1775; union established in Ireland, 1976; first U.S. vice province, 1979. Generalate, Kildare, Ireland; U.S. provincialate, 729 W. Wilshire Dr., Phoenix, AZ 85007, (602) 271-9687.

Providence, Daughters of Divine, F.D.P.: Founded 1832, Italy; in U.S., 1964. General motherhouse, Rome, Italy; U.S. address, 3100 Mumphrey Rd., Chalmette, LA 70043, (504) 279-4617.

Providence, Missionary Catechists of Divine, M.C.D.P.: Administrative house, 2318 Castroville Rd., San Antonio, TX 78237, (210) 432-0113.

Providence, Oblate Sisters of, O.S.P.: Founded 1829, in U.S., by Mother Mary Elizabeth Lange and Father James Joubert, S.S. First order of black nuns in U.S. General motherhouse, 701 Gun Rd., Baltimore, MD 21227, (410) 242-8500. Educational work.

Providence, Sisters of, S.P.: Founded 1861, in Canada; in U.S., 1873. General motherhouse, Our Lady of Victory Convent, 5 Gamelin St., Holyoke, MA 01040, (413) 536-7511, wwwsisofprov.org.

Providence, Sisters of, S.P.: Founded 1843, in Canada; in U.S., 1854. General motherhouse, Montreal, Canada; U.S. province, Mother Joseph Province, 506 Second Ave., #1200, Seattle, WA 98104, (206) 464-3394, www.sistersofprovidence.net.

Providence, Sisters of (of St. Mary-of-the-Woods), S.P.: Founded 1806, in France; in U.S., 1 Sisters of Providence, St. Mary-of-the-Woods, IN 47876, (812) 535-3131, www.sistersofprovidence.org.

Providence, Sisters of Divine, C.D.P.: Founded 1762, in France; in U.S., 1866. Generalate, Box 197, Helotes, TX 78023, (210) 695-8721. Educational, hospital work.

Providence, Sisters of Divine, C.D.P.: Founded 1851, in Germany; in U.S., 1876. Generalate, Rome, Italy. U.S. provinces: 9000 Babcock Blvd., Allison Park, PA 15101, (412) 931-5241; 3415 Bridgeland Dr., Bridgetown, MO 63044, (314) 524-3803; 363 Bishops Hwy., Kingston, MA 02364, (781) 585-7707. Educational, hospital work.

Providence, Sisters of Divine (of Kentucky), C.D.P.: Founded 1762, in France; in U.S., 1889. General motherhouse, Fenetrange, France; U.S. province, 1000 St. Anne Dr., Melbourne, KY 41059, (859) 441-0700, www.cdpkentucky.org. Education, social services, other ministries.

Redeemer, Oblates of the Most Holy, O.SS.R.: Founded 1864, in Spain. General motherhouse, Spain; U.S. foundation, 60-80 Pond St., Jamaica Plain, MA 02130, (617) 524-1640.

Redeemer, Order of the Most Holy, O.SS.R.: Founded 1731, by St. Alphonsus Liguori; in U.S., 1957. U.S. addresses: Mother of Perpetual Help Monastery, P.O. Box 220, Esopus, NY 12429, (914) 384-6533; Monastery of St. Alphonsus, 200 Ligouri Dr. Liguori, MO 63057, (636) 464-1093.

Redeemer, Sisters of the Divine, S.D.R.: Founded 1849, in Niederbronn, France; in U.S., 1912. General motherhouse, Rome, Italy; U.S. province, 999 Rock Run Road, Elizabeth, PA 15037, (412) 751-8600. Educational, hospital work; care of the aged.

Redeemer, Sisters of the Holy, C.S.R.: Founded 1849, in Alsace; in U.S., 1924. General motherhouse, Wurzburg, Germany; U.S. provincial house, 521 Moredon Rd., Huntingdon Valley, PA 19006, (215) 914-4100. Personalized medical care in hospitals, homes for aged, private homes; retreat work.

Reparation of the Congregation of Mary, Sisters of, S.R.C.M.: Founded 1903, in U.S. Motherhouse, St. Zita's Villa, Monsey, NY 10952, (914) 356-2011.

Reparation of the Sacred Wounds of Jesus, Sisters of, S.R.: Founded 1959 in U.S. General motherhouse, 2120 S.E. 24th Ave., Portland, OR 97214, (503) 236-4207.

Resurrection, Sisters of the, C.R.: Founded 1891, in Italy; in U.S., 1900. General motherhouse, Rome, Italy. U.S. provinces: 7432 Talcott Ave., Chicago, IL 60631, (773) 792-6363; Mt. St. Joseph, 35 Boltwood Ave., Castleton-on-Hudson, NY 12033, (518) 732-2226, www.resurrectionsisters.org. Education, nursing.

Rita, Sisters of St., O.S.A.: General motherhouse, Wurzburg, Germany. U.S. foundation, St. Monica's Convent, 3920 Green Bay Rd., Racine, WI 53404, (262) 639-5050, www.geocities.com/sistersofstrita.

Rosary, Congregation of Our Lady of the Holy, R.S.R.: Founded 1874, in Canada; in U.S., 1899. General motherhouse, Rimouski, Que., Canada; U.S. regional house, 20 Thomas St., Portland, ME 04102, (207) 774-3756; www.soeursdusaintrasaire.org/. Educational work.

Rosary, Missionary Sisters of the Holy, M.S.H.R.: Founded 1924, in Ireland; in U.S., 1954. Motherhouse, Dublin, Ireland; in U.S., 741 Polo Rd., Bryn Mawr, PA 19010, (610) 520-1974, www.icdc.com/~mshr. African missions.

Sacrament, Missionary Sisters of the Most Blessed, M.SS.S.: General motherhouse, Madrid, Spain; U.S. foundation, 1111 Wordin Ave., Bridgeport, CT 06605.

Sacrament, Nuns of the Perpetual Adoration of the Blessed, A.P.: Founded 1807 in Rome, Italy; in U.S., 1925. U.S. monasteries: 145 N. Cotton Ave., El Paso, TX 79901, (915) 533-5323; 771 Ashbury St., San Francisco, CA 94117, (415) 566-2743.

Sacrament, Oblate Sisters of the Blessed, O.S.B.S.: Founded 1935, in U.S. Motherhouse, St. Sylvester Convent, P.O. Box 217, Marty, SD 57361, (605) 384-3305. Care of American Indians.

Sacrament, Servants of the Blessed, S.S.S.: Founded 1858, in France, by St. Pierre Julien Eymard; in U.S., 1947. General motherhouse, Rome, Italy; American provincial house, St. Charles Borromeo Parish, 1818 Coal Pl. SE, Albuquerque, NM 87106, (505) 242-3692. Contemplative.

Sacrament, Sisters of the Blessed, for Indians and Colored People, S.B.S.: Founded 1891, in U.S., by St. Katharine Drexel. General motherhouse, 1663 Bristol Pike, P.O. Box 8502, Bensalem, PA 19020, (215) 244-9900, www.katharinedrexel.org.

Sacrament, Sisters of the Most Holy, M.H.S.: Founded 1851, in France; in U.S., 1872. Generalate, 313 Corona Dr. (P.O. Box 90037), Lafayette, LA 70509, (337) 981-8475.

Sacrament, Sisters Servants of the Blessed, S.J.S.: Founded 1904, in Mexico; in U.S., 1926. General motherhouse, Mexico; U.S. address, 215 Lomita St., El Segundo, CA 90245, (310) 615-0766.

Sacramentine Nuns (Religious of the Order of the Blessed Sacrament and Our Lady), O.S.S.: Founded 1639, in France; in U.S., 1912. U.S. monasteries: 235 Bellvale Lakes Rd., Warwick NY 10990; 2798 US 31 N, P.O. Box 86, Conway, MI 49722, (231)

347-0447. Perpetual adoration of the Holy Eucharist.

Sacred Heart, Daughters of Our Lady of the, F.D.N.S.C.: Founded 1882, in France; in U.S., 1955. General motherhouse, Rome, Italy; U.S. address, 424 E. Browning Rd., Bellmawr, NJ 08031, (609) 931-8973. Educational work.

Sacred Heart, Missionary Sisters of the (Cabrini Sisters), M.S.C.: Founded 1880, in Italy, by St. Frances Xavier Cabrini; in U.S., 1889. General motherhouse, Rome, Italy; U.S. provincial office, 222 E. 19th St., 5B, New York, NY 10003. Educational, health, social and catechetical work.

Sacred Heart, Society Devoted to the, S.D.S.H.: Founded 1940, in Hungary; in U.S., 1956. U.S. motherhouse, 9814 Sylvia Ave., Northridge, CA 91324, (818) 831-9710. Educational work.

Sacred Heart, Society of the, R.S.C.J.: Founded 1800, in France; in U.S., 1818. Generalate, Rome, Italy. U.S. provincial house, 4389 W. Pine Blvd., St. Louis, MO 63108, (314) 652-1500, www.rscj.org. Educational work.

Sacred Heart of Jesus, Apostles of, A.S.C.J.: Founded 1894, in Italy; in U.S., 1902. General motherhouse, Rome, Italy; U.S. motherhouse, 265 Benham St., Hamden, CT 06514, (203) 248-4225, www.ascjus.org. Educational, social work.

Sacred Heart of Jesus, Handmaids of the, A.C.J.: Founded 1877, in Spain. General motherhouse, Rome, Italy; U.S. province, 1242 S. Broad St., Philadelphia, PA 19146, (214) 468-6368. Educational, retreat work.

Sacred Heart of Jesus, Missionary Sisters of the Most (Hiltrup), M.S.C.: Founded 1899, in Germany; in U.S., 1908. General motherhouse, Rome, Italy; U.S. province, 51 Seminary Ave., Reading, PA 19605, (610) 929-5751. Education, health care, pastoral ministry.

Sacred Heart of Jesus, Oblate Sisters of the, O.S.H.J.: Founded 1894; in U.S., 1949. General motherhouse, Rome, Italy; U.S. headquarters, 50 Warner Rd., Hubbard, OH 44425, (330) 759-9329, www.oblatesistersofshj.com. Educational, social work.

Sacred Heart of Jesus, Servants of the Most, S.S.C.J.: Founded 1894, in Poland; in U.S., 1959. General motherhouse, Cracow, Poland; U.S. address, 866 Cambria St., Cresson, PA 16630, (814) 886-4223, www.nb.net/~sscjusa. Education, health care, social services.

Sacred Heart of Jesus, Sisters of the, S.S.C.J.: Founded 1816, in France; in U.S., 1903. General motherhouse, St. Jacut, Brittany, France; U.S. provincial house, 11931 Radium St., San Antonio, TX 78216, (210) 344-7203. Educational, hospital, domestic work.

Sacred Heart of Jesus and of the Poor, Servants of the (Mexican), S.S.H.J.P.: Founded 1885, in Mexico; in U.S., 1907. General motherhouse, Apartado 92, Puebla, Pue., Mexico; U.S. address, 3310 S. Zapata Hwy, Laredo, TX 78043, (956) 723-3343.

Sacred Heart of Jesus and Our Lady of Guadalupe, Missionaries of the, M.S.C.Gpe.: U.S. address, 1212 E. Euclid Ave., Arlington Heights, IL 60004, (708) 398-1350.

Sacred Heart of Jesus for Reparation, Congregation of the Handmaids of the, A.R.: Founded 1918, in Italy; in U.S., 1958. U.S. address, 36 Villa Dr., Steubenville, OH 43953, (740) 282-3801.

Sacred Heart of Mary, Religious of the, R.S.H.M.: Founded 1848, in France; in U.S., 1877. Generalate, Rome, Italy. U.S. provinces; 50 Wilson Park Dr., Tarrytown, NY 10591, (914) 631-8872, www.rshm.org; 441 N. Garfield Ave., Montebello, CA 90640, (323) 887-8821, www.rshm.org.

Sacred Hearts and of Perpetual Adoration, Sisters of the, SS.CC.: Founded 1797, in France; in U.S., 1908. General motherhouse, Rome, Italy; U.S. provinces: 1120 Fifth Ave., Honolulu, Hawaii 96816, (808) 737-5822 (Pacific); 35 Huttleston Ave., Fairhaven, MA 02719, (508) 994-9341 (East Coast). Varied ministries.

Sacred Hearts of Jesus and Mary, Sisters of the, S.H.J.M.: Established 1953, in U.S. General motherhouse, Essex, England; U.S. address, 2150 Lake Shore Ave., Oakland CA 94606, (510) 832-2935.

Savior, Company of the, C.S.: Founded 1952, in Spain; in U.S., 1962. General motherhouse, Madrid, Spain; U.S. foundation, 820 Clinton Ave., Bridgeport, CT 06604, (203) 368-1875.

Savior, Sisters of the Divine, S.D.S.: Founded 1888, in Italy; in U.S., 1895. General motherhouse, Rome, Italy; U.S. province, 4311 N. 100th St., Milwaukee, WI 53222, (414) 466-0810. Educational, hospital work.

Social Service, Sisters of, S.S.S.: Founded in Hungary, 1923, by Sr. Margaret Slachta. U.S. generalate, 296 Summit Ave., Buffalo, NY 14214, (716) 834-0197. Social work.

Social Service, Sisters of, of Los Angeles, S.S.S.: Founded 1908, in Hungary; in U.S., 1926. General motherhouse, 2303 S. Figueroa Way, Los Angeles, CA 90007, (213) 746-2117.

Teresa of Jesus, Society of St., S.T.J.: Founded 1876, in Spain; in U.S., 1910. General motherhouse, Rome, Italy; U.S. provincial house, 18080 St. Joseph's Way, Covington, LA 70435, (985) 893-1470, www.teresians.org.

Thomas of Villanova, Congregation of Sisters of St., S.S.T.V.: Founded 1661, in France; in U.S., 1948. General motherhouse, Neuilly-sur-Seine, France; U.S. foundation W. Rocks Rd., Norwalk, CT 06851, (203) 847-2885.

Trinity, Missionary Servants of the Most Blessed, M.S.B.T.: Founded 1912, in U.S., by Very Rev. Thomas A. Judge. General motherhouse, 3501 Solly Ave., Philadelphia, PA 19136, (215) 335-7550. Educational, social work, health services.

Trinity, Sisters Oblates to the Blessed, O.B.T.: Founded 1923, in Italy. U.S. novitiate, Beekman Rd., P.O. Box 98, Hopewell Junction, NY 12533, (914) 226-5671.

Trinity, Sisters of the Most Holy, O.Ss.T.: Founded 1198, in Rome; in U.S., 1920. General motherhouse, Rome, Italy; U.S. address, Immaculate Conception Province, 21281 Chardon Rd., Euclid, OH 44117, (216) 481-8232, www.srstrinity.org. Educational work.

Trinity, Society of Our Lady of the Most Holy, S.O.L.T.: Motherhouse, P.O. Box 189 Skidmore, TX 78389, (361) 287-3256.

Ursula of the Blessed Virgin, Society of the Sisters of St., S.U.: Founded 1606, in France; in U.S., 1902. General motherhouse, France; U.S. novitiate, 50 Linnwood Rd., Rhinebeck, NY 12572, (845) 876-2557, www.sistersofstursula.com. Educational work.

Ursuline Nuns (Roman Union), O.S.U.: Founded 1535, in Italy; in U.S., 1727. Generalate, Rome, Italy. U.S. provinces: 323 E. 198th St., Bronx, NY 10458, (718) 365-7410; 210 Glennon Heights Rd., Crystal City, MO 63019, (636) 937-6206, www.osucentral.org; 639 Angela Dr., Santa Rosa, CA 95401, (707) 545-6811; 45 Lowder St., Dedham, MA 02026, (781) 326-6219.

Ursuline Sisters of Mount Saint Joseph, O.S.U.: Founded 1535, in Italy; in U.S., 1727, in New Orleans. U.S. motherhouses: 20860 St, Rte. 251, St. Martin, OH 45118-9705, (513) 875-2020; 901 E. Miami St., Paola, KS 66071, (913) 557-2349; 3105 Lexington Rd., Louisville, KY 40206, (502) 896-3914, www.ursuineslou.org; 2600 Lander Rd., Cleveland, OH. 44124, (440) 449-1200, www.ursuline.edu/ursulines; 8001 Cummings Rd., Maple Mount, KY 42356, (270) 229-4103, www.ursulinesmsj.org; 4045 Indian Rd., Toledo, OH 43606, (419) 536-9587; 4250 Shields Rd., Canfield, OH 44406, (330) 792-7636; 1339 E. McMillan St., Cincinnati, OH 45206, (513) 961-3410.

Ursuline Sisters of the Congregation of Tildonk, Belgium, O.S.U.: Founded 1535, in Italy; Tildonk congregation, 1832; in U.S., 1924. Generalate, Brussels, Belgium; U.S. address, 81-15 Utopia Parkway, Jamaica, NY 11432, (718) 591-0681. Educational, foreign mission work.

Ursuline Sisters of Belleville, O.S.U.: Founded 1535, in Italy; in U.S., 1910; established as diocesan community, 1983. Central house, 1026 N. Douglas Ave., Belleville, IL 62220, (618) 235-3444. Educational work.

Venerini Sisters, Religious, M.P.V.: Founded 1685, in Italy; in U.S., 1909. General motherhouse, Rome, Italy; U.S. provincialate; 23 Edward St., Worcester, MA 01605.

Vietnamese Adorers of the Holy Cross, M.T.G.: Founded 1670 in Vietnam; in U.S. 1976. General motherhouse 7408 S.E. Adler, Portland, OR 97215, (503) 254-3284.

Vincent de Paul, Sisters: *See* Charity of St. Vincent de Paul, Sisters of.

Visitation Nuns, V.H.M.: Founded 1610, in France; in U.S. (Georgetown, DC), 1799. Contemplative, educational work. Two federations in U.S.

• First Federation of North America. Major pontifical enclosure. Pres., Mother Mary Jozefa Kowalewski, Monastery of the Visitation, 2055 Ridgedale Dr., Snellville, GA 30078, (770) 972-1060. Addresses of monasteries belonging to the federation: 2300 Springhill Ave., Mobile, AL 36607, (251) 473-2321; Beach Rd., Tyringham, MA 01264, (413) 243-3995; 12221 Bievenue Rd, Rockville, VA 23146, (804) 749-4885; 5820 City Ave., Philadelphia, PA 19131, (215) 473-5888; 1745 Parkside Blvd., Toledo, OH 43607, (419) 536-1343; 2055 Ridgedale Dr., Snellville, GA 30078-2443, (770) 972-1060.

• Second Federation of North America. Constitutional enclosure. Pres., Sr. Anne Madeleine Godefroy, Monastery of the Visitation, 3020 N. Ballas Rd., St. Louis, MO 63131, (314) 432-5353, www.visitation monastery.org/stlouis. Addresses of monasteries belonging to the federation: 1500 35th St., Washington, DC 20007, (202) 337-0305; 3020 N. Ballas Rd., St. Louis, MO 63131, (314) 432-5353; 200 E. Second St., Frederick, MD 21701, (301) 622-3322; Mt. de

Chantal Monastery of the Visitation, 410 Washington Ave., Wheeling, WV 26003, (304) 232-1283; 8902 Ridge Blvd., Brooklyn, NY 11209, (718) 745-5151, www.visitationsisters.org; 2455 Visitation Dr., Mendota Heights, St. Paul, MN 55120, (651) 683-1700.

Visitation of the Congregation of the Immaculate Heart of Mary, Sisters of the, S.V.M.: Founded 1952, in U.S. Motherhouse, 2950 Kaufmann Ave., Dubuque, IA 52001, (319) 556-2440. Educational work, parish ministry.

Vocationist Sisters (Sisters of the Divine Vocations), S.V.D.: Founded 1921, in Italy; in U.S., 1967

General motherhouse, Naples, Italy; U.S. foundation, Perpetual Help Nursery, 172 Broad St., Newark, NJ 07104, (973) 484-3535.

Wisdom, Daughters of, D.W.: Founded 1703, in France, by St. Louis Marie Grignion de Montfort; in U.S., 1904. General motherhouse, Vendee, France; U.S. province, 385 Ocean Ave., Islip, NY 11751, (631) 277-2660. Education, health care, parish ministry, social services.

Xaverian Missionary Society of Mary, Inc., X.M.M.: Founded 1945, in Italy; in U.S., 1954. General motherhouse, Parma, Italy; U.S. address, 242 Salisbury St., Worcester, MA 01609, (508) 757-0514.

ORGANIZATIONS OF RELIGIOUS

Conferences

Conferences of major superiors of religious institutes, dating from the 1950s, are encouraged by the Code of Canon Law (Code 708) "so that joining forces they can work toward the achievement of the purpose of their individual institutes more fully, transact common business and foster suitable coordination and cooperation with conferences of bishops and also with individual bishops." Statutes of the conferences must be approved by the Holy See "by which alone they are erected" (Canon 709). Conferences have been established in 24 countries of Europe, 14 in North and Central America, 10 in South America, 35 in Africa and 19 in Asia and Oceania.

Listed below are U.S. and international conferences.

Conference of Major Superiors of Men: Founded in 1956; canonically established Sept. 12, 1957. Membership, 269 major superiors representing institutes with a combined membership of approximately 24,000. President, Bro. Stephen Glodek, S.M.; executive director, Rev. Ted Keating, S.M. National office: 8808 Cameron St., Silver Spring, MD 20910, (301) 588-4030.

Leadership Conference of Women Religious: Founded in 1956; canonically established Dec. 12, 1959. Membership, nearly 1,000 (Dec. 31, 1996), representing approximately 400 religious institutes. Executive director, Sister Carole Shinnick, SSND. National office: 8808 Cameron St., Silver Spring, MD 20910, (301) 588-4955, www.lcwr.org.

Council of Major Superiors of Women Religious: Canonically erected June 13, 1992. Membership, 141 superiors of 103 religious congregations. Chairperson, Mother Mary McGreevy, R.S.M. National office: P.O. Box 4467, Washington, DC 20017-0467, (202) 832-2575; www.cmswr.org.

International Union of Superiors General (Women): Established Dec. 8, 1965; approved, 1967. General secretary, Sister Rita Burley, A.C.I. Address: Piazza Ponte S. Angelo, 28, 00186, Rome, Italy, 06-684-00-20.

Union of Superiors General (Men): Established in 1957. President, Father Alvaro Echeverria, F.S.C.; general secretary, Bro. Lino Da Campo, F.S.F. Address: Via dei Penitenzieri 19, 00193 Rome, Italy, 06-686-82-29.

Latin American Confederation of Religious (Confederacion Latinoamericana de Religiosos — CLAR): Established in 1959; statutes reformed in 1984. President, Sr. Carmen Margarita Fagot, R.S.C.J.; secretary general, Sr. Lurdes Cascho, C.F. Address:

Calle 64 No 10-45, Piso 5°, Apartado Aéreo 56804, Santafé de Bogotá, D.C., Colombia, (91) 31-00-392-31-00-481.

Union of European Conferences of Major Superiors (UCESM): Established Dec. 25, 1983. Permanent secretary, P. Jesús Maria Lecea Sainz, S.P. Rue Joseph II, 174, B-1000, Bruxelles, Belgium, 02-32-22-31.

Other Organizations

Institute on Religious Life (1974). To foster more effective understanding and implementation of teachings of the Church on religious life, promote vocations to religious life and the priesthood, and promote growth in sanctity of all the faithful according to their state in life. Executive director, Fr. Thomas Nelson, O.Praem.. National office, P.O. Box 41007, Chicago, IL 60641, (773) 267-1195, www.religiouslife.com; publishes *Religious Life* magazine and *Consecrated Life* periodical.

Religious Brothers Conference (1972): To publicize the unique vocations of brothers, to further communication among brothers and provide liaison with various organizations of the Church. Executive secretary, Br. Kenneth Pfister, F.S.C. National office, 1337 West Ohio, Chicago, IL 60622, (312) 829-8525, www.brothersonline.org.

National Black Sisters' Conference (1968): Black Catholic women religious and associates networking to provide support through prayer, study, solidarity and programs. President, Sr. Patricia J. Chappell, S.N.D.de N. Address: 101 G. St., NE, Washington, DC 20002, (202) 529-9370.

National Conference of Vicars for Religious (1967): National organization of diocesan officials concerned with relations between their respective dioceses and religious communities engaged therein. President, Sr. Therese Sullivan, S.P., 9292 Broadway, Merrillville, IN 46410; secretary, Eymard Flood, O.S.C. Address: 2811 East Villareal Dr., P.O. Box 14195, Orange, CA, 92863.

National Religious Vocation Conference (NRVC) (1988, with merger of National Sisters Vocation Conference and National Conference of Religious Vocation Directors): Service organization of men and women committed to the fostering and discernment of vocations. Executive director, Sr. Catherine Bertrand, S.S.N.D. Address: 5420 S. Cornell, #105, Chicago, IL 60615, (773) 363-5454, www.nrvc.net.

Religious Formation Conference (1953): Originally the Sister Formation Conference; membership includes women and men Religious and non-canonical groups. Facilitates the ministry of formation, both initial and ongoing, in religious communities. Executive director, Sister Janet Mock, C.S.J. National office: 8820 Cameron St., Silver Spring, MD 20910, (301) 588-4938, www.relforcon.org.

SECULAR INSTITUTES

(*Sources*: Catholic Almanac *survey; United States Conference of Secular Institutes*; Annuario Pontificio.)

Secular institutes are societies of men and women living in the world who dedicate themselves to observe the evangelical counsels and to carry on apostolic works suitable to their talents and opportunities in the areas of their everyday life.

"Secular institutes are not religious communities but they carry with them in the world a profession of evangelical counsels which is genuine and complete, and recognized as such by the Church. This profession confers a consecration on men and women, laity and clergy, who reside in the world. For this reason they should chiefly strive for total self-dedication to God, one inspired by perfect charity. These institutes should preserve their proper and particular character, a secular one, so that they may everywhere measure up successfully to that apostolate which they were designed to exercise, and which is both in the world and, in a sense, of the world" ("Decree on the Appropriate Renewal of Religious Life," No. 11; Second Vatican Council).

Secular institutes are under the jurisdiction of the Congregation for Institutes of Consecrated Life and Societies of Apostolic Life. General legislation concerning them is contained in Canons 710 to 730 of the Code of Canon Law.

A secular institute reaches maturity in several stages. It begins as an association of the faithful, technically called a pious union, with the approval of a local bishop. Once it has proved its viability, he can give it the status of an institute of diocesan right, in accordance with norms and permission emanating from the Congregation for Institutes of Consecrated Life and Societies of Apostolic Life. On issuance of a separate decree from this congregation, an institute of diocesan right becomes an institute of pontifical right.

Secular institutes, which originated in the latter part of the 18th century, were given full recognition and approval by Pius XII Feb. 2, 1947, in the apostolic constitution *Provida Mater Ecclesia*. On Mar. 25 of the same year a special commission for secular institutes was set up within the Congregation for Religious. Institutes were commended and confirmed by Pius XII in a *motu proprio* of Mar. 12, 1948, and were the subject of a special instruction issued a week later, Mar. 19, 1948.

The World Conference of Secular Institutes (CMIS) was approved by the Vatican May 23, 1974. Address: Via Tullio Levi-Civita 5, 00146 Rome, Italy.

The United States Conference of Secular Institutes (USCSI) was established following the organization of the World Conference of Secular Institutes in Rome. Its membership is open to all canonically erected secular institutes with members living in the United States. The conference was organized to offer secular institutes an opportunity to exchange experiences, to do research in order to help the Church carry out its mission, and to search for ways and means to make known the existence of secular institutes in the U.S. Address: P.O. Box 4556, 12th St. NE, Washington, DC 20017; (262) 547-7733; www.execpc.com/~uscsi. Pres., Carol Winkler.

Institutes in the U.S.

Apostolic Oblates: Founded in Rome, Italy, 1947; established in the U.S., 1962; for women. Approved as a secular institute of pontifical right Dec. 8, 1994. Addresses: 2125 W. Walnut Ave., Fullerton, CA 92633; 6762 Western Ave., Omaha, NE 68132, (402) 553-4418; 730 E. 87th St., Brooklyn, NY 11236, (718) 649-0324; www.prosanctity.org.

Apostolic Sodales: Founded in Rome, Italy, 1992 by Bp. Guglielmo; for priests. Established to promote a spirit of fraternity among diocesan priests gathered around their bishop in docile availability in the two-fold universal vocation — the call to holiness and brotherhood. Address: Rev. Michael F. Murphy, 655 C. Ave. Coronado, CA 92118-2299.

Caritas Christi: Originated in Marseilles, 1937; for women. Established as a secular institute of pontifical right Mar. 19, 1955. Address: P.O. Box 5162, River Forest, IL 60305. International membership.

Catechists of the Heart of Jesus (Ukrainian): Founded in Parana, Brazil, 1940 by Christoforo Myaskiv, OSBM; approved as Secular Institute of Pontifical Right, 1971; for women. Established for religious instruction, to assist clerics in missionary work, to help the Church, and to maintain the Ukrainian rite and culture. Address: 161 Glenbrook Rd., Stamford, CT 06902.

Company of St. Paul: Originated in Milan, Italy, 1920; for lay people and priests. Approved as a secular institute of pontifical right June 30, 1950. Address: Rev. Stuart Sandberg, 52 Davis Ave., White Plains, NY 10605.

Crusaders of St. Mary: Founded 1947 in Madrid, Spain; approved as a secular institute of diocesan right, 1988; for men. Address: 2001 Great Falls St., McLean, VA 22101, (703) 536-3546.

Diocesan Laborer Priests: Founded 1885 in Spain; approved as a secular institute of pontifical right, 1952. The specific aim of the institute is the promotion, sustenance and cultivation of apostolic, religious and priestly vocations. Address: Rev. Rutilio J. del Riego, 3706 15th St. N.E., Washington, DC 20017, (202) 832-4217.

Don Bosco Volunteers: Founded 1917 by Bl. Philip Rinaldi; for women. Approved as a secular institute of pontifical right Aug. 5, 1978. Follow spirituality and charism of St. John Bosco. Address: Cathy Sylvester, Don Bosco Volunteers, P.O. Box 588, Hawthorne, NJ 07507.

Don Bosco Institute: Founded in Rome on Sept. 12, 1994 by Fr. Egidio Viganó, rector major of the Salesians of Don Bosco, for celibate men. Recognized as public association of the faithful on May 24, 1998 by Cardinal Ignacio Velasco Garcia, abp. of Caracas, Venezuela. The association, which follows the spirit and charism of St. John Bosco, intends to become established juridically as a secular institute.

Address: 174 Filors Lane, Stony Point, NY 10980-2645, (845) 947-2200.

Family of Mary of the Visitation: Founded in Vietnam, 1976. Approved as a Secular Institute of Diocesan Right; intended to promote faith-filled vowed women, to help people protect their faith and to meet social needs. Address: Therese Chan Ngo, P.O. Box 441, Westminster, CA 92684.

Fr. Kolbe Missionaries of the Immaculata: Founded in Bologna, Italy, in 1954, by Fr. Luigi Faccenda, O.F.M. Conv.; for women. Approved as a secular institute of pontifical right Mar. 25, 1992. Live the fullness of baptismal consecration, strive for perfect charity and promote the knowledge and veneration of Mary. Address: 531 E. Merced Ave., West Covina, CA 91790.

Handmaids of Divine Mercy: Founded in Bari, Italy, 1951; for women. Approved as an institute of pontifical right 1972. Address: 2410 Hughes Ave., Bronx, NY 10458, (718) 295-3770.

Institute of Secular Missionaries: Founded in Vitoria, Spain, 1939; for women. Approved as a secular institute, 1955. Address: 2710 Ruberg Ave., Cincinnati, OH 45211, Attn.: E. Dilger.

Institute of the Heart of Jesus (Men): Originated in France Feb. 2, 1791; restored Oct. 29, 1918; for diocesan priests and laity. Received final approval from the Holy See as a secular institute of pontifical right Feb. 2, 1952. U.S. address, Rev. Francis X. Mawn, St. James Rectory, 6 Cottage St. Haverhill, MA 01830-4920, (978) 372-8537.

Institute of the Heart of Jesus (Women): Foundation stems from the Institute of the Heart of Jesus which originated in France Feb. 2, 1791. Established to help lay women live the Gospel radically in the modern worl by means of the evangelical counsels, to engage in group discernment and various forms of prayer. Address, Diana Bland, 417 N. Buena Vista St. Burbank, CA 91505-3208.

Jesu Caritas Fraternity: Founded in France, 1952. Approved as a Secular Institute of Diocesan Right, 1996. Established to form members in the contemplative tradition of Brother Charles de Foucauld, bringing God's love especially to his most neglected children; members strive in their daily life to live the Gospel message. Address: Mary D. Christensen, P.O. Box 92, Yonkers, N.Y. 10704.

Mission of Our Lady of Bethany: Founded in France, 1948; for women. Approved as a secular institute of diocesan right, 1965. Address: Estelle Nichols, 7 Locksley St., Jamaica Plain, MA 02130.

Missionaries of the Kingship of Christ the King: Under this title are included three distinct and juridically separate institutes founded by Agostino Gemelli, O.F.M. (1878-1959) and Armida Barelli (1882-1952). Two are active in the U.S.

(1) Women Missionaries of the Kingship of Christ: Founded in 1919, in Italy; definitively approved as an institute of pontifical right 1953. U.S. branch established 1950.

(2) Men Missionaries of the Kingship of Christ: Founded 1928, in Italy, as an institute of diocesan right. U.S. branch established 1962.

Addresses: Rev. Damien Dougherty, O.F.M., P.O. Box 278, Eime Rd., Dittmer, MO 63023 (for Men Missionaries); Rev. Dominic Monti, O.F.M., 10400 Lorain Ave., Silver Spring, MD, 20901 (for Women

Missionaries); (301) 593-4479, www.simkc.org.

Nuestra Señora de la Altagracia: Founded in Dominican Republic, 1956; approved as a secular institute of diocesan right, 1964; for women. Address: Ms. Christiana Perez, 129 Van Siclen Ave., Brooklyn, NY 11207.

Oblate Missionaries of Mary Immaculate: Founded, 1952; approved as a secular institute of pontifical right 1984; for women. Address: Oblate Missionaries of Mary Immaculate, P.O. Box 764, Lowell, MA 01853, inst-seculier-omni.com.

Opus Spiritus Sancti: Originated in West Germany, 1952; for diocesan priests and unmarried permanent deacons. Formally acknowledged by Rome as a secular institute of diocesan right, 1977. Address: Rev. James McCormick, 421 E. Bluff St., Carroll, IA 51401-3099; (712) 792-4386.

Schoenstatt Sisters of Mary: Originated in Schoenstatt, Germany, 1926; for women. Established as a secular institute of diocesan right May 20, 1948; of pontifical right Oct. 18, 1948. Addresses: W. 284 N. 404 Cherry Lane, Waukesha, WI 53188, (262) 542-4384; House Schoenstatt, 134 Front St., Rockport, TX 78382; (361) 729-2019.

Secular Institute of Pius X: Originated in Manchester, NH, 1940; for priests and laymen. Approved as a secular institute, 1959. Also admits married couples and unmarried men as associate members. Addresses: C.P. 7731, Charlesbourg, Quebec G1G 5W6, Canada; (418) 626-5881.

Secular Institute of Schoenstatt Fathers: Founded in Germany by Fr. Joseph Kentenich in 1965; for priests serving the International Schoenstatt Movement in over 20 countries. Approved as a secular institute of pontifical right, June 24, 1988. Address: W. 284 N. 746 Cherry Lane, Waukesha, WI 53188, (262) 542-4384.

Secular Institute of St. Francis de Sales: Founded in Vienna, Austria, 1940; for women. Pontifical right, 1964. Address: Thérèse Keyes, Dir., 87 Gerrish Ave., T2, East Haven, CT 06512; www.secularinstitutes.org/sfs.ht.

Society of Our Lady of the Way: Originated, 1936; for women. Approved as a secular institute of pontifical right Jan. 3, 1953. Address: 2339 N. Catalina, Los Angeles, CA 90027, (323) 665-0333; www.execpc.com/uscsi/index.html.

Voluntas Dei Institute: Originated in Canada, 1958, by Father L. M. Parent; for secular priests and laymen (with married couples as associates). Approved as a secular institute of pontifical right, July 12, 1987. Established in 21 countries. Address: Rev. George Hazler, 370 Emerald Bay Circle, N-7, Naples, FL 34110.

The *Annuario Pontificio* lists the following secular institutes of pontifical right which are not established in the U.S.:

For men: Christ the King; Institute of Our Lady of Life; Institute of Prado; Priests of the Sacred Heart of Jesus.

For women: Alliance in Jesus through Mary; Apostles of the Sacred Heart; Catechists of Mary, Virgin and Mother; Company of St. Ursula, Cordimarian Filiation; Daughters of the Nativity of Mary; Daughters of the Queen of the Apostles; Daughters of the Sacred Heart; Evangelical Crusade;

Faithful Servants of Jesus; Handmaids of Our Mother of Mercy; Institute of Notre Dame du Travail; Institute of Our Lady of Life; Institute of St. Boniface; Little Apostles of Charity.

Life and Peace in Christ Jesus; Missionaries of Royal Priesthood; Missionaries of the Sick; Oblates of Christ the King; Oblates of the Sacred Heart of Jesus; Servants of Jesus the Priest; Servite Secular Institute; Union of the Daughters of God; Workers of Divine Love; Workers of the Cross; Handmaids of Holy Church; Augustinian Auxiliary Missionaries; Heart of Jesus; Apostolic Missionaries of Charity; Combonian Secular Missionaries; Missionaries of the Gospel; Secular Servants of Jesus Christ Priest; Women of Schoenstatt; Missionaries of Infinite Love.

Associations

Association of Mary Help of Christians: Founded by St. John Bosco in Turin, Italy, in 1869 for men and women. Public association of the faithful. Members encourage participation in the liturgical life of the Church, emphasizing frequent reception of the Eucharist and the Sacrament of Reconciliation. They also live and spread devotion to Mary Help of Christians according to the spirit of St. John Bosco. Address: 174 Filors Lane, Stony Point, NY 10980-2645; (845) 947-2200.

Caritas: Originated in New Orleans, 1950; for women. Follow guidelines of secular institutes. Small self-supporting groups who live and work among the poor and oppressed; in Louisiana and Guatemala. Address: Box 308, Abita Springs, LA 70420, (985) 892-4345.

Daughters of Our Lady of Fatima: Originated in Lansdowne, PA, 1949; for women. Received diocesan approval, Jan., 1952. Address: Fatima House, Rolling Hills Rd., Ottsville, PA 18942, (215) 795-0924.

Focolare Movement: Founded in Trent, Italy, in 1943, by Chiara Lubich; for men and women. Approved as an association of the faithful, 1962. It is not a secular institute by statute; however, vows are observed by its totally dedicated core membership of 4,000 who live in small communities called Focolare (Italian word for "hearth") centers. There are 17 resident centers in the U.S. and four in Canada. GEN (New Generation) is the youth organization of the movement. An estimated 75,000 are affiliated with the movement in the U.S. and Canada; 2,000,000 worldwide. Publications include *Living City*, monthly; *GEN II* and *GEN III* for young people and children. Five week-long summer conventions, called "Mariapolis" ("City of Mary"), are held annually. Address for information: 204 Cardinal Rd., Hyde Park, NY 12538, (845) 229-0230 (men's or women's branch); www.rc.net/focolare.

Jesus-Caritas Fraternity of Priests: An international association of diocesan priests who strive to combine an active life with a contemplative calling by their membership in small fraternities. U.S. address for information: Rev. Greg Pawloski, St. Patrick's Church, P.O. Box 96, 126 E. 7th St., Imperial, NE 69033-0096, (308) 882-4995, www.rc.net/org/jesuscaritas.

Franciscan Missionaries of Jesus Crucified: Founded in New York in 1987; separate communities for women and men. Approved as an association of the faithful Jan. 7, 1992. To provide an opportunity for persons with disabilities to live a life of total consecration in the pursuit of holiness in the apostolate of service to the Church and to those who suffer in any way. Address: Louise D. Principe, F.M.J.C., 400 Central Ave., Apt. 3D, Albany, NY 12206; (518) 438-5887.

Holy Family Institute (aggregated to the Society of St. Paul): Founded by Fr. James Alberione in 1963 for married couples who wish to commit themselves to seeking evangelical perfection in marriage; definitively approved by the Holy See, 1993. First Americans professed, 1988. Address: 9531 Akron-Canfield Rd., Box 498, Canfield, OH 44406.

Madonna House Apostolate: Originated in Toronto, Canada, 1930; for priests and lay persons. Public association of the Christian faithful. Address: Madonna House, Combermere, Ontario, Canada KOJ ILO; (613) 756-3713; www.madonnahouse.org. Directors General: Jean Fox (women), Albert Osterberger (men), Fr. Robert Pelton (priests). International membership and missions.

Opus Spiritus Sancti: Originated in Germany; for women. An association of the faithful. Address: 103 Pine St., P.O. Box 518, Pawtucket, RI 02860, Attn.: Rev. Msgr. Jacques Plante, Reg. Coord., (401) 278-4515.

Pax Christi: Lay institute of men and women dedicated to witnessing to Christ, with special emphasis on service to the poor in Mississippi. Addresses: St. Francis Center, 708 Ave. I, Greenwood, MS 38930; LaVerna House, 2108 Altawoods Blvd., Jackson, MS 39204, (601) 373-4463.

Rural Parish Workers of Christ the King: Founded in 1942; for women. A secular institute of the Archdiocese of St. Louis. Dedicated to the glory of God in service of neighbor, especially in rural areas. Address: Rt. 1, Box 1667, Cadet, MO 63630, (636) 586-5171, www.web.jcn.net/rpwck.

Salesian Cooperators: Founded by St. John Bosco in Turin, Italy, in 1876; for lay men and women and diocesan clergy. A public association of the faithful, members commit themselves to apostolates in the local Church, especially on behalf of the young, in the Salesian spirit and style. Address: 174 Filors Lane, Stony Point, NY 10980-2645; (845) 947-2200; www.memorare.com.

Teresian Institute: Founded in Spain 1911 by Pedro Poveda. Approved as an association of the faithful of pontifical right Jan. 11, 1924. Mailing Address: 3400 S. W. 99th Ave., Miami, FL 33165, (305) 553-8567.

THIRD ORDERS

Third orders (commonly called secular orders) are societies of the faithful living in the world who seek to deepen their Christian life and apostolic commitment in association with and according to the spirit of various religious institutes. The orders are called "third" because their foundation usually followed the establishment of the first and second religious orders with which they are associated.

In addition to the recognized third orders, there are other groups of lay persons with strong ties to religious orders. Relationships of this kind serve the spiritual good of the faithful and also enrich the religious orders in a complementary fashion, with the mutual vitality of prayer in the cloister or convent and action in the marketplace.

Augustine, Third Order Secular of St.: Founded 13th century; approved Nov. 7, 1400.

Carmelites, Lay (Third Order of Our Lady of Mt. Carmel): Rule for laity approved by Pope Nicholas V, Oct. 7, 1452; new statutes, January, 1991. Addresses: 8501 Bailey Rd., Darien, IL 60561; P.O. Box 613, Williamston, MA 01267; P.O. Box 27, Tappan, NY 10983-0027. Approximately 270 communities and 10,000 members in the U.S. and Canada.

Carmelites, The Secular Order of Discalced (formerly the Third Order Secular of the Blessed Virgin Mary of Mt Carmel and of St. Teresa of Jesus): Rule based on the Carmelite reform established by St. Teresa and St. John of the Cross, 16th century; approved Mar. 23, 1594. Revised rule approved May 10, 1979. Office of National Secretariat, U.S.A.; P.O. Box 3079, San Jose, CA 95156-3079, (408) 251-1361. Approximately 24,445 members throughout the world; 130 groups/communities and 5,200 members in the U.S. and Canada.

Dominican Laity (Third Order of St. Dominic): Founded in the 13th century. Addresses of provincial promoters in the United States: Central Province, 1909 South Ashland Ave., Chicago, IL 60608-2994, (312) 666-3244; www.op.org/domcentral; Eastern Province, 487 Michigan Ave., N.E., Washington, D.C., 20017, (202) 529-5300; Southern Province, P.O. Box 12927, Raleigh, NC 27605, (919) 833-1893; Western Province,

2005 Berryman St., Berkeley, CA 94709, (510) 526-4811.

Franciscan Order, Secular (SFO): Founded 1209 by St. Francis of Assisi; approved Aug. 30, 1221. National Minister, William Wicks, SFO, 3307 Quail Meadows Dr., Santa Maria, CA 93455; International Secretariate, Via Pomponia Grecina, 31, 00145 Rome. *Tau USA*, quarterly. Approximately 780,000 throughout the world; 18,000 in U.S.

Mary, Third Order of (Marist Laity): Founded, Dec. 8, 1850; rule approved by the Holy See 1857. Addresses of provincial directors: Marist Laity Center, 1706 Jackson Ave., New Orleans, LA 70113, (504) 524-5192, www.maristsociety.org; Marist Fathers, 518 Pleasant St., Framingham, MA 01701; Marist Fathers, 2335 Warring St., Berkeley, CA 94704. Approximately 14,000 in the world, 5,600 in U.S.

Mary, Secular Order of Servants of (Servite): Founded 1233; approved 1304. Revised rule approved 1995. Address: National Assistant for the Secular Order, 3121 W. Jackson Blvd., Chicago, IL 60612.

Mercy, Secular Third Order of Our Lady of (Mercedarian): Founded 1219 by St. Peter Nolasco; approved the same year.

Norbert, Third Order of St.: Founded 1122 by St. Norbert; approved by Pope Honorius II in 1126.

Oblates of St. Benedict: Lay persons affiliated with a Benedictine abbey or monastery who strive to direct their lives, as circumstances permit, according to the spirit and Rule of St. Benedict.

Trinity, Third Order Secular of the Most: Founded 1198; approved 1219.

"STARTING AFRESH FROM CHRIST"

On June 14, 2002, the Congregation for Institutes of Consecrated Life and Societies of Apostolic Life published with the approval of Pope John Paul II the pastoral instruction "Starting Afresh from Christ: A Renewed Commitment to Consecrated Life in the Third Millennium."

In four parts, the instruction seeks to encourage women and men religious to live according to the Gospel and care for others as God does even in the face of difficulties such declining numbers, an increasing clash of cultures within religious communities, and a lack of appreciation on the part of the community at large. While making a number of practical recommendations, the document focuses chiefly on spirituality and the need to maintain a deep prayer life, individually and in religious communities. Some excerpts:

"Contemplating Christ's crucified and glorious face and witnessing to his love in the world, consecrated persons joyfully accept the Holy Father John Paul II's pressing invitation at the beginning of the third millennium to cast out into the deep: '*Duc in altum!*' (Lk 5:4).... *Consecrated persons are called by the Spirit to a continual conversion* to give new vigour to the prophetic dimension of their vocation....

"Consecrated life, in its continuous development and experience of new forms, is already in itself an eloquent expression of this very presence, almost a kind of Gospel spread out through the centuries. It appears in fact as a 'prolongation in history of a special presence of the Risen Lord....'

"Today's world is expecting to see in consecrated men and women the concrete reflection of Jesus' way of acting, of his love for every person without distinction or qualification....

"Consecrated persons — monks and nuns, contemplatives, religious dedicated to the works of the apostolate, members of Secular Institutes and Societies of Apostolic life, hermits and consecrated virgins — truly deserve the gratitude of the ecclesial community....

"Consecrated persons extend a persuasive invitation to reflect upon the primacy of grace and to respond to it through a generous spiritual commitment. Despite widespread secularization, there is a widespread demand for spirituality which is often expressed as a renewed need for prayer....

"... If, as is affirmed in some places, the third millennium will be the time of promotion of the laity, of associations, and of ecclesial movements, we can rightfully ask: what place will be reserved for the traditional forms of consecrated life? Consecrated life, John Paul II reminds us, still has a history to be written together with all the faithful . . .

"... In the Eucharist all forms of prayer come together, the Word of God is proclaimed and received, relationships with God, with brothers and sisters, with all men and women are challenged. It is the Sacrament of filiation, of communion and of mission. The Eucharist, the Sacrament of unity with Christ, is at the same time the Sacrament of Church unity and community unity for the consecrated person...."

Apostolates and Ministries

RIGHTS AND OBLIGATIONS OF ALL THE FAITHFUL

The following rights are listed in Canons 208-223 of the revised Code of Canon Law; additional rights are specified in other canons.

- Because of their baptism and regeneration, there is equality regarding dignity and action for the building up of the Body of Christ.
- They are bound always to preserve communion with the Church.
- According to their condition and circumstances, they should strive to lead a holy life and promote the growth and holiness of the Church.
- They have the right and duty to work for the spread of the divine message of salvation to all peoples of all times and places.
- They are bound to follow with Christian obedience those things which the bishops, as they represent Christ, declare as teachers of the faith or establish as rulers of the Church.
- They have the right to make known their needs, especially their spiritual needs, to pastors of the Church.
- They have the right, and sometimes the duty, of making known to pastors and others of the faithful their opinions about things pertaining to the good of the Church.
- They have the right to receive help from their pastors, from the spiritual goods of the Church and especially from the word of God and the sacraments.
- They have the right to divine worship performed according to prescribed rules of their rite, and to follow their own form of spiritual life in line with the doctrine of the Church.
- They have the right to freely establish and control associations for good and charitable purposes, to foster the Christian vocation in the world, and to hold meetings related to the accomplishment of these purposes.
- They have the right to promote and support apostolic action but may not call it "Catholic" unless they have the consent of competent authority.
- They have a right to a Christian education.
- They have a right to freedom of inquiry in sacred studies, in accordance with the teaching authority of the Church.
- They have a right to freedom in the choice of their state of life.
- No one has the right to harm the good name of another person or to violate his or her right to maintain personal privacy.
- They have the right to vindicate the rights they enjoy in the Church, and to defend themselves in a competent ecclesiastical forum.
- They have the obligation to provide for the needs of the Church, with respect to things pertaining to divine worship, apostolic and charitable works, and the reasonable support of ministers of the Church.
- They have the obligation to promote social justice and to help the poor from their own resources.
- In exercising their rights, the faithful should have regard for the common good of the Church and for the rights and duties of others.
- Church authority has the right to monitor the exercise of rights proper to the faithful, with the common good in view.

RIGHTS AND OBLIGATIONS OF LAY PERSONS

In addition to rights and obligations common to all the faithful and those stated in other canons, lay persons are bound by the obligations and enjoy the rights specified in these canons (224-231).

- Lay persons, like all the faithful, are called by God to the apostolate in virtue of their baptism and confirmation. They have the obligation and right, individually or together in associations, to work for the spread and acceptance of the divine message of salvation among people everywhere; this obligation is more urgent in those circumstances in which people can hear the Gospel and get to know Christ only through them (lay persons).
- They are bound to bring an evangelical spirit to bear on the order of temporal things and to give Christian witness in carrying out their secular pursuits.
- Married couples are obliged to work for the building up of the people of God through their marital and family life.
- Parents have the most serious obligation to provide for the Christian education of their children according to the doctrine handed down by the Church.
- Lay persons have the same civil liberty as other

citizens. In the use of this liberty, they should take care that their actions be imbued with an evangelical spirit. They should attend to the doctrine proposed by the magisterium of the Church but should take care that, in questions of opinion, they do not propose their own opinion as the doctrine of the Church.

- Qualified lay persons are eligible to hold and perform the duties of ecclesiastical offices open to them in accord with the provisions of law.
- Properly qualified lay persons can assist pastors of the Church as experts and counselors.
- Lay persons have the obligation and enjoy the right to acquire knowledge of doctrine commensurate with their capacity and condition.
- They have the right to pursue studies in the sacred sciences in pontifical universities or facilities and in institutes of religious sciences, and to obtain academic degrees.
- If qualified, they are eligible to receive from ecclesiastical authority a mandate to teach sacred sciences.
- Laymen can be invested by liturgical rite and in a stable manner in the ministries of lector and acolyte.

- Lay persons, by temporary assignment, can fulfill the office of lector in liturgical actions; likewise, all lay persons can perform the duties of commentator or cantor.
- In cases of necessity and in the absence of the usual ministers, lay persons — even if not lectors or acolytes — can exercise the ministry of the word, lead liturgical prayers, confer baptism and distribute Communion, according to the prescripts of law.
- Lay persons who devote themselves permanently or temporarily to the service of the Church are obliged to acquire the formation necessary for carrying out their duties in a proper manner.
- They have a right to remuneration for their service which is just and adequate to provide for their own needs and those of their families; they also have a right to insurance, social security and health insurance.

[See also the section on Canon Law for other details pertaining to the Code of Canon Law.]

SPECIAL APOSTOLATES AND GROUPS

Apostleship of the Sea (1920, Glasgow, Scotland; 1947 in U.S.): 3211 Fourth St. NE, Washington, DC 20017 (national office); (202) 541-3226; www.aos-usa.org. An international Catholic organization for the moral, social and spiritual welfare of seafarers and those involved in the maritime industry. Formally instituted by the Holy See in 1952 (apostolic constitution *Exul Familia*), it is a sector of the Pontifical Council for Migrants and Itinerant Peoples. Its norms were updated by Pope John Paul II in a *motu proprio* dated Jan. 31, 1997. The U.S. unit, an affiliate of the USCCB, serves port chaplains in 63 U.S. ports. Nat. Dir., Robert Mario Balderas, a permanent deacon.

Auxiliaries of Our Lady of the Cenacle (1878, France): 18 Sycamore Meadow Rd., Sunderland, MA 01375; www.cenaclesisters.org. An association of consecrated Catholic laywomen, under the direction of the Congregation of Our Lady of the Cenacle. They profess annually the evangelical counsels of celibacy, poverty and obedience and serve God through their own professions and life styles and pursue individual apostolates. Reg. Dir., Dr. Carolyn Jacobs.

Catholic Central Union of America (1855): 3835 Westminster Pl., St. Louis, MO 63108; (314) 371-1653; *Social Justice Review*, bimonthly. One of the oldest Catholic lay organizations in the U.S. and the first given an official mandate for Catholic Action by a committee of the American bishops (1936).

Catholic Medical Mission Board (1928): 10 W. 17th Street, New York, NY 10011; (212) 242-7757; www.cmmb.org. A charitable, non-profit organization dedicated to providing health care supplies and support for the medically disadvantaged in developing and transitional countries. CMMB depends upon the financial generosity of over 25,000 individual donors and through product contributions by major pharmaceutical corporations. In 2001, CMMB delivered more than $79 million in medicines, volunteer medical servies and healthcare programming to 59 countries and responded to emergencies across the globe.

Among recent relief efforts were earthquakes in El Salvador and Peru, a meningitis outbreak in Burkina Faso, devastating floods in India and the refugee situation in Afghanistan. The CMMB also placed long and short term volunteers in various countries and provided training of local health care workers. CMMB's medical program includes a placement service for health care specialists who volunteer at Catholic medical facilities in developing countries. Exec. Dir., Jack Galbraith.

Catholic Movement for Intellectual and Cultural Affairs: 3049 Fourth St., N.E., Washington, D.C., 20017, (202) 269-6672. The U.S. affiliate of *Pax Romana*-ICMICA (see International Catholic Organizations); *The Notebook*, quarterly. Pres., Joseph Kirchner.

Catholic Network of Volunteer Service (1963; formerly, International Liaison of Lay Volunteers in Mission): 1410 Q. St., N.W., Washington, DC 20009; (202) 332-6000; www.cnvs.org. Network for lay mission programs, coordinating and facilitating efforts of volunteer mission organizations. *The Response*, annual directory. Exec. Dir., James Lindsay.

Catholic Volunteers in Florida (1983): P.O. Box 702, Goldenrod, FL 32733; (307) 331-6444, www.cvif.org. Co-sponsored by the bishops of Florida to promote values of social justice by direct service to farm workers, homeless, hungry, low-income people, single mothers and others in need. Volunteers, 20 years of age and older, serve for a one-year period in urban and rural settings. Exec. Dir., Richard Galentino.

Center for Applied Research in the Apostolate (CARA): Georgetown University, Washington, DC 20057; (202) 687-8080; www.georgetown.edu/research/CARA. A non-profit research center serving the planning needs of the Catholic Church. CARA gathers empirical data for use by bishops, diocesan agencies, parishes, congregations of men and women religious and Catholic organizations. The *CARA Re-*

port, quarterly; *CARA Catholic Ministry Formation Directory*, annually. Exec. Dir., Bryan Froehle, Ph.D.

Christian Family Movement (CFM) (1947): National office, Box 272, Ames, IA 50010. Originated in Chicago to Christianize family life and create communities conducive to Christian family life. Since 1968, CFM in the U.S. has included couples from all Christian churches.

Christian Life Communities (1971, promulgation of revised norms by Pope Paul VI; originated, 1563, as Sodalities of Our Lady, at the Jesuit College in Rome): 3601 Lindell Blvd., Room 202, St. Louis, MO 63108 (national office); (314) 977-7370; the world CLC office is in Rome. Small communities of primarily lay persons who come together to form committed individuals for service to the world and the Church.

Cursillo Movement (1949, in Spain; in U.S., 1957): National Cursillo Center, P.O. Box 210226, Dallas, TX 75211. An instrument of Christian renewal designed to form and stimulate persons to engage in evangelizing their everyday environments.

Franciscan Mission Service of North America, an Overseas Lay Ministry Program (1990): P.O. Box 29034, Washington, DC 20017; (202) 832-1762. Lay missioners work with Franciscan sisters, brothers and priests for a minimum of three years in underdeveloped countries. Co-Dir. Joseph Nangle, O.F.M. and Megeen White.

Grail, The (1921, in The Netherlands, by Rev. Jacques van Ginneken, S.J.; 1940, in U.S.): Grailville, 932 O'Bannonville Rd., Loveland, Ohio 45140 (U. S. headquarters); Duisburger Strasse 442, 45478 Mulheim, Germany; international secretariat). An international movement of women concerned about the full development of all peoples, working in education, religious, social, cultural and ecological areas.

Jesuit Volunteer Corps (1956): 18th and Thompson Sts., Philadelphia, PA 19121 (address for information), (215) 232-0300, www.jesuitvolunteers.org. Sponsored by the Society of Jesus in the U.S. Men and women volunteers work throughout the U.S. serving the poor directly and working for structural change.

LAMP Ministries (Lay Apostolic Ministries with the Poor): 2704 Schurz Ave., Bronx, NY 10465; (718) 409-5062; www.lampministries.org. Missionary service of evangelization with the materially poor and homeless in the larger metropolitan New York-New Jersey area. Newsletter, two times a year. Directors, Drs. Tom and Lyn Scheuring.

Lay Mission-Helpers Association (1955): 3424 Wilshire Blvd., Los Angeles, CA 90010; Trains and assigns men and women for work in overseas apostolates for periods of two to three years. Approximately 700 members of the association have served in overseas assignments since its founding. Director, Msgr. Michael Meyers. **The Mission Doctors Association** (same address; 626-285-8868; www.mission doctors.org) recruits, trains and sends Catholic phy-

sicians and their families to mission hospitals and clinics throughout the world for tours of two to three years. Additionally, MDA has a short-term program for volunteer physicians with a term of service of 1-2 months. Program Dir., Elise Frederick.

Legion of Mary (1921, in Dublin, Ireland, by Frank Duff): P.O. Box 1313, St. Louis, MO 63188 (U.S. address), (314) 631-3447; De Montfort House, Dublin 7, Ireland (headquarters). Membership: active Catholics of all ages, under the direction of local bishops and priests, for the work of conversion, conservation and consolation.

*Movimiento Familiar Cristiano***-USA (MFC)** (1969): Movement of Catholic Hispanic families united in their efforts to promote the human and Christian virtues of the family so that it may become a force that forms persons, transmits the faith and contributes to the total development of the community. Address: 700 Waverly, San Antonio, TX 78201, (210) 736-5228. Rev. Clemente Barron, C.P., national spiritual director.

National Catholic Conference for Seafarers (affiliated with the Apostleship of the Sea in the U.S.): Apostleship of the Sea, P.O. Box 1387, Pt. Arthur, TX 77641, (409) 982-4501. Pres., Fr. Sinclair Aubre.

Pax Christi **USA** (1972): 532 W. 8th St., Erie, PA 16502; (814) 453-4955. Pax Christi (see International Catholic Organizations). Founded to establish peacemaking as a priority for the American Catholic Church. *Pax Christi USA*, quarterly; membership.

Schoenstatt Lay Movement (1914): International Schoenstatt Center, W284 N 698 Cherry Lane, Waukesha, WI 53188; (262) 547-7733. Lay movement founded in Germany by Fr. Joseph Kentenich. A Marian and apostolic way of life, Schoenstatt is present on all continents and includes people of all ages and walks of life, men and women, young and old, priests and laity. The Schoenstatt Shrine, dedicated to Mary, Mother Thrice Admirable, Queen and Victress of Schoenstatt, is an integral part of the spirituality of Schoenstatt. There are over 160 shrines around the world, 6 of them in the U.S., in Minnesota, New York, Texas, and Wisconsin.

Volunteer Missionary Movement (1969): 5980 W. Loomis Rd., Milwaukee, WI 53129. Independent lay international mission organization with origins in the Catholic tradition but ecumenical and open to all Christian denominations. *Bridges*, quarterly.

Volunteers for Educational and Social Services (VESS): 1625 Rutherford Lane, Bldg. D, Austin, TX 78754; (512) 339-7123. A program of the Texas Catholic Conference. Volunteers offer their services for a year at mission-sites throughout Texas as teachers, social workers, counselors, ESL instructors, immigration and refugee assistants, parish, youth and campus ministers, health care workers and nurses. The experience offers individuals the opportunity to acquire professional experience by ministering to the needs of parishes, agencies and schools that are economically disadvantaged. Dir., Michael G. Guerra.

CATHOLIC YOUTH ORGANIZATIONS

Camp Fire Boys and Girls: 4601 Madison Ave., Kansas City, MO 64112; (816) 756-1950; www.campfire.org. The National Catholic Committee for Girl Scouts and Camp Fire, a standing com-

mittee of the National Federation for Catholic Youth Ministry, cooperates with Camp Fire Boys and Girls.

Catholic Forester Youth Program, Catholic Order of Foresters: Naperville, IL 60566; (800) 552-

0145. To develop Christian leadership and promote the moral, intellectual, social and physical growth of its youth members. Catholic Forester. Membership: youth up to 16 years of age; over 19,046 in 610 local courts in U.S. High Chief Ranger-Pres., Robert Ciesla.

Catholic Youth Organization (CYO): Name of parish-centered diocesan Catholic youth programs throughout the country. CYO promotes a program of spiritual, social and physical activities. The original CYO was organized in 1930 by Archbishop Bernard Sheil, auxiliary bishop of Chicago.

Columbian Squires (1925): 1 Columbus Plaza, New Haven, CT 06510-3326; (203) 772-2130, www.kofc.org. The official youth organization of the Knights of Columbus. To train and develop leadership through active participation in a well-organized program of spiritual, service, social, cultural and athletic activities. Membership: Catholic young men, 12-18 years old. More than 25,000 in over 1,000 circles (local units) active in the U.S., Canada, Puerto Rico, Philippines, Mexico, the Bahamas, Virgin Islands and Guam. *Squires Newsletter*, monthly.

Girl Scouts: 830 Third Ave., New York, NY 10022. Girls from archdioceses and dioceses in the U.S. and its possessions participate in Girl Scouting through the collaboration of Girl Scouts of the U.S.A., with the National Catholic Committee for Girl Scouts and Camp Fire, a standing committee of the National Federation for Catholic Youth Ministry.

Holy Childhood Association (Pontifical Association of the Holy Childhood) (1843): 1720 Massachusetts Ave. N.W., Washington, DC 20036. The official children's mission-awareness society of the Church. Provides mission awareness for elementary-grade students in parochial schools and religious edu-cation programs and financial assistance to children in more than 100 developing countries. Publishes *It's Our World*, three times a year, in two grade levels. Nat. Dir., Rev. Francis W. Wright, C.S.Sp.

The National Catholic Committee on Scouting: P.O. Box 152079, Irving, TX 75015-2079, (972) 580-2114, www.catholic-church.org/catholicscouting. Works with the Boy Scouts of America in developing the character and spiritual life of members in units chartered to Catholic and non-Catholic organizations. National Committee Chairman, Robert Runnels of Leawood, KS. Admin. Sec., Barbara Nestel.

National Catholic Forensic League (1952): 21 Nancy Rd., Milford, MA 01757; (508) 473-0431. To develop articulate Catholic leaders through an interdiocesan program of speech and debate activities. Newsletter, quarterly. Membership: 925 schools; membership open to Catholic, private and public schools through the local diocesan league. Exec. Sec.-Treas., Richard Gaudette.

National Catholic Young Adult Ministry Association (1982): 1185 Van Buren Ave., St. Paul, MN 55104, (888) 629-2621, www.ncyama.org. A response to the needs of young adults, an invitation to share their gifts with the larger community and a challenge to live gospel values in the world. A national network for single and married young adults. Sec., Chris Zirker.

National Federation for Catholic Youth Ministry, Inc. (1981): 415 Michigan Ave., N.E., Washington, D.C. 20017; (202) 636-3825, www.nfcym.org. To foster the development of youth ministry in the United States. Exec. Dir., Robert McCarty.

Young Christian Students: 19646 W. Dunlap Rd., Dennison, IL 62423, (217) 826-5708. A student movement for Christian personal and social change.

CAMPUS MINISTRY

Campus ministry is an expression of the Church's special desire to be present to all who are involved in higher education and to further dialogue between the Church and the academic community. In the words of the U.S. bishops' 1985 pastoral letter entitled "Empowered by the Spirit," this ministry is "the public presence and service through which properly prepared baptized persons are empowered by the Spirit to use their talents and gifts on behalf of the Church in order to be sign and instrument of the Kingdom in the academic world."

Campus ministry, carried on by lay, Religious and ordained ministers, gathers members of the Church on campus to form the faith community, appropriate the faith, form Christian consciences, educate for justice and facilitate religious development.

The dimensions and challenge of this ministry are evident from, among other things, the numbers involved: approximately 550,000 Catholics on more than 230 Catholic college and university campuses; about four million in several thousand non-Catholic private and public institutions; 1,200 or more campus ministers. In many dioceses, the activities of ministers are coordinated by a local diocesan director. Two professional organizations serve the ministry on the national level:

The National Association of Diocesan Directors of Campus Ministry, Ms. Krista Bajoka, Contact Person, 305 Michigan Ave., Detroit, MI 48226; (313) 237-5962.

The Catholic Campus Ministry Association, with a membership of 1,200, 300 College Park, Dayton, OH 45469-2515; (937) 229-4648, www.ccmanet.org. Exec. Dir., Edmund Franchi.

COLLEGE SOCIETIES

Alpha Sigma Nu (1915): Marquette University, Brooks 201, P.O. Box 1881, Milwaukee, WI 53201-1881 (national headquarters); (414) 288-7542; www.alphasigmanu.org. National honor society of the 30 Jesuit institutions of higher education in the U.S. and a chapter at Sogany University in Korea; members chosen on the basis of scholarship, loyalty and service; 1,575 student and 38,000 alumni members. Member, Association of College Honor Societies.

Gamma Pi Epsilon (1925) merged with Alpha Sigma Nu in 1973 to form society for men and women. Exec. Dir., Peg Fennig.

Delta Epsilon Sigma (1939): Barry University, 11300 NE Second Ave., Miami Shores, FL 33161, (305) 899-3020, socrates.barry.edu\des. National scholastic honor society for students, faculty and alumni of colleges and universities with a Catholic tradition. *Delta Epsilon Sigma Journal*, three times a year. Membership: 60,000 in 116 chapters. Sec., Dr. J. Patrick Lee.

Kappa Gamma Pi (1926): KGP National Office, 10215 Chardon Rd., Chardon, OH, 44024-9700; (440) 286-3764, www.kappagammapi.org. A national Catholic college honor society for graduates who, in addition to academic excellence, have shown outstanding leadership in extra-curricular activities. *Kappa Gamma Pi News*, five times a year. Membership: more than 37,000 in 139 colleges; 20 alumnae chapters in metropolitan areas. Nat. Exec. Sec., Christine Walick.

Phi Kappa Theta: 3901 W. 86th St., Suite 425, Indianapolis, IN 46268. National social fraternity with a Catholic heritage. Merger (1959) of Phi Kappa Fraternity, founded at Brown University in 1889, and Theta Kappa Phi Fraternity, founded at Lehigh University in 1919. *The Temple Magazine*, semi-annually, and newsletters. Membership: 2,800 undergraduate and 50,500 alumni in 63 collegiate and 40 alumni chapters. Exec. Dir., Mark T. McSweeney.

National Catholic Student Coalition (1988); 6801 N. Yates Rd., Box 90A, Milwaukee, WI 53217, (414) 410-4251. National coalition of Catholic campus ministry groups at public and private institutions of higher education. Formed after National Newman Club Federation and the National Federation of Catholic College Students dissolved in the 1960s. The U.S. affiliate of Pax Romana-IMCS (see International Catholic Organizations). *The Catholic Collegian*, four times a year. Membership: 200 campus groups. Exec. Dir., Jamie Williams.

ASSOCIATIONS, MOVEMENTS, SOCIETIES IN THE U.S.

(*Principal source*: Catholic Almanac *survey*.)

Academy of American Franciscan History (1944): 1712 Euclid Ave., Berkeley, CA 94709, (510) 548-1755, www.aafh.org. To encourage the study of the Franciscan Order in the New World. Dir., Dr. John F. Schwaller.

Adoremus-Society for the Renewal of the Sacred Liturgy (1995): P.O. Box 3286, St. Louis, MO 63130, (314) 863-8385, www.adoremus.org. Promotes authentic renewal of Catholic liturgy in accordance with the Second vatican Council's Constitution of the sacred Liturgy, *Sacrosanctum Concilium*. Publishes *Adoremus Bulletin,* 10 times a year; editor, Helen Hull Hitchcock.

Aid to the Church in Need (1947): U.S. office, 378 Broome St., 3rd Floor, NY, NY, 10013, (212) 334-5340; www.acnusa.org. Assists the pastoral activities of the church in Third World countries, Eastern Europe and the former Soviet Union. *Mirror,* newsletter, 9 times a year. Pres./Exec. Dir., Joseph Donnelly.

Albanian Catholic Institute "Daniel Dajani, S.J." (1992): Xavier Hall, University of San Francisco, San Francisco, CA 94117; (415) 422-6966. To assist the rebuilding of the Catholic Church in Albania and to promote the dissemination of knowledge of Albania's national, religious and cultural heritage. Founder, Gjon Sinishta (1930-95) in memory of the martyr Daniel Dajani (d. 1946). Exec. Dir., Raymond Frost; Jesuit Community Liaison, Paul Bernardicou, S.J.

American Benedictine Academy (1947): Saint Meinrad Archabbey, 1 Hill Dr. Saint Meinrad, IN, 47577; (812) 357-6644. To promote Benedictine values in contemporary culture. Pres., Eugene Hensell, O.S.B.

American Catholic Correctional Chaplains Association (1952): 13934 Lemoli Ave., Hawthorne, CA 90250; (310) 676-2038. Pres., Rev. Mark Santo.

American Catholic Historical Association (1919): The Catholic University of America, Washington, DC 20064; (202) 319-5079. *The Catholic Historical Review*, quarterly. Sec.-Treas., Rev. Msgr. Robert Trisco.

American Catholic Philosophical Association (1926): Fordham University, 441 E. Fordham Rd., Bronx, NY, 10458, (718) 817-3295, www.acpa-main.org. *American Catholic Philosophical Quarterly*; *Proceedings*, annually.

American Committee on Italian Migration (1952): 352 W. 44th St., New York, NY 10036; (212) 5419; www.acimny.org. *ACIM Newsletter* and *ACIM Nuova Via*, 6 times a year.

American Friends of the Vatican Library (1981): 157 Lakeshore Rd., Grosse Point Farms, MI 48236. Sponsored by the Catholic Library Association. To assist in supporting the Vatican Library. *AMICI*, newsletter.

Ancient Order of Hibernians in America, Inc. (1836): 31 Logan St., Auburn, NY 13021. 120,000 members. *National Hibernian Digest*, bimonthly. Nat. Sec., Thomas McNabb.

Apostleship of Prayer (1844, France; 1861, U.S.): 3 Stephen Ave., New Hyde Park, NY 11040. Promotes Daily Offering and Sacred Heart devotion. Nat. Dir., Rev. John H. Rainaldo, S.J.

Apostolate for Family Consecration (1975): 3375 County Rd. 36, Bloomingdale, OH 43910; (740) 765-5500, www.familyland.org. Pope John Paul II Holy Family Center, known as Catholic Familyland, Pres., Jerome F. Coniker. To transform families and parishes and nourish families through the Catholic faith.

Archconfraternity of Christian Mothers (Christian Mothers) (1881): 220 37th St., Pittsburgh, PA 15201; (412) 683-2400; over 3,500 branches. Dir., Rev. Bertin Roll, O.F.M. Cap.

Archconfraternity of the Holy Ghost (1912): Holy Ghost Fathers, 2401 Bristol Pike, Bensalem, PA 19020, (215) 638-0232 (U.S. headquarters), Rev. Albert M. Seichepine, C.S.Sp.

Archdiocese for the Military Services Seminary Education Fund (1988): P.O. Box 4469, Washington, D.C., 20017-0469, (202) 269-9100, www.milarch.org.

Association for Spiritual, Ethical, and Religious Values in Counseling (ASERVIC): Dept. of Educational Psychology and Special Education, Southern Illinois University at Carbondale, Carbondale, IL 62901. Division of the American Counseling Association. *Counseling and Values*, 3 times a year.

Association for Social Economics (formerly the Catholic Economic Association) (1941): Marquette University, Milwaukee, WI 53233. 1,300 members. *Review of Social Economy*, quarterly.

Association of Catholic Diocesan Archivists (1979): 711 W. Monroe, Chicago, IL 60661; (312) 831-0711. To work for establishment of an archival program in every American diocese. *ACDA Bulletin*, quarterly. Pres., Charles Nolan.

Association of Marian Helpers (1944): Eden Hill, 2 Prospect Rd., Stockbridge, MA 01263; (413) 298-3691; www.marian.org; 900,000, mostly in U.S. To promote vocations to Church service and support worldwide apostolates of Marians of the Immaculate Conception. Exec. Dir., Rev. Joseph, M.I.C. *Marian Helpers Bulletin*, quarterly.

Assumption Guild — Mass Cards: 330 Market St., Brighton, MA 02135, (617) 783-0495, www.masscardsaa.com.

Beginning Experience (1974): International Ministry Center, 1247 171st Plc., Hammond, IN 46324; (219) 989-8915. Adult and youth programs to help divorced, widowed and separated start a new beginning in their lives. Pres., Kathleen Murphy.

The Blue Army of Our Lady of Fatima, USA (1947): P.O. Box 976, Washington, NJ 07882-0976; (908) 689-1701; www.bluearmy.com. U.S. branch of the World Apostolate of Fatima. Promote the Fatima Message. Fatima shrine; *Soul*, bimonthly; *Hearts Aflame*, quarterly. Nat. Pres., Most Rev. James S. Sullivan.

Calix Society (1947): 2555 Hazelwood St., St. Paul, MN 55109; Association of Catholic alcoholics maintaining their sobriety through 12-step program. Pres. Jim Billigmeier

Canon Law Society of America (1939): Catholic University, Caldwell Hall, 431, Washington, DC 20064; (202) 269-3491; www.clsa.org. To further research and study in canon law; 1,600 members. Exec. Coord., Arthur J. Espelage, O.F.M.

Cardinal Mindszenty Foundation (CMF) (1958): P.O. Box 11321, St. Louis, MO 63105, (314) 727-6279, www.mindszenty.org. To uphold and defend the Catholic Church, family life and freedom for all under God. *The Mindszenty Report*, monthly. Pres., Eleanor Schlafly.

Catholic Aid Association (1878): 3499 N. Lexington Ave. North, St. Paul, MN 55126, (651) 490-0170, www.catholicaid.com. Fraternal life insurance society. *Catholic Aid News*, monthly. Chairman of the Board and CEO, Michael McGovern.

Catholic Alumni Clubs International (1957): P.O. Box 2412, Youngstown, OH 44509. To advance social, cultural and spiritual well-being of members. Membership limited to single Catholics with professional education. 7,500 members in 48 clubs in U.S. Pres., Patricia Keller.

Catholic Answers (1982): 2020 Gillespie Way, El Cajon, CA 92020, (619) 387-7200, www.catholic.com. Apologetics and evangelization organization. *This Rock*, monthly. Founder and dir., Karl Keating.

Catholic Biblical Association of America (1936): The Catholic University of America, Washington, DC 20064, (202) 319-5519, www.cba.cua.edu. *The Catholic Biblical Quarterly*, *Old Testament Abstracts*, *CBQ* monograph series. Exec. Sec., Joseph Jensen, O.S.B.

Catholic Book Publishers Association, Inc. (1987): 8404 Jamesport Dr., Rockford, IL 61108; (815) 332-3245; www.cbpa.org. Exec. Dir., Terry Wessels.

Catholic Coalition on Preaching: Madonna University, 36600 Schoolcraft Rd. Livonia, MI 48150-1173; (734) 432-5538. Pres., Rev. Francis Tebbe, O.F.M.

Catholic Commission on Intellectual and Cultural Affairs (CCICA) (1946): LaSalle University, Philadelphia, PA 19141; 350 members. Exec. Dir., Bro. Daniel Burke, F.S.C.

Catholic Committee of Appalachia (1970): P.O. Box 662, Wheeling, WV 26288. Exec. Coord., Todd Garland.

Catholic Daughters of the Americas (1903): 10 W. 71st St., New York, NY 10023; (212) 877-3041; www.catholicdaughters.org. 125,000 members. *Share Magazine*. Nat. Regent, Eunice Riles.

Catholic Familyland (1975): 3375 County Rd. 36, Bloomingdale, OH 43910; (740) 765-5500, www.familyland.org. Canonically named the John Paul II Holy Family Center; functions under the auspices of the Apostolate for Family Consecration. Pres., Jerome F. Coniker.

Catholic Golden Age (1975): P.O. Box 3658, Scranton, PA 18505-0658; (800) 836-5699. *CGA World*, quarterly. For Catholics over 50 years of age.

Catholic Guardian Society (1913): 1011 First Ave., New York, NY 10022, (212) 371-1000. Exec. Dir., John J. Frein.

Catholic Home Bureau (1899): 1011 First Ave., New York, NY 10022, (212) 371-1000, www.catholichomebureau.com. Exec. Dir., Philip Georgini.

Catholic Home Study Service (1936): P.O. Box 363, Perryville, MO 63775, (573) 547-4084, www.amm.org/chss.htm. Provides instruction in the Catholic faith by mail free of charge. Dir., Rev. Oscar Lukefahr, C.M.

Catholic Interracial Council of New York, Inc. (1934): 899 Tenth Ave., New York, NY 10019; (212) 237-8600; www.amm.org/chss.htm. To promote racial and social justice.

Catholic Knights of America (1877): Publication Office, 1850 Dalton St., Cincinnati, OH 45214. 7,800 members. Fraternal insurance society. *C K of A Journal*, monthly.

Catholic Knights of Ohio (1891): 22005 Mastick Rd., Fairview Park, OH 44126; 8,000 in Ohio and Kentucky. Fraternal insurance society. Pres., Victor D. Huss. *The Messenger*, monthly.

Catholic Kolping Society of America (1849): 9 East 8th St., Clifton, NJ 07011-1101. International society concerned with spiritual and educational development of members. *Kolping Banner*, monthly.

Catholic Lawyers' Guild: Organization usually on a diocesan basis, under different titles.

Catholic League for Religious Assistance to Poland (1943): 984 N. Milwaukee Ave., Chicago, IL 60622-4199. Exec. Dir., Most Rev. Thad Jakubowski.

Catholic League for Religious and Civil Rights (1973): 450 Seventh Ave., 34th Floor, New York, NY 10123; (212) 371-3191; www.catholicleague.org; local chapters throughout U.S. Serves Catholic community as an anti-defamation and civil rights agency. *Catalyst*, league journal. Pres., William A. Donohue.

Catholic Library Association (1921): 100 North St., Suite 224, Pittsfield, MA 01201-5109; (413) 442-2252; www.cathla.org. *Catholic Library World*, *Catholic Periodical and Literature Index*, quarterlies. Exec.Dir., Jean R. Bostley, S.S.J.

Catholic Marketing Network (1955): 7750 N. MacArthur Blvd., Suite 120, PMB 323, Irving, TX 75063; (800) 506-6333, www.catholicmarketing.com.

A trade associaton founded to encourage the most effective production and distribution of Catholic goods and provide a common forum for mutual interchange of ideas. *Catholic Marketing Network*, quarterly. Exec. Dir., Cherylann Tucker.

Catholic Near East Welfare Association (1926): 1011 First Ave., Suite 1552, New York, NY 10022; (212) 826-1480, www.cnewa.org. A papal agency for humanitarian and pastoral support serving the churches and peoples of the Middle East, Northeast Africa, India and Eastern Europe, with offices in New York, Vatican City, Addis Ababa, Amman, Jerusalem and Beirut. Pres., Cardinal Edward Egan; Sec. Gen., Msgr. Robert L. Stern.

Catholic Order of Foresters (1883): 355 Shuman Blvd., P.O. Box 3012, Naperville, IL 60566, (800) 552-0145, www.catholicforester.com. 136,685 members. Fraternal insurance society. *The Catholic Forester*, bimonthly. High Chief Ranger, Robert Ciesla.

Catholic Press Association of the U.S. and Canada, Inc. (1911): 3555 Veterans Memorial Highway, Unit O, Ronkonkoma, NY 11779; (631) 471-4730, www.catholicpress.org. *The Catholic Journalist*, monthly; *Catholic Press Directory*, annually. Pres., Christopher J. Gunty; Exec. Dir., Owen P. McGovern.

Catholic Theological Society of America (1946), John Carroll University, 20700 North Park Blvd., University Hgts., OH, 44118, (216) 397-1631, www.bc.edu/ctsa. *Proceedings*, annually. Exec. Sec., Dolores Christie.

Catholic Union of Texas, The K.J.T. (1889): 214 E. Colorado St., La Grange, TX 78945, (979) 968-5877, www.kjtnet.org. 18,226 members. Fraternal and insurance society. *Nasinec*, weekly, and *K. J. T. News*, monthly. Pres., Elo J. Goerig.

Catholic War Veterans (1935): 441 N. Lee St., Alexandria, VA 22314, (703) 549-3622, www.cwv.org. 500 posts. *Catholic War Veteran*, bimonthly.

Catholic Worker Movement (1933): 36 E. 1st St., New York, NY 10003. Lay apostolate founded by Peter Maurin and Dorothy Day; has Houses of Hospitality in over 60 U.S. cities and several communal farms in various parts of the country. Promotes the practice of the works of mercy, nonviolence, personalism, voluntary poverty. *The Catholic Worker*, 8 times a year.

Catholic Workman (Katolicky Delnik) (1891): 111 West Main St., New Prague, MN 56071; (612) 758-2229. 16,405 members. Fraternal and insurance society. *Catholic Workman*, monthly.

Catholics Against Capital Punishment (1992), P.O. Box 5706, Bethesda, MD 20824; (301) 652-1125; www.igc.org/cacp. Promotes greater awareness of papal and episcopal statements against the death penalty. *CACP News Notes*, bimonthly. Nat. Coord., Frank McNeirney.

Catholics United for the Faith (1968): 827 N. Fourth St., Steubenville, OH 43952; (800) 639-8424. 23,000 members worldwide. Lay apostolic group concerned with spiritual and doctrinal formation of members. *Lay Witness*, monthly. Pres., Chris Erickson, Dir. of Communications.

Center of Concern (1971): 1225 Otis St., N.E., Washington, DC 20017; (202) 635-2757; www.coc.org. Exec. Dir., James E. Hug.

Central Association of the Miraculous Medal (1915): 475 E. Chelten Ave., Philadelphia, PA 19144; (800) 523-3674; www.cmphila.org/camm. *Miracu-*

lous Medal, quarterly. Dir., Rev. William J. O'Brien, C.M.

Chaplains' Aid Association, Inc. (1917): 3311 Toledo Terrace, Hyattsville, MD 20780. To receive and administer funds toward education of seminarians to become priest-chaplains in military services.

Christian Foundation for Children and Aging: One Elmwood Ave., Kansas City, KS 66103; (913) 384-6500; www.cfcausa.org. Grassroots movement dedicated to improving through sponsorship the lives of children and aging at Catholic mission sites around the world. Exec. Dir., Louis Finocchario.

Christophers, Inc., The (1945): 12 E. 48th St., New York, NY 10017; (212) 759-4050; www.christophers.org. Founded by Rev. James Keller, M.M. The Christophers stimulate personal initiative and responsible action in line with Judeo-Christian principles through broadcast of Christopher radio and TV programs; free distribution of *Christopher News Notes*, ten times a year; publication of a weekly Christopher column in over 200 newspapers; Spanish literature; annual media awards; youth outreach. Dir., Msgr. James P. Lisante.

Citizens for Educational Freedom (1959): 921 S. Walter Reed Dr., Suite 1, Arlington, VA 22204. Nonsectarian group concerned with parents' right to educational choice by means of tuition tax credits and vouchers. Exec. Dir., Patrick J. Reilly.

Confraternity of Bl. Junipero Serra (1989): P.O. Box 7125, Mission Hills, CA 91346; 3,500 in U.S. and foreign countries. Founded in Monterey (CA) diocese to help promote process of canonization of Bl. Junipero Serra and increase spiritual development of members. Dir., Rev. Thomas L. Davis, Jr.; Spiritual Dir., Rev. Noel F. Moholy, O.F.M.

Confraternity of Catholic Clergy (1976): 4445 W. 64th St., Chicago, IL 60629, (773) 581-8904. Association of priests pledged to pursuit of personal holiness, loyalty to the Pope, theological study and adherence to authentic teachings of the Catholic faith. Sec., Rev. L. Dudley Day, O.S.A.

Confraternity of Christian Doctrine, Inc.: 3211 Fourth St., N.E., Washington, DC 20017; (202) 541-3098, www.usccb.org. A distinct entity, separately incorporated and directed by a Board of Trustees from the United States Catholic Conference of Bishops. Its purpose is to foster and promote the teaching of Christ as understood and handed down by the Roman Catholic Church. To this end it licenses use of the Lectionary for Mass and the *New American Bible* (NAB), the Revised Psalms of the NAB and the Revised New Testament of the NAB, translations made from the original languages in accordance with the papal encyclical *Divino Afflante Spiritu* (1943) of Pope Pius XII.

Confraternity of the Immaculate Conception of Our Lady of Lourdes (1874): Box 561, Notre Dame, IN 46556. Distributors of Lourdes water.

Confraternity of the Most Holy Rosary: See **Dominican Rosary Apostolate.**

Couple to Couple League (1971), P.O. Box 111184, Cincinnati, OH 45211; (513) 471-2000, www.ccli.org. Founded to teach and promote marital chastity through Natural Family Planning. Exec. Dir., Mark Hayden.

Courage (1980): c/o St. John the Baptist Church and Friary, 210 West 31st St., New York, NY 10001; (212) 268-1010; www.couragerc.org. Ministry to men and women who experience same-sex attractions and desire to live Christian chastity in accordance with the teachings of the Catholic Church. Newsletter, 4 times a year. Nat. Dir., Rev. John F. Harvey, O.S.F.S.

CUSA (Catholics United for Spiritual Action, Inc.) — An Apostolate of the Sick or Disabled (1947): 176 W. 8th St., Bayonne, NJ, 07002-1227, (201) 437-0412, www.cusan.org. A group-correspondence apostolate for the disabled and chronically ill. Admin. Ms. Anna Marie Sopko.

Damien-Dutton Society for Leprosy Aid, Inc. (1944): 616 Bedford Ave., Bellmore, NY 11710; (516) 221-5829. 25,000 members. Provides medicine, rehabilitation and research for conquest of leprosy. *Damien Dutton Call*, quarterly. Pres., Howard E. Crouch; Vice Pres., Elizabeth Campbell.

Daughters of Isabella (1897): P.O. Box 9585, New Haven, CT 06535. 100,000 members. To unite Catholic women into a fraternal order for spiritual benefits and to promote higher ideals within society.

Disaster Response Office (1990): Catholic Charities USA, 1731 King St., Suite 200, Alexandria, VA 22314; (703) 549-1390; www.catholiccharitiesusa.org. Promotes and facilitates Catholic disaster response in the U.S. Dir., Jane A. Gallagher.

Dominican Rosary Apostolate (1806): 141 E. 65th St., New York, NY 10021. Dir., Rev. Edward L. Martin, O.P.

Edith Stein Guild, Inc. (1955): Church of St. John the Baptist, 210 W. 31st St., New York, NY 10001-2876, (212) 564-9070. Assists and encourages Jewish Catholics; fosters among Catholics a better understanding of their Jewish heritage; promotes spread of knowledge of life and writings of Bl. Edith Stein; fosters better understanding between Jews and Christians and supports the Church's spirit of ecumenism. Pres., Mrs. Cabiria Nardiello; Liaison, Rev. Philip F. Romano, O.F.M. Cap.

Enthronement of the Sacred Heart in the Home (1907): P.O. Box 111, Fairhaven, MA 02719; (508) 999-2680.

Federation of Diocesan Liturgical Commissions (FDLC) (1969): P.O. Box 29039, Washington, DC 20017; (202) 635-6990; www.fdlc.org. Voluntary association of personnel from diocesan liturgical commissions and worship offices. The main purpose is promotion of the liturgy as the heart of Christian life, especially in the parish community. Exec. Dir., Rev. Michael J. Spillane.

Federation of Seminary Spiritual Directors (1972): c/o Sacred Heart Major Seminary, 2701 Chicago Blvd., Detroit, MI, 48206; (313) 883-8540. Responsible for priestly spiritual formation in high school and college seminaries, novitiates, theologates and houses of formation in the U.S. Pres., Dan Trapp.

Fellowship of Catholic Scholars (1977): 124 Law School, Notre Dame, IN 46556; (219) 631-8385; 1,000 members. Interdisciplinary research and publications of Catholic scholars in accord with the magisterium of the Catholic Church. Pres., Prof. Gerard V. Bradley.

First Catholic Slovak Ladies' Association, USA (1892): 24950 Chagrin Blvd., Beachwood, OH 44122, (800) 464-4642, www.fcsla.com. 102,000 members.

Fraternal insurance society. *Fraternally Yours*, monthly. Pres., Mary Ann Johanek.

First Catholic Slovak Union (Jednota) (1890): FCSU Corporate Center, 6611 Rockside Rd., Independence, OH 44131, (216) 642-9406, www.fcsu.com. 96,206 members. *Jednota*, biweekly. Nat. Sec., Kenneth A. Arendt.

Foundation for the Family (1986): P.O. Box 111184, Cincinnati, OH 45211; (513) 471-2000, www.ccli.org. Established by Couple to Couple League (see entry above) to provide materials for family not relating to Natural Family Planning, Exec. Dir., Mark Hayden.

Foundations and Donors Interested in Catholic Activities, Inc. (FADICA) (1976): 1350 Connecticut Ave. N.W., Suite 303, Washington, DC 20036; (202) 223-3550; www.FADICA.org. A consortium of private foundations providing continuing education and research to members to make church-related philanthropy more effective. Pres., Francis J. Butler.

Franciscan Apostolate of the Way of the Cross (1949): P.O. Box 23, Boston, MA 02112, (617) 542-6659. Distributes religious materials to the sick and shut-in. Dir., Rev. Robert Lynch, O.F.M.

Free The Fathers (1983): 845 Oak St. Chattanooga, TN 37403; (423) 756-9660, www.ftf.org. To work for the freedom of bishops and priests imprisoned in China. Pres., John M. Davies.

Friends of the Holy Land, Inc. (1974): 347 Mile Square Rd., Yonkers, NY 10701; 300 members. To provide spiritual and material support for the Christian communities in the Holy Land. *Friends of the Holy Land Newsletter*. Gen. Dir., Ernest F. Russo.

Gabriel Richard Institute (1949): 3641 Estates Dr., Troy, MI 48084; (800) 382-8609. Conducts Christopher Leadership Course. Exec. Dir., Dolores Ammar.

Guard of Honor of the Immaculate Heart of Mary (1932): 135 West 31st St., New York, NY 10001, (212) 736-8500, www.friars.org. An archconfraternity approved by the Holy See whose members cultivate devotion to the Blessed Virgin Mary, particularly through a daily Guard Hour of Prayer. Dir., Rev. Cassian A. Miles, O.F.M.

Holy Cross Family Ministries (formerly The Family Rosary, Inc.) (1942): 518 Washington St., North Easton, MA, 02356-1200, (508) 238-4095, www.hcfm.org. Founded by Father Patrick Peyton, C.S.C. Encourages family prayer, especially the Rosary. Pres., Rev. John Phalen, C.S.C.

Holy Name Society: Founded in 1274 by Blessed John Vercelli, master general of the Dominicans, to promote reverence of the Holy Name of Jesus; this is still the principal purpose of the society, which also develops lay apostolic programs in line with directives of the Second Vatican Council. Introduced in the U.S. in 1870-71 by Dominican Father Charles H. McKenna, the society has about 5 million members on diocesan and parochial levels. With approval of the local bishop and pastor, women as well as men may be members.

Holy Name Society, National Association (NAHNS) (1970): P.O. Box 12012, Baltimore, MD 21281, (410) 276-1166, www.members.aol.com/nahns. Association of diocesan and parochial Holy Name Societies. *Holy Name Newsletter*, monthly.

Hungarian Catholic League of America, Inc. (1945): One Cathedral Sq., Providence, RI 02903; (401) 278-4520. Chair., Rev. Msgr. William I. Varsanyi.

International Catholic Stewardship Council (1962): 1275 K St. N.W., Suite 980, Washington, DC 20005-4006; (202) 289-1093, www.catholic stewardship.org. A professional association which fosters an environment in which stewardship is understood, accepted and practiced throughout the church. Nat. Dir., Matthew R. Paratore.

International Catholic Charismatic Renewal Services: Palazzo della Cancelleria, 00120 Vatican City; 39 06 698 87538; www.iccrs.org. The ICCRS provides leadership and vision to the Catholic Charismatic Renewal throughout the world in harmony with the Pontifical Council for the Laity which has established ICCRS as a Private Association of the Faithful. See also National Catholic Charismatic Renewal Services below.

Italian Catholic Federation (1924): 675 Hegenberger Rd., #110, Oakland, CA 94621; (888) 426-1924; www.home.earthlink.net/~icf1924.19,000 members. Fraternal organization of Italian-American Catholics.

John Carroll Society, The (1951): P.O. Box 50188, Washington, DC 20091, (703) 573-3043.

Judean Society, Inc., The (1966): 1075 Space Park Way No. 336, Mt. View, CA 94043.

Knights of Peter Claver (1909), and **Knights of Peter Claver, Ladies Auxiliary** (1926): 1825 Orleans Ave., New Orleans, LA 70116, (504) 821-4225, www.knightsofpeterclaver.com. Fraternal and aid society. *The Claverite*, biannually. National Chaplain, Most Rev. Curtis J. Guillory, S.V.D.

Knights of St. John, International Supreme Commandery (1886): 89 So. Pine Ave., Albany, N.Y. 12208; (518) 453-5675, www.members.tripod.com/ksji/knights/ksji.html. Supreme Sec., Maj. Gen. Joseph Hauser, Jr.

Ladies of Charity of the United States of America (1960): P.O. Box 31697, St. Louis, MO 63131; (314) 821-1296; 25,000 in U.S.; 250,000 worldwide. International Association founded by St. Vincent de Paul in 1617.

Latin Liturgy Association (1975): 3074 Hylan Blvd., Staten Island, NY 10306, (718) 979-6685, www.latinliturgy.com. 850 members. To promote the use of the Latin language and music in the approved rites of the Church. Quarterly journal. Chair., William J. Leininger.

Legatus (1987): 30 Frank Lloyd Wright Dr., P.O. Box 997, Ann Arbor, MI 48106; (734) 930-3854. To apply Church's moral teaching in business and personal lives of members. *Legatus Newsletter*, monthly.

Lithuanian Groups: **Ateitininkai**, members of **Lithuanian Catholic Federation Ateitis** (1910), 1209 Country Lane, Lemont, IL 60439. *Ateitis*, bimonthly. Pres., Juozas Polikaitis. **Knights of Lithuania** (1913): Roman Catholic educational-fraternal organization. *Vytis*, monthly. Pres., Evelyn Ozelis, 2533 W. 45th St., Chicago, IL 60632. **Lithuanian Catholic Alliance** (1886), 71-73 S.

Washington St., Wilkes-Barre, PA 18701. Fraternal insurance organization. Pres., Thomas E. Mack.

Lithuanian Roman Catholic Federation of America (1906): 4545 W. 63rd St., Chicago, IL 60629; (312) 585-9500. Umbrella organization for Lithuanian parishes and organizations. *The Observer*, bimonthly. Pres., Saulius Kuprys.

Lithuanian Roman Catholic Priests' League (1909): P.O. Box 1025, Humarock, MA 02047-1025, (781) 834-4079. Religious-professional association. Pres., Rev. Albert Contons.

Lithuanian Catholic Religious Aid, Inc. (1961): 351 Highland Blvd., Brooklyn, NY 11207, (718) 827-7932. To assist Catholics in Lithuania. Chairman and Pres., Most Rev. Paul Baltakis, O.F.M.

Little Flower Mission League (1957), P.O. Box 25, Plaucheville, LA 71362; (318) 922-3630. Sponsored by the Brothers of the Holy Eucharist. Dir., Bro. André M. Lucia, F.S.E.

Little Flower Society (1923): 1313 Frontage Rd. Darien, IL 60561. 200,000 members. Nat. Dir., Rev. Robert E. Colaresi, O. Carm.

Liturgical Conference, The: 415 Michigan Ave., NE, #65, Washington, DC 20017, (202) 832-6520, www.litconf.org. Liturgy, homily service. Education, research and publication programs for renewing and enriching Christian liturgical life. Ecumenical.

Loyal Christian Benefit Association (1890): P.O. Box 13005, Erie, PA 16514. Fraternal benefit and insurance society. *The Fraternal Leader*, quarterly.

Marian Movement of Priests (1972): P.O. Box 8, St. Francis, ME 04774-0008 (U.S.); (207) 398-3375; www.mmp-usa.net. International headquarters, Via Mercalli, 23, 20122 Milan, Italy. 4,000 clergy, 53,000 religious and laity (U.S.). Spiritual renewal through consecration to the Immaculate Heart of Mary. Nat. Dir., Rev. Albert G. Roux.

Mariological Society of America (1949): Marian Library, Box 1390, University of Dayton, Dayton, OH 45469; (937) 229-4294. Founded by Rev. Juniper B. Carol, O.F.M., to promote greater appreciation of and scientific research in Marian theology. *Marian Studies*, annually. Sec., Rev. Thomas A. Thompson, S.M.

Marriage Encounter, National: 4704 Jamerson Pl., Orlando, FL 32807. The national office of Worldwide Marriage Encounter is located at 2210 East Highland Ave., #106, San Bernardino, CA 92404; (909) 863-9963. Brings couples together for a weekend program of events directed by a team of several couples and a priest, to develop their abilities to communicate with each other as husband and wife.

Maryheart Crusaders, The (1964): 22 Button St., Meriden, CT 06450; (203) 239-5979, www.maryheartcrusaders.org. Pres., Louise D'Angelo.

Men of the Sacred Heart (1964): National Shrine of the Sacred Heart, P.O. Box 500, Harleigh, PA 18225, (570) 455-1162. Promotes enthronement of Sacred Heart.

Militia Immaculate National Center — Marytown (1917): 1600 W. Park Ave., Libertyville, IL 60048, (847) 367-7800, www.consecration.com. Canonically established with international headquarters in Rome. A pious association for evangelization and catechesis beginning with members' own total consecration to the Immaculate Virgin Mary.

Missionary Association of Catholic Women (1916): 3501 S. Lake Dr., P.O. Box 07212, Milwaukee, WI 53207-0912; (414) 769-3406.

Missionary Vehicle Association, Inc. (MIVA America) (1971): 1400 Michigan Ave., N.E., Washington, DC 20017-7234; (202) 635-3444; MIVAmerica@aol.com. To raise funds and distribute them annually as vehicle grants to missionaries working with the poor in Third World countries. Nat. Dir., Rev. Philip De Rea, M.S.C.; Exec. Dir., Rev. Anthony F. Krisak.

Morality in Media, Inc. (1962): 475 Riverside Dr., New York, NY 10115; (212) 870-3222; www.moralityinmedia.org. Interfaith national organization. Works by constitutional means to curb the explosive growth of hard-core pornography and to turn back the tide of grossly offensive, indecent media. A major project is the National Obscenity Law Center which provides legal information for prosecutors and other attorneys. Newsletter, bimonthly. Pres., Robert W. Peters.

National Assembly of Religious Women (NARW): 529 S. Wabash Ave., Suite 404, Chicago, IL 60605; (312) 663-1980. Founded as the National Assembly of Women Religious, 1970; title changed, 1980. A movement of feminist women committed to prophetic tasks of giving witness, raising awareness and engaging in public action and advocacy for justice in church and society.

National Association for Lay Ministry (1977): 5420 S. Cornell Ave., Chicago, IL 60615; (773) 241-6050; www.nalm.org. Acts as advocate and support for lay people who respond to a call to ministry in the Church.

National Association of Catholic Family Life Ministers: University of Dayton, 300 College Park, Dayton, OH 45469; (937) 229-3324, www.nacflm.org. Strives to be a voice and advocate for families and family ministry in Church and society. Co-Pres., Butch and Linda Moses.

National Association of Catholic Home Educators (1993): 6102 Saints Hill Lane, Broad Run, VA 20137, (540) 349-4314; www.nache.com. Promotion of home-schooling. *The Catholic Home Educator*, quarterly.

National Association of Church Personnel Administrators (1971): 100 E. 8th St., Cincinnati, OH 45202; (513) 421-3134; www.nacpa.org. Association for human resource and personnel directors dedicated to promotion and development of just personnel practices for all church employees. Exec. Dir., Sr. Ellen Doyle, O.S.U.

National Association of Diaconate Directors: 1204 N. Church St., Rockford, IL 61103; (815) 965-0075. Deacon Thomas C. Welch, Exec. Dir.

National Association of Diocesan Ecumenical Officers: 7800 Kenrick Rd., St. Louis, MO 63119, (314) 961-4320. Network of Catholics involved in ecumenical and interreligious work. Pres., Vincent A. Heier.

National Association of Pastoral Musicians (1976): 225 Sheridan St. N.W., Washington, DC 20011; (202) 723-5800, www.npm.org. 9,000 members. Dedicated to fostering the art of musical liturgy. *Pastoral Music*, six times a year. Exec. Dir., Dr. J. Michael McMahon.

National Association of Priest Pilots (1964): 481 N. Shore Dr., Apt. 301, Clear Lake IA, 50428-1368, (641) 435-2070. Pres., Rev. John Hemann.

National Catholic AIDS Network: P.O. Box 422984, San Francisco, CA 94142; (707) 874-3031; www.ncan.org. Exec. dir., Rev. Rodney DeMartini; Board Pres., Rev. Robert J. Vitillo.

National Catholic Band Association (1953): 3334 N. Normandy, Chicago, IL 60634, (773) 282-9153.

National Catholic Cemetery Conference (1949): 710 N. River Rd., Des Plaines, IL 60016; (847) 824-8131. Exec. Dir., Irene K. Pesce.

National Catholic Charismatic Renewal Services: P.O. Box 628, Locust Grove, VA 22508; (800) 338-2445; www.iccrs.org. The mission of the National Service Committee is "to stir into flame the grace of Pentecost within and beyond the Church, to broaden and deepen the understanding that baptism in the Holy Spirit is the Christian inheritance of all, and to strengthen the Catholic Charismatic Renewal."

National Catholic Conference for Interracial Justice (NCCIJ) (1960): 1200 Varnum St. N.E., Washington, DC 20017; (202) 529-6480. Exec. Dir., Rev. Mr. Joseph M. Conrad, Jr.

National Catholic Conference for Seafarers: 4219 Constance St., New Orleans, LA 70115; (504) 891-6677. Association of chaplains and laity serving in the pastoral care of seafarers.

National Catholic Conference of Airport Chaplains (1986): P.O. Box 66363, Chicago, IL 66363; (773) 686-2636. Provides support and communication for Catholics performing pastoral ministry to airport and airline workers and Catholic travelers; affiliated with Bishops' Committee on Migration, USCCB. Episcopal liaison, Most Rev. James C. Timlin. Pres., Rev. David J. Baratelli, Ed.S.

National Catholic Council on Alcoholism and Related Drug Problems, Inc.: P.O. Box 248, Lafayette, IN 47902; (765) 420-0129, www.ncca today.com. An affiliate of the USCCB. Committed to assisting members in a greater awareness of alcoholism, other chemical addictions and prevention issues.

National Catholic Development Conference (1968): 86 Front St., Hempstead, NY 11550; (516) 481-6000. Professional association of organizations and individuals engaged in raising funds for Catholic charitable activities. Pres., George T. Holloway.

National Catholic Ministry to the Bereaved (NCMB) (1990): 28700 Euclid Ave., Wickliffe, OH, 44092-2527, (440) 943-3480, www.griefwork.org. Offers ongoing education, resources and assistance to dioceses, parishes and caregivers in their ministry to the bereaved. Pres., Sr. Maureen O'Brien, O.P.

National Catholic Pharmacists Guild of the United States (1962): 1012 Surrey Hills Dr., St. Louis, MO 63117; (314) 645-0085. Publishes *The Catholic Pharmacist*. Co-Pres., Exec. Dir. and Editor, John P. Winkelmann.

National Catholic Society of Foresters (1891): 320 S. School St., Mt. Prospect, IL 60056; (847) 342-4500, www.ncsf@enteract.com. A fraternal insurance society. *National Catholic Forester*, quarterly. Pres. and CEO, Sue Koleczek.

National Catholic Women's Union (1916): 3835 Westminster Pl., St. Louis, MO 63108, www.social justice.org. 7,000 members.

National Center for the Laity (1977): P.O. Box

291102, Chicago, IL 60629; (773) 776-9036; www.laity-initiatives.org. To promote and implement the vision of Vatican II: That the laity are the Church in the modern world as they attend to their occupational, family and neighborhood responsibilities. *Initiatives*, six times a year.

National Center for Urban Ethnic Affairs (1971): P.O. Box 20, Cardinal Station, Washington, DC 20064; (202) 232-3600. Research and action related to the Church's concern for cultural pluralism and urban neighborhoods. An affiliate of the USCCB. Pres., Dr. John A. Kromkowski.

National Christ Child Society Inc. (1887): 5101 Wisconsin Ave. N.W., Suite 304, Washington, DC 20016; (800) 814-2149; www.NationalChrist ChildSoc.org. Founder, Mary V. Merrick. A non-profit Catholic association of volunteers of all denominations dedicated to the service of needy children and youth regardless of race or creed. Membership: approximately 7,000 adult members in 37 chapters in U.S. Exec. Dir., Margaret Saffell.

National Committee of Catholic Laymen, The (1977): 215 Lexington Ave., Fourth Floor, New York, NY 10016, (212) 685-6666. Lobbying and publishing organization representing "orthodox" Catholics who strongly support Pope John Paul II. *Catholic Eye*, monthly. Editor, Catholic Eye, Mrs. Anne Conlon.

National Conference of Catechetical Leadership (formerly, National Conference of Diocesan Directors of Religious Education) (1936): 3021 4th St. N.E., Washington, DC 20017; (202) 636-3826. 1,300 members. To promote catechetical ministry at the national diocesan and parish levels. Exec. Dir., Neil A. Parent.

National Conference of Diocesan Vocation Directors (NCDVD) (1961): P.O. Box 1570, Little River, SC 29566; (843) 280-7191. Professional organization for diocesan vocation personnel providing resources and on-going education in their promoting, assessing and forming of candidates for the diocesan priesthood.

National Council for Catholic Evangelization (1983): 905 E. 166th St., P.O. Box 1260, South Holland, IL 60473; (800) 786-NCCE. To promote evangelization as the "primary and essential mission of the Church," in accordance with *Evangelii Nuntiandi*, the 1975 apostolic exhortation of Pope Paul VI. Pres., Sr. Priscilla Lemire, R.J.M.

National Council of Catholic Men: 5664 Midforest Ln., Cincinnati, OH 45233. A federation of Catholic organizations through which Catholic men may be heard nationally on matters of common interest. NCCM is a constituent of the National Council of Catholic Laity.

National Council of Catholic Women (1920): 1275 K St. N.W., Suite 975, Washington, DC 20005; (202) 682-0334; www.nccw.org. A federation of some 7,000 organizations of Catholic women in the U.S. NCCW unites Catholic organizations and individual Catholic women of the U.S., develops their leadership potential, assists them to act upon current issues in the Church and society, provides a medium through which Catholic women may speak and act upon matters of common interest, and relates to other national and international organizations in the solution of present-day problems. It is an affiliate of the World Union of Catholic Women's Organizations. *Catholic Woman*, bimonthly. Exec. Dir., Annette P. Kane.

National Evangelization Teams (NET): 110 Crusader Ave., West St. Paul, MN 55118-4427; (651) 450-6833. Trains Catholic young adults to be evangelists to peers and high school/junior high youth through traveling retreat teams.

National Federation of Catholic Physicians' Guilds (1927): P.O. Box 757, Pewaukee, WI 53072; (262) 523-6201; www.cathmed.com. *Linacre Quarterly*. Exec. Dir., Robert H. Herzog.

National Federation of Priests' Councils (1968): 1337 West Ohio, Chicago, IL 60622-6490; (312) 226-3334; www.nfpc.org. To give priests' councils a representative voice in matters of presbyteral, pastoral and ministerial concern to the U.S. and the universal Church. Publishes *Touchstone*, quarterly, with a circulation of 25,000. Pres., Rev. Donald J. Wolf; Exec. Dir., Bro. Bernard Stratman, S.M.

National Institute for the Word of God (1972): 487 Michigan Ave. N.E., Washington, DC 20017; (202) 529-0001; www.niwg.op.org/niwg. For renewed biblical preaching, Bible sharing and evangelization. Dir., Rev. John Burke, O.P.

National Life Center, Inc.: 686 N. Broad St., Woodbury, NJ 08096; (856) 848-1819, (800) 848-LOVE, www.nationallifecenter.com. Interdenominational guidance and referral service organization offering pregnant women alternatives to abortion. Pres., Denise F. Cocciolone.

National Organization for Continuing Education of Roman Catholic Clergy, Inc. (1973): 1337 W. Ohio St., Chicago, IL 60622; (312) 226-1890. Membership: 152 dioceses, 66 religious provinces, 46 institutions, 49 individuals in U.S., 18 associates outside U.S. Pres., Rev. Francis S. Tebbe, O.F.M.

National Pastoral Life Center: 18 Bleecker St., New York, NY 10012-2404; (212) 431-7825, www.nplc.org. *Church*, quarterly. Dir., Msgr. Philip Murnion.

NETWORK, A Catholic Social Justice Lobby (1971): 801 Pennsylvania Ave. S.E., Suite 460, Washington, DC 20003; (202) 547-5556; www.network lobby.org. A national Catholic social justice lobby. *NETWORK Connection*, bimonthly. Nat. Coord., Kathy Thornton, R.S.M.

Nocturnal Adoration Society of the United States (1882): 184 E. 76th St., New York, NY 10021; (212) 288-5082. Nat. Dir., Rev. Mario Marzocchi, S.S.S.

North American Academy of Liturgy: c/o CSSR Executive Office, Valparaiso University, Valparaiso, IN 46383. Foster ecumenical and interreligious liturgical research, publication and dialogue on a scholarly level. *Proceedings*, annually. Pres., Alan Barthel.

North American Conference of Separated and Divorced Catholics (1972): P.O. Box 360, Richland, OR 97870; (541) 893-6089; www.nacsdc.com. Exec. Dir., Irene Varley.

North American Forum on the Catechumenate: 3033 Fourth St. NE, Washington, DC 20017; (202) 529-9493, www.naforum.org. An international network committed to the implementation of the Order of Christian Initiation of Adults. Exec. Dir., vacant.

Order of the Alhambra (1904): 4200 Leeds Ave., Baltimore, MD 21229; (410) 242-0660; www.Order Alhambra.org. 7,000 in U.S. and Canada. Fraternal society dedicated to assisting developmentally disabled and handicapped children. Supreme Commander, Angelo Miele.

Our Lady's Rosary Makers (1949): 4611 Poplar Level Rd., Louisville, KY 40233. 23,000 members. To supply missionaries with free rosaries for distribution throughout the world. *News Bulletin*, monthly. Pres., Michael Ford.

Paulist National Catholic Evangelization Association (1977): 3031 Fourth St., N.E., Washington, DC 20017-1102; (202) 832-5022; www.pncea.org. To work with unchurched and alienated Catholics; to develop, test and document contemporary ways in which Catholic parishes and dioceses can evangelize the unchurched and inactive Catholics. *Share the Word*, bimonthly magazine; *Evangelization Update*, bimonthly newsletter. Dir., Rev. Kenneth Boyack, C.S.P.

Philangeli (Friends of the Angels) (1949 in England; 1956 in U.S.): Viatorian Fathers, 1115 E. Euclid St., Arlington Heights, IL 60004.

Pious Union of Prayer (1898): St. Joseph's Home, P.O. Box 288, Jersey City, NJ 07303, (201) 798-4141. *St. Joseph's Messenger* and *Advocate of the Blind*, quarterly.

Polish Roman Catholic Union of America (1887): 984 N. Milwaukee Ave., Chicago, IL 60622; (773) 728-2600; www.prcua.org. *Narod Polski*, bimonthly. Fraternal benefit society.

Pontifical Mission for Palestine (1949): 1011 First Ave., New York, NY 10022, (212) 826-1480, www.cnewa.org. A papal relief and development agency of the Holy See for the Middle East, with offices in New York, Vatican City, Amman, Beirut and Jerusalem. Pres., Msgr. Archim. Robert L. Stern, J.C.D.

Pontifical Missionary Union (1916): 366 Fifth Ave., New York, NY 10001. To promote mission awareness among clergy, religious, candidates to priestly and religious life, and others engaged in pastoral ministry of the Church. Nat. Dir., Most Rev. William J. McCormack; Nat. Sec., Rev. Eugene LaVerdiere, S.S.S.

Priests' Eucharistic League (1887): Hampton House-Apt. 91, 5300 South Shore Dr., Chicago, IL 60615-5708. *Emmanuel*, 10 issues a year. Nat. Dir., Rev. Anthony Schueller, S.S.S.

Pro Ecclesia Foundation (1970): 350 Fifth Ave., New York, NY 10118. Publishes *Pro Ecclesia Magazine*. Pres., Dr. Timothy A. Mitchell.

Pro Maria Committee (1952): 22 Second Ave., Lowell, MA 01854-2808; (978) 453-5281. Promotes devotion to Our Lady of Beauraing (See Index).

Pro Sanctity Movement: Pro Sanctity Spirituality Center, 205 S. Pine Dr., Fullerton, CA 92833, (714) 956-1020; 730 E. 87th St., Brooklyn, NY 11236, (718) 649-0324, www.prosanctity.org; 6762 Western Ave., Omaha, NE 68132, (402) 553-4418, www.prosanctity.org; 1102 N. 204 St. Elkhorn, NE 68022, (402) 289-2670, www.prosanctity.org. Organized to spread God's call of all persons to holiness.

Project Children (1975): P.O. Box 933, Greenwood Lake, NY 10925, (845) 477-3472, www.inter webinc.com/children/. Nonsectarian volunteer group; provides children of Northern Ireland with a six-week summer vacation with host families in the U.S.

The Providence Association of the Ukrainian Catholics in America (Ukrainian Catholic Fraternal Benefit Society) (1912): 817 N. Franklin St., Philadelphia, PA 19123, (215) 627-4984.

Queen of the Americas Guild, Inc. (1979): P.O. Box 851, St. Charles, IL 60174; (630) 584-1822; 7,000 members. To build English information center and retreat center near Basilica in Mexico City and spread the message of Guadalupe. Pres., Frank E. Smoczynski.

Raskob Foundation for Catholic Activities, Inc. (1945): P.O. Box 4019, Wilmington, DE 19807-0019; (302) 655-4440, www.rfca.org. Exec. Pres., Frederick Perella, Jr.

Reparation Society of the Immaculate Heart of Mary, Inc. (1946): 100 E. 20th St., Baltimore, MD 21218. *Fatima Findings*, monthly.

Retrouvaille: P.O.Box 25, Kelton, PA 19346. A minstry to hurting marriages, Retrouvaille consists of a weekend experience with follow-up sessions designed to provide couples with ways and means of healing and reconciling. Emphasis is placed on communication, enabling husband and wife to rediscover each other and to examine their lives in a new and positive way. The ministry is neither a retreat nor a sensitivity group, nor does it include group dynamics or discussions. The program is conducted by trained couples and priests, with programs offered under the auspices of diocesan family life agencies. International Coordinating Team: Bill and Peg Swaan.

Sacred Heart League: 6050 Hwy 61 N, P.O. Box 190, Walls, MS 38680. Pres., Rev. Robert Hess, S.C.J.

St. Ansgar's Scandinavian Catholic League (1910): 28 W. 25th St., New York, NY 10010-2705, (212) 675-0400; www.neighborhorhoodlink.com/org/stansgar. 1,000 members. Prayers and financial support for Church in Scandinavia. *St. Ansgar's Bulletin*, annually. Pres., Astrid M. O'Brien.

St. Anthony's Guild (1924): Paterson, NJ 07509, (973) 777-3737; Promotes devotion to St. Anthony of Padua and support for formation programs, infirm friars and ministries of the Franciscans of Holy Name Province. *The Anthonian*, quarterly. Dir., Rev. Joseph Hertel, O.F.M.

St. Bernadette Institute of Sacred Art (1993): P.O. Box 8249, Albuquerque, NM 87198-8249; (505) 265-9126. To promote, initiate, encourage interest and sustain projects and persons engaged in sacred art.

St. Gregory Foundation for Latin Liturgy (1989): Newman House, 21 Fairview Ave., Mount Pocono, PA 18344; (570) 839-2185. To promote within the Church in the U.S. the use of the Latin language in the Mass in accordance with the teachings of Vatican II. Founder and Pres., Very Rev. Peter M.J. Stravinskas, Ph.D., S.T.D.

St. Jude League (1929): 205 W. Monroe St., Chicago, IL 60606; (312) 236-7782; www.stjude league.org. Promotes devotion to St. Jude; supports work of Claretian Missionaries throughout the world. Dir., Rev. Mark J. Brummel, C.M.F.

St. Margaret of Scotland Guild, Inc. (1938): Graymoor, P.O. Box 300, Garrison, NY 10524; (845) 424-3671. Moderator, Bro. Pius MacIsaac.

St. Martin de Porres Guild (1935): 141 E. 65th St., New York, NY 10021; (212) 744-2410; www.op-stjoseph.org. Dir., Rev. Raymond F. Halligan, O.P.

Serra International (1934): 220 S. State St., Suite 1703, Chicago, IL 60604; (312) 588-0700; www.serrainternational.org. 21,000 members in 673 clubs in 35 countries. Fosters vocations to the priesthood, and religious life, trains Catholic lay leadership. Formally aggregated to the Pontifical Society for Priestly Vocations, 1951. *Serran*, bimonthly.

Slovak Catholic Federation (1911): 915 Cornell St., Youngstown, OH, 44502-2765; (330) 788-5082. Founded by Rev. Joseph Murgas to promote and coordinate religious activities among Slovak Catholic fraternal societies, religious communities and Slovak ethnic parishes in their effort to address themselves to the special needs of Slovak Catholics in the U.S. and Canada. Pres., Rev. Msgr. Peter M. Polando.

Slovak Catholic Sokol (1905): 205 Madison St., Passaic, NJ 07055; (973) 777-2606; www.slovak catholicsokol.org. 38,000 members. Fraternal benefit society. *Slovak Catholic Falcon*, weekly.

Society for the Propagation of the Faith (1822): 366 Fifth Ave., New York, NY 10001; (212) 563-8725 (fax); www.propfaith.org. Established in all dioceses. Church's principal instrument for promoting mission awareness and generating financial support for the missions. General fund for ordinary and extraordinary subsidies for all mission dioceses. *Mission*, 4 times a year; *Director's Newsletter*, monthly. Is subject to Congregation for the Evangelization of Peoples. Nat. Dir., Rev. John Kozar.

Society of St. Monica (1986): 215 Falls Ave., Cuyahoga Falls, OH 44221. More than 10,000 members worldwide. Confident, daily prayer for the return of inactive Catholics and Catholics who have left the Church. Founder and Spir. Dir., Rev. Dennis M. McNeil.

Society of St. Peter Apostle (1889): 366 Fifth Ave., New York, NY 10001, (212) 563-8700, www.propfaith.org; all dioceses. Church's central fund for support of seminaries, seminarians and novices in all mission dioceses. Nat. Dir., Rev. John Kozar.

Society of the Divine Attributes (1974): 2905 Castlegate Ave., Pittsburgh, PA 15226; (412) 456-3114. Contemplative prayer society. 3,000 members worldwide (lay, clerical and religious). Spir. Dir. Rev. Ronald D. Lawler, O.F.M. Cap.

Spiritual Life Institute of America (1960): Box 219, Crestone, CO 81131, (719) 256-4778, www.spirituallifeinstitute.org. Forefront, seasonal. An eremetical movement to foster the contemplative spirit in America. Founder, Rev. William McNamara, O.C.D. Second foundation: Nova Nada, Primitive Wilderness Hermitage, Kemptville, Nova Scotia, Canada B0W 1Y0. Third foundation, Holy Hill Hermitage, Skreen, Co. Sligo, Ireland.

Support Our Aging Religious (SOAR) (1986): 1400 Spring St., Suite 320, Silver Spring, MD 20910, (301) 589-9811, www.soar-usa.org. Laity-led campaign to raise funds for retired religious.

Theresians of the United States (1961): 1237 W. Monroe, Springfield, IL 62704, (217) 726-5484, www.theresians.org. Spiritual, educational and ministerial organization of Christian women. Exec. Dir., Victoria S. Schmidt. International division: Theresian World Ministry (1971), same address.

United Societies of U.S.A. (1903): 613 Sinclair St., McKeesport, PA 15132. 3,755 members. *Prosvita-Enlightenment*, bimonthly newspaper.

United States Catholic Historical Society (1884): The Catholic Center, 1011 First Ave., New York, NY 10022; (718) 250-8753, www.uschs.com. President and Chairman, Brian Butler, K.M.; Exec Dir., Edward J. Thompson.

Western Catholic Union (1877): 510 Maine St., Quincy, IL 62301; (800) 223-4928; www.western catholicunion.org; 19,000 members. *Western Catholic Union Record*, quarterly. A fraternal benefit society. Pres., Mark A. Wiewel.

Women for Faith and Family (1984): P.O. Box 8326, St. Louis, MO 63132; (314) 863-8385, www.wf-f.org. 60,000 signers worldwide. An international movement to promote Catholic teachings especially on all issues involving the family and roles for women. Members sign an 8-point statement of fidelity to the Church. *Voices*, quarterly. Dir., Helen Hull Hitchcock.

Young Ladies' Institute (1887): 1111 Gough St., San Francisco, CA 94109-6606; (415) 346-4367; 13,000. *Voice of YLI*, bimonthly. Grand Sec., Frances Ridley.

Young Men's Institute (1883): 1625 "C" Palmetto Ave., Pacifica, CA 94044; (650) 738-3007, www.ymiusa.org. 4,500 members. *Institute Journal*, bimonthly. Grand Sec., Clifford C. Smethurst.

PERSONAL PRELATURE OF THE HOLY SEE: OPUS DEI

Founded in Madrid in 1928 by Msgr. Josemaría Escrivá de Balaguer (beatified in 1992 and scheduled for canonization in October 2002), Opus Dei has the aim of spreading throughout all sectors of society a profound awareness of the universal call to holiness and apostolate (of Christian witness and action) in the ordinary circumstances of life, and, more specifically, through one's professional work. On Nov. 28, 1982, Pope John Paul II established Opus Dei as a personal prelature with the full title, Prelature of the Holy Cross and Opus Dei. The 2002 edition of the *Annuario Pontificio* reported that the prelature had 1,763 priests (37 newly ordained) and 355 major seminarians. Also, there were 82,443 lay persons – men and women, married and single, of every class and social condition — of about 80 nationalities, as well as 1,684 churches and pastoral centers.

Further, the prelature operates the Pontifical University of the Holy Cross in Rome; it was established in 1985 and received approval as a pontifical instutution in 1995. Courses of study include theology, philosophy, canon law, and the recently established School of Social Communications.

In the United States, members of Opus Dei, along with cooperators and friends, conduct apostolic works corporately in major cities in the East and Midwest, Texas and on the West Coast. Elsewhere, corporate works include universities, vocational institutes, training schools for farmers and numerous other apostolic initiatives. Opus Dei information offices are located at: 99 Overlook Cir., New Rochelle, NY 10804; (914) 235-6128 (office of the New York chaplain); and 655 Levering Ave., Los Angeles, CA 90024; (310) 208-0941; www.opusdei.org.

KNIGHTS OF COLUMBUS

The Knights of Columbus, a fraternal benefit society of Catholic men, is a family service organization founded by Fr. Michael J. McGivney and chartered by the General Assembly of Connecticut on Mar. 29, 1982. Currently, there are over 1.6 million Knights of Columbus — more than ever before in the Order's history. Together with their families, the Knights are nearly 6 million strong. In addition, from the first local council in New Haven, the Order has grown to more than 12,000 councils in the United States, Canada, Mexico, the Philippines, Puerto Rico, Cuba, the Dominican Republic, Panama, the Virgin Islands, Guatemala, Guam and Saipan.

In keeping with their general purpose to be of service to the Church, the Knights and their families are active in many apostolic works and community programs.

The Knights cooperate with the U.S. bishops in Pro-Life activities and are engaged in other apostolic endeavors as well. According to the annual report of the Supreme Knight (August 2000), charitable contributions in 1999 exceeded $109 million; member Knights also contributed 55 million volunteer hours to charitable causes. In the decade of the 1990s, the Knights donated nearly $1 billion to numerous charitable causes and nearly 400 million hours of volunteer service.

In 2001, members raised and contributed to charity more than $125.6 million and volunteered more than 58.9 million hours of service. In 2000, the Knights raised and donated $116 million and 55.3 million volunteer hours. Twenty years ago, the Knights reported raising and donating to charity $52 million and volunteering 13.4 million hours of service.

The programmatic activities of the Knights remain much the same from one year to the next. The K of C funded the restoration of the *Maderno Atrium* of St. Peter's Basilica in Rome, named for the architect, Carlo Maderno (1556-1629). The atrium is the big "front porch" through which every visitor to St. Peter's passes. This is one of a series of projects for the restoration of St. Peter's funded by the Knights over the years: renovation of the roof of the Blessed Sacrament Chapel (1993); renovation of the Room of the Architects and Room of the Window Panes (1987-88); restoration of the facade (1985-86); construction of chapels in the grottoes (1981-82).

The Knights of Columbus headquarters address is One Columbus Plaza, New Haven, CT 06510-3326; (203) 772-2130; www.kofc.org. The Grand Knight is Carl Anderson.

LETTER OF JOHN PAUL II
TO THE SUPREME COUNCIL OF THE KNIGHTS OF COLUMBUS

In honor of their Annual Supreme Convention, held in Anaheim, California, Pope John Paul II sent a letter to the Knights of Columbus that was published on Aug. 6, 2002:

Once again I offer you my prayerful good wishes on the occasion of the Annual Supreme Convention, being held this year in Anaheim, California. This yearly assembly enables the Supreme Council to commit your Order ever anew to the noble ideals of fraternity and service of the Church laid down by your Founder, the Servant of God Father Michael McGivney. I pray that the meeting will provide inspiration and guidance to all the Knights of Columbus as they strive to bear witness to Christ by working zealously for the spread of his Kingdom on earth.

The theme of this 120th Supreme Convention – "Now is the Time for the Great Catch" – is a summons to ever deeper trust in the Lord's command to "put out into the deep" (cf. *Lk* 5:4) in obedience to his word. As I noted in my Apostolic Letter *Novo Millennio ineunte*, this invitation – *Duc in altum!* – is directed to the whole Church at the dawn of the third millennium. The years of spiritual preparation for the Great Jubilee, the immense outpouring of grace symbolized by the opening of the Holy Doors of the great Roman Basilicas, and the lively sense of mission which followed the experience of the Holy Year were an incentive to Christians everywhere "to remember the past with gratitude, to live the present with enthusiasm and to look forward to the future with confidence" (*ibid.,*1).

Now indeed is the time to "put out into the deep," without fear or hesitation! As the experience of the Great Jubilee made clear, at the heart of the new evangelization there must be a fresh blossoming of holiness in the Church (cf. *Novo Millennio ineunte*, 30-31). For this reason, I am most pleased that the Knights have continued to emphasize the need for profound spiritual renewal as the basis for the many and varied initiatives undertaken in support of the Church's mission....

... I express once more my gratitude for the Knights' unfailing commitment to promoting vocations to the priesthood and the religious life. Experience has shown that the more the lay apostolate develops, the more strongly the need for priests is felt; and the more the laity's own sense of vocation is deepened, the more deeply is the unique role of priests appreciated....

... I pray that the Knights of Columbus, in full fidelity to the vision of Father Michael McGivney, will make every effort to draw young people to Jesus Christ and help them to understand that the true meaning and value of life is found in the generous gift of self to God and to others. In this way a new generation will discover at the heart of the Church the spiritual resources necessary for building a society marked by authentic freedom, respect for the demands of truth and selfless concern for the good of all, especially the poor and the underprivileged.

With these sentiments I commend the deliberations of the Supreme Council to the loving intercession of Mary, Mother of the Church. To all the Knights and their families I cordially impart my Apostolic Blessing as a pledge of abiding joy and peace in our Lord Jesus Christ.

From the Vatican, July 10, 2002

Catholic Social Services

Catholic Charities USA (formerly National Conference of Catholic Charities): 1731 King St., Suite 200, Alexandria, VA 22314; (703) 549-1390; www.catholiccharitiesusa.org. Founded in 1910 by Most Rev. Thomas J. Shahan and Rt. Rev. Msgr. William J. Kerby in cooperation with lay leaders of the Society of St. Vincent de Paul to help advance and promote the charitable programs and activities of Catholic community and social service agencies in the United States. As the central and national organization for this purpose, it services a network of more than 1,400 agencies and institutions by consultation, information and assistance in planning and evaluating social service programs under Catholic auspices.

Diocesan member agencies provide shelter, food, counseling, services to children, teen parents and the elderly, and a variety of other services to people in need — without regard to religion, gender, age or national origin. Each year millions of people receive help from Catholic Charities; in 1995 (latest statistics available), more than 10 million turned to Catholic Charities agencies for help. In addition, Catholic Charities is an advocate for persons and families in need.

Catholic Charities USA serves members through national and regional meetings, training programs, literature and social policy advocacy on the national level. It is charged by the U.S. bishops with responding to disasters in this country. Catholic Charities USA's president represents North America before Caritas Internationalis, the international conference of Catholic Charities, and thus maintains contact with the Catholic Charities movement throughout the world. Publications include *Charities USA*, a quarterly membership magazine, and a directory of U.S. Catholic Charities agencies and institutions. Pres. of Catholic Charities USA: Rev. Fred Kammer, S.J.

Society of St. Vincent de Paul, Council of the United States (originally called the Conference of Charity): National Council, 58 Progress Parkway, St. Louis, MO 63043; (314) 576-3993; www.svdpus council.org. An association of Catholic lay men and women devoted to personal service to the poor through the spiritual and corporal works of mercy. The first conference was formed at Paris in 1833 by Bl. Frederic Ozanam and his associates.

The first conference in the U.S. was organized in 1845 at St. Louis. There are now approximately 4,400 units of the society in this country, with a membership of more than 60,000. The society operates world wide in more than 130 countries and has more than

800,000 members.

Besides person-to-person assistance, increasing emphasis is being given to stores and rehabilitation workshops of the society through which persons with marginal income can purchase refurbished goods at minimal cost. Handicapped persons are employed in renovating goods and store operations. The society also operates food centers, shelters, criminal justice and other programs. Publications include *The Ozanam News*, a biannual membership magazine, and *The United States Councilor*, a quarterly newsletter. Nat. Pres., Eugene Smith; Exec. Dir., Richard Hennicke.

Catholic Health Association of the United States (CHA): National Headquarters, 4455 Woodson Road, St. Louis, MO 63134; (314) 427-2500; www.chusa.org. Represents more than 1,200 Catholic-sponsored facilities and organizations, works with its members to promote justice and compassion in healthcare, influence public policy, shape a continuum of care through integraated delivery, and strengthen ministry presence and influence in the U.S. healthcare system. CHA supports and strengthens the Catholic health ministry by being a catalyst through research and development (leading edge tools for sustaining a faith-based ministry in price competitive markets), education and facilitation (annual assembly, conferences, and other methods for engaging the ministry), and advocacy (a united ministry voice for public policy). CHA members make up the nation's largest group of not-for-profit healthcare facilities under a single form of sponsorship.

National Association of Catholic Chaplains: 3501 S. Lake Dr., Milwaukee, WI 53207; (414) 483-4898. Founded in 1965. membership is over 3,500.

SOCIAL SERVICE ORGANIZATIONS
(See separate article for a listing of facilities for the handicapped.)

The Carroll Center for the Blind (formerly the Catholic Guild for All the Blind): 770 Centre St., Newton, MA 02158. The center conducts diagnostic evaluation and rehabilitation programs for blind people over 16 years of age, and provides computer training and other services. Pres., Rachel Rosenbaum.

International Catholic Deaf Association: 8002 S. Sawyer Rd., Darian, IL 60561; TTY (630) 887-9472. Established by deaf adults in Toronto, Canada, in 1949, the association has more than 8,000 members in 130 chapters, mostly in the U.S. It is the only international lay association founded and controlled by deaf Catholic adults. The ICDA publishes *The Deaf*

Catholic, bimonthly, sponsors regional conferences, workshops and an annual convention. Pres., Kathleen Kush.

National Apostolate for Inclusion Ministry (NAfIM): P.O. Box 218, Riverdale, MD, 20738; (800) 736-1280; www.nafim.org. Formerly known as the National Apostolate for Persons with Mental Retardation (NAPMR). Established in 1968 to promote the full participation by persons with mental retardation in the life of the Church. Exec. Dir., Barbara Lampe.

National Catholic Office for the Deaf: 7202 Buchanan St., Landover Hills, MD 20784; (301) 577-1684; www.ncod.org. Formally established in 1971, at Washington, D.C., to provide pastoral service to those who teach deaf children and adults, to the parents of deaf children, to pastors of deaf persons, and to organizations of the deaf. Exec.Dir., Arvilla Rank.

National Catholic Office for Persons with Disabilities (NCPD): 415 Michigan Ave., N.E., Washington, DC 20017; (202) 529-2933; www.ncpd.org. NCPD's mission is to provide resources and consultation to a national network of diocesan directors who oversee access and inclusion at the parish level; to collaborate with other national Catholic organizations, advocating for inclusion within all their programs and initiatives and to work with Catholic organizations addressing the concerns and needs of those with various disabilities. Established in 1982 as a result of the 1978 Pastoral Statement of the U.S. Catholic Bishops on People with Disabilities., the office continues to press for words and actions which promote meaningful participation and inclusion at all levels of the Church.

Xavier Society for the Blind: 154 E. 23rd St., New York, NY 10010-4595; (212) 473-7800. Founded in 1900 by Rev. Joseph Stadelman, S.J., it is a center for publications for the blind and partially sighted. Exec. Dir., Rev. Alfred E. Caruana, S.J.

OTHER SOCIAL SERVICES

Cancer Hospitals or Homes: The following homes or hospitals specialize in the care of cancer patients. They are listed according to state; capacities are in parentheses.

Our Lady of Perpetual Help Home, Servants of Relief for Incurable Cancer, 760 Pollard Blvd., S.W., Atlanta, GA 30315; (404) 688-9515 (52).

Rose Hawthorne Lathrop Home, Servants of Relief for Incurable Cancer, 1600 Bay St., Fall River, MA 02724; (508) 673-2322 (35).

Our Lady of Good Counsel Home, Servants of Relief for Incurable Cancer, 2076 St. Anthony Ave., St. Paul, MN 55104; (651) 646-2797.

Calvary Hospital, Inc., 1740 Eastchester Rd., Bronx, NY 10461; (718) 863-6900 (200). Operated in connection with Catholic Charities, Department of Health and Hospitals, Archdiocese of New York.

St. Rose's Home, Servants of Relief for Incurable Cancer, 71 Jackson St., New York, NY 10002; (212) 677-8132 (60).

Rosary Hill Home, Servants of Relief for Incurable Cancer, 600 Linda Ave., Hawthorne, NY 10532; (914) 769-0114 (72).

Holy Family Home, Servants of Relief for Incurable Cancer, 6753 State Rd., Parma, OH 44134; (440) 845-7700; www.cle-dioc.org (50).

Sacred Heart Free Home for Incurable Cancer, Ser-

vants of Relief for Incurable Cancer, 1315 W. Hunting Park Ave., Philadelphia, PA 19140; (215) 329-3222 (45).

Substance Abuse: Facilities for substance abuse (alcohol and other drugs) include:

Daytop Village, Inc., 54 W. 40th St., New York, NY 10018, (212) 354-6000, www.daytop.org. Msgr. William B. O'Brien, president. Twenty-eight residential and ambulatory sites in New York, New Jersey, Pennsylvania, Florida, Texas and California.

Good Shepherd Gracenter, Convent of the Good Shepherd, 1310 Bacon St., San Francisco, CA 94134; (415) 586-2822. Residential program for chemically dependent women.

New Hope Manor, 35 Hillside Rd., Barryville, NY 12719; fax (914) 557-6603. Residential substance abuse treatment center for teen-age girls and women ages 13-40. Residential; half-way house and aftercare program totaling 6 months or more.

St. Joseph's Hospital, L.E. Phillips Libertas Center for the Chemically Dependent, 2661 County Road, Hwy. I, Chippewa Falls, WI 54729; (715) 723-1811 (46). Residential and outpatient. Adult and adolescent programs. Hospital Sisters of the Third Order of St. Francis.

St. Joseph's Hospital (Chippewa Falls, WI) Libertas Center for the Treatment of Chemical Dependency, 1701 Dousman St., Green Bay, WI 54302 (23). Residental and outpatient adolescent programs. Hospital Sisters of the Third Order of St. Francis.

St. Luke's Addiction Recovery Services, 7707 NW 2nd Ave., Miami, FL 33150; (305) 795-0077; www.catholiccharitiesadm.org/stluke. A program of Catholic Community Services, Miami. Adult residential and family outpatient recovery services for drug, alcohol addiction and DUI.

Miami Substance Abuse Prevention Programs, 7707 N.W. Second Ave., Miami, FL 33150; (305) 795-0077; www.catholiccharitiesadm.org/stluke. Trains parents, youth, priests and teachers as prevention volunteers in the area of substance abuse.

Transitus House, 1830 Wheaton St., Chippewa Falls, WI 54729; (715) 723-1155. Two programs for chemically dependent: adult intensive residential (15 beds, women); adolescent intensive residential (5 beds, girls 15-18 yrs.). Hospital Sisters of the Third Order of St. Francis.

Matt Talbot Inn, 2270 Professor Ave., Cleveland, OH 44113; (216) 781-0288. Two programs: Chemical dependency Residential Treatment/Halfway House (capacity 27) and outpatient treatment/aftercare. Serves male clients 18 years and over.

Sacred Heart Rehabilitation Center, Inc., 2203 St. Antoine, Detroit, MI 48201 (admissions/assessment, outpatient); 400 Stoddard Rd., P.O. Box 41038, Memphis, MI 48041 (12 beds, detoxification; 70 beds residential treatment); 28573 Schoenherr, Warren, MI 48093 (outpatient). All facilities serve male and female clients 18 and over.

Straight and Narrow, Inc., 396 Straight St., Paterson, NJ 07501. Facilities and services include (at various locations): Straight and Narrow Hospital (Mount Carmel Guild), substance abuse, detoxification (20 beds); Alpha House for Drug and Alcohol Rehabilitation (women; 30 beds — 25 adults, 5 children), Dismas House for Drug and Alcohol Rehabilitation (men; 78 beds); The Guild for Drug and Alcohol Rehabilitation (men, 56 beds); juvenile residential units; outpatient services and facility; three halfway houses; counseling services; employment assistance; intoxicated driver's resource center; medical day care center (available to HIV infected persons and persons diagnosed with AIDS); methadone clinic.

The National Catholic Council on Alcoholism and Related Drug Problems, Inc., 1550 Hendrickson St., Brooklyn, NY 11234, offers educational material to those involved in pastoral ministry on ways of dealing with problems related to alcoholism and medication dependency.

Convicts: Priests serve as full- or part-time chaplains in penal and correctional institutions throughout the country. Limited efforts have been made to assist in the rehabilitation of released prisoners in Halfway House establishments.

Dining Rooms: Facilities for homeless: Representative of places where meals are provided, and in some cases lodging and other services as well, are:

St. Anthony Foundation, 121 Golden Gate Ave., San Francisco, CA 94102, (415) 241-2600; www.st anthonyfdn.org. Founded in 1950 by the Franciscan Friars. Multi-program social service agency serving people who are poor and homeless. Dining room serves up to 2,100 meals daily; more than 25 million since its founding. Other services include free clothing and furniture; free medical clinic; residential drug and alcohol rehabilitation programs; employment program; emergency shelter, housing and daytime facility for homeless women; residence for low-income senior women; free hygiene services; case management for seniors; social services.

St. Vincent de Paul Free Dining Room, 675 23rd St., Oakland, CA 94612, (510) 451-7676. Administered by Daughters of Charity of St. Vincent de Paul, under sponsorship of St. Vincent de Paul Society. Hot meals served at lunch time 7 days a week. Also provides counseling, referral/information services.

St. Vincent's Dining Room, P.O. Box 5099, Reno, NV 89513; (775) 329-5363.

St. Vincent Dining Room, 1501 Las Vegas Blvd., Las Vegas, NV 89101. Structured program for 275 men in which job development office works with homeless to enable them to find employment. For nonresidents, there is a hot meal every day at noon. Emergency overnight shelter facility for families, women and men.

Good Shepherd Center, Little Brothers of the Good Shepherd, 218 Iron St. S.W., P.O. Box 749, Albuquerque, NM 87103; (505) 243-2527.

Holy Name Centre for Homeless Men, Inc., 18 Bleecker St., New York, NY 10012. A shelter for alcoholic, homeless men. Provides social services and aid to transients and those in need. Affiliated with New York Catholic Charities.

St. Francis Inn, 2441 Kensington Ave., Philadelphia, PA 19125. Serves hot meals. Temporary shelter for men. Day center for women. Thrift shop.

St. John's Hospice for Men, staffed by Little Brothers of the Good Shepherd, 1221 Race St., Philadelphia, PA 19107. Hot meals served daily; 36-bed shelter; clothing distribution, showers, mail distribution, drug/alcohol rehabilitation and work programs. Good Shepherd Program of St. John's Hospice, 1225 Race St., Philadelphia, PA 19107. Ten-bed facility for homeless men with AIDS.

Camillus House, Little Brothers of the Good Shepherd, P.O. Box 11829, Miami, FL 33101; (305) 374-1065; www.camillus.org. Free comprehensive services for the poor and homeless including daily dinner; night lodging for 70; clothing distribution; showers; mail distribution; drug/alcohol rehabilitation program. Forty-eight units of single-room occupancy housing for employed formerly homeless women and men who have completed drug and alcohol rehabilitation programs.

Camillus Health Concern, P.O. Box 12408, Miami, FL 33101; (305) 577-4840. Free comprehensive medical and social services for the homeless.

Shelters: Facilities for runaways, the abused, exploited and homeless include:

Anthony House, supported by St. Anthony's Guild (see Index). Three locations: 38 E. Roosevelt Ave., Roosevelt, NY 11575 (with St. Vincent de Paul Society — for homeless men); 128 W. 112th St., New York, NY 10026 (emergency food and clothing); 6215 Holly St., P.O. Box 880, Zellwood, FL 32798 (for migrant workers and their families).

Good Shepherd Shelter-Convent of the Good Shepherd. Office, 2561 W. Venice Blvd., Los Angeles, CA 90019; (323) 737-6111. Non-emergency long-term shelter for battered women and their children.

Covenant House, 346 W. 17th St., New York, NY 10011, (212) 727-4973. President, Sister Mary Rose McGeady, D.C. Provides crisis care — food, shelter, clothing, medical treatment, job placement and counseling — for homeless youth without regard to race, creed, color and national origin. Locations: New York, New Jersey (Newark, Atlantic City), Houston, Ft. Lauderdale, New Orleans, Anchorage, Los Angeles, Detroit, Orlando, Washington, D.C.; Toronto (Canada), Tegucigalpa (Honduras), Guatemala City (Guatemala), Mexico City (Mexico).

Crescent House, 1000 Howard Ave., Suite 1200, New Orleans, LA 70113. Provides temporary shelter, counseling and advocacy for battered women and their children.

The Dwelling Place, 409 W. 40th St., New York, NY 10018; (212) 564-7887. For homeless women 30 years of age and over.

Gift of Hope, Missionaries of Charity, 724 N.W. 17th St., Miami, FL 33136; (305) 326-0032. Shelter for women and children; soup kitchen for men.

House of the Good Shepherd, 1114 W. Grace St., Chicago, IL 60613; (773) 935-3434. For abused women with children.

Mercy Hospice, 334 S. 13th St., Philadelphia, PA 19107, (215) 545-5153. Temporary shelter and relocation assistance for homeless women and children.

Mt. Carmel House, Carmelite Sisters, 471 G Pl., N.W., Washington, DC 20001. For homeless women.

Ozanam Inn, 843 Camp St., New Orleans, LA 70130. Under sponsorship of the St. Vincent de Paul Society. Hospice for homeless men.

St. Christopher Inn, P.O. Box 150, Graymoor, Garrison, NY 10524; (845) 424-3616, www.atone mentfriars.org. Temporary shelter (21 days) for alcohol- and drug-free homeless and needy men.

Siena-Francis House, Inc., P.O. Box 217 D.T.S., Omaha, NE 68102. Two units, both at 1702 Nicholas St., Omaha, NE 68101, (402) 341-1821: Siena House (for homeless and abused women or women with children; provides 24-hour assistance and advocacy services); Francis House (temporary shelter for homeless men). Also at this location:

a 50-bed residential substance abuse program.
Unwed Mothers: Residential and care services for unwed mothers are available in many dioceses.

FACILITIES FOR RETIRED AND AGED PERSONS

(*Sources:* Almanac *survey,* The Official Catholic Directory.)

This list covers residence, health care and other facilities for the retired and aged under Catholic auspices. Information includes name, type of facility if not evident from the title, address, and total capacity (in parentheses); unless noted otherwise, facilities are for both men and women. Many facilities for the aged offer intermediate nursing care.

Alabama: Allen Memorial Home (Skilled Nursing), 735 S. Washington Ave., Mobile 36603; (334) 433-2642 (119).

Cathedral Place Apartments (Retirement Complex), 351 Conti St., Mobile 36602; (334) 434-1590 (184).

Mercy Medical (Acute Rehabilitation Hospital, Skilled and Post-Acute Nursing, Hospice, Home Health and Assisted and Independent Living), P.O. Box 1090, Daphne 36526; (334) 626-2694 (162). Not restricted to elderly.

Sacred Heart Residence Little Sisters of the Poor, 1655 McGill Ave., Mobile 36604; (334) 476-6335 (84).

Seton Haven (Retirement Complex), 3721 Wares Ferry Rd., Montgomery 36193; (334) 272-4000 (114).

Arizona: Guadalupe Senior Village, 222 W. Thomas Rd., Ste. 214, Phoenix, 85103; (602) 406-6218.

California: Alexis Apartments of St. Patrick's Parish, 756 Mission St. 94103; 390 Clementina St., San Francisco 94103; (415) 495-3690 (240).

Casa Manana Inn, 3700 N. Sutter St., Stockton 95204; (209) 466-4046 (162). Non-profit housing for low-income elderly over 62.

Cathedral Plaza, 1551 Third Ave., San Diego 92101; (619) 234-0093 (222 apartments).

Garden Oaks, 3334 Wagner Heights, Stockton 95209; (209) 956-3401 (48).

Guadalupe Plaza, 4142 42nd St., San Diego 92105; (619) 584-2414 (147 apartments).

Jeanne d'Arc Manor, 85 S. Fifth St., San Jose 95112; (408) 288-7421 (145). For low income elderly and handicapped.

La Paz Villas, P.O. Box 1962, Palm Desert 92261; (760) 772-1382 (24 units).

Little Flower Haven (Residential Care Facility for Retired), 8585 La Mesa Blvd., La Mesa 91941; (619) 466-3163 (85).

Little Sisters of the Poor, St. Anne's Home, 300 Lake St., San Francisco 94118; (415) 751-6510 (90).

Little Sisters of the Poor, Jeanne Jugan Residence, 2100 South Western Ave., San Pedro, Calif. 90732; (310) 548-0625 (100).

Madonna Senior Center and Residence, 350 Golden gate Ave., San Francisco 94102; (415) 592-2864, www.stanthonysf.org (37).

Marian Residence (Retirement Home), 124 S. College Dr., Santa Maria 93454; (805) 922-7731 (32).

Mercy McMahon Terrace (Residential Care Facility), 3865 J St., Sacramento 95816; (916) 733-6510;

www.mercysacramento.org (118 units).

Mercy Retirement and Care Center, 3431 Foothill Blvd., Oakland 94601; (510) 534-8540 (59).

Mother Gertrude Home for Senior Citizens, 11320 Laurel Canyon Blvd., San Fernando 91340; (818) 898-1546 (98).

Nazareth House (Residential and Skilled Care), 2121 N. 1st St., Fresno 93703; (559) 237-2257 (65 residential; 39 skilled nursing).

Nazareth House (Residential and Skilled Nursing), 3333 Manning Ave., Los Angeles 90064; (310) 839-2361 (123).

Nazareth House (Retirement Home), 245 Nova Albion Way, San Rafael 94903; (415) 479-8282 (151).

Nazareth House Retirement Home, 6333 Rancho Mission Rd., San Diego 92108; (619) 563-0480 (354).

Our Lady of Fatima Villa (Skilled Nursing Facility), 20400 Saratoga-Los Gatos Rd., Saratoga 95070; (408) 741-2950 (85).

St. Bernardine Plaza (Retirement Home), 550 W. 5th St., San Bernardino 92401; (909) 888-0153 (150 units).

St. John of God (Retirement and Care Center), 2035 W. Adams Blvd., Los Angeles 90018; (323) 731-0641 (215).

Vigil Light Apartments, 1945 Long Dr., Santa Rosa 95405; (707) 544-2810 (54).

Villa Scalabrini (Retirement Center and Skilled Nursing Care), 10631 Vinedale St., Sun Valley 91352; (818) 768-6500, www.villascalabrini.com (130 residence; 58 skilled nursing).

Villa Siena (Residence and Skilled Nursing Care), 1855 Miramonte Ave., Mountain View 94040, (650) 961-6484 (56, residence; 20, skilled nursing care).

Colorado: Francis Heights, Inc., 2626 Osceola St., Denver 80212; (303) 433-6268 (384 units; 411 residents).

Gardens at St. Elizabeth (Congregate Housing and Assisted Living), 2835 W. 32nd Ave., Denver 80211; (303) 964-2005 (320).

Little Sisters of the Poor, 3629 W. 29th Ave., Denver 80211; (303) 433-7221 (70).

Connecticut: Augustana Homes (Residence), Simeon Rd., Bethel 06801; (203) 743-2508.

Carmel Ridge, 6454 Main St., Trumbull 06611; (203) 261-2229.

Holy Family Home and Shelter, Inc., 88 Jackson St., P.O. Box 884, Willimantic 06226; (860) 423-7719 (155).

Monsignor Bojnowski Manor, Inc. (Skilled Nursing Facility), 50 Pulaski St., New Britain 06053; (860) 229-0336 (60).

Notre Dame Convalescent Home, 76 West Rocks Rd., Norwalk 06851; (203) 847-5893 (60).

St. Joseph Living Center, 14 Club Rd., Windham 06280; (860) 456-1107 (120).

St. Joseph's Manor (Health Care Facility; Home for Aged), Carmelite Srs. for Aged and Infirm, 6448 Main St., Trumbull 06611; (203) 268-6204 (297).

St. Joseph's Residence, Little Sisters of the Poor,

1365 Enfield St., Enfield, Conn. 06082; (860) 741-0791 (84).

St. Lucian's Home for the Aged, 532 Burritt St., New Britain 06053; (860) 223-2123 (42).

St. Mary's Home (Residence and Health Care Facility) 2021 Albany Ave., W. Hartford 06117; (860) 570-8200 (26).

Delaware: The Antonian, 1701 W. 10th St., Wilmington 19805; (302) 421-3758 (136 apartments).

Jeanne Jugan Residence, Little Sisters of the Poor, 185 Salem Church Rd., Newark 19713; (302) 368-5886 (80).

Marydale Retirement Village, 135 Jeandell Dr., Newark 19713; (302) 368-2784 (118 apartments).

St. Patrick's House, Inc., 115 E. 14th St., Wilmington 19801; (302) 654-6908 (12).

District of Columbia: Jeanne Jugan Residence-St. Joseph Villa, Little Sisters of the Poor, 4200 Harewood Rd., N.E. Washington 20017; (202) 269-1831 (73).

Florida: All Saints Home, 5888 Blanding Blvd., Jacksonville 32246; (904) 772-1220 (118).

Casa Calderon, Inc. (Retirement Apartments), 800 W. Virginia St., Tallahassee 32304; (850) 222-4026 (111).

Haven of Our Lady of Peace (Assisted Living and Nursing Home), 5203 N. 9th Ave., Pensacola 32504; (850) 477-0531 (89).

Palmer House, Inc., 1225 S.W. 107th Ave., Miami 33174 (120 apartments).

St. Andrew Towers (Retirement Apartments), 2700 N.W. 99th Ave., Coral Springs 33065 (432).

St. Catherine Laboure (Skilled and Intermediate Care), 1750 Stockton St., Jacksonville 32204; (904) 308-4700 (239).

St. Dominic Gardens (Retirement Apartments), 5849 N.W. 7th St., Miami 33126 (149 apartments).

St. Elizabeth Gardens, Inc. (Retirement Apartments), 801 N.E. 33rd St., Pompano Beach 33064 (150).

St. John's Rehabilitation Hospital and Nursing Center, Inc., 3075 N.W. 35th Ave., Lauderdale Lakes 33311.

Stella Maris House, Inc., 8636 Harding Ave., Miami Beach 33141 (136 apartments).

Illinois: Addolorata Villa (Sheltered Intermediate, Skilled Care Facility; Apartments), 555 McHenry Rd., Wheeling 60090; (847) 808-6168 (100 apartments).

Alvernia Manor (Sheltered Care), 13950 Main St., Lemont 60439; (630) 257-7721 (50).

Carlyle Healthcare Center, 501 Clinton St., Carlyle 62231, (618) 594-3112 (131).

Carmelite Carefree Village, 8419 Bailey Rd., Darien 60561; (630) 960-4060 (98).

Cortland Manor Retirement Home, 1900 N. Karlov, Chicago 60639; (773) 235-3670 (48).

Holy Family Health Center, 2380 Dempster, Des Plaines 60016; (847) 296-3335 (362).

Holy Family Villa (Intermediate Care Facility), 12395 McCarthy Rd., Lemont 60439; (630) 257-7721 (50).

Jugan Terrace, Little Sisters of the Poor, 2300 N. Racine, Chicago 60614; (773) 935-9600 (50 apartments).

Little Sisters of the Poor, St. Joseph's Home for the Elderly, 80 W. Northwest Hwy., Palatine 60067; (847) 358-5700 (61).

Little Sisters of the Poor Center for the Aging, 2325 N. Lakewood Ave., Chicago, Ill. 60614; (773) 935-9600 (71).

Maria Care Center (Skilled Intermediary Facility), 350 W. S. First St., Red Bud 62278; (618) 282-3891 (115).

Marian Heights Apartments (Elderly, Handicapped), 20 Marian Heights Dr., Alton 62002; (618) 462-0363 (130).

Marian Park, Inc., 26 W. 171 Roosevelt Rd., Wheaton 60187; (630) 665-9100 (470).

Maryhaven, Inc. (Skilled and Intermediate Care Facility), 1700 E. Lake Ave., Glenview 60025; (847) 729-1300 (138).

Mayslake Village (Retirement Apartments), 1801 35th St., Oak Brook 60521; (630) 850-8232 (630 apartments).

Mercy Residence at Tolentine Center, 20300 Governors Hwy., Olympia Fields 60461; (708) 748-9500 (48).

Meredith Memorial Home, 16 S. Illinois St., Belleville 62220; (618) 233-8780 (86).

Merkle-Knipprath Countryside (Apartments and Nursing Facility), 1190 E. 2900 N. Rd., Clifton 60927; (815) 694-2306 (130).

Mother Theresa Home (Skilled, Intermediate and Sheltered Care), 1270 Franciscan Dr., Lemont 60439; (630) 257-5801; (150).

Nazarethville (Intermediate and Sheltered Care), 300 N. River Rd., Des Plaines 60016; (847) 297-5900; (83).

Our Lady of Angels Retirement Home, 1201 Wyoming, Joliet 60435; (815) 725-6631; (101).

Our Lady of the Snows, Apartment Community, 9500 West Illinois Highway 15, Belleville 62223; (618) 397-6700 (201).

Our Lady of Victory Nursing Home (Intermediate and Skilled Care), 20 Briarcliff Lane, Bourbonnais 60914; (815) 937-2022 (107).

Pope John Paul Apartments (Elderly and Handicapped), 1 Pope John Paul Plaza, Springfield 62703; (217) 528-1771; www.dio.org (160).

Provena Cor Mariae Center (Assisted Living and Nursing Home), 3330 Maria Linden Dr., Rockford 61107; (815) 877-7416 (146).

Provena St. Anne Center (Nursing Home), 4405 Highcrest Rd., Rockford 61107; (815) 229-1999 (179).

Provena St. Joseph's Home for the Aged, 659 E. Jefferson St., Freeport 61032; (815) 232-6181 (120).

Provena Villa Franciscan (Skilled Care), 210 N. Springfield, Joliet 60435; (815) 725-3400, www.provenahealth.com.

Queen of Peace Center, 1910 Maple Ave., Lisle 60532; (630) 852-5360; www.Qopc.net (32).

Resurrection Nursing Pavilion (Skilled Care), 1001 N. Greenwood, Park Ridge 60068; (847) 692-5600 (295).

Resurrection Retirement Community, 7262 W. Peterson Ave., Chicago, 60631; (773) 792-7930 (472 apartments).

Rosary Hill Home (Women), 9000 W. 81st St., Justice 60458; (708) 458-3040 (48).

St. Andrew Life Center (Retirement Residence),

7000 N. Newark Ave., Niles 60714; (847) 647-8332 (99).

St. Anne Place (Retirement Apartments), 4444 Brendenwood Rd., Rockford 61107; (815) 399-6167 (120).

St. Benedict Home, 6930 W. Touhy Ave., Niles 60714; (847) 647-0003; (99).

St. Elizabeth Home (Residence), 704 W. Marion St., Joliet 60436; (815) 727-0125 (11). Group living for Senior women.

St. James Manor, 1251 East Richton Rd., Crete 60417; (708) 672-6700 (110).

St. Joseph's Home (Sheltered and Intermediate Care), 3306 S. 6th St. Rd., Springfield 62703; (217) 529-5596 (110).

St. Joseph's Home (Sheltered and Intermediate Care), 2223 W. Heading Ave., Peoria 61604; (309) 673-7425 (200).

St. Joseph Home of Chicago, Inc. (Skilled Care), 2650 N. Ridgeway Ave., Chicago 60647; (773) 235-8600 (173).

St. Patrick's Residence, 1400 Brookdale Rd., Naperville 60563; (630) 416-6565, www.stpatricks residence.org

Villa Scalabrini (Sheltered, Intermediate and Skilled), 480 N. Wolf Rd., Northlake 60164; (708) 562-0040 (259).

Indiana: Albertine Home, 1501 Hoffman St., Hammond 46327; (219) 937-0575 (35).

Our Lady of Holy Cross Care Center (Comprehensive Nursing), 7520 S. US Hwy 421, San Pierre 46374; (219) 828-4111 (200).

Provena LaVerna Terrace, 517 N. Main St., Avilla 46710; (219) 897-2093 (51).

Provena Sacred Heart Home (Comprehensive Nursing), 515 N. Main St., Avilla 46710; (219) 897-2841, (133).

Regina Continuing Care Center (Intermediate Care Facility), 3900 Washington Ave., Evansville 47714; (812) 485-4226, www.stmarys.org (137).

St. Anne Home (Residential and Comprehensive Nursing), 1900 Randallia Dr., Ft. Wayne 46805; (219) 484-5555 (254).

St. Anthony Home, Inc., 203 Franciscan Rd., Crown Point 46307; (219) 757-6281 (219).

St. Augustine Home for the Aged, Little Sisters of the Poor, 2345 W. 86th St., Indianapolis 46260; (317) 872-6420; (92).

St. John's Home for the Aged, Little Sisters of the Poor, 1236 Lincoln Ave., Evansville 47714; (812) 464-3607 (70).

St. Paul Hermitage (Residential and Intermediate Care Nursing), 501 N. 17th Ave., Beech Grove 46107; (317) 786-2261 (100).

Iowa: The Alverno Health Care Facility (Nursing Care), 849 13th Ave. N., Clinton 52732; (319) 242-1521 (194).

Bishop Drumm Retirement Center, 5837 Winwood Dr., Johnston 50131; (515) 270-1100 (64).

Hallmar-Mercy Medical Center, 701 Tenth St. S.E., Cedar Rapids 52403, (319) 369-4638 (57).

Holy Spirit Retirement Home (Intermediate Care), 1701 W. 25th St., Sioux City 51103; (712) 252-2726 (95).

Kahl Home for the Aged and Infirm (Skilled and Intermediate Care Facility), 1101 W. 9th St., Davenport 52804; (319) 324-1621 (135).

The Marian Home, 2400 6th Ave. North, Fort Dodge 50501; (515) 576-1138 (110).

St. Anthony Nursing Home (Intermediate Care), 406 E. Anthony St., Carroll 51401; (712) 792-3581 (79).

St. Francis Continuation Care and Nursing Home Center, Burlington 52601; (319) 752-4564 (170).

Stonehill Adult Center (Day Care), 3485 Windsor, Dubuque 52001; (319) 557-7180 (35).

Kansas: Catholic Care Center (Skilled and Intermediate Care Facility), 6700 E. 45th St, Wichita 67226; (316) 744-2020 (294).

Mt. Joseph Senior Community (Intermediate Care Facility), 1110 W. 11, Concordia 66901; (785) 243-1347 (16 apartments).

St. Elizabeth Home Health Agency, 2225 Canterbury Rd., Hays 67601; (785) 628-8742 (43).

St. John Rest Home (Nursing Facility), 701 Seventh St., Victoria 67671; (785) 735-2208 (90).

St. John's New Horizons, 2225 Canterbury, Hays 67601; (785) 628-8742 (43).

Villa Maria, Inc. (Intermediate Care Facility), 116 S. Central, Mulvane 67110; (316) 777-1129 (99).

Kentucky: Bishop Soenneker Personal Care Home, 9545 Ky. 144, Knottsville, KY 42366; (270) 281-4881 (55).

Carmel Home (Residence, Adult Day Care, Respite Care and Nursing Care), 2501 Old Hartford Rd., Owensboro 42303; (270) 683-0227 (101).

Carmel Manor (Skilled, Intermediate and Personal Care Home), 100 Carmel Manor Rd., Ft. Thomas, 41075; (859) 781-5111 (145).

Madonna Manor Nursing Home, 2344 Amsterdam Rd., Villa Hills 41017; (606) 341-3981 (60).

Marian Home, 3105 Lexington Rd., Louisville 40206; (502) 893-0121 (69).

Nazareth Home, 2000 Newburg Rd., Louisville 40205; (502) 459-9681 (168).

St. Charles Care Center and Village, 500 Farrell Dr., Covington 41011 (606) 331-3224; www.stcharlescare.org (149). Nursing home; adult day health program. Independent living cottages (44). Assisted living (60). Independent living apartments (12).

Louisiana: Annunciation Inn, 1220 Spain St., New Orleans 70117; (504) 944-0512 (111).

Bethany M.H.S. Health Care Center (Women), P.O. Box 2308, Lafayette 70502; (337) 234-2459; (200).

Château de Notre Dame (Residence and Nursing Home), 2832 Burdette St., New Orleans 70125; (504) 866-2741 (103).

Christopher Inn Apartments, 2110 Royal St., New Orleans 70116; (504) 949-0312 (144).

Christus St. Joseph's Home (Nursing Home), 2301 Sterlington Rd., Monroe 71211; (318) 323-3426 (150).

Consolata Home (Nursing Home), 2319 E. Main St., New Iberia 70560; (337) 365-8226 (114).

Haydel Heights Apartments, 4402 Reynes St., New Orleans 70126; (504) 242-4438 (65 units).

Lafon Nursing Home of the Holy Family, 6900 Chef Menteur Hwy., New Orleans 70126; (504) 246-1100 (171).

Mary-Joseph Residence for the Elderly, 4201 Woodland Dr., New Orleans 70131; (504) 394-2200 (127).

Metairie Manor, 4929 York St., Metairie 70001; (504) 456-1467 (287).

Nazareth Inn, 9630 Hayne Blvd., New Orleans 70127; (504) 241-9630 (158).

Ollie Steele Burden Manor (Nursing Home), 4250 Essen Lane, Baton Rouge 70809; (225) 926-0091 (184).

Our Lady of Prompt Succor Home, 954 East Prudhomme St., Opelousas 70570 (337) 948-3634 (80).

Our Lady's Manor, Inc., 402 Monroe St., Alexandria 71301; (318) 473-2560 (114).

Place Dubourg, 201 Rue Dubourg, LaPlace 70068; (504) 652-1981 (115).

Rouquette Lodge, 4300 Hwy 22, Mandeville 70471; (504) 626-5217 (51).

St. John Berchmans Manor, 3400 St. Anthony St., New Orleans 70122; (504) 943-9343 (157).

St. Margaret's Daughters Home (Nursing Home), 6220 Chartres St., New Orleans 70117; (504) 279-6414 (139).

St. Martin Manor, 1501 N. Johnson St., New Orleans 70116; (504) 945-7728 (145).

Villa St. Maurice 500 St. Maurice Ave., New Orleans 70117; (504) 277-8477 (193).

Villa St. Maurice II, 6101 Douglas St., New Orleans 70117; (504) 277-8731 (80).

Village du Lac, Inc., 1404 Carmel Ave., Lafayette 70501; (337) 234-5106 (200).

Wynhoven Apartments and Wynhoven II (Residence for Senior Citizens), 4600-10th St., Marrero 70072; (504) 347-8442 (375).

Maine: Deering Pavilion (Apartments for Senior Citizens), 880 Forest Ave., Portland 04103; (207) 797-8777 (232 units).

Maison Marcotte (Independent Living Community), 100 Campus Ave., Lewiston 04240; (207) 786-0062 (128 apartments).

Mt. St. Joseph Holistic Care Community, Highwood St., Waterville 04901; (207) 873-0705 (138).

St. Andre Health Care Facility, Inc. (Nursing Facility), 407 Pool St., Biddeford 04005; (207) 282-5171 (96).

St. Joseph's Manor (Nursing Care Facility), 1133 Washington Ave., Portland 04103; (207) 797-0600 (200).

St. Marguerite D'Youville Pavilion, 102 Campus Ave., Lewiston 04240; (207) 777-4200 (280).

St. Xavier's Home (Apartments), 199 Somerset St., Bangor 04401; (207) 942-4815 (19 units).

Seton Village, Inc., 1 Carver St., Waterville 04901; (207) 873-0178 (140 housing units).

Maryland: Little Sisters of the Poor, St. Martin's Home (for the Aged), 601 Maiden Choice Lane, Baltimore 21228; (410) 744-9367 (104).

Sacred Heart Home, 5805 Queens Chapel Rd., Hyattsville 20782; (301) 277-6500 (102).

St. Joseph Nursing Home, 1222 Tugwell Dr., Baltimore 21228; (410) 747-0026 (51).

Villa Rosa Nursing Home, 3800 Lottsford Vista Rd., Mitchellville 20721; (301) 459-4700 (100).

Massachusetts: Catholic Memorial Home (Nursing Home), 2446 Highland Ave., Fall River 02720; (508) 679-0011 (300).

Don Orione Nursing Home, 111 Orient Ave., East Boston 02128; (617) 569-2100 (185).

D'Youville Manor (Nursing Home), 981 Varnum Ave., Lowell 01854; (978) 454-5681; www.dyouville.com (203).

Jeanne Jugan Pavilion, 190 Highland Ave., Somerville 02143; (617) 776-4420 (30).

Jeanne Jugan Residence, Little Sisters of the Poor (Home for the Elderly), 186 Highland Ave., Somerville 02143; (617) 776-4420 (84).

Madonna Manor (Nursing Home), 85 N. Washington St., N. Attleboro 02760; (508) 699-2740 (129).

Marian Manor, for the Aged and Infirm (Nursing Home), 130 Dorchester St., S. Boston, 02127; (617) 268-3333; www.marianmanor.org (366).

Marian Manor of Taunton (Nursing Home), 33 Summer St., Taunton 02780; (508) 822-4885 (184).

Maristhill Nursing Home, 66 Newton St., Waltham 02154; (781) 893-0240 (154).

MI Nursing/Restorative Center, Zero Bennington St., Lawrence 01841; (508) 685-6321 (335).

MI Residential Community, 189 Maple St., Lawrence 01841; (978) 682-7575 (35).

Our Lady's Haven (Nursing Home), 71 Center St., Fairhaven 02719; (508) 999-4561; www.dhfo.org (158).

Sacred Heart Home (Nursing Home), 359 Summer St., New Bedford 02740 (508) 996-6751; www.dhfo.org (217).

St. Joseph Manor Health Care, Inc., 215 Thatcher St., Brockton 02302; (508) 583-5834 (118).

St. Joseph's Nursing Care Center, 321 Centre St., Dorchester, Boston 02122; (617) 825-6320 (191).

St. Patrick's Manor (Nursing Home), 863 Central St., Framingham 01701 (508) 879-8000, www.stpatricksmanor.org (460).

Michigan: Bishop Noa Home for Senior Citizens (Nursing Home and Residence), 2900 3rd Ave. S., Escanaba 49829; (906) 786-5810 (123).

Lourdes Nursing Home (Skilled Facility), 2300 Watkins Lake Rd., Waterford 48328; (248) 674-2241, www.lourdescampus.com (108).

Marycrest Manor (Skilled Nursing Facility), 15475 Middlebelt Rd., Livonia 48154; (313) 427-9175; (55).

Ryan Senior Residences of the Archdiocese of Detroit:

Casa Maria, 600 Maple Vista, Imlay City 48444; (810) 724-6300 (84).

Kundig Center, 3300 Jeffries Freeway, Detroit 48208; (313) 894-0555 (160).

Lourdes Assisted Living Home, Inc., (Residence), 2450 Watkins Lake Rd., Waterford 48328; (248) 618-6361, www.lourdescampus.com (6).

Marian-Oakland West, 29250 W. Ten Mile Rd., Farmington Hills 48336; (248) 474-7204 (87).

Marian Place, 408 W. Front St., Monroe 48161; (734) 241-2414 (53).

Marydale Center, 3147 Tenth Ave., Port Huron 48060; (810) 985-9683 (56).

Maryhaven, 11350 Reeck Rd., Southgate 48195; (734) 287-2111 (90).

Mercy Madonna Villa 17825 Fifteen Mile Rd., Clinton Twp. 48035; (810) 792-0358 (86).

Stapleton Center, 9341 Agnes St., Detroit 48214; (313) 822-0397 (59).

Villa Marie, 15131 Newburgh Rd., Livonia 48154; (734) 464-9494 (86).

St. Ann's Home, (Residence and Nursing Home), 2161 Leonard St. N.W., Grand Rapids 49504; (616) 453-7715 (140).

St. Catherine House, 1641 Webb Ave., Detroit 48206; (313) 868-4505 (12).

St. Elizabeth Briarbank (Women, Residence), 1315 N. Woodward Ave., Bloomfield Hills 48304; (248) 644-1011 (44).

St. Francis Home (Nursing Home), 915 N. River Rd., Saginaw 48609, (517) 781-3150 (100).

St. Joseph's Home, 4800 Cadieux Rd., Detroit 48224; (313) 882-3800 (104).

Minnesota: Alverna Apartments, 300 8th Ave. S.E., Little Falls 56345; (320) 632-1246; (68).

Assumption Home, 715 North First St., Cold Spring 56320; (320) 685-4110 (34)

Divine Providence Community Home (Skilled Nursing Care) and Lake Villa Maria Senior Housing, 702 Third Ave. N.W., Sleepy Eye 56085; (507) 794-5333 (58).

Franciscan Health Community, 1925 Norfolk Ave., St. Paul 55116; (651) 696-8400 (223).

John Paul Apartments, 200 8th Ave. N., Cold Spring 56320; (320) 685-4429 (61).

Little Sisters of the Poor, Holy Family Residence (Skilled Nursing and Intermediate Care), 330 S. Exchange St., St. Paul 55102; (651) 227-0336 (73). Independent living apartments (32).

Madonna Towers (Retirement Apartments and Nursing Home), 4001 19th Ave. N.W., Rochester 55901; (507) 288-3911 (184).

Mary Rondorf Retirement Home of Sacred Heart Parish, Inc., 222 5th St., N.E., Staples 56479; (218) 894-2124 (45). Board and lodging with special services.

Mother of Mercy Nursing Home and Retirement Center, 230 Church Ave., Box 676, Albany 56307; (320) 845-2195 (114).

Regina Nursing Home and Retirement Residence Center, 1175 Nininger Rd., Hastings 55033; (651) 480-4336; www.reginamedical.com. (Nursing home (61); retirement home (43); boarding care (32).

Sacred Heart Hospice (Skilled Nursing Home, Adult Day Care, Home Health Care) 1200 Twelfth St. S.W., Austin 55912; (507) 433-1808 (59).

St. Ann's Residence, 330 E. 3rd St., Duluth 55805; (218) 727-8831; www.stanns.com (185).

St. Anne Retirement Community (Skilled Nursing Home), 1347 W. Broadway, Winona 55987; (507) 454-3621, www.saintannehosp.homestead.com (74).

St. Benedict's Center, 1810 Minnesota Blvd. S.E., St. Cloud 56304; (320) 252-0010 (198 bed skilled nursing care; adult day care, respite care). Benedict Village (Retirement Apartments), 2000 15th Ave. S.E., St. Cloud 56304; (320) 252-4380. Benedict Homes (Alzheimer Residential Care) and Benedict Court (Assisted Living), 1980 15th Ave. S.E., St. Cloud 56304; (320) 252-0010.

St. Elizabeth's Health Care Center, 626 Shields Ave., Wabasha 55981; (651) 565-3414 (106).

St. Elizabeth's Medical Center, 1200 Grant Blvd., W., Wabasha 55981; (651) 565-4531.

St. Francis Home, 501 Oak St., Breckenridge 56520; (218) 643-7661 (124).

St. Mary's Regional Health Center, 1027 Washington Ave., Detroit Lakes 56501, (218) 847-5611 (100).

St. Otto's Care Center (Nursing Home), 920 S.E. 4th St., Little Falls 56345; (320) 632-9281 (150).

St. William's Nursing Home, P.O. Box 30, Parkers Prairie 56361; (218) 338-4671 (90).

Villa of St. Francis Nursing Home, 1001 Scott Ave., Morris 56267; (320) 589-1133 (128).

Villa St. Vincent (Skilled Nursing Home and Residence), 516 Walsh St., Crookston 56716; (218) 281-3424. Skilled Nursing home (80); special care unit (24); apartments (27); board and care (34).

Westwood Senior Apartments, 925 Kenwood Ave., Duluth 55811; (218) 733-2238, www.westwood duluth.org (70).

Mississippi: Notre Dame de la Mer Retirement Apartments, 292 Hwy. 90, Bay St. Louis 39520; (228) 467-2885 (61).

Santa Maria Retirement Apartments, 674 Beach Blvd., Biloxi, 39530; (228) 432-1289 (223).

Villa Maria Retirement Apartments, 921 Porter Ave., Ocean Springs 39564; (228) 875-8811 (225).

Missouri: Cathedral Square Towers, 444 W. 12th St., Kansas City 64105; (816) 471-6555 (167).

Chariton Apartments (Retirement Apartments), 4249 Michigan Ave., St. Louis 63111; (314) 352-7600 (122 units; 143 residents).

LaVerna Heights Retirement Home (Women), 104 E. Park Ave., Savannah 64485; (816) 324-3185, www.sistersofstfrancis.org (57).

LaVerna Village Nursing Home, 904 Hall Ave., Savannah 64485; (816) 324-3185 (133).

Little Sisters of the Poor (Home for Aged), 3225 N. Florissant Ave., St. Louis 63107; (314) 421-6022 (114).

Mary, Queen and Mother Center (Nursing Care), 7601 Watson Rd., St. Louis 63119; (314) 961-8000 (230).

Mother of Good Counsel Home (Skilled Nursing, Women), 6825 Natural Bridge Rd., Northwoods, 63121; (314) 383-4765 (114).

Our Lady of Mercy Country Home, 2205 Hughes Rd., Liberty 64068; (816) 781-5711 (105).

Price Memorial Skilled Nursing Facility, Forby Rd., P.O. Box 476, Eureka 63025; (636) 587-3200 (120).

St. Agnes Home for the Elderly, 10341 Manchester Rd., Kirkwood 63122; (314) 965-7616 (124).

St. Joseph Hill Infirmary, Inc., (Nursing Care Facility, Men), St. Joseph Road, Eureka 63025; (636) 587-3661 (120).

St. Joseph's Home (Residential and Intermediate Care), 723 First Capitol Dr., St. Charles 63301; (314) 946-4140; (110).

St. Joseph's Home (Residential and Intermediate Care Facility), 1306 W. Main St., Jefferson City 65109; (573) 635-0166 (90).

Nebraska: Madonna Rehabilitation Hospital, 5401 South St., Lincoln 68506; (402) 489-7102; www.madonna.org (252).

Mercy Care Center (Skilled Nursing Facility for Chronic, Complex and Subacute Levels of Care and Rehabilitation), 1870 S. 75th St., Omaha 68124; (402) 343-8500 (246).

Mercy Villa, 1845 S. 72nd St., Omaha 68124; (402) 391-6224.

Mt. Carmel Home, Keens Memorial (Nursing Home), 412 W. 18th St., Kearney 68847; (308) 237-2287 (75).

New Cassel Retirement Center, 900 N. 90th St., Omaha 68114; (402) 393-2277; www.newcassel.org (165).

St. Joseph's Nursing Home, 401 N. 18th St., Norfolk 68701; (402) 371-9404 (99).

St. Joseph's Retirement Community, 320 E. Decatur St., West Point 68788; (402) 372-3477 (90).

St. Joseph's Villa (Nursing Home), 927 7th St., David City 68632; (402) 367-3045 (65).

New Hampshire: Mount Carmel Nursing Home, 235 Myrtle St., Manchester 03104; (603) 627-3811 (120).

St. Ann Home (Nursing Home), 195 Dover Point Rd., Dover 03820; (603) 742-2612 (54).

St. Francis Home (Nursing Home), 406 Court St., Laconia 03246; (603) 524-0466 (51).

St. Teresa Manor (Nursing Home), 519 Bridge St., Manchester 03104; (603) 668-2373 (5).

St. Vincent de Paul Nursing Home, 29 Providence Ave., Berlin 03570; (603) 752-1820 (80).

New Jersey: McCarrick Care Center, 15 Dellwood Lane, Somerset 08873; (732) 545-4200 (142).

Mater Dei Nursing Home, 176 Rt. 40, Newfield 08344; (856) 358-2061 (64).

Morris Hall (St. Joseph Skilled Nursing Center, St. Mary Residence), 1 Bishops' Dr., Lawrenceville 08648; (609) 896-0006, www.morrishall.org (100).

Mount St. Andrew Villa (Residence), 55 W. Midland Ave., Paramus 07652; (201) 261-5950 (55).

Our Lady's Residence (Nursing Home), 1100 Clematis Ave., Pleasantville 08232; (609) 646-2450 (236).

St. Ann's Home for the Aged (Skilled and Intermediate Nursing Care Home, Women), 198 Old Bergen Rd., Jersey City 07305; (201) 433-0950 (106).

St. Francis Health Resort (Residence), Denville 07834; (973) 625-9245 (150).

St. Joseph's Home for the Elderly, Little Sisters of the Poor, 140 Shepherd Lane, Totowa 07512; (973) 942-0300 (134).

St. Joseph's Rest Home for Aged Women, 46 Preakness Ave., Paterson 07522; (973) 956-1921 (35).

St. Joseph's Senior Residence (Sheltered Care), 1 St. Joseph Terr., Woodbridge, 07095; (732) 634-0004 (60).

St. Mary's Nursing Home, 210 St. Mary's Dr., Cherry Hill 08003; (856) 424-9521 (215). The Manor at St. Mary's, 220 St. Mary's Dr., Cherry Hill 08003; (856) 424-3817 (739).

St. Vincent's Nursing Home, 45 Elm St., Montclair 07042; (973) 754-4800 (220).

Villa Maria (Residence and Infirmary, Women), 641 Somerset St., N. Plainfield 07061; (908) 757-3050 (86).

New Mexico: Good Shepherd Manor (Residential Care for Aged Persons), Little Brothers of the Good Shepherd, P.O. Box 10248, Albuquerque 87184; (505) 898-0177 (40).

New York: Bernardine Apartments, 417 Churchill Ave., Syracuse 13205; (315) 469-7786.

Brothers of Mercy Sacred Heart Home (Residence) 4520 Ransom Rd., Clarence 14031; (716) 759-2644 (80). Brothers of Mercy Nursing Home, 10570 Bergtold Rd., Clarence 14031; (716) 759-6985; www.brothersofmercy.org (240). Brothers of Mercy Housing Co., Inc. (Apartments), 10500 Bergtold Rd., Clarence 14031; (716) 759-2122 (110).

Carmel Richmond Nursing Home, 88 Old Town Rd., Staten Island 10304; (718) 979-5000 (300).

Ferncliff Nursing Home, 52 River Rd., Rhinebeck 12572; (914) 876-2011 (328).

Franciscan Health System of New York, 2975 Independence Ave., Bronx 10463; (718) 548-1700.

Good Samaritan Nursing Home (Skilled Nursing), 101 Elm St., Sayville, N.Y. 11782; (631) 244-2400 (100).

The Heritage (Apartments with Skilled Nursing Care), 1450 Portland Ave., Rochester 14621; (716) 342-1700; www.stannsrochester.org (237)

Holy Family Home, 1740-84th St., Brooklyn 11214; (718) 232-3666 (200).

Holy Family Home (Adult Home), 410 Mill St., Williamsville 14221; (716) 634-5400 (85).

Kateri Residence (Skilled Nursing), 150 Riverside Dr., New York 10024; (212) 769-0744; www.catholic healthcaresystem.org/kateri (610).

Little Sisters of the Poor, Jeanne Jugan Residence (Skilled Nursing and Health Related; Adult Care), 3200 Baychester Ave., Bronx 10475; (718) 671-2120 (60).

Little Sisters of the Poor, Queen of Peace Residence, 110-30 221st St., Queens Village 11429; (718) 464-1800.

Mary Manning Walsh Home (Nursing Home), 1339 York Ave., New York 10021; (212) 628-2800 (362).

Mercy Healthcare Center (Skilled Nursing Facility), 114 Wawbeek Ave., Tupper Lake 12986; (518) 359-3355, www.muhc.org (80).

Mt. Loretto Nursing Home, (Skilled Nursing Home), Sisters of the Resurrection, 302 Swart Hill Rd., Amsterdam 12010; (518) 842-6790 (120).

Nazareth Nursing Home (Women), 291 W. North St., Buffalo 14201; (716) 881-2323 (125).

Our Lady of Consolation Geriatric Care Center (Skilled Nursing) 111 Beach Dr., West Islip 11795; (631) 587-1600 (450).

Our Lady of Hope Residence (Home for the Aged), Little Sisters of the Poor, 1 Jeanne Jugan Lane, Latham 12210; (518) 785-4551 (117).

Ozanam Hall of Queens Nursing Home, Inc., 42-41 201st St., Bayside 11361; (718) 423-2000 (432).

Providence Rest, 3304 Waterbury Ave., Bronx 10465; (718) 931-30000; www.chcn.org/providence (242).

Resurrection Nursing Home (Skilled Nursing Facility), Castleton 12033; (518) 732-7617 (80).

St. Ann's Community (Skilled Nursing Facility), 1500 Portland Ave., Rochester 14621; (716) 342-1216, www.stannscommunity.com (354).

St. Cabrini Nursing Home, 115 Broadway, Dobbs Ferry 10522; (914) 693-6800 (304).

St. Clare Manor (Nursing Home), 543 Locust St., Lockport 14094; (716) 434-4718 (28).

St. Columban's on the Lake (Retirement Home), 2546 Lake Rd., Silver Creek 14136; (716) 934-4515 (50).

St. Elizabeth Home (Adult Home), 5539 Broadway, Lancaster 14086; (716) 683-5150 (117).

St. Francis Home (Skilled Nursing Facility), 147 Reist St., Williamsville 14221; (716) 633-5400 (142).

St. Joseph Manor (Nursing Home), 2211 W. State St., Olean 14760; (716) 372-7810 (22).

St. Joseph Nursing Home, 2535 Genesee St., Utica 13501; (315) 797-1230; www.stjosephnh.org.

St. Joseph's Guest Home, Missionary Sisters of St. Benedict, 350 Cuba Hill Rd., Huntington 11743; (631) 368-9528.

St. Joseph's Home (Nursing Home), 420 Lafayette St., Ogdensburg 13669; (315) 393-3780, www.stjh.org (117).

St. Joseph's Villa (Adult Home), 38 Prospect Ave., Catskill 12414; (518) 943-5701.

St. Luke Manor, 17 Wiard St., Batavia 14020; (716) 343-8806 (20).

St. Mary's Manor, 515 Sixth St., Niagara Falls 14301; (716) 285-3236 (165).

St. Patrick's Home for the Aged and Infirm, 66 Van Cortlandt Park S., Bronx NY 10463; (718) 519-2800; www.hometown.aol.com/stpatshome/stp/ (264).

St. Teresa Nursing Home, 120 Highland Ave., Middletown 10940; (914) 342-1033; (98).

St. Vincent's Home for the Aged, 319 Washington Ave., Dunkirk 14048; (716) 366-2066 (40).

Terence Cardinal Cooke Health Care Center (Skilled Nursing), 1249 Fifth Ave., New York 10029; (212) 360-1000 (523).

Teresian House, 200 Washington Ave. Extension, Albany 12203; (518) 456-2000; www.teresian house.com (300).

Uihlein Mercy Center (Nursing Home), 420 Old Military Rd., Lake Placid 12946; (518) 523-2464 (220).

North Carolina: Maryfield Nursing Home, 1315 Greensboro Rd., High Point 27260; (336) 886-2444 (115).

North Dakota: Manor St. Joseph (Basic Care Facility), 404 Fourth Ave., Edgeley 58433; (701) 493-2477 (40).

Marillac Manor Retirement Center, 1016 28th St., Bismarck 58501; (701) 258-8702 (78 apartments).

St. Anne's Guest Home, 524 N. 17th St., Grand Forks 58203; (701) 746-9401 (86)

St. Vincent's Care Center (Nursing Facility), 1021 N. 26th St., Bismarck 58501; (701) 223-6888 (101).

Ohio: Archbishop Leibold Home for the Aged, Little Sisters of the Poor, 476 Riddle Rd., Cincinnati 45220; (513) 281-8001 (100).

The Assumption Village, 9800 Market St., North Lima 44452; (330) 549-0740 (120).

Francesca Residence (Retirement), 39 N. Portage Path, Akron 44303; (330) 867-6334; (40).

House of Loreto (Nursing Home), 2812 Harvard Ave. N.W., Canton 44709; (330) 453-8137 (76).

Jennings Hall, Inc. (Nursing Care), 10204 Granger Rd., Cleveland 44125; (216) 581-2900 (150).

Little Sisters of the Poor, Sacred Heart Home, 4900 Navarre Ave., Oregon 43616; (419) 698-4331 (81).

Little Sisters of the Poor, Sts. Mary and Joseph Home for Aged, 4291 Richmond Rd., Cleveland 44122; (216) 464-1222 (125).

The Maria-Joseph Living Care Center, 4830 Salem Ave., Dayton 45416; (937) 278-2692; www.maria joseph.org (440).

Mercy Franciscan Terrace, 100 Compton Rd., Cincinnati 45215; (513) 761-9036 (148).

Mercy St. Theresa Center, 7010 Rowan Hill Dr., Cincinnati 45227; (513) 271-7010, www.e-mercy.com (157).

Mercy Siena Woods (Nursing Home, Skilled and Intermediate Care, Alzheimer Center), 235 W. Orchard Spring Dr., Dayton 45415; (937) 278-8211 (99).

Mount Alverna (Intermediate Care Nursing Facility), 6765 State Rd., Cleveland 44134; (440) 843-7800; www.franciscanservices.com/facilities/ (203).

Mt. St. Joseph (Skilled Nursing Facility, Dual Certified), 21800 Chardon Rd., Euclid 44117; (216) 531-7426 (100).

Nazareth Towers, 300 E. Rich St., Columbus 43215; (614) 464-4780 (229).

St. Augustine Manor (Skilled Nursing Facility), 7801 Detroit Ave., Cleveland 44102; (216) 634-7400 (248).

St. Francis Health Care Centre, 401 N. Broadway St., Green Springs 44836; (419) 639-2626, www.sfhcc.org (186).

St. Francis Home, Inc. (Residence and Nursing Care), 182 St. Francis Ave., Tiffin 44883; (419) 447-2723 (173).

St. Joseph's Nursing Home and Assisted Living, 2308 Reno Dr., Louisville 44641; (330) 875-5562 (100, nursing home; 40 assisted living).

St. Margaret Hall (Rest Home and Nursing Facility), Carmelite Sisters for the Aged and Infirm, 1960 Madison Rd., Cincinnati 45206; (513) 751-5880 (133).

St. Raphael Home (Nursing Home), 1550 Roxbury Rd., Columbus 43212; (614) 486-0436 (78).

St. Rita's Home (Skilled Nursing Home), 880 Greenlawn Ave., Columbus 43223; (614) 443-9433 (100).

Schroder Manor Retirement Community (Residential Care, Skilled Nursing Care and Independent Living Units), Franciscan Sisters of the Poor, 1302 Millville Ave., Hamilton 45013; (513) 867-1300 (125).

The Villa Sancta Anna Home for the Aged, Inc., 25000 Chagrin Blvd., Beachwood 44122; (216) 464-9250 (68).

The Village at St. Edward (Apartments, Nursing Care and Assisted Living), 3131 Smith Rd., Fairlawn 44333; (330) 666-1183, www.vased.org (160).

Oklahoma: St. Ann's Home, 9400 St. Ann's Dr., Oklahoma City 73162; (405) 728-7888 (120).

Westminster Village, Inc. (Residence), 1601 Academy, Ponca City 74604; (580) 762-0927 (131).

Oregon: Benedictine Nursing Center, 540 S. Main St., Mt. Angel 97362; (503) 845-6841 (75). Home Health Agency, Outpatient Therapies. Benedictine Institute for Long Term Care. Child Development Center.

Evergreen Court Retirement Apartments, 451 O'Connell St., North Bend 97459; (541) 756-4466.

Maryville Nursing Home, 14645 S.W. Farmington, Beaverton 97007; (503) 643-8626 (156).

Mt. St. Joseph, 3060 S.E. Stark St., Portland 97214; (503) 535-4700 (347).

St. Catherine's Residence and Nursing Center, 3959 Sheridan Ave., North Bend 97459; (541) 756-4151 (200).

Pennsylvania: Antonian Towers, 2405 Hillside Ave., Easton 18042; (610) 258-2033 (50).

Ascension Manor I (Senior Citizen Housing), 911 N. Franklin St., Philadelphia 19123; (215) 922-1116.

Ascension Manor II (Senior Citizen Housing), 970 N. 7th St., Philadelphia 19123; (215) 922-1116.

Benetwood Apartments, Benedictine Sisters of Erie, 641 Troupe Rd., Harborcreek 16421; (814) 899-0088 (80).

Bethlehem Retirement Village, 100 W. Wissahickon Ave., Flourtown 19031; (215) 233-0998.

Christ the King Manor, 1100 W. Long Ave., Du Bois 15801; (814) 371-3180 (160).

D'Youville Manor (Residential Care Facility), 1750 Quarry Rd., Yardley 19067; (215) 579-1750 (49).

Garvey Manor (Nursing Home), 128 Logan Blvd., Hollidaysburg 16648; (814) 695-5571 (150).

Grace Mansion (Personal Care Facility), Holy Family Residential Services, 1200 Spring St., Bethlehem; (610) 865-6748 (33).

Holy Family Apartments, 330-338 13th Ave., Bethlehem 18018; (610) 866-4603 (50).

Holy Family Home, Little Sisters of the Poor, 5300 Chester Ave., Philadelphia 19143; (215) 729-5153 (105).

Holy Family Manor (Skilled and Intermediate Nursing Facility), 1200 Spring St., Bethlehem 18018; (610) 865-5595 (208).

Holy Family Residence (Personal Care Facility), 900 W. Market St., Orwigsburg 17961; (570) 366-2912 (85).

Immaculate Mary Home (Nursing Care Facility), 2990 Holme Ave., Philadelphia 19136; (215) 335-2100 (296).

John XXIII Home (Skilled, Intermediate and Personal Care), 2250 Shenango Freeway, Hermitage 16148; (724) 981-3200 (142).

Little Flower Manor (Residence, Women), 1215 Springfield Rd., Darby 19023; (610) 534-6000 (180).

Little Flower Manor Nursing Home (Skilled Nursing), 1201 Springfield Rd., Darby 19023; (610) 534-6000 (185).

Little Flower Manor of Diocese of Scranton, (Long-Term Skilled Nursing Care Facility), 200 S. Meade St., Wilkes-Barre 18702; (570) 823-6131.

Little Sisters of the Poor, 1028 Benton Ave., Pittsburgh 15212; (412) 761-5373, (40).

Little Sisters of the Poor, Holy Family Residence, 2500 Adams Ave., Scranton 18509; (570) 343-4065 (58).

Maria Joseph Manor (Skilled Nursing, Personal Care Facility and Independent Living Cottages), 875 Montour Blvd., Danville 17821; (570) 275-4221 (135).

Marian Hall Home for the Aged (Women), 934 Forest Ave., Pittsburgh 15202; (412) 761-1999 (49).

Marian Manor (Intermediate Care), 2695 Winchester Dr., Pittsburgh 15220; (412) 563-6866 (194).

Mount Macrina Manor (Skilled Nursing Facility), 520 W. Main St., Uniontown 15401; (724) 437-1400 (141).

Neumann Apartments (Low Income), 25 N. Nichols St., St. Clair 17970; (570) 429-0699 (25).

Queen of Angels Apartments, 22 Rothermel St., Hyde Park, Reading 19605; (610) 921-3115 (45 units).

Queen of Peace Apartments (Low Income), 777

Water St., Pottsville 17901; (570) 628-4504 (65).

Redeemer Village II, 1551 Huntingdon Pike, Huntingdon Valley 19006; (215) 947-8168; www.holyredeemer.com (151

Sacred Heart Manor (Nursing Home and Independent Living), 6445 Germantown Ave., Philadelphia 19119; (215) 438-5268 (171 nursing home; 48 personal care; 48 independent living).

St. Anne's Home and Village, 3952 Columbia Ave., Columbia 17512; (717) 285-5443 (121).

St. Anne Home (Nursing Facility), 685 Angela Dr., Greensburg 15601; (724) 837-6070 (125).

St. Ignatius Nursing Home, 4401 Haverford Ave., Philadelphia 19104; (215) 349-8800 (176).

St. John Neumann Nursing Home, 10400 Roosevelt Blvd., Philadelphia 19116; (215) 248-7200 (107).

St. Joseph Home for the Aged (Residential and Skilled Nursing Facility), 1182 Holland Rd., Holland 18966; (215) 357-5511 (76).

St. Joseph Nursing and Health Care Center (Skilled Nursing Facility), 5324 Penn Ave., Pittsburgh 15224; (412) 665-5100 (153).

St. Leonard's Home Inc. (Personal Care Facility), 601 N. Montgomery St., Hollidaysburg 16648; (814) 695-9581 (30).

St. Mary of Providence Center, R.D. 2, Box 145, Elverson 19520; (610) 942-4166 (52).

St. Mary's Home of Erie, 607 E. 26th St., Erie 16504; (814) 459-0621, www.stmaryshome.org (131).

Saint Mary's Manor (Residential, Personal Care, Short-Term Rehabilitation and Nursing Care), 701 Lansdale Ave., Lansdale 19446; (215) 368-0900 (200).

St. Mary's Villa Nursing Home, St. Mary's Villa Rd., Elmhurst 18416; (570) 842-7621; (112).

Trexler Pavilion (Personal Care Facility), 1220 Prospect Ave., Bethlehem 18018; (610) 868-7776 (30).

Villa Teresa (Nursing Home), 1051 Avila Rd., Harrisburg 17109; (717) 652-5900 (184).

Vincentian de Marillac Nursing Home, 5300 Stanton Ave., Pittsburgh 15206; (412) 361-2833 (52).

Vincentian Home (Nursing Facility), 111 Perrymont Rd., Pittsburgh 15237; (412) 366-5600 (217).

Rhode Island: Jeanne Jugan Residence of the Little Sisters of the Poor, 964 Main St., Pawtucket 02860; (401) 723-4314 (95).

Saint Antoine Residence (Skilled Nursing Facility), 10 Rhodes Ave., North Smithfield 02896; (401) 767-3500, www.stantoine.net (416).

St. Clare Home (Nursing Facility), 309 Spring St., Newport 02840; (401) 849-3204 (47).

St. Francis House, 167 Blackstone St., Woonsocket 02895; (401) 762-5255 (59).

Scalabrini Villa (Convalescent, Rest-Nursing Home). 860 N. Quidnessett Rd., North Kingstown 02852; (401) 884-1802; www.freeyellow.com/members3/scalabrini/ (175).

South Carolina: Carter-May Home, 1660 Ingram Rd., Charleston 29407; (843) 556-8314 (15).

South Dakota: Avera Brady Memorial Home (Skilled Nursing Facility), 500 S. Ohlman St., Mitchell 57301; (605) 966-7701 (83).

Mother Joseph Manor (Skilled Nursing Facility), 1002 North Jay St., Aberdeen 57401; (605) 622-5850 (81).

Prince of Peace Retirement Community, 4500 Prince of Peace Pl., Sioux Falls 57103; (605) 322-5600 (204).

St. William's Home for the Aged (Intermediate Care, 60), and Angela Hall (Assisted Living Center for Developmentally Handicapped Women, 22), 901 E. Virgil, Box 432, Milbank 57252; (605) 432-4538.

Tekakwitha Nursing Home (Skilled and Intermediate Care), 6 E. Chestnut, Sisseton 57262; (605) 698-7693 (101).

Tennessee: Alexian Village of Tennessee, 100 James Blvd., Signal Mountain 37377; (423) 886-0100 (277).

St. Mary Manor, 1771 Highway 45 Bypass, Jackson 38305; (731) 668-5633.

St. Peter Manor (Retirement Community), 108 N. Auburndale, Memphis 38104; (901) 278-8200.

St. Peter Villa (Intermediate and Skilled Care), 141 N. McLean, Memphis 38104; (901) 276-2021.

Villa Maria Manor, 32 White Bridge Rd., Nashville 37205; (615) 352-3084 (230).

Texas: Casa, Inc., Housing for Elderly and Handicapped, 3201 Sondra Dr., Fort Worth 76107; (817) 332-7276 (200).

Casa Brendan Housing for the Elderly and Handicapped (56 apartments) and Casa II, Inc. (30 apartments), 1300 Hyman St., Stephenville 76401; (254) 965-6964 (83).

John Paul II Nursing Home (Intermediate Care and Personal Care), 209 S. 3rd St., Kenedy 78119; (830) 583-9841.

Mother of Perpetual Help Home (Intermediate Care Facility), 519 E. Madison Ave., Brownsville 78520; (956) 546-6745; (38).

Mt. Carmel Home (Personal Care Home), 4130 S. Alameda St., Corpus Christi 78411; (512) 855-6243 (92).

Nuestro Hogar Housing for Elderly and Handicapped, 709 Magnolia St., Arlington 76012; (817) 261-0608 (63).

St. Ann's Nursing Home, P.O. Box 1179, Panhandle 79068; (806) 537-3194 (56).

St. Dominic Residence Hall, 2401 Holcombe Blvd., Houston 77021; (713) 741-8700 (149).

St. Francis Nursing Home (Intermediate Care Facility), 630 W. Woodlawn, San Antonio 78212; (210) 736-3177 (152).

St. Francis Village, Inc. (Retired and Elderly), 1 Chapel Plaza, Crowley 76036; (817) 292-5786 (420).

San Juan Nursing Home, Inc. (Skilled and Intermediate Care Facility), P.O. Box 1238, San Juan, 78589; (956) 787-1771 (127).

Villa Maria (Home for Aged Women-Men), 920 S. Oregon St., El Paso 79901; (915) 533-5152 (17 units).

Villa Maria, Inc. (Apartment Complex), 3146 Saratoga Blvd., Corpus Christi 78415; (361) 857-6171 (59).

Utah: St. Joseph Villa (Senior Care Complex), 451 Bishop Federal Lane, Salt Lake City 84115; (801) 487-7557 (300).

Vermont: Loretto Home for Aged, 59 Meadow St., Rutland 05701; (802) 773-8840 (57).

Michaud Memorial Manor (Residential Home for Elderly), Derby Line 05830; (802) 873-3152 (34).

St. Joseph's Home for Aged, 243 N. Prospect St., Burlington 05401; (802) 864-0264 (32).

Virginia: Madonna Home (Home for Aged), 814 W. 37th St., Norfolk 23508; (757) 623-6662 (16).

Marian Manor (Assisted Living, Nursing Care), 5345 Marian Lane, Virginia Beach 23462; (757) 456-5018 (100).

Marywood Apartments, 1261 Marywood Lane, Richmond 23229; (804) 740-5567 (126).

McGurk House Apartments, 2425 Tate Springs Rd., Lynchburg 24501; (804) 846-2425 (89).

Our Lady of the Valley Retirement Community, 650 N. Jefferson St., Roanoke 24016; (540) 345-5111.

Russell House Apartments, 900 First Colonial Rd., Virginia Beach 23454; (757) 481-0770 (126).

St. Francis Home, 2511 Wise St., Richmond 23225; (804) 231-1043 (34).

St. Joseph's Home for the Aged, Little Sisters of the Poor, 1503 Michael Rd., Richmond 23229; (804) 288-6245 (72).

St. Mary's Woods (Independent and Assisted Living Apartments), 1257 Marywood Lane, Richmond 23229; (804) 741-8624 (118 apartments).

Seton Manor (Apartments), 215 Marcella Rd., Hampton 23666; (757) 827-6512 (112).

Washington: Cathedral Plaza Apartments (Retirement Apartments), W. 1120 Sprague Ave., Spokane 99204 (150).

Chancery Place (Retirement Apartments), 910 Marion, Seattle 98104 (206) 343-9415.

The Delaney, W. 242 Riverside Ave., Spokane 99201, (509) 747-5081 (83).

Elbert House, 16000 N.E. 8th St., Bellevue 98008; (206) 747-5111.

Emma McRedmond Manor, 7960-169th N.E., Redmond 98052; (206) 869-2424 (31).

Fahy Garden Apartments, W. 1403-11 Dean Ave., Spokane 99201 (31).

Fahy West Apartments, W. 1523 Dean Ave., Spokane 99201 (55).

The Franciscan (Apartments), 15237-21stAve. S.W., Seattle 98166; (206) 431-8001.

Providence Mt. St. Vincent (Nursing Center and Retirement Apartments), 4831 35th Ave. S.W., Seattle 98126; (206) 937-3700 (174).

Tumwater Apartments, 5701-6th Ave. S.W., Tumwater 98501; (360) 352-4321.

West Virginia: Welty Home for the Aged, 21 Washington Ave., Wheeling 26003; (304) 242-5233 (46).

Wisconsin: Alexian Village of Milwaukee (Retirement Community/Skilled Nursing Home), 9301 N. 76th St., Milwaukee 53223; (414) 355-9300; www.alexianvillage.org (327).

Bethany-St. Joseph Health Care Center, 2501 Shelby Rd., La Crosse 54601; (608) 788-5700 (226).

Clement Manor (Retirement Community and Skilled Nursing), 3939 S. 92nd St., Greenfield 53228; (414) 321-1800 (162).

Divine Savior Nursing Home, 715 W. Pleasant St., Portage 53901; (608) 742-4131 (124).

Felician Village (Independent Living), 1700 S. 18th St., Manitowoc 54020; (920) 683-8811 (134 apartments).

Franciscan Care Center, 2915 North Meade St., Appleton 54911; (920) 831-8700 (215).

Franciscan Skemp Healthcare, Mayo Health System:

Arcadia Campus Nursing Home, 464 S. St. Joseph Ave., Arcadia 54612; (608) 323-3341 (75).

McCormick Memorial Home, 212 Iroquois St., Green Bay 54301; (920) 437-0883 (60).

Marian Catholic Home (Skilled Care Nursing Home), 3333 W. Highland Blvd., Milwaukee 53208; (414) 344-8100 (215).

Marian Franciscan Center, 9632 W. Appleton Ave., Milwaukee 53225; (414) 461-8850 (310).

Marian Housing Center (Independent Living), 4105 Spring St., Racine 53405; (262) 633-5807 (40).

Maryhill Manor Nursing Home (Skilled Nursing Facility), 501 Madison Ave., Niagara 54151; (715) 251-3178 (75).

Milwaukee Catholic Home (Continuing Care Retirement Community), 2462 N. Prospect Ave., Milwaukee 53211; (414) 224-9700 (131).

Nazareth House (Skilled Nursing Facility), 814 Jackson St., Stoughton 53589; (608) 873-6448 (99).

St. Ann Rest Home (Intermediate Care Facility, Women), 2020 S. Muskego Ave., Milwaukee 53204; (414) 383-2630 (50).

St. Anne's Home for the Elderly, 3800 N. 92nd St., Milwaukee 53222; (414) 463-7570; www.wahsa.org/st.anne/index.html (106).

St. Camillus Campus (Continuing Care Retirement Community), 10100 West Blue Mound Road, Wauwatosa 53226; (414) 258-1814, www.stcam.com (386).

St. Elizabeth Nursing Home, 502 St. Lawrence Ave., Janesville 53545; (608) 752-6709 (43).

St. Francis Home (Skilled Nursing Facility), 1416 Cumming Ave., Superior 54880; (715) 394-5591.

St. Francis Home (Skilled Nursing), 33 Everett St., Fond du Lac 54935; (920) 923-7980 (106).

St. Joseph's Home, 9244 29th Ave., Kenosha 53143; (262) 694-0080; www.sjosephs.com (93).

St. Joseph's Rehabilitation Center, 2902 East Ave. S., La Crosse 54601; (608) 788-9870 (80).

St. Joseph's Nursing Home of St. Joseph Memorial Hospital, P.O. Box 527, Hillsboro 54634.

St. Joseph Residence, Inc. (Nursing Home), 107 E. Beckert Rd., New London 54961; (920) 982-5354; (107).

St. Mary's Home for the Aged (Skilled Nursing, Alzheimer's Unit, Respite Care), 2005 Division St., Manitowoc 54220; (920) 684-7171 (266).

St. Mary's Nursing Home, 3515 W. Hadley St., Milwaukee 53210; (414) 873-9250 (88).

St. Monica's Senior Citizens Home, 3920 N. Green Bay Rd., Racine 53404; (262) 639-5050 (110).

St. Paul Home, Inc. (Intermediate and Skilled Nursing Home), 1211 Oakridge Ave., Kaukauna 54130; (920) 766-6020 (129).

Villa Loretto Nursing Home, N8114 Calvary St., Mount Calvary 53057; (920) 753-3100 (52).

Villa St. Francis, Inc., 1910 W. Ohio Ave., Milwaukee 53215; (414) 649-2888;. (142).

FACILITIES FOR CHILDREN AND ADULTS WITH DISABILITIES

(*Sources:* Catholic Almanac *survey;* The Official Catholic Directory.)

This listing covers facilities and programs with educational and training orientation. Information about other services for the handicapped can generally be obtained from the Catholic Charities Office or its equivalent (c/o Chancery Office) in any diocese. (See Index for listing of addresses of chancery offices in the U.S.)

Abbreviation code: b, boys; c, coeducational; d, day; g, girls; r, residential. Other information includes age for admission. The number in parentheses at the end of an entry indicates total capacity or enrollment.

Deaf and Hearing Impaired

California: St. Joseph's Center for Deaf and Hard of Hearing, 3880 Smith St., Union City 94587.

Louisiana: Chinchuba Institute (d,c; birth through 18 yrs.), 1131 Barataria Blvd., Marrero 70072.

Missouri: St. Joseph Institute for the Deaf (r,d,c; birth to 14 years), 1809 Clarkson Rd., Chesterfield, MO 63017; (314) 532-3211 (Voice/TDD).

New York: Cleary School for the Deaf (d,c; infancy through 21), 301 Smithtown Blvd., Nesconset, NY 11767-2077; (516) 588-0530, www.clearyschool.org, (70).

St. Francis de Sales School for the Deaf (d,c; infant through elementary grades), 260 Eastern Parkway, Brooklyn 11225; (718) 636-4573 (150).

St. Joseph's School for the Deaf (d,c; parent-infant through 14 yrs.), 1000 Hutchinson River Pkwy, Bronx 10465; (718) 828-9000 (140).

Ohio: St. Rita School for the Deaf (r,d,c; birth to 12th grade), 1720 Glendale-Milford Rd., Cincinnati 45215; (513) 771-7600; www.srsdeaf.org (130).

Pennsylvania: Archbishop Ryan School for Hearing Impaired Children (d,c; parent-infant programs through 8th grade), 233 Mohawk Ave., Norwood, PA 19074; (610) 586-7044 (49).

De Paul Institute (d,c; birth through 21 yrs.), 2904 Castlegate Ave., Pittsburgh 15226; (412) 561-4848 (77).

Emotionally and/or Socially Maladjusted

This listing includes facilities for abused, abandoned and neglected as well as emotionally disturbed children and youth.

Alabama: St. Mary's Home for Children (r,c; referred from agencies), 4350 Moffat Rd., Mobile 36618; (334) 344-7733.

California: Hanna Boys Center (r,b; 10-15 yrs. at intake; school, 4th to 10th grade), Box 100, Sonoma 95476; (707)996-6767 (107). Treatment center and therapeutic special school for boys with emotional problems, behavior disorders, learning disabilities.

Rancho San Antonio (r,b; 13-17 yrs.), 21000 Plummer St., Chatsworth 91311; (818) 882-6400.

St. Vincent's (r,d,g; 12-17 yrs.), 4200 Calle Real, P.O. Box 669, Santa Barbara 93102; (805) 683-6381.

Colorado: Mt. St. Vincent Home (r,c; 5-13 yrs.), 4159 Lowell Blvd., Denver 80211; (303) 458-7220; www.nahse.org/member/st.vincent.

Connecticut: St. Francis Home for Children (r,d,c; 4-17 yrs.), 651 Prospect St., New Haven 06511; (203) 777-5513.

Mt. St. John (r,b; 11-16 yrs.), 135 Kirtland St., Deep River 06417; (860) 526-1636, (77).

Delaware: Our Lady of Grace Home for Children (r,d,c; 6-12 yrs.), 487 E. Chestnut Hill Rd., Newark 19713; (302) 738-4658.

Seton Villa, Siena Hall and Children's Home (r,c; group home; 12-18 yrs,; mothers and their children), c/o 2307 Kentmere Pkwy, Wilmington 19806; (302) 656-2183.

Florida: Boystown of Florida (r,b; 12-16 yrs.; group home), 11400 S.W. 137th Ave., Miami 33186.

Georgia: Village of St. Joseph (r,c; 6-16 yrs.), 1961 Druid Hills Rd., Ste. 205-B, 30329; (404) 321-2900.

Illinois: Guardian Angel Home (d,c; r,b), 1550 Plainfield Rd., Joliet 60435; (815) 729-0930 (35).

Maryville Academy (r,c; 6-18 yrs.), 1150 North River Rd., Des Plaines 60016; (708) 824-6126.

Mission of Our Lady of Mercy, Mercy Home for Boys and Girls (r,d,c; 15-18 yrs.), 1140 W. Jackson Blvd., Chicago 60607; (312) 738-7560; www.mercyhome.org.

St. Joseph's Carondelet Child Center (r,b, 5-21 yrs.; d.c.,5-18 yrs., 739 E. 35th St., Chicago 60616; (773) 624-7443.

Indiana: Gibault School for Boys (r; 10-18 yrs.), 6301 South U.S. Highway 41, P.O. Box 2316, Terre Haute 47802; (812) 299-1156.

Hoosier Boys Town (r; 10-18 yrs.), 7403 Cline Ave., Schererville 46375; (219) 322-8614.

Kentucky: Boys' Haven (r; 12-18 yrs.), 2301 Goldsmith Lane, Louisville 40218; (502) 458-1171, www.boyshaven.org.

Louisiana: Hope Haven Center (r,c; 5-18 yrs.), 1101 Barataria Blvd., Marrero 70072; (504) 347-5581.

Maryland: Good Shepherd Center (r,g; 13-18 yrs.), 4100 Maple Ave., Baltimore, 21227; (410) 247-2770; www.goodshepherdcenter.com.

Massachusetts: The Brightside for Families and Children (r,d,c; 6-16 yrs.), 2112 Riverdale St., W. Springfield 01089; (413) 788-7366.

McAuley Nazareth Home for Boys (r; 6-13 yrs.), 77 Mulberry St., Leicester 01524 (16). Residential treatment center.

St. Vincent Home (r,c 5-22 yrs.), 2425 Highland Ave., Fall River 02720; (508) 679-8511.

Michigan: Boysville of Michigan, Inc. (r,d,c; 13-17 yrs.), Corporate offices, 8759 Clinton-Macon Rd., Clinton 49236; (517) 423-7451 (650). Facilities located throughout the state and northern Ohio.

Don Bosco Hall (r,b; 13-17 years.), 10001 Petoskey Ave., Detroit 48204; (313) 834-8677.

Vista Maria (r,g; 11-18 yrs.), 20651 W. Warren Ave., Dearborn Heights 48127; (313) 271-6250; www.community.milive.com/cc/girls.

Minnesota: St. Cloud Children's Home (r,c; 8-18 yrs.), RTC Campus, Bld. 4-D, P.O. Box 1006, Fergus Falls, MN 56538, (218) 739-9325. Day Treatment Program (d,c; 7-14 yrs.), same address.

St. Elizabeth Home (r,c; 18 yrs. and older), 306 15th Ave. N., St. Cloud 56301; (320) 252-8350.

Missouri: Child Center of Our Lady (r,d,c; 5-14 yrs.), 7900 Natural Bridge Rd., St. Louis, 63121 (314) 383-0200.

Marygrove (r,d,c; 6-21 yrs.) (97); intense treatment unit (r,b; 13-18 yrs) (13); overnight crises care (r,d,c; birth to 18 yrs.) (8), 2705 Mullanphy Lane, Florissant, 63031 (314) 837-1702, www.marygroveonline.org.

St. Joseph's Home for Boys (r,d,b; 6-14 yrs.), 4753 S. Grand Blvd., St. Louis 63111; (314) 481-9121.

Montana: Big Sky Ranch (r,g; 12-18 yrs.), P.O. Box 1128, Glendive 59330 (406) 687-3839.

Nebraska: Father Flanagan's Boys' Home (r,c; 10-

16 yrs.), 14100 Crawford St., Boys Town 68010; (402) 498-1000, www.boystown.org (556). Boys Town National Research Hospital (r,d,c; 1-18 yrs.), 555 N. 30th St., Omaha 68131; (402) 498-6511. Center for Abused Handicapped Children; diagnosis of speech, language and hearing problems in children. Boys Town also has various facilities or programs in Brooklyn, NY; Portsmouth, RI; Philadelphia, PA; Washington, DC; Tallahassee, Orlando and Delray Beach, FL; Atlanta, GA; New Orleans, LA; San Antonio, TX, Las Vegas, NV, and southern California.

New Jersey: Catholic Community Services/Mt. Carmel Guild, 1160 Raymond Blvd., Newark 07102; (973) 596-4084.

Collier High School (d,c; 13-18 yrs.), 160 Conover Rd., Wickatunk 07765; (732) 946-4771; www.collierservices.com.

Mt. St. Joseph Children's Center (r,d,b; 6-14 yrs.), 124 Shepherd Lane, Totowa 07512; (973) 595-5720.

New York: The Astor Home for Children (r,d,c; 5-12 yrs.), 36 Mill St., P.O. Box 5005, Rhinebeck 12572; (845) 876-4081, www.astorservices.org. Child Guidance Clinics/Day Treatment (Rhinebeck, Poughkeepsie, Beacon, Bronx). Head Start - Day Care (Poughkeepsie, Beacon, Red Hook, Dover, Millerton).

Baker Victory Services, 780 Ridge Rd. Lackawanna 14218; (716) 828-9500; www.ourladyofvictory.org.

Good Shepherd Services (r,d,c), 305 Seventh Ave., New York, NY 10001, (212) 243-7070, www.goodshepherds.org. City-wide residential programs or adolescents (12-21 yrs.), foster care and adoption services (infant-21 yrs.); training institute for human services workers; day treatment program (13-18 yrs.); community-based neighborhood family services in South Brooklyn Community (infant-adult),

LaSalle School (r,d,b; 12-18 yrs.), 391 Western Ave., Albany 12203; (518) 242-4731.

Madonna Heights Services (r,d,g; 12-18 yrs.), 151 Burrs Lane, Dix Hills 11746; (516) 643-8800 (110). Also conducts group homes on Long Island and out-patient programs.

Saint Anne Institute (r,d,g; 12-18 yrs.), 160 N. Main Ave., Albany 12206; (518) 437-6500.

St. Catherine's Center for Children (r,d,c; birth through 12 yrs.), 40 N. Main Ave., Albany 12203; (518) 453-6700; www.st-cath.org.

St. John's of Rockaway Beach (r,b; 9-21 yrs.), 144 Beach 111th St., Rockaway Park 11694, (718) 945-2800. Programs include Diagnostic centers and independent living programs.

North Dakota: Home on the Range (r,c; 10-18 yrs.), 16351 I-94, Sentinel Butte 58654; (701) 872-3745 (79). Residential and emergency shelter therapeutic programs.

Home on the Range-Red River Victory Ranch (r,b; 10-18 yrs.), P.O. Box 9615, Fargo 58106; (701) 293-6321, www.hotr.org (12). Residential chemical addictions program.

Ohio: St. Vincent Family Centers (d,c; preschool) Outpatient counseling program (c; 2-18 yrs.), 840 W. State St., Columbus 43222, (614) 252-0731; www.svfc.org.

Marycrest (r,g; 13-18 yrs.), 7800 Brookside Rd., Independence 44131.

Catholic Charities Services/Parmadale (r,c; 12-18 yrs.), 6753 State Rd., Parma 44134; (440) 845-7700.

Rosemont (r,g;d,c; 11-18 yrs.), 2440 Dawnlight Ave., Columbus 43211; (614) 471-2626.

Oregon: St. Mary's Home for Boys (r; 10-18 yrs.), 16535 S.W. Tualatin Valley Highway, Beaverton 97006; (503) 649-5651.

Pennsylvania: Auberle (r,c; 7-18 yrs.), 1101 Hartman St., McKeesport 15132-1500, (412) 673-5800, www.trfn.clpgh.org/auberle; (412) 673-5800 (181). Residential treatment for boys; emergency shelter care, foster care, group home for girls and family preservation program.

De LaSalle in Towne (d,b; 14-17 yrs.), 25 S. Van Pelt St., Philadelphia 19103; (215) 567-5500.

De LaSalle Vocational Day Treatment (b; 15-18 yrs.), P.O. Box 344, Bensalem 19020; (215) 464-0344.

Gannondale (r,g; 12-17 yrs.), 4635 E. Lake Rd., Erie 16511; (814) 899-7659.

Harborcreek Youth Services (r,d,c; 10-17 yrs.), 5712 Iroquois Ave., Harborcreek 16421; (814) 899-7664, www.hys-erie.org.

Holy Family Institute (r,d,c; 0-18 yrs.), 8235 Ohio River Blvd., Emsworth 15202, (412) 766-4030, www.hfi-pgh.org.

Lourdesmont Good Shepherd Youth and Family Services (r,g;d,c; 12-17 yrs.), 537 Venard Rd., Clarks Summit 18411; (507) 587-4741.

St. Gabriel's Hall (r,b; 10-18 yrs.), P.O. Box 7280, Audubon 19407; (215) 247-2776.

St. Michael's School (r,b; d,c; 12-17 yrs.), Box 370, Tuckhannock 18657; (570) 388-6155.

Texas: St. Joseph Adolescent and Family Counseling Center (c; 13-17 yrs.), 5415 Maple Ave., #320, Dallas 75235; (214) 631-TEEN.

Washington: Morning Star Boys Ranch (Spokane Boys' Ranch, Inc.), (r,b; 10-18 yrs.), Box 8087, Spokane 99203-0087, (509) 448-1411, www.morning starboysranch.org.

Wisconsin: North American Union Sisters of Our Lady of Charity Center (r,c; 10-17 yrs.), 154 Edgington Lane, Wheeling, WV, 26003-1535; (304) 242-0042.

St. Charles Youth and Family Services (r,d,b; 12-18 yrs.), 151 S. 84th St., Milwaukee 53214; (414) 476-3710.

Wyoming: St. Joseph's Children's Home (r,c; 6-18 yrs.), P.O. Box 1117, Torrington 82240; (307) 532-4197.

Developmentally Challenged

This listing includes facilities for children, youth, and adults with learning disabilities.

Alabama: Father Purcell Memorial Exceptional Children's Center (r, c; birth to 10 yrs.), 2048 W. Fairview Ave., Montgomery 36108; (334) 834-5590.

Father Walter Memorial Child Care Center (r,c; birth-12 yrs.), 2815 Forbes Dr., Montgomery 36110; (334) 262-6421.

California: Child Study Center of St. John's Hospital (d,c; birth-18 yrs.), 1339-20th St., Santa Monica 90404; (310) 829-8921.

St. Madeleine Sophie's Center (d,c; 18 yrs. and older), 2111 E. Madison Ave., El Cajon 92019.

Tierra del Sol Foundation (d,c; 18 yrs. and older), 9919 Sunland Blvd., Sunland 91040; (818) 352-1419; 14547 Gilmore St., Van Nuys 91411; (818) 904-9164.

Connecticut: Gengras Center (d,c; 3-21 yrs.), St. Joseph College, 1678 Asylum Ave., W. Hartford 06117.

Villa Maria Education Center (d,c; 6-14 yrs.), 161 Sky Meadow Dr., Stamford 06903; (203) 322-5886.

District of Columbia: Lt. Joseph P. Kennedy, Jr., Institute (d,c; 6 weeks to 5 yrs. for Kennedy Institute for Child Development Center; 6-21 yrs. for Kennedy School; 18 yrs. and older for training and employment, therapeutic and residential services). Founded in 1959 for people of all ages with developmental disabilities and their families in the Washington archdiocese. Heaquarters: 801 Buchanan St. N.E. Washington 20017; (202) 529-7600, www.kennedy institute.org. Other locations in District of Columbia and Maryland. No enrollment limit.

Florida: L'Arche Harbor House, (c; 20 yrs. and older; community home), 700 Arlington Rd., Jacksonville 32211; (904) 744-4435.

Marian Center Services for Developmentally Handicapped and Mentally Retarded (r,d,c; 2-21 yrs.), 15701 Northwest 37th Ave., Opa Locka 33054, (305) 625-8354. Pre-school, school, workshop residence services.

Morning Star School (d,c; 4-16 yrs.), 725 Mickler Rd., Jacksonville 32211; (904) 421-2144.

Morning Star School (d,c; school age), 954 Leigh Ave., Orlando 32804.

Morning Star School (d,c; 6-14 yrs.), 4661-80th Ave. N., Pinellas Park 33781; (813) 544-6036, www.morningstarschool.org.

Morning Star School (d,c; 6-16 yrs.), 210 E. Linebaugh Ave., Tampa 33612; (813) 935-0232.

Georgia: St. Mary's Home (r,c), 2170 E. Victory Dr., Savannah 31404; (912) 236-7164.

Illinois: Bartlett Learning Center (r,d,c; 3-21 yrs.), 801 W. Bartlett Rd., Bartlett 60103; (630) 289-4221.

Brother James Court (r, men over 18 yrs.), 2500 St. James Rd., Springfield 62707; (217) 544-4876.

Good Shepherd Manor (men; 18 yrs. and older), Little Brothers of the Good Shepherd, P.O. Box 260, Momence. 60954; (815) 472-6492; www.good shepherdmanor.org. Resident care for developmentally disabled men.

Misericordia Home South (r,c), 2916 W. 47th St., Chicago 60632; (773) 254-9595. For severely and profoundly impaired children.

Misericordia Home - Heart of Mercy Village (r,c; 6-45 yrs.), 6300 North Ridge, Chicago 60660; (773) 973-6300.

Mt. St. Joseph (developmentally disabled women; over age 21), 24955 N. Highway 12, Lake Zurich 60047; (847) 438-5050.

St. Coletta's of Illinois (r,d,; 6 to adult), 123rd and Wolf Rd., Palos Park 60464; (708) 448-6520.

St. Mary of Providence (r,women; 18 yrs. and older), 4200 N. Austin Ave., Chicago 60634; (773) 545-8300.

St. Vincent Community Living Facility (r,c; adults, over 18 yrs.) (20), and St. Vincent Supported Living Arrangement (r,c; adults, over 18 yrs.) (20), 659 E. Jefferson St., Freeport 61032; (815) 232-6181.

Springfield Developmental Center (m; 21 yrs. and over), 4595 Laverna Rd., Springfield 62707, (217) 525-8271.

Vocational Training

Indiana: Marian Day School (d,c; 6-16 yrs.), 700 Herndon Dr., Evansville 47711; (812) 422-5346.

Kansas: Lakemary Center, Inc. (r,d,c), 100 Lakemary Dr., Paola 66071; (913) 557-4000.

Kentucky: Pitt Academy (d,c), 4605 Poplar Level Rd., Louisville 40213; (502) 966-6979; www.pitt.com.

Louisiana: Department of Special Education, Archdiocese of New Orleans, St. Michael Special School (d,c; 6-21 yrs.), 1522 Chippewa St., New Orleans 70130.

Holy Angels Residential Facility (r,c; teenage, 14 yrs. and older), 10450 Ellerbe Rd., Shreveport 71106; (318) 797-8500.

Ocean Avenue Community Home, 361 Ocean Ave., Gretna 70053; (504) 361-0674.

Padua Community Services (r,c; birth-25 yrs.), 200 Beta St., Belle Chasse 70037.

St. Jude the Apostle, 1430 Claire Ave., Gretna 70053; (504) 361-8457.

St. Mary's Residential Training School (r,c: 3-22 yrs.), P.O. Drawer 7768, Alexandria 71306; (318) 445-6443.

St. Peter the Fisherman, 62269 Airport Dr., Slidell 70458; (504) 641-4914.

St. Rosalie (r; men 18 and up), 119 Kass St., Gretna 70056; (504) 361-8320.

Sts. Mary and Elizabeth, 720 N. Elm St., Metairie 70003; (504) 738-6959.

Maryland: The Benedictine School for Exceptional Children (r,c; 6-21 yrs.), 14299 Benedictine Lane, Ridgely 21660; (410) 634-2112.

Francis X. Gallagher Services (r) 2520 Pot Spring Rd., Timonium 21093.

St. Elizabeth School and Habilitation Center (d,c; 11-21 yrs.), 801 Argonne Dr., Baltimore 21218; (410) 889-5054, www.stelizabeth-school.org.

Massachusetts: Cardinal Cushing School and Training Center (r,d,c; 16-22 yrs.), Hanover 02339 (116 r; 28 d).

Mercy Centre (d,c; 3-22 yrs. and over), 25 West Chester St., Worcester 01605-1136; (508) 852-7165, www.mercycentre.com.

St. Coletta Day School (d,c; 3-22 yrs.), 85 Washington St., Braintree 02184.

Michigan: Our Lady of Providence Center (r,g; 11-30 yrs., d,c; 26 yrs. and older), 16115 Beck Rd., Northville. 48118; (734) 453-1300.

St. Louis Center and School (r,d,b; 6-18 yrs. child care; 18-36 yrs. adult foster care), 16195 Old U.S. 12, Chelsea 48118; (734) 475-8430.

Minnesota: Mother Teresa Home (r,c; 18 yrs. and older), 101-10th Ave. N., Cold Spring 56320.

St. Francis Home (r,c; 18 yrs. and older), P.O. Box 326, Waite Park 56387, (320) 251-7630.

St. Luke's Home (r; 18 yrs. and older), 411 8th Ave. N., Cold Springs 56320.

Missouri: Department of Special Education, Archdiocese of St. Louis, 4472 Lindell Blvd., St. Louis. 63108; (314) 533-3454. Serves children with developmental disabilities, mental retardation or learning disabilities; services include special ungraded day classes in 8 parish schools.

Good Shepherd Homes (residential for developmentally disabled men; 18 yrs. and up), The Community of the Good Shepherd, 10101 James A. Reed Rd., Kansas City 64134, (816) 767-8090.

St.Mary's Special School (r,c; 5-21 yrs.), 1724 Redman, St. Louis 63138; (314) 261-8533. St. Mary's Supported Living (r,c) (24); supervised homes for adolescents or adults. St. Mary's Early Intervention (d,c) (30); early intervention for toddlers.

Nebraska: Madonna School for Exceptional Children (d,c; 5-21 yrs.), 2537 N. 62nd St., Omaha 68104; (402) 556-1883, www.discoveromaha.com. Children with learning problems.

Villa Marie School and Home for Exceptional Children (r,d,c; 6-18 yrs.), P.O. Box 80328, Lincoln 68501; (402) 786-3625.

New Jersey: Archbishop Damiano School (d,c; 3-21 yrs.), 1145 Delsea Dr., Westville Grove 08093.

Catholic Community Services, Archdiocese of Newark, 1160 Raymond Blvd., Newark 07102.

Department of Special Education, Diocese of Camden, 1845 Haddon Ave., Camden 08101; (609) 756-7993. Services include: Archbishop Damiano School (above), and full time programs (d,c; 6-21 yrs.) at 4 elementary (96) and 2 high schools (60) and some religious education programs.

Department for Persons with Disabilities, Diocese of Paterson, 1049 Weldon Rd., Oak Ridge, N.J. 07438, (973) 697-4394, www.dpd.org. Services include 8 residential programs for adults, one adult training center, family support services.

Felician School for Exceptional Children (d,c; 5-21 yrs.), 260 S. Main St., Lodi 07644; (201) 777-0725.

McAuley School for Exceptional Children (d,c; 5-21 yrs.), 1633 Rt. 22 at Terrill Rd., Watchung 07060.

Mt. Carmel Guild Special Education School (d,c ; 6-21 yrs.), 60 Kingsland Ave., Kearny 07032, (201) 995-3280.

St. Anthony's Special Education School (d,c), 25 N. 7th St., Belleville 07109, (973) 844-3700.

Sister Georgine School (d,c; 6-17 yrs.), 544 Chestnut Ave., Trenton 08611; (609) 396-5444.

St. Patrick's Special Education School (d,c), 72 Central Ave., Newark 07102.

New York: Baker Victory Services (r), 780 Ridge Rd., Lackawanna, N.Y. 14218; (716) 828-9500. Residential care for handicapped and retarded children; nursery school program for emotionally disturbed preschool children.

Bishop Patrick V. Ahern High School (d,c; 15-21 yrs.), 100 Merrill Ave., Staten Island 10314.

Cantalician Center for Learning (d,c; birth-21 yrs.), 3233 Main St., Buffalo 14214; (716) 833-5353, www.cantalician.org. Infant and pre-school; elementary and secondary; workshop (426). Three group homes. Rehabilitation, day treatment and senior rehabilitation programs.

Catholic Charities Residential Services, Rockville Center Diocese, 269 W. Main St., Bay Shore 11706. Conducts residences for developmentally disabled adults (88).

Cobb Memorial School (r,d,c; 5-21 yrs.), 100-300 Mt. Presentation Way, Altamont 12009; (518) 861-6446.

Joan Ann Kennedy Memorial Preschool (d,c; 3-5 yrs.), 26 Sharpe Ave., Staten Island 10302.

L'Arche (r, adults), 1232 Teall Ave., Syracuse 13206 (12). Homes where assistants and persons with developmental disabilities share life, following the philosophy of Jean Vanier. Member of International L'Arche Federation.

Maryhaven Center of Hope (r,d,c; school age to adult), 450 Myrtle Ave., Port Jefferson 11777, (631) 474-4120.

Mercy Home for Children (r,c), 243 Prospect Park West, Brooklyn 11215; (718) 832-1075. Conducts six residences for adolescents and young adults who are developmentally disabled: Visitation, Warren, Vincent Haire, Santulli and Littlejohn residences (Brooklyn), Kevin Keating Residence (Queens).

Office for Disabled Persons, Catholic Charities, Diocese of Brooklyn, 191 Joralemon St., Brooklyn 11201; (718) 722-6000; www.ccbg.org. Services include: adult day treatment center; community residences for mentally retarded adults; special events for disabled children (from age 3) and adults.

Office for Disabled Persons, Archdiocese of New York, 1011 First Ave., New York 10022; (212) 371-1000. Services include consultation and referral, variety of services for deaf, blind, mentally retarded, mentally ill.

School of the Holy Childhood (d,c; 5-21 yrs.), 100 Groton Parkway, Rochester 14623.

Seton Foundation for Learning (d,c; 5-15 yrs.), 104 Gordon St., Staten Is. 10304; (718) 447-1750.

North Carolina: Holy Angels (r,c; birth to adult), 6600 Wilkinson Blvd., P.O. Box 710, Belmont 28012; (704) 825-4161, www.holyangelsnc.org.

North Dakota: Friendship, Inc. (r,d,c; all ages), 3004 11th St. South, Fargo 58103, (701) 235-8217.

Ohio: Julie Billiart School (d,c; 6-12 yrs.), 4982 Clubside Rd., Cleveland 44124; (216) 381-1191.

Mary Immaculate School (d,c; 6-14 yrs.), 3837 Secor Rd., Toledo 43623; (419) 474-1688.

OLA/St. Joseph Center (d,c; 6-16 yrs.), 2346 W. 14th St., Cleveland 44113; (216) 621-3451.

Rose Mary, The Johanna Graselli Rehabilitation and Education Center (r,c; 5 yrs. and older), 19350 Euclid Ave., Cleveland 44117.

St. John's Villa (r,c; continued care and training, 15 yrs. and over), P.O. Box 457, Carrollton 44615, (330) 627-9789.

Oregon: Providence Montessori School Early Intervention Program (d,c; 3-5 yrs.), 830 N.E. 47th Ave., Portland 97213; (503) 215-2409.

Pennsylvania: Clelian Heights School for Exceptional Children (r,d,c; 5-21 yrs.), R.D. 9, Box 607, Greensburg 15601; (724) 837-8120; (95). Also conducts re-socialization program (r,d,c; young adults).

Divine Providence Village (adults), 686 Old Marple Rd., Springfield 19064; (610) 328-7730.

Don Guanella Village: Don Guanella School (r,d,b; 6-21 yrs.) and C.K. Center (r; adults, post-school age), 1797-1799 S. Sproul Rd., Springfield 19064.

John Paul II, Center for Special Learning (d,c; 3-21 yrs.), 200 Reading Ave., West Reading 19611; (610) 373-5687.

McGuire Memorial (r,d,c; 18 mos. to adult.), 2119 Mercer Rd., New Brighton 15066.

Mercy Special Learning Center (d,c; 3-21 yrs. and early intervention), 830 S. Woodward St., Allentown 18103; (610) 797-8242.

Our Lady of Confidence Day School (d,c; 4½-21 yrs.), 10th and Lycoming Sts., Philadelphia 19140.

Queen of the Universe Day Center (d,c; 4½-16 yrs.), 2443 Trenton Rd., Levittown 19056; (215) 945-6090.

St. Anthony School Programs (d,c; 5-21 yrs.), 2718 Custer Ave., Pittsburgh 15227; (412) 882-1333.

St. Joseph Center for Special Learning (d,c; 4-21 yrs.), 2075 W. Norwegian St., Pottsville 17901; (570) 622-4638, www.pottsville.com/stjosephctr.

St. Joseph's Center (r,d,c; birth-10 yrs.), 2010 Adams Ave., Scranton 18509; (570) 342-8379; www.stjoseph center.org.

St. Katherine Day School (d,c; 4½-21 yrs.), 930 Bowman Ave., Wynnewood 19096; (610) 667-3958.

Tennessee: Madonna Learning Center, Inc., for Retarded Children (d,c; 5-16 yrs.), 7007 Poplar Ave., Germantown 38138.

Texas: Notre Dame of Dallas School (d,c; 3-21 yrs.), 2018 Allen St., Dallas, Tex. 75204; (214) 720-3911.

Virginia: St. Coletta School (d,c; 5-22 yrs.), 207 S. Peyton St., Alexandria, 22314; (703) 683-3686. For developmentally disabled. Services include: occupational, physical and language therapy; vocational program with job search, placement, training and follow-up services.

St. Mary's Infant Home (r,c; birth to 14 yrs.), 317 Chapel St., Norfolk 23504; (757) 622-2208. For multiple handicapped.

Wisconsin: St Coletta of Wisconsin, W4955 Hwy 18, Jefferson 53549, (920) 674-4330, www.stcoletta wi.org. Year-round special education programs for adolescents and adults; pre-vocational and vocational skills training; residential living alternatives. Young adult population. Employment opportunities for those who qualify.

St. Coletta Day School (c; 8-17 yrs.), 1740 N. 55th St., Milwaukee. 53208; (414) 453-1850.

Orthopedically/Physically Challenged

Pennsylvania: St. Edmond's Home for Children (r,c; 1-21 yrs.)., 320 S. Roberts Rd., Rosemont 19010; (610) 525-8800.

Virginia: St. Joseph Villa Housing Corp. (adults), 8000 Brook Rd., Richmond 23227; (804) 553-3283.

Visually Challenged

Maine: Educational Services for Blind and Visually Impaired Children (Catholic Charities, Maine), 1066 Kenduskeag Ave., Bangor 04401; 66 Western Ave., Fairfield 04937; 15 Westminster St., Lewiston 04240; 562 Congress St., Portland 04101, (207) 871-7440. Itinerant teachers, instructional materials center.

New Jersey: St. Joseph's School for the Blind (r,d,c; 3-21 yrs.), 537 Pavonia Ave., Jersey City 07306; (201) 653-8300.

New York: Lavelle School for the Blind (d,c; 3-21 yrs.), East 221st St. and Paulding Ave., Bronx 10469; (718) 882-1212. For visually impaired, multiple handicapped.

Pennsylvania: St. Lucy Day School (d,c; pre-K to 8th grade), 130 Hampden Rd., Upper Darby 19082, (610) 352-4550, www.stlucydayschool.org. For children with visual impairments.

RETREATS, SPIRITUAL RENEWAL PROGRAMS

There is great variety in retreat and renewal programs, with orientations ranging from the traditional to teen encounters. Central to all of them are celebration of the liturgy and deepening of a person's commitment to faith and witness in life.

Features of many of the forms are as follows.

Traditional Retreats: Centered around conferences and the direction of a retreat master; oriented to the personal needs of the retreatants; including such standard practices as participation in Mass, reception of the sacraments, private and group prayer, silence and meditation, discussions.

Team Retreat: Conducted by a team of several leaders or directors (priests, religious, lay persons) with division of subject matter and activities according to their special skills and the nature and needs of the group.

Closed Retreat: Involving withdrawal for a period of time — overnight, several days, a weekend — from everyday occupations and activities.

Open Retreat: Made without total disengagement from everyday involvements, on a part-time basis.

Private Retreat: By one person, on a kind of do-it-yourself basis with the one-to-one assistance of a director.

Special Groups: With formats and activities geared to particular groups; e.g., members of Alcoholics Anonymous, vocational groups and apostolic groups.

Marriage Encounters: Usually weekend periods of husband-wife reflection and dialogue; introduced into the U.S. from Spain in 1967.

Charismatic Renewal: Featuring elements of the movement of the same name; "Spirit-oriented," communitarian and flexible, with spontaneous and shared prayer, personal testimonies of faith and witness.

Christian Community: Characterized by strong community thrust.

Teens Encounter Christ (TEC), SEARCH: Formats adapted to the mentality and needs of youth, involving experience of Christian faith and commitment in a community setting.

Christian Maturity Seminars: Similar to teen encounters in basic concept but different to suit persons of greater maturity.

RENEW International: Spiritual renewal process involving the entire parish. Office, 1232 George St., Plainfield, NJ 07062; (908) 769-5400. Director, Msgr. Thomas A. Kleissler.

Cursillo: see separate entry.

Conference

Retreats International Inc.: National Office, Box 1067, Notre Dame, IN 46556; (219) 631-5320. An organization for promoting retreats in the U.S. was started in 1904 in New York. Its initial efforts and the gradual growth of the movement led to the formation in 1927 of the National Catholic Laymen's Retreat Conference, the forerunner of the men's division of Retreats International. The women's division developed from the National Laywomen's Retreat Movement which was founded in Chicago in 1936. The men's and women's divisions merged July 9, 1977. The services of the organization include an annual summer institute for retreat and pastoral ministry, regional conferences for retreat center leadership and area meetings of directors and key leadership in the retreat movement. The officers are: Episcopal advisor, Auxiliary Bishop Robert Morneau of Green Bay; Pres., Sr. Mary Elizabeth Imler, O.S.F.; Exec. Dir., Anne M. Luther.

HOUSES OF RETREAT AND RENEWAL

(*Principal sources:* Catholic Almanac *survey;* The Official Catholic Directory.)

Abbreviation code: m, men; w, women; mc, married couples; y, youth. Houses and centers without code generally offer facilities to most groups. An asterisk after an abbreviation indicates that the facility is primarily for the group designated but that special groups are also accommodated. Houses furnish information concerning the types of programs they offer.

Alabama: Blessed Trinity Shrine Retreat and Cenacle, 107 Holy Trinity Rd., Holy Trinity 36859, (334) 855-4474; Visitation Sacred Heart Retreat House, 2300 Spring Hill Ave., Mobile 36607, (334) 473-2321.

Alaska: Holy Spirit Center, 10980 Hillside Dr., Anchorage 99516, (907) 346-2343, home.gci.net/ ~hsrh.

Arizona: Franciscan Renewal Center, 5802 E. Lincoln Dr., Scottsdale 85253, (480) 948-7460; Holy Trinity Monastery, P.O. Box 298, St. David 85630, Benedictine community, self-directed/Spirit-directed monastic retreat, (520) 720-4642; Mount Claret Retreat Center, 4633 N. 54th St., Phoenix 85018, (602) 840-5066; Our Lady of Solitude House of Prayer, P.O. Box 1140, Black Canyon City 85324, (623) 374-9204; Redemptorist Picture Rocks Retreat House, 7101 W. Picture Rocks Rd., Tucson 85743, (520) 744-3400, www.desertrenewal.org.

Arkansas: Brothers and Sisters of Charity, Little Portion Hermitage, 350 C R 048, Barryville, 72616-

8505, (501) 253-7710, www.johnmichaeltalbot.com; Little Portion Retreat and Training Center, Rt. 4, Box 430, Eureka Springs 72632, (501) 253-7379; St. Scholastica Retreat Center, P.O. Box 3489, Ft. Smith 72913, (501) 783-1135, www.catholic-church.org/ scholastica; Hesychia House of Prayer, 204 St. Scholastica Rd., New Blaine, Shoal Creek, 72851, (501) 938-7375.

California: Angela Center, 535 Angela Dr., Santa Rosa 95403, (707) 528-8578; Christ the King Retreat Center, 6520 Van Maren Lane, Citrus Heights 95621, (916) 969-4706, www.passionist.org; Claretian Retreat Center, 1119 Westchester Pl., Los Angeles 90019, (323) 737-8464; De Paul Center, 1105 Bluff Rd., Montebello 90640, (323) 721-6060; El Carmelo Retreat House, P.O. Box 446, Redlands 92373, (909) 792-1047; Heart of Jesus Retreat Center, 2927 S. Greenville St., Santa Ana 92704, (714) 557-4538; Holy Spirit Retreat Center, 4316 Lanai Rd., Encino 91436, (818) 784-4515; Holy Transfiguration Monastery (m*), Monks of Mt. Tabor (Byzantine Ukrainian), 17001 Tomki Rd., P.O. Box 217, Redwood Valley 95470, (707) 485-8959; Jesuit Retreat House, 300 Manresa Way, Los Altos 94022, (650) 948-4491, www.elretiro.org; Madonna of Peace Renewal Center (y), P.O. Box 71, Copperopolis 95228, (209) 785-2157; Marian Retreat Center, 535 Sacramento St., Auburn 95603, (916) 887-2019; Mary and Joseph Retreat Center, 5300 Crest Rd., Rancho Palos Verdes 90275, (310) 377-4867, www.maryjoseph.org.

Marywood Retreat Center, 2811 E. Villa Real Dr.,

Orange 92867, (714) 282-2300, www.rcbo.org; Mater Dolorosa Retreat Center, 700 N. Sunnyside Ave., Sierra Madre 91024, (626) 355-7188, www.passion ist.org; Mercy Center, 2300 Adeline Dr., Burlingame 94010, (650) 340-7474, www.mercy-center.org; Mission San Luis Rey Retreat, 4070 Mission Ave., Oceanside, 92057-6402, (760) 757-3659, www.sanluisrey.org; Mount Alverno Retreat and Conference Center, 3910 Bret Harte Dr., Redwood City 94061, (650) 369-0798, www.mountalverno.com; New Camaldoli Hermitage, Big Sur 93920, (831) 667-2456, www.contemplation.com; Our Lady of the Oaks Villa, P.O. Box 128, Applegate 95703, (530) 878-2776.

Poverello of Assisi Retreat House, 1519 Woodworth St., San Fernando 91340, (818) 365-1071; Presentation Education and Retreat Center, 19480 Bear Creek Rd., Los Gatos 95033, (408) 354-2346, www.prescenter.org; Prince of Peace Abbey, 650 Benet Hill Rd., Oceanside 92054, (760) 430-1305; Pro Sanctity Spirituality Center, 205 S. Pine St., Fullerton 92633 (for day use); Sacred Heart Retreat House (w*), 920 E. Alhambra Rd., Alhambra 91801, (626) 289-1353; St. Andrew's Abbey Retreat House, 31001 N. Valyermo Rd., Valyermo 93563, (661) 944-2178, www.valyermo.com; St. Anthony's Retreat House, P.O. Box 249, Three Rivers 93271, (559) 561-4595, www.stanthonyretreat.org; St. Clare's Retreat, 2381 Laurel Glen Rd., Soquel 95073, (831) 423-8093, www.infoteam.com/nonprofit/stclaresretreat/ index.html; St. Francis Retreat, P.O. Box 970, San Juan Bautista 95045, (831) 623-4234, www.stfrancis retreat.com; St. Francis Youth Center (y), 2400 E. Lake Ave., Watsonville 95076; St. Joseph's Salesian Youth Center, P.O. Box 1639, 8301 Arroyo Dr., Rosemead 91770, (626) 280-8622; St. Mary's Seminary and Retreat House, 1964 Las Canoas Rd., Santa Barbara 93105, (805) 966-4829; San Damiano Retreat, P.O. Box 767, Danville 94526, (925) 837-9141, www.sandamiano.org.

San Miguel Retreat House, P.O. Box 69, San Miguel 93451, (805) 467-3256; Santa Sabina Center, 25 Magnolia Ave., San Rafael 94901, (415) 457-7727; Serra Retreat, 3401 S. Serra Rd., Box 127, Malibu 90265, (310) 456-6631, www.sbfranciscans.org; Starcross Community, 34500 Annapolis Rd., Annapolis 95412, (707) 886-1919, www.starcross.org; Villa Maria del Mar, Santa Cruz, 2-1918 E. Cliff Dr., Santa Cruz 95062, (831) 475-1236; Villa Maria – House of Prayer (w), 1252 N. Citrus Dr., La Habra 90631, (562) 691-5838.

Colorado: Benet Pines Retreat Center, 15780 Highway 83, Colorado Springs 80921, (719) 495-2574; Camp St. Malo Religious Retreat and Conference Center, 10758, Hwy. 7, Allenspark 80510, (303) 747-2892; Sacred Heart Retreat House, Box 185, Sedalia 80135, (303) 688-4198, www.gabrielmedia.org/shjrh; Spiritual Life Institute (individuals only), Nada Hermitage, P.O. Box 219, Crestone 81131, (719) 256-4778.

Connecticut: St. Edmund's Retreat, P.O. Box 399, Mystic 06355, (860) 536-0565, www.sse.org/enders; Emmaus Spiritual Life Center, 24 Maple Ave., Uncasville 06382, (860) 848-3427; Holy Family Retreat, 303 Tunxis Rd., Farmington 06107, (860) 521-0440; Immaculata Retreat House, P.O. Box 55, Willimantic 06226, (860) 423-8484, www.ntplx.net/ ~omict; Mercy Center at Madison, P.O. Box 191, 167 Neck Rd., Madison 06443, (203) 245-0401, www.mercyctmadison.com; My Father's House, Box 22, 39 North Moodus Rd., Moodus 06469, (860) 873-1906, www.myfathershouse.com; Our Lady of Calvary Retreat (w*), 31 Colton St., Farmington 06032, (860) 677-8519; Trinita Retreat Center, 595 Town Hill Rd., Rt. 219, New Hartford 06057, (860) 379-4329; Villa Maria Retreat House, 161 Sky Meadow Dr., Stamford 06903, (203) 322-5886; Wisdom House Retreat Center, 229 E. Litchfield Rd., 06759, (860) 567-3163, www.wisdomhouse.org.

Delaware: St. Francis Renewal Center, 1901 Prior Rd., Wilmington 19809, (302) 798-3360.

District of Columbia: Washington Retreat House, 4000 Harewood Rd. N.E., Washington 20017, (202) 529-1111.

Florida: Cenacle Retreat House, 1400 S. Dixie Highway, Lantana 33462-5492, (561) 582-2534; Dominican Retreat House, Inc., 7275 S.W. 124th St., Miami 33156, (305) 238-2711; Franciscan Center, 3010 Perry Ave., Tampa 33603, (813) 229-2695, www.fsalleh.org/franciscancenter.htm; John Paul II Retreat House, 720 N.E. 27th St., Miami 33137, (305) 576-2748, www.acu-adsum.org; Our Lady of Divine Providence, 702 S. Bayview Ave., Clearwater, 33759, (727) 797-7412, www.divineprovidence.org; Our Lady of Perpetual Help Retreat and Spirituality Center, 3989 S. Moon Dr., Venice 34292, (941) 486-0233, www.osphretreat.org; Saint John Neumann Renewal Center, 685 Miccosukee Rd., Tallahassee 32308, (850) 224-2971; St. Leo Abbey Retreat Center, P.O. Box 2350, St. Leo 33574, (352) 588-2009.

Georgia: Ignatius House, 6700 Riverside Dr. N.W., Atlanta 30328, (404) 255-0503.

Idaho: Nazareth Retreat Center, 4450 N. Five Mile Rd., Boise 83704, (208) 375-2932.

Illinois: Bellarmine Jesuit Retreat House (mc), 175 W. County Line Rd, Barrington 60010, (847) 381-1261; Bishop Lane Retreat House, 7708 E. McGregor Rd., Rockford 61102, (815) 965-5011; Cabrini Retreat Center, 9430 Golf Rd., Des Plaines 60016, (847) 297-6530; Carmelite Spiritual Center, 8433 Bailey Rd., Darien 60561, (630) 969-4141; Cenacle Retreat House, 513 Fullerton Parkway, Chicago 60614, (773) 528-6300; Cenacle Retreat House, P.O. Box 797, Warrenville 60555, (630) 393-1231, www.cenacle.org; King's House of Retreats, Henry 61537, (309) 364-3084, www.cdop.org.

La Salle Manor, Christian Brothers Retreat House, 12480 Galena Rd., Plano 60545, (630) 552-3224; Retreat and Renewal Center, 700 N. 66th St., Belleville 62223, (618) 397-0584; St. Mary's Retreat House, P.O. Box 608, 14230 Main St., Lemont 60439, (630) 257-5102; Tolentine Center, 20300 Governors Highway, Olympia Fields 60461, (708) 748-9500; Villa Redeemer Retreat Center, 1111 N. Milwaukee Ave., P.O. Box 6, Glenview 60025, (847) 724-7804.

Indiana: Archabbey Guest House, St. Meinrad Archabbey, St. Meinrad 47577, (800) 581-6905; Benedict Inn Retreat and Conference Center, 1402 Southern Ave., Beech Grove 46107, (317) 788-7581, www.benedictinn.org; Bethany Retreat House, 2202 Lituanica Ave., 46312, (219) 398-5047; Fatima Retreat House, 5353 E. 56th St., Indianapolis 46226-1486, (317) 545-7681, www.archindy.org; John XXIII Center, 407 W. McDonald St., Hartford City 47348, (765) 348-4008, www.netusa1.net/~john23rd; Kordes Retreat Center, 841 E. 14th St., Ferdinand 47532, (812) 367-2777, www.thedome.org/kordes.

Lindenwood, PHJC Ministry Center, P.O. Box 1, Donaldson 46513, (219) 935-1780; Mary's Solitude, St.Mary's, 100 Lourdes Hall, Notre Dame 46556, (219) 284-5599; Mount Saint Francis Retreat Center and Friary, 101 St. Anthony Dr., Mount Saint Francis 47146, (812) 923-8817, www.cris.com/~mtstfran; Our Lady of Fatima Retreat Center, P.O. Box 929, Notre Dame 46556, (219) 631-8288, www.nd.edu/~fatima; Sarto Retreat House, 4200 N. Kentucky Ave., Evansville 47724, (812) 424-5536.

Iowa: American Martyrs Retreat House, 2209 N. Union Rd., P.O. Box 605, Cedar Falls 50613, (319) 266-3543; Emmanuel House of Prayer Country Retreat and Solitude Center, 4427 Kotts Rd. N.E., Iowa City 52240; New Melleray Guest House, 6500 Melleray Circle, Dubuque 52068, (319) 588-2319; Shalom Retreat Center, 1001 Davis Ave., Dubuque 52001, (319) 582-3592, members.aol.com/dbqshalom.

Kansas: Heartland Center for Spirituality, 3600 Broadway, Great Bend 67530, (316) 792-1232; Manna House of Prayer, 323 East 5th St., Box 675, Concordia 66901, (785) 243-4428; Spiritual Life Center, 7100 E. 45th St., N. Wichita 67226, (316) 744-0167, www.feist.com/~spiritlife/index.html.

Kentucky: Bethany Spring, 115 Dee Head Rd., New Haven, 40051, (502) 549-8277; Catherine Spalding Center, P.O. Box 24, Nazareth 40048, (502) 348-1516, www.scnazarethky.org/csc; Flaget Center, 1935 Lewiston Dr., Louisville 40216, (502) 448-8581; Marydale Retreat Center, 945 Donaldson Hwy., Erlanger 41018, (606) 371-4224; Mt. St. Joseph Retreat Center, 8001 Cummings Rd., Maple Mount 42356, (502) 229-0200, www.msjcenter.org. Our Lady of Gethsemani (m, w, private), The Guestmaster, Abbey of Gethsemani, Trappist, 40051; Passionist Nuns, 8564 Crisp Rd, Whitesville 42378, (270) 233-4571.

Louisiana: Abbey Christian Life Center, St. Joseph's Abbey, St. Benedict 70457, (504) 892-3473; Ave Maria Retreat House, 8089 Barataria Blvd., Crown Point, 70072, (504) 689-3837; Cenacle Retreat House (w*), 5500 St. Mary St., P.O. Box 8115, Metairie 70011, (504) 887-1420, www.cenaclesisters.org/metairie.htm; Jesuit Spirituality Center (m,w; directed), P.O. Box C, Grand Coteau 70541, (337) 662-5251, members.aol.com/jespiritcen; Lumen Christi Retreat Center, 100 Lumen Christi Lane, Hwy. 311, Schriever 70395, (504) 868-1523; Magnificat Center of the Holy Spirit, 23629 Faith Rd., Ponchatoula 70454, (504) 362-4356.

Manresa House of Retreats (m), P.O. Box 89, Convent 70723, (225) 562-3596; Maryhill Renewal Center, 600 Maryhill Rd., Pineville 71360, (318) 640-1378, www.diocesealex.org; Our Lady of the Oaks Retreat House, P.O. Box D, 214 Church St., Grand Coteau 70541, (318) 662-5410, members.aol.com/olorhgc; Regina Coeli Retreat Center, 17225 Regina Coeli Rd., Covington 70433, (504) 892-4110; Sophie Barat House, 1719 Napoleon Ave., New Orleans 70115, (504) 899-6027.

Maine: Bay View Villa, 187 Bay View Rd., Saco 04072, (207) 286-8762; Marie Joseph Spiritual Center, RFD 2, Biddeford 04005, (207) 284-5671; Mother of the Good Shepherd Monastery by the Sea, 235 Pleasant Ave., Peaks Island 04108, (207) 766-2717; Notre Dame Retreat & Spiritual Center, P.O. Box 159, Alfred 04002, (207) 324-6160; St. Paul Retreat and Cursillo

Center, 136 State St., Augusta 04330, (207) 622-6235.

Maryland: Bon Secours Spiritual Center, Marriottsville 21104, (410) 442-1320, www.bonsecours.org/bssc; Christian Brothers Spiritual Center (m,w,y), P.O. Box 29, 2535 Buckeyestown Pike, Adamstown 21710, (301) 874-5180; Loyola on the Potomac Retreat House, Faulkner 20632, (301) 870-3515, www.loyolaretreat.org; Msgr. Clare J. O'Dwyer Retreat House (y*), 15523 York Rd., P.O. Box 310, Sparks 21152, (410) 666-2400; Our Lady of Mattaponi Youth Retreat and Conference Center, 11000 Mattaponi Rd., Upper Marlboro 20772, (301) 952-9074; Seton Retreat Center, 333 S. Seton Ave., Emmitsburg 21727, (301) 447-6021.

Massachusetts: Boston Cenacle Society, 25 Avery St., Dedham 02026; Calvary Retreat Center, 59 South St., P.O. Box 219, Shrewsbury 01545, (508) 842-8821, www.calvaryretreat.org; Campion Renewal Center, 319 Concord Rd., Weston 02193, (781) 788-6810; Community of teresian Carmelites, 30 Chrome St., 01613, (508) 752-5734; Don Orione Center, P.O. Box 205, Old Groveland Rd., Bradford 01835, (508) 373-0461; Eastern Point Retreat House, Gonzaga Hall, 37 Niles Pond Rd., Gloucester 01930, (978) 283-0013; Espousal Center, 554 Lexington St., Waltham 02452, (781) 209-3101; Esther House of Spiritual Renewal, Sisters of St. Anne, 1015 Pleasant St., Worcester 01602.

Franciscan Center - Retreat House, 459 River Rd., Andover 01810, (978) 851-3391, www.franrcent.org; Genesis Spiritual Life Center, 53 Mill St., Westfield 01085, (413) 562-3627; Glastonbury Abbey (Benedictine Monks), 16 Hull St.,Hingham 02043; Holy Cross Fathers Retreat House, 490 Washington St., N. Easton 02356, (508) 238-2051; La Salette Center for Christian Living, 947 Park St., Attleboro 02703, (508) 222-8530, www.ultranet.com/~lasalett; Marian Center, 1365 Northampton St., Holyoke 01040 (day and evening programs); Marist House, 518 Pleasant St., 01701, (508) 879-1620; Miramar Retreat Center, P.O. Box M, Duxbury, 02331, (781) 585-2460; Mt. Carmel Christian Life Center, Oblong Rd., Box 613, Williamstown 01267, (413) 458-3164.

Sacred Heart Retreat Center, Salesians of St. John Bosco, P.O. Box 567, Ipswich 01938; St. Benedict Abbey (Benedictine Monks), 252 Still River Rd., P.O. Box 67, Still River 01467, (978) 456-3221; St. Joseph Villa Retreat Center, Sisters of St. Joseph, 339 Jerusalem Rd., Cohasset 02025, (781) 383-6024; St. Joseph's Abbey Retreat House (m) (Trappist Monks), 167 North Spencer Rd., Spencer 01562, (508) 885-8710, www.spencerabbey.org; St. Stephen Priory Spiritual Life Center (Dominican), 20 Glen St., Box 370, Dover 02030, (508) 785-0124, www.ststephenpriory.org.

Michigan: Augustine Center, 2798 U.S. 31 North, Box 84, Conway 49722, (231) 347-3657; Capuchin Retreat, 62460 Mt. Vernon, Box 188, Washington 48094, (248) 651-4826; Colombiere Conference Center, Box 139, 9075 Big Lake Rd., Clarkston 48347, (248) 620-2534, www.colombiere.com; Manresa Jesuit Retreat House, 1390 Quarton Rd., Bloomfield Hills 48304, (313) 564-6455; Marygrove Retreat Center, Garden 49835, (906) 644-2771; Queen of Angels Retreat, 3400 S. Washington Rd., P.O. Box 2026, Saginaw 48605, (517) 755-2149, www.rc.net/saginaw/retreat.

St. Francis Retreat Center, Diocese of Lansing, 703

E. Main St., De Witt 48820, (517) 669-8321; St. Lazare Retreat House, 18600 W. Spring Lake Rd., P.O. Box 462, Spring Lake 49456, (616) 842-3370; St. Mary's Retreat House (w*), 775 W. Drahner Rd., Oxford 48371, (248) 628-3894; St. Paul of the Cross Retreat Center (m*), 23333 Schoolcraft, Detroit 48223, (313) 535-9563; Weber Retreat Center, 1257 Siena Hghts. Dr., Adrian 49221, (517) 266-4000.

Minnesota: Benedictine Center, St. Paul's Monastery, 2675 E. Larpenteur Ave., St. Paul 55109, (651) 777-7251, www.osb.org/spm; The Cenacle, 1221 Wayzata Blvd., Wayzata 55391; Center for Spiritual Development, 211 Tenth St. S., P.O. Box 538, Bird Island 55310, (320) 365-3644, www.centerbi.com; Christ the King Retreat Center, 621 First Ave. S. Buffalo 55313, (763) 682-1394; Christian Brothers' Retreat Center, 15525 St. Croix Trail North, Marine-on-St. Croix 55047, (651) 433-2486.

Franciscan Retreats, Conventual Franciscan Friars, 16385 St. Francis Lane, Prior Lake 55372, (952) 447-2182, www.franciscanretreats.net; Holy Spirit Retreat House, 3864 420th Ave., Janesville, 56048, (507) 234-5712; Jesuit Retreat House (m), 8243 DeMontreville Trail North, Lake Elmo 55042, (651) 777-1311; Maryhill (m,w*), 1988 Summit Ave., St. Paul 55105, (651) 696-2970, www.sdhm.net; Villa Maria Center, Villa Maria Center, 29847 County 2 Blvd., Frontenac 55026, (651) 345-4582.

Missouri: Assumption Abbey, Rte. 5, Box 1056, Ava 65608, (417) 683-5110; The Cenacle, 3393 McKelvey Rd., Apt. 211, Bridgeton, 63044, (314) 387-2211; Cordis House, 648 S. Assisi Way, Republic 65738, (417) 732-6684; Il Ritiro - The Little Retreat, P.O. Box 38, Eime Rd., Dittmer 63023, (636) 285-3759; La Salle Institute, 2101 Rue de la Salle, Wildwood 63038, (636) 938-5374; Maria Fonte Solitude (private; individual hermitages), P.O. Box 322, High Ridge 63049, (314) 677-3235.

Marianist Retreat and Conference Center, P.O. Box 718, Eureka 63025-0718, (636) 938-5390; Mercy Center, 2039 N. Geyer Rd., St. Louis 63131, (314) 966-4686; Our Lady of Assumption Abbey (m,w), Trappists, Rt. 5, Box 1056, Ava 65608-9142; Pallottine Renewal Center, 15270 Old Halls Ferry Rd., Florissant 63034, (314) 837-7100; members.aol.com/prcrenewal/home.html; Society of Opur Mother of Peace (private, individual hermitages), 12494 Hwy. T, Marionville 65705, (417) 744-2011; White House Retreat, 3601 Lindell Blvd., Ste. 204, St. Louis 63108, (314) 533-8903, www.gabrielmedia.org/whr; Windridge Solitude, 1932 W. Linda Lane, Lonedell 63060.

Montana: Sacred Heart Retreat Center, 26 Wyoming Ave., P.O. Box 153, Billings 59103, (406) 252-0322; Ursuline Retreat Centre, 2300 Central Ave., Great Falls 59401, (406) 452-8585.

Nebraska: Our Lady of Good Counsel retreat House, R.R. 1, Box 110, 7303 N. 112th St., Waverly 68462, (402) 786-2705.

Nevada: Monastery of Christ in the Mountains, P.O.Box 708, Caliente 89008, (775) 726-3669.

New Hampshire: Epiphany Monastery, 96 Scobie Rd., P.O. Box 60, New Boston 03070; La Salette Shrine (private and small groups), 410 NH, Route 4A, P.O. Box 420, Enfield 03748, (603) 632-7087.

New Jersey: Bethany Ridge, P.O. Box 241, Little York 08834, (908) 995-9758; Bethlehem Hermitage, 82 Pleasant Hill Rd., Chester 07930, (908) 879-7059; Carmel Retreat House, 1071 Ramapo Valley Rd., Mahwah 07430, (201) 327-7090; Cenacle Retreat House, 411 River Rd., Highland Park 08904, (732) 249-8100, www.cenacle.sisters.org; Emmaus House, 101 Center St., Perth Amboy 08861, (732) 442-7688; Father Judge Apostolic Center (young adults), 1292 Long Hill Rd., Stirling 07980; Felician Retreat House, 35 Windemere Ave., Mt. Arlington 07856, (973) 398-9806; John Paul II Retreat Center, 414 S. 8th St., Vineland 08360; Loyola House of Retreats, 161 James St., Morristown 07960, (973) 539-0740, www.loyola.org.

Marianist Family Retreat Center (families*), 417 Yale Ave., Box 488, Cape May Point 08212-0488; Maris Stella (Vacation Home for Sisters*), 7201 Long Beach Blvd., Harvey Cedars 08008, (609) 494-0499; Mount Paul Retreat Center, 243 Mt. Paul Rd., Oak Ridge 07438, (973) 697-6341; Mt. St. Francis Retreat House, 474 Sloatsburg Rd., Ringwood 07456, (973) 962-9778; Queen of Peace Retreat House, St. Paul's Abbey, P.O. Box 7, Newton 07860, (973) 383-2470; Sacred Heart Renewal Center, P.O. Box 68, Belvidere 07823, (908) 475-4694; Sacred Heart Retreat Center (y*, m,w), 20 Old Swartswood Rd., Newton 07860, (973) 383-2620; St. Joseph by the Sea Retreat House, 400 Rte. 35 N., South Mantoloking 08738, (732) 892-8494.

St. Pius X Spiritual Life Center, P.O. Box 216, Blackwood 08012, (856) 227-1436; San Alfonso Retreat House, P.O. Box 3098, 755 Ocean Ave., Long Beach 07740, (732) 222-2731, www.sanalfonso retreats.org; Sanctuary of Mary, Pilgrimage Place, Branchville 07826, (973) 875-7625; Stella Maris Retreat House, 981 Ocean Ave., Elberon 07740, (732) 229-0602; Villa Pauline Retreat House, 350 Bernardsville Rd., Mendham 07945, (973) 543-9058; Vincentian Renewal Center, 75 Mapleton Rd., P.O. Box 757, Plainsboro 08536, (609) 520-9626; Vocationist Fathers Retreat, 90 Brooklake Rd., Florham Park 07932, (973) 966-6262, www.vocationist.org; Xavier Retreat and Conference Center, P.O. Box 211, Convent Station 07961, (973) 290-5121.

New Mexico: Holy Cross Retreat, Conventual Franciscan Friars, P.O. Box 158, Mesilla Park 88047; Immaculate Heart of Mary Retreat and Conference Center, Mt. Carmel Rd., Santa Fe 87501, (505) 988-1975; Madonna Retreat Center, Inc., 4040 St. Joseph Pl., N.W., 87120, (505) 831-8196; Pecos Benedictine Abbey, Pecos 87552, (505) 757-6415, www.pecos abbey.org; Spiritual Renewal Center, 2348 Pajarito Rd., S.W., Albuquerque 87105, (505) 877-4211, www.christdesert.org/dominican; Sacred Heart Retreat, P.O. Box 1989, Gallup 87301.

New York: Bethany Retreat House, County Road 105, Box 1003, Highland Mills 10930, (845) 928-2213, www.rcnet/newyork/bethany; Bethlehem Retreat House, Abbey of the Genesee, Piffard 14533; Bishop Molloy Retreat House, 86-45 Edgerton Blvd., Jamaica 11432, (718) 739-1229; Blessed Kateri Retreat House, National Kateri Shrine, P.O. Box 627, Fonda 11432, (518) 853-3646; Cardinal Spellman Retreat House, Passionist Community, 5801 Palisade Ave., Bronx (Riverdale) 10471, (718) 549-6500, www.passionists.org; Cenacle Center for Spiritual Renewal, 310 Cenacle Rd., Lake Ronkonkoma 11779, (631) 588-8366.

Cenacle Retreat House, State Rd., P.O. Box 467, Bedford Village 10506, (914) 234-3344; Christ the

King Retreat and Conference Center, 500 Brookford Rd., Syracuse 13224, (315) 446-2680; Cormaria Retreat House, Sag Harbor, L.I. 11963, (631) 725-4206; Dominican Spiritual Life Center, 1945 Union St., Niskayuma 12309, (518) 393-4169; Don Bosco Retreat Center, 174 Filors Lane, Stony Point, 10980-2645, (845) 947-2200, www.marianshrine.org; Graymoor Spiritual Life Center, Graymoor, Route 9, P.O. Box 300, Garrison 10524; Jesuit Retreat House, Auriesville, (518) 853-3033; Monastery of the Precious Blood (w), Ft. Hamilton Parkway and 54th St., Brooklyn 11219 (single day retreats); Mount Alvernia Retreat House, Box 858, Wappingers Falls 12590.

Mount Irenaeus Franciscan Mountain Retreat, Holy Peace Friary, P.O. Box 100, West Clarksville, NY 14786, (716) 973-2470; Mount Manresa Retreat House, 239 Fingerboard Rd., Staten Island 10305, (718) 727-3844; Mt. St. Alphonsus Redemptorist Retreat Ministry, P.O. Box 219, Esopus 12429, (845) 384-8000, www.msaretreat.com; Notre Dame Retreat House, Box 342, 5151 Foster Rd., Canandaigua 14424, (716) 394-5700; Our Lady of Hope Center, 434 River Rd., Newburgh 12550, (914) 568-0780; Regina Maria Retreat House, 77 Brinkerhoff St., Plattsburgh 12901-2701, (518) 561-3421; St. Andrew's House, 257 St. Andrew's Rd., Walden 12586, (914) 778-5941; St. Columban Center, Diocese of Buffalo, 6892 Lake Shore Rd., P.O. Box 816, Derby 14047, (716) 947-4708, www.stcolumbacenter.org.

St. Francis Retreat, 1 Pryer Manor Rd., Larchmont 10538, (914) 235-6839; St. Gabriel Retreat House (y, mc), 64 Burns Rd., P.O. Box P, Shelter Island 11965, (631) 749-0850; St. Ignatius Retreat House, P.O. Box 756, Searingtown Rd., Manhasset 11030, (516) 521-8300; St. Josaphat's Retreat House, Basilian Monastery, East Beach Rd., Glen Cove 11542; St. Joseph Center (Spanish Center), 275 W. 230th St., Bronx 10463, (718) 796-4340; St. Mary's Villa, 150 Sisters Servants Lane, Sloatsburg 10974, (914) 753-5100; St. Paul Center, 21-35 Crescent St., Astoria 11105, (718) 932-0752; St. Ursula Retreat Center, P.O. Box 86, Middle Rd. and Blue Point Ave., Blue Point 11715, (631) 363-2422; Stella Maris Retreat Center, 130 E. Genesee St., Skaneateles 13152, (315) 685-6836; Tagaste Monastery, 220 Lafayette Ave., Suffern 10901; Trinity Retreat, 1 Pryer Manor Rd., Larchmont 10538, (914) 235-6839.

North Carolina: Avila Retreat Center, 711 Mason Rd., Durham 27712, (919) 477-1285; Madonna House, 424 Rose Ln., Raleigh 27610.

North Dakota: Presentation Prayer Center, 1101 32nd Ave. S., Fargo 58103, (701) 237-4857; Queen of Peace Retreat, 1310 Broadway, Fargo 58102, (701) 293-9286.

Ohio: Bergamo Center for Lifelong Learning, 4400 Shakertown Rd., Dayton 45430, (937) 426-2363, www.bergamocenter.org; Franciscan Renewal Center, Pilgrim House, 321 Clay St., Carey 43316, (419) 396-7970, www.olcshrine.com; Friarhurst Retreat House, 8136 Wooster Pike, Cincinnati 45227, (513) 561-2270; Jesuit Retreat House, 5629 State Rd., Cleveland 44134, (440) 884-9300; Loyola of the Lakes, 700 Killinger Rd., Clinton 44216, (330) 896-2315, www.lotljrh.com; Maria Stein Center, 2365 St. Johns Rd., Maria Stein 45860, (419) 925-7625, www.spiritualcenter.net; Milford Spiritual Center, 5361 S. Milford Rd., Milford 45150, (513) 248-3500, www.milfordspiritual

center.org; Our Lady of the Pines, 1250 Tiffin St., Fremont 43420, (419) 332-6522.

Sacred Heart Retreat and Renewal Center, 3128 Logan Ave., P.O. Box 6074, Youngstown 44501, (330) 759-9539; St. Joseph Christian Life Center, 18485 Lake Shore Blvd., Cleveland 44119, (216) 531-7370, www.stjosephchristianlife.com; St. Joseph Renewal Center, 200 St. Francis Ave., Tiffin 44883, (419) 443-1485.

Oklahoma: St. Gregory's Abbey, 1900 W. MacArthur, Shawnee 74804, (405) 878-5491, www.sgc.edu.

Oregon: Franciscan Renewal Center, 0858 S.W. Palatine Hill Rd., Portland 97219, (503) 636-1590; The Jesuit Spirituality Center, 424 S.W. Mill St., Portland 97201, (503) 242-1973; Mount Angel Abbey Retreat House, 1 Abbey Dr., St. Benedict 97373, (503) 845-3027, www.mtangel.edu; Our Lady of Peace Retreat, 3600 S. W. 170th Ave., Beaverton 97006, (503) 649-7127, www.geocities.com/ourladyofpeaceretreat; St. Rita Retreat Center, P.O. Box 310, Gold Hill 97525, (541) 855-1333; Shalom Prayer Center, Benedictine Sisters, 840 S. Main St., Mt. Angel 97362-9527, (503) 845-6773, www.open.org/shalom; St. Benedict Lodge, 56630 North Bank Rd., McKenzie Bridge 97413, (541) 822-3572; Trappist Abbey Guesthouse (m,w), 9200 N.E. Abbey Rd., Lafayette 97127, (503) 852-0107.

Pennsylvania: Avila Retreat Center, 61 E. High St., Union City 16438, (814) 438-7020; Dominican Retreat House, 750 Ashbourne Rd., Elkins Park 19027, (215) 782-8520; Ecclesia Center, 9101 Ridge Rd., Erie 16417, (814) 774-9691; Fatima Renewal Center, 1000 Seminary Rd., Dalton 18414, (570) 563-8500; Franciscan Spirit and Life Center, 3605 McRoberts Rd., Pittsburgh 15234, (412) 881-9207; Gilmary Diocesan Center, 601 Flaugherty Run Rd., Coraopolis 15108-3899, (412) 264-8400, www.diopitt.org.

Jesuit Center for Spiritual Growth, Box 223, Church Rd., Wernersville 19656, (610) 670-3642, www.jesuitcenter.webjump.com; Kearns Spirituality Center, 9000 Babcock Blvd., Allison Park 15101, (412) 366-1124, www.sistersofdivprovidence.org; Mariawald Renewal Center, P.O. Box 97 (1094 Welsh Rd.), Reading 19607, (610) 777-0135, www.hometown.aol.com/mariawald/index.html; Martina Spiritual Renewal Center, 5244 Clarwin Ave., Pittsburgh 15229, (412) 931-9766; St. Emma Retreat House, 1001 Harvey Ave., Greensburg 15601, (724) 834-3060, www.stemma.org; St. Francis Retreat Center (y*), c/o Dept. of Youth Ministry, 900 W. Market St., Orwigsburg 17961, (570) 366-1016; St. Francis Center for Renewal, Monocacy Manor, 395 Bridle Path Rd., Bethlehem 18017, (610) 867-8890, www.catholic-church.org/stfrancis-cfn; St. Francis Retreat House, 3918 Chipman Rd., Easton 18045, (610) 258-3053; St. Gabriel's Retreat House, 631 Griffin Pond Rd., Clarks Summit 18411, (570) 586-4957, www.intiques.com/cpnuns/.

St. Joseph's in the Hills, 313 Warren Ave., Malvern 19355, (610) 644-0400, www.st-joseph-in-the-hills.org; St. Paul of the Cross Retreat Center, 148 Monastery Ave., Pittsburgh 15203, (412) 381-7676; Saint Raphaela Center, 616 Coopertown Rd., Haverford 19041, (610) 642-5715; St. Vincent Summer Retreat Program (m,w,mc; summers only), Latrobe 15650, (724) 532-6600; Urban House of Prayer, 1919 Cambridge St., Philadelphia 19130,

(215) 236-8328; Villa of Our Lady Retreat Center (w, mc, y), HCR No. 1, Box 41, Mt. Pocono 18344, (570) 839-7217.

Rhode Island: Bethany Renewal Center, 397 Fruit Hill Ave., N. Providence 02911, (401) 353-5860; Father Marot CYO Center (y), 53 Federal St., Woonsocket 02895, (401) 762-3252; Our Lady of Peace Spiritual Life Center, 333 Ocean Rd., Box 507, Narragansett 02882, (401) 884-7676; St. Paul Priory Guest House, 61 Narragansett Ave., 02840, (401) 847-2423.

South Carolina: Sea of Peace House of Prayer, 59 Palmetto Pointe Rd., Edisto Island 29438, (843) 869-0513; Springbank Retreat Center,1345 Springbank Rd., Kingstree 29556, (800) 671-0361, www.spring bankretreat.org.

South Dakota: St. Martin's Community Center, 2110C St. Martin's Dr., Rapid City 57702, (605) 343-8011.

Tennessee: Carmelites of Mary Immaculate Center of Spirituality, 610 Bluff Rd., Liberty 37095, (615) 536-5177.

Texas: Benedictine Retreat Center, HC#2, Box 6300, Sandia 78383; Bishop DeFalco Retreat Center, 2100 N. Spring, Amarillo 79107, (806) 383-1811, www.bdrc.org; Bishop Rene H. Gracida Retreat Center, 3036 Saratoga Blvd., Corpus Christi 78415, (512) 851-1443; Catholic Renewal Center of North Texas, 4503 Bridge St., Ft. Worth 76103, (817) 429-2920; Cenacle Retreat House, 420 N. Kirkwood, Houston 77079, (281) 497-3131, www.cenacleretreat house.org; Christian Renewal Center (Centro de Renovacion Cristiana), Oblates of Mary Immaculate, P.O. Box 699, Dickinson 77539, (281) 337-1312.

Holy Family Retreat Center, 9920 N. Major Dr., Beaumont 77713-7618, (409) 899-5617; Holy Name Retreat Center, 430 Bunker Hill Rd., Houston 77024, (713) 464-0211; Holy Spirit Retreat and Conference Center, 501 Century Dr. S., Laredo 78040, (956) 726-4352, www.stjean.com/laredo/hsrc/holy.htm; Lebh Shomea House of Prayer, La Parra Ranch, P.O. Box 9, Sarita 78385; Montserrat Retreat House, P.O. Box 398, Lake Dallas 75065, (940) 321-6020, www.montserratretreat.org; Moye Center, 600 London, Castroville 78009, (830) 931-2233, www.moye center.org; Oblate Renewal Center, 5700 Blanco Rd., San Antonio 78216, (210) 349-4173.

Omega Retreat Center, 216 W. Highland Dr., Boerne 78006, (830) 816-8471; Our Lady of Mercy Retreat Center, P.O. Box 744, 19th & Division, Slaton 79364, (806) 828-6428; Prayer Town Emmanuel Retreat House, P.O. Box 17, Channing 79018, (806) 534-2312; San Juan Retreat House (St. Eugene de Mazenod Retreat Center), P.O. Box 747, San Juan 78589, (956) 787-0033.

Utah: Abbey of Our Lady of the Holy Trinity (m), 1250 S 9500 E, Huntsville 84317, (801) 745-3784, www.xmission.com/~hta; Our Lady of the Mountains, 1794 Lake St., Ogden 84401, (801) 392-9231.

Virginia: Benedictine Retreat and Conf. Center, Mary Mother of the Church Abbey, 12829 River Rd., 23233, (804) 784-3508; Dominican Retreat, 7103 Old Dominion Dr., McLean 22101-2799, (703) 356-4243; The Dwelling Place, 601 Holly Grove Ln., Richmond 23235, (804) 323-3360; Holy Family Retreat House, The Redemptorists, P.O. 3151, 1414 N. Mallory St., Hampton 23663, (757) 722-3997; Madonna House, 828 Campbell Ave., S.W., Roanoke 24016, (540) 343-8464; Missionhurst Mission Center, 4651 N. 25th St., Arlington

22207, (703) 525-6557, www.missionhurst.org. Retreat House, Holy Cross Abbey, Rt. 2, Box 3870, Berryville 22611, (540) 955-3124; Shalom House, P.O. Box 196, Montpelier 23192, (804) 883-6149; Tabor Retreat Center, 2125 Langhorne Rd., Lynchburg 24501, (804) 846-6475; The Well, 18047 Quiet Way, Smithfield 23430, (757) 255-2366, www.thewellretreatcenter.org.

Washington: Immaculate Heart Retreat Center, 6910 S. Ben Burr Rd., Spokane 99223, (509) 448-1224, www.ihrc.net; House of the Lord Retreat Center, P.O. Box 1034, Tum Tum 99034, (509) 276-2219; KAIROS House of Prayer, 1714 W. Stearns Rd., Spokane 99208, (509) 466-2187; Palisades Retreat House, P.O. Box 3739, Federal Way 98063, (206) 838-9583; St. Peter Retreat Center, 15880 Summitview Rd., Cowiche 98923, (509) 678-4935.

West Virginia: Bishop Hodges Pastoral Center, Rt. 1, Box 9D, Huttonsville, 26273, (304) 335-2165; Good Counsel Friary, 493 Tyrone Rd., Morgantown 26508, (304) 594-1714; John XXIII Pastoral Center, 100 Hodges Rd., Charleston 25314, (304) 342-0507; Paul VI Pastoral Center, 667 Stone and Shannon Rd., Wheeling 26003, (304) 277-3300; Priest Field Pastoral Center, Rt. 51, Box 133, Kearneysville 25430, (304) 725-1435; West Virginia Institute for Spirituality, 1414 Virginia St. E., Charleston, WV 25301, (304) 345-0926, www.wvis.ws.

Wisconsin: Archdiocesan Retreat Center, 3501 S. Lake Dr., P.O. Box 07912, Milwaukee 53207, (414) 769-3491, www.archmil.org; The Dwelling Place, 528 N. 31st St., Milwaukee 53208, (414) 933-1100; Franciscan Retreat Center, 503 S. Browns Lake Dr., Burlington 53105, (262) 763-3600; Franciscan Spirituality Center, 920 Market St., La Crosse 54601, (608) 791-5295, www.fspa.org; Holy Name Retreat House, Chambers Island, mailing address: 1825 Riverside Drive, P.O. Box 23825, Green Bay 54305, (920) 437-7531; Jesuit Retreat House, 4800 Fahrnwald Rd., Oshkosh 54902, (920) 231-9060, www.jr house.fp.execpc.com; Marywood Franciscan Spirituality Center (FSPA), 3560 Hwy. 51 N., Arbor Vitae 54568, (715) 385-3750, www.fspa.org.

Monte Alverno Retreat Center, 1000 N. Ballard Rd., Appleton 54911, (920) 733-8526; Mount Carmel Hermitage, 897 U.S. Hwy. 8, 54001, (715) 268-9313; Mount Tabor, 522 2 St., Menasha 54952, (920) 722-8918; Norbertine Center for Spirituality, St. Norbert Abbey, 1016 N. Broadway, De Pere 54115, (920) 337-4315, www.norbertines.org; Redemptorist Retreat Center, 1800 N. Timber Trail Lane, Oconomowoc 53066-4897, (262) 567-6900, www.redemptorist retreat.org; St. Anthony Retreat Center, 300 E. 4th St., Marathon 54448, (715) 443-2236, www.sar center.com.

St. Bede Retreat and Conference Center, 1190 Priory Rd., P.O. Box 66, Eau Claire 54702, (715) 834-8642; Saint Benedict Center (monastery and ecumenical retreat and conference center), P.O. Box 5070, Madison 53705-0070, (608) 836-1631; St. Clare Center for Spirituality, 7381 Church St., Custer 54423, (715) 592-4099; St. Joseph's Retreat Center, 3035 O'Brien Rd., Bailey's Harbor 54202, (920) 839-2391; St. Vincent Pallotti Center, N6409 Bowers Rd., Elkhorn 53121, (262) 723-2108, www.vpallelk@elknet.net; Schoenstatt Center, W. 284 N. 698 Cherry Lane, Waukesha 53188, (414) 547-7733.

Catholic Education

LEGAL STATUS OF CATHOLIC EDUCATION

The right of private schools to exist and operate in the United States is recognized in law. It was confirmed by the U.S. Supreme Court in 1925 when the tribunal ruled (Pierce v. Society of Sisters, see Church-State Decisions of the Supreme Court) that an Oregon state law requiring all children to attend public schools was unconstitutional.

Private schools are obliged to comply with the education laws in force in the various states regarding such matters as required basic curricula, periods of attendance, and standards for proper accreditation.

The special curricula and standards of private schools are determined by the schools themselves. Thus, in Catholic schools, the curricula include not only the subject matter required by state educational laws but also other fields of study, principally, education in the Catholic faith.

The Supreme Court has ruled that the First Amendment to the U.S. Constitution, in accordance with the No Establishment of Religion Clause of the First Amendment, prohibits direct federal and state aid from public funds to church-affiliated schools. (See several cases in Church-State Decisions of the Supreme Court.)

Public Aid

This prohibition does not extend to all child-benefit and public-purpose programs of aid to students of non-public elementary and secondary schools.

Statutes authorizing such programs have been ruled constitutional on the grounds that they:

- have a "secular legislative purpose"
- neither inhibit nor advance religion as a "principal or primary effect"
- do not foster "excessive government entanglement with religion."

Aid programs considered constitutional have provided bus transportation, textbook loans, school lunches and health services, and "secular, neutral or non-ideological services, facilities and materials provided in common to all school children," public and non-public.

The first major aid to education program in U.S. history containing provisions benefiting non-public school students was enacted by the 89th Congress and signed into law by President Lyndon B. Johnson on Apr. 11, 1965. The Elementary and Secondary Education Act was designed to avoid the separation of Church and state impasse which had blocked all earlier aid proposals pertaining to non-public, and especially church-affiliated, schools. The objective of the program, under public control, is to serve the public purpose by aiding disadvantaged pupils in non-public as well as public schools.

With respect to college and university education in church-affiliated institutions, the Supreme Court has upheld the constitutionality of statutes providing student loans and, under the Federal Higher Education Facilities Act of 1963, construction loans and grants for secular-purpose facilities.

Catholic schools are exempt from real estate taxation in all of the states. Since Jan. 1, 1959, nonprofit parochial and private schools have also been exempt from several federal excise taxes.

NCEA

The National Catholic Educational Association, founded in 1904, is a voluntary organization of educational institutions and individuals concerned with Catholic education in the U.S. Its objectives are to promote and encourage the principles and ideals of Christian education and formation by suitable service and other activities. The NCEA serves approximately 200,000 Catholic educators at all levels from pre-K through university. Its official publication is *Momentum*. Numerous service publications are issued to members. Bishop Robert J. Banks of Green Bay, chairman of the Board of Directors; Leonard F. DeFiore, president. Address: 1077 30th St. N.W., Washington, DC 20007; (202) 337-6232.

EDUCATIONAL VOUCHERS

Although 41 educational voucher programs funded by private philanthropy were operating in the United States by 1998-99, discussion of vouchers as a political, legal, and educational issue primarily concerns publicly-funded plans allowing parents to send their children to the school of their choice. At present there are three educational voucher programs of this kind — in Milwaukee, Cleveland, and the state of Florida.

The Vouchers Debate

Proponents of vouchers argue that they are not merely consistent with parental rights but an appropriate, even necessary, practical means of realizing them. In particular, it is said, they enable low-income parents to exercise a choice about schools. Another pro-vouchers argument is that they create an incentive for self-improvement by public schools that is lacking when they enjoy a near monopoly.

Arguments against vouchers are that they take funds away from public schools and encourage highly motivated parents and competent students to abandon failing public institutions in favor of private ones. Using vouchers at church-related schools also is said to violate the First Amendment ban on an establishment of religion. The chief opponents of educational vouchers are teacher unions — the National Education Association, the American Federation of Teachers, and their affiliates — and other public school groups, church-state separationists, and some mainline African American organizations. Phi Delta Kappa/Gallup polls in 1998 and 1999 found 51% of the respondents, including 60% of public school parents in the latter year, were in favor of total or partial government-paid tuition for children in private or church-related schools, although support declined when vouchers were specified.

Recent Developments

The Milwaukee Parental Choice Program began in 1990 and was expanded by the state legislature in 1995 to allow participation by religious schools. By 2000, about 6,000 low-income students were receiving vouchers worth $5,000 to attend non-public institutions. The state Supreme Court in June 1998 upheld including religious schools; in November of 1998 the U.S. Supreme Court refused without comment to consider an appeal from that ruling.

The Ohio legislature established the Cleveland Scholarship and Tutoring Program as a pilot program in March 1995. Some 3,800 low-income students take part. The participation of church-related schools was challenged from the beginning. On June 27, 2002, the U.S. Supreme Court upheld the constitutionality of the Cleveland voucher program. (For details, see under **New in Depth**.)

Florida enacted its voucher plan, the first statewide program in the country, in 1999. Students in public schools that fail to measure up to specified standards two years out of four are eligible. Despite predictions that as many as 150,000 of Florida's 2.3 million public elementary and secondary students might receive vouchers, only a tiny handful have up to now. A state judge held the program unconstitutional in March 2000, but allowed it to continue pending the outcome of the legal process.

On June 28, 2000, the U.S. Supreme Court handed down a decision that could have implications for the future of vouchers, ruling 6-3 (in *Mitchell v. Helms*, a case from Louisiana) that the government may pay for computers and other instructional items used by parochial students under a federal program dating back to 1965.

Writing for himself and for Chief Justice William Rehnquist and Associate Justices Antonin Scalia and Anthony Kennedy, Justice Thomas saw anti-Catholicism as the historical source of opposition to government aid to church-sponsored education; he blamed the Supreme Court for keeping prejudice alive by using the pejorative expression "pervasively sectarian" as code language to refer to Catholic schools.

In June 2001 the Democrat-controlled U.S. Senate defeated an effort by President George W. Bush to attach vouchers to the Education Reform Bill.

SUMMARY OF SCHOOL STATISTICS

Status and figures (as of Jan. 1) reported by *The Official Catholic Directory*.

Colleges and Universities: 238 (U.S., 233; outlying areas, 5).

College and University Students: 724,065 (U.S., 702,328; outlying areas, 21,737).

High Schools: 1,344 (786 diocesan and parochial; 557 private). U.S., 1,244 (728 diocesan and parochial; 473 private). Outlying areas, 100 (58 diocesan and parochial; 42 private).

High School Students: 691,456 (386,157 diocesan and parochial; 305,299 private). U.S., 651,181 (367,925 diocesan and parochial; 283,256 private). Outlying areas, 40,275 (18,232 diocesan and parochial; 22,043 private).

Public High School Students Receiving Religious Instruction: 766,754 (U.S., 745,469; outlying areas, 21,285).

Elementary Schools: 6,949 (6,623 diocesan and parochial; 326 private). U.S., 6,833 (6,550 diocesan and parochial; 283 private). Outlying areas, 116 (73 diocesan and parochial; 43 private).

Elementary School Students: 2,005,573 (1,918,853 diocesan and parochial; 86,720 private). U.S., 1,959,744 (1,896,067 diocesan and parochial; 63,677 private). Outlying areas, 45,829 (22,786 diocesan and parochial; 23,043 private).

Public Elementary School Students Receiving Religious Instruction: 3,547,478 (U.S., 3,522,410; outlying areas, 25,068).

Non-Residential Schools for Handicapped: 81 (U.S.). Students: 18,696 (U.S.).

Teachers: 176,088 U.S., 169,669 (lay persons 158,703; sisters, 7,934; priests, 1,806; brothers, 1,175; scholastics, 51). Outlying areas, 6,419 (lay persons, 6,001; sisters, 299; priests, 93; brothers, 19; scholastics, 7).

Seminaries: 200 (78 diocesan; 122 religious). U.S.: 180 (73 diocesan; 107 religious). Outlying areas: 20 (5 diocesan; 15 religious).

Seminarians: 4,719 (3,359 diocesan; 1,360 religious). U.S.: 4,619 (3,300 diocesan; 1,319 religious). Outlying areas: 100 (59 diocesan; 41 religious).

CATHOLIC SCHOOLS AND STUDENTS IN THE UNITED STATES

(Source: Official Catholic Directory, *2002; figures as of Jan. 1, 2002. Archdioceses are indicated by an asterisk.)*

State Diocese	Univs. Colleges	Students	High Schools	Students	Elem. Schools	Students
Alabama	1	1,003	8	3,175	39	10,912
*Mobile	1	1,003	3	1,487	19	5,479
Birmingham	-	-	5	1,688	20	5,433
Alaska	-	-	3	334	5	865
*Anchorage	-	-	2	104	3	407
Fairbanks	-	-	1	230	1	294Juneau
- -	-	-	1	164		
Arizona	-	-	11	6,159	47	16,010
Phoenix	-	-	5	4,227	25	10,095
Tucson	-	-	6	1,932	22	5,915
Arkansas						
Little Rock	-	-	6	1,795	31	6,507
California	13	41,260	115	72,191	608	180,183
*Los Angeles	5	10,523	51	30,201	236	68,496
*San Francisco	3	11,289	14	8,185	66	20,908
Fresno	-	-	2	1,402	23	5,404
Monterey	-	-	5	1,688	14	4,065
Oakland	3	5,030	9	6,521	51	14,657
Orange	-	-	6	5,704	38	14,485
Sacramento	-	-	7	4,412	46	13,107
San Bernardino	-	-	2	935	35	8,288
San Diego	1	7,062	5	3,611	44	14,061
San Jose	1	7,356	6	6,055	30	10,465
Santa Rosa	-	-	6	1,953	13	2,861
Stockton	-	-	2	1,524	12	3,386
Colorado	1	12,360	8	3,665	47	13,739
*Denver	1	12,360	5	3,117	38	11,126
Colorado Springs	-	-	1	396	5	1,508
Pueblo	-	-	2	152	4	1,105
Connecticut	5	17,422	23	11,177	128	32,215
*Hartford	2	5,938	9	5,097	71	17,621
Bridgeport	3	11,484	8	3,875	35	10,177
Norwich	-	-	6	2,205	22	4,417
Delaware, Wilmington	-	-	8	4,706	29	10,694
District of Columbia						
*Washington, DC	3	20,422	17	9,475	87	24,453
Florida	3	22,258	33	23,900	180	69,433
*Miami	2	12,327	13	11,996	57	25,445
Orlando	-	-	5	2,540	31	12,247
Palm Beach	-	-	3	2,267	16	6,214
Pensacola-Tallahassee	-	-	2	640	9	2,435
St. Augustine	-	-	2	1,857	24	8,121
St. Petersburg	1	9,931	5	2,959	34	11,245
Venice	-	-	3	1,645	9	3,726
Georgia	-	-	9	4,899	32	11,171
*Atlanta	-	-	4	3,032	16	6,563
Savannah	-	-	5	1,867	16	4,608
Hawaii, Honolulu	1	3,973	7	4,739	32	10,589
Idaho, Boise	-	-	1	695	13	2,532
Illinois	12	55,727	76	47,127	492	154,170
*Chicago	6	42,943	43	30,558	260	91,800
Belleville	-	-	3	1,715	36	6,765
Joliet	3	11,005	8	5,815	56	19,678
Peoria	1	150	7	2,680	46	11,791
Rockford	-	-	8	4,217	41	12,221
Springfield	2	1,629	7	2,688	53	11,915
Indiana	11	25,988	21	11,920	180	49,255
*Indianapolis	2	2,773	9	5,320	63	19,775
Evansville	-	-	4	1,620	24	6,226

State Diocese	Univs. Colleges	Students	High Schools	Students	Elem. Schools	Students
Indiana, cont.						
Ft.Wayne-S. Bend	5	14,945	4	2,993	41	11,122
Gary	1	978	3	1,623	29	7,310
Lafayette	3	7,292	1	364	23	4,822
Iowa	7	9,453	24	7,657	113	27,419
*Dubuque	3	4,227	7	2,779	53	12,936
Davenport	2	3,818	7	1,164	18	4,532
Des Moines	1	442	2	1,414	16	4,951
Sioux City	1	969	8	2,300	26	5,000
Kansas	4	4,622	16	6,536	98	23,376
*Kansas City	3	2,605	7	3,615	44	11,757
Dodge City	-	-	-	-	10	1,114
Salina	-	-	5	758	12	2,101
Wichita	1	2,017	4	2,163	32	8,404
Kentucky	5	6,958	25	11,676	122	34,023
*Louisville	3	4,563	10	6,369	59	18,334
Covington	1	1,555	9	3,315	30	9,014
Lexington	-	-	3	945	15	3,281
Owensboro	1	840	3	1,047	18	3,394
Louisiana	4	11,813	50	28,621	172	68,472
*New Orleans	3	10,759	23	16,568	81	34,498
Alexandria	-	-	3	578	9	2,549
Baton Rouge	1	1,054	8	4,419	25	11,688
Houma-Thib.	-	-	3	1,943	10	4,155
Lafayette	-	-	10	3,851	29	10,501
Lake Charles	-	-	1	572	7	2,540
Shreveport	-	-	2	690	9	1,918
Maine, Portland	1	3,879	3	1,068	18	4,153
Maryland,*Baltimore	4	11,671	22	11,424	75	25,706
Massachusetts	13	31,957	51	26,275	202	58,407
*Boston	7	21,520	35	17,670	128	38,985
Fall River	1	2,490	4	2,850	24	5,941
Springfield	2	1,062	4	1,425	26	7,168
Worcester	3	6,885	8	4,330	24	5,647
Michigan	8	25,649	54	20,093	292	72,826
*Detroit	4	20,728	34	13,396	131	41,646
Gaylord	-	-	4	675	16	2,769
Grand Rapids	1	2,571	4	1,919	41	7,545
Kalamazoo	-	-	3	808	23	3,964
Lansing	3	2,350	6	2,494	43	10,328
Marquette	-	-	-	-	10	1,585
Saginaw	-	-	3	801	28	4,989
Minnesota	7	24,871	23	11,031	195	44,909
*St.Paul and Minn.	3	17,110	13	8,094	96	28,262
Crookston	-	-	1	176	9	1,274
Duluth	1	2,231	-	-	12	1,999
New Ulm	-	-	3	643	18	2,470
St. Cloud	2	4,162	2	894	33	5,753
Winona	1	1,368	4	1,224	27	5,151
Mississippi	1	34	9	2,545	30	7,385
Biloxi	-	-	5	1,770	14	3,251
Jackson	1	34	4	775	16	4,134
Missouri	4	20,308	42	20,894	250	63,435
*St.Louis	2	14,000	30	15,457	156	42,721
Jefferson City	-	-	2	1,020	37	6,436
Kansas City-St. Joseph	2	6,308	7	3,510	35	10,546
Springfield-Cape Girar.	-	-	3	907	22	3,732
Montana	2	2,300	5	970	16	3,094
Great Falls-Billings	1	900	3	578	12	2,276
Helena	1	1,400	2	392	4	818
Nebraska	2	7,282	27	8,045	97	22,936
*Omaha	2	7,282	17	5,727	65	16,391
Grand Island	-	-	4	567	7	1,085
Lincoln	-	-	6	1,751	25	5,460

State Diocese	Univs. Colleges	Students	High Schools	Students	Elem. Schools	Students
Nevada	-	-	2	1,580	11	3,778
Las Vegas	-	-	1	959	7	2,623
Reno	-	-	1	621	4	1,155
New Hampshire						
Manchester	5	5,533	5	2,541	37	7,868
New Jersey	7	21,259	74	37,658	352	117,526
*Newark	4	16,996	37	16,196	139	42,338
Camden	-	-	10	6,195	57	16,031
Metuchen	-	-	6	3,574	44	13,735
Paterson	2	1,843	10	4,082	60	17,337
Trenton	1	2,420	11	7,611	52	28,085
New Mexico	1	1,700	4	2,067	30	6,148
*Santa Fe	1	1,700	2	1,788	16	4,171
Gallup	-	-	2	279	10	1,394
Las Cruces	-	-	-	-	1	355
New York	30	95,935	125	73,077	677	219,039
*New York	12	44,904	54	27,611	215	83,501
Albany	4	4,500	7	3,055	39	9,145
Brooklyn	3	22,323	20	17,519	154	53,585
Buffalo	7	15,416	17	6,048	92	21,363
Ogdensburg	-	-	2	561	23	3,651
Rochester	1	111	7	3,532	54	12,110
Rockville Centre	2	5,766	12	11,299	63	28,709
Syracuse	1	2,915	6	3,452	37	6,975
North Carolina	2	1,769	3	2,266	45	12,888
Charlotte	2	1,769	2	1,404	15	5,945
Raleigh	-	-	1	862	30	6,943
North Dakota	1	2,343	4	1,388	24	3,835
Bismarck	1	2,343	3	1,126	12	1,662
Fargo	-	-	1	262	12	2,173
Ohio	12	37,256	79	45,256	444	141,569
*Cincinnati	4	23,239	22	16,022	114	41,247
Cleveland	3	6,505	23	14,280	137	48,340
Columbus	1	2,197	11	4,985	46	14,214
Steubenville	1	2,208	3	753	17	2,390
Toledo	2	1,585	14	6,415	85	21,361
Youngstown	1	1,522	6	2,801	45	14,017
Oklahoma	1	805	4	2,286	30	7,899
*Oklahoma City	1	805	2	977	20	4,222
Tulsa	-	-	2	1,309	11	3,677
Oregon	2	5,144	10	4,962	46	9,855
*Portland	2	5,144	10	4,962	43	9,188
Baker	-	-	-	-	3	667
Pennsylvania	26	76,620	87	51,840	573	165,341
*Philadelphia	11	33,836	37	30,649	229	83,982
Allentown	2	3,660	9	4,129	52	13,430
Altoona-Johnstown	2	4,012	3	1,213	25	4,457
Erie	2	6,514	7	3,068	42	9,651
Greensburg	2	2,624	2	790	26	5,554
Harrisburg	-	-	7	3,816	42	11,054
Pittsburgh	3	13,871	11	4,107	110	26,103
Scranton	4	12,103	11	4,068	47	11,110
Rhode Island, Providence	2	7,557	12	6,021	53	13,204
South Carolina						
Charleston	-	-	4	1,358	25	6,782
South Dakota	2	1,783	5	1,420	23	5,061
Rapid City	-	-	2	392	2	706
Sioux Falls	2	1,783	3	1,028	21	4,355
Tennessee	2	2,768	11	5,020	43	11,368
Knoxville	-	-	2	1,072	8	2,650
Memphis	1	2,027	6	2,456	17	4,225
Nashville	1	741	3	1,492	18	4,493
Texas	8	23,618	47	17,642	228	65,767
*San Antonio	4	11,998	10	3,872	39	12,212

State Diocese	Univs. Colleges	Students	High Schools	Students	Elem. Schools	Students
Texas, cont.						
Amarillo	-	-	1	131	6	789
Austin	1	4,151	4	798	16	3,899
Beaumont	-	-	1	530	6	1,652
Brownsville	-	-	2	773	9	3,095
Corpus Christi	1	40	1	349	16	2,673
Dallas	1	3,119	8	3,758	33	11,728
El Paso	-	-	3	923	12	4,417
Fort Worth	-	-	4	1,550	15	5,337
Galveston-Houston	1	4,310	8	3,544	49	13,715
Laredo	-	-	1	645	6	1,803
Lubbock	-	-	-	-	2	388
San Angelo	-	-	-	-	3	785
Tyler	-	-	1	204	4	971
Victoria	-	-	3	565	12	2,303
Utah, Salt Lake City	-	-	3	1,646	10	3,739
Vermont, Burlington	3	3,261	2	714	15	2,724
Virginia	4	5,471	14	7,040	58	22,841
Arlington	4	5,471	6	4,219	35	13,458
Richmond	-	-	8	2,821	23	9,383
Washington	3	12,071	12	6,512	80	21,633
*Seattle	2	7,440	9	5,633	57	16,049
Spokane	1	4,631	2	712	16	3,701
Yakima	-	-	1	167	7	1,883
West Virginia, Wheeling-Charleston	1	1,658	8	1,852	26	5,282
Wisconsin	9	34,708	27	12,017	343	61,592
*Milwaukee	5	23,700	13	7,521	130	30,365
Green Bay	2	6,764	6	2,196	74	11,884
La Crosse	1	2,167	7	1,680	77	9,245
Madison	1	2,077	1	620	45	7,198
Superior	-	-	-	-	17	2,900
Wyoming, Cheyenne	-	-	1	46	6	892
EASTERN CHURCHES	-	-	3	599	24	4,001
*Philadelphia	-	-	1	365	8	1,418
St. Nicholas (Chicago)	-	-	1	76	2	380
Stamford	-	-	1	180	3	255
St. Josaphat (Parma)	-	-	-	-	2	298
*Pittsburgh	-	-	-	-	2	342
Parma	-	-	-	-	2	284
Passaic	-	-	-	-	1	124
Van Nuys	-	-	-	-	-	-
St. Maron (Maronites)	-	-	-	-	-	-
Our Lady of Lebanon (Maronites)	-	-	-	-	-	-
Newton (Melkites)	-	-	-	-	-	-
St. Thomas Apostle of Detroit (Chaldeans)	-	-	-	-	-	-
St. George Martyr (Romanians)	-	-	-	-	-	-
Armenians (Ap. Ex.)	-	-	-	-	4	976
SCHOOLS AND STUDENTS IN OUTLYING AREAS						
American Samoa	-	-	1	190	2	397
Caroline Islands	-	-	4	745	5	1,578
Guam	-	-	2	1,014	7	2,117
Marshall Islands	-	-	-	-	6	1,325
Marianas	-	-	1	207	3	365
Puerto Rico	5	21,737	90	39,093	90	29,995
Virgin Islands	-	-	2	233	3	584
TOTAL 2002	**238**	**724,065**	**1,344**	**691,456**	**6,949**	**2,005,573**
Total 2001	235	705,059	1,596	680,947	7,061	2,058,474
Total 1992	235	659,155	1,400	638,079	7,442	1,999,401

CATHOLIC UNIVERSITIES AND COLLEGES IN THE UNITED STATES

(*Sources:* Catholic Almanac *survey;* The Official Catholic Directory.)

Listed below are institutions of higher learning established under Catholic auspices. Some of them are now independent.

Information includes: name of each institution; indication of male (m), female (w), coeducational (c) student body; name of founding group or group with which the institution is affiliated; year of foundation; total number of students, in parentheses.

Albertus Magnus College (c): 700 Prospect St., New Haven, CT 06511; (203) 773-8550; www.albert us.edu. Dominican Sisters; 1925; independent (2,065).

Alvernia College (c): 400 Saint Bernardine St., Reading, PA 19607; (610) 796-8200; www.alvernia.edu. Bernardine Sisters; 1958 (2,033).

Alverno College (w): 3400 S. 43th St., P.O. Box 343922, Milwaukee, WI 53234; (414) 382-6000; www.alverno.edu. School Sisters of St. Francis; 1887; independent (1,940).

Anna Maria College (c): 50 Sunset Lane, Paxton, MA 01612; (508) 849-3300; www.annamaria.edu. Sisters of St. Anne;1946; independent (1,267).

Aquinas College (c): 1607 Robinson Rd. S.E., Grand Rapids, MI 49506; (616) 459-8281. Sisters of St. Dominic; 1922; independent (2,605).

Aquinas College (c): 4210 Harding Rd., Nashville, TN 37205; (615) 297-7545; www.aquinas-tn.edu. Dominican Sisters; 1961 (306).

Aquinas Institute of Theology (c): 3642 Lindell Boulevard, St. Louis, MO 63108; (314) 977-3869; www.op.org/aquinas. Dominicans, 1961; graduate theology; offers distance learning program in pastoral studies and specializations in preaching (200).

Assumption College (c): 500 Salisbury St., Worcester, MA 01615-0005; (508) 767-7000; www.assump tion.edu. Assumptionist Religious; 1904 (2,801).

Ave Maria School of Law (c): 3475 Plymouth Rd., Ann Arbor, MI 48105; (734) 930-4408.

Avila College (c): 11901 Wornall Rd., Kansas City, MO 64145-1698; (816) 942-8400; www.avila.edu. Sisters of St. Joseph of Carondelet; 1916 (1,412).

Barat College (c): 700 Westleigh Rd., Lake Forest, IL 60045; (847) 234-3000; www.barat.edu. Society of the Sacred Heart; 1919; independent (830).

Barry University (c): 11300 N.E. 2nd Ave., Miami Shores, FL 33161; (305) 899-3000; www.barry.edu. Dominican Sisters (Adrian, MI); 1940 (8,300).

Bellarmine College (c): 2001 Newburg Rd., Louisville, KY 40205; (502) 452-8211; www.bellar mine.edu. Louisville archdiocese; independent (2,214).

Belmont Abbey College (c): 100 Belmont-Mt. Holly Rd., Belmont, NC 28012; (704) 825-6700; www.belmontabbeycollege.edu. Benedictine Fathers; 1876 (925).

Benedictine College (c): 1020 N. Second St.,Atchison, KS 66002; (913) 367-5340; www.benedictine.edu. Benedictines; 1859; independent (1,4304).

Benedictine University (formerly Illinois Benedictine College) (c): 5700 College Rd., Lisle, IL 60532-0900; (630) 829-600 0; www.ben.edu. Benedictine Monks of St. Procopius Abbey; 1887 (2,860).

Boston College (University status) (c): Chestnut Hill, MA 02167; (617) 552-8000; www.bc.edu. Jesuit Fathers; 1863 (14,419).

Brescia University (c): 717 Frederica St., Owensboro, KY 42301; (270) 685-3131; www.brescia.edu. Ursuline Sisters; 1950 (750).

Briar Cliff College (c): 3303 Rebecca St., Sioux City, IA 51104; (712) 279-5405; www.briarcliff.edu. Sisters of St. Francis of the Holy Family; 1930 (949).

Cabrini College (c): 610 King of Prussia Rd., Radnor, PA 19087; (610) 902-8100; www.cabrini.edu. Missionary Srs. of Sacred Heart; 1957; private (2,534).

Caldwell College (c): 9 Ryerson Ave., Caldwell, NJ 07006; (973) 618-3000; www.caldwell.edu. Dominican Sisters; 1939 (2,104).

Calumet College of St. Joseph (c): 2400 New York Ave., Whiting, IN 46394; (219) 473-7770; www.ccsj.edu. Society of the Precious Blood, 1951 (978).

Canisius College (c): 2001 Main St., Buffalo, NY 14208; (716) 883-7000; www.canisius.edu. Jesuit Fathers; 1870; independent (4,861).

Cardinal Stritch University (c): 6801 N. Yates Rd., Milwaukee, WI 53217; (414) 410-4000; www.stritch.edu. Sisters of St. Francis of Assisi; 1937 (5,658).

Carlow College (w): 3333 5th Ave., Pittsburgh, PA 15213; (412) 578-6005; www.carlow.edu. Sisters of Mercy; 1929 (2,000).

Carroll College (c): Helena, MT 59625; (406) 447-4300. Diocesan; 1909 (1,292).

Catholic Distance University (c): 120 East Colonial Highway, Hamilton, VA 20158-9012; www.cdu.edu. Offers External Degree programs, including Masters degrees in Religious Studies (7,000).

Catholic Theological Union (c): 5401 South Cornell Ave., Chicago, IL 60615; (773) 324-8000; www.ctu.edu (348). Offers Graduate theological programs, including M.Div., M.A., M.A.P.S., and D.Min.

Catholic University of America, The (c): Michigan Ave. & Fourth St., NE, Washington, DC 20064; (202) 319-5000; www.cua.edu. Hierarchy of the United States; 1887. Pontifical University (5,930).

Chaminade University of Honolulu (c): 3140 Waialae Ave., Honolulu, HI 96816; (808) 735-4711; www.chaminade.edu. Marianists; 1955 (8,454).

Chestnut Hill College (w): 9601 Germantown Ave., Philadelphia, PA 19118; (215) 248-7000; www.chc.edu. Sisters of St. Joseph; 1924 (1,536).

Christendom College (c): 134 Christendom Dr., Front Royal, VA 22630; (540) 636-2900. Independent, 1977 (286).

Christian Brothers University (c): 650 E. Parkway S., Memphis, TN 38104; (901) 321-3000. Brothers of the Christian Schools; 1871 (2,055).

Clarke College (c): 1550 Clarke Dr., Dubuque, IA 52001; (563) 588-6300; www.clarke.edu. Sisters of Charity, BVM; 1843; independent (1,249).

Creighton University (c): 2500 California Plaza, Omaha, NE 68178; (402) 280-2700; www.creigh ton.edu. Jesuit Fathers; 1878; independent (6,237).

Dallas, University of (c): 1845 E. Northgate, Irving, TX 75062; (972) 721-5000. Dallas diocese; 1956; independent (3,738).

Dayton, University of (c): 300 College Park, Dayton, OH 45469-1660; (937) 229-1000; www.u dayton.edu. Marianists; 1850 (10,170).

DePaul University (c): One E. Jackson Blvd., Chicago, IL 60604; (312) 362-8000; www.depaul.edu. Vincentians; 1898 (20,500).

De Sales University (c): 2755 Station Ave., Center Valley, PA 18034; (610) 282-1100; www.desales.edu. Oblates of St. Francis de Sales; 1965 (1,272).

Detroit Mercy, University of (c): 4001 W. McNichols Rd., Detroit, MI, 48221; 8200 W. Outer Dr., Detroit MI 48219; (313) 993-1000. Society of Jesus and Sisters of Mercy; 1877; independent (6,500).

Dominican College (c): 470 Western Hwy., Orangeburg, NY 10962; (845) 359-7800; www.dc.edu. Dominican Sisters; 1952; independent (1,700).

Dominican University of San Rafael (c): 50 Acacia Ave., San Rafael, CA 94901-2298; (415) 457-4440; www.dominican.edu. Dominican Sisters; 1890; independent (1,480).

Dominican University (formerly Rosary College) (c): 7900 W. Division St., River Forest, IL 60305; (708) 366-2490; www.dom.edu. Sinsinawa Dominican Sisters; 1901 (2,360).

Duquesne University (c): 600 Forbes Ave., Pittsburgh, PA 15282; (412) 396-6000; www.duq.edu. Congregation of the Holy Ghost; 1878 (10,000).

D'Youville College (c): 320 Porter Ave., Buffalo, NY 14201; (716) 881-3200; www.dyc.edu. Grey Nuns of the Sacred Heart; 1908; independent (2,397).

Edgewood College (c): 1000 Edgewood College Dr., Madison, WI 53711; (608) 663-4861. Sinsinawa Dominican Sisters; 1927 (1,909).

Emmanuel College (w): 400 The Fenway, Boston, MA 02115; (617) 735-9715; www.emmanuel.edu. Sisters of Notre Dame de Namur; 1919; independent (1,630).

Fairfield University (c): 1073 North Benson Rd., Fairfield, CT 06430; (203) 254-4000; www.fair field.edu. Jesuits; 1942 (5,127).

Felician College (c): 262 S. Main St., Lodi, NJ 07644; (201) 559-6000; www.felician.edu. Felician Sisters; 1942; independent (1,400).

Fontbonne College (c): 6800 Wydown Blvd., St. Louis, MO 63105; (314) 862-3456; www.font bonne.edu. Sisters of St. Joseph of Carondelet; 1917; independent (2,060).

Fordham University (c): Fordham Rd. and Third Ave., New York, NY 10458; (718) 817-4925 (fax). Society of Jesus (Jesuits); 1841; independent (14,000).

Franciscan University of Steubenville (c): 1235 University Blvd., Steubenville, OH 43952; (740) 283-3771; www.franuniv.edu. Franciscan TOR Friars; 1946 (2,131). Also offers distance learning programs.

Gannon University (c): 109 University Square, Erie, PA 16541-0001; (814) 871-7000; www.gannon.edu. Diocese of Erie; 1933 (3,289).

Georgetown University (c): 37th and O Sts. NW, Washington, DC 20057; (202) 687-0100; www.george town.edu. Jesuit Fathers; 1789 (11,178).

Georgian Court College (w/c): 900 Lakewood Ave., Lakewood, NJ 08701; (732) 364-2200; www.georgian.edu. Sisters of Mercy; 1908 (2,420).

Gonzaga University (c): E. 502 Boone Ave., Spokane, WA 99258; (509) 328-4220. Jesuit Fathers; 1887 (4,515).

Graduate School of Theology (c): 5890 Birch Ct., Oakland, CA 94618; (510) 652-1651; www.sat gtu.org. Affiliate of the Graduate Theological Union.

Great Falls, University of (c): 1301 20th St. S., Great Falls, MT 59405; (406) 761-8210; www.ugf.edu. Sisters of Providence; 1932; independent (1,054).

Gwynedd-Mercy College (c): Gwynedd Valley, PA 19437; (215) 646-7300; www.gmc.edu. Sisters of Mercy; 1948; independent (1,819).

Hilbert College (c): 5200 S. Park Ave., Hamburg, NY 14075; (716) 649-7900; www.hilbert.edu. Franciscan Sisters of St. Joseph; 1957; independent (893).

Holy Cross, College of the (c): Worcester, MA 01610; (508) 793-2011; www.holycross.edu. Jesuits; 1843 (2,801).

Holy Family College (c): Grant and Frankford Aves., Philadelphia, PA 19114 and One Campus Dr., Newtown, PA 18940; (215) 637-7700; www.hfc.edu. Sisters of Holy Family of Nazareth; 1954; independent (2,637).

Holy Names College (c): 3500 Mountain Blvd., Oakland, CA 94619; (510) 436-1000; www.hnc.edu. Sisters of the Holy Names of Jesus and Mary; 1868; independent (947).

Immaculata College (w): Immaculata, PA 19345; (610) 647-4400; www.immaculata.edu. Sisters, Servants of the Immaculate Heart of Mary; 1920 (2,800).

Incarnate Word, University of the (c): 4301 Broadway, San Antonio, TX 78209; (210) 829-6000; www.uiw.edu. Sisters of Charity of the Incarnate Word; 1881 (3,702).

Iona College (c): 715 North Ave., New Rochelle, NY 10801; (914) 633-2000; www.iona.edu. Congregation of Christian Brothers; 1940; independent (4,897).

John Carroll University (c): 20700 North Park Blvd., Cleveland, OH 44118; (216) 397-1886; www.jcu.edu. Jesuits; 1886 (4,389).

King's College (c): 133 North River St., Wilkes-Barre, PA 18711; (570) 208-5900; www.kings.edu. Holy Cross Fathers; 1946 (2,207).

La Roche College (c): 9000 Babcock Blvd., Pittsburgh, PA 15237; (412) 367-9300; www.laroche.edu. Sisters of Divine Providence; 1963 (1,875).

La Salle University (c): 1900 W. Olney Ave., Philadelphia, PA 19141; (215) 951-1000. Christian Brothers; 1863 (5,376).

Le Moyne College (c): 1419 Salt Springs Rd., Syracuse, NY 13214; (315) 445-4100; www.lemoyne.edu. Jesuit Fathers; 1946; independent (approx. 3,129, full-time, part-time, graduate)

Lewis University (c): Romeoville, IL 60446; (815) 838-0500; www.lewisu.edu. Christian Brothers; 1932 (4,289).

Loras College (c): 1450 Alta Vista St., Dubuque, IA 52004; (319) 588-7100. Archdiocese of Dubuque; 1839 (1,725).

Lourdes College (c): 6832 Convent Blvd., Sylvania, OH 43560; (419) 885-3211; www.lourdes.edu. Sisters of St. Francis; 1958 (1,356).

Loyola College (c): 4501 N. Charles St., Baltimore, MD 21210; (410) 617-2000; www.loyola.edu. Jesuits; 1852; combined with Mt. St. Agnes College, 1971 (6,073).

Loyola Marymount University (c): 7900 Loyola Blvd., Los Angeles, CA 90045-2699; (310) 338-2700;

www.lmu.edu. Society of Jesus; Religious of Sacred Heart of Mary, Sisters of St. Joseph of Orange, 1911 (5,332).

Loyola University (c): 6363 St. Charles Ave., New Orleans, LA 70118; (504) 865-2011. Jesuit Fathers; 1912 (5,400).

Loyola University Chicago (c): 820 N. Michigan Ave., Chicago, IL 60611; (312) 915-6000; www.luc.edu. Society of Jesus; 1870 (12,604).

Madonna University (c): 36600 Schoolcraft Rd., Livonia, MI 48150; (734) 432-5300. Felician Sisters; 1947 (3,868).

Magdalen College (c): 511 Kearsarge Mountain Rd., Warner, NH 03278; (603) 456-2656; www.magdalen.edu. Magdalen College Corporation; 1973 (75).

Manhattan College (c): Manhattan College Pkwy., Bronx , NY 11201; (718) 862-7200; www.man hattan.edu. De La Salle Christian Brothers; 1835; independent (2,622). Cooperative program with College of Mt. St. Vincent.

Marian College of Fond du Lac (c): 45 S. National Ave., Fond du Lac, WI 54935; (920) 923-7600; www.mariancollege.edu. Sisters of St. Agnes; 1936 (2,243).

Marian College (c): 3200 Cold Spring Rd., Indianapolis, IN 46222; (317) 955-6000; www.marian.edu. Sisters of St. Francis (Oldenburg, IN); 1851; independent (1,787).

Marist College (c): Poughkeepsie, NY 12601; (914) 575-3000; www.marist.edu. Marist Brothers of the Schools; 1946; independent (4,300).

Marquette University (c): P.O. Box 1881, Milwaukee, WI 53201-1881; (414) 288-7250; www.mar quette.edu. Jesuit Fathers; 1881; independent (10,780).

Mary, University of (c): 7500 University Dr., Bismarck, ND 58504; (701) 255-7500; www.umary.edu. Benedictine Sisters; 1959 (2,115).

Marygrove College (c): 8425 W. McNichols Rd., Detroit, MI 48221; (313) 927-1200. Sisters, Servants of the Immaculate Heart of Mary; 1905; independent (4,906).

Marylhurst College (c): P.O. Box 261, Marylhurst, OR 97036-0261; (503) 636-8141; www.maryl hurst.edu. Srs. of Holy Names of Jesus and Mary; 1893; independent (1,876).

Marymount College (w): Tarrytown, NY 10591; (914) 631-3200; www.marymt.edu. Religious of the Sacred Heart of Mary; 1907; independent (842). Coed in weekend degree programs.

Marymount Manhattan College (w): 221 E. 71st St., New York, NY 10021; (212) 517-0400; www.cmsv.edu. Religious of the Sacred Heart of Mary; 1936; independent (2,330).

Marymount University (c): 2807 N. Glebe Rd., Arlington, VA 22207; (703) 522-5600; www.mary mount.edu. Religious of the Sacred Heart of Mary; 1950; independent (3,672).

Marywood College (c): Scranton, PA 18509; (570) 348-6211; www.marywood.edu. Sisters, Servants of the Immaculate Heart of Mary; 1915; independent (2,903).

Mercy College of Health Sciences (c): 928-6th Ave., Des Moines, IA 50309-1239; (515) 643-3180; www.mchs.edu. Srs. of Mercy of the Americas (432).

Mercyhurst College (c): 501 E. 38th St., Erie, PA 16546; (814) 824-2000; www.mercyhurst.edu. Sisters of Mercy; 1926 (3,026).

Merrimack College (c): North Andover, MA 01845; (978) 837-5000; www.merrimack.edu. Augustinians;1947 (2,100).

Misericordia (College Misericordia) (c): 301 Lake St., Dallas, PA 18612-1098; (570) 674-6400; www.miseri.edu. Religious Sisters of Mercy of the Union; 1924 (1,640).

Molloy College (c): 1000 Hempstead Ave., P.O. Box 5002, Rockville Centre, NY 11570-5002; (516) 678-5000. Dominican Sisters; 1955; independent (2,252).

Mount Aloysius College (c): 7373 Admiral Peary Hwy., Cresson, PA 16630; (814) 886-4131; www.mtaloy.edu. Sisters of Mercy; 1939 (2,000).

Mount Marty College (c): 1105 W. 8th St., Yankton, SD 57078; (800) 658-4552; www.mtmc.edu. Benedictine Sisters; 1936 (1,125).

Mount Mary College (w): 2900 N. Menomonee River Pkwy., Milwaukee, WI 53222; (414) 258-4810. School Sisters of Notre Dame; 1913 (1,319).

Mount Mercy College (c): 1330 Elmhurst Dr. N.E., Cedar Rapids, IA 52402; (319) 363-8213; www.mtmercy.edu. Sisters of Mercy; 1928; independent (1,363).

Mount St. Clare College (c): 400 N. Bluff Blvd., Clinton, IA 52732; (319) 242-4023; www.clare.edu. Sisters of St. Francis of Clinton, Iowa; 1918 (appr. 631).

Mount St. Joseph, College of (c): 5701 Delhi Rd., Cincinnati, OH 45233-1670; (513) 244-4200; www.msj.edu. Sisters of Charity; 1920 (5,741).

Mount Saint Mary College (c): Newburgh, NY 12550; (914) 561-0800; www.msmc.edu.. Dominican Sisters; 1954; independent (2,011).

Mount St. Mary's College (c): Emmitsburg, MD 21727; (301) 447-6122; www.msmary.edu. Founded by Fr. John DuBois, 1808; independent (1,716).

Mount St. Mary's College (w/c): 12001 Chalon Rd., Los Angeles, CA 90049 and 10 Chester Pl., Los Angeles, CA 90007 (Doheny Campus); (310) 954-4010; www.msmc.la.edu. Sisters of St. Joseph of Carondelet; 1925. Coed in music, nursing and graduate programs (1,398).

Mount Saint Vincent, College of (c): 6301 Riverdale Ave., New York, NY 10471; (718) 405-3200; www.cmsv.edu. Sisters of Charity; 1847; independent (1,580). Cooperative program with Manhattan College.

Neumann College (c): One Neumann Dr., Aston, PA 19014; (610) 459-0905; www.neumann.edu. Sisters of St. Francis; 1965; independent (1,659).

Newman University (c): 3100 McCormick Ave., Wichita, KS 67213; (316) 942-4291; www.new manu.edu. Sisters Adorers of the Blood of Christ; 1933 (1,005).

New Rochelle, College of (w/c): 29 Castle Pl., New Rochelle, NY 10805 (main campus); (914) 654-5000; www.cnr.edu. Ursuline Order; 1904; independent (6,514). Coed in nursing, graduate, new resources divisions.

Niagara University (c): Lewiston Rd. Niagara Univ., NY 14109-2015; (716) 285-1212; www.niagara.edu. Vincentian Fathers and Brothers; 1856 (3,146).

Notre Dame, College of (c): 1500 Ralston Ave., Belmont, CA 94002; (650) 593-1601; www.cnd.edu. Sisters of Notre Dame de Namur; 1851; independent (1,670).

Notre Dame, University of (c): (Full title: University of Notre Dame du Lac) Notre Dame, IN 46556; (219) 631-5000; www.nd.edu. Congregation of Holy Cross; 1842 (10,654).

Notre Dame College (c): 2321 Elm St., Manchester, NH 03104; (603) 222-7100; www.notredame.edu. Sisters of Holy Cross; 1950; independent (1,120).

Notre Dame College of Ohio (w): 4545 College Rd., Cleveland, OH 44121; (216) 381-1680; www.ndc.edu. Sisters of Notre Dame; 1922 (813).

Notre Dame of Maryland, College of (w): 4701 N. Charles St., Baltimore, MD 21210; (410) 435-0100; www.ndm.edu. School Sisters of Notre Dame; 1873 (3,193).

Oblate School of Theology (c): 285 Oblate Dr., San Antonio, TX 78216-6693; (210) 341-1366; www.ost.edu. Oblates of Mary Immaculate; 1903 (268). Graduate theology programs.

Ohio Dominican College (c): 1216 Sunbury Rd., Columbus, OH 43219-2099; (614) 253-2741; www.odc.edu. Dominican Sisters of St. Mary of the Springs; 1911 (2,135).

Our Lady of Holy Cross College (c): 4123 Woodland Dr., New Orleans, LA 70131; (504) 394-7744; www.olhcc.edu. Congregation of Sisters Marianites of Holy Cross; 1916 (1,233).

Our Lady of the Elms, College of (w): Chicopee, MA 01013; (413) 594-2761; www.elms.edu. Sisters of St. Joseph; 1928 (1,013).

Our Lady of the Lake College (c): 5345 Brittany Dr., Baton Rouge, LA 70808-4398; (225) 768-1710; www.ololcollege. Independent (1,047).

Our Lady of the Lake University (c): 411 S.W. 24th St., San Antonio, TX 78207; (210) 434-6711; www.ollusa.edu. Sisters of Divine Providence; 1895 (3,474).

Pontifical Catholic University of Puerto Rico (c): 2250 Avenida de las Americas, Ponce, PR 00717-0777; (787) 841-2000; www.pucpr.edu. Hierarchy of Puerto Rico; 1948; Pontifical University (10,365).

Portland, University of (c): 5000 N. Willamette Blvd., Portland, OR 97203; (503) 943-7911; www.up.edu. Holy Cross Fathers; 1901; independent (2,673).

Presentation College (c): Aberdeen, SD 7401; (605) 225-1634. Sisters of the Presentation; 1951 (462).

Providence College (c): 549 River Ave., Providence, RI 02918; (401) 865-1000; www.providence.edu. Dominican Friars; 1917 (5,673, day, evening, and graduate).

Queen of the Holy Rosary College (c): P.O. Box 3908, Mission San Jose, CA 94539; (510) 657-2468. Dominican Sisters of Mission San Jose, independent (199).

Quincy University (c): 1800 College Ave., Quincy, IL 62301; (217) 222-8020; www.quincy.edu. Franciscan Friars; 1860 (1,182).

Regis College (w): 235 Wellesley St., Weston, MA 02493-1571; (781) 768-7000; www.regiscollege.edu. Sisters of St. Joseph; 1927; independent (1,200).

Regis University (c): 3333 Regis Blvd. Denver, CO 80221; (303) 458-4100. Jesuits; 1887 (11,240).

Rivier College (c): Nashua, NH 03060; (603) 888-1311; www.rivier.edu. Sisters of the Presentation of Mary; 1933; independent (2,572).

Rockhurst College (c): 1100 Rockhurst Rd., Kansas City, MO 64110; (816) 501-4000; www.rockhurst.edu. Jesuit Fathers; 1910 (3,751).

Rosemont College of the Holy Child Jesus (w):

Rosemont, PA 19010-1699; (610) 526-2984; www.rosemont.edu. Society of the Holy Child Jesus; 1921 (1,198).

Sacred Heart University (c): 5151 Park Ave., Fairfield, CT 06432; (203) 371-7999; www.sacredheart.edu. Diocese of Bridgeport; 1963; independent (5,637).

St. Ambrose University (c): Davenport, IA 52803; (319) 333-6300; www.sau.edu. Diocese of Davenport; 1882 (3,011).

Saint Anselm College (c): Manchester NH 03102-1030; (603) 641-7000; www.anselm.edu. Benedictines; 1889 (1,985).

St. Basil College (m): 195 Glenbrook Rd., Stamford, CT 06902; (203) 324-4578; UkrCath Sem@aol.com; the Ukranian Catholic Dioeese of Stamford, 1939. (16).

Saint Benedict, College of (w): 37 S. College Ave., St. Joseph, MN 56374; (320) 363-5407; www.csbsju.edu. Benedictine Sisters; 1913 (2,024). Sister college of St. John's University, Collegeville (see below).

St. Bonaventure University (c): St. Bonaventure, NY 14778; (716) 375-2000; www.sbu.edu. Franciscan Friars; 1858; independent (2,800).

St. Catherine, College of (w): St. Paul: 2004 Randolph Ave., St. Paul, MN 55105; (651) 690-6000; Minneapolis; www.stkate.edu. Sisters of St. Joseph of Carondelet; 1905 (4,491).

St. Edward's University (c): 3001 S. Congress Ave., Austin, TX 78704; (512) 448-8400; www.stedwards.edu. Holy Cross Brothers; 1881; independent (3,669).

Saint Elizabeth, College of (w): 2 Convent Rd., Morristown, NJ 07960-6989; (973) 290-4000; www.st-elizabeth.edu. Sisters of Charity; 1899; independent (1,810). Coed in adult undergraduate and graduate programs.

St. Francis College (c): 180 Remsen St., Brooklyn Heights, NY 11201; (718) 489-5200. Franciscan Brothers; 1884; private, independent in the Franciscan tradition (2,505).

St. Francis University (c): P.O. Box 600, Loretto, PA 15940-0600; (814) 472-3000; www.sfcpa.edu. Franciscan Friars; 1847; independent (1,321).

St. Francis, University of (c): 500 N. Wilcox, Joliet, IL 60435; (815) 740-3360; www.stfrancis.edu. Sisters of St. Francis of Mary Immaculate (4,321).

St. Francis, University of (c): 2701 Spring St., Fort Wayne, IN 46808-3994; (219) 434-3100; www.sf.edu. Sisters of St. Francis; 1890 (1,629).

St. Gregory's University (c): 1900 W. MacArthur, Shawnee, OK 74801; (405) 878-5100; www.sgc.edu. Benedictine Monks; 1876 (755).

St. John's University (c): 8000 Utopia Pkwy., Jamaica, NY 11439 (Queens Campus); 300 Howard Ave., Staten Island, NY 10301 (Staten Island Campus); (718) 990-6161; www.stjohns.edu. Vincentians; 1870 (18,523).

St. John's University (m): Collegeville, MN 56321; (320) 363-2011; www.csbsju.edu. Benedictines; 1857 (2,020). All classes and programs are coeducational with College of St. Benedict (see above).

St. Joseph in Vermont, College of (c): 71 Clement Rd., Rutland, VT 05701; (802) 773-5900; www.csj.edu. Sisters of St. Joseph; 1950; independent (517).

Saint Joseph College (w/c): 1678 Asylum Ave.,

West Hartford, CT 06117-2700; (860) 232-4571; www.sjc.edu. Sisters of Mercy; 1932 (2,643). Women's college in undergraduate liberal arts. Coed in graduate school and Weekend College.

Saint Joseph's College (c): 278 Whites Bridge Rd., Standish, ME 04084-5263; (207) 893-7711; www.sjcme.edu. Sisters of Mercy; 1912 (3,941 total; 1,331 graduate). Offers extensive distance education programs.

Saint Joseph's College (c): P.O. Box 909, Rensselaer, IN 47978; (219) 866-6000; www.stjoe.edu. Society of the Precious Blood; 1891 (848).

St. Joseph's College (c): 245 Clinton Ave., Brooklyn, NY 11205; (718) 636-6800 and 155 W. Roe Blvd., Patchogue, NY 11772; (631) 447-3200; www.sjcny.edu. Sisters of St. Joseph; 1916; independent (1,352).

St. Joseph's University (c): 5600 City Ave., Philadelphia, PA 19131; (610) 660-1000; www.sju.edu. Jesuit Fathers; 1851 (6,350).

Saint Leo College (c): P.O. Box 6665, MC 2186, Saint Leo, FL 33574; (352) 588-8200; www.saint leo.edu. Order of St. Benedict; 1889; independent (8,270).

Saint Louis University (c): 221 N. Grand Blvd., St. Louis, MO 63103; (314) 977-2222; www.slu.edu. Society of Jesus; 1818; independent (11,112).

Saint Martin's College (c): 5300 Pacific Ave. SE, Lacey, WA 98503-1297; (360) 438-4311; www.stmartin.edu. Benedictine Monks; 1895 (1,033 main campus; 496 extension campuses).

Saint Mary, College of (w): 1901 S. 72nd St., Omaha, NE 68124; (402) 399-2400; www.csm.edu. Sisters of Mercy; 1923; independent (981).

Saint Mary College (c): Leavenworth, KS 66048; (913) 682-5151. Sisters of Charity of Leavenworth; 1923 (780).

Saint Mary-of-the-Woods College (w): St. Mary-of-the-Woods, IN 47876; (812) 535-5151; www.smwc.edu. Sisters of Providence; 1840 (1,439).

Saint Mary's College (w): Notre Dame, IN 46556; (219) 284-4556; www.saintmarys.edu. Sisters of the Holy Cross; 1844 (1,458).

Saint Mary's College (c): 3535 Indian Trail, Orchard Lake, MI 48324; (248) 683-0521; www.stmarys-avemaria.edu; 1885 (326).

St. Mary's College (c): Moraga, CA 94575; (510) 631-4000. Brothers of the Christian Schools; 1863 (4,060).

Saint Mary's University of Minnesota (c): 700 Terrace Heights, Winona, MN 55987-1399; (507) 452-4430; www.smumn.edu. Brothers of the Christian Schools; 1912 (1,364).

St. Mary's University of San Antonio (c): One Camino Santa Maria, San Antonio, TX 78228-8607; (210) 436-3011; www.stmarytx.edu. Society of Mary (Marianists); 1852 (4,137).

Saint Meinrad School of Theology (c): 200 Hill Dr., St. Meinrad, IN 47577; (812) 357-6611; www.saintmeinrad.edu. Benedictines (91 full- and part-time lay students.) Graduate-level theological studies.

St. Michael's College (c): Winooski Park, Colchester, VT 05439; (802) 654-2211; www.smcvt.edu. Society of St. Edmund; 1904 (2,635).

St. Norbert College (c): De Pere, WI 54115; (920) 403-3181; www.snc.edu. Norbertine Fathers; 1898; independent (2,000).

Saint Peter's College (c): 2641 Kennedy Blvd., Jersey City, NJ 07306; (201) 915-9000; www.spc.edu. Society of Jesus; 1872; independent (3,280).

Saint Rose, College of (c): 432 Western Ave., Albany, NY 12203; (518) 454-5111. Sisters of St. Joseph of Carondelet; 1920; independent (4,031).

St. Scholastica, The College of (c): 1200 Kenwood Ave., Duluth, MN 55811; (218) 723-6000. Benedictine Sisters; 1912; independent (2,100).

St. Thomas, University of (c): 2115 Summit Ave., St. Paul, MN 55105; (651) 962-5000; www.stthomas.edu. Archdiocese of St. Paul and Minneapolis; 1885 (11,435).

St. Thomas, University of (c): 3800 Montrose Blvd., Houston, TX 77006-4696; (713) 522-7911; www.stthom.edu. Basilian Fathers; 1947 (2,897).

St. Thomas Aquinas College (c): Sparkill, NY 10976; (914) 398-4000; www.stac.edu. Dominican Sisters of Sparkill; 1952; independent, corporate board of trustees (2,200).

St. Thomas University (c): 16400 N.W. 32nd Ave., Miami, FL 33054; (305) 625-6000; www.stu.edu. Archdiocese of Miami; 1962 (3,339).

Saint Vincent College (c): 300 Fraser Purchase Rd., Latrobe, PA 15650-2690; (724) 537-4592; www.benedictine.stvincent.edu/seminary. Benedictine Fathers; 1846 (1,206).

Saint Vincent's College (c): 2800 Main St., Bridgeport, CT 06606; (203) 576-5235; www.stvincents college.edu; (275).

St. Xavier University (c): 3700 W. 103rd St., Chicago, IL 60655; (773) 298-3000. Sisters of Mercy; chartered 1847 (4,100).

Salve Regina University (c): Ochre Point Ave., Newport, RI 02840-4192; (401) 847-6650; www.salve.edu. Sisters of Mercy; 1934 (1,489). Offers distance learning programs in graduate studies.

San Diego, University of (c): 5998 Alcala Park, San Diego, CA 92110; (619) 260-4600. San Diego diocese and Religious of the Sacred Heart; 1949; independent (6,806).

San Francisco, University of (c): 2130 Fulton St., San Francisco, CA 94117; (415) 422-5555. Jesuit Fathers; 1855 (7,948).

Santa Clara University (c): 500 El Camino Real, Santa Clara, CA 95053; (408) 554-4000; www.scu.edu. Jesuit Fathers; 1851; independent (7,668).

Santa Fe, College of (c): 1600 St. Michael's Dr., Santa Fe, NM 87505; (505) 473-6011. Brothers of the Christian Schools; 1947 (1,700).

Scranton, University of (c): Scranton, PA 18510; (570) 941-7533; www.uofs.edu. Society of Jesus; 1888; independent (4,615).

Seattle University (c): 900 Broadway, Seattle, WA 98122; (206) 296-6000; www.seattleu.edu. Society of Jesus; 1891 (5,829).

Seton Hall University (c): South Orange Ave., South Orange, NJ 07079; (973) 761-9000. Diocesan Clergy; 1856 (9,760).

Seton Hill College (w): Seton Hill Dr., Greensburg, PA 15601-1599; (724) 834-2200; www.setonhill.edu. Sisters of Charity of Seton Hill; 1883 (1,328).

Siena College (c): 515 Loudon Rd., Loudonville, NY 12211; (518) 783-2300; www.siena.edu. Franciscan Friars; 1937 (3,011).

Siena Heights University (c): 1247 E. Siena Heights Dr., Adrian, MI 49221; (517) 263-0731; www.sienahts.edu. Adrian Dominican Sisters; 1919 (1,994).

537

Silver Lake College of the Holy Family (c): 2406 S. Alverno Rd., Manitowoc, WI 54220-9319; (920) 684-6691. Franciscan Sisters of Christian Charity; 1935 (4,455).

Spalding University (c): 851 S. 4th Ave., Louisville, KY 40203; (502) 585-9911; www.spalding.edu. Sisters of Charity of Nazareth; 1814; independent (1,606).

Spring Hill College (c): 4000 Dauphin St., Mobile, AL 36608; (334) 380-4000; www.shc.edu. Jesuit Fathers; 1830 (1,003).

Stonehill College (c): North Easton, MA 02357; (508) 565-1000; www.stonehill.edu. Holy Cross Fathers; 1948; independent (2,165).

Thomas Aquinas College (c): 10000 N. Ojai Rd., Santa Paula, CA 93060; (805) 525-4417; www.thomas aquinas.edu. Founded 1971 (277).

Thomas More College (c): 333 Thomas More Pkwy., Crestview Hills, Covington, KY 41017; (859) 341-5800; www.thomasmore.edu. Diocese of Covington; 1921 (1,274).

Trinity College of Vermont (w): 208 Colchester Ave., Burlington, VT 05401; (802) 658-0337; www.trinityvt.edu. Sisters of Mercy; 1925 (200).

Trinity College (w): 125 Michigan Ave. NE, Washington, DC 20017; (202) 939-5000. Sisters of Notre Dame de Namur; 1897 (1,450). Coed in graduate school.

Ursuline College (w): 2550 Lander Rd., Pepper Pike, OH 44124; (440) 449-4200; www.ursuline.edu. Ursuline Nuns; 1871 (1,253).

Villanova University (c): Villanova, PA 19085; (610) 519-7499; www.villanova.edu. Order of St. Augustine; 1842 (10,019).

Viterbo College (c): 815 S. 9th, La Crosse, WI 54601; (608) 796-3000; www.viterbo.org. Franciscan Sisters of Perpetual Adoration; 1890 (2,106).

Walsh University (c): 2020 Easton St. N.W., North Canton, Ohio 44720-3396; (330) 490-7090; www.walsh.edu. Brothers of Christian Instruction; 1958 (1,580).

Washington Theological Union (c): 6896 Laurel Street NW, Washington, DC 20012-2016; (202) 726-8800; www.wtu.edu. Coalition of Religious Seminaries; 1968 (263).

Wheeling Jesuit University (c): 316 Washington Ave., Wheeling, WV 26003-6295; (304) 243-2000; www.wju.edu. Jesuit Fathers; 1954 (1,515).

Xavier University (c): 3800 Victory Pkwy., Cincinnati, OH 45207; (513) 745-3000; www.xu.edu. Jesuit Fathers; 1831 (2,504).

Xavier University of Louisiana (c): 1 Drexel Dr., New Orleans, LA 70125; (504) 486-7411; www.xula.edu. Sisters of Blessed Sacrament; 1925 (3,787).

Catholic Two-Year Colleges

Ancilla Domini College (c): P.O. Box 1, Donaldson, IN 46513; (219) 936-8898; www.ancilla.edu. Ancilla Domini Sisters; 1937 (473).

Assumption College for Sisters: Mendham, NJ 07945; (973) 543-6528. Sisters of Christian Charity; 1953 (33).

Chatfield College (c): St. Martin, OH 45118; (937) 875-3344; www.chatfield.edu. Ursulines; 1971 (452).

The College of St. Catherine-Minneapolis (c): 601 25th Ave. S., Minneapolis, MN 55454; (651) 690-7702. Sisters of St. Joseph of Carondelet (969).

Donnelly College (c): 608 N. 18th St., Kansas City, KS 66102; (913) 621-6070; www.donnelly.cc.ks.us. Archdiocesan College; 1949 (600).

Don Bosco Technical Institute (m): 1151 San Gabriel Blvd., Rosemead, CA 91770; (626) 307-6500; www.boscotech.tec.ca.us. Salesians; 1969 (1,122).

Holy Cross College (c): 54515 State Rd., 933 N., Notre Dame, IN 46556-0308; (219) 239-8400; www.hcc-nd.edu. Brothers of Holy Cross; 1966 (485).

Manor College (c): 700 Fox Chase Road, Jenkintown, PA 19046; (215) 885-2360; www.manor.edu. Sisters of St. Basil the Great; 1947.

Maria College (c): 700 New Scotland Ave., Albany, NY 12208. Sisters of Mercy; 1963 (815).

Marymount College Palos Verdes (c): 30800 Palos Verdes Dr., E., Rancho Palos Verdes, CA 90275-6299; (310) 377-5501; www.marymountpv.edu. Religious of the Sacred Heart of Mary; independent (739).

St. Catharine College (c): 2735 Bardstown Rd., St. Catharine, KY 40061; (606) 336-5082. Dominican Sisters; 1931 (509).

Springfield College in Illinois (c): 1500 N. Fifth St., Springfield, IL 62702-2694; (217) 525-1420; www.sci.edu. Ursuline Sisters; 1929 (308).

Trocaire College (c): 360 Choate Ave., Buffalo, NY 14220; (716) 827-2423; www.trocaire.edu. Sisters of Mercy; 1958; independent (746).

Villa Maria College of Buffalo (c): 240 Pine Ridge Rd., Buffalo, NY 14225; (716) 896-0700; www.villa.edu. Felician Sisters 1960; independent (408).

DIOCESAN AND INTERDIOCESAN SEMINARIES

(Sources: Catholic Almanac *survey;* The Official Catholic Directory*; Catholic News Service.)*

Information, according to states, includes names of archdioceses and dioceses, and names and addresses of seminaries. Types of seminaries, when not clear from titles, are indicated in most cases. Interdiocesan seminaries are generally conducted by religious orders for candidates for the priesthood from several dioceses. The list does not include houses of study reserved for members of religious communities. Archdioceses are indicated by an asterisk.

California: Los Angeles* — St. John's Seminary (major), 5118 Seminary Rd., Camarillo 93012-2599; (805) 482-2755. St. John's Seminary College, 5118 Seminary Rd., Camarillo 93012-2599; (805) 482-2755; www.west.net/sjsc.

San Diego — St. Francis Seminary (college and pre-theology formation program), 1667 Santa Paula Dr., 92111; (619) 291-7446.

San Francisco* — St. Patrick's Seminary (major), 320 Middlefield Rd., Menlo Park 94025; (650) 325-5621; www.stpatricksseminary.org..

Colorado: Denver* — St. John Vianney Theological Seminary (college and pre-theology formation program), 1300 S. Steele St., 80210; (303) 282-3427.

Connecticut: Hartford* — St. Thomas Seminary (college formation program), 467 Bloomfield Ave., Bloomfield 06002-2999; (860) 242-5573.

Norwich — Holy Apostles College and Seminary (adult vocations; minor and major), 33 Prospect Hill Rd., Cromwell 06416; (860) 632-3010; www.holy apostles.edu.

Stamford — Byzantine Rite: Ukrainian Catholic Seminary: St. Basil College Seminary (minor), 195 Glenbrook Rd., Stamford 06902-3099; (203) 324-4578.

District of Columbia: Washington, DC* — Theological College (national, major), The Catholic University of America, 401 Michigan Ave., NE 20017; (202) 756-4900; www.theologicalcollege.org.

St. Josaphat's Seminary, 201 Taylor St. NE, 20017; (202) 529-1177. (Major house of formation serving the four Ukrainian Byzantine-rite dioceses in the U.S.)

Florida: Miami* — St. John Vianney College Seminary, 2900 S.W. 87th Ave., 33165; (305) 223-4561.

Palm Beach — St. Vincent de Paul Regional Seminary (major), 10701 S. Military Trail, Boynton Beach 33436; (561) 732-4424.

Illinois: Chicago* — Archbishop Quigley Preparatory Seminary (high school), 103 East Chestnut St., Chicago 60611; (312) 787-9343; www.quigley.org. St. Joseph Seminary (college), 6551 N. Sheridan Rd., Chicago 60626; (773) 973-9700; www.st joseph.luc.edu. University of St. Mary of the Lake Mundelein Seminary (School of Theology), 1000 E. Maple Ave., Mundelein 60060; (847) 566-6401; www.vocations.org.

Indiana: Indianapolis* — Saint Meinrad Seminary, College and School of Theology (interdiocesan), St. Meinrad 47577; (812) 357-6611; www.saint meinrad.edu.

Iowa: Davenport — St. Ambrose University Seminary (interdiocesn), 518 W. Locust St., 52803; (319) 333-6151; www.davenportdiocese.org.

Dubuque* — Seminary of St. Pius X (interdiocesan), Loras College, 52004-0178; (319) 588-7782.

Louisiana: New Orleans* — Notre Dame Seminary Graduate School of Theology, 2901 S. Carrollton Ave., 70118; (504) 866-7426 St. Joseph Seminary College (interdiocesan), St. Benedict 70457-9999; (504) 892-1800; www.stjosephabbey.org.

Maryland: Baltimore* — Mount St. Mary's Seminary and University, 5400 Roland Ave., 21210; (410) 864-4000; www.stmarys.edu. Mount St. Mary's Seminary, Emmitsburg 21727-7797; (301) 447-5295; www.msmary.edu.

Massachusetts: Boston* — St. John's Seminary, School of Theology, 127 Lake St., Brighton 02135; (617) 254-2610; St. John's Seminary, College of Liberal Arts, 127 Lake St., Brighton 02135; (617) 746-5450. Pope John XXIII National Seminary (for ages 30-60), 558 South Ave., Weston 02943; (781) 899-5500; www.blessedjohnXXIII.org.

Newton — Melkite Greek Catholic: St. Gregory the Theologian Seminary, 3 VFW Parkway, Roslindale, MA 02131; (617) 323-9922. Seminary of St. Basil the Great, 30 East St., 01844; (978) 683-2471.

Michigan: Detroit* — Sacred Heart Major Seminary (college/theologate and institute for ministry), 2701 Chicago Blvd., Detroit 48206; (313) 883-8500. Sts. Cyril and Methodius Seminary, St. Mary's College (theologate and college) independent, primarily serving Polish-American community, 3535 Indian Trail, Orchard Lake 48324-1623; (248) 683-0500; home.earthlink.net/~sscyrilmethodiussem.

Grand Rapids — Christopher House, 723 Rosewood Ave., S.E., East Grand Rapids 49506; (616) 243-6538.

Minnesota: St. John's School of Theology and Seminary, St. John's University, P.O. Box 7288, Collegeville 56321-7288; (320) 363-2100; www.csbsju.edu/sot.

St. Paul and Minneapolis* — St. Paul Seminary School of Divinity, University of St. Thomas, St. Paul 55101; (612) 962-5050; www.stthomas.edu. St. John Vianney Seminary (college residence), 2115 Summit Ave., St. Paul 55105; (651) 962-6825; www.st thomas.edu/sjv.

Winona — Immaculate Heart of Mary Seminary, St. Mary's University, No. 43, 700 Terrace Heights, 55987; (507) 457-7373.

Missouri: Jefferson City — St. Thomas Aquinas Preparatory Seminary (High School Seminary), 245 N. Levering Ave., P.O. Box 858, Hannibal 63401; (573) 221-4330; www.members.sockets.net/~stasem.

St. Louis* — Kenrick — Glennon Seminary (St. Louis Roman Catholic Theological Seminary). Kenrick School of Theology and Cardinal Glennon College, 5200 Glennon Dr., 63119; (314) 644-0266.

Montana: Helena — Pre-Seminary Program, Carroll College, 59625; (406) 447-4300.

Nebraska: Seward — St. Gregory the Great Seminary (pre-theology), 1301 280th Rd., 68434; (402) 643-4052; www.stgregoryseminary.org.

New Jersey: Newark* — Immaculate Conception Seminary — college seminary; major seminary; graduate school — Seton Hall University, 400 South Orange Ave., South Orange 07079; (973) 761-9575; www.shu.edu.

New York: Brooklyn — Cathedral Seminary Residence of the Immaculate Conception (college and pretheology), 7200 Douglaston Parkway, Douglaston 11362; (718) 229-8001. Cathedral Preparatory Seminary, 56-25 92nd St., Elmhurst 11373; (718) 592-6800.

Buffalo — Christ the King Seminary (interdiocesan theologate), P.O. Box 607, 711 Knox Rd., East Aurora 14052-0607; (716) 652-8900.

New York* — St. Joseph's Seminary (major), 201 Seminary Ave., Dunwoodie, Yonkers 10704; (914) 968-6200. St. John Neumann Residence (college and pre-theology), 201 Seminary Ave., Yonkers, N.Y., 10704-1896; (914) 964-3025. Cathedral Preparatory Seminary, 946 Boston Post Rd., Rye 10580; (914) 968-6200; www.cathedralprep.com.

Rockville Centre — Seminary of the Immaculate Conception (major), 440 West Neck Rd., Huntington, 11743; (631) 423-0483.

St. Maron Eparchy, Brooklyn — Our Lady of Lebanon Maronite Seminary, 7164 Alaska Ave. N.W., Washington, DC 20012; (202) 723-8831; www.maroniteseminary.org.

North Dakota: Fargo — Cardinal Muench Seminary (interdiocesan high school, college and pre-theology), 100 35th Ave. N.E., Fargo 58102; (701) 232-8969; www.cardinalmuench.org.

Ohio: Cincinnati* — Mt. St. Mary's Seminary of the West (division of the Athenaeum of Ohio), 6616 Beechmont Ave., 45230; (513) 231-2223; www.mtsm.org..

Cleveland — St. Mary Seminary and Graduate School of Theology, 28700 Euclid Ave. Wickliffe 44092; (440) 943-7600.

Columbus — Pontifical College Josephinum (national), theologate and college, 7625 North High St., 43235-1498; (614) 885-5585; www.pcj.edu.

Oregon: Portland* — Mount Angel Seminary (interdiocesan, college, pre-theology program, graduate school of theology), 1 Abbey Dr., St. Benedict 97373; (503) 845-3951.

Pennsylvania: Erie — St. Mark Seminary, P.O. Box 10397, Erie 16514; (814) 824-1200.

Greensburg — St. Vincent Seminary (interdiocesan; pre-theology program; theologate; graduate programs in theology; religious education), 300 Fraser Purchase Rd., Latrobe 15650-2690; (724) 537-4592; www.stvincent.edu.

Philadelphia* — Theological Seminary of St. Charles Borromeo (College, pre-theology program, spirituality year pogram, theologate), 100 East Wynnewood Rd., Wynnewood 19096; (610) 667-3394; www.scs.edu.

Pittsburgh* (Byzantine-Ruthenian) — Byzantine Catholic Seminary of Sts. Cyril and Methodius (college, pre-theology program, theologate), 3605 Perrysville Ave., 15214; (412) 321-8383; www.byzcath.org/seminary.

Pittsburgh — St. Paul Seminary (interdiocesan, college and pre-theology), 2900 Noblestown Rd., 15205; (412) 921-5800; www.diopitt.org.

Scranton — St. Pius X Seminary (college and pre-theology formation; interdiocesan), 1000 Seminary Rd., Dalton 18414; (570) 563-1131. Affiliated with the University of Scranton.

Rhode Island: Providence — Seminary of Our Lady of Providence (House of Formation; college students and pre-theology), 485 Mount Pleasant Ave., 02908; (401) 331-1316; www.catholicpriest.com.

Texas: Dallas — Holy Trinity Seminary (college and pre-theology; English proficiency and academic foundation programs), P.O. Box 140309, Irving 75014; (972) 438-2212.

El Paso — St. Charles Seminary College, P.O. Box 17548, 79917; (915) 591-9821.

Galveston-Houston — St. Mary's Seminary (theologate), 9845 Memorial Dr., Houston 77024; (713) 686-4345.

San Antonio* — Assumption Seminary (theologate and pre-theology, Hispanic ministry emphasis), 2600 W. Woodlawn Ave., 78228; (210) 734-2324.

Washington: Spokane — Bishop White Seminary, College Formation Program, E. 429 Sharp Ave., 99202; (509) 326-3255.

Wisconsin: Milwaukee* — St. Francis Seminary, 3257 S. Lake Dr., St. Francis 53235; (414) 747-6400; www.sfs.edu. College Program, 2497 N. Murray Ave., Milwaukee, 53211; (414) 964-6982. Sacred Heart School of Theology (interdiocesan seminary for second-career vocations), P.O. Box 429, Hales Corners, 53130-0429; (414) 425-8300.

North American College

Founded by the U.S. Bishops in 1859, the North American College serves as a residence and house of formation for U.S. seminarians and graduate students in Rome. The first ordination of an alumnus took place June 14, 1862. Pontifical status was granted the college by Pope Leo XIII Oct. 25, 1884. Students pursue theological and related studies principally at the Pontifical Gregorian University and at the Pontifical University of Saint Thomas Aquinas (the Angelicum). The current rector is Msgr. Kevin McCoy. Address: 00120 Città del Vaticano; 011-39-06-684-931.

American College of Louvain

Founded by U.S. Bishops in 1857, the American College of Louvain, Belgium, is a seminary for U.S. students. It also serves as a community for English-speaking graduate-student priests and religious priests pursuing studies at the Catholic University of Louvain (*Université Catholique de Louvain*, founded 1425). The college is administered by an American rector and faculty, and operates under the auspices of a committee of the national Conference of Catholic Bishops. The rector is Rev. Kevin A. Codd. Address: The American College, Catholic University of Louvain, Naamsestraat 100, B-3000, Leuven, Belgium; 32-16-32-00-11.

WORLD AND U.S. SEMINARY STATISTICS

The 2000 *Statistical Yearbook of the Church* (the most recent edition) reports the following comparative statistics for the years 1990 to 2000 of candidates in Philosophy and Theology (major seminarians). World totals are given first; U.S. statistics are given in parentheses.

Year	Total Major Seminarians	Diocesan	Religious
1990	96,155 (5,552)	64,629 (3,676)	31,526 (1,876)
1991	99,668 (5,487)	66,305 (3,777)	33,363 (1,710)
1992	102,000 (5,380)	67,960 (3,645)	34,040 (1,735)
1993	103,709 (5,123)	68,829 (3,505)	34,880 (1,618)
1994	105,075 (5,100)	69,613 (3,526)	35,462 (1,574)
1995	106,346 (4,831)	69,777 (3,234)	36,569 (1,597)
1996	105,870 (4,785)	70,034 (3,268)	35,836 (1,517)
1997	108,517 (4,729)	70,534 (3,311)	37,983 (1,418)
1998	109,171 (4,830)	70,564 (3,436)	38,607 (1,394)
1999	110,021 (5,024)	70,989 (3,428)	39,032 (1,596)
2000	110,583 (5,109)	71,756 (3,479)	38,827 (1,630)

PONTIFICAL UNIVERSITIES

(*Principal source:* Annuario Pontificio.)

These universities, listed according to country of location, have been canonically erected and authorized by the Congregation for Catholic Education to award degrees in stated fields of study. New laws and norms governing ecclesiastical universities and faculties were promulgated in the apostolic constitution *Sapientia Christiana*, issued Apr. 15, 1979. Phone numbers are listed where possible.

Argentina: Pontifical Catholic University of S. Maria of Buenos Aires (June 16, 1960): Av. Alicia Moreau de Justo 1400, 1107 Buenos Aires.

Belgium: Catholic University of Louvain (founded Dec. 9, 1425; canonically erected, 1834), with autonomous institutions for French- (Louvain) and Flemish-(Leuven) speaking: Place de l'Universite I, B-1348 Louvain-La-Neuve (French); Naamsestraat 22/b, B-3000 Leuven (Flemish).

Brazil: Pontifical Catholic University of Rio de Janeiro (Jan. 20, 1947): Rua Marquês de São Vicente 225, 22451-000 Rio de Janeiro, RJ.

Pontifical Catholic University of Minas Gerais (June 5, 1983): Av. Dom José Gaspar 500, C.P. 2686, 30161-000 Belo Horizonte, MG.; (031) 319-1127.

Pontifical Catholic University of Parana (Aug. 6, 1985): Rua Imaculada Conceição, 1155, Prado Velho, C.P. 670, 80001-000 Curitiba, PR; (041) 223-0922.

Pontifical Catholic University of Rio Grande do Sul (Nov. 1, 1950): Av. Ipiranga 6681, C.P.1429,90001-000 Porto Alegre, RS.

Pontifical Catholic University of São Paulo (Jan. 25, 1947): Rua Monte Alegre 984, 05014-901 São Paulo SP.

Pontifical University of Campinas (Sept. 8, 1956): Rua Marechal Deodoro 1099, 13020-000 Campinas, SP.; (0192) 27-001.

Canada: Laval University (Mar. 15, 1876): Case Postale 460, Québec G1K 7P4.

St. Paul University (formerly University of Ottawa) (Feb. 5, 1889): 223 Rue Main, Ottawa, Ont. K1S 1C4;

University of Sherbrooke (Nov. 21, 1957): Chemin Ste.-Catherine, 2500, boulevard de l'Université, Sherbrooke, Qué. J1K 12R1.

Chile: Pontifical Catholic University of Chile (June 21, 1888): Avenida Bernardo O'Higgins, 340, Casilla 114D, Santiago.

Catholic University of Valparaíso (Nov. 1, 1961): Avenida Brasil 2950, Casilla 4059, Valparaíso.

Colombia: Bolivarian Pontifical Catholic University (Aug. 16, 1945): Circular 1a, N.70-01, Apartado 56006, Medellín.

Pontifical Xaverian University (July 31, 1937): Carrera 7, N. 40-62, Apartado 56710, Santafé de Bogota D.C.; Apartado 26239, Calle 18, N. 118-250, Cali (Cali campus).

Cuba: Catholic University of St. Thomas of Villanueva (May 4, 1957): Avenida Quenta 16,660, Marianao.

Dominican Republic: Pontifical Catholic University "Mother and Teacher" (Sept. 9, 1987): Apartado 822, Santiago de Los Caballeros.

Ecuador: Pontifical Catholic University of Ecuador (July 16, 1954): Doce de Octubre, N. 1076, Apartado 17-01-2184, Quito.

France: Catholic University of Lille (Nov. 18, 1875): Boulevard Vauban 60, 59016 Lille Cedex.

Catholic Faculties of Lyon (Nov. 22, 1875): 25, Rue du Plat, 69288 Lyon Cedex 02.

Catholic Institute of Paris (Aug. 11, 1875): 21, Rue d'Assas, 75270 Paris Cedex 06.

Catholic Institute of Toulouse (Nov. 15, 1877): Rue de la Fonderie 31, 31068 Toulouse.

Catholic University of the West (Sept. 16, 1875): 3, Place André Leroy, B.P. 808, 49005 Angers; 2-41-81-66-00.

Germany: Catholic University Eichstätt (Apr. 1, 1980): Ostenstrasse 26, D-85072, Eichstätt, Federal Republic of Germany; (08421) 201.

Guatemala: Rafael Landívar University (Oct. 18, 1961): Vista Hermosa III, Zona 16, Guatemala; (02) 69-21-51.

Hungary: Catholic University Pázmány Péter (March 25, 1999): Papnövelde Utea 7, H-1053 Budapest, Hungary; (01) 11-73-701.

Ireland: St. Patrick's College (Mar. 29, 1896): Maynooth, Co. Kildare.

Italy: Catholic University of the Sacred Heart (Dec. 25, 1920): Largo Gemelli 1, 20123 Milan.

Libera University Mary of the Assumption (Oct. 26, 1939): Via della Transpontina 21, 00193 Rome, Italy.

Japan: Jochi Daigaku (Sophia University) (Mar. 29, 1913): Chiyoda-Ku, Kioi-cho 7, Tokyo 102.

Lebanon: St. Joseph University of Beirut (Mar. 25, 1881): Rue de l'Université St.-Joseph, Boite Postale 293, Beyrouth (Beirut), Liban; (01) 42-64-56.

Netherlands: Catholic University of Nijmegen (June 29, 1923): P.B. 9102, Comeniuslaam 4, 6500 HC, Nijmegen.

Panama: University of S. Maria La Antigua (May 27, 1965): Apartado 6-1696, Panama 6.

Paraguay: Catholic University of Our Lady of the Assumption (Feb. 2, 1965): Independencia Nacional y Comuneros, Casilla 1718, Asunción; (021) 44-10-44.

Peru: Pontifical Catholic University of Peru (Sept. 30, 1942): Av. Universitaria, s/n. San Miguel, Apartado 1761, Lima 100.

Philippines: Pontifical University of Santo Tomás (Nov. 20, 1645): España Street, 1008 Manila.

Poland: Catholic University of Lublin (July 25, 1920): Aleje Racùawickie 14, Skr. Poczt. 129, 20-950, Lublin.

Catholic Theological Academy (June 29, 1989): Ul. Dewajtis 5, 01-815, Warsaw.

Pontifical Academy of Theology of Krakow (Dec. 8, 1981): Ul. Kanonicza, 25, 31-002 Kraków; (014) 22-33-31.

Portugal: Portuguese Catholic University (Nov. 1, 1967): Palma de Cima, 1 600 Lisbon.

Puerto Rico: Pontifical Catholic University of Puerto Rico (Aug. 15, 1972): 2250 Ave. Las Américas Suite 523, Ponce, Puerto Rico 00731-6382.

Spain: Catholic University of Navarra (Aug. 6, 1960): Campus Universitario, E-31080 Pamplona.

Pontifical University "Comillas" (Mar. 29, 1904): Campus de Cantoblanco, 28049 Madrid.

Pontifical University of Salamanca (Sept. 25, 1940): Compañía 5, 37002 Salamanca.

University of Deusto (Aug. 10, 1963): Avenida de las Universidades, 48, 48007 Bilbao o Apartado 1, 48080 Bilbao; 94-445-31-00.

Taiwan (China): Fu Jen Catholic University (Nov.

15, 1923, at Peking; reconstituted at Taipeh, Sept. 8, 1961): Hsinchuang, Taipeh Hsien 24205.

United States: The Catholic University of America (Mar. 7, 1889): 620 Michigan Ave. NE, Washington, DC 20064.

Georgetown University (Mar. 30, 1833): 37th and O Sts. NW, Washington, DC 20057.

Niagara University (June 21, 1956): Lewiston Rd., Niagara Falls, NY 14109.

Uruguay: Catholic University of Uruguay "Dámaso Antonio Larrañaga" (Jan. 25, 1985): Avda. 8 de Octubre 2738, 11.600 Montevideo.

Venezuela: Catholic University "Andrés Bello" (Sept. 29, 1963): Esquina Jesuitas, Apartado 29068, Caracas 1021; (02) 442-21-20.

ECCLESIASTICAL FACULTIES

(*Principal source*: Annuario Pontificio) These faculties in Catholic seminaries and universities, listed according to country of location, have been canonically erected and authorized by the Congregation for Catholic Education to award degrees in stated fields of study. In addition to those listed here, there are other faculties of theology or philosophy in state universities and for members of certain religious orders only.

Argentina: Faculties of Philosophy and Theology, San Miguel (Sept. 8, 1932).

Australia: Catholic Institute of Theology, Sydney (Feb. 2, 1954).

Austria: Theological Faculty, Linz (Dec. 25, 1978). International Theological Institute for Family Studies (Oct. 1, 1996).

Brazil: Philosophical and Theological Faculties of the Company of Jesus, Belo Horizonte (July 15, 1941 and Mar. 12, 1949).

Ecclesiastical Faculty of Philosophy "John Paul II," Rio de Janeiro (Aug. 6, 1981).

Cameroon: Catholic Institute of Yaoundé (Nov. 15, 1991).

Canada: College of Immaculate Conception — Montréal Section of Jesuit Faculties in Canada (Sept. 8, 1932). Suspended.

Pontifical Institute of Medieval Studies, Toronto (Oct. 18, 1939).

Dominican Faculty of Theology of Canada, Ottawa (1965; Nov. 15, 1975).

Regis College, Toronto Section of the Jesuit Faculty of Theology in Canada, Toronto (Feb. 17, 1956; Dec. 25, 1977).

Congo (formerly Zaire): Catholic Faculties of Kinshasa, Kinshasa (theology, Apr. 25, 1957; philosophy, Nov. 25, 1987).

Côte d'Ivoire (Ivory Coast): Catholic Institute of West Africa, Abidjan (Aug. 12, 1975).

Croatia: Philosophical Faculty, Zagreb (July 31, 1989).

France: Centre Sèvres, Faculties of Theology and Philosophy of the Jesuits, Paris (Sept. 8, 1932).

Germany: Theological Faculty of the Major Episcopal Seminary, Trier (Sept. 8, 1955).

Theological Faculty, Paderborn (June 11, 1966).

Theological-Philosophical Faculty, Frankfurt (1932; June 7, 1971).

Philosophical Faculty, Munich (1932; Oct. 25, 1971).

Theological Faculty, Fulda (Dec. 22, 1978).

Philosophical-Theological School of Salesians, Benediktbeuern (May 24, 1992).

Philosphical-Theological School, Vallendar (Oct. 7, 1993).

Great Britain: Heythrop College, University of London, London (Nov. 1, 1964). Theology, philosophy.

Hungary: Faculty of Theology (1635), Institute on Canon Law (Nov. 30, 1996), Budapest.

India: *Jnana Deepa Vidyapeeth* (Pontifical Athenaeum), Institute of Philosophy and Religion, Poona (July 27, 1926).

Vidyajyoti, Institute of Religious Studies, Faculty of Theology, Delhi (1932; Dec. 9, 1974).

Satya Nilayam, Institute of Philosophy and Culture. Faculty of Philosophy, Madras (Sept. 8, 1932; Dec. 15, 1976).

Pontifical Institute of Theology and Philosophy at the Pontifical Interritual Seminary of St. Joseph, Alwaye, Kerala (Feb. 24, 1972).

Dharmaram Vidya Kshetram, Pontifical Athenaeum of Theology and Philosophy, Bangalore (theology, Jan. 6, 1976; philosophy, Dec. 8, 1983).

Pontifical Oriental Institute of Religious Studies, Kottayam (July 3, 1982).

Faculty of Theology, Ranchi (Aug. 15, 1982).

St. Peter's Pontifical Institute of Theology, Bangalore (Jan. 6, 1985).

Indonesia: Wedabhakti Pontifical Faculty of Theology, Yogyakarta (Nov. 1, 1984).

Ireland: The Milltown Institute of Theology and Philosophy, Dublin (1932).

Israel: French Biblical and Archeological School, Jerusalem (founded 1890; approved Sept. 17, 1892; canonically approved to confer Doctorate in Biblical Science, June 29, 1983).

Italy: Theological Faculty of Southern Italy, Naples. Two sections: St. Louis Posillipo (Mar. 16, 1918) and St. Thomas Aquinas Capodimonte (Oct. 31, 1941).

Pontifical Theological Faculty of Sardinia, Cagliari, (Aug. 5, 1927).

Interregional Theological Faculty, Milan (Aug. 8, 1935; restructured 1969).

Faculty of Philosophy "Aloisianum," Gallarate (1937; Mar. 20, 1974).

Pontifical Ambrosian Institute of Sacred Music, Milan (Mar. 12, 1940).

Theological Faculty of Sicily, Palermo (Dec. 8, 1980). Theological Institute Pugliese, Molfetta (June 24, 1992). Theological Institute Calabro, Catanzaro (Jan. 28, 1993).

Theological Faculty of Central Italy, Florence (Sep. 9, 1997).

Japan: Faculty of Theology, Nagoya (May 25, 1984).

Kenya: Catholic Higher Institute of Eastern Africa, Nairobi (May 2, 1984).

Lebanon: Faculty of Theology, University of the Holy Spirit, Kaslik (May 30, 1982).

Madagascar: Superior Institute of Theology and Philosophy, at the Regional Seminary of Antananarivo, Ambatoroka-Antananarivo (Apr. 21, 1960).

Malta: Faculty of Theology, Tal-Virtù (Nov. 22, 1769), with Institute of Philosophy and Human Studies (Sept. 8, 1984).

Mexico: Theological Faculty of Mexico (June 29, 1982) and Philosophy (Jan. 6, 1986), Institute of Canon Law (Sept. 4, 1995), Mexico City.

Nigeria: Catholic Institute of West Africa, Port Harcourt (May 9, 1994).

Peru: Pontifical and Civil Faculty of Theology, Lima (July 25, 1571).

Poland: Pontifical Theological Faculty, Warsaw (May 3, 1988) with two sections: St. John Baptist (1837, 1920, Nov. 8, 1962) at the "Metropolitan Seminary Duchowne," and "St. Andrew Bobola" – "Bobolanum" (Sept. 8, 1932).

Philosophical Faculty, Krakow (1932; Sept. 20, 1984).

Theological Faculty, Poznan (1969; pontifical designation, June 2, 1974).

Spain: Theological Faculty, Granada (1940; July 31, 1973).

Theological Faculty of San Esteban, Salamanca (1947; Oct. 4, 1972).

Theological Faculty of the North, of the Metropolitan Seminary of Burgos and the Diocesan Seminary of Vitoria (Feb. 6, 1967).

Theological Faculty of Catalunya, (Mar. 7, 1968), with the Institutes of Fundamental Theology (Dec. 28, 1984), Liturgy (Aug. 15, 1986) and Philosophy (July 26, 1988), Barcelona.

Theological Faculty "San Vicente Ferrer" (two sections), Valencia (Jan. 23, 1974).

Theological Faculty "San Damaso" (Sept. 19, 1996), Madrid.

Switzerland: Theological Faculty, Lucerne (Dec. 25, 1973).

Theological Faculty, Chur (Jan. 1, 1974).

Theological Faculty, Lugano (Nov. 20, 1993).

United States: St. Mary's Seminary and University, School of Theology, Baltimore (May 1, 1822).

St. Mary of the Lake Faculty of Theology, Mundelein, IL (Sept. 30, 1929).

Weston Jesuit School of Theology, Cambridge, MA (Oct. 18, 1932).

The Jesuit School of Theology, Berkeley, CA (Feb. 2, 1934, as "Alma College," Los Gatos, CA).

Faculty of Philosophy and Letters, St. Louis, MO (Feb. 2, 1934).

St. Michael's Institute, Jesuit School of Philosophy and Letters, Spokane, WA (Feb. 2, 1934).

Pontifical Faculty of Theology of the Immaculate Conception, Dominican House of Studies, Washington, DC (Nov. 15, 1941).

Also located in the United States are:

The Marian Library/International Marian Research Institute (IMRI), U.S. branch of Pontifical Theological Faculty "Marianum," University of Dayton, Dayton, OH 45469 (affil. 1976, inc. 1983).

John Paul II Institute for Studies on Marriage and the Family, U.S. section of Pontifical John Paul II Institute for Studies on Marriage and Family at the Pontifical Lateran University, 487 Michigan Ave. NE, Washington, DC 20017 (Aug. 22, 1988).

Pontifical College Josephinum (Theologate and College) at Columbus, OH, is a national pontifical seminary. Established Sept. 1, 1888, it is directly under the auspices of the Vatican through the Apostolic Pro-Nuncio to the U.S., who serves as the seminary's chancellor.

Vietnam: Theological Faculty of the Pontifical National Seminary of St. Pius X, Dalat (July 31, 1965). Activities suppressed.

PONTIFICAL UNIVERSITIES AND INSTITUTES IN ROME

(*Source*: Annuario Pontificio.)

Pontifical Gregorian University (*Gregorian*) (1552): Piazza della Pilotta, 4, 00187 Rome. Associated with the university are: **Pontifical Biblical Institute** (May 7, 1909): Via della Pilotta, 25, 00187 Rome; **Pontifical Institute of Oriental Studies** (Oct. 15, 1917): Piazza S. Maria Maggiore, 7, 00185 Rome.

Pontifical Lateran University (1773): Piazza S. Giovanni in Laterano, 4, 00184 Rome. Attached to the university is the **Pontifical Institute of Studies of Marriage and the Family**, erected by Pope John Paul II, Oct 7, 1982; a section of the Institute was established at the Dominican House of Studies, Washington, DC, by a decree dated Aug. 22, 1988; sections were opened in Mexico in 1992 and Valencia, Spain, in 1994.

Pontifical Urbaniana University (1627): Via Urbano VIII, 16, 00165 Rome.

Pontifical University of St. Thomas Aquinas (*Angelicum*) (1580), of the Order of Preachers: Largo Angelicum, 1, 00184 Rome.

Pontifical University *Salesianum* (May 3, 1940; university designation May 24, 1973), of the Salesians of Don Bosco: Piazza dell'Ateneo Salesiano, 1, 00139 Rome. Associated with the university is the **Pontifical Institute of Higher Latin Studies**, known as the Faculty of Christian and Classical Letters (June 4, 1971).

Pontifical University *della Santa Croce* (of the Holy Cross) (Jan. 9, 1985), of the Personal Prelature of Opus Dei: Piazza S. Apollinare, 49, 00186 Rome.

Pontifical Athenaeum of St. Anselm (1687) of the Benedictines: Piazza Cavalieri di Malta, 5, 00153 Rome.

Pontifical Athenaeum *Antonianum* (of St. Anthony) (May 17, 1933), of the Order of Friars Minor: Via Merulana, 124, 00185 Rome.

Athenaeum *Regina Apostolorum* (Queen of the Apostles), of the Legionaries of Christ: Via Aurelia Antica, 460, 00165 Rome.

Pontifical Institute of Sacred Music (1911; May 24, 1931): Via di Torre Rossa, 21, 00165 Rome.

Pontifical Institute of Christian Archeology (Dec. 11, 1925): Via Napoleone III, 1, 00185 Rome.

Pontifical Theological Faculty *St. Bonaventure* (Dec. 18, 1587), of the Order of Friars Minor Conventual: Via del Serafico, 1, 00142 Rome.

Pontifical Theological Faculty, Pontifical Institute of Spirituality *Teresianum* (1935), of the Discalced Carmelites: Piazza San Pancrazio, 5-A, 00152 Rome.

Pontifical Theological Faculty *Marianum* (1398), of the Servants of Mary: Viale Trente Aprile, 6, 00153 Rome. Attached to the university is **The Marian Library/International Marian Research Institute** (IMRI), U.S. branch of Pontifical Theological Faculty *Marianum*, University of Dayton, Dayton, OH, 45469 (affil. 1976, inc. 1983).

Pontifical Institute of Arabic and Islamic Studies (1926), of the Missionaries of Africa: Viale di Trastevere, 89, 00153 Rome.

Pontifical Faculty of Educational Science *Auxilium* (June 27, 1970), of the Daughters of Mary, Help of Christians: Via Cremolino, 141, 00166 Rome.

Catholic Communications

CATHOLIC PRESS

Statistics

The *2002 Catholic Press Directory*, published by the Catholic Press Association, reported a total of 640 periodicals in North America, with a circulation of 26,805,268. The figures included 217 newspapers, with a circulation of 6,619,655; 243 magazines, with a circulation of 14,742,376; 136 newsletters, with a circulation of 4,290,253; and 44 other-language periodicals (newspapers and magazines), with a circulation of 1,152,984.

Newspapers in the U.S.

There were 205 newspapers in the United States, with a circulation 6,472,055. Six of these had national circulation totaling 220,411; 167 were diocesan newspapers with a total circulation of 5,899,420; 14 were Eastern Catholic Church publications with a total circulation of 82,579. Eighteen other publications were recently reclassified by the CPA from magazine to newspaper status to classify them correctly based on their actual format; they had a total circulation of 269,645.

National papers included: **National Catholic Register**, founded 1900; **Our Sunday Visitor**, founded 1912; **National Catholic Reporter**, founded 1964; **The Wanderer**, founded 1867; **The Adoremus Bulletin**, founded 1995; and the English-language weekly edition of *L'Osservatore Romano*, established in the U.S. in 1998.

The oldest U.S. Catholic newspaper is **The Pilot** of Boston, established in 1829 (under a different title).

Other diocesan newspapers: There were three other diocesan newspapers located outside continental North America (Samoa, U.S. Virgin Islands, West Indies), with a circulation of 20,700.

Magazines in U.S.

The Catholic Press Directory reported 228 magazines in the U.S., with a circulation of 13,952,792. In addition, there were 135 newsletters, with a circulation of 4,282,753.

America and **Commonweal** are the only weekly and biweekly magazines, respectively, of general interest.

The monthly magazines with the largest circulation are **Columbia** (1,497,206), the official organ of the Knights of Columbus, **Catholic Digest** (400,000) and **St. Anthony's Messenger** (339,000).

Other-language publications: There were an additional 30 publications (newspapers and magazines) in the U.S. in languages other than English, with a circulation of 894,984.

Canadian Statistics

There were nine newspapers in Canada with a circulation of 126,900. These included five national newspapers (**The Catholic Register**, founded 1893; **Catholic New Times**, founded 1976; **Restoration**, founded 1947; **The Catholic Times**, founded 1976; and **St. Vladimir's College Gazette**, founded 1998) and five diocesan. There were 15 magazines, with a circulation of 789,584; one newsletter, with a circulation of 7,500; and 14 publications in languages other than English, with a circulation of 258,000.

CATHOLIC NEWSPAPERS, MAGAZINES, AND NEWSLETTERS IN THE U.S.

(*Sources:* Catholic Press Directory; The Catholic Journalist; Catholic Almanac *survey; Catholic News Service.*) *Abbreviation code: a, annual; bm, bimonthly; m, monthly; q, quarterly; w, weekly; bw, bw.)*

Newspapers

Acadiana Catholic, m; 1408 Carmel Ave., Lafayette, LA 70501; (337) 261-5511; Lafayette diocese.

A.D. Times, bw; 2141 Downyflake Lane, Allentown, PA 18103-4724; (610) 797-3330; Allentown diocese.

Adoremus Bulletin, The, 10 times a year; P.O. Box 3286, St. Louis, MO 63130; (314) 863-8385; www.adoremus.org; national liturgical journal.

Agua Viva, m; 1280 Med Park Dr., Las Cruces, NM 88005-3239; (505) 523-7577; www.dioceseof lascruces.org; Las Cruces diocese.

Alaskan Shepherd, bm; 1312 Peger Rd., Fairbanks, AK 99709; (904) 474-0753; www.ptialaska.net/~cbna/; Fairbanks diocese.

America (Ukrainian-English), 2 times a week; 817 N. Franklin St., Philadelphia, PA 19123; (215) 627-4519; Providence Association of Ukrainian Catholics in America.

Anchor, The, w; P.O. Box 7, Fall River, MA 02722; (508) 675-7151; Fall River diocese.

Arkansas Catholic, w; P.O. Box 7417, Little Rock, AR 72217; (501) 664-0125; Little Rock diocese.

Arlington Catholic Herald, w; 200 N. Glebe Rd., Suite 607, Arlington, VA 22203; (703) 841-2590;

www.catholicherald.com; Arlington diocese.

Atchison Benedictines, q; Mount St. Scholastica Convent, 801 S. 8th St., Atchison, KS 66002; (913) 360-6200.

Bayou Catholic, The, w; P.O. Box 505, Schriever, LA 70395; (504) 850-3132; Houma-Thibodaux diocese.

Beacon, The, w; P.O. Box 1887, Clifton, NJ 07015-1887; (973) 279-8845; www.patersondiocese.org; Paterson diocese.

Bishop's Bulletin, m; 523 N. Duluth Ave., Sioux Falls, SD 57104-2714; (605) 988-3791; www.sfcatholic.org; Sioux Falls diocese.

Bolletino, m; 675 Hegenberger Rd., Suite 110, Oakland, CA 94621; (510) 633-9058; www.icf.org; Italian Catholic Federation.

Byzantine Catholic World, bw; 66 Riverview Ave., Pittsburgh, PA 15214; (412) 281-0380; Pittsburgh Byzantine archdiocese.

Catholic Accent, 40 times a year; 725 E. Pittsburgh St., Greensburg, PA 15601; (724) 834-4010; www.dioceseofgreensburg.org; Greensburg diocese.

Catholic Advance, The, w; 424 N. Broadway, Wichita, KS 67202-2377; (316) 269-3965; www.cdowk.org; Wichita diocese.

Catholic Advocate, The, w; 171 Clifton Ave., Newark, NJ 07104-9500; (973) 497-4200; www.catholic advocate@rcan.org; Newark archdiocese.

Catholic Aid News, m; 3499 N. Lexington Ave., St. Paul, MN 55126; (651) 490-0170; www.catholic aid.com.

Catholic Anchor, w; 225 Cordova St., Anchorage, AK 99501; (907) 297-7708; Anchorage diocese.

Catholic Calendar, semi-monthly; 411 Iris St., Lake Charles, LA 70601; (337) 439-7430; www.lcdiocese.org; one page in local newspaper twice a month; Lake Charles diocese.

Catholic Chronicle, bw; P.O. Box 1866, Toledo, OH 43603-1866; (419) 885-6397; Toledo diocese.

Catholic Commentator, The, bw; P.O. Box 14746, Baton Rouge, LA 70898-4746; (225) 387-0983; www.diobr.com; Baton Rouge diocese.

Catholic Connector, The, m; 660 Burton, SE, Grand Rapids, MI 49507; (616) 243-0491; www.dioceseofgrandrapids.org; Grand Rapids diocese.

Catholic Courier, w; P.O. Box 24379, Rochester, NY 14624-0379; (716) 328-4340; www.catholic courier.com; Rochester diocese.

Catholic East Texas, bw; 1015 ESE Loop 323, Tyler, TX 75701-9663; (903) 534-1077; Tyler diocese.

Catholic Explorer, w (bw July, Aug.); 402 S. Independence Blvd., Romeoville, IL 60446-2264; (815) 838-6475; www.dioceseofjoliet.org/explorer; Joliet diocese.

Catholic Exponent, bw; P.O. Box 6787, Youngstown, OH 44501-6787; (330) 744-5251; www.doy.org; Youngstown diocese.

Catholic Free Press, w; 51 Elm St., Worcester, MA 01609; (508) 757-6387; www.catholicfreepress.org; Worcester diocese.

Catholic Health World, semi-monthly; 4455 Woodson Rd., St. Louis, MO 63134-3797; (314) 427-2500; www.chausa.org; Catholic Health Association.

Catholic Herald, The, m; 29 W. Kiowa St., Colorado Springs, CO 80903; (719) 685-5202; Colorado Springs diocese.

Catholic Herald, w; P.O. Box 07913, Milwaukee, WI 53207-0913; (414) 769-3500; www.execpc.com/~chn; Milwaukee archdiocese. Also publishes editions for Madison and Superior dioceses.

Catholic Herald: Madison Edition, w; P.O. Box 44985, Madison, WI 53744-4985; (608) 821-3070; www.madisoncatholicherald.org; Madison diocese.

Catholic Herald: Superior Edition, w; P.O. Box 969, Superior, WI 54880; (715) 392-8268; www.catholic herald.org; Superior diocese.

Catholic Herald, bw; 5890 Newman Ct., Sacramento, CA 95819; (916) 452-3344; Sacramento diocese.

Catholic Islander, m; P.O. Box 301825, St. Thomas, USVI, 00803-1825; (340) 774-3166; Virgin Islands diocese.

Catholic Journalist, The, m; 3555 Veterans Highway, Unit O, Ronkonkoma, NY 11779; (631) 471-4730; www.catholicpress.org; Catholic Press Association.

Catholic Key, 44 times a year; P.O. Box 419037, Kansas City, MO 64141-6037; (816) 756-1850; www.catholickey.org; Kansas City-St. Joseph diocese.

Catholic Light, bw; 300 Wyoming Ave., Scranton, PA 18503; (570) 207-2229; www.dioceseof scranton.org; Scranton diocese.

Catholic Lighthouse, m; P.O. Box 4070, Victoria, TX 77903; (361) 573-0828; Victoria diocese.

Catholic Messenger, w; P.O. Box 460, Davenport, IA 52805; (563) 323-9959; Davenport diocese.

Catholic Mirror The, m; 601 Grand Ave., Des Moines, IA 50309; (515) 244-6234; www.dm diocese.org; Des Moines diocese.

Catholic Missourian, w; P.O. Box 1107, Jefferson City, MO 65102-1107; (573) 635-9127; Jefferson City diocese.

Catholic Moment, The, w; P.O. Box 1603, Lafayette, IN 47902; (765) 742-2050; www.dioceseoflafayette.org; Lafayette diocese.

Catholic New World, The, w; 721 N. La Salle St., Chicago, IL 60610; (312) 655-7777; www.catholic newworld.com; Chicago archdiocese.

Catholic New York, w; 1011 First Ave., New York, NY 10022; (212) 688-2399; www.cny.org; New York archdiocese.

Catholic News, w; P.O. Box 85, Independence Square, Port-of-Spain, Trinidad, West Indies; (868) 623-6093; www.trinidad.net/catholicnews.

Catholic News and Herald, The, w; P.O. Box 37267, Charlotte, NC 28237; (704) 370-3333; www.charlottediocese.org; Charlotte diocese.

Catholic Northwest Progress, The, w; 910 Marion St., Seattle, WA 98104; (206) 382-4850; www.seattle earch.org; Seattle archdiocese.

Catholic Observer, bw; Box 1730, Springfield, MA 01101-1730; (413) 737-4744; Springfield diocese.

Catholic Peace Voice, q.; 532 W. Eighth St., Erie, PA 16502-1343; (814) 453-4955; www.paxchristi usa.org; published by Pax Christi.

Catholic Post, The, w; P.O. Box 1722, Peoria, IL 61656; (309) 673-3603; www.cdop.org/post; Peoria diocese.

Catholic Register, bw; P.O. Box 413, Hollidaysburg, PA 16648; (814) 695-7563; Altoona-Johnstown diocese.

Catholic Review, w; P.O. Box 777, Baltimore, MD

21203; (410) 547-5380; www.catholicreview.org; Baltimore archdiocese.

Catholic San Francisco, bw; One Peter Yorke Way, San Francisco, CA 94109; (415) 614-5630; San Francisco archdiocese.

Catholic Sentinel, w; P.O. Box 18030, Portland, OR 97218-0030; (503) 281-1191; www.sentinel.org; Portland archdiocese, Baker diocese.

Catholic Spirit, The, w; 244 Dayton Ave., St. Paul, MN 55102-1893; (651) 291-4444; www.thecatholic spirit.com; St. Paul and Minneapolis archdiocese.

Catholic Spirit, The, w; P.O. Box 5247, Kendall Park, NJ 08824-5247; (732) 940-2111; www.catholic spirit.com; Metuchen diocese.

Catholic Spirit, The, m; P.O. Box 13327, Austin, TX 78711; (512) 476-4888; www.austindiocese.org; Austin diocese.

Catholic Spirit, The, m; P.O. Box 951, Wheeling, WV 26003-0119; (304) 233-0880; www.dwc.org; Wheeling-Charleston diocese.

Catholic Standard, w; P.O. Box 4464, Washington, DC, 20017; (202) 281-2410; www.cathstan.org; Washington archdiocese.

Catholic Standard and Times, w; 222 N. 17th St., Philadelphia, PA 19103; (215) 587-3660; www.arch diocese-phl.org/cs&t; Philadelphia archdiocese.

Catholic Star Herald, w; 1845 Haddon Ave., Camden, NJ 08103; (856) 756-7900; Camden diocese.

Catholic Sun, The, semi-monthly; P.O. Box 13549, Phoenix, AZ 85002; (602) 257-5565; www.catholic sun.org; Phoenix diocese.

Catholic Sun, The, w; 421 S. Warren St., Syracuse, NY 13202; (315) 422-8153; Syracuse diocese.

Catholic Telegraph, w; 100 E. 8th St., Cincinnati, OH 45202; (513) 421-3131; www.catholic cincinnati.org; Cincinnati archdiocese.

Catholic Times, w; 197 E. Gay St., Columbus, OH 43215-3229; (614) 224-5195; www.ctonline.org; Columbus diocese.

Catholic Times, The, w; P.O. Box 4248, Flint, MI 48504; (810) 659-4670; Lansing diocese.

Catholic Times, w; P.O. Box 3187, Springfield, IL 62708-3187; (217) 698-8500; Springfield diocese.

Catholic Transcript, w; 467 Bloomfield Ave., Bloomfield, CT 06002; (860) 286-2828; Hartford archdiocese; Bridgeport and Norwich dioceses.

Catholic Universe Bulletin, bw; 1027 Superior Ave. NE, Cleveland, OH 44114-2556; (216) 696-6525; www.catholicuniversebulletin.org; Cleveland diocese.

Catholic Virginian, bw; Box 26843, Richmond, VA 23220; (804) 359-5654; www.catholicvirginia.org; Richmond diocese.

Catholic Vision, m.; P.O. Box 31, Tucson, AZ 85702; (520) 792-3410; www.catholic-vision.org; Tuscon diocese.

Catholic Voice, The, bw; 3014 Lakeshore Ave., Oakland, CA 94610; (510) 893-5339; Oakland diocese.

Catholic Voice, The, bw; P.O. Box 4010, Omaha, NE 68104-0010; (402) 558-6611; www.tcv omaha.com; Omaha archdiocese.

Catholic War Veteran, bm; 441 N. Lee St., Alexandria, VA 22314-2344; (703) 549-3622; www.cwv.org.

Catholic Week, The, w; P.O. Box 349, Mobile, AL 36601; (334) 432-3529; Mobile archdiocese.

Catholic Weekly, The, w; 1520 Court St., Saginaw, MI 48602; (989) 793-7661; Saginaw diocese.

Catholic Weekly, The, w; P.O. Box 1405, Saginaw, MI 48602; (989) 793-7661; Gaylord diocese.

Catholic Witness, The, bw; P.O. Box 2555, Harrisburg, PA 17105; (717) 657-4804; Harrisburg diocese.

Catholic Women's Network, bm; 877 Spinosa Dr., Sunnyvale, CA 94087; (408) 245-8663; www.catholic womensnet.org.

Catholic Workman, m; P.O. Box 47, New Prague, MN 56071; (952) 758-2229; www.catholic workman.com.

Catolico de Texas, El (Spanish), m; P.O. Box 190347, Dallas, TX 75219; (214) 528-8792; Dallas diocese.

Centinela, El (Spanish), m; P.O.Box 18030, Portland, OR 97218-0300; (503) 281-1191.

Central Washington Catholic, bm; 5301-A Tieton Dr., Yakima, WA 98908; (509) 965-7117; Yakima diocese.

Chicago Catolico (Spanish), m; 721 N. La Salle St., 4th Floor, Chicago, IL 60610; (312) 655-7880; Chicago archdiocese.

Christian Renewal News, q; P.O. Box 547, Fillmore, CA 93016-0547; (805) 524-5890; www.theservantsandhandmaids.com; Apostolate of Christian Renewal.

Chronicle of Catholic Life, bm; 1001 North Grand Ave., Pueblo, CO 81003; (719) 685-5202; www.diocesenet.com; Pueblo diocese.

Church Today, twice a month; P.O. Box 7417, Alexandria, LA 71306-0417; (318) 445-2401; Alexandria diocese.

Church World, The, w; P.O. Box 11559, Portland, ME 04104; (207) 773-6471; Portland diocese.

Clarion Herald, bw; P.O. Box 53247, New Orleans, LA 70153; (504) 596-3035; www.clarionherald.org; New Orleans archdiocese.

Compass, The, w; P.O. Box 23825, Green Bay, WI 54305-3825; (920) 437-7531; www.gbdioc.org; Green Bay diocese.

Courier, The, m; P.O. Box 949, Winona, MN 55987-0949; (507) 454-4643; www.dow.org; Winona diocese.

Credo, bw; P.O.Box 504, Ann Arbor, MI 48106; (734) 930-3100.

Criterion, The, w; P.O. Box 1717, Indianapolis, IN 46206; (317) 236-1570; www.archindy.org/criterion; Indianapolis archdiocese.

Cross Roads, bw; 1310 W. Main St., Lexington, KY 40508-2040; (859) 253-1993; Lexington diocese.

Dakota Catholic Action, m (except July); P.O. Box 1137, Bismarck, ND 58502-1137; (701) 222-3035; www.bismarckdiocese.com; Bismarck diocese.

Denver Catholic Register, w; 1300 S. Steele St., Denver, CO 80210-2599; (303) 715-3215; www.archden.org; Denver archdiocese.

Dialog, The, w; P.O. Box 2208, Wilmington, DE 19899; (302) 573-3109; www.cdow.org; Wilmington diocese.

East Tennessee Catholic, The, bw; P.O. Box 11127, Knoxville, TN 37939-1127; (865) 584-3307; www.etcatholic.com; Knoxville diocese.

East Texas Catholic, semi-monthly; P.O. Box 3948, Beaumont, TX 77704-3948; (409) 832-3944; Beaumont diocese.

Eastern Catholic Life, bw; 445 Lackawanna Ave., W. Paterson, NJ 07424; (201) 890-7794; Passaic Byzantine eparchy.

Eastern Oklahoma Catholic, bw; Box 690240, Tulsa, OK 74169-0240; (918) 294-1904; Tulsa diocese.

Eternal Flame (Armenian-English), 110 E. 12th St., New York, NY 10003; (212) 477-2030; Armenian exarchate.

Evangelist, The, w; 40 N. Main Ave., Albany, NY 12203; (518) 453-6688; www.evangelist.org; Albany diocese.

Fairfield County Catholic, m; 238 Jewett Ave., Bridgeport, CT 06606; (203) 372-4301; Bridgeport diocese.

Florida Catholic, The, w; P.O. Box 609512, Orlando, FL 32860-9512; (407) 660-9141; Orlando diocese. Publishes editions for Miami archdiocese and Palm Beach, Pensacola-Tallahassee, St. Petersburg and Venice dioceses.

Florida Catholic: Miami Edition, w; 9401 Biscayne Blvd., Miami, FL 33138; (305) 757-6241; www.thefloridacatholic.org.

Florida Catholic: Palm Beach Edition, w; 9995 N. Military Trail, Palm Beach Gardens, FL 33410; (561) 775-9528; www.flcath.org

Florida Catholic: Pensacola-Tallahassee Edition, w; P.O. Drawer 17329, Pensacola, FL 32522; (904) 432-5215.

Florida Catholic: St. Petersburg Edition, w; P.O. Box 40200, St. Petersburg, FL 33743; (727) 345-3338; www.flcath.org.

Florida Catholic: Venice Edition, w; 1000 Pinebrook Rd., Venice, FL 34292; (941) 484-9543.

Four County Catholic, m; 1595 Norwich New London Turnpike, Uncasville, CT 06382; (860) 848-2237; www.norwichdiocese.org; Norwich diocese.

Georgia Bulletin, w; 680 W. Peachtree St. NW, Atlanta, GA 30308; (404) 877-5500; www.archatl.com; Atlanta archdiocese.

Glasilo KSKJ Amerikanski Slovenec (Slovenian), bw; 708 E. 159th, Cleveland, OH 44110; (216) 541-7243; American Slovenian Catholic Union.

Globe, The, w; P.O. Box 5079, Sioux City, IA 51102; (712) 255-2550; Sioux City diocese.

Good News for the Diocese of Kalamazoo, The, m; 215 N. Westnedge, Kalamazoo, MI 49007-3760; (616) 349-8714; www.dioceseofkalamazoo.org; Kalamazoo diocese.

Gulf Pine Catholic, w; P.O. Box 1189, Biloxi, MS 39533-1189; (228) 702-2127; Biloxi diocese.

Harvest, The, 121 23rd St. South, Great Falls, MT 59405; (406) 727-6683; www.dioceseofgfb.org; Great Falls diocese.

Hawaii Catholic Herald, bw; 1184 Bishop St., Honolulu, HI 96813; (808) 533-1791; Honolulu diocese.

Heraldo Catolico, El (Spanish), bw; 5890 Newman Ct., Sacramento, CA 95819; (916) 733-0680; Sacramento diocese.

Hlas Naroda (Voice of the Nation) (Czech-English), bw; 2340 61st Ave., Cicero, IL 60650; (708) 656-1050.

Holy Smoke: Our Lady of the Hills Church, six times a year; 2700 Ashland Rd., Columbia, SC 29210; (803) 772-7400.

Horizons, twice a month; 1900 Carlton Rd., Parma, OH 44134-3129; (216) 741-3312; www.parma.org; Parma Byzantine eparchy.

Idaho Catholic Register, twice a month; 303 Federal Way, Boise, ID 83705; (208) 342-1311; www.catholicidaho.org/icr.cfm; Boise diocese.

Inland Register, every 3 weeks; P.O. Box 48, Spokane, WA 99210; (509) 358-7340; www.diocese ofspokane.org; Spokane diocese.

Inside Passage, bw; 419 6th St., Juneau, AK 99801; (907) 586-2237; Juneau diocese.

Intermountain Catholic, w; P.O. Box 2489, Salt Lake City, UT 84110-2489; (801) 328-8641; www.icnp.com; Salt Lake City diocese.

Jednota (Slovak-Eng.), w; 6611 Rockside Rd., Independence, OH 44131; (216) 642-9406; First Catholic Slovak Union.

Lake Shore Visitor, w; P.O. Box 10668, Erie, PA 16514-0668; (814) 824-1160; www.eriecd.org; Erie diocese.

Leaven, The, w; 12615 Parallel Parkway, Kansas City, KS 66109; (913) 721-1570; www.the leaven.com; Kansas City archdiocese.

Long Island Catholic, The, w; P.O. Box 9000, Rockville Centre, NY 11575-9000; (516) 594-1000; www.licatholic.org; Rockville Centre diocese.

L'Osservatore Romano, w; P.O. Box 777, The Cathedral Foundation, Baltimore, MD, 21203; (410) 547-5380; www.catholicreview.org; English edition of the Vatican newspaper.

Maronites Today, m; 1320 East 51st St., Austin, TX 78723; (512) 458-3693; www.eparchyla.org; Maronite Epachy of Our Lady of Lebanon of Los Angeles.

Maronite Voice, The, m; 4611 Sadler Rd., Glen Allen, VA 23060; (804) 270-7234; www.stmaron.org; Eparchy of St. Maron of Brooklyn.

Message, The, w; P.O. Box 4169, Evansville, IN 47724-0169; (812) 424-5536; Evansville diocese.

Messenger, The, w; 2620 Lebanon Ave., Belleville, IL 62221; (618) 235-9601; www.belleville messenger.org; Belleville diocese.

Messenger, The, 45 times a year; P.O. Box 18068, Erlanger, KY 41018; (859) 283-6270; www.dioof covky.org; Covington diocese.

Michigan Catholic, The, w; 305 Michigan Ave., 4th Floor, Detroit, MI 48226; (313) 224-8000; Detroit archdiocese.

Mirror, The, w; 601 S. Jefferson Ave., Springfield, MO 65806-3143; (417) 866-0841; www.the-mirror.org; Springfield-Cape Girardeau diocese.

Mississippi Catholic, w; P.O. Box 2130, Jackson, MS 39225-2130; (601) 969-1880; www.mississippi catholic.com; Jackson diocese.

Monitor, The, w; P.O. Box 5147, Trenton, NJ 08638-0147; (609) 406-7404; www.dioceseoftrenton.org; Trenton diocese.

Montana Catholic, The, 16 times a year; P.O. Box 1729, Helena, MT 59624; (406) 442-5820; www.diocesehelena.org; Helena diocese.

Narod Polski (Polish Nation) (Polish-Eng.) semi-monthly; 984 Milwaukee Ave., Chicago, IL 60622; (773) 782-2600; www.prcua.com; Polish Roman Catholic Union of America.

National Catholic Register, w; 432 Washington Ave., North Haven, CT 06473; (203) 230-3800; www.ncregister.com; national.

National Catholic Reporter, w; P.O. Box 419281, Kansas City, MO 64141; (816) 531-0538; www.natcath.org; national.

National Jesuit News, m; 1616 P St. NW, Suite 400, Washington, DC 20036; (202) 462-0400; www.jesuit.org.

New Catholic Miscellany, The, w; 119 Broad St., Charleston, SC 29401; (843) 724-8375; www.catholic-doc.org; Charleston diocese.

New Earth, The, m; 244 Dayton Ave., St. Paul, MN 55102; (651) 291-4444; www.thecatholicspirit.com; Fargo diocese.

New Star, The, every 3 weeks; 2208 W. Chicago Ave., Chicago, IL 60622; (312) 772-1919; St. Nicholas of Chicago Ukrainian diocese.

NC Catholic, bw; 715 Nazareth St., Raleigh, NC 27606; (919) 821-9736; www.raldioc.org; Raleigh diocese.

North Country Catholic, w; P.O. Box 326, Ogdensburg, NY 13669; (315) 393-2540; www.north countrycatholic.org; Ogdensburg diocese.

North Texas Catholic, w; 800 West Loop 820 South, Fort Worth, TX 76108; (817) 560-3300; Fort Worth diocese.

Northwest Indiana Catholic, w; 9292 Broadway, Merrillville, IN 46410-7088; (219) 769-9292; www.nwic@dcgary.org; Gary diocese.

Northwestern Kansas Register, w; P.O. Box 1038, Salina, KS 67402; (785) 827-8746; www.salina diocese.org; Salina diocese.

Oblate World, The and Voice of Hope, twice a month; P.O. Box 680, Tewksbury, MA 01876; (978) 851-7258; www.omiusa.org; published by the Missionary Oblates of Mary Immaculate.

Observer, The, m; P.O. Box 2079, Monterey, CA 93942; (831) 373-2919; www.dioceseofmonterey.org. Monterey diocese.

Observer, The, m; 4545 W. 63rd St., Chicago, IL 60629; (312) 585-9500; Lithuanian Roman Catholic Federation of America.

Observer, The, twice a month; 921 W. State St., Rockford, IL 61102; (815) 963-3471; Rockford diocese.

One Voice, w; P.O. Box 10822, Birmingham, AL 35202; (205) 838-8305; Birmingham diocese.

Orange County Catholic, m.; P.O. Box 14195, Orange, CA 92863-1595; (714) 282-3023; Orange diocese.

Our Northland Diocese, semi-monthly; 1200 Memorial Dr., P.O. Box 610, Crookston, MN 56716; (218) 281-4553; www.crookston.org; Crookston diocese.

Our Sunday Visitor, w; 200 Noll Plaza, Huntington, IN 46750; (219) 356-8400; www.osv.com; national.

People of God, m; 4000 St. Joseph Pl. NW, Albuquerque, NM 87120; (505) 831-8188; Santa Fe archdiocese.

Pilot, The, w; 141 Tremont St., Boston, MA 02111-1209; (617) 482-4316; www.rcab.org; Boston archdiocese.

Pittsburgh Catholic, w; 135 First Ave., Suite 200, Pittsburgh, PA 15222-1506; (412) 471-1252; www.pittsburghcatholic.org; Pittsburgh diocese.

Prairie Catholic, m; 1400 6th St. North, New Ulm, MN 56073-2099; (507) 359-2966; www.dnu.org; New Ulm diocese.

Praxis Press, 10 times a year; P.O. Box 508, San Jose, CA 95103; (408) 450-9800.

Pregonero, El (Spanish), w; P.O. Box 4464, Washington, DC 20017; (202) 281-2440; www.elpreg.org; Washington archdiocese.

Providence Visitor, The, w; 184 Broad St., Providence, RI 02903; (401) 272-1010; www.providence visitor.com; Providence diocese.

Record, The, w; Maloney Center, 1200 S. Shelby St., Louisville, KY 40203-2600; (502) 636-0296; Louisville archdiocese.

Redwood Crozier, The, m; P.O. Box 1297, Santa Rosa, CA 95402; (707) 459-5710; Santa Rosa diocese.

Rio Grande Catholic, The, m; 499 St. Matthews St., El Paso, TX 79907; (915) 872-8414; El Paso diocese.

Saint Cloud Visitor, The, w; P. O. Box 1068, St. Cloud, MN 56302-1066; (320) 251-3022; www.stclouddiocese.org/visitor; St. Cloud diocese.

St. Louis Review, w; 462 N. Taylor Ave., St. Louis, MO 63108; (314) 531-9700; St. Louis archdiocese.

Seasons, q; 5800 Weiss St., Saginaw, MI 48603-2799; (989) 797-6666; www.dioceseofsaginaw.org; Saginaw diocese.

Slovak Catholic Falcon (Slovak-English), w; 205 Madison St., P.O.Box 899, Passaic, NJ 07055; (973) 777-4010; Slovak Catholic Sokol.

Sooner Catholic, The, bw; P.O. Box 32180, Oklahoma City, OK 73123; (405) 721-1810; www.sooner editor@ilinkusa.net; Oklahoma City archdiocese.

Sophia, q; 200 E. North Ave., Northlake, IL 60164; (708) 865-7050; Newton Melkite eparchy.

South Plains Catholic, twice a month; P.O. Box 98700, Lubbock, TX 79499-8700; (806) 792-3943; www.catholiclubbock.org; Lubbock diocese.

South Texas Catholic, twice a month; P.O. Box 2620, Corpus Christi, TX 78403-2620; (361) 882-6191; www.goccn.org; Corpus Christi diocese.

Southern Cross, semi-monthly; P.O. Box 81869, San Diego, CA 92138; (858) 490-8266; www.the southerncross.org; San Diego diocese.

Southern Cross, The, w; 601 E. Liberty Street, Savannah, GA 31401-5196; (912) 238-2320; www.dioceseofsavannah.org; Savannah diocese.

Southern Nebraska Register, w; P.O. Box 80329, Lincoln, NE 68501; (402) 488-0090; Lincoln diocese.

Southwest Catholic, The, m; P.O. 411 Iris St., Lake Charles, LA 70601; (337) 439-7430; www.lc diocese.org; Lake Charles diocese.

Southwest Kansas Register, bw; P.O. Box 137, Dodge City, KS 67801; (316) 227-1500; Dodge City diocese.

Sower (Ukrainian and English), bw; 14 Peveril Rd., Stamford, CT 06902; (203) 358-9905; the sower@att.net; Stamford Ukrainian diocese.

Spinnaker, 5 times a year; 610 W. Elm, Monroe, MI 48161; (313) 241-3660; IHM Sisters.

Star of Chaldeans (Arabic and English), bm; 25585 Berg Rd., Southfield, MI 48034; St. Thomas the Apostle Chaldean diocese.

Steubenville Register, bw; P.O. Box 160, Steubenville, OH 43952; (740) 282-3631; www.diosteub.org; Steubenville diocese.

Tablet, The, w; 310 Prospect Park West, Brooklyn, NY 11215; (718) 965-7333; www.tablet-brooklyn.com; Brooklyn diocese.

Tautai, bw; P.O. Box 532, Feiloaimauso Hall, Apia, Samoa; Samoa-Apia archdiocese.

Tennessee Register, The, bw; 2400 21st Ave. S., Nashville, TN 37212; (615) 783-0770; Nashville diocese.

Texas Catholic, bw; P.O. Box 190346, Dallas, TX 75219; (214) 528-8792; Dallas diocese.

Texas Catholic Herald, The, twice a month; 1700 San Jacinto St., Houston, TX 77001-0907; (713) 659-5461; Galveston-Houston diocese.

Tidings, 11 times a year; 153 Ash St., Manchester, NH 03105-0310; (603) 669-3100; www.diocese manch.org; Manchester diocese.

Tidings, The, w; 3424 Wilshire Blvd, Los Angeles, CA 90010; (213) 637-7360; Los Angeles archdiocese.

Times Review, The, w; P.O. Box 4004, La Crosse, WI 54602-4004; (608) 788-1524; www.diocese oflacrosse.com; La Crosse diocese.

Today's Catholic, w; P.O. Box 11169, Fort Wayne, IN 46856; (219) 456-2824; www.diocesefwsb.org; Fort Wayne-South Bend diocese.

Today's Catholic, bw; P.O. Box 28410, San Antonio, TX 78228-0410; (210) 734-2620; tcpaper@archdiosa.org; San Antonio archdiocese.

UNIREA (The Union) (Romanian) (10 times a year), P.O. Box 7189, Canton, OH 44714-0189; (330) 492-4086; Romanian diocese of Canton.

U. P. Catholic, The, semi-monthly; P.O. Box 548, Marquette, MI 49855; (906) 227-9131; www.diocese ofmarquette.org; Marquette diocese.

Valley Catholic, m; 900 Lafayette St., Suite 301, Santa Clara, CA 95050-4966; (408) 983-0260; www.dsj.org/vc/valley; San Jose diocese.

Verelk (Armenian-English), bm; 1237 Pleasant Ave., Los Angeles, CA 90033; (213) 267-1740.

Vermont Catholic Tribune, bw; P.O. Box 489, Burlington, VT 05402; (802) 658-6110; www.ver montcatholic.org; Burlington diocese.

Visitante de Puerto Rico, El (Spanish), w; Apartado 41305 – Minillas Sta., San Juan, PR 00940-1305; (787) 728-3710; www.elvisitante.com; Puerto Rican Catholic Conference.

Voice of the Southwest, m; 414 N. Allen, Farmington, NM 87401; (505) 325-9743; Gallup diocese.

Voz Catolica, La (Spanish); m; 9401 Biscayne Blvd., Miami, FL 33138; (305) 762-1201; www.voz cat.com; Miami archdiocese.

Wanderer, The, w; 201 Ohio St., St. Paul, MN 55107; (651) 224-5733; national.

Way, The (Ukrainian-Eng.), bw; 827 N. Franklin St., Philadelphia, PA 19123; (215) 922-5231; Philadelphia archeparchy.

West Nebraska Register, w; P.O. Box 608, Grand Island, NE 68802; (308) 382-4660; Grand Island diocese.

West River Catholic, m; P.O. Box 678, Rapid City, SD 57709; (605) 343-3541; Rapid City diocese.

West Tennessee Catholic, w; P.O. Box 341669, Memphis, TN 38184-1669; (901) 373-1213; www.cdom.org; Memphis diocese.

West Texas Angelus, m; P.O. Box 1829, San Angelo, TX 76902; (915) 651-7500; www.san-angelo-diocese.org; San Angelo diocese.

West Texas Catholic, bw; P.O. Box 5644, Amarillo, TX 79117-5644; (806) 383-2243; Amarillo diocese.

Western Kentucky Catholic, m; 600 Locust St., Owensboro, KY 42301; (270) 683-1545; Owensboro diocese.

Western New York Catholic, m; 795 Main St., Buffalo, NY 14203-1250; (716) 847-8727; www.wnycatholic.org; Buffalo diocese.

Witness, The, w; P.O. Box 917, Dubuque, IA 52004-0917; (319) 588-0556; Dubuque archdiocese.

Wyoming Catholic Register, m; P.O. Box 1468, Cheyenne, WY 82003; (307) 638-1530; Cheyenne diocese.

Magazines

AIM: Liturgy Resources, q; P.O. Box 2703, Schiller Park, IL 60176; (800) 566-6150.

America, w; 106 W. 56th St., New York, NY 10019; (212) 581-4640; www.americapress.org; Jesuits of U.S. and Canada.

American Benedictine Review, q; Assumption Abbey, Box A, Richardton, ND 58652; (701) 974-3315.

American Catholic Philosophical Quarterly (formerly **The New Scholasticism**), Fordham University, Bronx, NY 10458; (718) 817-4081; www.acpa-main.org; American Catholic Philosophical Assn.

The Annals of St. Anne de Beaupre, m; P.O. Box 1000, St. Anne de Beaupre, Quebec, GOA 3CO; (418) 827-4538.

Anthonian, The, q; c/o St. Anthony's Guild, Paterson, NJ 07509; (201) 777-3737; www.friars.org; St. Anthony's Guild.

Apostolate of the Little Flower, bm; P.O. Box 5280, San Antonio, TX 78201; (210) 736-3889; Discalced Carmelite Fathers.

Barry Magazine, 2 times a year; 11300 NE 2nd Ave., Miami Shores, FL 33161; (305) 899-3188; Barry University.

Be Magazine, 6 times a year; 2020 Gillespie Way, El Cajon, CA 92020; (619) 387-7200; www.catholic.com.

Benedictines, m., 44 N. Mill St., Kansas City, KS 66101; (913) 342-0938; www.mountsb.com.

Bible Today, The, bm; Liturgical Press, Collegeville, MN 56321; (320) 363-2213; www.litpress.org.

Bright Ideas; P.O. Box 432, Milwaukee, WI, 53201-0432; (800) 876-4574; www.exepc.com/~Lpi.

Carmelite Digest, q; P.O. Box 2178, Relands, CA 92373; (909) 793-0424.

Carmelite Review, 2 times a month; 1540 East Glenn St., Tucson, AZ 85719; (520) 326-4967; www.carmelites.org/review.htm; published by the Province of the Most Pure Heart of Mary of the Carmelite Order.

Catechist, The, 7 times a year; 2621 Dryden Rd., Dayton, OH 45439; (937) 293-1415; www.pflaum.com.

Catechumenate: A Journal of Christian Initiation, bm; 1800 N. Hermitage Ave., Chicago, IL 60622-1101; (773) 486-8970; www.ltp.org.

Catholic Answer, The, bm; 200 Noll Plaza, Huntington, IN 46750; (219) 356-8400; www.osv.com; Our Sunday Visitor, Inc.

Catholic Biblical Quarterly; Catholic University of America, Washington, DC 20064; (202) 319-5519; www.cua.edu/students/org/cbib; Catholic Biblical Assn.

Catholic Cemetery, The, m; 710 N. River Rd., Des Plaines, IL 60016; (847) 824-8131; National Catholic Cemetery Conference.

Catholic Connection, The, m.; 3500 Fairfield Ave., Shreveport, LA 71104; (318) 868-4441; www.dioshpt.org; diocese of Shreveport.

Catholic Digest, m; 2115 Summit Ave., St. Paul, MN 55105-1081; (651) 962-6730; www.catholicdigest.org.

Catholic Dossier, bm; P.O. Box 591120, San Francisco, CA 94159; (415) 387-2324; www.ignatius.com.

Catholic Faith, The, bm; P.O. Box 591090, San Francisco, CA 94159-1090; (415) 387-2324; www.ignatius.com.

Catholic Faith and Family, w.; 33 Rossotto Dr., Hamden, CT 06514; (203) 288-5600; national, established 1998.

Catholic Family News, m.; MPO Box 743, Niagara Falls, NY 14302; (905) 871-6292.

Catholic Historical Review, q; 620 Michigan Ave. NE, Washington, DC 20064; (202) 319-5079; research.cua.edu/acha.

Catholic International, m; Cathedral Foundation, P.O. Box 777, Baltimore, MD 21203; (410) 547-5380; www.catholicreview.org.

Catholic Knights of America Journal, m; 1850 Dalton St., Cincinnati, OH 45214; (513) 721-0781; Catholic Knights of America.

Catholic Lawyer, q; St. John's University, 8000 Utopia Parkway, Jamaica, NY 11439; (718) 990-6655; St. Thomas More Institute for Legal Research.

Catholic Library World, q; 100 North St., #224, Pittsfield, MA 01201-5109; (413) 443-2252; www.cathla.org; Catholic Library Association.

Catholic Near East Magazine, bm; 1011 First Ave., New York, NY 10022; (212) 826-1480; www.cnewa.org; Catholic Near East Welfare Assn.

Catholic Outlook, m; 2830 E. 4th St., Duluth, MN 55812; (218) 724-9111; www.dioceseduluth.org; Duluth diocese.

Catholic Parent, bm; 200 Noll Plaza, Huntington, IN 46750; (219) 356-8400; www.osv.com; Our Sunday Visitor, Inc..

Catholic Pharmacist, q; 1012 Surrey Hills Dr., St. Louis, MO 63119-1438; (314) 645-0085; National Catholic Pharmacists Guild.

Catholic Press Directory, a; 3555 Veterans Highway, Unit O, Ronkonkoma, NY 11779; (631) 471-4730; www.catholicpress.com; Catholic Press Assn.

Catholic Quote, m; Valparaiso, NE 68065.

Catholic Review (Braille, tape, large print), bm; 154 E. 23rd St., New York, NY 10010; (212) 473-7800; Xavier Society for the Blind.

Catholic Southwest: A Journal of History and Culture, a; 1625 Rutherford Lane, Bldg. D, Austin, TX, 78754-5105; (512) 339-9882.

Catholic Telephone Guide, a. 210 North Ave., New Rochelle, NY 10801; (914) 632-1220; www.catholicguides.com; published by The Catholic New Publishing Co.

Catholic Woman, bm; 1275 K St. NW, Suite 975, Washington, DC 20005; (202) 682-0334; www.nccw.org; National Council of Catholic Women.

Catholic Worker, 7 times a year; 36 E. First St., New York, NY 10003; (212) 677-8627; Catholic Worker Movement.

Catholic World Report, The, 11 times a year; P.O. Box 1328, Dedham, MA 02027 (editorial office); Ignatius Press.

Celebration, m; 115 E. Armour Blvd., Kansas City, MO 64111; (816) 531-0538; National Catholic Reporter Publishing Co.

Charities USA, q; 1731 King St., Suite 200, Alexandria, VA 22314; (703) 549-1390; www.catholiccharitiesusa.org.

Chicago Studies, 3 times a year; 1800 N. Hermitage Ave., Chicago, IL 60622-1101; (800) 933-4213.

Christian Renewal News, q.; P.O. Box 547, Fillmore, CA 93016-0547; (805) 524-5890; www.theservantsandhandmaids.net; published by The Servants and Handmaids of the Sacred Heart of Jesus.

Christianity and the Arts, q; P.O. Box 118088, Chicago, IL 60611; (312) 642-8606; www.christianarts.net.

Church, q; 18 Bleecker St., New York, NY 10012; (212) 431-7825; National Pastoral Life Center.

CNEWA World, bm; 1011 First Ave., New York, NY 10022; (212) 826-1480; www.cnewa.org; Catholic Near East Welfare.

Columban Mission, 8 times a year; St. Columbans, NE 68056; (402) 291-1920; www.st.columban.org; Columban Fathers.

Columbia, m; One Columbus Plaza, New Haven, CT 06510; (203) 772-2130; www.kofc.org; Knights of Columbus.

Commonweal, bw; 475 Riverside Dr., Room 405, New York, NY 10115; (212) 662-4200; www.commonwealmagazine.org.

Communio: International Catholic Review, q; P.O. Box 4557, Washington, DC 20017-0557; (202) 526-0251; www.communio-icr.org.

Company, q; P.O. Box 60790, Chicago, IL 60660; (773) 760-9432; www.companysj.com; Jesuit Magazine.

Consecrated Life, semi-annually; P.O. Box 41007, Chicago, IL 60641; (773) 267-1195; www.religiouslife.com; Institute on Religious Life. English edition of *Informationes*, official publication of Congregation for Institutes of Consecrated Life and Societies of Apostolic Life.

Consolata Missionaries, bm; P.O. Box 5550, Somerset, NJ 08875; (732) 297-9191; www.consolata.org.

Cord, The, m; P.O. Drawer F, St. Bonaventure, NY 14778; (716) 375-2160; www.franinst.sbu.edu; Franciscan Institute.

Counseling and Values, 3 times a year; Dept. of Educational Psychology and Special Education, Southern Illinois University, Carbondale, IL 62901; (618) 537-7791.

Crescat, 3 times a year; Belmont Abbey, Belmont, NC 28012; (704) 825-6707; Benedictine Monks.

Crisis, 11 times a year; 1814½ N St., NW, Washington, DC 20036; (202) 861-7790; Journal of lay Catholic opinion.

Cross Currents, q; College of New Rochelle, New Rochelle, NY 10805; (914) 235-1439; www.aril.org; interreligious; Association for Religion and Intellectual Life.

Crusade Magazine, bm; P.O. Box 341, Hanover, PA 17331; (717) 225-9177; Foundation for a Christian Civilization, Inc.

CUA Magazine, 3 times a year; 620 Michigan Ave. NE, Washington, DC 20064; (202) 319-5600; www.cua.edu; Catholic University of America.

Darbininkas (The Worker) (Lithuanian), w; 341 Highland Blvd., Brooklyn, NY 11207; (718) 827-1352; Lithuanian Franciscans.

Desert Call, q.; P.O. Box 219, Crestone, CO 81131-0219; (719) 256-4778; www.spirituallifeinstitute.org; published by the Spiritual Life Institute.

Desert Clarion, 10 times a year; 4519 Simmons St., North Las Vegas, NV 89031; (702) 657-0200; Las Vegas diocese.

Diakonia, 3 times a year; University of Scranton, Scranton, PA 18510-4643; (717) 941-6116; www.nyssa.cecs.uofs.edu/diaktoc.html; Center for Eastern Christian Studies.

Divine Word Missionaries, q; P.O. Box 6099, Techny, IL 60082; (847) 272-7600.

Ecumenical Trends, m (except Aug.); Graymoor, Route 9, P.O. Box 306, Garrison, NY 10524-0306; (845) 424-2109; www.atonementfriars.org; Graymoor Ecumenical Institute.

Eglute (The Little Fir Tree) (Lithuanian), m; 13648 Kikapoo Trail, Lockport, IL 60441; (708) 301-6410; for children, ages 5-10.

Emmanuel, 10 times a year; 5384 Wilson Mills Rd., Cleveland, OH 44143; (440) 449-2103; www.blessedsacrament.com; Congregation of Blessed Sacrament.

Envoy, bm; P.O. Box 640, Granville, OH 43023; (740) 264-2040; www.envoymagazine.com; Journal of Catholic apologetics and evangelization.

Extension, m; 150 S. Wacker Dr., 20th Floor, Chicago, IL 60606; (312) 236-7240; www.catholic-extension.org; Catholic Church Extension Society.

Faith, 300 W. Ottawa St., Lansing, MI 48933-1577; (517) 342-2595.

Faith and Family, bm; 432 Washington Ave., North Haven, CT 06473; (203) 230-3800; formerly Catholic Twin Circle.

Faith and Reason, q; 134 Christendom Dr., Front Royal, VA 22630; (540) 636-2900.

Family Digest, The, bm; P.O. Box 40137, Fort Wayne, IN 46804 (editorial address); (952) 929-6765.

Family Friend, q; P.O. Box 11563, Milwaukee, WI 53211; (414) 961-0500; www.cfli.org; Catholic Family Life Insurance.

Fidelity, m; 206 Marquette Ave., South Bend, IN 46617; (219) 289-9786.

F.M.A. Focus, q; P.O. Box 598, Mt. Vernon, NY 10551; (914) 664-5604; Franciscan Mission Associates.

Forum Focus, q.; P.O. Box 542, Hudson, WI 54016-0542; (651) 426-2812; www.wandererforum.org.

Franciscan Studies, a; St. Bonaventure, NY 14778; (716) 375-2105; www.franinst.sbu.edu; Franciscan Institute.

Franciscan Way, q; 1235 University Blvd., Steubenville, OH 43952; (740) 283-6450; www.franuniv.edu.

Fraternal Leader, q; P.O. Box 13005; Erie, PA 16514-1302; (814) 453-4331; Loyal Christian Benefit Association.

Fraternally Yours (Engish-Slovak), m; 24950 Chagrin Blvd., Beachwood, OH 44122; (216) 464-8015; First Catholic Slovak Ladies Assn.

Fuente de Misericordia, q; Eden Hill, Stockbridge, MA 01263; (413) 298-3691; www.marian.org; Congregation of Marians of the Immaculate Conception.

Glenmary Challenge, The, q; P.O. Box 465618, Cincinnati, OH 45246-5618; (513) 874-8900; www.glenmary.org; Glenmary Home Missioners.

God's Word Today, m; 2115 Summit Ave., St. Paul, MN 55105-1982; (651) 962-6738; www.godswordtoday.org; University of St. Thomas.

Good News, m; P.O. Box 432, Milwaukee, WI 53201-0432; (800) 876-4574; www.execpc.com/~lpi; Liturgical Publications.

Good News for Children, 32 times during school year; 330 Progress Rd., Dayton, OH 45449; (513) 847-5900.

Good Shepherd (Dobry Pastier) (Slovak-English), a; 8200 McKnight Rd., Pittsburgh, PA 15237; (412) 364-3000.

Greyfriars Review, 3 times a year; St. Bonventure University, St. Bonaventure, NY 14778; (716) 375-2105; Franciscan Institute.

Growing with the Gospel, w; Publications Division, P.O. Box 432, Wisconsin, WI, 53201-0432; (800) 876-4574; www.execpc.com/~lpi.

Guide to Religious Ministries, A, a; 210 North Ave., New Rochelle, NY 10801; (914) 632-1220; www.catholicguides.com.

Guide to Religious Ministries for Catholic Men and Women, A, a; 210 North Ave., New Rochelle, NY 10801; (914) 632-1220; www.catholicguides.com.

Health Progress, bm; 4455 Woodson Rd., St. Louis, MO 63134-3797; (314) 427-2500; www.chausa.org; Catholic Health Association.

Hearts Aflame, q; P.O. Box 976, Washington, NJ 07882; (210) 689-1700; www.ewtn.com/Bluearmy/; for youth, ages 13-23.

Homiletic and Pastoral Review, m; P.O. Box 591810, San Francisco, CA 94159-1810; (415) 387-2324.

Horizon, q; 5420 S. Cornell Ave., #105, Chicago, IL 60615-5604; (773) 363-5454.

Horizons, 2 times a year; Villanova University, Villanova, PA 19085; (610) 519-7302; College Theology Society.

Horizons/Crossroads with the Catholic Evangelist, five times a year; P.O. Box 2009, Tulsa, OK, 74101; (918) 587-3115.

Human Development, q; 5401 South Cornell Ave., Chicago, IL 60615-5698; (773) 684-8146; www.ctu.edu/cishs.html.

ICSC Resource; 1275 K St. NW, Suite 980, Washington, DC, 20005-4006; (202) 289-1093; www.catholicstewardship.org; published by International Catholic Stewardship Council.

Immaculata, bm; 1600 W. Park Ave., Libertyville, IL 60048; (847) 367-7800; www.marytown.com.

Immaculate Heart Messenger, q; P.O. Box 158, Alexandria, SD 57311-0158; (800) 271-6279; www.fatimafamily.org.

In a Word, m; 199 Seminary Dr., Bay Saint Louis, MS 39520-4626; (601) 467-1097; www.inaword.com; Society of the Divine Word.

Inside the Vatican: See under **International Catholic Periodicals**.

Jesuit Bulletin, 3 times a year; 3601 Lindell Blvd., St. Louis, MO 63108; (314) 977-7363; www.jesuitsmis.org; Jesuit Seminary Aid Association.

Jesuit Journeys, 3 times a year; 3400 W. Wisconsin Ave., Milwaukee, WI 53208-0287; (414) 937-6955; www.jesuitswisprov.org.

Josephite Harvest, The, q; 1130 N. Calvert St., Baltimore, MD 21202-3802; (410) 727-2233; Josephite Missionaries.

Jurist, The, semi-annually; Catholic University of America, Washington, DC 20064; (202) 319-5439; Department of Canon Law.

Kinship, q; P.O. Box 22264, Owensboro, KY 42304; (270) 686-8401; www.glenmarysisters.org; Glenmary Sisters.

Knights of St. John International, q; 89 South Pine Ave., Albany, NY 12208; (518) 453-5675; www.members.tripod.com/ksji/knights/ksji.html.

Law Briefs, m; 3211 Fourth St. NE, Washington DC 20017; (202) 541-3300; Office of General Counsel, USCCB.

Lay Witness, m; 827 North Fourth St., Steubenville, OH, 43952; (740) 283-2484; www.cuf.org; Catholics United for the Faith.

Leaflet Missal, 16565 South State St., S. Holland, IL 60473; (708) 331-5485; www.leafletmissal.com.

Leaves, bm; P.O. Box 87, Dearborn, MI 48121-0087; (313) 561-2330; www.rc.net/detroit/marianhill/leaves.htm; Marianhill Mission Society.

Liguorian, m; 1 Liguori Dr., Liguori, MO 63057; (636) 464-2500; www.liguori.org; Redemptorists.

Linacre Quarterly; P.O. Box 757, Pewaukee, WI 53072; (262) 523-6201; www.cathmed.org; Catholic Medical Association (National Federation of Catholic Physicians Guilds).

Liturgia y Cancion (Spanish and English), q; 5536 NE Hassalo, Portland, OR 97213; (800) 548-8749; Oregon Catholic Press.

Liturgy Planner, The, semi-annual; P.O. Box 13071, Portland, OR 97213; (503) 331-2965.

Living City, m; P.O. Box 837, Bronx, NY 10465; (718) 828-2932; www.rc.net/focolare.org; Focolare Movement.

Living Faith: Daily Catholic Devotions, q; 1564 Fencorp Dr., Fenton, MO 63026; (636) 305-9777; www.livingfaith.com.

Living Light, The, q; 3211 Fourth St. NE, Washington, DC 20017; (202) 541-3453; www.usccb.org/education/catechetics/livinglt.htm; Department of Education, USCCB.

Magnificat, m.; Dunwoodie, 201 Seminary Ave., Yonkers, NY 10704; (914) 377-8513; www.magnificat.net.

Marian Helper, q.; Eden Hill, Stockbridge, MA 01263; (413) 298-3691; www.marian.org.

Marriage, bm; 955 Lake Dr., St. Paul, MN 55120; (651) 454-7947; www.marriagemagazine; International Marriage Encounter.

Mary's Shrine, 2 times a year; 400 Michigan Ave. NE, Washington, DC 20017-1566; (202) 526-8300; www.nationalshrine.com; Basilica of National Shrine of the Immaculate Conception.

Maryknoll, m; Maryknoll, NY 10545-0308; (914) 941-7590; www.maryknoll.org; Catholic Foreign Mission Society.

Matrimony, q; 215 Santa Rosa Pl., Santa Barbara, CA 93109; (805) 965-9541; Worldwide Marriage Encounter.

Medical Mission News, q; 10 W. 17th St., New York, NY 10011; (212) 242-7757; www.cmmb.org; Catholic Medical Mission Board, Inc.

Medjugorje Magazine, q; 317 W. Ogden Ave., Westmont, IL 60559; (630) 968-4684; www.medjugor.com.

Migration World, 5 times a year; 209 Flagg Pl., Staten Island, NY 10304; (718) 351-8800; www.cmsny.org; Center for Migration Studies.

Ministry & Liturgy, m.; 160 E. Virginia St., #290, San Jose, CA 95112; (408) 286-8505; wwwrpinet.com.

Miraculous Medal, q; 475 E. Chelten Ave., Philadelphia, PA 19144; (215) 848-1010; www.cmphila.org/camm; Central Association of the Miraculous Medal.

Mission, q; 1663 Bristol Pike, Bensalem, PA 19020-8502; (215) 244-9997; www.katharinedrexel.org; Sisters of the Blessed Sacrament.

MISSION Magazine, q; 366 Fifth Ave., New York, NY 10001; (212) 563-8700; www.propfaith.org; Society for Propagation of the Faith.

Mission, The, q; 90 Cherry Lane, Hicksville, NY 11801-6299; (516) 733-7042; www.cc-li.org; Catholic Charities, Diocese of Rockville Center.

Mission Helper, The, q; 1001 W. Joppa Rd., Baltimore, MD 21204-3787; (410) 823-8585; Mission Helpers of the Sacred Heart.

Missionhurst, bm; 4651 N. 25th St., Arlington, VA 22207; (703) 528-3804; www.missionhurst.org.

Modern Schoolman, The, q; St. Louis University, P.O. Box 56907, St. Louis, MO 63156; (314) 997-3149; St. Louis University Philosophy Department.

Momento Catolico, El; 205 W. Monroe St., Chicago, IL, 60606; (312) 236-7782; www.hmrc.claretianpubs.org.

Momentum, q; Suite 100, 1077 30th St. NW, Washington, DC 20007-3852; (202) 337-6232; www.ncea.org; National Catholic Educational Association.

Mountain Spirit, The, bm; 322 Crab Orchard Rd., Lancaster, KY 40446; (606) 792-3051; www.chrisapp.org; Christian Appalachian Project.

My Daily Visitor, bm; 200 Noll Plaza, Huntington, IN 46750; (219) 356-8400; www.osv.com; Our Sunday Visitor, Inc.

My Friend, 10 times a year; 50 St. Paul's Ave., Jamaica Plain, Boston, MA 02130; (617) 522-8911; www.pauline.org; for children, ages 6-12.

National Apostolate for Inclusion Ministry, q; P.O. Box 218, Riverdale, MD, 20738; (301) 699-9500; www.nafim.org.

National Catholic Forester, q; 320 S. School

St., Mt. Prospect, IL 60056; (847) 342-4500.
National Catholic Rural Life, bi-annual; 4625 Beaver Ave., Des Moines, IA 50310; (515) 270-2634; www.ncrlc.com.
NCSC Resource, 1275 K St. NW, Suite 980, Washington, DC 20005-4006; (202) 289-1093; www.catholicstewardship.org.
NETWORK Connection, bm; 801 Pennsylvania Ave. SE, Washington, DC 20003; (202) 547-5556; www.networklobby.org; Network.
New Oxford Review, 10 issues a year; 1069 Kains Ave., Berkeley, CA 94706; (510) 526-5374; www.newoxfordreview.org.
Notebook, The, q; CMICA-USA, 3049 4 St. NE, Washington, DC 20017; (202) 269-6672; www.paxromana.org; Catholic Movement for Intellectual and Cultural Affairs.
Notre Dame Magazine, q; Notre Dame University, Notre Dame, IN 46556; (219) 631-5335; www.nd.edu/~mdmag.
Nova-Voice of Ministry, bm; P.O. Box 432, Milwaukee, WI 53201; (800) 876-4574; www.execpc.com/~lpi; Liturgical Publications.

Old Testament Abstracts, 3 times a year; 294 Leahy Hall, Catholic University of America, Washington, DC 20064; (202) 319-5519.
Origins, 48 times a year; 3211 Fourth St. NE, Washington, DC 20017; (202) 541-3284; documentary service.
Ozanam News, The, twice a year; 58 Progress Parkway, St. Louis, MO 63043-3706; (314) 576-3993; www.svduscouncil.org; Society of St. Vincent de Paul.

Palabra Entre Nosotros, La, bm; 9639 Dr. Perry Rd., Unit 126N, Jamesville, MD, 21754; (301) 831-1262; www.wau.org.
Parish Liturgy, q; 16565 S. State St., S. Holland, IL 60473; (708) 331-5485; www.parishliturgy.com.
Passionists' Compassion, The, q; 526 Monastery Pl., Union City, NJ 07087; (201) 864-0018; www.cptryon.org.
Pastoral Life, m; Box 595, Canfield, OH 44406; (216) 533-5503; www.albahouse.org; Society of St. Paul.
Pastoral Music, bm; 225 Sheridan St. NW, Washington, DC 20011-1452; (202) 723-5800; www.npm.org; National Association of Pastoral Musicians.
Philosophy Today, q; De Paul University, 2219 N. Kenmore Ave., Chicago, IL 60614-3504; (773) 325-7267; Philosophy Department.
PIME World, m (except July-Aug.); 17330 Quincy St., Detroit, MI 48221; (313) 342-4066; www.pimeysa.org; PIME Missionaries.
Pope Speaks, The: Church Documents Bimonthly; 200 Noll Plaza, Huntington, IN 46750; (219) 356-8400; www.osv.com; Our Sunday Visitor, Inc.
Poverello, The, 10 times a year; 6832 Convent Blvd., Sylvania, OH 43560; (419) 824-3627; www.sistersosf; Sisters of St. Francis of Sylvania.
Prayers for Worship, q; P.O. Box 432, Milwaukee, WI 53201; (800) 876-4574; www.execpc.com/~lpi.
Priest, The, m; 200 Noll Plaza, Huntington, IN 46750; (219) 356-8400; www.osv.com; Our Sunday Visitor, Inc.

Proceedings, a; Fordham University, Adm. Bldg., Bronx, NY 10458; (718) 817-4081; www.acpamain.org; Journal of the American Catholic Philosophical Association.
Promise, 32 times a year; 330 Progress Rd., Dayton, OH, 45449; (513) 847-5900.

Queen of All Hearts, bm; 26 S. Saxon Ave., Bay Shore, NY 11706; (631) 665-0726; www.montfort missionaries.com; Montfort Missionaries.

Reign of the Sacred Heart, q; 6889 S. Lovers Lane, Hales Corners, WI 53130; (414) 425-3383.
Religion Teacher's Journal, m (Sept.-May); P.O. Box 180, Mystic, CT 06355; (860) 536-2611; www.twentythirdpublications.com.
Religious Life, bm., P.O. Box 41007, Chicago, IL 60641; (773) 267-1195; www.religiouslife.com.
Renascence, q; P.O. Box 1881, Marquette University, Milwaukee, WI 53201-1881; (414) 288-6725.
Report on U.S. Catholic Overseas Mission, bi-annually; 3029 Fourth St. NE, Washington, DC 20017; (202) 832-3112; www.catholicmission.org; United States Catholic Mission Association.
Response: Directory of Volunteer Opportunities, a; 1410 Q St. NW, Washington, DC 20009; (202) 332-6000; www.cnvs.org; Catholic Network of Volunteer Service.
Review for Religious, bm; Room 428, 3601 Lindell Blvd., St. Louis, MO 63108; (314) 977-7363; www.reviewforreligious.org.
Review of Politics, q; Box B, Notre Dame, IN 46556; (219) 631-6623; www.nd.edu/~rop.
Review of Social Economy, q; Marquette University, Milwaukee, WI 53233; (414) 288-5438; Association for Social Economics.
Revista Maryknoll (Spanish-English), m; Maryknoll, NY 10545; (914) 941-7590; Catholic Foreign Mission Society of America.
RITE, 8 times a year; 1800 North Hermitage Ave., Chicago, IL 60622-1101; (773) 486-8970; www.ltp.org.
Roze Maryi (Polish), m; Eden Hill, Stockbridge, MA 01263; (413) 298-3691; www.marian.org; Marian Helpers Center.

Sacred Music, q; 134 Christendom Dr., c/o K. Poterack, Front Royal, VA 22630; (540) 636-2900.
St. Anthony Messenger, m; 28 W. Liberty St., Cincinnati, OH 45210-1298; (513) 241-5615; www.americancatholic.org; Franciscan Friars.
St. Augustine Catholic, bm (Sept-May); P.O. Box 24000, Jacksonville, FL 32241-4000; (904) 262-3200; www.staugcatholic.org; St. Augustine diocese.
St. Joseph's Messenger and Advocate of the Blind, bi-annual; St. Joseph Home, 537 Pavonia Ave., Jersey City, NJ 07303; (201) 798-4141.
St. Paul's Family Magazine, q; 14780 W. 159th St., Olathe, KS 66062; (913) 780-0405.
Salesian Directory, q; 148 Main St., P.O. Box 639, New Rochelle, NY 10802; (914) 636-4225; Salesians of Don Bosco.
Salesian Missions of St. John Bosco, q; 2 Lefevre Lane, New Rochelle, NY 10801-5710; (914) 633-8344; www.salesianmissions.org; Salesians of Don Bosco.
SALT/Sisters of Charity, BVM, q; 1100 Carmel Dr., Dubuque, IA 52001; (319) 588-2351; www.bvmcong.org.

Scalabrinians, q; 209 Flagg Pl., Staten Island, NY 10304; (718) 351-0257.

School Guide, a; 210 North Ave., New Rochelle, NY 10801; (914) 632-7771; www.schoolguides.com.

SCN Journey, bm; SCN Office of Communications, P.O. Box 9, Nazareth, KY 40048; (502) 348-1564; www.scnazarethky.org; Sisters of Charity of Nazareth.

Seeds, 32 times a year; 330 Progress Rd., Dayton, OH 45449; (513) 847-5900.

Serenity, q; 601 Maiden Choice Lane, Baltimore, MD 21228; (410) 744-9367; Little Sisters of the Poor.

Serran, The, bm; 65 E. Wacker Pl., #802, Chicago, IL 60601-7203; (312) 201-6549; www.serraus.org; Serra International.

Share Magazine, q; 10 W. 71st St., New York, NY 10023; (212) 877-3041; Catholic Daughters of the Americas.

Share the Word, bm; 3031 Fourth St. NE, Washington, DC 20017-1102; (202) 832-5022; www.sharetheword.net; Paulist Catholic Evangelization Association.

Silent Advocate, q; St. Rita School for the Deaf, 1720 Glendale-Milford Rd., Cincinnati, OH 45215; (513) 771-7600; www.srsdeaf.org.

Sisters Today, bm; Liturgical Press, St. John's University, Collegeville, MN 56321; (612) 363-2213; www.littpress.org.

Social Justice Review, bm; 3835 Westminster Pl., St. Louis, MO 63108-3409; (314) 371-1653; www.socialjusticereview.com; Catholic Central Union of America.

SOUL Magazine, bm; P.O. Box 976, Washington, NJ 07882; (908) 213-2223; www.bluearmy.com; The Blue Army of Our Lady of Fatima, USA, Inc.

Spirit, w; 1884 Randolph Ave., St. Paul, MN 55105; (612) 690-7012; www.goodgroundpress.com; for teens.

Spirit, bi-annually; Seton Hall University, South Orange, NJ 07079; (201) 761-9000.

Spirit & Life, bm; 800 N. Country Club Rd., Tucson, AZ 85716; (520) 325-6401; www.benedictine sisters.org; Benedictine Srs. of Perpetual Adoration.

Spiritual Life, q; 2131 Lincoln Rd. NE, Washington, DC 20002; (800) 832-8489; Discalced Carmelite Friars.

Star, 10 times a year; 22 W. Kiowa, Colorado Springs, CO 80903.

Studies in the Spirituality of Jesuits, 5 times a year; 3601 Lindell Blvd., St. Louis, MO 63108; (314) 977-7257.

Sunday by Sunday, w; 1884 Randolph Ave., St. Paul, MN 55105; (651) 690-7012; www.good groundpress.com.

Sword Magazine, 2 times a year; 2097 Town Hall Terrace, #3, Grand Island, NY 14072-1737; (716) 773-0992; Carmelite Fathers.

Theological Studies, q; Marquette University, 100 Coughlin Hall, Milwaukee, WI 53201-1881; (414) 288-3164; www.ts.mu.edu.

Theology Digest, q; P.O. Box 56907, St. Louis, MO 63156-0907; (314) 977-3410; St. Louis University.

This Rock Magazine, 10 times a year; 2020 Gillespie Way, El Cajon, CA 92020; (619) 387-7200; www.catholic.com.

Thomist, The, q; 487 Michigan Ave. NE, Washington, DC 20017; (202) 529-5300; Dominican Fathers.

Today's Catholic Teacher, m (Sept.-April); 2621 Dryden Rd., Dayton, OH 45439; (937) 293-1415; www.catholicteacher.com.

Today's Liturgy, q; 5536 NE Hassalo, Portland, OR 97213; (800) 548-8749.

Today's Parish, m (Sept.-May); P.O. Box 180, Mystic, CT 06355; (800) 321-0411; www.twentythird publications.com

Together in the Word, bi-annual; Box 577, Techny, IL 60082-0577; (708) 272-2700; www.divine word.org; Chicago province, Society of Divine Word.

The Tower, w; The Catholic University of America, University Center, W. Michigan Ave., Ste. 400 A, Washington, DC 20064; (202) 319-5778.

Tracings, q; Gamelin St., Holyoke, MA 01040; (413) 536-7511; www.sisofprov.org; Sisters of Providence.

Turnaround, The, five times a year; Cardinal Newman Society, 207 Park Ave., Ste. B-2, Falls Church, VA 22046; (703) 536-9585; www.rc.net/cardinalnewman/.

TV Prayer Guide, 19 Second Ave., P.O. Box 440, Pelham, NY 10803-0440; (914) 738-3344; www.the sundaymass.org.

Ultreya Magazine, bm; 4500 W. Davis St., P.O. Box 210226, Dallas, TX 75211; (214) 339-6321; Cursillo Movement.

L'Union (French and English), q; P.O. Box F, Woonsocket, RI 02895; (401) 769-0520.

Universitas, q; 221 N. Grand, Room 39, St. Louis, MO 63103; (314) 977-2537; www.slu.edu; St. Louis University.

U.S. Catholic, m; 205 W. Monroe St., Chicago, IL 60606; (312)-236-7782; www.uscatholic.org; Claretians.

Venture, 32 times during school year; 330 Progress Rd., Dayton, OH 45449; (513) 847-5900; intermediate grades.

Vida Catolica, La, m.; 40 Green St., Lynn, MA 01902; (781) 586-0197 www.la-vida.org/catolica; Boston archdiocese Hispanic community.

Vincentian Heritage, twice a year; 2233 N. Kenmore Ave., Chicago, IL 60614; (773) 325-7348; www.depaul.edu/~vstudies.

Vision, a, 205 W. Monroe St., Chicago, IL 60606; (312) 236-7782; www.visionguide.org; Claretian Publications in conjunction with National Religious Vocation Conference.

Vision, 3 times a year; 7202 Buchanan St., Landover Hills, MD 20784; (301) 577-1684; www.ncod.org; National Catholic Office for the Deaf.

Vision (Spanish-English), P.O. Box 28185, San Antonio, TX 78228; (210) 732-2156; www.mac csa.org; Mexican American Cultural Center.

Visions, 32 times during school year; 330 Progress Rd., Dayton, OH 45449; (513) 847-5900; for students in grades 7 to 9.

Vocations and Prayer, q; 6635 Tobias Ave., Van Nuys, CA 91405; (818) 782-1765; www.rcj.org; Rogationist Fathers.

Waif's Messenger, q; 1140 W. Jackson Blvd., Chicago, IL 60607; (312) 738-7565; Mission of Our Lady of Mercy.

Way of St. Francis, bm; 1500 34th Ave., Oakland,

CA 94601; (916) 443-5717; www.sbfranciscans.org; Franciscan Friars of California, Inc.

Wheeling Jesuit University Chronicle, 3 times a year; 316 Washington Ave., Wheeling, WV 26003; (304) 243-2295.

Word Among Us, The, m; 9639 Dr. Perry Rd., No. 126N, Jamesville, MD 21754; (301) 831-1262; www.wau.org.

Word and Witness, P.O. Box 432, Wisconsin, WI, 53201-0432; (800) 876-4574; www.execpc.com/~lpi.

World Lithuanian Catholic Directory, P.O. Box 1025, Humarock , MA 02407; (781) 834-4079.

Worship, bm; St. John's Abbey, Collegeville, MN 56321; (612) 363-3883.

YOU! Magazine, 10 times a year; 29963 Mulholland Highway, Agoura Hills, CA 91301; (818) 991-1813; www.youmagazine.com; Catholic youth magazine.

Newsletters

ACT, 10 times a year; Box 925, Evansville, IN 47706; (812) 962-5508; www.cfm.org; Christian Family Movement.

Action News, q; Pro-Life Action League, 6160 N. Cicero Ave., Chicago, IL 60646; (773) 777-2900; www.prolifeaction.org.

Annual Report, The, 2021 H St. NW, Washington, DC 20006; (202) 331-8542; Black and Indian Mission Office.

Archdiocesan Bulletin, bm; 827 N. Franklin St., Philadelphia, PA 19123; (215) 627-0143; Philadelphia archeparchy.

At Home with Our Faith, 10 times a year; 205 W. Monroe St., Chicago, IL 60606; (312) 236-7782.

Baraga Bulletin, The, q; 347 Rock St., Marquette, MI 49855; (906) 227-9117.

Benedictine Orient, twice a year; 2400 Maple Ave., Lisle, IL 60532; (630) 968-4264.

Brothers' Voice, 1337 W. Ohio St., Chicago, IL 60622-6490; (312) 829-8525.

Campaign Update, bm; 1513 Sixteenth St. NW, Ste. 400, Washington, DC 20036; (202) 833-4999; www.cathcamp.org; Catholic Campaign for America.

Capuchin Chronicle, q.; P.O. Box 15099, Pittsburgh, PA 15237-0099; (412) 367-2222; www.capuchin.org.

CARA Report, The, bm; Georgetown University, Washington, DC 20057-1203; (202) 687-8080; www.cara.georgetown.edu; Center for Applied Research in the Apostolate.

Caring Community, The, m; 115 E. Armour Blvd., Kansas City, MO 64111; (816) 531-0538; www.ncrpub.com.

Catalyst, 10 times a year; 450 Seventh Ave., New York, NY, 10123; (212) 371-3191; www.catholicleague.org; Catholic League for Civil and Religious Rights.

Catechist's Connection, The, 10 times a year; 115 E. Armour Blvd., Kansas City, MO 64111; (816) 531-0538; www.ncrpub.com.

Catholic Communicator, The, q; 120 East Colonial Hgwy., Hamilton, VA 20158-9012; (540) 338-2700; Catholic Distance University Newsletter.

Catholic Trends, bw; 3211 Fourth St. NE, Washington, DC 20017; (202) 541-3287; Catholic News Service.

Catholic Update, m; 28 W. Liberty St., Cincinnati, OH 45210; (513) 241-5615; www.americancatholic.org.

CCHD News, q; 3211 Fourth St. NE, Washington, DC 20017-1194; (202) 541-3210; www.usccb.org/cchd; Catholic Campaign for Human Development.

C.F.C. Newsletter, 5 times a year; 33 Pryer Terr., New Rochelle, NY 10804; (914) 636-6194; Christian Brothers.

Christ the King Seminary Newsletter, 3 times a year; 711 Knox Rd., Box 607, E. Aurora, NY 14052; (716) 652-8900.

Christian Response Newsletter, P.O. Box 125, Staples, MN 56479-0125; (218) 894-1165.

Christopher News Notes, 10 times a year; 12 E. 48th St., New York, NY 10017; (212) 759-4050; www.christophers.org; The Christophers.

Clarion, The, 5 times a year; Box 159, Alfred, ME 04002-0159; (207) 324-0067; Brothers of Christian Instruction.

CMSM Bulletin, m; 8808 Cameron St., Silver Spring, MD 20910; (301) 588-4030; www.cmsm.org.

Comboni Mission Newsletter, q; 8108 Beechmont Ave., Cincinnati, OH 45255-3194; (513) 474-4997; www.combonimissionaries.org.

Commentary, bm; 1119 K St., Second Floor, Sacramento, CA 95814; (916) 443-4851.

Context, 22 issues a year; 205 W. Monroe St., Chicago, IL 60606; (312) 236-7782; www.contextonline.org.

CPN Newsletter, 8108 Beechmont Ave., Cincinnati, OH, 45255-3194; (513) 474-4997; www.combonimissionaries.org.

Cross and Feathers (Tekakwitha Conference Newsletter), q; P.O. Box 6768, Great Falls, MT 59406; (406) 727-0417.

Crossroads, 8 times a year; 1118 Pendleton St., #300, Cincinnati, OH 45210; (888) 714-6631; www.ccmanet.org; Catholic Campus Ministry Association.

CRUX of the News, w; P.O. Box 758, Latham, NY 12110; (518) 783-0058.

CUF Links, q.; 827 North Fourth St., Steubenville, OH 43952; (740) 283-2484; www.cuf.org.

Cycles of Faith, P.O. Box 432, Milwaukee, WI 53201-0432; (800) 876-4574; www.execpcl.com/~lpi.

Damien-Dutton Call, q; 616 Bedford Ave., Bellmore, NY 11710.

Dimensions, m; 86 Front St., Hempstead, NY 11550; (516) 481-6000; www.amm.org/ncdc.htm; National Catholic Development Conference.

Diocesan Dialogue, two time a year; 16565 South State St., South Holland, IL, 60473; (708) 331-5485; www.acpress.org.

Diocesan Newsletter, The, m; P.O. Box 2147, Harlingen, TX 78551; (956) 421-4111; www.cdob.org; Brownsville diocese.

Environment and Art Letter, m; 1800 N. Hermitage Ave., Chicago, IL 60622-1101; (773) 486-8970.

Envisioning, 555 Albany Ave., Amityville, NY 11701; (631) 842-6030; www.molloy.edu/amityop/; Sisters of St. Dominic.

Ethics and Medics, m; 159 Washington St., Boston, MA 02135; (617) 787-1900; www.ncbcenter.org.

Eucharistic Minister, m; 115 E. Armour, P.O. Box 419493, Kansas City, MO 64141; (816) 531-0538; www.ncrpub.com.

Every Day Catholic, m.; 28 W. Liberty St., Cincinnati, OH 45210; (513) 241-5615; www.everyday catholic.org.

Explorations, q; American Interfaith Institute, 321 Chestnut St., Philadelphia, PA, 19106; (215) 238-5345.

Family Connection, The, bm; 3753 MacBeth Dr., San Jose, CA 95127; (408) 258-8534.

Father Flood, q; P.O. Box 432, Milwaukee, WI 53201; (800) 876-4574; www.execpc.com/~lpi.

Fellowship of Catholic Scholars Newsletter Quarterly, De Sales Univ., 2755 Station Ave., Center Valley, PA 18034; (219) 631-5825; www.4.allencoll.edu/~philtheo/fcs/quarterly.html.

Fonda Tekakwitha News, P.O. Box 627, Fonda, NY 12068; (518) 853-3636.

Food for the Poor, 3 times a year; 550 SW 12th Ave., Deerfield Beach, FL 33442; (954) 427-2222; www.foodforthepoor.org.

Foundations Newsletter for Newly Married Couples, bm; P.O. Box 1632, Portland, ME, 04104-1632; (207) 775-4757.

Franciscan Reporter, a; 3140 Meramec St., St. Louis, MO 63118-4399; (314) 353-3132; www.thefriars.org; Franciscan Friars of Sacred Heart Province.

Franciscan World Care, q; P.O. Box 29034, Washington, DC 20017; (202) 832-1762; Franciscan Mission Service.

Frontline Report, bm; 23 Bliss Ave., Tenafly, NJ 07670; (201) 567-0450; www.smafathers.org; Society of African Missions.

Graymoor Today, m; Graymoor, Garrison, NY 10524; (845) 424-3671; www.atonementfriars.org.

Guadalupe Missioners Newsletter, m; 4714 W. 8th St., Los Angeles, CA 90005; (213) 937-2780.

Happiness, q; 567 Salem End Rd., Framingham, MA 01702; (508) 879-2541; www.sonsofmary.com; Sons of Mary, Health of the Sick.

Harmony, 3 times a year; 800 N. Country Club Rd., Tucson, AZ 85716; (520) 325-6401; Benedictine Srs. of Perpetual Adoration.

Healing & Hope, 9480 North De Mazenod Dr., Belleville, IL 62223; (618) 398-4848; www.snows.org.

Heart Beats, 169 Cummins Hwy., Roslindale, MA 02131; (617) 325-3322.

HLI Reports, m; 4 Family Life, Front Royal, VA 22630; Human Life International.

HN People, bm; 127 W. 31st St., New York, NY 10001-3403; (212) 594-6224; www.friars.com; Franciscans of Holy Name Province.

HNP Today, w; 127 W. 31st St., New York, NY 10011-3403; (212) 594-6224; www.friars.com; Franciscans of Holy Name Province.

ICSC Commitment, 1275 K St. NW, Suite 980, Washington, DC 20005-4006; (202) 289-1093; www.catholicstewardship.org.

Immaculate Heart of Mary Shrine Bulletin, 3 times a year; Mountain View Road, P.O. Box 976, Washington, NJ 07882; (908) 689-1700; www.ewtn.com/bluearmy.

Initiatives, bm; P.O. Box 291102, Chicago, IL 60629; (773) 776-9036; www.centerforlaity.org; National Center for the Laity.

Interchange, Assisi Heights, 1001 14 St., NW, #100, Rochester, MN 55901; (507) 529-3523; Rochester Franciscan Sisters,

It's Our World, 4 times during school year; 1720 Massachusetts Ave. NW, Washington, DC 20036; (202) 775-8637; Young Catholics in Mission.

Journey, The, q; 210 W. 31st St., New York, NY 10001-2876; (212) 714-0950; www.capuchin.org; Province of St. Mary of Capuchin Order.

Joyful Noiseletter, The, m; P.O. Box 895, Portage, MI 49081-0895; (616) 324-0990; www.joyful noiseletter.com; Fellowship of Merry Christians.

Knightline, 18 times a year; 1 Columbus Plaza, New Haven, CT 06510-3326; (203) 772-2130; Knights of Columbus Supreme Council.

Laity and Family Life Updates, bm; 7800 Kenrick Rd., St. Louis, MO, 63119; (314) 961-4320.

Land of Cotton, q; 2048 W. Fairview Ave., Montgomery, AL 39196; (205) 265-6791; City of St. Jude.

Law Reports, q; 4455 Woodson Rd., St. Louis, MO 63134; (314) 427-2500; Catholic Health Association.

LCWR Update, m; 8808 Cameron St., Silver Spring, MD 20910; (301) 588-4955; www.lcwr.org; Leadership Conference of Women Religious.

Legatus, m; 30 Frank Lloyd Wright Dr., Ann Arbor, MI 48106; (313) 930-3854.

Let's Talk! (English edition), **Hablemos!** (Spanish edition), bm; 3031 Fourth St. NE, Washington, DC 20017-1102; (202) 832-5022; prison ministries of Paulist National Catholic Evangelization Assn.

Letter to the Seven Churches, bm; 1516 Jerome St., Lansing, MI 48912; (800) 837-2622.

Life at Risk, 10 times a year; 3211 Fourth St. NE, Washington, DC 20017; (202) 541-3070; Pro-Life Activities Committee, USCCB.

Life Insight, m; 3211 Fourth St. NE, Washington, DC 20017; (202) 541-3070; Committee for Pro-Life Activities, USCCB.

Liturgical Images, m; P.O. Box 2225, Hickory, NC 28603; (828) 327-3225.

Loyola World, 22 times a year; 820 North Michigan Ave., Chicago, IL, 60611; (312) 915-6157; www.luc.edu.

Magnificat, three times a year; Star Route 1, Box 226, Eagle Harbor, MI, 49950; (906) 289-4388 (fax); www.societystjohn.com.

Markings, m; 205 W. Monroe St., Chicago, IL 60606; (312) 609-8880.

Maronites Today, m; P.O. Box 1891, Austin, TX 78767-1891; (512) 458-3693; www.eparchyla.org; Eparchy of Our Lady of Los Angeles.

Medical Mission Sisters News, q; 8400 Pine Road, Philadelphia, PA 19111; (215) 742-6100; www.medicalmissionsisters.org.

Men of Malvern, q; Malvern, PA 19355-0315; (610) 644-0400; www.laymensretreat.org.

Messenger of St. Joseph's Union, The, 3 times a year; 108 Bedell St., Staten Island, NY 10309; (718) 984-9296.

Mission Messenger, The, q; P.O. Box 610, Thoreau, NM, 87323; (505) 862-7847; www.sbms.k12.nm.us; St. Bonaventure Indian Mission and School.

Missionaries of Africa Report, q; 1624 21st St. NW, Washington, DC 20009; (202) 232-5154; Society of Missionaries of Africa (White Fathers).

Mission Update, bm; 3029 Fourth St. NE, Washington, DC 20017; (202) 832-3112; www.uscatholic mission.org.

Mountain View, q.; 8501 Bailey Rd., Darien, IL 60561; (630) 969-5050; Lay Carmelite Headquarters.

National Holy Name Newsletter, bm; 1169 Market St., #304, San Francisco, CA 94103-1503; (415) 255-2368; www.members.aol.com/nahns.

NCPD National Update, q; 415 Michigan Ave. NE, #240, Washington, DC 20017; (202) 529-2933; www.ncpd.org; National Catholic Office for Persons with Disabilities.

Neighbors, Committee on Home Missions, q.; 3211 Fourth St. NE, Washington, D.C. 20017; (202) 541-5400; Bishops' Committee on Home Missions.

News and Ideas, q.; 9480 North De Mazenod Dr., Belleville, IL 62223; (618) 398-4848; www.snows.org; Missionary Oblates of Mary Immaculate.

News and Views, q; 3900 Westminster Pl., St. Louis, MO 63108; (314) 533-0320; www.sacredheart program.org; Sacred Heart Program.

Newsletter of the Bureau of Catholic Indian Missions, 10 times a year; 2021 H St. NW, Washington, DC 20006; (202) 331-8542.

Northern Nevada Catholic Newsletter, m; 290 S. Arlington Ave., #200, Reno, NV 89501; (775) 826-1010; Reno diocese.

Nuestra Parroquia (Spanish-English), m; 205 W. Monroe St., Chicago, IL 60606; (312) 236-7782; www.hmrc.claretianpubs.org; Claretians.

Oblate Mission-Friendship Club News, q; 9480 North De Mazenod Dr., Belleville, IL 62223-1160; (618) 398-4848; www.snows.org; Missionary Oblates of Mary Immaculate.

Oblates, bm; 9480 North De Mazenod Dr., Belleville, IL 62223-1160; (618) 398-4848; www.snows.org; Missionary Oblates of Mary Immaculate.

Origins, 48 times a year; 3211 Fourth St. NE, Washington, DC 20017; (202) 541-3284; Catholic News Service.

Overview, m; 205 W. Monroe St., 6th Floor, Chicago, IL 60606; (312) 609-8880; Thomas More Assn.

Pacer, m; P.O. Box 34008, Seattle, WA 98124; (206) 320-2402; Providence Medical Center.

Paulist, Today, q; 997 Macarthur Blvd., Mahwah, NJ 07656; (201) 818-4515; www.paulist.org.

Peace Times, 3-4 times a year; P.O. Box 248, Bellevue, WA 98009-0248; (425) 451-1770.

Pentecost Today, q; P.O. Box 628, Locust Grove, VA 22508-0628; (540) 972-0628; www.nsc-chariscenter.org.

Perspectives, q; 912 Market St., La Crosse, WI 54601; (608) 791-5289; www.fspa.org.

Pilgrim, The, q; 136 Shrine Rd., Auriesville, NY 12016; (518) 853-3033; Shrine of North American Martyrs.

Priests for Life, bm; P.O. Box 141172, Staten Island, NY 10314; (718) 980-4400; www.priestsfor life.org.

Proclaim, 10 times a year; 3211 Fourth St. NE, Washington, DC 20017-1194; (202) 541-3237; www.usccb.org.

Quarterly, The, q; 209 W. Fayette St., Baltimore, MD 21201; (410) 625-2220; www.catholicrelief.org; Catholic Relief Services.

Religious Life, m (bm, May-Aug.); P.O. Box 41007, Chicago, IL 60641; (312) 267-1195; www.ewtn.com/religiouslife; Institute on Religious Life.

RSCJ Newsletter, m; 1235 Otis St. NE, Washington, DC 20017-2516; (202) 526-6258; www.rscj.org; Religious of Sacred Heart.

St. Anthony's Newsletter, m; 103 St. Francis Blvd., Mt. St. Francis, IN 47146; (812) 923-5250; Conventual Franciscans.

St. Joseph's Parish Life Quarterly, q; 1382 Highland Ave., Needham, MA 02192; (617) 444-0245.

Sacred Ground, three times a year; 1 Elmwood Ave., Kansas City, KS 66103-3719; (913) 384-6500; www.cfcusa.org; Christian Foundation for Children.

San Francisco Charismatics, m; 2555 17th Ave., San Francisco, CA 94116; (415) 664-8481; www.sfspirit.com.

SCJ News, 9 times a year; P.O. Box 289, Hales Corners, WI 53130-0289; (414) 427-4266; Sacred Heart Fathers and Brothers.

SCRC Spirit, The, bm; 9795 Cabrini Dr., #105, Burbank, CA, 91504; (818) 771-1361; www.scrc.org.

Spirit & The Bide, The, m; 8300 Morganford Rd., St. Louis, MO 63123; (314) 792-7070; www.stl charismatic.org.

Spiritual Book Associates, 8 times a year; Notre Dame, IN 46556-0428; (219) 287-2838; www.spiritualbookassoc.org.

Squires Newsletter, m; One Columbus Plaza, New Haven, CT 06510-3326; (203) 772-2130; Columbian Squires.

SSpS Mission, q; P.O. Box 6026, Techny, IL 60082-6026; (847) 441-0126; Holy Spirit Missionary Sisters.

Tidings, Washington Theological Union, 3 times a year; 6896 Laurel St. NW, Washington, DC 20012; (202) 726-8800; www.wtu.edu.

Touchstone, q; NFPC Office, 1337 W. Ohio St., Chicago, IL 60622; (312) 226-3334; www.nfpc.org; National Federation of Priests' Councils.

Trinity Missions Report, q; 9001 New Hampshire Ave., Silver Spring, MD 20903; (301) 434-6761.

Triumph of the Past, m.; P.O. Box 29535, Columbus, OH 43229; (614) 261-1300.

Unda USA Newsletter, q; 901 Irving Ave., Dayton, OH 45409-2316; (937) 229-2303; www.unda usa.org.

USCCB Currents, 10 times a year; 3211 Fourth St. NE, Washington, DC 20017.

Vision: National Association of Catholic Chaplains, 10 times a year; P.O. Box 070473, Milwaukee, WI 53207-0473; (414) 483-4898; www.nacc.org.

Voices, 2 times a year; 1625 Rutherford Lane, Bldg. D, Austin, TX 78754-5105; (512) 339-7123; Volunteers for Educational and Social Services.
Voices in Mission and Ministry, q.; 1257 E. Siena Heights Dr., Adrian, MI 49221; (517) 266-3400; www.admc-op.org; Adrian Dominicans.

Woodstock Report, q; Georgetown University, Box 571137, Washington, DC 20057; (202) 687-3532; www.guweb.georgetown.edu/woodstock; Woodstock Theological Center.
Word One, 5 times a year; 205 W. Monroe St., Chicago, IL 60606; (312) 236-7782; www.wordone.org; Claretians.

Xaverian Missions Newsletter, bm; 101 Summer St., Holliston, MA 01746; (508) 429-2144; Xaverian Missionary Fathers.

Your Edmundite Missions Newsletter, bm; 1428 Broad St., Selma, AL 36701; (334) 872-2359; www.edmunditemissions.com; Southern Missions of Society of St. Edmund.
Youth Update, m; 1615 Republic St., Cincinnati, OH 45210; (513) 241-5615; www.american catholic.org.

Zeal Newsletter, 3 times a year; P.O. Box 86, Allegany, NY 14706; (716) 373-1130; Franciscan Sisters of Allegany.

BOOKS

The Catholic Almanac, a; Our Sunday Visitor, Inc., 200 Noll Plaza, Huntington, IN 46750; publisher; editorial offices, 9165 W. Desert Inn Rd., N-202, Las Vegas, NV 89117; (702) 254-2678; www.osv.com. First edition, 1904.
The Official Catholic Directory, a; P.J. Kenedy & Sons in association with R.R. Bowker, a Reed Reference Publishing Company, 121 Chanlon Rd., New Providence, NJ 07974; (847) 966-8278. First edition, 1817.

BOOK CLUBS

Catholic Book Club (1928), 106 W. 56th St., New York, NY 10019; (212) 581-4640; www.america press.org/cbc.htm; sponsors the Campion Award.
Catholic Digest Book Club (1954), 2115 Summit Ave., St. Paul, MN 55105-1081; (651) 962-6748.
Spiritual Book Associates (1934), Ave Maria Press Building, P.O. Box 428, Notre Dame, IN 46556; (219) 287-2838.
Thomas More Book Club (1939), Thomas More Association, 205 W. Monroe St., Sixth Floor, Chicago, IL 60606; (312) 609-8880.

CANADIAN CATHOLIC PUBLICATIONS

(*Principal source*: 2002 Catholic Press Directory.)

Newspapers

B. C. Catholic, The, w; 150 Robson St., Vancouver, BC V6B 2A7; (604) 683-0281; www.rcav.bc.ca.
Casket, The, w; 88 College St., Antigonish, NS B2G 2L7; (902) 863-4370.
Catholic New Times (national), bw; 80 Sackville St., Toronto, ON M5A 3E5; (416) 361-0761; www.catholicnewtimes.org.
Catholic Register, The (national), w; 1155 Younge St., Suite 401, Toronto, ON M4T 1W2; (416) 934-3410; www.catholicregister.org; lay edited.
Catholic Times, 10 times a year; 2005 St. Marc St., Montreal, QC H3H 2G8; (514) 937-2301.
Monitor, The, m; P.O. Box 986, St. John's, NF A1C 5M3; (709) 739-6553; www.delweb.com/rcec.
New Freeman, The, w; 1 Bayard Dr., St. John, NB E2L 3L5; (506) 653-6806.
Prairie Messenger, w; Box 190, Muenster, SK S0K 2Y0; (306) 682-1772; www.stpeters.sk.ca/prairie_messenger.
Restoration, 10 times a year; Madonna House, Combermere, ON K0J 1L0; (613) 756-3713; www.madonnahouse.org.
St. Vladimir's College Gazette, q; Box 789, Roblin, MB, R0L 1P0.
Teviskes Ziburiai (The Lights of the Homeland) (Lithuanian), w; 2185 Stavebank Rd., Mississauga, ON L5C 1T3; (905) 275-4672.
Western Catholic Reporter, w.; 8421 101 Ave. NW, Edmonton, AB T6A 0L1; (780) 465-8030; www.wcr.ab.ca.

Magazines, Other Periodicals

L'Almanach Populaire Catholique, a; P.O. Box 1000, St. Anne de Beaupre, Québec, G0A3C0; (418) 827-4538.
ANNALS of St. Anne de Beaupre, The, m; Box 1000, Ste. Anne de Beaupre, QC G0A 3C0; (418) 827-4538; Basilica of St. Anne.
Apostolat, bm; 8844 Notre-Dame Est, Montréal, QC H1L 3M4; (514) 351-9310; Oblates of Mary Immaculate, CMO (*Centre Missionnaire Oblat*).
Bread of Life, The, bm; 209 MacNab St. N, P.O. Box 395, Hamilton, ON L8N 3H8; (905) 529-4496.
Canadian Catholic Review, The, St. Joseph's College, University of Alberta, Edmonton, AB T6G 2J5; (403) 492-7681.
Canadian League, The, q; 1-160 Murray Park Rd., Winnipeg, Man. R3J 3X5; (204) 885-4856; www.cwl.ca; Catholic Women's League of Canada.
Caravan, q; 90 Parent Ave., Ottawa, ON K1N 7B1; (613) 241-9461; www.cccb.ca; Canadian Conference of Catholic Bishops.
Celebrate! (Novalis), bm; St. Paul University, 223 Main St., Ottawa, ON K1S 1C4; (780) 451-2228.
Chesterton Review, The, q; 1437 College Dr., Saskatoon, SK S7N 0W6; (309) 966-8962.
Companion Magazine, m; 695 Coxwell Ave., Suite 600, Toronto, ON M4C 5R6; (416) 690-5611; www.franciscan.on.ca; Conventual Franciscan Fathers.
Compass — A Jesuit Journal, bm (Jan.-Nov.); Box 400, Stn F, 50 Charles St. East, Toronto, ON M4Y 2L8; (416) 921-0653; www.io.org/ngvanv/compass/com-phome.html.
CRC Bulletin (French-English), q; 219 Argyle Ave., Ottawa, ON K2P 2H4; (613) 236-0824; www.crcn.ca/crcn; Canadian Religious Conference.
L'Église Canadienne (French), 11 times a year; 6255 rue Hutchison, Bureau 103, Montreal, QC H2V 4C7; (514) 278-3020; www.novalis.ca.
Fatima Crusader, q; P.O. Box 602, Fort Erie, ON L2A 4M7; (905) 871-7607; www.fatima.org.
Global Village Voice, q; 10 St. Mary St., Suite 420, Toronto, ON M4Y 1P9; (416) 922-1592; Canadian Organization for Development and Peace.

Kateri (English-French), q; P.O. Box 70, Kahnawake, QC J0L 1B0; (450) 638-1546.

Le Messager de Saint Antoine (French), 10 times a year; Lac-Bouchette, QC G0W 1V0.

Messenger of the Sacred Heart, m; 661 Greenwood Ave., Toronto, ON M4J 4B3; (416) 466-1195; Apostleship of Prayer.

Mission Canada, q; 201-1155 Younge St., Toronto, ON M4T 1W2; (416) 934-3424; www.mission canada.ca.

Missions Étrangères (French), bm; 180 Place Juge-Desnoyers, Laval, QC H7G 1A4; (450) 667-4190; www.smelaval.org.

Nouvel Informateur Catholiqué, Le, semimonthly; 6550 Rte 125, Rawdon, QC J0K 1S0; (450) 834-8503.

Oratory, bm; 3800 Ch. Queen Mary, Montreal, QC H3V 1H6; (514) 733-8211; www.saint-joseph.org.

Our Family, m; P.O. Box 249, Battleford, SK; S0M 0E0; (306) 937-7771; www.ourfamilymagazine.com; Oblates of Mary Immaculate.

Prêtre et Pasteur (French), m; 4450 St. Hubert St., #500, Montreal, QC H2J 2W9; (514) 525-6210.

Prieres Missionaires, m; Missionaires de la Consolata, 2505 Boulevard Gouin ouest, Montréal, QC H3M 1B5; (514) 334-1910; www.consolata.org.

Relations (French), 10 times a year; 25 Rue Jarry Ouest, Montreal, QC H2P 1S6; (514) 387-2541.

Reveil Missionaire, bm; Missionaire de la Consolata, 2505 Boulevard Gouin ouest, Montréal, QC H3M 1B5; (514) 334-1910; www.consolata.org.

La Revue d'Sainte Anne de Beaupre (French), m; P.O. Box 1000, Ste. Anne de Beaupre, Québec G0A 3C0; (418) 827-4538.

Scarboro Missions, 9 times a year; 2685 Kingston Rd., Scarboro, ON M1M 1M4; (416) 261-7135; www.web.net/~sfms.

Spiritan Missionary News, q; 121 Victoria Park Ave., Toronto, ON M4E 3S2; (416) 698-2003; www.spiritans.com.

Unity, q; 308 Young St., Montréal, Québec H3C 2G2; (514) 937-5973.

INTERNATIONAL CATHOLIC PERIODICALS

Principal source: Catholic Almanac survey. Included are English-language Catholic periodicals published outside the U.S.

African Ecclesial Review (AFER), bm; Gaba Publications, P.O. Box 4002, Eldoret, Kenya.

Australasian Catholic Record, q; 99 Albert Rd., Strathfield 2135, New South Wales, Australia.

Christ to the World, 5 times a year; Via di Propaganda 1-C, 00187, Rome, Italy.

Christian Orient, q; P.B. 1 Vadavathoor, Kottayam 686010, Kerala, India.

Doctrine and Life, m; Dominican Publications, 42 Parnell Sq., Dublin 1, Ireland.

Downside Review, q; Downside Abbey, Stratton on the Fosse, Bath, BA3 4RH, England.

East Asian Pastoral Review, q; East Asian Pastoral Institute, P.O. Box 221 U.P. Campus, 1101 Quezon City, Philippines.

Furrow, The, m; St. Patrick's College, Maynooth, Ireland.

Heythrop Journal, q; Heythrop College, Kensington Sq., London W8 5HQ, England (edito-

rial office). Published by Blackwell Publishers, 108 Cowley Rd., Oxford, OX4 1JF, England.

Holy Land Magazine, q; P.O. Box 186, 91001 Jerusalem, Israel. Illustrated.

Inside the Vatican, 10 times a year; Rome office: Via della Mura Aurelio 7c, 00165 Rome, Italy; U.S. office: St. Martin de Porres Community, 3050 Gap Knob Rd., New Hope, KY 40052; (270) 325-5499; www.insidethevatican.com. The only current journal that focuses exclusively on Rome, the impact of the papacy worldwide, and the functioning, travels, and activities of the Holy Father and the Roman Curia.

Irish Biblical Studies, The, q; Union Theological College, 108 Botanic Ave., Belfast BT7 1JT, N. Ireland.

Irish Journal of Sociology, The, a; St. Patrick's College, Maynooth, Ireland.

Irish Theological Quarterly, q; St. Patrick's College, Maynooth, Ireland.

L'Osservatore Romano, w; Vatican City. (See above under U.S. Newspapers.)

Louvain Studies, q; Peeters Publishers, Bondgenotenlaan 153, B-3000, Leuven, Belgium.

Lumen Vitae (French, with English summaries), q; International Center for Studies in Religious Education, 186, rue Washington, B-1050 Brussels, Belgium.

Mediaeval Studies, a; Pontifical Institute of Mediaeval Studies, 59 Queen's Park Crescent East, Toronto, ON M5S 2C4, Canada.

Month, m; 114 Mount St., London W1Y 6AH, England.

Music and Liturgy, bm; The Editor, 33 Brockenhurst Rd., Addiscombe Croydan, Surrey CRO 7DR, England.

New Blackfriars, m; edited by English Dominicans, Blackfriars, Oxford OX1 3LY, England.

Omnis Terra (English Edition), m; Pontifical Missionary Union, Congregation for the Evangelization of Peoples, Via di Propaganda 1/c, 00187 Rome, Italy.

One in Christ, q; Edited at Turvey Abbey, Turvey, Bedfordshire MK43 8DE, England.

Priests & People (formerly **The Clergy Review**), 11 times a year; Blackfriars, Buckingham Rd., Cambridge CB3 0DD, England.

Recusant History, bi-annual; Catholic Record Society, 12 Melbourne Pl., Wolsingham, Durham DL13 3EH, England.

Religious Life Review, bm; Dominican Publications, 42 Parnell Sq., Dublin 1, Ireland.

Scripture in Church, q; Dominican Publications, 42 Parnell Sq., Dublin 1, Ireland.

Southwark Liturgy Bulletin, q; The Editor, 10 Claremont Rd., Maidstone, Kent ME14 5L2, England.

Spearhead, 5 times a year; Gaba Publications, P.O. Box 4002, Eldoret, Kenya.

Spirituality, bm; Dominican Publications, 42 Parnell Sq., Dublin 1, Ireland.

Tablet, The, w; 1 King Street Cloisters, Clifton Walk, London W60QZ, England; 0181-748-8484.

Way, The, q; 114 Mount St., London W1Y6AN, England.

CATHOLIC NEWS AGENCIES

(Sources: International Catholic Union of the Press, Geneva; Catholic Press Association, U.S.)

Argentina: *Agencia Informativa Catolica Argentina* (AICA), av. Rivadavia, 413, 40 Casilla de Correo Central 2886, 1020 Buenos Aires.

Austria: *Katholische Presse-Agentur* (Kathpress), Singerstrasse 7/6/2, 1010 Vienna 1.

Belgium: *Centre d'Information de Presse* (CIP), 35 Chausée de Haecht, 1030 Brussels.

Bolivia: *Agencia Noticias Fides*, ANF, Casilla 5782, La Paz.

ERBOL, Casilla 5946, La Paz.

Chile: *Agencia informativa y de comunicaciones* (AIC Chile), Brasil 94, Santiago.

Croatia: *Christian Information Service*, Marulicev 14, PP 434, 410001 Zagreb.

Germany: *Katholische Nachrichten Agentur* (KNA), Adenauer Allee 134, 5300 Bonn 1.

Greece: *Agence TYPOS,* Rue Acharnon 246, Athens 815.

Hong Kong: *UCA-News*, P.O. Box 69626, Kwun Tong (Hong Kong).

Hungary: *Magyar Kurir*, Milkszath ter 1, 1088, Budapest.

India: *South Asian Religious News* (SAR-News), PB 6236, Mazagaon, Bombay 400 010.

Italy: *Servizio Informazioni Religiosa* (SIR), Via di Porta Cavalleggeri 143, I-00165 Roma.

Centrum Informationis Catolicae (CIC-Roma), via Delmonte de la Farina, 30/4, 00186 Roma.

Peru: ACI-PRENSA, A.P. 040062, Lima.

Switzerland: *Katholische Internationale Presse-Agentur* (KIPA), Case Postale 1054 CH 1701, Fribourg.

Centre International de Reportages et d'Information Culturelle (CIRIC), Chemin Clochetons 8, P.O. Box 1000, Lausanne.

United States of America: *Catholic News Service* (CNS), 3211 Fourth St. NE, Washington, DC 20017; (202) 541-3250; www.catholicnews.com.

U.S. PRESS SERVICES

Catholic News Service (CNS), established in 1920 (NC News Service), provides a worldwide daily news report by satellite throughout the U.S. and Canada and by wire and computer links into several foreign countries, and by mail to other clients, serving Catholic periodicals and broadcasters including Vatican Radio in about 40 countries. CNS also provides feature and photo services and a weekly religious education package, "Faith Alive!" It publishes "Origins," a weekly documentary service, and *Catholic Trends*, a fortnightly newsletter, the weekly *TV and Movie Guide* and *Movie Guide Monthly*. CNS maintains a full-time bureau in Rome. It is a division of the United States Catholic Conference, with offices at 3211 Fourth St. NE, Washington, DC 20017; (202) 541-3250; www.catholicnews.com. The director and editor-in-chief is Thomas N. Lorsung.

Spanish-Language Service: A weekly news summary provided by Catholic News Service, used by a number of Catholic newspapers. Some papers carry features of their own in Spanish.

Religion News Service (RNS) provides coverage of all religions as well as ethics, spirituality and moral issues. Founded in 1934 (as the Religious News Service) by the National Conference of Christian and Jews as an independent agency, RNS became an editorially independent subsidiary of the United Methodist Reporter, an interfaith publishing company, in 1983. It was acquired by Newhouse News Service in 1994. Address: 1101 Connecticut Ave. NW, Suite 350, Washington, DC 20036.

RADIO, TELEVISION, THEATER

(The following listings are as of June 1, 2002; sources, Catholic Almanac *survey, William Ryan, Communications, USCCB. Telephone and web addresses are listed as available.)*

Radio Stations and Networks

Catholic Family Radio (Catholic Radio Network): 8910 University Center Lane, Suite 130, San Diego, CA 92122-1016; (619) 784-6900; www.catholicfamilyradio.com; rapidly expanding network founded by Fr. Joseph Fessio and Nick Healy; launched in 1999.

Vatican Radio: See under Vatican City State.

WEWN Radio Network: Part of the Eternal Word Television Network (EWTN): 5817 Old Leeds Rd., Birmingham, AL 35210; (205) 271-2900; www.ewtn.com; the first 24-hour U.S. Catholic radio network; launched in 1996.

Programs

Catholic Views Broadcasts, Inc.: 10 Audrey Place, Fairfield, NJ 07004; (973) 882-8700. Produces weekly 15-minute program "Views of the News." Also operates Catholic community TV stations in Chicago and Minneapolis.

Christopher Radio Program: 14-minute interview series, "Christopher Closeup," weekly and "Christopher Minutes," daily, on 400 stations. Address: 12 E. 48th St., New York, NY 10017; (212) 759-4050; www.christophers.org.

Father Justin Rosary Hour (Radio): P.O. Box 454, Athol Springs, NY 14010; (716) 627-3861; www.franciszkanie.com/rosary.hour. Founded in 1931. Polish Catechetical Radio Network. Rev. Marion M. Tolczyk, O.F.M. Conv., director.

Journeys Thru Rock (Radio): Produced in cooperation with the Department of Communication, USCCB. A 15-minute weekly program currently employing a youth-oriented music and commentary format (ABC).

Radio Maria (Italian): Italian Catholic radio station founded in 1992, 352 W. 44th St., New York, NY 10036. Rev. Mariano Cisco, C.S., executive director.

Television and Communications Services

Catholic Communication Campaign (CCC): A U.S. Catholic bishops' program that produces, distributes and supports Catholic media projects, including a weekly television talk show, "Personally Speaking," television documentaries and public service messages. Ellen McCloskey, 3211 4th Street NE, Washington, DC 20017; (202) 541-3204; www.usccb.org/ccc.

Catholic Communications Foundation (CCF): A foundation established by the Catholic Fraternal Benefit Societies in 1966 to lend support and assistance to development of the communications apostolate of the Church. The CCF promotes the development of diocesan communications capabilities and funds a scholarship program at the Annual Institute for Religious Communications. CCF officers include Bishop Anthony G. Bosco, chairman of the board; 303 W. Lancaster Ave., PMB 333, Wayne, PA 19087.

Christopher TV Series, "Christopher Closeup": Originated in 1952. Half-hour interviews, weekly, on commercial TV and numerous cable outlets; 12 E. 48th St., New York, NY 10017; (212) 759-4050; www.christophers.org.

Clemons Productions, Inc.: Produces "That's the Spirit," a family show for television; "Thoughts for the Week," on the ABC Satellite Network and "Spirituality for Today" on the internet. Available to dioceses, organizations or channels; P.O. Box 7466, Greenwich, CT 06830; www.spirituality.org.

Eternal Word Television Network (EWTN): 5817 Old Leeds Rd., Irondale, AL 35210; (205) 271-2900; www.ewtn.com. America's largest religious cable network; features 24 hours of spiritual-growth programming for the entire family. Offers documentaries, weekly teaching series and talk shows, including the award-winning "Mother Angelica Live." Also features live Church events from around the world and devotional programs such as "The Holy Rosary." Mother M. Angelica, P.C.P.A., foundress.

Family Theater Productions: Founded by Father Peyton. Videocassettes, films for TV; 7201 Sunset Blvd., Hollywood, CA 90046; (323) 874-6633; www.familytheater.org. Nat. Dir., Rev. Wilfred J. Raymond, C.S.C.

Franciscan Communications: Producer of video and print resources for pastoral ministry; St. Anthony Messenger Press, 28 W. Liberty St., Cincinnati, OH 45210; (513) 241-5615; www.AmericanCatholic.org.

Hispanic Telecommunications Network, Inc. (HTN): Produces "Nuestra Familia," a national weekly Spanish-language TV series; 1405 N. Main, Suite 240, San Antonio, TX 78212.

Mary Productions: Originated in 1950. Offers royalty-free scripts for stage, film, radio and tape production. Audio and video tapes of lives of the saints and historical characters. Traveling theater company; Mary Productions, 212 Oakdale Dr., Tomaso Plaza, Middletown, NJ 07748; (732) 617-8144.

National Interfaith Cable Coalition: A 28 member consortium representing 64 faith groups from Roman Catholic, Jewish, Protestant and Eastern Orthodox traditions; works with faith groups to present programming on the Faith and Values Media; 74 Trinity Place, Suite 1550, New York, NY 10006; (212) 406-4121; www.faithandvalues.com.

Oblate Media and Communication Corporation: Producers, Broadcast syndicators and distributors of Catholic and value-centered video programming; 7315 Manchester Rd., St. Louis, MO 63143.

Passionist Communications, Inc.: Present Sunday Mass on TV seen in U.S. and available to dioceses and channels; publish "TV Prayer Guide," semi-annually; P.O. Box 440, Pelham, NY 10803-0440.

Paulist Media Works: Full service audio production in syndication to dioceses, religious communities and church groups; 3055 4th St. NE, Washington, DC 20017. Pres., Sue Donovan.

Paulist Productions: Producers and distributors of the INSIGHT Film Series (available for TV) and educational film series; 17575 Pacific Coast Hwy., Pacific Palisades, CA 90272; (310) 454-0688; www.paulistproductions.org.

Sacred Heart Program, Inc.: Produces and distributes free of charge the weekly "CONTACT" program in 30-, 15-, and 5-minute formats to more than 300 stations in North America; 3900 Westminster Pl., St. Louis, MO 63108; (341) 533-0320; www.sacred heartprogram.org/www.contactradio.org. Exec. Dir., Gary Kolarcik.

Telecare: Instructional TV operations or broadcasts of Masses have been established in the following archdioceses and dioceses; www.telecaretv.org. Archdioceses are indicated by an asterisk.

Boston,* MA: Rev. Francis McFarland, Director, P.O. Box 9109, Newton, 02160; (617) 965-0050.

Brooklyn, NY: Rev. Msgr. Michael J. Dempsey, Director, 1712 10th Ave., 11215.

Chicago, *IL: Mr. Joseph Loughlin, Director, Radio/TV Office, Archdiocese of Chicago, 155 E. Superior, 60611.

Corpus Christi, TX: Mr. Martin L. Wind, 1200 Lantana St., 78407.

Dallas, TX: Mr. Michael McGee, 3725 Blackburn, P.O. Box 190507, 75219.

Detroit,* MI: Mr. Ned McGrath, Director, 305 Michigan Ave., 48226.

Los Angeles,* CA: Mr. David Moore, 3424 Wilshire Blvd., 90010; (213) 637-7312; www.la-archdiocese.org.

New York,* NY: Mr. Michael Lavery, Director, 215 Seminary Ave., Yonkers, 10704; (914) 968-7800.

Oakland, San Jose, San Francisco,* CA: Shirley Connolly, Director, 324 Middlefield Rd., Menlo Park, 94025; (650) 326-4605 (fax); www.ctnba.org.

Orlando, FL: Rev. Robert Hoeffner. Director, P.O. Box 1800, 32802.

Rockville Centre, NY: Rev. Msgr. Thomas Hartman, Director, 1200 Glen Curtiss Blvd., Uniondale, 11553; (516) 538-4108.

San Bernardino, CA: Caritas Telecommunications, Clare Colella, Director, 1201 E. Highland Ave., 92404; (909) 475-5350; www.sbdiocese.org or www.caritastelecommunications.org. Youngstown, OH: Rev. James Korda, P.O. Box 430, Canfield, 44406.

Unda-USA: A national professional Catholic association for broadcasters and other allied communicators in church ministry; organized in 1972. It succeeded the Catholic Broadcasters Association of America that in 1948 had replaced the Catholic Forum of the Air organized in 1938. It is a member of Unda-International, the international Catholic association for radio and television (Unda is the Latin word for "wave," symbolic of air waves of communication). In addition to providing support and network opportunities in church communications the organization works to encourage the secular media to produce value-oriented programs and stories. Unda-USA sponsors an annual general assembly and presents the Gabriel Awards annually for excellence in broadcasting. It publishes six newsletters for its membership. President, Frank Morock; Unda-USA, 901 Irving Ave., Dayton, OH 45409; (937) 229-2303; www.UNDAUSA.org.

Theater

Catholic Actors' Guild of America, Inc.: Established in 1914 to provide material and spiritual assistance to people in the theater. Has more than 500 members; publishes *The Call Board*; 1501 Broadway, Suite 510, New York, NY 10036; (212) 398-1868 (fax).

FILM

Vatican List of the Greatest Films of the 20th Century

On the occasion of the one-hundredth anniversary of cinema in 1995, the Vatican compiled this list of "great films." The 45 movies are divided into three categories: "Religion," "Values," and "Art." Synopses courtesy of Our Sunday Visitor's Family Guide to Movies and Videos, edited by Henry Herx.

Religion

Andrei Rublev (1969); Babette's Feast (1988); Ben-Hur (1959); The Flowers of St. Francis (1950); Francesco (1989); The Gospel According to St. Matthew (1966); La Passion de Notre Seigneur Jesus-Christ (1905); A Man for All Seasons (1966); The Mission (1986); Monsieur Vincent (1947); Nazarin (1958); Ordet (1954); The Passion of Joan of Arc (1928); The Sacrifice (1986); Thérèse (1986).

Values

Au Revoir les Enfants (1988); The Bicycle Thief (1949); The Burmese Harp (1956) Chariots of Fire (1981); Decalogue (1988); Dersu Uzala (1978); Gandhi (1982); Intolerance (1916); It's a Wonderful Life (1946); On the Waterfront (1954); Open City (1945); Schindler's List (1993); The Seventh Seal (1956); The Tree of Wooden Clogs (1978); Wild Strawberries (1958).

Art

Citizen Kane (1941); 8-1/2 (1963); Fantasia (1940); Grand Illusion (1937); La Strada (1956); The Lavender Hill Mob (1951); The Leopard (1963); Little Women (1933); Metropolis (1926); Modern Times (1936); Napoleon (1927); Nosferatu (1922); Stagecoach (1939); 2001: A Space Odyssey (1968); The Wizard of Oz (1939).

CATHOLIC INTERNET SITES

Remember web site addresses change periodically. Find this list online at www.CatholicAlmanac.com.

Holy See Sites

Vatican: www.vatican.va
L'Osservatore Romano: www.vatican.va/news_services/or/or_eng/index.html
Vatican Radio: www.vatican.va/news_services/radio/index.htm

Catholic Megasites, Directories and Links

A la Padre: http://alapadre.net
Biblical Evidence for Catholicism: http://ic.net/~erasmus/erasmus.htm
Catholic Almanac: www.CatholicAlmanac.com
Catholic Canada: www.catholicanada.com
Catholic Community Forum: www:catholic-forum.com
Catholic Goldmine!: www.catholicgoldmine.com
Catholic Hotlinks: www.cathinsight.com
Catholic Information Center on the Internet: www.catholic.net/
Catholic Information Network: www.cin.org
Catholic Internet Directory: www.catholic-church.org/cid
Catholic Internet Yellow Pages: www.monksofadoration.org/directory.html
Catholic Life: www.diocese.net
Catholic Kiosk: www.aquinas-multimedia.com/arch/index.html
Catholic.Net Periodicals: www.catholic.net/RCC/Periodicals/index.html
Catholic Pages: www.catholic-pages.com
Catholic Press Association: www.catholicpress.org
Catholic Sites in Spanish: http://socrates.barry.edu/lib-poneill/cathspan.htm
Catholic Web: www.catholicweb.com
Catholicity Internet Directory: www.catholicity.com/airport
DioceseNet: www.diocesenet.com/index.html
Catholic Exchange: www.e3mil.com
Ecclesia Web Service for Catholics: www.catholic-church.org/
El Directorio Catolico en Internet: www.iglesia.org/
Our Sunday Visitor: www.OSV.com

Our Sunday Visitor Links Page: www.osvpublishing.com/links/view-links.asp
PetersNet: www.petersnet.net/
RCNet: www.rc.net
St. Jane's: www.stjane.org
The Internet Padre: www.internetpadre.com
Thelogy Library Search Engines: www.shc.edu/theolibrary/engines.htm
Totally Catholic Link Directory: www.tcld.net/

Catholic Internet Service Providers

Catholic Families Network: www.catholicfamilies.com
Catholic Online: www.catholiconline.com
FamiLink (ISP for the family): www.familink.com

Catholic Movements and Organizations

Adoremus: www.adoremus.org
Catholic Charismatic Center: www.garg.com/ccc
Catholic Doctrinal Concordance: www.infpage.com/concordance
Catholic Family and Human Rights Institute: www.c-fam.org/
Catholic Health Association USA: www.chausa.org/CHAHOME.ASP
Catholic League: www.catholicleague.org
CHA Wisconsin: www.execpc.com/~chaw
Focolare Movement: www.rc.net/focolare
Friendship House: www.friendshiphouse.org/
Madonna House: www.madonnahouse.org
Nat'l Bioethics Center: www.ncbcenter.org
Opus Dei: www.opusdei.org
Pax Christi International: www.paxchristi.net/
Pax Christi USA: www.paxchristiusa.org/
Saints Alive: www.ichrusa.com/saintsalive/
Schoenstatt (information): www.catholiclinks.org/schoenstattunitedstates.htm
Seton Home Study School: www.setonhome.org/

Catholic Newspapers and Magazines

Catholic Digest: www.catholicdigest.org
Catholic New York Online: www.cny.org
Catholic Worker: www.catholicworker.org
First Things: www.firstthings.com
Houston Catholic Worker: www.cjd.org
Our Sunday Visitor: www.osv.com
The Tablet, U.K.: www.thetablet.co.uk

The Universe, U.K.: www.totalcatholic.com/
The Wanderer: www.thewandererpress.com
  Religious Orders and Apostolates
Apostolates\Orders: www.catholic-forum.com/
  links/pages/Religious_Orders/
EWTN: www.ewtn.com
RCNet-Apostolates: www.rc.net/org
  Colleges and Universities (Links To)
Colleges: www.shc.edu/theolibrary/edu.htm
Assocation of Catholic Colleges and Universities:
  www.accunet.org/
  Useful and Informative Sites
Mass Times: www.masstimes.org
Mass in Transit: www.massintransit.com
Christworld: www.christworld.com
Catholic Web: www.catholicweb.com
Catholic-Pages: www.catholic-pages.com
Catholic U.S.A.: www.catholic-usa.com
PetersVoice: www.petersvoice.com
Rosary Center: www.rosary-center.org
Daily E-pistle (e-newsletter) Signup Page:

www.catholic-forum.com/e-pistle.html
Grace In Action Stewardship:
  www.GraceInAction.org
What the CHURCH Teaches:
  www.WhatTheCHURCHTeaches.com
  For Kids and Families
Catholic Kids Net: www.catholickidsnet.org/
Global Schoolhouse: www.gsn.org/
My Friend: www.myfriendmagazine.com
Teaching Catholic Kids:
  www.TeachingCatholicKids.com
Apostolate for Family Consecration:
  www.familyland.org
Catholic Family and Human Rights Institute:
  www.c-fam.org
Catholic Fathers: www.dads.org
Catholic Parent Magazine:
  www.CatholicParent.com
CatholiCity Men: www.catholicmen.com/
Natural Family Planning: www.ccli.org
Domestic Church: www.domestic-church.com/

DEVELOPMENTS IN COMMUNICATIONS 2001-2002

The following are significant developments in the field of Catholic Communications in 2001-2002.

"THE CHURCH AND INTERNET" AND "ETHICS IN INTERNET"

On Feb. 28, 2002, the Pontifical Council for Social Communications under Abp. John P. Foley issued two documents encouraging the Church to embrace the technology of the Internet and to help utilize it for the benefit of all humanity.

The two 27-page documents, "Ethics in Internet" and "The Church and Internet," provide assessments of the ethical demands of the Internet and the online pastoral opportunities of the World Wide Web. Russell Shaw, a U.S. journalist who serves as a consultor on the council, headed the drafting process. The following are excerpts from the two documents:

"The Church and Internet"

The Church's interest in the Internet is a particular expression of her longstanding interest in the media of social communication. Seeing the media as an outcome of the historical scientific process by which humankind "advances further and further in the discovery of the resources and values contained in the whole of creation," the Church often has declared her conviction that they are, in the words of the Second Vatican Council, "marvellous technical inventions" that already do much to meet human needs and may yet do even more....

The Church has a two-fold aim in regard to the media. One aspect is to encourage their right development and right use for the sake of human development, justice, and peace — for the upbuilding of society at the local, national, and community levels in light of the common good and in a spirit of solidarity. Considering the great importance of social communications, the Church seeks "honest and respectful dialogue with those responsible for the communications media"—a dialogue that relates primarily to the shaping of media policy....

Since announcing the Good News to people formed by a media culture requires taking carefully into account the special characteristics of the media themselves, the Church now needs to understand the Internet. This is necessary in order to communicate effectively with people—especially young people — who are steeped in the experience of this new technology, and also in order to use it well.

The media offer important benefits and advantages from a religious perspective.... It offers people direct and immediate access to important religious and spiritual resources — great libraries and museums and places of worship, the teaching documents of the Magisterium, the writings of the Fathers and Doctors of the Church and the religious wisdom of the ages. It has a remarkable capacity to overcome distance and isolation, bringing people into contact with like-minded persons of good will who join in virtual communities of faith to encourage and support one another. The Church can perform an important service to Catholics and non-Catholics alike by the selection and transmission of useful data in this medium.

The Internet is relevant to many activities and programs of the Church — evangelization, including both re-evangelization and new evangelization and the traditional missionary work *ad gentes*, catechesis and other kinds of education, news and information, apologetics, governance and administration, and some forms of pastoral counseling and spiritual direction....

Among the specific problems presented by the Internet is the presence of hate sites devoted to defaming and attacking religious and ethnic groups. Some of these target the Catholic Church. Like pornography and violence in the media, Internet hate sites are "reflections of the dark side of a human nature marred by sin." And while respect for free expression may require tolerating even voices of hatred up to a point, industry self-regulation — and, where required, intervention by public authority — should establish and enforce reasonable limits to what can be said.

The proliferation of web sites calling themselves Catholic creates a problem of a different sort. As we have said, church-related groups should be creatively present on the Internet; and well-motivated, well-informed individuals and unofficial groups acting on their own initiative are entitled to be there as well. But it is confusing, to say the least, not to distinguish eccentric doctrinal interpretations, idiosyncratic devotional practices, and ideological advocacy bearing a "Catholic" label from the authentic positions of the Church....

In concluding these reflections, therefore, we offer words of encouragement to several groups in particular — Church leaders, pastoral personnel, educators, parents, and especially young people.

To Church leaders. People in leadership positions in all sectors of the Church need to understand the media, apply this understanding in formulating pastoral plans for social communications together with concrete policies and programs in this area, and make appropriate use of media....

To pastoral personnel. Priests, deacons, religious, and lay pastoral workers should have media education to increase their understanding of the impact of social communications on individuals and society and help them acquire a manner of communicating that speaks to the sensibilities and interests of people in a media culture....

To educators and catechists. The Pastoral Instruction *Communio et Progressio* spoke of the "urgent duty" of Catholic schools to train communicators and recipients of social communications in relevant Christian principles. The same message has been repeated many times. In the age of the Internet, with its enormous outreach and impact, the need is more urgent than ever.

To parents. ... As far as the Internet is concerned, children and young people often are more familiar with it than their parents are, but parents still are seriously obliged to guide and supervise their children in its use If this means learning more about the Internet than they have up to now, that will be all to good.

To children and young people. The Internet is a door opening on a glamorous and exciting world with a powerful formative influence; but not everything on the other side of the door is safe and wholesome and true.... The Internet places in the grasp of young people at an unusually early age an immense capacity for doing good and doing harm, to themselves and others. It can enrich their lives beyond the dreams of earlier generations and empower them to enrich others' lives in turn. It also can plunge them into consumerism, pornographic and violent fantasy, and pathological isolation.

To all persons of good will. Finally, then, we would suggest some virtues that need to be cultivated by everyone who wants to make good use of the Internet; their exercise should be based upon and guided by a realistic appraisal of its contents.

"Ethics in Internet"

Today it takes no great stretch of the imagination to envisage the earth as an interconnected globe humming with electronic transmissions—a chattering planet nestled in the provident silence of space. The ethical question is whether this is contributing to authentic human development and helping individuals and peoples to be true to their transcendent destiny....

The Internet is the latest and in many respects most powerful in a line of media — telegraph, telephone, radio, television—that for many people have progressively eliminated time and space as obstacles to communication during the last century and a half. It has enormous consequences for individuals, nations, and the world.

In this document we wish to set out a Catholic view of the Internet, as a starting point for the Church's participation in dialogue with other sectors of society, especially other religious groups, concerning the development and use of this marvelous technological instrument. The Internet is being put to many good uses now, with the promise of many more, but much harm also can be done by its improper use. Which it will be, good or harm, is largely a matter of choice — a choice to whose making the Church brings two elements of great importance: her commitment to the dignity of the human person and her long tradition of moral wisdom....

Use of the new information technology and the Internet needs to be informed and guided by a resolute commitment to the practice of solidarity in the service of the common good, within and among nations. This technology can be a means for solving human problems, promoting the integral development of persons, creating a world governed by justice and peace and love.... This is an astonishing vision. The Internet can help make it real — for individuals, groups, nations, and the human race—only if it is used in light of clear, sound ethical principles, especially the virtue of solidarity....

The Internet has a number of striking features. It is instantaneous, immediate, worldwide, decentralized, interactive, endlessly expandable in contents and outreach, flexible and adaptable to a remarkable degree. It is egalitarian, in the sense that anyone with the necessary equipment and modest technical skill can be an active presence in cyberspace, declare his or her message to the world, and demand a hearing. It allows individuals to indulge in anonymity, role-playing, and fantasizing and also to enter into community with others and engage in sharing....

A number of concerns about the Internet are implicit in what has been said so far.

One of the most important of these involves what today is called the digital divide — a form of discrimination dividing the rich from the poor, both within and among nations, on the basis of access, or lack of access, to the new information technology. In this sense it is an updated version of an older gap between the "information rich" and "information poor".... We are particularly concerned about the cultural dimensions of what is now taking place.... Cultures have much to learn from one another, and merely imposing the world view, values, and even language of one culture upon another is not dialogue but cultural imperialism. Cultural domination is an especially serious problem when a dominant culture carries false values inimical to the true good of individuals and groups. As matters stand, the Internet, along with the other media of social communication, is transmitting the value-laden message of Western secular culture to people and societies in many cases ill-prepared to evaluate and cope with it....

The question of freedom of expression on the Internet is similarly complex and gives rise to another set of concerns.

We strongly support freedom of expression and the free exchange of ideas. Freedom to seek and know the truth is a fundamental human right, and freedom of expression is a cornerstone of democracy.... In light of these requirements of the common good, we deplore attempts by public authorities to block access to information — on the Internet or in other media of social communication — because they find it threatening or embarrassing to them, to manipulate the public by propaganda and disinformation, or to impede legitimate freedom of expression and opinion. Authoritarian regimes are by far the worst offenders in this regard; but the problem also exists in liberal democracies, where access to media for political expression often depends on wealth, and politicians and their advisors violate truthfulness and fairness by misrepresenting opponents and shrinking issues to sound-bite dimensions . . . The sheer overwhelming quantity of information on the Internet, much of it unevaluated as to accuracy and relevance, is a problem for many. But we also are concerned lest people make use of the medium's technological capacity for customizing information simply to raise electronic barriers against unfamiliar ideas....

Standing alongside issues that have to do with freedom of expression, the integrity and accuracy of news, and the sharing of ideas and information, is another set of concerns generated by libertarianism. The ideology of radical libertarianism is both mistaken and harmful — not least, to legitimate free expression in the service of truth....

It also can help men and women in their age-old search for self-understanding. In every age, including our own, people ask the same fundamental questions: "Who am I? Where have I come from and where am I going? Why is there evil? What is there after this life?" The Church cannot impose answers, but she can—and must—proclaim to the world the answers she has received; and today, as always, she offers the one ultimately satisfying answer to the deepest questions of life—Jesus Christ, who "fully reveals man to himself and brings to light his most high calling". Like today's world itself, the world of media, including the Internet, has been brought by Christ, inchoately yet truly, within the boundaries of the kingdom of God and placed in service to the word of salvation.

MESSAGE OF THE HOLY FATHER FOR THE 36TH WORLD COMMUNICATIONS DAY

On May 12, 2002, Pope John Paul II issued his annual message for the World Communications Day. His theme for 2002 was: "Internet: A New Forum for Proclaiming the Gospel." Following are excerpts from his message:

The Internet is certainly a new "forum" understood in the ancient Roman sense of that public space where politics and business were transacted, where religious duties were fulfilled where much of the social life of the city took place, and where the best and the worst of human nature was on display. It was a crowded and bustling urban space, which both reflected the surrounding culture and created a culture of its own. This is no less true of cyberspace, which is as it were a new frontier opening up at the beginning of this new millennium. Like the new frontiers of other times, this one too is full of the interplay of danger and promise, and not without the sense of adventure which marked other great periods of change. For the Church the new world of cyberspace is a summons to the great adventure of using its potential to proclaim the Gospel message. This challenge is at the heart of what it means at the beginning of the millennium to follow the Lord's command to "put out into the deep": *Duc in altum! (Lk. 5:4)*.

The Church approaches this new medium with realism and confidence. Like other communications media, it is a means, not an end in itself. The Internet can offer magnificent opportunities for evangelization if used with competence and a clear awareness of its strengths and weaknesses. Above all, by providing information and stirring interest it makes possible an initial encounter with the Christian message, especially among the young who increasingly turn to the world of cyberspace as a window on the world....

At a subsequent stage, the Internet can also provide the kind of follow-up which evangelization requires. Especially in an unsupportive culture, Christian living calls for continuing instruction and catechesis, and this is perhaps the area in which the Internet can provide excellent help. There already exist on the Net countless sources of information, documentation and education about the Church, her history and tradition, her doctrine and her engagement in every field in all parts of the world....

There are nevertheless certain necessary, even obvious, questions which arise in using the Internet in the cause of evangelization. The essence of the Internet in fact is that it provides an almost unending flood of information, much of which passes in a moment. In a culture which feeds on the ephemeral there can easily be a risk of believing that it is facts that matter, rather than values. The Internet offers extensive knowledge, but it does not teach values; and when values are disregarded, our very humanity is demeaned and man easily loses sight of his transcendent dignity....

The fact that through the Internet people multiply their contacts in ways hitherto unthinkable opens up wonderful possibilities for spreading the Gospel. But it is also true that electronically mediated relationships can never take the place of the direct human contact required for genuine evangelization....

There is no doubt that the electronic revolution holds out the promise of great positive breakthroughs for the developing world; but there is also the possibility that it will in fact aggravate existing inequalities as the information and communications gap widens. How can we ensure that the information and communications revolution which has the Internet as its prime engine will work in favour of the globalization of human development and solidarity, objectives closely linked to the Church's evangelizing mission?

Finally, in these troubled times, let me ask: how can we ensure that this wondrous instrument first conceived in the context of military operations can now serve the cause of peace? Can it favour that culture of dialogue, participation, solidarity and reconciliation without which peace cannot flourish? The Church believes it can; and to ensure that this is what will happen she is determined to enter this new forum, armed with the Gospel of Christ, the Prince of Peace.

HONORS AND AWARDS

Pontifical Orders

The Pontifical Orders of Knighthood are secular orders of merit whose membership depends directly on the pope.

Supreme Order of Christ (Militia of Our Lord Jesus Christ): The highest of the five pontifical orders of knighthood, the Supreme Order of Christ was approved Mar. 14, 1319, by John XXII as a continuation in Portugal of the suppressed Order of Templars. Members were religious with vows and a rule of life until the order lost its religious character toward the end of the 15th century. Since that time it has existed as an order of merit. Paul VI, in 1966, restricted awards of the order to Christian heads of state.

Order of the Golden Spur (Golden Militia): Although the original founder is not certainly known, this order is one of the oldest knighthoods. Indiscriminate bestowal and inheritance diminished its prestige, however, and in 1841 Gregory XVI replaced it with the Order of St. Sylvester and gave it the title of Golden Militia. In 1905 St. Pius X restored the Order of the Golden Spur in its own right, separating it from the Order of St. Sylvester. Paul VI, in 1966, restricted awards of the order to Christian heads of state.

Order of Pius IX: Founded by Pius IX June 17, 1847, the order is awarded for outstanding services for the Church and society, and may be given to non-Catholics as well as Catholics. The title to nobility formerly attached to membership was abolished by Pius XII in 1939. In 1957 Pius XII instituted the Class of the Grand Collar as the highest category of the order; in 1966, Paul VI restricted this award to heads of state "in solemn circumstances." The other three classes are of Knights of the Grand Cross, Knight Commanders with and without emblem, and Knights. The new class was created to avoid difficulties in presenting papal honors to Christian or non-Christian leaders of high merit.

Order of St. Gregory the Great: First established by Gregory XVI in 1831 to honor citizens of the Papal States, the order is conferred on persons who are distinguished for personal character and reputation, and for notable accomplishment. The order has civil and military divisions, and three classes of knights.

Order of St. Sylvester: Instituted Oct. 31, 1841, by Gregory XVI to absorb the Order of the Golden Spur, this order was divided into two by St. Pius X in 1905, one retaining the name of St. Sylvester and the other assuming the title of Golden Militia. Membership consists of three degrees: Knights of the Grand Cross, Knight Commanders with and without emblem, and Knights.

Papal Medals

Pro Ecclesia et Pontifice: This decoration ("For the Church and the Pontiff") had its origin in 1888 as a token of the golden sacerdotal jubilee of Leo XIII; he bestowed it on those who had assisted in the observance of his jubilee and on persons responsible for the success of the Vatican Exposition. The medal, cruciform in shape, bears the likenesses of Sts. Peter and Paul, the tiara and the papal keys, the words *Pro Ecclesia et Pontifice*, and the name of the present pontiff, all on the same side; it is attached to a ribbon of yellow and white, the papal colors. Originally, the medal was issued in gold, silver or bronze. It is awarded in recognition of service to the Church and the papacy.

Benemerenti: Several medals ("To a well-deserving person") have been conferred by popes for exceptional accomplishment and service. The medals, which are made of gold, silver or bronze, bear the likeness and name of the reigning pope on one side; on the other, a laurel crown and the letter "B." These two medals may be given by the pope to both men and women. Their bestowal does not convey any title or honor of knighthood.

Ecclesiastical Orders

Equestrian Order of the Holy Sepulchre of Jerusalem

The order traces its origin to Godfrey de Bouillon who instituted it in 1099. It took its name from the Basilica of the Holy Sepulchre where its members were knighted. After the fall of the Latin Kingdom of Jerusalem and the consequent departure of the knights from the Holy Land, national divisions were established in various countries.

The order was re-organized by Pius IX in 1847 when he reestablished the Latin Patriarchate of Jerusalem and placed the order under the jurisdiction of its patriarch. In 1888, Leo XIII confirmed permission to admit women — Ladies of the Holy Sepulchre — to all degrees of rank. Pius X reserved the office of grand master to himself in 1907; Pius XII gave the order a cardinal patron in 1940 and, in 1949, transferred the office of grand master from the pope to the cardinal patron. Pope John XXIII approved updated constitutions in 1962; the latest statutes were approved by Paul VI in 1977.

The purposes of the order are strictly religious and charitable. Members are committed to sustain and aid the charitable, cultural and social works of the Catholic Church in the Holy Land, particularly in the Latin Patriarchate of Jerusalem.

The order is composed of knights and ladies grouped in three classes: class of Knights of the Collar and Ladies of the Collar; Class of Knights (in four grades); Class of Ladies (in four grades). Members are appointed by the cardinal grand master according to procedures outlined in the constitution.

Under the present constitution the order is divided into national lieutenancies, largely autonomous, with international headquarters in Rome. Cardinal Carlo Furno is the grand master of the order.

There are nine lieutenancies of the order in the United States and one in Puerto Rico. Vice Governor General: F. Russell Kendall, 309 Knipp Rd., Houston, TX 77024; (713) 468-5602.

Order of Malta

The Sovereign Military Hospitaller Order of St. John of Jerusalem of Rhodes and of Malta traces its origin to a group of men who maintained a Christian hospital in the Holy Land in the 11th century. The group was approved as a religious order — the Hospitallers of St. John — by Paschal II in 1113.

The order, while continuing its service to the poor, principally in hospital work, assumed military duties in the twelfth century and included knights, chaplains and sergeants-at-arms among its members. All the knights were professed monks with the vows of poverty, chastity and obedience. Headquarters were located in the Holy Land until the last decade of the 13th century and on Rhodes after 1308 (whence the title, Knights of Rhodes).

After establishing itself on Rhodes, the order became a sovereign power like the sea republics of Italy and the Hanseatic cities of Germany, flying its own flag, coining its own money, floating its own navy, and maintaining diplomatic relations with many nations.

The order was forced to abandon Rhodes in 1522 after the third siege of the island by the Turks under Sultan Suleyman I. Eight years later, the Knights were given the island of Malta, where they remained as a bastion of Christianity until near the end of the 18th century. Headquarters have been located in Rome since 1834.

The title of Grand Master of the Order, in abeyance for some time, was restored by Leo XIII in 1879. A more precise definition of both the religious and the sovereign status of the order was embodied in a new constitution of 1961 and a code issued in 1966.

The four main classifications of members are: Knights of Justice, who are religious with the vows of poverty, chastity and obedience; Knights of Obedience, who make a solemn promise to strive for Christian perfection; Knights of Honor and Devotion and of Grace and Devotion — all of noble lineage; and Knights of Magistral Grace. There are also chaplains, Dames and Donats of the order.

The order, with six grand priories, three sub-priories and 40 national associations, is devoted to hospital and charitable works of all kinds in some 100 countries.

Under the provisions of international law, the order maintains full diplomatic relations with the Holy See — on which, in its double nature, it depends as a religious Order, but of which, as a sovereign Order of Knighthood, it is independent — and 68 countries throughout the world.

The Grand Master, who is the head of the order, has the title of Most Eminent Highness with the rank of Cardinal. He must be of noble lineage and under solemn vows for a minimum period of 10 years, if under 50.

The present Grand Master is Fra' Andrew Willoughby Ninian Bertie, member of the British aristocracy, who was elected for life Apr. 8, 1988, by the Council of State. His election was approved by the Pope.

On Dec. 6, 1999, John Paul Reiner, an attorney from Manhattan, was elected the new president of the American Association of the Knights of Malta.

The address of headquarters of the order is Via Condotti, 68, Palazzo Malta, 00187 Rome, Italy; (011) 3906-679-8851. U.S. addresses: American Association, 1011 First Ave., New York, NY 10022; Western Association of U.S.A., 465 California St., Suite 524, San Francisco, CA 94104; Federal Association of U.S.A., 1730 M St. NW, Suite 403, Washington, DC 20036; (202) 331-2494; www.smom.org.

Order of St. George

The Sacred Military Constantinian Order of St. George was established by Pope Clement XI in 1718. The purposes of the order are to work for the preaching and defense of the Catholic faith and to promote the spiritual and physical welfare of sick, disabled, homeless and other unfortunate persons. The principal officer is Prince Carlo of Bourbon-Two Sicilies, duke of Calabria. Addresses: Via Sistina 121, 00187 Rome, Italy; Via Duomo 149, 80138 Naples, Italy; Address of American Delegation, 302 Gessner Rd., Houston, TX 77024; (713) 888-0242.

2002 CATHOLIC PRESS ASSOCIATION AWARDS

Catholic Press Association Awards for material published in 2001 were presented at the annual Catholic Press Association Convention in Minneapolis from May 29-31, 2002. Awards included:

Newspapers — General Excellence

National Newspapers: *National Catholic Reporter*, First Place; *National Catholic Register,* Second Place; *The Catholic Register*, Third Place; *Our Sunday Visitor*, Honorable Mention.

Diocesan Newspapers, 40,001+ Circulation: *Western New York Catholic* (Buffalo, NY), First Place; *The Tidings* (Los Angeles, CA), Second Place; *Catholic Standard* (Washington, DC), Third Place; *Fairfield County Catholic* (Bridgeport, CT), Honorable Mention.

Diocesan Newspapers, 17,001-40,000: *The Catholic Universe Bulletin* (Cleveland, OH), First Place; *The Southern Cross* (San Diego, CA), Second Place; *The Catholic Herald* (Milwaukee, WI), Third Place; *North Texas Catholic* (Fort Worth, TX), and *The Catholic Free Press* (Worcester, MA), Honorable Mentions.

Diocesan Newspapers, 1-17,000: *The Catholic Spirit* (Metuchen, NJ), First Place; *Catholic Anchor*

(Anchorage, AK), Second Place; *The Florida Catholic* (Venice, FL), Third Place; *Catholic Sentinel* (Portland, OR) and *Today's Catholic* (Fort Wayne, IN), Honorable Mentions.

Magazines — General Excellence

General Interest: *Faith and Family* (North Haven, CT), First Place; *Catholic Parent* (Huntington, IN), Second Place; *U.S. Catholic* (Chicago, IL), Third Place; *Lay Witness* (Steubenville, OH) and *St. Augustine Catholic* (Jacksonvolle, FL), Honorable Mention.

Mission Magazines: *Mission* (New York, NY), First Place; *EXTENSION Magazine* (Chicago, IL), Second Place; *Columban Mission* (St. Columbans, NE), Third Place; *PIME World* (Detroit, MI), Honorable Mention.

Religious Order: *Roze Maryi* (Stockbridge, MA), First Place; *The Anthonian* (Paterson, NJ), Second Place; *Share Magazine* (New York, NY), Third Place; *Marian Helper* (Stockbridge, MA), Honorable Mention.

Professional/Special Interest: *Church Magazine* (New York, NY), First Place; *Faith Magazine* (Lansing, MI), Second Place; *Celebrate!* (Ottawa, Canada), Third Place; *CUA Magazine* (Washington, DC), *The Priest* (Huntington, IN), and *Today's Catholic Teacher* (Dayton, OH), Honorable Mentions.

Scholarly: *National Catholic Bioethics* Quarterly (Boston, MA), First Place; *Horizons* (Villanova, PA), Second Place; *Crisis* (Washington, D.C.), Third Place.

Prayer and Spirituality: *The Bible Today* (Collegeville, MN), First Place; *Spiritual Life* (Washington, DC), Second Place; *Share the Word* (Washington, DC), Third Place; *Queen of All Hearts* (Bay Shore, NY), Honorable Mention.

Newsletters

General Interest: *Every Day Catholic* (Cincinnati, OH), First Place; *Youth Update* (Cincinnati, OH), Second Place; *Sacred Ground* (Kansas City, KS), Third Place; *Catholic Update* (Cincinnati, OH), Honorable Mention.

Special Interest: *Call to Action*, First Place; *Context* (Chicago, IL), Second Place; *Comboni Mission Newsletter* (Cincinnati, OH), Third Place; *At Home with our Faith* (Chicago, IL), Honorable Mention.

Books — First Place Awards

Popular Presentation of the Catholic Faith: The Crossroad Publishing Co., Miriam Therese Winter, *Out of the Depths.*

Spirituality: **Softcover**: The Liturgical Press, Patricia McCarthy, *The Word of God — The Word of Peace.* **Hardcover**: Orbis Books, Henri Nouwen, *Jesus: A Gospel.*

Theology: Orbis Books, Jon Sobrino, *Christ the Liberator.*

Scripture: Orbis Books, Elisabeth Schussler Fiorenza, *Wisdom Ways.*

Liturgy: The Liturgical Press, Joyce Ann Zimmerman, Thomas A. Greisen, Kathleen Harmon, and Thomas Leclerc, *Living Liturgy.*

Pastoral Ministry: Twenty-Third/Bayard Publ., William J. Bausch, *Brave New Church: From Turmoil to Trust.*

Professional Books: The National Catholic Bioethics Center, Peter J. Cataldo and Albert S. Moraczewski, *Catholic Health Care Ethics: A Manual for Ethics Committees.* **Educational Books**: The Liturgical Press, Ronald D. Witherup, *Biblical Fundamentalism: What Every Catholic Should Know.*

Design and Production: Orbis Books, Henri Nouwen, *Jesus A Gospel.*

Children's Books: St. Anthony Messenger Press, Silvia Gastaldi, Claire Musatti, *People of the Bible.*

First Time Author of a Book: Orbis Books, Jeremy Langford, *God Moments.*

Family Life: Loyola Press, Denise Roy, *My Monastery is a Minivan.*

History/Biography: Orbis Books, Dale T. Irvin and Scott W. Sunquist, *History of the World Christian Movement.*

Gender Issues: The Liturgical Press, Kerrie Hide, *Gifted Origins to Graced Fulfillment.*

Spanish Language Titles: Liturgy Training Publications, Gabe Huck and Cerald T. Chinchar, *Liturgia con Estilo y Gracia.*

Reference: The Liturgical Press, Michael Walsh, *Dictionary of Christian Biography.*

2002 CHRISTOPHER AWARDS

Christopher Awards are given each year to recognize the creative writers, producers and directors who have achieved artistic excellence in films, books and television specials affirming the highest values of the human spirit. The 2002 awards were presented Feb. 28, 2002, in New York.

Books: *Nickel and Dimed* by Barbara Ehrenreich, *An Hour Before Daylight* by Jimmy Carter, *Freedom's Daughters* by Lynne Olson, *Choosing Mercy* by Antoinette Bosco, *Aging with Grace* by David Snowdon, Ph.D., and *John Adams* by David McCullough.

Books for Young People: Preschool: *Kiss Good Night* by Amy Hest, illustrated by Anita Jeram. Ages 6-8: *Beatrice's Goat* by Page McBrier, illustrated by Lori Lohstoeter. Ages 8-10: *Love That Dog* by Sharon Creech. Ages 10-12: *Uncle Daddy* by Ralph Fletcher.

Young Adult: *Soldier X* by Don Wulffson and *Witness* by Karen Hesse.

Television Specials: *The Lost Battalion* (Arts & Entertainment); *Band of Brothers* (HBO); *American Experience* — "Abraham and Mary Lincoln: A House Divided" (PBS/WGBH Boston); *Uprising* (NBC); *Wit* (HBO); *Taking Back Our Town* (Lifetime Television), "Mother Dolores" (ABC NEWS 20/20); *Jazz* (PBS/WGBH Boston).

Films: *A Beautiful Mind* (Imagine Entertainments); *Iris* (BBC, Miramax); *Shrek* (Dream Works, Pacific Data Images); *The Widow of Saint-Pierre* (La Veuve de Saint-Pierre, Cinémaginaire Inc., Epithète Films).

Leadership Award: Mayor Rudolph W. Giuliani.

Special Christopher Award: "ExxonMobil Masterpiece Theatre."

James Keller Award: Jacques d'Amboise, dancer/educator and founder of the National Dance Institute.

Ecumenism and Interreligious Dialogue

ECUMENISM

(Sources: Brother Jeffrey Gros, F.S.C. and Rev. Ronald Roberson, C.S.P., associate directors, Secretariat for Ecumenical and Interreligious Affairs, USCCB.)

The modern ecumenical movement, with roots in nineteenth-century scholars and individuals began its institutional life in 1910 among Protestants and Orthodox and led to formation of the World Council of Churches in 1948, developed outside the mainstream of Catholic interest for many years. It has now become for Catholics as well one of the great religious facts of our time.

The *magna carta* of ecumenism for Catholics is a complex of several documents which include, in the first place, *Unitatis Redintegratio*, the "Decree on Ecumenism," promulgated by the Second Vatican Council Nov. 21, 1964. Other enactments underlying and expanding this decree are *Lumen Gentium* ("Dogmatic Constitution on the Church"), *Orientalium Ecclesiarum* ("Decree on Eastern Catholic Churches"), and *Gaudium et Spes* ("Pastoral Constitution on the Church in the Modern World").

The Holy See has more recently brought together Catholic ecumenical priorities in *Directory for the Application of Principles and Norms on Ecumenism* (1993) and *The Ecumenical Dimension in the Formation of Pastoral Workers* (1998). These, in addition to Pope John Paul II's encyclical letter, *Ut Unum Sint* (1995), provide a guide for Catholic ecumenical initiatives.

VATICAN II DECREE

The following excerpts from *Unitatis Redintegratio* cover the broad theological background and principles and indicate the thrust of the Church's commitment to ecumenism, under the subheads: Elements Common to Christians, Unity Lacking, What the Movement Involves, Primary Duty of Catholics.

Men who believe in Christ and have been properly baptized are brought into a certain, though imperfect, communion with the Catholic Church. Undoubtedly, the differences that exist in varying degrees between them and the Catholic Church — whether in doctrine and sometimes in discipline, or concerning the structure of the Church — do indeed create many and sometimes serious obstacles to full ecclesiastical communion. These the ecumenical movement is striving to overcome (No. 3).

Elements Common to Christians

Moreover some, even very many, of the most significant elements or endowments which together go to build up and give life to the Church herself can exist outside the visible boundaries of the Catholic Church: the written word of God; the life of grace; faith, hope, and charity, along with other interior gifts of the Holy Spirit and visible elements. All of these, which come from Christ and lead back to Him, belong by right to the one Church of Christ (No. 3).

(In a later passage, the decree singled out a number of elements which the Catholic Church and other churches have in common but not in complete agreement: confession of Christ as Lord and God and as mediator between God and man; belief in the Trinity; reverence for Scripture as the revealed word of God; baptism and the Lord's Supper; Christian life and worship; faith in action; concern with moral questions.)

The brethren divided from us also carry out many of the sacred actions of the Christian religion. Undoubtedly, in ways that vary according to the condition of each church or community, these actions can truly engender a life of grace, and can be rightly described as capable of providing access to the community of salvation.

It follows that these separated Churches and Communities, though we believe they suffer from defects already mentioned, have by no means been deprived of significance and importance in the mystery of salvation. For the Spirit of Christ has not refrained from using them as means of salvation which derive their efficacy from the very fullness of grace and truth entrusted to the Catholic Church (No. 3).

Unity Lacking

Nevertheless, our separated brethren, whether considered as individuals or as Communities and Churches, are not blessed with that unity which Jesus Christ wished to bestow on all those whom he has regenerated and vivified into one body and newness of life — that unity which the holy Scriptures and the revered tradition of the Church proclaim. For it is through Christ's Catholic Church alone, which is the all-embracing means of salvation, that the fullness of the means of salvation can be obtained. It was to the apostolic college alone, of which Peter is the head, that we believe our Lord entrusted all the blessings of the New Covenant, in order to establish on earth the one Body of Christ into which all those should be fully incorporated who already belong in any way to God's People (No. 3).

What the Movement Involves

Today, in many parts of the world, under the inspiring grace of the Holy Spirit, multiple efforts are being expended through prayer, word, and action to attain that fullness of unity which Jesus Christ desires. This sacred Synod, therefore, exhorts all the Catholic faithful to recognize the signs of the times and to participate skillfully in the work of ecumenism.

The "ecumenical movement" means those activities and enterprises which, according to various needs of the Church and opportune occasions, are started and organized for the fostering of unity among Christians. These are:

- First, every effort to eliminate words, judgments, and actions which do not respond to the condition of separated brethren with truth and fairness and so make mutual relations between them more difficult.
- Then, "dialogue" between competent experts from different Churches and Communities (scholarly ecumenism).
- In addition, these Communions cooperate more closely in whatever projects a Christian conscience demands for the common good (social ecumenism).
- They also come together for common prayer, where this is permitted (spiritual ecumenism).
- Finally, all are led to examine their own faithfulness to Christ's will for the Church and, wherever necessary, undertake with vigor the task of renewal and reform.

It is evident that the work of preparing and reconciling those individuals who wish for full Catholic communion is of its nature distinct from ecumenical action. But there is no opposition between the two, since both proceed from the wondrous providence of God (No. 4).

Primary Duty of Catholics

In ecumenical work, Catholics must assuredly be concerned for their separated brethren, praying for them, keeping them informed about the Church, making the first approaches toward them. But their primary duty is to make an honest and careful appraisal of whatever needs to be renewed and achieved in the Catholic household itself, in order that its life may bear witness more loyally and luminously to the teachings and ordinances which have been handed down from Christ through the Apostles.

Every Catholic must aim at Christian perfection (cf. Jas. 1:4; Rom. 12:1-2) and, each according to his station, play his part so that the Church may daily be more purified and renewed, against the day when

Christ will present her to himself in all her glory, without spot or wrinkle (cf. Eph. 5:27).

Catholics must joyfully acknowledge and esteem the truly Christian endowments from our common heritage which are to be found among our separated brethren.

Nor should we forget that whatever is wrought by the grace of the Holy Spirit in the hearts of our separated brethren can contribute to our own edification. Whatever is truly Christian never conflicts with the genuine interests of the faith; indeed, it can always result in a more ample realization of the very mystery of Christ and the Church (No. 4).

Participation in Worship

Norms concerning participation by Catholics in the worship of other Christian Churches were sketched in this conciliar decree and elaborated in a number of other documents such as: the Decree on Eastern Catholic Churches, promulgated by the Second Vatican Council in 1964; Interim Guidelines for Prayer in Common, issued June 18, 1965, by the U.S. Bishops' Committee for Ecumenical and Interreligious Affairs; a Directory on Ecumenism, published in 1967, 1970 and 1993 by the Pontifical Council for Promoting Christian Unity; additional communications from the U.S. Bishops' Committee, and numerous sets of guidelines issued locally by and for dioceses throughout the U.S.

The norms encourage common prayer services for Christian unity and other intentions. Beyond that, they draw a distinction between separated churches of the Reformation tradition and of the Anglican Communion, and separated Eastern churches, in view of doctrine and practice the Catholic Church has in common with the separated Eastern churches concerning the apostolic succession of bishops, holy orders, liturgy and other credal matters.

Full participation by Catholics in official Protestant liturgies is prohibited, because it implies profession of the faith expressed in the liturgy. Intercommunion by Catholics at Protestant liturgies is prohibited. Under certain conditions, Protestants may be given Holy Communion in the Catholic Church (see Intercommunion). A Catholic may stand as a witness, but not as a sponsor, in baptism, and as a witness in the marriage of separated Christians. Similarly, a Protestant may stand as a witness, but not as a sponsor, in a Catholic baptism, and as a witness in the marriage of Catholics.

The principal norms regarding liturgical participations with separated Eastern Churches are included under **Eastern Ecumenism**.

DIRECTORY ON ECUMENISM

A Directory for the Application of the Principles and Norms of Ecumenism was approved by Pope John Paul II on Mar. 25, 1993, and published early in June. The Pontifical Council for Promoting Christian Unity said on release of the document that revision of Directories issued in 1967 and 1970 was necessary in view of subsequent developments. These included promulgation of the Code of Canon Law for the Latin Church in 1983 and of the Code of Canons of the Eastern Churches in 1990; publication of the *Catechism of the Catholic Church* in 1992; additional documents

and the results of theological dialogues. In 1998, *The Ecumenical Dimension in the Formation of Pastoral Workers* was published by the Holy See to give practical and detailed guidance in the implementation of Chapter 3 of the *Directory*.

The following excerpts are from the text published in the June 16, 1993, English edition of *L'Osservatore Romano*.

Address and Purpose

"The Directory is addressed to the pastors of the

Catholic Church, but it also concerns all the faithful, who are called to pray and work for the unity of Christians, under the direction of their bishops."

"At the same time, it is hoped that the Directory will also be useful to members of churches and ecclesial communities that are not in full communion with the Catholic Church."

"The new edition of the Directory is meant to be an instrument at the service of the whole Church, and especially of those who are directly engaged in ecumenical activity in the Catholic Church. The Directory intends to motivate, enlighten and guide this activity, and in some particular cases also to give binding directives in accordance with the proper competence of the Pontifical Council for Promoting Christian Unity."

Outline

Principles and norms of the document are covered in five chapters.

"I. The Search for Christian Unity. The ecumeni-cal commitment of the Catholic Church based on the doctrinal principles of the Second Vatican Council.

"II. Organization in the Catholic Church at the Service of Christian Unity. Persons and structures involved in promoting ecumenism at all levels, and the norms that direct their activity.

"III. Ecumenical Formation in the Catholic Church. Categories of people to be formed, those responsible for formation; the aims and methods of formation; its doctrinal and practical aspects.

"IV. Communion in Life and Spiritual Activity among the Baptized. The communion that exists with other Christians on the basis of the sacramental bond of baptism, and the norms for sharing in prayer and other spiritual activities, including, in particular cases, sacramental sharing.

"V. Ecumenical Cooperation, Dialogue and Common Witness. Principles, different forms and norms for cooperation between Christians with a view to dialogue and common witness in the world."

ECUMENICAL AGENCIES

Pontifical Council

The top-level agency for Catholic ecumenical efforts is the Pontifical Council for Promoting Christian Unity (formerly the Secretariat for Promoting Christian Unity), which originated in 1960 as a preparatory commission for the Second Vatican Council. Its purposes are to provide guidance and, where necessary, coordination for ecumenical endeavor by Catholics, and to establish and maintain relations with representatives of other Christian Churches for ecumenical dialogue and action.

The council, under the direction of Cardinal Walter Kasper (successor to Cardinal Edward I. Cassidy), has established firm working relations with representative agencies of other churches and the World Council of Churches. It has joined in dialogue with Orthodox Churches, the Anglican Communion, the Lutheran World Federation, the World Alliance of Reformed Churches, the World Methodist Council and other religious bodies. In the past several years, staff members and representatives of the council have been involved in one way or another in nearly every significant ecumenical enterprise and meeting held throughout the world.

While the council and its counterparts in other churches have focused primary attention on theological and other related problems of Christian unity, they have also begun, and in increasing measure, to emphasize the responsibilities of the churches for greater unity of witness and effort in areas of humanitarian need.

Bishops' Committee

The U.S. Bishops' Committee for Ecumenical and Interreligious Affairs was established by the American hierarchy in 1964. Its purposes are to maintain relationships with other Christian churches and other religious communities at the national level, to advise and assist dioceses in developing and applying ecumenical policies, and to maintain liaison with corresponding Vatican offices — the Pontifical Councils for Christian Unity and for Interreligious Dialogue.

This standing committee of the National Confer-ence of Catholic Bishops is chaired by Bishop Tod D. Brown of Orange (Bishop Stephen E. Blaire of Stockton will assume the chair in November 2002). Operationally, the committee is assisted by a secretariat with Rev. Arthur L. Kennedy, executive director; Dr. Eugene J. Fisher, executive secretary for Catholic-Jewish Relations; Dr. John Borelli, executive secretary for Interreligious Relations, the Rev. Ronald Roberson, C.S.P., and Brother Jeffrey Gros, F.S.C., associate directors.

The committee co-sponsors several national consultations with other churches and confessional families. These bring together Catholic representatives and their counterparts from the Episcopal Church, the Lutheran Church, the Polish National Catholic Church, the United Methodist Church, the Orthodox Churches, the Oriental Orthodox Churches, the Alliance of Reformed Churches: the United Church of Christ, the Presbyterian Church and Reformed Church in America, the North American Mission Board of the Southern Baptist Convention. (See Ecumenical Dialogues.)

The committee relates with the National Council of Churches of Christ, through membership in the Faith and Order Commission and through observer relationship with the Commission on Ecumenical Networks, and has sponsored a joint study committee investigating the possibility of Roman Catholic membership in that body in the 1970s. Collaboration in multiple areas of Church life have proved to be more fruitful than membership given the disparity of numbers and diversity of program priorities of the Bishop's Conference and the Council.

Advisory and other services are provided by the committee to ecumenical commissions and agencies in dioceses throughout the country.

Through its Section for Catholic-Jewish Relations, the committee is in contact with several national Jewish agencies and bodies. Issues of mutual interest and shared concern are reviewed for the purpose of furthering deeper understanding between the Catholic and Jewish communities.

Through its Section for Interreligious Relations, the

committee promotes activity in wider areas of dialogue with other religions, notably, with Muslims, Buddhists and Hindus. Offices of the committee are located at 3211 Fourth St. NE, Washington, DC 20017; www.usccb.org/seia/index.htm.

World Council of Churches

The World Council of Churches is a fellowship of churches which acknowledge "Jesus Christ as Lord and Savior." It is a permanent organization providing constituent members — 330 churches with some 450 million communicants in 100 countries — with opportunities for meeting, consultation and cooperative action with respect to doctrine, worship, practice, social mission, evangelism and missionary work, and other matters of mutual concern.

The WCC was formally established Aug. 23, 1948, in Amsterdam with ratification of a constitution by 147 communions. This action merged two previously existing movements — Life and Work (social mission), Faith and Order (doctrine) — which had initiated practical steps toward founding a fellowship of Christian churches at meetings held in Oxford, Edinburgh and Utrecht in 1937 and 1938. A third movement for cooperative missionary work, which originated about 1910 and, remotely, led to formation of the WCC, was incorporated into the council in 1971 under the title of the International Missionary Council.

Additional general assemblies of the council have been held since the charter meeting of 1948: in Evanston, Ill. (1954), New Delhi, India (1961), Uppsala, Sweden (1968), Nairobi, Kenya (1975), Vancouver, British Columbia, Canada (1983) and Canberra, Australia (1991). The 1998 general assembly was held in Harare, Zimbabwe, with the regular Catholic delegation in attendance, led by Bishop Mario Conti from St. Andrew's, Scotland.

The council continues the work of the International Missionary Council, the Commission on Faith and Order, and the Commission on Church and Society. The work of the council is carried out through four program units: unity and renewal; mission, education and witness; justice, peace and creation; sharing and service.

Liaison between the council and the Vatican has been maintained since 1966 through a joint working group. Roman Catholic membership in the WCC is a question officially on the agenda of this body. The Joint Commission on Society, Development and Peace (SODEPAX) was an agency of the council and the Pontifical Commission for Justice and Peace from 1968 to Dec. 31, 1980, after which another working group was formed. Roman Catholics serve individually as full members of the Commission on Faith and Order and in various capacities on other program committees of the council.

WCC headquarters are located in Geneva, Switzerland. The United States Conference for the World Council of Churches at 475 Riverside Drive, Room 915, New York, NY 10115, provides liaison between the U.S. churches and Geneva, and a communications office for secular and church media relations, and a publications office. The WCC also maintains fraternal relations with regional, national and local councils of churches throughout the world. The Rev. Konrad Raiser, a Lutheran from Germany, was elected general secretary, Aug. 24, 1992.

National Council of Churches

The National Council of the Churches of Christ in the U.S.A., the largest ecumenical body in the United States, is an organization of 35 Protestant, Orthodox and Anglican communions, with an aggregate membership of about 52 million.

The NCC, established by the churches in 1950, was structured through the merger of 12 separate cooperative agencies. Presently, the NCC carries on work in behalf of member churches in overseas ministries, Christian education, domestic social action, communications, disaster relief, refugee assistance, rehabilitation and development, biblical translation, international affairs, theological dialogue, interfaith activities, worship and evangelism, and other areas.

Policies of the NCC are determined by a general board of approximately 270 members appointed by the constituent churches. The board meets once a year.

NCC president: **Elenie K. Huszagh,** President in 2002-2003; **Bishop Thomas L. Hoyt, Jr.,** President Elect in 2004-2005. General Secretary: Rev. Dr. Robert W. Edgar. NCC headquarters are located at 475 Riverside Drive, New York, NY 10115; (212) 870-2141; www.ncccusa.org.

Consultation on Church Union

(Courtesy of Rev. David W.A. Taylor, General Secretary.)

The Consultation on Church Union, officially begun in 1962, is a venture of American churches seeking a united church "truly catholic, truly evangelical, and truly reformed." The churches engaged in this process, representing 25 million Christians, are the African Methodist Episcopal Church, the African Methodist Episcopal Zion Church, the Christian Church (Disciples of Christ), the Christian Methodist Episcopal Church, the Episcopal Church, the Presbyterian Church (U.S.A.); the United Church of Christ, the United Methodist Church and the International Council of Community Churches.

At a plenary assembly of COCU in December 1988, a plan of church unity was unanimously approved for submission to member churches for their action. The plan is contained in a 102-page document entitled "Churches in Covenant Communion: The Church of Christ Uniting." It proposes the formation of a covenant communion of the churches which, while remaining institutionally autonomous, would embrace together eight elements of ecclesial communion: claiming unity in faith, commitment to seek unity with wholeness, mutual recognition of members in one baptism, mutual recognition of each other as churches, mutual recognition and reconciliation of ordained ministries, celebrating the Eucharist together, engaging together in Christ's mission, and the formation together of covenanting councils at each level (national, regional, and local). At its January 1999 plenary in St. Louis, the churches proposed a 2002 decision to come into full communion as the *Churches Uniting in Christ.* This new step will be celebrated in Memphis, during the week of prayer, in Jan. 2002.

Vivian U. Robinson, Ph.D., a lay member of the Christian Methodist Episcopal Church, was elected president in 1988. The Rev. Rev. Michael Kinnamon is the general secretary. His Office is located at Edens Theological Seminary, 475 Lockwood Ave, St. Louis, MO 63119.

Graymoor Institute

The Graymoor Ecumenical and Interreligious Institute is a forum where issues that confront the Christian Churches are addressed, the spiritual dimensions of ecumenism are fostered, and information, documentation and developments within the ecumenical movement are published through *Ecumenical Trends*, a monthly journal. Director: The Rev. Elias D. Mallon, S.A. Address: 475 Riverside Dr., Rm. 1960, New York, N.Y. 10115-1999.

INTERNATIONAL BILATERAL COMMISSIONS

Anglican-Roman Catholic International Commission, sponsored by the Pontifical Council for Promoting Christian Unity and the Lambeth Conference, from 1970 to 1981; succeeded by a **Second Anglican-Roman Catholic International Commission**, called into being by the Common Declaration of Pope John Paul and the Archbishop of Canterbury in 1982.

The International Theological Colloquium between Baptists and Catholics, established in 1984 by the Pontifical Council for Promoting Christian Unity and the Commission for Faith and Interchurch Cooperation of the Baptist World Alliance.

The Disciples of Christ-Roman Catholic Dialogue, organized by the Council of Christian Unity of the Christian Church (Disciples of Christ) and the U.S. Bishops' Committee for Ecumenical and Interreligious Affairs, along with participation by the Disciples' Ecumenical Consultative Council and the Unity Council; since 1977.

The Evangelical-Roman Catholic Dialogue on Mission, organized by Evangelicals and the Pontifical Council for Promoting Christian Unity; from 1977. This dialogue is now sponsored by the World Evangelical Fellowship, on the evangelical side.

The Lutheran-Roman Catholic Commission on Unity, established by the Pontifical Council for Promoting Christian Unity and the Lutheran World Federation; from 1967.

The Joint International Commission for Theological Dialogue between the Orthodox Church and the Catholic Church, established by the Holy See and 14 autocephalous Orthodox Churches, began its work at a first session held at Patmos/Rhodes in 1980. Subsequent sessions have been held at Munich (1982), Crete (1984), Bari (1987), Valamo (1988), Freising (1990), Balamand (1993), and Emmitsburg, Maryland (2000).

Pentecostal-Roman Catholic Conversations, since 1966.

The Reformed-Roman Catholic Conversations, inaugurated in 1970 by the Pontifical Council for Promoting Christian Unity and the World Alliance of Reformed Churches.

The International Joint Commission between the Catholic Church and the Coptic Orthodox Church, since 1974. Established officially in the Common Declaration signed by Pope Paul VI and Coptic Pope Shenouda III in Rome in 1973.

The Joint International Commission between the Roman Catholic Church and the Malankara Orthodox Syrian Church, since 1989.

The Joint Commission between the Catholic Church and the Malankara Jacobite Syrian Orthodox Church, since 1990.

The Assyrian Church of the East-Roman Catholic Dialogue, officially established in the Common Declaration signed by Pope John Paul II and Mar Dinkha IV in November 1994. Has been meeting annually since 1995.

U.S. ECUMENICAL DIALOGUES

Representatives of the Bishops' Committee for Ecumenical and Interreligious Affairs, National Conference of Catholic Bishops, have met in dialogue with representatives of other churches since the 1960s, for discussion of a wide variety of subjects related to the quest for unity among Christians. Following is a list of dialogue groups and the years in which dialogue began.

Anglican-Roman Catholic Consultation, 1965; North American Orthodox-Catholic Theological Consultation, 1965; Joint Committee of Orthodox and Catholic Bishops, 1981; Lutheran Consultation, 1965; Oriental Orthodox Consultation (with Armenian, Coptic, Ethiopian, Indian Malabar and Syrian Orthodox Churches), 1978; Polish National-Catholic Consultation, 1984; Presbyterian/Reformed Consultation, 1965; Southern Baptist Conversations, 1969; United Methodist Consultation, 1966; Faith and Order National Council of Churches.

COMMON DECLARATIONS OF POPES, OTHER CHURCH LEADERS

(*Source: Secretariat of the Bishops' Committee for Ecumenical and Interreligious Affairs, United States Conference of Catholic Bishops.*)

The following Common Declarations, issued by several popes and heads, carry the authority given them by their signators.

Paul VI and Orthodox Ecumenical Patriarch Athenagoras I, First Common Declaration, Dec. 7, 1965: They hoped the differences between the churches would be overcome with the help of the Holy Spirit, and that their "full communion of faith, brotherly concord and sacramental life" would be restored.

Paul VI and Anglican Archbishop Michael Ramsey of Canterbury, Mar. 24, 1966: They stated their intention "to inaugurate between the Roman Catholic Church and the Anglican Communion a serious dialogue which, founded on the Gospels and on the ancient common traditions, may lead to that unity in truth for which Christ prayed."

Paul VI and Patriarch Athenagoras I, Second Common Declaration, Oct. 27, 1967: They wished "to emphasize their conviction that the restoration of full communion (between the churches) is to be found within the framework of the renewal of the Church and of Christians in fidelity to the traditions of the Fathers and to the inspirations of the Holy Spirit who remains always with the Church."

Paul VI and Vasken I, Orthodox Catholicos-Pa-

triarch of All Armenians, May 12, 1970: They called for closer collaboration "in all domains of Christian life. . . . This collaboration must be based on the mutual recognition of the common Christian faith and the sacramental life, on the mutual respect of persons and their churches."

Paul VI and Mar Ignatius Jacob III, Syrian Orthodox Patriarch of Antioch, Oct. 27, 1971: They declared themselves to be "in agreement that there is no difference in the faith they profess concerning the mystery of the Word of God made flesh and become really man, even if over the centuries difficulties have arisen out of the different theological expressions by which this faith was expressed."

Paul VI and Shenouda III, Coptic Orthodox Pope of Alexandria, May 10, 1973: Their common declaration recalls the common elements of the Catholic and Coptic Orthodox faith in the Trinity, the divinity and humanity of Christ, the seven sacraments, the Virgin Mary, the Church founded upon the Apostles, and the Second Coming of Christ. It recognizes that the two churches "are not able to give more perfect witness to this new life in Christ because of existing divisions which have behind them centuries of difficult history" dating back to the year 451 A.D. In spite of these difficulties, they expressed "determination and confidence in the Lord to achieve the fullness and perfection of that unity which is his gift."

Paul VI and Anglican Archbishop Donald Coggan of Canterbury, Apr. 29, 1977: They stated many points on which Anglicans and Roman Catholics hold the faith in common and called for greater cooperation between Anglicans and Roman Catholics.

John Paul II and Orthodox Ecumenical Patriarch Dimitrios I, First Common Declaration, Nov. 30, 1979: "Purification of the collective memory of our churches is an important fruit of the dialogue of charity and an indispensable condition of future progress." They announced the establishment of the Catholic-Orthodox Theological Commission.

John Paul II and Anglican Archbishop Robert Runcie of Canterbury, May 29, 1982: They agreed to establish a new Anglican-Roman Catholic commission with the task of continuing work already begun toward the eventual resolution of doctrinal differences.

John Paul II and Ignatius Zakka I, Syrian Orthodox Patriarch of Antioch, June 23, 1984: They recalled and solemnly reaffirmed the common profession of faith made by their predecessors, Paul VI and Mar Ignatius Jacob III, in 1971. They said: "The confusions and the schisms that occurred between the churches, they realize today, in no way affect or touch the substance of their faith, since these arose only because of differences in terminology and culture, and in the various formulae adopted by different theological schools to express the same matter. Accordingly, we find today no real basis for the sad divisions which arose between us concerning the doctrine of the Incarnation." On the pastoral level, they declared: "It is not rare for our faithful to find access to a priest of their own church materially or morally impossible. Anxious to meet their needs and with their spiritual benefit in mind, we authorize them in such cases to ask for the sacraments of penance, Eucharist and anointing of the sick from lawful priests of either of our two sister churches, when they need them."

John Paul II and Orthodox Ecumenical Patriarch Dimitrios I, Second Common Declaration, Dec. 7, 1987: Dialogue conducted since 1979 indicated that the churches can already profess together as common faith about the mystery of the Church and the connection between faith and the sacraments. They also stated that, "when unity of faith is assured, a certain diversity of expressions does not create obstacles to unity, but enriches the life of the Church and the understanding, always imperfect, of the revealed mystery.

John Paul II and Anglican Archbishop Robert Runcie of Canterbury, Oct. 2, 1989: They said: "We solemnly re-commit ourselves and those we represent to the restoration of visible unity and full ecclesial communion in the confidence that to seek anything less would be to betray our Lord's intention for the unity of his people."

John Paul II and His Holiness Mar Dinkha IV, Catholicos-Patriarch of the Assyrian Church of the East, Nov. 11, 1994: Following is the text of the "Common Christological Declaration" between the Catholic Church and the Assyrian Church of the East, signed Nov. 11, 1994, by Pope John Paul II and His Holiness Mar Dinkha IV, Catholicos-Patriarch of the Assyrian Church of the East. The declaration acknowledges that, despite past differences, both churches profess the same faith in the real union of divine and human natures in the divine Person of Christ. Providing background to the declaration was the Assyrian Church's adherence to the teaching of Nestorius who, in the fifth century, denied the real unity of divine and human natures in the single divine Person of Christ.

The text was published in the Nov. 16, 1994, English edition of *L'Osservatore Romano*:

"As heirs and guardians of the faith received from the Apostles as formulated by our common Fathers in the Nicene Creed, we confess one Lord Jesus Christ, the only Son of God, begotten of the Father from all eternity who, in the fullness of time, came down from heaven and became man for our salvation. The Word of God, second Person of the Holy Trinity, became incarnate by the power of the Holy Spirit in assuming from the Virgin Mary a body animated by a rational soul, with which he was indissolubly united from the moment of conception.

"Unity of Two Natures in One Person

"Therefore our Lord Jesus Christ is true God and true man, perfect in his divinity and perfect in his humanity, consubstantial with the Father and consubstantial with us in all things but sin. His divinity and his humanity are united in one person, without confusion or change, without division or separation. In him has been preserved the difference of the natures of divinity and humanity, with all their properties, faculties and operations. But far from constituting "one and another," the dignity and humanity are united in the person of the same and unique Son of God and Lord Jesus Christ, who is the object of a single adoration. Christ therefore is not an "ordinary man" whom God adopted in order to reside in him and inspire him, as in the righteous ones and the prophets. But the same God the Word, begotten of his Father before all worlds without beginning according to his divinity, was born of a mother without a father in the last times according to his humanity. The humanity to which the Blessed Virgin Mary gave birth always was that of the Son of God himself. That is the reason the Assyrian Church of the East is praying the Virgin Mary as 'the Mother of Christ our God and Savior.' In the light of this same faith the Catholic tradition addresses the Virgin Mary as 'the Mother of God' and also as 'the Mother of Christ.' We both recognize the legitimacy and rightness of these expressions of the same faith and we both respect the preference of each Church in her liturgical life and piety.

"Confession of the Same Faith

"This is the unique faith that we profess in the mystery of Christ. The controversies of the past led to anathemas, bearing on persons and on formulas. The Lord's Spirit permits us to understand better today that the divisions brought about in this way were due in large part to misunderstandings. Whatever our Christological divergences have been, we experience ourselves united today in the confession of the same faith in the Son of God who became man so that we might become children of God by his grace. We wish from now on to witness together to this faith in the One who is the Way, the Truth and the Life, proclaiming it in appropriate ways to our contemporaries, so that the world may believe in the Gospel of salvation. The mystery of the Incarnation which we profess in common is not an abstract and isolated truth. It refers to the Son of God sent to save us. The economy of salvation, which has its origin in the mystery of communion of the Holy Trinity — Father, Son and Holy Spirit — is brought to its fulfillment through the sharing in this communion, by grace, within the one, holy, catholic and apostolic Church, which is the People of God, the Body of Christ and the Temple of the Spirit.

"The Sacraments

"Believers become members of this Body through the sacrament of Baptism, through which, by water and the working of the Holy Spirit, they are born again as new creatures. They are confirmed by the seal of the Holy Spirit who bestows the sacrament of anointing. Their communion with God and among themselves is brought to full realization by the celebration of the unique offering of Christ in the sacrament of the Eucharist. This communion is restored for the sinful members of the Church when they are reconciled with God and with one another through the sacrament of Forgiveness. The sacrament of Ordination to the ministerial priesthood in the apostolic succession assures the authenticity of the faith, the sacraments and the communion in each local Church.

"Sister Churches But Not Full Communion

"Living by this faith and these sacraments, it follows as a consequence that the particular Catholic Churches and the particular Assyrian Churches can recognize each other as sister Churches. To be full and entire, communion presupposes the unanimity concerning the content of the faith, the sacraments and the constitution of the Church. Since this unanimity for which we aim has not yet been attained, we cannot unfortunately celebrate together the Eucharist which is the sign of the ecclesial communion already fully restored. Nevertheless, the deep spiritual communion in the faith and the mutual trust already existing between our Churches entitles us from now on to consider witnessing together to the gospel message and cooperating in particular pastoral situations, including especially the areas of catechesis and the formation of future priests.

"Commitment to Unity Efforts

"In thanking God for having made us rediscover what already unites us in the faith and the sacraments, we pledge ourselves to do everything possible to dispel the obstacles of the past which still prevent the attainment of full communion between our Churches, so that we can better respond to the Lord's call for the unity of his own, a unity which has of course to be expressed visibly. To overcome these obstacles, we now establish a Mixed Committee for theological dialogue between the Catholic Church and the Assyrian Church of the East. Given at Saint Peter's on Nov. 11, 1994."

Pope John Paul II with Ecumenical Orthodox Patriarch Bartholomew I, June 29, 1995: Pope John Paul and Ecumenical Orthodox Patriarch Bartholomew I, after several days of meetings, signed a common declaration June 29, 1995, declaring: "Our meeting has followed other important events which have seen our Churches declare their desire to relegate the excommunications of the past to oblivion and to set out on the way to establishing full communion. Our new-found brotherhood in the name of the Lord has led us to frank discussion, a dialogue that seeks understanding and unity. This dialogue — through the Joint International (Catholic-Orthodox) Commission — has proved fruitful and has made substantial progress. A common sacramental conception of the Church has emerged, sustained and passed on in time by the apostolic succession. In our Churches, the apostolic succession is fundamental to the sanctification and unity of the People of God. Considering that in every local church the mystery of divine love is realized and that this is how the Church of Christ shows forth its active presence in each one of them, the Joint Commission has been able to declare that our Churches recognize one another as Sister Churches, responsible together for safeguarding the one Church of God, in fidelity to the divine plan, and in an altogether special way with regard to unity."

Pope John Paul II with Anglican Archbishop George Carey, Common Ecumenical Declaration, Dec. 5, 1996: The pontiff and archbishop praised the work of the Anglican-Roman Catholic International Commission and stated that "In many parts of the world Anglicans and Catholics attempt to witness together in the face of growing secularism, religious apathy and moral confusion."

Pope John Paul II with Karekin I, Catholicos of All Armenians, Dec. 13, 1996.

Pope John Paul and His Holiness Karekin I, Supreme Patriarch and Catholicos of All Armenians, signed Dec. 13, 1996, signed a common declaration in which they said in part: "Pope John Paul II and Catholicos Karekin I recognize the deep spiritual communion which already unites them and the bishops and clergy and lay faithful of their churches. It is a communion which finds its roots in the common faith in the holy and life-giving Trinity proclaimed by the Apostles and transmitted down the centuries.... They rejoice in the fact that recent developments of ecumenical relations and theological discussions ... have dispelled many misunderstandings inherited from the controversies and dissensions of the past. Such dialogues and encounters have prepared a healthy situation of mutual understanding and recovery of the deeper spiritual communion based on the common faith in the holy Trinity that they have been given through the Gospel of Christ and in the holy tradition of the Church. "They particularly welcome the great advance that their churches have registered in their common search for unity in Christ, the Word of God made flesh. Perfect God as to his divinity, perfect man as to his humanity, his divinity is united to his humanity in the Person of the only-begotten Son of God, in a union which is real, perfect, without confusion, without alteration, without division, without any form of separation.

"The reality of this common faith in Jesus Christ and in the same succession of apostolic ministry has at times been obscured or ignored. Linguistic, cultural and political factors have immensely contributed toward the theological divergences that have found expression in their terminology of formulating their doctrines. His Holiness John Paul II and His Holiness Karekin I have expressed their determined conviction that because of the fundamental common faith in God and in Jesus Christ, the controversies and unhappy divisions which sometimes have followed upon the divergent ways in expressing it, as a result of the present declaration, should not continue to influence the life and witness of the Church today. They humbly declare before God their sorrow for these controversies and dissensions and their determination to remove from the mind and memory of their churches the bitterness, mutual recriminations and even hatred which have sometimes manifested themselves in the past, and may even today cast a shadow over the truly fraternal and genuinely Christian relations between leaders and the faithful of both churches, especially as these have developed in recent times. The communion already existing between the two churches and the hope for and commitment to recovery of full communion between them should become factors of motivation for further contact, more regular and substantial dialogue, leading to a greater degree of mutual understanding and recovery of the community of their faith and service."

Pope John Paul II with Aram I, Armenian Catholicos of Cilicia, Jan. 25, 1997: The common declaration stated, "the two spiritual leaders stress the vital importance of sincere dialogue…. The Catholic Church and the Catholicate of Cilicia also have an immense field of constructive cooperation before them."

Cardinal Edward Cassidy with Bishop Christian Krause, President of the Lutheran World Federation, Oct. 31, 1999: "Joint Declaration on Justification by Faith." (See **Special Section** below.)

Pope John Paul II with Karekin II, Catholicos of All Armenians, Nov. 10, 2000 in Rome: "His Holiness Pope John Paul II, Bishop of Rome, and His Holiness Karekin II, Supreme Patriarch and Catholicos of All Armenians, give thanks to the Lord and Savior Jesus Christ, for enabling them to meet together on the occasion of the Jubilee of the Year 2000 and on the threshold of the 1700th anniversary of the proclamation of Christianity as the state religion of Armenia.

"They also give thanks in the Holy Spirit that the fraternal relations between the See of Rome and the See of Etchmiadzin have further developed and deepened in recent years. This progress finds its expression in their present personal meeting and particu-

larly in the gift of a relic of Saint Gregory the Illuminator, the holy missionary who converted the king of Armenia (301 A.D.) and established the line of Catholicoi of the Armenian Church. The present meeting builds upon the previous encounters between Pope Paul VI and Catholicos Vasken I (1970) and upon the two meetings between Pope John Paul II and Catholicos Karekin I (1996 and 1999). Pope John Paul II and Catholicos Karekin II now continue to look forward to a possible meeting in Armenia. On the present occasion, they wish to state together the following.

"Together we confess our faith in the Triune God and in one Lord Jesus Christ, the only Son of God, who became man for our salvation. We also believe in One, Catholic, Apostolic and Holy Church. The Church, as the Body of Christ, indeed, is one and unique. This is our common faith, based on the teachings of the Apostles and the Fathers of the Church. We acknowledge furthermore that both the Catholic Church and the Armenian Church have true sacraments, above all — by apostolic succession of bishops — the priesthood and the Eucharist. We continue to pray for full and visible communion between us. The liturgical celebration we preside over together, the sign of peace we exchange and the blessing we give together in the name of our Lord Jesus Christ, testify that we are brothers in the episcopacy. Together we are jointly responsible for what is our common mission: to teach the apostolic faith and to witness to the love of Christ for all human beings, especially those living in difficult circumstances.

"The Catholic Church and the Armenian Church share a long history of mutual respect, considering their various theological, liturgical and canonical traditions as complementary, rather than conflicting. Today, too, we have much to receive from one another. For the Armenian Church, the vast resources of Catholic learning can become a treasure and source of inspiration, through the exchange of scholars and students, through common translations and academic initiatives, through different forms of theological dialogue. Likewise, for the Catholic Church, the steadfast, patient faith of a martyred nation like Armenia can become a source of spiritual strength, particularly through common prayer. It is our firm desire to see these many forms of mutual exchange and rapprochement between us improved and intensified.

"As we embark upon the third millennium, we look back on the past and forward to the future. As to the past, we thank God for the many blessings we have received from his infinite bounty, for the holy witness given by so many saints and martyrs, for the spiritual and cultural heritage bequeathed by our ancestors. Many times, however, both the Catholic Church and the Armenian Church have lived through dark and difficult periods. Christian faith was contested by atheistic and materialistic ideologies; Christian witness was opposed by totalitarian and violent regimes; Christian love was suffocated by individualism and the pursuit of personal interest. Leaders of nations no longer feared God, nor did they feel ashamed before humankind. For both of us, the 20th century was marked by extreme violence. The Armenian genocide, which began the century, was a prologue to horrors that would follow. Two world wars, countless regional conflicts and deliberately organized campaigns of extermination took the lives of millions of faithful. Nevertheless, without diminishing the horror of these events and their consequences, there may be a kind of divine challenge in them, if in response Christians are persuaded to join together in deeper friendship in the cause of Christian truth and love.

"We now look to the future with hope and confidence. At this juncture in history, we see new horizons for us Christians and for the world. Both in the East and in the West, after having experienced the deadly consequences of godless regimes and lifestyles, many people are yearning for the knowledge of truth and the way of salvation. Together, guided by charity and respect for freedom, we seek to answer their desire, so as to bring them to the sources of authentic life and true happiness. We seek the intercession of the Apostles Peter and Paul, Thaddeus and Bartholomew, of Saint Gregory the Illuminator and all Saintly Pastors of the Catholic Church and the Armenian Church, and pray the Lord to guide our communities so that, with one voice, we may give witness to the Lord and proclaim the truth of salvation. We also pray that around the world, wherever members of the Armenian and the Catholic Church live side by side, all ordained ministers, religious and faithful will 'help to carry one another's burdens, and in this way obey the law of Christ' (Gal. 6: 2). May they mutually sustain and assist one another, in full respect of their particular identities and ecclesiastical traditions, avoiding to prevail one over another: 'so then, as often as we have the chance, we should do good to everyone, and especially to those who belong to our family in the faith' (Gal. 6:10).

"Finally, we seek the intercession of the Holy Mother of God for the sake of peace. May the Lord grant wisdom to the leaders of nations, so that justice and peace may prevail throughout the world. In these days in particular, we pray for peace in the Middle East. May all the children of Abraham grow in mutual respect and find appropriate ways for living peacefully together in this sacred part of the world."

Pope John Paul II with Christodoulos, Archbishop of Athens, May 4, 2001:

"We, Pope John Paul II, Bishop of Rome, and Christodoulos, Archbishop of Athens and All Greece, standing before the bema of the Areopagus, from which Saint Paul, the Great Apostle to the Nations, 'called to be an Apostle, set apart for the Gospel of God' (Rom. 1:1), preached to the Athenians the One True God, Father, Son and Holy Spirit, and called them unto faith and repentance, do hereby declare:

"1. We give thanks to the Lord for our meeting and communication with one another, here in the illustrious City of Athens, the Primatial See of the Apostolic Orthodox Church of Greece.

"2. We repeat with one voice and one heart the words of the Apostle to the Nations: 'I appeal to you, brethren, by the name of our Lord Jesus Christ, that all of you agree and that there be no schisms among you, but that you be united in the same mind and the same judgment' (1 Cor. 1:10). We pray that the whole Christian world will heed this exhortation, so that peace may come unto 'all those who in every place call on the name of our Lord Jesus Christ' (1 Cor. 1:2). We condemn all recourse to violence, proselytism and fanaticism in the name of religion. We especially maintain that relations between Christians, in all their manifestations, should be characterized by honesty, prudence and knowledge of the matters in question.

"3. We observe that man's social and scientific evolution has not been accompanied by a deeper delving into the meaning and value of life, which in every instance is a gift of God, nor by an analogous appreciation of man's unique dignity, as being created according to the Creator's image and likeness. Moreover, economic and technological development does not belong equally to all mankind but belongs only to a very small portion of it. Furthermore, the improvement of living standards has not brought about the opening of men's hearts to their neighbours who suffer hunger and are naked. We are called to work together for the prevailing of justice, for the relief of the needy and for the ministry unto those who suffer, ever keeping in mind the words of St. Paul: 'the kingdom of God does not mean food and drink but righteousness and peace and joy in the Holy Spirit' (Rom. 14:17).

"4. We are anguished to see that wars, massacres, torture and martyrdom constitute a terrible daily reality for millions of our brothers. We commit ourselves to struggle for the prevailing of peace throughout the whole world, for the respect of life and human dignity, and for solidarity towards all who are in need. We are pleased to add our voice to the many voices around the world which have expressed the hope that, on the occasion of the Olympic Games to be held in Greece in 2004, the ancient Greek tradition of the Olympic Truce will be revived, according to which all wars had to stop, and terrorism and violence had to cease.

"5. We follow carefully and with unease what is referred to as globalization. We hope that it will bear good fruit. However, we wish to point out that its fruits will be harmful if what could be termed the "globalization of brotherhood" in Christ is not achieved in all sincerity and efficacy.

"6. We rejoice at the success and progress of the European Union. The union of the European world in one civil entity, without her people losing their national self-awareness, traditions and identity, has been the vision of its pioneers. However, the emerging tendency to transform certain European countries into secular states without any reference to religion constitutes a retraction and a denial of their spiritual legacy. We are called to intensify our efforts so that the unification of Europe may be accomplished. We shall do everything in our power, so that the Christian roots of Europe and its Christian soul may be preserved inviolate.

"With this Common Statement, we, Pope John Paul II, Bishop of Rome, and Christodoulos, Archbishop of Athens and All Greece, wish that 'our God and Father and our Lord Jesus direct our way, so that we may increase and abound in love towards one another and towards all men and establish the hearts of all unblamable in holiness before our God and Father, at the coming of the Lord Jesus with all his saints' (Cf. 1 Thess. 3:11-13) Amen. " Athens, at the Areopagus, 4 May 2001.

John Paul II and Karekin II, Catholicos of All Armenians, Sept. 27, 2001, in Etchmiadzin, Armenia:

"The celebration of the 1700th anniversary of the proclamation of Christianity as the religion of Armenia has brought us together — John Paul II, Bishop of Rome and Pastor of the Catholic Church, and Karekin II, the Supreme Patriarch and Catholicos of All Armenians — and we thank God for giving us this joyous opportunity to join again in common prayer, in praise of his all-holy Name. Blessed be the Holy Trinity — Father, Son and Holy Spirit — now and for ever.

"As we commemorate this wondrous event, we remember with reverence, gratitude and love the great confessor of our Lord Jesus Christ, Saint Gregory the Illuminator, as well as his collaborators and successors. They enlightened not only the people of Armenia but also others in the neighbouring countries of the Caucasus. Thanks to their witness, dedication and example, the Armenian people in A. D. 301 were bathed in the divine light and earnestly turned to Christ as the Truth, the Life, and the Way to salvation.

"They worshipped God as their Father, professed Christ as their Lord and invoked the Holy Spirit as their Sanctifier; they loved the apostolic universal Church as their Mother. Christ's supreme commandment, to love God above all and our neighbour as ourselves, became a way of life for the Armenians of old. Endowed with great faith, they chose to bear witness to the Truth and accept death when necessary, in order to share eternal life. Martyrdom for the love of Christ thus became a great legacy of many generations of Armenians. The most valuable treasure that one generation could bequeath to the next was fidelity to the Gospel, so that, with the grace of the Holy Spirit, the young would become as resolute as their ancestors in bearing witness to the Truth. The extermination of a million and a half Armenian Christians, in what is generally referred to as the first genocide of the twentieth century, and the subsequent annihilation of thousands under the former totalitarian regime are tragedies that still live in the memory of the present-day generation. These innocents who were butchered in vain are not canonized, but many among them were certainly confessors and martyrs for the name of Christ. We pray for the repose of their souls, and urge the faithful never to lose sight of the meaning of their sacrifice. We thank God for the fact that Christianity in Armenia has survived the adversities of the past seventeen centuries, and that the Armenian Church is now free to carry out her mission of proclaiming the Good News in the modern Republic of Armenia and in many areas near and far where Armenian communities are present.

"Armenia is again a free country, as in the early days of King Tiridates and Saint Gregory the Illuminator. Over the past ten years, the right of citizens in the burgeoning Republic to worship and practise their religion in freedom has been recognized. In Armenia and in the diaspora, new Armenian institutions have been established, churches have been built, associations and schools have been founded. In all of this we acknowledge the loving hand of God. For he has made his miracles visible in the continuing history of a small nation, which has preserved its particular identity thanks to its Christian faith. Because of their faith and their Church, the Armenian people have developed a unique Christian culture, which is indeed a most valuable contribution to the treasury of Christianity as a whole.

"The example of Christian Armenia testifies that faith in Christ brings hope to every human situation, no matter how difficult. We pray that the saving light of Christian faith may shine on both the weak and the strong, on both the developed and developing nations of this world. Particularly today, the complexities and challenges of the international situation require a choice between good and evil, darkness and light, humanity and inhumanity, truth and falsehood. Present issues of law, politics, science, and family life touch upon the very meaning of humanity and its vocation. They call today's Christians — no less than the martyrs of other times — to bear witness to the Truth even at the risk of paying a high price.

"This witness will be all the more convincing if all of Christ's disciples could profess together the one faith and heal the wounds of division among themselves. May the Holy Spirit guide Christians, and indeed all people of good will, on the path of reconciliation and brotherhood. Here at Holy Etchmiadzin we renew our solemn commitment to pray and work to hasten the day of communion among all the members of Christ's faithful flock, with true regard for our respective sacred traditions.

"With God's help, we shall do nothing against love, but 'surrounded by so great a cloud of witnesses, we shall lay aside every weight, and sin which clings so closely, and shall run with perseverance the race that is set before us' (cf. Heb. 12:1)

"We urge our faithful to pray without ceasing that the Holy Spirit will fill us all, as he did the holy martyrs of every time and place, with the wisdom and courage to follow Christ, the Way, the Truth and the Life." Holy Etchmiadzin, 27 September 2001.

Pope John Paul II and Ecumenical Patriarch Bartholomew I signed a Common Declaration on Environmental Ethics, June 10, 2002: "We are gathered here today in the spirit of peace for the good of all human beings and for the care of creation. At this moment in history, at the beginning of the third millennium, we are saddened to see the daily suffering of a great number of people from violence, starvation, poverty and disease. We are also concerned about the negative consequences for humanity and for all creation resulting from the degradation of some basic natural resources such as water, air and land, brought about by an economic and technological progress which does not recognize and take into account its limits.

"Almighty God envisioned a world of beauty and harmony, and He created it, making every part an expression of His freedom, wisdom and love (cf. Gen. 1:1-25).

"At the centre of the whole of creation, He placed us, human beings, with our inalienable human dignity. Although we share many features with the rest of the living beings, Almighty God went further with us and gave us an immortal soul, the source of self-awareness and freedom, endowments that make us in His image and likeness (cf. Gen. 1:26-31;2:7). Marked with that resemblance, we have been placed by God in the world in order to cooperate with Him in realizing more and more fully the divine purpose for creation.

"At the beginning of history, man and woman sinned by disobeying God and rejecting His design for creation. Among the results of this first sin was the destruction of the original harmony of creation. If we examine carefully the social and environmental crisis which the world community is facing, we must conclude that we are still betraying the mandate God has given us: to be stewards called to collaborate with God in watching over creation in holiness and wisdom.

"God has not abandoned the world. It is His will that His design and our hope for it will be realized through our co-operation in restoring its original harmony. In our own time we are witnessing a growth of an ecological awareness which needs to be encouraged, so that it will lead to practical programmes and initiatives. An awareness of the relationship between God and humankind brings a fuller sense of the importance of the relationship between human beings and the natural environment, which is God's creation and which God entrusted to us to guard with wisdom and love (cf. Gen. 1:28).

"Respect for creation stems from respect for human life and dignity. It is on the basis of our recognition that the world is created by God that we can discern an objective moral order within which to articulate a code of environmental ethics. In this perspective, Christians and all other believers have a specific role to play in proclaiming moral values and in educating people in ecological awareness, which is none other than responsibility towards self, towards others, towards creation.

"What is required is an act of repentance on our part and a renewed attempt to view ourselves, one another, and the world around us within the perspective of the divine design for creation. The problem is not simply economic and technological; it is moral and spiritual. A solution at the economic and technological level can be found only if we undergo, in the most radical way, an inner change of heart, which can lead to a change in lifestyle and of unsustainable patterns of consumption and production. A genuine conversion in Christ will enable us to change the way we think and act.

"First, we must regain humility and recognize the limits of our powers, and most importantly, the limits of our knowledge and judgement. We have been making decisions, taking actions and assigning values that are leading us away from the world as it should be, away from the design of God for creation, away from all that is essential for a healthy planet and a healthy commonwealth of people. A new approach and a new culture are needed, based on the centrality of the human person within creation and inspired by environmentally ethical behavior stemming from our triple relationship to God, to self and to creation. Such an ethics fosters interdependence and stresses the principles of universal solidarity, social justice and responsibility, in order to promote a true culture of life.

"Secondly, we must frankly admit that humankind is entitled to something better than what we see around us. We and, much more, our children and future generations are entitled to a better world, a world free from degradation, violence and bloodshed, a world of generosity and love.

"Thirdly, aware of the value of prayer, we must implore God the Creator to enlighten people everywhere regarding the duty to respect and carefully guard creation.

"We therefore invite all men and women of good will to ponder the importance of the following ethical goals:

"1. To think of the world's children when we reflect on and evaluate our options for action.

"2. To be open to study the true values based on the natural law that sustain every human culture.

"3. To use science and technology in a full and constructive way, while recognizing that the findings of science have always to be evaluated in the light of the centrality of the human person, of the common good and of the inner purpose of creation. Science may help us to correct the mistakes of the past, in order to enhance the spiritual and material well-being of the present and future generations. It is love for our children that will show us the path that we must follow into the future.

"4. To be humble regarding the idea of ownership and to be open to the demands of solidarity. Our mortality and our weakness of judgement together warn us not to take irreversible actions with what we choose to regard as our property during our brief stay on this earth. We have not been entrusted with unlimited power over creation, we are only stewards of the common heritage.

"5. To acknowledge the diversity of situations and responsibilities in the work for a better world environment. We do not expect every person and every institution to assume the same burden. Everyone has a part to play, but for the demands of justice and charity to be respected the most affluent societies must carry the greater burden, and from them is demanded a sacrifice greater than can be offered by the poor. Religions, governments and institutions are faced by many different situations; but on the basis of the principle of subsidiarity all of them can take on some tasks, some part of the shared effort.

"6. To promote a peaceful approach to disagreement about how to live on this earth, about how to share it and use it, about what to change and what to leave unchanged. It is not our desire to evade controversy about the environment, for we trust in the capacity of human reason and the path of dialogue to reach agreement. We commit ourselves to respect the views of all who disagree with us, seeking solutions through open exchange, without resorting to oppression and domination.

"It is not too late. God's world has incredible healing powers. Within a single generation, we could steer the earth toward our children's future. Let that generation start now, with God's help and blessing."
Rome — Venice, 10 June 2002

ECUMENICAL STATEMENTS

The ecumenical statements listed below, and others like them, reflect the views of participants in the dialogues which produced them. They have not been formally accepted by the respective churches as formulations of doctrine or points of departure for practical changes in discipline. (For other titles, see **U.S.**

Ecumenical Dialogues, Ecumenical Reports.)

• The "Windsor Statement" on Eucharistic doctrine, published Dec. 31, 1971, by the Anglican-Roman Catholic International Commission of theologians. (For text, see pages 132-33 of the 1973 *Catholic Almanac*.)

• The "Canterbury Statement" on ministry and ordination, published Dec. 13, 1973, by the same commission. (For excerpts, see pages 127-30 of the 1975 *Catholic Almanac*.)

• "Papal Primacy/Converging Viewpoints," published Mar. 4, 1974, by the dialogue group sanctioned by the U.S.A. National Convention of the World Lutheran Federation and the U.S. Bishops' Committee for Ecumenical and Interreligious Affairs. (For excerpts, see pages 130-31 of the 1975 *Catholic Almanac*.)

• An "Agreed Statement on the Purpose of the Church," published Oct. 31, 1975, by the Anglican-Roman Catholic Consultation in the U.S.

• "Christian Unity and Women's Ordination," published Nov. 7, 1975, by the same consultation, in which it was said that the ordination of women (approved in principle by the Anglican Communion but not by the Catholic Church) would "introduce a new element" in dialogue but would not mean the end of consultation nor the abandonment of its declared goal of full communion and organic unity.

• "Holiness and Spirituality of the Ordained Ministry," issued early in 1976 by theologians of the Catholic Church and the United Methodist Church; the first statement resulting from dialogue begun in 1966.

• "Mixed Marriages," published in the spring of 1976 by the Anglican-Roman Catholic Consultation in the U.S.

• "Bishops and Presbyters," published in July 1976 by the Orthodox-Roman Catholic Consultation in the U.S. on the following points of common understanding: (1) Ordination in apostolic succession is required for pastoral office in the Church. (2) Presiding at the Eucharistic Celebration is a task belonging to those ordained to pastoral service. (3) The offices of bishop and presbyter are different realizations of the sacrament of order. (4) Those ordained are claimed permanently for the service of the Church.

• "The Principle of Economy," published by the body named above at the same time, concerning God's plan and activities in human history for salvation.

• "Venice Statement" on authority in the Church, published Jan. 20, 1977, by the Anglican-Roman Catholic International Commission of theologians.

• "Response to the Venice Statement," issued Jan. 4, 1978, by the Anglican-Roman Catholic Consultation in the U.S.A., citing additional questions.

• "An Ecumenical Approach to Marriage," published in January, 1978, by representatives of the Catholic Church, the Lutheran World Federation and the World Alliance of Reformed Churches.

• "Teaching Authority and Infallibility in the Church," released in October 1978 by the Catholic-Lutheran dialogue group in the U.S.

• "The Eucharist," reported early in 1979, in which the Roman Catholic-Lutheran Commission indicated developing convergence of views.

• "The Holy Spirit," issued Feb. 12, 1979, by the International Catholic-Methodist Commission.

• A statement on "Ministry in the Church," published in March 1981 by the International Roman Catholic-Lutheran Joint Commission, regarding possible mutual recognition of ministries.

• The Final Report of the Anglican-Roman Catholic International Commission, 1982, on the results of 12 years of dialogue.

• "The Mystery of the Church and of the Eucharist in the Light of the Mystery of the Holy Trinity," issued by the Mixed International Commission for Theological Dialogue between the Catholic Church and the Orthodox Church at Munich, Germany, in July 1982.

• The Final Report of the Anglican-Roman Catholic International Commission, 1982, on the results of 12 years of dialogue.

• "Justification by Faith," issued Sept. 30, 1983, by the U.S. Lutheran-Roman Catholic dialogue group, claiming a "fundamental consensus on the Gospel."

• "Images of God: Reflections on Christian Anthropology," released Dec. 22, 1983, by the Anglican-Roman Catholic Dialogue in the United States.

• "The Journeying Together in Christ — The Report of the Polish National Catholic-Roman Catholic Dialogue (1984-89)."

• "Salvation and the Church," issued Jan. 22, 1987, by the Second Anglican-Roman Catholic International Commission.

• "Faith, Sacraments and the Unity of the Church," issued by the Mixed International Commission for Theological Dialogue between the Catholic Church and the Orthodox Churches in June 1987.

• "The Sacrament of Order in the Sacramental Structure of the Church, with Particular Reference to the Importance of Apostolic Succession for the Sanctification and Unity of the People of God," issued by the Mixed International Commission for Theological Dialogue between the Catholic Church and the Orthodox Church in Valamo, Finland, in 1988.

• "The Presence of Christ in Church and World" and "Toward a Common Understanding of the Church" (developed between 1984 and 1990), by the Reformed-Roman Catholic Conversations, under the auspices of the Pontifical Council for Promoting Christian Unity and the World Alliance of Reformed Churches.

• "The Church as Communion," issued by the Second Anglican-Roman Catholic International Commission, 1991.

• "Uniatism, Method of Union of the Past, and the Present Search for Full Communion," issued by the Mixed International Commission for Theological Dialogue between the Catholic Church and the Orthodox Church at Balamand, Lebanon, in 1993.

• "Life in Christ: Morals, Communion and the Church," issued by the Second Anglican-Roman Catholic International Commission, 1994.

• "Common Response to the Aleppo Statement on the Date of Easter/Pacha," issued by the North American Orthodox-Catholic Theological Consultation in Washington, D.C., Oct. 31, 1998.

• "The Gift of Authority," issued by the Second Anglican-Roman Catholic International Commission, May 12, 1999.

• "Baptism and 'Sacramental Economy'," issued by the North American Orthodox-Catholic Theological Consultation at Crestwood, New York, in June 1999.

• "Guidelines Concerning the Pastoral Care of Oriental Orthodox Students in Catholic Schools," issued by the Oriental Orthodox-Roman Catholic Theological Consultation in the United States at New Rochelle, New York, in June 1999.

• "Joint Declaration of the Catholic Church and the Lutheran World Federation on the Doctrine of Justification," issued July 8, 1999 by the International Roman Catholic-Lutheran Joint Commission.

• "Agreed Report on the Local/Universal Church," issued by the United States Anglican-Roman Catholic Consultation, Nov. 12, 1999.

• "Communion in Mission" and "Action Plan to Implement 'Communion in Mission,'" issued by a special consultation of Anglican and Roman Catholic bishops in Mississauga, Ontario, Canada, May 19, 2000.

• "Sharing the Ministry of Reconciliation: A Statement on the Orthodox-Catholic Dialogue and the Ecumenical Movement," issued June 1, 2000, by the North American Orthodox-Catholic Theological Consultation in Brookline, Massachusetts.

• "Doing the Truth in Charity," issued in July 2001 by the World Methodist Council and the Pontifical Council for Promoting Unity's Methodist-Catholic International Commission.

• "Interchurch Families: Resources for Ecumenical Hope," issued by the Catholic/Reformed Dialogue in the United States in 2002.

ANGLICAN-ROMAN CATHOLIC FINAL REPORT

The Anglican-Roman Catholic International Commission issued a Final Report in 1982 on 12 years of dialogue on major issues of concern, especially the Eucharist and ordained ministry.

In 1988 the Lambeth Conference called parts of the report on these two subjects "consonant in substance with the faith of Anglicans." In 1991 the Congregation for the Doctrine of the Faith and the Pontifical Council for Promoting Christian Unity called the Report a significant milestone not only in relations between the Catholic Church and the Anglican Communion but in the ecumenical movement as a whole. They said, however, that it was not yet possible to state that substantial agreement had been reached on all the questions studied by the commission, and that important differences still remained with respect to essential matters of Catholic doctrine regarding the Eucharist, ordination and other subjects. Clarifications were requested.

The Anglican-Roman Catholic Commission II responded in 1994, saying that its members were in agreement regarding:

• the substantial and sacramental presence of Christ in the Eucharist;

• the propitiatory nature of the Eucharistic Sacrifice, which can also be applied to the deceased;

• institution of the sacrament of order from Christ;

• the character of priestly ordination, implying configuration to the priesthood of Christ.

In 1994 Cardinal Edward I. Cassidy, president of the Pontifical Council for Interreligious Dialogue addressed a letter to the Catholic and Anglican co-chairmen of the commission, responding to the clarifications, stating that "no further work" seems to be necessary at this time on Eucharist and ministry. Questions still remained to be answered about a number of subjects, including the authority in the Church, ordination of women, infallibility and Marian doctrine.

JOINT DECLARATION ON JUSTIFICATION

(By Russell Shaw)

Hailed by Pope John Paul II as a "milestone" on the road to Christian unity, a Lutheran-Catholic Joint Declaration on the Doctrine of Justification was signed Oct. 31, 1999, in Augsburg, Germany, by representatives of the Catholic Church and the Lutheran World Federation.

"This document represents a sound basis for continuing the ecumenical theological research and for addressing the remaining problems with a better founded hope of resolving them in the future," Pope John Paul said the same day in Rome in a talk accompanying the recitation of the Angelus. "It is also a valuable contribution to the purification of historical memory and to our common witness."

The Joint Declaration states a "consensus" shared by the signers regarding the doctrine of justification. The key passage formulating this consensus says:

"In faith we together hold the conviction that justification is the work of the triune God. The Father sent his Son into the world to save sinners. The foundation and presupposition of justification is the incarnation, death, and resurrection of Christ. Justification thus means that Christ himself is our righteousness, in which we share through the Holy Spirit in accord with the will of the Father.

"Together we confess: By grace alone, in faith in Christ's saving work and not because of any merit on our part, we are accepted by God and receive the Holy Spirit, who renews our hearts while equipping and calling us to good works."

The signers of the Joint Declaration were Cardinal

Edward I. Cassidy, President of the Vatican's Pontifical Council for Promoting Christian Unity, and Bishop Christian Krause, President of the Lutheran World Federation, which represents 58 million of the world's 61 million Lutherans. Most of the churches within the federation have accepted the Joint Declaration.

Both the date and the place of the signing had symbolic significance. October 31 is observed by Protestants as Reformation Day, commemorating Martin Luther's nailing of his Ninety-five Theses on the castle church door in Wittenberg on that date in 1517. The city of Augsburg is associated with the Augsburg Confession, a document authored in 1530 by the Protestant Reformer Philipp Melancthon in an attempt to bring about a reconciliation between Lutherans and Catholics.

From a theological perspective, the doctrine of justification was of central importance in the Reformation and in the mutual condemnations exchanged by Catholics and Lutherans in the 16th century via the Council of Trent and the Lutheran Confessions.

The Joint Declaration stresses that the churches "neither take the condemnations lightly nor do they disavow their own past." But, it insists, as a result of ecumenical dialogue during the last 30 years, they have come to "new insights" that transcend the mutual polemics of the Reformation era and make it clear that neither party's understanding of justification, as it is expressed in the Joint Declaration, now merits condemnation by the other, while the differences about the doctrine that continue to exist between them "are acceptable."

The Council for Promoting Christian Unity and the Lutheran World Federation reached basic agreement on the document in June, 1998, but further clarifications were required on both sides before official approval was forthcoming. These clarifications are embodied in an "Annex" to the text.

Despite the harmonious tone of the document and the various statements that accompanied its signing, the Joint Declaration has been, and to some extent remains, a controversial document. Some Lutheran bodies, including the Lutheran churches of several countries, have not accepted it. Nor has an unknown number of individual Lutherans, theologians among them.

On the Catholic side, there has been criticism that the document does not go far enough in coming to terms with Lutheranism and, on the other hand, that it goes too far in papering over serious theological differences. According to the theologian Father Avery Dulles, S.J., it is "a bold statement, difficult to defend" to claim that the differing views still held by Catholics and Lutherans on various questions relating to the doctrine of justification really do "escape the condemnations" pronounced by each side on the other in the 16th century.

"But notwithstanding all the theological reservations on both sides," Father Dulles added in an October 1999 lecture at Fordham University, New York, reprinted in the magazine *First Things*, the signing of the Joint Declaration "can be a powerful symbolic event."

"It says clearly to a world that hovers on the brink of unbelief that the two churches that split Western Christendom on the issue of justification nearly five centuries ago are still united on truths of the highest import," he said.

The Joint Declaration has been hailed as the fruit of some 30 years of ecumenical dialogue between Lutherans and Catholics. The doctrine of justification was an issue in these conversations from the start. The 1972 report of the international Lutheran-Catholic dialogue included five paragraphs on the topic, and observed that "today … a far-reaching consensus is developing." This emerging consensus also was noted in 1980 and 1981 reports by the international dialogue.

The doctrine of justification was considered in reports from national Lutheran-Catholic dialogues in the United States ("Justification by Faith," 1985) and Germany ("The Condemnations of the Reformation Era. Do They Still Divide?" 1986). These reports from national dialogues contributed to a lengthy report developed by the third phase of the international dialogue and published in 1993 as "Church and Justification: Understanding the Church in the Light of the Doctrine of Justification." In 1993, at the request of the Lutheran World Federation and the Council for Promoting Christian Unity, a small Lutheran-Catholic working group was formed to begin work on what became the Joint Declaration.

While the document first of all marks a significant new stage in Lutheran-Catholic relations, it also has broader ecumenical significance, Cardinal Cassidy said in an article published in the Vatican newspaper *L'Osservatore Romano*.

"What has been achieved in this mutual agreement of the Joint Declaration surely is an historic develop-ment of particular importance in the history of Western Christianity, and indeed for the whole ecumenical movement as well, since it illustrates that ecumenical progress can be made on questions that are of central importance, and have long been seen as church-dividing issues," he wrote.

Cardinal Cassidy listed "three basic truths" that he said were central to the doctrine of justification and to the Lutheran-Catholic consensus expressed in the Joint Declaration. They are:

"Firstly, justification is a free gift bestowed by the Trinitarian God and centers on the person of Christ who became incarnate, died and rose. In being related to the person of Christ through the work of the Holy Spirit, we enter into a condition of righteousness.…

"Secondly, we receive this salvation in faith.…[T]he reality of justification is linked to faith, but not simply as an intellectual assent of the mind. Rather the believer is to give him/herself over to Christ in the renewal of life.

"Thirdly, justification points to the heart of the Gospel message, but must be seen in an organic unity with all the other truths of faith: Trinity, Christology, Ecclesiology and Sacraments."

The Joint Declaration begins with a Preamble that includes this statement of the document's intention: "… to show that on the basis of their dialogue the subscribing Lutheran churches and the Roman Catholic Church are now able to articulate a common understanding of our justification by God's grace through faith in Christ. It does not cover all that either church teaches about justification; it does encompass a consensus on basic truths of the doctrine of justification and shows that the remaining differences in its explication are no longer the occasion for doctrinal condemnations."

Following an overview of significant scriptural passages on the doctrine (section one), the document notes that, historically, justification has been an ecumenical problem between the Catholic Church and the Reformation churches and that differences focusing on it were the "principal cause" of their division and mutual condemnations in the 16th century. But in the ecumenical dialogue since the Second Vatican Council (1962-1965), it says, a "notable convergence" has emerged (section two).

The Joint Declaration then states the "consensus" on the basic truths of the doctrine, quoted above (section three). Justification is said to be "more than just one part of Christian doctrine. It stands in an essential relation with all truths of faith, which are to be seen as internally related to each other."

The fourth section of the Declaration ("Explicating the Common Understanding of Justification") is the document's longest section. It identifies, one by one, seven particular questions relating to the doctrine, states the consensus shared by Lutherans and Catholics regarding these seven questions, and then sets out distinctive Catholic and Lutheran perspectives on each.

The seven topics treated in this manner are: "Human Powerlessness and Sin in Relation to Justification," "Justification as Forgiveness of Sins and Making Righteous," "Justification by Faith and through Grace," "The Justified as Sinner," "Law and Gospel," "Assurance of Salvation," and "The Good Works of the Justified."

The Joint Declaration closes by once again underlining the "consensus in basic truths" regarding justification and stating its "significance and scope" (section five):

"In light of this consensus the remaining differences of language, theological elaboration, and emphasis in the understanding described in paragraphs 18 to 39 [section four] are acceptable. Therefore the Lutheran and Catholic explications of justification are in their difference open to one another and do not destroy the consensus regarding the basic truths.

"Thus the doctrinal condemnations of the 16th century, in so far as they relate to the doctrine of justification, appear in a new light. The teaching of the Lutheran churches presented in this Declaration does not fall under the condemnations from the Council of Trent. The condemnations of the Lutheran Confessions do not apply to the teaching of the Roman Catholic Church presented in this Declaration."

The document lists a number of other questions between Catholics and Lutherans that need clarification: the relationship between the Word of God and church doctrine, ecclesiology, ecclesial authority, church unity, ministry, the sacraments, and the relation between justification and social ethics. "We are confident that the consensus we have reached offers a solid basis for this clarification," it says.

An "Official Common Statement" of the Lutheran World Federation and the Catholic Church, issued at the time of the signing in Augsburg, commits both to continued ecumenical dialogue on outstanding questions regarding justification as well as the matters just mentioned. Such dialogue is necessary, it says, "in order to reach full church communion, a unity in diversity, in which remaining differences would be 'reconciled' and no longer have a divisive force."

In his article in *L'Osservatore Romano*, Cardinal Cassidy linked the signing of the Joint Declaration to the preparations for the third millennium of Christianity and the Great Jubilee of the Year 2000. In his 1994 Apostolic Letter *Tertio Millennio Adveniente* ("On the Coming of the Third Millennium"), he pointed out, Pope John Paul spoke of the scandal of Christian division and the need to work for unity in the new millennium. The Lutheran-Catholic accord marks important progress toward this goal, he suggested.

At the same time, the Cardinal acknowledged "the limits of our achievement" as represented in the Joint Declaration: "The declaration brings the Catholic Church and the member churches of the Lutheran World Federation which affirmed it a clear step closer to unity. They have not yet, however, achieved the goal of full, visible unity."

In particular, he said, "Catholics are not able to share the Eucharist with their Lutheran brothers and sisters....Our common participation in the Eucharist awaits the full ecclesial communion which we seek."

Nevertheless, Cardinal Cassidy added, the limitations of what has been accomplished in reaching this agreement should not cause it to be underestimated. "Serious difficulties remain, but they are secondary to what we hold in common. No longer may we look upon our different expressions of faith as being like two huge cannons drawn up in battle line and facing each other.... We need, above all, to give thanks to God for this achievement."

THE RELATIONSHIP OF ANGLICANS AND ROMAN CATHOLICS

(*By Dr. John Borelli, associate director, Secretariat for Ecumenical and Interreligious Affairs, National Conference of Catholic Bishops*)

A special consultation of Roman Catholic and Anglican bishops from thirteen regions around the world met in Mississauga, Ontario, May 14-20, 2000 to review and evaluate the accomplishment of thirty years of dialogue between the two traditions and to reflect on how the special relationship has been developing in various parts of the world. Bishops attended from New Zealand, Canada, England, United States, Ireland, India, Nigeria, Papua New Guinea, Southern Africa, Uganda, Australia, Brazil and the West Indies.

The meeting was convened by His Eminence Edward Cardinal Cassidy, President of the Pontifical Council Promoting Christian Unity, and His Grace Archbishop George Carey of Canterbury. Also participating were the two recently appointed co-chairman for the Anglican-Roman Catholic International Commission: the Most Rev. Frank T. Griswold, Presiding Bishop of the Episcopal Church (U. S.) and Most Rev. Alexander J. Brunett, Archbishop of Seattle.

The meeting grew out of the visit of Archbishop Carey with Pope John Paul II in Advent 1996 and was suggested in their Common Declaration of December 5, 1996, "it may be opportune at this stage in our journey to consult further about how the relationship between the Anglican Communion and the Catholic Church is to progress." With consensus yet to be achieved on authority in the church and with the new situation created by ordination of women as priests and bishops in some provinces of the Anglican Communion becoming increasingly evident, a certain amount of risk was involved in calling for a special consultation. The meeting could end in a standoff on certain issues and might even conclude with a simple acknowledgment of past achievements, current good will, and hope that the future will be brighter. These scenarios would be viewed as evidence that the dialogue is deadlocked or, at best, lost in a maze of seemingly endless study of details and differences and no certain direction towards reconciliation. Over three years were spent in preparations for the special consultation. Independent provinces of the Anglican Communion and national conferences of Catholic bishops were asked twice in the course of the planning to advise on agenda and other aspects of the proposed meeting. It was postponed once from May 1999 to May 2000 so that careful reflection and thorough preparation could take place first, and conveniently the meeting did not coincide with other developments related to restoration of unity between Anglicans and Catholics.

In the meantime, the Lambeth Conference met in July 1998. The Lambeth Conference is a meeting of Anglican bishops, currently from 36 provinces and other churches in the communion worldwide, and one of its actions in 1998 was to receive "the Virginia Report," prepared by the Inter-Anglican Theological and Doctrinal Commission. This study is a response to the particular need recognized by the Lambeth Conference of 1988 for exploration of the meaning and nature of communion and how the Anglican Communion makes authoritative decisions while maintaining unity and interdependence among the independent provinces. The Lambeth Conference of 1998 recommended the report for study throughout the Communion. Also, in May 1999, the Anglican-Roman Catholic International Commission released its third agreed statement on authority in the Church, "The Gift of Authority," which among other suggestions lists eleven advances points of consensus on authority (See page 102 of the 2000 *Catholic Almanac.*) In a dramatic gesture of unity, on Jan. 18, 2000, Archbishop Carey assisted Pope John Paul II in opening the holy door at St. Paul-Outside-the-Walls Basilica. Thus there was a certain momentum building up to the Mississauga meeting.

On May 20, 2000, Cardinal Cassidy and Archbishop Carey released two short documents resulting from the meeting and a press release: "Communion in Mission" and "Action Plan to Implement 'Communion in Mission.'" They reported that the bishops had spent a week in prayer together, worship, and reflection. They focused on the relationship between their communions which the Second Vatican Council said "occupies a special place" (*Decree on Ecumenism* 13). They also reported how the participants came to see that the relationship is no longer to be viewed in minimal terms but has reached a significant new place. The texts acknowledge unresolved differences and challenges, but they felt that these did not compare with all that Anglicans and Catholics hold in common. They also list the essentials of the faith and common practices to which the faithful hold fast and noted areas of theological convergence that have been achieved. They also express a common vision of full and visible unity.

The strength of the texts resulting from the special consultation lies in the recommendations. First, as a sign of the new stage in relations, they recommend the signing and celebration of a Joint Declaration of Agreement. This may turn out to be something on the scale of the joint declaration between Catholics and Lutherans on the doctrine of justification. To prepare the joint declaration and promote and monitor the reception of theological agreements, they recommend the formation of a Joint Unity Commission. They go into some detail how the bishops at the meeting believed the membership, accountability and mandate of the commission should be defined as well as how the participants themselves and how the Anglican-Roman Catholic International Commission or

dialogue might follow up to this meeting.

Some of the specific recommendations have been seen before in previous reports. For example, "the Malta Report" (1968) of the Joint Preparatory Commission, established by Pope Paul VI and Archbishop Michael Ramsey of Canterbury to work out the steps towards a formal theological dialogue, made several of recommendations that were repeated, in some way or another, in the Mississauga texts. The Anglican-Roman Catholic Consultation in the U.S. produced a twelve-year report in 1977 that contained similar recommendations. Also in 1981, a U.S. Anglican/Roman Catholic Leaders Conference proposed, on a smaller scale, that a Joint Commission be established to deal with specific areas, like pastoral ministry for Anglican-Catholic couples, and other recommendations requiring joint efforts and liaison. At best, these various recommendations were implemented sporadically. The difference with the steps taken at the Mississauga meeting is that accountability and responsibility for the implementation of these excellent recommendations lies with the Holy See's Pontifical Council for Promoting Christian Unity and the Inter-Anglican Standing Commission on Ecumenical Relations, a body established at the Lambeth Conference of 1998. The proposed Joint Unity Commission will report to these two high offices.

Much has been achieved in thirty five years of dialogue both on the international commission and on various national Anglican-Roman Catholic commissions, but now a special effort will be made to incorporate these theological agreements into the lives of the churches. Also, in more formal ways, Anglicans and Catholics will be encouraged to spend more time together in prayer, study, consultation, teaching, preparation of educational and liturgical materials, marriage preparation, and common action. Bishops of both churches will be asked to gather more frequently and to work together and consult more often, especially prior to one church making decisions on matters of faith and morals that would affect the other church. Catholics and Anglicans will be asked to live more visibly the unity they already share in service and witness to the gospel. As they strive to participate together in the mission of the church, Catholics and Anglicans will inevitably return to the unresolved differences and challenges and may be able to address them in a renewed spirit of unity and guided by the results of the ecumenical dialogue that will continue. The shape of how Anglicans and Catholics will live together in full visible unity has yet to be discerned fully, but for the present there seems to be a reinvigorated effort to live more visibly the unity they already have.

SEPARATED EASTERN CHURCHES

THE ORTHODOX CHURCH

This is a group of Eastern churches of the Byzantine tradition that were in full communion with Rome during the first millennium, and which all recognize the Patriarch of Constantinople as the first Orthodox bishop. In spite of the division between Catholics and Orthodox, often symbolized by the mutual excommunications of 1054, the Catholic Church considers

itself to be in almost full communion with the Orthodox Churches. According to Vatican II, they "are still joined to us in closest intimacy" in various ways, especially in the priesthood and Eucharist. The Orthodox Churches recognize the first seven ecumenical councils as normative for their faith, along with the Scriptures and other local councils that took place in later centuries.

The Orthodox Churches are organized in approximately 15 autocephalous (independent) churches that correspond in most cases to nations or ethnic groups. The Ecumenical Patriarch of Constantinople (modern Istanbul) has a primacy of honor among the patriarchs, but his actual jurisdiction is limited to his own patriarchate. As the spiritual head of worldwide Orthodoxy, he serves as a point of unity, and has the right to call Pan-Orthodox assemblies.

Top-level relations between the Churches have improved in recent years through the efforts of Ecumenical Patriarch Athenagoras I, John XXIII, Paul VI and Patriarch Dimitrios I. Pope Paul met with Athenagoras three times before the latter's death in 1972. The most significant action of both spiritual leaders was their mutual nullification of excommunications imposed by the two Churches on each other in 1054. Development of better relations with the Orthodox has been a priority of John Paul II since the beginning of his pontificate. Both he and Orthodox Ecumenical Patriarch Bartholomew have made known their commitment to better relations, despite contentions between Eastern Catholic and Orthodox Churches over charges of proselytism and rival property claims in places liberated from anti-religious communist control in the recent past.

The largest Orthodox body in the United States is the Greek Orthodox Archdiocese of America consisting of nine dioceses and an estimated membership of 1.9 million. Next is the Orthodox Church in America, with more than one million members; it was given autocephalous status by the Patriarchate of Moscow May 18, 1970, without the consent of the Patriarchate of Constantinople. An additional 650,000 or more Orthodox belong to smaller national and language jurisdictions. Heads of orthodox jurisdictions in this hemisphere hold membership in the Standing Conference of Canonical Orthodox Bishops in the Americas.

JURISDICTIONS

THE AUTOCEPHALOUS ORTHODOX CHURCHES

Patriarchate of Constantinople (Ecumenical Patriarchate), with jurisdiction in Turkey, Crete, the Dodecanese, and Greeks in the rest of the world outside Greece and Africa. Autonomous churches linked to the Ecumenical Patriarchate exist in Finland and Estonia. Several other jurisdictions of various ethnicities in the diaspora are also directly under the Patriarchate.

Patriarchate of Alexandria, with jurisdiction in Egypt and the rest of Africa; it includes a native African Orthodox Church centered in Kenya and Uganda.

Patriarchate of Antioch, with jurisdiction in Syria, Lebanon, Iraq, Australia, the Americas.

Patriarchate of Jerusalem, with jurisdiction in Israel and Jordan. The autonomous church of Mount Sinai is linked to the Jerusalem Patriarchate.

Russian Orthodox Church, the Patriarchate of Moscow with jurisdiction over most of the former Soviet Union. Autonomous churches in Japan and China are linked to the Moscow Patriarchate, and since the breakup of the Soviet Union, a certain autonomy has been granted to the Orthodox churches in the newly independent republics of Ukraine, Belarus, Estonia, Moldova and Latvia.

The Serbian Orthodox Church, a patriarchate with jurisdiction in all of former Yugoslavia, Western Europe, North America and Australia.

The Romanian Orthodox Church, a patriarchate with jurisdiction in Romania, Western Europe and North America.

The Bulgarian Orthodox Church, a patriarchate with jurisdiction in Bulgaria, Western Europe and North America.

The Georgian Orthodox Church, a patriarchate with jurisdiction in the republic of Georgia.

The Orthodox Church of Cyprus, an archbishopric with jurisdiction in Cyprus.

The Orthodox Church of Greece, an archbishopric with jurisdiction in most of Greece.

The Orthodox Church of Poland, a metropolitanate with jurisdiction in Poland.

The Orthodox Church of Albania, an archbishopric with jurisdiction in Albania.

The Orthodox Church in the Czech and Slovak Republics, a metropolitanate with jurisdiction in the Czech and Slovak Republics. Its autocephalous status was granted by Moscow in 1951 but by Constantinople only in 1998.

The Orthodox Church in America, a metropolitanate with jurisdiction in North America and a few parishes in Latin America and Australia. Its autocephalous status was granted by Moscow in 1970; Constantinople and most other Orthodox churches have not recognized this.

Population

The Division of Archives and Statistics of the Eastern Orthodox World Foundation reported a 1970 estimate of more than 200 million Orthodox Church members throughout the world. A contemporary estimate put the number close to 220 million. Many Orthodox today claim a total membership of about 300 million.

Standing Conference of Orthodox Bishops

The Standing Conference of Canonical Orthodox Bishops in the Americas was established in 1960 to achieve cooperation among the various Orthodox jurisdictions in the Americas. Office: 8-10 East 79th St., New York, NY 10021.

Member churches are the: Albanian Orthodox Diocese of America (Ecumenical Patriarchate), American Carpatho-Russian Orthodox Greek Catholic Diocese in the U.S.A. (Ecumenical Patriarchate), Antiochian Orthodox Christian Archdiocese of North America, Bulgarian Eastern Orthodox Church, Greek Orthodox Archdiocese of America (Ecumenical Patriarchate), Orthodox Church in America, Romanian Orthodox Archdiocese in America and Canada, Serbian Orthodox Church in the United States and Canada, Ukrainian Orthodox Church in the United States (Ecumenical Patriarchate), Ukrainian Orthodox Church of Canada (Ecumenical Patriarchate).

ANCIENT CHURCHES OF THE EAST

The Ancient Eastern Churches, which are distinct from the Orthodox Churches, were the subject of an article by Gerard Daucourt published in the Feb. 16,

1987, English edition of *L'Osservatore Romano*. Following is an adaptation:

By Ancient Eastern Churches one means: the Assyrian Church of the East (formerly called Nestorian), the Armenian Apostolic Church, the Coptic Orthodox Church, the Ethiopian Orthodox Church, the Syrian Orthodox Church (sometimes called Jacobite) and the Malankara Orthodox Syrian Church of India.

After the Council of Ephesus (431), the Assyrian Church of the East did not maintain communion with the rest of the Christian world. For reasons as much and perhaps more political than doctrinal, it did not accept the Council's teaching (that Mary is the Mother of God, in opposition to the opinion of Nestorius; see Nestorianism. For this reason, the Assyrian Church of the East came to be called Nestorian.) It is well known that in the 16th century a great segment of the faithful of this Church entered into communion with the See of Rome and constitutes today, among the Eastern Catholic Churches, the Chaldean Patriarchate. The Patriarch of the Assyrian Church of the East, His Holiness Mar Dinkha IV, in the course of his visit to the Holy Father and to the Church of Rome of 7 to 9 November, 1984, requested that people stop using the term "Nestorian" to designate his Church and expressed the desire that a declaration made jointly by the Pope of Rome and himself may one day serve to express the common faith of the two Churches in Jesus Christ, Son of God incarnate, born of the Virgin Mary. The labors of Catholic historians and theologians have, moreover, already contributed to showing that such a declaration would be possible.

The other Ancient Churches of the East (today known as the Oriental Orthodox Churches) for a long time have been designated by the term "Monophysite" Churches (see Monophysitism). It is regrettable to find this name still employed sometimes in certain publications, since already in 1951, in the encyclical *Sempiternus Rex*, on the occasion of the 15th centenary of the Council of Chalcedon, Pius XII declared with regard to the Christians of these Churches: "They depart from the right way only in terminology, when they expound the doctrine of the Incarnation of the Lord. This may be deduced from their liturgical and theological books."

In this same encyclical, Pius XII expressed the view that the separation at the doctrinal level came about "above all, through a certain ambiguity of terminology that occurred at the beginning." Since then, two important declarations have been arrived at in line with the ecumenical stance taken by the Church at the Second Vatican Council and the labors of the theologians (particularly in the framework of the Foundation "Pro Oriente" of Vienna). One was signed by Pope Paul VI and Coptic Patriarch Shenouda III on 10 May, 1973, and the other by Pope John Paul II and the Syrian Patriarch Ignatius Zakka II was, on 23 June, 1984. In both of these texts, the hierarchies of the respective Churches confess one and the same faith in the mystery of the Word Incarnate. After such declarations, it is no longer possible to speak in general terms of the "Monophysite" Churches. The Armenian Apostolic Church has communicants in the former Soviet Union, the Middle and Far East, the Americas. The Coptic Orthodox Church is centered in Egypt and has a growing diaspora overseas. The Syrian Orthodox Church has communicants in the Middle East, the Americas, and India. Members of the Assyrian Church of the East are scattered throughout the world, and the Patriarch now resides near Chicago, Illinois.

It is estimated that there are approximately 10 million or more members of these other Eastern Churches throughout the world. For various reasons, a more accurate determination is not possible.

EASTERN ECUMENISM

The Second Vatican Council, in *Orientalium Ecclesiarum*, the Decree on Eastern Catholic Churches, pointed out the special role they have to play "in promoting the unity of all Christians." The document also stated in part as follows.

The Eastern Churches in communion with the Apostolic See of Rome have a special role to play in promoting the unity of all Christians, particularly Easterners, according to the principles of this sacred Synod's Decree on Ecumenism first of all by prayer, then by the example of their lives, by religious fidelity to ancient Eastern traditions, by greater mutual knowledge, by collaboration, and by a brotherly regard for objects and attitudes (No. 24).

If any separated Eastern Christian should, under the guidance of grace of the Holy Spirit, join himself to Catholic unity, no more should be required of him than what a simple profession of the Catholic faith demands. A valid priesthood is preserved among Eastern clerics. Hence, upon joining themselves to the unity of the Catholic Church, Eastern clerics are permitted to exercise the orders they possess, in accordance with the regulations established by the competent authority (No. 25).

Divine Law forbids any common worship (*communicatio in sacris*) that would damage the unity of the Church, or involve formal acceptance of falsehood or the danger of deviation in the faith, of scandal, or of indifferentism. At the same time, pastoral experience clearly shows that with respect to our Eastern brethren there should and can be taken into consideration various circumstances affecting individuals, wherein the unity of the Church is not jeopardized nor are intolerable risks involved, but in which salvation itself and the spiritual profit of souls are urgently at issue.

Hence, in view of special circumstances of time, place, and personage, the Catholic Church has often adopted and now adopts a milder policy, offering to all the means of salvation and an example of charity among Christians through participation in the sacraments and in other sacred functions and objects. With these considerations in mind, and "lest because of the harshness of our judgment we prove an obstacle to those seeking salvation," and in order to promote closer union with the Eastern Churches separated from us, this sacred Synod lays down the following policy:

In view of the principles recalled above, Eastern Christians who are separated in good faith from the Catholic Church, if they ask of their own accord and have the right dispositions, may be granted the sacraments of penance, the Eucharist, and the anointing of the sick. Furthermore, Catholics may ask for these same sacraments from those non-Catholic ministers whose Churches possess valid sacraments, as often as necessity or a genuine spiritual benefit recommends such a course of action, and when access to a Catholic priest is physically or morally impossible (Nos. 26, 27).

Again, in view of these very same principles, Catholics may for a just cause join with their separated Eastern brethren in sacred functions, things, and places (No. 28). Bishops decide when and if to follow this lenient policy.

RECENT DOCUMENTS

Two recent documents of importance with respect to relations between Catholic and separated Eastern Churches are the apostolic letter, *Orientale Lumen*, issued May 5, 1995; and the encyclical letter, *Ut Unum Sint*, issued May 30, 1995, especially paragraphs 50-63.

In addition, the Pontifical Council for Promoting Christian Unity issued the following *Guidelines for Admission to the Eucharist between the Chaldean Church and the Assyrian Church of the East* on July 20, 2001, and made public on Oct. 25, 2001:

Given the great distress of many Chaldean and Assyrian faithful, in their motherland and in the diaspora, impeding for many of them a normal sacramental life according to their own tradition, and in the ecumenical context of the bilateral dialogue between the Catholic Church and the Assyrian Church of the East, the request has been made to provide for admission to the Eucharist between the Chaldean Church and the Assyrian Church of the East. This request has first been studied by the Joint Committee for Theological Dialogue between the Catholic Church and the Assyrian Church of the East. The present guidelines subsequently have been elaborated by the Pontifical Council for Promoting Christian Unity, in agreement with the Congregation for the Doctrine of Faith and the Congregation for the Oriental Churches.

1. Pastoral necessity

The request for admission to the Eucharist between the Chaldean Church and the Assyrian Church of the East is connected with the particular geographical and social situation in which their faithful are actually living. Due to various and sometimes dramatic circumstances, many Assyrian and Chaldean faithful left their motherlands and moved to the Middle East, Scandinavia, Western Europe, Australia and Northern America. As there cannot be a priest for every local community in such a widespread diaspora, numerous Chaldean and Assyrian faithful are confronted with a situation of pastoral necessity with regard to the administration of sacraments. Official documents of the Catholic Church provide special regulations for such situations, namely the Code of Canons of the Eastern Churches, can. 671, §2-§3 and the Directory for the Application of Principles and Norms of Ecumenism, n. 123.

2. Ecumenical rapprochement

The request is also connected with the ongoing process of ecumenical rapprochement between the Catholic Church and the Assyrian Church of the East. With the 'Common Christological Declaration', signed in 1994 by Pope John Paul II and Patriarch Mar Dinkha IV, the main dogmatic problem between the Catholic Church and the Assyrian Church has been resolved. As a consequence, the ecumenical rapprochement between the Chaldean Church and the Assyrian Church of the East also entered a further phase of development. On 29 November 1996 Patriarch Mar Raphaël Bidawid and Patriarch Mar Dinkha IV signed a list of common proposals with a view to the re-establishment of full ecclesial unity among both historical heirs of the ancient Church of the East. On 15 August 1997 this program was approved by their respective Synods and confirmed in a 'Joint Synodal Decree'. Supported by their respective Synods, both Patriarchs approved a further series of initiatives to foster the progressive restoration of their ecclesial unity. Both the Congregation for the Oriental Churches and the Pontifical Council for the Promotion of Christian Unity support this process.

3. The Anaphora of Addai and Mari

The principal issue for the Catholic Church in agreeing to this request, related to the question of the validity of the Eucharist celebrated with the Anaphora of Addai and Mari, one of the three Anaphoras traditionally used by the Assyrian Church of the East. The Anaphora of Addai and Mari is notable because, from time immemorial, it has been used without a recitation of the Institution Narrative. As the Catholic Church considers the words of the Eucharistic Institution a constitutive and therefore indispensable part of the Anaphora or Eucharistic Prayer, a long and careful study was undertaken of the Anaphora of Addai and Mari, from a historical, liturgical and theological perspective, at the end of which the Congregation for the Doctrine of Faith on January 17, 2001, concluded that this Anaphora can be considered valid. H.H. Pope John Paul II has approved this decision. This conclusion rests on three major arguments.

In the first place, the Anaphora of Addai and Mari is one of the most ancient Anaphoras, dating back to the time of the very early Church; it was composed and used with the clear intention of celebrating the Eucharist in full continuity with the Last Supper and according to the intention of the Church; its validity was never officially contested, neither in the Christian East nor in the Christian West.

Secondly, the Catholic Church recognises the Assyrian Church of the East as a true particular Church, built upon orthodox faith and apostolic succession. The Assyrian Church of the East has also preserved full Eucharistic faith in the presence of our Lord under the species of bread and wine and in the sacrificial character of the Eucharist. In the Assyrian Church of the East, though not in full communion with the Catholic Church, are thus to be found "true sacraments, and above all, by apostolic succession, the priesthood and the Eucharist" (U.R., n. 15). Secondly, the Catholic Church recognises the Assyrian Church of the East as a true particular Church, built upon orthodox faith and apostolic succession. The Assyrian Church of the East has also preserved full Eucharistic faith in the presence of our Lord under the species of bread and wine and in the sacrificial character of the Eucharist. In the Assyrian Church of the East, though not in full communion with the Catholic Church, are thus to be found "true sacraments, and above all, by apostolic succession, the priesthood and the Eucharist" (U.R., n. 15).

Finally, the words of Eucharistic Institution are indeed present in the Anaphora of Addai and Mari, not in a coherent narrative way and *ad litteram*, but rather in a dispersed euchological way, that is, integrated in successive prayers of thanksgiving, praise and intercession.

4. Guidelines for admission to the Eucharist

Considering the liturgical tradition of the Assyrian Church of the East, the doctrinal clarification regarding the validity of the Anaphora of Addai and Mari, the contemporary context in which both Assyrian and Chaldean faithful are living, the appropriate regulations which are foreseen in official documents of the Catholic Church, and the process of rapprochement between the Chaldean Church and the Assyrian Church of the East, the following provision is made:

1. When necessity requires, Assyrian faithful are permitted to participate and to receive Holy Communion in a Chaldean celebration of the Holy Eucharist; in the same way, Chaldean faithful for whom it is physically or morally impossible to approach a Catho-

lic minister, are permitted to participate and to receive Holy Communion in an Assyrian celebration of the Holy Eucharist.

2. In both cases, Assyrian and Chaldean ministers celebrate the Holy Eucharist according to the liturgical prescriptions and customs of their own tradition.

3. When Chaldean faithful are participating in an Assyrian celebration of the Holy Eucharist, the Assyrian minister is warmly invited to insert the words of the Institution in the Anaphora of Addai and Mari, as allowed by the Holy Synod of the Assyrian Church of the East.

4. The above considerations on the use of the Anaphora of Addai and Mari and the present guidelines for admission to the Eucharist, are intended exclusively in relation to the Eucharistic celebration and admission to the Eucharist of the faithful from the Chaldean Church and the Assyrian Church of the East, in view of the pastoral necessity and ecumenical context mentioned above.

CRISIS IN RELATIONS WITH THE MOSCOW PATRIARCHATE

On Feb. 11, 2002, it was made public that Pope John Paul II had elevated the four Apostolic Administrations in Russia to the status of dioceses. This precipitated a crisis in relations with the Moscow Patriarchate. On Feb. 12, 2002, Patriarch Aleksy II of Moscow and All Russia and the Holy Synod of the Russian Orthodox Church released the following statement:

It was announced on Feb. 11 in the Vatican that the Pope John Paul II of Rome decided to elevate the status of the administrative structures of the Roman Catholic Church in the territory of Russia to the level of dioceses. From now on the Vatican in its documents will name the territory of our country a "church province" led by a metropolitan.

The Russian Orthodox Church has been presented with a fait accompli, whereas such matters, in our opinion, require a preliminary discussion. We see this step as unfriendly and undermining the prospects for better relations between the two Churches.

Historically the Catholic Church in the territory of our country took pastoral care of the flock that traditionally belonged to it — Poles, Lithuanians, Germans, etc. Precisely for this reason the territory of Russia was not divided into Catholic dioceses and the Catholic ethnic parishes were part of the dioceses of Mogilev and Tiraspol. The establishment of a "church province," a "metropolitanate," means in fact the establishment of a national Catholic Church in Russia having its center in Moscow and claiming the Russian people, who are the flock of the Russian Orthodox Church culturally, spiritually and historically, as its flock.

The formation of such a church in Russia means in fact a challenge to Orthodoxy which has been rooted in the country for centuries. Nothing of this sort has ever happen in the history of our country. Moreover, this form of the organization of Catholic church life is atypical even of Catholic countries where there are no church provinces or dioceses governed actually by a metropolitan.

The fact should be pointed out that in taking care of its faithful in Catholic countries, the Russian Orthodox Church has never tried to establish church insti-

tutions parallel to Catholic ones. Our dioceses are established to take care of the Russian-speaking Orthodox diaspora, that is the children of the Russian Church who are far from their Motherland, not to carry out missionary work among the local population. If the Catholic Church worked in Russia with the same tact and good will as we do in Catholic countries, then no difficulties would arise in our relations.

We see as absolutely wrongful the references made by representatives of the Roman Catholic Church to the Catholic structures which existed in Russia before the 1917 Revolution and which they say they restore. Almost all the Roman Catholic dioceses that existed in the Russian empire by the early 20th century were in the territory of what today are Poland, Lithuania, Ukraine and Belorussia and did not have one center in the Russian capital city or any other city. The boundaries of our country as well as the ethnic and confessional composition of its population have considerably changed since. The number of Catholics in the present-day Russia is incomparably smaller than it was in the Russian Empire of the 20th century.

We are convinced that to take care of the Catholics who are not so many in our country it was not necessary to elevate the status of the already existing Catholic church structures, the more so to establish a special church division. Such actions of the Roman Catholic Church, not conditioned by any real pastoral needs, expose the missionary purposes of the changes made. This is corroborated by numerous facts of missionary work carried out by Catholic clergy among the Russian population. This is the activity we call proselytic and keep pointing to as one of the basic obstacles for improving relations between our two Churches.

It is especially regretful that the Vatican has taken this decision just before the next round of official talks between our Churches is to take place in the end of this February. As a result, a serious threat has emerged for the fragile negotiation process, which in its turn will make extremely difficult the settlement of problems and perplexities existing between us.

The leadership of the Roman Catholic Church is

now responsible before God and history for a sharp aggravation of our relations, for the frustration of the hope for their normalization that has just begun to shape. The Vatican's action has put in jeorpady the ability of the Catholic West and the Orthodox East to cooperate as two great civilizations for the benefit of Europe and the world. The opportunity for common Christian witness before divided humanity has been sacrificed for momentary benefits.

The question arises: Does the Vatican still regard its relations with the Orthodox Church as those of dialogue and cooperation, as it has continually stated, or it sees Orthodoxy as an undesirable rival? If the latter is the case, any agreement between us is out of question.

Nevertheless, we continue to remind the Vatican that at a time when the confused world expects the Orthodox and the Catholics to take common public action, we should work together rather than be at enmity. We still have good relations with dioceses, parishes and monasteries of the Catholic Church and cooperation with Catholic humanitarian organizations and educational institutions. These examples make it possible to hope that, whatever difficulties provoked by the Vatican's mistaken policy towards the Russian Orthodox Church, relations between the Orthodox and the Catholics will develop to become an important factor in the preservation of Christian values in the life of Europe and the world.

Addressing our flock, we call them to be faithful to Holy Orthodoxy. Let us respond calmly and peacefully but firmly to any attempts to divide our people spiritually. "Stand therefore, having your loins girt about with truth, and having on the breastplate of righteousness; and your feet shod with the preparation of the gospel of peace" (Eph. 6:14-15). Moscow Patriarchate Press Release, Feb. 12.

Archbishop Tadeusz Kondrusiewicz of the newly-created Archdiocese of the Mother of God in Moscow, issued the following statement on February 13:

1. We want to express our bewilderment and serious concern at the interference in the internal affairs of the Catholic Church in Russia which in the past few days has become more glaring. We would like to make our statement in the light of the following points:
- religious groups have the right to self government in accordance with their own hierarchical and organizational structure;
- it is the duty of the Apostolic Representation and the bishops of the Catholic Church to create normal conditions for the pastoral care of the faithful;
- according to Canon Law the normal structures of the Catholic Church are dioceses and metropolitan sees (ecclesiastical provinces);
- the setting up of temporary Russian Apostolic Administrations as regular dioceses which took place on 11th February 2002, does not contravene present Russian law;
- this essential step for Russian Catholics was carried out with notification to the government and ecclesiastical authorities of the Russian Orthodox Church in accordance with generally accepted international practice;

Furthermore we are convinced that the Catholics of the Russian Federation have the same rights as citizens professing other religions and that the lawful exercise of those rights must not in any way give rise to suspicion or be held subject to political speculation.

2. Moreover, we consider it our duty to publicly reject the unfounded assertions contained in the public Statement of the Patriarch of Moscow and of all Russia, Aleksy II, and of the Holy Synod of the Russian Orthodox Church dated 12th February 2002.

3. In that Statement it is alleged that "a form of Catholic Church life" has been founded in Russia which is "untypical even for Catholic countries where ecclesiastical provinces do not usually exist — that is dioceses administered by a Metropolitan."

This assertion is not correct. The Code of the Church's Canon Law states that for proper collegiate pastoral activity in different neighboring dioceses and for the proper collaboration between diocesan bishops and different neighboring dioceses, higher ecclesiastical authority is invested in ecclesiastical provinces, that is in metropolitan sees. (cf Canon 431)

The head of a metropolitan see is a metropolitan bishop, who is always a resident archbishop in the archdiocese governed by him. This authority is bound to an episcopal see which is created by the Roman Pontiff. Metropolitan sees exist for example, in Paris, Washington, Prague, Milan and Warsaw. (In Poland alone there are thirteen metropolitan sees.) At present they also exist in countries of the former Soviet Union, the metropolitan sees of Riga, Minsk-Mogiliev, Vilnius, Kaunas and Lvov.

Other dioceses within an ecclesiastical province are called "suffragan" sees. Canon law defines the authority of the metropolitan bishop in their regard:
- to assure the fullness of the faith and ecclesiastical discipline and to bring abuse to the attention of the Roman Pontiff (Canon 436 sect. 1)
- to conduct canonical visitation with the approval of the Apostolic See in the case of a suffragan bishop not administering his diocese (Canon 436 sect. 1)
- to appoint an administrator to a vacant episcopal see within eight days of its falling vacant (Canon 436 sect 1)
- A metropolitan does not have any other authority in his suffragan dioceses (Canon 436 sect.3)

4. In its Statement the ruling authorities of the Russian Orthodox Church state that "Russian territory was never divided into Catholic dioceses."

We must call to mind the following facts;
- Episcopal structures of the Catholic Church already existed in the south of Russia in the XIV-XV centuries.
- St Petersburg, the capital of the Russian Empire, was the center of the Mogiliev metropolitan diocese. Saratov was the seat of the Tiraspolis diocese. Besides this the diocese of Vladivostok was erected in 1922. The Archbishop of Mogiliev had the title of Metropolitan of all the Catholic churches in the Russian Empire.
- from the founding of the Metropolitan See of Mogiliev to its extinction at the expulsion from the country of its last occupant, Metropolitan Ian Tsepliak, the see of St Petersburg was occupied by twenty-seven bishops.

Therefore Catholic dioceses and metropolitan sees with their metropolitan and suffragan bishops have in fact existed within the present day boundaries of the Russian Federation.

5. Taking the above into consideration, we hold that the changes in the status of the Catholic Church in Russia and the erection of an ecclesiastical province cannot be described as establishing "a new Catholic structure, parallel to the Russian Orthodox Church." We would also like to make the following points:

Firstly, the dioceses do not take their names from the cities where they have their centers. There is no Metropolitan of Moscow or of Russia, instead there is a Metropolitan in Moscow.

Secondly, in the Russian Orthodox Church, there exists, for example, the Metropolitan of Vilnius and Lithuania and the Archbishop of Brussels and Belgium, of Berlin and Germany, and no-one in the Catholic Church is against these, since these metropolitan titles are the internal affair of the Russian Orthodox Church which names archbishops according to its needs:

Thirdly, a metropolitan does not have any real authority in different dioceses for they are autonomous and are governed by their own bishops.

6. In the Statement referred to above, mention is made in turn of multiple examples of missionary activity by Catholic clergy among the Russian population. "In fact, we describe this activity as 'proselytism' and continu-

ally indicate this as one of the outstanding reasons working against the improvement of relations between our two Churches" it is said in the document.

For our part we have repeatedly invited over a period of eleven years the leaders of the Russian Orthodox Church to discuss concrete details and to give hard facts of proselytism by Catholics in Russia. We want to know the facts of exactly who is involved or has been involved in proselytism, in what places, at what times and in what circumstances.

Unfortunately, we have not yet received any answer, neither have we received any response to our invitation "to sit at a round table to arrive at an agreement of the meaning of the term 'proselytism.' "

7. Despite the deterioration in the already strained situation in relations between the Catholic and Russian Orthodox Churches, I hope and pray to God that the dialogue will continue and be fruitful. I am convinced that the Catholic and Orthodox Churches can together respond to the calls of our age for the good of mankind and of civilization.

Statement distributed by the Information Center of the Conference of Catholic Bishops of the Russian Federation.

REFORMATION CHURCHES

LEADERS AND DOCTRINES OF THE REFORMATION

Some of the leading figures, doctrines and churches of the Reformation are covered below. A companion article covers **Major Protestant Churches in the United States**.

LEADERS

John Wycliff (c. 1320-1384): English priest and scholar who advanced one of the leading Reformation ideas nearly 200 years before Martin Luther — that the Bible alone is the sufficient rule of faith — but had only an indirect influence on the 16th century Reformers. Supporting belief in an inward and practical religion, he denied the divinely commissioned authority of the pope and bishops of the Church; he also denied the Real Presence of Christ in the Holy Eucharist, and wrote against the sacrament of penance and the doctrine of indulgences. Nearly 20 of his propositions were condemned by Gregory XI in 1377; his writings were proscribed more extensively by the Council of Constance in 1415. His influence was strongest in Bohemia and Central Europe.

John Hus (c. 1369-1415): A Bohemian priest and preacher of reform who authored 30 propositions condemned by the Council of Constance. Excommunicated in 1411 or 1412, he was burned at the stake in 1415. His principal errors concerned the nature of the Church and the origin of papal authority. He spread some of the ideas of Wycliff but did not subscribe to his views regarding faith alone as the condition for justification and salvation, the sole sufficiency of Scripture as the rule of faith, the Real Presence of Christ in the Eucharist, and the sacramental system. In 1457 some of his followers founded the Church of the Brotherhood which later became known as the United Brethren or Moravian Church and is consid-

ered the earliest independent Protestant body.

Martin Luther (1483-1546): An Augustinian friar, priest and doctor of theology, the key figure in the Reformation. In 1517, as a special indulgence was being preached in Germany, and in view of needed reforms within the Church, he published at Wittenberg 95 theses concerning matters of Catholic belief and practice. Leo X condemned 41 statements from Luther's writings in 1520. Luther, refusing to recant, was excommunicated the following year. His teachings strongly influenced subsequent Lutheran theology; its statements of faith are found in the Book of Concord (1580).

Luther's doctrines included the following: The sin of Adam, which corrupted human nature radically (but not substantially), has affected every aspect of man's being. Justification, understood as the forgiveness of sins and the state of righteousness, is by grace for Christ's sake through faith. Faith involves not merely intellectual assent but an act of confidence by the will. Good works are indispensably necessary concomitants of faith, but do not merit salvation. Of the sacraments, Luther retained baptism, penance and the Holy Communion as effective vehicles of the grace of the Holy Spirit; he held that in the Holy Communion the consecrated bread and wine are the Body and Blood of Christ. The rule of faith is the divine revelation in the Sacred Scriptures. He rejected purgatory, indulgences and the invocation of the saints, and held that prayers for the dead have no efficacy. Catholics clarified their positions at the Council of Trent. The 1999 Joint Declaration indicates that the condemnations of doctrine by the Council of Trent and the Book of Concord do not apply to present day Catholic and Lutheran teaching respectively.

Ulrich Zwingli (1484-1531): A priest who triggered

the Reformation in Switzerland with a series of New Testament lectures in 1519, later disputations and by other actions. He held the Gospel to be the only basis of truth; rejected the Mass (which he suppressed in 1525 at Zurich), penance and other sacraments; denied papal primacy and doctrine concerning purgatory and the invocation of saints; rejected celibacy, monasticism and many traditional practices of piety. His symbolic view of the Eucharist, which was at odds with Catholic doctrine, caused an irreconcilable controversy with Luther and his followers. Zwingli was killed in a battle between the forces of Protestant and Catholic cantons in Switzerland.

John Calvin (1509-1564): French leader of the Reformation in Switzerland, whose key tenet was absolute predestination of some persons to heaven and others to hell. He rejected Catholic doctrine in 1533 after becoming convinced of a personal mission to reform the Church. In 1536 he published the first edition of Institutes of the Christian Religion, a systematic exposition of his doctrine which became the classic textbook of Reformed — as distinguished from Lutheran — theology. To Luther's principal theses — regarding Scripture as the sole rule of faith, the radical corruption of human nature, and justification by faith alone — he added absolute predestination, certitude of salvation for the elect, and the incapability of the elect to lose grace. Calvin's Eucharist teaching, while affirming Christ's true presence, was not able to find agreement with that of Luther. However, in our own time, agreement has been reached between Lutherans and Reformed (Calvinists), and considerable progress has been made with Catholics and Orthodox toward a common understanding of Christ's presence in Communion.

CHURCHES AND MOVEMENTS

Adventists: Members of several Christian groups whose doctrines are dominated by belief in a more or less imminent second advent or coming of Christ upon earth for a glorious 1,000-year reign of righteousness. This reign, following victory by the forces of good over evil in a final Battle of Armageddon, will begin with the resurrection of the chosen and will end with the resurrection of all others and the annihilation of the wicked. Thereafter, the just will live forever in a renewed heaven and earth. A sleep of the soul takes place between the time of death and the day of judgment. There is no hell. The Bible, in literalist interpretation, is regarded as the only rule of faith and practice. About six churches have developed in the course of the Adventist movement which originated with William Miller (1782-1849) in the United States. Miller, on the basis of calculations made from the Book of Daniel, predicted that the second advent of Christ would occur between 1843 and 1844. After the prophecy went unfulfilled, divisions occurred in the movement and the Seventh Day Adventists, whose actual formation dates from 1860, emerged as the largest single body. The observance of Saturday instead of Sunday as the Lord's Day dates from 1844.

Anabaptism: Originated in Saxony in the first quarter of the 16th century and spread rapidly through southern Germany. Its doctrine included several key Lutheran tenets but was not regarded with favor by Luther, Calvin or Zwingli. Anabaptists believed that baptism is for adults only and that infant baptism is invalid. Their doctrine of the Inner Light, concerning the direct influence of the Holy Spirit on the believer, implied rejection of Catholic doctrine concerning the sacraments and the nature of the Church. Eighteen articles of faith were formulated in 1632 in Holland. Mennonites are Anabaptists.

Arminianism: A modification of the rigid predestinationism of Calvin, set forth by Jacob Arminius (1560-1609) and formally stated in the Remonstrance of 1610. Arminianism influenced some Calvinist bodies.

Baptists: So-called because of their doctrine concerning baptism. They reject infant baptism and consider only baptism by immersion as valid. Leaders in the formation of the church were John Smyth (d. 1612) in England and Roger Williams (d. 1683) in America.

Congregationalists: Evangelical in spirit and seeking a return to forms of the primitive church, they uphold individual freedom in religious matters, do not require the acceptance of a creed as a condition for communion, and regard each congregation as autonomous. Robert Browne influenced the beginnings of Congregationalism.

Disciples: From a nineteenth century revival movement and desire for the unity of the Christian churches, a network of congregations developed which desired to be called simply "Christian churches." These churches opened their communion and membership to all, celebrated the Eucharist each Sunday and baptized only adults. From this movement the Christian Church/Disciples of Christ, the Churches of Christ and the independent Christian Churches emerged.

Methodists: A group who broke away from the Anglican Communion under the leadership of John Wesley (1703-1791), although some Anglican beliefs were retained. Doctrines include the witness of the Spirit to the individual and personal assurance of salvation. The largest Methodist body in the United States is the United Methodist Church. There are three Black Methodist bodies: African Methodist Episcopal, African Methodist Episcopal Zion, and Christian Methodist Episcopal Churches. There are also several Holiness Churches in the Wesleyan tradition: i.e., Nazarene, Free Methodist, Wesleyan Church.

Pentecostals: Churches that grew up after the 1906 enthusiastic revival, accompanied by the phenomena of speaking in foreign tongues and the experience of baptism in the Holy Spirit. From this revival churches of a Methodist or Baptist theological emphasis emerged, such as the Church of God in Christ or the Assemblies of God. In the mid-twentieth century, the charismatic experience began to be shared by some members of the classical churches, including Roman Catholic.

Puritans: Congregationalists who sought church reform along Calvinist lines in severe simplicity. (Use of the term was generally discontinued after 1660.)

Presbyterians: Basically Calvinistic, called Presbyterian because church polity centers around assemblies of presbyters or elders. John Knox (c. 1513-1572) established the church in Scotland.

Quakers: Their key belief is in internal divine illumination, the inner light of the living Christ, as the only source of truth and inspiration. George Fox (1624-1691) was one of their leaders in England. Called the Society of Friends, the Quakers are noted for their pacifism.

Unitarianism: A 16th-century doctrine which rejected the Trinity and the divinity of Christ in favor of a uni-personal God. It claimed scriptural support for a long time but became generally rationalistic with respect to "revealed" doctrine as well as in ethics and its world-view. One of its principal early proponents was Faustus Socinus (1539-1604), a leader of the Polish Brethren. A variety of communions developed in England in the Reformation and post-Reformation periods.

Universalism: A product of 18th-century liberal Protestantism in England. The doctrine is not Trinitarian and includes a tenet that all men will ultimately be saved.

Anglican Communion: This communion, which regards itself as the same apostolic Church as that which was established by early Christians in England, derived not from Reformation influences but from the renunciation of papal jurisdiction by Henry VIII (1491-1547). His Act of Supremacy in 1534 called Christ's Church an assembly of local churches subject to the prince, who was vested with fullness of authority and jurisdiction. In spite of Henry's denial of papal authority, this Act did not reject substantially other principal articles of faith. Notable changes, proposed and adopted for the reformation of the church, took place in the subsequent reigns of Edward VI and Elizabeth, with respect to such matters as Scripture as the rule of faith, the sacraments, the nature of the Mass, and the constitution of the hierarchy. There are 27 provinces in the Anglican Communion. (See Episcopal Church, Anglican Orders, Anglican-Catholic Final Report.)

MAJOR PROTESTANT CHURCHES IN THE UNITED STATES

There are more than 250 Protestant church bodies in the United States. The majority of U.S. Protestants belong to the following denominations: Baptist, Methodist, Lutheran, Presbyterian, Protestant Episcopal, the United Church of Christ, the Christian Church (Disciples of Christ), Evangelicals.

See Ecumenical Dialogues, Reports and related entries for coverage of relations between the Catholic Church and other Christian churches.

Baptist Churches

Baptist churches, comprising the largest of all American Protestant denominations, were first established by John Smyth near the beginning of the 17th century in England. The first Baptist church in America was founded at Providence by Roger Williams in 1639.

Largest of the nearly 30 Baptist bodies in the U.S. are:

The Southern Baptist Convention, 901 Commerce St., Suite 750, Nashville, TN 37203, with 15.7 million members.

The National Baptist Convention, U.S.A., Inc., 915 Spain St., Baton Rouge, LA 70802, with 8 million members;

The National Baptist Convention of America, Inc., 1320 Pierre Ave., Shreveport, LA 71103, with 4.5 million members.

The American Baptist Churches in the U.S.A., P.O. Box 851, Valley Forge, PA 19482, with 1.5 million members.

The total number of U.S. Baptists is more than 29 million. The world total is 33 million.

Proper to Baptists is their doctrine on baptism. Called an "ordinance" rather than a sacrament, baptism by immersion is a sign that one has experienced and decided in favor of the salvation offered by Christ. It is administered only to persons who are able to make a responsible decision. Baptism is not administered to infants.

Baptists do not have a formal creed but generally subscribe to two professions of faith formulated in 1689 and 1832 and are in general agreement with classical Protestant theology regarding Scripture as the sole rule of faith, original sin, justification through faith in Christ, and the nature of the Church. Their local churches are autonomous.

Worship services differ in form from one congregation to another. Usual elements are the reading of Scripture, a sermon, hymns, vocal and silent prayer. The Lord's Supper, called an "ordinance," is celebrated at various times.

Christian Church (Disciples of Christ)

The Christian Church (Disciples of Christ) originated early in the 1800s from two movements against rigid denominationalism led by Presbyterians Thomas and Alexander Campbell in western Pennsylvania and Barton W. Stone in Kentucky. The two movements developed separately for about 25 years before being merged in 1832.

The church, which identifies itself with the Protestant mainstream, has nearly one million members in almost 4,000 congregations in the U.S. and Canada. The greatest concentration of members in the U.S. is located roughly along the old frontier line, in an arc sweeping from Ohio and Kentucky through the Midwest and down into Oklahoma and Texas.

The general offices of the church are located at 130 E. Washington St., Indianapolis, IN 46204. The church's persistent concern for Christian unity is based on a conviction expressed in a basic document, Declaration and Address, dating from its founding. The document states: "The church of Christ upon earth is essentially, intentionally and constitutionally one."

The Disciples have no official doctrine or dogma. Their worship practices vary widely from more common informal services to what could almost be described as "high church" services. Membership is granted after a simple statement of belief in Jesus Christ and baptism by immersion; most congregations admit un-immersed transfers from other denominations. The Lord's Supper or Eucharist, generally called Communion, is always open to Christians of all persuasions. Lay men and women routinely preside over the Lord's Supper, which is celebrated each Sunday; they often preach and perform other pastoral functions as well. Distinction between ordained and non-ordained members is blurred somewhat because of the Disciples' emphasis on all members of the church as ministers.

The Christian Church is oriented to congregational government, and has a unique structure in which three sections of polity (general, regional and congregational) operate as equals rather than in a pyramid of authority. At the national or international level, it is governed by a general assembly which has voting representation direct from congregations and regions as well as all ordained and licensed clergy.

Episcopal Church

The Episcopal Church, which includes 100 dioceses in the United States, Central and South America, and elsewhere overseas, regards itself as part of the same apostolic church which was established by early Christians in England. Established in this country during the colonial period, it became independent of the jurisdiction of the Church of England when a new constitution and Prayer Book were adopted at a general convention held in 1789. It has approximately 2.5 million members worldwide.

Offices of the presiding bishop and the executive council are located at 815 Second Ave., New York, NY 10017.

The presiding bishop is chief pastor and primate; he is elected by the House of Bishops and confirmed by the House of Deputies for a term of nine years.

The Episcopal Church, which is a part of the Anglican Communion, regards the Archbishop of Canterbury as the "First among Equals," though not under his authority.

The Anglican Communion, worldwide, has 70 million members in 36 self-governing churches.

Official statements of belief and practice are found in the Book of Common Prayer. Scripture has primary importance with respect to the rule of faith, and authority is also attached to tradition.

An episcopal system of church government prevails, but presbyters, deacons and lay persons also have an active voice in church affairs. The levels of government are the general convention, and executive council, dioceses, and local parishes. At the parish level, the congregation has the right to select its own rector, with the consent of the bishop.

Liturgical worship is according to the Book of Common Prayer as adopted in 1979, but details of ceremonial practice vary from one congregation to another.

Lutheran Churches

The origin of Lutheranism is generally traced to Oct. 31, 1517, when Martin Luther — Augustinian friar, priest, doctor of theology — tacked "95 Theses" to the door of the castle church in Wittenberg, Germany. This call to debate on the subject of indulgences and related concerns has come to symbolize the beginning of the Reformation. Luther and his supporters intended to reform the Church they knew. Though Lutheranism has come to be visible in separate denominations and national churches, at its heart it professes itself to be a confessional movement within the one, holy, catholic and apostolic Church.

The world's 61 million Lutherans form the third largest grouping of Christians, after Roman Catholics and Orthodox. About 57 million of them belong to church bodies which make up the Lutheran World Federation, headquartered in Geneva.

There are about 8.5 million Lutherans in the United States, making them the fourth largest Christian grouping, after Roman Catholics, Baptists and Methodists. Although there are nearly 20 U.S. Lutheran church bodies, all but 100,000 Lutherans belong to either the Evangelical Lutheran Church in America (with 5.2 million members and headquarters at 8765 W. Higgins Rd., Chicago, IL 60631), The Lutheran Church-Missouri Synod (with 2.61 million members and headquarters at 1333 S. Kirkwood Rd., St. Louis, MO 63122), or the Wisconsin Evangelical Lutheran Synod (with 420,000 members and headquarters at 2929 N. Mayfair Rd., Milwaukee, WI 53222).

The Evangelical Lutheran Church in America and the Lutheran Church-Missouri Synod carry out some work together through inter-Lutheran agencies such as Lutheran World Relief and Lutheran Immigration and Refugee Services; both agencies have offices at 390 Park Ave. South, New York, NY 10010.

The statements of faith which have shaped the confessional life of Lutheranism are found in the *Book of Concord*. This 1580 collection includes the three ancient ecumenical creeds (Apostles', Nicene and Athanasian), Luther's Large and Small Catechisms (1529), the Augsburg Confession (1530) and the Apology in defense of it (1531), the Smalkald Articles (including the "Treatise on the Power and Primacy of the Pope") (1537), and the Formula of Concord (1577).

The central Lutheran doctrinal proposition is that Christians "receive forgiveness of sins and become righteous before God by grace, for Christ's sake." Baptism and the Lord's Supper (Holy Communion, the Eucharist) are universally celebrated among Lutherans as sacramental means of grace. Lutherans also treasure the Word proclaimed in the reading of the Scriptures, preaching and absolution.

In the ELCA, the bishop is the minister of ordination. Much of Lutheranism continues what it understands as the historic succession of bishops (though without considering the historic episcopate essential for the church). All of Lutheranism is concerned to preserve apostolic succession in life and doctrine. Lutheran churches in Scandinavia and the Baltics, in the U.S., and in Canada have moved into full communion with their Anglican counterparts.

Lutheran jurisdictions corresponding to dioceses are called districts or synods in North America. There are more than 100 of them; each of them is headed by a bishop or president.

Methodist Churches

John Wesley (1703-1791), an Anglican clergyman, was the founder of Methodism. In 1738, following a period of missionary work in America and strongly influenced by the Moravians, he experienced a new conversion to Christ and shortly thereafter became a leader in a religious awakening in England. By the end of the 18th century, Methodism was strongly rooted also in America.

The United Methodist Church, formed in 1968 by a merger of the Methodist Church and the Evangelical United Brethren Church, is the second largest Protestant denomination in the U.S., with more than nine million members; its principal agencies are located in New York, Evanston, IL, Nashville, TN, Washington, DC, Dayton, OH, and Lake Junaluska, NC (World Methodist Council, P.O. Box 518 28745). The second largest body, with just under 2 million communicants, is the African Methodist Episcopal Church. Four other major churches in the U.S. are the African Methodist Episcopal Zion, Christian Methodist Episcopal, Free Methodist Church and the Wesleyan Church. The total Methodist membership in the U.S. is about 15.5 million.

Worldwide, there are more than 73 autonomous Methodist/Wesleyan churches in 107 countries, with a membership of more than 33 million. All of them participate in the World Methodist Council, which gives global unity to the witness of Methodist communicants.

Methodism rejects absolute predestination and maintains that Christ offers grace freely to all men, not just to a select elite. Wesley's distinctive doctrine was the "witness of the Spirit" to the individual soul and personal assurance of salvation. He also emphasized the central themes of conversion and holiness. Methodists are in general agreement with classical Protestant theology regarding Scripture as the sole rule of faith, original sin, justification through faith in Christ, the nature of the Church, and the sacraments of baptism and the Lord's Supper. Church polity is structured along episcopal lines in America, with ministers being appointed to local churches by a bishop; churches stemming from British Methodism do not have bishops but vest appointive powers within an appropriate conference. Congregations are free to choose various forms of worship services; typical elements are readings from Scripture, sermons, hymns and prayers.

Presbyterian Churches

Presbyterians are so called because of their tradition of governing the church through a system of representative bodies composed of elders (presbyters).

Presbyterianism is a part of the Reformed Family of Churches that grew out of the theological work of John Calvin following the Lutheran Reformation, to which it is heavily indebted. Countries in which it acquired early strength and influence were Switzerland, France, Holland, Scotland and England.

Presbyterianism spread widely in this country in the latter part of the 18th century and afterwards. Presently, it has approximately 4.5 million communicants in nine bodies.

The two largest Presbyterian bodies in the country — the United Presbyterian Church in the U.S.A. and the Presbyterian Church in the United States — were reunited in June, 1983, to form the Presbyterian Church (U.S.A.), with a membership of 2.7 million. Its national offices are located at 100 Witherspoon St., Louisville, KY 40202.

These churches, now merged, are closely allied with the Reformed Church in America, the United Church of Christ, the Cumberland Presbyterian Churches, the Korean Presbyterian Church in America and the Associate Reformed Presbyterian Church.

In Presbyterian doctrine, baptism and the Lord's Supper, viewed as seals of the covenant of grace, are regarded as sacraments. Baptism, which is not necessary for salvation, is conferred on infants and adults The Lord's Supper is celebrated as a covenant of the Sacrifice of Christ. In both sacraments, a doctrine of the real presence of Christ is considered the central theological principle.

The Church is twofold, being invisible and also visible; it consists of all of the elect and all those Christians who are united in Christ as their immediate head.

Presbyterians are in general agreement with classical Protestant theology regarding Scripture as the sole rule of faith and practice, salvation by grace, and justification through faith in Christ.

Presbyterian congregations are governed by a session composed of elders elected by the communicant membership. On higher levels there are presbyteries, synods and a general assembly with various degrees of authority over local bodies; all such representative bodies are composed of elected elders and ministers in approximately equal numbers. The church annually elects a moderator who presides at the General Assembly and travels throughout the church to speak to and hear from the members.

Worship services, simple and dignified, include sermons, prayer, reading of the Scriptures and hymns. The Lord's Supper is celebrated at intervals.

Doctrinal developments of the past several years included approval in May 1967 by the General Assembly of the United Presbyterian Church of a contemporary confession of faith to supplement the historic Westminster Confession. A statement entitled "The Declaration of Faith" was approved in 1977 by the Presbyterian Church in the U.S. for teaching and liturgical use.

The reunited church adopted "A Brief Statement of Reformed Faith" in 1991 regarding urgent concerns of the church.

United Church of Christ

The 1,501,310-member (in 1994) United Church of Christ was formed in 1957 by a union of the Congregational Christian and the Evangelical and Reformed Churches. The former was originally established by the Pilgrims and the Puritans of the Massachusetts Bay Colony, while the latter was founded in Pennsylvania in the early 1700s by settlers from Central Europe. The denomination had 6,362 congregations throughout the United States in 1988.

It considers itself "a united and uniting church" and keeps itself open to all ecumenical options. Its headquarters are located at 700 Prospect, Cleveland, OH 44115.

Its statement of faith recognizes Jesus Christ as "our crucified and risen Lord (who) shared our common lot, conquering sin and death and reconciling the world to himself." It believes in the life after death, and the fact that God "judges men and nations by his righteous will declared through prophets and apostles."

The United Church further believes that Christ calls its members to share in his baptism "and eat at his table, to join him in his passion and victory." Each local church is free to adopt its own methods of worship and to formulate its own covenants and confessions of faith. Some celebrate communion weekly; others, monthly or on another periodical basis. Like other Calvinistic bodies, it believes that Christ is spiritually present in the sacrament.

The United Church is governed along congregational lines, and each local church is autonomous. However, the actions of its biennial General Synod are taken with great seriousness by congregations. Between synods, a 44-member executive council oversees the work of the church.

Evangelicalism

Evangelicalism, dating from 1735 in England (the Evangelical Revival) and after 1740 in the United States (the Great Awakening), has had and continues to have widespread influence in Protestant churches.

It has been estimated that about 45 millon American Protestants — communicants of both large denominations and small bodies — are evangelicals.

The Bible is their rule of faith and religious practice. Being born again in a life-changing experience through faith in Christ is the promise of salvation. Missionary work for the spread of the Gospel is a normal and necessary activity.

Additional matters of belief and practice are generally of a conservative character. Fundamentalists, numbering perhaps 4.5 million, comprise an extreme right-wing subculture of evangelicalism. They are distinguished mainly by militant biblicism, belief in the absolute inerrancy of the Bible and emphasis on the Second Coming of Christ. Fundamentalism developed early in the 20th century in reaction against liberal theology and secularizing trends in mainstream and other Protestant denominations.

The Holiness or Perfectionist wing of evangelicalism evolved from Methodist efforts to preserve, against a contrary trend, the personal-piety and inner-religion concepts of John Wesley. There are at least 30 Holiness bodies in the U.S.

Pentecostals, probably the most demonstrative of evangelicals, are noted for speaking in tongues and the stress they place on healing, prophecy and personal testimony to the practice and power of evangelical faith.

Assemblies of God

Assemblies (Churches) of God form the largest body (more than 2 million members) in the Pentecostal Movement which developed from (1) the Holiness Revival in the Methodist Church after the Civil War and (2) the Apostolic Faith Movement at the beginning of the 20th century. Members share with other Pentecostals belief in the religious experience of conversion and in the baptism by the Holy Spirit that sanctifies. Distinctive is the emphasis placed on the charismatic gifts of the apostolic church, healing and speaking in tongues, which are signs of the "second blessing" of the Holy Spirit.

The Assemblies are conservative and biblicist in theology; are loosely organized in various districts, with democratic procedures; are vigorously evangelistic. The moral code is rigid.

INTERRELIGIOUS DIALOGUE

JUDAISM

Judaism is the religion of the Hebrew Bible and of contemporary Jews. Divinely revealed and with a patriarchal background (Abraham and Sarah, Isaac and Jacob), it originated with the Mosaic Covenant, was identified with the Israelites, and achieved distinctive form and character as the religion of the Torah (Law, "The Teaching") from this Covenant and reforms initiated by Ezra and Nehemiah after the Babylonian Exile.

Judaism does not have a formal creed but its principal points of belief are clear. Basic is belief in one transcendent God who reveals himself through the Torah, the prophets, the life of his people and events of history. The fatherhood of God involves the brotherhood of all humanity. Religious faith and practice are equated with just living according to God's Law. Moral conviction and practice are regarded as more important than precise doctrinal formulation and profession. Formal worship, whose principal act was sacrifice from the Exodus times to 70 A.D., is by prayer, reading and meditating upon the sacred writings, and observance of the Sabbath and festivals.

Judaism has messianic expectations of the complete fulfillment of the Covenant, the coming of God's kingdom, the ingathering of his people, and final judgment and retribution for all. Views differ regarding the manner in which these expectations will be realized — through a person, the community of God's people, an evolution of historical events, an eschatological act of God himself. Individual salvation expectations also differ, depending on views about the nature of immortality, punishment and reward, and related matters.

Sacred Books

The sacred books are the 24 books of the Masoretic Hebrew Text of The Law, the Prophets and the Writings (see The Bible). Together, they contain the basic instruction or norms for just living. In some contexts, the term Law or Torah refers only to the Pentateuch (Genesis, Exodus, Leviticus, Numbers, Deuteronomy); in others, it denotes all the sacred books and/or the whole complex of written and oral tradition.

Also of great authority are two Talmuds, which were composed in Palestine and Babylon in the fourth and fifth centuries A.D., respectively. They consist of the Mishna, a compilation of oral laws, and the Gemara, a collection of rabbinical commentary on the Mishna. Midrash are collections of scriptural comments and moral counsels.

Priests were the principal religious leaders during the period of sacrificial and temple worship. Rabbis were originally teachers; today they share with cantors the function of leaders of prayer. The synagogue is the place of community worship. The family and home are focal points of many aspects of Jewish worship and practice.

Of the various categories of Jews, Orthodox are the most conservative in adherence to strict religious traditions. Others — Reformed, Conservative, Reconstructionist — are liberal in comparison with the Orthodox. They favor greater or less modification of religious practices in accommodation to contemporary culture and living conditions.

Principal events in Jewish life include the circumcision of males, according to prescriptions of the Covenant; the bar and bat mitzvah which marks the coming-of-age of boys and girls in Judaism at the age of 13; marriage; and observance of the Sabbath and festivals.

Observances of the Sabbath and festivals begin at sundown of the previous calendar day and continue until the following sundown.

Sabbath: Saturday, the weekly day of rest prescribed in the Decalogue.

Sukkoth (Tabernacles): A seven-to-nine-day festival in the month of Tishri (Sept.-Oct.), marked by some Jews with Covenant-renewal and reading of The Law. It originated in agricultural feast at the end of the harvest and got its name from the temporary shelters used by workers in the fields.

Hanukkah (The Festival of Lights, the Feast of Consecration and of the Maccabees): Commemorates the dedication of the new altar in the Temple at Jerusalem by Judas Maccabeus in 165 B.C. The eight-day festival, during which candles in an eight-branch candelabra are lighted in succession, one each day, occurs near the winter solstice, close to Christmas time.

Pesach (Passover): A seven-day festival commemorating the liberation of the Israelites from Egypt. The narrative of the Exodus, the Haggadah, is read at ceremonial Seder meals on the first and second days of the festival, which begins on the 14th day of Nisan (Mar.-Apr.).

Shavuoth, Pentecost (Feast of Weeks): Observed 50 days after Passover, commemorating the anniver-sary of the revelation of the Law to Moses.

Purim: A joyous festival observed on the 14th day of Adar (Feb.-Mar.), commemorating the rescue of the Israelites from massacre by the Persians through the intervention of Esther. The festival is preceded by a day of fasting. A gift- and alms-giving custom became associated with it in medieval times.

Rosh Hashana (Feast of Trumpets, New Year): Observed on the first day of Tishri (Sept.-Oct.), the festival focuses attention on the ways of life and the ways of death. It is second in importance only to the most solemn observance of Yom Kippur.

Yom Kippur (Day of Atonement): The highest holy day, observed with strict fasting. It occurs 10 days after Rosh Hashana.

Yom HaShoah (Holocaust Memorial Day): Observed in the week after Passover; increasingly observed with joint Christian-Jewish services of remembrance.

CATHOLIC-JEWISH RELATIONS

The Second Vatican Council, in addition to the Decree on Ecumenism (concerning the movement for unity among Christians, stated the mind of the Church on a similar matter in *Nostra Aetate*, a Declaration on the Relationship of the Church to Non-Christian Religions. This document, as the following excerpts indicate, backgrounds the reasons and directions of the Church's regard for the Jews. (Other portions of the document refer to Hindus, Buddhists and Muslims.)

Spiritual Bond

As this sacred Synod searches into the mystery of the Church, it recalls the spiritual bond linking the people of the New Covenant with Abraham's stock.

For the Church of Christ acknowledges that, according to the mystery of God's saving design, the beginnings of her faith and her election are already found among the patriarchs, Moses, and the prophets. She professes that all who believe in Christ, Abraham's sons according to faith (cf. Gal. 3:7), are included in the same patriarch's call, and likewise that the salvation of the Church was mystically foreshadowed by the Chosen People's exodus from the land of bondage.

The Church, therefore, cannot forget that she received the revelation of the Old Testament through the people with whom God in his inexpressible mercy deigned to establish the Ancient Covenant. Nor can she forget that she draws sustenance from the root of that good olive tree onto which have been grafted the wild olive branches of the Gentiles (cf. Rom. 11:17-24). Indeed, the Church believes that by his cross Christ, our Peace, reconciled Jew and Gentile, making them both one in himself (cf. Eph. 2:14-16).

The Jews still remain most dear to God because of their fathers, for he does not repent of the gifts he makes nor of the calls he issues (cf. Rom. 11:28-29). In company with the prophets and the same Apostle (Paul), the Church awaits that day, known to God alone, on which all peoples will address the Lord in a single voice and "serve him with one accord" (Zeph. 3:9; cf. Is. 66:23; Ps. 65:4; Rom. 11:11-32).

Since the spiritual patrimony common to Christians and Jews is thus so great, this sacred Synod wishes to foster and recommend that mutual understanding and respect which is the fruit above all of biblical and theological studies, and of brotherly dialogues.

No Anti-Semitism

True, authorities of the Jews and those who followed their lead pressed for the death of Christ (cf. Jn. 19:6); still, what happened in his passion cannot be blamed upon all the Jews then living, without distinction, nor upon the Jews of today. Although the Church is the new People of God, the Jews should not be presented as repudiated or cursed by God, as if such views followed from the holy Scriptures. All should take pains, then, lest in catechetical instruction and in the preaching of God's Word they teach anything out of harmony with the truth of the Gospel and the spirit of Christ.

The Church repudiates all persecutions against any person. Moreover, mindful of her common patrimony with the Jews, and motivated by the Gospel's spiritual love and by no political considerations, she deplores the hatred, persecutions, and displays of anti-Semitism directed against the Jews at any time and from any source (No. 4).

The Church rejects, as foreign to the mind of Christ, any discrimination against men or harassment of them because of their race, color, condition of life, or religion (No. 5).

Bishops' Secretariat

The American hierarchy's first move toward implementation of the Vatican II Declaration on the Relationship of the Church to Non-Christian Religions (*Nostra Aetate*) was to establish, in 1965, a Subcommission for Catholic-Jewish Relations in the framework of its Commission for Ecumenical and Interreligious Affairs. Its moderator is Cardinal William H. Keeler of Baltimore. The Secretariat for Ecumenical and Interreligious Relations is located at 3211 Fourth St. NE, Washington, DC 20017. Its Catholic-Jewish efforts are directed by Dr. Eugene J. Fisher.

According to the key norm of a set of guidelines issued by the secretariat Mar. 16, 1967, and updated Apr. 9, 1985: "The general aim of all Catholic-Jewish meetings (and relations) is to increase our understanding both of Judaism and the Catholic faith, to eliminate sources of tension and misunderstanding, to initiate dialogue or conversations on different levels, to multiply intergroup meetings between Catholics and Jews, and to promote cooperative social action."

Vatican Guidelines

In a document issued Jan. 3, 1975, the Vatican Commission for Religious Relations with the Jews offered a number of suggestions and guidelines for implementing the Christian-Jewish portion of the Second Vatican Council's Declaration on Relations with Non-Christian Religions.

Among "suggestions from experience" were those concerning dialogue, liturgical links between Christian and Jewish worship, the interpretation of biblical texts, teaching and education for the purpose of increasing mutual understanding, and joint social action.

Notes on Preaching and Catechesis

On June 24, 1985, the Vatican Commission for Religious Relations with the Jews promulgated its "Notes on the Correct Way to Present Jews and Judaism in Preaching and Catechesis in the Roman Catholic Church," with the intent of providing "a helpful frame of reference for those who are called upon in the course of their teaching assignments to speak about Jews and Judaism and who wish to do so in keeping with the current teaching of the Church in this area."

The document states emphatically that, since the relationship between the Church and the Jewish people is one "founded on the design of the God of the Covenant," Judaism does not occupy "an occasional and marginal place in catechesis," but an "essential" one that "should be organically integrated" throughout the curriculum on all levels of Catholic education.

The Notes discuss the relationship between the Hebrew Scriptures and the New Testament, focusing especially on typology, which is called "the sign of a problem unresolved." Underlined is the "eschatological dimension," that "the people of God of the Old and the New Testament are tending toward a like end in the future: the coming or return of the Messiah." Jewish witness to God's Kingdom, the Notes declare, challenges Christians to "accept our responsibility to prepare the world for the coming of the Messiah by working together for social justice and reconciliation."

The Notes emphasize the Jewishness of Jesus' teaching, correct misunderstandings concerning the portrayal of Jews in the New Testament and describe the Jewish origins of Christian liturgy. One section addresses the "spiritual fecundity" of Judaism to the present, its continuing "witness — often heroic — of its fidelity to the one God," and mandates the development of Holocaust curricula and a positive approach in Catholic education to the "religious attachment which finds its roots in biblical tradition" between the Jewish people and the Land of Israel, affirming the "existence of the State of Israel" on the basis of "the common principles of international law."

WE REMEMBER: A REFLECTION ON THE SHOAH

On Mar. 16, 1998, the Commission for Religious Relations with the Jews under Cardinal Edward Idris Cassidy, issued a long-awaited white paper on the Holocaust, entitled "We Remember: Reflections on the Shoah."

The document offered repentance for the failures of many Christians to oppose the policies of Nazi Germany and to resist the extermination of the Jews during the years of the Third Reich. It analyzed the history of anti-Semitism in the Church, while distinguishing between the historical anti-Judaism of Christian teaching over the centuries and the modern, racial ideology of Nazism that climaxed with the Holocaust.

"We Remember" defends Pope Pius XII and his efforts on behalf of the Jews during World War II, and at the same time acknowledges the need for a "call to penitence" by the Church as a whole "for the failures of her sons and daughters in every age." Cardinal Cassidy, in an address given in May of 1998 to the American Jewish Committee responding to criticisms of the text, stated clearly that terms such as "sons and daughters" and "members of the Church" are not restricted to a single category, "but can include popes cardinals, bishops, priests and laity," and he acknowledged that Christian anti-Judaism paved the way for Nazi anti-Semitism, though distinct from it.

"We Remember" begins with a letter from Pope John Paul II expressing his hope that the document will indeed help to heal the wounds of past misunderstandings and injustices and enable memory to play its necessary part in the process of shaping a future in which the unspeakable iniquity of the Shoah will never again be possible."

The U.S. Conference of Catholic Bishops' Committee for Ecumenical and Interreligious Relations in 1998 published the text of "We Remember" along with the statements of European and American bishops' conferences similarly expressing repentance for Christian sins of omission and commission during the Shoah in a volume entitled, *Catholics Remember the Holocaust*. In 2001 the U.S. Bishops issued *Catholic Teaching on the Shoah: Implementing the Holy See's "We Remember"* urging and giving guidelines for Holocaust education in all Catholic schools, from elementary through college and university education.

Five-Part Document

"We Remember" begins with a letter from Pope John Paul II expressing his hope that the document "will indeed help to heal the wounds of past misunderstandings and injustices" and "enable memory to play its necessary part in the process of shaping a future in which the unspeakable iniquity of the Shoah will never again be possible."

Part I, "The Tragedy of the Shoah and the Duty of Remembrance," looks at the call by Pope John Paul II in *Tertio Millennio Adveniente*: "The Church should become more fully conscious of the sinfulness of her children," lamenting that the 20th century "has witnessed an unspeakable tragedy which can never be forgotten: the attempt by the Nazi regime to exterminate the Jewish people ... We ask all Christians to join us in meditating on the catastrophe which befell the Jewish people, and on the moral imperative to ensure that never again will selfishness and hatred grow to the point of sowing such suffering and death."

Part II, "What We Must Remember," declares that "such an event cannot be fully measured by the ordinary criteria of historical research alone," requiring a "reflection" on the conditions that made it possible. One important point is that the Shoah was perpetrated in Europe, raising the question of a relationship between Nazism and historical Christian anti-Semitism.

Part III, "Relations Between Jews and Christians," traces the "tormented" history of Christian-Jewish relations. The section explores the historical failure of Christians to follow Christ's teachings right up to the 19th century. It is noted that in that century, "there began to spread in varying degrees throughout most of Europe an anti-Judaism that was essentially more sociological and political than religious," in connection with ideas that "denied the unity of the human race." Of these, National Socialism was the most extreme expression, an ideology resisted, as the paper documents, by Church leaders in Germany and by Pope Pius XI.

Part IV, "Nazi Anti-Semitism and the Shoah," stresses that Nazism's anti-Semitism "had its roots outside of Christianity and, in pursuing its aims, it did not hesitate to oppose the Church and persecute her members also." Further, "the Nazi Party not only showed aversion to the ideas of divine Providence … but gave proof of a definite hatred directed at God … such an attitude led to a rejection of Christianity, and a desire to see the Church destroyed…."

Part V, "Looking Together to a Common Future," expresses Catholic hopes that by this act of repentance (teshuva), a new relationship will be possible. It calls upon all peoples to reflect upon the Shoah and resolve that "the spoiled seeds of anti-Judaism and anti-Semitism must never again be allowed to take root in any human heart."

PAPAL STATEMENTS

(Courtesy of Dr. Eugene Fisher, associate director of the Bishops' Committee for Ecumenical and Inter-religious Affairs.)

Pope John Paul II, in a remarkable series of addresses beginning in 1979, has sought to promote and give shape to the development of dialogue between Catholics and Jews.

In a homily delivered June 7, 1979, at Auschwitz, which he called the "Golgotha of the Modern World," he prayed movingly for "the memory of the people whose sons and daughters were intended for total extermination."

In a key address delivered Nov. 17, 1980, to the Jewish community in Mainz, the Pope articulated his vision of the three "dimensions" of the dialogue: (1) "the meeting between the people of God of the Old Covenant and the people of the New Covenant"; (2) the encounter of "mutual esteem between today's Christian churches and today's people of the Covenant concluded with Moses"; (3) the "holy duty" of witnessing to the one God in the world and "jointly to work for peace and justice."

On Mar. 22, 1984, at an audience with members of the Anti-Defamation League of B'nai B'rith, the Pope commented on "the mysterious spiritual link which brings us close together, in Abraham and through Abraham, in God who chose Israel and brought forth the Church from Israel." He urged joint social action on "the great task of promoting justice and peace."

In receiving a delegation of the American Jewish Committee Feb. 14, 1985, the Holy Father confirmed that Nostra Aetate "remains always for us a teaching which is necessary to accept not merely as something fitting, but much more as an expression of the faith, as an inspiration of the Holy Spirit, as a word of the divine wisdom."

During his historic visit to the Great Synagogue in Rome Apr. 13, 1986, the Holy Father affirmed that God's covenant with the Jewish people is "irrevocable," and stated: "The Jewish religion is not 'extrinsic' to us, but in a certain way is 'intrinsic' to our own religion. With Judaism, therefore, we have a relationship which we do not have with any other religion."

Meeting with the Jewish community in Sydney, Australia, Nov. 26, 1986, the Holy Father termed the 20th century "the century of the Shoah" (Holocaust) and called "sinful" any "acts of discrimination or persecution against Jews."

On June 14, 1987, meeting with the Jewish community of Warsaw, the Pope called the Jewish witness to the Shoah (Holocaust) a "saving warning before all of humanity" which reveals "your particular vocation, showing you (Jews) to be still the heirs of that election to which God is faithful."

A collection of Pope John Paul II's addresses, On Jews and Judaism 1979-1986, prepared by the NCCB Secretariat was sent to the Pope Aug. 12, 1987. In a response of Aug. 17, the Pope reiterated his Warsaw statement and added: "Before the vivid memory of the extermination (Shoah), it is not permissible for anyone to pass by with indifference. The sufferings endured by the Jews are also for the Catholic Church a motive of sincere sorrow, especially when one thinks of the indifference and sometimes resentment which have divided Jews and Christians."

In 1995, an updated edition of the collection of papal texts entitled Spiritual Pilgrimage won the National Jewish Book Award and became the third bestselling "Jewish" book, according to the Jewish Book News.

Meeting with Jewish leaders Sept. 11, 1987, in Miami, the Pope praised the efforts in theological dialogue and educational reform implemented in the U.S. since the Second Vatican Council; affirmed the existence of the State of Israel "according to international law," and urged "common educational programs on the Holocaust so that never again will such a horror be possible. Never again!"

In an apostolic letter on the 50th anniversary of World War II (Aug. 27, 1989), the Pope stressed the uniqueness of the Jewish sufferings of the Shoah, "which will forever remain a shame for humanity."

On Aug. 14, 1991, during a visit to his home town of Wadowice, Poland, the Pope recalled with sadness the deaths of his Jewish classmates at the hands of the Nazis during World War II: "In the school of Wadowice there were Jewish believers who are no longer with us. There is no longer a synagogue near the school. It is true that your people (the Jews) were on the front lines. The Polish Pope has a special relationship to that period because, together with you, we lived through all that in our Fatherland."

On Apr. 7, 1994, the eve of Yom HaShoah, the Jewish day of prayer commemorating the victims of the Holocaust, Pope John Paul II hosted a memorial concert at the Vatican. It was, he noted, a moment of "common meditation and shared prayer," as the Kaddish, the prayer for the dead, and the Kol Nidre, the prayer for forgiveness and atonement, were recited.

Speaking Apr. 10, 1997, to Aharon Lopez, Israel's second ambassador to the Holy See, the Pope said: "The Catholic Church as a whole is committed to cooperating with the State of Israel in combating all forms of anti-Semitism, racism and religious intolerance, and in promoting mutual understanding and respect for human life and dignity. There can be no question that in these areas more can and must be done. It is precisely such renewed efforts that will give to the Great Jubilee of the Year 2000 a truly universal significance, not limited to Catholics or Christians but embracing every part of the world."

The Pope addressed members of the Pontifical Biblical Commission Apr. 11, 1997, saying: "Jesus' human identity is determined on the basis of his bond with the people of Israel, with the dynasty of David and his descent from Abraham. This does not mean only a physical belonging. By taking part in the synagogue celebrations where the Old Testament texts were read and commented on, Jesus nourished his mind and heart with the.... From her origins, the Church has well understood that the Incarnation is rooted in history and, consequently, she has fully accepted Christ's insertion into the history of the people of Israel. She has regarded the Hebrew Scriptures as the perennially valid word of God addressed to her as well as to the children of Israel. It is of primary importance to preserve and renew this ecclesial awareness."

To the Jewish people of Sarajevo on Apr. 13, 1997, the Pope declared: "The great spiritual patrimony which unites us in the divine word proclaimed in the Law and the Prophets is for all of us a constant and sure guide.... We (together are) the witnesses of the Ten Commandments.... Let us therefore go forward courageously as true brothers and heirs of the promises on the path of reconciliation and mutual forgiveness. This is the will of God."

MILLENNIUM EVENTS

During 2000 the London Philharmonic conducted by Maestro Gilbert Levine played a special series of concerts of Haydn's "Creation" for interreligious audiences in Baltimore, Paris, Jerusalem and, finally in Rome to celebrate the Holy Father's 80th birthday.

Pope John Paul II determined that the year marking the beginning of the third millennium would be a year of repentance by the Church for the sins of its members during the second millennium. On the first Sunday of Lent, during Mass in St. Peter's, he lead the Church in a liturgy of repentance in seven categories of Christian sins, one of which was the mistreatment of Jews and Judaism over the centuries including, especially, the Shoah in the 20th century.

A high point of the millennium year was the pope's pilgrimage to the Holy Land. In Israel, he visited not only Christian holy places, but places central to Jewish memory as well. At Yad VaShem in Jerusalem, Israel's memorial to the six million Jews murdered by Nazi Germany, he prayed for the deceased and embraced Jewish survivors, some of them from his own home town of Wadowice. The prime minister of Israel, Ehud Barak, spoke movingly for his people and his country in a warm response. At the Western Wall (the Kotel, the last remnant of the ancient Temple of Jerusalem), the Pope not only prayed but inserted into the Wall a written petition just as the humblest of Jews have done ever since the Temple's destruction in 70 C.E. Its wording summarizes one of the major themes of the millennium year and of the remarkable pontificate of Karol Wojtyla. Addressing the "God of our fathers," the pope prayed in the name of the whole Church: "We are deeply saddened by the behavior of those who in the course of history have caused these children of yours to suffer and, asking your forgiveness, we wish to commit ourselves to genuine brotherhood with the People of the Covenant." The note was reverently taken from the wall for permanent display at Yad VaShem.

In 2002 the Pontifical Biblical Commission issued "The Jewish People and Their Sacred Scriptures in the Christian Bible," a 205-page volume fulfilling the pope's 1997 mandate to the Commission. The first section of the report stresses, contrary to Marcionism, that the Jewish Scriptures are a fundamental part of the Christian Bible. The second section shows how the New Testament attests "conformity" (continuity) to the Jewish Bible in "fulfilling the Scriptures" but also presents a "newness" ("discontinuity, progression") in the life and certain teachings of Christ (IIA). Still, major "fundamental themes" of revelation are shared by both testaments (II,B). Jewish readings of the Bible, from rabbinic times to the present, maintain their own integrity and validity based upon the integrity and validity of the Jewish Scriptures understood in their own terms.

The third section outlines the historical setting of the New Testament as a document of "post-exilic Judaism" (IIIA) and describes the portrait of Jews in each gospel (IIIB) and of Judaism in the Pauline Letters and other apostolic writings (IIIC). The document concludes with "pastoral orientations" urging Jews and Christians to continued dialogue over the "inexhaustible riches" of our shared sacred texts.

INTERNATIONAL LIAISON COMMITTEE

The International Catholic-Jewish Liaison Committee (ILC) was formed in 1971 and is the official link between the Commission for Religious Relations with the Jewish People and the International Jewish Committee for Interreligious Consultations. The committee meets every 18 months to examine matters of common interest.

Topics under discussion have included: mission and witness (Venice, 1977), religious education (Madrid, 1978), religious liberty and pluralism (Regensburg,

1979), religious commitment (London, 1981), the sanctity of human life in an age of violence (Milan, 1982), youth and faith (Amsterdam, 1984), the Vatican Notes on Preaching and Catechesis (Rome, 1985), the Holocaust (Prague, 1990), education and social action (Baltimore, Md., 1992), family and ecology (Jerusalem, 1994), the Catholic Church and the Shoah (Rome, 1998), and theological understandings of one another (New York, 2001).

Pope John Paul, addressing in Rome a celebration of *Nostra Aetate* (the Second Vatican Council's "Declaration on the Relationship of the Church to Non-Christian Religions") by the Liaison Committee, stated: "What you are celebrating is nothing other than the divine mercy which is guiding Christians and Jews to mutual awareness, respect, cooperation and solidarity. The universal openness of *Nostra Aetate* is anchored in and takes its orientation from a high sense of the absolute singularity of God's choice of a particular people. The Church is fully aware that Sacred Scripture bears witness that the Jewish people, this community of faith and custodian of a tradition thousands of years old, is an intimate part of the mystery of revelation and of salvation."

Family Rights and Obligations

The Liaison Committee, at its May 1994 meeting in Jerusalem, issued its first joint statement, on the family — in anticipation of the UN Cairo Conference subsequently held in September.

The statement affirmed that "the rights and obligations of the family do not come from the State but exist prior to the State and ultimately have their source in God the Creator. The family is far more than a legal, social or economic unit. For both Jews and Christians, it is a stable community of love and solidarity based on God's covenant."

Caring for God's Creation

During its March 23-26, 1998, meeting in the Vatican, the Liaison Committee issued its second joint statement, on the environment. Drawing deeply on the shared sacred text of Genesis, the Committee affirmed that "concern for the environment has led both Catholics and Jews to reflect on the concrete implications of their belief in God, creator of all things," especially "a recognition of the mutual dependence between the land and the human person." "Care for creation," the document concluded "is also a religious act."

In its April 2001 meeting, the Liaison Committee issued two statements, one affirming the need to preserve the sacred character of Christian and Jewish holy places, as well as the communities who give witness to them, and one urging review and revision where necessary of curriculum and course materials teaching about each other's traditions especially in institutions of theological education.

Protecting Religious Freedom and Holy Sites

At its May 2001 meeting in New York, the Liaison Committee issued a joint declaration on a subject of increasing concern, not only in the Middle East, but in Asia and Africa as well. With regard to the obligation of states, the document notes: "Government and political authorities bear special responsibility for protecting human and religious rights. Those responsible for law, order, and public security should feel themselves obligated to defend religious minorities and to use available legal remedies against those who commit crimes against religious liberty and the sanctity of holy places. Just as they are prohibited from engaging in anti-religious acts, governments must also be vigilant lest by inaction they effectively tolerate religious hatred or provide impunity for the perpetrators of anti-religious actions."

On Education in Catholic and Jewish Seminaries and Theological Schools

Also in New York, the Liaison Committee issued a statement calling on Catholic and Jewish seminaries to provide understanding of the other. In addition to expanding course work and examining existing courses for the treatment of the other, the statement concluded that "educational institutions in both our communities should make every effort to expose students to living Jewish and Christian communities through guest lecturers, field trips, involvement in local national and international dialogue groups and conferences."

Vatican-Israel Accord

On Dec. 30, 1993, a year of dramatic developments in the Middle East was capped by the signing in Jerusalem of a "Fundamental Agreement" between representatives of the Holy See and the State of Israel. The agreement acknowledged in its preamble that the signers were "aware of the unique nature of the relationship between the Catholic Church and the Jewish people, and of the historic process of reconciliation and growth in mutual understanding and friendship between Catholics and Jews." Archbishop (later Cardinal) William H. Keeler, president of the National Conference of Catholic Bishops, welcomed the accord together with the Israeli Ambassador to the United States at a ceremony at the NCCB headquarters in Washington. (See also News Events for recent developments.)

In 1996, the Anti-Defamation League published a set of documents related to the accord, entitled "A Challenge Long Delayed," edited by Eugene Fisher and Rabbi Klenicki.

U.S. Dialogue

The National Workshop on Christian-Jewish Relations, begun in 1973 by the NCCB Secretariat, draws more than 1,000 participants from around the world. Recent workshops have been held in Baltimore (1986), Minneapolis (1987), Charleston, S.C. (1989), Chicago (1990), Pittsburgh (1992), Tulsa (1994), Stamford (1996), and Houston (1999).

In October 1987, the Bishops' Committee for Ecumenical and Interreligious Affairs began a series of twice-yearly consultations with representatives of the Synagogue Council of America. Topics of discussion have included education, human rights, respect for life, the Middle East. The consultation has issued several joint statements: "On Moral Values in Public Education" (1990), "On Stemming the Proliferation of Pornography" (1993), "On Dealing with Holocaust Revisionism" (1994).

Ongoing relationships are maintained by the USCCB Secretariat with such Jewish agencies as the

American Jewish Committee, the Anti-Defamation League, B'nai B'rith International, and the National Jewish Council for Public Affairs.

In June 1988, the Bishops' Committee for Ecumenical and Interreligious Affairs published in Spanish and English Criteria for the Evaluation of Dramatizations of the Passion, providing for the first time Catholic guidelines for passion plays.

In January 1989, the Bishops' Committee for the Liturgy issued guidelines for the homiletic presentation of Judaism under the title, "God's Mercy Endures Forever."

When the Synagogue Council of America dissolved in 1995, the Bishops' Committee for Ecumenical and Interreligious Affairs initiated separate consultations with the new National Council of Synagogues (Reform and Conservative), chaired by Cardinal William H. Keeler, and the Orthodox Union/Rabbinical Council, chaired by Cardinal John J. O'Connor, of blessed memory. The bishops have issued three joint statements with the National Council of Synagogues: "Reflections on the Millennium" (1998), "To End the Death Penalty" (1999), and "Children and the Environment" (2001). Bishop William Murphy of the Diocese of Rockville Center has succeeded Cardinal O'Connor as co-chair of the dialogue with Orthodox Judaism.

Recent Developments

In December of 1999 the Holy See's Commission and the International Jewish Committee for Interreligious Consultations announced the establishment of a committee of three Catholic and three Jewish scholars to look into the many complex historical and moral issues involving the Church and the Shoah beginning with an analysis of the thousands of archival documents for the period of World War II already made public by the Holy See in its 12 volume *Actes et Documents* (1965-1980). The Committee met in New York in December of 1999, in London in May of 2000, in Baltimore in July of 2000, and finally in Rome in October of 2000, where it issued its "Preliminary Report." The report affirmed the objectivity of the original team of four Jesuit scholars who selected the tens of thousands of texts from the Vatican archives for inclusion in the 11 volumes of the *Actes et Documents du Saint Siege Relatives a la Seconde Guerre Mondiale* (Libreria Editrice Vaticana, 1965-1980), but also raised numerous questions for further study and documentation. The Joint Commission's Catholic Coordinator, Dr. Eugene Fisher praised the group's "achievement of so much consensus between Catholic and Jewish scholars on what are the questions that need to be faced today. Such solid consensus could by no means be presumed when the group started its work, so emotional and complex are the issues . . . The scholarly successors of this group will be forever in their debt" (*Catholic International*, May 2002, p. 68).

ISLAM

(*Courtesy of Dr. John Borelli, executive secretary for Interreligious Relations, USCCB.*)

Islam, meaning grateful surrender (to God), originated with Muhammad and the revelation he is believed to have received. Muslims acknowledge that this revelation, recorded in the *Qu'ran*, is from the one God and do not view Islam as a new religion. They profess that Muhammad was the last in a long series of prophets, most of whom are named in the Hebrew Bible and the New Testament, beginning with Adam and continuing through Noah, Abraham, Moses, Jesus and down to Muhammad.

Muslims believe in the one God, Allah in Arabic, and cognate with the Hebrew Elohim and the ancient Aramaic Elah. According to the *Qu'ran*, God is one and transcendent, Creator and Sustainer of the universe, all-merciful and all-compassionate Ruler and Judge. God possesses numerous other titles, known collectively as the 99 names of God. The profession of faith states: "There is no god but the God and Muhammad is the messenger of God."

The essential duties of Muslims are to: witness the faith by daily recitation of the profession of faith; worship five times a day facing in the direction of the holy city of Mecca; give alms; fast daily from dawn to dusk during the month of Ramadan; make a pilgrimage to Mecca once if possible.

Muslims believe in final judgment, heaven and hell. Morality and following divinely revealed moral norms are extremely important to Muslims. Some dietary regulations are in effect. On Fridays, the noon prayer is a congregational (juma) prayer which should be said in a mosque. The general themes of prayer are adoration and thanksgiving. Muslims do not have an ordained ministry.

The basis of Islamic belief is the *Qu'ran*, the created word of God revealed to Muhammad through the angel Gabriel over a period of 23 years. The contents of this sacred book are complemented by the Sunna, a collection of sacred traditions from the life of the prophet Muhammad, and reinforced by Ijma, the consensus of Islamic scholars of Islamic Law (*Shariah*) which guarantees them against errors in matters of belief and practice

Conciliar Statement

The attitude of the Church toward Islam was stated as follows in the Second Vatican Council's Declaration on the Relation of the Church to Non-Christian Religions (*Nostra Aetate*, No. 3).

"The Church has a high regard for the Muslims. They worship God, who is one, living and subsistent, merciful and almighty, the Creator of heaven and earth, who has also spoken to men. They strive to submit themselves without reserve to the hidden decrees of God, just as Abraham submitted himself to God's plan, to whose faith Muslims eagerly link their own. Although not acknowledging him as God, they venerate Jesus as a prophet, his virgin Mother they also honor, and even at times devoutly invoke. Further, they await the day of judgment and the reward of God following the resurrection of the dead. For this reason, they highly esteem an upright life and worship God, especially by way of prayer, alms-deeds and fasting.

"Over the centuries many quarrels and dissensions have arisen between Christians and Muslims. The sacred Council now pleads with all to forget the past, and urges that a sincere effort be made to achieve mutual understanding; for the benefit of all men, let them together preserve and promote peace, liberty, social justice and moral values."

Dialogue

Pope John Paul II has met with Muslim leaders and delegations both in Rome and during his trips abroad. He has addressed large gatherings of Muslims in Morocco, Indonesia, Mali and elsewhere. In *Tertio Millennio Adveniente*, he recommended for the year 1999 that "the dialogue with Jews and the Muslims ought to have a pre-eminent place" and "meetings in places of significance for the great monotheistic religions." On Feb. 24, 2000, John Paul II traveled to Egypt as part of his Jubilee Year pilgrimages and was received by Grand Sheik Mohammed Sayyid Tantawi at al-Azhar University, the most influential Islamic university in the world. The Pontifical Council for Interreligious Dialogue holds formal dialogues with several Islamic organizations on a regular basis. In the U.S., the bishops' Committee for Ecumenical and Interreligious Affairs holds consultations on relations with Muslims and several special dialogues with Muslims related to international issues. Dialogue with participation of Catholics and Muslims from several U.S. cities was initiated in October 1991. These continue on a regional basis. In 1996, an annual regional dialogue in the Midwest with the co-sponsorship of the Islamic Society of North America in Indianapolis was initiated. In 1998, an annual dialogue in the Mid-Atlantic region with the co-sponsorship of the Islamic Circle of North America in Queens, New York held its first meeting. In 1999, the West Coast Dialogue of Muslims and Catholics began meeting in Orange, CA, with the co-sponsorship of several Islamic councils. Also in 1996 a dialogue between representatives of the ministry of W.D. Mohammed and the National Conference of Catholic Bishops began.

In 1995, the American Muslim Council presented its Mahmoud Abu-Saud Award for Excellence to Cardinal William H. Keeler for his leadership in promoting Christian-Muslim relations during his term as president of the National Conference of Catholic Bishops/United States Catholic Conference.

MESSAGE FOR THE END OF RAMADAN 'ID AL-FITR 1422 A.H./2001 A.D.

Promoting Human Values in an Era of Technology

The following message was issued by Cardinal Francis Arinze, President of the Pontifical Council for Interreligious Dialogue, and was addressed to the Muslim community on the occasion of the observance of the Muslim feast of 'Id al-Fitr at the end of Ramadan, the month of fasting.

Dear Muslim Friends,

1. I am writing to you again this year on the occasion of the end of Ramadan to assure you that I share the joy you must feel at having completed the fast and come to the celebration of 'Id al-Fitr. I address this message to you as a sign of esteem and friendship on the part of the Catholic Church. Many Muslims write to us in reply to this annual message, to express their gratitude, but also to share their point of view on the reflections it proposes. We are sure that the positive reactions are not limited to those sent to us, but could also be found in many local situations where Muslims and Christians live and work together.

In addressing you at this moment, the end of the period in which you have been fulfilling a specific religious duty in order to come closer to the Most High, I cannot forget, in the first place, the dramatic events which our world is experiencing, events which affect in a particular way the hearts of believers belonging to the monotheistic religions. The faithful adorers of the One God are called to be in the world the artisans of a civilization founded on the perennial values of peace and justice, of unity and love, of dialogue and freedom, of cooperation and fraternity, between persons and among peoples. May expressions of solidarity and fraternity among believers and all people of good will lead society along new paths, in full respect for human values and in the promotion of these values.

2. This year it is precisely upon this theme of human values and their promotion in an era marked by great technological progress that I wish to reflect with you. We are living in an era of technology which touches all spheres of activity: transport, communications, information, medicine, genetics, etc. Technological advances are constantly transforming the face of the earth and even allowing human beings to reach out to conquer space. However the most exciting and at the same time controversial field of technology is genetics which touches human nature directly, as human beings try to pierce its mysteries with the aid of technology, with the risk that human life itself and the respect due to it are endangered.

3. Another area is that of information technology which, through the Internet, makes possible widespread and rapid communication. We can only praise the Creator for human genius which has invented these means of information, learning and communication. Here also, however, much depends on the use which human beings make of these means.

4. The Bible speaks of the human person as one who experiences temptation and sin. The human heart is inclined to pride, to hardness, to duplicity (cf *Proverbs* 21:4; *Job* 41:16; *Psalm* 11:3). Human relations cannot help being affected by this situation. The Qur'anic meditation on human nature also reminds us that human beings are always tempted to put themselves in the centre, forgetting the One who created them. The human person is prone to injustice, to unbelief (cf *Qur'an* 14:34). Yet true well-being lies in submission to the will of God.

Faced with the lights and shadows of our world, including the challenges of technology, the Second Vatican Council affirmed: "In the light of the foregoing factors there appears the dichotomy of a world that is at once powerful and weak, capable of doing what is noble and what is base, disposed to freedom and slavery, progress and decline, brotherhood and hatred. Man is growing conscious that the forces he has unleashed are in his own hands, and that it is up to him to control them or to be enslaved by them" (*Gaudium et Spes*, n.9 §4).

5. What can we do, Christians and Muslims, together with the believers belonging to other religions and other people of good will, to ensure that we make

good use of these new means at our disposal?

Can we not work together to protect the most important human values which are threatened by a world in continual transformation ? In the first place comes the right to life, to be protected from conception right up to natural death. For life comes from God and it is to Him that it must return, when He wills. Life is a most precious gift from God, the precondition for all other divine gifts. Next comes the dignity of the human person and the rights which flow from it; these we must promote for all. Social justice, peace and freedom are also major values that are necessary for a life worthy of human beings, a life which gives glory to God who created it.

6. How can we protect and promote these values together in this technological era? First of all through dialogue, which is an exchange characterized by openness and friendship. Such dialogue, which would be concerned essentially with the ethical dimensions of new discoveries, could lead naturally to collaboration in the fields already mentioned. This dialogue and collaboration are to be pursued at all levels, local, regional, national and world-wide. All are called to make a contribution, according to their particular responsibilities and capacities. The common action to which we are invited concerns the whole of humanity, considered as one large family, having God as its origin and end. Consequently, constant reference to God and a continual search to discern His will are of capital importance in our efforts to promote human values.

With the expression of my best wishes for peace and prosperity.

HINDUISM AND BUDDHISM

(Courtesy of Dr. John Borelli.)

In its Declaration on the Relation of the Church to Non-Christian Religions, the Second Vatican Council stated: "In Hinduism men explore the divine mystery and express it both in the limitless riches of myth and the accurately defined insights of philosophy. They seek release from the trials of the present life by ascetical practices, profound meditation and recourse to God in confidence and love." (2)

Catholics, especially in India, have sought good relations with Hindus and have engaged in numerous dialogues and conferences. In papal visits to India, Paul VI in 1964 and John Paul II in 1986 and 1999, popes have addressed words of respect for Indian, particularly Hindu, religious leaders. Pope John Paul II said to Hindus in India in 1986: "Your overwhelming sense of the primacy of religion and of the greatness of the Supreme Being has been a powerful witness against a materialistic and atheistic view of life." In 1987, he said of Hinduism: "I hold in esteem your concern for inner peace and for the peace of the world, based not on purely mechanistic or materialistic political considerations, but on self-purification, unselfishness, love and sympathy for all."

In 1995, the Pontifical Council for Interreligious Dialogue began sending a general message to Hindus on the occasion of Diwali, a feast commemorating the victory of light over darkness. In 1999, John Paul II was in India during the celebration and said these words to the religious leaders of India: "On the occasion of Diwali, the festival of lights, which symbolizes the victory of life over death, good over evil, I express the hope that this meeting will speak to the world of the things that unite us all: our common human origin and destiny, our shared responsibility for people's well-being and progress, our need of the light and strength that we seek in our religious convictions." In the United States, there are a few dialogues between Catholics and Hindus.

"Buddhism in its multiple forms acknowledges the radical insufficiency of this shifting world. It teaches a path by which men, in a devout and confident spirit, can either reach a state of absolute freedom or attain supreme enlightenment by their own efforts or by higher assistance." So stated the Second Vatican Council in its Declaration on the Relation of the Church to Non-Christian Religions.

Numerous delegations of Buddhists and leading monks have been received by the popes, and John Paul II has met with Buddhist leaders on many of his trips. Paul VI said to a group of Japanese Buddhists in 1973: "Buddhism is one of the riches of Asia: you teach men to seek truth and peace in the kingdom of the Eternal, beyond the horizon of visible things. You likewise strive to encourage the qualities of goodness, meekness and non-violence." In 1995, while in Sri Lanka, John Paul II said to Buddhists: "I express my highest regard for the followers of Buddhism … with its four great values of loving kindness, compassion, sympathy, and equanimity; with its ten transcendental virtues and the joys of the Sangha [the monastic community].… At the 1986 World Day of Prayer for Peace at Assisi, the Dalai Lama, principal teacher of the Gelugpa lineage, was placed immediately to the Holy Father's left. Numerous dialogues and good relations between Catholics and Buddhists exist in many countries.

In 1995, the Pontifical Council for Interreligious Dialogue organized a Buddhist-Christian colloquium hosted by the Fo Kuang Shan Buddhist order in Taiwan. A second colloquium was held in Bangalore, India, in 1998. These grew out of the perceived need for greater ongoing contact between the Pontifical Council and Buddhist leaders and scholars. Each of these meetings has produced a report. Also in 1995, the council began sending a message to Buddhists on the feast of Vesakh, the celebration of Gautama Buddha's life.

A meeting of great significance between Buddhist and Catholic monastics took place at Our Lady of Gethsemani Abbey, Kentucky, in July 1996, which was organized and facilitated by Monastic Interreligious Dialogue, a network formed in 1981 of mostly monasteries of men and women following the rule of St. Benedict. "The Gethsemani Encounter," the result of several formal visits and hospitality between Catholic and Buddhist monks and nuns, focused on various aspects of monastic life. There were twenty-five participants on each side with numerous observers. The Buddhists represented the Theravada, Tibetan, and Zen traditions.

In 1998, an ongoing dialogue between Buddhists and Catholics in Los Angeles hosted a retreat dialogue for 50 Catholic and Buddhist participants from different regions of the U.S. The retreat/dialogue was co-planned with the Faiths in the World Committee of the National Association of Diocesan Ecumenical Officers, a network of Catholic diocesan staff responsible for ecumenical and interreligious relations.

In 1996, Cardinal Arinze, in a letter to "Dear Buddhist Friends," wrote: "The pluralistic society in which we live demands more than mere tolerance. Tolerance is usually thought of as putting up with the other or, at best, as a code of public conduct. Yet, this resigned, lukewarm attitude does not create the right atmosphere for true harmonious coexistence. The spirit of our religions challenges us to go beyond this. We are commanded, in fact, to love our neighbors as ourselves." The cardinal wrote in the same vein to Muslims on the occasion of their 1996 celebration of Id al-Fitr.

Formal dialogues continue in the Archdiocese of Los Angeles and formal relations are developing in a few other dioceses. In 1989, the Bishops' Committee for Ecumenical and Interreligious Affairs convened its first national consultation on relations with Buddhists; a second consultation was held in 1990.

Message for the Feast of Diwali

Cardinal Francis Arinze sent this message on behalf of the Pontifical Council for Interreligious Dialogue to the Hindu faithful of the world on the occasion of the upcoming feast of Diwali.

"Hindus and Christians: educating their respective communities to dialogue."

Dear Hindu Friends,

1. As you celebrate the Feast of Diwali I send greetings and good wishes in my own name and on behalf of the Pontifical Council for Interreligious Dialogue. May your celebration bring you much joy and happiness.

2. Mutual respect and esteem for our respective religious traditions lead to a greater awareness of our responsibility to cooperate in promoting social peace and harmony. War and violence waged in the name of religion are contrary to the true spirit of religion and can endanger its very existence. Education for dialogue, greater communication and practical cooperation will contribute to overcoming the causes of violence and to promoting a spirit of mutual under-

standing and respect. I propose that we intensify our efforts to foster relations and promote dialogue between our communities.

3. This proposal echoes that of the representatives of various religious traditions at the Interreligious Assembly held in the Vatican in 1999: "Education is a key for promoting interreligious harmony, religious freedom and respect for people of different religious traditions ... Above all, education is committed to seeking truth, justice, peace and reconciliation. A very practical programme, which already exists in various places, is the joint examination of textbooks, not only of religion, but also — and perhaps especially — of history. The lamentable ignorance and misinformation with which we sometimes bring up our children concerning other people's religious traditions need to be rectified. We must strive to present all religious traditions in an objective manner so that individuals belonging to these traditions can recognize themselves in that representation" (*Final Report*, 28 October 1999).

4. Education and training in promoting better relations between the followers of religions is an urgent priority. Growing awareness of religious pluralism should not lead to indifference. Dialogue, while respecting the religious traditions of others, requires us to be firmly rooted in our own religious tradition and to acknowledge the objective differences between religions. Each religious community should devise its own approach to educating its followers in a spirit of dialogue, and indicate how they believe an attitude of dialogue could best be fostered in our respective communities. Furthermore, dialogue should be complemented by joint efforts to uphold the family, form the consciences of the young, defend fundamental moral and spiritual truths and values, increase the awareness of the need for a deeper spiritual life and promote exchange of accurate information about each other's beliefs and practices.

5. Together, let us look forward to the future with hope that it will bring lasting peace for all. Happy Diwali.

— Cardinal Francis Arinze, President

Index

ABOUT THE GENERAL EDITOR

Matthew Bunson was born in Germany and grew up in Hawaii. He is the author or co-author of more than 30 books, including *Our Sunday Visitor's Encyclopedia of Catholic History, Encyclopedia of the Roman Empire, Papal Wisdom, Words of Hope and Inspiration from Pope John Paul II, The Encyclopedia of Saints, The Catholic Almanac's Guide to the Church,* and *The Angelic Doctor: The Life and World of St. Thomas Aquinas.* He is also general editor *Our Sunday Visitor's Catholic Almanac.* In addition to delivering lectures on a variety of topics, he has appeared on many radio and television programs. He has a B.A. in history and an M.A. in theology.

Our Sunday Visitor . . .
Your Source for Discovering the Riches of the Catholic Faith

Our Sunday Visitor has an extensive line of materials for young children, teens, and adults. Our books, Bibles, booklets, CD-ROMs, audios, and videos are available in bookstores worldwide.

To receive a FREE full-line catalog or for more information, call **Our Sunday Visitor** at **1-800-348-2440**. Or write, **Our Sunday Visitor** / 200 Noll Plaza / Huntington, IN 46750.

- -

Please send me: __A catalog
Please send me materials on:
__Apologetics and catechetics   __Reference works
__Prayer books   __Heritage and the saints
__The family   __The parish
Name_____
Address_____Apt._____
City_____State_____Zip_____
Telephone (   ) _____

A29BBABP

- -

Please send a friend: __A catalog
Please send a friend materials on:
__Apologetics and catechetics   __Reference works
__Prayer books   __Heritage and the saints
__The family   __The parish
Name_____
Address_____Apt._____
City_____State_____Zip_____
Telephone (   ) _____

A29BBABP

- -

Our Sunday Visitor
200 Noll Plaza
Huntington, IN 46750
Toll free: **1-800-348-2440**
E-mail: osvbooks@osv.com
Website: www.osv.com